DATE DUE

DEMCO 38-296

AMERICAN NATIONAL BIOGRAPHY

AMERICAN
NATIONAL BIOGRAPHY

Published under the auspices of the
AMERICAN COUNCIL OF LEARNED SOCIETIES

General Editors

John A. Garraty

Mark C. Carnes

VOLUME 14

OXFORD UNIVERSITY PRESS

New York   1999   Oxford

OXFORD UNIVERSITY PRESS

Oxford   New York
Athens   Auckland   Bangkok   Bogotá
Buenos Aires   Calcutta   Cape Town   Chennai
Dar es Salaam   Delhi   Florence   Hong Kong   Istanbul
Karachi   Kuala Lumpur   Madrid   Melbourne   Mexico City
Mumbai   Nairobi   Paris   São Paulo   Singapore
Taipei   Tokyo   Toronto   Warsaw
and associated companies in
Berlin   Ibadan

Published by Oxford University Press, Inc.,
198 Madison Avenue, New York, New York 10016
http://www.oup-usa.org

Funding for this publication was provided in part by
the Andrew W. Mellon Foundation, the Rockefeller Foundation,
and the National Endowment for the Humanities,
a federal agency.

Library of Congress Cataloging-in-Publication Data

American national biography / general editors, John A. Garraty, Mark C. Carnes
p.   cm.
"Published under the auspices of the American Council of Learned Societies."
Includes bibliographical references and index.
1. United States—Biography—Dictionaries.   I. Garraty, John Arthur,
1920– .   II. Carnes, Mark C. (Mark Christopher), 1950–   .
III. American Council of Learned Societies.
CT213.A68   1998   98-20826   920.073—dc21   CIP
ISBN 0-19-520635-5 (set)
ISBN 0-19-512793-5 (vol. 14)

Printing (last digit): 9 8 7 6 5 4 3 2 1

Printed in the United States of America
on acid-free paper

L

LOVEJOY, Arthur O. (10 Oct. 1873–30 Dec. 1962), founder of the History of Ideas movement, was born Arthur Oncken Lovejoy in Berlin, Germany, the son of Wallace William Lovejoy, a physician, and Sara Oncken. His father was in Berlin pursuing medical research when Lovejoy was born. After the family returned home to Massachusetts, his mother died of an overdose of drugs when he was eighteen months old. In a crisis of grief, the young physician abandoned medicine and became a minister of the Protestant Episcopal church. Lovejoy grew up where his father served churches, in Ironton, Ohio; Palmyra and Trenton, New Jersey; Germantown, Pennsylvania, where he graduated from Germantown Academy; and Oakland, California, where his father was professor of the Old Testament at Pacific Theological Seminary.

Lovejoy entered the University of California at Berkeley in 1891. His father encouraged him to seek a clerical career, but Lovejoy sought the rational basis of theology; his driving force was a "quest for intelligibility," which he pursued with all the techniques of philosophy and history. His father's imperatives also included helping those in need, and so Lovejoy began as an undergraduate to work in settlement houses—a form of service common at the time and exemplified in Jane Addams's Hull-House. He helped establish a settlement house in Oakland and thus began his tradition of volunteer social service, which continued for twenty years, though the religious motive transmuted into a desire for the moral justification of human decency and American democracy.

At Berkeley Lovejoy fell under the influence of the idealist George Holmes Howison. After earning an A.B. in 1895, he entered graduate school at Harvard University, then in its Golden Age, with William James, Josiah Royce, and George Santayana among its faculty. Whereas Howison's idealism was pluralistic, insisting on the independence of many minds, Royce's version tended to regard all minds as parts of one cosmic Mind. Lovejoy could not accept Royce's proofs of such an Absolute Whole that is alone fully real and true. He trusted the commonsense experience of many things independent of thought, a form of realism.

After receiving an M.A. in philosophy in 1897, Lovejoy studied comparative religions at the Sorbonne; then, without a Ph.D., he began teaching philosophy at Stanford University in 1899. Over the next two years he formed his strongest scholarly conviction: that the academic life requires freedom.

Lovejoy resigned from Stanford in 1901 rather than serve a president who dismissed a colleague whose politics did not please the trustees. To his friend William Pepperell Montague, then an instructor at Berkeley, Lovejoy's "passionate and persistent concern for justice" and his willingness to sacrifice his interest rather than neglect his duty made him a hero. He gained the admiration of many who were to join with him fifteen years later in founding the American Association of University Professors (AAUP), but he also acquired the reputation of a troublemaker. The Harvard Department of Philosophy wanted to offer him a professorship, but he was denied the post by Harvard president A. Lawrence Lowell.

Lovejoy was professor of philosophy at Washington University in St. Louis (1901–1907), Columbia University (1907–1908), the University of Missouri at Columbia (1908–1910), and Johns Hopkins University (1910–1938). He never married. After his retirement he devoted his time to scholarship and public service. He died in Baltimore.

Lovejoy's books include two important works completed late in his career: *The Revolt against Dualism* (1930) and *The Great Chain of Being* (1936). Both came as a result of invitations to speak: the first—on theory of knowledge, or epistemology—addressed to philosophers as Carus Lectures at an annual meeting of the American Philosophical Association; the second as William James Lectures at Harvard in 1933, which attracted persons in literature and other disciplines of the humanities. He developed the ideas contained in the books in three hundred articles and reviews, and several later books as well.

In a paper titled "Temporalistic Realism" (1930), Lovejoy stated his position as an elaboration systematically and historically founded on "the most indubitable fact of our experience, namely that experience itself is temporal. That life is transition; that our existence is meted out to us in fragments which succeed and supplant one another."

Lovejoy believed that this "most indubitable fact" had been obscured by ancient, medieval, and early modern philosophers who regarded this world as mere transience, a changing copy of the unchanging source and model. Here there is largely opinion, but yonder, in what Leibniz called the Intelligible World, there was pure knowledge and truth. Life in time then could be little more than preparation for wisdom, which should be lived, as Spinoza said, under the aspect of eternity.

Lovejoy had great respect for colleagues who abandoned the active life and withdrew to contemplate the eternal verities. One such was Paul Elmer More, who practiced a Buddhist withdrawal for two years. There is no evidence that Lovejoy's purpose in studying Buddhist and Hindu wisdom was to find salvation in Nirvana or in union with Brahma. By 1909 he pronounced the search to be vain in an essay called "The Obsolescence of the Eternal."

Of greatest importance in confirming his concept of time were the biological sciences, being rethought after Darwin in evolutionary fashion, and the physical sciences, being rethought, after Einstein, in the relativistic mode. Lovejoy devoted many important papers to understanding these temporalistic revolutions in science, and he hoped that philosophers, following the lead of the sciences, would come to agreements that were beyond the idiosyncrasies of merely private temperament and taste ("On Some Conditions of Progress in Philosophical Inquiry"). He argued that the scientific philosopher should suspect his own passions, exercise great caution, cooperate with a community of inquirers, avoid edification, and seek above all "truths verifiable by the common reason."

In concentrating on methods, Lovejoy's philosophy resembles John Dewey's instrumentalism and various positivistic methods, but he distinguished himself sharply from both in not renouncing metaphysics. He criticized pragmatisms first, both that of his teacher William James and later that of his friend and academic ally Dewey. In his judgment, a most significant method of clarification is definition, and the worst abuse of language is the use of -ism terms. Lovejoy analyzes the ambiguities of James in a famous essay, "The Thirteen Pragmatisms" (1908), and in "Pragmatism *versus* the Pragmatist" (1920) tries to demonstrate that, against Dewey's confused metaphysics, what is true in what Dewey says is nothing more than what Lovejoy called "critical realism." Pragmatists themselves were extremely disturbed by Lovejoy's distinction between thought and thing, between unchanging past fact and the open alterable future, and other aspects of dualism. These are such distinctions that no reasoning can ever abolish. Using Lovejoy's own technique, one critic (Arthur E. Murphy) found in *The Revolt against Dualism* no less than seventeen varieties of dualism ("Mr. Lovejoy's Counter-Revolution," *Journal of Philosophy* 28, no. 2 [1931]: 29–42, and 28, no. 3 [1931]: 57–71).

Lovejoy's "temporalistic realism" was close in some respects to the emphasis on process that the pragmatists James and Dewey shared with Bergson and Whitehead. Nine essays on the distinctions Lovejoy found blurred in his colleagues are models of exact thought. These were published in 1963, the year after Lovejoy's death, in *The Thirteen Pragmatisms and Other Essays*. They make the point that the pragmatists, according to Lovejoy, had nothing new except their novel compounds of ideas, but their diverse borrowings are difficult to harmonize. The internal conflicts concerning meaning, truth, knowledge, and values were spelled out, as summarized by P. P. Wiener (the prime agent in the founding of, and close associate in the editing of, the *Journal of the History of Ideas* [1940]) in his essay "Pragmatism," which appears in *The Dictionary of the History of Ideas* (5 vols., 1968–1974), an encyclopedia of achievement edited by Wiener.

Lovejoy, more than any other major scholar of his generation, made every effort to breach the wall separating different branches of knowledge. In his graphic phrase, he cut doors through disciplinary walls. Ideas, he demonstrated, pay no attention to the domain of origin; they move quickly, from the astronomy of Ptolemy or Copernicus into poetry, from theology into politics; and therefore students of ideas should not be expected to confine their investigations within curricular boundaries. Historians and students of literature were drawn into Lovejoy's circle, and no one was excluded. The History of Ideas Club at Johns Hopkins led to the founding of the *Journal of the History of Ideas* and to *The Dictionary of the History of Ideas*.

The Great Chain of Being was Lovejoy's greatest success. It was hailed as the masterpiece of the History of Ideas movement and inspired hundreds of articles, particularly among students of literature. The chain metaphor was most appealing because it raised the issue of man's relation to the lower animals, and various levels of still lower rank, and to what is above man, particularly the dependence on a divine source. It puts that question in the broad context of ancient philosophers, in whose work aspects of the *Great Chain*—plenitude, continuity, and gradation—were initially formulated. Generations of neo-Platonic, medieval, and modern thinkers worked out implications, the most important one being that humans participate in two worlds: however similar to higher animals, in mind akin to angels. The book has drama because its thesis had become an axiomatic truth among leaders of the eighteenth-century Enlightenment, but went into rapid decline when the levels of timeless being were reread as stages of temporal development. Thus a false picture of the cosmos—false because it ignored temporality—led thinkers, most famous of whom was Darwin, to formulate a theory of evolution. The conclusion of the book is that this tradition, with powerful associations that stir our "pathos," must now be rejected. Evolution has replaced hierarchy. This is "the moral" Lovejoy drew, and both his handling of important chapters and the conclusion have frequently stirred controversies. Some students of the book have rejected Lovejoy's moral and tried to show that thinking of levels is necessary in order to understand nature, particularly the emergence of higher species.

By no means was Lovejoy an evolutionist in the sense of trusting that each successive stage must be higher, and although Lovejoy allied himself with the Unitarian movement, he was not sympathetic with the famous Unitarian expression of faith, "The Fatherhood of God and the Brotherhood of Man, onward and upward forever." In one of Lovejoy's last books, *Reflections on Human Nature* (1961), his view of human nature was closer to the Augustinian estimates of human sinfulness as adapted to political use by Reinhold Niebuhr.

Lovejoy was a deeply moral man who believed that one of the profound motives guiding human action was the need of approbation. He was brought up to seek to satisfy the Christian standards of his father, but as a philosopher he felt closest to the rationalists of the Enlightenment who heeded the imperative to use reason to curb excesses of power. If university presidents abuse their authority and do not heed the protests of individuals or learned societies, as he observed they often do not, then there must be an organization of all professors so strong that it can censure such administrations for violation of academic freedom.

Lovejoy the activist issued his appeal to form "a National Association of University Professors" in both *Nation* and *Science* in 1914. He served as first secretary and second president (after John Dewey) of the AAUP, formulated many of its early statements about rights and responsibilities, and wrote the classic article "Academic Freedom" (*Encyclopedia of the Social Sciences*, vol. 1 [1930], pp. 384–88). Josiah Royce, one of Lovejoy's most admired teachers, referred to the early AAUP as "the society of the united mice, organized for the belling of cats." Lovejoy was one of the academic mice who roared, taking part in many investigations of violations of academic rights.

The primary duty of a university professor in Lovejoy's view is to ensure that his or her search for truth leads toward the discovery of new truth. Therefore there should be no restrictions imposed by ecclesiastical, political, or economic authority. This freedom is not primarily for the benefit of scholars but is for the sake of knowledge itself and to satisfy the right of students to know all sides of every question. It is society that benefits when a professor is not regarded as an employee. Lovejoy compared professors to judges, who may be appointed by a president or a governor but then are to render judgment independent of all political considerations. Professors are also like physicians, who must tell their patients what they may not want to hear.

Following the logic of protecting professional impartiality, Lovejoy went further than other founders of the AAUP in advising academics to stay out of politics and not to be candidates for political office. But herein lies the irony of Lovejoy's career as an activist. During World War I, his early neutrality with regard to the Central Powers and the Allies gave way to warmest sympathy with Britain and France as defenders of the rule of law and constitutional government and to increasing hostility to the German Imperial government. He became convinced that America's interests lay with the Allies, and he urged President Woodrow Wilson to join in what Lovejoy called the most just of wars. When America entered the war, he teamed up with the historian Albert Bushnell Hart to publish *Handbook of the War for Readers, Public Speakers and Teachers*, which went into a second edition in 1918.

Lovejoy's defense of democracy did not allow toleration of pacifists, whose chief leader, Norman Thomas, had characterized their position in "The Religion of Free Men" (*New Republic* 11 [1917]: 109–11). In "To Conscientious Objectors" Lovejoy denied their right as citizens to exempt themselves from military duty (*New Republic* 11 [1917]: 187–89).

Lovejoy's critical rebuke to pacifists was not the sort of philosophizing that American students of later decades cared to hear. Having been drawn from his study into the public forum by the threat of the Kaiser, he was equally opposed to the rise of Hitler's war machine in the 1930s.

Lovejoy found Hitler's profession of pacifism utterly inconsistent with what he had written in *Mein Kampf*, and in 1933, at a time when a majority of Americans and Britons were unalarmed, Lovejoy told the Baltimore branch of the American Jewish Conference that Hitler was a grave menace to world peace and that the United States and other democracies must prepare to prevent aggression. He was referred to during the 1930s as a warmonger. Lovejoy was as active in preparing American public opinion for World War II as he had been for World War I, but in the second case he used his exacting scholarly standards to avoid becoming a propagandist. The laws then in force to keep America's neutrality were working in favor of the dictators and were denying aid or encouragement to the victims of aggression. Hence he appealed to Congress to alter the laws. His pamphlets "What Shall Be Done about Germany after the War?" and "Can We Prevent Future Wars?" present alternatives, then ask his reader, after taking into consideration the costs and benefits, to decide.

Lovejoy's practical activities during World War II, through numerous organizations, are those of a statesman exercising "detached criticism" rather than a politician inciting his listeners to join in a crusade.

Lovejoy was unlike many American antifascists in that he saw no commonality whatsoever between democracy and Soviet Communism. Although he tolerated intellectual Marxism as a possible alternative to the capitalist economic system, he came by 1941 to regard membership in the Communist party as incompatible with academic freedom and concluded that a younger colleague at Johns Hopkins who had become a functionary of the Communist Party of America should be excluded from the faculty.

It is debatable whether Lovejoy lapsed into the ideology of anticommunism, but his activities had nothing in common with the campaign of Senator Joseph McCarthy to rid government, education, and entertainment of those accused of un-American activities. Lovejoy's thinking can be examined in "Communism *versus* Academic Freedom," a careful contribution to *American Scholar* (18 [1949]: 332–37) written about the dismissal of several Communists. He had concluded by 1941 that the principles of academic freedom were as endangered by Communism as by Nazi or Italian Fascist loyalty to a dictator or party. That is, such a party member "is pledged to alter his professed conclusions, and his teaching on scientific or philosophic questions, at the dictates of an external, nonscientific organization" (letter to Frank N. Trager, 23 Oct. 1941, quoted in Wilson, *Arthur O. Lovejoy and the Quest for Intelligibility*, p. 201).

Lovejoy's disapproval of Communists on university faculties is not at all like the condemnation of pacifists twenty-two years earlier. The difference is that the pacifist was judged vicious for his neglect of his civic duty to bear arms to defend the state, and the Communist or fascist is guilty of neglecting "canons of academic responsibility."

The statesman Lovejoy restricts the question to current membership in the Communist Party of America, excluding any problem of past membership, and has no question about the civil right of anyone to belong to such a political party. It is only simultaneous membership in a university faculty that he questions, because of the nature of research and teaching. To report "*not the results of their own research and reflection and that of their fellow-specialists, but rather the opinion of others[s]*," is to him a perversion. Academic freedom "is as much an obligation as a right."

Lovejoy's "First Academic Commandment" was "Thou shalt not knowingly misrepresent facts, or tell lies." What offended this absolute was Lenin's commandment: "Use any ruse, cunning, unlawful method, evasion and concealment of the truth."

While in his public career Lovejoy was often the center of controversy, in his private life he compared himself to David Hume. He had moderate needs, held no strong doctrines, and cared mostly to study ideas. Like Hume, he contributed both to philosophy and to history but managed also to make a significant contribution to public life.

• Lovejoy's papers are in the archives of the Eisenhower Library, Johns Hopkins University. An excellent bibliography is Daniel J. Wilson, *Arthur O. Lovejoy: An Annotated Bibliography* (1983). Major works not mentioned in the text include *Essays in the History of Ideas* (1953), which includes a bibliography (pp. 339–53); *A Documentary History of Primitivism and Related Ideas* (1953); *The Reason, the Understanding and Time* (1961); and, with George Boas, *Contributions to the History of Primitivism, Primitivism and Related Ideas in Antiquity* (1965). For biographical information on Lovejoy, see Wilson, *Arthur O. Lovejoy and the Quest for Intelligibility* (1980); and Boas et al., "Arthur O. Lovejoy at Seventy-Five: 'Reason at Work,'" *Journal of the History of Ideas* 9, no. 4 (Oct. 1948): 403–46, has five articles that give a remarkably well-rounded picture of the man, his work, and his influence.

The secondary and critical literature about Lovejoy and his contribution is very rich. Consult John Herman Randall et al., eds., "A Symposium in Memory of Arthur O. Lovejoy," *Philosophy and Phenomenological Research* 23, no. 4 (June 1963): 475–537; and Boas, "A. O. Lovejoy: Reason-in-Action," *American Scholar* 29 (Autumn 1960): 535–42. Among some of the more recent collections of essays responding to Lovejoy's *Great Chain of Being* are Angela Ales Bello, *The Great Chain of Being from the Point of View of Phenomenology of Action* (1981); Donald R. Kelley, *This History of Ideas: Canon and Variations* (1990); Marion Leathers Kuntz and Paul Grimley Kuntz, *Jacob's Ladder and the Tree of Life: Concepts of Hierarchy and the Great Chain of Being* (1987); and Paul G. Kuntz, "Hierarchy Today," *Contemporary Philosophy* 13, no. 8 (Mar.–Apr. 1991).

PAUL G. KUNTZ

LOVEJOY, Elijah Parish (9 Nov. 1802–7 Nov. 1837), abolitionist editor and preacher, was born near Albion, Maine, the son of Daniel Lovejoy, a Congregational preacher and farmer, and Elizabeth Pattee. Lovejoy graduated from Waterville (now Colby) College in 1826 and a year later moved to St. Louis, Missouri,

where he conducted a private school and edited the *St. Louis Times*, an anti-Jacksonian paper. In 1832, under the influence of a religious revival, he resolved to become a preacher. Soon after graduation from Princeton Theological Seminary in 1833, he returned to St. Louis, organized a Presbyterian church on the outskirts of the city, and began editing a religious newspaper, the *Observer*. In 1835 he married Celia Ann French; they had two children.

From the first, the *Observer* reflected Lovejoy's affiliation with the New School faction of Presbyterianism and his predilection for the emerging reform movements. He focused in particular on condemning Sabbath breaking and such moral lapses as blasphemy and the use of tobacco and alcohol. As an evangelical Protestant, he editorialized against the growing influence of Catholicism in the city. Anti-Catholicism, a longtime cause of New England Protestants, took on new life in the early 1830s as Lyman Beecher and other religious leaders warned that the West was about to fall under papal control. Lovejoy imperiled his position in Missouri further by endorsing gradual emancipation of slaves. Even though his sentiments on slavery at that time were relatively moderate, many Missourians opposed any discussion of the subject, and some threatened violence against the *Observer*. Lovejoy reacted to this threat and to the wave of antiabolitionism that swept the nation at the time by asserting the right of free discussion, even of unpopular issues. His consistent stand on this principle would earn him his place in history and lead to his death.

In May 1836 Lovejoy protested the lynching of a free black man in St. Louis and castigated Judge Luke E. Lawless for seeming to condone the act. The judge, he wrote, was "a Papist; and in his charge we see the cloven foot of Jesuitism." The night after the article appeared, a mob damaged the *Observer*'s press. Lovejoy responded by moving to Alton, Illinois, but before his press could be unloaded there, a mob destroyed it. He would not again attempt to flee from opposition.

At a public meeting soon afterward, Lovejoy asserted that even though he was and would remain an "uncompromising enemy of Slavery," the *Observer* would not function in Alton as an abolitionist newspaper. His audience interpreted this statement as a pledge to cease agitating on the slavery issue. But Lovejoy, like many other moderate opponents of slavery, soon decided that the preservation of civil rights for white Americans required the immediate and unequivocal end of slavery. Thus, as he moved ever closer to full-fledged abolitionism, local opposition grew accordingly. Late in August 1837, a mob destroyed his second press and in September a third. Lovejoy and his supporters determined to use force to protect a fourth. After news of these events reached the East, Lovejoy, hitherto an obscure religious editor, became an object of intense interest among reformers.

In October 1837 Lovejoy issued a call to hold a convention to form a state auxiliary to the American Anti-Slavery Society. Local hostility became extreme, especially from those who were afraid that an antislavery reputation might have a negative effect on the city's commercial growth. Alton's prominent men met to request that Lovejoy leave town. He refused to do so, instead delivering an eloquent public defense of civil rights. He failed to persuade city leaders, however, and on 7 November a mob gathered outside the warehouse where the *Observer*'s fourth press was stored and demanded its surrender. Lovejoy and a band of supporters waited inside, armed to defend the press. When Lovejoy emerged from the building to try to prevent an incendiary from setting fire to the roof, he was shot and killed. Lovejoy was hailed by abolitionists as a martyr to their cause. At the same time, however, his decision to defend his press by use of force created intense controversy within the antislavery movement, many members of which adhered to the principle of nonresistance.

Lovejoy's persistence as an abolitionist editor places him among the leading defenders of a free press in American history. At the time, the Alton riots were used by abolitionists to support their contention that slavery menaced the liberties of all people. To that extent, Lovejoy's death contributed to the growth of the antislavery movement and of the sectional controversy.

• The major source of Lovejoy's papers is the Wickett-Wiswall Collection at Texas Tech University. Files of the *Observer* are available at the Chicago Historical Society and the Illinois State Historical Society. Modern biographies are John G. Gill, *Tide without Turning* (1958), and Merton L. Dillon, *Elijah P. Lovejoy, Abolitionist Editor* (1961). Contemporary sources include Joseph C. Lovejoy and Owen Lovejoy, *Memoir of the Rev. Elijah P. Lovejoy* (1838); Edward Beecher, *Narrative of the Riots at Alton* (1838); Henry Tanner, *History of the Rise and Progress of the Alton Riots* (1878); and William S. Lincoln, *Alton Trials* (1838).

MERTON L. DILLON

LOVEJOY, Esther Pohl (16 Nov. 1869–17 Aug. 1967), physician and medical administrator, was born Esther Clayson in a logging camp near Seabeck, Washington Territory, the daughter of Edward Clayson, a logging-camp operator, and Annie Quinton. During her childhood financial difficulties caused the family to move to Portland, Oregon, where they ran a hotel. As a young girl she watched as her mother nearly died following numerous pregnancies, but when a woman physician safely delivered her sister, Esther became intrigued with medicine. Acquaintance with a female medical student further inspired her to become a doctor.

Following brief schooling in Seabeck, Esther was tutored in Latin, history, and the classics by a professor who boarded at the hotel until the family moved to a farm. Two years later her mother, Esther, and her brothers returned to Portland to find work. In 1890 Esther saved enough money to attend the first term at the newly-established medical school of the University of Oregon. She dropped out to work for a year but managed to receive her M.D. in 1894 as the school's second female graduate; she received a medal for earn-

ing the highest grades over three years. A few weeks later she married Emil Pohl, a classmate and surgeon.

Esther Pohl became an obstetrician, and the couple set up separate practices and offices in their home. In 1896 they traveled to Chicago, Illinois, for postgraduate work at West Side Post-Graduate School, with Esther studying gynecology and obstetrics. In 1898 they set up practice in Skagway, Alaska, where Esther's brothers lived. With the help of area residents, they opened Union Hospital in 1898. Esther traveled long distances, sometimes by dogsled, to visit patients in their homes. Her brother's murder in Alaska, however, prompted Esther's return to Portland in 1899. She visited Alaska in the summers until her husband joined her in Portland on the birth of their son and only child in 1901.

In 1904 Esther Pohl attended a clinic in obstetrics and gynecology in Vienna, Austria. She became active in the women's suffrage movement about this time. Elected to the Portland Board of Health in 1905, she became its head in 1907, the first woman physician to attain this post in a large city. Realizing that many deaths among children and infants had been caused by contaminated milk, she waged a vigorous campaign to ensure milk purity and dairy inspections. Her fight was won when a milk ordinance was finally passed. She was largely responsible for the establishment of excellent health sanitation standards in Portland. Tragically, her own son died in 1908 of septic peritonitis, which she believed had been caused by tainted milk.

In 1909 Esther Pohl resigned from the Board of Health and joined a private practice with four other doctors. She also worked hard for woman suffrage, which was passed in Oregon in 1912, and was an ardent supporter of Prohibition. After her husband's death in 1911, she married a businessman, George A. Lovejoy, in 1913; they divorced in 1920.

America's entry into World War I diverted Esther Pohl Lovejoy's interests, and she moved to New York City, where she went to work for the American Medical Women's Association (AMWA). The AMWA's intention was to gain more credibility for female physicians, who at the time were restricted from serving in a military capacity. After offering to pay her own expenses, Lovejoy received permission to sail to France in 1917 under the auspices of the Red Cross. Her mission was to explore the possibilities of AMWA women becoming relief workers overseas. In Paris she saw devastation, food shortages, and sick and starving women and children. She traveled to the front lines, shocked at the hardships people endured. On her return to the United States in 1918, she recounted her war experiences in a book, *The House of the Good Neighbor* (1919).

In 1917 the American Women's Hospitals (AWH) was established by the AMWA and established its first hospital in France to provide war relief. After the war the AWH continued giving assistance to refugees and the sick in local wars, revolutions, and disasters both in the United States and abroad. It relied on a staff of volunteer female doctors. Lovejoy was its organization chairman from 1919 to 1920, after which she returned to Oregon. After an unsuccessful attempt to win a Democratic congressional seat, she was called back by the AMWA to head the AWH.

Lovejoy's leadership, persuasive speaking, and fundraising strategies raised funds to continue the AWH's successful operations. She oversaw AWH groups working with the Red Cross and other agencies to train local people and set up clinics, maternity shelters, and dispensaries. Lovejoy traveled to Smyrna, Greece, Serbia, and other countries to ensure that help was being given to people ravaged by war or epidemics. Her book *Certain Samaritans* (1927) described the problems encountered during the 1922 Christian exodus from Turkey to Greece. Calling for a worldwide coalition of medical women to exchange ideas and unite efforts, she helped to found the Medical Women's International Association and became its first president from 1919 to 1924. She also served as president of the AMWA (1932–1933).

Continually juggling medical relief to suit worldwide needs, Lovejoy directed the AWH's activities wherever disaster struck, from China to Appalachia. During the Great Depression, the AWH's attention shifted to the United States, until World War II drew its services once again to Europe. At war's end, AWH services extended to the Far East and South America. Lovejoy was widely recognized for her service: she was awarded the AMWA's Elizabeth Blackwell Medal (on two occasions), the French Legion of Honor, Yugoslavia's Gold Cross of Saint Sava, Jerusalem's Gold Cross of the Holy Sepulcher, and Greece's Gold Cross of the Order of George I. In 1959 the AWH became an independent corporation, the America Women's Hospital Service (AWHS). Lovejoy remained as its president until March 1967. She died five months later in New York City.

In the course of Lovejoy's work, she constantly urged women to become doctors, believing it was a woman's natural profession. She set up scholarships, designating that one-third of the funds be awarded to women. To further encourage women and provide role models, she wrote *Women Physicians and Surgeons* (1939) and *Women Doctors of the World* (1957), documenting the accomplishments of women physicians. Tragedy altered her life, but through adaptability, a passion for life, and a sense of humor, she put aside her troubles to help unfortunate people worldwide.

• Biographical information and other items relating to Lovejoy are in the University of Oregon Health Services Center in Portland, the archives of the Oregon Historical Society, and the AWHS in New York City. A biography is Olive W. Burt, *Physician to the World* (1973). Other writings by Lovejoy include "American Women's Hospitals: 'A Cullinan,'" *Medical Review of Reviews*, Feb. 1934, pp. 104–8; and "My Medical School, 1890–1894," *Oregon Historical Quarterly*, Mar. 1974, pp. 7–35. Additional information is in Marguerite Norris Davis, "Dr. Esther Lovejoy, State Pioneer Woman in Medicine," *Oregon Journal*, 14 Feb. 1968; Libman Block, "The Doctor Was an Adventuress," *Today's Health* 48 (Aug. 1970):

10, 70; "Esther Pohl Lovejoy," *New York State Journal of Medicine* 77 (June 1977): 1161–65; "In Recognition of Esther Pohl Lovejoy and the American Women's Hospitals," *Women and Health* 6 (Fall–Winter 1981): 89–92; and Ellen S. More, "A Certain Restless Ambition: Women Physicians and World War I," *American Quarterly* 41 (Dec. 1989): 636–59. An obituary is in the *New York Times*, 18 Aug. 1967.

MARILYN ELIZABETH PERRY

LOVEJOY, Owen (6 Jan. 1811–25 Mar. 1864), congressman and Congregational minister, was born in Albion, Maine, the son of Rev. Daniel Lovejoy, a Presbyterian minister, and Elizabeth Pattee. One of eight children of highly religious parents, Lovejoy entered Bowdoin College in 1830 but left in 1833 following the death of his father. He taught school to support himself in college and studied law. In 1836, having already become a convert to abolitionism, apparently influenced by Theodore Dwight Weld, he moved to Alton, Illinois, to study for the ministry under his brother Elijah P. Lovejoy. As tensions mounted with Elijah's vehement attacks on slavery, Owen urged his brother to persevere and defend his right to speak and publish his newspaper, the *Alton Observer*. After his brother's death in 1837 at the hands of a drunken antiabolition mob in Alton, Owen vowed to devote himself to "the cause that has been sprinkled with my brother's blood" (*Chicago Tribune*, 12 June 1874). The following year he and his brother Joseph Lovejoy coauthored a biography and tribute to Elijah that emphasized his commitment to abolition and freedom of the press.

Continuing his theological study, Lovejoy prepared first for Anglican ordination but refused to pledge himself never to discuss abolitionism, as the church demanded. He then assumed the pastorate at the Congregational church of Princeton, Illinois, thus returning to the church of his father, for to him, following his brother's violent death, the freedom to oppose slavery openly was far more significant than the differences in theology between the Anglican and Congregational churches. He held the Princeton pastorate for seventeen years and freely used his pulpit in vehement attacks on slavery, initially preferring the moral suasion approach of Weld. At first he impressed his listeners as a rugged but awkward and unkempt speaker, but he soon became a powerful and effective orator and antislavery advocate. During these years he assisted several fugitive slaves in their efforts to escape to freedom. In 1843 he was tried by county officials for harboring two slaves but was acquitted. In 1843 he married Eunice Storrs Denham, with whom he had seven children.

In the 1840s Lovejoy became an active political abolitionist, running unsuccessfully for Congress as a Liberty party candidate in 1846. In August 1848 he attended the Free Soil convention in Buffalo and again ran unsuccessfully as that party's candidate for Congress from Illinois's Fourth District. During these years he modified his antislavery stance, rejecting the argument of the more radical abolitionists that slavery should be attacked wherever it existed in favor of advocacy of the Wilmot Proviso, which would contain slavery and prevent its expansion into territories acquired during the Mexican War. With other Free Soilers, he opposed Stephen A. Douglas's Kansas-Nebraska Act in 1854 and joined in the unsuccessful efforts that year to form the Illinois Republican party. In doing so he urged antislavery radicals to moderate their demands to facilitate unity in a new party. He was elected to the state legislature that fall.

The Whig party in Illinois died more slowly than in many other northern states, and Lovejoy was among the most active in persuading members to join the new Republican organization rather than its rival, the antiimmigrant Know Nothing party. Among those he befriended in these efforts was Abraham Lincoln. In 1856 Lovejoy was a delegate to the state and national Republican conventions, and that fall he won a seat in Congress as a Republican, beginning eight years of antislavery agitation in the House of Representatives. His first efforts concentrated on preventing the admission of Kansas as a slave state, and he actively opposed southern efforts to annex Cuba as potential slave territory. He worked for Lincoln's election to the Senate in 1858 and won a national reputation as an outspoken opponent of the proslavery James Buchanan administration. He was also a strong advocate of a homestead law that would grant free farms to settlers in western territories.

Lovejoy campaigned actively in Illinois for Lincoln's election as president in 1860. A supporter of a vigorous prosecution of the war effort against the Confederacy, he sought to persuade President Lincoln and the Congress to move more quickly toward emancipation. He briefly served under General John C. Frémont as a colonel in the Western Department of the Army in Missouri. Determined to end slavery, on his return to Congress in late 1861 he told his constituents, "If we do not destroy it, it will destroy us" (*Bureau County Republican*, 5 Dec. 1861). His bill to free all slaves in the United States was defeated by two votes in the House (20 Dec. 1861). He also called for the use of black troops in Union armies and later fought for equal pay for black recruits. In these efforts he engaged in several highly publicized exchanges with conservatives in Congress.

In 1862 Lovejoy was elected to the House for the fourth time. He continued to work with abolitionist members in both houses, including Thaddeus Stevens and Charles Sumner, to weaken slavery and achieve a measure of equality for all blacks, proposing bills to abolish slavery in the District of Columbia and in the territories. Yet he staunchly defended Lincoln's hesitancy to move more rapidly against slavery, as long as the president continued to move in what Lovejoy considered to be the right direction. Disagreeing with Radicals like Stevens and Sumner, Lovejoy advocated a more lenient Reconstruction of the South. In 1862 he played a major role in the passage of a homestead act and the Pacific Railroad Bill, authorizing the building of the first transcontinental railroad. He gloried in Lincoln's Emancipation Proclamation of 1 January 1863 but did not live to see the enactment of the Thirteenth Amendment, abolishing slavery throughout the Union, in 1865.

When Lovejoy died in Brooklyn of Bright's disease, Lincoln eulogized him as "the *best* friend I had in Congress" (Francis B. Carpenter to Mrs. Owen Lovejoy, 18 May 1865, Owen Lovejoy Collection, Bureau County Historical Society). Lovejoy's significance was as a staunch opponent of slavery and supporter of the rights of African Americans. A close colleague of Lincoln, his support of the president was critical in the successful prosecution of the war.

• Lovejoy's papers are in the Bureau County Historical Society, Princeton, Ill. and the William L. Clements Library at the University of Michigan. His speeches are in the *Congressional Globe*, 35th–38th Congs. (1857–1864); and in the *Bureau County* (Ill.) *Republican*. With his brother Joseph Lovejoy, he wrote *Memoir of the Rev. Elijah P. Lovejoy; Who Was Murdered in Defence of the Liberty of the Press at Alton, Illinois, Nov. 7, 1837* (1838). A modern biography is Edward Magdol's laudatory *Owen Lovejoy: Abolitionist in Congress* (1967). Other studies of significance include Ruth E. Haberkorn, "Owen Lovejoy in Princeton, Illinois," *Journal of the Illinois State Historical Society* 36 (1943): 284–315; and Magdol, "Owen Lovejoy's Role in the Campaign of 1858," *Journal of the Illinois State Historical Society* 51 (1958): 403–16. Merton Dillon, *Elijah P. Lovejoy, Abolitionist Editor* (1961), is useful for Owen Lovejoy's early life, religious upbringing, and conversion to abolitionism.

FREDERICK J. BLUE

LOVEJOY, Owen Reed (9 Sept. 1866–29 June 1961), social worker and reformer, was born in Jamestown, Michigan, near Grand Rapids, the son of Hiram Reed Lovejoy and Harriett Helen Robinson. His parents' occupations are not known. He obtained a B.A. at Albion College in 1891 and married Jennie Evalyn Campbell the following year. They had five children, of whom only two survived to adulthood. Lovejoy became a Methodist minister, serving in a number of Michigan communities while also earning an M.A. from Albion in 1894.

In 1898 Lovejoy moved to a pastorate at the First Congregational Church of Mount Vernon, New York. While there he helped organize a Sociological Club, which invited leading authorities to speak on social and industrial questions of the day. When, at the request of a Mount Vernon community group, he visited the anthracite coal district of Pennsylvania during the 1902 strike, Lovejoy was shocked at the conditions of the workers' lives, and he galvanized others with his dramatic descriptions of what he had seen. The issue of child labor was drawing increasing attention during these years, and in 1904 a group of leading reformers organized the National Child Labor Committee (NCLC). That summer the NCLC commissioned Lovejoy to return to the Pennsylvania coalfields and survey the condition of child workers there. Once again, Lovejoy's sympathies were deeply stirred, especially by the children whom he saw toiling all day in the dark. He wrote later, "Sights like those cling to you. I dreamed about those boys."

When Lovejoy was offered a full-time position with the NCLC in October 1904, he left the ministry and embarked on the career that would engross him for the rest of his life. His initial assignment was to serve as one of the committee's two field representatives, covering the northern half of the country. In 1907 a debate broke out over the respective merits of working at the state level versus pushing for national child labor laws. When those arguing for state action prevailed, the NCLC secretary (who had backed the minority position) resigned, and Lovejoy replaced him. Convinced that work at the federal level would only antagonize the southern states, he wrote to a committee member, "My own feeling is that the less said about this matter of our relation to Federal regulation, the better."

Over the next several years, Lovejoy began to change his mind. There were complaints, for instance, that the NCLC's representative in the southern states had needlessly alienated local leaders; after investigating, Lovejoy concluded that accepting local manufacturers' dictates for the pace of change would mean no change at all. In addition, a multivolume report from the U.S. Bureau of Labor (1910–1913) provided ample documentation of child labor problems nationwide, and particularly in the South. Many states had passed child labor laws of some kind, but they were weakened by numerous loopholes and erratic enforcement. In addition, the hundreds of thousands of children working in agriculture, domestic service, street trades, and sweatshops remained unprotected. Reviewing a decade's effort in 1914, Lovejoy reported, "We have been disillusioned. More has been done than seemed possible within the period, but the field is immensely larger than was supposed." Concluding that working at the state level was not sufficient, the NCLC now joined the U.S. Children's Bureau in a campaign for federal child labor legislation. They succeeded in winning passage of the Keating-Owen Act in 1916, but, as Lovejoy observed, it covered less than 10 percent of the nation's working children. Even the limited progress represented by this law was reversed: in 1918 it was found unconstitutional, and two years later a proposed constitutional amendment went down to defeat. In 1924 an amendment passed Congress but failed to win ratification from the states.

Besides battling against child labor, Lovejoy spent these years crusading for many other reforms. A dynamic speaker and ardent advocate, he visited Lawrence, Massachusetts, during the 1912 textile workers' strike and spoke passionately on the workers' behalf. He was also an active member of the National Conference of Charities and Corrections, writing many papers for its meetings and chairing its Committee on Standards of Living and Labor, which worked for several years to develop a "platform of social standards." The economic and labor platform adopted by Theodore Roosevelt's Progressive party in 1912 was virtually identical with that recommended by Lovejoy's com-

mittee, although no direct connection has been documented. Lovejoy was elected president of the National Conference in 1920; however, because he had recently expressed sympathy for socialist Eugene V. Debs, his selection evoked the organization's first recorded protest to a nomination. Lovejoy also helped organize the American Association of Social Workers in 1921 and served as its second president.

By the mid-1920s, with the ultimately unsuccessful battle to ratify the child labor amendment still under way, Lovejoy resigned as director of the NCLC. He then became secretary of the Children's Aid Society of New York (1927–1935); he also remained on the NCLC board of trustees. In 1935 he became associate director of the American Youth Commission, an agency established by the American Council on Education; his field reports on the commission's work in Maryland, Indiana, and Texas won a wide readership in the profession.

Lovejoy's wife had died in 1929. In 1937 he married Kate Calkins Drake. After his retirement in 1939 they moved to a farm in Biglerville, Pennsylvania, where he died.

Lovejoy spearheaded the drive that pushed through child labor legislation in nearly every state, and though he himself was frustrated with the pace of progress, the efforts made by him and his allies did significantly help to reduce the level of child labor throughout the country. He built a strong staff of investigators, lobbyists, and volunteers, and he pioneered methods of public education—investigation by experts, photography, pamphlets, and mass mailings—that would be used by social advocates for generations thereafter. Lovejoy was, according to historian Frank J. Bruno "one of the unsung heroes of social work; a man who combined a singular purity of religious devotion with a loyalty to liberal philosophy."

• The NCLC Papers, in the Manuscript Division of the Library of Congress, include much information by and about Lovejoy. See also the committee's annual reports and other publications, including its periodicals *Child Labor Bulletin* and *American Child*. For material on Lovejoy's career, see Robert H. Bremner, ed., *Children and Youth in America: A Documentary History*, vol. 2 (1971); Frank J. Bruno, *Trends in Social Work, 1874–1956* (1957); Elizabeth Davidson, *Child Labor Legislation in the Southern Textile States* (1939); "The New Child Labor Secretary," *Charities and the Commons*, 2 Nov. 1907, pp. 951–52; *Survey* (July 1939); and Walter I. Trattner, *Crusade for the Children* (1970). An obituary is in the *New York Times*, 30 June 1961.

SANDRA OPDYCKE

LOVELACE, Francis (1618?–10 May 1683 or 1686), second royal governor of New York, was born in Hurley, Berkshire, England, the son of Sir William Lovelace, an army officer and member of Parliament, and Lady Anne Barne. An ardent royalist, he was a colonel in the forces of Charles I during the English civil wars. In 1644 he was appointed by the king to serve as governor of Carmarthen Castle in Wales. A year later he was compelled to surrender the castle to a Parliamentary army after losing his brother, William Lovelace, in the fighting. Thereafter he served for a time as a soldier in the armies of Louis XIV in France.

In 1650 Lovelace was permitted by Oliver Cromwell to join his sister Anne Gorsuch in Virginia. Two years later he joined Charles II as an exile in France, conveying information to the king about political conditions in the colonies. He returned to England in 1658 and rejoined the royalists in battling Parliamentary forces. In about 1659 he was married in secret to Blanche Talbot; they had two children. He was arrested by the Parliamentarians on 5 August 1659 and confined in the Tower of London but was released a year later when Charles II was restored to the throne. In the early 1660s Lovelace became a favorite of the king's brother, the duke of York, and on the strength of this connection the duke appointed him deputy governor of Long Island in either 1664 or 1665. In April 1667 he was appointed governor of New York, succeeding Richard Nicolls. Samuel Maverick, an eccentric New Englander whose bitter criticism of Puritan Massachusetts had earned him the respect of English royalists, recommended Lovelace to the earl of Clarendon, the king's first minister, for the position, declaring that Lovelace was "a pson euery way accomplished for such an Imploy and very well beloued in all those pts." On 13 June 1667 the king also commissioned Lovelace as the lieutenant colonel of a regiment of troops raised by Colonel Sir Walter Vane.

Lovelace arrived in New York in March 1668, and although Nicolls remained in the colony until August to instruct him in the intricacies of the office of governor, he immediately assumed full control. His difficult and complex assignment was to harmonize the interests of the Dutch, Swedish, and English populations of his colony with English authority. Instructed by the duke of York to continue all policies in effect when he took office, he acted with restraint so as not to exceed his mandate. His accomplishments were many. He was tolerant in religious matters, guaranteeing New Yorkers "liberty of conscience to all, provided they raise not fundamentalls." He paid more attention to his council than had his predecessor, holding regular meetings of his advisers to sound public opinion in the colony. New York prospered under Lovelace because of his emphasis on the development of better transportation facilities on land and water, the laying out of new towns, and the establishment of a merchants' exchange. He also started a regular postal service between New York and Boston and bought all Indian lands on Staten Island. He took a genuine interest in the Indians of his colony, attempting to convert them to Christianity by sending out missionaries. He saw to the defense of New York by establishing militia companies of infantry and cavalry and by improving the town's fortifications.

Although Lovelace was successful in many areas of his administration, he was not entirely so. He was vexed by Indian problems on his frontiers and on one occasion was compelled to send the garrison of New York to Esopus to ward off an Indian threat. He also was involved in boundary squabbles with neighboring colonies, a political rebellion in New Jersey in 1672, continuing cultural and religious tensions between the diverse nationalities in his own colony, and the perpetual danger of a Dutch invasion. Moreover, New Yorkers resented the taxes he imposed to pay for new military programs and were particularly outraged when in 1672 he ordered that a petition from some Long Islanders against the levies be publicly burned. Finally, he was politically high-handed, even though he called regular council meetings. He had a penchant for ignoring the colonists' advice, and he refused their demands for a popular assembly. His failure to heed the wishes of the Dutch residents hastened the collapse of his administration. War broke out between England and Holland on 10 March 1672, and while Lovelace was in New Haven, Connecticut, in July 1673, a hostile Dutch fleet sailed into New York harbor and demanded the surrender of Fort James. The Dutch inhabitants, rather than resisting, either cooperated by arming themselves to support the invaders or remained neutral. Surrendering the fort after only a brief exchange of cannon fire with the fleet, they renamed the colony New Netherlands and the city New Orange. Lovelace, while hastening back to New York, was arrested on Long Island and on 30 July 1673 was sent back to England. The colony was restored to English rule by the Treaty of Westminster, 19 February 1674.

Although the loss of New York was beyond Lovelace's ability to avoid, he was ruined both financially and politically by the debacle. He lost all of his property in New York to the Dutch, and later to creditors, and in England his erstwhile friend, the duke of York, seized Lovelace's estate as compensation for money owed to him. Other English creditors also sued Lovelace for the collection of unpaid debts, and he was enmeshed in court proceedings for many years thereafter. On 2 and 9 March 1674 he was questioned by the Privy Council at the Cockpit in Whitehall regarding the loss of New York. Although his interlocutors found his answers unsatisfactory, the Crown took no further actions against him at the time. Later that year he was captured by Algerians while traveling on the Mediterranean Sea and robbed of all his money and jewels. After being ransomed, he returned to England, only to be thrown into the Tower of London by the king for several months. Finally released, he retired to Woodstock, Oxfordshire, England, where he died.

• Lovelace's official correspondence is in the Colonial Office Papers, Public Record Office, Kew, Surrey, England. Printed materials are in Edward B. O'Callaghan, ed., *Documentary History of the State of New York*, vol. 1 (1849); O'Callaghan and Berthold Fernow, eds., *Documents Relative to the Colonial History of the State of New York*, vol. 2 (1858), and vols. 3–4, 9 (1854–1855); *The Colden Letters on Smith's History*, New-York Historical Society, *Collections*, 1868 (1869); *The Clarendon Papers*, New-York Historical Society, *Collections*, 1869 (1870); and Fernow, ed., *Records of New Amsterdam*, vols. 6–7 (1897). Proceedings of Lovelace's councils are in Victor H. Paltsits, ed., *Minutes of the Executive Council of the*

Province of New York: Administration of Francis Lovelace, 1668–1673 (2 vols., 1910). Other primary information is in Historical Manuscripts Commission, *The MSS. of H. S. Le Fleming, Esq., of Rydal Hall*, 12th report, app., pt. 7 (1890). Biographical and genealogical sketches are Elizabeth Doremus, *Lovelace Chart* (1900?); Edward C. Delavan, *Colonel Francis Lovelace and His Plantation on Staten Island* (1902); J. Hall Pleasants, "Francis Lovelace, Governor of New York, 1668–1673," *New York Genealogical and Biographical Record* 51 (1920): 175–94; and Florance Loveless Keeney Robertson, *The Lovelace-Loveless and Allied Families* (1952). His governorship is described in John R. Brodhead, *History of the State of New York*, vol. 2 (1871); Benson J. Lossing, *History of New York City*, vol. 1 (1884); Ellis H. Roberts, *New York: The Planting and the Growth of the Empire State*, vol. 1 (1892); Jacqueline Overton, *Long Island's Story* (1929); and Rodman Gilder, *The Battery* (1936).

PAUL DAVID NELSON

LOVELACE, William Randolph, II (30 Dec. 1907–12 Dec. 1965), surgeon and scientist in aviation and space medicine, was born in Springfield, Missouri, the son of Edgar Blaine Lovelace, a rancher, and Jewell Costley. Randolph was raised north of Sunnyside, New Mexico, where his father homesteaded. In September 1925 Lovelace entered Washington University in St. Louis, Missouri. After a poor performance in his freshman year, his outlook improved the next year, and in 1930 he completed a B.A. with a premedicine major, allowing his entrance into Washington University Medical School.

As an undergraduate, Lovelace had joined the U.S. Navy Reserve Officer Training Corps. Attending Great Lake's Naval Training Station, Illinois, in 1928, he received his pilot's license. Lovelace's passion for flight would dominate much of his career.

Restless, Lovelace transferred to medical schools at Cornell University in 1932, and then, Harvard University in September 1933. That same year he married Mary Easter Moulton; they had five children. Receiving an M.D. from Harvard in October 1934, he promptly entered a medical internship at Bellevue Hospital in New York City. A visit to the Mayo Clinic in Rochester, Minnesota, in 1935 made Lovelace eager to enter the Mayo Foundation for Medical Education and Research, a graduate program then affiliated with University of Minnesota. About a year later, he received a Mayo fellowship in surgery to start in July 1936.

At Mayo, Lovelace blossomed professionally. Besides receiving training in surgery, he worked with Dr. Walter M. Boothby, reviewing Boothby's studies of anoxia—the lack of oxygen in human tissues—and oxygen administration in Mayo's metabolism laboratory. After Northwest Airlines officials approached Boothby and Dr. Charles W. Mayo about an economical oxygen-delivery system for high-altitude flying, Boothby, aided by Lovelace and dentist Arthur H. Bulbulian, produced an oxygen mask, dubbed "B.L.B." after its originators. First reported in 1938, the B.L.B. mask proved effective in medicine and in aviation, especially in its World War II applications.

As a major contributor, Lovelace found his aviation medicine interests greatly stimulated. In 1940 President Franklin D. Roosevelt presented Boothby, Lovelace, and U.S. Army captain Harry G. Armstrong with the National Aeronautics Association's Collier Trophy, recognizing the mask's contributions to aviation safety.

Lovelace took a brief leave from his Mayo fellowship in early 1937, for flight surgeon training at the School of Aviation Medicine in Randolph Field, Texas. A recipient of Mayo's J. William White Scholarship in 1939, he spent three months visiting centers in surgery and aviation medicine in nine European countries, including Germany. Also in 1939 he received an M.S. in surgery from the University of Minnesota for his Mayo work. Lovelace then served at Mayo as first assistant in surgery, 1939–1940; assistant surgeon, 1940–1941; and staff surgeon and head of a section of surgery, from 1941 to 1946.

During World War II Lovelace went on leave to serve in the U.S. Army. Called to duty in February 1942 as a major in the Air Surgeon's Office, Washington, D.C., he moved in April to the Aero Medical Laboratory, Wright Field, Ohio, as chief of the Service Liaison Branch, and then, chief of the Oxygen Branch. Promoted to lieutenant colonel in early 1943, he made a record-breaking 40,200-foot parachute jump to test oxygen equipment on 24 June 1943. He was laboratory chief from September 1943 to December 1945, and became a colonel in 1944. Honored with the Distinguished Flying Cross (1943), he was also commended for his trips to European, Pacific, and Alaskan theaters of war to collect aviation medicine data firsthand. While supervising a research staff of several hundred, he helped assemble basic data and develop equipment to meet jet-aircraft flight stresses.

In March 1946 Lovelace returned to Mayo and shortly thereafter experienced two tragic events. The death in July of his five-year-old son of polio was followed in August by the death of his four-year-old son. Numbed, Lovelace and his family nevertheless remained in Albuquerque, where he decided to become a partner with his uncle William R. Lovelace I and Edgar T. Lassetter in the Lovelace Clinic. In September 1947 he helped establish the Lovelace Foundation for Medical Education and Research, a nonprofit corporation patterned after the Mayo Foundation, and reorganized the clinic into a voluntary association of physicians under a board of governors. Until his death he served on the clinic board and on the foundation's board of trustees, becoming clinic cochair in 1960 and foundation president in 1963. He was also director of the foundation. In addition, he was president after 1963. Throughout the 1950s Lovelace maintained a heavy surgical schedule and held several hospital staff appointments in Albuquerque and Los Alamos.

Lovelace's service to his country continued to grow, as he became a consultant, member, or chair of numerous advisory bodies dealing with aviation medicine, including the North Atlantic Treaty Organization from 1952 to 1964. In 1961 he became brigadier general in the U.S. Air Force Reserve, assigned to bioastronautics. He was prominent in the medical aspects of the U.S. space program and helped develop new methods of physical evaluation and biological monitoring for Mercury astronaut selection. Calling Lovelace "a true twentieth-century pioneer," President Lyndon B. Johnson named him director of space medicine of the National Aeronautics and Space Administration in 1964.

Over the course of his career, Lovelace held some twenty-two foundation and organization positions and some thirty-three association memberships. At home and abroad he received many recognitions of his aviation contributions. He prepared roughly ninety papers and articles, primarily on surgery of the neck and abdomen as well as oxygen therapy and aerospace medicine. He and his wife died in an airplane accident near Aspen, Colorado.

• The Lovelace collection of clippings and articles is in Lassetter-Foster Memorial Library, Lovelace Medical Center, Albuquerque, N.M. Among the important Lovelace publications are "Oxygen for Therapy and Aviation: An Apparatus for the Administration of Oxygen or Oxygen and Helium by Inhalation," *Proceedings of the Staff Meetings of the Mayo Clinic* 13 (1938): 646–54; "Oxygen in Aviation," *Journal of Aviation Medicine* 9 (1938): 172–98 (with W. M. Boothby); "Oxygen Therapy and Its Practical Use with Troops on Active Service," *Transactions, Tenth International Congress on Military Medicine and Pharmacy* 1 (1939): 319–63 (with C. K. Berle); "Biomedical Aspects of Orbital Flight," with A. S. Crossfield, in *Physics and Medicine of the Atmosphere and Space*, ed. O. O. Benson and H. Strughold (1960), pp. 447–63; "Human Factors in Space Exploration," *Advances in Ballistic Missile and Space Technology* 1 (1960): 38–48. The most complete assessment of Lovelace's life and work is Richard G. Elliott, "On a Comet Always," *New Mexico Quarterly* (1966): 351–87. An obituary is in the *New York Times*, 16 Dec. 1965.

CLARK W. NELSON

LOVELL, James (31 Oct. 1737–14 July 1814), revolutionary congressman, was born in Boston, Massachusetts, the son of John Lovell, the head of South Grammar School, and Abigail Green. His father, reportedly a stern, demanding but not unhumorous educator, supervised his son's formal training. From fairly comfortable if not affluent environs, James gravitated to the educated circles of the provincial urban society. He graduated from Harvard in 1756 and pursued a year's postgraduate studies in the classics. In 1757 he joined his father, the Latin School master, as an usher. For the next sixteen years they taught together until escalating hostilities in Boston closed the school. Meanwhile he moved in the city's social circles, dabbled in commercial affairs, tried his hand at farming, and invested his energies promoting the economic growth of the Boston area. As had his father, James gained public attention as an orator, first in 1760 for his eulogy of a revered Harvard tutor. In the same year he married Mary Middleton; they had nine children who survived to adulthood.

Between 1760 and 1775 James Lovell shared the sentiments of emerging Boston radicals such as the cousins John Adams (1735–1826) and Samuel Adams, Josiah Quincy, and James Warren. In 1771 the Boston town committee nominated Lovell to a position of high profile, choosing him to deliver the oration at the first anniversary of the Boston Massacre. Though his father, increasingly identified as a Loyalist, objected, he made the speech on 2 April 1771 to a crowd that had adjourned from Faneuil Hall to the larger Old South Church. Lovell's ringing rhetoric not only stimulated the local Sons of Liberty, but his words were widely distributed in published form.

By the time military hostilities superseded journalistic jousts and oratorical contests, Lovell had come to believe firmly that American rights must be defended at all costs. Delicate health kept him from enlisting in militia drills; a large family kept him rooted to Boston. Following the battle of Bunker Hill, the British discovered Lovell's accurate estimates of their troop strength on a paper found on the corpse of Joseph Warren. They arrested him on 27 June 1775 and detained him in Provost's Prison, where he suffered through the summer. The British refused to release Lovell or to bring him to trial. When they evacuated Boston, he was carted along to Halifax, Nova Scotia. There he shared a cell with a notable colleague, Ethan Allen. Ironically, his father, John Lovell, had fled to Halifax in the Tory exodus. In the fall of 1776 Generals George Washington and William Howe agreed to exchange Lovell for Philip Skene, the prominent New York Loyalist. On 3 November Lovell was set free, in New York, after a sixteen-month captivity. His patriotic fervor had not slackened.

While Lovell was traveling home to Boston the Massachusetts legislature elected him one of seven delegates to the Continental Congress. He accepted the call, forsaking his private affairs and family life. In the company of John Adams, Lovell journeyed to Congress in January 1777. He first attended on 4 February and thus began five years of continuous service, a record unmatched in the revolutionary legislature of the fledgling nation. Lovell's scholarly care for detail, his diligence, and most especially his fluency in French made him a prime candidate for key committee assignments. He was also a prime recruit for the more radical faction, formed behind Samuel Adams of Massachusetts and Richard Henry Lee of Virginia, early advocates of independence from Britain who sought to render reconciliation impossible.

As a congressional workhorse Lovell often functioned in a quasi-administrative capacity. Three specific areas beckoned. First he acted as a buffer among numerous French officers who appeared brandishing commissions from Silas Deane, congressional envoy to France, for high rank in the Continental army. Often brusquely Lovell deflated these aspirations. He was suspicious of foreign assistance, whether voluntary or not, as he believed patriotic virtue sufficient to sustain the revolutionary cause. Moreover he became the avid opponent, in 1778–1780, of the faction that supported

Deane, who had dispatched the Frenchmen and war material to America. Second, as an avid republican, Lovell persisted in readying the *Journals of the Congress* for publication. Third, as the most regular member of the Committee for Foreign Affairs, Lovell accepted incoming mail from the revolutionary "militia diplomats" scattered throughout Europe. More frequently he diligently dispatched official and personal correspondence to these envoys. He is credited with creation of ciphers for encoding official dispatches. An early partisan of Arthur Lee and John Adams, he was suspicious of Benjamin Franklin (1706–1790). After initial hesitation he came to admire the independence of John Jay. Known for his sarcasm and wit, Lovell often found himself at the center of factional disputes, such as the "Conway Cabal," the 1777 effort to replace Washington with Horatio Gates. Lovell was not so much a critic of Washington as he was adamant to reorganize the Continental army, do battle with the British, and elevate Gates. Lovell's gallant correspondence with Abigail Adams caused some contemporary commentary and later historical debates. After 1780 Lovell altered his regionally centered voting pattern as the war moved south and the nation's precarious finances worried Congress. While he served the interests of his home state—demanding access to Canadian fisheries be incorporated in peace treaties—he increasingly voted for national programs, such as the impost.

In January 1782 Lovell took a leave of absence to return home, amid some unsavory rumors. A New York Loyalist publisher printed an intercepted letter to Abigail Adams in the *Royal Gazette* in December 1781. This labeled Lovell "a telltale Scoundrel" and broadly hinted that Lovell was having an extramarital affair with his landlady in Philadelphia. Lovell then returned to Boston to his wife Mary and family; he decided personal affairs took precedence over congressional service. Robert Morris appointed him receiver of continental taxes in Massachusetts. In the postwar era he served as naval officer for the port of Boston and Charlestown under the Federalists and Republican-Democrats alike. His latter years proved more tranquil than his early career. He died in Windham, Maine, during a visit to relatives.

In late 1776 John Adams had described Lovell as "A Man of Spirit, Fortitude, and Patience, three Virtues the most useful of any in these times. And besides these he has Taste, Sense, and Learning." Lovell was indeed a useful public servant. The resistance movement in Boston pulled him out of the classroom into public demonstrations. He was caught up in, and contributed to, the drive to assert independence. During remarkable congressional service he sustained these drives for a virtuous citizenry and a republic free from foreign entanglements. His personal and public correspondence exhibit the sacrifices he made for these causes.

• Lovell's manuscripts are scattered among the collections of his correspondents. The microfilm publication of the Papers of the Continental Congress, Record Group 360, by the National Archives, through a thorough index, charts Lovell's sustained contributions. His letters on foreign affairs are found in Francis Wharton, ed., *The Revolutionary Diplomatic Correspondence of the United States* (1889). His political career and voting record are analyzed in Helen Frances Jones, "James Lovell in the Continental Congress 1777–1782" (Ph.D. diss., Columbia Univ., 1968). A well-focused essay is provided by Edith B. Gelles, "A Virtuous Affair: The Correspondence between Abigail Adams and James Lovell," *American Quarterly* 39 (Summer 1987): 252–69. Clifford K. Shipton, *Sibley's Harvard Graduates*, vol. 14 (1968), pp. 31–47, offers a general sketch of his life.

LOUIS W. POTTS

LOVELL, John (1 Apr. 1710–1778), educator, was born in Boston, Massachusetts, the son of John Lovell and Priscilla Gardiner. He entered the public Latin School in 1717 and was graduated from Harvard College in 1728. He became an usher of the Latin School in 1729 and was appointed its master in 1734. In 1734 or 1735 he married Abigail Green; they had two children.

Lovell instructed many students who later were to play prominent roles in the American Revolution and early republic, including Samuel Adams, James Bowdoin, Andrew Oliver, John Hancock, Henry Knox, Christopher Gore, and Harrison Gray Otis. Children entered the Latin School at seven years of age, and for the next seven years Lovell, a rigid disciplinarian, put them through a lengthy and demanding training. A pupil was expected to gain a mastery of Greek and Latin through reading the best writers in those tongues. Harrison Gray Otis remembered Master Lovell's instrument of punishment, the ferule. It "was a short, stubbed, greasy-looking article, which when not in use, served him as a stick of sugar candy. The lightest punishment was one clap, the severest four—the most usual two, one on each hand. The inflictions of the old gentleman were not much dreaded."

Lovell also demonstrated his involvement in the cultural life of Boston. He won renown as "a pleasing and elegant writer" for contributions to the *Weekly Rehearsal* (1731–1735). He delivered the first published address in Faneuil Hall, *A Funeral Oration Delivered at the Opening of the Annual Meeting of the Town, March 14th, 1742* (1743), occasioned by the death of the hall's donor, Peter Faneuil. Lovell hoped that "this hall may be ever sacred to the interests of truth, of justice, of loyalty, of honor, of liberty." He added, "And may loyalty to a king, under whom we enjoy this liberty, ever remain our character!" Lovell also contributed poetry to the *Pietas et Gratulatio Colleqii Cantabriqiensis apud Novamgios* (1761) and wrote *The Seasons, an Interlocutory Exercise at the South Latin School* (1765). Lovell was a member of the French Club, a group of prominent Bostonians who met periodically to converse in French.

On 19 April 1775 Lovell dismissed school by saying, "War's begun—school's done." His sympathies were with the British. In March 1776 he went to Halifax, Nova Scotia, where he lived until his death there. According to Henry F. Jenks, for nearly forty-two years Lovell had discharged the duties of master "with great skill and fidelity." He was schoolmaster to the revolutionary generation.

• Though no collection of papers or full-length biography is available, a valuable historical sketch appears in James Spear Loring, *The Hundred Boston Orators* (1852). Other sources of information include Henry F. Jenks, *Catalogue of the Boston Public Latin School* (1886), Robert Francis Seybolt, *The Public Schools of Colonial Boston, 1635–1775* (1935), and Justin Winsor, *The Memorial History of Boston* (1881). On the French Club, see *The Diary and Letters of His Excellency Thomas Hutchinson*, ed. Peter Orlando Hutchinson (1883), and *Letters and Diary of John Rowe*, ed. Anne Rowe Cunningham (1903). Lovell wrote *Freedom, the First of Blessings* (1754) about the Massachusetts Excise Bill. Typical of the biographies on Lovell's students are Samuel Eliot Morison, *Harrison Gray Otis, 1765–1848* (1969), and Helen R. Pinkney, *Christopher Gore, Federalist of Massachusetts, 1758–1827* (1969).

JACOB L. SUSSKIND

LOVELL, Joseph (22 Dec. 1788–17 Oct. 1836), military surgeon, was born in Boston, Massachusetts, the son of James S. Lovell and Deborah Gorham. He received the A.B. degree from Harvard College in 1807 and, after studying medicine as an apprentice to a local physician, received the M.D. degree in 1811, ranking first in the first class to graduate from the Harvard Medical School.

On 15 May 1812 Lovell joined the U.S. Army as surgeon to the Ninth Infantry Regiment, with which he served on the Niagara frontier. By the end of 1812 he was in charge of a newly established general hospital at Burlington, Vermont, a well-regarded facility that served the men of all units in the area rather than exclusively those of the Ninth Infantry. Subsequently he set up another general hospital at Williamsville, New York. After the end of the war in 1815, he was named chief medical officer of the Northern Department. He served with such success that in the spring of 1818, when Congress created a permanent medical department for the U.S. Army, President James Madison named Lovell to serve as its first surgeon general.

As head of the new organization, Lovell faced a formidable task. He needed not only to design and establish an entirely new organization but also to obtain the support of Congress, his military superiors, and the men who served under him. In creating regulations to guide the operations of the medical department, he successfully ignored Congress's plans, which would have created an organization so rigid that it would not be able to staff the larger general hospitals that a war might make necessary. Within a few years he had gained the legislature's tacit acknowledgement of his ability to deal with the assignments of army surgeons without its guidance. Despite his constant struggles to have more surgeons in his department, he was never able to persuade Congress to grant him a department of sufficient size to provide adequate medical care for all of the army posts scattered about the growing nation.

Lovell's concerns were scientific as well as administrative, and from the outset of his tenure as surgeon general he concerned himself with finding ways to improve the health of the nation's soldiers. Believing that humans were essentially herbivorous, he urged the army to provide less meat and more bread and to supplement the diet with vegetables. He deplored the way soldiers cooked their food and the amount of alcohol provided to them, urging that beer and molasses mixed with water be substituted for hard liquor.

Although Lovell apparently had little time as surgeon general for scientific research, he encouraged such efforts among his subordinates. In an attempt to discover the relationship between health and meteorological factors, he required his subordinates to submit regular reports concerning the diseases and the weather and climate that they encountered at the posts to which they had been sent, and to include data on the flora, fauna, and geological characteristics of the area as well. Using the data they sent him, he initiated two series of publications, *Meteorological Registers* and *Statistical Reports*. With his encouragement, medical officers also began submitting data and specimens of the animals and plants they encountered to nongovernment organizations.

Most famous among the army physicians to profit from Lovell's support and encouragement was William Beaumont, who in 1822 began studying the digestive processes of a patient with an unhealed wound that permitted a direct view of his stomach. Lovell put Beaumont in contact with renowned scientists both in the United States and abroad and arranged the young surgeon's assignments so that they did not conflict with his scientific researches. Lovell claimed no credit for the work of his subordinates, however; when a journal mistakenly attached his name to an article written by Beaumont but submitted through Lovell, Lovell required the publishers to print a correction.

Lovell worked unceasingly to guarantee that the physicians who joined the medical department were of the highest caliber. His efforts included mandatory professional examinations put into effect in 1832 for all who sought to enter the department. He was not successful in obtaining higher salaries for those who met his high standards until 1834, after years of campaigning.

Lovell's insistence on being allowed flexibility in assigning posts to his surgeons bore fruit in 1832 during the Black Hawk War, when he was required to provide medical care for units called together to defeat members of the Sac and Fox tribes attempting to return to their homelands east of the Mississippi. He called some post surgeons back from leave and temporarily reassigned others. He assigned one to serve as medical director under Major General Winfield Scott, leaving the specific assignments of the others up to the commanders in the field. Ironically, however, the greatest challenge these men faced proved to be a terrifying pandemic of cholera.

The conflict with the Seminoles and their allies that came to be known as the Second Seminole War was not a year old when Lovell unexpectedly died in Washington, D.C., only a short time after the death of his wife, Margaret Mansfield (date of marriage unknown), leaving eleven children.

Lovell set a high standard for future surgeons general of the army. He was strong enough to deal effectively with the difficulties of establishing a new organization and making its members work as a team. His insistence on and encouragement of high standards of professional competence and moral character served as a valuable precedent. Yet he remained personally modest and unassuming, respected both for his accomplishments as an administrator and for his "undeviating kindness" toward his subordinates.

• Lovell published nothing of significance in the journals of his time, although the National Library of Medicine holds a few of Lovell's papers. The largest number of his letters form part of RG 112, the Records of the Office of the Surgeon General, held by the National Archives in Washington, D.C., most of them in Entry 2, the Surgeon General's Letterbooks. A few letters can also be found in the multivolume *Papers of John C. Calhoun*, ed. Robert L. Meriwether and W. Edwin Hemphill (1959–). Biographical information is available in James M. Phalen, *Chiefs of the Medical Department, United States Army, 1775–1940* (1940); James E. Pilcher, *Surgeon Generals of the Army of the United States of America* (1905); and Mary C. Gillett, *The Army Medical Department, 1818–1865* (1987). An obituary is in the *National Intelligencer*, 19 Oct. 1836.

MARY C. GILLETT

LOVELL, Mansfield (20 Oct. 1822–1 June 1884), soldier and civil engineer, was born in Washington, D.C., the son of Dr. Joseph Lovell, surgeon general of the U.S. Army from 1818 to 1836, and Margaret Mansfield. Having entered West Point at the age of sixteen, he graduated in 1842 and was assigned to the Fourth Artillery Regiment as a second lieutenant. During the Mexican War he was wounded at the battle of Monterrey (18–21 Sept. 1846) and in the storming of Mexico City (13–14 Sept. 1847), in the process winning promotion to first lieutenant and being brevetted captain for gallantry in action. In 1849 he married Emily Plympton, the daughter of an army officer. In 1854, tiring of garrison duty along the frontier, he resigned from the army to take a position with the Cooper & Hewitt's Iron Works in Trenton, New Jersey. In 1858 he moved to New York City, where he was at first superintendent of street improvement, then deputy street commissioner under another future Confederate general, Gustavus W. Smith. His own entry into the Confederate service came exceptionally, and in the eyes of some southerners suspiciously, late, not occurring until September 1861, five months after the Civil War began. Even so, because of his high reputation in the "old army," he was appointed a major general on 7 October 1861 and placed in command of "Department No. 1"—New Orleans, the South's largest city and main port.

It was a highly important assignment but also a virtually impossible one. In essence the defense of New Orleans depended on two forts situated near the mouth of the Mississippi River about seventy miles below the city. Should a powerful enemy fleet succeed in passing these forts without suffering crippling damage, it then would have New Orleans, which was unfortified and very vulnerable to bombardment, totally at its mercy. Fully aware of this fact, Lovell did all he could to strengthen the forts, to erect obstructions in the river, and to hasten the construction of two ironclad ships that would be more than a match for the wooden vessels of the northern navy. Through no fault of his, these efforts proved futile. On 24 April 1862 Union warships commanded by Captain David G. Farragut got by the forts with minimal damage, penetrated the obstructions, and forced the Confederates to destroy the still unfinished ironclads. The following day Lovell and his small garrison evacuated the city, whose mayor thereupon surrendered it to Farragut. Lovell had no rational alternative to giving up the city, and a court of inquiry subsequently exonerated him of blame for its loss. Nevertheless he was subjected to much criticism in the southern press, some of it accompanied by innuendos against his loyalty to the Confederacy.

Lovell received an opportunity to redeem his professional and personal reputation when he participated in an attempt on 3–4 October 1862 by Major General Earl Van Dorn's Confederate army to retake the strategic railroad junction of Corinth, Mississippi, from a Federal force headed by Major General William S. Rosecrans. Prior to the battle, in which he commanded one of Van Dorn's three infantry divisions, Lovell asserted, "If we cannot succeed we had better lay down our arms and go home," a statement probably inspired by an erroneous belief among the Confederates that they outnumbered Rosecrans's troops. After performing well during the first day's fighting, on the second day Lovell ignored orders from Van Dorn to storm the Union fortifications and thus contributed to the bloody repulse of the other two Confederate divisions. Evidently Lovell, contrary to his earlier optimism, had concluded that an assault could not succeed and would only result in useless losses, an appraisal that in all likelihood was correct. Still this could not and did not excuse his failure to obey orders, so he was soon relieved of his command and, to use military parlance, "put on the shelf" without any assignment. There he remained for most of the rest of the war, even though his friend, General Joseph E. Johnston, on whose staff he served as a volunteer aide, requested both before and during the Atlanta campaign of 1864 that Lovell be given command of a corps in the Army of Tennessee. Finally, on 23 March 1865 General Robert E. Lee, by then commander of the entire Confederate army, ordered him to report for an assignment, presumably under Johnston. However, Lee's surrender on 9 April 1865, followed a few weeks later by Johnston's, rendered this order meaningless.

Following the war, Lovell failed as a rice planter in Georgia and then returned to New York, where he engaged in surveying and civil engineering. In the latter field he served as an assistant to a West Point classmate of his, Major General John Newton of the Corps of Engineers, in removing obstructions to navigation in the East River at Hell Gate. Somewhat ironically in view of southern wartime suspicions of Lovell's loyalty to the Confederacy, Newton was a native of Virginia who remained loyal to the Union. On the other hand, it was appropriate that upon his death Lovell was buried in a New York cemetery, for he served that northern city more than he had been able to serve the South.

Lovell no doubt was highly intelligent. Yet it was this very intelligence that caused him to evacuate New Orleans and disobey orders at Corinth, acts that ruined his Civil War career, a career that can be summed up as a case of being in the wrong places at the wrong times.

• The War of the Rebellion: A Compilation of the Official Records of the Union and Confederate Armies (128 vols., 1880–1901) and the Official Records of the Union and Confederate Navies in the War of the Rebellion (30 vols., 1894–1922) contain the reports, correspondence, and other documents pertinent to Lovell's attempt to defend New Orleans and his participation in the battle of Corinth. These sources, however, should be supplemented with Clarence C. Buel and Robert U. Johnson, eds., Battles and Leaders of the Civil War, vol. 2 (4 vols., 1884–1888), regarding New Orleans, and with Albert Castel, General Sterling Price and the Civil War in the West (1968), regarding Corinth. The basic facts concerning Lovell's personal life and nonmilitary activities appear in Clement A. Evans, ed., Confederate Military History: Maryland and West Virginia (1899).

ALBERT CASTEL

LOVELL, Solomon (1 June 1732–9 Sept. 1801), revolutionary general, was born in Abington, Massachusetts, the son of David Lovell, a schoolmaster, and Mary Torrey. When Solomon was not quite two years old his father died, and he went to live in Weymouth with his wealthy grandfather, Captain Enoch Lovell. He received his early education in the local schools and privately from the Reverend William Smith, father of Abigail Smith Adams. After the death of his grandfather, the fourteen-year-old Solomon chose his stepfather, Lieutenant Samuel Kingman, as his guardian, and it was under Kingman's supervision that Solomon learned husbandry. By the time he was twenty-four, Lovell was a wealthy farmer in Weymouth, living on lands he had inherited from his grandfather.

Lovell's military career began during the French and Indian war when he served in the 1756 expedition against Crown Point, on Lake Champlain, as the first lieutenant of Captain Samuel Thaxter's company under Colonel Richard Gridley. After his tour of nine months, he returned to Weymouth where he lived as a farmer. He married Lydia Holbrook in 1758; they had one surviving child before his wife's death in 1761. In May of the following year he married Hannah Pittey (Petty), with whom he had seven children, three of whom survived childhood. Lovell was a prominent Weymouth resident, active throughout his life in local and colony affairs. From his first appointment in 1771, he served many years as representative to the General Court. In 1775 he was chosen as a member of the Weymouth Committee of Correspondence. He also served on various town committees and held local offices such as justice of the peace and selectman.

Lovell continued to serve in the militia, having become a major of the Second Suffolk regiment in 1771. On 7 February 1776, one month before his regiment was ordered to join the rebel force that seized Dorchester Heights (south of Boston), he was commissioned as a colonel. The following year, on 24 June 1777, he was promoted to brigadier general of the Suffolk County militia.

Lovell's first major military challenge was as field commander of about 1,200 Massachusetts militia at the battle of Rhode Island in the summer of 1778. This was a joint Franco-American effort to regain control of Rhode Island from the British, who had captured Newport in December 1776. Though the action ended in stalemate, Lovell and his brigade earned the praise of Major General John Sullivan for their bravery and distinguished service.

The climax of his military career came the following year with his command of the land forces in the Penobscot expedition. On 17 June the British landed about 700 men under General Francis McLean on the peninsula of Bagaduce (now Castine) in Penobscot Bay, Maine (then part of Massachusetts), and made immediate preparations for establishing a fort, which they called Fort George. In response, the Massachusetts General Court ordered the dispatch of an expeditionary force to expel them, appointing Lovell to command the land forces and Dudley Saltonstall, captain of the frigate Warren, to command the naval forces. Within a month they had assembled the largest amphibious operation of the Revolution with nineteen armed vessels, twenty transports, 2,000 sailors and about 1,000 militia at a cost of £1,739,174 sterling ($8,500,000 currency). But in spite of this superior naval power—the American vessels mounted 300 guns to the British 38 guns—the expedition failed as a result of numerous delays and lack of a unified command. From the time of their arrival at Bagaduce on 24 July, Lovell and Saltonstall could not agree on strategy. Lovell's plan was for the naval forces to seize the three British sloops in the harbor while the land forces simultaneously captured the fort. However Saltonstall insisted that he maintain only maximum-range fire until Lovell had taken the fort, and then he would order his fleet into the harbor to destroy the British sloops. Instead of the swift victory that should have been theirs (McLean later wrote that he was prepared to surrender after "one or two guns"), the Americans lost their advantage and ended up in a stalemate that lasted through the first two weeks of August. The delay proved to be disastrous, because it gave the British command at New York time to prepare a naval task force to relieve Fort George. The arrival of the British men-of-war at Bagaduce shattered the Massachusetts expedition. All the American ships were destroyed, and the soldiers, dispersed on shore, were left to find their own way home. On 14 August Lovell wrote in his journal that it was a "terrible Day . . . to see four Ships pursuing seventeen Sail of Armed Vessells . . . Transports on fire, Men of War blowing up . . . and as much confusion as can possibly be conceived."

The Massachusetts General Court appointed a committee to investigate the causes of the failed expedition. After interrogating more than thirty witnesses, the committee fixed the entire blame for the fiasco on Saltonstall, who had "discouraged any enterprises or offensive measure on the part of our fleet." Saltonstall was relieved of his command and expelled from the navy. Lovell retained command of the Suffolk militia for the remainder of the war and resigned his commission in 1782.

Not much is known about Lovell's personal life, and there is little information concerning his life after the revolutionary war. In 1795 his wife Hannah died, and he remained unmarried until his death in Weymouth. Although Lovell is remembered primarily for his participation in the disastrous Penobscot expedition, he was an able military strategist and courageous officer.

• A small collection of Lovell papers is in the Massachusetts Historical Society, Boston. His original journal is in the Weymouth Historical Society; it is published as Gilbert Nash, *The Original Journal of General Solomon Lovell, Kept during the Penobscot Expedition, 1779, with a Sketch of His Life*, Weymouth Historical Society, *Publications*, no. 1 (1881). Very little has been written about Lovell. Biographical information can be found in Chester B. Kevitt, *General Solomon Lovell and the Penobscot Expedition 1779* (1976), and George W. Chamberlain, *History of Weymouth Massachusetts in Four Volumes*, vol. 3, *Genealogy of Weymouth Families* (1923), p. 399. Accounts of the Penobscot expedition are contradictory regarding some of the details of the engagement (e.g., number of American vessels) but contain much information about Lovell's participation. See Jon M. Nielson, "Penobscot: From the Jaws of Victory—our Navy's Worst Defeat," *American Neptune* 37 (1977): 288–305; Henry I. Shaw, Jr., "Penobscot Assault: 1779," *Military Affairs* 17 (1953): 83–94; John E. Cayford, *The Penobscot Expedition* (1976); and the more popular Charles B. Flood, *Rise and Fight Again: Perilous Times along the Road to Independence* (1976), which contains the best bibliography.

BARBARA DEWOLFE

LOVEMAN, Amy (16 May 1881–11 Dec. 1955), editor and literary critic, was born in New York City, the daughter of Adolph P. Loveman, a cotton broker, and Adassa Heilprin. In 1901 she received an A.B. from Barnard College. Remaining in New York City, she worked as a volunteer in a settlement house and as a tutor, then assisted Louis Heilprin, her uncle, in editing and revising reference books. In 1915 she began working at the *New York Evening Post*, first as a researcher assisting another uncle, Gustav Pollak, on a book marking the fiftieth anniversary of the *Nation*, then as an assistant librarian and book reviewer.

In 1920 Loveman joined the staff of a new weekly literary supplement that Henry Seidel Canby, an English professor at Yale University, had been asked to start for the *Evening Post*. She worked as an associate

editor with Canby, William Rose Benét, and Christopher Morley to establish the *Literary Review* as a successful enterprise that was respected for its high standards and the quality of its essays and reviews. Canby later referred to Loveman as "one of the ablest, certainly the kindest, assuredly one of the most useful women in New York," who was "soon more knowledgeable about contemporary books and authors than anyone else in town" (*American Memoir*, pp. 271, 274). Loveman collaborated with the other editors on *Saturday Papers: Essays on Literature from the Literary Review* (1921), which included one of her essays, "The Masquerading Tract." In it, she faulted contemporary writing for having "acquired a propagandist turn, and . . . serving the ends of particular theses rather than of universal art" (pp. 79–80). She argued against special pleading in literature and invoked Matthew Arnold's view that criticism must be disinterested.

In 1924 the *Post*'s new owners decided to end the literary weekly, and former publisher Thomas W. Lamont and Time Inc. founders Henry Luce and Briton Hadden provided backing for Canby to continue it as the *Saturday Review of Literature*. It debuted on 2 August 1924, with Loveman as associate editor. In her more than thirty years under four editors at the magazine, she ably handled a wide range of tasks that included assigning reviews, writing hundreds of reviews and editorial essays, reading proofs, dummying pages, supervising the closing of each issue, and answering office mail.

Her reviews, which earned Loveman respect and influence in the literary world, reflected "basic critical values carefully developed out of a remarkable working knowledge of the best in literature," *Saturday Review* editor Norman Cousins wrote in a tribute to her ("Amy Loveman," p. 21). She stated her policy, and the magazine's, on reviewing in an editorial in the 25 July 1931 issue: "We believe the cardinal sin of a reviewer to be the exploitation of himself instead of interpretation of his subject . . . the mere display of his own erudition, for the advancement of personal peccadilloes or the waging of personal controversies." She was not reluctant to find fault with a book, and she adhered uncompromisingly to high standards of literary value. But her tone was never unkind, and she insisted on trying to see the book in terms of the author's intentions, assessing it fairly and avoiding overemphasis on startling elements. Loveman avoided placing herself, instead of the author and the book, in the spotlight. Colleagues noted that she enjoyed working with new writers and helping them get their work published. "Her advice was precise, crisp, practical, built on a solid foundation of reasonable explanation," Cousins wrote. "And underlying everything else was an almost epic kindness. This combination of incisiveness and kindness characterized her entire life" ("Amy Loveman," p. 31).

Until 1937 Loveman also wrote the "Clearing House" department of the magazine, answering readers' queries about books. In 1936 she edited *I'm Looking for a Book*, a compilation of items from that feature. She also collaborated on *Designed for Reading: Anthology Drawn from the Saturday Review of Literature* (1934). In 1950 Loveman took on the additional job of poetry editor after Benét died. Her energy, dependability, and willingness to assume responsibilities did much to make the magazine a success. Further, Loveman "set the tone and spirit" for the *Saturday Review*, Cousins wrote (*Present Tense*, p. 8).

In addition to her magazine duties, Loveman worked with the Book-of-the-Month Club from its beginning in 1926 until her death. Until 1951 she headed first the reading (or "sifting") department, then the editorial department of the club, supervising the screening of hundreds of books each month. Harry Scherman, founder of the club, recalled that thousands of books submitted by publishers for club consideration went to her first. She herself read thirty to fifty of them each month. In 1951 Loveman was named to the club's board of judges. Clifton Fadiman, a board member, described her as "a perceptive and sensitive literary critic" who "spoke with a deceptive softness that concealed a vein of iron." He cited her dissent in 1955 on Robert Ruark's *Something of Value*, in which she insisted that the novel's shockingly violent content required a *caveat emptor* to club members. Her minority report, published in the April 1955 issue of the club's newsletter, caused a furor.

In the early 1950s Loveman supervised the compiling of *Varied Harvest: A Miscellany of Writing by Barnard College Women*, published in 1953 as part of the bicentennial of Columbia University. She maintained a full working schedule of magazine and book club work until five days before her death in New York City. She had never married or had children.

After her death colleagues remembered Loveman for her personal qualities, including her thoughtfulness and capacity for friendship, as well as for her skills as an editor, writer, and critic. Cousins wrote that Loveman seemed "to all who knew her, to represent the optimum in human graciousness, generosity of spirit, and personal splendor" (*Present Tense*, p. 72). Many recalled her positive view of life and her lack of patience with cynicism or defeatism. Cousins wrote, "Her nobility was a universe; and to know it was to soar inside it. . . . There were peace and purpose in her life and incredible strength, and it gave nourishment to others" ("Amy Loveman," p. 31).

• The Amy Loveman Correspondence at Columbia University Libraries comprises items from 1933 to 1943. Her memoir of the Book-of-the-Month Club is in the Oral History Collection of Columbia University. Book-of-the-Month Club records are in the Manuscript Division, Library of Congress. Norman Cousins, "Amy Loveman," *Saturday Review*, 24 Dec. 1955, pp. 20–32 (repr. in *The Saturday Review Gallery*, ed. Jerome Beatty, Jr., et al. [1959]), and "The World of Amy Loveman," *Saturday Review*, 31 Dec. 1955, pp. 19–21, with articles by several associates, are fond tributes. See also Henry Seidel Canby, *American Memoir* (1947); Cousins, *Present Tense: An American Editor's Odyssey* (1967); Bennett Cerf, "Trade Winds," *Saturday Review*, 27 June 1942; and Clifton Fadiman, "The Most Exclusive Lunch in Town," and Jack Newcombe, "A Half-Century Quest for the Best of Books," both in *Special 50th Anniversary Supplement to the April 1976 BOMC News* (1976). Obituaries are in the *New York Times*, 12 Dec. 1955, and *Publishers Weekly*, 17 Dec. 1955.

RONALD S. MARMARELLI

LOVESTONE, Jay (24 Dec. 1898–8 Mar. 1990), political and international trade union figure, was born Jacob Leibstein in Czarist Russian Lithuania. His parents' names are unknown. In 1907 Lovestone migrated with his family to New York, where his father obtained a position as a cantor. While attending the City College of New York during World War I, Lovestone became active in the Socialist party and the leader of the college's socialist club. In the aftermath of the Russian Revolution, he emerged at City College as an ardent supporter of Lenin's concept of a revolutionary vanguard party.

In the postwar Red Scare period, Lovestone became an important figure in the new Communist party, which was initially splintered into competing groups and forced underground by government repression. As such he served as editor of the party's underground journal, *The Communist*, in 1921. He later maneuvered himself into the Executive Committee of the Communist International or Comintern, and became a major figure in the Communist Party, USA (CPUSA), majority faction led by General Secretary Charles Ruthenberg, the former president of the Ohio Federation of Labor.

Following Ruthenberg's death in 1927, Lovestone emerged as the most powerful organizational figure in the Communist party. He quickly carried out a general purge of American adherents of Leon Trotsky and fought factional wars to isolate the party's most prominent trade union figure, William Z. Foster, and all others who resisted him.

As he consolidated his power, Lovestone began to revise Marxist-Leninist theory concerning imperialism and revolution into a doctrine later called "American exceptionalism," which predicted a long period of capitalist expansion in the United States. Based on this analysis, Lovestone called for Communists to advance nonrevolutionary policies in the labor movement and society at large.

When these positions produced major opposition within the ranks of U.S. Communists and were repudiated by the Comintern at its Sixth Congress in 1928, Lovestone and his loyal group of followers were defeated and expelled from the CPUSA in 1929. As the conflict developed, Lovestone flew to Moscow and made an unsuccessful attempt to get Soviet leader Joseph Stalin to intervene on his behalf. Called "the American Stalin" by many of his supporters, Lovestone accused Stalin of holding him captive in Moscow at the same time he privately told his supporters to prepare to seize Communist party buildings and assets in New York when he gave them the signal from Moscow.

Lovestone and his supporters, still considering themselves Communists, then spent the depression decade seeking unsuccessfully to win hegemony from the CPUSA in the labor and general radical movements. Called throughout this period "Lovestoneites," they formed an opposition group, the Communist Party (Majority), at the beginning of the depression, seeing themselves as the heirs of the Russian Bolsheviks, taking the name "majority" to distinguish themselves from their opponents. Later known more widely as the Communist Party Opposition, the Lovestoneites published the Marxist journal *Revolutionary Age*, sought influence in the Socialist party, and formed alliances with David Dubinsky, the anti-Communist president of the International Ladies Garment Workers Union (ILGWU), a major union in which they had some influence.

After failing in a 1938 attempt to take over the United Auto Workers and use it as a base to advance his faction, Lovestone, outraged also at the execution of Nikolai Bukharin and others in the Soviet leadership whom he regarded as allies, worked more closely with Dubinsky in the American Federation of Labor (AFL) against CPUSA influence in the Congress of Industrial Organizations (CIO).

After the outbreak of World War II Lovestone supported U.S. intervention in the war and worked for the ILGWU's international affairs program in campaigns to both rescue and recruit labor leaders from Axis-occupied countries. In December 1940 Lovestone's followers formally dissolved as an organized group—journalist I. F. Stone noted during World War II that Lovestone threatened to sue former supporters who called themselves Lovestoneites. Appointed by Dubinsky as director of the ILGWU's International Affairs Department in 1943, Lovestone cultivated the friendship of conservative AFL leader George Meany and in 1944 became director of the AFL's Free Trade Union Committee (FTUC), which pursued a "premature" Cold War policy by seeking to prevent Communists and other leftists from either gaining or regaining influence in labor movements in countries liberated from the Axis. Lovestone also worked in the 1940s with the Office of Strategic Services (OSS) and its postwar successor, the Central Intelligence Agency (CIA), which helped to subsidize FTUC activities.

In the postwar period, Lovestone used U.S. government and trade union money and power to build anti-Communist labor organizations throughout the world. He played a major behind-the-scenes role in the creation of the International Confederation of Free Trade Unions (ICFTU), the CIA–funded world labor group that continued the work of the FTUC in fighting the Communist and left-supported World Federation of Trade Unions (WFTU). He served as director of the ICFTU from its creation in 1949 until 1963. He also played a leading role in the creation of the American Institute for Free Labor Development (AIFLD) in 1961 to counter Communist influences in Latin America in the aftermath of the Cuban revolution.

After becoming director of the AFL-CIO's International Affairs Department in 1963, Lovestone continued to build regional anti-Communist labor federations and organizations to foster U.S.–style business unionism, most notably the Africa-oriented African-American Labor Center. By the time he retired as director of the AFL-CIO's International Affairs Department in 1974, he had in effect created a vast institutional network that had turned the U.S. labor movement, in its activities abroad, into an arm of U.S. Cold War policy.

Although international exposés of Lovestone's activities from the late 1960s on associated him with political plots and bribery scandals in Europe, Africa, Latin America, and Asia, he continued before and after his retirement to pursue a policy of inflexible anticommunism. In this regard he rallied AFL-CIO support for the Vietnam War and against the Nixon-Kissinger "détente" foreign policy of the 1970s. He also brought the AFL-CIO leadership together with military, corporate, and political figures to form the Committee on the Present Danger in the mid-1970s to advocate increased military spending and a more aggressive foreign policy, providing, through the splinter group Social Democrats USA, which the AFL-CIO leadership supported in the 1970s and 1980s, recruits for state department, foreign service, and United Nations staffs during the Reagan administration.

In the U.S. and world labor movements and in U.S. intellectual life, Jay Lovestone used political skills gained decades earlier in the Communist movement to develop and strengthen conservative principles and organization. Indeed, the neoconservative intellectuals who provided important legitimation for the Reagan administration were, in their foreign policy positions, proclaiming principles that Jay Lovestone, among others, had helped to develop since the 1940s.

Jay Lovestone had no known family life. In the years following his retirement in 1974 to his death in New York City sixteen years later, he continued to work as a consultant to the AFL-CIO and as a lecturer on labor and international affairs.

• Lovestone's papers are at the Hoover Institution on War, Revolution, and Peace at Stanford University. Materials relevant to Lovestone and the Lovestoneites appear in various ILGWU–related collections and the oral history of the left at the Tamiment Library, New York City; in the AFL Papers at the State Historical Society of Wisconsin, Madison; in the Labor Archives at Wayne State University; and in the archival materials on the history of the Communist Party, USA, at Emory University. Lovestone influence, particularly in the postwar world labor movement, is covered in a wide variety of sources, from Philip Agee's *Inside the Company: CIA Diary* (1972) to Ronald Radosh's scholarly treatment, *American Labor and United States Foreign Policy: The Cold War in the Unions from Gompers to Lovestone* (1969). For Lovestone and the Lovestoneites, see Robert J. Alexander, *The Right Opposition: The Lovestoneites and the International Communist Movement* (1981). See also Bert Cochran, *Labor and Communism: The Conflict That Shaped American Unions* (1977); Roger Keeran, *The Communist Party and the Automobile Workers Unions* (1978); and Harvey Levenstein, *Communism, Anti-*

Communism and the CIO (1981), for the internal conflicts and factionalism within American labor politics. For a sympathetic treatment of Lovestoneites and other Communists who became anti-Communists, see John Patrick Diggins, *Up from Communism: Conservative Odysseys in American Intellectual History* (1975). An obituary is in the *New York Times*, 9 Mar. 1990.

NORMAN D. MARKOWITZ

LOVETT, Robert Abercrombie (14 Sept. 1895–7 May 1986), under secretary of state and secretary of defense, was born in Huntsville, Texas, the son of Robert Scott Lovett, a lawyer, and Lavinia Chilton Abercrombie. Lovett's father, who represented the E. H. Harriman Railroad interests in Texas, became chief counsel and then president of the Union Pacific and Southern Pacific railroads. In 1909 the family moved to New York City, where Robert enjoyed the fruits of wealth and social standing. He entered Yale in 1914 and received his B.A. in 1918. After service as a navy pilot during World War I, he briefly studied law and business administration at Harvard. After his discharge from the navy in 1919, in April of that year he married Adele Brown, daughter of a senior partner in Brown Brothers, one of Wall Street's most prestigious firms. They would have two children. Two years later he joined that firm as a "runner." Owing to his intelligence, loyalty, preparedness, and willingness to take risks, he would likely have risen quickly even without his family connections. Within just five years, he was appointed a partner. In 1931 he merged his firm with the E. H. Harriman banking company, for whom his father had once overseen sizable financial interests in Texas.

While enrolled at Yale during the First World War, Lovett organized a corps of young men who became Naval Reserve pilots preceding their graduation. They saw considerable air combat in France during 1917 and 1918. Despite his later involvement in the world of finance, he never abandoned his interest in air warfare. This, combined with his Wall Street reputation, brought him to the attention of a former secretary of both the State Department and the War Department, Henry L. Stimson, and to the attention of Robert Patterson, one of Stimson's chief associates. When President Franklin D. Roosevelt in 1940 appointed the Republican Stimson to a second stint at the War Department, Patterson became his army under secretary. Patterson read Lovett's persuasive recommendations concerning aircraft readiness and invited Lovett to become his special assistant.

With the Second World War becoming likely, Lovett quickly became a key member of the defense team. In April 1941 Stimson elevated him to assistant secretary of war for air, where he forged a close relationship with General George C. Marshall, Roosevelt's military chief of staff. Working closely with Stimson and Marshall, Lovett effectively administered a vast plan for aircraft production. More than any other official, Lovett persuaded the president to give top priority to heavy bomber production, and Roosevelt's successor,

Harry Truman, later awarded Lovett the Distinguished Service Medal for this work.

Lovett returned to Wall Street after the Japanese surrender, but not for long. When President Truman appointed General Marshall as secretary of state in 1947, Marshall asked Lovett to become his under secretary. The two men maintained a remarkably close relationship. Lovett described himself as Marshall's "alter ego," and Marshall's biographer said they achieved a closeness similar to the mental processes of identical twins. Lovett served not only as Marshall's troubleshooter and chief liaison to Congress but as a key policy adviser in respect to some of the momentous issues of the early Cold War, including the recognition of Israel, the Marshall Plan, and the formation of the North Atlantic Treaty Organization (NATO). His conservatism (which was both temperamental and political), his rejection of isolationism, and his belief that international stability required both military and economic commitments for the United States mirrored the attitudes of his chief. For Lovett, no line separated America's strategic and economic interests. He was less enamored with international democracy than with stability, and his approach to the world was fundamentally pragmatic rather than ideological. He had little patience for either the idealism that led to the new United Nations (UN) or the rigid anticommunism of the political right.

Lovett left the State Department and returned to private business in 1949 after Marshall resigned, but he would soon return to Washington. When President Truman asked Marshall to become secretary of defense a few months after the Korean War began in June 1950, Lovett once more became Marshall's chief deputy. As during World War II, he focused on budget and procurement. Lovett emphatically backed the 1951 decision by Truman and Marshall to relieve General Douglas MacArthur as commander of UN troops, believing strongly in proper authority and in civilian control of the military.

Lovett succeeded Marshall who, under attack by anti-Communists led by Senator Joseph McCarthy, resigned from the Pentagon in September 1951 (Marshall had accepted the position only temporarily). Because Lovett already had assumed many of Marshall's responsibilities, his appointment represented continuity more than change. He was an effective secretary and, having returned to Washington during years when defense spending soared, directed his energies to coordinating a single defense budget since the armed services were in 1947 unified under the Defense Department. He cooperated closely with Dean Acheson, whom he deeply respected. He also expanded research into missile development and chemical and biological weapons. His influence in respect to the Korean War was surprisingly modest, never matching that of Secretary of Defense Robert McNamara during the Vietnam War. Lovett generally gave his commanders plenty of latitude in devising military strategy, and he watched sadly as the war settled into a frustrating stalemate. He proposed no notable initiatives other than favoring forced repatriation of prisoners of war in order to encourage North Korean leaders to conclude a truce. Truman, however, favored voluntary repatriation, and he prevailed.

Lovett left the Pentagon when Dwight Eisenhower became president in January 1953. Rarely consulted by the new administration, he returned to Wall Street, where he resumed his investment activity and served on the boards of numerous corporations. Although he was a Republican, Democrats often called on him for advice. In 1961 the newly elected president John F. Kennedy appealed for the support of the so-called "Establishment" by offering Lovett a cabinet position at state, treasury, or defense. Lovett declined on health grounds. He did, however, lend his counsel to Kennedy and helped bring Dean Rusk to the State Department, McNamara to the Defense Department, and Douglas Dillon to the Treasury. He also joined the Executive Committee of the National Security Council, known as ExCom, the president's circle of influential advisers that was formed during the 1962 Cuban missile crisis.

Lovett's influence in Washington waned after Kennedy's death. In some areas, including nuclear nonproliferation and NATO troop levels, the White House continued to solicit his advice. During the early 1970s, National Security Adviser Henry Kissinger and former secretary of state Acheson recruited him to support their efforts to keep American troops in Europe.

Lovett's voice lost resonance after the Vietnam era. With advancing age, he gracefully withdrew from public activity. As a man who always placed great stock in "character," he was pained by the scandals of the Richard Nixon administration. Lovett's own success owed much to his character. He was scrupulously honest, trustworthy, and loyal. Both reserved and shy, he nevertheless had a sharp sense of humor. He was bright, resourceful, and cautious. Eshewing publicity, he was the type of official who allowed others to take credit for his own accomplishments, including his considerable role in shaping the world of the Cold War. He died in Locust Valley, New York.

• Diaries are housed in the Brown Brothers, Harriman and Company Collection at the New-York Historical Society, and some microfilm papers for the years 1941 to 1943 and 1947 to 1949 are at the Harry S. Truman Library in Independence, Mo. An oral history is at the Truman Library. Lovett was so circumspect that both contemporaries and historians tended to overlook his significance. The best single book about him links biography and intellectual history in tracing an ideology of foreign policy that influenced Americans long after Lovett left public life: Walter Isaacson and Evan Thomas, *The Wise Men. Six Men and the World They Made: Acheson, Bohlen, Harriman, Kennan, Lovett, McCloy* (1986). Other important books dealing with Lovett include Clark Clifford, *Counsel to the President: A Memoir* (1991), written by Truman's chief adviser; Forrest C. Pogue, *George C. Marshall* (4 vols., 1963–1987), covering the man under whom Lovett served both during and after World War II; David McCullough, *Truman* (1992), Michael Sherry, *The Rise of American Air Power: The Creation of Armageddon* (1987); and David Halberstam, *The*

Best and the Brightest (1972), which highlights Lovett's immense influence by the early 1960s. A comprehensive obituary is in the *New York Times*, 8 May 1986.

GARY B. OSTROWER

LOVETT, Robert Morss (25 Dec. 1870–8 Feb. 1956), educator, writer, and reformer, was born in Boston, Massachusetts, the son of Augustus Sidney Lovett, an insurance broker, and Elizabeth Russell. Lovett grew up in the Roxbury section of Boston and then went to Harvard, where he graduated at the head of his class with an A.B. in English in 1892.

Lovett's teaching career began the fall after his graduation, when he served as an instructor in English at Harvard while pursuing graduate study in the same field. In 1893 he accepted a position as an instructor in rhetoric at the new University of Chicago. He taught and served as an administrator at the university for forty-three years. While teaching courses in writing and literature, Lovett served successively as special assistant to President William Rainey Harper, secretary of the English department, and dean of the junior college. He became a professor of English in 1909, and in that position he encouraged the careers of many writers and scholars. In 1895 he married Ida Campbell Mott-Smith, with whom he had three children.

Lovett's own writing was broad rather than profound and included a play, titled *Cowards* (produced 1914, published 1917); *History of English Literature* (1902) and *A First View of English Literature* (1905), both written with William Vaughn Moody; two novels, *Richard Gresham* (1904) and *A Winged Victory* (1907); *Edith Wharton: A Critical Biography* (1925); and *All Our Years* (1948), his autobiography. He compiled several books, including *Selected Poems of William Vaughn Moody* (1931), and worked with Howard Mumford Jones to compile *College Reader* (1936). Although a prolific writer and editor, Lovett felt that he was not a scholar, writing in *All Our Years*, "I have never made any contribution to knowledge. The chief value of my teaching has been in the organization of fields which I have seen my students enter with success" (p. 94). A writer in *Current Biography* (1943) was more generous, stating that Lovett's literary and political writings were "characterized by scholarly approach, by a sure background of facts presented with ease and clarity, and by a complete absence of emotionalism or hysteria."

In 1918 and 1919 Lovett served briefly as editor of *The Dial*, a controversial literary magazine. An active political progressive, Lovett wrote for and served on the editorial board of Herbert Croly's *New Republic* from 1921 to 1940. David Levy, Croly's biographer, has written that "Lovett, a sensitive and versatile professor of English literature, was hired to run the book pages, and he turned them into a consistently exciting forum for the leading ideas of the era."

Like John Dewey and others associated with the *New Republic*, Lovett initially supported America's entry into World War I. However, his oldest son was killed at Belleau Wood, and this tragedy no doubt strengthened Lovett's postwar interest in pacifism. Another influence that moved Lovett politically to the left and toward pacifism was his long association with Jane Addams and Hull House; for many years Lovett and his family lived at Hull House and were active in Addams's reform causes. He also served as an organizer, writer, and speaker on behalf of many organizations ranging from progressive to radical, including the American Civil Liberties Union, League for Industrial Democracy, Sacco-Vanzetti Defense League, International Labor Defense, League for Independent Political Action, League of American Writers, and American Peace Mobilization.

Lovett followed a policy that he described in his 1948 autobiography as "minimizing differences among liberals and radicals," and although he was critical of Communism and of the party's manipulative tactics, he unapologetically joined groups dominated by Communists. He wrote: "I still believe that liberals and Communists can work together for good in local causes, and both are deeply concerned with civil liberties in the United States, but . . . I am suspicious of organizations which enjoy their existence on sufferance and depend on the variable policies of a foreign power" (p. 291).

In 1935 Lovett's controversial associations led a conservative committee of the Illinois Senate to recommend, without success, that the University of Chicago dismiss him. Although Lovett criticized the New Deal from the left, Secretary of the Interior Harold Ickes, who had been one of Lovett's students at the University of Chicago, appointed him government secretary of the Virgin Islands in 1939. In this role Lovett worked vigorously to promote education and social welfare for the people of the islands. However, in 1943 the Un-American Activities Committee of the House of Representatives (the "Dies Committee") investigated Lovett and declared him to be subversive. After a hearing before a special subcommittee (the "Kerr Committee"), the House Appropriations Committee withheld Lovett's pay, along with that of two other suspected subversives. This move was later overturned by the Supreme Court as an unconstitutional bill of attainder. At the end of his career Lovett taught briefly at the University of Puerto Rico and Fisk University before retiring in 1947. He died in Chicago.

Like other academic progressives, Lovett struggled to make connections between academic and political life. Historian Robert Iversen called him "the academic fellow traveler pre-eminent," adding that "Lovett was a radical before there were Communists." He asked: "What can one say of this mellow man who, to the day of his death at age eighty-five, continued to sign every petition placed before him? . . . He failed to see that, despite temporary successes, the presence of the Communists bestowed upon each cause the kiss of death rather than the breath of life. . . . In Lovett's failure to see this even dimly through thirty-five years lies his deep tragedy" (Iversen, pp. 169–70).

Lovett would have disagreed. The true tragedy of his life was the loss of his son in World War I. Lovett certainly did not see his political embroilments as tragedies; he took pride and satisfaction in supporting causes he believed in and in confronting his conservative accusers. Lovett was far from alone among liberals in supporting, rather indiscriminately, a range of petitions and causes. Some of his political activities may be seen as errors rather than tragedies and must be weighed against his decades of exemplary service to major organizations working for peace, civil liberties, racial integration, and social and economic justice.

• Lovett's autobiography, *All Our Years* (1948), is a readable and dependable source. There is also incidental early autobiographical material in Lovett's preface to *Selected Poems of William Vaughn Moody* (1931), a volume that he edited. *Current Biography* for 1943 (pp. 461–65) has a long article on Lovett, providing extensive detail on the 1935 and 1943 controversies over his associations with various political groups. Robert Iversen, *The Communists and the Schools* (1959), places Lovett in the context of twentieth-century ideological disputes on the left. More balanced interpretations include Jefferson B. Fletcher, "Salute to Bob Lovett," *New Republic* 109 (27 Sept. 1943): 420–23, and Louis Filler, "An American Liberal," *Antioch Review* 7 (Sept. 1948): 377–79 (review of *All Our Years*). On some of Lovett's activities and associations in liberal journalism, see David Levy, *Herbert Croly of the New Republic* (1985). An obituary is in the *New York Times*, 9 Feb. 1956.

JAMES M. WALLACE

LOVEWELL, John (14 Oct. 1691–9 May 1725), frontier soldier, was born in what is now Nashua, New Hampshire, then part of Dunstable, Massachusetts, the son of John Lovewell and Anna Hassell, who were probably farmers. The elder John Lovewell had served with Cromwell's army before emigrating to New England and participated in the "Great Swamp Fight" during King Philip's War in 1675. The record discloses little of the younger John Lovewell's youth except that he was known as an eager and successful hunter and that he applied his wilderness skills to discovering "the lurking places of Indians" (Symmes, p. 7), probably during Queen Anne's War (1702–1713). When in 1722 a series of frontier disturbances in northern New England initiated what is known as "Dummer's War," Lovewell was working a modest farm in Dunstable with his wife, Hannah. The couple eventually had three children, the third born after the father's death.

An Indian attack on Dunstable in the autumn of 1724 prompted Lovewell to go to war. When Josiah Farwell, his brother-in-law, returned as one of the few survivors of a party that chased the raiders in the hope of recovering the two Dunstable captives, Lovewell joined Farwell and Jonathan Robbins in petitioning the Massachusetts General Court for authority to raise a company of rangers. Armed with authority to promise daily wages plus a bounty for scalps, they recruited thirty men. Having elected Lovewell captain, the company marched into the New Hampshire woods north of Lake Winnipesaukee. On 19 December they killed an Indian man and captured a teenaged boy and returned to Boston early in January with the scalp and the captive.

The modest success of Lovewell's first expedition aroused enough interest to swell the company's ranks to eighty-seven for a second foray in February. This time Lovewell's company surprised and killed all ten members of a sleeping Indian raiding party. Lovewell and his men were quickly becoming famous, especially after parading the scalps and captured weapons through the streets of Boston.

Lovewell's climactic expedition of forty-six men marched from Dunstable in the middle of April 1725. The destination was Pequawket, or Pigwacket (Evans lists sixty-eight variations of spelling, pp. 121–25), the main village of the northern New Hampshire and western Maine tribe of that name, on the Saco River. After leaving a sick comrade with attendants and guards at a makeshift fort at Ossipee Lake, Lovewell led his reduced force to Pequawket near modern Fryeburg, Maine. At about ten in the morning of 9 May, while Lovewell's company was pursuing a lone Indian who had been spotted at a distance, the Pequawkets ambushed them on the shore of what has since been named Lovewell's (or Lovell's) Pond. Lovewell was fatally shot at the outset, but "one of the most obstinate and deadly bush-fights in the annals of New England," as historian Francis Parkman called it, continued until evening. More than half of the thirty-four men that Lovewell had led into battle were either killed or seriously wounded. The larger Indian force suffered still more casualties.

The historic importance of "Lovewell's Fight," preserved in ballads, tradition, and in fiction (as the basis of Nathaniel Hawthorne's story "Roger Malvin's Burial"), almost justifies the lavish attention that the battle and its participants attracted on dramatic and romantic grounds during the nineteenth century. The Pequawkets thereafter remained peaceful, and the formal end of Dummer's War in 1726 opened the way for a new period of unmolested expansion of English settlement into northern New England.

• The account of Lovewell's campaigns from which most others are derived is that of Samuel Penhallow in *The History of the Wars of New England, with the Eastern Indians* (1726). A portion of Penhallow's text is printed in Colin Calloway, ed., *Dawnland Encounters: Indians and Europeans in Northern New England* (1991), which also provides useful context. The story has been retold many times, most elegantly by Francis Parkman in *A Half-Century of Conflict*, first published in two volumes in 1892. Fannie Hardy Eckstorm, "Pigwacket and Parson Symmes," *New England Quarterly* 9 (1936): 378–402, substantially revised some of the details of the traditional accounts of the Pigwacket fight, including its date, demonstrating somewhat convincingly that the "original account" of Thomas Symmes had been falsified to protect young Jonathan Frye, who served as the expedition's chaplain and was also killed in the battle, from the charge that he had gone "scalp-hunting for money on the Sabbath," which was 9 May, a Sunday. Eckstorm finds that to be the true date of the battle instead of 8 May, the date used by Symmes and Penhallow and nearly all of their successors. Eckstorm's findings are accepted here to date both the battle and Lovewell's death. See also Jeremy Belknap, *History of New-Hampshire* (1784–1792); George Hill Evans, *Pigwacket, Part I. Old Indian Days in the Valley of the Saco* (1939); Charles J. Fox, *History of the Old Township of Dunstable: Including Nashua, Nashville, Hollis, Hudson, Litchfield, and Merrimac, N.H.; Dunstable and Tyngsborough, Mass.* (1846); Frederic Kidder, *The Expeditions of Capt. John Lovewell and His Encounter with the Indians* (1865); Nashua History Committee, ed., *The Nashua Experience: History in the Making 1673/1978* (1978); and Thomas Symmes, *The Original Account of Capt. John Lovewell's "Great Fight" with the Indians, at Pequawket, May 8, 1725*, ed. Nathaniel Bouton (1861).

CHARLES E. CLARK

LOVING, Richard Perry (29 Oct. 1933–29 June 1975), construction worker and plaintiff in the Supreme Court case *Loving v. Virginia* (1967), was born in Caroline County, Virginia, the son of Twillie Loving, a lumber truck driver, and Lola Allen, a homemaker and midwife. He attended local schools, worked as a bricklayer, and was a drag racer in his spare time. In June 1958, in Washington, D.C., Loving, a white man, married Mildred Dolores Jeter, of mixed Native-American and African-American ancestry. They took up residence as newlyweds in her parents' home in Caroline County. Early one morning some weeks later, they awoke to find three police officers in their bedroom, and they were arrested for violating Virginia's laws against interracial marriage. In January 1959 they pleaded guilty, and the presiding judge, Leon Bazile, sentenced them each to a year in jail but suspended the sentence on condition that they leave the state and not return together for the next twenty-five years.

The couple moved to Washington, D.C., where they lived with one of Mildred Loving's cousins and his wife and Richard Loving worked as an automobile mechanic. They had three children, and Mildred Loving returned to her home in Virginia for the birth of each child. In 1963, after more than four years in exile, she wrote to Attorney General Robert F. Kennedy, seeking assistance. The Justice Department put the couple in touch with the American Civil Liberties Union, a group that had challenged antimiscegenation laws like Virginia's.

Virginia had first enacted legislation restricting interracial marriage in 1691, and at the time of the Civil War, a majority of all American states had antimiscegenation statutes in force. Faced with a challenge against the Alabama statute in 1883, the U.S. Supreme Court, in *Pace v. Alabama*, had ruled that they did not violate the Equal Protection Clause of the Fourteenth Amendment, and that approach governed the issue well into the twentieth century. In 1948 the Supreme Court of California had rejected that state's antimiscegenation law in *Perez v. Sharp*, but as late as the mid-1950s, in cases that arose in Alabama and Virginia, the U.S. Supreme Court avoided confronting the question.

A young lawyer in Alexandria, Bernard S. Cohen, took charge of reopening the Lovings' case in the Virginia courts. In 1964 Philip J. Hirschkop joined him in the effort and sought to move the case into federal court. While their case began making its way through the courts, the Lovings moved back to Virginia. In January 1965, with a three-judge federal panel due to intervene soon if he did not act, Judge Bazile finally rejected the Lovings' petition to set aside his original decision. By way of conclusion, Bazile explained, "Almighty God created the races white, black, yellow, malay and red, and he placed them on separate continents. . . . The fact that he separated the races shows that he did not intend for the races to mix." In March 1966 the Virginia Supreme Court of Appeals unanimously upheld the Virginia statutes against all constitutional challenges. In December 1966 the U.S. Supreme Court agreed to hear the case. In a unanimous decision in June 1967—nine years after the couple's wedding—the Court declared unconstitutional all laws restricting marriage on the basis of race.

In the decade between *Brown v. Board of Education* (1954) and the Civil Rights Act of 1964, federal policy had rejected every kind of Jim Crow legislation across the country except the laws banning interracial marriage. *Loving v. Virginia* brought an end to centuries of criminalization of marriage across racial lines. The Lovings had not intended, in 1958 or even in 1963, to embark on a crusade against Jim Crow. They meant only to end the obstacles to living in peace with their children in their home county and state. To do so, however, they had to put into play a case that had extraordinary consequences in American public law and private life. At the time of the adverse decision by the state supreme court and the resulting need to take the case to the U.S. Supreme Court, Richard Loving, a private and taciturn man, said, "We have thought about other people, but we are not doing it just because someone had to do it and we wanted to be the ones. . . . We are doing it for *us*—because we want to live here" ("The Crime of Being Married," *Life*, 18 Mar. 1966, p. 91). As their attorney Cohen told the Supreme Court in his oral argument, Richard Loving had said to him, "Mr. Cohen, tell the Court I love my wife, and it is just unfair that I can't live with her in Virginia."

Richard Loving knew his priorities. On the afternoon of his Supreme Court victory he told of his plans. "My wife and I plan to go ahead and build a new house now," he said, since they had secured permission now to live where they wished as Mr. and Mrs. Loving, and they did so. Richard Loving's new life in Virginia lasted only eight years, however. He died in a car crash just south of Bowling Green, Virginia, when a drunk driver ran a stop sign.

• The fullest account of Loving's Supreme Court case is Peter Wallenstein, "Race, Marriage, and the Law of Freedom: Alabama and Virginia, 1860s–1960s," *Chicago-Kent Law Review* 70 (1994): 371–437. News accounts of his life, his marriage, and his death are in the *Washington Post*, 30 June 1975 and 12 June 1992, and the *New York Times*, 13 June 1967 and 12 June 1992.

PETER WALLENSTEIN

LOW, Charles Porter (19 Sept. 1824–22 Feb. 1913), clipper ship captain, was born in Salem, Massachusetts, the son of Seth Low, a druggist, who later imported African and South American goods, and Mary Porter. The family moved to Brooklyn, New York, in 1828, and Charles's oldest brother, Abiel Abbot Low, after a trading stint in China, established in Manhattan A. A. Low & Brothers, a firm that imported Chinese tea and Japanese silk in its fast clipper ships. Although his uncle James Willis Low was a ship captain, Charles was the only one of his parents' twelve children to go to sea.

Low attended a school in Brooklyn, established by his father with teachers from Salem, before going to work at the age of fourteen. By his own account (in *Some Recollections*), his heart was never in his studies, because he wanted, throughout his childhood, to go to sea. "I was at a very early age, inclined to seek salt water." (At the age of twelve, Low and a friend attempted to run away after buying passage on a sailing ship bound for Savannah, Georgia; before the ship sailed, however, they lost their nerve and returned home.) His first job was working for a wholesaler of dry goods in Manhattan. Though his hours were long, Low found time to spend on the wharves, where many sailing ships were docked, and he could climb the rigging and gaze at the ocean.

When his employer's business failed, Low, at the age of fifteen, became a clerk for his father. Across the street from his father's store was a sailors' boardinghouse, where Low spent long hours listening to stories about the sea and learning to splice ropes, tie knots, and read a compass.

Though his family was anxious to keep him on dry land, claiming that the real money was to be made in the merchant trade, young Low was determined to go to sea. Before his twentieth birthday, Low tried to stow away on his brother's topsail schooner, the *Mazeppa*. He hid in a bread locker, where he nearly suffocated before being discovered, and, humiliated, he was sent home. After enrolling in navigation school, Low finally set sail on his first sea journey in 1842, as a cabin boy on board the family's China packet *Horatio*. Though he did an ordinary seaman's work, the position offered no wages; before departure, however, his father gave him $50 and a sailor's outfit. His second job, as a seaman on the *Toronto*, earned him $11 a month.

During several more voyages, on the *Courier* bound for Rio de Janeiro and on the *Houqua* sailing to Hong Kong, Low rose quickly to third mate, then second and first. He was given command of his first ship at the young age of twenty-three. The vessel, the *Houqua*, belonged to his family, and it was a well-designed, fast clipper ship, which he sailed from New York in November 1847. The voyage was a memorable one, as the ship encountered a typhoon in the Indian Ocean, a full month after such storms were usually expected. The young captain, alarmed by the falling barometer and uncertain how to proceed, ordered all sails down except for the close-reefed topsails. Then he decided to "scud," that is, to run before the wind. By his account, "The sky was covered with dense masses of black, smoky clouds filled with thunder and lightning, and all the mast-heads and yard-arms has composants, or balls of electricity, resting on them, as low down as the lower yards" (*Some Recollections*). The ferocious storm was devastating, destroying the rigging, sails, and spars, battering the masts and decks, and ripping away a quarter boat. Low was tossed overboard and survived only by grabbing a submerged line as the threatening waves carried him under. Even though all their tools except a hatchet and a gouge had been lost in the storm, Low and his crew concocted a jury-rig and sailed 3,000 miles to Hong Kong. While achieving this tour de force, he copied his ship's log to send with explanations to his oldest brother. When newspapers and marine journals published his account, Charles Low became a hero, with the five companies that had insured his cargo congratulating him on a silver plate attached to the eight-day chronometer they presented him for managing to save and sell his water-damaged cargo, thereby clearing more than $60,000.

Subsequent commands, while not so frightening, were still exciting; in 1850 Low sailed the *Samuel Russell* from New York to San Francisco in 109 days, the shortest voyage made to that date by twelve days. The young captain noted humbly, "As we entered the Golden Gate the wind increased rapidly, and we went in flying, and came to anchor just where I would have done if I had known all about it" (*Some Recollections*).

Low next captained a new clipper ship, the family's *N. B. Palmer*, in 1851. A year later, he married Sarah Maria Tucker in South Danvers, Massachusetts. The two took a honeymoon around the world on board the *Palmer*, a journey marked by a crewman's murder, an attempted mutiny, and the desertion of some twenty seamen in Valparaiso. Captain Low promptly hired a new crew, and the voyage continued. The first of the Lows' seven children was born on board ship in the South China Sea, a few hours after the vessel had run onto reefs, slashing a huge hole in its bow. Trying to attend to his wife while commanding the injured clipper, Low managed to anchor in shallow water just as his son was delivered. (Their second son was also born during the voyage, off Sandy Hook in New York just before the vessel's scheduled arrival in New York harbor.)

In 1864 Low decided to stay on dry land and go into business with his brothers in New York, where they built a store to sell teas and other Chinese goods. He moved his family to Brooklyn, New York, and the business prospered. In 1866 Low and several friends started New York's Atlantic Yacht Club. He purchased a sloop, the *Annie Laurie*, for pleasure trips on Long Island Sound. The financial crash of 1867 warned the Low brothers that business was precarious, and they decided to close the store. Low, already missing his life at sea, was asked to resume command of the *N. B. Palmer*, which he readily accepted, and he shipped off for Hong Kong.

Low finally gave up the sea in 1873 and returned home to New York. He retired to Santa Barbara, California, where he died, after writing, at the age of seventy-nine, colorful and articulate memoirs of his life as a clipper ship captain.

• Low's *Some Recollections* (1905) is a wonderful source for family information as well as details about specific ships and voyages; it is articulate and colorful. A. B. C. Whipple, *The Challenge* (1987), supplies interesting and amusing anecdotes about Low's early life as well as about his clippers and voyages. Abbot Low Moffat, *The Moffat-Low Genealogy* (1932), is an accurate list of family statistics for those interested in the whole Low family. Alexander Laing, *The American Heritage History of Seafaring America* (1974), includes a good description of the typhoon that threatened the *Houqua*. Robert Carse, *The Moonrakers: The Story of the Clipper Ship Men* (1961), is a good source of background information about the clipper ship era. An obituary is in the *Morning Press* (Santa Barbara, Calif.), 23 Feb. 1913.

ANN WHIPPLE MARR

LOW, Frederick Ferdinand (30 June 1828–21 July 1894), businessman, politician, and diplomat, was born in Frankfort (present-day Winterport), Maine, into a Penobscot Valley farming family. His parents' names are not known. Frederick Low attended public schools and Hampden Academy. At age fifteen he was apprenticed to Russell, Sturgis and Company, a Boston firm with a large China trade. He enriched his education by attending Fanuiel Hall and Lowell Institute lectures. Low completed his apprenticeship in 1849 and joined other Forty-niners in California. For three months he panned gold on the American River. Taking some $1,500 from his claim, he declared himself "satisfied" and returned to San Francisco to commence successful careers in business and government.

During the decade before the Civil War, California grew rapidly, as ships carrying people and merchandise sailed into San Francisco. Low developed essential banking and transportation enterprises. In 1850 he and two brothers formed a shipping partnership in San Francisco and Marysville, a busy interior trading town. Also that year Low married Mollie Creed. In 1854 he organized the California Steam Navigation Company, merging inland steamship lines in the San Francisco Bay area and along the Sacramento River, and he established a banking business in Marysville.

By the 1860s California was eligible for a third congressman. Low, elected as a Union Republican representative at large, took a seat in the Thirty-seventh Congress in June 1862. (Congress had convened in Dec. 1861, but his seating was delayed pending authorization of the additional seat.) Although not a prominent participant in debates, he showed his interest in California land titles, banking, and revenue bills. Low did not seek a second term but instead held an appointment as collector of the Port of San Francisco, June–September 1863.

Low's next political office was significant for the nation torn by the Civil War, because California's loyalty to the Union was critical but by no means certain. In

December 1863 Low became the state's first four-year governor, "perhaps one of the most difficult positions ever held by an executive in the state, for we had a large secession element here, and it required . . . good judgment to keep ourselves from being mixed up in broils" (*Reflections*, p. 12). With gubernatorial leadership, the state met the Lincoln administration's requests for financial assistance and also sent 16,000 volunteers to relieve army regulars. The state thus helped prevent the Confederacy from gaining a direct route to California through the Southwest and a foothold on the West Coast. In the 1864 presidential election, California supported Abraham Lincoln. Low's policies as governor included justice for Chinese immigrants, toward whom he felt state laws had been discriminatory and oppressive; measures leading to establishment of the University of California at Berkeley; preservation of land that became Golden Gate Park; and recommending ratification of the Fourteenth Amendment to the Constitution. In 1865 Low refused to become a candidate for the U.S. Senate.

Low's government service turned to diplomacy when President Ulysses S. Grant appointed him minister to China, a post he held from 1870 to 1874. While Low lacked diplomatic experience and had the nondiplomatic tendency to be outspoken and precise, he had knowledge of the Orient, good business sense, and concern for fairness. He supported a cooperative policy toward China—working with the Chinese in solving problems—in contrast to previous policies of coercion. In an early dispatch from Peking (Beijing) to Secretary of State Hamilton Fish, Low espoused this cooperative philosophy yet acknowledged, "It will require time and patience to work changes . . . by peaceful means" (Anderson, p. 243).

The Tientsin massacre, 21 June 1870, soon tested this policy. When a Chinese mob killed French officials and missionaries, Low condemned the murders and joined French demands for punishment and retribution. However, he criticized the French government and the Catholic church for causing Chinese hostility toward foreigners and for demanding 400 percent reparations for property damages. Low's policy was to seek payment equivalent to damages, urging that "foreigners conduct themselves properly towards this people" (Anderson, p. 246).

In his next year of Peking service, Low suffered disillusionment, and his actions turned to the gunboat diplomacy he had wished to avoid. In 1866 an American trading schooner *General Sherman* had been attacked in Korean waters, its crew presumably murdered by Koreans. Low, as minister to China, was instructed to go to the kingdom of Korea to negotiate a treaty for commerce and navigation and the protection of shipwrecked sailors. Korea's policy was to refuse contact with foreign governments, and Low anticipated failure. Accompanied by five warships commanded by Rear Admiral John Rodgers, the American party sailed to Korea and upriver toward Seoul, where it was fired on. Low and Rodgers sought an official apology for what they considered an unprovoked attack on the

honor of the United States. When unsuccessful, they resorted to force. Five forts were demolished and about 250 Koreans killed. American casualties were light, but the first three American soldiers killed in Korea were buried there in June 1871. The cooperative policy had failed in Korea, and Low became pessimistic about relations with the Orient.

Nevertheless, Low achieved a historic breakthrough in normalizing Western relations with China. He relentlessly insisted that Western diplomats be received as equals by the emperor, without the traditional kowtow ritual. Low had the respect of the Chinese and ultimately won his point. On 29 June 1873 he was one of the first foreigners to receive the desired audience with the emperor.

In 1874 Low resigned his diplomatic post, returning to his neglected businesses. During the next twenty years, he was joint manager of the Anglo-California Bank, a director of the California Steam Navigation Company, and a participant in sugar and lumber enterprises. Low died in San Francisco.

Low was by preference a businessman and did not seek public office. Yet his contemporary, historian Hubert Howe Bancroft, said Low was "one of the best types that the demands of our Republic produce" (*Reflections*, pp. ix–x). His election as governor and his appointments by the Lincoln and Grant administrations indicate the esteem he won in California and in Washington. He did not escape criticism from the American public for the Korean action, yet Low won respect from the Chinese and sincerely felt that contrasting cultures need not be conflicting cultures.

• Low's papers are in the Hubert Howe Bancroft Library, University of California, Berkeley. His governor's messages are in the *Journals of the California Senate and Assembly* (1863–1867), which may be located by contacting the state librarian, Sacramento, Calif. Low's diplomatic correspondence provides a detailed, forthright description of the complexities of America's China policy following the Civil War; see *Dispatches from United States Ministers (China)* and *Diplomatic Instructions of the Department of State (China)*, both on file at the National Archives, and *Foreign Relations of the United States* (covering 1870–1874). An important publication is *Some Reflections of an Early Governor Contained in a Short Dictated Memoir by Frederick Ferdinand Low, Ninth Governor of California, and Notes from an Interview between Governor Low and Hubert Howe Bancroft in 1883*, ed. Robert H. Becker (1959), whose notes enhance the text. Bancroft places Low within the context of events in his *History of California* (1890). A century after the Civil War, Leo P. Kibby analyzed the "Union Loyalty of California's War Governors," *California Historical Society Quarterly* 44 (1965): 311–21, disproving unchallenged skepticism about Calif.'s loyalty and describing Governor Low's importance. Tyler Dennett assessed the Korean expedition in *Americans in Eastern Asia: A Critical Study of United States' Policy in the Far East in the Nineteenth Century* (1922); a more recent and detailed discussion is William M. Leary, Jr., "Our Other War in Korea," *United States Naval Institute Proceedings* 94 (1968): 46–53. An evaluation of Low's dispatches during the Tientsin massacre is Paul H. Clyde, "Frederick F. Low and the Tientsin Massacre," *Pacific Historical Review* 2 (1933): 100–108. For a thorough discussion of Low's diplomatic service, well footnoted and citing many sources, see David L. Anderson, "Between Two Cultures: Frederick F. Low in China," *California History* 59 (1980): 240–54. An obituary is in the *San Francisco Chronicle*, 22 July 1894.

SYLVIA B. LARSON

LOW, Isaac (13 Apr. 1735–25 July 1791), merchant, early revolutionary leader, and later prominent Loyalist, was born near New Brunswick, New Jersey, the son of Cornelius Low, Jr., and Johanna Gouverneur (occupations unknown). Little can be ascertained about his early years. Low established himself as a merchant in New York City, rising to both fortune and political prominence. He became well enough off to marry Margarita Cuyler, daughter of the mayor of Albany, New York, in 1760. They had one child. Low was a founding member of the New York City Chamber of Commerce and became its president during the revolutionary war.

Low prospered in prerevolutionary New York. When he later sought compensation from the British after the revolutionary state government seized his estate, he estimated its value at £34,184 (N.Y. pounds). By independence he had invested most of his fortune in land, two-thirds of it in speculative shares outside New York City. Unlike other Loyalist merchants, he made no claims at all for the loss of bonds and notes or book debts. His portfolio suggests that when the Revolution brought an end to Low's New York career, he was abandoning the life of a merchant for that of a rentier gentleman.

The fortune that Low accumulated placed him in the upper ranks of colonial New York City's merchant leadership but nowhere near its absolute pinnacle. He might not have attracted historical attention at all had he not made a last-minute conversion from playing a very active part in the movement of resistance against Britain to rejection of the movement's consequence, American independence. Writing from exile to his patriot brother in 1787, Low declared that he would never "envy the Happiness of others who are advocates for republican Government. The height of my Ambition was and is to live and die a British subject." A British observer of New York City between 1765 and 1775 might have been pardoned for thinking otherwise.

Never a member of either the provincial council or the provincial assembly, Low emerged into public life through the irregular politics of committees, boycotts, mass meetings, and demonstrations. Although he took no apparent part in the Stamp Act crisis (1765–1766), he joined a panel of fellow merchants as a "committee of inspection" to enforce the boycott of British goods that was New York's response to the Townshend Acts (1767–1770). The committee was a coalition that included both New York's most militant traders, such as Isaac Sears, and cooler-headed men like Low.

That Low was already defining himself as cool to revolution was demonstrated early in 1770, when he allied with the "Friends of Liberty and Trade" rather than with the more militant "Sons of Liberty." Low's choice of political dining and drinking partners pre-saged his ultimate political position. In early 1770, however, the difference was losing its salience, since the Townshend Acts were nearing repeal and the nonimportation movement was nearing dissolution.

Low's next appearance in politics was almost four years later, at the end of 1773, as New York confronted the issue of admitting tea on which the last remaining Townshend Duty had been paid. He actively "solicited subscriptions" to a statement that dutied tea "ought not, on any account, to be suffered to be sold or purchased" and that "a firm and vigorous opposition ought to be given" to importers or vendors. That stance was enough to win him the chairmanship of a joint meeting of merchants and mechanics that picked the city's first committee of correspondence, consisting of twenty-five members. He was among the men chosen. He served as well on its successors, of fifty-one, sixty, and one hundred members, chairing both the Fifty-one and the One Hundred.

Committee service sent Low into higher revolutionary politics. He was elected to the First Continental Congress in 1774. He gave his support there to the Continental Association, which responded to Britain's punishment of Massachusetts for the Boston Tea Party by renewing the American boycott of British commerce. He declined a seat in New York's provincial convention that year, but he did go to the first of four provincial congresses. But though Low was willing enough to use economic pressure in defense of what he saw as colonial rights, he would go no further. He circulated a declaration during the Tea Crisis at the end of 1773 opposing "the landing or storing the said tea with force" on the ground that it would "hazard the peace of the city." Ultimately, opposition to American use of force was more important to him than opposition to British policy.

Low was not elected to the second provincial congress, which was chosen in November 1775. That event marked his rejection of revolutionary politics. He did not flee New York City when the British seized it in the autumn of 1776 but rather resumed trade. In 1779 the state legislature listed him among Loyalists whom it attainted by name, confiscating their estates and banishing them for life. After the war he received £5,667 compensation from Britain for his losses. Low died on the Isle of Wight eight years after he left the city with the departing British forces.

• Low's papers survive only in scattered form. His fullest statement is his claim for Loyalist compensation in the Public Record Office, London, Audit Office Papers, ser. 12, vol. 21, which reveals a great deal about his finances but very little about his actions or motivations. The fullest account of Low's political career during the Revolution can be pieced together from Carl Lotus Becker, *The History of Political Parties in the Province of New York, 1760–1776* (1909). Low's merchant career and fortune are considered in Edward Countryman, "The Uses of Capital in Revolutionary America: The Case of the New York Loyalist Merchants," *William and Mary Quarterly*, 3d ser., 49 (Jan. 1993): 3–28.

EDWARD COUNTRYMAN

LOW, Juliette (31 Oct. 1860–18 Jan. 1927), founder of the Girl Scouts of America, was born Juliette Gordon in Savannah, Georgia, the daughter of General William Washington Gordon, a former Confederate officer and cotton merchant, and Eleanor Kinzie. "Daisy," as she was known to friends and members of her family, was a "brilliant eccentric," according to her siblings. Juliette seems to have taken after her mother, a "Yankee" from Chicago, who was well known as a vivacious, energetic, independent woman who spoke her mind and generally belied the sentimental, passive ideal of antebellum women. Like her mother, Juliette, was frequently described by her friends and family in terms of her charm, wicked wit, vitality, enthusiasm, and devil-may-care attitude.

Juliette's father quickly recovered financial losses sustained during the war, and Juliette and her siblings were all provided expensive and stylish educations. Juliette attended private school in Savannah and then boarding school at Stuart Hall and Edge Hill in Virginia. She completed her education at Mesdemoiselles Charbonnier's, a select finishing school in New York City, where she acquired all the accomplishments necessary to a nineteenth-century debutante. Though Juliette proved quite talented at art and acquired a great interest in history and literature, her spelling remained notoriously poor and she commonly used malapropisms.

After graduation, Juliette embarked on a series of travels in the United States and Europe. In England she met William Mackay Low, the independently wealthy son of a family well established in English and Savannah society. As the only male heir to the multimillion-dollar English estate of Andrew Low, William hobnobbed with the highest members of British society, including the prince of Wales. After a long, secret engagement, William and Juliette were married on 21 December 1886 in Savannah. They spent most of their nine-year marriage in England, where they established several households but did not have children. Although Juliette Low apparently experienced some trepidation upon entering such aristocratic circles, she became a popular and talented hostess, joining the social circuit of hunts, balls, and events at court. The marriage, however, began to deteriorate. An earache, mistakenly treated with nitrate of silver, left Low with chronic hearing problems, and as they became worse it was impossible for her to continue horseback riding and hunting. Soon William Low was leaving his wife alone for long periods of time. He became involved with another woman and asked his wife for a divorce. Low consented, and the couple had a long and bitter separation. In 1905, before the divorce was finalized, William Low died, leaving the bulk of his estate to his mistress. For the next six years, a disheartened Low, burdened by wounded pride and chronic hearing problems, migrated back and forth from Europe to the United States visiting friends and family.

During her many travels, Low met General Sir Robert Baden-Powell, founder of the British Boy Scouts. The two struck up a warm friendship straightaway, based on mutual interests in sculpture and Low's immediate interest in scouting. They corresponded regularly for several years, and according to two of Low's biographers it was rumored that Baden-Powell had once proposed marriage. Allegedly the 51-year-old Low declined because she believed that having children was important to Baden-Powell, and she realized that she could no longer bear children. She did, however, develop a keen interest in the Girl Guides, the feminine equivalent of the Boy Scouts. In 1911 Low established her own troop among poor girls living around her Scottish home, then she formed two troops in London. She also brought the idea of the guides to the United States, organizing sixteen Savannah girls into a guide troop in 1912. Although Low's work promoting scouting was temporarily disrupted by the death of her father, she resumed enthusiastic promotion of the Girl Guides in 1913. Within a few years, Baden-Powell's speaking engagements in the United States and Low's efforts in Savannah had piqued national interest in the Girl Guides. During World War I membership in the scouts expanded dramatically.

Low threw her abundant energies into scouting, becoming an international leader and the guiding light of the American movement. She visited Washington, D.C., in 1913 to set up a national organization and traveled to Chicago and New England in 1914 to set up troops. During her travels, she recruited a number of prominent women to the cause, including Mina Edison, the wife of Thomas Edison, and Corinne Roosevelt Robinson, the sister of Theodore Roosevelt. Low also tried to combine the Girl Guides with the Campfire Girls, a group already established in the United States, but the plan fell through because of disagreements about the administration of the proposed union. By this time Low and her associates had begun to refer to the guides as Girl Scouts, a term that became permanent with the organization of the Girl Scouts of America in 1915. Low became the first president of the Girl Scouts, supervised the composition of a handbook, *How Girls Can Help Their Country*, and underwrote all the expenses of the administration and publicity herself. She served as president until 1920 and represented the American scouts at the first international gathering of Girl Scouts and Guides in 1919. In the final years of her life, Low suffered from cancer but continued to dedicate her time to the scouts and kept her illness largely a secret. One of her final services to the scouts was to aid in the organization of the world Girl Scout camp held in the United States in 1926.

As founder of the Girl Scouts, Low was truly tireless in her dedication to her young troops. Low's extraordinary efforts on the behalf of the scouts have elevated her to hero status in scout mythology. In a story much treasured in Girl Scout lore, and one that perhaps best captures Low's personality and contagious excitement, "Daisy" allegedly once stood on her head during an early scout board meeting to exhibit the newly designed Girl Scout shoe, which she had just happened to wear to the meeting. Such unbridled, unself-conscious enthusiasm and uncommon efforts made Low the leader of an extraordinarily successful movement. Low died in Savannah.

• The Gordon-Low family papers are housed in the Southern Historical Collection at the University of North Carolina at Chapel Hill and the Georgia Historical Society of Savannah. Among the several biographies about Low, one of the most discerning is Gladys Denny Shultz and Daisy Gordon Lawrence, *Lady from Savannah: The Life of Juliette Low* (1958). Based on family papers and reminiscences, it provides a thorough account of Low's family background, her childhood, and her personal life. Other useful sources include Anne Hyde Choate and Helen Ferris, eds., *Juliette Low and the Girl Scouts* (1928), a book of essays by friends and family members, and Mildred Mastin Pace's *Juliette Low* (1947), a biography produced for younger readers and approved by the national organization of the Girl Scouts. An obituary appears in the *New York Times*, 18 Jan. 1927.

MICHELLE BRATTAIN

LOW, Nicholas (30 Mar. 1739–15 Nov. 1826), merchant and speculator, was born at Raritan Landing, New Jersey, the son of Cornelius Low, Jr., and Johanna Gouverneur, descendants of English and Dutch settlers in New York. After education in New Jersey he moved to New York City to clerk for merchant Hayman Levy. Low established his own firm in 1774, primarily selling imported and manufactured goods.

As a patriot, Low left New York when the British arrived in 1776. His activities during the Revolution have not been firmly established. His brother Isaac and his brothers-in-law, Hugh and Alexander Wallace, married to Low's sisters, were wealthy merchants in New York City throughout the war. They left with the British in 1783, and possibly they put their city properties and merchandise into Nicholas's hands. Certainly he was far wealthier in 1784 than in 1776. One evidence of Low's new wealth and influence was his purchase of stock in the Bank of New York, organized in 1784 by his friend Alexander Hamilton and others. Low was a director of the bank from 1784 to 1792.

Low was an import and export merchant, as well as a retailer, in New York City. He imported Irish linens, salt, gunpowders, West Indian Products, dry goods, and wine, while he exported corn, wheat, tobacco, rice, cotton, staves, potash, and flaxseed. Low remained in close contact with Alexander Wallace, and Alexander's son William came to New York in the 1790s to work for his uncle, becoming a partner in Low & Wallace in 1796. Judging from his business correspondence, Low's interest in importing and exporting seemed to end about 1810. One aspect of Low's business was maintaining credit accounts for those who purchased goods. He acted as a banker and broker for clients, executing drafts for currency, lending money, and purchasing or selling securities on their behalf. This aspect of his business was particularly evident in the 1780s and 1790s.

Following the Revolution, Low became interested in politics. He served in the New York State Assembly in 1788 and 1789, as a representative from New York City. He was also elected to the Poughkeepsie Convention that ratified the U.S. Constitution in 1788. There is no evidence that he played a significant role in the debate, but he voted with the Federalists.

In the late 1780s Low speculated on the United States public debt, land warrants, and state debt securities. He used securities to purchase estates confiscated from his brother Isaac and Hugh Wallace, which he subsequently sold, giving the proceeds to their families. After Hamilton convinced Congress to adopt funding and assumption of the public debt, Low made a considerable profit on the securities he then held, funding $38,729 worth in 1790 and up to $20,000 later. Low used part of his profit to purchase stock in the new Bank of the United States. He was elected as one of its directors in 1791, but declined the honor because it would have required him to spend too much time in Philadelphia. Instead, he became a director of the New York branch of the bank, serving until 1799.

Low also used his profits to purchase land. By 1793 he had a residence on fashionable Broadway, and in 1799 he had a house and lot valued at £2,000 on Sloat Lane. More important, however, were his acquisitions in upstate New York. His largest holdings were in St. Lawrence, Saratoga, Lewis, and Steuben counties, but he also had land in Oneida, Onondaga, and Otsego counties. He sold to individual settlers, usually using a land agent to negotiate the contracts. A common contract required the settler to pay $3 an acre, with 10 percent down, and one-quarter of the remainder in two, three, four, and five years, with interest paid annually on the sums remaining. Contracts usually required the settler to clear four acres within one year. If the farmer did this and paid the first two installments on time, Low provided a deed, requiring a mortgage on the remainder due. In Ballston Spa and Lowville he made greater efforts to develop the communities by investing funds in buildings such as hotels, mills, and churches.

Low was active in several other enterprises. He was a director of the Society for the Establishment of Useful Manufactures in Paterson, New Jersey, becoming its governor in 1792. The Society attempted to establish Paterson as a site for cotton manufacturing, but the directors lacked experience in manufacturing cloth, and the Society's operations ended in 1796. After 1796 Low was president of the United Insurance Company, which issued ship and cargo insurance. He was a director of the Northern Inland Lock Navigation Company at the time of its creation in 1792 to connect the Hudson River to Lake Champlain; the company collapsed after a brief existence. In 1824 he signed a petition asking the governor to support a canal between Lake Champlain and the St. Lawrence River. Both projects would have increased the value of Low's lands and might have increased commerce through New York City.

In his fifties Low married a widow, Alice Fleming, with whom he had three children. Two of his children remained in New York City after Low's death there, while one son settled in Lowville. In spite of political differences with his brother and brothers-in-law, Low retained ties to their families.

In many ways Low was a typical New York merchant of this period. His business involved importing, exporting, and retailing a variety of goods as well as banking and brokering for his clients. However, Low was more successful than many others, having accumulated $40,000 worth of personal property by 1815. In short, Low was an excellent example of a wealthy and influential capitalist at work during the early years of the United States.

• For a detailed view of Low's life, consult papers of Nicholas Low, Special Collections and Archives, Rutgers University Libraries, New Brunswick, N.J.; papers and land records of Nicholas Low, Manuscripts and Special Collections, New York State Library, Albany; papers of Elkanah Watson, Burton Historical Collection, Detroit Public Library; and papers of William Bingham, Broome County Historical Society, Binghamton, N.Y. In addition, Low letters are scattered through other manuscript collections. For information on Low's family and early career, see Robert Dructor, "The New York Commercial Community" (Ph.D. diss., Univ. of Pittsburgh, 1975); Dixon Ryan Fox, *The Decline of Aristocracy in the Politics of New York* (1919); Joseph Scoville, *The Old Merchants of New York City* (1870; repr. 1968); and John Stevens, Jr., *Colonial Records of the New York Chamber of Commerce* (1867). For Low's speculation in securities, see James Ferguson, *The Power of the Purse* (1961), and Forrest McDonald, *We the People* (1958).

For his political career, see Francis Childs, *The Debates and Proceedings of the Convention of the State of New-York* (1788; repr. 1905), and *Civil List and Constitutional History of the Colony and State of New York* (1886). For information about his lands, see Frederick Collins, *Money Town* (1946); Fox (1919); Almon Lauber, "The Valleys of the Susquehanna and the Delaware," in *History of the State of New York*, ed. Alexander Flick (1934); James Grant Wilson, *The Memorial History of the City of New-York* (1893); and Harry Yoshpe, *The Disposition of Loyalist Estates in the Southern District of the State of New York* (1939). For his participation in other businesses, see Joseph Davis, *Essays in the Earlier History of American Corporations* (2 vols., 1916–1917); Henry Domett, *A History of the Bank of New York* (1884); Robert East, *Business Enterprise in the American Revolutionary Era* (1938); Fox (1919); Julius Goebel, Jr., ed., *The Law Practice of Alexander Hamilton* (1964); and Harold Syrett et al., eds., *The Papers of Alexander Hamilton* (1961–1979).

SUE C. PATRICK

LOW, Seth (18 Jan. 1850–17 Sept. 1916), reform mayor and university president, was born in Brooklyn, New York, the son of Abiel Abbot Low, a merchant, and Ellen Almira Dow. Low's mother died a week after his birth, and two years later his father married Ann Davison Bedell Low, the widow of Low's uncle. Low had all the advantages of wealth and social status: he enjoyed a home in fashionable Brooklyn Heights, summers spent in New England, and travel in Europe. After graduating first in his class from Columbia College

in 1870, he joined his father's tea and silk importing firm, A. A. Low and Brothers, eventually becoming a full partner. On 9 December 1880 he married Annie Wroe Scollay Curtis; they had no children.

Financially secure and without enthusiasm for a business career, Low turned to public service as a more rewarding vocation. In 1876 he did volunteer work for the Brooklyn County Commission of Charities, and two years later he cofounded and became the first president of the Brooklyn Bureau of Charities. He organized a campaign club in Brooklyn in 1880 to promote Republican James A. Garfield's presidential candidacy, and the next year he and other club members reorganized as the Brooklyn Young Republican Club in time to participate in Brooklyn's mayoral election. The 1881 election was the first under the city's new charter, which greatly enhanced mayoral power.

Although a political newcomer, Low plunged into the nominating process, emerging as the only candidate acceptable to both the Young Republican Club and the regular Republican organization. Enough independents and antimachine Democrats joined Republican voters to give him a victory of 45,434 to 40,937 votes over Democratic incumbent James Howell. Renominated in 1883, Low narrowly defeated his Democratic opponent.

Low occupied an office of rising importance, and he provided a generally nonpartisan, honest, and efficient administration. He restructured Brooklyn's tax system and reduced the city's debt, initiated franchise reform, brought municipal departments under civil service, began new school construction, established a normal school for teacher training, and informally achieved home rule by convincing state legislators to grant him veto power over laws affecting the city. He also allowed orderly saloons to remain open on Sunday despite sabbath laws.

Low's mayoral record, his participation in the Mugwump Revolt in 1884 against Republican presidential nominee James G. Blaine, and his numerous speeches and publications on municipal problems propelled him into the front ranks of Gilded Age urban reformers and theorists. "An American View of Municipal Government in the United States," a chapter he wrote for James Bryce's *The American Commonwealth* (1888), probably was his best-known essay. Low located "the problem of city government" largely in faulty municipal structures and administrative practices, and optimistically he believed that honest, efficient, and responsive government could be achieved through placing competent men in charge of institutionally reformed city governments. Low's urban reform agenda included increasing mayoral power, especially over appointments, separating city balloting from state and national elections, reforming the franchise, and establishing municipal civil service and home rule.

In 1888, after leaving the mayoral office, he liquidated the family business, which made him independently wealthy. His career changed drastically the next year when the Columbia College Board of Trustees, on which he had sat since 1881, appointed him president of the college. His eleven-year tenure (1890–1901) proved to be "the turning point in Columbia's history," according to Columbia faculty member John W. Burgess.

Under Low, Columbia developed new academic programs, raised degree requirements in law and medicine, expanded the number of colleges that made up the university, organized a faculty council, introduced sabbaticals and a pension plan for faculty, created twenty-four university fellowships and a university press, and established reciprocal relations with three theological schools. Against some opposition and a good deal of skepticism, Low took a financial leap of faith in moving the college from 49th Street and Madison Avenue to Morningside Heights in uptown Manhattan. In addition, he contributed the money for a new library and invested $1 million in university bonds.

Low encouraged the faculty to take part in city affairs, just as he was politically engaged throughout the nineties. Resisting pressure from reform forces to run for mayor in 1894 on an anti-Tammany fusion ticket, he enthusiastically supported millionaire dry-goods merchant William L. Strong. He helped write the charter and was involved in the politics that brought Greater New York City into being in 1898. In addition, he was a member of the Rapid Transit Commission, chaired the board of the University Settlement Society, worked with the Church Association for the Advancement of the Interests of Labor, served as an arbiter in labor disputes, and was a delegate on the U.S. Commission to the Hague Arbitration Conference in 1899.

His stature among New York's religious, professional, and business leaders active in municipal reform causes was sufficiently high in 1897 for him to be nominated for mayor by the Citizens' Union, a newly created independent party committed to political and social reform. Despite, in his words, "one of the most remarkable efforts of the civic spirit witnessed in our day in the City of New York," neither he, nor the Republican candidate, nor the candidate of the anti-machine Jeffersonian Democracy could defeat Tammany's man.

In 1901, after four years of corrupt and incompetent Tammany control, Low again agreed to run for mayor. This time he was endorsed by a broader anti-Tammany coalition spearheaded by a politically wiser Citizens' Union and a more cooperative Republican party. He was elected, defeating his Democratic opponent by 296,813 votes to 265,177. He staffed city departments with professionally trained employees, often reaching out for recruits to the city's civic and professional organizations. He also brought into his administration Italians, Jews, and blacks who were underrepresented in the city's political system. As he had done in Brooklyn, he opened municipal board meetings to the press and met weekly with administrators, who, in the main, ran their departments with competence and efficiency.

Low restructured the city's tax system, which allowed him to reduce the real estate tax rate, and by 1903 he cut the budget by more than $1 million. He opposed municipal ownership of utilities, alienating some reformers, but he secured better administrative control over and monetary compensation from the city's many lucrative franchise grants to private utility companies. His administration also provided middle-class as well as poorer New Yorkers with moderate social reforms and expanded government services. Part of his success stemmed from the achievements of the men he appointed to head several city departments: public health services improved dramatically, the quality of tenement houses was upgraded, and welfare abuses were reduced. In addition, his administration, in office for only two years because of the charter revisions of 1901, substantially increased city expenditures for municipal parks and buildings, rapid transit and bridge construction, and harbor, street, and water system improvements.

Despite Low's integrity, efficient administration, and moderate reform record, he was repudiated in his 1903 reelection bid. His aloofness, pedantic style, and refusal to build his own political organization hurt him with voters of all classes. His efficiency drives alienated city workers, while his department heads' zealous enforcement of regulatory laws turned those voters adversely affected against him. His inability to provide faster solutions to politically volatile problems, such as transit congestion, police corruption, and inadequate school facilities, tarnished his image as a problem-solver. And his switch from lax to rigid enforcement of the Sunday ban on liquor sales alienated supporters on both sides of that troublesome issue. Abandoned by many independent Democrats and other groups, and only lukewarmly supported by some within reform's ranks, Low, the patrician reformer, was no match for the energetic George B. McClellan (1865–1940), son of the Civil War general and the Democratic candidate for mayor. He was defeated by more than 62,000 votes.

After leaving the mayoralty, Low spent the rest of his life championing the rights of labor and minorities. In 1905 he joined the National Civic Federation (NFC), becoming its president in 1908. As head of this progressive association, organized to settle labor disputes and promote industrial harmony, he supported labor's right to organize, strike, and engage in collective bargaining. He and the NCF wrote and lobbied for uniform state workmen's compensation and other laws beneficial to working people, secured from Congress the Newlands Act (1913) that provided for mediation of labor-management disputes on the railroads, and supported passage of the Federal Trade Commission Act (1914).

Also in 1905 he was elected to the board of trustees of Tuskegee Institute, becoming board chair two years later and serving the college and its students with distinction. Nationally, Low opposed literacy tests and other immigration restriction laws. In May 1914 he was elected president of the New York State Chamber of Commerce, an office his father had held fifty years earlier. Before illness forced him to resign in 1916, he used this position to promote better employer-employee relations and secure federal help for the nation's merchant marine, hurt by World War I. He renewed his interest in municipal government in 1915, serving as a delegate to the New York State Constitutional Convention, at which he chaired a committee on cities. His last years marred by illness, he died at Bedford Hills, New York.

Low's remarkable public career intersected with the urban and industrial forces that transformed American society during the late nineteenth and early twentieth centuries. His lack of charisma and passive leadership style have partly obscured his achievements. However, scholars have begun to reassess his significant contributions to public life in the age of reform.

• Low's papers are at Columbia University; the official papers of his New York City mayoral administration are in the Municipal Archives and Records Center of the City of New York. For a further sampling of his political thought, see "The Problem of City Government," *Notes Supplementary to the Johns Hopkins University Studies in Historical and Political Science, No. 4* (1889). A listing of Low's writings can be found in the excellent bibliography by Gerald Kurland, *Seth Low: The Reformer in an Urban and Industrial Age* (1971), which is the only comprehensive account of Low's life and career. But see, too, Benjamin R. C. Low, *Seth Low* (1925); Steven C. Swett, "The Test of a Reformer: A Study of Seth Low, New York City Mayor, 1902–1903," *New-York Historical Society Quarterly* 44 (1960): 5–41; James Coviello, "Seth Low as Mayor of New York" (master's thesis, Columbia Univ., 1938); and Richard S. Skolnik, "The Crystallization of Reform in New York City, 1890–1917" (Ph.D. diss., Yale Univ., 1964).

AUGUSTUS CERILLO, JR.

LOW, Will Hickok (13 May 1853–27 Nov. 1932), artist and author, was born in Albany, New York, the son of Addison Low, a cabinetmaker and construction engineer, and Elvira Steele. Low's interest in art began when he was very young and never waned. He was first attracted to the profession of sign painter, but after meeting an English painter who decorated railroad cars, called "head-linings," Low became more interested in painting scenes and later assisted the Englishman. He also was led to the distinguished and kindly Albany sculptor Erastus Dow Palmer through Palmer's son Walter, a classmate of Low's. Low's first teacher did not believe in much guidance; his advice to Low and his son, who became a landscape artist, was simply "study nature."

Low's parents, whom he described as "gentle and cultured," were unenthusiastic about his decision to become an artist. Nonetheless, at age seventeen he went to New York City, where he supported himself with occasional sales of drawings and paintings and with illustration work. He remained there for only two years during which time he was denied admission to the National Academy of Design (NAD) school because the drawing he sent was executed in pencil rather than charcoal or crayon as the review committee

preferred. He later regretted his decision not to comply with the committee's rule but fortunately a windfall enabled him to make his first trip to Paris to study at the École des Beaux-Arts with J. L. Gérome and Carolus-Duran. In addition to this structured study, Low was influenced by Paul Baudry, whose large mural decoration for the foyer of the new opera building being built in Paris shaped his opinion of large-scale wall painting. Low related his early days in Paris in *A Chronicle of Friendships: 1873–1900* (1908), in which he described the artists' life in Paris and in the Paris suburb of Barbizon. The book, his first, was dedicated to Berthe Eugenie Marie Julienne, whom he met in Paris and married in 1875. Low's *Chronicle* also recounted his close friendship with Scottish writer Robert Louis Stevenson. Berthe J. Low translated Stevenson's *Dr. Jekyll and Mr. Hyde* into French and had plans to proceed with all of his works, but her death, in 1909, intervened. Later that same year Low married Mary Louise Fairchild, the former wife of sculptor Frederick William MacMonnies and a fine artist in her own right. No children resulted from either marriage.

Low's *Reverie—In the Time of the First Empire* was accepted in the Salon of 1876, even though he went against the advice of Carolus-Duran, who told him not to send it. *Reverie* was then submitted to the annual NAD exhibition the following year in New York and caused a controversy that, along with the NAD's rejection of Augustus Saint-Gaudens's work, resulted in June 1877, at the close of the exhibition, in the formation of the Society of American Artists. It also resulted in Low becoming friends with Saint-Gaudens. Among Low's other friends were painter Theodore Robinson and multimedia artist John La Farge, from whom he acquired his knowledge of stained glass.

Low called the drawings he did to illustrate an 1885 edition of John Keats's *Lamia* his first success. Later in life he described the venture as:

an incident in the life of a young artist who had followed many false routes, who had met with little encouragement, who had been despaired of by others, though at the worst he had kept alive some small faith in himself, and at last, taking, as the French say, his courage in both hands, had made an effort to break the bonds in which circumstance, partially created by his own mistakes, had enmeshed him. (*A Painter's Progress*, p. 241)

In addition, Low illustrated a collection of Keats's works called *Odes and Sonnets* (1888).

Low was awarded the silver medal for the drawings he exhibited at the 1889 Paris exhibition. In his student days he had admired the work of Jean-François Millet and other Barbizon artists. The conversations he had with Millet in the French painter's home so impressed Low that he likened them to holding "converse with Boaz, Biblical master of the harvest; or rather with some Virgilian demi-god of the fields."

One little-known artistic endeavor undertaken by Low was the design of U.S. bank notes. For many years stock portraits had been used to decorate paper money, but after government officials learned that

U.S. bills were looked down upon in foreign markets, they hired artists to design the notes. Although referred to by the *Toledo Blade* as "the star of the government artists" who were in charge of "making money," Low can only definitely be credited with the design of the 1896 dollar, called "History Instructing Youth."

Low's work was featured in An Exhibition of Decorative Works by Three American Painters, held at the City Art Museum in St. Louis, Missouri, after 1909 and in a one-man show held at the Art Institute of Chicago in 1902. His wall-painting designs included murals for the ladies' reception room, concert hall, and ballroom of the Waldorf-Astoria Hotel in New York (1892, 1897), the Essex County Court House in Newark, New Jersey (1907), the Luzerne County Court House in Wilkes-Barre, Pennsylvania (1908), the federal building in Cleveland, Ohio (1910), Saint Paul's Protestant Episcopal Church in Albany, New York (1912), the rotunda of the state education building and the frieze of the legislative library, both at the New York state capitol in Albany, as well as for several private residences. *Victory 1918*, a war picture, was painted for Columbia University. Low won numerous awards and medals, both at home and abroad, and he served as a teacher from 1882 to 1885 at Cooper Union in New York and from 1889 to 1892 at the National Academy of Design. The fifth annual Scammon Lectures, delivered by Low in 1910 to students of the Art Institute of Chicago, were published that same year as *A Painter's Progress*. A memoir of his life as an artist, the book featured Low's reminiscences of artists who had influenced him and on his own artistic development as well as his views on art, for example, the virtues of mural painting. In addition to his books, Low contributed numerous articles to *Scribner's, Century, McClure's*, and other noted periodicals.

Low spent the latter part of his life at his home in the Lawrence Park section of Bronxville, New York. He summered in Milton, Massachusetts, where an old tool house served as his studio. Although he was one of the first American artists to work in plein air, he was not interested in innovation merely for the sake of effect, and as an older artist he took little interest in the "new art" of the twentieth century. Before his death, at his home in Lawrence Park, he summed up his sentiments by saying, "I suppose movements like these serve their purpose of stirring up the goldfish."

• The major sources of information on Low's life and works are his two books, *A Chronicle of Friendships* (1908) and *A Painter's Progress* (1910). In addition he is the author of many articles, including a three-part series, "A Century of Painting," in *McClure's Magazine*, Sept. 1896, pp. 293–304; Oct. 1896, pp. 415–26; and Apr. 1897, pp. 472–82; "National Expression in American Art," *International Monthly* 3 (Mar. 1901): 231–51; "The Mural Painter and His Public," *Scribner's Magazine*, Feb. 1907, pp. 253–56; and "Carolus-Duran: An Appreciation," *Scribner's Magazine*, June 1917, pp. 771–74. Besides the entries in the standard biographical dictionaries devoted to American artists, see Laura Meixner, "Will Hickok Low (1853–1932): His Early Career and Barbizon Experience," *American Art Journal* 17 (Autumn 1985). For his work designing bank notes see the *Toledo* (Ohio) *Blade*, 22 Feb. 1896. An obituary is in the *New York Times*, 28 Nov. 1932.

MARIANNE BERGER WOODS

LOWDEN, Frank Orren (26 Jan. 1861–20 Mar. 1943), businessman, governor of Illinois, and agriculturist, was born near the village of Sunrise City, Minnesota, the son of Lorenzo Orren Lowden and Nancy Elizabeth Bregg, and grew up in central Iowa. His father, a restless and independent man, worked as blacksmith and farmer, then studied law while in his forties; he was also somewhat of a rebel and political activist, involved in the Grange and the Democratic and Greenback parties. Lowden studied at rural schools, became a teacher at the age of fourteen, and in 1881 entered the University of Iowa, where he graduated as valedictorian in 1885. He then moved to Chicago, where he studied law at the Union College of Law, graduating in 1887, and landed a position at a major law firm. In 1896 he married Florence Pullman, daughter of the extremely wealthy and powerful industrialist George M. Pullman. They had four children.

The combination of Lowden's own talents plus his wife's immense wealth and social position rapidly made him a leading figure in Chicago, both as a lawyer and an investor/businessman. He also entered Chicago politics in the 1890s as a moderately independent Republican, opposed to the spoils system and the local Republican "machine." In 1902 he and his family moved to their new, magnificent estate, "Sinnissippi," on the Rock River near Oregon, Illinois, where his agricultural interests began to develop. Over time, Lowden evolved from a "gentleman farmer" to a sophisticated agriculturist, focusing on dairy farming in Illinois but also owning extensive cotton acreage in Arkansas.

Lowden became increasingly active in Republican politics at the turn of the century. He was appointed to Congress in 1906 and then elected to the post in 1908. In Washington, as later in Springfield, Lowden was particularly adept in the area of administrative reform; he was not a leading figure, politically or in terms of policy, in the House. Finding himself appointed to the Foreign Affairs Committee (rather than the Agriculture Committee, which he wanted), an area in which he had little knowledge or experience, his main activities related to applying civil service principles to the State Department and providing sufficient funding to avoid making ambassadorial posts available only to the wealthy (the Embassy Bill, 1911). Lowden was very middle of the road on the central issues of progressivism (the tariff and banking control, for example) and was fiscally conservative. He did continue to support agriculture, however, and offered legislative initiatives for programs to provide federal funding for research into hog cholera and federal control of insecticides shipped in interstate commerce.

While sympathetic to federal support of agriculture, Lowden was leery of undue expansion of the federal government's role in economics generally, particularly if it threatened to unbalance the budget. He was neither notably pro- nor antilabor, somewhat reluctantly supported the income tax amendment, and shared the general sense that some large private interests were too rich and powerful. His support for progressive programs was limited by his primary concern with agricultural issues and his own background and contacts, which tended to be with conservative Republicans. Thus, while he was friendly with Theodore Roosevelt (1858–1919), he had no difficulty in supporting William Howard Taft in the 1912 presidential election. Although Lowden shared some characteristics and some interests with the progressives, he would never be clearly identified with or accepted by them.

Lowden decided not to run for reelection in 1910, for health reasons. He was frequently ill throughout his adult life, often with rather vague symptoms—fatigue, "frayed nerves," and so on—which were not uncommon to Victorians, and the extent to which they were psychological as much as physical is difficult to judge. He returned to his expansive business interests, primarily as an investor. He remained politically active, as Republican national committeeman for Illinois, and worked to reunite the Republican party after its 1912 splintering. In 1916 he was the successful Republican candidate for governor, defeating the Democratic incumbent, Edward F. Dunne. During his single term, Lowden focused primarily on administrative reform, particularly in introducing a budget system. He was more comfortable with progressive issues at the state level than he had been as a national legislator, supporting woman suffrage, civil service reform, an eight-hour day for female workers, and stronger workmen's compensation contributions from business. Like many other marginal progressives, he was open to some government regulation of business but strongly opposed to government ownership. Similarly, he resisted most government involvement in social problems, as in his vetoes of bills to control racially incendiary materials and to prohibit owners of public facilities from advertising that they did not admit persons of a given race, religion, or nationality. Lowden did not get directly involved in the great Chicago race riot of 1919, which was a loaded gun both politically and socially. He preferred that Chicago Mayor William Hale Thompson, with whom his political relationship was always touchy, bear the responsibility. Lowden did appoint the Chicago Commission on Race Relations to study the causes of the violence once the riot had ended.

As Lowden looked to his own political future, he had to maneuver within a highly factionalized Illinois Republican party, which reflected the progressive–old guard split and had numerous leaders (including Thompson, Charles S. Deneen, and Senator Medill McCormick) who were trying to build their own organizations for control of the party and of nominations.

The governorship was a good launching pad for the 1920 Republican presidential nomination, and Lowden became one of the main contenders. His major strength, in being closely identified with neither the weakened progressive wing nor the old guard wing of the party, was ultimately also a source of weakness. To the progressives, Hiram Johnson and General Leonard Wood were much preferred; to many conservatives they were not as well known and reliable as Senator Warren G. Harding; and to those fighting the League of Nations, Senator William Borah was clearly preferable. Thus the prize was denied Lowden.

Refusing to run again for governor or to accept cabinet and ambassadorial posts offered him by Harding and his successors, Lowden returned to private life in the 1920s. He did mount modest campaigns for the 1924 and 1928 Republican presidential nominations, but they were unsuccessful. In good part, that was because his main political interests in the 1920s, like his nonpolitical ones, revolved around agriculture. He became a leading figure in numerous agricultural organizations and, after first opposing it, ultimately became a strong advocate of the controversial McNary-Haugen plan for agricultural relief, particularly its equalization fee, which guaranteed minimum price levels to producers of major crops. He became head of the Country Life Commission in 1929, reflecting his concern with the social as well as economic status of American farmers.

Lowden strongly opposed President Herbert Hoover's agricultural policies, arguing that voluntary production controls were an inadequate solution to the problem of agricultural overproduction. He was sympathetic to the approach taken by the New Deal's Agricultural Adjustment Act, with its more effective production controls and its efforts to increase farmers' purchasing power and ease the problem of farm debt. However, that was not sufficient to overcome his generally conservative and Republican opposition to the major domestic programs of Franklin D. Roosevelt and the New Deal. In the later 1930s Lowden also became an isolationist and was involved in the America First Committee—another typical position for a person with his agricultural background and political interests.

Lowden's wife died in 1937, when he, too, was ailing, from both age and the variety of illnesses that had continually plagued him. He died in Tucson, Arizona.

• Lowden's personal papers are at the University of Chicago, and his official gubernatorial papers are at the Illinois State Library, Springfield. Only one serious study of Lowden's life exists, William T. Hutchinson, *Lowden of Illinois: The Life of Frank O. Lowden* (2 vols., 1957). His campaign for the presidential nomination is discussed in Joseph B. Miller, "A Rhetorical Analysis of the Campaign Speaking of Frank O. Lowden in Quest of the 1920 Republican Presidential Nomination" (Ph.D. diss., Case Western Reserve Univ., 1974); Randolph C. Downes, *The Rise of Warren Gamaliel Harding, 1865–1920* (1970); and Francis Russell, *The Shadow of Blooming Grove: Warren G. Harding in His Times* (1968). His role in the Chicago race riot is covered in William M. Tuttle, Jr., *Race Riot: Chicago in the Red Summer of 1919* (1970). There is a fairly complete obituary in the *Chicago Tribune*, 21 Mar. 1943.

JOHN M. ALLSWANG

LOWELL, A. Lawrence (13 Dec. 1856–6 Jan. 1943), university president, was born Abbott Lawrence Lowell in Boston, Massachusetts, the son of Augustus Lowell, a prominent businessman, and Katherine Bigelow Lawrence. Endowed with a lengthy legacy of achievement in the legal profession and business on both sides of his family, Lowell also had two siblings who achieved notable success; while his older brother Percival became a famous astronomer, his younger sister Amy gained recognition as a poet. After beginning his formal education at a local private academy founded by W. Eliot Fette, Lowell traveled with his family to Europe in the spring of 1864. Although the voyage was initiated in the hope of reviving his mother's failing health, it also gave Lowell and his brother the opportunity to attend a boarding school in Paris. Following two years at the school (which was run by a Mr. Kornemann), he returned with his family to Boston. At another local private academy (George W. C. Noble's), he completed his college preparations.

An indifferent student, Lowell nevertheless entered Harvard in the fall of 1873; he continued to achieve only mediocre academic success until his sophomore year. Mathematics proved to be his strongest subject, and under the guidance of noted instructor Benjamin Pierce he took second year honors in the subject. Although Lowell became a member of Hasty Pudding (famous for its comic theatricals), he was never admitted to any of the "final clubs" that claimed the cream of the Harvard student body and to which he might have (given his family background and social prestige) reasonably expected acceptance; instead he focused on his newly found interest in math. Always robust in constitution, he also excelled in intracollegiate running events.

After graduating cum laude in 1877, Lowell immediately entered Harvard Law School. At the time, the curriculum was in the process of expanding from two to three years, and students briefly possessed the opportunity of earning their third year's credit by examination. Lowell availed himself of this opportunity and graduated cum laude in 1880. He had previously, in June 1879, married Anna Parker Lowell, a distant cousin; the couple was to be childless. After clerking in the local law office of Russell and Putnam, Lowell gained admission to the Massachusetts bar in July 1880. That same year he formed a legal partnership with his brother-in-law Francis Cabot Lowell; the two were joined the following year by Frederic J. Stimson. Although all three men later achieved careers of distinction, Lawrence Lowell gained neither success nor wealth from his legal practice. He did, however, follow family tradition by entering public service. He became a member of the Corporation at the Massachusetts Institute of Technology in 1890 and in 1895 began a three-year term on the Boston School Committee.

Scholarship offered the young attorney additional outlets. His first book (coauthored with his brother-in-law) was *The Transfer of Stock in Private Corporations* (1884), which proved useful to practicing attorneys for a time. But Lowell's interests had already begun to shift. His second book, *Essays on Government* (1889), while little noticed, did attract the attention of Woodrow Wilson, who began corresponding with Lowell, and the two men soon forged a lasting friendship despite their differences over the relative merits of the English and American national governments. Lowell's third book, *Governments and Parties in Continental Europe* (2 vols., 1896), was better received; as the first comprehensive study of European governments by an American, it confirmed Lowell's reputation as a scholar and brought him an invitation to teach at his alma mater in 1897.

Although Lowell's appointment to teach Existing Political Systems was only temporary and part time, he immediately resigned from his legal practice and threw himself into teaching. A popular lecturer, he joined with Silas Macvane in 1898–1899 to teach Government I, a large introductory course. His scholarship in the meantime did not languish; in addition to producing two articles for the *Harvard Law Review*, he published *The Government of Dependencies* (1899) and *Colonial Civil Service* (1900). Appointed to a full-time academic appointment in 1900, Lowell became professor of the science of government; he also assumed full responsibility for teaching Government I, whose enrollment soon reached four hundred. Despite being a relative latecomer to academia—he was forty-one when first appointed to the Harvard faculty—Lowell did not shy away from aggressively seeking to improve the quality of undergraduate education at Harvard. As a leading member of the Committee on Improving Instruction in 1902–1903, Lowell drew on information gained from a set of questionnaires completed by both faculty and students; as a result of the committee's findings, residency requirements for a bachelor's degree were fixed at four years (students had previously held the option of taking their diploma after only three years' study). In 1908 Lowell chaired another committee that found undergraduate aspirations to academic achievement sadly wanting. Lowell's most significant scholarly work, *The Government of England* (1908), appeared at a fortuitous time for Lowell because Harvard president Charles W. Eliot had announced that he would retire at the end of the 1908–1909 academic year. By virtue of his scholarship, administrative committee work, and family position, Lowell (who had long aspired to the post) was the overwhelming choice to replace Eliot. Elected in January 1909, Lowell assumed his new duties in May of the same year.

On becoming president, Lowell immediately set out to rectify what he perceived to be the institution's shortcomings. Although the graduate and professional schools had flourished under his predecessor's long tenure (1869–1909), many people associated with Harvard felt that the quality of undergraduate instruction had slipped badly. Critics of the system focused much of their attention on Eliot's vaunted free elective system, which allowed a student complete freedom in selecting his courses. A radical innovation at the time of its inception, the elective system was felt by many to be out of control, with students selecting courses on the basis of their relative ease rather than their academic merits. Lowell was also troubled by what he perceived as increasing social segregation among the undergraduates, with wealthier students from exclusive preparatory school backgrounds congregating in a series of dwellings on Mount Auburn Avenue (the "Gold Coast") while their less genteel brethren had to make do with boarding houses and university dormitories of inferior quality.

Lowell first took on the matter of undergraduate course selection. Based largely on the results of his last committee assignment, the curriculum was reformed in 1910. Students were henceforth required to take a concentration of at least six courses in one field as well as at least six courses from a variety of the academic divisions. Long interested in increasing the number of students striving for academic honors, Lowell also instituted general examinations in most of the possible areas of concentration. In an effort to aid students in their studies, Lowell also set up a tutorial system that employed faculty members as student advisers in matters such as course coordination and outside readings. Because the new system (which drew heavily on the English systems at Oxford and Cambridge for inspiration) required so much additional effort and time, Lowell introduced yet another innovation: the "reading period," a three-week block of time at the end of each semester that allowed students the opportunity to coordinate and clarify their studies. Results were impressive; between 1922 and 1927 graduates with honors rose from 21 percent to 32 percent of the graduating class.

With his academic reforms well underway, Lowell turned his attention to the matter of student housing, having long been eager to see students from different backgrounds and locations living together and mixing socially. By 1914 the first new freshman dormitory at Harvard opened its doors, and mandatory freshmen residency had its beginnings. When the freshman residency plan proved successful, it provided further momentum toward another long-cherished vision of Lowell's: the formation of "houses" for the upperclassmen. In this endeavor he had the unlikely assistance of a Yale graduate, Edward Stephen Harkness, who had sought to donate sufficient funds to his own alma mater for such a purpose, only to experience delays and frustrations in having his gift accepted. Harness first approached Lowell with his proposition in November 1928 and ultimately donated $13 million to the project. The Harvard House Plan overcame sharp opposition among the undergraduates (mostly from final club men who feared its effect on their own organizations) and became a reality with the opening of the first two Houses in 1930 (five more Houses opened in the following year). Again taking his cue from Oxford and Cambridge, Lowell made sure that each House had its own dining room and library; staff consisted of resident tutors and a master.

Residential housing for students was only the most visible example of campus development that occurred during the Lowell administration. The overall number of students increased from 4,046 in 1909 to 8,227 in 1932, while the number of instructors and administrators rose from 743 to 1,635 in the same period. Although he disliked the sobriquet "The Builder," the physical growth of the campus during his administration was truly remarkable. Altogether sixty-seven structures were either built or modified during his tenure, Widener Library (1915) and the Fogg Art Museum (1927) being among the more prominent. Of course, such expansion required enormous amounts of capital, and during the Lowell presidency Harvard's endowment rose from $22.7 million to $128.5 million. Lowell claimed to be a miserable fundraiser, but he was fortunate in having numerous individuals provide generous support, as well as institutions such as the Carnegie Corporation and the General Education Board (wealthy in his own right, Lowell himself gave several million dollars to the university).

In the course of his many successes, Lowell also experienced failures along the way. Believing that two institutions offering similar instruction side-by-side were a waste of resources, he pushed long and hard for a merger between Harvard's engineering school and nearby Massachusetts Institute of Technology. The plan engendered enormous alumni resentment, and the merger was ultimately dissolved by court order in 1917. Lowell's undergraduate living program also produced one of the hotter controversies during his presidency. In 1922–1923, when Roscoe Conkling Bruce, Jr., son of an African American who had also attended Harvard, attempted to reside in the freshman halls, Lowell enforced an edict that disallowed racial mixing in the living quarters on campus. (Two decades before, Bruce's father did not face such an edict.) Claiming that he favored equal opportunity for all, Lowell nevertheless declared, "We have not thought it possible to compel men of different races to reside together" (qtd. in Sollors et al., p. 203). The issue became a matter of national debate. The Harvard Board of Overseers in fact overturned Lowell's decision, but for years thereafter African-American students were housed in out-of-the-way residential buildings. Even greater controversy was sparked by Lowell's attempt to reduce the number of Jewish students enrolling at Harvard. Lowell, who purported to be a thoroughgoing assimilationist, was especially alarmed by the rising percentage of Jewish students in the college. Although he contended that "excessive" numbers of Jews on campus would breed anti-Semitism, he failed to impose the kind of quota he thought desirable. The university's new commitment to a "national" student body, however, was aimed at broadening the demographic mix on campus, with the result that the number of Jewish students did decline.

On one issue, Lowell was a staunch defender of those who were not in the mainstream. His advocacy of academic freedom of speech first became prominent during World War I, when he stood up for Professor

Hugo Munsterberg's right to champion the German cause. At the time of the bitter Boston police strike of 1919, when Lowell urged Harvard students to act as strikebreakers, he defended before the Board of Overseers the right of Harold J. Laski, then an untenured lecturer, to express the opposite viewpoint. In 1921, when Professor Zechariah Chafee faced censure from the board for criticizing prosecutions conducted under the Espionage Act of 1918, Lowell again took up the cause of academic freedom of speech.

During the war years, Lowell was a member of the League to Enforce Peace, an organization founded in 1917 that antagonized other antiwar groups because of its willingness to see force used to bring about peace. Following the war, the group stood behind Woodrow Wilson's efforts to have the Versailles treaty and its League of Nations Covenant ratified by the U.S. Senate; Lowell was himself tireless in arguing for the League of Nations. But in October 1920 he helped write the "Statement of the Thirty-one Republicans," which urged the election of Warren Harding and a modified League of Nations.

The last major controversy in which Lowell became embroiled took place in 1927, when he was appointed to a commission charged with reviewing the case of Nicola Sacco and Bartolomeo Vanzetti, two Italian-born anarchists convicted of robbery and murder. The prosecution was held by many to have made the radicalism of the defendants the real basis for convicting them, and those who sympathized with Sacco and Vanzetti saw an insidious class bias at work. Because the review commission concluded that no legal basis for a retrial could be found, the governor of Massachusetts, Alvan T. Fuller, was deaf to international pleas on Sacco and Vanzetti's behalf. Following their execution in August 1927, Lowell was vilified; for the rest of his life, he was to receive hate mail on every anniversary of that event.

In declining health, Lowell resigned as Harvard president in 1933. Before he did so, he created the Society of Fellows, which provided the most promising graduate students with a three-year stipend and free access to university resources and came to carry great prestige. In retirement, Lowell published *At War with Academic Traditions in America* (1934) and *What a University President Has Learned* (1938). Opposed to much of Franklin D. Roosevelt's New Deal, he promoted in 1935 the creation of the Constitutional party from a fusion of conservative Democrats and Republicans, but he met with no success. He died in Boston.

A. Lawrence Lowell defies easy definition. Born into the Boston elite, he nevertheless worked to undercut the social elitism of Harvard College by urging the ideal of the "well-rounded man." Intelligent and undaunted by opposition, he was determined to make the university a haven for the highest academic achievement. But, in his view of people outside his milieu, he remained very much of his class and his time. While Lowell's contributions to Harvard continue to be acknowledged, few historians have forgiven him his prejudices.

• The papers of Abbott Lawrence Lowell are held at the Harvard University archives in Cambridge, Massachusetts. In addition to the texts already cited, Lowell was the author of *Public Opinion and Popular Government* (1913), *Public Opinion in War and Peace* (1923), and *Conflicts of Principle* (1932). The standard biography of Lowell is Henry A. Yeomans, *Abbott Lawrence Lowell, 1856–1943* (1948); while detailed and balanced in approach, it glosses over many of the more controversial aspects of his career. Still useful are Samuel Eliot Morison, ed., *The Development of Harvard University since the Inauguration of President Eliot, 1869–1929* (1930) and his *Three Centuries of Harvard, 1636–1936* (1936). Lowell has not been treated kindly by recent scholars; for an extremely negative view of his role in the Jewish controversy, see Marcia Graham Synnott, *The Half-Opened Door: Discrimination and Admissions at Harvard, Yale, and Princeton, 1900–1970* (1979). Regarding his treatment of African Americans, see Werner Sollors et al., eds., *Blacks at Harvard: A Documentary History of African-American Experience at Harvard and Radcliffe* (1993). His role in the peace movement is covered in Ruhl J. Bartlett, *The League to Enforce Peace* (1944). Literature on the Sacco and Vanzetti case abounds; among the best sources are David Felix, *Protest: Sacco-Vanzetti and the Intellectuals* (1965), and G. Louis Joughin and Edmund M. Morgan, *The Legacy of Sacco and Vanzetti* (1948). An obituary is in the *New York Times*, 7 Jan. 1943.

EDWARD L. LACH, JR.

LOWELL, Amy (9 Feb. 1874–12 May 1925), poet, critic, and lecturer, was born in Brookline, Massachusetts, the daughter of Augustus Lowell and Katherine Bigelow Lawrence. Both sides of the family were New England aristocrats, wealthy and prominent members of society. Augustus Lowell was a businessman, civic leader, and horticulturalist, Katherine Lowell an accomplished musician and linguist. Although considered as "almost disreputable," poets were part of the Lowell family, including James Russell Lowell, a first cousin, and later Robert Lowell.

As the daughter of a wealthy family, Lowell was first educated at the family home, "Sevenels" (named by her father as a reference to the seven Lowells living there), by an English governess who left her with a lifelong inability to spell. Her first poem, "Chacago," written at age nine, is testament to this problem. In the fall of 1883 Lowell began attending a series of private schools in Brookline and Boston. At school she was "the terror of the faculty" (Gould, p. 32). Even at Mrs. Cabot's school, founded by a Lowell cousin to educate her own children and the children of friends and relations, Lowell was "totally indifferent to classroom decorum. Noisy, opinionated, and spoiled, she terrorized the other students and spoke back to her teachers" (Heymann, p. 164).

During school vacations Lowell traveled with her family. She went to Europe and to New Mexico and California. On the latter trip she kept a travel journal. Lowell enjoyed writing, and two stories she wrote during this time were printed in *Dream Drops; or, Stories from Fairyland* (1887), by a "Dreamer." The volume was published privately by her mother, who also contributed material, and the proceeds were donated to the Perkins Institute for the Blind.

Lowell's schooling included the usual classes in English, history, French, literature, and a little Italian. As Lowell later noted, "My family did not consider that it was necessary for girls to learn either Greek or Latin" (Damon, p. 87). She would also describe her formal education as not amounting to "a hill of beans" (Benvenuto, p. 6). School ended in 1891, and Lowell made her debut. Described as the "most popular debutante of the season," she went to sixty dinners given in her honor. Her popularity was attributed to her skills in dancing and in the art of conversation, but her debut did not produce the expected marriage proposal.

Although Lowell had finished formal schooling, she continued to educate herself. Unfortunately, higher education was not an option for Lowell women. She put herself through a "rigorous" reading program, using her father's 7,000-volume library and the resources of the Boston Athenaeum (her great-grandfather was one of the founders). Later Lowell would successfully speak out against the proposed relocation of the Athenaeum; this would also become the subject of a poem. Lowell's love of books themselves began with her first "Rollo" book, *Rollo Learning to Read*, which her mother gave her when she was six. This gift marked the beginning of an enthusiasm for book collecting that would last throughout her life. In 1891 she made her first major purchase of a set of the complete works of Sir Walter Scott with money she had received as a Christmas gift. It was, however, her collection of Keatsiana, including a rare first edition of *Lamia* inscribed to F. B. from J. K. (Fanny Brawne from John Keats), that put her in the forefront of international book collectors.

Following her debut, Lowell led the life of a prominent socialite, visiting, going to parties and the theater, and traveling. Her mother, who had been an invalid for years, died in 1895. A disappointment in love prompted a winter trip to Egypt in 1897–1898. Lowell had accepted the proposal of a Bostonian whom she loved, but before the engagement was formally announced he "became entangled elsewhere" (Damon, p. 120). "The family could do nothing to protect her except guard tenaciously the name of the errant suitor" (Gould, p. 65). The trip was also for "health" reasons. Doctors felt Lowell's obesity could be cured by the Egyptian heat and a diet of nothing but tomatoes and asparagus. The regimen almost killed her and resulted in a "prolonged nervous collapse." In 1900 Lowell's father died, and she bought Sevenels. She also bought a summer home in Dublin, New Hampshire, that she named "Broomley Lacey." The area was home to the MacDowell Artists' Colony as well as to other notable painters and sculptors.

In Brookline Lowell assumed her father's civic responsibilities. Early in 1902 she spoke against the reappointment of the elderly superintendent of the Brookline public school system. She was the "first woman in the Lowell family to make a speech in public" (Gould, p. 77). Initially booed, Lowell continued to speak with her usual forthrightness and, at the end,

won applause as well as her point. Lowell became a member of the executive committee of the Brookline Education Society and chair of its Library Board.

In October 1902 Lowell became a poet. Her interest in verse had been growing beyond her childhood enthusiasm, fueled by her reading Leigh Hunt's *Imagination and Fancy; or, Selections from the English Poets*, which she had found "near the ceiling" in her father's library. The volume was a revelation to her, opening a "door that might otherwise have remained shut," Lowell remarked (Gould, p. 51). She had become enamored of poetry and the poets Hunt discussed, particularly Keats. After she saw Eleanora Duse perform one October night she wrote her first adult poem, "Eleanora Duse." Although some critics say that she was being too hard on herself, Lowell described the 71-line poem as having "every cliche and every technical error which a poem can have." Yet she also said, "It loosed a bolt in my brain and I found out where my true function lay" (Damon, p. 148). At age twenty-eight she had discovered her calling: to be a poet.

In 1910 four of Lowell's sonnets were accepted for publication by the *Atlantic Monthly*. "A Fixed Idea," published first, appeared in August of that year. By 1912 she had published her first book of poetry, *A Dome of Many-Coloured Glass*; the title came from Percy Bysshe Shelley's *Adonais*, his elegy for Keats. It was not well received by either the public or the critics. Louis Untermeyer wrote that the book "to be brief, in spite of its lifeless classicism, can never rouse one's anger. But, to be briefer still, it cannot rouse one at all" (Damon, p. 192).

Yet 1912 was also the year that Lowell met actress Ada Dwyer Russell. The friendship between the two women has been described as platonic by some, as lesbian by others; it was, in fact, a "Boston marriage." They lived together and were committed to each other until Lowell's death. Russell was Lowell's companion, providing love and emotional support, as well as the practical skill of organizing Lowell's busy life. Biographer Richard Benvenuto observed that Lowell's "great creative output between 1914 and 1925 would not have been possible without her friend's steadying, supporting presence" (p. 10).

The following year Lowell discovered some poems in *Poetry* by Hilda Doolittle, signed "H.D. Imagiste." Lowell felt an identification with the style of H.D.'s poetry and determined to discover more about it. Armed with a letter of introduction from *Poetry* editor Harriet Monroe, Lowell traveled to London to meet Ezra Pound, head of the imagist movement. In London Lowell not only learned about imagism and free verse from Pound, but she also met many poets, several of whom became lifelong friends. Over the years Lowell would develop many literary friendships that resulted in an enormous volume of literary correspondence, requiring Lowell to employ two full-time secretaries. Lowell not only supported and encouraged other poets with her writing, such as her favorable review of Robert Frost's *North of Boston* in the *New Republic* (20 Feb. 1915), but also with money and gifts.

Lowell's poems began to appear in increasing numbers in journals, and she was becoming a prolific writer of essays and reviews. Pound had requested the inclusion of her poem "In a Garden" in his anthology *Des Imagistes* (1914). Later Lowell and Pound would have a falling out over the direction of the imagist movement, and Pound would call the movement, as adapted by Lowell, "Amygism." Lowell became the spokesperson of imagism, leading the fight for the "renewal of poetry in her homeland" (Francis, p. 510), and her efforts were tireless. She traveled throughout the country, "selling" the new poetry.

Her own volume *Sword Blades and Poppy Seed* (1914), written in free verse and polyphonic prose, a Lowell invention, "brought her an instantaneous phenomenal rise to fame" (Gould, p. 139). Lowell's first book of criticism, *Six French Poets* (1915), based on a series of her lectures, was also well received.

Lowell was publishing a book a year, alternating between volumes of short verse and longer poems. *Men, Women and Ghosts* (1916) was highly regarded and contained "Patterns," one of her most famous poems. In it an eighteenth-century woman, walking in her garden, contemplates a future that has suddenly become empty because of the loss of her fiancé in battle; she mourns the fact that the "patterns" of her role required her to remain chaste before marriage. The next year she published another critical volume, *Tendencies in Modern American Poetry*, which included essays on six contemporary poets: Edwin Arlington Robinson, Robert Frost, Edgar Lee Masters, Carl Sandburg, H.D., and John Gould Fletcher. Lowell also published anthologies of imagist poets in 1915, 1916, and 1917. Her next volume of poetry, *Can Grande's Castle* (1918), included four long poems; the title was taken from the name of the refuge where Dante, the Florentine exile, wrote portions of his *Divine Comedy*. Inspired by her lifelong interest in the Orient, *Pictures of a Floating World* (1919) is a translation of the Japanese word *ukiyo-e*, a term commonly associated with a form of eighteenth-century Japanese painting. It includes 174 short, free verse lyrics, considered by some as "overtly erotic." For example, "A Decade" and "The Weather-Cock Points South" are described as a celebration of lesbian devotion. *Legends* (1921) contains eleven longer poems, and *Fir-Flower Tablets* (1921) is a collection of poems based on translations of ancient Chinese verse. Since Lowell did not read Chinese, she was dependent on English translations by Florence Wheelock Ayscough, which Lowell then turned back into poetry.

A Critical Fable (1922) is a long, humorous poem, evaluating the state of contemporary poetry. Originally published anonymously, the poem pokes fun at fellow poets and at Lowell herself in lines of rhymed couplets. The poem was modeled on James Russell Lowell's *A Fable for Critics* (1848).

Her last publication was the momentous biography *John Keats* (1925). In 1921 Lowell had given an address at Yale honoring Keats on the one-hundredth anniversary of his birth. The lecture stimulated her to write the book, which minutely examines Keats's life and corrects some long-standing misconceptions about him. Lowell was also the first biographer to see Fanny Brawne in a favorable light. The book was well received in the United States but not in Britain, where she was accused of writing "a psychological thriller" rather than a literary biography. Lowell was angry and heartbroken but in typical fashion determined to confront the critics on their own turf. Accordingly, she planned to travel to England. The journey was never made; Lowell died of a cerebral hemorrhage at Sevenels.

Posthumous publications, edited by Ada Dwyer Russell, are *What's O'Clock*, which won the Pulitzer Prize for poetry in 1925 and includes the frequently anthologized poem "Lilacs"; *East Wind* (1926); and *Ballads for Sale* (1927).

Perhaps Lowell's poetry was not sufficiently recognized during her lifetime, but she did write more than 650 poems, and she is now acknowledged as the first American woman poet to see herself as part of a feminine literary tradition, reflected in poems such as "The Sisters." What her contemporaries did realize was that Lowell made things happen for American poetry through her own innovations and her support of other poets. Lowell's lectures on the "new poetry" of imagism and free verse drew large crowds, and she was so persuasive that the public began accepting her literary judgments "as nothing less than gospel" (Heymann, p. 214). T. S. Eliot described her as a "demon saleswoman of poetry" (Heymann, p. 217), and Sandburg remarked on her forceful presence: "To argue with her is like arguing with a big blue wave" (Heymann, p. 217). Frost wrote in a tribute that she "helped to make it stirring times for a decade to those immediately concerned with art and to many not so immediately" (Francis, p. 512).

• Lowell's correspondence, private papers, and some manuscripts are in the Houghton Library at Harvard University. Her collection of rare books and manuscripts is also at Harvard. Brown has other manuscripts and pictures in the Harris collection. The Alderman Library at the University of Virginia has papers, and her letters to Harriet Monroe are at the University of Chicago. A complete list of her work is in the definitive biography by S. Foster Damon, *Amy Lowell: A Chronicle with Extracts from Her Correspondence* (1935). Other book-length biographies that include critical material are Richard Benvenuto, *Amy Lowell* (1985); Glenn Richard Ruihley, *The Thorn of a Rose: Amy Lowell Reconsidered* (1975); and Jean Gould, *Amy: The World of Amy Lowell and the Imagist Movement* (1975). Several books have chapters on Lowell. Particularly interesting are C. David Heymann, *American Aristocracy: The Lives and Times of James Russell, Amy, and Robert Lowell* (1980), and Cheryl Walker, "Women and Feminine Literary Traditions: Amy Lowell and the Androgynous Persona," in her *Masks Outrageous and Austere* (1991). Significant articles include Lesley Lee Francis, "A Decade of 'Stirring Times': Robert Frost and Amy Lowell," *New England Quarterly* 59 (Dec. 1986): 508–22; Andrew Thacker, "Amy Lowell and H.D.: The Other Imagists," *Women: A Cultural Review* 4 (Spring 1993): 49–59; Lillian Faderman, "Cigar-Smoking Sappho: Lesbian Laureate Amy

Lowell Took Her World by Storm," *Advocate*, 13 Feb. 1990; and Jane P. Ambrose, "Amy Lowell and the Music of Her Poetry," *New England Quarterly* 62 (Mar. 1989): 45–62. An obituary is in the *New York Times*, 13 May 1925.

MARCIA B. DINNEEN

LOWELL, Francis Cabot (7 Apr. 1775–10 Aug. 1817), textile manufacturer, was born in Newburyport, Massachusetts, the son of John Lowell, a judge, and Susanna Cabot. He enrolled in 1789 at Harvard College, where he was proficient at mathematics. He was rusticated during his senior year for starting a fire in the Yard and was required to study under the Reverend Zedekiah Sanger of nearby Bridgewater, Massachusetts, before graduating with his class in 1793. After graduation he began almost at once to work in an import-export company with William Cabot, an uncle. Lowell took business trips to Canada, France, and eastern seaboard states, establishing trade connections with Nathan Appleton, the wealthy Boston importer, and other men with commercial interests. He was particularly impressed with Boston merchant Uriah Cutting's promotion of public improvements. In 1798 Lowell married Hannah Jackson; they had four children. In 1802, when his father died, Lowell, his brother Charles Lowell, and his half brother John Lowell inherited an estate of $80,000, mostly invested in eight ships. By 1804 Lowell had a financial interest in a distillery, and in 1807 he was a proprietor, with Cutting and others, of holdings on Boston's India Street, including India Wharf.

By 1810 Lowell was moderately wealthy, partly as a result of the Canton trade and exporting flour to Spain. That year Lowell took his family to Edinburgh, Scotland, to improve his and his wife's ill health and also to observe power looms producing cotton fabric in Manchester and other locations. In 1811, while rendezvousing with Appleton in Edinburgh, Lowell revealed that he hoped to build a textile mill back home. He felt that New England would prosper only by supplementing its trade with manufacturing. During his years abroad Lowell by correspondence developed a commercial relationship in real estate and cloth-making ventures with his fiscally daring brother-in-law Patrick Tracy Jackson.

Returning to Massachusetts in 1812, Lowell was aware that the War of 1812 would cripple his overseas trade. He enlisted Jackson's cooperation, and the two spearheaded the establishment of the Boston Manufacturing Company in 1813. Although records are scant, it seems that Lowell took the lead in expanding the company during its early years. In February 1813 it was incorporated with a subscription of $100,000, including Lowell's $15,000, and chartered to capitalize at $400,000, which it soon did. To design a prototype loom, Lowell relied on his memory of machinery seen in Manchester, Lancaster, and elsewhere and on rough sketches smuggled out of patent-conscious England. In his Boston workshop he and Paul Moody, a brilliant mechanic from Amesbury, designed and built his model, which they successfully tested in November 1813. The two men then incorporated refinements machined by native toolmakers, carpenters, and millwrights. In the autumn of 1814 they showed their product to Appleton and then to other investors; immediately afterward Lowell and Jackson patented it. The company bought land along the Charles River at Waltham, Massachusetts, and later along the Merrimac River. In these ventures Lowell again proved essential, since he was experienced in land speculation in Maine. In 1814 the company erected several buildings at Waltham and fitted them with machines based on Lowell's model, powered by water. Lowell's mills were soon recognized as the first in the world capable of converting raw cotton into finished fabric under one roof, revolutionizing the entire textile industry.

In 1815, when the war ended and the embargo was lifted, American textile manufacturers were threatened by a flood of cheap textiles primarily from England but also from other European countries and India. British cotton cloth at 25 cents a yard was underselling American goods of comparable quality. Lowell went to Washington, D.C., and helped persuade John Caldwell Calhoun and William Lowndes, members of the U.S. House of Representatives, to include a minimum duty of 6.25 cents per yard on foreign cotton fabrics in the 1816 tariff act.

Lowell's brother Charles had been a university student in Edinburgh, and some of Charles's friends, especially the young scholars who founded the *Edinburgh Review* in 1802, helped Francis Lowell socially during his time in Scotland. Another indirect influence on Lowell, and more likely on his friend Appleton, might have been Robert Owen, the Welsh Socialist who sought to combine business and philanthropy to improve working conditions. Lowell may have visited Owen's social experiment at New Lanark, Scotland, and it is certain that he developed a paternalistic philosophy of labor. In addition, he felt that manufacturers and merchants, working in concert, could achieve reliable, ever-rising incomes. To narrow the gap between rich and poor and thus avoid political and social upheavals of the sort menacing England and the Continent, he envisioned the wealthy devoting much of their disposable capital to philanthropic purposes. In this he hoped the Lowell family would play a leading role. As early as 1805 he had set an example by raising funds for the Harvard Botanical Garden. Later the Lowell family wealth, undoubtedly including some bequests by Francis Lowell, provided support for the Athenaeum; Harvard College; the Massachusetts General Hospital, of which he was one of the original trustees; the Lowell Institute, founded by his son John Lowell; and the Massachusetts Institute of Technology.

In 1815 Lowell's wife died, and Lowell, who always overtaxed his limited physical strength, worked doubly hard to assuage his sense of loss. His last practical work, shortly before his death, was helping Moody perfect the "double speeder," which made possible "roving," a process enabling the spinning of threads straight onto spindles without preliminary winding.

Soon the Waltham mill could spin thirty miles of cloth a day. But before Lowell could see his innovation on to great commercial success, he became an invalid. Treatment at Ballston Spa, near Saratoga Springs, New York, only worsened his health, and he returned home to Boston, where he died of chronic nervous indigestion, perhaps compounded by tic douloureux and an inability to take nourishment.

Lowell remains a somewhat mysterious figure. Few of his personal papers are extant, and only one likeness of him, a silhouette, has survived. His inventive genius and his benevolent attitude toward labor had far-reaching consequences. In 1822 Appleton, Jackson, Moody, and others incorporated the Merrimac Manufacturing Company, and along the Merrimac, whose current was more powerful than that of the Charles, they built new mills that adapted much of Lowell's work and thought. In 1801 Lowell and his associates had located their headquarters in a little Massachusetts village with a carding mill built on the Merrimac. In 1826 the town was incorporated and named Lowell in honor of Francis Lowell, who, as Appleton wrote, was "the informing soul" of "the system which gave birth to the place." The town's nickname was "the Manchester of America."

• No account book or journal by Lowell is extant. His few surviving letters are in the Massachusetts Historical Society in Boston. George Sweet Gibb, *The Saco-Lowell Shops: Textile Machinery Building in New England 1813–1949* (1950); Robert Sobel, *Entrepreneurs: Explorations within the American Business Tradition* (1974); and Robert F. Dalzell, Jr., *Enterprising Elite: The Boston Associates and the World They Made* (1987), discuss Lowell's part in the development of the Massachusetts textile industry. Ferris Greenslet, *The Lowells and Their Seven Worlds* (1946), places him in the context of the distinguished Lowell family. Nathan Appleton, *Introduction of the Power Loom and Origin of Lowell* (1858), is an early, detailed history of the Waltham-Lowell factory system. Frances W. Gregory, *Nathan Appleton, Merchant and Entrepreneur, 1779–1861* (1975), suggests that Appleton may have been influenced by Robert Owen. Leon Stein and Annette K. Baxter, eds., *Women of Lowell* (1974), reprints nineteenth-century books and essays on textile factories in Lowell and nearby towns, on women workers there, and on regional factory magazines. Francis Cabot Lowell III, *Exercises at the Seventy-fifth Anniversary of the Incorporation of the Town of Lowell* (1901), includes a eulogy of Lowell.

ROBERT L. GALE

LOWELL, James Russell (22 Feb. 1819–12 Aug. 1891), author and diplomat, was born in Cambridge, Massachusetts, the son of Charles Lowell, a liberal Congregational minister, and Harriet Brackett Spence. Among New Englanders who were apt to take ancestry seriously, the Lowell family was already firmly established in the region's ecclesiastical and legal annals. During the nineteenth century the Lowell name became synonymous with manufacturing wealth and State Street trusts, but Charles Lowell's descendants benefited little from this tradition. Their area of prominence was in literature; both James Russell Lowell's sister Mary Lowell Putnam and brother Robert Traill

Spence Lowell were accomplished writers, though neither enjoyed the public recognition of their brother.

Lowell's early education in Cambridge met the best standards of the day, and he entered Harvard in 1834. His studies there were not particularly challenging, and he soon gave more attention to social and literary matters than his preceptors thought wise. Spoiled and immature, Lowell frequently ran afoul of the Harvard authorities; eventually his violation of college regulations and neglect of his studies led to his suspension several months before graduation, and he was sent to nearby Concord to finish his studies under the direction of the local minister. This was by no means severe punishment. Lowell's chief regret was that his enforced absence from Cambridge prevented him from fulfilling in person the office of class poet, an honor voted him by his classmates in recognition of his budding literary talents, which had already been displayed in essays and poems published in *Harvardiana*, the college magazine of which Lowell was an editor. But neither these pieces nor the *Class Poem* (1838) reveal a literary power altogether exceptional for the time. Even the ardent passion for literature displayed in this early work and the earnest satire that marks the best parts of the *Class Poem* are fairly typical of undergraduate performances of that day.

No matter how great Lowell's literary interests and talent were at the time of his graduation, they would not have been sufficient to ensure him a vocation in literature in the United States during these antebellum years; like others with similar tastes and desires, he was forced to earn his way in the world. Because the ministry, medicine, or business could not long hold his interest (though he considered all three), he finally settled on law. Awarded the bachelor of laws degree at Harvard's Dane Law School in 1840, and admitted to the Massachusetts Bar two years later, Lowell attempted to establish a legal practice in Boston, but within six months he became convinced that for him law was just as impractical as, and probably even more unprofitable than, a literary life, so he gave up his practice and turned to literature for support.

Periodical publication in America was making significant gains during the 1840s, and Lowell's poems found ready acceptance in the leading literary journals, such as the *Southern Literary Messenger, Graham's Magazine*, and the *United States Magazine and Democratic Review*. While the money paid for his work was small and irregular, the reputation Lowell won during these early years as a lyric poet lasted his lifetime. His first volume of verse, *A Year's Life* (1841), was followed soon after by *Poems* (1844), *Poems: Second Series* (1848), and the greatly popular *Vision of Sir Launfal* (1848). The critical response to Lowell's verse was unusually favorable, and N. P. Willis did not greatly exaggerate when he later called Lowell the best-launched poet of his generation. But this early recognition of Lowell's poetic talents was undiscriminating, far more patriotic than critical. Nor are the deficiencies that characterized these early poems—technical infelicities and irregularities, didacticism, obscurity, and affected literary tone—ever entirely absent even from his more mature performances, especially those written in the lyrical mode. Later Lowell did write some distinguished poetry in a philosophical, public vein, particularly *The Cathedral* (1870), the magisterial *Ode Recited at the Commemoration of the Living and Dead Soldiers of Harvard University* (1865), and the 1874 elegy occasioned by the death of his friend Louis Agassiz, but his achievement in serious verse is small. Lowell himself was aware of his limitations as a poet, and he increasingly expressed to friends his misgivings. His reference to the volume of poems *Under the Willows* (1869) as "Under the Billows or dredgings from the Atlantic" is not only a masterful pun (many of the poems having first appeared in the *Atlantic Monthly*), but also accurate in describing the forced quality of much of the book's contents.

Lowell soon discovered that his verse was not likely to provide him with a financial basis on which to build the life he desired, especially marriage to the poet Maria White of Watertown, Massachusetts, to whom he had become engaged in 1840. Hoping to profit from the burgeoning public interest in periodicals, Lowell, in partnership with his friend Robert Carter (1819–1879), founded a magazine of his own, the *Pioneer*, the first number appearing in January 1843. His expectations for the monthly, however, were more than just financial; as he wrote in the magazine's prospectus, it would provide "intelligent and reflecting" readers with something better than "the enormous quantity of thrice-diluted trash" that was the ordinary fare of magazines at the time. Lowell solicited and received contributions from an impressive group of writers, including Nathaniel Hawthorne, Edgar Allan Poe, Jones Very, John S. Dwight, and Elizabeth Barrett in England, but an eye problem that required his absence from Boston and financial misunderstandings with the magazine's publisher caused the venture to fail within three months. After such an ambitious beginning, the failure of what he had envisioned to be the great American magazine was an enormous disappointment, especially since the debt he incurred delayed his marriage to Maria White until December 1844.

No doubt Lowell's defeat in the economic chance-world of periodical publishing contributed to his growing political radicalism; and though Maria White was not the source of his antislavery sentiments, as was sometimes claimed, she did encourage her fiancé to take a more active role in reform movements, bringing Lowell increasingly into the public arena. He became a chief editorial writer in the 1840s for the *Pennsylvania Freeman* and the *National Anti-Slavery Standard*, and during that decade he published scores of prose articles and poems in support of abolition and other liberal causes. Generally in sympathy with the Garrisonian wing of the antislavery movement, Lowell attacked not only slavery, but also the church, the Constitution, and, on occasion, even the Union itself. But his tolerance for human frailty and his sense of irony

and humor prevented him from being as unrelenting a reformer as many of his compatriots thought desirable. His shrewdness and wit found their natural expression in satire, which was as likely to be turned against the reformers as against the objects of their zeal. Humorous satire, Lowell believed, was a means to establish equilibrium in a world out of balance. He looked on creation with a laughing eye, a point of view not generally favored by polemicists. In his best poetry and essays, even in the stories remembered and told afterward about him, humor is never absent, and its range is as varied as the occasions that elicited it, witty and learned at times, boisterous and close to bawdy at others.

Nowhere is Lowell's humor better revealed than in *The Biglow Papers* (1848), a curious little masterpiece of political satire occasioned by the war with Mexico (1846–1848). In the beginning the book was no more than some clever newspaper verses written in Yankee dialect and printed under the name of Hosea Biglow, an upcountry farmer whose practical good sense far outshines the patriotic cant of the supporters of the war (which Biglow, like Lowell, saw as an imperialistic drive to expand westward the area of slavery). The Yankee oracle, a regional variety of the cracker-barrel philosopher so popular in the Jacksonian era, was by no means new to American literature, though he spoke generally in prose rather than verse. Lowell's contribution to the tradition was in turning this rustic figure into an effective and memorable poet, in raising the vernacular voice to a level not only of trenchant political satire but of high artistic expression. Immediately successful, the verses were copied and quoted, imitated and admired, even by those out of sympathy with Lowell's politics, a response that led Lowell to decide to make a book out of the Biglow material. For this he created two other Yankee voices: the picaresque Birdofredum Sawin, a townsman of Hosea who has hurried off to enlist, assured by the promise of wealth and adventure to be had in Mexico, and Homer Wilbur, a pedantic but well-meaning Congregational minister whose job it is to bring the verses before the public in proper form. The result is a work that transcends generic categories: a medley of voices and moods, prose and verse, classic English, Yankee speech, and tortured Latin. Some of it is dated, as one would expect of occasional satire, but much is timeless, classic, the finest political satire of nineteenth-century America.

By the time of the Compromise of 1850 Lowell had largely withdrawn from active participation in reform movements, though his sympathies could still be stirred by the tide of liberalism that was then redefining the relationship between individuals and their societies in Europe and the United States. But like many others, most notably his friend Ralph Waldo Emerson, he believed that reform must first be manifested within the self. Lowell was also still determined to find within the structures of American economic life a way to maintain his and his family's well-being through a devotion to literature, if not solely as a poet, then as a man of letters. He had made his debut as a serious critic of literature in a collection of prose essays titled *Conversations on Some of the Old Poets* (1845), but far more popular was *A Fable for Critics* (1848), a satiric jeu d'esprit in verse surveying the state of letters in the United States.

The sale of some land Maria Lowell had inherited allowed the couple to sail in July 1851 to Europe, where they remained fifteen months. In part these travels were to advance Lowell's literary ambitions, but the Lowells also hoped that the mild climate of Rome, where they spent the winter, would benefit Maria Lowell's health, which, never strong, now grew worse. Back in Cambridge in 1852, Lowell continued his studies, worked over some of the impressions gathered during his European trip (later included in *Fireside Travels* [1864]), and enjoyed the friendships in which his life was extraordinarily rich, relationships maintained over the years by a correspondence not only entertaining but of significant literary merit. Underneath the happy surface, however, was sadness. Three of the four children born to the Lowells between 1845 and 1850 did not survive their second year; only their second daughter lived to maturity. Then in 1853 Maria Lowell died, leaving her husband distraught. Lowell published little during these years; instead, he made his library a place of refuge where he commonly spent twelve to fifteen hours a day at work. The range of his reading was enormous, including the major modern languages as well as the classics, and his mastery of what he read was thorough. He did see through to press popular editions of Dryden, Donne, Marvell, Keats, Wordsworth, and Shelley, and in January 1855 he delivered a series of lectures on the English poets before the Lowell Institute, the influential lyceum association in Boston. His success in these lectures led Harvard to offer Lowell the chair in modern literature that had been Longfellow's, which Lowell accepted on the condition that he first be given a year to study in Germany and Italy. He assumed the post in the autumn of 1856. Lowell's tenure as a Harvard professor coincided with the period of that school's transformation from a small, provincial college to a modern university. Though he was not a principal architect of this great change, Lowell did play an important role in guiding the university in its development during the two decades he spent on the faculty.

Two events in 1857 did much to renew Lowell's outlook: his marriage to Frances Dunlap of Portland, Maine, and his editorship of the *Atlantic Monthly*, a new monthly that promised to fulfill his early dream of a magazine that, under his guidance, would not compromise in political or artistic matters. Even in the 1840s, when literary nationalism was most intense, Lowell had known that the basis for a great American literature was to be found in neither "sublime spaces" nor "democracy," but rather in economic and social compensation for authors. Now his editorial position would make a difference. Although somewhat wanting in matters of business and editorial routine, he more than compensated in his literary taste and editorial judgment. He was able during the magazine's impor-

tant early years to maintain that difficult balance between commercial and aesthetic demands, and he did so without sacrificing political responsibility. At his insistence, the *Atlantic* was one of the first important American periodicals to take a decided stand against slavery; it also engaged in political controversy of other kinds, and under Lowell's stewardship the *Atlantic* became a leading voice in national debate. Lowell's own political writings began appearing in its pages during his tenure as editor, essays in support of the emerging Republican party and, long before most other New Englanders had measured his greatness, its leader, Abraham Lincoln. Even after his resignation from the *Atlantic* editorship in 1861, Lowell continued to be one of its most valued writers, especially on political questions during the Civil War. It was then, too, that he again assumed the personae of Hosea Biglow and his down-east friends. The appearance of these new "Biglow Papers" in the *Atlantic* (1862–1866) met with considerable success, especially verses, such as "Sunthin' in the Pastoral Line," in which Lowell achieves an admirable ironic detachment and lyrical simplicity, a thorough mastery of vernacular art. But, as a book, *The Biglow Papers: Second Series* (1867) lacks the harmonious design of the first series.

In 1864 Lowell was named coeditor with Charles Eliot Norton of the *North American Review*, a position he held until 1868. While the actual editorial duties fell mostly on Norton, much of the best writing in the journal was Lowell's, both his political pieces, now supporting a more moderate approach to Reconstruction than that desired by the radical wing of the Republican party, and his literary essays, certainly his greatest achievement during the postwar years. Unburdened by a philosophical system or program, Lowell as a critic possessed a scholar's care for detail and a stylist's delight in expression, and his major essays, such as "Chaucer" (1870), "Spenser" (1875), and "Dante" (1872), remain durable pieces of critical exposition, informed by an appreciation of the literary text in both its historical and linguistic complexities. These, along with many of his other prose pieces, were collected in *Among My Books* (1870), *My Study Windows* (1871), and *Among My Books: Second Series* (1876); not only did they establish beyond question Lowell's reputation as the nation's leading man of letters, but they were also among the most popular of his books, much more so than the poetry he published after the war, *The Cathedral, Three Memorial Poems* (1877), and *Heartsease and Rue* (1888).

Lowell might have spent the rest of his days reasonably content as a professor of literature at Harvard and a much-sought-after essayist for the leading magazines; at least he did not seem to himself any better off when he took a two-year leave in Europe from 1872 to 1874. His interest in politics continued, though the causes that he now supported, most often in the *Nation*, were far less noble than those that had motivated him during his youth; now it was the reform of government, especially the civil service, and the recognition in the United States of international copyright.

The political verse he published in the *Nation*, humorous and satirical short pieces, along with his more serious political essays, earned him great respect in the world of affairs, a far more important sphere than literature in the American sense of things. A delegate from Massachusetts to the Republican convention in 1876, he was one of his state's presidential electors later that year. His support for Rutherford B. Hayes in that disputed election undoubtedly contributed to his being appointed U.S. minister to Spain in 1877. Three years later he became U.S. minister at the Court of St. James, a post he held with considerable acclaim until 1885 when, the Democratic party having gained power at home, he was recalled. Alone again following the death of his wife in 1885, Lowell continued as long as his health allowed to spend part of each year in England, where he was in demand as a speaker and a friend, an ambassador of goodwill between the two English-speaking nations, great in the public view, a triumph of style and character. Shortly before his death from cancer in Cambridge, Massachusetts, Lowell was able to see into press the ten-volume Riverside Edition of his *Writings* (1890). Later, Charles Eliot Norton issued several more volumes of essays and poems, *Latest Literary Essays and Addresses* (1892), *The Old English Dramatists* (1892), and *Last Poems* (1895), and he edited the first collection of Lowell's *Letters* (1894). But by the time Norton came out with the expanded sixteen-volume Elmwood Edition of Lowell's *Complete Writings* in 1904, literary fashion had lost most of its interest in Lowell, which subsequent years have done nothing to change. But this neglect of Lowell in the twentieth century does not invalidate his importance to his own time; and no understanding of the cultural life of America in the nineteenth century can be complete without recognition of Lowell's centrality and versatility.

• The major depository for Lowell's letters and manuscripts is the Houghton Library, Harvard University. Other important collections are at the Library of Congress; the Massachusetts Historical Society; the Pierpont Morgan Library; the Berg Collection, New York Public Library; the University of Texas Library; and the Clifton Waller Barrett Library at the University of Virginia. These materials are the basis of several biographical studies of Lowell, including Martin Duberman, *James Russell Lowell* (1966), and Leon Howard, *Victorian Knight-Errant: A Study of the Early Career of James Russell Lowell* (1952). The standard edition of Lowell's *Letters* was assembled by Charles Eliot Norton (3 vols., 1904). See also M. A. DeWolfe Howe, ed., *New Letters* (1932). Other printed gatherings of letters, as well as other primary and secondary materials, are listed in Robert A. Rees's bibliographical essay on Lowell in Rees and Earl N. Harbert, eds., *Fifteen American Authors before 1900* (1984).

THOMAS WORTHAM

LOWELL, John (17 June 1743–6 May 1802), politician and judge, was born in Newbury, Massachusetts, the son of the Reverend John Lowell, a Congregational minister, and Sarah Champney. After graduating from Harvard College in 1760, he studied law with Oxenbridge Thacher of Boston and was admitted to the bar in 1763. After his marriage in 1767 to Sarah Higginson, daughter of Stephen Higginson of Salem and his wife Elizabeth Cabot, Lowell returned to his native parish, which had separated in 1764 to become the town of Newburyport. There his legal practice flourished, he became active in town affairs as a selectman, committeeman, and justice of the peace, and he built a large mansion, which John Adams (1735–1826) described as "the Palace of a Nobleman." The Lowells had three children, including the lawyer John Lowell (1769–1840), prior to Sarah Lowell's death in 1772.

Affiliated with many who later became Loyalists, Lowell in 1774 placed himself under the same suspicion by signing the address to Governor Thomas Hutchinson after his departure from the province and the welcoming address to General Thomas Gage. However, with the advent of the Boston Port Bill, Lowell publicly recanted his support of the Hutchinson regime (*Essex Journal*, 4 Jan. 1775), was reelected as a selectman, and served as both a member of the town's Committee of Safety, Correspondence, and Inspection and as a major in the local militia company. In 1774 Lowell married Susanna Cabot, daughter of Francis Cabot, another Salem merchant, and his wife Mary Fitch; she died in 1777. There were two children, including Francis Cabot Lowell, the textile manufacturer.

In May 1776 the town meeting of Newburyport elected Lowell to represent them in the provincial legislature, but at the end of that session he moved his home and office into Boston. There he developed a large legal practice as a successful criminal lawyer and with a lucrative trade in privateering cases. In 1778 he was married a third time, to Rebecca (Russell) Tyng, widow of James Tyng. They had four children, including Charles Lowell, father of James Russell Lowell and Robert T. S. Lowell.

In 1778 Lowell was returned to the House of Representatives, this time as a delegate from Boston. In 1780 he was a member of the constitutional convention that effectively ended slavery in Massachusetts. After the convention Lowell publicly offered his services to represent anyone being held as a slave.

In 1782 Lowell went to Philadelphia as the successor to John Adams in the Continental Congress but served only the balance of the remaining term and did not stand for reelection. Instead, he returned to Boston and resumed his seat in the state legislature and his legal practice, which after the war included many of the large London merchant companies. He also took on a number of law students, including Harrison Gray Otis. When Congress created a new court of appeals on admiralty cases, Lowell was elected to the bench (in Dec. 1782), and, as Clifford Shipton commented, "it was soon evident that in the magistracy he had found his metier" (p. 656). He also served as a commissioner on the New York and Massachusetts boundary settlement in 1784.

In addition to the duties of the bench, Lowell was active in the wide array of organizations that the new republic offered. He was a founding member of the American Academy of Arts and Sciences (1780), a member of the American Philosophical Society, the Society for Propagating the Gospel among the Indians, the Massachusetts Charitable Society, and the Massachusetts Society for Promoting Agriculture, deputy grand master of the Freemasons' Grand Lodge of Massachusetts, a fellow of the Corporation of Harvard College, a founder of the Massachusetts Bank, and a director of the Boston branch of the Bank of the United States. In politics, Lowell was associated with the Essex Junto, which long dominated Federalist politics in eastern Massachusetts.

In 1789 Lowell became a judge in the newly created federal court for the district of Massachusetts. In 1801 with the passage of the Judiciary Act he became chief justice of the First Circuit, which included Maine, Massachusetts, New Hampshire, and Rhode Island, as one of the "midnight judges." The Jefferson administration promptly repealed the act, Judge Lowell left the law, and died shortly thereafter at Roxbury, Massachusetts, where he maintained a large residence.

• There are several copies of a portrait of Lowell painted by John Johnson extant, and a miniature of him painted by Charles Willson Peale is now at the Museum of Fine Arts, Boston. His manuscripts are at the Massachusetts Historical Society. Clifford K. Shipton's sketch of Judge Lowell appears in *Sibley's Harvard Graduates*, vol. 14 (1968), pp. 650–61. Charles Deane, "Judge Lowell and the Massachusetts Declaration of Rights," in Massachusetts Historical Society, *Proceedings* 13 (1875): 299–304, and 14 (1876): 108–9, discusses the apparently inaccurate claim that Judge Lowell introduced in the declaration the phrase "men are born free and equal," which was later used as a determinate in excluding slavery from the state. The family history is told in narrative form in Ferris Greenslet, *The Lowells and Their Seven Worlds* (1946). A discussion of the Essex Junto can be found in David H. Fischer, "The Myth of the Essex Junto," *William and Mary Quarterly*, ser. 3, 21 (1964): 191–235.

EDWARD W. HANSON

LOWELL, John (11 May 1799–4 Mar. 1836), philanthropist and businessman, was born in Boston, Massachusetts, the son of Francis Cabot Lowell, one of the nation's first great cotton manufacturers, and Hannah Jackson. Lowell, whose family generally called him John, Jr., was born prematurely and was sickly as a boy. In 1810 he accompanied his family on an extended trip to Europe. While Lowell attended school in Edinburgh, Scotland, his father studied the new English power looms, surreptitiously gathering enough information to launch mechanized cotton weaving in the United States. The next year the family moved to Paris, where Lowell again attended school. Sailing home on an American ship in the midst of the War of 1812, they were captured by the British and detained in Halifax, Nova Scotia, before finally arriving back in Boston.

Lowell entered Harvard in 1813, but he was lonely and unhappy there and withdrew after two years. Telling his father that he wanted to become a sea captain and "come forward in the world in that way," he made one voyage to Batavia (present-day Indonesia) and another to India. However, when his father died in 1817, he returned home and entered his father's firm. He helped finance the construction of huge cotton mills in nearby Chelmsford (renamed Lowell in 1825) and was among the investors in the Boston & Lowell Line, one of the first railroads in the country. Lowell also read widely and built a large personal library, helped found the Boston Society for the Diffusion of Useful Knowledge, and served two terms on the city council and one in the state legislature. In 1825 he married Georgiana Amory, with whom he had two children.

Lowell's pleasant way of life was destroyed in 1830–1831, when within eighteen months he lost his wife and then both daughters to scarlet fever. After a long trip west, Lowell returned having made two decisions. First, he would undertake an even longer trip, starting in Europe and then moving on to the Far East; he would not come home, he told a friend, "till I see the circle of the earth." Second, he would leave half of his estate to establish an institute that would promote popular education in Boston. Having written his will and discussed his plans with his cousin and executor, John Amory Lowell, he sold his Boston properties and set sail in November 1832.

Lowell spent the next year in a round of social activity in Paris, London, Ghent, Florence, and Rome. He then moved on to Sicily, Greece, and Turkey, studying several languages, absorbing the historic sights at every stop, and mixing convivially with local notables. In Rome he engaged Gabriel Gleyre, a young Swiss watercolorist, to accompany him on his travels and paint the things they saw. Lowell also documented his experiences in his journal, which provides a lively record of his political, social, and artistic observations.

In the fall of 1834 Lowell and Gleyre sailed through the Greek Islands to Alexandria and then traveled to Cairo. There they engaged a riverboat on which they spent most of the following year, progressing slowly up the Nile. Along the way Lowell shipped back to Boston a valuable collection of Egyptian antiquities, including two huge statues. Traveling conditions were very difficult, and he suffered periodically from fever, dysentery, and a painful disease of the eyes, but an outbreak of plague in Cairo made it dangerous for Lowell to return the way he had come. He therefore decided to press on to Nubia and then to the African coast, where he could get a ship to India. After a grueling trip by camel across the desert, the exhausted travelers reached Khartoum in October 1835. There Lowell and Gleyre parted company, having quarreled over the ownership of Gleyre's pictures. Lowell moved on to the coast, where he set sail across the Red Sea for Mocha. When the ship began to sink, he prevented the crew at gunpoint from abandoning him and then escaped to safety with them on a raft. Reaching Mocha on New Year's Day 1836, Lowell immediately took a ship to India. He was desperately ill by the time he landed in Bombay, and he died there three weeks later.

About a year before his death, while in Luxor, Lowell had written a codicil to his will to guide his cousin in establishing his proposed institute. He observed that since New England's prosperity could not come from its barren soil, it must come from the morality and intelligence of its people. Accordingly, he urged that besides presenting lectures "on the historical and internal evidences in favor of Christianity," the institute should offer courses in physics, chemistry, zoology, geology, literature, language, and any other subjects that, in the trustee's opinion, "the wants and taste of the age may demand." There would be only one trustee, and each would designate his successor, preferably from among the male Lowells. To keep the endowment growing, the institute was to reinvest 10 percent of its income each year; no funds were to be spent on acquiring property. Lectures were to be free or very inexpensive, but those attending must behave and dress respectably.

The Lowell Institute opened on 31 December 1839. It was an immediate success, and by the next season the demand for seats was so intense that the pressure of the crowd broke the ticketshop windows. Lowell's $250,000 legacy, multiplied by reinvestment, enabled the institute to attract distinguished lecturers in the years that followed and also to rent an elegant building. The programs as well as the atmosphere remained relatively conservative; Henry David Thoreau condemned the institute for excluding "the ignorant and critical classes of society." Nevertheless, it was enormously successful, presenting in its first twenty years more than a hundred lectures to several hundred thousand people. By 1860 the institute had overshadowed every other lecture organization in Boston. More than a century later, it was still thriving. During the 1990s the institute sponsored lectures and courses in more than two dozen museums and colleges around Boston. It also supported the evening school at the Massachusetts Institute of Technology, the university extension program at Harvard University, and New England's leading public television station, WGBH, and its affiliate, WGBH Radio. The vision that Lowell worked out by the Nile in 1835 has outlasted all the commercial ventures for which his family was known during his lifetime.

• Lowell correspondence is in the Francis Cabot Lowell (b. 1799) Papers in the Massachusetts Historical Society. The fullest recent sketch of Lowell's life appears in Edward Weeks, *The Lowells and Their Institute* (1966). See also Ferris Greenslet, *The Lowells and Their Seven Worlds* (1946); Ronald Story, *The Forging of an Aristocracy: Harvard and the Boston Upper Class, 1800–1870* (1980); and C. David Heymann, *American Aristocracy: The Life and Times of James Russell, Amy and Robert Lowell* (1980). Earlier accounts include Edward Everett, *Memoir of Mr. John Lowell, Jr.* (1840), and Harriette Knight Smith, *The History of the Lowell Institute* (1898).

SANDRA OPDYCKE

LOWELL, Josephine Shaw (16 Dec. 1843–12 Oct. 1905), charity worker and reformer, was born in West Roxbury, Massachusetts, the daughter of Francis George Shaw, a merchant who had retired from business to pursue literary and philanthropic interests, and Sarah Blake Sturgis. Josephine's grandfathers, Robert Shaw and Nathaniel Sturgis, earned fortunes in real estate and trade with the West Indies and China. Because both of her parents came from large families, Josephine had eighty-five first cousins linking her to prominent New England families. Francis Shaw helped finance the communitarian experiment at Brook Farm. The Shaws, Unitarian in religion, were radical abolitionists and counted Theodore Parker, William Lloyd Garrison, Harriet Beecher Stowe, and Lydia Maria Child as close friends.

In 1848 Josephine's family moved to Staten Island, New York. Between 1851 and 1856 the Shaws lived abroad, mainly in Italy. Josephine attended schools in Paris and Rome, and after the family's return to Staten Island she continued her education at private schools in New York City and Boston. A stimulating home environment, involving lively discussions among family members, relatives, and guests, seems to have been as important as formal schooling in her intellectual development.

In July 1863 Lowell's brother, Colonel Robert Gould Shaw, was killed in action leading the first regiment of African-American volunteers in an attack on Fort Wagner, near Charleston, South Carolina. The family elected to treat his death not as a personal loss, but as a contribution to a noble cause.

During the war Lowell worked with the Women's Central Association of Relief, which coordinated soldiers' aid societies in the New York City area. On 31 October 1863 she married Colonel Charles Russell Lowell, nephew of the poet James Russell Lowell and grandson of the founder of the first power loom cotton mill in the United States. In October 1864 Colonel Lowell died of wounds suffered in battle. Josephine Lowell gave birth to their daughter six weeks after her husband's death. The loss of both her husband and brother, combined with the satisfaction derived from her own work during the war, were among the factors influencing Lowell's subsequent commitment to public service.

After the war Lowell inspected and supervised the hiring of teachers for schools for freedmen in Virginia and served on the Richmond County (Staten Island) visiting committee of the Prison Association of New York. In 1873 she joined the State Charities Aid Association, a watchdog agency founded by her friend Louisa Lee Schuyler. Lowell's incisive reports on able-bodied paupers and conditions in county poorhouses led to her appointment by Governor Samuel J. Tilden as the first woman member of the State Board of Charities.

In thirteen years on the state board (1876–1889), Lowell displayed keen powers of observation and the ability to report her findings cogently. Believing that "vicious and pauper women" became mothers of "vicious and pauper children," she worked for the removal of girls and women of childbearing age from poorhouses to asylums and reformatories staffed by women. She criticized the system of providing subsidies from public funds to denominational institutions for children. The practice, she asserted, enabled parents to shift the burden and expense of caring for their children to taxpayers without the stigma attached to public relief, prolonged institutionalization, and in many cases, failed to prepare children for responsible citizenship. Her report on waste and duplication of effort by private charities in New York City brought about the formation in 1882 of the New York Charity Organization Society (COS), which she guided for many years. Under her leadership COS progressed from its initial preoccupation with "scientific philanthropy"—that is, rigorous administration of private charity to discourage mendicity and minimize the need for public relief—to support for legislation and regulations intended to improve the health, sanitary, and living conditions of the poor.

A product of wealth and leisure, Lowell aligned herself with the self-reliant workers whose pockets, in her opinion, were plundered by tax-supported programs to assist the less industrious and successful. The latter might need aid, but she believed it should come from private rather than public sources. In 1889 she resigned from the state board, declaring that helping workers "before they go under" was better than "fishing them out when they are half drowned and taking care of them afterward!" (Stewart, p. 359).

During the 1890s Lowell demonstrated her support for workers in numerous ways. She founded the Consumer's League of New York (1890) to enlist shoppers in efforts to improve working conditions in stores and assisted in the formation of women's trade unions. She organized work relief for the unemployed in New York City (1893–1894), endorsed the rights of labor in strikes, advocated industrial conciliation and arbitration, and supported adoption of the living wage. Long active in civil service reform, she devoted much of her energy in the last years of her life to opposing American imperialism in the Philippines and Caribbean.

After 1874 Lowell lived with her daughter in a house on East 30th Street in Manhattan that became a meeting place for men and women active in social reform and civic betterment. After several years of failing health she died in New York City. She was buried beside her husband in Mount Auburn Cemetery, Cambridge, Massachusetts.

Augustus Saint-Gaudens's bas-relief portrait of Lowell, rendered in 1899, shows a serene and gentle countenance. Although possessed of a keen sense of humor, her underlying seriousness and dedication made a friend say it was impossible to be with her without seeing "the halo upon her brow" (Stewart, p. 544). Throughout her life she showed an ability to examine problems objectively, to learn from others, and to accept and apply new ideas. Her creed of responsible individualism led her to emphasize the needs of working people and helped direct the organized charity of the 1880s toward the social reform movements of the Progressive Era.

• Lowell's letters and reports relating to the COS are in the Community Service Society Collection, Butler Library, Columbia University. Her reports for the New York State Board of Charities are in the *Annual Reports* of that body; those in the volumes for 1880, 1882, 1886, and 1887 are of particular interest. She was the author of *Public Relief and Private Charity* (1884) and of numerous articles including "Methods of Relief for the Unemployed," *Forum*, Feb. 1894, pp. 655–62, and "The True Aim of Charity Organization Societies," *Forum*, June 1896, pp. 494–500. Many of her articles are included in William Rhinelander Stewart, *The Philanthropic Work of Josephine Shaw Lowell* (1911; repr. 1974), which also contains a chronological bibliography of Lowell's writings and a topical index to them. Joan Waugh, "Unsentimental Reformer, The Life of Josephine Lowell" (Ph.D. diss., UCLA, 1992), the first full-length biography, identifies important manuscript sources and covers all aspects of Lowell's career in an exemplary way. Russell Duncan, ed., *Blue-Eyed Child of Fortune: The Civil War Letters of Colonel Robert Gould Shaw* (1992), contributes information on Shaw family relationships. Edward Waldo Emerson, *Life and Letters of Charles Russell Lowell* (1907), contains letters from Colonel Lowell to his wife. The biographical sketch by Barbara S. Beatty in Walter Trattner, ed., *Biographical Dictionary of Social Welfare* (1986), provides an excellent summary and evaluation of Mrs. Lowell's career from the standpoint of modern social work. An obituary is in the *New York Tribune*, 14 Oct. 1905; the journal *Charities and the Commons* published a memorial issue, 2 Dec. 1905.

ROBERT H. BREMNER

LOWELL, Maria White (8 July 1821–27 Oct. 1853), poet, was born Anna Maria White in Watertown, Massachusetts, the daughter of Abijah White, a prosperous cattle-trading merchant, and Anna Maria Howard. She was educated in her Unitarian home by a governess and then attended the fashionable Ursuline Convent School in nearby Charlestown until a mob of anti-immigrant, anti-Catholic arsonists destroyed it in 1834. In 1839 Maria White joined a high-minded group led by Margaret Fuller, the Transcendalist reformer, for the purpose of conversing about moral regeneration. Maria participated in the same manner in the "Band," an informal association comprised mainly of Harvard students and their sisters. One such Harvard student was James Russell Lowell, who was introduced to her in 1839 by her brother, one of Lowell's classmates at Harvard. Lowell was instantly attracted to her, admiring her physical appearance, her demeanor, and her mind. She was delicately beautiful, with large, luminous eyes; had a low, gentle voice and a fragile physique; was usually demure; sewed well; drew competently; recited and wrote poetry; and could read German. Contemporaries were complimenting her when they regularly described her as "spiritual." She was responsible for helping Lowell become both less shallow in the style and more liberal in the content of his writings. In the fall of 1840 she and Lowell, who had earned a bachelor of laws degree at Harvard that summer, became engaged.

In the early 1840s Maria wrote, raised money, and even publicly demonstrated—once in a white dress and an oak-leaf garland—for temperance and abolitionist causes. In the summer of 1843 she contracted influenza, which left her with a troublesome cough. By 1844 James Lowell was sufficiently successful as an author, though never as a lawyer, to enable the two to get married. Maria's father reluctantly helped with some of their expenses. They moved to Philadelphia, where they hoped for a milder winter. They returned to Boston early in 1845, and Maria began to have babies in rapid and unhappy succession. Her first daughter was born in 1845 and died two years later. Her second daughter was born in 1847. Her third daughter was born in 1849 and died the following year. Her fourth and last child, a son, was born in 1850. In 1851 the Lowells grew alarmed because of Maria's health, since she suffered not only from her persistent cough but also from deep depression. Her father had died in September 1845, leaving her some land and an annual income of $500. In 1851, in the hope that Maria's health would improve, the Lowells sold some of her acreage, reckoned that they could live on $1,500 annually, and set sail for Italy.

They lived briefly in Florence, saw the sights there with American painter William Page, went on to Rome, and socialized with William Wetmore Story, the American sculptor and writer, and with British poets Robert Browning, Elizabeth Barrett Browning, and Walter Savage Landor, among other expatriates. Maria could not socialize energetically, although she did seem to be in better health. But then her son died suddenly in June 1852. The bereft family made quick stops in Venice, Paris, Switzerland, and England and then sailed for Boston. The Lowells arrived in Boston in November 1852.

Maria was relieved to be home again. She watched over her surviving daughter with unnecessary alarm, continued to write a little, and was happy that James Lowell himself socialized frequently with other Boston intellectuals. However, in the spring of 1853 she grew ill again, was better and then worse, then died, probably of tuberculosis. On the day of her death, a baby was born to their neighbors Henry Wadsworth Longfellow and his wife, Frances Appleton. This coincidence Longfellow celebrated in "The Two Angels." In this sentimental poem the angel with "asphodels" brings the Longfellows new life even as the angel "crowned with amaranth, as with flame," takes Maria away.

Maria Lowell published some sixteen poems, in the abolitionist periodical *Liberty Bell*, *Putnam's Monthly Magazine*, and Rufus Griswold's anthology *The Female Poets of America*. In 1855 James Russell Lowell privately published *The Poems of Maria Lowell* in fifty copies, as gifts for friends. Maria's reputation was significantly aided when Thomas Wentworth Higginson suggested in 1870 that Emily Dickinson might profit from reading Maria Lowell's poetry. In 1907 a new printing of her 1855 collection was issued, and Amy Lowell, the early twentieth-century poet and James Russell Lowell's cousin, praised it widely. Amy Lowell's close friend S. Foster Damon helped see into

print the definitive edition of Maria Lowell's work in 1936.

Much of Maria's poetry is too saccharine for modern taste. For example, in "The Morning-Glory" the poet compares her daughter to the "smil[ing] . . . flower" but soon sees both child and blossom wither and die. The poet takes some comfort in new blooms but more in knowing that her infant is now "twin[ing] . . . round our dear Lord's knee." The martyr in "Rouen, Place de la Pucelle" is Joan of Arc, "who meekly wore / Alike the gilded mail and peasant gown" and who at the stake receives the "honor" of a "fiery crown." "An Opium Fantasy" startlingly describes the half-conscious state of a patient in pain but soothed by "the opiate in the brain" and imagining "distance" unrolling "Like silver balls, that, softly dropped, / Ring into golden bowls." The persona in "The Slave-Mother" hopes that her tiny daughter will be freed at once, by death, from a life of "infamy and sin." In "Africa," perhaps Maria Lowell's finest poem, the dark continent is imaged as an enthroned and brooding queen, "rigid and black, as carved in stone," proud of her past, deploring the enslavement of her children across "the great sea," but expecting the slow hand of fate to "lift me from my sunken state." The three-line stanzas, each rhyming *aaa* and in somber iambic tetrameter, are effective from beginning to end.

• Maria White Lowell's papers are in the Houghton Library at Harvard University. The definitive edition is *The Poems of Maria Lowell, with Unpublished Letters and a Biography*, ed. Hope Jillson Vernon, with an introduction by S. Foster Damon (1936). Ferris Greenslet, *The Lowells and Their Seven Worlds* (1946), and Martin Duberman, *James Russell Lowell* (1966), include details concerning Maria White Lowell. Thomas Buchanan Read, ed., *The Female Poets of America* (1857), and Cheryl Walker, ed., *American Women Poets of the Nineteenth Century: An Anthology* (1992), reprint several of Lowell's best poems. Newton Arvin, *Longfellow: His Life and Work* (1963), explicates Longfellow's "The Two Angels" expertly.

ROBERT L. GALE

LOWELL, Percival (13 Mar. 1855–12 Nov. 1916), astronomer and writer, was born in Boston, Massachusetts, the son of Augustus Lowell, a president of cotton companies and director of banks, and Katharine Bigelow Lawrence, daughter of Abbott Lawrence, a textile manufacturer and founder of the city of Lawrence, Massachusetts. His brother Abbott Lawrence Lowell served Harvard University as president from 1909 to 1933, while a sister, Amy Lowell, helped introduce new poetry into America. More distant relations included the poet James Russell Lowell and Francis Cabot Lowell, who organized the finances and designed the machinery that launched the modern American textile industry with manufacture of cotton cloth on a large scale, and for whom the town of Lowell, Massachusetts, was named.

Lowell graduated from Harvard in 1876 with distinction in mathematics. He then took the customary grand tour of Europe, though he traveled farther than most—all the way to Syria. He then returned to Boston and settled down to work in the office of his grandfather, John Amory Lowell, handling finances for cotton mills and for a time serving as executive head of a large cotton mill. Shrewd investments soon freed Lowell from the daily tedium of business. Lowell traveled to the Far East several times and was so well received that he was appointed foreign secretary and counselor for a special Korean diplomatic mission to the United States in 1883 (Korea could not afford to carry out the task). He wrote articles for the *Atlantic Monthly* and four books about the region, one of which (*The Soul of the Far East* [1888]) may have helped persuade Lafcadio Hearn to go to Japan.

Lowell was deeply interested in astronomy; his Harvard commencement speech had been on the nebular hypothesis, explaining the origin of the solar system, and he sometimes took a telescope on his travels. One story has Lowell learning in 1893, while returning from Japan, that the eyesight of the Italian astronomer Giovanni Schiaparelli, observer of "canali" on Mars, was failing. Lowell, his eyesight the keenest a leading ophthalmologist had ever examined, now supposedly decided that it was his manifest destiny to continue Schiaparelli's work. (Schiaparelli's eyesight was deteriorating, but he may not have realized it; neither, consequently, would Lowell have known about the deterioration until years later.)

In 1894 Lowell established an observatory at Flagstaff in the Arizona Territory and began searching for signs of intelligent life on Mars. In 1895 he published his controversial hypothesis in a series of articles in the *Atlantic Monthly* and in the book *Mars*. From visible changes, including changes in the polar cap and seasonal changes in the tint of dark areas, Lowell concluded that Mars had both an atmosphere and water and thus could support life. Seemingly there were signs of actual inhabitants: an apparent irrigation system of straight canals (visible to Lowell and some others but not to all observers) radiating from central points. For Lowell it was enough that the theory might be true, but professional scientists envisioned alternative explanations and returned a verdict of "not proven." Furthermore, scientists were expected to observe first and theorize secondly, if at all. William Wallace Campbell at the Lick Observatory objected that "Mr. Lowell went direct from the lecture hall to his observatory, and how well his observations established his pre-observational views is told in his book."

Scientists generally responded negatively to Lowell's work, but many readers responded enthusiastically to his entertaining and informative prose. For example, he described Mars as "a great red star that rises at sunset through the haze about the eastern horizon, and then, mounting higher with the deepening night, blazes forth against the dark background of space with a splendor that outshines Sirius and rivals the giant Jupiter himself." Lowell was a poet turned physicist applying his New England intellectual heritage to science. Emphasizing that something was possible rather than that it was not proved, legitimizing inferences,

and intelligently anticipating new developments, he replaced sane but unsensational astronomy with more imaginative thought. Furthermore, Lowell had taken the popular side of the most popular question afloat. Tenantless globes would be an affront to the sense of the rational in creation, while the discovery of intelligent life on other planets would increase reverence for the Creator. There would also be enlightening social results because cooperation was seemingly a distinctive feature of life on Mars, where the civilization did not have wars. Mars and its inhabitants had perhaps developed earlier and thus further than had humans on earth, in accord with Darwinian theory. Mars revealed the future of the earth, with an advanced science and technology and also an ebbing of life-sustaining resources.

Lowell's purported observation of canals on Mars is now thoroughly discredited. Partly the product of a psychological inclination to connect minute details too small to be separately and distinctly defined, it is also an instance of preconception influencing observation. In his obituary of Lowell, the Princeton astronomer Henry Norris Russell warned that "if the observer knows in advance what to expect . . . his judgment of the facts before his eyes will be warped by this knowledge, no matter how faithfully he may try to clear his mind of all prejudice. The preconceived opinion unconsciously, whether he will or not, influences the very report of his senses."

Nervous exhaustion slowed Lowell's pace for several years, but by 1901 he was back observing. He also gave two series of popular lectures at the Massachusetts Institute of Technology, in 1902 on the solar system and in 1909 on the evolution of worlds, and a series of lectures at the Lowell Institute in 1906 on Mars as the abode of life. All three series were published in book form, and the 1906 lectures also appeared in the *Century Magazine*. Lowell married Constance Savage Keith, a long-time Boston neighbor, in 1908; they had no children.

To explain the origin of the solar system, Lowell in his 1908 *Mars as the Abode of Life* chose Pierre-Simon Laplace's older nebular hypothesis (in which rings of gas shed by the contracting sun condensed to form planets) over its new rival, the Chamberlin-Moulton hypothesis (in which the solar system was formed by a collision between a small nebula and the periphery of a large nebula). Eliot Blackwelder, professor of geology at the University of Wisconsin (where Thomas Chrowder Chamberlin had been president), characterized Lowell's book as fancy foisted upon a trusting public. Misbranding intellectual products was as immoral as misbranding manufactured products, and "censure can hardly be too severe upon a man who so unscrupulously deceives the educated public, merely in order to gain a certain notoriety and a brief, but undeserved, credence for his pet theories." The quarrel escalated in an entertaining if unseemly manner, with Forest Ray Moulton calling Lowell "that mysterious 'watcher of the stars' whose scientific theories, like Poe's vision of the raven, 'have taken shape at midnight.'"

In his 1902 lectures on the solar system, Lowell had casually predicted the existence and eventual detection of another planet. He began searching for it in 1905, directing assistants at Flagstaff to take sets of photographs, each set of the same region of the sky but at different times, and then to compare photographs within each set, looking for objects that had changed position over time. Stars show no such movement, but a planet does, as do comets and asteroids, which Lowell Observatory astronomers found in abundance. But no new planet was detected. In 1908 Lowell plunged vigorously into mathematical calculations of the position of a trans-Neptunian planet from perturbations in Uranus's motion, and followed up with a systematic photographic search of regions of the sky suggested by his several solutions to the mathematical problem. But his death in Flagstaff (at the observatory) preceded success.

Lowell left more than $1 million in trust for the observatory to ensure continuation of his work, but his widow instituted litigation that dragged on for more than a decade. Planning for an expensive new photographic telescope and for another search for Planet X began in 1927, the search itself began in 1929, and by March 1930 the planet was found. Continuing the tradition of naming planets for Roman gods, Vesto M. Slipher, the director of the observatory, chose the name Pluto, god of the regions of darkness, and ℙ, Percival Lowell's superposed initials, for the planetary symbol. The remarkable resemblance between Pluto's orbit and Lowell's prediction probably is a coincidence, since Pluto's mass is now known to be too small to have caused the perturbations in Uranus's orbit used by Lowell to calculate Pluto's position.

Little of Lowell's scientific work has survived history's cruel critique. Yet his scientific bequest—the distinguished and continuing efforts of many astronomers at the Lowell Observatory, which he founded and funded—is as formidable as his family heritage.

• Documentary material on Lowell's scientific life, including correspondence, drafts and texts of articles, and newspaper clippings, is preserved at the Lowell Observatory. The letters are available in a microfilm edition, *The Early Correspondence of the Lowell Observatory 1894–1916* (1973). Lowell's books not mentioned in the text are *Chosön, the Land of the Morning Calm: A Sketch of Korea* (1886); *Noto: An Unexplored Corner of Japan* (1891); *Occult Japan; or, The Way of the Gods: An Esoteric Study of Japanese Personality and Possession* (1894); *The Solar System: Six Lectures at the Massachusetts Institute of Technology in December, 1902* (1903); *Mars and Its Canals* (1906); and *The Evolution of Worlds* (1909). His scientific reports appeared primarily in publications of his observatory: *Annals of the Lowell Observatory, Lowell Observatory Bulletins,* and *Memoirs of the Lowell Observatory.* A biography, with many excerpts from Lowell's writings but little insight into his character, was compiled by his brother, A. Lawrence Lowell, *Biography of Percival Lowell* (1935). Quotations from his letters, chosen by his long-time secretary to display his personality and varying moods, are presented in Louise Leonard, *Percival Lowell: An Afterglow* (1921). A thorough command of archival material at the Lowell Observatory is evident in the excellent depictions of Lowell's work by Wil-

liam Graves Hoyt, *Lowell and Mars* (1976) and *Planets X and Pluto* (1980). The crucial role of the Harvard College Observatory in the founding of the Lowell Observatory, revealed in the correspondence in the Harvard University Archives, is detailed by David Strauss, "Percival Lowell, W. H. Pickering and the Founding of the Lowell Observatory," *Annals of Science* 51 (Jan.-Feb. 1994): 37–58. A sketch of his life appears in Ferris Greenslet, *The Lowells and Their Seven Worlds* (1946).

On the debate over life on Mars, see Michael J. Crowe, *The Extraterrestrial Life Debate 1750–1900: The Idea of Plurality of Worlds from Kant to Lowell* (1986), in particular chapter 10. Lowell's observations of Mars are examined in chapter 5 of Norriss S. Hetherington, *Science and Objectivity: Episodes in the History of Astronomy* (1988). Other aspects of Lowell's work are examined in Hetherington, "Lowell's Theory of Life on Mars," *Astronomical Society of the Pacific Leaflet* 501 (Mar. 1971): 1–8; and "Percival Lowell: Professional Scientist or Interloper?" *Journal of the History of Ideas* 42 (1981): 159–61. Related topics are discussed in George E. Webb, "The Planet Mars and Science in Victorian America," *Journal of American Culture* 3 (1980): 573–80, and in Hetherington, "Amateur versus Professional: The British Astronomical Association and the Controversy over Canals on Mars," *Journal of the British Astronomical Association* 86 (1976): 303–8. On Lowell's study of East Asia, see David Strauss, "The 'Far East' in the American Mind, 1883–1894: Percival Lowell's Decisive Impact," *Journal of American–East Asian Relations* 2 (Fall 1993): 217–41.

NORRISS S. HETHERINGTON

LOWELL, Ralph (23 July 1890–15 May 1978), banker and civic leader, was born in Chestnut Hill, Massachusetts, the son of John Lowell, a lawyer, and Mary Emlen Hale. Bearing one of the Bay State's most distinguished family names, Lowell was brought up amid material comfort and dedication to community service. He graduated from Harvard College in 1912 with a Phi Beta Kappa key that he wore thereafter on his vest pocket chain. Lowell majored in anthropology and always maintained a keen interest in the Indians of the American Southwest.

In 1913, after a ten-month postgraduation tour of Europe and Asia, Lowell launched his career in finance, starting as a clerk in a small Boston brokerage firm. Three years later he became an assistant to the president of the First National Bank of Boston, the largest commercial bank in New England.

Even as Lowell's business career advanced, however, he was involved with public issues. Prior to U.S. involvement in World War I, Lowell, like many of his social class, joined the movement to prepare for American belligerency. He attended the civilian military training camp at Plattsburg, New York, in 1915 and 1916. On entering active service in the war in May 1917 as first lieutenant in the infantry, he was assigned to stateside training of officer candidates. He was discharged in December 1918 as a lieutenant colonel. Lowell helped recruit officers for the U.S. Army during the 1920s and was an advocate of universal military training in the 1940s.

In 1917 Lowell married Charlotte Loring, also of Boston's elite. They had seven children, the first of whom died in an automobile accident at age eight. In the mid-1930s the family moved into the eighty-acre Loring estate in suburban Westwood, and thereafter Lowell commuted to Boston by public transportation and later by hired car. Neither of the Lowells learned to drive; nor did they ever fly.

In 1919 Lowell became manager of a small stock brokerage department at the Boston investment banking house of Lee, Higginson & Co.; he was made a partner in 1929. Three years later the firm collapsed, the victim of its dealings—of which Lowell had no part except as a deceived bond purchaser—with the unscrupulous Swedish "match king," Ivar Kreuger. Lowell endured an unsatisfying decade during the 1930s directing the Boston office of a minor New York stock brokerage firm. His fortunes rose in 1943, however, when friends engineered his election as chairman of the Boston Safe Deposit & Trust Company, the state's largest independent trust company. Over the next fifteen years Lowell guided the company to high levels of profitability and public visibility.

Lowell's civic activities increased markedly in the 1940s and 1950s. Long associated with social welfare and health-related philanthropies, Lowell gained stature in 1940 by being chosen a trustee of Massachusetts General Hospital. In 1943 Lowell was elected to the first of two six-year terms on the Harvard Board of Overseers; in 1957–1958, he served as its president. Named a trustee of Boston's Museum of Fine Arts in 1943, Lowell became president in 1951, a post he held until 1968.

In 1943 Lowell succeeded his cousin, former Harvard president A. Lawrence Lowell, as trustee of the Lowell Institute. Founded in the 1830s to promote adult education, the institute was renowned for its free public lectures. Encouraged by Harvard president James Bryant Conant, Ralph Lowell moved the institute into the new field of educational broadcasting and became one of the medium's pioneers.

Lowell and Conant in 1946 brokered creation of the Lowell Institute Cooperative Broadcasting Council, which linked Harvard, the Massachusetts Institute of Technology, Boston College, Boston University, Tufts University, and Northeastern University in the production of educational programs for Boston's commercial radio stations. Five years later the council, through its corporate entity, the WGBH Educational Foundation, started its own radio station, WGBH-FM. Lowell joined the national movement to reserve television channels for educational broadcasters and helped gain Federal Communications Commission approval in 1952 both for the general policy and for reservation of Channel 2 in Boston. In 1953 the WGBH Educational Foundation was awarded Channel 2, and in 1955 the station went on the air. WGBH-TV quickly emerged as a leader among educational broadcasting operations.

Lowell was a founding board member in 1952 of the Educational Television and Radio Center, an enterprise underwritten by the Fund for Adult Education and the Ford Foundation to supply programming to educational stations, and served as chair from 1955 to 1962. In 1964, urged on by WGBH general manager Hartford Gunn, Lowell pressed for a national commission to study long-term financing of educational television. Within a year the Carnegie Commission on Educational Television was established. Passage of the Public Broadcasting Act of 1967, creating the Corporation for Public Broadcasting (CPB), flowed directly from the Carnegie group's work. The Ralph Lowell Award, given annually by CPB for an individual's "outstanding contribution to the cause of educational television," was established by his family in 1970 to commemorate Lowell's own achievements.

Lowell also played a prominent role in Boston's urban renaissance. The ancient and bitter hostility between the Irish-Catholic Democratic politicians who controlled Boston's City Hall and the Anglo-Protestant Republican businesspeople who dominated the city's economic life was a major factor in Boston's marked economic decline in the decades after World War I. Not until 1959, with the downtown commercial district badly deteriorated and the municipality nearly bankrupt, were the old antagonists prepared to cooperate for their mutual benefit and that of the city. Winning an upset victory in the mayoralty election that year, maverick Democrat John Collins sought a partnership with the Brahmin elite, and they accepted his challenge. Because of his reputation for philanthropy and his success with WGBH, Lowell was chosen to chair the business community's new group, known formally as the Coordinating Committee but usually referred to as the "Vault" because its meetings were held in a boardroom next to the vault at Boston Safe Deposit. Together, Collins and the Vault charted the physical development of the "New Boston."

Lowell fared less well in recharging Boston's social climate. Amid ethnic, religious, and cultural divisions, he personally practiced toleration and understanding. It was said that Ralph Lowell talked not only "to the Cabots, but also to the Kellys and Cohens." However, if the old tears in Boston's social fabric were mended somewhat because of Lowell's example, he could do little about the racial divisions that surfaced in the 1960s. Lowell was sympathetic to the objectives of the civil rights struggle. In 1964 he was a member of the special state commission that recommended action to end the de facto segregation of Boston's public schools, but the last years of Lowell's life were marked by worsening racial discord as Boston struggled to satisfy legislative and court orders to implement this recommendation.

By the mid-1960s, Lowell had gained national recognition and local sainthood. On the national level he was known for contributions to educational broadcasting and as the "nation's busiest executive" based on his first-place ranking in an annual compilation of memberships on boards of directors. Closer to home, Lowell's civic involvement earned him the title, "Mr. Boston." Lowell, whose final years were physically painful because of injuries suffered in a fall in 1973, died in a Boston-area hospital of complications resulting from an automobile accident. Not an original thinker and conservative by nature, Lowell had nonetheless served as a bridge between Boston's past and its future by helping to weaken the parochialism that had long plagued the "Hub of the Universe."

• The Ralph Lowell Manuscripts at the Massachusetts Historical Society contain his diaries (1907–1976, with gaps), a small collection of his correspondence, and scrapbooks of newspaper clippings. The Charlotte Loring Lowell Manuscripts also at the Massachusetts Historical Society are devoted to her husband's career; the collection mainly includes printed materials, although there are some letters. A 1964 interview with Lowell focusing on the Lowell Institute and its broadcasting activities is contained in the Columbia University Oral History Collection. Lowell wrote about himself in the reports of his Harvard class, particularly the *Twenty-fifth Anniversary Report of the Class of 1912* (1937) and the *Fiftieth Anniversary Report of the Class of 1912* (1962). A sketch of Lowell's life is contained in Edward Weeks, *The Lowells and Their Institute* (1966). A lengthy obituary is in the *Boston Globe*, 16 May 1978.

MARK I. GELFAND

LOWELL, Robert (1 Mar. 1917–12 Sept. 1977), poet, was born Robert Traill Spence Lowell IV in Boston, Massachusetts, the son of Robert Traill Spence Lowell III, an engineer in the U.S. Navy, and Charlotte Winslow. Lowell's ancestors on his father's side included poets James Russell Lowell and Amy Lowell as well as Civil War colonel Charles Russell Lowell, Harvard president Abbott Lawrence Lowell, and astronomer Percival Lowell. On his mother's side, he counted as ancestors colonial patriarchs Edward Winslow and Josiah Winslow and revolutionary war general John Stark. Robert Lowell felt these ancestors to be as much a moral burden as a point of pride. He wrote numerous poems expressing guilt for his ancestors' crusades against various opponents including Native Americans, political dissidents, and the natural environment. He even expressed disdain for his poetic forerunners, calling James Russell Lowell a poet "pedestalled for oblivion" and Amy Lowell "a scandal, as if Mae West were a cousin."

The Lowell family's notable, if often guilty, past collided with its present straightened and conflicted obscurity. Despite benefiting from a sizable inheritance, Lowell's father failed in both his naval career and his subsequent attempts to establish himself as a stockbroker. Moreover, Lowell's mother and father perpetually quarreled. Young Lowell endured the irony of possessing a celebrated family name but a pedestrian and even tortured and ignominious family reality. He grew up haunted and repelled by his familial and cultural history, as works such as "At the Indian Killer's Grave," "The Quaker Graveyard in Nantucket," "Salem," "Mr. Edwards and the Spider," "Charles Russell Lowell," and his dramatic trilogy, *The Old Glory*, attest. He was equally obsessed and horrified by his experience of family and national life. His witty, pained, and revealing autobiographical lyrics—appearing most memorably in his 1959 "Life Studies" se-

quence—formed the spine of his poetic identity and achievement.

Lowell grew up in Boston after spending brief, unsettled periods in Washington, D.C., and Philadelphia. In Boston he attended the Episcopalian prep school St. Mark's, where his antisocial behavior earned him the sobriquet of "Cal," short for both "Caligula," the Roman tyrant, and "Caliban," the beastman of Shakespeare's *Tempest*. Lowell then studied for two years at Harvard (1935–1937), where his incipient poetic gifts went unrecognized and where his sullenness and anger only grew. After a violent quarrel with his father—memorialized in a series of guilt-ridden poems written throughout his career—Lowell drove to Clarksville, Tennessee, to introduce himself to the Fugitive poet and critic Allen Tate. Tate became Lowell's first and most important poetic mentor, changing and perhaps saving Lowell's life.

Tate recognized Lowell's talent and gave that talent direction. After buying a tent at a local department store, Lowell camped out on Tate's lawn for a summer, spending his days composing poems and talking poetry with Tate. In fall 1937 Lowell enrolled at Kenyon College in Ohio to study with Tate's friend and fellow poet John Crowe Ransom. Among the other students at Kenyon, Lowell met a lifelong friend, Randall Jarrell, who eventually became another prominent member of Lowell's "Middle Generation" of poets. Lowell excelled in his classes, wrote impassioned poems on classical and Christian themes that were published in the school literary journal *Hika*, and graduated summa cum laude in classics in 1940.

Soon after graduation Lowell married his first wife, Jean Stafford, who was just beginning her illustrious career as a writer of fiction. They had no children. He then commenced graduate study at Louisiana State University with two of the most prominent New Critics, Cleanth Brooks and Robert Penn Warren. Lowell at that time converted to Roman Catholicism, influenced by Gerard Manley Hopkins, Etienne Gilson, and other Catholic writers and philosophers and impelled as well by his dark moods and what his wife termed "fire-breathing righteousness." This religious conversion strongly shaped the character of his first two books of poetry. Lowell left graduate school in September 1941 to work briefly at the New York publishing house Sheed and Ward. His poetic career resumed when he returned with Stafford for a year's stay with Tate and his wife, novelist Caroline Gordon, in Monteagle, Tennessee. There Lowell wrote most of the highly rhetorical religious and social poems that appeared in his first published book, the privately printed *Land of Unlikeness* (1944).

Although Lowell had volunteered and been rejected for military service in the Second World War, when he was inducted in 1943, he refused to serve. He based his refusal partly on a newfound but principled pacifism, partly on political opposition to President Franklin D. Roosevelt's demand for Germany's unconditional surrender, partly on a congenital rebelliousness, and perhaps partly on barely conscious fascist sympathies he had acquired both from his upbringing and as a self-conceived inheritor of a certain variety of high Modernism. His mentors Tate and Ransom also opposed U.S. participation in the war, as did such Modernist luminaries as Ezra Pound and, to a lesser extent, Wallace Stevens. As a conscientious objector, Lowell served five months in West Street Jail in New York City and in federal prison at Danbury, Connecticut, an experience he later represented in poems such as "In the Cage" and "Memories of West Street and Lepke." Upon release, Lowell returned, with renewed inspiration and dedication, to his poetic vocation. He composed thirty-two new poems, revised ten previously published poems, and published them all in the book that made him famous, *Lord Weary's Castle* (1946). This volume won rave reviews by many of the most prominent poets and critics of the time, and it won the first of Lowell's two Pulitzer Prizes. His friend Randall Jarrell, the nation's leading poetry reviewer at the time, wrote in the *Nation*,

When I reviewed Mr. Lowell's first book I finished by saying, "Some of the best poems of the next years ought to be written by him." The appearance of *Lord Weary's Castle* makes me feel less like Adams or Leverrier than like a rain-maker who predicts rain and gets a flood which drowns everyone in the country. (18 Jan. 1947, p. 77)

Lord Weary's Castle, moderating and perfecting the rhetoric of Lowell's first book, lambastes the violence, opportunism, greed, and egotism that Lowell saw pervading the American past and present. According to "Children of Light," our Puritan ancestors "fenced their gardens with the red man's bones." In "At the Indian Killer's Grave," Lowell has the murdered Indian King Philip arise to condemn the Puritan elders to hell for having "hurled / Anathemas at nature and the land." In "Concord," Lowell scorns twentieth-century Americans who have replaced the Puritans' religious zealotry with consumerist conformity: "Ten thousand Fords are idle here in search of a tradition." The volume's longest and most harrowing poem, "The Quaker Graveyard in Nantucket," laments all that American seamen of the nineteenth century "lost / In the mad scramble of their lives." The poem even more intensely mourns present-day losses, implicitly those resulting from World War II, in imagery that echoes and alters that of *Moby-Dick* (among other texts): "The bones cry for the blood of the white whale." Throughout "The Quaker Graveyard in Nantucket" and *Lord Weary's Castle*, Jesus Christ and the Virgin Mary are presented as the sources of salvation. But it is the prolonged anguish of the narrating subject rather than his occasional half-vision of redemption that governs this poetic discourse: "I am a red arrow on this graph / Of Revelations." Moving American poetry to a new plateau of linguistic energy and complexity, *Lord Weary's Castle* brings to a triumphant climax one variety of poetic Modernism, especially as constructed by New Critical reading strategies. The volume also culminates a tradition of apocalyptic cultural critique that

may be traced back through T. S. Eliot, Pound, William Butler Yeats, and Hopkins to Matthew Arnold, Robert Browning, Percy Bysshe Shelley, and John Milton.

For all its impact, *Lord Weary's Castle* was more an ending than a beginning. Lowell's Modernist and Christian loyalties consumed themselves in the process of articulation, leaving Lowell's career momentarily in ashes. American poetry, of which his work seemed to some exemplary, found itself at a confused moment as well. Lowell's poetic drive sputtered on, producing one additional volume, *The Mills of the Kavanaughs* (1951). Although this volume included several interesting narrative poems, it was pervaded by a sense of anticlimax, devitalization, and even indifference.

Then followed a thundering silence, a period of transition marked by few poems and tumultuous personal changes. Lowell had divorced Jean Stafford in 1948 and married essayist and novelist Elizabeth Hardwick the following year. The couple had one child. He had also lost his Roman Catholic faith; he had acquired a politics Stanley Kunitz characterized as "conventionally liberal" (though it was striated with conservative and radically leftist strands); and he began to experience a series of manic-depressive episodes that left him periodically disabled, hospitalized, and medicated throughout the rest of his life. Moreover, this was a period in which both of Lowell's parents died. His ineffectual, ambivalently loved father died in 1950, and his demanding, frustrated, brilliant, and even more ambivalently loved mother died in 1954. Lowell spent much of 1955 in mental hospitals. By 1957 he was back in Boston, living with Hardwick and their newborn daughter and teaching poetry part-time at Boston University. He was attempting to write a prose autobiography, and he was publishing nothing. On a West Coast reading tour, he thought that his old poems "seemed like prehistoric monsters dragged down by their ponderous armor" (*Prose*, p. 227). Feeling that most of what he knew about writing poetry was a hindrance, he determined to start over.

Influenced by the friendship and poetic examples of William Carlos Williams, Elizabeth Bishop, and W. D. Snodgrass—and perhaps, though he denied it, by the popular success of Allen Ginsberg—Lowell began writing autobiographical and domestic poems that were elegiac and self-deprecating, painful and comic. In these poems about his parents, his upbringing, his marriage, and his mental breakdown, Lowell came down off his rhetorical stilts and pondered, in Yeats's phrase, "old bones, old rags." He wanted to see "how much of my personal story and memories I could get into poetry" (Meyers, p. 85). He hoped that "each poem might seem as open and single-surfaced as a photograph" (Meyers, p. 158). Gone was the prophetic, intricately crafted discourse of *Lord Weary's Castle*. In its place were free-verse lyrics that adopted a tone "that sounded a little like conversation" (Meyers, p. 79). The poems were written "rather directly with hidden artifice" (Meyers, p. 75), forging a dialectic of "actual experience" and "something invented" (Meyers, p. 94). Including both a fullness of human representation and a maximum of linguistic ingenuity, these were poems in which characters spoke, felt, and acted and in which language self-reflexively played.

Chronicling a family's decline while commenting ironically on class, race, gender, sexuality, and American nationality from the 1920s to the end of the Dwight Eisenhower era, *Life Studies* (1959) was Lowell's second great success. The volume won wide notice, impressive reviews, and the 1960 National Book Award for poetry. It changed the course of poetry in the United States, ushering out what Lowell called the "symbol hanging on a hatrack" (Meyers, p. 169) and ushering in the family plot. The book's key "Life Studies" sequence commences with memory poems about growing up in a family whose dominant notes were conflict, failure, separation, loss, and death. The sequence concludes with poems depicting the narrator's own discordant marriage, his descent into mental illness, and his partial and perhaps temporary recovery. The final poem, "Skunk Hour," breaks irretrievably with the Modernist principles of objectivity, unity, and impersonality: "I myself am hell; nobody's here." The ambiguous concluding lines depict a mother skunk who, implicitly like the narrating subject himself, "will not scare." Brilliantly deploying the signs of his own life and those of his culture, Lowell accomplished a memorable and influential de-idealization and de-centering of personal being, family, nation, and poetic language itself.

In the years that followed, Lowell modified and expanded the personal lyric without ever quite abandoning it. He felt that after *Life Studies*, "continuous autobiography was impossible" (Meyers, p. 156). He and his family moved from Boston to New York, and he began to focus more on his nation's intellectual and historical life and less on his family relationships. He published a volume of creative translations, *Imitations* (1960), and then a volume of new poems, *For the Union Dead* (1964). Although not as cohesive or compulsively readable as *Life Studies*, the latter volume concludes with one of Lowell's most justly celebrated poems, "For the Union Dead." Employing an astonishing array of echoing images and words, this poem moves effortlessly between personal-seeming memory and cultural critique. It juxtaposes a heroic black Union army regiment with the integration battles of African Americans in the 1950s, and it counterpoises Hiroshima with parking structures, advertising, TV news, and societal amnesia. On the basis of this poem, Richard Poirier labeled Lowell "our truest historian."

Lowell continued to write poems of political resistance and historical memory throughout the rest of the 1960s. His dramatic trilogy, *The Old Glory* (1965), reimagines stories by Nathaniel Hawthorne and Herman Melville in order to critique the uneasy alliance of idealism and violence in the American past and present. Regarding violence as "*the* hellfire" (Meyers, p. 164), Lowell dramatizes crucial moments in seventeenth-, eighteenth-, and nineteenth-century America as filtered through an awareness of twentieth-century racism and imperialism.

In 1965 Lowell protested the Vietnam War by publicly declining President Lyndon Johnson's invitation to a White House arts festival. This controversial act plunged him into active politics for the first time since he had refused the draft twenty-two years before. The connecting thread between these acts of resistance was his horror of war. He spent the last half of the 1960s participating in antiwar demonstrations and Senator Eugene McCarthy's 1968 presidential campaign. Lowell's retelling of Aeschylus's *Prometheus Bound* (1969) and especially his brief collection of poems titled *Near the Ocean* (1967) reflect and extend this political engagement. Both books question the kind of patriarchal authority that precipitates war abroad and inequity at home. "Central Park," in *Near the Ocean*, portrays an America wracked by poverty, crime, class distinction, and brutality. "Waking Early Sunday Morning," in the same volume, represents President Johnson justifying international violence yet secretly "sick / of his ghost-written rhetoric!" This poem concludes with an eloquent lament for a human race made abject by its own violent desires: "Pity the planet."

Lowell's political and moral concerns reached a climax in an experimental volume of sonnetlike poems that attempted to mix "the day-to-day with the history." Initially titled *Notebook 1967–68* (1969), it was revised and republished twice, first as an expanded *Notebook* (1970) and then as a much-altered *History* (1973). *History* removes the personal sonnets from *Notebook*, adds some additional sonnets about history and politics, and arranges the whole chronologically. It plunges readers into a verbal labyrinth of tyrants, heroes, artists, wars, artworks, and quotations, all tied together with bent epigrams and accompanied by the insistent sounds of death. The book sums up the poet's obsession with the public life and cultural past—and perhaps liberates him from it.

Lowell rearranged and republished the more personal sonnets of *Notebook* in *For Lizzie and Harriet* (1973). As a counterpoint to that book, which focuses on his second marriage, Lowell also wrote *The Dolphin* (1973), which constructs a fissured narrative of his 1972 divorce from Hardwick, his marriage later that year to his third wife, Caroline Blackwood, and the birth of their son. Perhaps more importantly, the volume creates a space in which to chart the interactions of love and art, of human experience and poetic language. The "dolphin" of the title is alternatively erotic love and poetic voice and vocation. Thus, if *History* forms the capstone of Lowell's public meditations, *The Dolphin* culminates his domestic and aesthetic ones. Although attacked by some readers for violating privacies as well as venerated notions of poetic language and form, *The Dolphin* earned Lowell his second Pulitzer Prize.

In his final years Lowell was plagued by worsening physical and psychological debilities. His heart was failing, his third marriage was dissolving, and his depression grew increasingly constant. In 1970 Lowell had moved to England, where he fell in love with Blackwood, but in 1977 the marriage failed and he returned to Elizabeth Hardwick in the United States. Lowell died of congestive heart failure in a New York City taxi on his way back from a last, unhappy visit with Blackwood in Ireland. Weeks earlier his final book of poetry, *Day by Day* (1977), had appeared. It included a complex Homeric narrative of domestic tension called "Ulysses and Circe"; a final political poem, juxtaposing Richard Nixon with mad King George, called "George III"; and a poignant sequence of autobiographical poems haltingly describing a downward descent. In almost his last composed poem, an *ars poetica* called "Epilogue," Lowell wrote, "Pray for the grace of accuracy." The poet, who had devoted his life to exploring the uncertain borders dividing the literary and the lived, left as his final words an evocation of that quest in the form of a prayer.

• Lowell's papers are collected at Harvard University. A second major collection is housed at the University of Texas, Austin. Other papers are at Yale University; Princeton University; the University of California, Riverside; the University at Buffalo; Kenyon College; and Washington University. A well-chosen but ultimately inadequate selection of Lowell's poems appears in *Selected Poems*, rev. ed. (1977). His essays and autobiographies have been collected in *Collected Prose*, ed. Robert Giroux (1987). Lowell's major interviews appear in *Robert Lowell: Interviews and Memoirs*, ed. Jeffrey Meyers (1988). A bibliography of primary works is the very early Jerome Mazzaro, *The Achievement of Robert Lowell, 1939–1959* (1960). The most complete bibliography of secondary materials is Steven Gould Axelrod and Helen Deese, *Robert Lowell: A Reference Guide* (1982). Major biographies are Ian Hamilton, *Robert Lowell* (1982), which focuses on misdeeds and scandals in an often superficial manner; Paul Mariani, *Lost Puritan: A Life of Robert Lowell* (1994), which provides the best and most complete life history to date; and Richard Tillinghast, *Robert Lowell's Life and Work: Damaged Grandeur* (1995), a revealing critical memoir. Early critical studies of Lowell include the following works, all published while Lowell was in mid-career: Hugh Staples, *Robert Lowell: The First Twenty Years* (1962), which takes a New Critical stance; Jerome Mazzaro, *The Poetic Themes of Robert Lowell* (1965), which provides multiple cultural and literary contexts for reading the early volumes; Richard J. Fein, *Robert Lowell* (1970; rev. ed., 1979), which explicates the poems in terms of both a private and a common world; Marjorie Perloff, *The Poetic Art of Robert Lowell* (1973), which provides an essential starting point for theoretically sophisticated readings of Lowell; Alan Williamson, *Pity the Monsters: The Political Vision of Robert Lowell* (1974), which initiates both a psychoanalytical and a cultural studies approach to Lowell; and Stephen Yenser, *Circle to Circle: The Poetry of Robert Lowell* (1975), which gives Lowell's poetry intensive aesthetic scrutiny. Since 1977, critical books have been able to consider Lowell's career in its entirety. Steven Gould Axelrod, *Robert Lowell: Life and Art* (1978), provides a biography of Lowell's imagination as well as sustained readings of all of his major poems and a positioning of his work within a fabric of influences that includes Allen Tate and William Carlos Williams. Vereen Bell, *Robert Lowell: Nihilist as Hero* (1983), presses the case for Lowell's chronic pessimism. Katharine Wallingford, *Robert Lowell's Language of the Self* (1988), offers a reading of Lowell's oeuvre in terms of the process of Freudian psychoanalysis. Terry Witek, *Robert Lowell and "Life Studies": Revising the Self* (1993), offers an intensive reading of Lowell's autobiographical volume. Henry Hart, *Robert Lowell and the Sublime* (1995), provides multiple perspectives on Lowell's tropes of sublimity. Two notable collections of essays are Steven Gould Axelrod and Helen Deese, eds., *Robert Lowell: Essays on the Poetry* (1986), and Harold Bloom, ed., *Robert Lowell* (1987). Obituaries are in the *New York Times*, 13 Sept. 1977, and *The Times* (London), 14 Sept. 1977.

STEVEN GOULD AXELROD

LOWELL, Robert Traill Spence (8 Oct. 1816–12 Sept. 1891), Episcopal priest, educator, and author, was born in Boston, Massachusetts, the son of the Reverend Charles Lowell, a Unitarian minister, and Harriett Brackett Spence. He attended the Round Hill School, Northampton, Massachusetts, 1823–1828, where he studied with Joseph Green Cogswell, the founder of the school, and George Bancroft, the great historian. Many years later, Lowell dedicated a book of poems to Cogswell with "love and reverence." From Round Hill he went to Harvard College, where he graduated in 1833. He then studied medicine at Harvard, 1833–1836, but never practiced. In 1836 he went into business with his oldest brother, Charles, but gave this up in 1839 in order to study for the ministry of the Episcopal church. He went to Schenectady, New York, to study with Alonzo Potter, whom he had known in Boston when Potter was the rector of St. Paul's Church. After two years of theological study with Potter, the bishop of Newfoundland, whom Lowell had met in Boston, arranged for him to go to Bermuda to do missionary work. On 4 December 1842 he was ordained deacon by Bishop Aubrey George Spencer of Newfoundland, when Spencer was in Bermuda, and in March 1843 he was ordained priest by Spencer. In Bermuda he served as a domestic chaplain to the bishop.

In late 1843 Lowell went to Bay Roberts, Newfoundland, where he was a missionary for the Society for the Propagation of the Gospel. On a trip back to Boston in 1845, he married Mary Ann Duane, later Marianna, and they had seven children. She was from Duanesburg, New York, and was very wealthy. After five years of service at Bay Roberts, during which he and his family were among those who suffered through a winter famine and he was the chairman of the relief committee, he returned to Boston in 1847 in broken health. After several months he became a missionary in a poor section of Newark, New Jersey, where he established Christ Church. It was a free church, that is, it had no pew rents, and it had a weekly Eucharist every Sunday and Morning and Evening Prayer, Monday through Saturday. He served there until 1859.

From 1859 until 1868, Lowell was the rector of Christ Church, Duanesburg, New York. Christ Church had been built in 1793, by Judge James Duane, the grandfather of Lowell's wife. While rector of Christ Church, Lowell was offered several professorships, including professor of belles-lettres at Racine College, Racine, Wisconsin, but he declined all of them. In 1869 he went to Southborough, Massachusetts, where he served for four years as the headmaster of St. Mark's School. In 1873 Lowell became professor of Latin language and literature in Union College, Schenectady, New York, and remained there until he retired in 1879.

Lowell is more widely known for his work as a writer and poet than for his work as a priest. His work as a poet and writer is, however, overshadowed by that of his brother, James Russell Lowell. In 1858 Lowell published one of his most successful works, *The New Priest in Conception Bay*. This was based on his experience at Bay Roberts, the "Petersport" of *New Priest*, and all of the characters in the book, except one, are based on persons in Bay Roberts. While in Newark, Lowell had a friendly publishing controversy with a Roman Catholic priest, and this person was probably the model for Father Terence in *New Priest*. In 1858 Lowell published his most popular poem, "Relief of Lucknow," in the February issue of *Atlantic Monthly*, which was edited by his brother James. That poem was also in *Fresh Hearts That Failed Three Thousand Years Ago; with Other Things* (1860). "Relief of Lucknow" was read frequently on public occasions by Ralph Waldo Emerson. On 9 April 1865 General Lee surrendered at Appomattox, and late in May the president and fellows of Harvard College appointed 21 July a day to commemorate the young men who had died for the Union cause. The hymn sung that day was "Thy Work, O God, Goes On in Earth," which was written by Lowell. *Antony Brade, a Story of a Schoolboy Life* (1874), his book for boys, grew out of Lowell's experiences at St. Mark's School. On 19 September 1877 he wrote "Burgoyne's Last March. Poem For the Celebration of the Hundredth Year of Bemis Heights," and it was published in that year. It was read at the Saratoga County centennial celebration. His last book was *A Story or Two from an Old Dutch Town* (1878), which described his time in Schenectady. Lowell also published short stories, sermons, and addresses.

Lowell never attained the fame and recognition of his brother James Russell Lowell; in fact, when James died, the obituary in the *New York Times* stated that "Mrs. Burnett was his only near relative, except a brother Robert, whose whereabouts are uncertain." While his work is not as significant as that of James, Robert Lowell was a skillful writer and a poet of repute. Lowell died in Schenectady, New York.

• Lowell's papers are in the Archives of Harvard University. Information about him must be obtained from works about James Russell Lowell or about the Lowell family. Helpful in this regard are Ferris Greenslet, *The Lowells and Their Seven Worlds* (1946), and Horace Elisha Scudder, *James Russell Lowell: A Biography* (2 vols., 1901). There is also some information about Lowell in Martin Duberman, *James Russell Lowell* (1966). There are two letters to Robert in *Letters of James Russell Lowell*, ed. Charles Eliot Norton (2 vols., 1894). The reference to "Robert, whose whereabouts are un-

known," was in "Mr. Lowell's Elder Brother," *New York Times*, 3 Sept. 1891. The most complete obituary is in the *Churchman*, 19 Sept. 1891.

DONALD S. ARMENTROUT

LOWENSTEIN, Allard Kenneth (16 Jan. 1929–14 Mar. 1980), lawyer, congressman, and political agitator, was born Allard Augustus Lowenstein in Newark, New Jersey, the son of Gabriel Abraham Lowenstein, a medical school teacher who turned restaurateur, and Augusta Goldberg. Lowenstein later chose Kenneth to replace Augustus, his given middle name. Only a year old when his mother died he was not told at first that his stepmother was not his birth mother, which he discovered when he was thirteen. In 1945 Lowenstein graduated from Horace Mann School in New York City and four years later graduated from the University of North Carolina. At North Carolina he succeeded in ending the practice of pairing Jewish students as roommates and gained them access to campus fraternities, and when the student state legislature met in Chapel Hill in December 1945 he got a resolution passed opening it up to black participation. Becoming a powerful personality on campus, Lowenstein found a hero and friend in the school's president, Frank Porter Graham. When Graham was appointed to fill a vacancy in the U.S. Senate in 1949, Lowenstein worked for him in Washington and the next year helped run his unsuccessful campaign to retain his Senate seat.

After serving as president of the U.S. National Student Association, 1950–1951, Lowenstein entered Yale University law school and in 1952 was the national chairman of Students for Adlai Stevenson. To gain student support for Stevenson's bid for the presidency, Lowenstein took part in debates on college campuses around the country and spoke at the National Press Club. Upon receiving his Yale law degree in 1954, he served two years as an enlisted man in the U.S. Army, stationed mainly in Germany. During 1956–1957 he was educational consultant to the American Association for the United Nations, where he worked with Eleanor Roosevelt, who with Graham and Norman Thomas, the Socialist leader, formed his trinity of heroes. The following year he worked as a foreign-policy assistant to Senator Hubert Humphrey. In 1959 Lowenstein gathered information in South-West Africa (or Namibia), at the request of its representatives, for a report to the United Nations (UN), *Brutal Mandate: Journey to South-West Africa* (1962), on apartheid and living conditions in that area dominated by South Africa. While practicing law in New York in 1960, he was active in civil rights and Democratic politics.

Lowenstein's reputation as a Pied Piper for college students and the "supreme agitator" of the 1960s began at Stanford University, where he became an assistant dean and a political science lecturer in 1961 and remained for the academic year. Although he began teaching at North Carolina State University in Raleigh in the fall of 1962 and spearheaded local integration attempts there, part of his spirit remained at Stanford, where some of the students were still called "Al People." They played an important role in registering black voters in Mississippi during the 1963 Freedom Vote and the 1964 Freedom Summer, which he helped organize.

Despite the fact that Lowenstein's civil rights work attracted numerous other students, many from the University of North Carolina and Yale, the Stanford students, including activist Dennis Sweeney, became more radicalized by their Student Nonviolent Coordinating Committee (SNCC) associates and, as a result, were more difficult for Lowenstein to influence. Siding with SNCC in its conflict with Lowenstein over civil rights strategy, Sweeney discussed with his Stanford colleagues reasons for his disillusionment with his former mentor and found that others had shared his experience. Many "Al People" found objectionable Lowenstein's scheming to be physically close to his young male associates. Often he contrived to sleep with them and hug them, though apparently he did not initiate genital contact. Refusing to consider these encounters homosexual, Lowenstein seemed to draw comfort from them, but they often confused and sometimes angered his companions.

In the 1964 voter registration drive, all the civil rights organizations were united in their tactics and goals. Lowenstein worked to promote cooperation between blacks and (to prevent) tensions from flaring between the SNCC and the National Association for the Advancement of Colored People, the group with whom his ties were closest. Fearful of criticisms that Communists had infiltrated the civil rights movement, he questioned the participation of the National Lawyers' Guild and the Southern Conference Education Fund. In so doing, he raised the hackles of SNCC workers, who did not want to lose the support of these organizations and who did not want Lowenstein to determine policy. Although Lowenstein briefly left Mississippi, deciding that the movement had become too radicalized, he rushed back to the state after the disappearance in June of civil rights workers Michael Schwerner, Andrew Goodman, and James Chaney. Norman Thomas insisted that Lowenstein return, since it was he who had recruited the students. Lowenstein's relationship with the SNCC ended at the Democratic National Convention in Atlantic City later that summer. Working within the system and emphasizing gains rather than losses, he counseled accepting the compromise seating offer made to the Mississippi Freedom Democratic party delegation, even while calling it inadequate.

In 1965 Lowenstein became active in the early teach-ins and protests against the Vietnam War. The next year he married Jennifer Lyman; they had three children before divorcing in 1979.

In 1966 Lowenstein lost a bid for the Democratic congressional nomination in the primary in Manhattan's Nineteenth District. The next year, while teaching at City College of the City University of New York, he organized the national "Dump Johnson" movement to deny Lyndon Johnson renomination as the Democratic presidential candidate and became a one-man search committee for an alternative candidate. Unable to draft Robert F. Kennedy, who had become another of his heroes, or George McGovern, he settled for Eugene McCarthy. Lowenstein again played the Pied Piper in successfully attracting droves of college students to work in McCarthy's campaign. When, to everyone's surprise, Lowenstein's plan worked and Johnson declared he would not seek reelection following McCarthy's good showing in the New Hampshire Democratic primary, Kennedy belatedly entered the race. Lowenstein continued to back McCarthy, but McCarthy suspected that Lowenstein preferred Kennedy. To get away from this unpleasant muddle, Lowenstein ran for Congress in Long Island's Fifth District and won. The next year he entered the House as a folk hero who had unseated a president and, as Congressman Jonathan Bingham attested, made more of an impression there than had any freshman since Henry Clay.

In 1970 Lowenstein was denied reelection when his district was redrawn to favor Republicans, and for the rest of his life he focused on winning election to Congress. He chaired Americans for Democratic Action for two terms beginning in 1971. In 1972 he lost in a disputed Democratic primary in Brooklyn's Fourteenth District, in 1974 and 1976 he lost in his old Long Island district, and in 1978 he again lost in the Democratic primary in Manhattan's Nineteenth District. When not running for office, he taught, lectured, and agitated for peace and racial justice, winning the number seven place on President Richard Nixon's list of political enemies.

In 1977 and 1978, as the U.S. representative to the United Nations Commission on Human Rights and his country's alternate representative for UN special political affairs, Lowenstein traveled widely and, as the *New York Times* reported on 15 March 1980, exhibited "a remarkable ability to talk to both sides in almost any diplomatic dispute." As a special ambassador, he in 1979 again went to southern Africa, and purportedly, "No other foreigner had as full an understanding of the South African Scene." Months later the British used his plan of economic pressure to break the Rhodesian deadlock between white minority rulers and black guerrillas, resulting in the birth of Zimbabwe.

Lowenstein's life ended when Dennis Sweeney, in a meeting in Lowenstein's law office, talked with him briefly, then fired seven shots, hitting him five times. Sweeney had become a "paranoid schizophrenic of the chronic type" (Harris, p. 293). He had trailed and threatened another former associate, who he was convinced, along with Lowenstein, had wrecked the civil rights movement. While surgeons worked to keep Lowenstein alive, his family and friends formed a vigil in another part of the Manhattan hospital, and some sang civil rights songs. By the time the weary doctors announced that Lowenstein was dead, Senator Edward Kennedy had arrived. In a memorial oration, Kennedy aptly described Lowenstein as "a portable and powerful lobby for progressive principles," a man with "electricity in his thought, and eloquence in his words," and a man who truly made "a difference" (Stone and Lowenstein, p. 329).

• Lowenstein's papers are in the Southern Historical Collection, Wilson Library, University of North Carolina at Chapel Hill. Tapes and transcripts of numerous interviews with Lowenstein's family and associates conducted by William H. Chafe are at the University of North Carolina at Chapel Hill and the Columbia University Oral History Collection, Butler Library. For careful documentation of every aspect of Lowenstein's life and career, see Chafe, *Never Stop Running: Allard Lowenstein and the Struggle to Save American Liberalism* (1993). For a collection of his speeches and writings, contemporary writings about him, and a chronology of his life, see Gregory Stone and Douglas Lowenstein, eds., *Lowenstein: Acts of Courage and Belief* (1983), for which Arthur Schlesinger, Jr., wrote the foreword and James A. Wechsler wrote the introduction. See also Richard Cummings, *The Pied Piper: Allard K. Lowenstein and the Liberal Dream* (1985), and David Harris, *Dreams Die Hard* (1982), a highly critical view by an associate of both Lowenstein and Sweeney. On his Brooklyn defeat for Congress, see Lanny J. Davis, "Why Lowenstein Lost: Ethnics, Crooks, and Carpetbaggers," *Washington Monthly* 4 (Sept. 1972). An obituary and a related article on Sweeney are in the *New York Times*, 15 Mar. 1980.

OLIVE HOOGENBOOM

LOWENTHAL, Marvin Marx (6 Oct. 1890–15 Mar. 1969), writer and Zionist organizer, was born in Bradford, Pennsylvania, the son of Louis S. Lowenthal, a jeweler, and Pauline Marx. At the age of fifteen he went to work in a local silk mill. Having risen from bobbin boy to assistant superintendent within six years, Lowenthal quit his job to enroll at the University of Wisconsin at Madison. In February 1912 Lowenthal embarked on a rigorous course of humanistic studies and graduated with the class of 1915.

Although Lowenthal and his parents belonged to Bradford's Jewish Reform Temple, he was not religious. In Wisconsin a skeptical Lowenthal joined the Menorah Society, an intercollegiate Jewish cultural organization (founded at Harvard in 1906). He only joined because he had won first prize in the society's essay contest and felt that for the lavish prize money of 100 dollars (Lowenthal's rent was two dollars a week) he should attend at least one meeting. Lowenthal's condescending attitude toward Jewish history and culture changed completely when he met the philosophy professor Horace Kallen in November 1912. Kallen had studied at Harvard under Josiah Royce and George Santayana, written his dissertation under the direction of William James, and participated in the founding of the Menorah Society. When Lowenthal met him, Kallen was working on his theory of American cultural pluralism but was nevertheless deeply committed to Zionism. Entirely under Kallen's spell, Lowenthal began to study Zionism in 1914, won another Menorah essay contest with an article on Zionism, and from 1915 became a regular contributor to the *Menorah Journal*, an important cultural journal for American-Jewish intellectuals before the founding of *Commentary* in 1945.

Following Kallen's advice, Lowenthal enrolled at Harvard University to pursue a master's degree in philosophy, which he obtained in 1916, and became part of a tight network of committed Zionists that included Louis Brandeis. In 1916 Brandeis asked Lowenthal to head the Zionist Bureau of the Pacific Coast in San Francisco. Lowenthal accepted and worked effectively as a fundraiser until the Zionist Organization of America (ZOA) moved him to its New York bureau in 1919. A year later Lowenthal decided to leave the ZOA to become a full-time writer. Working as a part-time editor at the *Menorah Journal* to support himself and his wife, Sylvia Mardfin, whom he had married in 1918, Lowenthal began to produce a steady stream of articles on Jewish cultural affairs. However, it was not until the couple moved to Europe in February 1922 and lived for a year in Florence, London, and Berlin, that Lowenthal found the subject that turned him from a two-cents-a-word journalist into a writer—the fate of the Jews of Europe.

With astonishing perspicacity Lowenthal described in the early 1920s the rise of European fascism as a threat to Jewish life and spotted in Adolf Hitler and his fringe party the most virulent and deadly enemy of the Jews. Alienated by an "atmosphere so thick with hatred against the Jews," as Lowenthal wrote to a friend, he and his wife left Europe in February 1923 only to return to Paris in the fall of 1924 because Lowenthal was restless in America and felt too far away from the subject he cared about. During the next decade, while traveling through Europe, Palestine, and North Africa on journalistic assignments or as representative of the Jewish minority interests at the League of Nations (1927–1931), Lowenthal laid the intellectual foundations for his major works that were to appear in rapid succession in the early 1930s.

In 1932 Lowenthal published his translation of the seventeenth-century *Memoirs of Glückel of Hameln*, which was followed by *A World Passed By* in 1933, an intellectual Baedecker of Jewish Europe and North Africa. Seeking refuge from Europe's bleak political scene, Lowenthal had early on turned to the writings of Montaigne, and in 1935 he published *The Autobiography of Michel de Montaigne*, culled from Montaigne's essays. In 1936 Lowenthal published his most important book, *The Jews of Germany: A Story of Sixteen Centuries*. It was also his most painful work because he was certain that that story was rapidly coming to an end. Although Lowenthal had left Europe and resettled in America in 1934, he followed the events in Germany closely and was deeply disturbed by the passing of the Nuremberg Laws in September 1935, which deprived the German Jews of their citizenship.

The Jews of Germany left Lowenthal exhausted. His journal of the time is filled with literary fragments, essay sketches, and writing plans, but no finished product materialized. In 1941 Lowenthal returned to the only spark of hope in a world that had darkened for the Jews—the men and women committed to Zionism. He wrote and edited *The Life and Letters of Henrietta Szold* (1942), the founder of the women's Zionist organization Hadassah. As America was waging war in Europe and the Pacific, Lowenthal collaborated with Frank Monaghan on *This Was New York: The Nation's Capital in 1789*, a volume clearly designed to instill Americans with a sense of pride in their country. From 1946 to 1949 Lowenthal served on the Zionist Advisory Committee, and from 1952 to 1954 he edited the *American Zionist*. He then began his last major work, a one-volume edition and translation of *The Diaries of Theodore Herzl* (1956). Lowenthal's editorial comments show reverence for the man whose ideas (mediated by Kallen) had persuaded him to put his talents at the service of the Jewish people. Lowenthal died in New York City in 1969.

• Lowenthal's papers are deposited in the archives of the American Jewish Historical Society in Waltham, Massachusetts. An appreciation of Lowenthal's life and a detailed summary of his work are in Charles Madison, "Marvin Lowenthal, 1890–1969," *Jewish Book Annual* 28 (1970–1971): 94–98. A biographical essay by Susanne Klingenstein, "'Not the Recovery of a Grave, but of a Cradle': The Zionist Life of Marvin Lowenthal," is in *The "Other" New York Jewish Intellectuals*, ed. Carole S. Kessner (1994).

SUSANNE KLINGENSTEIN

LOWE-PORTER, H. T. (15 June 1876–26 Apr. 1963), translator and writer, was born Helen Tracey Porter in Towanda, Pennsylvania, the daughter of Henry Clinton Porter, a pharmacist, and Clara Holcombe. A prominent aunt, Charlotte Endymion Porter, editor of William Shakespeare, Robert Browning, and the Boston literary magazine *Poet Lore*, acted as her role model and had a strong sway on the young Porter. She attended her aunt's alma mater, Wells College in Aurora, New York, and became an editor for the college's literary magazine, the *Wells College Chronicle*, which Charlotte Porter had helped to found. After graduating in 1898, Helen Porter went to work for *Poet Lore*, and it was here that her translations of plays by Henrik Ibsen and Gerhart Hauptmann made their first appearance. Additionally she assisted her aunt in preparing folio editions of Shakespeare and Browning.

In 1906–1907 Porter visited her sister who was in Germany training to become a singer. There she met Elias Avery Lowe, an American studying at the University of Munich. They were married in Switzerland in 1911 and eventually had three daughters. Elias Lowe was one of the preeminent paleographers of the twentieth century. He taught at Oxford University, and the couple made their home in Oxford until 1936, when Elias Lowe was offered a position at the Institute for Advanced Study at Princeton University in Princeton, New Jersey.

At Oxford, shortly after the German publication of Thomas Mann's *Buddenbrooks* (1901), publisher William Heinemann invited Lowe-Porter to translate Mann's novel. Although Heinemann did not publish the translation, it appeared in 1924 among the Borzoi Books of the publishing firm of Alfred Knopf. Lowe-

Porter then published all of her Mann translations—up to *The Holy Sinner*—with Knopf.

In 1925, just a few months after the German publication of *Der Zauberberg*, Mann sent a copy of the book to Lowe-Porter, who was then living in Paris. Although she at first enthusiastically accepted the challenge of translating the unprecedented work, she later decided the task was too great for her and set the intricate novel aside. But after both Blanche Knopf and Mann himself encouraged her to continue, she resumed her work, and her translation, *The Magic Mountain*, was published in 1927. This English-language version received warm praise and was hailed as one of the masterpieces of modern literature, winning the Nobel Prize in 1929.

Mann was very demanding of his translator and kept a sharp eye directed toward any work in progress. Lowe-Porter once commented that Mann's negative criticism was usually more helpful than his positive suggestions. "He'd feel correctly when something was wrong, but he would be unable to give me the right solution," she once explained (*New York Times*, 27 Apr. 1963). Clearly their relationship was not an easy one, and, according to the same *New York Times* article, Mann once called Lowe-Porter "a sociological bird, not a literary one." Nevertheless, Mann allowed her to translate most of his works, the notable exception being *Die Betrachtungen eines Unpolitischen*, which he refused to have translated by anyone. She displayed expansive energy and tenacity in preparing her translations. For the Joseph novels, for example, she studied Egyptian archaeology and learned special terminology in English relating to the field. Lowe-Porter believed in close cooperation between the author and the translator; Mann would send her all the books and research materials he used in preparing his novels before she ever received the manuscript. Once a work was translated, Mann would read the draft and comment extensively, asking questions and offering suggestions. In addition to her translations of Thomas Mann, she also translated works by Lion Feuchtwanger, Bruno Frank, Frank Thiess, Franz Werfel, and Mme. A. Bulteau. A polyglot by anyone's definition, Lowe-Porter mastered not only German and French but also Dutch, Italian, and Latin, the latter being the language in which she was able to aid her husband and his career.

Besides her many translations, Lowe-Porter was a writer in her own right, and recognition for her own work was one of her great ambitions. Her efforts included poetry, fiction, nonfiction prose, and plays. Much of this went unpublished, but her blank-verse drama, *Abdication*, the story of the renunciation of the throne by Edward VIII of England written in the manner of a Shakespearean tragedy, received good reviews when it was performed at the Gate Theatre in Dublin in 1948. The play was then published as a book in 1950. In 1957 Oxford University Press published *Casual Verse*, a small book of her poetry. She wrote many essays on political, social, and literary subjects, though only her essays concerning Mann were ever published.

H. T. Lowe-Porter, as she signed her name, retired from her translation work in 1951 in order to devote complete attention to her own original writing, but health problems intervened. She spent the last six years of her life in a nursing home in Princeton, New Jersey, where she died.

Her contribution to the world of literature is a substantial one, for literary translation is an art that is complex, demanding, and yet often overlooked. Her high regard for Mann was so enduring that it supported her through the truly impressive task of handling his sophisticated and unwavering pen.

• Correspondence between Helen Tracy Lowe-Porter and Thomas Mann addressing her translations are at Beinecke Library at Yale University. Bibliographical information dealing with Lowe-Porter can be found in John C. Thirlwall, *In Another Language* (1966), which also includes correspondence and two of her essays. Hans Burgin, *Das Werk Thomas Manns: eine Bibliographie* (1959), lists all of her translations. E. Koch Emmery, "Thomas Mann in English Translation," in *German Life and Letters* (July 1953), is a general review essay. Also see Klaus W. Jonas, "In Memoriam: Helen T. Porter Lowe," *Monatshefte* (Nov. 1963). An obituary is in the *New York Times*, 27 Apr. 1963.

ROBERT C. FUHRMANN

LOWERY, Ellin Prince. *See* Speyer, Ellin Prince.

LOWES, John Livingston (20 Dec. 1867–15 Aug. 1945), literary scholar, was born in the newly settled village of Decatur, Indiana, the son of Abraham (or Abram) Brower Lowes, a Presbyterian minister, and Mary Bella Elliott. Though there was still something of a frontier atmosphere in the village at that time, his father encouraged him to learn both Hebrew and Greek as well as Latin. He received a scholarship at Washington and Jefferson College (A.B., 1888) in Washington, Pennsylvania, where he concentrated on science and mathematics as well as continuing his study of languages. Because of his learning and interest in biblical studies, he received a further scholarship to the Presbyterian Western Theological Seminary in Pittsburgh, Pennsylvania (1891–1893). After a year's study of theology in Germany at the universities of Leipzig and Berlin (1894–1895), he taught at Hanover College in Indiana as a professor of ethics, to which was later added the title of professor of English. In 1897 he married Mary Cornett, with whom he had one child.

Virtually self-taught in literature, Lowes, now in his early thirties, felt he at last had found the career to which he wished to devote himself, and in 1902 he enrolled as a graduate student in English at Harvard. When in three years he received his Ph.D. (1905), his oral examination was described by his examiners as "a true conference of scholars." While professor of English at Swarthmore College (1905–1909) and Washington University, St. Louis (1909–1918), he wrote a series of more than twenty important articles on Chaucer and the influences on his genius of earlier authors—

classical, French, and Italian—and also of scientific writers. The search for "influences" and "sources" was at this time becoming one of the principal aims of literary scholarship and led to innumerable studies of almost intolerable dullness. But Lowes transformed this pursuit because his primary interest was in the development of imaginative genius as revealed in its use of materials. After coming to Harvard in 1918, he wrote his popular book *Convention and Revolt in Poetry* (1919) and became a friend of Amy Lowell and a champion of the new kind of poetry—imagism and free verse—in which she was a leader. He was turning now to the great English Romantics, especially Coleridge and Keats, and in 1927 published his famous *The Road to Xanadu*.

The Road to Xanadu was unquestionably the best-known work of literary scholarship in the period from 1900 to 1960, for two reasons. One was the engaging and lucid style of which Lowes was a master. The second was its unrivaled brilliance as a literary "detective" or "sleuthing" story. For two of Coleridge's best-known poems, "The Rime of the Ancient Mariner" and "Kubla Khan," Lowes tracked down the origin of almost every image, allusion, and even phrasing in Coleridge's omnivorous reading in travel books, scientific treatises, histories, philosophy, and theology and showed them coalescing in Coleridge's imagination and unconscious mind to form these two poems. Though "source studies" had become common in literary scholarship from the 1890s to the 1920s, nothing like *The Road to Xanadu* had ever been seen to compare with it in the combination of range of erudition, narrative skill, and sheer readability. Several imitations followed this admired work, most of them forgotten except by specialists, while *The Road to Xanadu* remains unique as the masterpiece of this form of scholarship.

After the publication of *The Road to Xanadu*, Lowes's teaching at Harvard concentrated mainly on the English Romantic poets, who were the subject, in alternate years, of his noted lecture course, English 50. He always lectured without notes, having before him only the text of the writer discussed and drawing on his capacious memory of detail. His enthusiasm for poetry was contagious, and, having an excellent ear for cadence and an imaginative appreciation for the magic and power of expression, he unfolded the beauty of poetic style to students. A very small man (less than five feet tall), he had a deep and resonant voice. Between 150 and 250 students would be present at his lectures, including undergraduates and advanced Ph.D. candidates, many of whom later became noted scholars. Alternating with English 50 was his lecture course in sixteenth-century English poetry, and every year he joined his colleague F. N. Robinson in giving the main course in Chaucer, English 15.

Meanwhile, he served as dean of the graduate school (1924–1925) and chairman of the English department (1924–1926). He served as the first George Eastman Visiting Professor at Oxford University (1930–1931) and returned to Harvard to succeed Bliss Perry as

Francis Lee Higginson Professor of English. In 1932 he published his *Geoffrey Chaucer and the Development of His Genius*, which still remains authoritative. Other publications, aside from several articles, include two admirable volumes of essays: *Of Reading Books* (1929) and *Essays in Appreciation* (1935). The latter contains his famous essay, often anthologized, on the King James version of the Bible, "The Noblest Monument of English Prose." He had hoped to deal with Keats as he had with Coleridge in *The Road to Xanadu* and collected a mass of materials for this purpose. But his health was failing. By the late 1930s, when he was approaching seventy, his short-term memory was declining. Only later was this understood with the discovery of Alzheimer's disease. When it was brought to his attention that he was occasionally repeating lectures in the same class, he retired at age seventy-one but continued for a while to attend the weekly meetings of the Harvard Society of Fellows, in which he served as senior fellow, along with Abbott Lawrence Lowell, philosopher Alfred North Whitehead, and historian Samuel Eliot Morison. He died in Cambridge, Massachusetts.

• Lowes's papers, including manuscripts and research notes, are in the Houghton Library, Harvard University. For biographical information, consult W. J. Bate et al., eds., *Harvard Scholars in English, 1890 to 1990* (1992), and, for commentary, Thomas McFarland's introduction to the 1986 edition of *The Road to Xanadu*.

LARRY BENSON
W. JACKSON BATE

LOWIE, Robert Harry (12 June 1883–21 Sept. 1957), anthropologist, was born in Vienna, Austria, the son of Samuel Lévai (originally Lővi), a merchant in Budapest, and Ernestine Kohn. Lowie spent his childhood in Vienna, living with his mother and sister at the home of his maternal grandfather, Dr. Israel Kohn, in the borough of Leopoldstadt. The influence of Dr. Kohn, a physician, on his grandchild was of paramount importance to Lowie throughout his life. Lowie's determined and coherent agnostic attitude vis-à-vis any religious faith, as well as his abiding and deeply felt love of German literature and culture, can only be understood in relation to the years spent with *Grosspapa*, in whose personal library he read practically every day. Lowie attended the *Czerninschule* and had already passed his entrance examination to the classical Gymnasium when, in the fall of 1893, he moved with his mother and sister to New York to join his father, who had been in business there for several years.

Lowie's life in the United States was divided between his thoroughly Germanic household and the outside world of America. He attended Public School No. 83 in Manhattan and the College of the City of New York, where he received an A.B. in 1901. His father's declining financial situation delayed the start of his studies at Columbia for three years. During that time, Lowie earned tuition money by working as a substitute public school teacher. Discarding several other possibilities, such as law and chemistry, he decided, in 1904, to study anthropology under Franz Boas, because "he represented German science and culture, words of mystic potency" (Lowie papers). At the suggestion of one of his professors, anthropologist Livingston Farrand, and the subsequent invitation by curator of anthropology Clark Wissler, Lowie began a collaboration with the American Museum of Natural History. Under those auspices, he made his maiden journey, in 1906, to conduct ethnographic research among the Lemhi Shoshone of Idaho; this was followed by a field trip in 1907 to the Stoney Assiniboine of Alberta and to the Crow of Montana. In 1908 he received a Ph.D. from Columbia in anthropology with a dissertation on "The Test-Theme in North American Mythology."

For several years, Lowie's summers were devoted to the study of Native Americans—chiefly his beloved Crow but also the Hopi of the Southwest (1915–1916). A stream of distinguished papers began to flow from his field research; these dealt chiefly with the ethnography of the Plains Indians but also covered topics of a more theoretical nature, such as kinship terminologies and the matrilineal complex. In 1914 and 1917 he delivered a series of public lectures at the American Museum of Natural History; the latter constituted his first book, *Culture and Ethnology* (1917).

Lowie spent 1917–1918 as a visiting associate professor at the University of California at Berkeley. He found the campus atmosphere to be much more exciting and intellectually nourishing than that of the museum, and the year at Berkeley became a watershed in his life. His classes on social organization provided the foundation for the book he began to write on his return to New York. Written between December 1918 and September 1919, even though Lowie did not sign a contract with a publisher until May 1919, *Primitive Society*, based on concrete data and logical analysis, systematically criticized the hypothetical reconstruction of the stages of the evolution of civilization as postulated by Lewis H. Morgan. For almost thirty years, Lowie's work was the beacon in the field of social organization, the only clear and well-argued overview available in America or Europe. Scholars whose theoretical approaches differed substantially from those of Boas praised *Primitive Society*. Alfred Reginald Radcliffe-Brown recommended it to his students in Cape Town, as did Bronislaw Malinowski at the London School of Economics. Its French translation, *Traité de Sociologie Primitive* (1935), had considerable impact in Europe and was instrumental in converting Claude Lévi-Strauss from philosophy to anthropology. But its most astonishing influence was acknowledged by a German interned by the French after the outbreak of hostilities in September 1939. In a letter to Lowie, dated 15 October 1943, the Swiss anthropologist Alfred Métraux wrote: "He [Erwin H. Ackerknecht] told me that his interest in anthropology was mainly stimulated by the French version of 'Primitive Society'; your book was one of the few he took with him to a concentration camp, where he made a long sojourn. [Up to February 1940] 'Primitive Society' was very popular among the prisoners and for many of them who were staunch Marxists it was a revelation and a challenge. Your statements were briskly discussed in miserable sheds by the light of candles after a day of hard labor."

Primitive Society is also noteworthy for a short sentence in its concluding paragraph (p. 441), which refers to "that thing of shreds and patches called civilization." This seemingly simple sentence was submitted to incessant criticism for over seventy years, by nearly every major scholar, among them, Radcliffe-Brown, Malinowski, Alfred Louis Kroeber, George P. Murdock, and Edmund R. Leach. In formulating their criticisms, however, these scholars largely ignored the background and context of the passage. As Lowie made clear in his review of Malinowski's *A Scientific Theory of Culture and Other Essays* (*American Anthropologist*, n.s., 48 [1946]: 119) and in his preface to the 1947 reprinting of *Primitive Society*, the sentence makes sense *not* as a theory of culture but rather as a sad commentary on the depressing state of affairs in Europe following the disastrous experience of World War I.

Lowie was a scholar but also a man of action. Like Boas, he could take a courageous stand on political matters, even at a heavy personal cost. During the First World War he argued against the rising tide of anti-German prejudice, wrote papers with a pro-German point-of-view, and delivered a lecture on "Anthropology and War" in October 1917 at Berkeley. As late as 1923 his appointment to a full professorship at the University of Michigan was denied because he had not been "wholly loyal" during the war. Like Boas, John R. Swanton, and Paul Radin, he had definite socialist sympathies. In 1921 he was let go by the American Museum of Natural History and began his permanent teaching career in the Department of Anthropology at the University of California, in company with Kroeber. In the 1920s he published *Primitive Religion* (1924), *The Origin of the State* (1927), and *Are We Civilized?* (1929). The first was a critique of the major theories of religion; the second tackled the complex problem of sorting out the various factors that led to the emergence of centralized political authority; the third was a summary of the technological progress of mankind since prehistory as contrasted with the abysmal moral decay of Western civilization, for which he chiefly blamed those wartime intellectuals whom he called "the worst delinquents" (p. 296).

Like Kroeber, Lowie trained many outstanding students at Berkeley, but the importance of his scientific contributions shows also in the influence and inspiration he provided to those who did not actually study under him. This influence was warmly acknowledged by Métraux, who referred to Lowie as "Tu, magister carissime" ("You, dearest teacher"). Lowie's classes and seminars in the 1930s spawned three books: *An Introduction to Cultural Anthropology* (1934), a comprehensive ethnography of *The Crow Indians* (1935), and *The History of Ethnological Theory* (1937).

Lowie's disillusionment with contemporary Western civilization grew even deeper with Hitler's rise to power in 1933. That same year he married Luella W. Cole, the former Mrs. Sidney L. Pressey, who wrote several books on psychological topics. They had no children. The worsening of the European situation under the growing Nazi cloud, the invasion of his native Austria in 1938, the outbreak of World War II in 1939, and the persecution and extermination of European Jewry saddened him considerably.

During World War II, American universities tried to provide soldiers bound for the European battlefield with as much knowledge as possible about the countries of the Old World. Berkeley focused on Germany and the Balkans. Although well read in Balkan history and culture, Lowie concentrated on his native Austria and Germany, in whose language and literatures he was fluent. When the Nazi regime was approaching its end and the prospect of a renovated and united Europe loomed larger, Lowie turned his attention more vigorously to his own roots. In 1945 he wrote a booklet called *The German People: A Social Portrait to 1914*. Three years later, he traveled to England, Belgium, France, and Austria, and he carried out field work in 1950–1951 in Germany and Austria. His data were published in *Toward Understanding Germany* (1954), a remarkable work for its depth of enquiry. It embraced methods ranging from participant observation and interviews to the systematic combing of daily newspapers, magazines, and other rich literary sources. Lowie's efforts and the assistance of his wife and sister Risa produced an unprecedented study of the development of the German family during the preceding two centuries. More important, Lowie succeeded in maintaining an objective view despite the burning heritage of the Holocaust and the historical relationship between German Christians and German Jews. As an Austro-American Jewish scholar, many of whose Hungarian relatives had perished in the extermination camps, he nonetheless drew an admirably balanced, thoroughly documented, and humane portrait. In reply to a one-sided and polemic evaluation of his book in the *Times Literary Supplement* of London (31 Dec. 1954), he calmly stated that he had not made any apologies for Nazi Germany.

Meanwhile, Lowie maintained his interest in the field of kinship and social structure. Because *Primitive Society* had become outdated by subsequent field work and related theoretical advances, he decided to write a completely new book, *Social Organization* (1948). The ethnographic illustrations include American, Melanesian, and African societies, together with "Imperial Austria." Thus, the book ends with Lowie's homeland during the time it was divided into four Allied occupation zones. Like Stefan Zweig's *The World of Yesterday*, Lowie's work was a tribute to a body politic that no longer existed.

Near the end of his life, Lowie returned his attention to his favorite ethnographic area of study. *Indians of the Plains* (1954) is an excellent summary of the knowledge concerning those tribes, useful to specialists as well as to the general public, written in Lowie's clear, jargon-free language. In September 1957, the day before his death in Berkeley, Lowie began writing *Jung Büffel* (Young buffalo), a literary piece based on Indian ethnography and a testimony to his lifelong interest.

Among the outstanding features of Lowie's scientific labors was the painstaking accuracy of the record. Although his interpretations of the information might have sometimes been mistaken, the accuracy of his data will support different conclusions in the future. As he grew older, Lowie acknowledged more and more the value of old sources, too frequently ignored and denigrated just because data were gathered by traders, travelers, or missionaries. The clarity of Lowie's thought undoubtedly owes much to his interest in philosophy, and the philosophy of science in particular. His concern with questions of scientific method stemmed from his incessant reading of the works of Austrian physicist and philosopher Ernst Mach, *Die Mechanik in ihrer Entwicklung historisch-kritisch dargestellt* (The science of mechanics), *Erkenntnis und Irrtum* (Knowledge and error), and, above all, *Beiträge zur Analyse der Empfindungen* (The analysis of sensations). Although anthropology could never be a natural science, its methods, Lowie believed, should be as rigorous and logical as those of any other branch of knowledge. This idea suffused his writing and teaching. In his autobiography, published posthumously in 1959, he wrote that he had never tried to establish a school of anthropology or to have disciples; independence of thought was more important to him. It is worth remembering the tribute paid to Lowie by psychologist-anthropologist George Devereux in a letter of 16 November 1954: "I *hope* I will always recall at the crucial moment that an idea which seems 'all my own' was picked up in your writings. The will to acknowledge the debt is always there—if I ever fail to remember, I hope you will know that it is not intentional—that it simply shows the teaching was so good as to become second nature."

• Lowie's papers are held by the Bancroft Library, University of California at Berkeley. His field work notes are in the Department of Anthropology, American Museum of Natural History, New York City. His autobiography is *Robert H. Lowie, Ethnologist: A Personal Record* (1959). Alan Dundes edited *The Complete Bibliography of Robert H. Lowie* in 1966. A short biography is Robert F. Murphy, *Robert H. Lowie* (1972). The most comprehensive and accurate obituary of Lowie was written by Paul Radin in *American Anthropologist* 60 (1958): 358–61.

PIERO MATTHEY

LOWNDES, Rawlins (Jan. 1721–24 Aug. 1800), South Carolina legislator, was born on the island of St. Kitts, British West Indies, the son of Charles Lowndes, a plantation owner, and Ruth Rawlins, the daughter of a plantation owner. The Lowndes family left the island for the colony of South Carolina in 1730. Following financial difficulties and a legal separation from his wife, Charles Lowndes killed himself. His widow and

eldest son went back to St. Kitts while the two younger sons, Charles and Rawlins, stayed in South Carolina and were raised to adulthood by Robert Hall, the provost marshal, or high sheriff, of the colony. Hall also supervised the boys' education.

Hall died in 1741, and by the summer of 1745 Lowndes had become provost marshal. He raised himself to gentry status in South Carolina through his marriage to Amarinthia Elliott in 1748 and his election to the general assembly of the colony in 1749. His wife died in 1750 (the couple had no children), and in 1751 he married Mary Cartwright, with whom he had seven children. With the exception of a year spent in England (1754–1755), Lowndes was deeply involved in the law, politics, and government of the colony until 1775. His second wife died in 1770, and in 1773 he married Sarah Jones. The couple had three children.

Lowndes served as Speaker in the general assembly twice (1763–1765, 1772–1775). He won the favor of the populace through his actions on several occasions: he declined to uphold the Stamp Act in 1765; he resisted two royal governors (William Henry Lyttelton and Charles Greville Montagu) whose actions were seen by Lowndes and others as arbitrary; and in 1773 he ruled that the governor's council could not serve as an upper house for the legislature in the manner that the House of Lords did in England. The last action, known as the Thomas Powell case, established Lowndes as a favorite among the political elements in the colony that favored some type of separation from Great Britain.

Following the Powell case, Lowndes watched helplessly as the colony drifted into rebellion. On 31 August 1775 the last session of the colonial legislature ended. Lowndes transferred his allegiance to the Committee of Safety and the Provincial Congress of South Carolina. He was one of the eleven men who wrote the provisional state constitution (adopted on 26 Mar. 1776), and in September he took his seat in the new general assembly of the state of South Carolina.

Lowndes became president of South Carolina on 12 March 1778 following a political crisis that had been initiated by the resignation of John Rutledge, who had served as the first president of the state (1776–1778). In his new position as chief executive, Lowndes was out of his political depth. A moderate by disposition and a judicial conservative from his early days, Lowndes was ill suited to lead South Carolina during the trying period of 1778–1779. British forces invaded sections of the state, and Lowndes proved unable to cope with the combination of political and military vicissitudes that accompanied his term in office. He did not seek reelection in 1779; instead he retired to his plantation seat, "Crowfield," on Goose Creek.

On 10 May 1780 Charles Town surrendered to the British forces led by General Henry Clinton. Lowndes was in the city when it yielded, and he remained there for several months, during which time he, among many other South Carolinians, petitioned the military government of the town to be restored to the rights of British subjects. Lowndes acted in response to the pillaging of his plantation (he lost much property and upwards of seventy slaves during the war), but his action was resented by many patriotic South Carolinians who thought it was unseemly that the former chief executive should make such a petition to the British.

With the end of the revolutionary war in 1783, Lowndes sought to restore his fortunes. He petitioned the new state government for restoration of his citizenship in South Carolina, which he received in the summer of 1783. He worked to rebuild his plantation at "Horseshoe," but he sold his Crowfield estate in 1784, painful evidence of the decline of his status.

In February 1787 Lowndes returned to public service, representing Charleston (it had been renamed in 1783) in the South Carolina assembly. In January 1788 he led the faction that opposed ratification of the proposed U.S. Constitution. Lowndes made four significant objections to the document: he believed the Senate would have too much power in regard to treaties; he believed that the southern states were too small in population to ever elect a president; he resented the agreement that would prohibit the slave trade after twenty years' time; and he stated that the northern, commercially oriented states would dominate the southern, agriculturally oriented ones. Lowndes concluded his speeches against ratification with the statement that he desired no epitaph other than "Here lies the man that opposed the Constitution, because it was ruinous to the liberty of America" (Vipperman, p. 251). Lowndes's speeches were in the long run ineffective, and South Carolina voted for ratification.

Lowndes closed his career by serving as intendant, or mayor, of Charleston, 1789–1790. He recouped many of his financial losses during the last decade of his life and died in Charleston a wealthy man.

Lowndes was a tidewater aristocrat who swayed between strict allegiance to his class and a belief that the rights of political minorities should be protected. A truly self-made man who had risen in the law and in politics through merit, he became righteous and sensitive of his dignities as he advanced in years. His most successful political activity came in the years just before the Revolution; his political theory led him to support the revolutionary trend even though he was at heart a conservative. His term as president of South Carolina was a debacle, and his request for British citizenship could have been held against him much more strongly than was the case. Only in the last years of his political career did Lowndes regain what might be called an authentic political voice; he chose at that time to represent the interests of the South against what he felt would surely be tyranny. Although not strong of will in his political views and a poor chief executive of his state, Lowndes had a prophetic political vision; he foresaw the conflicts that would arise between North and South, and he was in many ways an advance herald of the movement for states' rights that would culminate in the speeches of John C. Calhoun.

• Most of Lowndes's papers were destroyed by fire around 1783. Those that survived are in the Southern Historical Collection at the University of North Carolina, Chapel Hill, and in the Library of Congress. The most valuable and up-to-date source is Carl J. Vipperman, *The Rise of Rawlins Lowndes, 1721–1800* (1978). See also W. Roy Smith, *South Carolina as a Royal Province* (1903), and M. Eugene Sirmans, *Colonial South Carolina: A Political History, 1663–1763* (1966).

SAMUEL WILLARD CROMPTON

LOWNDES, William Jones (11 Feb. 1782–27 Oct. 1822), statesman, was born in the Colleton District of South Carolina, the son of Rawlins Lowndes, former president of South Carolina and soon to be the chief Antifederalist in the South Carolina ratification contest, and Sarah Jones. At age seven Lowndes went to England for a three-year stay at a boarding school. After his return to South Carolina he briefly attended the College of Charleston, then followed his favorite teacher to the Athenian Academy in Charleston. Lowndes's education at the academy ended when, at the age of sixteen, he was told by his teacher, a former University of Paris professor, that he should study on his own.

Lowndes had suffered exposure to cold while in England, and he spent the rest of his life emaciated and weak. Although six feet, six inches tall, he was slightly stooped and small in the chest. Acquaintances believed his inability to engage in boyhood diversions was the catalyst of his remarkable intellectual growth. Lowndes married Elizabeth Pinckney, daughter of eminent Federalist Thomas Pinckney, in 1802.

Lowndes was taken on as a partner in 1804 by city attorney John Cogdell, who trained him in the law. In 1805, when his duty as an attorney jarred with his sense of right, Lowndes entered politics. He was elected to the South Carolina House in 1804 and was reelected in 1806; he did not run in 1808. During his early political career, South Carolina was a state in transition from dominance by George Washington's party to fealty to Thomas Jefferson's, and Lowndes was independent. He authored the famous constitutional adjustment of 1808, by which a political equilibrium was established between the upcountry and the older, more settled low country districts, pleasing Republicans; however, he opposed President Jefferson's mercantile policies in the conflict with Great Britain. Among the positions Lowndes took in the legislature was his support of efforts in 1804 and 1805 to close the slave trade. The measure passed in the lower (Lowndes's) house but was killed in the upper. Despite opposing the international slave trade, Lowndes, as was typical of South Carolina's ruling elite, bought and sold slaves, as economic conditions indicated, throughout his adult life. His income was derived mainly from agriculture, which he pursued on a large low country plantation.

Lowndes was outraged over the 1805 *Two Friends* incident, in which a French privateer captured an American ship off the Charleston bar. He blamed President Jefferson's lax military policy. Elected to Congress in 1810, Lowndes became a leader of the faction known as the "War Hawks," a group of young congressmen committed to forcing a resolution of the

Anglo-American naval disputes. They soon helped push President James Madison into war.

In tandem with Speaker of the House Henry Clay and John C. Calhoun, Lowndes supported measures to augment the Republic's military prowess. While the Madison administration's ineptitude undercut U.S. military prospects, the War Hawks insisted that the energy of the general government must be great enough to meet future contingencies. Like most of the War Hawks, Lowndes held the vindication of American honor, not military victory, the leading motive for the American war effort, saying, "If war should last many years I believe that the nation possesses resources which may enable it to support it with honor" (Vipperman, *William Lowndes and the Transition of Southern Politics*, p. 117). At various times during the war, Lowndes was chairman of the Committees on Ways and Means and Naval Affairs and held posts on the Committees on Commerce and Manufactures and Military Affairs. One of the administration's most dependable advocates in Congress during the war, his only major deviation from Madison's war agenda was his opposition to the reimposition of an embargo.

During the War of 1812, Lowndes helped craft the statute establishing a second national bank, and he defended that bank when it came under attack years later, when he was receiving loans on preferential terms. While Lowndes was chairman, the Ways and Means Committee reported out a plan in 1817 to pay off the national debt, and Congress adopted it. The plan was fulfilled, and the debt was extinguished in 1835, after Lowndes's death. At that time Calhoun said, "For this important step at so early a period the country is indebted to my friend, now unfortunately no more." Lowndes also supported the postwar adoption of moderate protective duties and a broad construction of the general government's powers regarding internal improvements, each of which positions would have fateful consequences for South Carolina. In time, as Clay's "American System" took shape, Lowndes opposed farther-reaching protective duties.

On the inauguration of James Monroe as president in 1817, Lowndes was offered the position of secretary of war. He rejected it, saying he would be more useful in the House. Over the remainder of his life, he was offered several other positions by President Monroe, but he always gave the same answer. As chairman of the Committee on Ways and Means and as a figure respected by politicians of all stripes, Lowndes wielded great influence.

In Monroe's first term, Clay wanted the House to go on record in support of the rebellious Spanish colonies of the New World, and Lowndes made his mark by arguing that such issues were the responsibility of the president. The House sided overwhelmingly with Lowndes. When in 1818 General Andrew Jackson invaded Spanish Florida without congressional consent, Lowndes remained consistent with his prior position. Although he admired Jackson, Lowndes took Jackson and the executive to task.

Lowndes and Clay led the House group that insisted Missouri be allowed to decide the issue of slavery within its borders for itself. In the House they were the main advocates of the simultaneous admission of Maine and Missouri, and in the end they had their way. Lowndes was drafted as a candidate for Speaker in 1820, and he failed to be elected by one vote. He read the result, coming in the wake of the Missouri conflict, as an omen of sectional division to come.

Soon after the resolution of the Missouri issue, the South Carolina legislature nominated Lowndes for president. Lowndes, a Calhoun supporter, was unhappy with the blow to Calhoun's prospects. Lowndes's health, failing from the spring of 1821, deteriorated steadily in 1822. He died en route to England, where he was headed in search of a healthier climate, and was buried at sea.

• The bulk of Lowndes's public papers were destroyed in the Charleston fire of 1861, and most of his private papers were systematically destroyed by Lowndes himself. His granddaughter, Mrs. St. Julien Ravenel, published a biography, *Life and Times of William Lowndes of South Carolina: 1782–1822* (1901), based in large part on papers still in the family at that time. Carl Jackson Vipperman wrote a good treatment, "William Lowndes: South Carolina Nationalist, 1782–1822" (Ph.D. diss., Univ. of Virginia, 1966), published as *William Lowndes and the Transition of Southern Politics, 1782–1822* (1989), which unfortunately strives for cosmic significance. For the Missouri Controversy generally, the leading, though dated, work remains Glover Moore, *The Missouri Controversy, 1819–1821* (1953). In regard to the War of 1812, see Ralph Ketcham, *James Madison: A Biography* (1971). For the "mind of South Carolina" in the period before the war, see Margaret Latimer, "South Carolina—A Protagonist of the War of 1812," *American Historical Review* 61 (July 1956): 914–29, and *Papers of John C. Calhoun*, vol. 1, *1801–1817*, ed. Robert Meriwether (1959). For the significance of the constitutional adjustment of 1808, see Rachel Klein, *The Unification of a Slave State: The Rise of the Planter Class in the South Carolina Backcountry, 1760–1808* (1990).

K. R. CONSTANTINE GUTZMAN

LOWRY, Edith Elizabeth (23 Mar. 1897–11 Mar. 1970), interdenominational leader in home mission work, was born in Plainfield, New Jersey, the daughter of Robert H. Lowry, Jr., a banker, and Elizabeth Darling. Majoring in languages, she earned an A.B. at Wellesley College in 1920. After two years of tutoring and substitute teaching, she launched her professional career as a staff member of the Board of National Missions of the Presbyterian church in the U.S.A., though she chose to retain her church membership all her life in the congregation in which she had been raised, the First-Park Baptist Church of Plainfield.

In 1926 Lowry entered ecumenical work as assistant both to the executive director and to the director of work with agricultural migrants of the Council of Women for Home Missions (CWHM), an organization backed by the women's national mission societies of some twenty Protestant denominations. Well before there was general public awareness of the extreme difficulties faced by migrants and their families, she strove to deal with the needs of the roving, ill-housed, minimally paid, seasonal laborers, and in three years she was elevated to the directorship of the migrant program. Her annual reports reflected the growth and spread of her work. In referring in 1931 to just one of the six areas in California where the program she directed was carrying on its work, namely the cotton field migrant camps of the San Joaquin Valley, she said: "Four large new camps were included, which meant that Miss Eva Barnes, our registered nurse, visited regularly twenty-three camps, varying in size from eight shacks to one hundred and seventy-five. Over three thousand calls were made during these months 'in cotton' and almost every disease from mumps and measles to diphtheria and smallpox was treated. Through the 'Jesus nurse,' as Miss Barnes is called, the mortality rate in San Joaquin Valley was reduced sixty percent" (CWHM Annual Report, pp. 11–12).

Her leadership skills flowered as she developed and promoted the work through the terrible years of the Great Depression. Traveling frequently, visiting camps, observing the harshness of the life of the migrants, she made many speeches and wrote effective articles about their plight, even as she directed an expanding regular and volunteer staff of social workers, nurses, ministers, and teachers. She compiled a widely circulated booklet, *They Starve That We May Eat* (1938), and with others edited *Tales of Americans on Trek* (1940). Through her efforts the plight of migrants became known to many outside of the churches. In the course of her remarkable leadership she was the first woman to occupy the National Radio Pulpit, a pioneer effort in religious broadcasting sponsored by the then leading cooperative agency of many Protestant denominations, the Federal Council of Churches (FCC), speaking on "Women in a Changing World" in 1939.

In 1936 Lowry became executive secretary of the CWHM, and when that agency merged four years later with the general Home Missions Council of North America (HMCNA), she retained her title as part of a dual coordinate secretaryship of the unified agency. She continued to direct the migrant work in addition to the other responsibilities given to her. In the tense days of World War II, many avenues of service for cooperative home mission work increased, often as developments from the migrant program's years of effort. In the 1940s she was instrumental in establishing many new day care centers for the children of migrants. When Lowry looked back in 1950, she noted that the State War Council in New York had discovered that the HMCNA was the only agency doing anything significant in maintaining day care centers for migrant children and helped it to secure funds to expand that program. She explained that "as a result of our pioneering in public health services in migrant camps through missionary nurses, various public health and welfare officials credit the Home Missions Council with being the forerunner of their departments. Our circulating library and audio-visual aids

program has interested libraries and schools in an extension of such services. The State Child-Care program in New York is an outgrowth of our child-care centers established in that state in 1931" (HMCNA Annual Report of Committees, n.p.).

In 1950 the HMCNA united with other interdenominational organizations to form the National Council of Churches, which she served as one of two coordinate executive secretaries of the division of home missions. In this role her responsibilities involved attention to the many aspects of cooperative home mission work, including concern in both rural and urban areas for such minority groups as Native Americans, Alaskans, Hispanic Americans, and Japanese Americans. She retained directorship of the migrant program, taking steps to reach migrants in more inaccessible areas and leading a drive to inform all migrants about their eligibility for Social Security benefits.

When Lowry had taken over leadership in cooperative church migrant work in 1929, the permanent staff devoted to the program was three, serving in five states. When the fortieth anniversary of the program was celebrated in 1960, it was operating in thirty-four states with a permanent staff of 40, augmented not only by 500 seasonal workers—doctors, nurses, teachers, and students—but also by an estimated 8,000 community volunteers.

Two years after that anniversary, the even-tempered, alert woman with a ready smile who had been a firm yet gentle leader of the many women and men ministering to migrants for more than thirty years retired. Lowry continued to be in demand; in 1962 through 1964 she served as part-time consultant to the National Council on Agricultural Life and Labor in Washington, a coordinating agency for thirty-five private organizations dealing with the problems of farm labor. Her last five years were spent in a Perkinsville, Vermont, farmhouse that she had refurbished. She died in nearby Claremont, New Hampshire.

• Lowry's papers in the archives of the Federal/National Council of Churches at the Department of History, Presbyterian Church (U.S.A.), Philadelphia, contain letters and memoranda, drafts of speeches, articles, and reports. There is also a file of clippings on her at the Wellesley College Alumnae Association. Virginia L. Munford prepared an informative biobibliography, which lists articles by and about Lowry; a copy is in the Schlesinger Library of Radcliffe College. References to her work and its institutional settings are in Robert T. Handy, *We Witness Together: A History of Cooperative Home Missions* (1956); she was interviewed by the author several times. See also Louisa R. Shotwell, *The Harvesters: The Story of the Migrant People* (1961). Obituaries are in the Plainfield, N.J., *Courier-News*, 13 Mar. 1970, and the *New York Times*, 14 Mar. 1970.

ROBERT T. HANDY

LOWRY, Robert (10 Mar. 1829?–19 Jan. 1910), governor of Mississippi and lawyer, was born in Chesterfield District, South Carolina, the son of Robert Lowry, a merchant, and Jemima Rushing. The family moved to West Tennessee in the early 1830s and then to Tishomingo County, Mississippi, in 1840. At the age of thirteen, Lowry went to live with his uncle, James L. Lowry, a probate judge and merchant in Smith County, Mississippi. After working for his uncle as clerk and bookkeeper, Lowry subsequently became his partner in the mercantile business, first in Raleigh and then in Brandon, Mississippi. In 1849 he married Maria M. Gammage; they had eleven children before she died in 1873. In 1854, seeking better economic opportunities, Lowry moved to Arkansas, where he studied law and was admitted to the bar. In 1859 he returned to Brandon, Mississippi, where he established a law practice. When the Civil War began, he enlisted as a private in the Confederate army and quickly assumed command of a Mississippi regiment. Recognized in a letter written by Thomas B. Sykes as "a cool gallant leader in the field, amid shot and shell" (27 Apr. 1893), Lowry rose to the rank of brigadier general in the Army of Tennessee before the war ended. After the war he returned to Brandon and his law practice.

In the postwar era Lowry became active in Mississippi politics. After winning a legislative seat in 1865, he served on a commission with Giles M. Hillyer in Washington to seek the pardon and release of the Confederate president, Jefferson Davis. A leader in the state Democratic party during Reconstruction, he advocated moderate, conservative policies that accepted the results of the war and the legality of the Fourteenth and Fifteenth Amendments. Lowry opposed violence and the abuse of blacks. He believed that preservation of law and order, along with limited accommodation of black suffrage, would hasten the economic recovery of the state and enable native whites to regain control of state and local government. In the 1875 legislative elections, he canvassed the state in the Democrats' successful and notably violent campaign to overthrow Republican rule. Six years later, as the Democratic nominee for governor, he defeated the candidate of a Greenback-Republican coalition in the general election. Commenting on his victory, the *New Orleans Daily Picayune* (19 Nov. 1881) declared that Mississippi could now move "further and faster to the road of good legislation, civil order, and industrial advancement." In 1885 he encountered little opposition in winning a second four-year term.

Lowry and his Democratic colleagues believed that intelligent white rule would bring peace and prosperity to the state. In his inaugural address in 1882, he urged Mississippians of all races to work together to solve the state's problems, and he pledged to protect the rights of all citizens. An advocate of the New South economic program advanced by Atlanta newspaper editor Henry Grady, Lowry encouraged diversification of agriculture along with industrial development to overcome the state's dependence on the sluggish cotton economy and remained hostile to corporate regulation. Lowry regarded railroads as the "great moral agents of prosperity," and his administration granted liberal tax exemptions to railroad corporations and other industrial enterprises. During his two terms, railroad track mileage and the number of manufacturing establishments more than doubled in the state. He vigorously supported successful efforts to secure federal funds for agricultural experiment stations and for flood control work in the counties bordering the Mississippi River. Appropriations for public education increased during his administration, but they fell short of meeting the needs of the state's dual system of racially segregated schools. In 1884 he approved legislation to establish the Industrial Institute and College (later Mississippi University for Women) to educate white females in the arts and sciences and train them to become schoolteachers.

Lowry opposed a constitutional convention in 1888, arguing that amendments submitted by the legislature would be a wiser course than drafting a new constitution amidst the unsettled politics of a presidential election year. He believed too much legislation had "been the bane of the country" and change was "not always improvement" (Lowry, "The Needs of the South," *North American Review*, Apr. 1890, p. 445). With no interest in seeking a third term, he opposed the move for constitutional suffrage restrictions on the grounds that many poor whites would be disfranchised along with most blacks. In his final message to the legislature, he pointed out that he had held the governorship for eight consecutive years, longer than any of his predecessors.

After leaving office in January 1890, Lowry remained in Jackson and practiced law. He waged several campaigns for the U.S. Senate but never won another elective post. Friends recommended him for a diplomatic appointment, but he declared that he had "at all times been distinctly averse to an unseemly and persistent scramble for public position" (letter to Charles B. Howry, 20 Mar. 1894). He and William H. McCardle, the editor of a Vicksburg newspaper, were coauthors of *A History of Mississippi* (1891), which they later revised for use in the schools. He served as commander of the Mississippi Division of United Confederate Veterans for seven years (from 1903 until his death). Having devoted most of his life to public service, he never accumulated much personal wealth. He died at the home of a granddaughter in Jackson.

Steeped in the traditions of the Old South, Lowry believed, "If the Negro was let alone by the politicians . . . he would be a better laborer, and more contented; and, with the advantages of education, time would increase his appreciation of citizenship" ("The Needs of the South," p. 442). Believing that universal suffrage would only be tolerable with universal education, he asserted that white leaders "should generously unite in contributing to his [the black's] mental elevation and moral training, and thus fit him for greater efficiency in agricultural pursuits" as well as industrial skills (Lowry, "The Negro as a Mechanic," *North American Review*, Apr. 1893, p. 476). He expressed dismay that "sectional animosities caused by slavery should be kept alive" so long after the institution had been abolished. Prior to Lowry's inauguration as governor in

1882, a Mississippi newspaper editor praised him for his progressive and moderate views: "He has been credited in certain quarters with being a Bourbon, but if that term is intended to designate an irreconcilable politician, who chafes under the amendments to the Federal constitution and [bears] an irrepressible antagonism to any class or color, it does not describe the man" (*Brookhaven Ledger*, 15 Dec. 1881).

• Letters, newspaper clippings, and other material relating to Lowry are in the Governors' Records, the Robert Lowry Papers, and the Robert Lowry–Joseph M. Jayne Papers at the Mississippi Department of Archives and History (MDAH). Kate Markham Power, "Mistresses of the Governor's Mansion" (c. 1903), in the MDAH, provides details of Lowry's family life. Lowry wrote *Elements of Civil Government* (1892), and he and William H. McCardle coauthored *A History of Mississippi for Use in the Schools* (1892). Biographical sketches are in Dunbar Rowland, *The Official and Statistical Register of the State of Mississippi* (1917), and Clayton Rand, *Men of Spine in Mississippi* (1940). Rowland, *Mississippi*, vol. 2 (1907); Rowland, *History of Mississippi, the Heart of the South*, vol. 2 (1925); and Edward Mayes, *Lucius Q. C. Lamar: His Life, Times and Speeches, 1825–1893* (1896), are other sources of information. See also William C. Harris, *The Day of the Carpetbagger: Republican Reconstruction in Mississippi* (1979), on his early political career. Thomas N. Boschert, "A Family Affair: Mississippi Politics, 1882–1932" (Ph.D. diss., Univ. of Mississippi, 1995), and Stephen Cresswell, *Multi-Party Politics in Mississippi, 1877–1902* (1995), discuss his gubernatorial administration and subsequent political activities. An obituary is in the *New York Times*, 20 Jan. 1910; more comprehensive obituaries are in the *Jackson (Miss.) Clarion-Ledger* and the *Memphis (Tenn.) Commercial Appeal*, both 20 Jan. 1910.

THOMAS N. BOSCHERT

LOWRY, Thomas (27 Feb. 1843–4 Feb. 1909), businessman, was born in Logan County, Illinois, the son of Sam R. Lowry and Rachel Bullock, farmers. He grew up near Pleasant View in Schuyler County, Illinois, and attended Lombard University in Galesburg. He left Lombard after two years, suspected of having tuberculosis, traveled to regain his health and visited Minneapolis. Upon returning home he studied law at the offices of Judge John C. Bagby in nearby Rushville. Lowry was admitted to the Illinois bar in 1867, and that year he moved to Minneapolis to establish a law practice.

Shortly after Lowry's arrival, a revolution in milling technology took place in Minneapolis that made the city the flour-milling center of the United States. The consequent expansion in the population and wealth of the city provided an opportunity for risk takers like Lowry to build substantial fortunes. Between 1868 and 1875 he and his associates purchased extensive tracts of real estate fanning out east, south, and west from the center of the city. One of his helpful associates was Calvin G. Goodrich, medical doctor and real estate investor, whose sixteen-year-old daughter Beatrice married Lowry in 1870 and whose son Calvin, Jr., joined Lowry in the street railway business in 1878. The Lowrys had one child.

In 1873 Lowry served as the lawyer in organizing the Minneapolis Street Railway Company, but the effort collapsed with the panic of that year. Lowry came back into the enterprise two years later with William S. King, a local newspaperman and political figure. Both men saw urban transit as the way to increase the value of their extensive real estate holdings. The capital for the revived company came principally from investors in Ilion, New York, associated with Philo Remington, the arms manufacturer, whose company diversified into streetcar and farm implement manufacture after the Civil War. Lowry traveled to Ilion to secure financing, and in subsequent years he became a familiar figure on Wall Street and in Boston as he raised capital for his street railway and other Upper Midwest enterprises. In 1878 Lowry formed a syndicate with four other Minneapolis businessmen. They exchanged a good deal of Minneapolis real estate to buy out the Ilion investors, and they secured controlling interest in the street railway, of which Lowry became president.

In 1881 Lowry became the sole owner of the Minneapolis Street Railway, and he soon extended his interest in mass transit to St. Paul and Duluth. In 1882 he became one of the new owners of the financially troubled St. Paul City Railway Company. By 1883 all but one of the St. Paul directors had resigned, and the new board, dominated by Minneapolitans, elected Lowry president. In 1886 he acquired a 20-percent interest in the Duluth Street Railway Company, and in 1889 he set out to replace all of his horsecars in the Twin Cities with newly invented electric trolley cars. The following year he secured financing to electrify the Duluth system. Because bonds to modernize the Minneapolis streetcars sold better than those for St. Paul, Lowry combined the two companies into the interurban Twin City Rapid Transit Company in 1891. Over the next fifteen years Lowry extended the tracks twenty-four miles east to Stillwater in the scenic valley of the St. Croix River on the Wisconsin border, and he purchased an amusement park halfway in between. He built tracks eighteen miles west to the resort communities on Lake Minnetonka, constructed a fleet of boats, and built another amusement park on an island in the lake. A shop was established in 1898 to build more rugged equipment for the Twin City's climate and to supply streetcars for the Duluth-Superior system. Lowry's Twin City Rapid Transit Company came to be regarded as one of the most comprehensive in the nation, and it lasted until 1970, when it was taken over by the publicly owned Metropolitan Transit Commission.

In 1883 Lowry was one of the founders of the Minneapolis, Sault Ste. Marie & Atlantic Railway, more commonly known as "the Soo Line." The company was originally financed solely by Minneapolis businessmen to provide an eastbound rail route for local products, particularly flour and wheat, that would bypass the discriminatory rates set by the Chicago railroad interests. In late 1887 the Soo Line was completed with tracks running northeast from Minneapolis to join the Canadian Pacific tracks at Sault Ste. Marie, Michigan. The Soo Line came under the control of Canadian Pacific Railway interests and was consolidated with three other lines, and Lowry became president. He headed the renamed Minneapolis, St. Paul & Sault Ste. Marie Railway from 1889 until his death, except for an interruption in 1890, when he took his family on a tour of Europe and the Middle East. During Lowry's years as president, the Soo Line trackage was extended into North Dakota and Montana, providing Minneapolis interests with an alternative to the railroad network dominated by James J. Hill and the Canadian Pacific investors with a subsidiary line that tapped the resources of the Upper Midwest and Northern Plains states. Alert to possible profits in connection with those developments, Lowry invested in building a stockyard northeast of Minneapolis, and in the early 1890s he purchased land for the development of a nearby residential community named Columbia Heights, which was linked to Minneapolis by his electric streetcar system by 1904.

Lowry's success was attributed to his ability to convey confidence in the great potential of the Upper Midwest, his unfailingly affable disposition, and his detailed knowledge of real estate and mass transit. He was always ready to contribute time and money to Minneapolis civic projects and was a major figure in the development of the Minneapolis library and park systems. In addition, he was involved in hydroelectric power development at St. Anthony Falls on the Mississippi River; the opening of a teaching hospital and a bank; and the construction of several office buildings and the Minneapolis Exposition Building, a hall that showcased local enterprises and housed the 1892 Republican National Convention.

With a tall silk hat to accentuate his six-foot-two-inch height, a friendly demeanor, and a fund of stories, he modeled himself after his father's lawyer, Abraham Lincoln. In 1905 he brought Lincoln's funeral car to Minnesota to attract land buyers to Columbia Heights. It became a central attraction for the 1908 Encampment of the Grand Army of the Republic in Minneapolis and was then returned to Columbia Heights, where it remained until it was destroyed by a grass fire in 1914. In the last years of his life he developed tuberculosis, spent his winters in the Southwest, and worked on a short book titled *Personal Reminiscences of Abraham Lincoln*, which was privately published in 1910. He died in Minneapolis.

• The manuscript collections of the Minnesota Historical Society in St. Paul contain the papers of several individuals who discuss Thomas Lowry as well as the Russell Olson Papers, which contain extensive material on the Twin City Rapid Transit Company. In addition it is the repository for the Soo Line Railroad Papers. The only biography of Lowry is by his grandson Goodrich Lowry, *Streetcar Man* (1979). For works on some of Lowry's business activities see Russell L. Olson, *The Electric Railways of Minnesota* (1976); Stephen A. Kieffer, *Transit and the Twins* (1958); Marion E. Cross, *Pioneer Harvest: Farmers and Mechanics Savings Bank* (1949); John Gjevre, *Saga of the Soo* (1973); and Patrick C. Dorin, *The Soo Line* (1979).

THOMAS C. BUCKLEY

LOY, Matthias (17 Mar. 1828–26 Jan. 1915), Lutheran church leader and editor, was born in rural Cumberland County, Pennsylvania, the son of Matthias Loy, a farmer and shopkeeper, and Christina Reaver. An impoverished childhood prevented Loy from attending school regularly, and in 1847 he was apprenticed to a printing firm in Harrisburg, Pennsylvania. While employed there, he learned to read and write German and English and attended the Harrisburg Academy. During his youth Loy was exposed to "American Lutheranism," a movement within the Lutheran church that promoted revivalism and urged a revision of the sixteenth-century Lutheran confessions, and he was converted at a revival in a Lutheran church in Harrisburg in 1843. Although a local pastor urged him to enroll at Gettysburg Seminary and prepare for the ministry, Loy's poor health and finances would not allow this, and instead in 1847 he left for Ohio. However, he was still interested in the ministry, and the Lutheran Joint Synod of Ohio gave him a small scholarship to attend the seminary in Columbus, Ohio, where he studied from 1847 to 1849.

At Columbus, Loy was strongly influenced by the confessional Lutheranism of his teachers, William Lehmann and Christian Spielmann, and by the writings of Missouri theologian Carl F. W. Walther. This type of Lutheranism stressed a return to the confessional theology of the sixteenth century, rejecting revivalism in favor of baptismal regeneration and employing the traditional liturgical formulas of Lutheranism. In 1849 Loy was ordained by the Joint Synod of Ohio and accepted a call to St. Mark Lutheran Church in Delaware, Ohio. At St. Mark he introduced strict confessional Lutheran theology and practice, completely separating this congregation from an associated Reformed congregation. Loy's congregation flourished, and he became a leader among the strict confessional wing of the Joint Synod of Ohio. In December 1853 Loy married Mary Willey; they had seven children. He served as president of the Joint Synod from 1860 to 1878, and again from 1880 to 1894, and became the dominant force behind that organization. In 1864 he became editor of the synod's periodical, the *Lutheran Standard*, a position he continued until 1891.

In 1865 Loy was called to be professor of theology at Capital Seminary in Columbus, Ohio, where he taught until retiring in 1902. From 1881 to 1890 he also served as president of Capital University. He was influential in moving the seminary and university to a stricter confessional Lutheranism and was the guiding force of these institutions during the latter part of the nineteenth century as they grew.

Under Loy's leadership, the Joint Synod of Ohio become a national force within American Lutheranism, generally along confessional Lutheran lines. In

1867 he prevented the synod from becoming a part of the General Council of the Evangelical Lutheran Church in North America. He believed that the General Council was not strict enough because it did not forcefully reject premillenialism (chiliasm, or the belief that the end of the world was imminent and that that it would usher in a climactic battle between God and the forces of evil); at times allowed non-Lutherans to receive communion and to preach; and did not condemn those who held membership in secret societies or lodges. The General Council's response did not satisfy Loy, so in 1871 he took the Ohio Synod into an affiliation with the Synodical Conference, a group dominated by the Missouri Synod. In 1881, however, Loy broke with Missouri theologian Walther over the issue of predestination, which erupted into a national theological battle and resulted in Ohio's withdrawal from the Synodical Conference that same year. The bitter battle over predestination involved the question of whether God predestines a believer to faith or whether God foresees that a person will have faith and "elects" that person to salvation, "in view of his faith." Walther and the Missouri Synod held to the former idea; Loy, along with other theologians of the Ohio, Iowa, and Norwegian Synods held to the latter. Although in his early years Loy had been greatly influenced by Walther, he came to feel during this controversy that Walther had become a theological "dictator," allowing no discussion. Loy believed that while the General Council was too lenient theologically, Walther and the Missouri Synod expected confessional theological agreement beyond what was reasonable.

In 1881 Loy founded the *Columbus Theological Monthly* and used the journal as a forum for strong attacks on Walther's views on predestination and on his leadership; he edited the journal until 1888. After his break with Missouri and the Synodical Conference, Loy and the Ohio Synod moved toward the Iowa Synod; negotiations for a closer relationship between the two synods began in 1883, but it was not until 1930 that the two groups formally merged.

Loy was a prolific writer, especially during his long term as editor of two periodicals; most of his polemical writing is in these journals. His publications include *The Doctrine of Justification* (1869) and *Essays on the Ministerial Office* (1870), which were especially aimed against the General Council and "American Lutheranism." *The Fallacy of Liberalism* (1883) was a general attack on modern trends, which Loy bitterly opposed. *The Augsburg Confession* (1908) was a theological and historical introduction to the primary Lutheran confession of the sixteenth century. A number of volumes of his collected sermons were widely circulated. He was also active as a hymn writer and translator, writing over twenty hymns and translating many more.

In 1902, because of heart problems, Loy retired as professor at Capital Seminary, but he was active in retirement, writing a number of books and articles. He died at his home in Columbus.

Loy's legacy is in the institutions he shaped—the Joint Synod of Ohio and Capital Seminary—and in his writings. The length of his service to the Ohio Synod and his influence on that group were remarkable, as was his place within American Lutheranism.

• Loy's papers are in the Archives of Capital University, Columbus, Ohio. His autobiography, *The Story of My Life* (1905), is a valuable source of information, as is Charles G. Fry, "Matthias Loy, Patriarch of Ohio Lutheranism, 1828–1915" (Ph.D. diss., Ohio State Univ., 1965). For a selection of his writing, see Theodore Tappert, *Lutheran Confessional Theology in America, 1840–1880* (1972). For a history of the Ohio Synod, see Clarence V. Sheatsley, *History of the Joint Synod of Ohio* (1919), and Willard D. Allbeck, *A Century of Lutherans in Ohio* (1966). On Capital Seminary, see Donald Huber, *Educating Lutheran Pastors in Ohio* (1989).

MARK GRANQUIST

LOY, Mina (27 Dec. 1882–25 Sept. 1966), poet and artist, was born Mina Gertrude Lowy in London, England, the daughter of Sigmund Lowy, a tailor, and Julia Bryan. Loy received little formal education but at seventeen was sent to art school in Munich. In 1901–1902 she returned to England, where she studied with the English painter Augustus John and began to exhibit her painting. It was also during this time that she met her first husband, art student Stephen Haweis (Hugh Oscar William Haweis). In 1903 Loy moved to Paris to study painting, married Haweis, and changed her name to Loy, a change, she remembered, that she "adopted in a spirit of mockery," in response to her husband's old and distinguished family name, which was pronounced "Hoyes" (Burke, pp. 67, 97). Loy and Haweis had three children; the first daughter died in infancy, the one son in his teens.

In Paris Loy became acquainted with leading modernists and was elected a member of the Salon d'Autumne for 1906. She and Haweis then moved to Florence, Italy, and joined the city's Anglo-American community. Loy's friendships and romances with the Italian Futurists became fodder for her satires of machismo, but the Futurists helped to shape her revolutionary poetic. The tone and rhetoric of their manifestos encouraged her rejection of poetic convention, while Filippo Tommaso Marinetti's "parole in liberta" encouraged her experiments with typography and free verse.

In 1915 Loy began to consider a trip to the United States to obtain a divorce and earn a living as a designer. Her arrival in New York City in December 1916 was preceded by the appearance of her poems in the American little magazines *Trend*, *Rogue*, and *Others*. She introduced herself in *Camera Work* (Jan. 1914) with "Aphorisms on Futurism." Declaring that "TODAY is the crisis in consciousness," this manifesto of psychic liberation anticipated Loy's designation as the "Modern Woman" by the *New York Evening Sun* (Feb. 1917). Her divorce from Haweis was final in 1917.

Among the artistic expatriates from World War I gathered in New York, Loy met proto-Dadaist Arthur

Cravan (Fabian Avenarius Lloyd). Loy and Cravan married in Mexico City in January 1918; in November he disappeared, having ventured out to sea in a sailboat from Salina Cruz, Mexico, and was never seen again. After the birth of their daughter, Loy searched for Cravan in Europe and the United States and then became a notable figure in Paris in the 1920s.

Loy drew on her family life and marriages to express her modernism, which originated in her rebellion against late-Victorian gender definitions, whereby oppressed mothers enforced patriarchal repression on defenseless daughters. In her satire on gender and genre expectations, the poetic allegory *Anglo-Mongrels and the Rose* (1923–1925), she is Ova, the mongrel daughter of Exodus, son of a Hungarian Jewish immigrant, and Alice, his disillusioned English "Rose"; Haweis is Esau Penfold, the "Infant Aesthete"; and Cravan is Colossus, the pugilistic *enfant terrible*.

Loy had already made innovations in poetic form, as exemplified in "Parturition" (*Trend*, Nov. 1914), a startling verbal and rhythmic rendering of birth and rebirth that had a shocking effect at the time it was published. On the page, it typographically depicts consciousness moving on waves of pain between animality and metaphysical analysis. Loy's poetry is distinguished by a verbal virtuosity that Ezra Pound labeled "logopoeia" and defined as "a dance of the intelligence among words and ideas and modification of ideas and characters." Its movement between abstraction and vivid image suggests the French philosopher Henri Bergson's theory of consciousness as the flux between intellection and intuition, a theory in which Loy had immersed herself.

Loy's most notorious poem is *Love Songs* or *Songs to Joannes* (*Others*, Apr. 1917), a thirty-four-poem collage of failed love that satirizes the male love-song tradition. The first four poems created a small scandal when they launched *Others*, edited by Alfred Kreymborg, in July 1915. *Love Songs* follows Christina Rossetti's *Monna Innominata* in letting the beloved woman speak. Loy's "I" objectifies, however, the male lover with an un-Rossettian irreverence. The popular love poetry of the time, as in the work of Sara Teasdale and Edna St. Vincent Millay, pales to sentimental cliché before the *Love Song*'s eroticism and deflation of romantic love:

> Pig Cupid   his rosy snout
> Rooting erotic garbage

Loy expressed her preoccupation with self-realization through the image of "I-eye." The eyes in the poems of the 1910s belong to dissatisfied women: "A thousand women's eyes / Riveted to the unrealizable." In the 1920s they are the unflinching visionary eyes of admired artists: Gertrude Stein, James Joyce, Constantin Brancusi, and Wyndham Lewis. In a tightening of her free verse line, Loy structures these portraits as concise, visually brilliant stanzas that Yvor Winters called "images that have frozen into epigrams." A memorable example comes from "Lunar Baedeker," a satire of failed artistic vision. Many of these art poems appeared in the prominent American literary monthly

The Dial and were collected with earlier poems in *Lunar Baedecker* [*sic*] (1923). The title alludes to the Baedecker travel guides used throughout Europe; Loy was mapping a journey to sites of the imagination beyond the poetic loci honored by tradition.

In 1936 Loy joined her daughters Joella and Fabi in New York, having become haunted by the specter of German expansionism and, being of Jewish birth, fearful of the Nazis' lethal anti-Semitism. Care-worn, she felt alien in the American metropolis. One of her few friendships of this period was with the artist Joseph Cornell, creator of exquisite, enigmatic box constructions, some of which Loy helped to inspire. Increasingly reclusive, Loy moved in 1949 into the Bowery, lower Manhattan's skid row. Her few published poems of this period pursue the theme of unrealized vision. Her subjects are often society's rejects, like her Bowery neighbors in the poem "Hot Cross Bum" (*New Directions in Prose and Poetry* 12 [1950]). They are "misfortune's monsters," betrayed by alcohol into a false "Elysium." Her artistic interest then centered on collages created from objects found in the city's streets. These were exhibited as "Constructions" at New York's Bodley Gallery in 1959.

A forgotten participant in the American poetry revolution of 1912 to 1925, Loy was known among contemporaries for her startling free verse analysis of sexuality, her beauty, and her dramatic life. The rediscovery of her radical modernism, signaled by Jonathan Williams's 1958 collection of her poetry, *Lunar Baedeker & Time-Tables*, has continued in feminist challenges to the high modernist canon.

Neglect of Loy's poetry has lent qualified support to revisionist claims that leading male modernists like T. S. Eliot, Pound, and Joyce defined modernism so as to marginalize writers whose poetics and politics threatened their own largely conservative stance. However, Eliot and Pound praised Loy's work. In the Prologue to *Kora in Hell* (1920), William Carlos Williams singles out Loy and Marianne Moore as the South and North poles of the poetry landscape. High modernist champions of technical innovation and intellectual rigor could not accuse Loy of formal conservatism or sentimentality. Literary historians may have marginalized Loy by making her a modernist icon, woman-as-Dada, while relegating her writing to avant-garde obscurity; but equally relevant is Loy's lessened attention to her poetry in later life. When she died in Aspen, Colorado, where she had lived with her daughters since 1953, she was known mostly through the memoirs of her contemporaries. Renewed interest in her poetry belongs to the recovery of the neglected, multiple aspects of early modernism. In *The Autobiography of Alice B. Toklas* (1933), Stein, whom Loy praised as "Curie / of the laboratory / of vocabulary," offers a definitive tribute to Loy's artistic vision. Recalling Loy's first husband's plea that she punctuate the long sentences without commas in *The Making of Americans* (1925), Stein notes that "Mina Loy . . . was able to understand without the commas. She has always been able to understand."

• Loy's papers are in Yale University's Beinecke Library. Published works not mentioned above include *Auto-Facial-Constructions* (1919), *Psycho-Democracy* (1920), and a 1930s novel, *Insel* (1991), about the German surrealist painter Richard Oelze. Roger L. Conover edited a Jargon Press edition of the poetry, *The Last Lunar Baedeker* (1982), and an edition published by Farrar, Strauss & Giroux, *The Last Lunar Baedeker: Poems of Mina Loy* (1996); Conover has also edited *The Autobiography of Mina Loy: "Anglo-Mongrels and the Rose" and "Colossus"* (1998). The first half of *Anglo-Mongrels and the Rose* originally appeared in the *Little Review* 9 (Spring 1923): 10–18, and 9 (Autumn-Winter 1923–1924): 41–51; the second half in *Contact Collection of Contemporary Writers* (1925). Early critical commendations of her poetry include Ezra Pound, "Others," *Little Review* 4 (Mar. 1918): 56–58, and Yvor Winters, "Mina Loy," *Dial* 80 (June 1926): 496–99. Kenneth Rexroth reclaimed Loy for the modernist canon in "Les Lauriers Sont Coupés: Mina Loy," *Southern Review* 3 (July 1967): 597–607. The first book on Loy's life and poetry was Virginia M. Kouidis, *Mina Loy: American Modernist Poet* (1980). Another biography is Carolyn Burke, *Becoming Modern: The Life of Mina Loy* (1996). An obituary is in the *Aspen Times*, 29 Sept. 1966.

VIRGINIA M. KOUIDIS

LOY, Myrna (2 Aug. 1905–12 Dec. 1993), actress and political activist, was born Myrna Adele Williams in Radersburg, Montana, the daughter of David Franklin Williams, a cattle rancher, and Della Mae Johnson, a singer. After her father's death in the 1918 influenza epidemic, the family moved to Culver City, California. While attending high school, Loy auditioned for movie studios and helped support her family by teaching children's dancing classes and working as an assistant film cutter at Horsley Studios. She also danced in the prefeature chorus line at Grauman's Chinese Theater before coming under contract to Warner Brothers. Her first role was a "human chandelier" in *Pretty Ladies* (1925). She adopted the name "Loy" at the suggestion of a friend, who believed it sounded more exotic and interesting than the Welsh family name of Williams.

A role as an exotic mistress in *Ben Hur* (1925) resulted in Loy's being typecast as a predatory vamp, usually Oriental or of mixed blood. During the following years she appeared in sixty films and eventually started playing leading roles and being cast as an Occidental. She also displayed a talent for sophisticated comedy in films such as *Love Me Tonight* (1932), *Penthouse* (1933), and *Topaze* (1933). Recalling her early years at the movie studios, she later stated: "They worked us to death. You'd go from one picture to another without rehearsal. . . . We were little more than chattels, really, but it was valuable experience. You didn't need acting school; you learned on the job, and if they decided to build you, they built you to last" (*Myrna Loy*, p. 85).

Full stardom arrived the following year, while Loy was under contract to Metro-Goldwyn-Mayer (MGM). Critics and the public praised her work as Clark Gable's lover in *Manhattan Melodrama* (1934). This caused director Woodbridge Strong Van Dyke to cast her opposite William Powell in the role of Nora Charles for *The Thin Man* (1934). Although budgeted

and quickly produced as a typical "B" movie, the film became an enormous box office success. Nick and Nora Charles became the epitome of witty, urbane, and quite frequently tipsy sophistication.

Loy and Powell went on to make a series of sequels in the following decade: *After the Thin Man* (1936); *Another Thin Man* (1939); *Shadow of the Thin Man* (1941); *The Thin Man Goes Home* (1944); and *Song of the Thin Man* (1947). The pair also worked together in other popular MGM films, including *Libeled Lady* (1936) and *The Great Ziegfeld* (1936). Loy also continued to appear with Clark Gable in *Wife versus Secretary* (1936), *Test Pilot* (1938), and *Too Hot to Handle* (1938). During 1937 and 1938 the Motion Pictures Exhibitors Association named her as one of the ten most popular film stars.

Loy's personal life was not as successful as her film career. Her marriage in 1936 to film producer Arthur Hornblow, Jr., ended in divorce in 1942. Six days later she married advertising executive John Daniel Hertz, Jr.; they were divorced in 1944.

After Pearl Harbor was attacked in 1941, Loy temporarily stopped making movies and moved to New York City, where she worked for the Red Cross as assistant director of its welfare activities in the New York area. She also did volunteer work in military canteens and organized entertainment for military hospitals. Her only movie work during World War II was a picture in *The Thin Man* series, which she performed in exchange for being released from her contract with MGM.

One of Loy's last roles for MGM—as the wife of a returning air corps veteran in William Wyler's *The Best Years of Our Lives* (1946)—earned her an award for best actress at the Brussels World Film Festival. As an independent actress, she continued to perform in comedies, including *The Bachelor and the Bobby-Soxer* (1947) and *Mr. Blandings Builds His Dream House* (1948), but she also sought more serious roles such as efficiency engineer Lillian Gilbreth in *Cheaper by the Dozen* (1950) and the ranch mother in *The Red Pony* (1949).

Most of Loy's energies in the postwar period were taken up by political causes. She ascribed her political liberalism to her late father, a state legislator who had strongly supported the League of Nations. Loy became a close friend of Eleanor Roosevelt and was a strong supporter of the United Nations. Her support of liberal causes and political candidates resulted in an accusation by labor leader Matthew Woll in 1946 that Loy was sponsoring communist-front organizations. After Loy filed a lawsuit for libel, Woll retracted his accusations. The following year Loy became one of the few leading actors to protest the congressional investigations into alleged communist influence in Hollywood and the movie industry. She helped organize the Committee of the First Amendment, which sought the abolition of the House Committee on Un-American Activities.

In 1946 Loy married producer Gene Markey, but this marriage ended in divorce in August 1950. In June 1951 she married H. Howland Sergeant, a member of the U.S. State Department who served as assistant secretary of state for public affairs under President Harry S. Truman. The couple divorced in 1960. Loy had no children. She was an active member of the American Association for the United Nations and was an American delegate to the 1948 Pacific Regional Conference of the United Nations Educational, Scientific, and Cultural Organization (UNESCO). In 1949 Loy was appointed a film adviser to the U.S. delegation to UNESCO, a role she occupied until 1954.

During most of the 1950s and 1960s Loy had few film roles and none at all between her appearances in *Belles on Their Toes* (1952) and *The Ambassador's Daughter* (1956), in which she performed in a supporting role rather than as the star. She later recalled: "Despite the subterfuges of men who operate them, cameras really don't lie. In the end, an actress has only two ways to go: quit at the top, like Garbo, or shift into character parts, as I did" (*Myrna Loy*, p. 269). She alternated subsequent movie roles with occasional television shows and started summer-stock stage appearances in 1960 that eventually led to a Broadway performance in a revival of *The Women* (1973). Her final film role was in *Just Tell Me What You Want* (1980), and she appeared opposite Henry Fonda in the critically acclaimed television movie *Summer Solstice* (1981).

Loy's final years brought critical praise for her work in film. The National Board of Review of Motion Pictures gave her the first David Wark Griffith Award in 1980, and Lauren Bacall hosted a 1985 tribute to her at Carnegie Hall sponsored by the movie community. In 1991 the Motion Picture Academy of Arts and Sciences gave her an honorary Oscar. She died in New York City.

• Loy's papers are part of the Twentieth Century Archives at Boston University. "Reminiscences of Myrna Loy," a transcript of an oral history interview, is at the Oral History Research Office, Columbia University. Loy's memoir, written with James Kotsilibas-Davis, is *Myrna Loy: Being and Becoming* (1987), and she was profiled in the *New York Times*, 3 Feb. 1980. She is discussed in Jane Ellen Wayne, *Gable's Women* (1987), and James Harvey, *Romantic Comedy in Hollywood: From Lubitsch to Sturges* (1987). See also Lawrence J. Quirk, *The Films of Myrna Loy* (1980). Obituaries are in the *New York Times* and the *Washington Post*, both 16 Dec. 1993, and *Variety*, 27 Dec. 1993.

STEPHEN G. MARSHALL

LOZIER, Clemence Sophia Harned (11 Dec. 1813–26 Apr. 1888), physician and reformer, was born in Plainfield, New Jersey, the daughter of David Harned, a farmer and Methodist, and Hannah Walker, an informal medical practitioner and Quaker. As a child Clemence acquired an interest in medicine from her physician brother and from her mother, who had learned traditional healing practices from American Indians. Her mother, realizing that her daughter had a quick mind, began teaching her healing skills. The lessons ended when her mother died and eleven-year-old Clemence was sent to school at Plainfield Academy.

At age sixteen Clemence married Abraham Witton Lozier, an architect and builder. Only one of their children survived infancy. Her husband's failing health led Clemence Lozier to support the family by opening a school for girls in her home in 1832. She introduced subjects such as physiology, anatomy, and hygiene to her students. Her husband died in 1837; Lozier's school remained open until 1843.

As a Methodist, Lozier opened her home weekly for prayer meetings, and she worked toward social reform as a member of the New York Moral Reform Society. She wanted to prevent prostitution and rehabilitate women, and as a Society "visitor" she went into the homes of the poor and the ill. Her mother's medical teachings and Lozier's own observations in her visits, as well as her care of her sick husband, gave her the knowledge to advise students and others. Around 1844 she moved to Albany, and then to Webster, New York (outside Rochester), where she continued visiting the sick and lectured in churches on physiology and hygiene. She also married John Baker; she divorced him in 1861 and resumed the surname Lozier. No children resulted from this marriage, and little is known about this period in her life.

Although Lozier desired to practice medicine, no medical schools then admitted women, so her physician brother became her tutor. In 1849 she was finally permitted to attend lectures at Central Medical School in Rochester, New York. The school was "eclectic," offering general courses not of the same caliber as those in medical colleges for men. She attained the highest honors on her graduation in 1853 from its successor, the Syracuse Medical College. After graduation she went to New York City, where she set up a private practice and became interested in homeopathic treatments.

Lozier's practice became quite lucrative, although she sometimes offered free services to the destitute. Called Madame Lozier by her patients—many of them former students—she specialized in gynecology and obstetrics, seeing as many as fifty patients a day. Although trained in the homeopathic school, Lozier never held to any one theory of treatment but employed new methods and techniques. She performed both minor and major surgical procedures, including the removal of tumors. She was reported to have earned a substantial income of $25,000 and to have owned two homes.

In addition to her medical practice, Lozier lectured to women in her home from 1860 to 1863. These popular lectures were attended by women interested in general health information as well as by those who wished to become doctors. The lectures resulted in the establishment of a women's medical library association; they also gave Lozier the idea to found a medical school for women. Assisted by Elizabeth Cady Stanton and other women in the suffrage movement, Lozier in 1863 obtained the necessary charter to found the New York Medical College and Hospital for Women, a homeopathic institution. A branch of the Homeopathic Medical College of New York, the college was the first women's medical school in New York State. Lozier provided financial backing for the school, which opened in 1863 with seven students taught by four male and four female physicians. Her school so impressed A. K. Gardner, a doctor previously opposed to female physicians, that he wrote in *Frank Leslie's Illustrated Newspaper* that women should be allowed to "study medicine as thoroughly and as freely as men" and "stand equal with male doctors."

Lozier taught at the college until the end of the Civil War. In 1867 she traveled to Europe for additional medical studies and to research the building and administration of foreign hospitals. On her return the same year, she resumed her private practice and became the school's dean and professor of gynecology and obstetrics, holding those titles until 1887. She secured new equipment and expanded the curriculum. A move to a new and more expensive building, undertaken against her advice, created financial problems for Lozier since her physician's income still largely supported the institution. She declared bankruptcy in 1878. The college nonetheless survived and became nationally recognized; in 1918 it became part of the New York Medical College of the Flower and Fifth Avenue Hospitals.

Well connected with others in the suffrage movement, Lozier was president of the New York City Woman Suffrage Society from 1873 to 1886 and president of the National Woman Suffrage Association from 1877 to 1878. In addition, she helped to finance Susan B. Anthony's newspaper, *Revolution*. On behalf of the National Workingwomen's League Lozier investigated and testified for a young woman accused of infanticide, helping the woman to win a pardon. During the 1862 draft riots her home became an asylum for African Americans.

Lozier was the first woman to read a paper before the New York State Medical Society. She aided in bringing the study of physiology into public schools, spoke at clinics, and wrote papers on education. She published a short pamphlet, *Child-Birth Made Easy* (1870), which offered general rather than specialized information, while *Dress* (date unknown) emphasized the danger of wearing tight-fitting clothes. At the time of her death in New York City, 200 women had graduated from the college she established. Forty-eight of them attended her funeral; six were her own relatives.

A gentle woman with tireless energy, Lozier fought for women's rights to cast a vote and to attain a medical education. In 1885 she tried to register to vote, and it was her desire to "live long enough to cast one vote." An 1895 *New York Times* article described Lozier as a "pioneer" and "a clever practitioner" who "has probably done more to advance the 'cause of woman' and smooth her thorny path than any one other woman of any age or clime." A valiant fighter and ardent advocate of suffrage, temperance, and a number of other moral reforms, Lozier not only provided good medical care but also encouraged women to become physicians themselves, sometimes securing positions for them across the country and abroad.

• There is no known collection of Lozier's papers. The best biographical source is *In Memoriam: Mrs. Clemence Sophia Lozier, M.D.* (1888). See also Caroline H. Dall, *The College, the Market, and the Court* (1867); James Parton et al., *Eminent Women of the Age* (1869), pp. 517–22; Elizabeth Cady Stanton et al., *History of Woman Suffrage*, vol. 3 (1886); Susan B. Anthony and Ida Husted Harper, *The History of Woman Suffrage*, vol. 4 (1902); Mary Ormsbee Whitton, *These Were the Women: U.S.A. 1776–1860* (1954); Esther Pohl Lovejoy, *Women Doctors of the World* (1957); Alma Lutz, *Created Equal: A Biography of Elizabeth Cady Stanton* (1974); Blanche Glassman Hersh, *The Slavery of Sex: Feminist Abolitionists in America* (1978); William Leach, *True Love and Perfect Union: The Feminist Reform of Sex and Society* (1980); Virginia G. Drachman, *Hospital with a Heart* (1984); Elisabeth Griffith, *In Her Own Right* (1984); and Regina Markell Morantz-Sanchez, *Sympathy and Science: Women Physicians in American Medicine* (1985). Obituaries are in the *New York Times*, 28 Apr. 1888, and *Woman's Journal*, 5 May 1888.

MARILYN ELIZABETH PERRY

LUAHINE, Iolani (31 Jan. 1915–10 Dec. 1978), kuma hula (hula master teacher), dancer, and chanter, was born Harriet Lanihau Makekau at Napoopoo near Kealakekua Bay on Hawaii (meaning the Big Island), the daughter of Manasseh Makekau and Koolani (maiden name unknown). In the traditional belief that the exchange of children strengthened *ohana* (family) ties, she was *hanaied* (adopted) at birth by her great-aunt, Keahi Luahine, who also taught her to dance. She was raised on Kauai island by the Luahine family. The name Iolani, which in Hawaiian means hawk (a symbol of royalty), was given to her by a *kahuna nui* (high priest) after she had fallen ill as a child and lost her sight. The priest inquired about the name Harriet and remarked that it was not the right name for her; after he renamed her Iolani, her sight returned.

Luahine's grandmother was Kalei-Hulu-Mamo, a court dancer on Kauai. Also a dancer, Keahi, the great-aunt who adopted her, took Iolani with her to Honolulu where she went to practice and revive the art of hula with King Kalakaua's support—extended after his queen, Kapiolani, observed Keahi's dancing and invited her to teach and perform at court in Honolulu. From age four, Luahine was trained by Keahi in the ancient hula, but the family wisely also wanted a well-rounded academic education for their protégé. She first attended Kamehameha School for Girls, which was founded by Bernice Bishop through her Bishop Estate trust. But when Keahi learned that the school prohibited the teaching and practice of the standing hula because it was too suggestive or lewd in the eyes of the missionaries, Luahine was withdrawn and enrolled in St. Andrew's Priory, a school for outstanding native Hawaiian young ladies.

From childhood when she first learned to dance, Luahine dedicated herself to Laka, the Hawaiian goddess of the hula. Inspired no doubt by her grandmother's and great-aunt's interests in traditional dance, Luahine would dedicate her life to the study of the ancient dances and folkways and become widely regarded as a repository of authentic hulas. In the 1970s she was credited with encouraging reinterest in ancient Hawaiian culture. It was also during this Hawaiian Renaissance that she was viewed as the foremost expert in the ancient hula dance steps, and she taught hula on the Waianae coast of Oahu to Hawaiians who would carry on her knowledge.

Luahine began performing professionally in the 1930s, first with David K. "Daddy" Bray at the Royal Hawaiian Hotel and later with Alfred Apaka at the Alexander Young Hotel. With both troupes she danced comic hulas similar to Hilo Hattie (also known as Clara Nelson) as well as the more religious and sacred dances of the past. As her reputation grew she decided to drop the humorous hulas and to add more sacred hulas to her repertoire. For more than thirty years she was widely acclaimed for teaching and performing the ancient dances. In 1940, 1946, and 1971 Luahine represented Hawaii at the National Folk Festival in Washington. After the death of her great-aunt in the late 1940s, Luahine studied under Mary Kawena (Wiggin) Pukui, who was associated with the Bishop Museum. Pukui passed along her knowledge of the Hawaiian chants that often accompanied the hulas, as well as her discernment of the plants and costumes appropriate to the sacred ancient hulas. In 1947 Luahine opened a *halau* (hula school) of her own and became a professional hula teacher. In her halau she continued the authentic training passed to her through her forebears. She received praise and renown from hula colleagues as well as from visitors such as the famous dancer Ted Shawn, who remarked that Luahine was "an artist of world stature."

Luahine seemed to embody all the ancient spirits of the famed kuma hulas of the past. Through her the hula became an art form rather than something cheap and sexy, or something for nightclub acts. She always performed with the greatest dignity and demanded respect from her audiences. Shawn observed that "Iolani can and does show the world that the hula is a noble art, rich, beautiful and with great dignity, and a fitting expression of a noble race."

Luahine danced to support herself after a failed marriage (1951–1953) to James McMahon, a painter; they had no children. She appeared in Honolulu, at the Queen's Surf, Don the Beachcomber's, Duke Kahanamoku's, and the Niumalu Hotel, where she continued her sacred dances. She was considered such an authority on hula that she served with Henry Pa as consultant and choreographer of the hula dances for the film *Bird of Paradise* (1950).

In 1956 she returned to the island of Hawaii where she became curator of the Hulihee Palace in Kailua-Kona (the site of the early capital before the capital became Honolulu during the reign of Kamehameha II). She returned later to Oahu to be the curator of the Royal Mausoleum, where Hawaii's royal figures are buried. While in Honolulu she continued to teach and perform the ancient hulas, and several of her students—Beverly Noa, Pele Pukui Suganuma, and especially her niece Hoakalei Kamauu—went on to achieve distinction under her instruction. Throughout her life-

time she trained over three hundred students. These students became the archivists of Luahine's special style and grace. In 1966 she returned to her roots to occupy her family's 100-year-old home at Napoopoo and, just before her death in Honolulu, she returned to Hulihee Palace to resume curating. She attended the installation ceremony of the president of Nauru in the mid-1960s to compare dance steps and to recapture more of the sacred hulas and chants of that South Pacific island.

By the early 1970s native Hawaiians realized they were losing their rich traditions as Hawaiian youths were becoming increasingly westernized and inattentive to preserving the old dances, chants, music, and life-style of ancient Hawaii. Luahine was poised to become an original leader of the Hawaiian Renaissance that was to recapture the ancient Hawaiian culture to preserve it for posterity. Luahine realized this trend as early as 1969 and called a seminal meeting of all of Hawaii's kuma hulas on the Waianea coast at Nanakuli, and she taught them all that she knew, hoping they would continue recovering, restoring, and teaching ancient hula. Other Hawaiian artists and artisans were inspired to come together to slow the erosion of their culture, eventually establishing the State Council on Hawaiian Heritage, which provided grants and workshops for recovering Hawaiian culture. In 1970 the State of Hawaii awarded Luahine its prestigious Order of Distinction for Cultural Leadership. Numerous nonprofit organizations were formed to further the renaissance, such as the Hawaiian Music Foundation (1971) and the Kamehameha Day Hula Kahiko (ancient hula) competition (1972). *National Geographic* filmed Luahine, who had been named a Living Treasure in the Islands in 1976, and produced two films illustrating her chanting and dancing, *Hula Hoolaulea: The Traditional Dances* 1961 and *Iolani Luahine: Hawaiian Dancer* (1976). Brigham Young University at Laie, on Oahu, also recorded her dances and chants on film for archival purposes.

• Additional information on Luahine can be found in John Thomson Faris, *Paradise of the Pacific* (1939), and in "Sunday Afternoon in a Hilo Bar and a Talk with a Legend," *Honolulu Star Bulletin*, 13 Sept. 1973. Also see the *Honolulu Star Bulletin*, 24 Oct. 1947; the *Honolulu Advertiser*, 22 Sept. 1947 and 1 Apr. 1978; the Kenneth Emory MS at the Bishop Museum library, Honolulu; interview with Keahi Luahine Sylvester Gomes; the Hawaiian Music Foundation records; and the archives of Brigham Young University at Laie, Oahu. Another portrait can be found in Jerry Hopkins, "Iolani Luahine," in *Notable Women of Hawaii*, ed. Barbara Bennett Peterson (1984). Obituaries are in the *Honolulu Advertiser* and the *Honolulu Star Bulletin*, 11 Dec. 1978.

BARBARA BENNETT PETERSON

LUBBOCK, Francis Richard (16 Oct. 1815–22 June 1905), governor of Texas, was born in Beaufort, South Carolina, the son of Henry T. W. Lubbock, a physician, steamboat owner, planter, and merchant, and Susan Ann Saltus. His family sent him to private schools at Beaufort and Charleston until he was fourteen, when his father's death forced him to go to work. He clerked in a hardware store in Charleston for three years and then moved to Hamburg, where he managed a cotton warehouse. In 1834 he moved to New Orleans, Louisiana, and with a partner opened a drugstore. After its failure in 1836 he sold jewelry and dealt in military goods. In New Orleans he married Adele Baron in 1835. It is not known if the marriage produced any children.

In 1836 Lubbock went to the Republic of Texas, searching for his brother Thomas S. Lubbock, whom he found in Velasco. Liking the town, Lubbock decided to move there himself, and he opened a store. His interests quickly strayed from storekeeping, however, and he became involved in the politics of the new republic. In 1837 he received an appointment as assistant clerk and then clerk of the Texas House of Representatives of the Second Congress. The same year President Sam Houston appointed him comptroller of the Treasury. During this period he moved to Houston, where he started a drugstore and a mercantile business, invested in land, and engaged in farming and ranching.

As his businesses prospered, Lubbock remained active in politics. In 1841 he ran successfully for district clerk of Harris County and subsequently held that position for sixteen years. By the mid-1850s he was a prominent leader in the state Democratic party and, in the face of the Know Nothing challenge, helped to revitalize it by shifting the nominating process from party caucuses to open conventions. Lubbock was elected lieutenant governor of the state in 1857 but was defeated for reelection in the 1859 elections, which saw a Unionist ticket headed by Houston and Edward Clark victorious. Lubbock, a slave owner, was a delegate to the Democratic National Convention in 1860 and during the political crisis was a strong secessionist.

Lubbock ran for governor in 1861 and won, obtaining 21,854 votes to Clark's 21,730 and Thomas J. Chambers's 13,759. Lubbock took office on 7 November 1861 and found the state facing a crisis. The governor suggested that the legislature create a state military board to organize, equip, and finance state military organizations, on which he would serve along with the comptroller and treasurer. Among the board's initiatives were the sale of U.S. bonds acquired as a part of the Compromise of 1850 and the development of trade in cotton through Mexico. To provide war matériel for the army, the board established a cloth and shoe factory at the state penitentiary, a state foundry, and a percussion-cap factory. Lubbock also encouraged private firms to manufacture arms. The governor dealt vigorously with dissent, pursuing Unionists and draft dodgers and supporting the suspension of the writ of habeas corpus and imposition of martial law. He successfully pushed the legislature to raise a mounted regiment for frontier defense.

Lubbock was also responsible for calling a conference of governors of the Trans-Mississippi region to coordinate their activities and encourage greater interest in their affairs by the Richmond government, specifically calling for a branch of the Treasury to be established in the western Confederacy and encouraging the Confederate government to insure supplies and men for their defense. The governors' conference was at least in part responsible for President Jefferson Davis's extension of greater autonomy to the Trans-Mississippi District and the naming of General Theophilus H. Holmes to command it in July 1862.

Lubbock declined to run for reelection in 1863. Instead he joined the staff of General John Bankhead Magruder at Galveston as a colonel. He served with General John A. Wharton in the Red River campaign in the spring of 1864 and took part in the cavalry pursuit of General Nathaniel Banks's retreating Federal force. That summer Lubbock went to Richmond, where he joined the staff of President Davis as an adviser on Trans-Mississippi affairs. He fled Richmond with Davis and was with him at the time of his capture. Lubbock was imprisoned at Fort Delaware but was released by order of President Andrew Johnson on 24 November 1865 and returned home.

In Texas Lubbock returned to ranching, opened commission houses in Houston and Galveston, and invested in various economic endeavors. The collapse of one of these investments, a beef packing business, practically destroyed him financially. In addition to his business activity, he remained a stalwart in Democratic politics. He was tax collector at Galveston and in 1878 was elected state treasurer, a post he held until 1891. His last public position was during the administration of Governor James S. Hogg, who named him a member of the state board of pardons. Following the death of his first wife, he married twice more, to Sarah E. Black Porter in 1883 and to Lue Scott in 1903. Lubbock died in Austin.

• Lubbock's papers are in the American History Center, University of Texas at Austin, and in the Archives, Texas State Library. Lubbock wrote an autobiography, *Six Decades in Texas; or, Memoirs of Francis Richard Lubbock*, ed. C. W. Raines (1900). A modern biography is a short essay in James T. DeShields, *They Sat in High Places: The Presidents and Governors of Texas, 1836–1939* (1940). An obituary is in the *Dallas Morning News*, 23 June 1905.

CARL H. MONEYHON

LUBELL, Samuel (?3 Nov. 1911–16 Aug. 1987), author and political analyst, was born Samuel Lubelsky in Poland, the son of Mollie Reitkop and Louis Lubelsky. He immigrated to the United States at the age of two with his parents and settled in New York, where he later adopted the shorter name. He explained later that, required to specify a birthday at age six and knowing only the month and year of his birth, he had picked that year's election day. He began working for the *Long Island Daily Press* as early as 1925. He studied evenings between 1927 and 1931 at the College of the City of New York (now City University of New York) and then transferred to Columbia University, graduating in 1933 with a B.S. from the School of Journalism.

Travel and writing occupied Lubell in the 1930s. A hitchhiking trip in summer 1930 took him to Canada, Mexico, California, and Florida. After graduation from Columbia he traveled around the country with a classmate, Walter Everett, while writing occasional pieces. In late 1933 Columbia's School of Journalism awarded him a Pulitzer Traveling Scholarship that took him to Europe for two years. He returned to his old newspaper on Long Island in 1936 but soon moved to Washington, D.C., where he reported on the U.S. Army and Navy and wrote the column "The Federal Diary" for the *Washington Post*. During most of 1937 he worked in Virginia at the copy desk and as labor reporter for the *Richmond Times-Dispatch*. Returning to the nation's capital, he worked for the *Washington Herald* for some months before leaving in 1938 to travel across the country again, this time with Everett and Everett's wife. Intent on trying their hands at freelance writing, the two men hit paydirt. They were in Arkansas when the *Saturday Evening Post* accepted an article they wrote together, "Rehearsal for State Medicine," which appeared in December 1938. Lubell and Everett jointly published other pieces in *The Nation*, *Collier's*, and *Reader's Digest*, but Lubell increasingly worked alone. The *Saturday Evening Post* asked him to analyze Franklin D. Roosevelt's victory in the 1940 presidential election, and Lubell gained his first taste of public opinion polling for that piece, published in January 1941 as "Mostmortem: Who Elected Roosevelt?" He married Helen Sopot in 1941, and they had two children.

World War II brought new venues and new responsibilities. In December 1941 Lubell began writing for the Office of Facts and Figures (later the Office of War Information). He served in 1942 as general secretary to the Rubber Survey Committee, headed by Bernard M. Baruch. He also assisted Baruch on the advisory committee for war and postwar adjustment policies in the Office of War Mobilization, and he assisted James F. Byrnes, director of the Office of Economic Stabilization. In 1944 he left government and went to Asia as war correspondent for the *Saturday Evening Post* in China and India. Following the war he spent much of 1946 in Europe as a correspondent for the *Providence Journal* and the North American Newspaper Alliance. Along the way he published essays about international developments in *Collier's*, *Commentary*, *Current History*, *Harper's*, and other periodicals.

Lubell became best known as a book writer and political analyst. The *Saturday Evening Post* asked him to analyze President Harry S. Truman's surprise victory over Thomas E. Dewey in 1948, and Guggenheim Fellowships in 1951 and 1954 facilitated the writing of his first books. *The Future of American Politics* (1952) combined a social history of twentieth-century American politics with a prescient prediction that Dwight D. Eisenhower and the Republicans would take back the White House that year. He analyzed the voting public in terms of group interests, whether sectional, economic, religious, or racial and ethnic. He perceived that the very success of New Deal programs had great-

ly enlarged the American middle class, and this new affluence made many of those programs less compelling and the New Deal constituency less cohesive. The book earned him the American Political Science Association's Woodrow Wilson Award for 1952. It also led to his work as a commentator on radio and television for NBC and CBS during the national elections of 1952 through 1960.

Lubell was often described as a short pudgy man with a disarming grin and an enormous capacity for work. In his efforts to identify public opinion, he would stroll up to a stranger and explain, "My name is Sam Lubell, and I'm trying to report the political campaign by talking to the voters" ("The Doorbell Ringer," *Time*, 15 Oct. 1956, p. 84. During each presidential campaign he continued his characteristic approach by traveling widely, ringing doorbells, and talking directly to voters about what they saw as the crucial issues and how they planned to vote. In particular he identified what he determined to be key precincts, analyzed voter concerns and behavior there, and used the results to discern national trends. Why, he wanted to know, did people change their votes, particularly in precincts that in the past had shown consistency? He spoke to voters but avoided politicians, especially the candidates themselves, and he steered clear of local journalists. To maintain his emotional balance while seeking to understand the major trends and issues that were shaping national politics, he stopped voting, registering, or even hoping for any particular electoral outcome.

Subsequent books reflected Lubell's keen interest in and acute perceptions of American politics and international relations. *The Revolution in World Trade and American Economic Policy* (1955), which built on his travels in and reporting on Asia and Europe during the 1930s and 1940s and his wartime work in Washington, analyzed trends in world trade and the place of the United States in the emerging world order. *Revolt of the Moderates* (1956) continued through President Eisenhower's first term the analysis of domestic politics Lubell had begun in *The Future of American Politics*. *White and Black: Test of a Nation* (1964) focused on the crucial domestic question of the early 1960s, and *The Hidden Crisis in American Politics* (1970) dissected the political volatility of the late 1960s. Lubell's final book, *The Future While It Happened* (1973), took the story through the 1972 election.

An innovative analyst and one of America's premier journalists in any medium, Lubell merged the roles of historian, political scientist, reporter, and commentator. He was a member of the National Press Club. At Columbia's Graduate School of Journalism he organized the Opinion Reporting Workshop in 1958 and directed it until 1968. He also taught courses at American University in Washington, D.C., and was a Kennedy Fellow at Harvard University. His column "The People Speak," which he wrote for many years for the United Features Syndicate, exemplified his ability to speak effectively to scholars and general newspaper readers alike. Lubell retired in 1976 after a serious stroke and moved to Los Angeles, where he died.

• The Samuel Lubell Papers, mostly interview materials and data files on each state, are at the Lauinger Library at Georgetown University. Accounts of Lubell are in *Current Biography*, 1956, and "Keeping Posted," *Saturday Evening Post*, 30 Nov. 1940, p. 6. Several assessments appear in Alexander Lamis et al., "Symposium on the Work of Samuel Lubell," *PS: Political Science and Politics* 23 (June 1990): 184–90. Obituaries are in the *New York Times*, 21 Aug. 1987; the *Washington Post*, 23 Aug. 1987; *Time*, 31 Aug. 1987; and *Current Biography*, 1987.

PETER WALLENSTEIN

LUBIN, David (10 June 1849–1 Jan. 1919), merchant, agricultural reformer, and pioneer internationalist, was born in the Jewish settlement of Klodowa in Russian Poland, the son of Simon Lubin and Rachel Holtz. While David was still an infant, his father died of cholera. His mother soon married Solomon Weinstock, a peddler, who, following an anti-Jewish pogrom, fled with his new family to London, England, before eventually coming to the United States in 1855. Settled in New York City, Lubin attended public schools until the age of twelve, when he became an apprentice jeweler in North Attleboro, Massachusetts.

In 1865 Lubin moved to San Francisco, where he worked for several months before moving to Los Angeles and then to Arizona in 1868. For the next three years he prospected for gold and labored at the Vulcan Mine near Wickenburg. Failing to strike it rich, Lubin went back to New York and spent another three years as a traveling salesman for a lamp manufacturer. In 1874 he returned to San Francisco and, with his younger half brother Harris Weinstock, formed a brief partnership in a dry-goods store started by his widowed sister, Jeanette Levy.

Soon dissatisfied with the local trade, Lubin left San Francisco in October 1874 and opened his own store in Sacramento. There he quickly demonstrated his business acumen and his penchant for innovation. Discarding the traditional but time-consuming practice of bargaining with customers over the price of each item sold, Lubin helped pioneer "single price" retailing. Lubin's method featured fixed prices for goods that were clearly marked, openly displayed, and completely nonnegotiable. An instant success, single pricing, combined with aggressive advertising, caused trade to boom and encouraged Weinstock to leave San Francisco and become Lubin's partner. By 1881 their Mechanic's Store, rechristened Weinstock, Lubin, and Company, ranked among the premier department stores of the Pacific Coast and boasted the nation's largest mail-order business. Meanwhile, in 1875 Lubin married Louisa Lyons, with whom he eventually had five children.

The tremendous success of Weinstock, Lubin, and Company enabled its founders to retire early and devote the rest of their lives to public service. Lubin resigned from active management of the store in 1894, and Weinstock followed in 1908. Together with Lu-

bin's eldest son, Simon J. Lubin, they formed a trio of prominent California progressives who focused their efforts on solving the problems of farmers and farm laborers. Weinstock and Simon Lubin received important appointments in Governor Hiram Johnson's administration after 1911, while David Lubin moved on from state and national issues to the causes of international peace and agricultural reform.

Convinced that he was destined for future greatness, Lubin was driven by ambition and his belief that, as a Jew, he had a duty to act as "a Servant unto the Nations of the Earth." This sense of individual and ethnic mission had been nurtured by his strong-willed mother and reinvigorated by a trip Lubin took with her to Palestine in 1884. By that time, this urban Jewish immigrant and merchant had become something of a latter-day Jeffersonian who believed that a healthy democracy required a prosperous yeomanry and that agriculture was the primary industry on which all else in civilization rested. Arguing that high wages, thriving businesses, and flourishing cities all depended ultimately on the purchasing power of farm families, Lubin saw the agricultural crisis of the late nineteenth century as the most critical issue facing Western civilization. Lubin believed that if the fundamental problem of falling farm prices and profits could be solved, global prosperity, and therefore peace, could be ensured. Lubin's grand but idiosyncratic vision of achieving world peace through international agricultural reform became the lodestar of his entire career following his return from Palestine.

Desiring practical experience in farming and agricultural marketing, Lubin, in association with Weinstock, purchased a 300-acre fruit orchard near Sacramento in 1885 and began growing wheat on two sections of land in Colusa County. That year Lubin and Weinstock helped launch the California Fruit Union, one of the first grower-owned cooperatives designed to market California produce east of the Rockies. Meanwhile, to address the concerns of U.S. wheat growers competing in the international market, Lubin joined the Grange and began to promote his innovative plan for tariff reform.

A Republican who favored high protective tariffs, Lubin recognized that taxes on foreign imports did little to aid farmers growing export crops like wheat and cotton. To make the tariff work for them, Lubin proposed that the federal government use tariff revenues to subsidize the transportation costs of farm exports by paying a bounty to overseas shippers. Anticipating the controversial McNary-Haugen farm export plans of the 1920s, the Lubin Plan won the enthusiastic endorsements of state Grange affiliates from California to Pennsylvania during the depression of the early 1890s. Interest in Lubin's proposal dwindled rapidly, however, after its rejection by the National Grange in 1894.

Three more years of intense campaigning not only failed to revive the idea, which finally perished on the floor of Congress in 1897, but nearly ruined Lubin's health and destroyed his marriage. Divorced in 1896, Lubin remarried in 1897 and moved back to San Francisco, where he opened a second branch of Weinstock, Lubin, and Company. With his second wife, Florence Platnauer, he had three more children.

In 1904 Lubin departed for Europe to promote yet another idea first formulated in 1896: his proposal for a "world chamber of agriculture" designed to fulfill his vision of securing world peace by fostering rural prosperity. Having been rebuffed by the U.S. Department of Agriculture, Lubin, like a twentieth-century Columbus in search of a royal patron, peddled his project from one capital to another before arriving in Rome, where he secured an audience with King Victor Emmanuel III on 24 October. Remarkably, Lubin won the support of the king and Prime Minister Giovanni Giolitti, who, in May 1905, sponsored an international conference attended by delegates from more than forty nations, including the United States. On 7 June 1905 the conferees signed a formal protocol establishing the International Institute of Agriculture (IIA). Sixty-three nations eventually ratified the treaty and joined the institute. Endowed by the king with a permanent headquarters in Rome, the IIA began functioning in May 1908.

A bicameral body, the IIA comprised a permanent committee composed of delegates from each participating government and a general assembly that met periodically to bring together representatives of private farm organizations and cooperatives. Its official duties were to collect and disseminate global crop and market data and to study the common problems facing farmers throughout the world. Though it had no legislative powers, the IIA was authorized to advise member governments regarding farm policy and to submit formal recommendations for their approval.

For Lubin, the IIA represented the first major step toward a "United States of the World, [a] world where swords and spears will be beaten into plowshares and pruning hooks" (Agresti, p. 297). Appointed in 1906 by Theodore Roosevelt as the U.S. delegate to the permanent committee, Lubin remained the guiding spirit of the IIA for thirteen more years until his death in Rome.

Although Lubin had apparently favored merging the IIA with Woodrow Wilson's proposed League of Nations, the institute retained its independence after his death and did not begin working closely with the league until 1932. Following the establishment of the United Nations at the end of World War II, the IIA was absorbed by the UN's Food and Agricultural Organization (FAO) in 1946. In 1952 the FAO established the David Lubin Memorial Library to honor this pioneer of international government and cooperation.

• Collections of Lubin's papers are housed at the Western Jewish History Center of the Judah L. Magnes Museum in Berkeley, Calif., and at the David Lubin Memorial Library of the United Nations Food and Agricultural Organization in Rome. Lubin papers can also be found at the American Jewish Archives in Cincinnati. Books and pamphlets published by Lubin include *A Novel Proposition: Revolutionizing the Distribution of Wealth: Farm Products Moved as Mail Matter* (1893); *Protection for Agricultural Staples by an Export Bounty* (1896); and *Let There Be Light* (1900).

The most important secondary source remains Olivia Rossetti Agresti, *David Lubin: A Study in Practical Idealism* (1922). Azriel Eisenberg, *Feeding the World: A Biography of David Lubin* (1965), is essentially an undocumented historical novel. Whatever factual material it contains is derived almost exclusively from Agresti's book. On Lubin's efforts during the 1890s to resettle Jewish refugees from eastern Europe, see Norton B. Stern, "The Orangevale and Porterville, California, Jewish Farm Colonies," *Western States Jewish Historical Quarterly* 10 (1978): 159–67. Regarding Lubin and the IIA, refer to Asher Hobson, *The International Institute of Agriculture* (1931).

Important information and insights on Lubin can also be obtained by examining the careers of Harris Weinstock and Simon J. Lubin. The Western Jewish History Center and the Bancroft Library of the University of California at Berkeley each have Weinstock and Simon Lubin manuscript collections. The Bancroft also possesses the papers of the Simon J. Lubin Society, established in 1936 to aid California's migrant farm workers.

MICHAEL MAGLIARI

LUBIN, Isador (9 June 1896–6 July 1978), economist and government official, was born in Worcester, Massachusetts, the son of Lithuanian and Polish Jewish immigrants Harris Lubin and Hinda Francke. His father owned a store in Worcester that sold work clothes on credit. While attending high school and Clark University in Worcester, from which he graduated with a bachelor's degree in 1916, Lubin worked for his father as a bill collector. This experience showed him the vicissitudes of industrial labor and the need for unemployment insurance. Frequently, his father's customers could not pay because of seasonal mill layoffs. In college, Lubin became intrigued with the writings of Thorstein Veblen. Deciding he would study with him, Lubin, in 1916, on a graduate fellowship, entered the University of Missouri, where Veblen was then teaching. Veblen became his mentor, major influence on his economic thought, and close friend.

In 1918 Lubin left the university with Veblen to work first as a statistician for the U.S. Food Administration and then as a special expert for the War Industries Board. Lubin found wartime Washington stimulating, meeting brilliant young economists and political scientists. Many became his friends and later colleagues in the administration of Franklin D. Roosevelt.

With the war and his job ended, Lubin departed in 1919 for the University of Michigan to continue his graduate studies, and he became assistant professor of economics. In 1922 the newly established Brookings Institution lured him back to Washington with an offer to join its staff as an economist specializing in labor's economic problems. Lubin also taught at its Robert Brookings Graduate School and in 1926 received his Ph.D. in economics from the institution. He married a graduate student at George Washington University, Alice E. Berliner, in 1923. They had one child before divorcing in 1928.

Lubin's research at Brookings convinced him as early as 1927 that although the American economy appeared robust, it had a hidden but growing unemployment problem. His study of this issue brought him to the attention of the U.S. Senate Committee on Education and Labor, chaired by Senator James Couzens (R.-Mich). In 1928, when the committee began hearings on unemployment, he served as its adviser. After the 1929 crash the ranks of the jobless swelled, and Lubin counseled New York senator Robert Wagner and Wisconsin's Robert La Follette, Jr., as they investigated depression suffering and suggested legislative remedies. These included unemployment insurance and major public works spending, which President Herbert Hoover rejected. In 1932 Lubin wed Ann Shumaker, editor of an education journal.

The next year, on Senator Wagner's recommendation, President Roosevelt's secretary of labor, Frances Perkins, hired Lubin as U.S. commissioner of labor statistics. The soft-spoken, scholarly Lubin won respect from both labor and management for his meticulously compiled and analyzed figures on employment, wages, hours, prices, and other key indicators published in the *Monthly Labor Review* and for the Consumer Price Index, which he refined and popularized. However, Lubin's influence extended well beyond data collection. He had a hand in drafting the National Industrial Recovery Act and from 1933 to 1939 served as labor consultant on the Federal Emergency Administration of Public Works, advising on wages and projects. A member of the President's Economic Security Committee (1934), Lubin assisted in the creation of the unemployment insurance part of the Social Security Act, and he helped get the 1938 Fair Labor Standards Act through Congress. Personal tragedy struck Lubin in 1935, when his second wife died shortly after the birth of their child.

Lubin and other Keynesians in the administration believed that the 1937 "Roosevelt Recession" resulted from wages that were too low, a price structure too high due to monopolistic practices in business, and too much cutback in government spending. Working mostly through Harry Hopkins, who had the president's ear, they urged stepping up deficit spending (Lubin emphasized spending that stimulated private investment) and launching the Temporary National Economic Committee (TNEC) to investigate monopoly in the United States.

Composed equally of congressmen and administration members, including Lubin, the TNEC between 1938 and 1941 conducted a thoroughgoing investigation of the economic and financial structure of American business but produced a final report with few legislative suggestions. Lubin and TNEC executive secretary Leon Henderson signed a minority statement pointing out monopolistic practices that ought to be outlawed, but the administration, preoccupied with World War II, had lost interest in trustbusting.

Lubin, too, became increasingly absorbed in defense. In 1940 Roosevelt made him deputy director of the labor division of the Office of Production Manage-

ment. The following year Lubin moved into the White House as economic assistant to the president, his job to keep track of, assemble, and interpret for Roosevelt the statistics on all war programs. Lubin's knack for presenting voluminous data concisely and clearly (Roosevelt once said "Lube's" statistical reports were the only ones he understood) led other executive officials to depend on him as well. He directed the statistical branch of the Combined Chiefs of Staff, headed the statistical staff of Hopkin's Munitions Assignment Board, and traveled to London, where he developed with his British counterpart a common statistical reporting system to facilitate planning between Roosevelt and Winston Churchill. In March 1945 Roosevelt assigned "his favorite economist" to lead the American delegation to the Allied Reparations Commission scheduled to meet in Moscow.

President Harry S. Truman subsequently named his own political appointee, Edwin W. Pauley, chief of the delegation but asked Lubin to stay on as associate representative. After months of fruitless wrangling with the Soviets, Lubin prepared a final report to Truman on the commission's failure and resigned. As an assistant secretary of state for economic affairs in 1949–1950, Lubin advised on details of the Marshall Plan. Between 1950 and 1953 he served as American minister to the United Nations Economic and Social Council, where he advocated land reform and action against international cartels. In 1952 Lubin married Carol Riegelman, who had worked for the International Labor Organization. They had no children. They originally met when President Roosevelt named Lubin America's first representative to that body in 1935. Lubin's last government position was New York State industrial commissioner, 1955–1959, under Governor Averell Harriman.

Through the 1960s and 1970s Lubin remained active. He was a member of the board of directors of the New School for Social Research and consulted for the Twentieth Century Fund and on programs in Israel for the Jewish Agency. He died in Annapolis, Maryland.

• The Isador Lubin Papers are in the Franklin D. Roosevelt Library in Hyde Park, N.Y. Two "Reminiscences of Isador Lubin" are in the Columbia University Oral History Collection. One dates from 1957 and covers his life and career to that point; the other, from 1965, is a part of the "Social Security Project" and concentrates on Lubin's role in the creation of the 1935 system.

Monographs and reports written by Lubin include *Government Control over Prices*, with Paul Willard Garrett and Stella Stewart (1920); *Miners' Wages and the Cost of Coal* (1924); *The British Coal Dilemma*, with Helen Everett (1927); *The Absorption of the Unemployed by American Industry* (1929); *The British Attack on Unemployment*, with A. C. C. Hill, Jr. (1934); *Report on German Reparations to the President of the United States, February to September 1945*, with Edwin W. Pauley (1946); *The United States Proposes United Nations Action on Cartels* (1951); and *Our Stake in World Trade*, with Forrest D. Murden, Jr. (1954).

Brief biographical sketches are in Forest Davis, "Minister to Moscow," *Saturday Evening Post*, 16 June 1945, pp. 17,

81–83; *United Nations Bulletin*, 11 Feb. 1947, p. 119, and 15 Feb. 1951, p. 171; and Spencer Calhoun, "Biggest Bill Collector," *Collier's*, 2 June 1945, pp. 17, 27. An excellent discussion of the Keynesian economists in the administration, including Lubin, and their influence on Roosevelt in 1937–1938 is in Joseph P. Lash, *Dealers and Dreamers: A New Look at the New Deal* (1988). An obituary is in the *New York Times*, 8 July 1978.

BARBARA BLUMBERG

LUBITSCH, Ernst (28 Jan. 1892–30 Nov. 1947), motion picture director and actor, was born in Berlin, Germany, the son of Simon Lubitsch, owner of a small clothing shop, and Anna Lindenstedt. Ambitions to become an actor led him to drop out of high school at age sixteen. While working in his father's shop, he studied acting with a well-known stage comedian, Victor Arnold, and began performing nights in cabarets and music halls. In 1911, Arnold, a member of the Max Reinhardt theater company, introduced Lubitsch to the celebrated German director, who employed him, chiefly in small roles, until 1917. Hired by Union-Film in Berlin as a comic actor in 1913, Lubitsch achieved a fair measure of popularity over a six-year period by acting in and then directing a series of broad comedies, usually appearing as a stereotypically Jewish character. By 1918, when he moved into feature film production, he gave up acting for the most part.

Lubitsch's success as a comic performer remained a local phenomenon. It was rather as a director of dramatic films that he attracted international attention, achieving a reputation in the United States as "the [D. W.] Griffith of Europe." From 1918 to 1923 Lubitsch directed a series of grand romantic tragedies, generally with a historical or exotic setting, most of them starring Polish actress Pola Negri, whom Lubitsch had introduced to German audiences. *Madame Dubarry* (1919), Lubitsch's third film with Negri, was released in the United States in 1920, becoming the first film to break an unofficial ban of German films after World War I. Under the title *Passion*, it achieved a critical and popular success that prompted the release of the earlier Lubitsch-Negri collaborations. Lubitsch continued to work in comedy as well, often alternating the tragic films with comic features that starred Ossi Oswalda, an actress he had discovered. Although Oswalda was billed as "the German Mary Pickford," these films were not released in the United States.

In their much-lauded handling of crowd scenes and spectacular sets, the historical dramas clearly revealed the influence of Max Reinhardt on Lubitsch, but the films' more intimate aspects won the most praise, gaining for Lubitsch renown as a "humanizer" of history. In these dramas he imported the deflating ironies of his comedies to create a distinctive keyhole view of history as something determined by what happened in the bedrooms of important personages. Much as these personages governed other people, they themselves were governed by the same libidinal drives that ruled their subjects.

If Lubitsch created a German Mary Pickford in Oswalda, Mary Pickford herself helped create the American Lubitsch by inviting him to direct her in a film in the United States. Lubitsch thus became the first of the many Germans who left their native industry for Hollywood throughout the 1920s and 1930s. After directing the historical costume drama *Rosita* (1923) for Pickford, Lubitsch struck out in a new direction when he signed a four-year contract with Warner Bros., then a small company specializing in action films, which hoped Lubitsch would bring it some prestige. Under the acknowledged influence of Charles Chaplin's *A Woman of Paris* (1923), Lubitsch created in his first Warners film, *The Marriage Circle* (1924), the kind of intimate and sophisticated romantic comedy that he would work with for the remainder of his American career.

Lubitsch returned briefly to the tragic mode with three films in the late 1920s, but it was in the series of comedies that he directed for Warner Bros. from 1924 until 1926 and in the musicals and comedies directed chiefly for Paramount from 1929 through the 1930s that Lubitsch fully established his own distinctive dramatic and visual style. These films became a major influence on other notable directors, ranging from Billy Wilder, William Wyler, and Preston Sturges to François Truffaut and Alain Resnais. When Lubitsch died, *Variety* noted he was one of the few directors whose name on the marquee could itself attract audiences. This reputation developed because the style of his films was sufficiently different that it led to coinage of the critical catchphrase "the Lubitsch touch." What the term chiefly meant was the stunning indirection of Lubitsch's camera, which announced itself by focusing on seemingly irrelevant objects to the point of obscuring narrative events, looking at a door, for example, instead of the highly dramatic actions taking place behind the door. In *Trouble in Paradise* (1932), one of Lubitsch's most stylish comedies, an entire evening's romantic encounter is shown through a series of clocks seen in close-up as the soundtrack presents snippets of dialogue between two would-be lovers.

Much as the distancing character of Lubitsch's camera encased his comedies in an insistently ironic tone, it also achieved something more that represents the most distinctive achievement of his art. The *looking away* from the main action created irony, but the *looking at* something else created metaphor. The clocks in *Trouble in Paradise*, for example, are part of a temporal metaphor that runs throughout the film and defines the nature of the love affair that is just beginning. It is this brilliant conjoining of irony and metaphor that is most characteristic of Lubitsch's films and unexpectedly blends lightness of tone with depth of meaning, a surface simplicity with a subterranean complexity.

As the United States moved from depression to World War II, Lubitsch's comedies underwent striking changes that lent his later work a greater gravity. The straightforward political content of such films as *Ninotchka* (1939) and *To Be or Not to Be* (1942) provides a historical view of the characters' lives that enriches the comic form by recalling the historical dimension of Lubitsch's German dramas. These later comedies, along with *The Shop around the Corner* (1940), *Heaven Can Wait* (1943), and *Cluny Brown* (1946), are among the most enduring of Lubitsch's films, emotionally rich and dramatically complex.

Although Lubitsch rarely enjoyed a major commercial success in the sound period, he continued to work in Hollywood and exert an influence on other directors until his death. In 1934 he was appointed head of production at Paramount Pictures, the only time in the sound era that a creative artist held the top production position at a major studio. The experience was not a happy one for either Lubitsch or the studio, but it represents an indication of the regard with which he was held. He was able to work throughout his American career with absolute independence, whether his home studio was Warner Bros., Paramount, Metro-Goldwyn-Mayer, or Twentieth Century–Fox.

Lubitsch became an American citizen in 1933. He was married twice. His 1922 marriage to Leni Kraus, a widow with two children, ended in divorce in 1930 when she became involved with Hans Kraly, a screenwriter Lubitsch had brought from Germany to work on his American films. In 1935 he married Sania Bezencenet, who worked as a literary agent under the name Vivian Gaye. They had his only child before they divorced in 1943. Suffering a debilitating heart attack in 1943, Lubitsch had to greatly curtail his activities, completing direction on only one more film, *Cluny Brown*. He died in Beverly Hills following another heart attack about halfway through *That Lady in Ermine* (1948). Although Lubitsch never won an Academy Award in competition, he was given a special Oscar eight months before his death for his contributions to the industry in twenty-five years as a director.

• Major critical studies of Lubitsch include Leland A. Poague, *The Cinema of Ernst Lubitsch* (1978), which provides an overview of Lubitsch's American films from silents to sound; William Paul, *Ernst Lubitsch's American Comedy* (1983), which focuses on Lubitsch's films from 1932 to 1948; and Sabina Hake, *Passions and Deceptions: The Early Films of Ernst Lubitsch* (1992), which discusses the films through 1932, paying particular attention to Lubitsch's work in Germany. For biographical information, see Herman G. Weinberg, *The Lubitsch Touch* (1977), and Scott Eyman, *Ernst Lubitsch: Laughter in Paradise* (1993). Barry Sabbath and Robert Carringer, *Ernst Lubitsch: A Guide to References and Resources* (1978), provides a complete filmography as well as background information on all Lubitsch films and an extensive bibliography of published writings by and about Lubitsch. Obituaries are in the *New York Times*, 1 Dec. 1947, and *Variety*, 3 Dec. 1947.

WILLIAM PAUL

LUBOFF, Norman (14 May 1917–22 Sept. 1987), choral director and arranger, was born Norman Kador Luboff in Chicago, Illinois, the son of Julius Luboff, an insurance salesperson, and Rose (maiden name unknown). Even though his parents discouraged him from entering the field of music, Norman was happily surrounded with music throughout his childhood and adolescence, enjoying his family's amateur vocal harmonizing and his membership in his high school's orchestra and choir. Foreshadowing events to come, he even organized a small choir of his teenage peers whom he taught by rote to sing in four-part harmony. However, he did not consider music as a profession until 1935, after entering Chicago's Central Y.M.C.A. College (later renamed Roosevelt University), from which he received a bachelor of arts degree in music in 1939. During these formative years Luboff's influential teachers included Richard Bloch, Alexander Vivaiski, Norman Lockwood, and Leo Sowerby.

In order to help finance his higher education, Luboff sang professionally for funerals and in church choirs, for Christmas caroling "gigs" and vaudeville theaters, for workshops with choral music education pioneer Noble Cain, and for radio broadcasts. Following his graduation, Luboff was hired by WGN of Chicago to sing in the chorus of popular radio programs. Recognized for his innate musicality, he was soon asked by the radio station's production staff to assist in the generation and preparation of music for its broadcasts. Here, Luboff developed and honed his skills as a composer and musical arranger.

In 1942 Luboff married Marilyn Pearson and was drafted into the armed services, serving in the Army Signal Corps. His marriage lasted only a few months, and in 1943, following his military tour of duty, Luboff moved to New York City where he thrived as a singer, composer, arranger, and choral director for many top radio programs, including "The Fred Allen Show," "Your Hit Parade," and "The Milton Berle Show." In 1945 he retired from his active singing career in order to concentrate more on conducting, composing, and arranging. During this time period Luboff studied composition with Aaron Copland—an endeavor that revealed Luboff's desire to maintain high standards of excellence, even in his primary field of popular music.

In November 1944 Luboff married Betty Mulliner, a professional singer, who subsequently sang for many of his shows and recordings. They had one son and one daughter. This second marriage ended in divorce in 1966.

In August 1948 Luboff moved his family to Los Angeles, where he was the choral arranger and conductor of NBC's radio show "The Railroad Hour," starring Gordon McRae in a program of light classics and popular music. Luboff gained fame from this program because the listening audience associated his name with the featured Norman Luboff Choir. Hollywood beckoned in 1951 when Warner Bros. appointed Luboff as its chief choral director; he produced choral music for films such as *Where's Charlie?*, *The Desert Song*, *The Jazz Singer*, and *Mister Roberts*. In his responsibility to rehearse and coach principal singers, Luboff worked with several well-known stars, including Bing Crosby, Frank Sinatra, and Doris Day.

Luboff also became increasingly active in the recording industry during his early years in Los Angeles. In 1951 his first album with Columbia Records, "Lullabye of Broadway with Doris Day," with the Norman Luboff Choir, was released. Luboff's total output of more than 130 recordings includes albums of the Norman Luboff Choir, often with featured artists on a variety of record labels such as RCA Victor, Decca, and Capitol. This body of recorded sound included many records for children (in collaboration with figures such as Danny Kaye and Bing Crosby) as well as theme albums on subjects including Christmas, Broadway hits, the American South, operetta, cowboy songs, hymns, Walt Disney movies, and Latin and calypso music. Luboff's copyrighted "Yellow Bird" was the most noted song of this last category, popularized by singer Harry Belafonte. What distinguished Luboff's choral music albums from others of the time was that they consisted almost exclusively of his own arrangements, which represented a vast amount of creative work.

Largely because he wished to publish his vocal arrangements himself, Luboff formed the Walton Music Corporation with cofounder Arthur Shimkin in the mid-1950s, enabling him to collect publisher's fees from performances of his music for radio and television broadcasts, films, and recordings. Subsequently, Luboff guided the growing company into the publishing of classical choral works of other composers in addition to his own arrangements of folk and popular music. Luboff's goal was to build a catalog of quality choral music from the United States and Europe, regardless of its difficulty or likelihood to be commercially successful. In particular, Walton's catalog would eventually include a large amount of Scandinavian choral music as a result of Luboff's great interest in Northern Europe and in the work of many Danish, Swedish, and Norwegian composers.

In the late 1950s and early 1960s the Luboffs lived for short periods of time in France and England as well as in Los Angeles, where he worked in the television industry on programs such as "The Dinah Shore Show" and "The Jerry Lewis Show" and continued his active recording career. In 1963 he organized a tour for the Norman Luboff Choir, the first of twenty-four such annual tours that continued until Luboff's death. Tours lasted as short as two weeks and as long as four months, depending on the particular year. Substantial amounts of classical music as well as Luboff's trademark arrangements were included in the choir's concerts, which were performed in small towns as well as major cities.

In the mid-1960s Luboff became increasingly active in visiting schools and universities, serving as a guest conductor, clinician, and workshop leader. In 1970 he and Bernie Fisher cofounded Choral Associates, an organization that featured several choral experts in summer workshop settings held across the United States. These five-day clinics promoted the publications of Walton Music Corporation, but they also presented sessions in choral rehearsal techniques and literature.

In the early 1970s he further developed his Scandinavian ties and musical interests, traveling to Sweden for a wide range of conducting engagements.

The year 1973 marked Luboff's marriage to Gunilla Marcus of Stockholm. A television producer and director, Marcus had met Luboff in 1971 in Sweden while filming a documentary on him. They resided in New York City and on Long Island except when taking their annual vacations at their summer home on the Baltic Sea island of Gotland. The final fifteen years of Luboff's life were largely spent successfully touring with his professional choir, guest conducting a wide variety of ensembles, teaching at choral workshops, and maintaining his strong connection with Scandinavian music and musicians.

Luboff was the recipient of a Grammy Award for his 1960 album "Songs of the West" and was a Grammy nominee in 1961 and 1962. In 1985 he became the first foreigner to receive the Swedish honor of the Hugo Alfven Award, honoring his championing of the music of Sweden. He died in Bynum, North Carolina.

Luboff was a significant contributor to the growth and rising popularity of choral music, introducing it to a vast audience through his broadcasts, recordings, concerts, teaching, compositions and arrangements, and publications. He was highly instrumental in broadening the awareness of Scandinavian music in the United States and in fostering the performance of the folk music of many countries, including his own. As an ardent and visible advocate of the choral art in general, Luboff stands as an important figure on a national and international scale.

• Virtually all of Luboff's published compositions and arrangements are part of the catalog of the Walton Music Corporation. Some 1,500 of his unpublished works are held by the Library of Congress, and most of his commercial recordings have remained out of print. The best source on details of his life and work is Julie Lane Carter, "Norman Luboff: His Life, Career, and Professional Choir" (Ph.D. diss., Arizona State Univ., 1993), which includes an extensive bibliography. An obituary is in the *Chicago Tribune*, 24 Sept. 1987, and two tributes are in the *Choral Journal* (Feb. 1988).

STEPHEN COKER

LUCAS, Frederic Augustus (25 Mar. 1852–9 Feb. 1929), naturalist and museum administrator, was born in Plymouth, Massachusetts, the son of Augustus Henry Lucas, a clipper ship captain, and Eliza Oliver. Until age eighteen Lucas lived in Plymouth, where he attended public schools. At the age of six he crossed the Atlantic on his father's ship for the first time. Thereafter he often sailed with his father, circling the globe twice. He had no intention, however, of making sailing a career. At an early age he developed a keen interest in natural history, particularly in collecting birds, a common avocation of the period. On voyages he often caught seabirds and stuffed them, and he took advantage of time ashore in foreign lands to study local natural history. He was particularly adept at working with tools and innovating when appropriate tools were not available. He also kept detailed notes and developed exceptional artistic skills, abilities that served him well throughout his life. When he was eighteen, his skills, enthusiasm, and understanding of natural history led to employment at Henry A. Ward's Natural Science Establishment in Rochester, New York. He remained there for eleven years (1871–1882), acquiring broad knowledge of vertebrate anatomy and learning many museum skills, specializing in the cleaning and articulation of skeletons. His scientific, administrative, and teaching efforts led to his being put in charge of the preparation of museum exhibits at Ward's, where he influenced many workers who went on to become prominent figures in American museums.

Lucas left Ward's to accept a position as osteologist (1882–1887) at the U.S. National Museum in Washington, D.C., where he later became assistant curator in the Division of Comparative Anatomy (1887–1893), then curator (1893–1904). By 1902 his duties at the National Museum included simultaneously serving as curator of comparative anatomy, curator of fossil vertebrates, and staff member in charge of exhibits and the children's room.

In 1904 Lucas left the National Museum to become curator in chief of the Museum of the Brooklyn Institute of Arts and Sciences (later the Brooklyn Museum), an institution that was acknowledged to be in chaos. His efforts brought order, exemplary exhibits of educational value to the public, and further recognition within the museum community as a strong but kind leader who could win controversies without losing friends. In 1911 he became director of the American Museum of Natural History in New York City, then the major natural history museum in the United States. He served in that position until 1923, then as honorary director until his death.

Lucas's work reflected his belief that a museum should be an educational institution, not merely a repository for curiosities. He sought educational value in exhibits through carefully selected and mounted specimens and meticulously prepared labels. Many of his osteological and paleontological displays were enjoyed for many decades by visitors to the museums where he was employed, as well as at several museums where he provided technical assistance in exhibit development.

Lucas served as acting president (1913–1918) of the National Association of Audubon Societies after William Dutcher was incapacitated by a stroke and the Audubon Board refused to name a new president while he was alive. He also served the society as second vice president (1912 and 1919–1929). Lucas was active in the Biological Society of Washington, serving as secretary, vice president, and president (1901–1902). He was an honorary member of the Historical Society of St. Louis and a fellow of the New York Academy of Science and American Ornithologists' Union (AOU). He also served on the board of directors of the Explorers Club and as a council member of the AOU (1905–1929).

Lucas was clearly a well-rounded naturalist, but birds remained a focus of his research throughout his life. Mammals were also of great interest to him, and he was particularly proud of the Hall of Mammals at the American Museum, which was at one time named the Lucas Hall. Although adept at fieldwork and often involved in obtaining anatomical and paleontological specimens in the United States, he participated in only three major expeditions. The first (1887) was to Funk Island off the coast of Newfoundland to collect skeletal material of the extinct great auk. The second (1896–1897) was as a member of a U.S. commission to investigate the condition of the fur seal herd in the Pribilof Islands, which continued to dwindle even after sealing on the island was prohibited. His anatomical studies determined that seals killed on the high seas were from the Pribilofs; as a result, the killing of seals on the high seas was banned, settling this international controversy in the favor of American claims. His last major expedition (1903) was to Newfoundland for the National Museum, to obtain a cast and skeleton of the blue whale.

Lucas was a prolific author, producing more than 360 papers and two books, *Animals of the Past* (1901) and *Animals before Man in North America* (1902). He wrote extensively for popular audiences and had a gift for interpreting science for the public. The breadth of his knowledge of natural history allowed Lucas to contribute numerous zoological entries to the *Universal Cyclopedia* and the *International Encyclopedia*. He was among the first to study variability in avian anatomy, and his studies of the tongues and skeletons of birds culminated in publications that contributed greatly to the understanding of systematic relationships among birds. In his writing and dealings with colleagues, Lucas often displayed a sense of humor—at times sardonic, as in his well-known regulations for the conduct of modern museums: "A Museum is an institution for the preservation and display of objects that are of interest only to its owners. It is also a place where paintings, bric-a-brac, trophies of the chase, etc., may be deposited whenever their owner wishes to have them stored temporarily without expense to himself."

On 13 February 1884 Lucas married Annie J. Edgar; they had two daughters. He died at his home in Flushing, Long Island, New York.

• Collections of Lucas's papers are in the archives at the Smithsonian Institution and the American Museum of Natural History, and manuscripts are at the New York Botanical Garden. For information about Lucas's tenure at the American Museum, see Geoffrey Hellman, *Bankers, Bones and Beetles* (1968, 1969). An autobiography and bibliography were published by the American Museum of Natural History, *Fifty Years of Museum Work* (1933). Obituaries include those by Charles H. Townsend, *Science* 69 (1929): 445–56, and *Auk* 47 (1930): 147–58, and Robert Cushman Murphy, *Natural History* 29 (1929): 211–14, as well as the *New York Times*, 10 Feb. 1929.

JEROME A. JACKSON

LUCAS, Howard Johnson (7 Mar. 1885–22 June 1963), organic chemist, was born in Marietta, Ohio, the son of William Lucas, a telegraph operator, and Marian

Curtis. After completing his high school education in Columbus, he entered Ohio State University, receiving bachelor's and master's degrees in chemistry in 1907 and 1908. His chemistry teacher, a University of Chicago Ph.D., urged him to continue his studies at Chicago. After one year, however, his hopes for a Chicago doctorate were dashed when he had to leave school because of his father's death and the family's financial difficulties. The U.S. Department of Agriculture employed Lucas from 1910 to 1913 in its Bureau of Chemistry. The bureau's task was to develop standards and tests for food purity following the enactment of the Pure Food and Drug Act. Lucas analyzed the composition of commercial food products and tested for adulterants. His duties took him to the agricultural experiment station in Puerto Rico for one year to study the Puerto Rican dairy industry.

In 1913 Lucas moved to southern California hoping that this region of expanding population might offer a teaching opportunity. Throop College of Technology, a small Pasadena school, hired him, and he remained there until his retirement in 1955. Following a reorganization in 1920 the college became the California Institute of Technology, a novel hybrid of university and research organization that aimed to do path-breaking research and be on the cutting edge of science. Lucas was only to teach organic chemistry to undergraduates. However, he proved to be highly original and stimulating in both teaching and research and many talented students earned their doctorates under his direction.

For one-half of his Caltech career Lucas was the only organic chemist on a faculty that included some of the world's most eminent scientists. He spent ten years developing a curriculum with extremely high standards, and he inspired gifted students to choose organic chemistry despite the presence at Caltech of physical chemists with stronger reputations and better funding. William G. Young and Saul Winstein were the best known of his Ph.D. students; they later created at the University of California at Los Angeles one of the world's foremost centers for physical organic chemistry.

Lucas rose slowly through the professorial ranks, serving as an associate professor from 1915 to 1940 before becoming a full professor. Because he lacked a Ph.D., both promotion and recognition of the importance of his research came late in life. Only after his retirement was he elected to the National Academy of Sciences. His devotion to teaching resulted in two books for undergraduates. He created the model for all modern organic chemistry textbooks with his *Organic Chemistry* (1935). Now a classic with its novel electronic interpretations of structures and reactions, it was the first text to introduce modern electronic theories of valency and the chemical bond. In 1949 he wrote the widely used *Principles and Practice in Organic Chemistry* with David Pressman, a former student and head of immunochemistry at the Sloan-Kettering Institute for Cancer Research. He also was a consultant to the Kelco Company in San Diego from 1932 to 1940. Based on Lucas's patent, Kelco manufactured sodium alginate, the gelatinous substance in kelp and other seaweeds, for use in food products, especially ice cream.

Lucas was central to the development of physical organic chemistry in the United States. To elaborate a physical approach to traditional qualitative organic chemistry he applied the ideas of three major scientists: Gilbert N. Lewis of the University of California at Berkeley, his Caltech colleague Linus Pauling, and the British chemist Christopher Ingold. His starting point was the electronic theory of valency of Lewis, who in 1916 proposed the electron-shared or covalent bond. Electron-sharing enabled Lucas to explore and interpret relationships between organic structure, reactivity, and the course of reactions. In the 1930s Pauling developed the resonance theory, whereby electron-sharing is delocalized because of the wave nature of electrons. Lucas found this conception essential to understanding a variety of structures and reactions. Ingold used chemical kinetics and physical measurements to unravel the intermediate steps in organic reactions. Few American organic chemists appreciated how significant these new conceptions and approaches could be for organic chemistry. Lucas did, and he made the first clear use of them in interpreting the behavior of organic substances. Beginning in 1924 he published papers explaining the course of many fundamental organic reactions, combining modern chemical theories with rigorous and careful experimentation using pure substrates, precise analytical techniques, and physical measurements.

Lucas's most important research contributions were accomplished between 1935 and 1945, especially those in collaboration with Winstein. They produced a series of elegantly conceived and executed investigations that provided evidence for the existence of new types of cyclic ions formed as intermediates in organic reactions. They demonstrated the necessity of these in order to account for the stereospecificity of the reactions and the products formed. The Lucas and Winstein studies greatly expanded the use of physical methods in organic chemistry, the cyclic ions being part of a scheme in which kinetics, mechanisms, and stereochemistry converged to provide penetrating insights into the nature of organic reactions.

The reaction mechanisms proposed by Lucas often involved Pauling's resonance theory. A striking instance of such was a series of papers by Lucas and Winstein on the formation of metallic ion-unsaturated complexes with the metallic ion embedded in the electron cloud of the double bond and not strictly covalently bonded to either carbon atom. Measurement of physical constants documented their formation and illustrated the role of resonating wave forms in stabilizing the structures. Although Lucas here utilized the new ideas of Pauling as he also did extensively in his 1935 book, he remained throughout his life an independent thinker who kept abreast of current developments in chemical theory and used whatever he found valuable.

In a 1939 paper Lucas and Winstein discussed neighboring-group participation, finding that substituents near to but not connected to the reactive center of a molecule can play a major role in a reaction by forming an intermediate that determines the stereochemical configuration and direction of the reaction and products. Furthermore, they proved that neighboring-group participation was common in organic reactions. It was a significant contribution, relevant to carbohydrate, steroid, and heterocyclic chemistry, to the synthesis of such natural products as hormones and vitamins, and to the question of how enzymes and substrates interact in living systems.

Lucas died in Pasadena; he had never married. He was an active outdoorsman, mountain climber, camper, and hiker. Easygoing, affable, and modest, Lucas had to endure the snobbery of some of the Caltech faculty who looked down on him for his lack of a doctorate. His alma mater, Ohio State, did award him an honorary doctorate in 1953. His contributions are often overlooked by writers on Caltech and on American chemistry. Lucas pioneered the physical approach to organic chemistry in his teaching, writing, and research. With Young and Winstein he made southern California a center for research on reaction mechanisms. His own research was important in gaining recognition of physical organic chemistry. After World War II all areas of traditional organic chemistry and of biochemistry were affected by the new field, which proved to be enormously fruitful, especially in revolutionizing organic synthesis by showing how to control the stereochemical direction of reactions through knowledge of intermediates and mechanisms.

• The Caltech Archives have only a small amount of material relating to Lucas; his papers were collected after his death but were subsequently lost. Young and Winstein wrote the biography of their mentor for the National Academy of Sciences, *Biographical Memoirs* 43 (1973): 163–76, which contains a bibliography of his ninety-three publications. Brief accounts of his career are in *Chemical and Engineering News*, 23 Feb. 1953, p. 778, and in the Caltech publication, *Engineering and Science*, Mar. 1953. Leon Gortler portrays Lucas's role in "The Development of a Scientific Community: Physical Organic Chemistry in the United States, 1925–1950," in *Essays on the History of Organic Chemistry*, ed. James Traynham (1987), pp. 95–113. An obituary is in the *New York Times*, 25 June 1963.

ALBERT B. COSTA

LUCAS, Jonathan (1754–1 Apr. 1821), millwright, was born in Cumberland, England, the son of John Lucas and Ann Noble. His mother's family owned mills in Whitehaven, and he learned that trade in his youth. He married Mary Cooke in 1774; they had five children. After she died, sometime between 1783 and 1786, he married Ann Ashburn of Whitehaven.

Lucas migrated to Charleston, South Carolina, in about 1786 and sought employment in his trade. Gideon Dupont had recently perfected a system of flooding the Carolina ricefields with tidal flows, and this system was being adopted by more and more planters. How-

ever, they had difficulty removing the husks from the increasing volume of rice. From the late 1690s on the South Carolina Assembly had issued various patents for pecker-type rice mills powered by animals, but none had been very successful.

Recruited by a Santee rice-planter, Lucas immediately began to experiment with wind and water as sources of power. Before long he had developed a new kind of pounding mill; initially it seems to have been powered by wind, but before long water became the source of energy, with the mill being driven by a large, undershot water-wheel. The earliest recorded mill built by Lucas was that of J. Bowman of Peach Island Plantation on the North Santee River in 1787; the water was drawn from a backwater reserve. Lucas's first tidal mill, operating automatically with each ebb tide, was built for Andrew Johnstone at Millbrook Plantation on the North Santee in 1791. He constructed a tidal mill with a better design for Henry Laurens's plantation on the west branch of the Cooper River in 1793. This mill, equipped with rolling screens, elevators, and packers, was so efficient that only three people were needed to run it; it could beat from sixteen to twenty barrels on a strong tide. The threshed rice was carried in buckets on a revolving belt to screens for removing sand and trash, and then moved to hoppers above five-foot rotating millstones, which removed the husks. The rice was next struck several dozen times a minute by 200-pound iron pestles in mortars, where the fine covering of the rice grain was removed. After this a rolling screen removed the flour, a fan blew off the rest of the chaff, revolving drums with prepared sheepskins polished the rice, and the packers put the clean rice into barrels. Lucas and his son, Jonathan, Jr., installed mills throughout the Coastal Carolina rice region.

In 1803 Lucas bought a plantation on Shem Creek in Christ Church Parish, where he set up a combined rice and saw mill called Greenwich Mills. Then, with two carpenters, he bought land in Charleston and built more rice mills. In 1817 Lucas constructed his first steam-driven rice mill. His plans served as the models for all later rice mills.

Lucas died in Charleston. Jonathan Lucas, Jr. later constructed a number of rice mills in London and Liverpool, England, where unpolished Carolina rice—which stood the Atlantic passage better—was cleaned. Another son, William Lucas, became the largest rice planter in Charleston District.

• There are a number of Lucas papers held by the South Carolina Historical Society in Charleston. For a review of Lucas's construction of rice mills in South Carolina, see "A Lucas Memorandum," *South Carolina Historical Magazine* 69 (1968): 193. See also David Doar, *Rice and Rice Planting in the South Carolina Low Country* (1936); George C. Rogers, *The History of Georgetown County, South Carolina* (1970); and Joyce E. Chaplin, *An Anxious Pursuit: Agricultural Innovation and Modernity in the Lower South, 1730–1815* (1993), with accounts of mills constructed by Lucas. There is an obituary in the *Charleston Mercury*, 2 Apr. 1821.

JAMES M. CLIFTON

LUCAS, Robert (1 Apr. 1781–7 Feb. 1853), congressman, governor of Ohio, and territorial governor of Iowa, was born at Shepherdstown, Jefferson Country, Virginia, the son of William Lucas, a land owner, and Susannah Barnes. Born into a family of some wealth and social standing, Lucas was educated in surveying and mathematics by a Scottish private tutor. In 1800 the family moved to Scioto County, Northwest Territory (later Ohio). Lucas's emerging career exemplified the opportunities offered on the frontier: he was the county surveyor after Ohio statehood in 1803, justice of the peace for Scioto County, and an officer in the state militia. His rapid rise from lieutenant in 1804, to colonel in 1809, and to brigadier general by 1810 testified to the expanding militia in Ohio as well as to the influence of Lucas's friends. In 1810 he married Elizabeth Brown, who died in 1812; the couple had one child.

At the outbreak of the War of 1812, Lucas served as messenger and liaison to General William Hull. Although sufficiently detached to escape connection with Hull's disastrous invasion of Canada and his subsequent surrender of Detroit, Lucas recorded in his journal one of the most complete accounts of the ill-fated campaign. Declining two commissions in the regular army, he passed the remainder of the war as a recruiter and staff officer in the militia.

With the end of the war, Lucas became actively involved in state politics. He had previously served in the lower house (1808–1809); he subsequently represented his district in the state senate (1814–1822, 1824–1828, 1829–1830) and again in the lower house (1831–1832). He strongly supported Andrew Jackson, attracted by Jackson's western origins, patriotism, and military achievements as well as his political principles. Throughout this time, Lucas lived in Piketon (Pike County), where he ran a general store. As a legislator, Lucas vigorously supported canal construction in Ohio and the expansion of public education.

Lucas married Friendly Ashley Sumner in 1816. Her skills as a hostess and her quick wit were important sources of support in his political ambitions. They had five children, and the family lived in a large, two-story brick house on 437 acres that bore Lucas's wife's name, "Friendly Grove." He united with the Methodist church in 1819 and strongly supported this denomination for the rest of his life. The family home hosted Methodist circuit riders as well as local and state political figures.

In 1830 Lucas, who had achieved a considerable reputation in Ohio politics, was nominated for governor on the Democratic ticket. Although he lost narrowly to Duncan McArthur, he was nominated again and elected in 1832 and reelected in 1834. The office of governor of the state of Ohio under the constitution of 1803 was a weak one. The salary was only $1,000 per annum. The governor had no veto power and almost no authority in appointments, giving the legislature a dominant voice in state affairs. In his first term, Lucas threw the limited weight of his office behind the expansion of the state's internal improvements; in the second, he was largely preoccupied with the boundary controversy between Ohio and Michigan known as the "Toledo War."

In 1838 President Martin Van Buren appointed Lucas governor of the newly established Iowa Territory. Lucas's governorship was marked by partisan and personal disputes with the legislature and other officials. Although the immediate issue was territorial expenses, Lucas and the legislature were more generally at odds over the authority of the governor in a newly organized territory in an age of increasing popular participation. Lucas, veteran of a time of greater deference to authority and steeped in a military service that emphasized loyalty and obedience, vigorously stood by the governor's authority. These powers of absolute veto, sole authority in appointments, control over expenditures, and command of the militia seemed excessive and arbitrary to a younger generation of ambitious political figures who recognized the real source of authority in a widening franchise rather than in officials in Washington, D.C. Nor did Lucas's personality soften the clash, for he was imperious in manner, intense in his convictions, and generally stern and unbending in his policies. This conflict overshadowed what was, in many respects, a capable and even farsighted administration that dealt effectively with many of the problems facing a new territory and its people, including inexperienced legislators, border disputes, and the need to defend against possible Indian attacks.

When William Henry Harrison appointed the Whig John Chambers as the new governor of Iowa Territory in 1841, Lucas retired to his estate "Plum Grove" near Iowa City. He remained active in the causes of temperance and public education until his death at Plum Grove.

• Manuscripts, letters, and papers of Robert Lucas are at the State Historical Society of Iowa, Iowa City. For published writings, see John C. Parish, ed., *The Robert Lucas Journal of the War of 1812* (1906), and Betty Hall, comp., *Personal Letters of Robert Lucas, Governor of Iowa, and of His Sister Lavisa Steenbergen, 1809–1863* (1990). Parish also wrote a biography, *Robert Lucas* (1907). Additional family information can be found in Anne Beiser Allen, "Friendly's Frontier; Images from the Life of Friendly Lucas, Iowa's 'First Lady,'" *Palimpsest* 73 (Spring 1992): 18–31.

MALCOLM J. ROHRBOUGH

LUCAS, Scott Wike (19 Feb. 1892–22 Feb. 1968), lawyer and U.S. senator, was born in Chandlerville, Illinois, the son of William Douglas Lucas, a tenant farmer, and Sarah Catherine Underbrink. After attending public schools in Bath, Illinois, Scott graduated from high school in nearby Virginia, Illinois, in 1911. With the advice and financial assistance of an older brother, he entered Illinois Wesleyan University, where he studied law, graduating in 1914. As his family was of modest means, Lucas worked his way through college with a variety of jobs, including playing baseball in the summers with the Peoria, Illinois, team in the Triple I League (Ind., Ill., and Iowa). A popular student, he played on the varsity football and basketball teams, sang in the glee club, and participated in various student activities. Following graduation, he taught for a year in a one-room schoolhouse. In 1915 he passed the bar exam and opened a law practice in Havana, Illinois, a tough town on the Illinois River. In 1917 he entered the army as a private and attained the rank of lieutenant by the end of World War I. His unit was awaiting shipment overseas when the war ended. Returning to Havana, he resumed his law practice and won election in 1920 as state's attorney for Mason County. He served one four-year term before returning to private practice. In 1923 he married Edith Biggs; they adopted a son.

In 1932 Lucas sought the Democratic party's nomination for the U.S. Senate; however, he was defeated in the primary by the forces of the powerful Kelly-Nash political machine, which then dominated Chicago and Cook County. The following year Governor Henry Horner, a reform-minded Democratic opponent of the machine, appointed Lucas as chairman of the State Tax Commission. In 1934, with Horner's urging, Lucas successfully sought the U.S. House seat left vacant by the death of Speaker of the House Henry T. Rainey, who had been Lucas's idol. In 1938, after two terms in the House, Lucas once again challenged the Kelly-Nash machine for the party's Senate nomination, this time with the support of Governor Horner. He defeated the machine candidate in the primary and won election to the Senate. Following his primary victory, he mended his fences with the Kelly-Nash forces and thereafter received the machine's full support. He won reelection to the Senate in 1944 and in 1946 was elected Democratic whip by his Senate colleagues. In 1949 he became Senate majority leader, succeeding Alben Barkley, who had been elected vice president.

Throughout his legislative career, Lucas enthusiastically supported the New Deal of President Franklin Delano Roosevelt and the Fair Deal of President Harry S. Truman. Considered an expert on farm policy, he was frequently consulted by the White House on agricultural matters. In 1940 he supported President Roosevelt's efforts to prepare for war and in 1941 backed the lend-lease program. During World War II Lucas advocated a larger international role for the United States and sought to rally support in Illinois for a more internationalist foreign policy. In 1944, speaking before the Illinois American Legion, he urged his fellow veterans, who had once elected him their state commander, to abandon isolationism. Arguing in support of a strong postwar world organization, he stated: "The world does not ask for a debating society of nations. We can not have another League of Nations without teeth to enforce its mandates" (*New York Times*, 23 Feb. 1968). With the onset of the Cold War, Lucas backed the Truman administration's containment policies, including the Marshall Plan, the North Atlantic Treaty Organization (NATO), and American involvement in the Korean War. Although a party loyalist, Lucas at times differed with both Roosevelt and Truman. In 1937 he denounced Roosevelt's Supreme

Court reorganization plan to "pack" the Court with justices favorable to the New Deal. He called Roosevelt's scheme "full of destruction" and considered his address on the Senate floor regarding the issue as "perhaps the greatest speech of my career." Lucas's sharp disagreement with Roosevelt on the Supreme Court issue may have caused the president to bypass him as a possible running mate in 1940 and again in 1944. Lucas later differed with Truman on the need for national health insurance.

As Senate majority leader, Lucas was popular with his colleagues. Nevertheless, he controlled only forty of the fifty-four Democratic votes in the Senate. A moderate liberal, he sought to advance President Truman's Fair Deal agenda but was often defeated by a coalition of conservative southern Democrats and Republicans who opposed proposed legislation on civil rights, public housing, federal aid to education, and national health insurance, an issue Lucas personally opposed. Like most moderate liberals, he was placed on the defensive in February 1950 by the allegations of Senator Joseph McCarthy that the Truman administration had knowingly tolerated Communists in the State Department. In an unsuccessful strategy to discredit McCarthy, Lucas appointed a Senate investigating committee, headed by Senator Millard E. Tydings of Maryland, but McCarthy frustrated their attempt to secure any substantiation of his charges. Thus, the issue of Communist sympathizers in the government remained a powerful one for Republicans in the 1950 election campaign.

Over six feet tall, trim and fit even in his later years, Lucas was an outstanding golfer and loved fishing and duck hunting. He was an expert marksman and once earned entry into the *Guinness Book of World Records* for downing three ducks with a single shot. He enjoyed playing poker and liked "plain, solid food, good Bourbon, and male talk" (*New York Times*, 23 Feb. 1968). Raised a Baptist, Lucas considered himself an agnostic in his adult years. A sharp dresser who favored double-breasted suits, he had a charming and gracious manner and was a captivating storyteller. His hunting and fishing companions nicknamed him the "Old River Pirate," and throughout his career he was known for giving free legal advice "to any farmer, ballplayer or war veteran" (Schapsmeier and Schapsmeier, "Scott W. Lucas of Havana," p. 304).

In the 1950 campaign Lucas was challenged by former U.S. congressman Everett McKinley Dirksen, who successfully made the Illinois Senate race a referendum on Truman's liberal programs and internationalist foreign policy. Lucas's candidacy was hindered moreover by the adverse publicity of Senator Estes Kefauver's Committee to Investigate Organized Crime in Interstate Commerce, which conducted hearings into police corruption in Cook County, Illinois. Lucas's defeat by 294,000 votes was nonetheless primarily caused by Truman's general unpopularity and voter apprehension about American involvement in the Korean War. Lucas regularly supported the president but was not always in complete agreement with him. During the campaign Lucas wrote to a constituent: "You must remember as Majority Leader I am compelled to reconcile some of my viewpoints with those of the president. . . . I have flexed my conscience a bit on some things" (Schapsmeier and Schapsmeier, "Scott W. Lucas of Havana," p. 314).

Following his election defeat, Lucas unsuccessfully sought the position of commissioner of major league baseball. He returned to his legal practice, maintaining offices in Washington, D.C., and Illinois. He also worked as a lobbyist in Washington, representing major corporations, commercial associations, and the Republic of Panama. He remained active in Democratic politics and maintained a regular correspondence with Truman. He supported the Great Society of President Lyndon Johnson and believed his administration was following a proper cause in the Vietnam War and other Cold War confrontations. In 1966 he wrote Johnson, "I have complete faith in your ability to see that this country of ours is ultimately victorious in the troublesome problems you have on foreign soil."

During his Senate career, Lucas had suffered from heart problems, and in 1966 complications from diabetes caused circulatory problems necessitating the amputation of his left leg above the knee. He died in Rocky Mount, North Carolina, while on a train destined for Florida.

• The Lucas papers are in the Illinois State Historical Library in Springfield. Also see Edward L. Schapsmeier and Frederick H. Schapsmeier, "Scott W. Lucas of Havana: His Rise and Fall as Majority Leader in the United States Senate," *Journal of the Illinois State Historical Society* 70 (Nov. 1977): 302–20, and the same authors' *Dirksen of Illinois: Senatorial Statesman* (1985). Obituaries are in the *New York Times* and the *Chicago Tribune*, 23 Feb. 1968.

MICHAEL J. DEVINE

LUCE, Clare Boothe (10 Apr. 1903–9 Oct. 1987), writer and political figure, was born Ann Clare Boothe in New York City, the daughter of William F. Boothe, a businessman and pit-orchestra violinist, and Ann Clare Snyder, a former dancer. She spent her childhood in Chicago and Memphis and also lived for a year in France with her mother after her parents separated. She attended several private schools, including St. Mary's in Garden City, Long Island, from 1915 to 1917, and then Miss Mason's School in Tarrytown, New York, from which she graduated in 1919. As a child, Clare Boothe had briefly been an understudy to Mary Pickford in a stage play and a bit player in a motion picture. Determined to become an actress, after graduating from secondary school she became a student at Clare Tree Major's School of the Theatre in Manhattan. After only a few months, however, she withdrew to accompany her mother and stepfather on a trip to Europe.

During her visit abroad, Clare Boothe met New York society matron Mrs. O. H. P. Belmont. Belmont, an active campaigner for woman suffrage, inspired Boothe's interest in women's rights. She also introduced the young woman to her future husband,

New York clothing manufacturer George Tuttle Brokaw. The couple married in 1923 and had one child. After their divorce in 1929, Boothe resumed her maiden name.

In 1930 Boothe joined the staff of *Vogue*, the fashion magazine, as an editorial assistant. A year later she became an associate editor at *Vanity Fair* and began contributing short satirical sketches to the magazine; these were collected and published as *Stuffed Shirts* in 1931. Boothe became managing editor of *Vanity Fair* in 1933 but left the magazine a year later to write plays.

Boothe made her debut as a playwright in November 1935 with a Broadway production of *Abide with Me*, a psychological drama about an abusive husband that received mostly negative reviews. That same month she married Henry Robinson Luce, the editor and publishing executive who had founded *Time* magazine a decade earlier and later created *Life*—reportedly at his wife's suggestion—and *Fortune*. Clare Luce continued to write plays, and her second Broadway production, *The Women*, opened in December 1936. Critics dismissed this satirical play about rich women as "brittle" and "superficial," but audiences loved it. It ran for 657 performances, later toured the United States and eighteen foreign countries, and was eventually made into a motion picture.

Luce's next play, *Kiss the Boys Goodbye*, a comedy that premiered in 1938, was also well received by audiences. Two years later she had still another popular success with her third Broadway production, *Margin for Error*, a comedy-melodrama that concerned the murder of a Nazi agent. Like *The Women*, these plays were eventually made into motion pictures. By now, however, Luce had turned her attention from playwrighting to public affairs.

In the spring of 1940, soon after the outbreak of World War II, Luce traveled to Europe as a *Life* journalist to report her observations of daily life in Italy, France, Belgium, and the Netherlands. The material that she collected proved too extensive for a magazine article, and it was published later that year as a book under the title *Europe in the Spring*.

Luce became active in Republican party politics in the summer of 1940, when she declared her support for presidential candidate Wendell Willkie. In campaign appearances on behalf of Willkie she denounced President Franklin D. Roosevelt for failing to prepare the United States for war. She continued to follow the international situation closely, and in 1941, during a trip through China with her husband, she sent back dispatches to *Life* describing that country's war with Japan. In early 1942, after the United States had entered World War II, Luce undertook an extensive tour of Africa, India, China, and Burma, interviewing a number of prominent figures, including the Chiang Kai-sheks, Jawaharlal Nehru, and General Joseph Stilwell, for *Life*.

In the summer of 1942, after Luce returned to the United States, the Connecticut Republican party named her to run as a nominee for representative from that state's fourth congressional district, which included Fairfield County, where the Luces maintained a country home. Luce cited her firsthand acquaintance with international affairs as an important qualification. She won the nomination handily over six opponents and went on to defeat the Democratic candidate in the fall election, campaigning on a platform that called for a hard-line approach to the war effort.

In Washington, D.C., the new congresswoman received a coveted appointment to the powerful House Military Affairs Committee. She attracted wide attention with her maiden speech on the House floor, in which she attacked Vice President Henry Wallace for proposing a so-called freedom-of-the-air policy for postwar America to maintain international peace. Denouncing Wallace's ideas as "globaloney," she endeared herself to isolationists and other conservatives by calling for "civilian, as well as military, control of the air." In answer to criticism, Luce maintained that she was not championing universal American control but reciprocal arrangements that would ensure each nation's control over its own skies.

Luce continued to attract national attention through numerous speeches and radio broadcasts. In many of them, as well as in debate on the House floor, she took a strongly partisan line in attacking the Democratic administration's foreign policy, although for the most part she voted to support it. By 1944 her speaking ability had made Luce one of her party's leading luminaries, and in June of that year she gave the keynote address at the Republican National Convention, which nominated Thomas E. Dewey as the party's presidential candidate.

Dewey lost that election to Roosevelt, but Luce was reelected to a second term in Congress. She spent Christmas 1944 with American troops in Italy, and, when she returned, she urged Congress to appropriate aid for Italian war victims. In 1945 Luce began warning against what she perceived as a growing Communist threat internationally; her anti-Communist stance became increasingly pointed in the years that followed. During her second term in Congress she also served as a member of the Joint Committee on Atomic Energy and strongly supported the creation of the Atomic Energy Commission to bring atomic energy under civilian control.

In 1946 Luce announced that she would not seek reelection. Earlier that year she had made a widely publicized conversion to Roman Catholicism, the consequence of a spiritual journey begun two years earlier following the accidental death of her only child. Luce claimed that she now wanted to devote more time to writing, on both secular and religious issues. In 1947 she contributed a series of articles to *McCall's* magazine on her conversion, and in the following years she wrote numerous other articles for both religious and secular journals. She received an Academy Award nomination in 1949 for the screenplay of *Come to the Stable* and two years later wrote another play, *Child of the Morning*. At this time Luce began collecting and editing a series of essays on various saints; titled *Saints for Now*, it was published in 1952. During these years

Luce was often mentioned as one of the world's most admired women, and many former critics noted that her self-centeredness had been supplanted by unselfishness and compassion.

Luce reentered politics in the spring of 1952, when she announced her support of General Dwight D. Eisenhower for the Republican presidential nomination. She also made an unsuccessful attempt to secure her party's nomination for U.S. senator from Connecticut. During Eisenhower's successful fall campaign, Luce made nearly fifty radio and television speeches on his behalf. Rewarding her for this support, in early February 1953 President Eisenhower named Luce ambassador to Italy. Although some conservative Protestant groups in the United States opposed her nomination, fearing that, as a Catholic, she would undertake secret diplomatic relations with the Vatican, she successfully laid such concerns to rest during her confirmation hearings, expressing her firm support for "the American tradition of separation of church and state." Confirmed in early March, a month later she moved to Rome, accompanied by her husband.

During her three years as ambassador to Italy, Luce carried out her diplomatic duties with vigor. She was a forthright opponent of Communism and warned that American aid to Italian industry would be cut off if left-wing forces in the labor movement gained control. She resigned from the post in 1956, after battling a mysterious illness that was finally diagnosed as arsenic poisoning caused by flakes of paint from her bedroom ceiling.

Three years later President Eisenhower nominated Luce as ambassador to Brazil, and she was confirmed despite the persistent opposition of Senator Wayne Morse of Oregon. When Luce, in a parting shot, said that Morse's behavior was caused by his being "kicked in the head by a horse," a public uproar resulted, and at the urging of her husband Luce resigned from the post.

Luce continued to be active in Republican politics, becoming increasingly identified with the conservative wing of the party. In 1964 she seconded the nomination of Arizona senator Barry Goldwater as the Republican presidential candidate, and later that summer she announced that she would run as a Conservative party candidate for the U.S. Senate from New York. Under pressure from both liberal Republicans and Senator Goldwater, Luce resigned from the race shortly before the Conservative party convention. Henceforth, she spent more time at a house owned by the Luces in Phoenix, where she enjoyed an active social life and devoted much of her time to needlepoint, painting, and creating mosaics. She also continued to write articles as well as another play, *Slam the Door Softly* (1970).

After Henry Luce's death in 1967, Clare Boothe Luce moved to Honolulu. In 1983 she moved to an apartment in the Watergate complex in Washington, D.C., where she died.

• Clare Boothe Luce's papers are housed in the Manuscript Division of the Library of Congress. Biographical information can be found in Wilfrid Sheed, *Clare Boothe Luce* (1982), and in Ralph G. Martin, *Henry and Clare: An Intimate Portrait of the Luces* (1991). For detailed information on Luce's plays and their production, see Mark Fearnow, *Clare Boothe Luce: A Research and Production Sourcebook* (1995). An obituary is in the *New York Times*, 10 Oct. 1987.

ANN T. KEENE

LUCE, Henry Robinson (3 Apr. 1898–28 Feb. 1967), journalist and publisher, was born in Tengchow, China, the son of Henry Winters Luce, a missionary and educator, and Elizabeth Middleton Root, formerly a social worker for the Young Women's Christian Association. Although their income was limited, the Luces lived well in China. They maintained a devout Presbyterian home, and young "Harry" Luce displayed a precocious interest in sermons; even as an adult, he prayed on his knees before going to sleep. Luce also shared his parents' faith in America and its global destiny; Theodore Roosevelt was his lifelong hero.

Luce was an intelligent, determined young man. Though afflicted with a stammer, he did not let the fear of ridicule impede his performance at the Hotchkiss School, which he attended from 1913 to 1916. At Yale College, Luce helped to edit the *Daily News* and was an enthusiastic advocate of U.S. entry into World War I. After a stint in the Reserve Officers Training Corps at Yale, the army sent him to boot camp near Columbia, South Carolina. Late in 1918 Luce received his commission as a second lieutenant in the U.S. Army. The Armistice prevented him from serving in Europe, so Luce returned to college in 1919. His peers voted him the "most brilliant" member of his graduating class (1920). After receiving his B.A., Luce sailed to England to study at Oxford University. After his return to the United States he worked at mundane jobs with newspapers in Chicago and Baltimore.

Briton Hadden, whom Luce had known at Hotchkiss, Yale, and in the army, shared his friend's enthusiasm for journalism. At boot camp they had discussed the possibility of starting a new kind of publication. The two men wrote a prospectus for potential backers and planned to call their magazine *Time*. Luce and Hadden intended to rewrite newspaper articles and wire reports into brief, snappy stories. The new magazine, they argued, would appeal to busy people eager to gain insights into a rapidly changing world. In 1921 and 1922 Luce and Hadden were actively promoting their project, for which they raised $86,000. The first issue of *Time* was dated 3 March 1923, and the magazine had about 12,000 initial subscribers. The same year Luce married Lila Ross Hotz; they had two sons.

After initial difficulties, *Time* and its parent Corporation, Time, Inc. (Luce and Hadden soon dropped the comma), attracted a growing readership. The "book," as Luce called it, prided itself on solid research. *Time* offered compelling human interest stories and shared the values of its largely middle-class, well-educated readers. Its editors tried to explain a fast-moving, complicated world in simple terms—some said too simple. Cofounder Luce, however, was quite different from the product he sold: a complex, intense, humorless man, with work at the heart of his life. He had little small talk and lacked social graces. *Time*, by contrast, was sometimes too slick and clever; it made mistakes (eagerly pounced on by critics), but its more serious flaw was an editorial tendency to ignore or suppress inconvenient facts.

Luce freely admitted that he rejected the classic definition of journalistic objectivity. In his view, an editor needed to reveal his values to his readers. Then the editor would weigh both sides in a dispute and tell readers which argument best reflected the values presumably shared by readers and editors. *Time* was thus in favor of civil rights and against the Ku Klux Klan and racism; in favor of Charles Darwin and opposed to fundamentalists; supportive of capitalism and hostile to Communism; in favor of repeal and derisive of Prohibition; sympathetic to Christianity (religion was a "goddam good thing," said Luce) and against atheism.

Luce walked a fine line between the smart-aleck and the sophisticate; *Time*'s irreverence, snideness, and cleverness increased its readership. Thanks to Briton Hadden, coinages like "cinemactor," "tycoon," "socialite," and "kudos" quickly made their way into the American language. Nobody had ever seen anything like this readable, spunky magazine. Luce maintained his balance, however, and in 1927 *Time* turned a small profit.

After the death of Hadden in 1929, Luce was depressed. He quickly pulled himself together, however, and returned to his new project, *Fortune* magazine. Luce felt that businessmen failed to understand how their work affected and reflected the complexities of a modern, changing society. *Fortune*, he declared proudly, would provide entrepreneurs with a literature of their own. He insisted that his new publication be superbly researched and lavishly produced. *Fortune* cost an enormous sum—one dollar per issue.

Luce, a good advertisement for what he later called the "American proposition," had become a millionaire by 1929. Despite the onset of the Great Depression, he insisted on bringing out *Fortune* in 1930. It made Luce an important figure on Wall Street. He did not rest on his laurels, and in 1932 Time Inc. purchased *Architectural Forum*. In 1935 the company inaugurated a documentary film series, "The March of Time." These newsfilms, the most imaginative of the era, soon appeared in thousands of theaters worldwide.

In 1935 the Luces divorced, and later that year Luce married Clare Boothe Brokaw, an editor and aspiring playwright. Bright, beautiful, and sometimes acerbic, Clare Boothe Luce avidly sought the personal publicity her husband shunned. After a few years their marriage became troubled, but they eventually settled into a friendly rivalry, a partnership between two brilliant but very different people.

When Harry Luce wed Clare Boothe Brokaw, he was heavily involved in a major new project. Luce wanted to start a pictorial magazine, although others had failed in the attempt, and he bought the rights to a defunct magazine, *Life*. The first issue appeared late in 1936, and *Life* quickly won the affection of millions of weekly readers. Its stories ranged from the maudlin to the spectacular, and scenes of tragic accidents appeared side by side with tales of great human achievements. With its marvelous photographs and snappy captions, *Life* was the television of its era. Luce liked to say that *Time* made enemies, while *Life* made friends. With *Life* Luce gained a mass readership, sometimes estimated at 20 million per week. He was more than an entertainer, however; he was a kind of lay evangelist whose magazines were his pulpit. Luce intended to profit from people's curiosity about the world, but he also wished to edify and uplift. Using the latest techniques in photojournalism, *Life* featured stories on painters like Rembrandt and lavish celebrations of Christmas. Soon, long, serious, well-edited essays began to appear in some issues.

By 1937 Luce believed that the world was headed for a disaster that only the United States could prevent. He rushed to support China's resistance to the Japanese invasion. Time Inc.'s media publicized Japanese atrocities; Luce himself organized United China Relief (1941–1946), which funneled millions of dollars in private donations to the besieged regime of Chiang Kai-shek. Luce was also a generous supporter of the Yale-in-China Association and of Christian colleges in China, and later of United Service to China. He did not remain indifferent to the dire events in Europe, either; he watched Hitler's Germany with growing concern.

Though not immune to the prejudices common to his elite social class, Luce supported *Fortune*'s pioneering study of anti-Semitism in America. He also visited Nazi Germany before war erupted and returned to the United States convinced that a new world war would soon come and that an awakened America could determine its outcome. Although he mistrusted President Franklin D. Roosevelt and much of his New Deal, Luce supported the president when he seemed to be helping the Allies and rearming the United States. After France fell in 1940 Luce met with Roosevelt on 25 July. He urged that the president dispatch over-age U.S. destroyers to Britain in return for the use of naval and air bases in the Western Hemisphere. During the next months Time Inc.'s media strongly supported conscription and the Lend-Lease Bill. Isolationists reviled Luce as a warmonger, especially after he published his famous essay, "The American Century," in *Life* in the winter of 1941. The editorial argued that the United States could determine the outcome of the war, then build a free and orderly world after an Allied victory.

During the war Time Inc. grew ever more influential. Luce's reach extended beyond the world of journalism. In 1940 he virtually created the presidential candidacy of Republican Wendell L. Willkie. Russell W. Davenport, managing editor of *Fortune*, ran Willkie's campaign and wrote his major addresses. Luce and his circle helped to move the Republican party away from isolation, enraging isolationists, but no partisan Republican could complain about Luce's adversarial coverage of Roosevelt.

Luce's relationship with the Democratic president had again grown sour, in part because Time Inc.'s partisan and personal jibes at Roosevelt enraged the president. Roosevelt refused to let the publisher visit his beloved China and even denied a Silver Star medal to *Time*'s John Hersey, because the correspondent worked for Luce. Despite this enmity, Time Inc. flourished in wartime.

Throughout the war Luce was troubled by the agony of China. His chief correspondent in Chungking, Theodore H. White, warned Luce that *Time* was giving Americans an excessively optimistic view of Chiang and his war effort: the Communists were growing stronger, thanks largely to the corruption and incompetence of Chiang's regime. Luce refused to heed the warnings. He was the impresario of Madame Chiang Kai-shek's spectacular U.S. visit in 1943, when Luce and his network helped turn the Chiangs into national celebrities. After the Allied victory Luce returned to China, where he again found grounds for optimism. American aid and good will, he believed, could save China from civil war. Another visit late in 1946 left him troubled, realizing that China was heading for civil war. He saw the Communists under Mao Tse-tung as the culprits, but Luce also blamed the Russians for Chiang's troubles. In his view, the Soviet Union and its friends around the world were maligning Chiang and advancing the Marxist cause of his enemies. Luce, who had visited the Soviet Union in 1932, came home convinced that Communism was a collectivist nightmare. As tensions between Joseph Stalin's regime and the West troubled Europe after 1945, Luce became an early advocate of massive U.S. resistance to Soviet expansion in both Europe and Asia. Hersey and White refused to share Luce's views on Russia and China and departed from Time Inc. in 1945 and 1946, respectively. Luce, who had a paternalistic view of his company, saw departures as disloyalty.

In 1947 a grateful Chinese government bestowed the Order of the Auspicious Star on Luce, but he did not really understand the China of poor peasants and desperate city dwellers. As an adult Luce knew little Chinese and visited China as the guest of its fading elite. He saw China through a missionary lens crafted by his father.

When things went badly for the Nationalists after 1947, the Luce media refused to blame Chiang or his American friends for the debacle. Instead, *Time* asked, "Who lost China?" To Luce, the answer was clear: liberals and Communist sympathizers had given the U.S. administration bad advice; American failure, compounded by Soviet treachery, had brought about Chiang's expulsion in 1949. Clare Boothe Luce, who served two terms in the U.S. House of Representatives (1943–1947), became a vocal part of the "China lobby," which argued against the recognition of Communist China and for the dispatch of military and economic aid to Chiang on Taiwan.

Luce's efforts on behalf of anti-Communism in Asia were tireless. He helped to fund and lead the China Institute in America and the Committee to Aid Refugee Chinese Intellectuals, and he was an active member of the Committee of One Million Against the Admission of Communist China to the United Nations.

Although Luce and *Time* were early critics of the demagogic Senator Joseph R. McCarthy, they were equally hostile to McCarthy's targets in the Harry Truman administration. Given Truman's failure in Asia, Luce awaited the day when his beloved Republican party ("my second church") would return to power. In 1951 and 1952 he helped engineer the nomination and election as president of General Dwight D. Eisenhower.

Luce was victorious, but in the process he enraged both liberals and conservatives. The followers of Senator Robert A. Taft, whom Eisenhower had defeated for the nomination, often blamed Luce and his allies for their hero's downfall. They resented *Time*, which had effectively accused the Taft forces of "stealing" several southern delegations. In the 1952 campaign *Time* so savaged Democratic candidate Adlai E. Stevenson that its senior editor, Thomas S. Matthews, a friend and admirer of Stevenson, left the magazine. But Luce finally had a good friend in the White House, and the grateful Eisenhower named Clare Boothe Luce ambassador to Italy.

Henry Luce hoped that Secretary of State John Foster Dulles, whom *Life* had helped to promote since 1944, would lead a new crusade to roll back Communism in Europe and eastern Asia. Luce was disappointed when Truman's containment policy continued, but in public his criticism of Eisenhower and Dulles remained discreet.

These were good years for Luce and Time Inc. In the 1930s *Life*'s vision of a future consumer's paradise had brightened the spirits of weary Americans. During the 1950s Luce celebrated postwar American civilization as humane, reverent, and prosperous. By the end of the Eisenhower era, Time Inc.'s prosperity reflected that of the nation: *Life* was selling almost 6 million copies a week, and *Time* about 2 million. In 1954, hoping to profit from the population's search for leisure and pleasure, Luce started the successful magazine *Sports Illustrated*. Time Inc. earned revenues of more than $200 million in 1955.

By this time many prominent people, both in the United States and abroad, viewed Luce as a kind of private head of state. Foreign leaders and journalists often assumed that his magazines spoke for the Eisenhower administration—and they sometimes did. When he traveled abroad to meet prime ministers and kings, Luce received treatment often accorded only to leading statesmen. Administrations sought his support for intervention in foreign lands, and *Time* provided plausible cover for U.S. intervention in places like Iran, Guatemala, and Lebanon.

Liberals were appalled by Luce's influence, but even angry subscribers found themselves compelled to read *Time*, which offered insights and details that escaped most daily newspapers. Sophisticated readers discounted *Time*'s bias and enjoyed it, in part because Luce had an extraordinary ability to find editorial talent. He paid high wages and knew how to extract the last ounce of energy and intelligence from his staff. He drove people by his own example. Though gruff and sometimes withdrawn, he liked to argue, before deciding that his opinion had carried the day. He rarely gave direct orders, but everyone knew who ran the company.

An ardent advocate of civil rights for all Americans, Luce was anxious to right historic wrongs. He opposed the powerful Ku Klux Klan in the 1920s. In the 1930s *Time*'s persistent documentation of lynchings enraged southern segregationists. Luce was a major supporter of the Urban League and an early backer of the United Negro College Fund.

In the 1960 presidential election Time Inc. was remarkably even-handed, thanks to Luce's friendship with Ambassador Joseph P. Kennedy. Luce, who had promoted young John F. Kennedy's book *Why England Slept* in 1940, liked the Democratic candidate and had easy access to him after his election. Asia was still very much on his mind; after an encounter with Luce, President Kennedy decided not to change U.S. policy toward Communist China. At the same time the Luce publications emphasized the American stake in Vietnam. Luce patronized the American Friends of Vietnam, and between 1954 and 1963 Time Inc. favored President Ngo Dinh Diem with enormous publicity. As the United States became more entangled in the jungle war ravaging Vietnam, Luce remained an ardent supporter of President Lyndon Johnson's failing venture. *Time*'s strident support for the war, maintained for three years after Luce retired in 1964, hurt the magazine's credibility.

There was bad news on another front as well. The growing attraction of television to advertisers undermined *Life*, but Time Inc. as a whole continued to be immensely prosperous during and after Luce's retirement. Luce died in Phoenix, Arizona.

Robert M. Hutchins, perhaps the most important university educator of his day, argued that Luce's magazines did more to shape the American character than "the whole education system put together." The poet Carl Sandburg called Luce the "greatest journalist of all time." Even Luce's enemies agreed. Franklin Roosevelt saw Luce as a dishonest troublemaker capable of undermining his foreign policy, and Harry Truman denounced the Luce press as too big, partisan, and powerful.

When many Americans were confused about a troubling issue, they often looked to the Luce media for guidance, especially in small towns with weak newspapers. By promoting the candidacies of Willkie and Eisenhower, Luce helped to move a moribund Republican party toward internationalism, moderation, and victory. In his "American Century," Luce espoused an ideology of optimism and globalism that many Americans adopted from the 1940s through the mid-1960s. His ceaseless insistence that the United States prevent the spread of Communism in Asia helped to prepare the public for the Vietnam War, and his "China network" worked effectively for U.S. assistance to Taiwan, South Korea, and South Vietnam.

Luce changed the world of journalism. *Time* created the newsmagazine; *Fortune* changed business journalism; the "March of Time" was the best newsfilm of its era; and *Life* revolutionized and dominated photojournalism. These achievements show Luce to have been the most innovative and influential American journalist and publisher during the first half of the twentieth century.

• Luce's papers are in the Manuscript Division of the Library of Congress; much material relevant to his life is also in the papers of Clare Boothe Luce in the same repository. Other collections with relevant materials include the papers of John Shaw Billings at the South Caroliniana Library, Columbia, S.C.; materials in the Archives Department at Time Inc.; and the papers of Daniel Longwell and W. A. Swanberg, both in the Rare Books and Manuscripts Library at Columbia University. For Luce's important speeches, see John K. Jessup, ed., *The Ideas of Henry Luce* (1969). A standard source on both Luce and Time Inc. is the three-volume, authorized history of the company: Robert T. Elson, *Time Inc.: The Intimate History of a Publishing Enterprise*, vol. 1, *1923–1941* (1968), and vol. 2, *1941–1960* (1973), and vol. 3, by Curtis Prendergast and Geoffrey Colvin, *1960–1980* (1986). Biographies of Luce include W. A. Swanberg, *Luce and His Empire* (1972); James L. Baughman, *Henry R. Luce and the Rise of the American News Media* (1987); and Robert E. Herzstein, *Henry R. Luce: A Political Portrait of the Man Who Created the American Century* (1994).

ROBERT EDWIN HERZSTEIN

LUCE, Molly (18 Dec. 1896–16 Apr. 1986), painter, was born Marian C. Luce in Pittsburgh, Pennsylvania, the daughter of Artemus Barrett Luce and Celia Clark. Shortly after her birth, Luce moved with her parents to Bethlehem, Pennsylvania, and then to Glen Ridge, New Jersey, where she graduated from high school in 1914. She spent her childhood summers and many vacations well into her married life with the families of her maternal and paternal grandparents in northeastern Ohio—especially in the town of Kingsville. Luce had wanted to be an artist from the time of her high school graduation, but her parents persuaded her that two years of a liberal arts program at Wheaton College in Norton, Massachusetts, would provide her with a broader education before art school. After graduating from Wheaton with the class of 1916, she enrolled in the Art Students League in New York City and took classes from 1916 through 1922 in painting with F. Luis Mora, George Bellows, and Kenneth Hayes Miller, in drawing with Boardman Robinson, George Bridgman, and Solon Borglum, in composition with Jay Hambidge, and in color with H. G. Maratta.

A yearlong European tour that began in the fall of 1922 gave Luce the opportunity to visit historic collections in France, Italy, Switzerland, and England and to settle into work in St. Paul du Var and Paris. Europe allowed her style and subject matter to come together as well as fostering a conviction that, in her words, "as much as I enjoyed looking at sixteenth-century Europe, I believed that it was more important for me, at least, to paint twentieth-century America." She returned to the United States with a portfolio of paintings, one of which she exhibited at the Whitney Studio Club in May 1924. Reviews were excellent, and she was nominated by fellow artist and associate director of the club, Alexander Brook, for her first solo show that fall. The reviews were again excellent and referenced, as they would throughout the 1920s, Sinclair Lewis's *Main Street*. The *New York Herald Tribune* wrote that she "makes mild caricatures of 'Main Street' life and character" (30 Nov. 1924), while the *New York Evening Post* commented, "It is a pretty severe indictment she makes in her hideous Main Streets and straggling villages" (8 Jan. 1927). Her affectionate yet critical view of small town and rural America was in harmony with the art public and art critics alike for the next quarter-century, as they embraced regionalism, realism, and paintings of the American scene as the major forces in "modern" American art.

In 1925 Luce began a romance with fellow Art Students Leaguer Alan Burroughs, who was a painter, budding art historian, curator, and soon to be the developer of X-ray technology as a tool for investigation of works of art. Burroughs was also a member of a prominent art family: his father was chief curator of the Metropolitan Museum and a successful painter, his mother Edith Woodman Burroughs had been a respected sculptor who had exhibited in the Armory Show of 1913, and his sister Betty, a sculptor in her own right, was the first wife of painter Reginald Marsh. Luce had been married briefly to a fellow student at the Art Students League, Ernest Stock, but while the divorce was pending she accompanied Burroughs to his new job as curator at the Minneapolis Institute of Art. The couple married in Greenwich in 1926; they would remain childless, but Molly Luce acquired a stepson, Bruce Burroughs, from Alan's first marriage. The success of his X-ray film technique was such that Burroughs received an appointment at the Fogg Art Museum at Harvard. The young couple had barely unpacked in Boston before they took off in the summer of 1926 for a research trip to Europe.

Luce suggested that the success of her 1924 exhibitions and the disruptions of moving and travel sent her into an artistic slump: "Although I painted not more than three pictures which showed distinct progress in the next three years, I saw more paintings and more picture galleries than most artists see in their lifetimes. And I saw them, literally, from the inside." However, in 1927 she returned to the United States and held a series of well-received exhibitions in New York, where she was compared for the first time with Charles Burchfield: "Miss Luce amplifies the powerful and acrid vision of a Charles Burchfield with an unreserved, if slightly amused, love of that scene's raw beauty" (*New York Times*, 6 Feb. 1927).

In 1926 the Whitney had acquired one of Luce's paintings, and shortly it and the Metropolitan Museum each had two of Luce's works in their permanent collections. Luce was a regular participant in the 1920s, 1930s, and 1940s in traveling exhibitions that went to the majority of the major U.S. museums that were interested in contemporary American art; she also participated in the major annual juried exhibitions.

From 1925 until 1929 Luce experimented with precisionism, an American style that paralleled cubism's sharp geometric divisions with rulered lines and angled compositions, but in the 1930s her canvases grew larger and bolder as she entered the mainstream of the regionalists. By the mid-1930s she was regularly showing her work alongside that of Grant Wood, John Steuart Curry, Thomas Hart Benton, Joe Jones, and others at the most prominent New York galleries dealing in contemporary American art. The Burroughses in 1928 moved from Boston to Belmont, Massachusetts, and in 1931 they bought a summer house, "Threeways," in Little Compton, Rhode Island. Burroughs retired from Harvard in 1941, and the couple moved the next year to Little Compton permanently.

Although she had had a close relationship with the Whitney, the last painting Luce exhibited there was in 1950, as it was for many of her colleagues, because the tide of taste had changed toward more abstract forms of art. She had few venues for her painting over the next quarter-century, but she continued to paint and develop entirely new ways of expressing herself. Nature had always been a love of hers, and she was an avid gardener, birdwatcher, and all-around naturalist. Her new paintings were increasingly glorifications of nature; people and their works appear only occasionally in the later paintings. Most remarkably, she poured out an enormous volume of work during a period when she received almost no recognition from the art establishment.

In 1980, however, a retrospective traveling museum exhibition of more than fifty paintings opened at the Museum of Our National Heritage in Lexington, Massachusetts, and went on to more than a dozen other American museums. Once again public interest in scene painting increased, and she was able, in the last years of her life, to see appreciation from a public that included museum goers as well as prominent critics. She died in Little Compton.

Luce's friend and fellow student at the Art Students League, art historian Lloyd Goodrich, wrote in the foreword to *Molly Luce: Eight Decades of the American Scene* (1980):

From her very first painting, Molly Luce was herself. Through her five years at the League, her stay in Italy and France, and her and Alan's many friends in the art worlds of New York and Boston, she was fully aware of current trends, traditional and advanced, representational and abstract; but from the beginning her dominant interest was in the American Scene, pictured naturalistically. There was no trace of chauvinism in this,

as with the Mid-West regionalists of the time; she simply wanted to paint the world she knew and loved, truthfully, with humor (but not satire), and often with an element of imaginative fantasy. Her subject matter has been centered on country and village life in America, specifically in New England, and more specifically, in Little Compton. Few painters have captured so authentically the character and flavor of rural New England.

Luce enriched the painted view of America in more than eighty years of painting and more than 1,000 canvases and panels that give great critical insight into the mores and foibles of her fellow citizens and the joys of and dangers to the natural world. She has been called the most important woman painter of the American scene and the most important New England regionalist; in the mid-1920s she was given the sobriquet the "American Brueghel" by Henry McBride of the *New York Sun*, and she is credited by Robert McGrath with being the leader of the small but influential group of "American Brueghelists."

• The most complete primary source is Luce's unpublished autobiography, "An Artist's Angle" (c. 1952), a copy of which is at Arents Library, Syracuse University. D. Roger Howlett and Lloyd Goodrich, *Molly Luce: Eight Decades of the American Scene* (1980), is a thorough exhibition catalog. Deborah J. Wilk, "Molly Luce: Landscape and American Culture, 1920–1939" (master's thesis, Univ. of Wisconsin, Milwaukee, 1994), discusses the cultural iconography of two decades of Luce's work. Robert L. McGrath, *Paul Sample: Painter of the American Scene* (1988), has a section on the Brueghel Revival in regionalist painting and makes the case for Luce anticipating other painters in using Pieter Brueghel the Elder as a model. Edward J. Sozanski, "Welcome Back, Molly, You've Been Missed," *Providence Sunday Journal Magazine*, 17 Aug. 1980, is an affectionate portrait of the artist with good insights into her paintings based on interviews. Robert Taylor, "The Ordinary, the Fantastic," *Boston Globe Magazine*, 26 Oct. 1980, contains a fine analysis of Luce and other painters of the American scene and is especially good as criticism of her late work. Obituaries are in the *Boston Globe*, the *Boston Herald*, and the *Providence Journal-Bulletin*, all 17 Apr. 1986; and *Antiques and the Arts Weekly*, 25 Apr. 1986.

D. ROGER HOWLETT

LUCE, Stephen Bleeker (25 Mar. 1827–28 July 1917), rear admiral in the U.S. Navy, was born in Albany, New York, the son of Vinal Luce, a druggist, and Charlotte Bleeker. In 1835 Stephen's family moved to Washington, D.C., where his father had obtained a position as a clerk in the Treasury Department.

In 1841 Luce was appointed a midshipman. After six months of training he joined the frigate *Congress* on duty in the Mediterranean and then in South American waters. While on that station Luce saw his first, but inglorious, naval action, during which Commodore Philip Voorhees had an entire Argentine naval squadron seized. Returning to New York in 1845, Luce was stationed on the 74-gun ship of the line *Columbus*. The *Columbus* sailed for the Far East, where it was based until being called home upon the outbreak of the war with Mexico.

After the war Luce attended the U.S. Naval Academy in Annapolis, Maryland, which had opened in 1845. While there, he was falsely implicated in a disturbance and reduced in seniority by seventy-two numbers. This injustice was not rectified until 1862, despite the fact that he passed his examinations at the top of his class. Luce graduated in 1849, and in August of that year he reported to the sloop of war *Vandalia*. In May 1853 Luce joined the steamer *Vixen* and served briefly with the Home Squadron in Pensacola. He then received orders to the U.S. Coast Survey for a three-year tour of duty. In 1854 Luce married Eliza Henley, a childhood friend. They had three children.

Luce served from 1857 to 1860 in the sloop of war *Jamestown* with the Home Squadron in the West Indies and off the coast of Central America. In May 1860 he reported to Annapolis, where he accepted an assignment as instructor in seamanship and gunnery. This shore duty allowed Luce his first opportunity to write for publication. In 1862 he revised a short gunnery manual, *Instruction for Naval Light Artillery, Afloat and Ashore*, first written in 1859 by Lieutenant William H. Parker, who had since joined the Confederate States navy. Next he began to compile a textbook on seamanship, but he had to abandon the project when ordered to report to the screw frigate *Wabash*, the flagship of the Atlantic Blockading Squadron under Rear Admiral Silas H. Stringham. In January 1862 Luce returned to the staff of the Naval Academy and resumed work on his unfinished textbook, *Seamanship*. The book went through nine editions and was the standard American manual on the subject in the late nineteenth century.

In the summer of 1863 Luce received his first command, the academy practice ship *Macedonian*. After a cruise in European waters he submitted a report on European naval training and later used the information in articles in the *Army and Navy Journal* that recommended a training system for the U.S. Navy. Luce's next assignments were the monitor *Nantucket*, the *Sonoma* in 1864, and the *Pontiac*. In June 1865 he returned to the Naval Academy as a commandant of midshipmen. In September 1868 Luce returned to sea duty and remained in this capacity until September 1872, when he became equipment officer of the Boston Navy Yard, moving up to captain of the yard shortly after his promotion to captain. Luce became increasingly interested in naval training. In 1873 he delivered a lecture to the newly established Naval Institute titled "The Manning of the Navy and the Mercantile Marine," which was published as the first article of the first issue for the Naval Institute's *Proceedings* in 1874.

In late 1874 Luce supervised the fitting out of the sloop of war *St. Mary's* to become the New York State Maritime School. For use in this school and others like it, Luce prepared a textbook, *The Young Seaman's Manual* (1875). While in command of the naval training ship *Minnesota*, Luce initiated a system of annual awards of medals and prizes for proficiency in training. In April 1881 Luce was promoted to commodore and was appointed commander of the U.S. Naval Training Squadron.

After working to secure the permanent acquisition of Coaster's Harbor Island for the navy, Luce worked to establish a school for the advanced education of naval officers in the highest aspects of their profession: diplomacy, strategy, tactics, international law, and logistics. In March 1884 he approached Secretary of the Navy William Chandler, who appointed Luce to head a board to consider the proposal. Chandler formally approved the establishment of the Naval War College in October 1884, appointing Luce its first president. The college opened a year later for a month-long series of lectures. Luce recruited Lieutenant Tasker Bliss of the army and Professor James Soley as the college's first faculty members. For the following year Captain Alfred Thayer Mahan prepared lectures linking naval history to international affairs, and the lectures were published as *The Influence of Sea Power upon History, 1660–1783* (1890).

In June 1886 Luce left the Naval War College to resume command of the North Atlantic Squadron. While in this capacity he became involved in the Canadian-American fisheries dispute, a complex issue involving party politics in Congress as well as foreign relations. Luce found himself heavily criticized in Washington for his role in the controversy. Leading Republican congressmen attacked the administration for their stand on the issue, and the secretary of the navy reprimanded Luce for dealing directly with Canadian officials. A year later, however, the State Department commended Luce for his tact, judgment, and discretion in conducting negotiations in Haiti over the steamer *Haitian Republic*. While he was serving as the senior officer in the navy, Luce was the president of the Naval Institute from 1887 to 1889. He retired from active duty on 1 February 1889.

Settling in Newport, Rhode Island, Luce remained active in the life of the Naval War College, frequently lecturing and writing. In 1892 he served as commissioner general of the U.S. Commission for the Columbian Historical Exposition in Madrid, Spain. In 1901 the Navy Department ordered Luce to return to active duty at the Naval War College, where he remained a member of the staff until 1910. During this period President Theodore Roosevelt appointed him to the commission headed by Secretary of the Navy Dwight Moody to consider how to reorganize the Navy Department in a way that best reflected its military character. Luce died at his home in Newport.

Luce was the foremost intellectual leader and the catalyst for the development of professional education, training, and thought in the U.S. Navy from the 1860s to about 1910. He was a key leader during the period of innovation, reform, and revitalization in the 1880s and 1890s.

• For manuscript collections, see the guide to the collection at the Library of Congress, *David Foote Sellers and Stephen B. Luce: A Register of Papers*; and the guide to the collections at the Naval War College, Evelyn M. Cherpak, comp., *Register* of the Papers of Stephen B. Luce. The major published works are Albert Gleaves, *The Life and Letters of Rear Admiral Stephen B. Luce* (1925); John D. Hayes and John B. Hattendorf, *The Writings of Stephen B. Luce* (1975); Hattendorf et al., *Sailors and Scholars: The Centennial History of the Naval War College*, chs. 1–4 (1984); and Hattendorf, "Luce's Idea of the Naval War College," *Naval War College Review* (Sept.–Oct. 1984). For his experiences in the *Columbus* in 1845–1848, see Hattendorf's annotated edition of Charles Nordhoff, *Man of War Life* (1985), which includes an article by Luce as an appendix. An obituary is B. A. Fiske, "Stephen B. Luce: An Appreciation," U.S. Naval Institute *Proceedings* 43 (Sept. 1917): 1935–40.

JOHN B. HATTENDORF

LUCHESE, Thomas (1 Dec. 1899–13 July 1967), garment manufacturer and criminal entrepreneur, was born Gaetano Luchese in Palermo, Sicily. While neither the names nor occupations of his parents is known, they immigrated to New York in 1911, bringing their son with them. The family settled among other Sicilians in the predominantly Italian sections of East Harlem. Luchese learned the rudiments of reading and writing and became a plumber's helper and apprentice machinist. Sometime between 1915 and 1919 he lost his right index finger in an ammunition plant accident. In 1921, when Luchese was first arrested, a policeman jokingly referred to him as "Three-Finger Brown," an allusion to a well-known baseball player, Mordecai "Three-Finger" Brown. Much to Luchese's discomfort, the nickname stuck, and he himself sometimes used the name "Thomas Brown."

As a young man, the 5′2″ Luchese frequently attracted the attention of law enforcement agents. His 1921 arrest, for automobile theft, took place at a Long Island bootleggers' hangout, and it led to a conviction and a three-year sentence in a New York penitentiary. Luchese became involved in the Italian lottery in East Harlem and was twice arrested (but not convicted) for receiving stolen property. In 1928 and 1930 he was charged (but not indicted) in murder cases. He was, moreover, rumored to have assisted Charles "Lucky" Luciano in the mysterious gangland murder of Salvatore Maranzano in 1931. Luchese appeared frequently with entertainment, sporting, and underworld figures. In 1931 police detained him and Luciano in Cleveland, Ohio, where the two were attending the Stribling-Schmeling prizefight. Luchese had grown up in the same neighborhood in East Harlem as Frank Costello and Carlo Gambino, later major underworld figures. The Luchese and Gambino families had known one another in Sicily. Luchese was the godfather of Carlo Gambino's son, who later married Luchese's daughter.

In the mid-1930s Luchese began to prosper. By 1931 he had married Kitty (maiden name unknown), with whom he had two children. He labored as a window cleaner, then became involved in construction and trucking operations in the New York garment district. He appears to have been most successful in the garment center, where violence and union racketeering were commonplace. Ultimately he became principal owner of Braunell, Ltd., which produced a respected line of women's clothing. During World War II Luchese obtained contracts for military uniforms. Afterward he was associated with a construction company that built tract houses in upstate New York.

Luchese pursued an upwardly mobile, conservative lifestyle. He purchased exclusive homes in suburban New York and dressed in well-cut business suits. In 1943 he was naturalized in a federal court in Newark, New Jersey, and in 1950 he obtained a certificate of good conduct from the New York State Parole Board, removing the bar his 1921 felony conviction had placed on his right to vote. Luchese successfully lobbied Congressman Vito Marcantonio (who had also grown up in Luchese's neighborhood) to nominate his son for an appointment to the U.S. Military Academy. Apparently without telling them of his criminal record, Luchese began to court a variety of aspiring politicians, prosecutors, and judicial officials. One judge remembered him as "an agreeable little man who rarely said anything."

Luchese's political activities became a significant issue in the 1950 mayoral campaign in New York. Republican candidate Edward Corsi claimed that both Tammany Democrat Ferdinand Pecora and independent Vincent Impellitteri were tools of the underworld, with Costello backing Pecora and Luchese supporting Impellitteri. Indeed, Corsi argued that Luchese in 1945 had dictated the selection of Impellitteri as city council president.

When Impellitteri won the election, Luchese came under intense scrutiny. In 1951 a special committee chaired by Senator Estes Kefauver heard testimony that Corsi had vastly overstated Luchese's political influence, but Rudolph Halley, the committee's chief counsel, resigned his position to launch a political career based in part on the claim that Luchese had replaced Costello as New York's dominant underworld political power. A New York state crime commission in 1952 held extensive hearings into Luchese's background and political contacts. Most of the political figures involved professed not to have known of Luchese's past. Certainly, Luchese had retained contact with prominent figures in the underworld. He angrily protested, however, the suggestion that he was involved in the narcotics traffic. "Any man who got a family should die before he goes into any of that kind of business," he asserted (*New York Times*, 22 Nov. 1952).

In the late 1950s and early 1960s concern over organized crime continued to mount. While Luchese was not arrested at the celebrated gathering of underworld figures at Apalachin, New York, in 1957, his name was publicly linked with the meeting. In 1958 he was questioned by a select Senate committee about his ties to union violence and corruption. Most sensational of all, in 1963 underworld figure Joseph Valachi, who had known Luchese in the early 1930s, testified about the inner workings of organized crime. Valachi maintained that a highly structured Italian-American cartel known as La Cosa Nostra dominated the underworld. Luchese, he claimed, had been an "underboss" in one of New York's five organized crime "families" from the time of the Maranzano murder in 1931 until 1953, when he had taken over as "boss." Luchese also supposedly served as a ranking member of "the Commission," which oversaw syndicate activities around the country.

Largely taken uncritically, the Valachi testimony had a profound impact on law enforcement, policymakers, and popular culture. Luchese himself told one prosecutor, "Valachi's crazy. I know nothing about any Cosa Nostra. The only thing I belong to is the Knights of Columbus" (*New York Times*, 14 July 1967). Despite Luchese's protests, law enforcement officials and writers soon produced a massive but largely speculative literature on the structure of organized crime and the role Luchese had supposedly played in its development. By 1965 Luchese was hospitalized, undergoing surgery for a brain tumor and treatment for a heart ailment. He died at his home in Lido Beach, Long Island, New York.

• The best short biographical sketches are Ralph Salerno and John S. Tompkins, *The Crime Confederation: Cosa Nostra and Allied Operations in Organized Crime* (1969), and Virgil W. Peterson, *The Mob: 200 Years of Organized Crime in New York* (1983). Peter Maas details the accusations of the 1960s in *The Valachi Papers* (1968). Useful testimony on the 1950 elections can be found in Special Committee to Investigate Organized Crime in Interstate Commerce (U.S. Senate, 82d Cong., 2d sess.), *Hearings*, pt. 7. Dwight C. Smith, Jr., presents an indispensable corrective to the popular literature on organized crime in *The Mafia Mystique* (1975). The *New York Times* provides detailed excerpts of Luchese's testimony before the New York State Crime Commission on 15 and 22 Nov. 1952 and an obituary on 14 July 1967.

WILLIAM HOWARD MOORE

LUCIANO, Lucky (11 Nov. 1897–26 Jan. 1962), founder of the Mafia in the United States, was born Salvatore Lucania in Lercara Friddi, Sicily, the son of Antonio Lucania, a miner and day laborer, and Rosalia Capporelli. Luciano's family immigrated to the United States in 1906 and settled on the Lower East Side of Manhattan. His attendance in school was erratic, and he was sent to a special school for truants in Brooklyn for two months in 1914. After his release, he dropped out of school with the equivalent of five years of education and became a delivery boy for a hat manufacturer—his only legitimate employment.

In June 1916 Luciano was arrested, pleaded guilty for opium trafficking, and was sentenced to one year in prison. After his release, Luciano formed a gang with Frank Costello, Meyer Lansky, Benjamin Siegel, Joe Adonis, and Vito Genovese to rob pawnshops, moneylenders, and banks on the Lower East Side. During Prohibition, the gang's fortunes grew dramatically. Luciano entered the bootlegging business with the financial backing and patronage of Arnold Rothstein, whose mythic reputation included unfounded claims that he had fixed the 1919 World Series. Luciano reinvested his bootlegging profits in a variety of other il-

legal enterprises, including labor racketeering and gambling.

Luciano's rising fortunes gained the attention of New York's two Sicilian crime bosses, Giuseppe Masseria and Salvatore Maranzano, both of whom wanted a share of his bootlegging business. In 1927 Luciano sided with Masseria, becoming his chief lieutenant. It was while working for Masseria that Lucania, also called Charlie, adopted the names Lucky and Luciano. In the fall of 1928 he was arrested for robbery and used the alias Luciano. When he discovered that the police had less trouble pronouncing the alias than his real name, he adopted Luciano. The following year he was abducted, badly beaten, and left for dead in a deserted part of Staten Island. His wounds included a knife scar across his face that caused his eye to droop and gave him a sinister appearance. Because Luciano was the only person ever known to have survived the gangland ritual of being "taken for a ride," he adopted the nickname Lucky. Luciano never revealed the details of the incident, although many speculated that his attackers included Maranzano.

In 1931 Luciano seized on the growing rivalry between Masseria and Maranzano to enlarge his own power base. During the so-called Castellammarese wars, Luciano arranged the murders of both Masseria and Maranzano. He then took over the Italian underworld, setting up a syndicate that later became mythologized as the Mafia. In fact, Luciano's empire consisted of a series of informal relationships and business dealings with other underworld figures, mostly limited to gambling and part ownership in clubs at Sarasota Springs, rather than the formal structure described by law enforcement officials, who labeled him the "boss of bosses."

The first law enforcement official who had a vested interest in portraying Luciano as the nation's leading crime boss was Thomas E. Dewey, who in 1935 was appointed a special district attorney in Manhattan. Dewey launched his reputation as the nation's most fearless racket buster by prosecuting Luciano in 1936 for running a prostitution ring. Although the evidence was weak and Dewey's techniques were questionable, he won a conviction because of the charged atmosphere of the era. Luciano was given a thirty-to-fifty-year sentence, the longest for that type of crime in New York State history.

World War II broke out while Luciano was serving his sentence at the Dannemora prison in upstate New York. Naval intelligence authorities, concerned about German espionage along the docks of New York City, sought Luciano's help in gathering information among dockworkers. Luciano was transferred to the state penitentiary at Comstock near Albany so that he could consult with his allies, including Joseph "Socks" Lanza, the labor racketeer who controlled the Fulton Fish Market. The most visible success of the underworld operation was the arrest in June 1942 of eight German agents, who had been landed by U-boats. The agents had explosives, $170,000 in cash, and maps and plans for a two-year attack on defense plants, railroads, and bridges along the East Coast. Luciano also provided names of sources who helped the Allied invasion forces in Sicily. All this was later denied by the U.S. government for political reasons.

In exchange for Luciano's cooperation with the navy, Dewey, who had since become New York's governor, granted him executive clemency. Luciano, who never became a U.S. citizen, was deported to Italy on 10 February 1946. A year later he moved to Cuba, where Lansky and other allies owned gambling casinos. Federal authorities, led by U.S. Bureau of Narcotics director Harry Anslinger, pressured Cuban authorities to send Luciano back to Italy, which they did in March 1947. Anslinger claimed that Luciano was a major drug trafficker who hoped to use Cuba as a base for shipping heroin into the United States. Anslinger continued to insist that Luciano headed an international drug syndicate that shipped heroin into the United States, but Luciano was never tried on the charges.

Luciano died in Naples. Some newspapers claimed he had married Iges Lissoni, a dancer, in 1949, but the evidence for that remains questionable. Luciano's siblings brought his body back to the United States and interred it in the family vault at St. John's Cemetery in Queens in February 1962.

Luciano's importance stems in part from his larger-than-life persona as the founder and supposed head of the Mafia in the United States. In fact, organized crime always has been loosely structured, localized, and more ethnically diverse than the stereotypes suggest. Sicilians were just one ethnic group involved in organized crime, as Luciano's own links with Jews, such as Lansky and Siegel, indicate. Chroniclers also have credited Luciano with being the first crime boss to create modern rackets, organized along corporate lines with layers of middlemen. In fact, the trend toward modernization began much earlier. Rothstein, for example, organized his gambling and bootlegging operations using business techniques before Luciano. Still, Luciano and his partners furthered these trends, in part because of the fortunes they amassed during Prohibition. In the process, they created powerful crime syndicates that also played an important part in the nation's folklore.

• A number of films have been made and two anecdotal and unreliable biographies have been written about Luciano. See Sid Feder and Joachim Joesten, *The Luciano Story* (1960), and Martin Gosch and Richard Hammer, *The Last Testament of Lucky Luciano* (1974). More credible evidence can be found in Mary M. Stolberg, "Political Justice" (Ph.D. diss., Univ. of Virginia, 1991), and Robert Lacey, *Little Man: Meyer Lansky and the Gangster Life* (1991). An obituary is in the *New York Times*, 27 Jan. 1962.

MARY M. STOLBERG

LUCKIESH, Matthew (14 Sept. 1883–2 Nov. 1967), physicist and illuminating engineer, was born in Maquoketa, Iowa, the son of John Luckiesh, a groundskeeper at the Maquoketa Academy, and Frances "Fannie" Root Sumek. He attended Iowa State College of Agriculture and Mechanic Arts (now Iowa State University) in Ames and in 1909 received his B.S. in Electrical Engineering at Purdue University in West Lafayette, Indiana. In 1911 he received an M.S. in physics from the State University of Iowa, Iowa City. In 1912 Iowa State College awarded him the degree of electrical engineer.

Luckiesh began his career with the National Electric Lamp Association (NELA) of Cleveland, Ohio, in 1910 as an assistant physicist and stayed with this company through its various transformations until he retired in 1949. He married Frances T. Clark in 1913; she died in 1925, and in 1928 he married Helen Pitts, with whom he had two children.

Luckiesh initially used his training in physics to study physiology and physiological optics as part of NELA's physical laboratory, which had been established by Edward P. Hyde. This knowledge was meant to broaden and deepen the understanding of the nascent field of illuminating engineering, then only sketchily understood as the combination of science and art necessary to put a specific amount of light on a certain object. Following Hyde's lead, Luckiesh tirelessly researched and promoted not only better lighting techniques but also ways to establish an objective basis for connecting particular levels and types of light with optimal visual conditions. His studies came to define the notoriously complex intersection of the physics of electric light, the physiology and psychology of human beings, and the aesthetics of the built environment. Touted as being free of commercial objectives, this research actually became the foundation for broad practical applications. The reflective quality of different materials, the absorption of light by different colors, the visibility of different typefaces, and even the effects of ultraviolet radiation were all within Luckiesh's purview. In January 1914, at Luckiesh's urging, Hyde expanded the physical laboratory to include not only pure science, which came under the direction of Ernest F. Nichols, but also applied physics, which Luckiesh was asked to direct. Six years later each section was expanded again to become a full laboratory, and Luckiesh became director of applied science. In 1924 he was named director of the Lighting Research Laboratory, the position he held until his retirement.

While Luckiesh's duties expanded, NELA underwent dramatic redefinition. Initially projected as a consortium of independent electric lamp companies, in 1911 an antitrust suit exposed General Electric (GE) as NELA's dominant stockholder. NELA then became the National Quality Lamp Division of General Electric Company, one of many name changes. At the same time, at Hyde's urging, NELA moved from a cramped setting in industrial Cleveland to a relatively rural site east of the city. What became known as Nela Park was a very early version of the modern corporate campus, with stylish buildings and expansive grounds. Just as this research center came to be appreciated as the "University of Light," in contrast to GE's industrial sites elsewhere, Luckiesh's research came to complement the scientific study of electricity carried out by Charles P. Steinmetz, as well as technical research exemplified by the development of ductile tungsten by William D. Coolidge, both of whom worked at GE's Schenectady plant. Luckiesh's work increasingly equaled if not usurped the promotional power held by the Illuminating Engineering Laboratory run by Walter D'Arcy Ryan at Schenectady. Whereas Ryan showed the sophisticated effects light could have in different physical settings, Luckiesh emphasized the effect light had on the human eye and thus on physical and mental well-being. Just at the time that spectacular lighting had reached its peak, lighting designed for heightened standards of health and productivity became an increasingly widespread imperative.

The success of this campaign rested on its combination of scientific and popular appeal. Luckiesh demonstrated an evangelistic fervor for conducting and disseminating scientific research. His work reached out through professional channels, particularly in the areas of illuminating engineering and optometry, but it also followed numerous less technical routes, such as *Electrical Merchandising*, *Architectural Record*, and *Good Housekeeping*. His scientific abstracts mingled with inspirational articles like "Light, Life and Happiness," in the *Transactions of the Illuminating Engineering Society* (20, no. 8 [Oct. 1925]), and his many technical monographs shared the shelf with romantic books like *The Torch of Civilization: The Story of Man's Conquest of Darkness* (1940). Ultimately, his twenty-five books, several hundred articles, and eleven scientific instruments formed a monument to a driven individual and a fertile profession. His work adds to scientific understanding of light and shows a deep emotional identity with light's meanings and values.

Luckiesh's ability to encourage professional development as well as lighting sales through scientific and popular avenues exposed him to criticism for skewing scientific fact with commercial zeal. In particular, he was slow to reconsider assertions he made concerning light's ability to increase worker output. Numerous studies demonstrate how GE's fierce competitive drive and marketing savvy drove them to fabricate a variety of images for their products and services to appeal to diverse audiences. Some were more accurate than others.

Although the scientific veracity of GE claims might at times seem tainted, Luckiesh's investigative skills ranged far more widely. One characteristically novel investigation concerned the development of airplane camouflage, carried out as part of the NELA's efforts during World War I. Luckiesh jumped into open-cockpit airplanes, logged thousands of airborne hours, and analyzed the visual qualities of the earth and sky as a study in light, color, and brightness. This led to the first scientifically determined application of patterns and colors for airplanes, ships, and land vehicles. Ships, formerly painted white or black, were painted various shades of the now characteristic steel gray as a result of Luckiesh's research. The studies also resulted in the development of an instrument for determining brightness. A paper Luckiesh published in the *Journal of the Franklin Institute*, "Visibility of Airplanes," resulted in his being given the Edward Longstreth Medal by the Franklin Institute on 7 April 1920.

One of Luckiesh's most significant and lasting contributions linked the physiology of the eye, the physics of light and lighting, and the definition of specific "tasks" or challenges faced in vision. He called this process the "Science of Seeing." In 1934 the basic concept became the foundation of the National Better Light–Better Sight Bureau, a nonprofit organization ostensibly concerned only with education and social services but having undeniable commercial aspects. The *Better Light–Better Sight News* circulated for thirty-eight years to 20,000 readers, primarily teachers and administrators, until it ceased operation in 1979.

Luckiesh retired from GE in 1949 and became director of research and development for the Foster and Davies Advertising Agency and published sporadically in the *Consumers Research Bulletin*. In addition to two honorary degrees, he received recognition for his work from numerous societies, including presidency of the Illuminating Engineering Society (1925–1926), election to the American Association for the Advancement of Sciences (1929), a commendation from the Academy of Motion Picture Arts and Sciences (1928), fellowship in and a gold medal from the Distinguished Service Foundation of Optometry (1930, 1932), as well as fellowship in the Institute of Electrical and Electronic Engineers (1940) and the Illuminating Engineering Society (1944). He died of cancer of the pancreas in Cleveland, Ohio.

• A full biography of Luckiesh is Edward J. Covington, *A Man from Maquoketa: A Biography of Matthew Luckiesh* (1992). Nela Park is described in Hollis L. Townsend, *A History of Nela Park, 1911–1957* (c. 1957). Information on the physical laboratory is in E. P. Hyde, "The Physical Lab of the National," *Transactions of the Illuminating Engineering Society* 4, no. 7 (Oct. 1909): 631–37, and in *Abstract-Bulletin of the Physical Laboratory* (1913–1925). A useful statement of the philosophy of the physical laboratory when Luckiesh was hired is in Hyde's presidential address for the Society of Illuminating Engineers, "The Goal of Illuminating Engineering," *Transactions of the Illuminating Engineering Society* 5, no. 7 (Oct. 1910): 539–45. Works on the context of GE lamp production include T. K. Quinn, *Giant Business: Threat to Democracy, The Autobiography of an Insider* (1953); Leonard S. Reich, "Lighting the Path to Profit: GE's Control of the Electric Lamp Industry, 1892–1941," *Business History Review* 66, no. 2 (Summer 1992): 305–34; and David E. Nye, *Image Worlds: Corporate Identities at General Electric, 1890–1930* (1985). On misrepresentation of lighting's effects, see Charles D. Wrege, *Facts and Fallacies of Hawthorne: A Historical Study of the Origins, Procedures and Results of the Hawthorne Illumination Tests and Their Influence upon the Hawthorne Studies* (1961; rep. 1986). Matthew Luckiesh's monographs include *Color and Its Applications* (1915, 1921); *Lighting the Home* (1920); *Light and Color in Advertising and Merchandising* (1923); *Light and Work: A Discussion of Quality and Quantity of Light in Relation to Effective Vision and Efficient Work* (1924; German translation 1926); and *The Science of Seeing*, with Frank K. Moss, (1937).

E. G. DAVES ROSSELL

LUDLAM, Charles (12 Apr. 1943–28 May 1987), playwright, director, actor, and artistic director, was born in Floral Park, New York, the son of Joseph William Ludlam, a plasterer, and Marjorie Braun. Although Ludlams had been among the earliest settlers of Long Island, Charles's family lived modestly in a working-class neighborhood, across the street from a movie theater. There Charles and his mother saw two feature films each week. These, the puppet show that he wandered into at the Mineola fair, and television's "Kukla, Fran and Ollie" all influenced six-year-old Ludlam to create his own puppet shows and to enlist neighborhood children to stage his first scripts. After appearing in plays at school and apprenticing to the Red Barn Theater in 1958, a trip to Manhattan to see productions by the Living Theatre prompted him to found, with Christopher Scott, the Students Repertory Theatre in Northport, an enterprise that he had to close when he enrolled at Hofstra University in 1961. He studied acting, directing, playwriting, and dramatic literature—but specialized, even then, in hyperbole—and in 1965 took his B.A. and his mastery of theater history and its craft to Manhattan, where he finally enjoyed an opportunity to fully explore without impediment his homosexuality.

Living first on the Lower East Side and then in several apartments a few blocks north in the East Village, Ludlam soon met director John Vaccaro and playwright Ronald Tavel, who in 1966 formed the Play-House of the Ridiculous. In that nascent company's first production of a full-length play, *The Life of Lady Godiva* (1966), Ludlam made his New York debut as Peeping Tom. He took his first drag role at the same theater in *Screen Test* (1966), where he created his own version of Gloria Swanson's Norma Desmond, the washed-up actress in *Sunset Boulevard*. When Tavel left the Ridiculous, Ludlam wrote for Vaccaro, first the pastiche of others' work known as *Big Hotel* (1966) and then his spoof of Marlowe's *Tamburlaine* and other classics, which he titled *Conquest of the Universe* (1967). But in 1967 during rehearsals for the latter, the director fired Ludlam. Outraged that Ludlam should be thrown out of his own play and already intensely loyal to his genius, most of the ensemble quit. Later that year, together they founded the Ridiculous Theatrical Company, a name that conveyed their adherence to the "ridiculous" aesthetic of hyperbole (that is, farcical exaggeration and gay "camp"), their dedication to old-fashioned theatrical conventions, and their continuation of the company of actors who had performed for Vaccaro. While Vaccaro, using the new name Theater of the Ridiculous, presented *Conquest of the Universe*, Ludlam's group staged the same script as *When Queens Collide* (1967).

Through the rest of the 1960s Ludlam made theater by night and supported himself by clerking in stores and doing other odd jobs by day. In 1970, however, his farce *Bluebeard* (about a mad scientist striving to invent a third gender) achieved such success that he won a Guggenheim Fellowship in playwriting, began touring both in the United States and abroad, and

started teaching at the first of several prestigious universities. The 1970s saw him working particularly with actors Bill Vehr, Black-Eyed Susan (with whom, when she was known as Susan Carlson, he had acted at Hofstra), John Brockmeyer, and Lola Pashalinski. In 1976 he cast Everett Quinton, with whom he had been living since the previous September, in *Caprice*. The pair shared their lives and work and Ludlam's West Village apartment until Ludlam's death from acquired immunodeficiency syndrome (AIDS). As Ludlam had insisted, Quinton assumed the artistic directorship of the theater. Although he was not a matinee idol, an athlete, or a politician, the *New York Times* reported Ludlam's passing on its front page.

During his first few years in New York Ludlam moved from loosely knit, even anarchic works based largely on others' creations to more original scripts more classical in structure. Ultimately his dialectical impulses led him to evolve a hallmark style—of acting, directing, writing, and design—grounded in paradoxes. He created a new avant-garde theater based in old theatrical strategies and devices, including commedia dell'arte, ventriloquism, quick-change, magic, footlights, a wind machine, and thunder sheets. He wedded pathos and hilarity, physicality and verbal dexterity, sincerity and camp, originality and parody, reverence and ridicule. He raided the classics, some of them obscure, while employing his equally broad knowledge of life to create accessible comedies for a popular audience. While romping through rowdy, often raunchy action, he avoided sloppy clowning around, reaching instead a high degree of professionalism. When he cast against type, which he loved to do, he balanced realistic performances with careful reminders that he or some other cast member performed a role in drag. He contrasted biting satire and witty barbs with humane laments of barbaric cruelty or scary moments (as in the thriller *The Mystery of Irma Vep*) that left spectators gasping. His female impersonations often proved at least as touching as they were humorous; while spectators laughed at his dying Camille, he wept. He appreciated the importance of melding laughter and tears and denied that comedy and melodrama need be polar opposites.

Although in his own plays Ludlam often flouted strictures of good taste, moderation, or subtlety, he performed, with an absolute conviction that seemed hyperreal, every character he undertook, including the title role in *Hedda Gabler* for the American Ibsen Theater, parts in several films (such as the southern lawyer in *The Big Easy*) and television shows (such as "Miami Vice"). Toward the end of his life he was beginning to direct elsewhere as well—a production of *The Country Wife* at Carnegie-Mellon University and, in two successive seasons, at the Santa Fe Opera House. Always he surprised; after ridiculing conservative norms in *Utopia, Incorporated*, he adapted, directed, and starred in a perfectly straightforward production of Dickens's *A Christmas Carol*. A master of slapstick and parody, he nevertheless revered Maria Callas in his "tragic" *Galas*.

Unlike such twentieth-century giants as Eugene O'Neill, Tennessee Williams, Arthur Miller, and Neil Simon, Ludlam left a repertory company that for twenty years had devoted itself exclusively to presenting his plays. He also left thirty scripts, several of which have made him one of the most-produced American playwrights. His theater continued to flourish on what New York City renamed Charles Ludlam Lane in Greenwich Village until June 1995, eight years after Ludlam's death, when the company began searching for a new home.

• Ludlam's papers are in the Billy Rose Theatre Collection of the New York Public Library for the Performing Arts. They include, in the words of the catalog, "diaries, notebooks, scripts, set and costume designs, clippings, transcripts of interviews, and manuscript pages" from Steven Samuels's *The Complete Plays of Charles Ludlam* (1989). Samuels's companion volume, *Ridiculous Theatre, Scourge of Human Folly: The Essays and Opinions of Charles Ludlam* (1992), provides the other readily available source of Ludlam's work, much of it lifted from interviews of Ludlam but rearranged in thematically related segments. For accounts of his early career, see Stefan Brecht, *Queer Theatre* (1986), and Calvin Tomkins, "Profiles: Ridiculous," *New Yorker*, 15 Nov. 1976, pp. 55–98. David Kaufman, "From the Ridiculous to the Sublime," *Interview* 19 (Dec. 1989): 78–84, 120, may prove useful, as well as Tish Dace, "Rampantly Ridiculous," *Other Stages*, 19 Oct. 1978, pp. 3–4, and, on design, her "From the Ridiculous to the Sublime," *Theatre Crafts* 20 (Mar. 1986): 34–37, 67–70. For a critical overview, see Dace, "Charles Ludlam," *International Dictionary of Theatre*, vol. 2, *Playwrights* (1994). The files of the New York Public Library for the Performing Arts contain numerous reviews of Ludlam's productions. Jeremy Gerard's obituary in the *New York Times*, 29 May 1987, provides details of Ludlam's last months.

TISH DACE

LUDLOW, Daniel (2 Aug. 1750–26 Sept. 1814), merchant and banker, was born in New York City, the son of Gabriel Ludlow, a merchant, and Elizabeth Crommelin. In 1765 Ludlow's father sent him to Amsterdam, Holland, to enter the counting house of Crommelin and Zoon, where his grandfather Charles Crommelin was a principal. During his five year stint with the firm, young Ludlow learned banking, French, German, and of course Dutch. After returning to New York around 1770, Ludlow joined his father's mercantile business, which he took over after the latter's death in 1773. In October of that same year Ludlow married Arabella Duncan. The couple had five children before Arabella's death in 1803. Ludlow, a Loyalist during the Revolution, joined the Chamber of Commerce in 1783. Shortly thereafter, on 1 January 1784, he entered into a partnership with Edward Goold. Their first advertisement, a circular letter, was rather vague about their line of business, promising "to contribute to the Success of whatever Concerns may be entrusted to our Charge." They probably imported goods on commission and on their own account. Manuscript evidence suggests that they were also involved in marine insurance. The partnership

dissolved in 1790, when Ludlow joined with his nephew Gulian Ludlow under the name Daniel Ludlow & Company. This firm, a major importer of East India goods and a marine insurer, stayed together for fifteen years. The firm experienced significant underwriting losses during the 1798 Quasi-War with France, but soon recovered with aid from Ludlow's new banking concern.

Ludlow, who owned two shares in the Bank of New York in the late 1780s, embarked on his banking career in the spring of 1799, helping Aaron Burr and others form the Manhattan Company. Ostensibly a private water company, its charter contained a clause allowing it to employ its excess capital in banking or other "monied transactions." Ludlow, who was not initially a major subscriber, was most likely voted director and president of the new institution because of his European training and his reputation for conservatism. Under Ludlow's leadership the Manhattan Company established a bank of discount and deposit in early September 1799. New York State's first Republican-controlled bank, Ludlow's Manhattan Company did well, both politically and economically. By funding Aaron Burr's campaigns during New York's crucial assembly elections, the bank also played a key role in the U.S. presidential election of 1800. The bank's stock sold for 24 to 46 percent above par during Ludlow's tenure, averaging 7 percent in annual dividends.

As a reward for Ludlow's services, and to make his own patronage policies seem less partisan, Jefferson appointed the former Loyalist a navy agent in April 1801. Despite the fact that Federalists made Ludlow's allegedly poor performance as navy agent an election issue in 1802, Ludlow stayed in this post throughout Jefferson's two terms. In 1803 Federalists again made Ludlow's performance a campaign issue, alleging he and three other Manhattan Company directors unfairly borrowed $160,000 from their own bank to finance a trading excursion to Calcutta.

The following year Ludlow spearheaded the movement to stop the charter of a rival institution, the Merchants' Bank. Ludlow, who backed Morgan Lewis for governor during the spring of 1804, teamed up with Manhattan Company cashier Henry Remsen and powerful politicians DeWitt Clinton and William Few, also directors, in an effort to block the charter and gain passage of the infamous Restraining Act of 1804. This act, designed to eradicate the Merchants' Bank and future competitors, forbade unincorporated associations from banking in New York. Though the act was not overturned, New York's 1805 assembly ultimately chartered the Merchants' Bank despite Ludlow's continued opposition.

Although a member of the merchant elite, Ludlow eventually grew quite close to Jefferson. In June 1805, for example, he paid William Hazards an advance of more than $200 "from his Excellency Thomas Jefferson." Ludlow was not reimbursed for his loan for over a week and apparently received no interest for such aid. Ludlow could well afford it, however; his company continued to thrive. In these prosperous years Ludlow was also a director of the Harlem Bridge Company.

By 1807, however, the trade dislocations of the Napoleonic Wars, exacerbated by Jeffersonian economic warfare, bankrupted Daniel Ludlow & Company. Ludlow lost his summer house on the East River, his marble home on Broadway, his bank stock, and of course the presidency of the Manhattan Company. His ability to continue his hospitable and generous social lifestyle also gone, Ludlow moved to Skaneateles, New York, where he resided until his death there. After his first wife's death in 1803, Ludlow later married a Mrs. Van Horne.

Though a member of New York City's merchant elite, Ludlow was one of several dozen important Loyalists to join the Republican party. His European bank training helped him to become one of the nation's first "expert" bankers as he forged the Manhattan Company into a powerful economic tool for the Republican party. Like many older merchants, however, the economic dislocations of the new and changing century doomed his far-flung personal concerns, eventually forcing him out of active life.

• The Ludlow Family Papers are at Columbia University, where evidence of Daniel Ludlow's loan to Thomas Jefferson can be found in the Charles Ludlow Papers. His stock holdings in the Bank of New York are in the James O. Wettereau Papers, also at Columbia University. For information concerning the financial condition of the Manhattan Company under Ludlow, see the institution's first ledgers at the Chase-Manhattan Bank Archives. Ludlow's petition in the Merchants' Bank controversy is in the *Journal of the Assembly of the State of New York*, 27th sess. (1804). Short biographical sketches appear in the *New York Genealogical and Biographical Record* (Jan.–Apr.1919), and Edmund N. Leslie, *Skaneateles: History of Its Earliest Settlement and Reminiscences of Later Times* (1902). For information concerning Ludlow's role in New York City politics, see the *Minutes of the Common Council of the City of N.Y.* (1784–1831), especially vol. 1. For his early role in the Chamber of Commerce, John Austin Steven, Jr., *Colonial Records of the New York Chamber of Commerce, 1768–1784* (1867), remains the best source. An analysis of Ludlow's leadership appears in Gregory Hunter, *The Manhattan Company: Managing a Multi-Unit Corporation in New York, 1799–1842* (1989). Finally, for his importance as an "expert" banker, see Fritz Redlich, *Molding of American Banking: Men and Ideas* (1947; repr., 1968). An obituary is in the *New York Evening Post*, 6 Oct. 1814.

ROBERT E. WRIGHT

LUDLOW, Gabriel George (16 Apr. 1736–12 Feb. 1808), Loyalist soldier and politician, was born in Queens County, Long Island, New York, the son of Gabriel Ludlow, a wealthy merchant, and Frances Duncan. His grandfather immigrated to New York from England in 1694 and established the family's wealth by operating a successful coasting trade out of New York City and acquiring vast land holdings on the west side of the Hudson River. The Ludlows were prosperous members of New York's colonial gentry.

A staunch Anglican, in 1760 Ludlow became governor of King's College (now Columbia University), although his own education was acquired through private tutors. In 1760 he married Ann ver Planck, a descendant of a New Netherland family who brought an inheritance of 17,000 acres in Ulster County to the marriage. They had four children. Ludlow pursued a genteel existence, buying and refurbishing a 140-acre estate in Hempstead, Long Island, tending his real estate and business interests in the coastal trade, and earning a local reputation as a generous, stylish host. He was not as prominent as his brother, George Duncan Ludlow, a justice of the supreme court of New York, nor as active in international trade as his half-brother, Daniel Ludlow, but his appointment as justice of the peace and colonel of the local militia in 1775 testify to his status in Queens County.

Queens County became the storm center of Loyalism at the outbreak of the American Revolution. When American rebel forces occupied Long Island in 1775, Lieutenant Governor Cadwallader Colden organized Tory resistance in Queens, with the Ludlow brothers serving as his key lieutenants. Partisan warfare between Whigs and Tories was ferocious. Ludlow and his brother George was leading 700 men to the battle of Long Island when they were informed it was over. "A universal hunt after Loyalists took place," according to Loyalist historian Thomas Jones, and Ludlow went into hiding as "the Loyalists were pursued like wolves and bears, from swamp to swamp, from one hill to another, from dale to dale, and from one copse of wood to another" (Jones, vol. 1, p. 109). He emerged in 1776 with the arrival of British troops and began raising a battalion of 700–800 men, who formed the Third Battalion of De Lancey's Brigade with Ludlow as their colonel. This unit stayed on Long Island throughout the war, protecting the residents and the refugee camps against incessant raiding parties and coastal attacks by rebel forces. Thus, although he and his family were exposed to constant danger from the marauders, Ludlow saw no formal military action during the Revolution. He did form close friendships with other Loyalist military officers and with the British high command, often entertaining them in his home at Hempstead. Ludlow was sufficiently notorious to be attainted for treason by the New York State assembly in 1779, which also confiscated his estate, although the confiscation was not implemented until after the British evacuation. When he left for England at the end of the war, the state seized his property and forced his wife to pay rent in order to continue living there, an act of revenge that the victors savored and the victims deeply resented.

Ludlow was doubtless astonished by the results of the war, but he moved swiftly to salvage his fortune and his status. In particular he and such Loyalist friends as Ward Chipman and Joshua Upham used their connection with Sir Guy Carleton, the British military commander in New York at the end of the war, to great advantage. They personally lobbied the Colonial Office and all sympathetic English officials for financial compensation for "the suffering Loyalists" and posts for themselves in the postwar imperial establishment. After an intricate transatlantic campaign, involving most of the Loyalist military officers, they persuaded the government to establish the province of New Brunswick as a special Loyalist asylum, where they could restore their battered fortunes and build a new British colonial society that would be, in the words of Ludlow's comrade Edward Winslow, "the envy of the American states" (Condon, p. 39).

Ludlow's New Brunswick years began unfavorably when the ship bringing his wife up from New York to join him was wrecked, and all their worldly goods were lost. Nonetheless, he resumed his merchant career and held several important public posts that made him one of the key government leaders in the new colony. He was appointed a member of the council in 1784 and judge of the vice admiralty court in 1785. His most important post was that of mayor of St. John, an office modeled on colonial New York City's mayoralty and deliberately vested by Governor Thomas Carleton with strong discretionary powers to offset the tendency of the city's population toward popular protest. Ludlow built a grand house in West St. John and participated enthusiastically in the frequent civic ceremonies that enabled the Loyalists to express their sense of heroic sacrifice and their vision for the colony. Ludlow achieved the rank of brigadier general in the provincial militia. He also served as one of three agents appointed by the governor to oversee the emigration of black Loyalists from the province to Sierra Leone. The high point of his mayoralty was doubtless the opportunity in 1794 to entertain Prince Edward, the son of the king he had supported so loyally. He resigned this post later in 1794 to express his anger at Governor Carleton for appointing his political enemy Elias Hardy to be city recorder instead of Ludlow's son Gabriel. Ludlow's son thereupon left for New York City, where he married into the powerful Federalist Hunter family and successfully practiced law, all the while continuing to collect half pay from the British government for his service in opposing American independence. After 1795 Ludlow led an increasingly secluded life. He was called on in 1808 to serve as president of the council in the governor's absence and to call up the militia against a threatened American invasion. Ludlow did his duty and then promptly died, having as his last official act prepared to renew the conflict with his old foes.

The lack of personal documents limits our knowledge of Ludlow's personality. His portrait shows him coiffed in an elaborate wig, suggesting a man who enjoyed display and high style. He was one of those rare Loyalists who was able to enjoy a very comfortable life in exile, thanks to his half pay, the fees from the vice admiralty court, the slaves he had brought with him from New York, and the compensation of £1,450 sterling that the British Claim Commission had awarded him in response to his claim of £2,500. While it is true that the Ludlows who stayed in America achieved greater wealth and distinction in subsequent generations, Ludlow may be admired for his spirited defense of his conservative convictions and the stylish way he accepted his exile and built a new life in British North America.

• Ludlow left no personal records, and he is mentioned only occasionally in official documents pertaining to the war. Contemporary Loyalist records that single Ludlow out include Thomas Jones, *The History of New York during the Revolutionary War*, ed. George F. DeLancey (2 vols., 1879); William Smith, Jr., *Historical Memoirs . . . of William Smith*, ed. William H. W. Sabine (3 vols., 1956–1971); Henry Onderdonk, Jr., comp., *Documents and Letters Intended to Illustrate the Revolutionary Incidents of Queens County* (1970); and W. O. Raymond, ed., *The Winslow Papers* (1901). Two detailed articles have been written by Joseph S. Tiedemann on the war in Queens County, "Patriots by Default: Queens County, New York and the British Army, 1776–1783," *William and Mary Quarterly*, 3d ser., 43 (1986): 35–63, and "A Revolution Foiled: Queens County, New York, 1775–1776," *Journal of American History* 75 (1988): 417–44. Ludlow's claim to the Loyalist Claims Commission is in Alexander Fraser, ed., *The Second Report of the Bureau of Archives for the Province of Ontario* (1905). Additional information on his New Brunswick years is in Ann Gorman Condon, *The Envy of the American States: The Loyalist Dream for New Brunswick* (1984). His portrait and his work as mayor of St. John are reproduced in Eric Teed, *Canada's First City: Saint John, the Charter of 1785 and Common Council Proceedings under G. G. Ludlow* (1962).

ANN GORMAN CONDON

LUDLOW, George Duncan (1734–13 Nov. 1808), judge and Loyalist official, was born in Queens County, Long Island, New York, the son of Gabriel Ludlow, a wealthy merchant, and Frances Duncan. The family was well established in the province, with strong ties to the Anglican church and to the powerful De Lancey political faction. George Ludlow's younger brother was Gabriel George Ludlow, a merchant and also a Loyalist who, like his brother, went into exile after the American Revolution and resettled in New Brunswick.

George Ludlow received most of his education from private tutors, although his neighbor and fellow judge, Thomas Jones, said that he did attend college. Initially he trained to be an apothecary rather than studying law. Lorenzo Sabine attributes this choice to a speech handicap: "In consequence of sickness, his tongue was too large and his speech defective." Jones adds that Ludlow soon abandoned the apothecary trade and turned to the law: "By dint of hard study, constant application, retentive memory, and a most brilliant genius he in a short time made an amazing proficiency" (Sabine, vol. 1, p. 431). By his thirtieth year, Ludlow had been admitted to the bar and was involved in a large commercial practice. In 1758 he married his cousin Frances Duncan; they had three children.

In 1768 Ludlow was appointed to the council of New York, thanks to the patronage of Lieutenant Governor Cadwallader Colden, and in 1769 he was raised to the provincial supreme court. Although never overtly involved in the political disputes of the era, Ludlow's well-known Tory connections were resented in New York City, and in the mid-1770s he felt compelled to leave his town house and take up residence at his country estate in Hempstead.

When hostilities broke out in 1775 Ludlow and his brother worked covertly under the direction of Colden to unite the Tories in Queens County and mount a firm resistance to the patriot invaders. In August 1776 the brothers were "reportedly leading about seven hundred county residents to the battlefield," when news of Sir William Howe's quick victory in the battle of Long Island reached them. George Washington evacuated Long Island immediately after, so that "the battle that had raged between Whigs and Tories for the allegiance of county residents was over at last" (Tiedemann, "Revolution Foiled," p. 441).

In 1778 Ludlow hoped to be appointed chief justice of the supreme court and was so disappointed when the post went to William Smith, Jr., that he resigned from the court entirely. To win back the support of such an important Loyalist, Governor James Robertson in 1780 appointed Ludlow master of the rolls and superintendent of police for Long Island, two powerful and very lucrative posts. Ludlow's discharge of his duties has been a source of controversy ever since. Jones, who was both a Loyalist and a fellow justice on the supreme court, felt that Ludlow's exorbitant fees and unnecessary harshness alienated the population and led to a precipitate decline in support for the British cause. He asserts that Ludlow and Governor Robertson used these posts to participate in the lucrative smuggling trade between New York and New England and to increase the amount of land confiscated from the rebels. Furthermore all police functions on Long Island were centralized in the superintendent's office, which operated under military rules. Joseph Tiedemann estimates that the court of police collected about £7,660 during its thirty-five months of existence, and that Ludlow personally received "more than £1,825 for working one day a week for thirty-five months" (Tiedemann, "Patriots by Default," p. 62).

Chief Justice Smith agreed with Jones's harsh criticism of Ludlow, as have most modern historians. Yet the British commander Sir Guy Carleton and Loyalist military officers like Edward Winslow were lavish in their praise of his service to the cause. The controversy turns less on Ludlow than on the wisdom of continuing military rule in British-occupied New York. General Henry Clinton, Ludlow himself, and the Loyalist military officers deemed martial law essential for British victory; Jones and the more moderate Tories believed the absence of civil government in British territories contributed substantially to British defeat. In the bitter history of the war that Jones wrote in exile, he dubbed Ludlow "the tyrant of Long Island" (Jones, vol. 2, p. 12). The label may not be entirely fair, but it has stuck. Yet Ludlow was not always a hard-liner, as he proved when he resigned in protest of the role taken by the Board of Associated Loyalists in the execution of the prisoner Joshua Huddy.

As a highly public Loyalist, who had been attainted for treason and deprived of his property by the New York legislature, Ludlow had no choice but to go into exile at the war's end. With his brother and other ranking Loyalists, he went to London and campaigned to get the British government to establish a new province in British North America that would provide government posts for the many office-seeking Loyalists. He also filed a claim for property losses amounting to £7,000 and received compensation of £2,500 from the claims commission. When the province of New Brunswick was set up in 1784, Ludlow was appointed a member of the council and chief justice of the supreme court, posts he retained until his death.

Ludlow's independence of mind can be seen in his major judicial decisions. A slaveowner himself, he showed compassion to the black woman Nancy Mozely in 1787, when he reduced the charge of murdering her husband to manslaughter and her sentence to a thumb brand. In 1787, to the outrage of the local bar, he lowered the table of legal fees by one-half, on the grounds that a young province could not support the level of expense customary in more developed societies. In a second slave case in 1800, however, he upheld the legality of slavery in New Brunswick, in sharp contrast to the abolitionist trends in the other British colonies. Finally, in 1807, Ludlow laid down a landmark decision sharply reducing the rights of property owners, when he declared the Bay of Fundy waters open to all fishermen up to the high-water mark, not just to those who owned shoreline property.

Ludlow's personal style also set him apart from other Loyalist leaders. He lived on a 1,500-acre estate above Fredericton, called "Spring Hill" in honor of Colden's old home. When the Scottish immigrant agent Patrick Campbell visited Ludlow, he was delighted to note that all the furniture in the house was made of North American woods—spruce, maple, pine—instead of the imported mahogany that was a status symbol for most of the Loyalist elite. His portrait also suggests a dignified simplicity, showing a slender figure, plainly dressed and wigless. Ludlow's legal contribution is recognized in the naming of Ludlow Hall, the home of the University of New Brunswick Law School built in the 1960s, and in the portraits of him that hang in the library of the Law School and the chambers of the supreme court building. All in all, Ludlow made a remarkably smooth transition from the inner circles of Tory New York to the unsettled wilderness of Loyalist New Brunswick and in the process used his extensive professional experience to establish the legal foundations of the exile community. He died in Fredericton, New Brunswick.

• No significant collection of Ludlow papers exists. The best contemporary, if highly opinionated, account is Thomas Jones, *The History of New York during the Revolutionary War*, ed. Edward F. De Lancey (2 vols., 1879). Ludlow's claim for losses during the Revolution is reprinted in Daniel P. Coke, *The Royal Commission on the Losses and Services of American Loyalists*, ed. Hugh E. Egerton (1915), p. 212. For his controversial role as superintendent of police on Long Island, in addition to the account by Jones, see K. G. Davies, "The Restoration of Civil Government by the British in the War of Independence," in *Red, White & True Blue: The Loyalists in the Revolution*, ed. Esmond Wright (1976); Milton M. Klein, "An Experiment That Failed: General James Robertson and Civil Government in British New York, 1779–1783," *New-York History* 61 (1980): 229–54; and two articles by Joseph S. Tiedemann, "Patriots by Default: Queens County, New York and the British Army, 1776–1783," *William and Mary Quarterly*, 3d ser., 43 (1986): 35–63, and "A Revolution Foiled: Queens County, New York, 1775–1776," *Journal of American History* 75 (1988): 417–44. The Huddy affair is discussed in Edward A. Tebbenhoff, "The Associated Loyalists: An Aspect of Militant Loyalism," *New-York Historical Society Quarterly* 63 (1979): 115–44. For a more general account of the Loyalist experience in N.Y., see Philip Ranlet, *The New York Loyalists* (1986).

Lorenzo Sabine, *Biographical Sketches of Loyalists of the American Revolution* (1864), mentions Ludlow's speech defect. Henry Onderdonk, Jr., comp., documents the plunder of his house in 1779 in *Documents and Letters Intended to Illustrate the Revolutionary Incidents of Queens County* (1970).

Loyalist life in New Brunswick is memorably recorded in W. O. Raymond, ed., *The Winslow Papers* (1901), and Patrick Campbell, *Travels in the Interior Inhabited Parts of North America in the Years 1791 and 1792*, ed. Hugh H. Langton and William F. Ganong (1937). A comprehensive scholarly survey is Ann Gorman Condon, *The Envy of the American States: The Loyalist Dream for New Brunswick* (1983). His decisions on slave cases can be followed in Robin Winks, *The Blacks in Canada* (1971); James W. St. G. Walker, *The Black Loyalists: The Search for a Promised Land in Nova Scotia and New Brunswick, 1783–1870* (1976); and William A. Spray, *Blacks in New Brunswick* (1972). Adrien G. W. Gilbert, "New Brunswick's First Chief Justice," *University of New Brunswick Law Journal* 11 (1958): 29–32, and David G. Bell, "Slavery and the Judges of Loyalist New Brunswick," *University of New Brunswick Law Journal* 31 (1982): 9–42, assess Ludlow's legal contribution.

ANN GORMAN CONDON

LUDLOW, Noah Miller (3 July 1795–9 Jan. 1886), actor and theater manager, was born in New York City, the son of John Ludlow, a farmer, and Phebe Dunham. Hoping that he would become a merchant, his mother placed him, at a very early age, in a mercantile house where he remained until he was eighteen years of age. Soon after his father died in 1813, he moved to Albany, New York, to be with his brother Joseph. There he made the acquaintance of some actors and eventually played some small parts. In the spring of 1815 he joined the company of Samuel Drake, Sr., an early pioneer theatrical manager. The company, en route to Kentucky, and using every method of transportation then available in the West, visited numerous towns presenting a variety of plays.

Ludlow left the company in June 1817 and set out for Nashville, Tennessee, where he organized his own dramatic company that included a widow, "Miss Wallace," the professional name of the soon-to-be Mrs. Ludlow—Mary Maury Squires (or Squire). They were married on 1 September 1817 and together had eight children. Ludlow soon went to Natchez, Mississippi, where his company gave the first performance by a professional company in that city around 15 November 1817. In the same year the company traveled to New Orleans, Louisiana, where Ludlow claimed to have presented the first performance in the English language staged in that city. James H. Caldwell, another theatrical pioneer, arrived two years later in 1819. Caldwell's arrival began a protracted struggle for theatrical supremacy between Ludlow and Caldwell in the West and the South.

Ludlow and his company subsequently traveled to and performed in several communities including Huntsville, Alabama, in December 1818, and St. Louis, Missouri, in March 1820. Often the cities they visited had not previously seen a professional theater company. On 24 December 1824 Ludlow opened a new theater in Mobile, Alabama, the first built in that city, with Ludlow playing one of his favorite parts, Rolando in *The Hangmen*. As an actor, he played primarily high comedy parts, such as Young Marlowe in *She Stoops to Conquer* and Scamper in *The Promissory Note*.

After several successful seasons, Ludlow set out for New York City to recruit new members for the company. During the trip, he made his New York debut at the Chatham Theatre on 29 June 1826 as Young Wilding in *The Liar*. While in New York, he managed to engage ten professionals and six novices to help in another very ambitious theatrical foray in Mobile, Nashville, and Montgomery, Alabama. Following the close of the season in Mobile, he took his company to New York and took residence at the Chatham Theatre on 15 September 1828.

On 2 May 1829 Ludlow opened a new theater in Mobile after fire destroyed his original theater. Here, according to Ludlow, began six or seven years of financial setbacks. Despite their ongoing struggles for theatrical dominance, Ludlow went to Natchez in 1831 for James Caldwell on a theatrical mission to obtain performers for Caldwell's company. It was there that he met his future partner, Solomon F. Smith, for the first time. Even though they disputed over roles for the first Mrs. Smith (Martha Theresa Mathews), Ludlow and Smith formed a partnership in 1835 that lasted eighteen years. Sometime later, Ludlow independently secured the financial help of two St. Louis men to build a theater in St. Louis. Until that theater was built, theatrical performances were held in Caldwell's "old salt house." The foundation stone for the theater was laid in 1836. As part of the partnership agreement, at least in the early years, Smith was the primary agent in St. Louis while Ludlow managed the Mobile operation. At one time Ludlow and Smith controlled theaters in St. Louis, New Orleans, and Mobile. In 1843, after Ludlow and Smith constructed the New St. Charles Theatre in New Orleans, Caldwell retired from the business. After the 1848–1849 season, they abandoned the Mobile theater venture.

The Ludlow and Smith organization remains as one of the most intriguing partnerships in theatrical history. That these two men, so disparate in temperament and abilities, could rule the theatrical world in the South and then the West seems inexplicable. However, one element continued to tie them together—money. Ludlow alone—and later as a partner—was scrupulous about paying company members even when he was personally disadvantaged. But compared with Smith, Ludlow was financially unskilled, stiff, formal, and introverted. "I didn't fancy Mr. Ludlow at first," wrote actress Clara Fisher Maeder in her memoir, *Autobiography of Clara Fisher Maeder* (1897), "and wrote home that he looked to me as if he had swallowed a poker." Ludlow was apparently an unhappy man. His wife's alcoholism no doubt contributed to his gloom.

The partners closed their theater in St. Louis in 1851 and dissolved the partnership in 1853. The final break in their relationship occurred as a result of a long-standing loan obligation by Ludlow to Smith and the stance of the men during the Civil War when Ludlow supported the South and Smith stood by the Union. During his long retirement, Ludlow wrote an important theatrical autobiography, *Dramatic Life as I Found It* (1880; repr. 1966), and appeared in benefit performances. He died in St. Louis, Missouri.

Ludlow was a pioneer theatrical manager who brought theater and other amusements to a frontier fraught with assorted dangers. He, and later he and Smith together, presented a wide assortment of entertainments to the West and the South, including many of Shakespeare's works. They brought stars from the East and encouraged a reverse migration of popular players from the West and the South to New York City and other eastern cities. Such luminaries as Junius B. Booth, Charles and Ellen Kean, James Murdoch, J. W. Wallack, Jr., the Batemen children, Charles Burke, Dan Marble, John "Irish" Collins, "Jim Crow" Rice, Anna Cora Mowatt, James H. Hackett, George F. "Yankee" Hill, and George Holland graced the stages of Ludlow's and Smith's theaters, which were known as no-nonsense operations that emphasized scrupulous adherence to respectability and dignity.

• Ludlow's letters, diaries, and other records are in the Missouri Historical Society, St. Louis. W. G. B. Carson, *The Theatre on the Frontier* (1932; repr. 1965) and *Managers in Distress* (1949) along with Larry E. Grisvard, "The Final Years: The Ludlow and Smith Theatrical Firm in St. Louis, 1845–1851" (Ph.D. diss., Ohio State Univ., 1965) are important sources. See also Solomon F. Smith, *Theatrical Management in the West and South for Thirty Years* (1868; repr. 1968).

LARRY E. GRISVARD

LUDLOW, Roger (c. 1590–c. 1664), colonial official and jurist, was the son of Thomas Ludlow of Maiden Bradley, Wiltshire, and Jane Pyle. Educated at Balliol College, Oxford in 1610 and the Inner Temple in 1612, he married Mary Endicott, the sister of John Endicott, an early governor of Massachusetts Bay. The couple had at least six children. In early 1630 Ludlow was elected an assistant of the Bay company, at which time he removed himself and his family to the new colony, helping to establish the town of Dorchester. Regularly reelected an assistant, Ludlow was chosen deputy governor in 1634. He was left out of office in 1635, apparently because of differences with more liberal political developments in the colony concerning the popular election of magistrates, and perhaps because of his plans to move again, this time

to the Connecticut River along with other Massachusetts settlers. One of the founders of Windsor, he served during the next year (1636–1637) under the authority of a Massachusetts commission as presiding magistrate for the three towns that were forming the nucleus of Connecticut: Windsor, Hartford, and Wethersfield. He was reelected a magistrate or assistant for the next seventeen years, except when in 1642 and 1648 he served as deputy governor of Connecticut.

As an accomplished lawyer, magistrate, and colony official, Ludlow is credited with putting Connecticut's first instrument of government, the Fundamental Orders of 1639, into final form. Influenced by Massachusetts colony and trading company experiences, and informed by the Puritan partiality for covenants and compacts, the Orders determined how Connecticut's government was to be elected and defined the compass of its authority. Given his apparent earlier difficulties with a more popular exercise of political power in Massachusetts, Ludlow's participation in drawing up the Fundamental Orders suggests a coming to terms with the Hartford minister Thomas Hooker's recently voiced sentiments concerning a more democratic-like election of magistrates and limitations on government. Modified several times over the next twenty-three years, the orders served as a model for Connecticut's royal charter of 1662, a document that in turn endured as Connecticut's instrument of government until 1818.

At the request of the colony government, Ludlow also compiled Connecticut's earliest extant law code. Officially adopted in 1650, Ludlow's Code, or the Code of 1650, drew heavily on Massachusetts law, especially the Laws and Liberties of 1648 and, to a lesser extent, the Body of Liberties of 1641. Of the seventy-eight provisions in Ludlow's Code, twenty were original, while the others were copied exactly or modified slightly from the Massachusetts models. Given his continuous service as an assistant or magistrate, especially as a member of Connecticut's Particular Court, a quarterly court composed of the governor and several magistrates, Ludlow was well positioned to understand the actual or practical legal needs of the colony.

By 1639 Ludlow had moved again, this time to the southwestern reaches of the colony where he was a founder of Fairfield and a purchaser of the land that in 1651 would become Norwalk. His farming and trading endeavors, along with his government service, did not prevent him from serving Connecticut in other important capacities, especially as a colony representative. He was one of Connecticut's three delegates to the Cambridge Synod of 1637, which dealt with Anne Hutchinson and her Antinomianism. As one of the colony's representatives in 1643 he also helped negotiate the formation among Connecticut, Massachusetts, New Haven, and New Plymouth of the first intercolonial confederation, the United Colonies of New England. Ludlow served several times as a Connecticut commissioner to this confederation, in 1648, 1651, and 1653. During 1653 Ludlow participated in a bitter squabble between a refractory Massachusetts and its nervous fellow colonies over a prospective declaration of war against the Dutch in nearby New Netherland. Alarmed at the perceived Dutch and Indian threat, and tiring of the Bay's refusal to go to war, Fairfield named the elderly Ludlow commander of its own forces. The end of the first Anglo-Dutch War in 1654 rendered the intercolonial dispute moot before Fairfield could take the field, but not before Ludlow had moved on once again. By the fall of 1654 he was in Dublin as a member of a Cromwellian commission regarding the disposition of forfeited lands in Ireland, a service he continued until at least 1659. He was alive in England in 1660, and possibly as late as 1664.

Ludlow was a man of talent and temper, a public-spirited colonial leader and an able jurist who helped to create the legal, political, and territorial foundations of Massachusetts and especially Connecticut. He was consistently recognized for twenty-five years by pioneering generations in two English colonies as an individual who possessed and exercised the courage and stamina of a successful pioneer. Ludlow was an extraordinary but by no means singular figure in an emerging seventeenth-century Anglo-American world. Men such as Ludlow were the able and resourceful, transatlantic citizens who linked the old and new worlds, welcome in both.

• Ludlow manuscripts are scattered throughout the Connecticut Archives (Connecticut State Library, Hartford). Printed materials appear in several of the early volumes of the *Winthrop Papers* (5 vols., 1929–1947) and in a number of volumes in the Massachusetts Historical Society *Collections* (1792–). The only biography of Ludlow is John M. Taylor, *Roger Ludlow, the Colonial Lawmaker* (1900), which may be supplemented by two small works by R. V. Coleman, *Roger Ludlow in Chancery* (1934) and *Mr. Ludlow Goes for Old England* (1935); an article by Arthur L. Shipman, "Connecticut's First Lawyer," *Connecticut Bar Journal* 1 (1927); and Thomas J. Farnham, *Fairfield: The Biography of a Community, 1639–1989* (1988). Ludlow's Connecticut career may be followed in J. Hammond Trumbull, ed., *The Public Records of the Colony of Connecticut*, vol. 1 (1850), and in *Records of the Particular Court of Connecticut, 1639–1663*, vol. 22 of the Connecticut Historical Society *Collections* (1928). Two contemporary histories of Connecticut provide necessary context as well as discussion of Ludlow, Mary Jeanne Anderson Jones, *Congregational Commonwealth: Connecticut, 1636–1662* (1968), and Robert J. Taylor, *Colonial Connecticut: A History* (1979).

THOMAS W. JODZIEWICZ

LUDWELL, Philip (c. 1638–c. 1723), governor of the Carolinas and colonial Virginia official, was the son of Thomas Ludwell and Jane Cottington of Bruton Parish, Somersetshire, England. By 1660 Philip and his brother Thomas were living in Virginia, where Thomas was a member of the Council. The governor, Sir William Berkeley, was also from Bruton Parish; hence, the Ludwells had easy access to his intimate circle, becoming his friends and staunch political allies. Philip Ludwell acquired "Fairfield Plantation" in Gloucester County, and by October 1667 he was married to Lucy Higginson, the daughter of Robert and Joanna Tokesey Higginson and the widow of Lewis

Burwell and Colonel William Bernard. Lucy was the mother of Ludwell's two children. After 1678 the Ludwells moved to the James City County plantation "Rich Neck," which he inherited from his brother.

Appointed to the Council in 1675, Philip Ludwell also was deputy secretary of state (1675–1677) for his brother and later served briefly as secretary of state. During Bacon's Rebellion in 1676, Ludwell, a colonel of the militia, arrested Giles Bland and other Baconites and was involved in the trials of the rebels. The rebellion and Berkeley's heavy-handed punishment of the participants resulted in the governor's recall and replacement by Herbert Jeffreys. At the heart of the local Virginia power structure, Ludwell resented and clashed with the policies of Jeffreys, who had been directed to bring order to the colony. Characterized by the governor as "rash and fiery," Ludwell was removed from the Council in 1679.

Having been a widower since 1675, in October 1680 Ludwell married Lady Frances Culpeper (1634–1690), daughter of Thomas Culpeper (Lord Culpeper), a proprietor of the Northern Neck, a vast proprietary grant on the peninsula between the Rappahannock and Potomac rivers. Lady Frances was the widow of Samuel Stephens (d. 1670), a governor of Albemarle County, Carolina, and most recently the widow of Sir William Berkeley, who had died in 1677. Through this marriage Ludwell acquired Berkeley's "Green Spring" plantation near Jamestown. Lady Frances had inherited a Carolina proprietorship from Sir William, but Ludwell persuaded her to sell it in 1684.

Ludwell was restored to the Council in 1681 by Governor Lord Culpeper, a relative of Lady Frances, and was a key member of the group of planters called "irreconcilables," who were unalterably opposed to the royal governor's efforts to weaken the power of the local aristocracy and bring the colony under royal authority. Bitter confrontation surfaced under the imperious Francis Howard, Baron Howard of Effingham, governor from 1684 to 1689. Accused by the governor of having "rudly and boldly disputed the King's authority," Ludwell was again suspended in 1687 from all offices and then dismissed from the Council the next year. He was elected to the House of Burgesses but was not allowed to take his seat. The next year he went to England to present grievances from the House of Burgesses against the governor. Effingham's biographer, Warren M. Billings, has characterized Ludwell as "a man of large abilities" with "the restless spirit of a freebooter." Ludwell's zeal for vengeance likely contributed to the failure of his mission to unseat the governor, but the concerns of a distant colony seemed of little importance in an England stirred by the Glorious Revolution.

While in London, Ludwell, who was already known to the Carolina proprietors, evidently conferred with them about the troubled state of affairs in their southern colony of Albemarle County, whose citizens had recently deposed their governor, the proprietor Seth Sothel. Apparently impressed with the abilities of

Ludwell, on 5 December 1689 the proprietors appointed him governor of "that part of our province of Carolina that lieth north and East of Cape Fear." This was the first territorial delineation of what would become North Carolina.

When Ludwell arrived in Albemarle County in May 1690, he was challenged by Colonel John Gibbs of Virginia, a cacique in the Carolina nobility. According to the Fundamental Constitutions, when there was no resident governor or proprietor, members of the nobility were next in line of succession. Gibbs threatened to contest Ludwell's right to the governorship and led a brief violent attempt to break up a local court; however, he rallied little support among the colony's citizens. Both Ludwell and Gibbs traveled to London, seeking proprietary support for their claims, and Ludwell was confirmed as governor.

The next year, to prevent further turmoil, the proprietors suspended the colony's constitution because Sothel had gone to southern Carolina and claimed the governorship. To settle the confusion in Charles Town, the proprietors on 2 November 1691 commissioned Ludwell governor of all of Carolina, with authority to name a deputy governor for the northern colony. Ludwell qualified as governor in Charles Town in April 1692. Sothel departed quietly, but Ludwell was unable to solve the long-term bitter factional struggle that had wracked the southern colony for several years. He is credited, however, with handling Indian affairs well. In contrast, northern Carolina was effectively governed through local deputy governors, entering a politically peaceful decade.

Ludwell headed for Virginia in May 1693, and by November the proprietors had appointed a successor as governor. The proprietors retained Ludwell as the governor of their northern colony for two more years. In this area Ludwell was successful in solving a major problem in land policy and quitrents by supporting the colonists' view that their 1668 agreement for a more liberal policy was valid. After his return to Virginia, Ludwell was Speaker of the House of Burgesses in 1695 and continued to serve as a burgess until 1698. He left Virginia for England about 1700 and never returned to America. He apparently lived quietly in England and is buried at Stratford-le-Bow Church in Middlesex.

Although Ludwell did not dominate Virginia politics in his day, he was an important figure for two decades. His confidence in taking on the Stuart-appointed royal governors is an indication of his firm position at the center of the Virginia power structure. His tenures as governor of both of the Carolinas were at least partially successful. Although he was able to deal only with minor problems in the southern colony, he left the northern colony pacified, ending years of political in-fighting and turmoil.

• Official papers of Ludwell are in "Philip Ludwell's Account [of Bacon's Rebellion]," *Virginia Magazine of History and Biography*, 1 (Oct. 1893); H. R. McIlwaine, ed., *Minutes of the Council and General Court of Colonial Virginia* (1929; 2d ed.,

1979), and *Journals of the House of Burgesses in Virginia, 1659/60–1693* (1914); Mattie E. E. Parker, ed., *North Carolina Higher-Court Records* vol. 1, *1670–1696* (1968) and vol. 2, *1697–1701* (1971); W. Noel Sainsbury, ed., *Calendar of State Papers, Colonial Series, America and West Indies, 1677–1680* (1896) and *1685–1688* (1899); and William L. Saunders, ed., *The Colonial Records of North Carolina*, vol. 1 (1896). Biographical information is in Cassius F. Lee, Jr., "Ludwell Genealogy," *New England Historical and Genealogical Register*, 33 (Apr. 1879): 220–22; Edmund J. Lee, *Lee of Virginia, 1642–1892* (1974); "Ludwell Family," *William and Mary Quarterly*, 1st ser., 19 (Jan. 1911): 199–214; Fairfax Harrison, *The Proprietors of the Northern Neck: Chapters of Culpeper Genealogy* (1926); and Nell M. Nugent, comp., *Cavaliers and Pioneers*, vol. 1 (1934). Ludwell's public career is included in Warren M. Billings, *Virginia's Viceroy: Their Majesties' Governor General Francis Howard, Baron Howard of Effingham* (1991); Edward McCrady, *The History of South Carolina under the Proprietary Government, 1670–1719* (1897); and M. Eugene Sirmans, *Colonial South Carolina: A Political History, 1663–1763* (1966).

LINDLEY S. BUTLER

LUDWIG, Christoph (17 Oct. 1720–17 June 1801), baker and philanthropist, was born in Gießen, Hesse-Darmstadt. Little is known of his childhood, including the names of his parents. His father was a baker from whom he learned the trade that was to garner him fame in the Continental army. He attended a free school at the age of fourteen and by the age of seventeen joined the ill-fated army of the Holy Roman Emperor in the 1736–1739 renewed war against the Ottoman Empire that lost all of the Balkan territories acquired up to the treaty of Passarowitz (1718). Ludwig made his way back from Turkey to Vienna. He nearly starved to death on the way, and in his old age he included Roman Catholic institutions of charity in his will in remembrance of the Catholic peasants who gave him enough to eat and sufficient clothing to return to Vienna. Scarcely had he and his fellow soldiers recuperated but their further journey homeward was interrupted at Prague, where the French laid siege to the city in the War of Austrian Succession.

A year later, in 1741, Ludwig enlisted in the Prussian Army, which in alliance with the French was now fighting the Habsburgs. At war's end in 1748, Ludwig made his way to London, exploring the capital of Austria's recent allies. He signed on as ship's baker on the *Duke of Cumberland* and spent the next three and one-half years in service in the East Indies. Returning to London in 1745, he collected his wages of about £117 and returned to visit his family in Gießen, where he learned of his father's death. Selling his paternal inheritance in land and goods for 400 Gulden (about £188), he apparently squandered the sum in good living in Britain, finally of necessity putting to sea again on voyages between 1745 and 1752 that took him to the Netherlands, Ireland, and the West Indies.

At the age of thirty-two Ludwig changed his habits, investing the £25 he had saved from these voyages in ready-made English clothes. The following year he made his first voyage to the mainland British colonies and landed at Philadelphia, where he sold the finished goods for a handsome profit of 300 percent. Returning to London he invested his wealth in turning his basic knowledge of the baker's trade to mastery of the more difficult and elite arts of sugar confection and gingerbread baking. Armed with these new skills, Ludwig returned to Philadelphia in 1755, where he began a rapid economic and social rise among the German-speaking settlers in Pennsylvania. He married Catharine English, a widow, in 1755; they had no children together. By the 1770s, his fortune included £3,500 Pennsylvania current money earning interest for him, as well as a farm in Germantown and nine houses in Philadelphia. He was a member and elder of St. Michael's and Zion Lutheran Church in Philadelphia, a signer of its church order of 1762, and he and his wife were regular contributors. He loaned the church during the 1760s some £400 when internal strife undercut attendance and financial contributions. The Philadelphia tax rolls for 1772 show him to have been assessed for £85 and the owner of two slaves he later emancipated before his death.

As the imperial crisis of the 1770s deepened, Ludwig served on various revolutionary committees and put his considerable wealth at the disposal of the patriot cause. He subscribed £200 for firearms and volunteered his service as a baker without pay for the American forces in 1776. Because of his Hessian background, he was sent disguised as a deserter to the Hessian mercenaries on Staten Island, where his fulsome description of the possibilities of land ownership, the beauty of the German-American churches, and the delights of eating as much beef as one could imagine lured away hundreds of deserters, who were then placed under his protection by the Continental Congress.

On 3 May 1777 Congress made Ludwig superintendent of bakers and director of baking for the Continental army. George Washington expressed his hope to John Hancock and the Continental Congress that Ludwig's probity would put an end to the "many abuses" that had occurred in the army "for want of some proper regulations." During the course of the war, Washington came to value Ludwig's honesty and to refer to him as his "honest friend." In his correspondence, and to contemporaries, Ludwig became known as "Baker General," most probably because his official title of superintendent would have confused fellow German-speakers who knew this title to mean one exercising regional authority over the European state churches. Ludwig was warmly regarded by Congressional members who accepted his insistence on providing the correct 135 pounds of bread for every 100 pounds of flour provided instead of the one-to-one ratio they had proposed.

At the war's end, Ludwig returned to his farm near Germantown, his home having been plundered by the British and his estates laid waste. Since he had rescued his inlaws from financial ruin, and been paid in depreciated money for his services, his payment of the bakers under him from his own personal funds left him financially ruined. He prepared a memorial to Congress asking for the land bounty being offered to other officers in the Continental army. Refusing to borrow or buy on credit, he obtained an attestation from Washington in 1785 of his patriotism and was awarded $200 by Congress for his losses. He quickly began to rebuild his fortune and by the late 1780s divided his time between his Germantown residence and Philadelphia, where he also continued to worship at St. Michael's and Zion Lutheran Church.

Ludwig's first wife died in 1795 and Ludwig sold his Germantown farm, moving to Philadelphia where he boarded for a time with Frederick Fraley, who had learned the baker's trade under Ludwig. He remarried in 1798, this time to Sophia Binder, a widow. Two years later, as yellow fever gripped the city, Ludwig volunteered to work with Fraley in baking bread for the poor. The following year, in 1798, he moved to 176 North Fifth Street, only a few blocks from his parish church, St. Michael's Lutheran. He had begun to consider how to support various charities during 1797 and endowed his own church as well as the German Reformed, St. Michael's Lutheran in Germantown, the German Society of Pennsylvania, the University of Pennsylvania, and the Roman Catholic, Episcopal, African, and Presbyterian churches with funds to support the needy poor with bread and to provide poor children with a free education.

His will stipulated that schools for poor children should be established without regard to denomination within five years of his death. In this, he frustrated the objectives of his own pastor at St. Michael's and Zion in Philadelphia, J. H. C. Helmuth, who had begun a charity school project of his own in the early 1780s but within the context of the Lutheran parochial system. The Philadelphia Society for the Establishment and Support of Charity Schools opened a night school for poor children in 1799 and a few years later was able to secure a total of $13,000 as the result of Ludwig's charitable interests. Ludwig died in Philadelphia and was buried in St. Michael's Lutheran churchyard. The effects of his charitable intents are still felt in the late twentieth century as the funds established by his will are administered by the Board of City Trusts, which continues to support the charitable work for which Ludwig was justly celebrated by his contemporaries.

• There is no collection of Ludwig papers; various letters survive in the Library of Congress, the Historical Society of Pennsylvania, the Philadelphia Board of Trust, and the Lutheran Archives Center, Philadelphia, which has acquired the original of Ludwig's will. The older accounts of his life include the unique recollections of Benjamin Rush, *An Account of the Life and Character of Christopher Ludwick* (1831), originally published in *Poulson's American Daily Advertisor* (Philadelphia, 30 June 1801); see also John C. Fitzpatrick, ed., *The Writings of George Washington from the Original Manuscript Sources*, vol. 8 (1933), pp. 16, 475; W. W. Abbott et al., eds., *The Papers of George Washington*, Confederation ser., vol. 2 (1992), pp. 471–72.

A. G. ROEBER

LUFBERY, Gervais Raoul Victor (14 Mar. 1885–19 May 1918), aviator, was born in Clermont, France, the son of Edward Lufbery, a stamp dealer, and Annette Vessieres. His father was probably an American citizen, although accounts vary; his mother was French. When his mother died in 1886, he was sent to live with a family in the Auvergne Mountains. In 1890 his father remarried and in 1891 moved to Wallingford, Connecticut, leaving Raoul and his two brothers with their grandmother in France. After his stepmother died in 1901, Lufbery went to work in a chocolate factory in Blois to help support his family.

In 1904 he decided to see the world, traveling to Algiers, Tunis, Egypt, and then to Constantinople, where he worked as a waiter. He was later employed by a German steamship line plying between Hamburg and German South Africa. In 1906 he went to Wallingford to visit his father, who, unfortunately, had sailed the same day for Europe. After two years in Wallingford, in 1908 Lufbery yielded again to wanderlust, visiting Cuba, working in a bakery in New Orleans and then as a waiter in San Francisco, and then joining the army. After two years in the Philippines with the U.S. Army and receiving U.S. citizenship as a result of his service, he went to China, where he worked for the Chinese Customs Service, and then to India, where he found employment as a ticket agent in Bombay.

In Calcutta he met Marc Pourpe, an early barnstorming pilot, and became his mechanic, partner, and close friend. The two were in France in 1914 to obtain a new airplane when World War I broke out. Pourpe immediately enlisted in the Service Aeronautique; Lufbery, an American citizen, enlisted in the Foreign Legion on 24 August and was detached on 31 August to serve as Pourpe's mechanic.

When Pourpe was killed in a flying accident, Lufbery determined to avenge his death by becoming a pilot. He was sent to aviation school at Chartres. Breveted on the Maurice Farman bomber on 29 July 1915, he was sent to the front on 7 October 1915 to join VB 106, flying Voisin bombers.

On 10 April 1916, at Lufbery's own request, he was transferred to a depot at Le Plessis-Belleville for training as a *pilote de chasse*—a fighter pilot. He found it difficult to adapt to the sensitive controls of scout-type aircraft after flying bombers and nearly "washed out," but he completed the course on 22 May and joined the Lafayette Escadrille at Bar-le-Duc on 24 May 1916, only five weeks after it had been organized.

Lufbery scored his first victory on 30 July, his second the next day, the next two on 4 and 8 August, and on 12 October he became the first American "ace" with five confirmed aerial victories. He eventually won seventeen confirmed victories, the largest number attained by any member of the Lafayette Flying Corps (an organization larger than the Escadrille). According to his squadron mates, he won many more that occurred too far behind German lines for confirmation.

Like other Allied aces such as Albert Ball, William Avery Bishop, and Georges-Marie Guynemer, Lufbery was a loner in the air, often returning with his aircraft badly shot up. Between flights he enjoyed hunting mushrooms and playing practical jokes, and despite a severe case of rheumatism he loved to frolic with "Whiskey" and "Soda," the squadron's two African lion mascots. Even so, he did not always manage to avoid getting into fistfights.

After America joined World War I and sent aviation units to France, Lufbery was transferred to the U.S. Air Service. He was commissioned a major (he had been a *sous-lieutenant*) on 10 January 1918 and was named commanding officer of the 95th Pursuit Squadron, but it existed only on paper. His complaints to higher authority resulted in his being declared "not suitable for command." He was sent to Issoudon, a training base, to sit at a desk, an assignment for which he was utterly ill suited. On 21 January he was assigned to the 94th Pursuit Squadron, only to find that the unit had few airplanes and no guns. Undeterred, Lufbery began a training program for the green Americans, and when they were finally combat ready, he led the first combat patrol on 10 April 1918.

On 19 May Lufbery took off alone in another pilot's aircraft and attacked a German reconnaissance airplane flying over his field. As his squadron mates watched, his aircraft was struck by enemy fire and burst into flames. Lufbery jumped, fell, or was thrown from the airplane, landing in a flower garden at Maron (Merthe-et-Moselle), just north of Nancy. (Parachutes were not issued to Allied pilots at the time.) Villagers carried his body to the town hall and covered it with flowers, where his squadron mates found it. His final resting place is the Lafayette Escadrille Memorial at Villeneuve.

Although aviation made at best a modest contribution to the outcome of World War I, before his death Lufbery had won the Legion d'Honneur, the Medaille Militaire, the Croix de Guerre with ten palms, and the British Military Medal. He was described by General Joseph Joffre, marshal of France, as a "model of skill, of sang-froid, of courage."

• A file of biographical material on Lufbery is at the public library in Wallingford, Conn. An excellent source of information on Lufbery is *The Lafayette Flying Corps* (2 vols., 1920) by James N. Hall and Charles B. Nordhoff, themselves members of the corps. Also see Edwin C. Parsons, *I Flew with the Lafayette Escadrille* (1963), originally published as *The Great Adventure* (1937). Two more recent and carefully researched books are Herbert M. Mason, Jr., *The Lafayette Escadrille* (1964), and Philip M. Flammer, *The Vivid Air: The Lafayette Escadrille* (1981). Accounts of Lufbery's death and burial are in the *New York Times*, 21–23 May 1918.

VINCENT P. NORRIS

LUGOSI, Bela (20 Oct. 1882–16 Aug. 1956), actor, was born Béla Ferenc Dezsö Blaskó in Lugos, Hungary, the son of István Blaskó, a baker and banker, and Paula Vojnits. His father died and left the family impoverished while Lugosi was young, so he quit school to train as an ironworker. In 1901 he decided to become an actor and started playing roles in provincial theaters and singing in operas and musical comedies. He used several different stage names, including Ariztid Olt and Bela Lugossy.

In 1913 Lugosi joined the National Theater of Hungary, where he had small roles in several dozen plays. After the outbreak of World War I in 1914, Lugosi joined the Royal Hungarian Infantry. He served as a lieutenant on the Russian and Serbian fronts. Badly wounded in 1916, he left the service and returned to the National Theater. He made his film debut the following year in *The Leopard* and played in several other Hungarian films in subsequent months. In 1917 he married Ilona Szmik, the daughter of a Budapest banker.

After the war ended, a Communist revolution led by Béla Kun briefly established a socialist regime in Hungary and was then violently suppressed. Lugosi had supported the revolution and had taken an active role in organizing an actors' union, so he fled to Vienna and then Berlin. His wife accompanied him to Vienna but then returned to Hungary and obtained a divorce.

Lugosi appeared in several German films and then immigrated to the United States in 1921. He initially toured as a leading man of a small Hungarian-language troupe that played to American-Hungarian audiences. The same year he married actress Ilona Montagh de Nagybányhegyes; the marriage ended in divorce in 1924. His third marriage, to Beatrice Woodruff Weeks in 1929, also ended in divorce. After Lugosi left the troupe, he played several character roles on Broadway: a Parisian criminal in *The Red Poppy* (1922), a sheik in *Arabesque* (1925), and an evil monk in *The Devil in the Cheese* (1926). He also appeared in several films produced on the East Coast, starting with Fox's *The Silent Command* (1923). Although he often played romantic leads on the stage, he was cast as a villain in most of his films.

His career began to take off in 1927, when he played the lead in *Dracula*, an English play brought over to Broadway. After a year's run in New York, he toured with the play for two additional years. The play's success prompted Universal Studios to purchase the film rights, and they cast Lugosi in the lead in the 1931 film version. He was a great success with critics and the public.

Universal next slated Lugosi to appear in *Frankenstein* (1932), but he declined in favor of what became a less successful film, *Murders in the Rue Morgue* (1932). Boris Karloff took the lead in *Frankenstein* instead and became prominent as Lugosi's rival as top horror star. In 1933 Lugosi married his secretary, Lillian Arch, who continued to act as his business manager. The couple had one son and were divorced in 1953.

During the following decade Lugosi appeared in numerous films, usually as the villain in horror movies, including *White Zombie* (1932), *The Black Cat* (1934), *The Return of Chandu* (1935), *The Raven* (1935), *The Invisible Ray* (1936), and *Son of Frankenstein* (1939). He was cast against type as a Communist commissar in Greta Garbo's comedy hit, *Ninotchka* (1939), and then returned to horror films such as *The Ghost of Frankenstein* (1942), *Frankenstein Meets the Wolfman* (1943), and *The Return of the Vampire* (1943).

He returned to the stage in productions of *Dracula* and *Arsenic and Old Lace* in the late 1940s. He also toured and performed in a revue consisting of portions of *Dracula* and brief comedy skits in which he parodied himself. He returned to movies in *Abbott and Costello Meet Frankenstein* (1948) and, after touring England with a stage production of *Dracula*, played the Count for the last time in *Old Mother Riley Meets the Vampire* (1953).

Lugosi's movie roles grew smaller, less lucrative, and less frequent after the end of the war. He started to use narcotics, beginning with morphine prescribed for his sciatica, and then methadone and meperidine. An operation eventually cured the medical condition, but he had become addicted to the drugs. In April 1955 he publicly announced his addiction and had the courts commit him to the California State Hospital at Norwalk. Declared cured and released several months later, he found the attendant publicity had attracted offers of roles in several movies. He appeared in *Bride of the Monster* (1956) and *The Black Sleep* (1956). In 1955 he married for the fifth time, to Hope Lininger, a longtime fan who had moved to Hollywood in order to be near him.

Lugosi died in Los Angeles during the filming of Edward Wood's *Plan 9 from Outer Space* (released in 1959). Pursuant to his wishes, he was buried in his Count Dracula cape.

Count Dracula was the role of a lifetime. It branded Lugosi into the public's mind but also smothered his opportunities to become known as a comedic and romantic actor. Lugosi's persona as Count Dracula implied unbelievable horror hidden behind a cultured facade imbued with subtle sexual overtones. The continuing public fascination made the merchandising of Lugosi's likeness on masks, t-shirts, and other pop culture items a very profitable business. Lugosi's son became a lawyer in 1964 and instituted a lawsuit that demanded that Lugosi's estate be paid compensation for the film company's use of Lugosi's likeness. The lawsuit, *Lugosi v. Universal Studios* (1979), resulted in one of the first rulings on legal rights to use of the likeness of a dead person.

• There are no Lugosi papers or memoirs. He is the subject of a biography, Arthur Lennig, *The Count: The Life and Films of Bela "Dracula" Lugosi* (1974), and the papers collected by Lennig about Lugosi are located at the Special Collections Archives, Brigham Young University, Provo, Utah. A transcript of an oral history interview of his fourth wife, Lillian Lugosi Donlevy, is at the Oral History Project of Brigham Young University. Lugosi is discussed in John Brosnan, *The Horror People* (1976), and Clive Hirschhorn, *The Universal Story* (1983). Gary J. Svehla and Susan Svehla, eds., *Bela Lugosi* (1995), examines his films. The postmortem litigation over the image of Lugosi and other celebrities is discussed in the *New York Times*, 8 Nov. 1994. An obituary is in the *New York Times*, 17 Aug. 1956.

STEPHEN G. MARSHALL

LUHAN, Mabel Dodge (26 Feb. 1879–13 Aug. 1962), writer and patron, was born in Buffalo, New York, the daughter of Charles Ganson and Sarah Cook, members of the upper class who lived on inherited wealth. Like most Victorian women of her class, Luhan was educated to charm and groomed to marry. Stultified emotionally and intellectually at home and at the various finishing (or boarding) schools she attended, she worked throughout her life to create a world that would simultaneously establish her identity and serve as a model for the larger European and American communities that surrounded her. She moved from one "cosmos," as she called them, to the next, with the expectation that each would provide the answer to her own and her contemporaries' need to connect with something larger than the dying legacy of individualism left them by late Victorian culture.

After the accidental hunting death of her first husband, John Evans, whom she had married in 1900 and who was the father of her only child, Luhan was sent to Paris by her family, who were also eager to get her away from the prominent Buffalo gynecologist with whom she was having an affair. In 1904 she met and married Edwin Dodge, in Paris, soon moving with him to Florence, where he purchased a Medicean villa that they jointly reconstructed. She devoted the next eight years of her life to realizing her dream of creating an identity by reconstructing the Renaissance and collecting famous guests to grace her salon and share her table—Gertrude Stein and Leo Stein, Paul Draper and Muriel Draper, Eleonora Duse, Bernard Berenson, and Arthur Rubinstein among them.

When the past failed Luhan as a means to establish her identity, she returned to the United States in 1912. Soon after settling in Washington Square, she separated from her husband because he stood between her and "real life." (They were divorced in 1916.) In Europe Dodge had provided a safe background against which she could play out her unfulfilled romantic dreams. In the shock of her uprooting, as she plunged into the many new freedoms offered by the radical activists and avant-garde aesthetes of Greenwich Village, she no longer wanted or needed him as a stabilizing force. In the Village she established one of the most successful salons in U.S. history, incorporating the diverse social, artistic, and political rebellions of the time and attempting to direct them through her liberated life force. Her openness to the ideas and issues that played out before her in her living room—birth control, woman suffrage, peace, socialism, anarchism, postimpressionism, psychoanalysis—allowed her to taste and influence rich and variegated slices of the intellectual and cultural life of her times and to meet and learn from such luminaries as Walter Lippmann, Emma Goldman, Lincoln Steffens, and Margaret Sanger. Indeed, historian Frederick Hoffman said of her that she "all but established the pattern of the 'freelance intellectual' of the early twentieth century" (*Freudianism and the Literary Mind* [1945], pp. 56–57). In January 1913 Luhan helped raise funds for the Armory Show, the first major exhibition of postimpres-

sionist art in the United States. It was there that Gertrude Stein was introduced to American audiences through her "Portrait of Mabel Dodge at the Villa Curonia," which Luhan had bound and printed and circulated at the exhibition. She gave room and board to avant-garde artists Marsden Hartley and Robert Edmond Jones; posted bail for imprisoned socialists; and helped to mount the Paterson strike pageant with her lover, radical journalist John Reed. She wrote for Alfred Stieglitz's journal *Camera Work* and for the *Masses*, the best left-wing magazine of the day, and through her syndicated column in the Hearst papers, "Mabel Dodge Writes," she helped to popularize Freudian psychology. As a leading advocate of modernism in all its forms, Luhan represented, according to a Chicago newspaper reporter, "the most peculiar common denominator that society, literature, art and radical revolutionaries ever found in New York and Europe," a reputation enhanced by the numerous appearances of her life and character in the art and fiction of her peers—including Carl Van Vechten, Neith Boyce, Max Eastman, Gertrude Stein, Jacques Emile-Blanche, Jo Davidson, Andrew Dasburg, and, later, after her move to New Mexico, D. H. Lawrence.

In December 1917, recently remarried, to artist Maurice Sterne, Luhan went to New Mexico seeking a "Change." The capital "C" denoted, in the fourth and final volume of her published memoirs, that more than boredom had brought her to New Mexico. "My life broke in two right then, and I entered the second half, a new world that replaced all the ways I had known with others, more strange and terrible and sweet than any I had ever been able to imagine" (*Edge of Taos Desert*, p. 6). Not long after her arrival, she began to imagine that world as a center for the rebirth of Anglo-American civilization.

Among the scores of East and West Coast writers and artists who moved to Santa Fe and Taos after World War I, Luhan took the leading role in promoting the utopian myth of the Southwest as a Garden of Eden, where the climate, terrain, and indigenous peoples offered a neurotic and mechanized white civilization a model for its aesthetic and spiritual renewal. She did this not only through her extensive correspondence and published articles and essays in such magazines as *Theatre Arts Monthly*, the *Dial*, and *Creative Arts*, but also by attracting to Taos an extraordinary array of painters, writers, ethnologists, musicologists, and reformers to help her celebrate and preserve the lands and culture of what John Collier, her friend and a future commissioner of Indian affairs, called "the Red Atlantis." Among the more prominent visitors whose lives and works were influenced by their visits to Luhan and by the Taos landscape are D. H. Lawrence, Georgia O'Keeffe, Ansel Adams, John Marin, Jean Toomer, Elsie Clews Parsons, Dorothy Brett, Leopold Stokowski, and Frank Waters. Both in her own right, as writer and publicist, as well as a hostess to important artists and thinkers of her time, Luhan played a significant role in the revitalized cultural life of the Southwest.

Luhan believed that among the Pueblo Indians she had at last found a world in which love, rather than power, was the basis of human relationships. The Pueblos attracted her because theirs was a culture of seemingly timeless and stable values that offered what no twentieth-century society was able to: an integration of personal, social, and work life with religious and aesthetic expression. Taos became her final home, and Taos Pueblo Indian Antonio Luhan, whom she married in 1923, became her final husband. (After a lengthy separation she and Sterne had divorced in 1922.) Luhan hoped that she and "Tony" could articulate the ancient doctrines of Pueblo life in terms that could effectively persuade modern men and women to reintegrate their minds and bodies and learn to live with respect for the land. She dreamed of making her home, and its compound of six guesthouses, a model for a "new world plan" that would bring about a transformation of values in which native cultures and ecological principles formed the basis for a vital and pluralist national culture.

Motivated by her desire to convince others of the decline and fall of Western civilization and its potential for rebirth in the American Southwest, Luhan wrote four volumes of published memoirs. Her most important contribution to American social and cultural history, they offer a rich and often insightful (if sometimes overwritten) portrait of American life among the upper classes and the intelligentsia from the late nineteenth through the early twentieth century. Her legacy as a patron of artists and Native-American cultures is more mixed, as she is responsible for helping to purvey the myth of the exotic Indian "other," a romantic construct that has more to do with the needs of the dispossessed Anglo elite than with the real lives and needs of America's native peoples. Yet the interest that she and her friends took in Native-American life and culture resulted in positive movements to protect their lands and culture and in a renewed respect for the contributions of America's indigenous peoples to the making of American civilization.

Mabel Dodge Luhan died in Taos. During the 1940s and 1950s she had receded from the national public eye, devoting most of her time to New Mexican and Indian affairs, as Taos had come to be more of a refuge for individuals in search of physical and spiritual renewal. During this period Luhan published *Taos and Its Artists* (1947), one of the earliest histories of the art colony. Despite her mythologizing of its "spirit of place," Luhan did not exaggerate when she wrote in the introduction to her last book that Taos had served the artists who had come there over a forty-year period as "a fabulous honeycomb, irresistible and nourishing."

• Luhan's papers are at the Beinecke Library, Yale University. Her most important publications are her four volumes of memoirs, which were published as *Background* (1933), *European Experiences* (1935), *Movers and Shakers* (1936; repr. 1985), and *Edge of Taos Desert: An Escape to Reality* (1937; repr. 1987) under the general title *Intimate Memories*. The most complete biography is Lois Rudnick, *Mabel Dodge Luhan: New Woman, New Worlds* (1984). See also Rudnick, "The Male-Identified Woman and Other Anxieties: The Life of Mabel Dodge Luhan," in *The Challenge of Feminist Biography*, ed. Sara Alpern et al. (1992). Other biographical works include Emily Hahn's anecdotal *Mabel: A Biography of Mabel Dodge Luhan* (1977) and Christopher Lasch, "Mabel Dodge Luhan: Sex as Politics," in his *The New Radicalism in America (1899–1963): The Intellectual as a Social Type* (1965). An obituary is in the *New York Times*, 14 Aug. 1962.

LOIS PALKEN RUDNICK

LUKE, Keye (18 June 1904–12 Jan. 1991), actor, was born in Canton, China, the son of Lee Luke, an exporter of objects to the United States, and Tseng Shih. The family migrated permanently to the United States when Keye was three years old. In Seattle, Washington, his father became an importer at the retail level. Luke graduated from high school in Seattle, planning to matriculate as an architecture student at the University of Washington, but he was unable to do so following the death in 1923 of his father. He supported his mother and four younger siblings as a skillful commercial artist. He moved to Hollywood, where beginning in 1930 he worked as an artist, a billboard designer, and a caricaturist for Fox Films. He did publicity artwork for Fox in connection with several early Charlie Chan movies, beginning in 1931. He also did newspaper artwork for movies produced by RKO Radio Pictures, including *King Kong* and *Flying Down to Rio* (both 1933). RKO promised Luke an acting role opposite Anna May Wong in *Ho for Shanghai*, a sequel to *Flying Down to Rio*, but studio infighting caused its cancellation. His acting career began when a Metro-Goldwyn-Mayer director needed a Chinese actor who could speak cultured English as a Chinese doctor in *The Painted Veil*. Luke got the part in the movie, which was released in 1934 and starred Greta Garbo. Thereafter, Luke appeared in upwards of a hundred movies in a career spanning more than five decades.

The role for which Luke was most famous was created in 1935. The first Charlie Chan movie had been *Charlie Chan Carries On* (1931), with Warner Oland as Chan. After five more Chan movies, all of them popular, *Charlie Chan in Paris* came out in 1935 and first featured Luke as Lee Chan, Charlie's "Number One Son." The warm blend of inscrutable father and clean-cut son was an instant hit. Nine more movies in the series followed in the 1930s, all with Oland and seven with Luke: *Charlie Chan in Shanghai* (1935); *Charlie Chan at the Circus* (1936, with Luke first displaying talent as a comic actor and relishing work with the midget couple George and Olive Brasno); *Charlie Chan at the Race Track* (1936); *Charlie Chan at the Opera* (1936, with Luke partly in chorus-boy disguise); *Charlie Chan at the Olympics* (1937, featuring Boris Karloff); *Charlie Chan on Broadway* (1937); and *Charlie Chan at Monte Carlo* (1937). When Oland, who appeared in sixteen Chan movies (for Fox, then 20th Century–Fox), died in 1938, Sidney Toler replaced him in twenty-two subsequent movies (half 20th Century–Fox, then half Monogram Pictures). For a long while Luke was not interested in participating, and his connection with the series came to a temporary end. Sen Yung (later calling himself Victor Sen Young) and Benson Fong became Son Number Two and Son Number Three, respectively. Luke did act, however, as Lee Chan in *Mr. Moto's Gamble* (1938), which Fox reworked from the canceled *Charlie Chan at Ringside* and which starred Peter Lorre. Interestingly, Luke's brother Edwin Luke played Charlie Chan's Number Four Son, Eddie Chan, in *The Jade Mask* (1945), starring Toler as Charlie.

Meanwhile Luke had demonstrated versatility in other movies in the 1930s. He was something of a victim of Hollywood's then-notorious racial stereotyping but rose above it with great dignity. He enjoyed minor roles in *Oil for the Lamps of China* (1935) and *The Good Earth* (1937), in the latter working most enjoyably with Irving Thalberg. Luke replaced Karloff in *Phantom of Chinatown* (1940), the sixth and last Mr. Wong mystery movie, and he appeared as the fighting servant Kato in *The Green Hornet* and *The Green Hornet Strikes Again* (both 1940). Notable among other appearances in the 1940s were those in *Across the Pacific* (1942, as a menacing Japanese agent) and *Dragon Seed* (1944). He married Ethel Davis in 1942 and adopted her daughter. In 1944 Luke became a naturalized American citizen. During these years he also acted in a few of the Hardy family movies. More importantly, he played Dr. Lee Won How, the dedicated intern in some of the Dr. Gillespie movies spun off the Dr. Kildare series. When Toler died in 1947, Roland Winters took over as Charlie Chan in six more Monogram movies. In the last two—*The Feathered Serpent* (1948) and *The Sky Dragon* (1949)—Luke reprised his Lee Chan role. Continuing to demonstrate skill as a Hollywood pictorial artist, he created murals for *The Shanghai Gesture* (1941) and *Macao* (1950).

The most important of Luke's roles in the 1950s were in *Love Is a Many Splendored Thing* (1955), *Around the World in 80 Days* (1956), and the British *Yangtse Incident* (1957; American title: *Battle Hell*). In 1958–1959 Luke had a baritone role as a Chinese-American family patriarch in *The Flower Drum Song*, the musical by Richard Rodgers and Oscar Hammerstein. In the 1960s and 1970s he appeared in few movies, most of them poor, including *The Most Dangerous Man in the World* (British, 1969; U.S. title: *The Chairman*) and *Won Ton Ton, the Dog Who Saved Hollywood* (1976). Branching into television work, he was most endearing in "Kung Fu," the western series (1972–1975), in which he played Master Po, the blind martial-arts monk. This was his favorite role, because his lines included quotations from Confucius, Mencius, and other Chinese philosophers. He was Dr. Fong in "Harry O," the popular TV series (1974–1976), and had guest television roles as well, in such series as "Magnum, P.I.," "Mike Hammer," and "Trapper John, M.D." He acted in many unsold television pilots, including *Judge Dee* (1974, set in seventeenth-century China); *Lester Hodges and Dr. Fong* (1976, a

failed spinoff from "Harry O"); *Fly Away Home* (1981, about Vietnam); *Unit 4* (1981, about antiterrorism); *Kung Fu: The Next Generation and Warriors* (1987–1988, a failed "Kung Fu" spinoff); and *T. J. Hooker: Blood Sport* (1986, a failed revival of the 1982–1985 "T. J. Hooker" series). Luke's voice, as that of Charlie Chan, was effective in the cartoon series *The Amazing Chan and the Chan Clan* (1972–1974).

In the late 1980s Luke enjoyed a screen comeback. He appeared in a few movies, including *A Fine Mess* (1986, a slapstick) and *Dead Heat* (1988, a science-fiction horror film). Better were *Gremlins* (1984), in which he played the owner of a Chinatown curio shop and the keeper of the original Mogwai, and its sequel, *Gremlins 2: The New Batch* (1990). Most delightful was his portrayal of the weird herbalist Dr. Yang in Woody Allen's *Alice* (1990).

Luke was one of the several founders of the Screen Actors Guild in 1933, was honored with the first Lifetime Achievement Award by the Association of Asian/Pacific American Artists in 1986, and had a sidewalk star placed for him in the Hollywood Hall of Fame in 1990. Through tolerance, intelligence, and ability, he helped Asian-American actors and actresses break down the stereotypes of the Chinese laundryman or Confucian guru and the Japanese gardener or evil fighter pilot and step into the mainstream of America. Luke died in Whittier, California.

• Larry Langman and Daniel Finn, *American Crime Films of the Thirties* (1995), includes plot summaries of eight Charlie Chan movies in which Luke appeared. A complete list of Charlie Chan movies, with copious commentary on and quotations from Luke, is in Ken Hanke, *Charlie Chan at the Movies: History, Filmography, and Criticism* (1989). John Walker, ed., *Halliwell's Film Guide: Leslie Halliwell* (1995), provides facts on all movies in which Luke appears. He is mentioned in Lee Goldberg, *Unsold Television Pilots 1955 through 1988* (1990), and in Vincent Terrace, *Fifty Years of Television: A Guide to Series and Pilots, 1937–1988* (1991). Background information pertinent to Luke's career can be found in Richard Oehling, "The Yellow Menace: Asian Images in American Film," in *The Kaleidoscopic Lens: How Hollywood Views Ethnic Groups*, ed. Randall M. Miller (1980). Obituaries are in the *Los Angeles Times*, 15 Jan. 1991, the *New York Times*, 16 Jan. 1991, and *Variety Obituaries 1991–1992* (1993).

ROBERT L. GALE

LUKENS, Henry Clay (18? Aug. 1838–1900?), humorist and journalist, was born in Philadelphia, Pennsylvania, where he attended the public schools. (Nothing is known about his parents.) He began writing for local papers when he was fifteen. For a year, between 1858 and 1859, he served as associate editor of the *School Journal*, a nonprofessional publication.

In his twenties, Lukens ceased being a writer and became a trader, a steadier and more lucrative occupation. For the next decade or so, he shifted back and forth between writing and trading. Business trips included travel to South America, but he could not completely leave newspapering behind: in 1874–1875, while touring Atlantic seaports on business, Lukens reported for a weekly illustrated paper in London on governmental upheavals in Uruguay, specifically the overthrow of its president and the violence in Montevideo, the capital city.

When Lukens returned to the United States, he reconnected with the merchant trade. But on the side, in 1870, he wrote *Lean 'Nora*, a parody subtitled "A Supernatural, though Sub-pathetic Ballad a Good Long Way (almost ninety-seven years) after The German of Gottfried August Bürger by Henrich Yalc Snekul." His playfulness with the pseudonymic author's names, two of which are anagrams of his own, suggests the level of his humor. Henry Wadsworth Longfellow did not like the parody.

Also in 1870 Lukens, using the name of Vernon L. Kingsbury, edited *Don't Give It Away*, an anthology of what he subtitled "American humor, bathos, and philosophy and spirited vignettes," although it is not certain if the book reached critics because of the dearth of extant commentary. In 1877 Lukens returned to New York City to write full time. One of his assignments was to write columns for the *Danbury (Conn.) News* using the pseudonym "Erratic Enrique," later "Enrique the Word-Maker." That same year, he came on board the editorial staff of the *New York Daily News*, for which he continued to write quotable "wisdom" in the form of epigrams, such as "Pretty girls at masquerade balls are blessings in disguise." Lukens also employed a pseudonym for *Jets and Flashes*, which he wrote in 1883; this small book is a compendium of lampoons.

In the latter part of the 1880s Lukens served as recordskeeper for the New York Press Club, and, starting in May 1886, he and Allan Forman coedited *The Journalist*. Lukens's name does not appear on the masthead, although his firm signature—his own name—follows his columns and his light verse; examples of the latter reappeared in the special anniversary issue, *Journalist: A Souvenir*, published in 1887.

In an unbylined blurb in *The Journalist* (22 Oct. 1887), titled "Enrique, the Word-Maker," Lukens is called "a prominent newspaper man." He is credited with—which is to say, Lukens credits himself with—inventing "home-made" words such as "Ulysseum" to label a series of pictures of U. S. Grant, "Metropolis" for New York City, and "festivious" for "unbounded hilarity."

His light style applied equally to poems as well as to profiles of fellow humorists. For example, Lukens praises Robert J. Burdette, an editor of the *Burlington (Iowa) Daily Hawk-Eye*, in a profile originally published in the *Ladies' Home Journal* (8 Oct. 1887) and republished in *The Journalist*. Lukens underpins his airy style with respect not only for Burdette's work as a humorist but also for the domestic trials Burdette suffered with his beloved, invalid wife.

Lukens's verse in *The Journalist* often referred to his own wife Kate (about whom little is known, not even a wedding date). He praised her in an apostrophe with Shakespearean allusions in "Homage and Holly-Leaves" (*The Journalist*, 18 Dec. 1887): "Then kiss me, Kate, while 'neath the Christmas holly / We stand, as erst we stood, fond lovers, twain!" The subtitle of the poem, "A Modern Geographic Christmas Carol," shows Lukens's silly touch with lines that sing like lyrics. For example, he refers to far-flung places: "No woman, fair, in Delhi or in Denver, / Could chain my heart so tight." He even manages to tuck Yuba Dam and Yonkers into the same line. This poem, like many others, bubbles with alliteration: "Coal-color curls," "guise of guile," "boyish baskers," and "beggar bold." Another poem, titled "Her Little, Loving Hand" (28 Jan. 1888), praises Kate; it, too, is littered with alliteration—"I worship winsome Kate, my wedded mate . . . " *The Journalist* poems are witty—that is, both intelligent in allusion and amusing in purpose—and even sweet, without rancor or acid.

Not just a humorist himself, Lukens also chronicled America's humor. For the April 1890 issue of *Harper's*, Lukens wrote uncritically of American funnymen who preceded him, starting from the 1600s. In "American Literary Comedians," he defined "humor" as a "truthful mirroring of the odd or laughter-provoking in ourselves." Lukens credited the source of America's humor to the citizenry: "The population of a land made up, as ours is, of immigrants from every older nation and remote corner of the world, has elements as curious as they are variable, incongruous, and grotesque." However, he distinguished between the delightful and the profane: "There is a wide and steadily widening difference between pure, rippling, unexpected, welcome, exhilarating newspaper humor and the coarse, inane paragraphic cackle or vulgar guffaw of numerous mis-named fun-makers."

Lukens followed his definitions with a thirteen-page litany of humorists—all men, unless women lie hidden behind initials. Among the regionalists, Lukens cites George Lanigan, "a jovial son of Aesop," and Thomas W. Eichelberger, "the constitutional wag of Keokuk." Lukens refers to humorists who have maintained a place in the canon of American literature—Benjamin Franklin, Washington Irving, and James Russell Lowell. He mentions "Mark Twain" (his quotations). He does not leave out James Fenimore Cooper or Nathaniel Hawthorne, introducing them with the statement "Our applauded storytellers have not scorned to delve in humor's golden-veined mine." Lest anyone had forgotten, Lukens even includes John Quincy Adams—"quite proficient as a constructor of humorous verse."

In his closing paragraph for the Burdette profile, Lukens had expressed his own attitude—and legacy—as a humorist: "For us (the fools of the lighter sort) the earth is fairer and the stars are brighter. To us the sunlight is not hateful; to our ears and hearts, alike, the song of the summer birds are [*sic*] sweeter. There is laughter and music in the air around us, and, as our own hearts are lighter, the world about us is made better. Let us persist in our folly."

Lukens spent his last years in Jersey City, New Jersey, separated from New York City publishers.

• Information about Henry Clay Lukens, his life, and philosophy can be gleaned mainly from his own verse and articles. His compendium in *Harper's* is listed in *Native American Humor*, ed. Walter Blair (1960).

MARTHA K. BAKER

LUKENS, Rebecca Webb Pennock (6 Jan. 1794–10 Dec. 1854), pioneering iron manufacturer, was born in West Marlboro Township, Chester County, Pennsylvania, the daughter of Isaac Pennock, an iron manufacturer, and Martha Webb. The oldest surviving child in a family of nine, she enjoyed a happy childhood in a Quaker household that emphasized both discipline and learning. Her formal schooling, which consisted of several years at two private academies, began at the age of twelve. Lukens received a good education for the time, and while she excelled in all her classes, French and chemistry proved to be her favorite subjects.

As Lukens continued her education, her father, who began operating the Federal Slitting Mill (later the Rokeby Works) at Buck Run in Chester County in September 1793, expanded his ironmaking operations in July 1810 with the purchase of the Brandywine Mill in newly-founded Coatsville, Pennsylvania. While visiting Philadelphia with him, she met Dr. Charles Lukens. Romance blossomed between the two, and they subsequently married in 1813. The couple had six children, three of whom reached maturity.

Impressed by the potential of the iron industry, Dr. Lukens soon forsook his medical practice and formed the partnership of Pennock and Lukens with his father-in-law. After several years at Buck Run, the couple moved to the Brandywine Mill. Dr. Lukens leased the facility from his father-in-law, and in anticipation of the growing demand for so-called "Charcoal" iron, proceeded to convert the mill to rolling boiler plates for both locomotives and ship engine boilers.

Although the firm received a huge order (to produce plates for the "Codorus," the first iron-hulled vessel in the United States), tragedy soon struck the firm, and set the course of the rest of Rebecca Lukens's life. Her father died in 1824 and left a will that was ambiguous at best. The greatest blow occurred in the summer of the following year, however, when her husband died. Now alone with five children to raise (and pregnant with a sixth), Lukens faced a daunting challenge. The recent expansion of operations had left the Brandywine Mill heavily in debt, and although she wished to honor her dying husband's request to keep the mill running, her task was further complicated by her late husband's intestate status, which left her with a clouded title to the property.

Despite the daunting challenges that she faced, Lukens was determined to carry on; writing at the time that "Necessity is a stern taskmistress; and my every responsibility gave me courage. I had my promise made to my husband. I had my duty to my children." She also possessed practical knowledge of ironmaking from working with her father and husband, as well as a better-than-average education for women of her day.

After engaging brother-in-law Solomon Lukens to oversee production in the Mill, Lukens undertook to manage all commercial aspects of the firm. In addition to purchasing supplies, executing contracts, and establishing prices, Lukens also faced transportation problems. River traffic proved impossible during winters, and teamsters hauling freight to Philadelphia by wagon charged a prohibitive four dollars a short ton as their fee. This problem was not fully resolved until 1834, when the advent of rail lines made it possible for Lukens to expand her sales efforts beyond a seventy-five mile range.

Dependent upon water as a power source, Brandywine Creek itself provided additional challenges for Lukens. The advent of drought conditions forced her to curtail operations, and she incurred additional litigation at the hands of an upstream competitor when efforts to repair her mill dam caused the water level to rise and back up against the plaintiffs' property. Still more litigation occurred following her mother's death in 1844. Despite these difficulties, the quality of her product caused an increase in demand, and her operation became a success. Well known to steam engineers across the country, her mill produced plate for boilers in Albany, New York City, Baltimore, and New Orleans. Although Lukens achieved a personal net worth of $60,000 by 1844, advancing age was beginning to take its toll. She entered into a copartnership with son-in-law Abraham Gibbons, Jr., in October 1847, and she began to withdraw from active management of the firm, now known as A. Gibbons Jr. & Co. Another son-in-law, Charles Huston, gained admittance to the firm in 1849. Although overweight and troubled with asthma in her later years, Lukens gained the satisfaction of seeing an end to the litigation that had plagued the firm since her assumption of its management; a generous payment to her father's heirs resulted in her acquisition of a clear title to the firm in 1853. She died the following year at her home near Coatsville.

Forced by circumstances beyond her control into the management of her family's business, Rebecca Lukens achieved notable success against occasionally daunting odds at a time when few women worked outside the home, let alone in manufacturing. Her legacy is her firm, which was renamed Lukens Iron Works (later known as Lukens Steel) in 1859.

• The papers of the Lukens Steel Company are held at the Eleutherian Mills Historical Library in Wilmington, Del. The best modern secondary source on Lukens's life and career is Robert W. Wolcott, *A Woman In Steel—Rebecca Lukens (1794–1854)* (1940). Dated but still useful are J. B. Pearse, *A Concise History of the Iron Manufacture of the American Colonies up to the Revolution and of Pennsylvania until the Present Time* (1876), and J. M. Swank, *History of the Manufacture of Iron in All Ages* (1884). An obituary appeared in the *(Philadelphia, Pa.) Friend*, 28 Apr. 1855.

EDWARD L. LACH, JR.

LUKS, George Benjamin (13 Aug. 1867–30 Oct. 1933), artist and teacher, was born in Williamsport, Pennsylvania, the son of Emil Charles Luks, a physician and apothecary, and Bertha von Kraemer. Prior to becoming a painter, he costarred in a vaudeville act, "Buzzy and Anstock," with his younger brother Charles, but his career in theater lasted only a year. In 1883 a fire swept through Williamsport, and he and his brother returned home to Pennsylvania to assist in the rebuilding of their parents' home. Luks did not return to the stage but instead enrolled at the Pennsylvania Academy of Fine Arts in 1884, taking classes under Thomas Anschutz. He did not remain at the academy for long, departing for Europe the next year; he studied first in Dusseldorf, then in Munich, Paris, and London. Luks made few comments about his time in Europe other than that he had "studied" with Lowenstein, Jensen, and Gambrinus (all brands of German beer) and with some now-unidentified French painters.

By 1893 Luks returned to Philadelphia, where he worked as an illustrator for the *Philadelphia Press*. To save money he shared a room with fellow staff member and aspiring artist Everett Shinn. During this time both men began to attend Robert Henri's Tuesday evening classes at the Pennsylvania Academy, along with fellow *Press* artist William Glackens and *Philadelphia Inquirer* artist John Sloan. In 1895 Luks left the *Press* for the *Evening Bulletin*; the following year the newspaper sent him to Cuba to illustrate Maurice O'Leary's coverage of the Cuban Insurrection. Although Luks never went near the battlefield, he executed twenty-nine sketches based on verbal reports. The *Evening Bulletin* fired Luks in 1897 for failure to forward his work, so he left for New York City, where he shared a room with William Glackens upon the latter's return from Paris. The *New York World* hired Luks to replace the cartoonist Richard Felton Outcault, who had left the paper for the *New York Morning Journal*. Although Outcault had taken with him his popular comic strip, "The Yellow Kid," a replacement strip of the same title, later known as "Hogan's Alley" and "McFadden's Flats," continued to run in the *World*, with Luks as the new artist.

The next year Glackens persuaded Luks to begin oil painting—ink and charcoal had been Luks's choice of medium for most of his early career. Gravitating toward an urban realist style similar to that of Henri and Sloan, the artist executed his works with broad, fluid strokes of paint. Luks's rapid manner imparts a sketchlike quality to his paintings, capturing the character of his subjects at that moment. This journalistic impulse to capture the "reality" of the event depends in part on Luks's occupational history, but he also counted the loose painting style of the Dutch master Frans Hals as inspiration. In addition, he felt that the appearance of his style depended on his feelings toward the New York City streets and slums he chose as subjects. The artist attempted to invest his brushwork with same vitality he perceived in New York City life, and he consciously sought out subjects that possessed what he called "edge," or character. Because of his interest in the candid aspects of New York City, critics labeled Luks, along with Henri and Sloan, as members of the "Ash Can" school, so named for their sordid depictions of the city's less appealing side.

Luks's new interest in oil painting led him to make a second trip to Paris in 1902. There he painted several scenes of the Parisian cityscape and its inhabitants. Returning to New York in the late months of 1903, Luks had several of his works selected for Henri's group exhibition of American paintings at the National Arts Club in 1904.

The following year Luks began to sell paintings through William Macbeth's gallery, allowing the artist enough financial support to give up illustration. In 1906, Henri encouraged Luks to submit a number of works to the winter exhibition at the National Academy of Design, but all of Luks's Works were rejected on the basis of his "unrefined" style and subjects. At the 1907 spring exhibition, his single entry, *Pawn Broker's Daughter* (Metropolitan Museum of Art, New York City), was also rejected. However, Henri appealed the decision, and the jury subsequently accepted the painting with at least one-third of members voting in favor of it. Despite this promising turn, the hanging committee chose not to hang *Pawn Broker's Daughter*, claiming that there was no longer room for the canvas. When Henri pointed out an empty space, the painting was hung momentarily but removed the next day when several academicians claimed that Luks's painting disrupted the mural effect of the wall. Henri's continued arguments on Luks's behalf were in vain, and he consequently withdrew his own paintings from the exhibition in protest.

Sloan, Glackens, Arthur B. Davies, and Ernest Lawson joined Luks and Henri in withdrawing from the National Academy exhibition and decided to hold an independent show. The group, joined later by Shinn and Maurice Prendergast, rented the Macbeth Galleries for February 1908. The press quickly nicknamed the group "The Eight" and advanced them as rebels who heralded a new, distinctively American art. These claims were fueled in part by the painters' own statements, and Luks himself commented in the *New York Daily Tribune*, "We want a true American art and not bad copies of foreign artists. It will give the people of this city a chance to see true American art" (15 May 1907). He hung six paintings at the exhibition but sold only one, *Woman with a Goose* (Whitney Museum of American Art, New York City), to Gertrude Vanderbilt Whitney.

In the years following the Macbeth exhibition and the subsequent nine-city tour, Luks's reputation as an artist improved substantially, and he was increasingly sought after as a portraitist. With his sales increasing, Luks received his first one-man show at the Macbeth Galleries in 1910, which led him to decline the first Independent exhibition that same year. The Independent exhibition of 1910, organized by members of The Eight as well as a number of other artists, constituted one of the first major displays of American art outside the control of the National Academy of Design. As an unjuried exhibition, the organizers placed no restrictions in terms of style or subject matter on participating artists. The exhibition proved successful, and Luks chose to enter the second annual the next year. He also entered several works in the American section of the 1913 International Exhibition of Modern Art, later called the Armory Show. Intended to expose American audiences to the latest currents of European modernism, the Armory Show proved extremely important for the development of vanguard styles such as cubism and futurism in the United States.

During the next several years Luks experimented with watercolor, while still using his preferred medium of oil paint. He also expanded his repertoire to include landscape painting. His new interest in both watercolor and landscape led to his first major award in 1916 from the New York Watercolor Club (of which he was a member) for *On the Marne* (location unknown). Luks continually entered exhibitions thereafter—often with favorable results. He took the fourth place William A. Clark Prize and Honorable Mention at the 1917 exhibition at the Corcoran Gallery of Art and received the Temple Gold Medal from the Pennsylvania Academy of Fine Arts the following year.

Although Luks remained active in the studio with commissions, in 1920 he accepted a teaching position at the Art Students League, where he taught painting courses for the next four years. His career continued to meet with success; in 1920 he won the Logan Medal from the Art Institute of Chicago for his portrait *Otis Skinner in "The Honor of the Family"* (Phillips Collection, Washington, D.C.). His paintings of a Pennsylvanian mining community met with critical acclaim as well, with his portrait *The Miner* (1925; National Gallery of Art, Washington, D.C.) earning the Logan Medal in 1926. After he concluded his tenure at the Art Students League, Luks briefly operated his own school.

Despite his successful career as a painter, much of Luks's reputation and popularity rested on his eccentric personality. He often distorted his personal history with fictional events to such an extent that even his close friends sometimes questioned his veracity. His contemporaries commented on his clever albeit arcane wit and his fondness for alcohol. Often the local speakeasy provided the perfect forum for Luks's stories of his mythical accomplishments, such as his successful boxing career under the name "Chicago Whitey." He considered drinking to be essential for a successful life and told the abstemious Shinn that he would never be a successful artist unless he picked up a bottle.

Luks was equally vocal concerning his talents for painting. He often claimed that he could "paint with a shoestring dipped in pitch and lard" and that there were only two great painters in the world: Frans Hals and George Luks. However, many of his friends noted that Luks compromised his own abilities by his excessive drinking habits and that his best efforts emerged during his sober periods. Works such as *The Wrestlers* (1905–1907; Museum of Fine Arts, Boston) display Luks's talent for anatomy and his vigorous painting style.

This dynamic character also made Luks a lively subject in paint. Glackens made the first attempt to capture Luks's boisterous personality in 1899 (National Portrait Gallery), when the two shared a room. Henri followed suit in 1904 (National Gallery of Canada, Ottawa), and Jo Davidson cast a bronze bust (National Portrait Gallery). Only one self-portrait, dating from 1930, has been reproduced (location unknown, last listed with Frank K. M. Rehn Galleries, New York City).

Luks's final achievement came in 1932, when he won the first place William A. Clark Prize and the Corcoran Gold Medal for *Woman with a Black Cat* (Corcoran Gallery of Art). The next year Luks was found dead on a doorstep in New York City—presumably from injuries he received in a bar room fight. Friends surmised that the 72-year-old artist had apparently angered someone with his abrasive wit.

Luks was survived by his wife Mercedes, a native of Cuba whom he had married in the early 1920s. He had been married twice before, although the exact dates of these marriages remain in question. Luks and his first wife (name unknown) were divorced by 1906. She remarried Frank Crane, Luks's former editor at the *New York World*; Crane adopted Luks's only child, a son who was unaware until the age of eighteen that Luks was actually his father. By 1906 Luks had married Emma Louise Noble, whom he called "Babe." The two divorced in the late 1910s or early 1920s.

As a member of The Eight, Luks has received credit for challenging the authority of the National Academy of Design and consequently providing the possibility for the jury-free independent exhibitions. With the success of the 1908 Macbeth exhibition, Luks and his colleagues became cultural heroes of the nationalistic cause of developing a unique American art.

• Luks left no collection of manuscripts or letters. Only the letters he sent to his close friends and colleagues survive, and those may be found in their respective papers. A brief biographical sketch is in Judith Hansen O'Toole, "George Luks: The Watercolors Rediscovered," *American Art Review* 7 (1995): 98–101, 160, and *George Luks: Expressionist Master of Color—The Watercolors Rediscovered* (1995), by the same author. Luks's involvement with The Eight is well documented in Elizabeth Milroy, *Painters of a New Century: The Eight and American Art* (1991). Details concerning Luks's life are also in Ira Glackens, *William Glackens and the Ashcan Group: The Emergence of Realism in American Art* (1957), and Bruce St. John, ed., *John Sloan's New York Scene from the Diaries, Notes and Correspondence 1906–1913* (1965). Bennard B. Perlman, *The Immortal Eight* (1962), offers anecdotal information concerning Luks based on personal conversations with living friends of the artist, although he provides no documentation. An obituary is in *Art Digest* 8 (1933): 5–6.

MARK ANDREW WHITE

LUMAN, Bob (15 Apr. 1937–27 Dec. 1978), rockabilly musician, was born Robert Glynn Luman in Blackjack, Texas, near the Louisiana state line (although he generally stated that he was from Nacogdoches, Texas), the son of Joe G. Luman, a school custodian and farmer, and Lavine (maiden name unknown). Luman developed an early fascination with both music and baseball. He got his first guitar when he was thirteen and learned the basic chords from his father, who played country music at home on the fiddle, harmonica, and guitar.

Luman was trying for a baseball career as well as playing in an amateur country band when he went to see Elvis Presley in Kilgore, Texas, in 1955. "That was the last time I tried to sing like Webb Pierce or Lefty Frizzell," he told journalist Paul Hemphill. Luman entered a Future Farmers of America music talent contest and beat out Mac Curtis (who later recorded rock 'n' roll for King Records) for first place. With Curtis's band behind him, Luman made his first recordings for Jim Shell in Dallas in 1956, which were unissued at the time. Luman still saw baseball as his first career choice and had been summoned to the Pittsburgh Pirates spring training camp when he received an invitation to replace the departing Johnny Cash on the Louisiana Hayride, broadcast over KWKH in Shreveport, Louisiana.

In early 1957 Luman joined his Louisiana Hayride costars David Houston and Slim Whitman on Imperial Records, based in Hollywood, California. The label had a small country roster, and Luman was the only rockabilly act. Luman was managed by Louisiana Hayride program director Horace Logan, who took him to California. He recorded his first session for Imperial in February 1957 with the band he had assembled in Shreveport, which included guitarist James Burton, James Kirkland on bass, and Butch White on drums. It was at this first session that Luman recorded "Red Cadillac and a Black Mustache." Although it did not become a hit, it is regarded by many as an essential rockabilly recording, and the song has since been revived by many artists. Luman and his band also made an appearance that year in a rock 'n' roll exploitation movie, *Carnival Rock*.

One of those who heard Luman's work was future teen-pop star Ricky Nelson, who also recorded for Imperial Records. "I was sitting in [Imperial president] Lew Chudd's office and I heard this voice and a band playing, particularly an unbelievable guitar player. Bob and these guys had all driven out to Los Angeles together. James Kirkland played the slap bass in a way I particularly liked. That was rock and roll as far as I was concerned," said Nelson. He quickly co-opted Luman's band, which left Luman in California by himself. Johnny Cash stepped in with an offer of work on his show for fifty dollars a week.

Luman signed with Capitol Records in April 1958 but remained very much an artist on the sidelines. After leaving Cash's revue, he performed at the Showboat in Las Vegas with cowboy singer Tex Ritter between 1958 and 1960, but—without a hit—he was unable to strike out on his own. He was signed to the relatively new record division of Warner Bros. in 1959, but after his first two singles failed to sell in appreciable quantities, Luman decided that he would try to resume his baseball career. He later told interviewers that he was at the point of asking the Pittsburgh

Pirates if he could try out for the team again. "After Vegas I went back to Hollywood," Luman told Hemphill. "I was back on 'Town Hall Party' and the Everly Brothers were in town. Don called me and asked me to come see him . . . [He] told me about a song in Nashville they thought I could do. I told them I was through with the business. I was going into the service and then back to baseball. . . . Well, they . . . insisted I should go to Nashville and record this song" (Hemphill, p. 192).

The song was "Let's Think about Living." It had been written by Boudleaux and Felice Bryant as a response to the craze for sick records that dealt with violent and often premature death like "Tell Laura I Love Her" and "Endless Sleep." Luman recorded "Let's Think about Living" in July 1960, and it became a Top-Ten pop and country hit in the fall of that year. Just as it was peaking, Luman was inducted into the army reserves, which he later insisted stalled his career at a critical juncture.

In 1963 Luman's Warner Bros. contract was picked up by Hickory Records, the record label owned by the Acuff-Rose publishing company in Nashville. Luman had returned to Las Vegas to play at the Showboat in 1962, but he quit in 1964 to lead his own roadshow after he began scoring a steady flow of country hits, first for Hickory, then for the Epic division of Columbia Records (starting in 1968), and then for Polydor Records (starting in 1977). He moved to Nashville in 1965 and joined the Grand Ole Opry in August of that year. Despite the switch to country music, Luman liked to think that he was still introducing a little rock 'n' roll into his act. "I got the dust out of the cracks that settled when Hank Williams died," he told Hemphill.

Luman and his wife Barbara, whom he had married in 1964 and with whom he subsequently had two children, bought a property in Hendersonville, Tennessee, near Johnny Cash's estate. His first serious illness, an ulcer, came in 1971, and in February 1976 he was hospitalized with a ruptured blood vessel in his esophagus. He fell ill again with pneumonia in mid-December 1978. He went into the hospital on 19 December 1978 and died in Nashville, Tennessee, eight days later.

Luman's filmed appearance in *Carnival Rock* is curiously static, but he became an accomplished and personable stage performer, specializing in comedy routines and imitations. Although his early rock 'n' roll recordings for Imperial Records are well thought of among collectors, his 1970s country recordings, although more commercially successful, fell victim to overproduction. In many ways, Luman's career was a template for what happened to many first-generation rock 'n' roll singers, such as Conway Twitty and Jerry Lee Lewis, who made the same transition from rock 'n' roll to country music.

• Paul Hemphill's portrait of Bob Luman appears in *The Nashville Sound: Bright Lights and Country Music* (1970), pp. 191–98. Luman has been covered in several articles: David

McGee, "Dialog with Ricky Nelson," *Record World*, 21 Mar. 1981; Tom Grein, "Rock-a-Billy Bob Luman," *Music City News*, Oct. 1968; Andy Jackson, "Mr. Music's Almanac," *KBUC Kicker*, Aug.–Sept. 1972; and Doug Green, "Bob Luman (April 15, 1937–December 27, 1978): A Retrospective," *Country Music*, Apr. 1979.

COLIN ESCOTT

LUMBROZO, Jacob (?–between 17 Nov. 1665 and May 1666), physician and accused blasphemer, also known as John Lumbrozo, was a Portuguese Jew from Lisbon. A court record describes Lumbrozo as being "black," suggesting that he was a Moor. His parents are unknown, but he had a sister living in Holland in 1665.

When Lumbrozo immigrated to Maryland in 1656, he was among a minority of settlers at the time who arrived as freemen rather than as bound servants. He purchased land in Charles County and probably engaged in agriculture on at least a small scale. Lumbrozo's principal occupation, however, was as a physician and surgeon, a high-status profession in the sparsely settled colony. Lumbrozo also appeared in court as an attorney. This title did not connote formal legal training in seventeenth-century Maryland; rather, it indicated a person who had the education, experience, and confidence necessary to represent the interests of another before a court.

Aside from his education and professional status, there is little besides his religion to set Lumbrozo apart from the thousands of others who immigrated to seventeenth-century Maryland. He bought and sold land, appeared before the county court as both plaintiff and defendant in suits for debt, served on juries, and appraised the estates of deceased fellow colonists. He married, fathered at least two children, and, again typical of most colonists, died within a decade of his arrival in Maryland, leaving behind personal property worth very little.

What makes Lumbrozo worthy of note are his brushes with the law in matters both civil and religious. In 1663 Lumbrozo married Elizabeth Weale, his indentured servant, to prevent her from testifying against him before the Charles County Court. Depositions filed with the court charged that Lumbrozo had fathered a child with Weale and had given her a drug that had induced an abortion. After telling several neighbors what had happened, Weale tried to recant the story, but the county court indicted them both. Lumbrozo's marriage to Weale thwarted the prosecution, since a wife could not testify against her husband.

Lumbrozo appeared before the court again shortly before his death. A Charles County planter, Thomas Allcock, accused Lumbrozo of receiving goods stolen from Allcock's house. In an arbitrated settlement, Lumbrozo agreed to pay Allcock 900 pounds of tobacco and to return the property he had received.

Lumbrozo's religion figured in a case that came before the Provincial Court in February 1658 (O.S.). Depositions filed with the court alleged that Lumbrozo had stated that Jesus was a man and that his mir-

acles were "Art Magick." In responding to the charge of blasphemy, Lumbrozo stated that he was a Jew and that he had answered questions about his religion to those who asked. He insisted, however, that he had "sayd not any thing scoffingly or in derogation of him, Christians acknowledge for their Messias" (*Archives of Maryland* 41:203).

The court ordered Lumbrozo held in custody until its next meeting, at which he was to answer the charge "concerning those blasphemous words & speeches." Lumbrozo could secure his release on bail by posting security "Body for Body," meaning that he would have to find someone who agreed to stand trial and to receive sentence in his stead if he failed to appear before the court. Blasphemy was a capital crime, and the requirement of "Body for Body" security indicates that the court did not consider the charge against Lumbrozo frivolous.

The Provincial Court heard few cases involving Maryland's unusual policy of religious toleration, and Lumbrozo was the only non-Christian charged with blasphemy. From the beginning of the colony, the Roman Catholic proprietor, Cecil Calvert, second Lord Baltimore, had insisted that his government and his colonists adhere to an informal policy of religious toleration. In 1649, anticipating the Puritan ascendancy in England, Lord Baltimore asked the Maryland Assembly to mandate religious toleration. The result was passage of the Act Concerning Religion, the first law in any English colony guaranteeing freedom of religion for Christians. The act set penalties ranging from fines to death for those guilty of violating its provisions.

Puritan victory in the English Civil War spawned a revolt in Maryland. In 1655 Puritans defeated Lord Baltimore's forces and took control of the Maryland government. The first Puritan assembly revoked the Act Concerning Religion, but when Lord Baltimore secured the return of his colony in 1658, he immediately ordered the act's reinstatement. Ironically, it was a provision of this reinstated act, which provided the most liberal protection for freedom of conscience in the English-speaking world, that Lumbrozo was charged with violating.

As a Jew, Lumbrozo was outside the pale of the Act Concerning Religion, which guaranteed freedom of religion to Christians. It is unlikely, however, that in limiting the act Lord Baltimore intended to discriminate against Jews. Instead, he probably meant to distinguish the religious beliefs of his settlers, virtually all of whom were Christian, from those of the Native Americans. Lord Baltimore wanted to convert the Indians, not to extend respect and protection to their "heathen" religious beliefs.

How Lumbrozo, a Jew, would have fared at his prosecution on the charge of blasphemy remains a matter of speculation. Shortly after Lumbrozo first appeared before the court on the charge, Governor Josias Fendall, in honor of Richard Cromwell's ascension as lord protector of England, pardoned everyone the Provincial Court had indicated, convicted, or condemned to die.

Nothing in the record after Lumbrozo's pardon indicates that his religion interfered further with his life in Maryland. The colony's general assembly granted him denization—a form of naturalization—in 1663, and thereafter he sat on juries and served in other capacities in local government. The Council issued him a license to trade with the Indians, and the Provincial Court granted him a license to keep an ordinary, actions that suggest his religion posed no impediment to his ambitions. Perhaps Lumbrozo had learned from his near prosecution for blasphemy that getting along in Lord Baltimore's colony did not depend on the statutory protection for freedom of conscience, but on simply keeping quiet about one's religious views.

Lumbrozo wrote his will in September 1665 and was dead within eight months. After his death, his widow bore a son, an heir he may not have even known had been conceived. Elizabeth married and was widowed again, and married once more before her own death in 1671, testimony to the high mortality and rigors of life in seventeenth-century Maryland.

Unlike his wife, Jacob Lumbrozo was a well-educated and able individual who did not have to endure years of servitude as his introduction to the colony. That he was a Jew, a rarity in seventeenth-century Maryland, seems to have been more an object of curiosity to his fellow colonists than an impediment to his career. Although Lumbrozo probably did not reach his full potential in the New World, his failure was due not to his religion but to that stumbling block for so many early settlers in Maryland, premature death.

• None of Jacob Lumbrozo's personal papers are known to survive, and no biography of him has been published. The outlines of his career in Maryland must be pieced together from scattered references in early provincial and Charles County records located at the Maryland State Archives in Annapolis, Md., and from records of the Council and Provincial Court published in William Hand Browne et al., eds., *Archives of Maryland* (72 vols., 1883–1972). The biographical details given above are based on research in these sources by Lois Green Carr, historian, St. Mary's City Commission, St. Mary's City, Md. Her research report, "Jacob, Alias, John Lumbrozo," is in the files of the commission.

LOIS GREEN CARR
GREGORY A. STIVERSON

LUMMIS, Charles Fletcher (1 Mar. 1859–25 Nov. 1928), author, editor, and explorer, was born in Lynn, Massachusetts, the son of Henry Lummis, a teacher and Methodist clergyman, and Harriet Waterman Fowler. A sickly child, he was tutored at home, attended Harvard intermittently from 1877 to 1881, but left without a degree. He was a reporter for and then the editor of the weekly Scioto *Gazette*, in Chillicothe, Ohio, from 1882 to 1884. When offered a position on the Los Angeles *Daily Times*, he walked indirectly from Cincinnati to Los Angeles—covering, he averred, an astonishing 3,507 miles in 143 days—sending newspaper reports along the way to the *Ga-*

zette and the *Daily Times*. He served as the city editor of the *Daily Times* from 1885 to 1887. Los Angeles was his residence thereafter. He was a correspondent for his newspaper during the 1886 Apache War. He was partially paralyzed by a stroke in 1887.

To aid in his slow recovery, which took five years, Lummis moved to a friend's New Mexican ranch and also lived among Native American Pueblos, in Isleta, on the Rio Grande south of Albuquerque. While in that region, he collected native folktales and old Spanish songs, explored archaeological locales with historian and anthropologist Adolph Bandelier, and wrote articles and fiction for *Harper's Weekly* and *Scribner's Magazine*. In 1892–1894 he accompanied Bandelier on an ethnological expedition to Bolivia and Peru. He grew eager to preserve the old Spanish missions from ruin and sites in California from exploitation, including the Pala, San Juan Capistrano, and San Fernando missions. In 1894 Lummis returned to Los Angeles, began to surround himself with a literary group, and became editor of the *Land of Sunshine*, which started as a publication to promote southern California commerce but which he expanded to include belles lettres. (In 1900 it was retitled *Out West*.) Lummis, who edited the journal until 1909, accepted works by Mary Austin, Sharlot Mabridth Hall (part of the time his co-editor), Robinson Jeffers, Jack London, Edwin Markham, Washington Matthews, Joaquin Miller, and Eugene Manlove Rhodes. In 1895 Lummis cofounded the Landmarks Club, to advance the cause of historic preservation. In 1897 Princeton professor William Libbey ascended the 400-foot Acoma mesa and concluded that there were no signs of human life at the top. This negated data in "The Enchanted Mesa," a 1892 essay by Lummis, who quickly—and repeatedly—countered in print. When some 300 Native Americans were expelled from their homes by court order, he established the Sequoya League in 1902 to help in their resettlement, which was accomplished in 1903. In 1903 Lummis also cofounded and was secretary of the Archaeological Institute of America's Southwest Society. He worked as chief librarian of Los Angeles Public Library from 1905 to 1910, making it a resource center for scholars of Western Americana.

Lummis's publications may be divided into poetry, fiction and folktales, autobiography and biography, and travel and geopolitical books. His verse is assembled in *Birch Bark Poems* (1879)—printed on twelve pages of birch bark—which enjoyed fine reviews and good sales, and *A Bronco Pegasus* (1928). His fiction and folktales appeared in *A New Mexico David and Other Stories and Sketches of the Southwest* (1891), *The Man Who Married the Moon and Other Pueblo Indian Folk-Stories* (1894), *The Gold Fish of Gran Chimú* (1896), *The King of the Broncos and Other Stories of New Mexico* (1897), *The Enchanted Burro and Other Stories* (1897), and *Pueblo Indian Folk-Stories* (1910) (a new edition of *The Man Who Married the Moon*). *The Gold Fish of Chimú*, his only novel, combines realistic descriptions of Lummis's Peruvian archaeological locales and a melodramatic plot featuring a digger and his son opposed by armed villains and confiscatory government agents. Lummis's autobiographical and biographical works are *A Tramp across the Continent* (1892) and *My Friend Will* (1911). *A Tramp*, which is a collection of his newspaper letters, includes tour-guide commentary, describes his evolving respect for Hispanics and Native Americans, and touches up some of his experiences into fiction. *My Friend Will* tells how by willpower he conquered paralysis. His travel and geopolitical essays are in *Some Strange Corners of Our Country* (1892), *The Land of Poco Tiempo* (1893), *The Spanish Pioneers* (1893), *The Awakening of a Nation: Mexico of To-day* (1898), *Mesa, Cañon and Pueblo: Our Wonderland of the Southwest* (1925; a revision and expansion of *Some Strange Corners of Our Country*), and *The Spanish Pioneers and the California Missions* (1929; a revision and expansion of *The Spanish Pioneers*). In *Some Strange Corners* Lummis describes southwestern scenery, including geological formations and archaeological sites, and analyzes the clash of native and Spanish cultures. *The Land of Poco Tiempo* discusses the life and beliefs of New Mexico Indians and includes a description of Los Hermanos Penitentes' scary rituals. *The Awakening of a Nation* presents a corrective geography and history of Mexico and lauds José de la Cruz Porfirio Díaz, Mexican general and president.

Lummis recorded almost a thousand old Spanish and Native-American songs, the latter in thirty-seven languages. In 1915 he was made a knight of the Order of Isabel the Catholic by King Alphonso XIII of Spain for his distinguished work. His *Spanish Songs of Old California* (1923) made use of the latest technology and is considered authentic and of enduring value. Lummis was married three times: to (Mary) Dorothea Roads of Ohio from 1880 until their divorce in 1890, to Eve (Eva) Frances Douglas, of New Mexico, in 1891 (the couple had four children and were divorced in 1911), and to Gertrude Redit of Los Angeles in 1915. Suffering from cancer in 1928, Lummis worked feverishly in his Los Angeles home until he finished revising *Spanish Pioneers*, soon lapsed into a partial coma, and died a few weeks later. Some years after his death, many of his 1880 and 1890s articles were collected in *General Crook and the Apache Wars* (1966), *Bullying the Moqui* (1968), and *Dateline Fort Bowie* (1979). These books, the first of which was edited by Lummis's daughter Turbesé Lummis Fiske, reveal the author's respect for Apache and also Moqui (that is, Hopi) culture and courage, in ways that have gained him respect from the most liberal of recent historians. Lummis, who wasted much energy writing undistinguished poetry and fiction, will be remembered and esteemed for his pioneering editorial work, for preserving and popularizing southwestern legends of several sorts, and for presenting vivid word-pictures of a now bygone era.

• Most of Lummis's papers, which are widely scattered, may be found at the University of Arizona, the California Historical Society in San Francisco, Occidental College in Los Angeles, and the Southwest Museum Library in Los Angeles.

Mary A. Sarber, *Charles F. Lummis: A Bibliography* (1977), is useful. The following books are of biographical and critical value: Edwin R. Bingham, *Charles F. Lummis: Editor of the Southwest* (1955); Dudley Gordon, *Charles F. Lummis: Crusader in Corduroy* (1972); Turbesé Lummis Fiske and Keith Lummis, *Charles F. Lummis: The Man and His West* (1975); and Robert E. Fleming, *Charles F. Lummis* (1981). Obituaries are in the *Los Angeles Times* and the *New York Times*, both 26 Nov. 1928.

ROBERT L. GALE

LUMPKIN, Grace (c. 1900–23 Mar. 1980), novelist, was born in Milledgeville, Georgia, the daughter of Colonel William Wallace Lumpkin and Annette Morris. After graduating from Brenau College in Gainesville, Georgia, in 1911 Lumpkin went to France where she worked as a recreation director, first for American nurses and later for French girls in industry. She also served as YWCA director in Roanns. Lumpkin returned to the United States around the end of 1920 and began working with farmers and cotton mill employees. She organized and taught night school for farm men and women and continued working within the YWCA until she decided that unions would better answer these people's needs. Around 1926 she moved to New York City where she took writing courses at Columbia University.

Lumpkin picketed for the Sacco-Vanzetti Defense Committee in August 1927 and in 1928 became involved with the Communist party, though she was never actually a member. Her first story was published in *New Masses*, and a small group of Communists gathered regularly in her apartment. She married Michael Intrator around 1931; they had no children. At this time, her roommate married active party member Whittaker Chambers, who later resigned from the party and convinced Lumpkin to distance herself from it.

Lumpkin's first novel, *To Make My Bread* (1932), is one of several fictionalized accounts of the 1929 textile mill strikes in Gastonia County, North Carolina. The winner of the Maxim Gorky Award for the best labor novel of 1932, it is considered by several critics to be the best of the novels based on the Gastonia strikes. The novel centers around the McClures, who are tricked into selling their land to a lumber company and then forced to pay rent to continue living on it, after which they are easily enticed to move from their mountain home to a mill town where high-paying jobs are promised. The novel's protagonists, the youngest McClure children Bonnie and John, go to school for a while but eventually must quit to work in the mill. Dissatisfied with his family's treatment by the mill owners and managers, John seeks information about unions and, with help from outside sympathizers, leads the people in a strike that culminates in Bonnie's murder. The novel ends with no resolution: "This is just the beginning," John Stevens, a Marxist union strike organizer, tells John at the novel's close. *To Make My Bread* was translated and printed in Russia. It was also adapted for the stage by Albert Bein and was produced under the title *Let Freedom Ring*, first at the Broadhurst Theater in New York, where it opened on 6 November 1935, moving later to the City Repertory Theater, where it played until April 1936.

Lumpkin continued to express Communist party propaganda in her second novel, *A Sign for Cain* (1935), though the central concern of this novel is its criticism of the continuing caste system and racial oppression in the South. The main family of the novel is the aristocratic Gaults, whose fortunes may be declining but whose position remains prominent. Youngest son Jim, in need of money, murders his aunt, but two black men are charged with raping as well as murdering her and are tortured while the novel's hero, Bill Duncan, a local Communist, tries to get party help. Before the two victims are tried, Jim—playing the vigilante defender of his aunt's honor—murders them.

Lumpkin's third book, *The Wedding* (1939), is a novel of manners rather than a proletarian treatise. It covers the day before and the wedding day of Jennie Middleton and Dr. Shelley Gregg, but it flashes back to fill in the reader on their backgrounds and courtship. The novel's central conflict is that the two have quarreled and Jennie has called the wedding off. The basis of the quarrel is each intended's desire to maintain some of his or her independence even while bonding to the other. Family members and the best man struggle in the course of the novel to mend the rift, and the wedding proceeds as planned.

In 1941 Lumpkin gave up communism and also resumed her Christian faith. Her last novel, *Full Circle* (1962), a semiautobiographical account of her involvement with and later rejection of the party, harshly critiques communism. The action is focused on the narrator Ann Braxton's attempts to discover the cause of her catatonic daughter Arnie's breakdown. In flashbacks, Ann reviews her own and Arnie's affiliation with the Communist party in New York, while in the novel's present she seeks out party members to find out what happened to Arnie after she left her daughter and returned home to South Carolina. Ultimately it is revealed that Arnie has suffered heartbreak and disillusionment, having been betrayed by jealous fellow party members. This is Lumpkin's weakest novel, the purpose of which seems only to be the writer purging herself of Communist affiliation. It follows by almost a decade Lumpkin's declaration to the Senate Permanent Investigating Sub-Committee "that she had written Communist propaganda into [*A Sign for Cain*] after being told that Communist book reviewers would 'break' her literary career if she did not" (*New York Times*, 3 Apr. 1953, p. 10). Apparently she was not questioned at that time about and did not remark upon the sympathetic portrayal of communism in *To Make My Bread*.

Although Lumpkin's novels are no longer in print or widely read, even in academic circles, she does hold a position in American literary history. *To Make My Bread* has been praised both for its proletarian purpose as an exposé on the working conditions that led to the Gastonia strikes and for its success in raising social awareness of and sympathy for the plight of the workers involved. Lumpkin once remarked that "a writer must have some idea to present. For myself this idea is the one that humanity is making progress . . . that a new step is to be taken, and that only the working class and those sympathetic with that class can lead to this new step . . . [i]n one form or another, without distorting character or truth, I hope to present this idea in whatever I write" (quoted in *Contemporary American Authors* [1940], p. 459). Lumpkin died in a nursing home in Columbia, South Carolina.

• Lumpkin's papers, including manuscripts and correspondence, are in the University of South Carolina Caroliniana Library in Columbia. Besides novels, Lumpkin published short stories, including "The Bridesmaids Carried Lilies," published in the *North American Review* in 1937, and "The Treasure," which is included in the *O. Henry Memorial Award Stories of 1940*. *To Make My Bread* has received the most critical attention of all of her works; see John M. Reilly, "Images of Gastonia: A Revolutionary Chapter in American Social Fiction," *Georgia Review* 28 (1974): 498–517; Sylvia Jenkins Cook, *From Tobacco Road to Route 66: The Southern Poor White in Fiction* (1976); Joseph R. Urgo, "Proletarian Literature and Feminism: The Gastonia Novels and Feminist Protest," *Minnesota Review* 24 (1985): 64–84; and Candida Ann Lacey, "Engendering Conflict: American Women and the Making of Proletarian Fiction" (Ph.D. diss., Univ. of Sussex, 1986). *The Wedding* was reprinted by Southern Illinois University Press in 1976 in the Lost American Fiction series with an afterword by Lillian Barnard Gilkes that provides some facts about Lumpkin's family background. A book by Lumpkin's sister, Dr. Katherine Du Pre Lumpkin, *The Making of a Southerner* (repr. 1991), also provides family history. Very little is known about Lumpkin's personal life, and there is some question as to the exact dates of certain events in her life, beginning with the year of her birth. An obituary is in the *Columbia (S.C.) State*, 24 Mar. 1980.

MARGARET D. BAUER

LUMPKIN, Joseph Henry (23 Dec. 1799–4 June 1867), jurist and reformer, was born near Lexington in Oglethorpe County, Georgia, the son of John H. Lumpkin and Lucy Hopson, planters. At age seventeen Lumpkin entered the University of Georgia, but because the school soon fell on hard times he left to complete his studies at the College of New Jersey (later Princeton), where he graduated with honors in 1819. Afterward he returned to Oglethorpe County, where he studied law with Judge Thomas W. Cobb, established a law practice in Lexington in 1820, and married Callendar Cunningham Grieve, a native of Scotland, in 1821. Over the next several years, Lumpkin made a name for himself as a talented lawyer and an exceptional orator. He served a single term in the Georgia General Assembly in 1824–1825, founded a literary and oratorical society at the University of Georgia in 1825, and helped rewrite his state's penal code in 1833.

Lumpkin's religious beliefs and reform activities constituted the most significant aspect of his early career. Inspired after his religious conversion at a Methodist camp meeting sometime in the early 1820s, Lumpkin went on to serve as an elder in the Presbyterian church and spent much of his life engaged in temperance reform. He took a pledge of abstinence from alcohol in 1828 and the following year was elected president of the Oglethorpe County Temperance Society. Over the next two and a half decades Lumpkin emerged as the preeminent voice in Georgia's temperance movement, as he traveled across the state speaking against the evils of strong drink. In 1832 he became third vice president of the state temperance society and in 1833 represented Georgia at the National Temperance Convention in Boston, where he was elected one of sixteen vice presidents and expressed antislavery sentiments in a meeting with fellow reformers. During the late 1830s, at the peak of the antebellum temperance movement's success, Lumpkin joined Methodist Josiah Flournoy in leading a campaign to repeal Georgia's licensing laws in order to end the sale of spirituous liquor. Wary voters, however, rejected legal prohibition in Georgia.

The 1840s brought enormous changes to Lumpkin's career. In 1842 he and his family moved to Athens in neighboring Clarke County, and two years later he became president of the State Temperance Convention, a post he held for the next decade. In the meantime, overwhelming responsibilities and physical exhaustion prompted Lumpkin to take an extended vacation in Europe during much of 1845–1846. While he was out of the country, Georgia legislators created a state supreme court and elected him one of its three justices. Lumpkin's efforts on behalf of the temperance movement, his reputation as an orator, and his record as a legal advocate had earned him the respect of both the state legislature and the legal profession. In 1846 he began serving as a justice of the Georgia Supreme Court and that same year declined an appointment as chair of oratory and rhetoric at the University of Georgia.

As the leader of the court for the next twenty-one years, and after 1863 as its chief justice, Lumpkin wrote more than 2,000 opinions on issues ranging from contracts and economic development to slavery and manumission. On economic matters, Lumpkin believed in the inherent importance of upholding contractual relationships, and he usually sided with creditors and sellers to protect business investment. At the same time he willingly undermined private contracts when he felt it served the public interest, as in *Shorter v. Smith* (1851), a case involving Shorter's supposedly exclusive rights to operate a toll bridge. Like Chief Justice Roger B. Taney in the landmark decision *Charles River Bridge v. Warren Bridge* (1837), Lumpkin rejected the claim to monopoly privileges, permitted the construction of a new bridge, and eloquently championed technological advancement. In general, Lumpkin's judicial decisions on economic matters reflected his desire for the South to diversify economically through industrial development, a theme he often sounded in his speeches and writings.

On the issue of slavery, Lumpkin's evangelical Christian sensibilities largely shaped his judicial decisions. As the threat of northern abolitionism increased during the antebellum period, Lumpkin and other southern evangelicals came to embrace the proslavery argument. By 1850, in contrast to his previous sympathy for the antislavery position, he boldly noted that "the conscience of the whole South . . . has become thoroughly satisfied that this institution . . . is of God." As the decade progressed Lumpkin worked both to degrade the legal standing of free blacks and to restrict opportunities for the manumission of slaves. In *Bryan v. Walton* (1853), for example, he ruled that the act of manumission conferred neither "citizenship, nor any powers, civil or political, incident to citizenship," while in *Adams v. Bass* (1855) he cleverly interpreted a testator's will to disallow the manumission of his slaves in the North. Lumpkin's evangelical belief in the social benefits of slavery for both blacks and whites made him one of the most proslavery state judges in the Old South.

Lumpkin was the most important legal figure in nineteenth-century Georgia, and he gained national recognition from his contemporaries. In 1855 President Franklin Pierce offered him a seat on the newly created federal court of claims in Washington, D.C., but he declined the appointment to remain in service to his home state. Four years later Lumpkin assisted in founding the law school at the University of Georgia, originally named the Lumpkin Law School, where the justice himself taught constitutional law. He also served as a trustee of the university (1854–1867) but refused the position of chancellor when it was offered to him in 1860. Lumpkin continued in his duties as a law teacher and state supreme court justice through the Civil War and until his death in Athens.

The Lumpkins were one of the state's most prominent families, and Joseph Henry Lumpkin's historical significance stems nearly as much from his family's fame as from his own accomplishments. He was the younger brother of Wilson Lumpkin, the governor of Georgia during the 1830s. Joseph Henry Lumpkin and his wife had eleven children, and their oldest daughter Marion married Thomas R. R. Cobb, the famous treatise writer on slavery and architect of secession in Georgia. Moreover, two of Lumpkin's grandsons, Samuel Lumpkin and Joseph Henry Lumpkin II, served as justices of the Georgia Supreme Court during the late nineteenth century.

Lumpkin was both the typical southern gentleman and the atypical social reformer. His life and career fused traditional southern gentility with a forward-looking zeal for social and economic change. Although he epitomized southern orthodoxy in his commitment to slavery, Lumpkin envisioned an economically independent South built on the pillars of slavery and industrialization, cotton and cotton mills. His most lasting overall achievement was his judicial service, for he almost single-handedly fashioned the Georgia Supreme Court during his twenty-one years as a justice.

• A relatively good collection of Lumpkin's personal papers—mostly letters to his daughter Callie and his wife—are at the University of Georgia Law School Library. A smaller collection of Lumpkin papers are held by the Hargrett Rare Books and Manuscripts Library at the University of Georgia, while a few of his letters are published in U. B. Phillips, ed., *The Correspondence of Robert Toombs, Alexander H. Stephens, and Howell Cobb* (1913). Lumpkin's judicial opinions can be found in the *Georgia Reports*, vols. 1–31.

For general biographical information see W. T. Brantly, *Life and Character of Joseph Henry Lumpkin, an Oration Delivered in Athens, Ga. before the Phi Kappa Society, August 5, 1867* (1867), and his memorial in the *Georgia Reports*, vol. 31. On his reform activities, see Timothy S. Huebner, "Joseph Henry Lumpkin and Evangelical Reform in Georgia: Temperance, Education, and Industrialization, 1830–1860," *Georgia Historical Quarterly* 75 (Summer 1991): 254–74; on his judicial record, see Huebner, "Encouraging Economic Development: Joseph Henry Lumpkin and the Law of Contract, 1846–1860," *Georgia Journal of Southern Legal History* 1 (Fall/Winter 1991): 357–75; and Mason D. Stephenson and D. Grier Stephenson, "To Protect and Defend: Joseph Henry Lumpkin, the Supreme Court of Georgia and Slavery," *Emory Law Journal* 25 (1976): 579–608.

TIMOTHY S. HUEBNER

LUMPKIN, Katharine Du Pre (22 Dec. 1897–5 May 1988), reformer and author, was born in Macon, Georgia, the daughter of William Wallace Lumpkin, a railroad employee, and Annette Caroline Morris. Both parents were the offspring of planters who lost their fortunes in the Civil War. Annette Lumpkin had taught school briefly before she married, and her learning, Katharine wrote later in *The Making of a Southerner* (1947), was "a proud family possession" (p. 185). William Lumpkin read for the bar but finally had to take a position as a railroad commission agent. The family moved often, finally settling in Columbia, South Carolina, where William devoted himself to the movement to enshrine the memory of the Lost Cause.

Shortly before Katharine's twelfth birthday, the Lumpkins moved to the Sand Hills, South Carolina's most desolate region. There, for the first time, she came into intimate contact with the black and white rural poor. There too her father died. Confronted with the hard work of farming and freed from her father's influence, Katharine's romantic views of antebellum plantation life crumbled. By the time she left for college in 1912, she was, as she remembered it, a skeptic, a Democrat, and an aspiring intellectual. "Right in the bosom of our family," she wrote, doubts about her heritage had sprung (p. 185).

That skepticism deepened at Brenau College in Gainesville, Georgia (B.A., 1915), where a history professor taught her to "go to the sources" (p. 186) and where the Young Women's Christian Association (YWCA) introduced her to the Social Gospel. In 1918 she went north to study at Columbia University, hoping "to unravel the mysteries of why men behaved as they did and perhaps what could make them behave differently" (p. 203). Disappointed by academic sociology, she struck out on her own, beginning a pattern she would follow throughout her life. At Columbia she wrote a master's thesis in political science on the "Social Interests of the Southern Woman" (1919); during that period she also took courses at the YWCA National Training School. In 1920 she became the YWCA's national student secretary for the southern region. Her mission was to implement a new program of "interracial education," first by exposing white students to the Social Gospel and then by encouraging black and white students to "think, study, discuss, work together." Forging a partnership with black staff members, she helped to organize an interracial Southern Regional Council, plant interracial study groups on college campuses, and fight for full integration of the YWCA. She also cooperated with the Y's industrial secretaries and worked briefly in a factory. Her involvement with the industrial department was critical, for it was by confronting the ways in which manmade economic arrangements doomed the poor of both races to destitution that Lumpkin was finally able to rid herself of the assumption that black poverty was somehow inevitable or innate.

Lumpkin left the South again in 1925, this time to pursue her twin interests, labor and race, at the University of Wisconsin (Ph.D., 1928). She studied with some of progressivism's leading lights, including Selig Perlman, the founder with John R. Commons of the Wisconsin school of labor history, and Edward Alsworth Ross, under whose direction she wrote a dissertation in sociology on delinquent girls. As at Columbia, however, Lumpkin did not find in the classroom the knowledge she sought. "In despair of finding it anywhere," she remembered, "I undertook my own self-education in what science had to offer on race, while continuing to carry out the necessary requirements for my doctorate."

After a year as an instructor at Mount Holyoke (1928–1929), followed by a year of research supported by a Social Science Research Council postdoctoral fellowship, Lumpkin took a job as director of research for the newly established Council of Industrial Studies at Smith College (1932–1939). Under her guidance, a series of women graduate students conducted studies of workers and industrialization in the Connecticut Valley. Their projects departed from the institutional labor history taught by Commons and Perlman at Wisconsin, foreshadowing instead the concern with family and community that characterized the new labor history of the 1970s. Budget cuts forced Lumpkin to leave the council in 1939. From 1940 to 1953 she served as research director of the independent Institute of Labor Studies in Northampton, Massachusetts, which tracked World War II developments in labor relations.

Increasingly, Lumpkin turned from academic sociology to social critique. Her first book, *The Family: A Study of Member Roles* (1933), attributed family problems to the booms and busts of a capitalist economy. In *Shutdowns in the Connecticut Valley: A Study of Worker Displacement in the Small Industrial Community* (1934), she pursued her interest in the effect of unemployment on families and communities. In 1937 she joined forces with the radical economist Dorothy Wolff Douglas, with whom she lived for many years, to write *Child Workers in America*, attacking the exploitation of children in domestic and agricultural labor and making a case for a child labor amendment. In *The South in Progress* (1940), Lumpkin drew not on the statistical sources and case records on which she had based her earlier studies but on such left-wing sources as the *Daily Worker* and the *New Masses* as well as the publications of southern liberals and radicals. She condemned segregation, argued for New Deal programs, and portrayed interracial industrial unions as the best hope for regional change.

Lumpkin's move to the left was shared—and influenced by—a network of radical intellectuals stretching back to her days in the YWCA. Her sister Grace Lumpkin had gained recognition as a proletarian writer after 1932, when she published *To Make My Bread*, a novel based on the Gastonia, North Carolina, strike of 1929. Perhaps most important to Katharine Lumpkin's evolution, however, was her relationship with Dorothy Douglas. The two women raised Douglas's four children, traveled to observe the revolutionary ferment in Mexico and the Soviet Union, and pursued their interest in labor issues. Douglas, however, was the more outspoken activist, while Lumpkin returned to her early preoccupation with the South and mined her own experience for political ends.

Lumpkin's *The Making of a Southerner* (1947) was one of a spate of autobiographies published by white southerners in the 1930s and 1940s, but it did not conform to either of the two dominant molds. Neither elegiac reminiscence nor savage attack, *The Making of a Southerner* showed how a child absorbed her society's assumptions about race, class, and gender and how change could occur from within. Autobiography as a genre is premised on the notion of a unique, individual self; by contrast, Lumpkin evoked a powerful sense of history, family, and place. Indeed, she departed almost entirely from autobiographical convention by devoting the first half of her book to events that took place before she was born, relying on a blend of memory, family lore, and historical research to portray the paternalistic slaveholding society of her Georgia ancestors and the world of segregation and disfranchisement into which she was born. Even her liberation, as she represented it, depended not on a rejection of her regional heritage, but on a rereading of southern history that stressed dissent, conflict, and change. "It was the dynamics of the South itself in its glaring incongruities," she wrote, that "in the end drew me towards my refashioning" (p. 239).

The publication of *The Making of a Southerner* marked the high point of Lumpkin's career. Reviewed favorably in both the South and the North and chosen as a Book-of-the-Month Club selection, the book's success helped Lumpkin win a Houghton Mifflin Literary Fellowship to write a historical novel from the point of view of a black Reconstruction leader. The manuscript, however, was rejected by Houghton Mifflin, and she finally put it aside. McCarthyism compounded her difficulties. In 1953 Robert Gorham Davis, a Smith College English professor, testified before the House Committee on Un-American Activities that Lumpkin and Douglas had been members of a Communist party faction within the American Federation of Teachers. Subpoenaed by the committee, Douglas cited the Fifth Amendment.

Lumpkin never spoke publicly about this experience, but it seems to have been shattering. Both women left Northampton, and the two parted ways. Lumpkin wanted to return to the South, but she was unable to secure a position in a black college and was unwilling to teach in a segregated institution. In 1957 she joined the sociology department at Wells College in Aurora, New York, where she taught until 1967. Upon retirement she and her companion, Elizabeth Bennett, moved to Charlottesville, Virginia, and then to Chapel Hill, North Carolina.

In 1974 Lumpkin published a biography of Angelina Grimké, a feminist abolitionist from South Carolina. A pioneering work in women's history, the biography was begun in the 1950s at a time when both feminism and interest in women's history were at a low ebb. Unlike *The Making of a Southerner*, which dealt gently with the conflict between family and self, this last work probed the guilt, jealousy, and emotional violence that blunted a rebel's power and cut short her public life.

Like many exiled southern intellectuals, Lumpkin could neither embrace the region she loved nor feel at home anywhere else. Similarly, like most women social scientists of her generation, she never held a position in a research university. She pursued her career on the margins, as a research director, an independent scholar, and a teacher in women's colleges. Yet these two forms of marginality—as a southern intellectual outside the South and as a woman in a male-dominated profession—had their advantages, for they inspired her to abandon conventional academic writing, find her own, more original voice, and put her intellectual training at the service of her social concerns.

Lumpkin died in Chapel Hill.

• Lumpkin's papers, including an interview by Jacquelyn Hall, are in the Southern Historical Collection, University of North Carolina at Chapel Hill. Her sister Grace Lumpkin's papers are in the South Caroliniana Library of the University of South Carolina in Columbia. Publications not listed above include *The Emancipation of Angelina Grimké* (1974); "Factors in the Commitment of Correctional School Girls in Wisconsin," *American Journal of Sociology* 37 (Sept. 1931): 222–30; "Parental Conditions of Wisconsin Girl Delinquents," *American Journal of Sociology* 38 (Sept. 1932): 232–39; with Dorothy Wolff Douglas, "The Effect of Unemployment and Short-time during 1931 in the Families of 200 Alabama Child Workers," *Social Forces* 9 (May 1933): 548–58; "The Child Labor Provisions of the Fair Labor Standard Act," *Law and Contemporary Problems* 6 (1939): 391–405; and "The General Plan Was Freedom: A Negro Secret Order on the Underground Railroad," *Phylon* 28 (Spring 1967): 63–67. Little has been written about Lumpkin's career, but for recent attention see Darlene Clark Hine's foreword to a reprint of *The Making of a Southerner* (1991); Elizabeth Fox-Genovese, "Between Individualism and Community: Autobiographies of Southern Women," in *Located Lives: Place and Idea in Southern Autobiography*, ed. J. Bill Berry (1990), pp. 20–38; and Frances Sanders Taylor, "'On the Edge of Tomorrow':

Southern Women, the Student YWCA, and Race, 1920–1944" (Ph.D. diss., Stanford Univ., 1984). On the links between the Smith College Council of Industrial Studies and the new labor history, see Jill Ker Conway's preface to *The New England Working Class and the New Labor History*, ed. Herbert G. Gutman and Donald H. Bell (1987). An obituary is in the *Chapel Hill Newspaper*, 6 May 1988.

JACQUELYN D. HALL

LUMPKIN, Wilson (14 Jan. 1783–28 Dec. 1870), politician, was born in Pittsylvania County, Virginia, the son of John Lumpkin, a jurist, and Lucy Hopson. Within a year of Lumpkin's birth the family moved to Wilkes County, Georgia, in the region that later became Oglethorpe County, where he lived until he established a permanent home in Morgan County in 1814. As a boy Lumpkin worked on his father's farm and attended the local common schools before studying law and working as an assistant to his father in the county clerk's office between 1799 and 1804. In 1803 he briefly taught school; the following year, he was admitted to the bar. That year he also began his political career with his election at age twenty-one to the state legislature. By this time he had established a family with his marriage in 1800 to Elizabeth Walker, with whom Lumpkin had eight children before her death in 1819. In 1821 he married Annis Hopkins, with whom he had four children.

For most of the next forty years Lumpkin was involved in public affairs. In addition to ten years (1804–1812, 1819–1821) of service as a legislator, he served six years in Congress (1815–1817, 1827–1831), two consecutive terms as Georgia's governor (1831–1835), and four years in the U.S. Senate (1837–1841). He began his career as a moderate on good terms with the two chief rivals for dominance of Georgia politics, the Troup and Clark factions. In the mid-1820s he became one of the first advocates in Georgia of Andrew Jackson's election to the presidency, and by the 1830s he was a loyal supporter of Jackson's Democratic party. Despite his votes in 1816 for a protective tariff and for the charter of the Second Bank of the United States, Lumpkin was known as an earnest advocate of a strict construction of the Constitution. He later explained that he was misinformed on the tariff issue, and he endorsed Jackson's campaign against the bank. Likewise, although a firm defender of states' rights, he opposed South Carolina's attempt to "nullify" federal law on the ground of state interposition; during the Nullification crisis, he was elected governor as the candidate of the Unionist party.

Lumpkin was also known as a champion of internal improvements, especially the construction of railroads. As a member of the Georgia Board of Public Works, he participated in an 1825 survey with state engineer Hamilton Fulton to determine the feasibility of building either a canal or a railroad through northern Georgia to connect the Chattahoochee and Tennessee rivers. Lumpkin's experience on this tour convinced him of the advantages of a railroad, and the path suggested by his and Fulton's report ultimately became the route of the state-owned Western and Atlantic Railroad. Sixteen years later, after his retirement from the Senate, Lumpkin became disbursing agent for the company building the road. In this position he took charge of the company's reorganization, and his success in helping the company eliminate its debt and resume construction earned him the popular title of "father of the Western and Atlantic line."

Lumpkin's fame stemmed chiefly from his ardent promotion of the removal of the Cherokee Indians from northwestern Georgia to the territory west of the Mississippi River. He had considerable exposure to Native American tribes in his youth on the frontier, during the survey for a railroad route, and on an earlier tour of the Southern states. This experience confirmed for him the popular view that isolation from white civilization was the only way to prevent the Indian people's extinction. At the same time, he frankly stated his belief that the Indians' presence blocked the progress of Georgia and of the United States; advocacy of removal, meanwhile, made "excellent politics" that provided an issue "ideally suited to advance his political fortunes" (Vipperman, pp. 300–301). Thus, on his return to Congress in 1826 he spoke frequently on the importance of removal and played a leading role on the House Committee on Indian Affairs that drafted the bill eventually passed as the Indian Removal Act of 1830. As governor, Lumpkin refused to send representation for the state in the Supreme Court's hearing of *Worcester v. Georgia* (1832), and he ignored, with President Jackson's tacit consent, the court's ruling that Georgia had no authority over the Indians' lands. Instead, Lumpkin promoted and secured legislative approval for a survey of the Cherokee lands, for the creation of new counties in the region, and for a lottery to distribute the land to white settlers as a way to encourage the Indians' migration. When the signing of the Treaty of New Echota in 1835 formally provided for removal, Lumpkin, on finishing his term as governor, became a commissioner to oversee the treaty's enforcement. When he entered the Senate two years later, he continued to keep Indian removal at the center of public attention; he also advised General Winfield Scott on ways to carry out the terms of the New Echota treaty. No other politician in the Jacksonian period deserved greater responsibility for the tragedy of the Trail of Tears.

During his career, Lumpkin accumulated a sufficient amount of land and slaves so that he could retire comfortably to his plantation outside of Athens. Until his death there, he spent his retirement working on his memoirs and serving as a trustee for the University of Georgia. His later years were marred by Georgia's secession, which he supported, and the experience of Civil War and Reconstruction.

• Lumpkin's memoirs, published as *The Removal of the Cherokee Indians From Georgia* (1907), contain, in addition to an autobiography, a collection of speeches, and public and personal letters and papers. The manuscript for the memoirs, dated 1852 and entitled "Incidents Connected With the Life of Wilson Lumpkin," as well as his personal papers, are held in the University of Georgia Library in Athens. Additional papers are held in the Georgia Department of Archives and History, Atlanta. Good scholarly treatments of Lumpkin are Carl J. Vipperman, "The 'Particular Mission' of Wilson Lumpkin," *Georgia Historical Quarterly* 66 (Fall 1982): 295–316; and Robert G. McPherson, "Wilson Lumpkin" in *Georgians in Profile*, ed. Horace Montgomery (1958). Biographical sketches are in Josephine Mellichamp, *Senators from Georgia* (1976); and James F. Cook, *The Governors of Georgia, 1754–1995* (1995). Lumpkin's role in the confrontation over removal between Georgia and the federal government is discussed in Richard E. Ellis, *The Union at Risk: Jacksonian Democracy, States' Rights and the Nullification Crisis* (1987); and in John Ehle, *Trail of Tears: The Rise and Fall of the Cherokee Nation* (1988).

JONATHAN M. ATKINS

LUMSDEN, Leslie Leon (14 June 1875–8 Nov. 1946), epidemiologist and public health administrator, was born in Granite Springs, Virginia, the son of James Fife Lumsden, a merchant and farmer, and Martha Ann Hillman. His early education took place at private schools in Virginia. He gained admission to the Medical School of the University of Virginia without an undergraduate degree (a common practice at American medical schools well into the early twentieth century) and graduated with an M.D. in 1894. Lumsden secured an internship at the newly established Johns Hopkins Hospital, which with the related Baltimore medical school was setting a new American standard for excellence in medical education. His stint at Hopkins and two additional internships at New York hospitals gave Lumsden four years of postgraduate medical training. In March 1898 he was awarded a commission in the U.S. Public Health Service (then the Marine Hospital Service) after passing a series of rigorous examinations.

Lumsden began his work for the federal government by serving as medical officer aboard a troop transport during the Spanish-American War, which started a month after the young physician received his commission and ended four months later. Over the next several years Lumsden held a number of assignments, including the operation of quarantine stations in San Francisco, California, and San Juan, Puerto Rico; medical inspection of incoming immigrants at Ellis Island, New York; and a cruise aboard a training ship for coast guard recruits. In June 1906 Lumsden was transferred to Washington, D.C., to work in the Public Health Service's (PHS) Hygienic Laboratory, a small research facility that decades later evolved into the National Institutes of Health. Only weeks after Lumsden's arrival in Washington, District of Columbia officials asked the PHS to identify the cause of recurrent local outbreaks of typhoid. Lumsden was one of three Hygienic Laboratory staff members assigned to carry out this task. The intensive five-year epidemiological investigation that ensued was a formative experience for Lumsden. Even after he had achieved high recognition for his work in public health, he would still identify himself with pride as a "shoe-leath-

er epidemiologist." Lumsden married Alfreda Blanche Healy in 1902; she died childless in 1908.

Lumsden made a pioneering contribution to public health administration with the investigation of another typhoid outbreak in Yakima County, Washington, in 1911. Lumsden's investigation pointed to unsanitary privies as the primary problem; he recommended improvement of the county's sanitation facilities and called for the creation of a full-time county health department. Local leaders accepted his recommendations, establishing in 1911 the Yakima County Department of Health, staffed by several full-time employees, including a physician (who served as director), a bacteriologist, a public health nurse, and an office clerk. It was one of the nation's first county public health departments. The reforms that Lumsden had inspired in Yakima brought important results: locally, the incidence of typhoid fell to less than one-tenth the levels experienced during previous summers; nationally, the Yakima County Department of Health served as a model for the development of similar agencies as part of the growing rural sanitation movement.

Lumsden went on to supervise sanitation surveys in rural areas around the country, especially in the South. In the years preceding World War I a group of dedicated junior PHS officers—who referred to Lumsden as "Chief" and themselves as "Lumsden's Boys"—carried out rural public health surveys in places such as Dorchester County, Maryland; Bedford County, Indiana; Edgecombe County, North Carolina; Union County, Mississippi; Clay County, Mississippi; Walker County, Alabama; Cumberland County, Illinois; Hill County, Texas; Okmulgee County, Oklahoma; and Mason County, Kentucky. An article on the growing rural sanitation movement that appeared in the *Saturday Evening Post* (19 Aug. 1916) described Lumsden as possessing "a sort of apostolic fervor—teaching the people of the United States the elemental facts as to the disposal of the wastes of the human body" (quoted in Williams, "Leslie L. Lumsden, MD," p. 466).

World War I brought some interruption to Lumsden's work in rural sanitation, but he played a pivotal role in preventing the complete absorption of the PHS into the U.S. military machine. As the patriotic ardor of Americans increased during the spring and summer of 1917, a growing number of PHS officers became eager to don military uniforms. In November 1917 four members of a five-member committee chosen by PHS officers to consider the role of the PHS in the war signed a resolution urging President Woodrow Wilson to transfer the federal health agency to the army or the navy for the duration of the war. Lumsden, the only dissenting member of this committee, argued with thinly veiled ferocity that the PHS should not abandon its mission to preserve and protect the health of the entire American populace, and he stressed the military significance of this function in war time.

This acrimonious debate was resolved at the cabinet level, generally in favor of Lumsden's position. PHS officers, including Lumsden, did engage in some important work directly related to the military, such as sanitary inspection of troop cantonments and the immediate surrounding regions, but the PHS was not transferred to a branch of the military during the war, and the agency was not entirely diverted from the pursuit of public health. Even after the war, however, Lumsden's conflicts with his colleagues on the proper wartime function of the PHS continued to affect his standing in the agency. He narrowly missed being chosen to replace outgoing Surgeon General Rupert Blue in 1920; the officer chosen for the job was Hugh S. Cumming, who had been among the four officers whose resolution Lumsden had bitterly opposed in 1917.

After the war and his failure to be named surgeon general, Lumsden continued his efforts to foster the rural sanitation movement. By 30 June 1930 "Chief" Lumsden and his "boys" were operating cooperative rural sanitation demonstration projects in 202 counties across twenty-four states. In 1930 Lumsden began to lobby Congress for funds to convert the federal government's involvement in rural public health from a demonstration program to a system with permanent financial support. Surgeon General Cumming, who was seeking the presidency of the American Medical Association at the time, did not approve of this scheme, which the AMA viewed nervously as leading toward federal involvement in the delivery of health care. In November 1930 Cumming removed Lumsden from his position at the head of the Office of Rural Sanitation and assigned him to a largely ceremonial position in New Orleans as medical director of PHS operations in eight southern states. Lumsden perceived this transfer—accurately, it seems—as an attempt by Cumming quietly to banish an old rival who had become an uncomfortable threat.

Lumsden remained in New Orleans for the remainder of his career with the PHS. In the years before he reached mandatory federal retirement age in 1939 he returned to his old role as an epidemiologist, investigating diseases such as typhoid, tuberculosis, poliomyelitis, and epidemic encephalitis. He married Flora Elizabeth Dick in 1937; despite his age, they had two children. Lumsden died in New Orleans.

Ralph Chester Williams, who had joined the PHS as a medical officer in 1917, when he "came under the spell of [Lumsden's] very dynamic personality," summed up his mentor's legacy by stating that he "quite properly can be regarded as the father of local public health work in the United States."

• The best biographical account is Ralph Chester Williams, "Leslie L. Lumsden, MD: Pioneer in Rural Sanitation and Early Epidemiology in the United States," *Southern Medical Journal* 67 (Apr. 1974): 463–73. Williams also noted Lumsden's PHS career in his *The United States Public Health Service, 1798–1950* (1951). Two other books devoted to the general history of the PHS give extensive but intermittent attention to Lumsden: Bess Furman, *A Profile of the United States Pub-lic Health Service, 1798–1948* (1973), and Fitzhugh Mullan, *Plagues and Politics: The Story of the United States Public Health Service* (1989).

JON M. HARKNESS

LUNA Y ARELLANO, Tristan de (1514?–16 Sept. 1573), explorer and colonizer of La Florida, was born in Borovia, Soria province, Spain, the son of Don Carlos de Luna y Arellano, marshal of Castile and lord of Ciria and Borobia, and his second wife, Doña Juana Dávalos. Nothing is known of his childhood or education. Luna first went to New Spain in 1530 in the retinue of Hernán Cortés, whose wife, Doña Juana de Zuñiga, was Luna's cousin. Returning to Spain, Luna next voyaged to New Spain in 1535 with another cousin, Don Antonio de Mendoza, the first viceroy of Mexico. When Mendoza organized the Francisco Vázquez de Coronado expedition to explore New Mexico (1540–1542), Luna was appointed captain of cavalry but soon rose to the rank of brigadier general (*maestre de campo*) when the holder of that position fell ill and could not continue. Luna's principal duty was to lead the main body of the army while Coronado explored in the van. Luna accompanied Coronado on the journey in search of Quivira and claimed credit for preparing the winter supplies and camp for 1542.

Three years after his return to Mexico Luna married Isabel de Rojas, a wealthy twice-widowed woman from Oaxaca. Her properties and encomiendas made his fortune. They had two children. She was to die by 1558.

In 1548 Viceroy Mendoza appointed Luna commander of a force sent to repress an uprising of the Coatlan and Tetiapa Indians in the mountains of Oaxaca. He imposed a peace that lasted for a decade. In 1551 he was named administrator of the estates of the marques del Valle de Oaxaca, Hernán Cortés's son, a position he held for a number of years.

When the regency government in Spain approved plans to found a Spanish colony on the northern shore of the Gulf of Mexico, then Viceroy Luis de Velasco named Luna as commander. The colony was to be a base from which shipwrecked persons might be rescued, from which missionaries might reach the numerous Indian groups reported by the de Soto expedition as resident in the interior of the American Southeast, and from which a string of Spanish towns might be established along a road that would reach the Atlantic coast at the Punta de Santa Elena (present-day Tybee Island, Ga.) via Coosa and Cofitachequi.

As was customary, Luna used his fortune and mortgaged his children's inheritance properties (from their mother) to help pay some of the expedition's expenses. In addition, the royal treasury and many of the persons who went on the expedition put substantial sums into its outfitting. Some 500 soldiers and other persons sailed from San Juan de Ulua on 11 June 1559 expecting to find a land rich in agricultural products and filled with Indians who could be distributed in encomiendas.

The Luna expedition proved to be a failure in spite of the elaborate preparations and Viceroy Velasco's keen interest in it. The landing of the expedition at Ochuse (present-day Pensacola Bay) on 14 August was followed on 19 August by a tropical storm that sank many of the ships and their cargoes of supplies. While awaiting replacement supplies, Luna moved the expedition to Nanipacana, an Indian town on the Alabama River. Believing the tales of Coosa's abundance that the survivors of de Soto's expedition had spread in New Spain, in April 1560 Luna sent Captain Mateo del Sauz to find that place, which he did after some difficulty. Sauz reported that Coosa had food but that only some of the residents of the towns were present, the rest evidently having retired to the forests to avoid the Spaniards. Meanwhile, the expedition returned to Pensacola Bay and received supplies sent from Cuba and Mexico. Heartened by Sauz's report, Luna wanted to move the expedition to Coosa but was prevented from doing so by his officers. Discouraged by hardships already suffered, they and the Dominican friars in the expedition lobbied Viceroy Velasco to replace Luna as its commander and withdraw it from Florida. Velasco, meanwhile, had received preemptory orders from Philip II to send a party from Ochuse to the Punta de Santa Elena. In response, Luna ordered his nephew Martín Díaz to lead three ships to the Punta de Santa Elena, but storms forced two of them into Havana, whence they returned to Mexico, as did the third.

Velasco, meanwhile, appointed Angel de Villafañe to replace Luna as governor and captain general of Florida. His orders called for allowing the discontented to return to New Spain, leaving a small garrison at Ochuse, and then taking the remaining men to occupy the Punta de Santa Elena. Villafañe arrived at Ochuse on 8 April 1561.

Luna sailed to Spain to defend his record, seek compensation for his services to the crown, and attempt to ensure that he would inherit the title of marshal of Castile from his older brother, who had no heirs. He was disappointed on all counts. The title passed to his son, Don Carlos de Arellano (1575). After his return to Mexico in 1564, Luna lived an impoverished life until his death in the Mexico City home of a longtime friend, Don Luis de Castilla.

• The classic treatment of Luna and his expedition is Herbert I. Priestley, ed., *The Luna Papers* (2 vols., 1928). Other accounts are in Woodbury Lowery, *The Spanish Settlements within the Present Limits of the United States, 1513–1561* (1901); Robert Weddle, *Spanish Sea* (1985); and Paul E. Hoffman, *A New Andalucia and a Way to the Orient: The American Southeast during the Sixteenth Century* (1990). Luna's genealogy is found in Ricardo Ortega y Pérez Gallardo, *Historia genealógica de las familias más antiguas de Mexico* (1908), vol. 2, pt. 1, portfolio 8; Jorge Ignacio Rubio Mañe, *Introducción al estudio de los virreyes de Nueva España, 1535–1746*, vol. 2 (1955), pp. 74–81; and Peter Boyd-Bowman, *Indice geobiográfico de 40,000 pobladores españoles de America en el siglo XVI*, vol. 2 (1964), p. 179.

PAUL E. HOFFMAN

LUNCEFORD, Jimmie (6 June 1902–12 July 1947), jazz and popular bandleader, was born James Melvin Lunceford in Fulton, Missouri, the son of a choirmaster. His parents' names are unknown. Before he enrolled in high school the family moved to Denver, Colorado, where he studied reed instruments, flute, guitar, and trombone under Wilberforce James Whiteman (father of Paul Whiteman).

Lunceford first worked professionally in the society dance orchestra of violinist George Morrison, with whom he traveled to New York City in 1922 for performances at the Carlton Terrace and for recordings. Soon afterward, he entered Fisk University in Nashville, Tennessee, where he excelled in basketball, football, and track while earning a bachelor's degree in music education (c. 1926). During summer vacations he worked in Deacon Johnson's band in New York, and early in 1926 he was regularly with banjoist Elmer Snowden's band at the Bamville Club in Harlem, playing saxophone and trombone alongside pianist Bill (later Count) Basie and trumpeter Bubber Miley.

After taking some graduate courses at City College of New York, Lunceford went to Memphis, Tennessee, in fall 1926 to teach physical education and music at Manassa High School, where he organized a jazz band including bassist Moses Allen and drummer Jimmy Crawford. During the summers of 1928 and 1929 they played in Lakeside, Ohio, and during the 1929 season the band included alto saxophonist and singer Willie Smith, pianist Ed Wilcox, trombonist and singer Henry Wells (all three having been Fisk students), Allen, and Crawford. Wilcox also recalled summer engagements at Belmar, New Jersey, and the following year at Asbury Park, the years unspecified. In Memphis the group played professionally at the Hotel Men's Improvement Club Dance Hall and the Silver Slipper night club, broadcasting on WREC from the latter venue.

Finally, Lunceford abandoned education for the entertainment field. Around 1929 or 1930 the group suffered through an early winter in Cleveland, Ohio, struggling for work. They found a job in Cincinatti, Ohio, and in June 1930 recorded as the Chickasaw Syncopators. After touring in 1931, Lunceford made Buffalo, New York, the group's home base for about three years. In 1932 two additional Fisk alumni joined, trumpeter Paul Webster and baritone saxophonist Earl Carruthers. In summer 1933 the band performed at the Lake Caroga resort in upstate New York, and that year Lunceford hired trumpeter Tommy Stevenson and the man who would become his finest soloist, tenor saxophonist Joe Thomas.

Up to this point the group had been structured as a cooperative held among Smith, Wilcox, and Lunceford, but when Harold F. Oxley took over management of the band in 1933, questions of business reverted to Lunceford and Oxley alone. By mid-decade the two men had expanded their domain, with Lunceford Artists, Inc., managing other orchestras as well as their own.

Arranger, trumpeter, and singer Sy Oliver joined the band in Buffalo, shortly before an engagement at the Lafayette Theater in Harlem in September 1933. The performance was a disaster, this being the first time that Lunceford's men had played for a choreographed show rather than for dancing, but they survived the experience, toured New England, and returned to New York to record their first well-received recordings, "White Heat" and "Jazznocracy," and more significantly, to follow Cab Calloway's big band as the resident group at the Cotton Club. By January 1934 trumpeter and singer Eddie Thompkins (often misspelled Tompkins) joined; he was another of Lunceford's men who doubled as a glee club singer in the band.

Lunceford's men broadcast nightly from the Cotton Club for roughly half a year. The band then embarked on years of regular national touring—as well as a Scandinavian tour in February 1937—while recording prolifically. Three titles associated with Duke Ellington, including Smith's arrangements of "Sophisticated Lady" and "Mood Indigo," show off the virtuosity of the saxophone section and the band's strong independence from Ellington's conception, other bands of that era having found it quite difficult to perform Ellington's music in an original manner. For this same session of September 1934 Lunceford himself made a rare contribution, his zany and technically demanding composition "Stratosphere." In general his musical involvement was directed toward inspiration and organization rather than the nuts and bolts of playing and writing.

Later sessions exemplify the band's bouncy dance music, including Oliver arrangements of his own composition "Stomp It Off," Wilcox's arrangement of "Rhythm Is Our Business" (1934), and Oliver's versions of the popular songs "Four or Five Times," "My Blue Heaven" (1935), and "Organ Grinder's Swing" (1936). The band may be seen in action in the film short "Jimmie Lunceford and his Dance Orchestra" (1936).

Arranger, trombonist, and guitarist Eddie Durham had joined in 1935 and contributed scores to the band but without making the impact that he earlier had with Bennie Moten and soon would have with Basie. In the fall of 1937 trombonist Trummy Young replaced Durham and alto saxophonist Ted Buckner joined; both men are featured on "Margie" (1938). Further hits by Oliver included his compositions and arrangements of "For Dancers Only" (1937) and "Le Jazz Hot" (1939) and his arrangement of " 'Tain't What You Do (It's the Way That You Do It)" (1939). In 1937 Lunceford had married Crystal Tally.

In 1939 Snooky Young replaced Thompkins, and late that year he was featured with Smith on "Uptown Blues." In mid-1939 trumpeter Gerald Wilson and arranger Billy Moore collectively took Oliver's place, and Moore soon gave Lunceford a hit record with his version of "What's Your Story, Morning Glory?" (1940). In its last great moment, Lunceford's orchestra was featured in the movie *Blues in the Night* (1941), its title track providing a hit song for Lunceford and others, including Hot Lips Page with Artie Shaw, Woody Herman, and Jo Stafford with Tommy Dorsey.

By 1940 Lunceford's men were discontented. Crawford claimed that Oxley doled out insufficient salaries. Moore complained that Lunceford routinely appropriated royalty rights for his arrangers' scores, and that the leader and Oxley paid the band as little as possible: "He was an inspiring leader, from a distance, and he did mould his men into a most effective orchestra; he kept the men on their toes and maintained a fine public image. But he failed to reward the musicians who were mostly responsible for his huge success. . . . Meanwhile Lunceford bought himself a Lincoln Continental, and then his own plane, which he piloted" (Feather, pp. 170, 172). Considering these and other remembrances, writer Albert McCarthy speculated that "no musicians of any other major band of the swing era seem to have received such parsimonious salaries as those who worked with Lunceford." Snooky Young, Moses Allen, Smith, and Wilson quit in 1942, Crawford and Trummy Young in 1943. The band continued for several years, but the spark was gone. While signing autographs at a music store in Seaside, Oregon, Lunceford collapsed and soon died of a heart attack. Wilcox and Thomas, and then Wilcox alone, kept the group going for nearly three years before it finally disbanded permanently.

Lunceford's big band may be rated a notch below the greatest ensembles of the swing era, owing to the absence of highly original improvisers or a consistently original approach to arrangement (Oliver's best scores excepted). The group excelled in its delivery of a relaxed swing beat for dancing, in its presentation of novelty vocal trios (usually sung by Wells, Smith, and Oliver) that became very popular with college students (especially "My Blue Heaven"), and, above all, in its showmanship. Writer George T. Simon reports that among twenty-eight bands playing fifteen-minute sets at the Manhattan Center on 18 November 1940, including those of Benny Goodman, Glenn Miller, Count Basie, Les Brown, and Guy Lombardo, Lunceford's was the only one given such an overwhelming reception that they played beyond their alloted time. They owed this success to their superior antics: "The trumpets would throw their horns in the air together; the saxes would almost charge off the stage; . . . the trombones would slip their slides toward the skies; and . . . the musicians would be kidding and shouting at one another, projecting an aura of irresistible exuberance" (Simon, p. 329).

• Photos, scores, including that of "Stratosphere," and clippings are among the Lunceford items in the Sy Oliver Collection at the New York Public Library for the Performing Arts, Lincoln Center. Surveys of Lunceford's career include George Hoefer, "Hot Box: Jimmie Lunceford," *Down Beat*, 24 Sept. 1964, pp. 35–36; Gene Fernett, *Swing Out: Great Negro Jazz Bands* (1970); Ian Crosbie, "Lunceford: Message from Memphis," *Jazz Journal* 25 (Jan. 1972): 2–5 and (Feb. 1972): 26–29; and Albert McCarthy, *Big Band Jazz* (1974). See also Ralph J. Gleason, *Celebrating the Duke, and Louis,*

Bessie, Billie, Bird, Carmen, Miles, Dizzy, and Other Heroes (1975); George T. Simon, *The Big Bands*, 4th. ed. (1981); and Bruce Crowther, "Jimmie Lunceford and the Harlem Express," *Jazz Journal International* 41 (Dec. 1988): 12–13. Smith, Wilcox, and Oliver recall the band in Stanley Dance, *The World of Swing* (1974), Wilcox's portion repr. as "Lunceford Days," *Jazz Journal International* 30 (July 1977): 6–8. Moore's recollections are in Leonard Feather, *The Jazz Years: Earwitness to an Era* (1986). For musical analysis, see Gunther Schuller, *The Swing Era: The Development of Jazz, 1930–1945* (1989); David Ives, "Elmer Snowdon [*sic*]," *Jazz Journal* 16 (Jan. 1963): 26; and Mike Hennessey, *Klook: The Story of Kenny Clarke* (1990). A catalog of recordings is Charles Garrod's *Jimmie Lunceford and His Orchestra* (1990). An obituary is in the *New York Times*, 14 July 1947.

BARRY KERNFELD

LUND, Art (1 Apr. 1915–31 May 1990), singer and actor, was born Arthur Earl Lund, Jr., in Salt Lake City, Utah, the son of Arthur Earl Lund and Lilie Golberg. At Westminster College in Salt Lake City (1933–1935), he demonstrated a wide range of athletic abilities that won him an athletic scholarship to attend Eastern Kentucky State Teachers College, where he lettered in seven sports and was a Little All-American football player and a Golden Gloves boxer (B.S., 1937). During his college years, he also began singing with local bands. While coaching high school football in Maysville, Kentucky, in the late 1930s, he took summer engagements singing in nightclubs, under the stage name Art London. He toured with the Jimmy Joy orchestra in 1939–1941. In later 1941, still billing himself as Art London, he moved to New York City to become a lead singer with the Benny Goodman band, sharing vocal duties with Peggy Lee in regular broadcasts from the Terrace Room of the Hotel New Yorker as well as in recording sessions. He recorded a duet with Lee, "Winter Weather," in 1941. In 1940 Lund married Kathleen Virginia "Tiny" Bolanz; she died in 1969. The couple had two children.

Lund's professional career was interrupted in 1942 when he enlisted in the U.S. Navy. He earned a master's degree in aerological engineering from the U.S. Naval Academy in 1943 and subsequently saw duty in the South Pacific. After his discharge in 1946 he rejoined the Benny Goodman band. That same year he made the first of his five gold records: *Blue Skies* and *On the Alamo*. Leaving Goodman, he went solo. In the next few years, several of his recordings for the MGM, Paramount, and Coral labels made the top twenty. His hits included "My Blue Heaven" (1946), "Peg O' My Heart" and "Mimi" (1947), "On a Slow Boat to China" (1948), "Cherokee" (1949), and "Mona Lisa" (1950). His recording of "Mam'selle" (1947) went to number one.

A tall (6′4″), ruggedly athletic, blond man with a pleasing, lusty baritone voice and a forceful stage presence, Lund turned to the Broadway stage as the swing era ended. He won a Tony nomination for the role of Joey in Frank Loesser's *Most Happy Fella* (1956), which he created in 1956 and later reprised in London. He also costarred with Eddie Foy in *Donnybrook* (1961) and toured in *Wonderful Town, Fiorello, No Strings, Decisions, Decisions,* and *Destry Rides Again*. His portrayal of the simple-minded Lennie in an off-Broadway musical version of Steinbeck's *Of Mice and Men* (1958) was called "tremendously effective" by the *New York Times* reviewer Louis Calta.

By 1968 he had moved to Hollywood, where he played Frazier, the burliest of the Molly Maguires in the picture of that name. Other films include *The Last American Hero* (1973), *Black Caesar* (1973), *Baby Blue Marine* (1976), and *It's Alive III: Island of the Alive* (1987), among others. He appeared frequently on television, including two years on the Ken Murray show and in such dramas as "Gunsmoke" (1955), "The Rockford Files" (1974), and "Wagon Train" (1957). Lund married Janet Burris Chytraus in 1989. He moved from Sherman Oaks, California, to Holliday, Utah, a suburb of Salt Lake City, shortly before his death.

• For additional information, see D. Russell Conner, *Benny Goodman: Listen to His Legacy* (1988). Obituaries are in the *New York Times*, 6 June 1990; the *Washington Post*, 7 June 1990; and the *Salt Lake City Deseret News*, 2 June 1990.

LOUIS E. AULD

LUNDBERG, Emma Octavia (26 Oct. 1881–17 Nov. 1954), child welfare leader, was born in Västergötland, Sweden, the daughter of Frans Vilhelm Lundberg, a machine hand, and Anna Kajsa Johanson. The family emigrated from Sweden in 1884 and settled in Rockford, Illinois, where Emma attended public school. She graduated from Rockford High School in 1901. She then worked as a bookkeeper and secretary for the next two years. With the money she saved, in 1903 she enrolled at the University of Wisconsin at Madison, where she worked as the secretary for the dean of the medical school. She earned a bachelor's degree in English in 1907 and a master's degree in 1908.

After graduation, while she was still deciding on a career in social work, Lundberg conducted a cost-of-living survey in Buffalo, New York, the first of many studies she would conduct over the course of her long career. From 1908 to 1910 she worked in a number of positions, including one at the United States Immigration Commission, through which she conducted surveys of immigrants in several urban areas. During this time period she also served as a visitor on the staff of the United Charities of Chicago, where she worked with and attended lectures by some of the early social thinkers and activists, and she lived for brief spans of time in several settlement houses. From 1910 to 1912 she worked as an executive secretary with Associated Charities in Madison, Wisconsin, and then went on to Associated Charities in Milwaukee. Following that, she became a deputy at the Wisconsin Industrial Commission. It was in 1913, in this position, that she met Katharine Fredrica Lenroot, a recent graduate of the University of Wisconsin at Madison, who was hired as Lundberg's assistant. The two women became very close, working and living together for much of the next three decades.

In 1914 Julia Lathrop, chief of the newly created United States Children's Bureau, named Lundberg director of the bureau's new Social Services Division, a position she held until 1925. In this capacity Lundberg, assisted by Lenroot, directed studies on illegitimacy, juvenile delinquency, the care of mentally deficient children, and state child welfare laws; many were published as Children's Bureau publications. *Illegitimacy as a Child Welfare Problem*, a two-part study written with Lenroot, was published in 1920 (n. 66) and 1922 (n. 75).

After leaving the Children's Bureau, Lundberg joined the Child Welfare League of America, a federation of institutions for children and child-placing agencies, where she became director for studies and surveys. Her surveys conducted there resulted in the book *Child Dependency in the United States: Methods of Statistical Reporting and Census of Dependent Children in Thirty-One States*, which was published in 1933. Not long after she joined the New York State Temporary Emergency Relief Administration in 1931, Lundberg became its director for research and statistics. Over the next four years she also served as a consultant for other public agencies, producing *Unmarried Mothers in the Municipal Court of Philadelphia* (1933) for *Social Welfare in Florida* (1934) for the Philadelphia Bureau of Municipal Research and the State Board of Public Welfare of Florida. In 1934 Lenroot was appointed chief of the Children's Bureau. At her request, Lundberg returned to the bureau in 1935 as assistant director of the Child Welfare Division. Part of her duties entailed organizing the child welfare provisions of the Social Security Act of 1935. In 1942 she became the bureau's consultant in social services for children.

Over the course of her career, Lundberg was involved in three White House Conferences on Children. At the 1919 Conference on Child Welfare Standards, she organized the work for the section on children in need of special care. At the 1930 Conference on Child Health and Protection, she was the research secretary of the handicapped section. At the 1940 Conference on Children in a Democracy, she served as assistant secretary, was responsible for the administrative work, and contributed to the follow-up program for the conference.

In 1947, two years after Lundberg retired from the Children's Bureau because of ill health, she published *Unto the Least of These*. Her best-known work, it traces the development of social services for children in the United States. In 1951, the year Lenroot retired from the bureau, the two women moved to Hartsdale, New York, where they lived until Lundberg's death there.

At a time when social work and child welfare were fledgling movements, Lundberg's studies helped to shape child welfare services at the federal, state, and local levels. The data published in *Child Dependency in the United States*, collected from state welfare agencies rather than the Bureau of the Census, prompted state and local agencies to change and improve their collection and interpretation of data on dependent and neglected children. Her studies on illegitimacy showed a correlation between illegitimacy and infant mortality, delinquency, and child neglect. However, based on her research, Lundberg contended that illegitimate children who were left in their mother's care and were nursed by their mothers had a much lower infant mortality rate than did those who were separated from their mothers. She also contended that the father should be held responsible for financial support of the child when possible. Lundberg was a proponent of mothers' pensions or mother's aid, public money distributed to needy mothers with dependent children, contending that it would help keep families together and thus enable a normal home life for the child. Some of her claims were relatively new ideas in the field of child welfare, but Lundberg's prominence added to the weight of her findings.

• A collection of Lundberg's papers, predominantly professional in content, is at the Butler Library at Columbia University. *The Reminiscences of Katharine Lenroot*, in the Oral History Collection of Columbia University, contains some useful information. The Rockford, Illinois, Public Library has a small file of local newspaper clippings and obituaries on Lundberg. The University of Wisconsin, Madison, confirmed the dates of her A.B. and A.M. degrees, which occasionally are listed incorrectly. Article-length publications that provide biographical information include Katharine Lenroot, "Emma Octavia Lundberg," *Child Welfare* 34 (Jan. 1955): 19–20, and Emma O. Lundberg, "A Man of Good Will," *The Family* 27 (Mar. 1946): 9–11. An obituary is in the *New York Times*, 18 Nov. 1954.

CONNIE L. PHELPS

LUNDEBERG, Harry (25 Mar. 1901–28 Jan. 1957), labor leader, was born Harald Olaf Lundeberg in Oslo, Norway, the son of Karl Lundeberg, a small businessman, and Alette Koffeld. Lundeberg's parents were activists who championed the rights of women and labor. He completed secondary school and then went to sea, shipping under nine different flags. He belonged to Norwegian, British, and Australian seafarers' unions and was influenced by Spanish syndicalism and the Industrial Workers of the World (IWW). After the early 1920s, he shipped out of Seattle, Washington, and joined the Sailors' Union of the Pacific (SUP). Founded in 1885, the SUP had wielded significant influence in Pacific Coast maritime labor relations before World War I, but it lost nearly all its contracts, and most of its members, in the early 1920s. Lundeberg became an American citizen in 1933, by which time he was a boatswain—the most proficient and highest-paid classification for a deckhand—and was also licensed as a mate.

In 1933 Lundeberg won election as SUP patrolman in Seattle (similar to a business agent). Soon after, in May 1934, Pacific Coast longshoremen, organized in the International Longshoremen's Association (ILA), went on strike. Maritime workers quickly followed, and Lundeberg became chair of the SUP strike committee in Seattle. The strikes lasted for three months, ending in arbitration. Lundeberg emerged from the strike with both a reputation for militancy and a wide following among northwestern seamen.

In April 1935 Pacific Coast maritime unions formed the Maritime Federation of the Pacific (MFP). Harry Bridges, a longshoreman close to the Communist party, had come out of the 1934 strike as the most prominent maritime labor leader on the Pacific Coast. At the MFP's founding convention, Bridges championed Lundeberg for the MFP presidency. Lundeberg won, amid expectations he would be Bridges's reliable ally, if not his puppet. Lundeberg, however, set his own course.

From his new position, Lundeberg challenged the ineffectual SUP leadership. In December 1935 he won election as secretary-treasurer, the SUP's executive officer, and he resigned as MFP president. Leaders of the International Seamen's Union (ISU), the SUP's parent body, fearing a challenge from Lundeberg, contrived charges to justify rescinding the SUP charter. Refusing to accommodate, Lundeberg piloted the SUP to an independent course outside the American Federation of Labor (AFL).

Relations between the two largest MFP affiliates, the SUP and ILA, soon soured over "quickie" job actions (spontaneous small strikes, often involving a single ship), jurisdictional issues, and the handling of cargo from ships declared "unfair." Though the MFP ran a joint strike in late 1936 and early 1937, antagonism increased between the SUP and ILA and between Bridges and Lundeberg. Lundeberg also became increasingly critical of Communist influence in the maritime unions.

The Congress of Industrial Organizations (CIO) initially attracted Lundeberg, and John L. Lewis of the CIO considered the SUP a progressive union and a likely CIO recruit. By mid-1937 the CIO had chartered both the National Maritime Union (NMU), led by Joseph Curran, which overwhelmed the ISU in representational elections among Atlantic and Gulf Coast seamen, and also the International Longshoremen's and Warehousemen's Union (ILWU), formerly the Pacific Coast division of the ILA, headed by Bridges. Lundeberg now held back from the CIO, due partly to a concern over Communist influence in both the NMU and ILWU and partly to a fear that, if the SUP joined the CIO, it would be submerged into the much larger NMU and lose its autonomy. The SUP remained independent. Then, in April 1938, ILWU members slugged their way through an SUP picket line marking a jurisdictional dispute with the NMU. Afterward, the SUP withdrew from the MFP, and Lundeberg convinced his members to approve rejoining the AFL. A veteran poker player, Lundeberg held one of his strongest hands, for AFL leaders had no viable alternative to the SUP for organizing seafarers. In October 1938 the AFL chartered a new union, the Seafarers' International Union (SIU), with the SUP as its core and Lundeberg as its president.

Well over six feet tall and burly, Lundeberg earned a reputation as an outspoken anticommunist who never backed away from a fight. Seeking to recapture Atlantic and Gulf coast seamen lost to the NMU, SIU organizers included SUP veterans, conservative former ISU members, left-wing anticommunists (including Trotskyists and IWW-style syndicalists), and a few unsavory waterfront characters. Lundeberg and his union became known for strong-arm tactics, with Lundeberg himself acknowledging that organizing seamen sometimes involved "goon squads, gun-play, black jacks, etc." In 1940 his jaw was broken when he led an SUP attack on an ILWU picket line. The SUP newspaper, *West Coast Sailor*, which Lundeberg edited, was also blunt and hard-hitting, unmercifully lambasting employers and labor opponents. Those not sharing his own staunch anticommunism received Lundeberg's special vitriol and were likely to be labeled "commies."

During World War II expansion of the American merchant marine brought a surge in SIU membership to a high of 250,000. At the war's end, Lundeberg convinced SUP members to spend most of the huge bank account generated by wartime dues on a monumental headquarters building in San Francisco that would also memorialize merchant seamen killed in the war. In 1946 Lundeberg married Ida Warner. They had three children. Major strikes in 1946 and 1952 served to retain and extend wartime gains in wages and conditions for the SIU's 80,000 peacetime members. With the merger of the AFL and CIO, Lundeberg, in 1955, became president of the AFL-CIO Maritime Trades Department.

By the 1950s Lundeberg had become a conservative Republican, bluntly informing the California Labor Federation in 1952 that he would vote for Dwight Eisenhower regardless of their endorsement of Adlai Stevenson. Lundeberg also defended the longstanding SUP exclusion of Asians and blacks on the grounds that "my men don't want them."

Throughout his career as a union officer, Lundeberg drew a salary no greater than that of the best-paid boatswain in the SUP. He expected officials of his union periodically to work aboard ship, and he did so himself, even working his way from New York to Norway and back. He swore like a sailor but eschewed alcohol and tobacco. He disdained "tuxedo unionism" and always wore black jeans and an open-necked shirt. Seamen labeled his ever-present short-billed cap the "Lundeberg homburg." He died from a heart attack in a hospital in Burlingame, the San Francisco suburb where he lived with his family.

• Lundeberg's most important papers are held by the SUP at its headquarters in San Francisco. Another important source is the *West Coast Sailor*, the SUP's newspaper. Information also appears in histories of the SUP or maritime unionism, including Joseph Goldberg, *The Maritime Story* (1958); Bruce Nelson, *Workers on the Waterfront: Seamen, Longshoremen, and Unionism in the 1930s* (1988); and Stephen Schwartz, *Brotherhood of the Sea: A History of the Sailors' Union of the Pacific, 1885–1985* (1986). See also Frank J. Taylor, "Roughneck Boss of the Sailors' Union," *Saturday Evening Post* (18 Apr. 1953), and Curtis Fields, Jr., "A Labor Boss

Signs On—and Off," *Washington Post*, 7 Sept. 1947). Obituaries are in the *New York Times*, 29 Jan. 1957, and *San Francisco Chronicle*, 29 Jan. 1957.

ROBERT W. CHERNY

LUNDEEN, Ernest (4 Aug. 1878–31 Aug. 1940), congressman and senator, was born at Beresford, South Dakota, the son of Charles Henry Lundeen, a Methodist minister, and Christine Peterson. He was first raised in a two-room house built by his father, but after twelve years he moved with his family to Dayton, Iowa. During the Spanish-American War, he served as a private with Company B of the Twelfth Minnesota Volunteers. Shortly after his discharge, he entered Carleton College, graduating with a B.A. in 1901. For the next three years, he studied law at the University of Minnesota. In 1906 he was admitted to the bar, beginning a law practice in Minneapolis that he resumed intermittently much of his life. In 1919 he married Norma Matheson Ward; they had two children.

A heavyset, humorless man, Lundeen entered politics as a progressive or "La Follette" Republican. Representing in particular the immigrant Swedish and Norwegian workers of south Minneapolis, he served in the Minnesota House of Representatives from 1911 to 1915. In 1916, running in the Fifth Minnesota District, he was elected to the U.S. House of Representatives. He voted against U.S. entry into World War I. Speaking in opposition, he warned, "Our fixed determination is to thrust bayonets down the throats of unwilling people." He opposed conscription as "always distasteful to a free people." Seeking legislation to abolish war profits, he said, "If you conscript men for war, conscript wealth for war." Because of Lundeen's isolationist opinions, he and Representative Charles H. Dillon (R.-S.D.) were banned from British battlefields during a congressional tour of the front.

In 1918 Lundeen lost his congressional seat to Walter H. Newton. In February 1919, while a lame-duck congressman, he introduced a bill calling for a national referendum on the League of Nations. "We have announced," he said, "the policy of self-determination for others. The American people want self-determination for themselves." While attempting to make an antileague address, he was ridden out of Ortonville, Minnesota, in a locked refrigerator car.

Joining the Farmer-Labor party, Lundeen ran unsuccessfully under its banner for governor in 1928 and U.S. senator in 1930. From 1933 to 1935 he was U.S. congressman at large, and in 1935 he was returned to the House from Minnesota's Third District, which encompassed north Minneapolis. In June 1935, along with four other congressmen, he called for a new party that, in its call, would be "based upon a fundamental program striking at the root of the profit system." He withdrew, however, from a planning session in Chicago in opposition to a proposed ban on Communists. In August 1936, upon the death of Farmer-Labor senatorial candidate Floyd B. Olson, then Minnesota's governor, the party chose Lundeen as the new senatorial standard-bearer. The state's Democrats also backed

Lundeen, who defeated Republican nominee Theodore Christianson in the general election. That year Lundeen supported the Union party candidate, Congressman William Lemke of North Dakota, for president.

While in Congress Lundeen remained consistently radical on domestic policy. In 1934 the Communist-controlled Unemployment Councils persuaded him to introduce a bill providing unemployment benefits for all workers at prevailing wages. The program would be administered by a commission chosen from rank-and-file members of labor and farm organizations and funded by taxes on inheritances, gifts, and individual and corporate income over $5,000 a year. In 1939 he introduced a resolution backed by the Townsend National Recovery Plan, an organization led by Long Beach physician Francis Townsend, that called for a constitutional amendment to grant Congress the power to levy taxes for old-age assistance. Lundeen sought moratoriums on farm debts, the nationalization of banking, and bonuses for veterans. In protest against Supreme Court rulings against major New Deal legislation, he called for enlarging the Court to eleven members. In 1938 he urged the federal government to establish a five-member U.S. railroad service to assume "operation, control and ownership" of all railroads that grossed over a million dollars in 1935.

Always an isolationist, Lundeen opposed naval appropriations, aid to the Allies, and the Conscription Law of 1940. The United States, he repeatedly urged, should take over the hemispheric possessions of European states that refused to pay their war debts. Referring to islands owned by Great Britain and France, he threatened that unless the debts were paid, "we will send our armed forces to seize them." In December 1940 he announced the formation of the Make Europe Pay War Debts Committee, later the Islands for War Debts Defense Committee, of which he was national chairman. The group was fostered by German-American propagandist George Sylvester Viereck and received money from the German government. Lundeen also endorsed American purchase of the Dutch West Indies and Greenland.

Lundeen died in an air crash a mile and a half from Lovettsville, Virginia. Columnists Drew Pearson and Robert Allen claimed that at the time of his death Lundeen was being followed by agents of the Federal Bureau of Investigation as a Nazi sympathizer, but Attorney General Robert H. Jackson issued an "emphatic denial" that Lundeen was under investigation by the Department of Justice.

• The Lundeen papers are at the Hoover Institution on War, Revolution, and Peace, Stanford, Calif. Harvey Klehr, *The Heyday of American Communism: The Depression Decade* (1984), delves into his relations with the Communists. Klehr puts to rest the accusation of Benjamin Gitlow, a top Communist official turned strongly anti-Communist, in *The Whole of Their Lives* (1948), that Lundeen was a paid undercover agent of the party. For accusations that Lundeen was an unwitting tool of the German government, see O. John Rogge, *The Official German Report* (1961). An obituary is in the *New York Times*, 1 Sept. 1940.

JUSTUS D. DOENECKE

LUND-QUIST, Carl Elof (19 Sept. 1908–26 Aug. 1965), Lutheran clergyman and international Lutheran administrator, was born near Freemount, Kansas, the son of Emanuel Elof Lundquist and Alida Larson, farmers. Lund-Quist, the fourth of five siblings, was born and raised in a rural area settled by Swedish immigrants. So close was the family to its European roots that when Lund-Quist began elementary school his first language was Swedish. His mother died when he was eight years old, leaving his father with responsibility for five young children. Carl's grandmother Anna Rodell Lundquist, who often stayed with the family, exerted a strong religious influence on him. He preached his first sermon at the age of seventeen. The economic hardships endured by his family worsened during Lund-Quist's college years because of the depression, drought, and grasshopper invasions that began in 1929 and continued throughout the 1930s. Thus Lund-Quist's higher education was not achieved without financial difficulty. Instead of living on campus at Bethany College in Lindsborg, where he began studies in 1927, he had to stay at home and drive about ten miles to attend classes.

At Bethany Lund-Quist earned a reputation as a skilled debater. He also was early recognized as a leader and was elected vice president of the student council. Between his sophomore and junior years (1929–1930) he attended the Lutheran Bible Institute in Minneapolis, Minnesota. The legalism he encountered there repelled him, but during that time he came into contact with a chapter of the Lutheran Student Association of America (LSAA) on the campus of the University of Minnesota. This was the beginning of his lifelong interest in the LSAA. Between 1930 and his graduation from Bethany College in 1932, he actively participated in the organization's conventions.

In the autumn of 1932 Lund-Quist entered the Augustana Theological Seminary, a Swedish Lutheran school in Rock Island, Illinois. During his first year there, while serving as national president of the LSAA, Lund-Quist began to realize that the Lutheran church went far beyond the boundaries of the Augustana Synod, which had been organized by Swedish immigrants in 1860. Through his work with the LSAA he met representatives from conferences and synods of Danish, German, and Norwegian origins. He also began to develop the administrative skills for which he would become known. It probably was at seminary that he changed the spelling of his name from Lundquist to Lund-Quist. During this period many young pastors with Swedish names altered the spelling of their names in order to distinguish themselves from so many others with the same last name. Lund-Quist's change, however, retained an obvious link to his Swedish heritage.

After he was ordained in the spring of 1936, Lund-Quist traveled to Europe, where he began to see the church not simply as denominational but also as interdenominational and international. In Oslo, Norway, he attended a convention of the World Student Sunday School Association and was elected president of its youth council. While in Scandinavia he took the opportunity to visit Sweden. In Geneva, Switzerland, he attended a convention of the World Student Christian Federation (WSCF)—he would later become a member of its executive committee—and an ecumenical seminar at the University of Geneva. Among the prominent church leaders he met in Geneva was Hans Lilje, secretary in Germany of the WSCF. In later years Lund-Quist would work closely with Lilje when he was president of the Lutheran World Federation and Lund-Quist was general secretary.

In the autumn of 1936 Lund-Quist became pastor of Concordia Lutheran Church in Chicago, Illinois. During his five-year pastorate, membership more than doubled and the Sunday school more than tripled in size. He had been called to Concordia, in part, because he could preach in Swedish, but by the end of his ministry there in 1941, he had changed the language of worship to English, another indication of the developing Americanization of the Augustana Synod even as it retained basic elements of its Swedish Lutheran heritage, among them the form of worship.

From 1941 until 1946 Lund-Quist served as the first full-time pastor to Lutheran students at the University of Minnesota. He was also active ecumenically by participating on the University Religious Council.

In 1946 Lund-Quist became director of public relations of the National Lutheran Council. Formed in 1917, it brought together nine Lutheran bodies in origin: one Danish, one Finnish, four German, two Norwegian, and one Swedish. As director of public relations Lund-Quist helped organize the 1947 meeting, held in Lund, Sweden, at which the Lutheran World Federation (LWF) was formed with the goals of integrating and uniting world Lutheranism through theological study and of strengthening relief efforts to fellow Lutherans who had suffered the devastation of war in Europe. A year later, in 1948, he became assistant executive secretary of the LWF and, in 1952, its executive secretary, a post he held until 1960, when declining health forced him to resign.

As executive secretary Lund-Quist provided leadership in reconstructing European churches in the postwar years, a monumental task that included not only rebuilding structures but also providing for the education and re-education of pastors and students through seminars and exchange scholarships and for the provision of literature. Thousands of refugees also were helped to find new homes in other countries, including the United States, and 850,000 Arabs received gifts of food and clothing in the camps where they were forced to reside. An important and often hazardous part of Lund-Quist's work was negotiating with Lutheran churches behind the iron curtain. Although he was able to secure the necessary visas for travel to various countries, at times he had to ride in Red Cross trucks, and he knew he was under constant surveillance. During his tenure as executive secretary Lund-Quist traveled more than 150,000 miles and with the exceptions of China and Russia, where entry was prohibited, visited all of the thirty-one countries with Lutheran churches. By the time of the LWF's third assembly, held in Minneapolis in 1957, fifty million Lutherans were members of the federation.

In late October 1960, following his resignation the previous August, Lund-Quist suffered a massive stroke. From then until his death nearly five years later, he was incapable of caring for himself and had difficulty speaking. He spent his last three years in Fairview Hospital in Minneapolis, where he died. He had never married.

Lund-Quist's contributions were considerable. His leadership in the reconstruction, development, and maintenance of communications among the churches, and in the relief and relocation of victims of war, as well as his extensive travels, helped to form a fellowship network among the churches as a result of their greater knowledge of one another. The mergers that took place later in the 1960s in the formation of the American Lutheran Church and the Lutheran Church in America were no doubt much affected by his work.

• The chief repository of Lund-Quist papers is the archives of the Lutheran World Federation, Geneva, Switzerland. Other materials are in the archives of the Lutheran Church in America, Rosemont, Ill., and the Lutheran Theological Seminary, St. Paul, Minn. Lund-Quist's writings include "A Divided Church and Unity," *American Lutheran*, Aug. 1957, pp. 9–10; "Dr. Lund-Quist Describes Urgent Questions Facing Federation," *LWF News Release*, no. 22 (1956); "The Hannover Assembly," 18 Mar. 1952; "The Lutheran World Federation Today," address presented at the Second Conference of Lutherans of the South American Conference, Petropolis, Brazil, July 1954; "Served Better by Laymen," *National Lutheran*, souvenir ed., third assembly of the Lutheran World Federation (1957), pp. 23–24, 39, all available from LWF headquarters, Geneva; and "The Tasks of the Lutheran Churches of the World," *Augustana Seminary Review* 9 (Third Quarter 1957): 3–10. For additional biographical information see Emmet E. Eklund and Marion Lorimer Eklund, *He Touched the Whole World: The Story of Carl E. Lund-Quist* (1992); William H. Gentz, "Carl E. Lund-Quist—Lutheranism's Man of the Hour," *Lutheran Herald*, 13 Aug. 1957, pp. 750–53; and Willmar Thorkelson, "From Farm Boy to Church Diplomat," *Lutheran Standard*, 13 Sept. 1957, pp. 18–19, and "Dr. Lund-Quist: His Parish Covers the Entire World," *Minneapolis Star*, 31 July 1957. An obituary is in the *National Lutheran*, Oct. 1965.

EMMET E. EKLUND

LUNDY, Benjamin (4 Jan. 1789–22 Aug. 1839), antislavery editor, was born in Sussex County, New Jersey, the son of Joseph Lundy and Elizabeth Shotwell, farmers. The Lundy family had been Quakers for many generations, and Lundy maintained close ties with other Quakers throughout his life.

Lundy had little formal education. At the age of nineteen, while working as a saddler's apprentice in Wheeling, Virginia, he was so distressed by the sight of coffles of slaves that he vowed to make antislavery his life's work. In 1815 he married Esther Lewis; they had five children. The couple settled in southeastern Ohio, where Lundy founded the Union Humane Society, dedicated to aiding free blacks. Soon he began assisting in the publication of the *Philanthropist*, a local Quaker journal. In the winter of 1819 he traveled to Missouri to campaign, unsuccessfully, for an antislavery state constitution.

In 1821 he founded the *Genius of Universal Emancipation* in Mount Pleasant, Ohio, and subsequently published it in Greeneville, Tennessee (1822–1824), Baltimore (1824–1830), and Washington, D.C. (1830–1833). He spent most of his career addressing his antislavery arguments chiefly to nonslaveholding white southerners in the Upper South, who, he believed, might be persuaded to end slavery by political means. Although this major goal was not achieved, the *Genius* did succeed in tying together a network of antislavery activists by providing information and a forum for discussion at a time when no other such source existed. In 1828 Lundy traveled to New England and New York in an effort to mobilize antislavery sentiment. On this trip he met abolitionist William Lloyd Garrison, who in 1829 joined him in Baltimore as coeditor of the *Genius*. With the *Genius* facing increasingly serious financial difficulties, Garrison and Lundy dissolved their partnership, and Garrison returned to Boston to agitate for immediate emancipation through his newspaper, the *Liberator*, which began publication in January 1831. Meanwhile, mounting southern hostility and declining financial support plagued the *Genius*. After 1831 it was published only sporadically and with lengthy interruptions.

Unlike later, more doctrinaire abolitionists, Lundy welcomed the discussion of a variety of antislavery arguments and emancipation plans—both immediate and gradual—in his newspaper. Although deeply troubled by the immorality and cruelty of slavery, he believed it would most likely not be abolished unless white citizens became convinced that it damaged their own interests. Therefore, the *Genius* emphasized the danger of slave insurrections, the aristocratic and tyrannical inclinations of slave owners, and the unprofitability of slave labor.

Lundy also supported the free produce movement, which advocated the boycott of all goods produced by slave labor. Although the movement enjoyed a certain vogue, especially in the late 1820s, it did little to hasten the demise of slavery. As a way to demonstrate the superiority of free labor while also aiding a few black people, he spent many years trying, with little success, to establish black settlements in Haiti, Upper Canada, and the then-Mexican province of Texas. Most followers of Garrison rejected his emigration plans on the grounds that they failed to confront slavery as a moral issue and seemed to imply that African Americans should be removed from the United States. While Lundy was on a mission to Haiti in 1826, his wife died, effectively making orphans of their young children since Lundy's wide-ranging travels prevented him from caring for them himself. The children were reared by relatives.

While negotiating a land grant in Mexico, Lundy witnessed the early phases of the Texas Revolution, an event that he believed was part of a southern conspiracy to expand and safeguard slavery (which the Mexican government had outlawed). He set forth this view in a widely circulated pamphlet, *The War in Texas* (1836), which John Quincy Adams (1767–1848), with whom he frequently corresponded, used in the U.S. Congress to oppose the annexation of Texas. Lundy's interpretation, generally accepted by abolitionists and others in the North, helped delay annexation and contributed to the growth of antisouthern sentiment in the North.

In 1836 Lundy began publishing the *National Enquirer* in Philadelphia to agitate for antislavery political action, a course that set him still further apart from the followers of Garrison. In 1838 he moved to Putnam County, Illinois, where some of his children lived. His plans to resume publication of the *Genius* and to take part in the local antislavery movement were cut short by his death from a fever less than a year later.

• Lundy's letters are in the Benjamin Lundy Papers at the Ohio Historical Society, the Benjamin Lundy and Paxson Vickers Collection in the Library of Congress, the Adams Family Papers at the Massachusetts Historical Society, the Pennsylvania Abolition Society Manuscript Collection in the Historical Society of Pennsylvania, and the Elizabeth Margaret Chandler Papers in the Bentley Historical Library at the University of Michigan. A nearly complete file of the *Genius of Universal Emancipation* is in the Johns Hopkins University Library. An early collection of documents is [Thomas Earle, comp.], *The Life, Travels, and Opinions of Benjamin Lundy* (1847). For a modern biography, see Merton L. Dillon, *Benjamin Lundy and the Struggle for Negro Freedom* (1966). A shorter account is in Jane H. Pease and William H. Pease, *Bound with Them in Chains* (1972).

MERTON L. DILLON

LUNSFORD, Bascom Lamar (21 Mar. 1882–4 Sept. 1973), folk performer, folk song collector, and festival promoter, was born in Mars Hill, North Carolina, the son of James Basset Lunsford, a teacher and schoolmaster, and Louarta Leah Buckner. Both of his parents were descended from pioneer settlers in the area. Though the entire Lunsford family had varying degrees of formal education, James Lunsford encouraged his six children to take seriously the rich folk culture of the mountains. By the time he was ten years old, Bascom Lunsford and his brother Blackwell were adept on the fiddle and were performing for schoolhouse functions.

Lunsford was educated at rural one-room schoolhouses and at Camp Academy in Leicester, North Carolina. He apparently stayed there only a year and then turned to teaching; in the off-season he traveled around selling fruit trees and for a time ran a commercial beekeeping business. In the meantime Lunsford began to collect old ballads and fiddle and banjo tunes

of the area, the same region that later would yield so many ballads for folk song collectors like Cecil Sharp. In 1906 Lunsford married his childhood sweetheart, Nellie Triplett, and moved to Connelly Springs, North Carolina, where he attended nearby Rutherford College, graduating in 1909. Next he enrolled in the law school at Trinity College (now Duke University) and passed the bar exam in 1913. During the next few years Lunsford continued to teach and give lectures on folk music, worked as a county solicitor, and during World War I served as an agent of the U.S. Justice Department chasing down draft evaders. His family continued to grow, and by 1925 he and Nellie had six daughters and a son.

Lunsford's performing career went into high gear on 15 March 1924, when he became one of the first old-time singers to make commercial phonograph records; for the OKeh Company he recorded the ballad "Jesse James" and the mountain lyric "I Wish I Was a Mole in the Ground." The latter would become his best-known song and was associated with him throughout his long career. In August 1925 Lunsford recorded two more songs for OKeh, and then in 1928 he did a major session for the Brunswick Company; these won him a nationwide reputation and included the familiar comic song "Mountain Dew." In 1929 he appeared in a Fox Movietown newsreel playing his fiddle and clog dancing. As early as 1922 folklorists such as Frank C. Brown began recording Lunsford's folk music on wax cylinders, discs, and tape. In 1935 Lunsford traveled to Columbia University to record 317 items from his personal "memory collection." A second mammoth recording session took place at the Archive of American Folk Song for the Library of Congress in 1949, yielding another 350 items. He also made commercial recordings in the 1950s.

Lunsford pioneered another key innovation on the traditional music scene, the folk festival. Asked by the Asheville, North Carolina, Chamber of Commerce to organize a festival that would help lure tourists to the city, he founded in 1928 the Mountain Dance and Folk Festival, which remained an annual affair through the 1990s. Lunsford continued to be active in the festival throughout his life, and during the 1930s and 1940s he assisted in the development of parallel festivals around the country. In 1929 he shared some of his songs with classical composer Lamar Stringfield, resulting in the book *30 and 1 Folk Songs from the Southern Mountains* (1929). By 1939 Lunsford's fame was such that he was invited to appear at the White House for the visiting king and queen of England.

Though disabled by a stroke in 1965, Lunsford continued to promote and attend his beloved festival until his death in Asheville. Not only did he preserve hundreds of Appalachian songs and tales, but he was a pioneer promoter and advocate of venues in which to celebrate these songs. Unlike many such collectors, Lunsford came from and remained a part of the culture he celebrated, becoming one of the most passionate and articulate advocates of authentic mountain culture.

• A sampling of his Library of Congress recordings, with an extensive booklet of notes, is *Bascom Lamar Lunsford* (Smithsonian Folkways CD 40082, 1996). A biography is Loyal Jones, *Minstrel of the Appalachians: The Story of Bascom Lamar Lunsford* (1984).

CHARLES K. WOLFE

LUNT, Alfred (12 Aug. 1892–3 Aug. 1977), and **Lynn Fontanne** (6 Dec. 1887–30 July 1983), actors and producers. Lillie Louise Fontanne, known from childhood as Lynn, was born in Woodford, Essex, England, the daughter of Jules Pierre Antoine Fontanne, a printer, and Frances Ellen Thornley Barnett. Lynn demonstrated theatrical aptitude at an early age and was recommended by a family friend to Ellen Terry, England's foremost actress, who occasionally gave lessons to talented aspirants. Partly as a result of Terry's training, Fontanne was given secondary roles in plays in London and on tour throughout England from 1905 to 1916, at which time she emigrated to the United States, accepting an offer to perform in a company headed by Laurette Taylor. Fontanne played in support of Taylor for two years, then struck out on her own in 1918, demonstrating her versatility in a series of supporting roles.

Alfred David Lunt, Jr., was born in Milwaukee, Wisconsin, the son of Alfred David Lunt, a lumberman and land agent who achieved considerable wealth, and Harriet Washburn Briggs. The senior Lunt died in 1894, leaving more than $500,000 to his family. However, his wife, whose eccentricities included a complete lack of interest in financial matters, gradually lost all the money, forcing them to move to the smaller city of Waukesha, where the family ran a boardinghouse, with Alfred assuming most of the responsibility. Alfred, who had become fascinated with the theater at an early age, began performing in high school and at Carroll College in Waukesha. He transferred to the Emerson College of Oratory in Boston in 1912 but rarely attended classes, having found a job as a minor actor and assistant stage manager with the Castle Square Theatre in Boston. Subsequently, Lunt performed minor roles in vaudeville in support of Lillie Langtry, with Margaret Anglin's classical repertory company, and elsewhere. In 1917 he made his Broadway debut. He then appeared with Fontanne in a Washington, D.C., summer stock company, where they fell in love. Lunt's first leading role was in New York in *Clarence* (1919), a play Booth Tarkington tailored to the actor's talents. In 1922 Lunt and Fontanne were married; they had no children.

Fontanne's rise in stature as a performer was slower than Lunt's, but a progression of plays on Broadway led to her first leading role, in *Dulcy*, in 1921. From then on, Lunt and Fontanne were established as major performers in New York, each pursuing a separate career.

That changed in 1924 when both were hired by the Theatre Guild, which staged plays on Broadway but defied Broadway conventions by offering serious and innovative plays that were regularly rejected by commercial managements. The Lunts acted together in Ferenc Molnár's *The Guardsman* that season, establishing themselves as brilliant light comedians. Subsequent productions for the Theatre Guild enhanced their reputations and demonstrated their remarkable versatility. Furthermore, their styles complemented one another perfectly. In 1928 they made it a condition of their employment with the guild that they must always act together. Thus began the greatest acting partnership that the United States, and perhaps the world, has ever known. Neither ever appeared separately on the stage again. Only in her last performance on television (in *Anastasia*, in 1967) did Fontanne appear in a production without her husband. In all, the Lunts appeared together in twenty-seven plays, three films, and four television programs, winning Tonys for their stage presentations, Emmys for their television performances, and Oscar nominations for their only sound film appearance (*The Guardsman*, 1931). As a tribute to their achievements, they were jointly awarded the Presidential Medal of Freedom in 1964.

The Lunts maintained an estate in Genesee Depot, Wisconsin, to which they returned every summer. This pattern was broken during World War II, as Fontanne believed that she should share the hardships of her family and friends in England. Thus, the Lunts lived in England, appearing in plays for soldiers and for the British public, from 1943 to 1945.

Following the war, the Lunts, who had in earlier times appeared in as many as five plays a year, slowed their pace appreciably. They acted in generally mediocre comedies to enthusiastic audiences in New York, London, and throughout the United States, but their penchant for choosing plays of inferior quality diminished their reputations among serious theatergoers. However, their appearance in Friedrich Dürrenmatt's mordant satire *The Visit* in 1958 decisively reconfirmed their positions as peerless artists. Following the tour of that production, the Lunts retired from the stage, acting occasionally on television and finally settling into retirement in 1967.

Lunt, who suffered from various diseases throughout his life, gradually went blind; he died in Chicago. Fontanne, who was honored at the Kennedy Center in 1980 for lifetime achievement in the performing arts, died in Genesee Depot.

Despite their success in the electronic media, the Lunts preferred the challenges and rewards of the stage. Their almost unbroken line of successes can be attributed largely to their inextinguishable drive for perfection. They were legendary for their fierce dedication to achieving the best production they could offer. No effort was too great, no rehearsal too long, no detail too small in their unceasing attempt to give the finest possible performances on every occasion. They made no distinction between the first performance of a play and the three hundredth; it made no difference whether they were acting on Broadway or playing a one-night stand in what might have been regarded by others as unlikely theatrical territory. Seldom have performers brought such undiminished enthusiasm to every performance of every play, each of which was looked upon not as mere repetition but as an opportunity to improve on the performance given the night before.

Their attitude was exemplified by Fontanne's remark on the Lunts' closing night in Noel Coward's *Design for Living* in 1933: the play had been running for months in New York when the last two performances arrived, on Saturday afternoon and evening. During the matinee, Fontanne finally managed to get a laugh she had been striving for since the play opened. She came offstage flushed with victory, thrilled at having finally achieved the desired effect. Coward, who was also acting in the play, was puzzled at the extent of her enthusiasm and asked her if it wasn't a bit late to be experimenting. "Why, *no!*" she answered, equally perplexed by his reaction. "There's still tonight, isn't there?" With the Lunts it was taken for granted that improvements could always be made. Regardless of how good today's performance had been, tomorrow's might be better. As a result, their productions consistently improved rather than deteriorated the longer they ran.

The Lunts limited their social lives, using their offstage hours to perfect what they hoped to accomplish onstage, rehearsing endlessly. Thus, their performances presented a theatrical reality that was more vital and more convincing than most other actors could achieve because their portrayals were filled with a wealth of fascinating details that filled out the characters they played in subtle, apparently effortless ways.

But the quality of effortlessness they projected was only an illusion. Their method was to try out hundreds of ideas, then select only those that showed the most promise and rehearse them painstakingly until the whole process seemed to the viewer to be effortless. One actor recalled watching the Lunts work out the details of a single entrance for more than six hours, during which they subtly varied each detail until they found precisely the mood, the tone, the attitudes they wanted to convey.

The Lunts experimented with techniques once considered too risky to attempt. They perfected the use of overlapping dialogue, for example, improving on a technique that Fontanne had begun to explore in her performances with Laurette Taylor. The Lunts saw to it that although both actors were speaking at the same time, the audience would not miss a word spoken by either. Great skill was required in order to bring off this effect successfully. Lunt spoke in a slightly different rhythm and at a slightly different pitch than Fontanne; each modulated his or her volume level to accommodate the other; and, perhaps most difficult of all, they made the effect sound perfectly natural. As a consequence, the Lunts' scenes together often seemed more vivid, more *real* than those of other actors.

When Lunt was beginning his professional career, turning one's back to the audience was unheard of, and, when attempted, severely frowned upon. But Lunt believed that under certain circumstances an actor could communicate feeling and emotion as effectively with his back as with his facial expressions. Eventually he proved it, thus adding another weapon to every actor's arsenal. The Lunts often appeared in sparkling comedies, and for thousands of theatergoers they personified wit and urbanity. Fontanne, whose beauty was often remarked on (she retained a youthful appearance until well into her fifties), was the ideal partner for Lunt, handsome and tall at 6'3". Both were noted for the elegance of their movement as well as for vocal clarity, variety, and precision. Fontanne always spoke with a British accent, irrespective of the character she was playing, while Lunt generally employed a cultivated Americanized English.

The Lunts' eminence as actors had the almost inevitable result of leading them into directing: other actors, admiring the Lunts' achievements, eager to listen to and learn from them, willingly accepted their authority in all artistic matters. As a director Lunt was regarded as one of the best in America. And, as the Lunts extended their concern from their own performances to the performances of all the actors with whom they were working, they became eager to assume the producer's function as well: to select the members of their companies, choose and shape the plays in which they would appear, and determine where, when, and under what conditions they would perform. Their company, Transatlantic Productions, offered presentations on its own and in collaboration with the Theatre Guild.

Lunt and Fontanne attempted to reestablish repertory—the system of alternating productions under which the companies of Shakespeare and Molière had operated successfully hundreds of years before—as a viable theatrical system in New York. Their attempt, which clashed too jarringly with the commercial necessities of Broadway, was ultimately unsuccessful, but it had a significant impact nevertheless, for they played *The Sea Gull, Amphitryon 38*, and *Idiot's Delight* in repertory on tour throughout the United States in the late 1930s. They also wished to maintain an ensemble company, a group of actors who would remain with the Lunts play after play, season after season, thus assuring a unity of performance that could not be matched by actors unfamiliar with one another's idiosyncrasies. In this they were successful for years, despite the fact that the ensemble system is complex and expensive.

One of their most significant accomplishments was their successful struggle to maintain the interest of audiences outside New York City in the legitimate theater. The Lunts invariably toured the country in the productions that had achieved fame in New York. Often they played in high school gymnasiums and other ill-equipped structures, as well as in lavishly furnished theaters. Their devotion to touring was physically and emotionally wearing and brought no greater financial reward than playing in New York would have done. But they felt a responsibility to playwrights to keep their works and the underlying themes of their plays before the public for as long as possible. They also felt a responsibility to theatergoers outside New York, believing that the residents of Seattle or Houston or Minneapolis had as much right to see first-rate theater as those who happened to live in (or could afford to travel to) New York.

In their time, no performers were more influential or more highly respected. Some of that respect can be traced to longevity: few theatrical personalities practice their professions over as long a period. Lunt's career as an actor spanned fifty-three years, from 1912 until 1965; Fontanne was active for a remarkable sixty-two years, not giving her last performance until 1967. Furthermore, the Lunts often appeared in outstanding plays, *The Guardsman*, *The Doctor's Dilemma* (1927), *The Taming of the Shrew* (1935 and 1940), *Amphitryon 38* (1937), *The Sea Gull* (1938), and *The Visit* among them. Before arranging to act together in all plays, Lunt appeared in *Volpone* (1928) and Fontanne in *Pygmalion* (1926) and *Strange Interlude* (1928). (Lunt did join Fontanne for the national tour of *Pygmalion* after the New York run ended.)

The Lunts' achievements as actors induced dramatists to craft plays especially for them, such as S. N. Behrman's *The Second Man* (1927), Noel Coward's *Design for Living*, and Robert E. Sherwood's *There Shall Be No Night* (1940), among others.

Together, the Lunts brought a sense of wit, style, and grace to every play with which they were associated. They brightened even the most somber dramas with moments of humor and invested the most frivolous comedies with a depth that could not have been suspected from a reading of the script.

• *The Fabulous Lunts*, by Jared Brown (1986), is the most recent and most complete biography of the Lunts, quoting extensively from their correspondence and other unpublished sources. Maurice Zolotow, *Stagestruck: The Romance of Alfred Lunt and Lynn Fontanne* (1965), was written before the end of the Lunts' careers, as was George Freedley, *The Lunts* (1958), which is more a collection of photographs than a biography. Philip M. Runkel, *Alfred Lunt and Lynn Fontanne: A Bibliography* (1978), is a useful compilation of sources. The Lunts' ideas about acting are quoted in *Actors on Acting*, ed. Toby Cole and Helen Krich Chinoy (1970); Morton Eustis, *Players at Work: Acting According to the Actors* (1937); and *Actors Talk about Acting* (1961), ed. Lewis Funke and John E. Booth. Valuable information about the Lunts' lives and careers is included in Noel Coward, *Present Indicative* (1937), Lawrence Langner, *The Magic Curtain* (1951), Randolph Goodman, *Drama on Stage* (1961), and Roy S. Waldau, *Vintage Years of the Theatre Guild: 1928–39* (1972). Articles written by Lunt appeared in *Theatre Arts* (Feb. 1950), the *New York Times*, 16 Nov. 1930, *Billboard*, 26 Dec. 1936, and *Theatre Guild Magazine*, 1928 Nov. Obituaries of Lunt are in the *New York Times*, 6 Aug. 1977; the *Chicago Tribune*, 8 Aug. 1977; and *Variety*, 24 Aug. 1977. Obituaries of Fontanne are in the *New York Times*, 31 July 1983, and the *Christian Science Monitor*, 21 Nov. 1983.

JARED BROWN

LUNT, George (31 Dec. 1803–16 May 1885), lawyer and author, was born in Newburyport, Massachusetts, the son of Abel Lunt, a sea captain, and Phoebe Tilton. As a youth Lunt attended Phillips Academy at Exeter, New Hampshire. Then, having graduated from Harvard College in 1824, the young scholar returned to Newburyport, where he taught school before reading law with a local attorney, Asa W. Wildes. In 1831 Lunt passed the Massachusetts bar and entered private practice. During this period the young lawyer began a lifelong pursuit of belles lettres, publishing several mostly neglected collections of poetry, including *The Grave of Byron, with Other Poems* (1826), *The Age of Gold, and Other Poems* (1843), and *The Dove and the Eagle* (1851), among others. None of Lunt's poetry achieved contemporary popularity, perhaps owing in part to his antique style, especially his eschewal of romantic sentiment. Prose also drew Lunt's attention. His *Eastford; or, Household Sketches* (1855) and *Old New England Traits* (1873) are characteristic examples of mid-nineteenth-century Yankee "local color" novels, while *Three Eras of New England, and Other Addresses* (1857) suggests the author's oratorical appeal. Not content with literary endeavor, the Newburyport lawyer also entered politics, serving several terms as a Whig legislator in the Massachusetts Senate (1835, 1836) and House of Representatives (1837, 1841, 1847). In 1848 he moved to Boston and, as reward for supporting Zachary Taylor's successful bid for president, was appointed U.S. attorney for the district of Massachusetts, a position he held until 1853. When, soon afterward, the Whig party disbanded in the wake of antislavery agitation and passage of the Kansas-Nebraska Act, Lunt cast his lot with the conservative wing of the Democratic party.

An essential conservatism marked Lunt's character until his dying day. His poetry always tended toward the chaste and formal, reflecting classical and neoclassical models; his prose, often tinged with nostalgia for bygone New England, eschewed sensation; and when the author addressed contemporary social issues, he invariably abetted the cause of tradition. Having seen his beloved Newburyport eclipsed in New England's march toward an urban and industrial society, Lunt became convinced that his era's vaunted "progress" was illusory; this was no "Golden age," he lamented in one characteristic poem, but an "age of Gold" lost to self-seeking aggrandizement and political scheming. It was also, he once complained, the "Age of Twaddle," with "Humbug" ascendant in the form of women's rights and abolitionist sentiment. This last reform impulse especially pained Lunt because by the 1850s it threatened to destroy the tradition-bound Union that he held dear. As editor of the Democratic *Boston Daily Courier* (a position he occupied from the mid-1850s through the Civil War), Lunt roundly condemned the so-called "self-seeking and ambitious demagogues" whom he charged with dragging the nation willy-nilly toward dissolution. Not surprisingly, such sentiments gained him an arguably deserved reputation as a proslavery apologist. Nor did the war change Lunt's tune; barely a year after Robert E. Lee's surrender, the conservative Bostonian publicly urged swift restoration of the defeated South's political powers and the denial of voting rights to freedmen, whom he branded, in his extensive polemic *The Origin of the Late War* (1866), a "subordinate people" wholly unsuited to civic equality. Like the Federalist politician Fisher Ames, whose life and works he admired, Lunt embodied the impulses of an older order intent on the rule of a "cultured elite," dismayed by social innovation, and dedicated to Union above all. Ames's reputed deathbed sentiment, "The Union must be preserved; things are bad enough; but anything is better than dissolution," could as easily have been Lunt's.

Though perhaps happiest when contemplating his New England boyhood, Newburyport's famous son was by no means unhappy in private life. Lunt was married three times—in 1834 to Sarah Miles Greenwood; in 1845 to Emily Ashton; and in 1864 to Adeline Parsons—and fathered six children. Most of Lunt's later years were spent in Scituate, Massachusetts, where his civic exertions brought much-needed improvements to the local harbor. He died in Boston.

• Lunt's extant papers are scattered; the largest collections are at the Massachusetts Historical Society, Boston Public Library, and the Houghton Library of Harvard University. Biographical data appears in D. Hamilton Hurd, *History of Essex County, Massachusetts*, vol. 1 (1888), p. xli; John James Currier, *History of Newburyport*, vol. 2 (1909), pp. 281–82; Massachusetts Daughters of the American Revolution, Chief Justice Cushing chapter, *Old Scituate* (1921); and T. S. Lunt, *A History of the Lunt Family in America* (1914). Lunt's contribution to Yankee literature is briefly cited in Perry D. Westbrook, *The New England Town in Fact and Fiction* (1982), pp. 121–22. The author is also mentioned in W. S. Tryon, *Parnassus Corner: A Life of James T. Fields, Publisher to the Victorians* (1963), p. 103. The best introduction to Lunt's political and social philosophy is through his own poetry and prose. Obituaries are in the *Boston Daily Courier*, 24 May 1885; the *Boston Daily Advertiser*, 18 May 1885; and the *Newburyport Herald*, 19 May 1885.

THOMAS N. BAKER

LUNT, Orrington (24 Dec. 1815–5 Apr. 1897), merchant and philanthropist, was born in Bowdoinham, Maine, the son of William Webb Lunt, a merchant and state legislator, and Ann Matilda Sumner. After receiving a meager education in local schools, he entered his father's store at the age of fourteen and by the age of twenty-two had become a partner in the enterprise. He achieved sufficient local stature to serve as both town clerk and treasurer, and upon his father's retirement from the business he carried on the firm's affairs in partnership with a brother. Following the panic of 1837, business conditions steadily deteriorated, and Lunt, like so many of his countrymen, turned his sights westward.

In January 1842 Lunt married Cornelia A. Gray, with whom he had four children. He then sold what remained of his father's business at a loss and headed west. He arrived in Chicago in November of that year, bearing little more than letters of introduction and hope for a better future. His wife became seriously ill shortly after their arrival, and as a result the Lunts returned east. They again traveled to Chicago the following summer, however, and soon entered into the

general commission business in a rented wooden storehouse on the banks of the Chicago River. Lunt then ventured into the grain trading business in the spring of 1844. Farmers soon learned to trust Lunt, who had a well-deserved reputation for honesty, and his business grew apace. By November 1845 Lunt was able to sell a large quantity of grain, which netted a profit of $10,000. The gaudy profit proved to be a mixed blessing, however, because Lunt, emboldened by his newfound success, soon turned to reckless price speculation. Within a year his entire fortune had been lost. Undaunted, Lunt continued in the grain business (albeit on a more conservative track) and soon recouped his lost funds.

With his fortune now secured, Lunt explored other business opportunities. In 1849 he was one of the founders of the Galena & Chicago Union Railroad, which he later served in the multiple roles of trustee, auditor, and vice president (the last position for two years) before the line merged with the Chicago & Northwestern. Immediately following the outbreak of the Civil War, Lunt took a leading role in the Committee of Safety and War Finance in Chicago, which produced the first regiment of federal troops from the city. He served from 1855 to 1861 as water commissioner of the southern district of Chicago. His health declined in 1862, and Lunt retired from active business. In 1865 he undertook an extensive trip around the world with his family, visiting parts of Europe and Asia. In constant demand as a treasurer due to his high reputation for honesty, upon his return to Chicago Lunt served as president and treasurer of the newly established Board of Public Works and also took a leading part in the formation of Chicago's first Board of Trade.

With his business reputation and personal fortune both secure, Lunt devoted the latter portion of his life to the area for which he is best remembered—philanthropy. A devout Methodist, Lunt joined the Clark Street Methodist Church soon after his arrival in Chicago. There he met Grant Goodrich, a young and ambitious lawyer who would later work extensively in partnership with Lunt to form Northwestern University. Lunt served as a trustee of the Clark Street Church for twenty years and in 1848 purchased a lot at State and Harrison Streets with a view toward the establishment of a second Methodist church. He also donated heavily to the Quinn Chapel, a local African-American Methodist church. The Clark Street Church also provided a fortuitous meeting with Mrs. Augustus Garrett, a wealthy widow of a Chicago mayor who sought to memorialize her late husband. Numerous meetings between Garrett, Lunt, and other parties resulted in the 1853 founding of the Garrett Biblical Institute, a theological school charged with the training of ministers. Lunt served the institute from the beginning as both secretary and treasurer and also sat on its board of trustees for many years. In 1854 Lunt (in partnership with Jabez Botsford, another leading Chicago citizen) contributed $20,000 toward the completion of a building for the Chicago Orphan Asylum.

Lunt's greatest charitable endeavor (and the one for which he is best known) resulted in the founding of Northwestern University. He was present at the initial meeting in May 1850 when plans were formed regarding "a university in the Northwest under the patronage of the Methodist Episcopal Church." Upon the granting of a university charter by the Illinois state legislature on 28 January 1851, Lunt, along with his friends Goodrich and Dr. John Evans, was named to the first board of trustees. Lunt immediately donated $5,000 to the fledgling enterprise and was named to a committee charged with finding a location for the school. At the suggestion of the school's first president, Clark Titus Hinman, Lunt and Evans concentrated their search on the suburbs of Chicago, with a view toward purchasing a block of land sufficient to allow for the future development of both the university and the surrounding community. After viewing property as far south as the Indiana border and as far north as Winnetka Lunt finally chose a 379-acre lakefront parcel near Jefferson Park. The property, which also benefited from the proximity of the projected Chicago-Milwaukee Railroad, was purchased by the trustees in October 1853. With Dr. Evans's advancement of the purchase downpayment, Lunt, with characteristic modesty, concurred with the other trustees in their decision to name the new village "Evanston."

Lunt moved his residence to Evanston in 1874 and provided quiet but active support for Northwestern University for the rest of his life. His most notable contribution was the new Orrington Lunt Library, which opened on the campus in the fall of 1894. He also continued to be active in church work, serving as a member of the Methodist Ecumenical Council, which was held in London in 1881. Lunt died at his home in Evanston.

Lunt's life and career paralleled that of many self-made men in the nineteenth century. Rising from modest beginnings, he acquired a fortune through hard work and entrepreneurial skill. His devotion to the Methodist church and other philanthropic endeavors provided an outlet for his wealth; the growth and development of Northwestern University is the most prominent of his legacies.

• Save for a small amount of miscellaneous material held at the Northwestern University archives, no collection of Lunt's papers has survived. The best secondary source of information on his life and career is Harold F. Williamson and Payson S. Wild, *Northwestern University: A History, 1850–1975* (1976). Dated, but still useful, are J. S. Currey, *Chicago: Its History and Its Builders*, vol. 4 (1912), and E. F. Ward, *The Story of Northwestern University* (1924). Obituaries are in the *Chicago Daily Tribune* and the *Chicago Times-Herald*, 6 Apr. 1897.

EDWARD L. LACH, JR.

LUPINO, Ida (4 Feb. 1918–3 Aug. 1995), film actor, producer, and director, was born in London, England, the daughter of Stanley Lupino, a comedian and playwright, and Connie Emerald, a musical-comedy performer. At an early age, Ida and her younger sister Rita began appearing on stage, and Ida studied at the Royal Academy of Dramatic Art. According to Hollywood legend, Lupino's film career began at age fourteen, when she accompanied her mother to an audition for director Allan Dwan, who hired her, not her mother, for his British production, *Her First Affaire* (1933).

Promoted as "the English Jean Harlow," Lupino signed her first Hollywood contract with Paramount in 1933. While still a teenager, she began to play "older" women in B and minor A pictures, including *Peter Ibbetson* (1935), with Gary Cooper, and *The Adventures of Sherlock Holmes* (1939), which marked Basil Rathbone's initial film portrayal of the great detective. In 1938 Lupino married actor Louis Hayward. She also found time to craft a musical score that was performed by the Los Angeles Philharmonic Orchestra.

In 1940 Lupino's film career, propelled by roles in *The Light That Failed* (1939) and *They Drive by Night* (1940), suddenly blossomed. Lupino enjoyed her greatest success as an actor while at Warner Bros. during the early 1940s. She costarred with Humphrey Bogart in *High Sierra* (1941); with Edward G. Robinson and John Garfield in *The Sea Wolf* (1941); and with Dennis Morgan and Jack Carson in *The Hard Way* (1942), a performance for which the New York Film Critics awarded her best actress. During the Second World War, while Hayward served in the marines, Lupino played an active role in Hollywood's own war effort. Wartime service, however, took a psychological toll on Hayward, and the couple divorced in 1945.

During the war, Lupino also began to consider how she might expand her motion picture career. In a 1945 interview she talked about "directing or producing or both. I see myself developing new talent" because "I am more genuinely interested in the talent of others than I am in my own." When Lupino expressed these aspirations, there were no women, for the first time in many years, employed as Hollywood directors.

Although Lupino continued to appear before the cameras in films such as *Road House* (1948), she did move on to producing and directing. She was an uncredited coproducer on an independent film, *War Widow* (1946), and coproduced *The Judge* (1948), a quirky thriller reputedly written in two days and shot in five. In 1948 she married Collier Young, who had been a producer at Columbia. Later, Lupino and TV producer Anson Bond formed Emerald Productions, which was named after Lupino's mother. The company (which was reorganized as the Filmakers in 1950) released its first feature, *Not Wanted*, in 1949, a picture cowritten, coproduced, and anonymously directed by Lupino after the film's credited director, Elmer Clifton, suffered a heart attack.

Not Wanted, a social-problem melodrama with touches of film noir, set the tone for seven other films, six of which were directed by Lupino, produced by the Filmakers. Narrated in flashback form, *Not Wanted* focuses on an unmarried woman who is arrested for trying to kidnap an infant; subsequently, it is revealed that she had given up the child for adoption. Lupino's second film, *Never Fear* (1950) featured the story of a young dancer whose career plans are threatened when she is stricken with polio. (Lupino herself had overcome polio during the late 1930s.) Other films directed by Lupino during this period include *Outrage* (1950), the story of a traumatized rape victim; *Hard, Fast, and Beautiful* (1951), a melodrama about a young woman who is pushed into a tennis career by a dominating mother; and two noir classics, the *Hitch-Hiker* (1953) and *The Bigamist* (1953). Lupino's status as a director received confirmation when she was selected to present the award for best film direction at the 1950 Academy Awards ceremony. The Filmakers' productions never returned significant profits, however, and the company was dissolved by 1954. After the collapse of the Filmakers, Lupino only directed one more Hollywood feature, *The Trouble with Angels* (1966), a movie that was dismissed by reviewers in the mid-1960s but has become of interest to film scholars because of Lupino's directorial style.

Indeed, during the 1980s and 1990s, scholarly interest in post–World War II cinema and in films by female directors prompted a broad reassessment of Lupino's directing work. Film scholars linked Lupino's work with that of other maverick directors, such as Nicholas Ray and Samuel Fuller, and praised her ability to make tightly budgeted, socially conscious films on the margins of the Hollywood studio system. Lupino often employed location shooting; much of *Never Fear*, for example, was shot in a polio rehabilitation hospital. In addition, Lupino's films invariably focused on the traumatic aspects of everyday life in Cold War America. Her characters generally seemed dazed, confused, passively inept, and profoundly inarticulate in the face of cultural and social changes. Finally, feminist critics began to consider the ways in which Lupino's films sympathetically explored, often obliquely and with contradictory discourses, issues related to women's limited public roles and to gender politics.

Lupino also continued to act—most notably in noirs such as *On Dangerous Ground* (1951), *Beware My Lovely* (1952), and her own *The Bigamist*—and often costarred with her third husband Howard Duff. Her second marriage had ended in divorce in 1950, and she had married Duff the following year. They had one daughter. She and Duff were featured in "Mr. Adams and Eve," a TV comedy series about two movie stars, in 1957–1958. Lupino and Duff coproduced the series, and she received two Emmy nominations for her acting. She continued to act, intermittently, during the 1960s and 1970s, most notably in Sam Peckinpah's *Junior Bonner* (1972). One of her last film appearances came in *The Food of the Gods* (1976), a low-budget horror film, and her final TV appearance was in an episode of "Charlie's Angels."

Meanwhile, Lupino returned to directing, this time for television, and remained one of TV's busiest directors for nearly a decade, from about 1959 to 1969. Her credits include "The Donna Reed Show," "Have Gun Will Travel," "Alfred Hitchcock Presents," "General Electric Theater," "The Untouchables," "The Fugitive," and even "Gilligan's Island." Ironically, Lupino, who had often been criticized as a slow-working actor, became known for a quick, no-nonsense approach to TV production. She also developed the reputation of being an expert in "action" films, a status confirmed by the large number of westerns she was hired to direct.

After separating from Duff in the early 1970s—their divorce was not final until 1984—Lupino, who had been active in liberal political causes, gradually retreated into an intensely private life. Her reactions toward her directorial work, when she was interviewed, varied from curt dismissals to cautious pride. But toward the end of her life, as museums and film societies mounted retrospectives of her motion-picture and television productions, Lupino began to respond more extensively to inquiries about her directing career and declared that she had derived more satisfaction from directing than from acting. She died in Los Angeles. Ida Lupino achieved considerable acclaim in her own time as one of Hollywood's most skilled performers but only scant attention (primarily as an anomaly) for her directorial efforts. After her retirement, however, as the study of popular film gained prominence, Lupino's career as a director increasingly came to overshadow her work in front of the cameras.

• Print and visual sources on Lupino's work, as both an actor and a director, are available at a variety of different archives, including the Wisconsin Center for Film and Theater Research, the University of Southern California Cinema-Television Library, the UCLA Film and Television Archive, and the Margaret Herrick Library of the Academy of Motion Picture Arts and Sciences in Beverly Hills, Calif.

William Donati, *Ida Lupino: A Biography* (1996), is a careful, admiring account of Lupino's life and career. The essays in Annette Kuhn, ed., *Queen of the 'B's: Ida Lupino Behind the Camera* (1995), offer scholarly appraisals of Lupino's directorial work, and most of these address filmic and feminist issues. The volume also contains a useful bibliography, compiled by Kuhn, that lists many popular magazine stories about and interviews with Lupino. Karyn Kay and Gerald Peary, eds., *Women and the Cinema: A Critical Anthology* (1977), contains an "Interview with Ida Lupino," by Debra Weiner. Lucy Stewart, *Ida Lupino as Film Director, 1949–1953: An "Auteur" Approach* (1980), is a reprint of a doctoral dissertation. Although E. Ann Kaplan, ed., *Women in Film Noir* (1980), contains nothing specifically on Lupino's work in the noir cycle, it does offer a broad context, as does Elizabeth Cowie, "*Film Noir* and Women," in *Shades of Noir*, ed. Joan Copjec (1993).

NORMAN L. ROSENBERG

LURIA, Salvador Edward (13 Aug. 1912–6 Feb. 1991), geneticist, was born in Turin, Italy, the son of David Luria, an accountant and printer, and Ester Salvadore. After receiving his early education in local schools in Turin, Luria enrolled in the medical school of the University of Turin in 1929. At the Turin Medical School, while studying anatomy under Giuseppi Live, Luria developed a technical facility for cultivating living cells. He was a medical officer in the Italian army for three years after receiving his medical degree summa cum laude in 1935. While in the army, Luria began studying physics and mathematics, and upon discharge from the army he continued this interest by studying medical physics and radiology for a time at the Curie laboratory at the Radium Institute in Paris.

Around 1938 Luria became interested in studying the production of mutations in viruses and bacteria by irradiation. When it became evident that Italy was going to ally with Germany in 1940, Luria left his home country and returned to France. From France he went to the United States, where he accepted an appointment as research assistant at the College of Physicians and Surgeons at Columbia University in New York City. He began a collaboration with Max Delbruck after they met at a 1941 meeting of the American Physical Society. They planned a series of experiments, and in 1942 and 1943 Luria was awarded a Guggenheim fellowship, which enabled him to spend some time working at Princeton University and the remainder at Vanderbilt University in Nashville, Tennessee, where he continued his work with Delbruck. In 1943 Luria was appointed instructor in the Department of Bacteriology at Indiana University in Bloomington. In 1945 he was appointed assistant professor. He married Zella Hurwitz that same year; they had one child. He was elevated to associate professor in 1947.

In his work with Delbruck, Luria studied whether bacterial resistance resulted from spontaneously arising mutants or whether the cells became resistant as a result of an action of the phage on otherwise normal bacteria. Luria's solution for the problem originated at the Bloomington Country Club, where he watched a colleague playing a slot machine at a party. As Luria watched the wheels with the lemons, oranges, and cherries spin, it occurred to him that there was an analogy between the slot machine's payoff mechanism and the clustering of mutant bacteria. He reasoned that a slot machine returned money put into it at random, sometimes a few coins at a time or, on rare occasion, a great many coins at once. In a similar manner, bacterial cultures are clustered in groups of one, two, four, or eight or occasionally larger colonies, "the jackpot." The size of each cluster was caused by a mutation that occurred some generation earlier than might be expected by chance. From this observation, Luria developed an experiment to distinguish whether resistance is induced or is the product of a spontaneous mutation that occurred in a previous generation. This experiment, the so-called fluctuation test, was published in 1947 with Delbruck; it was the first evidence presented for bacterial mutation. Overnight this experiment made bacteria choice organisms for genetic research, superior to fruit flies or molds because of the speed of their reproduction.

At this time, Luria and Delbruck began a collaboration with Alfred Hershey, a biologist working with phage at Washington University in St. Louis. This association resulted in the formation of the core of the "Phage Group." The first step was to agree that they would work on only seven strains of bacteriophage that infect the colon bacillus *Escherichia coli* strain B. This agreement was made so that the results from sev-

eral laboratories could be reliably compared. In 1950 Luria was appointed professor of bacteriology at the University of Illinois at Champaign-Urbana. The next year he published unequivocal proof that bacteriophage and viral genes undergo spontaneous mutations in a process similar to that of bacteria. Luria had planned to present a paper in 1953 at the meeting of the Society for General Microbiology in England, but James A. Watson, a former student, had to present this work. Luria was denied a visa because Senator Joseph McCarthy's committee suspected him of being a communist. In this paper Luria skillfully set forth his belief that phage protein rather than DNA carried the genetic information, a belief widely held in the scientific community that was later proven to be in error.

In 1959 Luria was appointed professor and chair of the Department of Microbiology at the Massachusetts Institute of Technology (MIT). He was named Sedgwick Professor of Biology at MIT in 1964, and in the following year he became a resident member of the Salk Institute in San Diego, California. He shared the 1969 Nobel Prize with Max Delbruck and Alfred Hershey for their discoveries on the regulatory mechanisms and the genetic structure of viruses. Luria was appointed Institute Professor of Biology at MIT, and in 1974 he was made director of the Center for Cancer Research.

In his retirement Luria worried about the application of biology to destructive purposes. In this vein he donated a portion of his Nobel Prize money to support antiwar groups. He died in Lexington, Massachusetts.

• Luria's papers are preserved at the American Philosophical Society. Important books by Luria are *Virology* (1953), *Life the Unfinished Experiment* (1973), and *Thirty-six Lectures in Biology* (1975). Representative papers are "Interference between Bacterial Viruses," *Archives of Biochemistry* 1 (1943): 111–41; "Mutations of Bacterial Viruses Affecting Their Host Range," *Genetics* 30 (1945): 84–99; "Reactivation of Inactivated Bacteriophage by Transfer of Self-Replicating Units," *Proceedings of the National Academy of Sciences* 33 (1947): 253–64; and "Colicins and Energetics of Cell Membranes," *Scientific American* 233 (1975): 30–37. He also published an autobiography, *A Slot Machine, a Broken Test Tube, an Autobiography* (1984). G. Bertani wrote a short biography of Luria for *Genetics* 131 (1992): 1–4, as did H. F. Judson for *Lancet* 337 (1991): 605. An anonymous short biography is in *Nobel Prize Winners* (1987), pp. 648–49. An obituary is in the *Boston Globe*, 7 Feb. 1991.

DAVID Y. COOPER

LURTON, Horace Harmon (26 Feb. 1844–12 July 1914), U.S. Supreme Court justice, was born in Newport, Kentucky, the son of Lycurgus Leonidas Lurton, a physician and Episcopalian minister, and Sarah Ann Harmon. While Lurton was still a child, his family moved to Clarksville, Tennessee, the town Lurton ever after regarded as home. In 1861 he was studying at Douglas University in Chicago but left school upon the outbreak of the Civil War to enlist in the Confederate army. Taken prisoner at the battle of Fort Donelson, he escaped and promptly reenlisted. Serving under General John Hunt Morgan during the spectacular but futile raid into Ohio, Lurton was again captured; this time he gained release as one of numberless youths who were allegedly paroled by President Abraham Lincoln in response to a mother's plea. After the war the young veteran entered law school at Cumberland University and graduated in 1867. In September of the same year he married Mary Frances Owen; they had four children.

Admitted to the Tennessee bar in 1867, Lurton returned to Clarksville, where he practiced law until 1875, when the governor appointed him chancellor of the state's Sixth Chancery Division, to fill a vacancy. At the age of thirty-one, Lurton was the youngest man ever named a chancellor in Tennessee. Running as the incumbent in 1876, he was elected to a regular term but resigned in 1878 to resume the practice of law in Clarksville, where he formed a partnership with Charles G. Smith and served as president of a local bank. Elected to the Tennessee Supreme Court on the Democratic ticket in 1886, he became chief justice in January 1893 but resigned in March of that year to accept appointment by President Grover Cleveland to the U.S. Circuit Court for the Sixth Circuit, which was centered in Cincinnati. There Lurton developed a warm friendship with the presiding judge, William Howard Taft. Settling in 1898 in Nashville, Tennessee, Lurton combined active judicial service with teaching law at Vanderbilt University, where he lectured on constitutional law and federal procedure. He became dean of its law department in 1905. He also served as a trustee of the University of the South at Sewanee, Tennessee, from 1882 to 1914. The convivial Lurton became well known locally for what he called his "tobacco congress," meetings in his law chambers on mornings when he was not in court at which he discoursed with his friends on literature and philosophy, probably expressing views of the utmost conventionality.

In December 1909 Lurton's career entered its final phase when his old friend Taft, now president of the United States, named him to the U.S. Supreme Court. Only a few months short of his sixty-sixth birthday, Lurton was the oldest man ever to have been appointed. A Southern Democrat and Confederate veteran who had been a prisoner of war, he seemed a surprising choice for a Republican president. In fact, as Taft knew, Lurton shared the president's cautious conservatism on social and economic issues. Moving to Washington, Lurton and his wife quickly became prominent on the capital's social scene and offered southern hospitality at their numerous entertainments.

Lurton served on the Supreme Court for the rest of his life. Soon after his appointment he addressed a joint meeting of the Maryland and Virginia Bar Associations. His speech, "A Government of Law or a Government of Men?" (*North American Review* 193 [1911]: 9–25), was an uninspired restatement of conservative judicial values that eschewed liberal construction of the Constitution, judicial lawmaking in the interests of social advancement, and infringements on states' rights and was spiced with expressions of nativist fears of foreign immigrants. His opinions as an associate justice during his brief tenure were equally conservative and pedestrian. Although he tolerated some "trust busting," as his opinion for the court indicated in *United States v. Terminal Railroad Association of St. Louis* (1912), his dissent (without opinion) in the Shreveport Rate Case, *Houston, East and West Texas Railway Co. v. United States* (1914), demonstrated his unwillingness to accept substantial regulation. He never expressed, perhaps because his tenure was so brief, a consistent theory of the constitutional limitations on economic regulation.

In December 1913 illness forced Lurton to withdraw from judicial duties, and rumors of his impending retirement were widespread, but he rejoined the court in April 1914, seemingly restored to health. His death came suddenly three months later, while he was vacationing at Atlantic City, New Jersey; his body was returned for burial to his beloved Clarksville. Even his eulogist confessed that he had rendered "no startling or sensational decisions" (*U.S. Reports*, p. xviii). Perhaps his most significant contribution was as principal drafter of the 1912 Federal Equity Rules, which governed practice and procedure in that branch until the merger of law and equity in the 1938 Federal Rules of Civil Procedure.

A Cleveland Democrat who reached the Supreme Court during an era of Republican ascendancy, Lurton typified the consensus that underlay party differences. An upholder of the verities of small-town America, above all individualism, Lurton was one of a generation of judges who retarded needed reforms, not least by the charm and transparent honesty with which he maintained traditional values.

• Lurton's papers, a 300-item collection of correspondence, are in the Library of Congress. The most complete modern assessment is by James F. Watts, Jr., in *The Justices of the United States Supreme Court*, ed. Leon Friedman and Fred L. Israel, vol. 3 (1969), pp. 1847–63. Memorial proceedings in the U.S. Supreme Court, including a eulogy by Attorney General Thomas Watt Gregory, are in *U.S. Reports* 237 (1915): v–xxv. An obituary is in the *New York Times*, 13 July 1914.

JOHN V. ORTH

LUSCOMB, Florence Hope (6 Feb. 1887–27 Oct. 1985), white social and political activist, was born in Lowell, Massachusetts, the daughter of Otis Luscomb, an artist, and Hannah Skinner Knox. Luscomb's mother left her husband and son before Florence was two. A small inheritance enabled Hannah Luscomb to raise Florence alone and to contribute time and money to labor and woman suffrage organizations. By accompanying her mother to meetings and rallies, young Luscomb received an education in activist philosophies and techniques that she would put to use in a career that spanned seventy years.

Luscomb graduated from the Massachusetts Institute of Technology with an S.B. in architecture in

1909. During college and while working as an architect, she devoted her free time to the campaign for woman suffrage. She was a partner in Ida Annah Ryan's firm in Waltham, Massachusetts, until 1917, when she became the paid executive secretary of the Boston Equal Suffrage Association for Good Government. She was among the younger generation of suffragists inspired by the radical tactics used by English suffragettes. In a time when women of her social class were expected to be demure, Luscomb gave open-air speeches, hawked the *Woman's Journal* on the Boston Common, and canvassed door-to-door across Massachusetts and in other states.

After she cast her newly won vote for socialist Eugene Debs in 1920, Luscomb continued to be an activist. She began a life dedicated to a variety of progressive movements that, as she put it, were not yet "wholly proper." Indeed, particularly after she became more radical in the late 1920s, she often not only tested the bounds of respectability but also remained a step ahead of most left-wing political activists. From 1920 into 1933, in addition to volunteer work, Luscomb held paid positions with organizations such as the Boston League of Women Voters; the Joint Board of Sanitary Control, where she policed factory safety through tactics such as bringing upper-class women on inspections; and the Massachusetts branch of the Women's International League for Peace and Freedom. When her mother died in 1933, she decided to live on her small inheritance rather than take paid jobs away from those who needed them.

From the 1920s through the 1970s, Luscomb served on the boards of, and was active in, many civil liberties, civil rights, labor, peace, and other activist organizations, most in the Boston area. Many of the groups with which she worked survived only as long as the cause was current; others still exist. She was a leader in the Civil Liberties Union of Massachusetts and was active in the National Association for the Advancement of Colored People (Boston). In addition to picketing for several labor unions, she helped organize and was president of the Boston local of the United Office and Professional Workers of America. Her opposition to fascism and imperialism led to her involvement in groups such as the Joint Anti-Fascist Refugee Committee and those formed against the Vietnam War. In addition to participating in organizations, Luscomb went on marches, attended rallies, wrote leaflets and letters to periodical editors, made small financial contributions, and gave speeches.

Luscomb's work for peace and her curiosity about other political systems led her to the Soviet Union (1935, 1962), Cuba (1961), and China (1962); she traveled to Western Europe several times, once for an international suffrage conference (1911). By working with third parties, such as the U.S. Progressive party, she joined others attempting to expand the U.S. electoral system and educate voters. She also ran for public office, unsuccessfully, at least four times. She was narrowly defeated for Boston City Council in 1922. She ran for a seat in the U.S. House of Representatives on the People's Labor party ticket (1936) and again on the slate of the Progressive party of Massachusetts (1950). In 1952 she joined the Massachusetts gubernatorial race as part of the Progressive party's presidential campaign.

Her activities in the 1950s may best characterize her commitment to social change. At a time when even many left-wing activists were supporting Cold War ideology, Luscomb was among the minority who not only refused to support anticommunism but also fought to defend the civil liberties of those attacked. Although she never joined the Communist party, she was staunchly opposed to capitalism because it interfered with true democracy by wresting power from the people and placing it in the hands of an unelected elite. She was called before state investigations in Massachusetts and New Hampshire in 1955, refused to cooperate, and used the incidents to further publicize the outrage of "fascism" in the United States. The same factors that empowered Luscomb to fight anticommunism enabled her to be a lifelong activist: a strong will, an independent income (which meant she could not be fired), no family reputations to protect, and a network of devoted, like-minded friends who did not desert her.

Luscomb worked long enough to see at least one issue come full circle, when women's rights returned to the public agenda in the 1970s. An inspiring "foremother," her speeches to members of the women's movement urged them to encompass the needs of all women. As she had earlier reminded union audiences that "labor" included women, she reminded feminists that "women" included poor and African-American women.

Luscomb lived with her mother in the Boston area until Hannah died. From the 1950s until the mid-1970s she lived in cooperative houses with people much younger than she. She spent most summers in a rustic cabin she designed in Tamworth, New Hampshire, in the 1940s. Luscomb had close relationships with men and women but chose to remain single; her sexual preference is not clear. She died in a nursing home in Watertown, Massachusetts.

Although her activities may appear disparate, Luscomb knew her causes to be inextricably linked. She firmly believed in every country's right to self-determination, the fundamental equality of all people, the need to overcome capitalism, and that the world should be based on some form of socialist cooperation. She thought that in the United States democracy was the avenue through which progressive change would occur; the struggle required educating people about democracy's potential. Her steadfast idealism led her to believe that, bit by bit, people would demolish the barriers (such as the military-industrial complex) that blocked democracy from living up to its promise of equality and justice.

• Florence Luscomb's papers, which include her short "Progressive Movements and What They Did to Me: A Mental Autobiography" (1957), are in the Schlesinger Library on the

History of Women in America, Radcliffe College, Cambridge, Mass. Luscomb is also represented in several other manuscript collections at the Schlesinger Library. The only biography currently available is Sharon Hartman Strom, "Florence Luscomb: For Suffrage, Labor, and Peace," in *Moving the Mountain: Women Working for Social Change*, ed. Ellen Cantarow (1980). For a discussion of Luscomb's suffrage work, see Strom, "Leadership and Tactics in the American Woman Suffrage Movement: A New Perspective from Massachusetts," *Journal of American History* 62 (Sept. 1975): 296–315. For an oral history with Brigid O'Farrell that covers her work with the Women's Trade Union League, see the Institute of Labor and Industrial Relations (University of Michigan—Wayne State University), Program on Women and Work, *Twentieth Century Trade Union Woman: Vehicle for Social Change Oral History Project* (1978). An obituary is in the *Boston Globe*, 28 Oct. 1985.

KIMBERLY HAYDEN BROOKES

LUSH, Jay Laurence (3 Jan. 1896–2 May 1982), animal scientist and geneticist, was born in Shambaugh, Iowa, the son of farmers (names unknown). He studied animal husbandry at Kansas State Agricultural College (now Kansas State University), receiving a B.S. in 1916 and an M.S. in 1918, with a year off in between to teach high school. After brief stints in the U.S. military and at another Kansas high school, he entered the University of Wisconsin in 1919 to continue graduate study in genetics. After earning a Ph.D. in 1922, he researched animal husbandry at the Texas Experiment Station for eight years, until he joined the faculty of Iowa State College (now University) in 1930. He married Adaline Lincoln, a second cousin once removed of Abraham Lincoln who earned a master's degree at the University of Chicago at age seventeen, in 1923. They had two children.

Although Lush technically concentrated on physiology as a graduate student, he was already applying statistical tools to animal breeding in his Ph.D. thesis, "The Possibility of Sex Control by Artificial Insemination with Centrifuged Spermatozoa" (published in *Journal of Agricultural Researches* 30 [1925]: 893–913). He continued to take a statistical approach in his work in animal production and breeding at the Texas Agricultural Experiment Station. His 1923 paper "The Influence of Individuality, Age and Season upon Weights of Fleeces Produced by Range Sheep," published with J. M. Jones as *Texas Agricultural Experiment Station Bulletin 311*, is considered to be an early classic in the field. By utilizing statistics in the measurement of animal development, in this case the weight of sheep fleece, Lush was beginning to establish a mathematical approach to animal science, in which genetics played a central role. During this time, Lush began to be influenced by the writings of University of Chicago geneticist Sewall Wright, as he realized that Wright's tools of statistical genetics had potential use in animal breeding. Yet, during his tenure at College Station, Texas, Lush also published papers on traditional topics, such as inheritance and performance evaluation.

When Lush moved to Iowa State, he conducted pig inbreeding experiments in closed herds. He compared intense and mild inbreeding in pigs, finding that the optimum structure was the subdivision of breeds into many lines descended from carefully selected ancestors. In these and related experiments, he began to collect mass data in commercial conditions and devise more accurate statistical methods for measuring characteristics. During these years he also traveled to Chicago frequently in order to study under Wright, began to train graduate students in earnest (he only had one student in Texas), and wrote his textbook, *Animal Breeding Plans* (1937). It went through three editions and was translated into at least four languages. In this reference for students and commercial breeders, Lush characterized a breed as a population. He established the necessity of using statistical averages and variability measurements as the basis of breeding decisions in order to create the most precise genetic changes.

Lush's particular problem-solving approach is perhaps best revealed by a 1947 paper, "Family Merit and Individual Merit as Bases for Selection," published in two parts in *American Naturalist* (81 [1947]: 241–61, 362–79). He started each of his studies with an actual or practical problem and developed it into a larger question, the solution of which contributed to theoretical understanding. Lush used the fundamental principles of genetics as well as the statistical tools of population and biometrical genetics. In his research, Lush believed it important to account for the role of chance in addition to other factors, including financial limits, the role of mutations, and varying effects of selection. His 1947 paper dealt additionally with the broader problem of ascertaining the relative importance allotted to various factors in a study. It also showed that Lush had an entirely different way of thinking about animal breeding than others of his time. The statistical tools Lush developed in the paper, including the analysis of variance and intraclass correlations and regression equations for predicting the breeding value of an individual, were later used by geneticists, animal and plant breeders, statisticians, sociologists, and anthropologists.

Lush's teaching abilities were widely applauded by his contemporaries and students. His approach emphasized both the proper technical conduct of research and the mastery of verbal skills for reporting and teaching results, one of Lush's own most appreciated talents. While he valued undergraduate education and taught many introductory breeding courses, over the course of his career he also trained twenty-six master's and 124 doctoral students, such as R. R. Shrode, R. W. Touchberry, and Arthur B. Chapman. In fact, many of the important researchers in animal breeding in the second half of the twentieth century, including Wright, A. E. Freeman, E. N. Wentworth, and R. A. Fisher, were linked to him academically or intellectually. Several of these people honored him with a 1972 symposium at Virginia Polytechnic Institute.

After Lush retired from Iowa State in 1966, he continued to do research, focusing on the inheritability of disease. He traveled widely advising researchers around the world, helped establish U.S. Department of Agriculture regional laboratories for animal breeding research, and participated in the formation and conduct of National Poultry Breeders' Round Table Sessions. Despite his achievements, Lush always viewed his career modestly. In a 1967 statement to the National Academy of Sciences, he described his discoveries as "minor innovations." Lush's lifelong goal was to improve plant and animal breeding through the more efficient use of genetics.

Lush received several honorary doctorates and numerous awards; some of the most prestigious included election to the National Academy of the Sciences in 1967, a 1968 National Medal of Science, and a 1979 Wolf Foundation Agricultural Award. Throughout his career, Lush brought the science of genetics to bear on animal breeding, transforming this field of study from a qualitative to a quantitative discipline in the process. In dedicating the 1972 Animal Breeding and Genetics Symposium to Lush, Lush's former student R. R. Shrode, a professor of animal science at the University of Tennessee, cited Lush's "unequaled ability to communicate ideas by verbalizing them, supplementing mathematical statements with understandable verbal sentences, often with effective analogies skillfully woven into them," and concluded that Lush had "contributed more than any other individual, directly and indirectly through his many students, toward the continuing evolution of Animal Breeding from an art into a science" (*Proceedings of the Animal Breeding and Genetics Symposium in Honor of Dr. Jay L. Lush* [1973]: iii).

• Lush's papers are in the Special Collections of the library at Iowa State University. In addition to the works mentioned above, especially well-known publications by Lush include "The Number of Daughters Necessary to Prove a Sire," *Journal of Dairy Science* 14 (1931): 209; *Linebreeding: Iowa Agricultural Experiment Station Bulletin No. 301* (1933); the second and third editions of *Animal Breeding Plans* (1943 and 1945); and "The Genetics of Populations," a 1948 mimeograph, published in 1994 as *Iowa Agricultural and Home Economics Experiment Station Special Report 94*. A list of most of his nearly 200 papers appears in Arthur B. Chapman, "Jay Laurence Lush," National Academy of Sciences, *Biographical Memoirs* 57 (1987): 277–306. Obituaries are Chapman, "Jay Laurence Lush, 1896–1982: A Brief Biography," *Journal of Animal Science* 69 (1991): 2671–76, and in the *Des Moines Register*, 4 May 1982.

AMY ACKERBERG

LUSK, Georgia Lee Witt (12 May 1893–5 Jan. 1971), congresswoman and educator, was born in Carlsbad, Eddy County, New Mexico, the daughter of George Witt, a surveyor and rancher, and Mary Isabel Gilbreath. She graduated from New Mexico State Teachers College (now Western New Mexico University) in 1914 and also attended New Mexico Highlands University and Colorado State Teacher's College (now the University of Northern Colorado). She taught in southeastern New Mexico for one year before her marriage in 1915 to Dolph Lusk, a rancher and banker. The Lusks lived on a ranch in southeastern New Mexico near the community of Lovington. The couple had two sons, and Georgia was pregnant with their third son when Dolph died in 1919. Newly widowed with three small children, Lusk returned to teaching and at the same time managed the ranch she had inherited from her husband.

In 1924 Lusk began a 35-year political career under the aegis of the Democratic party. Women in New Mexico had held few statewide offices since they received the right to vote, though school board posts and other education offices were the exception. It was through education that Georgia Lusk was able to make her entrée into politics. She was elected superintendent of Lea County schools in 1924, and in 1930 she successfully ran for state superintendent of public instruction. Lusk was elected to the post five more times throughout the years, a feat unequaled by any other state superintendent in New Mexico history prior to Lusk. During her years as state superintendent of public instruction, she led educational improvement in New Mexico. She focused on upgrading teacher qualifications, increasing teacher salaries, and improving the science curriculum, and she was a firm believer in bilingual education for all New Mexico children at a time when bilingual education was not popular. Lusk helped spearhead successful drives for increased Indian education and federal school-lunch funding. She also worked for an increased number of accredited high schools and a program for physical education and recreation for elementary and secondary schools, and she was instrumental in consolidating a number of small school districts in the state.

Lusk imparted her interest in education to her sons, all three of whom graduated from college. During World War II her oldest son was killed in an airplane accident while serving in the army air corps, and Lusk established the Virgil Lusk Scholarship at New Mexico Military Institute to honor his memory. After her son's death and the maturing of her other children who left home by 1943, Lusk sold the family ranch and devoted her energies to winning a seat in the U.S. Congress, a major highlight of her political career. She ran for the U.S. House of Representatives on the Democratic ticket in 1946 and outdistanced all other candidates in the general election, receiving more votes than the experienced Hispanic congressman Antonio Fernandez. Her election to the U.S. Congress was not only a milestone in her political career but a singular achievement for all women in her state.

Georgia Lusk indicated both the direction of her congressional work and the major influences in her life when she wrote to the chairman of the Committee on Ways and Means before she arrived in Washington, D.C. She asked to be assigned to the Committee on Education, the Committee on Veterans' Affairs, or the Committee on Public Lands, in that order. She was appointed to the Committee on Veterans' Affairs and worked to increase veterans' benefits. As a Democrat, she voted in support of President Harry S. Truman's foreign policy, including foreign aid and military assistance for Greece and Turkey. Her other congressional votes included her long-standing support of federal aid to education and school lunch programs. She did, however, oppose the president when she voted for what would become the Taft-Hartley Act and then voted to override Truman's veto.

In 1948 Lusk lost her bid for reelection to Congress by coming in third in the Democratic primary. Ironically, the major Democratic primary winner was another education innovator, John E. Miles. Lusk's political career was not over, however. President Truman appointed her to the War Claims Commission in July 1949. As vice chairman of the committee, she assisted in the distribution of liquidated enemy assets to persons who had been prisoners of war during World War II. Lusk's work on the War Claims Commission included a visit in November 1951 to the Philippines, where she spoke to church groups and civilian citizens who had either lost property or been incarcerated during the Japanese occupation of the Bataan peninsula. In December 1953 Republican president Dwight D. Eisenhower notified Lusk that he was removing her and other members of the War Claims Commission in order to nominate his own committee members. She initially refused to resign, saying she still had much to do, but eventually she stepped down from her position on the commission.

Lusk continued her political career back in New Mexico. She once again ran successfully for state superintendent of public instruction and served from 1955 to 1959. Her last active political endeavor was assisting her son Eugene during his years as a state senator and in his unsuccessful bid to become governor of New Mexico in 1966. Two years later, after learning he was terminally ill, he committed suicide.

Even though she suffered the loss of a young husband and two adult sons, Georgia Lusk's political and personal life were both active and fulfilling. She was a member of diverse organizations such as the New Mexico Cattle Grower's Association, Delta Kappa Gamma (an educational honorary fraternity), Gold Star Mothers of America, the Parent-Teacher Congress, the American Legion Auxiliary, and the General Federation of Women's Clubs. These organizations represented the three major facets of her public life: education, veterans' affairs, and ranching.

Lusk died in Albuquerque. Her career as a wife, mother, educator, and politician spanned more than fifty years. The significance of her career lies in much more than the fact that until at least the late 1990s she remained the only woman elected to the U.S. Congress from New Mexico. As an elected official, she worked for her constituents and for those issues that were significant to her throughout her life. She made major contributions to the modernization of education in her home state, and she worked in Congress to assure veterans' benefits for all who deserved them.

• Many primary sources are available in the Georgia L. Lusk File at the State Record and Archives Center, Santa Fe, which includes records of the War Claims Commission and numerous scrapbooks containing letters and news clippings. A biography of Lusk is by Roger D. Hardaway, "Georgia Lusk of New Mexico: A Political Biography" (M.A. thesis, New Mexico State Univ., 1979). See also Hardaway's article on Lusk's election to Congress, "New Mexico Elects a Congresswoman," *Red River Valley Historical Review* (Fall 1979). Obituaries are in the *New York Times* and the *Albuquerque Journal*, both 6 Jan. 1971.

JUDITH BOYCE DeMARK

LUSK, Graham (15 Feb. 1866–18 July 1932), physiologist and biochemist, was born in Bridgeport, Connecticut, the son of William Thompson Lusk, an obstetrician, and Mary Hartwell Chittenden. Having impaired hearing, young Lusk followed his father's advice not to become a physician and instead studied chemistry at the Columbia School of Mines in New York, graduating with a Ph.B. in 1887. To study the biological sciences, Lusk traveled to Europe; in the next few years he worked first in Leipzig under the famous physiologist Carl Ludwig and then in Munich under the physiological chemist Carl Voit. In 1891 he received his Ph.D. from the University of Munich and returned to America full of enthusiasm for the Voit-Rubner doctrines in nutrition, which held that the energy derived from the metabolism of the three groups of foodstuffs—carbohydrate, fat, and protein—was exchangeable in the body in accordance with caloric equivalence. Voit and Rubner also stated that the metabolic rate was related to the body surface area of the individual.

Lusk's first academic appointment, in 1891, was as instructor in physiology at the Yale Medical School. In 1892 he became assistant professor and in 1895 full professor. He was invited in 1898 to be professor of physiology at the recently reorganized University and Bellevue Hospital Medical School, affiliated with New York University Medical School. He held this appointment until 1909, when he assumed the chair of physiology vacated by Austin Flint at the Cornell University Medical School. He held this chair until he retired a few years before his death. He married May W. Tiffany of New York in 1899; they had three children.

Lusk's work on experimental diabetes induced by the chemical phlorihizin began while he was at Yale, initiating a prolonged investigation of the sources of glucose in the body. These studies, originally done in animals, were extended to humans when Lusk came to New York. His work demonstrated there was a definite relationship between dextrose formed in the organism and the protein metabolized, as indicated by nitrogen excretion in the urine. When he studied the effect of administering various amino acids on the dextrose-nitrogen ratio, he was able to determine the amounts of carbohydrate derived from the various amino acids.

When he moved to Cornell, Lusk was offered the opportunity to construct a respiration calorimeter of the Atwater-Rosa-Benedict type that was large enough to study metabolism in dogs. This allowed him to study the hourly changes in metabolism of carbohydrate, fat, and protein.

In 1912 Lusk became director of the Russel Sage Institute of Pathology. With this position and the institute's affiliation with the Second Medical (Cornell) Division of Bellevue Hospital, he was able to find sufficient funds to construct a human calorimeter. Over the next twenty years Lusk was able to experiment on dogs and compare these results with those from both normal humans and those with diabetes. He demonstrated clearly that large amounts of glucose could be derived from the breakdown (metabolism) of protein, while little could be derived from the breakdown of fat, an important finding in understanding the metabolic disturbances in diabetes. Lusk devoted great effort to measuring the increased heat production (specific dynamic action) of various foodstuffs (carbohydrate, fat, and protein). Although his carefully planned experiments produced much useful data, he never was able to explain his results with existing theories. He maintained his allegiance to the theory that body surface area was of great significance in determining basal metabolism. Lusk was interested in the respiratory quotient (amount of carbon dioxide produced divided by amount of oxygen consumed); he was responsible for demonstrating the knowledge that can be obtained from respiratory quotients measured under the proper conditions.

Lusk devoted great effort to teaching, and although many students found his lectures daunting, they were also stimulated by them. He presented the details of the classical experiments on which the science of nutrition is founded in a clear, concise manner. Lusk was always ready to help deserving younger workers, and when he coauthored papers with his younger collaborators, his name, if present, was always last.

Lusk enjoyed scientific meetings and played a significant role in the founding of the Harvey Society of New York, which invites distinguished medical scientists to give lectures on clinical and scientific topics. Lusk also played a role in founding the Society for Experimental Biology and Medicine and the American Society of Biological Chemists. He had a keen sense of humor combined with a buoyancy of spirit and cheerfulness, which earned him many friends. Even though he was hearing-impaired from youth, he was a good conversationalist and an effective public speaker.

Throughout Lusk's life he was a storehouse of knowledge, which he synthesized for the public in his textbook *The Elements of the Science of Nutrition*, which appeared in four editions between 1906 and 1928. He respected the work of his predecessors and never made enemies of those with whom he disagreed, although he was emphatic and fearless in disputes. He made a vigorous although only partially successful effort to improve the compensation of professors. At one time he thought that medical school teachers should teach full time to strengthen departments, but he later altered his views and opposed rigid adherence to the full-time program when it interfered with academic freedom. He was a strong supporter of the freedom of faculties and fought any movement that he felt dangerous to the vital spirit of universities. Lusk died in New York after a brief illness.

• Lusk's papers in the archives of the Cornell Medical Center, New York City, include letters, manuscripts, reprints, photographs, and an unfinished history of nutrition. John R. Murlin, "Graham Lusk: A Brief Review of His Work," *Journal of Nutrition* 5 (1932): 527–28, and Eugene DuBois, "Obituary: Graham Lusk," *Science* 76 (1932): 113–15, are important sources. *Addresses Given at a Memorial Meeting at the New York Academy of Medicine, December 10, 1932*, gives a clear picture of Lusk's personality, integrity, and scientific capabilities as witnessed by his colleagues. See also "Biographical Memoir of Graham Lusk," National Academy of Sciences, *Biographical Memoirs* 21 (1941): 95–142. George B. Wallace, *Graham Lusk and the Harvey Society* (1932), describes Lusk's role in scientific societies and the founding of the Harvey Society. An obituary is in the *New York Times*, 19 July 1932.

DAVID Y. COOPER

LUTHER, Seth (1795–29 Apr. 1863), carpenter and labor activist, was born in Providence, Rhode Island, the son of Rebecca and Thomas Luther. His mother's maiden name is not known. His father, a veteran of the revolutionary war, was a tanner and currier. Seth Luther received a common school education and served an apprenticeship to become a house carpenter. In 1815 he was received into the First Baptist Church, but in 1824 the fellowship of the church was withdrawn from him for "disorderly walking." He never married. In 1817 he undertook the first of many journeys to the West, and by the end of his peripatetic life he claimed to have traveled 150,000 miles, mostly on foot. In 1823 he successfully petitioned the Rhode Island legislature for release from debtors' prison.

His mission in life was rooted in the stark contrast he perceived between, on the one hand, his encounters with egalitarian frontier hospitality and the rhetoric of the Revolution ("all men are created equal") and, on the other, the class inequalities of the northeast. He perceived a great dissonance between the squalid lives of the nascent working class and his idealization of his father's generation, which had fought the revolutionary war. He joined the Jackson-era labor movement and the movement against property qualifications for voting in his native Rhode Island. "Those who build houses today," he said in an address to working men in Brooklyn, "have none of their own and are dependent on a combination of landlords for shelter. . . . It was not so before the revolution and I expect another revolution will be necessary before the rights of the people are respected."

In 1832 he was in a delegation of workers which called on the governor of Rhode Island in support of the ten-hour day. That year he traveled extensively and made speeches in support of Boston workers striking for shorter hours. He became a correspondent and salesman for the *New England Artisan*, a labor paper. During one of his stops in Providence that year, he was assaulted and battered by one of his enemies and wrote of his injuries in the Providence *Republican Herald*, "I glory in these wounds knowing they would not have been inflicted, had I not advocated the cause of the suffering children incarcerated in the cotton mills of our once happy New England." The following year (1833), he claimed in his *Address on the Right of Free Suffrage* that "many in the community entertain bitter prejudice against me. . . . First I am charged with the unpardonable sin of being a poor man. But that would not have been so heinous if I had made no exertions against the oppression under which poor men, women and children labor."

In 1834 Luther was one of the founders of the Trades Union of Boston and Vicinity and became a leader of the short-lived National Trades Union. His attitude toward workers' self-organization was epitomized in the statement that "the mechanic or laborer who opposes Trades Unions is either ignorant, foolish or wicked. He is a kind of suicide." (*Address Delivered before the . . . Working-Men of . . . Brooklyn*).

In 1841 the Rhode Island free suffrage movement, which sought repeal of a state constitutional provision imposing a property qualification of $134 or more for the franchise, engaged Luther's services as a lecturer. This movement established a People's party that conducted a referendum ratifying a manhood-suffrage constitution under which Thomas W. Dorr was made governor. There were then two state governments and the abortive confrontation between them, remembered as the 1842 Dorr War, led to Luther's imprisonment. Charged with "wickedly devising and intending the peace of said State to disturb . . . to raise and levy war, insurrection and rebellion against said State . . . and to overthrow and destroy the government and laws thereof," he was jailed in Newport. At one point during his incarceration he set fire to his cell and escaped, but was quickly apprehended.

After the Whig authorities released him in 1843, Luther traveled to Baltimore, where supporters, including Justice Roger Taney, raised a fund which enabled Luther to travel to Illinois to recuperate from his ordeal. He had traveled widely in the West since 1817 and presumably knew someone in Bond County who put him up. In the summer of 1844 he made speeches in the Polk presidential campaign in Ohio, Indiana, and Illinois, calling for the release of Dorr, who had been sentenced to life imprisonment. The realities of party politics drove victims of the Whigs, like Luther, into the waiting arms of the Democrats. Earlier he had cast aspersions on both major parties as inimical to the interests of working people: "The pretended representatives of the people of *all parties* have for years been pursuing a cause of self-aggrandisement and ruinous corruption, while the workingmen have been deceived and juggled out of their rights by the cry of Whigism or Democracy triumphant, as the case may be" (*Address Delivered before the . . . Working-Men of . . . Brooklyn*).

His last active involvement in the labor movement was his participation in a March 1846 conference in support of the ten-hour day. After war was declared against Mexico two months later, Luther's hope of serving as a clerk in the army or navy was thwarted when he was arrested for trying to rob a bank in Boston. He had demanded $1,000 "in the name of President Polk." He was committed in June 1846 and spent the rest of his life in various asylums. It was an age when the diagnostic categories of psychiatry were even less scientific than those of a later age, and the records of Butler Hospital in Providence, where he spent ten years, merely described him as "demented when he entered. Not violent, nor mischievous but occasionally noisy." Although he had three brothers as well as nieces and nephews, the hospital's records note that in ten years he had no visitors. In 1858 he was transferred to Vermont Asylum in Brattleboro, where he died.

A scurrilous obituary in the perennially anti-labor *Providence Journal*, while conceding his "considerable talent for both writing and speaking," denounced him as a "natural radical" who had just concluded his "worse than useless life." In rebuttal, a *Providence Daily Post* obituary lauded his dedicated struggles against oppression. Eccentric or not, Luther's championing of working-class rights and his leadership in the ten-hour and free-suffrage movements of the 1830s and 1840s have earned him an important place in the history of the early American labor movement.

• Seven letters from Luther are in the John Hay Library of Brown University and one, to President Polk, is in the National Archives (RG 107). Luther's printed works include *An Address to the Working Men of New England* (1832); *An Address on the Right of Free Suffrage* (1833); *An Address on the Origin and Progress of Avarice* (1834); and *An Address Delivered Before the Mechanics and Working-Men of the City of Brooklyn on the Celebration of the Sixtieth Anniversary of American Independence* (1836). Obituaries are in the *Providence Journal*, 4 May 1863, and the *Providence Daily Post*, 7 May 1863. See also Louis Hartz, "Seth Luther: The Story of a Working-Class Rebel," *New England Quarterly* 13 (1940): 401–18; Carl Gersuny, "A Biographical Note on Seth Luther," *Labor History* 18 (1977): 239–48; and Mark S. Schantz, *Piety in Providence: The Class Dimensions of Religious Experience in Providence, Rhode Island, 1790–1860* (1991).

CARL GERSUNY

LUTZ, Frank Eugene (15 Sept. 1879–27 Nov. 1943), entomologist, was born in Bloomsburg, Pennsylvania, the son of Martin Peter Lutz, an insurance agent, and Anna Amelia Brockway. As a boy, he enjoyed exploring the outdoors. He attended public schools and Bloomsburg State Normal School. When he entered Haverford College, Lutz initially planned to major in mathematics at his father's urging. But in his third year he turned to biology, with the intention of going into medicine, and received his A.B. in 1900. A biology professor advised him to go into statistical work in biology.

Lutz spent the summer of 1900 at Cold Spring Harbor, New York, where University of Chicago zoologist Charles Benedict Davenport conducted a summer biological laboratory. The young man published a short paper on variations in the number of grooves on the shell of a species of *Pecten*, which was instrumental in his receiving a scholarship to the University of Chicago. He received his A.M. in 1902 and that summer worked as a biologist conducting mosquito control for the North Shore Improvement Association of Long Island, New York. He spent the college year of 1902–1903 studying in England and Germany and then returned to the University of Chicago.

When Davenport established the Station for Experimental Evolution at Cold Spring Harbor in 1904, Lutz was hired there as a resident investigator. He married Martha Ellen Brobson in December 1904; they had four children. He received his Ph.D. from the University of Chicago in 1907, with a thesis, "The Variation and Correlation of Certain Taxonomic Characters of *Gryllus*" (a genus of cricket), in which he noted that many of the named species were merely geographic or morphological variants.

Lutz continued at the Cold Spring Harbor station until 1909, publishing several papers on inheritance in various animals, on biometry, and on the effect of environment on animals. He went on a collecting expedition to Cuba and Mexico. At the station, where much work on genetics was beginning, he observed a white-eyed form of the fruit fly *Drosophila* and gave that strain to Thomas Hunt Morgan, who soon began genetic studies with it that led to the insect's enormous use for research.

In 1909 Lutz was hired at the American Museum of Natural History as assistant curator in the department of invertebrate zoology. He advanced to associate curator in 1917, and in 1921 he became curator of the newly established department of insects and spiders. Lutz held that position until his death, and through the years he increased the staff considerably. From 1925 to 1928 he was in charge of the museum's Station for Study of Insects at Tuxedo, New York.

At the museum, Lutz's interest turned almost exclusively to insects and somewhat to spiders. He participated in many field expeditions, including travels to the West Indies, British Guiana, Panama, Puerto Rico, and much of the United States. For trips to western states he equipped an automobile as a van for his collecting equipment and camping supplies. His collecting, plus purchases and donations, doubled the museum's collection of insects to about two million specimens.

Lutz planned exhibits of insects at the museum, including the stimulating and informative Hall of Insect Life in 1915. Later he created habitat groups of insects, including live exhibits of insects, spiders, and scorpions, which portrayed many aspects of this large group. He also published many papers on the biology and behavior of insects, including geographic distribution, adaptations of insects, their sounds, their flight in relation to wind, the diurnal rhythm of some, the sensory behavior of bees, insects in hot springs, galls, and spider webs. He recorded insect sounds and interpreted their function. Even though he encouraged others in taxonomy, Lutz took great pride in the fact that he never named a new species. His interest was especially in the behavior of the animals and was not directed to economic entomology.

Among Lutz's significant observations was that some flowers have a color pattern invisible to the human eye but visible through ultraviolet to insects. He determined this by photography with the aid of color filters. His essay, "The Colors of Flowers and the Vision of Insects with Special Reference to Ultraviolet," was awarded the A. Cressy Morrison prize of the New York Academy of Sciences in 1923.

In 1918 Lutz published *Field Book of Insects* for popular use, partly to answer frequently asked questions. It was widely sold and much appreciated. He revised it in 1921 and 1935. His final book, *A Lot of Insects* (1941), dealt with ones of special interest to himself. In it Lutz emphasized the insects of his own backyard and nearby surroundings in Ramsey, New Jersey. The book included "his sound and humorous entomological philosophy—all expressed interestingly and in a lucid style," according to his biographer Harry B. Weiss. He was called "a champion of insects for the large part they play in our everyday life," and he enjoyed pointing out the good traits of many of them.

Lutz served as editor of the museum's publications from 1917 to 1929. He was a member of many scientific societies, including charter membership in the Entomological Society of America, of which he was president in 1927.

Lutz created the concept of nature trails in parks, beginning with one at Harriman State Park in New York in 1925, and the idea has become widely used. National and local parks and youth organizations often called on him for advice. He also chaired a committee on biological relations between flowers and insects for the National Research Council. Lutz died in New York City.

• Some of Lutz's archival records are at the American Museum of Natural History. In addition to the books cited above, he wrote more than 100 papers, many scientific and others for a lay audience. Biographies are by Harry B. Weiss, in the *Journal of the New York Entomological Society* 52 (1944): 63–73, with selected bibliography; Herbert F. Schwarz, *Entomological News* 55 (1944): 29–32; Alfred E. Emerson, *Science* 99 (1944): 233–34; and W. J. Gertsch, *Annals of the Entomological Society of America* 37 (1944): 133–35.

ELIZABETH NOBLE SHOR

LYBRAND, William Mitchell (14 Aug. 1867–19 Nov. 1960), certified public accountant, was born in Philadelphia, Pennsylvania, the son of George W. Lybrand, a Methodist Episcopal minister, and Sara Aldred. After completing two years of study at Philadelphia High School, Lybrand took a position as a clerk in a tool-building company. At a time when opportunities for formal professional education were limited, apprenticeships in the machine tool industry represented a primary entry point for those aspiring to careers in manufacturing. He gradually focused his educational endeavors on cost accounting, which was becoming a vital adjunct to engineering as American industry responded to important managerial and technological advances. Moreover, Philadelphia was the home of Frederic Winslow Taylor's scientific management movement, which emphasized the need for the precise measurement and tight control of costs in business operations. In the midst of these momentous changes, Lybrand in 1887 joined one of the earliest public accounting firms organized in the United States, Heins and Whelen in Philadelphia.

In 1898 Lybrand formed his own firm, Lybrand, Ross Brothers and Montgomery (now Coopers and Lybrand), with three other junior partners from Heins and Whelen: T. Edward Ross, Adam Ross, and his brother-in-law Robert H. Montgomery. The date of Lybrand's marriage to Lenore Montgomery is not known. They had no children.

Like other successful pioneers in the new profession of public accountancy, Lybrand recognized the importance of establishing a solid reputation for competency in key aspects of accounting. Three such specializations helped to propel Lybrand's career. The first, cost accounting, allowed him to become an implementer for his firm's clients of the standard cost systems and other control techniques that the Taylorites had long advocated. The second, municipal accounting, helped him to develop standardized reporting formats to satisfy the informational needs of the *U.S. Census of Municipal Finance*. The third specialization, holding company accounting, became important as industrial concentration created a need for better methods to present the financial position and results of complex business consolidations.

Lybrand's professional leadership was also shown by the prominent role he played in associational affairs. In 1897 he helped to form the Pennsylvania Institute of Public Accountants (now the Pennsylvania Institute of Certified Public Accountants, PICPA) after practitioners in New York state succeeded in securing licensing legislation for "certified public accountants." Lybrand served initially as the treasurer of his state's association (1897–1901) when it successfully agitated for public accountancy legislation in Pennsylvania in 1899. During Lybrand's tenure as its president, from 1902 to 1904, the Pennsylvania body joined the Federation of Societies of Public Accountants in the United States (later the American Association of Public Accountants, AAPA), a national confederation of practitioner groups that sought to promote professional licensing and to assure the consistency of professional governance nationwide.

Lybrand also played an important role in the formation of an associational framework for cost accounting. Although the AAPA was primarily a public accounting organization, its membership initially included a smattering of industrial accountants, educators, and controllers. The status of these latter professional groups was downgraded to nonvoting associates in 1917 when the AAPA was superseded by the American Institute of Accountants (AIA), a more centrally controlled organization that promoted greater uniformity in professional standards and governance. Because of this change, Lybrand and others who shared

his belief that a need existed for a representative body for the growing numbers of cost accountants founded, in 1919, a new association, the National Association of Cost Accountants (NACA, now the Institute of Management Accountants). Lybrand served as the new association's president from 1920 to 1922. Through its meetings and its publication, the *NACA Bulletin* (now *Management Accounting*), NACA became an important source of information about advances in industrial cost accounting. In 1947 the association also recognized Lybrand's strong contribution to the professionalization of cost accounting by establishing an award in his name for the best technical manuscript submitted each year to the *NACA Bulletin*.

Although he began to defer after 1905 to Montgomery as the firm's representative in public accountancy organizations, Lybrand's expertise in cost accounting indirectly helped to draw the profession closer to the administration of President Woodrow Wilson in 1916. Following the advice of presidential adviser Louis D. Brandeis, the Wilson administration abandoned a proposed requirement, strongly opposed by many business leaders, for uniform corporate financial reporting through the Federal Trade Commission (FTC). Instead, FTC chair Joseph E. Davies and commissioner Edwin N. Hurley embraced an alternate proposal advanced by the AAPA's committee on federal legislation (chaired by Montgomery) to provide cost accounting studies for small businesses, a strong constituency of the Democratic regime. The accountants contended that the studies were both prerequisites to any system of uniform financial accounting and an effective means for promoting more efficient business management. To advance its program the AAPA drew on the expertise of members with strong backgrounds in cost accounting, like Lybrand, and was able to develop guidelines for lithographers, typesetters, pipe manufacturers, paper and pulp processors, chair manufacturers, and retail merchants.

Lybrand also promoted education and technical publishing. He supported an early professional journal, the *Public Accountant*, which was eventually discontinued after the AAPA began to sponsor in 1905 the *Journal of Accountancy*, which became the leading practitioner publication. In addition, Lybrand played a leading role in 1902 in the PICPA's effort to provide evening training courses for junior accountants. In 1904 Lybrand helped to persuade Professor E. S. Meade, father of anthropologist Margaret Meade, to take over this training through the evening division of the Wharton School of Business at the University of Pennsylvania.

Besides these professional achievements, Lybrand and his partners embarked on a program of practice development that led eventually to the formation of one of the nation's largest, or so-called Big Eight, public accounting firms. Although the firm initially operated through a single office in Philadelphia, in 1902 the partners decided to send Montgomery to open a second office in New York City. The decision coincided with a boom in corporate consolidation activity that had created wider opportunities for public accountants to serve investment bankers in the nation's financial capital. Underwriters, who were eager to build public confidence in the companies they assisted in funding, engaged well-known public accounting firms to certify the financial statements included in their offering prospectuses. Although Lybrand's firm was not well known at that time outside of Philadelphia, its leaders were able to build a favorable reputation in New York City by their activism in professional affairs and public service and by the high quality of the professional services they rendered. This drive was so successful that Lybrand relocated his office from Philadelphia to New York City in 1908. Subsequently, the firm developed an extensive branch office network to serve giant business clients whose operations were widely scattered across the continent.

By the time of his death in Stamford, Connecticut, Lybrand had witnessed an enormous increase in the size and influence of the two organizations he had helped to establish for ordering professional affairs in both public and cost accounting. A second lasting monument to his foresight and energy was the creation of the international professional services company that continues to bear his name.

• Information about Lybrand's life is in his "As I Look Back over Half a Century," *L. R. B. & M. Journal* (Jan. 1938), and his "History of the Firm," in the same journal (Feb., Mar., May, and Nov. 1920). Some of Lybrand's technical articles include "Accounting for Industrial Enterprises," *Journal of Accountancy* (Dec. 1908): 111–21, and (Jan. 1909): 224–36; "Accounts of Holding Companies," *Accounting and Business Management* 4 (1920): 203–32; "Municipal Accounting in the City of Philadelphia," *Journal of Accountancy* (Aug. 1906): 275–79; "Relation of Cost Accounting to Business Management—From the Viewpoint of the Professional Accountant," National Association of Cost Accountants, *NACA Yearbook* (1920), pp. 65–75; and "Stock Accounts and Book Inventories," *Journal of Accountancy* (Feb. 1906): 293–300. His ideas about the early development of the profession of public accountancy were communicated in "Development of Accounting in the United States," *Canadian Chartered Accountant* (Nov. 1924): 168–82. He is noted in the writings of his partners; see T. Edward Ross, *Pioneers of Public Accounting in Pennsylvania* (1940), and Robert H. Montgomery, *Fifty Years of Accountancy* (1939). A memorial by T. Edward Ross et al., "William M. Lybrand—In Memoriam," is in the *Lybrand Journal* (Jan. 1961). An obituary is in the *New York Times*, 21 Nov. 1960.

PAUL J. MIRANTI, JR.

LYDENBERG, Harry Miller (18 Nov. 1874–16 Apr. 1960), librarian, was born in Dayton, Ohio, the son of Wesley Braxton Lydenberg, a Civil War veteran, and Mariana Miller. His father died of war wounds when Lydenberg was only five years of age, leaving the family in relative poverty. Lydenberg worked several jobs to support his family, including as a page in the Dayton Public Library. He continued to work in the library at Harvard College, where he received a Bowditch Scholarship in 1893. Four years later he received the B.A. magna cum laude.

Lydenberg found work in 1896 as a cataloger in the New York Public Library (NYPL), which was beginning to develop into one of the major research libraries in the United States as a result of a merger between several private libraries. Lydenberg gave most of his life to developing the NYPL, especially its research collection. He moved up the ladder quickly because of his energy and diligence and with the help of mentors such as John Billings and Edward H. Anderson.

Lydenberg was promoted to reference librarian in 1908 and by 1928 was running the entire research collection. In 1928 he was selected as the assistant director, and from 1934 to 1941 he directed the entire NYPL.

Lydenberg led the NYPL in its continued mission to become a national library, even making trips to Europe and the Soviet Union in 1923 and 1924 to acquire research materials. Lydenberg was a pioneer in the preservation of library materials. He wrote and spoke on this, and established a preservation laboratory. He also made early advances in use of microfilm and Photostat copiers to provide preservation and access for researchers.

Lydenberg married NYPL librarian Madeliene Rogers Day in 1912, and they had two children. Lydenberg was recognized as a leader of libraries, serving as president of the American Library Association from 1932 to 1933, as well as the Bibliographical Society of America (1929–1931). He also served as secretary-treasurer of the American Council of Learned Societies from 1937 to 1941.

Following Lydenberg's retirement from the NYPL, he worked on international issues in librarianship. He set up the Biblioteca Benjamin Franklin, which was a joint ALA-governmental attempt to expand American influence in Mexico at the dawn of World War II. Two years later he ran the ALA International Relations Office. In 1946 he again was in Europe for six months analyzing the situation of publishers and libraries in postwar Europe, as well as acquiring works for American libraries. Through the IRO, he also was active in Latin America, helping to rebuild Peru's National Library. The IRO also helped establish bibliographic international cooperation, which was taken over by UNESCO. In 1946 Lydenberg retired from library work, although he continued to do research and publish for more than a decade before he died in Westerville, Ohio.

Researchers who have used the NYPL will understand why Keyes Metcalf called Lydenberg the "greatest librarian" during his sixty years of library work. Its comprehensive stacks have remained evidence of his foresight in collecting unique materials. Lydenberg also should be appreciated as a true pioneer of research library cooperation efforts for preservation and acquisition.

• Lydenberg's papers are in the Manuscript Division, New York Public Library. Other materials may be found in the American Library Association Archives at the University of Illinois Archives, Champaign. His major publications can be divided into several areas: library histories, conservation, and print history. The first category includes his comprehensive *History of the New York Public Library* (1923) and his biography of the NYPL director, *John Shaw Billings* (1924). The various editions of *Care and Repair of Books* (1931-), coauthored with John Archer, expressed his pioneering practical interest in the preservation of books. Lydenberg also furthered American understanding of printing history with his translations of Andre Blum's *On the Origin of Paper* (1934) and *The Origins of Printing and Engraving* (1940). His publications are listed in bibliographies published by David H. Stam in the *Bulletin of the NYPL* (1960) and by George L. McKay in *Bookmen's Holiday* (1943).

Phyllis Dain "Harry M. Lydenberg and American Library Resources: A Study in Modern Librarianship," *Library Quarterly* 47 (1977): 451–69, is an outstanding resource. Her study of the New York Public Library updates Lydenberg's own work and places him in context. A festschrift in his honor titled *Bookmen's Holiday* (1943), published by the NYPL on his retirement, contains additional biographical information. An obituary is in the *New York Times*, 17 Apr. 1960.

ANDREW B. WERTHEIMER

LYDSTON, G. Frank (3 Mar. 1858–14 Mar. 1923), urologist and transplant surgeon, was born George Frank Lydston in Jacksonville, California, the son of George Nelson Lydston, an entrepreneur and investor, and Lucy McGowan. From California George N. Lydston took his family to his native Maine in 1865 and then to Chicago, Illinois, in 1869. Young Lydston completed his secondary education and then studied medicine in Chicago under F. B. Norcom from 1876 to 1879. He attended Rush Medical College in Chicago in 1877–1878 and attended Bellevue Hospital Medical College in New York City, where he obtained his M.D. in February 1879.

At Bellevue, Lydston had a six-month tutorship under Joseph W. Howe, clinical professor of surgery. He then won an eighteen-month internship at Charity Hospital in New York City. Afterward he worked briefly there and at the Penitentiary Hospital and New York State Emigration Hospital and Refuge. These experiences gave him an understanding of the criminal and poor classes that he later brought to both his medical and literary writings.

In August 1881 Lydston returned to Chicago, where his parents and mentor still lived. There he began practice as a general physician but gradually specialized in the new field of urology. Any physician wishing to specialize successfully at this time could do so only with solid experience in general medicine. Lydston's interest in urology had been kindled by his association in New York with William H. Van Buren, a pioneer in this field. From 1882 to 1913 Lydston taught at the College of Physicians and Surgeons (later the College of Medicine of the University of Illinois). In 1883 Lydston had married one of his early patients, sixteen-year-old Josie M. Cottier; the couple had two daughters.

Lydston developed or improved many urological instruments. However, he firmly believed that in diagnostic procedures the physician should use the five senses first and then draw on instruments as they could add to this knowledge. Lydston the teacher and compassionate practitioner is revealed in this response to students who sought advice about proficiency in the use of urological instruments. "My personal opinion is that *no man is competent to pass an instrument upon a patient until he has practiced the maneuver upon himself a few times*" (*Stricture of the Urethra* [1893], p. 40).

Lydston's prolific career in medical literature began in 1880 with a brief anatomical paper. As his interests turned toward urology he did substantial work in several areas. For example, he pioneered in perineal prostatectomy and in 1905 constructed a replacement penile urethra from scrotal tissues. His new method for anastomosing the vas deferens was known for some time as the Lydston operation. Lydston was author of some 250 articles and pamphlets and nineteen books, and his major medical work was *The Surgical Diseases of the Genito-Urinary Tract* (1899; rev. ed., 1904).

During the Spanish-American War Lydston volunteered as a military surgeon. Although he did not see foreign action, he wrote several practical articles on the medical and military effects of modern gunfire.

Lydston was often outspoken and sarcastic in his writings and speeches. The American Urological Association, founded in 1902, waited nearly twenty years to elect him a member, despite his standing as a pioneer in the field. The Chicago Urological Society, founded in 1903, did not accept him until 1919.

Sex gland transplantation in humans was the field in which Lydston made his most widely known contribution. His interest was stimulated by the recent growth of knowledge about internal secretions. To perform the actual transplantation he had to overcome two major problems: obtaining a suitable subject and a surgeon qualified to do the operation. He resolved both quandaries in typical fashion by deciding to operate on himself. On 16 January 1914 Lydston transplanted into his own scrotum a testis from a young man who had recently committed suicide. Lydston's 32-page report, containing a review of the literature and accounts of his self-operation and six later operations on others, appeared serially in four issues of the *New York Medical Journal* (17, 24, and 31 Oct. and 7 Nov. 1914). Max Thorek, a surgical colleague, verified the presence of the self-transplanted testis five years later. Lydston continued his work in this field and performed other operations, several of which appeared to be successful. In 1982 John R. Herman, professor of urology at Einstein Medical College, commented that "Lydston, unlike many others in this field, was not one for publicity . . . his work was a true contribution."

Lydston's firm belief in the importance of sex education for the general public is exemplified by his book *Sex Hygiene for the Male and What to Say to the Boy* (1912) and several articles and pamphlets. In addition to his medical writings Lydston drew on his broad social and anthropological interests in such books as *The Diseases of Society (The Vice and Crime Problem)* (1904) and in many articles. For many years he served as professor of criminal anthropology at the Kent College of

Law. He also wrote about sports and physical training, emphasizing individual rather than team activities.

Lydston built up a large and lucrative practice, moving his medical office several times so that it would be in a prestigious section of the city. He was well aware of the importance of efficient business methods, and his articles and pamphlets on the subject were widely read.

Lydston's combative nature reached a peak during his battles (1899–1918) with the American Medical Association and its spokesman, George Simmons. Lydston objected to the fact that Simmons simultaneously held the positions of editor, secretary, and manager. With other physicians Lydston also opposed the 1901 reorganization of the AMA that removed the right of individual members to elect officers and to participate in various activities at the general meeting, assigning these responsibilities to the new House of Delegates.

Among Lydston's literary works were *Poker Jim, Gentleman, and Other Tales and Sketches* (1906), which contains a searing essay on the 1903 fire in the Iroquois Theater that took 600 lives, and a novel, *Trusty Five-Fifteen* (1921), which included some of his forward-looking views on the justice and penal systems. These views included an emphasis on prevention of crime rather than punishment for it, opposition to capital punishment, and more efforts for rehabilitation.

Well known for his skill as a surgeon, his popularity as an author and speaker on medical, literary, and social topics, and his lively though sometimes mordant attitude toward life, Lydston contributed to the growth of his chosen field, urology, and to a broader understanding of those he referred to as the underdogs in society. Lydston died in Hollywood, California, where he and his wife had been living since 1920.

• No collection of Lydston's personal papers is known to exist. Lydston's book *Panama and the Sierras* (1900) contains much on his early years and a full account, with pictures, of his trip in that area just before its publication. William K. Beatty, "G. Frank Lydston—Urologist, Author, and Pioneer Transplanter," *Proceedings of the Institute of Medicine of Chicago* 43, no. 2 (Apr.–June 1990): 35–69, is the most thorough account of Lydston's life and work (portrait on p. 35) and describes his basic arguments with the American Medical Association. John R. Caulk writes of Lydston's pioneering in perineal prostatectomy in Edgar G. Ballenger, ed., *History of Urology*, vol. 2 (1933), and John Herman discusses Lydston's work on sex gland transplantation in the *New York State Journal of Medicine* 82, no. 12 (1982): 1731–39.

WILLIAM K. BEATTY

LYMAN, Charles Parker (1 Sept. 1846–1 Feb. 1918), educator and veterinarian, was born in New York City, the son of Jabez Whiting Lyman, a partner in a Boston dry goods store, and Mary Ainsworth Parker. Lyman married Lucy E. Pope in 1868; they had a son and a daughter. He graduated from the Veterinary College (Edinburgh, Scotland) in 1874 and then returned to the United States to establish a practice in Springfield, Massachusetts. Between 1877 and 1879

he taught veterinary courses at the Massachusetts Agriculture College (now the University of Massachusetts, Amherst). During these same two years he also served as president of the U.S. Veterinary Medical Association. In 1880, for U.S. commissioner of agriculture William G. Le Duc, he undertook an extensive study of contagious bovine pleuro-pneumonia, one of several animal diseases (epizootics) threatening the beef and dairy industries. This work took him to most East Coast stockyards and seaports. In addition he traveled to Great Britain in order to persuade officials there to lift their embargo on imported cattle from the United States. Although unsuccessful in this part of his task, his four reports on this economically devastating disease were widely disseminated and served to convince the public, livestock owners, and politicians that bovine pleuro-pneumonia was, indeed, contagious. An unusual feature of Lyman's published report was a thematic map showing that the epizootic appeared only in contiguous counties on the Atlantic seaboard. This added visual proof, or so Lyman thought, that the country was, indeed, facing a contagious disease. In 1879 and 1880 Lyman traveled to Great Britain and—by examination—became a member (1879) and then a fellow (1880) of the Royal College of Veterinary Surgeons (London).

In 1882 Harvard University appointed Lyman professor of veterinary medicine in its School of Veterinary Medicine, then being formed, and in 1886 named him dean. Working under the direction of university president Charles W. Eliot, Lyman organized a curriculum and oversaw the construction of classrooms and an animal hospital on Village Street near the center of Boston. This was the fourth veterinary school established in the United States but the first integrated fully into a university. Veterinary colleges had hitherto been independent institutions where laboratories and classrooms were few and where instruction was superficial because faculty members taught part-time without pay while engaged in busy practices. As a consequence, veterinary degrees, or diplomas, barely distinguished their holders from veterinarians who were self-taught or had undergone an informal apprenticeship. Under Lyman, the Harvard Veterinary School changed all of that, for it drew on the university's Medical School for most of its teachers, establishing rigorous admission standards, building a three-year graded curriculum with a nine-month school year (when the norm was two-year curricula with six-month school years), and requiring a course of study heavily weighted with scientific subjects. Although Lyman was not the first veterinary educator with this vision, he was the first to achieve it. As a result, Harvard's veterinary graduates received comprehensive and rigorous training, which earned them a creditability no other veterinary graduates in the United States could claim. Following in Harvard's footsteps, the University of Pennsylvania established its veterinary school on the same model (1884), as did Ohio State University (1885) and Cornell (1896); eventually all veterinary schools became part of a university or closed.

Although the school showed great promise in the 1880s, it began to falter during the 1890s, as did other veterinary schools in the United States and Canada. The economic turmoil of that decade and an oversupply of veterinary school graduates led to a decline in all veterinary school enrollments, forcing several to close. Harvard's high admission standards and its rigorous and long curriculum made it especially vulnerable to a decline in student numbers. As a result, by the end of the decade its already small student body fell to unacceptable levels. This, together with the lack of an endowment and President Eliot's resistance to state funding for higher education, led to the school's demise in 1901.

During the 1890s, while serving as dean of the Veterinary School, Lyman continued his fight against epizootics by joining the Massachusetts Board of Cattle Commissioners as its secretary. During his term (May 1892 to Sept. 1896), he and his protégé, Frederick H. Osgood, the chairman, reorganized the commissioners (who were responsible for all contagious animal diseases in the state, including rabies in dogs and glanders in horses), increased the number of animal and meat inspectors, made inspection more rigorous, and introduced tuberculin as a test for bovine tuberculosis.

Lyman retired from the Harvard faculty in 1902 but continued practicing veterinary medicine in Boston with his son (Richard P. Lyman) and two other graduates of the Harvard Veterinary School. Because of poor health he wintered in Whittier, California, and died in Los Angeles in 1918.

Lyman's first achievement was as a veterinarian and sanitarian who joined the contagionist side in fighting epizootics at national and state levels at a time when many farmers, livestock owners, politicians, and even some veterinarians still held anti-contagionist views. But his most lasting achievement was as dean of the Harvard Veterinary School, where the faculty trained veterinarians in scientific subjects with a rigor comparable to that received by medical doctors.

• Although Lyman left no personal papers, the Harvard University Archives has much material about the Harvard School of Veterinary Medicine and Lyman's relationship with Charles W. Eliot. His four reports on contagious bovine pleuro-pneumonia were published by the U.S. Department of Agriculture in *Contagious Diseases of Domesticated Animals* (Special Reports 22 and 34; 1880 and 1881) and in its *Annual Reports* for 1880 and 1881. His work on animal diseases in Massachusetts appears in the lengthy *Annual Reports of the Massachusetts Board of Cattle Commissioners* for 1892 through 1896 and in a pamphlet for farmers and livestock owners, *Tuberculosis in Cattle* (1893), that can be found in the National Agriculture Library, Beltsville, Md.

PHILIP M. TEIGEN

LYMAN, Eugene William (4 Apr. 1872–15 Mar. 1948), philosopher of religion and theologian, was born in Cummington, Massachusetts, the son of Darwin Eugene Lyman and Julia Sarah Stevens. His "public-minded" father owned the village store and served for a time in the state legislature; his mother operated a millinery shop in connection with her husband's store. Regularly, Julia Lyman read biblical stories, John Bunyan's *Pilgrim's Progress*, John Milton's *Paradise Lost*, and a wide range of novels aloud to her children. Young Lyman received a common school education, but no high school was located nearby. While teaching school to raise money for college, he prepared for it on his own and with private tutors. Lyman recalled the Congregational church, the local town meeting, and the *Springfield Republican* as other formative influences. At church, ministers in the liberal evangelical tradition of Horace Bushnell made a strong impression on him, and he read the books of Washington Gladden, a theologian of the social gospel, and Theodore Thornton Munger, an admirer of Bushnell.

Entering Amherst College in 1890, Lyman studied philosophy with Charles Edward Garman, whose Socratic pedagogy and philosophical idealism made a lasting impression on him. After graduating from Amherst with an A.B. in 1894, Lyman taught Latin for a year at Williston Academy in Easthampton, Massachusetts, and for a year at the Lawrenceville School in Lawrenceville, New Jersey. Entering seminary at Yale University in 1896, Lyman studied with F. C. Porter, whose treatment of Christianity as a historical religion he found convincing. After graduating from Yale with a B.D. three years later, Lyman married Bertha Burton Thayer in 1899. They became the parents of two adopted children. Lyman's academic performance in seminary won a Hooker Fellowship for two years of theological study at the Universities of Halle, Berlin, and Marburg in Germany.

In 1901 Lyman was ordained in the ministry of the Congregational church and was appointed professor of philosophy at Carleton College in Northfield, Minnesota, the first of a series of academic appointments over the next seventeen years. In 1904–1905 he was professor of systematic theology and philosophy of religion at the Congregational Church College of Canada in Montreal. From 1905 to 1913 he was professor of systematic theology at Bangor Theological Seminary in Maine. While there, he gave the Nathaniel Taylor Lectures at Yale in 1909–1910, which were published as *Theology and Human Problems* (1910). The lectures examined four "highways of thought" among contemporary philosophers of religion: supernaturalism, absolute idealism, neo-Kantianism, and pragmatism. Lyman acknowledged his lingering debt to both idealism and neo-Kantianism, but he found in a "higher pragmatism" the most likely avenue for future work in the field. After spending six months in postgraduate study at the Universities of Heidelberg, Jena, and Paris in the 1911–1912 academic year, he taught philosophy of religion, systematic theology, and Christian ethics in the Oberlin College Graduate School of Theology from 1913 to 1918.

In 1918 Lyman accepted an appointment to the chair in philosophy of religion at Union Theological Seminary in New York City. His influence was limited by reactions against theological liberalism in academic circles, but he continued to teach at Union for the rest of his academic career. Within a theological faculty of strong personalities, social activists, and dynamic lecturers, Lyman earned his reputation as an outstanding classroom teacher by inviting students to engage in philosophical dialogue directed to the resolution of a problem. He was neither a political activist nor a theoretical pacifist, but he opposed U.S. entry into World War I, joined the pacifist Fellowship of Reconciliation, and, when the Union Seminary faculty debated about American foreign policy in the 1930s, was inclined to oppose intervention abroad. A consistent supporter of the social gospel, he criticized some aspects of capitalism as "deeply immoral" and was known among the seminary's African-American students as one of its few empathetic faculty members. Lyman's 1928 Ingersoll Lecture at Harvard was published as *The Meaning of Selfhood and Faith in Immortality* (1928), but his magnum opus was *The Meaning and Truth of Religion* (1933). In it, Lyman moved beyond advocating pragmatism as a vehicle for a philosophy of religion to espouse theological realism. Defining God as a purposive "cosmic creative spirit," Lyman's theological realism affirmed the independent reality of divine revelation, natural objects, and moral values that were known by intuition.

Lyman's wife died in 1924. In 1926 Lyman married Mary Redington Ely. A former student of her husband at Union Seminary and the top scholar in the class of 1919 who was not allowed to sit with her male classmates at graduation, Mary Lyman was an able theologian in her own right. She held a doctorate from the University of Chicago, taught at Vassar and Barnard Colleges, and published five books, primarily on the Gospel of John, between 1925 and 1960. When Eugene Lyman retired from the Union Seminary faculty in 1940, they moved to Virginia, where Mary Lyman became dean and professor of religion at Sweet Briar College. In 1946 Lyman, the "dean's husband" and unofficial philosopher in residence, suffered a stroke. After having almost fully recovered, he died suddenly in Sweet Briar, Virginia.

• No known collection of Lyman's papers exists, but transcripts of William R. Hutchison's oral interviews with Mary Ely Lyman and John C. Bennett, a colleague at Union Theological Seminary, are deposited at Union Seminary. Lyman, "Christian Theology and a Spiritualistic Philosophy," in *Contemporary American Theology*, ed. Vergilius Ferm (1933), is his intellectual autobiography. Beyond those mentioned in the text, Lyman's books included *The Experience of God in Modern Life* (1918) and *Religion and the Issues of Life* (1943). For a nearly complete bibliography of his published work, see David E. Roberts and Henry P. Van Dusen, eds., *Liberal Theology, an Appraisal: Essays in Honor of Eugene William Lyman* (1942). For appraisals of Lyman's theological enterprise, see Ernest Leon Snodgrass, "Naturalism and Supernaturalism in E. W. Lyman's Philosophy" (Ph.D. diss., Univ. of Chicago, 1937); Walter Marshall Horton, "Eugene W. Lyman: Liberal Christian Thinker," in *Liberal Theology*, ed. Roberts and Van Dusen (1942); Kenneth Cauthen, *The Im-*

pact of American Religious Liberalism (1962); and Hutchison, *The Modernist Impulse in American Protestantism* (1976). An obituary is in the *New York Times*, 16 Mar. 1948.

RALPH E. LUKER

LYMAN, Mary Redington Ely (24 Nov. 1887–9 Jan. 1975), minister and biblical scholar, was born in St. Johnsbury, Vermont, the daughter of Henry Guy Ely, a factory manager, and Adelaide Newell. Mary grew up in the Congregational church, where she was active in the Society of Christian Endeavor. Her mother was frequently ill during Mary's childhood, so that when she went away to Mount Holyoke College, she felt it to be "the open door on life for me." After graduating in 1911, she taught high school for two years, served as general secretary of the YWCA at Mount Holyoke, and conducted evening Bible study classes before entering Union Theological Seminary in New York City in 1916.

Lyman received her B.D. from Union in 1919, the only woman in her class. Although she graduated as the top-ranking student, she was not allowed to participate in her own graduation ceremony except as a balcony spectator because she was a woman. She published her first book, *Paul the Conqueror*, that same year. A prestigious scholarship allowed her to spend two years of study at Cambridge University in England, yet once again she encountered gender discrimination, as the university refused to grant a theological degree or even issue a transcript to a woman. In 1924 she received her Ph.D., magna cum laude, from the University of Chicago, and a year later her dissertation was published as *Knowledge of God in Johannine Thought*. In 1924 she married Eugene W. Lyman, Marcellus Hartley Professor of the Philosophy of Religion at Union, and taught at Vassar and Barnard colleges for the next fifteen years. After her husband's retirement in 1940, Mary Lyman became dean of Sweet Briar College in Virginia.

In 1949, shortly after her husband died, Lyman was ordained a Congregationalist minister in Cummington, Massachusetts, where she and Eugene had spent their summers. Returning to Union Seminary the next year, she was installed as the Morris K. Jesup Professor of the English Bible, the first woman to hold a faculty chair at Union and the first woman to serve as full professor at an American seminary. She served also as dean of women students, a position that enabled her to advise the growing numbers of women who were entering theological schools at that time. She was appointed to the World Council of Churches Commission on the Life and Work of Women in the Churches, a position that allowed her to expand the opportunities for religious vocations for women. Union president Henry Pitney Van Dusen described Lyman as "one of the ablest teachers of the English Bible in the United States, a distinguished New Testament scholar, and a leader in all matters connected with the life and work of women in the church" (Burke Library, folder 14).

Lyman retired from Union in 1955 and traveled around the world to learn more about the global expansion of Christianity, while preaching and lecturing on a variety of topics. She wrote to her friends about the terrible poverty in Hong Kong yet was heartened to see "all the helpful ways in which our National Council of Churches in U.S.A. [sic] is trying to relieve the dreadful conditions." She also supported the efforts of the National Council of Churches on behalf of the farmers of Okinawa, noting, "We were all mighty glad the American churches had stood up" for the farmers (Burke Library, folder 14).

Lyman published numerous books, articles, and pamphlets between 1919 and 1960. Interested in making the findings of biblical criticism widely accessible to lay people, she wrote *The Fourth Gospel and the Life of To-day* (1931), *The Christian Epic: A Study of New Testament Literature* (1936), and *Jesus* (1937). In her own words, "Scholarship has made available much that allows a reconstruction of the world that produced the Gospel [of John], but this material has not been appropriated by those most to be benefited by it, those who love the Gospel and want to use it, but who feel baffled by the many questions which a little knowledge of its origin has raised" (*The Fourth Gospel*, pp. 5–6). After her retirement from Union, she wrote *Death and the Christian Answer* (1960) and *In Him Was Life: A Study Guide on the Gospel of John* (1960). Working in the tradition of theological liberalism, she sought to make biblical scholarship accessible and relevant to a wide range of religious believers.

One of the recurrent themes in Lyman's writings on New Testament literature is the apparent conflict between the limitations and inconsistencies of the early Christian writings in light of modern scientific and historical methods. As she observed in *Jesus*, "If in the light of modern knowledge and in comparison with modern values, Jesus' ideal seems inadequate or outmoded, then we should be willing to acknowledge its failure, and start new with some new ideal worthy of the task to which it must be set" (p. 49). Having been educated in the latest findings of biblical criticism, Lyman sought to sustain, even heighten, the relevance of the New Testament for modern people, interpreting Jesus as a great ethical teacher and, more significantly, "the concrete embodiment of the ideal in living, that carries over these centuries an enthusiasm, a winsomeness, a power that no system of ethics could ever give" (*Jesus*, p. 53). Lyman challenged those who reacted fearfully to biblical criticism and tried to make of the New Testament a rigid bulwark against thorough inquiry. In analyzing the Book of Revelation, she averred that "many of its beliefs we cannot hold today," even as she deftly explicated its powerful appeal to generations of artistically minded Christians (*Christian Epic*, p. 207). What she affirmed in place of a retrogressive doctrine of infallibility was the "heroic quality" of the early Christian writings, the "transcendent creative personality of Jesus" as their source, and the life-changing transformative power of the faith, attested by the longevity and ardency of the historic Christian community (*Christian Epic*, p. 257). Lyman's foremost contribution as a scholar and as a

teacher, then, was to animate the far Christian past and illuminate, with keen acuity and vigor, its lasting ethical and religious import.

In 1961 Lyman moved to Pilgrim Place in Claremont, California, where she could live in community with other retired church workers. Until the end of her life she continued to give public talks, write religious and scholarly articles, and participate in the life of the church through Bible study groups and worship services. Inspiring as a model for younger women interested in ministry, scholarship, and seminary teaching, she supported the needs of women entering those fields and in so doing opened the doors of opportunity to new generations of church women.

• Various materials pertaining to Lyman are in the Burke Library at Union Theological Seminary. Along with sermon and lecture notes and the memorial written by Paul Hoon, these materials primarily comprise correspondence between Lyman and Union Seminary presidents Henry Sloan Coffin, Henry Pitney Van Dusen, and John Bennett. Lyman's books, beyond the ones mentioned above, include *Into All the World* (1956). She contributed an essay, "The Liberal Spirit in the New Testament," to *Liberal Theology: An Appraisal*, ed. David E. Roberts and Henry P. Van Dusen (1942), and contributed several articles to *Advance*, the Congregational church journal. Her inaugural address at Union is in a special issue of the *Union Seminary Quarterly Review* (Jan. 1951): 21–31. An obituary is in the *New York Times*, 11 Jan. 1975.

R. MARIE GRIFFITH

LYMAN, Phineas (1715–10 Sept. 1774), provincial general and colonizer, was born in Durham, Connecticut, the son of Noah Lyman, a weaver, and Elizabeth (maiden name unknown). Lyman's exact birthdate is unknown; he was baptized 6 Mar. 1715. After abandoning weaving, his father's craft, Lyman studied to enter Yale, graduated in 1738, and stayed on as a tutor and part-time law student until 1742. In that year he married Eleanor Dwight; they had five sons and two daughters. Lyman moved to Suffield, Connecticut, where he practiced law, held a militia commission, and became prominent in provincial politics. In 1747 he was appointed to initiate the ultimately successful process to obtain recognition that Suffield was in Connecticut, rather than Massachusetts, a province with an equally, and perhaps more, plausible claim to the town. Lyman served briefly as a deputy, one of two elected by the freemen of Suffield to the General Court of Connecticut. In 1752 he was chosen for its upper house. As one of the most active of the twelve assistants elected annually, until 1758 he negotiated with other colonies and the London government about Connecticut's wartime roles. Military duties began to divert him in 1755. War with France interrupted another of Lyman's interests, his close involvement in the schemes for westward settlement of the Susquehannah Company.

He campaigned throughout the French and Indian War. Beginning in 1755 as a major general commanding all Connecticut troops, Lyman would end his military career as commander of all provincial troops on an overseas expedition. Also in 1755 Lyman oversaw the building of Fort Edward (initially named Fort Lyman) on the Hudson River and began to construct Fort William Henry on Lake George. Connecticut troops campaigned in the vicinity of these forts through most of the war. He won acclaim in 1756 for his role in the battle of Lake George, where he converted a rout into successful resistance to the French, whose commander, Baron Dieskau, was made prisoner. Although the royal authorities in London rewarded his nominal superior (the wounded William Johnson) for the victory, Lyman gained much local credit.

His chaplain deplored Lyman's drinking on Sundays and his tolerance for his officers' foul language, but Lyman was basically a disciplinarian, insistent on clean muskets and uniforms and orderly behavior. Unlike some of his colonial peers, he saw no reason why provincial troops should not serve under regular officers nor why there should not be a standing colonial army. British officers thought well of him, as evidenced by the high provincial commands, including in 1762 the highest, with which they entrusted him, though he was never allowed to fulfill an ambition to dress as an Indian and lead a ranger unit. At Ticonderoga, where the French repeatedly threw back costly frontal attacks, many provincials sought to abandon the battlefield. Lyman's Connecticut line, by contrast, remained resolute. He took command at Ticonderoga in the following year after the French abandoned its fort. He and his men also took part in the successful campaigns against Fort Levis and Montreal in 1760. It was probably a reputation for reliability, bolstered by an excellent working relationship with Jeffrey Amherst, the British commander in chief, rather than flair for combat that caused Lyman to be given the supreme provincial command and second in command overall in the expedition against Havana in 1762.

Connecticut survivors of the victorious, but costly, Havana campaign looked to Lyman to see that land grants would reward their military service, a prospect that Amherst had encouraged and to the best of his ability supported. Lyman became spokesman for the Company of Military Adventurers, which was founded in 1763, with the purpose of obtaining enough land for a new colony in land ceded by Britain's Bourbon enemies.

Lyman sailed at once for England, where he helped secure just payments to Connecticut veterans of the prize money due for the conquest of Havana. By his own account, he was also influential in raising the northern boundary of West Florida to include the area where the Adventurers would settle. Although the 150,000 acre land grant he sought for the Adventurers eluded him, the king made him a personal grant of 20,000 acres in 1770.

The aging general lingered in England. Perhaps the most important reason for his return to Connecticut in 1772 was the fall from office of the secretary for American affairs, Lord Hillsborough, whose obdurate opposition to western settlement had stymied the ambitions of the Adventurers. Other inducements included the offer from Peter Chester, West Florida's new governor, of favorable fees to Adventurers in acquiring land, and Lyman's knowledge that his personal grant would be legally void if he did not settle it within three years.

Back in Hartford, Lyman revived the moribund Company of Military Adventurers, which dispatched two emigrant ships to the Mississippi in December 1773. Lyman was aboard and settled briefly on his plantation, "Nanachay," on the Bayou Pierre, a tributary of the Mississippi north of Natchez, before he died there of a now unidentifiable fever.

Lyman gave up a lucrative legal practice to become a soldier. His reliability and insistence on discipline earned him the respect of superior officers. At home, and eventually in England as well, he was recognized as Connecticut's premier soldier. He may not have embraced the comparatively ill-paid military career for celebrity so much as to fulfill a vision of himself as leader of a community of veterans from land-poor Connecticut. No revolutionary, although he denounced the Stamp Act, Lyman wrote of England as his mother country and saw Britain as the sole means to fulfill his vision. He did not live to see how short-lived his colonizing achievement would be; he died after successfully promoting, through his dedication and example, the largest implemented scheme for settling on the Mississippi in the revolutionary era.

• No collection of Lyman's papers is known. Details of his and his wife's forebears may be found in Lyman Coleman, *Genealogy of the Lyman Family in Great Britain and America* (1872), and William Fowler, *History of Durham, Connecticut* (1866). For Lyman at Yale, see Frank B. Dexter, *Biographical Sketches of the Graduates of Yale College with Annals of the College History, October 1701 to September 1815*, vol. 1 (1885). Information about his political life may be gleaned from Charles H. Hoadly, ed., *The Public Records of the Colony of Connecticut* (1876–1887). References to Lyman's connection with the Susquehannah Company are in Julian Boyd, ed., *Susquehannah Company Papers*, vols. 1–3, (1930–1971).

Something of Lyman's military career may be found in Lawrence H. Gipson, *The Great War for the Empire* (1949–1956), and *The Papers of Sir William Johnson*, ed. James Sullivan (1921–1965). For a chaplain's view, see John Graham's diary in *Magazine of American History* 8 (1882): 206–13. More comprehensive on Lyman himself is Delphina L. H. Clark, *Phineas Lyman: Connecticut's General* (1964).

There is information on the Havana expedition and on Lyman's settlers' organization in Albert C. Bates, *The Two Putnams: Israel and Rufus in the Havana Expedition, 1762, and in the Mississippi Exploration, 1772–1773, With Some Account of the Company of Military Adventurers* (1931). His ideas on new colonies may be found in Clarence Alvord and Clarence Carter, eds., *The New Régime, 1765–67* (1916). A secondary source relating to Lyman's Mississippi settlement is Robin F. A. Fabel, *The Economy of British West Florida, 1763–1783* (1988).

ROBIN F. A. FABEL

LYMAN, Theodore (23 Aug. 1833–9 Sept. 1897), zoologist, was born in Waltham, Massachusetts, the son of Theodore Lyman, a wealthy Bostonian political figure, and Mary Elizabeth Henderson. He received a genteel upbringing; his early formal lessons were administered in his home by private tutors, and he toured Europe from 1847 to 1849. After receiving his A.B. from Harvard College in 1855, he enrolled in Harvard's Lawrence Scientific School, where he studied corals and birds under Louis Agassiz, the noted natural scientist. In 1856 he married Elizabeth Russell, with whom he had three children. He received his S.B. from Lawrence in 1858.

In 1859 Lyman became a trustee of the Reform School, a state-run facility for wayward boys that had been endowed generously by his father. Although his formal connection with the school lasted only one year, he convinced his fellow trustees that it should be made into an institution for true reform rather than a holding pen for vicious youths. That same year he was appointed to the board of trustees of Harvard's new Museum of Comparative Zoology; he remained actively involved in the museum's affairs for almost thirty years.

By this time Lyman's research interest had shifted to serpent stars, marine invertebrates related to starfish but with arms that are much longer and more snake-like. Between 1859 and 1865 he published six papers on these deep-sea creatures, including an illustrated catalog published by the museum. From 1861 to 1863 he traveled throughout Europe collecting specimens for the museum. Upon his return he accepted a position as instructor in zoology.

Shortly thereafter, however, Lyman joined the Union army as a lieutenant colonel and served in the Army of the Potomac as an aide-de-camp to General George C. Meade. The letters he sent home, edited and published in 1922 by George R. Agassiz in *Meade's Headquarters, 1863–65: Letters of Col. Theodore Lyman from the Wilderness to Appomattox*, offer much valuable information on the daily activities and positions of the Army of the Potomac from the beginning of General Ulysses S. Grant's advance on Richmond to the surrender of General Robert E. Lee's Army of Northern Virginia at Appomattox.

After the war Lyman resumed his teaching duties at the museum and also became its treasurer, a position he held until 1872 and then again from 1874 to 1876. In 1866 he became the first chairman of the Massachusetts Commission of Inland Fisheries, an unremunerated position he held until 1883. Between 1867 and 1870 he published several studies of migratory river fish, particularly salmon, shad, and perch; in later years he reported on the possible exhaustion of sea fisheries and the progress of fish-breeding in New England's inland waters. From 1868 to 1880 and from 1881 to 1888 he served as an overseer at Harvard; in this capacity he argued emphatically that students should attend Sunday church services regularly and that they should be allowed a considerable amount of freedom when choosing their individual courses of study.

Lyman continued to study serpent stars and wrote the preliminary report on specimens of these creatures dredged up during a voyage of deep-sea exploration between Cuba and the Florida Reef in 1869. In 1875 he produced an illustrated catalog of serpent stars dredged up by American marine zoologist William Stimpson off Grand Manan Island in the Bay of Fundy in 1849 and in the North Pacific Ocean between 1853 and 1856. In 1878 and 1882 he produced similar catalogs of the serpent stars collected between 1872 and 1876 by the Challenger Expedition, a major event in the history of deep-sea exploration. In 1880 he published a list of the known genera and species of serpent stars, their similarities and differences, and the localities and depths at which they had been found. These publications established his reputation as one of the world's foremost authorities on these creatures.

Lyman was a founder and vice president of the Massachusetts Reform Club, a nonpartisan group that advocated civil service reform. In 1882 he was elected to the U.S. House of Representatives as an independent and served a single term. In 1883 he began to suffer from degenerative disease that gradually robbed him of his strength and mobility while leaving his mental faculties intact. As a result, he retired from politics at the end of his term in the House, and in 1887 he also retired from his teaching and administrative positions at the museum. Although forced to spend his remaining years as a semireclusive invalid, he continued to communicate through a secretary with his many scientific, social, and political friends until his death in Nahant, Massachusetts.

Lyman was elected to the American Academy of Arts and Sciences in 1859 and served as its treasurer from 1877 to 1883. He was elected to the National Academy of Sciences in 1872, and in 1884 he was elected president of the American Fish Cultural Association. He was also an honorary member of the New York Academy of Sciences and presided over the affairs of Boston's Thursday Evening Club for many years.

Lyman contributed to American society in several ways. As a soldier he participated in the struggle to preserve the Union, and as an amateur historian he provided much useful firsthand information on the Civil War. As a politician he sought to minimize corruption in the federal government. As a zoologist he made important contributions to the scientific body of knowledge concerning serpent stars, migratory river fish, and pisciculture.

• Lyman's papers are in the archives of the Museum of Comparative Zoology at Harvard University and the Massachusetts Historical Society. A biography and bibliography appear in Henry P. Bowditch, "Theodore Lyman," National Academy of Sciences, *Biographical Memoirs* 5 (1905): 141–53. An obituary is in the *Boston Transcript*, 10 Sept. 1897.

CHARLES W. CAREY, JR.

LYMAN, Theodore (23 Nov. 1874–11 Oct. 1954), experimental physicist, was born in Boston, Massachusetts, the son of Theodore Lyman and Elizabeth Russell. He came from a line of monied Bostonians; his great-grandfather established the family fortune through trade, and his public-spirited grandfather was variously an author, a general in the Massachusetts militia, and a mayor of Boston. Lyman's father dabbled in marine biology, served briefly as a mugwump congressman, and throughout his life busied himself with good works. His mother's family had no less distinguished a background; her father was prominent in the China trade, and her grandfather had served as minister to Sweden.

Although fascinated by electrical and mechanical gadgets, the teenage Lyman showed no especial aptitude for physics before coming under the influence of Professor Wallace C. Sabine at Harvard. Having taken his A.B. degree cum laude in 1897, Lyman was encouraged by Sabine to stay on for a Ph.D. and also suggested the topic of ultraviolet spectroscopy. His Ph.D. completed in 1900, Lyman studied at Cambridge, England, under Sir Joseph John Thomson and at Göttingen before returning to Harvard in 1902. He was to spend the rest of his life there, living unmarried on the Brookline estate built by his grandfather. Assistant professor in 1907 and full professor in 1917, Lyman was made Hollis Professor of Mathematics and Natural Philosophy in 1921. He resigned the chair in 1925, but as an emeritus professor he continued to work and teach.

Lyman devoted his research to a study of the ultraviolet, a region of the spectrum that poses severe practical difficulties. With decreasing wavelength, few substances transmit electromagnetic radiation adequately. Even fluorite, used for prisms and lenses in the pioneering work of Viktor Schumann, is inefficient and in addition had such a poorly known refractive index that accurate spectroscopy was impossible. Lyman's solution—suggested by Sabine—was to use the relatively new Rowland concave reflecting grating, which could both disperse and focus the ultraviolet light with a minimum loss of intensity. The grating was not without its own problems, however; Lyman's Ph.D. thesis and first paper presented a study of spurious spectral lines—subsequently called "Lyman ghosts"—introduced by periodic irregularities in the ruling. Strong absorption of the air presented another obstacle. Vacuum technology was still in its infancy, and all Lyman's equipment leaked. Moreover, ultraviolet light is invisible, making alignment difficult and necessitating photographic plates for detection. Yet Lyman persevered, working methodically to optimize his experiments. By 1917 he had measured hundreds of lines and extended the spectrum down to 500 Å. His most significant discovery was a series of lines in the hydrogen spectrum, today called the Lyman series, which he announced in 1914. The wavelengths of these lines fit a formula derivable from the atom structure model proposed by Niels Bohr a year previously. Lyman's work thus provided important empirical support for the fledgling quantum theory and helped establish spectroscopy as an American specialty.

Lyman's sense of gentlemanly obligation characterized his approach to the war. From 1915 to 1917 he put his money and energies into the Harvard Training Corps. In late 1917 he set out as a captain in the Signal Corps for France, where he studied sound and flash ranging for the artillery. He saw front-line service, and by his return in 1919 he was a major.

From 1919 until the end of his work as an experimentalist in the late 1930s, Lyman measured spectral lines, particularly of helium and molecular hydrogen, investigated optical properties of substances in the ultraviolet, and gradually improved the apparatus. His search for a transmitter better than fluorite was fruitless, and no major improvement in the photographic emulsions he used for ultraviolet detection occurred during his lifetime. However, with better vacuums he was able to develop his discharge source significantly, and he made many improvements in the experimental geometry.

Lyman's academic activities were not confined to research. He taught extensively and supervised graduate work, continuing both long after his official retirement, and he took a keen responsibility for the welfare of his graduate students and staff. The aptitude for organization he had demonstrated in the army served him in good stead as, with increasing seniority and the prompting of colleagues, he assumed more administrative duties. From 1910 until 1947 he was director of Harvard's Jefferson Physical Laboratory, and in the late 1920s he was tireless in his efforts to raise money for a new building. The building, which he also helped design, was completed in 1931 and renamed the Lyman Laboratory of Physics upon his retirement as director in 1947.

Between academic terms Lyman used family money to travel. Initial jaunts were primarily for amusement—he journeyed widely and was particularly proud of shooting lions in Africa. Zoologists participated in later expeditions, and although Lyman's interests remained with hunting rather than studying game, a species of stoat collected during a trip to Siberia and Mongolia was named after him.

Like his father and grandfather, Lyman was deeply aware of the duties of his social station. Much of his time was occupied with philanthropic works around the community. He served on the board of trustees of both the local hospital and lending library, donated to numerous charities, and even helped graduate students in straitened circumstances. Since he was independently wealthy, Lyman felt free to forgo pay for his work in the physics department and the Jefferson laboratory. A private and reserved man, he kept these acts of generosity to himself.

Throughout his life Lyman suffered from a frail constitution and never fully recovered from a ruptured appendix suffered while sailing to Europe in 1930. The conditions of his work left him with poor eyesight and a painful radiation burn on his hand. He led a productive life nevertheless, not content with the life of ease his wealth could have provided him. He died in Brookline, Massachusetts.

Lyman was a fellow of the National Academy of Sciences and the American Philosophical Society (Cresson Medal, 1930). He served as president of both the

American Physical Society (1921–1922) and the American Academy of Arts and Sciences (1924–1927; Rumford Medal, 1918). He was an honorary member of the Optical Society of America (Ives Medal, 1931) and the Royal Institution and was a fellow of the Royal Geographical Society.

• All Lyman's published work concerned the vacuum ultraviolet. He wrote about forty scientific papers, the most important of which are "An Explanation of the False Spectra from Diffraction Gratings," *Physical Review* 16 (1903): 257–66; "The Spectrum of Hydrogen in the Region of Extremely Short Wave Lengths," *Astrophysical Journal* 23 (1906): 181–210; and "The Spectrum of Helium in the Extreme Ultra-Violet," *Astrophysical Journal* 60 (1924): 1–14. The "Lyman series" work was announced at the Washington meeting of the Physical Society in April 1914. The abstract of this paper, "An Extension of the Spectrum in the Extreme Ultra-Violet," appeared in *Nature* 93 (1914): 241 and *Physical Review* 3 (1914): 504–5. The latter is reprinted in H. Henry Stroke, ed., *The Physical Review: The First Hundred Years* (1995). Lyman also wrote a book on the subject, *The Spectroscopy of the Extreme Ultra-Violet* (1914; 2d ed., 1928).

The most complete study of Lyman is by the physicist philosopher Percy W. Bridgman, in National Academy of Sciences, *Biographical Memoirs* 30 (1957): 237–56, which concludes with an extensive bibliography. Also noteworthy are shorter appreciations from F. A. Saunders, *Science* 121 (1955): 187–88; Otto Oldenberg, *Journal of the Optical Society of America* 45 (1955): 586–87; and John H. Van Vleck, *American Philosophical Society Yearbook, 1954* (1955).

DAVID HOWIE

LYNCH, Charles (1736–29 October 1796), planter and the man whose name probably gave rise to the phrase "lynch law," was born in Virginia (town unknown), the son of Charles Lynch and Sarah Clark, Quakers who had immigrated to Virginia from Ireland. The city of Lynchburg, Virginia, which is located at the site of Lynch's ferry over the James River, was named for a member of the family, probably his brother John Lynch. As a young man, Charles Lynch served as clerk of the Friends' South River monthly meeting, but he probably did not share the antipathy to slavery that Quakers increasingly manifested during the latter portion of the eighteenth century, and he did not scruple in April 1767 to take the oaths to qualify as a justice of the peace of Bedford County, Virginia. For taking the oaths and attempting to justify his conduct, the South River monthly meeting disowned him on 20 December 1767. Lynch lived in the portion of Bedford County that became Campbell County in 1781, and he served as a justice of the peace in the new county too. In 1755 he married Anne (or Anna) Terrell, who was also a Quaker and according to her gravestone remained a member of the Society of Friends until her death. The couple had five children.

Lynch represented Bedford County in the House of Burgesses from 1769 until the outbreak of the Revolution. He sat in the convention of 1776 that voted for independence and adopted both the Virginia Declaration of Rights and the first constitution of Virginia. He remained a member of the general assembly until January 1778. He became a colonel in the militia early in that year and served in the field under General Nathanael Greene during the closing months of the war. After the Revolution, Lynch represented a four-county district in the Virginia Senate from 1784 to 1789.

In addition to being a planter and investor in frontier lands, though never very wealthy, Lynch played an important role in the early industrial history of southwestern Virginia. In 1775 he discovered a large natural outcropping of saltpeter and erected one of the first mills on the frontier for the production of gunpowder. During the Revolution he was also partly responsible for operating the public lead mines, located in what is now Wythe County, from which a large quantity of lead was extracted, refined, and shipped to the armies in the East. The labor force at the mines consisted of a mixture of free white men from Virginia, experienced miners from Wales, hired slaves, criminals serving their sentences as miners, and slaves who had been confiscated from the estates of Loyalists.

Lynch's greatest notoriety stems from his role in 1780 in helping put down a threatened uprising in the area that is now southwestern Virginia, where fears of cooperation among English agents, Loyalists, slaves, and Indians kept the settlers in a more or less constant state of fear. One of the proximate causes of the disorder was a strike by some of the Welsh miners. In several separate incidents, Lynch and other prominent men from the region, including Robert Adams, James Callaway, and William Preston, all of whom were justices of the peace and high-ranking militia officers, rounded up suspects and gave them summary trials before informal courts. They punished some of the leaders at the whipping post, forced some of their followers into the army, extracted oaths of allegiance under duress, and in at least one instance looked aside as a group of angry settlers plundered the property of suspected Loyalists. On 24 December 1782 the general assembly of Virginia passed a special act that specifically named Lynch and the other three leading men and retroactively legitimized their proceedings. It is generally thought that the organized but extralegal punishment carried out by these men gave rise to the phrase "Lynch's Law" and all the subsequent permutations of that into the phrases "lynch law" and "judge lynch" and the verb "to lynch." The phrases initially and generally signified only organized, unauthorized punishment of reputed miscreants.

Lynch himself, so far as is known, never took credit for the term, but two years later in describing the incident he used the phrase "Lynch.s Law." It had clearly gained such currency by then that Lynch did not think that he needed to explain it; nor, evidently, did one of the state's purchasing agents when he later sent Lynch's letter to Governor Benjamin Harrison. Within a generation or two the phrases derived from "Lynch's Law" became universally known in the United States, and during the 1850s they became standard entries in both British and American dictionaries of the English language. There is, however, an alternative story about the origin of the terms. In 1780 William Lynch and several other men of Pittsylvania County, Virginia, are supposed to have signed a pact by which they pledged themselves to track down and punish a band of outlaws who were operating in that county and across the border in North Carolina. William Lynch later moved to South Carolina and in 1811 told a visitor that his participation in the Pittsylvania group had provided the basis for the phrase, which by then was famous (see Catherine Van Courtlandt Mathews, *Andrew Ellicott, His Life and Letters* [1908], pp. 220–22). What was purported to be the text of the Pittsylvania agreement was later printed in the *Southern Literary Messenger* (2 [May 1836]: 389). However, the Pittsylvania County alliance, if it was formed at all, was so obscure compared to the well-known suppression of the uprising in southwestern Virginia that Charles Lynch's use of the phrase makes it seem most probable that it was derived from his actions, not from William Lynch's.

Lynch died at his home, "Avoca," in Campbell County, Virginia.

• Reasonably accurate biographies of Lynch appear in Howell Colston Featherston, "The Origin and History of Lynch Law," *Green Bag* 12 (1900): 150–58; Thomas Walker Page, "The Real Judge Lynch," *Atlantic Monthly*, Dec. 1901, pp. 731–43; and Pauline Edwards, *Lest It Be Forgotten: A Scrapbook of Campbell County, Virginia* (1976), pp. 124–27. The family history and other useful records from the Cedar Creek and South River monthly meetings are abstracted in William Wade Hinshaw et al., eds., *Encyclopedia of American Quaker Genealogy*, vol. 6 (6 vols., 1936–1950), pp. 258, 289–90, 329–30. The events and context of the 1780 uprising are in Emory G. Evans, "Trouble in the Backcountry: Disaffection in Southwest Virginia during the American Revolution," in *The Uncivil War: The Southern Backcountry during the American Revolution*, ed. Ronald Hoffman et al. (1985), pp. 179–212, and Albert H. Tillson, *Gentry and Common Folk: Political Culture on a Virginia Frontier, 1740–1789* (1991), pp. 101–16. The 1782 act of indemnity is in William Waller Hening, ed., *The Statutes at Large of Virginia*, vol. 11 (13 vols., 1809–1823), pp. 134–35. Lynch's description of the strike at the lead mines and his use of the phrase "Lynch.s Law" are in Lynch to David Ross, 11 May 1782, now attached to William Hay to the governor, 10 June 1782, RG 3, Executive Department, Letters Received, Library of Virginia; it is not included in the microfilm edition. An abstract of the letter that does not clearly indicate who used the phrase is in William P. Palmer and Henry W. Flournoy, eds., *Calendar of Virginia State Papers and Other Manuscripts*, vol. 3 (11 vols., 1875–1893), pp. 189–90. A useful early essay is Albert Matthews, "The Term Lynch Law," *Modern Philology* 2 (Oct. 1904): 173–95.

BRENT TARTER

LYNCH, James (8 Jan. 1839–18 Dec. 1872), minister, editor, and politician, was born in Baltimore, Maryland, the son of Benjamin Lynch, a merchant and minister, and Benjamin's wife, a former slave purchased by her husband. Her name is not known. Lynch attended the elementary school operated by the Reverend Daniel A. Payne of Bethel African Methodist Episcopal (AME) Church in Baltimore. When Payne moved on in 1852, Lynch enrolled in the Kimball Union Academy in Meriden, New Hampshire.

After about two years, he later testified, his father's business failed and "we were cut short in our pursuit for knowledge by pecuniary disability" (*Christian Recorder*, 16 Feb. 1867). He taught school on Long Island for a year and then studied for the ministry with a Presbyterian minister in Brooklyn. Struggling with the decision about his future, Lynch moved to Indianapolis to work with Elisha Weaver, an AME minister with whom he would later cross paths, and occasionally swords, at the *Christian Recorder*. Grateful for his Indiana experience, Lynch committed himself to the ministry, was licensed to preach, and was assigned a small church in Galena, Illinois. In 1860 the now Bishop Payne took him east, where Lynch served a District of Columbia church and completed his studies leading to ordination. Two years later he moved to Baltimore as minister of the Waters Chapel Church, and also that year he married Eugenia Rice.

Lynch's return to the East Coast energized his editorial and speaking talents and brought him denominational attention. Challenging fellow ministers in 1862 to place the care of freedmen above petty theological disputes, he later responded to Bishop Payne's call for southern missionaries, landing in South Carolina in May 1863. His first opportunity to preach to freedmen came after a mass baptism on Hilton Head Island. He recalled, "My heart was so full I felt like it was overflowing, and there was no trouble for tears and words to run" (*Christian Recorder*, 6 June 1863).

During the next two years, Lynch established churches in South Carolina and Georgia, ministered informally and occasionally to several black regiments, including the famous Massachusetts Fifty-fourth, and helped to start schools for freedmen and their children (his sister, Jane Margaret Lynch, taught in one). Elected secretary of the AME's first southern conference, he traveled incessantly, preached and baptized, chastised and reconciled, introduced parliamentary procedure, and licensed local ministers and exhorters. After the war, Lynch faced threats of violence from defeated rebel forces and grappled with the trauma of hungry, sick, and homeless freedmen. "They need all the help, protection, advice, and prayer, that the Government, philanthropists, and Christians, can grant," he told the *Christian Recorder* (1 July 1865). He had both defamers and defenders; many in the black community believed, as one black minister wrote the same paper, "that Rev. James Lynch has done more for the elevation of the colored people in this department, than any other man" (19 Aug. 1865).

Lynch was appointed editor of the *Christian Recorder* in February 1866 and moved his family to Philadelphia. During his sixteen months with the *Christian Recorder*, it became a lively, issue-oriented paper. Early in 1867, worried by the intransigence of the Methodist Episcopal (ME) Church, South, and fearful of AME's structural weakness, Lynch tendered his services to the ME Church, North, as a southern missionary.

The AME church did not give up without a struggle; it offered him the pulpit of the mother church, Bethel Church in Philadelphia, in addition to his editorship, two highly prized and influential positions. He refused both invitations, "because I have convictions of duty to my race as deep as my soul" to go south (*Christian Recorder*, 8 June 1867). News of Lynch's denominational switch was slow to reach the faithful, but his appointment as a Republican activist, arranged by party notables, was reported within weeks.

In Mississippi, the twin challenge of evangelicalism in religion and politics suited Lynch to perfection. The ME church provided opportunities, he believed, "where white and black can meet as equals around God's altar," and he asserted that blacks wanted to work with whites but needed the franchise and equality before the law for their own protection (Gravely, *Gilbert Haven*, p. 183). Elected permanent vice president of the Mississippi Republican Convention in September 1867, he found his moderate views placed him between the Radicals, who wanted to disfranchise former rebels, and the conservatives, who resented blacks as voters and in positions of authority. During 1868, as Republican factions squabbled about proscribing whites and integrating schools, Lynch maintained his stance against proscription and integration. He started the *Colored Citizen Monthly* to appeal to blacks and stayed with the less extreme wing of the party. By mid-1869, as executive council member and vice president of the July convention, Lynch was the foremost African-American politician in the state. The convention platform represented his views, endorsing "universal amnesty and universal suffrage," free schools, and free speech.

At the same time, pressured by envious associates, he resigned as the Freedmen's Bureau state assistant superintendent for education before taking up his duties. He refused a nomination as lieutenant governor from the party's splinter wing and accepted the mainstream party's nomination for secretary of state. After a grueling fall campaign, Lynch became the first elected black official in Mississippi. In office he demonstrated his abilities as a responsible and responsive elected official. Besides handling routine duties, he began to unravel the public land confusion, a product of twenty years of neglect, to enable the state to identify taxable lands for schools and internal improvements. As a member of the Mississippi Board of Education, he played a key role in the development of a public school system that rapidly achieved success. Unwilling to depend solely on political solutions to race problems, he denounced the sharecrop system and its credit burden, which, he explained in February 1871, "leaves the laborer at the mercy of the planter, the merchant, and his own ignorance and improvidence" (quoted in Harris, 1971, p. 56). Lynch urged planters to sell surplus lands to blacks, since some planters were already seeking white purchasers for part or all of their holdings.

Lynch did not neglect his denomination. As presiding elder of the Jackson District, he saw a four-year, fourfold increase in membership, even as new districts compressed his own. He was active in the ME's 1872 national conference, opposing a proposal to create a separate conference for Georgia and Alabama blacks and urging that black ministers be considered for the episcopate. "The spirit of the age," he affirmed, demands that we "ignore all questions of color or caste" (*New York Tribune*, 5 June 1872).

His moderation and his prominence within and without the party exposed Lynch to bitter personal accusations of rape and excessive drinking, the first a specious and the second a probable charge. He consequently failed to win the party's nomination for Congress from the Jackson-Vicksburg district, yet he was reelected secretary of state and remained the state's leading African American. A delegate to the 1872 Republican National Convention, he afterward campaigned for the Grant-Wilson ticket in Indiana. Rejecting rumors of political independence, Lynch protested his loyalty, saying that Republicans represent "the only safeguard for the rights of colored people and the only real hope . . . for prosperity" (*New York Times*, 14 Sept. 1872).

Lynch's death in Jackson, from a bronchial infection and Bright's disease, was sudden and unexpected. "He lived exactly at the right time," his eulogist declaimed, since opportunities to serve his race, his country, and his God could not have been more tailored to his talents. His successor editor at the *Christian Recorder* called him "exceptionally talented—the most far-seeing man of his age we ever knew." Lynch was a builder whose forward-looking posture and performance helped a race and a region and presaged twentieth-century positions that engaged the allies of Booker T. Washington and W. E. B. Du Bois.

• No corpus of Lynch papers exists. A speech he made on 4 July 1865 was printed as a pamphlet, *The Mission of the United States Republic . . . Augusta, Georgia* (1865). William B. Gravely has edited six Lynch letters in "A Black Methodist on Reconstruction in Mississippi . . . ," *Methodist History* 11 (1973): 3–18, and "The Decision of A. M. E. Leader, James Lynch, to Join the Methodist Episcopal Church: New Evidence . . . ," *Methodist History* 15 (1977): 263–69. Daniel A. Payne included seven Lynch essays in his *The Semi-Centenary and the Retrospection of the African Methodist Episcopal Church* (1866; repr. 1972). Aside from Lynch's occasional letters to New York and Jackson, Miss., newspapers, the major source for his writing is the *Christian Recorder*, 1862–1867, especially during his editorship, Feb. 1866–June 1867. William C. Harris and Gravely have produced the best accounts of Lynch's service. Harris published "James Lynch: Black Leader in Southern Reconstruction," *Historian* 34 (1971): 40–61, followed by *The Day of the Carpetbagger: Republican Reconstruction in Mississippi* (1979). Gravely, "James Lynch and the Black Christian Mission during Reconstruction" is a chapter in *Black Apostles at Home and Abroad*, ed. David W. Wills and Richard Newman (1982). Gravely, *Gilbert Haven: Methodist Abolitionist* (1973), and Clarence Walker, *A Rock in a Weary Land: The African Methodist Episcopal Church during the Civil War and Reconstruction* (1982), add light to Lynch's denominational switch. Robert C. Morris, *Reading, 'Riting, and Reconstruction: The Education of Freedmen in the South, 1861–1870* (1981), is helpful in that area. Useful obituaries are in the *Christian Recorder*, 28 Dec. 1872, 16 Jan. 1873; and the *New National Era*, 21 Dec. 1872. A southern white opponent's tribute is in the *Jackson Weekly Clarion*, 26 Dec. 1872.

LESLIE H. FISHEL, JR.

LYNCH, James Mathew (11 Jan. 1867–16 July 1930), labor leader, was born in Manlius, New York, the son of James Lynch and Sarah Caulfield. Lynch attended the local public schools until 1884 and then, entering the trade with which he would be associated the rest of his life, became a printer's devil at the *Syracuse Evening Herald*. When he completed his apprenticeship three years later, he formed another lifelong association by joining the Syracuse local of the International Typographical Union (ITU). He was elected to two terms as local president, starting in 1889, and then seven terms as president of the Syracuse Central Trades and Labor Assembly.

Lynch was an officer of the Wahnetas, the secret society within the ITU that dominated the union, and in 1898 he was elected first vice president of the ITU. Moving to Indianapolis, the union headquarters, he married Letitia C. McVey in 1899; they had nine children. In 1900 he was elected to the first of seven two-year terms as ITU president. Lynch proved to be an able and hardworking leader. Many printing-related crafts had left the ITU to form their own unions during the decade before he took office. Under Lynch, the typesetters, who had remained in the ITU, joined the other crafts in 1911 to form the International Allied Printing Trades Association, whose label the ITU adopted. It was also during his tenure that the union established a pension system for its members, reorganized its apprenticeship system, won the eight-hour day, and expanded its retirement facility, the Union Printers' Home in Colorado Springs, Colorado. All these activities helped to double the union's membership and strengthen its finances during Lynch's years in office.

Both in his relations with management and in his politics, Lynch belonged to the more conservative wing of the labor movement. Like Samuel Gompers, the head of the American Federation of Labor (AFL), he was committed to business unionism, to the idea that labor's interests could best be served by disciplined negotiations over bread-and-butter issues like wages and working conditions, rather than by more radical schemes of political reform. Lynch served on the National Civic Federation, an organization designed to promote dialogue between management and labor. Within his own union, he went to considerable lengths to prevent confrontations with employers, drawing upon Gompers's support and even threatening his members with expulsion when they engaged in what he regarded as unjustified strikes. Lynch also worked closely with the Democratic party and in 1911 joined the Militia of Christ, an organization formed to combat socialist influence among Catholic workers.

With the backing of the New York State Federation of Labor, Lynch was nominated by Governor William Sulzer in 1913 to be New York's commissioner of labor. The state senate rejected him, but when Sulzer was impeached a few months later Lynch was renominated by the new governor and this time was confirmed. Resigning the ITU presidency in January 1914, Lynch moved his family to Syracuse, although the commissionership required him to spend most of his time in Albany. Once in office Lynch soon came under pressure from reform groups to convert a number of top positions in the department to civil service and to justify his appointments of certain unionists whom they regarded as unqualified. Lynch gave no ground, and the reformers grew increasingly critical of his management of the department. In this they received little support from their usual allies in the labor movement. The State Federation had helped put Lynch in the commissionership (along with another labor representative, John Mitchell, as head of Workmen's Compensation), and it was reluctant to criticize either man.

When the departments headed by Lynch and Mitchell merged with others to form the state Industrial Commission in 1915, both men were appointed to the five-person board heading the new commission. Later that year an investigation of a fire in a Brooklyn candy factory revealed serious flaws in the commission's enforcement and record keeping. As the official most directly responsible for the enforcement of labor laws, Lynch once again drew the criticism of reformers; this time they demanded that he be passed over when he came up for reappointment the following year. The State Federation, however, continued to value Lynch as one of the first high state officials drawn from the labor movement, and they helped ensure that he was reappointed in 1916. Even when Lynch and Mitchell took positions that organized labor had long opposed—such as their 1916 draft legislation permitting women to work more hours than the current law allowed—the State Federation continued to support them. Lynch did take some progressive stands, including supporting early efforts to establish state health insurance and pension programs. He was appointed to another term by Governor Alfred E. Smith in 1919, but he lost his position when the Industrial Commission was reorganized in 1921.

After an unsatisfying year as president of the American Life Society, an insurance company, Lynch once again became ITU president in 1924, elected as a member of the Administration party, an expanded version of the old Wahnetas faction. He served only one term, however. By this time a formal opposition party had developed within the union. This Progressive party, advocating a more militant approach to collective bargaining, had won the ITU presidency for the first time in 1922, lost it to Lynch in 1924, but defeated him when he ran for reelection in 1926. Lynch became ill shortly thereafter and suffered a heart attack in 1928, but he returned to public life in 1929 when Governor Franklin D. Roosevelt appointed him to the state Old Age Security Commission. As a member of this board, Lynch helped draw up the pension bill, which later became state law. He had written many articles for the press in the course of his life, and in 1930 he also began editing a labor newspaper, the *Syracuse Advocate*. He died in Syracuse later that year.

Lynch was a frequent traveler and enthusiastic joiner, widely known in labor circles for his portly presence, bald head, convivial manner, and fervent public speaking. In many ways he exemplified the conservative Gompers style of trade unionism, with his commitment to craft traditions and cautious politics. Yet his work for occupational safety, health insurance, and state pension laws reflected a broader view of public responsibility, one to which the labor movement would give increasing support in the years ahead.

• Papers of the International Typographical Union are in the Southern Labor Archive at Georgia State University in Atlanta. A biographical sketch of Lynch's life appears in Gary Fink, ed., *Biographical Dictionary of American Labor Leaders* (1974). See also *American Labor Legislation Review* 20, no. 3 (Sept. 1930): 236, and the files of *Typographical Journal*, particularly Aug. 1930. Information about his union can be found in Fink's *Labor Unions* (1977), 403–6, and in Seymour Lipset et. al., *Union Democracy: The Internal Politics of the International Typographical Union* (1956). A negative assessment from the left is in William Z. Foster, *Misleaders of Labor* (1927). For material on his association with the Industrial Commission, see Irwin Yellowitz, *Labor and the Progressive Movement in New York State, 1897–1916* (1965), and George Martin, *Madam Secretary: Frances Perkins* (1976). See also Marc Karson, *American Labor Unions and Politics, 1900–1918* (1958).

SANDRA OPDYCKE

LYNCH, John Roy (10 Sept. 1847–2 Nov. 1939), U.S. congressman, historian, and attorney, was born on "Tacony" plantation near Vidalia, Louisiana, the son of Patrick Lynch, the manager of the plantation, and Catherine White, a slave. Patrick Lynch, an Irish immigrant, purchased his wife and two children, but in order to free them, existing state law required they leave Louisiana. Before Patrick Lynch died, he transferred the titles to his wife and children to a friend, William Deal, who promised to treat them as free persons. However, when Patrick Lynch died, Deal sold the family to a planter, Alfred W. Davis, in Natchez, Mississippi. When Davis learned of the conditions of the transfer to Deal, he agreed to allow Catherine Lynch to hire her own time while he honeymooned with his new wife in Europe. Under this arrangement, Catherine Lynch lived in Natchez, worked for various employers, and paid $3.50 a week to an agent of Davis, keeping whatever else she earned.

On Davis's return, he and Catherine Lynch reached an agreement that her elder son would work as a dining-room servant and the younger, John Roy, would be Davis's valet. Catherine accepted these conditions, recognizing that she had no alternative. Under this arrangement, John Roy Lynch studied for confirmation and baptism in the Episcopal church, but the Civil War intervened. Lynch attended black Baptist and Methodist churches during and after the war. Because of a falling out with Davis's wife, Lynch briefly worked on a plantation until he became ill.

When Union forces reached Natchez in 1863, they freed Lynch, who was sixteen years old. He was visiting relatives at Tacony when Confederate troops overran the plantation and began seizing the ex-slaves as captives. Lynch convinced the troops that the workers had smallpox, which was a ruse, and the military released them.

Lynch worked at several jobs from 1865 to 1866, including dining-room waiter at a boarding house, cook with the Forty-ninth Illinois Volunteers Regiment, and pantryman aboard a troop transport ship moored at Natchez. Eventually he became a messenger in a photography shop, where he learned the photographic developing process as a "printer." He continued that line of work with another shop, and in 1866 he took over the full management of a photography shop in Natchez. Briefly attending a grammar school operated by northern teachers, he learned to read by studying newspapers, reading books, and listening to classes given in a white school near his shop. One of the books he studied was on parliamentary law, which fascinated him.

In 1868 Lynch gave a number of speeches in Natchez before the local Republican club in support of the new Mississippi state constitution. The constitution legitimized all slave marriages, including that of his mother and father. In his autobiography Lynch noted that the later constitution, passed by Democrats in 1890, did away with the feature that had legitimized marriages between whites and African Americans but not retroactively.

In 1869 the Natchez Republican club sent Lynch to discuss local political appointments with the state's military governor, Adelbert Ames. Impressed with Lynch's presentation, Ames appointed him justice of the peace, a position Lynch had not sought. Later that year Lynch was elected to the Mississippi House of Representatives, where he served through 1873. In his first term he sat on the Judiciary Committee and the Committee on Elections and Education. In his last term he served as Speaker of the house and earned recognition and praise from Republican and Democratic legislators and the local press. During this period he formed an alliance with Governor James L. Alcorn, a white Republican who urged his party to make common cause with black voters. Lynch worked closely with other African-Americans in the Mississippi Republican party, especially Blanche K. Bruce and James Hill. Later he fell into disagreement with Hill, who opposed Lynch's influence in the party.

Lynch was elected to Congress in 1872 and was reelected in 1874. In Congress, he impressed his colleagues with his knowledge of parliamentary procedure, unusual among the small contingent of southern African-American Republican members of Congress. Arguing forcefully for the Civil Rights Act of 1875, he called it "an act of simple justice" that "will be instrumental in placing the colored people in a more independent position." He anticipated that, given more civil rights, blacks would vote in both parties and not depend entirely on the Republican party.

Defeated in the 1876 congressional election, Lynch charged his opponent with fraud. In the election in 1880, through a series of dishonest practices, including lost ballot boxes, miscounts, and stuffed boxes, at least 5,000 votes for Lynch were wrongfully thrown out. General James R. Chalmers, a Democrat, claimed victory, but Lynch contested the election. Finally seated late in the term, Lynch served in 1882–1883. Although he was defeated for reelection in 1882 by Henry S. Van Eaton, Lynch was regarded as a political hero by the Republican party. He was the keynote speaker and temporary chairman of the 1884 national convention. Lynch was the last black keynote speaker at a national political convention until 1968.

In 1884 Lynch married Ella W. Somerville. They had one child before divorcing in 1900. From 1869 through 1905 he was successful in buying and selling real estate, including plantations, in the Natchez region. In 1889 President Benjamin Harrison appointed Lynch fourth auditor of the Treasury for the Navy Department, and he served to 1893.

In 1890 Lynch protested strongly against the "George" scheme, which, under the new Mississippi state constitution, required a literacy test for voting. An "understanding" clause also allowed registrars to pass whites and deny registration to African Americans who could not satisfactorily demonstrate an understanding of the state constitution.

In 1896 Lynch and Hill led competing delegations to the Republican National Convention. Both factions were committed to William McKinley, and through a compromise, delegates from both groups were seated at the convention. One of Hill's delegates bolted the McKinley slate, reducing the influence of the Hill "machine." After the election, McKinley gave Lynch partial control over the distribution of political patronage in the state.

Lynch began to study law in the 1890s and was admitted to the Mississippi bar in 1896. He subsequently obtained a license to practice law in Washington, D.C., where he opened an office with Robert H. Terrell, who had worked with him in the Treasury Department. He continued with this practice into 1898.

With the outbreak of the Spanish-American War, McKinley selected Lynch as an additional paymaster of volunteers with the rank of major in the army. In 1900 Lynch was again a delegate to the Republican National Convention, serving on the Committee on Platform and Resolutions and as chair of the subcommittee that drafted the national platform.

After the war Lynch remained with the army and received a regular commission in 1901. For three years he was assigned to Cuba, where he learned Spanish, then he was stationed for three and a half years in Omaha, Nebraska, and for sixteen months in San Francisco. In 1907 he sailed for Hawaii and the Philippines. In the Philippines a medical examiner claimed that Lynch had a serious heart condition and was therefore unfit for service with only a few months to live. Suspecting racial discrimination, Lynch protested directly to Washington and was reassigned to California.

Lynch retired from the army in 1911 and moved to Chicago. In 1912 he married Cora Williamson, who was twenty-seven years younger than he. They had no children. Admitted to the Chicago bar by reciprocity in 1915, he practiced law for over twenty-five years. During these years he began writing about the Reconstruction period. An early revisionist, he anticipated the later writings of W. E. B. Du Bois and the post–World War II historians, who looked at the achievements of African-American politicians in the 1860s and 1870s with more objectivity than prior historians. Lynch published several well-documented works, beginning with *The Facts of Reconstruction* (1914). Initially rejected by several presses, his critique of James Ford Rhodes's history was published in 1917 and 1918 as two articles in the *Journal of Negro History* and was republished in 1922 entitled *Some Historical Errors of James Ford Rhodes*. He also criticized as full of errors Claude G. Bowers's work *The Tragic Era* (1920). He later incorporated a large section of his 1913 history of Reconstruction in his autobiography, *Reminiscences of an active Life*, completed shortly before his death in Chicago but not published until 1970, edited by John Hope Franklin.

An accomplished African-American author and politician, Lynch was representative of a small group who worked with some success within the existing political and patronage structure to create opportunities for themselves and to fight for blacks' civil rights. Considering his childhood as a slave and his lack of formal education, his achievements as a politician, statesman, and historian are notable.

• Some Lynch correspondence is in the papers of Carter Woodson in the Manuscripts Division of the Library of Congress. Other sources include Frank C. Bell, "The Life and Times of James R. Lynch: A Case Study 1847–1939," *Journal of Mississippi History* 38 (Feb. 1976): 53–67; and Kenneth E. Mann, "John Roy Lynch, U.S. Congressman from Mississippi," *Negro History Bulletin* 37 (Apr. 1974): 239–41. An obituary is in the *New York Times*, 3 Nov. 1939.

RODNEY P. CARLISLE

LYNCH, Patrick Neison (10 Mar. 1817–26 Feb. 1882), Roman Catholic bishop, was born in Kilberidogue, Clones, County Monaghan, Ireland, the son of Conlaw Peter Lynch and Eleanor McMahon Neison, farmers. In 1819 the Lynches emigrated to Cheraw, South Carolina. Ten years later Patrick entered St. John the Baptist Seminary in Charleston. In 1833 he was sent to the Urban College of Propaganda in Rome, where on 5 April 1840 he received a doctorate in divinity and his priestly ordination. Returning to Charleston, he was named an assistant at the Cathedral of St. Finbar, editor of the diocesan newspaper, the *U.S. Catholic Miscellany*, and professor at St. John's Seminary. In 1845 he was appointed pastor of St. Mary Church in Charleston. Meanwhile he was assigned with two other priests to collect the writings of the first bishop of Charleston, John England. From 1847 to 1857 he was rector of the cathedral and of the seminary, which closed in 1851. In 1850 he began the supervision of the erection of a new cathedral and was appointed vicar general. In 1852 he was treasurer and chaplain to St. Mary's Relief Hospital for yellow fever victims.

Because of the ill health of Bishop Ignatius Reynolds, Lynch was named diocesan administrator in November 1854, and after Reynolds's death he was consecrated bishop of Charleston, on 14 March 1858. At that time the diocese comprised fourteen parishes scattered throughout North and South Carolina. By the end of 1861, Lynch had founded a school in Columbia, South Carolina, and three new parishes, but progress was stifled by the outbreak of war, the adverse effects of which occupied him for the remainder of his episcopacy.

The Charleston fire of December 1861 destroyed the new cathedral, the bishop's residence, St. John's Seminary, and five other Catholic institutions, along with about 600 Charleston homes, businesses, and public buildings. Later, while the city was under siege in 1863, Lynch successfully negotiated a prisoner exchange. In April 1864 the Confederate government named Lynch "special commissioner" with the task of securing Papal recognition, but by the time he reached Rome the Confederacy's cause was on the wane, and he never attempted to fulfill his diplomatic mission. As a Confederate agent, to be allowed to return to the United States after Appomattox Lynch would need a presidential pardon, which he received in August 1865. He found his diocese in a shambles: virtually every diocesan institution was defaced or destroyed, and diocesan indebtedness amounted to more than $376,000. As he wrote of the situation in 1865, "Rich have become poor, and the poor have sunk into misery." For the next seventeen years Lynch tried to raise money in northern urban parishes. His fundraising was so successful that, by the time of his death, only a small portion of the debt remained, and all diocesan institutions had been restored.

Like his contemporary in Florida, Bishop Augustin Verot, Lynch had written (in 1864) a prosouthern tract (*Letter of a Missionary on Domestic Slavery in the Confederate States of America*) opposing the immediate abolition of slavery but outlining the duties of masters toward their slaves. After the war, Lynch expressed deep concern for the fate of newly freed blacks, and in 1868 he established St. Peter Church in Charleston, the first black parish in the South. Despite a shortage of money and personnel, in January 1866 he initiated a plan to establish an educational, religious, and economic preserve (modeled after the Jesuit "reductions" in seventeenth- and eighteenth-century South America) for families of freedmen on Folly Island, led by two Belgian Capuchins. The hapless experiment, called the "Paraguay Village of Catholic Negroes," was defunct by early 1867 since the Capuchins returned to Europe because the colony attracted too few blacks. Lynch's Lenten Pastoral Letter of 1867 reiterated his concerns for freedmen but also frustration over his own economic inability to implement a plan for their pastoral care.

His other postwar activities included the publication of several scholarly articles on Catholic piety, Christology, ecclesiology, and even astronomy, which were published in several popular Catholic journals. He also attended the Second Plenary Council of Baltimore (1866), helped constitute the Vicariate of North Carolina (1868), and attended Vatican Council I (1869–1870). After two serious operations in 1877, his health declined. He died in Charleston.

• There is no biography of Lynch, but primary sources on him can be found in the Lynch papers and the *U.S. Catholic Miscellany*, Archives of the Diocese of Charleston. In addition to his 1864 *Letter of a Missionary . . .* , he wrote letters from Vatican I, *Catholic World* 21–22 (1869–1870), and articles on theology in *American Catholic Quarterly Review*, 1 (1876) and 7 (1882). See also the following secondary works about Lynch: Richard Madden, "Lynch, Patrick N.," *New Catholic Encyclopedia*, vol. 8 (1967), pp. 1111–12; Jeremiah Joseph O'Connell, *Catholicity in the Carolinas and Georgia* (1879); Richard C. Madden, *Catholics in South Carolina: A Record* (1985); Michael J. McNally, "A Peculiar Institution: A History of Catholic Parish Life in the Southeast, 1850–1980," in *The American Catholic Parish*, ed. Jay Dolan, vol. 1 (1987); James J. Hennesey, *The First Council of the Vatican: The American Experience* (1963); Hugh McElrone, "Bishop Lynch," *Catholic World* 35 (Apr.–Sept. 1882): 160–69; and Willard E. Wight, ed., "Some Wartime Letters of Bishop Lynch," *Catholic Historical Review* 43 (1957–1958): 20–37.

MICHAEL J. MCNALLY

LYNCH, Thomas (1727–Dec. 1776), member of the Continental Congress, was born in South Carolina, the son of Thomas Lynch and Sabina Vanderhorst, planters. Presumably educated in the colony, he inherited several productive rice plantations in the late 1730s, to which he added land grants totaling more than 10,000 acres. Most of his holdings were in the northeastern part of the province near Georgetown, but he owned land in Georgia and Florida as well as a house in Charleston. He was primarily a rice and indigo planter, but his diverse economic interests included rental property and shares in three vessels. First elected to the South Carolina Commons House in 1752, he served in the legislature thereafter (with the exception of 1761 when he declined to take his seat) until his death. Throughout this period—during most of which he represented the parish of Prince George Winyah—his frequent appointment to important committees marked him as one of the most active and influential members of the house.

Lynch's commitment to the local legislature also made him a staunch defender of its rights and privileges. Thus when Parliament imposed a stamp tax on the colonists, the South Carolina Commons House chose him as one of its three representatives to the Stamp Act Congress that met in New York in 1765; his fellow delegates were Christopher Gadsden and John Rutledge. Because Lynch apparently opposed an implicit acknowledgement of Parliament's jurisdiction over the colonies, he believed that the meeting should address only the Crown. But he served on—and probably acted as chairman of—the committee that drafted the petition to the British House of Commons requesting repeal of the Stamp Act. Three years later, during the crisis over the Townshend duties, Lynch became one of the organizers of the movement in South Carolina against Parliament's next attempt to tax the colonists. A member of the general committee to oversee a nonimportation agreement, Lynch favored strict enforcement of its terms. His stance appealed more to the artisans than to the merchants of Charleston, and the former helped to elect him when in July 1774 a general meeting of the populace chose representatives to the First Continental Congress.

Lynch served in both the First and Second Continental Congresses. At the former, he vehemently denied the right of Parliament to regulate colonial trade; but as a realist, he had little patience with enthusiasts like his colleague at the Second Continental Congress, Christopher Gadsden, who had gone back to South Carolina, Lynch reported, "to Command our Troops, God Save them" (Smith, vol. 3, p. 126). Lynch himself, who appeared a decade older than he was, impressed others as a "firm, judicious Man" (J. Adams, *Diary*, vol. 2, p. 117). Sam Adams termed him virtuous, and another delegate to the First Continental Congress, Silas Deane, stated that Lynch was "above Ceremony, and carries with him more Force in his very appearance, than most powdered Folks, in their Conversation" (Smith, vol. 1, p. 34). "Very obstinate" was the description preferred by British officials.

As late as January 1776 Lynch remained flexible enough to engage in serious but unsuccessful talks with Thomas Lord Drummond, a Scotsman who acted as an unofficial intermediary between British authorities and several members of Congress. Reported to have observed that if negotiations with the British failed, "we shall be obliged to set up a Republic"—the governmental form "best in Idea, [but] bad in Experiment" (Klein, p. 365)—Lynch would obviously have preferred a compromise solution to the imperial crisis that would have preserved colonial rights within the empire. In the interim, however, he sent his son instructions for making gunpowder and served on several congressional committees charged with the oversight of military affairs. Lynch suffered a stroke on 20 February 1776. An acquaintance who visited him several months later observed that it was "shocking to see a man whose opinion at one moment swayed Millions & the next he himself under the direction of Doctors & Nurses" (Rogers, p. 112). Lynch died in Annapolis while attempting to return to South Carolina. His son, Thomas Lynch, Jr., who had also been elected to the Continental Congress, signed the Declaration of Independence.

Lynch's private life is less well documented. His first marriage to Elizabeth Allston occurred in 1745; they had three children. After Elizabeth's death, Lynch in 1755 married Hannah Motte, whose father was the provincial treasurer. Lynch and his second wife had one child. That Lynch sent his son to England for schooling and stipulated in his will that his plantation was to remain forever in the family—heirs always to take the name of Lynch—reveal some of his personal values. But it was his public role that made Lynch important to his contemporaries, for they clearly considered him to have been one of the most influential advocates of American rights in prerevolutionary South Carolina.

• No substantial collection of Lynch papers survives, but scattered correspondence appears in Paul H. Smith, ed., *Letters of Delegates to Congress, 1774–1779*, vols. 1–3 (1976–1978). The *Diary and Autobiography of John Adams*, ed. L. H. Butterfield (4 vols., 1962), also mentions him frequently. Useful secondary works include Milton M. Klein, "Failure of a Mission: The Drummond Peace Proposal of 1775," *Huntington Library Quarterly* 35 (1972): 343–80, and George C. Rogers, Jr., *The History of Georgetown County, South Carolina* (1970).

ROBERT M. WEIR

LYND, Helen Merrell (17 Mar. 1896–30 Jan. 1982), sociologist and social philosopher, was born in LaGrange, Illinois, the daughter of Edward Tracey Merrell and Mabel Waite. After serving briefly as the editor of a small Congregationalist journal, her father moved from one nondescript job to another, while her mother supplemented his meager income by taking in boarders. Raised a strict Congregationalist, Lynd rebelled against her parents' narrow provincialism, especially concerning sexual behavior. Throughout her later work, a former colleague later commented, Lynd ran a protest against "cautious . . . Protestant forebears, who interpreted Christianity as a restraint on her vitality." But Lynd herself also remembered her parent's opposition to social injustice in their small midwestern town. Their vision of humanity, without regard to race, class, or nation, laid a basis for a holistic vision of human behavior that profoundly shaped her later thought. After the family moved to Framingham, Massachusetts, Lynd attended nearby Wellesley College (B.A. 1919), where she was especially influenced by Mary S. Case, who introduced her to philosophy, particularly Hegel. "Miss Case with my father," she later reminisced in an interview, "were the great influences in my life."

After teaching school for two years, Lynd began graduate work at Columbia, where she eventually earned an M.A. (1922) and Ph.D. (1944) in history. In 1921 she married Robert S. Lynd, a divinity student at Union Theological Seminary and later a distinguished sociologist, with whom she collaborated on the two studies of Muncie, Indiana, for which they were best known: *Middletown: A Study in Contemporary American Culture* (1929) and *Middletown in Transition: A Study of Cultural Conflicts* (1937). Climaxing work in the social survey tradition, *Middletown* broke new ground by applying methods derived from recent British and American anthropology to a contemporary American community. Although the sponsoring committee, the Rockefeller Foundation's Institute of Social and Religious Research, repudiated the project, judging the initial manuscript to be too diffuse and possibly irreligious, it was soon hailed as a classic of sociological research. For her part in the project, Helen Lynd joined her husband and three other researchers in Muncie from January 1924 through June 1925 and later contributed to the analysis and writing to a point where it was difficult to distinguish her contribution from his (even though, in awarding Robert a Ph.D. in 1931 for the work, Columbia required him to pencil out the portions she had written). Although Helen Lynd did not return to Muncie for the follow-up study in the summer of 1935, she helped analyze the findings and contributed substantially to the writing of *Middletown in Transition*.

With a versatility increasingly rare in academia, Lynd during the 1940s and 1950s turned from sociology to history, psychology, and social philosophy. In *England in the Eighteen Eighties* (1945), a study inspired by work under Columbia historian Carleton J. H. Hayes, she described the shift in English opinion during that decade from a negative to a positive conception of freedom to be realized through vigorous state action. Applying to an entire country and an earlier period the methods of social analysis developed in the Middletown studies, Lynd challenged conventional portraits of the decade as one of political reaction. In *Field Work in College Education* (1945) she argued that "field work," as exemplified by students at Sarah Lawrence who developed off-campus projects in the arts and the social and natural sciences, was an essential component of a liberal education, opposing it to the "great books" curriculum at St. John's College (Annapolis) and to narrowly conceived "practical" and "technical" work.

In *On Shame and the Search for Identity* (1958) and numerous reviews during the 1950s, Lynd continued to criticize the growing cult of "conformity" and "adjustment" as represented in psychology by Harry Stack Sullivan and other contemporary psychologists, who, she alleged, treated human personalities as separate entities while ignoring the dynamic relations among them. Her starting point was a distinction between guilt and shame: the first the result of violating a specific code, the second of a wound to one's self-esteem. Experiences of shame, however painful, she argued, provided insight into unrecognized aspects of society and the world. Shame thus could provide clues not to what a person is, but what he or she might become. In exploring the problems of identity in modern society, one reviewer noted, the book joined the distinguished company of Erich Fromm's *Escape from Freedom*, Erik Erikson's *Childhood and Society*, and David Riesman's *The Lonely Crowd*.

From 1928 to 1965 Lynd taught social philosophy at Sarah Lawrence. The prefix "social," she later explained, allowed her to "follow any possible road to discovery." It also signaled her own commitment to social activism. During the McCarthy era, she came under attack from the local American Legion, who demanded that Sarah Lawrence fire her for alleged communist sympathies. By her own later account, the only evidence was various petitions she had signed and the fact that for several years she had served as possibly the only nonparty member of New York Teachers Union. In March 1953 she was also summoned, along with twelve other members of the Sarah Lawrence Faculty, before Senator William Jenner's Internal Security Subcommittee, where, to her later regret, she testified that she had not been a Communist party member rather than decline to answer on Constitutional grounds. Writing in the *American Scholar* four years earlier, she already had condemned the dismissal of several faculty members at the University of Washington for alleged communist sympathies. In one of the reviews collected in *Toward Discovery* (1965), she wrote that freedom "in a democracy is not a dispensable luxury to be enjoyed at such times as the society is secure and untroubled, but rather, is itself the basis of security and survival." In other essays and public addresses she elaborated the theories of society and education that informed her scholarly work, insisting always on the human potential for self-discovery and development and on the importance of seeing issues in ever larger contexts. Learned as well as humane, Lynd illustrated her points with copious references and quotations from European philosophy and literature.

Although Lynd rarely if ever addressed issues of feminism or the situation of women in her published work, she was an important representative of the generation of American women professionals whose careers spanned the decades from the 1920s through the 1950s. The tensions inherent in this role were, for Lynd, a source of creativity and insight. Her work, remarked political scientist Susanne Hoeber Rudolph, was distinguished by a "sensory concreteness," an attention to "the feeling tone of any situation as much or more as its factual or logical side," the former being "a kind of knowing which some would say is purely feminine." Reviewing her own life, Lynd likewise saw herself torn between a quest for "largeness and relatedness" and "concentration on detail." Praising her combination of sympathy and analysis, historian Bert James Loewenberg observed that she "transformed openness to experience into a rigorous analytical discipline." Although Lynd's professional reputation remained inextricably bound up with that of her husband on the Middletown studies, the tension between personal understanding and meticulous scholarship in *On Shame and the Search for Identity* and her other published work earned her a distinct if minor place among the social theorists of her generation.

Dedicated to her family no less than to her career, Lynd remained married to Robert until his death in 1970. They had two children, one of whom (Staughton) gained prominence as an historian and social activist during the 1960s. She died in Warren, Ohio.

• The Manuscript Division of the Library of Congress holds a collection of the papers of Robert S. and Helen Lynd. The Oral History Archive at Columbia contains interviews with Helen Lynd, a version of which is printed in Helen M. Lynd, *Possibilities* (1983). Selections from Lynd's published and previously unpublished work are collected in *Toward Discovery*, ed. Bert James Loewenberg (1965). Although no formal study of Lynd's career exists, her work in connection with the

Middletown studies is discussed in passing in Maurice R. Stein, *The Eclipse of Community* (1960), and Dwight W. Hoover, *Middletown Revisited* (1990). Obituaries are in the *Chicago Tribune*, 2 Feb. 1982, and the 15 Feb. 1982 issues of *Newsweek*, *Time*, and *AB Bookman's Weekly*.

ROBERT C. BANNISTER

LYND, Robert Staughton (26 Sept. 1892–1 Nov. 1970), sociologist and social commentator, was born in New Albany, Indiana, the son of Staughton Lynd, a banker, and Cordelia Day. Lynd grew up in Louisville, Kentucky. He attended Princeton University and, on his graduation in 1914, took a job as an assistant editor of *Publishers Weekly*. After four years at the magazine, Lynd served in the field artillery in World War I but failed to see combat. He was hospitalized for unidentified reasons, and while recovering he appears to have resolved that his calling was to help people. The experience in the ward, he recalled in an anonymous *Harper's* magazine article of 1921, "'sold' me completely—in the lingo of business—on the satisfactoriness . . . of service directly among people."

After the war Lynd resumed work in publishing, first at Charles Scribner's Sons and then at the *Freeman Magazine*. He entered Union Theological Seminary in 1920, declaring himself a Unitarian in contrast to his family's traditional Presbyterianism. He studied under the preacher Harry Emerson Fosdick, among others, and took a course at Columbia University with philosopher John Dewey, whose ideas about collective experience and social learning shaped his thinking long afterward. In 1922 Lynd married Helen Merrell, who later worked closely with him on the community studies in Muncie, Indiana; they had two children. Lynd received a D.D. from Union in 1923.

During the summer of 1921 Lynd worked as a missionary preacher in Elk Basin, Montana, and developed the participant-observer persona that would characterize his sociological fieldwork. Two published accounts of the experience present contrasting impressions: "Crude Oil Religion" (*Harper's*, Sept. 1922, pp. 425–34) portrays a ditch-digging preacher who praises the roustabouts' friendliness, while "Done in Oil" (*Survey Graphic*, Nov. 1922) is an exposé of oil-field conditions and practices.

In 1922 the Committee on Social and Religious Surveys (later the Institute of Social and Religious Research) sponsored an investigation of the social and religious life of an as-yet-unnamed small city. Appointed director of the study in 1923, Lynd completed the research with his wife the following year. Although their emphasis on an anthropological rather than religious orientation concerned many of their colleagues, the institute finally agreed to endorse *Middletown*'s publication in 1929. In the meantime Robert Lynd had become an administrator at the Social Science Research Council in New York in 1927.

Middletown, the Lynds' functionalist study of Muncie, Indiana, presented the overwhelmingly white town as a representative community, a depiction that conflicted with the urban ethnic diversity more common elsewhere. The small-town world of the 1890s was counterpoised to that of the 1920s in the areas of work, leisure, religion, social life, and material consumption. Time after time the authors concluded that the earlier era had supported collective harmony and individual identity while the later period showed that the forces of mass marketing and industrial standardization had exacted a severe toll. According to the Lynds, conformity and material consumption mattered more to Middletowners than ideas, beliefs, or collective identity.

The book sold well and was taken by many to endorse the view of small-town middle provincialism that novelist Sinclair Lewis had popularized in *Babbitt* (1922) and *Main Street* (1920). H. L. Mencken titled one of his two reviews "A City in Moronia," and delighted in the evidence that he believed the Lynds had lent to his critique of the "booboisie." While the Lynds were critical of their subjects, the endorsement of such a perspective does not appear to have been their goal. The success of *Middletown* led to Lynd's appointment as Giddings Professor of Sociology at Columbia University in 1931, a title that he held until 1960. Earlier that year Columbia had granted him a Ph.D. after submission of portions of *Middletown* as a dissertation and then hired him in the hope that his survey methodology could rejuvenate the department. Lynd began two other projects but neither saw completion, in part because Lynd neither endorsed the statistical approach favored by many sociologists of the time nor proposed an alternative course.

The return of the Lynds to Muncie in 1935 in order to add an appendix to *Middletown* resulted in the full-length *Middletown in Transition* (1937). Reinforcing the view of the earlier book, the work pointed up repeated instances of nativism, conformity, and anti-intellectualism. The close and supportive community of the 1890s, which was held up as a prospect for renewal in *Middletown*, does not figure in the later volume, leaving the impression of hopelessness on the authors' part. They conclude the book with an image, borrowed from the historian R. H. Tawney, of the city walking "reluctantly backwards into the future, lest a worse thing should befall them."

Lynd changed direction in his next and final book. Originally given as the Stafford Little Lectures at Princeton University in 1938, *Knowledge for What?* (1939) issued a challenge to American social science. It called for increased activism, fewer fact finders, more problem-centered investigative organization, and less disciplinary purity. In sum, the work endorsed the social engineering perspective that was distrusted by Lynd's department chair Robert MacIver and absent only a decade before in *Middletown*. Believing that experts could enhance the lives of the masses, Lynd called on social scientists to investigate the "large and pervasive extension of planning and control to many areas now left to casual individual initiative" (p. 209).

In all of his work Lynd sought to analyze society for the purpose of changing it. Paradoxically, after giving up formal religion early on, he spent his life searching for a secular system of meaning to replace the church. And although he moved easily among elites, the implications of class differences informed his scholarship. His egalitarian politics, however, never extended to the Marxism of his Columbia colleague C. Wright Mills. In spite of his pioneering work in *Middletown*, Lynd spawned no "school" of sociology. He continued to write on questions of political power and the place of technology in modern society, but published no books after 1939. His own ambivalence about the masses notwithstanding, Lynd remained committed to the idea of social betterment even as he was unsure about the possibilities for its realization. He died in Warren, Connecticut.

• Lynd's papers are in the Library of Congress. Records that relate to his work under the auspices of the Institute of Social and Religious Research are at the Rockefeller Archive Center, Pocantico Hills, N.Y. For biographical details, see Richard Wightman Fox, "Epitaph for Middletown: Robert S. Lynd and the Analysis of Consumer Culture," in *The Culture of Consumption: Critical Essays in American History, 1880–1980*, ed. Fox and T. J. Jackson Lears (1983), pp. 101–41. A special issue of *Journal of the History of Sociology* 2 (Fall-Winter 1979–1980) is devoted to Lynd. The entire issue of *Indiana Magazine of History* 74 (Dec. 1979) discusses the Lynds and Muncie. An obituary is in the *New York Times*, 3 Nov. 1970.

JOHN M. JORDAN

LYNDE, Benjamin (5 Oct. 1700–5 Oct. 1781), jurist, was born in Salem, Massachusetts, the son of Benjamin Lynde, Sr., a jurist, and Mary Browne. His father was a justice (1712–1729) and chief justice (1729–1745) of the Superior Court of Judicature for Massachusetts. Lynde entered Harvard in 1714, graduated four years later, and received his M.A. in 1721. He studied law with an uncle, Judge Samuel Browne. Lynde early held various local offices, including moderator of the town meeting in Salem and town treasurer. From 1721 to 1729 he was naval officer for the port of Salem, and in 1729 he was made a justice of the peace for Essex County. He served three annual terms in the Massachusetts legislature, the General Court, 1728–1731, during which time he was a member of a committee for retaining John Wilkes as an agent for the colony in London. In 1731 Lynde married Mary Bowles Goodridge; they had three children.

On 28 June 1734 Lynde was appointed special judge of the Inferior Court of Common Pleas for Suffolk County. In 1739 he switched over to the same position for Essex County, where he stayed until elevated to the colony's highest court in 1746. He was an agent lobbyist representing Massachusetts at a conference of royal commissioners that met in September 1737 in Hampton, New Hampshire, to arbitrate the boundary dispute between Massachusetts and New Hampshire.

Lynde was elected a member of the Massachusetts Council on 25 May 1737 by the colony's General Court. When supporters of the Land Bank (a scheme to issue bills of credit secured by borrowers' land) gained control of the Massachusetts legislature in the election of 1740, sixteen of eighteen Massachusetts councilors lost their seats, including Lynde, who had joined Governor Jonathan Belcher's opposition to the bank. The Land Bank scheme soon collapsed and was declared illegal by the British government. In the controversy Lynde sided with the merchant-creditor interest versus the small landholders, and he recovered his council seat in 1743.

Whether councilor or judge, Lynde had a reputation of being consistently a "prerogative" man—one who sided with the royal governor and unquestioningly upheld Crown authority. In 1748 Governor William Shirley sent Lynde and three others to the lower house (the house of representatives) to solicit approval for censorship of a newspaper, the *Independent Advertiser*, which had attacked the governor's war policies. The lower house flatly rejected this proposal.

Lynde was commissioned a superior court justice on 24 January 1746 and filled a seat that had become vacant with the death of his father the year before. The superior court was almost entirely appellate, having original jurisdiction only in cases that involved the Crown. Lynde and Thomas Hutchinson were among the judges who, as John Adams described in March 1817, "in their new fresh Robes of Scarlet English Cloth . . . and immense judicial Wiggs," rendered the verdict upholding the use of writs of assistance in Massachusetts at the 1761 trial made famous by James Otis, who opposed the writs.

As a jurist Lynde sought to avoid confrontation with the legislature. During the Stamp Act crisis, the house of representatives declared that the courts should remain open, even without use of the stamps for judicial documents required by the Stamp Act. The council refused to concur until the superior court made a decision on the issue. Undoubtedly reflecting the influence of Lynde, the superior court, in its March 1766 session, merely went through the motions of business, hearing only one case and postponing all others. The question became moot when news arrived in May 1766 of the repeal of the Stamp Act. Councilors frequently served in other government capacities, and in 1766 this plural officeholding came under fire. When the popular faction in the house of representatives succeeded in removing the attorney general, the secretary, and the treasurer of the province from the council, Lynde anticipated his own removal and resigned from the council.

In October–December 1770, at the trials of the British soldiers involved in the Boston Massacre, Lynde served as the presiding judge in place of Lieutenant Governor and Chief Justice Hutchinson, who had removed himself from the court because he was acting governor. Lynde twice tried to resign rather than sit on these trials, but Hutchinson persuaded him to stay on. Hutchinson considered Lynde a "timid" person and thought that "little matters as well as great frighten Lynde" (Wroth and Zobel, vol. 3, p. 14). Although Adams's defense is credited as the major factor in the acquittal of murder charges for all the accused and only manslaughter convictions for two of the soldiers,

Judge Lynde contributed to the outcome by charging the jury that the soldiers could be held accountable individually rather than collectively. He reminded the jury in addition that the soldiers had been lawfully assembled and provoked by a mob. At the trial of Captain Thomas Preston, Lynde was "deeply affected, that this affair turns out so much to the disgrace of every person concerned against him [the defendant], and so much to the shame of the town in general" (Wroth and Zobel, vol. 3, p. 98).

When Hutchinson's appointment as governor became official, Lynde was commissioned chief justice on 21 March 1771. He served in this capacity less than a year, resigning from the superior court because at age seventy-two he considered himself too old to "ride the Circuit." He also did not like being at the center of the controversy over payment of judges' salaries directly by the Crown instead of by the previous method, appropriation of the legislature. On 15 January 1772 he accepted appointment to the less demanding post of judge of probate for Essex County, an office he held until the beginning of the American Revolution. During the Revolution, Lynde, though sympathetic to the Loyalists, kept a neutral position. For their better protection, he moved his family in January 1777 to live with Israel Smith's family in Danvers for the duration of the war.

Known for his learning, Lynde was a contributor to Thomas Prince's *Chronological History of New England* (1736), and he was a ruling elder of the First Church in Salem. Also noted for his charity, he provided a fire engine for Salem, held membership in a society that employed poor people in Boston to manufacture linen, donated a year's salary as town treasurer for the improvement of education, and presented six folio volumes of the "Statutes of England" to the legislature. Lynde had substantial real estate holdings, including a mansion in Salem and a summer home on a rocky prominence south of the town, where he also had an observatory. He owned part of Thompson Island in Boston harbor, owned a farm in Brimfield (through his wife's inheritance), and was one of twenty proprietors of the Lincolnshire Company, which owned the Muscongus Patent in Maine.

Lynde died in Salem, Massachusetts, from injuries inflicted by a kick of a horse. His was a life in the law. Much respected as a judge, he nevertheless remains obscure because of his reticence to enter the political debates of the revolutionary era and because he produced no body of public writings.

• Records relating to Lynde as a member of the Massachusetts high court are in the clerk's office, Massachusetts Supreme Judicial Court for Suffolk County, Boston, and selectively in L. Kinwin Wroth and Hiller B. Zobel, eds., *Legal Papers of John Adams* (3 vols., 1965). Biographical sketches are in F. E. Oliver, ed., *The Diaries of Benjamin Lynde and of Benjamin Lynde, Jr., with an Appendix* (1880), John H. Sibley, *Biographical Sketches of Those Who Attended Harvard College*, vol. 6 (1873; repr. 1942); and A. C. Goodell, "A Biographical Notice of the Officers of Probate in Essex County from the Commencement of the Colony to the Present Time," *Historical Collections of the Essex Institute* 3 (Aug. 1861): 149–52. William T. Davis, *History of the Judiciary of Massachusetts* (1900), has fragmentary mention of Lynde. Regarding the best-known cases, see M. H. Smith, *The Writs of Assistance Case* (1978), and Zobel, *The Boston Massacre* (1970). Implications of the political context for Lynde's roles as judge and councilor are noted in John A. Schutz, *William Shirley: King's Governor of Massachusetts* (1961); Malcolm Freiberg, *Prelude to Purgatory: Thomas Hutchinson in Provincial Massachusetts Politics, 1760–1770* (1990); Francis G. Walett, "The Massachusetts Council, 1766–1774: The Transformation of a Conservative Institution," *William and Mary Quarterly* 6 (1949): 605–27: and Thomas Hutchinson, *The History of the Province of Massachusetts Bay*, vol. 3, *1749–1774* (1828; repr. 1972). A death notice is in the *Salem Gazette*, 18 Oct. 1781.

HARRY M. WARD

LYNDE, Paul (13 June 1926–9 Jan. 1982), actor and comedian, was born Paul Edward Lynde in Mount Vernon, Ohio, the son of Hoy C. Lynde, a butcher shop owner, and Sylvia Bell. His adolescent years included some time spent working for his father beheading and plucking chickens. His father, mother, and a brother died within a three-month span while Lynde was still a schoolboy. A high school teacher recognized his theatrical talents and encouraged him to pursue an acting career. In 1944 he enrolled in the Speech and Drama School at Northwestern University, where, he would later tell interviewers, he found that every time he tried to perform serious drama he drew unwanted laughs from his classmates. He thus made comedy his lifetime specialty. At graduation in 1948 he was named Best Student Actor of the Year.

Bachelor's degree in suitcase, Lynde moved to New York City and took up residence in a decidedly unposh hostel with a communal kitchen. He lived hand-to-mouth for a couple of years, receiving some money from home, clerking at B. Altman's, lining up with the winos to sell blood for $5 every six weeks, and doing other odd jobs as he could find them. Then in late 1950 he entered an amateur contest at the nightclub Number One Fifth Avenue with an original comic monologue depicting a tattered tourist just back from an African safari who, despite getting clawed and gored and losing his wife to a waterfall, was happy because "it didn't rain and I got some *dandy* snapshots." This would launch him on the first stage of his professional career. Not only did he win the contest and get an engagement, but he also performed that piece on "The Ed Sullivan Show" and in Leonard Sillman's revue *New Faces of 1952*, which was adapted in 1954 into a movie in which Lynde appeared. This, alongside the summer stock circuits and some additional sketch-writing work with Sillman, characterized the takeoff of Lynde's professional life throughout the 1950s.

Another high point was his performance as Henry MacAfee, the beleaguered father of a starry-eyed teenager and reluctant host to the eponymous rock idol in the Broadway hit *Bye, Bye Birdie* (1960). "Paul Lynde," wrote Brooks Atkinson in a *New York Times* review of the show, "contributes to the merriment of the nation by simulating indignation and provincial fatuity." He repeated the role in the 1963 movie version. He also appeared in several other movies in the 1960s, including *Under the Yum-Yum Tree* (1963), *Send Me No Flowers* (1964), and *How Sweet It Is* (1968). In 1968 he bought the Hollywood mansion that had once been Errol Flynn's.

Several memorable television characters became associated with Paul Lynde in the 1960s and 1970s. On "Bewitched," he was the mischievous warlock Uncle Arthur. On "The Paul Lynde Show," which lasted a single season in 1972, he was attorney Paul Simms, perpetually pitted against his save-the-earth hippie son-in-law Howie in the classic intergenerational conflict of the era. "He was, in fact, getting laughs out of straight lines," *Variety* critic Bob Knight wrote, so well had he perfected "his fussy, prissy caricature of the horrified square adult." Lynde starred as the snarling hospital administrator Dr. Mercy on the short-lived "Temperature's Rising." He was also seen regularly in the center spot of the giant tic-tac-toe board of "Hollywood Squares," and his voice could be heard as the nefarious Hooded Claw on "The Perils of Penelope Pitstop" and Templeton the rat in the animated movie *Charlotte's Web* (1973). During those years he never gave up performing nationally on live stages. The American Guild of Variety Artists honored him as Entertainer of the Year for 1975. At the time of his death, there was talk of another television series in which he would play a TV gossip columnist.

Unfortunately, Paul Lynde had a drinking problem through stretches of his life and occasionally got his name in the papers for skirmishes with law-enforcement officers. He identified himself as a confirmed bachelor and at times spoke to interviewers of his difficulties with personal relationships. He died in bed from a massive heart attack at the age of fifty-five. But for all the sorrows of his personal life, he succeeded in being best known for his faith in the power of comedy. "The way things are today," he was quoted as saying, "we live in a world that needs laughter, and I've decided if I can make people laugh, I'm making [an] important contribution."

• A clipping file on Lynde is at the Billy Rose Theatre Collection at the New York Public Library for the Performing Arts, Lincoln Center. A lengthy entry on him appears in the Nov. 1972 edition of *Current Biography*. He also had a listing in the 1978–1979 edition of *Who's Who in America*. Articles on Lynde appeared in the *New York Sunday News*, 28 Aug. 1960, the *New York World Telegram and Sun*, 20 May 1961, and the *Wilmington (Del.) Evening Journal*, 12 Sept. 1972. An obituary is in the *New York Post*, 12 Jan. 1982.

BEN ALEXANDER

LYNES, George Platt (15 Apr. 1907–6 Dec. 1955), publisher and photographer, was born in East Orange, New Jersey, the son of Joseph R. Lynes, a clergyman, and Adelaide Sparkman. Aspiring to a literary career, at age eighteen Lynes wrote to Gertrude Stein, beginning a long correspondence. In 1925 he visited her and

Alice B. Toklas at Stein's summer residence in Bilignin, France. Lynes memorialized the visit in a photograph, while Stein referred to Lynes in her book *The Autobiography of Alice B. Toklas* (1933). Stein encouraged Lynes and introduced him to literary and artistic members of the avant-garde of New York and France. When he returned to the United States in 1926, he spent a year at Yale but became disenchanted with formal education. With the help of patrons Edith Finch and Jane Heap, he started a publishing company, As Stable Publications, and printed Stein's *Descriptions of Literature* and Ernest Hemingway's first play, *Today Is Friday*.

Lynes changed the object of his attention to photography, and in 1927 he worked as an assistant to a (now unknown) photographer in Englewood, New Jersey. His first photographs were of friends and family. That year Lynes also opened Park Place Book Shop in Englewood, which was funded by Finch. In 1928 Lynes traveled to Villefranche-sur-Mer, France, with writer Glenway Wescott and publisher Monroe Wheeler. Lynes's photographic documentation of the artists and patrons he met during this trip was the beginning of his career in portraiture. His experimental techniques showed the influence of surrealism. Since Lynes's sitters were acquaintances, friends, and lovers, he was often able to evoke personality in his portraits. According to James Crump, "It was to his credit that Lynes often succeeded in transcending simply the biographical information about his sitters, leaving a visually stunning image resonating with psychological intensity" (p. 142).

Lynes took Stein's portrait in 1928; in 1931, frustrated with Man Ray, she appointed Lynes her official photographer. Some of Lynes's other subjects include Colette (1930), Jean Cocteau (1936), E. M. Forster (1936), George Balanchine (1941), Dorothy Parker (1943), Tennessee Williams (1944), Katherine Anne Porter (1945), and e. e. cummings (1947).

Lynes's career took off in 1931, when Julien Levy included his work in the first American exhibition of surrealist work, "Newer Super-Realism." Afterwards Levy featured Lynes's work in an exhibition at his New York gallery. Levy's support led in 1932 to the inclusion of Lynes's modernist photographs in "Murals by American Painters and Photographers," the first exhibition of photography at the Museum of Modern Art. Lynes's contribution, "Landscape," was an eight-by-sixteen-foot surrealist mural of a natural landscape superimposed on two male nudes posing as classical Greek statues. In 1932 Lynes had his first solo exhibition at the Leggett Gallery; it was followed by a two-man show with Walker Evans at the Julien Levy Gallery. Levy included Lynes in the "International Photographers" exhibition at the Brooklyn Museum and in his exhibition "New York by New Yorkers." In 1936 Lynes was firmly identified as a surrealist with the inclusion of his "The Sleepwalker" in the Museum of Modern Art exhibition "Fantastic Art, Dada, Surrealism." In 1941 200 of his photographs were exhibited at the Pierre Matisse Gallery in New York.

Lynes received the attention of fashion editors, who from 1934 onward commissioned him for accounts with Henri Bendel, Bergdorf Goodman, Hattie Carnegie, and Saks Fifth Avenue, providing Lynes with a much-needed steady income. Lynes brought to fashion shoots the same talent he had for portraits. His fashion studies appeared in *Harper's Bazaar, Town and Country, Camera, Vogue, Life,* and other national magazines. Even his photographs of the senior women at Vassar for the 1935 yearbook *Vassarion* display his theatrical use of light and positioning, which enabled him to draw from his subjects something particular to them. In 1934 Lynes expressed the poetry of dance with his photographs of choreographer Frederick Ashton and his three principal performers from the opera *Four Saints in Three Acts,* a collaboration between Virgil Thomson and Gertrude Stein. From 1935 until his death Lynes was the official photographer for Lincoln Kirstein's American Ballet (later New York City Ballet) company. He took promotional photographs of the repertory and principal dancers and, with the assistance of director and choreographer George Balanchine, re-created moments from performances. According to Balanchine, Lynes could capture the "atmosphere" and "intentions" of a ballet like no other photographer or film producer. Photographer Martha Swope declared that no one could match Lynes when it came to the creative use of lighting for dance photography. Notable among others is his studio nude photo of Francisco Moncion and Nicholas Magallanes embracing as the Dark Angel and Orpheus from the 1950 Balanchine, Igor Stravinsky, and Isamu Noguchi production of *Orpheus.*

Although Lynes had to rely on his fashion photography to earn a living, his main interest was experimenting with techniques to create homoerotic images of the nude male, many of them in a surrealistic manner with mythological themes. Painter Pavel Tchelitchev, whom Lynes met through Stein in France, often provided backgrounds for these photographs. However, Lynes risked hurting his professional career by exhibiting these images, since some of the leading figures of surrealism were outspoken homophobics. Laws against homosexuality meant imprisonment for Lynes if he exhibited his work in public. When in the 1950s Lynes sold some photographs to Dr. Alfred C. Kinsey, author of *Sexual Behavior in the Human Male* (1948), he avoided the mail, not wanting to risk government confiscation. Lynes found an avenue for exhibiting the photographs he prized most in the Swiss gay magazine *Der Kreis,* first under his own name and later under the pseudonym Roberto Rolf.

In 1945 Lynes went to Hollywood for three years as chief photographer for *Vogue's* Hollywood Studios. While there he lived beyond his means and went into debt. By the time he returned to New York in 1948, other fashion photographers had been given his accounts. Toward the end of his life Lynes twice filed for bankruptcy. It was partly owing to financial problems that Lynes sold more than 600 vintage silver prints and several original negatives to Kinsey, who was conducting research on homosexual male eroticism for his research institute. Lynes destroyed several hundred of his homoerotic photographs before his death; however, because of Kinsey's interest, a large collection exists, providing a twenty-five year history of male homoeroticism in the United States. The first monograph of his work, *George Platt Lynes: Photographs 1931–1955,* published in 1981 by Jack Woody, as well as an exhibition at Boston's Institute of Contemporary Art, showcased the full range of Lynes's work, inspiring renewed interest in his photography. In 1993, partly owing to the breakthrough work of followers such as Robert Mapplethorpe, Lynes's pioneering homoerotic male images were shown at New York University's Grey Art Gallery in an exhibition titled "George Platt Lynes: Photographs from The Kinsey Institute." Lynes was sharing an apartment with his brother Russell, a social historian and writer, when he died in New York City.

• The Kinsey Institute for Research in Sex, Gender, and Reproduction at Indiana University in Bloomington possesses the George Platt Lynes Collection of photographs as well as the correspondence between Lynes and Alfred C. Kinsey from 1949 to Lynes's death. Lynes's photographs appear in a number of museum collections, including the Museum of Modern Art, New York City; the Metropolitan Museum of Art, New York City; the Smithsonian Institution, Washington, D.C.; and the Art Institute of Chicago. The New York Public Library for the Performing Arts at Lincoln Center has a collection of Lynes's photographs of dancers and dance performances in its Dance Collection. For a complete list of collections containing Lynes's photographs, see *Index to American Photographic Collections,* 3d enlarged ed. (1995). The Yale University Beinecke Rare Book and Manuscript Library holds Lynes's correspondence with Gertrude Stein in its Collection of American Literature. See Lincoln Kirstein's memoir *The New York City Ballet* (1973) for dance photographs taken by Lynes. James Crump provides the most extensive information about Lynes (with the use of an unpublished memoir of Lynes written by his brother Russell) in his two articles accompanying *George Platt Lynes: Photographs from The Kinsey Institute* (1993): "Photography as Agency: George Platt Lynes and the Avant-Garde," pp. 137–47, and "Iconography of Desire: George Platt Lynes and Gay Male Visual Culture in Postwar New York." The selected bibliography included in the Kinsey book is an invaluable guide to further research on Lynes. Mindy Aloff reviews Lynes's dance photography and his association with Balanchine and Kirstein in *Dance Magazine,* Apr. 1982, pp. 46–49. For a discussion of Lynes's photography, see also Ann E. Berman, "George Platt Lynes Reconsidered: The Photographer's Mastery of Psychology and Light," *Architectural Digest,* Sept. 1993, pp. 60ff. Jeffrey Wechsler places Lynes in the context of American surrealism in *Surrealism and American Art: 1931–1947* (1976). An obituary is in the *New York Times,* 7 Dec. 1955.

BARBARA L. CICCARELLI

LYON, Ben (6 Feb. 1901–22 Mar. 1979), entertainer and film executive, was born in Atlanta, Georgia, the son of Benjamin Lyon, a furniture salesman, and Alvina (maiden name unknown). Raised in a family devoted to amateur music and theatrics, Lyon abandoned thoughts of a physician's career when he received $5 for a film bit part. At seventeen he played juvenile leads on Broadway. In 1923 he went to Hollywood to perform in films produced by Samuel Goldwyn at $400 weekly. Soon he was making $2,000. He appeared in at least thirty silent films. Tall and handsome in an open-faced way, Lyon proved a matinee idol, though for five years he was confined mainly to trivial romantic comedies.

In 1927 Lyon won his permanent place in silent film lore as Briton Monte Rutledge in Howard Hughes's World War I film, *Hell's Angels*. In the movie, Lyon piloted his own aircraft, dueling with a German zeppelin. The two painstaking years Hughes used shooting *Hell's Angels* coincided with the rise of talking pictures, and it became necessary to replace the original female lead, whose accent was unsuitable. Lyon was credited with "discovering" her replacement, an extra, Jean Harlow, who became Hollywood's reigning sex symbol of the 1930s. Released in 1930, *Hell's Angels* was a landmark for action and frankness.

Lyon married actress Bebe Daniels that year; they had two children. Their joint film career began in 1930 and continued for more than twenty-five years.

In 1931 Lyon made his first film musical, *The Hot Heiress* (the title dealt with a fire in the boudoir of the heiress, played by Ona Munson). Otherwise undistinguished, the picture was also Richard Rodgers and Lorenz Hart's first film score. In 1933 the celebrity Lyons toured British theaters. He made seven British films. In 1936 the couple formed a variety act and became the first American stars to appear on incipient British television.

When war broke out in September 1939 the Lyons decided to stay in England because the "British had been so wonderful to us, we couldn't run out on them when they were in trouble." They made their London home a haven for British—and later American—servicemen and women. In response to broadcasts from Germany by the turncoat Lord Haw Haw, in December 1939 they appeared in a London stage revue, *Haw Haw*. Although Daniels was the star, Lyon amiably partnered her in duets. From then on, to the British public they were simply "Bebe and Ben."

Lyon is credited with inventing "Hi, Gang!" a morale-building BBC radio program that developed from late-night shows at the American Eagle Club. "Hi, Gang!" (Lyon spoke these words after the opening theme on every show) was an action and wisecrack-filled variety show, the first BBC offering to run fifty-two weeks without a break, thirty months in all, ending only when Lyon enlisted in the U.S. Army Air Corps late in 1942. Heard in the occupied countries, "Hi, Gang!" was allegedly on Hitler's "list." Its studios were bombed out once and often strafed by German planes.

In 1941 the Lyons began "The Stars and Stripes in Great Britain," a BBC program spotlighting American servicemen that was beamed to North America throughout the war. In another London revue with Daniels, *Gangway* (1941), Lyon soloed and wisecracked. Running forty-seven weeks, the show was a glamorous tribute to escapism and stiff-upper-lipness. The Lyons toured Great Britain, entertaining American and British troops.

Lyon flew combat missions and lobbied for daylight bombing of Europe. He became a lieutenant colonel. Fifteen days after the Allied invasion in 1944, Lyon flew Daniels to Normandy, where she interviewed American wounded six hundred yards behind the front lines. In the United States she later was awarded the Medal of Freedom, he the Legion of Merit.

After the war Lyon joined Twentieth Century-Fox in London as a casting executive. He returned to Hollywood, and in 1947 he claimed credit for discovering Marilyn Monroe. He wrote, "It's Jean Harlow all over again." In 1948 the Lyons returned to London, where he headed a talent agency and joined a television production firm. In 1950 he conceived a radio series designed to help Britons laugh through the austerity years, "Life with the Lyons." It ran for ten years on radio and eight on television. Daniels wrote the scripts. They said of the Lyon family here portrayed: "It was us, but a little crazier." The show, prefiguring American TV comedies, featured a vague and sentimental mother, an idiotic father, a teenaged daughter's catchline, "I'll die, I'll just die," and a son repeatedly rushing up and down stairs, followed by Lyon's "What kept you, son?"

The series spawned a stage version and two theatrical films. Lyon and Daniels made seven royal command performances. After Daniels's death in 1971, Lyon returned to California. In 1975 he married Marion Nixon, one of his costars from silent films, and they settled in Beverly Hills. In 1977 he was awarded the Order of the British Empire by Queen Elizabeth II for his services in World War II. He died en route to Honolulu aboard the *Queen Elizabeth II*.

• Lyon and Daniels jointly wrote *Life with the Lyons* (1953), a straightforward and unliterary presentation of primary sources collected throughout their lives in case they wanted to write more formal autobiographies. In its clumsy authenticity it is more useful than *Bebe and Ben* (1975), by Jill Allgood, a dual biography written by a British friend, which adds details after 1953.

JAMES ROSS MOORE

LYON, Irving Whitall (19 Oct. 1840–4 Mar. 1896), antiquarian, author, and physician, was born in Bedford, New York, the son of Solomon Lyon and Hannah Rundell. He graduated from the Lawrenceville (Pa.) Preparatory School, the Vermont Medical College, and the College of Physicians and Surgeons in New York City. Lyon practiced medicine for a brief period with the Union army during the Civil War, followed by work at the Bellevue Hospital in New York City (1864–1866). In 1866 he turned to private practice and relocated to Hartford, Connecticut, where he worked for the remainder of his life. In addition to publishing numerous articles on medicine and surgery, Lyon was also medical examiner for the Hartford Life and Annuity Company. At the time of his death, he was serving an extended term as president of the Hartford County Medical Society. He married Mary Elizabeth Tucker of New York; the couple had three children.

In 1877 Lyon began to actively collect antiques with a special focus on Pilgrim century furniture produced in and around Hartford. His collection, which eventually numbered several hundred pieces, was the catalyst for a lifelong interest in early furniture. Lyon's curiosity about early American furniture, coupled with a lack of published information about early Americana, led him to begin documenting the collections of his fellow antiquarians. In addition, he sought out clues about the dates of specific furniture forms through the study of wills, inventories, and other documents. In the process of examining these early collections and primary records, Lyon discovered a number of errors in the common wisdom about seventeenth- and eighteenth-century furniture. To clarify the subject, he began work on a book that "included among other things an examination of specimens; an inquiry into what others knew or had written; and an examination of old records" (*The Colonial Furniture of New England*, pp. iii–iv). In 1891 this, Lyon's only published work, was printed in a limited edition of 750 by Houghton Mifflin and Company under the title *The Colonial Furniture of New England: A Study of the Domestic Furniture in Use in the Seventeenth and Eighteenth Centuries*. The work was reprinted in a larger edition by Houghton Mifflin in 1924 and again by E. P. Dutton in 1977. Lyon's publication includes a large number of photographs (approximately 113) drawn mostly from his own collection as well as from those of his friends. Arranged according to furniture forms (chairs, tables, chests), Lyon utilized a multidisciplinary approach to the study. He analyzed objects by their form within the context of construction, provenance, and relationships to other known pieces. In addition, he included tremendous amounts of documentation from primary sources to augment his own detailed examinations of individual forms.

The scope of Lyon's analysis of primary documentary materials still marks this work as being of seminal importance in material culture studies. While primarily researching and documenting southern New England furniture, Lyon examined a wide range of colonial American decorative arts. His discovery of a July 1736 Philadelphia inventory that included a Windsor chair belonging to Hannah Hodge is regarded as the earliest documented reference to that furniture form in the United States (Lyon, p. 176). Another pioneering effort by Lyon was the inclusion of European precedents in forms and decoration as a method for understanding American furnishings. This approach was in stark contrast to subsequent decorative arts scholarship, which sought to establish the complete and total distinctiveness of American furniture from its European predecessors. With the limited publication of his book and the subsequent popularization of several "coffee table" volumes on furniture, Lyon's work remained underutilized for sixty years. Lyon's correspondence with German and English furniture schol-

ars preceded John T. Kirk's *American Furniture and the British Tradition to 1830* (1982) by almost one hundred years.

In a review of Lyon's book in the *Magazine Antiques*, editor Homer Eaton Keyes wrote, "It is to be borne in mind, further, that the author was an inquirer rather than a dogmatist" ("Review of *Colonial Furniture of New England*," *Magazine Antiques* 6, no. 4 [Oct. 1924]: 210–11). Lyon's emphasis on the factual study and interpretation of primary materials (objects as well as documents) is still regarded as the first such type of study in the history of material culture scholarship. Regrettably, the limited publication of his work meant that few scholars had access to his research until the 1924 edition. In the years between the two editions a cottage industry sprang up in the mass publication of books on American antiques. Most of these works fell into the category of visual encyclopedias of form (for example, Wallace Nutting, *American Furniture Treasury* [1928]), which compared hundreds of photographs of similar forms of furniture. Lyon's limited number of photographs attracted far less attention. Further, Lyon's focus solely on early New England furniture meant that the work had a far more limited appeal than Nutting's publications, which spanned all geographic regions and periods. Interpretively, the accompanying text in many of these photo treasuries generally stressed the aesthetic differences of quality between each piece as a way of comparing styles. This was in contrast to Lyon's historical and documentary approach to the subject. Further, by focusing on a specific period and locale, Lyon was able to more closely identify regional variations.

Rediscovered in the 1970s by a new generation of material culture scholars, Lyon's work received a significant reappraisal by both collectors and researchers. His broad use of primary documents coupled with a close examination of forms became a model for the study of material culture, and his work is now regarded as the authoritative study of early New England furniture.

Lyon was working on an untitled book on colonial architecture when he died at his home in Hartford. His two sons, Irving Phillips Lyon and Charles Woolsey Lyon, continued the family tradition of interest in the decorative arts. Both extensively collected and dealt in antiques and Irving Phillips Lyon published a large number of articles on early southern New England joinery.

• Of primary interest are Lyon's own publications, "The Oak Furniture of Ipswich, Massachusetts," *Magazine Antiques* 32, no. 5 (Nov. 1937): 230–33; "Square Post Slat Back Chairs," *Magazine Antiques* 10, no. 4 (Oct. 1931): 210–16; "The Cupboard of Ephraim and Hannah Foster of North Andover, Massachusetts," *Oldtime New England* 28 (1938); and "A Pedigreed Cupboard Dated 1681 and Initialed IAE for Elizabeth Appleton of Ipswich, Massachusetts," *Oldtime New England* 28 (1938). Gerald W. P. Ward, *Perspectives on American Furniture* (1988), has important essays on the historiography of decorative arts scholarship and places Lyon in context; Benno Foreman, *American Seating Furniture: 1630–*

1730 (1988), carries on many ideas suggested by Lyon and reflects the most recent scholarship on Pilgrim century furniture.

PETER SWIFT SEIBERT

LYON, Mary (28 Feb. 1797–5 Mar. 1849), educator, was born in Buckland, Massachusetts, the daughter of Aaron Lyon and Jemima Shepard, farmers. The family farmed 100 rocky acres on a hillside near Baptist Corner, where many relatives lived and worshiped in that faith. Lyon's father died before her sixth birthday, and until her mother remarried in 1810, the family worked together to sustain the farm. When Lyon's mother relocated with her new husband to Ashfield, Massachusetts, Lyon stayed behind to support her brother Aaron in running the farm. Aaron paid her one dollar per week for her household management. After Aaron married, Lyon remained on the farm but was then better able to renew her intermittent attendance at local schools.

Lyon's lifelong commitment to education started with the district schools in Buckland and Ashfield. She occasionally boarded with friends or relatives to permit attendance at schools some distance from home, a practice she continued in her teens and twenties. Her quick mind and sharp memory distinguished her early, and a teacher helped secure Lyon her first teaching job in Shelburne Falls in the summer of 1814. For the next ten years she alternated between teaching and her own schooling, a role not unusual in the early nineteenth century, when male and female teachers were often itinerant students paying their way through school.

In 1817 Lyon enrolled at the new Sanderson Academy in Ashfield, where she met Amanda White, an important friend whose family welcomed Lyon and long served as supporters. Over the next few years, Lyon taught and attended both Sanderson and Amherst academies.

In 1819 Aaron Lyon's family moved to Stockton, New York, in hopes of better farming. Lyon thus was separated from the last of her family and spent the next years boarding with friends, relatives, and employers. In 1821 she and White entered Byfield Seminary, in eastern Massachusetts, run by the creative and influential teacher Rev. Joseph Emerson. Lyon's experience at Byfield was one of the most significant in her life, introducing her to intellectual challenge paired with Christian commitment—a combination she would later instill at Mount Holyoke Female Seminary.

Emerson was unusual in his support for the education of women, considering them men's intellectual equals. Moreover, his commitment to evangelical religion was paramount, born during the Second Great Awakening in New England, a period from the 1820s through the 1830s of intense religious revivalism that encouraged individual religious conversion. Emerson's attention to religion was welcomed by Lyon, whose Baptist upbringing stressed the importance of conversion. Although she had felt some surge of religious belief by 1816, it was 1822 before Lyon was formally baptized into the Congregational church.

Emerson gave Lyon another focus, however, by joining religious commitment to women's emerging role as teachers. In the decades after the American Revolution, women's public roles had been reconceived by a notion that historians term "Republican motherhood." In this view, women's presumed natural superiority in matters of morality and child care overcame societal concerns about their public activity, and women were increasingly viewed as "natural" teachers for America's youth. During her career, Lyon would join other pioneers of women's education in advancing this view by providing an important educational model for training women as teachers.

At Byfield, Lyon also became fast friends with Emerson's dynamic assistant, Zilpah Polly Grant, who would become Lyon's partner in educational efforts from 1823 to 1833. After Byfield, Lyon first taught at Sanderson Academy but soon pursued a wish to open her own school in Buckland, which she ran for ten-week winter terms between 1824 and 1830. For friendship's sake, Lyon soon joined Grant at a new school, the Adams Female Academy in Londonderry, New Hampshire. Grant was hired as preceptress; Lyon, although formally a teacher, exercised considerable influence on the curriculum. The pair ran Adams for three years (1824–1827), while Lyon continued her prospering winter school in Buckland. In 1828 the Adams trustees, unhappy with the school's strong evangelical focus, pushed Grant to resign by insisting that dancing be added to the curriculum.

Committed to their view of female education, Grant secured financial support from a group of investors to create Ipswich Female Seminary, initially bringing Lyon as a teacher for the summer terms. After a few exhausting years splitting her time between Buckland and Ipswich, Lyon agreed to join Grant full-time in 1830. Grant's health had always been a concern, and she needed Lyon to help with her administrative and pedagogical work during Grant's frequent health setbacks and travels, tasks that Lyon assumed with energy and good humor.

Ipswich was a strong success, prompting Lyon and Grant to conceive a plan to secure permanent funding for their work. When no support developed for endowing Ipswich, the two proposed a new establishment: The New England Female Seminary for Teachers, which could be located wherever support was strongest. This idea fared no better. The failure of the plans initially discouraged but did not deter Lyon in her belief that a seminary must be able to "outlive its present teachers"; in fact, Lyon's efforts to endow the schools clarified her plan for Mount Holyoke Female Seminary.

Lyon believed in the curriculum of history, science, math, and philosophy that she and Grant had developed. She also supported the mission of preparing Christian female teachers. However, she wanted a wider body of students to enjoy the opportunities of strong female seminaries, wishing that daughters of the "middling classes" might afford schools like Ipswich. After the failure of their endowment plan, Lyon began to separate from Grant. Grant was frequently ill, often leaving Lyon in charge of all aspects of their joint endeavors. Contributing more to their separation, however, was Lyon's belief that daughters of poorer families were the most necessary objects of female education. Grant had always relied on people of means for financial support and for providing students. Lyon had traveled during 1833, visiting schools around the country, laying her own plans. By 1834 she began her campaign to endow a seminary that would operate modestly enough to bring the best teacher training to poorer women.

Like other female school founders, Lyon turned to influential men to help her raise money and defend her ideas before a sometimes skeptical establishment. Her early supporters were longtime friend Edward Hitchcock, the Reverend Theophilus Packard, and Roswell Hawks, who became Mount Holyoke's paid agent. In addition to these traditional methods, however, Lyon soon realized the potential in female organizations, especially those created to support education. In the 1820s and 1830s women had frequently started their own groups as well as female auxiliaries of organizations like the American Education Society, which raised money to support college men pursuing ministry training. Lyon's unique contribution lay in realizing that these women, through small donations but long-term support, could serve as vital advocates for women's education. Between 1834 and 1837, either with Hawks or alone, Lyon visited dozens of towns, raising money, support, and consciousness. In two years, she raised $15,000 from "the Christian public," with gifts from more than 1,800 people in ninety towns. Building began in South Hadley, Massachusetts; the single large, all-purpose building was opened in 1837 to the seminary's first class of eighty students.

Mount Holyoke grew steadily over its first decade, soon filling its capacity of 200. Once finances were stable, Lyon could attend to her ongoing concern: raising academic standards. As applications rose, she tightened entrance requirements and kept the minimum admission age at sixteen. One feature that did not change, however, was commitment to low tuition. Lyon's seminary charged only $60 annually, one-third the cost of Ipswich. Some controversy surrounded Lyon's methods of keeping low costs, however, with critics challenging her requirement of daily domestic work by all students and very low wages for her teachers, whom she viewed as "missionaries" to the cause of education.

Any difficulties that Mount Holyoke might have experienced as a new institution did not hinder its general strong progress. Lyon was frequently disheartened when one of her able assistant teachers left for other work or marriage. The biggest setback was a typhoid epidemic in the third year that struck forty of 120 students, killing nine.

The daily curriculum of the school was built on intellectual challenge and moral purpose, with Lyon as prime model. A list of seventy rules was reviewed daily by students and staff, with each student "self-reporting" her progress to a "section" of fifteen or twenty colleagues. The day was strictly governed by schedules, and students were always under the watchful eyes of teachers, who lived in the same building with them.

Lyon led Mount Holyoke for only a dozen years. She died in South Hadley from erysipelas, a streptococcal infection of the skin and subcutaneous tissue. The disease hit her after a particularly hard period, after several family deaths.

Lyon joined other nineteenth-century advocates of education for women in creating new models for their education and their careers as teachers. Her unique contributions lay in demonstrating how an endowed institution for women (rather than one based on subscriptions or trustee contributions) could sustain itself and in organizing that institution to include women of the middle classes. Mount Holyoke experienced the permanence and growth that had eluded most other nineteenth-century women's schools. Lyon's commitment to training teachers was well realized; between 1838 and 1850 more than three-quarters of graduates became teachers. The strength of the Holyoke model was demonstrated in the numerous daughter colleges that appeared in the midwestern United States and abroad, all consciously following Lyon's model. In creating this unique and effective model, Lyon followed her belief that her institution must "penetrate far into futurity," and that its "great work of renovating a world" required permanence and financial endowment.

• The Mount Holyoke College Archives and Special Collections is the single best source of material on Lyon. The collection includes holograph and typed copies of letters and other documents. Lyon's only publications were *A Missionary Offering* (1843), a plea for financial support of the widespread missionary movement, and seven versions of circulars promoting Mount Holyoke (1834–1839), which present her educational philosophy in crisp form.

In 1858 Lyon's friend Edward Hitchcock, with the help of Zilpah Grant Banister, Eunice Caldwell Cowles, M. C. Eddy, and Hannah White published *The Power of Christian Benevolence: Illustrated in the Life and Labors of Mary Lyon.* This book contains hundreds of excerpts of Lyon's letters over her lifetime; however, her friends edited some material rather heavily, and many originals do not survive. Later biographies are Fidelia Fiske, *Recollections of Mary Lyon, with Selections from Her Instruction to the Pupils in Mount Holyoke Female Seminary* (1866); Beth Bradford Gilchrist, *The Life of Mary Lyon* (1910); and Marion Lansing, ed., *Mary Lyon through Her Letters* (1937). Sarah D. Locke Stow wrote an early history of the school, *History of Mount Holyoke Seminary, South Hadley, Mass., during Its First Half-Century, 1837–1887* (1887).

A good modern biography is Elizabeth Alden Green's *Mary Lyon and Mount Holyoke* (1979); a biographical essay with attention to wider educational issues is Susan McIntosh Lloyd's "Mary Lyon" in *Women Educators in the United States, 1820–1993,* ed. Maxine Schwartz Seller (1994). Recent scholarly appraisals of Lyon's contributions include Kathryn Kish Sklar, "The Founding of Mount Holyoke College," in Carol Ruth Berkin and Mary Beth Norton, *Women of America: A History* (1979); and Helen Lefkowitz Horowitz, *Alma Mater: Design and Experience in the Women's Colleges from Their Nineteenth-Century Beginnings to the 1930s* (1984).

LINDA EISENMANN

LYON, Matthew (14 July 1749–1 Aug. 1822), congressman, soldier, and entrepreneur, was born in Wicklow County, Ireland. Little information about Lyon's parents has survived, and most of the information about Lyon's youth is derived from the recollections of a grandson who read Lyon's memoirs before they were mutilated by attic mice.

In Ireland Lyon obtained a basic education, including some Latin, before being apprenticed to a Dublin printer. At age fifteen he left his master and a widowed mother to sail for America as a redemptioner. Before his term of indenture expired, Jabez Bacon, a Woodbury, Connecticut, merchant, sold him for a pair of stags. Local legend claims that he freed himself from his second master by throwing a mallet at him and then running away.

By 1772 Lyon had acquired sufficient income to buy land in Cornwall, Connecticut; the next year he married Mary Hosford, a relative of Ethan Allen. Later in 1773 he bought land in the Hampshire Grants from the Allen brothers, and in 1774 he moved his family to that northern frontier region between New Hampshire and New York that had been claimed by both colonies. He immediately joined the Green Mountain Boys, a militia formed to prevent "the landed aristocracy of New York" from taking possession of the land small farmers had purchased from the Allen brothers. The brothers had speculated in thousands of acres of questionable land titles, granted by the colony of New Hampshire before the Royal Privy Council ruled in 1764 that the land in question belonged to the colony of New York. As a colonel in the Green Mountain Boys, Lyon played an important role in the capture of Fort Ticonderoga in May 1775. After the signing of the Declaration of Independence, he joined the Continental army on 19 July 1776 and served as a second lieutenant under General St. Clair's command in the Northeast. According to Lyon's own account, while guarding the northern boundary his troops mutinied and forced their officers to seek shelter because of the threat of an attack by nearby Indians. For complying, Lyon and his superior officers were court-martialed and dishonorably discharged. Several months later, however, General St. Clair recommended Lyon to serve as scout and guide to General Schuyler during Burgoyne's Invasion. Schuyler promoted Lyon to captain and paymaster of Colonel Seth Warner's regiment. During the battle of Saratoga in 1778, Lyon served as a volunteer and "had the honor and pleasure" of seeing Burgoyne's forces surrender. When Colonel Warner's regiment was ordered south, Lyon resigned his commission to turn his full attention to the problems of the war-ravaged Green Mountain region.

Lyon had been active in the political upheaval taking place in the Hampshire Grants from the beginning of the Revolution. He was a delegate to the Second Dorset Convention, which voted to form the Grants into a separate district on 24 July 1776. Shortly afterward, the settlers of the Grants declared their independence from New York and established their district as the new state of Vermont. Lyon became a member of the Allen-Chittenden inner circle of revolutionary Vermont's government, serving as deputy secretary of the governor and council, clerk of the court of constitution, and representative in the state assembly. By the end of the Revolution, he later said, "I had so attended to my affairs, that I was able under the most favorable circumstances to set a going a number of mills and manufactures which made me rich" (Lyon to Armisted C. Mason, 16 Jan. 1817, James Monroe Memorial Foundation).

In 1782 Lyon's first wife died, leaving him with four children. By the time in late 1783 that he moved to Fairhaven, the manufacturing town he founded, he had married Governor Thomas Chittenden's daughter, Beulah Chittenden. They would have eight children.

His 400 acres of land in Fairhaven were rich in iron, timber, and water power. Among the enterprises he built were saw, grist, and paper mills, an iron foundry, a blast furnace, and a tavern. During the 1780s he was an Antifederalist, but immediately after the Constitution was adopted he began running for office in the federal government. His bitterest political opponents were lawyers whom he charged "are inclined to stand up for the claims of landjobbers in preference to the poorer sort of people" (*Farmer's Library*, 19 Aug. 1794). When he realized that "Tory doctrines were flowing freely from the favored presses of Vermont" (Lyon to Mason), he started a newspaper of his own, the *Farmer's Library*, in 1793. Since paper from cloth did not meet his publishing needs, he invented a process of making paper from basswood and published his formula rather than copyright it. His *Farmer's Library* advocated direct representation, sympathized with the French Revolution, and opposed the domestic fiscal policies of Alexander Hamilton. He later boasted of the role his press played in spreading "Republican doctrines," thus helping lay the groundwork for the emergence of the Jeffersonian Republican party and, ultimately, a two-party system.

After running for the House of Representatives in three elections, Lyon finally won his seat in 1796. Once in Congress, he was treated with contempt as the symbol of "raw" democracy. Federalists ridiculed his Irish origins and former lowly indentured servant status. Connecticut Federalist Roger Griswold badgered him about being dishonorably discharged from the Continental army. Lyon, in turn, spat in Griswold's face. Several days later Griswold hit Lyon on the head with a cane; Lyon then grabbed a pair of fire tongs and engaged Griswold in a fencing match. Such riotous activities on the floor of Congress led the Federalist press to fill its pages week after week with cartoons, columns, and poems satirizing "The Lyon of Vermont."

During his campaign for reelection in 1798, Lyon made clear the real issue that prompted the Federalists' attack. He warned his constituents of the Federalists' pro-British sympathies, which were leading them to arm the United States and prepare for war with France. This was the thrust of his attack upon President John Adams, whom he also accused of having "an unbounded thirst for ridiculous pomp" (*Spooners Vermont Journal*, 31 July 1798).

For expressing these views, Lyon was indicted under the Sedition Act of 1798. During his trial Lyon served as his own attorney, defending his right and duty as a congressman to convey to his constituents his critical opinions of government policies. Nevertheless, Associate Justice William Paterson found him guilty under the Sedition Act of maligning the government and bringing it into disrepute. Paterson fined Lyon $1,000 and sentenced him to four months in jail.

During his internment Lyon wrote articles defending his Democratic-Republican views in a new magazine, which he titled the *Scourge of Aristocracy*. Outraged by the attempt to silence Lyon and convinced by his arguments, his constituents reelected him while he was still in jail. Upon his release hundreds followed him on a triumphal tour from Vermont to Congress. There the Federalists attempted to bar him from his seat because of his jail sentence, but the Jeffersonian Republicans defended his innocence with arguments that refined and clarified the concept of free speech. They contended that only statement of false facts, and not of opinion, could be considered libelous. The role of Lyon's case in advancing America's doctrine of civil liberties was reflected in Congress's action in 1840, when it voted to remit Lyon's $1,000 fine to his heirs on the grounds that the Sedition Act of 1798 was unconstitutional (*Congressional Globe*, 26th Cong., 1st sess., pp. 410–14, 478).

In the election of 1800 the tie between Jefferson and Aaron Burr in the electoral college vote threw the election into the House. There Lyon crowned his career as Vermont congressman by casting the deciding vote for Thomas Jefferson.

Immediately thereafter Lyon moved his family to Kentucky, where he founded the town of Eddyville on the Cumberland and Ohio rivers. At age fifty-two, he started a new entrepreneurial career as merchant and shipbuilder. He used both free and slave labor but allowed his slaves to purchase their freedom. He also resumed his congressional career, serving in the House from 1803 to 1811. His most notable positions involved upholding the government's duty to honor its contractual obligations in the Yazoo land controversy, testifying unfavorably against James Wilkinson and exposing his role in the Burr conspiracy, and opposing measures leading to the War of 1812. Lyon behaved more like a Federalist seeking to protect his interests as a merchant during his Kentucky years. Through his connections he obtained several public contracts that enhanced his Kentucky enterprises.

Because of Lyon's opposition to the War of 1812, his Republican constituents did not reelect him to the Twelfth Congress. Thereafter he also suffered business reverses. Lyon appealed several times for a federal appointment and President James Monroe appointed him U.S. factor to the Cherokee Indians in Spadra Bluff, Arkansas, in 1820. There, at the age of seventy-one, he led a Spartan life managing the Cherokees' trading activities. He attempted to obtain a cotton gin, hoping to start productive agriculture among the Cherokees. These attempts were thwarted shortly before his death in Spadra Bluff.

Lyon represented a new type of American, a self-made man whose ability to rise above his family status was a product of the social movement of the American Revolution. His life as an entrepreneur and public servant exemplified two divergent strands in the heritage of the American Revolution: concern for the individual's rights of property and the pursuit of happiness, concerned with the well-being of the social community.

• The following manuscript collections contain papers relating to Lyon's life: Matthew Lyon Collection, Vermont Historical Society, which contains an insubstantial collection of miscellaneous papers gathered by an admirer of Lyon; Matthew Lyon Miscellaneous Papers, New York Public Library; John Messenger Papers, Illinois State Historical Society; Revolutionary War Pension Files of Matthew Lyon 36 689, Division of Veterans Records, National Archives, which contain Lyon's detailed account of his military service during the revolutionary war; and Colonel Thomas L. McKinney Papers, Records of the Bureau of Indian Affairs, which consist of correspondence between the superintendent of Indian trade and Lyon. The following government publications contain Lyon's speeches in Congress and describe his political activities in Vermont: *Annals of the Congress of the United States 1789–1824*, 4th–6th Cong., 8th–11th Cong., 16th Cong. (42 vols.); *State Papers of Vermont*, vols. 3–5, 8, 10–13; and *Records of the Governor and Council of the State of Vermont* (4 vols., 1873–1876), the first volume of which contains a biographical sketch of Lyon.

The most comprehensive, modern scholarly biography is Aleine Austin, *Matthew Lyon: "New Man" of the Democratic Revolution* (1981). An earlier uncritical biography, J. Fairfax McLaughlin, *Matthew Lyon: The Hampden of Congress* (1900), contains much salient source material. Two other early accounts that impart useful information about Lyon's Vermont years are Andrew N. Adams, *A History of the Town of Fairhaven, Vermont* (1870), and Pliny H. White, *The Life & Services of Matthew Lyon* (1858). Lyon's daughter wrote recollections of the family's social life in Kentucky and described in detail relations with individual slaves in Elizabeth A. Roe, *Aunt Leanna; or, Early Scenes in Kentucky* (1855).

ALEINE AUSTIN

LYON, Nathaniel (14 July 1818–10 Aug. 1861), U.S. Army officer, was born in rural Ashford (later Eastford), Connecticut, the son of Amasa Lyon, a farmer and local lawyer, and Kezia Knowlton. Lyon received a common school education and in 1837 gained entrance to West Point, from which he was graduated in 1841, eleventh in his class of fifty-two.

Choosing the infantry over more prestigious branches of military service, Lyon was assigned to the Second U. S. Infantry in Florida. After participating in campaigns against the Seminoles, he was transferred in 1842 to Sackets Harbor, New York. Lyon had a violent, hair-trigger temper and while there was court-martialed for the brutal beating and torture of an unruly enlisted man. A sworn bachelor, he proved himself a contentious and nearly unpromotable subordinate in peacetime, but he also proved an able leader in war. In the Mexican War, he fought at Contreras and Churubusco, was wounded, and received promotion to brevet captain for gallantry.

Lyon's unique beliefs about religion caused him to believe himself the Creator's chosen instrument for meting out punishment. Always rigid, after returning from Mexico he began to demonstrate a nearly psychopathic appetite for inflicting pain. Transferred to California, Lyon led an expedition in 1850 to seek out and punish local Indians accused of murdering three white residents. The action resulted in the extermination of two complete tribes. Moreover, Lyon's draconian punishments of enlisted men became notorious. Convinced of his own moral righteousness, Lyon questioned authority at all levels. After he was transferred to Kansas in 1854, he caused the court-martial of a superior officer and the removal from office of the territory's first governor by exposing a fraudulent land sale involving government property near the first territorial capital of Pawnee.

In Kansas Lyon witnessed firsthand the violence that erupted over the government's attempt to settle the issue of slavery by means of the Kansas-Nebraska Act. He attributed the territory's bitter strife to the "contemptible arrogance" of its proslavery faction. Accusing the federal government of "subserviency to the slave interest," Lyon resolved to use all means to thwart the slavocracy, which he regarded as the source of the nation's woes. He allowed soldiers at Fort Riley to vote illegally in a territorial election, assisted free-state "Jayhawkers" to escape arrest, and, though not an abolitionist, used government horses to assist fugitive slaves. By 1860 Lyon had become a strident adherent to the Republican party and wrote newspaper editorials supporting presidential candidate Abraham Lincoln and condemning the Democratic party, which he had formerly supported.

In January 1861 Lyon and two companies of infantry received transfer orders to St. Louis as part of an effort to bolster the defenses of the city's federal arsenal. Although Missouri voted to maintain neutrality, it boasted an active secessionist minority, which included the governor and much of the legislature. Arriving on 6 February, Lyon believed the city's military leadership to be of dubious loyalty and feared an attack upon the arsenal from the city's secessionists. He quickly acquainted himself with Congressman Frank P. Blair (1821–1875), leader of St. Louis's radical Republicans, brother of one of Lincoln's cabinet members, and son of one of the party's founders. In return for rifles to arm the city's large German population,

which ardently supported the federal government, Blair offered Lyon immunity from the administration for any actions he might take in attempting to protect the arsenal. Together they forced the removal of Lyon's moderate department commander, General William S. Harney. Lyon then assumed charge of both the department and the arsenal. He enlisted into federal service several thousand Home Guard militia, mostly Germans, and on 10 May captured the state militia encampment located on the city's outskirts, where many of the secessionists had gathered. While returning to the arsenal, after being fired upon by a civilian mob, Lyon's untrained Home Guards opened fire indiscriminately upon the crowd of spectators lining the street, killing at least twenty-eight, most of whom were unarmed. Several days of riots ensued, causing thousands to flee the city. Lyon's actions hastened thousands of recruits to flock to State Guard camps around the state and caused a jittery state legislature to pass a military bill providing Governor Claiborne F. Jackson with unprecedented power to arm the state for war.

The day following the fracas, Harney was reinstated as commander of the department. In an effort to preserve peace, he and former governor Sterling Price, commander of the State Guard, drafted and published an agreement stating that the state forces would assume responsibility for keeping order in Missouri. Believing the Harney-Price agreement a mere subterfuge to afford the governor time to arm the state troops, Lyon—newly commissioned brigadier general of volunteers—and Blair obtained an order from Lincoln that relieved Harney of command for the second time. Again, Lyon assumed temporary command of the department.

On 11 June, Jackson and Price met with Lyon and Blair at the Planters' House hotel in St. Louis. After four hours Lyon abruptly ended the conference by declaring, "This means war." Within forty-eight hours he launched an expedition up the Missouri River toward Jefferson City. After occupying the state capital, Lyon pressed on toward Boonville, where State Guard forces were concentrated. On 16 June his troops easily scattered the Guardsmen, who joined with Confederate forces in Arkansas under Brigadier General Ben McCulloch to form a force more than double the size of Lyon's. When Price learned that Lyon was at Springfield, he convinced McCulloch to move north into Missouri. Continuing south, Lyon skirmished with the Confederates at Dug Springs, then withdrew to Springfield. McCulloch and Price encamped on Wilson's Creek, south of the city.

Losing troops daily to enlistment expiration, most of whom were St. Louis Home Guard, Lyon feared the loss of his entire force without giving battle. He agreed to a rash plan of one of his subordinates, Colonel Franz Sigel, popular leader of Lyon's German troops, and divided his force for a surprise pincer attack. At dawn on 10 August, Lyon and Sigel struck the encamped Confederates. At the battle's height, Lyon was shot through the heart and killed. After four hours of pitched fighting, the federal force withdrew. In defeat, he became the North's first battlefield hero, its first general to fall. After a whistle-stop train procession, he was buried in Phoenixville, Connecticut.

• Letters written by Lyon are rather few and are scattered about in a number of collections. The largest collection is located at the American Antiquarian Society, while other smaller collections are found in the Archives, History and Genealogy Unit, of the Connecticut State Library; in the Thomas J. Sweeny Papers in the Henry E. Huntington Library, San Marino, Calif.; at the Connecticut Historical Society; the Kansas State Historical Society; the Western State Historical Manuscript Collection/State Historical Society of Missouri Manuscripts; the Western Reserve Historical Society, Cleveland, Ohio; the New-York Historical Society; the Wilson's Creek National Battlefield Park Archives and Library; and the Eastford, Connecticut, Historical Society. Lyon's newspaper articles are published in *The Last Political Writings of General Nathaniel Lyon, U.S.A.* (1861). The most recent and complete biography is Christopher Phillips, *Damned Yankee: The Life of General Nathaniel Lyon* (1990). See also Ashbel Woodward, *Life of General Nathaniel Lyon* (1862); James Peckham, *General Nathaniel Lyon and Missouri in 1861* (1866); Hans Christian Adamson, *Rebellion in Missouri, 1861: Nathaniel Lyon and His Army of the West* (1961); and Richard Scott Price, *Nathaniel Lyon: Harbinger from Kansas* (1990).

CHRISTOPHER PHILLIPS

LYONS, Jimmy (1 Dec. 1931 or 1933–19 May 1986), jazz alto saxophonist, was born James Leroy Lyons in Jersey City, New Jersey, the son of a shipyard worker. Reference works and the usually reliable *Cadence* magazine give his birth year as 1933, but writer Stanley Crouch claims 1931 in the obituary in the *Village Voice*. His parents, whose names are unknown, separated when he was a child, and from around 1941 he was raised by his grandmother, who owned the Chicken Shack restaurant franchise at the Hotel Woodside in Harlem, where Count Basie and many other jazz musicians often stayed.

From around 1945 or 1946 Lyons was once again living with his mother, an amateur pianist, now in the Bronx, where he attended parochial school. His uncle, a drummer, showed him some basic percussion techniques that he practiced by playing along with tenor saxophonist Lester Young's recordings. He also met pianists Elmo Hope and Bud Powell, who practiced in his neighbor's apartment. Clarinetist Buster Bailey helped Lyons's mother pick out an alto sax for him. Soon he had an opportunity to practice with pianists Hope and Thelonious Monk, who told him that he had a good ear but needed to learn music theory. Both because of and despite these distinguished opportunities for apprenticeship, Lyons's mother dissuaded him from becoming a jazz musician: "She'd look at a man like Bud Powell, playing the way he was at that time, and the financial situation he was in then—you know, to have nothing. The clothes he had on were raggedy, been slept in for days, and as beautifully as he played, my mother said it would be a crime if I turned out to be a musician."

Lyons finished school and attended college for two years (details are unknown) while also serving in the army in Korea for three years; in the course of sixteen months of combat he earned two bronze stars. Returning to Harlem, he played professionally on rare occasions but supported himself by working in the post office. Around 1958 or 1959 he studied with alto saxophonist Rudy Rutherford.

In the summer of 1961 Lyons played five or six nights per week with bassist Ali Richardson in Greenwich Village at Raphael's, where free jazz pianist Cecil Taylor was working on weekends with drummer Dennis Charles and tenor saxophonist Archie Shepp. That summer Lyons became a member of Taylor's group, rehearsing and then performing at the Five Spot. At this point many of his musical friends left him for having turned away from the bop tradition to Taylor's radical music; in particular he avoided meeting Hope, who was bitter about this stylistic change and whom he wished not to confront because he honored Hope's former friendship and musical tutoring. That fall he made his first recordings with Taylor, filling one side of the album *Into the Hot*, which was issued under arranger Gil Evans's name (although Evans did not participate in the music making) in an unsuccessful effort by Evans to gain greater public acceptance for Taylor's music.

In 1962 Lyons, Taylor, and drummer Sunny Murray performed in Scandinavia for six months. In Copenhagen the trio recorded *Cecil Taylor Live at the Cafe Montmartre*, and they worked with tenor saxophonist Albert Ayler at the cafe. They returned to find scarcely any musical work at home. Lyons rehearsed with Taylor twice a week but worked perhaps only once every two months over the next decade, including jobs in New York with Ayler, bassist Henry Grimes, and Murray in 1963. In 1966 he recorded Taylor's critically acclaimed free jazz albums *Unit Structures* and *Conquistador!*

To survive through the 1960s Lyons held jobs outside of music. Taylor brought him out of hard labor at a Chicago copper mill for a few musical jobs, including a residency in 1969 at the Maeght Foundation in Paris, where for the first time Lyons recorded an album of his own, *Other Afternoons*, with trumpeter Lester Bowie, bassist Alan Silva, and drummer Andrew Cyrille. While Taylor was on the music faculty at the University of Wisconsin during the academic year 1970 to 1971, Lyons taught music for the Narcotic Addiction Control Commission, a drug treatment center on the Lower East Side in New York. Writer Valerie Wilmer reports that "Lyons found acceptance among streetpeople who thought he must be an addict and offered him narcotics whenever they saw his horn. He had to fake a habit in order to keep their respect" (*As Serious as Your Life*, p. 135).

Lyons, Taylor, and Cyrille were appointed artists in residence at Antioch College from 1971 to 1973, and the following year Lyons made tours of Japan, Europe, and America with Taylor. In 1975 he directed the Black Music Ensemble at Bennington College and played with Taylor at the Five Spot and at European festivals. Further albums with Taylor included *Dark to Themselves* (1977) and *One Too Many, Salty Swift, and Not Goodbye* (1978).

From 1978 Lyons often performed with his own groups, which recorded the albums *Push Pull* (1978), *Jump up/What to Do about* (1980), *Wee Sneezawee* (1983), and *Give It Up* (1985). Apart from Lyons's preference for working with bassoonist Karen Borca, whose instrument gave the ensemble a somewhat distinctive sound, Lyons in his work as a leader continued to pursue the timbres and procedures developed by Taylor. A heavy smoker, he died in New York City of lung cancer.

Taylor told writer Brian Auerbach that he had often been asked by younger saxophonists if they might join his group, but he always refused, "Because they don't understand the position of Jimmy Lyons within my music. Until that happens, I'm not interested." Writer Gary Giddins offers perhaps the best description of this approach:

Lyons developed a style that incorporated both the increased fragmentation and permutation of line in the new music with a rhythmic bias derived from Parker, and because he sustained Parker's relative sweetness of tone in the middle register, . . . he brought an unexpected lyricism to Taylor's mercurial writing. His bright, dancing sound provides an unmistakable link with jazz tradition, a link not nearly as accessible in Taylor's piano playing.

• A number of sources contain information on Jimmy Lyons's life and work. They include Robert Levin, "The Third World," *Jazz and Pop* 9 (Aug. 1970): 16–17 (repr. in Levin, "The Emergence of Jimmy Lyons," in *Music & Politics*, ed. John Sinclair and Levin [1971]); Valerie Wilmer, "Jazzscene: In the Lyons Den . . . ," *Melody Maker*, 15 May 1971, p. 32; Gugliermo Lattanzi and Dino Giannasi, "Due chiacchiere con Andrew Cyrille e Jimmy Lyons," *Musica Jazz* (Dec. 1975): 18–19, 48; John B. Litweiler, "Profile: Jimmy Lyons," *Down Beat*, 16 Jan. 1975, p. 34; and Wilmer, *As Serious as Your Life: The Story of the New Jazz* (1977; rev. ed., 1980). See also Gary Giddins, "Jimmy Lyons: A Sideman's Self," *Village Voice*, 18 Dec. 1978, pp. 94, 96; Bob Rusch, "Jimmy Lyons: Interview," *Cadence* 4 (Oct. 1978): 23–24, 26–28; Bert Vuijsje, *De Nieuwe Jazz* (1978); and Kevin Whitehead, "Call and Response: Letters," *Cadence* 12 (Aug. 1986): 92. For musical analysis, see Ekkehard Jost, *Free Jazz* (1974; repr. 1981). Obituaries are in *Down Beat* 53 (Aug. 1986): 12, *Village Voice*, 19 Aug. 1986, and *Coda*, no. 209 (Aug.–Sept. 1986): 7.

BARRY KERNFELD

LYONS, Ted (28 Dec. 1900–25 July 1986), baseball player, was born Theodore Amar Lyons in Lake Charles, Louisiana, the son of A. F. Lyons, the owner of a large rice farm. His mother's name is unknown. Lyons grew up in nearby Vinton, hunting and fishing in the bayous and helping out on the family farm. At Vinton High School he was a good student and a talented baseball and basketball player. While still in school, he frequently played in the infield for local semiprofessional teams. He graduated in 1919 and was immediately admitted to Baylor University on a baseball scholarship. Lyons planned to become a lawyer, but the Baylor baseball coach persuaded him to try pitching, and the change permanently altered Lyons's life.

At Baylor, Lyons continued to make good grades, played center on the basketball team, and was elected president of the senior class. But it was on the pitching mound that he made his name, and when major league scouts began to follow his career, he gave up dreams of law school. In 1923 the Chicago White Sox held spring training in Seguin, Texas, and played some games at Waco. Lyons's coach got him a tryout with Ray Schalk, the White Sox catcher, and the team was impressed with his poise, maturity, and fastball. He accepted the club's offer of a $1,000 bonus and a salary of $300 a month.

Lyons joined the White Sox for a game in which the team was trailing badly against the St. Louis Browns. In the late innings manager Kid Gleason sent him in as a relief pitcher, and he retired the only three batters he faced. By appearing, he was one of the first players not only to go directly from college to the major leagues but to pitch in the first major league game he had seen. During his long career Lyons never played an inning in the minors.

Lyons's signing supplied Chicago with more than a new pitcher. The White Sox also needed a new image to repair the damage done by the Black Sox scandal of 1919 in which eight players were banished from organized baseball for life on charges of throwing the World Series. The pressures on Lyons were considerable, but almost at once he became a local hero. Some years later, a newspaper poll found him to be the most popular White Sox player from the 1920s until World War II.

His career accomplishments were praiseworthy, especially considering that he played exclusively for the White Sox, and in sixteen of his twenty-one active seasons the team finished in the bottom half of the eight-team league standings and never above third place. In 1925, while the White Sox finished in fifth place, he tied for the league lead with 21 wins. In 1926 he threw a no-hitter against the Boston Red Sox. Perhaps his greatest season was 1927 when he won 22 and lost 14, while completing 30 of 34 starts, to lead the American League in both victories and innings pitched.

In his career Lyons won 260 and lost 230 games. Never noted for his strikeouts, he had excellent control, walking 1,121 men in 4,161 innings. His control and workmanlike pitching style resulted in fast games, averaging about one hour and forty minutes, and once taking only an hour and eighteen minutes—unbelievable by today's standards. In 1931 he injured his arm, which caused him to lose some speed on his fastball. In its place, he taught himself to use the knuckleball almost exclusively and became a master of the pitch. When the depression cut into baseball attendance, the White Sox solution to coping with the slump was to make a Sunday pitcher out of Lyons, capitalizing on his popularity and prolonging his career. Amid publicity, in Chicago or on the road, he would start against the best pitchers of the time—a Lefty Grove, Lefty Gomez, or Bob Feller. Some of the games became memorable, with large crowds and happy owners. Curiously, Lyons's record for his final four seasons surpassed that of his younger days. From 1939 to 1942 he won 52 and lost only 30, completing 72 out of 85 starts, and he was chosen for the 1939 American League All-Star team. In 1942, at age forty-two, he recorded 14 wins, 6 losses, a league-leading earned run average of 2.10 (his best), and completed every game that he started, while the White Sox, the league's weakest-hitting team, finished in sixth place.

In the autumn of 1942 Lyons enlisted as a private in the U.S. Marine Corps and returned, three years later, a captain with service in the Pacific. At age forty-six he started—and completed—five games for the White Sox; he then was named manager and never pitched again. His managerial record was poor: fifth place in 1946, sixth place in 1947, and last place in 1948, with an overall .430 won-lost record. He was released as manager after the 1948 season, and he turned to coaching and scouting. After six years, although he continued scouting until 1966, he retired to help oversee his family rice farm and to run a hunting and fishing lodge. He was elected to the National Baseball Hall of Fame in 1955.

During his last years Lyons spent much of his time answering letters and autographing items for fans. He never married and kept the family farm as his permanent residence. In interviews other players called him the "classiest" man they had ever known. He died in Lake Charles, Louisiana.

• A valuable collection of Lyons material is the vast assortment of papers gathered by Thad Johnson in Reeves, Louisiana. For biographical accounts, see Thomas L. Karnes, "Theodore Amar Lyons," in *Biographical Dictionary of American Sports: Baseball*, ed. David L. Porter (1987); Karnes, "The Sunday Saga of Ted Lyons," *Baseball Research Journal* (1981); and Lowell Reidenbaugh, *Cooperstown: Where Baseball's Legends Live Forever* (1983). Much of the material used here is from interviews with Lyons and from players who knew him well. A clippings file is in the National Baseball Library, Cooperstown, New York.

THOMAS L. KARNES

LYTTELTON, William Henry (24 Dec. 1724–14 Sept. 1808), royal colonial governor and member of the British Parliament, was born in the parish of St. Martin's-in-the Fields, the sixth son of Sir Thomas Lyttelton, a baronet, and Christian Temple, daughter of Sir Richard Temple, a baronet. He attended Eton College and St. Mary Hall, Oxford, without completing a degree but was later awarded an honorary D.C.L. in 1781, having been called to the bar at the Middle Temple in 1748. From 1748 to 1755 he served in Parliament as a representative of the borough of Bewdley, Worcestershire. His impressive family connections included relation by birth to the Grenville family and by marriage to the Pitt family. Lord George Lyttelton, his older brother, was chancellor of the exchequer, and William Henry himself claimed as a personal friend the earl of

Halifax, who was president of the Board of Trade. Through these connections he was appointed royal governor of South Carolina in 1755 but was delayed in reaching Charleston until 1 June 1756 because of the French capture of his ship and his detention as a prisoner of war.

Great Britain had declared war on France in the Seven Years' War in May of the same year. Governor Lyttelton was, therefore, able to obtain greater support from the South Carolina General Assembly for defense and for building a fort among the Cherokee Indians than had his predecessor, Governor James Glen, who had quarreled for years with the assembly over the royal prerogative. Following Crown instructions for disposition of the Acadians (French Catholics deported from Canada for refusal to take the oath of allegiance to the British), Lyttelton and the assembly mandated their dispersal throughout the colony, with some adults and children being forced into contracts of indenture. The governor eventually clashed with the assembly over the royal prerogative relative to such matters as control of Indian affairs and governmental appointments. He also had a sharp conflict with Councilor William Wragg, who denounced a wartime embargo as unconstitutional and objected to the plan for dispersal of the Acadians. Wragg's vigorous opposition resulted in his suspension from the council by Lyttelton, an act upheld by the Board of Trade and Privy Council following distorted criticisms by Lyttelton. This action seriously diminished the status of the Council, enhanced the power and prestige of the Commons House, and resulted in the appointment of an unprecedented number of placemen to the Council and the refusal by many native South Carolinians to serve as councilor.

Lyttelton's severest test came when the Cherokee murdered what the governor estimated to be twenty-four Englishmen along the Broad and Pacolet rivers, then the frontier. When a Cherokee delegation led by Oconostota (Great Warrior) appeared in Charleston in 1759 for peace talks with the governor, Lyttelton declined negotiations because of questions about the official status of the Indians. Upon mixed advice from his Council on a four-to-four split, he proceeded in October with a military expedition, eventually totaling 1,700 men, to Fort Prince George along the Keowee River in present Pickens County, taking the Indian delegation with him. In negotiations he demanded twenty-four Cherokee (later reduced to twenty-one) for execution to atone for the dead colonists and then decided to hold this number from the delegation accompanying him as hostages. He then pressured six Cherokee headmen, including Attakullaculla (Little Carpenter), to agree to a "Treaty of Peace and Friendship." Renewing the general agreements of the treaty of 1730 in London with the Cherokees, the new treaty also provided that the twenty-four guilty murderers be surrendered to South Carolina officials and that the hostages be detained and released one by one only upon receipt of the guilty Indians. Licensed traders were to return to their trading posts, French emissaries to the Cherokees were to be put to death, and any white man or Indian attempting to promote conflict between the English and Cherokees was to be turned over to the governor. Lyttelton returned to Charleston on 8 January 1760 with his expedition weakened by measles and smallpox and with a false sense of accomplishment. This became very evident a little over a month later when soldiers murdered all of the Indian hostages at Fort Prince George following a fatal ambush of its commander, Lieutenant Richard Coytmore, by Cherokees concealed in nearby thickets upon signal from Oconostota.

As the Cherokee War erupted, Lyttelton received word in February 1760 of his promotion to royal governor of Jamaica. He departed for England on 4 April, leaving imperial forces under Colonel Archibald Montgomery and a second expedition under Lieutenant Colonel James Grant along with provincial troops to attack the errant Cherokees. In England Lyttelton married Mary Macartney in 1761; they had one son. Mary died in 1765.

Lyttelton arrived in Jamaica on 20 January 1762 and served for four years, successfully defending the island during the Seven Years' War and securing the area from possible slave insurrections. He encountered serious conflicts with the assembly, however, over the right of privilege of individual assembly members and their freedom from legal arrest and over the Crown's exercise of vetoes of colonial legislation. Controversy over these issues became so intense that the Jamaica Assembly vigorously asserted its inherent rights comparable to those of both the British House of Lords and House of Commons. Lyttelton's Jamaican experience proved even more contentious than in South Carolina as he attempted to follow royal mandates based upon the imperial theory of colonial dependency, which assumed that the power of the assembly originated with the Crown and was to be implemented by the governor's commission and royal instructions.

Lyttelton left Jamaica in 1766 and served until 1771 as ambassador to Portugal. He returned to England and again served in Parliament as a representative of Bewdley from 1774 to 1790. In 1774 he married Caroline Bristowe, who survived him; they had one son. On 29 July 1776 he was raised to the peerage in Ireland as Baron Westcote of Ballymore, County Longford, and on 13 August 1794 he achieved the same status in Great Britain as the first Baron Lyttelton of Frankley, County Worcester. As a minor writer he published "An Historical Account of the Constitution of Jamaica," which first appeared as a prefix to *The Laws of Jamaica* (1792) and was republished the following year as an appendix to Bryan Edwards's *History, Civil and Commercial, of the British Colonies in the West Indies*, vol. 1, pp. 238–48. He also composed *Trifles in Verse*, printed in fifty-two pages for private circulation in 1803. He died at "Hagley," the Lyttelton country estate, near Stourbridge, Worcestershire, England.

Lyttelton received favored appointments through family connections. While possessing attractive personal qualities of poise and tact, he was also ambitious. In the absence of full reports of all activities in the colonies, the Board of Trade gave him greater approval of his colonial administration than the actual record supported, particularly in South Carolina. He had some success in attempts to uphold the royal prerogative, but like many other royal governors he had great difficulty confronting the vigorous assertion of inherent rights by colonial assemblies.

• The William Henry Lyttelton Papers, containing primarily letters to Lyttelton from 1751 to 1760, are in the William L. Clements Library, Ann Arbor, Mich. Microfilm of Lyttelton's three letterbooks as governor of South Carolina, 1756–1760, is available at the South Carolina Department of Archives and History, Columbia. The most extensive secondary study of Lyttelton that compares his administrations in South Carolina and Jamaica in sympathetic terms is Clarence John Attig, "William Henry Lyttelton: A Study in Colonial Administration" (Ph.D. diss., Univ. of Nebraska, 1958). George Edward Cokayne et al., *The Complete Peerage or a History of the House of Lords and All Its Members from the Earliest Times*, vol. 8 (1932), pp. 312–13, provides family background. The most extensive coverage of the general histories of South Carolina is M. Eugene Sirmans, *Colonial South Carolina: A Political History, 1663–1763* (1966); see also Robert M. Weir, *Colonial South Carolina: A History* (1983), and David Duncan Wallace, *The History of South Carolina*, vol. 2 (1934). Additional information on complex Indian problems is in John Richard Alden, *John Stuart and the Southern Colonial Frontier: A study of Indian Relations, War, Trade, and Land Problems in the Southern Wilderness, 1754–1775* (1944). The best coverage of the Jamaican administration is in George Metcalf, *Royal Government and Political Conflict in Jamaica, 1729–1783* (1965).

W. STITT ROBINSON

M

MAAS, Anthony John (23 Aug. 1858–20 Feb. 1927), Jesuit priest and teacher, was born in Bainkhausen, Westphalia, the son of John Maas and Elizabeth Peetz. After attending private schools in Hellefeld and Stockum, Maas fled Germany to avoid military conscription and to ensure a quick entrance into religious life. He arrived in the United States in April 1877 and immediately applied for admission to the Society of Jesus (Jesuits). After an interview with Charles Charaux, superior of the Jesuits in New York and Canada, Maas was admitted to the novitiate at West Park, New York, on 9 April 1877.

Maas excelled in his studies at both the novitiate and juniorate (college) at West Park, and in September 1880 he enrolled at the College of the Sacred Heart in Woodstock, Maryland, to continue the traditional Jesuit course of studies in philosophy. Maas's superiors recognized his ability and assigned him to teach Greek and Latin to the juniors and novices in Frederick, Maryland. After this interruption he returned to his own studies at Woodstock and was ordained a priest in 1887. While at Woodstock, Maas was taught by Salvatore Brandi, the conservative Italian Jesuit theologian who would later play a prominent role in the "Americanist" controversy, in which liberal members of the Catholic hierarchy and priesthood sought more openness in the American Catholic church.

Upon ordination, Maas stayed on at Woodstock as both professor and librarian. In addition to teaching classical languages, he also began to teach scripture. In 1890 he published *The Life of Jesus Christ According to the Gospel History*, a chronological harmonization and commentary on the events in Christ's life using all four gospels. The work rejected new movements in scriptural exegesis that held for different sources, each with its own theology. Instead Maas took a conservative approach to the study of scripture, also rejecting the possibility of multiple authors. This position became the standard Catholic approach well into the twentieth century. In 1893 Maas went to Manresa, Spain, to finish his Jesuit formation by completing his tertianship and pronouncing the fourth and final Jesuit vow. In 1894 he returned to Woodstock, continued teaching, and in 1897 was named the prefect of studies.

In 1905 Maas was named editor of the *Messenger of the Sacred Heart*, a popular Jesuit magazine published for a lay audience, which prompted a move to Kohlmann Hall in New York City. Maas's time there was short-lived, and in 1907 he returned to Woodstock as rector of the college and consultor to the provincial. On 4 October 1912 Maas was named provincial of the Maryland–New York Province of the Society of Jesus with more than 800 Jesuits under his jurisdiction, along with the province's numerous colleges, high schools, parishes, and other institutions. With U.S.

entrance into the First World War, Maas's German background might have become a liability for the Jesuits, but he was well liked as provincial and was known for his kindness and understanding to everyone. Nevertheless, at his own request, his successor in 1918 was an American-born Jesuit.

At the end of his term as provincial, Maas began teaching tertians (young Jesuit priests) at St. Andrew's-on-the-Hudson in Poughkeepsie, New York. While there he also worked on revisions of Jesuit governance documents, in 1923 traveling to Rome in connection with this work. Maas authored more than 100 articles for the sixteen-volume *Catholic Encyclopedia* (1907–1914) and contributed articles to *America*, the Jesuit weekly magazine, as well as the *American Catholic Quarterly Review* and the *American Ecclesiastical Review*. A hardworking priest and a prolific writer, Maas died at St. Andrew's, after having helped to solidify and strengthen Jesuit influence in the Catholic church in the United States.

• Maas's published works include *The Life of Jesus Christ According to the Gospel History* (1890), *Enchiridion ad Sacrarum Disciplinarum Cultores* (1892), *A Day in the Temple* (1892), *Christ in Type and Prophecy* (2 vols., 1893–1896), and *A Commentary on the Gospel of St. Matthew* (1898). For a hagiographical but factually accurate account of Maas's life see an article by Raphael V. O'Connor, S.J., in *The Woodstock Letters* 58 (Oct. 1929): 408–16. Maas and his work in scripture are discussed in Gerald P. Fogarty, S.J., *American Catholic Biblical Scholarship: A History from the Early Republic to Vatican II* (1989).

ANTHONY D. ANDREASSI

MABIE, Hamilton Wright (13 Dec. 1845–31 Dec. 1916), editor and author, was born in Coldspring, New York, the son of Levi Jeremiah Mabie, a businessman in the lumber industry and later in the shoe industry, and Sarah Colwell. Mabie lived with his parents in Coldspring and then in Buffalo and Brooklyn. He was tutored for college, read for the law in a Brooklyn attorney's office, and entered Williams College in 1863. While there, he read voraciously, wrote for and edited the *Williams Quarterly*, and established lasting friendships with several other ambitious young men. Three such friends who later went on to distinguished careers were the Honolulu lawyer Sanford Ballard Dole, the psychologist and philosopher G. Stanley Hall, and Francis Lynde Stetson, an attorney for John Pierpont Morgan. Mabie graduated from Williams in 1867. After receiving a law degree from Columbia and being admitted to the bar in 1869, he practiced law conscientiously but with no love for the profession. He married Jeannette Trivett, an Episcopalian clergyman's daughter from Poughkeepsie, in 1876, which encouraged him to consider the life of a conventional man of letters, even though he continued to practice law until 1879.

Through his friendship with Edward Eggleston, the influential pastor and editor, Mabie met Lyman Abbott, another pastor and the editor of the conservative *Christian Union*. In 1879 Abbott hired Mabie as editor for the *Christian Union's* church-news department; Mabie was associated with the magazine, the name of which was changed to *The Outlook* in 1893, until his death. For five years, Mabie served an extended apprenticeship in his new field. He conscientiously read manuscripts for his supervisors, reviewed books, conducted a dull, gossipy religious column, edited *The Portrait Gallery of Eminent Lawyers* (1880), and assembled *Norse Stories Retold from the Eddas* (1882). In 1884 he was elected to the Author's Club; cofounded two years earlier, it included established men of letters such as Richard Watson Gilder, Brander Matthews, and Edmund Clarence Stedman, with all of whom Mabie was happy to associate. In 1884 Abbott made him his associate editor. Gaining a greater measure of confidence, Mabie began to publish critical essays, often with a religious orientation. Over the years, these pieces appeared in the *Andover Review*, the *Chautauquan*, *Forum*, *Harper's Monthly*, *International Monthly*, *Munsey's*, and the *North American Review*. His first such essay was "A Typical Novel" (*Andover Review*, Nov. 1885). It was an attack on William Dean Howells for the alleged falsification of reality, lack of spiritual values, and indifference to ideality in his novel *The Rise of Silas Lapham*. In later essays, Mabie slowly swung over to the side of genteel realism—at first timorously and then more energetically.

From 1888 Mabie, his wife, and their two daughters lived in a large Victorian house in Summit, New Jersey. There followed an unremitting stream of books, until his total output numbered twenty-six. The titles of several indicate their general contents: *My Study Fire* (1890), *Our New England* (1890), *Short Studies in Literature* (1891), *Essays in Literary Interpretation* (1892), *My Study Fire: Second Series* (1895), *Books and Culture* (1896), *Essays on Nature and Culture* (1896), *Essays on Work and Culture* (1898), *The Life of the Spirit* (1899), *William Shakespeare: Poet, Dramatist, and Man* (1900), *Works and Days* (1902), *Backgrounds of Literature* (1903), and *The Writers of Knickerbocker New York* (1912). In the 1890s Mabie became a popular lecturer, going on tour and appearing at commencements as principal speaker. Mark Twain knew Mabie, admired him extravagantly as a speaker, and complimented him—though not *Outlook*—in a couple of essays. His unoriginal but popular book on Shakespeare caused Mabie to be invited to give several lectures at Johns Hopkins University in 1901. From 1905 to 1910 Mabie edited a series of books for children on fairy tales, myths, legends, heroes, famous stories, essays, and folktales "that every child should know" (the second part of the title of each of these books—the first being *Fairy Tales That Every Child Should Know* [1905]).

In 1912 Mabie began the most momentous experience of his professional life. He was chosen by the Carnegie Endowment for International Peace to go to Japan as an unofficial ambassador; he resided in Japan in 1912 and 1913 and succeeded to a commendable degree in explaining American social, cultural, and spiritual values in a series of ten lectures to hospitable Japanese audiences. Mabie's *American Ideals, Character and Life* (1913) and *Japan To-Day and To-Morrow* (1914) were the published results of this experience. Two years after his return home, he suffered debilitating writer's cramp and then a heart attack. He died in Summit, New Jersey.

Essays in Literary Interpretation (dedicated to Hall and Stetson), though weakened by simplistic approaches to such difficult authors as Robert Browning, Dante, and John Keats, was Mabie's most strenuous effort to its date. In one part, Mabie praises the Naturalists for honestly presenting what is filthy in reality, even as he naively misunderstands their motivation. *Books and Culture* (dedicated to Stedman) is designed to help ambitious readers understand the Bible and such literary giants as Homer and Johann Wolfgang von Goethe, among others. In *Backgrounds of Literature* (dedicated to Abbott) Mabie neatly relates the social and cultural ambience of several distinguished authors—among them Ralph Waldo Emerson, Nathaniel Hawthorne, Washington Irving, and Walt Whitman—to their works.

Once extolled for his genteel, serene personality and earnest, delicate style, Mabie has long since been downgraded as conventional, sentimental, and superficial. Recent attempts by critics to show that some of his insights seem prophetic of middle-of-the-road revaluations of Naturalism are only partially persuasive.

• Most of Mabie's widely scattered papers are at Amherst College, the American Academy of Arts and Letters in New York City, Columbia University, Harvard University, Johns Hopkins University, the Library of Congress, Louisiana State University in Baton Rouge, the New-York Historical Society, and Trinity College in Hartford, Conn. David J. Rife, "Hamilton Wright Mabie: An Annotated Bibliography of Primary and Secondary Materials," *American Literary Realism* 9 (Autumn 1976): 315–80, is thorough and valuable. Edwin W. Morse, *The Life and Letters of Hamilton W. Mabie* (1920), is the standard biography but is too general and laudatory. Frank Luther Mott, *A History of American Magazines 1865–1885*, discusses Mabie's editorial work for *Outlook*. Howard Mumford Jones in *The Theory of American Literature* (1948) praises Mabie's vitalist theory of life as guided by love of great books; Van Wyck Brooks, however, in *The Confident Years: 1885–1910* (1952) ridicules Mabie for flaccidly purveying facile sweetness and light. A funeral notice is in the *New York Times*, 4 Jan. 1817. An obituary is in *Outlook*, 10 Jan. 1917.

ROBERT L. GALE

MABLEY, Moms (19 Mar. 1894?–23 May 1975), comedienne, was born Loretta Mary Aiken in Brevard, North Carolina, the daughter of Jim Aiken, a businessman and grocer. Her mother's name is not known. Details of her early life are sketchy at best, but she maintained in interviews she had black, Irish, and Cherokee ancestry. Her birth date is often given as sometime in 1897. Her grandmother, a former slave, advised her at age thirteen "to leave home if I wanted to make something of myself." However, she may have been unhappy over an arranged marriage with an older man. Mabley stated in a 4 October 1974 *Washington Post* interview, "I did get engaged two or three times, but they always wanted a free sample." Her formative years were spent in the Anacostia section of Washington, D.C., and in Cleveland, Ohio, where she later maintained a home. She had a child out of wedlock when she was sixteen. In an interview she explained she came from a religious family and had the baby because "I didn't believe in destroying children." Mabley recalled that the idea to go on the stage came to her when she prayed and had a vision. But in a 1974 interview she said she went into show business "because I was very pretty and didn't want to become a prostitute." Another time she explained, "I didn't know I was a comic till I got on the stage."

In 1908 she joined a Pittsburgh-based minstrel show by claiming to be sixteen; she earned $12.50 a week and sometimes performed in blackface. By 1910 she was working in black theatrical revues, such as *Look Who's Here* (1920), which briefly played on Broadway. She became engaged to a Canadian named Jack Mabley. Though they never married, she explained she took his name because "he took a lot off me and that was the least I could do."

In 1921 Mabley was working the "chitlin circuit," as black entertainers referred to black-owned and managed clubs and theaters in the segregated South. There, she recalled, she introduced a version of the persona that made her famous, the weary older woman on the make for a younger man. The dance duo Butterbeans and Suzie (Jody and Susan Edwards) caught her act and hired her, polishing her routines and introducing her to the Theater Owners Booking Association, or TOBA—black artists said the initials stood for Tough on Blacks. She shared bills with Pigmeat Markham, Tim "Kingfish" Moore, and Bill "Bojangles" Robinson.

In the late 1920s when Mabley struggled to find work in New York, black comedienne Bonnie Bell Drew (Mabley named her daughter in her honor) became mentor to Mabley, teaching her comedy monologues. Soon Mabley was working Harlem clubs such as the Savoy Ballroom and the Cotton Club and Atlantic City's Club Harlem. She appeared on shows with Bessie Smith and Cab Calloway (with whom she had an affair), Louis Armstrong, Count Basie, Duke Ellington, and even Benny Goodman orchestras. During the depression, when many clubs closed, she worked church socials and urban ghetto movie houses, such as Washington's Howard and Chicago's Monogram and Regal Theatres, where she later returned as a headliner.

Mabley had bit parts in early talkies made in the late 1920s in New York. She played a madam in *The Emperor Jones* (1931), based on the Eugene O'Neill play

and starring Paul Robeson. In 1931 Mabley collaborated on and appeared in the short-lived Broadway production *Fast and Furious: A Colored Revue in 37 Scenes* with flamboyant Harlem Renaissance writer Zora Neale Hurston. In the late 1920s she appeared in a featured role on Broadway in *Blackbirds*. She played Quince in *Swinging the Dream* (also featuring Butterfly McQueen) in 1939, a jazz adaption of *A Midsummer Night's Dream*. Other films include *Killer Diller* (1947), opposite Nat "King" Cole and Butterfly McQueen; *Boardinghouse Blues* (1948), in which she played a role much like her stage character; and *Amazing Grace* (1974), in which McQueen and Stepin Fetchit had cameos. It was drubbed by critics but did well at the box office.

The most popular Mabley character was the cantankerous but lovable toothless woman with bulging eyes and raspy voice who wore a garish smock or rumpled clothes, argyle socks, and slippers. Though she maintained, "I do the double entendre . . . and never did anything you haven't heard on the streets," the nature of her material, more often than not off-color, was such that, in spite of the brilliance of her comic timing and gift of ad-libbing, she was denied the route comics such as Flip Wilson, Dick Gregory, and Bill Cosby took into fine supper clubs and Las Vegas. A younger brother, Eddie Parton, wrote comedy situations for her, but most of her material was absorbed from listening to her world. Offstage Mabley was an avid reader and an attractive woman who wore furs, chic clothes, and owned a Rolls Royce, albeit an inveterate smoker, a card shark, and a whiz at checkers.

In 1940 she broke the gender barrier and became the first female comic to appear at Harlem's Apollo Theatre, where her act, which included song and dance, played fifteen sold-out weeks. Mabley was mentor to young Pearl Bailey and befriended by Langston Hughes, who wrote a friend that he occasionally helped Mabley financially. Legend has her acquiring the nickname "Moms" because of her mothering instincts toward performers.

Her first album, *Moms Mabley, the Funniest Woman in the World* (1960; Chess), sold in excess of a million copies. In 1966 she was signed by Mercury Records. She made over twenty-five comedy records, many capturing her live performances; others, called "party records," had laugh tracks. She said black and white comics stole her material, then forgot her when they became famous.

Television was late to discover Mabley. Thanks to fan Harry Belafonte, she made her TV debut in a breakthrough comedy he produced with an integrated cast, *A Time for Laughter* (1967), as the maid to a pretentious black suburban couple. Merv Griffin invited her on his show, and appearances followed with Mike Douglas and variety programs starring Flip Wilson, Bill Cosby, and the Smothers Brothers. Mabley had been known mainly to black audiences. Of this late acceptance, she mused, "It's too bad it took so long. Now that I've got some money, I have to use it all for doctor bills." Mabley was not always career savvy. She passed up an appearance on CBS's top-rated *Ed Sullivan Show*, saying, "Mr. Sullivan didn't want to give me but four minutes. Honey, it takes Moms four minutes just to get on the stage."

Because of her influence with African Americans, Mabley was seriously courted by politicians such as Adam Clayton Powell, whom she called "my minister." She did not aggressively support the 1960s civil rights movement, and she expressed outrage at the riots in Harlem. She was invited to the White House by Presidents John F. Kennedy and Lyndon Johnson. Of the latter event, she told a (fictional) joke about admonishing Johnson to "get something colored up in the air quick" (a black astronaut). She said, "I happen to spy him [and] said, 'Hey, Lyndon! Lyndon, son! Lyndon. Come here, boy!'" She brought the house down merely by the gall in her delivery. Mabley maintained she corresponded with and met Eleanor Roosevelt to "talk about young men."

Various articles, which say nothing of a first husband—if there was one—note that Mabley had been separated from her second husband, Ernest Scherer, for twenty years when he died in 1974. The comedienne had three daughters and adopted a son, who became a psychiatrist.

Late in her career, Mabley played Carnegie Hall on a bill with singer Nancy Wilson and jazz great Cannonball Adderley, the famed Copacabana, and even Washington's Kennedy Center (Aug. 1972).

During the filming of her last movie, Mabley suffered a heart attack, and production was delayed for her to undergo surgery for a pacemaker. Her condition weakened on tours to publicize the film, and for six months she was confined to her home in Hartsdale, in New York's Westchester County. She died at White Plains Hospital. Her funeral at Harlem's Abyssinian Baptist Church drew thousands of fans.

• The Schomburg Center for Research in Black Culture (New York Public Library) and the New York Public Library for the Performing Arts maintain research files. Elsie A. Williams, *The Humor of Jackie "Moms" Mabley: An African-American Comedic Tradition* (1995), an analysis of Mabley's humor, contains a 28-page biographical section. Mabley is featured in Mel Watkins, *On the Real Side, Laughing, Lying, and Signifying: The Underground Tradition of African-American Humor That Transformed American Culture, from Slavery to Richard Pryor* (1994); June Sochen, *Women's Comic Visions* (1991); Ted Fox, *Showtime at the Apollo* (1983); Donald Bogle, *Brown Sugar: Eighty Years of America's Black Female Superstars* (1980); and Henry T. Sampson, *Blacks in Black and White: A Source Book on Black Films* (1977). A biographical play, *Moms*, by Alice Childress and starring Clarice Taylor, opened off-Broadway in 1987. Insightful information can be found in the following articles: David Hinckley, "The Other MM: Moms Mabley Was a Tiffany Talent in a Goodwill Dress," *New York Daily News*, 18 Feb. 1987; Leslie Bennett, "The Pain behind the Laughter of Moms Mabley," *New York Times*, 8 Aug. 1976; Mark Jacobson, "Amazing Moms," *New York Magazine*, 14 Oct. 1974; and Sidney Fields, "Moms the Word," *New York Daily News*, 29 Oct. 1974. Mabley's genius as a stand-up comedienne, though strictly adult, may be

sampled on CD reissues of recordings, such as *Moms the Word* (1964; Mercury) and *The Best of Moms Mabley* (1965; Chess). An obituary is in the *New York Times*, 25 May 1975.
ELLIS NASSOUR

MACALISTER, James (24 Nov. 1859–13 Jan. 1915), educator and first president of Drexel University, was born in Glasgow, Scotland, the son of John MacAlister and Agnes Robertson. After the death of his father, and then of his paternal grandfather, MacAlister immigrated with his mother and two sisters to the United States in 1850 and settled in Wisconsin. MacAlister received his primary education in Scotland and later obtained an A.B. at Brown University, from which he graduated in 1856. He then returned to Wisconsin and taught school in Milwaukee. Finding promise in the legal profession, he attended the Albany Law School, graduating with an LL.B. in 1864. In 1866 he married Helen Lucretia Brayton of Aztalan, Wisconsin; they had one daughter. After a period of practicing law (1866–1873), he returned to what became his permanent calling, education. A keen interest in public affairs and a well-honed talent for speechmaking led to his appointment as a regent of the Wisconsin Normal Schools, a position in which he served from 1878 to 1883.

MacAlister's growing prominence in educational circles led to his appointment in 1873 as superintendent of schools in Milwaukee. As superintendent, he worked for the inclusion of both modern classics and technical training within the system curriculum. His success in Milwaukee brought him an offer of the same position in Philadelphia in 1883. Up until his arrival in Pennsylvania later that year, Philadelphia public schools had been administered at the local (ward) level. This management format had not only proved inefficient, it had also easily led to partisan political involvement in school administration. Under the new system administered by MacAlister, a delegate from each ward was named to a centralized board of education headed by MacAlister. Here, as in Milwaukee, he advocated the cause of technical education. Not content with leading by example within his administrative role, MacAlister tirelessly promoted, through speeches and the written word, his progressive educational program to all audiences. In an address to the Modern Language Association meeting at the University of Pennsylvania in 1887, he urged that the works of Cervantes, Dante, Goethe, and Shakespeare be added to the traditional and increasingly obsolete classical curriculum then being offered in American schools. In addition to numerous articles, he wrote *Manual Training in the Public Schools of Philadelphia* (1890) and *Art Education in the Public Schools* (1893).

By virtue of his local prominence and position, MacAlister was selected as president of the newly created Drexel Institute of Art, Science, and Industry in 1890. The institute had been founded by Philadelphia banker and philanthropist Anthony Joseph Drexel and his friend *Philadelphia Public Ledger* publisher George W. Childs in order to provide both technical and classical training for men and women alike. Following in the footsteps of institutions such as Cooper Union in New York City and the Pratt Institute in Brooklyn, Drexel Institute also sought to provide cultural and educational activities for the community at large as well as for the student body. Subcollegiate in curriculum during the administration of President MacAlister, the institute sought to provide solid vocational training (at modest cost) in preparation for employment in the burgeoning number of jobs that required technical knowledge at the end of the nineteenth century. The main building (located at the corner of Thirty-second and Chestnut streets) was dedicated before a horde of dignitaries on 17 December 1891, and MacAlister, having resigned as school superintendent in 1890, assumed his presidential duties on 1 January 1892.

Opening for classes with 1,600 students (a huge enrollment for the times) in early 1892, MacAlister shrewdly allocated the resources of the school on the basis of student demand for courses. Eleven departments were established, with staffing levels based on student registration. This radical approach (most colleges were only then beginning to come to grips with the concept of electives) served the institute well. Instruction was offered in art, mechanic arts, domestic economy, business, physical training, teacher education, and library science. Evening classes and lectures were held for the benefit of the public; the institute also provided the citizens of Philadelphia with choral concerts, organ recitals, a museum, and an art gallery.

The death of Anthony Drexel in June 1893 (followed shortly by that of George Childs) dealt a severe blow to the institute. Under MacAlister, who had been accustomed to meeting with the two men informally on an almost daily basis, the institute nevertheless survived and continued to grow. MacAlister selected new faculty members and oversaw reorganization of the board of trustees. Ever flexible in meeting the needs of his students, MacAlister added, dropped, and merged classes and departments freely. In recognition of his achievements, he received membership in the American Philosophical Society and was an Officier d'Académie Français. From 1885 to 1897 he also served as a trustee of the University of Pennsylvania.

Failing health prompted MacAlister's resignation as Drexel's president on 5 June 1913. Named president emeritus by the board of trustees, he died of heart failure the following December at sea while on a voyage to Bermuda.

MacAlister's legacy can be seen in the continued growth and development of today's Drexel University. He was a leader in the late nineteenth-century movement to expand educational opportunities in both scope and content for students of both sexes and from all walks of life.

• The fate of MacAlister's papers is uncertain; they may be in a body of unprocessed material currently held at Drexel University, Philadelphia, Penn. The best source of information on his life and career is Edward David McDonald, *Drexel Institute of Technology, 1891–1949: A Memorial History* (1942). An obituary is in the *Philadelphia Public Ledger*, 13 Dec. 1913.

EDWARD L. LACH, JR.

MACARTHUR, Arthur (2 June 1845–5 Sept. 1912), army general, was born in Springfield, Massachusetts, the son of Judge Arthur MacArthur and Aurelia Belcher. Soon after his birth, his family moved to Milwaukee, where his father then served as lieutenant governor and governor of Wisconsin.

MacArthur was commissioned a first lieutenant in the Twenty-fourth Wisconsin Volunteer Regiment in August 1862 and given the post of regimental adjutant. In his first combat experience, the battle of Perryville, Kentucky, October 1862, he was cited for gallantry in action and promoted to captain. At the battle of Stones River (Murfreeshore, Tenn.), December 1862–January 1863, MacArthur took command when the Twenty-fourth's commander was wounded; he won high praise for his valor. At the battle of Missionary Ridge, south of Chattanooga, November 1863, MacArthur led a daring regimental charge that routed the Confederates; for this feat he was promoted to major and eventually was awarded the Congressional Medal of Honor. Soon after he became a lieutenant colonel and was given command of the Twenty-fourth Wisconsin.

MacArthur led his regiment in thirty battles en route from Tennessee to Atlanta during the summer of 1864. In the battle of Kenesaw Mountain, June 1864, he was shot in the arm and chest. His wounds took him out of the battle, but he returned to his regimental command later in the summer. At the battle of Franklin, Tennessee, November 1864, MacArthur's regiment restored a critical break in the Union's lines and, according to a general's report to the secretary of war, probably turned the tide of battle. Also, MacArthur's corps commander reported that MacArthur's leadership resolved "the most important crisis of the battle." During the battle MacArthur was shot in the leg and chest; this time his wounds were serious enough to terminate his combat service. His leadership at Franklin was cited conspicuously in his promotion to brevet colonel in March 1865. That May he was promoted to the permanent volunteer rank of lieutenant colonel.

For a year MacArthur studied law, at his father's urging, but in July 1866 he joined the regular army, accepting a commission as a captain in the Thirty-sixth Infantry Regiment. He remained a captain for the next twenty-three years, serving briefly on Reconstruction duty in the South but mostly at isolated frontier posts in the West. In the Southwest he served as a company commander in operations against Geronimo's Apaches.

He married Mary Hardy of Norfolk, Virginia, in 1875. They had three sons; the youngest, Douglas MacArthur, went on to become a five-star general.

Shortly after the Spanish-American War erupted in 1898, MacArthur was commissioned a brigadier general of volunteers; he commanded a brigade in the capture of Manila in August. When the Philippine Insurrection began in early 1899, MacArthur, now a major general, headed the Department of North Luzon in operations against the Filipino insurgents. In May 1900 he was made overall commander of American forces in the Philippines and military governor.

The Philippine-American War, as it has been more accurately termed, evolved into a struggle between regular American troops and Filipino guerrillas that was extremely costly in lives on both sides. The main Filipino resistance leader, Emilio Aguinaldo, was captured by MacArthur's forces in 1901. Two years later the War Department officially but prematurely declared the rebellion to be suppressed, but combat in the southern Philippines, notably Mindanao and Jolo, continued for many years. Far more American forces and firepower were used in the Philippines' fighting than earlier in the Spanish-American War, and the casualties were much higher: 4,200 American troops killed and 2,800 wounded, together with 16,000 Filipino combatants killed and about 100,000 dead from famine in war-ravaged areas. As in most guerrilla wars, atrocities by both sides were common, and during MacArthur's command his forces were sometimes criticized for excessive brutality, including several alleged massacres of Filipino civilians.

MacArthur's aggressive campaigns ultimately broke the main rebel resistance. At the same time, he instituted enlightened civil reforms, such as habeas corpus, public schools, and more humane laws. When William Howard Taft arrived as civil governor, however, the two leaders developed sharp personal and policy differences. MacArthur, seeing that his troops still faced combat on various islands, favored at least a decade of military occupation before the Philippines could be considered pacified. On the other hand, Taft insisted on a rapid transition to civilian government. MacArthur was recalled to the United States in 1901; Taft later became his superior as secretary of war and then, in 1909, as president.

MacArthur headed a succession of regional army departments in the United States, besides serving as an observer in the Russo-Japanese War and touring defense systems in various Asian nations thereafter. He was promoted to lieutenant general in 1906; he thus became the army's highest ranking officer at the time but was denied the post of chief of staff. He retired in June 1909 and died a few years later in Milwaukee while addressing a reunion of veterans of his Civil War regiment. He chose to be buried in Milwaukee rather than in Arlington National Cemetery.

Arthur MacArthur demonstrated traits of versatility and aristocratic bearing similar to those displayed by his father and later by his son Douglas. He excelled as a combat leader and as an officer in charge of occupation and civil-affairs functions. He possessed high professional standards, drive, and superior intellect. He was an elitist who was always dignified, usually formal, and sound of character. But he also possessed two liabilities that, unhappily, Douglas would also display: contemptuousness bordering on insubordination for

civilian officials who interfered in his domain and outspokenness on matters beyond his knowledge and authority.

• The papers of Arthur MacArthur are in the MacArthur Memorial in Norfolk, Va. Records of the units with which he served are in the National Archives. An excellent biography is Kenneth R. Young, *The General's General: The Life and Times of Arthur MacArthur* (1994). MacArthur is mentioned in various volumes of *The War of the Rebellion: A Compilation of the Official Records of the Union and Confederate Armies* (128 vols., 1880–1901). See also Douglas MacArthur, *Reminiscences* (1964); D. Clayton James, *The Years of MacArthur*, vol. 1: *1880–1941* (1970); John M. Gates, *Schoolbooks and Krags: The United States Army in the Philippines, 1898–1912* (1973); Stuart C. Miller, *Benevolent Assimilation: The American Conquest of the Philippines, 1899–1903* (1982); and Rowland T. Berthoff, "Taft and MacArthur, 1900: A Study in Civilian-Military Relations," *World Politics* 5 (Jan. 1953): 196–233. An obituary is in the *Milwaukee Journal*, 6 Sept. 1912, and a news article about his death is in the *New York Times*, 6 Sept. 1912.

D. Clayton James

MACARTHUR, Charles Gordon (5 Nov. 1895–21 Apr. 1956), playwright, screenwriter, and journalist, was born in Scranton, Pennsylvania, the son of William Telfer MacArthur, an evangelical preacher, and Georgeanna Welstead. When MacArthur was in his teens the family settled in Nyack, New York. There his father enrolled him in Wilson Memorial Academy, a school that prepared its students for the ministry. The young man's talents lay elsewhere, however. Persuaded by one of his teachers to enter a literary contest at the school, he discovered that he had a flair for writing. That was to be his life's work.

The starting point of MacArthur's progress as a man of letters was the Midwest. In quick succession while still in his teens he worked as a reporter for *Oak Leaves*, a newspaper published in Oak Park, Illinois, by his elder brother Telfer, and for the Chicago City News Bureau. Major Chicago papers soon beckoned, and from 1914 to 1923 he held jobs first at the *Herald and Examiner* and later at the *Tribune*. He was the first reporter in the city to receive a weekly salary of $100.

MacArthur enjoyed the rough-and-tumble rivalry of big-city journalism and the camaraderie of such hard-working colleagues as Ben Hecht and Gene Fowler. One means of release from the tension of meeting deadlines and winning bylines was a lusty intake of alcohol, and MacArthur could match anyone drink for drink. Heavy drinking became a lifelong habit, ultimately to the dismay of his associates. On the positive side were his wit, good looks, and joie de vivre. He also was something of a prankster who knew that his assets of personality would keep him out of serious trouble. As Anita Loos, one of his many admirers, wrote of him: "The world to Charlie was one big playground of intriguing devices for fun." Even so, he could be relied on to complete the work at hand. In the words of another friend, Nunnally Johnson, "when it came to writing, he was Prince Charming who had a job."

In 1916 MacArthur interrupted his career in journalism to enlist as a cavalry trooper in the Mexican border campaign. One year later he went to France as a soldier in World War I. His experience in the war resulted in a satirical book of reminiscences. *A Bug's-Eye View of the War*, privately printed in 1920 and revised for commercial publication as *War Bugs* in 1929. During World War II he sought and received an army commission and served as assistant to the chief of chemical warfare.

In 1920, while at the *Herald and Examiner*, MacArthur married Carol Frink, another of the paper's writers. This marriage ended in divorce in 1926. Meanwhile, in 1923, he moved to New York City to take up a post as a reporter for the Hearst organization. It was in New York in 1924 that he met the young actress Helen Hayes, whom he married in 1928. It was also in New York that he took up a new career: writing for the stage. With Edward Sheldon, his relation by marriage and an established dramatist, he wrote *Lulu Belle*, a sensational melodrama on the life of a black prostitute. Produced in 1926, it was an immediate hit. With Sidney Howard, another popular dramatist, he collaborated less successfully in 1928 on *Salvation*, the saga of a female evangelist. In the same year in collaboration with Ben Hecht, he wrote *The Front Page*, a raucous farce on the unending efforts of members of the Chicago press corps to scoop one another on a major story. The play, an outstanding success that has been revived repeatedly and filmed three times, was the first of many Hecht-MacArthur collaborations. Their other Broadway plays were *Twentieth Century* (1932), also a frequently revived farce; *Jumbo* (1935), a musical with songs by Richard Rodgers and Lorenz Hart; the less successful *Ladies and Gentlemen* (1939), a vehicle for Helen Hayes; and *Swan Song* (1946), a suspense play with comic dialogue typical of the authors. To encourage American intervention in World War II, they also wrote a pageant, *Fun to Be Free* (1941). Alone, MacArthur wrote *Johnny on a Spot* (1942), a poorly received political farce. With Nunnally Johnson he worked on a comedy, *Stag at Bay*, at intervals from 1939 to 1951. It was produced posthumously in Florida in 1974. At the time of his death, MacArthur was reported to have been writing a play for Helen Hayes with Anita Loos and Ludwig Bemelmans.

While maintaining an increasingly busy pace that included an active social life with literary and theatrical celebrities, in 1930 MacArthur undertook a new career as a screenwriter. For Metro-Goldwyn-Mayer he wrote, among other films, *The Sin of Madelon Claudet* (1931), which starred Helen Hayes, and *Rasputin and the Empress* (1932, nominated for an Academy Award), which starred Ethel Barrymore, Lionel Barrymore, and John Barrymore. In 1934 he and Hecht accepted an offer from Paramount Pictures to both write and produce films in Astoria, Long Island. Of their four productions under this arrangement, the most popular was *The Scoundrel* (1935), starring Noël Coward. For its script the authors received an Academy Award. Their antics in the film world were amusingly satirized by Bella Spewack and Samuel Spewack in *Boy Meets Girl* (1935), a long-running Broadway farce that later was made into a successful film.

Among still other Hecht-MacArthur films were the popular *Gunga Din* and *Wuthering Heights* (both 1939, the latter nominated for an Academy Award). MacArthur's last film, *The Senator Was Indiscreet*, a tepid satire on politics at the federal level, was released in 1947. In the same year he was invited to return to journalism as the editor of a venerable monthly, *Theatre Arts*. He accepted and remained at the magazine until 1950.

The center of the MacArthurs' domestic life was a comfortable home in Nyack on land sloping down to the Hudson River. There they raised two children, a daughter, Mary, and an adopted son, James, both of whom became actors. James appeared frequently in films and on television, but in 1949, when only nineteen, Mary died of polio at the outset of a promising career. To the detriment of his already impaired health, this severe blow only increased MacArthur's dependence on alcohol—"the fire that wouldn't go out," as Hecht described it. While being treated for a dire combination of ulcers, nephritis, and anemia in a New York hospital, he suffered a fatal internal hemorrhage.

• The New York Public Library for the Performing Arts has MacArthur's scrapbook of clippings as well as a folder of miscellaneous clippings and the scrapbooks of Helen Hayes, which contain photographs of MacArthur and clippings about his career. *The Stage Works of Charles MacArthur* (1974) includes brief forewords by Helen Hayes, Nunnally Johnson, and MacArthur's younger brother, John. No authoritative, full-length biography of MacArthur has yet appeared. The high points of his life are reported with affection by Ben Hecht in *Charlie: The Improbable Life and Times of Charles MacArthur* (1957). Hecht also offers memories of MacArthur in *A Child of the Century* (1954), *Gaily, Gaily* (1963), and *Letters from Bohemia* (1964). Gene Fowler mentions him in *Skyline* (1961). Helen Hayes reminisces about her life with him in *A Gift of Joy* (1965), *On Reflection* (1968), and *My Life in Three Acts* (1990). A brief sketch of MacArthur by Anita Loos, "To Charlie," appeared in *Theatre Arts*, June 1957. An obituary is in the *New York Times*, 22 Apr. 1956.

MALCOLM GOLDSTEIN

MACARTHUR, Douglas (26 Jan. 1880–5 Apr. 1964), commander of the Southwest Pacific Area Theater during the Second World War, supreme allied commander in occupied Japan, and commander of U.S. and United Nations forces during the first ten months of the Korean War, was born in Little Rock, Arkansas, the son of Arthur MacArthur, a soldier, and Mary Pinckney Hardy. He was raised on a series of army posts in Texas and the Southwest. Like his father, a decorated Civil War veteran who eventually became one of the U.S. Army's highest ranking officers, Douglas chose a military career. After graduating from West Point with highest honors in 1903, he served as an engineering officer in the United States, in the Philippines, and in Panama, eventually joining the War

Department general staff in 1913. He also took part in the 1914 occupation of Veracruz, Mexico, by U.S. Army forces.

Following American entry in the First World War in April 1917, MacArthur fought in France with the 42d Division in the Champagne-Marne, St. Mihiel, and Meuse-Argonne campaigns. His aggressiveness, bravery, and unusual flair earned several decorations, much publicity, and promotion to the rank of brigadier general. Following the armistice, he briefly commanded American occupation troops in Germany.

In 1919 MacArthur began a three-year term as a reform-minded superintendent of the military academy at West Point. During the 1920s he spent two tours of duty in the Philippines, earning promotion to major general in 1925. While serving in the Philippines, MacArthur became a close friend of Manuel Quezon. On the basis of his social relations with such elite Filipinos, MacArthur proclaimed himself an expert on "Oriental psychology," a claim he frequently cited when others criticized his ideas. In 1922 he married Louise Cromwell Brooks, a wealthy socialite. The marriage ended in divorce seven years later; the couple had no children.

President Herbert Hoover (1874–1964) appointed MacArthur army chief of staff in 1930, a post he held through 1935. The depression severely limited military appropriations, and MacArthur spent most of his energy trying to preserve the nucleus of a modern fighting force amidst budget cuts. His reputation was severely tarnished in July 1932 when he supervised the army's violent dispersal of several thousand peaceful World War I veterans, the so-called Bonus Marchers, who had gathered in Washington, D.C., to appeal for early government pensions. Despite his friendship with Hoover, his espousal of conservative values, and the widespread criticism resulting from the rout of the demonstrating veterans, MacArthur was retained by President Franklin D. Roosevelt as army chief of staff. Although Roosevelt voiced criticism of the general's conservative ideas and privately described MacArthur as one of the "three most dangerous men in America," they cooperated closely in establishing the Civilian Conservation Corps, one of the first and most popular New Deal relief programs. Throughout the New Deal period, MacArthur received all of his promotions with the approval of Roosevelt.

In 1935 MacArthur stepped down as chief of staff to become military adviser to the Philippine Commonwealth government, led by President Manuel Quezon. For the next six years, assisted much of the time by Major Dwight D. Eisenhower, MacArthur labored to develop a Filipino army capable of protecting the country from Japan. In December 1937 he retired from the U.S. Army but continued working as a private military adviser to Quezon. That same year he married Jean Faircloth during a brief trip to the United States, his only visit until 1951. They had one son.

Despite his optimism and energy, a chronic lack of money, equipment, or a well-defined mission led to MacArthur's failure to organize an effective Filipino defense force. Scarce funds and growing skepticism in Manila and Washington about the Philippines' ability to resist Japan led most American military planners to disparage MacArthur's effort. By the summer of 1941 he felt despondent and planned to return to the United States as a private citizen. Japan's aggressive moves in Southeast Asia, however, including its occupation of French Indochina, and President Roosevelt's desire to do something to deter Japan, thrust MacArthur back into the limelight.

On July 26 the War Department recalled MacArthur to active duty at the temporary rank of lieutenant general. As commander of U.S. Army forces in the Far East, he presided over both regular American army troops in the Philippines and the Filipino forces he had trained. MacArthur, like Roosevelt and Secretary of War Henry Stimson, hoped this command, assisted by a large number of advanced B-17 bombers and the Asiatic Fleet, would either deter or defeat any further Japanese thrust in Southeast Asia. Convinced that no invasion would come before April 1942, MacArthur boldly predicted that his forces would "crush Japanese troops on the beaches" if they dared approach the Philippines. Japan's assault on 8 December 1941 shattered this illusion.

Japanese airplanes attacked the Philippines about nine hours after the debacle at Pearl Harbor. Despite the prior warning, MacArthur and his subordinate commanders were no better prepared than their Hawaiian counterparts. In the initial wave, the Japanese destroyed most of the American air force around Manila. Two weeks later Japanese troops landed on Luzon virtually unopposed. American and Filipino troops hastily withdrew to the Bataan Peninsula and Corregidor Island, where they fought under siege until April 1942.

Although the American public received heroic press reports about the resistance to the Japanese invaders, many top military and civilian officials questioned MacArthur's competence. They were appalled by the loss of his air force and later by his initial endorsement of Quezon's proposal to "neutralize" the Philippines by negotiating a truce with Japan. MacArthur's decision in February 1942 to accept a $500,000 personal payment from Quezon led some officials in Washington to charge he accepted a bribe.

Following orders from Roosevelt, on 17 March 1942 MacArthur, his family, and his staff left Corregidor via PT boats and later airplanes for an arduous journey to Australia. Following his arrival, Roosevelt appointed MacArthur commander of the Southwest Pacific Area Theater (SWPA), one of two Pacific war theaters. Although Roosevelt and General George C. Marshall, army chief of staff, privately criticized MacArthur's performance in the Philippines, they approved awarding him a Congressional Medal of Honor. Marshall justified the award as an effort to "offset any propaganda by the enemy," while Roosevelt described it as "pure yielding to congressional and public opinion." The White House hoped to counter Republican demands for a "Pacific first" strategy by granting

MacArthur a Pacific war theater, even one secondary to the Pacific Ocean Area Theater commanded by Admiral Chester W. Nimitz.

Promoted to the rank of full general by the time he reached Australia and took command of SWPA, MacArthur devoted himself during the next thirty months to fulfilling his pledge, "I shall return [to liberate the Philippines]." The effort began with a counteroffensive in New Guinea in the summer of 1942 and continued with a number of successful amphibious operations during 1943 and 1944. American and Australian units in SWPA took control of all New Guinea, the Admiralties, western New Britain, and Morotai—all envisioned as stepping stones to the Philippines.

Throughout this period MacArthur complained that Roosevelt and the Joint Chiefs of Staff starved his operations, giving preference to both the war in Europe and the central Pacific drive under Admiral Nimitz. "Some people in Washington," he told his staff, "would rather see MacArthur lose a battle than America win a war." He countered with public criticism of the Joint Chiefs and exaggerated accounts of his own accomplishments, often filtered through anti–New Deal newspapers and members of Congress. Possibly to press Roosevelt to support his claims, MacArthur tacitly encouraged an ultimately abortive effort by conservative Republicans to nominate him for president in 1944. Nevertheless, as in their earlier relationship, Roosevelt seemed unconcerned by MacArthur's politics and approved his promotion to five-star General of the Army in 1944. The following spring MacArthur became commander of all American army forces in the Pacific. As a result of his genuine achievements in the Pacific war as well as his excessive public relations effort, in later years many Americans credited him with Pacific victories won not only by his forces, but by the navy and marines under separate command.

Recent assessments of MacArthur's campaigns during World War II call into question his claim that he accomplished much with minimal resources. In fact, from mid-1942 on he controlled far more extensive resources than the Japanese. Until the invasion of the Philippines in October 1944, his casualties remained low in part because the Joint Chiefs prevented him from carrying out several dangerous operations. His own theater played only a supporting role, subordinate to the navy, in defeating Japan.

In autumn 1944 Roosevelt and the Joint Chiefs of Staff approved a major invasion of the Philippines. MacArthur anticipated crushing Japanese forces quickly, cutting Japan's links to Southeast Asia and thereby forcing Tokyo to surrender quickly. The operation failed to achieve its promised results. Fighting in the Philippines continued right up until August 1945 when the use of atomic bombs and the entry of the Soviet Union into the Pacific war made the campaign irrelevant. The ten-month battle for the Philippines devastated the islands and resulted in some of the Pacific war's highest casualty rates, but it had little effect on Japan's decision to surrender.

Nearly all biographers agree that the most positive period of MacArthur's professional life coincided with his service as occupation commander in Japan. President Harry Truman privately derided the general as "Mr. Prima Donna, Brass Hat, Five-Star MacArthur" and complained that only political pressure from Republicans led him to send the war hero to Tokyo. However, MacArthur proved well suited for the job of overseeing the restructuring of America's wartime enemy.

Working under guidelines developed in Washington, the "Allied" occupation was virtually an American monopoly. The general, widely referred to by his acronym SCAP (supreme commander for the Allied powers), presided over a complex process of demilitarizing and democratizing an authoritarian state. Occupation authorities administered policies and implemented reforms in both military and nonmilitary affairs. Although policies for Japan were technically to be formulated by the U.S. government and its wartime Allies, MacArthur usually ignored the Allies and often informed Washington of actions only after they had taken place.

Under the supreme commander's direct if autocratic leadership, the SCAP bureaucracy supervised the demobilization of millions of Japanese soldiers and sailors, conducted a limited purge of militarists and extreme nationalists from public life, promoted the growth of a trade union movement, encouraged an effective land reform, championed women's legal rights, restructured the education and police systems, and made a tentative effort to control the nation's dominant business combines, the *zaibatsu*.

MacArthur was especially proud of imposing an American-written constitution in 1947. It incorporated liberal western political forms, such as universal suffrage, and abolished Japan's right to maintain armed forces or conduct war. Observers noted, however, that democratic forms did not automatically assure democracy. The decision by both Truman and MacArthur to preserve a modified emperor system blocked a complete democratic change. Japan's prewar conservative political parties, along with most bureaucrats, largely escaped the purge and quickly mastered the new system. Political parties financed by large business enterprises dominated Japanese politics during the occupation and have continued to for nearly all the period since.

Neither MacArthur nor other American policy makers found it easy to cope with the virtual collapse of the Japanese economy. Initially, Japan was expected to emerge from American control as a modest industrial power alongside a revitalized China and Southeast Asia. However, civil war in China and anticolonial uprisings in Southeast Asia confounded Washington's hope that a stable, pro-American China would replace Japan as a U.S. regional proxy. The likely victory of the Chinese Communists, coupled with deteriorating Soviet-American relations in Europe, led Washington to reassess Japan's importance. By 1948 the Truman administration initiated a "reverse course," a policy centered on rebuilding Japan's industrial base while holding back on further social reform.

MacArthur, despite his personal conservatism, resisted pressure to reverse occupation reforms. He had decided to seek the Republican presidential nomination in 1948 and considered Washington's new interest in Japan really an attempt to undermine his status and accomplishments as occupation commander. The general stubbornly resisted the new agenda despite demands from the Truman administration. Ironically, MacArthur hoped to win credit from liberal Americans for his belated support for an antimonopoly program in Japan. Following the general's defeat in several Republican presidential primaries early in 1948, he abandoned his candidacy and accepted the so-called reverse course in Japan. With Truman returned to the White House, MacArthur relinquished effective control of economic policy in Japan to emissaries from Washington.

During 1949 and 1950, MacArthur emerged as a leading critic of the Truman administration's China policy. Even as the president and Secretary of State Dean Acheson tried to limit American support for the crumbling Chinese Nationalist (Kuomintang) government of Chiang Kai-shek (Jiang Jieshi), MacArthur warned in both secret dispatches and public statements that a Chinese Communist victory would endanger all Asia. When Chiang established a rump government on the island of Taiwan in 1949, the general urged Truman to protect the island and develop it as a base for future attacks on the Chinese mainland. MacArthur focused his attention so much on Taiwan that he advocated withdrawing American military forces from South Korea in 1948 and opposed any U.S. commitment to defend the government of South Korean strongman Syngman Rhee.

The outbreak of fighting in Korea on 25 June 1950 led MacArthur to dramatically change his assessment of American security priorities in East Asia. In spite of his earlier misgivings about the value of the South Korean regime, he advocated committing U.S. ground troops to Korea on 30 June, as soon as it became clear that the collapse of South Korean forces would result in a quick North Korean victory. Between 27 June and 30 June, President Truman resolved to defend South Korea and shield Taiwan from attack, and he named MacArthur commander of U.S. forces fighting on the Korean Peninsula. In July the president appointed MacArthur head of the United Nations military command, composed mainly of American troops.

From July 1950 on, MacArthur consistently pressed for a full commitment of U.S. military power to the Korean conflict. His forceful personality convinced the reluctant Joint Chiefs of Staff—who feared that the operation risked the safety of nearly all the nation's combat-ready troops—to authorize a daring amphibious counterattack behind enemy lines at Inchon on 15 September 1950. Its success resulted in the rapid defeat of most North Korean forces south of the 38th parallel (which divided the two Koreas) and the recapture of Seoul, South Korea's capital. Securing the 38th parallel fulfilled the original war aims of both the United States and the United Nations.

At this point, however, the Truman administration decided to expand the war by entering North Korea, destroying its government, and unifying the peninsula. Even though MacArthur vigorously supported these goals, he came into increasing conflict with civilian and military leaders in Washington because of his public calls to widen the war by assisting Chinese Nationalist forces on Taiwan in attacking the Chinese mainland. During a visit to Taiwan at the beginning of August and in a message to the Veterans of Foreign Wars a few weeks later, MacArthur demanded that Truman help the Nationalists land in China in order to relieve pressure on Korea, weaken the Beijing government, and turn back the Communist threat throughout Asia. These calls contradicted the ongoing efforts of Truman and Acheson to separate the Korean conflict from the Chinese civil war and risked, in their opinion, bringing Chinese Communist or even Soviet forces into the Korean War.

During September and October 1950, as MacArthur's forces pressed northward toward the North Korean–Chinese border along the Yalu River, the general minimized the danger of provoking Chinese intervention. At the Wake Island Conference on 15 October he assured a nervous Truman that the Chinese threat to intervene if U.S. forces moved into North Korea was a bluff. Even if they did so, he declared, they would easily be crushed by superior American power. Privately, in words to his staff, MacArthur appeared to savor the prospect of Chinese intervention in the Korean War as it would provide a justification for American attacks on China and greater assistance to Taiwan.

Despite the general's assurances to Truman, Chinese "volunteers" undertook a massive intervention in Korea at the end of November, just as MacArthur prepared to announce military victory in the campaign. During December 1950 and January 1951, the Chinese pushed U.S. forces south of the 38th parallel in a costly and humiliating retreat. Describing the situation as an "entirely new war," MacArthur blamed his battlefield problems on restrictions against attacking China. He rejected the administration's idea of seeking an armistice that merely restored the prewar boundary along the 38th parallel. Nor did he agree with the views of Truman and most military officials that expanding the war in Korea would make Western Europe, America's top security priority, more vulnerable to Soviet attack. The general insisted that his unique mastery of what he called "Oriental psychology" enabled him to dismiss the dangers of provoking a world war.

As MacArthur issued increasingly shrill warnings of imminent defeat, the Joint Chiefs of Staff discovered that he routinely exaggerated the danger to his troops and fought the war more vigorously in press releases than on the battlefield. In contrast to his dire predictions of defeat unless he received permission to attack China, battle lines stabilized near the 38th parallel in

March 1951. That month, just before President Truman planned to present a cease-fire proposal to North Korean and Chinese leaders, MacArthur sabotaged the effort by issuing a public demand that Chinese forces surrender at once to him or risk attacks upon their homeland.

On 5 April Republican congressman Joseph Martin released a letter sent to him earlier by MacArthur in which the general endorsed Martin's charge that Truman was guilty of appeasement and responsible for thousands of American deaths. There was, the letter insisted, "no substitute for victory." By calling for a wider war whose dimensions and consequences could not be gauged and by openly attacking the president, MacArthur sealed his fate. Some evidence suggests that the general actually hoped to goad Truman into firing him so that he could escape responsibility for the earlier battlefield reverses and the emerging stalemate in Korea. In any case, on 11 April 1951, after getting the approval of nearly all his senior military, diplomatic, and political advisers, an angry Truman relieved MacArthur of all his military commands.

MacArthur returned to a hero's welcome in the United States. The public outpouring reflected many things besides agreement with his call for a wider war. As the last major commander of the Second World War to return home, MacArthur symbolized the great victories in that struggle, which had united, rather than divided, Americans. The general made a dramatic speech to Congress on 19 April 1951 in which he falsely denied advocating that American troops be used to fight China but advocated, nevertheless, a wider war to assure military victory. He closed his address by citing the words from an old army song: "Old soldiers never die. They just fade away."

Clearly, the old general did not expect to fade away. He testified for several days during spring 1951 before congressional panels, trying to persuade the legislators of the wisdom of his strategy. However, nearly all senior military commanders refuted his call for a wider war. In the memorable words of General Omar Bradley, a conflict with China would involve the United States in the "wrong war, at the wrong place, at the wrong time, and against the wrong enemy." The public, which adored the general's sense of the dramatic, never voiced much interest in widening the Korean War.

MacArthur tried to recover momentum by making a series of nationwide speeches denouncing both Korean War strategy and the liberal domestic policies of the Truman administration. His hyperbolic, partisan attacks soon bored the public, and interest in his message faded when Korean armistice talks began late in the summer of 1951.

MacArthur tried to rekindle interest in his candidacy for the presidency by delivering the keynote address at the 1952 Republican nominating convention. The delegates cheered dutifully but then nominated another war hero, General Dwight D. Eisenhower. A disappointed MacArthur abandoned politics and dropped out of public life.

In 1952 MacArthur accepted the largely honorary position of board chairman of Remington Rand, later Sperry-Rand. He made occasional speeches but lived a generally secluded life in New York City. Shortly before his death in Washington, D.C., he published a memoir, *Reminiscences*, and from his hospital bed warned President Lyndon Johnson against committing troops to a land war in Asia, a war he felt would be unwinnable and unpopular. Following a state funeral in Washington, D.C., he was buried in Norfolk, Virginia.

MacArthur left an ambiguous legacy. Admiration for his World War II victories, supervision of occupied Japan, and eloquent rhetoric on the themes of duty, honor, and country must be tempered by his performance during the Korean War. His public challenge of civilian authority and accusations against the Truman administration contributed to the appeal of Senator Joseph R. McCarthy's charges that Communist subversion undermined American security.

• The Douglas MacArthur Papers are in the MacArthur Memorial Archives in Norfolk, Va. Secondary sources include D. Clayton James, *The Years of MacArthur* (3 vols., 1970–1985); Carol M. Petillo, *Douglas MacArthur: The Philippine Years* (1981); and Michael Schaller, *Douglas MacArthur: The Far Eastern General* (1989). See also, William McLeary, ed., *We Shall Return: MacArthur's Commanders and the Defeat of Japan* (1988).

MICHAEL SCHALLER

MACARTHUR, John D. (6 Mar. 1897–6 Jan. 1978), insurance executive and billionaire, was born in Pittston, Pennsylvania, the son of William Telfer MacArthur, a farmer and Presbyterian minister, and Georgiana Welstead. Dropping out of public school after the eighth grade, MacArthur worked for a time with his brother Charles on the staff of the *Chicago Herald* and the *Chicago Examiner*. In 1919 MacArthur married Louise Ingalls; they had two children, one of whom, J. Roderick MacArthur, independently established himself as a millionaire by selling commemorative plates through mail order. In 1928, with the financial assistance of his brother Alfred, MacArthur paid $7,500 for the Marquette Life Insurance Company. Despite the failure of many insurance businesses in the Great Depression, his survived by offering policies to low-income clients at premiums that the larger companies considered not worth the effort of collecting. In 1935 he purchased Bankers Life and Casualty Corporation, another small insurance company, for $2,500. Bankrupt at the time of purchase, the acquired company almost proved to be MacArthur's ruin; within one month of purchase, four major death claims were filed against it. In August 1938, after divorcing his first wife, MacArthur married his secretary, Catherine Hyland; they had no children. By 1940 MacArthur's insurance business was valued at over $1 million. By the mid-1950s he was considered by *Fortune* magazine to be one of America's wealthiest men.

At about this time MacArthur began investing in real estate in Florida. He bought more than 25,000 acres in Palm Beach County alone, as well as extensive tracts of land on both coasts, real estate holdings that totaled more than 100,000 acres. As one of Florida's major developers, MacArthur's attitudes toward environmental protection had a large impact on the state. At first he was lauded for his responsible policies, which included the widespread replanting of trees and rerouting roads when they threatened naturally beautiful or ecologically important areas. However, MacArthur's patience with conservationists soon wore thin. When protests arose that his development endangered the habitat of the alligator, MacArthur retorted, "Has anyone ever justified the existence of an alligator? They eat cattle and dogs. When they start eating kids the public is going to feel different about them. Let's stuff a few and put them in a museum and get rid of the rest."

MacArthur also was sole owner of the Citizens Bank and Trust Company, the largest Illinois bank not based in Chicago, with assets estimated at $365 million. He acquired extensive real estate in New York City, including the Gulf and Western Building, the Lincoln Tower apartment buildings, and two office buildings at 535 and 545 Fifth Avenue, and he obtained controlling interest in companies like the Royal American Industries, Inc., and the Southern Realty and Utility Company. In addition to his investments, MacArthur spent a portion of his time during the 1950s editing the magazine *Theatre Arts*. In 1965 MacArthur paid the $25,000 ransom for the DeLong star ruby, which had been stolen from New York's Museum of Natural History. When asked about the incident, he shrugged it off, saying "I've played hands of poker for more than that."

Known as an eccentric, MacArthur brought upon himself later in life adverse public comment. When his grandson Greg de Cordova-MacArthur disappeared in 1973 while hitchhiking in Mexico, MacArthur refused to help in the search efforts, saying "I have so many grandchildren." MacArthur, who died in West Palm Beach, had stated that he wished "to spare my friends and relatives the inconveniences involved in attending a funeral," and none was held. In his will, MacArthur directed that his fortune be used to set up two charitable foundations, the Retirement Research Foundation and the John D. and Catherine T. MacArthur Foundation.

Starting from almost nothing, MacArthur became one of the richest men in the United States. Because his companies were entirely privately owned, the full extent of his wealth is difficult to ascertain. He always refused to comment on the exact sum, saying "Anyone who knows what he's worth isn't worth very much." Remarkably thrifty in his lifestyle, MacArthur did not employ any servants and flew economy class on airplanes.

• For further information on MacArthur, see Jon Nordheimer, "John D. MacArthur: Accessible Billionaire," *New York Times*, 3 June 1973; William S. Hoffman, *The Stockholder* (1969); Lewis Bemen, "The Last Billionaires," *Fortune*, Nov.

1976; John D. and Catherine T. MacArthur Foundation, *John D. MacArthur* (1978–1988); and MacArthur Foundation, *John D. MacArthur, the Man and His Legacy: The First Ten Years* (1989). An obituary is in the *New York Times*, 7 Jan. 1978.

ELIZABETH ZOE VICARY

MACARTHUR, Robert Helmer (7 Apr. 1930–1 Nov. 1972), ecologist, was born in Toronto, Ontario, Canada, the son of John Wood MacArthur, a college professor, and Olive Turner. Much of his childhood was spent rambling through the woods of Ontario and Vermont, where he developed a fascination for the many different species of birds that live there. In 1947, after completing his early education in Toronto's public schools, he matriculated at Marlboro College in Vermont, one of two schools at which his father taught genetics; he received his B.A. degree four years later. In 1951 he began his graduate work at Brown University, receiving his M.S. degree in mathematics in 1953. He married Elizabeth Bayles Whittemore in 1952; they had four children.

MacArthur chose to complete his graduate work in ecology rather than in mathematics and attended Yale University for a year before entering the U.S. Army as a mathematician. While in the service he developed a method to measure the stability of a species in a given geographic area by applying probability theory to frequency sightings, a method he published in 1955. In 1956 he returned to Yale and completed his dissertation on five closely related species of warblers that seemed to occupy the same ecological niche in the spruce forests of New England. According to the niche theory's competitive exclusion principle, one or more of these species should have become extinct, yet all five thrived. By demonstrating that these warblers manage to coexist because each one hunts for food in a different part of the spruce tree, MacArthur earned the Ecological Society of America's Mercer Award in 1958, the year his dissertation was published, and the year after he received his Ph.D. in biology from Yale.

MacArthur then spent a year in England studying field ornithology at Oxford University. During this stay he developed the "broken stick" model, which postulated that when competing species of birds coexist in the same community, they divide that community among themselves in ways that, like the pieces of a broken stick, are both randomly sized and mutually exclusive. Although this theory was later rejected by a number of ecologists—including MacArthur himself—on the grounds that it did not apply to large or heterogeneous populations of species, it stimulated the development of more sophisticated models, such as the lognormal, logseries, and geometric distributions; it thus constituted a giant step forward in terms of understanding species distribution.

In 1958 MacArthur returned to the United States to accept a position as an assistant professor of biology at the University of Pennsylvania. Although primarily interested in birds up to this point, he now began to seek patterns that applied to a multitude of other species as well—an endeavor that had been neglected by most ecologists because they were more interested in describing and cataloging nature than in interpreting it. In 1959 he proposed models for understanding differences in size distribution among animals, as well as the apparent lack of aggressive behavior between many competing species. In 1960 he focused on the causes of species abundance and the varying degrees of rareness among species in a given habitat, as well as the relationship between niche size and species diversity (the number of different but related species in a given population). Over the next few years he made several important contributions. First he addressed the population effects of natural selection and undertook a study of the significance of niche overlap as a contributor to species diversity in tropical climates. In 1962 he showed that the basic theorems of natural selection apply to species without regard to individual size, environment, life expectancy, or rates of growth, reproduction, or mortality. Next he developed a method to represent graphically the interactions between a predator and its prey. A 1964 paper suggested ways in which simple ecological systems could be understood by means of computer simulation and analysis. Although many of these contributions gained acceptance slowly among ecologists because they seemed to strip away much of the mystique of nature and to oversimplify its many nuances, they nonetheless stimulated much thoughtful discussion and led to the development of more sophisticated and useful models.

Despite having become a full professor at Pennsylvania, in 1965 MacArthur left to join the biology department at Princeton University. With Joseph H. Connell, a professor of biology at the University of California at Santa Barbara, he coauthored *The Biology of Populations* (1966), a textbook treatment of population biology. That discipline attempts to recognize the patterns of time and space within which a particular population exists, to trace the evolution of that population via natural selection, and to understand how its species grow, interact, and regulate the population's size.

Shortly thereafter MacArthur and Edward O. Wilson of Harvard coauthored *The Theory of Island Biogeography* (1967), a full-blown presentation of the theory of species equilibrium that the two had first published in a relatively brief article four years earlier. According to this theory, a given island can support only a fixed number of species; any new species that migrates to an island in a state of species equilibrium and succeeds in becoming part of that island's population must necessarily cause a resident species to become extinct. The number of species is kept in equilibrium, even though the actual species are in constant flux. Therefore, the factors that determine species equilibrium are the rate of extinction, in large part a function of the size of the island (smaller islands can support fewer species), and the rate of immigration, in large part a function of the distance of the island from the mainland. By checking their theory against observations of the floral and faunal recolonization of Krakatoa after

its volcanic destruction in 1883, MacArthur and Wilson demonstrated that species extinction occurs much more frequently than biologists had previously believed. The species equilibrium theory shook the discipline of biogeography (the study of the geographic distribution of plants and animals) to its roots. Previously, the few active biogeographers had concentrated on observing and cataloging rather than predicting, mostly because they lacked good quantitative models. The species equilibrium theory provided them with just such a model, and before long more sophisticated versions of the theory were being developed and applied to a variety of discrete ecological communities or "habitat islands," such as mountaintops, lakes, coral reefs, and even bottles of water.

In 1968 MacArthur was appointed the Henry Fairfield Osborn Professor of Biology at Princeton. The next year he developed the concept of foliage height diversity, which explained why more species of birds live in a complex habitat like a forest than in a simple one like a field. He offered a mathematical equation for predicting how many species of birds could be supported by a given habitat, based on the height of its vegetation. That same year he also offered a hypothesis as to why some species eat only one kind of food and presented the concept of species packing. The latter theory, perhaps MacArthur's most important contribution to the development of ecology, postulated that a given habitat can support a number of species equal to the number of its niches that can be exploited by those species. The theory suggested that ecologists could manipulate a community so that its habitat could support more species than the ones that had migrated to it largely by chance. The species packing theory was a major development in ecology because it stimulated ecologists to think of themselves as potential managers of the environment rather than mere spectators.

In 1971 MacArthur, at the peak of his creative powers as an ecologist, discovered that he had an incurable case of renal cancer. Consequently he determined to weave together the many threads of investigation that had been his life's work. The result was *Geographical Ecology: Patterns in the Distribution of Species* (1972), a compendium of his ideas on a wide range of biogeographical topics including environment structure, species morphology and behavior, and the dynamics of population change. Written entirely from memory during a few months in a secluded part of Vermont, the book was published shortly before he died in Princeton, New Jersey.

In addition to his official duties at Princeton, MacArthur was also a research associate of the Smithsonian Tropical Research Institute and often visited its station on Barro Colorado Island in the Panama Canal Zone. Despite the significance of his contributions to the development of ecology as a scientific discipline, he received almost no major awards; however, these contributions did not go unrecognized by his peers, who elected him to the American Academy of Arts and Sciences and the National Academy of Sciences.

MacArthur possessed the observational skills of a naturalist and the pattern-making skills of a mathematician, abilities that made him unique among ecologists. By employing these skills to the fullest, he was able to develop a plethora of mathematical models that explained in relatively simple and quantitative terms many of the complexities of nature. He played a major role in transforming ecology in general, and biogeography in particular, from disciplines that primarily described rather than predicted into sciences that seek not only to recognize broad patterns but also to develop tools with which environments can be managed intelligently for the good of all species.

• A good biography of MacArthur is Edward O. Wilson and Evelyn G. Hutchinson, "Robert Helmer MacArthur," National Academy of Sciences, *Biographical Memoirs* 58 (1989): 319–27. Martin L. Cody and Jared M. Diamond, eds., *Ecology and Evolution of Communities* (1975), presents additional useful biographical information, with a complete bibliography of MacArthur's work and an evaluation of its significance. An obituary is in the *New York Times*, 2 Nov. 1972.

CHARLES W. CAREY, JR.

MACARTNEY, Clarence Edward Noble (18 Sept. 1879–19 Feb. 1957), Presbyterian pastor, was born in Northwood, Ohio, the son of John L. McCartney, a pastor in the Reformed Presbyterian church and professor of science in Geneva College, and Catherine Robertson, a writer. Macartney, who altered the spelling of his surname from that of his parents, moved with his family in his early years from Ohio to Pennsylvania, California, Colorado, and Wisconsin.

In 1901 Macartney earned his B.A. from the University of Wisconsin, where he became an accomplished debater under the tutelage of the future senator Robert M. La Follette. After a brief bout of vocational indecision, he entered Princeton Theological Seminary, where he adopted the conservative Princeton Theology, which affirmed a strict doctrine of biblical inerrancy. He received an M.A. from Princeton University in 1904 and graduated from Princeton Seminary in 1905.

Macartney was ordained to the pastorate of the First Presbyterian Church of Paterson, New Jersey, in 1905 and led a revitalization of that downtown congregation. In 1914 he moved to the Arch Street Presbyterian Church in Philadelphia and eventually earned a reputation as the city's foremost preacher. While at the Arch Street church he broadcasted worship services on local radio and frequently lectured on homiletics at Princeton Seminary.

In 1922 Macartney led the conservative Presbyterian response to Harry Emerson Fosdick's sermon, "Shall the Fundamentalists Win?" in which Fosdick contrasted liberal and conservative theological views and pled for tolerance for liberals in the church. Macartney's sermon, "Shall Unbelief Win?," challenged Fosdick's liberal views as irreconcilable with Presbyterian doctrinal standards and encouraged evangelical Christians to fight for the faith. He inaugurated disciplinary action that finally resulted in Fosdick's resignation from his position at the First Presbyterian Church in New York City.

In 1924 Macartney, then the acknowledged leader of the fundamentalist party in the Presbyterian church, was elected moderator of the General Assembly, the highest elective office of the church, from which he worked to advance the fundamentalist cause. Despite his efforts, the Presbyterian church by 1927 decided to tolerate liberals in the church in order to preserve a united mission.

In 1926 Macartney, feeling called to remain in the pastorate, declined an appointment to the chair of apologetics and Christian ethics at Princeton Seminary and in 1927 accepted a call to the prestigious First Presbyterian Church in Pittsburgh.

From 1927 to 1929 Macartney unsuccessfully opposed plans to reorganize the administration of Princeton Seminary in order to still unrest between moderate and conservative members of the faculty and administration. Upon the reorganization of the school in 1929, he declined an invitation to serve on the board of trustees. Instead, Macartney became a trustee of the newly founded Westminster Seminary in Philadelphia, which sought to preserve the traditions of the "old Princeton."

Nonetheless, in 1936 Macartney resigned from the Westminster board because of disagreements with the Westminster faculty, most notably J. Gresham Machen, over the wisdom of founding an independent board for Presbyterian foreign missions. Likewise, when Machen and others seceded from the Presbyterian church in 1936 to form the Orthodox Presbyterian church, Macartney chose to remain in the denomination to work for reform of the church from within.

From 1936 until his retirement in 1953 Macartney focused his energies on the First Presbyterian Church in Pittsburgh. His Sunday morning congregation consistently numbered from 1,200 to 1,600. He founded a Tuesday Noon Club for Businessmen that averaged an attendance of more than 800 and directed a popular Wednesday evening service. At the same time, Macartney advanced conservative Christianity by nurturing a number of assistant pastors, including Harold J. Ockenga, founder of the National Association of Evangelicals, and through leadership of the conservative "League of Faith."

In the course of his career Macartney authored fifty-seven books, most of which were collections of sermons. He specialized in biographical sermons, such as those published in *Great Women of the Bible* (1943) and *The Greatest Men of the Bible* (1941), and preached his most famous sermon, "Come Before Winter," a discourse on the right use of opportunity, every autumn from 1915 until his retirement.

Macartney lectured widely on college and seminary campuses, including the Princeton and Fuller seminaries. He traveled repeatedly to the Middle East in order to trace Paul's missionary journeys. He also cultivated a passionate interest in the Civil War, visiting many of the conflict's battlefields and authoring numerous studies of the war, including *Lincoln and His Generals* (1925) and *Lincoln and the Bible* (1949).

Throughout his ministry Macartney sought to advance orthodox Calvinism in the church and promote Christianity's influence on American culture. His theology stressed the sovereignty of God, the substitutionary atonement and bodily resurrection of Christ, and the inerrancy of Scripture. Profoundly disturbed by the social and cultural changes that transformed America after World War I, he opposed divorce, birth control, Sabbath desecration, the teaching of biological evolution, the use of alcoholic beverages, and the decline of family worship.

A lifelong bachelor, Macartney was a dignified and cultured preacher. In significant ways he embodied the ideas and ideals of Presbyterian fundamentalism of the 1920s. In the wake of the fundamentalist-modernist conflicts he sought to maintain a conservative theological witness in the church and culture. He died in the family home in Beaver Falls, Pennsylvania.

• Macartney's papers are housed in the McCartney Library, Geneva College, Beaver Falls, Pa. Important works by Macartney not mentioned above include *Things Most Surely Believed* (1930) and *The Christian Faith and the Spirit of the Age* (1940). Autobiographical reflections by Macartney are in "Warm Hearts and Steady Faith," *Christian Century* 56 (Mar. 1939): 315–19, and in *The Making of a Minister*, ed. J. Clyde Henry (1961). Chapters addressing Macartney's life and role in the fundamentalist-modernist conflicts may be found in Bradley J. Longfield, *The Presbyterian Controversy: Fundamentalists, Modernists, and Moderates* (1991), and Charles A. Russell, *Voices of American Fundamentalism* (1976). An obituary is in the *New York Times*, 21 Feb. 1957.

BRADLEY J. LONGFIELD

MACAULEY, James Alvan (17 Jan. 1872–16 Jan. 1952), business executive, was born in Wheeling, West Virginia, the son of James A. Macauley, a civil servant, and Rebecca Jane Mills. Macauley's father, an Irish immigrant, fought in the Civil War, lost an arm, and spent nine months in a Confederate prison camp. After the war he became West Virginia's first secretary of state. Alvan, as the son preferred to be called, attended Lehigh University and graduated from Columbian College (later George Washington University) with a law degree in 1892. He worked as an attorney in Washington, D.C., and in 1895, the year he married Estelle Littlepage, he became a patent attorney with the National Cash Register Company.

In 1901 Macauley moved to St. Louis to head American Arithmometer, the forerunner of Burroughs Adding Machine Company. Macauley rebuilt the firm but in 1905 quarreled with the city government over expansion plans. He then found suitable quarters for his company in Detroit, loaded his entire factory into boxcars at night, and moved out of St. Louis. Five years later, Henry Bourne Joy, president of the Packard Motor Car Company hired Macauley as general manager.

In 1916 Macauley became the president of Packard, and in that capacity he built a record of continued expansion. He hired Jesse Vincent, a brilliant engineer, to spearhead the company's technical developments. Vincent put the company on the map in 1915 with his "twin six," a twelve-cylinder car. Large, smooth, and powerful, the new auto set Packard above the competition. During World War I the company manufactured Liberty aircraft motors. Throughout the 1920s Packard prospered and added to its growing reputation. Macauley, ever the innovator, replaced the twin six with an eight-cylinder car in 1923. His cars sold worldwide and became the favorites of European royalty and the so-called lap robe trade at home. Production rose from 15,377 autos in 1922 to 47,855 in 1929. The money flowed in; from 1925 through 1929, Macauley's Packard earned the company $86 million. The price of its stock rose from a little over $5 a share in 1922 to a high of over $153 a share in 1929.

The luxury market never accounted for more than 10 percent of national car sales, however, and during the depression it melted away to nothing. Macauley's production fell only to 6,265 cars in 1934. He always tried to build a moderately priced Packard, to give his factory volume, and also make the more expensive Packards that maintained his company's reputation. He repeated that magic in the 1930s when he hired experts on mass production, many from the Big Three's ranks, to produce the 120 in 1935, a car that Packard could sell for as little as $980, or $6,500 less than the firm's most expensive model. The cheaper car was a smashing success; the factory had 10,000 orders before production began, and it ended the firm's financial losses. Macauley also reintroduced the twin six in 1932 to retain the manufacturer's cachet.

Macauley retired as president in 1939 but remained chairman of the board for another nine years. During the postwar period, the managers he had brought in to build the 120 concentrated on the medium-priced market with the Clipper, a streamlined, modern car introduced in 1941. Macauley became upset, however, when his company lost its lead in the growing luxury market to Cadillac. After failing to oust Packard's president, George Christopher, in 1948, Macauley resigned in disgust.

During his long career, Macauley was also active outside his company. He was president of the Automobile Manufacturers Association, sat on the Detroit Board of Commerce, and during World War II was president of the Automotive Council for War Production. He died in Clearwater, Pennsylvania.

Macauley was a man of foibles and passions, but throughout his career he maintained a reputation as one of the few gentlemen in the auto industry. He built cars for an elite class of discerning people who demanded the best of everything and who lived the way Macauley did; he understood their desires and temperaments. He disliked people who jingled coins or had gold fillings or awkward names; he shortened his own. He was an avid golfer, fisherman, and hunter, and crafted fine furniture in his woodworking shop. Even in the 1930s he lived the good life; he belonged to numerous private clubs, went to Florida every winter, and to Europe at least once a year. He was famous for the sign over his office door that proclaimed "Important If True," and his truths were the only ones that counted at Packard for a quarter of a century.

• Macauley's papers, if he left any, have not been found. He was on *Time* magazine's cover on 22 July 1929, and again on 4 Nov. 1935. Both issues have interesting, detailed articles on him and his place in the auto industry. A hagiographic biography by Morton H. Jaffe, *Alvan Macauley: Automotive Leader and Pioneer* (1957), was privately printed.

JAMES A. WARD

MACBETH, William (9 Aug. 1851–10 Aug. 1917), art dealer, was born in Madden, (Northern) Ireland, the son of Robert Macbeth, a schoolteacher, and Marry Haffey. For a brief while after his father's death in 1868, Macbeth took over his classes. In 1871 he was given a clerical position in the clearing house of the banks of the city of Dublin. He left the clearing house in 1873 to come to New York City, where his brother James was established as a successful businessman. Within a month of his arrival, he found a job at $5.00 a week in the gallery of Frederick Keppel, a dealer in fine prints, at 66 Beekman Street. This was his introduction to the art trade. "Think I will like it here," he noted in his diary on 3 November.

Macbeth had good reason to be happy in his position. Keppel, who was senior to Macbeth by only six years, thoroughly enjoyed his trade and was easy to work with. As Macbeth's diary makes clear, Keppel and his wife looked after him with the care they might have lavished on a younger brother. From almost the start of his employment, Macbeth was a valued member of the staff. A mere two months after he was hired, he was given the responsibility of managing the gallery entirely by himself while Keppel was in Europe on business. Macbeth received raises frequently, and in 1883, at the conclusion of his first ten years with the firm, he was given a partnership.

Macbeth's diversions from his duties at Keppel's gallery included faithful attendance at Episcopal services in Brooklyn, where he lived, the teaching of a Sunday school class, and visits to exhibitions held by such organizations as the National Academy of Design and the Society of American Artists. Brooklyn remained his principal place of residence throughout his life. In 1883 he married Jessie Walker. The couple had three children.

Although his position with Keppel was financially rewarding, Macbeth ultimately decided to establish a gallery of his own. The opening took place in April 1892. Among his chief assets was abundance of goodwill from Keppel; the two men remained friends until Keppel's death in 1912. They were never rivals in business; although Macbeth included prints in his inventory, his principal interest lay in oils, watercolors, and drawings. He determined that his gallery, unlike Keppel's, was to sell only American art. Macbeth had not only visited exhibitions of American art during his years with Keppel, but after becoming a partner he organized shows of American watercolors in the gallery. Macbeth sensed that the time was ripe for a distinctly American gallery. He was proud that his was the first gallery to specialize in American art and referred to it as such in *Art Notes*, an occasional publication of the Macbeth Gallery. Nevertheless, for the first six years he offered annual exhibitions of European paintings, mainly Dutch, and employed agents to scout the European market for him. The proceeds from the sale of European works helped to keep the gallery afloat at a time when the depressed national economy frightened many collectors away from art lacking the cachet of European origin.

Among the many artists whose work Macbeth successfully exhibited in the early years were Arthur B. Davies, Charles H. White, Homer Dodge Martin, Alexander H. Wyant, George Inness, Winslow Homer, and the older painters of the Hudson River School. As American impressionist painting grew increasingly popular at the turn of the century, it became one of Macbeth's preferred schools.

Although he was endowed with enough of the pioneer spirit to specialize in the art of his adopted country, Macbeth never revealed wholehearted enthusiasm for the cutting edge of American art. He took his boldest step in 1908, when he offered a show of sixty-three works by Davies, William J. Glackens, Robert Henri, George Luks, Ernest Lawson, Maurice Prendergast, Everett Shinn, and John Sloan. Following the exhibition, the group came to be known as the Eight and also, because of the unromantic cityscapes depicted by some of them, Luks and Sloan especially, as the Ashcan School. As measured by the crowds of visitors, the press coverage, and the sale of seven pictures, the show was a success. Macbeth believed that more pictures would have sold had not the stock market been weak at the time. Yet he never showed the Eight as a group again, although he did occasionally stock pictures by some of them.

Macbeth may have lacked the daring of certain other dealers of his day—Alfred Stieglitz, most notably, who showed modernist drawings, prints, and paintings at his gallery at 291 Fifth Avenue—but he nonetheless gave the public much to enjoy. Art lovers from across the country had opportunities to see works from Macbeth's inventory. He quickly became the leading figure in an informal network of dealers in American art, some of whom followed his example and stocked nothing else. In search of works that would please their clients, the firms frequently traded with one another; thus pictures found by Macbeth were shown in major cities from Massachusetts to California.

For a dealer so conservative, Macbeth showed surprising tolerance for the controversial International Exhibition of Modern Art, which opened at the 69th Regiment Armory in New York on 17 February 1913 and has gone down in history as "the Armory Show." He praised the project in its planning stages and after the opening wrote in *Art Notes* for April 1913, "On examining the pictures through several visits, my pleasure was in no measure marred because I found a few score of them to be utterly absurd, and, from my point of view, to bear no relation to art, except, possibly, in some cases, as decorations of a certain disagreeable sort." He concluded by saying "Hats off" to the show's organizers.

In *Art Notes* for April 1917, twenty-five years after the opening of his gallery, Macbeth described the event as "a rash venture under existing conditions, and disaster was frequently predicted." But, as he said in effect, the power of friendship had seen him through. More important, although he did not say so, was his keen eye and his understanding of the public for art. Four months later Macbeth died, in Southampton, New York. His gallery, a component of the national art market far too important and lucrative to be abandoned, continued in business until 1954, directed first by his son, Robert, and later by his nephew Robert McIntyre.

• Macbeth's diary and the correspondence, publications, scrapbooks, and ledgers of the Macbeth Gallery are in the collection of the Archives of American Art, Smithsonian Institution. On Macbeth and the Eight, see Bennard B. Perlman, *The Immortal Eight* (1979), and Elizabeth Milroy, *Painters of a New Century: The Eight & American Art* (1991). An obituary is in *American Art News*, 18 Aug. 1917.

MALCOLM GOLDSTEIN

MACCALLUM, William George (18 Apr. 1874–3 Feb. 1944), pathologist, was born in Dunnesville, Ontario, Canada, the son of George Alexander MacCallum, a physician, and Florence Octavia Eakins, a musician. Educated at home until age nine, and then at the public lower school and high school in Dunnesville, MacCallum enrolled in 1890 at the University of Toronto. He graduated in 1894 with a B.A. in the classics. Having developed an interest in parasites through the influence of a biology professor, he then entered Johns Hopkins Medical School, from which he received an M.D. in 1897. During the summer of 1897, while studying the malarial parasites in the blood of a crow, MacCallum identified the "flagellated form of the avian parasite as the agent of sexual conjugation." This discovery led to later work in the reproductive cycle of the human malarial parasite. On completion of his internship in 1898, MacCallum became an assistant in the Johns Hopkins pathological laboratory of William Henry Welch.

In 1900 MacCallum went to Germany to work in the pathological laboratory of Felix M. Marchand in Leipzig. He returned in 1901 to Johns Hopkins, where he was made resident pathologist. In 1902 MacCallum published two crucial papers elucidating the microscopic anatomy of the lymphatic system. The first paper demonstrated that lymphatic vessels had "complete endothelial linings and comprised a closed continuous vascular system similar to that of the arteries and veins." The second paper demonstrated how the red blood cells were actually absorbed into this "closed" system. His study of the lymphatic system had begun in Leipzig, but he completed his work under the tutelage of his colleague and close friend, Welch. He was shortly elevated to associate professor of pathology, and in 1908 he was appointed professor of pathology. In 1909 MacCallum filled the chair of pathology at Columbia University and he held this position as well as that of pathologist at the Presbyterian Hospital until 1927.

During his first fifteen years in Baltimore, spent teaching and researching in Welch's laboratory, MacCallum had a close association with William Osler, Simon Flexner, William Stewart Halsted, Eugene Opie, and Harvey Cushing, all prominent physicians. MacCallum's relationship with Halsted, the subject of a later biography by MacCallum (William Stewart Halsted, Surgeon [1930]), led to the latter's interest in complications stemming from thyroidectomie treatment. In 1905, along with pharmacologist Carl Voegtlin, MacCallum distinguished the autonomous function of the thyroid and parathyroid glands and showed the role of the parathyroid hormone in controlling calcium exchange in the body. The two also demonstrated that tetany could be prevented after the removal of the parathyroid gland by injecting a solution of calcium salts.

These theories were crucial in the safety of thyroid surgery and explained basic physiology as it related to pathologic conditions. MacCallum extended his studies on tetany to the investigation of gastric tetany, which occurs with pyloric obstruction in children as well as adults. In this condition he found the nervous excitability that resulted was due to a different cause: electrolyte loss. He also conducted ingenious experiments on the physiological effects of diseased heart valves on the circulation of dogs. Using special hooks and curved knives in a method he pioneered called duct-ligation, he was able to isolate lesions encountered in heart disease in man. By reproducing the lesion found in a disease at autopsy, MacCallum studied the effects of valvular abnormality on the mechanics of circulation in experimental animals.

MacCallum's move to New York brought new responsibilities, such as participation in the arrangements for the 1909 affiliation of the Presbyterian Hospital with Columbia's College of Physicians and Surgeons. In 1916 he was persuaded to write a *Textbook of Pathology*, which for the first time classified disease on the basis of etiology. He broke disease down into laymen's terms and discussed the "general principles underlying pathological changes." His textbook went through seven editions between 1916 and 1940, and its general principles remained in use throughout the century.

When Welch retired as chair of pathology at Johns Hopkins Medical School in 1917, MacCallum filled it as the Bixby Professor at the John Hopkins Medical School and pathologist to the Johns Hopkins Hospital. During World War I, MacCallum acted as pathologist for a commission that studied pneumonia in army camps (1914–1917).

In 1929 Johns Hopkins's department of pathology's facilities were destroyed by fire. This enabled MacCallum to design new laboratories suitable for modern studies of the pathology of humans, plants, and animals. He built rooms designed to demonstrate models of diseases in their stages of development, allowing students to concentrate on one disease at a time. MacCallum used clinical pathological conferences to integrate basic science with clinical teaching. Richard Cabot had pioneered this method at Massachusetts General Hospital in Boston with great success; its only drawback appeared to be a disproportionate focus on physical findings of diseases.

An avid medical history buff, MacCallum wrote numerous papers for the Johns Hopkins Hospital Historical Club, including "The Teaching of the Pathological Physiology" (1908); "On the Relation of the Islet of Langerhans to Glycosuria" (1909); "The Internal Secretion of the Pancreas" (1911); and "The Function of the Parathyroid Glands." He was president of the Historical Club in 1940–1941. MacCallum, a respected teacher, was known for his keen conversational skills and his quick sense of humor. Shy and somewhat moody, he remained a bachelor all of his life. He was also an enthusiastic traveler. He died in Baltimore from a stroke.

An ardent medical enthusiast, MacCallum dedicated his life to the science of pathology and the revelations it yielded, making tremendous contributions to his field. In addition to conducting early investigations on malarial parasites, he was a pioneer in the pathologic physiology of valvular heart disease, the relationship between the Islet of Langerhans and diabetes, and thyroid and parathyroid tetany. He also invented an operative technique—duct ligation—that was later used to isolate insulin. The principles set forth in his influential *Textbook of Pathology* continue to be referred to.

• Many of MacCallum's papers are available at Johns Hopkins Medical Hospital. Other papers are available through the *Journals of the American Medical Association*. MacCallum's *Textbook of Pathology* (1916) demonstrates his tremendous clarity of thought and understanding of pathogens. A biography is Warfield Longcope, "William George MacCallum," National Academy of Sciences, *Biographical Memoirs* 23 (1945). An obituary is in the *New York Times*, 4 Feb. 1944.

DAVID Y. COOPER
MICHELLE E. OSBORN

MACCAMERON, Robert Lee (14 Jan. 1866–29 Dec. 1912), figure and portrait painter, was born in Chicago, Illinois, the son of Thomas MacCameron (profession unknown), and Hattie (maiden name unknown). Named after his distant cousin General Robert E. Lee, MacCameron grew up in the backwoods of Wisconsin. An encounter with an itinerant French drawing instructor encouraged his move to Chicago, where he studied at the local Young Men's Christian Association. His formal art training began during the late 1880s in New York, under the tutelage of William M. Chase, probably at the Art Students League, and in Paris first at the Académie Julian in 1890 with Jean-Joseph Benjamin-Constant and Jean-Paul Laurens. In

late 1891 he entered the studio of Jean-Léon Gérôme, and at the end of the decade he attended James McNeill Whistler's school, the Académie Carmen. Around 1903 he received criticism from Raphael Collin, portrait painter and professor of drawing at the École des Beaux-arts. During these early years MacCameron supported himself as an illustrator, and a staff position on the London children's magazine *Boy's Own Annual* enabled him to raise funds for Paris studies.

MacCameron was academically trained to be a figure painter. Little from the 1890s—a few studies of Indians and blacks, scenes of the theater, and landscapes—has survived. Often dissatisfied with his art, MacCameron destroyed many of his early canvases. Poverty also haunted him during much of these years. However, his career changed dramatically during the first decade of the twentieth century.

MacCameron first won public recognition in 1904 at the salon of the Société des Artistes Françaises for *Mid-Lent* (destroyed). It was the first of a series of café scenes, including *The Daughter's Return* (1909, Metropolitan Museum of Art) and *The Absinthe Drinker* (1909, Memorial Art Gallery, University of Rochester), that over the next years won MacCameron repeated honors at the salon, including *hors-concours* status in 1906 for *Group of Friends* (Corcoran Gallery of Art, Washington, D.C.). In these genre paintings, the artist focused entirely on the indigent of Paris and London. MacCameron felt a strong bond with the common man because of his boyhood in Wisconsin, lumberjack experience as an adolescent, and years of deprivation and struggle as a young artist. In the tradition of Edgar Degas, Pablo Picasso, and a host of lesser-known turn-of-the-century painters, MacCameron portrayed the café as a place of refuge, the poor men and women crowded together in small groups around a table, their bodies exhausted, their faces devoid of any feelings of hope. Solace for these downtrodden men and women consisted of a glass of absinthe at the local bar. The flickering of a few candles, casting long murky shadows, provided the only illumination. By painting entirely with broad generalized brushwork and in a dark, eerie palette of black, brown, green (the color of absinthe), and maroon, MacCameron used color as a symbolist would to convey the oppressiveness of poverty. The artist found his models among street people, choosing them according to their resemblance to Christ, the Madonna, and other religious figures. While MacCameron remained an academic realist, his genre scenes were haunting and infused with so many mystical and religious overtones that one New York critic referred to them as "dramatic psychological" pictures (*New York Times*, 13 Mar. 1910). Nowhere was this more obvious than in *People of the Abyss* (1912, Musée Luxembourg, Paris), named after Jack London's novel.

The genre paintings were a respite from his portrait work, for MacCameron became an internationally famous portraitist during this period. In 1902 he married Louise Van Voorhis of Rochester, New York, and subsequently had two children. The connection with his wife's prominent family opened doors to him, and consequently his portrait trade prospered. He painted famous residents of Rochester as well as people of national and international renown, including Presidents William McKinley (Union League of Philadelphia) and William H. Taft (National Portrait Gallery, Washington, D.C.), Mrs. John Astor (location unknown), and Gustav Mahler (preparatory sketch, collection of the MacCameron family, Buffalo). MacCameron was a better-than-average portraitist with a facile handling that flattered his sitters. His portraits were the antithesis of his low-life scenes, projecting a sense of elegance that wealthy American businessmen, as well as French and English aristocrats, found appealing. So often did he cross the Atlantic Ocean to satisfy commissions that he maintained studios in Paris, London, and New York, often summering in Europe and wintering in America.

MacCameron's close colleagues included the wealthy American society artists Henry Clews, Jr., and Robert Chandler. Clews, a sculptor and friend of Auguste Rodin, probably encouraged MacCameron and Chandler to visit the great French master, for in 1910, the two first met Rodin. Rodin's confidant, the American-born duchesse de Choiseul, hoped to popularize the Frenchman's art in her native country, so she asked MacCameron to write an article about the sculptor. MacCameron complied, and the article appeared in *Town and Country* on 4 February 1911. Simultaneously, the Metropolitan Museum of Art in New York was negotiating the purchase of a number of Rodin's works; when the Metropolitan Museum's Rodin Gallery opened in 1912, MacCameron's portrait of the French sculptor was included.

In 1912 MacCameron returned to New York from abroad to satisfy a commission for a portrait of his friends the Goelets. Having suffered from heart problems for several years, he died in New York City suddenly thereafter. Not long before his demise, the artist was made a chevalier of the Legion of Honor and a knight of the Order of La Mancha. The year following MacCameron's death, memorial exhibitions were held in New York and Rochester, and in 1925 the Albright Art Gallery in Buffalo honored him with a retrospective. A self-portrait (c. 1910) is in the National Academy of Design, New York.

• MacCameron's private journal is owned by the family in Buffalo, while photographs of his works and letters (1904–1909) are held by the Rush Rhees Library, University of Rochester. His correspondence with the duchesse de Choiseul is in archives of the Musée de Rodin, Paris. The artist is interviewed in "Change in Our Skyline Foretells a New Art," *New York Times*, 5 Jan. 1913. The "Biographical Sketch of Robert Lee MacCameron, American Artist (1866–1912)" (typescript; 1965, rev. 1979), by the artist's son, Robert F. MacCameron, lists works still owned by the family. The earliest substantial discussions of the artist are Marc Legrand, "MacCameron, peintre," *Revue Moderne des Arts et de la Vie* 2–3 (1 July 1908): 10–12, and Charles H. Caffin, "Some New American Painters in Paris," *Harper's Magazine* 118 (Jan.

1909): 284–93. See also Briggs Davenport, "Making of a Salon Picture," *Harper's Weekly*, 8 Feb. 1913, pp. 7–8, for a first-hand account of the artist's working method, and Sadakichi Hartmann (pseudonym Sidney Allan), "Masterpieces of American Portraiture," *Bulletin of Photography* 17 (21 July 1915): 73–74, on his portraiture. Ilene Susan Fort, "Robert Lee MacCameron's *Portrait of Rodin* and the formation of the Metropolitan Museum of Art's Rodin Collection" (typescript; 1983), is in the collection of the author. Obituaries are in *American Art News* 11 (4 Jan. 1913): 8, and the *New York Times*, 30 Dec. 1912.

ILENE SUSAN FORT

MACCAULEY, Clay (8 May 1843–15 Nov. 1925), Unitarian clergyman and missionary, was born in Chambersburg, Pennsylvania, the son of Isaac H. MacCauley, a businessman, and Elizabeth Maxwell. A student at Dickinson College at the outbreak of the Civil War, he enlisted as a private in the Chambersburg Company and served with some distinction, rising to second lieutenant by 1863. He was captured at the battle of Chancellorsville and was interned briefly in Libby Prison before being paroled. He completed his undergraduate degree at Princeton in 1864 and served two summers in military hospitals as part of the U.S. Christian Commission.

In 1864 he joined his parents, who had moved to Chicago, Illinois, to attend Northwestern Theological Seminary. Upon graduation in 1867 he was deemed unacceptable for ordination by the Presbyterians because of his liberal views on the atonement, derived from his reading of Horace Bushnell, an influential liberal Congregationalist theologian. His fiancée, Annie Cleveland Deane (whom he married in 1867; they had no children), was connected to a Unitarian Church in Bangor, Maine, under the ministerial leadership of C. C. Everett. Everett introduced him to the Unitarians in Chicago.

After brief and unsatisfying ministries in the Unitarian churches in Detroit, Michigan, and Rochester, New York, MacCauley served in First Parish, Waltham, Massachusetts, in 1869. He left Waltham in 1873 for study in Germany, underwritten by a Waltham parishioner, studying philosophy and theology in Heidelberg, Leipzig, and Dresden. He was especially attracted to the philosophy of Karl C. F. Krause, a follower of Fichte who formulated a semipantheism, stating that nature and human consciousness are part of Absolute Being but the Absolute is not identical with them. In 1877, two years after his return from Germany, he was called to First Unitarian (later All Souls) Church in Washington, D.C. Although he led a successful reorganization and building program, he had a serious disagreement with the congregation over how to deal with indebtedness and resigned in 1880.

During the next nine years MacCauley tried various occupations. He worked for the Smithsonian Institute, studying the Menominee, Cherokee, and Seminole tribes. An illness (probably malaria) led to travels in Italy, Sicily, Montana, and Minnesota seeking a healthier climate. In 1885 he served Unity Church in St. Paul, Minnesota, and in 1886 he edited the *Minne-*

apolis Commercial Bulletin, a reform newspaper. His wife's death in 1887 added to his unsettledness. Despite his intellectual gifts and energy, he had not yet found his calling.

In 1886 some Japanese contacted Harvard University for help in transforming Keio Commercial College into a university and the American Unitarian Association for help in promoting an enlightened, modern religion. The Reverend Arthur May Knapp, who was sent to survey the situation, returned with an encouraging report, and the association undertook to establish a mission in Japan. Led by Knapp, a party of eight set out in September 1889. It included three university professors, two with wives, a young Japanese man educated at Meadville Theological Seminary, and MacCauley, who had been recruited by the American Unitarian Association. Knapp stayed only a year, so the leadership of the mission soon fell to MacCauley. As the professors returned to America one by one, he became the sole American member of the mission.

The Unitarians were not intending to convert Japanese but rather "to express the sympathy of Unitarians in America for progressive religious movements in Japan." Nevertheless there was some preaching and congregation forming, most successfully done by local Japanese associates of the mission, although MacCauley did some preaching through interpreters. He was especially involved in educational work, lecturing in rented halls to audiences mostly consisting of university students. He founded a magazine, *Shūkyo* (Religion), which continued under various names for over thirty years. His pride was the School for Advanced Learning, a kind of graduate institution for philosophy and religion, which he established and taught in. It lasted less than a decade, closing in 1899. When Unity Hall was built in 1894 it served as the focus of the mission and, after 1900, of the Japanese Unitarian Association.

The mission was always underfunded, and in 1900 American Unitarian interest waned. It was declared that the mission had accomplished its goal, and the work was handed over to the Japanese Association. MacCauley returned to the United States.

While he was in Japan MacCauley had become a figure of some importance in the foreign community and among "modern" Japanese. He began to see himself as a bridge between the West and Japan. He was a correspondent for the *Boston Transcript* and a regular contributor to English-language papers in Japan. Back in the United States, he concentrated on interpreting Japan to Americans; he wrote and spoke often on Japan as "the standard-bearer of Western Civilization in Asia." The Russo-Japanese War (1904–1905) occasioned many opportunities to promote Japan, and MacCauley attended the peace conference in Portsmouth in September 1905 as an honored friend of most of the participants. From 1902 until 1904 he was minister at Bell Street Chapel in Providence, Rhode Island.

When it appeared that the Japanese Unitarian Association was turning to a Buddhist viewpoint, the American Unitarians sent MacCauley back to Japan in 1909 to straighten things out. He stayed until 1919. He held positions in many intellectual and service societies, including vice president of the Asiatic Society of Japan, vice president of the Japanese Humane Society, councilor of the American Association, and trustee of the School for American Children. He was twice decorated by the Japanese emperor—with the Order of the Rising Sun (1909) and the Order of Sacred Treasure (1918)—for his services to Japan.

In this second term as missionary MacCauley helped turn the Unitarian headquarters into a kind of "settlement house" and participated in the organization of the "Friendly Society." This was a rudimentary labor union and was the beginning of the labor movement in Japan. In 1919 he left Japan for the last time, living in retirement in Berkeley, California, until his death.

Although the Unitarians were a tiny group in Japan, both in MacCauley's day and after—and are of no significance today—the mission and the Japanese Unitarian Association can be seen as forces in westernizing and secularizing Japan. In the United States, MacCauley was an apologist for Japan. He was one of the voices raised unsuccessfully in the early twentieth century for the orientation of U.S. government Asian policy toward Japan instead of China. Unlike many of the Japanophiles, he was not drawn to "traditional" Japan, but saw—and approved of—Japan as a rising modern nation.

• MacCauley's papers were briefly examined in the 1980s but have since been lost. In his retirement years he wrote a sort of autobiography, *Memories and Memorials* (1914), containing anecdotes from his life; selected items of his writings and speeches, including reports from the Japanese mission; and an eighty-page typescript describing his work there. Among the twenty books he wrote are religious works for the mission such as *Christianity in History* (1891) and *The Faith of the Incarnation* (1913). Some books are on contemporary culture, like *Thought and Fact for Today* (1911) and *Looking Before and After: Some Wartime Essays* (1919). He is credited with writing *Introductory Course in Japanese* (1896; 2d ed., 1906), a pioneering language book, but evidence suggests that the real work was done by Japanese staff at the mission and put out under his name. His final book was *Karl Christian Friedrich Krause: Heroic Pioneer for Thought and Life* (1925). The fullest biographical treatment is in Samuel A. Eliot, ed., *Heralds of a Liberal Faith*, vol. 4 (1952). He was the subject of a lengthy article in the *Christian Register*, 26 Nov. 1925, following his death.

THOMAS E. GRAHAM

MACCRACKEN, Henry Mitchell (28 Sept. 1840–24 Dec. 1918), educator and clergyman, was born in Oxford, Ohio, the son of John Steele MacCracken, a Presbyterian clergyman, and Eliza Hawkins Dougherty Welch, a teacher. He attended Miami University at Oxford (1852–1857) and taught school before entering United Presbyterian Seminary at Xenia (1860–1862). After graduating from Princeton Theological Seminary in 1863, he became a minister of the Presbyterian Church in the USA. In 1867 MacCracken traveled to

Europe where he studied theology and philosophy at the Universities of Berlin and Tübingen before returning to pastoral and synodal duties in 1868. His letters from Europe were printed in the Cincinnati *Daily Gazette*, his Toledo sermons in *The Toledo Blade*, and his first book, in part a translation, was published in 1879, *The Lives of the Leaders of the Church Universal*. In 1872 he married Catherine Hubbard, daughter of the Reverend Thomas Swan Hubbard of Rochester, Vermont. The couple had four children; two of their sons, John Henry MacCracken and Henry Noble MacCracken, became presidents of Lafayette and Vassar colleges, respectively.

MacCracken became professor of philosophy and chancellor of the Western University of Pennsylvania (now the University of Pittsburgh) in 1881. He soon became convinced that universities belonged in cities, where they could offer study "towards the limit of ultimate knowledge" and also "train men and women for some of the learned professions." MacCracken also came to believe that "Wherever intellect embodied in a wide group of men was married to a great city . . . a university was brought forth." Buoyed by those beliefs, in 1884 MacCracken became professor of philosophy at the small and financially beleaguered University of the City of New-York, founded in 1831, which had been housed since 1835 in a Gothic marble building on Washington Square. After he accepted the post of vice chancellor in 1885 under a caretaker chancellor, the Reverend John Hall, MacCracken became the university's sixth chancellor on 1 June 1891.

MacCracken's expansive vision of a university system encompassed advanced graduate study, as in Europe; training in teaching, business, law, and medicine in order to produce professionals for the commercial city that co-mingled with the university at Washington Square; residential halls, playing fields, and laboratories for undergraduates in arts and science; and centralized governance and administration of the colleges. Not long after becoming chancellor MacCracken described his idea of a modern university as "a group of faculties of schools devoted to higher learning, under the direction of a single corporation which confers the various degrees" ("A Metropolitan University," 5 May 1892, p. 3; repr. in *The Christian at Work*). His focused approach inaugurated the founding of the Graduate School of Arts and Science in 1887, which by 1888 had sixty-four students, including the university's first female Ph.D. graduate; the founding of the Schools of Pedagogy and Commerce, in 1890 and 1900; the merger of the law department with the Metropolitan Law School in 1895; and the merger of the Medical College with Bellevue Hospital Medical College in 1898; all admitted women. Beginning in 1896, the year in which the institution became known as New York University (NYU), the professional schools and their libraries were housed on the upper floors of a new building on the site of the 1835 building, designed by Alfred Zucker.

Also in his early years as chancellor, MacCracken initiated "the uptown movement," which gradually financed a spacious second campus in what came to be called University Heights. Located in the Bronx, on the eastern slope of the Harlem River overlooking the northern tip of Manhattan and rival Columbia University, the campus of manor houses, stables, and orchards opened in 1894; it gradually expanded via construction and the acquisition of real estate parcels, including Ohio Field, the latter funded by MacCracken's Ohio associates. The campus's attractive setting, combined with the extension of interborough railways, fueled the growth of the all-male residential arts and science undergraduate college and the expansion of engineering into a separate school in 1899. MacCracken hoped to preserve for arts and sciences the intimate classroom instruction he had experienced at his alma mater while also expanding classes and opportunities in the more populous professional schools at Washington Square.

MacCracken fostered a communal life at the University Heights campus, but faculty also taught downtown at the Square and at the Extra-Mural Division, located in Newark, New Jersey, in an effort "to bring the University out of cloistered life into nearness to the community and the nation." As first president of the Bronx Society of Arts and Sciences, he ceremonially presented Edgar Allan Poe's Bronx cottage in 1909 to the city of New York. In December 1905, following a number of deaths from football injuries, MacCracken met with other college presidents and administrators. Out of this initial meeting developed, in 1910, the National Collegiate Athletic Association, which encouraged institutional control of sports competition and player eligibility as well as the abandonment of dangerous plays, such as the flying tackle.

MacCracken was the first NYU chancellor to utilize large-scale benevolence and financing for physical expansion and faculty growth. According to Bayrd Still, while MacCracken was still vice chancellor he "sought contact" with entrepreneur and tycoon Jay Gould, who died in 1890, before making an anticipated financial commitment. Gould's daughter, Helen Miller Gould Shepard, later gave more than $2 million in his memory. Other substantial gifts, of $300,000 and $900,000, were given in 1906 and 1910 by Margaret Olivia Slocum Sage, the widow of Russell Sage, and by bequest of Emma Baker Kennedy, daughter of a faculty member. These and other prominent women, through the Women's Advisory Committee, founded in 1890, worked with MacCracken and the university council to develop educational opportunities and scholarships for women. Their efforts, however, failed to establish a women's college or the regular admission of women to the colleges at the University Heights campus.

MacCracken, who continued to teach during his chancellorship, conducted himself easily with students, making a point of learning their names early on. He took cheerful pride in his Scotch-Irish ancestry as well as the Presbyterian emphasis on "a school by every church," even venturing to suggest that the Scotch-Irish wholeheartedly adopted America because "they had long ago lost hold of Scotland" and "been denied a place in Ireland." A favored project was the patriotic Hall of Fame for Great Americans, an arcaded walk with statues that connected as of 1900 the Stanford White buildings of the quadrangle at the University Heights campus. When MacCracken resigned his office and active duties in 1910, his university system was in place: virtually mortgage-free with an enrollment of 4,000 students. Describing himself as reverent but not unduly orthodox, MacCracken never abandoned his clerical calling, articulating it most forcefully in his efforts to improve university education and to meld intellectual life with the life of the city. He died in Orlando, Florida.

• MacCracken's family and personal papers include published and unpublished writings, sermons, and speeches and are in the New York University Archives along with his administrative records; the unpublished finding aid for the Chancellor's Records contains an account of his administration by Bayrd Still. MacCracken's publications include, with Ernest G. Sihler, "New York University," in *Universities and Their Sons: New York University*, ed. Joshua L. Chamberlain (1901); addresses, sermons, and monographs, including "The Hall of Fame" (1901); and portions of T. F. Jones, ed., *New York University, 1832–1932* (1933). A critical biography has yet to be published, but see John Henry MacCracken's account, with others, in *Henry Mitchell MacCracken: In Memoriam* (1923); Henry Noble MacCracken, *The Family on Gramercy Park* (1949); and Walter Havighurst, *Men of Old Miami, 1809–1873: A Book of Portraits* (1974). An obituary is in the *New York Times*, 25 Dec. 1918.

MARILYN HILLEY PETTIT

MACCRACKEN, Henry Noble (19 Nov. 1880–7 May 1970), educator and college president, was born in Toledo, Ohio, the son of the Reverend Henry Mitchell MacCracken, a Presbyterian minister and educator, and Catherine Almira Hubbard. MacCracken graduated in 1900 from New York University, of which his father was chancellor, with a degree in English literature. After serving a three-year instructorship at the Syrian Protestant College in Beirut, he received a master's degree in English from NYU in 1904, another master's from Harvard in 1905, and a Ph.D. from Harvard in 1907.

After marrying Marjorie Dodd in June 1907, MacCracken pursued postgraduate studies in England. He became assistant professor of English at the Sheffield Scientific School of Yale University in 1909 and in 1913 accepted a professorship of dramatic literature at Smith College in Northampton, Massachusetts. The next year, in December, he was chosen to be the first lay president of Vassar College in Poughkeepsie, New York, during the same week that his brother John MacCracken, who had also been a candidate for the Vassar position, was named president of Lafayette College in Easton, Pennsylvania.

Inaugurated in October 1915, MacCracken rapidly modernized Vassar over the next decade with a series of bold initiatives that included admission, curricular, and extracurricular reform; a governance assuring academic freedom; and the encouragement of links between the college and the larger community. Treating students as adults, he gave them responsibility to set their goals within the framework of a revised curricular system of majors and distribution requirements. Unlike his predecessor, James M. Taylor, he thought that liberal education should do more than acquaint students with their academic heritage; it should motivate them to be useful citizens of their communities. He thus promoted the addition of experiential dimensions, such as field work, community research, and courses with a focus on the present.

The day after his inauguration in 1915, MacCracken invited the presidents of Smith, Mt. Holyoke, and Wellesley colleges to collaborate, especially to develop more uniform procedures for admitting the most qualified students from secondary schools. Thus he laid the groundwork for future cooperation among an enlarged group of women's colleges, which in 1926 officially became the "Seven Sisters" organization.

A pacifist, MacCracken worked unceasingly for peace throughout his life. Nevertheless, he effectively presided over the college during two world wars and fostered the college's contribution to the war effort, introducing, during World War II, various emergency measures, including an optional shortened degree requirement. In September 1917 he was appointed chief of the Division of instruction of the New York State Council of Defense and simultaneously organized and directed the American Junior Red Cross. By 1918 his Vassar reforms precipitated a crisis of confidence between him and some of the old-guard trustees who took steps to have him fired. He fought back, however, and with hearty support from faculty, other trustees, alumnae, and students retained his presidency.

Eager to experiment, in 1923 MacCracken established an undergraduate program in "euthenics" (a word coined by Ellen Swallow Richards, an 1870 alumna, to mean "the science of controllable environment"). This program, which subsequently attracted national recognition as a seminal adult summer school—the Vassar Summer Institute of Euthenics (1924–1958)—studied the family, society, and the community through a variety of disciplines. Early in his administration MacCracken also inaugurated the Vassar Experimental Theatre, under the direction of Hallie Flanagan, who later, on leave from Vassar in the mid-1930s, headed the Federal Theater program of Franklin D. Roosevelt's WPA (Works Progress Administration). MacCracken performed leading roles in numerous plays, among them that of Hippolytus in *Hippolytus*, produced in 1932 in the original Greek. MacCracken and his wife Marjorie had five children, of whom one died in infancy. As a couple, they fostered the college's intellectual life, encouraging artists, politicians, and alumnae to visit and share their thinking.

MacCracken founded and was president of the first county health organization in the United States in Dutchess County in 1916. In 1922, during a leave from Vassar, he made a tour of new universities in central Europe, taking special interest also in the republic of Czechoslovakia under Tomáš Masaryk. Thereafter he pioneered in bringing central European students to Vassar and other American colleges. In the wake of Adolf Hitler's rise in Germany, MacCracken's Vassar became primary host to many refugee professors. In 1925 MacCracken founded the Kosciuszko Foundation for the promotion of intellectual and cultural relations between Poland and the United States, remaining its president until 1955. He was also a founding director of the National Conference of Christians and Jews.

In 1926, sensing an opportunity for a new educational experiment in the junior college movement, MacCracken collaborated with millionaire William Lawrence of Bronxville, New York, in founding Sarah Lawrence College. Serving from 1926 to 1936 as chairperson of its board of trustees and nominating several Vassar trustees and faculty members to serve on its board, he developed a linkage between Vassar and the new college that helped it gain stature.

Throughout his career, MacCracken consistently engaged in both grass-roots and global humanitarian enterprises. During the depression he became head of New York State TERA (Temporary Emergency Relief Association) and secretary of the Dutchess County Works Administration (part of the Federal Works Administration). An outspoken proponent of student involvement in public affairs, MacCracken invited Eleanor Roosevelt to give the keynote address and participate in the deliberations of the Second World Youth Congress, which met on the Vassar campus in August 1938 to consider the student role in achieving world peace.

After his retirement from Vassar in 1946, MacCracken continued to live in Poughkeepsie until his death there. He wrote and published several popular books on local and family history and gave more than 350 radio talks on a variety of subjects. A gifted raconteur and folklorist as well as actor, he enjoyed entertaining audiences. He was a complex and urbane man with multiple interests.

MacCracken's Vassar offered newly enfranchised women after World War I opportunities for self-realization. As he wrote in 1930, Vassar was a college where "total learning" could take place twenty-four hours a day. During his 31-year tenure, he dispelled the concept of the college as an ivory tower and stressed its communality.

• The Vassar College Library houses MacCracken's papers, both personal and presidential. They are indexed and contain both published and unpublished manuscripts, speeches, texts for radio addresses, photographs, organizational papers, and memorabilia. He edited scholarly editions of Shakespeare, Chaucer, Lydgate, Gower, and works for the Early English Text Society. He published two light-hearted autobiographical works, *The Family on Gramercy Park* (1949) and *The Hickory Limb* (1950). After retirement in 1946, he published two books of local history, *Old Dutchess Forever! The Story of an American County* (1956) and *Blithe Dutchess, the Flowering of an American County from 1812* (1958). The

first published biography of MacCracken is Elizabeth A. Daniels, *Bridges to the World: Henry Noble MacCracken and Vassar College* (1994).

ELIZABETH A. DANIELS

MACDONALD, Betty (26 Mar. 1908–7 Feb. 1958), author and farmer, was born Anne Elizabeth Campbell Bard in Boulder, Colorado, the daughter of Darsie Campbell Bard, a mining engineer, and Elsie Tholimar Sanderson, an artist. Until she was nine, when her family settled in Seattle, MacDonald moved with her family from one mining project to another in the Far West and Mexico.

MacDonald attended the University of Washington, planning to major in art, but she was married in 1927 to Robert Eugene Heskett, an insurance salesman who yearned to be a farmer. For $450 they bought a chicken farm in Chimacum, Washington, which she called "the most untamed corner of the United States." There, she survived primitive living conditions with good humor and determination, although she said, "By the end of the second spring I hated everything about the chicken but the egg."

The Hesketts' marriage ended in divorce in 1935. Meanwhile, in 1931 after separating from her husband, Betty had moved back to Seattle and with two small daughters faced the hard times of the Great Depression. She held a series of secretarial and government jobs, including a position as the only woman labor adjuster in the National Recovery Administration. However, she contracted tuberculosis in 1938 and spent a year in a sanatorium, later recounting her struggle with the disease in her narrative *The Plague and I* (1948).

In 1942, after her recovery, she married Donald Chauncey MacDonald, a realtor, and they bought a rambling old house on Vashon Island, Washington. There she wrote her most successful book, *The Egg and I* (1945), which fictionalized her desperate but often amusing earlier adventures in chicken farming. (It was first serialized in the *Atlantic Monthly*—an event that, she said, "represented for me the ultimate in literary achievement.") It sold more than two million copies and also brought MacDonald $100,000 for the film rights. The 1947 production starred Claudette Colbert and Fred MacMurray. The comic characters in the novel (neighbor Ma Kettle was known for saying, "I itch—so I scratch—so what?") formed the basis for the Ma and Pa Kettles that appeared from 1949 through 1957.

Next, MacDonald completed two further autobiographical works, *Anybody Can Do Anything* (1950), based on her older sister's irrepressible work ethic, and *Onions in the Stew* (1955), containing anecdotes of her island life. In 1956 the MacDonalds moved to a cattle ranch in Carmel Valley, California, where she pursued hobbies of gardening, painting, and music and wrote children's stories based on the character of Mrs. Piggle-Wiggle, who specializes in concocting cures for bad habits. In 1958 MacDonald returned to

Seattle for cancer treatment and died there after a brief illness.

MacDonald wrote, "My family possessed a great capacity for happiness." She credited her fame and commercial success to her family as well as to her own confidence, optimism, and perseverance. By revealing the frustrations of domesticity and ill health in her semiautobiographical narratives, she provided encouragement and humorous diversion to readers with similar everyday hardships. Like Betty Smith, author of *A Tree Grows in Brooklyn*, MacDonald's life and work testify to the talent and resilience of ordinary people and to their necessary reliance on one another.

• There is little critical comment available on Betty MacDonald, perhaps because her life and views are chronicled in her own writing. Further information can be found in James D. Hart, *The Popular Book* (1950), and in a newspaper article by Don Duncan, "Betty MacDonald's Scramble to the Top," *Seattle Times*, 11 Mar. 1973. Obituaries appear in the *New York Times* and the *Seattle Times*, 8 Feb. 1958.

HARRIET L. KING

MACDONALD, Charles Blair (14 Nov. 1855–21 Apr. 1939), amateur golfer and golf course designer, was born in Niagara Falls, Ontario, Canada, the son of Godfrey Macdonald, a wealthy Scottish-born merchant, and Mary Blakewell. He was raised in Chicago. Macdonald attended St. Andrews University in St. Andrews, Scotland, from 1872 to 1874. After returning to Chicago in September 1874, he worked as a stockbroker and became a member of the Chicago Board of Trade. In 1884 he married Frances Porter; they had two daughters. The family moved to Garden City, New York, in 1900, when Macdonald became a partner in the brokerage firm of C. D. Barney & Co.

Macdonald was described as a "daring speculator," but his real passion was golf. His love of the game began in St. Andrews, where he became an accomplished player under the tutelage of his grandfather William Macdonald. He also watched and competed against some of the game's greatest figures, including Old Tom Morris, Young Tom Morris, and David Strath. To Macdonald the years following his return to Chicago were "the Dark Ages." Although golf clubs and balls had been introduced to America in the mid-eighteenth century, and isolated individuals continued to practice with them, the first true courses and organized clubs did not appear until the late 1880s. Macdonald therefore met his craving for the game during periodic business trips to Britain in the late 1870s and 1880s and by knocking balls around a deserted Civil War training camp. In 1892, however, he laid out seven short holes on the estate of U.S. senator Charles B. Farwell. At the request of members of the Chicago Club, he then set up a nine-hole course in suburban Belmont. He added nine holes the following spring, making it the nation's first eighteen-hole course. In 1895 the club moved to Wheaton, where Macdonald became its captain and sculptured a more challenging eighteen holes that ranked with the best inland courses abroad.

Macdonald, one of the better American amateur golfers, loudly claimed he was the best. He lost, however, on the eighteenth hole of the final in a match play tournament hosted by the St. Andrew's club in October 1894 to determine America's best amateur player. Macdonald then claimed it was just another tournament and that only an official association of clubs could host a true championship. To placate Macdonald and ease tensions between the East and the West, two delegates each from the nation's five most prestigious clubs—Newport, Shinnecock Hills, The Country Club, St. Andrew's, and Chicago Golf—met at the Calumet Club in New York on 22 December 1894 to form a national governing body for American golf. Named the Amateur Golf Association of the United States, and then the American Golf Association, the organization officially became the U.S. Golf Association (USGA) when its constitution was adopted in February 1895. One of Chicago Golf's delegates, Macdonald was chosen second vice president. He became the primary figure on the committees that drew up the organization's constitution and bylaws and decided on playing rules. At the new organization's first amateur championship, held in October 1895 at Newport, Macdonald defeated C. E. Sands twelve holes ahead with eleven holes left to play in the 36-hole final.

Besides winning several lesser tournaments, Macdonald subsequently was a medalist in two other U.S. Amateurs and twice made it as far as the semifinals. Although low amateur in the 1900 U.S. Open, he finished a distant forty-one strokes behind the winner, Harry Vardon. The game was attracting more skilled players, including his son-in-law H. J. Whigham, and spreading beyond the narrow circle of gentlemen clubs, and Macdonald became less of a threat in major competitions after 1900. He entered his last U.S. Amateur in 1912.

The egotistic Macdonald thought he knew more about the game and its traditions than anyone else, and, at 6′2″ and 220 pounds, he could be physically as well as intellectually intimidating. He was a USGA vice president from 1894 to 1898, ad hoc adviser to it afterward, and a member of Britain's Royal and Ancient Golf Club's powerful rules of golf committee from 1908 to 1926. He proved a fierce traditionalist who energetically sought to keep the game true to its Scottish roots, or what he called "the spirit of the game." He fought successfully attempts to abolish the distinction between the elite and more ordinary clubs, was instrumental in making the definition of "amateur" more restrictive, and resisted the upstart Western Golf Association's call for "Americanization" of the game and its resultant challenges to the USGA's authority. He could not, however, prevent a break between golf's two ruling bodies in 1911. Despite his pleas for unification and further discussion, the USGA refused to accept the British association's ban on the Schenectady, center-shafted mallet putter, a ban Macdonald also thought unwise.

Although John Reid, founder and president of St. Andrew's, the first permanent golf club in America, was called the "Father of American Golf," a title Macdonald thought should have been his, Macdonald was unchallenged as the "Father of American Golf Architecture." Golf design, however, remained an avocation for him. He never accepted a fee for his services and was involved in the construction of fewer than twenty courses, all designed for his own enjoyment and that of his rich and socially prominent friends.

By 1902 Macdonald had decided to build the nation's first world class course, with each of the eighteen holes a "shrine" in its own right. He made several trips to Great Britain to accumulate surveyors' maps and sketches of the great courses of Scotland and England. A syndicate of seventy wealthy friends each contributed $1,000 to finance the project. The National Golf Links in Southampton, Long Island, opened to immediate acclaim in 1911 and remains Macdonald's masterpiece. Macdonald's work was inspired by, but did not slavishly copy, European originals. At times, his versions of classic holes actually improved on their counterparts. Other holes, like the widely copied, crescent-shaped "Cape Hole," which allowed the golfer to chance as large a carry over water as he thought able, were entirely original, owing more to the nature of the terrain than to any existing model. As president of the National, he controlled everything on and off the course.

The Lido Golf Club (opened 1917 in Long Beach, Long Island), one of his most challenging designs and certainly, at an unprecedented cost of $750,000, his most noteworthy engineering achievement, no longer exists. Other venues, since lengthened and modified slightly, still rank among the best courses in the world. These include the Chicago Golf Club, the National, the Greenbrier's Old White (1915, W.Va.), the Mid-Ocean (1924, Bermuda), and the Yale University course (1926, New Haven). In most of this work, Macdonald was aided by Seth Raynor and his two assistants, Charles Banks and Ralph Barton. Skilled in construction techniques, these men soon became noted architects in their own right and in turn trained another generation of architects.

Macdonald also influenced course construction with his extensive writings, most notably his memoir, and by sponsoring a contest in *Country Life* magazine to choose the best design for a par four hole at the proposed Lido club. The winner, English physician Alister Mackenzie, soon switched occupations and became arguably the game's greatest architect.

Macdonald spent his last decade protesting tendencies he thought were corrupting the game. Ironically, the man who had learned the game on the democratic links of St. Andrews came to personify, as player, administrator, and architect, the elitist nature of early American golf. He died in Southampton, New York.

• There is no collection of Macdonald papers, but some of his correspondence is in the Papers of the United States Golf Association, Golf House, Far Hills, N.J. Many of his course maps are at the National Golf Links, Southampton, N.Y. The best introduction to Macdonald is his classic memoir *Scotland's Gift: Golf* (1928), which conveys his love for the game of golf and its traditions and thoroughly, if self-servingly, chronicles his career as player, administrator, and architect. For the most authoritative biographical treatments, see James R. Knerr, "Charles Blair Macdonald: The First Great Influence on American Golf," *Golfiana* 6, no. 4 (1994): 9–20, and Howard Rabinowitz, "Golf's Aspiring Autocrat," *Golf Journal* 48 (May 1996): 36–39. Herbert Warren Wind, *The Story of American Golf*, 3d ed. (1975), ably assesses the impact of Macdonald and his contemporaries. An obituary in the *Times* (London), 13 May 1939, captures the essence of the man. An obituary is also in the *New York Times*, 22 Apr. 1939.

HOWARD N. RABINOWITZ

MACDONALD, Dwight (24 Mar. 1906–19 Dec. 1982), critic and editor, was born in New York City, the son of Dwight Macdonald, an attorney, and Alice Hedges, the daughter of a successful Brooklyn merchant. Though his family was primarily middle class, Macdonald attended Phillips Exeter Academy and Yale University, from which he graduated in 1928 with a B.A. degree. The circumstances of Macdonald's family were reduced in 1926 when his father died, but the new monthly magazine *Fortune* hired Macdonald as an associate editor in 1929, at the onset of the Great Depression. He later claimed that his journalistic encounters with capitalism pushed him to the left, indeed even to the far left, as the system of private enterprise struck him as both unjust and doomed. He resigned from *Fortune* in 1936 in protest against editorial tampering with his article on the U.S. Steel corporation.

In 1937 Macdonald became one of the six editors of the revived and independent *Partisan Review*, a "little magazine" whose influence among intellectuals soared as a result of its modernism in the arts and radicalism in politics. Though he was less important to the success of the *Partisan Review* than its founders, Philip Rahv and William Phillips, Macdonald became its most politicized editor, detecting in cultural expression signs of social decay. Among the most militant of leading "New York intellectuals" in the era when that group exhibited its greatest creativity, Macdonald became a Trotskyist, joining the Socialist Workers party in the fall of 1938. The group soon split over the issue of support for the Soviet Union, when that "degenerated workers' state" (in the exiled Leon Trotsky's definition) made peace with Hitler's Third Reich and then invaded Finland. Siding with Max Shachtman and the faction that condemned the invasion of Finland, Macdonald was part of the breakaway Workers party until the spring of 1941. Though remaining implacably anti-Communist, Macdonald made his Trotskyist interlude his last venture in "revolutionary" politics, or indeed in any political movement.

Macdonald also broke with the influential *Partisan Review* in 1943, as the magazine continued its "critical support" of the Allied cause during World War II. The Western democracies, he asserted, could not crush the Axis powers without dramatic internal reform, which would make the postwar environment far more livable. Anti-Stalinist, anti-Fascist, and anti–New Deal, Macdonald founded *Politics* (1944), the magazine that solidified his fame. The magazine's business manager was Nancy Gardiner Rodman, whom he had married in 1935; Macdonald himself served as its owner and publisher, as well as editor, proofreader, and most prolific contributor. *Politics* cultivated a stance that was anarchist and later pacifist as well, opposing the militarization of the modern state, reexamining the inherited categories of Marxist thought, and forsaking automatic allegiance to the working class, particularly to trade unions. The monthly (and later quarterly) also defined the depersonalization of an apathetic citizenry as an evil that an invigorated radicalism must combat. *Politics* enlisted important contributions from French anti-Fascist intellectuals, like Simone Weil and Albert Camus; from refugees from nazism who had come to the United States, such as Bruno Bettelheim and Lewis Coser; and from native-born mavericks, like C. Wright Mills and Paul Goodman. Incisive and lively, the journal was considered among the best the Left had produced. Hannah Arendt, not a contributor but later Macdonald's literary executor, expressed admiration for the magazine's "extraordinary flair for significant fact and significant thought."

But by 1949 the Cold War had sapped much of Macdonald's dissidence, and publication of *Politics* ceased. There was such widespread concurrence that the Soviet Union had become the chief threat to peace and liberty that even an ornery radical found little fresh to say about it. By the early 1950s Macdonald had virtually abandoned his interest in politics. He and Nancy Rodman were divorced in 1950; they had two children.

In 1954 he married Gloria Lanier. From 1951 until 1971 Macdonald wrote on general cultural and literary subjects for the *New Yorker*, a magazine he had earlier disdained as "bourgeois." Based in London, he also was a special editor of *Encounter* (1956–1957). And from 1960 until 1966 Macdonald served as a film critic for *Esquire*, returning to an earlier fascination and becoming a prominent analyst of the cinema.

In the late 1960s the United States' deepening intervention in Vietnam revived Macdonald's political instincts. His unqualified opposition to American involvement in Vietnam began early and was reflected in piercing political columns in *Esquire* (1967–1969) and in antiwar demonstrations, including the October 1967 march on the Pentagon. Macdonald also championed the student rebels at Columbia University in 1968 and the sometimes turbulent activities of the Students for a Democratic Society. In *Politics*, a generation earlier, he had formulated and sponsored the anarcho-pacifism these students embraced, and he recognized that he was indirectly responsible for their actions. Awarded an honorary degree by Wesleyan University in 1964, Macdonald was a visiting professor from 1956 to 1977 at several American universities, including Northwestern, the University of Texas

at Austin, Yale, and the University of California, San Diego. He was a member of the American Academy of Arts and Sciences and was elected to the National Institute of Arts and Letters in 1970. A striking figure, more than six feet tall, Macdonald sported a goatee and often wore colorful shirts and ties. He spent his final years in New York, where he died.

Despite his place among American intellectuals, Macdonald never wrote a full-scale book advancing an argument or grounded in substantial scholarly research. A learned and high-brow journalist rather than a sustained thinker, he responded directly to political events and cultural moments. The seven volumes that are his most accessible legacy all appeared originally as magazine articles, such as *Henry Wallace: The Man and the Myth* (1948) and the utopian *The Root Is Man* (1953), both excavated from *Politics*, and *The Ford Foundation* (1956), which had appeared in the *New Yorker* a year earlier. Macdonald's best-known books are miscellanies of reprinted pieces. *Memoirs of a Revolutionist* (1957) retraces his steps in politics (and mostly in *Politics*), and *On Movies* (1969) is drawn from four decades of film reviews and articles. Claiming "I know what I like and why," Macdonald presents himself as "a congenital critic," eschewing theory. Two other anthologies, *Against the American Grain* (1962) and *Discriminations* (1974), solidify his reputation for exposing what is central and meretricious in American politics and culture, subjects he wrote about equally well. The lead essay in *Against the American Grain* launches an attack on "Masscult and Midcult," in which Macdonald finds defective both the vulgar and commercial popular culture that replaced folk art and the works that partake of the prestige but not the complexity of genuine creativity and originality. *Discriminations* bears the impact of the politics of the 1960s, including Macdonald's *New Yorker* review of Michael Harrington's *The Other America* (1962). That critique, called "Our Invisible Poor," is the most influential piece Macdonald ever wrote. It drew the attention of President John F. Kennedy and helped inaugurate Lyndon Johnson's "war on poverty."

Macdonald had a flair for seizing a bone of contention and classifying it in a paleontology of nonsense, for piecing together seemingly disparate parts into the looming presence of a dinosaur with a disproportionately small brain. His participation in a controversy meant that systematic political error could be inferred from apparently unexceptionable statements and that a general cultural lapse could be found in seemingly random defects in style. When Irving Howe, a former editorial assistant, cracked that if Jesus Christ were to deliver again the Sermon on the Mount, "Dwight Macdonald would write that while 'Mr. Christ makes some telling points,' they suffer from syntactical confusion and 'a wooly, pretentious style.'" Macdonald responded: "Were the Sermon on the Mount wooly and pretentious in style, that would indeed be my reaction and I should be right, since in that case the Sermon would not be the great moral message it is but a botch, and not only in style." Though often accused of inconsistency, Macdonald displayed certain patterns in his career. He was baptized a Presbyterian but was a nonbeliever and indeed a habitual skeptic. In politics he was never a liberal, though he remained a Democrat and a libertarian. In the arts he was never a formalist; he was conservative and classical in his tastes. By temperament he was an empiricist immunized against theory. Whether a Trotskyist, anarchist, pacifist, or mugwump (as he labeled himself in his later years), Macdonald exhibited keen intelligence, bite, and wit.

• Macdonald's papers are deposited at the Sterling Library at Yale University. In 1968 the Greenwood Reprint Corporation immortalized in four volumes the complete file of his magazine *Politics*. Its editor's political career is partly treated in the autobiographical introduction ("Politics Past") to *Memoirs of a Revolutionist: Essays in Political Criticism* (1957). The fullest account of Macdonald's life, though omitting his contributions as a cultural and film critic, is Stephen J. Whitfield, *A Critical American: The Politics of Dwight Macdonald* (1984). Other biographical studies include Michael Wreszin, *A Rebel in Defense of Tradition: The Life and Politics of Dwight Macdonald* (1994), and Gregory D. Sumner, *Dwight Macdonald and the* Politics *Circle* (1996). Macdonald's personal importance is recounted in the memoirs of several "New York Intellectuals," such as William Barrett, *The Truants* (1982); Irving Howe, *A Margin of Hope* (1982); and Sidney Hook, *Out of Step* (1987). Macdonald's film criticism is analyzed in Edward Murray, *Nine American Film Critics* (1975). An obituary appears in the *New York Times*, 20 Dec. 1982.

STEPHEN J. WHITFIELD

MACDONALD, Jeanette (18 June 1903–14 Jan. 1965), movie actress and lyric soprano, was born Jeannette Anna McDonald in West Philadelphia, Pennsylvania, the daughter of Daniel McDonald, a salesman for a woodworking factory, and Anna May Wright. (The revised spelling of MacDonald's name for professional purposes occurred as early as 1909 but did not hold until the mid–1920s.) The youngest and most driven of three talented daughters, MacDonald's earliest musical training came from her sisters, Elsie and Blossom. By age four she was being hired to sing at neighborhood church and lodge functions and was locally dubbed "Baby Jenny Lind." Her earliest documented performance was in a children's opera, *Charity*, staged at Philadelphia's Academy of Music on 15 February 1909.

MacDonald studied song and dance with ex-vaudevillian Al White, who put her in his touring act, the "Six Sunny Songbirds." In the fall of 1919 MacDonald left West Philadelphia High School for Girls to join her sister Blossom as a Ned Wayburn dancer in *The Demi Tasse Revue*, a lavish stage show at the Capitol Theatre, then New York City's grandest movie palace. During the next ten years the vivacious redhead rose from the chorus in Jerome Kern's *Night Boat* to featured roles in *The Magic Ring* and George Gershwin and Ira Gershwin's *Tip-Toes* to leads in *Yes, Yes, Yvette* (1927) and such Shubert Brothers musical productions as *Sunny Days* (1928) and *Boom Boom* (1929).

MacDonald's fervent goal was to train her voice for opera. In 1923 she began lessons with Ferdinand Torriani, a maverick who emphasized "vitalization of the muscles at the tip of the chin" rather than deep breathing from the diaphragm. When Torriani died in 1924, his associate, Grace Adele Newell, became MacDonald's lifelong voice teacher.

Movie director Ernst Lubitsch discovered MacDonald while searching for a singing actress to play opposite Maurice Chevalier in *The Love Parade* (1929), Lubitsch's first sound film. Viewing a screen test she had made for Paramount in 1928, Lubitsch shouted: "That's enough, I've found my queen!" The pairing of MacDonald as a sexual tease and Chevalier as a roué to be tamed was repeated in a series of bubbly bedroom farces: Lubitsch's *One Hour with You* (1932); Rouben Mamoulian's *Love Me Tonight* (1932); and the most sparkling of adapted screen operettas, Lubitsch's *The Merry Widow* (1934). Although Chevalier received top billing and salary in this country, the French were more taken with MacDonald, who endeared herself to them by her arch blend of Continental sophistication and American wholesomeness and by her uncommon ability to sing fluently in French. In this period MacDonald regularly removed clothes in front of the camera and became known as the "Lingerie Queen of the Talkies." Other early landmark films included Paramount's Technicolor operetta, *The Vagabond King* (1930), and the Lubitsch-directed *Monte Carlo* (1930), where she introduced a major song hit, Richard Whiting's "Beyond the Blue Horizon," sung in a railroad car sequence famous for its innovative fusion of sound and image.

In 1931 a rumor spread in Europe alleging that MacDonald had been involved in a love affair with Italy's Crown Prince Umberto and that the prince's wife, Marie-José of Belgium, had murdered the actress out of jealousy. Many European theater owners were outraged and threatened to boycott the pictures of the supposed royal housebreaker. In order to prove she was very much alive and to regain her favor with Europeans, MacDonald decided to make a concert tour abroad. Her success in London was so enormous that a cocktail was named in her honor. During a second European tour, in 1932–1933, Irving Thalberg sought to sign her for his independent production unit at Metro-Goldwyn-Mayer. But MacDonald's manager and fiancé, Robert Ritchie, advised her to hold out for an offer from studio chief Louis B. Mayer, which was soon forthcoming. In the years that followed Mayer often cast himself as MacDonald's protector and father confessor.

With the censorship guidelines of the Motion Picture Production Code now being enforced in matters of sexual explicitness, Mayer convinced MacDonald to team with Nelson Eddy, a blond baritone from the classical concert circuit whose persona was as downhome as Chevalier's was worldly. The bravura vocalism of the MacDonald-Eddy duo in *Naughty Marietta* (1935) took depression-era America and much of the world by storm. MacDonald appeared opposite more dramatically convincing actors, such as Clark Gable in the high-grossing *San Francisco* (1936) and Allan Jones in the epic *The Firefly* (1937), but the public vociferously demanded more Jeanette and Nelson, now known as "America's Singing Sweethearts." Their lyric duets—Victor Herbert's "Ah! Sweet Mystery of Life," Rudolf Friml's "Indian Love Call," Sigmund Romberg's "Will You Remember?"—became etched in the American consciousness as the greatest screen expressions of romantic yearning through song. *Maytime* (1937), MacDonald's personal favorite, showcased her dramatic range to best advantage and was infused with more operatic singing than any commercial film up to that time. The effervescent *Sweethearts* (1938) was MGM's first three-color Technicolor musical.

Lauded by the *Los Angeles Times* in 1937 as "the greatest singing-actress since Mary Garden" and voted "Queen of the Screen" by newspaper polls conducted in 1937 and 1939, MacDonald was Hollywood's highest-paid actress in 1939, the year in which she renegotiated her MGM contract and began a decade-and-a-half of concert tours in this country and abroad. In 1941 she made a song-filled remake of *Smilin' Through*, opposite Brian Aherne and husband Gene Raymond, whom she married in 1937. (The couple had no children). During World War II she became known for auctioning off encores to help the Army Emergency Relief fund. In 1943 MacDonald made her opera debut in Gounod's *Roméo et Juliette* at His Majesty's Theatre in Montreal, opposite tenor Armand Tokatyan and bass Ezio Pinza. Following her American opera debut with the Chicago Opera Company in 1944 in Gounod's *Faust*, Claudia Cassidy, music critic for the *Chicago Tribune*, called her "America's Princess of Opera." However, negotiations for a contract with the Metropolitan Opera fell apart when general manager Edward Johnson intimated that the Met's board of directors deemed the glamorous singer too "Hollywood."

The wartime move toward the democratization of popular culture lessened the mass appeal of MacDonald's "aristocratic" style of screen singing. Her last feature film (her twenty-seventh) was *The Sun Comes Up* (1949), with Lassie, Claude Jarman, Jr., and a music score by André Previn. In the 1950s, a time of rapidly changing tastes in popular music, MacDonald remained the country's most prominent exponent of semiclassical vocalism, working tirelessly in television, theater, concerts, and nightclubs; she continued to record for RCA Victor; and she described her cultural mission as "fighting like mad for melody." MacDonald died in Houston.

The subject of numerous parodies throughout the 1960s and 1970s, MacDonald continues to exercise a spell on receptive audiences through video and audio recordings. Many historians extol her naughty pre–Hays Code films at the expense of the post-Code favorites, but the later films have remained popular. In both periods, MacDonald's major appeal was her celebration of emotion in song, combining winking sophistication with unabashed sentiment.

• MacDonald's papers, including an unpublished autobiography, are in the possession of Gene Raymond. An important repository of primary documentation is the archive of the Jeanette MacDonald International Fan Club, Topeka, Kans. The Shubert Archive in New York City is a major source for material on MacDonald's Broadway years during the mid to late 1920s. The transcript of a taped interview from 1959 is part of the Popular Arts Project of the Oral History Collection, Columbia University. Useful biography files are found at the theater collections of the Free Library of Philadelphia and the New York Public Library. Comprehensive materials on MacDonald's films are housed at the Doheny Library of the University of Southern California, the Herrick Library of the Academy of Motion Picture Arts and Sciences, and the Louis B. Mayer Library of the American Film Institute. Scrapbooks that focus on her opera and concert tours are at the Arts Library–Special Collections of the University of California, Los Angeles.

Published materials include Eleanor Knowles, *The Films of Jeanette MacDonald and Nelson Eddy* (1975); James Robert Parish, *The Jeanette MacDonald Story* (1976); Lee Edward Stern, *Jeanette MacDonald* (1977); De Witt Bodeen, "Jeanette MacDonald," *Films in Review* (Mar. 1965): 129–44; and James Harvey, *Romantic Comedy in Hollywood, from Lubitsch to Sturges* (1987). MacDonald's passport and death record give her birth year as 1907. At the same time, many standard film reference works have 1901. However, the *Register of Baptisms, 1888–1911* of the Olivet Presbyterian Church (Philadelphia), pp. 468–69, the *Thirteenth Census of the United States: 1910*, and the records of Washington Irving and Julia Richman High Schools in New York City all give the birth year as 1903. No birth certificate is available. An obituary is in the *New York Times*, 15 Jan. 1965.

EDWARD BARON TURK

MACDONALD, John D. (24 July 1916–28 Dec. 1988), suspense and mystery writer and novelist, was born John Dann MacDonald in Sharon, Pennsylvania, the son of Eugene Andrew MacDonald, a business executive, and Marguerite Grace Dann. MacDonald was educated in Utica, New York, at the Utica Free Academy. He entered the University of Pennsylvania's Wharton School of Finance in 1934, but transferred in 1936 to the Syracuse University School of Business Administration, receiving a B.S. there in the spring of 1938. In July he married Dorothy Prentiss, an artist and fellow Syracuse graduate; they were to have one son. That fall he enrolled in the Harvard Graduate School of Business Administration, where he earned an M.B.S. in 1939.

After two failed attempts to start a career in the business world, MacDonald was commissioned a lieutenant in the U.S. Army in 1940. During World War II he served in the China-India-Burma theater, at the New Delhi headquarters. He was recruited in 1941 by the Office of Strategic Services (later to become the Central Intelligence Agency) and sent to Colombo, Ceylon (now Sri Lanka). In order to write more freely to his wife while under strict military censorship, he sent letters to her in the form of short stories. She sold one of these pieces, "Interlude in India," to *Story Magazine* for $25 while MacDonald was still in the service; it was his first publication, appearing in the July–August 1946 issue. Before his honorable discharge in 1946, MacDonald was promoted to lieutenant colonel.

Back in the United States, encouraged by his first success, MacDonald wrote indefatigably. For three months in the summer of 1946 he held a job with the Utica Taxpayers' Research Bureau, but after selling a few more stories he resigned to become a full-time writer. Establishing the schedule he was to follow for the rest of his career, he worked every day for at least eight hours, producing more than 12,000 revised and polished words a week. He turned out a wide range of fiction—from mystery stories to sports tales to science fiction and fantasy—which he regularly published in *Dime Detective*, *Black Mask*, *Shadow Mystery Magazine*, and other pulp magazines of that time, as well as in such widely circulated periodicals as *Collier's*, *Esquire*, *Cosmopolitan*, and *Liberty*. Among the many pseudonyms he used was "Scott O'Hara," acknowledging two of the most important influences on his developing style, F. Scott Fitzgerald and John O'Hara. In 1949 MacDonald moved with his family to Florida; for the rest of his life he divided his time between the southwest Florida Keys and upstate New York, where Dorothy MacDonald owned a house on Piseco Lake, forty miles from Utica.

The pulp magazine fiction market contracted dramatically in the 1950s, and MacDonald, like many of his contemporaries—Jim Thompson, David Goodis, and Charles Williams among them—shifted to producing detective, crime, and suspense novels that appeared only in paperback editions. MacDonald's first novel, *The Brass Cupcake*, was published in 1950 under the Fawcett Gold Medal imprint. It subsequently sold approximately 900,000 copies. From then until the mid-1960s, he published an average of more than two novels a year, primarily with Fawcett, in addition to many pieces of short fiction. He eschewed the whodunit style of mystery story, preferring to deal with urban crime, murder, police work, and the pressures of modern life on ordinary people. The Gold Medal originals became a learning process for him, in which he developed his skills as a storyteller and functional stylist. He experimented with multiple points of view to tell one story and set narrative problems for himself to solve. His efforts were clearly influenced by such detective novelists as Dashiell Hammett and Raymond Chandler and by such naturalistic writers as James M. Cain, Erskine Caldwell, and Horace McCoy.

With the appearance of each early novel, including *Murder for the Bride* (1951), *Judge Me Not* (1951), and *The Damned* (1952), MacDonald's reading audience expanded, as did his critical reputation. Noted mystery-story critics such as Anthony Boucher started to pay attention to his works. Boucher viewed MacDonald as "the John O'Hara of the crime-suspense story" and remarked on his "vivid dialogue" and "sharp observation." His story "The Bear Trap," which appeared in the May 1955 issue of *Cosmopolitan*, received

that year's Ben Franklin Award for the best story published in a popular magazine. His 1958 novel *The Executioners* was filmed in 1962 as *Cape Fear*, starring Gregory Peck and Robert Mitchum, one of many adaptations of his work for movies and television. In 1962 he was elected president of the Mystery Writers of America, the first paperback writer to be named to this office. MacDonald was successful internationally as well as in America; the French translation of his 1962 novel *A Key to the Suite* received the Grand Prix de Littérature Policière in 1964.

In 1964 MacDonald published *The Deep Blue Goodbye*, the first of a widely popular series of twenty-one novels, each with a different color in its title, that feature as their protagonist the private investigator Travis McGee. McGee, who lives on a houseboat in a Fort Lauderdale marina, recovers lost and stolen property through legal and extralegal means. He is a reluctant hero, maintaining a wry awareness of his own limits and expressing regret at the violence he is sometimes forced to use; at the same time, however, he is characterized as agile, physically imposing, and highly effective against attackers. A loner, he has one friend, Meyer, an economist and fellow houseboat-dweller, but enjoys the company of many female lovers who are attracted by his chivalric, sympathetic manner. MacDonald, a committed environmentalist, also gave McGee a strong social conscience, writing long asides in which the hero laments the destruction of the Florida Everglades due to overdevelopment.

In 1972 MacDonald was given a Grand Master Award from the Mystery Writers of America in recognition of his lifetime achievement. In 1973 his books began appearing in hardback as well as in Fawcett paperbacks, starting with *The Turquoise Lament* (1973), published by J. P. Lippincott. Later hardbacks were published by Harper & Row, Knopf, and Random House. The transition to hardback publishing qualified MacDonald's novels for inclusion on the *New York Times* bestseller list and adoption by commercial book clubs; most of his subsequent works achieved these distinctions.

In 1978 the first annual John D. MacDonald Conference on Mystery and Detective Fiction was held at the University of South Florida in Tampa; there, MacDonald was presented with the Award of Merit from the Popular Culture Association of the United States. *The Green Ripper*, a 1979 Travis McGee mystery, won the American Book Award in 1980. Although the McGee books, which he turned out regularly through the rest of his life, became his most famous work, he continued to write in other genres, including novels, science fiction, and nonfiction. At the time of his death in Milwaukee, he had just finished editing a volume of his correspondence with the comedian Dan Rowan. During his lifetime, more than eighty million copies of his books were published in nineteen languages. In recognition of his contribution to the literary culture of Florida, the John D. MacDonald Award for Excellence in Florida Fiction was established in 1994, while the John D. MacDonald Environmental Award, created to honor his efforts on behalf of the Florida ecosystem, was first given in 1996.

• MacDonald published more than seventy-five books and wrote over six hundred short stories. His papers as well as manuscripts and first editions of his books have been collected at the library of the University of Florida at Gainesville. The *JDM Bibliophile*, a journal devoted to MacDonald criticism and bibliography, is published biannually. David Geherin, *John D. MacDonald* (1982), is a valuable resource, with a good bibliography. Other useful works include Frank D. Campbell, *John D. MacDonald and the Colorful World of Travis McGee* (1977), and Edgar W. Hirshberg, *John D. MacDonald* (1985). Obituaries are in the *Los Angeles Times*, 29 Dec. 1986; the *New York Times*, 29 Dec. 1986; *Publisher's Weekly*, 9 Jan. 1987; and *Time*, 12 Jan. 1987.

ROBERT MIRANDON
SARAH WALL

MACDONALD, Ross (13 Dec. 1915–11 July 1983), detective novelist, was born Kenneth Millar in Los Gatos, California, the son of John Macdonald Millar, a journalist-printer, and Anne Moyer, a nurse. In 1919, when Macdonald's father abandoned the family in Vancouver, British Columbia, mother and son were left in such destitution, Macdonald later recalled, that he soon was in the streets begging for food and money. His mother, a partial invalid unable to work, returned with him to her native Ontario, where at one point she prepared to place the boy in an orphanage, being dissuaded only by his pleas at the gates of the institution. Until he graduated from high school, he and his mother lived either in rented rooms or in the homes of various relatives on whose charity they depended. With these experiences—and the resulting humiliation and alienation—Macdonald never came to terms, despite writing about them obsessively through the formal refraction of the detective novel.

In 1932 an insurance benefit from his father's death allowed Macdonald to enter the University of Western Ontario, where he studied English and history and, under the impetus of his ambition to be a writer, published short pieces in the college newspaper's literary supplement. After his mother's death in 1935, he traveled for a year in Europe, then returned to complete his degree, which he earned in 1938; in June of that year he married a high-school classmate, Margaret Sturm, herself an aspiring writer. The following year Macdonald took education classes at the University of Toronto; after the birth of his only child, Linda, for two years he taught high school English and history while publishing poems and short fiction in area newspapers and magazines. From 1941 to 1944 he did graduate work in English at the University of Michigan, leaving to accept a commission in the U.S. Naval Reserve and serve in the Pacific. Discharged in 1946, he settled with his family in Santa Barbara.

Macdonald's first four novels—two espionage stories, a "hard-boiled" thriller, and a psychological mystery—were published between 1944 and 1948 under the name Kenneth Millar. In 1949 he returned to Michigan to complete his degree, and he published

The Moving Target, a Chandleresque detective novel narrated by private investigator Lew Archer. The first Archer novel appeared under the pseudonym John Macdonald; the next two, under John Ross Macdonald. In 1952, after earning his Ph.D., Macdonald returned with his family to California, where he taught part time at Santa Barbara City College and quickly published three more detective novels and a volume of short stories. In 1956 *The Barbarous Coast* appeared under the name that would soon be recognized as that of the most significant detective novelist of his generation—Ross Macdonald.

From 1958 to 1968 Macdonald published nine more novels, all but one—*The Ferguson Affair* (1960)—featuring Lew Archer. His work had long had a secure following among readers of detective fiction as well as several admiring critics; however, these newer novels attracted a more serious criticism and a wider audience. *The Chill* (1964) and *The Far Side of the Dollar* (1965) received awards from the British Crime Writers Association, and Macdonald was elevated by reviewers to the triumvirate of "Hammett, Chandler, and Macdonald" atop the genre of the hard-boiled detective novel. In 1969 came the critical and popular success of *The Goodbye Look*; the novel was reviewed on the front page of the *New York Times Book Review*, which no doubt helped boost it onto the *Times* bestseller list, where it remained for over three months. With the 1971 publication of *The Underground Man* and a *Newsweek* cover story, Ross Macdonald entered the national consciousness. In 1974 he received the Grand Master Award of the Mystery Writers of America.

In 1956 Macdonald had undergone psychotherapy, and in 1959 he was hospitalized for hypertension and began to suffer attacks of gout. However, through the 1960s Macdonald lived in good health and modest comfort, produced increasingly good novels, and engaged in local literary and environmental activities. By most accounts a reserved, carefully spoken, occasionally irascible man, Macdonald apparently was difficult to know well; nevertheless, in his few intimates he effected a deep respect and loyalty. The 1970s brought unqualified professional success but also serious familial and personal problems: the death of his daughter, the failing eyesight of his wife, and, finally, the first symptoms of Alzheimer's disease. Ross Macdonald published his last novel in 1976. He died in Santa Barbara.

Several critics and reviewers have hailed Macdonald as "a major American novelist." Few readers of the Archer books would agree. However, few would disagree that Macdonald was an excellent writer who produced the most significant body of work in the hard-boiled or American detective genre. Several of his early Archer novels—*The Way Some People Die* (1951), *The Ivory Grin* (1952), and *The Doomsters* (1958)—remain satisfying fictions in the hard-boiled mode. The best of his later work—*The Zebra-Striped Hearse* (1962), *Black Money* (1966), *The Goodbye Look*, and *The Underground Man*—are superior novels by any literary standard.

While his fictional achievement was considerable, Macdonald is also important because of the transformation he effected in the genre in which he chose to work. As Raymond Chandler almost single-handedly rescued the hard-boiled detective novel from the pulp-magazine hacks, so Ross Macdonald saved it from Chandler's paperback epigones. Indeed, over his career Macdonald developed the detective novel into a form capable of combining aesthetic pleasure with moral seriousness. Shifting the narrative focus from the criminal class, he concentrated on middle-class families, on parents and children caught up in their own psychodramas of love and guilt. And he did so through an art that exercised all the technical skill and thematic subtlety associated with the best contemporary novelists. By developing the genre's potential, he created new possibilities for it—for both readers and writers.

• Some of Macdonald's papers are housed at the University of California, Irvine. In addition to the works noted above, Ross Macdonald/Kenneth Millar published the following novels: *The Dark Tunnel* (1944), *Trouble Follows Me* (1946), *Blue City* (1947), *The Three Roads* (1948), *The Drowning Pool* (1950), *Meet Me at the Morgue* (1953), *Find a Victim* (1955), *The Galton Case* (1959), *The Wycherly Woman* (1961), *The Instant Enemy* (1968), *Sleeping Beauty* (1973), and *The Blue Hammer* (1976). Other publications include a volume of short stories, *The Name Is Archer* (1955), which was republished, with two additional stories, as *Lew Archer, Private Investigator* (1977); the chapbooks *On Crime Writing* (1973) and *A Collection of Reviews* (1979); and a collection of essays edited by Ralph B. Sipper, *Self-Portrait: Ceaselessly into The Past* (1981). The standard bibliography is Matthew J. Bruccoli, *Kenneth Millar/Ross Macdonald: A Descriptive Bibliography* (1983). There have been four book-length studies of Macdonald and his work: Peter Wolfe's *Dreamers Who Live Their Dreams: The World of Ross Macdonald* (1976) and three titled *Ross Macdonald*—Jerry Speir's (1978), Bruccoli's (1984), and Bernard A. Schopen's (1990). An interesting and helpful volume, which includes material by both Macdonald and those who knew him, is Ralph B. Sipper, *Inward Journey: Ross Macdonald* (1984). The best critical essays on Macdonald's work are George Grella, "Evil Plots," *New Republic*, 26 July 1975, pp. 24–26; Sheldon Sacks, "The Pursuit of Lew Archer," *Critical Inquiry* 6 (Winter 1979): 231–38; and T. R. Steiner, "The Mind of the Hardboiled: Ross Macdonald and the Roles of Criticism," *South Dakota Review* 24 (Spring 1986): 29–54.

BERNARD A. SCHOPEN

MACDONALD, Thomas Harris (23 July 1881–7 Apr. 1957), highway engineer and public official, was born in Leadville, Colorado, the son of John MacDonald, a grain and lumber merchant, and Elizabeth Harris. The family soon moved to Montezuma, Iowa, where MacDonald attended public schools and the Iowa State Teachers College in 1899 before entering Iowa State College of Agricultural and Mechanic Arts, from which he graduated with a bachelor's degree in civil engineering in 1904. MacDonald married Elizabeth Dunham of Ames, Iowa, in 1907, and the couple had two children before her death in 1935.

As a student of noted engineering professor Anson Marston, MacDonald prepared a thesis on agricultural road traffic and calculated the horsepower needed to pull farm wagons. He also worked for the Chicago and Northwestern Railroad before graduation. But Marston, strongly committed to road improvement, lobbied successfully for legislation in 1905 creating the Iowa State Highway Commission. The commission was housed in the engineering college, with Marston a commissioner; MacDonald was appointed assistant professor of civil engineering for highway investigations but worked strictly on highway commission business. This arrangement typified Progressive Era reforms that relied on experts to eliminate corruption and promote efficiency. Named state highway engineer in 1907 and chief engineer under a revamped commission in 1913, MacDonald organized a state road system and prepared uniform standards for bridge construction and road maintenance that won him regional and national recognition.

In 1919 MacDonald was named chief of the U.S. Department of Agriculture's Bureau of Public Roads (BPR). Established in 1893 to advise states on road improvement practices and materials, the BPR administered funds provided to the states beginning with the Federal-Aid Highway Act of 1916. Under the law's structure of shared authority, the states built and maintained a system of rural roads designated for mail delivery, while the federal government provided up to 50 percent of the cost. In return, the BPR could inspect and approve the organization of state highway departments, construction standards, project plans, and completed construction. MacDonald inherited a difficult situation at the BPR, for some state highway engineers and congressmen were unhappy at the slow pace of work on federal-aid roads. World War I had halted construction, while the BPR struggled to administer expenditures that increased from $5 million in 1916 to $25 million in 1920. MacDonald eased friction by working closely with state highway departments and Congress, countering attacks on the federal-aid system as well as legislative proposals for a national highway department. At his urging, Congress in 1921 reaffirmed the federal-aid approach to highway building, although eligibility shifted from rural post roads to what became the U.S. numbered highway system. In short, Congress and state road officials both accepted MacDonald's vision of highway policy.

MacDonald was so influential, paradoxically, because he embraced cooperation. He never dictated policy, but most supporters of road construction deferred to the Bureau's superior technical expertise, a stance evident in the label universally applied to MacDonald—"The Chief." For example, he ran the BPR with the advice of only a couple of trusted associates but whenever possible used the American Association of State Highway Officials (AASHO) as a conduit for putting BPR proposals on highway building or appropriations before the states or Congress. MacDonald worked in a similar fashion with trade and professional groups such as the National Automobile Chamber of

Commerce; he also maintained close ties to congressional committees, which often invited him to help mark up bills. More than once, individual congressmen suggested that thorny problems be left for MacDonald to resolve. Five presidents also followed MacDonald's advice. Herbert Hoover, for example, expanded MacDonald's road program for public works jobs as the depression deepened through 1932, while New Dealers such as Harold Ickes praised the BPR's efficiency. Rexford Tugwell, another New Deal brain truster, stated, "Thomas MacDonald . . . was assiduous in educating me, and through me, Roosevelt. . . . [MacDonald] was there both before and after me, shaping, through one Presidency after another, and one Congress after another, the nation's highway policy." MacDonald was, without doubt, the arbiter of the nation's highway policy, yet his role was consistently veiled by cooperative mechanisms.

Several features of American highway policy reflected MacDonald's influence. For example, his opposition to private toll bridges led to restrictions on the use of federal-aid funds on approaches to toll bridges in the 1920s. His commitment to research enabled the states to build laboratories with federal money. MacDonald maintained the Progressive style of apolitical, expert decision-making, which may have been most evident in his effort to base general policy and construction priorities on statistical analysis of economic, traffic, and highway use data, not political expediency. In the 1920s BPR engineers started tabulating the economic cost of bad roads, considering the time lost in travel and smaller loads, and pioneered origin/destination surveys. Federal statistical data guided American road-building efforts into the 1960s, reflecting both the enormous popular support for highways and the unchallenged deference to technical expertise. And as the data showed changes in traffic patterns, MacDonald began urging Congress to include in the federal-aid highway program roadways reaching into cities (1934) and a system of secondary roads (1936).

MacDonald's most important legacy may have been laying the groundwork for the interstate highway system. This started after 1935, when congressmen first proposed grand schemes for toll-financed cross-country superhighways. Roosevelt requested a BPR study, which appeared as *Toll Roads and Free Roads* in 1939; the report proposed an expanded intercity road network but opposed toll financing. The BPR assumed—incorrectly this time—that motorists would shun roads like the Pennsylvania Turnpike, which opened in 1939. World War II temporarily put the issue on hold, as the BPR worked on roads to defense plants and planning the Alaska and Interamerican highways. The National Interregional Highway Committee, appointed by FDR in 1941 and chaired by MacDonald, resumed talking about postwar roads and endorsed the BPR's approach; this report informed the 1944 highway bill that authorized a system of interstate highways. This legislation, which increased federal highway funding to $500 million per year, was intended to solve the nation's road problems. But no one projected the flood of postwar traffic, which soon had supporters of rural, urban, and intercity highways fighting one another for more money. The resulting policy stalemate, prolonged by the Korean War, lasted through the early 1950s. Thus federal engineers approved a 37,700-mile system of intercity highways in 1947, but no funds appeared until 1952.

MacDonald, in his late sixties, could not provide the dynamic, unchallenged leadership of earlier years during this period of political chaos. He wanted to retire in 1948, remaining only at President Harry Truman's request. In 1953 Dwight Eisenhower accepted MacDonald's resignation after thirty-four years as head of the BPR. Yet even the 1956 highway bill that finally created the National System of Interstate and Defense Highways at a projected cost of $25 billion (the final cost was more than ten times that amount) showed the continuing influence of the BPR and MacDonald. The routes chosen and the high-level construction standards imposed (these were to be high-speed, multilane limited access superhighways), the rationale of serving traffic first, the retention of federal-aid procedures, the reliance on engineering experts, and the creation of a funding mechanism insulated from political influence all reflected enduring positions for MacDonald and the BPR.

Interstate highways made real the dream of some road engineers that motorists would travel cross-country without meeting a traffic signal. More importantly, perhaps, this system of less than 1 percent of the nation's total road mileage soon carried as much as 10 percent of the total traffic. The impact of these roads has been enormous. It hastened the demise of railroad passenger service, altered the nation's freight-shipping patterns, and assisted in the growth of suburbs and the flight from the cities. Modern automobile culture rests on this road network. Paradoxically, they also brought an end to a period of overwhelmingly popular, unchallenged highway construction projects, by prompting opposition to some segments, notably in cities. The interstate system proved even more important to American life than MacDonald had envisioned.

In retirement, MacDonald became the first holder of the Thomas MacDonald Chair of Highway Engineering at Texas A&M University and head of the Texas Transportation Institute. The day he left government service, he married his longtime Washington secretary, Carolyn Fuller. He died in College Station, Texas.

Few federal officials have enjoyed MacDonald's influence. While aided by longevity, his credibility rested most firmly on a reputation for honesty, hard work, and apparently incorruptible engineering expertise immune to narrow politics. He was involved in almost every major national and international body dealing with highways, ranging from the Pan-American highway congresses to the National Safety Council. Deeply respected by his peers, he received numerous honors, including Iowa State University's Marston Award for engineering achievement in 1939. Yet MacDonald was a stereotypical engineer—modest, a poor public speaker, and devoted to his work. One friend later recalled he had few entertainments apart from cooking, photography, and reading Arthur Conan Doyle and Arnold Toynbee. Robert Moses noted in 1949, "There is no better example of nonpolitical, effective, and prudent Federal, State and local cooperation than that afforded by the Public Roads Administration for almost 30 years under the respected leadership of Commissioner Thomas H. MacDonald" (Lind, p. 103). An editorial writer for *Roads and Streets* added, "Few men in contemporary public life have left greater tangible monuments, few have left a greater impress on the Nation's economic and social life."

• Several archival collections contain information about MacDonald. The Records of the Bureau of Public Roads, RG-30 in the National Archives, Washington National Records Center, Suitland, Md., are the official papers of the BPR, and MacDonald's work is visible throughout, especially in the voluminous correspondence files. The papers of Thomas H. MacDonald, University Archives, Texas A&M University, College Station, contain a small collection of personal papers, while the Reports of Thomas H. MacDonald, Bentley Historical Library, University of Michigan, Ann Arbor, has printed copies of many of his talks and published articles. See also William E. Lind, "Thomas H. MacDonald" (M.A. thesis, American Univ., 1965). MacDonald is the central figure in a history of the Bureau of Public Roads from 1893 to 1956 by Bruce E. Seely, *Building the American Highway System: Engineers as Policy Makers* (1987). Shorter comments can be found in memoirs by New Deal officials, including Rexford G. Tugwell, *Roosevelt's Revolution: The First Year—A Personal Perspective* (1977), pp. 152–53. A thorough biographical sketch can be found in U.S. Department of Transportation, Federal Highway Administration, *America's Highways, 1776–1976: A History of the Federal-Aid Program* (1976), pp. 176–79; see also "Mr. Highway," *Roads and Streets* 96 (May 1953): 60–61, and *Proceedings of the Twenty-sixth Annual Meeting, Highway Research Board* (1957), frontispiece. An obituary is in the *New York Times*, 8 Apr. 1957.

BRUCE E. SEELY

MACDONOUGH, Thomas (31 Dec. 1783–10 Nov. 1825), naval officer, was born at "The Trap," New Castle, Delaware, the son of Thomas Macdonough, a physician and major in the Delaware militia during the Revolution, and Mary Vance. Macdonough's older brother James served as a midshipman aboard the *Constellation* during its engagement with the French frigate *L'Insurgente* (9 Feb. 1799). During the fight he lost a foot and was sent to convalesce at home. Shortly thereafter Thomas Macdonough asked permission to join the navy. Through family influence he managed to secure appointment as a midshipman on 5 February 1800.

On 15 May 1800 Macdonough joined the ship *Ganges* bound for its station in the West Indies, where it was under orders to protect American shipping from French attack. He stayed with the *Ganges* for a year, during which time the ship captured three prizes. Also during this voyage, Macdonough came down with yellow fever and had to be hospitalized in Havana. He returned home with his ship in September. In January

1801 Macdonough sailed again on the *Ganges* for a brief cruise in the West Indies. On its return in June the *Ganges* was sold, and Macdonough was ordered to the frigate *Constellation* bound for the Mediterranean, where war had recently erupted in Tripoli.

Macdonough spent a year with the *Constellation*, sailing the Mediterranean protecting American shipping against attacks from the Barbary corsairs. He returned to the United States in May 1803 and was almost immediately reassigned to the frigate *Philadelphia* under orders to proceed to the Mediterranean. On 23 August en route to its station, the *Philadelphia* captured the Tripolitan vessel *Mirboka*. Macdonough was put aboard as part of the prize crew. It was a lucky move: for while he was tending to the *Mirboka*, the *Philadelphia* was captured by the Tripolitans. Later, on 16 February 1804, Macdonough was part of the expedition led by Stephen Decatur that successfully boarded and destroyed the *Philadelphia* in the harbor at Tripoli. During this time Commodore Edward Preble took command of the Mediterranean squadron. Under his tutelage Macdonough and many of his fellow officers came to professional maturity and took pride in being counted among "Preble's boys."

After the peace with Tripoli (3 June 1805) Macdonough remained for some time in the Mediterranean as a lieutenant aboard the schooner *Enterprise*. He returned to the United States in 1806, and in October of that year he was ordered to Middletown, Connecticut, to superintend the construction of gunboats.

From 1806 to the beginning of the War of 1812 Macdonough held a variety of posts. He served as lieutenant aboard the *Wasp*, carrying dispatches to Europe as well as patrolling the coast enforcing the Embargo Act. With little prospect of advancement or adventure Macdonough requested and received a furlough from the service to allow him to take command of a merchantman bound on an East Indies voyage. He returned from his voyage and resumed active duty at the opening of the War of 1812.

On 17 July 1812 Macdonough was ordered to the frigate *Constellation*, then undergoing repairs at the Washington Navy Yard. The work was so far from being completed that he asked for and received a new assignment. The secretary of the navy, Paul Hamilton, ordered him to take command of a division of gunboats at Portland, Maine. His stay at Portland was brief. On 28 September 1812 he was ordered to take command of a small naval force on Lake Champlain.

Lake Champlain was a vital waterway. From their base in Canada the British planned to use the western shore of the lake as an avenue of invasion. It was Macdonough's mission to deny the enemy control of the lake. Before traveling north Macdonough stopped in Middletown, Connecticut, where on 12 December he married Lucy Ann Shaler. From Middletown he and his new bride rode to Burlington, Vermont, where he established his headquarters. Through the winter of 1812–1813 he oversaw the construction of vessels for service on the lake. In July 1813 one of Macdonough's subordinates lost two vessels to the British, endangering the American position. Macdonough, however, was able to replace the lost vessels and thereby prevent the British from seizing control.

Oliver Hazard Perry's victory on Lake Erie (10 Sept. 1813) persuaded the British to shift their emphasis from the Great Lakes to Lake Champlain. In the spring, under the direction of General Sir George Prevost, the British began preparations for an invasion. In August 1814 the expedition got underway. Fourteen thousand troops marched south while a naval squadron under the command of Captain George Downie sailed down the lake, covering the advance.

Macdonough prepared to meet the British squadron at Plattsburgh, New York, positioning his squadron in such a way that Downie was forced to attack. Macdonough's dispositions were exceedingly well thought out and the British were overwhelmed in the battle that followed on 11 September. Within the first few minutes of the battle Downie was killed. Macdonough's victory forced Prevost to withdraw and left the Americans in nearly undisputed control of Lake Champlain. It also made Macdonough a national hero. Congress voted him their thanks and presented him with a gold medal.

Following the end of the war Macdonough was posted to command the navy yard at Portsmouth, New Hampshire, where he remained until 1818 when he was dispatched to Boston to take charge of the frigate *Guerriere*. He made a voyage to the Baltic and the Mediterranean and returned to the United States in 1820.

From 1820 until 1824 Macdonough remained ashore, spending a good deal of his time with his family in Middletown. On 23 May 1824 he was ordered to the *Constitution* and assigned as commodore of the Mediterranean squadron. While en route home from the Mediterranean on board the merchant brig *Edwin*, Macdonough died, apparently from respiratory complications.

• A chronology of Macdonough's service is in the Naval Historical Center "Z" files. A biography is Rodney Macdonough (his grandson), *Life of Commodore Thomas Macdonough* (1909). For additional information about Macdonough's naval career, see Harrison Bird, *Navies in the Mountains: The Battles of Lake Champlain and Lake George, 1609–1814* (1962); William M. Fowler, Jr., *Jack Tars and Commodores: The American Navy, 1783–1815* (1984); and Theodore Roosevelt, *The Naval War of 1812* (2 vols., 1902).

WILLIAM M. FOWLER

MACDOWELL, Edward (18 Dec. 1861–23 Jan. 1908), composer, was born in New York City, the son of Thomas MacDowell, a businessman, and Frances M. Knapp. MacDowell grew up in New York in comfortable middle-class surroundings, cultivating interests in literature, painting, music, and languages. His mother especially promoted involvement in the arts and, recognizing young Edward's talent, hoped her son would achieve fame as a concert pianist. MacDowell would indeed develop considerable pianistic talents, but he never really enjoyed performing.

When MacDowell was fifteen his mother took him to Europe to study at the Paris Conservatoire. Once enrolled he felt comfortable neither with the Conservatoire nor with Paris more generally. At the Conservatoire the large number of mechanical exercises required of him and the heavy emphasis on rote memorization were not to MacDowell's liking, though he excelled at both and ranked at the top of his class. MacDowell also disagreed with the concept of pedagogical divisions drawn between the realm of performance and that of theory and composition; they accentuated his ambivalence toward performing.

In Germany MacDowell found teachers as well as an environment that were more suited to his intellect and temperament. Consequently, after two years in Paris, MacDowell moved to Frankfurt am Main. There his talents were noticed by various conservatory masters, notably by the composer Joachim Raff. When Carl Heymann, a piano professor at Frankfurt, retired in 1880, he recommended that MacDowell succeed him. However, the conservatory board did not approve. MacDowell was then but nineteen years old.

It was during his studies in Germany that MacDowell's composition talents became apparent. Raff was impressed with MacDowell's compositions and referred him to Franz Liszt. Liszt was also impressed and secured concert stages for MacDowell to present his works. Increasingly successful, MacDowell remained in Germany for eight years, writing music and teaching piano. In 1884 he married Marian Griswold Nevins, one of his American students. They had no children. Liszt recommended MacDowell to the prestigious Leipzig publishing house Breitkopf and Härtel, which published several of his compositions, notably two piano suites, written in 1882 and 1884, and three orchestral tone poems: *Lancelot and Elaine* (1886), based on Tennyson's Arthurian poem, *Hamlet*, and *Ophelia* (both 1885). These works won the plaudits of European and American conductors and critics and established MacDowell as a composer of international renown.

The MacDowell's lived happily in a small cottage in the woods outside the city of Wiesbaden. They traveled widely and enjoyed the company of other Americans, notably the composer George Templeton Strong. With international fame secured, MacDowell returned to the United States in 1888, settling in Boston. For eight years he enjoyed great success there performing, teaching, and, most of all, composing. Particularly joyous and productive were the MacDowells' summers spent at a small home they bought outside Peterborough, New Hampshire.

MacDowell's compositions appealed to the tastes of the arts public in late nineteenth-century America. His orchestral works exude a fervent Romantic quality with lilting melodic lines and surging dynamics, all conveying rich emotional content. Often his orchestral tone poems were based on literary texts and poetry, particularly Keltic legends, which audiences found both pleasant and accessible. Harmonically, MacDowell's music fit within the norms of the late nineteenth-century symphonists. He did not venture heavily into the realms of dissonance that were beginning to create discomfort among some audiences and critics. Among the composers of the era, MacDowell ranked highly. One conductor, Anton Seidl, while director of the Metropolitan Opera, proclaimed MacDowell to be the superior of Brahms. While no one else placed him quite that high, MacDowell was warmly received and critically respected in both Europe and the United States, on a par with the likes of Edvard Grieg, Frederic Delius, and César Franck.

MacDowell was the best and most internationally renowned American composer of the late nineteenth century. While MacDowell's fame was considerable in his day, it has faded in the twentieth century for reasons that have little to do with any of the inherent qualities of his music. Several American critics and admirers tried to make a point of MacDowell's being a great *American* composer. Certain pieces, like his *Indian Suite* (1895) and *Woodland Sketches* (1896), refer to American events and scenery. He also marked some orchestral movements in English rather than in the customary Italian ("fast" rather than "allegro," for example). But MacDowell repeatedly rejected the idea that his music was specifically American. He felt that the issue of national identity was peripheral and, when imposed upon music, could distort listeners' responses. Americans, he contended, mistakenly believed that Europeans looked down on them. Nationalism in the arts, to MacDowell, created conflicts and allegiances for which there was no musical basis. Nationalism, he wrote, "has no place in art for its characteristics may be duplicated by anyone who takes the fancy to do so." He wanted Americans to progress in all areas of musical composition and performance and worked in all ways to foster this by advising young American colleagues and reviewing their work. But although MacDowell was supportive of many young artists, he would never lend his name to concerts devoted solely to American music. He believed himself to be a composer who simply happened to be American.

MacDowell's unwillingness to assert himself as a distinctly American composer contributed to the decline of his music's popularity in the early twentieth century. Had MacDowell also lived longer and written in cognizance of changing aesthetics, as he always did, his development would have cast his work differently. But as he died in 1908, the work of an artist appeared embedded in a bygone era and faced the music of overtly nationalistic rivals of subsequent generations like Charles Ives, Aaron Copland, and Roy Harris. Their precepts placed MacDowell ever further into the background, making him seem a mere curio of a former age. The composer and critic Virgil Thomson predicted that in time MacDowell's music would rebound and rank above Ives's as the greatest the nation has produced, but never in the twentieth century did such a reassessment occur.

The fate of MacDowell's music, savaged by fundamentally artless forces, was sadly mirrored elsewhere in the last decade of his life. In 1896 Columbia University president Seth Low persuaded MacDowell to move from Boston to New York and become the university's first professor of music. His teaching was highly successful, though some students found him overly refined and intellectual. New York City's rapid pace wore on him, however, and he was cut down by some nasty university politics. For three years he was Columbia's only music professor, and every detail involved in the creation of a new department fell on him: purchasing pianos and stationery, designing a curriculum, handling all correspondence, and, of course, doing virtually all the teaching. Had MacDowell had an experienced assistant and consistently sympathetic administrators, matters might have gone better. But in 1901, when Low left Columbia to become the city's mayor, Nicholas Murray Butler succeeded to the presidency. Butler and MacDowell clashed over the composer's conception of an interdisciplinary fine arts program. MacDowell felt that education in the arts was as necessary for undergraduates as training in mainstream letters and sciences. Butler, however, preferred traditional, discrete departments and resisted the idea of instituting an undergraduate requirement in fine arts. Butler also expressed his approval of the policy that relegated professors in the arts to non-voting status. These stances won Butler the political support of the most solidly entrenched in established departments, and he had his way, instituting his preferences while MacDowell was on sabbatical. Upon his return MacDowell expressed displeasure over the state of affairs at Columbia to students. After Butler had disregarded all his inquiries, MacDowell made the same problems known to several New York papers. Butler seized upon this as evidence of unprofessional behavior, and he discreetly leaked memoranda implying that MacDowell had been derelict in meeting his teaching duties. Hurt and angered by such academic warfare, for which he had neither taste nor temperament, MacDowell resigned from Columbia in February 1904.

MacDowell was greatly depressed over the Columbia debacle. This depression was aggravated by a deep malaise that came from being struck by a cab on Broadway. These injuries and depression triggered in MacDowell a general aphasia and with it a physical and emotional decline. Photographs of MacDowell taken in 1898 and 1906 reveal rapid aging. Learning of MacDowell's decline, Mayor Low sent Marian MacDowell $2,000 and confessed to her, "I feel partly responsible for this." "O! If we had never left Boston!" MacDowell lamented to his wife. His decline proceeded unabated. Doctors were powerless. Even visits to his beloved Peterborough home could not rally him. Scarcely a month after his forty-sixth birthday MacDowell passed away in New York City. Marian MacDowell maintained the Peterborough home and soon began a colony for artists there. She ran it until after World War II, and the MacDowell Colony continues to be a monument to its namesake and a haven for unfettered work in the creative arts.

• Despite the stature of MacDowell in the annals of western music, there is not yet a thorough biography of him, nor a systematic study of all his music. Two biographies based on personal memories and journalistic sources appeared shortly after the composer's death: Lawrence Gilman, *Edward MacDowell* (1906), and John F. Porte, *Edward MacDowell* (1922). Two contemporaries wrote personal memories of MacDowell's life and work: T. P. Currier, *Edward MacDowell (As I Knew Him)* (1915), and W. H. Humiston, *MacDowell* (1924). Marian MacDowell similarly published *Random Notes on Edward MacDowell and His Music* (1950). Some sentimental works have appeared on MacDowell: Elizabeth Page, *Edward MacDowell, His Works and Ideals* (1910); Opal Wheeler, *Edward MacDowell and His Cabin in the Pines* (1940); and Abbie Brown, *The Boyhood of Edward MacDowell* (1924). W. J. Baltzell edited some of MacDowell's writings about music in *Critical and Historical Essays: Lectures of Edward MacDowell Delivered at Columbia University* (1912). Beyond these works there are but chapters in texts and sections in musical dictionaries and encyclopedias, the best of which is the *New Grove's Dictionary of Music and Musicians.* Systematic work on MacDowell has been meager, in part, because MacDowell's papers were closed until 1992. They were finally opened that year at the Library of Congress.

ALAN LEVY

MACDOWELL, Katherine Sherwood Bonner. *See* Bonner, Sherwood.

MACDOWELL, Marian Griswold Nevins (22 Nov. 1857–23 Aug. 1956), founder and supporter of the MacDowell Colony, was born in New York City, the daughter of David N. Nevins (occupation unknown) and Cornelia Leonard Perkins. When she was ten years old, her mother died, and her father moved his four children to Waterford, Connecticut. There, Marian took piano lessons from her aunt, Mrs. Roger Perkins. At eighteen, she traveled to Frankfurt, Germany, to study music with renowned pianist Clara Schumann. Upon learning that she would first have to spend a year under the tutelage of Clara's daughter, Marian opted instead for instruction at the Darmstadt Conservatory, under American composer Edward MacDowell. They married in 1884 in Waterford. Upon inheriting $5,000, she abandoned her own musical career to support her husband's ambitions as a composer. They lived in Wiesbaden (1884–1888), Boston (1888–1896), and New York City (1896–1904), where he headed Columbia University's music department. During vacations they retreated to an eighty-acre summer home in Peterborough, New Hampshire. Edward resigned from Columbia over differences over music training with President Nicholas Murray Butler and soon fell ill with a sickness, generally reported to be an obscure incurable brain disease, that would take his life in 1908.

Edward's musical friends in New York City established a fund for Marian's support, even before she was widowed, but she applied the money to establish the MacDowell Association. In memory of her husband, she established an artists' colony on the New Hampshire property, for the use of American writers, visual artists, and composers. Here, she hoped, the artists could withdraw from worldly concerns to concentrate on their creative work. Over the next forty years, she would tour the country, playing four hundred concerts of her husband's compositions, to raise $100,000 to expand the colony; she did this despite a lifelong series of back injuries that sometimes left her bedridden or on crutches for long periods of time. She was particularly successful at winning financial support from women's music clubs affiliated with the National Federation of Music Clubs. By the time of Marian MacDowell's death, the MacDowell Colony consisted of six hundred acres of land with thirty-three buildings, mostly studios in which artists could work for the summer, uninterrupted even by meals, which were delivered to their cottage doorsteps. After a hard day's work, colonists were invited to congregate for conversation and a sharing of their work; on Sundays, MacDowell invited them to her home for dinner.

The first two colonists came in 1908, writer Mary Mears and sculptor Helen Farnsworth Mears. By 1923, three hundred applicants competed for fifty awards, and many colonists distinguished themselves by winning Pulitzer Prizes for their efforts, including composer Aaron Copland and writers Willa Cather, Edwin Arlington Robinson, and Thornton Wilder. Among other colonists were composers Mabel Daniels, Amy Beach, Roy Harris, and Lukas Foss and writers Elinor Wylie and Stephen Vincent Benét. MacDowell enjoyed acclaim in her lifetime for her efforts. She received several honorary degrees and a $5,000 prize in 1925 from the *Pictorial Review* "for the most distinctive achievement through individual effort in the field of art, industry, literature, music, drama, education, science or sociology," a sum that paid some colony debts. (Finances were a regular headache, for the colony constantly expanded in acreage and the physical plant was improved.) In her later years, she wintered in Los Angeles with companion Nina Maud Richardson, and she died there. She was buried at the colony alongside her husband.

MacDowell's greatest contribution to the MacDowell Colony was as a fundraiser, but she also socialized with the creators selected to come there and made every effort to attend to their particular needs, determined to make their visit productive, comfortable, and congenial. Her tenacity at establishing and developing a colony to facilitate the work of American men and women in the arts was a genuine contribution to the cultural life of the nation.

• Marian MacDowell's papers and those of the MacDowell Colony are in the Manuscript Division, Library of Congress. The Special Collections Department of the University of New Hampshire also has some material, mostly on the last years of her life. The MacDowell Colony has a small file on its history; Marian MacDowell wrote a personal account, *The First Twenty Years of the MacDowell Colony: A Sketch* (1951). See also Nancy McKee, *Valiant Woman* (1962); Gladys Livingston Graff, "The Most Outstanding American Woman," *Lyre: The Magazine of Alpha Chi Omega* 28 (Mar. 1925): 348–54; Jerome Beatty, "Pilot on the Glory Road," *Reader's Digest*, Oct. 1937, pp. 55–58; Robert Sabin, "MacDowell

Colony Notables and Neighbors Honor Founder," *Musical America*, Sept. 1952, pp. 3, 23, 33–34; Rollo Walter Brown, "Mrs. MacDowell and Her Colony," *Atlantic Monthly*, July 1949, pp. 42–46; Ronald Eyer, "Great Lady of Music," *Musical America*, Sept. 1956, p. 5; and "Peterborough," *American Magazine of Art* 8 (Aug. 1917); 396–401. Obituaries are in *Musical America*, Sept. 1956, p. 32; the *Manchester* (N.H.) *Union Leader*, 25 Aug. 1956; and the *New York Times* and *New York Tribune*, 30 Aug. 1956.

KAREN J. BLAIR

MACE, Aurelia (6 Mar. 1835–30 Mar. 1910), Shaker trustee, was born in Strong, Maine, the daughter of Marquis de LaFayette Mace, a Universalist minister, and Sarah Norton Flint. Aurelia, the youngest of six girls and two boys, was brought to the United Society of Believers in Christ's Second Appearing by her family when she was just one year old. Although her father chose not to join the Shaker society, her mother and three sisters joined the Believers, and all remained in the Shaker community until their deaths.

Mace officially joined the Society of Believers in Sabbathday Lake, Maine, signing the covenant when she was twenty-three. From 1853 through 1880 she taught school while simultaneously serving as second eldress from 1860 to 1866 and from 1869 to 1880. Mace eventually became in 1896 a trustee, dealing with the "world's people" and wielding considerable financial control, after working in the office for six years. She acted in that capacity until her death. In addition to the active role she played in establishing the Shaker brush industries, she is also credited with introducing the Shakers' lemon syrup and balsam pillows to the public.

Mace found popular fame when she mistook the famous jeweler Charles Lewis Tiffany for an unemployed tramp in the summer of 1900. Tiffany, age eighty-eight at the time, had gotten lost during a walk in the countryside, and he arrived at the Shaker community looking worn and hot, simply seeking a glass of water. Mace gave him lemonade, brushed off his clothing, insisted he sit with them for the noon meal, and encouraged him to thank God he still had his strength and health even though he was out of work. Despite his protestations, she sent him off with an immense boxed lunch and best wishes that he would find work soon. Several days later Mace was surprised to receive a set of silver spoons, forks, and knives, engraved "Aurelia," with a thank-you note from Tiffany. The story appeared in newspapers and, later, a book, and Mace delighted in telling it.

Mace is best known as a religious thinker and writer. She wrote regularly for the *Shaker Manifesto* and engaged in lively correspondence with many individuals, including Leo Tolstoy, the Russian writer. *The Aletheia: Spirit of Truth*, a collection of some of her letters, most of which were published in the *Messenger* (1883–1884), and essays, some of which had been printed in the *Manifesto*, was published in 1899, with a second edition printed in 1907. One of many Shakers who believed that the tenets of spiritualism in its pure sense were essential to an understanding of Shakerism, Mace also kept a journal, which included descriptions of meetings during the 1870s when sisters and little girls of the Sabbathday Lake community met to sing, dance, and speak. During these meetings Mace recorded the spiritual experiences of the participants, who were often overwhelmed when "many from beyond the veil would come into their midst" and "a flow of Divine Inspiration would reach their spirits which they would feel at no other time" (Humez, p. xxvi).

The Shaker vision of deity as both feminine and masculine was essential to Mace's beliefs, and she endorsed it by including Theodore Parker's statement "God is our Infinite Mother; She will hold us in her arms of blessedness and beauty forever and ever," on the title page of *The Aletheia*. Mace also expected that the Shaker community would reflect the beliefs she felt Mother Ann Lee, the founder of Shakerism, had inspired, including equality for men and women. Dismayed by the society's reluctance to do so, she wrote in her journal that a "great 'He' Spirit" had entered the community in 1883, when a building was constructed with only one door that the men always entered first. Mace viewed the practice of the sisters "coming over behind the little boys" as the demise of one of the great principles of the "New Creation" that was Shakerism, the equality of the sexes (Morse, p. 103).

Mace was among a number of Shakers who, in the 1890s, began referring to themselves as "Alethians," or "Truth-followers." Mace, Eldress Anna White, and Elder Alonzo Hollister were just a few of the Shakers who felt they were inspired by the Spirit to speak for tolerance of divergent religious beliefs and freedom of thought. They urged their sisters and brothers to abandon the Shakers' formal name, United Society of Believers in Christ's Second Appearing, and to take the name Alethians because what they referred to as the Christ Consciousness had manifested itself on earth many times. Mace was preoccupied with articulating the many ways in which the Christ Spirit appeared, writing in 1896 that "Christ had appeared in thousands before our Mother lived, and also before the days of Jesus" (*Manifesto* 26, no. 4: 45–46). Mace spoke to many groups outside of the Shaker community, including a Ba'hai audience gathered at "Greenacre" in Eliot, Maine, in July 1904. The text of that lecture "The Mission and Testimony of the Shakers of the Twentieth Century to the World," appears in the second edition of *The Aletheia*. Aurelia Mace died at the Sabbathday Lake community in New Gloucester, Maine.

• Mace's papers are housed at the United Society of Believers' Library, New Gloucester, Maine. Many books mention Mace and deal with ideas and issues important to her. See Stephen J. Stein, *The Shaker Experience in America* (1992); Robley Edward Whitson, *The Shakers: Two Centuries of Spiritual Reflection* (1983); Sally L. Kitch, *Chaste Liberation: Celibacy and Female Cultural Status* (1989); Flo Morse, *The Shakers and the World's People* (1987); and Jean M. Humez, *Mother's First-born Daughters* (1993).

ERIKA M. BUTLER

MACELWANE, James Bernard (28 Sept. 1883–15 Feb. 1956), geophysicist and Jesuit priest, was born near Port Clinton, Ohio, the son of Alexander Macelwane, a fisherman and farmer, and Catherine Agnes Carr. He obtained his early education on the benches of a rural schoolhouse, often interrupted by seasonal chores to assist the frugal fortunes of his family. In response to his desire to become a priest and missionary, his parents managed to enroll him at age eighteen in St. John's College in Toledo. Two years later, in 1903, he entered the Society of Jesus, where he followed the usual course of studies in the humanities, science, and theology.

He received an M.A. in 1911 and an M.S. in physics in 1912, both at Saint Louis University. He was ordained a priest in the Catholic church in St. Louis, Missouri, in 1918. Shortly thereafter he attended the University of California, where he obtained his Ph.D. in physics in 1923 under Professor Elmer E. Hall with a dissertation on a seismological topic. Impressed by Macelwane, Andrew C. Lawson, then chair of the Department of Geological Sciences, invited him to stay on at Berkeley, to take charge of the seismographic stations, and to organize an academic program in seismology.

During his tenure as an assistant professor of geology, Macelwane initiated the development of a chain of seismographic stations throughout northern California and began instrumental study of the small to moderate earthquakes that occur in the region with the intent of keeping as complete a record as possible of the seismicity of the Bay Area and northern California. He also recruited Perry Byerly as his first doctoral student. Byerly subsequently became his successor as director of the seismographic stations and director of the program in geophysics at the University of California.

Two years later, in 1925, Macelwane returned to Saint Louis University, where he founded the Department of Geophysics, the first in the nation, retaining the position of director of the department for the remainder of his life. In St. Louis, Macelwane set about developing a graduate program in geophysics, much as he had done at Berkeley, and establishing a regional network of seismographic stations.

More broadly, at the instigation of Harry Wood of the National Research Council and of Arthur L. Day, chairman of the Advisory Committee on Seismology of the Carnegie Institution of Washington, Macelwane became instrumental in the revitalization of the Jesuit Seismological Service, a network of seismographic stations that had been established at sixteen Jesuit institutions in 1910 and 1911. When first established this group of stations was the first network of similarly instrumented seismographic stations deployed over a region of continental dimensions. For a number of reasons several of these stations had languished. Macelwane saw to their reorganization as the Jesuit Seismological Association with a central station and research center at Saint Louis University.

A principal activity of the association, in cooperation with Science Service and the U.S. Coast and Geo-

detic Survey, was a routine, independent determination of the epicenters of the larger earthquakes each year. The results were published in a *Preliminary Bulletin* that was distributed to other national and international institutions and to governmental seismological agencies. This program continued into the 1960s, when the advent of computer processing of data and determination of epicenters rendered the service no longer useful.

Working with his students and colleagues at Saint Louis University, Macelwane instituted a study of the earthquakes that occur in the New Madrid seismic zone in southeastern Missouri, the site in 1811 and 1812 of three of the largest earthquakes to have occurred in North American history. Research into the seismicity of the area, and the related seismic hazard, remains an area of primary interest to the department. Other students of Macelwane engaged in studies of travel times of seismic waves, constructing travel time curves and investigating the character of the crust-mantle boundary or presenting evidence for second-order discontinuities within the mantle. In about 1935 his attention turned to the study of microseisms, continuous trains of seismic waves recorded at seismographic stations. By study of the passage of these waves across small triangular networks, he established their speed of propagation and direction of approach, relating them to storms at sea. While the exact mechanism of generation was never fully established, together with J. Emilio Ramirez, later director of the Geophysical Observatory of the Colombian Andes in Bogota, he endeavored (in the days before radar and before visual overflights by aircraft) to use the recording of these waves as a method of tracking storms at sea. With the help of the U.S. Navy Macelwane set up several stations in the West Indies to detect and track hurricanes.

Throughout his career Macelwane remained interested in geophysical education and in the training of young scientists. As chairman of a committee of the National Research Council he brought out in 1933 the volume *Seismology* in the *Physics of the Earth* series. He was a member of a similar committee and contributed "Evidence of the Interior of the Earth Derived from Seismic Sources" to another volume, the *Internal Constitution of the Earth*, which appeared in 1939. In 1936 he published his *Introduction to Theoretical Seismology*, part 1: *Geodynamics*, long a favorite textbook on the theory of elastic waves, bridging the gap between Augustus E. H. Love's more abstract *Theory of Elasticity* and the minds of American students. He was active in the Society of Exploration Geophysicists and in the American Institute of Mining and Metallurgical Engineers, serving on the Committees on Education for each of these societies.

Macelwane is perhaps best known for the part he played in national and international associations of seismology and geophysics. He was a life member and served as a director of the Seismological Society of America from 1925 till his death and was its president in 1928–1929. He was a member of the American Geophysical Union from 1925 onward, vice chairman of the Section on Seismology from 1935 to 1938, and section president from 1938 to 1941. He was elected president of the Union in 1953 and was in the third year of his term at the time of his death in St. Louis. He was similarly active and held appointments in the International Union of Geodesy and Geophysics.

Macelwane was called on to serve on many scientific advisory boards, such as the Research and Development Board of the Department of Defense and the Scientific Advisory Board of the U.S. Air Force. He was a member of the National Science Board and chairman of the Technical Panel for Seismology and Gravity of the U.S. National Committee for the International Geophysical Year. He was a fellow of the Geological Society of America, the American Association for the Advancement of Science, the American Physical Society, and the American Geographical Society and held membership in numerous other societies.

He was elected a member of the National Academy of Science in 1944. In 1948 he was awarded the Bowie Medal of the American Geophysical Union. Its motto reads, "Unselfish Cooperation." This same society honored his memory and paid tribute to his interest in the development of young scientists by naming in his honor the Macelwane Award, given annually to a young geophysicist of exceptional promise and accomplishment.

The geophysical sciences are relatively young disciplines that developed extensively over the twentieth century. Macelwane was one of the players, among a handful of others, who stood at the threshold of this era of growth and who by his dedication and cooperative spirit helped form the foundation on which others have built.

• Macelwane's papers are preserved in the archives of the Pius XII Library of Saint Louis University. His scientific publications include "Revised Travel-Time Tables," *Bureau Central Seismologique International, Series A, Travaux Scientifiques* 15 (1937): 3–8, and "The Problem of Microseisms and Ocean Storms," *Bulletin of the Seismological Society of America* 36 (1946): 81–82. He published other work principally in *Transactions of the American Geophysical Union, Bulletin of the Geological Society of America, Physical Review,* and *Geophysics.* His life and contributions are memorialized in National Academy of Sciences, *Biographical Memoirs* 31 (1958): 254–81, and in *Proceedings Volume of the Geological Society of America, Annual Report for 1956* (Sept. 1957): 159–64.

WILLIAM STAUDER

MACFADDEN, Bernarr (16 Aug. 1868–12 Oct. 1955), physical culturist and publisher, was born Bernard Adolphus McFadden near Mill Spring, Missouri, the son of William R. McFadden and Mary Miller, farmers. A weak and sickly boy, he was virtually abandoned after his mother divorced her often drunken and violent husband. Both parents died before he was eleven, his father of alcoholism, his mother of tuberculosis. After serving on an Illinois farm, he worked in a Chicago hotel and in the St. Louis area as delivery boy, clerk, bookkeeper, and farm and construction laborer, and for a short time co-owned a St. Louis laundry.

Macfadden strengthened his body with Indian clubs and other gymnasium equipment, became a wrestler, coached teams at military schools, and opened a physical culture studio in St. Louis. His crude novel, *The Athlete's Conquest* (1892), combined physical culture with romance. In 1893, at the World's Columbian Exposition in Chicago, he was so impressed with the dramatic highlighting of strongman Eugen Sandow that he had himself similarly photographed in classical poses. He moved to New York City and changed his name to Bernarr Macfadden, believing his new name to sound stronger and more unique, and distinguishing himself from the many McFaddens. In 1894 he established an exercise studio. In 1899 he started a monthly magazine, *Physical Culture.*

As a health promoter in the tradition of Sylvester Graham, Macfadden believed that poor hygiene led to ill health. He condemned corsets and advocated vigorous activity, adequate rest, fresh air, and a diet of natural foods, well-chewed. He disapproved of coffee, tea, liquor, and tobacco. He fasted frequently, maintaining that it rested the digestive organs and rid the body of poisons. He often walked barefoot, believing that it enabled the body to absorb the earth's magnetic force. With little education, he claimed to cure numerous diseases by natural methods, rejected the germ theory, condemned vaccination, regarded physicians as needless diagnosticians and drugs as poison. He waged a lifelong battle against the American Medical Association, describing it as a self-interested monopoly.

Applying his theory of natural healing, Macfadden operated several physical culture sanatoriums, the first in Kingston, New York (1901), followed by others at Lake Ronkonkoma, Long Island, Battle Creek, Michigan, and Chicago. Later in New York State he acquired a health resort in Dansville (1929) and a tuberculosis sanatorium in Liberty (1939). He also established inexpensive health food restaurants in New York City, Brooklyn, Philadelphia, and Chicago and other cities; by 1911 there were twenty such restaurants.

Macfadden was a prolific writer. His second novel portrayed a hopeless invalid whose conversion to a wholesome life-style enabled him to become *A Strenuous Lover* (1904). Macfadden's health doctrines were expounded in more than a hundred books ranging from hair culture, *Strength from Eating* (1901), and body-building, *Building of Vital Power* (1904), to sexual prowess, *Man's Sex Life* (1935). Between 1911 and 1912 he published a five-volume *Encyclopedia of Physical Culture*, a collaborative work superseded in 1931 by a revised eight-volume *Encyclopedia of Health and Physical Culture.*

A talented showman, Macfadden delighted in the display of the human body and sponsored exhibitions featuring contests of scantily clad men and women at Madison Square Garden. Posters advertising his 1905 exhibition—showing women in union suits and a man in leopard-skin and breechcloth—were seized by vice crusader Anthony Comstock; Macfadden was arrested but released, and the ensuing publicity led to an overflow crowd.

In 1905 Macfadden founded Physical Culture City, a health community near Spotswood, New Jersey, where 200 settlers wore minimal clothing. The experiment collapsed around 1908 after Macfadden was sued by the Spotswood postmaster for circulating through the mail an "obscene" story in *Physical Culture* about a drunken teenager who fornicated, got venereal disease, and had himself burned alive. A federal court convicted the publisher, who paid a $2,000 fine, but in 1909 President William Howard Taft pardoned the two-year prison sentence on the advice of Attorney General George W. Wickersham that in this case the law had been stretched.

Macfadden achieved a mass readership for *Physical Culture* shortly before incorporating Macfadden Publications in 1924. *True Story* (1919) was the pioneer confession magazine, featuring tales of love and romance. The first national publication to use photography successfully, it dealt openly with sexuality. Eventually it circulated more than two million copies and was widely imitated. Other flourishing ventures were *True Romances*, founded in 1923, and *True Detective Mysteries*, the first crime and detection magazine, premiered in 1924. *Liberty*, acquired in 1931, became Macfadden's editorial mouthpiece. One of his several newspapers, the tabloid *New York Evening Graphic*, which he published from 1924 to 1932, featured lurid accounts of sex, violence, and crime—some illustrated with faked photographs. Through his publishing empire Macfadden reached a vast audience; total circulation of his publications was estimated at 35 million to 40 million a year, and by 1930 he was worth $30 million.

In 1931 he created the Bernarr Macfadden Foundation with a $5 million endowment. It subsidized his Physical Culture Hotel in Dansville (1932), a military academy, several other schools, and a summer camp.

Macfadden had political ambitions but never won office. Convinced that the president needed a secretary of health, he saw himself as the logical choice. Although in 1932 he supported Franklin D. Roosevelt, he turned against the New Deal, seeing it as bureaucratic regimentation of government, and hoped to become the Republican nominee for president in 1936. Leasing a Miami Beach hotel, he ran for U.S. senator from Florida (1940), governor of Florida (1940, 1948), and mayor of New York City (1953). Stockholders of Macfadden Publications charged him with squandering corporation funds for political and personal expenses, and he was ousted from its presidency in 1941. He had no further connections with the company, which later changed its name to Macfadden Holdings, but he did publish a health magazine under several titles until at least 1953.

Macfadden's marital relations were unhappy. His marriage to Tillie Fontain in 1898 or 1899 soon ended; in 1901 he wed Marguerite Kelly, a Canadian nurse, who bore him one child before their divorce in 1911. While lecturing in England in 1912–1913 he conducted a contest for "the most perfect specimen of English womanhood," based on health, muscular development, and beauty. The winner was Mary Williamson, a carpet mill worker and champion swimmer, to whom he was married in 1913. Their "physical culture family," which included seven children, ended in divorce in 1946. In 1948 Macfadden married Johnnie Lee; they separated in 1954. Because of a much-reduced income, he failed to pay alimony to two wives, leading to brief jail sentences. At his death Macfadden's assets were reported as worth less than $5,000. He died in Jersey City, New Jersey.

Macfadden's muscular body was supported by a frame five and a half feet tall. He was an intuitive, shrewd, and eccentric egotist. He led well-publicized group hikes, piloted his own plane, and in his eighties celebrated his birthdays doing parachute jumps. He was an ardent champion of sexual vigor as essential to health and well-being. One of a long line of naturopathic health reformers, he was a flamboyant challenger of conventional medicine. As a publisher he was an influential innovator in journalism for the masses.

• There is no collection of Macfadden papers. Materials bearing on Macfadden as a publisher can be found in the papers of his chief editor, Fulton Oursler, in the Fordham University Library and in the Fulton Oursler Memorial Collection in the Georgetown University Library. The Bernarr Macfadden file of the American Medical Association contains many letters criticizing Macfadden. The most complete biography is Robert Ernst, *Weakness Is a Crime: The Life of Bernarr Macfadden* (1991), which includes a lengthy bibliography. Popularly written but less thorough is William R. Hunt, *Body Love: The Amazing Career of Bernarr Macfadden* (1989). For a vivid but biased account by Macfadden's estranged third wife see Mary Macfadden and Emile Gauvreau, *Dumbbells and Carrot Strips: The Story of Bernarr Macfadden* (1953). Obituaries are in the *New York Times* and the *Rochester Times-Union*, both 13 Oct. 1955, and *Time*, 24 Oct. 1955.

ROBERT ERNST

MACFARLANE, Catharine (7 Apr. 1877–27 May 1969), physician and educator, was born in Philadelphia, Pennsylvania, the daughter of John James Macfarlane and Henrietta Ottinger Huston, educators. Macfarlane was encouraged by her mother to pursue a career in science: "My choice of medicine as a profession was influenced almost entirely by my mother, a woman of rare wisdom and judgment," she wrote in 1947. At the age of fifteen Macfarlane was sent to Germany to attend the Girls' School in Leipzig. Upon her return to Philadelphia in 1893, she entered the University of Pennsylvania, from which she received a certificate in biology in 1895. In 1898 Macfarlane earned her M.D. from the Woman's Medical College of Pennsylvania (WMCP) in Philadelphia, after which she served a one-year internship at the Woman's Hospital of Philadelphia, followed by postgraduate study in gynecological urology at Johns Hopkins University. Further education included study with several of the most prominent figures in obstetrics and gynecology of her time at the Royal Charité, Berlin (obstetrics); Frauenklinik, University of Vienna (gynecology); and Radium Hemmet, Stockholm (radiology).

Macfarlane spent her career in medical education and research at the Woman's Medical College of Pennsylvania. In 1898 she became an instructor in obstetrics at the college; by 1922 she was made professor of gynecology and, in 1942, research professor of gynecology. In addition to her faculty appointments, she served briefly in 1940 as interim dean of the college and in 1946 became vice president of the Board of Corporators. Macfarlane's research activities centered on her Cancer Control Research Project, which she began in 1938 with WMCP colleagues Faith Fetterman and Margaret Castix Sturgis. This project, one of the first of its kind in the United States, established a cancer-screening program in Philadelphia designed to detect uterine cancer in its earliest stages.

Throughout her career, Macfarlane combined her research and teaching activities with a gynecological practice in the Germantown section of Philadelphia. She first made her rounds to patients' homes on a bicycle, later graduating to a horse and buggy, and finally to an electric car. At various times in her practice she shared an office and stayed overnight with other female physicians working in Center City Philadelphia, thereby maintaining two offices. Macfarlane continued to practice medicine to the end of her life, performing surgery with apparent success into her nineties.

Macfarlane was a highly-trained physician quick to credit good female teachers who had taught and inspired her. She actively supported the causes of women throughout her life by training women physicians; by fostering the advancement of women in medicine through her presidency in 1936 of the American Medical Women's Association; by conducting research on women's health problems; and by promoting the right of women to obtain birth control, a cause for which she appeared on the platform with Margaret Sanger at the first Pennsylvania State Conference on Birth Control, held in Philadelphia in 1922. Macfarlane also supported passage of the Nineteenth Amendment and spoke frankly on the issue during World War I, declaring that "while brave men fought in Europe to make the world 'Safe for Democracy,' brave and determined women strove in America to make democracy fair to women." She was the recipient of numerous awards and honors for her research and teaching, including the Gimbel Award (1949) and the Lasker Award (1951), and she was the first woman member (1932) of the College of Physicians of Philadelphia and the first woman president (1943) of the Obstetrical Society of Philadelphia.

Macfarlane was known by her colleagues as a woman of vision and action as well as a determined woman of hot temper. In a tribute to her some ten years after her death, Katharine Sturgis, a former student and colleague of Macfarlane's, called her "a woman of dignity and temper, but with a warm and loving core."

Macfarlane, who died in Philadelphia, never married and lived a significant portion of her life with her mother, who died in 1957.

• Manuscripts and a complete bibliography of Macfarlane's publications, correspondence, faculty minutes and minutes from her term as interim dean, data from the cancer-screening project, and other papers related to her work are in the Archives and Special Collections on Women in Medicine, the Medical College of Pennsylvania. The original handwritten manuscript of her autobiography is located at the College of Physicians of Philadelphia. Macfarlane's writings include *Reference Hand-Book of Gynecology for Nurses* (1908; 6th ed., 1934), and numerous articles in the field of obstetrics and gynecology, especially detection and treatment of cancer of the uterus, including "The Treatment of Precancerous Lesions of the Cervix," *Surgical Clinics of North America* 19 (1939): 1465–77; "An Experiment in Cancer Control," *American Gynecological and Obstetrical Journal* (1940); and "Control of Cancer of the Uterus: Report of a Ten Year Experiment," *Journal of the American Medical Association* 138 (27 Nov. 1948): 941–43. See also the memoir by Katharine B. R. Sturgis, "First Woman Fellow of the College of Physicians of Philadelphia: Memoir of Catharine Macfarlane, 1877–1969," *Transactions and Studies of the College of Physicians of Philadelphia* 38 (1971): 157–60. An obituary is in the *Philadelphia Evening Bulletin*, 28 May 1969.

SANDRA L. CHAFF

MACGAHAN, Januarius Aloysius (12 June 1844–9 June 1878), war correspondent, was born on a farm near New Lexington, Ohio, the son of Irish immigrants James MacGahan and Esther Dempsey. The MacGahan family moved to Huntington, Indiana, where Januarius worked as a grocer's clerk, a schoolteacher, and a sometime writer for the *Huntington Democrat*.

In 1868 MacGahan, then working as a stationery store clerk in St. Louis, Missouri, met General Philip H. Sheridan, an Ohio friend of the family. Perhaps through Sheridan's influence, MacGahan traveled to Europe late in 1868. He studied French and discovered a facility for languages that would prove invaluable in his journalistic career. He traveled the continent and lived for a time in an art colony at Ecouen, near Paris, where he taught English.

France had been at war with Prussia nearly six months when, toward the end of 1870, General Sheridan, serving as an American observer of the war, appears again to have assisted MacGahan by introducing him to Dr. George Hosmer, European agent for the *New York Herald*. The meeting resulted in MacGahan's gaining "special correspondent" credentials for the *Herald*.

Like other news reports of this era, MacGahan's work appeared without a byline. He covered the last-gasp campaign of the French Army of the East near the Swiss frontier and probably wrote of the battle at Villersexel, near Montbeliard in the Vosges Mountains, in January 1871; he was present at the fall of Paris, interviewed such eminent Frenchmen as Adolphe Thiers and Victor Hugo, and, during the seventy-day Commune of Paris, rode with the Polish nobleman Dombrowski and witnessed that officer's death on the barricades of the commune on 23 May 1871. MacGahan was taken prisoner briefly by Parisian police and released only after the intervention of U.S. Minister Elihu Washburne.

MacGahan's work in the war pleased the *Herald* management to the extent that he was given a "roving commission," between the fall of 1871 and the spring of 1873, to visit the great cities of Europe and write occasional pieces for the newspaper. He wrote about the Russian royal family vacationing in Yalta, covered the Crimean tour of General William Tecumseh Sherman, and reported on the *Alabama* claims arbitration in Geneva, in which the U.S. government sought compensation from Great Britain for damages caused by British-made Confederate warships.

In the spring of 1873 the *Herald* sent MacGahan to Central Asia to observe and write on the Russian incursion into Turkestan, specifically a campaign by a Russian army to subjugate the Turkoman tribes and to conquer the walled citadel of Khiva. In a harrowing twenty-nine days, and in defiance of the Russian commander's order that he not proceed, MacGahan crossed the Kyzil Kum desert and intercepted the Russian column, which welcomed him into its ranks as a *molodyetz* (brave fellow). He observed the fall of Khiva, sympathetically interviewed Muhamed Rahim Bogadur, the khan of Khiva, and rode with Cossacks. Out of his experiences MacGahan wrote the first of his two, full-length books of his adventures, *Campaigning on the Oxus and the Fall of Khiva* (1874).

The Carlist War in Spain provided MacGahan a six-month *Herald* assignment in 1874. He rode with the Carlist forces, wearing the red *boina* (beret) of the Pretender's army, interviewed Don Carlos on several occasions, and wrote fervently and often wrongheadedly of the futile Carlist cause, predicting great victories for the Pretender when none were in the offing.

In the spring of 1875 MacGahan accompanied the expedition of Captain Sir Allen Young on HMS *Pandora* to arctic waters, a voyage that was to attempt the fabled Northwest Passage and to locate traces of the lost expedition of Sir John Franklin, which had disappeared in the arctic fastness thirty years earlier. The expedition failed on both its missions, but MacGahan produced a charming book from the experience, *Under the Northern Lights* (1876).

Reports of savage Turkish reprisals for peasant insurrections in the Balkan provinces of the Ottoman Empire had appeared desultorily and without detail in British papers in the spring of 1876. MacGahan sensed the importance of the rumors but failed to interest the *Herald* in the story. The *Times* of London also refused to hire him, fearing his proclivity for "sensational reportage." Each was to regret its decision. MacGahan's incendiary reports for the London *Daily News* from the villages of Bulgaria were pitilessly detailed accounts of torture, mutilation, rape, and murder, the wholesale slaughter of an estimated 15,000 Bulgars, and the destruction of entire villages. These dispatches (later collected in pamphlet form and widely sold in England) were credited as a factor in the toppling of the pro-Turkish Disraeli ministry, in changing England's posture of supporting the Turks (in the interest of keeping Russia out of Eastern Europe), and in bringing former prime minister William Ewart Gladstone out of retirement. Archibald Forbes, MacGahan's *Daily News* colleague, went a step further, crediting his American friend as being "the virtual author of the Russo-Turkish War."

Russia declared war on Turkey in April 1877, and MacGahan was present at most of the key battles, including those of Plevna and the Shipka Pass, writing brilliant dispatches under the terrible hardships of battle conditions, a broken ankle that failed to heal, intermittent fever, and physical and mental exhaustion.

In Constantinople in the spring of 1878 to cover the signing of the Treaty of San Stefano, which followed the Turkish surrender, MacGahan contracted typhus and succumbed to a virulent fever in the British hospital in Galata, three days before his thirty-fourth birthday. He was survived by his wife, Varvara (called "Barbara") Nicholavna Elaguine, a widely published newspaper and magazine writer who was the daughter of a wealthy Russian landowner. They had married in Paris in 1873 and had one child.

MacGahan was buried in the cemetery at Pera, outside Constantinople. In 1884 his remains were exhumed and returned to the United States and then reburied in the Maplewood Cemetery in New Lexington, Ohio, near his birthplace. In 1911 a huge marble stone was placed on the grave. The inscription on the marker reads: "MacGahan—Liberator of Bulgaria."

MacGahan's brief career as a "special" correspondent remains one of the most extraordinary in the history of journalism. In seven and a half years of hectic work for two major newspapers he wrote eyewitness accounts of wars and battles in France, Central Asia, Spain, and the Balkans, participated in an arctic expedition, and wrote two books on his adventures. Even after the passage of more than a century, his partisan, first-person, unbylined reportage, scrawled hastily under the severest of battlefield conditions, retains a curious power. His dispatches from the villages of Bulgaria in 1876 are horrifying in their meticulous cataloguing of the Turkish atrocities.

Virtually forgotten in his own country, MacGahan is remembered in Bulgaria as a hero of the 1876 insurrection against Ottoman rule. There is a bust of him at a museum in Batak, a street named for him in Sofia, and long accounts of his life in Bulgarian history books and encyclopedias.

• The MacGahan papers, including those of his wife, Barbara Elaguine, are in the possession of MacGahan's grandchildren. These papers include a fragment of a diary of MacGahan's (covering the period 1871–1873), correspondence, scrapbooks, photographs, expense accounts, book contracts, and a few of MacGahan's handwritten newspaper dispatches. In addition to insightful memoirs by MacGahan's wife, the papers contain a narrative written about 1873 by an unknown Russian officer in the army commanded by General Constantine von Kaufmann after the conquest of Khiva.

The only biography of MacGahan is Dale L. Walker, *Januarius MacGahan: The Life and Campaigns of an American War Correspondent* (1988). Walker had full access to the MacGahan family archives. Other published sources on the correspondent include fragmentary pieces in the several war correspondent memoirs of MacGahan's London *Daily News* colleague Archibald Forbes and in histories of war correspondence and journalism such as F. Lauriston Bullard, *Famous War Correspondents* (1914); Rupert Furneaux, *The Breakfast War* (1958) and *News of War* (1965); and Louis L. Snyder and Richard B. Morris, eds., *A Treasury of Great Reporting* (1949).

DALE L. WALKER

MACGOWAN, Kenneth (30 Nov. 1888–27 Apr. 1963), drama critic, director/producer, and theater educator, was born in Winthrop, Massachusetts, the son of Peter Stainforth Macgowan and Susan Arletta Hall. Before he graduated from Harvard in 1911 he was already working as an assistant drama critic for the *Boston Transcript*, where he remained until 1914. In that year Macgowan became the drama, literary, and motion-picture critic for the *Philadelphia Evening Ledger*. In 1917 he moved to New York City, becoming the drama critic for the *Evening Globe* (later the *New York Globe*). Macgowan had married Edna Behre in 1913; they had two children.

As the First World War ended and American theater began to mature and attract serious international attention, Macgowan broadened his range of activities. While drama critic for the *New York Globe*, he was also on the staff of *Theatre Arts* magazine, initially in 1919 as drama critic, then as vice president and editor of that influential magazine.

The year 1920 was a major turning point for Macgowan. He became drama critic for *Vogue*, a position he would fill for the next four years, and, more significantly, he began his association with playwright Eugene O'Neill. After writing a favorable review in the *Globe* of O'Neill's *The Emperor Jones*, Macgowan became a friend and confidant of the dramatist, who came to trust Macgowan's theatrical judgment and opinions. Finding himself in the center of an explosion of innovative and exceptional American theatrical activity, Macgowan came to know and work with many of the most influential theater artists of the time. In 1921 he published his first book on this exciting work, *The Theatre of Tomorrow*.

Macgowan became fascinated with the "new stagecraft," the European anti-realistic design movement that began with the work of theorist and designer Edward Gordon Craig and architect Adolphe Appia. In 1922 he and stage designer Robert Edmond Jones spent ten weeks traveling throughout Europe, seeing plays in France, Sweden, Germany, Czechoslovakia, and Austria. As they experienced the new stagecraft in all its various aspects, Jones made sketches of the exciting stage designs they saw. The same year they published their impressions in *Continental Stagecraft*, one of the most influential books written on the subject.

The next year, 1923, held other changes for Macgowan. His interest in anthropology led to a collaboration with Herman Rosse that resulted in the book *Masks and Demons*. It was also the year that O'Neill asked him to take over direction of the Provincetown Players. This organization, begun in 1916 in Provincetown, Massachusetts, as an experimental group of playwrights, actors, and other artists that included Susan Glaspell and Robert Edmond Jones, had launched O'Neill's career. In 1918 they had opened the Provincetown Playhouse on Macdougal Street in New York City's Greenwich Village with the intention, according to the group's credo, of giving "American playwrights a chance to work out their ideas in freedom." There was a good deal of bickering among the group's members as to how the organization should be run, and the decision to bring Macgowan in as a director provided a much needed sense of direction.

Devoting most of his time to the Provincetown Players, Macgowan gradually dropped his work as drama critic, leaving the *Globe* in 1923, *Vogue* in 1924, and his office at *Theatre Arts* magazine in 1925. Together with O'Neill and Jones, Macgowan operated the Greenwich Village Theatre from 1925 through 1927, directing a number of New York's most inventive productions, including O'Neill's *All God's Chillun Got Wings*, *Desire under the Elms*, and *The Great God Brown*. In 1927 the Actor's Theatre joined this group under Macgowan's direction.

Macgowan now moved on to become a producer, losing touch with O'Neill as their paths diverged. He imported a number of English plays in collaboration with Joseph Verner Reed and left the Provincetown Players to move uptown to Broadway, where he produced another thirty-five plays.

In 1929 he wrote *Footlights across America*, but with the great stock market crash and ensuing depression Macgowan found New York theater less rewarding, and in the early 1930s he made another career change, moving to Hollywood. He became first a story editor for RKO and then a producer of motion pictures for RKO, 20th Century–Fox, and Paramount. His first film credit as an associate producer came in 1932 with *The Penguin Pool Murder*. He received an Academy Award for his 1934 short, *La Cucaracha*. Among the forty-five pictures he produced was *Becky Sharp* (1935), the first Technicolor motion picture. He also wrote a lively history of motion pictures, *Behind the Screen* (1965). Also, long interested in archaeology, in 1946 Macgowan became president of the Southern California Society of the Archeological [*sic*] Institute of America.

Macgowan's last career change came in 1947, when he became founder and chair of the theater arts department at the University of California at Los Angeles; he retired in 1958. UCLA's theater arts building is named Macgowan Hall in his honor. He died in West Los Angeles.

Kenneth Macgowan was a pivotal figure in the development of the modern American theater both through his critical assistance to playwrights, notably O'Neill, and through his fostering of American design in the manner of the new stagecraft.

• Macgowan's papers pertaining primarily to the theater are in a collection at Wayne State University, Detroit, Mich. His other writings include a number of theater texts such as *Drama in the High School* (1929), *A Primer of Playwrighting* (1951), *The Living Stage* (1955), and *Golden Ages of the Theater* (1959; rev. ed., 1979). Macgowan's important place in American theater history is discussed in Thomas Alan Bloom, *Kenneth Macgowan and the Aesthetic Paradigm for the New Stagecraft in America*, New Studies in Aesthetics, vol. 20 (1994). Works dealing with O'Neill frequently refer to Macgowan, most notably Jackson R. Bryer, ed., with the assistance of Ruth M. Alvarez and an introductory essay by Travis Bogard, *"The Theatre We Worked For": The Letters of Eugene O'Neill to Kenneth Macgowan* (1982). Articles written by Macgowan are often included in works on Jones; see especially Ralph Pendleton, ed., *The Theatre of Robert Edmond Jones* (1958). Macgowan's anthropological and archaeological works begin with *Masks and Their Meanings* (1923) and continue through the revision of his popular *Early Man in the New World* (1962). An extensive obituary is in the *New York Times*, 29 Apr. 1963.

CARY CLASZ

MACHEBEUF, Joseph Projectus (11 Aug. 1812–10 July 1889), Roman Catholic clergyman, was born in Riom, France, the son of Michael Anthony Machebeuf, a baker, and Gilberte Plauc. Machebeuf's early education was completed at a private school, a Christian Brothers' college, and the Oratorian College of Riom. He went on to attend the Sulpician Seminary in Montferrand, although illness periodically interrupted his studies there.

After his ordination in December 1836, Machebeuf first served as a curate in Cendre, France. Inspired by his contact with the missionaries J. M. Odin and Bishop B. J. Flaget, Machebeuf, along with his close friend Abbé John Baptist Lamy and mentors Bishop John Purcell and Flaget, left France for the United States in 1839. He worked in the Ohio towns of Tiffin, Lower Sandusky (Fremont), and Sandusky City, preaching to railroad workers and laborers and helping in the construction of three churches. In search of financial support and missionary volunteers, Machebeuf traveled to Montreal, Rome, and France, returning in June 1845 with a sisterhood of nuns.

When Lamy was made the vicar apostolic of New Mexico in 1850, Machebeuf traveled with him to Santa Fe. Learning Spanish along the way, Machebeuf went on through the Southwest, preaching and ministering to a large but geographically diffuse population. His courage and indefatigable spirit eventually earned the respect of the initially skeptical Mexicans, Indians, and settlers. Although primarily an itinerant preacher, he took responsibility for the vicariate in the event of Lamy's absence, held pastorships at Santa Fe and Albuquerque, New Mexico, and served at missions at Arroyo Hondo and Taos, New Mexico. In 1860 Lamy sent Machebeuf and John B. Raverdy to Denver to provide for the religious needs and the general welfare of Catholics in Colorado, then primarily a mining region. Machebeuf bought cheap tracts of land on which to build churches and to farm. His purchases put the church on firm economic footing and showed that the

mountainous region, which hitherto had been used only for mining, was also agriculturally viable. He was responsible for the construction of churches in Central City and Golden in 1863, in Trinidad in 1865, and in numerous smaller agricultural and mining towns in Colorado. He also helped religious communities such as the Sisters of Charity, the Sisters of Loretto, and the Sisters of St. Joseph with the creation of hospitals and schools in Central City, Denver, and Pueblo, Colorado.

In August 1868 Machebeuf was appointed vicar apostolic of Colorado and Utah, a position that conferred the title of bishop of epiphania. Earlier that year he had journeyed to the eastern United States on an unsuccessful mission to recruit volunteers to join him; the following year he returned to France for the same purpose, this time arriving back with four priests. He founded St. Joseph's Hospital in Denver in 1873 and a Catholic church in Colorado Springs three years later. In the early 1880s Machebeuf's earlier financial security began to crumble and, in danger of bankruptcy caused partly by creditors' panic, he traveled to Rome in 1887 to offer his resignation. Not only was the resignation refused, but the vicariate of Colorado was made into a diocese and Machebeuf made its bishop. He returned to Colorado, and in time his financial difficulties resolved themselves. Despite failing health and numerous injuries incurred while traveling, Machebeuf remained active in missionary work until the end of his life. In 1888 he helped found the College of the Sacred Heart (later Peter Regis College) in Denver, Colorado's first Catholic college for men. The same year Machebeuf attended the inauguration of the Catholic University of America in Washington, D.C. Also in 1888 his close friend Lamy died; Machebeuf, who survived him by less than a year, died in Denver.

Machebeuf played a significant role in the settlement of Colorado, both in the spread of Catholicism in the state and in the civic development of the region. He is primarily responsible for establishing the Catholic educational system in the state. At the time of Machebeuf's death, his diocese had 102 churches and chapels, sixteen parish schools, ten hospitals, nine academies, an orphanage, a protective home, a college for men, and over 40,000 Catholics. Known for his warmth, honesty, and temperamental simplicity, Machebeuf was widely respected by his parishioners and fellow priests. His sermons were straightforward and practical, without rhetorical or intellectual ostentation. Although not financially astute, Machebeuf was honest and responsible in his management of church funds.

• A good biographical source is W. J Howlett, *Life of the Rt. Rev. Joseph P. Machebeuf* (1908). See also J. G. Shea, *History of the Catholic Church in the U.S.*, vol. 4 (1892); Shea, *The Hierarchy of the Catholic Church* (1886); and R. H. Clarke, *History of the Catholic Church in the U.S. with Biographical Sketches of the Living Bishops*, vol. 2 (1890).

ELIZABETH ZOE VICARY

MACHEN, J. Gresham (28 July 1881–1 Jan. 1937), educator and theologian, was born John Gresham Machen in Baltimore, Maryland, the son of Arthur Webster Machen, a lawyer, and Mary Gresham. Machen grew up in a prominent and affluent family that was part of a circle of southern gentry who had moved to Baltimore after the Civil War. In this setting Machen developed a deep affection for classical literature, rare books, and the heritage of the Old South. The Machen home also fostered a strong allegiance to the faith and practice of southern Presbyterianism even though the piety of Baltimore's wealthy Presbyterians was a good deal more genteel than the spirituality of previous generations.

Machen deepened his appreciation for classical Greek during undergraduate studies at Johns Hopkins University where Basil Gildersleeve, the renowned American classicist, inspired many students to go on to graduate work in philology. After graduating first in the class of 1901, Machen stayed at Hopkins for a year of advanced study in Gildersleeve's graduate seminar. Uncertainty about a career prompted Machen to try the course of instruction at Princeton Theological Seminary, the leading institution for training ministers in the northern Presbyterian church. Machen did not find the courses at the seminary to be challenging and so also studied philosophy at Princeton University, earning in 1904 an M.A. Nevertheless, he did finish the course of instruction at the seminary and in 1905 received a bachelor of divinity degree.

One area that did interest Machen at seminary was New Testament studies. He won several academic prizes for seminar papers and developed a strong friendship with William Park Armstrong, another southerner and professor of the New Testament at Princeton Seminary. Park recognized the young student's abilities and advised Machen to study in Germany. During the academic year 1905–1906, Machen attended the universities in Marburg and Göttingen. In the summer of 1906, still uncertain about a career, he reluctantly accepted an offer from Park to become instructor in the New Testament department at Princeton Seminary.

Machen's reluctance stemmed from religious doubts as well as dissatisfaction with the low regard for biblical studies within American learning. He gradually resolved these misgivings and in 1914 was ordained a minister in the northern Presbyterian Church, U.S.A. (PCUSA) at his home church in Baltimore. Following his ordination, a requirement for being a voting member of the faculty, Machen was appointed assistant professor of the New Testament at Princeton Seminary.

The years between 1914 and 1920 were Machen's most productive as a scholar. They were interrupted by service from 1917 to 1919 as a Young Men's Christian Association secretary in France during World War I. Machen's early studies as a seminarian and then as a member of the Princeton faculty were the narratives of Christ's birth in the Gospels. With considerable skill he used philological, historical, and lin-

guistic evidence to argue that the New Testament birth narratives could not be explained away as mythological accretions from later centuries but extended back to the turn of the second century A.D. and, therefore, were part of the belief of the original Christian community. His argument, first published in scholarly articles and finally as a book in 1930, *The Virgin Birth of Christ*, was also intended to discredit the thesis of contemporary biblical scholars that interpreted the supernatural elements of the New Testament as merely symbolic of the early church's faith.

Machen also devoted considerable attention to the faith and writings of the apostle Paul. As he had in his studies of Christ's birth, Machen showed the inconsistencies of the dominant interpretations of his day, which traced Pauline theology to the culture of the Greco-Roman world, thereby denying the apostle's own account of Christianity as supernaturally derived. In *The Origin of Paul's Religion*, published in 1921, Machen argued, again with impressive knowledge of the scholarly literature, that the apostle's faith was best explained by the historicity of supernatural events surrounding Christ and the early church.

Despite his decidedly conservative conclusions, Machen's scholarship was well received by other scholars in his field. In fact, his work was the last of a well-informed and yet traditional approach within professional biblical studies that did not survive the polarization that erupted during the fundamentalist controversy, an ecclesiastical and cultural dispute between conservatives who championed a literalistic reading of the Bible and liberals who favored figurative interpretations of Scripture. Ironically, Machen himself was a leading figure in the fundamentalist movement. After 1920 he devoted more and more of his energies to driving Protestant liberalism out of the northern Presbyterian church. In *Christianity and Liberalism* (1923), Machen summarized his chief objections to theological liberalism. Christianity and "its chief modern substitute," liberalism, he argued, were two entirely different religions, the former stressing human sinfulness and divine grace, the latter appealing to human goodness and moralism. Machen believed that the best solution to the controversy was for liberals and conservatives to separate and form their own churches, a suggestion that drew praise from a number of intellectuals, including Walter Lippmann and H. L. Mencken.

Machen's candor, however, ran directly counter to the ecumenical efforts among major Protestant denominations after World War I. As a result, Machen spent the last ten years of his life battling the Presbyterian leadership, first about the character of Princeton Seminary and then about the soundness of the denomination's foreign missions board. In each case, Machen lost and formed separatist institutions: in 1929 Westminster Theological Seminary (Philadelphia) and in 1933 the Independent Board for Presbyterian Foreign Missions. Machen's continual opposition finally resulted in his being tried and expelled in 1936 from the ministry of the Presbyterian church. With the support of a small number of conservatives based primarily in southeastern Pennsylvania, Machen formed in that same year the Presbyterian Church of America, later the Orthodox Presbyterian church. A lifelong bachelor, he died of pneumonia only six months later during a trip to rally support for the new denomination in Bismarck, North Dakota.

Though his scholarly contributions inspired and became a model for a later generation of evangelical Protestants, some of whom studied with him, Machen's effort to preserve a Presbyterian faith and practice that would withstand the acids of modernity has been obscured by his reputation as a fundamentalist. Nevertheless, he gave intellectual credence to a movement deemed by many to be anti-intellectual and anticipated the criticism of mainstream Protestant acculturation that would achieve greater popularity through neo-orthodoxy, a movement that gained momentum in the 1940s and that criticized the optimism and sentimentality of liberal Protestant theology.

• Machen's papers, which include virtually all his correspondence and manuscripts, as well as documents relevant to the fundamentalist controversy in the northern Presbyterian church, are held at Westminster Theological Seminary (Philadelphia, Pa.). Representative semipopular books by Machen are *What Is Faith?* (1925), *The Christian Faith in the Modern World* (1936), and *The Christian View of Man* (1937), published posthumously. In addition to the conventional biography by Ned B. Stonehouse, *J. Gresham Machen: A Biographical Memoir* (1954), D. G. Hart, *Defending the Faith: J. Gresham Machen and the Crisis of Protestantism in Modern America* (1994), puts Machen's career and thought into the broader context of American culture. Mark A. Noll, *Between Faith and Criticism: Evangelicals, Scholarship, and the Bible in America* (1986), provides a good historical context for understanding Machen's biblical scholarship. Bradley J. Longfield, *The Presbyterian Controversy: Fundamentalists, Modernists and Moderates* (1991), gives a balanced treatment of Machen's involvement in Presbyterian disputes. Obituaries are in the *New York Times*, the *Herald Tribune*, and the Baltimore *Evening Sun*, all 2 Jan. 1937.

D. G. HART

MACHIN, Thomas (20 Mar. 1744–3 Apr. 1816), revolutionary war engineer and artillery officer, was born near Wolverhampton, in Staffordshire, England, the son of John Machin, the eminent English astronomer and mathematician; his mother's name is unknown. His father died when Thomas was seven years old. At the age of fifteen he was enrolled by his mother as a cadet in the British army. During the Seven Years' War he fought against the French (1759) at Minden, in Germany.

After the war Machin apprenticed himself as an assistant surveyor to James Brindley, the English canal pioneer who was constructing the country's first barge canal to carry coal forty miles from the Worsley mines to Manchester. Eventually establishing himself as a consulting engineer, Machin sailed for the East Indies. From there he went on to evaluate copper deposits in northern New Jersey sometime around 1770. He finally settled in Boston, and was caught up in the prerevolutionary ferment.

Machin joined the Sons of Liberty and went out on 16 December 1773 with the Boston Tea Party. He enrolled in Henry Knox's militia artillery company and, after hostilities commenced at Lexington and Concord, laid out the fortification lines on Bunker (Breed's) Hill on 17 June 1775. Following the battle, in which Machin was wounded, he was made a lieutenant in Gridley's Regular Massachusetts Artillery Regiment, serving with that unit until the end of the year. On 10 December 1775 Machin was commissioned a second lieutenant in Knox's artillery regiment in the new Continental army. Machin impressed Washington when he helped Knox quickly emplace the cannon from Ticonderoga on Boston's frozen Dorchester Heights. When the outmaneuvered British withdrew from Boston in March 1776, Machin was put to work obstructing the harbor channels. Soon he was surveying a canal route across the neck of Cape Cod to protect coastal shipping from the Royal Navy.

Machin was called away from the canal project by an urgent 10 June 1776 summons from George Washington, then in New York, to help organize the installation of a large chain across the Hudson River at Fort Montgomery—the southern entrance to the Hudson Highlands. "Lieutenant Machin," Washington explained to the New York legislature, "is as proper a person as any I can send, Being an ingenious faithful hand, and one that has considerable experience as an engineer." Machin was ordered to report to Colonel James Clinton at Fort Montgomery, where he immediately laid out the lines for a new adjoining work—Fort (George) Clinton.

Machin spent the fall of 1776 assembling used and new iron links into a 1,650-foot chain, designed to float on huge pine-log rafts across the Hudson between Fort Montgomery and Anthony's Nose. Cannon on both river banks would pound any British warship slowed by the obstruction. In November 1776 two attempts to install the chain ended in failure; weak links snapped under the enormous Hudson River tidal pressures. Efforts were put off until the following spring, while Machin inspected and repaired the linkage, reassuring Washington that the strategy was still sound. Before the month was out, Machin was promoted to first lieutenant, and by March 1777, with ice gone from the river, he was able to report to his commander in chief that the Fort Montgomery chain was securely in place.

For the next seven months, no enemy captain appeared willing to risk his warship against the obstruction. Instead, on 6 October 1777, Sir Henry Clinton launched a land-based attack on Forts Montgomery and Clinton, successfully outflanking the chain, which the enemy immediately demolished. Machin was again wounded but managed to escape. Failing to relieve Burgoyne at Saratoga, Sir Henry withdrew from the Hudson Highlands. A slowly recovering Machin was promoted (1 Jan. 1778) to provisional captain lieutenant in the Second Continental Artillery.

Machin was soon back at work designing a far heavier chain to be floated across the Hudson at a far more strategic spot—West Point—which, because of its seemingly impregnable position, the British were now calling "The Key of America." Smelted at Peter Townsend's Sterling Furnace and assembled at Brewster's Forge on the Hudson below Newburgh, the new chain for West Point was completed, during one of the cruelest winters of the Revolution, in only six weeks. At a cost of $92,000, Townsend's workmen forged and assembled the massive iron chain, which weighed almost 50 tons. Finished nine-link sections were joined together and affixed to the giant rafts to float the chain at the river's surface. Machin also devised the procedure by which the West Point Chain could be removed from the Hudson every winter, to prevent it being carried away by the ice. The finished obstruction, containing about 800 iron links, weighing about 115 pounds each, was winched 1,500 feet across the Hudson from West Point to Constitution Island on 30 April 1778. The Board of War immediately confirmed Machin's provisional captaincy.

In 1779 Machin joined General John Sullivan's campaign against the Iroquois. He used the impounded waters of Lake Otsego to float General James Clinton's brigade down the half-dry upper Susquehanna River to a rendezvous with Sullivan at Tioga. The summer after the expedition, Machin was promoted (21 Aug. 1780) to captain of artillery. It was no surprise that in 1781 Washington accorded Machin the honor of sighting the first cannon to be fired in the siege of Yorktown. Machin served until the end of the war and was discharged in June 1783.

After the American Revolution Machin settled near Newburgh, New York, where he established a water mill to mint copper and silver coins, before the advent of a national coinage. By then he had married and was raising several children. A son, Thomas, Jr., was a brigadier general of New York militia in the War of 1812. Machin patented a large tract of Oneida County land and in 1797 moved to Mohawk, New York, where he took up surveying. He died in Charleston, Montgomery County, New York.

Evaluating Machin's major revolutionary war achievement, it may be fairly said that his design and installation of the Great Chain at West Point—escaping Benedict Arnold's 1780 treachery—effectively played a role in impeding the British military during the critical years of the revolutionary war.

• A number of Machin's personal letters are in the collections of the New-York and Chicago Historical Societies. His military correspondence is in the National Archives. His military record during the Revolution is in Francis B. Heitman, *Historical Register of Officers of the Continental Army* (1914). Material relating to Machin's participation in the 1779 Sullivan expedition against the New York Iroquois is in *Journals of the Military Expedition of Major General John Sullivan against the Six Nations of Indians in 1779*, ed. Frederick Coole (1887). Lincoln Diamant, *Chaining the Hudson* (1989), offers an overview of Machin's role in obstructing navigation on the Hudson River.

LINCOLN DIAMANT

MACHITO (16 Feb. 1908?–15 Apr. 1984), salsa and jazz bandleader, singer, and percussionist, was born Frank Raúl Grillo in Tampa, Florida, the son of Rogelio Grillo, formerly a cigar maker and then a grocery store owner, and Marta Amparo. In his oral history Machito claimed that 1908 was his year of birth, but in the same interview he claimed to be two years older than Mario Bauzá, which would make 1909 the correct date; 1912, given in some sources, seems less likely (though not impossible), since Machito was already an experienced professional musician in 1928. While he was still an infant his family moved to Havana, Cuba, where his father ran two restaurants. He was nicknamed Macho because he was the first son after three daughters, one of whom, Graciela, would figure prominently in his career. Immersed in Afro-Cuban music from childhood, he began his career as a singer and maracas player with the group Los Jovenes de Rendición. From 1928 to 1937 he performed in Cuba with María Teresa Vera's El Sexteto Occidente, El Sexteto Agabama, El Sexteto Universo, Ignacio Piñero, and El Sexteto Nacional. During this period he married Luz María Pelgrino. They had one child.

In 1937 Grillo came to New York, where he joined Mulato's quartet Las Estrellas Habañeras (Stars of Havana). After holding a residency at the Cadillac Hotel in Detroit, the quartet returned to New York, where Grillo first recorded with vocalist Alfredito Valdez and Graciela, the latter then in New York as a member of the all-woman group El Septeto Anacaona. Grillo then recorded with El Quarteto Caney, El Conjuncto Moderno, and La Orquesta Hatuey, and he sang with the bands of Noro Morales and Augusto Coen. In 1939 Grillo and Mario Bauzá, his friend from the late 1920s and now a veteran of New York big bands, formed their first Afro-Cuban band to perform at a new nightclub, La Conga. The job fell through for want of a fuse to power the lights. Bauzá joined Cab Calloway, while Grillo sang with Alberto Iznaga and his Orchestra Siboney and also recorded with Xavier Cugat (1939–1940).

Divorced, Grillo married Hilda Esther Porres, from Puerto Rico, in April 1940. They had five children. Grillo modified his nickname from Macho to Machito, and with Bauzá as musical director he re-formed the Afro-Cubans in July 1940. The ten-man orchestra comprised Machito as singer, two trumpeters, two saxophonists, a pianist, a string bassist, and four percussionists (the leader playing maracas and his sidemen on timbales, bongos, and conga). The Afro-Cubans performed at the Park Palace Ballroom in Spanish Harlem, began an engagement at La Conga on 20 December 1940, and signed a recording contract with Decca. "Sopa de Pichón" (Pigeon soup) and "Tingo Talango," recorded in 1941, became hit songs.

Drafted into the army in 1943, Machito handed the group over to Graciela, who had performed in France, Colombia, and Puerto Rico before returning to Cuba as a member of El Trio García. Now married to Bauzá, she made her debut with the Afro-Cubans during a radio broadcast from La Conga. Machito's position was filled by singer Polito Galindez, but Machito soon returned, having received an honorable medical discharge after suffering a leg injury. Meanwhile, under Bauzá's influence, the band had begun to blend Afro-Cuban dance rhythms with jazz improvisation and techniques of big band arrangements, notably in its theme song from 1943, "Tanga." The Afro-Cubans recorded regularly from that year onward.

Sharing the stage with Stan Kenton's orchestra, Machito's band was featured at the first Latin jazz concert, given at Town Hall in New York on 24 January 1947. He began recording with guest jazz soloists, including tenor saxophonist Flip Phillips on "No Noise, Part 1," "Caravan," and "Tanga," alto saxophonist Charlie Parker on "No Noise, Part 2," "Mango Mangue," and "Okiedoke" (all from Dec. 1948–Jan. 1949), and trumpeter Howard McGhee and tenor saxophonist Brew Moore on "Cubop City" (Apr. 1949). The trumpet and saxophone sections grew in size, each routinely utilizing three or four players, and, with jazz musicians incorporated into the band, the Afro-Cubans were billed in alternation with bop groups at Bop City, the Royal Roost, and Birdland in New York, and the Harlem Club in Philadelphia. McGhee, Phillips, and vibraphonist Milt Jackson were recorded with Machito at the Royal Roost in the spring of 1949. Parker, Phillips, and drummer Buddy Rich were added for a performance of composer and arranger Chico O'Farrill's *Afro-Cuban Suite* on 21 December 1950.

Most of the aforementioned Afro-Cuban jazz pieces offer more of a superimposition of genres than a blending, and they are surpassed by recordings of 1948 to 1949 that Machito and his orchestra made on their own. "Vaya Niña," composed by Chico O'Farrill, demonstrates the characteristically repeated and interlocking syncopated instrumental patterns of Latin jazz. Also typical is René Hernandez's piano solo, played in octaves and built in a relaxed but staggered fashion. This track utilizes the mambo dance rhythm, as do several others, including "Tumba el Quinto" and "Llora Timbero," both sung by Machito. O'Farrill's "Gone City," without singing, melds together bop and Cuban styles. The group presents a slower, crisper dance, of the sort that would come to be known as cha-cha-cha, on "Un Poquito de Tu Amor" and "Vive Como Yo," both featuring Graciela, whose voice on these recordings is as bright and cutting as the tone of the Afro-Cuban trumpeters. An outstanding, uncredited arrangement of "The World Is Waiting for the Sunrise" shows how the genre of American popular song might be tastefully Latinized. Here, on these and associated titles, is the Afro-Cuban style that was popularized as salsa in the 1970s, already in full flower roughly a quarter century earlier.

Machito frequently performed at New York's Palladium ballroom from the late 1940s through the 1950s, and his band made annual tours to Venezuela for fifteen years beginning in 1950. A national craze for mambo also brought steady work in Miami and at resorts in the Catskills as well as a cross-country tour,

billed as "Mambo U.S.A.," together with the band of Joe Loco (1954–1955). From this time onward, if not earlier, Machito was giving considerable time to community work in New York. For the LP *Kenya* (1957; reissued as *Latin Soul Plus Jazz*) he brought in further guest artists, including Doc Cheatham, Joe Newman, Johnny Griffin, Herbie Mann, and Cannonball Adderley. Griffin, Mann, and trombonists Curtis Fuller and Sonny Russo contributed to the LP *Afro Jazziac* (1958).

Machito's group toured Japan (1962), Colombia (1965), Panama (1966), Peru (1968), Haiti (1969), and Puerto Rico (1970). In the mid-1970s the popularization of salsa brought him to the attention of a wider and younger audience, for whom he became one of the style's elder statesmen. He performed in New York City's Latin clubs, such as the Cork and Bottle, the Corso, Barney Googles, and El Chico East, and he regularly toured Europe from 1975 onward. In his capacity as a community leader, Machito headed Project Return, which endeavored to rehabilitate drug addicts and juvenile delinquents; he also served as project coordinator for the SCOUT program (Senior Citizens Outreach Unit Team), and he gave concerts for retarded children and adults.

Machito's album *Afro Cuban Jazz Moods*, including O'Farrill's "Oro, Incienso y Mirra," written for Gillespie with Machito's orchestra, was recorded in June 1975 in a nostalgic and unsuccessful attempt to re-create their early achievements. In December, following a personal disagreement, Bauzá left the band after thirty-five years. He was replaced by Machito's son Mario Grillo. Graciella retired in the late 1970s, and Machito's daughter Paula Grillo took her place. Machito again toured Japan, where in testimony to his international influence the Afro-Cubans appeared with the Tokyo Cuban Boys around 1980. His big band performed at President Ronald Reagan's inaugural ball in January 1981, and that summer he was honored with a concert at City Hall Plaza in New York. The finest album from his last years is *Machito and His Salsa Big Band 1982*, made in the Netherlands during a European tour; it won a Grammy award. While on yet another European tour, he died in London five days after suffering a stroke. His life was celebrated in the documentary film *Machito: A Latin Jazz Legacy*, completed posthumously and released in 1987.

Machito gave a penetrating description of a difference between Afro-Cuban dance music and jazz: "In Cuban music we never complicate the melody. It is the rhythm that is rich. But in jazz you have all the interest on top of the rhythm" (Woolley [1977], p. 37). His Afro-Cubans are significant historically as the pioneering ensemble in bringing these two musical streams together. Still more significantly, this was arguably the best Afro-Cuban orchestra, rivaled only briefly by Gillespie's big band of the late 1940s.

• A fine survey by Joe Conzo serves as the source for most published accounts of Machito's life; written as liner notes for the LP *Mucho Macho* (1978), the essay has been reissued as a

CD pamphlet under the same title. In May 1980 Max Salazar interviewed Machito for the Jazz Oral History Project housed at the Institute of Jazz Studies, Newark, N.J. Published interviews are by Dom Cerulli, "Machito Maps an Attack on Delinquency," *Down Beat*, 25 Jan. 1956, p. 11; Arnold Jay Smith, "Sounds from the Salsa Source: Tito and Machito," *Down Beat*, 22 Apr. 1976, pp. 16, 42; Stan Woolley, "Machito: Making Musical Earthquakes," *Jazz Journal International* 30 (Nov. 1977): 36–37; Larry Birnbaum, "Machito: Original Macho Man," *Down Beat*, Dec. 1980, pp. 25–27; and Enrique Fernandez, "Little Big Macho Man," *Village Voice*, 19 Oct. 1982, pp. 72–73. *Current Biography 1983*, while following Conzo and the interviews to some extent, additionally supplies valuable information not published elsewhere. For overviews of Machito's place in Latin music and jazz, see Jim Burns, "Lesser Known Bands of the Forties: Illinois Jacquet, Roy Porter, Machito," *Jazz Monthly* 164 (1968): 7–9; John Storm Roberts, *The Latin Tinge: The Impact of Latin American Music on the United States* (1979); Woolley, "The Spanish Tinge," *Jazz Journal International* 38 (July 1985): 8–10; and Jesse Hamlin, "Film: Life and Times of a Latin Musical Giant," *San Francisco Chronicle Datebook*, 16 Aug. 1987, p. 39. Obituaries are in the *New York Times*, 17 Apr. 1984, and *Jazz Journal International* 37 (June 1984): 7.

BARRY KERNFELD

MACHLUP, Fritz (15 Dec. 1902–30 Jan. 1983), economist, was born in Wiener Neustadt, Austria, the son of Berthold Machlup, an owner of a cardboard-manufacturing business, and Cecile Heymann. He entered the University of Vienna in 1920, where he studied under Friedrich von Wieser and Ludwig von Mises. His dissertation on the gold-exchange standard was completed under von Mises in 1923 and published in 1925 as *Die Goldkernwährung*. He married Marianne "Mitzi" Herzog in 1925; they had a son and a daughter.

Machlup became a partner in an Austrian cardboard-manufacturing firm in 1922 and helped form a paperboard corporation in Hungary in 1923. From 1929 to 1931 he was a member of the council of the Austrian Cardboard Cartel. Machlup also served as the treasurer and later the secretary of the Austrian Economic Society, and he participated from 1923 to 1933 in the famous seminar of von Mises and from the early 1920s to 1933 in the interdisciplinary seminar, the Geistkreis.

As an academic in Austria, Machlup published a book titled *Die neuen Wahrungen in Europa* in 1927 on the adoption of the gold-exchange standard in Europe, two important articles on the effects of German war reparations payments, and an important book on the stock market and capital formation titled *Borsenkredit, Industriekredit und Kapitalbildung* in 1931. As Austria and the world slipped deeper into depression, Machlup wrote 150 newspaper articles advocating liberal free-market economic policy.

In 1933 Machlup accepted a Rockefeller fellowship that took him to Columbia, Harvard, and Stanford Universities and the University of Chicago and put him into contact with most of the leading members of the American economics profession. He immigrated to the United States in 1935 and held a professorship at

the University of Buffalo until 1947. He also served in visiting positions at Cornell University (1937–1938), Northwestern University (1939), the University of California at Berkeley (1939), the University of Michigan (1941), Harvard (1934–1935 and 1938–1939), and Stanford (1940 and 1947). In the war effort Machlup served as a special consultant to the Post-War Labor Problems Division of the U.S. Department of Labor (1942–1943) and as a division chief in the Office of Alien Property while a part-time visiting professor at American University (1943–1946). During this period he wrote extensively, producing seminal papers on the supply and demand of foreign exchange and an influential book titled *International Trade and the National Income Multiplier* (1943), which exposed the limitations of the Keynesian multiplier approach to foreign exchange and national income. In 1946 Machlup defended economic theory in research on industrial organization and examined the problems of using questionnaires in empirical research.

In 1947 Machlup became a professor of political economy at the Johns Hopkins University. His 1949 book on the basing-point system that was published in the wake of the Supreme Court's decision against basing-point pricing was a tour de force, and it is credited with influencing President Truman's subsequent veto of further attempts to legalize the practice. His work in industrial organization continued with two books in 1952, *The Political Economy of Monopoly* and *The Economics of Sellers' Competition*, in which he established the primacy of theory and demonstrated that a purely "factual" approach in economics contained undisclosed theory. He served as a visiting professor at Columbia University (1948), the University of California at Los Angeles (1949), and Kyoto and Doshisha Universities of Japan (1955), and he was a Ford Foundation research fellow (1957–1958).

Machlup began an investigation of innovation and knowledge in 1950 that led to the publication of *The Economic Review of the Patent System* (1958), important articles in 1958 and 1960, *The Production and Distribution of Knowledge in the United States* (1962), and *Education and Economic Growth* (1970). He published the three-volume work, *Information through the Printed Word: The Dissemination of Scholarly, Scientific, and Intellectual Knowledge* (1978), and the first three volumes of the projected ten-volume series, *Knowledge: Its Creation, Distribution, and Economic Significance* (1980, 1982, 1983).

Machlup was the Walker Professor of Economics and International Finance and the director of the International Finance Section at Princeton University from 1960 to 1971. He was a visiting professor at City University of New York (1963–1964), New York University (1969–1971), Osaka University (1970), and the University of Melbourne (1970), and he was a consultant to the U.S. Treasury (1965–1977). He had worked on international monetary economics throughout the 1950s and provided a comprehensive assessment of the looming international monetary problems in the early 1960s. In 1963 he formed an organization of academics known as the Bellagio Group to study this problem, develop an academic consensus, and offer practical solutions. His success in this venture attracted the attention of governments and central bankers and resulted in the publication of numerous books and articles on the international currency crisis and its solutions. Robert Triffin dubbed him "the unquestioned intellectual leader and mentor of our vain efforts to reform the crumbling international monetary system." Ironically Machlup's dismissal of the traditional gold standard as a possible solution on the grounds of political impracticality led to a temporary split with his mentor, Ludwig von Mises.

In 1971 Machlup began commuting to New York University, giving him a chance to indulge his lifelong love of the opera. He published *Optimum Social Welfare and Productivity* with Jan Tinbergen, Abram Bergson, and Oskar Morgenstern in 1972. While continuing his massive projects on the international monetary system and the economics of knowledge, he published *A History of Thought on Economic Integration* (1977) and *Methodology of Economics and Other Social Sciences* (1978).

In addition to his offices in the Austrian Economic Society, Machlup served as president of the Southern Economic Association (1960), vice president (1956) and president (1966) of the American Economic Association, and president of the International Economic Association (1971–1974). He was also an active member of the American Association of University Professors, contributing articles to its *Bulletin* on academic freedom, tenure, and the business of education. He served as president of the association from 1962 to 1964. In his free time he was an enthusiastic fencer and downhill skier. Machlup was very influential on the development of economics by making contributions in nearly every field and by making crucial clarifications in methodology, theory, and policy. The Nobel committee listed his name several times as a candidate, and Nobel laureate Theodore Schultz said that he was "every inch an economist." He died in Princeton, New Jersey, shortly after finishing the third volume of *Knowledge*.

• Machlup's papers are in the Hoover Institution on War, Revolution, and Peace Archives at Stanford University. His early work on the language of economics is collected in Merton H. Miller, ed., *Essays in Economic Semantics* (1963; rev. eds., 1967, 1975). His most important papers include "The Commonsense of the Elasticity of Substitution," *Review of Economic Studies* 2 (1935); "The Theory of Foreign Exchanges," *Economica*, n.s. 6 (1939), and *Economica*, n.s. 7 (1940); "Elasticity Pessimism in International Trade," *Economia Internazionale* 3 (1950); "Concepts of Competition and Monopoly," *American Economic Review* 45 (1955); "The Problem of Verification in Economics," *Southern Economic Journal* 22 (1955); "Relative Prices and Aggregate Spending in the Analysis of Devaluation," *American Economic Review* 45 (1955); and "Theories of the Firm: Marginalist, Managerial, Behavioral," *American Economic Review* 57 (1967). Much biographical information is contained in Jacob S. Dreyer, ed., *Breadth and Depth in Economics: Fritz Machlup—The Man and His Ideas* (1978). A bibliography of his work is contained in George Bitros, ed., *Selected Economic Writings of Fritz Machlup* (1976).

MARK THORNTON

MACINNES, Helen (7 Oct. 1907–30 Sept. 1985), author, was born in Glasgow, Scotland, the daughter of Donald MacInnes and Jessica McDiarmid. After graduation from Glasgow University in 1928, MacInnes studied librarianship in London before marrying Oxford classicist Gilbert Highet in 1932. They had one son. MacInnes's first published writings were two translations from German on which she collaborated with her husband: Otto Kiefer's *Sexual Life in Ancient Rome* (trans. 1934) and Gustav Mayer's *Friedrich Engels: A Biography* (trans. 1936).

The couple immigrated to the United States in 1937 to allow Highet to accept a position at Columbia University, where he remained on the faculty for the rest of his professional life. Although it was only after the move to New York that MacInnes began to write fiction, her first novel had a Central European setting and was inspired by her husband's wartime service with British intelligence. *Above Suspicion* (1941) takes place in the summer after the Munich agreement and thus, by definition, takes place before World War II, but it is unambiguously a wartime spy story. MacInnes honed her craft through writing this novel, and in some ways it is the most immediately moving and suspenseful of her twenty works in this genre, dramatizing as it does the contradictions between personal loyalties—human decency—and corrupt political forces.

During the war and in the immediate postwar period, MacInnes published three more spy novels with anti-Nazi themes, *Assignment in Brittany* (1942), *While Still We Live* (1944; British ed., *The Unconquerable*, 1944), and *Horizon* (1945). In each of these, MacInnes contrasts the freedom of the individual under Western-style democracy with the mechanistic thought control imposed by the Nazis; and, in each, as in *Above Suspicion*, she addresses how the ideology and the system of fascism combine to make a treacherous monster out of someone that the novel's decent people expect to find on their own side.

Although her subsequent thrillers are often brilliantly plotted and researched, contain rich description of exotic locales, and make reference to the literature, art, and music MacInnes loved, they lack the same level of political and emotional involvement of her earlier works. After a brief postwar hiatus in which she published two works of "mainstream" fiction, MacInnes returned to the spy novel, committing her pen to the cause of the West in the Cold War. In one sense, she was merely filling the "enemies" slot in the stylized structure of the genre she had chosen, replacing the now-defeated Nazis and their collaborators with the Communists and their allies. In another sense, however, she was consciously enlisting in the propaganda war against the Soviets, whom she saw as representing a "totalitarianism" indistinguishable from that of the Nazis.

In orienting her later novels this way, MacInnes apparently believed she was emulating George Orwell. Her own convictions and the limitations of her genre, however, combined to eliminate from her work all the "gray areas" that enriched Orwell's analysis of Western society. The spy novel—at least in its early form—had to have "good guys" as well as "bad guys." Rather than entering into the ambiguities of international spying by having her Western protagonists be cloak-and-dagger professionals, she makes them decent, principled amateurs; she is thus able to attribute their decency to the political "side" to which their adventures contribute.

MacInnes's first Cold War novel, *Neither Five nor Three* (1951), is set in New York and, in the name of Western freedoms, supports McCarthy-style witchhunts in publishing and the academy. Thereafter, however, MacInnes's Communists are Soviets or their European allies, and her settings are appropriately exotic. *North from Rome* (1958), set in Italy, implicates the Communists in international drug trafficking. *Decision at Delphi* (1960) pits Greek anarchists against the rightful (conservative) authorities, with a subplot involving Communist atrocities during the Greek civil war.

In *The Venetian Affair* (1963) MacInnes introduces Third World revolutionaries, as she was later to introduce New Left activists and other non-Soviet agents, including various "terrorists," in order to display their "manipulation" by the Communists. This theme of manipulation allowed MacInnes to bring political events of the 1960s and 1970s into her work without dealing with Communist claims about the world or otherwise altering her essential vision of the two sides in a global conflict. This vision was reinforced in a number of her novels by the identification of Nazism with Communism—that is, the revelation that a former Nazi war criminal is now working for the KGB. *The Salzburg Connection* (1968) is perhaps the best known of the novels using this device.

MacInnes's spy novels were enormously successful, remaining on the bestseller lists for months and in print for years. Her commercial success enabled her to buy a house in Connecticut, where she and Highet spent weekends and vacations, and to travel extensively. The detailed description of exotic locales that appear in many of MacInnes's novels is one result of these travels.

In addition to the thrillers, MacInnes wrote one far less successful play in this period, *Home Is the Hunter* (1964), whose subtitle characterizes it as *A Comedy in Two Acts.* Set in ancient Greece, it draws on themes from *The Odyssey* for a plot centered on Ulysses's return to Ithaca after the Trojan War. MacInnes and Highet lived and traveled together until his death in 1978, and MacInnes continued to write suspense fiction until she died in New York City.

• MacInnes's major novels not cited above are *Friends and Lovers* (1947), *Rest and Be Thankful* (1949), *I and My True Love* (1953), *Pray for a Brave Heart* (1955), *The Double Image*

(1966), *Message from Malaga* (1971), *The Snare of the Hunter* (1974), *Agent in Place* (1976), *Prelude to Terror* (1978), *The Hidden Target* (1980), *Cloak of Darkness* (1982), and *Ride a Pale Horse* (1984). There is little on MacInnes in the way of biographical articles, aside from entries in the standard reference works. The most complete of these is Gina Macdonald's entry in the *Dictionary of Literary Biography*, vol. 87 (1989), pp. 284–94. See also comments on MacInnes in John M. Reilly, *Twentieth Century Crime and Mystery Writers* (1985), J. F. Baker, "Helen MacInnes," *Publishers Weekly*, 17 June 1974, pp. 10, 22, Roy Newquist, *Counterpoint* (1964), and Robert Van Gelder, *Writers and Writing* (1946), pp. 304–7. An obituary is in the *New York Times*, 1 Oct. 1985.

LILLIAN S. ROBINSON

MACINTOSH, Douglas Clyde (18 Feb. 1877–6 July 1948), Baptist minister and theologian, was born in Breadalbane, Ontario, Canada, the son of Peter Macintosh and Elizabeth Charlotte Everett, farmers. Raised in an evangelical home and especially influenced by the piety of his mother, he experienced a religious awakening when he was ten years old and a conversion at fourteen that led to his joining the local Baptist church. He taught in country schools for a time, and in 1897 he served a mission congregation in Marthaville, Ontario, and did evangelistic work among churches in the Baptist Convention of Ontario and Quebec. His self-guided readings included the works of Augustus H. Strong, the Rochester Baptist theologian, and Adoniram J. Gordon, the popular Boston Baptist pastor and Bible teacher. In 1899 Macintosh entered McMaster University, a Baptist institution in Toronto, Ontario, with the personal objective of subjecting his religious convictions to rigorous intellectual scrutiny. He studied the sciences and philosophy and read widely. At McMaster his mentors were professors O. C. S. Wallace, James TenBroeke (a devotee of the German metaphysician Lotze), and George Moore Cross. He graduated with a B.A. in 1903 in philosophy. Cross advised Macintosh to pursue modern theology in graduate studies, especially the German theologians.

Macintosh's education at McMaster influenced his career transition from the pastoral ministry to higher education. In 1904 he entered the University of Chicago, where for three years he studied with members of the so-called Chicago School, including J. H. Tufts, Addison Webster Moore, George Herbert Mead, Gerald Birney Smith, and George Burman Foster. He later characterized McMaster as having a conservative approach to Christian theology, which caused him to be radical. Yet Chicago's radicalism left him comparatively conservative and constructive. He was influenced by the thought of Albrecht Ritschl as well as the writings of Ernst Troeltsch. Macintosh devoted his doctoral dissertation to the relationship of metaphysics to theology and argued that theology must be grounded in metaphysics. He received his Ph.D. in 1909 and his dissertation was published as *The Reaction against Metaphysics in Theology*, in 1911.

While in Chicago, Macintosh was active in the local church and was ordained to the Baptist ministry at

Hyde Park Baptist Church, despite his open antagonism to orthodox Baptist doctrine. For two years (1907–1909) he served as professor of biblical and systematic theology at Brandon College in Manitoba, Canada, where he organized the Department of Theology to serve the western Baptist churches of Canada. In 1909 he went to Yale University where he taught systematic theology, becoming in 1916 the Dwight Professor of Theology at the Divinity School. In 1919 and again in 1923 he taught theology at the University of Chicago. He married Emily Pouell in 1921; she died the following year. Four years later, in 1925, he married Hope Griswold Conklin. In 1933 he moved to graduate studies in religion at Yale and was professor of theology and philosophy of religion until his retirement in 1942. As chair of the Department of Religious Studies (1920–1938), he guided the direction of graduate studies in religion at Yale, establishing philosophy of religion as a strength.

Macintosh dealt with two essential problems in his work. First was the nature of religious experience. Here he wished to offer a response to philosophical skepticism and historical uncertainty through empirical theology. In his book *Theology as an Empirical Science* (1919), he asserted that God could be universally understood by principles from religious experience similar to the way in which the natural and social sciences derive hypotheses. His theological system involved an organized body of experiential religious data, a set of laws defining how God responds to faithful human behavior, and theories about God's nature that are pragmatically related to religious experience. "Personal religion"—his designation of religious experience—was a self-surrender to God to allow God's will to be accomplished in one's life. Macintosh desired to utilize the benefits of the sciences in theological discourse, thus becoming a radical empiricist; his pragmatic bent was seen in his defense of human freedom and immortality, which justify moral intuition.

His second major interest was apologetics. Unconvinced by orthodox defenses of Christianity, he believed that the world could and should be improved by the goodwill of humans and that Jesus exemplified the pattern. While well-informed of the German approach to historical criticism and the comparative approach to religions, Macintosh was unsatisfied with the relativism and skepticism he found in his teacher, George Burman Foster. Instead, he taught that it was not necessary to establish absolute historical validity for the life of Jesus because the figure and symbol of Jesus were relevant for religious reasons. "If God was Christlike," he wrote, "then Christ was Godlike." The essence of Christianity lay apart from particular facts of history.

Issues of world affairs and personal struggles helped to shape Macintosh's thinking. The death of his first wife led him to a certitude of the goodness and sufficiency of God. Military service as a chaplain in World War I in France and England for the Canadian Expeditionary Forces taught him that war was not a solution to the problem of international conflict. He also questioned the depth of loyalty to one's national identity. In an address before the Philadelphia (Pennsylvania) Baptist Minister's Conference in 1932, Macintosh asserted that no one has the right to pledge his loyalty to any government except as it may be under God. He believed there were great dangers in the use of military force, which may involve selfish motives, and preferred to suffer injustices rather than cause the injustices and dreaded consequences of war. What the world needed most, he wrote, was international leadership that was interested in the highest well-being of all mankind, plus the scientific means to establish goodwill.

As a Baptist thinker, Macintosh held that religious liberty is freely rendered obedience to the will of God; the church of Christ is a fellowship of the regenerate and a spiritual democracy. Above all else, Christian experience is superior to ordinances (sacraments), and faith is a characteristic indispensable to fellowship in a Christian church.

Macintosh hoped for a church union that would be based on principles of religious liberty and spirituality, rather than on legalisms. His Baptist background guaranteed local congregations their rights and liberty within a national fellowship. Moreover, he felt the church should have nothing to do with preparing people for the world to come. Rather the church should actively apply Christian principles to social needs and problems. Weary of the contemporary fundamentalist attacks upon liberal Christian thought, he asserted that there should be no rivalry between evangelism and application of the gospel to social problems; he inveighed against individualism and called for a more enlightened evangelism that bridged the social chasm he perceived in his social context.

Toward the end of his career, Macintosh became interested in the dialogue of Christianity with other religions. Influenced by his Yale colleagues Kenneth Scott Latourette and Roland Bainton, Macintosh pursued the concept of a league of religions that would follow upon historical evolution and genuine religious toleration. In 1928 he gave the Stephanos Nirmalendu Ghosh Lectures at the University of Calcutta. Philosophy, he thought, could be an aid to the discovery of universal validity in religion, as it had been in his personal pilgrimage.

In 1930 Macintosh applied for U.S. citizenship and became involved in a celebrated case. When asked to take the oath of citizenship, which called for him to affirm his loyalty to the United States and to bear arms in case of war, he refused on the grounds that a Christian was ultimately loyal to the will of God alone. The U.S. Supreme Court denied his appeal in 1931. Remaining a Canadian citizen, he died in Hamden, Connecticut.

One of the most pivotal figures in the American liberal tradition, Macintosh was also recalled as a blunt person who could be uncompromising with his students. He is best remembered for his attempts to make theology an empirical science.

• Macintosh's papers are in the Yale University Archives, the American Baptist Historical Society in Rochester, N.Y., and the Canadian Baptist Archives at McMaster University in Hamilton, Ontario. Besides those works cited above, Macintosh's writings include *The Reaction against Metaphysics in Theology* (1911), *The Problem of Knowledge* (1915), *Theology as an Empirical Science* (1919), *The Reasonableness of Christianity* (1925), and *The Pilgrimage of Faith in the World of Modern Thought: The Stephanos Nirmalendu Ghosh Lectures for 1928* (1931). Much is revealed of Macintosh's person in Eugene G. Bewkes et al., *The Nature of Religious Experience: Essays in Honor of Douglas Clyde Macintosh* (1937), and there are autobiographical insights in Virgilius Ferm, ed., *Contemporary American Theology: Theological Autobiographies* (1932), and "Conscience and War," *Crozer Bulletin* (July 1932): 133–40. Assessments of his work are in W. Kenneth Cauthen, *The Impact of American Religious Liberalism* (1962); William R. Hutchison, *The Modernist Impulse in American Protestantism* (1976); and S. Mark Heim, "The Path of a Liberal Pilgrim: A Theological Biography of Douglas Clyde Macintosh," *American Baptist Quarterly* 2, no. 3 (Sept. 1983): 236–56.

WILLIAM H. BRACKNEY

MACIVER, Robert Morrison (17 Apr. 1882–15 June 1970), social scientist and humanist, was born in Stornoway, Scotland, the son of Donald MacIver, a merchant in the Harris tweed trade, and Christine Morrison. As a child he lived with four brothers and a sister on Lewis, the largest island in the Outer Hebrides. The region was noted for its commercial herring fishing, but textiles became more important in the years of MacIver's youth and helped the family business prosper. He married Ethel Marion Peterkin in 1911; together they raised three children.

MacIver earned M.A. (1903) and D. Phil. (1905) degrees from the University of Edinburgh in classics before moving to Oxford, where he received a double first in 1907 in "greats," the popular name for the honors degree in *Literae Humaniores*. He returned to Scotland as a lecturer at the University of Aberdeen, giving courses in political science from 1907 until 1915 and in sociology from 1911 until 1915. In that year MacIver emigrated to Canada to become professor of political science at the University of Toronto. He served as vice chairman of the Canadian War Labor Board from 1917 until 1919, returned to teaching, and was promoted to the head of the political science department in 1922.

In 1927 MacIver moved to Barnard College, where he headed the department of economics and sociology until 1936. Despite recruiting Robert Lynd to New York, MacIver expressed disappointment at his administrative impact and did not regard himself as an empire-builder. Columbia named him the Lieber Professor of Political Philosophy and Sociology in 1929, and he held that chair until his retirement in 1950. Among his many students was the similarly eclectic social theorist Daniel Bell.

MacIver worked on a variety of institutional research projects through the 1950s and from 1956 to 1961 directed a study for the city of New York of its juvenile delinquency programs. In April 1963 MacIver's friend Alvin Johnson, the former president of the New School for Social Research, persuaded him to accept a position as interim president of that institution, on whose board MacIver sat. With considerable help from Johnson, the New School weathered the financial crisis that had prompted MacIver's hiring, and he moved to the newly created position of chancellor for the 1965–1966 term.

MacIver's adolescent rebellion from the Presbyterian piety of his father was an early indication of a lifelong distrust of orthodoxy, both religious and social. His training in the classics grounded his later social thought in Plato and Aristotle rather than in more recent sociological theories deriving from Auguste Comte. The works of Emile Durkheim, Georg Simmel, and Lucien Levy-Bruhl, encountered at Oxford, also made a lasting impact.

Over the years of his career MacIver taught courses in sociology, political science, and political philosophy, having been academically trained in none of these areas. In contrast to increasingly dominant notions of professionalism, specialization, quantification, behaviorism, and positivism, MacIver's scholarship stressed human agency, methodological diversity, and ethical issues. He noted in his autobiography that the title of his first major book, *Community—A Sociological Study* (1917), "was prophetic of a life interest." MacIver sought to define an integrated social science that could comprehend people in their interactively economic, political, and social aspects. He used the notion of community to differentiate a group in search of collective meaning from mere aggregations of voters, subjects, buyers, workers, or individuals.

MacIver distinguished between conceptions of this group and the institutional arrangements governing its members. Accordingly, the state needed to be understood in terms of multiple relations of force and legitimacy; he applauded democracy not as a perfect system but as the best extant balance of centralized power with public accountability. As he contended, again in his autobiography, "the virtue of democracy is that it has placed limits on the absoluteness of power." In such governments the drive to rule was most successfully counteracted by the pursuit of liberty.

Beginning in 1914, MacIver opposed social scientific emphases on quantitative methods, contending that too many academics saw empirical data as an end in itself rather than as a prompting to causal explanations. In contrast to many of his professional colleagues, he was "firmly convinced that social science will never advance except by freeing itself from subjection to the methods and formulae of both physical and biological science." He maintained this outlook throughout his career, remarking much later that "there is no MacIver Neurotic Inventory, no MacIver Index of Morale, no MacIver Hidden Attitude Analysis." He distrusted inappropriate quantification, believing that scholars could only measure what they could not comprehend. Because humanity sought not only facts but also meanings, measurement failed to answer the fundamental questions of a society. "The only things we know as immutable truths," he once argued, "are the things we do not understand. The only things we understand are mutable and never fully known."

MacIver's scholarship reflected his education in the classics, his pursuit of complex explanations, and a deep concern for humanistic values. His intellectual code is spelled out most systematically in *Community: The Modern State* (1926), *Social Causation* (1942), *The Web of Government* (1947), and *The Elements of Social Science* (1949). Especially in the books he wrote after his retirement, MacIver ruminated on such humanistic questions as academic freedom, happiness, democracy, and even, in 1960, *Life: Its Dimensions and Its Bounds.*

Concerned with the fate of society, MacIver eschewed quantitative sociology. Seeking to analyze democracy, his interests in the ethical aspects of power alienated him from political scientists pursuing objectivity. Attempting to construct a coherent understanding of democratic society, he had no place in a philosophy profession largely wedded to logical positivism and linguistic turns. In the end he was a generalist in an age of specialization and a humanist among scholars looking to science as a social paradigm.

MacIver received eight honorary degrees, including one from Harvard at its tercentenary. He was a fellow of the American Academy of Arts and Sciences, the American Philosophical Society, and the British Academy. He resided in Palisades, New York, and died at the Columbia Presbyterian Medical Center in New York City.

• MacIver's papers, numbering about 5,000 items, and an oral history reminiscence dating from 1962 are held by Columbia University. MacIver's autobiography is entitled *As a Tale That Is Told* (1968). His other major works include *Leviathan and the People* (1939), *Towards an Abiding Peace* (1935), *The More Perfect Union* (1949), *Democracy and the Economic Challenge* (1952), *Academic Freedom in Our Time* (1955), *The Pursuit of Happiness* (1955), *The Challenge of the Passing Years* (1962), *Power Transformed* (1964), and *The Prevention and Control of Delinquency* (1966). For assessments of MacIver, see George Kateb, "R. M. MacIver," *New York Review of Books,* 25 Mar. 1965, and the biographical entry in the *International Encyclopedia of the Social Sciences,* vol. 9, pp. 513–15. One of MacIver's students, David Spitz, wrote a useful introduction to a selection of MacIver's essays entitled *Politics and Society* (1969). This volume also includes a complete bibliography of MacIver's writings. *Freedom and Control in Modern Society,* ed. Morroe Berger et al. (1954), considers MacIver's social and political thought. An obituary is in the *New York Times,* 16 June 1970. The most complete and insightful obituary, by MacIver's former student Mirra Komarovsky, is in *American Sociologist* 6 (1971): 51–53.

JOHN M. JORDAN

MACK, Connie (22 Dec. 1862–8 Feb. 1956), baseball player, manager, and owner, was born Cornelius McGillicuddy in East Brookfield, Massachusetts, the son of Michael McGillicuddy, a wheelwright, and Mary McKillop, both Irish immigrants. Mack quit school in the sixth grade to work in a shoe factory, but baseball was his first love.

A catcher (his position from the start), Mack wore a thin, fingerless buckskin glove with a slab of raw steak for padding when his town team won the state championship in 1883. Overcoming his mother's objections—she thought professional baseball was populated with gamblers, drinkers, and brawlers—he signed with Meriden of the Connecticut State League for $90 a month in 1884. But Mack promised his mother that he would not fall prey to vice and bad manners, and throughout his career he remained a gentleman, an exemplar for the sport.

In 1886 Mack was sold to Washington of the National League, and the next year he married his hometown sweetheart, Margaret Hogan. Five years later she died, leaving him with three children, who were raised by his mother.

Although later a staunch defender of club owners' interests, Mack in 1890 helped lead a players' revolt against the National League's arbitrary salary limit. A trade war broke out when the players formed their own league. Mack invested his savings in the Buffalo club, but the Players League folded at the end of the 1890 season, and Mack was assigned to Pittsburgh of the National League. A light-hitting but crafty catcher, he was noted for such tricks as tipping bats and chatting with batters to distract them. Although his peppery style of field leadership earned him the manager's job in 1894, front office interference caused him to look elsewhere, and in 1896 Ban Johnson, who was building a minor league in the West, enticed Mack to Milwaukee as manager and part owner. From 1897 to 1900 Mack directed the team on and off the field, mastering the business side of the game.

Another trade war was launched in 1901 when Johnson's newly named American League invaded eastern cities that had National League teams. Mack served as one of Johnson's lieutenants, recruiting star National League players and lining up suitable playing grounds. Awarded the American League's Philadelphia franchise as manager and 25 percent owner, he secured the backing of Ben Shibe, a partner in the A. J. Reach sporting goods company, and built the most successful expansion team in baseball history. The Philadelphia Athletics won the American League's second pennant and six of the first fourteen titles. Mack built his early champions around future Hall of Famers Rube Waddell, Frank "Home Run" Baker, Eddie Plank, Chief Bender, and Eddie Collins. In 1909 the Athletics built Shibe Park, the first modern steel and concrete stadium in the nation, triggering a building boom of new ballparks.

Mack, an innovator and a keen judge of young players, introduced "skull" sessions and pregame meetings. He coordinated pitching with defense; knowing how his pitcher would pitch to each batter, he positioned his fielders uncannily. From his first day in Philadelphia, he no longer wore a uniform and remained on the bench. He used a scorecard to wave his fielders into position, a signal that became his trademark.

Mack scouted colleges and high schools for players. He sought young, intelligent athletes who could develop plays such as double and triple steals and defenses against those tactics when used by other teams. His players were required to be well behaved, and he addressed them by their proper names, sometimes even prefaced by "Mister." (Players invariably called him "Mister Mack.") He rarely visited the clubhouse after a game or reprimanded a player in front of the others. At the time, the typical player and manager was a profane, tobacco-chewing umpire baiter. The soft-spoken Mack, however, sat in a dugout on the hottest days in a navy blue suit, high starched collar, and tie.

Mack attended Mass every Sunday, sometimes taking along young players he spotted in the hotel lobby. Throughout the nation, Catholics were his biggest fans and a fertile source of tips on prospects. Many of his early stars became college baseball coaches. They, too, sent many of their graduates to Mack.

The complex Mack was generous, patient, and kind, but he could be petty, tightfisted, sarcastic, impetuous, and stubborn. No destitute old-timer left his office empty-handed, but active players sometimes had difficulty squeezing a $500 raise out of him. His patience and courtliness impressed strangers who approached him.

To Mack, baseball remained primarily a business. He possessed no outside income or capital. If the team lost money, salaries were cut. He operated in a small blue-collar market with National League competitors and no Sunday games until 1934, when Pennsylvania finally legalized Sunday baseball.

In 1910 Mack married Katherine Hallahan. They had five children.

After Philadelphia won four pennants in five years from 1910 to 1914, the organizers of the new Federal League began raiding the rosters of the other two leagues. With huge bankrolls to spend, the new teams wooed Mack's top stars. This forced Mack to sell his great second baseman, Eddie Collins, to the Chicago White Sox because he could not match the Feds' offer to Collins. The Athletics then finished last the next seven years.

After Babe Ruth changed baseball from being predominantly a game of strategy to being more a contest of batting power, Mack spent freely to obtain hitters as well as canny base runners. He bought or developed future Hall of Famers Jimmie Foxx, Al Simmons, Mickey Cochrane, and Lefty Grove, and he dethroned the mighty New York Yankees with three league championships from 1929 to 1931. However, the highest payroll in the business and the Great Depression resulted in dwindling income and large bank loans, which forced Mack again to sell his stars.

In 1930 Mack received the Bok Award, an honor previously given to statesmen and cultural leaders for outstanding service to the city of Philadelphia. Five years later the press pilloried him as a tightwad because he broke up another winning team for financial reasons. His standing in Philadelphia, however, never dimmed. Over the next twenty years he tried many different combinations of players but never put together another winner.

In 1950 the 88-year-old manager was honored with a day in every major league ballpark. He received a scroll in Philadelphia signed by more than one million people and a telegram from President Harry Truman: "May your shadow never grow less."

At the end of that season he resigned as manager. During the twentieth century no other manager has come close to equaling his tenure in the major leagues. Under Mack, Philadelphia won nine pennants and finished last seventeen times. Because of his professional longevity (53 years) he managed more games (7,755), won more (3,731), and lost more (3,948) than any other manager ever may. Ever unemotional, he made no farewell speech and said no goodbyes to his team. He remained as club president but left the daily operation to his three sons. The Athletics floundered in the cellar, strapped for cash and deep in debt. The brothers could not work together, forcing the sale of the team. Despite Mack's pleas that the Athletics remain in Philadelphia, the American League refused to approve the purchase of the club by a local group. In 1954 the Athletics were sold to Arnold Johnson, who moved the team to Kansas City.

Mack, who had watched his first opening game when Grover Cleveland was president and his last when Dwight D. Eisenhower was in the White House, died in Germantown, Pennsylvania.

• The papers associated with Connie Mack and the Philadelphia Athletics disappeared somewhere during the team's moves to Kansas City and Oakland. Mack's life is portrayed in Frederick G. Lieb, *Connie Mack* (1945), and Connie Mack, *My 66 Years in the Big Leagues* (1950). See also the Mack file in the National Baseball Hall of Fame Library, Cooperstown, N.Y. An obituary appears in the *New York Times*, 9 Feb. 1956.

NORMAN L. MACHT

MACK, Julian William (19 July 1866–5 Sept. 1943), lawyer, judge, and Zionist leader, was born in San Francisco, California, the son of William Jacob Mack, an immigrant from Bavaria who prospered as a dry goods merchant, and Rebecca Tandler. Julian was the second of thirteen children born to the couple. Because of health reasons, William Mack resettled the family in Cincinnati in 1870, and there young Julian came under the influence of Rabbi Isaac Mayer Wise, the leading figure in American Reform Judaism.

A bright lad who graduated from high school with honors in just three years, he did not go to college but entered the Harvard Law School in 1884. Harvard at the time was a center of intellectual ferment, and Mack found himself exhilarated by it, and especially by James Barr Ames, who would have enormous impact not only on Mack, but on generations of Harvard students. "I owe to him," Mack later wrote when he established a fund to honor Ames, "whatever measure of love for legal science and interest in law I may have."

In his third year, Mack was one of the founders of the *Harvard Law Review* and served as a member of its board and as its first business manager. He also won the Parker Travelling Fellowship, which allowed him to go to Europe to study at the Universities of Berlin and Leipzig and to tour the Continent. He returned to the United States in the fall of 1890 and settled in Chicago, where he began his practice of law with Julius Rosenthal, then a leader of the city's Jewish community. Julian stayed with Rosenthal for three years and then opened his own office with two other young lawyers. Although he enjoyed some success, he eagerly accepted an offer in 1895 from the new law school at Northwestern University. The salary, while not large, allowed Julian to marry Jessie Fox in 1896; their one child was to become a prominent psychoanalyst (under the name Ruth Mack Brunswick).

In 1902 Mack left Northwestern to join the University of Chicago Law School, where he quickly gained prominence as a teacher. Jerome Frank considered Mack the best teacher at the school, one who had "helped him most and who gave the best understanding of the law in practical operation and effect." Even after he became a judge, Mack retained his teaching position with the Chicago Law School almost until his death.

In these years Mack, like many young lawyers, became caught up in the various reform movements of the Progressive Era. He got to know Jane Addams and other leading progressives, and through them he was drawn into a number of labor-related reforms. But as the son of a Jewish immigrant, he paid particular attention to the plight of Chicago's immigrant community and before long had become the directing official of Jewish charities in the city as well as adviser to Julius Rosenwald of Sears, Roebuck, the community's leading philanthropist.

The growing Jewish population of Chicago soon caught the attention of the city's Democratic leaders. In his bid for reelection, Mayor Carter Harrison, Jr., sought Jewish votes, and to show his gratitude he decided to name a Jewish lawyer to the office of civil service commissioner, a stepping stone to a judgeship. Rosenwald put forward Mack's name, Harrison made the offer, and Mack accepted; three months later the Democrats named Mack as their candidate for Cook County Circuit Court judge, and in 1903 he was elected, making him one of the first—if not the first—Jewish judge in Chicago.

Although in his long judicial career Judge Mack would hear many types of cases, it was in his work as a juvenile court judge in Cook County that he derived his greatest satisfaction. At the time juvenile court was an unpaid sideline of the circuit court, yet Mack willingly took on the responsibility and introduced many of the same types of reforms that are often credited to Ben Lindsey in Denver. Rather than try juvenile offenders as criminals, Mack insisted that they be treated as wards of the state and that every effort be made to rehabilitate them rather than send them to prison. His work with children soon won him the plaudits not only of Jane Addams, but of social reformers across the country. Theodore Roosevelt (1858–1919) named

him as one of the three vice chairmen of the first White House Conference on the Care of Dependent Children in 1909, and he was elected president of the National Conference of Social Workers in 1911.

Although Mack was a Democrat, William Howard Taft named him to the newly created commerce court in 1911; it turned out to be a less than happy experience for Mack because of the poor performance of some of his colleagues. The Democratically controlled Congress abolished the commerce court at the end of 1913 but converted the appointments of Mack and one other judge to the rank of circuit court judge. This placed Mack in the highest judicial position held by a Jew to that time. Mack greatly enjoyed the variety of cases he heard at the circuit court of appeals level, and he served on that bench until his retirement in 1941.

Aside from his judicial work, Mack served as a member of the Harvard Board of Overseers from 1919 to 1933 and again from 1937 to 1941. While in his first term, President A. Lawrence Lowell tried to impose a quota on Jewish students at the university, a policy Mack vigorously opposed and which, in the end, the overseers rejected.

Mack also remained active in Jewish affairs. In 1906 he was one of the founders of the American Jewish Committee, composed primarily of upper-class Jews of German origin pledged to oppose anti-Semitism and to work for the assimilation of Jews into American society. Most of them opposed Zionism because they saw the drive to reestablish a Jewish homeland in Palestine as threatening their status as American citizens. Mack was one of the few members of the committee to openly support Zionism, and when Louis Brandeis took over the leadership of the American Zionist movement in 1914 Mack became one of his chief lieutenants.

In 1918, two years after Brandeis went onto the Supreme Court, Mack became president of the Zionist Organization of America and also of the first American Jewish Congress. He went to the Paris Peace Conference as chairman of the Comité des Délégations Juives and helped arrange for the award of the League of Nations Mandate over Palestine to Great Britain. In 1921 he, along with the other Brandeisians, resigned from their positions of leadership in the dispute with Chaim Weizmann over the future policy of the Zionist movement. Whereas the Brandeisians wanted to emphasize the practical work of building the Jewish homeland in Palestine, the Europeans believed that a great deal of political negotiation had to be completed before any "practical" measures could be taken.

Mack remained active in Jewish affairs throughout the 1920s and 1930s and also presided over a number of important trials, including the antitrust suit against the Sugar Institute; that decision, upheld by the Supreme Court, became a landmark in antitrust law for its ruling regarding cartel pricing policies and information exchange.

His first wife died in 1938, and two years later Mack married Cecile Blumgart, his daughter Ruth's mother-in-law. His eyes had begun to give him trouble, and his vision problems led him to resign from the bench a few weeks before his remarriage. He lived out the remainder of his life quietly, dying peacefully in New York.

• The Julian W. Mack Papers are in the Zionist Archives and Library in New York City. The only biography is that by Harry Barnard, *The Forging of an American Jew: The Life and Times of Judge Julian W. Mack* (1974), but see also Horace M. Kallen, "Julian William Mack," *American Jewish Year Book* 46 (1944–1945): 35–46, and Melvin I. Urofsky, *American Zionism from Herzl to the Holocaust* (1975). An obituary is in the *New York Times*, 6 Sept. 1943.

MELVIN I. UROFSKY

MACKAY, James (1759?–16 Mar. 1822), explorer and surveyor, was born in the Parish of Kildonan, county of Sutherland, Scotland, the son of George Mackay, a judge, and Elizabeth McDonald. A surveyor by trade, he was well educated, fluent in both French and Spanish, and played the violin. In 1776 he left Scotland for Canada, where he became a fur trader for the North West Company. Under the employ of the English he explored the upper lakes and Western region of Canada and stayed for a time at Fort Espérance (in Saskatchewan), near the Qu'Appelle and Assiniboine rivers. In 1787 Mackay, along with an expeditionary force of a few men, went south to the Mandan Indian towns, where they spent ten days. It was apparently one of the first contacts that the Mandans had with white men. The Mandans honored Mackay and his party by carrying them on buffalo robes into their earthen towns. During his travels he mapped the area toward the Rockies. These maps would be of great benefit to later explorations. After returning to Canada, sometime between 1792 and 1794, Mackay went on to St. Louis, where he was one of the first English-speaking settlers of Upper Louisiana. In St. Louis he became a Spanish subject.

Because of his "honesty and intelligence" and his impressive reputation as a trader, he was hired by the Missouri Company, a Spanish commercial concern, to make a third expedition into the territory west of the Mississippi. Two previous excursions sent out by the company to explore the Missouri River region and determine a route to the Pacific Ocean had been failures. Baron de Carondelet appointed Mackay director of the company's operations in the Indian country and instructed him to drive the British from the Mandan villages and establish a chain of forts in the territory. He was to be paid a sum of 400 pesos a year and a share of the profits. If the party reached the Pacific Ocean they would receive a bonus of 3,000 pesos. Accompanying Mackay was John Evans, a 25-year-old Welshman who sought to find the Welsh Indians, fabled descendants of Prince Madoc of Wales, whom he thought to find among the Mandans.

In August 1795 Mackay and Evans left St. Louis with thirty-three men and four pirogues carrying goods. Stopping in northeastern Nebraska, Mackay built an outpost that he called Fort Charles in honor of King Carlos IV of Spain. Mackay remained behind to establish relations with the local Omaha Indian tribe and its chief Blackbird. He sent John Evans ahead with a small group to seek out trade, make alliances with Indians, and find the route to the Pacific Ocean.

The Spanish government spent 104,000 pesos for the two-year expedition, which proved to be invaluable, because it yielded new geographic and scientific information about the upper Missouri. Mackay and Evans kept journals that detailed the tributaries and the curving course of the Missouri, showing the distances, navigability, and length and telling of the tribes living in the vicinity. They described the Rocky Mountains as having a multiple-ridged topography instead of being a single range. Mackay's twelve-page *Notes on Indian Tribes* summarized his experiences with Piegans and Mandans and included information on burials and religion and descriptions of the construction of earth lodges, town layouts, and patterns of farming and hunting. This information helped bring success to the Lewis and Clark expedition in the following decade.

After returning home in 1797, Mackay, also known as Don Santiago Mackay, was elevated to the position of deputy surveyor by the Spanish surveyor general, Antoine Soulard. In 1798 Governor General Manuel Gayoso de Lemos gave him the title of captain of the militia and first commandant of San Andrés del Misuri (St. Andrews), a settlement twenty-four miles west of St. Louis on the south bank of the Missouri River. He also received 30,000 arpens of land. Within a short time, he and twenty-nine American families, mostly settlers from Kentucky, had cleared the land and were growing a large quantity of grain. Mackay recruited more families to the area and protested when Gayoso attempted to prevent any further immigration at the century's end. In 1800 Mackay married Isabella Long in St. Charles, Missouri; they had nine children. He remained commandant until 1804 when Missouri became a possession of the United States, and thereafter the settlement deteriorated. In 1811 naturalist John Bradbury reported that the town had been abandoned.

After the change of hegemony, Mackay was appointed one of the judges of the court of quarter sessions. He became a member of the legislature of Missouri Territory from St. Louis County in 1816 and also served as major of the militia. He died in St. Louis. Commended by Gayoso for his services of instituting military and civil regulations and for the opening of roads in the area, Mackay was described as "an officer of knowledge, zealous and punctual." Mackay's greatest accomplishments remained his ability to survey the land and the knowledge he passed on to other explorers. On 10 January 1804 he met with William Clark at Camp Dubois, where Mackay gave the explorer critical information on Indian-white relations, the opposition that might be encountered, and the geography to the west. Through verbal and written data, Mackay became a vital source for the Lewis and Clark expedition. The two explorers were able to anticipate the native peoples they would encounter, the landscape of the Rocky Mountains, and the Yellowstone, Big

Horn, and Powder rivers that lay beyond the bend of the Missouri River.

• The Mackay papers and documents from Spain are in the possession of the Missouri Historical Society. His journal can be found in *The Spanish Régime in Missouri*, vol. 2 (1909), pp. 181–94. Biographies of Mackay can be found in Abraham P. Nasatir, "James Mackay," in *The Mountain Men and the Fur Trade of the Far West*, vol. 4 (1965); and William S. Bryan and Robert Rose, *A History of the Pioneer Families of Missouri* (1977). Other helpful sources are Louis Houck, *A History of Missouri*, vols. 2 and 3 (1908); *Missouri Historical Society Collections*, vol. 4 (1912), pp. 20–21; Frederic L. Billon, *Annals of St. Louis*, vol. 1 (1886), p. 367; *American Historical Association Report 1908*, vol. 1 (1909); Annie H. Abel-Henderson, "Mackay's Table of Distances," *Mississippi Valley Historical Review* (Mar. 1924): 428–46; *St. Louis Enquirer*, 23 Mar. 1822; and William E. Foley, *Genesis of Missouri* (1989). Additional information on the exploration of the region and the relevance of Mackay's maps and journals are in Nasatir, ed., *Before Lewis and Clark: Documents Illustrating the History of the Missouri 1785–1804* (1952); and John Logan Allen, *Passage through the Garden: Lewis and Clark and the Image of the American Northwest* (1975).

MARILYN ELIZABETH PERRY

MACKAY, John Alexander (17 May 1889–9 June 1983), missionary and theological educator, was born in Inverness, Scotland, the son of Duncan Mackay, a prosperous tailor and clothing merchant in Inverness, and Isabelle Macdonald. The family belonged to the Free Presbyterian Church of Scotland, a denomination known for its strict doctrine and pietistic practices. Mackay and his family attended three services each Sunday—two in Gaelic and one in English. In his teens he applied several times for membership before he was finally accepted.

In his early teens Mackay had what he described as an "ecstatic" experience of Jesus Christ as "a living reality." He stated that he fell in love with the Bible and resolved, to his father's pleasure, to become a minister. He received an M.A. from the University of Aberdeen in 1912 and immigrated to the United States to study at Princeton Theological Seminary. His decision to enter Princeton was motivated largely by contact with the American Presbyterian missionary leader, Robert E. Speer, who left a profound imprint on Mackay's life.

Mackay completed his study at Princeton in 1915 and won a fellowship to study theology overseas. Because of the war, Princeton professor Benjamin B. Warfield encouraged him to study in Spain. There Mackay read the Spanish mystics and met the famous Spanish philosopher, Miguel de Unamuno, who introduced him to the writings of Søren Kierkegaard. Fascinated by Unamuno's mysticism and existentialism, Mackay later declared that he had been influenced more by Unamuno than any other secular thinker.

Returning briefly to Scotland in 1916, Mackay married Jane Logan Wells; they had four children. They shared a common interest in missionary work, especially in Latin America. Resigning from the Free Presbyterian church because of its doctrinal rigidity,

Mackay was ordained in 1916 by the Free Church of Scotland and sent to Lima, Peru, as that church's first missionary to Latin America.

Mackay's Latin American missionary experience was pivotal in shaping his future ministry. Fluent in Spanish, he wrote several books, the most notable being *The Other Spanish Christ* (Eng. ed., 1932), an interpretation of the Christian spirituality of Spanish culture. He was the founder and principal of the Anglo-Peruvian College in Lima and was named to the chair of metaphysics at the University of San Marcos in Lima in 1925. He built strong alliances with intellectuals and political dissidents in Peru and throughout Latin America as he opposed the domination of Latin American societies by the Roman Catholic church and the landed classes.

From 1926 to 1932 he was based in Montevideo, Uruguay, and then Mexico and traveled widely as a lecturer and writer for the South American Federation of the YMCA. In 1932 he was invited by Speer to come to New York as the secretary for Latin America and Africa in the Board of Foreign Missions of the Presbyterian Church in the U.S.A.

In 1936 Speer and the board of Princeton Theological Seminary invited Mackay to become president of the seminary, which had been devastated by the fundamentalist controversy. This battle pitted theological conservatives who wanted to define strict doctrinal standards against those who were willing to allow some theological differences in the Presbyterian church. Mackay initially refused and then accepted, seeing the possibilities of extending his missionary work through theological education.

Mackay served for twenty-three years and led Princeton Seminary not only through a period of healing, but also expansion and growth. During his presidency, he abolished the eating clubs, which he felt were divisive in the student body. The campus center with a common dining hall now bears his name. Under his leadership, Princeton launched the Summer Institute of Theology, an annual ten-day continuing education program for ministers; founded *Theology Today*, the most widely circulated quarterly journal of theology in the world; initiated a school of Christian education; established a doctoral program; consolidated and built Speer Library, named after Mackay's friend and mentor; diversified the student body by admitting more women and blacks; and expanded and improved the quality of the faculty.

Even as Mackay was rebuilding Princeton and making it a prominent institution of theological education, he began to emerge as a significant theological voice in American Protestantism and ecumenical Christianity. The eclectic theological influences in his life make it difficult to categorize him. He had some affinities with the neoorthodox movement in Protestantism and gave it one of its most famous slogans: "Let the Church be the Church." He was sharply critical of pre–Vatican II Roman Catholicism, primarily because of his experience with the Latin American church, but his theology drew deeply on Spanish Catholic mysticism. He was a vocal critic of Marxism and totalitarianism, but his open letter to Presbyterians in 1953 criticizing McCarthyism was widely publicized and helped turn public opinion against Senator Joseph R. McCarthy and the anticommunist crusade.

Mackay was both an ecumenical leader and an ecumenical theologian, participating in international church conferences and shaping ecumenical thought. He initiated the shift in terminology from "international" church discussions to "ecumenical" dialogue, arguing that the Greek-derived term better captured the biblical idea of the unity of the church as the body of Christ.

Both Mackay and his interpreters agree that he was driven by images and symbols. He always tried to formulate his ideas in compelling metaphors. He was fond of quoting Unamuno: "Get a great idea, marry it, found a home with it, and raise a family." At the center of his thought were two unifying themes—the nature of Jesus Christ and the doctrine of the church. One of his most popular images drew on his Spanish experience—the balcony and the road. The church, he argued, must always be on the road, never observing life from the balcony. Even in the closing years of his life, he continued to argue for the importance of Latin America for the United States and identified the Pentecostal-charismatic movement as a powerful force that churches should recognize.

After he retired in 1959, Mackay continued to lecture and write, including what is probably his most significant English work, *Ecumenics: The Science of the Church Universal* (1964), a study of the church's global mission. He died in Princeton.

• The Mackay papers are in Speer Library at Princeton Theological Seminary. The seminary also has an unpublished bibliography, "The Writings of Dr. John A. Mackay." Also see Stanton R. Wilson and William O. Harris, "John Mackay: Bibliographical Resources for the Period, 1914–1992," *Studies in Reformed Theology and History* 1 (1993): 1–58. The only book-length biography is John H. Sinclair, *Juan A. Mackay: Un Escoces con alma Latina* (John A. Mackay: A Scot with a Latin soul) (1991). An oral history is Gerald W. Gillette, "John A. Mackay: Influences on My Life," *Journal of Presbyterian History* 56 (1978): 20–34. See John A. Mackay, "Let Us Remember," *Princeton Seminary Bulletin* 45 (1972): 25–32. English-language sources include Pedro N. Cintrón, "The Concept of the Church in the Theology of John Alexander Mackay" (Ph.D. diss., Drew Univ., 1979); Samuel Escobar, "The Legacy of John Alexander Mackay," *International Bulletin of Missionary Research* 16 (July 1992): 116–22; James Leo Garrett, "John A. Mackay on the Roman Catholic Church," *Journal of Presbyterian History* 50 (1972): 111–28; Thomas W. Gillespie, "John Alexander Mackay: A Centennial Remembrance," *Princeton Seminary Bulletin*, n.s., 10 (1989): 171–81; H. McKennie Goodpasture, "The Latin American Soul of John A. Mackay," *Journal of Presbyterian History* 48 (1970): 265–92; Janet Harbison, "John Mackay of Princeton," *Presbyterian Life*, 15 Sept. and 1 Oct. 1958, pp. 6–11, 15–17, 34; Hugh T. Kerr, "John A. Mackay: An Appreciation," in *The Ecumenical Era in Church and Society*, ed. Edward J. Jurji (1959); David Wesley Soper, *Men Who Shape Belief: Major Voices in American Theology*, vol. 2 (1955), pp. 42–59; and Stanton R. Wilson, "Studies in the Life and Work of an Ecumenical Churchman" (master's thesis, Princeton Theological Seminary, 1958). Substantive obituaries are in the *Princeton Seminary Bulletin* 5 (1984): 41–43 and *Theology Today* 40 (1984): 453–56.

JOHN M. MULDER

MACKAYE, Hazel (24 Aug. 1880–12 Aug. 1944), women's rights activist and writer and director of pageants, was born in New York City, the daughter of James Morrison Steele MacKaye, a playwright and theatrical innovator, and Mary Medbery, a writer and actress. Her brothers Benton, Robert, and Percy MacKaye all became well-known authors.

MacKaye's first theatrical experiences were as an actress in her brother Percy's plays, touring with the Coburn Players, and working with producer Winthrop Ames at the Castle Square Theatre in Boston. An honorary member of the 1910 Radcliffe class, she briefly attended Harvard professor George Pierce Baker's playwrighting course in the fall of 1906. This class experience, reinforced by her family background and her acting experience, encouraged her to pursue further theatrical work as a director, writer, and stage manager.

Her first major production was *Allegory*, a suffrage pageant, which she wrote and directed. Commissioned by the National American Woman Suffrage Association's congressional committee, it was performed on 3 March 1913, the eve of Woodrow Wilson's inauguration, on the steps of Washington, D.C.'s imposing U.S. Treasury building for 3,000 seated dignitaries and a mass public audience. Featuring symbolic glorification of the American woman, MacKaye's pageant was followed by a suffrage parade during which the marchers were harassed by male and female opponents of woman suffrage, resulting in significant publicity for the suffrage cause.

Her next suffrage pageant, *Six Periods of American Life* (1914), sometimes referred to as *Woman in America*, was produced under the auspices of the Men's League for Woman Suffrage in collaboration with the Equal Franchise Society and was performed at New York City's Seventy-first Regiment Armory with 500 participants and 2,500 viewers. It portrayed women burdened by oppression and concluded with a stirring call to acknowledge women's right to vote and their equality in all spheres of life. *The Pageant of Susan B. Anthony* (1915), commissioned by the National Women's Party and performed in Washington, D.C.'s Convention Hall, brought together 400 actresses, a chorus of sixty, and a twenty-five-piece orchestra. The most popular of MacKaye's pageants, it was performed in other cities as well and was considered an important contribution to the suffrage movement. Consisting of ten scenes portraying Susan B. Anthony's fight for equal rights for women, the pageant pointed out that although several states had granted women the right to vote, there was still much to be done to ensure women's full participation in public affairs.

In 1915 MacKaye directed *Pageant of Athena*, written by Vassar students, for the college's fiftieth anniversary. In that year, she collaborated with another woman, Christian D. Hemmick, on an antiwar piece, *War and Woman's Awakening: Peace Tableaux*, which was produced under the auspices of the Washington branch of the Women's Peace Party. Her pageant *Portals of Light*, written for the YWCA's Jubilee celebration, was presented in 1916 at the Seventy-first Regiment Armory in New York. She became the first woman to write a pageant on industrial themes when her script *The New Vision: A Masque of Modern Industry* was performed by the employees of the Larkin Company in Buffalo, New York, in 1916. MacKaye assisted her brother Percy with the 1916–1917 productions of his play *Caliban* in New York and at Harvard, acting as a community liaison, marshaling and organizing all the volunteer committees for performance and production, and even designing some of the sets. From 1918 to 1920 she served as the director of the Board of Pageantry and the Drama for the National Board of the YWCA.

In 1923 the National Women's Party commissioned MacKaye to stage her most ambitious and spectacular production, *Equal Rights Pageant*, to commemorate the seventy-fifth anniversary of the Seneca Falls Women's Rights Convention. The pageant, which was performed at a National Women's Party conference in Seneca Falls, featured a thousand actresses depicting the history of the struggle for women's rights, a parade of barges on Seneca Falls Lake, and a large sign with the words "Declaration of Principles" in electric lights. Coming after the passage of the suffrage amendment, this pageant was celebratory in tone rather than persuasive. A great success, it was revived later that year in Colorado Springs, and again at the 1924 conference of the National Women's Party in Westport-on-Lake Champlain, New York, where it was called *Forward Into Light*.

MacKaye's literary and community activities were extensive, and her writing reveals a powerful individual artistic voice. Her peers considered her a pioneer writer and director of powerful political pageants and a champion of theater as a populist enterprise for artists and audiences. She retired in 1914 and devoted herself to the care of her ailing mother. She, too, had always suffered from frail health, and she spent her last years in a convalescent home in Monterey, Massachusetts. She died in Westport, Connecticut.

• The major repository for material on MacKaye is in the MacKaye Family Collection in Baker Library at Dartmouth College. Additional material can be found in the Harvard Theatre Collection, Harvard University, and in the Langdon Collection, John Hay Library, Brown University. Other sources on MacKaye include Edwin Osgood Grover, ed., *Annals of an Era: Percy MacKaye and the MacKaye Family, 1826–1932* (1932); Percy MacKaye, *Epoch: The Life of Steele MacKaye* (1927); Naima Prevots, *American Pageantry: A Movement for Art and Democracy* (1990); and Karen J. Blair, "Pageantry for Women's Rights: The Career of Hazel MacKaye, 1913–1923," *Theatre Survey* 31 (May 1990): 23–46. See also Durward Howes, ed., *American Woman: The Official Who's Who among the Women of the Nation* (1935). Obituaries are in the *New York Times*, 14 Aug. 1944; the *New York Herald Tribune*, 14 Aug. 1944; the Fitchburg, Mass., *Sentinel*, 26 Aug. 1944; and *Driftwood, a Magazine of Poetry*, Oct. 1944.

NAIMA PREVOTS

MACKAYE, Percy (16 Mar. 1875–31 Aug. 1956), poet and playwright, was born Percy Wallace MacKaye in New York City, the son of James Morrison Steele MacKaye, an actor-dramatist, and Mary Keith Medbery, a writer. MacKaye was schooled chiefly at home and in public schools in New York City, though he also attended Lawrence Academy in Groton, Massachusetts, for a short time.

In 1897, at his undergraduate convocation from Harvard University, MacKaye addressed the assembly with a paper titled "The Need for Imagination in the Drama of Today." He married Marion Homer Morse, his third cousin, in 1898; they had three children. Unable to secure a teaching post, he traveled for two years with her in Europe. On returning, MacKaye taught at the Craigie School for Boys in New York City from 1900 to 1904.

The American actor E. H. Sothern commissioned MacKaye to write *The Canterbury Pilgrims* (published in 1903, but not performed by Sothern) and *Fenris, the Wolf* (published in 1905). Both in verse, the former dramatized *The Canterbury Tales*, the latter a Scandinavian folk tale. The first of MacKaye's plays to receive a professional performance was *Jeanne d'Arc*, also in verse. It was produced by Sothern and Julia Marlowe at the Lyric Theatre in Philadelphia on 15 October 1906.

For *Sappho and Phaon*, produced in 1907, MacKaye engaged a University of Michigan professor, Albert A. Stanley, to compose the music for his lyrics and choruses. MacKaye's *The Scarecrow*, a prose drama inspired by Nathaniel Hawthorne's "Feathertop," was first produced by the Harvard Dramatic Club in 1909 and staged in New York two years later. Its success earned MacKaye productions in England (by the Theatre Royal, Bristol), Germany (by Max Reinhardt), and Russia (by the Moscow Art Theater).

Not content with publishing and producing drama alone, MacKaye wrote and performed commemorative poems in the hope that poetry might regain its oral importance in American culture. In a typical recitation, he read his epic poem "Ticonderoga" for the 1909 tercentenary celebration of the discovery of Lake Champlain, New York. Satirizing misappropriators of Henrik Ibsen and other modern thinkers, MacKaye wrote *Anti-Matrimony*, produced first in Ann Arbor, Michigan, in 1910 and staged later that year in New York. The 1912 publication of his drama on eugenics, *To-morrow*, provoked a mixed critical response to the topic and to his treatment of it; it was produced the following year in Philadelphia.

As MacKaye's theater work gained recognition, his concurrent efforts to formulate a theory of the role of participatory drama in democracy also received more attention. The principles in his *The Civic Theatre, in Relation to the Redemption of Leisure* (1912) were esteemed in civic and artistic quarters by such readers as President Woodrow Wilson and the theater theorist and practitioner Edwin Gordon Craig. The work of his suffragist sister Hazel, conservationist brother Benton, and economist-philosopher brother James informed some of the principles of his dramatic theories and the themes in his plays and masques.

Many of his works suited the time and place in which they were first produced, drawing on local history or topical contemporary issues for their appeal. For the 150th anniversary of St. Louis, Missouri, MacKaye organized an open-air civic performance, *Saint Louis, a Masque of American Civilization*, involving a cast of 8,000 citizens and playing before audiences of more than one million people during its run from 28 May to 1 June 1914. *Caliban, by the Yellow Sands*, his masque to celebrate the Shakespeare tercentenary while Great Britain was involved in World War I, dramatized the evolution of democratic and peaceful community drama. It included designs by Robert Edmund Jones, folk dances by the British ethnographer Cecil Sharp, an opening dance by Isadora Duncan, and an amateur cast of 2,500 when it opened in New York in 1916. A 1917 revival of *Caliban* at the Harvard Stadium in Boston involved a cast of 5,000. In 1920 Miami University in Oxford, Ohio, awarded MacKaye the first American fellowship in poetry, a chair of creative literature with no formal teaching duties.

With the momentum of the civic drama movement broken by World War I, MacKaye's theoretical treatises on the power of drama to "redeem leisure" and to serve as a "substitute for war" also lost favor. Masque-making by pageant societies became a segregated and formulaic practice of questionable artistic quality as fewer professionals devoted their efforts to them. Mac-Kaye, who had idealized the transformative powers of participatory civic drama, failed to find sponsors for his urban masques and pageants.

Inspired by Cecil Sharp, MacKaye turned his dramatic and poetic talents to depictions of the people and landscape of rural America. In 1921 he and his wife spent a summer in Kentucky collecting Appalachian folktales. Affecting the mountain dialect, MacKaye produced a biting three-act comedy, *This Fine-Pretty World* (1924); an edition of three short plays, *Kentucky Mountain Fantasies* (1928); a poem, "The Gobbler of God" (1928); and a collection of twelve stories, *Tall Tales of the Kentucky Mountains* (1926). He also published poems on New England.

MacKaye devoted the years 1923 to 1927 chiefly to compiling a two-volume biography and bibliography about his father titled *Epoch*. During this period Mac-Kaye experienced bouts of ill health, and in the 1930s he had a series of heart attacks. In 1932 his *Wakefield*, a federally sponsored masque to honor the 200-year anniversary of George Washington's birth, was produced at Constitution Hall in Washington, D.C., and in 1949 the Pasadena Playhouse produced his tetralogy, *The Mystery of Hamlet*. He published two tales for children in 1951 and 1952 and continued to write poet-

ry until his death at his home in Cornish, New Hampshire.

The large casts of his pageants and the specific locales or occasions required to produce them make MacKaye's works unlikely candidates for theatrical revivals. However, his transition away from classical themes and pageantry toward American folk and historical subjects, his use of American dialects, his integration of poetry, music, and dance, and his theories of community drama make him an important precursor in the emergence of American performing art forms.

• The MacKaye Family Papers at Dartmouth College include materials before 1932; papers of the MacKaye family and of George Pierce Baker in the Harvard University Theater Collection are also valuable. Edwin Osgood Grover, *Annals of an Era: Percy MacKaye and the MacKaye Family, 1826–1932* (1932), includes a narrative biography, indexes, and writings by and about MacKaye. See also the reminiscence by Mac-Kaye's daughter Arvia MacKaye Ege, *The Power of the Impossible: The Life Story of Percy and Marion MacKaye* (1992). Critical assessments by MacKaye's contemporaries include "The Playwright as Pioneer," in Thomas H. Dickinson, *Playwrights of the New American Theatre* (1925), and Arthur Hobson Quinn, "Percy MacKaye as a Dramatist of Revolt," *English Journal* 12, no. 10 (Dec. 1923). David Glassberg, *American Historical Pageantry* (1990), places MacKaye's work in the national movement toward community drama. An obituary appears in the *New York Times*, 1 Sept. 1956.

LIBBY SMIGEL

MACKAYE, Steele (6 June 1842–25 Feb. 1894), playwright, actor, and director, was born James Morrison Steele McKay in Buffalo, New York, the son of James Morrison McKay, a lawyer and president of Western Union, and Emily Steele. It is not known when he changed his name from McKay to MacKaye. In his youth MacKaye's life was one of privilege, ease, and opportunity. At the age of sixteen he was sent to study in Paris at the École des Beaux Arts to develop his talent and interest in painting. He returned to the United States in 1859. At the outbreak of the Civil War Mac-Kaye enlisted in the Union Army, and while his regiment was stationed in Baltimore he and fellow soldiers produced several amateur theatrical events. MacKaye seems to have been the star, playing Othello, Shylock, and Hamlet, among other roles, and playing them so impressively that he was offered but declined a professional engagement by John T. Ford, proprietor of theaters in Baltimore and Washington, D.C.

In 1862 MacKaye married Jennie Spring, but they were soon divorced, and in 1865 he wed Mary Keith Medbery. They had two children; one son, Percy, became a popular playwright. In 1868 or 1869 MacKaye made another trip to Paris, this time to study with François Delsarte, who had recently introduced a new approach to acting based on action and gesture. Mac-Kaye returned to the United States and lectured on the new form of expression in New York and Boston and at Harvard University. He founded his own New York acting company based on the form, and made his New

York debut in January 1872 at the St. James Theatre, with his own students in supporting roles. The play he chose to feature this new style was called *Monaldi*, which he co-wrote with Francis Durivage. Some critics thought the play had artistic merit, but it failed commercially, as did a second MacKaye play, *Marriage*, also produced during that season.

Perhaps because of these failures MacKaye headed back to Paris for more study, this time at the Comédie Française. In late 1872 he played Hamlet in French at the Paris Conservatoire and the following spring he reprised the role in English in London, becoming the first American to portray Hamlet in England. This marked the high point in his acting career and the end of his focus on it. Instead, while in England he concentrated on writing for the theater, collaborating on plays with Tom Taylor and Charles Reade. When he returned to the United States his adaptation of Ernest Blum's *Rose Michel* was produced in 1875 and became his first hit, running an impressive 121 performances at New York's Union Square Theatre. He wrote or adapted several other plays during the late 1870s, including the farce-comedy *Won at Last*, produced with success in 1877 at Wallack's Theatre in New York. This piece, about a woman who marries for love only to discover that her husband is cynical about it, moved away from melodrama and toward realism in its characters and settings. MacKaye successfully revived *Won at Last* in 1879 to feature his new dramatic company, trained in the principles of Delsarte.

After this production, MacKaye rethought the entire process of running a stock company. To secure the best possible players he proposed to divide 20 percent to 30 percent of the profits among a core of actors, making them feel a part of the venture. To secure the best plays he proposed to offer high royalties to the playwrights who would allow their works to be produced by him. These innovations took place in a new location, a simple but elegant auditorium ventilated by a system that anticipated air conditioning. A double stage facilitated noiseless scene changes in forty seconds, and inventive stage illumination placed less emphasis on footlights and concentrated on light from above. He opened this new space, called the Madison Square Theatre, on 4 February 1880 with his play *Hazel Kirke*. The plot concerns a father who has chosen a man for his daughter to marry, but she has fallen in love with someone else. He curses her: "May my eyes never more behold thee." After many melodramatic complications the daughter, Hazel, returns contrite to her now-blind father, falls into the millrace, is saved from drowning by her true love, and is forgiven by her father. The play became a major hit, running longer than any other nonmusical to that date (nearly 500 performances), then sending out fourteen touring companies. MacKaye could have made his fortune on *Hazel Kirke*, but because he had signed an ill-considered contract with partners, saw almost no profits and left the theater well before the play ended its run.

In the fall of 1884 MacKaye undertook another major project when he and prominent producers the Frohman brothers built the Lyceum Theatre. The auditorium with 614 seats (smaller than the Madison Square) was simply designed and intimate. MacKaye invented an early form of folding theater seats, for easy access and egress, and illuminated the auditorium and stage with electric lights made and installed by Thomas Edison. A permanent company acted in the plays produced at the Lyceum, supplemented by students from the Lyceum School of Acting, another of MacKaye's innovations. The theater opened on 6 April 1885 with *Dakolar*, which MacKaye adapted from the French. The innovative theater received praise, but the play failed, and by the following autumn, after quarreling with the Frohmans, MacKaye resigned his position at the Lyceum. He continued to write plays, including *In Spite of All*, an adaptation of Sardou's *Andrea* produced at the Lyceum by Minnie Maddern Fiske in September 1885, and *Paul Kauvar*, a story of the French Revolution, presented at the Standard Theatre in New York in December 1887.

Also in 1887 MacKaye wrote *The Drama of Civilization*, the scenario for one of Buffalo Bill Cody's wild west shows. In this uncharacteristic work MacKaye moved away from intimate melodrama and toward his last great project, the Spectatorium. MacKaye designed the Spectatorium building for the Chicago World's Fair in 1893 to house his drama/spectacle *The World Finder*, the story of Columbus's journey to the Americas. This theatrical adventure called for monumental scenic elements, and MacKaye attempted to provide them by constructing a huge 10,000-seat, six-story structure, 480 feet wide and 311 feet deep, with a proscenium opening 150 feet wide and 70 feet high. In this gigantic space the scenery, including ships sailing in real water, moved panoramically before the audience, and two tremendous light sources representing the sun and the moon moved along arcs to approximate day and night. This extraordinary effort to reproduce nature was never completed, however. The enterprise went into bankruptcy and construction was stopped. Determined to prove that his visions could be carried out, MacKaye built a scaled-down version early in 1894 called the Scenitorium, which the *Chicago Times* labeled "new, startling, and beautiful" (6 Feb. 1894). The work on this exhibition exhausted MacKaye, and he died less than a month later on a train near Timpas, Colorado.

• MacKaye's papers, including contracts, specifications of his inventions, and manuscripts of many of his plays, are in the collection of the Dartmouth College Library. Debra J. Woodard, "The MacKaye Collection: A Wealth of Americana," *Theatre Survey* 23 (May 1982): 108–10, offers a detailed description of the holdings. Several of MacKaye's plays are available in *America's Lost Plays*, vol. 2 (1940–1941), and *Hazel Kirke* has been anthologized frequently, for example, in Arthur Hobson Quinn, *Representative American Plays* (1917). MacKaye's son Percy MacKaye's *Epoch: The Life of Steele MacKaye* (2 vols., 1927) is the most comprehensive biography, if somewhat subjective, well supplemented by William Winter, *The Life of David Belasco* (2 vols., 1918), and by I. F. Marcosson and Daniel Frohman, *Charles Frohman, Manager and Man* (1916). Modern assessments focus on MacKaye's acting style in Garff B. Wilson, *A History of American Acting* (1966); his technical prowess in Tim Fort, "Steele MacKaye's Lighting Visions for *The World Finder*," *Nineteenth Century Theatre* 18 (Summer–Winter 1990): 35–51; his directing and management style in Wade Curry, "Steele MacKaye: Producer and Director," *Educational Theatre Journal* 18 (Oct. 1966): 210–15; and his attempts at realistic drama in Richard Moody, *America Takes the Stage: Romanticism in American Drama and Theatre, 1750–1900* (1955), and in Kathleen A. McLennon, "A Woman's Place: *Marriage* and America's Gilded Age," *Theatre Journal* 37 (Oct. 1985): 345–46. Obituaries in the *New York Times* and the *New York Herald Tribune*, both 26 Feb. 1894, offer contrasting views of his work.

JACK HRKACH

MACKELLAR, Patrick (1717–22 Oct. 1778), military engineer, was born probably in Scotland. (To date, no information on his parents has been found.) His training, which began in 1735 at Woolwich, continued on Minorca, where he was appointed, by the Board of Ordnance of the British army, in 1742 practitioner engineer, in 1743 engineer extraordinary, and in 1751 engineer in ordinary. Following twelve years of experience there on permanent masonry fortifications, he was sent to North America in 1754 as deputy to chief engineer James Montresor, under the command of Major General Edward Braddock. In 1755 he built roads and bridges in the wilderness in advance of the army's extraordinarily arduous march from tidewater Virginia over the Alleghanies toward the French Fort Duquesne in the Ohio country. Wounded in the ensuing battle of the Monongahela, he drew and captioned two field maps that are indispensable to the story of Braddock's disastrous defeat.

Sent to Oswego, New York, in 1756, Mackellar obtained approval for urgent major reconstruction of Forts Oswego, George, and Ontario but was given neither adequate funds nor manpower for the purpose; nor had he time to do more than begin work before Montcalm's force of French regulars, Canadians, and Indian allies attacked. His journal of the siege, otherwise a most accurate chronicle accompanied by good maps, neglected to mention some British tactical shortcomings that his French counterpart, Desandrouins, perceived as military ineptitude. In discussing the lack of preparedness, Mackellar overlooked the British gunners' failure to foresee a possible attack from the rear. The decision to bid for surrender ("if there was a Chance for any Terms, it must be before an assault was made") stemmed undoubtedly from the hope of French protection from an Indian massacre afterward; Mackellar, however, apparently saw nothing premature in asking for terms while British artillery was severely pounding the attackers. Finally, he was silent as to why the defenders made no attempt to pick off or harass "a great Body of French and Indians [who] had crossed [the Oswego River] at the Rift in order to surround us."

Taken prisoner at the capitulation of Oswego, Mackellar was confined at Quebec and Montreal until he was released in 1757 as part of an exchange. Following a brief tour of duty in Scotland, during which he was commissioned captain, he was promoted major and returned to North America as second engineer to Colonel John Henry Bastide at the siege of Louisbourg (June and July 1758). When Bastide (who knew the terrain well from having been engineer in the siege of 1745) was taken prisoner, Mackellar's conduct earned him an appointment as James Wolfe's chief engineer in the ensuing expedition against Quebec. He was not, however, spared criticism for what Wolfe perceived as slowness at Louisbourg.

Mackellar's report in 1757 to the Board of Ordnance on the defenses of Quebec must have been the best information available to Wolfe two years later, but having been based in part on P. F. X. de Charlevoix's *Histoire et description générale de la Nouvelle France*, published in 1744, it had not taken into account renovations made in and after 1745. The report's basic premise, however, was persuasive: "An Attack by Land is the Only Method that promises Success against the High Town and in all Probability it Could hold out but a very few Days against a Sufficient Force properly Appointed." Lower Town was a different matter. It was reduced to ruins in July 1759 by fire from batteries Mackellar had built on the Island of Orleans, but if it had been taken he was certain it could never have been held. He was wounded in an unsuccessful attack from Montmorency on 31 July. It is uncertain that Mackellar counseled either place or time in Wolfe's decision to scale the cliffs from the Anse du Foulon on 13 September.

Following the taking of Quebec, Mackellar, as chief engineer under James Murray, placed the city in a state of defense for the winter. As a result, the Chevalier de Lévis was unable, after defeating the British at Sainte Foy in April 1760, to effect a breach before the siege was raised. In November, following his recovery from wounds sustained at Sainte Foy, Mackellar was appointed chief engineer at the Halifax citadel, remaining there for a year until joining Robert Monckton's expedition against Martinique. Mackellar besieged Fort Royal, which fell in February 1762. Promoted lieutenant colonel, he successfully conducted very intricate siege operations against Havana, at the end of which he was dangerously wounded. In 1763 he returned to Minorca as chief engineer. He was married, probably after his return, to Elizabeth Basaline of the island; they had two children. In 1777 he was promoted to colonel and director of engineers, and he died in Minorca while still in service.

Mackellar left a legacy of £33,000, in addition to substantial property. His share of prize money from the fall of Havana amounted to £565. Research to date has provided no answer to the question of whether he received a great deal of additional booty on that occasion, as his family implied, or if he, like some other military engineers, transacted lucrative private commerce from the vantage point of his official posts. Perhaps the best opportunity for the latter would have been during the last fifteen years of his life.

"Obscurity and incompetence," wrote Douglas W. Marshall in 1973, "shrouded the reputation of the British engineers in the eighteenth century." To be sure, the British suffered by comparison with the reputations of French, Dutch, and German engineers, but Mackellar's competence was on a par with that of the foreign "imports" who served on the British side in North America. He made a solid contribution to the defeat of France, which freed the Anglo-American colonies from their dependence on Great Britain.

• Mackellar's maps of the battle of the Monongahela and his journal and maps of the siege of Oswego are published in Stanley Pargellis, ed., *Military Affairs in North America* (1936; repr. 1969). His 1757 assessment of Quebec is published in A. G. Doughty, ed., [Captain John Knox's] *An Historical Journal of the Campaigns in North America*, vol. 3 (1916; repr. 1968), pp. 151–60. The same editor published Mackellar's journal of the 1759 siege in *The Siege of Quebec and the Battle of the Plains of Abraham*, vol. 5 (1901), pp. 33–58. His work at Halifax is reported in the correspondence from May to Aug. 1761 within the Amherst papers, Public Record Office, London, WO34/14, which are available at the National Archives of Canada, Ottawa (microfilm). Mackellar's will, and a few other matters related to him, are discussed in Douglas W. Marshall, "The British Military Engineers, 1741–1783: A Study of Organization, Social Origin and Cartography" (Ph.D. diss., Univ. of Michigan, 1976); see also Marshall, "The British Engineers in America, 1755–1783," *Journal of the Society for Army Historical Research* 207 (1973): 155–63. Details of Mackellar's career are found in Whitworth Porter, *History of the Corps of Royal Engineers* (2 vols., 1889). For the judgment of an adversary at Oswego and Sainte-Foy, consult Abbé C. N. Gabriel, *Le Maréchal de Camp Desandrouins, 1729–1792* (1887). A recent assessment of Mackellar is contained in C. P. Stacey, *Quebec 1759: The Siege and the Battle* (1959 and subsequent editions).

FREDERICK J. THORPE

MACKENZIE, Alexander Slidell (6 Apr. 1803–13 Sept. 1848), naval officer and author, was born Alexander Slidell in New York City, the son of John Slidell, a merchant, and Margery Mackenzie. Alexander went by the family name until midlife, when, in 1838, he successfully petitioned the New York legislature to change his surname to Mackenzie, in order to benefit from a legacy that a childless maternal uncle provided.

As a child Alexander was stirred, like multitudes of his countrymen, by the navy's heroism in the War of 1812, and so on 1 January 1815, while that war was still in progress, the eleven-year-old boy entered the navy as a midshipman. For the next decade Slidell served on various ships in the Caribbean and the Pacific. He was aboard the *Macedonian* in the Pacific from 1818 to 1821. In 1822 he took leave from the navy to experience his first command, as captain of a merchant vessel. Returning to the navy, he served aboard the *Terrier*, suppressing piracy in the Caribbean in 1824, an incident of note in light of his reactions during the tragedy that would later envelop his career.

Early in 1825 Slidell was promoted to the rank of lieutenant, and soon after he was granted another extended leave, during which he traveled in Europe. He was that rarity, a studious officer who used his off-duty hours to improve himself by reading widely. Thus in the course of his travels, his culture and amiability caused him to be befriended in Madrid, Spain, by Washington Irving and by the young Henry Longfellow. Both friendships lasted until death severed them.

Slidell's colorful experiences in the Iberian Peninsula formed the basis of his first book, *A Year in Spain* (1829), a vivid, sharply observed travel account published first in Boston and subsequently, to considerable notice, in England. Irving had secured John Murray as his friend's English publisher and had written favorably of the work in the *Quarterly Review* (Feb. 1831).

Now with something of a literary name, Slidell resumed serving in the navy, while simultaneously pursuing his writing career. He cruised aboard the *Brandywine* in the Mediterranean in the early 1830s and, on his return to New York, published his second book, *Popular Essays on Naval Subjects*, in 1833. A tour of England and another visit to Spain provided material for two more books, the pallid *The American in England* (1835) and *Spain Revisited* (1836). In 1835 Slidell married Catherine Alexander Robinson of New York City. They had four children. In 1837–1838 Slidell served as first lieutenant aboard the *Independence* on a cruise to Russia; it was after his return during the latter year that he changed his name.

Now Lieutenant Mackenzie, he commanded the *Dolphin* in 1839 in Brazilian waters. Back in the United States before the year was out, Mackenzie devoted much of his time to writing *The Life of Commodore Oliver Hazard Perry* (1840) and *The Life of John Paul Jones* the following year. During that period he was also working closely with his brother-in-law, Commodore Matthew Perry, commandant of the New York Navy Yard and brother of the late hero of Lake Erie. Matthew Perry and Mackenzie were both much interested in reforming conditions in the navy, and—in hopes of providing means of training personnel more efficiently—Mackenzie, now promoted to commander (Sept. 1841), undertook the command of the new training vessel *Somers*. The brig sailed with a crew of young apprentices on a training mission to Africa in September 1842.

The cruise proved a fateful one. The crossing to Liberia was made without incident, but on the return passage the captain was informed of a mutiny being planned among the crew. He ordered his officers to investigate and on the basis of their findings proceeded to hang at the yardarm three of the alleged ringleaders: two seamen and an eighteen-year-old midshipman named Philip Spencer. At the time of the hanging, the vessel was some two days east of the Virgin Islands. After the burials at sea, the *Somers* put into port briefly at Charlotte Amalie and set course posthaste for New York, arriving battered and exhausted 14 December 1842.

The hanged midshipman was the son of Secretary of War John Spencer. President John Tyler's cabinet officer was overwhelmed by what Mackenzie had done and sought to have the commander tried in a civil court for murder. The navy forestalled that effort, conducting first a court of inquiry into the events aboard the *Somers* and then a court-martial, which dragged on for eight weeks during early 1843. Feelings ran high on both sides, and to this day opinions differ as to the necessity for Mackenzie's actions. Richard Henry Dana and the young lawyer Charles Sumner argued eloquently in the press in the commander's defense. James Fenimore Cooper and Thomas Hart Benton were equally eloquent and thorough in demonstrating that the execution had been an overreaction and that the so-called mutiny, never overt, was only idle chatter and could have been dealt with effectively without loss of life.

On 28 March 1843 the court-martial finally returned a finding of not proven, but thereafter Mackenzie's career in the navy was stalled. He withdrew on leave to his home and family in Tarrytown, near his friend Irving at "Sunnyside" and his brother-in-law Perry, and devoted himself to writing *The Life of Stephen Decatur* (1846). U.S. senator John Slidell of Louisiana, Mackenzie's brother, sought to intervene on his behalf, and other friends interested themselves in his languishing career. As a result, President James K. Polk in 1846 agreed to send the officer on a mission to Havana to negotiate with Santa Anna, who was seeking to return to power in Mexico. Mackenzie's fluency in Spanish stood him in good stead on this trip. Again, during the Mexican War, he acted as interpreter at the surrender of Veracruz and later commanded artillery at the second attack on Tabasco. His last shipboard service was as captain of the steamer *Mississippi* in 1847–1848.

Mackenzie's final days were spent with his wife and children at their modest home on the Hudson. He died while on a solitary horseback ride in Tarrytown, six years to the day after the *Somers* had set sail from Brooklyn on its controversial cruise.

• Alexander Slidell Mackenzie's papers are dispersed, most lost; a few letters are in the Houghton Library, Harvard University. After his death, Mackenzie's wife provided a seventeen-page sketch of her husband's life, published in Evert A. Duyckinck and George L. Duyckinck, *Cyclopaedia of American Literature* (1866). Reports of Mackenzie's naval trials are in *Proceedings of the Court of Inquiry Appointed to Inquire into the Intended Mutiny on Board the United States Brig of War Somers . . .* (1843) and *Proceedings of the Naval Court Martial in the Case of Alexander Slidell Mackenzie . . .* (1844). Bound with the latter volume is James Fenimore Cooper's devastating critique of Mackenzie's decision to execute young Spencer. Documents pertaining to the episode have been collected in Harrison Hayford, ed., *The Somers Mutiny Affair* (1959). The most telling later defense of Mackenzie's actions aboard the *Somers* is in Samuel Eliot Morison, *"Old Bruin": Commodore Matthew C. Perry, 1794–1858* (1967). The fullest modern account of Mackenzie's life, with emphasis on the mutiny and its aftermath, is Philip McFarland, *Sea Dangers* (1985). An obituary is in the *New York Herald*, 14 Sept. 1848.

PHILIP MCFARLAND

MACKENZIE, Jean Kenyon (6 Jan. 1874–2 Sept. 1936), Presbyterian missionary and author, was born in Elgin, Illinois, the daughter of Reverend Robert Mackenzie, who immigrated to the United States from Scotland in 1866, and Lydia Ann McLeod, a native of Novia Scotia. Mackenzie's father was a Presbyterian clergyman and founder and president of the theological seminary at San Anselmo, California. Mackenzie was educated in San Francisco. She attended the Van Ness Seminary in San Francisco from 1888 to 1890, then studied at the Sorbonne in Paris from the fall of 1890 to the spring of 1892. From 1895 to 1896 she was a student at the University of California.

In 1902, when her father became pastor of the Rutgers Presbyterian Church, Mackenzie's family moved to New York City. At this time she expressed a desire to join the West Africa Mission and volunteered for missionary service under the Presbyterian Board of Foreign Missions. In 1904 she was sent to the German colony of Kamerun, where she served for the next ten years at four different stations in the interior of Africa. Three of the stations were located in bush towns, where travel was still by foot, canoe, or other difficult means. Mackenzie soon became loved by the Africans that surrounded her.

As Mackenzie grew accustomed to her new home, she learned the native customs and languages. At one of the coast stations, she spent many hours learning the folklore and stories of the older people. She would later use these stories as material for some of her books.

Mackenzie retired from missionary service in 1914 due to health problems. She returned home to New York, where she devoted her time to writing about Africa, its people, and her mission. Her first publication outlining her life in Africa, *Black Sheep: Adventures in West Africa*, was published in 1916.

At the outbreak of World War I, the mission staff requested that Mackenzie return to Africa. In 1916 Kamerun had been captured from the Germans by France. Native resistance to the French threatened the continued existence of the Presbyterian mission in Africa. Mackenzie's fluency in French and her experiences in Africa, America, and France were thought to be valuable. Accordingly, she agreed to return to help establish Presbyterian missionary work under the new regime and reconcile the Bantu natives to the French.

During her journey to Africa, Mackenzie was detained for six weeks at Las Palmas on the Canary Islands, where ships were being torpedoed outside the harbor. Mackenzie finally reached Kamerun three months later. When she arrived she found that the Bantu and the French were unable to negotiate because of language differences. She interpreted between the French regime and the Bantu tribes and helped restore peace. While in Africa she published *An African Trail* (1917) through the Central Committee on the United Study of Missions. Its purpose was to guide future missionaries in their teaching of the gospel to the African people.

In 1918 Mackenzie returned to New York. She continued to write about her adventures and experiences in Africa in articles and essays that appeared in the *Atlantic Monthly*. Her next book, *The Story of a Fortunate Youth*, was published in 1920. It was her father's biography, a tribute to a man she deeply admired. Portions of the book also appeared in the *Atlantic*.

Mackenzie continued to develop as a writer during the 1920s. Her study *African Clearings* (1924) was praised in the *Atlantic Monthly* and the *New York Times*. Her subsequent book was a collection of love poems titled *The Venture* (1925). *The Trader's Wife* (1930) was well received and highly praised by critics of the day.

From 1932 to 1936 Mackenzie was part of the editorial staff of *Listen*, a magazine for Africans. The articles she published in *Listen* were later republished in the British magazine *Talking Woman*. And during these years her poems and essays were included in anthologies for use in high schools.

Mackenzie continued her church work while she wrote. Among other church duties, she taught a class of girls in the Sabbath school at Rutgers Church and wrote the devotional studies for *Women and Missions*. In 1923 she was elected a member of the Board of Foreign Missions. Three years later she was appointed as a special representative to the international and interdenominational conference in La Zoute, Belgium. The purpose of the conference was to discuss the future of mission work in Africa in light of the rapidly changing economic and social conditions there.

In addition to her writing and missionary work, Mackenzie was a member of the Women Geographers and the Cosmopolitan Club and spoke frequently at churches, colleges, and clubs until poor health overtook her in the early 1930s. She died in New York City.

Although Mackenzie held the patronizing view that missionaries should enlighten the primitive people of Africa, her writing contributed to the genre of mission literature and to the general understanding of a changing continent and its people.

• Other works by Mackenzie include *African Adventures* (1917), *Friends of Africa* (1928), and numerous essays, articles, and poems in the *Atlantic Monthly*. The story "Exile and Postman," *Atlantic Monthly*, Jan. 1917, pp. 22–26, became a minor classic. Fuller accounts of Mackenzie can be found in *Missionary Review of the World*, Dec. 1936, pp. 589–92, and *Women and Missions*, Oct. 1936. An obituary is in the *New York Times*, 3 Sept. 1936.

ELIZABETH ARCHULETA
SUSAN E. GUNTER

MACKENZIE, Murdo (24 Apr. 1850–30 May 1939), cattleman, was born near Tain, Scotland, the son of David Mackenzie and Jessie Mackenzie. As a youth Mackenzie attended the parish school at Balnagown, and in 1869 he graduated from the Royal Academy at Tain. He then served a one-year apprenticeship in a law office, after which he was employed as a clerk in the Tain bank and subsequently as assistant factor on the estate of Sir Charles Ross near Balnagown. He married Isabella MacBain of Tain in 1876; they had five children. He then returned to the local bank as an insurance agent, where he was employed for the next nine years. In 1885 the governing board of the five-year-old Prairie Cattle Company, Ltd., of Edinburgh, Scotland, was seeking a new manager. These businessmen met 35-year-old Mackenzie, noted his excellent skills and background, and hired him to fill the position.

Later that year Mackenzie came to the United States and settled with his family in Trinidad, Colorado, to manage the American operations of the company, the first British ranching corporation to operate in the American West. His duties included overseeing the firm's three divisions with extensive ranges and cattle herds in Colorado, New Mexico, and Texas; shipping and selling its livestock; and protecting the firm's general interests in America. Despite a strong endorsement by the board of directors, he resigned in 1890 because of opposition to some of his management decisions by one of the firm's influential owners.

In 1891 he became American manager of the Matador Land and Cattle Company, Ltd., of Dundee, Scotland, which owned a large range in the Texas Panhandle. He immediately moved the firm's headquarters from Fort Worth, Texas, to Trinidad. Over the years he hired a number of Scottish-immigrant assistants who possessed his preferred work ethic and who already knew about aspects of the cattle business because of their previous agricultural experience. Without carrying a gun, he imposed strict rules on the Matador's cowboys, including bans on gambling and drinking. To protect the firm against drought and ensure a sufficient supply of natural-grass ranges for the livestock, he obtained additional Texas acreage and leased land in Wyoming, the Dakotas, and Saskatchewan.

In 1892 he began to greatly expand the company's controlled breeding activities through acquisitions of purebred Hereford bulls and cows and reduced the herd's size by eliminating all scrub cattle from the firm's fenced ranges. His success in upgrading the Matador cattle began to receive recognition in 1902, and for many years these animals, especially in the carload lot category, won a number of prizes at livestock shows in Chicago, Kansas City, and Denver. Many commercial feeders preferred to buy Matador calves and yearlings—famous for their high quality—to finish for the slaughter market. The firm's cattle brought top prices when they were sold for beef (and occasionally for breeding). In recognition of Mackenzie's important leadership in improving the quality of livestock in the commercial beef-production business, the members of the American Hereford Cattle Breeders' Association elected him in 1910 to their board of directors.

He was elected president of the Texas and Southwestern Cattle Raisers' Association for three terms beginning in 1901. In 1905 he became president of the Colorado-based American Cattle Growers' Association, which became the American National Live Stock Association in 1906. Mackenzie became its first president and was elected to a second term in 1907. In 1896 he began to represent several cattlemen's associations, achieving success in obtaining reduced railroad rates for livestock shipments and in lobbying the federal government for an enlarged and more powerful Interstate Commerce Commission, eventuating in passage of the 1906 Hepburn Act. Because of Mackenzie's support of federal regulation of public land use, his friend President Theodore Roosevelt appointed him to the National Conservation Commission in 1908. From 1923 until 1935 he was a director of the Federal Reserve Bank of Denver.

In early 1912, at the age of sixty-one, Mackenzie moved his family to São Paulo, Brazil, where he was manager of the newly formed Brazil Land, Cattle, and Packing Company, which owned 2.5 million acres, large cattle herds, packing houses, and its own extensive railroad. After successfully completing his employment in South America, Mackenzie and his family returned to the United States in 1918, and in 1922 they settled permanently in Denver, where the Matador company reappointed him as American manager, the position he retained until his retirement in 1937. He also served on the firm's board of directors from 1918 until his death in Denver.

The Mackenzie homes in Trinidad (1885–1911), São Paulo (1912–1918), and Denver (1922–1939) were important centers of social life where many business associates and friends were entertained. On these occasions Mackenzie enjoyed playing his violin, preferring Scottish tunes and dances. For many years he owned a small ranch thirty miles west of Trinidad on the upper Purgatoire River, where he indulged his love of fishing, hunting, and fine horses. The Mackenzies' three sons worked for their father and for the firms he managed.

In recognition of his lifetime of leadership in the cattle business, Murdo Mackenzie was admitted to the Hall of Fame of the Great Westerners at the Cowboy Hall of Fame and Western Heritage Center in Oklahoma City in 1981.

• Records of the Prairie Cattle Company are in the Western Range Cattle Industry Study collection at the State Historical Society of Colorado. Mackenzie's correspondence and the Matador company records are in the Southwest Collection of Texas Tech University, Lubbock. He occasionally published insights into his own work or the livestock business. For example, see his article "The Matador Ranch," *Panhandle-Plains Historical Review* 21 (1948): 94–105, originally completed in 1932, and his articles in the *Breeder's Gazette* (Chicago), e.g., 15 Dec. 1909, p. 1270; 20 Dec. 1911, pp. 1282–83; 26 Dec. 1918, p. 1259; 15 Sept. 1921, p. 369. Mackenzie's early years as American manager of a cattle company are discussed in Albert W. Thompson, "The Great Prairie Cattle Company," *Colorado Magazine* 22 (1945): 76–83. Mackenzie is compared to other western cattlemen in Lewis Atherton, *The Cattle Kings* (1961). The most informed accounts of the Scotsman's life and career are found in three works by William M. Pearce: "The Road to Stability: A Decade in the History of the Matador Ranch, 1891–1900," *Panhandle-*

Plains Historical Review 26 (1953): 1–39; "Murdo Mackenzie," *Dictionary of American Biography*, vol. 22 (1958), pp. 416–17; and *The Matador Land and Cattle Company* (1964). Two studies about important dimensions of Mackenzie's management leadership are Averlyne M. Hatcher, "The Water Problem of the Matador Ranch," *West Texas Historical Association Yearbook* 20 (Oct. 1944): 51–76; and the entry on Mackenzie in Donald R. Ornduff, *The First 49 Personalities in the Honor Gallery of the AHA's Hereford Heritage Hall* (1981), pp. 100–107.

LARRY A. MCFARLANE

MACKENZIE, Ranald Slidell (27 July 1840–19 Jan. 1889), army officer, was born in New York City, New York, the son of Alexander Slidell Mackenzie, a naval officer, and Catherine Alexander Robinson. Raised in Morristown, New Jersey, Ranald began his university education at Williams College and enrolled at the United States Military Academy in 1858. He graduated first in his West Point class of 1862 and was commissioned second lieutenant in the Corps of Engineers. Serving with the Army of the Potomac on the eastern front, he was wounded at the second battle of Manassas. Mackenzie remained with the engineers at the battles of Fredericksburg, Chancellorsville, and Gettysburg, receiving regular promotions to first lieutenant and captain. Wounded several times during the 1864 Petersburg campaign (including the loss of two fingers, which later led Indians to label him "Bad Hand"), he was given the colonelcy of the Second Connecticut Heavy Artillery in July. After participating in the defense of Washington during Jubal Early's raid, he took command of the Second Brigade, First Division, in the Army of the Shenandoah. Mackenzie again distinguished himself at the battle of Cedar Creek where he suffered another wound but won appointment to brigadier general of volunteers. He rejoined the Army of the Potomac in time for the final siege and capture of Petersburg. Mackenzie was breveted brigadier general and major general of volunteers for his brilliant war services.

Following the Confederate collapse, Mackenzie served fourteen months as an engineer at Portsmouth, New Hampshire. He was promoted in March 1867 to colonel of the Forty-first Infantry Regiment, which was dispatched to Fort Brown, Texas. In 1869 army reorganization consolidated the Thirty-eighth and Forty-first regiments (both of which included all-black enlisted personnel) to form the Twenty-fourth Infantry, of which Mackenzie assumed command. Like many white officers, he sought to leave his black unit; in December 1870 he was transferred to command of the Fourth Cavalry Regiment. Taking station with his new unit at Fort Richardson, Texas, Mackenzie soon established himself as one of the Indian-fighting army's most capable officers. Although field operations in northern Texas in 1871 proved discouraging, on 29 September 1872 Mackenzie and 284 troopers razed a Kwahadi Comanche village at McClellan's Creek. His men killed twenty-four Indians and captured another 124; although the cavalrymen burned about one hundred lodges, they lost about three thousand captured ponies the following night to an Indian counterstrike.

The success at McClellan's Creek led the army to transfer Mackenzie and his veteran Fourth to Fort Clark, just north of the Rio Grande, where border raids had become increasingly common. In an April 1873 meeting at the post, General Philip Sheridan authorized his young colonel to use whatever means he deemed necessary to quell the violence, suggesting that President Ulysses S. Grant would also back Mackenzie's judgment. During the night of 17 May, Mackenzie and over 400 scouts and cavalrymen splashed across the Rio Grande. Forty miles inside the Mexican border, they burned several Lipan Apache and Kickapoo villages near Remolino, then returned to the United States on 19 May. The raid pleased Sheridan and seemed to reduce the border incursions for several years but drew the obvious wrath of the Mexican government. Many within the army, including commanding general William T. Sherman, privately criticized the action. In September rheumatism forced Mackenzie to take a leave of absence until January 1874. His return came in time for the colonel to assume a leading role in the Red River War later that year. Among the army's converging columns was Mackenzie's from Fort Concho, which boasted thirteen companies of regulars and thirty-one Tonkawa Indian auxiliaries. Pushing north toward the headwaters of the Red River, on 28 September Mackenzie surprised a large encampment of Kiowa, Cheyenne, Arapaho, and Comanche Indians at Palo Duro Canyon in the Texas panhandle. Almost all of the Indians escaped, but the cavalrymen seized virtually the entire pony herd. Mackenzie distributed about 350 horses to his scouts; then, he ordered the remainder shot.

The destruction of the pony herd after Palo Duro Canyon proved a major factor in convincing the southern Plains tribes to surrender to federal authorities. In 1875, in recognition of his effective campaigning, Mackenzie was given command of strategic Fort Sill in the Indian territory, from which he could force many of the tribes to remain on their reservations. With the destruction of much of George Custer's Seventh Cavalry at the Little Bighorn the following year, Mackenzie and his veteran Fourth were transferred to Camp Robinson, Nebraska. The colonel then commanded the advance guard for George Crook's Powder River expedition in November 1876. His men struck Dull Knife's Northern Cheyenne village on the 25th, where, though the army burned most of the lodges and captured many ponies, Mackenzie blamed himself for not having secured a decisive victory. Returning to the Southwest the following year, Mackenzie led two expeditions across the Mexican border in pursuit of Kickapoo Indians and cattle thieves in 1878. During the first raid, he skirmished with Mexican troops. In 1880 and 1881 he helped remove the Ute Indians from their homelands to reservations in Colorado and Utah, and was then assigned command of the District of New Mexico. He was appointed brigadier general on 26 October 1882 and the following November assumed command of the Department of Texas.

Mackenzie's war wounds and painful bouts with rheumatism had long threatened his health. Sensitive to criticism and frustrated by the slow rate of promotion that so divided the post–Civil War army, Mackenzie was seen by some as becoming increasingly unstable. Upon moving to Fort Sam Houston, Texas, he encountered an old acquaintance, Florida Tunstall, now widowed. She and Mackenzie became engaged, but before the two could exchange vows, the general, whose erratic behavior had alarmed his subordinates, was spirited away to the Bloomingdale Asylum in New York. Diagnosed as suffering from paresis, Mackenzie was found incurably insane by an army board, which officially retired him from military service in March 1884. Though hopeful of returning to duty, he lived with a sister in Morristown, New Jersey, for most of the remainder of his life and died at Staten Island, New York. Army doctors attributed Mackenzie's condition either to his having suffered sunstroke as a child or to a fall from a wagon at Fort Sill in 1875; subsequent biographers have suggested that his symptoms might very well have been caused by syphilis.

Mackenzie was seen by contemporaries as a strict disciplinarian whose Fourth Cavalry was widely considered the best mounted unit in the postwar army. Texans in particular demanded that he be stationed along their borders. Irritable and ambitious, he was among the most controversial officers of his day. Yet Ulysses S. Grant regarded him "as the most promising young officer in the army" (*Personal Memoirs* vol. 2 [1885–1886] p. 541), and consensus has placed Mackenzie alongside George Crook and Nelson Miles as the most effective Indian-fighters of the late nineteenth century.

• Some of Mackenzie's papers may be found at the U.S. Army Military History Research Institute, Carlisle Barracks, Pa., and in Ernest Wallace, ed., *Ranald Mackenzie's Official Correspondence Relating to Texas, 1871–1873* (1967), and *1873–1879* (1968). Biographies include Lessing H. Nohl, Jr., "Bad Hand: The Military Career of Ranald Slidell Mackenzie, 1871–1889" (Ph.D. diss., University of New Mexico, 1962); Ernest Wallace, *Ranald Mackenzie on the Texas Frontier* (1964); and J'Nell L. Pate, "Ranald S. Mackenzie," in *Soldiers West: Biographies from the Military Frontier*, ed. Paul A. Hutton (1987). Brief service records may be found in Mark M. Boatner, III, *Civil War Dictionary* (1959; rev. ed., 1988), and Francis B. Heitman, *Historical Register and Dictionary of the United States Army, from Its Organization . . . to 1903* (1903).

ROBERT WOOSTER

MACKENZIE, Robert Shelton (22 June 1809–21 Nov. 1881), author and journalist, was born at Drew's Court, County Limerick, Ireland, the son of Maria Shelton and Captain Kenneth Mackenzie of the Kaithness Fencibles. Until his late teens, Robert lived with his parents at Fermoy, a small garrison town for which his father acted as postmaster. But before long, young Mackenzie left his first job as a local schoolteacher for the lure of the literary world. While conducting a country journal at Hanley, in Staffordshire, England, the precocious Irish writer issued his maiden book, a volume of poems entitled *Lays of Palestine* (1828). Fifteen years were to intervene before the three-volume historical novel *Titian: A Romance of Venice* (1843) once again staked his claim to belles lettres.

In the meantime, economic demands were making another sort of litterateur of Mackenzie. After moving to London in 1830, the young man languished for some time before finding adequate literary employment. Even then, writing pocket biographies for the *Georgian Era* evidently did not provide sufficient income to keep Mackenzie in the nation's metropolis, as he soon returned to the provinces to edit the *Derbyshire Courier* (from 1831 to 1833). Over the next ten years the Irish-born journalist oversaw a string of papers—among them the fledgling *Liverpool Journal* (beginning in 1834), the *Liverpool Mail* (in the late 1830s), and the *Salopian Journal* (1840 to 1843)—and contributed poems and reviews to several others. In this period Mackenzie also edited a collection of the *Dramatic Works of J. S. Knowles* (1838). This journeyman labor had its rewards. In April 1834 Glasgow University awarded Mackenzie an honorary LL.D. in recognition of his literary attainments, after which he was pleased to claim himself to be the "youngest Doctor of Law in the Empire" (Mackenzie to Sydney, Lady Morgan, Liverpool, 17 Sept. 1834, Sydney, Lady Morgan Collection, Beinecke Rare Book and Manuscript Library, Yale University, New Haven, Conn.). But, aside from developing a network of literary contacts, his work ferreting out biographical lacunae for a projected *Dictionary of Living Authors* came to nought; by the late 1840s Dr. R. Shelton Mackenzie (as the would-be compiler hereafter styled himself) was engaged in the prosaic task of editing a railway journal. Then, having lobbied in support of Lord Brougham's Law Amendment Society, Mackenzie was appointed an official assignee of the Manchester bankruptcy court. No doubt glad of a steady income, he continued in this position until October 1852, when his term of office expired.

All along, Mackenzie had shown an unusual regard for the commercial and aesthetic potential of American as well as British letters; it was in this connection that he was to make his greatest mark. As an early overseas correspondent for the *New York Evening Star* (beginning in 1834), he could (and did) claim to be the first regular British contributor to an American newspaper. Whatever the merits of this claim, Mackenzie's transatlantic connections quickly proved their significance. For, along with publishing literary news in the *Star* and poems and stories in the *New York Mirror*, the *Liverpool Journal*'s chief had also busied himself with charting the progress of the *Mirror*'s celebrated traveling editor, Nathaniel P. Willis, for the folks at home. When word of Willis's gossipy letters of British high society got back to England, the news sparked an international incident that led the young author of *Pencillings by the Way* (1835)—as his letters were entitled in book form—to the brink of a duel even as it estab-

lished him as a perennial fixture on the Anglo-American literary scene. With journalists like Mackenzie reporting the news, the transatlantic culture of celebrity was ever after to be a two-way street.

As for Mackenzie's American connections, in the mid-1830s they had only just begun to bear fruit. For years he kept up his employment as a foreign correspondent. Then, in 1851, he married Georgiana Dickinson, and together they had a child. But when Mackenzie's new wife died tragically soon after, the widower, facing financial troubles, immigrated to the United States. In New York City Mackenzie earned his keep by reviewing literature and drama for several metropolitan newspapers. More important, he parlayed his wide, if anecdotal, knowledge of British literary affairs into a series of edited projects for the publishing house of J. S. Redfield. The most substantial and enduring of these several works were Mackenzie's five-volume compilation of the *Noctes Ambrosianae* (1854), the famous fictive colloquy long featured in *Blackwood's Edinburgh Magazine*, and a five-volume set of the *Miscellaneous Writings of the Late Dr. Maginn* (1855–1857), the irrepressible Irish Tory wit. In each case, Mackenzie supplemented his reprinted material with copious annotations and extensive biographical data, all of which served to accord these volumes definitive status. Yet the emigré editor was not averse to courting sensation; much of the appeal of the *Noctes* collection and the *Writings of Maginn* lay in their free rehearsals of once-libelous writings—like the infamous "Chaldee Manuscript"—that many Americans had probably heard of but perhaps never seen. Nor was Mackenzie above hackwork. His *Bits of Blarney* (1854) and their like were clearly dashed off with an eye toward profit. After his move to Philadelphia in 1857, this breezy quality predominated in Mackenzie's productions. As an editor he often contributed little but window dressing to the many popular volumes that traded on his name. So, too, was his anecdotal *Life of Charles Dickens* (1870) notable primarily as a five-week wonder whose claim that Boz had plagiarized the concept of *Oliver Twist* from the caricaturist Cruikshank was quickly repudiated by more careful scholars. A master of literary gossip, Mackenzie did not age well.

Still, the emigré doctor struck a substantial figure in his adoptive land. A family man (having had three children with his second wife, the German-born author Adelheid Zwissler, whom he had married in 1858), Mackenzie helped to organize the Philadelphia Dental College (now part of Temple University) around this time, afterward serving as the institution's secretary. For twenty years he also presided as the literary editor and drama critic of the *Philadelphia Press*, before ending his career as the literary editor for the *Philadelphia Evening News*. He died in Philadelphia. Though never able to establish entirely convincing claims to eminence in belles lettres, Mackenzie nonetheless proved that the business of literature could offer its more assiduous chroniclers considerable income and a serviceable reputation.

• Mackenzie's extant papers are few and far-flung; the Houghton Library at Harvard University and the Historical Society of Pennsylvania own the largest collections of his correspondence. For Mackenzie's correspondence with British authors, see *The Letters of William and Dorothy Wordsworth*, ed. Alan G. Hill, 2d ed., vols. 5 and 6 (1982); *The Letters of Charles Dickens*, vols. 2, 3, and 5 (1969); David W. Tutein, "Benjamin Disraeli and R. Shelton Mackenzie: Unpublished Letters," *Victorian Newsletter* 31 (Spring 1967): 42–44; and David Bonnell Green, "Elizabeth Barrett and R. Shelton Mackenzie," *Studies in Bibliography* 14 (1961): 245–50. Contemporary appreciations provide much of our knowledge of Mackenzie. See *Ballou's Pictorial Drawing-Room Companion*, 12 Jan. 1856; *Philadelphia Public Ledger*, 22 Nov. 1881; W. C. B., "Robert Shelton Mackenzie," *Notes and Queries*, 28 Sept. 1907, p. 247; and *New York Evening Star*, 15 Oct. 1835. On Mackenzie and Willis, see Thomas N. Baker, "The Trials of Celebrity: Nathaniel Parker Willis and American Culture, 1820–1870" (Ph.D. diss., Univ. of North Carolina, Chapel Hill, 1995). For Mackenzie and Dickens, see John Forster, *The Life of Charles Dickens* (1874).

THOMAS N. BAKER

MACKENZIE, William (30 July 1758–23 July 1828), bibliophile and book collector, was born in Philadelphia, Pennsylvania, the son of Kenneth Mackenzie and Mary Thomas, whose family came from Barbados. William Mackenzie was admitted as a student to the Philadelphia Academy in 1766 by a Captain Morrell, implying that Mackenzie's father may have died before this time. After leaving the academy, Mackenzie entered the offices of John Ross, one of the city's most prominent shipping merchants at the time. There he prospered, gaining an extensive knowledge of accounting and mercantile affairs.

Successful at business and rumored to have inherited a sizable income in his thirties, Mackenzie was "easy in his circumstances" and retired young to pursue a life of scholarship and book collecting. He never married, and by the time of his death in Philadelphia, he had assembled one of the largest libraries in the United States, "by far the most valuable collection of antiquarian and modern books up to then gathered by an American" (Wolf, p. 23). In his will he bequeathed the entire collection, partly in gift and partly under very favorable terms of purchase, to the Library Company of Philadelphia—a total of 7,051 volumes. Such a large bequest to a public library was almost unheard of at the time, and Mackenzie's generosity aroused a great deal of attention in the local press.

Mackenzie was a retiring man who left behind almost no trace of his life aside from his exceptional library. A collector of unusual depth and breadth for his day, he often is referred to as America's first rare book collector. Earlier American book collectors, such as James Logan, William Byrd, Isaac Norris, and Cotton Mather, had more practical, if no less emotional, reasons for creating their libraries: books to them were scholarly, religious, and practical sources, items to be read and studied and used. While collecting on this level, Mackenzie also followed the lead of a growing number of European collectors, who were creating libraries based on aesthetic sensibility and bibliophilic taste.

The dispersal of hundreds of monastic and aristocratic libraries during the French Revolution and the Napoleonic wars created an unprecedented opportunity for collectors such as Mackenzie, who were able to acquire a far greater amount of much older and rarer material on the open market than had previous generations. While few sources for Mackenzie's purchases have been identified, it is known that he bought at local bookstores. He probably frequented the shop of Philadelphia's most literate bookseller of the time, Thomas Dobson, who would have been the only person in town making readily available the wide array of books Mackenzie sought. It is likely that he had a European agent looking out for his interests. His library excels in fine incunables and early sixteenth-century books, a number of which are the only copies known in America. Among them are a copy of Pliny's *Natural History* in Italian, printed by Nicolas Jenson in 1476, on vellum with elaborate illuminations; the first Bible printed in Italy, produced by Sweynheym and Pannartz in 1471; and the first English edition of Jacobus de Voragine's *Golden Legend*, printed by William Caxton around 1485, probably the first Caxton to reach America. Mackenzie favored fine examples of printing and the related arts of engraving and binding; some of his acquisitions, such as John Baskerville's 1757 deluxe edition of Virgil and Jean-Baptiste Oudry's rococo masterpiece of design, La Fontaine's *Fables choisies* (1755–59), are universally acknowledged as epitomes of the printing arts. Mackenzie had a particular fondness for both fine French printing and early literature. His library contains a number of outstanding works of the fifteenth-century printers Guillaume Le Roy and Antoine Verard and the rare first complete edition of Spenser's *Faerie Queen* (1596). But Mackenzie did not limit himself to acquiring old books. His library is rich in Americana, much of it printed while he was collecting. He was the single largest buyer at the sale of the libraries of both William Byrd and Benjamin Franklin; included in these purchases are Byrd's own manuscript library catalog and Franklin's copy of a 1702 emblem book by Joachim Camerarius, used by Franklin and the Continental Congress in designing the first American paper money.

Mackenzie's library is as much his portrait as is the painting of him by John Neagle, presented by James Abercrombie to the Library Company. They both reveal a gentleman of leisure, refinement, and scholarship. Mackenzie became a member of the Library Company in 1786 and was an active philanthropist. The only intimate personal friendship he developed was with Abercrombie, a classmate at the Philadelphia Academy who later was associate pastor of Christ Church. Abercrombie said of his friend that "he believes he never had an enemy, at least, from the purity of his principles and correctness of his conduct, I am sure he never deserved one." In his will Mackenzie bequeathed over $20,000 to individuals and charitable institutions. Among the former were friends such as

Abercrombie, household servants, relatives, and a number of previous residents of Barbados. Institutional beneficiaries included the St. Andrew's Society, the city's charitable organization for Scottish immigrants, which suggests that his father may have been of Scottish birth. Another bequest, demonstrating Mackenzie's continued appreciation of his earliest vocation, went to the Society for the Relief of Poor, Aged and Infirm Masters of Ships. The author of the short introduction to the 1829 printed catalog of his library (probably the printer, Thomas Dobson's son Judah, who was also a coexecutor and beneficiary of Mackenzie's estate) wrote: "His constitution, though vigorous, was not robust, his manners plain and conciliatory, his hand and his purse were ever open and ready to relieve individual and domestic distress, and contribute to public requisitions; in short, in every relation which he bore to society, he exhibited a truly estimable and exemplary character.... He was an accomplished Belles Lettres and classical scholar, and the tenor of his life was an uniform illustration of his principles and the benevolence of his heart." In these modest terms is described the man who, in collecting rare books as such, heralded a new age in American book collecting.

• Archival material relating to Mackenzie can be found in the Philadelphia City Archives, the archives of the University of Pennsylvania and Christ Church, and the Historical Society of Pennsylvania. Contemporary printed sources are the *Catalogue of the Books, Belonging to the Loganian Library*, vol. II (1829) and the *Eighth Supplement to Volume II–Part I of the Catalogue of Books, Belonging to the Library Company* (1829). Secondary sources include Edwin Wolf II, "Great American Book Collectors to 1800," *Gazette of the Grolier Club* 16 (June 1971): 3–70; Marie Korey, "Three Early Philadelphia Book Collectors," *American Book Collector* 2 (Nov.–Dec. 1981): 2–13; and *Quarter of a Millennium: The Library Company of Philadelphia 1731–1981* (1981). Obituaries are in the Philadelphia *Daily Chronicle*, 24 and 28 July 1828, and the Philadelphia *Democratic Press*, 29 July 1828.

KAREN NIPPS

MACKEY, Biz (27 July 1897–22 Sept. 1965), Negro League baseball player and manager, was born James Raleigh Mackey in Eagle Pass, Texas, the son of J. Dee Mackey and Beulah Wright. Mackey was raised in Luling, Texas, where he and his brothers Ray and Ernest played for the Luling Oilers in the Prairie League, and where he learned the art of switch-hitting. In 1918 he began his professional career with the San Antonio Black Aces as a catcher. Two years later, when the Negro National League was organized, C. I. Taylor, manager of the Indianapolis ABCs, purchased Mackey's contract. In March 1922 Mackey played briefly for the Colored All-Stars against a white major league all-star team, led by Babe Ruth and Bob Meusel. Mackey batted .333 (11 hits in 33 at-bats) with two doubles and a triple. In 22 games that he would play against white major league teams, he hit .326 (27 hits in 82 at-bats).

When the Eastern Colored League was formed in 1923, Mackey was traded to Ed Bolden's Philadelphia Hilldale Giants of Darby, Pennsylvania. He led the Hilldale club to three successive league pennants in 1923, 1924, and 1925, hitting .364, .355, and .354, respectively. In 1925, behind Mackey's clutch .375 hitting, the Hilldale club won their first black world series title, beating the Kansas City Monarchs in six games.

A master practitioner behind the plate, Mackey was known for his ability to "call" a game and frame pitches to influence an umpire's decision. He possessed a powerful throwing arm, using a "snap throw" release, which became popular with catchers in the latter part of the twentieth century. He was strong enough to throw to second base from a sitting position, as he routinely did in pre-inning warm ups. Although he stood 6′1″ and weighed between 220 and 245 pounds, he was surprisingly agile behind the plate but lacked speed on the base paths.

In 1927 Mackey made a historic trip to Japan with Lonnie Goodwin's Philadelphia Royal Giants, the first black American team to visit Asia. Mackey became an instant favorite of Japanese fans when he hit the first home run in Tokyo's newly built Meiji Shrine Stadium. Mackey hit three home runs during the Giants' 48-game tour, as they showcased creative gamesmanship to their Japanese counterparts. The diplomatic tour by the black Americans, which took place three years before a similar tour led by Babe Ruth, has been credited by Japanese baseball historian Kazuo Sayama with inspiring the birth of professional Japanese baseball.

Following the demise of the Hilldale Giants, Mackey began playing for the Baltimore Black Sox in 1929. In 1933 he joined Bolden's new team, the independent Philadelphia Stars. Although the Stars were not a member of the Negro National League, Mackey was voted as a starting catcher, ahead of Josh Gibson, to the first East-West All-Star classic in Chicago's Comiskey Park. Mackey would play in five more all-star games in 1935, 1936, 1938, 1941, and 1947, when he received a ceremonial walk at the age of 50. In 1934 the Stars joined the Negro National League, and Mackey helped them beat the Chicago American Giants in the playoffs, four games to three, for the league title. Mackey delivered the game-winning hit in the seventh game.

After three seasons with the Stars, Mackey joined the Washington Elite Giants in 1936. When the Elite Giants moved to Baltimore in 1938, he became player-manager and tutor to a promising athlete named Roy Campanella. "Biz was a great, great catcher in his day," recalled Campanella. "I gathered quite a bit from Mackey, watching how he shifted his feet for an outside pitch, how he threw with a short, quick, accurate throw without drawing back. I didn't think Mickey Cochrane really was the master of defense that Mackey was."

In 1939 Baltimore owner Tom Wilson, satisfied with the progress of the young Campanella, traded the

41-year old Mackey to Effa Manley's Newark Eagles. Although by this time he was past his prime, Mackey was still a bona fide force in the game, hitting over .300 as a part-time catcher from 1940 to 1943. He became the Eagles' manager in 1946. That year, the Eagles won both halves of the Negro National League season, earning the right to challenge the Negro American League champs. With clutch hitting from future major leaguers Monte Irvin and Larry Doby, and superior pitching by Leon Day and Rufus Lewis, they defeated the favorite Kansas City Monarchs, in a hard-fought seven-game series. Retiring from baseball in 1949, Mackey finished his 31-year playing career with an unofficial .350 average.

In a 1952 poll conducted by the *Pittsburgh Courier* newspaper, Mackey was voted the greatest catcher in black baseball by his peers, edging out slugger Josh Gibson as well as Louis "Big Bertha" Santop and Bruce Petway. "For combined hitting, thinking and physical endowment, there has never been another Biz Mackey," recalled Cumberland Posey, who had managed Gibson yet rated Mackey as the best catcher on his all-time team. Posey added, "He was a tremendous hitter, a fierce competitor, although slow afoot, he is the standout among catchers who have shown their wares in this nation." Cool Papa Bell, a teammate of Gibson, once said, "As much as I admired Campanella as a catcher, and Gibson as a hitter, I believe Biz Mackey was the best all-around catcher I ever saw."

A confirmed bachelor, Mackey was a nonsmoker and nondrinker. After retiring from professional baseball he became a fork-lift operator for the Stauffers Chemical Company in Los Angeles, California, where he died. In 1959, at a celebration in his honor in Los Angeles, Campanella spoke highly of his mentor, saying, "I couldn't carry his glove or his bat." The likable, cherub-faced, and good-natured Raleigh "Biz" Mackey was arguably the finest catcher to ever play in the Negro Leagues.

• A file on Mackey is in the National Baseball Library, Cooperstown, N.Y. Mackey is mentioned in complete works by John Holway, *Voices from the Great Black Baseball Leagues* (1975); and Dick Clark and Larry Lester, *The Negro Leagues Book* (1994). Other sources include Larry Barbier, "Do You Remember Biz Mackey?" *Negro Digest*, Feb. 1951, pp. 35–36; John Holway, *Blackball Stars: Negro League Pioneers* (1988); and Larry Lester, "Biz Mackey," in *The Ballplayers*, ed. Mike Shatzkin (1990).

LARRY LESTER

MACKIN, J. Hoover (16 Nov. 1906–12 Aug. 1968), geologist, was born Joseph Hoover Mackin in Oswego, New York, the son of William David Mackin, the owner of a flour mill, and Mary Hoover. Mackin's father died when his son was only seven, so Hoover, as he invariably styled himself, was raised by his mother and his six siblings. He graduated from Oswego High School in 1924 and attended the Oswego Normal School for two years. Entering New York University in 1926, he abandoned an initial interest in journalism after taking George I. Finley's geology course. Stimu-

lated by contact with Douglas Johnson and William Morris Davis he ultimately decided to specialize in geomorphology. After completing his B.S. in 1930, he transferred to Columbia University to complete his M.S. in 1932 and his Ph.D. in 1937. Mackin married Esther Fisk in 1930; they had one daughter and one son.

He was an undergraduate employee in the geology department at New York University from 1928 to 1931 and received a fellowship at Columbia in 1933. He also worked as an assistant to Douglas Johnson. In 1934 he left the Columbia campus after finishing all requirements except his thesis and accepted an assistant professorship in geology at the University of Washington. He was promoted to associate professor in 1940 and to professor in 1946. Resigning in 1961, he accepted the Farish Professorship of Geology at the University of Texas, where he remained for the rest of his career. He held visiting lectureships at the University of Michigan in 1956 and at Stanford University in 1960.

From 1943 to 1954 he investigated mineral deposits as a part-time geologist in the U.S. Geological Survey. From 1955 through 1957 he consulted with the Atomic Energy Commission, again involved in mineral exploration. He was a consultant to the Electricity Authority of Iceland in 1959 and with the U.S. National Aeronautics and Space Administration in 1963. He also consulted with governmental agencies, state highway departments, and businesses on problems of engineering geology. After 1950 he was widely consulted on hydroelectric projects in the United States.

Mackin was primarily a geomorphologist but made significant contributions to economic geology resulting from his wartime and postwar service with the U.S. Geological Survey and the Atomic Energy Commission. A study of iron deposits in the Iron Springs District, Utah, was Mackin's major research effort in economic geology. His investigation clearly established the source of the iron, its mode of accumulation, and its relationship to the geologic history of the region. It is generally considered one of the best studies of its kind. Mackin also became interested in the relationships between extrusive volcanic deposits in the Great Basin and uranium accumulation. To attack this problem he and his students mapped about 10,000 square miles, some of it in detail and some in reconnaissance, and determined for the first time the very great aerial extent of individual ignimbrite deposits. Ignimbrites are fine-grained volcanic rocks deposited as incandescent ash after volcanic explosions. Mackin developed techniques for recognizing rocks resulting from individual eruptions and thus was able to trace them over thousands of square miles and place them in temporal sequence. His work was unprecedented in scale and revolutionized the geological study of such phenomena.

Mackin's study of gravel-capped terraces in the Big Horn Basin of Wyoming introduced the concept of their origin through lateral planation by streams essentially at grade rather than by downward erosion by streams dissecting older alluvial deposits. His paper

"Concept of the Graded River" (*Bulletin of the Geological Society of America* 59 [May 1948]: 463–511) discusses how streams immediately react, both upstream and downstream, to damming or diversion. This establishes the scientific basis for predicting altered stream conduct resulting from disturbing the natural equilibrium of a stream.

Mackin was active in professional affairs as a fellow of the Geological Society of America and a member of the Society of Economic Geologists, the American Association for the Advancement of Science, the American Geophysical Union, the American Association of Petroleum Geologists, the British Glaciological Society, the Society of Mining Engineers, the New York Academy of Science, and Sigma Xi. He was chair of the Cordilleran Section of the Geological Society in 1950 and councillor of the Geological Society from 1950 to 1953. He was a distinguished lecturer of the American Association of Petroleum Geologists in 1953 and a national lecturer for Sigma Xi in 1963. He was chair of the Division of Earth Sciences, National Research Council, in 1963–1965. He was a member of the National Academy of Sciences and of the Cosmos Club. Mackin died in Austin, Texas.

• A collection of Mackin's field notes is at the U.S. Geological Survey Library, Denver, Colo. A biographical sketch of Mackin by Harold L. James in National Academy of Sciences, *Biographical Memoirs* 45 (1974): 349–62, concisely outlines Mackin's career and contributions. See also a memorial by James Gilluly in *Proceedings of the Geological Society of America for 1968* (1971): 206–11.

RALPH L. LANGENHEIM, JR.

MACKINTOSH, Ebenezer (20 June 1737–1816), shoemaker and mob leader, was born in Boston, Massachusetts, the son of Moses Mackintosh, who served on occasion as a soldier during the 1730s and 1740s, and Mary Everet. The family name has also been spelled MacIntosh, McIntosh, and McKintosh. Mary died in 1751, and Moses left town, leaving young Ebenezer in the care of his uncle Ichabod Jones, a shoemaker to whom he was apprenticed. Ebenezer enrolled in the militia in 1754 and served on the British-colonial expedition to Fort Ticonderoga in 1758.

In 1760 the young cordwainer joined Fire Engine Company No. Nine in Boston's South End. In that capacity he rose to be leader of the South End Mob, which each year on 5 November—Guy Fawkes Day or "Pope's Day"—fought with the rival North End Mob over their respective effigies of the Pope, which the winners burned. The riot of 1764 was unusually violent, resulting in many injuries and the death of a young boy whose head was crushed by a cart bearing a "pope." Mackintosh and others were arrested but never tried, their bonds provided by members of the Loyal Nine, a political club that soon played a key role in Boston's revolutionary movement as a liaison between the crowd and upper- and middle-class groups like merchants' associations and the Sons of Liberty. In addition to escaping punishment for the Pope's Day violence, in 1765 Mackintosh was elected sealer of leather, an unpaid town office. Eager to ensure crowd leaders' loyalty to the cause, former tax collector Samuel Adams sued the shoemaker for approximately £12 in back taxes in July 1765, perhaps to remind Mackintosh that he needed the patriots to keep him out of legal trouble. The debt was not collected.

Mackintosh more than repaid the debt by his leadership of the Stamp Act mobs. On 14 August 1765 he probably headed the mob that pulled down a small building that Andrew Oliver, recently chosen stamp master of the province, had erected on Oliver's Wharf. Oliver was then compelled to declare that he would not exercise his office. Twelve days later, Mackintosh was present when a mob destroyed the Boston mansion of Lieutenant Governor Thomas Hutchinson, forcing him to flee for his life, dismantling his possessions, stealing his money, and scattering his collection of manuscripts and his uncompleted history of Massachusetts in the streets. The offices and residences of customs officials William Story and Benjamin Hallowell were also vandalized. Historians have disputed whether Mackintosh and his fellows acted autonomously, moving beyond the orderly protests favored by leading citizens, or whether upper and lower orders acted in tandem, as Loyal Nine member and merchant Henry Bass suggested when he wrote: "We do everything in order to keep this . . . private, and are not a little pleased to hear that Mackintosh has the credit of the whole affair" (Massachusetts Historical Society, *Proceedings* 44 [1910–1911]: 609). In any case, prominent Whigs prevented Suffolk County sheriff Stephen Greenleaf from holding Mackintosh after his arrest by promising that order could be maintained in Boston, but only if Mackintosh were free.

Later that year, the North and South End mobs, led by "General" Mackintosh, combined forces to parade rather than riot, discarding their popes for effigies of contemporary representatives of tyranny such as the Earl of Bute and George Grenville, author of the Stamp Act. In December Oliver's written resignation as stamp master being deemed insufficient, Mackintosh and his followers escorted Oliver to the Liberty Tree and forced him to abjure his office publicly. Observers noted that the town militia refused to protect Oliver and that many of them marched in the procession headed by Mackintosh, "arm in arm" with Colonel William Brattle, the militia's commander.

Mackintosh, it seems, could command a crowd with a whisper or gesture, and, in order to demonstrate the popular will, sometimes marched as many as 2,000 people in orderly, quiet files past the general court while it sat. Peter Oliver, Andrew's brother, fellow loyalist, and justice of the superior court, remarked that Mackintosh was "sensible and manly" and, referring to the town's radical leaders, said he "performed their dirty jobs for them with great éclat." Lieutenant Governor Hutchinson termed him "a bold fellow and as likely for a Massianello [a Sicilian revolutionary] as you can well conceive. When there is occasion to hang or burn effigies or pull houses these [the "rabble"] are employed" (Hutchinson to Thomas Pownall, 8 Mar. 1766, Massachusetts Archives 26: 207–14).

However, though the town meeting again elected him sealer of leather in 1766, 1767, and 1768, Mackintosh by 1769 had been eclipsed as a crowd leader. The reasons are unclear, but George Mason, a British informer, suggested his relationship with the revolutionary leadership had soured. Because Mackintosh knew "more of their Secret Transactions than the whole of what they call the Torys put together," Mason claimed that leaders of the Sons of Liberty, had "threatened [Mackintosh] with Death in case he should inform (qtd. in Anderson, "A Note," pp. 360–61). Mackintosh was not reelected sealer of leather in 1769, spent time in debtors' prison the following year, and eventually disappeared. Peter Oliver thought him dead. But in fact he had moved to Haverhill, New Hampshire, where he was living by September 1774. He served that town in his old position as sealer of leather (1782–1784), having enlisted for two months in the army to oppose British General John Burgoyne's invasion of New York in 1777.

Mackintosh had married Elizabeth Maverick in August 1766; his seventeen-year-old brother-in-law, Samuel, was one of the Boston Massacre's victims in 1770. The couple had two children, one of whom, Paschal (or Pasquale) Paoli, was named for the Corsican freedom fighter then leading his ethnically Italian island in revolt against the French. Elizabeth died in 1784; Mackintosh subsequently married a widow, Elizabeth Chase, with three children. Three more children followed. A number of Mackintosh's progeny moved to Ohio. At age sixty-five, he walked there and back to visit them. In old age he claimed to have led the Boston Tea Party, which is unlikely, given his earlier rift with the patriots, but not impossible. Ironically, this fighter for liberty had to sell his services to the overseer of the Haverhill poor farm in 1810–1811 in order to survive. When he died in Haverhill, New Hampshire, he was buried in the local cemetery, where he is erroneously identified as Philip McIntosh and credited with leading the Boston Tea Party.

An obscure shoemaker who briefly made history in 1765 and 1766, Mackintosh's leadership shaped crowd violence in prerevolutionary Boston. Called a dupe by the loyalists, he nevertheless seems to have been a sincerely committed patriot, as the naming of his son in 1770 suggested. Director and symbol of the lower-class Bostonians without whom the American Revolution would never have occurred, he deserved better than the poverty and mislabeled tombstone that marked the end of his days.

• Two articles by George Pomeroy Anderson, "Ebenezer Mackintosh: Stamp Act Rioter and Patriot," and "A Note on Ebenezer Mackintosh," in Colonial Society of Massachusetts, *Publications* 26 (1924–1926): 15–64 and 348–61, constitute remarkably thorough pieces of historical detective work. A surprisingly sympathetic sketch appears in Peter Oliver, *Origin and Progress of the American Rebellion*, ed. Douglass Adair and John A. Schultz (1961). See also Dirk Hoerder, *Crowd Action in Revolutionary Massachusetts, 1765–1780* (1977),

and, for the Stamp Act riots, Edmund S. Morgan and Helen M. Morgan, *The Stamp Act Crisis: Prologue to Revolution* (1953).

WILLIAM PENCAK

MACKLIN, Madge Thurlow (6 Feb. 1893–14 Mar. 1962), medical scientist, was born in Philadelphia, Pennsylvania, the daughter of William Harrison Thurlow, a stationery engineer, and Margaret De Grofft. She received an A.B., Phi Beta Kappa, in 1914, at Goucher College, Baltimore.

In the summer of 1914 Macklin first demonstrated her passion for social justice by volunteering to address the public on street corners and at open-air meetings in and around Baltimore on behalf of woman suffrage. That experience of recognizing social injustice motivated her to become a physician, in which capacity she felt she could be more effective.

After completing a fellowship in physiology (1914–1915) at Johns Hopkins University, she attended Johns Hopkins Medical School, from which she graduated cum laude in 1919. While at Johns Hopkins she met Charles Macklin, a young Canadian anatomist who had come to Johns Hopkins in 1914 as an instructor in anatomy. In the summer of 1916 they went to Philadelphia, where for several months they stayed with her parents and carried out research at the Wister Institute. There they investigated whether a certain dye would be incorporated into new bone and thereby provide a method of measuring the fate of bone grafts. This resulted in their first joint publication, in 1918, while Madge was still a medical student. That same year she married Charles Macklin. After receiving her M.D. in 1919, Madge Macklin worked as an instructor at the School of Hygiene of Johns Hopkins University.

In 1921 Charles Macklin accepted an offer to become head of the Department of History and Embryology at the University of Western Ontario in London, Canada. Madge Macklin was appointed an instructor in the same department at a nominal stipend, which was rescinded for several years during the depression. She taught histology and embryology, and her earliest publications, several coauthored with her husband, were in the field of microscopic anatomy. By 1926, however, Macklin had become interested in medical genetics, the discipline in which she would earn her reputation. Her nearly 200 publications in this field were concerned with the hereditary aspects of abnormalities of the eye, hemophilia, cancer, and mental retardation. The latter focus led to her becoming an outspoken eugenicist in the 1930s; she was executive secretary of the Eugenics Society of Canada between 1932 and 1935, and its director in 1935.

Using data from mental hospitals in Ontario from 1891 to 1934 gathered on both mentally ill (i.e., psychotic) and mentally retarded individuals, she predicted a continued increase in these groups, with startling repercussions: "the steadily falling birth rate noticeable chiefly among the more intelligent classes . . . the greater fecundity of the classes producing mental defectives . . . can lead to only one end, complete submersion and disappearance of the normal stock" (*Eugenical News*, July–Aug. 1934, p. 99). In another paper in the *Canadian Medical Association Journal* in the same year she wrote that she was not presenting propaganda for or against sterilization of mental defectives but simply demonstrating "scientific data which deal with the genetic aspects of the question." At the conclusion of this paper she wrote "although I am strongly in favour of sterilization of the mentally unfit, the above figures and the above genetical analysis of the situation are not the ideas of a propagandist; they are incontrovertible scientific facts" (30 [1934]: 13). She is careful to add that her arguments apply only if the defects are inherited and not environmental in character. Indeed, more than one subsequent generation of geneticists has tried to grapple with the difficulties of disentangling the relative importance of nature versus nurture.

As Canada's most scientific defender of the rationality of eugenics in the 1930s, Macklin advocated the inclusion of medical genetics in the medical school curriculum. She wrote several papers emphasizing the reasons why genetics should be part of the education of every medical student. Her first significant public address on this subject was to the Association of American Medical Colleges in November 1932. The response to her appeal, however, appears to have been indifference; for several years thereafter the only school with a course in medical genetics remained Ohio State University.

The mother of three daughters, Macklin later boasted, "I have lost one period of four months, one of two months and another of three weeks from teaching and research while I had the three daughters" (Soltan, p. 16). Although she had a housekeeper, she went home each day at lunch and was present when the children returned at the end of the afternoon. Thus, she adumbrated most impressively the modern woman's juggling of career and family.

In 1945 Macklin was informed by the administration at the University of Western Ontario that her sessional appointment, for which she received only $700 a year, would not be renewed. Clashes with some of her colleagues and perhaps her earlier involvement with eugenics, by then completely discredited, in large part by the taint of Nazi Germany's espousal of the eradication of mental defectives, contributed to the reasons for her summary dismissal.

In 1946 Macklin was appointed cancer research associate at Ohio State University and finally was able to give a course in medical genetics. During the next thirteen years her research and publications focused on heredity and cancer, particularly cancer of the breast. In one six-year study, begun in 1946, she found that relatives of women with breast cancer had breast cancer with a frequency significantly greater than that of women in the general population.

In 1957 Macklin received the Elizabeth Blackwell Award for her distinguished career and in 1959 realized her crowning achievement, the presidency of the American Society of Human Genetics.

During the thirteen years from 1946 to 1959 she traveled monthly from Columbus, Ohio, to London, Ontario, where her husband had remained and where she resumed her domestic chores for a few days. Not long after her retirement in 1959 her husband died, and Macklin moved to Toronto, to the home of her eldest daughter, where she died.

Madge Macklin was a distinguished scientist, recognized internationally by her peers but ultimately treated shabbily by her own faculty of medicine. Her reputation rests mainly on her tireless efforts to encourage recognition of the importance of medical genetics. She was prophetic in 1938, when, lamenting that only one medical school in North America had a compulsory course in medical genetics, she predicted that in twenty-five years every first-class medical school would have a curriculum in which students would be exposed to the fundamentals of genetics and the application of genetics to the practice of medicine.

• Selected papers from Macklin's extensive list of publications include seven sequential papers on "Hereditary Abnormalities of the Eye" in the *Canadian Medical Association Journal* 16 (1926): 1340–42 and 17 (1927): 55–60, 327–31, 421–23, 697–702, 937–42, 1191–97, 1336–42, 1493–98; "Mongolian Idiocy: The Manner of Its Inheritance," *American Journal of Medical Science* 178 (1929): 315–38; "The Teaching of Inheritance of Disease to Medical Students: A Proposed Course in Medical Genetics," *Annals of Internal Medicine* 6 (1933): 1335–43; "Genetic Aspects of Sterilization of the Mentally Unfit," *Canadian Medical Association Journal* 30 (1934): 190–95; "The Role of Heredity in Disease," *Medicine* 14 (1935): 1–75; "Erythroblastosis Foetalis: A Study of Its Mode of Inheritance," *American Journal of Diseases of Children* 53 (1937): 1245–67; "The Use of Monozygous and Dizygous Twins in the Study of the Mode of Inheritance," *American Journal of Obstetrics and Gynecology* 59 (1950): 359–64; and "Comparison of the Number of Breast Cancer Deaths Observed in Relatives of Breast Cancer Patients and the Numbers Expected on the Basis of Mortality Rates," *Journal of the National Cancer Institute* 22 (1959): 927–51. For further information on Macklin and her work, see H. C. Soltan, ed., *Medical Genetics in Canada: Evolution of a Hybrid Discipline* (1992), and Angus McLaren, *Our Own Master Race: Eugenics in Canada, 1885–1945* (1990).

PETER A. RECHNITZER

MACLAY, Samuel (17 June 1741–5 Oct. 1811), surveyor and politician, was born in Lurgan Township, Franklin County, Pennsylvania, the son of Charles Maclay and Eleanor Query, both immigrants from Ireland. The details of his childhood are unknown, except that he was educated at the classical school of the Reverend Dr. Alison. During 1767–1768 Maclay was an assistant to his brother William Maclay, who had been appointed deputy surveyor of Cumberland County, Pennsylvania. In 1769 he assisted William in the surveys of the "Officer's Tract," land awarded to officers who had served under the colonial government, in Buffalo Valley, largely in Mifflin County. Maclay became a large landowner there and made his lifelong home in Buffalo Valley. In 1773 he married Elizabeth Plunkett, granddaughter of John Harris, the founder of Harrisburg. They had nine children.

Although busy with both farming and surveying, Maclay became a leader in the public affairs of his community. As the American Revolution approached, he joined the local Committee of Correspondence. When war broke out, Maclay was commissioned a lieutenant colonel in a battalion of "associators," or state militia. On 4 July 1776 he was a delegate to the convention at Lancaster, Pennsylvania, that organized the associators. During the war he saw active service.

With the war over, he began his political career. In 1787 he was elected to the lower house of the state legislature, where he served until 1791. On 9 April 1790 the Supreme Executive Council of Pennsylvania commissioned Maclay, Timothy Matlack, and John Adlum to explore the headwaters of the Susquehanna River and the streams of the New Purchase, the northwestern portion of the state recently purchased from the American Indians. They were also to survey for a possible route for a road to connect the waters of the Allegheny River and the West Branch of the Susquehanna. Maclay kept a journal, beginning 20 April, detailing the weather, landscape, canoes, illnesses, guides, and food.

In February 1792 Maclay was appointed one of the associate judges for Northumberland County, and he held this position until his election to the Fourth U.S. Congress in the fall of 1794. He won his congressional seat by a large majority in an overwhelmingly Republican area, where he was widely respected for his character and abilities. However, a local Presbyterian minister, the Reverend Hugh Morrison, was adamantly opposed to the Jeffersonians and lectured Maclay from his pulpit. Maclay then left the congregation, and many of its members followed him. Morrison attempted a slander suit, which was discontinued and merely served to increase Maclay's popularity.

In Congress during the 1795–1797 term, Maclay took part in an unsuccessful attempt to defeat the proposed Jay Treaty and embarrass the George Washington administration. The Jeffersonian opposition bitterly resented this agreement, reached in 1794 with England. Maclay stated on the House floor that he could not "discover those merits in the Treaty which other gentlemen cried up" (*Annals of Congress* [Apr. 1796], p. 974). His opposition to the treaty further increased his popularity with his constituents at home.

The remarks of Congressman Maclay also revealed his experiences on the frontier, the influence of his classical education, and his continuing habit of wide reading. For example, during the House of Representatives' discussion on the distribution of national lands, he wished to be fair to both "moneyed men and men of small property." He contended that the land to be disposed of was a "great common right to which every citizen . . . was entitled to a share" (*Annals of Congress* [Feb. 1796], pp. 346–47). It would, therefore, be unjust to allow all of the land to go on the market at once, to be grabbed up by the wealthy; some must be set aside for those who might be able to afford it later.

Maclay returned to the Pennsylvania state legislature's lower house in 1797, and he served in the upper house from 1798 to 1802. He was elected Speaker of the state senate in 1801 and 1802. On 14 December 1802 he was chosen U.S. senator, and as Speaker of the state senate, he signed his own election certification. Maclay retained the Speakership, presiding over a judicial impeachment trial in January 1803, and did not resign the Speakership until 16 March 1803. He held onto his state senate seat until 2 September 1803.

On 4 March 1803 Maclay began his term as U.S. senator from Pennsylvania, representing his state as a Republican in the Eighth Congress. Senator Maclay was not prominent in debates, but he did propose three amendments to the U.S. Constitution. He was faithful to the Republican administration of Thomas Jefferson, and when Senator John Smith of Ohio was charged in connection with the Aaron Burr conspiracy, Maclay introduced the resolution to investigate Smith.

On 4 January 1809, before his term was concluded, Maclay resigned his Senate seat. His health was not good, and he returned to private life on his farm in Pennsylvania. Not quite three years after retiring from the U.S. Senate, he died at his farm in Buffalo Valley.

Maclay's classical education extended throughout his life, as he acquired and enjoyed a large library of many valuable books. He was a "good scholar and efficient writer," and his notebooks from his surveying expeditions "indicate a cultivated hand" (Linn, pp. 401–2). Contemporaries spoke of him as being a popular person. He was "of the people and for the people, plain and simple in his manner" and "one of the ablest statesmen of Pennsylvania" (Meginness, p. 5).

• John F. Meginness published and annotated Maclay's *Journal of Samuel Maclay while Surveying the West Branch of the Susquehanna, the Sinnemahoning and the Allegheny Rivers, in 1790* (1887), which details this arduous expedition and also contains a biographical sketch. The remarks of Congressman Maclay are in the *Annals of Congress* (Mar. 1795–Mar. 1797), 4th Cong., 1st sess., pp. 346, 347, 974. Biographical sketches of Maclay are in Edgar S. Maclay, *The Maclays of Lurgan: Being a Biographical Sketch of the Descendants of Charles and John Maclay Who Came to America in the Year 1734* (1889), which also gives genealogical backgrounds in England, Ireland, and Scotland; and John Blair Linn, collator, *Annals of Buffalo Valley, Pennsylvania, 1775–1855* (1877). For background on the Jay Treaty see Samuel Flagg Bemis, *Jay's Treaty: A Study in Commerce and Diplomacy* (1923; repr., 1962). Also of interest are H. V. Ames, "The Proposed Amendments to the Constitution of the United States during the First Century of Its History," *Annual Report of the American Historical Association for the Year 1896*, vol. 2 (1897); and F. J. Turner, "Correspondence of the French Ministers to the United States, 1791–1797," *Annual Report of the American Historical Association for the Year 1903*, vol. 2 (1904). An obituary is in *Annals of Buffalo Valley, Pennsylvania, 1755–1855*.

SYLVIA LARSON

MACLAY, William (20 July 1737–16 Apr. 1804), surveyor, legislator, and diarist, was born in New Garden Township, Chester County, Pennsylvania, the son of Charles Maclay and Eleanor Query, farmers, both of whom had emigrated from Lurgan in County Antrim, Ireland, three years earlier. In 1742 the family moved to what became Lurgan Township in Franklin County, three miles north of what is now Shippensburg. John Blair presided over an academy there at which William began his formal education. To further his studies he was sent to Samuel Finley's academy at West Nottingham in Chester County.

The imposing 6′3″ Maclay probably began his military career as early as 1755 as an ensign in the Third Pennsylvania Battalion of the British army. In 1758 he was commissioned a lieutenant and assisted in the survey and construction of a road across the western Pennsylvania mountains. Before he returned to active duty in the Indian campaigns of 1763 and 1764, Maclay studied law and opened a practice at Carlisle, the seat of Cumberland County. Between the two Indian campaigns Maclay traveled to London to visit Thomas Penn, proprietor of Pennsylvania, seeking land grants for the Pennsylvania officer corps. He so impressed Penn that Maclay was in 1764 appointed deputy land surveyor for Cumberland County. By the time Maclay ceased surveying in the 1790s, his surveys had become the basis for land titles in a half-dozen of Pennsylvania's present-day counties. His own extensive landholdings and financial independence resulted primarily from this work during the decade preceding the War for Independence.

In April 1769 Maclay married Mary Harris, the eldest daughter of John Harris, Jr.; between 1770 and 1787 they had eleven children, all but three of whom survived infancy. The couple settled at the site of Mifflintown on the Juniata River, where they resided until 1772. In that year they moved to Fort Augusta (now Sunbury) in newly created Northumberland County. This remained Maclay's home and political base for the next twenty years. County government consisted of twelve appointed justices. From 1772 until 1786, except when he represented the county in the assembly, Maclay held one of these positions. In addition, he served as prothonotary, register, recorder, and clerk of the county court, lucrative offices that he was appointed to in 1772.

A supporter of the Declaration of Independence, Maclay served on the Northumberland Committee of Safety and offered to assist in the manufacture of flints. Maclay advocated the use of trained dogs against the British army; despite the ridicule of friends, he sent the idea to the new state government, which transmitted it to Commander in Chief George Washington. Early in 1779 he became an assistant commissary for purchase. He was particularly active in supplying General John Sullivan's successful expedition against the Iroquois in July 1779. In 1782 he performed similar functions for the state.

The independent-minded Maclay spent fifteen of the last twenty-five years of his life as an elected member of a legislative body. As a legislator he had a high sense of self-sacrifice and duty to the public interest. He was economy-minded, democratic, uncompromising, suspicious of motive, incapable of placing party loyalty first, and deeply concerned for—and defensive of—his own reputation and that of the state he represented. First elected to the Pennsylvania assembly in October 1781, Maclay was reelected in 1782. It is likely he ran for reelection in 1784 and lost. Disputed elections in 1783 and 1785 were resolved in his favor. In the spring of 1786, however, the Constitutionalists prevented him from assuming a seat. In October 1786 he was elected to represent Northumberland and adjoining counties for a three-year term on the supreme executive council. Maclay differed with the majority of his constituents in supporting the Pennsylvania Republican, or Anti-Constitutionalist, party and showing great sympathy for Philadelphia and its interests. His last major involvement in state politics was the petition drive by Republicans for the calling of a convention to draft a new state constitution.

Maclay's public life during the 1780s was not limited to popularly elected office. Pennsylvania frequently turned to him to fulfill a variety of special commissions related to inland navigation, land purchases from the Indians, and state boundaries. His absence from the Treaty of Fort McIntosh in January 1785 lends credence to the story that he traveled to England in that year to meet with the Penns, for whom he continued to act as an agent. Between 1783 and 1785 Maclay assisted his father-in-law, Harris, in the creation of Dauphin County and the survey, platting, and establishment of Harrisburg as its seat. Maclay also surveyed and platted Maclaysburg on part of a 200-acre tract he owned on the northern border of Harrisburg. Both developers set aside land to be purchased by the state should it decide to move its capital there.

When the U.S. Constitution was proposed in 1787, Maclay, like many of his fellow Pennsylvania Republicans, became a Federalist. He was actively involved in organizing the state nominating convention at Lancaster that recommended a slate of Federalists for election to the first U.S. House of Representatives. On 30 September 1788 he became the first person elected to a seat in the U.S. Senate. There he aggressively opposed titles for federal officials as un-American and Alexander Hamilton's plans for funding the revolutionary war debt as anti-agrarian and as a welfare program for the rich. His most important contribution was the keeping of a diary, which provides insight into the politics of the First Federal Congress as it implemented the Constitution as well as into the personality of the man who kept it. It marks him as one of the first Federalists to break with the party. Since Maclay drew a two-year term in the first Senate, he had to stand for reelection in 1790. No candidate could muster a majority vote and the seat remained vacant during the Second Congress.

Sometime in 1791 the family moved to Maclaysburg. Efforts to elect him to either the U.S. House or Senate as a Democratic-Republican failed in 1792 and

1793. In October 1795 Maclay began three terms in the Pennsylvania House of Representatives, representing Dauphin County. He supported dozens of internal improvement bills to aid the growing population in the area where he had been a wilderness surveyor thirty years earlier. While in the house he voted in favor of term limits for U.S. senators and against an address expressing regret at the retirement of Washington as president. His most controversial action was the introduction of a resolution that declared Pennsylvania's opposition to war except in cases of invasion. This cost him reelection. Maclay served as a Jefferson presidential elector in 1796.

Between 1798 and 1801 Maclay held no office, and between 1801 and 1803 he held only Dauphin County judicial offices. In October 1803 Dauphin sent him back to the Pennsylvania House of Representatives, where he found himself in the unusual position of senior statesman of the majority Democratic-Republican party. Both political friends and enemies believed that he had returned to the legislature solely for the purpose of moving the state capital to more centrally located Harrisburg, an event that occurred a few years after his death. A lifelong Presbyterian, Maclay, who died in Harrisburg, was buried at that city's Paxtang Church.

• Most of Maclay's papers have disappeared. Various editions of the manuscript diary are at the Library of Congress. The modern edition, *The Diary of William Maclay and Other Notes on Senate Debates*, vol. 9 of *The Documentary History of the First Federal Congress, 1789–1791* (1988), contains a long biographical sketch as well as information about the diary and Maclay's papers. The most complete account of his life is Heber G. Gearart, "The Life of William Maclay," Northumberland County Historical Society, *Proceedings* 2 (1930): 46–73.

KENNETH R. BOWLING

MACLAY, William Brown (20 Mar. 1812–19 Feb. 1882), congressman and state legislator, was born in New York City, the son of recent Scottish immigrants, the Reverend Archibald Maclay, pastor of the Mulberry Street Church (Baptist), and Mary Brown. In 1836 Maclay graduated with highest honors from the University of the City of New York. Attracted to books, scholarship, and the world of the intellect, he accepted a position at his alma mater teaching Latin (language and literature) and also became associate editor for the *New York Quarterly Review*. Although he soon determined to make law his career, he always valued education and learning highly and served on his university's board of trustees from 1838 until his death.

In 1838 Maclay married Antoinette Walton; they had three children. In 1839 Maclay was admitted to the bar and formed a partnership with his brother-in-law, Isaac P. Martin. Seeking public office was a way for young lawyers to become better known in a large city like New York, and in 1839 Maclay ran successfully as a Democrat for the state assembly. He was reelected in 1840 and 1841. Despite his comparative youth Maclay assumed a leadership position, especial-

ly on matters related to New York City. His associates credited him with developing the statutes that reorganized the superior and common pleas courts of New York City and County. Most significantly, he authored a bill passed in 1842 that resolved a longstanding dispute over the control of public education in New York City, which had been simmering since 1839 when Whig governor William Henry Seward had first proposed reforms to encourage greater school attendance by the children of Catholic immigrants. A quasipublic organization, the Public School Society, had previously directed the schools and, according to Catholics, used them as instruments for Protestant indoctrination. Under Maclay's legislation, commissioners would be elected from each ward to form a public school board (similar to the practice in the remainder of the state), and these ward representatives could decide on the texts to be used in the schools in their wards. Although the religious issue was highly controversial and divided both parties, the Whigs on balance endured the greater damage, because Seward had raised the issue, and Maclay won the gratitude of many Catholic voters.

Maclay exhibited his intellectual interests in his efforts to preserve New York's heritage. He successfully advocated publication of the *Journals of the Provincial Congress . . . of New York*, which finally appeared in 1842 and contained important primary sources from the era of the American Revolution.

In the fall of 1842 the Democrats selected Maclay to run for Congress, and he sat in the Twenty-eighth through the Thirtieth Congresses (1843–1849). Although he served on comparatively important committees and was diligent in performing his duties, the issues at the national level did not seem to attract him as much as those closer to home. He introduced minor bills, such as an unsuccessful one to help the heirs of John Paul Jones (1747–1792), but most often simply vigorously affirmed in debate his party's positions on the issues of the 1840s: expansion into the Southwest and Oregon, the acquisition of Texas, and the Mexican War. He kept a low profile on the divisive issue of slavery in the newly acquired territories. The spread of knowledge still interested him. He advocated reduced postal rates and financial support for the development of the telegraph.

At the close of his third term Maclay himself decided to seek new opportunities in the West. He moved his family to tiny Mount Palatine in central Illinois. The move proved disastrous for the urbane New Yorker. His wife succumbed to cholera, and even the family's hasty retreat to New York did not save his daughter from also dying of the disease.

Maclay did not return to politics for some time. As hostility to foreigners and especially Catholics spilled over in the formation of the American (Know Nothing) party in the 1850s, New York Democrats sought to run Protestants with a record of fairness toward Catholics to minimize their losses on either side. Maclay was elected to the Thirty-fifth and Thirty-sixth Congresses (1857–1861), unseating a Know Nothing.

He attacked nativism in Congress as divisive to the country, once again ignoring the divisiveness of slavery. He also supported homesteads for western settlers. Maclay did not seek reelection in 1860. Big city politics, which increasingly involved bruising confrontations and the growth of political machines, had moved beyond the ken of this erudite, genteel scholar. Retiring to private life, he retained an interest in religious topics, writing frequently for the *Baptist Weekly*. He died in New York City.

• There are no Maclay manuscripts, although he published *A Selection of Letters Written on Various Public Occasions* (1859). See also Orrin B. Judd, *Maclay Memorial: Sketching the Lineage, Life and Obsequies of Hon. William B. Maclay* (1884). An obituary is in the *New York Times*, 20 Feb. 1882.

PHYLLIS FIELD

MACLEAN, John (1 Mar. 1771–17 Feb. 1814), chemist and physician, was born in Glasgow, Scotland, the son of John Maclean, a surgeon, and Agnes Lang. Both Maclean's parents died when he was very young, and a family friend, George Macintosh, acted as his guardian and guided his education. Following studies at the Glasgow Grammar School, he entered the university at the age of thirteen. Maclean's major interest was in chemistry, but being of a practical nature he also studied medicine and anatomy in order to qualify as a surgeon. To broaden his chemical knowledge further, Maclean spent the years from 1787 to 1790 studying at Edinburgh, London, and Paris. This period coincided with the definitive phase of the chemical revolution.

Maclean's particular motive for going to Edinburgh was to attend the lectures of Dr. Joseph Black, the most eminent chemist in Britain and a famously precise experimentalist. In Paris Maclean was exposed to the new system of chemistry of Antoine Lavoisier, which rejected the phlogiston concept. Phlogiston was thought to be a material substance and was used to explain a variety of phenomena including combustion, acidity, basicity, chemical reactivity, and composition. Without the defeat of the phlogiston concept, chemistry could not be put on a quantitative and theoretically consistent basis. Lavoisier's textbook, *Traite Elementaire de Chemie*, which was published in 1789, summarized the new chemistry that used oxygen as the source of combustion and acidity. A new system of nomenclature was provided, as well as an operational definition of an element. Maclean became a firm adherent and proponent of the new system of chemistry.

Returning to Glasgow in 1790, Maclean finished his medical studies and was appointed a member of the faculty of physicians and surgeons of Glasgow University. While practicing medicine, he continued his chemical studies and carried out some experimental work. Deciding that the United States offered important professional opportunities as well as a better political climate, he arrived in New York in May 1795. Traveling on to Philadelphia, he was advised to settle in Princeton, home of the College of New Jersey (later

Princeton University), where a man with his unique credentials as a physician and chemist could thrive.

Maclean quickly established a medical practice and offered a series of lectures on the new chemistry. These were so favorably received that on 1 October 1795 he was offered the chair of mathematics, natural philosophy, and chemistry at the college. With this appointment he became the first professor of chemistry in America who was not associated with a medical school. Maclean abandoned all further thoughts of practicing medicine and devoted the rest of his all-too-short life to teaching chemistry. Maclean married Phebe Bainbridge in 1798; they had one son. He left Princeton in 1812 for the College of William and Mary, but after one year his health failed. He returned to Princeton in 1814, where he died.

Maclean's two significant achievements in the United States were his advocacy of Lavoisier's new system of chemistry as well as his insistence that students could learn chemistry by actual experimentation and not solely by demonstration. As Maclean wrote in a letter to the president of the College of New Jersey in 1801: "the objects of chemistry are innumerable and very minute, so that no description can be given of even the most simple of its principles which will convey an adequate idea of it to a person who has never seen it performed." Maclean offered the first laboratory course of instruction in chemistry in America; it may in fact have been the first such course. This insistence on the need for students to have laboratory experience exerted a profound influence on the direction of the development of chemical education in America. His contributions were recognized by his election in 1805 to the American Philosophical Society.

By the time Maclean began his teaching career, most European chemists had abandoned the phlogiston theory. However, its influence was still strong in America due to the influence of Joseph Priestley's seminal work in defense of the phlogiston theory, "Considerations on the Doctrine of Phlogiston and the Decomposition of Water," which was published as a monograph in Philadelphia in 1796.

Maclean's reply to Priestley, also in the form of a monograph, was published in Philadelphia in 1797. "Two Lectures on Combustion . . . Containing An Examination of Dr. Priestley's Considerations on the Doctrine of Phlogiston . . . " included the texts of lectures Maclean had presented in Princeton. In the preface he states that the purpose of these lectures was to put students " . . . on your guard against falling into even that temporary delusion, which an erroneous opinion is so apt to produce, when supported by a celebrated name." He then completely discredits Priestley's empirical arguments in favor of the phlogiston doctrine.

A major point of the phlogiston theory was the contention that metals were actually compounds of the metal and phlogiston, rather than simple substances, as the antiphlogistonists maintained. Lavoisier and his contemporaries had both qualitatively and quantitatively shown that when a metal such as mercury, for example, is heated in air, it combines with the oxygen in the air to form the compound mercury oxide. Upon treatment at high temperatures, mercury oxide will decompose to form mercury and oxygen. Priestley cited experiments, later shown to be faulty, that claimed that upon decomposition mercury was not formed. Maclean cited the various experiments of Lavoisier to show that Priestley's contention regarding the complex nature of metals was false.

Another source of debate was the question of the action of hydrogen in the decomposition of metal oxides. In the mind of phlogistonists, hydrogen was a good source of phlogiston. Thus, when an oxide was decomposed to the metal from which it had been formed, hydrogen essentially put back the phlogiston that had been lost upon heating in air. Maclean showed that the role of hydrogen was to act as a reducing agent to combine with the oxygen to form water. Thus, Maclean contended, "If two portions of matter exhibit the same phenomena in all chemical operations, they ought most certainly be considered as the same substance; and as mercury revived from its oxyds by a mere increase in temperature, possesses all the properties of that revived by the assistance of hydrogen gas, etc., it cannot be in any respect deficient."

The issue of the composition of water and its origin in many processes was a major point of contention between Priestley and the antiphlogistonists. Maclean devoted a complete lecture to arguing the water problem and presenting all the experiments that show that it is formed by the union of hydrogen and oxygen. Nevertheless, Priestley held fast to his theory of phlogiston for the rest of his life, while Maclean and other antiphlogistonists promoted the growth of the new system of chemistry in America.

Benjamin Silliman recorded the following remarks about Maclean: "Dr Maclean was a man of brilliant mind, with all the acuteness of his native Scotland; and a sparkling wit gave variety to his conversation" (quoted in *Two Lectures on Combustion* [1929]).

• Maclean published several papers in the *New York Medical Reporter* while at Princeton. His most enduring work was his monograph, *Two Lectures on Combustion and an Examination of Doctor Priestley's Considerations on the Doctrine of Phlogiston*, republished and edited with a sketch of Maclean's life and work by William Foster (1929). See also William Foster, "Doctor Maclean and the Doctrine of Phlogiston," *Journal of Chemical Education* 2 (1925): 743–47.

MARTIN D. SALTZMAN

MACLEAN, Norman (23 Dec. 1902–2 Aug. 1990), educator and writer, was born Norman Fitzroy Maclean in Clarinda, Iowa, the son of John Norman Maclean, a Scotch Presbyterian minister, and Clara Evelyn Davidson. The family, including a younger brother, moved to Missoula, Montana, in 1909. The father tutored young Norman in literature, writing, religion, and fly-fishing. He began to attend public schools only in 1913, worked summers for the U.S. Forest Service commencing in 1917, and entered Dartmouth College in 1920. In 1922 he and his father built a cabin near

Seeley Lake, northeast of Missoula, and he enjoyed many summer vacations there. After graduating from Dartmouth College (B.A., 1924), Maclean was a teaching assistant in the English department there for two years. He worked for the forest service in Montana again (summers, 1926–1928), during which time he also hired on in logging camps.

In 1928 Maclean began teaching in earnest as a graduate assistant while he pursued doctoral studies at the University of Chicago. In 1931 he was promoted to instructor and, with his father officiating as minister, married Jessie Burns; Maclean and his wife had two children. He received his Ph.D. in English literature in 1940. Thereafter, his academic rise was steady: he was assistant professor (1941–1944), dean of students (1942–1945), coauthor of a military manual on maps and aerial photographs (1942), acting director for the Institute on Military Studies (1943–1945), associate professor (1944–1954), and professor (1954–1973). He won three awards for excellence in undergraduate teaching (1932, 1940, 1973) and was installed as the William Rainey Harper Professor of English Literature (1962–1972). He minimally fulfilled the university's academic publishing requirements with two solid critical essays: "From Action to Image: Theories of the Lyric in the Eighteenth Century," concerning the ode as validating pertinent critical theory, and "Episode, Scene, Speech, and Word: The Madness of Lear." Both essays were published in *Critics and Criticism, Ancient and Modern* (1952), a well-received volume of essays edited by Ronald S. Crane. Maclean's long span of years spent in teaching was darkened by the unsolved murder of his brother Paul, when Paul was a newspaperman in Chicago, in 1938, and by the lingering death from cancer of Maclean's wife in 1968.

Following his retirement from academe at the age of seventy, Maclean began a second career. He turned out a moderate flow of little essays and exciting fiction. Minor essays include a witty autobiographical piece on teaching (*University of Chicago Magazine* 66 [Jan.–Feb. 1974]: 8–12); a sketch on billiards and the Nobel Prize winner Albert Michelson, a University of Chicago scientist (*University of Chicago Magazine* 67 [Summer 1975]: 18–23); a humorous essay on Maclean's father and duck dogs (*Esquire*, Oct. 1977, pp. 14–22); an autobiographical essay on writing and rhythm (*Chicago*, Oct. 1977, pp. 208–19, 248–51); an essay on craftsmanship in teaching, baseball, and backpacking (*Association of Departments of English Bulletin* 61 [May 1979]: 3–5); and an autobiographical sketch (*American Dreams, Lost and Found*, ed. Studs Terkel [1980]). In addition, Maclean let his friend Ron McFarland publish four of his essays in *Norman Maclean* (1988), a book McFarland and Hugh Nichols edited. These essays concern forest-fire fighting, Montana frontier storytelling, the writing process, teaching, and fiction writing.

More significant is Maclean's fiction. *A River Runs through It and Other Stories* (1976) contains the title novella, now a classic, and two lesser efforts, "Logging and Pimping and 'Your Pal, Jim'" and "USFS 1919:

The Ranger, the Cook, and a Hole in the Sky." "A River Runs through It" is Maclean's fictionalized reminiscence of his father, mother, and brother Paul. The scene is set in and near Missoula, Montana; the year, 1937. The father is now retired: he still reads his Bible in Greek but can no longer fish vigorously. The narrator's fussy, loving mother especially dotes on Paul, a reporter now visiting from Helena; he drinks, gambles, is sexually promiscuous, but is a "beautiful" trout fisherman. The narrator is married to a puzzled wife with dour Scotch relatives living too close by and also an affected, hypocritical brother named Neal. Paul is briefly jailed after he slugs a drunk who seemed to insult his American Indian girlfriend. Neal goes fishing with the brothers and though hungover brings along a prostitute named Old Rawhide. The two of them lag behind, drink the foursome's beer, have sex in the sand, fall asleep exposed, and get embarrassingly sunburned. Maclean's humor is Faulknerian here, although everywhere else it is muted and deadpan, both in and out of the apt laconic dialogue. The brothers and their father go fishing memorably for what is to be a last time. Later, it is reported that Paul has been killed in a fracas during which he valorously fought back. The novella is unified by Montana's Big Blackfoot River, which is both real and metaphoric: a source of challenging sport, an arena of rugged competition, evidence of nature's sacred beauty and varied power, and a symbol of the divine and rhythmic flux. The best parts of "A River Runs through It" are Maclean's wise generalizations about how hard it is to help a loved one who needs, indirectly calls for, but stubbornly rejects help.

"Logging" is based on Maclean's activities in and near a lumber camp in the summer of 1927. "USFS 1919" makes disjointed but absorbing fiction out of his work, three earlier summers, with the forest service.

Maclean died at his home in Chicago and was thus prevented from completing what might have been a monumental account of the Mann Gulch forest fire in Montana that killed thirteen of a fifteen-man team of forest service "smokejumpers" on 5 August 1949. Maclean researched the dreadful event for many years, repeatedly hiking over its charred locale, interviewing survivors and other witnesses, studying contradictory reports, and consulting fire-science publications. He left incomplete manuscript sections of what his editors assembled and published as *Young Men and Fire* (1992). In addition to being a hypnotic narrative and documentary account, the book is a philosophical treatise attempting to explore how "good" firefighters could come to such a "bad" end. Partial answers that Maclean suggests are these: they sought to aid others, they heroically faced danger, the event contains lessons from which future firefighters may profit, and the pity and terror of it all is cleansing.

• Maclean's papers are at the University of Chicago library. The best book about Maclean is Ron McFarland and Hugh Nichols, eds., *Norman Maclean* (1988), which reprints short works by Maclean, two interviews with him, seven critical essays about him (including one by Glen A. Love and another by Wallace Stegner), and a primary and secondary bibliography. McFarland's *Norman Maclean* (1993) provides excellent biographical and critical coverage. Several journal articles concentrate on specific fictional works by Maclean. Helen Lojek in "Casting Flies and Recasting Myths with Norman Maclean," *Western American Literature* 25 (Aug. 1990): 145–56, downgrades "A River Runs through It" for being reductively macho. James E. Ford in "When 'Life . . . Becomes Literature': The Neo-Aristotelian Poetics of Norman Maclean's 'A River Runs through It,'" *Studies in Short Fiction* 30 (Fall 1993): 525–34, sees Paul's story as history and the narrator's story as literature. In "The Achievement of Norman Maclean," *Yale Review* 82 (Apr. 1994): 118–31, Marie Borroff, a former student, reminisces about Maclean and analyzes *Young Men and Fire* as narrative art. O. Alan Weltzien, "The Two Lives of Norman Maclean and the Text of Fire in *Young Men and Fire*," *Western American Literature* 29 (May 1994): 3–24, considers *Young Men and Fire* as both autobiography and history. An obituary is in the *New York Times*, 3 Aug. 1990. *A River Runs through It*, a movie directed by Robert Redford, was released in 1992.

ROBERT L. GALE

MACLEISH, Archibald (7 May 1892–20 Apr. 1982), poet and playwright, was born in Glencoe, Illinois, the son of Andrew MacLeish, a prosperous dry-goods merchant, and Martha Hillard, a college professor. Andrew MacLeish was a reserved, stern father whose lack of attention to his son may have generated Archibald's fierce drive to succeed. The influence of Martha MacLeish, who worked to develop her four children's sense of social responsibility, helps account for Archibald's intense involvement in American public life as well as his concern for those in personal or political trouble.

MacLeish spent his childhood on a seventeen-acre estate on Lake Michigan. He was a somewhat rebellious though industrious child who needed, his mother judged, the discipline of a private school; he therefore attended Hotchkiss from 1907 to 1911. At Yale (1911–1915) he majored in English, wrote poetry, and was heavily involved in campus literary, social, and athletic activities. After graduating from Yale, he entered Harvard Law School in the fall of 1915. In June 1916 he married Ada Taylor Hitchcock; they had four children, three of whom survived infancy.

MacLeish's first volume of poetry, *Tower of Ivory*, appeared late in 1917 shortly after he had left for France and World War I to serve in the Yale Mobile Hospital Unit. He soon transferred to artillery school and eventually saw action in the second battle of the Marne, commanding Battery B of the 146th Field Artillery. He was then ordered back to the United States to instruct draftees in artillery use and was there, a first lieutenant, when the war ended. MacLeish became embittered toward the war when his brother Ken, a fighter pilot, died in combat, but this disillusionment (best expressed in the poem "Memorial Rain" [1926]) would not prevent his appreciating the need to oppose fascism in the thirties.

Returning to Harvard Law School, MacLeish graduated at the head of his class in 1919. He then taught law courses for a semester in Harvard's government department but turned down an offer to teach at the Harvard Law School; he worked briefly, instead, as an editor for the *New Republic*. In September 1920 he joined the Boston law firm of Choate, Hall and Stewart. He was a successful lawyer, but feeling confined by the profession and craving time to write poetry, he quit the firm on the same day he was offered a partnership in February 1923.

Though he always felt an obligation to society, MacLeish believed at this time that he could pay his debt simply by creating poetry: "it was the art I owed," he recalled in *Riders on the Earth*. In September 1923 the MacLeishes headed for Paris, he hoping to become an accomplished poet and she to become a professional singer. There they joined the expatriate literary community, meeting writers such as E. E. Cummings, John Dos Passos, Scott and Zelda Fitzgerald, James Joyce, and Ernest Hemingway. With Hemingway, MacLeish began a long and close though difficult friendship.

Always an organized worker, he established a program of reading to develop poetic style and technique. Perhaps he studied too well, for during the Paris period he wrote several long poems, which sounded much like T. S. Eliot, Ezra Pound, and other pioneering modernists (*The Pot of Earth* [1925], *Nobodaddy* [1926], *Einstein* [1926, in *Streets in the Moon*], and *The Hamlet of A. MacLeish* [1928]). But he also wrote short poems equally notable for lyrical grace and a tone of muted horror at the human experience of spinning on our small planet through the dark and empty universe, as in "You, Andrew Marvell."

This poem and other lyrics—such as "Ars Poetica," "The End of the World," "Eleven," and " 'Not Marble Nor the Gilded Monuments' "—have long been the source of MacLeish's poetic reputation.

The MacLeishes returned to the United States in 1928 and bought a farm in Conway, Massachusetts. "American Letter" in *New Found Land* (1930) asserts his commitment to the United States, despite the pull of Europe. The long poem *Conquistador* (1932) presents Cortes's conquest of the Aztecs as symbolic of the American experience. In 1933 *Conquistador* won the Pulitzer Prize, the first of three awarded to MacLeish.

MacLeish worked for Henry Luce's new magazine *Fortune* from 1929 to 1938, writing voluminously on the American and international scenes. His production of poems, essays, and plays was also prolific. In them MacLeish carried on a debate with himself about the relation between art and society. He rejected the modernist emphasis on the private individual's experience and the poet's alienation from society. The poet, he came to believe, was inevitably involved in society. Poetry, especially in a tumultuous time like the thirties, should be "public speech." His stage and radio plays of the thirties, notably *Panic* (1935), *The Fall of the City* (1937), and *Air Raid* (1938) aimed at and sometimes reached a wide audience.

MacLeish was strongly criticized during the thirties not only for specific opinions, but for apparent inconsistency. He argued each position as though it were eternal truth, yet from poem to essay to play both his political views and his sense of the writer's social role varied as he worked out, in print, what he believed. By the late thirties he had achieved a consistent position, a vision of human freedom, dignity, and solidarity that was inevitably at odds with fascism, communism, and the excesses of American capitalism. What was wrong with America, MacLeish decided, was that Americans lacked a clear vision of their human potential as well as their national goals. But he believed that poetry could supply it. At times he argued that *only* poetry could provide a unifying cultural vision. He tried to capture it in poems, plays, and a book of photographs, *Land of the Free* (1938), for which he supplied the text, but none of his formulations of "an image of mankind in which men can again believe" (*Poetry* 38 [1931]: 216) caught the public imagination.

He did catch, however, the scorn of modernists for ignoring the supposed separation of art and politics and writing "public poetry" about the need for brotherhood and a common cultural vision. He was criticized also for transforming his poetic theory and practice from the vintage modernism expressed in "Ars Poetica"—"a poem should not mean / but be"—to a public poetry that commented directly on social and political issues, as if the Great Depression and the rise of fascism might not give one second thoughts about fundamentals.

Politically during the thirties MacLeish was developing a liberal humanism that made him admire Franklin D. Roosevelt, for whom he later wrote speeches. Along the way he took hits from all sides; the Left attacked him as an "unconscious fascist" and the Right as an associate of communists. In 1939 J. Parnell Thomas coined the term "fellow traveler" with specific reference to MacLeish on the occasion of his nomination by President Roosevelt to become librarian of Congress. In this position he applied his formidable administrative talents to reorganizing and modernizing the inertia-bound Library of Congress. He also directed an information/propaganda agency called the Office of Facts and Figures in 1941. The agency lasted less than a year and lacked the authority to accomplish much. MacLeish then became assistant director of the Office of War Information (1942–1943). He wrote little poetry during this period but in essays and speeches continued to argue for freedom and communal solidarity, not just to overcome fascism but to promote and exercise the freedoms on which the United States was based.

In 1944 MacLeish resigned from the library and prepared to return to private life. Roosevelt, however, appointed him assistant secretary of state for cultural and public affairs. In 1945 he resigned this position and led the U.S. delegation to the organizational meeting of UNESCO, and in 1946 he served as assistant head of the U.S. delegation to UNESCO. Only after that did he return to private life.

Actfive and Other Poems (1948), MacLeish's first poetic volume since *America Was Promises* (1939), contained public poems and private lyrics. The hortatory, activist stance of the thirties was gone, replaced by disillusionment with the political world. *Actfive* asserts that in the failure of the state, science, industry, heroes, and "the Crowd," nevertheless "The heart persists. The love survives." There remains the impulse to be "beautiful and brave," "dutiful and good."

MacLeish became the Boylston Professor of Rhetoric and Oratory at Harvard in 1949. He held this position, teaching a seminar in creative writing and a lecture course in poetry, until mandatory retirement in 1962. Teaching only in the fall semesters, he had ample time to write. During the fifties he achieved gratifying successes and a balance between his public and private work. *Collected Poems 1917–52* (1952) brought not only his second Pulitzer Prize, but Hayden Carruth's apology for the past carping of critics (*Nation*, 31 Jan. 1953). MacLeish was elected president of the American Academy of Arts and Letters in 1953. He tried unsuccessfully to involve the academy in confronting the anti-Communist hysteria of the time. He fought McCarthyism during those years in essays, poems, and the play *The Trojan Horse* (broadcast and published in 1952) and by standing up for those whom Senator Joseph R. McCarthy threatened. After visiting Ezra Pound in 1955, MacLeish worked tirelessly to obtain Pound's release from St. Elizabeths hospital, a goal accomplished in 1958. That same year he published *J.B.*, his reworking of the story of Job that, as a book and as a Broadway play, became his greatest popular success. *J.B.* brought MacLeish his third Pulitzer.

After his retirement from Harvard in 1962, MacLeish, always an energetic person, slowed his pace only gradually. He was a public resource in politics as well as literature, writing often for public celebrations and commemorations. And he accomplished a long-frustrated goal, locating in 1968 a vision of human existence that had a broad public impact, when he reflected for the *New York Times* on the first photograph of the earth taken from beyond the moon (the Apollo 8 voyage). It was an image with whose help "man may discover what he really is": "To see the earth as we now see it, small and blue and beautiful in that eternal silence where it floats, is to see ourselves as riders on the earth together, brothers on that bright loveliness in the unending night—brothers who *see* now they are truly brothers (*Riders on the Earth*, p. xiv).

In his later years MacLeish wrote excellent lyric poems that reflect in a direct, personal tone on love and aging. Not that he lost the desire to advise and exhort; the play *Herakles* (1967) warns of the destructive potential of science. But the short lyrics constitute his best poetry after *J.B.* It can be argued that these later poems are as good as his famous poems of the twenties. He died in Boston.

Once considered a major modernist poet of the generation that followed Pound and Eliot, MacLeish remains notable as one of those who influenced the development of modern poetry. With his sensitivity to technique and his lyrical gift, he expressed common existential anxieties of the time. And no poem has expressed the modernist sense of art so well as "Ars Poetica" (1926) with its signature statement: "A poem should not mean / but be."

MacLeish's reputation began to decline partly because he rejected the orthodox modernist position when he accepted the poet's complicity in society and politics. Another reason was that his sensitivity to styles and fashions exposed him to charges of derivativeness. But this receptiveness was also a strength, for time and again his instinct for finding the sources of power and vitality led him to the centers of influence and activity: Paris in the twenties, New York in the thirties, Washington in the forties, Harvard in the fifties. If he followed trends, he also innovated in his cultural poetics, in poetry and drama, and in creative uses of media (radio, television, film, the photographic essay). Craving success, he also dedicated himself to the common good and dedicated his energies to public purposes. He had a message for Americans, for everyone, and the medium was his art. "Ars Poetica" notwithstanding, even a poem had to *mean*.

• The Library of Congress is the major source of unpublished materials, including notebooks and correspondence. For other sources of the voluminous MacLeish materials, including many tape-recorded interviews with and about MacLeish, see the acknowledgments and bibliography in Scott Donaldson, in collaboration with R. H. Winnick, *Archibald MacLeish: An American Life* (1992). This biography is the definitive and indispensable work on MacLeish. The most convenient and complete edition of MacLeish's poems is *Collected Poems 1917–1982* (1985), which includes poems that MacLeish declined to publish during his lifetime; the most convenient edition of his major plays is *Six Plays* (1980). Of MacLeish's several collections of essays, the most rewarding today are *A Continuing Journey* (1968) and *Riders on the Earth: Essays and Recollections* (1978). R. H. Winnick, ed., *Archibald MacLeish: Letters 1907–1982* (1983), is invaluable, and two volumes of conversations and interviews are useful: Warren V. Bush, ed., *The Dialogues of Archibald MacLeish and Mark Van Doren* (1964), and Bernard A. Drabeck and Helen E. Ellis, eds., *Archibald MacLeish: Reflections* (1986). Edward J. Mullaly, *Archibald MacLeish: A Checklist* (1973), is an exhaustive bibliography. An obituary and an editorial tribute are in the *New York Times*, 21–22 Apr. 1982.

DAVID BARBER

MACLEISH, Martha Hillard (17 Aug. 1856–19 Dec. 1947), religious and educational leader, was born in Hadlyme, Connecticut, the daughter of Elias Brewster Hillard, a Congregational minister, and Julia Whittlesey. After graduating from Vassar College in 1878 she taught school in Connecticut and spent three years at Vassar as a mathematics teacher. In 1884 she became principal of Rockford (Ill.) Seminary, whose founder had recently retired. Rockford, like Mount Holyoke Seminary, which it resembled, was in the process of becoming a genuine college. MacLeish raised academic standards, introduced an honors system, built a gymnasium, and increased social ties with the nearby men's college, Beloit. She left Rockford in 1888 to become the third wife of Andrew MacLeish, a partner in the Chicago department store Carson, Pirie Scott. The couple had five children, including the poet Archibald MacLeish. After 1891 they made their home in Glencoe, Illinois.

Like other women of her generation, MacLeish saw the home and motherhood as important sources for the moral and spiritual improvement of society, and she felt that to be most effective women needed an education in the science of childraising. "What would the world be," she wrote, "if we could have one generation of thoroly [sic] prepared and responsible fathers and mothers? Would it not almost mean the millenial [sic] dawn?" (*Kindergarten Magazine*, June 1904, p. 584). Ever an educator, MacLeish became excited about new trends such as progressive education and the child study movement. When her children were young she joined a mother's class at the Kindergarten Training School run by Elizabeth Harrison. She also regularly observed John Dewey's experimental school at the University of Chicago. She belonged to the Illinois Child Study Society and published several articles on child study, including one based on observations of her daughter Ishbel and another on reading literature to children.

After 1907 she involved herself in the Baptist women's foreign missions effort, becoming president of the western society based in Chicago. When a 1913 merger joined this society with its eastern counterpart to form the Woman's American Baptist Foreign Missionary Society, she served as home vice president, part of the "triumvirate" that included the prominent missionary leaders Helen Barrett Montgomery as president and Lucy W. Peabody as foreign vice president. In 1915 she joined the executive committee of the Northern Baptist Convention.

MacLeish's gifts for administration and education came into full play in her efforts for the Baptists. She worked successfully for better cooperation between the Baptist women's home and foreign missionary efforts, drew up the plan of merger for the eastern and western societies, wrote for Baptist publications, and helped launch the World Wide Guild and the Children's World Crusade, organizations designed to interest young women and children in foreign missions. In the mid-1920s MacLeish, occupied with the illnesses of her husband and daughter, withdrew from active leadership in the missions effort. She became president of the Chicago Woman's Club in 1927 and in 1935 helped found the National Conference of Christians and Jews.

MacLeish's writings are filled with terms like "ideals," "character," and "service." For example, in a 1920 Easter editorial she wrote of those who had died in World War I (including her son Kenneth):

They have a place in the "cloud of witnesses" surrounding us, waiting to see how we "carry on" for the completion of the task begun by the heroes of the war. How they must rejoice if they see us rising above personal sorrow and out of indulgence of self to do a full soldier's part in meeting the new and boundless opportunities which God has put before us this Easter Day (*Baptist*, 27 Mar. 1920, p. 299).

She knew who she was: a "Connecticut Yankee" proud of her nation and her family (her ancestors included Pilgrim William Brewster [1576–1644]) and well aware of her civic responsibilities. Though not a self-declared feminist, she expected women to play significant public roles (as long as children and husbands did not suffer). A liberal in religion, and tolerant of other communions, she was nevertheless unwavering in her personal piety and in her belief in a benevolent God and personal immortality. She died in Chicago.

• MacLeish's autobiography is *Martha Hillard MacLeish* (1949). Her articles include "The Need of Reverence: How to Develop It," *The Outlook*, 11 May 1897, pp. 214–16; "Observations on the Development of a Child During the First Year," *Transactions of the Illinois Society for Child-Study*, vol. III, no. 2, pp. 109–124; "Has Not the Time Come When Education Should Prepare for Parenthood?" *Kindergarten Magazine*, June 1904, pp. 579–90; "Mothercraft in the Land of Confucius," *The Baptist*, 31 Jan. 1920, p. 17; "Two Thoughts for Easter," *The Baptist*, 27 Mar. 1920, pp. 298–99; "Our Debt to the Women of the Past," *The Baptist*, 18 Jun. 1921, pp. 623–25. Of related interest are Andrew MacLeish, *Life* (1929); *Letters of Archibald MacLeish, 1907 to 1982*, ed. R. H. Winnick (1983); and *Archibald MacLeish: Reflections*, ed. B. A. Drabeck and H. E. Ellis (1986). For her work at Rockford see Sally Lou Coburn, *Profiles of the Principals of Rockford Seminary* (1947), and C. Hal Nelson, ed., *Rockford College: A Retrospective Look* (1980). For her missionary activities see Louise Armstrong Cattan, *Lamps Are for Lighting* (1972); Robert G. Torbet, *Venture of Faith* (1955); and William B. Lipphard, "Who's Who among Baptists," *Baptist*, 27 Mar. 1920, p. 303. An obituary is in the *New York Times*, 20 Dec. 1947.

VIRGINIA LIESON BRERETON

MACLEOD, Colin Munro (28 Jan. 1909–11 or 12 Feb. 1972), medical scientist, was born in Nova Scotia, Canada, the son of John Charles MacLeod, a Presbyterian minister, and Lillian Munro, a schoolteacher. His early schooling is remarkable because he skipped so many grades during his elementary education that on its completion he was too young to be admitted to McGill College. He therefore spent a year as a sixth-grade schoolteacher before entering college. He graduated from McGill School of Medicine in 1932 and after two years of residency training joined the Rockefeller Institute for Medical Research in New York.

MacLeod's career as a medical scientist was of extraordinary breadth, with notable achievements in medical research, in medical education, and in administration in a variety of settings—university, private foundations, and government. His success in research began in 1934 at Rockefeller, where he joined O. T. Avery's laboratory devoted to a study of bacterial pneumonia.

In addition to clinical studies in which MacLeod participated, the Avery laboratory had been interested for several years in a phenomenon referred to as the transformation of pneumococcal types. The name "pneumococcus" was used for the most prevalent agent causing bacterial pneumonia, and the phenomenon involved a permanent change in one type of pneumococcus induced by material extracted from a second type. The process thus appeared to transfer genetic information from one cell to another. Not long before MacLeod's arrival, others in the laboratory had succeeded in preparing cell-free extracts that would induce the transformation, and he took on the assignment of trying to determine the nature of the substance that was responsible for the change.

For a variety of reasons this research proved to be a challenging task, and it was almost ten years later that MacLeod was able to report, with Avery and Maclyn McCarty, that this transforming substance was deoxyribonucleic acid, or DNA. This research provided the first experimental evidence indicating that genes are made of DNA. Although this finding was not immediately accepted by all biologists, it is now recognized as the initial step in the development of modern molecular biology and genetics and one of the most important discoveries in biology in the twentieth century.

Thus, MacLeod began his career in research with an outstanding contribution that has had a profound influence on the development of biomedical research in the last fifty years. Although he continued to participate in productive research for many years, MacLeod's activities diversified rapidly after leaving Rockefeller, leading to notable contributions in other areas as well. MacLeod married Elizabeth Randol in 1938, while he was at Rockefeller. They had one daughter.

His departure from the Rockefeller Institute took place in 1941, when he became chair of the Department of Microbiology at the New York University School of Medicine. He maintained close contact with the progress of the completion of the research on transformation at Rockefeller and at the same time initiated research projects with collaborators at NYU, including some pioneering studies on the development of a successful vaccine for pneumococcal pneumonia. In this new setting he also began to demonstrate his talents in other areas, building one of the strongest medical microbiology departments in the country and playing a major role in the remarkable growth of the school into a leading medical institution.

MacLeod became a U.S. citizen in 1941, and with the country's entry into World War II he soon added service to the government to his busy schedule, first as consultant to the secretary of war and as director of the Commission on Pneumonia of the Army Epidemiological Board of the War Department from 1941 to 1946. In 1946 he became president of the board, which became the Armed Forces Epidemiological Board (AFEB) after unification of the services. He had outstanding success in initiating and guiding the activities of the board and its commissions, facilitated by his ability to enlist the active and enthusiastic cooperation of the other members. AFEB research areas included work on vaccines for measles and other viral diseases and the use of penicillin therapy to help prevent rheumatic fever. He continued to serve in these activities after stepping down as president in 1955.

In 1956 MacLeod left NYU to become the John Herr Musser Professor of Research Medicine at the University of Pennsylvania. While this move was designed to provide more time for research by relieving him from his duties as head of a teaching department, he characteristically participated actively in the affairs of the medical school at Penn and continued his government activities. During this period he also became involved in a notable experiment in municipal support of medical research by participating in the founding of the Health Research Council of the City of New York, which he served as executive secretary from 1958 to 1960 and as chair from 1960 to 1970.

In 1960 MacLeod returned to NYU as professor of medicine and developed a division of medical genetics within the department. Three years later he took a leave of absence in order to assume his first full-time position in government as deputy director of the Office of Science and Technology, part of the Executive Office of the President. In this position he organized new programs such as the U.S.–Japan Cooperative Program in the Medical Sciences, which he continued to serve for the rest of his life.

On returning to New York in 1966, MacLeod moved to the position of vice president for medical affairs at the Commonwealth Fund for his first activity with a private foundation. After a brief return to NYU in 1969, he became president of the Oklahoma Medical Research Foundation and devoted his energy to strengthening this institution. He died in a motel at a London airport while en route to Bangladesh as a consultant for the Cholera Research Laboratory in Dacca, one of the activities that he had continued from his Washington years.

MacLeod was widely admired and respected for his manifold activities and contributions to medical science. He acquired a host of warm friends throughout the world and received numerous honors, including election to the National Academy of Sciences and the American Philosophical Society.

• MacLeod's research on DNA as genetic material is found in O. T. Avery, et al., "Studies on the Chemical Nature of the Substance Inducing Transformation of Pneumococcal Types. Induction of Transformation by a Deoxyribonucleic Acid Fraction Isolated from Pneumococcus Type III," *Journal of Experimental Medicine* 79 (1944): 137–58. A biography of MacLeod, written by Walsh McDermott, appears in National Academy of Sciences, *Biographical Memoirs* 54 (1983): 183–219.

MACLYN MCCARTY

MACLURE, William (27 Oct. 1763–23 Mar. 1840), scientist and educational reformer, was born in Ayr, Scotland, the son of David McClure, a merchant, and Ann Kennedy. Originally named James McClure, he changed his name at some point in early manhood. After receiving a classical education from private tutors, Maclure chose a career in commerce. Following a journey to the United States in 1782, he became a partner in the American firm of Miller, Hart & Co. in London. After several short stays in the United States, Maclure moved permanently to Philadelphia in 1796 and became an American citizen.

In 1797 Maclure retired on his substantial earnings and soon developed an interest in science, especially in mineralogy and geology. Philadelphia was then the cultural capital of the United States, and Maclure rapidly rose to an eminent position, joining the American Philosophical Society in 1799. However, he moved back to Europe in 1799 and traveled throughout the Continent collecting mineral specimens and taking notes for a geological survey. Geology was then dominated by two opposing systems: one, proposed by Abraham G. Werner, held that rock strata were successively precipitated from a primal sea; the other, championed by James Hutton, held that subterranean heat acted in concert with surface erosion to produce the earth's crust. Although Maclure initially adopted Werner's Neptunian system of rock classification, his doubts about its validity led him to favor an empirical approach. In 1811, after visiting the lakes around Neuchâtel, Maclure ruminated that "the changes on our globe depend more on the coincidence of a great many partial causes and changes rather than on any one great sweeping agent" (Doskey, p. 343). Maclure's plan for a geological map of Europe was defeated by the complexity and extent of the mountain ranges; however, he was able to use his experience and knowledge in the construction of a geological survey that extended over the eastern half of the United States.

Maclure returned to North America in 1808 and traveled from Maine to Georgia in his effort to encompass the territory then occupied by the United States. His work during this time, published in the *Transactions of the American Philosophical Society* in 1809 as "Observations on the Geology of the United States, Explanatory of a Geological Map," immediately made his reputation as the preeminent American geologist of his day. Maclure had by this time become almost an agnostic in geological systems: he used Neptunian nomenclature but claimed that his map was more a record than a theoretical exegesis. His principal contribution was the quadripartite division of the United States: according to Maclure, primitive rocks, such as granite and gneiss, appear in New England and New York State; transition rocks, most commonly greywacke, characterize the Appalachians; secondary rocks—sandstone and limestone—cover the area west of the Appalachians; and alluvial rocks—sand and gravel—constitute a coastal plain from Massachusetts to Florida and extend as far as the mouth of the Mississippi.

Maclure returned to Europe in November 1809 for a journey through Norway, Sweden, Finland, and Russia; from 1811 to 1814 he visited Belgium, France, Switzerland, and Italy. In 1815 Maclure, together with his amanuensis, Charles-Alexandre Lesueur, left Paris for England where he sailed for Barbados; here he observed the geology of the lesser Antilles before sailing on to New York City. After arriving in the United States in May 1816, Maclure traveled through New England, Pennsylvania, New York, Maryland, and Delaware to gather additional information for a revision of his geological survey of the United States.

In October 1816 Maclure and Lesueur settled in Philadelphia, where they became associated with the Academy of Natural Sciences, an organization founded in 1812 by a small group of naturalists who had decided to create a specialized society for the study of natural history. The academy, together with its sister organization in New York, the Lyceum of Natural History, quickly won leadership within the American scientific community over the emerging specialties of natural history, most notably zoology, botany, and ornithology. Nevertheless, in its first five years the academy maintained a threadbare existence, unable to publish a regular journal, expand its museum collections, or purchase its own building. With Maclure's arrival the academy's position rapidly changed. The *Journal of the Academy of Natural Sciences* appeared in 1817, many valuable books were soon added to the library, and Maclure donated specimens for the geological and botanical collections gathered on field trips to the West Indies in 1816–1817 and to Florida in 1817–1818. The academy's debt of $1,000 was paid off by Maclure, and in 1826 he provided the funds that enabled the academy to move to a building purchased from the Swedenborgian church. Maclure's munificence was rewarded in 1817 by his election to the presidency of the academy, a position he held until his death. More significantly, his patronage was central to the further development of American science—the academy quickly became the most important scientific institution in the United States, at least until the establishment of the Smithsonian Institution in 1846. Its success, at a time when scientific research and teaching within the United States were conducted primarily in a handful of medical schools, was crucially dependent on Maclure's support particularly with regard to his financial backing of the academy's *Journal*. By way of contrast, the Lyceum of Natural History did not win any significant financial support and as a result led a fitful and penurious existence for many decades.

Maclure's support of science was contiguous with his patronage of educational reform: both reflected a belief in Enlightenment ideals. He had witnessed the French Revolution firsthand and always claimed to have been inspired by the American Revolution. Maclure combined an enthusiasm for republican democracy with a belief in the centrality of the working class in remaking society and a faith in the necessity of universal education to create that new society. During his European travels Maclure visited the school conducted by Johann Heinrich Pestalozzi in Yverdon, Switzerland, and was so impressed by the emphasis placed on the development of the individual and practical education that he financed several Pestalozzian schools in Europe and America, most notably the school opened by Joseph Neef in Philadelphia in 1809. Maclure's European travels focused increasingly on a concern with educational and political developments. In 1820, disillusioned with the wave of reactionary politics then sweeping across the Continent, he traveled to Spain, where he hoped to establish Pestalozzian academies and agricultural schools. Encouraged by the inauguration of a liberal regime, Maclure invested heavily in land. Unfortunately the revolutionary government was overthrown by a royalist counterrevolution, and Maclure was forced to leave Spain in October 1823.

In July 1824 Maclure visited Scotland, where he met Robert Owen, who showed Maclure the model factory and school at New Lanark. Maclure and Owen found they had much in common, and in a subsequent meeting in London, Maclure fell in with Owen's plan to purchase land at New Harmony, Indiana, in order to establish a socialist community. In July 1825 Maclure arrived in the United States, where he decided to follow Owen's example by investing substantial sums of money in New Harmony, and in December Maclure traveled with a small group of naturalists from the Academy of Natural Sciences to Indiana. In May 1826 the educational program at New Harmony was organized under the aegis of a School Society; Maclure, who assumed financial control of the School Society, anticipated that education in the sciences would proceed under the leadership of the scientists from Philadelphia. As New Harmony gradually fell apart, Maclure won complete control over the School Society and transformed it into a significant center for scientific research. Maclure established a journal, the *Disseminator of Useful Knowledge*, in January 1828, and the School Press published several landmark works in the history of American science, most notably Lesueur's *American Ichthyology* (1827), Thomas Say's multivolume *American Conchology* (1830–1838), and François André Michaux's *North American Sylva* (1841). Despite Maclure's departure in 1828 to Mexico, the scientific community remained at New Harmony, where it continued to benefit from Maclure's financial support.

Maclure spent the remainder of his life in Mexico, where he devoted his dwindling energy to recouping the losses he had suffered over his purchases of land in Spain. He also continued to support science and education at New Harmony and Philadelphia. The Working Men's Institute Library at New Harmony and the Academy of Natural Sciences received substantial sums of money until Maclure's death in San Angel, Mexico. Maclure never married, and because he had no descendants, his estate was divided among the scientific and educational projects with which he had been associated in Europe and the United States.

• The largest collection of Maclure's papers and correspondence, including a set of twenty diaries of his European travels, is located at the Working Men's Institute Library at New Harmony, Ind. Correspondence with American and European scientists is also contained in the Eli Kirk Price Papers and the Samuel George Morton Papers at the American Philosophical Society; the Robert Owen Papers at the Cooperative Union, Manchester, England; the Parker Cleaveland Papers

at Bowdoin College; the Benjamin Silliman Papers at Yale University; the New Harmony Collection at the Indiana Historical Society; and the Biographical Papers Collection at the Academy of Natural Sciences. Maclure's views on politics, economics, and society are conveniently presented in his *Opinions on Various Subjects* (1831). A biography by his contemporary Samuel George Morton is *A Memoir of William Maclure* (1841); the most authoritative account of Maclure's life is John S. Doskey's introduction to *The European Journals of William Maclure* (1988). A detailed biography that provides valuable commentaries by Maclure's contemporaries is J. Percy Moore, "William Maclure: Scientist and Humanitarian," *Proceedings of the American Philosophical Society* 91 (1947): 234–49. Maclure's contributions to nineteenth-century geology are assessed in Dennis R. Dean, "New Light on William Maclure," *Annals of Science* 46 (1989): 549–74. An accurate account of Maclure's association with New Harmony is in Arthur Bestor, *Backwoods Utopias: The Sectarian Origins and the Owenite Phase of Communitarian Socialism in America, 1663–1829* (1970). Maclure's thoughts on the New Harmony experiment are revealed in abundant detail in Arthur Bestor, ed., *Education and Reform at New Harmony: Correspondence of William Maclure and Marie Duclos Fretageot, 1820–1833* (1948). Maclure's financial support for the Academy of Natural Sciences is discussed in Patsy A. Gerstner, "The Academy of Natural Sciences of Philadelphia, 1812–1850," in *The Pursuit of Knowledge in the Early American Republic: American Scientific and Learned Societies from Colonial Times to the Civil War*, ed. Alexandra Oleson and Sanborn C. Brown (1976), and Patricia Tyson Stroud, *Thomas Say: New World Naturalist* (1992).

SIMON BAATZ

MACMONNIES, Frederick William (28 Sept. 1863–22 Mar. 1937), sculptor and painter, was born in Brooklyn, New York, the son of William David MacMonnies, a grain broker, and Juliana Eudora West, a grandniece of painter Benjamin West. Young Willie determined to be a sculptor and made clever figures from clay and dough. Because the Civil War bankrupted the family, as a teenager MacMonnies left school, taking odd jobs before becoming choreboy in the New York studio of Augustus Saint-Gaudens, then on the threshold of becoming the leading sculptor of America's Gilded Age. MacMonnies's talents were recognized, and he became assistant, then secretary to the sculptor, studying evenings at the National Academy of Design and the Art Students League. Under Saint-Gaudens, the fledgling sculptor worked on monuments and decorations for mansions and was educated by studio life, a continuing symposium of sculptors, artists, architects, men of letters, and their patrons.

In 1884 MacMonnies was well grounded in his craft and ready for Europe: he sampled Paris, studied in Munich, and traveled in Italy before returning to New York for another year with Saint-Gaudens. In 1886 he returned to France, which was to be his home for thirty years.

Accepted at the École des Beaux-Arts, MacMonnies became a pupil of Alexandre Falguière, from whom he learned modeling *à la boulette*: building a figure with small pellets of clay or wax so the finished cast would have a slightly uneven surface that caught light and added liveliness. Falguière and, with Antónin Mercié, with whom MacMonnies also worked, favored Renaissance styles over classical and bronze over marble, and both also painted, traits absorbed by MacMonnies. In 1887 Falguière encouraged MacMonnies to open his own studio and begin working with architects. Charles McKim and Stanford White became generous sponsors, commissioning decorative statues (*Diana*, *Pan*, *Young Faun with Heron*) for the homes of wealthy clients. By 1890 came public commissions, life-sized bronzes of James S. T. Stranahan, "the Baron Haussmann of Brooklyn," and a Nathan Hale memorial for City Hall Park in New York City. MacMonnies's concept of the lone youth disdainful of impending death caught the imagination. Paris awarded it a Salon medal, and Americans encouraged the young and personable sculptor to greater efforts. He was selected to create the central fountain for the 1893 World's Columbian Exposition in Chicago. MacMonnies and his assistants rapidly fabricated *The Barge of State*, Columbia enthroned with Fame and Father Time, rowed by eight maidens personifying Arts and Industries, attended by tritons, sea horses, and putti. Made of staff (plaster and straw), MacMonnies's extravaganza barely lasted the occasion, but it made its creator famous. His *Bacchante with Infant Faun* (1893) was deemed infamous. Installed in the Boston Public Library, it was interpreted as a drunken mother corrupting her child. The work found a more congenial home in the Metropolitan Museum of Art in New York City. *Bacchante*, *Nathan Hale*, *Pan*, *Diana*, and others were also issued in editions of small-scale parlor pieces and garden ornaments.

MacMonnies at thirty had an international reputation and substantial patronage; his fourth decade brought prodigious accomplishments, especially for a sculptor supervising his own studio and with the added complications of working across an ocean. He produced a bronze of Sir Henry Vane for the city of Boston (1894) and, for the Library of Congress, a bronze of Shakespeare (1896) and bronze doors and typanum (1896). For Prospect Park in Brooklyn he created the bronze reliefs *Army* and *Navy* and a quadriga for the Soldiers' and Sailors' Memorial Arch (1901), two monumental *Horse Tamers* groups for the park entrance (1899), and an equestrian statue of General Henry Slocum (1905); for the realism he desired MacMonnies had horses brought to his studio's courtyard where he could study them. He also created *Fame* for the U.S. Military Academy at West Point (1896), spandrels for Washington Square Arch in New York City (1895), and pediment figures for the Bowery Savings Bank, New York City (1894). *Venus and Adonis* (1895), in veined red marble, was another *succès de scandale*, requiring draperies when first exhibited in the United States (after 1959, Brookgreen Gardens, S.C.).

"Mac," as MacMonnies was commonly known, was a vivid character, constantly in motion, working amid a crowd of family, friends, models, and devoted students. Briefly in 1898 he and James McNeill Whistler

conducted an art school in Paris. MacMonnies's fame amounted to notoriety, and his large income supported homes and studios in Paris and Giverny.

Early in the new century MacMonnies declared himself "suffering so from an indigestion of sculpture and hard work" that he turned to painting. He and his wife, American painter Mary Fairchild, whom he had married in Paris in 1888, retired to Giverny to paint and to teach. Their home, a restored medieval priory ("the MacMonastery"), was a center for visiting artists, friends, and students. Behind its sheltering walls, they sketched and painted the effects of garden light on models clothed and nude. MacMonnies's colorful paintings possess atmosphere, weight, and telling detail. His critics were not impressed, though later judges more generously place him among American impressionists. MacMonnies and Fairchild had two daughters before their 1909 divorce; in 1910 he married his painting student Alice Jones. They had no children.

The Giverny sculpture studio had a track for moving works out of doors to test daylight effects; here the sculptor worked on an equestrian *General McClelland* for the nation's capital (1907) and, for Denver, a *Pioneer Monument* fountain (1906–1911), designing the entire ensemble himself. After 1909 MacMonnies worked with New York architectural firm Carrère and Hastings on two fountain figures, *Truth* and *Beauty*, for the facade of the New York Public Library (1909–1921) and on the *Princeton Battle Monument* (1908–1922), a fifty-foot limestone pier backing a deeply cut frieze of Washington and Victory encouraging the revolutionaries.

Civic Virtue, designed for City Hall Park in New York City (1909–1922), became another controversy. Early designs show Civic Virtue as female, and the finished statue is a Wagnerian hero escaping mermaidlike sirens of civic corruption, a concept badly received, especially by suffragists, as denigrating to women. This unpopular image was later removed to Queens.

Returning to the United States in 1915, MacMonnies accepted one last commission, a gift from America to France (an exchange for the Statue of Liberty), the *Battle of the Marne Memorial* (1917–1932). MacMonnies's design, executed onsite at Meaux by his former student Edmondo Quattrocchi, is a more than seventy-foot tower of figures, France defiant sheltering victims of war. Atlantic City, New Jersey, has a ten-foot 1929 version, *Liberty in Distress*. MacMonnies died in New York City.

"No American has made a greater contribution to the development of the art of sculpture in this land," concluded Lorado Taft in 1930. While MacMonnies lacks the depth and scope of Daniel Chester French or Saint-Gaudens, he earns a high place in American sculpture for his prolific and exciting inventions and vigorous craftsmanship. MacMonnies found in Europe a respect for the beautiful, "the things that count," and did his best to translate that atmosphere to America's City Beautiful programs.

• The Archives of American Art has microfilmed selected correspondence, scrapbooks, a travel diary, exhibition catalogs, photographs (of paintings), and a lengthy 1927 interview with MacMonnies by DeWitt McClellan Lockman, as well as obituaries and memorials. For a discussion of MacMonnies within the history of American sculpture, see Wayne Craven, *Sculpture in America* (1968); for contemporary appraisals of him in his prime, see Charles H. Caffin, *American Masters of Sculpture* (1913); Royal Cortissoz, *American Artists* (1923); Lorado Taft, *The History of American Sculpture* (1903; rev. ed., 1930), and Christopher Brinton, "Frederick MacMonnies," *Munsey's Magazine* 34 (1906): 415–22. Late twentieth-century renewal of interest in MacMonnies is demonstrated by two exhibition catalogs: E. Adina Gordon, *Frederick MacMonnies and Mary Fairchild MacMonnies: Two American Artists in Giverny* (1988), and Robert Judson Clark, *Frederick MacMonnies and the Princeton Battle Monument* (1984); in both, footnotes and references are excellent. Comprehensive obituaries are in the *New York Times* and the *New York Herald-Tribune*, both 23 Mar. 1937.

MARIANNE CLARK GREY

MACMURRAY, Fred (30 Aug. 1908–5 Nov. 1991), actor, was born Frederick Martin MacMurray in Kankakee, Illinois, the son of Frederick MacMurray, a concert violinist, and Maleta Martin. Shortly after their son's birth the MacMurrays returned to their home in Beaver Dam, Wisconsin (MacMurray's father had been giving a concert in Kankakee). When MacMurray was a small child his parents divorced, and his father died a short time later. MacMurray's mother worked as stenographer to support her son, who attended local schools except for one unhappy year (1918–1919) spent at the Shattuck Boys' School, a military academy in Quincy, Illinois. The young MacMurray excelled as a student athlete and musician; he formed his own band, Mac's Melody Boys, that played local Beaver Dam area engagements. He attended Carroll College in Waukesha , Wisconsin, from the fall of 1925 to the spring of 1926 on an athletic scholarship, but the scholarship was not renewed because of MacMurray's substandard performances both in the classroom and on the football field. MacMurray then spent time in Chicago, working in a department store, singing and playing saxophone with local bands, and taking classes at the Art Institute of Chicago (with a career as a commercial artist in mind).

In 1928 MacMurray moved with his mother to Los Angeles, California, where other relatives were living. Suspecting that his musical ability might land him some part-time work in the rapidly growing medium of sound pictures, MacMurray registered at the Central Casting Agency. Tall and athletically built, with blue eyes and wavy brown hair, MacMurray's looks, rather than his musical talent, drew the attention of Hollywood executives. His first film role was a nonspeaking part as a college boy in the Fox Pictures movie *Girls Gone Wild* (1929). Still considering himself a musician and singer rather than an actor, MacMurray joined the musical variety band The California Collegians. The band had already signed a contract to appear in the Broadway revue *Three's a Crowd*, and the

show opened at New York's Selwyn Theatre in October 1930 with saxophonist MacMurray participating in musical numbers. He also had a small role in the revue as a young merchant seaman who resists the romantic advances of the show's star, torch singer Libby Holman. The California Collegians also appeared in the Otto Harbach–Jerome Kern musical *Roberta*, which opened at the New Amsterdam Theatre in November 1933. While appearing in *Roberta* MacMurray made a screen test for Paramount Pictures. When a call from Hollywood came MacMurray, who was never comfortable performing before a live audience, gave his notice to the producers of *Roberta*.

For his first job under his Paramount contract, MacMurray was loaned to RKO to play a supporting role in the little-noticed *Grand Old Girl* (1935), starring May Robson. It was *The Gilded Lily* (1935) that gave MacMurray his first significant attention. In this comedy he played the loyal newspaper reporter boyfriend of actress Claudette Colbert. She is temporarily infatuated with dashing Englishman Ray Milland but returns to the faithful MacMurray at the film's end. Handsome but somewhat lacking in sex appeal, MacMurray was well suited to this "regular guy" type of role. His good looks and mastery of understated reaction made him an excellent leading man to more charismatic female stars. Though never a top box-office attraction in his own right, MacMurray was much in demand for both comedic and dramatic roles. He appeared six more times with Colbert, most notably in the popular comedy *The Egg and I* (1947). He also made four films with Carole Lombard, three with Barbara Stanwyck, two with Rosalind Russell, and he played opposite other female stars such as Jean Arthur, Alice Faye, Irene Dunne, and Marlene Dietrich. Katharine Hepburn requested that MacMurray play her love interest in *Alice Adams* (1935), a very successful adaptation of the Booth Tarkington novel, directed by George Stevens. Among MacMurray's other notable films are *Captain Eddie* (1945), in which he stars as World War I flying ace Eddie Rickenbacker, and *The Miracle of the Bells* (1948), a religious drama with Frank Sinatra.

Despite his many affable, "regular guy" roles, MacMurray's most memorable screen performances were as a villain. He surprised filmgoers with his chilling portrayal of an insurance man duped into murder in *Double Indemnity* (1944), a film noir classic directed by Billy Wilder. In *The Caine Mutiny* (1954), an adaptation of Herman Wouk's bestselling novel, MacMurray plays a cowardly and embittered lieutenant who plots against his commanding officer, played by Humphrey Bogart. As a philandering, middle-aged business executive in the black comedy *The Apartment* (1960), MacMurray's character coldly toys with the affections of a young elevator operator, played by Shirley Maclaine.

In 1936, not long after the start of his film career, MacMurray married actress-model Lillian Lamont, whom he had met when they worked together in *Roberta*. The happily married couple adopted two children and took little interest in Hollywood high life.

Modest and easy-going MacMurray enjoyed camping, fishing, and cooking. He readily acknowledged that his success in the movie industry was probably based more on luck than on extraordinary talent or ambition: "I'm just a displaced saxophone player" is the way he summed up his acting career. MacMurray was careful with his money (realizing that the large paychecks might someday disappear) and hired a financial manager to make conservative investments, including a cattle ranch in northern California that became the family's second home. Sound financial planning and a comfortable but unextravagant personal life made MacMurray one of the wealthiest people in show business.

From 1960 to 1972 MacMurray starred in the television series "My Three Sons," playing a widower with three rambunctious offspring. His movie star presence gave distinction to the mildly amusing but durable situation comedy. Never a smash hit, "My Three Sons" drew moderately sized audiences during its unusually long run on American television and was popular in the world market. MacMurray was unwilling to submit to the rigor of a weekly series, and his contract stipulated that his duties on "My Three Sons" would require working no more than three months per year (his scenes for the entire season were shot in one batch and fitted into episodes completed later by the rest of the cast). This schedule left MacMurray free to pursue big-screen assignments at the Walt Disney studios. The first of these Disney projects was *The Shaggy Dog* (1959), starring MacMurray as a befuddled father whose son has turned into a canine. That film was followed by *The Absentminded Professor* (1961), *Bon Voyage* (1962), *Son of Flubber* (1963), *Follow Me, Boys!* (1966), *The Happiest Millionaire* (1967), and *Charley and the Angel* (1973). MacMurray's work in Disney's family films, along with his long-running television series, made him a familiar face to a new generation.

Left a widower by the death of Lamont in 1953, MacMurray married actress June Haver the following year. Haver, a star of musical films, gave up her career when they married. She and MacMurray adopted twins. MacMurray's final acting appearance was a brief turn in the star-studded disaster film *The Swarm* (1978). He died in Santa Monica, California.

• For a first-person account of MacMurray's life and career, see MacMurray (as told to Pete Martin), "I've Been Lucky," *Saturday Evening Post*, 24 Feb. 1962, pp. 36, 40, 44. James R. Parish and Don E. Stanke, *The All-Americans* (1977), offers a detailed biographical chapter on MacMurray. See also June Haver MacMurray, "The Magic of a Good Marriage," *Good Housekeeping*, Oct. 1971, pp. 94, 176–83; Dwight Whitney, "The Anatomy of Success," *TV Guide*, 31 July 1965, pp. 15–18; Cleveland Amory, "Hollywood's Ho-Hum Boy," *Saturday Evening Post*, 3 Mar. 1945, pp. 17, 97–98; and Kyle Crichton, "Star without Limousine," *Collier's*, 20 June 1936, pp. 16, 48. An obituary is in the *New York Times*, 6 Nov. 1991.

MARY C. KALFATOVIC

MACNEVEN, William James (21 Mar. 1763–12 July 1841), physician, professor, and Irish-American nationalist, was born on a small estate in Ballynahowne, County Galway, Ireland, the son of James MacNeven and Rosa Dolphin. William's mother died when he was young, and he and his three brothers were raised by their aunt. At age ten or eleven William was sent to Prague to live with his uncle Baron William O'Kelley MacNeven, a court physician to Empress Maria Theresa. Following a classical education, William attended university in Prague and went on to study medicine at the University of Vienna, from which he graduated in 1783. In 1784 MacNeven returned to Dublin, where he established a medical practice.

MacNeven took an early interest in chemistry and mineralogy. In 1788 he translated and wrote a preface for Geiss's *Essay on the Construction and Use of a Mine Auger*. At about this same time MacNeven also became an active participant in the Catholic Emancipation movement. Representing Meath at the Catholic Convention in 1792, he supported the extension of the forty-shilling freehold to Catholics. By 1797 MacNeven engaged in even more radical political action and joined the United Irish movement. He quickly rose to a position in its directory. MacNeven traveled to Hamburg in 1797 to assist in negotiations with the French for an invasion of Ireland as part of a general rebellion there. Passport difficulties prevented him from reaching France. Upon returning to Ireland, MacNeven and the other United Irish leaders were arrested and jailed in Kilmainham prison. To prevent further bloodshed, MacNeven, Thomas Addis Emmet, and Arthur O'Connor agreed to the "Kilmainham Treaty." Under its terms they were to provide a full account of the United Irish movement and accept banishment to a country at peace with Great Britain. MacNeven and Emmet chose the United States, but Rufus King, U.S. minister to England, branded them "malcontents" and raised objections. The British feared the prisoners' continued influence on Irish affairs and therefore moved them to Fort George, Inverness, Scotland, for four additional years of imprisonment. MacNeven was released in 1802 under the Treaty of Amiens. He traveled to the Continent and spent the next several months on a walking tour of Switzerland, an account of which he published in 1803 as *A Ramble through Swisserland in the Summer and Autumn of 1802*. Still hopeful of a French invasion of Ireland, MacNeven served as a captain in the Irish Brigade of the French army from 1803 to 1805. However, he became disillusioned by a lack of commitment from the French, and so he sailed for New York, where he landed on 4 July 1805.

MacNeven gained rapid acceptance in New York society because of Emmet's political and professional connections and his own excellent credentials. In 1807 he gave a series of lectures at the College of Physicians and Surgeons and that same year published *Pieces of Irish History*, which contains MacNeven's version of his secret testimony before a committee of Parliament during his imprisonment. In the book MacNeven claims King "sinned against the letter and spirit" of the Constitution in denying them entry to the United States. MacNeven was appointed professor of obstetrics at the College of Physicians and Surgeons in 1808, while also giving clinical lectures under David Hosack at the New York Almshouse. With the reorganization of the college, MacNeven was made professor of chemistry in 1811. A chemical laboratory was constructed under MacNeven's direction, which allowed his students to conduct experiments. He married Jane Margaret Riker Tom in 1810. The couple had four children. From 1808 to 1811 MacNeven coedited the *New York Medical and Philosophical Journal* with Hosack and Hugh Williamson. Between 1819 and 1821 MacNeven published three important scientific works. *An Exposition of the Atomic Theory*, published in 1819, was one of the earliest works in America in support of John Dalton's atomic theory and the notion that "substances enter into chemical combinations in definite proportions." A year later the first American edition of W. T. Brande's *Manual of Chemistry* was published, with notes and emendations by MacNeven. In *A Tabular View of the Modern Nomenclature*, published in 1821, MacNeven reported the latest developments in chemical classification in a clear and concise format for a knowledge-hungry audience.

MacNeven remained active on behalf of his fellow Irish immigrants to the United States. He was a co-founder of the Irish Emigrant Association, which in 1816 petitioned Congress to set aside lands in the Illinois Territory where Irish immigrants could settle so that they might become "respectable and independent." A decade later MacNeven established a free labor office to direct immigrants to jobs on road and canal projects, and he offered immigrants guidance in a pamphlet, *Directions or Advice to Irishmen Arriving in America*.

From the middle of the 1820s through the 1830s MacNeven turned his attention to organizing and directing campaigns to support and raise "rent" for political causes in Ireland, such as emancipation and repeal. In 1826, in his *Address to the People of Ireland*, MacNeven urged greater independence for Ireland within the imperial relationship. His suggestions were rebuffed by Daniel O'Connell, an important Irish nationalist leader. From 1828 to 1829 MacNeven served as president of the Friends of Ireland in New York, and while involved in controversy regarding Ireland he was also embroiled in a local controversy relating to his professional responsibilities. MacNeven and four other professors at the College of Physicians and Surgeons resigned when accused by members of the county medical society of excessive fee taking and favoritism toward their private students. Along with David Hosack, Valentine Mott, and John W. Francis, MacNeven founded a rival medical school (1826) under the auspices of Rutgers College. Though successful, under legal challenge the school was forced to close by the New York State Regents in 1829. During the cholera epidemic of 1832 MacNeven was appointed special medical council and advised increased sanitary efforts

to stop the spread of the disease. Due to illness MacNeven retired from medical practice in 1836.

MacNeven felt that the Irish in America should be cohesive but that they should not vote as a bloc: "We have no pretense of confederating as Irishmen upon American politics" (Potter, p. 228). Philosophically a Jeffersonian Republican, in practical terms MacNeven was involved in Tammany politics, having served a term as alderman for the Fourteenth Ward. Though an Andrew Jackson supporter, MacNeven publicly disagreed with the party over the Second Bank of the United States, believing the Jackson policy would adversely affect the poor. For his apostasy MacNeven suffered the wrath of the mob. He later forgave his fellow immigrants, believing they had been misled.

MacNeven was an officer or founding member of several cultural societies. In keeping with the spirit of the age for the practical application of science, MacNeven gave an "Introductory Discourse to a Few Lectures in the Application of Chemistry to Agriculture, Delivered before the New York Athenaeum in the Winter of 1825", and he hosted many meetings of the Literary and Philosophical Society of New York. MacNeven was elected a member of the American Philosophical Society in 1823.

MacNeven's contribution lies in his lifelong commitment to the cause of freedom for the people of Ireland as well as his solicitude for the plight of the Irish immigrant in America. He translated his republican principles into practice with his efforts to improve the social, economic, and even physical lives of his less-fortunate countrymen. MacNeven believed that the Irish in the United States could play a role in effecting change in Ireland and that their example could serve as a model for the Irish people. Though he died just prior to the large influx of his fellow Irish Catholics to the United States in the 1840s, MacNeven helped lay the organizational groundwork that would aid the immigrants' transition to American society. As a scientist and teacher MacNeven was instrumental in elucidating for his students and the general public in the new nation the latest advances from Europe in chemical classification, mineral analysis, and scientific method.

MacNeven died in New York City. A large monument to him in St. Paul's churchyard in Lower Manhattan stands in tribute to his patriotic and scientific achievements.

• The fullest biographical account is found in R. R. Madden, *The United Irishmen, Their Lives and Times* (1843), which includes a memoir by MacNeven's daughter. An appreciation may be found in Thomas Addis Emmet, Jr., *Incidents of My Life* (1911). A detailed account of MacNeven's United Irish activities is in Marianne Elliot, *Partners in Revolution: The United Irishmen and France* (1982). John C. Greene examines MacNeven's contribution to American chemistry in *American Science in the Age of Jefferson* (1984), but this should be supplemented by Deasmumhan O'Raghallaigh, "William James MacNeven," *Irish Studies* 30 (June 1941): 247–59, and for his medical career by Byron Stookey, "William James MacNeven (1763–1841)," *Bulletin of the New York Academy of Medicine* 41 (Oct. 1965): 1037–51. Victor R. Greene, *American Im-

migrant Leaders, 1800–1910: Marginality and Identity (1987), makes the case for MacNeven's leadership of the American Irish community, while George Potter, *To the Golden Door* (1960), describes MacNeven's domestic political activities. An obituary is in the *New York Tribune*, 14 July 1841.

EMIL J. HAFNER

MACNIDER, Hanford (2 Oct. 1889–17 Feb. 1968), businessman and army officer, was born Hanford McNider in Mason City, Iowa, the son of Charles Henry McNider, a banker, and May Cordelia Hanford. As a teenager, MacNider resumed the old family spelling, inserting the *a* in *Mac*. After attending Milton Academy in Milton, Massachusetts, MacNider enrolled at Harvard, receiving his B.A. in 1911. Returning to Mason City, he joined his father's bank, First National, as an apprentice bookkeeper.

A second lieutenant in Company A of the Iowa National Guard, "Jack" (as he was called) MacNider was sent in June 1916 to Brownsville, Texas, to patrol the Mexican border during the imbroglio with the Mexican guerrilla leader Pancho Villa. Once the United States entered World War I, MacNider enlisted in the regular army, joining the Ninth Regiment of the Second (Indianhead) Division as provisional second lieutenant. Because of a minor infraction of an enlisted man under his command, MacNider was placed under garrison arrest, but the penalty was not enforced and had no impact on his service. Once in France he served as instructor at the Army Candidate School at Langres. Anxious for combat, he broke all regulations by returning, without authorization, to the Ninth as adjutant. (Later, when he occupied high position, he destroyed all records containing charges of insubordination.)

MacNider participated in major offensives at Château-Thierry, Soissons, St.-Mihiel (where he was slightly wounded), Blanc Mont Ridge, and the Meuse-Argonne. On 12 September 1918 he was delivering instructions to the front when he captured a German gun nest. In November he was ordered to establish a bridgehead across the Meuse River, but knowing that the armistice had been signed, he saved the lives of two battalions, some 2,000 men, by defying the order. The commanding general later told him, "This doesn't make sense, but I seem to be glad you did it." Discharged as a lieutenant colonel in 1919, he bore more decorations than any other man except John J. Pershing.

In 1920 MacNider was elected Iowa state commander of the American Legion and a year later became national commander. He traveled throughout the nation advocating "adjusted compensation" for veterans, popularly called the "bonus." Embodied in the Legion Four-Fold Bill, the plan included aid for education, farms, home buying, and land settlement and a fixed adjusted service pay of $1.50 per day of service. "These men have first rank on the citizenship of America," he said. Although passed by Congress in 1922, it was attacked by the nation's leading business groups, opposed by Treasury secretary Andrew Mellon, and

vetoed by President Warren Harding. During the debate, MacNider returned an appointment to the U.S. Senate by Governor Note Kendall so as not to compromise his cause. Only in 1924, after MacNider's legion term was over, did a bonus bill become law. In 1925 he married Margaret Elizabeth McAuley; they had three children.

As chairman of the Republican Service League, MacNider was influential in gaining veterans' votes for his party in the 1924 and 1928 presidential elections. In 1925 President Calvin Coolidge appointed him assistant secretary of war. For the next three years he supervised procurement, developed industrial mobilization plans, and often served as acting secretary, thereby attending cabinet meetings. Such top-ranking World War II officers as Dwight D. Eisenhower, Leonard Gerow, and Mark Clark served in his office.

From 1930 to 1932 MacNider was American minister to Canada. President Herbert Hoover gave him the specific task of negotiating a treaty to develop the St. Lawrence Seaway. It took two years to conclude the agreement, and because of the intransigence of opponents in the U.S. Senate, the seaway project was not approved for twenty years.

All this time MacNider was engaged in numerous business enterprises, particularly after the death of his father in 1928. He launched the Northwest Bancorporation, a holding company that controlled more than a hundred banks in the Upper Mississippi Valley. Reorganizing the Northwestern States Portland Cement Company, a major family holding, he turned the firm into one of the nation's largest producers.

In 1940 MacNider was a "favorite son" candidate for the Republican presidential nomination, and he turned down feelers to become the running mate of the eventual nominee, Wendell Willkie. In 1941, critical of both the New Deal and the interventionist foreign policy of Franklin D. Roosevelt, MacNider was made national vice chairman of the America First Committee (AFC), which lobbied the public and the Congress to support noninvolvement in the raging war in Europe. In this capacity he testified before congressional committees against President Roosevelt's controversial Lend-Lease Bill. Four days before the Pearl Harbor attack, MacNider, always a staunch Republican, resigned from the AFC because of his objection to the committee's plans to support anti-interventionist congressional candidates irrespective of party.

When the United States entered World War II, MacNider returned to active military duty and was assigned to the Southwest Pacific. Made brigadier general in 1942, he commanded a task force against Buna in New Guinea. "We had only what weapons we could carry on our backs," he said. Hit by an enemy grenade on 23 November 1942, he was the first American general to be wounded in the war. Despite hospitalization, including a series of eye operations in New York, MacNider was soon back in the field, commanding the 158th Regimental Combat Team. He helped consolidate the American hold on Numfoor Island off Dutch New Guinea and participated in the assault on Lingayen and Legaspi in the Philippines. One enlisted man commented on MacNider's energy, "He can out-climb, out-walk, out-talk, and probably out-fight any man in the outfit."

After the war MacNider returned to Mason City, where he pursued his many business interests and rose to the rank of major general of the 103rd Infantry Reserve Division. In 1948 he participated in the short-lived effort by conservative Republicans to nominate General Douglas MacArthur for president. Always on the right, he supported the activities in the 1950s of Senator Joseph R. McCarthy in questioning the loyalty of liberal Democrats and attempting to purge the government of "subversives." In the 1960s, during the Vietnam War, he said the United States should either "stomp hell out of them and get it over with, or get out." He died in Sarasota, Florida.

• MacNider's papers are in the Herbert Hoover Presidential Library, West Branch, Iowa. Biographical articles include Joan Liffring, "The Many Lives of Hanford MacNider," *Iowan* 13 (Dec. 1967): 34–52, and Dorothy H. Rankin, "Hanford MacNider," *Annals of Iowa* 33 (Apr. 1956): 233–67. MacNider's involvement with the bonus issue is discussed in Robert E. Seifert, "The American Legion, Hanford MacNider and the Fight for Adjusted Compensation 1919–1924" (M.A. thesis, Univ. of Akron, 1975). References to MacNider's post–World War II political positions are in Justus D. Doenecke, *Not to the Swift: The Old Isolationists in the Cold War Era* (1979). For a superior journalistic account, see the *Des Moines Sunday Register*, 24 Oct. 1965. An obituary is in the *New York Times*, 18 Feb. 1968.

JUSTUS DOENECKE

MACNIDER, William De Berniere (25 June 1881–31 May 1951), physician and medical educator, was born in Chapel Hill, North Carolina, the son of Virginius St. Clair MacNider, a physician, and Sophia Beatty Mallett. MacNider was keenly interested in natural history and science during his childhood, and the university environment at Chapel Hill undoubtedly strengthened his desire for a career in the biological sciences. After attending public schools in Chapel Hill, he enrolled at the University of North Carolina in 1898. His father and grandfather were both physicians, and their influence probably contributed to his choice of a medical career; while an undergraduate, he resolved to become a medical researcher. His abilities were soon recognized by the faculty, and he was hired during his graduate study years as an assistant in biology from 1899 to 1900, as assistant in anatomy from 1900 to 1902, and as assistant in clinical diagnosis from 1902 until 1905. MacNider graduated in 1903 with the first class of the University of North Carolina Medical School to receive the M.D. degree. He subsequently received additional research and clinical training at the University of Chicago and at Case Western Reserve University in Cleveland. During these formative years MacNider benefited significantly from the mentorship of such prominent biologists and medical scientists as H. V. Wilson and Richard Whitehead of Chapel Hill,

George Neil Stewart of Case Western Reserve University, and William S. Thayer and William Osler of Johns Hopkins University.

MacNider returned to the University of North Carolina in 1905 to establish its department of pharmacology. He was professor of pharmacology until 1918, when he was named Kenan Professor of Pharmacology. MacNider married Sarah Jane Foard of Davie County, North Carolina, in 1918; they had one child. In 1919 he became Kenan Research Professor at the university, and he served in this capacity until 1937. That year Charles S. Magnum retired as dean of the School of Medicine; MacNider was appointed to the position, which he held until 1940. Although an able administrator, MacNider preferred research and teaching. He continued as chairman of the pharmacology department until 1943 and as Kenan Research Professor until retiring in 1950 as professor emeritus.

MacNider was best known for his research in pharmacology, toxicology, and gerontology. He was particularly interested in renal and hepatic diseases, including acute and chronic nephritis, the toxicity of general anesthetics on the kidney, and the effects of alcohol on the liver. Other investigations for which he was noted involved disorders of acid-base and electrolyte metabolism, the process of repair and regeneration in damaged liver cells, and cellular aspects of the aging process. MacNider published hundreds of major studies and notes; he also served as associate editor of a number of journals, including the *Proceedings of the Society for Experimental Biology and Medicine*, the *Journal of Pharmacology and Experimental Therapeutics*, and the *Quarterly Journal of Alcohol Study*.

MacNider was well recognized for his scientific contributions during his lifetime, receiving the New York Academy of Science's Gibbs Prize for Medical Research (1930–1931), the Southern Medical Association's Research Medal (1933), and the Association of American Physicians' Kober Medal (1941). He also was honored with a number of lectureships during his later years, including the Harvey Society Lecture (1928–1929), the Smith-Reed-Russell Lecture at George Washington University (1938), the Brown-Sequart Lecture at the Medical College of Virginia (1938), and the Mayo Foundation Lecture (1939). He served as physician in chief pro tem at Peter Bent Brigham Hospital, Boston, in 1925, and he was a lecturer at both Duke University Medical School and Columbia University.

MacNider was actively involved in many scientific and professional organizations and was elected to leadership roles. He served as president of the Elisha Mitchell Scientific Society, of the Medical Society of North Carolina (1925–1926), of the American Society for Pharmacology and Experimental Therapeutics (1932–1934), of the International Anesthesia Research Society (1934–1935), and of the Society for Experimental Biology and Medicine (1941–1942). MacNider was also chairman of several national committees and advisory groups, including the Gerontology Society, the Division of Pharmacology and Therapeutics of the

American Medical Association, the National Board of Medical Examiners, and the International Club for Research on Aging. He was a gerontology consultant for the National Institutes of Health and a member of the National Red Cross Committee on nutritional aspects of aging, the Executive Committee and the Cellular Physiology Committee of the National Research Council, and the Research Committee of the National Anesthesia Society. Among his many honors was election to the National Academy of Sciences, the American Philosophical Society, and the Harvard Society, as well as the American Association for the Advancement of Science, the American Academy of Arts and Sciences, and the American College of Physicians. MacNider died in Durham, North Carolina.

• Most of MacNider's professional papers are in the William de B. MacNider Collection at the Manuscript Department of the University of North Carolina, Chapel Hill. Major sources on MacNider include W. C. George, "William de Berniere MacNider: 1881–1951," *Science* 115 (1952): 489–90; the same article appeared in the *North Carolina Medical Journal* 13 (1952): 165–66. See also W. W. McLendon and S. G. Cochrane, eds., *The Good Doctor* (1953), and W. Reece Berryhill et al., eds., *Medical Education at Chapel Hill: The First Hundred Years* (1979).

MARCUS B. SIMPSON, JR.

MACOMB, Alexander (3 Apr. 1782–25 June 1841), soldier, was born at Detroit, Michigan Territory, the son of Alexander Macomb, a successful merchant, and Catharine Navarre, daughter of a former French official. The family relocated to New York City shortly after the Revolution, and Macomb attended primary schools in Newark, New Jersey. In 1798, at the age of sixteen, he joined a city militia unit and subsequently received a commission as coronet of light dragoons in the regular army under the auspices of Alexander Hamilton. Macomb advanced to second lieutenant on 2 March 1799 and following the Quasi-War with France was discharged on 15 June 1800. He reenlisted as a second lieutenant, Second Infantry, on 16 February 1801 and became secretary to General James Wilkinson. In this capacity Macomb conducted several tours of the southeastern frontier, becoming first lieutenant on 12 October 1802. That year he also became one of two students selected for instruction at the nascent U.S. Military Academy. In 1803 he married Catharine Macomb, a cousin, with whom he had several children (the exact number is unknown). Macomb remained at West Point until 1805, when he was appointed captain in the newly created Corps of Engineers on 11 June. He was deployed as chief engineer of coastal fortifications in Georgia and the Carolinas and garnered promotion to major on 23 February 1808 and to lieutenant colonel on 23 July 1810. He compiled and published *A Treatise on Martial Law and Courts Martial* in 1809, which was the first study of its kind in army history. On the eve of war with Great Britain, Macomb repaired to Washington, D.C., to assume responsibilities as adjutant general, one of the military's senior administrative positions.

Following the onset of hostilities, Macomb sought transfer out of the engineers in order to secure a field command. On 6 July 1812 he became colonel of the newly raised Third Artillery Regiment and spent several months as garrison commander at strategic Sackets Harbor, New York. Macomb participated in the 27 May 1813 capture of Fort George, Upper Canada, and subsequently commanded the reserves during General Wilkinson's ill-fated St. Lawrence expedition. He handled his soldiers adroitly on both occasions and on 24 January 1814 advanced to brigadier general attached to the Right Division at Plattsburg, New York. In late August 1814 the divisional commander, Major General George Izard, was ordered to march the bulk of his command westward to Niagara. Macomb's brigade of 1,500 regular soldiers and 3,000 militia remained at Plattsburg to defend it against an army of 10,000 veteran British troops under Governor General Sir George Prevost. On 11 September 1814 Macomb's troops bravely withstood Prevost's attack from within their fortifications while an American fleet under Commodore Thomas Macdonough decisively defeated a British squadron on nearby Lake Champlain. This event halted Prevost's land attack, and he immediately withdrew back to Lower Canada. For his determined resistance in the face of overwhelming numbers, Macomb was honored by a gold coin, the Thanks of Congress, and promotion to brevet major general.

Macomb was retained in the service after the war and served on a board of general officers charged with effecting the army's peacetime reduction. He also commanded military districts at New York and Detroit until 1 June 1821, when military cutbacks reduced him in grade to colonel of engineers. Macomb accepted his demotion quietly, and when the commanding general of the army, Jacob Jennings Brown, died in 1828, Macomb was chosen to succeed him in preference to Winfield Scott and Edmund Pendleton Gaines, who were feuding. As commanding general, Macomb proved himself a vigorous and farsighted leader. He sought to clarify and centralize a sometimes ambiguous chain of command by bringing all staff branches and bureaus under his immediate control. This move culminated in the 1830 court-martial of Adjutant General Roger Jones, who sought to maintain the autonomy of his department. Macomb then sought to centralize state militia administration and to abolish the whiskey ration; he also published several treatises, including *The Practice of Court Martials* (1840), and a play, *Pontiac; or, The Siege of Detroit* (1835). His first wife having died, Macomb married the widow Harriet Balch Wilson in 1826. He continued implementing effective military policy until his death by illness in Washington, D.C.

Macomb, while not a brilliant soldier, was a capable career officer possessing organizational and administrative talent. His efforts to streamline and systematize military procedures both epitomized and facilitated the growth of professionalism throughout the postwar period. His thirteen-year tenure as commanding general was marked by good relations with the executive and legislative branches of government and a trend toward modern administration. By taming and rationalizing the military bureaucracy, he laid the groundwork for the army's brilliant success in the Mexican War, a scant five years after his passing.

• Macomb's personal papers are in the Burton Historical Collection, Detroit Public Library. Collections of War of 1812 correspondence are at the Manuscript Department, New York State Library; the Historical Society of Pennsylvania; the Clements Library, University of Michigan; and the Feinstein Library, State University of New York, Plattsburg. Scattered materials also exist in the Clarke Library, Central Michigan University; the Lilly Library, University of Indiana; the Massachusetts Historical Society; and the Manuscript Division, New York Public Library. Published correspondence is in various volumes of *American State Papers: Military Affairs* (1832), and Clarence E. Carter, ed., *Territorial Papers of the United States* (25 vols., 1946–1954). Laudatory attempts at biography are "A Biographical Sketch of General Alexander Macomb," *Military and Naval Magazine* 5 (May 1835): 161–73, and "Biographical Sketch of Alexander Macomb," *United States Military Magazine* 2 (June 1841): 89–96. See also George H. Richards, ed., *Memoir of Alexander Macomb* (1833). The most modern interpretation remains Allan S. Everest, *The Military Career of Alexander Macomb* (1989). For analysis of his reform efforts consult William B. Skelton, "The Commanding General and the Problem of Command in the United States Army, 1821–1841," *Military Affairs* 34 (Dec. 1970): 117–22, and Patrick J. Hughes, "The Adjutant General's Office, 1821–1861" (Ph.D. diss., Ohio State Univ., 1977). An eyewitness of field activities is John T. Sprague, "Macomb's Mission to the Seminoles," *Florida Historical Quarterly* 35 (Oct. 1956): 130–96. Finally, an excellent overview of the officer corps in Macomb's day is William B. Skelton, *An American Profession of Arms* (1992).

JOHN C. FREDRIKSEN

MACON, Nathaniel (17 Dec. 1758–29 June 1837), politician, was born in Edgecombe (now Warren) County, North Carolina, the son of Gideon Macon and Priscilla Jones, planters. In 1774 Macon entered the College of New Jersey (now Princeton University), where he studied for two years. At the outbreak of the revolutionary war in 1776, he served with the New Jersey militia but left the army a year later and returned to North Carolina. In 1780 he reenlisted in a company led by his brother in time to fight as a private at the battle of Camden (16 Aug. 1780). In a democratic gesture that would come to characterize both his public and private lives, Macon refused a commission as an officer. In 1783 he married Hannah Plumer, who died seven years later, leaving Macon with three children. A slaveholder and planter of moderate means, Macon worked alongside his slaves until he began to complain of the heat at the age of sixty-seven. His plantation "Buck Spring" was situated on the Roanoke River in north central North Carolina, a fertile tobacco-growing region that sustained a wealthy and politically influential planter class.

Macon's political career was characterized by a commitment to the principles of states' rights and limited government. He entered politics in 1781, when he was

elected to the state senate in North Carolina. In the legislature, Macon came under the influence of Willie Jones, a staunch anti-federalist whose opposition to the proposed federal Constitution of 1787 was largely responsible for the failure of the first attempt at ratification in North Carolina. Macon brought this suspicion of a strong central government into the national political arena in the 1790s. Elected to the national House of Representatives in 1791, he joined the opposition to the Federalists that was coalescing around Thomas Jefferson and James Madison. Macon opposed Alexander Hamilton's program of economic nationalism and the Federalist-sponsored Jay Treaty with Great Britain. In North Carolina, Macon was instrumental in the growth of the Jeffersonian Republican party. He directed the "Warren Junto," a group of politicians that included David Stone of Wake County and James Turner of Warren County. In 1799 Macon sponsored the *Raleigh Register* as the official organ of the North Carolina Jeffersonians.

After Jefferson's election as president in 1800, Macon was elected Speaker in 1801 and became one of the leading Republicans in the House. During Jefferson's first administration, Macon remained an outspoken advocate of the rights of the states and a consistent opponent of a strong central government. Based on a strict construction of the Constitution, Macon opposed banks, paper money, and tariffs. He even objected to the buildup of national armed forces, fearing that the military would become an instrument of despotism. Ironically, Macon's fervent devotion to Jeffersonian doctrines eventually led him into opposition to the president. In 1806 he joined John Taylor of Virginia in what became known as the "Tertium Quids," a group of conservative congressmen who fought against what they saw as the corrupting influence of power in the Republican administration. Macon lost the Speakership in 1807.

Macon's name is also associated with the foreign policy of the early republic. The North Carolina representative supported Republican diplomacy during the global conflict between Great Britain and France, which began in 1803. The putative trade regulations of both European nations caused harm to the agricultural interests of Macon's tobacco-producing district. As chair of the Foreign Affairs Committee, Macon reported a bill in December 1809 (Macon's Bill Number 1) that closed American ports to the shipping of both England and France, promising to remove this provision if either power rescinded its decrees. In May 1810 Macon's Bill Number 2 repealed all measures of commercial retaliation and restored complete freedom of trade, adding that the president could reinstate a nonintercourse decree against either power if the other should cease its violations of American commerce. Although Macon was reluctant to go to war against Great Britain, he supported the War of 1812 in the belief that a nation must fight to protect its sovereignty.

In 1815 Macon was elected to the U.S. Senate, where he continued to support the principles of the "Old Republicans." He opposed measures such as a national bank, a protective tariff, and internal transportation improvements that were all part of the postwar nationalist program of economic growth. Once again, he argued that the government should not take any step beyond the Constitution. Macon became one of the first southerners to realize that the expansion of federal power posed a lethal threat to slavery, claiming, "If Congress can make canals they can with more propriety emancipate" (Sellers, p. 142). During the Missouri controversy of 1819–1820, Macon openly defended slavery on the floor of Congress. Anticipating the proslavery argument of the antebellum era, he argued that slaves were more kindly treated and better cared for than any poor people in the world. He was the only southerner to vote against the final admission of Missouri, determined that this slave state should be admitted without any provisions regarding the peculiar institution.

Macon continued to carry the banner of Jeffersonian principles during the 1820s. In the presidential contest of 1824, Macon endorsed William H. Crawford, the states' rights candidate from Georgia, and then he opposed the nationalizing policies of President John Quincy Adams. Though Macon refrained from openly supporting Andrew Jackson in the election of 1828, he supported the new president in the nullification controversy. While Macon disapproved of South Carolina's attempt to nullify the federal tariff law, he insisted on the constitutional right of secession as a safeguard against federal usurpation of power.

After serving thirty-seven years in Congress, Macon resigned from the Senate in 1828 and retired to his plantation home in North Carolina. He remained a committed Jeffersonian, supporting the principle of annual elections during the North Carolina constitutional convention of 1835. Macon is best remembered, in the words of one historian, as "the incarnation of Jeffersonian simplicity" (Schlesinger, p. 27). His political career, resting on a faithfulness to the ideals of limited government and states' rights, illustrates the origins of southern conservatism. In addition, Macon's joining of Jeffersonian principles to the defense of slavery foreshadowed one of the main themes of antebellum southern sectionalism. He died in his home in Warren County, North Carolina.

• The primary collections of Macon's manuscript papers are at the North Carolina Department of Archives and History and in the State Senators' Papers, 1779–1946, at Duke University. Additional Macon letters are in the Thomas Worthington Papers in the State Library of Ohio. For published primary sources, see *Letters of Nathaniel Macon, John Steele, and William Barry Grove*, ed. K. P. Battle, James Sprunt Historical Monograph no. 3 (1902), and *Some Unpublished Letters of Nathaniel Macon*, ed. John S. Bassett, in Trinity College Historical Papers, 6th ser. (1906). An older biography of Macon is William E. Dodd, *Life of Nathaniel Macon* (1903). A brief but penetrating sketch of Macon is in Arthur M. Schlesinger, Jr., *The Age of Jackson* (1945). On Macon's political ideas, see Noble E. Cunningham, Jr., "Nathaniel Macon and the Southern Protest against National Consolidation," *North Carolina Historical Review* 32 (July 1955):

376–84. The political context of Macon's career is fully described in Norman K. Risjord, *The Old Republicans: Southern Conservatism in the Age of Jefferson* (1965). For the foreign policy of the Jefferson and Madison administrations, see Bradford Perkins, *Prologue to War: England and the United States, 1805–1812* (1961). On the politics of the 1820s, consult Glover Moore, *The Missouri Controversy, 1819–1821* (1953); Charles S. Sydnor, *The Development of Southern Sectionalism, 1819–1848* (1948); and Charles G. Sellers, *The Market Revolution: Jacksonian America, 1815–1846* (1991).

MITCHELL SNAY

MACON, Uncle Dave (7 Oct. 1870–22 Mar. 1952), banjoist and singer, was born David Harrison Macon in Smart Station, near McMinnville, Warren County, Tennessee, the son of Captain John Macon, a merchant and distiller, and Martha Ann Ramsey. The Macon family had deep roots in the county, having first settled there in 1830 through a revolutionary war land grant. The youngest of nine children, Macon grew up during the hard times of Reconstruction, during which his father's family lost many of their landholdings and stores in the area. This eventually led to the family's relocating in nearby Nashville in about 1883; there Macon's mother operated the Broadway Hotel, which catered to the many theater performers traveling through Nashville.

Macon spent his teenage years in the urban part of Nashville near the Cumberland River docks, where he attended Hume Fogg High School and heard the folk songs of the black stevedores as well as the vaudeville jokes and banjo songs of the professional entertainers who stayed at his mother's hotel. He was fascinated by the show-off banjo styles popular on the stage in the 1880s, and by the time he was fourteen he had talked his mother into buying him a banjo. He also watched the revival meetings of the evangelist Sam Jones, who would soon convert Tom Ryman, the notorious riverboat captain who built the Ryman Auditorium—later the home of the Grand Ole Opry.

This fascinating world came to an end in 1886, when Captain John Macon was stabbed and killed on the street in front of the hotel by an old enemy. The Macon family vowed vengeance and pressed charges against the suspect; after a series of legal maneuvers, a jury found him innocent. At this point the family split up. Macon and his mother moved to the small hamlet of Readyville on the Rutherford-Warren County line, where she opened a boardinghouse for stagecoach travelers. Macon had continued to play the banjo and to learn songs of all sorts from traditional singers in the area, as well as from sheet music from Nashville. His main job in Readyville was to change and water the stagecoach horses, but he soon built an improvised stage on the barn from which he would entertain passengers with his banjo.

In about 1899 Macon courted and married Matilda Richardson; they had seven sons. The couple moved to her hometown of Kittrell. About this time Macon started a freight-hauling company with a neighbor, Hatton Sanford, calling it the Macon Midway Mule and Transportation Company. This would be his primary vocation for the next two decades, until the advent of gasoline-powered cars and trucks made mule power obsolete.

When he was about fifty, Macon began to accept offers to play and sing professionally. In 1924 he joined forces with Sid Harkreader, a young fiddler and guitarist from Wilson County, Tennessee. While playing at a convention of furniture dealers in Chattanooga, a representative of the Sterchi Brothers Furniture Company, the local distributor for Vocalion Records, offered to send the pair to New York City to make records. In July 1924 they went to New York to record some of the first country records made—fourteen sides that included such signature songs as "Keep My Skillet Good and Greasy," "Chewing Gum," "Jonah and the Whale," and "All I've Got's Gone." The records sold very well and formed the foundation for the pair's recording career, which would eventually include a total of 180 sides covering every major record company.

In January 1925 Macon and Harkreader began a series of personal appearances for Loew's Theaters, a national chain; their first stand was in Birmingham, Alabama, where they created a sensation and extended their stay for five weeks. Similar runs in Memphis and Nashville followed, and finally longer runs as far away as Boston and Florida. The Loew's experience, combined with the records, won for Macon a national reputation: he was a skilled and versatile banjo player (using as many as sixteen different picking styles), a strong singer, a consummate comedian, and a "trick" player who twirled his banjo, tossed it into the air, and danced around it. "He may not have been the best banjo player or the best singer," recalled his friend Bradley Kincaid, "but he sure was the best something."

In 1925 Macon also made it on to the radio, becoming, with Uncle Jimmy Thompson, one of the first two original stars of WSM-Nashville's Grand Ole Opry. In fact, he was about the only early member of the Opry troupe that had had any meaningful professional experience as an entertainer. Although he only appeared on the Opry intermittently in the 1920s (he soon learned he could make more money doing theater tours), he did become a regular by the 1930s. Prior to the coming of Roy Acuff in 1938, he was one of the most popular performers on the show. He soon dropped Harkreader for more skilled musical companions; two of these were guitarist Sam McGee and his brother, fiddler Kirk McGee. Sam McGee, one of the first country guitarists to do serious finger picking as opposed to strumming, was one of the prime instrumentalists in his generation and a serious challenge for Macon. Recordings like "Late Last Night When Willie Came Home" and "Wreck of the Tennessee Gravy Train," both done with McGee, demonstrated the kind of dense instrumental interplay that prefigured bluegrass. By the mid-1930s Macon was touring and recording with fellow Opry stars Alton and Rabon Delmore, both excellent songwriters and harmony singers.

In 1940 Macon appeared in the film *Grand Ole Opry* and became a regular on the NBC network portion of the Opry radio show. By now he was in his seventies and content to tour on package shows led by other Opry stars, including Acuff, Bill Monroe, Jamup and Honey, the Bailes Brothers, Curly Fox and Texas Ruby, and others. Although his complex and dexterous banjo playing was now simplified, his singing and comedy remained as effective as ever. His grief at the death of his wife in 1939 caused him to temporarily abandon his music; but he soon was performing again, often with the guitar accompaniment of his youngest son, Dorris. His last commercial recordings, for Victor-Bluebird, were made in 1938. He continued to make private recordings, however, and in 1950 he made his first tape recordings for folklorist Charles Faulkner Bryan.

The Macon repertoire ranged from blues he had learned from rural musicians in Middle Tennessee to old ragtime pieces like "Oh Babe, You Done Me Wrong." They included favorites like "The Death of John Henry," "Bully of the Town," "Eleven Cent Cotton and Forty Cent Meat," and his theme song, "How Beautiful Heaven Must Be." More than almost any other country performer, he bridged the old vaudeville and traditional tunes of the nineteenth century with the more modern country tunes of the twentieth century. Many of his records remain in print in various forms, and one of the South's largest old-time and bluegrass music festivals is held annually in his honor at Murfreesboro, Tennessee, where he died.

• For further information on Macon see Ralph Rinzler and Norm Cohen, *Uncle Dave Macon: A Bio-Discography* (1970); Charles K. Wolfe, "Uncle Dave Macon," in *Stars of Country Music*, ed. Judith McCulloh and Bill C. Malone (1975); and Wolfe, "Uncle Dave Macon," *Rutherford County Historical Society Publications*, no. 35 (1996).

CHARLES K. WOLFE

MACPHAIL, Larry (3 Feb. 1890–1 Oct. 1975), baseball executive, was born Leland Stanford MacPhail in Cass City, Michigan, the son of Curtis W. MacPhail, an investment banker, and Catherine Ann MacMurtrie. He was raised in Ludington, Michigan, and attended Staunton Military Academy in Virginia. At age sixteen he passed the entrance exam for the U.S. Naval Academy but chose instead to attend Beloit College in Wisconsin. He later attended the University of Michigan, Georgetown University, and George Washington University, playing both baseball and football. In 1910 MacPhail received a law degree from George Washington University and joined a law firm in Chicago, where he spent nearly five years. Also in 1910 he married Inez Thompson, with whom he would have three children. After a brief period as sales manager for the Rich Tool Company, in 1915 he became president of Huddleston-Cooper Company, a leading department store in Nashville, Tennessee.

During World War I MacPhail enlisted as a private in a Tennessee volunteer regiment and advanced to captain. While in France MacPhail was wounded and gassed; he was also part of an aborted attempt to kidnap the Kaiser from the castle of Count von Bentinck in Holland. During this episode MacPhail managed to pilfer the Kaiser's ashtray, which he proudly displayed on his desk for the remainder of his life.

Following the armistice, MacPhail settled in Columbus, Ohio, where he became distributor for Willys-Overland automobiles and simultaneously organized Standard Corporation, a glass manufacturing firm, with Walter Jones. He pursued his sporting interests as a college football referee and was active in the Central Ohio District Golf Association, in which he held leadership positions.

MacPhail's entrance into baseball came in January 1931, when he headed a syndicate that purchased the Columbus franchise of the American Association for $100,000. MacPhail then sold a controlling interest in the team to the St. Louis Cardinals, who appointed him president of the Columbus team. Columbus had consistently lost both on the field and in the account books for over a decade, but the franchise showed a profit in MacPhail's first season, as he successfully marketed the team. During the second season, with the opening of a new stadium, the installation of lights for night baseball, and a host of innovative promotional activities, the Columbus Red Birds drew 310,000 paying customers and was the only team in the league to show a profit. That same year MacPhail served as the chairman of the Executive Committee of the American Association. Despite this success, Branch Rickey, the Cardinals' general manager, maneuvered MacPhail out of his position as club president beginning in May 1933, following a dispute over the movement of player personnel from Columbus to St. Louis.

By November 1933 MacPhail was back in baseball when a Cincinnati bank, which held the controlling stock of the financially troubled Reds, appointed him vice president, director, and general manager. Here MacPhail earned his reputation as a great innovator and marketing genius, as he, along with Branch Rickey, was the first to develop "general manager" into a significant position in the business of baseball.

First, MacPhail persuaded radio magnate Powel Crosley to purchase the Reds, pour money into player acquisition and development, and revamp team operations. Then, with Crosley's money behind him, MacPhail developed a pattern of innovation and marketing that would be his trademark and his legacy to baseball over the next two decades. His first concern was to make the fans comfortable. The park was painted and repaired, uniformed usherettes were hired, and cigarette girls circulated through the stands wearing attractive red bloomers. To build fan interest he allowed unrestricted broadcasting of Reds games and brought in Red Barber to provide the play-by-play of home and away games on Crosley's station. The Reds were the first team to travel by air and the first major league team to play at night. To inaugurate night baseball, MacPhail arranged for President Franklin D. Roosevelt to "turn on" the lights by activating a telegraph key in the White House. Over 20,000 fans attended the first of seven night games that season, 24 May 1935. Marching bands and fireworks added to the festivities.

After the 1936 season MacPhail and Crosley parted company, as their differences in personality and policy reached an impasse. MacPhail returned to Michigan to try his hand at investment banking with his father. But in January 1938 the Brooklyn Trust Company turned to Larry MacPhail to save the financially troubled Dodger franchise. In Brooklyn he followed the same pattern: player acquisition and development, a face lift for the ball park, the installation of lights, and the use of radio. The first night game in Brooklyn came on 15 June 1938, when Johnny Vander Meer of the Reds pitched his second consecutive no-hitter, a unique feat. During the 1938 season, attendance increased by 250,000, and by 1941 the Dodgers were National League champions.

In 1939, at the end of a five-year agreement among the Dodgers, Giants, and Yankees banning radio play-by-play, MacPhail summoned Red Barber to Brooklyn and opened the New York radio market. That same year MacPhail approved the first telecast of a major league game on 26 August. It was transmitted from Ebbets Field to the NBC studios in Manhattan and to the television exhibit at the New York World's Fair.

In 1941 MacPhail and his wife separated, and four years later they were divorced. He then married, in 1945, Jean Bennett Wanamaker; they had one child.

During World War II MacPhail returned to military service as special assistant to the undersecretary of war. Near the end of the war he seized an opportunity to purchase the Yankees from the estate of Colonel Jacob Ruppert for the bargain price of $2.8 million. MacPhail's only problem was lack of money, but he convinced Dan Topping, a former owner of the Brooklyn Dodgers football team and tenant of MacPhail's at Ebbets Field, to join him. They contacted Bing Crosby, who recommended Phoenix real estate tycoon Del Webb as the third member of the Yankee ownership team.

MacPhail applied his earlier successful marketing techniques to the Yankees, including night games. Further innovations were the creation of a Stadium Club, Old-Timers Day, and the concept of season and combination ticket schemes. By 1947 the Yankees were back as World Series champions. MacPhail announced his retirement during the post–World Series celebrations that year, following a row with George Weiss, Yankee farm director. Topping and Webb bought out MacPhail for a reported $1.5–$2 million, and at age fifty-seven Larry MacPhail, baseball's most innovative executive, moved on to a new life.

MacPhail did not leave with an unblemished record. He was noted for his volatile temper, and many owners felt threatened by his innovations. Some may have been jealous of his success. His outspokenness irritated many, as did his steamroller manner.

More serious than his personal style was MacPhail's role in the desegregation of baseball: here he abandoned his innovator's hat and took on the role of obstructionist. At a joint NL-AL steering committee meeting in 1946, for instance, MacPhail attacked the advocates of integration as being ignorant as well as being political opportunists. He questioned the value of increased black attendance at major league games, suggesting that white attendance would correspondingly decrease. He went on to belittle the black athletes who, he wrote, had great natural ability, but lacked technique, coordination, a competitive attitude, and discipline. MacPhail warned that integration would kill the Negro leagues and in turn hurt the major league teams that rented their ball parks to Negro league teams. He was critical of Branch Rickey for signing Jackie Robinson, and he called on all major league teams to respect Negro league contracts. Furthermore, like many in baseball who wanted to delay desegregation, MacPhail claimed that his scouts could not find any Negro League players worthy of signing by the Yankees.

After leaving baseball MacPhail "retired" to his Bel Air, Maryland, farm, where he raised Black Angus cattle, bred horses, built a golf course, and became active in horse racing. He headed a syndicate that purchased Bowie Race Track and was given total control of operations. He revitalized the moribund track and achieved great success in the breeding business. He died in a veterans' hospital in Miami, Florida. He was inducted in the Baseball Hall of Fame on 7 August 1978.

Although Larry MacPhail was a successful businessman, his most significant contributions were to baseball. His marketing innovations, his receptivity to new technology, and his concerns for the comfort of the fans were all marked changes in the way the baseball business was conducted. MacPhail, with Branch Rickey, turned the position of general manager into a major figure in the direction of a baseball franchise. He transformed the game wherever he went.

Larry MacPhail's legacy continues not only via his innovations, but through the work of his son, Leland Stanford ("Lee") MacPhail, Jr., who has been a general manager, the president of the American League, and the director of the Player Relations Committee of Major League Baseball, as well as his grandson Andy MacPhail, the highly successful general manager of the Minnesota Twins.

• Don Warfield, *The Roaring Redhead: Larry MacPhail, Baseball's Greatest Innovator* (1987), is the only biography of MacPhail. There is no repository of MacPhail's personal papers, and the family has very little in its possession. The National Baseball Library in Cooperstown, New York, has a file of material that includes several unsigned biographical sketches and several clippings on MacPhail. These include interviews with and profiles of him from his postbaseball career; the best of these are from *Sports Illustrated* and the *Sporting News*.

Secondary works that treat certain facets of MacPhail's baseball career are Red Barber, *The Broadcasters* (1970), Richard C. Crepeau, *Baseball: America's Diamond Mind, 1919–1941* (1980), and Jules Tygiel, *Baseball's Great Experi-*

ment: *Jackie Robinson and His Legacy* (1983). Bits and pieces can also be found in numerous franchise histories, biographies, and autobiographies.

RICHARD C. CREPEAU

MACRAE, Gordon (12 Mar. 1921–24 Jan. 1986), singer and actor, was born Albert Gordon MacRae in East Orange, New Jersey, the son of William Lamont MacRae, a manufacturer, and Helen Sonn. MacRae spent a comfortable childhood in Syracuse, New York, where his father operated a profitable tool making business. After he graduated from the Deerfield Academy, he won a singing contest at the 1939–1940 World's Fair in New York City, and his prize was a two-week engagement with the Harry James band. He followed the stint with a summer of stock theater in Roslyn, New York, where he met Sheila Stephens, whom he married in 1941. They had four children. He left performing temporarily for a job as a page at NBC. A talent scout there overheard his singing in the men's room and booked him as the featured vocalist with Horace Heidt's Musical Knights. In 1944, after two years with the band, he joined the army air corps as a navigator.

Discharged from the service in 1945, MacRae found work on radio shows and was cast in the Broadway revue *Three to Make Ready* (1946). He began recording with Capitol Records in 1947 and had hits with "A Fellow Needs a Girl" and "Body and Soul." In 1948 he signed a motion picture contract with Warner Bros., and the same year he began hosting a long-running musical variety radio program, "The Railroad Hour."

MacRae's first film at Warners, *The Big Punch* (1948), was a fight melodrama. Later that year he costarred with June Haver in *Look for the Silver Lining* (1949), a musical biography of actress Marilyn Miller. Following in quick succession in 1950 were *The Daughter of Rosie O'Grady*, the mystery film *Backfire*, and *Return of the Frontiersman*, a nonmusical western with singer Julie London.

Although James Cagney was the star of *The West Point Story* (1950), MacRae and fellow band singer Doris Day were the romantic leads. The team clicked, and Warners cast MacRae and Day in three more well-received musicals: *Tea for Two* (1950), inspired by the play *No, No, Nanette*; *On Moonlight Bay* (1951), a syrupy musical based on a Booth Tarkington novel; and its sequel, *By the Light of the Silvery Moon* (1953). MacRae also appeared in *Starlift* (1951), with Day; *About Face* (1952), a musical version of the 1938 film starring Ronald Reagan, *Brother Rat*; and *The Desert Song* (1953), with Kathryn Grayson, the third film version of Sigmund Romberg's operetta.

In 1953 MacRae left his Warners contract two years before it was due to expire, forfeiting nearly $3,000 a week in salary. He freelanced at RKO Pictures in *Three Sailors and a Girl* (1953), based on George S. Kaufman's play *The Butter and Egg Man*, and again musicalized a role earlier played by Ronald Reagan in *An Angel from Texas* (1937).

From 1954 through 1955 MacRae hosted NBC's "The Colgate Comedy Hour," scheduled opposite the hugely popular "Ed Sullivan Show." The television program alternated between a variety and a book musical format and included a full re-creation of the musical *Roberta* in which MacRae starred. He was nominated for Emmy awards as best male singer in 1954 and 1955 but was beaten both years by Perry Como.

In 1954 MacRae appeared with such major stars as Mary Martin and Yul Brynner in a television salute to composers Richard Rodgers and Oscar Hammerstein II, opening the show with "Oh, What a Beautiful Mornin'" from *Oklahoma*. Because of this appearance, he was cast in the lead of the much-anticipated film version of the show. The role of the farmhand Curly was a prize—among the many actors also considered were MGM singing star Howard Keel (who had played the part in the London stage production) as well as dramatic actors James Dean and Paul Newman. *Time* (24 Oct. 1955) wrote that "hero Gordon MacRae acts with a winning warmth and naturalness and shows a voice as clear and flexible as any in Hollywood."

Oklahoma's success led 20th Century–Fox to plan a screen version of Rodgers and Hammerstein's darker musical *Carousel*, starring MacRae's *Oklahoma* costar Shirley Jones as the innocent factory worker and Oscar-winner Frank Sinatra as the vain and abusive carny whom she loves. Sinatra quit the film after disagreements over location and an involved shooting schedule, and MacRae replaced him with excellent, if surprising, results. According to author David Shipman, "Carousel was his, in a convincing strong portrayal of fair barker Billy Bigelow, big head and all-time heel."

MacRae followed *Carousel* with *The Best Things in Life Are Free* (1956), a light musical loosely based on the lives of the songwriting team de Sylva, Brown, and Henderson. It was his last major film. A combination of personal problems and the demise of the movie musical ended his big-screen career. In 1954 he and his wife were slapped with a tax lien, and in December 1955, only two days after being glowingly profiled by the *New York Times*, he was arrested on suspicion of drunk driving.

MacRae continued to perform frequently on television in such vehicles as "The Gordon MacRae Show" (1956); "The Lux Video Theatre" (1956–1957), a dramatic anthology series that he hosted; "The Voice of Firestone" (1958–1959), which alternated operatic and classical singers with popular vocalists such as MacRae and recording partner Jo Stafford; and "The Gift of the Magi" (1958), costarring Sally Ann Howes and Beatrice Arthur.

MacRae also continued to record, and duet albums with Stafford and operatic soprano Dorothy Kirsten sold well. In the late 1950s and early 1960s Gordon and Sheila MacRae toured with a popular cabaret act, which was the basis for a television special in which they starred in 1960. The MacRaes were also frequent guests on such television game shows as "Password" and "I've Got a Secret," and they performed with their children in stage musicals such as *Annie Get Your Gun* (1960). In 1967 the couple divorced, and that same year he took over Robert Preston's role in the Broadway musical *I Do, I Do* and married Elizabeth Lambert Schrafft. In 1968 their daughter was born.

Though MacRae continued to perform in concerts and on television, his drinking worsened. In 1977 he canceled a show because he was too drunk to perform, and two weeks later he sought treatment for alcoholism. By decade's end he was the honorary chairman of the National Council on Alcoholism.

MacRae's final screen appearance was a supporting role in *The Pilot* (1979). In 1982 he suffered a stroke, which kept him from performing for nearly a year and cost him the use of his left arm. In 1983 he was one of the *Great Stars of the Silver Screen*, a nostalgic touring stage revue. He continued to perform sporadically, though much of his energy went toward promoting alcohol dependency treatment and awareness. He hosted the Las Vegas–based Gordon MacRae Celebrity Golf Classic, which benefited the National Council on Alcoholism, and in 1984 he wrote the foreword to *The Courage to Heal—Personal Conversations about Alcoholism with Dennis Wholey*. MacRae died in Lincoln, Nebraska.

• Biographical sources include Sheila MacRae and H. Paul Jeffers, *Hollywood Mother of the Year* (1992); Stanley Green, *Encyclopedia of the Musical Film* (1981); David Shipman, *The Great Movie Stars: The Golden Years*, new rev. ed. (1979); and Ephraim Katz, *The Film Encyclopedia* (1994). Information on MacRae's television work can be found in Tim Brooks and Earle Marsh, *Complete Directory of Prime-Time Network and Cable TV Shows; 1946–Present* (1995), and details on aspects of MacRae's radio career are available in Frank Buxton and Bill Owen, *The Big Broadcast* (1972). Profiles of MacRae appeared in the *New York Times*, Frank Buxton and Bill Owen, 11 Dec. 1955; the *Boston Globe*, 30 Oct. 1981; and the *Philadelphia Inquirer*, 27 Nov. 1981. Obituaries are in the *Los Angeles Times* and the *San Jose Mercury*, both 25 Jan. 1986, and on the United Press International (UPI) wire, 24 and 28 Jan. 1986.

DIANA MOORE

MACSPARRAN, James (10 Sept. 1693–5 Dec. 1757), clergyman of the Church of England and missionary of the Society for the Propagation of the Gospel in Foreign Parts (SPG) to Rhode Island, was probably born in Dungiven, County of Derry, Ireland. His parents are unknown, but he was the nephew of the Reverend Archibald MacSparran, a Presbyterian minister and well-to-do landowner in Ireland who emigrated with others of his family from the west of Scotland during the persecution of Presbyterian ministers in the 1670s and 1680s.

MacSparran was admitted to the University of Glasgow when he was fifteen years old. In following years he appears to have received his credentials for the licentiate of the Presbyterian ministry under the guidance of his uncle Archibald. Arriving in Boston in June 1718, MacSparran was invited to become the Congregational minister in Bristol, Rhode Island, in

December. His "unguarded remarks" and rumored salacious nature caused Cotton Mather to dislike him and suggest that his ministerial papers were fraudulent. A council of the Bristol church investigated Mac-Sparran. Although he was exonerated in May 1719, suspicions about his ministerial legitimacy persisted, and he was urged to return to Ireland for confirmation of the credentials. Instead, MacSparran went to England, where he was ordained deacon in the Church of England in August 1720 and presbyter in September. He returned to New England in April 1721 as a licensed missionary of the SPG. There is no evidence that he had leaned toward conformity before 1720.

As rector of St. Paul's Church in Narragansett Country, MacSparran doubled the size of his parish in two years and held services in Bristol, Freetown, Swansea, and Little Compton, attracting many of the powerful families of Rhode Island to the Church of England. In 1722 he married Hannah Gardiner, a member of the colonial aristocracy, and baptized her younger brother, Silvester Gardiner, future surgeon and Loyalist in the Revolution. MacSparran founded the Episcopal church in New London, Connecticut. In 1731 Oxford conferred on him an honorary S.T.D.

MacSparran's political efforts to increase the prestige of the Church of England in his colony were less successful than his pastoral ones. He created enmity between himself, Quakers, and Independents. For thirty years he engaged in intricate, legal maneuverings against Joseph Torrey, Congregational minister and physician, for control of the Pettaquamscutt Purchase, a tract of 300 acres set aside in 1658 for the use of "an orthodox minister." While six of the seven original purchasers of the glebe intended it for the use of a Congregational, "Massachusetts orthodox," minister, MacSparran argued that "orthodox" meant Anglican. It was a flimsy claim. Nonetheless he traveled to England, where from June 1736 to August 1737 he pressed his case. In 1752 the Narragansett glebe lands case finally reached the Privy Council and was decided in favor of "the dissenting teacher," Joseph Torrey. In addition neither the SPG nor the archbishop of Canterbury supported MacSparran's claim. The case was of great importance in confirming the government's and the Church of England's commitment to the toleration of dissent in America.

But MacSparran was not through. In the same year he expressed his views in a tract, *The Sacred Dignity of the Christian Priesthood Vindicated* (1752). Intended to correct "irregularities" among colonial Anglican clergy, the tract instead raised a storm of protest from nonconforming ministers in New England, who understood it—correctly—as an indictment of their own ministries. MacSparran found Puritan Independents and Quakers as a whole "stuffed with odious Cant [and] at this Day offensive to a loyal and pious Ear," while "Papists are Christians, and to be preferred to many Protestant Heretics I could name."

By disparaging American ways in another tract, *America Dissected* (1753), MacSparran sought to further in the colonies the cause of England's established church. He extolled the advantages of a class-conscious society supported by religious uniformity and denounced pluralism and liberty of conscience. With the goal of an American episcopate and his own consecration into that office, he again traveled to England in 1754. But, in view of the church's attitude in the case of the glebe lands, it seemed unlikely that "during his stay in London the American bishopric was offered him." Once again his quest was in vain. Sorrow was added to disappointment when in London in 1755 his wife died of smallpox. MacSparran returned to America in February 1756 and died in South Kingston, Rhode Island.

A large man with a hot temper, MacSparran was an imperial-minded high churchman of the first British empire who disliked America and yearned to live in Britain. Like his aristocratic neighbors, he was an owner of both black and Native American slaves. It has been suggested that the MacSparrans treated their slaves like the children they never had, that treatment varying considerably between harshness and affection. Conscious of colonial mistreatment of other races, MacSparran made a point of taking his frequent visitor and fellow countryman, George Berkeley, philosopher and future bishop of Cloyne, to see firsthand the condition of nearby Indian tribes. As a result, the famous report made to the SPG by Berkeley stung British consciences. MacSparran was himself a faithful catechist of all the races. His preaching was eloquent and simple, both in churches and often at public executions, where he availed himself of the opportunity to be heard by dissenters.

MacSparran willed his house and farm for the use of an American bishop. The particular volumes from his library that he chose to bequeath to his successor indicate a theology based on the official documents of the English Reformation but with an added and not entirely compatible high church Arminianism. Most prominent were the *Book of Homilies* (1547; 1571), Tory Bishop John Pearson's learned *Exposition of the Creed* (1659), Whig Bishop Gilbert Burnet's *Exposition of the XXXIX Articles* (1699), and Arminian, rational supernaturalist Daniel Whitby's *Paraphrase and Commentary on the New Testament* (2 vols., 1703).

• A few manuscript sermons are in the Records of the Episcopal Church in Rhode Island, MSS. Group #41, University of Rhode Island, Kingston. Portions of other sermons are found in Wilkins Updike, *A History of the Episcopal Church in Narragansett, Rhode Island*, ed. Daniel Goodwin (3 vols., 1907); vol. 3 contains *America Dissected* (1753). James MacSparran's *A Letter Book and Abstract of Out Services, Written during the Years 1743–1751* has been edited by Daniel Goodwin as *MacSparran's Diary* (1899). Biographical material is also found in Delbert W. Tidesley, *St. Michael's Church in Bristol Rhode Island, 1718–1983* (1989), in Sydney V. James, *Colonial Rhode Island* (1975), in E. B. Carpenter, *South County Studies* (1924; 1971), and in W. B. Sprague, *Annals of the American Pulpit* (1857–1869) vol. 5, pp. 44–47. John Smibert's portrait of James MacSparran is owned by Bowdoin College, Brunswick, Maine; a copy of the portrait is in the Rhode Island Historical Society, Providence. Smibert's portrait of Hannah MacSparran is in the Museum of Fine Arts, Boston.

JOHN F. WOOLVERTON

MACUNE, Charles William (20 May 1851–2 Nov. 1940), agrarian and monetary reformer, was born in Kenosha, Wisconsin, the son of William Macune, a blacksmith and itinerant Methodist preacher, and Mary Almira McAfee. His father died in 1852 as the family trekked to California. Returning to Illinois that year, Macune attended school until the age of ten and then provided for his mother and sisters by farming a small family plot. Leaving home after the Civil War, he ranched and drove cattle in California and Kansas. In 1871 he made frontier Texas his home, and he studied and practiced both law and medicine. He also ran a hotel, which went bankrupt in the panic of 1873, painted houses, and edited local newspapers. In 1876 he married Sally Vickery; they had two sons and three daughters.

The agrarian depression that spread across Texas in the 1880s and 1890s engulfed Macune in 1885. Southern and western farmers faced plummeting cotton prices, deflated currency, exorbitant railroad rates, increased fertilizer costs, and spiralling debts to merchants. Organizations such as the Grange and the Farmer's Alliance attempted to confront these problems with calls for improved scientific farming, government control of railroads, and formation of farmers' cooperatives that would enable farmers to control their own banks, stores, and processing plants. As a newspaper editor in Milam County, Texas, Macune listened to farmers' complaints and began to formulate his own agenda for reform. He spoke at local Alliance meetings, where his personal magnetism captured farmers' imaginations. Increasingly, farmers turned to him to articulate their mounting rage and despair. In 1885 he joined the Texas Farmer's Alliance, and the next year he was elected chair of its executive committee.

Macune became an evangelist for the agrarian cause. He constantly exhorted farmers to mobilize, recruited and supervised hundreds to join as agrarian apostles, and edited newspapers, almanacs, and pamphlets on behalf of agrarianism. He traveled tirelessly throughout the South, urging other state alliances to join the Texas movement. Often elected to chair state and local conventions, he had a masterful ability to pull disparate groups together and keep the Alliance movement united. He was, by 1887, the Texas mastermind of an organization whose membership included over 100,000 Texas farmers.

Sensing that farmers would remain mired in debt if an economic alternative could not be formulated, Macune supported establishment of a farmers' cooperative that would circumvent merchants and allow farmers to purchase supplies and food on credit from an alliance-operated store. The cooperative would also store the farmers' crops until it was advantageous to sell. Macune believed that banks had to be co-opted if farmers were ever to escape poverty and debt, and he proposed a "sub-treasury plan" to create a government-subsidized agency that would make credit available to farmers.

Such challenges to the foundations of capitalism were not greeted kindly by merchants and bankers. A disgruntled economic elite spread rumors maligning Macune's integrity. He moved to Washington, D.C., in 1889, and while editing the *National Economist*, the Alliance national newspaper, Macune was accused of absconding with thousands of dollars of Alliance dues. Sharecroppers and tenants were warned to stay away from Alliance rallies, and churches split over Alliance affiliations. When over 750,000 members had joined the Alliance movement by the autumn of 1889, captains of industry and U.S. bankers worried that their hegemony might be slipping away.

However, the basic structures of capitalism thwarted Macune's plans and kept the oligarchy that controlled the economy of the United States after the Civil War in power. Funding the Texas cooperative proved impossible. Although Macune solicited over $100,000 from Texas banks as the cooperative movement started, bankers soon grew less enamored of Macune's charm, and their support dried up. Although Texas farmers pledged $200,000 in support of the cooperative movement, less than $80,000 was collected. By 1889 creditors foreclosed on Alliance buildings, and the cooperative venture had failed.

As farmers consistently saw their dreams blocked by the economic elite, they increasingly turned to politics to voice their discontent, and Macune joined in this political movement. He was elected president of the National Alliance movement at conventions held in Shreveport, Louisiana, in 1887 and in Meridian, Mississippi, in 1888. He became chairman of the National Executive Board of the National Alliance in 1889. As the movement grew, factions inevitably emerged, dividing the membership. The *Southern Mercury*, a major Alliance newspaper, became increasingly anti-Macune. An October 1888 editorial warned: "Brother Macune, step down and out. . . . You are a stumbling block in the way of unity, good fellowship, and success in our order."

While many Alliance members thought it necessary to create a new third party to counter the lethargy of the Democratic and Republican parties, others, including Macune, disagreed. Loyal to the Democratic party, Macune urged farmers to work within the two-party system. By the 1892 Alliance convention held at Memphis, Tennessee, he could see that the new Populist party had captured the Alliance movement, and he resigned all of his offices. Although he decided to help organize the People's party in Texas and other southern states, he did not work as diligently for that movement, nor did he gain as much power in it. In 1893 his newspaper, the *National Economist*, folded. He was seldom seen or heard in the subsequent Populist movement, which culminated in 1896 in William Jennings Bryan's race for the presidency.

Returning to Texas in 1893, Macune published a local newspaper, which was unsuccessful. In 1900 he became an itinerant Methodist preacher and reestablished his medical practice. Working alongside his son, the Reverend Dennis Macune, he often provided health care for the destitute. Nearly four decades later, Macune, before his death in Fort Worth, Texas, believed he saw realized in Franklin Delano Roosevelt's New Deal at least a glimpse of his vision for governmental aid to the poor.

• Macune's unpublished memoirs, "The Texas Alliance," are at the University of Texas Library at Austin, Tex. His speeches and analytical papers are in N. A. Dunning, ed., *The Farmer's Alliance History and Agricultural Digest* (1975), and W. Scott Morgan, *History of the Wheel and Alliance and the Impending Revolution* (1891; repr. 1968). The most insightful analysis of Macune's life and economic philosophy is in Lawrence Goodwyn, *Democratic Promise: The Populist Movement in America* (1976). Other helpful sources include Ralph Smith, "'Macuneism,' or the Farmers of Texas in Business," *Journal of Southern History* 13 (May 1947); Smith, "The Farmer's Alliance in Texas, 1875–1900: A Revolt against Bourban and Bourgeois Democracy," *Southwestern Historical Quarterly* 48 (Jan. 1945); Donna Barnes, *Farmers in Rebellion: The Rise and Fall of the Southern Farmer's Alliance and People's Party in Texas* (1984); and Robert C. McMath, Jr., *Populist Vanguard: A History of the Southern Farmer's Alliance* (1975). An obituary of Macune is in the *Fort Worth Star-Telegram*, 3 Nov. 1940.

RANDY FINLEY

MACURDY, Grace Harriet (12 Sept. 1866–23 Oct. 1946), classicist, was born in Robbinston, Maine, the daughter of Simon Angus Macurdy, a carpenter, and Rebecca Thomson. When she was a girl, the family moved to Watertown, Massachusetts, where Macurdy received her high school education. She entered Radcliffe College in 1884 and received an A.B. degree in Greek in 1888. Her teaching career began immediately thereafter at the Cambridge School for Girls, where she taught classics from 1888 to 1893, the year she was appointed instructor in Greek at Vassar College in Poughkeepsie, New York.

During the year 1899–1900, while pursuing graduate work at Columbia University, Macurdy studied at the University of Berlin on a fellowship from the Boston Women's Educational Association. In 1903 she received a Ph.D. in Greek from Columbia, with a dissertation directed by Mortimer Lamson Earle entitled "The Chronology of the Extant Plays of Euripides." This work, published as a monograph in 1905, involved incisive study of metrical and linguistic elements in the Euripidean plays whose dates were in doubt and formed a solid foundation for dating that has not been seriously challenged (though all her dates have not been accepted by all scholars). Conferral of the doctorate in 1903 resulted in an immediate promotion at Vassar from instructor to associate professor of Greek. It was unusual to bypass the assistant professor rank, but her excellence as a classroom teacher and promise as a scholar made her exceptional in the eyes of the Vassar administration. She was promoted to

professor of Greek in 1916 and in 1920 became chairman of her department, a position she held continuously until her retirement. From 1908 to 1918 Macurdy taught courses in Greek language and literature at the Columbia University summer sessions. In addition to her year in Berlin, later in her career she had two leaves of absence from Vassar, in 1922–1923 and 1929–1930, devoted to study and travel in Europe, a practice that also characterized almost all her summers. Her research was conducted in the British Museum, at Oxford University and in Greece, France, Italy, and Austria.

In 1924 Macurdy moved into the newly built Williams Hall, a campus apartment building for unmarried women professors, most of them fast friends who dined together each evening. She soon became a "legend" at Vassar in the eyes of her grateful students, a status she maintained throughout her career. One student remembered, "Her white hair was flying all around; she had . . . a beautiful blue chain of stones around her neck which exactly matched her eyes (not that she had planned this, for she never thought about herself as far as we could see)." Never married, she resided in Williams throughout the remainder of her Vassar career.

Macurdy's outgoing personality and inquiring nature shaped her scholarly life and won her many classicist friends. In particular, she was close to Gilbert Murray, perhaps the most prominent classicist of the time, and Lady Mary Murray. An affectionate correspondence documents their decades-long relationship, and she stayed with the Murrays on several occasions in Oxford. She also corresponded with other well-known classical philologists, archaeologists, and historians, including W. W. Tarn, Lewis Farnell, F. M. Cornford, J. A. K. Thompson, and Jane Ellen Harrison. If Jane Harrison was the most celebrated British woman classicist of the first half of the twentieth century, Grace Macurdy could well be placed among a handful of American women of similar distinction.

Although her philological writings are competent, they do not open new fields of inquiry in the way her historical work does. The book that bridges her earlier interest in literary subjects and her more accomplished historical scholarship is *Troy and Paeonia* (1925), a collection of essays dealing with literary allusions in Homer to the culture and religion of Balkan tribes. In investigating the role of women in the Hellenistic Greek world, she was a pioneer in feminist studies, even if such a term would probably have been alien to her. Her most important work, *Hellenistic Queens* (1932), brought a new approach to the study of Macedonia, Seleucid Syria, and Ptolemaic Egypt by concentrating on the power of women and how they achieved and kept it. Macurdy approached the subject of these influential women of antiquity in a new way, studying them not as appendages to their husbands, fathers, or brothers, but on their own terms. She used phrases, like "woman-power," that were novel in classical history in the early decades of the twentieth century and anticipated the feminist historians of antiquity who came many years later. *Vassal Queens and Some Contemporary Women in the Roman Empire* (1937), was another such study of women in antiquity that was ahead of its time. For the seventy-fifth anniversary of Vassar she produced *The Quality of Mercy* (1940), a rather conventional study of humanity in Greek literature that was praised at the time it was published. She published seventy articles and book reviews. Fittingly, her final publication, "Prologue to a Study of the Tragic Heroine," *Classical Weekly*, 22 May 1944, had a feminist theme.

A member of Phi Beta Kappa, the American Philological Association, the Archaeological Institute of America, the American Linguistic Society, the Hellenic Society (Great Britain), and the American Association of University Professors, Macurdy also served, from 1922 to 1937, on the managing committee of the American School of Classical Studies at Athens. She retired in 1937 but continued to live in Williams Hall. Naming her professor emeritus, Vassar president Henry Noble MacCracken declared, "No description in words can fittingly portray the service which Miss Macurdy has rendered to the life of Vassar." During World War II, much of her time was devoted to Greek and British war relief. In July 1946 she was awarded the King's Medal "for Service in the cause of Freedom" by the British government. She died in Poughkeepsie.

• Most of the manuscripts of Macurdy's scholarly works seem to have been dispersed, but there is a collection of some of her papers in special collections at the Vassar College Library. A few of the letters she received from British classicists and other friends are there, although most of her correspondence with Gilbert Murray is in the Bodleian Library, Oxford, England. A full list of Macurdy's publications was prepared at the time of her death by the Vassar College Library and can be found in her file. A biographical sketch was published in the *Vassar Alumnae Magazine*, Jan. 1936; another, in her file, was written by Theodore H. Erck at an unspecified date, and a glowing account of her contributions to Vassar exists in Henry Noble MacCracken, *Report of the President of Vassar College* (1937). Obituaries are in the *New York Times*, the *New York Herald-Tribune*, and the *Poughkeepsie New Yorker*, 24 Oct. 1946. There are also obituaries in the *Radcliffe Quarterly*, May 1947, and in the *Annual Report of the Carnegie Foundation for the Advancement of Teaching* (1946–1947).

ROBERT L. POUNDER

MACVEAGH, Franklin (22 Nov. 1837–6 July 1934), merchant and secretary of the treasury, was born near Phoenixville, Chester County, Pennsylvania, the son of John MacVeagh, a farmer and local politician, and Margaret Lincoln, a distant cousin of Abraham Lincoln. He was educated by private tutors, attended Freeland Seminary (now Ursinus College), and graduated from Yale College in 1862. He received an LL.B. from Columbia University in 1864, read law briefly in the office of Judge John Worth Edmonds in New York City, and was admitted to the bar. In 1865 he entered practice in West Chester, Pennsylvania, with his brother, Isaac Wayne MacVeagh, but left after a year because of poor health.

MacVeagh moved to Chicago, Illinois, in 1866 and became a partner in the wholesale grocery house of Whitaker and Harmon. In 1868 he married Emily Eames, the daughter of the founder and longtime president of the Commercial National Bank of Chicago. They had five children. In 1871 the great Chicago fire destroyed MacVeagh's firm, but he was able to feed many victims of the fire and served on the relief committee. With the aid of insurance funds soon after the fire he formed Franklin MacVeagh and Company, which became one of America's largest wholesale grocery establishments, operating until 1932.

As his business grew, MacVeagh became active in Chicago reform politics. He helped to organize and later became president of the Citizens' Committee of 1874, which reorganized the fire department, unified city government, and enlarged the city's water supply. He served as vice president of the Civil Service Reform League of Chicago (1884–1885), president of the Chicago Bureau of Charities (1896–1904), and a trustee of the University of Chicago (1901–1913). MacVeagh became a director of the Commercial National Bank in 1881, serving until 1909.

Although he was a Republican, MacVeagh's interest in tariff revision caused him to support Grover Cleveland's presidential candidacies in 1884, 1888, and 1892. He was nominated by the Democratic state convention of Illinois for U.S. senator in 1894 but, despite a vigorous campaign, lost to the Republican incumbent Shelby M. Cullom. An opponent of "free silver," MacVeagh refused to support William Jennings Bryan in 1896 and left the Democratic party. He did not return until 1928, when he supported Alfred E. Smith for president.

In 1909 President William Howard Taft appointed MacVeagh secretary of the treasury. As secretary, he was an advocate of the central bank program recommended by the National Monetary Commission in 1910 and presented to Congress as the Aldrich Bill in 1911. MacVeagh worked to allay the fears that westerners and small bankers had of Senator Nelson Aldrich's plan by opposing the concentration of money and power in a few banks. The secretary advocated equal membership of all banks and called for the elimination of interlocking directorates from the program. However, partisan politics and differing views of the nation's financial needs defeated the Republican efforts at banking reform; the bill never passed, although it influenced the Federal Reserve Act of 1913.

MacVeagh favored lowering the tariff. While his efforts were ultimately unsuccessful, he did help to create the "scientific tariff board" that President Taft established in 1911. He continued the investigations of customhouse frauds that the Roosevelt administration had begun, and he recovered more than $8 million in lost tariff revenues. Perhaps his most meaningful work was done in shaping and supporting Taft's budgetary program, which would have given the president considerable power over expenditures. While not accepted by Congress at the time, it was approved in the Budget and Accounting Act of 1921.

MacVeagh supported the Taft administration's increase of the civil service list, classifying many jobs in the treasury department. He also reorganized the department, using a board of experts to eliminate 540 jobs in Washington, D.C., and 1,915 positions nationwide. He increased the department's efficiency, claiming that none of his actions were at the expense of providing adequate services. In each of his annual reports MacVeagh recommended the creation of a pension system for department employees. He did this while opposing a demand for expanded pensions for veterans of the Civil War, a position that drew fire from the Grand Army of the Republic veterans' organization. Taft ultimately did not endorse MacVeagh's position for political reasons.

Some Republicans resented MacVeagh's appointment to the cabinet because of his former associations with the Democratic party. He was not particularly active in the administration's political problems but believed that Taft should incorporate more progressive Republicans into his body of advisers. MacVeagh's support of Senator Albert J. Beveridge, who stood for reelection in 1910, angered Taft, who was displeased with Beveridge's legislative opposition to administration programs. Perplexed by his secretary's actions, Taft described MacVeagh as "tinged with insurgency" (Butt, p. 355). MacVeagh also championed Henry L. Stimson's appointment as secretary of war after Jacob M. Dickinson resigned in 1911. He viewed the selection as a conciliatory gesture toward Republican liberals and progressives.

Although MacVeagh supported President Taft in his struggle against Theodore Roosevelt in 1912, his role was inconsequential in the Republican split, which led to the defeat of Taft and the party in the general election. After leaving office MacVeagh returned to his business and civic affairs in Chicago. Having traveled widely in Europe, he became deeply interested in the study of architecture and was a founder and for many years president of the Municipal Art League of Chicago. He was active in a variety of social and educational groups and an accomplished speaker. He also published several articles in scholarly journals on governmental and historical topics. MacVeagh was considered a good companion, an intelligent conversationalist, and a gentle person. He died in Chicago.

• MacVeagh's papers are located at the Library of Congress and the University of Illinois at Urbana-Champaign. MacVeagh's articles include "Banking and Currency Reforms," *Journal of Political Economy* 19 (1911): 809–18; "Civil Service Pension," *Annals of the American Academy of Political and Social Sciences* 38 (1911): 3–5; and "How President Taft Has Followed the Roosevelt Policies—or Improved upon Them," *Outlook*, 18 May 1912, pp. 110–16. Information about his early life is in Robert I. Vexler, *The Vice-Presidents and Cabinet Members*, vol. 2 (1975). On his career as secretary of the treasury, see *Annual Report of the Secretary of the Treasury on the State of the Finances, 1909, 1910, 1911, 1912*; Archibald W. Butt, *Taft and Roosevelt: The Intimate Letters of Archie Butt* (2 vols., 1930); Donald F. Anderson, *William Howard Taft: A Conservative's Conception of the Presidency* (1973); Paolo E. Colletta, *The Presidency of William Howard Taft* (1973); Henry F. Pringle, *The Life and Times of William Howard Taft* (2 vols., 1939); Hildreth M. Allison, "Dublin Greets a President," *Historical New Hampshire* 35 (1980): 202–6; and [anon.], "MacVeagh, the Administration's Political Equilibrator," *Current Literature*, Feb. 1911, pp. 147–50. An obituary is in the *New York Times*, 7 July 1934.

ROBERT S. LA FORTE

MACVEAGH, Isaac Wayne (19 Apr. 1833–11 Jan. 1917), lawyer, diplomat, and political reformer, was born near Phoenixville, Pennsylvania, the son of Major John MacVeagh and Margaret Lincoln, hotelkeepers. Margaret was a relative of Abraham Lincoln. Isaac, known as Wayne, attended Freeland Seminary (later Ursinus College) for two years before entering the junior class at Yale College, graduating in 1853. In 1856 he married Letitia Minor Lewis, who died in 1862. The couple had three children, one of whom died in infancy. In 1866 MacVeagh married Virginia Rollette Cameron, daughter of Simon Cameron, a Pennsylvania Republican leader. They had two children in a marriage of more than fifty years.

MacVeagh was admitted to the bar in 1856 and began practice in West Chester, Pennsylvania. He moved to Harrisburg in 1871, and in 1876 he relocated to Philadelphia, where he made his reputation, rising to prominence in the Philadelphia bar. His successful corporate practice included a career-long association as general counsel and solicitor for the Pennsylvania Railroad, and he frequently argued cases before the United States Supreme Court. In 1897 he moved his practice to Washington, D.C. The American Bar Association recognized MacVeagh's stature within his profession in 1901, when it invited him to participate in its observance of the one-hundredth anniversary of John Marshall's appointment as chief justice. MacVeagh eulogized Marshall in a keynote address before an audience in the House of Representatives that included the president and his cabinet, justices of the Supreme Court, and members of both houses of Congress.

MacVeagh combined his legal career with an active interest in political affairs. Opposition to the expansion of slavery drew him to the Republican party in 1856, and he was an uncompromising defender of the Union cause. As chairman of the Republican State Committee, responsible for achieving the reelection of Pennsylvania governor Andrew Curtin in 1863, MacVeagh was in the small group that accompanied Lincoln to Gettysburg when the president delivered his immortal address at the dedication of the battlefield cemetery. President Ulysses S. Grant appointed MacVeagh U.S. minister to Turkey (1870–1871).

In 1877 President Rutherford B. Hayes appointed MacVeagh to a commission sent to Louisiana to seek a settlement between rival Republican and Democratic state governments that would permit withdrawal of federal occupation troops. Concluding that the Democratic government enjoyed wider popular support, the commission negotiated the dissolution of the Republican legislature, with inclusion of some of its members in the Democratic body, and recommended recognition of the Democratic regime and troop withdrawal. Hayes acted promptly on the recommendations, thereby ending Reconstruction in Louisiana. This outcome raised suspicions that the commission's objective had been to complete a bargain related to Hayes's "disputed" election (1876) in which Louisiana (and other southern) Democrats had accepted the election of the Republican Hayes in return for promises that included troop withdrawal and control of local affairs. MacVeagh maintained that the committee had achieved the most practical settlement, and he vehemently rejected allegations of wrongdoing by himself or the committee. President James A. Garfield named MacVeagh U.S. attorney general in 1881, but he resigned shortly after Garfield's assassination because of political differences with his successor, President Chester A. Arthur.

MacVeagh belonged to the reform faction of the Republican party. The party's tolerance of political corruption and catering to business interests during the Gilded Age annoyed him greatly. As a member of the civil service reform movement he supported efforts leading to passage of the Pendleton Act in 1883, but he was reluctant to desert his party. Although he supported their proposed reforms, he did not join the Liberal Republicans who backed Democratic candidate Horace Greeley in 1872 or the Mugwumps who supported Democrat Grover Cleveland in 1884. Upset by the high tariff and inflationary monetary policies of Republican president Benjamin Harrison, MacVeagh defected in 1892 and announced his support of Cleveland, whose views on the tariff and currency were close to his own and whom he regarded as more committed to serving the public interest. He campaigned aggressively and successfully for Cleveland, who appointed him ambassador to Italy (1893–1897). Bryanism, however, particularly the silver issue, drove him back into Republican ranks by the next election.

After reaching retirement age, MacVeagh resolved to go "at a more relaxed pace," but he remained active. He cultivated a circle of friends that included Mark Twain, Henry Adams, Andrew Carnegie, and Presidents Theodore Roosevelt and William Howard Taft. In 1903 Roosevelt appointed MacVeagh chief counsel for the United States and Venezuela in an arbitration before the Hague Court. In 1902 Great Britain, Germany, and Italy had used a naval blockade to force a defaulting Venezuela to assign customs revenues to pay debts and demanded payment ahead of other creditors. MacVeagh presented the case for the United States and Venezuela (not a member of the court) advocating equal treatment of all creditors and arguing that an award of preferential payments would encourage the use of force to collect debts. MacVeagh's participation in the arbitration was a fitting complement to his legal career, even though the court decided in

favor of the blockading powers. The case was the first before the Hague Court to involve a majority of the major European powers.

MacVeagh was particularly in tune with the spirit of the Progressive Era and frequently voiced his opinions in articles for the *North American Review* and other periodicals. He advocated taxes on incomes and inheritances to redistribute wealth and relieve the lot of the poor. He urged the wealthy to accept greater responsibility for social ills and appealed to his friend, President Taft, to "consider the poor." He feared that without such redistribution the poor would lose respect for law and overturn the social order, but his appeals were prompted by more than fear. He genuinely sympathized with the plight of poor Americans, and he was optimistic that the democratic system and the American people would respond to the challenges of his day.

MacVeagh was a complex man, combining aristocratic tastes and scholarly interests with political activitism and a penchant for publicly voicing his opinions on contemporary issues. He was not always consistent. He opposed the spoils system but received his father-in-law Simon Cameron's assistance for his first diplomatic appointment (Cameron had used his influence with President Grant to help MacVeagh secure the appointment to Turkey) and accepted his second foreign mission as a reward for supporting President Cleveland. His work as a corporation lawyer also seemed inconsistent with reform. Such behavior, however, was not necessarily hypocritical. MacVeagh was a patrician reformer who regarded men of his background as best qualified to serve and thought that he exercised a beneficial influence on his corporate employers. If political foes tired of MacVeagh's sermon-like admonitions and questioned his actions, his friends never doubted his intentions or integrity. He was a spokesman for efficiency, honesty, and justice in national life and an advocate of reform to establish those principles. Editor George Harvey of the *North American Review* termed him "an unquenchable spirit" and concluded that few Americans served as "trusted advisor" to so many presidents.

World War I prompted MacVeagh's last public comments. He initially counseled noninvolvement, but he became alarmed by German actions and impatient with President Woodrow Wilson's neutral stance. Writing again in the *North American Review* in 1916, on the anniversary of the *Lusitania* disaster, he harshly condemned German "atrocities" and called Wilson's "mere words" in the face of them cowardly. MacVeagh died at his Washington residence a few months before Wilson's declaration of war.

• MacVeagh's papers are in the Historical Society of Pennsylvania (Philadelphia) and the Wayne MacVeagh Letter Collection in the Chester County Historical Society (West Chester). Many MacVeagh letters are in the papers of Franklin MacVeagh and Simon Cameron, both in the Library of Congress, and in the papers of every U.S. president from Abraham Lincoln to Woodrow Wilson. The papers of Rutherford B. Hayes (Hayes Library, Fremont, Ohio, and the Library of Congress), and the James A. Garfield and Grover Cleveland papers, both in the Library of Congress, are particularly useful. U.S. Department of State, *Despatches from United States Ministers to Turkey, 1818–1906*, vols. 21, 22, 23 (1870–1871), Record Group 59, National Archives and U.S. Department of State, *Despatches from United States Ministers to the Italian States, 1832–1906*, vols. 28, 29, 30 (1894–1897), Record Group 59, National Archives, record his diplomatic service.

MacVeagh recounted his experience with Lincoln at Gettysburg in "Lincoln at Gettysburg," *Century Magazine*, Nov. 1909, pp. 20–23. MacVeagh's other writings include "Ethical Ideals in American Politics," *Arena*, Oct. 1901, pp. 337–61; and, all in the *North American Review*, "The Value of the Venezuelan Arbitration," Dec. 1903, pp. 801–11, "An Appeal to Our Millionaires," June 1906, pp. 801–23, "An Appeal to President Taft," Feb. 1911, pp. 161–79, "The Impassable Chasm," July 1915, pp. 26–34, and "'Lusitania Day': May 7, 1916," June 1916, pp. 814–20.

J. Smith Futhey and Gilbert Cope, *History of Chester County Pennsylvania with Genealogical and Biographic Sketches* (1881), contains a biographical sketch of MacVeagh. Contemporary portraits of MacVeagh are in "Portrait," *Arena*, Aug. 1905, p. 140; "The Rapier-like Mr. MacVeagh," the *Nation*, 29 July 1915, pp. 140–41; and George Harvey, "A Passionate Patriot," *North American Review*, Mar. 1917, pp. 337–44. Ari Hoogenboom, *Outlawing the Spoils: A History of the Civil Service Reform Movement, 1865–1883* (1961), and C. Vann Woodward, *Reunion and Reaction: The Compromise of 1877 and the End of Reconstruction* (1956), are important sources for these two issues with which MacVeagh had an important relationship. Warner B. Berthoff and David B. Green, "Henry Adams and Wayne MacVeagh," *Pennsylvania Magazine of History and Biography*, 19 Oct. 1956, pp. 493–512, describes the long MacVeagh-Adams friendship. Obituaries are in the *Philadelphia Inquirer* and the Washington *Evening Star*, 12 Jan. 1917. See also *Obituary Records of Graduates of Yale University* (1917).

ROBERT C. OLSON

MACVEAGH, Lincoln (1 Oct. 1890–15 Jan. 1972), diplomat and publisher, was born in Narragansett Pier, Rhode Island, the son of Charles MacVeagh, a diplomat, and Fanny Davenport Rogers. The MacVeagh family had distinguished itself in public service; his father served as ambassador to Japan during the Calvin Coolidge administration; his grandfather, Wayne MacVeagh, as President James Garfield's attorney general; and his great-uncle, Franklin MacVeagh, as President William Howard Taft's secretary of the treasury.

In 1909 MacVeagh graduated from the Groton School and went on to Harvard, graduating magna cum laude in 1913. His affinity for languages took him to the Sorbonne from 1913 to 1914, where he also studied philosophy. MacVeagh was proficient in French, Spanish, Latin, German, Italian, and Greek, a skill that proved invaluable in his diplomatic career.

Returning to the United States, MacVeagh was employed for a year by the United States Steel Products Company and then worked for the Henry Holt Publishing Company. In May 1917 he enlisted in the U.S. Army and was commissioned a first lieutenant two days prior to his marriage to Margaret Charleton Lewis in August 1917. They had one child, Margaret Ewen. Assigned to the Eightieth Division, the newly promoted Captain MacVeagh was deployed to Europe where he served as an aide to the commanding general. He participated in actions on the Artois front, at St. Mihiel, and the Meuse-Argonne offensive. After service with the Sixth and Ninth Army Corps, he was assigned to the general staff of the American Expeditionary Forces (AEF) in the historical section. Leaving the military as a major in July 1919, he was cited for "exceptionally meritorious and conspicuous service by General John J. "Blackjack" Pershing, commanding general of the AEF.

MacVeagh returned to Holt Publishing until 1923, when he formed Dial Press Incorporated in New York City. At Dial, he served as president, secretary, treasurer, and publisher of *Dial* magazine until his appointment as minister to Greece in 1933. Although not a politically active Democrat, MacVeagh and his family were close to the Roosevelt family, which enhanced his chances for the appointment. President-elect Franklin D. Roosevelt was aware of his fellow Groton and Harvard alumnus's knowledge of Greece and its people when he made the appointment. MacVeagh and his family arrived in Athens in September 1933. After presenting his credentials to the president and foreign minister, he read a short prepared speech in classical Greek, which few understood, but all applauded.

One of MacVeagh's first tasks was to influence the government of Greece to extradite Samuel Insull, a notorious American financial speculator, who had sought refuge in Greece. Subtly working behind the scenes, he facilitated Insull's return to the United States to stand trial for mail fraud. This caliber of work typified MacVeagh's performance as ambassador, along with his lengthy and informative dispatches. Until the advent of World War II, MacVeagh's reports received wide circulation not only for their wit but also for their comprehensiveness and professionalism. As the war clouds gathered around Greece, his messages were relegated to telegraph and took on a more somber and succinct form.

MacVeagh's love of Greece continued to flourish in spite of his heavy diplomatic responsibilities. In 1936 his excavation site at the Acropolis uncovered numerous shards, dated about 1000 B.C., which were presented to the National Museum in Athens. His extensive travel throughout Greece made him an authority on that country, causing even the Greeks to call upon him for detailed geographical information.

Returning to the United States in 1941, after the Greek government went into exile to flee Nazi occupation, MacVeagh was quickly appointed as the first minister to Iceland. In his short stay, he successfully aided in the settling of numerous diplomatic and labor problems that had plagued the construction of the large military airfield at Keflavik. Another brief assignment awaited him in South Africa in 1942, where as minister he essentially established his own diplomatic agenda and priorities. In November 1943 he became the ambassador to the Greek and Yugoslav governments in exile, quartered in Cairo, Egypt. Typical of his assignments in South Africa and Cairo, Mac-Veagh received little guidance in his actions, but his astute performance merited him several commendations for his part in South Africa's shift to greater emphasis on production of raw material in support of the war and the king of Greece's decision to acquiesce to the desires of the people in regard to his position in a postwar Greek government.

Prior to returning to Athens in the fall of 1944, Mac-Veagh wrestled with the problem of Soviet influence in both Yugoslavia and Greece. His accurate predictions that turmoil would follow the war in both countries were conveyed to Roosevelt, but little resulted because of the relative global insignificance of the two countries.

The battle between the royalist, liberal, and communist parties for control in Greece occupied much of MacVeagh's time in the postwar era. The Truman administration, concurring in MacVeagh's assessment of a possible Communist takeover, formulated many of his earlier suggestions of aid to Greece into the Truman Doctrine.

The year 1947 was turbulent for MacVeagh. U.S. aid to Greece became bogged down because of tension between warring Greek parties until finally resolved by the Sophoulis-led coalition government in September. Differences arose between Dwight Griswold, administrator of the aid program, and MacVeagh, because of the former's infringement on embassy authority. MacVeagh's wife died during this period after a prolonged illness, but he continued his duties until he took her home for burial.

MacVeagh was reassigned to Portugal rather than returning to Greece even though differences with Griswold had reportedly been reconciled. He remained in Portugal until 1952 when he was reassigned to Spain to negotiate the acquisition of military bases with the Franco government.

Retiring in 1953, MacVeagh lived in Portugal with his second wife, Virginia Ferrante Coats, whom he had married in May 1955, and his stepson, Colin. Illness brought MacVeagh back to the United States in 1971, where he died in Adelphi, Maryland, bringing to a close a distinguished career.

MacVeagh's perceptive analysis of postwar Southeastern Europe and his ability to articulate the problems in his dispatches and testimony to the Senate Committee on Foreign Relations aided significantly in preventing a complete Communist takeover in this strategic area. Generally unheralded, particularly after the death of his friend, President Roosevelt, Mac-Veagh was a reliable, highly competent diplomat who appears to have been held in higher esteem by the Greeks than by those he served.

• MacVeagh's diaries are in the possession of his family. His diplomatic correspondence is held in the files of the Department of State. Letters to Presidents Roosevelt and Truman are located in their respective libraries. The most important source in the study of MacVeagh is John O. Iatrides's compilation of his diary entries and letters, *Ambassador MacVeagh*

Reports: Greece, 1933–1947 (1980). Howard Jones, "*A New Kind of War": America's Global Strategy and the Truman Doctrine in Greece* (1989), and Lawrence S. Wittner, *American Intervention in Greece, 1943–1949* (1982), provide a view of MacVeagh's contributions to the overall Truman strategy as well as his participation in American diplomacy during the mid-1940s. See also "National Affairs," *Time*, 24 Mar. 1947, pp. 20–21, and "People of the Week," *U.S. News and World Report*, 8 Nov. 1940, pp. 36–37, for additional activities in Greece. Records maintained by the National Archives provide very little information on his military career. An obituary is in the *New York Times*, 17 Jan. 1972.

HAROLD R. KLOBE

MACY, Anne Sullivan (14 Apr. 1866–20 Oct. 1936), special educator, was born Johanna Mansfield Sullivan in Feeding Hills (near Springfield), Massachusetts, the daughter of Thomas Sullivan and Alice Cloesy, farmers. She was known throughout her life as Anne or Annie. Her parents (both immigrants from County Limerick, Ireland) were illiterate, and her childhood was marred by both poverty and misfortune. An attack of trachoma around the age of five left her virtually blind, and she was subjected to frequent beatings at the hands of her alcoholic father. In 1874 her mother died, and two years later her father abandoned his three living children. While her sister Mary was sent to live with relatives, Anne and her brother Jimmie (crippled from a bout with tuberculosis) were sent to the state almshouse in Tewksbury, where Jimmie died a few months later.

Devastated by her brother's death, Sullivan was miserable at Tewksbury. The facility was filthy, badly overcrowded, and provided no educational facilities. She learned of the Perkins Institute for the Blind in Boston, and when a commission headed by state board of charities chairman Frank Sanborn visited Tewksbury for an inspection Sullivan literally threw herself at him and cried out "Mr. Sanborn, I want to go to school!" Arrangements were made shortly, and she entered Perkins in October 1880. Her childhood and almshouse experiences left their mark on Sullivan, who never quite overcame the feelings of shame and inferiority that she acquired as a result.

Despite her total lack of formal education, Sullivan prospered at Perkins. She regained some of her sight through an operation in 1881, and she graduated from the school in 1886 as class valedictorian. Uncertain as to her future vocation, she learned of a governess position through Perkins's director (and son-in-law of its founder, Samuel Gridley Howe), Michael Anagnos. Arthur H. Keller of Tuscumbia, Alabama, had contacted Anagnos to see if anyone was willing to attempt to teach his daughter Helen, a seven-year-old girl who had lost both her sight and hearing at the age of nineteen months. After studying Howe's notes (who taught Laura Bridgeman, a similarly afflicted girl), Sullivan accepted the position with some trepidation and arrived in Tuscumbia in March 1887.

Upon her arrival, Sullivan found Helen to be a willful, spoiled, and moody child. As her behavior was completely uncontrolled, Sullivan made instruction in obedience her first priority. Realizing that Helen possessed great intelligence in spite of her isolation, she attempted to communicate with her through a manual method—"finger spelling"—in which letters to words were articulated into a pupil's hand. After weeks of frustration, Sullivan spelled out the word "water" while pumping water over her pupil's hand. Keller recognized the connection, and her link to the outside world was restored. Insatiable for knowledge, she made rapid progress. The two visited Perkins in the spring of 1888, stopping en route to meet with inventor and deaf educator Alexander Graham Bell, who shared the astonishment felt by nearly all who came into contact with Keller regarding her progress.

Sullivan remained with Keller for the rest of her life. The pair traveled widely as their fame spread, and they enjoyed the philanthropy of individuals such as industrialists Andrew Carnegie, Henry H. Rogers, and John Spaulding. She attended Keller's classes at Wright-Humason oral speech school in New York City (1894–1896), the Cambridge (Mass.) School for Young Ladies (1896–1897), and finally Radcliffe College (1900–1904). Assisting Keller in her schoolwork exhausted Sullivan, and the resulting overwork proved disastrous for her already frail eyesight. Sullivan also came into frequent conflict with school administrators. Fiercely protective of Keller and resentful of attempts to separate them (a prevalent rumor was that Sullivan was either "controlling" or "using" Keller), Sullivan experienced estrangement from both Anagnos and Arthur Gilman (the head of the Cambridge School). Insecure and often petulant in behavior, Sullivan also suffered the slights of a society that (she often felt) fawned over Keller while largely ignoring or discounting her own contributions to Keller's development.

Following Keller's graduation from Radcliffe, the pair relocated to farm in Wrentham, Massachusetts. A frequent visitor there was John Albert Macy, a youthful Harvard instructor who had assisted the pair in preparing Keller's biography. Despite misgivings (Sullivan feared the marriage's effect on Keller; Macy was also eleven years her junior), the two married (with Keller's blessing) in 1905. Although the three lived together in harmony for a time, marital strains created a separation by 1912, when John Macy, an aspiring writer, left to work for the mayor of Schenectady. No children resulted from the marriage, which was never formally terminated despite the couple's failure to reconcile.

Anne Macy and Keller moved to Forest Hills, New York, in 1917. In constant demand as lecturers and as potential fundraisers, the pair had to balance the public's desire to hear their story with their own financial constraints. Charitable to a fault, they were in constant need of supplementing their income. While a trip to Hollywood in 1918 to produce the movie *Deliverance* came to naught—the film flopped—a stint on the vaudeville circuit (1919–1921) proved more lucrative. Although Macy's failing health took them off the tour by the latter year, the pair undertook fundraising tours

on behalf of the newly formed American Foundation for the Blind (1924–1927).

Despite their worldwide fame, Macy's final years were painful. She hated fundraising and lost an eye through surgery in 1929. Totally blind at the end, she did not adapt well to her encumbrance. Nevertheless, long-overdue recognition came her way. Awarded an honorary doctor of humane letters from Temple University in 1931, she stubbornly refused to accept it until the following year. She and Keller also became honorary fellows of the Educational Institute of Scotland (1933) and received medals from the Roosevelt Memorial Foundation (1936). Vacations in search of health failed to raise Macy's spirits, and she died at her home in Forest Hills after a long period of decline.

Although occasionally controversial, "Teacher" (as Keller inevitably referred to her) achieved remarkable success with her one and only pupil. Though she possessed only minimal training, her tireless and creative efforts resulted in the gift of Helen Keller to the world. If her life apart from Keller was largely unsuccessful, Anne Sullivan Macy still merits the recognition that she was so often denied in life.

• Anne Sullivan Macy's papers are held at the Perkins Institute for the Blind, Watertown, Mass.; the American Antiquarian Society in Worcester, Mass.; and the Volta Bureau in Washington, D.C. Scholarship on Macy includes Joseph P. Lash, *Helen and Teacher: The Story of Helen Keller and Anne Sullivan Macy* (1980), which is often critical of Macy. Dated but still useful is Nella Braddy, *Anne Sullivan Macy* (1933). Helen Keller, *Teacher: Anne Sullivan Macy* (1955), is valuable but marred by Keller's defensiveness on her subject. An obituary is in the *New York Times*, 21 Oct. 1936.

EDWARD L. LACH, JR.

MACY, John Williams, Jr. (6 Apr. 1917–22 Dec. 1986), federal administrator, was born in Chicago, Illinois, the son of John W. Macy, an advertising executive, and Juliette Moen. He attended the North Shore Country Day School in Winnetka, Illinois, then entered Wesleyan College, where he majored in government, graduating Phi Beta Kappa in 1938. After college he served as an intern with the National Institute of Public Affairs from 1938 to 1939 in a program designed to introduce the brightest young minds to the idea of a career in government.

Macy served as administrative assistant for the Social Security Board (1939–1940) and as a civilian employee with the War Department (1940–1943). During World War II he enlisted in the Army Air Force and served in China, rising to the rank of captain. In 1944 he married Joyce Hagan; the couple had four children. After retiring from the military in 1946, he returned to the War Department as a civilian. In 1947 he became the director of personnel and organization for the Atomic Energy Commission–Los Alamos Project, a position he held until 1951, when he became special assistant to the secretary of the army.

In 1953, President Dwight Eisenhower appointed Macy executive director of the Civil Service Commission (CSC). This was part of a shake-up of the CSC, aimed at increasing its efficiency. Macy's appointment was considered a victory for broad, people-oriented principles of personnel management, versus a narrower orientation that emphasized bureaucratic regimen. With the support of the CSC chairman, Philip Young, former head of Columbia University's College of Business, Macy turned the commission into an activist agency, reforming the bureaucracy and directly assisting the president on personnel matters. He rejuvenated the government's college recruiting program, pioneered in new fringe benefits for federal employees, and initiated a merit system for superior job performance. When President Eisenhower replaced Young in 1957 with a defeated congressman, Harris Ellsworth, the commission was simultaneously weakened and politicized, and in 1958 Macy resigned.

After twenty years in government service, Macy returned to Wesleyan College to become executive vice president. He remained there until 1961, when President John F. Kennedy appointed him chair of the CSC, a position he held until 1969. During this period Macy made his greatest impact on the executive branch and on the federal bureaucracy in general, both because of his influence over appointments and because he modernized personnel methods. Macy became the personnel adviser first to President Kennedy and then to President Lyndon Johnson, with whom he enjoyed a particularly close relationship. Johnson referred to Macy as "my talent scout" and extolled the chairman as "the best there is." For senior appointments Macy submitted a list of three or four candidates from his computerized data bank of over 20,000 highly qualified potential appointees. In part Macy's influence led the White House to accept merit rather than partisan affiliation as the primary criterion for second-level appointments and promotions, reflected in the 1965 appointment of the Republican John W. Gardner as secretary of health, education, and welfare. Macy estimated that in those years he spent about one-third of his time at the White House and two-thirds handling the personnel needs of the executive branch. He also convinced Johnson to approve a major training program designed to improve the skills of federal employees and to introduce them to the latest concepts in management. By 1966 65,000 federal employees were participating in these classes. In addition, Macy founded the Federal Executive Institute to foster management expertise and leadership qualities among government managers. Another example of the role Macy played in the federal government came during the Vietnam War, when he recognized the growing demand for civilian workers in the military. Requesting manpower estimates from the Department of Defense and finding none, Macy took the initiative and established a joint CSC/Defense task force. This commission conducted the necessary analysis and planning and thus averted a crisis.

In 1969 President Richard Nixon appointed Macy the first president of the Corporation for Public Broadcasting, where he fostered the rise of public broadcasting. Among the notable programs that originated and were nurtured during his term was "Sesame Street," the acclaimed children's television show. Macy also helped create the Public Broadcast Laboratory, the Children's Theatre Workshop, and the New York Television Theatre. Macy resigned in 1972 as a result of disputes with the Nixon administration over the level of funding for public broadcasting, the content of public-affairs programs, and the balance between centralized programming versus locally initiated projects.

Macy then served in a variety of posts, including president of the Council of Better Business Bureaus (1973–1975) and project manager and president of the Development and Resources Corporation (1975–1979). In 1979 President Jimmy Carter asked Macy to return to government as director of the Federal Emergency Management Administration. Resigning this post two years later, Macy became vice president of the National Executives Service Corps, a position he held until his death in McLean, Virginia.

• John W. Macy, Jr., wrote numerous works on government, including *Public Service: The Human Side of Government* (1971); *To Irrigate a Wasteland* (1974); and, with Bruce Adams and J. Jackson Walter, *America's Unelected Government: Appointing the President's Team* (1983). He appeared prominently in and provided a brief introduction to Donald Harvey, *The Civil Service Commission* (1970). Frank Sherwood, "The Legacy of John W. Macy, Jr.," *Public Administration Review* 47 (May–June 1987): 221–26, serves as both eulogy and critique of Macy's career. An obituary is in the *New York Times*, 25 Dec. 1986.

ROBERT A. SLAYTON

MADDEN, John Edward (28 Dec. 1856–3 Nov. 1929), racehorse breeder and trainer, was born in Bethlehem, Pennsylvania, the son of Irish immigrants Patrick Madden, a zinc worker, and Catherine McKee. Patrick Madden died when John was four years old, leaving his wife and three children to support themselves. Working in the steel mills as a boy, Madden developed great strength and endurance; he became an outstanding athlete and captained the Bethlehem East End baseball team. As a teenager, he began earning a living on the midwestern county fair circuit, running footraces, boxing, and driving in harness horse races.

Once he had amassed some savings, Madden invested in trotters, buying cheap horses and trading up in class. In 1884 he traded for Class Leader and, through a unique exercise program of alternating hard and easy days, trained the gelding into a respectable trotter, eventually selling him for $10,000. In 1889 Madden went to England in search of Warlock, whose bloodlines were popular in America. He bought the standardbred for $4,000, transported him to the United States, and sold him for $15,000. In a similarly wise venture, he bought Geneva S. for $1,500, then sold her for $15,000 when her pedigree became popular. Madden invested some of his capital in breeding stock in 1890, paying $33,250 for the nineteen-year-old standardbred stallion Robert McGregor, who later sired the world champion harness racer Cresceus. In June 1890 Madden married Ann Louise Megrue of

Cincinnati, Ohio. They had two sons and divorced in 1906.

In 1890, two years after buying his first thoroughbred, Madden won his first thoroughbred stakes, the Great Western, with Dundee. He bought another thoroughbred, Harry Reed, for $400 in 1893 and sold him for $10,000 after he won the 1894 Van Nest Stakes. Madden's Amanda V. won three stakes races in 1895. Impressed by her performance and bloodlines, he paid $1,200 for her half-brother, Hamburg. In 1897 Madden raced the two-year-old sixteen times, with a record of twelve wins, three second places, and a third. Marcus Daly, owner of the Anaconda copper mine and a key figure in Montana racing, paid Madden a record sum of $40,001 for Hamburg.

Madden's reputation as a horse speculator had grown, and it soon became difficult for him to purchase bargains. Figuring that he could breed good horses more cheaply than he could buy them, he used the profit from the sale of Hamburg to buy "Overton Place," a farm near Lexington, Kentucky, in 1897. Renaming it "Hamburg Place," he expanded the farm as his breeding operation grew. It eventually consisted of 2,300 acres, with distinctive black fences, black barns trimmed in red, a special stable for retired racehorses, and an equine cemetery. In 1898 Madden's mare Iolanthe produced Clashful, the first thoroughbred stakes winner that Madden bred.

In 1898 Madden established a lasting professional relationship with William Collins Whitney, a wealthy corporate lawyer, former secretary of the navy, and transit tycoon who bought from Madden the Kentucky Derby winner Plaudit for $25,000. When Plaudit finished a disappointing second in his next two races, Madden bought him back for $12,000. He went on to sell other horses to Whitney, including Kilmarnock and Ballyhoo Bey. In 1901 Madden led all trainers in race earnings and was second only to W. C. Whitney in earnings among owners. The next year Madden established the trainer's earnings record at $150,476.

In addition to Plaudit, Madden's famous thoroughbred stallions at Hamburg Place included Ogden, Sir Martin, and Star Shoot. He also maintained his interest in standardbreds; besides Robert McGregor, his standardbred stallions included Siliko, winner of the 1906 Kentucky Futurity and sire of Periscope, winner of the major three-year-old races of 1919, the Kentucky Futurity, the Horseman Futurity, the Matron Stake, and the Review Futurity. Madden used races to showcase his homebred horses, most notably in the 1908 racing season. At the beginning of the season he had fifty-four two-year-olds in training; by the end of the year he had sold them all. That year he ranked second among owners in victories and earnings and second among trainers in earnings. The *Thoroughbred Record* noted that during this period Madden was "the only millionaire breeder of Thoroughbreds who trains, develops, and races his own horses." Fastidious about horses' feet, Madden often quoted the advertising slogan "No foot, no horse" and insisted on the highest standard of care from his farriers. He turned

this to his profit in 1909, after he balanced the troublesome standardbred Hamburg Belle's feet, trained her to run the mile in a record 2:01¼, and sold her for a record $50,000.

Madden was well known for his aphorisms, the most often-repeated of which was "Better to sell and regret than to keep and regret." He had ample opportunity to test this advice, having sold the young gelding Exterminator in 1918 for $9,000, only to see him win the Kentucky Derby in his first start for his new owner and eventually earn $252,996. Although a successful breeder, he valued training over pedigreed bloodlines, maintaining that "The best-bred horse in any race is the winner. And if he wins often enough, the experts will find plenty of reasons why he is the best-bred horse in the world" (Bob Moore, "The Madden Legend," *Horseman's Journal* [Jan. 1972]: 73).

From 1898 through 1929 Madden bred 182 American stakes winners, including six Kentucky Derby winners (Plaudit, 1898; Old Rosebud, 1914; Sir Barton, 1919; Paul Jones, 1920; Zev, 1923; and Flying Ebony, 1925) and five Belmont Stakes winners. Sir Barton was the first American Triple Crown winner. Zev became the greatest money-winning colt of the era, with earnings of $313,369, and Madden also bred the most lucrative filly of the time, Princess Doreen, who won $174,745. He was America's leading breeder of winners from 1917, the first year official breeding statistics were compiled, through 1927. In 1921 and 1923 horses he had bred won more than 400 races, a feat unduplicated until 1977. Madden, who had risen from poverty through hard work and intelligence, left an estate valued at over $9 million when he died in New York City. He was elected to both the Hall of Fame of the Trotter and the National Horse Racing Hall of Fame.

• Madden wrote two books, *The Trotters at Hamburg Place, Lexington, Ky., USA* (1911) and *Madden's Stallion Record of Horses Not Well Known Whose Pedigrees Appear in Many of Our Present Day Great Trotters* (1917). An article he wrote on training methods appears in the *Thoroughbred Record* 89 (1919): 126. Kent Hollingsworth wrote an extensive biography of Madden, "Wizard of the Turf," serialized in *Bloodhorse* 88 (1964) and 89 (1965); another biographical series, by Neil Newman, is in the *Thoroughbred Record* 146 (1947). Contemporary articles on Madden, his career, and his breeding and training techniques appear in the *Thoroughbred Record* 85 (1917): 140 and 107 (1928): 327, and *Kentucky Farmer and Breeder* 2 (1905): 1, 4. See also Hollingsworth, *The Kentucky Thoroughbred* (1976). Obituaries are in the *Thoroughbred Record* 110 (1929): 286–87; and the *Lexington Herald* and the *New York Times*, both 4 Nov. 1929.

STEVEN P. SAVAGE

MADDEN, Owen Victor (18 Dec. 1891–24 Apr. 1965), criminal entrepreneur, was born in Leeds, England, the son of Irish immigrants Francis Madden, a factory laborer, and Mary (maiden name unknown). After Madden's father died, in 1902 his mother moved the family to New York, where they settled in the West Side Irish slum area known as Hell's Kitchen. As a teenager Madden became an archetypical delinquent, combining mugging, burglary, and racketeering with gang battles to build a reputation as a fearsome street fighter. First as a member and then a leader of the Gophers, a major Irish gang in Hell's Kitchen, Madden's skill with firearms earned him the nickname "The Killer." He was responsible for at least three murders by 1914. Madden was one of several New York City street toughs who managed to build successful careers in bootlegging and entertainment (including nightclubs, prizefighting, and gambling) during the first half of the twentieth century. While still a gang member he married Dorothy Roberts in 1911. A daughter was born before they separated in 1913 (they were divorced in 1934).

Although members of the Gophers enjoyed a degree of protection from Tammany Hall because of their help in winning elections on the West Side, the gang's notoriety eventually was its undoing. Madden's personal immunity ended in 1915 with his conviction on a charge of first-degree manslaughter. Sentenced to serve ten to twenty years, Madden's good behavior while in Sing Sing prison earned him an early release in 1923.

Madden had missed the early days of Prohibition, but a combination of good luck, a shrewd business sense, and a reputation as an honest man (among his criminal peers) enabled him to build a very successful career in bootlegging and associated enterprises during the 1920s. Forming a long-term partnership with George Jean DeMange, another West Side street tough, Madden began his bootlegging career as a highjacker of other people's liquor supplies. He quickly moved on, however, to other areas in the business of bootlegging, joining a partnership with Bill Dwyer and Frank Costello that smuggled whiskey from England and rum from the West Indies into New York. He also established an illegal brewery to manufacture beer.

Unlike some of his criminal contemporaries, Madden also displayed a flair for legal and quasi-legal business activities. Bootleggers were avid customers for the numerous nightclubs that proliferated in New York during the 1920s, a fact that Madden used to his advantage. In a partnership with DeMange and Arnold Rothstein (a major underworld figure of the era), Madden bought a nightclub in Harlem called the Club DeLuxe. Renaming it the Cotton Club, Madden turned it into one of the era's most famous entertainment centers. By the end of the 1920s Madden owned interests in several other major nightclubs, and he had become an important benefactor in show business, sponsoring figures such as George Raft, Mae West, and Duke Ellington.

Madden simultaneously pursued another passion, prizefighting. During the 1920s he invested in partnerships that controlled the careers of five championship boxers, including Primo Carnera and Maxie Rosenbloom, both of whom became world champions.

Madden's connections with Hot Springs, Arkansas, which would become the focus of his post-Prohibition career, began in the spring of 1931. He had come under increasing scrutiny from diverse law enforcement agencies, including Judge Samuel Seabury, who was investigating corruption in New York City, and the New York State Parole Board, which was under political pressure to investigate whether or not Madden had violated the terms of his parole. These inquiries into his affairs may have prompted Madden to think of safer places to conduct his business, and Hot Springs had a long-deserved reputation for providing political protection to its local gambling and prostitution entrepreneurs who catered to the town's many tourists. On this first visit he met Agnes Demby, the daughter of the local postmaster, in her tourist shop. Madden and Demby married in 1934; they had no children.

In the summer of 1932 the parole board sent Madden back to Sing Sing for a year. After his release, he launched a new career as an investor in major gambling operations, following an emerging national pattern among ex-bootleggers. He moved to Hot Springs, where he became the local representative of an investment syndicate composed of himself, Frank Costello, and probably Meyer Lansky in several Hot Springs casinos. Madden also invested in race tracks in California and Florida.

The remainder of his career was comparatively peaceful and, no doubt, profitable. A steady stream of entertainment and underworld friends visiting from Hollywood, New York, and Chicago guaranteed his local celebrity status and helped sustain Hot Springs's reputation as a major tourist attraction through the mid-1940s. He also spent considerable time cultivating a good reputation with the local citizens through charitable contributions. In the early 1940s he became a U.S. citizen.

Beginning in 1947, a decade-long struggle between reformers and corrupt politicians made prosperity somewhat more difficult and less predictable for Hot Springs's underworld, but Madden proved adroit at maintaining good relations with whomever happened to be in charge of local government.

In the late 1950s the slow decline of Hot Springs as a tourist attraction combined with national indignation over corrupt relations between the underworld and local politicians to force Madden out of business. Like many of his ex-bootlegger peers, Madden was getting old; his generation was passing from the scene, and it probably did not require much thought for him to decide to retire. He sold his remaining gambling interests in 1961 and spent the remaining four years of his life quietly in Hot Springs, where he died.

Although Madden never gained national notoriety of the sort associated with men like Bugsy Siegel or Frank Costello, he exemplified a particular kind of criminal entrepreneur. Criminals like Madden, who had reputations for toughness and honesty, built very successful careers by satisfying public demands for legal and illegal entertainment during and after Prohibition.

• Madden has not received as much attention as several of his contemporaries. A full-length study of his career, Graham Nown, *The English Godfather* (1987), is a very sympathetic portrait that needs to be used cautiously. Madden is mentioned in Stephen R. Fox, *Blood and Power: Organized Crime in Twentieth-century America* (1989). An obituary is in the *New York Times*, 24 Apr. 1965.

DAVID R. JOHNSON

MADDISON, Isabel (13 Apr. 1869–22 Oct. 1950), mathematician and administrator, was born in Cumberland, England, the daughter of John Maddison, a civil servant, and Mary Anderson. Maddison studied for four years at the University College of South Wales and Monmouthshire in Cardiff under Principal Viriamu Jones and Professor H. W. Lloyd Tanner. In 1889 she matriculated at Girton College, Cambridge, with a scholarship from the Clothworkers' Guild.

At Girton, Maddison was supervised by John Dodds, Arthur Berry, Alfred North Whitehead, and William Henry Young. She was a classmate of Grace Chisholm and attended the mathematical lectures of Professors Arthur Cayley and Robert Webb. Maddison earned a first class on the 1892 Cambridge Mathematical Tripos. Her examination was judged to be equal to that of the male examinee who placed twenty-seventh. She was the twelfth woman to earn a first class since Charlotte Scott first did so in 1880. Maddison also took a second class Mathematical Honor School Examination at Oxford University in 1892.

Maddison received a grant to undertake graduate studies in mathematics for the academic year 1892–1893 at Bryn Mawr College, where she studied under the supervision of Professors James Harkness, A. Stanley Mackensie, and Charlotte Scott. Scott described Maddison as having a "powerful mind" and regarded Maddison's training at Girton as having been excellent. Much of Maddison's early work concentrated on recent developments in modern and linear algebra made by Arthur Cayley and James Joseph Sylvester. Her interests then shifted to analysis, and she began work under Scott's supervision on singular solutions of differential equations of the first order in two variables. This work would form the basis for her doctoral dissertation. In 1893 Maddison passed an examination permitting her to receive an "external" bachelor of science degree, with honors, from the University of London. Neither Cambridge nor Oxford granted degrees to women at the time. Maddison was awarded the Resident Mathematical Fellowship, enabling her to continue her studies at Bryn Mawr for the academic year 1893–1894.

Maddison was awarded Bryn Mawr's first Mary E. Garrett European Fellowship of $500 and used it to travel to Germany during 1894–1895. At Göttingen, along with Grace Chisholm and Mary Winston (later Newson), she attended the lectures of Felix Klein, David Hilbert, and Heinrich Burkhardt and took part in the work of the Mathematical Seminary. Maddison returned to Bryn Mawr and served as an assistant to Bryn Mawr's president, M. Carey Thomas, while she completed work on her thesis under Scott's supervision. In 1896 she was awarded a Ph.D. and took a position as reader in mathematics. In 1904 she was promoted to associate professor. She was awarded Bryn Mawr's Gambel Prize for a paper based on her thesis that appeared in the *Quarterly Journal of Pure and Applied Mathematics*. She spoke before Bryn Mawr's Mathematical Journal Club in 1897 on limit sets of Kleinian and Fuchsian groups. The topic, a precursor to complex dynamics, was one she had studied at Göttingen.

A subscriber to the *Educational Times*, Maddison between 1887 and 1889 posed one problem and submitted thirteen solutions to its mathematical section. In 1887 she was elected to membership in the American Mathematical Society and the London Mathematical Society. She was an active member of the former and published a number of book reviews and articles in its *Bulletin*. In 1905 Maddison traveled to Dublin, Ireland, to receive an external bachelor of arts degree from Trinity College.

In her position as assistant to the president at Bryn Mawr she was responsible for much of the routine administration of the college. Her papers contain a myriad of memos concerning college-related matters, including committee assignments, requests for course titles, replies to job interviews, student illness, and information regarding student transcripts. She organized student registration, classroom assignments, menus for college functions, and itineraries for guest lectures and distributed faculty course schedules. She corresponded with publishers, sent out information to prospective students, planned itineraries for the president, and conducted interviews with candidates for the secretarial staff. In 1910 she took on the additional responsibility of recording dean and continued in both administrative positions until her retirement in 1926.

Maddison's *Handbook of Courses Open to Women in British, Continental, and Canadian Universities* (1896) was informative and went through several editions. In 1917 Maddison published a statistical study for the American Association of University Women of the health, marital status, children, occupations, financial status, and education of children of women college graduates between 1869 and 1898. Her administrative work made it virtually impossible for her to pursue mathematical research. She later admitted that, even though she had not lost her interest in mathematics, she felt a bit "ashamed of having deserted mathematics for a less rarified atmosphere of work among people and things" (Women in Mathematics questionnaire [1937], Helen Brewster Owens Collection, Schlesinger Library).

Maddison was a member of the Daughters of the British Empire. After retiring from Bryn Mawr she migrated to England for a time. She returned to Pennsylvania and devoted much of her time to writing poetry, most of which went unpublished. She died at The Croft, Martin's Dam, Wayne, Pennsylvania. She had never married. In her will she bequeathed $10,000 to Bryn Mawr in memory of M. Carey Thomas for use as a pension fund for nonfaculty staff members. Colleagues remembered her for her "natural and gentle sweetness, her love of youth, and her sensitivity" (minutes, Board of Directors, 21 Dec. 1950, Miriam Coffin Canaday Library).

• Maddison's papers are in the Miriam Coffin Canaday Library at Bryn Mawr College. Other references to Maddison can be found in the Helen Brewster Owens and Mary Williams Collections at the Schlesinger Library, Radcliffe College, Cambridge, Mass. For further bibliographic information, see Betsey Whitman's article on Maddison in *Women of Mathematics: A Biobibliographic Sourcebook*, ed. L. Grinstein and P. Campbell (1987). An obituary is in the *New York Times*, 24 Oct. 1950.

JAMES J. TATTERSALL
SHAWNEE L. McMURRAN

MADISON, Dolley (20 May 1768–12 July 1849), first lady, was born near Guilford, North Carolina, the daughter of John Payne, an unsuccessful merchant and planter, and Mary Coles. When Dolley was one year old the Paynes left North Carolina and moved back to rural eastern Virginia, settling with the Coles family. There she grew up in comfort; throughout her life she defined herself as a Virginian. Her family were Quakers, and in 1783 her father manumitted his slaves and moved his wife and eight children to Philadelphia. There he opened a starch business, which failed in 1789. His wife then supported the family by converting her home into a boardinghouse. Dolley Payne came of age during difficult years; she saw her father slide into debt, expelled from his Quaker congregation, and die a broken man, leaving her mother and her sisters in severely reduced circumstances.

Dolley Payne achieved financial security by twice marrying well. In 1790 she wed a young Quaker lawyer from Philadelphia, John Todd. They quickly had two children. In 1793, however, both her husband and her infant son succumbed to a yellow fever epidemic that swept Philadelphia, leaving her a widow with one young son, John Payne Todd.

In May 1794 Aaron Burr introduced Dolley Payne Todd to James Madison, a 43-year-old bachelor from a successful planter family in Orange County, Virginia. He had played a major role in drafting the U.S. Constitution and the Bill of Rights, and by 1794 he was a leader of the emerging Republican party. In anticipation of their first meeting, she wrote to a friend, "Aaron Burr says that the great little Madison has asked to be brought to see me this evening." It proved a successful match, and they were married on 15 September 1794. She thus became the wife of a leading American politician, a successful Virginia planter, and an Episcopalian; the Quakers disowned her. For the next three years the Madisons lived much of the time in Philadelphia, the new nation's capital. After James Madison's departure from Congress in 1797, however, they retired to the Madison plantation, "Montpelier."

The Madisons reentered public life in 1801 when James Madison took up the post of secretary of state in Thomas Jefferson's administration. Washington was then an ungainly village where the few brick houses of the wealthy squatted amid the wooden hovels of the numerous poor. Washington high society was composed of a small group of southern planters, the few foreign diplomats sent to the new nation, a handful of civil servants, and a scattering of politicians who brought their families with them when Congress was in session. The social forms of this new city were still fluid, and the political elite set the city's pace and tone.

During the years that her husband served as secretary of state (1801–1809) Dolley Madison became the city's most important hostess. There were many reasons for her success. She was a Virginian in a small southern town. She had spent her youth in Philadelphia, the largest and most elegant American city. She had only one child and therefore had time to devote to entertaining. Her manner was open-hearted, without pretension to European graces. Generous by nature, she was also eager to please. "I confess," she once wrote, "I do not admire contention in any form, either political or civil. I would rather fight with my hands than my tongue." Her friend Margaret Bayard Smith commented in her diary (later published as *The First Forty Years of Washington Society* [1906]) that Dolley Madison was "a foe to dullness in every form, even when invested with the dignity which high ceremonial could bestow."

On 4 March 1809 James Madison became the fourth president of the United States, and Dolley Madison the nation's third first lady. The demands of official entertainment had become increasingly complex over the preceding few years as the U.S. government attempted to remain neutral in the Napoleonic wars, and as political conflicts between Republicans and Federalists grew in intensity. The Madisons had to receive all—French and British, Republican and Federalist, warhawk and antiwar. Unable to use the informal, often all-male forms of official entertaining that the widower Jefferson had employed between 1801 and 1809, Dolley Madison refashioned the formal dinner parties and weekly open houses that Martha Washington and Abigail Adams had hosted in Philadelphia in the 1790s. In doing so, however, she took a strikingly central and conspicuous role. She placed herself at the head of the White House dinner table, and her cousin and the president's secretary, Edward Coles, at the foot; her husband—content to be relieved of the social obligations of host—sat at the side of the table.

Dolley Madison crafted a middle path between European elegance and domestic republican simplicity. The British held the American "court" in disdain; American men, they complained, too often came to the White House wearing dirty linen and boots. Republican congressmen, on the other hand, worried that White House evenings were too refined. Some accused the first lady of acting like a queen. Symbolically, they insisted on their right to wear plain boots—good republican footwear—to any occasion.

Dolley Madison loved high fashion, especially any article of clothing from Paris. She wrote to the wife of the American minister in France, Ruth Barlow, asking her to send hats and gloves and stockings, for "you [in Paris] have everything that is beautiful; we nothing." Nevertheless, in her drawing room she effectively conveyed a commitment to republican virtues. As Jonathan Roberts, a congressman from Pennsylvania, wrote to his brother after reluctantly attending a White House dinner, "My impressions respecting the deportment of Mrs. Madison & the whole arrangement of the feast is that it was conducted with much ease and plainness. Nor do I think the sternest democrat amongst us would be dispos'd to condemn the practice with much severity were he to witness it."

During the first two years of the Madison administration, Dolley Madison decorated the White House with the help of the architect Benjamin Latrobe. Congress allocated the money, and she and Latrobe constructed an important American public space. Jefferson had furnished the building in a casual and personal style, bringing his own things from "Monticello." James Madison delegated the job of redecorating to his wife. She chose high-quality, American-made furniture. Here again, she found a middle ground between Republican simplicity and Federalist high fashion. The White House became a presidential palace fine enough for the new nation's international image, yet simple enough to soothe Republican fears.

The Madisons, however, did not spend all eight years of his presidency at the White House. On 17 August 1814 the British landed troops thirty-five miles from the capital city and began marching toward it. A few days later the president left Washington to review American troops while Dolley Madison guarded the White House. By the afternoon of 24 August the British advance could no longer be disregarded. Dolley Madison packed a wagon with valuables and sent it to be stored at the Bank of Maryland. She then decided she had to save the portrait of General Washington. "I have ordered the frame to be broken, & the canvass taken out," she recorded in a letter to her sister. "It is done . . . & now, dear sister I must leave this house, or t[he] retreating army will make me a prisoner in it." She thus became known as one of the heroes of the War of 1812. After the war was over, the first couple initially moved into the Octagon House, but after less than a year they moved again, to a house on the corner of Nineteenth and Pennsylvania Avenue, where Dolley Madison continued to entertain with great energy and style.

In 1817 the Madisons retired to Montpelier, where they remained until James Madison's death on 28 June 1836. Dolley Madison stayed there one more year. Her niece Anna Payne became her companion and continued in this role until Dolley Madison's death. Increasingly Madison felt the burden of isolation and debts, especially those piled up by her wayward son, Payne Todd. In 1837 she sold a portion of her husband's papers and moved back to Washington, to a house on Lafayette Square, across from the White House. She took up her old life as doyenne of Washington as best she could, receiving in the afternoon, holding dinner parties and evening parties, going out

with regularity, sustaining old friendships and forging new ones.

As the wife of a Virginia congressman who went on to become secretary of state and president of the United States—and on her mother's side a cousin of respectable Virginia planter families such as the Winstons and the Coles—Dolley Madison had an extraordinarily wide range of friends and connections. She knew every president from Washington to Zachary Taylor. Her sister Lucy married a nephew of Washington; her cousin Angelica Singleton wed a son of President Martin Van Buren. Madison counted among her companions and acquaintances politicians such as Henry Clay and Daniel Webster, writers such as Margaret Bayard Smith, Lydia Howard Huntley Sigourney, and Harriet Martineau, and foreign dignitaries such as the marquis de Lafayette. She acted as hostess for sixteen years at the White House and received scores of visitors for many more years at Montpelier. On 7 February 1849—five months before her death—President James K. Polk wrote in his diary of a large party at the president's mansion. There "toward the close of the evening I passed through the crowded rooms with the venerable Mrs. Madison on my arm."

Madison continued to entertain and be entertained, the last living icon of the Early Republic. But she became poorer and poorer. She mortgaged her house and tried to sell more Madison papers, offering them first to private buyers, then in the winter of 1843–1844 to Congress. She sold off parts of Montpelier and rented out the house. Finally she felt forced to liquidate the whole estate. "No one," she wrote a friend, "I think can appreciate my feelings of grief and dismay at the necessity of transferring to another a beloved home."

Though sinking deeper into poverty, Madison lived on in Washington, "the same good-natured, kindhearted, considerate, stately person that she had been in the heyday of her fortunes." Her son, still accumulating debts and drinking to great excess, continued to make her life miserable. Dolley Madison died in Washington. Her funeral was a state occasion.

Dolley Madison transformed the role of the first lady. She could not copy the Federalist forms of Martha Washington and Abigail Adams, nor take up the bachelor style of Thomas Jefferson. She found that she needed to create new ceremonial models and a new public setting for the republic. She did so with modesty, flair, charm, and skill. She was not an appendage to her powerful husband; she constructed, instead, a kind of third world between public and private. The drawing rooms of the White House were hers, and she presided over her world as no first lady had done before. In doing so she created a precedent that her successors would follow.

• The largest collection of Dolley Madison papers is in the Papers of James Madison, Alderman Library, University of Virginia, Charlottesville. There are also Dolley Madison papers in the Library of Congress and at the Greensboro Historical Museum, Greensboro, N.C. There are a number of related collections, especially the papers of her brother-in-law John G. Jackson at Indiana University; the diary of her friend Anna Marie Thornton at the Library of Congress; and the letters of Margaret Bayard Smith in the J. Henley Smith Papers at the Library of Congress. The papers of Benjamin Latrobe are at the Maryland Historical Society in Baltimore, and there is a three-volume edition of the Latrobe papers edited by John C. Van Horne (1986). There are a number of biographies of Dolley Madison, as well as children's books and biographical novels. The first two biographies were written as the "life and letters" of Madison: Lucia B. Cutts, *Memoirs and Letters of Dolly Madison* (1886), and Allen C. Clark, *Life and Letters of Dolly Madison* (1914); both are heavily bowdlerized. Other biographies include Maud W. Goodwin, *Dolly Madison* (1896), and Ethel Stephens Arnett, *Mrs. James Madison: The Incomparable Dolley* (1972). On decorating the White House see Conover Hunt-Jones, *Dolley and the "Great Little Madison"* (1977), and on entertaining see Barbara G. Carson, *Ambitious Appetites: Dining, Behavior, and Patterns of Consumption in Federal Washington* (1990).

HOLLY COWAN SHULMAN

MADISON, Helene Emma (19 June 1913–25 Nov. 1970), swimmer, was born in South Bend, Washington, the daughter of Charles William Madison and Cecilia Helene Ensby. During her childhood the family moved to Seattle, Washington, where her father operated a dry-cleaning business. At age five Helene learned to swim the dog paddle and then the crawl in Green Lake. In 1927 she won her first race, a 50-yard sidestroke event, at a Seattle Parks meet. Switching her practice sessions from Green Lake to Seattle's Crystal Pool, she improved her abilities gradually. She finished second in a 100-yard freestyle competition at the 1928 state championships. Impressed by Helene's potential, Ray Daughters, the swim coach at Crystal Pool, began teaching her the six-beat crawl stroke and other techniques that shortly transformed her into a champion.

At the 1929 Amateur Athletic Union (AAU) junior outdoor championships in Detroit, Michigan, Madison won the 100-yard freestyle race, but her 1:15.2 time was disappointing because her practice times had been far better. In August, in San Francisco, California, she lost a 100-meter duel by a small margin to Albina Osipowich, the 1928 Olympic champion, but pushed Osipowich to a 1:09.4 world record. This performance convinced Madison she possessed superior ability and gave her the confidence to utilize it. She never lost another freestyle contest, at any distance.

In March 1930 Madison accompanied a Pacific Coast swim team to Florida. At Palm Beach, she set two new American freestyle records; at Miami Beach, in the AAU senior indoor championships, she won the 100-, 220-, and 500-yard freestyle titles, each time defeating Josephine McKim, a 1929 AAU champion; and at Jacksonville she set six more American records. In July 1930, at the AAU senior outdoor championships in Long Beach, California, she amazed everybody by winning the 100-meter, 440-yard, 880-yard, and one-mile freestyle titles, again defeating McKim each time. A week later, in Vancouver, British Colum-

bia, Canada, she set unofficial world records in the 50- and 100-yard events, and in the latter race her 59-second time made her the first woman to better one minute. By the year's end Madison had set twenty-six American freestyle records in distances up through one mile. In the James E. Sullivan Memorial Award voting by sports experts to name the outstanding American amateur athlete of 1930, Madison placed fourth, behind Bobby Jones, Clarence De Mar, and Helen Wills Moody.

When Seattle's Washington Athletic Club (WAC) was established in 1930, Daughters became its swim coach and Madison followed her there. In April 1931 at the AAU indoor championships in New York City, she again captured the 100-, 200-, and 500-yard titles and, with WAC teammates Lucy Schacht, Edna McKibben, and Dawn Gilson, won the 400-yard freestyle relay. She finished third in the 100-yard backstroke behind Eleanor Holm and Joan McSheehy, but in doing so still increased WAC's team points. After graduating from Lincoln High School in Seattle, Madison, in the AAU outdoor meet at Bronx Beach, New York, triumphed in the same four events she won the year before. Now holding ten world records, she was credited by the AAU with establishing 26 American best marks by the end of 1931. In the Sullivan Award voting that year, she trailed the winner, track and field star Barney Berlinger, by only two votes; the Associated Press named her the female athlete of the year.

At the 1932 AAU indoor meet, Madison again won the 100-, 220-, and 500-yard freestyles and, as anchor, the 400-meter relay with teammates Olive McKean, Patricia Linton, and McKibben. Only the 100-yard race was close, with McKim only a foot behind. At the U.S. Olympic tryouts that year in Jones Beach, New York, Madison won the 100- and 400-meter freestyle events easily and was named to the 400-meter freestyle relay team. At that time the Olympic program did not include longer-distance races, which Helene dominated.

At the 1932 Olympic Games, in Los Angeles, California, Madison immediately set a new 100-meter record of 1:08.9 in a preliminary heat, but it was quickly shattered in another heat by Eleanor Garrati Saville of the United States with 1:08.5 and in a semifinal by Willemijntje den Ouden of Holland with 1:07.6. In the final, Madison flashed to victory in 1:06.8, with den Ouden a second behind, Saville third, and McKim fourth. In the 400-meter final, Madison and fellow American Lenore Kight had "never more than a foot between . . . them from the initial dive . . . until Miss Madison hit the end wall in front" (*New York Times*, 14 Aug. 1932). Both broke the 5:39.3 world record—Madison in 5:28.5, Kight in 5:28.6. The U.S. relay team of McKim, Saville, Helen Johns, and Madison outclassed the field by almost ten seconds and bettered the existing record by 9.5 seconds. Only American swimmer Ethelda Bleibtrey in 1920 had won three Olympic women's swimming gold medals before Madison did it.

As her brief, scintillating swimming career ended, Madison, still a teenager, owned three Olympic records, 17 of 18 world records, and 45 American records in various length pools, from 100 yards to one mile. From 1930 through 1932, in five national AAU meets, the Olympic tryouts, and the 1932 Olympic finals, she won all 26 freestyle events in which she raced. At 5′10¾″ and 154 pounds, with broad shoulders, slim hips, and supple muscles, Madison continuously exhibited great energy, strength, and stamina. Characterized as happy-go-lucky, she enjoyed her races thoroughly. Daughters attributed her dominance to "the most wonderful complex of anyone I have ever coached—a competitive complex . . . a certain amount of fear of losing that makes her extend herself. That's what makes her a champion" (*New York Times*, 19 Apr. 1931).

Shortly after the Olympics, Madison became a professional by accepting pay for an exhibition swim at Seattle's Playland Amusement Park. In September 1932 she signed a motion picture contract but had only one minor role, in *The Warrior's Husband* (1933). Subsequently, she swam in exhibitions, taught swimming at the Moore Hotel in Seattle, worked in a sporting goods store, and served a term as a probationary nurse. In 1937 she married Luther C. McIver, a Puget Sound Power & Light Company official; they had one daughter before they divorced in 1958. The following year she married William Kappahan; they were divorced in 1961, and she reverted to using her maiden name. During her final years she suffered from diabetes and cancer, and she died in Seattle. In 1950 a panel named her one of the ten best swimmers, male or female, of the half-century. In 1960 she was elected to the Washington State Athletic Hall of Fame and, in 1966, to the International Swimming Hall of Fame. The Washington Athletic Club pool and a City Parks Department pool in north Seattle were both named in her honor.

• Doris H. Pieroth, *Their Day in the Sun: Women of the 1932 Olympics* (1996), is an excellent book that draws in part on interviews with Madison's daughter; it also contains a bibliography. Brief biographical sketches appear in Pat Besford, *The Encyclopedia of Swimming* (1971); Buck Dawson, *Weissmuller to Spitz . . . An Era to Remember* (1987); Ralph Hickok, *A Who's Who of Sports Champions* (1995); and Howard Plossell, "Helene Madison," in *The Blue Book of Sports* (1931). An expert critique of Madison's swimming technique is provided in Louis deBreda Handley, "Players of the Game: Miss Helene Madison—Record-Breaker Extraordinary," *New York Times*, 1 Dec. 1930; and "Records Beware! You're Fragile Stuff to Helene," *Literary Digest*, 15 Aug. 1931. Royal Brougham provided a local Seattle perspective in "Miss Madison Was Greatest," *Seattle Post-Intelligencer*, 1 Dec. 1975. Obituaries are in the *Seattle Times*, 26 Nov. 1970, and the *New York Times* and the *Seattle Post-Intelligencer*, both 27 Nov. 1970. The *New York Times* obituary and other sources incorrectly state that Madison was born in Madison, Wis.

FRANK V. PHELPS

MADISON, James (27 Aug. 1749–6 Mar. 1812), college president and first bishop of the Episcopal church in Virginia, was born near the town of Staunton, Virginia, the son of John Madison, a planter, and Agatha Strother. A second cousin of U.S. president James Madison, he spent his early childhood at his father's plantation in Augusta County. He attended school in Maryland and entered the College of William and Mary in 1768. There he served as writing master and displayed great promise as a student of science. He graduated in 1772, a winner of the Botetourt Medal. Although he prepared for the law under the noted Williamsburg legal scholar George Wythe and was admitted to the bar, he never practiced. Instead, in 1773 he became professor of natural philosophy and mathematics at William and Mary. In 1775 he sailed to England, where he was ordained an Anglican priest. Returning to William and Mary the following year, he accepted appointment as the college's president for the term of one year in the spring of 1777. In fact, he would retain that post until his death.

Madison became president of William and Mary at a difficult time for the college, which had begun in 1693 as an Anglican school and stood to lose greatly, perhaps to be dissolved altogether, during the revolution. Madison's immediate predecessor, John Camm, had been an outright Loyalist who considered William and Mary inextricably bound to the Church of England and to Great Britain. Madison, on the other hand, was so well known as an advocate of the American cause that the British government had considered him a potential spy while he was in England. The most immediate problem for the new president was money. William and Mary had lost its income from both royal land grants in Virginia and traditional sources in England, forcing Madison to sell college holdings in land and slaves and to seek funds from the state legislature. During this time he also cooperated with Thomas Jefferson's well-intentioned, though generally unsuccessful, attempts to reform the college between 1776 and 1779. In the latter year Madison married Sarah Tate of Williamsburg; they had two children.

Madison succeeded in keeping William and Mary functioning more or less normally until late 1780, when the threat from British forces under the command of Benedict Arnold led many professors and students to seek safer quarters. He officially closed the school in June 1781 after Lord Cornwallis arrived with a much larger British army. First the British, then the Americans and their French allies occupied the college until July 1782, when the last French troops finally withdrew, and Madison was able to advertise an October 1782 reopening of classes.

From the time of his appointment as professor until shortly before his death, Madison published steadily on science, politics, and religion. He was also at the forefront of the creation of the Episcopal church out of what remained of the Church of England after the revolution. In 1785 he presided at the first convention of the Episcopal Diocese of Virginia, and in 1790 he journeyed to England to be consecrated a bishop by the archbishop of Canterbury. The Anglican church in Virginia was in decline even before the revolution owing both to rising anti-British sentiment and to the successes of the dissenters during the Great Awakening. Madison had little success in rehabilitating his church after independence, and his dual role as bishop of what had been the English state church and as president of a college that still existed on the authority of a charter issued by an English monarch made it doubly difficult to keep William and Mary afloat financially. Although he remained at his post, he considered leaving for another, such as the presidency of Columbia College in New York or that of Transylvania College in Kentucky, both offered to him as William and Mary sank completely to its knees around the turn of the century. It is likely that declining health in the form of heart disease kept Madison in Williamsburg, where he was also an active member of the governing board of the state asylum for the insane. Toward the end of 1811 his condition deteriorated markedly, and he died in Williamsburg.

• There are collections of Madison's papers at both the College of William and Mary and the Colonial Williamsburg Foundation. Madison is well represented in the extant archival material for the school during the period from the onset of the struggle for independence through 1812. That material, along with many other primary sources, is synthesized in the excellent history of the college by Susan H. Godson et al., *The College of William and Mary: A History* (2 vols., 1993). On Madison as college president, see Jack E. Morpurgo, *Their Majesties' Royall Colledge: William and Mary in the Seventeenth and Eighteenth Centuries* (1979). On Madison as a republican clergyman and theorist, see Charles R. Crowe, "Bishop James Madison and the Republic of Virtue," *Journal of Southern History* 30 (1964): 58–70. On his church career, see William Meade, *Old Churches, Ministers, and Families of Virginia* (2 vols., 1857), and Edward Lewis Goodwin, *The Colonial Church in Virginia . . .* (1927).

CAROLYN S. WHITTENBURG

MADISON, James (5 Mar. 1751–28 June 1836), "the father of the Constitution" and fourth president of the United States, was born in King George County, Virginia, the oldest child of James Madison, Sr., and Nelly Conway, who was visiting her mother's estate on the Rappahannock River. The senior Madison, a vestryman, a justice of the peace, and Orange County's leading planter, was the master of 4,000 acres and perhaps 100 slaves. Although without a formal education of his own, he was determined to provide his namesake with the training and accomplishments appropriate for one who was expected to assume a place among the great Virginia gentry. In 1762, at age eleven, the younger Madison (who would subscribe himself "James Madison, Jr.," until his father's death in 1801) began five years of study at Donald Robertson's boarding school in King and Queen County. From there, encouraged by the Reverend Thomas Martin, who gave him two more years of tutoring at home, he traveled north to Princeton, where he passed examinations with the freshman class in September 1769 and completed the next three years in two.

The Madisons, like Martin, were enthusiastic Whigs, and James matured with the American Revolution. In 1765, while he was learning Greek and Latin at the Scotsman's school, Patrick Henry opened the revolt against the Stamp Tax. Politics, together with the rising reputation of the institution, may have influenced his selection of the College of New Jersey, where President John Witherspoon (1723–1794), another immigrant from Scotland and a future signer of the Declaration of Independence, directed a curriculum that may have been the most progressive and exciting on the seaboard. At Princeton, patriotic students dressed in homespun, mustered in their academic garb to demonstrate against the relaxation of nonimportation, and spoke at their commencements on "The Rising Glory of America" or on the circumstances under which oppression could be rightfully resisted. After graduating in September 1771, Madison stayed in Princeton through the winter, mending his debilitated health and reading law, theology, and Hebrew under Witherspoon's direction. He returned to the plantation in the spring, two years before Parliament responded to colonial resistance with the infamous Coercive Acts. As Orange County mobilized for war, he joined his father on the local Committee of Safety, practiced with a rifle, and drilled with the county militia. As he put it late in life, "he was under very early and strong impressions in favor of liberty both civil and religious."

Civil and religious liberty were intimately linked in Madison's career and thinking. His intense involvement in the early Revolution is a necessary starting point for understanding his distinctive role among the major framers of the Constitution. Although religious topics disappear from his surviving papers after 1776 and his mature convictions are unknown, he was an earnest Christian on the eve of independence and, throughout his long career, a dedicated champion of the Enlightenment's most forward-looking stance on freedom of religion. His earliest involvement in Virginia's politics, in 1774, was to denounce the jailing of unlicensed preachers in neighboring Culpeper County. When his feeble health defeated plans for active military service, the gratitude of Baptist neighbors may have helped him win election to the state convention of 1776, which framed one of the earliest, most widely imitated revolutionary constitutions. In this convention, he made his first important contribution to the revolutionary reconstruction: an amendment that replaced a reference to religious "toleration" with a recognition of an equal, universal right to freely exercise religion and wrote into Virginia's Declaration of Rights a standard that no society had ever recognized in its organic law. He also gave his full support to Thomas Jefferson's attempts to liberalize the state's religious statutes.

Defeated at the next election—he would not provide the customary treats for voters—Madison was soon selected by the legislature as a member of the executive Council of State, where he served with Governors Henry and Jefferson. Two years later, in December 1779, the legislature picked him as a delegate to Congress. In that body, where he set an unexampled record for attendance, he acquired a continental reputation for his mastery of legislative business. Seated in the spring of 1780, Madison was instrumental in Virginia's cession of its claims to the old Northwest, which paved the way to ratification of the Articles of Confederation and the creation of a national domain. Soon regarded as the most effective member of the Congress, he appealed repeatedly to his Virginia friends for full compliance with congressional requests, favored the creation of executive departments, and supported Robert Morris's (1734–1806) attempts to bring more rationality to the Department of Finance. At the conclusion of the war, when angry grumblings in the unpaid army posed a crisis, he introduced the compromise that ended in the congressional recommendations of 18 April 1783, which called upon the states for an amendment to the Articles permitting Congress to impose a 5 percent duty on foreign imports, for the completion of their western cessions, and for other revenues required to pay the interest on the continental debt. He retired from Congress in November 1783 and stood immediately for reelection to the state assembly.

When Madison returned to the Virginia House of Delegates in April 1784, he was the commonwealth's most knowledgeable authority on federal affairs, accepted from the outset as a major legislative leader. He supported the reforms of April 1783. He was an advocate, as well, of granting Congress power to retaliate against British restrictions on the country's foreign trade. He hoped that peace would make it easier for states to meet their federal requisitions, that better times and quick adoption of these limited reforms would make it possible for Congress to fulfill its obligations and restore its faltering prestige. However, he had learned that absolute dependence on the states for revenues, as well as for enforcement of its treaties, rendered the Confederation government unequal to its tasks and could endanger its existence. Thus, he watched the nation's progress from an apprehensive, continentalist perspective, convinced that revolutionary liberty could not survive disintegration of the continental union, which protected the republican experiment from foreign intervention and secured the states against the rivalries and fragmentation that had splintered Europe and condemned its peoples to oppressive taxes, swollen military forces, tyranny, and wars.

Peace, however, was succeeded by a sharp postwar depression. The states did not approve amendments to the Articles of Union. Most of them were late or short in meeting their federal requisitions. Animosities between them rose to dangerous extremes as several tried, by separate legislation, to retaliate against restrictions on their trade, only to be baffled by conflicting regulations by their neighbors. Deprived of steady revenues, the Continental Congress failed to manage its domestic debt and found it ever harder to secure the European loans with which it met its foreign obligations. In 1786, as Madison prepared for the Annapolis Convention, northerners and southerners clashed bitterly in Congress over the negotiation of a commercial treaty with Spain. Deadlocked on this issue and unable to agree on new proposals for a federal power over commerce, members from both sections talked about a speedy separation into smaller, regional confederations.

Madison had never been an unreserved enthusiast for extralegal meetings, and a convention to consider better means of regulating trade had won his backing only after other motions were defeated. At Annapolis, however, Madison and others gathered in a context of profound, immediate concern for the survival of the union. More in desperation than with any real conviction that the measure would succeed, the dozen delegates on hand agreed upon the most decisive action circumstances would permit, recommending the appointment of another general convention to consider all of the "exigencies" of the Confederation. From September forward, Madison was thoroughly committed to this course.

By 1786, moreover, Madison no longer hoped that a revision of the Articles could solve the country's problems. Neither was he worried solely by the peril of disunion. In all the states, the legislatures were attempting to protect their citizens from economic troubles. Many of their measures—paper money, laws suspending private suits for debts, postponements of taxation, and continued confiscations of the Loyalists' estates—interfered with private contracts, threatened people's right to hold their property secure, or robbed the states of the resources necessary to fulfill their individual and federal obligations. To Madison, the multiplicity, the mutability, and the injustices of local laws were challenging the basic premise of republics: that private rights and public good could both be best protected by the body of the people.

Virginia managed to avoid the worst abuses of the middle 1780s, but Madison was thinking continentally. During the fall of 1786, correspondents warned him of increasing disillusionment with popular misgovernment, especially in Massachusetts, where Shays's Rebellion climaxed in the winter. Virginia's own immunity from insurrection or abuses seemed increasingly in doubt. The legislature had refused to call for a revision of Virginia's constitution. Madison had often been defeated when he moved for major state and federal reforms. His single greatest triumph, the enactment of the Statute for Religious Freedom (19 Jan. 1786) had been won, in his opinion, only after jealousies between Virginia's multiplicity of sects had blocked the passage of a bill providing tax support for teachers of religion, which would have been a devastating blow to freedom of religious conscience. Fearful and disgusted, Madison was even more afraid that the revulsion from abuses in the states could spread in time to growing numbers of the people, whose commitment to the revolutionary enterprise was threatened by a governmental system that could not advance their interests or protect their fundamental rights. An effectual reform, he told one correspondent, must "perpetuate the union." More than that, it must "redeem the honor of the republican name."

No one played so critical a part in the developments that followed. Returning from Annapolis to the Virginia state assembly, Madison secured the legislature's quick endorsement of the plan for a convention, wrote the resolutions that announced the state's profound commitment to the project, and helped persuade George Washington to lead a delegation whose quality encouraged other states to send distinguished men as well. Selected for the delegation, he was also reelected now that he was eligible again, to his familiar place in the Confederation Congress. Rushing to New York, he helped complete the groundwork for a well-attended meeting. By this time, he may already have prepared his notes on other ancient and modern confederations. In April 1787 he also wrote a formal memorandum on the "Vices of the Political System of the United States." Here and in his letters to his friends, he argued that the mortal ills of the Confederation government and the concurrent crisis in the states demanded the abandonment of the existing federal system and the substitution of a national republic that would derive directly from the people, would possess effective, full, and independent powers over matters of general concern, and would incorporate so many different economic interests and religious sects that popular majorities could seldom form "on any other principles than those of justice and the public good." Urging other members of Virginia's delegation to arrive in Philadelphia in time to reach agreement on some introductory proposals for the meeting, he arrived, himself, the best prepared of all who gathered for the great convention.

Madison made numerous distinctive contributions to the writing of the Constitution. To begin with, he was certainly the major author of the resolutions introduced by Edmund Randolph (1753–1813) on 29 May: the propositions that initiated the convention's sweeping reconsideration of the federal system and served throughout the summer as the outline for reform. In the early weeks of the deliberations, he and other advocates of this "Virginia Plan" persuasively explained why no reform could prove effective if it left the central government dependent on the states. With other members from the larger states, he argued stubbornly for proportional representation in both houses of the Congress, popular ratification of the new federal charter, and a careful balance of authority between a democratic House of Representatives and branches less immediately responsive to majority demands. Most distinctively of all, he urged the other members not to limit their attention to the weaknesses of the Confederation but to come to grips as well with the vices of republican government as these had been revealed in the revolutionary states. A sound reform, he argued, had to grant the central government the powers necessary to perform its delegated tasks. A sound reform would also have to overcome the doubts engendered by majority abuses, both by placing limitations on the states and by correcting the mistakes of governmental structure common to the early revolutionary constitutions. In all these ways, Madison pushed the convention toward a thoroughgoing reconsideration of the nature of a sound republic, even as the other members were compelling him to reconsider his initial thoughts about the character of federal reform. The finished Constitution differed in a number of significant respects from his original proposals. Nevertheless, by general agreement of his peers and modern scholars, he was unmistakably the most important of its framers.

The federal convention ended on 17 September. Before returning to Virginia, where his leadership was crucial to defeating Henry and other Antifederalists, Madison resumed his seat in the Confederation Congress, helped provide some central guidance for the ratification contest, and joined with Alexander Hamilton (1755–1804) to write *The Federalist*, the most important exegesis and defense of the completed Constitution. Madison's numbers of *The Federalist*, regarded to this day as probably the greatest classic in the history of American political thinking, justified the compromises made by the convention, explained the partly national and partly federal government created by the charter, and in doing so, contributed as surely to the shaping of the Constitution as the work of the convention. Almost from the start, *The Federalist* was recognized as an essential source for understanding the intentions of the framers, and Madison's great theme—that the completed Constitution was entirely faithful to the principles of 1776, a necessary, democratic remedy for the diseases most destructive to republics—was only one of his enormous contributions to the document's success.

The newly constituted government assembled in New York in April 1789. As everyone expected, Madison immediately assumed a leading role in the First Federal Congress. He drafted Washington's inaugural address, prepared the reply of the House of Representatives, and helped defeat proposals to address the president as "highness"—important contributions to the early effort to define the protocol between the branches and to set the democratic tone he wanted for the new regime. He introduced the resolutions that resulted in the first federal tariff and took the lead in the creation of executive departments, successfully insisting that the president alone should have the power to remove executive officials. Most importantly of all, he drafted the constitutional amendments that became the Bill of Rights.

Through much of 1788, while the adoption of the Constitution was in doubt, Madison had disapproved of the demand for these amendments. He argued that the powers of the federal government were limited to matters that did not involve the fundamental rights protected by the constitutions of the states. He warned that an insistence on a federal bill of rights might threaten the essential liberties that its proponents wanted to protect; an inadvertent error or omission could become the basis for a claim to powers not intended by the Constitution. At the Virginia state convention, nonetheless, the Federalists were forced to promise that amendments would be added once the

Constitution was approved; and Madison repeated this commitment during his campaign for a position in the House. Politics were not his only reason.

Throughout the course of constitutional reform, Madison's insistence on a stronger federal system had been linked to a commitment to a form of government that would remain responsive to the people. Even as he worried over popular abuses, he reminded correspondents of the dangers that could rise from rulers who were able to escape a due dependence on the people; and even as he argued that the central government would have to be released from its dependence on the states, he recognized that too much power could be placed in federal hands. In *The Federalist* he described the new regime as neither wholly national nor strictly federal in structure, but as an unexampled compound under which concurrent state and central governments would each be limited to the responsibilities that each was best equipped to meet, while each would check intrusions by the other. These ideas, together with his recognition that a Bill of Rights could reconcile the opposition and become a bulwark for the courts, enabled him to change his mind and persevere in overcoming stout congressional resistance to amendments.

The same ideas can also help account for the "reversal" of positions many analysts associate with Madison's career. As early as the second session of the new Congress, Madison became alarmed about the sectional inequities and other dangers that appeared to him inseparable from Hamiltonian finance. Among these, as he saw it, was the broad construction of the Constitution used by Hamilton to justify his economic program. In 1791, when Secretary of the Treasury Hamilton proposed creation of a national bank, Madison protested that the chartering of corporations went beyond the powers granted by the Constitution and that bold reliance on a doctrine of implied authority could rapidly transmute a limited, republican regime into a system that could undermine the Revolution. Soon thereafter, he and Jefferson encouraged the establishment of Philip Freneau's *National Gazette*, a semiweekly watchdog over governmental usurpations. To this paper, even as he organized an opposition in the House, Madison contributed a string of unsigned essays seeking to arouse the people to the danger. Before the end of 1792, he and Jefferson were the acknowledged leaders of a movement that would soon become a true political party.

Jefferson resigned as Washington's secretary of state in December 1793. Madison continued in the House of Representatives, as leader of the party, until adjournment of the Fourth Congress in March 1797. He declined reelection. On 15 September 1794, after a courtship of four months, the longtime bachelor had married the attractive young widow, Dolley Payne Todd (Dolley Payne Madison) whose husband and one of their two children had been victims of the yellow fever epidemic of 1793. Madison himself would have no children. The same year saw the loss of Madison's brother, Ambrose Madison, who had carried much of the responsibility for managing the family plantation. With his father in declining health and Jefferson returning to the seat of government as vice president, Madison decided that his long public service entitled him to withdraw to "Montpelier."

The retreat to private life proved brief. To Madison's disgust, the Washington administration had escaped a crisis in its relationship with Britain by concluding a commercial treaty that the Jeffersonians regarded as a sacrifice of vital national interests. Damaged and offended by this treaty, revolutionary France, at war with most of Europe since the execution of King Louis XVI, began to prey on U.S. merchant shipping. President John Adams (1735–1826) sought to solve the crisis with a combination of negotiations and increased appropriations for defense, but the negotiations stalled when unofficial agents of the French foreign minister—referred to in American dispatches as X, Y, and Z—informed the American commissioners that nothing could be done until they paid a bribe to Charles-Maurice de Talleyrand-Périgord, apologized for Adams's belligerent remarks, and consented to a large American loan to the French republic. In April 1798 Adams publicized the XYZ affair, and patriotic fury focused both on France and on its Jeffersonian supporters. Seizing on this panic, the Federalist-dominated Congress launched a naval war on France, together with a program intended to crush domestic opposition. The Alien and Sedition Acts unleashed a bloodless reign of terror on the opposition press.

From the beginning of the war in Europe, Jeffersonians had feared that their opponents were conspiring to subvert the Revolution. Hamiltonian finance and broad construction of the Constitution seemed deliberately designed to concentrate all power in the distant central government and most of that in branches least responsive to the people. The foreign policy of Federalist administrations seemed to sympathize with European despots and to yearn for an alliance, maybe a reunion, with the British. Now, the Quasi-War with France, the effort to intimidate domestic opposition, the enlargement of the army, and a measure authorizing the enlistment of a larger force of 50,000 men (which was to take the field in the event of an invasion) seemed abundant proof that this conspiracy had burst into the open. While Republicans in Congress blasted the repressive legislation as a patent violation of the First Amendment and a potent danger to the people's underlying right to criticize official acts and change their government through free elections, Jefferson and Madison decided to arouse the states. Each drafted secret legislative resolutions condemning the Alien and Sedition Acts. Madison gave his to John Taylor (1753–1824) of Caroline, Virginia's agricultural thinker and an influential party pamphleteer. Jefferson slipped his to John Breckinridge (1760–1806) of Kentucky. On 16 November 1798 Kentucky's legislature resolved that the repressive laws were unconstitutional, "void and of no force." On 24 December Virginia voted a similar condemnation and called upon the other states to join the protest.

All the other states refused to join Virginia and Kentucky on a path that led, much later, to nullification and secession. Their responses to the resolutions prompted Madison to stand for reelection to the state assembly in 1799 and to prepare his Report of 1800, which explained the compact theory of the Constitution and initiated modern, literalist interpretations of the First Amendment as proscribing any governmental interference with the free development and circulation of opinion. The Kentucky and Virginia resolutions also opened the campaign of 1800, which carried the Republicans to power.

Madison returned to federal office as his old collaborator's first lieutenant. From 1801 to 1809, he served not only as the new administration's secretary of state, but also as a principal adviser on the range of policies that followed from the president's determination to restore the federal balance and withdraw the central government to the limits that the Jeffersonians believed had been intended when the people ratified the Constitution.

The victory of 1800, as the Jeffersonians conceived it, rescued the Republic from a plot that might have ended in subversion of the Constitution and a reintroduction of hereditary rule. Nonetheless, a party victory was not enough without a change of governmental measures. Hamilton and his successors had supported rapid economic growth, envisioning the quick emergence of an integrated state in which the rise of native manufactures would provide materials for export and a large domestic market for the farmers. Republican ambitions focused more upon the West, where a republic resting on the sturdy stock of independent farmer-owners could be constantly revitalized as it expanded over space. The Federalists had been intent on the creation of a modern nation-state, which could compete with European empires on the Europeans' terms. Jefferson and his lieutenants hoped to free the country's oceanic commerce and provide new markets for its agricultural producers, but they also meant to keep the federal government within the limits of the Constitution. Hamilton had seen the national debt as an advantage for the country, because it could be used to back a stable currency supply. The Jeffersonians were willing to subordinate much else to the reduction of the debt as quickly as the public's contracts would permit, believing that the interest payments transferred wealth from the productive to the nonproductive classes while creating a corrupting link between the federal government and special-interest factions. In foreign policy, moreover, they intended to pursue a policy of genuine neutrality between Great Britain and the French republic, not the national subservience to Britain that had seemed to them the policy of Washington and Adams.

The "revolution of 1800," as Jefferson described it, was amazingly successful. From 1801 to 1803, the only interlude in twenty years of constant European warfare made it possible for the Republicans to concentrate on their domestic program, which consolidated their support among the people. In 1803 Napoléon

Bonaparte's resumption of the war prepared the way for the Louisiana Purchase and the doubling of the size of the United States. Although he was a strict constructionist in general, Madison conceded that contingencies could sometimes justify departures from the letter of the Constitution. He defended the Louisiana Purchase on these grounds and by suggesting that a power to acquire new territory was inherent in a sovereign nation. As Jefferson's successor, he would act upon the basis of implied authority again in ordering the occupation of West Florida, where the United States and Spain had overlapping claims; and he would also recommend rechartering the national bank, maintaining that repeated acts of every part of government, repeatedly approved of by the people, had overruled his earlier opinion. Nevertheless, his leadership as president was marked by deep respect for both the letter and the spirit of the Constitution. This was, at once, his weakness and his strength.

When Madison succeeded Jefferson in 1809, like Adams, he inherited a crisis. This one, in substantial measure, was a product of his own ideas. By 1805 Napoléon controlled the whole of western Europe. Britain ruled the seas. Both powers were determined to deny their enemy the benefits of neutral commerce, trapping the United States between the tiger and the shark. By 1807, France or Britain had condemned some 1,500 U.S. ships and passed decrees that threatened most of its remaining commerce. Jefferson's administration faced the crisis in the way that Madison had always recommended. Throughout the 1790s, he and Jefferson had both maintained that the United States possessed a weapon that could guarantee its national interests as effectively as war. That weapon was its trade. Most American exports, as the Jeffersonians conceived it, were necessities of life: raw materials and food on which the Europeans and their island colonies were vitally dependent. Most American imports, they believed, were "niceties" or "luxuries" that the United States could either do without or manufacture on its own. Accordingly, in any confrontation with the Europeans (and especially the British), the United States could force the enemy to terms by a denial of its trade; and it could do so while avoiding higher taxes, swollen military forces, rising debts, and all the other dangers to a sound republic that appeared inherent in a war.

In 1807 Jefferson's administration answered French and British depredations by imposing a complete embargo on the nation's trade. By early 1809, as Jefferson prepared to turn his office over to his friend, the embargo had resulted in a sharp depression, a revival of the Federalists, and an enforcement policy so fierce that it endangered the Republicans' commitment to protecting civil rights. With neither Jefferson nor Madison approving of the action, but with neither intervening with his party, the embargo was repealed. Congress substituted legislation limiting nonintercourse to trade between the United States and the belligerents alone.

The new administration was confronted from the start with problems it was poorly suited to resolve. A principled proponent of substantial legislative independence, Madison was different in his relationships with Congress, where rifts among Republicans had opened as the Federalists lost strength. The program of commercial confrontation was relaxed as Congress fruitlessly attempted to apply it in a manner that would hurt the Europeans more than it was hurting the United States itself. In 1810 nonintercourse was ended, and a bill was passed providing that restrictions would be reimposed on either European power if the other would respect the nation's neutral rights. Napoléon delivered an ambiguous announcement, which suggested that he might exempt Americans from his decrees. Madison decided to interpret the announcement as fulfilling the American demands and called upon the British to respond in kind. When they refused, he reimposed nonintercourse with Britain.

By the winter of 1811–1812, commercial warfare had been pressed, in one form or another, for a full four years. The people were becoming restless under policies that damaged their prosperity without compelling any action by the British. The Federalists were winning state elections. Hostilities continued with the northwest tribes, which were encouraged and supplied by British officials in Canada. Thus, before the Twelfth Congress met, the president reluctantly decided that his only choices were submission to the British or a war. On 18 June, in what was basically a party vote, a declaration passed the Congress.

The War of 1812 consigned the Madison administration to a mediocre rank in modern ratings of the presidents' successes. Although its chief had recommended stronger preparations as the war approached, the United States embarked upon the conflict with a fleet of fourteen warships and an army that mustered less than 7,000 well-trained troops. After years of economic confrontation, the United States was so divided that New England governors refused to let the country's best militia march beyond the borders of their states, and western forces met with only limited success before the battle of New Orleans. Congressional refusal to preserve the national bank had crippled the treasury, and the president deliberately attempted to conduct the war at minimal expense to the republican and federal nature of the country. The consequence was thirty months of warfare, during which it was uncertain whether the United States would manage to survive intact, followed by a peace (agreed upon at Ghent, Belgium, on 24 December 1814) that settled none of the disputes about which fighting had begun.

Contemporaries, nonetheless, were more impressed with the administration's conduct and achievements than historians have been. Adams wrote that Madison had won more glory and secured more union than all of the preceding presidents combined. Certainly, the presidency ended in a brilliant burst of national harmony and pride and with important readjustments to the lessons of the war. On 5 December 1815, in his final annual message, the great coarchitect of Jeffersonian beliefs proposed a federal program of internal improvements, modest tariff protection for the infant industries that had sprung up during the war, and the creation of a new national bank. Early in 1816, with the Federalists collapsing, Congress enacted all of his proposals, although the president refused to sign the bill for internal improvements until a constitutional amendment clearly authorized the federal government to act. The readjustment hardly constituted a complete surrender to the Federalists' ideas. Madison believed that education, an enormous reservoir of western lands, and the continued leadership of the legitimate defenders of the people's Constitution might preclude the civic evils he and Jefferson had long associated with these programs. Nevertheless, his willingness to borrow from his old opponents helped legitimate the other side of a debate that had embroiled the nation since adoption of the Constitution. Within four years of Madison's retirement, the triumph of the Jeffersonian Republicans was practically complete. With James Monroe's essentially unanimous election to a second term, the country entered on a period of single-party rule.

Retiring to his Orange County home, Madison reassembled his surviving letters, aided Jefferson in the creation of the University of Virginia, and lived as a revered, though troubled, oracle on the creation and interpretation of the Constitution. His final years were haunted by his own insistence that the federal charter was a compact among the sovereign peoples of the several states, who were the only power capable of making a definitive decision on its meaning. This compelled him to combat the southern use of the Virginia and Kentucky resolutions to elaborate a doctrine of interposition and nullification. It compelled him also to resist the broad constructions of the Marshall Court. The Constitution could be stretched beyond endurance, he believed, much as it could be constricted to the point that the United States would once again be faced with problems of the sort that had destroyed the old Confederation. Preservation of the continental union was, as always, at the center of his hopes. As always, too, he argued to the last that only a capacity for mutual conciliation and restraint—the spirit that had marked the great convention—could preserve what he and other founders had constructed. Madison died at breakfast at Montpelier days before the sixtieth anniversary of independence. He was the last, as he had once been first, among the framers of the Constitution.

• A definitive modern edition of William T. Hutchinson et al., eds., *The Papers of James Madison* (1962–), is currently complete in seventeen volumes to 1801. Students must turn for the years after 1801 to Gaillard Hunt, ed., *The Writings of James Madison* (9 vols., 1900–1910), and to William C. Rives and Philip R. Fendall, eds., *Letters and Other Writings of James Madison* (1865), which is less complete but fuller on the years of Madison's retirement. There are three superb biographies of nicely varied length: Irving Brant, *James Madison* (6 vols., 1941–1961); Ralph Ketcham, *James Madison: A Biography* (1971); and Jack N. Rakove, *James Madison and the Creation of the American Republic* (1990). Topical studies of the founder's thought and contributions include Lance Banning, *The Sacred Fire of Liberty: James Madison and the*

Founding of the Federal Republic (1995); Drew R. McCoy, *The Elusive Republic: Political Economy in Jeffersonian America* (1980); Robert A. Rutland, *The Presidency of James Madison* (1990); and Drew R. McCoy, *The Last of the Fathers: James Madison and the Republican Legacy* (1989).

LANCE BANNING

MADJECKEWISS. *See* Matchekewis.

MAEDER, Clara Fisher (14 July 1811–12 Nov. 1898), actor, was born in Brighton, England, the daughter of Frederick George Fisher, a librarian and auctioneer, and his wife (name unknown). Three of Fisher's five siblings also worked on the professional stage. Under her father's tutelage, Clara began performing for relatives and friends at age four. At six she debuted at Drury Lane (10 Dec. 1817), performing the title role in the final act of *Richard III* and the prime minister of Lilliput in Garrick's *Gulliver*, two productions cast with children. An instant success with a London public enamored of several child stars, Fisher repeated her roles at Covent Garden to wider applause. During the next decade she performed at several provincial theaters, broadening her repertory to include Shylock, Dr. Pangloss, Sir Peter Teazle, and Young Norval, and amazing audiences with her ability to enact several diverse characters in the same play.

In 1827 her father arranged with theater manager Edmund Simpson for Fisher's debut in New York City, where she followed in the wake of several English stars who had profited from the desire among elite American theatergoers to see London-approved talent. Fisher's debut at the Park Theatre and her tour to other theaters in the East and South, along with Simpson's manipulation of the press, created a Clara Fisher sensation in 1827–1828. Spectators in New York, Philadelphia, New Orleans, and Baltimore crowded box offices, named steamboats after her, and competed for the honor of inviting her into their homes. Elite males, charmed by her buoyant and vulnerable characterizations, published poetry to her in newspapers. Theater managers and stage mothers, hoping to duplicate Fisher's success, placed their protégés and daughters on stage in hastily arranged debuts in roles made famous by the star. Playwrights used the situations and devices of plays she had starred in to fashion new vehicles for her and for other juvenile prodigies vying for some of her reflected limelight. In 1829 *New York Mirror* critic William Cox summed up the appeal of the eighteen-year-old star: "In form and feature, Clara Fisher is neither dignified nor beautiful, but she is irresistibly [*sic*] fascinating. . . . She is one of nature's actresses. Perhaps no one ever so completely possessed the faculty of mobility or entered with more keen enjoyment into the spirit of the part represented. Her whole soul appears to be in everything she does, and we believe it is not only so in seeming, but in reality" (Young, pp. 373–74). An 1828 portrait by Henry Inman shows her with bobbed hair, large eyes, a chubby physique, and a tomboyish smile.

Under Simpson's management in the late 1820s and early 1830s, she played fewer men's roles than before, specializing in parts written for boys or young girls. Ophelia, Viola, Lady Teazle, Little Pickle in *The Spoiled Child*, and the title role in *Clari; or, The Maid of Milan* were among her most celebrated roles. Audiences also applauded her singing in melodramas, operettas, and vaudevilles, more for her energy and sincerity, however, than for her voice, which was clear but light in timbre, with a range adequate for most ballads but few operatic roles. Even after she reached maturity, Americans preferred her in childlike parts, cherishing her mobile plasticity, spunky assertiveness, and charming vulnerability.

Clara Fisher's popularity plummeted after her marriage in 1834 to James Gaspard Maeder, an Irish-American composer. After she and her husband lost their savings in the depression of 1837–1844, the elite of New York City sponsored a benefit for her and her oldest sister, Jane Vernon, where Fisher reprised many of the juvenile parts that had made her famous. Now using her married name professionally, Maeder continued to perform with a variety of stock companies, including Brougham's Lyceum in New York, the Globe Theatre in Boston, and the Arch Street in Philadelphia. She gradually left behind her youthful roles and finally assumed the "old lady" line of business, continuing to gain applause as Juliet's Nurse and as Mrs. Candour in *The School for Scandal*. Fisher retired from the stage in 1889 and died nine years later in Metuchen, New Jersey. She was the mother of seven children, three of whom enjoyed successful careers on the stage.

Apart from her abilities, her popularity in the late 1820s owed much to the social needs of her public. Older male theatergoers, their control of their families increasingly questioned in the late 1820s and 1830s, could imagine themselves as moral, benevolent, and commanding when Fisher appeared in any of several roles as virtuous, sprightly, and finally obedient. However, her star status crashed abruptly when audiences no longer saw an unwed, vulnerable daughter as a believable part of her public image. The length of her remaining career, however, attests to her considerable talent and training.

• The most complete source on Maeder's life is her *Autobiography of Clara Fisher Maeder* (1897), which includes portraits and an introduction by Douglas Taylor. See also the sketch by J. N. Ireland in *Actors and Actresses of Great Britain and the U.S.*, ed. Brander Matthews and Lawrence Hutton (1886), vol. 3, pp. 259–72; and the entry in *Famous Actors and Actresses of the American Stage*, ed. William C. Young (1975), vol. 1, pp. 270–74. For a modern interpretation of her popularity, see Bruce A. McConachie, *Melodramatic Formations: American Theatre and Society, 1820–1870* (1992). An obituary appears in the *New York Times*, 13 Nov. 1898.

BRUCE A. McCONACHIE

MAES, Camillus Paul (13 Mar. 1846–11 May 1915), Roman Catholic bishop, was born in Courtrai, Belgium, the son of Jean Baptiste Maes, who served in the royal

Belgian Regiment d'Élite, and Justine Ghyoot. Both the Maes and Ghyoot families were noted for their distinguished clergymen and their interest in Louvain University. Maes was educated at St. Aloysius Preparatory School and in 1859 was admitted to St. Amandus College, Courtrai. The death of his father in 1861 compelled him to interrupt his studies and become a clerk in the office of a local civil engineer while also studying with a Courtrai architect. After the death of his mother in 1862, he resided with a maternal uncle and that autumn returned to St. Amandus. After graduating the next year, he entered the seminary preparatory to the priesthood in the Diocese of Bruges. His growing interest in the American missions attracted the attention of a visiting bishop, Peter P. Lefevre, of the Diocese of Detroit, who successfully asked for the seminarian's transfer to his diocese. On 6 October 1867 Maes entered the American College of Louvain to prepare for his work in the Diocese of Detroit, for which he was ordained a priest on 19 December 1868.

Maes left Courtrai for Detroit on 18 April 1869 and arrived at his destination on 14 May. Within a month he was appointed associate pastor of St. Peter's Church, Mount Clemens, Michigan, and after the death of the congregation's elderly pastor, the 23-year-old Maes was appointed as successor 26 November 1869. He soon built a parish school and staffed it with religious sisters from Monroe, Michigan. On 3 March 1871 he was appointed pastor of the French- and English-speaking parish of St. Mary in Monroe. Directed by the bishop to organize an English-speaking parish, Maes did so and then erected a church, for which he became pastor on 3 July 1873. During his seven years at this new St. John parish, he became an American citizen, on 17 December 1875. He also wrote and published (Cincinnati, 1880) a biography of Reverend Charles Nerinckx, an early missionary to Kentucky. Maes was made chancellor and secretary to Bishop Caspar Borgess of Detroit on 21 March 1880. In this role he attended the Provincial Council of Bishops in Cincinnati in 1882; founded the Catholic Young Men's Union; was chaplain of the Sisters of the Good Shepherd, whose property he had advantageously negotiated; participated in preaching missions to the Flemings and the Hollanders in Detroit; and also handled well the business of the Diocese of Detroit as it was entrusted to him.

When Bishop Augustus M. Toebbe of Covington, Kentucky, died on 2 May 1884, Pope Leo XIII selected Maes as successor (1 Oct. 1884). While he was still bishop-elect, Maes went to Baltimore for the Third Plenary Council of American Bishops, held from 9 November to 7 December 1884. He favored the decisions to issue a new catechism, encourage the founding of Catholic schools, and inaugurate the Catholic University of America. Maes was consecrated the diocese's third bishop on 25 January 1885 and, accordingly, became responsible for the Catholic church in the eastern third of Kentucky. In addition, he eventually served on the board of trustees of the Catholic University of America, Washington, D.C.; the governing board of the American College of Louvain University; and, from 1905 to 1915, the governing board of the Catholic Church Extension Society. The banking failures of 1873 and the ensuing depression in the United States notwithstanding, Maes began to enlarge the diocesan Catholic school system and to this end brought to the United States in 1889 the Sisters of Divine Providence from Alsace-Lorraine. The diocese already had some flourishing parish schools and girls' academies, but the ever-growing population necessitated more educational establishments. Maes dreamed of new special institutions for boys. Several times he tried in vain to found at least a junior college for them but never succeeded.

It is evident that Maes did not favor the Faribault plan of Archbishop John Ireland of St. Paul, Minnesota, to have Catholic schools become public institutions with religion taught outside the regular school hours. On the other hand, he and Ireland remained personal friends, and both supported the Americanist stand on teaching religion in English rather than in some ethnic language in the Catholic schools. Both bishops remained loyal in word and deed to the authority of the pope.

In between his many labors, Bishop Maes wrote the "History of the Catholic Church in Monroe City and County" (unpublished but printed in part in the *United States Catholic Historical Magazine*, Apr. 1888, pp. 1–40).

Some of Maes's most fruitful years came after the celebration of his silver jubilee of priesthood on 10 December 1893. He began a diocesan newspaper, the *New Cathedral Chimes*, which was issued from May 1894 to April 1896 and was succeeded by the *Christian Year*, a paper published from 1 January 1912 to 20 January 1916. To deepen the spirituality of his priests, Maes introduced the Priests' Eucharistic League on 7 March 1894 and fostered eucharistic congresses. Maes founded and edited from 1895 to 1903 the spiritual periodical *Emmanuel*, which has continued to be published. To ensure appropriate supplies and vestments for church services he founded, in 1907, the Diocesan Tabernacle Society.

The most outstanding project of the Maes episcopacy was the building of St. Mary Cathedral, for which ground was broken in Covington on 1 May 1894 and the cornerstone laid on 8 September 1895. The interior of this Gothic structure was modeled on St. Denis, Paris, and the exterior was inspired by Notre Dame Cathedral, also in Paris. The architect was Leon Coquard of Detroit. The large oil paintings of the eucharistic chapel were the work of Frank Duveneck, a European-trained native of Covington. The handsome façade, designed by David Davis of Newport, Kentucky, and graced by the sculpture of Clement Barnhorn, was structurally finished in time for the silver jubilee of the episcopacy of the bishop in 1910, but he did not live to see Barnhorn's magnificent tympanum over the main door, which was not finished and blessed until 14 October 1917.

One of the bishop's projects that did not succeed was the establishment of a priests' "Evangelist Home" in Richmond, Kentucky. Maes inaugurated such a home in 1905. A substantial building was purchased, and missionary priests of the diocese occupied it briefly and from it fanned out to more remote parts of the diocese. But the illness and death of many parish priests in and near Covington forced the closing of the home, as such, in 1909. Some of the bishop's highest hopes for reaching scattered mountain areas with the faith were thereby curtailed.

At Maes's death in Covington after a thirty-year episcopacy, he was remembered as a pious, devoted, cultured, and dignified pastor; a writer of distinction; and the builder of the architectural jewel of northern Kentucky, St. Mary Cathedral, which has since been elevated to the rank of a basilica.

• Maes's papers and bound correspondence in English, French, Latin, and some Flemish are in the Archives of the Diocese of Covington. The fourteen volumes of the Maes bound correspondence have been translated and transcribed (but not published) by Mary Philip Trauth (1993). A bibliography of the bishop's published works can be found in J. Bittermieux and J. Van der Heyden, "The Right Reverend Camillus P. Maes," *Records of the American Catholic Historical Society* 33 (June 1922): 139–43. In 1917 the Sisters of Divine Providence produced *Character Sketches of the Rt. Rev. C. P. Maes, D.D., Late Bishop of Covington*, a laudatory account of his life and work. A brief biographical sketch and suggestions for an elaborated "hidden history" as adumbrated in the Maes archival collection is in Trauth, "A New American Catholic History: The Hidden History," *U.S. Catholic Historian* 8 (Fall 1989): 174–84. The *History of the Diocese of Covington, Ky.*, by Paul E. Ryan (1953), is a full-length history of the diocese.

MARY PHILIP TRAUTH

MAFFITT, John Newland (28 Dec. 1794–28 May 1850), Methodist preacher, was born in Dublin, Ireland, to a middle-class family that belonged to the Church of Ireland, a branch of the Anglican church. Information about Maffitt's family background and early life is decidedly spotty: his parents' names are unknown, although we do know that his father died when Maffitt was twelve and that his mother shortly thereafter attempted to establish him in a mercantile establishment devoted to tailoring. One account claims he graduated from Trinity College. The teenage Maffitt indulged a love of reading novels and historical romances, however, until a conversion experience in a Methodist meeting at age eighteen or nineteen—accounts conflict on this score—convinced him to become a preacher. The Irish Methodist church did not recognize him as a licensed preacher, and his sporadic attempts at evangelical work both in and beyond Dublin were a mixed success at best. Even so, he displayed a highly melodramatic style, which would personify his later career in the United States. He married Ann Carnic at age twenty. They had seven children; the oldest son, John Newland Maffitt, Jr., attained notoriety as a Confederate blockade runner during the Civil War.

The would-be preacher also floundered financially. Maffitt's autobiography, *Tears of Contrition* (1821), at no point mentions his profession as a tailor, although Maffitt stated that the family business failed. In any event, business reversals in 1819 left the Maffitts in straitened circumstances and prompted Maffitt to go to America that year, encouraged by his brother William, a physician, who had originally planned the journey. Unable to gain the confidence of Manhattan Methodists, Maffitt worked briefly as a tailor in New York before heading to Connecticut in 1819 to speak at a camp meeting. He established himself as a charismatic preacher of the first order. His musical voice and poetic phrases produced large turnouts and increased membership in Methodist churches during the next few years.

Maffitt's behavior in and away from the pulpit, however, attracted criticism, much of which focused on his foppish behavior, unusual gallantries to female admirers, contradictory statements about his tailoring past, and meager intellectual attainments. Attacks against Maffitt on these grounds in the *New England Galaxy*, a Boston newspaper edited by Joseph T. Buckingham, a newsman known for barbed commentary, led to a slander suit by Maffitt in 1822. Buckingham highlighted the preacher's denial and later admission of his tailoring background, reported that he plagiarized a sermon, and suggested that he enticed young women to his bedchamber during a "pretended" sickness (Buckingham, pp. 105–6). The ensuing trial in Boston redefined the course of libel law in the United States when the judge, Josiah Quincy, Jr., permitted the truth as a basis for the newspaper's defense. This threw out the common law tradition in such cases, and Maffitt lost his suit against Buckingham. Fellow Methodists exonerated Maffitt from serious wrongdoing, preferring to blame his youth and ignorance of social conventions. Nevertheless, as one journalistic critic later noted, "Mr. Maffitt's style was still as ornate as the tail of a peacock" (Congdon, p. 46).

Accepted as a fully licensed preacher by the New England Methodist Conference in 1822, Maffitt rebuilt his preaching career in towns in New Hampshire and Massachusetts, typically serving one or two years in particular locations under the authority of the conference. He remained a popular speaker. Indeed, speaking engagements before varied audiences of churchgoers often resulted in publication of his sermons during the 1820s and 1830s. The criticism of the past, although never totally forgotten, remained submerged given Maffitt's ability to further the Methodist cause. An 1828 revival in New York City demonstrated his skills as listeners packed churches to hear him speak. His personal life, meanwhile, suffered from marital discord, and financial difficulties compelled Maffitt to send his oldest son to live with his brother William in North Carolina in 1824. Domestic trouble in 1831 probably spurred Maffitt to abandon the Northeast and "locate," a Methodist term meaning that he had removed himself from the ranks of active circuit riders to become a local preacher, in 1932. As such, Maffitt could select where he spoke provided he maintained his preaching license. The Maffitts separated and divorced sometime in the 1830s.

As a freelance revivalist during the 1830s and 1840s Maffitt cultivated his preaching persona and attained widespread attention, traveling across the United States to speak before enthusiastic and curious audiences. Paid speaking engagements provided him with a constant source of revenue. Described by one admirer as the "Beau Brummel of preachers" (Nichols, p. 231), the nattily attired, unusually handsome minister captivated audiences much as before. He was especially popular in the southern and western states. In 1833 or 1835 he helped found the *Western Methodist*, a Nashville-based weekly journal, and in 1837 he held a chair in elocution and belles lettres at La Grange College in Alabama. An 1838 camp meeting near Nashville, Tennessee, where Maffitt preached for two weeks, had one observer recall how "grey-headed men might be seen trembling like leaves in a rushing wind; and beautiful maidens, with jewelled hair, were heard to shriek as if in the presence of a ghost from eternity" (Elsemore, p. 11). Critics assailed him as a theological lightweight, and some Methodist preachers privately voiced criticism of his flamboyant style, but many people admired his orations, regardless of their thin intellectual caliber. Even William Henry Harrison, who encountered Maffitt in Cincinnati in the winter of 1840–1841 before going to Washington, D.C., for his inauguration, was converted by the preacher. Southern and western congressmen lined up in 1841 to select Maffitt as congressional chaplain, a position that marked the height of his fame during his two-year term in the post.

Maffitt's preaching career fell apart in the Northeast during the mid-1840s, however. A literary and religious monthly, the *Calvary Token*, founded by him in Auburn, New York, lasted no more than two years between 1845 and 1846, while accusations of unprofessional behavior centered on drinking and womanizing increasingly clung to Maffitt. Complaints in 1846 against the revivalist by a Methodist family in New York City led to an ecclesiastical investigation. Although Maffitt dismissed the complaint as involving no more than a young black servant girl seeing him respond to a call of nature in the bedroom, the Methodist authorities, who never publicly detailed the incident, obviously thought it a serious breach of professional etiquette. Maffitt refused to appear before his colleagues, moving to Brooklyn to avoid their jurisdiction, so the conference stripped him of his preaching license, for nonattendance, in March 1847. Maffitt's marriage that month to Frances Pierce, a seventeen-year-old woman, added to the negative publicity and almost caused a riot at the church. The death of his first wife that year produced an additional backlash, augmented further by a marital rift between Maffitt and his second wife. New York City tabloids spun exaggerated stories about the couple when Fanny left her husband in late 1847. Stories about an attempted drunken seduction by the minister and an abortion performed on Fanny appeared in the *Police Gazette*. Maffitt was unable to refute the charges, and the doors of Methodist churches were closed to him without a preaching license. He relocated to Arkansas in 1848, was accepted into the Methodist Episcopal Church South, and again preached at different churches as a freelance speaker. His subsequent southern career, more modest than before, ended with his death in Mobile, Alabama, due to heart trouble.

Maffitt's career rivaled better known evangelicals such as Lyman Beecher and Charles G. Finney, combining a charismatic presence with a dramatic flair that transformed him into a popular religious figure. Scorned for his limited intellectual range, his career nonetheless shows how the Second Great Awakening permitted ordinary individuals to develop into religious celebrities with sizable followings. His troubled personal life ultimately doomed his ministry with both the Methodist church and the general public and relegated him to obscurity in later church histories.

• The United Methodist Archives at Drew University, Madison, N.J., contain some letters written by Maffitt, but surviving correspondence is limited. Maffitt authored innumerable sermons and published several sketches, essays, and a dictionary. His autobiography, *Tears of Contrition* (1821), only covers his very early life and is selective about what it details. Additional biographical information is available in Moses Elsemore, *An Impartial Account of the Life of the Reverend John N. Maffitt* (1848), together with shorter accounts from the *American Cyclopaedia*, vol. 10 (1875), and William Sprague, *Annals of the American Pulpit*, vol. 7 (1865). Emma Martin Maffitt, *The Life and Service of John Newland Maffitt* (1906), a biography of her husband, the Confederate blockade runner, has some material on the elder Maffitt also. Accounts about Maffitt's disputes with New York City Methodists can be found in George Peck, *Life and Times of Rev. George Peck* (1874), which is an anti-Maffitt account, and Rufus B. Hibbard, *Startling Disclosures Concerning the Death of John N. Maffitt* (1856), a pro-Maffitt account. Useful contemporary works that mention the preacher include Joseph T. Buckingham, *Personal Memoirs and Recollections of Editorial Life* (2 vols., 1852); Charles T. Congdon, *Reminiscences of a Journalist* (1880); Thomas L. Nichols, *Forty Years of an American Life, 1821–1861* (1937); and B. F. Tefft, *Methodism Successful and the Internal Causes of Its Success* (1860).

ROBERT E. CRAY, JR.

MAFFITT, John Newland (22 Feb. 1819–15 May 1886), American and Confederate naval officer, was born at sea while his mother, Ann Carnic, was en route from Ireland to the United States to join her husband, John Newland Maffitt, a Methodist minister. In 1824 Dr. William Maffitt, young Maffitt's uncle, took pity on the modest circumstances of his brother's family and offered to take charge of his nephew. Maffitt went to live with his uncle near Fayetteville, North Carolina. He attended school in Fayetteville and White Plains, New York, until age thirteen, when his family obtained a midshipman's commission for him. For the next ten years he spent much of his time at sea, including service on board the frigates *Constitution* and *Macedonian*. In 1840, while stationed at Pensacola,

Florida, Maffitt married Mary Florence Murrell. This marriage ended in somewhat cloudy, but most certainly unhappy, circumstances in 1844. In 1852 he was married again, to Caroline Laurens Read. She died in 1859.

In 1842 Maffitt was posted to the United States Coast Survey. For the next sixteen years he spent his professional life surveying the Atlantic Coast and adjacent areas. In 1858 he was detached from the Survey, given command of the brig *Dolphin*, and ordered to cruise the coast of Cuba. One year later he was transferred to the U.S. steamer *Crusader* and ordered to patrol the same waters. The *Crusader* returned to New York in late February 1861. Understanding the crisis at hand, Maffitt left the *Crusader* and traveled to Washington, D.C. He was there when the Civil War began. Along with many other southern officers Maffitt, who considered himself a North Carolinian submitted his resignation to the secretary of the navy, and he traveled south to join the Confederate cause in May 1861.

Maffitt's first assignment was to join the staff of General Robert E. Lee. In January 1862 he was given command of the blockade runner *Cecile*, and in April he took command of another, the *Nassau*. Because of his success as a blockade runner, the Confederate Navy Department gave Maffitt command of the C.S.S. *Oreto*. Built in Liverpool, England, the *Oreto* had been brought secretly to Nassau, where it was armed and renamed *Florida*. The *Florida* left Nassau on 17 August 1862. The crew, however, were stricken with yellow fever, and the vessel limped into Cárdenas, Cuba. At the request of the Spanish authorities, Maffitt brought the *Florida* to Havana harbor, where it remained until 1 September. Unable to recruit enough crew members for an extended voyage, Maffitt left Havana, and in a daring venture the *Florida* managed to sail north and dash past the Union blockade into Mobile, Alabama. On the morning of 16 January 1863, *Florida* ran out of Mobile and headed to sea.

After returning to Nassau for coal, *Florida* cruised the western Atlantic. During the next six months the vessel managed to capture or destroy more than twenty Union vessels and sent many more scurrying for cover. Maffitt was promoted from lieutenant to commander on 29 April 1863. On 6 May *Florida* captured the small brig *Clarence*. Maffitt armed the vessel and put it under the command of Lieutenant C. W. Read. At Maffitt's orders, Read cruised independently and managed to capture more than half a dozen Union vessels. After cruising for more than six months, *Florida* needed considerable repair; late in August 1863 Maffitt took *Florida* into the port of Brest, France, for repair. While at Brest Maffitt became ill and asked to be relieved of his command. Regaining his health, Maffitt traveled to Bermuda to take command of the blockade runner *Lillian* and ran the vessel into Wilmington, North Carolina. In June 1864 Maffitt was posted to command the C.S.S. *Albemarle*, a ram stationed at Plymouth, North Carolina. Fearing that the *Albemarle* might be captured by a stronger Union force, Confed-

erate authorities kept the ram confined close to base. Maffitt found it a disappointing command, and he was pleased in September 1864 to be relieved of the *Albemarle* and dispatched to command the blockade runner *Owl*. Maffitt's last command, the *Owl* made several successful runs through the blockade, the last being at Galveston. At the end of the war the *Owl* and Maffitt were in Liverpool.

For two years after the war Maffitt commanded the British merchant steamer *Widgeon*. In 1867 he returned to the United States. Shortly after his return he bought a farm near Wilmington, North Carolina, which he named the "Moorings." On 23 November 1870 Maffitt married Emma Martin. With his three wives he had seven children and three stepchildren. Maffitt spent the remainder of his life at the Moorings as a gentleman farmer and author. He wrote a novel, *Nautilus, or Cruising under Canvas* (1871), and many magazine articles recalling his service, and that of other Confederate naval officers, in the war. Maffitt tried unsuccessfully in 1884 to secure an appointment to the Wilmington customhouse from President Grover Cleveland. His health deteriorated due to Bright's disease, and he died in Wilmington.

Like other Confederate high seas raiders, John Newland Maffitt both embarrassed and damaged the northern war effort. His destruction of Union shipping removed tonnage from service and at the same time forced Union ship owners to pay ever higher insurance premiums. His success, and that of other Confederate high seas raiders, forced the Union navy to divert much needed resources away from the blockade to the task of chasing these will-o'-the-wispish sea rovers.

• Two biographies of Maffitt have been written: Edward C. Boykin, *Sea Devil of the Confederacy: The Story of the Florida and Her Captain, John Newland Maffitt* (1959), and Emma Martin Maffitt, *The Life and Services of John Newland Maffitt* (1906). Maffitt himself wrote a good deal about his experiences; these articles may be found in various issues of the *Confederate Veteran* and *United Service*. *The Official Records of the Union and Confederate Navies in the War of the Rebellion* also contain important information.

WILLIAM M. FOWLER, JR.

MAGALLANES, Nicholas (27 Nov. 1922–1 May 1977), ballet dancer, was born in Camargo, Mexico, the son of Philip Magallanes and Vicenta Holquin. When he was five years old, the family moved to New Jersey and subsequently to New York City, where Magallanes graduated from De Witt Clinton High School.

Magallanes first saw a ballet at age fifteen and thereupon decided to become a dancer. He began training at the School of American Ballet, receiving instruction from George Balanchine, Pierre Vladimirov, Anatole Obukhov, and Muriel Stuart. Magallane's professional debut occurred in 1940 with Lincoln Kirstein's Ballet Caravan, performing at the New York World's Fair Ford Pavilion in the ballet *A Thousand Times Neigh!* A year later the young dancer was touring South America with Ballet Caravan, appearing as a soloist in Balanchine's *Ballet Imperial* (1941); he then danced with the Catherine Littlefield Ballet in 1942, followed by engagements with the Ballet Russe de Monte Carlo. During this period, he performed in works choreographed by Balanchine for the Ballet Russe. He was Cleonte in *Le Bourgeois Gentilhomme* (1944), Jean de Brienne in *Raymonda* (Danilova version, 1946), and he created the role of the Poet in *Night Shadow* (later called *La Sonnambula*, 1946), partnering Alexandra Danilova.

Magallanes's primary affiliation was with the companies of Balanchine and Kirstein. In 1946 he joined the Ballet Society, which became the New York City Ballet in 1948. His early roles included Bacchus in *The Triumph of Bacchus and Ariadne* (1948), the First Movement in *Symphony in C* (the new version of *Le Palais de Cristal*, 1948), and the title role in *Orpheus* (1948), portraying the lyre-playing poet. His exotic looks and romantic presence were used to great effect by Balanchine.

These same qualities were called upon when Magallanes was again cast as a poet in *Illuminations*, which Frederick Ashton created for the New York City Ballet. The choreographer wanted to have elements of French writer Arthur Rimbaud's life depicted in the ballet as well as some of his poetry. Ashton gave Magallanes books to read in preparation for a role demanding a high degree of dramatic interpretation. The work itself also formed part of the New York City Ballet's most ambitious programs, premiering on 2 March 1950 at the City Center of Music and Drama. Lillian Moore reported in the *Dancing Times* that Magallanes "has drawn just about the best performance of his career. . . . Magallanes demonstrates in the scene of Anarchy (where he carries on a single-handed revolution against existing order) that his dancing can be fluid and forceful as well as technically facile" (Apr. 1950).

Magallanes's association with Balanchine continued with successive roles created for him, but it was in two works by Jerome Robbins that his dancing talents were further stretched. In 1951 he appeared as an Intruder in *The Cage* (1951), a fiercely dramatic work in which a female insect swarm's novice learns to destroy potential mates, and he was principal dancer in *The Pied Piper*. The latter was an abstract work that included a lyric pas de deux danced by Magallanes and Diana Adams. The dance was in a very slow tempo and had a dreamy quality; the male dancer lifted the ballerina high into the air, continually changing the positions by slow turns and expansive assisted leaps.

Ballerinas rely on their male partner's strength and artistry for support in performing particular movements and balletic poses. In this context, Magallanes was a favorite among his female colleagues. Dance critic Arlene Croce noted that "he was a model partner, strong and gallant yet unobtrusive; he could set off a ballerina like black velvet under a diamond" (Croce, p. 23). This perfectly suited Balanchine's choreography as he brought out Magallanes's talent, emphasizing his beautiful grace and lyricism. Through-

out the 1950s and 1960s, he created principal roles in Balanchine's *Caracole* and *Metamorphoses* (both 1952); *Valse Fantaisie* (1953); *Opus 34*, *The Nutcracker*, and *Western Symphony* (all 1954); *Allegro Brillante* and *Divertimento No. 15* (both 1956); *Square Dance* (1957); *Episodes II* (1959); *Liebeslieder Walzer* (1960); *A Midsummer Night's Dream* (1962); and *Don Quixote* (1965).

The role with which Magallanes was most associated was that of the principal male dancer in *Serenade*, and he was featured in this work on the front cover of the celebratory book commemorating the first twenty-five years of the New York City Ballet.

As the company developed and a new generation of male dancers advanced, Magallanes was cast in essentially character roles, for which he felt unsuited. He thus retired from the company in 1973. His last public appearance was in the eponymous mime role in a staging of *Don Quixote* in 1976. Magallanes died of cancer at his home in North Merrick, Long Island, New York.

A principal with the New York City Ballet for many years, Magallanes was praised for his stylish and romantic presence on stage, despite a lack of technical virtuosity, and for his secure and self-effacing partnering. Magallanes's career spanned a period of vital development for dance in the United States, as strong foundations were laid and new companies formed.

• Resources on Magallanes, including photographs, are held at the Dance Collection at the New York Public Library for the Performing Arts, Lincoln Center. Contemporary reflections are in Anatole Chujoy, *The New York City Ballet* (1953), and Lillian Moore, "Ashton's New Ballet—New York Notes," *Dancing Times*, Apr. 1950, pp. 410–11, 416. Later considerations of Magallanes's dancing may be found in Martha Bremser, ed. *International Dictionary of Ballet* (1933); Arlene Croce, *Going to the Dance* (1982); Lincoln Kirstein, *Thirty Years: Lincoln Kirstein's The New York City Ballet* (1979); and David Vaughan, *Frederick Ashton and His Ballets* (1977). An obituary is in the *New York Times*, 5 May 1977.

MELANIE TRIFONA CHRISTOUDIA

MAGEE, Sherry (6 Aug. 1884–13 Mar. 1929), baseball player and umpire, was born Sherwood Robert Magee in Clairton, Warren County, Pennsylvania, the son of James S. Magee, an oil field worker, and Drusilla Hall. Nothing is known of his early life or education. Magee began his professional baseball career at Allentown, Pennsylvania, in 1903. The 5′11″, 180-pound right-hander played in the outfield for Carlisle, Pennsylvania, until June 1904, when Philadelphia Phillies' scout James Randall signed him. Magee joined the Phillies, starting a sixteen-year major league career. In 1905 he married Edna May Cary; they had three children.

An excellent all-around player, Magee proved a solid hitter in the dead-ball era and a fine defensive left fielder with unusual speed and a powerful throwing arm. He was a fine base stealer and set a Phillies' season record—55 stolen bases in 1906—that stood for more than seven decades.

Magee's best seasons came from 1904 through 1914, all with the Phillies. During that decade he led the National League in seven offensive categories—runs scored, runs batted in (four times), hits, on-base percentage, slugging average (twice), doubles, and batting average. In 1910 he won the National League batting title with a .331 average, while also pacing the league with 110 runs scored, 123 runs batted in, a .445 on-base percentage, and a .507 slugging average. Four years later, he led the National League in hits (171), doubles (39), runs batted in (103), and slugging percentage (.509). He once (1912) led league outfielders in fielding percentage (.981).

After serving as field captain for the Phillies, Magee expected to be named manager in 1914. However, Pat Moran was appointed. Magee demanded a trade, and in December 1914 he was sent to the World Champion Boston Braves. He played for the Braves until August 1917, when his contract was waived to the Cincinnati Reds; with the Reds he led the National League in runs batted in with 76 during the war-shortened season of 1918. Magee finished his major league career in 1919. He played for Cincinnati in the infamous "fixed" World Series of 1919 when the Reds defeated the Chicago "Black Sox."

From 1920 through 1926, Magee played in the minor leagues. In 1927 he umpired in the New York/Pennsylvania League, and the next season National League president John Heydler promoted him to his umpiring staff. Magee was prepared to begin his second year as a major league umpire when he was stricken with pneumonia and died in West Philadelphia.

Magee had a legendary temper. A notorious bench jockey, he needled friends and foes alike. A long-running feud with teammate Dode Paskert led to a brawl in the Phillies' dugout. But the most famous example of Magee's temper came during a July 1911 game. After umpire Bill Finneran called him out on strikes, Magee charged the umpire and knocked him senseless. The National League fined Magee $200 and suspended him for the rest of the season, a penalty later reduced to thirty-six days.

Magee, a prototypical baseball player in the days when the sport was young and tough, performed well in the dead-ball era. If not in the same class as Ty Cobb, Honus Wagner, or Walter Johnson, he played just a notch below them. A lifetime .291 hitter, he had 2,169 hits, 1,182 runs batted in, 1,112 runs scored, 425 doubles, and 441 stolen bases during his major league career.

• Information on Magee is scarce. Frank Bilovsky and Rich Westcott's *The Phillies Encyclopedia*, 2d ed. (1993) contains a sketch of his career as well as his Phillies ranking in various categories. Also see Frederick G. Lieb and Stan Baumgartner, *The Philadelphia Phillies* (1953). The *Philadelphia Evening Bulletin* obituary, 14 Mar. 1929, provides a solid overview of his achievements.

JOHN P. ROSSI

MAGIC SAM (14 Feb. 1937–1 Dec. 1969), blues singer and guitarist, was born Samuel Gene Maghett in Grenada, Mississippi, the son of Jessie Maghett and Hetha Anna Henderson, farmers. His mother died when he was still a child. Raised eight miles east of Grenada in a community known as Redgrass, he showed an early aptitude for music, constructing a one-string guitar at age ten. He helped his father farm until he was thirteen, at which time he and a brother were sent to Chicago to live with an aunt. In Chicago he became deeply involved with music. A local gambler, James "Shakey Jake" Harris, encouraged Maghett to keep practicing and to work on his singing instead of concentrating solely on guitar.

Becoming more confident as a musician in his late teens, Maghett began singing in a family gospel group in South Side churches while also playing guitar with Shakey Jake, by now a blues singer and harmonica player. Shakey Jake hired Maghett and Mack Thompson to back him at a club called the Wagon Wheel around 1954. In 1955 Maghett auditioned at the 708 Club, which then featured Muddy Waters. The owner promptly booked him to follow Waters, a job that allowed Maghett—or "Good Rocking Sam" as he was billed—to begin expanding his repertoire and developing his own sound.

In 1956 Maghett made his recording studio debut, playing as a sideman on two sides for the short-lived ABCO label, operated by Eli Toscano. Within months he was back in the studio, this time as a featured artist for Toscano's new Cobra label. With the new name of Magic Sam, his first single, "All Your Love" backed by "Love Me with a Feeling," was a substantial regional hit. There were three follow-up singles on Cobra, but the records did little to advance Magic Sam's career; he continued to make his main mark in Chicago's blues clubs. Cobra folded in 1959, and that same year Magic Sam was drafted into the army. He deserted and returned to Chicago but was captured and imprisoned for six months. Fellow musicians felt the hiatus hurt his career, affecting both his physical and mental health. As guitarist Luther Allison recalled, "The people seemed [like] they had forgotten about him" (Iglauer and O'Neal, p. 7).

Sam resumed steady work in Chicago's clubs in the early 1960s, sharing billings with Muddy Waters, Howlin' Wolf, or Otis Rush, among others. He became a regular in the guitar "cutting" contests that were popular in West Side clubs, trying to out-play guitar slingers like Mighty Joe Young, Freddie King, or Allison. He resumed recording, too, with several sessions for the German L+R label in 1963 and 1964 and a single on Crash in 1966.

The major event of Magic Sam's career came in 1967 when he recorded an album for the Chicago-based Delmark label, *Magic Sam Blues Band: West Side Soul*. The album, which showcased Sam's instrumental versatility and his soul vocal stylings, earned a five-star review from *Downbeat* magazine and is considered one of the best urban blues recordings of all time. The album caught the attention of the rock world, leading to bookings far beyond the Chicago club scene. Suddenly Magic Sam was playing rock palaces on both coasts and touring on the college concert circuit. A follow-up album, *Black Magic*, was re-corded on Delmark in the fall of 1968, although it was not released until the next year.

Fueled by the reviews and recognition generated by *West Side Soul*, 1969 began as Magic Sam's most suc-cessful year. *Rolling Stone* magazine reviewed his work, and several major labels were said to be eager to sign him. A rigorous schedule, put together by his manager Denny Bruce, kept him on the road, and a European tour with the American Folk Blues Festival was set for later that year. In August he performed at the Ann Arbor Blues Festival, a set so memorable it elicited comparisons to rock legend Jimi Hendrix. With Sam finally nearing stardom, though, his health began to deteriorate under the strain of travel, heavy drinking, and an ongoing heart problem. Collapsing after a concert in Kentucky, he returned to Chicago to recuperate, reportedly spending a week in the hospi-tal. Warned to stop drinking, he went on the Europe-an tour, after which he returned to the states and made a trip to California. Back in Chicago in the fall of 1969, he suffered a heart attack in his home and was pro-nounced dead at St. Anthony Hospital. He was buried in Restvale Cemetery in Worth, Illinois. At the time of his death, his finances were in disarray, supposedly because of union problems, and a benefit concert was held on the West Coast to help his common-law wife, Leola, and their four children.

Magic Sam embodied what became known as the "West Side Sound," a modern blues style based around three pieces: guitar, bass (or a second guitar), and drums. Simple economics dictated the three-piece format because West Side clubs paid relatively little for live entertainment. The style demanded strong vo-cals and instrumental virtuosity, and Sam excelled at both. He possessed an outstanding, soaring blues voice, dramatically effective due to his affinity for mi-nor-chord blues and his soul/gospel vocal inflections. He once told researcher Jim O'Neal, "I'm a modern type of bluesman, I can play the soul stuff, too," im-plying that unlike some older artists, he could still ap-peal to contemporary African-American audiences. As a guitarist, he employed tremolo heavily, played with his fingers instead of a pick, and displayed a talent for lightning-fast melodic invention within the tight con-fines of the blues format.

As a writer, Sam was fond of sixteen-bar blues but was equally at home with primitive boogies. He drew material from sources as diverse as Lowell Fulsom, J. B. Lenoir, and Louis Jordan, but he always re-shaped the material with his own signature sound. Un-like earlier artists such as Muddy Waters or Howlin' Wolf who brought fully developed musical traditions from Mississippi to Chicago, Magic Sam developed an urban sound a generation removed from his Mississip-pi birth.

• For additional information, see Sheldon Harris, *Blues Who's Who: A Biographical Dictionary of Blues Singers* (1979; repr. 1989), and Steve Franz, "Magic Rocker: The Life and Music of Magic Sam," *Living Blues* 125 (Jan.–Feb. 1996): 32–44. For an appreciation from fellow musicians, see Bruce Iglauer and Jim O'Neal, "Remembering Magic Sam," *Living Blues* 1, no. 1 (Spring 1970): 2–10. For a discussion of his music, see Robert Cappuccio, "The Magic of Magic Sam," *Living Blues* 13 (Summer 1973): 13. For a discography, see Mike Leadbitter et al., *Blues Records 1943–1970: "The Bible of the Blues*," vol. 2: *L–Z* (1994). For a sample of his music, try *Magic Sam Blues Band: West Side Soul*, Delmark 615; *Black Magic: Magic Sam Blues Band*, Delmark 620; and *Mag-ic Sam Live*, Delmark 645/646. (The live recordings are tech-nically flawed but convey a sense of his on-stage presence.)
BILL MCCULLOCH
BARRY LEE PEARSON

MAGILL, Edward Hicks (24 Sept. 1825–10 Dec. 1907), second president of Swarthmore College, was born in Bucks County, Pennsylvania, the son of Mary Watson and Jonathan Paxson Magill, Quaker farmers. Magill received a Quaker education at the local monthly meeting school and then at the prestigious Westtown School near Philadelphia. After graduation he taught elementary school for seven years before continuing his education at Williston Seminary in Easthampton, Massachusetts. He spent a year at Yale College (1850–1851) before transferring to Brown College, where he completed his degree in 1852. After graduation Magill married Sarah Warner Beans; they had five children. Remaining in Providence, he served for seven years as principal of the classical program in the high school. He moved to Boston in 1859 to teach Latin and French at the famous Public Latin School. Although he had studied under the innovative President Francis Way-land (1796–1865) at Brown, the experience seemed to have little influence on Magill, who taught languages by traditional drills.

After a year of travel and study in Europe, Magill returned to Pennsylvania and became the first princi-pal of the preparatory department at Swarthmore Col-lege, which had been founded in 1869 as the first col-lege of the Hicksite wing of Quakerism. The Hicksites had split with Orthodox Quakers in 1827, and the schism endured for nearly a century. Traditional Hicksites were predominantly rural, culturally more traditional, and slower to develop denominational in-stitutions than their Orthodox rivals were. They fol-lowed the doctrine of simplicity, continuing plain speech and, often, plain dress into the twentieth centu-ry. They avoided holiday celebrations and distrusted music, art, and modern literature. Not having retreat-ed to rural isolation as the Mennonites had, the Hick-sites relied on "guarded education" to protect their children from "the world" and to pass on their life style and values. To create a protected environment, Swarthmore was one of the few colleges that required all students to live on the campus.

Like many other colleges of the time, Swarthmore had more secondary (or preparatory) students than collegians. Magill's preparatory students numbered about three-quarters of Swarthmore's initial 170 stu-dents. The college president, Edward Parrish, came from the Hicksite wing that included Lucretia Mott and John Hicks. Parrish soon lost favor as the board of managers fell under the control of traditionalists who demanded that Swarthmore provide a "guarded education" that promoted their distinct life style. Magill, with his background as a disciplinarian in secondary schools and his commitment to Hicksite distinctiveness, better fit the traditionalists' desires. Elevated to the presidency after Parrish was pushed out in 1871, Magill fulfilled the managers' demands by creating 100 rules to prevent conduct that would offend either Hicksite or Victorian sensibilities.

But Magill's educational ambitions conflicted with the managers' values. Many of them were more interested in using Swarthmore to provide secondary education and to train teachers for Quaker schools than in having a true college. Given the Quaker distrust of the classics and the absence of a need to train clergy, the school lacked two of the normal incentives for attaining collegiate standards. Magill, however, harbored a desire for respect in the broader academic world and for a prosperous institution. Throughout his presidency he fought to include non-Quaker students and faculty because Hicksites alone could not fill the school. He also fought to reduce the secondary and normal programs in deference to baccalaureate studies. By the end of his presidency in the late 1880s the preparatory classes were being phased out, and a teacher training program, which briefly threatened to replace collegiate studies, had been eliminated. Magill's papers reveal a virtuoso president who dealt with a variety of issues that in the twentieth century would be turned over to administrators. Every admissions, financial aid, and disciplinary case passed through his office. He also continued to carry a heavy burden of teaching Latin and French throughout his presidency.

At Swarthmore Magill presided over one of the first coeducational colleges in the East. This experiment was based on a Hicksite belief in the intellectual equality of the sexes. The board of managers statutorily had the same number of men and women, although the former normally exercised more power. Magill always supported coeducation, and his 100 rules helped reduce embarrassing incidents for the institution, though many students resented the straitlaced social life.

His greatest educational achievement may have been inadvertent. In 1887 he initiated the founding of the College Association of Pennsylvania to discuss the relationship of private colleges and state government. As its focus shifted to relations with high schools and its geographic scope broadened, it became the Association of Colleges and Preparatory Schools of the Middle States and Maryland. This group created the powerful College Entrance Examination Board at the turn of the century.

Magill retired as president in 1888 but continued to teach until he was seventy-five. As president he had helped maintain collegiate standards at an institution that in the twentieth century would lose its Quaker distinctiveness and become an elite college that embraced "the world." Magill probably would have been delighted by Swarthmore's educational success, but disconcerted by the cultural and social changes. He died in New York City.

• Among the most useful sources on Magill are his autobiography, *Sixty-five Years in the Life of a Teacher: 1841–1906* (1907), and the Magill Presidential Papers at the Friends Historical Library at Swarthmore College. Homer E. Babbidge, "Swarthmore College in the Nineteenth Century" (Ph.D. diss., Yale Univ., 1953), has an excellent history of the Magill years. Richard J. Walton, *Swarthmore College: An Informal History* (1986), is a good brief history. W. Bruce Leslie, *Gentlemen and Scholars: College and Community in the "Age of the University," 1865–1917,* puts Magill's Swarthmore in a comparative perspective.

W. BRUCE LESLIE

MAGINNIS, Charles Donagh (7 Jan. 1867–15 Feb. 1955), architect, was born in Londonderry, Ireland, the son of Charles Maginnis and Bridget McDonagh. After attending Cusack's Academy in Dublin, he obtained his first semiprofessional training at London's South Kensington Museum School of Art, where he won the Queen's Prize in math and drawing. Turning down a British civil service position, Maginnis emigrated in 1885 with his mother, brothers, and sister. Accounts of his early years in North America are sketchy and conflicting: some place him in Toronto, Canada, from 1885 to 1888, and others in Boston, Massachusetts, in William P. Wentworth's architectural firm.

By 1891 Maginnis had joined the office of Edmund M. Wheelwright, city architect, whose buildings typified the eclecticism popular in turn-of-the-century Boston. Wheelwright designed in numerous styles, from Georgian to Oriental, and his important commissions included the Boston Fire Department, modeled after the Palazzo Vecchio in Florence. As head draftsman in this firm, Maginnis gained a reputation for his perspective drawings, published a book, *Pen Drawing* (1898), and taught at Cowles Art Club and the Boston Architectural Club. Maginnis emerged from Wheelwright's office with drawing skills and a knowledge of historical styles that proved a solid base for his later work.

In 1898 Maginnis formed a partnership with Matthew Sullivan, who also worked in Wheelwright's office, and Timothy F. Walsh, a draftsman for Peabody & Stearns. (Sullivan left the firm in 1908 to start his own practice.) The firm of Maginnis, Walsh, & Sullivan received its first commission in 1898 for St. Patrick's Church in Whitinsville, Massachusetts. The commission resulted from Maginnis's article for a local church magazine criticizing American Catholic ecclesiastical buildings. According to Maginnis, cathedral models were much too ambitious for most parish budgets. He called for a return to the style of Italian medieval brick churches, writing in the pamphlet "Catholic Church Architecture" (1906) that "An unpretentious brick church, with the mark of a gifted hand upon it, may have more artistic value than the cathedral." Maginnis and Walsh sought to reform Catholic architecture by using Lombard Romanesque churches like San Pietro in Toscanella as a model. This style permitted economic, simple forms and a flexibility of motifs and materials yet was still part of the Catholic tradition, like the more popular Gothic style. Churches designed by Maginnis and Walsh such as St. John's Seminary Chapel in Brighton (1899–1902) and St. Catherine of Genoa in Somerville (1907–1916) brought the architects into prominence in Boston archdiocesan circles. The firm went on to design hundreds of churches in the Boston area and to become the leading Roman Catholic architectural firm in the United States in the first part of the century. Their better-known national projects include the altar and bronze doors of St. Patrick's Cathedral in New York (1942) and the National Shrine of the Immaculate Conception in Washington, D.C. (1919–1959).

Maginnis and Walsh also worked on at least twenty-five Catholic colleges and universities, planning individual buildings and entire campuses. Their first college commission was Boston College: they designed a long-range plan for the new Chestnut Hill campus in 1909 and designed at least eleven buildings from 1909 to 1959. Boston College ranks as one of the earliest collegiate Gothic designs of the modern period along with the University of Chicago (1892) and Princeton University (1909). Boston College also served as a model for many of the firm's later collegiate works, such as the University of Notre Dame (Notre Dame, Ind., 1929–1953). Maginnis & Walsh's work can also be seen on the campuses of the Catholic University of America (Washington, D.C.), College of the Holy Cross (Worcester, Mass.), Fordham University (N.Y.), and St. Thomas College (St. Paul, Minn.).

In sum, Maginnis and Walsh served as architects for the expanding Roman Catholic church in America. The firm's eclectic style suited its traditional patron well: the architects worked, as needed, in the Gothic, Lombard Romanesque, Byzantine, classical, and Spanish mission styles. The firm received numerous awards for its designs, including two gold medals from the American Institute of Architects (AIA)—one for the Carmelite Convent in Santa Clara, California (1925), and another for Trinity College Chapel in Washington, D.C. (1927). Maginnis, who served as AIA president from 1937 to 1939, received the Gold Medal for Outstanding Service to American Architecture from this organization in 1948.

Often overlooked by historians of twentieth-century architecture, who have focused on modernist design, Maginnis was a traditionalist working in an age of innovation. As an architect for the Roman Catholic church, Maginnis's projects were immersed in that religious tradition. Holding to an earlier approach to architecture, he sought to integrate buildings with nature and their environment and to preserve the architect's role as overseer of every detail of the building. His choice of material also referred to the past: he preferred masonry architecture and saw limitations in new materials, such as the steel and concrete being used by modern architects like Walter Gropius.

In obituaries, contemporaries characterized Maginnis as a world-famous architect who brought about a regeneration of ecclesiastic architecture. In his many articles on Catholic art and its place in the twentieth century, Maginnis complained about the low quality of Catholic art in the United States and criticized mass-produced statuary, decoration, and pattern-book church plans. He projected a renaissance of Catholic architecture in the country, writing in his 1906 pamphlet, "The hope may indeed seem visionary that, with modern methods of art production, the church will again inspire an artistic manifestation approaching the Gothic tradition in beauty of thought or in sublimity of power." Maginnis's buildings are evidence of his desire to rejuvenate American Catholic architecture and rival past monuments.

In 1907 Maginnis married Amy Brooks, with whom he had five children. He was known as charming and modest, displaying wit and facility in his speeches and writings and generosity as a teacher. Hardly an artistic or political radical, Maginnis was an activist in the community in true liberal fashion, working for numerous art, civic, and religious organizations in the Boston area. He died in Brookline, Massachusetts, where he had lived for many years.

• The Maginnis & Walsh Collection, which includes a commission list, drawings, plans, full-scale details, and photographs, as well as memorabilia donated by Alice Maginnis Walsh, is located at the print department of the Boston Public Library. For Maginnis's writings see Charles D. Maginnis, *A Selection of His Essays and Addresses*, ed. Robert P. Walsh and Andrew W. Roberts (1956). Sylvester Baxter, "A Selection from the Works of Maginnis and Walsh," *Architectural Record* 53 (Feb. 1923): 93–113, is perhaps the most comprehensive account of the firm's projects and includes illustrations of its major designs to that date. J. Sanford Shanley and John La Farge, "Charles D. Maginnis 1867–1955: A Tribute," *Liturgical Arts* 23, no. 4 (Aug. 1955): 151–55, is a good starting place to study Maginnis, as it contains a biographical sketch, an outline of his career and major works, a list of Maginnis's writings, and a bibliography of material written about the architect. Other articles include Donna M. Cassidy, "The Collegiate Gothic Designs of Maginnis & Walsh," *Studies in Medievalism* 3, no. 2 (Fall 1990): 153–85; and Douglass Shand Tucci, "The Other Gothic Revival—The Work of P. C. Keely and Maginnis and Walsh," *Drumlin* 1 (Mar. 1976): 4–5.

DONNA M. CASSIDY

MAGNES, Judah Leon (5 July 1877–27 Oct. 1948), rabbi, communal leader, and first chancellor and first president of the Hebrew University in Jerusalem, was born in San Francisco, California, the eldest of five children of David Magnes and Sophie Abrahamson. His father had emigrated from Poland at age fifteen in 1863 and his mother from eastern Prussia in 1872. When Magnes was five, the family moved to nearby Oakland, California, where his father opened a dry-goods store. The Magneses were a close-knit family. English was the language of the home, although Magnes's mother and maternal grandmother insisted that the children learn German. The family belonged to the local Reformed congregation, where Magnes received his early religious education. From his father he gained an empathy for the Jewish religious traditions and Yiddish culture of Eastern Europe and from his mother a grounding in German culture. In later life his appreciation for both religious-cultural strands in American Jewish life made him an ideal mediator between the two.

In 1894 Magnes entered the Hebrew Union College in Cincinnati, Ohio, and at the same time began his studies at the University of Cincinnati. He received his B.A. in 1898 and his rabbinical ordination in 1900. Magnes continued his studies in Germany. He received his Ph.D. in Semitics and philosophy from the University of Heidelberg in 1902 after spending a year at the University of Berlin and the Lehranstalt fuer die Wissenschaft des Judentums. The three years in Germany were critical in shaping his outlook and career. He established ties with a group of young European Jewish intellectuals who shared the Zionist ideals of rebuilding a national home in Palestine and reviving Hebrew culture.

Magnes's public career in the United States lasted from 1904 to 1922, when he and his family settled in Jerusalem. For only eight of these years did he occupy a pulpit. From 1904 to 1906 he served Temple Israel in Brooklyn, New York, and in 1907 he was called to New York City's most prestigious and wealthy Reformed congregation, Temple Emanuel. In 1910 Magnes, whose brilliant and controversial sermons won him a citywide following, resigned his position when the congregation refused to accept his program for the "reconstruction of Reformed Judaism," which called for a return to more traditional observance and a more intensive Hebraic religious school curriculum. He briefly held the pulpit of the Conservative B'nai Jeshurun congregation of New York, his last.

Magnes's marriage to Beatrice Lowenstein in 1908 strengthened his ties to the German-Jewish elite who dominated the temple and Jewish communal life during the early decades of the century. Beatrice Magnes's sister was married to Louis Marshall, an eminent lawyer and a founder and then president of the American Jewish Committee, the most important Jewish community-relations organization at the time. Throughout his life Magnes was held in high esteem by the patrician Schiff, Warburg, Straus, Guggenheim, Lehman, Wertheim, and Sulzberger families, the sources of his power in Jewish affairs. The Magneses had three children. Jonathan, the middle son, became a professor of physiology and dean of the medical school of the Hebrew University.

In 1905 Magnes was elected secretary (executive director) of the Federation of American Zionists, a post he held until 1908. He was the most popular Zionist speaker of the day, esteemed by the Jewish immigrant masses no less than by upper-class Americanized audiences. He mixed with Yiddish writers and intellectuals and brought them to the notice of the English-speaking public. Magnes belonged to a circle of Zionists that included Solomon Schechter, Israel Friedlaender, and Mordecai M. Kaplan (all members of the faculty of Conservative Judaism's Jewish Theological Seminary), and Henrietta Szold. They held that Zionism had a dual purpose: to serve as a bulwark against assimilation and as a force for group survival wherever Jews lived and to support Zionist settlement in Palestine for Jews needing or wishing to make their home there. They believed the national home would become the center of a Jewish cultural renaissance for the benefit of world Jewry.

Magnes's alarm over the assimilatory trends among Americanized Jews and the social disarray among New York's Jewish immigrants led him to advocate a comprehensive communal organization of New York Jews. In 1909 the New York Kehillah (Jewish community) was established to coordinate and improve Jewish educational, philanthropic, religious, and social welfare services. Magnes was elected chair and headed the Kehillah until its demise in 1922. Through professional bureaus, the Kehillah was active in the areas of religious education, labor arbitration, and crime prevention. Magnes attracted a talented group of professional educators, social workers, and lay leaders and brought together acculturated "uptown" German Jews and "downtown" Jewish immigrants. He presented the Kehillah as a model for ethnic organization and formulated the notion of America as a "Republic of Nationalities," the title of a sermon he delivered in 1909 in which he anticipated Horace Kallen's better-known 1915 pronouncement on ethnic pluralism. Too ambitious in scope for the resources at hand and addressing a culturally, ideologically, and socially fragmented Jewish population, the Kehillah began its precipitous decline in 1917. Magnes's position was also severely compromised by his outspoken pacifism when the United States entered the war, his civil libertarian advocacy, and his pro-Soviet position. He won the admiration of American liberals and radicals, including Roger Baldwin, Morris Hillquit, Scott Nearing, Norman Thomas, and Oswald Garrison Villard, with whom he collaborated.

The failure of the Kehillah and Magnes's pacifism estranged him from the Jewish community. He looked for solace in an extended stay in Jerusalem, which he had visited alone in 1907 and with his wife in 1912. However, soon after his arrival he was co-opted to the planning committee of the Hebrew University, a Zionist-sponsored project to establish a university in Jerusalem that he had long supported. His ties with his American philanthropist friends, especially with banker Felix Warburg, enabled the university to begin operations in 1925. In no small measure Magnes's American connections led to his election as chancellor (1925–1935). Beginning with three research institutes in the sciences and Jewish studies, the university grew steadily under Magnes's guidance. Its scientists, in addition to basic research, applied their skills to the practical needs of the country and the region. Magnes also believed that the institutes of Jewish and Islamic studies would create a bridge of goodwill between East and West. After ten years as spokesman, academic planner, and money-raiser, he was elected to the honorary position of president (1935–1948). During his long tenure, he maintained close ties with the American scene through fundraising trips and by hosting important American guests in his office atop the library building, with its biblical view of Jerusalem and the Judean Desert.

Magnes reentered the political arena following the 1929 Arab anti-Jewish riots in Palestine. He had long viewed an accommodation with the Arabs as essential for building the homeland. The Zionists, he insisted, should forgo their goals of a Jewish state and a Jewish majority in exchange for guarantees for continued Jewish immigration and land settlement. The large increase in immigration in the 1930s, mostly refugees from Nazi Germany, sparked an armed Arab revolt. Magnes intensified his efforts to mediate between Arab and Zionist leaders, winning no concessions from the former and alienating the latter. In 1942, when the Zionist movement committed itself to establishing a Jewish commonwealth at the conclusion of the war, Magnes viewed the policy as leading to a war between Arabs and Jews. He organized a political party in Palestine, the Ihud (Unity) Association for Jewish-Arab Rapprochement, to promote his binational formula that called for political parity between Arabs and Jews and allowed for Jewish immigration until numerical parity with the Arabs was achieved. The association remained small, and Magnes became increasingly estranged from the Zionist establishment.

Magnes died in New York City while on a political mission. He arrived in April 1948, invited unofficially by the State Department to win Jewish support for a United States–supported, United Nations–imposed truce in the Arab-Jewish fighting that had erupted in January 1948 as British forces withdrew from Palestine in accordance with the UN decision to partition Palestine into Arab and Jewish states. In an interview with President Harry Truman in early May, Magnes urged the imposition of an economic blockade on both sides to end the fighting and pressed for American support of a temporary UN trusteeship. Zionists considered his actions traitorous. Following Israel's proclamation as an independent state on 15 May, Magnes spent the remaining months of his life lobbying for a confederation of sovereign Arab and Jewish states and calling on the Israeli government to repatriate Arab refugees.

Magnes is best remembered as founder of the New York Kehillah and the Hebrew University in Jerusalem. The Kehillah experiment underscored the limits of ethnic community but also served as a benchmark in the continuing efforts to forge a viable American Jewish communal order to assure Jewish group continuity. Magnes's stewardship of the university was characterized by his insistence that university policy be shielded from political considerations and that academic freedom be protected. Notable were his efforts to absorb German refugee professors in the 1930s. In politics, Magnes played the maverick. His pacifism in America and his nonconformist search for a political accommodation with the Arabs in Palestine antagonized the Jewish communal and Zionist establishments, although few questioned his integrity and ethical motives.

Magnes was buried in New York, and his remains were reinterred in Jerusalem in 1955. The Hebrew University established a chair in biblical studies in his name and also named the university press in his honor. In 1962 the Judah L. Magnes Museum was opened in Berkeley, California.

• The major collection of Magnes's papers is in the Central Archives for the History of the Jewish People in Jerusalem, Israel. Smaller collections are located at the Judah L. Magnes Memorial Museum, Berkeley, Calif., and the American Jewish Archives, Cincinnati, Ohio. Magnes published four collections of essays, *War-time Addresses* (1923), *Like All the Nations?* (1930), *Addresses by the Chancellor of the Hebrew University* (1936), and *In the Perplexity of the Times* (1946). With Martin Buber, Magnes edited *Arab-Jewish Unity: Testimony before the Anglo-American Committee* (1947). Norman Bentwich, *For Zion's Sake: A Biography of Judah L. Magnes* (1954), is a sympathetic biography written by a friend. *Dissenter in Zion: From the Writings of Judah L. Magnes*, edited and with an introduction by Arthur A. Goren (1982), is a collection of his journals, letters, and unpublished speeches. For various aspects of his career, see Goren, *New York Jews and the Quest for Community: The Kehillah Experiment, 1908–1922* (1970); Herbert Parzen, *The Hebrew University, 1925–1935* (1974); and William M. Brinner and Moses Rischin, eds., *Like All the Nations? The Life and Legacy of Judah L. Magnes* (1987).

ARTHUR A. GOREN

MAGNIN, Edgar Fogel (1 July 1890–17 July 1984), rabbi and communal leader, was born Edgar Isaac Magnin in San Francisco, California, the son of Samuel Magnin, who managed one of the family's stores, and Lillian Fogel. His paternal grandfather was Isaac Magnin, whose name eventually became the moniker of I. Magnin, a large department store chain. Magnin's parents divorced when he was a small child, and he was raised in the home of his maternal grandfather, George Fogel, who owned a small clothing store. Although totally estranged from his father after the divorce, young Magnin maintained relationships with his paternal grandparents and cousins. Magnin subsequently adopted Fogel as his middle name (dropping Isaac) in tribute to his mother's side of his family. Reflecting back on family influences, Magnin liked to attribute his practical abilities to the Magnins and his human skills to the Fogels.

Magnin attended John Swett Elementary School and Lowell High School in San Francisco. Although he often maintained that he could not recall why he decided to study for the rabbinate, his career aspirations were undoubtedly affected by the pervasive Jewish atmosphere of George Fogel's home as well as the traditional religious training that Magnin received from Rabbi Meyer S. Levy at Congregation Beth Israel. In 1907 Magnin went to Cincinnati to study for the rabbinate at the Hebrew Union College (HUC). He later recalled being deeply impressed during his student years by the distinguished Rabbi Emil G. Hirsch of Chicago. Hirsch, a prominent communal leader and social activist, captivated Magnin with his brilliance, clarity of expression, and seriousness of purpose. "That's the kind of man I'd like to be," Magnin concluded.

Magnin received his baccalaureate degree from the University of Cincinnati in 1913 and, upon receiving his rabbinic ordination in 1914, returned to his native state to become the rabbi of Temple Israel in Stockton, California. The fundamental character of his rabbinate took shape during his tenure in Stockton. Convinced that "the common people build up a temple," Magnin established warm and personal relationships with the members of his congregation. He succeeded in bringing people into the temple and to Judaism by means of his tremendous personal magnetism. In an effort to build good relations between the Jews and non-Jews of Stockton, Magnin began to write articles for the local newspaper and to conduct a children's story hour at the public library. He devoted himself to the task of providing an array of social and community services for adults and children in the region. Magnin's forceful, direct, and folksy style of oratory attracted a large and regular attendance at worship services and educational lectures.

Word of the young rabbi's success came to the attention of the members of the B'nai B'rith Temple (after 1929, Wilshire Boulevard Temple) in Los Angeles, and in 1915 Magnin accepted the congregation's invitation to become Rabbi Sigmund Hecht's associate. The following year he married Evelyn Rosenthal, with whom he would have two children, a son and daughter. When Hecht retired in 1919, Magnin became the congregation's rabbi and remained in that pulpit for six-and-a-half decades until his death. Magnin's long tenure at the Wilshire Boulevard Temple coincided with the dramatic transformation of Los Angeles from a small city to the second largest population center in North America. His congregation, made up of barely four hundred families when he arrived, eventually grew to become one of the country's largest Reform synagogues, its roster comprising more than twenty-seven hundred families. With financial support from Hollywood moguls such as Irving G. Thalberg, Louis B. Mayer, and the Warner brothers, Magnin oversaw construction of the congregation's enormous facility in the Wilshire district of Los Angeles.

As the Jewish community of Los Angeles burgeoned, Magnin skillfully divided his time and energies between the demands of a rapidly growing congregation and the extensive program of civic activities in which he was involved. He quickly established himself as one of the city's leading rabbis by serving on the board of virtually every major Jewish communal agency in the city, including B'nai B'rith, the Jewish Welfare Board, and the Rabbinical Association. Working with the USO and under the auspices of the National Conference of Christians and Jews, Magnin traveled to combat zones during World War II as a representative of the Jewish Welfare Board. After the war he served as the first president of the College of Jewish Studies in Los Angeles, a school that later became the Hebrew Union College–Jewish Institute of Religion's Rhea Hirsch School of Education. From 1934 to 1955 he lectured on Judaism at the University of Southern California. Magnin played an active leadership role as well in numerous civic organizations, such as the Hollywood Bowl, the Los Angeles World Affairs Council, the local chapter of the Red Cross, and Cedars of Lebanon Hospital. He was also a founder of the National Council on Alcoholism. Thousands read his weekly newspaper columns in the *Los Angeles Herald Examiner* and the Wilshire Boulevard Temple *Bulletin* and listened to his radio broadcasts, which, especially during the turbulent years preceding World War II, promoted religious tolerance. By the late 1950s Magnin had become a ubiquitous presence in Los Angeles and one of the most prominent Jewish spokesmen in the region.

Magnin's fundamental religious values—the Ten Commandments, honesty, and decency—were emblematic of the religious liberalism that typified Reform Jewish thought during the early decades of the twentieth century. He repeatedly defined himself as a "*Jew*-manist," a humanist with Jewish roots. "Judaism is basically a simple religion," Magnin wrote in the Temple's *Bulletin*, "consisting mostly of observing humanitarian and moral commandments." By means of his colorful, outspoken rhetoric, he tried to make Jewish worship services more interesting to his congregants. He wanted them to leave the temple "not only feeling glad to be alive but to be Jews and human beings." His book, *How to Live a Richer and Fuller Life* (1951), typified the practical idealism that was characteristic of the popular psychological writings of that era. A compendium of Magnin's columns was published posthumously under the title *365 Vitamins for the Mind* (1984).

Dismissing the notion of retirement, Magnin remained active into his nineties when, as the legendary patriarch of Los Angeles Jewry, he received numerous awards and honorary doctorates. He was criticized during the 1970s for emphasizing public relations at the expense of the more salient concerns of American Jewry: the oppression of Soviet Jewry, the upsurge in the rate of intermarriage, and the need to press the lessons of the Holocaust. Magnin shrugged off the disapproval by insisting that "people around me know how I feel, and they know I always try to do the right thing" (Wixen, p. 56). Magnin's boundless energy and earthy charm had made him the preeminent Jewish leader in Los Angeles. After his death in Beverly Hills, loved by generations of congregants and venerated by the city's communal leaders, Magnin was hailed as "California's outstanding Jew" (Marcus, p. 298).

• Magnin's papers, including his scrapbooks, are in the Jacob Rader Marcus Center, the American Jewish Archives, Cincinnati, Ohio. Additional material can be found in the Judah L. Magnes Museum, Berkeley, California. For a transcription of Magnin's oral memoirs, see Malca Chall, *Rabbi

Edgar Fogel Magnin: Leader and Personality (1975). Helpful biographical sources include Dianne W. Morris, "Wilshire Boulevard Temple and the Golden Age of Hollywood" (M.A. thesis, UCLA, 1996). On Magnin's years in Stockton, see William M. Kramer and Reva Clar, "Rabbi Edgar F. Magnin in Stockton (1914–1915): Rehearsal for Los Angeles," *Western States Jewish History* 17 (1985): 99–121. See also Deborah Dash Moore, *To the Golden Cities: Pursuing the American Jewish Dream in Miami and L.A.* (1994), and Max Vorspan and Lloyd P. Gartner, *History of the Jews of Los Angeles* (1970). On Magnin's Hollywood associations, see Neal Gabler, *An Empire of Their Own: How the Jews Invented Hollywood* (1988). For additional biographical information, see Joan S. Wixen, "65 Years in the Pulpit," *Modern Maturity*, Dec. 1980–Jan. 1981, pp. 55–57; John Dart, "Rabbi Magnin Nears 90, Goes Like 60," *Los Angeles Times*, 28 May 1980; and "Rabbi Edgar F. Magnin: True Jewish Legend in His Time," *B'nai B'rith Messenger*, 23 May 1980. See also Jacob Rader Marcus, "Edgar Fogel Magnin," *CCAR Yearbook* 95 (1985): 298–99. A lengthy obituary is in the *Los Angeles Times*, 18 July 1984.

GARY P. ZOLA

MAGNUSON, Warren Grant (12 Apr. 1905–20 May 1989), U.S. senator, was born in Moorhead, Minnesota. Nothing is known about his biological parents. Orphaned in infancy, he was adopted by William G. Magnuson, a Moorhead banker, and Emma Anderson. Warren Magnuson was raised in Minnesota and North Dakota, working in Young Men's Christian Association (YMCA) camps and on wheat farms. After briefly attending the University of North Dakota and North Dakota State College, Magnuson traveled by boxcar to Seattle in the early 1920s. He labored at several jobs to earn tuition for the University of Washington, where he obtained a B.A. in 1926 and a law degree in 1929. He practiced law in Seattle and worked in the King County prosecuting attorney's office; in 1933 he became an assistant U.S. district attorney.

Magnuson's nearly half-century in political office began during the Democratic landslide of 1932, when Seattle voters elected him to the previously Republican-dominated Washington State House of Representatives. The young legislator was reportedly moved by unemployed and homeless persons who set up a tent city near the capitol building in Olympia, and he helped secure passage of early unemployment compensation and old age pension laws. In 1934 Magnuson was elected prosecuting attorney for King County, which encompasses Seattle. However, legislating was of greater interest than prosecuting, and two years later the suicide of a Seattle congressman propelled Magnuson to run for his seat. Successful, he served eight years in the U.S. House of Representatives (1937–1944). A naval reserve officer, he spent eight months on active duty during World War II.

In 1944 Magnuson was elected decisively to the U.S. Senate, replacing his mentor, Senator Homer T. Bone, recently appointed a federal judge. A gubernatorial appointment shortly after the election gave Magnuson advantageous seniority over other newly elected senators. Although his first senatorial campaign focused on foreign policy, he built a powerful political base in his home state that embraced labor, shipping and agricultural interests, and public power advocates. He was reelected five times, occasionally defeating prominent Republicans including three-term governor Arthur B. Langlie. Magnuson's Senate seniority allowed him to serve on influential committees, chair those on commerce (1955–1979) and appropriations (1977–1981), and gain commensurate power. He held the largely honorary position of Senate president pro tempore during his final two years.

Entering Congress during the heyday of Franklin D. Roosevelt, Magnuson was a loyal supporter of New Deal programs, which set the direction he followed throughout his life. As a young representative, Magnuson helped create the National Cancer Research Institute (1937), and he continued to exercise leadership in matters concerning public health, sometimes spurred on by wartime exigencies. In 1948 he cosponsored the bill creating the National Institute of Health, which gave the federal government a central role promoting health care and medical research. A later Magnuson effort established the National Science Foundation. After his appointment to the Appropriations Committee, he used his increasing power to help fund additional institutes, research divisions, and grant programs and to create a network of advocates and health professionals that helped bring about Medicare and Medicaid. When Republican administrations sought to decrease funds for health care, highlighted by plans to close public health hospitals, Magnuson's influence and these lobbyists posed an effective counter. In 1974 Magnuson coauthored *How Much for Health?*, which outlined current health issues and advocated expanding programs on fire control, food safety, and product manufacture.

Magnuson's narrowest election victory occurred in 1962, when a young, little-known challenger exploited the senator's age and pork barrel politics. Disenchantment following the Cuban missile crisis and the threat of nuclear war also aroused strong conservative sentiments, especially in eastern Washington. Likely chastened by this near defeat, Magnuson spearheaded reforms on consumer-related issues from his Commerce Committee post. In 1968 he coauthored *The Dark Side of the Market Place*, which sought to increase consumer awareness of issues, such as health, safety, and public welfare. Subcommittee hearings prompted legislation on package labeling, advertising, generic drugs, poison prevention, cigarette labeling and advertising, automobile safety, product warranties, and—in a highly publicized campaign—the use of flammable fabrics for children's sleepwear. He helped create the Consumer Products Safety Commission in 1972 and an agency to assist citizens in hearings before federal agencies and courts. Partially because of White House strategies that operated through the Commerce Committee, Magnuson played an influential role in passage of the Civil Rights Act of 1964.

Magnuson concentrated more on domestic and social issues than on foreign affairs, a field favored by his junior colleague from Washington, Henry M. Jackson. Yet, as the senior senator from a Pacific Coast state and one who had visited China during his youth and served in the Pacific theater during World War II, Magnuson was well versed in matters relating to the Pacific Rim. He dealt with maritime and fisheries issues, fostered programs to aid Alaska, worked to promote transpacific trade, and early on favored recognition of the People's Republic of China. Although not an early opponent of American ventures in Southeast Asia, by the late 1960s he was urging a halt to the bombing of North Vietnam and favoring a negotiated settlement of the conflict.

Less a national figure than Jackson, Magnuson was equally well regarded throughout his home state for attending to local and regional needs, and he frequently acted in harmony with Republicans in the state and in the congressional delegation. As chairman of the Appropriations Committee, he held reins on federal spending, but he was not hesitant to assist Washington State industries, including Boeing, major shipyards, and agriculture. He secured funds for highway construction, dams and hydroelectric power projects, military bases, replacement of several Puget Sound bridges, and world's fairs held in Seattle (1962) and Spokane (1974). He developed concerns for environmental issues, such as oil pollution on Puget Sound, and he secured almost $100 million to alleviate the effects of the 1980 eruption of Mount St. Helens. Senatorial punsters noted that his middle name was "Grant," and Vice President Walter Mondale allegedly quipped that the Appropriations chair scrupulously divided federal funds 50-50, "half for Washington State and half for the rest of the country." The local perception that "Maggie" took care of his own ensured reelection support from powerful interests and large majorities of Washington voters.

In the 1980 Ronald Reagan landslide, Magnuson lost to Washington attorney general Slade Gorton. The age and health of the 75-year-old incumbent were whispered factors among such outward economic issues as inflation and declines in traditional Northwest industries.

The senator was a convivial man of the people who nevertheless allowed others the spotlight. Powerful behind the scenes, he was adept at wheeling and dealing with congressional colleagues while quietly slipping favored items into larger bills. He was not an outstanding orator, but his deep, gravelly voice conveyed a sense of abiding earnestness and sincerity. He surrounded himself with bright and devoted staffers, many of whom regarded him as their mentor as they went on to hold influential positions at national and state levels. He died at his Seattle home.

A 1928 marriage to Eleanor Peggine Maddieux ended in divorce in 1935. For many years Magnuson played the role of an eligible bachelor, often linked with movie starlets. In 1964 he married Jermaine Peralta, with his former Senate colleague, President Lyndon Johnson, serving as best man. Magnuson had no children; he had one step-child, Jermaine's daughter.

• The Warren G. Magnuson Papers are in the Manuscripts and Archives Division, University of Washington Libraries, Seattle. Magnuson figures prominently in Eric Redman, *The Dance of Legislation* (1973), an account of the creation of the National Health Service Corps by a one-time staff member (see especially pp. 189–209). An obituary is in the *Seattle Times/Seattle Post-Intelligencer*, 21 May 1989.

CHARLES P. LEWARNE

MAGOFFIN, Beriah (18 Apr. 1815–28 Feb. 1885), governor of Kentucky, was born in Harrodsburg, Kentucky, the son of Beriah Magoffin and Jane McAfee, farmers. After graduating from Centre College in 1835, Magoffin completed the law program at Transylvania College in 1838. He began to practice law in Jackson, Mississippi, but became ill and returned to Kentucky, where he opened a successful practice in Harrodsburg. On 21 April 1840 he married Anna Nelson Shelby; ten of their children survived infancy. Although a strong Democrat, Magoffin was appointed as Harrodsburg police judge in 1840 by a Whig governor. He was a delegate to several Democratic National Conventions and was elected to the state senate in 1850. After declining a nomination for Congress in 1851, he ran for lieutenant governor in 1855 but lost to a Know Nothing candidate. A presidential elector in 1856, he was elected governor in 1859, 76,187 to 67,283, over his Whig opponent, Joshua Bell.

Magoffin's administration was dominated by the secession crisis and the Civil War. Prosouthern in his sentiments, he accepted slavery and the right of a state to secede, but he believed that if the slave states presented collective demands the North would have to accept them. In a circular letter of 9 December 1860 to the slave state governors, he suggested calling a conference that would insist on strict enforcement of the Fugitive Slave Act, a division of the territories between slave and free at the thirty-seventh parallel, and a constitutional provision that would allow the South to protect its interests, perhaps by requiring a two-thirds Senate majority to pass legislation pertaining to slavery. If this proposal failed, Magoffin believed that Kentucky would join the other slave states in leaving the Union.

In response to a secessionist appeal from the Alabama governor, Magoffin replied on 28 December 1860 that "the mode and manner of defense and redress should be determined in a full and free conference of all the Southern States, and that their mutual safety requires full co-operation in carrying out the measures there agreed upon." This cooperative movement was to be completed before Abraham Lincoln's inauguration in March 1861.

In a special legislative session that he called for 17 January 1861, Magoffin admitted that he had not been able to arrange a conference of the slave states. While he recommended Kentucky's participation in a border states convention scheduled for Baltimore in February and endorsed the compromise proposals of John J. Crittenden, the governor asked for a state convention to determine Kentucky's course of action. Such a sovereignty convention was required for secession, and Unionists, by refusing to convene it, blocked any attempt by Magoffin to take Kentucky out of the Union. When the war started at Fort Sumter, Magoffin rejected Lincoln's call for troops, and in his 7 May message to a special legislative session he blamed the Republicans for starting the war. He also refused a request from Confederate president Jefferson Davis (1808–1889) for troops. The legislators again denied the governor's request for a state convention, and they established a six-man commission, on which Magoffin served, to determine policy for the state. With opinion sharply divided, the immediate solution was to declare neutrality, which Magoffin proclaimed on 20 May 1861. No other state tried such a policy, and it was actually no more legal than was secession. Both Union and Confederate recruiters violated the state's neutrality, and a pro-Union Home Guard was formed to counter the State Guard that was largely pro-Confederate.

Legislative elections on 5 August gave Unionists a better than two-thirds majority in both houses, and thereafter the governor's vetoes of measures that he believed favored the Union were swiftly overridden. "My functions are purely executive," he declared, "and I am bound by my oath of office to carry out the lawful will of the people, whether the policy they prefer accords with my own views or not." Magoffin was careful to execute laws of which he disapproved after they had been passed over his veto, but the Unionists did not trust him. After neutrality ended in September 1861, when Confederate forces entered the western part of the state, he was pressured to resign. Even his condemnation of the Confederate government of Kentucky that was organized at Russellville in November 1861 and admitted into the Confederate States of America on 10 December 1861 did not reassure his opponents. That government did not represent the wishes of a majority of the people of the state, and he would not recognize it. Shorn of most of his powers, Magoffin complained in July 1862, "I am without a soldier or a dollar to protect the lives, property, and liberties of the people." He complained that military officers, such as Brigadier General Jeremiah T. Boyle, were violating the civil rights of Kentuckians by making arbitrary arrests of suspected Confederate sympathizers, interfering with elections, and curbing freedom of speech and press.

His position became increasingly untenable, and on 16 August 1862 Magoffin indicated a willingness to resign if, despite being a Unionist, his successor was a "conservative, just man." The office of lieutenant governor was vacant, and the Speaker of the senate, who was next in line of succession, was more radical in his views than the governor would accept. In an arranged sequence of events, the Speaker resigned, and James F. Robinson, who had Magoffin's approval, was elected Speaker. Magoffin resigned on 18 August 1862, Robinson became governor, and the previous Speaker of the senate was reelected to that position.

Magoffin retired quietly to his Mercer County farm and his lucrative legal practice, and he participated little in events during the rest of the war. In 1867 he was elected to the Kentucky House of Representatives, where he advocated acceptance of the results of the war, much to the dismay of many fellow Democrats. He favored extension of civil rights to blacks and ratification of the Thirteenth Amendment to the federal constitution, which the legislature had rejected. He did not seek reelection. Magoffin made shrewd land investments in the Chicago area, and when he died on his beloved farm he was one of Kentucky's wealthiest citizens. By the time of his death, much of the wartime animosity had dissipated, and Magoffin was recognized as a man of principle who had tried to fulfill the duties and responsibilities of the governorship, even when he disagreed with the prevailing opinion in the state.

• Magoffin's state papers are in the Kentucky State Archives, Frankfort. A number of his messages and official letters are in the Kentucky Senate and House *Journals* (1859–1862) and *The War of the Rebellion: A Compilation of the Official Records of the Union and Confederate Armies* (128 vols., 1880–1901). E. Merton Coulter, *The Civil War and Readjustment in Kentucky* (1926), contains a detailed account of his wartime problems. Michael T. Dues, "The Pro-Secessionist Governor of Kentucky: Beriah Magoffin's Credibility Gap," *Register of the Kentucky Historical Society* 67 (1969): 221–31, and Lowell H. Harrison, "Governor Magoffin and the Secession Crisis," *Register of the Kentucky Historical Society* 72 (1974): 91–110, are more recent articles. Harrison, ed., *Kentucky's Governors* (1985), has a sketch of his career. An obituary is in the Louisville *Courier-Journal*, 1 Mar. 1885.

LOWELL H. HARRISON

MAGONIGLE, Harold Van Buren (17 Oct. 1867–29 Aug. 1935), architect and critic, was born in Bergen Heights, New Jersey, the son of John Henry Magonigle, the business manager for actor Edwin Booth, and Katherine Celestine Devlin. Magonigle attended public school until the age of thirteen, when, because of financial troubles, his father apprenticed him as a student draftsman to the firm of Vaux & Radford. For almost twenty years he worked as a draftsman in various architectural offices, including Charles C. Haight (1882–1887), Rotch & Tilden (1893), and McKim, Mead & White (1887–1892 and 1896–1897). Magonigle won the Rotch Travelling Scholarship in 1894, which afforded him two years of study in Europe. In 1897 he entered into partnership with the architect Evarts Tracy; from 1899 to 1901 he was the head designer and draftsman for Schickel & Ditmars; and from 1901 to 1904 he practiced with the architect Henry W. Wilkinson. He opened his own office in New York in 1904. He married the painter and designer Edith Marion Day in 1900; they had no children.

Magonigle's first major commission was the memorial tomb for President William McKinley. In 1904 he won the two-year, two-stage open competition for the McKinley National Memorial against dozens of other architects, including some of the leading firms in

America. His monument, erected in McKinley's home town of Canton, Ohio, is a cylindrical, domed, granite mausoleum, which stands on a conical terraced hill ascended by a grand flight of stairs. The landscape plan combines a sword and a cross, symbolizing the union of military strength and Christian piety in the person of McKinley. Inside, a massive double sarcophagus containing the bodies of the president and his wife rises overhead. The tomb recalls a multitude of sources, from the fifth-century tomb of Theodoric in Italy to the 1897 Grant monument in New York, among others. Magonigle successfully united and transformed these images into an entirely new synthesis, suited for the leader of an emerging international power.

The McKinley monument was the first in a long series of memorial designs for which Magonigle became celebrated. In 1910 he won the competition for the Robert Fulton Memorial Watergate in New York City with an immense classical colonnade that was to house Fulton's tomb, a museum, and reception rooms; the monument, however, was never built. Magonigle designed the National Maine Monument in 1911, a classical pylon on Central Park South carrying inscriptions and surrounded by allegorical bronze sculptures by Attilio Piccirilli. His winning entry in the competition for the Liberty Memorial, a national World War I monument in Kansas City, Missouri (1921), abstracts the classical column: its 217-foot-high limestone-clad shaft is composed of projecting vertical members, some of which terminate in allegorical figures. For this memorial Magonigle also designed the landscape and two statues of shrouded sphinxes, representing *Memory* and the *Future*; the large sculptural frieze on the podium is by Edward Amateis. Among Magonigle's many other memorials are the Mason Monument in Detroit, Michigan (1907), the Firemen's Memorial in New York City (1911), and the Burritt Memorial in New Britain, Connecticut (1911). He entered, but did not win, the competitions for the Perry Victory and International Peace Memorial in Ohio (1911–1912) and the New York State Theodore Roosevelt Memorial (1926).

Magonigle designed a wide range of other buildings during his long career. He created "Victory Way," the extensive street decorations for New York City's 1918 Victory Loan Drive. He was the architect of Mrs. Dow's School in Briarcliff Manor, New York (1904) and the Arsenal Technical Schools in Indianapolis, Indiana (1919), as well as estates for former governor Franklin Murphy in Mendham, New Jersey (1908–1915) and Isaac Guggenheim in Port Washington, New York (1916). With Robert W. McLaughlin, he designed the First Plymouth Congregational Church, in Lincoln, Nebraska (1929) and, with Antonin Raymond, the U.S. embassy complex in Tokyo, Japan (1929).

Magonigle was an influential member of many professional associations, including the American Institute of Architects, becoming a fellow of the AIA in 1907 and designing its seal and the cover and title page of its *Journal*. Magonigle received many honors, win-

ning the Gold Medal of the Architectural League of New York in 1889 and the Medal of Honor of the New York chapter of the AIA in 1930.

A prolific designer, Magonigle embodied the beaux-arts ideal of a union of the arts: he was a sculptor, painter, and landscape architect; a designer of inscriptions, typography, and book and magazine covers; and a writer, who staunchly defended historicist architecture in numerous books and articles. In the 1930s he wrote two columns in *Pencil Points*, "A Half Century of American Architecture" and "'The Upper Ground': Being Essays in Criticism." His writings emphasized the value of competitions, the need to uphold professional standards in architectural practice, and the importance of keeping architecture a creative art founded on a broad knowledge of historical design. He derided modernism's disavowal of history and its belief that architecture resulted primarily from a simplistic manipulation of materials and construction. He wrote: "I respect and admire progressive design which neither rejects structural and aesthetic standards, nor stupidly plagiarizes the work of the living or the dead. I like very few modernistic designs because most of them do both" (*Pencil Points*, Sept. 1935). After his death, the view of architecture as a process of continual, gradual adaptation for which he was a leading spokesman was almost wholly supplanted by modernist doctrine. Magonigle died in Vergennes, Vermont.

• The Magonigle Collection in the Avery Library, Columbia University, contains most of the architect's drawings, paintings, and sketchbooks, many of which have been put on video. Magonigle's other articles include "The Values of Tradition," *Pencil Points* 10 (Jan. 1929): 17–23; and "What Is an Architect?" *American Architect* 143 (July 1933): 30–32. He wrote several books, among them *Architectural Renderings in Wash* (1921) and *The Nature, Practice and History of Art* (1924); he also wrote the essay "The Renaissance," in *The Significance of the Fine Arts* (1923).

Most of Magonigle's important designs and competition entries were published in contemporary architectural periodicals. Francis S. Swales included Magonigle in his series of essays on leading *beaux-arts* practitioners: "Master Draftsmen, X: Harold Van Buren Magonigle," *Pencil Points* 6 (Mar. 1925): 46–66. Philip Langdon and Thomas Fisher, "The Debate Goes On: Nelson and Magonigle," *Progressive Architecture* 76 (Apr. 1995): 66–69, contrasts Magonigle's writings in *Pencil Points* (which later became *Progressive Architecture*) with those of his contemporary George Nelson, a supporter of modernism. Obituaries are in the *New York Times*, 30 Aug. 1935, and *Pencil Points* 16 (Oct. 1935): 521–22.

KAY FANNING

MAGOON, Charles Edward (5 Dec. 1861–14 Jan. 1920), lawyer and public servant, was born in Steele County, Minnesota, the son of Henry C. Magoon and Mehitable W. Clement. Magoon moved with his family to Platte County, Nebraska, shortly after the end of the Civil War. He studied in various programs at the University of Nebraska at Lincoln for three years in the late 1870s, leaving without a degree to study law in the firm of Mason and Whedon, which became Whedon and Magoon shortly after his admission to the bar in 1882. A respected member of the local legal community, Magoon often commented on legal issues for the *Daily Nebraska State Journal*, and he wrote a work of local significance, *The Municipal Code of Lincoln* (1889). He also joined several local service organizations and the Nebraska National Guard, in which he was a major and judge advocate.

In 1899 Magoon became law officer of the Bureau of Insular Affairs of the Department of War, advising the William McKinley administration on legal issues arising from the U.S. occupation of former Spanish colonies. The appointment resulted from the intercession of a friend, Assistant Secretary of War George D. Meiklejohn. Pleased with his work, Magoon's superiors appointed him general counsel to the Isthmian Canal Commission in 1904, a member of the commission itself in 1905, and both U.S. minister to Panama and governor of the Canal Zone from May 1905 to September 1906. He returned to the United States in September 1906 to await a new assignment.

Magoon arrived home at a propitious moment. That same month the Theodore Roosevelt administration used U.S. troops to suppress an uprising in Cuba at the request of President Tomás Estrada Palma. Within days Estrada Palma ceded authority to the Roosevelt administration, which organized a provisional government to secure public order and prepare for credible elections. Recognizing the value of Magoon's experience in Panama and with the War Department, Roosevelt appointed him provisional governor of Cuba rather than sending him to the Philippines as he had originally planned. Expectations of Magoon ran very high. Each Cuban political faction looked to him for reform and protection, while the Roosevelt administration desired not only an efficient administration but a speedy end to the occupation under conditions that would make future interventions unnecessary.

Magoon served as provisional governor of Cuba from 13 October 1906 to 28 January 1909. During his tenure, he oversaw an energetic campaign against yellow fever and an unprecedented public works program intended to remedy Cuba's chronic cyclical unemployment. In order to foster U.S.–Cuban amity, he appointed many Cubans, most of them opponents of Estrada Palma, to high positions within his administration. The most important legacy of the U.S. occupation, however, was the creation of a Cuban army. Wanting to leave Cuba with the capacity to keep order without U.S. intervention, the U.S. Army trained and equipped a professional, nonpartisan army. By the 1930s this army had become a major influence in Cuban politics.

Historical assessment of Magoon's administration is mixed. Supporters emphasize his efficiency, incorruptibility, and willingness to cooperate with Cubans. His critics, however, consider him an agent of American empire whose efforts kept Cuba politically and economically subservient to U.S. political and economic interests. Certainly Magoon considered U.S. influence over Cuba beneficial and believed it was only natural that the older, more successful Republic should teach its younger neighbor the precepts of representative government—administrative efficiency, fair elections, respect for private property, and public order. That Magoon never looked beyond these shibboleths to examine the way they perpetuated Cuba's economic and political inequities is unfortunate but not surprising.

Following a peaceful presidential election, Magoon departed Cuba. Residing principally in Washington, D.C., thereafter, he apparently made no serious return to the practice of law but lapsed into the quiet life of a gentleman of means. He died in Washington from complications resulting from an operation for appendicitis. He never married.

• The vast majority of Magoon's papers were destroyed upon his death. No organized, public collection exists. Nevertheless, information regarding both Magoon and the Cuban occupation are in the Enoch Crowder Papers, Ellis Library, University of Missouri; and the Robert Lee Bullard Papers, Manuscripts Division, Library of Congress. Magoon wrote three official reports often cited by historians, *Report on the Law of Civil Government in Territory Subject to Military Occupation by the Military Forces of the United States* (1902), *Report of the Provisional Administration: From December 1st, 1907 to December 1st, 1908* (1909), and *Supplemental Report, Provisional Governor of Cuba, for the Period December 1, 1908 to January 28, 1909* (1909). He also published an address, *What Followed the Flag to the Philippines* (1904). For an informative account of Magoon's background and career see David Lockmiller, *Magoon in Cuba* (1938). Allan Millett, *The Politics of Intervention* (1968), offers a more thorough account of the intervention itself but less on Magoon. A short description of Magoon's career in Panama is in David McCullough, *The Path between the Seas* (1977). Dana Munro, *Intervention and Dollar Diplomacy in the Caribbean, 1900–1921* (1964), provides a positive assessment of Magoon and of U.S. foreign policy. More critical assessments of U.S. policy are in Louis A. Pérez, Jr., *Cuba under the Platt Amendment* (1986), and José M. Hernández, *Cuba and the United States: Intervention and Militarism* (1993).

JOSEPH J. GONZALEZ

MAGOUN, George Frederic (29 Mar. 1821–30 Jan. 1896), clergyman and college president, was born in Bath, Maine, the son of David Crooker Magoun, and Hannah Webb. His father was a merchant and bank president and served as a member of the Maine state legislature. In 1837 Magoun graduated from Bath Academy and completed a degree at Bowdoin College in 1841. He attended Yale Divinity School and received a degree in theology from the Andover Theological Seminary in 1847. In that same year, he married Abby Anne Hyde; they had nine children, five of whom died in infancy. Abby died in Lyons, Iowa, in 1864, and in 1870 Magoun married Elizabeth E. Earle in Waterbury, Connecticut. He and Elizabeth had three children.

George Magoun was ordained a Congregational minister in 1848 in Shullsburg, Wisconsin. While he lived in Shullsburg, Magoun was responsible for founding a home-mission Congregational church. For the next several years, he served as a clergyman, first as the pastor of the Second Presbyterian Church at Galena, Illinois, for three years and then as the pastor at Congregational churches in Davenport and Lyons, Iowa.

Magoun began a lifelong association with a small midwestern college in 1856 when he became a trustee of Iowa College in Davenport. The college had been founded in 1846 by a group from New England who had moved to the Midwest and who had strong social reform and Congregational church backgrounds. The school was moved to Grinnell, Iowa, in 1859. (The name of the college was changed to Grinnell College in 1909.) In 1862 George Magoun was elected president of the college. The student body and teaching faculty decreased during the Civil War as students and teachers alike served in large numbers in the Union army. Because there was little to do at the college during the war years, Magoun continued his work as a minister at the Congregational church in Lyons. When his wife died in 1864, Magoun moved to Grinnell and became a full-time college president.

In addition to his administrative duties, Magoun was active in other facets of academic life. He taught moral and mental philosophy. "Moral philosophy" would in today's colleges be labeled "philosophy of the mind" and, according to other biographers, Magoun probably taught this course with a metaphysical bent as he had a lifelong interest in metaphysics. "Mental philosophy" would today be called ethics. Magoun also wrote several articles and one book. He continued to preach and give public addresses, including a series of talks known as the Boston Lectures that he began in 1872. Magoun was also known as a tireless fundraiser for Grinnell College, a particularly important part of the duty of a college president. This part of his job was especially significant after the burning of one of the college's two buildings in 1871 and the destruction of the other building in 1872 in a cyclone.

Magoun was involved in politics and several reform causes. He was a Republican and had been active in the formation of the party in 1854. He was particularly devoted to the causes of temperance, antislavery, and, after the U.S. Civil War, world peace. From 1877 to 1879, Magoun lectured on home missions at the Andover Theological Seminary. He was a delegate to three of the Peace Congresses in Europe. In 1882 he represented Congregationalists in the Midwest at the semicentennial Congregational Union of England and Wales.

Magoun retired from the presidency of Grinnell College in 1884. He continued to teach until 1890. He died in Grinnell, Iowa. While George Magoun was not a prolific writer or a well-known American educational figure, he is considered the first president of Grinnell College by the college itself, and his work for education and social reforms, often behind the scenes, makes him typical of those who devote their lives to the progress of others, and for this Magoun should be remembered.

• A helpful collection of material on Magoun is in the archives of Grinnell College. A list of Magoun's publications and addresses can be found in Alice Marple, *Iowa Authors and Their Works* (1918). He wrote a biography of one of the religious and educational pioneers of the West titled *Asa Turner, a Home Missionary Patriarch and His Times* (1889). Biographies of Magoun can be found in such books as *Portrait and Biographical Record of Johnson, Poweshiek and Iowa Counties, Iowa* (1893) and J. B. Grinnell, *Men and Events of Forty Years* (1891). Both of these works are housed in the Special Collections Library of Grinnell College. See also John Nollen, *Grinnell College* (1953), and Joseph Wall, *Grinnell College in the 19th Century* (1997). An obituary is in the *Iowa State Register*, 31 Jan. 1896.

JUDITH BOYCE DEMARK

MAGOUN, Horace Winchell (23 June 1907–6 Mar. 1991), neuroscientist and educator, was born in Philadelphia, Pennsylvania, the son of Roy Winchell Magoun, an Episcopal clergyman, and Minnie Sheida. Nicknamed "Tid" by his baby sister, he grew up mostly in Rhode Island, where during the First World War his father founded and directed the Seaman's Church Institute. After graduating in 1929 from Rhode Island State College, Magoun did graduate work at Syracuse University, New York (M.S., 1931), and Northwestern University Medical School, from which he received a Ph.D. in anatomy in 1934. He married Jeanette Jackson in 1931; they had three children.

Magoun's graduate research at Syracuse, involving the study of embryogenesis of nerve cells controlling equilibrium in a fresh water eel, provided his initiation into the field of neuroscience. His nascent career in this field began to flourish when he joined Stephen Walter Ranson's group at the Institute of Neurology at Northwestern, where he researched postural control by structures below the brain surface of experimental animals. The Horsley-Clarke sterotoxic instrument, designed in England, was the foundation for the research at the institute. Its three-dimensional coordinates precisely position electrodes to record or stimulate small regions within the brain. Magoun's chief responsibility was to operate the apparatus and to train students, postdoctorate fellows, and visiting scientists, keeping the instrument involved in projects on the role of the hypothalamus and lower brain stem and the way it operated on all levels.

After Ranson's unexpected death, the Institute of Neurology was dismantled and Magoun moved to the Department of Anatomy. His research included, but was not limited to, collaboration with the group headed by Warren McCulloch at the Illinois Neuropsychiatric Institute. He was joined in late 1948 by Giuseppe Moruzzi from Pisa, Italy. Their studies in lightly anesthetized animals identified a brain stem reticular core, stimulation of which brought about arousal and a pattern of brain waves characteristic of the alert state. Regardless of modality of stimulation, the effect was to diffuse impulses throughout the cerebrum and along pathways in the thalamus in contrast to the classic, nondiffuse projection of the incoming sensory impulses along lateral paths to specific regions of the brain. The concept of brainstem activation was developed in Magoun's *Harvey Lectures* (ser. 47 [1952], pp. 53–71) and more fully in his *The Waking Brain* (1958; rev. ed., 1963). He observed, "These nonspecific mechanisms are distributed widely through the central core of the brainstem, and as spokes radiate from the hub of a wheel to its peripheral working rim, so functional influences of these central systems can be exerted in a number of directions. . . . Just as all spokes move together in the turning of a wheel, though they may bear weight sequentially, so the variously directed influences of these nonspecific reticular systems are closely interrelated in normal function" (p. 20).

In 1950 Magoun became founding chairman of the Department of Anatomy at the nascent School of Medicine, University of California, Los Angeles. He subsequently organized the Brain Research Institute there. During the 1950s, evidence supporting the concept of the ascending arousal system accumulated, not only from Magoun's temporary laboratories at the Long Beach Veterans Administration Hospital but also from international groups, including Moruzzi's in Pisa. As a result of this evidence, Magoun increasingly was invited to give talks and receive awards. He was elected to the National Academy of Sciences in 1955.

The 1950s also saw the organization and planning for the Brain Research Institute, which took all of Magoun's persuasive eloquence to bring to fruition in a ten-story building occupying a corner of UCLA's medical school. In *An American Contribution to Neuroscience: The Brain Research Institute, UCLA, 1958–1984* (1984), coauthored with John D. French and John B. Lindsley to celebrate the institute's twenty-fifth anniversary, Magoun described his wide participation in committees and councils of federal agencies supporting brain research and the BRI's outstanding role in interdisciplinary training at graduate and postdoctorate levels. In 1962, as a consequence of the institute's increasing preoccupation with research training, he became dean of its graduate division, a position he held until 1972. Immediately thereafter, as director of the Fellowship Office of the National Research Council in Washington, D.C., Magoun demonstrated his dedication to representation of women and minorities on panels and committees. Those endeavors echoed his earlier active recruitment of neuroscientists from abroad, especially from Japan, to the highly diversified and productive research and training programs of the Brain Research Institute. Japan acknowledged his efforts in 1971 by conferring the emperor of Japan's award of the Order of the Sacred Treasure, Second Class.

In 1958 Magoun began writing on the early development of ideas relating the mind to the brain; this was perhaps an outgrowth of his thought in *The Waking Brain*, which was later translated into Russian, Polish, Japanese, and Spanish. He continued to publish during the 1960s on the role of the brain stem reticular formation in processes such as emotion, stress, learning, and mental derangement, while also producing a steady stream of articles on graduate training and science personnel needs. Finally, in the next decade, he authored a collaborative chapter and monograph-length manuscript (unpublished) on American neuroscience, demonstrating his growing preoccupation with history and culminating in a series of posters on brain history that form the framework of a posthumous publication, *Discoveries in the Human Brain: Neuroscience Prehistory, Structure, and Function* (1998). Forty-five years after its discovery, brainstem activation of the cortical processes promises to lead to new data on several aspects of cortical information processing.

Following his brief tenure at the Fellowship Office of the National Research Council (from 1972 to 1974), he was recalled to UCLA, where he served as professor of psychiatry until 1989. He also assisted in the organization of that department's Division of Behavioral Sciences. He died in Los Angeles.

One of the great conceptualists in the research on brain structure and function, Magoun made significant and lasting contributions to knowledge of brain processes. His pioneering work on brainstem activation, modality of stimulation, and embryogenesis of nerve cells have secured him a place in American medical history.

• Magoun's papers are at the Neuroscience History Archives of the Brain Research Institute, University of California, Los Angeles. The best biographical information is given in his "The Northwestern Connection with the Reticular Formation," *Surgical Neurology* 24 (1985): 250–52, and a 1978 video recording (57 minutes) produced by the National Medical Audiovisual Center, Atlanta, Ga. An early study by Magoun is, with R. Rhines, "An Inhibitory Mechanism in the Bulbar Reticular Formation," *Journal of Neuroscience* 9 (1946): 165–71. On the observation and presentation of the ascending reticular formation, see Giuseppe Moruzzi and Magoun, *Electroencephalography and Clinical Neurophysiology* (1949), pp. 455–73. His writings on science include "Education of the Negro American in the Emancipation Century," in *Proceedings of the . . . Council of Graduate Schools in the United States* (1964); and, with E. Shooter, "Survey of Manpower for Research and Teaching in Neuroscience," *Experimental Neurology* 49 (1975): 35–59. Among his major historical publications are "Development of Concepts of Organization and Function in the Brain," in *Research Approaches to Psychiatric Problems*, ed. Tourlentes, Pollach, and Himwich (1962), pp. 1–32; and "John B. Watson and the Study of Human Sexual Behavior," *Journal of Sex Research* 17 (1981): 368–78.

LOUISE MARSHALL
MICHELLE OSBORN

MAGRUDER, Calvert (26 Dec. 1893–22 May 1968), judge and legal educator, was born in Annapolis, Md., the son of Daniel Randall Magruder, an appellate judge, and Rosalie Eugenia Stuart. Calvert Magruder graduated from St. John's College, Annapolis (A.B., 1913), and Harvard Law School (LL.B., 1916). He began his career as a law clerk in 1916–1917 to Justice Louis D. Brandeis of the U.S. Supreme Court. During that year he earned an M.A. degree from St. John's College. In 1917 he entered the U.S. Army, serving until 1919 when he received an honorable discharge with the rank of second lieutenant. In 1919–1920 he was a lawyer with the U.S. Shipping Board in Washington, D.C. Magruder married Anita Saltonstall Ward in 1925. They had three children.

Magruder was appointed assistant professor of law at Harvard Law School in 1920, professor in 1925, and vice dean in 1930, a post he held until 1939. Magruder specialized in the law of torts (civil wrongs) and partnerships. Among other works, he wrote a classic law review article in 1935 on intentional infliction of emotional distress. He was the coauthor of the *Law of Partnerships* (1923), a leading case book, and he wrote a graceful review of his judicial work, "The Trials and Tribulations of an Intermediate Appellate Court" (1958). During the 1930s Magruder also served the Roosevelt administration in various posts. In 1934–1935 he was general counsel to the National Labor Relations Board and played a principal role in drafting the Wagner Labor Relations Act. In 1938–1939 he was general counsel to the Wage and Hour Division of the Department of Labor.

In 1939 President Franklin D. Roosevelt appointed Magruder judge of the U.S. Court of Appeals for the First Circuit, which includes Maine, Massachusetts, New Hampshire, Rhode Island, and Puerto Rico. Because of rapid turnover among his colleagues, in 1940 he became chief judge, a post he held until his retirement in 1959. According to Judge Ammi Cutter of the Massachusetts Supreme Judicial Court, Magruder "gave [the court] an impulse and a new way of thinking which was very much to the benefit of the bar" (quoted in Dargo, p. 243). Magruder developed a close relationship to the Commonwealth of Puerto Rico, and beginning in 1950 his court annually heard appeals in San Juan "as an altogether proper manifestation of respect for the people of Puerto Rico and their local bar" (Dargo, p. 244).

Magruder was best known for his decisions in torts, taxation, and labor law, and he decided many cases under the newly enacted Federal Rules of Civil Procedure and Administrative Procedure Act. His opinions concerning state prisoners seeking release under habeas corpus in federal court because of alleged constitutional violations won renown for their sensitivity both to individual rights and the conflicts of authority in a federal union.

One of Magruder's earliest opinions involved two complex issues arising from the 1938 decision of the Supreme Court in *Erie R.R. Co. v. Tompkins*, which held that a federal court whose jurisdiction depended on the diversity of citizenship of plaintiff and defendant had to follow the "substantive" law of the state in which it was sitting in order to avoid applying different legal rules depending on which court system was involved. In *Sampson v. Channell* (1940), Magruder concluded that both burden of proof and conflict of laws were "substantive" issues under *Erie*; two years later the Supreme Court vindicated his position.

In an important constitutional decision, *Crown Kosher Supermarket of Mass., Inc. v. Gallagher* (1959), Magruder ruled that the Massachusetts "closing law"

that banned the conduct of business on Sunday violated the First Amendment's establishment clause because, as applied to a kosher supermarket, the Christian roots of the law meant that the state was preferring one religion over another. Although the Supreme Court reversed this decision, Justice Hugo Black said that "[t]he Magruder opinion will last . . . whatever may be the fate of the holding" of the Supreme Court.

Magruder's judicial performance was unusually nonideological. Professor Frank E. A. Sander, a former law clerk, described how "a student at Harvard Law School who was well-schooled in the labels of the day asked me 'was he a liberal or a conservative?' I have thought for a long time about this question and I guess I still don't know the answer. That, too, says a lot about Judge Magruder" (Proceedings of the presentation of the portrait of Judge Magruder at Harvard Law School, 6 May 1980; quoted on p. 8 of the booklet of the proceedings).

A feature of Magruder's opinions, almost invariably commented on by those appraising his work, was their grace and informality. Justice Felix Frankfurter described the opinions as "the colloquial talk of a cultivated man." Warren A. Seavey, a leading scholar, wrote that Magruder's "clarity of expression is as important as the striking and quotable phrases of Cardozo, the pungent brevity of Holmes, or the deeply philosophical approach of Learned Hand." Magruder himself said, "I don't know anything about syntax or grammar. It is all in the sound."

Magruder took on several special assignments during and after his period as chief judge. He served on the Emergency Court of Appeals, which Congress set up during World War II to administer the complicated wartime price control system. In 1943 he headed the American section of the Joint Bolivian–United States Labor Commission to investigate labor unrest in Bolivia that threatened the smooth production of tin that was essential to the war effort. And in January 1961, newly inaugurated President John F. Kennedy appointed Magruder chairman of a panel on conflicts of interest and ethics. The Magruder Commission's report established a set of internal guidelines for the Kennedy administration. In all his activities Magruder exercised unusually effective leadership without apparent effort. His intellectual prowess was complemented by his southern charm and a riveting presence, owing to his piercing blue eyes and elegant sartorial style.

Magruder was widely honored for his years of judicial service. According to Frankfurter, he "set a standard of intelligence, fairness, integrity and realism." Justice Brandeis praised Magruder's prowess when he wrote that "[a]mong all my law clerks Magruder was the best critic I had." Professor Milton Katz, a former student and colleague of Magruder's at Harvard Law School, said that "The sharp edge of his intelligence was sheathed in matter-of-fact simplicity; and he applied his power with a lightness of manner that cleansed it of any suggestion of roughness or violence, but in no way diminished its effect." Upon Magruder's retirement Justice William O. Douglas told him, "You have written yourself a wonderful record."

After his retirement, Magruder moved to San Francisco, where he taught torts at Hastings College of Law and occasionally sat on cases in the federal courts of appeal. Magruder died in Newton Centre, Massachusetts.

• The Magruder papers are in the library of Harvard Law School. His philosophy of judging is concisely expressed in his article, "The Trials and Tribulations of an Intermediate Appellate Court," *Cornell Law Review* 44 (Fall 1958): 1–13. See articles by Felix Frankfurter, Paul A. Freund, Ernest J. Brown, Warren A. Seavey, and Harry H. Wellington, *Harvard Law Review* 72, no. 7 (May 1959), which is dedicated to Magruder. See also George Dargo, "Calvert Magruder of the First Circuit: The Law Professor as Judge," *Massachusetts Law Review* 74 (1989): 239–46. An obituary is in the *New York Times*, 24 May 1968.

NORMAN DORSEN

MAGRUDER, John Bankhead (1 May 1807–18 Feb. 1871), Confederate soldier, was born at Port Royal, Virginia, the son of Thomas Magruder, a lawyer, and Elizabeth Bankhead. Admitted to the U.S. Military Academy at West Point in 1826, Magruder displayed a fondness for drink and came within four demerits of expulsion in his final year. He also became a cadet captain, graduating fifteenth of forty-two in the class of 1830. Assigned to the Seventh Infantry as a second lieutenant on 1 July 1830, Magruder transferred on 11 August 1831 to the First Artillery. In 1831 he married Henrietta Von Kapff; they had three children. Promoted to first lieutenant on 31 March 1836, he served in Florida against the Seminoles in 1837–1838. A solid performance in the battle of Palo Alto during the war with Mexico advanced Magruder to captain on 18 June 1846. Brevet ranks of major and lieutenant colonel, to date from 18 April and 13 September 1847, rewarded his contributions at the battles of Cerro Gordo and Chapultepec.

The last dozen antebellum years took Magruder to California, Texas, Rhode Island, and elsewhere. He served at Fort Leavenworth in 1859–1860 as commander of the post and of the Artillery School for Instruction. During this period, he also enhanced his reputation as a generous host whose flamboyant dress, polished manners, and flair for the dramatic prompted the sobriquet "Prince John." Money from his wife helped support his lifestyle; however, Henrietta Magruder moved with the children to Europe in 1850. Magruder's spendthrift ways and drinking likely contributed to his wife's decision to leave the United States.

Although not a secessionist, Magruder resigned from the U.S. Army on 20 April 1861. Commissioned a Confederate colonel on 21 May (to date from 16 Mar.), he took charge of troops defending the Virginia Peninsula. On 10 June a portion of his command won a skirmish at Big Bethel. Magruder played scarcely any role in the triumph but trumpeted it as a decisive engagement. Newspapers praised him lavishly, and he

soon ranked behind only P. G. T. Beauregard as a Confederate military idol. He was promoted to brigadier general on 17 June and to major general on 7 October 1861.

Magruder oversaw an excellent defense of the lower Peninsula against George B. McClellan's army in April 1862. He constructed earthworks, dammed streams to flood lowlands, and conducted an effective game of bluff that prompted McClellan to waste a month at Yorktown while Joseph E. Johnston shifted his Confederate army from northern Virginia to the Peninsula. Johnston, who unfairly criticized Magruder's defensive line as too long and claimed the flooded areas prohibited offensive action, assigned him the right wing of the army. Magruder reported directly to Major General Gustavus W. Smith, with whom he immediately began a pattern of bickering that culminated in his requesting reassignment. He received word on 23 May of his appointment to command the Trans-Mississippi Department. Pleased with this news, Magruder asked Secretary of War George Wythe Randolph to postpone the transfer until after the current campaign had ended, a request Randolph granted over Johnston's objection.

Given a secondary role by Johnston at the battle of Seven Pines on 31 May–1 June, Magruder found himself in the same position when Robert E. Lee opened his offensive against McClellan in the battles of Mechanicsville and Gaines' Mill on 26–27 June. In both instances, Magruder occupied McClellan's attention while other Confederates assaulted fragments of the Union army. He performed his tasks so adeptly that McClellan labeled his feints on 27 June a major Confederate attack.

The battle of Savage Station on 29 June marked a turning point. Ordered to strike McClellan's rear guard expeditiously, Magruder waited until late afternoon to mount an anemic assault. "I regret very much that you have made so little progress today in pursuit of the enemy," a disappointed Lee wrote him. Relegated to a supporting role on 30 June, Magruder exhibited marked nervousness and never got his troops into action. He told a staff officer he had been ill and had reacted badly to prescribed medicine. He also had lost "so much sleep it affects me strangely." The sad climax of Magruder's service during the Seven Days' battles came on 1 July at Malvern Hill. After another virtually sleepless night, he again reached the battlefield late. A witness observed, "The wild expression in his eyes and his excited manner impressed me at once with the belief that he was under the influence of some powerful stimulant, spirits or perhaps opium." Magruder eventually committed about one-third of his men to the disastrous Confederate attacks Lee had ordered.

Rumors that Magruder had been inebriated at Malvern Hill circulated widely. Robert H. Chilton of Lee's staff recommended the revocation of his assignment to the Trans-Mississippi, and Jefferson Davis held up the transfer until charges against Magruder were dismissed. On 10 October 1862 Magruder received orders to assume command of the District of Texas, New Mexico, and Arizona rather than the entire Trans-Mississippi theater.

Magruder served competently in the western Confederacy. Orchestrating the recapture of Galveston on 1 January 1863, he earned plaudits from Davis and Texas governor Francis Lubbock. He took command of the District of Arkansas in September 1864, returning in the spring of 1865 to Texas, where he surrendered on 2 June 1865 at Galveston.

Magruder joined a number of Confederates emigrating to Mexico in June 1865. He became a naturalized Mexican citizen and in September 1865 was appointed chief of the Land Office of Colonization in Ferdinand Maximilian's puppet government with the goal of attracting former Confederates to Mexico. Few immigrated, however, and Magruder found himself without a job in April 1866. He left Mexico in mid-November 1866, stopped briefly in Havana, and returned to the United States in early 1867. Settling in New York City, he practiced law before moving in late 1868 to New Orleans to pursue a brief career as a public lecturer. Magruder subsequently lived in Houston, Texas, where he died.

• No substantial body of Magruder's private papers has survived, but manuscripts relating to his antebellum and Confederate military service are in various collections at the National Archives. The best biographical study is Thomas Michael Settles, "The Military Career of John Bankhead Magruder" (Ph.D. diss., Texas Christian Univ., 1972). Also useful is A. L. Long, "Memoir of General John Bankhead Magruder," *Southern Historical Society Papers* 12 (Jan.–Feb. 1884): 105–10. Joseph Lancaster Brent, *Memoirs of the War between the States* (1940), and Douglas Southall Freeman, *Lee's Lieutenants: A Study in Command* (1942–1944), contain useful material on Magruder's career in Virginia during 1861 and 1862. Obituaries are in the *Galveston News* and the *New York Herald*, both 21 Feb. 1871.

GARY W. GALLAGHER

MAGRUDER, Julia (14 Sept. 1854–9 June 1907), author, was born in Charlottesville, Virginia, the daughter of Allan Bowie Magruder, a lawyer, and Sarah Gilliam. When she was three years old the family moved to Washington, D.C., where her father established a law firm. Except for a short time living in Virginia while her father served the Confederacy during the Civil War, Washington remained her home. Taught by governesses and with access to her father's bountiful library, Magruder excelled in languages and literature, often engaging in lively literary discussions with her father. Exposed to many writers and ideas, she was especially influenced by George Eliot, Ralph Waldo Emerson, and James Martineau and began early to write stories and sketches. At seventeen she won first place for the best serial story in a competition sponsored by the *Baltimore Sun*. She became well known in international society and spent much time abroad in Scotland, Italy, and France. Among her close friends were Amélie Rives (Princess Troubetzkoy) and F. Marion Crawford, both novelists.

The problems of the post–Civil War nation absorbed Magruder; she strongly opposed sectionalism and worked toward breaking down the prejudices that northerners and southerners held against each other. In 1885 her first novel, *Across the Chasm*, was published anonymously. Early in the novel she mentions these dual prejudices and of "healing an old breach," using Margaret, a strong-minded young southern woman, and Louis, a hard-working young man steeped in northern traditions, to symbolize that healing. Toward the end of the novel, in a discussion of the differences between the North and South, Margaret says to Louis, "If only we could both get rid of our prejudices! Just think what a people we might be, if we were kneaded together, each willing to assimilate what is best in the other. But I suppose that is a utopian dream." Certainly it was Magruder's dream, expressed clearly when Margaret, in agreeing to marry Louis, says, "such a Yankee and such a Rebel, as you and I! Let us set an example of letting bygones be bygones and shake hands across the bloody chasm!" This first novel caused quite a stir, and the author's identity was soon discovered. The *New York Times* (10 June 1907) said that it "soon earned the reputation of being the best of the year."

One of the early voices that spoke out against sectionalism, Magruder believed in the necessity of change and progress, championed the rights and dignity of the working man, and urged more opportunities for women. In *A Sunny Southerner* (1901), when Chiltern Hall, the protagonist's family home, is destroyed by fire, the heroine insists that it be rebuilt, not as an exact replica of the old one as the other family members would prefer, but with modern, forward-looking ideas. Several times the character Honora speaks of social evolution, calling it "the most interesting idea in life." Honora deplores the artificiality of the divisions between the classes and asserts that aristocratic ancestors signify nothing without work. Through the actions and words of her women characters, Magruder expressed her feelings about the need for equality of opportunity for women, such as when Honora rails against the "belief that domestic life and neighborhood intercourse were all that a woman should desire," and when she says, "a new woman is what I want to be for my future." In a discussion about the lack of opportunities for women, Honora refers to the pearl-diver who endures many failures trying for the perfect pearl: "The pearl-diver is happier, after all, than he who, knowing that the pearl is in the sea, is bound hand and foot, and may not even dive for it."

Magruder wrote several more novels, among them *A Magnificent Plebian* (1888), *A Realized Ideal* (1898), *A Heaven-Kissing Hill* (1899), and *The Princess Sonia* (1895), which she is said to have written in eighteen three-hour sessions. Her other works include *Miss Ayr of Virginia and Other Stories* (1896), a collection of short stories; and *Child-Sketches from George Eliot* (1895), most first published in *St. Nicholas* magazine. She expressed the hope that the sketches would interest young people in the study and appreciation of George Eliot's "magnificent works of English fiction."

During her last illness Magruder completed her final novel, *Her Husband: The Mystery of a Man*, published posthumously in 1911 after first appearing as a serial in *Ladies' Home Journal*. Shortly before her death Magruder received word that the French Academy had awarded her the Order of the Palm, a literary honor rarely given to Americans. She died in Richmond, Virginia.

• A collection of Magruder's letters is at Duke University, Durham, N.C.; a manuscript book is at the Virginia Historical Society. Biographical sources include Alice Archer Graham, "Julia Magruder, 1854–1907" (Master's thesis, George Washington Univ., 1934); Elizabeth W. P. Lomax, "Julia Magruder," in *Library of Southern Literature*, vol. 8 (1907), pp. 3321–24; and *The American Authors of the South* (1893). Obituaries are in the *New York Times* and the *Richmond Times-Dispatch*, both 10 June 1907.

BLANCHE COX CLEGG

MAGUIRE, Patrick (5 Dec. 1838–28 Nov. 1896), machine politician, was born in County Monaghan, Ireland. His parents' identities and the circumstances of his early childhood are lost in the mists of Irish rural poverty. At age seven he emigrated to Prince Edward Island, Canada, where he apprenticed in the printer's trade. He moved to Boston in 1852 in search of better opportunities and set type for several Democratic newspapers in the city through the 1850s. In 1859 he won a seat on the Democratic City Committee, which he held for the rest of his life. Membership on this committee, which controlled the party's mayoral nominations, brought him close to other upwardly mobile Irish Americans, including liquor dealer Michael Doherty, treasurer of the committee and Maguire's main political mentor.

By 1865 Maguire had left the printer's case to go into real estate. Speculation in the expanding streetcar suburbs south of Boston, including Roxbury where he ultimately made his home, brought him wealth and community prestige. He clinched his political clout in 1876 by swinging the city committee behind the mayoral nomination of Yankee Democrat Frederick O. Prince, a Harvard blue blood committed to integrating the city's Irish-American politicians with the state and national party structure through patronage and personal favors.

Prince's election established Maguire's authority as Boston's leading backroom political manager, a status he managed to retain against insurgent rivals for the next two decades. Through Prince he ingratiated himself to the Tilden wing of the national party, and in 1884 he threw his strength to presidential nominee Grover Cleveland despite Greenback candidate Ben Butler's popularity among Boston's Irish Americans. Thereafter Maguire struck up a quiet working alliance with Cleveland's Yankee supporters in the city, including the volatile Mugwump reform faction. He confirmed this alliance by consenting to Cleveland's choice of Leverett Saltonstall to be collector of the Bos-

ton Customs House, the most important federal patronage post in the city. Together Saltonstall and Maguire managed to use job distribution to maintain an uneasy balance among Irish and Yankee aspirants for party places.

In December 1884 Maguire engineered the election to city hall of Hugh O'Brien, Boston's first Irish-American mayor. With this victory Maguire's central role in the city's governance became an acknowledged fact, though he shunned elective public office for himself. The New York *Irish-American* applauded, "We can fancy our friend Maguire, leaning up against the 'Old South,' and bidding the Hub and the rest of mankind to bring on some more political worlds for him to conquer" (quoted in Boston *Republic*, 20 Dec. 1884). Maguire's power in fact depended on his calculated deference to Yankee Democrats seeking success for Cleveland's style of conservative reformism and on his own appeals to aspiring assimilationist values among Boston's growing Catholic middle class. He used the editorial columns of his weekly newspaper, the *Republic*, founded in 1882, to promote these values.

When Mayor O'Brien lost a reelection bid in 1888, owing in part to an ugly surge of anti-Catholicism among evangelical Protestant school reformers in Boston, Maguire revived the politics of Irish deference to upper-class Yankee Democratic leadership to protect his earlier gains. His choice for mayor in 1890, Harvard-educated Nathan Matthews, restored Democratic control at city hall and imposed a strong, austere business efficiency on the city's governance. When the depression of the 1890s unstrung Matthews's mayoralty, Maguire's deferential tactics met increasing resistance from ambitious Irish-Catholic ward bosses like Martin Lomasney and John F. Fitzgerald, who now challenged Maguire's citywide organization in order to promote greater Irish-American autonomy and broader access to city patronage. Maguire responded by urging the mayoral nomination in 1895 of Josiah Quincy (1859–1919), the most liberal Yankee politician of the decade.

Quincy's mayoralty (1896–1900) proved to be the last product of Maguire's twenty-year control of Boston's Irish-Catholic political machine. In the disruptive presidential campaign of 1896, Maguire—plagued by rheumatism in his body and factional splintering in his party—sacrificed his cherished friendship with Cleveland in the name of party loyalty despite his dislike for the Democratic candidate, William Jennings Bryan. Maguire died in Roxbury from a stroke three weeks after the election. He was survived by three children, his wife having died in 1893. (The date of his marriage and his wife's name are unknown.) His funeral cortege stretched over a half-mile on Boston's city streets.

The staid *Boston Evening Transcript*, journal of record for its Yankee readers, observed on the day of Maguire's funeral, "He was a man of many admirable qualities, and the danger now is that his successor, whoever he may be, will not use the same questionable power with equal moderation, honesty, and regard for the public service" (30 Nov. 1896). Maguire had imposed conservative control on the most crucial power transfer in the city's political history, a shift from Yankee to Irish-American hegemony taut with resentments over ethnic, religious, and class differences. His passing released Boston's Irish Democrats to pursue the tactics of fratricidal factionalism that marked the city's governance well into the twentieth century.

• A long interview with Maguire is in the Boston *Record*, 15 June 1895. Succeeding issues of Maguire's Boston *Republic* reflect the social and political attitudes of its owner. His career is analyzed in Geoffrey Blodgett, *The Gentle Reformers: Massachusetts Democrats in the Cleveland Era* (1966), and John T. Galvin, "Patrick J. Maguire: Boston's Last Democratic Boss," *New England Quarterly* 55 (Sept. 1982): 392–415. Maguire's obituaries, dated 29 Nov. 1896, are in all Boston papers, including the *Boston Globe*, the *Boston Evening Transcript*, the *Boston Herald*, and the *Daily Advertiser*, as well as the *New York Times*.

GEOFFREY BLODGETT

MAHAN, Alfred Thayer (27 Sept. 1840–1 Dec. 1914), naval officer and author, was born in West Point, New York, the son of Dennis Hart Mahan, a professor of military engineering and dean of faculty at the U.S. Military Academy, and Mary Helena Okill. Raised in a household run on two guiding principles, strict military obedience and a stern literalist and fundamentalist form of Episcopalianism that emphasized constant prayer, Mahan did not have a happy childhood. In his autobiography, *From Sail to Steam* (1907), he scarcely mentioned his parents or his youth.

Mahan's career at the U.S. Naval Academy, which he entered in 1856 following two years at Columbia College, was also unhappy. He had open contempt for the academy's anti-intellectual curriculum and boasted that he did not really have to study at all. Still he graduated second in his class in 1859, and while there he grew to be a tall, handsome, brilliant, enormously vain, and pompous man, self-assured to the point of arrogance. He thus made no close friends either at the academy or within the operational navy, in which he spent thirty-seven years. He was, his daughter Ellen later observed, "The Cat That Walked by Himself." Further, Mahan was prone to seasickness, was deathly afraid of the sea, and hated sea duty so much that he sought assiduously to avoid it whenever confronted by it. He also suffered various mishaps to ships he later commanded.

Mahan served ingloriously throughout the Civil War on blockade duty and obscurely in the antiquated vessels and boring shore stations of the small postwar wooden navy. In 1872 he married Ellen Lyle Evans; they had three children. By 1872 he had reached the rank of commander, and in 1885 he was promoted to captain.

At no time during the 1880s, however, did Mahan participate publicly in the debate in the navy, the press, and the Congress that centered on the building of a "New Navy" of modern steel ships to protect the nation's presumed need for the expansion of its foreign

trade and the protection of its naked coasts. Nonetheless, in 1883, while serving in the Brooklyn Navy Yard, he was asked by the Charles Scribner's Sons publishing house in New York to produce a book for their new series, *The Navy in the Civil War*, suggesting only that it be completed as quickly as possible. Working at fever pitch at night and on weekends, Mahan completed the task in just under five months, and *The Gulf and Inland Waters* appeared in June 1883. While it contained no hint of the sea power hypothesis that would make him famous, it did demonstrate that Captain Mahan could write passable historical prose. Most important, in 1884 the book caught the eye of Captain Stephen B. Luce, founder and president of the new U.S. Naval War College in Newport, Rhode Island. Luce secured Mahan's appointment to the college to write and teach naval history, which Mahan did and did well. In 1890 he published his class lecture notes under the title *The Influence of Sea Power upon History, 1660–1783*. The book electrified foreign offices and war departments all over the world. A sequel was published in two volumes, *The Influence of Sea Power upon the French Revolution and Empire, 1793–1812* (1892).

In the first *Influence* book, Mahan argued that great navies and related merchant marines were the primary factors enabling Spain, Holland, England, and France to win wars that permitted them to seize overseas colonies, close them to their enemies, and exploit their natural resources and populations. Both *Influence* books appeared at the time when the great European powers were busily carving up Africa and, together with Japan, were contemplating a similar fate for China and East Asia. In the United States they were read by nationalists and expansionists in and out of Congress, men like Theodore Roosevelt, Henry Cabot Lodge, and John Hay, who were beginning to argue that the nation was at an economic and political disadvantage internationally unless it abandoned the isolationist foreign policy of its post–Civil War years. For this and other reasons they sought to increase the export of the nation's overly abundant production of agricultural and manufactured goods into overseas markets, especially those in East Asia. It was an anticipated expansion that would also require the protective shield of a respectable modern steam and steel navy and an improvement of diplomatic relations with Great Britain.

Americans embracing such dreams, unrealistic as they turned out to be, thought they had found in Mahan and his books a prophet who could show them the way to the international respectability due a great economic, military, and imperial power. They misread him. In the introductory chapter of his first *Influence* book, Mahan treated the United States only briefly and peripherally. He did not call for colonies, or for a policy of massive exports abroad, or a great navy to shepherd a growing merchant marine to service those markets. True, he was an exponent of free trade, but by free trade he meant trade not subsidized by the government or its gunboats.

However, he did advocate in 1890 a navy large enough, and related coaling stations available and commodious enough, to establish, patrol, protect, and maintain two discreet defensive perimeters that would make militarily secure to Americans their Gulf and Caribbean coasts and their sparsely populated West Coast. He was certain that a canal would soon pierce Central America and would attract the world's naval and merchant shipping like a giant magnet. He was therefore convinced that the United States must eventually own or control and be able militarily to defend such a canal. A defensive perimeter in the eastern Pacific, he argued, would prohibit any foreign state, especially Japan, from establishing "a coaling station within three thousand miles of San Francisco—a distance which includes the Hawaiian and Galapagos islands and the coast of Central America."

Mahan, in sum, was thinking in defensive terms. Since a canal through Central America that was not controlled by the United States would nonetheless still hurl the nation into the vortex of European international power politics and treaty alignments, he joined those Americans who advocated building a modern navy (size negotiable), the acquisition of a Panama or Nicaragua canal, and the annexation of Hawaii.

The Hawaiian matter persuaded the isolationist second Grover Cleveland administration to order Mahan to sea in May 1893 as commanding officer of the partially protected armored cruiser *Chicago*. Happily for Mahan, it carried him to England, where he received a tumultuous reception in British naval and political circles as the brilliant author of the *Influence of Sea Power* volumes. This reception raised Mahan's already considerable Anglophilia to prodigious heights. Since the British well understood the importance of sea power in their own imperial history, they roundly cheered the now famous American who wholly agreed with them.

By the time Captain Mahan returned to New York in March 1895, he was determined to resign from the navy. He had decided to gamble on the possibility that his annual retirement pay ($3,375) supplemented by royalty income from books as well as magazine articles (at five to seven cents a word) would enable him to provide inheritances for his two unmarried daughters, maintain a summer home in Quogue, Long Island, and a winter residence in New York City, support four house servants, travel occasionally in Europe, and in general lead a comfortable life. In sum, he would write his way into a well-paid retirement, as indeed he did.

Not surprisingly, Mahan's enormous literary output was often as long-winded as it was voluminous. He published twenty-one books, eleven of them reprintings of various of his 137 magazine articles. He also penned 107 letters (some for pay) to newspaper editors on various naval and diplomatic topics, many of them contentious. The Sino-Japanese, Spanish-American, Boer, Russo-Japanese, and Balkan wars were financial godsends to him. The rise of German and Japanese naval powers in the 1900–1914 period and their potential threats to Britain and the United States were steady providers of income. Indeed, Mahan's numerous gratuitous warnings to the English that the growing German navy was a clear and present danger to their nation and empire, together with his advice on the strategies that would best thwart Berlin's evil designs, was a recurring theme.

Also repetitive in his books and articles were his closely interrelated theological, historical, and historiographical convictions. They can be summed up as follows:

1. While war was inherent in human history, God had placed in the hands of Christian warriors the corrective that was the "Just War," an instrument by which such warriors could abolish slavery, crush tyrants, and otherwise right the earth's numerous wrongs.
2. Arms limitations treaties, international arbitration courts, and other well-meaning "rules of war" notions were all dangerous in that they compromised the necessity of entering and fighting just wars and bringing them to speedy and victorious conclusions.
3. Sea power had an enormous influence on the course of human history and was one of the numerous natural laws that God, in creating the universe, had suffused into it. It was also a law that the Creator had revealed to Mahan.
4. The law of "tactical concentration," which the correct prosecution of naval war absolutely required, demanded that the ships of one's own fleet be maneuvered in such manner as to concentrate their combined firepower on weaker firepower units of the enemy—this especially during the decisive "Big Battle" that usually ended wars at sea.
5. Sound historical analysis required the employment of a proper historiographical methodology based on the "subordination" of carefully arranged relevant facts to a central historical theme. "Facts won't lie if you work them right," Mahan wrote, "but if you work them wrong, a little disposition in the emphasis, a slight exaggeration of color, a little more or less limelight on this or that part of the grouping and the result is not truth, even though each individual fact be as unimpeachable as the multiplication table."

In spite of Mahan's theoretical, tactical, strategical, and theological interest in war, his personal involvement in American imperialism in the 1898–1914 period was minimal. Although most historians have linked him with the imperialists of 1898–1904, he had virtually nothing to do with the onset of the war with Spain or the contingency planning of it. He was recalled to active duty from a vacation trip in Europe to serve on the Naval War Board in Washington, but his membership on it was largely a public relations gesture. So instead of worrying much about the brief and unequal war, he began gathering materials for what would become a profitable book, *Lessons of the War with Spain* (1899).

At the same time, however, he cheered the annexation of Hawaii, it being the key to his eastern Pacific defense-perimeter proposal, and he approved the annexation of Puerto Rico as a future contribution to his

Gulf and Caribbean defense-perimeter concept. Only reluctantly did he accept the annexation of the Philippines. Indeed, he argued (presciently) that the navy simply could not defend that distant archipelago in the event of a war with Japan. The embarrassing outbreak of the Philippine Insurrection (1899–1901) so dismayed him that he wrote not a word about it. Instead, he brought out a poorly received book on the Boer War, in which he upheld the British explanation of its necessity as being legally and morally justified.

Nor in 1898–1902 did Mahan have any particular interest in the markets of China, save to suggest that American businessmen could probably function there adequately on a free trade basis if the European powers already resident surrendered their spheres of influence, which of course they did not. He saw nothing to applaud in Secretary of State Hay's Open Door policy initiatives in 1899 and 1900, which urged international respect for the administrative and territorial integrity of China. The main thing that truly interested Mahan about China was his hope and expectation that more Christian missionaries would soon enter the country and uplift the natives spiritually. He was thus particularly outraged by the wanton slaughter of missionaries by Boxer Rebellion mobs in 1900 and urged military retaliation. He believed, too, that the Open Door in China and the Monroe Doctrine in the Western Hemisphere, taken together, overextended U.S. involvement in world affairs. He therefore suggested that the nation reduce its overseas commitments by confining the applicability of the Monroe Doctrine to the area north of the Amazon valley.

As for the Caribbean sector of Latin America, Theodore Roosevelt's crude "Big Stick" interventions in Panama in 1903 and the Dominican Republic in 1904 initially elicited only pained silence from Mahan. It was years before he could even bring himself to write about either operation, when he considered them in the broader context of the nation's diplomatic problems and related naval capabilities. Further, he was highly critical of Roosevelt's support of the navy's all-big-gun battleship building program in 1906–1914, which produced ships of the HMS *Dreadnought* type armed with 12-inch and 14-inch guns. He argued instead that the batteries on the new vessels should be varied in size and range. The ordnance argument within the navy, which Mahan lost, virtually ended a close personal Roosevelt-Mahan relationship, which turned principally on naval matters. As for naval technology in general, Mahan's failure to see the tactical or strategic importance of the submarine, wireless telegraphy, and the airplane had already marked him as a "back number" among the navy's senior officers when World War I commenced three months before his death in Washington, D.C.

Whatever Mahan's reputation as a historian and a prophet might be in the years ahead, it now seems that he was not much of an imperialist in the years 1890–1914; nor do his letters, papers, and publications lend much support to Marxist interpretations of his beliefs or Freudian analyses of his personality. On the other hand, his insistence that the United States must become and remain a sea power has surely been his greatest contribution to national survival in the twentieth century.

• Mahan's papers have been published in Robert Seager II and Doris D. Maguire, eds., *Letters and Papers of Alfred Thayer Mahan* (3 vols., 1975). Mahan's other writings include "Subordination in Historical Treatment," *Annual Report of the American Historical Association for the Year 1902* 1 (1903): 47–63, which was reprinted as "The Writing of History," *Atlantic Monthly*, Mar. 1903, pp. 289–98; and *The Harvest Within: Thoughts on the Life of a Christian* (1909). See also John B. Hattendorf and Lynn C. Hattendorf, comps., *A Bibliography of the Works of Alfred Thayer Mahan* (1986); Philip A. Crowl, "Alfred Thayer Mahan: The Naval Historian," in *Makers of Modern Strategy from Machiavelli to the Nuclear Age*, ed. Peter Paret (1986); William E. Livezey, *Mahan on Sea Power* (1947); Seager, *Alfred Thayer Mahan* (1977); Seager, "Ten Years before Mahan: The Unofficial Case for the New Navy, 1880–1890," *Mississippi Valley Historical Review* 40 (Dec. 1953): 491–512; Seager, "Alfred Thayer Mahan: Christian Expansionist, Navalist, and Historian," in *Admirals of the New Steel Navy: Makers of the American Naval Tradition, 1880–1930*, ed. James C. Bradford (1990); Richard W. Turk, *The Ambiguous Relationship: Theodore Roosevelt and Alfred Thayer Mahan* (1988); Paul A. Varg, *The Making of a Myth: The United States and China, 1897–1912* (1968); David F. Trask, *The War with Spain in 1898* (1981); Julius W. Pratt, "The 'Large Policy' of 1898," *Mississippi Valley Historical Review* 19 (Sept. 1932): 219–43; Pratt, *Expansionists of 1898: The Acquisition of Hawaii and the Spanish Islands* (1936); and James A. Field, Jr., "American Imperialism: The Worst Chapter in Almost Any Book," *American Historical Review* 83 (June 1978): 644–68.

ROBERT SEAGER II

MAHAN, Dennis Hart (2 Apr. 1802–16 Sept. 1871), military engineer, was born in New York City, the son of John Mahan, a carpenter, contractor, and real estate agent, and Mary Cleary. Recent emigrants from Ireland, Mahan's parents settled in Norfolk, Virginia, soon after Dennis's birth. Mahan entered the U.S. Military Academy at West Point in 1820. In November 1821 he became acting assistant professor of mathematics to teach underclass cadets. Mahan graduated in 1824 as the top graduate in his class and was commissioned a second lieutenant in the corps of engineers. The only field duty of his career came during a three-month survey in Baltimore immediately after graduation. After this he returned to West Point as assistant professor in mathematics and a year later became an assistant in engineering. At that time cadets were placed in sections by ability and the professor taught the first section with the best students. Junior officers, the assistants, taught the other sections.

In 1826 Mahan began a leave of absence for health reasons in France. His stay gradually extended to four years, during which he examined military institutions and public works. During 1829 and early 1830 he attended the Military School of Application for Engineers and Artillerists at Metz, the premier military school in the world with a faculty of French scientists and veterans of the Napoleonic Wars.

Mahan returned to West Point in 1830 as assistant professor of civil and military engineering. After one year as acting professor, in 1832 he resigned his commission (still a second lieutenant) to become professor of engineering, a post he held until his death. Mahan immediately set out to reform the teaching of engineering at the academy. He brought back a lithographic press from France to print notes and books for his courses, which he later expanded into published books. In 1839 Mahan married Mary Helena Okill. They had two daughters and three sons.

During Mahan's tenure about two thousand cadets graduated, and every cadet took Mahan's demanding course on field operations, fortification, and leadership during his final year at the academy. Mahan published three main texts, expanding his influence beyond the military academy. The *Treatise on Field Fortification* first appeared in 1836, with a half-dozen editions selling more than 10,000 copies. *Field Fortification* was used extensively in both the Mexican and Civil wars. In 1847 Mahan published *Advanced Guard, Outpost, and Detachment Service of Troops*, which was greatly expanded in 1862 and sold more than 8,000 copies. The *Army and Navy Journal* observed that the expanded book would better have been titled *An Elementary Treatise on the Art of War*. When the publisher would not sell copies to the Confederacy, both books were reprinted in the South. The Federal army had been dispersed as small units along the frontier prior to the Civil War, and Mahan's books provided an important blueprint on how to mobilize into a large force. A two-volume *Elementary Course of Military Engineering* appeared in 1866–1867, combining the *Field Fortification* and *Permanent Fortification* (1850).

Mahan's *Course of Civil Engineering* first appeared in 1837 and was revised until 1868, selling more than 15,000 copies. Primarily descriptive in the first edition, the work became more theoretical, especially in mechanics of materials, from Mahan's familiarity with French work. He also published the American edition of *Mosley's Mechanical Principles of Engineering and Architecture* (1856 and 1869 editions) and *Industrial Drawing* (1853).

In addition to his teaching, Mahan served as mentor for the young corps of engineers officers assigned as his assistant professors. After an 1857 clash with the superintendent of the academy, Mahan personally taught very little; he viewed his role as supervising the assistant professors and ensuring that all cadets learned from his courses, and not just those in the first section. Mahan inspired many junior officers at West Point in the Napoleon Club, a semi-official organization that sought to instill professionalism in the years before the Civil War.

Mahan was a prodigious letter writer, both to individuals and to contemporary periodicals. He stressed loyalty to the military academy, the army, and the nation, and although a proud Virginian he did not join the Confederacy. He corresponded with many Union generals during the war, especially William T. Sherman. The constant theme of his writing was the need for military professionalism, defined as vocational expertise and high standards of performance and behavior.

By force of will and personality, Mahan dominated the academy during his long tenure. He influenced all discussion on the curriculum, maintaining the need for a strong technical background for all graduates. Mahan became the example to cadets of the disciplined officer and high-toned gentleman, strictly enforcing military protocol. While tradition credits Alfred Thayer as the father of the U.S. Military Academy, Mahan's long tenure ensured that Thayer's principles endured.

In 1871 the academy's board of visitors recommended that Mahan retire. President Ulysses S. Grant was an old student, and Mahan expected to have the recommendation overturned. Mahan brooded over publication of the recommendation and followed the advice of family and friends to consult his doctor in New York City. En route on the Hudson River he committed suicide by stepping off the boat into the path of the waterwheels.

Reflecting his national reputation, Mahan was among the original fifty incorporators of the National Academy of Sciences. He was an educator and popularizer. He helped develop and mold the U.S. Military Academy as an educational institution. His engineering texts brought new principles to a wider audience as other colleges joined West Point in teaching engineering. Finally, he was the conscience of military professionalism in the years before the Civil War; by personal example, published writings, and personal letters he influenced most of the key officers who fought the Civil War.

• The West Point archives has a collection of material related to Mahan's service and his prodigious letter writing. Robert Seager II's biography of Mahan's son, *Alfred Thayer Mahan* (1977), includes some information on Mahan himself. Thomas E. Griess, "Dennis Hart Mahan: West Point Professor and Advocate of Military Professionalism, 1830–1871" (Ph.D. diss., Duke Univ., 1969), would be the starting point for any future work on Mahan. Major obituaries are in the *New York Times* and the *New York Herald*, both 17 Sept. 1871, and the *Army and Navy Journal*, 7 Oct. 1871.

PETER L. GUTH

MAHLER, Margaret S. (10 May 1897–6 Oct. 1985), physician and psychoanalyst, was born in Sopron, Hungary, the daughter of Gusztav Schonberger, a physician, and Eugenia Wiener. Her father, a prominent public health officer, encouraged her scientific aptitude and interests. She attended the medical schools of the universities of Budapest, Munich, and Jena, graduating in 1922, after which she practiced pediatrics and child psychoanalysis in Vienna. She married Paul Mahler in 1936 (they would have no children) and moved to New York City in 1938; there she became well known as a gifted clinician, teacher, and researcher.

In her practice in Vienna as a pediatrician and analyst working with psychotic children, Mahler became impressed with the fact that neither the very young child nor the psychotic child was really tuned into the world of reality: they did not seem to know where they began and where another person left off. In other words, they seemed to live in a symbiotic orbit that encompassed the mother and the infant, or the psychotic child, in one common boundary. Neither seemed to be psychologically born.

These impressions, strengthened by her work in New York, led Mahler to undertake a research study of symbiotic infantile psychosis, followed in 1962 by a research project planned to investigate the mechanisms or steps by which the vast majority of infants gradually emerge from the state of human symbiosis, learning how normal children separate their self-images from the images of their mothers—how they go through the gradual process of psychological birth. Mahler called this process the separation-individuation process, a term referring to the stages marking the infant's gradual intrapsychic separation from the mother and his or her simultaneous acquisition of an understanding of himself or herself as a distinct individual with a subjectively felt sense of identity.

Unlike other workers who formed theories about the first years of life on the basis of clinical psychoanalytic work with older children and adults, Mahler felt that her views could be addressed only through the observational research study of children in the first three years of life in a naturalistic setting. The research was guided by the belief that although the intrapsychic process of separation-individuation could not be directly observed, it could be inferred from behaviors that were observable. This emphasis on an intrapsychic process distinguishes Mahler's work from that of most other theorists and researchers in the field.

Mahler explained the particular line her research studies took in 1962: "At an advanced stage in their life work some psychoanalysts seek to come closer to the actual fountainhead of their reconstructive efforts." Her aim was to seek preverbal and verbal observational data in the first three years of life that could be compared with the reconstructive inferences about these years derived from the psychoanalytic treatment of adult and child patients.

Mahler had a creative gift as a researcher. Rather than organizing the behavioral data according to what was already known, she was receptive to new organizations of ideas when observations presented them to her. Rather than thinking in terms of broad patterns, she preferred an impassioned study of the data in microscopic detail, as did Freud in his intensive study of dreams. Her understanding of the details of the normal process of separation-individuation led to major contributions to the theory of normal development and of clinical psychopathology.

Mahler's work was distinguished by a rare originality in observing essential phenomena in children's behavior and by a talent in formulating original hypotheses and in verifying or modifying these in research

studies. These studies added a new dimension to the understanding of psychological development in the first three years of life. They also showed how development may go wrong; how it influences subsequent stages in development; and ultimately how it contributes to personality traits, character formation, and emotional disorders in the adult.

Mahler showed an unswerving and independent singleness of purpose, youthful curiosity, intellectual alertness, and an ability to open up new avenues for understanding the human mind. These same traits made her an excellent teacher of psychoanalytic candidates in training, of young psychiatrists, and of psychologists, social workers, and others interested in child development.

Mahler died in New York City. She had been a major player on the world stage of psychoanalysis and had made important contributions to the understanding of the human condition, especially in her theory of the psychological birth of the human infant.

• Mahler's major papers on infantile psychosis and on the separation-individuation process are collected in *The Selected Papers of Margaret Mahler* (1979). Her studies on infantile psychosis culminated in the publication of *On Human Symbiosis and the Vicissitudes of Individuation: The Infantile Psychosis* (1968). She is best known as the author of *The Psychological Birth of the Human Infant* (1975). Her memoirs were published as *Memoirs of Margaret S. Mahler*, comp. and ed. Paul E. Stepansky (1988). Other sources include Anni Bergman, "Tribute to Margaret S. Mahler," *Psychoanalytical Inquiry* 7 (1987): 307–10; and Fred Pine, "Margaret S. Mahler, M.D.: In Memoriam," *Psychoanalytical Psychology* 3 (1986): 101–4. An obituary is in the *New York Times*, 3 Oct. 1985.

JOHN B. MCDEVITT

MAHON, George Herman (22 Sept. 1900–19 Nov. 1985), lawyer and member of Congress, was born in Mahon, Louisiana, the son of John Kirkpatrick, a cotton farmer, and Lola Willis Brown. His family moved to Loraine, Texas, located between Big Spring and Abilene in the western part of the state, when Mahon was eight. Educated locally, he also taught at a grammar school during his senior year in high school, riding fourteen miles by bicycle. He graduated from Simmons University (now Hardin-Simmons) in 1924. He received a law degree from the University of Texas at Austin in 1925. Mahon married Helen Stevenson in 1923; the couple had one child. The voters chose Mahon as county attorney for Mitchell County in 1926. Ten months later the governor appointed him district attorney of the Thirty-second Judicial District. He served from 1927 to 1933.

In 1934 the Nineteenth Congressional District was created. Mahon led a field of eight candidates in the first primary and easily won the Democratic runoff with a 16,000-vote margin. After that, he faced serious contests only in the 1946 primary and in the 1976 general election. Mahon was an effective advocate for the economic interests of his district over the years. By the mid-1970s, his district, which included the city of Lubbock, was receiving several hundred million dollars a year from Washington, much of it for cotton stabilization payments and a variety of federal government facilities. Mahon gained a seat on the powerful Appropriations Committee in 1939 and began acquiring the seniority that would make him a power in the House two decades later. He supported the foreign and defense policies of Franklin D. Roosevelt and also endorsed the agricultural programs of the New Deal. He told reporters that he picked 100 pounds of cotton annually himself "so that I won't forget that living on a farm is a very strenuous life" (*Current Biography*, p. 271). Mahon was invariably charming and gracious in his personal dealings.

Mahon's speeches on the floor of the House were few. He opposed civil rights legislation and endorsed measures, such as the Taft-Hartley Act of 1947, to restrict the power of organized labor. He developed a reputation as a quiet, hard-working legislator who avoided the dictatorial style of some of his more flamboyant colleagues. During the presidency of Harry S. Truman, Mahon achieved his goal of chairing the Defense Appropriations Subcommittee of the larger Appropriations panel.

Mahon was a strong proponent of defense spending during the 1950s and 1960s. While doing so, he also championed savings through careful management of military appropriations. In 1964, after the death of Representative Clarence Cannon, Mahon became chairman of the Appropriations Committee. He did not support the 1964 Civil Rights Act, the 1965 Voting Rights Act, or other Great Society programs such as medicare and aid to depressed areas.

Long friendly with Lyndon B. Johnson, Mahon endorsed the Vietnam policies of the mid-1960s. He helped to restrain those in the House who sought a more aggressive posture toward the war in Southeast Asia, and he also restrained members who wanted to oppose the president. By 1967, however, he noted that he and his colleagues were not "entirely happy with the progress of the war, or all of the tactics being followed, but we are in support of the overall objectives of the nation" ("Excerpts from Statements by George Mahon," Mahon biographical file, Univ. of Texas).

As the 1960s progressed, Mahon became more and more concerned about the impact of government spending on the nation's future. "Money doesn't grow on trees," he said in 1967, and, he complained, "We're doing all these things for the poor and the needy in the face of the threat of a $30 billion deficit" ("Excerpts from Statements," Mahon biographical file, Tex.). Privately, he told a White House aide that liberals "are just for money for poor people" (Liz Carpenter memorandum, 13 Mar. 1968, Lyndon B. Johnson Library).

Mahon used his power as Appropriations Committee chairman to reflect his policy views. He placed liberals on the Foreign Relations Subcommittee in 1965 to curb the influence of Congressman Otto Passman of Louisiana. Two years later he selected conservatives for the Labor-Health, Education, and Welfare Subcommittee to limit the power to enact Great Society legislation. The disgruntled subcommittee chairman

told the White House that "Mahon intends to press for budget cuts every inch of the way" (John Gardner memorandum to Lyndon Johnson, 2 Mar. 1967, LBJ Library). Despite Mahon's opposition to much of Johnson's programs, he remained friendly with the president and his family because of Mahon's kindly personal manner and the emotional links that had been forged before Johnson came to the White House.

During the Richard Nixon and Gerald Ford presidencies, Mahon retained his influence in Washington. To court Mahon's support, the Nixon administration retained his nephew in the choice patronage position of United States attorney for Lubbock rather than replace him with a Republican appointee. Despite his great power, however, Mahon was largely unknown outside of Washington. "I never was a grandstand type and I'm not now," he said toward the end of his public career (undated clipping in Mahon biographical file, Tex.). Mahon retired in 1978 after forty-four years in the House of Representatives. He died in San Angelo.

Reporters rarely covered Capitol Hill in depth during Mahon's career, and his influence on the legislative history of his time has not yet been charted. He conceded that he was not "a headline man" in terms of public visibility. A commitment to both lower government spending in general and a strong national defense was the keynote of his public agenda. The existing evidence indicates that a careful survey of Mahon's work in the House will reveal him to have been one of the most important lawmakers within the southern Democratic bloc that wielded such influence in Washington from 1940 to 1980.

• Mahon's extensive and well-organized personal papers are in the Southwest Collection, Texas Tech University, Lubbock. There is also information about Mahon's legislative role in the Wright Patman Papers and the Lyndon Johnson Papers at the Lyndon B. Johnson Library, Austin. Other information exists at the Harry Truman Library, the Dwight D. Eisenhower Library, the John F. Kennedy Library, and the Nixon papers project, Washington, D.C. For Mahon's own views, see "George Mahon Talks on Spending," *Nation's Business* 52 (Aug. 1964): 32–33, 56, 58, 60; "We're Spending Our Way to Disaster," *Nation's Business* 60 (Apr. 1972): 34–36; and his speeches in the *Congressional Record* (1935–1979). There is no biography of Mahon. A useful biographical file at the Center for American History, University of Texas at Austin, has clippings and a few public documents. Dale Pullen, *George H. Mahon: Democratic Representative from Texas* (1972), is a lengthy and well-documented analysis done for the Ralph Nader Congress Project. See also, Julius Duscha, "George Mahon: Tall Tight-fisted Texan," *Washingtonian Magazine*, Sept. 1969, pp. 23, 26. Also useful is the sketch in *Current Biography 1958*, pp. 270–71. For obituaries, see the *New York Times*, 21 Nov. 1985, and the *Sherman Democrat*, 20 Nov. 1985.

LEWIS L. GOULD

MAHONE, William (1 Dec. 1826–8 Oct. 1895), soldier, railroad executive, and politician, was born in Monroe, Virginia, the son of Fielding Mahone, a merchant, and Martha Drew. After studies at Littletown Academy, William entered the Virginia Military Institute in 1844. He graduated in 1847 and afterward taught at the Rappahannock Academy. At the end of the 1848–1849 academic year, he was appointed surveyor of the Orange and Alexandria Railroad. He remained in this post until 1852, when he was appointed chief engineer of the Fredericksburg and Valley Plank Road. He left that company one year later to accept the post of chief engineer of the Norfolk and Petersburg Railroad; in April 1860 he was elected president of the company. In 1855 he married Otelia Butler. Only three of the couple's thirteen children reached maturity.

At the outbreak of the Civil War, Mahone participated in the seizure of the Gosport Navy Yard at Norfolk, after which he was commissioned a lieutenant colonel in the Virginia volunteer service on 29 April 1861. Less than a week later he was promoted to colonel. On 16 November 1861 he became a brigadier general and was given command of a brigade near Norfolk. Following the evacuation of Norfolk in May 1862, Mahone's brigade assisted in the construction of batteries along the James River before joining the main Confederate army on the Virginia Peninsula. He participated in the battle of Seven Pines and the Seven Days' battles, then was wounded at the battle of Second Manassas (Second Bull Run). Although forced to miss the Maryland campaign of September 1862, he recovered in time to see action at Fredericksburg and Chancellorsville, but he took no active part at Gettysburg.

In May 1863 Mahone was elected to the Virginia Senate. He did not take his seat until March 1864, and only two months later he returned to the army. Promoted to division command on 17 May, Mahone earned his greatest fame during the fighting around Petersburg in 1864. His most distinguished service took place on 30 July 1864 at the battle of the Crater, where he led the counterattack that restored a badly broken Confederate line. This performance led General Robert E. Lee, already an admirer of Mahone, to personally order his promotion to major general, the rank he held when the army surrendered at Appomattox.

After the war Mahone returned to his post as president of the Norfolk and Petersburg Railroad. His success directing the reconstruction of that road led the stockholders of the adjoining South Side Railroad to offer him in December 1865 the presidency of their line as well, which he accepted. Mahone subsequently decided to consolidate the two roads with the Virginia and Tennessee, but he failed to persuade that company's stockholders to merge. He then turned to the state legislature for assistance. The legislature passed the Southside Consolidation Act of 1867, permitting the consolidation. Although pleased, Mahone spent the rest of the year purchasing Virginia and Tennessee stock to strengthen his control of that line. On 12 November 1867 his efforts bore fruit when the stockholders elected him president of the Virginia and Tennessee, giving him control over all rail traffic from Norfolk, Virginia, to Bristol, Tennessee.

The 1867 Consolidation Act lapsed when certain financial arrangements mandated by the law were not completed by 1 May 1868. However, fear that failure to pass consolidation would allow northern capitalists to extend their control over Virginia railroads and the fact that the three railroads involved were already de facto consolidated and prospering facilitated passage of a new consolidation bill. On 17 June 1870 Governor Gilbert C. Walker signed a bill authorizing the formation of the Atlantic, Mississippi, and Ohio Railroad Company. Mahone was formally elected president of the company in November.

The depression that followed the panic of 1873, however, took a severe toll on the company, and on 8 May 1880 a decree of foreclosure and sale was issued. This gave northern interests the opportunity they had sought to wrest control of the railroad from Mahone. On 4 April 1881 the final sale was confirmed, and its new owners rechristened it the Norfolk and Western.

By this time Mahone was deeply involved in state politics. He had played a key role in Walker's election to the governorship in 1869, and in 1877 Mahone unsuccessfully sought the Conservative nomination for governor. He subsequently organized and assumed leadership of the "Readjuster" movement in the state. During the 1870s Virginia raised taxes and cut spending on public schools in an effort to reduce the state's $40 million debt. The Readjusters denounced this approach and called for repudiation, or readjustment, of approximately one-third of the public debt and the restoration of funds for public schools. This platform found strong support among Virginia's traditional "out" groups—blacks, poor whites, and residents of the mountain regions.

Under Mahone's leadership, the Readjusters won decisive victories in the 1879 and 1881 elections, seizing control of every branch of the state government. While in power, they reformed the state tax system by increasing corporate taxes and giving tax relief to poor farmers. The Readjusters restored funds for education and successfully turned a third of Virginia's prewar debt over to West Virginia. Mahone won election to the U.S. Senate in 1880. Internal divisions quickly emerged, particularly over whether the Readjuster movement should seek allies among Republicans and blacks. In 1880 the Democratic National Committee clearly aligned itself with Mahone's rivals in the "Funder" faction in choosing the state's electors for the presidential contest. Mahone consequently moved toward the National Republican party, which helped attract black votes but cost him and the movement much white support. With the defection of Readjusters, conservative elements in the state regained power. In 1889 Mahone was decisively defeated in his race for governor. Although he continued to dominate the state's Republican party, he never again held elective office. He died in Washington, D.C.

Discontent with Bourbon rule was not confined to Virginia during the years after the restoration of home rule in the South. Yet only in the Old Dominion did the solid South crack, albeit briefly. He was not a physically imposing man, but Mahone's forceful and dynamic personality, status as a war hero and successful railroad magnate, and leadership abilities made possible what success the Readjuster movement enjoyed in Virginia.

• A substantial collection of Mahone's papers and other materials related to his life and career are located at the Duke University Library. The standard biography is Nelson M. Blake, *William Mahone of Virginia: Soldier and Political Insurgent* (1935). Mahone's service in the Civil War is traced in U.S. War Department, *The War of the Rebellion: A Compilation of the Official Records of the Union and Confederate Armies* (128 vols., 1880–1901), and Douglas Southall Freeman, *Lee's Lieutenants: A Study in Command* (3 vols., 1942–1944). Allen W. Moger, "Railroad Practices and Policies in Virginia after the Civil War," *Virginia Magazine of History and Biography* 59 (1951): 423–57; Charles C. Pearson, *The Readjuster Movement in Virginia* (1917); James Tice Moore, *Two Paths to the New South: The Virginia Debt Controversy* (1974); and Brooks Barnes, "Triumph of the New South: Independent Movements in the 1880s" (Ph.D. diss., Univ. of Virginia, 1991), all contain valuable information on Mahone's postwar career.
ETHAN S. RAFUSE

MAHONEY, John Friend (1 Aug. 1889–23 Feb. 1957), medical researcher and public health administrator, was born in Fond du Lac, Wisconsin, the son of David Mahoney, a locomotive engineer, and Mary Ann Hogan. He graduated from public high school in Fond du Lac in 1908 and worked for a year as a truck farmer before enrolling at Milwaukee University, from which he received an S.B. in 1910. He then undertook medical studies at Marquette Medical College in Milwaukee and earned an M.D. in 1914.

After medical school Mahoney held internships at both Milwaukee County Hospital (1914–1915) and Chicago Lying-In Hospital (1915–1916). In 1917 he accepted a commission as an officer in the U.S. Public Health Service (PHS). After serving in several routine positions, Mahoney's superiors detailed him to the U.S. Foreign Service in 1925. The following year he married Leah Ruth Arnold; they had two children. Mahoney remained with the Foreign Service through January 1929, working as a public health adviser in Dublin, Ireland; Liverpool, England; and Bremen, Germany. In addition to fulfilling his routine obligations, Mahoney spent much of his time overseas visiting leading European laboratories and clinics engaged in research on, and treatment of, venereal diseases.

After returning from his foreign assignments, Mahoney was appointed clinical director and executive officer of PHS's Marine Hospital on Staten Island, New York. In addition to carrying out his administrative duties, he was able to devote a large portion of his energy to laboratory research on syphilis. Initially, Mahoney conducted his investigations in a small, poorly equipped room. Over the next twenty years, however, the Public Health Service provided him with expanded facilities for research. Designated the Venereal Disease Research Laboratory, the facility attracted a number of young, talented medical researchers

who joined Mahoney in his laboratory and clinical studies. Mahoney and his collaborators at the Staten Island laboratory had much research success, beginning with their first great triumph, in 1937, when they convincingly demonstrated the effectiveness of sulfa drugs in the treatment of gonorrhea.

Several years later Mahoney also played a central role in establishing a relatively simple cure for the other major venereal disease that had afflicted men and women for centuries: syphilis. Early in World War II Allied medical researchers embarked on a massive effort to develop techniques that would allow for the production of penicillin on an industrial scale. Military and medical leaders alike recognized that success in this undertaking would mark a major advance in the treatment of infected wounds. Mahoney and some of his immediate co-workers thought that this remarkable antibiotic might also cure syphilis—a less heroic but highly significant problem in military medicine.

Early in 1943 Mahoney obtained a small sample of penicillin, which federal science administrators were distributing with miserly care because large-scale production of the antibiotic had not been achieved. Preliminary experiments with animals at the Venereal Disease Research Laboratory quickly suggested to Mahoney that penicillin might successfully attack the syphilis spirochete. In June 1943 he initiated a clinical trial of the drug with four men suffering from the early stages of syphilis. Four months later Mahoney reported before an annual meeting of the American Public Health Association that this first trial had shown tremendous promise: penicillin seemed to kill the microorganisms that caused syphilis without harming the patient, and the treatment regimen lasted for only eight days. This discovery marked a monumental medical advance. Earlier in the century, German researchers had established a treatment for syphilis that required repeated injections of toxic arsenic compounds and salvarsan over an eighteen-month period. However, this therapeutic ordeal was so lengthy and unpleasant that most patients abandoned the regimen before its conclusion.

By 1944 other Allied scientists and engineers, working with millions of dollars of government support (mainly from the United States), had begun the industrial production of penicillin. Mahoney went on to play an integral role in a large, coordinated effort to confirm the successful first test of penicillin at the Venereal Disease Research Laboratory, and he was widely recognized as the pioneer in developing this amazingly effective treatment. He was one of the five people presented with a Lasker Award by the American Public Health Association in 1946, the inaugural year of this prestigious prize.

After more than three decades as a PHS officer, Mahoney retired from federal service in December 1949 and began several years of high-level service to New York City. In 1949 he served briefly as director of the Bureau of Laboratories in New York's Department of Health, but after only four days, the newly elected mayor, William O'Dwyer, chose Mahoney as New

York City's Health Commissioner. As expected, venereal disease control was one of the major thrusts of Mahoney's term as Health Commissioner, and his department achieved such success with the introduction of penicillin treatment for venereal diseases at public clinics that he was able to close the city's largest VD clinic in 1951. During his term, among other contributions, Mahoney fostered an initiative to prevent childhood lead poisoning, worked to introduce isoniazid chemotherapy for tuberculosis at public clinics, and worked toward the fluoridation of the city's drinking water.

In 1954, when Mayor O'Dwyer was defeated at the polls, Mahoney stepped down as health commissioner and returned to his former position as director of the health department's laboratories. He died in Staten Island, New York, while still serving in this position.

• An excellent general history of venereal disease in the United States that gives some attention to Mahoney is Allan M. Brandt, *No Magic Bullet* (1985; repr. 1987). The development of penicillin treatment for syphilis during World War II is covered in some detail in the chapter titled "Venereal Disease" in *Advances in Military Medicine*, ed. E. C. Andrus (1948). Sources of biographical information include *Journal of Social Hygiene* 32 (1946): 155–57; *American Journal of Public Health* 40 (Feb. 1950): 240; and Ralph Chester Williams, *The United States Public Health Service, 1798–1950* (1951), pp. 387–90. Obituaries are in the *New York Times*, 24 Feb. 1957; *Time*, 4 Mar. 1957; *British Medical Journal* (23 Mar. 1957): 708–9; and *Journal of the American Medical Association* 164 (18 May 1957): 313.

JON M. HARKNESS

MAHONY, Marion. *See* Griffin, Marion Lucy Mahony.

MAIER, Walter Arthur (4 Oct. 1893–11 Jan. 1950), radio minister and seminary professor, was born in Boston, Massachusetts, the son of Emil William Maier, a piano and organ builder, and Anna Katharine Schad, a grocer. Raised in the Lutheran Church-Missouri Synod, Maier was educated at Concordia Collegiate Institute in Bronxville, New York, between 1906 and 1912 and received his B.A. in 1913 after a year's study at Boston University. He earned his B.D. at Concordia Theological Seminary in St. Louis, where he was enrolled between 1913 and 1916. Maier also studied at Harvard Divinity School (1916–1918) and at the Harvard Graduate School (1918–1929), from which he earned an M.A. in 1920 and a Ph.D. in Old Testament studies in 1929. Ordained to the ministry in 1917, he served as pastor of Zion Church in Boston and provided pastoral care to German soldiers at a nearby prisoner-of-war camp during World War I. In June 1924 he married Hulda Augusta Eickhoff, a former schoolteacher, with whom he had two children.

Maier's career as a national religious figure began in 1920, when he became the first executive secretary of the Missouri Synod's youth auxiliary, the Walther League. Although the Missouri Synod maintained a strong German ethnic identity and was the least assimilated branch of American Lutheranism in the early twentieth century, Maier broadened the League's outlook and helped its membership to double during the two years he led the organization. He also edited the *Walther League Messenger* and, despite becoming professor of Old Testament at Concordia Seminary in 1922, kept that position until 1945. He published several hundred articles and increased the magazine's circulation from 7,000 to 80,000 during his time as editor.

Although radio broadcasting was still in its infancy in the 1920s, Maier recognized its potential as a means of mass communication and evangelism. Episcopalians in Pittsburgh had started the first religious programming in 1921, and Maier was determined to use radio to strengthen the ministry of his denomination as well. He obtained financial support from the Walther League and from the Lutheran Laymen's League, and on 14 December 1924 station KFUO at Concordia Seminary went on the air. Known as "The Gospel Voice," KFUO was successful enough to expand its operation from two hours a week in 1924 to thirty hours a week three years later. Maier served on the seminary's radio committee and planned the construction of permanent broadcasting facilities, which were completed in 1927. Besides offering Concordia chapel services and a Sunday *Vespers* series, the station featured Maier's regular commentary on current events and church affairs.

Maier further expanded his radio ministry in 1930, when he accepted an invitation to speak each week on a new CBS series, *The Lutheran Hour*, sponsored by the Laymen's League of the Missouri Synod. Despite financial difficulties that forced the program to suspend operation in June 1931, Maier's enthusiasm was never dampened, and he was able to begin broadcasting again in 1935. *The Lutheran Hour* won plaudits from a wide variety of religious people and grew steadily in popularity over the next decade. While Maier remained on the faculty of Concordia Seminary during that period, the program demanded more and more of his time. Finally, in 1944 he was forced to take what proved to be a permanent leave of absence from his teaching responsibilities and began to concentrate his energies exclusively on the radio ministry. *The Lutheran Hour* eventually went on television in 1949, and by 1950 the radio program was broadcast regularly in fifty-five countries, with an audience of approximately 20 million people.

Maier combined Lutheran orthodoxy and a general doctrinal conservatism with an appealing manner and distinctive preaching style. He consistently attacked modern secular culture and liberal theology, but he avoided the bigotry and extreme positions adopted by other radio preachers in the 1930s and 1940s. Maier remained true to traditional Missouri Synod emphases on biblical inerrancy and justification by faith, and his Lutheran background and academic studies kept his message free of the anti-intellectualism, ahistoricism, and nondoctrinal biblicism then common in American fundamentalist circles. He had a rapid-fire delivery, and his voice conveyed a sense of moral urgency. Each week he began with a brief prayer, spoke for twenty minutes, and ended by asking his listeners to surrender their lives to Jesus Christ. In his sermons he commented on both biblical themes and events in the news; he communicated a genuine pastoral concern to his audience. He employed a large staff to handle the mail he received from his enthusiastic public and responded personally to each letter that asked him for advice. Maier died in St. Louis. Although he did not live to experience the church revival that took place in the United States during the 1950s, the popularity of his ministry on *The Lutheran Hour* exemplified the later growth of widespread interest in religious topics in American society.

As one of the early figures in what is now called the "electric church," Maier had a significant impact on American popular religion in the mid-twentieth century. He not only pioneered the use of the radio as an evangelistic tool but also helped lead the Lutheran Church-Missouri Synod out of the narrow ethnic base in which it had been confined prior to World War I. Although Maier was a self-described fundamentalist, his academic training and irenic temperament enabled him to communicate with a broad spectrum of the American public and advanced the cause of conservative Protestantism in the United States.

• Materials relating to Maier's *Lutheran Hour* ministry and a list of his periodical articles are at the Concordia Historical Institute in St. Louis, Missouri. Maier published thirty-one books, mostly collections of his radio sermons. His major works include *The Lutheran Hour* (1931), *Christ for Every Crisis* (1935), *The Airwaves Proclaim Christ* (1948), and *One Thousand Radio Voices for Christ* (1950). An anthology issued more recently is *The Best of Walter A. Maier* (1981). The most comprehensive biography is by his son, Paul L. Maier, *A Man Spoke, A World Listened: The Story of Walter A. Maier and the Lutheran Hour* (1963). Milton L. Rudnick, *Fundamentalism and the Missouri Synod: A Historical Study of Their Interaction and Mutual Influence* (1966) contains an extensive analysis of the significance of Maier's work.

GARDINER H. SHATTUCK, JR.

MAIN, Charles Thomas (16 Feb. 1856–6 Mar. 1943), mechanical engineer, was born in Marblehead, Massachusetts, the son of Thomas Main, Jr., a mechanic, and Cordelia Green Reed. Main graduated from the Massachusetts Institute of Technology (MIT) in 1876 with a B.S. in mechanical engineering. Because of an economic depression at the time of his graduation and a lack of available jobs, he delayed embarking on his career for three years, taking advanced classes and working at MIT as an assistant instructor. In 1879 he was hired as a draftsman by the Manchester Mills textile factory in Manchester, New Hampshire. He remained there until 1881, when he was hired as an engineer by the Lower Pacific textile mills in Lawrence, Massachusetts. Main was married in 1883 to Elizabeth F. Appleton; they had three children.

Main was promoted to assistant superintendent at Lower Pacific in 1886, and that same year he prepared a series of four lectures, titled "Notes on Mill Construction." These were later printed in textbook form and used for course work at MIT. He was made superintendent of Lower Pacific in 1887. In 1889 he was issued a patent for a device designed to regulate the pressure in exhaust receivers of compound steam engines. The invention had widespread use in factories, for at the time steam was the predominant power source.

Main's reputation as an expert on power systems and the solutions of associated problems grew when the management of Lower Pacific permitted him to serve as a consultant at other textile mills. In 1891 he wrote the first of his many papers presented to his fellow engineers. That year he outlined the then-novel idea of bleeding steam from factory power systems for use in manufacturing processes. In a presentation titled "Value of a Water Power," Main described the process of evaluating all aspects of developing water power for industrial use. The principles set forth in this seminal paper were so universal that they remained in use for decades. He continued in the employ of Lower Pacific until late 1891, when he resigned and entered private practice collaborating with architect Frank P. Sheldon of Providence, Rhode Island, on the design and construction of several large factory buildings.

In 1893 Main moved to Boston, where he entered a partnership with Francis W. Dean, a prominent consulting engineer and expert on steam power. The office of Dean and Main began by specializing in the design of textile mills. Gradually the scope of their work broadened to include the design and construction of large steam- and water-powered plants. In 1894 they designed the first of a number of municipal lighting plants when they produced plans for systems at Marblehead and Lynn, Massachusetts. The partnership was dissolved in 1907 and Main again opened his own office. During his time with Dean, Main formed the first of several long-lasting associations with clients. The engineering construction firm of Stone & Webster was one such firm that relied on his service as a consulting engineer for many years.

Main worked as a consultant, designer, and supervisor of construction, and the projects he undertook were varied and located in all parts of the United States. They included industrial plants of all types including milling and soap making, entire facilities such as those built for Wood Worsted and Ayer Mills, and hydroelectric installations such as that built for the Montana Power Company. As he further refined his skills, his work became international in scope. Main was a recognized specialist in the valuation of industrial properties, and on occasion he was called upon as an expert witness or arbitrator in legal matters in which engineering was involved.

During World War I Main served as a consultant to the construction division of the Quartermaster Corps of the U.S. Army, and at the request of the secretary of war, Newton D. Baker, he served as a consultant on war-related boards. His firm was responsible for the construction of several military installations. Following the war, Main was a member of a delegation of American engineers who inspected war-damaged areas and made recommendations to the French government on their reconstruction. Main was elected a member of the American Society of Mechanical Engineering (ASME) in 1885. He served as a manager from 1914 to 1917 and became the president of the society in 1918. He also held memberships in the American Society of Civil Engineers, the American Institute of Consulting Engineers, the National Association of Cotton Manufacturers, and the American Association for the Advancement of Science.

Main set high standards for himself and those with whom he worked. He had deep concern for the engineering profession and placed great importance upon professional ethics. Therefore, in 1919 he sponsored the creation of the ASME Charles T. Main Award, a cash award and certificate given to the young engineer who wrote the best paper on the influence of the engineering profession on public life.

Main's growing business and his concern for his colleagues and workers led him to incorporate the business in 1926. In that way he believed that the organization might continue to function and provide a public service without his involvement. He held the office of president until 1938 and continued as the chairman of the board until his death.

Main had a strong sense of civic obligation and believed in public service. As a result of his involvement in an 1891 movement aimed at government reform, he was elected and served three years as an alderman in Lawrence, Massachusetts. In addition to serving on the board of directors of several companies, he was a member of the sewer and water board of Winchester, Massachusetts. Main was dedicated to his alma mater and served not only as a member of the Corporation of MIT, but he also held a life membership on its executive committee. He died in Winchester, Massachusetts.

Main conducted his business in an exemplary manner. He stressed the need to treat clients fairly and if at all possible to give them more than they expected. He also believed in being honest with them: if they wanted something that Main felt was unsafe, he would recommend that they go elsewhere. His employees were held in high regard, and he believed that they should be paid as much as possible and that their good work should be recognized.

• When Main was elected president of the American Society of Mechanical Engineers an account of his life appeared in the ASME *Transactions* 40 (1918). His role in the newly defined field of industrial engineering was discussed in "Charles T. Main: Industrial Engineer," *Power*, 25 May 1920. The most extensive biographical sketch of Main's life is William F. Uhl, *Charles T. Main (1856–1943): One of America's Best* (1951), which was prepared for the Newcomen Society. An obituary is in the *New York Times*, 7 Mar. 1943.

WILLIAM E. WORTHINGTON, JR.

MAIN, John Hanson Thomas (2 Apr. 1859–1 Apr. 1931), educator, was born in Toledo, Ohio, the son of Hezekiah Main and Margaret Costello, farmers. Main's mother died when he was an infant, and he was raised by an aunt near Fremont, Ohio. He graduated from Moore's Hill College with a bachelor of science in 1880 and earned a master of arts there in 1883. Main became a professor of ancient languages at Moore's Hill College in 1880 and was appointed vice president of the college. Moore's Hill College, located in Moore's Hill, Indiana, was a coeducational institution founded by the Methodist church in 1853. It is no longer in existence. Main married Emma Myers in 1881; they had no children. After receiving his master's degree, he taught public school for a short time. He served as an assistant professor of Greek and Latin at Baltimore College for Women (now Goucher College) from 1889 until 1890. The following year he became a senior fellow of Greek at Johns Hopkins.

Upon completing his Ph.D. in classical languages in 1892 at Johns Hopkins University, Main was hired as a professor of Greek at Iowa College (now Grinnell College). He served as acting president from 1900 to 1902 and was named dean of the faculty in 1902. In 1906 Main became president of Grinnell College, a position he retained for the next twenty-five years, the longest administration in the history of the college.

During his tenure as president, Main made a significant contribution to Grinnell College in several areas, including administration, architecture, and academics. Several new buildings were added to the campus, including dormitories designed by Main for students who had formerly been housed in private community residences. President Main also became well known for his fundraising, which brought large sums of money to the college, including major grants from the Rockefeller Foundation. He was also instrumental in the permanent name change of the college from Iowa College to Grinnell College in 1909.

Main is considered an early advocate of the modernization of higher education. In 1913 he initiated the Grinnell in China program, which sent graduates to Shantung province to help run schools for Chinese students. He was responsible for beginning the Gates Memorial Lectureship, a series of lectures, named in honor of former college president and proponent of the Social Gospel George A. Gates, that brought several speakers to campus, and he initiated an annual lecture exchange with Harvard University in 1912. With an interest in liberal arts, he added new departments, including business administration, art, drama, journalism, and physical education. Although Grinnell College remained quite small during his tenure, Main was able to double the student enrollment in the first twenty years of his administration, and he instituted the offices of dean of men and dean of women.

Main's presidency also focused on the religious and moral education of students. Shortly after Main assumed the presidency of the college, he initiated a Sunday vesper service, which became a forty-year tradition at Grinnell. In conjunction with the vesper service, Main was responsible for the building of Herrick Chapel, the purchase of a new organ, and the growth of the men's and women's glee clubs, which regularly performed during vespers.

Grinnell College grew steadily in the early years of President Main's tenure, until World War I brought a temporary drop in student enrollment. During this period the Student Army Training Corps had a branch at the college. In 1917 the young men in the corps were exposed to the worldwide influenza epidemic, and many recruits lost their lives while at the college. Main contributed to the postwar relief effort by working from late 1918 until the summer of 1919 as a member of a commission appointed by the Near East Committee of New York to investigate famine conditions in Armenia and Syria, and he served as a commissioner for the American Committee for Syrian and Armenian Relief from 1919 to 1924. His interest in that area of the world was partly due to a friendship with a Grinnell graduate, the Reverend George E. White, who became president of Anatolia College in Turkey. Main was a trustee of the Carnegie Foundation from 1924 until his death, and he was also a member of the American Philological Association and the Archaeological Institute of America.

When Main died in Grinnell, Iowa, he was still serving as president of the college. Friends and colleagues had asked him to retire to preserve his health, but this dedicated administrator stayed at his beloved college until his death.

Main was a hard-working college administrator who brought many changes to the small, religiously based college at Grinnell, Iowa. The reforms he initiated at Grinnell College were typical of the changes being enacted at other progressive institutions in the Midwest in the early twentieth century. While initiating such programs as international studies and adding new departments, he also ensured that Grinnell maintained its focus on religious and moral education. Without the guidance and leadership of Main, the changes might not have occurred when they did.

• Main's papers are cataloged in the Records of the Office of the President, RG A, at the Grinnell College Archives, Grinnell, Iowa. For a more detailed understanding of Main's educational philosophy, see his early presidential address entitled "What Should the College Contribute to Its Students?" in Grinnell College, *Fifth Annual Report of President Main, September 1, 1911–September 1, 1912* (1912). John S. Nollen's history of the college, *Grinnell College* (1953), contains a chapter on Main's administration. Obituaries are in the *New York Times*, 2 and 3 Apr. 1931.

JUDITH BOYCE DEMARK

MAINER, J. E. (20 July 1898–20 June 1971), musician, was born Joseph Emmett Mainer in Asheville, North Carolina, the son of Joseph Mainer and Polly Arwood, farmers. Mainer was born in a one-room log cabin in the Blue Ridge Mountains on a farm that could not support the family, so at age ten he went to work in a cotton mill. Soon after his twelfth birthday he left home to work at the Brook Side Cotton Mill in Knox-

ville, Tennessee, and each week he sent two dollars to his father to help support the family. Over the next dozen years, Mainer's residence alternated between Knoxville and his family's home in North Carolina. While working in Knoxville, he taught himself to play the banjo and fiddle and with his brother-in-law, fiddler Roscoe Banks, began his musical career playing fiddle and banjo at square dances. In 1922 Mainer moved to Concord, North Carolina, where he secured employment in a local mill and established his permanent home. The same year, he married Sadie Gertrude McDaniel, with whom he had eight children; one was adopted.

Mainer's fiddling ability developed quickly during his late adolescence and early adulthood, and eventually he became one of the most popular fiddlers in the Blue Ridge area. He formed a small band with his brother Wade and guitarist-vocalist John Love. The three were in great demand at bluegrass and fiddlers' conventions, which were popular events throughout the South during those years. Mainer won numerous fiddling competitions and talent contests as he gained a reputation for transforming old-time fiddle playing into a polished, virtuosic style of bluegrass fiddling.

In 1932 the Crazy Water Crystals Company invited Mainer and his brother to become regular guests on a program that aired on WBT radio in Charlotte, North Carolina. John Love and Claud "Zeke" Morris joined the brothers in 1934 to form J. E. Mainer's Mountaineers, with Mainer serving as manager. The group performed on more than two hundred radio stations throughout the eastern United States and Mexico, and in August 1935 in Atlanta they made their first recording, for the Bluebird label. Among the songs recorded at that session was Mainer's "Maple on the Hill," for which he would be known—and acclaimed—for the rest of his life. Mainer's Mountaineers also recorded for RCA Victor (1935–1938), King (1941–1945), Blue Jay (1965–), and Rural Rhythm (1967–). Their recordings of "Maple on the Hill" and "Take Me in the Life Boat" (also 1935) were bestselling records for more than two years; their live performances attracted record crowds; and they were recognized by the National Broadcasting Company as the performing group to receive the most fan mail during that era—more than 11,000 letters in one shipment.

While being noted as a gifted bluegrass fiddler and singer, Mainer also gained respect and popularity as a songwriter. Many of his tunes and song texts, such as "Oh, My Lord, Won't You Show Me the Way" (1935), "Maple on the Hill" (1935), and "You Will Always Be Mine" (1938), have become bluegrass standards. His secular songs often were recitations of true stories or love ballads; many paid tribute to his parents. His sacred songs were expressions of faith and hope. His fiddling tunes, high-spirited melodies with fast dance rhythms suited for square dancing and clogging, contain fast sixteenth-note passages that require strong finger technique and quick bowing skills. His other recorded hits included "John Henry" (1936) and "City Called Mt. Zion" (1937).

Mainer performed with some of the best-known bluegrass and country performers, including the Carter family, Bill and Charlie Monroe, and the Blue Sky Boys, and was widely recognized for his musicianship. In 1941 he was invited to perform for President Franklin D. Roosevelt at the White House. He was included in the 1966 edition of *Who's Who in Country Music*, and in 1967 he received a gold trophy presented by the Mooresville (N.C.) Lions Club, which, along with a congratulatory letter from Congressman James T. Broyhill of North Carolina, recognized Mainer's fifty-year career in country music. In 1969 he was inducted into the Country Music Hall of Fame.

During the 1950s Mainer stayed close to his Concord home and tended to confine his public performances to the Carolinas, Tennessee, and Virginia. By then, most of his children had established careers of their own and moved away. Much of his time was spent in his private music shop, where he repaired and built fiddles. His limited number of recording sessions in these years included a series of albums for Uncle Jim O'Neal's Rural Rhythm label (1967), and he often appeared as a guest on the WWVA (Wheeling, W.Va.) Jamboree. He remained active, performing in local churches and participating in community activities, until his death at his Concord home.

In the late 1960s a fiddler's convention was organized in Mainer's honor. The convention, sponsored by the East Lincoln Optimist Club, has since become an annual event held in Denver, North Carolina, with all proceeds going to various community organizations. The J. E. Mainer Memorial Award (named for Mainer after his death) is given each year to a person "making significant contributions to old-time country and bluegrass music." During his lifetime, Mainer often presented one of his self-crafted fiddles to the recipient of this award. His obituary in the Concord newspaper referred to Mainer as "the number-one fiddler in the nation." Inspiring other musicians to continue in the traditions of bluegrass music, he spent his life and talents promoting and preserving the particularly American heritage of bluegrass music.

• Biographical information on Mainer can be found at the Country Music Hall of Fame Library in Nashville. On file there, in addition to letters and newspaper articles, is *Songs as Sung by J. E. Mainer and His Mountaineers*, a short collection of texts that includes a summary of his life and career. The two-volume record album *J. E. Mainer's Mountaineers* (1967–1968) includes an autobiography containing accounts of Mainer's struggles and achievements in the early part of his career. A biographical sketch is also included in Barry McCloud, *Definitive Country* (1995). Significant information for this article was provided by J. E. Mainer, Jr.

LINDA P. SHIPLEY

MAIN POC (c. 1765–1816), Potawatomi war leader and shaman, was born probably in southern Michigan. His parentage is unknown, but he was the son of a Potawatomi war chief. His name is also rendered as Man Pock, Mar Pock, and other misspellings of the French nickname Main Poche meaning Puckered Hand. Main

Poc received his French nickname from the deformed, clublike left hand he was born with, missing fingers and thumb. He claimed the deformity was a special gift from the spirits, while his followers believed him an ancient warrior reborn and invulnerable to injury. A huge, muscular man, Main Poc was the most influential of the Potawatomi *wabenos* or sorcerers in the first decade of the nineteenth century. *Wabenos* were "fire handlers" who could hold hot coals, place their hands in campfires, and even breathe flames from their mouths and nostrils. *Wabenos* could also assume the shape of animals and could use their power to cure diseases, bring about changes in the weather, and sometimes predict the future.

Main Poc grew to manhood hating Americans, and sometime after the treaty of Greenville he established a village at the mouth of Rock Creek on the Kankakee River in northern Illinois. The treaty of Greenville, negotiated in 1795 following the defeat of the Indians of the Old Northwest at Fallen Timbers in 1794, promised protection of Indian landholdings against growing American expansion and brought peaceful relations for a time with the tribes of the area, including the Potawatomi. Main Poc, however, continued leading raids against the Osage villages west of the Mississippi as a means of gaining prestige for himself and young warriors. His raids on the growing American settlements near St. Louis and Vincennes brought him to the attention of American authorities and into the historical record.

Soon after the purchase of the Louisiana Territory in 1803, Governor William Henry Harrison began pushing rapid land cessions throughout the Indiana and Illinois Territory. American bribery of chiefs and the spread of alcohol along with aggressive trading practices and efforts to induce Indians to take up Euro-American style agriculture led to much unease among tribes. At a conference in St. Louis in October 1805, American authorities tried but failed to establish an end to the intertribal raids led by Main Poc. Main Poc did not attend the conference, and a month later ambushed an Osage encampment, killing thirty-four women and children and taking some sixty captives.

Main Poc responded strongly to the teachings of the Shawnee prophet Tenskwatawa, who rejected American technology and called for a return to older native beliefs. He spent nearly two months with Tenskwatawa at Greenville in late 1807. He accepted the prophet's doctrines against using Euro-American technology but rejected abstinence from alcohol and the belief that all Indians were brothers, insisting that he would continue to raid Osage villages. The addition of the greatly feared and respected war chief to the prophet's cause increased the chances of a breakup of the pro-American tribes in the Northwest.

Rushing to counter resistance he had aroused among the warriors of many tribes by pushing land cession treaties, Governor Harrison tried to detach Main Poc from Tenskwatawa. In December 1807 William Wells invited Main Poc to Fort Wayne, where he was Indian agent, and lavished gifts on him and his followers for two months. Main Poc was not won over to the American side, however, and soon resumed raids on the Osages and threatened the government trader at Chicago because he believed prices were too high and the guns supplied in trade inferior.

In 1808 President Thomas Jefferson invited Main Poc to Washington, hoping to wean him from the constant raiding that disrupted commerce on the Mississippi and Missouri rivers and hindered the development of Illinois Territory. Jefferson encouraged a policy of "civilization," the assimilation by Indians of Euro-American style agriculture and the concept of private property in order to free tribal land for white settlement. Jefferson's message was lost on one whose life was equally devoted to leading warriors and drinking heavily. Main Poc rejected Jefferson's suggestions that the Potawatomi "cultivate the earth and raise domestic animals" and told him he had no intention of making peace with the Osages.

In the fall of 1809 Governor Harrison sought a new treaty that would encourage settlement of Indiana Territory in anticipation of statehood. The Miami, not wishing to cede any more land, opposed the treaty for a time and forced Harrison to disavow the support of Little Turtle, by then a staunchly pro-American chief. The treaty greatly increased Indian opposition to pro-American chiefs and encouraged support for Tecumseh among warriors. American authorities countered with increased recruiting of local militia. During the summer of 1810, Main Poc visited Tecumseh at Prophetstown on the Tippecanoe River near present-day Lafayette, Indiana, and joined in plans to attack various American posts. He moved his village to western Illinois, where his followers skirmished with local militia units and he again led raids on the Osages. To the amazement of his followers, he was seriously wounded during one raid and spent the winter of 1810–1811 recovering from his wounds. He assured his followers that his medicine remained strong and claimed he could still see the bullets fired by his enemies.

By the spring of 1811, Main Poc had reestablished a village at Crow Prairie, north of Lake Peoria, and began a series of attacks that spread panic among the white settlers in southern Illinois. He traveled among the Potawatomi, Sac, and Kickapoo villagers in Illinois who were engaged in constant skirmishes with invading Americans, encouraging them to raid Osage and American settlements. He did not participate in the raids, instead moving in June from Crow Prairie to establish a new camp on the Huron River east of Detroit opposite the British Indian agency at Amherstburg, where British officials warmly received him. Matthew Elliott, the British Indian agent, believed Main Poc was the greatest of all war leaders of the Potawatomi. He spent the fall and winter of 1811–1812 trying to draw Odawa and Ojibwa bands into support of the British and sent messengers among Potawatomi villages in Illinois and Indiana, urging attacks on Americans.

Blackbird and Mad Sturgeon, Main Poc's brother-in-law, joined him in opposing Americans. On 19 July Main Poc was painfully wounded in a skirmish near Fort Malden. On 9 August he participated in an ambush of an American supply column and inflicted heavy casualties. After the fighting died down, Main Poc vented his anger on an American prisoner, tomahawking the man against the pleas of British officers. On 16 August 1812, General William Hull, leader of American forces, surrendered Detroit in the face of successful Indian attacks.

After the defeat of the British and their Indian allies at the Battle of the Thames on 5 October 1813, General Harrison found most of the Indians gathered at Detroit ready to make peace. Main Poc signed the 14 October armistice document but had no intention of honoring the agreement. He and his followers continued to carry intelligence to the British, and Harrison feared they would renew warfare in the spring. The following July, Main Poc and most Potawatomi refused to attend the peace conference held at Greenville, Ohio. Only after the winter of 1814–1815 did most Potawatomi warriors become anxious to make peace with American officials when they realized they would get no further aid from the British.

Main Poc carried on resistance against the United States even after news of the Treaty of Ghent and the end of the War of 1812 reached his camp in March 1815. He called for warriors and tried to attack American settlements near Vincennes but was unsuccessful. He died near Manistee, Michigan Territory, in the spring of 1816, still unalterably opposed to American authority. Details regarding his family life and place of death are not known.

Though far less well known than Tecumseh, Tenskwatawa, Little Turtle, Winamek, and other Indian leaders of the Old Northwest, Main Poc emerged as a key figure in Indian-white relations in the region during the period up to the end of the War of 1812. His unalterable hatred of Americans and his uncompromising resistance to American settlement and political domination set him aside from leaders who accommodated themselves to American expansion and efforts to force acculturation.

• Main Poc's life is discussed most fully in David Edmunds, *The Potawatomi* (1978), *Tecumseh* (1984), and "Main Poc: Potawatomi Wabeno," *American Indian Quarterly* 9 (1985): 259–72, and in James A. Clifton, *The Prairie People* (1977). There are scattered references to this elusive Indian war leader in the National Archives, Records of the Secretary of War Relating to Indian Affairs, Letters Sent, 1800–1824, RG 75. References are also scattered through Logan Esarey, ed., *Messages and Papers of William Henry Harrison* (1922); Clarence E. Carter et al., eds., *Territorial Papers of the United States*, vols. 7 (1939), 13 (1948), and 16 (1948); and *Michigan Pioneer and Historical Society*, historical collections, vols. 11 (1888), 15 (1889), and 16 (1910).

STEWART RAFERT

MAISCH, John Michael (30 Jan. 1831–10 Sept. 1893), pharmacist and teacher, was born in Hanau, Hesse, Germany, the son of Conrad Maisch, a retailer of very modest means, and Agnese Louise Liebtreu. Educated in the local schools and taken under the wings of teachers who recognized his special abilities and gave him private tutelage, he gained free admittance to the Oberrealschule (a nonclassical upper high school). He studied languages, botany, zoology, mineralogy, and chemistry and was introduced to the microscope. Ill health, however, thwarted his hope to attend a Gymnasium to pursue a university education. He turned his attention to pharmacy, but involvement with the revolutionary Turners gymnast club of Hanau led to his capture at Sinsheim in 1849. He was imprisoned but escaped with the help of friends and fled to the United States. He arrived in Baltimore in September 1849.

Maisch was alone, almost penniless, and lacked advanced formal education when he arrived. Yet he soon won two silver medals (one dated 1853) for chemical presentations at exhibitions of the Maryland Institute for the Promotion of the Mechanical Arts and the Metropolitan Mechanics Institute in Washington, D.C. The training he had received, his intelligence, his studies, and his industry were to bring him to the forefront of American academic and organizational pharmacy.

After arriving in Baltimore he worked as a factory hand but eventually found employment as a pharmacy clerk in drugstores in Baltimore, Washington, New York, and Philadelphia. Even in these journeyman years he had begun to contribute to the literature of pharmacy. An article by him, "On the Adulteration of Drugs and Chemicals," was the first of two that appeared in the *American Journal of Pharmacy* in 1854; five appeared in 1855, followed by a constant flow of contributions from his pen throughout his career. Indeed, altogether more than 400 contributions to the pharmaceutical literature were made by Maisch, mainly in the *American Journal of Pharmacy* but also in the *Proceedings of the American Pharmaceutical Association* and in the German *Repertorium für die Pharmacie*. Although his papers covered a wide range of materia medica, chemistry, botany, and pharmacy, he was mainly concerned with the materia medica. Maisch was the pioneer American pharmacognosist, and his work led to the introduction of a course in the field in the better American colleges of pharmacy. He was the first in the country to recognize the value of the microscope in the study of drugs and adulterants.

Maisch moved to Philadelphia in 1856, and his final post as a pharmacy employee was in the shop of E. B. Garrigues and Robert Shoemaker & Co. So impressive were his accomplishments that in 1859 Edward Parrish asked Maisch to teach a course in practical pharmacy and supervise a laboratory for practical and analytical chemistry at Parrish's School of Practical Pharmacy. Thus began Maisch's academic career. Also in 1859 Maisch married Charlotte Justine Kuhl, with whom he had eight children. In 1861 he accepted the chair of materia medica and pharmacy in the College of Pharmacy of the City of New York. While in New York he also found employment in the laborato-

ries of E. R. Squibb and so impressed Squibb that when the U.S. Army Laboratory was opened in Philadelphia in 1863, Maisch was named superintendent on Squibb's recommendation. In the two and a half years to the end of the Civil War, the profits from the laboratory under Maisch's management were estimated as saving the U.S. government more than $750,000.

At the close of the war Maisch opened his own pharmacy and ran it until 1871, when other obligations demanded his attention. In 1866 he had accepted the post of professor of pharmacy at the Philadelphia College of Pharmacy and the next year had transferred to the position of professor of materia medica and botany. He spent the rest of his life on the faculty of the college and was dean from 1879 until his death. Maisch's attachment to the college preceded his appointment to the faculty, which he had joined in 1859. Maisch became a member of the board of trustees of the college in 1860, and through his initiative, personal expense, and fundraising, the college procured a microscope the same year. As a faculty member he was a delegate of the college to the pharmacopoeial revision convention in 1870 and served on the revision committee of that convention through three decennial revisions. In addition, from 1871 until his death he was editor of and a prolific contributor to the *American Journal of Pharmacy*.

Maisch's activity at the Philadelphia College of Pharmacy was but one facet of his career. In 1857 he had joined the American Pharmaceutical Association. In 1860 he was chosen as chairman of the committee on the progress of pharmacy and two years later as corresponding secretary. In 1863 he was elected first vice president and in 1864 chairman of the executive committee. The meteoric rise reflected both his ability and his willingness to work. All this culminated in his appointment as permanent secretary in 1865, a position that was essentially executive officer of the association and that included supervising publication of the association's *Proceedings*. He held the post for the rest of his life.

Maisch's writings in pharmacy went beyond his contributions to the journal literature. In 1862 he edited and revised a translation of Rochleder's *Proximate Analysis of Plants and Vegetable Substances*, and in 1874 he revised the third edition of Griffith's *Universal Formulary*. His major contributions were his coauthorship, with Alfred Stillé, of the *National Dispensatory* and his own *Manual of Organic Materia Medica*. Maisch was responsible for the chemical, botanical, and pharmaceutical portions of the former, which went through five editions between 1879 and 1894, the last appearing after Maisch's death. The *Manual*, essentially a handbook of pharmacognosy, went through five editions from 1882 to 1892 and was continued by his son, Henry C. C. Maisch, for two further editions (1895, 1899).

Perhaps Maisch's most pervasive influence on American pharmacy and American society was his advocacy of legislation regulating the education and examination of pharmacists and the practice of pharmacy. His survey in 1868 under the aegis of the American Pharmaceutical Association indicated that such legislation was virtually nonexistent; in 1869 he presented a model state law, and thereafter he pointed up the need for the organizing of state pharmaceutical associations to obtain the necessary state legislation. By the end of the century state pharmaceutical associations and state laws regulating pharmacy were to be found in virtually every jurisdiction. No fewer than fifteen state associations elected Maisch to honorary membership.

Maisch's honors went beyond those presented by state pharmaceutical associations. Professional bodies in Australia, Canada, Mexico, Great Britain, Belgium, Switzerland, and Germany paid him homage. His highest honor was the bestowal in 1893 of the Hanbury Gold Medal, presented by the Pharmaceutical Society of Great Britain for distinguished research in the natural history and chemistry of drugs. Maisch was too ill to attend the joint meeting of the American Pharmaceutical Association and the International Pharmaceutical Congress in Chicago at which the medal was presented. He was the first American to receive the honor. He died in Philadelphia.

• Some Maisch papers, including a field book kept on herborizing expeditions, and a good deal of memorabilia are in the Archives of the Philadelphia College of Pharmacy and Science. The chief biographies are Frederick Hoffmann, "Johann Michael Maisch," *Pharmazeutische Rundschau* 11 (1893): 223–27, which includes Maisch's 1879 autobiographical sketch; J. P. Remington, "Prof. J. M. Maisch," *American Journal of Pharmacy* 66 (1894): 1–9; M. L. Wilbert, "John Michael Maisch: An Ideal Pharmacist," *American Journal of Pharmacy* 75 (1903): 351–77, which includes a list of Maisch's writings and awards; and G. Urdang, "The Fiftieth Anniversary of the Death of John Michael Maisch," *American Journal of Pharmacy* 116 (1944): 14–24.

DAVID L. COWEN

MAJOR, Charles (25 July 1856–13 Feb. 1913), novelist, was born in Indianapolis, Indiana, the son of Stephen Major, a lawyer and judge, and Phoebe Gaskill. His father was prominent as an attorney and as a judge of the Fifth Judicial Circuit of Indiana. When Charles was thirteen, the family moved to Shelbyville, Indiana. After graduating from the University of Michigan in 1875, he read law in his father's office, was admitted to the Shelby County bar in 1877, was elected city clerk in 1885, and served one term as a Democrat in the Indiana legislature in 1886–1887 but declined to run again. He married Alice Shaw of Shelbyville in 1885; they had no children.

Though he devoted himself mostly to his law practice, Major read omnivorously in English and French history of the Renaissance, sometimes sending to England for materials unavailable elsewhere. He was intrigued by the account that when Mary Tudor, sister of Henry VIII of England, married Louis XII, king of France, she was really in love with Charles Brandon, a friend of Henry. After Louis died, Mary wrote to Brandon, saying that if he still wanted to marry her, he should come to Paris without the knowledge of Henry,

who might otherwise prevent the marriage. From this fascinating story arose Major's first and best novel, *When Knighthood Was in Flower*, which he wrote in the evenings and on Sunday afternoons in his law office. The story is supposedly told by the master of the dance at the court of Henry VIII, Sir Edwin Caskoden, a pseudonym used by Major. The manuscript was rejected by Harper and Brothers. However, he then gave it to a salesman from the Bowen-Merrill Publishing Company of Indianapolis, who had come to Major's office to sell him some law books. Bowen-Merrill changed Major's original title from "Charles Brandon, Duke of Suffolk" to the present title and published the novel in 1898. It achieved such sudden success, both from critics and from readers, that Major, a studious and rather shy person, found himself the famous author of a bestseller. It remained a bestseller for fourteen months, selling 200,000 copies in two years. The novel was later dramatized by Paul Kester and played to capacity audiences in America and in London with the famous Shakespearean actress, Julia Marlowe, as Mary and in Australia with Nellie Stuart taking the lead. When it played at English's Opera House in Indianapolis, a special train was run from Shelbyville to Indianapolis for the performance on "Shelbyville night." After the cast took their curtain calls at the conclusion of the play, Julia Marlowe led Major from the wings to receive the applause of the crowd. About 10,000 people saw the play in one week at English's. Later the book was issued as a comic opera and made into a motion picture.

After this success Major tended to do less legal work, though he continued to write his other books in his law office, sometimes being harried by the curious, who wanted to see or photograph a celebrity. *Dorothy Vernon of Haddon Hall* (1902), another love story set in the time of Queen Elizabeth I and Mary, queen of Scots, was next in popularity to *Knighthood* and was converted into a popular play by Paul Kester. Less successful romances followed: *Yolanda, Maid of Burgundy* (1905); *A Gentle Knight of Old Brandenburg* (1909); *The Little King, a Story of the Childhood of Louis XIV, King of France* (1910); and *The Touchstone of Fortune, Being the Memoir of Baron Clyde, Who Lived, Thrived, and Fell in the Doleful Reign of the So-Called Merry Monarch, Charles II* (1912). In all these romances, Major repeated his favorite formula of placing obstacles in the path of a romantic couple, who eventually triumph over them, and using mostly stock types instead of individualized characters. Yet, these tales were immensely popular.

Major wrote three books about Indiana: *The Bears of Blue River* (1901); *Uncle Tom Andy Bill* (1908); and *A Forest Hearth; a Romance of Indiana in the Thirties* (1903). The first two are full of action and adventure, but the last was practically a failure because of Major's attempt to transplant the machinery and elevated dialogue of European romance to frontier Indiana. His last book, *Rosalie*, was published posthumously in 1925. The story of a faithless priest and lack of ethics in the medical profession, it was an anticlimax to the success of his romances. His most famous books are *When Knighthood Was in Flower, Dorothy Vernon of Haddon Hall*, and *The Bears of Blue River*.

Though Major maintained that a historical novelist should use the real life of the people as his guide, not simply political history, and should not attempt to utilize the language of the period, his works lack a true depiction of social history, and he seems to violate his own definition of historic atmosphere as "the application of realism to historical fiction" (*Scribner's*, June 1900). Nevertheless, his accurate use of political history and his high-spirited romances gave the public what it then wanted. Actually he made no lasting contribution to the rise of the historical novel, which was already much in vogue at the turn of the century. Yet, as a contemporary Indiana writer, Meredith Nicholson, said, "[Major's] *When Knighthood Was in Flower* gave a great impetus to historical romance and numbers of writers imitated the style of this book" (*Indianapolis News*, 13 Feb. 1913).

• The best collection of materials on Charles Major is in the Purdue University Library, which contains the manuscripts of his ten principal works in holograph and typescript, corrected galley and page proofs, his personal library, and all materials by and concerning him up to 1925, as well as newspaper articles and recent reprints of some of his novels. See William M. Hepburn, *The Charles Major Manuscripts in the Purdue University Libraries* (1946), reprinted from the *Indiana Quarterly for Bookmen* 2, no. 3 (July 1946): 71–81. Major's article, "What Is Historic Atmosphere?," is in *Scribner's*, June 1900, p. 753. Howard Baetzhold, "Charles Major: Hoosier Romancer," *Indiana Magazine of History*, Mar. 1955, pp. 31–42, gives a good overview of Major. Maurice Thompson, "The Author and the Book," often unsigned, is included in several editions of *When Knighthood Was in Flower* and adds information about the novel. Meredith Nicholson, *The Hoosiers* (1900), offers an early appraisal. See also J. P. Dunn, *Indiana and Indianans* (1919); J. M. Purcell, "The Hoosier Period in American Literature," *Indianapolis Star*, 20 Jan. 1929; and the *Bookman*, Nov. 1900, p. 206, in which an anonymous author reveals the real Charles Brandon of history as something less than noble. An obituary is in the *Indianapolis News*, 13 Feb. 1913.

ARTHUR W. SHUMAKER

MAJOR, Ralph Hermon (29 Aug. 1884–15 Oct. 1970), physician and historian of medicine, was born in Clay County, Missouri, the son of John Sleet Major, a banker, and Virginia Anderson. After completing his A.B. degree at William Jewell College in Liberty, Missouri, in 1902, he traveled in Europe for three years. There he became proficient in German, French, Italian, and Spanish, adding to his knowledge of Greek and Latin. Back in America, he studied medicine at Johns Hopkins University in Baltimore, obtaining his M.D. degree in 1910. He remained at Johns Hopkins for two years of postgraduate training in internal medicine before returning to Europe to spend 1912–1913 at the clinic of Friedrich Müller in Munich, Germany.

In 1913 Major accepted a position in the Department of Pathology at Stanford University, but one year later he returned to the Midwest and the School of Medicine, University of Kansas, Kansas City, where he would work for most of his career. He began as professor and chair of the Department of Pathology and Bacteriology (1914–1919). In 1915 he married Margaret Norman Jackson; they would have three children. He served nearly three decades as professor and chairman of the Department of Medicine (1921–1950); finally he became chairman of the Department of the History of Medicine (1950–1955). Upon his retirement in 1955, he became professor emeritus. The only hiatus in his lengthy service to the university was a two-year absence, when he held a temporary appointment at Henry Ford Hospital in Detroit (1919–1921).

Major was a good internist and teacher, and his facility with languages, together with his appreciation for European culture, served him in his professional life in both clinical medicine and medical history. Former students and associates were quick to identify the influence of Johns Hopkins medical founder, William Osler, in his love of physical diagnosis and its history and in his ability to combine the two at the bedside by recalling the discoveries of diseases and of the signs used to detect them. Major admired Osler's philosophy, but he also considered Müller to have had a profound effect on his appreciation of clinical diagnosis.

Major published 184 articles and several books. His textbook, *Physical Diagnosis* (1937), ran to nine editions, the last two of which were published posthumously; it was translated into Japanese, Persian, Portuguese, and Spanish. Conforming to the new style of medical pedagogy, it was amply illustrated with photographs of patients from his own practice, but it also made reference to classic descriptions from medicine's past, which he had collected for many years.

The most enduring of Major's publications has proven to be his *Classic Descriptions of Disease* (1932), an anthology of original clinical descriptions, spanning medical practice from antiquity to the twentieth century, in English translation. *Classic Descriptions* remained in print more than six decades after it first appeared, and it continued to be the most frequently cited of his publications.

Major also wrote for lay audiences, producing several works that combined medicine and history. Among them, his *Faiths that Healed* (1940) was a study of famous miracle healings and the potential scientific explanations for them. He was fascinated by the intriguing influence of faith and psyche over soma, but he seemed to favor material explanations of mysteries.

As Major approached retirement, he presided over the American Association of the History of Medicine (1950–1952) and prepared his two-volume *History of Medicine* (1954). This textbook took a chronological approach to history and emphasized the biographical details of his subjects. From 1954 until his death the University of Kansas honored him annually with presentation of the "Gold-Headed Cane" and a series of lectures by visiting dignitaries.

In 1965 Major was saddened by the death of his first wife. He married Wanda E. Graham in 1967, but he fell ill soon after with a series of strokes that left him comatose for the last eight months of his life. He died in Kansas City.

Major was a gentle, patient teacher, well liked by his students and colleagues, and he was one of the rare individuals who successfully combined a distinguished career in clinical medicine with an equally distinguished career in medical history. For him diseases were concrete entities that lay hidden under a clinical facade awaiting discovery by astute clinicians. His positivistic writings display little awareness of the rising cultural relativism that would come to pervade historical writing about disease in the decades following his death. Nevertheless, his broad clinical acumen, his attention to detail, and his care to uncover sources in their original form continue to make his contributions in both medicine and history both lucid and reliable.

• For information on Major's life and contributions, see the tributes of his former associates, Robert P. Hudson, "Ralph H. Major, 1884–1970," *Bulletin of the History of Medicine* 45 (1971): 283–86; Mahlon Delp, "Ralph Hermon Major, M.D.," *Transactions of the American Clinical and Climatological Association* 83 (1972): 46–47; William S. Middleton, "Intellectual Crossroads—An Appreciation of Ralph H. Major," *Perspectives in Biology and Medicine* 14 (Summer 1971): 651–58.

JACALYN DUFFIN

MAJORS, Monroe Alpheus (12 Oct. 1864–10 Dec. 1960), physician, civil rights activist, and writer, was born in Waco, Texas, the son of Andrew Jackson Majors and Jane Barringer. In 1869 his family moved to Austin, Texas. After attending public schools in Austin, Majors studied at West Texas College, Tillotson Normal and Collegiate Institute, Central Tennessee College, and finally Meharry Medical College in Nashville, Tennessee, from which he graduated in 1886.

After medical school Majors practiced medicine in Brenham, Dallas, and Calvert, Texas; he was the first African American doctor in Calvert. In 1886 he also established the Lone Star State Medical Association for African-American physicians in response to the exclusionary policies of the American Medical Association. Because of his prominence as a black doctor and his support of civil rights for African Americans, Majors became a target of racist threats. In 1888 he moved to Los Angeles to escape the rising antiblack violence in Texas and to further his medical career. In Los Angeles Majors participated in various medical societies and was probably the first African American to present lectures at the Los Angeles Medical College. In 1889 he passed the California board medical examination, the first African American to do so. Majors continued his agitation for civil rights while in California. He served as an editor of the *Los Angeles Western News*, through which he successfully encouraged the appointment of African Americans to several civil service positions, including police officers. In 1889 Majors married Georgia A. Green, a fellow native Texan; they had one daughter.

In 1890 Majors returned to Waco, where he practiced medicine until 1895. He also lectured at Paul Quinn College (1891–1894), edited the *Texas Searchlight* (1893–1895), helped build a hospital, and opened the first black-owned drugstore in the southwestern United States. In 1893 Majors's *Noted Negro Women*, a biographical encyclopedia that was the first of its kind, was published in Chicago. In the mid-1890s Majors wrote several articles for African-American newspapers, most notably the *Indianapolis Freeman*, for which he prepared a weekly column. In his journalism he covered numerous topics, including the Ku Klux Klan, black intellectualism, slavery, crime, medicine, and practical advice for African Americans.

In 1898 Majors moved to Decatur, Illinois, where he continued to practice medicine and participate in political reform movements. As a successful black physician, Majors incurred the enmity of the town's white doctors. His life was threatened after he publicly denounced a lynching that had taken place in Decatur shortly before his arrival. Majors then moved to Indianapolis, where he worked as the associate editor of the *Indianapolis Freeman* until 1899.

In 1899 Majors moved back to Texas. For two years he served as superintendent of the Waco hospital he had helped build. Once again Majors faced racist reaction, including death threats, and in 1901 he moved to Chicago, Illinois, where he lived for thirty-two years. In Chicago Majors continued to practice medicine and wrote articles and poetry for several African-American newspapers, including the *Broad Ax*, the *Chicago Defender*, the *Washington Bee*, the *Peoples Advocate*, and the *Colored American*. From 1908 to 1910 he served as editor of the *Chicago Conservator*. In 1921 Majors's *First Steps to Nursery Rhymes* appeared, a book that is generally considered one of the first publications specifically written for African-American children. Having divorced his wife in 1908, Majors married Estelle C. Bond the following year; the couple had one daughter. He later married twice more and had three sons.

In the 1920s failing eyesight curtailed Majors's activities. He discontinued his medical practice in Chicago in 1923 and largely retired from writing. In 1933 he moved back to Los Angeles, where he resumed his medical practice for sporadic periods. Majors died in Los Angeles.

A man of remarkable accomplishments, Majors managed to combine a pioneering career in medicine with substantial contributions to African-American journalism and politics. He is credited with inventing the medical term "paralysis diabetes."

• Hightower T. Kealing wrote an introduction to Majors's *Noted Negro Women* (1893) that contains a useful but brief biographical sketch. For information on Majors's medical career, see Herbert M. Morais, *The History of the Negro in Medicine* (1967).

THADDEUS RUSSELL

MAKEMIE, Francis (1658?–c. July 1708), Presbyterian minister, was born near Ramelton, County Donegal, Ireland, of Scottish ancestry; his parents are unknown. He was enrolled in the University of Glasgow in 1676, presented as a candidate for ordination to the Presbytery of Laggan, Ireland, on 28 January 1680, licensed to preach in late 1681 or early 1682, and ordained in 1682.

A combination of restrictive laws against Presbyterians in Ulster and a letter to Ireland from a member of third Lord Baltimore's council, Colonel William Stevens, brought Makemie to the Chesapeake region in 1683. There he joined another Ulster minister, William Trail, who had probably preceded him by several months. Makemie itinerated along the coasts of Maryland, Virginia, and North Carolina but by 1687 had taken up residence in Accomack County, Virginia. There he began to acquire land in order to engage in trade, in addition to exercising his ministry. As early as 1689 he traveled to London, where he consulted with English dissenting ministers. By this time he had established trading interests in Barbados, as well as serving as a minister there from as early as 1690. Although he retained a residence in Accomack County, he appears to have remained in Barbados most of the period until 1698.

Sometime between 1687 and 1698 Makemie married Naomi Anderson, the daughter of William Anderson, a wealthy merchant and landowner in Accomack. She was ten years Makemie's junior and bore two daughters. Upon Anderson's death in 1698, Makemie and his wife inherited extensive properties. He proved to be adept at plantation management and trade, and in his pamphlet *A Plain and Friendly Persuasive to the Inhabitants of Virginia and Maryland, for Promoting Towns and Cohabitation* (1705) he expressed concern about the lack of commerce in the Chesapeake region. He called for the formation of towns and centers of commerce, which would cause self-interest to "truckle to the Common Good." A more cosmopolitan environment in the Chesapeake, he reasoned, would encourage cultural, economic, and religious interests.

In 1704 Makemie once again sailed to England. Along with looking after his trading interests, the main purpose of this journey was to secure ministerial assistance. Several years earlier he had written *Truths in a True Light* (1699), which called for Protestant unity in the face of Roman Catholicism and stressed the closeness of Presbyterianism to Anglicanism. Now, however, he was increasingly concerned about growing Anglican activity in America. The Society for the Propagation of the Gospel, organized in 1701, appeared to be attempting to draw non-Anglicans into conformity; clearly, the society was active in seeking to establish by law the Church of England in the colonies. By 1705 Makemie had returned to the Chesapeake with two new ministerial recruits, only to face increasing Anglican hostility. He proceeded quickly to organize the first American presbytery, which met in Philadelphia in the spring of 1706 and was composed of the seven Presbyterian ministers then laboring in Maryland, Virginia, Delaware, and Pennsylvania. Makemie was elected their first moderator. By drawing these ministers and their congregations into an authoritative church judicatory, opposition to Anglican aggressiveness would be strengthened.

In early 1707, Makemie and one of his ministerial colleagues visited New York to attempt to broaden the scope of the presbytery. There they were confronted by the royal governor, Edward Hyde (1661–1723), Lord Cornbury, whose regular practice of parading through the streets of New York dressed in women's clothes may not have been to Makemie's taste. Cornbury, who had been actively opposing the rights of dissenting ministers in New York, had the two arrested for preaching without his permission. Makemie was imprisoned for six weeks and used the time to prepare for publication *A Good Conversation* (1707), the sermon that had been the immediate cause of his arrest. In June, he appeared in court to defend his actions. The thrust of his argument was that although he was fully protected as a dissenting minister by England's 1689 Toleration Act, he had come to believe that the establishment of the Church of England did not extend to the colonies. Therefore, said Makemie, there was no need for "toleration." The presiding judge noted that this was the first such trial in the American colonies. The jury, relishing the opportunity of striking out at Cornbury, found Makemie innocent of any crime; when the court affixed on him the entire costs of the trial, the New York assembly passed an act that made illegal the assessing of an innocent party for such expenses. Cornbury fumed, calling Makemie a "Jack of all Trades he is a Preacher, a Doctor of Physick, a Merchant, an Attorney . . . and, which is worse of all, a Disturber of Governments." From Boston, Cotton Mather viewed the trial with a different eye:

That brave man, Mr. Makemie, has after a famous Trial at N. York . . . triumphed over the Act of Uniformity, and the other Poenal Lawes for the Ch. of England. Without permitting the Matter to come so far as to Pleading the Act of Toleration, he has compelled an Acknowledgement that those Lawes aforesd, are but Local ones, and have nothing to do with the Plantations.

Immediately after the trial, Makemie published his last and most important work, *A Narrative of a New and Unusual American Imprisonment of Two Presbyterian Ministers: And Prosecution of Mr. Francis Makemie* (1707). He died probably at or in the vicinity of his home in Accomack, Virginia. The second largest landholder in the county, his estate comprised well over 5,000 acres of land, together with thirty-three slaves.

Makemie was Presbyterianism's chief exponent in the early colonial period as well as its leading literary apologist, the main defender of its liberties, and the foremost overseer of its congregations. His theology was rigidly orthodox, in the style of seventeenth-century Calvinism.

• In addition to the works already mentioned, Makemie published *An Answer to George Keith's Libel* (1694), an unpleasant and verbose theological diatribe against Pennsylvania Quakers. Earlier he had published a catechism for young people, but no copy is known to have survived. All Makemie's extant writings, including his letters, are reprinted in Boyd S. Schlenther, *The Life and Writings of Francis Makemie* (1971). See also Char Miller, "Francis Makemie: Social Development of the Colonial Chesapeake," *American Presbyterians: Journal of Presbyterian History* 63 (1985): 333–40.

BOYD STANLEY SCHLENTHER

MALAMUD, Bernard (26 Apr. 1914–18 Mar. 1986), writer, was born in Brooklyn, New York, the son of Max Malamud, a grocer, and Bertha Fidelman. Both parents were Jewish immigrants to the United States from Russia. Bernard Malamud received the B.A. from the City College of New York in 1936 and the M.A. in English from Columbia University in 1942, with a thesis on Thomas Hardy's *Dynasts*. He was a clerk for the Bureau of the Census in Washington, D.C., in 1940 and thereafter taught English in evening high schools in New York City from 1940 to 1949, including his own high school, Erasmus Hall in Brooklyn, from which he had graduated in 1932. He married Ann de Chiara, an Italian American, in 1945; they had two children. He taught English at Oregon State University from 1949 to 1961, rising to the rank of associate professor. In 1956–1957 he spent a sabbatical year chiefly in Rome. From 1961 to his death he taught in the Division of Languages and Literature at Bennington College in Vermont. He was a visiting lecturer at Harvard from 1966 to 1968. He was elected to the National Institute of Arts and Letters in 1964 and the American Academy of Arts and Sciences in 1967. He won the National Book Award for *The Magic Barrel* (1958) and *The Fixer* (1966), for which he also won the Pulitzer Prize in 1967.

Malamud's first book, *The Natural* (1952), was a novel about baseball. Its hero (or antihero) is Roy Hobbs, a naturally gifted player who is corrupted by the American myth of success. Hobbs resembles Shoeless Joe Jackson, and the events of the Black Sox scandal of 1919 are echoed in the novel, which also has affinities with the Grail story of Percival and his attempt to heal the Fisher-King. In Roy Hobbs, Malamud establishes a typical protagonist: an innocent outsider who is unable to cope with an alien society.

Malamud's next novel, *The Assistant* (1957), is one of his most memorable works. He explores his most characteristic theme of what it means to be Jewish, and the novel ends with Frankie Alpine, the Italian assistant in the grocery store, circumcising himself and converting to Judaism. Malamud is drawing on his own experiences in his parents' grocery store in Brooklyn, a marginal and failing enterprise. There is a great emphasis on ritual and ceremony in the novel, which recalls Malamud's own description, in conversation, of his father performing the rite of bar mitzvah for him later in his life.

The Magic Barrel, a collection of thirteen short stories, was published in 1958. The stories mingle naturalistic and fantastic detail in the best tradition of the Yiddish folktale as represented in such writers as Sholom Aleichem, I. L. Peretz, and Isaac Bashevis Singer.

In "Angel Levine," for example, a Jewish tailor named Manischevitz is made to believe that he must seek out his black Jewish guardian angel, Alexander Levine, in Harlem.

The novel *A New Life* (1961) is based on Malamud's own experiences as a professor of English at Oregon State University, although it quickly gets beyond the grounds of an academic novel to an exploration of Arcadian, Edenic myths of the West. Seymour Levin, the professor, is an archetypal Malamud hero as schlemiel, who manages to triumph over a series of academic and erotic disasters. For Levin, a former drunk and the son of a thief, the new pastoral life of the American frontier is ironically unsatisfying and must be rejected.

Idiots First (1963), a collection of twelve stories, is again centered on the schlemiel figure, who manages to acquire dignity and status in his confrontation with adverse circumstance. There are some curious, allegorical stories in this collection, including "The Jewbird," about a crow named Schwartz, and "Black Is My Favorite Color," about a Jewish liquor dealer in Harlem named Nat Lime. This story confronts the ambiguities of Jewish-black relations without trying to simplify the issues and anticipates the novel *The Tenants* (1971).

The Fixer (1966) may be Malamud's most compelling novel. It is based on the Mendel Beiliss case in Kiev in 1913, in which Beiliss was tried and acquitted of the charge of ritual murder of a Christian child whose blood was supposedly used in the baking of matzoh for Passover. This is a legendary anti-Semitic accusation that dates back to the Middle Ages. Yakov Bok, the handyman, explores his Jewishness while he is in prison, especially through his reading of Spinoza, who seems to promise an escape from the ineluctability of Jewish history. Bok is the scapegoat—*bock* is goat in German—a sacrificial figure like Christ the carpenter who will be resurrected. The novel has apocalyptic overtones.

In *Pictures of Fidelman: An Exhibition* (1969) Malamud uses three previously published stories and three new ones to explore Arthur Fidelman's burlesque and pointless search for artistic fulfillment in Italy. Malamud is preoccupied with the tragic conflict, echoed from Nathaniel Hawthorne, between the artist's egoistic pursuit of his art and his detachment from life and human experience, which should be the source of his artistic inspiration. Fidelman abandons painting and ends as a glass blower in Venice, thereby recovering his relation to love and to his inner life. Incidentally, Fidelman is the maiden name of Malamud's mother.

The Tenants (1971) is Malamud's bleakest novel, with a white Jewish novelist, Harry Lesser, pitted against Willie Spearman, an angry black squatter in the same, almost empty building. This is a reflexive novel about the writing of a novel and the ambiguous relations of art to life. As the landlord Levenspiel says, "Art my ass, in this world it's heart that counts" (p. 22). So Lesser destroys himself by substituting writing for living.

Rembrandt's Hat (1973) is another collection of short stories, some on the theme of art and life. In "Man in a Drawer," Feliks Levitansky is a Russian-Jewish writer whose work cannot be published in his country, but his manuscript is heroically smuggled out by an American, Howard Harvitz (a play on the word "Harvard"?).

In the novel *Dubin's Lives* (1979) the art-life theme is continued. Dubin is a professional biographer who is currently writing *The Passion of D. H. Lawrence*, a writer who has a broken and fragmented sensibility like Dubin, torn between calculating rationality and unthinking sensuality. Dubin, approaching sixty, is having an affair with the young, romantic Fanny Bick, but he is so immersed in the lives of colorful literary figures that he finds it difficult to live his own life: "You see in others who you are" (p. 130). This is Malamud's only novel that is set in Vermont in a rural atmosphere like that of Bennington.

Malamud's last novel, *God's Grace* (1982), is freely apocalyptic and allegorical. It is a fantasy of some time in the future after the thermonuclear war between the Djanks and the Druskies. Calvin Cohn, a paleologist, is the sole survivor, and he mates with Mary, a chimpanzee, to produce a humanoid progeny. Malamud projects his novel as a biblical fable, with Cohn as a Christ figure who is martyred at the end as the forces of violence and chaos take over.

Malamud has said, "All men are Jews except they don't know it." He himself was not an observant Jew, yet he believed that being a Jew was essential for understanding and accepting the human condition. He associates Judaism with suffering, which defines what it means to be a human being. In this sense, Malamud is close to the Russian novelists of the nineteenth century, whom he read so avidly. Everyone has a moral obligation to his fellow human beings and to the community in which they live. This is the heart of *menschlichkeit*, being human. We must accept responsibility for our fellow humans and be involved in the suffering of others. This is what is meant by *rachmones*, or the Jewish idea of compassion and mercy. One learns from the sufferings of others, but even more important one learns from one's own sufferings. In this way one realizes one's full humanity and becomes what in Yiddish is called flatteringly a "mensch." Malamud is a Jewish-American novelist who goes beyond specifically ethnic themes to explore the darker moral paradoxes of American writers such as Hawthorne and Melville and Russian novelists such as Dostoyevsky.

• Most of Malamud's manuscripts are in the Library of Congress, including the typescripts and proofs of *The Natural*, *The Assistant*, *A New Life*, *The Fixer*, *Pictures of Fidelman*, parts of *The Magic Barrel* and *Idiots First*, and various short stories. Malamud's last, unfinished novel, *The People*, and sixteen short stories are collected and edited by Robert Giroux in *The People and Uncollected Stories* (1989). Lawrence M. Lasher assembles an excellent collection of interviews in *Conversations with Bernard Malamud* (1991). Critical essays on Malamud are collected by Leslie A. Field and Joyce W.

Field in *Bernard Malamud and the Critics* (1970) and in the Twentieth Century Views volume, *Bernard Malamud: A Collection of Critical Essays* (1975). See also Richard Astro and Jackson J. Benson, eds., *The Fiction of Bernard Malamud* (1977); Joel Salzberg, ed., *Critical Essays on Bernard Malamud* (1987); and Harold Bloom, *Modern Critical Views: Bernard Malamud* (1986). *A Malamud Reader*, with an introduction by Philip Rahv (1967), is a useful compilation.

Among critical studies, see Sidney Richman's book in the Twayne's United States Authors Series, no. 109 (1966); Sheldon J. Hershinow, *Bernard Malamud* (1980); Jeffrey Helterman, *Understanding Bernard Malamud* (1985); Robert Solotaroff, *Bernard Malamud: A Study of the Short Fiction* (1989); and Edward A. Abramson, *Bernard Malamud Revisited* (1993). Of special interest is Iska Alter, *The Good Man's Dilemma: Social Criticism in the Fiction of Bernard Malamud* (1981). The best of the bibliographical guides are Salzberg, ed., *Bernard Malamud: A Reference Guide* (1985), continued in Richard O'Keefe, "Bibliographical Essay: Bernard Malamud," *Studies in American Jewish Literature* 7 (1988): 240–50; and Rita N. Kosofsky, *Bernard Malamud: A Descriptive Bibliography* (1991). An obituary is in the *New York Times*, 20 Mar. 1986.

MAURICE CHARNEY

MALBONE, Edward Greene (Aug. 1777–7 May 1807), miniature portrait painter, was born Edward Greene in Newport, Rhode Island, the son of John Malbone, a merchant and brigadier general in the Rhode Island militia, and Patience Greene, his common-law wife. His childhood was spent in modest circumstances, and by October 1794 he had assumed his father's last name. Malbone consistently described himself as a self-taught artist, although he may have received some instruction from Samuel King, a Newport instrument maker and miniature painter who may have provided prints for Malbone to copy. At age seventeen Malbone went to Providence, Rhode Island, to establish himself as a miniature portrait painter, and from the start he seems to have attained considerable success. His career was marked by sojourns in the major urban centers along the eastern seaboard, where he developed an impressive clientele. After spending two years in Providence, Malbone moved to Boston, then to Philadelphia, and then to New York; he arrived in Charleston, South Carolina, in 1801.

In the spring of that year Malbone departed for London with noted Boston painter Washington Allston, with whom he had been friends for several years. While in London, Malbone was impressed by the fashionable oil portraits by Sir Thomas Lawrence and was influenced by the miniatures of Samuel Shelley and Richard Cosway. Although he is known to have drawn at the Royal Academy, Malbone does not seem to have received formal instruction in London nor to have shown much interest in old masters or contemporary history painting. Malbone's own portraits were admired by American painter Benjamin West, president of the Royal Academy.

In December 1801 Malbone returned to the United States and adopted an itinerant lifestyle that, from 1802 to 1804, took him to Charleston, Philadelphia, Boston, Newport, and New York. He spent 1804–

1805 in Boston, and by the winter of 1805–1806 he had returned to Charleston. Suffering from tuberculosis, Malbone sought a variety of ways to improve his health, including a trip to Jamaica, which was not to his liking. In 1807 when he returned to the United States, Malbone moved to Savannah, Georgia, where he lived at the home of his cousin Robert Mackay until his death. Malbone never married or had children and died before this thirtieth birthday.

During the early years of the American Republic, miniature portraits were a popular art form, often used to commemorate such important personal events as courtships and marriages. Because of their small size (Malbone's usually measure 2¹⁵⁄₁₆″ by 2⁵⁄₁₆″), their delicate technique (watercolor on ivory), and their often precious settings (gold lockets, sometimes set with semiprecious stones and accompanied by locks of hair), miniatures were ideal expressions of affection.

Over the twelve years of his career, Malbone's style evolved from somewhat dark, convention-driven portraits to fresher likenesses. Malbone capitalized on the translucency of his medium, creating expansive and airy portraits. The hallmark of his style—something his imitators never fully captured—is a delicate system of hatching and cross-hatching, usually most visible in his backgrounds.

Malbone successfully obtained commissions in each of the cities he frequented. He often advertised in the local press, and word of his availability spread among prospective clients. Among his patrons Malbone could claim distinguished members of the social aristocracy, as in Charleston, where members of the Pinckney, Izard, Manigault, Rutledge, and Poinsett families sat for him. Malbone generally received $50 for his portraits, occasionally $100 for larger ones. Malbone's sitters invariably appear self-assured, well bred, and handsome. More often than not the subjects were young. Malbone is credited with creating pleasing likenesses, as noted by Allston and recorded by William Dunlap: "He had the happy talent among his many excellencies, of elevating the character without impairing the likeness, this was remarkable in his male heads, and no woman ever lost any beauty from his hand, nay, the fair would often become still fairer under his pencil" (*History*, vol. 2, p. 16).

Several American artists known for painting oil portraits, including John Singleton Copley, Charles Willson Peale, and Henry Benbridge, also painted miniatures. Malbone, however, remained committed to one medium; perhaps this contributed to his success in the genre. (Ironically, the only known self-portraits by Malbone were done in oil; they are housed in the Corcoran Art Gallery in Washington, D.C., and in the Providence Athenaeum.) Respected by patrons and peers alike, Malbone influenced other American artists working in miniatures, including Anson Dickinson, Charles Fraser, and Richard Morrell Staigg. In Charleston Fraser followed Malbone's example by presenting his patrons with luminous, flattering likenesses. Working primarily in New England, Dickinson emulated the delicacy of Malbone's portraits,

while Staigg in Newport simultaneously imitated and simplified his predecessor's style.

In the obituary that appeared in the *Charleston Times*, Fraser wrote the following evaluation of Malbone's portraits: "He imparted such life to the ivory, and produced always such striking resemblances, that they will never fail to perpetuate the tenderness of friendship, to divert the cares of absence, and to aid affection in dwelling on those features and that image which death has forever wrested from it. His style of painting was chaste and correct, his coloring dear and judiciously wrought, and his taste altogether derived from a just contemplation of nature." Malbone's career as a miniature portrait painter seems to have been well suited to his temperament and talents. Active in the field for less than twelve years, Malbone nevertheless achieved national acclaim and continues to rank as the finest American miniature portrait painter. His output, which is estimated to have been about 720 portraits, was prodigious, especially given his poor health and peripatetic lifestyle.

• Miniature portraits by Malbone can be found in the Museum of Fine Arts, Boston; the Metropolitan Museum of Art; the National Museum of American Art, Smithsonian Institution; the Carolina Art Association/Gibbes Museum of Art, Charleston; and the Mead Art Museum, Amherst College, Amherst, Mass., among others. William Dunlap, *A History of the Rise and Progress of the Arts of Design in the United States* (1918; repr. 1969), written during the 1830s, contains important primary source material about Malbone, including correspondence from Fraser and Allston and a reminiscence by Malbone's sister. Henry Tuckerman, *Book of the Artists* (1867), discusses Malbone and praises him as an exceptional miniature painter. Malbone is treated in the two major surveys of miniatures: Theodore Bolton, *Early American Portrait Painters in Miniature* (1921), and Harry B. Wehle, *American Miniatures, 1730–1850* (1927). Malbone was the subject of a 1929 exhibition at the National Gallery of Art that included eighty examples of his work. Ruel P. Tolman published several articles about Malbone in *Antiques* magazine: "Newly Discovered Miniatures by Edward Greene Malbone," Nov. 1929, pp. 373–80; "Malbone's 'Hours,'" Dec. 1931, pp. 508–9; "Other Malbone Miniatures," Apr. 1933, pp. 120–31; and "Edward Greene Malbone's Self-Portraits," Dec. 1942, pp. 306–8. Tolman, *The Life and Works of Edward Greene Malbone, 1777–1807* (1958), remains the most complete discussion of Malbone and benefits from the inclusion of many illustrations and a facsimile of an account book kept by Malbone. Malbone's miniatures have been included in a variety of museum publications and catalogs, including Martha R. Severens, *The Miniature Portrait Collection of the Carolina Art Association* (1984), and Dale T. Johnson, *American Portrait Miniatures of the Manney Collection*, which accompanied an exhibition of miniatures at the Metropolitan Museum of Art in 1990. An obituary is in the *Charleston Times*, 27 May 1807.

MARTHA R. SEVERENS

MALCOLM, Norman Adrian (11 June 1911–5 Aug. 1990), philosopher, was born in Selden, Kansas, the son of Charles Malcolm, a druggist, and Ada Wingrove, a teacher. He entered the University of Nebraska in 1929, intending to study law, but was attracted into philosophy by Oets Bouwsma. After receiving his

B.A. from Nebraska in 1933, he began graduate work at Harvard, receiving his M.A. in 1938. Through Bouwsma he had become interested in the philosophy of G. E. Moore. In 1938 he studied at Cambridge, on a Harvard traveling fellowship where he worked with Moore, who also supervised his doctoral dissertation. Although he formed a close personal and philosophical relationship with Moore, the chief philosophical influence on Malcolm at Cambridge was Ludwig Wittgenstein, with whom he became friends. His association with Wittgenstein, which he vividly and movingly described in *Ludwig Wittgenstein: A Memoir* (1958), had a profound influence on his subsequent career.

In 1940 Malcolm returned to the United States and completed his doctorate at Harvard. From 1940–1942 he taught at Princeton University. When the United States entered World War II, he joined the U.S. Navy, where he served from April 1942 to December 1945. After briefly commanding an escort vessel in the Carribean, he became executive officer and navigator on a destroyer escort on the Atlantic. In February 1944 he married Leonida Morosova. They had two children.

After the war he resumed his instructorship at Princeton, and in 1946 he returned to Cambridge on a Guggenheim fellowship and renewed his association with Wittgenstein.

In 1947 Malcolm joined the faculty of Cornell University as an assistant professor. Max Black had joined the Cornell faculty a year earlier, and the two put Cornell's philosophy department and its *Philosophical Review* at the center of philosophical activity in the United States.

In the summer of 1949 Wittgenstein came to visit Malcolm in Ithaca, and stayed several months. During his stay, he and Malcolm had a number of conversations about G. E. Moore's defense of common sense and his "proof" of the existence of the external world. In "Moore and Ordinary Language" (in *The Philosophy of G. E. Moore*, ed. Paul A. Schilpp [1942]), Malcolm had interpreted Moore's defense of common sense as a defense of ordinary language, but in his "Defending Common Sense" (*Philosophical Review* 58 [1949]: 201–20) he argued that Moore's famous "two hands" proof of the external world involved a misuse of the word "know." Malcolm's and Wittgenstein's discussions provided the stimulus for the work by Wittgenstein that was eventually published as *On Certainty* (1969) and Malcolm's influential paper "Knowledge and Belief" (*Mind* 61 [1952]; subsequently published in his essay collection *Knowledge and Certainty* [1963]).

Wittgenstein died in 1951, and two years later his *Philosophical Investigations* was published. Malcolm's critical notice, "Wittgenstein's Philosophical Investigations" (*Philosophical Review* 63 [1954]: 530–59) was a highly influential exposition and discussion of Wittgenstein's later philosophy, and especially of his "private language argument." It established him as the foremost American interpreter and advocate of Wittgenstein's philosophy.

Malcolm was promoted to associate professor in 1950, and to full professor in 1955. In 1964 he was appointed Susan Linn Sage Professor of Philosophy. He was chair of the Cornell philosophy department from 1965–1970.

Malcolm's earliest papers—"The Verification Argument" (in *Philosophical Analysis*, ed. Max Black [1950]) and "Knowledge and Belief" are among the best known—deal with issues about knowledge and skepticism. After the publication of Wittgenstein's *Philosophical Investigations*, his work became more centered in the philosophy of mind. Probably the most controversial of his writings of this period was his book *Dreaming* (1959), in which he argued that dreams do not have genuine duration or temporal location and do not involve the having of genuine experiences.

Another provocative work of this period was his "Anselm's Ontological Arguments" (1960), in which he defended a version of the ontological argument for the existence of God. This grew out of a graduate course he taught on the philosophy of Descartes—as did some of his views on dreaming. He also taught courses on Descartes, Spinoza, Leibniz, Freud, and Moore. Increasingly Malcolm's teaching concentrated on Wittgenstein, his early philosophy (the *Tractatus* and the *Notebooks*) as well as such later works as the *Investigations*, *Zettel*, and *On Certainty*.

By the mid-1950s Malcolm had become the most influential teacher of philosophy at Cornell and his style had given Cornell philosophy its distinctive tone. The pace in his classes and at the meetings of the Cornell Discussion Club, which he dominated, was sometimes excruciatingly slow, but the intellectual atmosphere could be electrifying. The refrain was "What d'you mean?" pronounced in the Nebraska accent Malcolm never lost. He was tenacious, blunt, and sometimes gruff, but his single-minded devotion to getting at the truth and exposing confusion commanded respect. His seriousness was tempered by a sense of the ridiculous, a knack for devising apt and amusing examples, and personal warmth. Malcolm once wrote that the qualities contributing to G. E. Moore's philosophical eminence were "complete modesty and simplicity, saving him from the dangers of jargon and pomposity; thorough absorption in philosophy, which he found endlessly exciting; strong mental powers; and a pure integrity that accounted for his solidity and his passion for clarity." As the Finnish philosopher George Henrik von Wright remarked in a memorial statement, Malcolm's description of Moore could serve as a self-characterization.

In the fall of 1952 Malcolm was Hebben Research Fellow at Princeton, and the following year he was on leave in Oxford. During 1960–1961 he was a Fulbright Research Fellow at the University of Helsinki, where he had extensive discussions with Jaakko Hintikka and George Henrik von Wright on the topic of memory (on which Malcolm had taught seminars at Cornell). These led to three lectures on memory delivered at Princeton University in 1962 (subsequently published in *Knowledge and Certainty*). Later he returned to this topic in *Memory and Mind* (1977). There he criticized both philosophical and psychological theories of memory and argued that the notion of a memory trace "is not a scientific discovery . . . [but] a product of philosophical thinking, of a sort that is natural and enormously tempting, yet thoroughly muddled" (p. 228).

A recurrent theme in Malcolm's writing and teaching was the idea that in order to achieve philosophical understanding one must get to the root of the temptations to advance philosophical doctrines. That accomplished, one will see the philosophical doctrines as confused or nonsensical. Although he was convinced that dualism and other Cartesian views about the mind were thoroughly confused, he thought no better of contemporary materialist and functionalist views, or of current theorizing in psychology and linguistics (one of his papers is titled "The Myth of Cognitive Processes and Structures," in *Cognitive Development and Epistemology*, ed. T. Mischel [1971]). He shared with Wittgenstein an antipathy to scientism, and with Moore an antipathy to obscurantism. A number of his papers in philosophy of mind were republished in a volume titled *Thought and Knowledge* (1977). An influential paper not republished in any of his books is "The Conceivability of Mechanism" (*Philosophical Review* 77 [1968]: 45–72), in which he argues that once an action has been explained in terms of its physiological causal antecedents, it is no longer open to us to explain it in terms of the agent's reasons.

In 1964 Malcolm was Visiting Flint Professor at the University of California, Los Angeles. In 1968–1969 he was a fellow at the Center for Advanced Research in the Behavioral Sciences in Stanford, California. In 1972 he was President of the Eastern Division of the American Philosophical Association. He was elected to the American Academy of Arts and Sciences in 1975, and in 1975–1976 he held a National Endowment for the Humanities Fellowship. He spent that year in London, during which he wrote *Memory and Mind*.

By this time his first marriage had ended in divorce. While in London he became acquainted with Ruth Riesenberg, a Chilean psychoanalyst practicing in London. They were married in Ithaca in 1976. After his retirement in 1978, they settled in a flat in London.

In England Malcolm served as a visiting professor at King's College, London, and shortly before his death was appointed a fellow of the college. According to his obituary in the London *Times*, his seminars at King's were "renowned for their lucidity, depth and intellectual honesty. . . . He set a shining example as a teacher; and his high standards of philosophical clarity, his contempt for pretentiousness and his striving for truth and understanding affected all who worked with him."

During his last years he also continued to write and publish. In 1984 he and David Armstrong coauthored *Consciousness & Causality: A Debate on the Nature of Mind*, to which Malcolm's contribution was a wholesale rejection of the materialist/functionalist approach

to the philosophy of mind represented by Armstrong. His *Nothing Is Hidden: Wittgenstein's Criticism of His Early Thought* (1986) examines the relations between Wittgenstein's earlier and later philosophies.

Malcolm died in London. His years there are thought by some of his friends to have been the happiest of his life. He took full advantage of the cultural resources of the city. He ran daily in Hampstead Heath. And he remained actively involved in philosophy to the end.

Malcolm made significant contributions to the discussion of a number of philosophical topics (including knowledge, memory, other minds, and the mind-body problem), and to the understanding of Wittgenstein's philosophy. What was most distinctive about him was his philosophical character and style of doing philosophy—a style characterized by independence of mind, directness, lucidity, and vividness.

• Malcolm's other works include *Problems of Mind* (1971), an introductory book on philosophy of mind, and the posthumously published *Wittgenstein: A Religious Point of View?*, ed. Peter Winch (1994), which was the last work he completed before his death. A collection of the essays he wrote after 1977 was edited by George Henrik von Wright, *Wittgensteinian Themes* (1995). For a complete bibliography up to 1983, see *Knowledge and Mind*, ed. Carl Ginet and Sydney Shoemaker (1983), a volume of essays honoring Malcolm. Obituary notices about Malcolm are in London newspapers, the *Times*, 16 Aug. 1990, and the *Guardian*, 17 Aug. 1990. Memorial notices by Peter Winch and George Henrik von Wright are in the journal *Philosophical Investigations*, July 1992.

SYDNEY SHOEMAKER

MALCOLM X (19 May 1925–21 Feb. 1965), African-American religious and political leader also known as el-Hajj Malik el-Shabazz, was born Malcolm Little in Omaha, Nebraska, the son of Earl Little and Louise (also Louisa) Norton, both activists in the Universal Negro Improvement Association established by Marcus Garvey. Earl Little, a Georgia-born itinerant Baptist preacher, encountered considerable racial harassment because of his black nationalist views. He moved his family several times before settling in Michigan, purchasing a home in 1929 on the outskirts of East Lansing, where Malcolm Little spent his childhood. In 1931 the elder Little was run over by a streetcar and died. Although police concluded that the death was accidental, the victim's friends and relatives suspected that he had been murdered by a local white supremacist group. This incident led to a severe decline in the family's economic fortunes and contributed to Louise Little's mental deterioration. In January 1939 she was declared legally insane and committed to a Michigan mental asylum, where she remained until 1963.

Although Malcolm Little excelled academically in grammar school and was popular among classmates at the predominately white schools, he also became embittered toward white authority figures. In his autobiography he recalled quitting school after a teacher warned that his desire to become a lawyer was not a "realistic goal for a nigger." As his mother's mental health deteriorated and he became increasingly incorrigible, welfare officials intervened, placing him in several reform schools and foster homes. In 1941 he left Michigan to live in Boston with his half sister, Ella Collins.

While in Boston and New York during the early 1940s, Malcolm held a variety of railroad jobs while also becoming increasingly involved in criminal activities such as peddling illegal drugs and numbers running. During this period he was often called Detroit Red because of his reddish hair. Arrested in 1946 for larceny as well as breaking and entering, he was sent to prison in February 1946.

While in Concord Reformatory in Massachusetts, Malcolm X responded to the urgings of his brother Reginald and became a follower of Elijah Muhammad (formerly Robert Poole), leader of the Temple of Islam (later Nation of Islam—often called the Black Muslims), a small black nationalist Islamic sect. Attracted to the religious group's racial doctrines, which categorized whites as "devils," he began reading extensively about world history and politics, particularly concerning African slavery and the oppression of black people in America. After he was paroled from prison in August 1952, he became Minister Malcolm X, using the surname assigned to him in place of the African name that had been taken from his slave ancestors.

Malcolm X quickly became Elijah Muhammad's most effective minister, bringing large numbers of new recruits into the group during the 1950s and early 1960s. By 1954 he had become minister of New York Temple No. 7, and he later helped establish Islamic temples in other cities. In 1957 he became the Nation of Islam's national representative, a position of influence second only to that of Elijah Muhammad. In January 1958 he married Betty X (Sanders), also a Muslim; the two had six daughters.

Malcolm's forceful, cogent oratory attracted considerable publicity and a large personal following among discontented African Americans. In his speeches he urged black people to separate from whites and win their freedom "by any means necessary." In 1957, after New York police beat and jailed Nation of Islam member Hinton Johnson, Malcolm X mobilized supporters to confront police officials and secure medical treatment. A 1959 television documentary on the Nation of Islam called *The Hate That Hate Produced* further increased Malcolm's notoriety among whites. In 1959 he traveled to Europe and the Middle East on behalf of Elijah Muhammad, and in 1961 he served as Muhammad's emissary at a secret Atlanta meeting seeking an accommodation with the Ku Klux Klan. The following year he participated in protest meetings prompted by the killing of a black Muslim during a police raid on a Los Angeles mosque. By 1963 he had become a frequent guest on radio and television programs and was the most well-known figure in the Nation of Islam.

Malcolm X was particularly harsh in his criticisms of the nonviolent strategy to achieve civil rights reforms advocated by Martin Luther King, Jr. His letters seeking King's participation in public forums were generally ignored by King. During a November 1963 address at the Northern Negro Grass Roots Leadership Conference in Detroit, Malcolm derided the notion that African Americans could achieve freedom nonviolently. "The only revolution in which the goal is loving your enemy is the Negro revolution," he announced. "Revolution is bloody, revolution is hostile, revolution knows no compromise, revolution overturns and destroys everything that gets in its way." Malcolm also charged that King and other leaders of the recently held March on Washington had taken over the event, with the help of white liberals, in order to subvert its militancy. "And as they took it over, it lost its militancy. It ceased to be angry, it ceased to be hot, it ceased to be uncompromising," he insisted. Despite his caustic criticisms of King, however, Malcolm nevertheless identified himself with the grass-roots leaders of the southern civil rights protest movement. His desire to move from rhetorical to political militancy led him to become increasingly dissatisfied with Elijah Muhammad's apolitical stance. As he later explained in his autobiography, "It could be heard increasingly in the Negro communities: 'Those Muslims *talk* tough, but they never *do* anything, unless somebody bothers Muslims.'"

Malcolm's disillusionment with Elijah Muhammad resulted not only from political differences but also his personal dismay when he discovered that the religious leader had fathered illegitimate children. Other members of the Nation of Islam began to resent Malcolm's growing prominence and to suspect that he intended to lay claim to leadership of the group. When Malcolm X remarked that President John Kennedy's assassination in November 1963 was a case of the "chickens coming home to roost," Elijah Muhammad used the opportunity to ban his increasingly popular minister from speaking in public.

Despite this effort to silence him, Malcolm X continued to attract public attention during 1964. He counseled boxer Cassius Clay, who publicly announced, shortly after winning the heavyweight boxing title, that he had become a member of the Nation of Islam and adopted the name Muhammad Ali. In March 1964 Malcolm announced that he was breaking with the Nation of Islam to form his own group, Muslim Mosque, Inc. The theological and ideological gulf between Malcolm and Elijah Muhammad widened during a monthlong trip to Africa and the Middle East. During a pilgrimage to Mecca on 20 April 1964 Malcolm reported that seeing Muslims of all colors worshiping together caused him to reject the view that all whites were devils. Repudiating the racial theology of the Nation of Islam, he moved toward orthodox Islam as practiced outside the group. He also traveled to Egypt, Lebanon, Nigeria, Ghana, Senegal, and Morocco, meeting with political activists and national leaders, including Ghanian president Kwame Nkrumah. After returning to the United States on 21 May, Malcolm announced that he had adopted a Muslim name, el-Hajj Malik el-Shabazz, and that he was forming a new political group, the Organization of Afro-American Unity (OAAU), to bring together all elements of the African-American freedom struggle.

Determined to unify African Americans, Malcolm sought to strengthen his ties with the more militant factions of the civil rights movement. Although he continued to reject King's nonviolent, integrationist approach, he had a brief, cordial encounter with King on 26 March 1964 as the latter left a press conference at the U.S. Capitol. The following month, at a Cleveland symposium sponsored by the Congress of Racial Equality, Malcolm X delivered one of his most notable speeches, "The Ballot or the Bullet," in which he urged black people to submerge their differences "and realize that it is best for us to first see that we have the same problem, a common problem—a problem that will make you catch hell whether you're a Baptist, or a Methodist, or a Muslim, or a nationalist."

When he traveled again to Africa during the summer of 1964 to attend the Organization of African Unity Summit Conference, he was able to discuss his unity plans at an impromptu meeting in Nairobi with leaders of the Student Nonviolent Coordinating Committee. After returning to the United States in November, he invited Fannie Lou Hamer and other members of the Mississippi Freedom Democratic Party to be guests of honor at an OAAU meeting held the following month in Harlem. Early in February 1965 he traveled to Alabama to address gatherings of young activists involved in a voting rights campaign. He tried to meet with King during this trip, but the civil rights leader was in jail; instead Malcolm met with Coretta Scott King, telling her that he did not intend to make life more difficult for her husband. "If white people realize what the alternative is, perhaps they will be more willing to hear Dr. King," he explained.

Even as he strengthened his ties with civil rights activists, however, Malcolm acquired many new enemies. The U.S. government saw him as a subversive, and the Federal Bureau of Investigation initiated efforts to undermine his influence. In addition, some of his former Nation of Islam colleagues, including Louis X (later Louis Farrakhan), condemned him as a traitor for publicly criticizing Elijah Muhammad. The Nation of Islam attempted to evict him from the home he occupied in Queens, New York. On 14 February 1965 Malcolm's home was firebombed; although he and his family escaped unharmed, the perpetrators were never apprehended.

On 21 February 1965 members of the Nation of Islam shot and killed Malcolm as he was beginning a speech at the Audubon Ballroom in New York City. On 27 February more than 1,500 people attended his funeral service held in Harlem. Although three men were later convicted in 1966 and sentenced to life terms, one of those involved, Thomas Hagan, filed an affidavit in 1977 insisting that his actual accomplices were never apprehended.

After his death, Malcolm's views reached an even larger audience than during his life. *The Autobiography of Malcolm X*, written with the assistance of Alex Haley, became a bestselling book after its publication in 1965. During subsequent years other books appeared containing texts of many of his speeches, including *Malcolm X Speaks* (1965), *The End of White World Supremacy: Four Speeches* (1971), and *February 1965: The Final Speeches* (1992). In 1994 Orlando Bagwell and Judy Richardson produced a major documentary, *Malcolm X: Make It Plain*. His words and image also exerted a lasting influence on African-American popular culture, as evidenced in the hip-hop or rap music of the late twentieth century and in director Spike Lee's film biography, *Malcolm X* (1992).

• In addition to the works mentioned in the text, see Clayborne Carson, *Malcolm X: The FBI File* (1991); Michael Friedly, *Malcolm X: The Assassination* (1992); and Bruce Perry, *Malcolm: The Life of a Man Who Changed Black America* (1991). An obituary is in the *New York Times*, 22 Feb. 1965.

CLAYBORNE CARSON

MALCOM, Daniel (1725–23 Oct. 1769), mariner and merchant, was born in Georgetown, Maine, the son of Michael Malcom and Sarah (maiden name unknown). His parents arrived in America from Northern Ireland a few years before his birth. Daniel Malcom married Ann Fudge (date unknown); they had four children.

Malcom began as a sea captain in the coastal trade, particularly in voyages "down east" of Boston to Maine, Newfoundland, and Quebec. Eventually, he graduated to the more lucrative transatlantic routes to Ireland and the west of England. By the 1760s he began to acquire property in Boston, styled himself a merchant, and became the junior warden of Christ Church, the Anglican parish in Boston's North End. Early in the decade, Malcom joined a number of Boston merchants in their defense of the town's notoriously corrupt collector of customs, Benjamin Barons, against the accusations of the recently arrived governor Francis Bernard and other members of the customs establishment.

Out of the Barons controversy emerged the famous case of the writs of assistance (general search warrants) argued by James Otis before the superior court, Chief Justice Thomas Hutchinson presiding. Malcom signed a petition to the Massachusetts General Court objecting to the use of writs of assistance in January 1761. He was also a charter member of the Boston Society for Encouraging Trade and Commerce, which later petitioned against both the Sugar Act and the Revenue Act of 1766.

On 24 September 1766 Benjamin Hallowell, comptroller of customs at Boston, and William Sheaffe, the deputy collector, appeared at Malcom's house with a writ of assistance demanding admittance and claiming they had information that smuggled wines were stored there. Malcom first showed them an outbuilding on his property, then several rooms of the house itself before coming to the cellar. One section of the cellar had been partitioned off, and when Hallowell and Sheaffe demanded the key, Malcom replied that it was in the possession of his business partner William Mackay, to whom he had leased that portion of the cellar. Sheaffe went to Mackay's house for the key. Mackay denied having the key and returned with him to Malcom's. When Hallowell and Sheaffe began to talk of breaking down the door to the inner cellar, Malcom grabbed his pistols and his sword and swore that "the first Man that would break open my House without having Legal Authority for the same, I would kill him on the spot" (Smith, p. 444).

After remonstrating with Malcom, Hallowell and Sheaffe retreated to seek reinforcements and the advice of the governor and council. The patriot-dominated council, loathe to become involved, shifted responsibility to Stephen Greenleaf, the sheriff of Suffolk County. When Hallowell and Sheaffe returned with Greenleaf, they found Malcom's gate locked and his windows shuttered. An angry crowd had begun to gather outside the house as well. A standoff ensued until nightfall when the warrant was no longer valid.

The sheriff and customs officers reappeared before the council on the next day when depositions about the affair were taken down to be sent to England. Because misrepresentations based on ex parte evidence were so much a part of the Barons controversy, a committee appointed by the town meeting soon began soliciting counterdepositions (presumably arranged by Otis, Malcom's attorney). British authorities did not act on the case until January 1767. Unfortunately for those eager to punish Malcom, Attorney General William De Grey ruled that the superior court of Massachusetts did not have authority to issue writs of assistance despite that court's previous rulings to the contrary. Malcom again aroused the suspicions of the customs authorities in February 1768, when it was rumored he had run ashore sixty pipes of wine from a schooner moored among the islands of the outer harbor (a favorite unloading point for smugglers) and brought them the five miles distance to town in wagons guarded by men with clubs.

Four months later Malcom figured prominently in the riot that ensued following the seizure of John Hancock's sloop *Liberty*. Hancock had declared only twenty-five pipes of wine at the customs house, whereas rumor had it a far larger quantity remained on board. A tide waiter stationed on the vessel to prevent the unloading of any undeclared cargo was allegedly forced below while a great noise was heard on deck that sounded like the hoisting out of large casks. Based on the tide waiter's evidence, the Board of Customs Commissioners ordered the *Liberty* seized. When marines from HMS *Romney* attempted to carry out the seizure, a riot broke out. Popular feeling in Boston was so intense against the Board of Customs Commissioners that they fled for safety to Castle William in the harbor. News of the *Liberty* riot led directly to Whitehall's decision to send two regiments of British troops to Boston.

In the investigation that followed, Malcom's name figured prominently, prompting Governor Bernard to describe him as "the famous Captain Malcom, who having twice in a forcible Manner set the Laws of Trade at Defiance with Success, has thereby raised himself to be a Mob Captain" (Wolkins, "Seizure," p. 256).

Bernard and the customs authorities finally struck back on 29 October 1768 when Advocate General Jonathan Sewall filed suit for £9,000 each against Malcom, Hancock, and four other merchants, treble damages in the alleged landing of 100 pipes of wine from the *Liberty*. This was the first prosecution under a provision of the Sugar Act, which allowed for fines in such staggering amounts, far beyond the capacity of anyone but Hancock to pay. The widely publicized trial dragged on for five months before the suit was withdrawn on 25 March 1769. Malcom died in Boston just seven months later at the age of forty-four. His tombstone in Copp's Hill Burial Ground describes Malcom as "a true Son of Liberty, a Friend to the Publick, an Enemy to oppression, and one of the foremost in opposing the Revenue Acts on America."

• Papers with information on Malcom may be found in the Georgetown, Maine, town records; the Suffolk County Deeds, the Suffolk County Probate Files, no. 14,571, and the Christ Church records, all in Boston; and the Thwing file, Massachusetts Historical Society. See also G. G. Wolkins, "The Seizure of Hancock's Sloop *Liberty*," Massachusetts Historical Society, *Proceedings* 55 (1922): 239–84; Wolkins, "Daniel Malcom and the Writs of Assistance," Massachusetts Historical Society, *Proceedings* 58 (1924): 5–84; M. H. Smith, *The Writs of Assistance Case* (1978), pp. 443–53; and Oliver M. Dickerson, *The Navigation Acts and the American Revolution* (1951), pp. 241–45.

JOHN W. TYLER

MALIN, James Claude (8 Feb. 1893–26 Jan. 1979), historian, was born near Edgeley, North Dakota, the son of Jared Nelson Malin, a farmer and farm implement salesman, and Emma Jane McCristy. In 1903 the family joined relatives in Edwards County, Kansas. At Baker University in Baldwin, Kansas, Malin completed majors in history, philosophy, and science. Following his 1914 graduation he began teaching high school, but within a year he enrolled in summer graduate courses in history at the University of Kansas. Malin received his M.A. in 1916. Four years later he married Pearl Ethel Keene, they had one child. In 1921 Malin completed his doctorate and accepted an instructorship in the Department of History at Kansas. (He remained at his alma mater for forty-two years, until his retirement in 1963.) From his adviser and colleague Frank Heywood Hodder he absorbed a scientific approach to history and an interest in the politics of the Kansas Territory.

Malin, a soft-spoken, conversational young lecturer, at first taught courses on subjects ranging from English history to the contemporary United States. Building on his own research, he soon developed unique offerings in the history of the trans-Mississippi West and in the history of Kansas. Malin, twice president of the Kansas History Teachers Association, shaped his state's teacher corps by supervising nearly

100 master's theses. Given his university's small Ph.D. program, Malin directed only seven doctoral candidates. Nevertheless, his convention papers and scholarly publications earned him a national reputation. Numerous graduate students from other universities, including the young Allan G. Bogue and Lee Benson, journeyed to Lawrence to study with Malin or sought his advice.

Although later Malin would be regarded by some of his peers in the profession as a maverick, before the mid-1940s he enjoyed a conventional and extraordinarily promising academic career. By 1930 he had published his dissertation, *Indian Policy and Westward Expansion* (1921), and two well-received surveys of twentieth-century U.S. history. During the Great Depression limited travel funds and the opportunity to serve as associate editor of the *Kansas Historical Quarterly* induced Malin to explore local history. He produced a striking series of articles based on careful, intensive research. Malin's 1935 article on the turnover of the farm population in Kansas pioneered the use of the manuscript federal and state censuses to analyze population mobility. His methodology initially influenced agricultural historians. Two decades later it stimulated the quantitative studies of a rising generation of social historians interested in explaining the development of both rural and urban communities. In 1941 Malin served as president of the Kansas State Historical Society. By 1943 he was president of the Agricultural History Society, and he also served on the editorial board of the *Mississippi Valley Historical Review*.

After 1940 Malin increasingly turned his attention to the philosophy of history. *Essays in Historiography* (1946), *Essays, on the Nature of History* (1954), and *The Contriving Brain and the Skillful Hand* (1955) reflected the concerns of a man passionately committed to the integrity of his discipline. Dedicated to pursuing objectivity in his own work, Malin perceived himself at war with those historians whom he termed "subjective-relativists." He openly criticized the work of such leading figures as Charles Beard, Carl Becker, and Merle Curti. Malin's radical faith in individualism caused him to reject New Deal social and economic planning, and he branded supporters of a more powerful federal government "totalitarian liberals."

In 1945 a disagreement with the editor of the University of Kansas Press over how to revise a manuscript had fueled Malin's growing lack of confidence in the peer review system and helped convince him to self-publish his subsequent books. Friends feared that Malin's unorthodox publishing mechanism would reduce his audience, but they admired his fearlessness and respected his social science methods. Critics, however, found him cranky. His opaque writing style, his conclusions about the origins of dust storms, his evaluation of Kansas Populists, and his revisionist interpretation of John Brown's role in Kansas politics all drew criticism, as did his sometimes intemperate historiographical essays. Malin persisted, and, with the

support of his family, he continued to write and publish prolifically until his death in Lawrence.

During his lifetime and afterward Malin's influence derived from his innovative research. His rambling, unedited prose did not camouflage his diligence or his remarkably creative mind. Malin read so deeply in such subjects as geography, soil science, and ecology that he earned the respect of scientists in those fields. As early as 1940 he wrote of history written "from the ground up," meaning history that considered geology and climate, described soil and plants, investigated the choices made by individuals, and evaluated the influence of technology. Malin's most important book, *The Grassland of North America: Prolegomena to Its History* (1947), demonstrated the utility of his interdisciplinary orientation and sketched an imposing agenda for future agricultural and western historians. In a May 1950 essay in *Scientific Monthly*, he asserted that the proper task of historians was "the study of organisms in all their relations, living together, the differences between plant, animal, and human ecology or history being primarily a matter of emphasis" (p. 295). His ecological approach to the grasslands prefigured the work of later environmental historians.

Unlike the best-known western historians of his time, Frederick Jackson Turner and Walter P. Webb, Malin perceived no closed frontier. The optimistic Kansan, ever the independent product of his state's wide-open spaces, repeatedly argued for the power of individuals to change and to adapt to "open" systems. A truly original thinker who wrote eighteen books, more than eighty articles, and dozens of book reviews, Malin mined state and local subjects to make durable, albeit controversial, contributions to western, agricultural, and antebellum political history.

• Malin's papers are at the Kansas State Historical Society in Topeka. The University of Kansas Archives, Lawrence, also holds a copy of the transcript of Malin's 29 March 1972 oral history interview housed in the oral history collection at Cornell University. Essential to understanding Malin's scholarly range are his *John Brown and the Legend of Fifty-Six* (1942); *Winter Wheat in the Golden Belt of Kansas* (1944); *Grassland Historical Studies*, vol. 1 (1950); and *The Nebraska Question, 1852–54* (1953). Malin, "The Historian and the Individual," in *Essays on Individuality*, ed. Felix Morley (1958), reveals much about Malin's basic assumptions. The most accessible introduction to Malin's work in grassland history is Robert P. Swierenga, ed., *James C. Malin: History and Ecology, Studies of the Grassland* (1984), which contains a thoughtful introduction by Swierenga, excerpts from Malin's publications, and a useful selected bibliography. For a complete bibliography, see "Appendix A—Publications of James C. Malin," in *Essays in American History in Honor of James C. Malin*, ed. Burton J. Williams (1973). Malin's most influential article was "The Turnover of Farm Population in Kansas," *Kansas Historical Quarterly* 4 (Nov. 1935): 339–72. Allan G. Bogue, "James C. Malin: A Voice from the Grassland," in *Writing Western History*, ed. Richard W. Etulain (1991), precisely and sympathetically analyzes Malin's contributions to western history. For evidence of Malin's continuing influence, see also Bogue, "The Heirs of James C. Malin: A Grassland Historiography," *Great Plains Quarterly* 1 (Spring 1981): 105–31.

JULIENNE L. WOOD

MALINA, Frank Joseph (2 Oct. 1912–9 Nov. 1981), aeronautical engineer, was born in Brenham, Texas, the son of Czech immigrants Frank Malina, a musician, and Caroline Marek. After graduating from Texas A&M University in 1934, Malina received a fellowship from the California Institute of Technology, where he quickly became involved with its Guggenheim Aeronautical Laboratory (GALCIT). He earned an M.S. in mechanical engineering in 1935 and a second M.S. in aeronautical engineering in 1936. He received a Ph.D. magna cum laude in aeronautics in 1940. In his dissertation he examined the problems of rocket propulsion and sounding rocket flight performance. Malina served as an assistant professor at CIT from 1942 until 1946. He married Marjorie Duckworth, his second wife, in 1949; they had two children.

Aerodynamicist Theodore von Kármán, director of GALCIT and doctoral adviser to Malina, had encouraged Malina to pursue rocket research, and Malina and von Kármán developed a close, lifelong working relationship. Malina later became recognized as a founder of modern rocketry. In 1936, with von Kármán's blessing, Malina and a small group of men interested in rockets founded the GALCIT Rocket Research Project. From 1940 to 1944 Malina was the chief engineer of the Air Corps Jet Propulsion Research Project of GALCIT; in 1944 these projects became the Jet Propulsion Laboratory (JPL), a somewhat independent research facility attached to the California Institute of Technology. JPL later developed lunar and planetary spacecraft under contract to the National Aeronautics and Space Administration.

In the 1930s and early 1940s rocketry and rocket propulsion were popularly associated with radio, movie, and comic strip portrayals of space travel by fictional characters like Buck Rogers and Flash Gordon. To distance its rocket research from such fiction, in 1944 JPL was not named the "Rocket Propulsion Laboratory." In fact many scientists did not believe that rocket propulsion had a future; one scientist even encouraged Malina to pursue other interests. Rocketry had such a bad reputation that institutional funding of research was unavailable. Possible military use of rockets also limited the sharing of research results, especially between nations during World War II. Despite these limitations, in 1936 Malina and his associates conceived of using a liquid-fueled motor to power a high-altitude sounding rocket. In 1937 they made limited progress in actually running such a motor.

Robert Goddard's earlier experimental rockets had been propelled by liquid oxygen, a difficult to handle and store oxidizer, whose use therefore seemed impractical. Looking for propellant combinations that were easier to use, more reliable, and practical, Malina led a group of researchers, including John W. Parsons

at the Rocket Research Project of GALCIT, in testing many liquid fuels. They developed red fuming nitric acid (RFNA) and aniline, a propellant combination that achieved great use in American rocketry. RFNA and aniline ignited spontaneously, yet were reliable and storable.

Malina and another researcher, H. S. Tsien, also continued a theoretical study of the thermodynamic characteristics of rocket motors. Although they initially thought their research in rocket propulsion would be applied to upper atmosphere sounding rockets, its first use occurred in assisting aircraft takeoff. In 1941 a small airplane—the Ercoupe—took off at March Field near Riverside, California, assisted by solid-fuel rockets. This was the first successful American use of solid fuel JATOs (jet-assisted takeoff). A year later, a liquid-fuel JATO assisted a light bomber, the Douglas A-20a, to take off at the Army Air Corps Bombing and Gunnery Range at Muroc, California, another American first. Under Malina's direction, researchers also developed and patented a hydrazine-nitric acid fuel. This mixture was later used to propel the engines for the Apollo Service and Lunar Excursion Modules. Malina, von Kármán, Jack Parsons, Ed Forman, Martin Summerfield, and Andrew Haley founded the Aerojet Engineering Corporation in 1942 to build JATOs.

In the summer of 1944, prompted by 1943 British intelligence reports on German advancements in rocketry, Malina and his associates began developing a series of rockets that eventually led to an American version of the German V-2. Their first effort—the ten-mile-range solid fuel Private A—was an experimental missile stabilized with fixed fins, boosted out of a rail-type launcher by a quick-burning JATO unit. The successful launches of Private A made it a distance predecessor of the Minuteman and other American composite solid-propellant rockets. Malina and his associates added wings to the Private A to create the Private F, theorizing that range would increase by 50 percent with a reduced payload. Instead, the Private F had only limited success, with each test round going into a tailspin.

While slow progress was made on the large liquid-propelled missile named Corporal, Malina built a model Corporal, the WAC Corporal, to be used as a high-altitude scientific sounding rocket. The launch of the sixteen-foot-tall WAC Corporal in 1945 crowned Malina's rocket career. Fueled by RFNA and aniline, the WAC Corporal was boosted out of a 100-foot-tall launch tower by a modified ballistic armament rocket. The WAC Corporal met its performance expectation and in 1949, when boosted on the nose of a captured V-2, became the first man-made object to reach outer space.

Malina made a number of other important contributions to rocketry during his career. With von Kármán, he developed in 1940 the theory of constant-thrust long-duration solid fuel rocket motors. In 1942 he and another associate, Mark Mills, designed and patented a safety pressure relief valve for solid propellant rocket motors. In 1943, with Martin Summerfield, Malina introduced and patented improvements in methods of applying rocket propulsion to flying boats. In 1946 they formulated the "Malina-Summerfield Criterion" for step-rockets. This criterion stated that each step of the optimum step-rocket has an equal ratio between its payload mass and the total mass of the step-rocket propelling that payload.

In 1944 and in 1946 Malina worked with the U.S. War Department for European Missions, traveling to Britain and France as a scientific consultant. He studied British rocket developments and the remains of a German V-2 rocket, which had landed in Sweden. His trip to France included inspection of German V-1 and V-2 launching sites in the Pas-de-Calais region. He also traveled often to Washington, D.C., to obtain funding for JPL rocket programs and as a consultant to the U.S. National Defense Research Committee.

In 1947 Malina left JPL to work on the United Nations Educational, Scientific, and Cultural Organization in Paris. He sought to increase international cooperation in scientific studies, having experienced firsthand the limiting nature of international conflict and competition. He was first assigned to study ways to decrease national barriers to allow the free movement of scientists and their equipment. He also worked on the Arid Zone Research Program, one of UNESCO's major projects at the time. Malina was a counselor in the Natural Sciences Department at UNESCO in 1947–1948, becoming the deputy director of this department in 1948 and later serving as the head of the Division of Scientific Research from 1951 to 1953. The International Astronautical Federation named him their permanent representative to UNESCO in 1959.

In 1953 Malina resigned from his post at UNESCO to become a studio artist. While living in Paris, he developed kinetic sculpture that linked art, science, and technology. His more that 250 works used electric light in motion and were exhibited in Paris and other cities in Europe and around the world. Malina founded *Leonardo*, a magazine of the contemporary arts, in 1967–1968 and acted as editor.

In the late 1950s, at the request of his mentor von Kármán, Malina returned to rocketry and helped found the International Academy of Astronautics. Created to promote international cooperation in astronautics, a close match in its intent to Malina's previous UNESCO work, the academy was remarkable in that it transcended Cold War barriers and brought Eastern European and Soviet scientists together with Western scientists. Between 1960 and 1965 Malina was one of four coeditors of *Astronomica Acta*, a publication of the academy.

Malina presented several professional papers related to his work at GALCIT and JPL between 1936 and 1946. The first of these was "The Jet Propulsion Laboratory: Its Origins and First Decade of Work" (*Spaceflight*, 6 [Sept. 1964]: 160–65 and [Oct. 1964]: 193–97). In 1967 Malina prepared a paper for the First International Symposium on the History of Astronautics in Belgrade that later appeared as "The Rocket Pioneers: Memoirs of the Infant Days of Rocketry at Caltech [1934–1939]" in *Engineering and Science* (31 [Feb. 1968]: 9–13, 30–32).

As an early pioneer in the field of rocketry and propulsion, Malina made many valuable contributions. His innovations in long-duration propulsion and solid and liquid fuel propellants were particularly important. According to a 1958 letter to Malina from Rear Admiral D. S. Fahrney, U.S.N. (retired), "It was based on your findings that we produced the first jet propelled guided missile in this country." Malina promoted international cooperation in the sciences, especially astronautics, and was admired for his efforts. He was a member of the American Academy of Arts and Sciences, the French Aeronautics Society, the British Interplanetary Society, Sigma Xi, the New York Academy of Sciences, and the International Academy of Astronautics and was a fellow at the American Astronautics Society and the American Institute of Aeronautics and Astronautics. Malina died at his home in Boulogne-sur-Seine, near Paris.

• Malina's papers are at the Library of Congress, with a microform copy at the California Institute of Technology Archives. A more detailed biography of Malina, a longer bibliography of his works, and copies of most of his scientific studies are available at the JPL Archives. Malina described the military application of rockets and the accompanying research and development in which he engaged during World War II in "The US Army Air Corps Jet Propulsion Research Project, GALCIT Project No. 1, 1939–1946: A Memoir," *Proceedings of the Third International History Symposium of the International Academy of Astronautics, 1969* (1973). He recalled the work JPL did for the U.S. Army Ordnance Corps involving rockets in a presentation at the International Academy of Astronautics Symposium on the History of Astronautics in Brussels in Sept. 1971 that was later published as "America's First Long-Range Missile and Space Exploration Program," *Spaceflight* 15 (Dec. 1973): 442–56. General summary articles by Malina that describe his experiences as an artist include "Some Reflections on the Differences between Science and Art," in *Data: Directions in Art Theory/Aesthetics*, ed. Anthony Hill (1968), pp. 134–49, and "Electric Light as a Medium in the Visual Fine Arts: A Memoir," *Leonardo* 8 (1975): 109–19.

JOHN BLUTH

MALINOWSKI, Bronislaw Kasper (7 Apr. 1884–16 May 1942), social anthropologist, was born in Cracow, Austrian Poland, the only child of Lucjan Malinowski, a professor of Slavonic philology, and Józefa Łącka. Both parents were Roman Catholics and somewhat impoverished members of a landed gentry (*szlachta* class). At the time of Malinowski's upbringing, Cracow was an important intellectual and artistic center.

Malinowski was, in his own words, "drawn early into the realm of learning despite a vexatiously sickly constitution" (Ellen et al., p. 196). His attendance at the Sobieski Gymnasium in Cracow was interrupted by persistent illness and severe eye problems, and much of his early education was imparted at home. Despite these handicaps he was a brilliant student.

Following the death of his father in 1898, Malinowski's mother, a highly cultivated woman, took him on long recuperative trips to warmer climes: to Italy, Dalmatia, the Mediterranean, North Africa, and the Canary Islands. By the time he was sixteen, Malinowski had begun to develop a cosmopolitan outlook.

In 1902 Malinowski began to study physics, mathematics, and philosophy at the Jagiellonian University in Cracow. In 1906 he completed a brilliant doctoral dissertation in philosophy dealing with the so-called second positivism of Ernst Mach. *On the Principle of the Economy of Thought* contains the germ of Malinowski's "functionalism," the methodological doctrine for which he was to become famous. The conviction that facts and theory are interdependent and mutually conditioned; the mathematical concept of function as the key scientific tool; the epistemological tenet that synchronic functional explanations should take precedence over diachronic ones of cause and effect: these ideas formed the basis of Malinowski's later view of human culture as an instrumental apparatus, which, whatever else it does, ultimately serves man's biological and psychological needs. To this Machian source too can be traced Malinowski's profound suspicion of history and his empirical view of the past as a "charter" for present practices.

At the Jagiellonian, Malinowski had also studied Nietzsche, and dreamed romantically of self-improvement by managing his wayward emotions through the exercise of will. In 1908 he was awarded the highest academic honor in the Hapsburg Empire, the doctorate *sub auspiciis Imperatoris.*

Between 1908 and 1910 Malinowski spent three terms at the University of Leipzig, where he studied *Völkerpsychologie* (psychological anthropology) under Wilhelm Wundt and economic history under Karl Bücher. His scientific interests were turning inexorably toward anthropology (initially inspired by a reading of Sir James Frazer's *The Golden Bough*). When not in Leipzig, Malinowski stayed in Cracow or Zakopane amid a circle of aspiring young artists and writers. Among them was his close friend, Stanislaw Ignacy Witkiewicz, who became one of Poland's most celebrated surrealist painters and dramatists. Influenced by fin de siècle Western Europe, these young men shared their thoughts, their girlfriends, and a romantic fascination for the exotic.

In late 1910 Malinowski went to London, possessed by what he called "a highly developed Anglomania" (Wayne, *American Ethnologist* 12:532). There he joined an older woman (a South African pianist), with whom he had begun an affair in Leipzig, and continued his studies in anthropology at the London School of Economics under the supervision of Charles G. Seligman and Edward Westermarck. Malinowski also came under the influence of A. C. Haddon and W. H. R. Rivers, who, like Seligman, were veterans of the pioneering Cambridge University Torres Strait Expedition of 1898–1899.

From 1911 to 1913 Malinowski divided his time between London, Zakopane, and Warsaw, where he lectured on anthropological topics and completed a number of essays in Polish. In 1913 he published *The Family among the Australian Aborigines*, a critique of evolutionist theories of the family.

A decisive moment in Malinowski's career occurred when he was appointed secretary to Section H (Anthropology) of the British Association for the Advancement of Science, which was to convene in Australia in mid-1914. Seligman had secured him grants to conduct fieldwork in Papua (ex-British New Guinea and since 1906 an Australian colony). War was declared in Europe as the congress was about to begin, but Malinowski, though technically an "enemy alien," was permitted by the Australian authorities to proceed with his plans.

Over the next four years Malinowski dedicated himself to creating a social anthropology based on meticulous field studies conducted through "participant observation" and a mastery of the vernacular (his remarkable facility for languages was crucial to this methodological innovation). Few other anthropologists had spent so long in one spot and tilled the same field so deeply, and none could have formulated the goal of ethnography as Malinowski now saw it: "to grasp the native's point of view, his relation to life, to realize *his* vision of *his* world" (*Argonauts*, p. 25).

Anthropology in Britain had been based on a division of labor: desk-bound scholars synthesized ethnographic information collected by explorers, missionaries, and colonial officers. But by the turn of the century, Malinowski's mentors had begun to professionalize the discipline and urge the intensive study of limited areas. The "survey anthropology" yielded ethnographic monographs of considerable scope but little depth.

Malinowski's apprentice fieldwork among the Mailu people of southern Papua in late 1914 was of the survey type, but he soon appreciated its deficiencies. Returning to Australia for several months in early 1915, he published a detailed ethnographic report, *The Natives of Mailu*, which he privately disparaged, though it gratified his various sponsors and secured him funding from the Australian government; together with his book on the Aborigines it also earned him a D.Sc. from the University of London in 1916.

Two years of intensive fieldwork followed. On his return to eastern Papua in mid-1915 Malinowski settled in the Trobriand Islands and there put his methodological ideas into practice. The ethnographer's essential task, he believed, was to observe and describe customs in their natural contexts. He pitched his tent "right among the natives," learned their language, investigated all aspects of everyday village life, elicited vernacular texts, and drew up "synoptic charts" of each social institution. Malinowski's fieldwork in the Trobriands became a "charter myth" for subsequent generations of anthropologists.

Fieldwork by total immersion in an alien society was not without its psychic traumas. Malinowski's posthumously published field diaries reveal something of the ordeal he suffered. Although many readers were scandalized by his forthright expressions of racism, sexual longing, and self-contempt, *A Diary in the Strict Sense of the Term* (1967) is an intriguing document, an introspective, profoundly ambivalent yet therapeutic "rubrication" in which Malinowski kept a ledger of his daily achievements, failings, and moral dilemmas.

In 1919, shortly after returning to Melbourne, Malinowski married Elsie Rosaline Masson, with whom he had three children. In 1920 the couple left Australia and, after spending six months in England and Scotland, settled for a year in the Canary Islands, where Malinowski completed his classic work *Argonauts of the Western Pacific* (1922), a richly textured study of canoe-borne trade and the ceremonial exchange of armshells and shell necklaces that linked the Trobriands to other island groups of eastern New Guinea. The work has never been out of print and is probably *the* bestselling anthropological monograph ever to be published. Although Malinowski never achieved the literary grace of his admired compatriot and fellow exile Joseph Conrad, his stylistic combination of scientific observation, methodological prescription, and literary romanticism was compellingly fresh and vivid.

In 1922 the Malinowskis visited Poland, where he declined a professional appointment at the Jagiellonian. For the next sixteen years Malinowski was based in London. For the sake of his own and his wife's fragile health they spent vacations and sabbaticals at their villa in the Italian Tyrol to which they frequently invited graduate students. His rise to eminence at the University of London was swift: from lecturer in 1922 he became foundation professor of social anthropology by 1927. Though frequently sick and physically absent from the university, he worked ferociously hard, teaching, writing, and propagating his progressive views on every contemporary social issue, from birth control, marriage, and the family to religion, morals, race, and warfare. As a polemical essayist, broadcaster, and pundit, he won the kind of popular recognition Margaret Mead was later to enjoy in the United States.

During these prolific London years Malinowski produced a spate of influential books, pamphlets, and articles, including "Magic, Science and Religion" (in J. A. Needham, ed., *Science, Religion and Reality* [1925]), *Crime and Custom in Savage Society* (1926), *Myth in Primitive Psychology* (1926), *Sex and Repression in Savage Society* (1927), *The Father in Primitive Psychology* (1927), *The Sexual Life of Savages in Northwestern Melanesia* (1929), *Coral Gardens and Their Magic* (2 vols., 1935), and *The Foundations of Faith and Morals* (1936). In addition, Malinowski promoted his theories in innumerable essays, in lengthy forewords to his students' books, and in magisterial encyclopedia articles.

Malinowski soon gained a reputation as a stimulating Socratic teacher, one who made his students think for themselves by what Firth called "intellectual shock tactics." Students were attracted to Malinowski's electrifying seminar from every continent and from many different academic disciplines; there was much cross-fertilization of ideas. There can be no facts without theories to give them meaning, he taught. Look for the use of a custom or institution in the present, then you will have an explanation for its existence. Using his methods and treating the field as a "natural laboratory," Malinowski's students completed the revolution he had begun by occupying powerful positions in the universities from the 1940s until the early 1970s. Malinowski thus seeded a whole generation of influential anthropologists worldwide.

Malinowski made his first visit to the United States in 1926 as a Laura Spelman Rockefeller Memorial Fellow. He traveled the continent, lecturing, visiting the Hopi Indians, and debating eminent American colleagues. Although few senior American anthropologists were receptive to his messianic message, Rockefeller officials were impressed, and Malinowski won their support for his new vision of a "practical anthropology" concerned with race relations, the administration of colonial possessions, and the study of culture change. By the late 1920s Malinowski was the undisputed leader of British anthropology and American funding was essential to his success. With Rockefeller funds and the sponsorship of the International African Institute, Malinowski launched a batch of talented researchers into the African field. In 1934 he visited his students working among the Swazi, the Bemba, the Bantu Kavirondo, and the Chagga and conducted some fieldwork of his own.

In 1933 Malinowski had delivered the Messenger Lectures at Cornell University and in 1936 attended the Harvard tercentenary celebrations. In 1938 he took sabbatical leave in the United States, where after the outbreak of war in Europe he decided to remain for the duration. In 1939 he became Bishop Museum Visiting Professor at Yale University and was appointed professor of cultural anthropology there early in 1942. Although he taught at Yale for two-and-a-half years, he did not find it as congenial as the London School of Economics. His wife died in 1935, and he married Valetta Swann in 1940. They had no children together.

In the summer of 1940, accompanied by his new wife, Malinowski began a brief but fruitful period of fieldwork in Mexico's Oaxaca Valley with Julio de la Fuente. This collaboration resulted in a pioneering study of the function of rural markets, and was published in Spanish (1957) and in English (1982) as *The Economics of a Mexican Market System*.

Even before the outbreak of hostilities in Europe, Malinowski had begun to speak and write on war, totalitarianism, and internationalism. The war revived his latent Polish nationalism, and he helped to establish the Polish Institute of Arts and Sciences in New York City. A few hours after giving his inaugural address as newly elected president of this institute, he suffered a heart attack and died at his home in New Haven. Some of his many uncompleted manuscripts were published posthumously by his widow: *A Scientific Theory of Culture* (1944), *Freedom and Civilization* (1944), *The Dynamics of Culture Change* (1945), and his fieldwork diaries (1967).

Malinowski was an intensely passionate man, and he provoked strong passions in others. His humor was often self-mocking, but his sharp wit could be unkind; he gave generously but demanded absolute loyalty in return. He was regarded by some as arrogant, vain, petulant, even anti-Semitic, but by others as magnanimous, sensitive, and charming. None denied his dynamism and intellectual brilliance. As his youngest daughter observed, he "was strongly influenced by women all his life" (Wayne, p. 529). Unusual for his time, he treated women as intellectual equals, and many of his female students became distinguished anthropologists.

Malinowski's achievements have been frequently evaluated. His doctrinal hegemony in Britain hardly survived his departure for America, but his reputation was revived in the later decade of the twentieth century, and there is now a more settled consensus concerning his international stature as a creative founder of modern anthropology.

As a consummate ethnographer his reputation was always secure. His Trobriand corpus remains one of the most comprehensive and most widely read in world ethnography. At a clinical level, his methodological functionalism provided a valuable set of directives for field research in preliterate tribal societies; however, its status as a grand theory is largely discredited. His vision of an integrated study of man was never realized, and his own followers soon abandoned it to pursue their exclusively sociological concerns.

Malinowski's theorizing about the relationship of the particular to the general in the context of specific "institutions" (itself a concept that Malinowski vitalized) provided a more permanent legacy. Many of his ideas have been absorbed by the discipline, notably in the fields of kinship, marriage, and the family; in economic anthropology, ceremonial exchange, and land tenure; in the anthropology of law; in linguistics; and in magic, mythology, and ritual. Some of the apt phrases he coined still retain their currency: "sociological paternity," "dogma of procreation," "principle of legitimacy," "biographical method," "reciprocal obligation," "mythical charter," "phatic communication," "context of situation," and many more. A pioneer of applied anthropology and the study of culture change, he exerted an influence extending to sociology, psychology, law, and linguistics, while his challenge to psychoanalysis (notably in *Sex and Repression*) has continued to be debated.

• Malinowski's papers are in the British Library of Political and Economic Science, the London School of Economics, and the Sterling Memorial Library, Yale University. Letters between Malinowski and his first wife have been published in a work edited by their daughter Helena Wayne (Malinowska), *The Story of a Marriage: The Letters of Bronislaw Malinowski and Elsie Masson* (2 vols., 1995). In addition to his books mentioned in the text there are two useful collections of his essays, *Magic, Science and Religion and Other Essays* (1948) and *Sex, Culture and Myth* (1962). For his works in Polish, see P. Skalnik and Robert J. Thornton, eds., *The Early Writings of Bronislaw Malinowski* (1993). His fieldwork

in Mailu is dealt with in Michael W. Young, *Malinowski among the Magi* (1988), and in Oaxaca in Susan Drucker-Brown, *Malinowski in Mexico* (1982). For two digests of his Trobriand writings, see Young, ed., *The Ethnography of Malinowski* (1979), and Ivan Strenski, *Malinowski and the Work of Myth* (1992).

On his Polish roots, see Roy Ellen et al., eds., *Malinowski between Two Worlds* (1988). Valuable biographical essays are Raymond Firth, "Bronislaw Malinowski," in *Totems and Teachers*, ed. Sydel Silverman (1981), and Helena Wayne (Malinowska), "Bronislaw Malinowski: The Influence of Various Women on His Life and Works," *American Ethnologist* 12 (1985): 529–40; see also K. Symmons-Symonolewicz, "Bronislaw Malinowski: An Intellectual Profile," *Polish Review* 3, no. 1 (1958): 55–76. The best introduction to his work is Raymond Firth, ed., *Man and Culture* (1957), a posthumous festschrift containing critical essays by twelve of Malinowski's most distinguished pupils. A modern British assessment is in Adam Kuper, *Anthropology and Anthropologists*, rev. ed. (1983); see also Michael W. Young, "Malinowski and the Function of Culture," in *Creating Culture*, ed. Diane J. Austin-Broos (1987). The most comprehensive historical evaluations of Malinowski's work are by George W. Stocking, Jr.: "The Ethnographer's Magic," in *Observers Observed*, History of Anthropology, vol. 1 (1983); "Radcliffe-Brown and British Social Anthropology," in *Functionalism Historicized*, HOA, vol. 2 (1984); "Anthropology and the Science of the Irrational," in *Malinowski, Rivers, Benedict and Others*, HOA, vol. 4 (1986); and "Maclay, Kubary, Malinowski," in *Colonial Situations*, HOA, vol. 7 (1991). For thoughtful obituary statements, see those by M. F. Ashley Montague in *Isis* 34 (1942): 146–50; Clyde Kluckhohn in *Journal of American Folklore* 56 (1943): 208–19; George P. Murdoch in *American Anthropologist* 45 (1943): 441–51; and Audrey I. Richards in *Man* 43 (1943): 1–4.

MICHAEL W. YOUNG

MALKIEL, Theresa Serber (1 May 1874–17 Nov. 1949), trade union leader, woman suffragist, publicist, and educator, was born in Bar, Russia. In 1891 she emigrated with her parents to the United States.

Soon after her arrival, Theresa Serber became a pioneer in the Jewish workers' movement and socialist labor agitation in New York City. Employed in the garment industry, she joined the Russian Workingmen's Club in 1892. In October 1894 she was among a group of seventy women who founded the Infant Cloak Makers Union (ICMU). Although it was a depression year, she and her associates decided not to accept wage cuts and deteriorating labor conditions any longer. Their action was front-page news. Eventually the ICMU became part of the Socialist Trades and Labor Alliance. In 1896, Serber was among the delegates to the first convention of the latter alliance; in 1899, along with many others, she broke with labor leader Daniel DeLeon and joined the Socialist Party of America.

In 1900 Serber married Leon Malkiel, a lawyer and activist in the Socialist Labor Party, the Socialist Party of America, and the Women's Trade Union League; they had one child. Marriage led her to give up her job in the garment trades but did not deter her from political pursuits. After the couple moved from Manhattan to Yonkers, Theresa Malkiel founded the Women's Progressive Society of Yonkers, which became Branch

One of the Socialist Women's Society of Greater New York.

Coming from a strongly class-oriented perspective, Malkiel and others like her, such as Rose Schneiderman and Clara Zetkin, brought a strategy to women's political work unfamiliar to most American-born women's-rights activists. Malkiel argued that women's consciousness needed to become one with their class consciousness: "The working woman must learn how to share the burden of her brothers and together work for the common emancipation of mankind—the socialist regime—the only true exponent of complete equality and complete economic independence" (Buhle, p. 184).

Malkiel's interest later returned to labor organizing. She was active among the garment workers and helped to organize the 1909 strike of shirtwaist makers. She believed in a strike not only as a means to obtain immediate goals, but also as a consciousness-raising movement. During the 1909 strike, Malkiel felt that women "who had gone through life in a trance had with one gigantic effort torn asunder the fetters of ancient custom and tradition determined for this once to wage an earnest battle for the right to live." She believed that "the very spontaneity of the strike brought about a revolution in their minds" (Buhle, p. 197). In 1910 she published a short novel on the events of that strike, *The Diary of a Shirtwaist Striker*. An exposé on the labor conditions for women in New York's garment industry, the book contributed to the reform of the state's factory laws.

Malkiel strongly opposed the cooperation between working-class women and the upper-class women represented in the Women's Trade Union League. Firmly committed to a class-conscious vision of labor organizing, she resented what she regarded as a condescending attempt at sisterhood, and she abhorred "the pretended friendship of the Miss Morgans, who come down from the height of their pedestals to preach identity of interest to the little daughters of the people" (Buhle, p. 200).

While she pursued her commitment to labor organizing, Malkiel became increasingly active in the woman suffrage movement. On 19 December 1909 she took part in a meeting of woman suffrage activists at the Labor Temple on East Eighty-fourth Street. Against her arguments, the attending socialists agreed to cooperate with the middle-class and upper-class women, such as Alva Belmont. When the New York state legislature decided to have a voters' referendum on woman suffrage in 1915, Malkiel was entrusted with leading the socialist campaign forces in New York City. Since 1910 she had formed Socialist Suffrage clubs in the Lower East Side, Brooklyn, Harlem, the Bronx, and Queens. Owing to her campaigning and organizing, the Socialist party experienced a 25 percent increase in membership. When the referendum failed, however, the party withdrew its funds, despite Malkiel's pleas to continue support for her organizational work. In 1920 she ran for the New York state assembly but lost by a small margin.

Malkiel was also the author of *Women and Freedom* (1915) and *Woman of Yesterday and Today* (1915). She also wrote for the *German-American Volkszeitung*, *Everybody's Magazine*, and *McClure's*. With her husband, Leon Malkiel, she founded the New York *Call*.

After 1920 Malkiel's interests turned toward adult education. She organized an Adult Students' Association after New York cut its adult education budget. In 1932 she founded a women's adult-education summer camp in Long Branch, New Jersey, which she ran until her death in New York City.

• For biographical information see her obituary in the *New York Times*, 18 Nov. 1949; William Stewart Wallace, *A Dictionary of North American Authors Deceased before 1950* (1968), p. 293; Sally M. Miller, "From Sweatshop Worker to Labor Leader: Theresa Malkiel, a Case Study," *American Jewish History* 68 (Dec. 1978): 189–205; Françoise Basch, "Malkiel, Theresa Serber," in *Encyclopedia of the American Left*, ed. Mari Jo Buhle et al. (1990), p. 446. Malkiel is mentioned in the context of women's and socialist politics in Buhle, *Women and American Socialism, 1870–1920* (1981). For background on the assimilation of Russian Jewish women in America in the context of labor and politics, see also Susan Anita Glenn, *Daughters of the Shtetl: Life and Labor in the Immigrant Generation* (1990). Malkiel's best-known work, *The Diary of a Shirtwaist Striker*, was reissued, edited with an introductory essay by Françoise Basch (1990).

THOMAS WINTER

MALL, Franklin Paine (28 Sept. 1862–17 Nov. 1917), embryologist and anatomist, was born near Belle Plaine, Iowa, the son of Franz Mall, a farmer, and Louise Christine Miller, both natives of Germany. Mall's mother died when he was ten years old, and his father remarried a woman who was unaffectionate toward Franklin. As a consequence, Mall had a difficult, unhappy youth and could not find an outlet for his creative mind. Mall's whole attitude was changed by his boarding school teacher, Jack McCarthy, who showed Mall that the source of his disdain for school was not the subjects themselves, but rather the method by which they were taught, which stressed memorization without comprehension. McCarthy's strong influence on Mall was evident in Mall's later attempts to reform university science teaching.

Mall entered the medical department of the University of Michigan in 1880. While there he was greatly influenced by Professors Victor C. Vaughan and Henry Sewall, who taught him that the only way to acquire true knowledge of a subject was to perform firsthand investigations and experiments. After receiving an M.D. from Michigan in 1883, Mall left for Germany, where he spent a year in Heidelberg studying the nervous system and the eye with the intention of specializing in ophthalmology. In 1884 Mall went to Leipzig to work under Wilhelm His, considered to be the "most outstanding anatomist of his day" (Sabin, p. 73). Although relatively inexperienced in research and a true novice in embryology, Mall made keen observations and developed a well-supported conclusion that the thymus originated from the endoderm of the pharynx, a finding that contradicted earlier conclusions reached by His. While in Leipzig Mall developed what would become close, lifelong friendships with His and William H. Welch, another American postgraduate student who later became dean of the Johns Hopkins University School of Medicine. Following His's suggestion, Mall applied for a position in Carl Ludwig's laboratory in Leipzig, where he reconfirmed his earlier findings about the development of the thymus and studied the blood vessels and lymphatics of the small intestine.

Mall returned to the United States in 1885, and the following year he was appointed the first fellow of pathology at Johns Hopkins Hospital, where he worked under William Welch, who had several years earlier organized the Department of Pathology. Mall was named instructor of pathology in 1888. While at Johns Hopkins, Mall investigated the fermentative powers of various species of bacteria on different tissues. Working with surgeon William S. Halsted, Mall discovered that results of intestinal surgery were improved when the sutures entered but did not penetrate the submucosal layer because the submucosa's white fibrous tissue was strong enough to hold the sutures. Mall spent additional time studying intestinal contraction, intestinal anastomosis, and the circulation of blood through the stomach. He received wide acclaim for the series of reports on intestinal contraction published in the *Johns Hopkins Hospital Reports* (1 [1889]: 37–110).

Mall accepted an adjunct professorship in anatomy at Clark University in Worcester, Massachusetts, in 1889. He spent three productive years there, studying the reticulum, as well as conducting experiments that demonstrated the existence of vasomotor nerves of the portal system, and devoted the majority of his research to embryology. In 1892 Mall, displeased with the administration of Clark University, left Massachusetts for a professorship in anatomy at the University of Chicago, taking with him several faculty members from Clark University. Although Mall remained there for only one year, he actually founded Chicago's Department of Anatomy and developed the plans by which each university department could form an institute with an emphasis on both faculty and student research.

Offered the opportunity to quickly organize a department in which he could concentrate on research, Mall accepted the professorship of anatomy at Johns Hopkins University in 1893, the same year its new medical school was opened. The following year he married Mabel Stanley Glover, one of three women students in his first class at Johns Hopkins; they had two daughters. While at Johns Hopkins, Mall's collection of human embryos, begun as a postgraduate student in Leipzig, had become large enough to strain the university's resources. In 1913 he persuaded the Carnegie Institution of Washington, D.C., to create an entire department of embryology at the Johns Hopkins Medical School around his collection, the largest in the world at the time. He was appointed in 1914 director of the embryology department, a position he held until his death.

Mall spent his mature years in Baltimore working in embryology, specifically studying ways in which the structure of organs in adult organisms had adapted specific functions. Among his most widely received studies were those on the development of the diaphragm, the ventral abdominal walls, the body cavities, and the loops of the intestine. Mall also devised a formula for estimating the age of a human embryo. He argued in *A Study of the Causes Underlying the Origin of Human Monsters* (1908) that abnormally developed humans, or "monsters," developed from the faulty implantation of a normal egg. His description of the arrangement of blood vessels in the spleen underlies the current conception of the spleen as a storage place of blood. He also conceived of the liver as divided into structural anatomical units and applied this system to other organs. Mall's colleague and biographer, Florence Sabin, described him as "a great scientific investigator. As such his work was thorough: he touched no subject on which his investigations did not throw light and in most cases he left the subject standing clearly, the obscurities gone" (W. T. Councilman, "Franklin Paine Mall, 1862–1917," *Proceedings of the American Academy of Arts and Sciences* 57 [1922]: 495).

Mall's contributions to anatomy and embryology went beyond his own laboratory and classroom. In 1901 he helped found the *American Journal of Anatomy*, which he published from his laboratory for eight years and which he edited until his death. He served as coeditor of the journal and also of the *Journal of Morphology* and the *Anatomical Record*. He served as president of the American Association of Anatomists in 1905–1906 and successfully revitalized it to European standards. As a leading member of the Wistar Institute of Anatomy in Philadelphia, Mall broadened its international and national exposure. He served as trustee of the Marine Biological Laboratory in Woods Hole, Massachusetts. Mall was also a member of the International Association of Academies, the American Academy of Arts and Sciences, the National Academy of Sciences, the American Physiological Society, the American Society of Morphologists, the American Zoological Society, the American Association for the Advancement of Science, and the Society of Biology and Experimental Medicine. Together with Franz Keibel, he also edited a *Manual of Human Embryology* (German ed., [1910–1911]: American ed., [1910–1912]), to which he contributed several chapters, and the first six of nine volumes of the Carnegie Institution's *Contributions to Embryology* (1915–1920).

Mall is credited with revolutionizing medical education in the United States. He was a chief proponent of the concentration system, in which students studied no more than two subjects concurrently for a long period, as opposed to the common system of the time, in which students studied several concurrently taught subjects. This system, begun at Johns Hopkins, was subsequently adopted by medical schools throughout the United States. Mall was also a leader in the movement to enable teachers of clinical medicine to devote their full time to teaching, research, and patient care in a hospital setting without having to carrying on a private practice on the side. Mall's own department of anatomy at Johns Hopkins University was exemplary as the first in the United States to bring into one discipline the studies of cytology, histology, embryology, and adult structure. Mall died in Baltimore, Maryland.

• A collection of Mall's personal papers is at the Johns Hopkins Hospital Archives. Mall's research in Leipzig resulted in a publication from each of the two laboratories he worked in: "Die Blut-und Lymphwege im Dunndarm des Hundes," *Archiv für Anatomie und Entwickelungsgeschichte* (1887): 1–34, and "Entwickelung der Branchialbogen and Spalten des Hundes," *Abhandlungen des mathematisch-physischen Classe der koniglichen sachsischen Gessellshaft der Wissenchaften* 14 (1887): 153–89. Florence R. Sabin appended a list of 104 of Mall's written contributions to her memoir of Mall in the National Academy of Sciences, *Biographical Memoirs* 16 (1934): 65–122. Sabin also wrote a more extensive biography, *Franklin Paine Mall, the Story of a Mind* (1934) Other interesting insights into Mall are made by G. Carl Huber in "Franklin Paine Mall 1862–1917. In Memoriam," *Anatomical Record* 14 (Jan. 1918): 3–17, and by William H. Welch and others in "Memorial Services in Honor of Franklin Paine Mall, Professor of Anatomy, Johns Hopkins University, 1893–1917," *Johns Hopkins Hospital Bulletin* 29 (1918): 109–23.

PHILIP K. WILSON

MALLARY, Rollin Carolas (27 May 1784–15 Apr. 1831), politician and lawyer, was born in Chesire, Connecticut, the son of Daniel Mallary and Martha Dutton. His family moved to Poultney, Vermont, in 1795, and Mallary matriculated at Middlebury College. Following his graduation in 1805. He read law with Horatio Seymour in Middlebury and Robert Temple in Rutland, Vermont; he also served a one-year preceptorship at Castleton Seminary in Castleton, Vermont, in 1806–1807. In October 1806 he married Ruth Stanley, with whom he would have three children, and in March 1807 he was admitted to the bar of Rutland County, Vermont.

Mallary began practicing in Castleton, and in October 1807 he was appointed secretary to the governor and council, a position he also held from 1809 to 1812 and from 1815 to 1819. He served Rutland County as its state's attorney from 1810 to 1813 and from 1815 to 1816. In 1818 he moved his practice to his childhood home of Poultney.

At that time the U.S. congressional race that would define Mallary's career was already in progress. In the fall of 1817 the Republican state caucus had made the curious decision to dump two incumbents and a regional caucus winner from their ticket in favor of three others, including Mallary. A splinter faction picked up the three discards, and the remnants of the Federalists also decided to field candidates, so there were twelve contenders for the state's six congressional seats. As several other small states did at the time, Vermont elected its representatives in a statewide general election, regardless of region, meaning that the six

candidates with the most votes would go to Washington.

The election was held on 1 September 1818, but the votes were not tallied until the state legislature convened over a month later. After the votes of six towns were thrown out on technicalities, Mallary was announced as finishing eighth, with congressional incumbent Orsamus C. Merrill given the sixth and final seat. The votes of the six deleted towns would have made Mallary sixth, but Merrill's father-in-law was chairman of the canvassing committee, and a resolution of protest came to nothing.

Merrill officially took his seat in March 1819, but since Congress did not convene until December, Mallary had to wait fifteen months from the election to challenge the results, and committee consideration by the House took an additional month. On 5 January 1820 the House unseated Merrill, but his counterprotest consumed another week of debate before being defeated 116–47. Mallary officially became a representative on 13 January, and would hold the seat until his death.

Mallary earned immediate notice by speaking against the admission of Missouri as a slave state in the debates that resulted in the Missouri Compromise. He befriended John Quincy Adams, to whom he reported the political dispositions of members of Congress on the eve of the presidential race of 1824. A minor controversy ensued when Mallary and fellow Vermont congressman William C. Bradley each tried to convince Adams that the other was supporting William H. Crawford.

As a strong spokesman for regional interests, particularly manufacturing and industry, Mallary continually championed high tariffs to protect New England products in competition with imports. He gained considerable power to control related interests in 1827 when he was appointed chairman of the Committee on Manufactures, and he used his position to organize support for stronger tariffs. England, he claimed, was trying to monopolize the woolen industry, and American manufacturers needed government intervention to be able to continue to compete. Mallary helped frame the famous Tariff of 1828, known in the South as the "Tariff of Abominations," and worked vigorously to insure its passage.

By the time southern reaction to the more stringent tariff, particularly in South Carolina, had thrown the country into what became known as the nullification crisis, however, Mallary was dead. During the 1830–1831 winter session of Congress, overwork and stress left Mallary in poor condition. When the session ended he went to Baltimore, Maryland, to receive care from relatives; he did not recover, however, and died in Baltimore. The official cause of death is not known, but it was probably heart-related. His body was returned to Poultney for burial.

Mallary is remembered primarily for his aggressive representation of regional interests, with his roles in the writing and the passage of the Tariff of 1828 the most prominent aspect of his abbreviated public career.

• A few Mallary papers can be found at the Vermont Historical Society in Montpelier. A published speech is *An Oration Pronounced at the Republican Celebration of Our Independence at Poultney, Vt., July 4, 1810* (1810). Walter H. Crockett, *Vermont: The Green Mountain State*, vols. 3 and 5 (1921–1923), has biographical information. A good summary of the election controversy is Kevin Graffagnino, "'I saw the ruin all around' and 'A comical spot you may depend'; Orasmus C. Merrill, Rollin C. Mallary and the Disputed Congressional Election of 1818," *Vermont History* 49 (Summer 1981): 159–68. Primary materials on the case are published in Committee on Elections, *Report of the Committee of Elections on the Petition of Rollin C. Mallary, Contesting the Election of Orasmus C. Merrill* (n.d.), and United States, *Debates and Proceedings of the Congress of the United States . . . Sixteenth Congress* (1855). Several mentions of Mallary are made in Charles Francis Adams, ed., *Memoirs of John Quincy Adams* (12 vols., 1877). An obituary appeared in *Niles' Weekly Register*, 23 April 1831.

KENNETH H. WILLIAMS

MALLERY, Garrick (23 Apr. 1831–24 Oct. 1894), army officer and ethnologist, was born in Wilkes-Barre, Pennsylvania, the son of Garrick Mallery, a jurist and state legislator, and Catherine J. Hall. The young Mallery studied at Yale University (A.B., 1850) and the University of Pennsylvania (LL.B., 1855).

Mallery practiced law in Philadelphia until June 1861, when he volunteered for service as a private in the Civil War. Soon afterward he was commissioned a captain in the Seventy-eighth Pennsylvania Infantry and later a lieutenant colonel in the Thirteenth Pennsylvania Cavalry. After the war he was commissioned as a regular army officer and assigned to the Forty-third Infantry. During Reconstruction he was judge advocate of the First Military District in the South and at times served as acting secretary of state and acting adjutant general of Virginia.

In 1870 Mallery married Helen W. Wychoff. In the same year he became an aide to the chief officer of the Signal Corps and was involved in meteorological work. In 1876 he was sent to Ft. Rice, in Dakota Territory, where he began to study American Indian sign language and the pictographs of Plains Indian tribes. The following year, at John Wesley Powell's request, Mallery was detailed to the U.S. Geographical and Geological Survey of the Rocky Mountain Region to study a collection of American Indian drawings assembled by Powell and the survey staff. In 1879, when Powell's organization was transformed into the Bureau of Ethnology (later the Bureau of American Ethnology, or BAE), Mallery retired from the military and joined the staff of the new organization as an ethnologist.

Mallery worked for the BAE mainly in Washington, D.C., and was assisted for several years by ethnologist W. J. Hoffman. Their sources were in part book-length circular questionnaires completed by army officers, federal agents, missionaries, and others who were living among the American Indians. Mallery was also assisted by American Indians themselves, some encountered in the field but more met in the nation's capital where they had arrived to deal with the government. In addition Mallery drew information from the Tenth Census, which included a statistical study of American Indians. On occasion, when Powell and his more immediate aides were otherwise occupied, Mallery was left in charge of the Bureau of Ethnology office.

Mallery was a much admired and trusted aide to his superiors. He also had a strongly social side that he tended to combine with his intellectual interests. He was active in several organizations, including the Philosophical Society of Washington, of which he was president in 1888. He was a founding member of the Anthropological Society of Washington in 1879 and served as its president in 1893. That same year he became the president of the Literary Society of Washington. Mallery died in Washington, D.C.

An unidentified friend wrote that Mallery "was the gallant soldier with a stainless record; the scholar largely read in the literature of his own and other times; the man of science who has left an imperishable record of ingenious and far-reaching research; the trusted councilor in the societies which honored him with their highest dignities; the genial companion; the affectionate husband; the staunch friend; the high-bred gentleman" (*Sixteenth Annual Report of the Bureau of American Ethnology*, 1897). These were qualities Mallery demonstrated throughout his life, and they served him well in the work for which he is mainly remembered: compilations that are primary source materials for important aspects of American Indian life. These were timely studies because at the time Mallery carried them out, the traditions were still strong in Indian life.

• Mallery's papers concerning American Indian sign language and pictographs are at the Smithsonian Institution National Anthropological Archives. The archives also include a few other manuscripts and letters. Robert Fletcher ed., *Brief Memoirs of Colonel Garrick Mallery* (1895), consists of remarks read before the Philosophical Society of Washington in 1895. Reports of Mallery's work for the Bureau of American Ethnology appear in the administrative sections of its annual reports. Obituaries are in *American Anthropologist*, o.s., 18, no. 2 (1895): 79–80; the *Bulletin of the Philosophical Society of Washington* 12 (1892–1894): 464–71; and the *Washington Evening Star*, 25 Oct. 1894.

JAMES R. GLENN

MALLET, John William (10 Oct. 1832–7 Nov. 1912), chemist, was born in Dublin, Ireland, the son of Robert Mallet and Cordelia Watson. Under the guidance of his father, a fellow of the Royal Society and owner of one of the largest engineering works in Ireland, John developed a taste for scientific studies at an early age. He made use of his father's extensive library and conducted experiments in a private laboratory that his father provided. At the age of sixteen he attended the chemical lectures of Dr. James Apjohn at the Royal College of Surgeons of Ireland, who also provided

Mallet with private laboratory instruction. This association led to the publication of his first paper in 1850, on the "Notice of a New Chemical Examination of Killinite" (*Journal of the Geological Society of Dublin*, 4 [1848–1850]). In 1849 he entered Trinity College in Dublin and graduated in 1853 with an A.B. degree. He conducted a series of experiments on the transmission of shock waves from gunpowder explosions through different materials. From 1852 to 1854 he assisted his father in preparing an extensive catalog of the earthquakes that took place from 1606 B.C. to A.D. 1850.

In 1851–1852 Mallet worked in the laboratory of Friedrich Wöhler at the University of Göttingen, where he received his Ph.D. in 1852. Wohler's chemical laboratory attracted many English-speaking students who sought instruction in experimental chemistry by working in a laboratory. Mallet's thesis involved the first chemical examination of ancient Celtic ornaments from the Museum of the Royal Irish Academy of Dublin. Through his detailed analysis of these specimens, Mallet attempted to elucidate the history of the ancient arts by which these implements were produced, thereby contributing to the study of Irish history and prehistory.

Mallet came to the United States in 1853 to collect information for his father on the Ericsson "caloric engine." John Ericsson, a Swedish-American inventor and engineer, had designed and constructed a "caloric engine" based on the theory that superheated air would have the driving power of steam. He also designed the ironclad USS *Monitor*, which had the first armored revolving gun turret. Instead of returning to Ireland he accepted a position at Amherst College in Massachusetts, where in 1854 he was appointed professor of analytical chemistry. The following year he was appointed chemist to the Geological Survey of Alabama and professor of chemistry at the University of Alabama, where he remained until 1861. The next year he published a book on cultivation of cotton, a crop of great economic importance to the southern states. *The Science of the Culture of Cotton* included a detailed study of the chemical and physical properties of soils, plants, and rocks collected from three continents. In 1857 he married Mary Ormond, the eldest daughter of John Ormond, a former judge of the Alabama Supreme Court; they had three children. Mallet's wife died in 1886, and in 1888 he married Mrs. Joséphine (Pagès) Burthe.

When the Civil War broke out in 1861 he enlisted as a private in the Confederate cavalry and was soon commissioned lieutenant and made aide to General Robert E. Rodes. Although Mallet remained a British citizen all his life, his sympathies were with his southern friends. In 1862 General Josiah Gorgas, chief of the Ordnance Department of the Confederate States, appointed Mallet superintendent of the Confederate States Ordnance Laboratory. He took charge of the production of ammunition, reorganized southern arsenals and depots, and planned the new central ordnance laboratory at Macon, Georgia. At Macon he developed standards for the production of a uniform caliber of ammunition and experimented with new types of powder, shells, rockets, and other pieces of ordnance. Mallet is credited with solving many of the problems associated with shortages of materials that were essential to the South, such as potassium nitrate, lead, iron, copper, mercury, and mineral acids. With great ingenuity and technical skills Mallet and the Confederate Ordnance Department created foundries, rolling mills, niter refineries, iron furnaces, and munition plants, which contributed greatly to the southern war effort.

After the war Mallet became professor of chemistry at the medical department of the University of Louisiana, where he devoted much time to the study of medicine. In 1868 he joined the University of Virginia and taught analytical, industrial, and agricultural chemistry. He remained there for the next forty years, except for brief periods at the University of Texas (1883–1884) and the Jefferson Medical College in Philadelphia (1884–1885). He organized the School of Analytical and Industrial Chemistry, which served the purpose of educating men for the needs of agriculture and industry. His course in industrial chemistry was one of the first courses in the United States to employ technological specimens, models, and instruments to illustrate chemical manufacturing processes. His lectures included instruction on the production of materials such as metals and alloys, the manufacture of acids and alkalies, and the chemistry of agriculture, building materials, explosives, paints, varnishes, and fuels. In the laboratory students were trained in the qualitative and quantitative analysis of ores, soils, manures, and technical products, and they also conducted original research. In the years that Mallet was associated with the university he became a leader in the development of chemical education and research in the United States. His reputation firmly established, Mallet was widely sought after as a consultant and as an expert witness in cases involving toxicological and industrial disputes.

Mallet's honors include his elections as fellow of the Chemical Society of London in 1857 and fellow of the Royal Society of London in 1877. He was a member of more than twenty scientific societies in the United States, Great Britain, Germany, and Mexico and was one of the founders of the American Chemical Society in 1876, serving as its president in 1882. He held several patents on chemical manufacturing processes and published more than 100 papers on a variety of subjects connected with the investigation of the chemical and physical properties of elements and compounds. His most notable research was his pioneer work in the determination of the atomic weights of aluminum, lithium, and gold. The determination of accurate atomic weights was an important goal of analytical chemists during the latter half of the nineteenth century, since reliable atomic weights were needed for a sound system of classification of the elements. His most lasting influence, however, was in the field of chemical education. William H. Echols, a colleague at the university, stated in a 1913 memorial that "generations of his students testify to the remarkable excellence of the lectures he gave in chemistry. . . . The lecture was always a marvel of precision and continuity." As a scientist and teacher, his powers of observation, broad knowledge, patience, dignity, and kindness won the respect of his students and peers alike. He continued as professor of chemistry until he was seventy-six, when he published his last paper on the interaction of mercury with alloys of other metals. He became professor emeritus in 1908 and died four years later at his residence in Charlottesville. His memory was preserved in the naming of Mallet Hall, a fitting testimony to his forty-year association with the University of Virginia.

• The main body of Mallet's papers is found in the University of Virginia Library, Manuscripts Department, Charlottesville. Mallet donated his Confederate military papers to the War Department in 1899, and they are housed in the National Archives. His major published papers include "Report on the Chemical Examination of Celtic Antiquities from the Museum of the Royal Irish Academy," *Transaction of the Royal Irish Academy* 22 (1853): 313–42; "On the Atomic Weight of Lithium," *American Journal of Science and Arts* 28 (1859): 349–54; "Revision of the Atomic Weight of Aluminum," *Philosophical Transactions of the Royal Society* 171, part 3 (1880): 1003–35; "Determination of Organic Matter in Potable Water," *American Chemical Journal* 4 (1882): 241–63, 5 (1883): 334–56, and 6 (1883): 426–39; and "Revision of the Atomic Weight of Gold," *Philosophical Transactions of the Royal Society* 180 (1889): 395–441. Biographical treatments include William H. Echols, "John W. Mallet: Scholar, Teacher, Gentleman," *University of Virginia Alumni Bulletin*, 3d ser., 4, no. 1 (1913): 3–47, which includes a complete listing of public lectures and publications; Francis P. Dunnington, "A Sketch of Dr. John William Mallet, as a Chemist and a Teacher," *Journal of Chemical Education* 5, no. 2 (1928): 183–88; and Desmond Reilly, "John William Mallet: His Earlier Work in Ireland," *Journal of Chemical Education* 25 (1948): 634–36. Obituaries are in the *Richmond Times-Dispatch* and the *New York Times*, 8 Nov. 1912.

JOHN B. SHARKEY

MALLINCKRODT, Edward (21 Jan. 1845–1 Feb. 1928), chemical manufacturer and philanthropist, was born Edward Theodor Mallinckrodt in St. Louis, Missouri, the son of Emil Mallinckrodt, a horticulturist and real estate developer, and Eleanor Didier Luckie. Edward's father was in the first generation of Mallinckrodts to emigrate to the United States, from Westphalia, Germany. The Mallinckrodt family did a great deal of traveling, both to escape the hot summers of St. Louis and to maintain close ties to family residing in Germany. On returning from an extended stay in Germany (1850–1855), Edward's father purchased forty acres of farm land approximately ten miles west of St. Louis, where the family then resided. Early in his life Edward discovered his father's chemistry books, and his father encouraged this interest by building a laboratory for him in an outbuilding.

From 1862 to 1864, while his parents and sisters visited Germany, Mallinckrodt remained in St. Louis to oversee the farm and his father's interests in the city, and to care for his younger brother. Spending most days working on and improving the farm as well as experimenting in his laboratory, he stated in a letter to his father that "during the day I generally employ myself with work and if melancholy overcomes me in the evening I take up my chemistry, which soon quiets my troubled mind; it is to me what the bible is to a Christian" (18 Sept. 1863). His brother Gustav noted his generally somber mood and urged their father to allow Edward and their younger brother Otto to travel to Germany to finish their education in chemistry. The brothers had already developed a plan for entering the chemical industry. In May 1864 Edward and Otto arrived in Germany and, after studying chemistry at Wiesbaden under Professor Karl Fresenius, took apprenticeships, with Edward learning the trade at de Haën Chemical Works.

Immediately upon returning to St. Louis in September 1867, the three brothers set up their chemical factory. Beginning with only one permanent structure, a number of small wooden sheds, and the borrowed sum of $10,000, G. Mallinckrodt and Company (named for the eldest brother), the first chemical company west of Philadelphia, was born. The first years were difficult, as competition from the already firmly entrenched eastern companies almost forced the fledgling company into bankruptcy. A number of wise decisions by the brothers enabled them to flourish, however, precipitating expansion in 1870 and virtually every year or so thereafter. The brothers had chosen to focus on the production of high purity chemicals, including distilled acids and nitrous ether, and were among the first to produce refined chemical salts in granulated form, which were easy to pour and use. Among the other products permitting the company's rapid growth was anhydrous ammonia, an artificial refrigerant in high demand in the 1880s. In 1882 Edward incorporated the company and changed its name to Mallinckrodt Chemical Works, Inc. It became the country's largest producer of this chemical, instigating the formation of the National Ammonia Company in 1889 as a cooperative enterprise involving the top five manufacturers of anhydrous ammonia. Edward was elected as the cooperative's first president and general manager, which procured for him national recognition in the chemical trade.

By the time the National Ammonia Company was formed, a great many changes had taken place in Mallinckrodt's life. In June 1876 he had married Jennie Anderson; they had one son. The couple's happiness was short-lived, however, as Edward's brother Otto died suddenly of pneumonia in December of that same year, and Gustav succumbed to consumption the following June, leaving the Chemical Works under the sole direction of Edward. Now responsible for all aspects of the business, Edward leapt into the improvement of the company and quickly expanded the number of products and factories while maintaining the highest standards of quality. By 1884, Mallinckrodt Chemical had a sales office and warehouse in New

York and, by 1887, had expanded chemical production beyond that of the continually growing St. Louis plant to a facility in New Jersey.

Even though Edward Mallinckrodt had attained national recognition, in St. Louis he was still predominantly affiliated with the German community. This was all changed by an 1889 law permitting the organization and operation of trusts in St. Louis. Established in 1890, the Union Trust Company of St. Louis was the second trust formed under the law, and its board consisted of prominent businessmen of the day, including G. A. Madill, Robert S. Brookings, W. K. Bixby, and William Taussig. Mallinckrodt was elected to membership in 1891 and to the trust's executive committee two years later. In 1901 the two major trusts consolidated, and Mallinckrodt and his closest friends became the "group which profoundly influenced the industrial, commercial, and financial development of the city" (Stout, p. 64). Through this group, Mallinckrodt's interests diversified to include real estate, philanthropy, and education. Around 1901 he astutely purchased an area of land for commercial development, which soon was encompassed by the growing downtown area, an example of his excellent ability to predict demand. He also began actively supporting Washington University, where Brookings had been elected president in 1895.

In 1899 Mallinckrodt gave his first substantial donation to the university, which he repeated in 1906 and 1909. Elected to the board of trustees in 1902, he took a keen interest in the Medical School when plans for its reorganization were developed around 1910. He contributed one-third of the private funds needed for the establishment of full-time departments of surgery, medicine, and pediatrics and subsequently endowed the chair of the pathology department. In 1916 he established an endowment fund for Children's Hospital in honor of his wife, who had died suddenly that February. He also provided an endowment for the Department of Pediatrics (1916) and funds to establish a Department of Pharmacology (1919). His greatest donation to Washington University Medical School was a pledge in 1927 that the Mallinckrodt family would donate the money for a building to house an Institute of Radiology. The building was completed in 1930 following the donation of more funds by his son, Edward, Jr., to increase the size of the facility. Mallinckrodt Institute of Radiology has since evolved into a leading force in computer tomography, magnetic resonance imaging, positron emission tomography, and the development of radioactive pharmaceuticals for therapy and diagnostic imaging. Prominent scientists affiliated with the institute over its history include Jean Kieffer, Carl Vernon Moore, Sherwood Moore, Martin Kamen, Hugh Wilson, Wendell G. Scott, Michel M. Ter-Pogossian, William Powers, Juan M. Taveras, and James Potchen.

In the early 1890s Mallinckrodt had selected Harvard University for his son's education in chemistry, because of the quality of the faculty, particularly T. W. Richards, and in spite of its insufficient laboratory facilities. Following his son's graduation, Edward provided $500,000 to initiate the construction of a new chemistry building. Although he never desired public recognition for these donations, he could be convinced of the necessity of crediting him in order to elicit funds from other sources.

Mallinckrodt served on the boards of numerous civic organizations in St. Louis, including the St. Louis Art Museum, Shaw's Gardens, and St. Luke's Hospital. A toast on his eightieth birthday, given by Harvard chancellor-emeritus Edwin Herbert Hall, characterized the tenacious and farsighted Mallinckrodt: "Sagacious in business, Artistic in taste, Generous and warm-hearted in philanthropy, Honored citizen of St. Louis, And, with it all, most unassuming, Edward Mallinckrodt" (Stout, p. 84). At the time of his death in St. Louis, Mallinckrodt Chemical Works had an estimated value of $17 million.

• The Missouri Historical Society's archives hold some of Emil Mallinckrodt's correspondence and other family information. A thorough biography is George Dumas Stout, *Edward Mallinckrodt: A Memoir* (1933). Anita M. Mallinckrodt, a distant relative, provides a detailed history of the Mallinckrodt family, going back to the Middle Ages, in *From Knights to Pioneers: One German Family in Westphalia and Missouri* (1994). This work also includes an extensive bibliography and sources of family correspondence. A brief description of both Edward Mallinckrodt and Edward Mallinckrodt, Jr., is in *Mallinckrodt Institute of Radiology: Fiftieth Anniversary* (1981). An obituary is in the *New York Times*, 2 Feb. 1928, and editorial comments are in the *St. Louis Post-Dispatch*.

JOANNA B. DOWNER

MALLINCKRODT, Edward, Jr. (17 Nov. 1878–19 Jan. 1967), chemical manufacturer and chemist, was born in St. Louis, Missouri, the son of Edward Mallinckrodt, a chemical manufacturer, and Jennie Anderson. Mallinckrodt's father, a leader of the large St. Louis German community, was owner of Mallinckrodt Chemical Works, a firm founded in 1867, and the family was well-to-do by midwestern standards. Mallinckrodt graduated from Smith Academy, a local preparatory school. He pursued a B.A. in chemistry at Harvard University, graduating cum laude in 1900. He remained at Harvard, studying with the renowned chemist Theodore W. Richards and was awarded his M.A. in 1901.

When Mallinckrodt returned to St. Louis, he joined the family firm, which was known nationally for the purity of its fine chemicals and pharmaceuticals and as a manufacturer of liquid ammonia for refrigeration and chemicals used in photography. Mallinckrodt brought with him from Harvard four associates, Arthur C. Boylston, Frederick W. Russe, Wilfred N. Stull, and Harold W. Simpkins, whose scientific expertise and leadership were to help him create the Mallinckrodt Chemical Company of the twentieth century. Emphasis was placed on basic research and the development of new products; new laboratories and administration buildings were built; and expansion into Canada was achieved. Commitment to maintaining the quality of the company's products was continued. Mallinckrodt himself began research on diethyl ether, commonly used as an anesthetic. Problems involving impurities and explosive decomposition products, such as peroxides, were solved. He developed a new continuous distillation process and packaging to prevent changes during storage. As a result of this research Mallinckrodt published several journal articles and was awarded sixteen patents. He married Elizabeth Baker Elliot, the daughter of a prominent St. Louis businessman, in 1911. The couple had three children.

During World War I Mallinckrodt served on the Committee on Chemicals of the Advisory Commission of National Defense, chairing the subcommittee on miscellaneous chemicals. Until his father's death in 1928, Mallinckrodt was primarily responsible for the technical activities of the company. During this period he initiated the manufacture of stearates, gelling agents widely used in paper manufacture, in paints, and for general waterproofing. A major application of these compounds was for the manufacture of laboratory greases, the antichatter oils used in Model T Fords.

In 1923, at the request of his friend, the famed surgeon Evarts A. Graham, Mallinckrodt began to produce X-ray contrast media, particularly iodides, that were used to examine the gall bladder. He also initiated the development of turf fungicides, primarily to improve the appearance of golf courses. In 1928 Mallinckrodt succeeded his father as chairman of the board. His devotion to his employees was such that, by reducing hours and finding alternate jobs, no one was laid off during the depression. During the 1930s the company continued to expand by developing a method to purify alkaloids from opium and a product to simplify the etching of photographic plates. With Powers-Weightman-Rosengarten and Merck, Mallinckrodt Chemical was one of the "big three" in the manufacture of fine chemicals.

In April 1942, because of its reputation for pure products and previous experience in the separation of metals, Mallinckrodt Chemical was asked by Arthur H. Compton, F. H. Spedding, and Norman Hilberry to assist the Manhattan Project by producing very high quality uranium compounds to be used at the University of Chicago in the first atomic pile. The request was put to Mallinckrodt on a park bench in Forest Park, safe from possible prying of enemy agents. The metallic uranium and uranium dioxide used to fuel the first self-sustaining nuclear reaction on 2 December 1942 were a result of this project. By 1945 production levels reached one ton per day. After the war, Mallinckrodt began to manufacture pure raw materials commercially for the Atomic Energy Commission and nuclear fuel for atomic submarines and power plants.

During the Korean War, a process to separate columbium and tantalum from their ores was developed, producing metals that could withstand the high temperatures within nuclear reactors. During the 1950s Mallinckrodt oversaw a physical expansion of the company and several expensive and risky research projects that led to the loss of the company's competitive edge. Mallinckrodt Chemical went public in 1954 and 1956 and, after approving a reorganization of the company's structure, Mallinckrodt retired in December 1965 and was named honorary chairman of the board. In 1952 he received the prestigious Midwest Award for Excellence in Chemistry presented by the St. Louis section of the American Chemical Society.

Mallinckrodt was a dedicated outdoorsman, a skilled huntsman, particularly of big game, and an avid mountain climber. His interest in photography led to the production of some of the earliest films of wildlife. His scientific curiosity was not abandoned on his expeditions; he once sent back bear fat to be analyzed in his laboratory. As a dedicated conservationist he was interested in the Dinosaur National Monument (Colo. and Utah) and land preservation in the Adirondacks. Because of his work in conservation he received the Horace Marden Albright Medal, awarded by the American Scenic and Historic Preservation Society in 1962, for leadership in "scientific preservation."

Mallinckrodt's philanthropic activities were widespread and varied. At Washington University in St. Louis, he gave to improve the chemistry building, to better the Engineering Development Fund, and to underwrite research in fluid science. In memory of his father, he endowed the Mallinckrodt Institute of Radiology, which is a pioneer in research on medical imaging. He established chairs of anesthesiology at both Washington University and Harvard and contributed to the Shields Radiation Research Laboratory in Boston. Mallinckrodt gave to the Harvard Divinity School, allowing it to increase its influence in religious studies. He endowed Ward 4 at Massachusetts General Hospital for the study of baffling diseases. In his will he left large bequests to Washington University and to Harvard. Mallinckrodt's donations were often made anonymously, and in 1962 he received the St. Louis Humanistic Award for his "enduring love and compassion for mankind."

Mallinckrodt died in his home in St. Louis after a long life of service to chemistry and humanity. Because of editorial error, some sources indicate that Mallinckrodt died in a plane crash. This was the fate of two sons, Edward III in 1952 and George in 1968. He changed the emphasis of the family firm to make it more research oriented. His development of diagnostic imaging materials is the basis of current technology. His service to the nuclear effort in war and peace was indispensable to the nation. And his gifts of millions of dollars were vital in the areas of chemistry, medicine, and conservation.

• Information on Edward Mallinckrodt, Jr., can be found in the archives of Washington University, the University of Missouri at St. Louis, and Christ Church Cathedral, St. Louis. His articles include E. Mallinckrodt, Jr., and A. D. Alt, "The Determination of Small Amounts of Alcohol and Water in Ether for Anesthesia," *Journal of Industrial and Engineering Chemistry* 8 (1916): 807–12; and Mallinckrodt, "Reaction of Anesthetic Ethers with KOH and with Hg and the Test for Foreign Odors," *Journal of the American Chemical Society* 49

(1927): 2655–66. Mallinckrodt was awarded the following U.S. patents for the manufacture, storage, and purification of ether: 1,461,539; 1,508,563; 1,697,320; 1,807,598; 1,828,117; 1,829,529; 1,814,718; 1,881,783; 1,881,784; and 1,961,936. See also Wyndham D. Miles, ed., *American Chemists and Chemical Engineers* (1976); Williams Haynes, *The American Chemical Industry: A History* (1945–1954), vol. 2, pp. 45, 348; vol. 3, p. 292; vol. 4, pp. 287–88; vol. 5, pp. 258, 406; and vol. 6, pp. 256–58; and the History Factory, *Mallinckrodt, 125th Year Anniversary* (1992). The most accessible obituaries are in the *New York Times*, 20 Jan. 1967, and *Chemical and Engineering News* 45 (6 Feb. 1967): 112.

JANE A. MILLER

MALLON, Mary (23 Sept. 1869–13 Nov. 1938), domestic cook and first identified healthy carrier of typhoid fever in North America, known as "Typhoid Mary," was born in Cookstown, County Tyrone, Ireland, the daughter of John Mallon and Catherine Igo. She immigrated to the United States in 1883 and lived in New York City with an aunt. She had some schooling, but the level of her education is not known.

As a young adult Mallon worked as a cook in the homes of New York's elite. Sometimes she boarded with her employers, and at other times she lived with friends, including an A. Briehof, whose name she was known to have used. She earned high wages and had a reputation as a good cook. In the summer of 1906 she took a job in the Oyster Bay, Long Island, rented home of the Charles Henry Warren family, where in late August six people in the eleven-person household contracted typhoid fever. The owner of the home hired a sanitary engineer, George Soper, to determine the cause of the outbreak.

An accomplished epidemic investigator, Soper soon eliminated the usual causes of typhoid fever—contaminated water or food and contact with people suffering from the disease—and turned his attention to the possibility that a healthy person might be responsible. The theory that healthy nonsymptomatic people could transmit disease was still very new. No specific healthy carrier of typhoid fever had yet been identified and traced in North America. Soper used common epidemiological methods to track the Warrens' cook, Mary Mallon, who had left the family at the end of the summer. He discovered that typhoid fever had broken out in the families of seven of her last eight employers. Even though typhoid fever was common at the time—between 3,000 and 4,500 new cases were reported in New York every year—Soper suspected that Mallon harbored typhoid bacilli in her body and could be implicated in the domestic outbreak he was hired to investigate.

Soper spent some months finding Mallon, then employed by the Walter Bowen family on Park Avenue. In March 1907 Soper appeared at the Bowen brownstone and accused the cook of causing disease in twenty-two people whose food she had prepared. He claimed that he was "diplomatic" in his initial approach, but Mallon nonetheless found no reasonableness in his request that she give him samples of her blood, urine, and feces. Possessing none of the knowl-

edge that led him to suspect her of being a carrier, Mallon brandished a carving fork and threw Soper out of the house. After another unsuccessful attempt to gain Mallon's cooperation, this time at the apartment she shared with Briehof, Soper turned the case over to the New York City health department for further action.

Physician S. Josephine Baker, a health department medical inspector, approached Mallon in the Park Avenue home with a similar request for specimens; when rebuffed, she returned with five police officers. The ensuing chase and capture resulted in forcing an unwilling Mallon into a city ambulance, where Baker literally sat on the confused and resistant woman for the ride to the hospital. Laboratory tests proved Soper's theory that Mallon carried typhoid bacteria in her gallbladder, excreted them in her feces, and through unwashed hands transmitted typhoid to people who ate her food. The health department removed Mallon, disbelieving and uncooperative, to North Brother Island in the East River, where officials kept her isolated in a one-room cottage.

Two years later Mallon obtained a lawyer, probably with the help of the Hearst newspaper *New York American*, and filed a writ of habeas corpus seeking release from her forced isolation. At this time the public learned Mallon's identity, but most referred to her as Typhoid Mary, a phrase used before her name was known. In July 1909 a New York Supreme Court judge ruled that he was convinced by the health officials' argument that Mallon posed a danger to the public's health. Although allowing other healthy carriers to walk the streets of New York, health officials returned Mallon to her island custody. In February 1910 officials finally freed her.

Back in New York City, Mallon contemplated suing the city for damages and tried to earn a living away from cooking, as she had promised; but, unable to earn good wages in another occupation, after four years she went back to cooking. In March 1915 the city again accused her of spreading typhoid fever and apprehended her at her place of employment. Health officials sent her back to North Brother Island. By this time most medical professionals were convinced that healthy carriers could endanger the public's health, but most lay people remained skeptical. Despite the numerous healthy carriers in the population—many of whom were similarly disbelieving and uncooperative, and some of whom were temporarily quarantined—Mallon was the only one officials forcibly isolated for life.

Over the years of Mallon's life and since her death, the phrase "Typhoid Mary" has entered the American cultural lexicon, often in a figurative sense. In medical texts, plays, novels, artwork, newspapers, and popular writing, Mary Mallon, the historical figure, has been replaced by Typhoid Mary, an inhuman monster who used her body to inflict harm on others. The term has become a metaphor for pollution and for the evil one person can inflict on society. Some modern writers have tried to evoke sympathy and understanding in their telling of Mallon's story; others remained harsh in their judgment.

Health authorities attributed forty-seven cases of typhoid fever and three deaths to Mallon, fewer than they traced to some other carriers, but Mallon remained unconvinced that she, a healthy woman, could have caused sickness in another person. Throughout her involuntary isolation she felt deeply wronged and continued to hope that she would "get justice, somehow, sometime." After suffering a stroke in 1932, Mallon was hospitalized on North Brother Island until her death.

• The New York County courthouse holds the habeas corpus hearing records, and Mary Mallon's last will and testament is available at the Surrogate's Court of Bronx County, N.Y. Despite the common usage of the term "Typhoid Mary," there has been little historical scholarship on Mallon. The one comprehensive study is Judith Walzer Leavitt, *Typhoid Mary: Captive to the Public's Health* (1996). For briefer historical treatment see Alan Kraut, *Silent Travelers: Germs, Genes, and the "Immigrant Menace"* (1994). George Soper's perspective can be found in "The Curious Career of Typhoid Mary," *Bulletin of the New York Academy of Medicine* 15 (1939): 698–712.

JUDITH WALZER LEAVITT

MALLORY, Frank Burr (12 Nov. 1862–27 Sept. 1941), physician, was born in Cleveland, Ohio, the son of George Burr Mallory, a sailor and ship's captain, and Anna Faragher. He attended Harvard College (A.B., 1886; A.M., 1890) and the Harvard Medical School (M.D., 1890). In 1891 he joined the pathological laboratory at the Boston City Hospital as assistant to William T. Councilman, newly elected Shattuck Professor of Pathology at Harvard. In 1893–1894 he studied with Hans Chiari in Prague and Ernst Ziegler in Freiburg, leading exponents of the new medical discipline of histopathology. There, in addition to gross observations on the bodies of the dead, pathologists examined tissue under the microscope to define the cellular patterns of disease. On his return he was appointed instructor in pathology at Harvard; he was made assistant professor in 1896 and associate professor in 1901. He resigned from the Harvard faculty in 1919, returning as professor in 1928. He formally retired from all positions in 1932 but continued to be active in the laboratory until just months before his death in Boston. He had married Persis McClain Tracy in 1893. They had two sons; both became pathologists and students of their father.

Mallory spent his entire career at the Boston City Hospital, serving as pathologist from 1908 to 1932. As a student, he pursued Councilman's interests in the microscopic pathology of infectious diseases such as typhoid, diphtheria, and scarlet fever, but in his mature career Mallory focused on studies of chronic liver disease (cirrhosis) and cancer. Although he was an expert clinical pathologist, particularly skilled at distinguishing benign from malignant (neoplastic) conditions, Mallory's greatest contributions were developing new staining techniques for the visualization of microscopic tissue lesions; founding an Ameri-

can "school" of pathology; writing, with his junior colleague Homer Wright, the first American manual on histologic techniques, *Pathologic Technique* (1897); and training more than 125 men and one woman during his forty years at Boston City Hospital. Many of his trainees went on to academic leadership positions of their own in pathology and clinical medicine. Both his *Principles of Pathologic Histology* (1914) and his first text, with Wright, which went through eight editions and was the leading text in its field for more than forty years, were tremendously influential.

An organizer of the American Association of Pathologists and Bacteriologists in 1900 and of the American Association for Cancer Research in 1907, Mallory was important in making university pathology departments active loci of medical research in the first half of the twentieth century. Not himself a leading creative investigator, Mallory consolidated his important role in American medical research through his position as editor in chief from 1923 to 1940 of the *Journal of Medical Research* (later the *American Journal of Pathology*). In 1933, in recognition of his role in the development of modern pathology as an academic discipline, the new pathology facilities at Boston City Hospital were named the Mallory Institute of Pathology.

Mallory was a quiet man but an enthusiast about his work. He worked extremely hard himself, abhorred sloppiness, and expected the same from his students, in whom he took a paternal interest, maintaining close ties with many even after they left his laboratory. In many ways, Mallory's scientific career was not in step with the most advanced trends in medical science. He emphasized the older microscopic pathology over the newer bacteriology and had little involvement with the important advances in chemistry and immunology. Nor were his own researches themselves, other than his development of tissue-specific stains, of major scientific import. Rather, his most important roles in the development of modern scientific medicine were as a builder of institutions essential for the development of a community of medical scientists—professional societies and medical research journals—and as an educator. He educated a generation of physician leaders not only in the technical practices but also in the mental attitudes of scientific medicine, emphasizing that the study of the cause and development of disease be approached with a "critical attitude in accepting so-called 'facts' without proof " (Freeman, p. 828) characteristic of the scientific ethos. In addition, Mallory's morphologic approach to disease reflected a lifelong orientation to the visual in medicine, as shown by his use as early as 1901 of photomicrographs in illustrating his scientific papers. Throughout his career Mallory helped to create the social and mental underpinnings of twentieth-century scientific medicine.

• Mallory's scientific papers have not been collected but are found principally in the *Journal of Medical Research* and its successor the *American Journal of Pathology*. His Shattuck Lecture summarizing his work on cirrhosis of the liver is in the *New England Journal of Medicine* 206 (1932): 1231–39.

For Mallory's understanding of the meaning of academic medicine, see his "The Present Needs of the Harvard Medical School," *Science*, n.s., 24 (1906): 334–38. H. K. Beecher and M. D. Altschule, *Medicine at Harvard* (1977), discuss his career in some detail. One of Mallory's pupils, Timothy Leary, places him in the context of pathology at the Boston City Hospital in "Frank Burr Mallory and the Pathological Department of the Boston City Hospital," *American Journal of Pathology* 9, supp. (1933): 659–72, which includes a photograph of Mallory at his microscope. A valuable discussion of his career as a teacher as well as a practicing pathologist is William Freeman, "Frank Burr Mallory: A Doctor of Physicians," *New England Journal of Medicine* 231 (1944): 824–28.

PAUL J. EDELSON

MALLORY, Molla Bjurstedt (6 Mar. 1884–22 Nov. 1959), tennis player, was born Anna Margrethe Bjurstedt in Oslo, Norway, the daughter of a Norwegian army officer (parents' names are unknown), and grew up in Christiana, Norway. She began playing tournament tennis at age ten, and in a country where few people participated in the sport, she won the Norwegian national women's singles championship eight times between 1904 and 1914. In 1904 she entered the world mixed doubles championship in Stockholm with Swedish crown prince Gustav Adolph as her partner, but they lost in the first round of the tournament. Mallory attended a private school in Wiesbaden, Germany, to learn German and later went to school in Paris to learn French. She also studied massage therapy at the Orthopedic Institute in Christiana and went to London in 1908 to work as a masseuse. There, she played in several London tournaments without success, finding the competition much keener than in Norway. In the summer of 1911, Mallory and her sister, Valborg, played in several tournaments in Germany, gaining experience that helped Mallory win a bronze medal in outdoor tennis at the 1912 Olympic Games in Stockholm. She played well but lost to Marguerite Broquedis of France, the gold medalist, in the semifinals, 6–3, 2–6, 6–4. When she left Norway for the United States in 1914, she held the women's singles championship and, with her sister, the Norwegian women's doubles championship.

After her arrival in the United States in October 1914, Mallory worked as a masseuse in New York and was unknown in the American tennis world when she entered the women's national championship tournament in 1915. She won every preliminary tournament she entered in the summer of 1915 and then beat Hazel Hotchkiss Wightman, the favorite, to become national women's singles champion. The following year, she won the title over Isabel Ashwell Raymond, 6–0, 6–1, in a match in Forest Hills, New York, that took just twenty-two minutes. Over the next eleven years, she won the national championship six times and was runner-up twice, losing both times to Helen Wills, who succeeded her as the dominant woman tennis player in the United States. In 1919 she married Franklin I. Mallory, a New York stockbroker, in a civil ceremony witnessed by Hazel Wightman and Julian Myrick, the president of the American Lawn Tennis Association.

In addition to her success in singles competition, Mallory was a skilled doubles player, winning the women's doubles championship in 1916 and 1917 with Eleanora Sears as her partner, and the mixed doubles championship with Irving C. Wright in 1917 and with William Tilden in 1922 and 1923. She also won the national indoor singles championship five times (1915–1916, 1918, 1921–1922), the indoor women's doubles once (1916), and the indoor mixed doubles twice (1921–1922). Between 1915 and 1927 the United States Lawn Tennis Association never ranked her lower than third nationally.

Mallory's most celebrated match occurred in the semifinals of the 1921 national women's championship when she faced Suzanne Lenglen of France, who had beaten her decisively in a match earlier that year. Lenglen's flamboyant lifestyle and dizzying pace of play had made her the best-known woman tennis player in the world; but Mallory's steady strokes quickly wore Lenglen down, and the Frenchwoman retired after losing the first set and the first two games of the second set. Although Lenglen claimed to be sick from bronchitis and the effects of having just arrived from France, many observers felt that Mallory was the superior player that day.

In 1926, at age 34, Mallory won the national women's singles championship for the final time in a match at Forest Hills with Elizabeth Ryan, who had beaten her in each of eight previous matches. Mallory lost the first set 6–4, won the second by the same score, and then fell behind, 0–4, in the decisive third set. But she stormed back, pulled even with Ryan at six games each, and won the set 9–7 to take the title.

Mallory's style of play was based on her strength and stamina. She drove the ball powerfully with an excellent forehand and once said the secret of her success was to hit the ball with topspin just before it reached the top of its bounce. Her backhand was described as steady, but her net game was considered weak. Mallory was among the most popular players of her day, free and generous with advice to younger players and never disposed to argue with a linesman's call. A knee injury ended her competitive career in 1929.

After 1929 Mallory lived in New York City. Her husband died in 1934, and she never remarried. She had no children. During World War II she worked in the Office of Censorship, using her fluency in French, German, and the Scandinavian languages to censor mail, radio transmissions, and films. After the war she worked as a salesperson for Lord & Taylor, a New York department store. She was elected to the International Tennis Hall of Fame in 1958. She died in Stockholm.

• The Tennis Hall of Fame in Newport, R.I., has a clipping file and a photo file on Mallory. An autobiographical account of Mallory's early years is in Molla Bjurstedt, *Tennis for Women* (1916). Her career highlights were covered in the newspapers and popular magazines of the day, notably *Outlook* and *Literary Digest*, and such books as Ralph Hickock, *Who Was Who in American Sports* (1971): United States Lawn Tennis Association, *Official Encyclopedia of Tennis* (1972), and Bud

Collins and Zander Hollander, *Bud Collins' Modern Encyclopedia of Tennis* (1980), give summaries of her career. Obituaries are in the *New York Times*, 23 Nov. 1959, and the *Times* (London), 24 Nov. 1959.

JOHN E. FINDLING

MALLORY, Stephen Russell (c. 1811–9 Nov. 1873), U.S. senator and Confederate secretary of the navy, was born in Trinidad, the son of John Mallory, an engineer, and Ellen Russell. Shortly after his birth, Mallory's parents moved to Key West. After his father died in 1822, Mallory helped his mother operate a boardinghouse there. From 1826 to 1829 Mallory received his only formal education when he attended a Moravian-run school at Nazareth, Pennsylvania. He returned to Key West, where he studied law and served as inspector of customs (1830), town marshal (1832), fire department director (1835), and collector of customs (1845). He also served in the Florida militia during the Seminole War (1836–1838).

In July 1838 Mallory married Angela Moreno. The couple had six children, four of whom lived to adulthood. His eldest son, Stephen Russell Mallory, Jr., served in both the U.S. House and the U.S. Senate.

Hard-working and honest, Mallory soon gained a statewide reputation. A staunch member of the Democratic party, he was elected in 1850 as an alternate to the Nashville Convention, and in 1851 he was elected by the Florida legislature to the U.S. Senate. As a senator, Mallory worked to establish in Florida naval bases, railroads, and marine hospitals. He also called for the removal of the Seminole. In 1853 he was made chairman of the Naval Affairs Committee and sponsored the Naval Reform Act of 1855 that resulted in the construction of new warships. He also championed ironclad vessels, screw propellers, and modern ordnance. His most controversial contribution was the establishment of the Naval Retiring Board that dropped from active duty incompetent, overaged, and otherwise impaired naval officers.

Though an enthusiastic and tireless worker on naval affairs, Mallory never lost sight of national politics. He defended the rights of southerners to expand slavery into the territories, demanded the enforcement of the Fugitive Slave Law, and called for the annexation of Cuba. Offered the ambassadorship to Spain in 1858, Mallory, worried over sectional disputes, refused.

During the secession crisis Mallory joined other southern senators in trying to gain a peaceful separation between North and South, and he helped arrange a truce between the Federal garrison at Fort Pickens and the Florida troops at Pensacola. He resigned on 21 January 1861 and returned to his home in Pensacola. On 21 February Jefferson Davis appointed Mallory the Confederacy's secretary of the navy.

In his new position Mallory faced a nearly impossible task, but he approached the work with his usual optimism and energy. He first tried to build a navy of wooden gunboats but soon dropped this program for the construction of ironclads, both at home and abroad. Under Mallory's direction the Confederacy employed commerce raiders, which forced northern merchantmen to seek the protection of neutral flags. He also backed the development of rifled cannon, mines, torpedo boats, and submarines. To pay for his overseas ventures Mallory became the first Confederate cabinet officer to use cotton as a medium of exchange.

A close friend of Jefferson Davis, Mallory was often a target of the administration's critics. In March 1862 he was investigated by a joint committee of Congress for the fall of New Orleans and the loss of the ironclads *Mississippi* and *Louisiana*. Though Mallory was cleared of any mismanagement, his programs never achieved the desired results. His under-powered and crudely constructed ironclads never successfully challenged the blockade or Union ironclads, his commerce raiders did nothing to affect the war's outcome, and there were never enough torpedoes or heavy cannon to make a difference. Still, the fact that any of these programs were even started is a testament to Mallory's determination and resourcefulness.

In April 1865 Mallory fled Richmond with the Confederate cabinet. He resigned his post on 2 May 1865 and joined his family at La Grange, Georgia. Arrested by Federal forces, Mallory was imprisoned at Fort Lafayette, New York City, from June 1865 until March 1866. After his release he returned to Pensacola where he practiced law until his death.

• The largest collection of Mallory papers, including his diary, are in the Southern Historical Collection, University of North Carolina, Chapel Hill, while a number of letters are still retained by family members in Pensacola, Fla. Vital sources to Mallory's activities with the Confederacy are the *War of the Rebellion: A Compilation of the Official Records of the Union and Confederate Armies* and *Official Records of the Union and Confederate Navies in the War of the Rebellion*. The only comprehensive biography of Mallory is Joseph T. Durkin, *Confederate Navy Chief: Stephen R. Mallory* (1954; repr. 1987). An excellent overview of Mallory's service as secretary of the navy can be found in Frank E. Vandiver, *Rebel Brass: The Confederate Command System* (1956; repr. 1969). Other important source material can be found at the Pensacola Historical Society.

STEPHEN R. WISE

MALO, Davida (18 Feb. 1795–21 Oct. 1853), native Hawaiian scholar and counselor of the high chiefs, also known as David, was born in Keauhou, North Kona, Hawaii, the son of Aoao, a warrior in the court of high chief Kamehameha the Great, and his wife, Heone. During Malo's youth, which was the early postcontact period, after 1778, he was trained as a traditional court genealogist under the island's foremost genealogist, Auwae Kaaloa. Malo became intimate with much of the traditional culture of Hawaiian chiefly society, particularly its worldview, religion, and politics during a period of transition due to the immense influence of Western (Euro-American) explorers and adventurers and the internal struggles for the unification of the island under one sovereign.

When the American missionaries, members of the American Board of Foreign Missions of the Congregational Church, arrived in 1820 to the very court of the high chief with which Malo was associated, Malo became one of the earliest native students to study at the mission and to assist in the translation of the Bible into Hawaiian. His mission education revealed a worldview and skills remarkably different from those he possessed. Although he never did master the English language, Malo excelled at the mission high school or seminary at Lāhaināluna on the island of Maui, which was the first such school west of the Rocky Mountains when it was established in 1831. The introduction of literacy increased Malo's special interest in the missionaries' desire to record traditional history and culture, the very subject in which he himself was already well versed.

Malo's personal skills of observation, memory, and deduction also endeared him as a counselor and confidant to the ruling king and chiefs of the islands. He was an early entrepreneur. The American explorer Captain Charles Wilkes wrote that Malo "sets an example of industry, by farming with his own hands, and manufactures from his own sugar cane an excellent molasses" (quoted in Malo, *Hawaiian Antiquities*, p. xiv). Malo not only served as a schoolmaster for the mission high school (c. 1835), but he also devoted much of his career to government service. He was appointed general school agent for the island of Maui (1841) and the first superintendent of schools for the kingdom (1841–1845), and he was elected to the first house of representatives of the kingdom (1841). He was well known as a champion for the rights of the commoner and continually advocated, as a counselor to the kingdom, a cautious immigration and foreign policy out of fear of having the small island kingdom "swallowed up" by foreigners.

Malo once wrote to the chiefs (18 Aug. 1837; quoted here in translation) that "The ships of the foreigners have come and smart people have arrived from the large nations. . . . They know our people are few, living in a small nation; they will eat us up, such has always been the case with large nations, the small ones have been gobbled up." Opinions like these led even his mission friends, such as the Reverend Lorrin Andrews, a mission historian, to comment in print that he saw Malo as someone "standing between the chiefs and the common people" and that "as a politician, Davida Malo is considered by the chiefs as rather *ultra* and is so treated at the present time. For he urges improvements which the King and the chiefs do not yet see to be necessary, yet for patriotism, pure devotion to the welfare of the Hawaiian Government and a willingness to make sacrifices for it, there is probably not his superior in the nation" (Lorrin Andrews, *Hawaiian Spectator*, Apr. 1839). Andrews's observations came to pass in the late 1840s, when Malo "was accused of helping to incite a 'revolution' against the Kingdom on the island of Maui. The cause for such alarm was the indignation of Hawaiians at the growing influence and numbers of foreigners in the government and those buying land. Although Malo's friends in the mission and government intervened on his behalf, in the end lands belonging to Malo were confiscated without notice or opportunity to appeal" (Chun, p. 6).

During the later part of his life, after he left the high school and government service, Malo's skills as a native scholar of his history and culture were recognized. With only encouragement from friends in the government and church, Malo began the task of recording the history of the Hawaiian people. The kingdom's foreign minister Robert C. Wyllie wrote, "I hear the Reverend Armstrong and him [Mr. Richards, the chief justice] regretting that if Davida Malo should die, much information respecting the ancient history of the Islands, the genealogy and rank of the chiefs, the customs and usages in regard to land, trial and punishment of crimes, etc., would be lost forever" (Wyllie to Baldwin, 12 Mar. 1847, Mission Children's Library, Honolulu). The manuscript he completed ranges in subject matter from the geographic formation and the different flora and fauna of the islands to various aspects of native Hawaiian material culture and society, including specific information on religions and rituals and governance and politics. His account was once perceived as a rambling collection of ethnographic topics unlike later chronological histories published by the missionaries, the government, and other native scholars. Critics and historians have come to believe, however, that "Malo's work is the most important source on ancient Hawaiian culture" because Malo had written a history true to the perspective of his own culture and he "never mixed ancient traditions with biblical stories" (Valeri, p. xxiv). The following excerpts from Malo's manuscript are examples of his observations and comments on Hawaiian traditions (translations from Chun MS):

Several ia [marine life, mostly fish] were made kapu for women to eat as was Puaa [pig], Maia [banana], and Niu [coconut]. If a large ia was brought ashore, with a piece of wood surrounded with iron on it, then these things were sacrifice to the akua kii(s). (chap. 38)

If a person turned his or her face towards where the sun set, it would soon be realized that his hema [left-hand] side was toward Kūkulu hema [south] and his ākau [right-hand] side was toward Kūkulu ākau [north]. These terms were only used in reference to the heavens and not to the sides of the islands. (chap. 5)

When the people were ready the kahuna nui [high priest] came. He had the responsibility of the luakini and he appeared with a bunch of Pala ferns in his hand and [wearing] a large malo kea [white loincloth]. He was accompanied by a person who carried (*halihali*) a human skull (*iwi pūniu poo kanaka*). There was sea water (*kai*) inside of this skull and the kahuna pule began to lead the praying (*a he kai no ka ke kahuna pule*). This pule was called kaiopōkeo. It was a long pule. (chap. 37)

While Malo struggled to complete the manuscript, he was also working to obtain his lifelong goal of becoming an ordained Christian minister. The missionary church, with its idealistic standards of baptism and church membership, placed many obstacles in his way, but he was finally ordained in 1852. Malo married three times. His first wife, Aalaioa, died childless sometime before 1822, and his second wife, Batesepa (Bathsheba) Pāhia, who was also childless, died in 1845. His last marriage was to Lepeka (Rebecca), a woman much younger than Malo. They had a daughter, Aalaioa, whose Christian name was Emma. Their marriage was not happy. Malo died at Lāhainā, on Maui.

While the account of his own life reveals the challenges and successes of a native Hawaiian during a period of great transition and tribulation, Malo's greater legacy was realized in the copying and later publication of his manuscript in 1903. He did not live to see it in print, but his work was later praised as excelling that of other native scholars (*Honolulu Advertiser*, 31 Mar. 1866). As a person who said he had only "treasured up" the traditional songs and genealogies and who was an "eye and ear witness" of events that radically changed the history of the Hawaiian islands, his account of the traditions of the Hawaiian people remains one of the classic, primary resources about early postcontact life in Hawaii.

• Davida Malo's manuscript was published as *Hawaiian Antiquities (Moolelo Hawaii)*, trans. Nathaniel B. Emerson (2d ed., 1971). More information on Malo is in Malcolm Nāea Chun, *Nā Kukui Pio Ole, the Inextinguishable Torches: The Biographies of Three Early Native Hawaiian Scholars, Davida Malo, S. N. Haleole and S. M. Kamakau* (1993) and "Moolelo Hawaii, *Hawaiian Traditions*" (MS); Valerio Valeri, *Kingship and Sacrifice, Ritual and Society in Ancient Hawaii*, trans. Paula Wissing (1985); and Charles Wilkes, *Narrative of the United States Exploring Expedition during the Years 1833–42* (1845).

MALCOLM NĀEA CHUN

MALONE, Annie Turnbo (9 Aug. 1869–10 May 1957), African-American businesswoman, manufacturer, and philanthropist, was born in Metropolis, Illinois, the daughter of Robert Turnbo and Isabella Cook, farmers. Little is known of the early childhood of Annie Turnbo Malone, except that she was second youngest of eleven children. Her parents were former slaves in Kentucky. Her father joined the Union army during the Civil War, and her mother escaped to Illinois with her small children. After the war, Robert Turnbo joined his family at Metropolis, where he became a farmer and landowner. Following the death of both parents, Annie went to live with older brothers and sisters in Metropolis and, later, Peoria and Lovejoy, Illinois. She completed public school education in Metropolis and attended high school in Peoria. Because of ill health, she did not complete her high school education. In these early years, Malone dreamed of making products to enhance the beauty of black women. She experimented with chemistry while in high school,

and believing that "woman's crowning glory is her hair," she developed a scalp treatment solution to grow and straighten hair.

In 1900 Malone, with assistance from her sister Laura Turnbo Roberts, began to manufacture hair products from the rear of a small building in Lovejoy. Her customers experienced amazing results through the treatments, and Malone's fame spread across the river to St. Louis. In 1902 Malone moved her growing business to 2223 Market Street in St. Louis. Plans were under way for the world's fair in that city. Malone realized that thousands would visit the fair, and she sensed greater demands for her preparations. She began canvassing house-to-house to advertise her work and enlist customers. She held press conferences with representatives of the Associated Negro Press, and orders came from faraway states.

In 1906 Malone copyrighted her products under the trade name Poro. The business moved to larger facilities at 3100 Pine Street in 1910, and four years later it was considered one of the largest black enterprise in St. Louis.

Malone had constructed a new three-story building at St. Ferdinand and Pendleton streets, where she opened Poro College in November 1918. Black beauticians came from all over the country to study hairdressing. Her business now consisted of a factory and a store for hair and cosmetic products, a hairdressing school, a dormitory and a business office, plus a large 500 capacity auditorium and dining room that served as a community center for religious, fraternal, civic, and social organizations.

Malone promoted her business by placing ads in black publications and by touring the South to demonstrate her products. In 1912 she created an exhibit of her beauty aids for display at the exposition in Chicago, Illinois. Poro College established branch offices in principal cities throughout the United States. Her products were sold not only in the United States, but in other countries as well. By 1920 some 200 employees worked at Poro College and in the large mail-order department.

A brief marriage for Malone in 1903 ended when she thought her husband began to interfere in her business affairs. In 1914 she married Aaron E. Malone, a former schoolmate and school principal. Thirteen years later, however, that marriage, too, ended in a stormy divorce. Legal entanglements between the two threatened to destroy Poro College, but Malone managed to keep her business intact.

Malone may well have exerted the greatest economic and social influence of any individual in St. Louis's black community during the early twentieth century. Her beautiful building, located in the center of the business district, encouraged others in the neighborhood to clean and refurbish their homes and businesses. Malone said, "Poro College is an industrial effort of the Colored people . . . and the education we have to offer is the education of example."

In addition to her business responsibilities, Malone participated and held offices in the Colored Women's

Federated Clubs of St. Louis, the National Negro Business League, the St. Louis Community Council, the Commission of Inter-Racial Cooperation, and the Woman's Christian Temperance Union.

Deeply religious all her life, she established daily chapel services for her students and employees. At age sixteen she began teaching Sunday school classes and represented the African Methodist Episcopal church at several state conventions during these early years. At a young age Malone joined the temperance forces and signed the WCTU pledge, which she kept throughout her life.

Because of her interest in young people, Malone gave generous financial assistance to the St. Louis Maternity Hospital, St. Louis Children's Hospital, the YMCA, St. James AME Church, and the St. Louis Colored Orphans' Home. For the latter, she donated $10,000 to purchase land on which to build the orphanage. In 1920 she spearheaded a fund drive for construction of the building. The drive raised $60,000 in nine days. She served as board president of the home from 1919 until 1943 and returned regularly to its May Day celebrations. The orphanage was named for her in 1946. Malone was also generous to her employees and students at Poro College and to members of her family. Following the St. Louis tornado disaster of 1927, Poro College, as one of the relief units of the American Red Cross, fed, sheltered, and clothed thousands of sufferers.

In 1930 Malone moved her business to Chicago, where she purchased a complete city block from 44th to 45th streets on South Parkway, a main thoroughfare on Chicago's thriving South Side. By this time she was considered one of the world's wealthiest black women. Poro College continued to operate in Chicago, but it did not attain its former prominence. The St. Louis building was sold in 1937 under foreclosure to the Mississippi Valley Trust Company of St. Louis. Poor bookkeeping had resulted in income tax problems. A large percentage of unemployed blacks during the depression and the aggressive promotion of the hair straightener by white manufacturers caused Poro College business to decline.

Always interested in education, Malone made large financial contributions to Howard University in Washington, D.C., and Wilberforce University in Ohio.

At the time of her death in Chicago, Poro colleges still operated in over thirty cities. Malone's nephews had operated her business in later years.

Malone's life provided inspiration to young black people, particularly women. She exemplified to them the traditional spirit of American business, as he rose from meager circumstances to a position of affluence through remarkable executive power and business acumen. Her accomplishments were remarkable for a black woman of her time.

• Biographical and business promotional material about Annie Turnbo Malone and Poro College are in the Chicago Historical Society and in the Western Historical Society Manuscript Collection, University of Missouri–St. Louis. Biographical sketches featuring Malone appear in Mary K. Dains, ed., *Show Me Missouri Women: Selected Biographies* (1989), and Dains, "Missouri Women in History," *Missouri Historical Review* 67 (July 1973): inside back cover. Black St. Louis newspapers, the *St. Louis American* and the *St. Louis Argus*, provide business and personal reference data. Obituaries are in the *St. Louis Post-Dispatch*, 12 May 1957; *St. Louis American*, 16 May 1957; and *St. Louis Argus*, 17 May 1957

MARY K. DAINS

MALONE, Dudley Field (3 June 1882–5 Oct. 1950), lawyer and government official, was born in New York City, the son of William C. Malone and Rose McKinney. He attracted public attention as a gifted orator and advocate of liberal causes, but relatively little is known of him. His father was probably also a lawyer, naming his son after the renowned attorney and pioneer of legal reform David Dudley Field. The family lived in reasonably affluent circumstances on Manhattan's West Side. Dudley graduated from Francis Xavier College in 1903 with a major in French and earned a law degree from Fordham University in 1905. In 1908 he married Mary P. O'Gorman, the daughter of Senator James O'Gorman. They had no children, and the marriage ended in divorce in 1921.

Malone soon became active in Democratic politics, aligning himself with the opponents of Tammany Hall. This brought him to the attention of Governor Woodrow Wilson of New Jersey, and he became an active member of Wilson's presidential campaign team in 1912. His efforts in the campaign were initially rewarded by appointment as third assistant secretary of state, a position that made him the department's personnel officer. Since the secretary of state, William Jennings Bryan, took a direct and major role in the staffing of the department, Malone's role was rather limited, and he continued to devote much of his time and interest to New York City politics. He was especially interested in creating an organization to contest the domination of New York City politics by Tammany Hall.

To further this effort Wilson shifted Malone to the position of collector of the Port of New York, a major patronage-dispensing job that he held for nearly four years. Following the outbreak of war in Europe in 1914, control of the port became a highly sensitive position, because it was the collector's responsibility to enforce the provisions of the Neutrality Law as they applied to shipping passing through the city's port facilities. Malone was frequently in the news.

Malone's visibility increased as he began to side publicly with underdog groups and causes. He often appeared at rallies in support of such issues as women's rights and Irish independence. In late 1917 he resigned his government position in protest of the mistreatment of demonstrating suffragettes by the District of Columbia police. After Prohibition became law, he was a cofounder of the Association against the Prohibition Amendment. He continued to identify himself with the Democratic party but ran for governor of

New York in 1918 on the (Progressive) Farmer-Labor ticket. He later supported non-Democratic candidates for office, and in 1932, still calling himself a Democrat, he actually supported Herbert Hoover for president. In 1921 he married Doris Stevens, an active leader of the women's movement. They had no children and divorced in 1929.

By the time of Hoover's election, Malone was an expatriate, and many of his associates were now wealthy men of business. It is unclear exactly when and why he decided to move away from New York, but by 1921 he was living in Paris, where he built a lucrative divorce practice, catering mainly to rich Americans. Oddly enough, this career change mirrored the life of the man he was named for, Field. Malone continued to support liberal causes and traveled to New York or other American cities to speak for such causes. He continued to be much in demand as a public speaker. One of his most widely noted public appearances was in the 1925 trial of John T. Scopes for violation of the Tennessee law prohibiting the teaching of evolution in the public schools. Malone assisted Clarence Darrow in the conduct of the defense; his eloquence drew applause even from his principal courtroom opponent (and Malone's onetime superior in the State Department) William Jennings Bryan.

In 1930 he married Edna Louise Johnson, an actress; they had one son. In 1940, after war had broken out in Europe, Malone returned to the United States. He spent the last ten years of his life in the Los Angeles area, much of the time as general counsel of 20th Century–Fox Film Studios. He was a frequent participant in a broad range of radio programs, mostly on cultural and literary issues. Bearing a strong physical resemblance to Winston Churchill, Malone portrayed the British leader in the 1943 film *Mission to Moscow*. The *New York Times* (6 Oct. 1950) noted, "He was known on two continents for his charm as a raconteur and for his wit as a speaker and phrasemaker." He died in Culver City, California.

• Apparently Malone's personal and professional papers were not preserved. Malone published a compilation of some of his speeches, *Unaccustomed As I Am . . .* (1931). See also John Reddy, "The Most Unforgettable Character I Ever Met," *Reader's Digest*, Aug. 1956, pp. 85–88. Obituaries are in the *New York Times* and the *Los Angeles Times*, 6 Oct. 1950.

FRANCIS H. HELLER

MALONE, Dumas (10 Jan. 1892–27 Dec. 1986), historian and biographer, was born in Coldwater, Mississippi, the son of John Wesley Malone, a Methodist minister and college president, and Lillian Kemp, a teacher. Malone graduated from Emory College at Oxford, Georgia (now Emory University at Atlanta), in 1910. After teaching in high school and junior college, he entered Yale University Divinity School (B.D., 1916). His thesis examined the controversy between Jesus and the Pharisees. He discovered that he was "relatively indifferent" to formal philosophy and systematic theology but had a love for history. His interest in people and his desire to write in narrative form drew him early to historical biography.

During World War I (1917–1919) Malone served as a private and later as a second lieutenant in the U.S. Marines. After the war he returned to Yale to study history under Allen Johnson (A.M., 1921; Ph.D., 1923). His dissertation was a biography of Thomas Cooper. In 1925 Malone married Elisabeth Gifford; the couple had two children.

From 1919 until 1926 Malone taught American and European history, largely to undergraduates. He was an instructor at Yale from 1919 to 1923. He then went to the University of Virginia as associate professor of history (1923–1926) and professor of history (1926–1929). During this period he began to explore the possibility of writing a biography of Thomas Jefferson. When he sought advice on the Jefferson biography in 1926, Johnson urged Malone to undertake a comprehensive study of Jefferson. He warned Malone against settling for another political biography. He should interest himself in "science, ethics, in architecture, in horticulture, and in many other interests which Jefferson professed." Though Johnson doubted that Malone knew enough about the sciences, he urged the young man to "select a field which would eventually produce a magnum opus." *Jefferson and His Time* actually occupied his interest for fifty-five years.

In 1926 Malone became a visiting professor of history at Yale. The next year he held a Senior Sterling (traveling) Fellowship. He used that fellowship in France, studying Jefferson's travels in that country.

In 1929, at the invitation of Johnson, Malone became editor of the *Dictionary of American Biography*, sponsored by the American Council of Learned Societies. When Johnson was killed in an accident in 1931, Malone was named editor in chief. He completed the 20-volume work in 1936. In 1981 he told his friend and library colleague Anne Freudenberg that his experience as editor of the *Dictionary of American Biography* had taught him to focus attention and to demand the precision and accuracy that characterized his own work. His sketch of Jefferson in the *Dictionary* forecast his later and larger work. His editorial career continued as director of the Harvard University Press (1936–1943). In 1945 he became professor of history at Columbia University. In 1959 he retired from Columbia and returned to the University of Virginia, as Thomas Jefferson Memorial Foundation Professor of History. In 1962 he was appointed Thomas Jefferson Memorial Foundation biographer-in-residence at the University of Virginia, the post he held until his death.

While working on volume six of his Jefferson biography, *The Sage of Monticello*, Malone became almost totally blind. He depended heavily on the help of his assistant, Steven H. Hochman, and his secretary, Katherine Sargeant. Hochman did the library research and read documents directly to him or taped them. To write, Malone used a video magnifier through which he could see only two or three words at a time. Laborious as the effort was, he saw positive advantages for euphony, noting that the ear catches some things the eye would not get, such as repetition of a word or a too-lengthy sentence.

Malone believed that a biographer needs to study the subject's opponents to appreciate his actions and his statements. He claimed that he probably knew Jefferson's mind better than had any of Jefferson's family or associates. None of them had done what Malone had done, read all of Jefferson's writings and those of many of his contemporaries. Malone served as a member of the advisory committees on the publication of the papers of Jefferson, and also those of Hamilton and Madison.

Though some scholars considered Malone an apologist for Jefferson, his description of Jefferson's "blunders," "gullibility," "fanaticism," and "obsessive" fears showed that he was not blind to Jefferson's faults. Malone acknowledged Jefferson's growing fatalism and pessimistic attitude toward slavery. He argued that Jefferson was born into the world of rural Virginia where slaves were treated as members of the family, yet that Jefferson recognized that slavery as an institution was wrong. Malone did not hesitate to write of Jefferson's increasing ambivalence, silences, and evasions on issues related to slavery and race, especially in later life.

Malone thought Jefferson was unduly optimistic about the power of reason, but he believed that Jefferson is best remembered for his daring transformation of enlightenment philosophy to public policy. He refused to impose ideological models on his subjects. Instead, he left Jefferson's complexities, inconsistencies, and contradictions for all to see. Malone called the role of the biographer, "not to prettify or deflate but to portray character plausibly, in the round." He tried to see historical figures in their own times and cultures.

Later biographers of Jefferson have turned their attention to social and moral issues that Jefferson never resolved and that continue to plague American society. They attacked Jefferson for not becoming a martyr or at least a personal witness to the rights of African Americans. Yet Malone described Jefferson's dependency on slavery and his views on differences between the races, and he acknowledged Jefferson's omission of women in his educational schemes. But these subjects were treated with the same evenhandedness that he gave to issues of public affairs and farm management.

The historian Eugene Genovese neatly summed up Malone's contribution, "Above all, [Malone] has taught us that history, whatever its claim to science, remains part of the humanities and demands a confrontation with moral values." His work was "a proper combination of respect for hard facts, a gentle skepticism toward all attempts to impose an interpretation upon resistant materials, a decent respect for alternative points of view, and a ruthless refusal to suppress unpleasant data."

Malone received the Thomas Jefferson Award for Distinguished Service to the University of Virginia in 1964. In 1984, the Society of American Historians awarded him the first Bruce Catton Prize for Lifetime Achievement in the writing of American history. He received the Phi Beta Kappa Award for Distinguished Service to the Humanities. He received a Pulitzer Prize in 1975, and he was awarded the Presidential Medal of Freedom by President Ronald Reagan in 1983. Malone died at his home in Charlottesville, Virginia.

• Malone's papers and manuscripts were deposited in the University of Virginia library. See "Reflections," *Virginia Magazine of History and Biography* 93, no. 1 (Jan. 1985): 3–13, for an autobiographical summary of Malone's career and views on historical biography. A useful but incomplete bibliography of his writings appears in Steven H. Hochman, *Dumas Malone: A Select Bibliography* (1981), issued by Malone's editorial assistant to commemorate the publication of *The Sage of Monticello*. Also commemorating the publication of the last volume of Malone's life of Jefferson was Anne Eugenie Herndon Freudenberg, *Malone and Jefferson: The Biographer and the Sage* (1981). See also Edmund Fuller, "A Conversation with Dumas Malone," *University of Virginia Alumni News*, July–Aug. 1977, pp. 16–18; C. Vann Woodward, "Thomas Jefferson: The Hero of Independence," *New York Times Book Review*, 5 July 1981; Charles McDowell, "Dumas Malone on a Library," *Richmond Times-Dispatch*, 25 June 1978, which summarizes Malone's story of Jefferson's sale of his library to the Library of Congress; "Dumas Malone and Jefferson," *Richmond Times-Dispatch*, 30 Dec. 1986; John J. Reardon, "The Years at Monticello: For a Monumental Biography—A Grand Finale," *Christian Science Monitor Monthly Book Review*, 10 Aug. 1981, a book review of *The Sage of Monticello*; Edwin M. Yoder, "For a Heroic Biography, a Heroic Biographer," *Richmond Times-Dispatch*, 2 Jan 1987; Elizabeth Wilkerson, "Mr. Malone and Mr. Jefferson," *University of Virginia Alumni News*, July–Aug. 1981, p. 3; and Henry Mitchell, "Appreciation: The Gentleman Historian," *Washington Post*, 4 Jan. 1987. An obituary is in the *New York Times*, 28 Dec. 1986.

O. ALLEN GIANNINY

MALONE, John Walter (11 Aug. 1857–30 Dec. 1935), Quaker minister and educator, was born near Marathon, Clermont County, Ohio, the son of John C. Malone and Mary Ann Pennington, farmers. When he was young, his family moved to the strongly Quaker community of New Vienna, Ohio. He attended public schools there and spent one term at Earlham College, a Quaker school in Richmond, Indiana, before entering the Chickering Institute, a preparatory school in Cincinnati. He graduated in 1877.

In 1880 Malone moved to Cleveland, where he would spend the rest of his life. He entered the building stone business as an assistant to, and later a partner with, his older brother Harry. Within a few years they had become one of the largest suppliers of building stone in the Midwest, providing Malone with considerable personal wealth that he used for his religious work.

Malone was born into a Quaker family at a time when Quakerism in the United States was undergoing radical change. His ties were with Gurneyite Friends, the largest of the American Quaker groups and the one closest to the dominant evangelical Protestant culture of the United States, bound to it especially through mutual participation in reform and humanitarian causes. In the 1870s most Gurneyite Friends were caught up in a wave of revivalism that swept away most traditional Quaker peculiarities and brought singing and pastors to their congregations. At the heart of this transformation was a group of aggressively evangelical young Quaker ministers who had been deeply influenced by the interdenominational holiness movement. They emphasized complete sanctification, or holiness, as an instantaneous second experience following conversion.

One of the most influential Quaker proponents of holiness was Dougan Clark, a minister and former Earlham professor. In 1882 Clark came to the small Quaker meeting in Cleveland to serve as its pastor. Clark's preaching made a deep impression on Malone who, under Clark's leadership, experienced sanctification himself. Thereafter he resolved to devote an increasing proportion of his wealth to religious work. He began by teaching in the Cleveland Friends Sunday School, which, under his leadership, increased dramatically in attendance. In 1886 Malone married Emma I. Brown of Cleveland, who would be closely associated with him in his work. They had six children.

By 1892 the Malones had decided to give their lives entirely to religious education and evangelism by founding the Friends Bible Institute and Training School, later the Cleveland Bible Institute. They modeled the school at least partially on the Moody Bible Institute in Chicago. It was in fact a Bible college very similar to others being founded in these years. Its impact on Quakerism, both in the United States and abroad, was considerable. While the Quaker colleges were increasingly emphasizing academic professionalization, the Malones' school was set up to provide practical training for aspiring missionaries and ministers. In the first half of the twentieth century it produced more Quaker pastors than any other school. Its graduates were central to the introduction of Quakerism to East Africa, India, China, and South America. It also spawned similar Quaker Bible schools, staffed by Cleveland alumni or former faculty, in Westfield, Indiana; Haviland, Kansas; Portland, Oregon; and Huntington Park, California.

Malone's influence also grew through his publications. In the 1890s he became the largest stockholder in the Chicago-based Quaker journal *Christian Worker* and played a leading role in its merger with the Philadelphia *Friends' Review* to form the *American Friend*. Later he began publishing a small religious journal, the *Bible Student*. In 1902 it became a weekly, the *Soul Winner*. He changed the name again in 1905 to the *Evangelical Friend*. It put Malone in the center of the modernist-fundamentalist controversy among American Quakers.

In the 1890s a small but articulate and influential group of modernists, committed to critical scriptural study and the social gospel and skeptical about revivalism, appeared among Gurneyite Friends. Its chief figure was Rufus Jones, a Haverford College professor and editor of the *American Friend* who made the journal an influential medium for modernist views. At first Malone was a Jones supporter, but by 1898 he was increasingly concerned about the course of the *American Friend*. Like many other Gurneyite Friends with views akin to those of the emerging fundamentalist movement, Malone saw modernism as a threat to Christian truth. Malone and the faculty at Cleveland became some of the most articulate critics of modernist Quakerism, and the *Evangelical Friend* led the battle against the *American Friend*; it was especially critical of the modernist tendencies in some of the Quaker colleges. The Cleveland Bible Institute in turn became the favorite school of fundamentalist-leaning Friends because of its unquestioned "soundness."

Even as much of his energy went into the school, Malone was actively involved in other projects. He took particular interest in orphanages and institutions for homeless men and women. Sympathetic in many ways with the Progressive movement, he criticized monopolies and the concentration of wealth. He also held to traditional Quaker pacifism. For almost a quarter of a century, from 1886 to 1917, he served as the pastor of the Cleveland Friends Church, which under his and his wife's leadership became one of the largest Quaker congregations in Ohio. From 1891 to 1904 he also served as the superintendent of the Gurneyite Ohio Yearly Meeting, presiding over its transition into the pastoral system.

For the last two decades of his life, poor health plagued Malone. He gave up the presidency of the Cleveland Bible Institute in 1918. After 1923 he was an invalid from Parkinson's disease. He died in Cleveland.

• Miscellaneous manuscripts written by Malone are at Malone College in Canton, Ohio, the successor institution to the Cleveland Bible Institute. Materials at Malone also include a considerable body of oral history collected from relatives and former students by John W. Oliver. Important Malone letters are in the Rufus M. Jones Papers at Haverford College and the Allen Jay Papers and Elbert Russell Papers at Earlham College. Oliver has edited an incomplete Malone autobiography, *J. Walter Malone: The Autobiography of an Evangelical Quaker* (1993). Considerable material on Malone and his wife appears in Byron Osborne, *The Malone Story* (1970). Other useful treatments include Oliver, "J. Walter Malone: *The American Friend* and an Evangelical Quaker's Social Agenda," *Quaker History* 80 (1991): 63–84; Thomas D. Hamm, *The Transformation of American Quakerism: Orthodox Friends, 1800–1907* (1988); and the essays in David L. Johns, ed., *Hope and a Future* (1993).

THOMAS D. HAMM

MALONE, Sylvester (8 May 1821–29 Dec. 1899), Catholic priest and community activist, was born in Trim, County Meath, Ireland, the son of Laurence Malone, a civil engineer and surveyor, and Marcella Martin. He received his early education in a classical academy directed by two Protestant schoolmasters who catered to a mixed clientele of Catholic and Protestant students.

As a result, Malone later boasted that, in contrast to many Irish Catholics of his generation, his "early life was toned by [congenial] associations with non-Catholics." In 1838 Malone met the Reverend Andrew Byrne, a New York priest (and future Bishop of Little Rock, Ark.), and accepted his invitation to emigrate to the United States and to study for the priesthood in the Diocese of New York. After five years of seminary studies, Malone was ordained a priest by coadjutor Bishop John McCloskey on 15 August 1844 in old St. Patrick's Cathedral in New York City.

The Diocese of New York was then ten times the size of the present Archdiocese of New York and included all of New York State and the northern half of New Jersey. Malone's first assignment was to the pastorate of St. Mary's Church in the village of Williamsburg, Long Island, directly across the East River from the Lower East Side of Manhattan. In 1847 the area became part of the new Diocese of Brooklyn, and in 1854 it was incorporated into the city of Brooklyn. Malone remained pastor of the same parish from 1844 until his death fifty-five years later. In 1848 he replaced the original St. Mary's Church with a new Gothic structure and changed the name of the parish to that of Saints Peter and Paul. As architect of his new church building, Malone commissioned a young Irish immigrant, Patrick C. Keely, who subsequently designed more than 500 Catholic churches in the United States. Malone later claimed credit for launching Keely on his career.

Although Malone never occupied any more important church post than that of a Brooklyn pastor, he became a well-known public figure because of his involvement in numerous civic and patriotic activities. At the outbreak of the Civil War, Malone, a moderate abolitionist and Republican, dramatized his support of the Union cause—and risked the ire of his Irish Democratic parishioners—by flying the American flag from the spire of his church. After the war, his efforts on behalf of black southerners led Bishop John McGill of Richmond to denounce him for "negrophily."

Malone was equally outspoken and unusual in his advocacy of better relations between Catholics and non-Catholics. He was a personal friend of several Protestant ministers, and on the first Memorial Day, 30 May 1868, he boldly shared a platform in Cypress Hills cemetery with three Protestant ministers. In 1873 he told a Brooklyn Jewish leader: "The prejudices engendered in minds that come among us from the other side of the Atlantic, prejudices of race and creed, should have no recognition among the citizens of this free republic."

Malone was a close friend of the Reverend Thomas Farrell, a Manhattan pastor who founded the so-called *Accademia*, a loose association of progressive New York priests such as *Edward McGlynn* and Richard Burtsell, who questioned the value of religious orders, Latin liturgy, clerical celibacy, and other traditional Catholic practices. Although Malone was a member of this group and openly defended the excommunicated McGlynn against Archbishop Michael Corrigan of New York, he himself escaped any formal ecclesiastical censure for his avant-garde views. Like McGlynn, Malone was also a vigorous supporter of the Irish Land League and helped raise funds for Irish nationalist leader Charles Stewart Parnell. Malone's closest brush with church authority came in 1894 when he ran successfully against Bishop Bernard McQuaid of Rochester for election to the board of regents of the University of New York, the state's highest-ranking educational authority. Malone's election as the Republican candidate angered New York's Catholic bishops and the state's Democratic politicians.

That same year, Malone's lavish celebration of his golden jubilee as a priest brought to his Brooklyn church the leading figures in the Americanist or liberal wing of the U.S. hierarchy, who, in opposition to the conservative majority, believed that the American way of life presented the ideal environment for manifesting the ideals and principles of the church. Bishop John Keane, rector of the Catholic University of America, hailed Malone as one "who has fought the good fight of true liberalism." Archbishop John Ireland (1838–1918) of St. Paul predicted that "the future success of the Catholic Church in America will be measured by its fidelity to the lines suggested by the record and lifework of Father Malone." From Rome, Monsignor Denis J. O'Connell, rector of the North American College, wrote to Malone that "the national interest taken in your Jubilee attests the deep impression you have made on your age and country." Malone lived just long enough to see the Americanist views of himself and his friends called into question by Pope Leo XIII in his apostolic letters *Testem Benevolentiae*, which the pontiff sent to James Cardinal Gibbons of Baltimore on 22 January 1899, eleven months before Malone's death in Brooklyn. Although the pope condemned no one by name, leading Americanists like Ireland and Malone came under suspicion in many quarters.

• The chief source for Malone's life is the *Memorial of the Golden Jubilee of the Rev. Sylvester Malone* (1895), which contains a shamelessly laudatory autobiographical sketch and the text of numerous speeches and letters from admirers. See also Denis R. O'Brien, "The Centenary of Rev. Sylvester Malone, Great Catholic and Great Citizen," *The Journal of the American-Irish Historical Society* 20 (1921): 179–92, and John K. Sharp, *History of the Diocese of Brooklyn, 1853–1953* (2 vols., 1954).

THOMAS J. SHELLEY

MALONE, Walter (10 Feb. 1866–18 May 1915), judge and poet, was born in De Soto County, Mississippi, the youngest of the twelve children of Franklin Jefferson Malone, a surgeon, and Mary Louisa Hardin. His father was an army surgeon during the Mexican War and later was a member of the Mississippi Constitutional Convention in 1868. As a boy Malone showed an interest in writing, publishing several articles in the Louisville *Courier-Journal* when he was thirteen and fourteen. He also began writing poetry around this time and, at sixteen, published his first book, the 300-page *Claribel, and Other Poems* (1882).

As a result of the attention he attracted selling subscriptions to this book, Malone, by this time fatherless, was awarded a scholarship for orphan boys to the University of Mississippi; he entered the university in 1883 to study law. In his fourth year he became editor in chief of the college magazine. During this period he also published his second book, *The Outcast, and Other Poems* (1885), which was praised by Oliver Wendell Holmes (1809–1894), and which John Greenleaf Whittier found promising, though immature.

Malone graduated in 1887 and soon after was admitted to the bar at Oxford, Mississippi. He moved to Memphis, Tennessee, that year and practiced law with his older brother James, who was later elected mayor of Memphis (1905–1910). In addition to his legal work, Malone became city editor of the daily newspaper the *Memphis Public Ledger* in 1888. His law practice kept him from writing poetry until 1891, when he began his next book, *Narcissus, and Other Poems* (1892), followed by *Songs of Dusk and Dawn* (1895). After his short volume, *Songs of December and June* (1896), Malone published a collection of eight short stories, *The Coming of the King* (1897), which was highly praised by such writers as Thomas Bailey Aldrich and Charles Dudley Warner. Malone's poetry did not rely on such attention-getting devices as humor or dialect, which were then in vogue, but was instead serious in nature. Consequently, it was not read by a broad audience. According to the contemporary critic M. W. Connolly, Malone's works had "long been known to the . . . discerning few; and through these his works have filtered down to the masses."

Malone then decided to leave his lucrative law practice and move to New York, where he could devote himself exclusively to writing. However, the move proved to be a disappointment, in part because of a change in the public's literary taste: the Spanish-American War had created a market for jingoist popular writing, and Malone found he was unable to sell his verses depicting life in the South.

Malone returned in 1900 to Memphis and the law. In *Songs of North and South* (1900), he published the poems he had worked on during his three years in New York. This collection also introduced him to readers in Great Britain, where he was favorably reviewed. In fact, he was able to number among his admirers Israel Zangwill and poet laureate Alfred Austin, who found in Malone's verse "deference to the best traditions of English poetry" (quoted in Hood, p. xxii). Malone's collected verse, *Poems*, appeared in 1904, and in March 1905 he published in *Munsey's Magazine* what became his most famous and popular poem, the inspirational "Opportunity," which he wrote to refute the commonplace notion that opportunity knocks only once. The following year he brought out *Songs of the East and West*, a collection of twenty-seven poems, many of which were set in Europe, California, Florida, Cuba, and Mexico.

In 1905 Malone was appointed judge of the newly added second division of the Shelby County (Tenn.) Circuit Court. He was later elected to that position, which he held until his death from a stroke in Memphis. He never married. During his ten years as a judge, Malone was respected by his colleagues as much for his encyclopedic knowledge of the law as for his compassion and modesty.

While Malone also tried his hand at fiction and even drama, his chief literary interest was in poetry, and he devoted nearly seven of the last eight years of his life to his 631-page epic poem in blank verse, *Hernando De Soto* (1914), which he continued to revise until shortly before his death. This work concerned the Spanish explorer's march across America during the years 1539 to 1541 and his eventual discovery of the Mississippi River at Memphis. The epic's narrative focused on De Soto's heroic struggle across the raw continent where one, as Malone maintained, "can never negotiate" with nature: "there can be no cessation of hostilities."

Malone's poetry is generally distinguished by his steady refusal to rely on such popular devices as black and Appalachian dialect, unlike many of his southern contemporaries. Instead, in his often-idealized emphasis on setting, his work places him among a small number of poets who used local color to write wholly in the grain of the American southern post-bellum experience. Indeed, M. W. Connolly viewed Malone as a pioneer in his reliance on "nature as she appears in the South alone." Malone frequently extolled aspects of what he saw as his region's appeal, including the brown-winged wood thrush, Florida's "lemon orchards, starred with blooms," and even a Mississippi swamp where, "like a jeweled necklace swings a snake / From dead limbs where a fallen cypress sank." In *De Soto*, his major opus, Malone's achievement lay in his capacity to identify material of epic potential within American history and to develop this imaginative concept at such ambitious length.

• The most significant collection of Malone's manuscripts and letters is in the John Brister Library, Memphis State University. Other collections of papers are at Houghton Library, Harvard University; the Newberry Library, Chicago; Butler Library, Columbia University; the Tennessee State Library and Archives, Nashville; Burke Library, Hamilton College, Clinton, N.Y.; Perkins Library, Duke University; and the Beinecke Rare Book and Manuscript Library, Yale University.
M. W. Connolly contributed a sketch of Malone's life and career to the *Library of Southern Literature*, vol. 8, ed. by E. A. Alderman and Joel Chandler Harris (1909). Other assessments include Frazer Hood, "Walter Malone—His Life and Works," in Malone, *Selected Poems* (1919). See also J. P. Young, *Standard History of Memphis, Tennessee* (1912); J. T. Moore, *Tennessee: The Volunteer State, 1769–1923* (1923); and Alfred Holden, "Mississippi Farm Boy, Who Became Editor, and Then Judge and Poet, Buried in Elmwood," Memphis *Commercial Appeal*, 18 Sept. 1932. An obituary is in the Memphis *Commercial Appeal*, 19 May 1915.

FRANCIS J. BOSHA

MALTBY, Margaret Eliza (10 Dec. 1860–3 May 1944), physicist, college professor, and administrator, was born on the family farm in Bristolville, Ohio, the daughter of Edmund Maltby and Lydia Jane Brockway. She graduated with a bachelor of arts degree from Oberlin College in Ohio in 1882 and spent the next year in New York City at the Art Students League. She then returned to Ohio and taught in high schools for four years.

Maltby enrolled at the Massachusetts Institute of Technology in 1887 after deciding to pursue a career in science rather than the arts or music, in which she also had considerable knowledge and interest. Also in that year she began her college teaching career as an instructor in physics at Wellesley College, where she stayed from 1887 to 1893. She received a bachelor of science degree in physics from MIT and a master's degree from Oberlin, both in 1891.

In 1893 Maltby received a two-year fellowship from MIT to study in Germany. Under the direction of Eduard Riecke, professor of physics, and Walther Nernst, professor of chemistry and later Nobel laureate, Maltby investigated the electrochemistry of dilute aqueous solutions, using results of Friedrich Kohlrausch's research on conductivity. As one of the foremost scientists investigating fundamental concepts concerning the conductivity of electrolyte solutions, Kohlrausch standardized concentration measurements, determined molecular conductivity, and discovered the law of independent migration of ions. Maltby's research was published in *Zeitschrift für physikalische Chemie*, one of the leading scientific journals of the time. She earned a doctorate in 1895 from Göttingen University, one of the most prestigious universities at that time for training the physical sciences. Since universities in the United States in the late 1800s did not yet offer advanced study or research in the sciences, most American men who aspired to be scientists went abroad for advanced study, especially to German universities. Thus, Maltby was clearly a pioneer and role model for other women of her time who desired professional careers in the sciences, and she may have been the first woman to receive a Ph.D. in physics from any German university, a claim difficult to verify. Nevertheless, Maltby did break new ground as the first American woman to receive a Ph.D. from Göttingen University. With the aid of a European fellowship sponsored by the organization that later became the American Association of University Women (AAUW), Maltby stayed in Göttingen another year for postdoctoral work, an important research opportunity for her as the only woman in the laboratory.

In 1896 Maltby went back to Wellesley College and was head of the physics department there for a year before returning to Ohio to teach physics and mathematics at Lake Erie College in Painesville, not far from her family home. In 1898 she was invited by Kohlrausch, who had become president of the Physikalisch-Technische Reichsanstalt in Charlottenburg, Germany, to act as his research assistant, the first woman to be granted that position and title at the insti-

tute. She accepted this invitation for one year, 1898–1899, and carried out a series of very accurate measurements of conductivity in dilute aqueous solutions that became part of the evidence used by Kohlrausch in claiming that conductivity reaches a limiting value at infinite dilution. This and other research distinguished her as one of the 150 most eminent physicists in the country, an honor accorded to her in the first seven editions of *American Men of Science*.

Back in the United States, Maltby worked in theoretical physics at Clark University with A. G. Webster for one year, 1899–1900. She then went to Barnard College as an instructor of chemistry in 1900 and the following year adopted Philip Randolph Meyer, the four-year-old orphaned child of a friend. In 1903 the anticipated position in physics opened at Barnard, and Maltby was promoted to adjunct professor of physics. Ten years later she was promoted to associate professor and became chair of the department, a position she held for the remainder of her professional life. During these years Maltby devoted her time and energy to administrative duties, service, and teaching in its broadest application, from new course development to mentoring women in physics and in higher education. She is said to have regretted having little time left to continue her own research but realized the importance of promoting education for women. From 1912 until 1929 she worked diligently in the AAUW, acting as chair of the fellowship committee from 1913 to 1924, when she helped establish invaluable policies and guidelines for selection. In 1926, in recognition of her major contributions, including her efforts to advance the higher education of women, the AAUW named a fellowship in her honor.

Maltby was known as a meticulous researcher as well as a demanding and dedicated teacher who kindly and willingly gave of her time and energy to help students and colleagues. Late in her career she developed one of the first courses on the physics of music. She retired in 1931 to spend more time on her many interests, including music. Until severe arthritis in her last few years interfered, Maltby, who never married, was an avid concert goer, traveler, and frequent visitor to the home of her adopted son and his family, with whom she remained close throughout her life. She died in New York City.

• Maltby papers are located in the archives at both Oberlin College and Barnard College. The most complete bibliography of her scientific work, as well as the fullest biographical sketch, is by Shirley W. Harrison for *Women in Chemistry and Physics*, ed. Louise S. Grinstein et al. (1993). E. Scott Barr wrote a brief piece on Maltby in "Anniversaries in 1960 of Interest to Physicists," *American Journal of Physics* 28 (May 1960): 474–75, which includes a photograph. Obituaries are in the *New York Times*, 5 May 1944, and the *AAUW Journal* 37 (Summer 1944): 245–46.

JOANNE A. CHARBONNEAU

MALTER, Henry (23 Mar. 1864?–4 Apr. 1925), scholar, author, and teacher, whose given name is rendered in Hebrew as Tsvi, was born in Banse, near Zabno, Galicia, then part of Austria, the son of Solomon Malter, a scholarly man of modest means, and Rosa, whose maiden name, according to some American sources, was also the rather common name of Malter. Under his father's tutelage, Malter became thoroughly grounded in Talmudic studies by early adolescence. The Hebrew weekly *Ha-Maggid*, of the Haskalah, that is, Jewish enlightenment, movement, sparked his ardent interest in Jewish studies broadly defined and in the relation between Jewish and secular studies. Consequently, at age sixteen, he walked to Lyck, the town in eastern Prussia where *Ha-Maggid* was published.

At eighteen, Malter undertook secular studies in Berlin to qualify for university admission, and in 1889 he began four years of study at the University of Berlin, which had a large Jewish enrollment. Supporting himself as a teacher of Hebrew and focusing his study on Semitic languages and philosophy, he earned a Ph.D. cum laude from the University of Heidelberg in 1894. Meanwhile, he studied medieval philosophy at the Lehranstalt (later Hochschule) fuer die Wissenschaft des Judentums, Berlin, under Martin Schreiner, receiving his rabbinical diploma in 1898. From 1890 to 1898 he had also been continuing his Jewish studies at the Veitel Heine-Ephraimsche Lehranstalt, Berlin. There he was one of the favorite students of the renowned scholar and bibliographer, Moritz Steinschneider, whose guidance proved to be decisive in Malter's development as a scholar. For the topic of Malter's dissertation, Steinschneider suggested a Muslim philosophical work known in Hebrew translation from an Arabic original, which Malter attempted to reconstruct and published as *Abhandlung des Abû Hâmid al-Gazzâlî* in 1896. He also produced a Hebrew translation and enlargement of Steinschneider's bibliographic work on medieval Jewish literature, *Juedische Literatur* (1850), titled *Sifrut Yisrael* (1897; 2d ed., 1923). Malter's bibliographic expertise helped him become the librarian of the Berlin Jewish community's new library in 1899. In September 1900 he married Bertha Freund.

That same year Malter became a faculty member at Hebrew Union College, Cincinnati, Ohio, where he taught medieval Judeo-Arabic philosophy, Bible, Ethiopic language, and rabbinic law and literature. In 1902 he assumed responsibilities as rabbi of She'erith Israel congregation in Cincinnati. Promoted to full professor in 1904, he was highly esteemed for his skills as an Arabist and for his vast knowledge of medieval Jewish literature. Nevertheless, his Zionism and his strong views on Jewish culture and nationalism brought him into conflict with Kaufmann Kohler, president of the college. The college represented Reform Judaism, and Kohler had strong support on theological issues. Inadequately paid and critical of the basics of Reform theology, Malter resigned his post, departing in 1907 with no prospect of a comparable teaching position. He moved to New York City and collaborated with Judah D. Eisenstein as an editor of the Hebrew encyclopedia *Otsar Yisrael* (1907–1913), for which he also wrote a number of articles, but some

time after Malter arrived, the project was temporarily suspended. From 1907 to 1909 he served as principal of the Hebrew School of the Hebrew Orphan Asylum.

In 1909 Malter was elected professor of rabbinical literature at the newly founded Dropsie College of Hebrew and Cognate Learning in Philadelphia, Pennsylvania. He taught there for the rest of his life. During this period, Malter wrote four major works. His consummate achievement, *Saadiah Gaon: His Life and Works* (1921), treats the most illustrious gaon, or great rabbinical scholar, exhaustively. Saadia held the office of gaon in tenth-century Babylonia and to a large extent created medieval Judaism. Far from being dry, this book engages and stimulates the reader in a lively way. Two other major works, published posthumously, involve Malter's design of a method of textual criticism to be applied to the Talmud. *The Treatise Ta'anit of the Babylonian Talmud* (1928) is the fruit of his method, and *The Treatise Ta'anit of the Babylonian Talmud . . . Provided with Notes Containing the Critical Apparatus as well as Discussions and Explanations of the Text* (1930) presents his method and rationale. His final major project was to reconstruct an influential Hebrew translation by Judah Ibn Tibbon of Saadia's *Emunoth we-Deoth* (Beliefs and Views), an attempt to reconcile Arabic philosophy and Judaism. When he died in Philadelphia, Malter left his reconstructed Hebrew translation in manuscript form with revision almost complete. He wrote for many scholarly journals and popular periodicals in English, Hebrew, and German, as well as for Hastings's *Encyclopaedia of Religion and Ethics* and *The Jewish Encyclopedia* (12 vols., 1901–1906).

Admired as a gifted teacher of the Talmud, Malter was characteristically thorough, painstaking, and precise in his work. His strength lay in his passion for knowledge, his convictions, and his well-considered opinions. Frail in health and by nature reserved, melancholic, and pessimistic, he was frequently a lonely sufferer.

During the nineteenth century and the first half of the twentieth, the growth of Jewish studies in America was sustained by a stream of scholars and publications from Europe. Malter was prominent and influential among those who came to America during his era. Thus he helped bring about a shift in the center of gravity of Jewish studies toward the United States, both enabling it to become a self-sustaining enterprise of high quality on American soil and continuing its development from European schools. The history of Islamic philosophy and Arabic studies also owe much to his labors.

• Malter's library and papers are in the library of the Center for Judaic Studies of the University of Pennsylvania in Philadelphia. Malter's letters to Alexander Marx are in the archives of the library of the Jewish Theological Seminary, New York City. Malter and Alexander Marx coedited a collection of their teacher's writings, *Gesammelte Schriften von Moritz Steinschneider* (1925; repr. 1980), of which only the first volume was published. For a partial list of the periodicals in which Malter's articles appeared, see the brief article on Malter by Cyrus Adler, the first president of Dropsie College, under whose leadership Malter served, in *The Jewish Encyclopedia*, vol. 8 (1906). The main source on Malter's life is the article by his lifelong friend, Alexander Marx, "Henry Malter," *American Jewish Year Book* 28 (1926): 260–72; repr. in *Studies in Jewish History and Booklore* (1944), pp. 409–16, and in Marx's *Essays in Jewish Biography* (1947), pp. 255–64. Marx reveals that Malter wrote only the first two brief chapters of an autobiography. The *American Jewish Year Book* also provides other information on Malter; see *American Jewish Year Book Index to Volumes 1–50, 1899–1949* (1967), p. 203. On Malter's departure from Hebrew Union College, see Herbert Parzen, "The Purge of the Dissidents, Hebrew Union College and Zionism, 1903–1907," *Jewish Social Studies* 37 (1975): 291–322. Other information on Malter is found in D. Druck's articles in *Der Amerikaner*, 28 Apr. and 5 May 1922. Obituaries are in the Hebrew weekly *Ha-Doar* (New York), 24 Apr. and 8 May 1925; the *Jewish Daily Bulletin* (New York), 7 Apr. 1925; the *Jewish Exponent* (Philadelphia), 10 Apr. 1925; and the *Jewish Tribune* (New York), 24 Apr. 1925.

LAWRENCE J. MYKYTIUK

MALTZ, Albert (28 Oct. 1908–26 Apr. 1985), fiction writer and screenwriter, was born in Brooklyn, New York, the son of Bernard Maltz, a builder, and Lena Sherry. After graduating with honors from Columbia College in 1930, Maltz spent two years at the Yale School of Drama, where he wrote his first plays and also began writing short fiction. His first two plays, *Merry Go Round* (1932) and *Peace on Earth* (1933), were coauthored with George Sklar and professionally produced. Maltz's proletarian drama, *The Black Pit*, was produced by the Theatre Union in New York in 1935, the same year he joined the Communist party.

In the late 1930s Maltz was active as a writer in many genres—plays, short stories, and novels. His first collection of short fiction, *The Way Things Are* (1938), contained "Man on a Road," which was first published in the *New Masses* in 1935 and included in *The Best Short Stories of 1936*. The fact that *The Way Things Are* was issued by International Publishers, the Communist party publishing house, and "Man on a Road" first appeared in a communist magazine suggests the close relationship that was possible in the 1930s between left-wing politics and respected mainstream literature. "The Happiest Man," a story that Maltz published in *Harper's* in June 1938, won first prize in that year's O. Henry Memorial Award competition. Maltz also taught writing during this period, working at New York University's School of Adult Education and at the summer Rocky Mountain Writers' Conference.

Maltz married Margaret Larkin in 1937; they had two children. In 1941 the family moved to Los Angeles, where Maltz worked as a screenwriter until he was blacklisted in the late 1940s. His Hollywood screen credits from this period include *This Gun for Hire* (1942), *Moscow Strikes Back* (1942), *Destination Tokyo* (1943), *The House I Live In* (1945), *Pride of the Marines* (1945), *Cloak and Dagger* (1946), and *The Naked City* (1948). He also wrote the original screenplay for *The Robe*, although he received no credit because of

the blacklist. Maltz's two Academy Award–winning scripts, *Moscow Strikes Back* (the American version of a Soviet documentary) and *The House I Live In* (a short), both products of wartime "united front" politics, are his most patently ideological work for the screen. Most of his screenplays were for action-adventure films, some of them war films and others in the detective genre, and they bear few, if any, marks of Maltz's left-wing views. By contrast, *Moscow Strikes Back* is a strong plea for support for our Soviet allies and *The House I Live In* celebrates an Americanism based on the country's racial and religious diversity and tolerance. During the Hollywood years, Maltz also wrote a bestselling historical novel, *The Cross and the Arrow* (1944).

Maltz's most dramatic confrontation with party discipline occurred shortly before the blacklist crisis. He published an article, "What Shall We Ask of Writers?," in the February 1946 *New Masses*, believing that he was participating in a forum on the social role of the artist and, in particular, the meaning of the term "art is a weapon." Instead, his article was attacked by influential Communist cultural figures, including his Hollywood comrades Alvah Bessie and John Howard Lawson, and he was forced to recant his position that art is not only a weapon. There is no indication that this heavy-handed imposition of the party line had any effect on Maltz's beliefs or his loyalty.

In 1947 Maltz was one of the screenwriters and directors who made up the Hollywood Ten, "unfriendly witnesses" who refused to cooperate with the House Un-American Activities Committee when it investigated Communist influence in the movie industry. For refusing to tell the committee whether he was a member of the Communist party, Maltz was convicted of contempt of Congress and sentenced to serve a year in federal prison.

While his case was making its way through the appeals process, Maltz's third novel, *The Journey of Simon McKeever* (1949), was published. He served his prison term in Mill Point, West Virginia, from 1950 to 1951 and, on his release, joined a community of McCarthy-era expatriate writers who had settled in Cuernavaca, Mexico. In the post-Hollywood years, his published work included *A Long Day in a Short Life* (1957), *A Tale of One January* (1966), and *Afternoon in the Jungle: The Selected Short Stories of Albert Maltz* (1970). He also published a collection of stories, *Abseits von Broadway/Off Broadway* (1960), in East Germany. In his study of Maltz's fiction, Jack Salzman suggests that this volume and *A Long Day in a Short Life*, which was published by International, had to be brought out under Communist auspices because no commercial publisher in the United States would violate a "second blacklist" by featuring Maltz's work. Maltz's only screen credit after the blacklist was for the 1970 production *Two Mules for Sister Sara*, a film whose background is the Mexican revolutionary struggle.

Maltz's marriage survived the stress of his political troubles, imprisonment, and expatriation but ended in divorce in 1963. The next year, he married Rosemary Wylde, who died in 1968. His third and final marriage, in 1969, was to Esther Engelberg. Contemporaries often described Maltz as "rigid" in his ideological and personal style, but at least one of them adds that he was also capable of "the most extraordinary compassion." It is this compassion that gives life to his ideologically based fiction, which often focuses on the helpless plight of a poor or working-class individual caught in a larger system of economic and racial injustice. Maltz died in Los Angeles.

• Maltz's papers are distributed among a number of different collections. The Wisconsin Center for Theatre Research has the typescript of his early play *Merry Go Round* as well as materials relating to the Theatre Union. Other material is in the Albert Maltz Collection, State Historical Society of Wisconsin, Madison; the Department of Special Collections at the University of California at Los Angeles; and the Library of Performing Arts, University of Southern California. The Columbia University Library has source material for *A Tale of One January*. Maltz's major publications not mentioned above include *The Underground Stream: An Historical Novel of a Moment in the American Winter* (1940) and *The Citizen Writer: Essays in Defense of American Culture* (1950). Biographical material can be found in Bernard F. Dick, *Radical Innocence: A Critical Study of the Hollywood Ten* (1989), and Jack Salzman, *Albert Maltz* (1978), as well as Victor Navasky's study of the McCarthy-era hearings, *Naming Names* (1980).

LILLIAN S. ROBINSON

MALVIN, John (1795–30 July 1880), abolitionist and political leader, was born in Dumfries, Prince William County, Virginia, the son of a slave father (name unknown) and a free Negro mother, Dalcus Malvin. By virtue of his mother's status Malvin was born free. As a boy, he was apprenticed as a servant to a clerk of his father's master; he later learned carpentry from his father. An elderly slave taught him to read, using the Bible as his primary text. Malvin became a Baptist preacher and later, after moving to Cincinnati, was licensed as a minister, although he never held a permanent position in a church.

In 1827 Malvin moved to Cincinnati, where two years later he married Harriet Dorsey. They had no children. During his four years in Cincinnati, Malvin was active in the antislavery movement and personally helped several escaped slaves find their way north on the Underground Railroad. He agitated against the state's Black Laws, which, among other things, restricted black immigration and prohibited black public education and court testimony. Unable to secure their repeal, however, he organized a committee of Cincinnati African Americans to seek permission to resettle in Canada. While he was living in Cincinnati, a vicious race riot took place, in which many blacks were attacked and terrorized by whites. In 1831, during a visit to Louisville, Kentucky, Malvin was arrested as a suspected fugitive slave. Although his "freedom papers" secured his release, this experience and the generally hostile racial climate in Cincinnati led Malvin and his wife to make preparations to move to

Canada. Upon learning that conditions for African Americans were much better in northern than southern Ohio, however, they decided in 1831 to move to Cleveland. Malvin remained in Cleveland for the rest of his life, becoming one of the city's most influential black leaders.

In Cleveland, Malvin worked a variety of occupations, including cook, sawmill operator, carpenter, and captain of barges operating on Lake Erie and the Ohio Canal between Cleveland and Marietta. He also served as an agent for two early black newspapers, the *Colored American* (1837–1842) and *Palladium of Liberty* (1843). Malvin bought one lake vessel and later sold it at considerable profit. He was successful enough as a businessman to be able to purchase the freedom of his father-in-law, Caleb Dorsey, from Dorsey's master in Kentucky.

In 1832, at a time when the state Black Laws did not authorize public funding for educating African Americans, Malvin helped organize Cleveland's first private school for this purpose. As a result of this success, in 1835 he helped set up the School Fund Society to promote black education throughout the state. Under its auspices schools were organized in Columbus, Cincinnati, and Springfield. Malvin continued to assist escaped slaves in securing safe passage to Canada. He was a leading member of the Cleveland Anti-Slavery Society and became well known as a speaker at meetings protesting slavery and the Black Laws; in 1858 he was elected vice president of the Ohio Anti-Slavery Society. Malvin was also active in the Negro Convention movement. In 1843 Malvin and another Clevelander represented the city at the National Convention of Colored Citizens in Buffalo; they were the first black Clevelanders to attend such a convention. The following year he helped organize the Ohio State Convention of Colored Citizens in Columbus, an influential organization whose meetings he regularly attended during the late 1840s and 1850s.

In 1833 Malvin and his wife were among the founding members of Cleveland's First Baptist Church, and two years later Malvin participated in the construction of the church's first permanent home. At that time he was successful in preventing the establishment of a separate "colored gallery" for black members of the church, a practice that was common in the North before the Civil War.

In April 1861, shortly after the Civil War began, Malvin called a meeting of black Clevelanders to organize a black military company. The governor of Ohio refused their offer of enlistment, however, and some of the volunteers from Cleveland went to Massachusetts, where black regiments were being organized. Ohio did not create its own military units for African Americans until 1863. After the war, Malvin remained active in the struggle for racial equality, opposing discriminatory state legislation and speaking out in support of the constitutional amendments of the Reconstruction era. After the passage of the Fifteenth Amendment in 1870, he was named chairman of the

Cleveland Colored Republican Club, the first political organization of African Americans in the city.

Malvin was a militant and articulate leader whose career illustrates the high degree to which successful African Americans were integrated into the social, economic, and political life of Cleveland during the first three-quarters of the nineteenth century. In 1879 Malvin published his *Autobiography*, in which his recounting of stirring events seemed to justify the author's faith in the triumph of racial justice over oppression during his lifetime. The decline of racism in the North since 1860 had convinced Malvin that racial prejudice in the United States "cannot be lasting, and must sooner or later succumb to the dictates of reason and humanity" (*Autobiography*, p. 86). At the time of his death in Cleveland he was affectionately known as "Father John" by many Clevelanders, who saw him as a symbol not only of personal achievement but of progress for African Americans as a group.

• The primary source for information on Malvin is his forty-two page *Autobiography of John Malvin* (1879). A modern reprint, *North into Freedom: The Autobiography of John Malvin, Free Negro, 1795–1880* (1966), ed. Allan Peskin, is annotated and contains a useful introduction by Peskin. For additional details on Malvin, see Harry E. Davis, "John Malvin, A Western Reserve Pioneer," *Journal of Negro History* 23 (1938): 426–34, and Kenneth L. Kusmer, *A Ghetto Takes Shape: Black Cleveland, 1870–1930* (1976), which places Malvin in the context of the black community of Cleveland.

KENNETH L. KUSMER

MAMOULIAN, Rouben (8 Oct. 1898–4 Dec. 1987), stage and film director, was born in Tiflis (now Tbilisi) in the Russian province of Georgia, the son of Zachary Mamoulian, a military officer and bank director, and Virginia Kalantarian, an actress and president of the Armenian theater in Tiflis. Mamoulian's Armenian parents benefited from the largess of his mother's wealthy family and spent a few years in Paris during his boyhood. While studying criminal law at Moscow University, the young Mamoulian became involved in the Moscow Art Theater under Evgeny Vakhtangov, an early associate of Stanislavsky. He left Russia in 1920 following the revolution, joining his sister and parents in London. There he became active in the theater, directing a play with a Russian setting titled *The Beating on the Door*, which opened at the St. James Theatre in 1922. Following this experience he received two very promising offers, one from Jacques Hébertot to direct at the Théàtre de Champs Elysées in Paris, the other from George Eastman to direct at the American Opera Company, which Eastman was forming in Rochester, New York. Mamoulian chose the Eastman offer, presumably because he saw a promising career in store for him in the United States.

Mamoulian's work on *The Beating on the Door* allowed him to experiment with the naturalistic style of the Moscow Art Theater, but he subsequently rejected this approach in favor of what he called "stylization." His remaining films and theatrical productions were distinguished not by the attention to quotidian settings and the inner life of the characters typical of Moscow Art Theater–trained creators but rather by their emphasis on lavish spectacle and rhythmic lyricism.

From 1923 to 1926 in Rochester, Mamoulian staged numerous one-act operas and opera excerpts along with other brief entertainments that were performed during film intermissions by students from the Eastman School of Music. In 1926 he began an association with the Theatre Guild in New York City, staging productions in their schools in Scarborough and New York. In 1927 he was given the opportunity to direct the Theatre Guild's professional production of Dorothy Heyward and DuBose Heyward's *Porgy*, a story of impoverished blacks in the rural South, which met with great critical and commercial success. Mamoulian was praised for his ability to capture a segment of American folk culture and, in particular, for his rhythmic opening in which the town slowly awakens. Other Broadway productions followed, including Eugene O'Neill's *Marco Millions*, along with *These Modern Women*, *Congai*, and *Wings over Europe*, all in 1928; *The Game of Love and Death* in 1929; and in 1930, Ivan Turgenev's *A Month in the Country*, Lawton Campbell's *Solid South*, Lawrence Stallings's adaptation of Ernest Hemingway's *A Farewell to Arms*, and a revival of Karl Capek's *R.U.R. (Rossum's Universal Robots)*. In 1930 Mamoulian also directed a production of Arnold Schönberg's *Die Glückliche Hand* (The hand of fate) for the Metropolitan Opera.

During this period movie companies were aggressively recruiting Broadway talent to help integrate the new sound technology into the storytelling art of motion pictures. Mamoulian accepted a directing offer from Adolph Zukor, Jesse Lasky, and Walter Wanger at Paramount Pictures and chose a project titled *Applause*, which was hailed for its pioneering use of dual microphones and its orchestration of the new sound technology with moving camera shots. Though a critical success, *Applause*, released in 1929, failed at the box office, and Mamoulian did not receive another directing assignment until 1931, when he directed *City Streets*, again for Paramount. With *City Streets*, a crime drama starring Gary Cooper from a story by Dashiell Hammett, Mamoulian introduced filmgoers to the technique of voice-over narration. Mamoulian remained at Paramount through the early thirties, following *City Streets* in 1931 with *Dr. Jekyll and Mr. Hyde*, sometimes considered his greatest achievement. In *Jekyll and Hyde* Fredric March's transformations from the respectable Dr. Jekyll to the satanic Mr. Hyde are handled largely without editing by the use of special make-up and a series of colored filters, another of Mamoulian's many innovations. Mamoulian followed *Jekyll and Hyde* in 1932 with *Love Me Tonight*, in which Maurice Chevalier and Jeanette MacDonald performed songs by Rodgers and Hart. This production revealed the director's flair for musicals, which showcased his taste for lavish spectacle, playful eroticism, and rhythmic movement. The film features an opening in which the city of Paris slowly awakens in a musical sequence that is often compared to the opening Mamoulian had previously devised for *Porgy*.

In 1933 Mamoulian became the only filmmaker to direct both of the screen's reigning love goddesses: Marlene Dietrich in *Song of Songs* for Paramount and Greta Garbo in *Queen Christina* for MGM. Mamoulian's next film, *We Live Again*, was adapted by Maxwell Anderson from Tolstoy's *Resurrection*, and in 1935 Mamoulian completed a pioneering feature using the new Technicolor process, *Becky Sharp*, adapted from William Makepeace Thackeray's *Vanity Fair*. Mamoulian's talent for color compositions stood out in this production, particularly in his striking use of red to signal approaching danger at the Duchess of Richmond's ball just before Waterloo. This film marked the end of what most commentators see as Mamoulian's most artistically significant Hollywood period. During the mid-1930s Mamoulian was also active in the formation of the Screen Directors Guild (now the Directors Guild), which promoted the cause of artists' rights for Hollywood filmmakers.

After *Becky Sharp*, Mamoulian returned to Broadway to direct George Gershwin's folk opera *Porgy and Bess*, adapted from the director's first great Broadway success, *Porgy*. Again, the production, which opened in 1935, garnered accolades, though Gershwin received most of the credit. Mamoulian resumed his career in Hollywood with *The Gay Desperado* in 1936; *High, Wide and Handsome*, with music and script by Jerome Kern and Oscar Hammerstein II, in 1937; and *Golden Boy*, adapted from the play by Clifford Odets, in 1939.

During the 1940s Mamoulian completed only four films, none of which have elicited great critical interest: two costume dramas with Tyrone Power and Linda Darnell, *The Mark of Zorro* in 1940 and *Blood and Sand* in 1941; a comedy, *Rings on Her Fingers*, in 1942; and *Summer Holiday*, a musical based on Eugene O'Neill's *Ah! Wilderness* and created under the auspices of the famed production unit headed by Arthur Freed at MGM, in 1946. In addition, Lucian Ballard, the cinematographer of *Laura* (1944), the widely praised romantic film noir, claimed that Mamoulian shot three-quarters of the picture before being replaced as director by Otto Preminger.

By contrast, on Broadway the 1940s were arguably Mamoulian's greatest period, beginning in 1943 with *Oklahoma!*, which ran for 2,248 performances and was universally hailed for its seamless synthesis of music and story. In 1944 he directed *Sadie Thompson*, which failed at the box office and was widely criticized for having bloated production values. But Mamoulian had another triumph in 1945 with *Carousel*, again collaborating with choreographer Agnes de Mille and the composer-librettist team of Rodgers and Hammerstein. In 1946 Mamoulian directed yet another all-black production, *St. Louis Woman*, following this with a few less notable efforts: *Leaf and Bough* and Maxwell Anderson's *Lost in the Stars*, both in 1949; and *Arms and the Girl* in 1950. In 1945 Mamoulian married the Washington socialite and portrait painter Azadia Newman. They had no children but cared for an increasingly large menagerie of cats in their Beverly Hills home.

Mamoulian's career during the 1950s consists of a series of revivals of his earlier Broadway successes, *Oklahoma!* and *Carousel*. His last film, *Silk Stockings*, was a 1957 musical remake of the Garbo-Lubitsch hit *Ninotchka*, again produced by the Freed unit at MGM. In 1966 the University of Kentucky staged Mamoulian's updated version of Shakespeare's *Hamlet*. The director devoted the remainder of his long life to appearing at retrospectives of his work at film festivals around the world.

As a creator working in the popular arts of Broadway theater and Hollywood cinema, Mamoulian enjoyed the advantage of a cosmopolitan background that allowed him to draw on the high-art traditions of European culture to invigorate the mass-entertainment forms in which he worked. He spoke eight languages and maintained a keen interest in the arts, especially music and painting. He is celebrated in particular for the technical innovations he devised for his stage and screen productions, most notably his pioneering work with sound and color in the Hollywood films he made in the early and mid-1930s and the integration of story and music he achieved in the Broadway productions he directed during the 1940s. The decline of his career during the 1950s and beyond is often explained with reference to the lack of new opportunities for innovation during this time; to quote Andrew Sarris's widely cited appraisal, Mamoulian was "an innovator who ran out of innovations." He died in Los Angeles.

At the heart of Mamoulian's art as a filmmaker lies a fascination with the human body. He once claimed that "through many centuries of development the human race, in its search for beauty and its desire to express it in a concrete visual form, has always chosen for its medium the form of the human body" (Spergel, p. 252). Dancing and bodily display of all kinds abound in his films, which often center on entertainers or athletes whose livelihood depends on physical accomplishment. Statues, mirror images, and shadows proliferate images of the human form. For Mamoulian, the beauty of the body was inextricably linked to its sexuality. He was adept at creating an aura of sophisticated erotic titillation through the use of motifs such as stripteases and double-entendres (for which he was repeatedly threatened with censorship). He created seductive vehicles for many of Hollywood's most alluring stars, including Greta Garbo, Marlene Dietrich, Gene Tierney, Gary Cooper, Tyrone Power, and Rita Hayworth, and his love of spectacle often found expression in provocative costumes and glamorous interior settings that maximized the charms of these romantic idols. Mamoulian's much-lauded talent for conceiving compelling rhythmic patterns can be viewed in this context as well. Tom Milne, in his book on the director, summed up Mamoulian's style by pointing to the connection between his interest in the erotics of the body and his gift for rhythmic effects when he commented, "Mamoulian films have as their real distinguishing mark their unerring sense of rhythm in exploring the sensuous pleasures of movement."

• The most exhaustive information on Mamoulian is contained in Mark Spergel's critical biography, *Reinventing Reality: The Art and Life of Rouben Mamoulian* (1993). This book contains a complete filmography and stageography along with an extensive bibliography of secondary sources and interviews. In addition, Spergel includes complete information about the whereabouts of production files and other relevant material on Mamoulian's films and plays. Spergel also lists a collection of Mamoulian's private papers and his mother's private diary among his sources, but though he quotes from these documents extensively, he does not specify where they may be located. The most important earlier work on the director is Tom Milne, *Mamoulian* (1969), and the brief but influential appraisal in Andrew Sarris, *The American Cinema* (1968).

VIRGINIA WRIGHT WEXMAN

MANA-ZUCCA (25 Dec. 1885–8 Mar. 1981), pianist, singer, and composer, was born Gizella Zuccamanov in New York City, the daughter of Samuel Shepard Zuccamanov (later changed to Zuccaman) and Yachnia (later changed to Jasmine; maiden name unknown), both émigrés from Poland. At the time of her birth, the Zuccamans lived in the Harlem section of Manhattan. Mana-Zucca showed an interest in music at a very early age. Given a toy piano at the age of three, she could not play the half tones, which she found upsetting. Her parents were anxious to let her study piano, and her first studies were with a Russian neighbor named Patotnikoff. After some initial lessons with him, she continued with a Russian immigrant by the name of Platon Brounoff and at the age of three and a half gave her first recital at a small neighborhood social hall. Shortly thereafter, her father took her to audition at the National Conservatory of Music (New York City), where at the age of four she was admitted on scholarship. Her first teachers at the conservatory were the Misses Margulies and Okell. Her first professional engagement was in Stamford, Connecticut, at the home of Dr. and Mrs. Phillips, who paid her $10 as a concert fee.

At the age of seven Mana-Zucca began to study piano with the eminent Polish pianist and pedagogue Alexander Lambert, who taught at the New York College of Music. Lambert was not only her teacher but also her concert manager and mentor. Her practice regime, dictated by Lambert, was rigorous. So that he could make sure she kept to her schedule, Mana-Zucca lived with Lambert all the while that her career as a child prodigy flourished. The two remained very close friends throughout his lifetime. Lambert suggested that she take the stage name of Augusta, which she used for a while but did not like and later dropped in favor of Mana-Zucca, a rearrangement of her surname.

Mana-Zucca was engaged to play Beethoven's Concerto in C Major with the New York Philharmonic at Carnegie Hall, under the baton of Walter Damrosch, at the age of eight. That same concert was presented also in the 20,000-seat Exposition Hall in Pittsburgh, after which Damrosch wired Lambert and asked to sign Mana-Zucca for a series of fourteen concerts. At the same time that Mana-Zucca studied piano with Lambert, she also studied harmony and composition with Herman Spielter. Her first published work, *Moment Musicale*, for violin and piano, was composed when she was only seven years old. Her *Etude de Concert* was written when she was eight. Her first art song, *Frage*, was published by Rudolph Schirmer, as were *Moment Triste* and *Moment Orientale*, both composed when she was nine, followed by a large number of other works composed in her lifetime.

As Mana-Zucca approached her early teens, she sailed to Europe with her elder sister Beatrice, better known as Bess. They settled in Berlin, Germany, and she soon became part of that city's busy and exciting cultural milieu. Mana-Zucca's debut in Berlin, at the Bechstein Saal, was highly acclaimed and opened doors for other engagements throughout Europe. Given the opportunity to play with famous Spanish violinist Juan Manon, she performed with him in several successful concerts before signing a contract to play sixty concerts with him over a three-year period; they appeared together throughout Germany and Russia.

While in Berlin, Mana-Zucca studied the works of Brahms with the eminent pedagogue Josef Weiss, and later she was accepted for study in the master classes of the great Ferruccio Busoni, which she attended for eight months. She received private instruction from Leopold Godowsky and also attended master classes that he conducted for selected students. In addition, while in Berlin she studied voice with a Fraulein van Gelder, and later, in London, she studied with Raimond von zur Muhlen, a famous singer of *lieder* and a much-sought-after voice teacher.

Following their stay in Berlin, Mana-Zucca and her sister spent several years in London, where she concertized, appeared in the musical comedy *The Count of Luxembourg*, and also appeared as a singer with the London Symphony Trio. Her wide acceptance as a singer made it difficult at times for her to choose among musical careers. After returning to the United States around 1915, Mana-Zucca accepted roles in several musical comedies, including Daphne in *The Rose Maid* and O Mimosa San in *The Geisha*. Later, tiring of these, she returned to serious music and composing.

A new phase in Mana-Zucca's life began when she accepted the marriage proposal of Irwin M. Cassel, a gentleman she had known since her youth. The couple eloped on 21 September 1921. Cassel promised his new wife that they would spend seven months of each year in New York City and the remaining five months in Miami, Florida, where he made his home. Cassel supported Mana-Zucca's musical career and even wrote the lyrics to the now-famous song "I Love Life" (1923), which has been performed by celebrated singers such as John Charles Thomas and Lawrence Tibbet. Ultimately, and especially after the birth of her only child, a son, in 1926, Miami became her permanent residence. She spent many happy hours there composing and presenting musicales in her home, "Mazica Hall." She died in Miami.

Mana-Zucca had three distinct but interconnected careers: as a concert pianist of great renown, as a singer who performed leading roles in musical comedy, and as a prolific composer. Her brochure of published music totals more than four hundred works. These include music for piano, orchestra, and voice. In addition, she also composed music for young students.

• All of Mana-Zucca's music and memorabilia is in the possession of her son, Marwin Cassel of Miami. A manuscript autobiography is in the possession of the author. For Mana-Zucca's musical opinions, see M. Stanley, "Mana-Zucca Tells Why *Rachem* Was Written," *Musical America* 31, no. 4 (1919): 19, and H. Brower, "American Women Pianists: Their Views and Achievements," *Musical America* 28, no. 26 (1918): 18. Also see "Mana-Zucca, Humorist," *Musical Courier* 73, no. 3 (1917): 42, and Sharon Leding Lawhon, "A Performer's Guide to Selected Twentieth-century Sacred Solo Art Songs Composed by Women from the United States of America" (Ph.D. diss., Southern Baptist Theological Seminary, 1993). An obituary is in the *New York Times*, 11 Mar. 1981.

TOMMIE EWERT CARL

MANCINI, Henry (16 Apr. 1924–14 June 1994), composer and conductor, was born Henry Nicola Mancini in Cleveland, Ohio, the son of Quinto Mancini, a steelworker, and Anna Pece. Mancini's father was an amateur musician, and he made his son start studying the flute and piccolo at the age of eight. While in high school in Aliquippa, Pennsylvania, Mancini began studying music under Max Adkins, the arranger and conductor of the house orchestra at Pittsburgh's Stanley Theater. Mancini briefly attended the School of Music at the Carnegie Institute of Technology in Pittsburgh and then transferred to the Juilliard School of Music in New York. His formal studies ended when he was drafted in 1943.

During the war Mancini served with the U.S. Army infantry and the Army Air Corps, where he met several members of Glenn Miller's Army Air Corps Band. After being discharged in 1946 he became a pianist and arranger with the new Glenn Miller Band, which was reorganized (after Miller's wartime death) by Tex Beneke. He left the band in 1947 and moved to Hollywood. In September 1947 Mancini married Virginia "Ginny" O'Connor, a singer with the Mello-Larks, who accompanied the band. The couple had three children, two of whom became musicians.

In Hollywood, Mancini began private music studies with composers Mario Castelnuovo-Tedesco, Ernst Krenek, and Alfred Sendrey. He also began writing music for radio programs, including "The F.B.I. in Peace and War," and composing arrangements for singers' and musicians' nightclub acts.

In 1952 Mancini joined the music department of Universal-International Studios in Hollywood, where he composed music for scores and songs used in nearly 250 films during the next six years. His music was used in comedies, horror films, dramas, and musicals, including *Abbott and Costello Meet Dr. Jekyll and Mr. Hyde* (1953), *Creature from the Black Lagoon* (1954), *Touch of Evil* (1958), and *The Glenn Miller Story* (1954). His score for the last film won him his first Academy Award nomination in 1954. Mancini later referred to Universal as a "salt mine" but added that "it was a good salt mine, and younger composers today do not have access to that kind of on-the-job training. Being on staff there I was called upon to do everything. . . . Whenever they needed a piece of source music, music that comes from a source in the picture, such as a band, a jukebox, or a radio, they would call me in."

Competition from television caused Universal financial problems in the 1950s, and in 1958 they disbanded their music department. Blake Edwards, a producer at Universal, was also leaving in order to produce a television detective series, "Peter Gunn." He asked Mancini to write the score. In doing so, Mancini used a heavy jazz idiom and won many favorable reviews from the critics. RCA-Victor subsequently released the album *Music from Peter Gunn*, and it won Mancini two Grammy Awards from the National Academy of Music Arts and Sciences in 1958 for best album and best arrangement. The album sold more than a million copies, as did a sequel, *More Music from Peter Gunn*.

Edwards produced another television detective series the following year, "Mr. Lucky," and he asked Mancini to collaborate again on the program's music. Both the show and its music were popular hits. The album *Music from Mr. Lucky* was another bestseller and garnered Mancini two more Grammy Awards in 1960 for best arrangement and best performance by an orchestra. Mancini also won a third Grammy that same year for another album, *The Blues and the Beat.* He would eventually write music for more than a dozen other television programs.

Mancini returned to writing music for motion pictures in 1960 as a freelance composer not under contract to any one studio. His music for Edwards's *Breakfast at Tiffany's* (1961) won him five more Grammys and also his first two Oscars from the Academy of Motion Picture Arts and Sciences. One was for best original score and the other for best song, which was his lilting ballad "Moon River." Another of his songs, "Bachelor in Paradise," was also nominated in the best-song category.

In 1962 Mancini provided music for Howard Hawks's *Hatari*, whose theme "Baby Elephant Walk" won him another Grammy, and for Edwards's *Experiment in Terror.* He also wrote *Sounds and Scores: A Practical Guide to Professional Orchestration* (1962), which was published by Northridge Music Publishing, a firm Mancini had founded in the late 1950s. During the early 1960s he also began to conduct orchestras in a series of live performances in the United States and abroad.

In 1962 the Edwards-Mancini collaboration led to the music for *Days of Wine and Roses*, whose theme song had the same name and won him another Oscar for best song. In 1963 Mancini's theme song "Charade," for Stanley Donen's romantic mystery of the same name, earned him another Oscar nomination for best movie song. Mancini also composed the music for Edwards's *The Pink Panther* (1964), the first in a series of comedies that featured Peter Sellers and that used variations on Mancini's quirky theme.

Mancini continued to compose movie music for the next twenty-five years, frequently for films directed by Edwards or Donen, but few of the films or their music became very popular: *The Great Race* (1965); *Arabesque* (1966); *The Molly Maguires* (1970); *The Night Visitor* (1970); *Sometimes a Great Notion* (1971); *Oklahoma Crude* (1973); *The Great Waldo Pepper* (1975); *The Silver Streak* (1976); *Who Is Killing the Great Chefs of Europe?* (1978); *S.O.B.* (1981); *Mommie Dearest* (1981), which was a moderate success; *Harry and Son* (1983); *A Fine Mess* (1986); *The Glass Menagerie* (1987); *Sunset* (1988); *Physical Evidence* (1989); *Ghost Dad* (1990); and *Switch* (1991).

The music in Edwards's *Victor/Victoria* (1982) won Mancini his fourth Oscar, for best score, in 1982. The music for that film, as well as for Edwards's *The Man Who Loved Women* (1983), contained the same type of haunting melodies that had characterized his music for the films of the 1960s.

During the early 1990s Mancini and Edwards collaborated again, on a stage version of *Victor/Victoria*. Before his death in Los Angeles, Mancini wrote music for twenty-five new songs for the Broadway show, which opened in New York in 1995.

Mancini was a prolific composer whose successful career spanned four decades, although he was best known for his work in the late 1950s and early 1960s. His instrumentals, the theme music for "Mr. Lucky," "Peter Gunn," "The Richard Boone Show," and *The Pink Panther*, and his songs "Moon River," "Charade," "Dear Heart," and "Days of Wine and Roses" were some of the best known tunes of the period and became established musical standards. But as the 1960s progressed, popular tastes changed. Audiences became younger and more interested in rock music, which emphasized rhythm and loudness rather than melody and subtle orchestration. Although Mancini was not as much in the public eye during his last two decades, his talent and craftsmanship still resulted in a steady demand for his participation in Hollywood's film and television productions.

• Mancini published an autobiography, with the assistance of Gene Lees, *Did They Mention the Music?* (1989). A large selection of his work is contained in Milton Okun, ed., *Henry Mancini Songbook* (1981). Interviews are included in Tony Thomas, ed., *Film Score: The View from the Podium* (1979); Joe Smith, with Mitchell Fink, ed., *Off the Record: An Oral History of Popular Music* (1988); and Fred Binkley, "Henry Mancini's Movie Manifesto," *Down Beat*, 5 Mar. 1970; repr. July 1994. See also Chuck Berg, "Henry Mancini: Sounds in the Dark," *Down Beat*, 7 Dec. 1978; Peter Lehman and Wil-liam Luhr, *Blake Edwards* (1981); and Joseph Andrew Casper, *Stanley Donen* (1983). Obituaries appear in the *New York Times*, 15 June 1994; *Variety*, 20 June 1994; *Billboard*, 25 June 1994; and *Down Beat*, Sept. 1994.

STEPHEN G. MARSHALL

MANDELBAUM, Maurice H. (9 Dec. 1908–1 Jan. 1987), philosopher and teacher, was born in Chicago, Illinois, the son of Maurice H. Mandelbaum and Ida Mandel. He earned his A.B. from Dartmouth College in 1929. While working on a master's degree at Dartmouth, he was also an assistant professor, teaching biography and comparative literature from 1931 to 1932. After receiving his master's degree in 1932, he went to Yale University to study for a doctorate in philosophy. In October 1932 he married his first wife, Gwendolyn Norton; they had two children. They later divorced, and in March 1949 he married Alice L. Moran. In 1934 he became an associate professor of philosophy at Swarthmore College in Pennsylvania. Two years later he received his Ph.D. from Yale.

Mandelbaum's dissertation was published in 1938 as *The Problem of Historical Knowledge: An Answer to Relativism*. This book firmly established him as one of the most influential driving forces in the field of philosophy of history, at a time when Anglo-American philosophers were generally uninterested in the subject. Mandelbaum argues against three relativists in his book: two Germans, Wilhelm Dilthey and Karl Mannheim, and the Italian, Benedetto Croce. With the publication of Mandelbaum's book, along with the publication of Carl Hempel's 1942 article "The Function of General Laws in History" and R. G. Collingwood's *The Idea of History* (1946), Anglo-American philosophers became more and more concerned with the problems of historicism and more sensitive to a historical approach rather than the historical approach that was in vogue at the time because of the influence of the logical positivists.

Mandelbaum maintained the general position outlined in *The Problem of Historical Knowledge* for the rest of his career. Against the three historical relativists, Croce, Dilthey, and Mannheim, he argued for the objectivity of history. When new developments in historical relativism gained an influential following with the publication of works such as Thomas S. Kuhn's *The Structure of Scientific Revolutions* (1962), Mandelbaum restated his objectivist position in "Some Instances of the Self-Excepting Fallacy" (1962), "Objectivism in History" (1963), a reprint of *The Problem of Historical Knowledge* (1967), "A Note on Thomas S. Kuhn's 'The Structure of Scientific Revolutions'" (1977), and "Subjective, Objective, and Conceptual Relativisms" (1979).

Mandelbaum was a Guggenheim Fellow in 1946 and then accepted a position as a professor of philosophy at his alma mater, Dartmouth. Over the next ten years he published numerous articles as well as his second monograph, *The Phenomenology of Moral Experience* (1955). The book is the final product of his studies as a Guggenheim Fellow.

Mandelbaum's attempt to ground an ethical theory upon a phenomenological analysis of moral experience was unique among the more logical and epistemological approaches by his contemporaries. Like his 1938 book that foreshadowed and in part precipitated the growth of philosophy of history in English-speaking universities, his 1955 book on metaethics foreshadowed the drift of English-speaking philosophers away from a logico-analytic approach to ethics. The dozen or so articles he published while at Dartmouth reveal his continuing interest and expertise in the philosophy of history and historiography. An examination of the methodology of historical studies naturally led him to issues in the philosophy of social science such as human freedom, determinism, methodological individualism, and societal laws. His work did not go unnoticed by the philosophical community. He was invited to the University of Michigan as visiting professor in 1950–1951 and Harvard University in 1957–1958.

Mandelbaum became professor of philosophy at Johns Hopkins University in 1957. He stayed there twenty years, the first ten of which he served as chairman of the philosophy department. He continued publishing at a prodigious rate while also becoming intricately involved with establishing the structure of the American Philosophical Association. Mandelbaum's colleague, Lewis White Beck, noted that he "was primarily responsible for the maturation of the American Philosophical Association during the years of his chairmanship of its Board of Officers (and a few years before and after his term of office)."

Having established his reputation as a philosopher, Mandelbaum then went on to serve the community of scholars and higher education. He was president of the Eastern Division of the American Philosophical Association in 1962 and delegate of the American Philosophical Association to the American Council of Learned Societies (1964–1968 and 1978–1981). He was also a member of the Council of Philosophical Studies (1969–1972), served on the National Board of Graduate Education (1971–1975), and was a member of the Maryland Committee on the Humanities and Public Policy (1974–1977).

While at Johns Hopkins, Mandelbaum authored more than thirty publications on the philosophy of history, ethics, the philosophy of social science, epistemology, and the history of philosophy. His presidential address to the American Philosophical Association, "Philosophy, Science, and Sense-Perception" was developed into a monograph and published in 1964 as *Philosophy, Science, and Sense-Perception: Historical and Critical Studies*. In the interest of defending a philosophical theory of perception/epistemology known as "critical realism," Mandelbaum, in characteristic historical fashion, goes back to the philosophy of the seventeenth and eighteenth centuries. He thoroughly examines the relationship of John Locke's epistemological realism with the sciences of his day, as exemplified in Boyle and Newton. Mandelbaum then goes on to critically assess Berkeley's and Hume's contributions to epistemology. Mandelbaum was careful to distinguish his critical realism from the direct realism defended by G. E. Moore and Gilbert Ryle in the twentieth century.

In 1967 Mandelbaum was named Andrew W. Mellon Professor of Philosophy at Johns Hopkins and was a fellow of the Center for the Advanced Study of the Behavioral Sciences, Palo Alto, California (1967–1968). His time spent at the center allowed him to finish work on a book that he had begun in 1953. Having devoted attention to the philosophy of the seventeenth and eighteenth centuries in *Philosophy, Science, and Sense-Perception*, he published *History, Man, and Reason: A Study in Nineteenth-Century Thought* (1971). In it he discusses social science as well as philosophy, demonstrating how "certain common beliefs and attitudes regarding history, man, and reason, came to pervade a great deal of nineteenth-century thought."

In his next book, *The Anatomy of Historical Knowledge* (1977), Mandelbaum turned back to the issues that occupied him in his first book, *The Problem of Historical Knowledge*. He calls attention to the sheer variety of approaches to historical inquiry that a philosopher of history in the late twentieth century grappled with. He spells out his views on historical explanation and gives his most detailed account of the important role that causation must play in any such explanation. In addition, he describes the level of objectivity one can expect from historical knowledge, given its reliance on causation and given the degree of trust that historians can reasonably put in causal laws.

During the last decade of his life, Mandelbaum published a half-dozen scholarly papers, a collection of previously published essays titled *Philosophy, History, and the Sciences: Selected Critical Essays* (1984), and the monograph *Purpose and Necessity in Social Theory* (1987). Mandelbaum's last monograph, *Purpose and Necessity in Social Theory* (1987), completed when he was a Mellon Senior Fellow at the National Humanities Center in 1986, gives his final word on necessity, chance, and choice in human affairs.

Mandelbaum retired from Johns Hopkins in 1974 but taught there part time until 1978. He decided to resume teaching and went back to Dartmouth, where he taught as an adjunct professor of philosophy from 1979 to 1983. In April 1981 he married Leland Barbee Hill, six years after the death of his second wife. He was named visiting scholar at Dartmouth in 1983 and retained that position until his death in Hanover, New Hampshire.

• Besides those works mentioned above, Mandelbaum, along with Francis W. Gramlich and Alan Ross Anderson, edited *Philosophic Problems: An Introductory Book of Readings*. The book became popular for classroom use and a second edition was issued in 1967. He coedited with Edward N. Lee *Phenomenology and Existentialism* (1967), and with Eugene Freeman, *Spinoza: Essays in Interpretation* (1975). An obituary is in *The Proceedings and Addresses of the American Philosophical Association* 60 (1987) and the *Boston Globe*, 3 Jan. 1987.

JOHN M. MIZZONI

MANDELL, Sammy (5 Feb. 1904–7 Nov. 1967), professional boxer, was born Samuel Mandella at Plana de Grece, Italy. (The names of his parents are not known.) At age two he was brought to the United States by his father. He grew up in Rockford, Illinois, where he attended high school and participated in athletics, especially basketball.

Mandell was introduced to boxing by an older brother, Joe, a professional boxer during World War I, who used him as his sparring partner. In 1920 Mandell made his professional debut as a bantamweight at Camp Grant, Illinois, near Rockford; he was fighting semifinals and main events by the end of the year. From the first he possessed natural hand and foot speed and boxing skills. Although not a devastating puncher, he hit sharply, accurately, and frequently, and he knocked out some of his opponents.

From 1920 to 1924 Mandell fought seventy-six times. Many of these fights had no official decision, but unofficial winners were designated by newspaper reporters, and Mandell lost only five times including newspaper verdicts. His only serious setback in that time was in a fight with Joey Sangor in Minneapolis in which Mandell was knocked down, rose too quickly, and immediately went back down to take a longer count. However, he was considered knocked out for dropping to the canvas without being hit. Mandell defeated many excellent fighters during this period: Babe Herman, Johnny Dundee, Jack Wolfe, Eddie Anderson, and Sangor. By 1925 he was recognized as a leading lightweight contender.

In that year a series of elimination fights were held in New York City to find a champion to replace the retired Benny Leonard. Mandell defeated the highly regarded Sid Terris in the first round of eliminations, but he lost his match with Jimmy Goodrich on a foul in a fight that he otherwise would have won. Mandell then began a string of victories that led to a lightweight title fight with the champion, Rocky Kansas, in 1926. In that fight, held in Chicago, the faster, quicker, and more skillful Mandell defeated the aggressive, harder-hitting Kansas.

Mandell was a strikingly handsome young man who kept his features intact with clever defensive boxing. His extraordinary reflexes allowed him to avoid his opponents' punches by quick head movements, and his graceful footwork usually kept him out of range. Nicknamed "Rockford Sheik," he married Elizabeth Hemming of Rockford in 1926; they had one child. Mandell was originally managed by Teddy Bodkins, a Rockford meat dealer; he later was handled by the knowledgeable Eddie Kane and Eddie Long and was trained by Jack Blackburn, who became famous as heavyweight champion Joe Louis's trainer.

Although Mandell continued to box often and win consistently, it was not until 21 May 1928 in New York City that he first defended the lightweight title. His opponent, Jimmy McLarnin, an excellent puncher and future welterweight champion, was unable to land a decisive blow, and Mandell boxed his way to an impressive victory. Soon afterward, in Flint, Michi-

gan, Mandell had a second unlucky loss to Goodrich in a nontitle fight, suffering a fractured collarbone that forced him to withdraw in the second round.

On 2 August 1929 in Chicago, Mandell successfully defended his title against Tony Canzoneri in a close fight. Once again his outstanding defensive work and clever boxing made the difference. Later that year he lost a nontitle return fight to an improved and heavier McLarnin. From 1926 until 1930 Mandell had sixty-three fights, defeating many strong opponents, including Billy Petrolle by newspaper decision and Jackie Fields, Phil McGraw, Joey Goodman, Tommy Herman, and Harry Brown by official decisions, in nontitle fights.

Mandell's four-year reign as lightweight champion ended on 17 July 1930 at Yankee Stadium in New York City when he was surprisingly knocked out in the first round by Al Singer. After that defeat he began to lose frequently, although he continued to be active until 1934, suffering defeats by many opponents he would have beaten easily before his reflexes and quickness declined. In all, he fought 187 times, losing only twenty-six, most of his defeats coming after he relinquished the lightweight title. He fought thirteen world champions and title claimants.

After his retirement, Mandell worked as a bank security guard in Chicago, but he also managed fighters and staged boxing promotions. In 1957 he suffered a stroke that left him an invalid. He died in Oak Park, Illinois.

• An accurate and complete record for Mandell appeared in the 1986–1987 edition of *The Ring Record Book and Boxing Encyclopedia*, ed. Herbert G. Goldman, although his birthplace is mistakenly given as Rockford, Illinois. The most authoritative and informative source on his early career is Robert Soderman, "Sammy Mandell, "*Newsletter #20 of the International Boxing Research Organization*, Oct. 1985, based on contemporary newspaper accounts. A four-part biography by Mike Murphy appeared in the *Chicago Daily News*, starting 20 July 1929. Detailed accounts of his major fights are found in the *Chicago Tribune*, the *New York Times*, and other newspapers. A detailed obituary appeared in the *Rockford Star*, 8 Nov. 1967.

LUCKETT DAVIS

MANDERSON, Charles Frederick (9 Feb. 1837–28 Sept. 1911), lawyer and U.S. senator, was born in Philadelphia, Pennsylvania, the son of John Manderson and Katherine Benfer. Charles graduated from high school in Philadelphia and then moved to Canton, Ohio, where he studied law. In 1859 he was admitted to the bar and the following year was elected city solicitor of Canton. At the outbreak of the Civil War, he joined the Union army, serving four years as an officer in the Nineteenth Ohio Infantry. Severely wounded during William T. Sherman's Georgia campaign, Manderson was unable to return to battle and forced to resign from the army in April 1865. Before resigning, however, he was brevetted brigadier general and for the rest of his life was referred to as General Manderson. Having returned to Canton, he married Rebecca

S. Brown in 1865. Moreover, Manderson was elected prosecuting attorney of Stark County, Ohio, and in 1867 he lost the Republican nomination for a seat in the U.S. House of Representatives by a single vote.

In 1869 Manderson left Canton and moved to Omaha, the chief city of the new state of Nebraska. He quickly established himself both as a leader of the Republican party and of the local bar, serving as city attorney for six years. As a delegate to the state constitutional conventions of 1871 and 1875, he played a major part in the debates over the state's fundamental law. In the 1871 convention he was a leading proponent of woman suffrage. Outraged that only males were allowed to elect convention delegates, Manderson told his colleagues, "We should have today on this floor those who were sent here to represent the women of our state." Manderson and his fellow delegates had "no more right to represent the women here than a man in Iowa has a right to go to the Congress of the United States and presume to represent Nebraska there." In part because of Manderson's efforts, a woman suffrage proposal was submitted to Nebraska voters in 1871, but it suffered defeat. Though somewhat radical on women's rights, Manderson was to become known as Nebraska's leading defender of the established social and economic order. At the constitutional conventions, and throughout his career, Manderson earned a reputation as a polished, cultivated conservative, wary of crude western radicals who threatened monied interests.

In 1883, after two weeks of deliberation and seventeen ballots, the Nebraska legislature elected Manderson as U.S. senator. A loyal member of that bulwark of veterans interests, the Grand Army of the Republic, Manderson was notably solicitous of the welfare of old soldiers and dedicated himself to securing pensions for those who had fought to preserve the Union. As a member of the Military Affairs Committee, he also sought to strengthen the existing army, and as a stalwart Republican he embraced high protective tariffs and the gold standard. With unusual foresight, in 1892 he proposed the creation of a system of national highways for the vehicles of the future. "By some system of electric accumulators or storage batteries light vehicles will be propelled at a wonderful rate of speed over these highways," he told his fellow senators.

In 1889 Nebraska's legislators reelected Manderson to the Senate on the first ballot. Two years later Manderson earned another distinction when he was elected president pro tempore of the Senate, a position he held until 1893, when the Democrats took control of the upper house. As president pro tempore, Manderson had the duty of presiding over the Senate when the vice president was absent.

During his second term in the Senate, the Populist rebellion was stirring in Nebraska, threatening the political hegemony of such pillars of Republicanism as Manderson. Perhaps because of this new opposition, in 1895 Manderson chose to retire from the Senate. Returning to private life, he became chief counsel for the Burlington Railroad. The remainder of his life was devoted to law and to serving corporate interests. In 1900 he was elected president of the American Bar Association, a bastion of corporation lawyers. During these later years he did find time to write *The Twin Seven-Shooters* (1902), a work based largely on his Civil War experiences. In 1911 he traveled to Europe to restore his declining health but died on shipboard when returning to the United States.

A Civil War general who devoted himself to soldiers' pensions, railroad corporations, high tariffs, and the gold standard, Manderson was a stereotypical Republican politician of the late nineteenth century. As such, he represented everything his fellow Nebraskan William Jennings Bryan would lead a nationwide revolt against. "His somewhat ostentatious aristocratic demeanor and associations," observed one Nebraska critic, could "be overlooked for the good it accomplished in demonstrating that Nebraska was not inimical to gentlemen, and that they might be bred here as successfully as hogs and corn." But, according to this observer, "Manderson's mistake and misfortune lay in not being amenable . . . to inevitable social, and especially, political progress along democratic lines. In his attitude toward capitalism, corporations, and class distinction he remained to the end a bourbon, though always a gentleman bourbon" (Morton and Watkins, pp. 288–89).

• Thomas W. Tipton, *Forty Years of Nebraska at Home and in Congress* (1902), offers a summary of Manderson's career in the Senate. Julius Sterling Morton and Albert Watkins, *History of Nebraska* (1913), and Addison E. Sheldon, *Nebraska: The Land and the People* (1931), provide some additional information on Manderson. Short biographical sketches are found in W. A. Howard, comp., *Biographical Sketches of the Nebraska Legislature and National and State Officers of Nebraska* (1895), and Alfred Sorenson, *History of Omaha from the Pioneer Days to the Present Time* (1889). Obituaries are in the *New York Times* and the *Washington Post*, both 29 Sept. 1911.

JON C. TEAFORD

MANEY, George Earl (24 Aug. 1826–9 Feb. 1901), soldier, lawyer, and diplomat, was born in Franklin, Tennessee, the son of Thomas Maney and Rebecca Southall, occupations unknown. Maney attended the Nashville Seminary and graduated from the University of Nashville in 1845. He served in the Mexican War as a second lieutenant in the First Tennessee Infantry from 28 May 1846 until honorably discharged on 7 September 1846 and as a first lieutenant in the U.S. Infantry and the Third U.S. Dragoons from 6 March 1847 until honorably mustered out on 31 July 1848. The Third Dragoons participated in General Winfield Scott's march on Mexico City.

Maney passed the Tennessee bar examination in 1850 and practiced law until the outbreak of the Civil War. He married Betty C. Crutcher in 1853; they had five children. Maney sided with the Confederacy, joining its army as captain in the Eleventh Tennessee Infantry, and he became the colonel of the First Regiment, Tennessee Infantry, on 8 May 1861. He fought in West Virginia in the Cheat Mountain campaign under General Robert E. Lee in September 1861 and at Bath, Hancock, and Romney under General Thomas J. "Stonewall" Jackson. In February 1862 he asked to be sent to defend Tennessee and fought at Shiloh, Perryville, Murfreesboro, Chickamauga, Chattanooga, and the Atlanta campaign. His able command at Shiloh earned him promotion to brigadier general on 16 April 1862 and command of the Second Brigade of General Benjamin Franklin Cheatham's division in General Leonidas Polk's (1806–1864) corps. Maney was wounded at Chattanooga and commanded a division in General William Hardee's corps during the Atlanta campaign until his capture in August 1864. He was released but saw no further action in the war. He surrendered and was paroled at Greensboro, North Carolina, on 1 May 1865.

In 1868 Maney began nine years as president of the Tennessee and Pacific Railroad. That same year he joined several former Confederate generals, including Nathan Bedford Forrest and Gideon Pillow, in condemning the violent verbal attacks on the Ku Klux Klan by Tennessee politicians, such as Parson William G. Brownlow. Later, he joined and was active in the Republican party. His nomination in 1875 to serve as minister to Ecuador was withdrawn before the Senate could act on it. In 1876 he was a Republican candidate for governor; he withdrew his name but still received 10,436 votes. He served in the state legislature.

On 19 May 1881 President James A. Garfield appointed Maney minister resident to Colombia. When French engineer Ferdinand de Lesseps's canal company acquired isthmian canal rights in the late 1870s, U.S.–Colombian relations became very important, but Maney had little to do with this matter because the negotiations were conducted in Washington and Paris. President Chester Arthur's administration recalled him on 19 July 1882 but sent him as minister resident and consul general to Bolivia. Chile defeated Bolivia and Peru in the War of the Pacific, 1879–1880, after which the U.S. government urged a peace settlement. The initial two-year diplomatic effort led by U.S. minister to Chile Thomas A. Osborn and special envoy William H. Trescot failed to persuade Chile to make concessions that would not dismember Peru. In 1882 Trescot, Osborn, and the U.S. ministers to Peru and Bolivia returned to the United States. Maney replaced the minister in Bolivia but was subordinated to Cornelius Ambrose Logan, the new minister to Chile. The State Department admonished Maney for arriving in La Paz two months after Logan and U.S. minister to Peru James Partridge had reached their posts, because his tardiness delayed negotiating efforts. Under Logan's direction, Chile and Peru signed an agreement that provisionally separated Tacna and Arica from Peru. A final resolution of this matter waited until 1929, however. Maney served until about 1 June 1883, when he returned to Tennessee, apparently practicing law in the mid- and late 1880s. He was a delegate to the Republic National Conventions in 1884 and 1888.

On 20 June 1889 Maney was appointed minister resident to Paraguay and Uruguay and was promoted on 23 September 1890 to be the first U.S. diplomat to serve as envoy extraordinary and minister plenipotentiary to Paraguay or Uruguay. No significant problems arose between the United States and Paraguay and Uruguay during Maney's tour. After his recall on 30 June 1894, he retired to Washington, D.C., where he lived until his death there. Maney is chiefly recognized for his able and reliable military service during the Mexican and Civil wars.

• No Maney papers exist, but material on the Maney family of Tennessee is in the John Kimberly Papers, Southern Historical Collection, University of North Carolina at Chapel Hill, and material on the Maney family of Franklin, Tenn., is in the Douglass-Maney Family Papers, Tennessee State Library and Archives. Documents about his Confederate military service are printed in *The War of the Rebellion: A Compilation of the Official Records of the Union and Confederate Armies* (128 vols., 1880–1901). The U.S. State Department's microfilmed records contain his official correspondence from Colombia (microfilm T33, reels 35 and 36), Bolivia (microfilm T51, reel 9), and Paraguay and Uruguay (microfilm M128, reels 7 and 8). There is no book-length or article-length biography. Sketches of Maney are in Clement A. Evans, ed., *Confederate Military History*, vol. 9 (1899); Ezra J. Warner, *Generals in Gray: Lives of the Confederate Commanders* (1959); and Jon Wakelyn, *Biographical Dictionary of the Confederacy* (1977). Nathaniel Cheairs Hughes, Jr., *General William J. Hardee: Old Reliable* (1965), and Thomas Lawrence Connelly, *Autumn of Glory: The Army of Tennessee, 1862–1865* (1971), devote some attention to his service in the Confederate army. His diplomatic role in the War of the Pacific is mentioned in Herbert Millington, *American Diplomacy and the War of the Pacific* (1948), and David Pletcher, *The Awkward Years: American Foreign Relations under Garfield and Arthur* (1962). Obituaries are in the *Washington Post*, 10 Feb. 1901, and the *Nashville Banner*, 11 Feb. 1901.

THOMAS SCHOONOVER

MANEY, Richard (11 June 1891–30 June 1968), theatrical press agent, was born in Chinook, Montana, the son of John Maney and Elizabeth Bohen, farmers and ranchers. Maney spent his early childhood in a four-room log house three miles outside of Chinook, where he and his sister Loretta had regular household chores but were packed off to school every day by parents who, though not formally educated themselves, determined that their children would be.

After a series of floods and droughts, along with a blizzard that killed off their newborn livestock, John Maney gave up the ranch and moved his family into Chinook. They remained there until 1906 when they moved west to Seattle. At Broadway High School Richard developed an enthusiasm for literature and a talent for writing. Later, at the University of Washington, where as a journalism major he aspired to be a sports writer, Maney discovered the theater. Impressed that an acquaintance who was a volunteer usher at the Moore Theatre was entitled to see performances free, Maney volunteered. Soon he too was sporting the black bow tie and jacket with crimson lapels of a Moore volunteer usher. It was a first, tentative step that would eventually lead him to Broadway.

Theater flourished in Seattle during this time, and many touring companies played the Moore. Maney became increasingly involved in this new world and took on full-time paying jobs at the theater, becoming head usher, then ticket taker, and finally doorman. He saw George M. Cohan in *George Washington, Jr.*, David Warfield in *The Music Master*, James K. Hackett in *Monsieur Beaucaire*, and Viola Allen in *The White Sister*. In addition to viewing other productions, including *The Merry Widow*, *The Chocolate Soldier*, and *Twin Beds*, he heard John McCormack, Calvé, Melba, and Tetrazzini in concert. Maney gave less and less time to university studies; he missed classes, his marks slid, and he did not earn a degree.

In 1913 John Cort, proprietor of the Moore, hired Maney as one of the advance press agents for a national tour of *Anna Held and Her All Star Jubilee* at $40 per week. After a less than successful fifteen-week tour, Maney landed in New York, jobless, and was forced to take whatever employment he could get—theater ticket taking, operating an electric baseball scoreboard in a West Side saloon, and editing the *American Angler*, a monthly publication for fishermen. Maney knew nothing about fishing, which eventually was his undoing, but the job provided opportunities for writing articles, editing copy, and learning the behind-the-scenes procedures of a publication—valuable experience for a press agent. Five years later he landed a job as a publicist for *Frivolities 1920*, a song-and-dance show produced by Broncho Billy Anderson. Although it flopped on Broadway, Anderson decided to send the production out on tour. During its Boston run, Maney met the Shubert theaters' powerful press agent A. Toxen Worm, a master practitioner of publicity, from whom the neophyte learned the finer points of his profession.

For the next forty-six years, until his retirement in 1966, Maney was an increasingly visible and successful publicist of the Broadway scene. He represented some 300 of its theatrical productions, including *Desire under the Elms* (1925), *The Front Page* (1927), *The Royal Family* (1927), *Coquette* (1927), *Fifty Million Frenchmen* (1929), *Twentieth Century* (1932), *The Little Foxes* (1938), *Watch on the Rhine* (1940), *The Male Animal* (1940), *The Corn Is Green* (1941), *Arsenic and Old Lace* (1941), *The Skin of Our Teeth* (1942), *Come Back, Little Sheba* (1950), *Private Lives* (1931), *Dial M for Murder* (1952), *My Fair Lady* (1956), and *Camelot* (1960).

Maney used his early enthusiasm for the written word to beat the drum for his clients. His personal style, professional skill, and outspokenness soon won him a following among the professionals of the theater world. In the 1932 comedy *Twentieth Century*, playwrights Charles MacArthur and Ben Hecht modeled their truculent press agent character after Maney. Many actors and actresses insisted on him in their contracts, and a *Time* magazine article of 8 January 1940 characterized him as a special breed of press agent

"with one foot in the theatre and the other in a newspaper office . . . Irish-tongued, Scotch drinking, . . . hardboiled, . . . sociable and smart. . . . He scorns the usual props: high pressuring, dancing attendance on people, buttering his employers."

Throughout his career Maney wrote articles on theater and subjects relating to theater for publications such as *Theatre Arts*, the *New York Times Magazine*, the *New York Herald Tribune*, *Saturday Evening Post*, and the *Brooklyn Daily Eagle*, as well as reviews of books about the world of theater. He also wrote his autobiography, *Fanfare: The Confessions of a Press Agent*, which was published by Harper in 1957. *New York Herald Tribune* columnist John Crosby described it as "the record of a sort of Broadway that is hard to find anymore. Maney, whose crushing candor has paralyzed some of the most monumental egos in the theatre, expresses his opinions and tells his tales with ringing authority" (15 Nov. 1957). About the book, the *New York Times*'s Lewis Nichols wrote, "Press agent Maney has enormous gusto. He also has humor and sanity. His booming laugh can be heard throughout *Fanfare*" (17 Nov. 1957). Maney was forthright about his chosen profession, defining a press agent as a "fusion of midwife, clairvoyant, public-address system and hypnotist. He is also akin to the smuggler, since there are those who look upon his traffic as illicit" (New York Post, 1 July 1968). Maney also asserted, "I have yet to find an actor, producer or stagehand who did not like to see his name in print" (*Time*, 8 Jan. 1940).

Producers sometimes fell short of Maney's expectations, and he did not remain silent in his disappointment. Playwright and producer Russel Crouse wrote, "The hands that feed Maney . . . are practically porous with Maney's teeth marks. He has corrected Gilbert Miller's English, questioned Orson Welles's veracity, blithely deflated Jed Harris and publicly derided Billy Rose, all the while being paid by them" (*Life*, 14 May 1945, pp. 55–62). In his own way, however, Maney was fond of his clients, as he made clear in *Fanfare*, saying, "Despite the pettiness, the egomania and the persecution complexes of stage folk, they are more amusing, more generous and more stimulating than any other professional group."

Maney had married Frances O'Hara in 1916. They were divorced in 1931, and that year he married Elizabeth Breuil. He had no children. He died in Norwalk, Connecticut. In a *New York Times* column after his death, Tallulah Bankhead wrote of Maney, her press agent for more than twenty years, "No one could copy Dick because he couldn't be copied. He was generous, innately kind, erudite and gifted in his profession." Maney was passionate about the theater, urging critics in a newspaper article to "bat the ears off cheap and vulgar plays."

• The Billy Rose Theatre Collection at the New York Public Library for the Performing Arts, Lincoln Center, is a rich source of newspaper clippings and magazine articles on Maney. *Current Biography* (1964) provides useful information. See also Wolcott Gibbs's profile of Maney, "The Customer Is Always Wrong," *New Yorker*, 11 Oct. 1941, pp. 27–38, and "Portrait of a Press Agent," *Time*, 8 Jan. 1940, pp. 44–45. A detailed obituary is in the *New York Times*, 2 July 1968.

ADELE S. PARONI

MANGAS COLORADAS (1790?–18 Jan. 1863), Chiricahua Apache chief, was probably born in southwestern New Mexico, a member of the Chihenne band. Likely known as Fuerte until 1840, he was prominent in Chiricahua-Mexican affairs as early as 1814. He was a leader in the 1831 Apache uprising against Mexico, remaining at war with the Mexicans for most of the next thirty years. His militancy gained him allies among warlike Chiricahua bands, and he became the greatest Chiricahua leader of the mid-1800s. During his long life, Mangas had perhaps twelve children, many of whom became prominent members of the tribe after his death. He formed alliances by marrying several of his daughters to Apache chiefs, including Cochise. A giant among his people, he was a powerfully built man of well over six feet who combined physical courage with a keen intellect.

He became known as Mangas Coloradas (Red Sleeves) around 1840 and by the summer of 1842 was recognized as the leader of the hostile Chiricahuas. On 30 March 1843, Mangas agreed to an armistice with the Mexicans at Janos, Chihuahua. The truce lasted only until May, at which time war resumed. In July 1844 Mangas led a large war party that annihilated a force of twenty-nine Sonorans near Santa Cruz. Mangas became even more hostile toward Mexico after a massacre of 130 Chiricahuas near Galeana, Chihuahua, in July 1846.

In October 1846, after the outbreak of war between Mexico and the United States, Mangas pledged friendship to American troops near Santa Rita del Cobre, New Mexico. For the next decade, he remained at war with Mexico, leading war parties of two or three hundred warriors that devastated the Mexican countryside and spread terror. Mangas's greatest victory came on 20 January 1851 when he led a large war party that defeated a Sonoran army of 100 under Ignacio Pesqueira, killing 26 and wounding 46.

That summer he met John Russell Bartlett, the head of a U.S. commission sent to establish the boundary between Texas and Mexico after the end of the Mexican War, near Santa Rita, New Mexico, and relations, for the most part, were amicable. He signed a peace treaty with Americans at Acoma, New Mexico, in July 1852, an agreement he kept throughout the 1850s, although he continued to lead incursions against his enemies south of the border. In early 1857, concerned about an American campaign against Apaches, Mangas made peace with the Mexicans and took his people to Janos, Chihuahua. He returned to New Mexico that fall, however, after members of the band were killed by poisoned rations issued by the Mexicans.

In the spring of 1858, Mangas led another campaign against Sonora to avenge the deaths of two of his sons, who had been killed there in a fight with Mexicans. After miners in Pinos Altos, New Mexico, launched an unprovoked attack on his people, he joined Cochise in the war against Americans in the spring of 1861. At the battle of Apache Pass on 15 July 1862, Mangas was wounded. On 17 January 1863, he was tricked by Americans into meeting near Pinos Altos, captured, and subsequently executed, an incident remembered by the Chiricahuas as "the greatest of wrongs."

• Sources on Mangas Coloradas include Edwin R. Sweeney, *Cochise: Chiricahua Apache Chief* (1991), and Dan L. Thrapp, *Victorio and the Mimbres Apaches* (1974).

EDWIN R. SWEENEY

MANGELSDORF, Paul Christoph (20 July 1899–22 July 1989), botanist, geneticist, and agronomist, was born in Atchison, Kansas, the son of August Mangelsdorf, a commercial seed merchant, and Marie Brune. Mangelsdorf later recalled that he had developed an intense curiosity about corn (*Zea mays*) and other plants at a very early age. In 1921 he graduated with a degree in agronomy from Kansas State Agricultural College, where he worked under John H. Parker, an early expert on corn and small grains.

In 1921 Mangelsdorf joined the Connecticut Agricultural Experiment Station as a graduate assistant to Donald F. Jones, one of the inventors of hybrid corn. With Jones, Mangelsdorf delved into the practical knowledge of maize varieties and the experimental production of hybrid corn, gaining a graduate education that was of fundamental importance to his later contributions. During the winters, he studied at Harvard University's Bussey Institution under Edward M. East. In Cambridge, Mangelsdorf explored the major questions of theoretical genetics and evolution and developed a combination of both practical and theoretical interests that remained with him throughout his professional career. In 1923 he married Helen Parker; they had two children.

Harvard awarded Mangelsdorf an M.S. in botany in 1923 and an Sc.D. in applied biology in 1925. In 1927 he accepted an offer from the Texas Agricultural Experiment Station to become an agronomist, a position he held until 1940. During his years at Texas, Mangelsdorf conducted an extensive range of experiments on corn and supervised the breeding work on wheat, barley, and oats. Although this practical work was important to him, his intellectual commitment centered on the evolutionary origins of the corn plant. With his colleague, cytologist Robert G. Reeves, he prepared *The Origin of Indian Corn and Its Relatives* (1939). In this monograph, Mangelsdorf and Reeves argued that modern corn originated from a wild form of "pod corn," which has seed covers like wheat or rice rather than husks.

Mangelsdorf's work on the origins of corn led to his 1940 invitation to become professor of botany and assistant director of the Botanical Museum in Harvard

University. In Cambridge he continued his studies on the evolution of corn and became closer to colleagues in archaeology. He also began an important association with the Rockefeller Foundation, with which his first assignment in 1941 was as a member of the Agricultural Commission to Mexico along with Elvin C. Stakman, chair of the commission and a plant pathologist from the University of Minnesota, and Richard Bradfield, a soil scientist from Cornell University.

At the time of the foundation's mission to Mexico, relations between the United States and Mexico had become quite strained. Mexican seizure of oil properties and agricultural land claimed by Americans had created severe tension between the two countries between 1934 and 1940. Manuel Avila Camacho's rise in 1940 to the presidency of Mexico and the outbreak of the Second World War in Europe created the conditions for a reconciliation. Vice President–elect Henry A. Wallace attended Avila Camacho's inauguration and, while in Mexico City, began a series of conversations that led the new Mexican government to invite the Rockefeller Foundation to inaugurate an agricultural research program. The concept appealed to both President Avila Camacho, who wanted more efficient agricultural production as an aid to industrialization, and President Franklin D. Roosevelt, who was anxious to end the rancor over seized properties and solidify Mexico as a clear ally in the midst of the Second World War.

Based on their extensive travels in Mexico, the Agricultural Commission recommended that the Rockefeller Foundation initiate a program, housed in the Mexican Ministry of Agriculture, that would reform the agricultural science establishment of Mexico. Avila Camacho's government accepted the plan and invited the foundation to send a team of scientists to Mexico to advise the minister of agriculture on scientific matters; conduct experiments on corn, beans, and wheat; and train Mexicans in the techniques of modern agricultural science. When activities began in 1943, Mexico became the first locus of a foundation program on agriculture and food supplies.

Mangelsdorf's career changed in two important ways as a result of his involvement with the Mexican Agricultural Commission. First, he substantially added to the information base for his studies on the origins of corn. Asked in 1943 by the foundation to do some preliminary collections of Mexican corn varieties, Mangelsdorf began work that was continued by E. J. Wellhausen, the corn geneticist hired to work full time for the foundation in Mexico. By 1948 Wellhausen, Mangelsdorf, and their colleagues had gathered nearly 2,000 varieties. This collection of contemporary varieties of corn not only served the practical purpose of providing resources for the improvement of corn in Mexico, it also immensely increased the evidence on which to base speculations of corn evolution.

Second, Mangelsdorf became a part of the movement that created the "green revolution" through his work with the Rockefeller Foundation. In 1944 foundation geneticist Norman E. Borlaug began work on wheat in Mexico. A decade later Borlaug and his colleagues were successful in producing varieties of wheat that were well adapted to Mexican conditions and remarkably higher yielding than traditional varieties. In the 1960s semi-dwarf wheats bred in Mexico were successful there and were exported to Pakistan, India, Chile, and elsewhere. Considerable controversy still surrounds the green revolution, because adoption of the high-yielding practices was associated with dislocations of traditional farmers and the encouragement of greater social inequities in rural areas. Nevertheless, the new varieties substantially increased the world's grain harvest. Mangelsdorf, Stakman, and Bradfield recounted this story and their role in it in *Campaigns against Hunger* (1967).

Mangelsdorf successfully bred varieties of wheat that are resistant to plant diseases. He also developed corn varieties without tassels, which made the production of hybrid corn cheaper and faster. Thus, though his first love was the evolutionary theory on the origins of corn, Mangelsdorf also contributed in major ways to the less visible scientific changes that have made modern agriculture possible. Few scientists have been able to contribute both practical and theoretical findings of such significance.

During his lifetime, Mangelsdorf was honored with a number of honorary degrees, was elected to the National Academy of Sciences, and served as president of several scientific societies. He died in Chapel Hill, North Carolina.

• Mangelsdorf provided an autobiographical statement in his last complete monograph on the origins of corn, *Corn: Its Origin, Evolution, and Improvement* (1974). He also left an oral history document, which is in the Rockefeller Foundation Archives, North Tarrytown, N.Y., and in a collection of his papers at the Harvard University Archives, Cambridge, Mass. An obituary is in the *New York Times*, 28 July 1989.

JOHN H. PERKINS

MANGIN, Joseph François (17 Dec. 1764–after 1818), engineer and architect, was born in Chalons-sur-Marne, France, the son of Joseph-Denis Mangin, surgeon, and Jeanne-Marie-Anne Morin Delaterasse. He served as engineer in the French army, spending eight years mapping the northern part of Santo Domingo until the revolt of 1793. He was married to Theresa Bulland; they had one child.

Mangin's first work in the United States was mapping and fortifying the harbor of New York, then threatened by both sides in the war between England and France. In 1795 he was placed in charge of planning and constructing facilities that, in two phases (1794–1796, 1798–1799), included Fort Jay on Governor's Island and batteries on Long Island and Bedloe's and Ellis islands. An arsenal and batteries also were established on Manhattan Island. In 1799 and 1800 Mangin designed and prefabricated eight blockhouses that were shipped to Antigua. In 1801 and in 1813, during the war with England, he was again planning harbor fortifications.

Mangin also practiced architecture, working in the early years in New York with his brother Charles Nicolas. In 1795 they designed Park Theatre, opened in 1798, sometimes attributed erroneously to Mark Isambard Brunel. An engraving shows an arcaded lower story and pedimented upper stories with tall Corinthian pilasters.

In 1796 the Mangin brothers projected an improvement of the sewage-filled Collect Pond by converting it into an inland harbor. After receiving U.S. citizenship on 7 May 1796, and being named Freeman of New York two days later, Mangin was appointed a city surveyor (1796–1804, 1810–1818). He performed numerous routine jobs and a major one, drawing an official city map with indications of lines of future growth. This work began late in 1797 with Casimir T. Goerck, who died within a year, and was completed in 1799; the engraved map was published in 1803.

Mangin designed and constructed the New York State Prison (1796–1797) at Greenwich, Christopher, and Front streets. Except for small Doric columns flanking the entrance, its austerity was relieved only by an allegorical sculpture in the tympanum. Mangin invented and received two patents (1796, 1797) for stone cutting and polishing machines, used probably in construction of the prison building and in the workshops provided in response to a Quaker prison commissioner's encouragement of rehabilitation through gainful employment. In 1802, with John McComb, Jr., he designed New York City Hall; it was built by McComb from 1803 to 1811. Mangin was responsible for the overall disposition—a long main block with advancing wings, a central pavilion with portico, attic, and tower—and the decoration with Ionic columns and pilasters. Its French architectural sophistication provided the young nation with an alternative to the English tradition.

His last buildings were ecclesiastical; they included St. Patrick's Roman Catholic Cathedral (1809–1815) and the Wall Street or First Presbyterian Church (1810–1811). Intended to have two towers, the cathedral was the first Gothic Revival style building in New York; twice burned and restored, the original walls still stand. The church burned in 1834 and again in 1860. It had two-story Doric pilasters across the front and, breaking through the pediment, a domed tower.

Mangin's writing and his clear and reasonable arguments suggest that he received an excellent French education. His often imaginative designs were presented in a skillful, distinctly French drawing technique. He achieved respect but no great financial success, nor was his style emulated in New York. The old-fashioned, French character of the design of the city hall evoked scorn from architect Benjamin Henry Latrobe (1764–1820). That Mangin's taste was formed in prerevolutionary France is shown by his use of the orders to express the purposes of the three secular structures—Doric for the utilitarian prison, Ionic for the local governmental building, and Corinthian for the theater. Today Mangin and McComb's city hall ranks among the most important buildings of the Federal period.

• Elevation and plan drawings of the prison are in the Schuyler papers, New York Public Library; letters and maps concerning fortifications are in the New-York Historical Society; and further documents are in the Alexander Hamilton Papers, Library of Congress, and in the Military and Cartographic Records Divisions, National Archives, Washington, D.C. For Mangin's work on fortifications, see Willard B. Robinson, *American Forts* (1977). The records of New York City supplied numerous references in I. N. Phelps Stokes, *The Iconography of Manhattan Island, 1498–1910* (1915–1928). Accounts of Mangin's architecture appear in Thomas Eddy, *An Account of the State Prison or Penitentiary House in the City of New York* (1801); Talbot Hamlin, *Greek Revival Architecture in America* (1944); and Damie Stillman, "New York City Hall: Competition and Execution," *Journal of the Society of Architectural Historians* 23 (1964): 129–42.

ROBERT L. ALEXANDER

MANGRUM, Lloyd Eugene (1 Aug. 1914–17 Nov. 1973), golfer, was born in Trenton, Texas, the son of James S. Mangrum, a truck farmer, and Etta Hudgens. In 1919 his family relocated to Dallas, where his financially strapped father began operating a boardinghouse. Within a few years he was exposed to golf through caddying at the Stevens Park municipal course. As a teenager Mangrum attended school infrequently, did odd jobs, and learned the game at Cliff-Dale Country Club. In 1930, at age sixteen, Mangrum turned professional. In that same year he and his older brother Ray, already an accomplished player who would win several titles, headed west to southern California, which offered competition and tournament purses.

In and around Los Angeles, Mangrum eked out a living caddying at various country clubs, hustled bets with amateurs, and observed and adapted the techniques of leading players such as Harry Cooper, Horton Smith, and Sam Snead. In 1934 he married Eleta P. (maiden name unknown), a beautician and widowed mother of two daughters and one son, the couple's only children. Two years later he began playing the emerging Professional Golfers' Association (PGA) tour and enjoyed meager success until winning the Pennsylvania Open in 1938. His first official tour win came at the 1940 Thomasville (Ga.) Open, which entitled him to play in that year's Masters Tournament, where he finished second and established a single-round record 64 that remained unbroken until 1986. By the end of 1942, the first full year of the country's involvement in World War II, he was the second-ranked tour player, behind Ben Hogan, and had won five times. In 1943, just as he was beginning to prosper, he was inducted into the army.

Unlike many of his contemporaries, the great majority of whom saw no frontline duty, Mangrum experienced the war in Europe firsthand, with the Ninth Infantry of the Third Army. Assigned to a reconnaissance unit, he was among the first ashore on Utah Beach during the Normandy (D-Day) Invasion and then saw action in the battle of the Bulge and in Czechoslovakia. He sustained two shrapnel wounds and a crushed upper left arm and shoulder, which doctors mistakenly believed would end his career. Wartime experience left him with multiple battle stars and Purple Hearts. "I don't suppose," he reflected, "that . . . golfers who were [in] combat . . . will soon be able to think of a three-putt green as one of the really bad troubles of life" (Sampson, p. 82).

At the end of the war Mangrum assumed a leading role in a transitional period in American golf, particularly professional tournament golf. The years from 1945 to 1960 introduced the modern era. Fueled by postwar affluence that generated tremendous growth and commercialization, the forties and fifties blended the early rush of talent from college ranks, represented by players such as Gene Littler and Arnold Palmer, with Mangrum and other tour pioneers of the thirties. A women's organization, the Ladies' Professional Golf Association (LPGA), and the tournament circuit took hold. Television brought big-time golf to middle America and financial rewards to professionals. The total PGA purse rose from $454,200 in 1946 to $1,527,849 in 1960.

As the game flourished, Mangrum's career blossomed. His double-playoff triumph in the 1946 U.S. Open and his 1956 Los Angeles Open victory framed a decade of competitive excellence. He won eight tournaments in 1948, led the PGA in earnings in 1951, and garnered the Vardon Trophy (for the best per-round average) in 1951 and 1953. In 1947, 1949, 1951, and 1953 Mangrum's solid play justified his inclusion on the American Ryder Cup team, once as captain, in biennial matches against premier British professionals. He also lent his name to two uninspiring instructional books, *Golf: A New Approach* (1949), and, with Otis Dypwick, *How to Break 90 at Golf* (1952), both of which also hinted at Mangrum's dislike for teaching.

From 1946 to 1959 Mangrum ranked third on the PGA tour, based on his top twenty-five finishes in medal play tournaments. Only Cary Middlecoff and Snead performed better. From 1916 through 1988 he was in seventh position, behind Snead, Jack Nicklaus, Palmer, Hogan, Billy Casper, and Byron Nelson. With his thirty-six official PGA titles, through 1993 Mangrum remained tenth among all-time winners, but his total, counting unofficial events, exceeded forty. He also stood twelfth among top-ten finishers in the so-called "majors," the British and U.S. opens, the Masters, and the PGA championship.

By the late 1950s heart disease had curtailed Mangrum's career and influenced his relocation to California's high desert. During his later years he affiliated with an Apple Valley golf development and died there. He was voted into the PGA Hall of Fame in 1964 and posthumously inducted into the Texas Golf Hall of Fame in 1984.

Mangrum's public persona conflicted with his standing among fellow competitors. Tall, dark, sporting a thin mustache and an omnipresent cigarette, he was described by journalists as a "tough guy" or a "riverboat gambler," a label he abhorred. His often grave countenance and uneasiness with interviewers caused his brilliant record to be overlooked. At Mangrum's death, Jim Murray of the *Los Angeles Times* (21 Nov. 1973) called him the "Forgotten Man of Golf." Tour professionals regarded him as unrelenting but considerate and sociable, although a friend admitted that he took "a lot of knowing" (Stump, p. 188). He was admired for a superb touch with his "Blue Goose" mallet putter and his imperturbability as in, for example, winning the 1951 St. Paul Open despite receiving a telephone death threat (probably from gamblers trying to shake his confidence in order to make money if he lost), which necessitated a police cordon during the final round. Mangrum regarded tournament golf as a matter of percentages and the course as his everyday workplace, where he earned his livelihood. As he told golf writer Charles Price, "If I can't come in first, I try to come in second . . . [or] third or fourth—or twentieth. The point is, I try to get in the money. After all, that's what a pro is supposed to be playing for" (*Saturday Evening Post*, 16 June 1956, p. 105).

• The contours of Mangrum's life and career are developed in a chapter in Al J. Stump, *Champions against Odds* (1952), and in a somewhat autobiographical piece (as told to Charles Price), "I Say Pro Golf Isn't So Tough," *Saturday Evening Post*, 16 June 1956, pp. 31, 101–2, 104–5; both works reveal Mangrum's character, outlook, and image. Also useful is Robert Scharff, ed., *Golf Magazine's Encyclopedia of Golf* (1970). The setting for Mangrum's achievements is detailed in Herbert Warren Wind, *The Story of American Golf: Its Champions and Its Championships*, 4th ed. (1986); Herb Graffis, *The PGA: The Official History of the Professional Golfers' Association of America* (1975); and two volumes by Al Barkow, *Golf's Golden Grind: The History of the Tour* (1974) and *The History of the PGA Tour* (1989). Barkow's 1989 work, impressive for its statistical breadth, provides individual records and rankings and can be supplemented by *The Golf Digest Almanac, 1984* (1984) and "1994 Record Book," *Golf Digest*, Jan. 1994, pp. 165–66. Information on Mangrum's instructional publications is in Joseph S. F. Murdoch, comp. and annot., *The Library of Golf, 1743–1966: A Bibliography . . .* (1968), and Don Kennington, ed., *The Sourcebook of Golf* (1981). See also Jim Murray, "Only One Mangrum," *Los Angeles Times*, 21 Nov. 1973; Charles Price, "The Last of the Tough Guys," *Golf Digest*, Oct. 1990, pp. 34, 36, 38, 40; and Curt Sampson, *Texas Golf Legends* (1993), illus. Paul Milosevich.

JAMES A. WILSON

MANGUM, Willie Person (10 May 1792–7 Sept. 1861), U.S. congressman and senator, was born in Orange (now Durham) County, North Carolina, the son of William Person Mangum, a farmer and merchant, and Catharine Davis. Willie (pronounced "Wylie") received a bachelor of arts degree from the University of North Carolina in 1815. He studied law under Duncan Cameron and began practice in 1817. He was awarded a master of arts from the state university in 1818. A year later he married Charity Alston Cain; they had five children.

Mangum served two terms in the House of Commons (1818–1819), where he championed the causes of public education, constitutional reform, and state-financed internal improvements. In December 1819 he was elected by the legislature to the state superior court, but he resigned the following year, citing poor health as his reason. He resumed the practice of law and won election to the U.S. House of Representatives in 1823. Despite his Federalist antecedents, he endorsed William H. Crawford for the presidency and voted for him when the election was decided in the House in February 1825. Mangum was reelected to the U.S. Congress in 1825, but soon afterward he informed his wife that he was "very tired of this place, & feel but little pleasure in any of my employments" (*Mangum Papers*, vol. 1, p. 268). On 18 August 1826 his close friend Governor Hutchins Gordon Burton appointed him to another term on the superior court. However, Mangum did not immediately give up his seat in Congress, preferring to serve the remaining few months of his term before assuming the judgeship. That attitude engendered considerable criticism, and he was finally pressured into resigning his House seat. An unforgiving general assembly refused to confirm the judicial appointment.

Mangum served as an elector for Andrew Jackson in the presidential campaign of 1828 and was elected without opposition to the superior court the following December. He remained there until December 1830, when the general assembly elected him to the U.S. Senate after the two leading contenders failed to win a majority. Entering that body in the midst of the nullification controversy, he gained a reputation as a vocal opponent of the protective tariff. In a speech in February 1832, he denounced the tariff as unjust and inexpedient but stopped short of explicitly endorsing nullification, which was unpopular in his home state.

Jackson's coercive policies toward South Carolina together with his removal of the deposits from the Bank of the United States resulted in a break between Mangum and the administration. Although he had voted against the bank recharter bill in July 1832, Mangum believed that Jackson had exceeded his powers by transferring the federal revenues to state banks without congressional authorization. Announcing his defection on 3 February 1834, he declared that the issue was no longer "bank or no bank" but rather "law or no law—constitution or no constitution." On 28 March he joined Henry Clay, John C. Calhoun, and other opposition senators in voting to censure the president for removing the deposits.

In North Carolina Mangum quickly became the focal point for both sides in the bank war. His supporters, now calling themselves "Whigs," organized meetings that passed resolutions praising his conduct, while administration loyalists staged similar meetings to denounce him. By thus extending their organizational efforts to the grassroots, the leaders of both factions stimulated the formation of mass-based political parties. In December 1834 the Democratic legislature passed resolutions instructing Mangum either to vote

for expunging the censure resolutions or to resign. He refused to acknowledge the right of the general assembly to instruct him but resigned his seat after Martin Van Buren carried North Carolina in the presidential election of 1836. Mangum received the eleven electoral votes of South Carolina for president.

An unsuccessful candidate for the House of Commons in 1838, Mangum returned to the state legislature in 1840. As chair of the Senate Committee on Education, he played an important role in preparing legislation that established the public school system in North Carolina. Shortly thereafter, he was elected to another term in the U.S. Senate and was reelected in 1846. In the Senate Mangum achieved a reputation as a hard worker and an effective parliamentarian. Although he participated in the running debates, he seldom delivered set speeches. A man of imposing physical appearance, refined manners, and great personal charm, he exerted considerable influence in party councils and was frequently mentioned as a candidate for president or vice president. As president pro tempore of the Senate from May 1842 until March 1845, he was, in effect, the acting vice president and next in line for the presidency. In 1852 he was formally offered the vice-presidential nomination on the ticket headed by Winfield Scott, but he declined in favor of William A. Graham.

A warm personal friend of Clay, Mangum supported the Kentuckian for the presidency at the Harrisburg convention in December 1839 and joined him in his break with John Tyler (1790–1862) in September 1841, introducing resolutions in the Whig caucus that effectively read Tyler out of the party. Although he was initially associated with the states' rights wing of the Whig party, Mangum's views on public policy became increasingly nationalistic during the 1840s. He voted for the recharter of the national bank in 1841, supported increases in the tariff duties in 1841 and 1842, and opposed the Democratic-sponsored Walker Tariff in 1846. In foreign policy matters, he also followed the lead of Clay, opposing the annexation of Texas and the war with Mexico and speaking out against the James K. Polk administration's bellicose policy toward Great Britain on the Oregon issue.

Mangum adopted Clay's moderate approach toward the issue of slavery expansion. In 1850 he served as a member of the Committee of Thirteen and spoke out in favor of Clay's compromise measures. In 1852 he supported Scott's presidential candidacy, despite the refusal of Scott to publicly endorse the Compromise of 1850. On 20 April 1852 Mangum presided over a stormy session of the Whig congressional caucus, in which he ruled out of order several motions that would have committed the party to withhold its support from any presidential aspirant who failed to endorse the compromise. His controversial decision led to the walkout of thirteen southern congressmen.

Mangum's unpopular ruling along with the belief that he had been neglecting his constituents at home cost him considerable support among the North Carolina Whigs. He did not seek reelection in 1852, returning instead to the practice of law. He campaigned for the American party ticket in the presidential election of 1856 but soon afterward suffered a stroke that impaired his power of speech and prevented him from walking. His health deteriorated rapidly after his only son was killed at Manassas in July 1861. Suffering a second stroke, he died at "Walnut Hall," his plantation in Orange County. Mangum's significance lies in his role as a founder of the Whig party in North Carolina during the 1830s and as a leader of the national party during the 1840s.

• Most of Mangum's correspondence and other personal papers have been published in Henry T. Shanks, ed., *The Papers of Willie Person Mangum* (5 vols., 1950–1956). Numerous references to him are also in J. G. de Roulhac Hamilton and Max R. Williams, eds., *The Papers of William Alexander Graham* (8 vols., 1957–1992). The fullest accounts of his career are the introduction by Shanks in *Mangum Papers*, vol. 1; and the essay by Stephen B. Weeks in *Biographical History of North Carolina*, vol. 5, ed. Samuel A. Ashe et al. (1905–1917). For Mangum's role in the formation of the N.C. Whig party, see William S. Hoffmann, *Andrew Jackson and North Carolina Politics* (1958) and "Willie P. Mangum and the Whig Revival of the Doctrine of Instructions," *Journal of Southern History* 22 (1956): 338–54. For a detailed assessment by a contemporary, see the obituary by William A. Graham in the *Raleigh Register*, 18 Sept. 1861.

THOMAS E. JEFFREY

MANIGAULT, Arthur Middleton (26 Oct. 1824–16 Aug. 1886), Confederate general, was born in Charleston, South Carolina, the son of Joseph Manigault, a wealthy rice planter, and Charlotte Drayton, a member of one of Charleston's oldest families. Privately educated, he did not attend college; instead, after making a European "grand tour" he was preparing to enter the export business when the Mexican War began in 1846. During that conflict he was a first lieutenant in South Carolina's Palmetto Regiment and participated in most of the major battles of Winfield Scott's campaign to capture Mexico City, an experience he subsequently described as "perhaps the happiest and most romantic period of my life." Upon returning to civilian life in 1848 he engaged in the commission business in Charleston until 1856, then became a rice planter in Georgetown County, South Carolina, where he had inherited considerable property from his parents. Meanwhile, in 1851, he married Mary Procter Huger, likewise of a prominent Charleston family, a union that produced five children.

Following South Carolina's secession in December 1860, Manigault again strapped on his sword, first as captain of the North Santee Mounted Rifles, then as an aide to General P. G. T. Beauregard, in which capacity he was present at the bombardment of Fort Sumter (12–14 Apr. 1861), the beginning of the Civil War. For awhile he remained on Beauregard's staff as an inspector general, having received a South Carolina commission as lieutenant colonel, but he left it after being elected colonel of the Tenth South Carolina Volunteers. Through the rest of 1861 and during early 1862 he trained his regiment and commanded the First Military District of South Carolina, an assignment in which his prime responsibility was coastal defense. In April 1862 he and his regiment were transferred to Corinth, Mississippi, to reinforce what would become known as the Army of Tennessee following its bloody defeat at Shiloh. During the year that ensued he took part in the defense and evacuation of Corinth, Braxton Bragg's invasion of Kentucky, and the battle of Stones River (Murfreesboro), much of the time as an acting brigade commander. Early in July 1863 he received a long-overdue promotion to brigadier general (commission dated 26 Apr. 1863) and took permanent command of what was officially designated, in accordance with Confederate practice, Manigault's Brigade.

Starting in the late summer of 1863 and continuing until the late fall of 1864, his brigade fought well and suffered heavy casualties at Chickamauga, at Missionary Ridge, during the Atlanta campaign, and in John B. Hood's Tennessee campaign. Most notably, at the battle of Atlanta (22 July 1864) Manigault's Brigade took advantage of an unfortified railroad cut to penetrate the Union lines and seize a number of enemy cannons, a success that, if it could have been exploited, might have transformed this battle into a Confederate victory rather than defeat. Manigault's wartime career ended on 30 November 1864 at the battle of Franklin, Tennessee, where he suffered a severe head wound that incapacitated him until the conclusion of the war in April 1865.

With the return of peace, Manigault resumed his life as a rice planter. During Reconstruction he, like almost all of his class, bitterly resented "carpetbag rule" and supported all efforts, including the use of violence, to overthrow it. In 1880, "home rule" (that is, white, Democratic domination) having been restored in South Carolina, he was selected adjutant and inspector general of the state, a position he retained until his death at his plantation, a relatively early demise that in part was attributable to the lingering consequences of his wound at Franklin.

Brave and intelligent, energetic and enterprising, Manigault was a highly capable brigadier with a combat record that was as distinguished as it was long. Yet historically his chief importance lies in the memoirs he wrote shortly after the Civil War describing his experiences and observations in that conflict and the Mexican War. Not published until 1983, they immediately became what they always will remain, one of the classics of Civil War military literature, for they provide a well-written and realistic insider's view of the Confederate Army of Tennessee and offer much valuable information about the Civil War in the West not to be found in any other source, such as the role of musicians as medics, the organization and functioning of the supply services in the Confederate Army of Tennessee, and the performance and personality of other generals.

• The best sources of information on Manigault's life are the introduction, editor's preface, notes, and appendices in R. Lockwood Tower, ed., *A Carolinian Goes to War: The Civil War Narrative of Arthur Middleton Manigault, Brigadier General, C. S. A.* (1983), which also contains Manigault's account of his Mexican War experiences. With regard to the Civil War, Manigault's memoirs should be supplemented by his reports in *The War of the Rebellion: A Compilation of the Official Records of the Union and Confederate Armies* (128 vols., 1880–1901). In addition, much useful information about Manigault and his Civil War career will be found in Cornelius Irvine Walker, *Historical Sketch of the Tenth Regiment, So. Ca. Volunteers* (1881), and Clement A. Evans, ed., *Confederate Military History: South Carolina* (1899). The most detailed accounts of Manigault as a combat leader appear in Peter Cozzens, *This Terrible Sound: The Battle of Chickamauga* (1992), and in Albert Castel, *Decision in the West: The Atlanta Campaign of 1864* (1992).

ALBERT CASTEL

MANIGAULT, Gabriel (21 Apr. 1704–5 June 1781), merchant and planter, was born in Charleston, South Carolina, the son of Pierre Manigault and Judith Giton. Manigault's father, an immigrant Huguenot, had engaged in farming in the Georgetown area before moving to Charleston. There, after several years as a cooper and victualer, he turned to distilling brandy and rum and then to merchandising, laying the foundation before his death in 1729 of what was to become, under Gabriel Manigault, the largest fortune in South Carolina (and quite possibly in America) before the Revolution. Manigault (without formal college training) became a wealthy merchant, operating in a number of markets, especially the West Indies and the northern mainland colonies. He exported in his own fleet of ships regional items such as rice, naval stores, lumber, shingles, leather, deerskins, corn, beef, peas, and pork and imported such commodities as rum, sugar, wine, oil, textiles, and wheat flour. He was also a private banker, lending vast sums from his great personal resources.

As early as the mid-1730s Manigault began acquiring land and slaves to engage in rice planting—eventually he would own 43,532 acres. While he would become one of the largest slaveholders in South Carolina, he was very much opposed to the importation of slaves, engaging only minimally in the slave trade. Over the years his slave numbers on his plantations grew from 86 to 270, with only twelve to fourteen purchased. His principal plantation was "Silk Hope" (of some 3,500 acres, about forty miles up the east branch of the Cooper River from Charleston), acquired in the purchase of the Seewee Barony of 5,518 acres in 1739. Silk Hope had been established by Governor Nathaniel Johnson at the turn of the century, where he failed to produce silk but grew the first successful crop of rice in South Carolina. Contrary to family tradition, Manigault did not retire from his commercial interests in the 1750s to look after Silk Hope. Rather, he was involved in business affairs as late as 1766, when he retired mainly because of old age. Thereafter he would spend much of his time on the plantation. In addition to his plantations and slaves, Manigault owned stores on Tradd Street in Charleston, his own fleet of ships, several lots in the city, and a pew in St. Philips Church (he also worshiped in the French Huguenot church).

Manigault entered public service in 1731 when St. Philips Parish elected him to the Ninth Royal Assembly in a special election. He was reelected (1733) to the Tenth Royal Assembly; however, he resigned to become public treasurer on 29 March 1735, which position he held until 23 March 1743, when he retired because of personal business. Feeling that advancement came through public service, he accepted election (1745) by St. Philips Parish to the Fourteenth Royal Assembly and by St. Thomas and St. Dennis Parish (1748) to the Seventeenth Royal Assembly. He would be elected by this parish (1751) to the Twentieth Royal Assembly. He was recommended by Governor William Bull to the governor's council twice, but he declined both times.

Manigault held a number of other positions throughout his life, such as tax assessor for St. Philips Parish, vestryman for St. Philips, justice of the peace for Berkeley County (where Silk Hope was located), and commissioner of Indian trade. He was both president and vice president of the Charleston Library Society, providing quarters for its books for twenty-one years.

Manigault's generosity and philanthropy rose in accordance with his great fortune. He gave £3,500 to help poor French immigrants to come to South Carolina; £5,000 to the South Carolina Society (Huguenot), the interest of which was to be used to educate a number of children; £500 to help found the College of Charleston and £700 to the College of Philadelphia. Most important, he loaned $220,000 for the support of the American side in the Revolution in South Carolina, from which he realized only $44,000, since he was repaid in indents.

In 1730 Manigault married Ann Ashby; they had one child. Ann's father was John Ashby, a cacique of Carolina (a hereditary title of nobility under the Lords Proprietors' Fundamental Constitutions), who owned a barony of 24,000 acres—there were only thirteen of these in South Carolina. Her mother was Constantia Broughton, a sister of Thomas Broughton, a former governor of South Carolina. This union provided important political and social connections for Manigault, whose home soon became a gathering place for governors, members of the council, the local gentry, and foreigners of distinction. Mrs. Manigault kept a diary from 1754 to 1781 that is a veritable mine of information on the social, political, cultural, and economic trends of the day.

Manigault died in Charleston and was buried in the Manigault vault at the French Huguenot church. He was one of the greatest South Carolinians during the colonial and revolutionary periods, probably having had a greater influence on merchandising than any other individual and being fully supportive of the American position in the crises with Great Britain in the 1760s and 1770s. He was a generous benefactor of social and cultural causes and gave the largest financial support of anyone in South Carolina to the American cause in the Revolution.

• The best study of the Manigaults is Maurice A. Crouse, "The Manigault Family of South Carolina, 1685–1783" (Ph.D. diss., Northwestern Univ., 1965). The principal Manigault papers are in the South Carolina Historical Society (Charleston), with some in the South Caroliniana Library of the University of South Carolina (Columbia). See Crouse, "Gabriel Manigault, Charleston Merchant," *South Carolina Historical Magazine* 68 (1967): 220–31, and J. C. Furnas, *The Americans: A Social History of the United States, 1587–1914* (1969). See also George C. Rogers, *Charleston in the Age of the Pinckneys* (1969); Joyce E. Chaplin, *An Anxious Pursuit: Agricultural Innovation and Modernity in the Lower South, 1730–1815* (1993); Edward McCrady, *The History of South Carolina under the Royal Government* (1899); W. R. Smith, *South Carolina under the Royal Province* (1903); David Ramsay, *The History of South Carolina*, vol. 2 (1809); Jon Butler, *The Huguenots in America, a Refugee People in New World Society* (1983); Stuart Stumpf, "The Merchants of Colonial Charleston, 1680–1766" (Ph.D. diss., Michigan State Univ., 1971); Leila Sellers, *Charleston Business on the Eve of the American Revolution* (1934); and Philip Hamer et al., *The Papers of Henry Laurens* (14 vols., 1968–). An obituary is in the *South Carolina Gazette*, 8 June 1781.

JAMES M. CLIFTON

MANIGAULT, Gabriel (17 Mar. 1758–4 Nov. 1809), architect, was born in Charleston, South Carolina, the son of Peter Manigault, a lawyer, and Elizabeth Wragg. From 1777 to 1779 Manigault studied law. On returning from England in 1780 he helped defend Charleston against a British attack, but after the city fell he swore allegiance to the Crown. From 1785 to 1794 he served in the general assembly, and in 1788 he was a member of the South Carolina convention to ratify the U.S. Constitution. He resigned from the legislature because of poor health and began spending part of each year in the North. In 1804–1805 he offered his South Carolina property for sale, including 27,495 acres of agricultural land and 281 slaves, and he moved permanently to the North, where he resided primarily in New York (1805–1807) and in Philadelphia (1807–1809). In 1785 he married Margaret Izard, the daughter of U.S. Senator Ralph Izard, and they had at least seven children.

Manigault is best known for his achievements as an amateur architect, but professionally he was a lawyer and a planter. He could well afford to pursue his avocation in preference to his professions, having inherited one of the largest fortunes in the United States from his paternal grandfather and namesake. As an architect Manigault was primarily influenced by Charles Bulfinch. While traveling in 1793 he met Bulfinch in Boston and saw examples of his attenuated version of the Adam style. Although little information is available about Manigault's work as an architect, the few buildings he is known to have designed indicate that he had uncommon ability. His obituary noted that "several public buildings in Charleston testify that his talents were judiciously employed," but did not specify which buildings. He is known to have won a competition for the design of South Carolina Hall in April 1801. The meeting room of this building is generally considered the finest Adamesque interior in Charleston, and the entire building has survived essentially intact behind a portico added by another architect, Frederick Wesner, in 1825. Apart from this design, the attributions of other buildings to Manigault are based primarily on an 1896 statement by his grandnephew, Gabriel E. Manigault, who credited him with the design of "his own dwelling . . . and his brother's . . . He also furnished the plans for the Orphan Asylum Chapel . . . the South Carolina Hall . . . the building now the City Hall, which was at first a bank, and he offered a plan for a large public building in New York City." This account is consistent with nearly all other evidence, including the stylistic evidence of the buildings themselves.

The cornerstone for the Orphan House Chapel was laid in 1801, and Manigault provided funds so the chapel could be stuccoed. This nationally important example of the Adam style was demolished for a parking lot in 1953. The bank attributed to Manigault was built as a branch of the Bank of the United States, but it has served as Charleston's City Hall since 1818. A newspaper account in 1800 referred to its carpenters as architects. They sometimes were but were probably not the designers of this building, which has a number of unusual features used in other buildings assignable to Manigault (including a stair tower and circular windows in the ground floor). Manigault built a house for himself on a lot he purchased in 1793, and in 1926 it was demolished for a service station. Architectural fragments from his house were used to build three service stations, one of which survives at the northeast corner of Meeting and Chalmers Streets. The house he designed for his brother Joseph was completed by 1806. It has been widely published as one of the outstanding examples of the Adam style in the United States, and it has been restored as a historic house of the Charleston Museum. Its exterior is almost unornamented, and the walls have a characteristic Adamesque flatness. The interiors have the type of low reliefs that Robert Adam designed late in his career. The plan includes apse-ended rooms and a cantilevered circular staircase.

No buildings by Manigault are known to have been constructed outside Charleston. Although his reputation as an architect depends on a small number of buildings, it is securely based on the high quality of the designs. He has been credited with having introduced the Adam style to Charleston, and he may have done so, but there were other able amateur architects such as Thomas Pinckney working in this style at about the same time and possibly earlier. Manigault's work unquestionably contributed to the widespread adoption of the style, which was used almost exclusively in Charleston for all types of buildings from 1790 to 1820.

• Letters and diaries by Manigault and his relations are well represented in the papers of the Manigault and Izard families at the South Carolina Historical Society, Charleston, and the South Caroliniana Library, Columbia. Several volumes of his wife's diaries are in the Hagley Museum and Library, Wilmington, Del. The most comprehensive biography of Manigault is a chapter in Beatrice St. Julien Ravenel, *Architects of Charleston* (1945).

GENE WADDELL

MANIGAULT, Peter (10 Oct. 1731–12 Nov. 1773), planter and legislator, was born in Charleston, South Carolina, the son of Gabriel Manigault, a merchant and planter, and Ann Ashby. His early studies were in a classical school in Charleston, whence he went to England for further training, entering the Inner Temple in 1752. Two years later he was called to the English bar. During his stay there he was introduced by his tutor, Thomas Corbett, to English cultured society and engaged in considerable travel on the continent. Manigault returned to South Carolina and was admitted to the bar there on 16 December 1754. In 1755 he married Elizabeth Wragg, the daughter of Joseph Wragg and Judith DuBose. They had seven children, but only four reached maturity. All the children married into leading South Carolina families: Gabriel, into the Izard family; Joseph and Anne, into the Middleton family; and Harriet, into the Heyward family.

The practice of law Manigault did not find fully satisfying, so in 1763, within a few years of establishing a practice in Charleston, he was engaged in business activities, managing Ralph Izard's rice and indigo plantations in Goose Creek on the Cooper River and representing English firms that had business affairs in South Carolina. He became briefly involved in the South Carolina slave trade, importing a shipload of slaves in 1768.

Before long Manigault's interests turned to planting. Between 1763 and 1772 he acquired through land grants 5,961 acres in Berkeley, Colleton, and Craven counties and about 200 slaves. At his death in 1773 he operated several plantations, mainly in Goose Creek. Manigault was one of the most cultured and sophisticated gentlemen in South Carolina, possessing the largest and finest library there—valued at £3,000 sterling. Additionally he had much fine furniture and silver and numerous oil paintings. His probated estate in 1774—of almost £28,000—was the largest in the country on the eve of the Revolution. This was more than twice as large as that of the next wealthiest man—from Massachusetts—which explains why other Americans regarded South Carolinians as extremely wealthy.

It is in the political arena, however, that Manigault is chiefly remembered. He entered politics soon after his return to South Carolina, elected by St. Philips Parish in a special election to the Twenty-first Royal Assembly and qualified 14 January 1756. Henceforth, from the Twenty-second Royal Assembly to the Thirty-second (1757–1772) he, however, represented St. Thomas and St. Dennis Parish. Manigault served as speaker of the Twenty-seventh, Twenty-eighth,

Twenty-ninth, Thirtieth, and Thirty-first Royal Assemblies (1765–1772). Poor health forced him to resign the speakership on 28 October 1772; consequently, he did not qualify for the Thirty-second Royal Assembly before it dissolved. In the assembly Manigault served on a committee of correspondence with the colony's agent in London and as speaker, voiced strong opposition to the Stamp Act of 1765. He also as speaker had to deal with the Townshend Act of 1767, which put additional British tariff duties on imported paint, paper, glass, and tea, and allowed South Carolina ship captains charged with smuggling to be tried in Halifax, Canada, with no jury.

Manigault was very much interested in educational and cultural causes. He served on the committee to plan the establishment of the College of Charleston and in 1770 became a trustee of the college. He also contributed £147 to the College of Philadelphia. He served as justice of the peace for Berkeley County and as a commissioner for establishing an Exchange and Customs House in Charleston. Manigault served as both junior and senior warden and steward of the South Carolina Society (Huguenot).

On 16 May 1773 Manigault sailed for England in the hope that the temperate climate there would halt the fevers that were attacking him. However, such was not to be, for he died at the London home of fellow South Carolinian Benjamin Stead. His remains were returned to Charleston and buried in the Manigault vault at the Huguenot Church. Manigault was one of the major political figures of colonial South Carolina. Few others enjoyed as long a period of parliamentary service or provided the kind of leadership in the clashes with the British in the 1760s and 1770s.

• The surviving papers of Peter Manigault (especially the Peter Manigault Letterbook, 1763–1773) are in the South Carolina Historical Society. See Maurice A. Crouse, "The Manigault Family of South Carolina, 1685–1783" (Ph.D. diss., Northwestern Univ., 1965); Crouse, ed., "The Letterbook of Peter Manigault, 1763–1773," *South Carolina Historical Magazine* 70 (1969): 79–95, 177–95; and Walter B. Edgar, "Notable Libraries of Colonial South Carolina," *South Carolina Historical Magazine* 72 (1971): 105–10. See also George C. Rogers, *Charleston in the Age of the Pinckneys* (1969); Joyce E. Chaplin, *An Anxious Pursuit: Agricultural Innovation and Modernity in the Lower South, 1730–1815* (1993); E. A. Jones, *American Members of the Inns of Court* (1924); Jon Butler, *The Huguenots in America: A Refugee People in New World Society* (1983); Alice Hanson Jones, *Wealth of a Nation To Be: The American Colonies on the Eve of the American Revolution* (1980); Jack Greene, *The Quest for Power: The Lower Houses of Assembly in the Southern Royal Colonies, 1689–1776* (1963); Robert M. Weir, "Liberty and Property and No Stamps; South Carolina and the Stamp Act Crisis" (Ph.D. diss., Western Reserve Univ., 1966); Weir, *Colonial South Carolina—A History* (1983); and Weir, *"A Most Important Epoch": The Coming of the Revolution in South Carolina* (1970).

JAMES M. CLIFTON

MANKIEWICZ, Herman Jacob (7 Nov. 1897–5 Mar. 1953), screenwriter, was born in New York City, the son of Franz Mankiewicz, a reporter for a German-language newspaper, and Johanna Blumenau, a dress-maker. Both parents were German immigrants and non-practicing Jews. In 1904 Mankiewicz moved with his family to Wilkes-Barre, Pennsylvania, where his father spent two years as editor of the *Demokratischer Wächter* and then became an instructor of modern languages at Hillman Academy, from which Mankiewicz graduated at age fourteen. Too young to enter college, he worked for a year as a surveyor's assistant at a coal mine.

In 1913 the family returned to New York, where Mankiewicz entered Columbia University and his father became a public school teacher (and later a professor at City College). At Columbia the blond and stockily built Mankiewicz exhibited the quick, cynical wit that would become his greatest strength as a writer. He also showed a prodigious capacity for drink; alcohol problems would plague him throughout his life. In 1916 Mankiewicz graduated from Columbia with a degree in English and German. The following year, after a brief stint studying English at Columbia's graduate school, Mankiewicz became a reporter and theater critic for the *American Jewish Chronicle*. In February 1918 he joined the U.S. Army Air Corps but did not make it through aviation training. He then joined the U.S. Marines and spent several months in Europe. Leaving the military in the summer of 1919, Mankiewicz worked for the press department of the American Red Cross in Paris. He then returned to the United States, where he married Shulamith Sara Aaronson of Washington, D.C., in July 1920. The couple had three children.

Immediately after his marriage, Mankiewicz moved with his wife to Berlin, Germany, where he worked as a correspondent for *Women's Wear Daily*, the *Chicago Tribune*, and the *New York Times*. Returning to New York in 1922, Mankiewicz worked for a short time as a general assignment reporter for the *New York World*, then moved to the *New York Times* as an assistant to drama editor George S. Kaufman, with whom he later collaborated on the unsuccessful Broadway play *The Good Fellow* (1926). Mankiewicz's extraordinary talent as a conversationalist made him a popular figure in theatrical and literary circles. He became a member of the Algonquin Round Table, the celebrated collection of wits that included Dorothy Parker, Robert Benchley, Alexander Woollcott, and Marc Connelly. With Connelly, Mankiewicz wrote another unsuccessful play, *The Wild Man of Borneo* (1927). "Mank was a wonderfully entertaining companion but he was a coffee-klatcher who confused talk about what he wanted to do with work done," said Connelly, who claimed to have written most of the play (Paul T. Nolan, *Marc Connelly* [1969], p. 61). In 1925 Mankiewicz was hired as drama critic for the newly founded magazine the *New Yorker*. He was fired from the position in early 1926, when editor Harold Ross became fed up with his tendency toward intellectual arrogance.

In July 1926 Mankiewicz moved to Hollywood to work for Paramount Pictures as a title writer for silent films. He had spent a brief period in Hollywood dur-ing the previous year, contributing an original story to *The Road to Mandalay* (1926), starring Lon Chaney. Among the films for which Mankiewicz wrote titles are *The City Gone Wild* (1927), *The Last Command* (1928), and *Three Week Ends* (1928). The introduction of sound films made Mankiewicz's theatrical experience and skill at writing dialogue extremely valuable. In the late 1920s and early 1930s he was one of the busiest and most influential screenwriters in Hollywood. He is credited with bringing a Broadway sensibility to motion pictures and for encouraging other New York writers, such as Ben Hecht, to come to Hollywood. "Mankiewicz spearheaded the movement of that whole Broadway style of wisecracking, fast-talking, cynical-sentimental entertainment onto the national scene," wrote Pauline Kael (*Citizen Kane Book*, p. 18). Alone or in collaboration, Mankiewicz wrote scripts for numerous films including *The Dummy* (1929), *Laughter* (1930), *The Royal Family of Broadway* (1930), and *Man of the World* (1931). He also supervised production and did uncredited script work on the Marx Brothers' films *Monkey Business* (1931), and *Horse Feathers* (1932). Moving to Metro-Goldwyn-Mayer Pictures (MGM) in 1933, he enjoyed a major success with *Dinner at Eight* (1933).

Still harboring ambition to be a playwright and feeling that his intellectual gifts were being wasted, Mankiewicz belittled his success in films and showed contempt for the motion picture industry. Nevertheless, he enjoyed a busy Hollywood social life, including tennis games with Greta Garbo, dinners at Chasen's, and visits to "San Simeon," the country estate that newspaper publisher William Randolph Hearst shared with his mistress, actress Marion Davies. He also indulged in high-stakes gambling, which left him perpetually in debt. By the mid-1930s Mankiewicz's alcoholism, tendency to lose interest in a project before it was completed, and general instability had tarnished his reputation. Though his talent was still highly regarded, many producers, including MGM's powerful Irving Thalberg, did not want to work with him, and his screenwriting assignments dwindled to a trickle. In 1939 his contract with MGM was severed after he failed to make good on a promise to studio chief Louis B. Mayer to stop gambling.

Mankiewicz made a comeback through his involvement with *Citizen Kane* (1941), the story of a powerful but pathetically lonely newspaper magnate based on the life of Hearst, with whom Mankiewicz had long been fascinated. Produced and directed by Orson Welles, who also played the title character, the film was a box office failure but was praised by critics and has come to be seen as one of the finest American films ever made. Mankiewicz shared the screenwriting credit with Welles, and their screenplay won the film's only Academy Award. The primary authorship of *Citizen Kane* has been long disputed. Mankiewicz maintained that he had written almost the entire script and that Welles, who had made only minor changes, insisted on a writing credit in order to be seen as a total filmmaker. Though some scholars believe Mankiewicz's assertion is exaggerated, there is general agreement that his contributions to the screenplay—including the use of the Kanes' sled, "Rosebud," as a connecting theme—were more important than Welles led others to believe.

The critical success of *Citizen Kane* revived Mankiewicz's career, but he never regained the eminence he had enjoyed a decade earlier. His screenplay with Jo Swerling for *The Pride of the Yankees* (1942), a biography of baseball star Lou Gehrig, received an Academy Award nomination. He also wrote *Christmas Holiday* (1944), *The Enchanted Cottage* (1945), *The Spanish Main* (1945), and *A Woman's Secret* (1949). In the course of his career, Mankiewicz worked on countless other screenplays that were never produced and completed films for which he received no credit.

By the early 1950s Mankiewicz's health had begun to decline owing to long years of alcoholism. He became depressed and reclusive and often disparaged himself for never returning to the East Coast literary environment. His sense of failure was exacerbated by the success of his younger brother, writer and director Joseph L. Mankiewicz. His final screenplay was *The Pride of St. Louis* (1952), a biography of baseball pitcher Dizzy Dean. Mankiewicz died in Hollywood of uremic poisoning.

• Good sources on Mankiewicz's career are Richard Meryman's biography, *Mank: The Wit, World, and Life of Herman Mankiewicz* (1978), and Pauline Kael, *The* Citizen Kane *Book* (1971), which examines his contribution to *Citizen Kane*. See also Ian Hamilton, *Writers in Hollywood, 1915–1951* (1990), and Robert L. Carringer, "Who Really Wrote *Citizen Kane*?" *American Film*, Sept. 1985, pp. 42–49, 70. An obituary is in the *New York Times*, 6 Mar. 1953.

MARY C. KALFATOVIC

MANKIEWICZ, Joseph Leo (11 Feb. 1909–5 Feb. 1993), scriptwriter and movie director, was born in Wilkes-Barre, Pennsylvania, the son of Frank Mankiewicz, a language instructor and the editor of *Modern Language Studies*, and Johanna Blumenau. Mankiewicz studied languages and literature at Columbia University and graduated in 1928. At his father's insistence he enrolled at the University of Berlin for graduate study, but after arriving in Germany he started working as a correspondent for the *Chicago Tribune* and a stringer for *Variety*. He also worked at Universum-Film Aktien-Gesellschaft (UFA), Germany's largest film company, writing English subtitles for their silent films.

In 1929 Mankiewicz's elder brother Herman got him a job at Paramount Studios, writing subtitles for sound movies that were shown in theaters lacking sound equipment. He soon graduated to writing dialogue, then entire screenplays, and received his first Oscar nomination as screenwriter for *Skippy* (1931). The following year's work included two classic comedies starring W. C. Fields, *Million Dollar Legs* and *If I Had a Million* (both 1932), in which Fields first uttered his famous salutation, "My little chickadee."

In 1933 Mankiewicz was hired by Metro-Goldwyn-Mayer (MGM), where his first project was to co-script *Manhattan Melodrama* (1934). It achieved notoriety as the film John Dillinger viewed just before his death and also won Mankiewicz his second Oscar nomination. In addition to his work for MGM, Mankiewicz wrote the screenplay (for a nominal fee) for King Vidor's *Our Daily Bread* (1934). In 1934 Mankiewicz married actress Elizabeth Young. The couple had two children before their divorce in 1937.

After writing the screenplays for several popular MGM comedies, Mankiewicz asked Louis B. Mayer, the head of the studio, to allow him to direct films. Mayer instead offered him a job as a producer, telling him, "You have to learn to crawl before you can walk." Although Mankiewicz considered this "about as good a definition of a producer as any," he accepted the offer. His first production was *Fury* (1936), directed by Fritz Lang, and was followed by several Joan Crawford comedies and the war movie *Three Comrades* (1938). The latter's screenplay was written by novelist F. Scott Fitzgerald and extensively revised by Mankiewicz, who said, "Some novelists cannot write dialogue and Scott Fitzgerald was one of them." Mankiewicz later commented, "If I go down in literary history, in a footnote, it will be as the swine who rewrote F. Scott Fitzgerald."

In 1939 Mankiewicz married actress Rosa Stradner. One of the couple's two children, Tom Mankiewicz, also became a movie screenwriter. Rosa Mankiewicz committed suicide in 1958.

Most of Mankiewicz's productions for MGM were competent but forgettable. The two exceptions (he also contributed to the scripts) were *The Philadelphia Story* (1940) and *Woman of the Year* (1942). The former was the film version of Philip Barry's popular play, in which Cary Grant, Katharine Hepburn, Celeste Holm, and James Stewart gave brilliant performances in a classic comedy of manners. The latter film was another witty and sophisticated comedy and featured the first screen pairing of Hepburn and Spencer Tracy.

In 1943 Mankiewicz left MGM, following a row with Mayer concerning Mankiewicz's affair with starlet Judy Garland. He joined 20th Century–Fox, where he produced *Keys to the Kingdom* (1944) and replaced the ailing Ernst Lubitsch as director of *Dragonwyck* (1946). He later told an interviewer that the job of directing was easy for a scriptwriter, because he had already directed the film in his head while writing the screenplay. His initial films as a director, *Somewhere in the Night* (1946), *The Late George Apley* (1947), and *The Ghost and Mrs. Muir* (1947), were profitable, but *Escape* (1948) was a flop at the box office.

The following year, however, Mankiewicz wrote and directed *Letter to Three Wives* (1949), which was a hit both at the box office and with the critics. It earned him two Oscars, for best screenplay and best direction. Mankiewicz scored again the following year with *All About Eve* (1950), which won the Academy Award for best picture. Mankiewicz again won two Oscars for his writing and direction, the first person to do so two years in a row. Both films were variants of the comedy of manners, the first examining suburban marriages within and across class lines, the second focusing on the rise to stardom in the theatrical world. Both films had similar intricate structures, involving multiple flashbacks and frequent off-camera narration. The dialogue in *Eve* included Bette Davis's frequently quoted line, "Fasten your seat belts. It's going to be a bumpy night."

The two films that followed, *People Will Talk* (1951) and *Five Fingers* (1952), were less popular, and Mankiewicz considered leaving Hollywood for work in the New York theater. He revised his plans when MGM asked him to direct a film version of Shakespeare's *Julius Caesar* (1953), with John Houseman as producer. The film met with lukewarm reviews and a poor box office, prompting Mankiewicz to head to New York. He directed a production of the opera *La Bohème* for the Metropolitan Opera, but this also met with mixed reviews.

After the disappointing response in New York, Mankiewicz decided to return to filmmaking. He then produced his first film as writer, director, and producer, *The Barefoot Contessa* (1954). This satire on the rise to stardom within the movie industry seemed to most American audiences and critics simply a poor remake of *All About Eve*. European critics and filmmakers, however, hailed it as brilliant, and Federico Fellini later claimed it was the inspiration for his own masterpiece, *La Dolce Vita*.

During the filming of *The Barefoot Contessa* Mankiewicz met Rosemary Matthews, a member of the production staff who later became his personal assistant. The couple were married in 1962 and had one child.

Mankiewicz's next film, *Guys and Dolls* (1955), was a popular musical comedy based on the stories of Damon Runyon. Its success prompted the National Broadcasting Company (NBC) to purchase a one-half interest in Mankiewicz's independent production company, Figaro, Inc., for $1 million. This enabled Mankiewicz to finance and direct a theatrical venture, *The Square Root of Wonderful* by Carson McCullers. The play opened at Broadway's National Theater on 31 October 1957, received poor reviews, and closed eight weeks later. Mankiewicz returned to Hollywood, where he filmed Graham Greene's novel *The Quiet American* (1958) and then collaborated with Gore Vidal in writing the screenplay for the film version of Tennessee Williams's *Suddenly, Last Summer* (1959), which Mankiewicz also directed. It starred Katharine Hepburn and Elizabeth Taylor, who both won Oscar nominations, and was successful with audiences but not with the critics.

Mankiewicz then began working with 20th Century–Fox on an adaptation of Lawrence Durrell's four-novel series *The Alexandria Quartet*. But after spending more than a year adapting *Justine*, the first novel of Durrell's tetralogy, for film, he dropped the project in order to take over the direction of *Cleopatra* (1963).

The film had begun under the direction of Rouben Mamoulian, but his ill health and numerous other problems had delayed production and escalated the budget well beyond its original $6 million limit.

When Mankiewicz agreed to take over the direction he had hoped to conclude his work in fifteen weeks, but it was eighteen months before the film was completed. During that period the head of the movie studio was replaced by Darryl F. Zanuck, who subsequently fired, and then rehired, Mankiewicz, who did not have any say in the film's final cut. He later said that "*Cleopatra* was first conceived in emergency, shot in hysteria, and wound up in blind panic." The film's final cost of $35 million was more than that of any other previous movie. Critics panned the film, and the audience response was lukewarm. Both the studio and the film's stars attempted to deflect criticism by creating a scapegoat: they blamed all the picture's faults on Mankiewicz.

The *Cleopatra* debacle prevented Mankiewicz from producing another Hollywood film for nearly a decade. In 1964 he directed a television movie, *A Carol for Another Christmas*, for American Broadcasting Companies (ABC). His next work was in England, where he directed a joint Anglo-American production, *The Honey Pot* (1967), and then a documentary jointly directed with Sidney Lumet, *King: A Final Record . . . Montgomery to Memphis* (1970). His two final films were a western, *There Was a Crooked Man* (1970), and a mystery based on a popular stage play, *Sleuth* (1972).

Mankiewicz's best films had been marked by literate and witty dialogue as well as subtle, complex structures. The box-office success of *Sleuth* revived critics' respect for Mankiewicz's career. Even *Cleopatra* was seen in fresh perspective. French filmmakers Luc Beraud and Michel Ciment made him the subject of a documentary, *All About Mankiewicz* (1983), and in 1986 the Directors' Guild gave him the D. W. Griffith Award for lifetime achievement. In 1987 the Venice Film Festival awarded him a Golden Lion for lifetime achievement. In 1991 the Motion Picture Academy of Arts and Sciences honored him with a special tribute, cosponsored by the Museum of Modern Art American Cinematheque and the Directors of America. Mankiewicz characterized this latter tribute as his "longevity award." He died in Bedford, New York.

• Random House has published Mankiewicz's screenplay, *All About Eve* (1951); others are in the archives of Fox, MGM, and Paramount. Mankiewicz and Gary Carey coauthored *More About All About Eve: A Colloquy* (1972). Mankiewicz and his films are discussed in Kenneth L. Geist, *Pictures Will Talk: The Life and Films of Joseph L. Mankiewicz* (1978); Bernard F. Dick, *Joseph L. Mankiewicz* (1983); John Springer, "The Films of Joseph L. Mankiewicz," *Films in Review*, Mar. 1971, pp. 153–57; and Andrew Sarris, "Mankiewicz of the Movies," *Show*, Mar. 1970, pp. 23–30, 78. See also Stephen Farber and Marc Green, *Hollywood Dynasties: The Ruling Families and the Legacy of Fame and Fortunes* (1984), Richard Meryman, *Mank: The Wit, World, and Life of Herman Mankiewicz* (1978), and Philip Dunne, *Take Two: A Life in Movies and Politics* (1980). Obituaries are in the *New York Times*, 6 Feb. 1993, and *Variety*, 15 Feb. 1993.

STEPHEN G. MARSHALL

MANKIN, Helen Douglas (11 Sept. 1894–25 July 1956), lawyer and legislator, was born Helen Douglas in Atlanta, Georgia, the daughter of Hamilton Douglas and Corinne Williams, lawyers and educators. Mankin's parents had earned law degrees together at the University of Michigan and then moved to Atlanta, where Mankin's father practiced law and helped found Atlanta Law School. Denied admission to the Georgia bar because of her sex, Corinne Douglas became a teacher and a pioneer in the education of women.

Mankin earned an A.B. at Rockford College in Illinois in 1917. During 1918–1919 she worked with suffragists in wartorn France, driving an ambulance for American Women's Hospital No. 1, a medical unit supported by suffragists, and in 1920 she earned an LL.B. from Atlanta Law School. She and her mother, then sixty-one years old, were together admitted to the Georgia bar in 1921, the ban on women having been lifted by the state legislature four years earlier. Both later joined the Douglas family firm.

In Atlanta, a woman practicing law was still an oddity and Mankin decided to explore possibilities for relocating her life and career. In May 1922 she and her sister Jean set out on a 13,000-mile automobile tour of North America, "a 1922 touring record for women drivers" (*Los Angeles Times*, 31 Aug. 1922). Douglas kept a journal of their tour, which was published in the *Atlanta Georgian*. After further travel in Europe, she ceased searching for a new home and resettled in Atlanta, opening her own law office in 1924.

Mankin's practice was small, and many of those she served were poor and not a few of them were African Americans. She early supplemented her income by lecturing at the Atlanta Law School. In 1927 she became active in city politics, serving as woman's manager of Isaac N. Ragsdale's successful mayoral campaign. The Atlanta Women's Club recognized her that year as "a pioneer among women in the profession of law."

In 1927 she married Guy Mark Mankin, a mechanical engineer and widower with a seven-year-old son, acquiring the name by which she became known. They had no children together. Guy's work required frequent relocations for the first five years of their marriage, and they lived in Cuba, Brazil, Argentina, and later New York and Chicago.

In 1933 the couple returned to Atlanta, where Mankin resumed her legal career. In 1935, after unsuccessfully lobbying the Georgia legislature for ratification of a child labor amendment to the federal Constitution, she decided to try for the legislature herself. Running against five men in the 1936 Democratic primary, she won a two-year term as state representative from Fulton County and was reelected four times, serving from 1937 to 1946. Of the five other women who had been state legislators until then, none served as long as Mankin.

Besides being physically imposing, Mankin was independent, forthright, and abrasive, the Georgia legislature's first "strong" woman member. With the powerful governor Eugene Talmadge she maintained an adversarial relationship while promoting electoral reform, child welfare, labor causes, and improvements in the educational and prison systems. After the liberal Ellis Arnall became governor in 1943, she championed his repeal of the poll tax and enfranchisement of eighteen-year-olds.

When U.S. congressman Robert Ramspeck, from the Fifth District, resigned in 1946, Governor Arnall called a special election in February to fill the unexpired term. Mankin left the legislature to seek the Ramspeck seat. In 1944 the southern Democratic white primary, long tantamount to election in the region's one-party states, was outlawed by the U.S. Supreme Court, and Georgia, which claimed immunity from the decision, by 1946 was defendant in a lawsuit for full implementation of the decision's intent. In this special election, however, primary rules were inapplicable, and blacks, holding new hope for the franchise, had doubled their registration for it. Mankin was the only candidate of the seventeen in the race who actively sought their support, and she won, 11,099 votes to 10,329 for her nearest opponent. Until the heavily black precinct 3-B on Ashby Street reported, the last to do so, Mankin had been narrowly behind, but 3-B delivered Mankin 963 of its 1,039 votes, a winning margin. "The Negro vote did it," said *Time* (25 Feb. 1946).

Later, when Talmadge campaigned to regain the governorship, he called her "the Belle of Ashby Street" and scornfully deplored "the spectacle of Atlanta Negroes sending a Congresswoman to Washington." Mankin refused to repudiate her black constituency, declaring, "I'm proud of every one of those votes and I hope I'll get them again." She also drew support from white progressives and the CIO and its union members, becoming the focus of a black-white voting alliance that Georgia's dominant groups had feared since the Populist uprising of the 1890s.

Mankin was regarded in Congress as a Georgia maverick. Consistently supporting Harry S. Truman's administration, she was among the few southerners who voted to uphold Truman's veto of the Case antistrike bill, a bill that labor strongly opposed.

In April 1946 the Supreme Court opened Georgia's Democratic primary to African Americans, and in the party's July primary Mankin was renominated to Congress by 53,611 votes to 42,482 for her principal opponent, James C. Davis, but under Georgia's county unit system, Davis was declared the winner. Designed to favor rural areas, the county unit system had not been used in the Fifth District since 1932, and it was resurrected to nullify the black vote and "to beat Mrs. Mankin—nothing else," declared W. Schley Howard, a former congressman. Under this system, the candidate receiving a plurality of a county's popular vote was awarded all its assigned unit votes; the one with the most county units won the election. Though gaining a large popular majority, Mankin won only the six unit votes of Fulton County, losing to Davis the winning eight unit votes of the district's other, smaller counties. The Georgia Democratic Executive Committee was loyal to outgoing governor Arnall, and when Mankin challenged the outcome, both candidates were placed on the general election ballot for that November, a rare procedure.

Supporters of Talmadge, who had won the party nomination for governor (also by county unit vote rather than by popular vote), promptly removed Mankin's name when the governor-elect, empowered by his primary victory, inherited control of the state committee from Arnall's forces before the general election. Mankin hastily solicited write-in votes but this eleventh-hour effort encountered violent opposition from a white supremacy group known as the Columbians, which worked closely with Davis's staff. Despite the obstacles, Mankin earned 19,527 votes to Davis's 31,444; she challenged Davis's right to a seat, but the Eightieth Congress upheld him.

Racial unrest flared in the South in 1946, prompting national demands for civil rights legislation, and since Mankin's public positions had placed her among the advocates of racial justice, she was a magnet for the resentment provoked by these demands in her region. When she ran against Davis again in 1948, the atmosphere was heavily charged, and this time she was decisively defeated.

Mankin never again held public office. She initiated a federal suit against the county unit system in 1949 (*South v. Peters*). The U.S. Supreme Court ruled against her, holding that the system was a political issue in which federal courts were powerless to intervene, a ruling that was later reversed in 1962 in *Baker v. Carr*, the court's "one man, one vote" case.

Helen Mankin did not live to see the reversal. Her election had inspired an upsurge in black voter registration and participation and, as the *Atlanta Constitution* said, "Georgia politics haven't been the same since." In an era of great political change, change accompanied often by fear and violence, Mankin left a legacy of courage and conviction. She died in Atlanta from injuries suffered in an automobile accident.

• Taped interviews on Mankin with Ellis Arnall, former governor, G. Everett Millican, former state senator, and James A. Mackay and James C. Davis, former congressmen, are available through the Georgia Government Documentation Project, Special Collections, Georgia State University, Atlanta. The interviews were used in the most complete account of Mankin's life and career, Lorraine Nelson Spritzer, *The Belle of Ashby Street: Helen Douglas Mankin and Georgia Politics* (1982). Mankin's accounts of her travels appeared in the *Atlanta Georgian* and *Sunday American*, May–Nov. 1922 and July–Dec. 1923, and are available on microfilm at the Atlanta Public Library. Articles about her political activities appeared in the *Atlanta Constitution* and the *Atlanta Journal*, 1936–1948. Her congressional electoral struggle is documented in *Hearings, Contested Election Case of Helen Douglas*

Mankin v. James C. Davis from 5th Cong. Dist. of Ga., 1947, available from the United States Archives. Anna Holden, "Race and Politics: Congressional Elections in the 5th Dist. of Ga., 1946–1952" (master's thesis, Univ. of North Carolina, 1955), also contains useful information on the same subject. Clarence A. Bacote, "The Negro in Atlanta Politics," *Phylon, the Atlanta University Review* 16, no. 4 (1955), provides a black's view of Mankin. Useful sources also are Supreme Court decisions *Cook v. Fortson*, 329 U.S. 675, *South v. Peters*, 339 U.S. 276, *Gray v. Sanders*, 372 U.S. 368, and *Baker v. Carr* 369 U.S. 186. Obituaries are in the *Washington Post*, 28 July 1956, and the *Washington Evening Star*, 27 July 1956. Mankin's birth date is given as 1896 in printed sources. The 1894 date is confirmed by the 1900 U.S. Census and by her sister, Jean Douglas Smith.

LORRAINE NELSON SPRITZER

MANLEY, John (Aug. 1732?–12 Feb. 1793), naval officer and privateer, was born apparently near Torquay, England, the son of Robert Manley. His mother's name is unknown. By 1757 he was living in Boston and was a captain in the merchant marine. In 1763 he married Hannah Cheevers. As of 1768 Manley was master of a vessel called the *Little Fortescue*. He also seems to have served some time in the British navy.

In August 1775 George Washington, commanding the Continental forces besieging British-occupied Boston, began purchasing merchant schooners, mounting guns on them, and setting them loose in Massachusetts Bay with orders to capture any merchant ship that was headed for Boston. The command of the *Lee*, one of the first vessels in "George Washington's Navy," went to Manley.

The *Lee* sailed on its first cruise on 28 October 1775. The complex legal environment made it almost impossible to define what constituted an "enemy" ship. Manley quickly seized three merchantmen, but their owners convinced the local authorities that the vessels were "not proper prizes."

On 29 November the *Lee* captured the brig *Nancy*, the first legitimate prize taken by a Continental warship. The *Nancy*'s cargo included two thousand muskets, thirty-one tons of musket balls, and a brass mortar. Over the next few weeks Manley took five more ships and became the first American naval hero of the Revolution. On 1 January 1776 Washington put him in command of a slightly larger schooner, the *Hancock*, and appointed him commodore of the fleet.

Later that month Manley captured two merchantmen, fended off an attempt by a British tender to rescue them, and escorted them to Plymouth. Early in February the British naval brig *Hope* chased the *Hancock* for four hours, after which Manley deliberately beached his ship near Scituate. A British prize crew boarded the *Hancock* and tried to destroy it but was driven off by Manley, his crew, and a local militia unit.

At the end of February, Manley put together a squadron of four schooners, the *Hancock*, *Franklin*, *Lee*, and *Lynch*. On 10 March they captured a merchantman called the *Stakesby*, but that night both the

Stakesby and the *Hancock* ran aground. The *Hancock* survived the episode but the prize was wrecked.

By the time Manley's ship had been repaired the British had begun to evacuate Boston. On 2 April the *Hancock*, *Lee*, and *Lynch* took the brig *Elizabeth*, which was headed for Canada laden with Loyalists and British soldiers, as well as merchandise they had looted from the Boston warehouses.

For some time Manley had been complaining that he and his men had been denied their fair share of the prizes they had taken. He also wanted a larger command, and in mid-April he announced that, unless he obtained one, he would not make another cruise. Manley undoubtedly knew that a more prestigious position was waiting for him. In April 1776 the Continental Congress announced the appointment of twenty-four captains in the new Continental navy. Manley's name was second on the list, and he was given command of a 32-gun frigate under construction at Newburyport, Massachusetts.

The new ship, like Manley's previous command, was to be named the *Hancock*. The task of equipping it for sea was complicated by the presence of another frigate, the *Boston*, which was fitting out at Newburyport at the same time. For almost a year Manley and the *Boston*'s captain, Hector McNeill, competed for the few seamen, guns, and other supplies available.

The *Hancock* and the *Boston* sailed from Boston on 21 May 1777, with orders to destroy British warships off New England and Canada. On 8 June the Americans captured HM frigate *Fox* and added it to their fleet. During the next month, as the enlarged squadron cruised around the Grand Banks, the relationship between McNeill and Manley, already strained, deteriorated further.

On 7 July the *Hancock*, *Boston*, and *Fox* encountered two British warships, the 44-gun *Rainbow* and the frigate *Flora*. The Americans held the advantage in both numbers and firepower, but by this time neither Continental captain was willing to support the other. The *Flora* recaptured the *Fox*; the *Rainbow*, after a running fight of thirty-nine hours, caught up with the *Hancock* on the morning of 9 July and forced Manley to surrender. The *Boston* escaped.

Manley remained a prisoner in British-occupied New York until he was exchanged in March 1778. That summer he was court-martialed for the loss of the *Hancock*; though he was acquitted, Congress had no command for him. He thereupon embarked on a career as a privateer, making a successful cruise in a vessel called the *Marlborough*. In January 1779 Manley sailed for the West Indies in the privateer *Cumberland* but encountered a British frigate and had to surrender. Four months later he escaped from a Barbados prison and made his way to Boston, where he took command of the privateer *Jason*. On his second cruise he was captured for a third time and sent to Mill Prison in England, where he spent two years before he was exchanged again. Congress then appointed him to the frigate *Hague*, which he commanded until the end of the war.

After the Revolution Manley apparently lived a peaceful life in Boston. His first wife died in 1786; five years later he married Friswith Arnold. Since Manley's death, which occurred in Boston, three ships of the U.S. Navy have been named after him.

James Warren, then a member of the Marine Committee of the Continental Congress, described Manley as "a Blunt, Honest, and I believe Brave Officer. . . . He is extreemly popular with Officers, and Seamen, and can Man a Ship with dispatch." His rivals, including McNeill and John Paul Jones, claimed he owed his rise in the navy to politics; Jones asserted that "he is Altogether Unfit to Command a Frigate of thirty two Guns." Manley's record is one of extraordinary energy and an audacity bordering on recklessness. The American Continental navy equated those qualities with heroism, but in that service Manley was unable to demonstrate his potential as a naval officer.

• Most of the extant papers relevant to Manley's career appear in William Bell Clark and William James Morgan, eds., *Naval Documents of the American Revolution* (9 vols., 1964–). Isaac Greenwood's full-length biography, *Captain John Manley* (1915), is dated. The best modern account of Manley's career in the Continental navy is contained in Philip Chadwick Foster Smith's narrative of the battle in which the frigate *Hancock* was lost, *Fired by Manley Zeal: A Naval Fiasco of the American Revolution* (1977). William Bell Clark, *George Washington's Navy: Being an Account of His Excellency's Fleet in New England Waters* (1960), details Manley's activities under Washington's command. See also William M. Fowler, Jr., *Rebels under Sail: The American Navy during the Revolution* (1976), William James Morgan, *Captains to the Northward: The New England Captains in the Continental Navy* (1959), and Gardner W. Allen, *A Naval History of the American Revolution* (2 vols., 1913).

JOHN A. TILLEY

MANLY, Basil, Jr. (19 Dec. 1825–31 Jan. 1892), Baptist minister, was born in Edgefield District, South Carolina, the son of Basil Manly, a Baptist minister, and Sarah Murray Rudulph. In 1843 Manly graduated with first honors from the University of Alabama. After one year of graduate study at Newton Theological Seminary in Newton, Massachusetts, Manly enrolled in Princeton Theological Seminary, where he learned Old School Calvinism and conservative methods of biblical criticism from Charles Hodge and J. A. Alexander before graduating in 1847.

Ordained in 1848, Manly accepted the pastoral charge of three churches, two in Alabama and one in Mississippi, preaching at each once or twice monthly. Believing that his duties had ruined his health, he resigned his pastorates after one year. He recovered his health and spent the next two years pursuing surveying and mining interests in addition to frequent preaching. During this time he edited, with his father's assistance, the *Baptist Psalmody* (1850). He later estimated that the hymnal sold fifty or sixty thousand copies over twenty-five years. In the fall of 1850 Manly accepted the pastorate of the First Baptist Church of Richmond, Virginia, the largest white Baptist congregation in the South. In 1852 he married Charlotte Ann Elizabeth Smith, who died at the age of thirty-four in 1867; the two had eleven children, three of whom died in early childhood. Although he was a successful preacher and pastor, Manly resigned his position in 1854 to become the founding principal of the Richmond Female Institute. In addition to teaching and fundraising, he served as pastor of two country churches and in 1856 edited the monthly *American Baptist Memorial*, a national magazine featuring Baptist history and news.

Manly began what he considered his life's great work in 1859, when he became a founding member of the faculty of the Southern Baptist Theological Seminary in Greenville, South Carolina. Along with fellow professors James P. Boyce and John Broadus and a few others, Manly had long promoted a southern theological school for Baptists. Support was tepid, however, and the school survived the disruptions of the Civil War and indifference and suspicion within the denomination largely through the sheer determination of Manly and his colleagues.

Opposing higher critical views of the Bible, Manly taught biblical introduction, Old Testament, and Hebrew throughout his career, occasionally adding Assyrian, Homiletics, or polemics. Although he was not an original thinker, Manly assimilated a wide range of scholarship and earned the respect of students and colleagues for both his knowledge and his piety. His chief theological work was *The Bible Doctrine of Inspiration* (1888). Like Princeton's Hodge, he defended the plenary inspiration view that "every part of Scripture" is a "union of absolute truth and divine authority" (p. 59).

Manly made two more enduring contributions to the seminary. He wrote the "Seminary Hymn" for the first commencement in 1860, and it has been sung at every one since. The opening lines of the hymn express his conviction that doctrine gives the church power to accomplish its mission: "Soldiers of Christ, in truth arrayed, / A world in ruins needs your aid." Manly also composed the seminary's official confession of faith, the "Abstract of Principles." After the founders decided that only a detailed creed would assure the orthodoxy of the faculty, Manly, relying on seventeenth-century Baptist creeds, crafted the Abstract as a Calvinistic Baptist statement.

Manly's teaching career at the seminary was twice interrupted. When the school closed its doors between 1862 and 1865 during the Civil War, Manly left Greenville to manage his newly acquired plantation in the Abbeville District and to preach at three churches in the area. He also led Southern Baptists to establish the denominational Sunday School Board, and he served as its first president from 1863 to 1868. In 1869 he married Hattie Summers Hair, with whom he had seven children, only three of whom survived childhood. His distaste for Republican rule in Reconstruction South Carolina induced him in 1871 to accept the presidency of Georgetown College in Kentucky. During his eight-year tenure he reformed the curriculum by introducing the elective system. In 1879 he moved to Louisville, Kentucky, to resume his post on the faculty of the Southern Baptist Theological Seminary, which had moved there in 1877. He replaced C. H. Toy, whom the faculty and trustees had forced out for teaching critical theories that assumed the existence of errors in the Bible. Manly taught at the seminary until his death. In this period he produced another hymn book, *Manly's Choice* (1891), and edited a Sunday school paper, the *Kind Words Teacher* (1887–1888). He died in Louisville.

Late in his life Manly regretted his failure to narrow the sphere of his activity, observing that "the things I know nothing about are few; there is nothing I know all about" (letter to George Manly, 28 Sept. 1878). Yet his diverse activity elicited from colleague John Broadus the assertion that Manly was "the most versatile man I ever met" (*Seminary Magazine*, Mar. 1892, p. 314). He reserved his greatest efforts for the institution he loved most—the seminary he helped to establish—and his talents in teaching, administration, and fundraising had a steadying influence on the struggling school. Manly combined gentleness with a firm commitment to doctrinal orthodoxy, a combination that gave credibility to the seminary and encouraged many Southern Baptists to surrender their suspicions and lend it their support.

• Manly's papers, consisting of two journals, twenty-one volumes of correspondence, manuscript sermons, sermon notes, and lecture notes, are in the library of the Southern Baptist Theological Seminary, Louisville, Ky. Additional papers are in the Manly collections of Samford University and Furman University. Louise Manly, *The Manly Family* (1930), is an important biographical source. The only thorough study is Joseph P. Cox, "A Study of the Life and Work of Basil Manly, Jr." (Ph.D. diss., Southern Baptist Theological Seminary, 1954), which includes a good bibliography. Also helpful are John Broadus, *Memoir of James Petigru Boyce* (1893); A. T. Robertson, *Life and Letters of John Albert Broadus* (1901); and William A. Mueller, *A History of Southern Baptist Theological Seminary* (1959). On Manly's contributions to hymn writing, composing, and editing see Paul A. Richardson, "Basil Manly, Jr.: Southern Baptist Pioneer in Hymnody," *Baptist History and Heritage*, Apr. 1992, pp. 19–30.

GREGORY A. WILLS

MANLY, John Matthews (2 Sept. 1865–2 Apr. 1940), philologist and educator, was born in Sumter County, Alabama, the son of the Reverend Charles Manly, a Baptist minister and educator, and Mary Esther Hellen Matthews. The Manlys were a prominent southern family, and John Matthews's grandfather, Basil Manly, his uncle, Basil Manly, Jr., and his father, Charles, were leading preachers and educators among the Southern Baptists. John Matthews Manly received his early education at several public and private schools, including the Staunton Military Academy in Virginia and the Greenville Military Institute in South Carolina. He graduated from Furman University with a master's degree in 1883 and then taught mathematics for several years before moving on to Harvard University, where he received his Ph.D. in philology in 1890.

While at Harvard, Manly studied with Edward Stevens Sheldon, whom he later acknowledged as the most important influence in his education there.

In 1891 Manly was made associate professor at Brown University and was soon made full professor. He stayed at Brown until 1898, when he moved to the University of Chicago, where he was professor and head of the English department and made his reputation as a Chaucer scholar. He remained at Chicago for more than thirty years, with a break in 1917, when he enlisted in the military. During World War I, Manly was commissioned as a captain assigned to the Military Intelligence Division, where he helped with the encoding and decoding of messages and the deciphering of enemy codes. He was discharged in 1919 as a major. This military service reflected Manly's interest in language and intellectual problems in etymology. He returned to the University of Chicago and continued to work and teach until 1933. His devotion to teaching and scholarship was repaid in respect and gratitude from students and colleagues alike, who in 1923 presented him with a volume of research titled "The Manly Anniversary Studies in Language and Literature," which included a bibliography of his own work.

Manly dedicated his life to the study of Chaucer and *Piers the Plowman*, while his active and far-reaching mind allowed him to produce publications in a variety of fields of study, including several major contributions to Chaucerian study. In his 1926 edition of a series of lectures delivered at the Lowell Institute, *Some New Light on Chaucer*, Manly argued that Chaucer had given the characters in his tales the attributes of living people that he knew. Two years later, Manly's textbook edition of the tales offered more fresh interpretation, while his critical study *The Text of the Canterbury Tales*, published in 1940 and coauthored with Edith Rickert, was a line-by-line examination of Chaucer's most famous work. His painstaking efforts, which tried to include every possible variant in the text, resulted in the most complete and nearest to the original volume of the tales produced up until that time.

In addition to his philological contributions to Chaucerian studies, Manly was also dedicated to education. This interest led to the publication of many textbooks for all levels of education, from the early grades through graduate school. His devotion to literature and education combined in his editing of anthologies, which Manly argued were valuable tools for teaching literature, making the texts themselves available to students.

Manly never married and was often accompanied on his many trips to England by his sisters, Anne and Hellen. These travels and the influence of his work on Chaucer made him figure in international literary circles and brought more recognition and responsibilities. He served as president of the Modern Language Association, the Mediaeval Academy, and the Modern Humanities Research Association of England and as vice president of the British Shakespeare Association. He was given five honorary degrees during the course of his career and was honored by the University of Chicago with the creation of a chair bearing his name, which continues to carry on Manly's legacy as a scholar.

Manly died in Tucson, Arizona, where he was staying with a sister. His major contributions were in the study of Chaucer, but his influence in the many organizations of which he was a member and his devotion as a thinker and teacher rank him with the finest names in the American academy.

• The best biographical sources on Manly include Louise Manly, *The Manly Family* (1930); *Modern Philology* (Aug. 1940); and *American Philosophical Society Yearbook* (1940). Publications of his important works as well as edited and coedited anthologies include *Specimens of the Pre-Shaksperean Drama* (1897; repr. 1967); *English Poetry, 1170–1892* (1907); *English Prose, 1137–1890* (1909); *The Piers Plowman Controversy* (1910); *The Poems and Plays of William Vaughn Moody* (1912); *Contemporary British Literature* (1921); *The Writer's Index of Good Form and Good English* (1923); *The Writing of English* (1923); *Chaucer and the Rhetoricians* (1926); *Some New Light on Chaucer* (1926); and *The Text of the Canterbury Tales, Studied on the Basis of All Known Manuscripts* (1940).
A. JAMES FULLER

MANLY, William Lewis (6 Apr. 1820–5 Feb. 1903), author, was born near St. Albans, Vermont, the son of a farmer whose name is unknown and Phoebe Calkins. Manly sometimes spelled his name Manley, and a Manly family historian said the name should be spelled that way (Johnson and Johnson, p. xv). But Manly is the commonly recognized spelling and the one on the title page of *Death Valley in '49* (1894), the book that established Manly's fame as a writer and as a California pioneer. Early in Manly's childhood his father "got the Western fever," sold his farm in Vermont, and moved to the Michigan territory. There were regular epidemics of "fever and ague and bilious fever" in the region, and when Manly himself became ill he said he "felt so miserable that I began to think I had rather live on the top of the Rocky Mountains and catch chipmunks for a living than to live here and be sick."

At the age of twenty, Manly set out for the Wisconsin territory, where he lived off and on for the next nine years, supporting himself by hunting, trapping, and working in lead mines. When news of the California gold rush arrived, he set out to seek his fortune. He met another man, John H. Rogers of Tennessee, at Council Bluffs, Iowa, and they both served as ox drivers on a wagon train headed for California. In what is now southwest Wyoming, Manly's employer realized he was too late to cross the Sierra Nevada before the winter snows, so he notified his drivers that they would have to winter in Salt Lake City with no opportunity for work or for continuing to the goldfields. Manly, Rogers, and five others decided to leave "the heated trail," and they began to float down the Green River in an abandoned ferryboat in the hopes of eventually reaching the Pacific Ocean. A series of hardships and the warnings of a Ute Indian chief about dangers ahead on the river convinced Manly to lead his men overland toward Salt Lake City. Before arriving there, they met a rendezvous of more than 100 wagons heading south on the Old Spanish Trail from Hobble Creek, Utah, for Los Angeles. The group organized under the name of the Sand Walking Company.

Near Enterprise, Utah, all but seven of the wagons headed west into unknown territory, lured on by a map that indicated that there was a shortcut that would take 300 to 500 miles off their journey to the California goldfields. About seventy-five of the wagons turned back after three days because of rugged terrain. The remaining group splintered even further; Manly scouted for the Asabel Bennett/John Arcane party, which included at least twenty-four men, women, and children. Food and water were in desperately short supply. When the party reached Death Valley and realized that they could not get over the Panamint Range with their wagons, the members asked Manly and Rogers to seek relief on foot. Instead of the ten days they expected to be gone, it took them nearly a month to reach Rancho San Francisco, north of Mission San Fernando, and return with sorely needed food and supplies to lead the stranded families safely to Los Angeles.

Manly continued to the northern California goldfields, where he staked a claim before returning to Wisconsin in 1851 via Panama, Havana, and New Orleans. Later that year he returned to California, where he mined for several years. Manly apparently kept a diary during his travels, and he first recorded a narrative account of his journey in a 300-page letter to his parents in 1851, based on his diary. In 1859 he settled on a farm near San Jose. In the winter of 1861, he and two other men retraced the forty-niners' route back to the Panamints, to rescue a companion who had been prospecting for gold the previous year. In 1862 Manly married Mary Jane Woods of Woodbridge, California. He lived in Santa Clara County for forty years and dealt in real estate in association with Dan Porter of Porter and Manly.

From June 1887 to July 1890 Manly published a serialized account of his travels, "From Vermont to California," in the newspaper *Santa Clara Valley*. These short sketches formed the basis for the book *Death Valley in '49* (1894). Scholars generally agree that *Death Valley in '49* was at least partly ghostwritten, but they disagree over who Manly's "editor" was. His writings helped reinforce a negative image of the American desert as lifeless, vacant, and inhospitable. He emphasized "the dreadful sands and shadows of Death Valley, its exhausting phantoms, its salty columns, bitter lakes, and wild, dreary sunken desolation." Yet he also appreciated the desert's "grand desolation." He marveled at the clear atmosphere and the stretching vistas of alkali flats.

Death Valley in '49 records one of the most dramatic incidents in the California gold rush, but Manly says the book was meant not as entertainment but as "a plain, unvarnished tale of truth." As Lawrence Clark Powell notes, Manly's "chronicle of death and disaster, survival and heroism" is distinguished "by narrative power, specific event, and precise observation." Manly's straightforward narrative style and his eye for detail memorably evoke the pioneers' despair, exhaustion, and helplessness during their ordeal and the euphoria of arrival. Manly and Rogers are forced to eat crows and hawks and to sleep cramped together "spoon fashion" in order to share the one blanket they have. At another point they are so dehydrated they cannot swallow meat. But their loyalty to their friends stranded in the desert is unwavering. *Death Valley in '49* is not only a drama of endurance, hardship, and survival but of sacrifice, selfless privation, and personal courage on behalf of others.

Despite Manly's title, "the riches of the book," in Powell's words, are not limited to the chapters on Death Valley. "Literary power and human interest" mark the narrative throughout and Manly records many of the complex interactions between whites, Mexicans, and indigenous tribes on the American frontier. *Death Valley in '49* was praised when it first appeared, and it remains an important piece of western Americana, both as a historical account and as a literary work.

Manly died in San Jose and is buried in the Woodbridge Cemetery near Lodi, California. Manly Pass and Manly Peak in the Slate Range in southern California are named after him.

• Manly's letters and maps are housed in the Palmer and Jayhawker collections at the Huntington Library. Manly's diary and a 300-page letter to his parents were destroyed in a fire. *The Jayhawkers' Oath and Other Sketches*, ed. Arthur Woodward (1949), contains sketches Manly contributed to the *San Jose Pioneer* during the 1880s and 1890s. Leroy Johnson and Jean Johnson reprint the California desert sections of "From Vermont to California" in *Escape from Death Valley* (1987). The Johnsons' book also contains the most accurate retracings of Manly and John Rogers's routes through the desert. Lawrence Clark Powell has a chapter on Manly in *California Classics: The Creative Literature of the Golden State* (1971). Patricia Nelson Limerick, *Desert Passages: Encounters with the American Deserts* (1989), compares Manly's work to other depictions of the desert. Manly is also the subject of a novel by George Snell Dixon, *And—If Man Triumph* (1938).

MICHAEL KOWALEWSKI

MANN, Ambrose Dudley (26 Apr. 1801–15 Nov. 1889), diplomat, was born of unknown parentage at Hanover Court House, Virginia. Educated at rural schools in Virginia and Kentucky, he briefly attended the U.S. Military Academy in 1823 but left West Point to marry Hebe Grayson Carter and embark on a mercantile career. The couple would have one child. He also read law and speculated in real estate, but over a period of almost two decades, his business ventures all eventually failed. Active in the Kentucky Democratic party, he was rescued from financial distress in 1842, when President John Tyler (1790–1862) appointed him U.S. consul at Bremen in Germany.

After completing his consular service in 1845, Mann became a roving diplomatic agent of James K. Polk's administration. It was on Mann's advice that the United States precipitately opened diplomatic relations with the abortive "Federal Government of Germany" at Frankfort, and it was owing to his efforts that commercial treaties were signed with several small German states. Meanwhile he traveled throughout western Europe in 1847, accumulating a huge body of information to help formulate an immigration policy for the United States. He was enthusiastic about the 1848 republican revolution in Germany, of which he was an eyewitness, and bitterly disappointed when it failed.

While an attaché at the American legation at Paris in 1849, Mann was sent by Secretary of State John M. Clayton on a secret mission to grant diplomatic recognition to the regime of Lajos Kossuth in Hungary, which was crushed by the Austrians before Mann arrived. His instructions fell into the hands of the Austrian foreign minister, whose remonstrances provoked spirited rejoinders from Clayton's successor, Daniel Webster, creating serious tension between the two governments. Mann was sent to Bern to negotiate a convention establishing diplomatic relations between the United States and Switzerland, which the Senate ratified in March 1851.

For the next two years Mann served as a peripatetic commercial agent to various German states; then from April 1853 until 8 May 1855 he occupied the newly created position of assistant secretary of state in Franklin Pierce's administration. After he violated instructions not publicly to support the annexation schemes of southern slaveholders directed primarily against the Spanish colony of Cuba, which were revealed in embarrassing newspaper stories discussing the Ostend Manifesto of October 1854, he was dismissed by Secretary of State William Marcy, carrying into retirement letters of praise from several of Marcy's predecessors.

From 1855 to 1861 Mann sought to further the economic autonomy of the southern slave states by working to establish a steamship connection between Virginia and Europe. He avidly pushed this project both in pamphlets and in articles in *DeBow's Review*. Although the Virginia legislature actually chartered a corporation to establish this "ocean ferry," the scheme was never carried out.

Mann's experience as a trade negotiator in Europe and his interest in maritime commerce were probably what led to his appointment as a Confederate special commissioner to Europe in 1861, along with William L. Yancey and Pierre A. Rost. Prior to his arrival in England, Mann was reported by the British consul at Charleston to be of questionable moral character, apparently because of his history of business failures, which may have adversely affected his reception by Her Majesty's government. A secretary at the U.S. legation in London described him from close observation as "thick, short and rather heavy," speaking softly and slowly "with a decided southern accent," and looking more distinguished than he was. Frank Owsley, a close student of Mann's labors as a Confederate

diplomatic envoy, described him as "full of words and wind," possessing "great vanity and ego," but also exuding social charm that won him many "friends in high places" (*King Cotton Diplomacy*, 2d ed. [1959], p. 52).

Replaced in London by James M. Mason early in 1862, Mann produced no significant achievements in his year there nor in his subsequent three years in Belgium. Intrigue and exhort as he might, he could not shake the resolution of the British and Belgian governments to remain neutral in regard to the American Civil War. Nor did a journey by Mann to Rome in November 1863 as a special envoy to try to persuade the pope officially to recognize the southern Confederacy succeed.

After the war ended in 1865, Mann expressed no interest in returning to the reunited states. Instead he settled in Paris, where he entertained southern visitors and maintained a voluminous correspondence but otherwise lived in the retirement of old age until his death there.

• In his old age Mann wrote an account of his diplomatic career, but it was never published, and its whereabouts is unknown. Portions of his correspondence during the Civil War years may be found in the Records of the Confederate States of America ("Pickett Papers"), the James Murray Mason Papers, and the Henry Hotze Papers, all at the Library of Congress. Many of these communications have been printed in *The Official Records of the Union and Confederate Navies in the War of the Rebellion*, ser. 2, vol. 3 (30 vols., 1894–1922), and James D. Richardson, ed., *The Messages and Papers of Jefferson Davis and the Confederacy Including Diplomatic Correspondence, 1861–1865*, vol. 2 (1905; repr. 1966). Some of Mann's wartime letters to Jefferson Davis are in the Emory University Library. Missives from the postwar period may be found in John Preston Moore, ed., *"My Ever Dearest Friend": The Letters of A. Dudley Mann to Jefferson Davis, 1869–1889* (1960), which also contains the best available biographical sketch of Mann. A fuller biographical treatment has not yet been published. Brief summaries of all four of Mann's major missions in Europe for the U.S. government are in Henry M. Wriston, *Executive Agents in American Foreign Relations* (1929; repr. 1967). A physical description of Mann may be found in Sarah A. Wallace and Frances E. Gillespie, eds., *The Journal of Benjamin Moran, 1857–1865*, vol. 1, p. 799. (1949). Mann's obituary is in the *New York Daily Tribune*, 1 Dec. 1889.

NORMAN B. FERRIS

MANN, Erika Julia Hedwig (9 Nov. 1905–27 Aug. 1969), writer and actress, was born in Munich, Germany, the eldest daughter of Thomas Mann, Nobel Prize–winning writer, and Katia Pringsheim. Despite Mann's many achievements, she is still better known as the daughter of Thomas Mann and sister of Klaus Mann, author of *Mephisto*. Her family included many other celebrated writers, including uncle Heinrich Mann (*The Blue Angel*), maternal great-grandmother Hedwig Dohm (*Sibilla Dalmar*), and Mann's poet-husband W. H. Auden (*The Age of Anxiety*). As a child Mann moved in the circles of the brightest, wealthiest, and most famous. She paid little heed to formal education and barely passed her *Abitur* (college entrance) examination in 1924; instead, she cultivated artistic circles and notoriety by exploiting public interest in the Mann family. While still in her teens, Mann began a prolific and highly publicized acting career with Germany's most prominent director, Max Reinhardt, in Berlin.

Mann's early life and much of her adulthood can scarcely be considered apart from those of her brother Klaus, with whom she shared an extraordinarily close, probably incestuous, bond. The siblings emphasized their androgyny and falsely proclaimed themselves "twins." Several of Klaus Mann's fictional characters are modeled on his sister, most notably Barbara Bruckner of his novel *Mephisto*. The Hendrik Höfgen character of the same novel closely resembles Mann's first husband, Gustaf Gründgens, a then-unknown actor whom she impulsively married on 24 July 1926 and who reached prominence during the Third Reich. Their personal, professional, and ideological paths soon diverged, and they divorced in January 1929.

During the 1920s Mann had little sense of political, familial, or social responsibility. Her writings of that period betray a complete failure to grasp the nature of social inequity and oppression (the very crux of her mature writings), and her interest in her father's 1929 Nobel Prize for Literature centered on how the prize money would pay off her debts. Her major works of this period, coauthored with brother Klaus, were accounts of their flamboyant travels around the world (*Rundherum*, 1929) and to the Riviera (*Das Buch von der Riviera*, 1931).

The political upheaval of 1933 caused Mann to make fundamental changes in her life and public image. Her books, essays, and lectures evolved into passionate defenses against fascism, and the literary/political cabaret that she founded along with actress Therese Giehse, "Die Pfeffermühle," created a sensation with its biting attacks on the Nazi regime. After leaving Germany on 13 March 1933, the cabaret troupe traveled through Europe and played a crucial role in uniting the exile community, highlighting the dangers of German national socialism and introducing political dimensions to European cabaret. Recognizing a powerful threat to the image of their regime abroad, the Nazis tried to prevent the cabaret's performances with diplomatic and physical force. Eventually Mann was forced to leave Europe and begin her career anew in the United States. Her expatriation from Germany became official on 8 June 1935. Exactly one week later Mann entered into a marriage of convenience with the poet W. H. Auden in order to obtain a British passport. Their marriage, which lasted to the end of Mann's life, resulted in a lasting friendship and a rich literary symbiosis.

In September 1936 Mann emigrated to the United States. Her cabaret, now called "The Pepper Mill," was not well received in Manhattan and ultimately folded, despite sparkling translations by Auden and musical adaptations by Aaron Copland. Switching from the stage to the lectern, Mann quickly became a much-sought-after lecturer during the war years and beyond. Her commanding (5'9") presence, combined with her clear and forceful messages, mesmerized audiences. She lectured on the evils of nazism and campaigned for U.S. intervention in World War II. Fellow exile novelist Joseph Roth wrote that Mann did "more to combat the barbarism [of Hitler's Germany] than all writers put together." She initially stressed the existence of a better, "other" Germany that would bring about Hitler's downfall. Her confidence in a German resistance movement ebbed, however, and her later journalism was marked by extreme bitterness toward her native land. Mann insisted that the Allied occupation should reeducate the German people completely to cleanse them of deeply ingrained fascist thinking. Her controversial standpoint made her the target of attacks but also won her admiration and praise. Her friends and collaborators in the United States included Franklin D. Roosevelt and Eleanor Roosevelt, Dorothy Thompson, and Carson McCullers.

Mann's 1938 book *School for Barbarians*, which described the miseducation of German youth under nazism, sold over 40,000 copies within three months of publication. The strength of this work lies in its ability to analyze a broad spectrum of problems that resulted from Hitler's dictatorship, beyond the obvious imperialism and racism that framed his program, including for example, the linguistic deterioration that took place in Germany. Two political analyses coauthored with brother Klaus depicted the situation in Germany (*The Other Germany*, 1940) and of those who left (*Escape to Life*, 1939). The political prescience and linguistic nuance of her journalism, which appeared regularly in such publications as the *New York Herald Tribune*, *Vogue*, *Liberty*, and the *Toronto Star*, assured her a devoted readership. In June and July of 1938 Mann reported from the front lines in Spain on the antifascist army's struggle against Franco; in the 1940s her work as an accredited American war correspondent led her throughout war-torn Europe. She was granted assignments of unusual sensitivity, such as interviewing the major war criminals on trial in Nuremberg.

Despite her firm identification with the United States, Mann never established a permanent domicile in this country, but choosing instead an itinerant life with extended stays at the Hotel Bedford in New York City, the Princeton and Pacific Palisades residences of her parents, and a series of upper berths in Pullman trains as she traveled to her many speaking engagements. Mann stated her intention of becoming an American citizen from the time of her arrival in the United States, and in the mid-1940s she initiated the formal application process. She volunteered her services to the FBI in identifying Nazis posing as German refugees. By December 1950, however, she withdrew her citizenship application because of the political climate of the McCarthy era, which in her case resulted in extended, grueling interrogations of her circle of acquaintances and herself by the FBI, with its unfounded suspicions of Mann's links to communist groups. These investigations led to doubts concerning her integrity, brought her career as a lecturer to a standstill, robbed her of her professional credibility and financial security, and altered her status from prominent member of American society to humiliated and suspect alien. Deeply disillusioned by both her native and adopted homelands, she, along with her parents, returned permanently to their original station-in-exile, Zurich, where Erika Mann remained until her death.

A combination of resignation, cynicism, and poor physical health prevented Mann from writing in the 1950s and 1960s; she devoted herself instead to editing and ensuring publication of the works of her aging father and her brother Klaus, who had committed suicide in 1949. During Thomas Mann's last years, Erika Mann structured, edited, and revised his works; she also wrote screenplays for and supervised cinematic versions of nine of his novellas and novels. After her father's death in 1955, Mann edited his letters in three volumes and wrote innumerable tributes to him, most notably her last major work, *The Last Year: A Memoir of My Father* (1958).

Thomas Mann scholars are sharply divided in their assessments of Erika Mann's supervisory role in molding her father's image for posterity. Most have lauded her mammoth project of compiling and annotating Thomas Mann's massive correspondence into what continues to be the standard edition; others have attacked her for suppressing unfavorable aspects of a man whose complex development included flirtations with hawkishness and bigotry. Her own many writings, some hastily composed, others finely polished, all impassioned appeals for human dignity and freedom, stand as compelling documents of literary and historical interest. Her greatest contribution was without doubt her skilled use of a variety of media to educate and mobilize a European and then an American public to take a firm and interventionist stand against Hitler.

• The Erika Mann Archives are located in the Handschriftenabteilung der Stadtbibliothek München (Manuscript Division of the Munich Municipal Library). In addition to her major works mentioned above, Mann edited the following volumes: *Klaus Mann zum Gedächtnis* (1950), *Thomas Mann Briefe* (3 vols. 1961–1963), *Thomas Mann, Autobiographisches* (1968), and *Thomas Mann, Eine Auslese* (1969). She also wrote a series of children's books: *Stoffel fliegt übers Meer* (1932), *Muck, der Zauberonkel* (1934), *A Gang of Ten* (1942), *Unser Zauberonkel Muck* (1952), *Christoph fliegt nach Amerika* (1953), and the *Zugvogel* tetralogy (1953–1955). An example of her regular contributions to newspapers, journals, and anthologies is her essay on the dangers Hitler posed to America, "Don't Make the Same Mistakes," in *Zero Hour: A Summons to the Free* (1940), pp. 13–76. The most comprehensive account of Mann's life and writings emerges from her letters, published in two volumes as *Erika Mann, Briefe und Antworten*, vols. 1 and 2 (1984–1985), edited by Anna Zanco Prestel. Other valuable sources include Ursula Hummel and Eva Chrambach, *Klaus und Erika Mann: Bilder und Dokumente* (1990), and Helga Keiser-Hayne's overview of the Pfeffermühle cabaret in *Beteiligt euch. Es geht um eure Erde* (1990). Two articles on Erika Mann in English, both by Shelley Frisch, are "'Alien Homeland': Erika Mann and the Adenauer Era," *Germanic Review* 6, no. 4 (1988): 172–82, and "The Pfeffermühle: Political Dimensions of a Literary Cabaret," in *Exile Literature and the Other Arts* (1990), pp. 141–53. See also Walter Berendsohn, *Thomas Mann und die Seinen* (1973), and Marcel Reich-Ranicki, *Thomas Mann and His Family* (1989), as well as Katia Mann, *Unwritten Memories* (1975). An obituary is in the *New York Times*, 3 Sept. 1969.

SHELLEY FRISCH

MANN, Frank Charles (11 Sept. 1887–30 Sept. 1962), experimental physiologist and physician, was born in Adams County, Indiana, the son of Joseph E. Mann and Louisa Kiess. Mann's parents were homesteaders on the Hoosier frontier, and his early rearing consisted of chores around the family farm. His interest in medicine arose early in childhood. "By the time I was six years of age," Mann wrote in his autobiography, "I had determined to be a doctor" (p. 2). He attended high school in Decatur, Indiana, and then Marion Normal College and Indiana University. From the latter institution, Mann received a B.A. in 1911. Although accepted by the medical school at the Johns Hopkins University, Mann attended Indiana's medical school for financial reasons. In 1913 Indiana awarded him an M.D. and the following year an M.A. for his work on surgical shock.

Mann's career in medical research began during his medical education at Indiana, with the repetition of J. S. Edkins's experiments on gastric secretin. Mann made extracts of secretin from the gastric mucosa of more than a dozen animal species and observed secretion of acidic gastric juice in cats, upon intravenous injection of the extracts. Although he had a prolific career in experimental medicine, Mann's first interest in medicine was surgery. "At the end of my junior year in medicine," he wrote again in his autobiography, "I knew I was going to be a surgeon" (p. 3). However, his first employment opportunity came from the Mayo Clinic in Rochester, Minnesota. On 10 April 1914 Mann began at the clinic as chief of the Laboratory of Experimental Surgery and Pathology. That July he married Velma J. Daniels; the couple would have three children. The following year the University of Minnesota incorporated the Mayo Foundation, and Mann became an assistant professor of experimental surgery at the university. In 1916 the American Physiological Society elected him to membership.

During the First World War, Mann was a second lieutenant in the Medical Corps and conducted experiments on surgical shock. His early research at the Mayo also included work on hemorrhage, endocrinology, gastroenterology, and other related topics. In 1918 the university promoted him to associate professor. The subject on which Mann spent most of his career, however, was hepatic physiology. The impetus for his studies on the liver arose from an autopsy report that he had read serendipitously: "if a human being could live with such a small amount of hepatic tissue," reasoned Mann, "it might be possible for an animal to live without any liver tissue" (Mann, p. 8). In 1921 Mann published his first paper in which he removed the liver from dogs. The effect of the hepatectomy was hypoglycemic shock and death—results that, according to Mann, surprised him. Injection of glucose into comatose dogs led to their dramatic resuscitation, indicating the importance of the liver in carbohydrate metabolism. Success with the studies on the liver also forced him to recognize, wrote Mann later, that his career was experimental medicine and not surgery. He was appointed, in 1921, full professor of experimental surgery at the university and then full professor of experimental medicine six years later. During his career Mann promoted the combination of surgical (ablation) and chemical techniques to elucidate the physiological functions of organs, particularly the liver.

In 1924 Mann became director of the newly created Institute of Experimental Medicine by the Mayo Foundation. He played a prominent role in establishing the Mayo as an institution where surgeons could be trained for careers in experimental medicine. On 9 December 1927 Mann delivered a Harvey Lecture, "The Relation of the Liver to Metabolism," in which he reported on the role of the liver in the maintenance of life through carbohydrate, protein, and lipid metabolism. In his 1936 Mellon Lecture, Mann again stressed the importance of the liver's role in the maintenance of life, a role he designated as the "Commissariat of the Body." In 1932 the Philadelphia Pathological Society bestowed on Mann its William Wood Gerhard Gold Medal. The next year the Mayo Foundation appointed him to its board of governors, on which he remained until 1948. Mann served for several years as secretary of the American Physiological Society before being elected president of the society for the year 1936–1937. He was active in the preparations for the semicentennial celebrations of the society in 1938. Involved in founding the editorial board of the *Annual Review of Physiology* in 1939, he served as its chair for an extended term. He also contributed several reviews on liver physiology to the periodical. In 1942 he was honored with the establishment of a lectureship bearing his name, at Indiana University, by the medical fraternity Phi Beta Pi.

During World War II, Mann worked on the National Research Council's Surgical Shock Subcommittee. After the war he served on the Physiology Study Section of the National Institutes of Health, until his retirement in 1952. In 1950 the National Academy of Sciences elected him a member of the academy. From 1951 to 1953 he also served on the National Advisory Council's Gastrointestinal Cancer Committee. Mann retired from the Mayo Clinic and Foundation in September 1952, at which time the Frank C. Mann Hall in the new Mayo Medical Sciences Building was dedicated to him. The following year the American College of Surgeons elected him an honorary member. In 1953 Mann published his last review on hepatic physiology in collaboration with his eldest son, capping a publication total of more than 400 papers. The American Gas-

troenterological Association awarded Mann in 1955 the Julius Friedenwald Medal. Mann died in Rochester, Minnesota. His work in experimental pathology, particularly with the liver, has assured his position in the history of scientific medicine in the United States.

• Mann's Papers are housed privately at the Mayo Historical Unit, Mayo Foundation, Rochester, Minn. His autobiographical account is "To the Physiologically Inclined," *Annual Review of Physiology* 17 (1955): 1–15. For a comprehensive biographical account and an extensive list of his writings, see Maurice B. Visscher, "Frank Charles Mann, 1887–1962," National Academy of Sciences, *Biographical Memoirs* 30 (1965): 161–204. For shorter biographical accounts, see Charles W. Greene, "The American Physiological Society: History of the Second Quarter Century," in *History of the American Physiological Society Semicentennial, 1887–1937* (1938); Hiram E. Essex, "Dr. Frank C. Mann," *Physiologist* 6 (1963): 66–69; and Toby A. Appel and Orr E. Reynolds, "Presidents, 1888–1962," in *History of the American Physiological Society: The First Century, 1887–1987* (1987). An obituary is in the *New York Times*, 2 Oct. 1962.

JAMES A. MARCUM

MANN, Horace (4 May 1796–2 Aug. 1859), educator and social reformer, was born in Franklin, Massachusetts, the son of Thomas Mann and Rebecca Stanley, farmers. Although earlier historical accounts that described his childhood as impoverished are inaccurate (his family was moderately prosperous), they are correct in their assertion that Mann's values were shaped during childhood by his family, his community, and in no small part by his relations with the local Congregationalist preacher, Nathaniel Emmons. After a lengthy struggle with the minister's undiluted Calvinism, Mann ultimately rejected orthodox religious dogma when, following the accidental drowning of his brother Stephen in 1810, Emmons relegated his brother to the ranks of the eternally damned. Unwilling to farm for a living, Mann determined to escape Franklin's narrow confines.

While college offered a means of advancement, Mann's limited secondary education (received in doses of a few weeks each winter at a nearby district school) presented an obstacle. He entered into a period of self-preparation in Latin and at nineteen took instruction in Greek from Samuel Barrett, an itinerant schoolmaster. Mann received further instruction, in mathematics, from the Reverend William Williams, a Baptist minister in nearby Wrentham. In the fall of 1816 Mann journeyed to Providence, Rhode Island, and gained admittance to the sophomore class at Brown. By dint of hard work, he not only overcame his remaining deficiencies but flourished. Eventually named president of the United Brothers, a literary society, Mann graduated at the top of his class in 1819. Determined to enter the legal field, he then read law in the office of Josiah J. Fiske back in Wrentham. Mann missed the mental stimulation of his Brown classmates and quickly became bored with the dull routine of office work. He had decided to enter Judge Tapping Reeve's renowned law school in Litchfield, Connecticut, when he received an offer to return to his alma mater as a tutor; after weighing his options, he returned to Brown in early 1820.

Mann found that life on the other side of the desk at Brown held few fascinations for him. Following his earlier intentions, he entered Litchfield law school in early 1822. As New England suffered from a surfeit of lawyers, graduation from the school provided no guarantee of employment. After considering various locations, Mann moved to the town of Dedham, Massachusetts, where he read law for almost another year in the office of attorney James Richardson before passing the Norfolk County bar in December 1823.

Although Mann's practice grew slowly at first (he often served as a collection agent for rural creditors), honors began to come his way. Asked to deliver Dedham's annual Fourth of July oration in 1823, he made such an impression that he was asked to give another speech in July 1826 commemorating Thomas Jefferson and John Adams, both of whom died on 4 July of that year. He started receiving business from Boston firms and was sufficiently successful to lend money on the side. In addition, he entered a business partnership with another brother, Stanley, in a series of textile mills. He also entered public life, beginning as the moderator of the Dedham Town Meeting, and in May 1827 was elected to the Massachusetts General Court (the lower house of the state legislature). His most significant effort as an elected representative was to back the move to provide state support for the construction of a private railroad line between Boston and New York's Hudson River. With the passage of the legislation, Mann gained his first experience in harnessing the power of the state to achieve reform; it would not be his last. In the midst of his legislative dealings, Mann married Charlotte Messer, the daughter of Brown University president Asa Messer, in Providence in September 1830; the couple had no children.

In the same year as his marriage Mann for the first time took a leading part in the reform movement that so characterized the era and that was to hold him in its sway for the rest of his life. Following reports of the shameful conditions under which the insane of Massachusetts often lived, Mann shepherded a bill through the legislature (signed into law in March 1830) that provided for the construction of a state insane asylum. Located in Worcester and possessing a capacity for 120 persons, the facility was a vast improvement over the filthy jail cells that had been the standard lot for the commonwealth's less fortunate citizens. Although totally unschooled in social work, architecture, and facility management, Mann and his fellow commissioners oversaw all facets of the facility's construction and selected its first superintendent, Dr. Samuel B. Woodward, as well.

Although the new facility opened amid acclaim in January 1833, Mann was in no mood to celebrate. His wife's health, never robust, had earlier collapsed, and in August 1832 she died. Mann immediately went into an emotional tailspin from which he was years in recovering. Adding to his distress was the impending failure of his brother's businesses, for which he had cosigned several notes. After moving to Boston, he briefly lived in a boardinghouse (where he met and befriended the Peabody sisters, Mary and Elizabeth—then engaged in editing as well as keeping school) before moving his belongings into his office in a further attempt to reduce his expenses. Attempts on the part of friends to revive his spirits met with only fleeting success. Although Mann remained busy, even his work brought him little solace.

Mann had long been involved with the temperance movement and by the mid-1830s had become a leader of that movement's moderate faction, which sought to eliminate alcohol abuse by use of logic and moral suasion. Having left the state legislature in 1832, he was urged by friends to return to public life. He briefly led a committee investigating the burning of the Ursuline convent of Cambridge in August 1834, only to have to resign when his health failed. Mann then reluctantly allowed his name to be placed in nomination as a Whig candidate for the state senate that fall. Elected in the Whig landslide, he became senate president in the following year.

Upon returning to the legislature, Mann initially focused on reforming debtor laws. His greatest endeavor, however, began with the passage of an act creating a state board of education in April 1837. Providing for a ten-member board (consisting of the governor, lieutenant governor, and eight appointed citizens), the bill also mandated the hiring of a secretary, who was to make annual reports to the legislature. Although the sponsor of the bill, James G. Carter, was expected to be appointed to the position, Mann was chosen instead. Many of Mann's friends were openly dubious about his giving up a senate seat and a possible chance at the governorship for an enterprise that seemed nebulous at best. Mann, however, was undismayed. While he remained ambitious, his wife's death caused him to lose all interest in material attainments by this time, and he seized upon this opportunity to make his mark in service to others.

The task that awaited him was daunting. Although Massachusetts had had a school district system in place since 1789, in reality the public schools were a disgrace. Exceptions existed, but classes were generally conducted in poorly equipped buildings during short, erratic wintertime sessions by teachers whose preparation for their task was as poor as their salaries. No formal teacher training programs existed on any level, and textbooks were equally varied in both content and quality. Mann viewed the establishment of a public school system as an opportunity for the uplifting of all individuals within society; indeed, in the face of increased immigration and the movement of individuals from the farm to the factory, he viewed the creation of such a system as vital to society's very survival. In his attempt to create a system of public schools that would equalize educational opportunity as well as mold individuals into more productive members of society, Mann brooked no opposition to his vision.

Those who did try to thwart his quest were deemed by him ignorant, ill informed, or narrowly partisan.

What Mann possessed in enthusiasm was unmatched by authority; his secretaryship, which paid a mere $1,000 annually, empowered him only to collect and disseminate information. Having gathered statistical data from around the state by circulating a written questionnaire, Mann set out on a series of local meetings across the commonwealth during his first year in office. While responses varied from location to location, he was generally successful in arousing the interest of locally influential citizens. Not content with personal appearances to advance his arguments, he began the *Common School Journal*, a twice-monthly magazine, in 1838 and remained its editor for ten years. As a means of informing the public, however, his twelve annual reports (1837–1848) while secretary were unsurpassed. Chock full of statistical data, the reports—which were widely read and circulated—presented the problems of the common schools as well as possible solutions.

Mann viewed improved teacher training as a priority. Blessed with a gift of $10,000 from education benefactor Edmund Dwight, Mann anonymously presented the donation to the state legislature with the proviso that the state match the amount in providing for teacher training facilities. Local municipalities soon clamored to be chosen for the new experiment, and in January 1839 the nation's first "normal" school opened its doors in Lexington; two more such institutions soon were established in Barre and Bridgewater. Noting that many current teachers could not afford to attend the normal schools, Mann set up local two-week training institutes as well as annual county educational conventions that allowed teachers and administrators to meet and exchange ideas.

Mann's attempts at such radical reform inevitably led some to question both his motives and purpose. By seeking to create nonsectarian school systems with centralized administrations, Mann was accused on several occasions of instituting "Godless" schools. One such controversy erupted in 1844, when a group of thirty-one schoolmasters from Boston published a sharply worded critique of his seventh *Annual Report*. Attacking Mann's recommendations for teacher training as well as his opposition to corporal punishment among other targets, the group soon faced Mann's wrath in the form of written rejoinders. A group of Mann's allies were elected to the Boston School Committee, and in the following year they issued a report that devastated the schoolmasters' position. Given the scope of Mann's exertions, however, it is surprising that he encountered as little overall resistance as he did. Although contemporary and later biographers cast the controversies that did erupt as pitting an enlightened Mann and his supporters against the reactionary orthodox clergy of his day, in reality Mann's proposals enjoyed a broad base of support among both orthodox and liberal clerics.

In May 1844 Mann married Mary Peabody, with whom he was to have three children. The newlyweds sailed for Europe, accompanied by Mann's longtime friend and noted educator of the blind Samuel Gridley Howe. Mann was eager to learn as much as possible about local school systems abroad, particularly the vaunted Prussian system. On his return to the United States in November 1844 Mann set out to merge the best that he found in European educational systems with the principles of the growing American common school movement. Within a few years, the results were remarkable. Having already succeeded at increasing the term of the school year to six months in 1839, Mann oversaw the expenditure of more than $2 million by the state in pursuit of better schoolhouses and equipment. Teacher salaries improved by more than 50 percent, and fifty new high schools opened during his tenure as secretary. Desiring uniform instructional materials, the board of education commissioned a Boston publisher to print 100 different titles of common school textbooks. Concerned with the physical condition of the students, Mann made sure that at least an hour a day was devoted to exercise and health education.

While Mann had been occupied with the development of public schools, political controversies such as the potential spread of slavery within the United States continued to mount on the national level. Following the death of Representative John Quincy Adams, the former president, in February 1848, Mann was elected that April to the U.S. House of Representatives to complete the remainder of Adams's term while remaining as secretary of the Massachusetts Board of Education. Elected with the support of both Conscience Whigs (antislavery) and Cotton (those willing to equivocate on the issue) Whigs, Mann sought to tread a fine line in Congress. Opposed to slavery—though not an abolitionist—and the Mexican War, Mann feared that entering into partisan debates would harm not only his work on behalf of public education but would erode his attempts to check the advance of slavery as well. His efforts to rise above the fray pleased neither half of his constituency, and he added to his workload by agreeing to direct the legal defense of Daniel Drayton and Edward Sayers, who were charged with aiding escaped slaves in the District of Columbia. Although initially convicted, the two men were eventually released after lengthy appeals. After being reelected to the House in the fall of 1848, Mann prepared his twelfth and final report as school secretary and resigned the post shortly thereafter.

During his first full congressional term, Mann was appointed a visitor at West Point and tried to assist Nathaniel Hawthorne, his wife's brother-in-law, when the author lost his position at the Salem (Mass.) Custom House. The slavery issue, however, would not go away, and by placing himself in opposition to Henry Clay's Compromise of 1850 Mann alienated many in the Whig party, none more than Senator Daniel Webster, whose support of the compromise floored Mann. Forced out of the Whig party by Webster's supporters, Mann sought vindication under the banner of the Free Soil party in 1850. Narrowly reelected, he was unable to mount an effort to repeal the odious fugitive slave law of 1851; the following year he failed to win the Massachusetts governorship as the Free Soil candidate.

Content to leave the turmoil of Congress behind him, Mann, after considerable thought, accepted the presidency of the newly founded Antioch College in Yellow Springs, Ohio. Founded by a religious group called the Christian Connexion, the college was to be coeducational as well as nonsectarian, making it doubly unusual for the time. When he arrived on campus in September 1853, he faced as great a challenge as any he had encountered. Most of the students were ill prepared for college, and the school's physical facilities were barely half-completed. Because the president's house was unfinished as well, Mann and his family temporarily lived in a dormitory without running water. Worst of all was the abysmal state of the college's finances. Shoddy accounting by the school's treasurer was compounded by the school's ill-advised attempts to raise money by selling scholarships to potential students to the college at a pittance ($100 for perpetual rights) that did not even begin to cover the college's expenses. Doomed to endless struggle to pay even faculty salaries, Mann was forced to travel constantly on behalf of the school in a largely fruitless effort to raise additional funds.

Despite the financial burdens, Mann was determined to mold the college after his own ideas. He himself taught courses in political economy and moral philosophy and insisted that all faculty members actually teach, rather than deliver memorized recitations as was then common in American higher education. Accordingly, he made the inclusion of teacher education courses a priority at the school. More unusual still was the practice of allowing students to select courses that interested them after they had completed a basic core curriculum. Perhaps most typical of Mann was his firm intention that a diploma from Antioch would stamp its holder as both a moral and an educated human being.

The years of financial struggle led, however, to the college being sold at auction and reorganized in 1859. Exhausted by his protracted burdens, Mann gave what was probably his greatest speech at the commencement exercises that year. After exhorting the graduates to aim at self-improvement and service on behalf of others, he closed by imploring the graduates to "be ashamed to die until you have won some great victory for humanity." Mann became ill shortly after commencement day and died at his home in Yellow Springs.

Known as the "father of the American public school," Mann was worthy of that title. In an era when the perfectibility of man was a widely shared dream, Mann was a leading prophet. Obsessed with reform, he made contributions in many areas and by example encouraged others (such as Henry Barnard) to undertake like-minded reforms in other parts of the United States. Although modern-day failings in the public education system have led some to criticize Mann as the creator of an institution that stifles, rather than rewards, creativity and initiative, he nevertheless deserves a great deal of credit for bringing about badly needed reforms in a number of areas of American life.

• The papers of Horace Mann are divided among several repositories. The largest collection is held by the Massachusetts Historical Society, Boston; smaller collections are held at the Dedham Historical Society; Houghton Library, Harvard University; Chicago Historical Society; Horace Mann School, New York City; the Library of Congress; and Brown University archives. Mann wrote *Letters on Education* (1845) and *Slavery: Letters and Speeches* (1851). The best contemporary work on him is *Life and Works of Horace Mann*, ed. Mary T. Mann and George Combe Mann (5 vols., 1865–1891). The most comprehensive recent study is Jonathan Messerli, *Horace Mann: A Biography* (1972); also useful are R. B. Downs, *Horace Mann: Champion of the Public Schools* (1974), and Carl F. Kaestle and Maris A. Vinovskis, *Education and Social Change in Nineteenth-century Massachusetts* (1980). An obituary is in the *New York Times*, 3 Aug. 1859.

EDWARD L. LACH, JR.

MANN, James (22 July 1759–7 Nov. 1832), physician and military surgeon, was born in Wrentham, Massachusetts, the son of David Mann and Anna (maiden name unknown). After graduating from Harvard in 1776, Mann studied medicine with Dr. Samuel Danforth of Boston. He joined the Continental army on 1 July 1779 as a surgeon of the 4th Massachusetts Regiment. In 1781 he was captured and imprisoned on Long Island by the British for two months. The following year, having resigned from military service because of ill health, he opened a private practice in Wrentham. In 1788 he married Martha Tyler, with whom he had five children. At this time he began writing the first of the many scientific articles he was to publish in the course of his lifetime. His contributions to medical literature during this period twice brought him Harvard's Boylston prize, in 1803 for a paper on children's diseases and in 1806 for an article on dysentery. He became a member of the Massachusetts Medical Society in 1803.

With the outbreak of the War of 1812, Mann resumed his career as an army surgeon. He managed a series of hospitals in New York State and Vermont, where he gained an enviable reputation for his administrative skill. His opinions on hospital design came to be particularly highly regarded. His experiences in the War of 1812 were the subject of his best-known publication, *Medical Sketches of the Campaigns of 1812, 13, 14, to which are added Surgical Cases, Observations on Military Hospitals; and Flying Hospitals Attached to a Moving Army, Also An Appendix*, which appeared in 1816. This volume covered the challenges Mann encountered in caring for military patients who, exposed to the rigors of winter without adequate blankets, bedding, or shelter, suffered from pneumonia as well as from the fevers, dysentery, and hepatitis endemic among the civilians living nearby, for whom he also cared.

Despite the recommendation of the head of the wartime medical department, James Tilton, Mann's position as the department's most senior surgeon, and the award of an honorary M.D. degree by Brown University, his request to remain in the service was denied when the Army was reduced in size after the end of hostilities in 1815. The next year, however, pleas addressed to influential political figures, including President James Madison (1751–1836), finally bore fruit. Mann was taken back into the army and was assigned as one of four hospital surgeons in the northeast.

Repeated reductions in the number of physicians in the army effectively eliminated the possibility of promotion for Mann. That a physician of obvious and well-recognized professional and administrative skill should be content to spend the rest of his life serving in a relatively humble capacity in the peacetime army is to a degree surprising. In this position, however, he was guaranteed the steady income that many in private practice could not achieve, and as one of the eight consulting physicians at the Massachusetts General Hospital in 1819 and as a member of such learned societies as the American Academy of Arts and Sciences, he enjoyed continued association with other noted scientists of his day. He was assigned first to Fort Independence in Boston harbor and then to Governor's Island in New York harbor, where he was serving as an assistant surgeon at the time of his death.

Although the era of modern medicine has long since transformed the scientific achievements of physicians of his era into curiosities, the respect owed to those who display courage and administrative ability on the scale achieved by Mann during the War of 1812 is unchanged by time.

• Mann is perhaps best known through his own writings, in particular his *Medical Sketches of the Campaigns of 1812, 13, 14* (1816). Many details about his work during the War of 1812 can also be found in Mary C. Gillett, *The Army Medical Department, 1776–1818* (1987). Willard Irving Tyler Brigham's *The Tyler Genealogy, the descendants of Job Tyler of Andover Massachusetts 1619–1700*, vol. 1 (1912), has a short overview of his life, and a brief mention of his work in Boston can be found in Nathaniel I. Bowditch, *A History of the Massachusetts Hospital* (1872). An obituary is in the *New York American*, 8 Nov. 1832.

MARY C. GILLETT

MANN, James Robert (20 Oct. 1856–30 Nov. 1922), congressman, was born near Bloomington, Illinois, the son of William Henry Mann, a horticulturist, and Elizabeth Abraham. Mann graduated from the University of Illinois at Urbana in 1876 and from Union College of Law (Chicago) in 1881. Admitted to the bar in 1881, he practiced law in Chicago in the firm of Mann & Miller. In 1882 he married Emma Columbia. Active in real estate in Hyde Park, he gained independent wealth that permitted him to turn to politics.

A Republican, he became attorney for the Hyde Park commissioners and the South Park commissioners of Chicago. His ability to bring the 1893 World's Columbian Exposition to Hyde Park resulted in his being sent to the Chicago Common Council, where he served for four years. Mann chaired the Republican County Conventions at Chicago in 1895 and 1902 and the Illinois State Republican Convention in 1897. He was elected to Congress in 1897, serving thirteen terms from the First Illinois District (1897–1922).

Mann possessed an acid wit, which he used with telling political effect to embarrass his opponents. His seniority in Congress and his association with Joseph Cannon, Speaker of the House, placed him in the center of congressional politics. Noted for his industry, he aspired to be Speaker of the House but was defeated by James Beauchamp "Champ" Clark. In 1912, when the Republicans lost control of the House, he became minority leader and resisted Democratic programs with diligence.

Mann was associated with much legislation during his long tenure in Congress. The White Slave Traffic Act of 1910, commonly known as the Mann Act, is his best-known legacy. The Mann-Elkins Act (1910) extended the regulatory authority of the Interstate Commerce Commission to include telephone, telegraph, and cable companies and authorized the establishment of a commerce court. He was instrumental in the passage of the Pure Food and Drugs Act (1906); was noted for tariff legislation, voting against the Paine-Aldrich Act of 1909 and opposing restrictions on Canadian paper and pulp; and contributed to the Bureau of Corporations Act, submitting a bill, in 1910, allowing corporations to seek federal registration under the act but leaving jurisdiction over corporations to individual states.

The Mann White Slave Traffic Act was considered "drastic and revolutionary" by the minority opposing it. Ostensibly written to stop the traffic in women and children for purposes of prostitution, it also contained the expression "for immoral purposes." As champion of this cause, Mann was responding to his Chicago constituents associated with the Chicago Vice Commission in 1909. Edwin W. Sims, the U.S. attorney from Chicago, wrote the first legislative draft. In 1913 the *Caminetti-Diggs* case (California) provided the U.S. Supreme Court the opportunity to establish the constitutionality of the act's novel use of the interstate commerce clause and provided a basis for regulating other moral behavior. Mann denounced President Woodrow Wilson and Attorney General James Clark McReynolds, linking them with Anthony Caminetti for their slowness in prosecuting the case.

Two years before his death, Mann had a nervous breakdown from which he never fully recovered. He faithfully attended congressional sessions despite his failing health.

Mann was noted for his attention to detail. An expert parliamentarian, he served as minority leader from the Sixty-second through the Sixty-fifth Congresses. Although his name is closely associated with the "white slave" law, he actively participated in the legislative process. Mann died at his home in Washington, D.C.

• James Mann destroyed his personal correspondence. The Library of Congress holds a voluminous collection, published in thirty-five volumes, of newspaper clippings and a scattering of letters. Brief sketches of his career are contained in *Biographical Directory of the American Congress* (1928); *Memorial Addresses Delivered in the House of Representatives . . . ,* 14 Jan. 1923 (1924); *New York Times,* 3 and 10 Dec. 1922; *Chicago Tribune* and *Evening Star* (Washington), 1 Dec. 1922. The Mann Act is dealt with in Norbert MacDonald, "The *Diggs-Caminetti* Case of 1913 and Subsequent Interpretation of the White Slave Trade Act," *Pacific Historian* 29, no. 1 (1985): 31–39; Marlene D. Beckman, "The White Slave Traffic Act: Historical Impact of a Federal Crime Policy on Women," *Women and Politics* 4, no. 3 (1984): 85–101; and William Seagle, "The Twilight of the Mann Act," *American Bar Association Journal* 55, no. 7 (1969): 641–47.

DAVID J. PIVAR

MANN, Klaus Heinrich Thomas (18 Nov. 1906–21 May 1949), writer, was born in Munich, Germany, the son of Thomas Mann, Nobel Prize-winning author, and Katia Pringsheim. The second child and eldest son, Mann felt oppressed by his father's celebrity, yet he exploited Thomas Mann's connections and finances throughout his life. His only lasting emotional bond was with his sister Erika Mann, on whom he was desperately dependent throughout his life. The contents of Mann's fiction and his life were nearly indistinguishable, and his many romans à clef gave literary form to familial and societal conflicts.

From his earliest childhood, Mann wrote poetry and plays, although he spurned formal education and did not complete high school. As a teenager, Mann organized his siblings and neighbors into an amateur acting troupe that performed classical theater as well as Mann's first known play, a drama in verse called *Ritter Blaubart* (Bluebeard the Knight). In the 1920s, a series of plays he wrote and produced created scandals throughout Germany, beginning with *Anja und Esther* (Anja and Esther, 1925). The media focused on this play because of its celebrity cast (Klaus and Erika Mann, the playwright Frank Wedekind's daughter Pamela, and Gustaf Gründgens) and its lesbian theme. Two additional plays, *Revue zu Vieren* (Four in Revue) and *Geschwister,* (Siblings) titillated audiences with thinly veiled portraits of the author and his sister, particularly in the case of *Geschwister,* which depicted sibling incest. An assignment as theater critic brought Mann to Berlin, where he frequented the city's many transvestite bars. Mann revealed his homosexuality quite openly in his life and also in his literary works, beginning with his earliest stories and particularly in his first novel, *Der fromme Tanz* (The Pious Dance, 1925).

Mann was an early and outspoken opponent of fascism. He left Germany on 13 March 1933 in protest of Hitler's rise to power and never returned to live there. Mann appeared on the Third Reich's first list of banned authors, issued on 23 April 1933. He spent the next few years in transit, living primarily in Paris and Amsterdam before he resettled in the United States. The main characters of Mann's polemical novels of this period, *Flucht in den Norden* (Journey into Freedom, 1934), *Mephisto* (1936), and *Der Vulkan* (The Volcano, 1939), grapple with the conflicting demands of personal fulfillment and political integrity during the years of the Third Reich. He was officially expatriated from Germany on 1 November 1934 but was granted Czech citizenship on 25 March 1937. Six years later, on 25 September 1943, Mann became a citizen of the United States.

In September 1933, Mann published the first issue of his literary and political journal *Die Sammlung* (The Collection) in Amsterdam; the journal became a leading voice of the early German exile. Its original patrons included Aldous Huxley, André Gide, and Mann's uncle Heinrich Mann. *Die Sammlung* printed viewpoints of a great variety of writers and thinkers from Albert Einstein to Ernest Hemingway. After the journal folded in August 1935, Mann devoted increasing attention to collaboration with Erika Mann on her literary cabaret *Die Pfeffermühle* (The Peppermill), for which he composed songs and sketches, until he emigrated to the United States in 1938.

Unlike many of his fellow émigrés, Mann acquired complete fluency in English soon after his arrival in the United States and became a highly paid and well-regarded lecturer and journalist. He was coauthor, with Erika Mann, of *Escape to Life* (1939) and *The Other Germany* (1940). As Mann's sense of commitment to the antifascist movement deepened, he turned increasingly to the publication of nonfiction political statements bearing directly on current events. He lectured widely on political themes, published essays in *Esquire* and the *Nation,* reported from the front lines in Spain in July 1938, and founded the English-language journal *Decision* in 1941, whose fusion of literary and political pieces took up the goals of *Die Sammlung.* Its illustrious contributors included W. H. Auden, Sherwood Anderson, Somerset Maugham, Stephen Spender, and Jean-Paul Sartre. The journal succumbed to financial difficulties barely one year after its promising debut.

In December 1942, Mann was inducted into the U.S. Army after prolonged unsuccessful applications; only later did he discover that he had been denounced as a homosexual and a communist and had been trailed by the FBI since 1940. Mann's 1944 tour of duty as army sergeant included North Africa and Italy, where he worked for the psychological warfare branch of military intelligence, composing propaganda leaflets and appearing at the front with loudspeaker in hand, calling on the Germans to surrender. After the war ended, Mann retained his military affiliation by signing on as intelligence officer and staff writer for the American military journal *Stars and Stripes.*

Mann had a penchant for committing even the minutest details of his life to paper, completing no fewer than three book-length autobiographies. The first, *Kind dieser Zeit* (Child of This Era), was published when he was only twenty-six. The second, *The Turning Point* (1942), which he wrote in English, was perhaps his finest work; Milton Rugoff of the *New*

York Herald Tribune compared its style and language to Marcel Proust and Thomas Wolfe. Like his father, Mann recorded particulars of his life in a diary kept over the course of decades. Moreover, Mann's biographies of Alexander the Great (1930), Tchaikovsky (1935), King Ludwig II of Bavaria (1937), and Gide (1943) revealed nearly as much about their author as their ostensible subject. Even his novels contained an unusual degree of self-portraiture. In *Treffpunkt im Unendlichen* (Meeting Point in Infinity, 1932) alone, Mann created three fictional counterparts for himself: the characters Sebastian, Peti, and Richard. Richard's suicide in France prefigured Mann's suicide seventeen years later under eerily similar circumstances.

The novel that assured Mann's place in literary history was *Mephisto*, a scathing attack on what had become of Germany and the Germans under Hitler. This novel later entered the international limelight because of its Academy Award–winning cinematic rendition by the Hungarian director István Szabó (1981). Subtitled "Novel of a Career," the book told of an opportunistic actor, called "Hendrik Höfgen," who betrayed moral and political principles to rise to the top of the theater world during the Nazi dictatorship. Mann intended to paint a general picture of life in Germany, but the central character inescapably reminded readers of Mann's former brother-in-law Gustaf Gründgens, whose most famous stage role was Mephistopheles in Goethe's *Faust*. Gründgens formed a personal and professional alliance with Hermann Goering so that he might remain center stage in the theaters of Germany. Mann roundly condemned Gründgens's complicity with the Nazis in his fictional and nonfictional works. *Mephisto*, with its thinly disguised portrait of Gründgens and other well-established artists of the Nazi era, became a test case for the postwar German acceptance of exile literature. After a series of libel suits in the 1960s and 1970s, *Mephisto* became the only book to be prohibited from publication in the Federal Republic of Germany. The publisher Rowohlt defied this prohibition by printing the novel in 1981 without legal incident; it became a runaway bestseller. Technically, however, the prohibition of this novel had not been repealed by the end of the twentieth century.

Mann's last known project was tellingly titled *The Last Day*; it remained a fragment. His outline indicated that the protagonist would take his own life to protest the political climate of the Cold War. Despondent over the unwillingness of German publishers to print his books, overwhelmed with loneliness, rootlessness, and despair about the political situation in Germany, and crippled by drug dependency, Mann committed suicide in Cannes with an overdose of sleeping pills. As if to confirm his isolation, neither his sister nor his father attended his funeral.

• The Klaus Mann Archives are located in the Manuscript Division of the Munich Municipal Library. For a comprehensive annotated listing of all published and unpublished works by Mann, see Michel Grunewald, *Klaus Mann 1906–1949: Eine Bibliographie* (1984). An edition of Mann's fictional and nonfictional works, a two-volume edition of his letters, and a six-volume edition of his diaries have been published by Edition Spangenberg im Ellermann Verlag (Munich); titles that have appeared in recent English-language editions are *Mephisto* (1977), *The Turning Point* (1984), *Pathetic Symphony* (1985), *The Pious Dance* (1987), and *Siblings and the Children's Story* (1991). The most detailed biography is Fredric Kroll, *Klaus-Mann-Schriftenreihe* (3 vols., 1976–1979). An obituary is in the London *Times*, 7 June 1949.

SHELLEY FRISCH

MANN, Louis (20 Apr. 1865–15 Feb. 1931), actor and playwright, was born in New York City, the son of Daniel Mann and Carolina Hecht. At age three, he made his first stage appearance in *Snowflake*, a Christmas pantomime performed at the Stadt Theatre in New York. Educated in the New York public school system, Mann enrolled in the University of California, but he never finished a course. Instead, he dropped out of school and joined the McCullough & Barrett Stock company in San Francisco where he played boys' parts. On his Sundays off from McCullough & Barrett he played with the General Stock Company. During this time he also performed with many of the leading performers who toured through San Francisco, including Edwin Booth, Tomasso Salvini, Marie Prescott, and Lewis Morrison. Eventually Mann made his way to New York, and in 1883 he appeared at the Union Square Theatre as the page in Oscar Wilde's first play, *Vera, the Nihilist*. At the Union Square Theatre Mann continued to learn the craft of acting from prominent actors E. H. Sothern and Cyril Maude. He toured with the theater's company in *Called Back* and *Last*.

In 1887 he toured with D. E. Bandmann in *Dr. Jekyll and Mr. Hyde* and the following year started his own company, which toured playing *Lady Audley's Secret* with Mann in the role of Robert Audley. In 1892 he scored his first big hit in a leading role playing Dick Winters in *Incog.*, which opened at the Bijou Theatre on 22 February. The following year Mann toured with G. W. Lederer's Company playing in *Nothing but Money* and other plays. In 1894 Mann once again toured across country with his own troupe—he had married actress Clara Lipman just prior to the tour and she costarred with him in *The Laughing Girl* and *Hannah*, two plays that Mann also authored.

Back in New York Mann starred as Svengali in *The Merry World*, which opened at the Casino Theatre on 8 June 1895. That same year he made a hit as Herr Von Moser in *The Strange Adventures of Miss Brown*, which opened at the Standard Theatre on 2 December. In his next three productions Mann performed with his wife: Hans in *The Girl from Paris*, Hans Nix in *The Telephone Girl*, and Le Bardy in *The Girl in the Barracks*. On 2 September 1900 Mann starred as Franz Hochstuhl in *All on Account of Eliza* at the Garrick and on 1 January 1906 he appeared as Jean Poujol in *Julie Bon-Bon*, a play written by his wife, at Field's Theatre and later took the show to the Waldorf Theatre in London, where it had a moderate success.

Mann worked continually for the next twenty years gradually taking on supporting roles when leading roles were offered less and less frequently as he grew older. A few of his most important performances during this time included John Krauss in *The Man Who Stood Still*, which opened at the Circle Theatre in 1908; Godfried Plittersdorf in *The Cheater*, a play authored by Mann that opened at the Lyric Theatre in June of 1910; and Charles Sample in *Elevating a Husband*, which opened on the road in 1911 and then settled in for a long run at the Harris Theatre in 1912. In 1918 Mann appeared in his most popular and critically successful role—Karl Pfeiffer in *Friendly Enemies* by Samuel Shipman. The wartime comedy is about a man who is pro-German until his son is killed by Germans, but who changes his mind again when his son is found alive. It also starred Samuel Bernard and played for more than a year at the Hudson Theater in New York and then went on tour across the country. The *New York Times* called the audience reaction to the players "tumultuous" (23 Mar. 1918). In 1920 Mann played Hyam Saloman in *The Unwritten Chapter*, which opened at the Astor Theatre on 19 October. Alexander Wollcott, critic for the *New York Times*, commented that Mann gave "an expert and dignified performance" (20 Oct. 1920). Mann followed this successful performance with the role of Karl Bauer, a supporting role in *The Whirl in New York*, which opened at the Winter Garden in June 1921. The following fall he appeared at the Apollo Theatre as Carl Schnitzler in *Nature's Nobleman*. The role gave Mann "but few opportunities to display his skill as an actor," according to the *New York Times* (15 Nov. 1923). His last two important roles were David Milgrim in *Milgrim's Progress*, which opened at Wallack's Theatre in December of 1924 and Karl Kraft in *That French Lady*, costarring his wife, which opened at the Ritz in March of 1927. According to the *New York Times* in his portrayal of Milgrim he addressed the comic scenes "expertly" (23 Dec. 1924), but three years later, in reference to his performance in *That French Lady*, the *New York Times* critic commented that Mann "acts strenuously in two keys—choleric and sentimental" (16 Mar. 1927). Mann completed a brief tour of *Thieves' Paradise*, a play he also co-wrote, before retiring in 1928. A year before his death, Mann returned to the stage to reprise his role in *Friendly Enemies* at a brief engagement in Philadelphia opposite the nephew of Samuel Bernard.

Active in political organizations, Mann helped found the Actor's Fidelity League, which opposed many of the demands made by Actors' Equity Association, during the actors' strike of 1919. Mann served as vice president of the organization for ten years. Mann was also an active member of the Broadway Association and the Jewish Theatrical Guild, and he served as vice president for the Grand Street Boys' Association. Mann died in New York City after lapsing into a coma during surgery for an intestinal ailment. As testament to his popularity and standing in the New York community, his pallbearers included the mayor of New York City, the governor and lieutenant governor of New York, William Randolf Hearst, Al Jolson, Eddie Cantor, George M. Cohan, and Lee Shubert.

With a theatrical career that lasted more than half a century, Mann was one of the most well-known and noted comedians of his time. His obituary in the *New York Times* stated that as "one of America's most beloved comedians" Mann "excelled in whatever part he took, but his best and most frequent characterization was that of a kindly, opinionated, stubborn, and thoroughly entertaining German-American." Mann almost always played characters that spoke in a dialect—accounting for the large number of characters with European names in his repertoire—and was famous for his starched "bat-wing" collars. Perhaps Mann's greatest contribution to the American theater was his endeavor to create topical theater, such as *Friendly Enemies*, which was both relevant and, through his comedic talents, uplifting and hopeful for the audience.

• Information on Mann's career may be gleaned from clippings in the Billy Rose Theatre Collection at the New York Public Library for the Performing Arts, Lincoln Center. Mann is also included in the *Biographical Encyclopedia and Who's Who in the Theatre* (1981) and *Who Was Who in the Theatre* (1979). An obituary is in the *New York Times*, 16 Feb. 1931.

MELISSA VICKERY-BAREFORD

MANN, Thomas (6 June 1875–12 Aug. 1955), writer, was born Paul Thomas Mann in Lübeck, Germany, the son of Senator Thomas Johann Heinrich Mann, a patrician merchant, and Julia da Silva-Bruhns, to whose Portuguese-Creole background Mann attributed his artistic temperament. Adamantly averse to the German educational system, Mann barely squeaked through high school with a non-college–track diploma. After his father's death in 1891, Mann's family relocated to Munich the next year, and he joined them in 1894 after completing high school in Lübeck.

Mann showed early prowess in writing and published his first collection of short stories, *Der kleine Herr Friedemann* (*Little Mr. Friedemann*), in 1898. His first novel, *Buddenbrooks*, appeared in two volumes in 1901. This multilayered work describes the decline of the bourgeois Buddenbrook family, and by extension the crisis of the merchant bourgeoisie, against a backdrop of Schopenhauerian pessimism. Both epic and autobiographical, the novel portrayed in often unflattering detail members of Mann's extended family and residents of Lübeck, some of whom accused him of libel. In 1929 *Buddenbrooks* earned Mann the Nobel Prize for literature, five years after he had published the more profound and polished novel *Der Zauberberg* (1924; *The Magic Mountain*). *The Magic Mountain* is the story of a naive, mildly tubercular young patient in a Swiss sanatorium, torn between the life-affirming and nihilistic philosophies of his fellow patients until a vision in a snowstorm inspires him to embrace life. Mann published numerous shorter prose works, notably *Tonio Kröger* (1903), *Tristan* (1903), *Der Tod in Venedig* (1912; *Death in Venice*), *Unordnung und frühes Leid* (1926; *Disorder and Early Sorrow*), and *Mario und der Zauberer* (1930; *Mario and the Magician*), as well as essays and lectures on a wide array of literary and political themes. However, Mann's preferred form was the long novel, as evidenced by the tetralogy *Joseph und seine Brüder* (1933–1943; *Joseph and His Brothers*) and the novels *Doktor Faustus* (1947; *Doctor Faustus*), *Der Erwählte* (1951; *The Holy Sinner*), and the fragmentary *Bekenntnisse des Hochstaplers Felix Krull* (1954; *Confessions of Felix Krull, Confidence Man*).

A primary theme of Thomas Mann's words is the isolated status of the artist, who may be applauded by society but is never fully accepted. The conflict between artists and others dogged Mann throughout his life, and found literary expression particularly in the years preceding his marriage. For example, the title character of *Tonio Kröger* craves the blond, blue-eyed normality of his classmates Hans Hansen and Ingeborg Holm, and curses his exotic heritage and exotic bent. Kröger declares toward the end: "I stand between two worlds. I am at home in neither."

Mann married Katia Pringsheim, the daughter of a wealthy Jewish family in Munich, in 1905. He celebrated their union with *Königliche Hoheit* (1909; *Royal Highness*), a cautiously optimistic novel of a physically handicapped and financially strapped prince who weds a prosperous princess and achieves the dubious pleasure of "austere happiness."

The undisputed masterpiece of this period was Mann's lyrical novella *Death in Venice*, in which the celebrated but solitary writer Gustav von Aschenbach degenerates and dies when overwhelmed with passion for a young Slavic boy whose beauty incarnate belies the aging writer's noble but sterile art. Here Mann introduced the technique of verbal leitmotiv, derived from Wagner's music dramas, in which an object or phrase assumes structural and symbolic significance.

The contrast of heterosexual obligation in *Royal Highness* and unbridled homosexual passion of *Death in Venice* reflects an ongoing conflict in Mann's self-definition and in his writings. Mann's sexual identity has been the subject of much speculation. Although married and the father of six children, Mann was preoccupied with homoeroticism. His literary characters, from Gustav von Aschenbach in *Death in Venice* to Lord Kilmarnock in *Felix Krull*, are drawn to beautiful young men, as was Mann. Since the publication of Mann's copious diaries, which, at his wish, remained sealed until twenty-five years after his death, scholars have reassessed the autobiographical basis of Mann's fictional writings.

Mann's early forays into politics during World War I had him supporting conservative, nationalistic views. His major political treatise of this period, *Betrachtungen eines Unpolitischen* (1918; *Reflections of a Non-Political Man*), pitted Germany, the land of purportedly profound culture, against France, the land of supposedly superficial civilization. By 1922, however, Mann had moved away from bombastic nationalism

and toward a democratic model in his lectures *Von deutscher Republik* (1922; *The German Republic*) and *Deutsche Ansprache: Ein Appell an die Vernunft* (1930; *An Appeal to Reason*).

Shortly after Adolf Hitler assumed power on 30 January 1933, Mann embarked on a European lecture tour. He settled in the town of Küsnacht, Switzerland, until his move to the United States in 1938. In his early years of exile, Mann wavered in his loyalties and continued to publish in Germany. Under pressure from his children Erika and Klaus and the course of events in Germany, Mann formally allied himself with the exile community and attacked the Nazi regime in an open letter of 3 February 1936. On 2 December 1936 the Nazi government revoked Mann's German citizenship after confiscating his house and money. The retraction of his citizenship from Germany elicited no public reaction from Mann, in part because he had been granted Czech citizenship on 18 August 1936 by special dispensation of President Edvard Benes. The loss of his honorary doctorate from the University of Bonn was another matter. His 1937 response to the dean's letter remains one of his most compelling and well-known essayistic writings. To explain his separation from Germany and his rejection of its destructive regime, he used a phrase that has since often been adopted to describe him: "I'm born to be a representative rather than a martyr." This letter was translated into nearly every European language and came to be seen as the clearest formulation of anti-Nazi sentiment after 1933.

In the United States his status as the "representative German" was confirmed. Mann had influential contacts throughout the country, from Agnes E. Meyer, wife of the owner of the *Washington Post*, to President Franklin D. Roosevelt, who conferred with Mann on matters pertaining to Germany. His books were quickly translated by Helen T. Lowe-Porter, sometimes while he penned them. The publisher Alfred A. Knopf was eager to publish every manuscript he completed. Mann's comfortable financial circumstances and solid reputation allowed him to bypass many of the difficulties that beset other exiles; even his elaborate furnishings followed him from Munich to Switzerland to the United States. Mann quickly garnered a string of American honorary doctorates, which more than compensated for the German one he had lost.

Mann spent his first American years lecturing at Princeton University. He also held the title of consultant in German literature of the Library of Congress (a sinecure provided by a well-connected American friend) and lectured from coast to coast. Beginning in October 1940 he recorded broadcasts for the "Deutsche Hörer" (Listen, Germany) series of the British Broadcasting Corporation, which were transmitted across enemy lines to the Germans. But as always he kept to his disciplined schedule and continued to publish literary works, such as *Lotte in Weimar* (1939; *The Beloved Returns*), a novel of homage to Mann's literary forebear Johann Wolfgang von Goethe. In 1942 Mann moved to Pacific Palisades, California, where he lived in the vicinity of many other prominent exiles from Germany and Austria, including an old Munich neighbor, the conductor Bruno Walter, and the composer Arnold Schoenberg. In June 1944 Mann became an American citizen. While in California, Mann completed his mammoth tetralogy *Joseph and His Brothers*, a recounting of the biblical story Mann had begun to write in 1926 when the threat of fascism started to loom larger in Germany. Mann considered Joseph the voice of humanism and a possible antidote to the angry rhetoric of his day.

From 1943 to 1947 Mann worked on his epic novel *Doctor Faustus*. This novel vented Mann's anger and dashed hopes for Germany. Reprising his early theme of the artist as sinister intruder, *Doctor Faustus* tells the story of the musician Adrian Leverkühn, whose twelve-tone compositions are thrillingly demonic. Their very genius signals doom for the society that has produced this dangerous artist. Here and throughout many of his works (notably *Buddenbrooks*, *Tristan*, and *Death in Venice*), music invokes and celebrates the irrational.

Mann completed the first volume of his final novel, *Felix Krull*, in the year preceding his death. Three decades earlier he had begun the composition of this work, a picaresque novel of a petty swindler who charms his way up the social ladder, but he found the novel's uncharacteristically light vein difficult to sustain. After considerable coaxing from and collaboration with his daughter Erika Mann, he saw the first volume of this whimsical work through to completion. However, Mann repeatedly expressed the wish that he had ended his writings with *Doctor Faustus*, which had captured his despair at the human condition.

Mann's postwar reception in Germany was sharply polarized. He was honored with the Goethe Prize in Frankfurt and similarly celebrated in Weimar when he came to visit both Germanies in 1949. However, resentment among Germans for his having left the country, coupled with an extended public controversy with a group of self-styled "inner emigrants," writers who had remained in Nazi Germany but claimed to have resisted Hitler more effectively than those who had left, confirmed Mann's resolve not to move back. Life in the United States was becoming untenable for Mann as well. Suspected of communist affiliations, defamed in the press, and tailed by the Federal Bureau of Investigation, he felt compelled to return to Switzerland in 1952, where he spent the remaining years of his life. He died in Kilchberg, near Zurich.

No other German writer of the twentieth century has had as large and devoted a readership as Mann. Celebrated around the world, often more than in his native Germany, the dazzling scope of his writings, which interweave music, science, mythology, theology, and metaphysics with haunting imagery, have elevated Mann to the status of Olympian author.

• The Thomas Mann Archives are in Zurich, Switzerland. The standard edition of Mann's complete works is *Gesammelte Werke* (1960). A three-volume selection of his copious correspondence was compiled by Erika Mann as *Briefe* (1961). As per his instructions, Mann's diaries were kept sealed for twenty-five years following his death but are now available in a multivolume edition, *Tagebücher* (1977). A single English-language volume containing a selection of the early entries is *Thomas Mann Diaries, 1918–1939* (1982). Readers of English will find Mann's major stories in *Stories of Three Decades* (1936) and his essays in *Essays of Three Decades* (1947), both translated by H. T. Lowe-Porter, who also translated Mann's major novels. Mann also wrote two brief autobiographical accounts: *Lebensabriß* (1930; *A Sketch of My Life*) and *Die Entstehung des Doktor Faustus: Roman eines Romans* (1949; *The Story of a Novel: The Genesis of Dr. Faustus*).

A definitive Thomas Mann biography remains to be written. A lengthy account of Mann's early life can be found in two volumes by Peter de Mendelssohn, both titled *Der Zauberer: Das Leben des deutschen Schriftstellers Thomas Mann*. The first volume (1975) covers the years through 1911, and the second (1992) describes two turbulent years in Mann's life and in German politics, 1919 and 1933. A partial biography in English covering the same years as de Mendelssohn's first volume is Richard Winston, *Thomas Mann: The Making of an Artist, 1875–1911* (1981). Nigel Hamilton, *The Brothers Mann* (1978), is a dual biography of Mann and his elder brother Heinrich. Hans Bürgin and Hans-Otto Mayer, *Thomas Mann: A Chronicle of His Life* (1969), provides an invaluable chronology of Mann's life. Erika Mann devoted a book to Mann's final year: *Das letzte Jahr: Bericht über meinen Vater* (1956; *The Last Year of Thomas Mann*), which is available in English translation. Three of Mann's other children allotted substantial portions of their memoirs to discussions of their father; all are available in English editions: Klaus Mann, *The Turning Point* (1942); Monika Mann, *Vergangenes und Gegenwärtiges* (1960; *Past and Present*); and Golo Mann, *Erinnerungen und Gedanken: Eine Jugend in Deutschland* (1986; *A Youth in Germany*). Katia Mann, *Ungeschriebene Memoiren* (1974; *Unwritten Memories*), chronicles her marriage to Mann. Mann's younger brother Viktor Mann describes the siblings' childhood in *Wir waren fünf* (1949).

There are countless critical studies of Mann's literary and essayistic writings. Two classic studies of his literary works in English are Erich Heller, *The Ironic German* (1958), and T. J. Reed, *Thomas Mann: The Uses of Tradition* (1974). Among the many studies of Mann's sexuality that have appeared since the publication of his diaries is Gerhard Härle, *Männerweiblichkeit* (1988). Mann's political development is examined by Kurt Sontheimer in *Thomas Mann und die Deutschen* (1965). His position as a cultural conservative is critically analyzed by Dagmar Barnouw in *Weimar Intellectuals and the Threat of Modernity* (1988), pp. 121–50. An obituary is in the *New York Times*, 13 Aug. 1955.

SHELLEY FRISCH

MANNE, Shelly (11 June 1920–26 Sept. 1984), jazz drummer, was born Sheldon Manne in New York City, the son of Max Harold Manne, a professional percussionist, and Anna Cozlin. He attended New York City public schools. Manne's first instrument was the saxophone, which, encouraged by percussionist/teacher Billy Gladstone, he traded for a drum set at age eighteen. A self-taught musician, Manne displayed talent as a jazz performer when he frequently sat in at Fifty-second Street jazz clubs in the 1940s. Earlier he gained playing experience on cruise ships traveling the Atlantic, then joined Kenny Watts and His Kilowatts, a hokum band that included a rhythm section and three kazoo players, playing arrangements styled after the Count Basie band. On the recommendation of drummer Ray McKinley, Manne was hired for his first big band job by trombonist Bobby Byrne. After filling in for Dave Tough with the Benny Goodman band, he joined clarinetist Joe Marsala at the Hickory House, recording with Marsala in 1941. A year later, he replaced McKinley with the Will Bradley band after having appeared in bands led by Raymond Scott and Bob Astor. He played briefly with Les Brown before joining the U.S. Coast Guard Reserve (1942–1945). In 1943 Manne married Florence "Flip" Butterfield, a Radio City Music Hall rockette. They had no children.

Manne's early career was limited by the musicians' union recording ban (1942–1943), but in late 1943 he made several records with tenor saxophonist Coleman Hawkins, including a famous Hawkins rendition of "The Man I Love." During this period Manne frequently worked with bebop musicians, including Dizzy Gillespie, Dexter Gordon, Don Byas, and Oscar Pettiford, all of whom he recorded with in the mid-1940s.

In 1946 Manne joined Stan Kenton's band, a move that brought him national attention and recognition as a jazz drummer. He made numerous recordings with the band, some of which are considered Kenton classics. During his time with Kenton, Manne played and recorded with a wide variety of musicians, including Johnny Bothwell (1946), George Shearing and Charlie Ventura (both 1947), Bill Harris (1948–1949), and Woody Herman (1949). He also toured with Jazz at the Philharmonic in 1948–1949.

When he left the Kenton band in 1952, Manne settled in California where he became a leading figure in what has been called the "West Coast" school of jazz. This movement, influenced in part by Miles Davis's album *Birth of the Cool* (1949–1950), emphasized tonal color, subtle harmonic textures, and sometimes classical music compositional techniques in contrast to the hard, rhythmically angular bebop style played by many East Coast musicians. Although Manne's earlier playing owes much, at least conceptually, to the bop innovations of Max Roach and other New York drummers, his later style epitomizes the melodic approach mirrored in the playing of several of his West Coast contemporaries, including Mel Lewis, Chico Hamilton, and Don Lamond. Manne's melodic approach to playing drums was based on the concept that the sonorous quality of the drum set plays a part equal to or greater than the rhythmic emphasis preferred by earlier drummers. While drummers did not tune their drums to fit specific chord patterns, they did borrow melodic ideas stated by other performers or improvised new ones during solo and accompaniment sections of the arrangement.

Throughout his career in California, Manne worked primarily as a studio drummer in film and television. And from 1955 until the 1970s he was the drummer on call for Contemporary Records. Manne played on several highly popular jazz albums for Contemporary, including *My Fair Lady*, with pianist André Previn and bassist Leroy Vinnegar, and on tenor saxophonist Sonny Rollins's *Way Out West* (1957), as well as the 1959 recording, directed by Henry Mancini, of music from the popular television show "Peter Gunn." In 1959 Manne recorded the album *Tomorrow Is the Question* with avant-garde saxophonist Ornette Coleman. He also appeared playing in a handful of well-known films, among them *The Man with the Golden Arm* (1955), *I Want to Live* (1958), *The Five Pennies* (1959), and *The Gene Krupa Story* (1959). His scores for film and television include *The Proper Time* (1961), *Clarence the Cross-Eyed Lion* (1965), *Young Billy Young* (1969), "Trial of the Catonsville Nine" (1972), and *Trader Horn* (1973). Manne was also a contributing composer for the 1960s television series "Daktari."

From 1955 through the 1960s Manne toured with his own California-based groups, which at different times included jazz musicians Stu Williamson, Russ Freeman, Victor Feldman, Bill Holman, Charlie Mariano, Joe Gordon, Richie Kamuca, Monty Budwig, Conte Condoli, and Gary Barone. In 1960 he opened his own jazz club in Hollywood, Shelly's Manne-Hole. The club featured his own small group and became a showplace for up-and-coming jazz artists. After the club closed in 1974, Manne replaced Chuck Flores with the L.A. Four, an eclectic ensemble consisting of flutist/saxophonist Bud Shank, guitarist Laurindo Almeida, and bassist Ray Brown; Manne recorded with them in 1975–1976. He led his own group, which included saxophonist Lew Tabackin, in 1978, and in 1980 he toured Japan with the Gentlemen of Swing, which included Benny Carter, Harry Edison, Teddy Wilson, and Milt Hinton. In the early 1980s Manne formed a trio with pianist Frank Collett and bassist Monty Budwig. He appeared at the Olympic Arts Festival in New York City in August 1984 and was honored by Los Angeles mayor Tom Bradley, who declared 9 September 1984 "Shelly Manne Day." Manne died of a heart attack in Sun Valley, California.

Manne gathered many awards during his career, winning readers' polls conducted by *Down Beat*, *Metronome*, *Playboy*, and the British jazz journal *Melody Maker*. His playing style was subtle, favoring musicality over technique, a characteristic he shared with Jo Jones and Dave Tough, both of whose influence he readily admitted. His earliest recordings demonstrate that his style was rooted in swing era drumming techniques, which he frequently called on throughout his career. However, he easily adapted to the bop techniques of his contemporaries (Roach, Kenny Clarke, Shadow Wilson), modifying his approach for either big band or small group performances. His affiliation with the Kenton band during its heyday and his film and TV performances encouraged him to experiment with the tone colors he could derive from the drum set. His melodically based solos are original and highly creative. Manne said in a 1981 interview, "Instead of letting the rhythm imply its own melody, my concept is to play melodically and allow the melody to create rhythm. My ideas are linearly conceived and executed, often in opposition to the structure of the bar lines. Improvisation is the result of melodic, not rhythmic thinking."

• Among the most informative and useful articles about Manne are "The Shelly Manne Story," as told to Sinclair Traill, *Jazz Journal International* 32, no. 8 (1979): 21–26; Dave Levine, "Shelly Manne" (an interview), *Modern Drummer*, Oct. 1981; and Charles M. Bernstein, "Shelly Manne: The Last Interview," *Modern Drummer*, Jan. 1985. Details about Manne's personal and professional life can be found in *Annual Obituary 1984* (1985). Recordings representative of his output include *Shelly Manne and His Men*, vols. 1–3 (Contemporary, 1953–1955), *Shelly Manne and His Men at the Manne-Hole*, (Contemporary, 1961), and *The L.A. Four* (Concord, 1976). A discography of important recordings by Manne appeared in Levine, "Shelly Manne: A Selected Discography," *Modern Drummer*, Jan. 1985. Obituaries are in the *Los Angeles Times* and the *New York Times*, both 27 Sept. 1984.

T. DENNIS BROWN

MANNERS, John Hartley (10 Aug. 1870–19 Dec. 1928), actor and playwright, was born in London, England, of Irish parentage. Little is known of his parents or his youth, but he was raised a Catholic, received a private education, and, in spite of his mother's wish that he become a priest, entered the British civil service. Manners soon tired of that life and became an actor, making his first appearance in Melbourne, Australia, on 19 February 1898. He played small roles for a season and apparently wrote his first play, never produced because the immensely popular Victorien Sardou wrote a piece on the same subject for Sir Henry Irving that overshadowed the fledgling Manners's effort. By April 1899 he had returned to London, performing with George Alexander's company at the St. James's Theatre and later with Johnston Forbes-Robertson's troupe, where he played Laertes to that star's Hamlet. In 1899, while acting in London, he wrote another play, a one-act for two characters called *The Queen's Messenger*, which became very popular, running for two years and for several years after frequently produced.

In 1902 Manners was commissioned to write a play for one of the most famous actresses of the era, Lily Langtry. She took this play, titled *The Crossways*, on her American tour, bringing Manners on his first trip to the United States as a member of the acting company. He continued this dual career, acting and writing for the theater, until 1905, when his play *Zira* was produced in New York by Henry Miller. *Zira* introduced Margaret Anglin as a new American star and convinced Manners to become a full-time playwright. He began writing at least one play a year, and by 1910 three Manners plays, *The Patriot, The Great John Ganton,* and *The House Next Door,* were running simultaneously in New York.

Manners's greatest theatrical achievement came in 1912 when he wrote *Peg o' My Heart*. This sentimental comedy became the longest-running nonmusical play of its time, with 101 performances in Los Angeles, then 604 in New York. Eight touring companies performed it, and the play enjoyed a year's run in London, accumulating a record 5,987 performances. The *New York Herald Tribune* pronounced it "one of the most popular plays ever produced in the United States" (20 Dec. 1928). The play's popularity was due in part to Manners's smartly written story of Peg, a young Irish-American heiress, who is brought to meet the Chichesters, her haughty but recently impoverished British relatives. The Chichester family will see a portion of the inheritance only if they teach Peg how to be a lady. This premise sets up a series of comic trials and tribulations that ends happily for Peg, who finds that "there's nothing half so sweet in life as love's young dream."

Clever as it was, the plot set up a variation on a frequently explored comic theme, and the play might have had a short life except for what proved to be the inspired casting of Laurette Taylor in the title role. Taylor, an actress with some experience on the New York stage, had appeared in at least one other Manners play, but she became a major star with this performance. In 1912 Manners and Taylor were married before *Peg* played New York, and their lives became intertwined on- and offstage, Manners writing plays almost exclusively as vehicles for Taylor and she performing almost exclusively in those plays. The couple had no children of their own, although Taylor had a daughter from a previous relationship. The general critical assessment of this pairing, based largely on Taylor's later great success as Amanda Wingfield in Tennessee Williams's *The Glass Menagerie*, holds that her strong performances propped up Manners's weak vehicles and hindered her career as a serious actress. Indeed, the critics, unkind to *Peg o' My Heart*, were even less charitable toward the playwright's subsequent work. John Corbin, writing in the *New York Times*, commented that although *Peg* had defied the critics, Manners's later efforts, such as *The Harp of Life* (1916), *Out There* (1917), and *Happiness* (1914, 1917) were pale imitations of the kind of formula that made *Peg* such a hit, substituting "tame, lymphatical fat" for "full-blooded vigor" (13 Jan. 1918). Manners was given equal space on the same page, and he responded with a defense of his writing on two counts. He placed character over plot, arguing that *Happiness*, far from formless, "has the only real form I feel disposed to recognize in the theatre—the consistent development of character. Let situation take care of itself. Character makes situation." And he upheld delicate, moral dramas against "the plethora of crook dramas and indecent farces" and, worse, "the play of indecent suggestion, marital infidelity, and the exploiting of women's frailty" so popular on the stage. Although critics almost universally opposed them, several Manners plays were quite successful, perhaps partially because of his dramatic theory, but almost certainly because of his wife's performances. Taylor and Manners spent time in Hollywood, where films were made of several of his scripts, including *Peg o' My Heart* (1922) and *Happiness* (1923), both directed by King Vidor and starring Taylor. Manners remained popular during his lifetime, writing or collaborating on more than thirty plays, including a musical version of *Peg* called *Peg o' My Dreams* (1924), but he is remembered only for *Peg o' My Heart*. He died in New York City of cancer of the esophagus.

• The Robinson Locke Collection of the New York Public Library for the Performing Arts contains clippings files under Manners's name and more under Laurette Taylor's that often refer to Manners. For biographical information on Manners, see *Who Was Who in the Theatre, 1912–1976* (1978). The most detailed biographical account of Manners can be found in Marguerite Courtney, *Laurette* (1955), a memoir by Taylor's daughter and Manners's stepdaughter. John Corbin's essay in the *New York Times*, 13 Jan. 1918, expresses the critical consensus on Manners; Manners's response on the same page is titled "The Freedom of the Dramatist: A Defense and a Plea." Bennett Cerf and Van Cartwell in *S.R.O.: The Most Successful Plays on the American Stage* (1945), provide biographical information and a critical assessment in their introduction to *Peg o' My Heart*. Obituaries are in the *New York Herald Tribune* and the *New York Times*, both 20 Dec. 1928.

JACK HRKACH

MANNES, Clara Damrosch (12 Dec. 1869–16 Mar. 1948), pianist and educator, was born in Breslau, Germany (now Wroclaw, Poland), the daughter of Leopold Damrosch, a conductor, composer, and violinist, and Helene von Heimburg, a singer. The family, including three older children and an aunt, emigrated to New York City in 1871, when Leopold accepted the offer of the music directorship of the Arion Society, one of a large number of singing groups active in New York at that time.

Clara was educated at private schools and began keyboard studies at an early age. Her teachers included Clara Gross and Jessie Pinney. In 1888 she traveled to Dresden with her mother and younger sister Elizabeth ("Ellie") to spend eight months studying theory with Johannes Schreyer and studying piano. She also pursued studies in sketching, another area in which she showed talent.

On her return to New York she began teaching piano privately and singing with her father's Oratorio Society. In 1897 she returned to Germany to study piano with Ferruccio Busoni in Berlin. David Mannes, a violinist in the New York Symphony Orchestra, conducted by her father, traveled on the same boat to Germany to study violin with Carl Halíř. During that summer she decided to give up sketching and make her career in music. She also returned to New York engaged to David. They were married in 1898 in Middle Granville, New York, at the home of her sister, Elizabeth Seymour. They had two children.

In 1903 the family traveled to Brussels so Mannes's husband could study with Eugène Ysaÿe. Privately Mannes worked on repertoire so that she and her husband could pursue a performing career as a violin-piano duo on their return to the United States.

During the winter of 1903–1904 the Manneses performed a series of concerts to benefit the Music School Settlement (later the Third Street Music School Settlement). They attracted the attention of a professional agent. From 1904 through 1917 they gave forty to fifty concerts each year throughout the United States and Canada. In 1913 the duo gave a series of three afternoon recitals at Bechstein (later Wigmore) Hall in London. The favorable reaction to their performances encouraged them to pursue an international career; however, the imminent war prevented them from following through with that idea.

By 1915 the Manneses decided to open a music school. Although they decided to name it the David Mannes School of Music, Mannes was an equal partner in the project. Their goal was to educate both amateurs and professionals. The school opened on the East Side of New York City in 1916.

The Manneses continued to perform together during the early years of the school. In addition to their recitals, other musicians, including Pablo Casals, joined them in performance in support of the school.

Mannes's services as an artist and educator were recognized by the French government's Ministry of Public Education and Fine Arts awarding her the rosette of Officier de l'Instruction Publique in 1926. This award was rarely given to a foreigner and less often to a woman.

At the school Mannes was responsible for administrative matters in addition to teaching chamber music to advanced students and supervising the ensemble department. She has been credited with ensuring the school's survival during her years of management because of her ability to deal effectively with committees, trustees, and donors.

An important aspect of the school was the development of a theory program that was particularly innovative for its time. This was accomplished by hiring Hans Weisse, a protégè of the Austrian theorist Heinrich Schenker. The subsequent appointment of Felix Salzer, another Schenkerian, brought about the development of a rigorous curriculum incorporating ear training, theory, harmony, dictation, and analysis.

Mannes died in New York City. Her life was her music: performing and teaching. Her life's work culminated in the creation, with her husband, of the Mannes College of Music.

• Mannes's correspondence is housed at the Library of Congress. George Martin, *The Damrosch Dynasty* (1983), is the most extensive source documenting her life. See David Mannes, *Music Is My Faith* (1949), for a personal view of her life and influence. See also Marya Mannes, *Out of My Time* (1971), for an interesting commentary on growing up in a musical family. Obituaries are in the *New York Times* and the *New York Herald Tribune*, both 18 Mar. 1948, and the *Musical Courier*, 1 Apr. 1948.

DEBORAH GRIFFITH DAVIS

MANNES, David (16 Feb. 1866–25 Apr. 1959), violinist, conductor, and educator, was born in New York City, the son of Henry Mannes, a merchant, and Nathalia Wittkowsky. Mannes's parents and elder brother had immigrated to the United States in 1860. With financial help from a cousin, Mannes's father had opened a clothing store on Seventh Avenue in New York City. Mannes was born in the impoverished family's home above the store. As a young child Mannes created his first violin from a cigar box, a piece of wood, and a string. His parents, hoping to encourage him, bought him a cheap violin and arranged for his intermittent studies. One of his earliest and most influential teachers was John Douglas, an African-American violinist, who had studied in Dresden with Eduard Rappoldi. Douglas was a talented, European-trained violinist who was never able to secure a chair in a symphony orchestra in the United States; he refused to charge Henry Mannes for David's lessons. In New York, Mannes also studied violin with August Zeiss, Herman Brandt, concertmaster of the New York Philharmonic, and Carl Richter Nicolai, Brandt's successor as concertmaster of the Philharmonic. As a young adult Mannes traveled to Germany to study with Heinrich de Ahna, second violin of the Joachim Quartet, and Karel Haliř, a violin professor at the Hochschule für Musik. His violin studies culminated in six months in Brussels with celebrated violinist Eugène Ysaÿe.

Mannes's formal education was limited. He left school at fifteen to play in dance and theater orchestras. In 1891 he auditioned for Walter Damrosch, who was creating a permanent orchestra for the Symphony Society in the newly built Carnegie Hall. Mannes was appointed concertmaster in 1903. He reluctantly left in 1912 due to health problems and to devote more time to his educational interests.

Mannes married pianist Clara Damrosch, sister of Walter Damrosch, in 1898. Her piano teachers included Ferruccio Busoni. Although Mannes and his wife had vowed never to perform together in public, they eventually formed a violin-piano duo and gave forty to fifty recitals per year throughout the United States, England, and Canada from 1904 through 1917. They had two children.

Although Mannes taught privately, his lifelong interest in education, particularly that of children, led him to teach first, in 1900, at the College Settlement on Rivington Street and then, in 1901, at the Music School Settlement (later the Third Street Music School Settlement). He became director of the latter in 1910 and remained there until 1916. In 1912 he founded the Music Settlement for Colored People in Harlem in memory of John Douglas. Mannes's interest in the education of African Americans prompted his service on the board of trustees of Fisk University from 1928 to 1951.

In 1916 the Manneses opened the David Mannes Music School in New York City. As Mannes wrote in his autobiography, the purpose of the school was "not to be just another good school, nor just a better school—but a very different kind of school. It was to become a veritable center of musical activity; embracing under the same roof not only the intense development of the potential professional, but the efforts of those who wanted merely to enrich themselves

through a better understanding or playing of music without the responsibilities of a career" (p. 234). Mannes accomplished this by hiring a first-rate faculty. Theory and composition teachers included composers Rosario Scalero, Ernest Bloch, and Hans Weisse. Weisse, a protégé of Heinrich Schenker, established the study of Schenkerian analysis at the school, rendering it the first American institution to offer this approach to music theory. This method utilizes a specialized vocabulary and notation to reveal the structure of tonal works through their linear connections. The school was also the first in the United States to introduce the study of solfège, a solmization system for teaching basic music skills. Other important faculty members included George Szell, Felix Salzer, Georges Enesco, and Bohuslav Martinů.

In 1948, following his wife's death, Mannes stepped down as director of the school but remained honorary director until his death. Mannes's son, Leopold, his co-director, assumed control of the day-to-day running of the school in 1948 and was named president in 1950. In 1953 the New York State Board of Regents granted a charter to the school that enabled it to offer courses leading to an academic degree. At that time the David Mannes Music School's name was changed to the Mannes College of Music.

David Mannes's other long-standing musical interest was conducting. He conducted children's orchestras during his tenure at the two settlement schools. From 1918 to 1947 he conducted the David Mannes Free Concerts at the Metropolitan Museum of Art. The museum's trustees, including John D. Rockefeller, Jr., bore the cost of the orchestra and rehearsals, and Mannes donated his services as conductor. It is estimated that over a thirty-year period two million people attended the series of concerts. Mannes thus achieved his goal of establishing a place where people could listen to fine music without the formal constraints of a concert hall: "where they could arrive when they chose and leave when they chose, and where, the tickets costing nothing, there would be no economic or social barrier to their coming" (*Music Is My Faith*, p. 244).

Mannes died in New York City. In his lifetime he greatly affected the cultural life of New York City through his performing, conducting, and educational activities. His chief legacy is the Mannes College of Music. Although his initial intention was to create a music school for the serious amateur, Mannes's foresight in hiring Schenker protégé Hans Weisse and, later, Felix Salzer to teach composition and analysis propelled the Mannes College of Music into a position of dominance as the premier institution teaching Schenkerian analysis and training professional musicians for orchestras and opera companies worldwide.

• Mannes's personal papers are housed in the Music Division of the Library of Congress in the Mannes-Damrosch collection. Mannes's autobiography, *Music Is My Faith* (1938; 2d ed., 1949), is an essential source. See also George Martin, *The Damrosch Dynasty: America's First Family of Music*

(1983), for an assessment of his life and relationship to the Damrosch family; Robert F. Egan, *Music and the Arts in the Community: The Community Music School in America* (1989), for his involvement in the settlement school movement; and Boris Schwarz, *Great Masters of the Violin* (1983), for a brief overview of his life and career. Obituaries are in the *New York Times* and the *New York Herald Tribune*, both 25 Apr. 1959.

DEBORAH GRIFFITH DAVIS

MANNES, Leopold Damrosch (26 Dec. 1899–11 Aug. 1964), pianist, educator, and scientist, was born in New York City, the son of David Mannes and Clara Damrosch, musicians. Mannes's musical precociousness became apparent at age three. According to his mother, Eugène Ysaÿe called the youngster "the reincarnation of Mozart." However, his parents carefully prevented his exploitation as a child prodigy. While he studied the piano in New York City with Elizabeth Quaile and Guy Maier, he also developed an avid interest in photography. In his last year of attending Riverdale Country School, he met Leopold Godowsky, Jr., a violinist and the son of the famous pianist, who also shared his keen interest in photography. Together they began physics experiments with color photography at the school and at the Mannes home. While attending Harvard College Mannes studied physics and music and continued his photography experiments.

Mannes graduated from Harvard in 1920 and traveled to Paris to study piano with Alfred Cortot. Upon his return to New York, he studied composition with Rosario Scalero at his parents' school, the David Mannes School of Music, and with Percy Goetschius at his uncle Frank Damrosch's Institute of Musical Art. Scalero's musical influence was the greater of the two and Mannes's study of sixteenth-century style is reflected in his compositions, which in 1923 included choral preludes, motets, and madrigals.

In 1922 Mannes debuted as one of the two pianists performing with the New York Symphony at Aeolian Hall with his uncle Walter Damrosch conducting the New York premiere of Camille Saint-Saëns's *Carnival of the Animals*. In that same year Mannes and Godowsky increased their experimentation with color photography. To patent their work they needed to discover a method of developing the film with one-step processing, and in 1923 they demonstrated for the patent office a method of controlled diffusion or differential depth bleach. When Lewis L. Strauss of the investment house of Kuhn, Loeb & Co. viewed a demonstration of their work, he offered to provide a loan in exchange for future royalties. Another viewer, Kenneth Mees, the director of research at Eastman Kodak, provided specially coated two-layer plates of film in exchange for progress reports.

During this time Mannes continued composing. In 1925 he was awarded a Pulitzer Traveling Scholarship ($1,500) for his Suite for Orchestra, and his work was published for the first time (Petite suite pour deux pianos, dedicated to Cortot). In 1925 Mannes also gave the American premiere of Randall Thompson's Suite for Pianoforte at the Mannes School, a work dedicated to Mannes.

Mannes completed his Quartet in C Minor and published his Orchestra Suite in revised form in 1926. That same year he married Edith Vernon Simonds, and they moved to Rome on a Guggenheim Fellowship that Mannes was awarded for his string quartet. They returned to New York City in 1927, and he began teaching theory at the Mannes School.

In 1930 Mannes and Godowsky became contractual employees of Kodak. Although they retained all rights to patents filed before their contract date, all patents filed after became the property of the company. By 1931 Mannes had joined Godowsky in Rochester, New York, working at Eastman Kodak's research laboratory.

Mannes and his wife divorced in 1933. That year his experiments with Godowsky resulted in the creation of a two-color film. By 1935 they had developed a three-color 16mm film suitable for amateur movie cameras, which was marketed under the trade name Kodachrome. In 1936 Kodak was able to offer the public 35mm rolls for still processing.

Mannes returned to New York City at the end of 1939 to compose, perform, and teach at the Mannes School. He completed his Suite for Two Pianos, and he performed in recital with the cellist Luigi Silva at Town Hall in 1941. In 1940 Mannes married Evelyn Sabin, a former dancer who had studied with Martha Graham and was an original member of the Graham Trio; they had one daughter.

In 1941, during World War II, Mannes worked on problems with haze in aerial photography, first at Eastman Kodak in Rochester and then at Wright Field in Dayton, Ohio. By 1948 Mannes had returned to New York City and had assumed the position of chief executive officer of the Mannes School. He also formed the Mannes Trio with Silva and violinist Vittorio Brero. In the trio's second season, Bronislav Gimpel replaced Brero, and the group was renamed the Mannes-Gimpel-Silva Trio.

In 1950 Mannes assumed the presidency of the Mannes School from his father. During his tenure the school was accredited by the State Board of Regents as a college. By allowing students to earn degrees, this change afforded the school's graduates the opportunity of earning graduate degrees at universities. During this time Mannes was also active in the Prades Festival, initiated by Pablo Casals in 1950 at a small Catalan village in France.

By 1955 the Mannes-Gimpel-Silva Trio had disbanded. Although Mannes continued to perform at the college, he discontinued all other public performances. He devoted his time and the money that he earned from photography royalties to the support of the college, which faced a severe financial crisis in 1959. But the difficulty eased when the college merged with the Chatham Square Music School in 1960 and gained a small endowment for the first time.

In 1961 Mannes was elected as the president of the Walter W. Naumberg Foundation. The following year he served on the jury of the first Van Cliburn International Piano Competition at Fort Worth, Texas. Mannes was named the chairman of the music panel of the cultural presentations program of the U.S. State Department in 1963. He died on Martha's Vineyard, Massachusetts.

Mannes was greatly admired for his musicianship, his scientific work, and his role as an educator. He also continued the work begun by his parents with the creation of the Mannes College of Music. At his grave, his sister Marya Mannes said: "Leopold was a universal man—as much at home with the structure of the atom as with the form of a fugue; a man of limitless intelligence, a playful wit, and a deeply generous spirit. He gave far more to the world than he received from it" (*Out of My Time*, p. 224). These words truly express the persona of this contemporary Renaissance man.

• Mannes's music manuscripts are in the Harry Scherman Library at the Mannes College of Music. George Martin, *The Damrosch Dynasty* (1983), contains comprehensive coverage of both the Mannes family and the history of the Mannes College of Music. See Marya Mannes, *Out of My Time* (1971), for a personalized view of life in the Mannes family. See also Edward John Wall, *The History of Three-Color Photography* (1925), for a description of Mannes's and Godowsky's method of controlled diffusion or differential depth bleach as discovered in their experiments in color photography. Obituaries are in the *New York Times* and the *New York Herald Tribune*, 12 Aug. 1964.

DEBORAH GRIFFITH DAVIS

MANNING, Daniel (16 May 1831–24 Dec. 1887), secretary of the treasury, was born in Albany, New York, the son of John Manning, a laborer, and Elizabeth Oley. Manning left school at age eleven to assist his widowed mother in supporting the family. In 1841 he secured a job as a page for two sessions in the New York State Assembly. The following year he began his long relationship with the *Albany Atlas* (later the *Albany Argus*), where, after being an office boy and printer, he became a reporter in 1856. In 1853 Manning married Mary Lee Little, with whom he had four children. Ten years later, in 1863, the Associated Press selected him to report the proceedings of the state legislature. He was also a legislative correspondent for the *Brooklyn Eagle*.

Manning rose rapidly in journalism and business. From 1858 to 1871 he reported the proceedings of the New York State Assembly for the *Argus*, and after 1865 he was associate editor, part owner, and business manager of the paper. He assumed the presidency of the *Argus* in 1873, the same year he was made director of the National Commercial Bank of Albany. In 1881 he was chosen vice president of the National Bank of Albany and became that institution's president the next year. He was a director of the Albany Electric Illuminating Company and a director representing the city in the Albany and Susquehanna Railway Company. He earned a reputation as a shrewd and capable Albany businessman, and during this time he established the *Argus* as a political power in the state.

Manning's experience in journalism, banking, and business proved valuable for his role in politics. A political lieutenant and close friend of Governor Samuel J. Tilden, Manning was a member of the Democratic State Committee from 1874 to 1884, serving as its secretary in 1879. He chaired the state committee from 1881 to 1884 and attended the party's state conventions, where he opposed the attempts of Tammany Hall, the powerful Democratic political organization in New York City, to control the state's politics. During the late 1860s and early 1870s he fought the Tweed Ring, named for William Marcy Tweed, a political boss. Participating in the Democratic National Conventions of 1876, 1880, and 1884, Manning worked tirelessly to promote the presidential nominations of Governor Tilden and Governor Grover Cleveland of New York.

After Tilden withdrew as a presidential possibility in 1884, Manning turned to Cleveland, promoting the governor as Tilden's natural heir. Chairman of the New York delegation at the 1884 Democratic National Convention in Chicago, Manning opened headquarters in that city for the governor and contributed to the Cleveland campaign fund. In a gentleman's agreement, he promised Representative Samuel J. Randall of Pennsylvania, former Speaker of the U.S. House of Representatives, virtual control over patronage in his state if he joined the Cleveland bandwagon by contributing Pennsylvania's votes for the New York governor. Manning's efforts greatly contributed to Cleveland's victory in 1884 as the Democratic presidential standard-bearer. He believed it was essential to success for Democrats to select a New York citizen for the presidency because of the state's large number of electoral votes. Near the close of the campaign Manning, fearing ballot-box stuffing and corruption at the polls on the part of the Republicans, joined others in sending telegrams to prominent Democrats across the nation warning them to be vigilant on Election Day. In 1884 Manning, whose first wife had died in 1882, married Mary Margaretta Fryer, an attractive and ambitious woman much younger than Manning. They had no children, but they were active in Washington's social life.

Heeding the advice of Tilden, Cleveland appointed Manning to his cabinet as secretary of the treasury, in which capacity he served from 1885 to 1887. Cleveland chose Manning for a variety of reasons. He valued Manning as a trusted friend whose hard work during the campaign merited a reward. Manning represented the Tilden wing of the party and was also a person of driving ambition who had risen from a newsboy to positions of wealth and authority. Moreover, Cleveland recognized that Manning possessed a knowledge of financial principles and held views on the leading issues that reflected his own.

A quiet man who had not sought public office, Manning was a good political manager and party conciliator. Knowledgeable on financial matters, he was a good adviser and surfaced as a valuable member of Cleveland's administration. A conservative Democrat who championed sound money principles, a noninflationary currency, low taxation, tariff reform, and the retirement of the greenbacks, he wrote cogent annual reports on the nation's fiscal affairs. He was a person of strong opinions, and he never hesitated to express them. He labeled free coinage a dangerous fraud and characterized high tariffs as robbery. Wanting the government to cease its purchase of silver, he argued with free-silverites, who accused him of subserviency to Wall and Lombard streets. Manning scoffed at their complaints, preferring instead to build up the gold reserves. He also opposed extravagant governmental appropriations as a means to reduce the surplus in the Treasury. Above all, Manning remained loyal to Cleveland.

The pressures of office ultimately came to a head for Manning in 1886 and 1887. Exhausted from overwork and long hours and weakened by worry, he journeyed to Bournemouth, England, to recuperate from a breakdown. His condition seemed to improve with rest, and he returned to Washington. On 23 March 1887, after attending a cabinet meeting, he fell as he walked up the stairs to his office in the Treasury Building, and physicians discovered that a blood vessel had burst at the base of the brain. He resigned from the cabinet, effective 31 May 1887. In one of his last political acts, Manning strongly advised Governor David B. Hill of New York to avoid rivalry with Cleveland in 1888 for the party's presidential nomination. After his resignation from the Treasury Department, Manning accepted the presidency of the Western National Bank in New York City. He died of a heart ailment in Albany, New York.

Manning excelled in journalism, business, and politics. He was a hard-working individual who as secretary of the treasury labored long hours at his desk in Washington. His blunt frankness combined with a determined courage and dogmatic persistence gave him an edge over political opponents.

• Manning left no collection of personal papers. His letters are in the manuscript collections of contemporaries, including those of Grover Cleveland, William C. Whitney, and Daniel S. Lamont in the Manuscript Division of the Library of Congress and those of Samuel J. Tilden in the New York Public Library. His official papers are in the General Records of the Office of the Secretary of the Treasury in the National Archives. Books containing information about Manning are Allan Nevins, *Grover Cleveland: A Study in Courage* (1932); Richard E. Welch, Jr., *The Presidencies of Grover Cleveland* (1988); George F. Parker, *Recollections of Grover Cleveland* (1909); and H. C. Thomas, *The Return of the Democratic Party to Power in 1884* (1919). Obituaries are in the *Albany Argus* and the *New York Times*, 25 Dec. 1887.

LEONARD SCHLUP

MANNING, Eleanor. *See* Howe, Lois Lilley, Eleanor Manning, and Mary Almy.

MANNING, Isaac Hall (14 Sept. 1866–12 Feb. 1946), physician, medical educator, and medical care administrator, was born in Pittsboro, North Carolina, the son of John Manning, a state legislator, congressman, law professor, and founder of the University of North Carolina Law School, and Louisa Hall. Manning attended the University of North Carolina from 1886 to 1891, including the then one-year medical program (he received no degrees). For four years he was an industrial chemist in Wilmington, North Carolina. In 1894 he enrolled in the Long Island College Hospital in Brooklyn, where he received the doctor of medicine degree in 1897.

Following a stint as a railroad surgeon for the Atlantic Coast Line, Manning returned to the University of North Carolina in 1901 as the third full-time faculty member in the now two-year medical school and remained in Chapel Hill the rest of his life. To prepare himself to teach physiology and physiological chemistry, he spent summer sessions studying physiology in laboratories at the University of Chicago and at Harvard University. In 1905 he succeeded Richard H. Whitehead as dean of the medical school. Manning was married in 1906 to Martha Battle Lewis, who died the following year. In 1911 he married Mary Best Jones; they had three children.

The major issue confronting Manning throughout his deanship was the survival of the UNC medical school as a two-year program. (An underequipped clinical campus in Raleigh, loosely affiliated with the university and with a separate dean, had closed in 1910 after graduating seventy-six students in its eight years of operation.) By this time most American schools had adopted the German model of two basic science years followed by two clinical years. "Half schools" like UNC did not award degrees but arranged for the transfer of their students to four-year schools. As dean and sole admissions and placement officer, Manning struggled each spring to find places for his forty students, all the while recognizing that the school's reputation depended on their subsequent performances in the relatively few degree-granting schools that accepted transfers.

During 1921 and 1922 Manning prepared an extensive report for university president Harry Woodburn Chase and the trustees, making the case for expanding to a four-year medical school. The board approved Manning's report and recommended an expanded medical school and teaching hospital in Chapel Hill, whereupon Governor Cameron Morrison appointed a committee to develop the recommendations further. The committee included Manning's longtime rival, pharmacology professor William deBerneire MacNider. Two of the committee's trustee members, legislators from Charlotte, favored locating the school in that city; MacNider favored locating it in Durham; the others wanted it in Chapel Hill.

Meanwhile, William Preston Few, president of Trinity College in Durham (a Methodist institution that had not yet been granted the portion of the Duke fortune that would change its name) offered a proposal to the committee: a clinical campus could be built in Durham, funded partly by the state and partly by an unnamed private source—presumably the Duke family—and controlled jointly by Trinity and UNC. Chase and the governor were agreeable, but the Charlotte constituency was not, nor were others on the committee, to whom a coalition between a religious institution and the state was an anathema, as it was to many North Carolinians.

The trustees decided ultimately against accepting Few's proposal and in 1923 voted to request funds from the general assembly to establish a four-year school in the university, without, however, specifying the location. The legislature disallowed the request. The organization of a new Duke University medical school in 1925 (opened in 1930) effectively prevented the realization of Manning's dream during his lifetime.

Manning was a private man with few outside interests beyond the medical school, his family, and his students, to whom he was devoted. An undergraduate student at the university, who had been a patient in the student health service, remembered him as a "bluff, kindly, careful doctor, not given to over-much talk." To his medical students he was tenacious, bluntly honest, taciturn, but kindly. His professional colleagues knew him for his personal and intellectual integrity and his frankness and fairness.

In 1933 Manning's deanship ended when university president Frank Porter Graham overruled him and ordered the admission of a fifth Jewish applicant, one beyond Manning's self-imposed restriction of no more than 10 percent of each class (the same informal quota that many American medical schools tacitly adopted during the 1920s). Graham, whose well-known moral and social convictions guided his presidency, told the dean that he would not approve a policy of institutionalized discrimination. Manning described to Graham the difficulty faced in placing Jewish students in four-year medical schools, adding that "the Medical School had just as well close its doors, as with a preponderance of Jews in the School the Gentiles would not come to it, and if such a policy was insisted upon [he] would be forced to resign." Despite a show of support from the medical school faculty for Manning's position, Graham insisted, whereupon Manning resigned. The episode was reported in newspapers throughout the state and nation. Most of the editorial comment, while regretting the medical school dean's resignation and commending his long record of service, praised President Graham's action. Manning continued as professor of physiology until his retirement in 1939.

At the time of his resignation Manning had already become involved in the emerging hospital pre-payment movement (later known as "Blue Cross"). In his 1934 presidential address to the North Carolina Medical Society, Manning called on the profession to exert its leadership in advancing hospitalization insurance. He was also careful to endorse organized medicine's position condemning insurance coverage for physicians' services. Manning's leadership was key in establishing the statewide Hospital Savings Association, one of two competing Blue Cross programs in North Carolina. He served as the association's first president from 1935 until 1941 and thereafter as chairman of the board and medical director. He died in Chapel Hill.

Manning was not celebrated for any scientific accomplishments, and he shunned the limelight of national professional circles. Throughout his twenty-eight years as dean of the UNC School of Medicine he worked quietly to protect its position and in the process succeeded in raising it from relative insignificance to high esteem by expanding and strengthening the faculty, library, physical facilities, and opportunities for faculty research. His unsuccessful attempt to add a hospital and clinical faculty was an important precursor of the post–World War II North Carolina Good Health Movement, which resulted finally in a full medical campus at the University of North Carolina. Manning is also credited for his pioneering role in establishing North Carolina Blue Cross–Blue Shield, which became the state's largest purveyor of health insurance.

• Manning's personal views of the significant events of his deanship are scattered throughout his unpublished history of the University of North Carolina School of Medicine titled "History of the U.N.C. School of Medicine, 1879–1937" (1940), which is housed in the Southern Historical Collection, University of North Carolina at Chapel Hill (no. 4369). This work was the basis of a chapter on the UNC medical school co-written with Walter Reece Berryhill, "Medical Education at the University of North Carolina," in *Medicine in North Carolina: Essays in the History of Medical Science and Medical Service, 1524–1960*, ed. Dorothy Long, vol. 2 (1972). It also served as the basis of a formal history of the school co-written with Berryhill and William B. Blythe, *Medical Education at Chapel Hill: The First Hundred Years* (1979). An independent account of Manning's attempt to expand the medical school is in Louis R. Wilson, *The University of North Carolina, 1900–1930: The Making of a Modern University* (1957). Manning's undergraduate years at Chapel Hill are mentioned in Kemp P. Battle, *History of the University of North Carolina* (1907; repr. 1974). The most expansive version of the episode that precipitated Manning's resignation as dean is in Edward C. Halperin, "Frank Porter Graham, Isaac Hall Manning, and the Jewish Quota at the University of North Carolina Medical School," *North Carolina Historical Review* 67 (4 Oct. 1990): 385–410. For another account see Warren Ashby, *Frank Porter Graham: A Southern Liberal* (1980). Manning's "President's Address" to the Medical Society of the State of North Carolina appeared in *Southern Medicine and Surgery* 46 (May 1934): 199–202. The history of the Hospital Savings Association is chronicled in V. K. Hart, "The History of Blue Cross and Blue Shield in North Carolina," in *Medicine in North Carolina: Essays in the History of Medical Science and Medical Service, 1524–1960*, ed. Dorothy Long, vol. 1 (1972). For depictions of Manning's personality see Robert B. House, *The Light that Shines: Chapel Hill, 1912–1916* (1964); Edward C. Halperin's article in the *North Carolina Historical Review* cited earlier; and a remembrance by Betty Smith, "Dr. Manning," *Chapel Hill Weekly*, 15 Feb. 1946. The same issue contains Manning's obituary. Obituaries in the state's major daily newspapers, including the *Durham Morning Herald* and the *Raleigh News and Observer*, appeared on 13 Feb. 1946. An official faculty memorial, written by Walter Reece Berryhill et al., "Memorial to Isaac Hall Manning, Presented to the General Faculty on May 31, 1946," is in the minutes of the general faculty of the University of North Carolina at Chapel Hill.

DONALD L. MADISON

MANNING, James (Oct. 1738–29 July 1791), Baptist clergyman and founding president of Rhode Island College (now Brown University), was born in Elizabeth Township, New Jersey. The first names and occupations of his parents are uncertain. Manning attended Hopewell Academy, a Baptist grammar school in New Jersey. After completing the course of study at Hopewell, he entered the College of New Jersey (later Princeton University), where he studied under Samuel Davies. In September 1762 he graduated second in his class.

After completing college, Manning was ordained a minister at the Scotch Plains Baptist Church in Elizabeth Township. In 1763 he married Margaret Stites; they had no children. In 1764 the couple moved to Warren, Rhode Island, where he founded a Latin school and a Baptist church. While on a preaching mission to Nova Scotia the previous July, he stopped at Newport, Rhode Island, to deliver a proposal from leaders of the Philadelphia Baptist Association to establish a Baptist college in Rhode Island. The Baptists of Newport requested that Ezra Stiles, a Congregational pastor in Newport who would later serve as president of Yale College, write the charter for them. Because Baptist leaders in the Rhode Island Assembly felt that Stiles's proposed charter would have given effective control of the college to the Congregationalists, the provincial assembly modified it to give the Baptists greater control. Although Manning played no apparent part in the charter revision, the rancorous debates in the provincial assembly concerning these modifications left Stiles and many Congregationalists opposed to the college and to Manning. The assembly finally approved the charter for Rhode Island College in 1764.

The Fellows of Rhode Island College chose Manning to be president of the college, which was organized in Warren in 1765. A Calvinist with an evangelistic spirit, he was more suited to action than to scholarship. However he taught classical languages, moral philosophy, and rhetoric. In 1769 the first class graduated with seven members. Shortly thereafter the college's financial problems led to its relocation to Providence in 1770.

Under Manning's leadership Rhode Island College accommodated several religious minorities. Seventh-day Baptists and Jews were not required to attend Sunday worship, for example. Jews were exempted from having to affirm the inspiration of the New Testament. Also, Quakers could wear hats in college buildings.

By organizing the Warren Baptist Association in 1767, Manning attempted to unite New England Baptists on a Calvinistic plan using a Baptist version of the Westminster Confession. His arrival in Providence occasioned a schism in the Baptist church there. When the pastor and part of the congregation withdrew, Manning became the pastor of Providence Baptist Church, where he served from 1770 until 1791. Under his leadership, the church reintroduced congregational singing, expanded the terms of communion to include more Baptists, and moved to a more Calvinistic theology.

Manning's involvement in Baptist affairs also included working to end taxation of Baptists to support Congregationalist churches and ministers in Massachusetts. As representatives of the Warren Association in 1774, he and Isaac Backus petitioned the Massachusetts delegates to the Continental Congress, requesting relief from this burden. The incident caused John Adams, Ezra Stiles, and others to accuse him of disloyalty to the American cause.

These attacks on Manning's patriotism were unfair. Although he regretted having to suspend classes and resented the damage done to college property by the French who used it as a hospital, he maintained the trust and cooperation of the New England civil and military authorities. His early wartime correspondence with English Baptists does, however, suggest that initially he was neutral in the conflict.

Despite his expressed disdain for politics, the Rhode Island Assembly unanimously elected Manning to Congress under the Articles of Confederation in 1786. He actively worked for the ratification of the U.S. Constitution both in Massachusetts and Rhode Island. His influence among Massachusetts Baptists helped provide the margin of victory there.

Manning was one of the earliest New England Baptists to become involved in the abolitionist movement. Despite having earlier owned a slave, in 1789 he joined the abolitionist society of Moses Brown. His support of gradual emancipation alienated some Baptist merchants. In April 1791 he resigned as pastor of Providence Baptist Church and requested that the college find a new president. He was still serving as president in July 1791 when he was struck by a fatal attack of apoplexy at his home.

Although Manning is primarily known as the founding president of Brown University, his greatest significance lies in his contribution to the institutional development of the Baptist denomination. While the college became a focus of Baptist identity, Manning helped develop Baptist identity in other areas. He worked to remove barriers to communion among the diverse New England Baptists. His influence helped reestablish Calvinism as the theological standard among New England Baptists, providing the basis for cooperation with the Philadelphia Association. This Calvinism was not a theological straitjacket, but served as a common reference around which disparate New England Baptists could coalesce and from which they could evolve.

• The only collection of Manning's papers consists of one oversized box in the Brown University Archives in the John Hay Library at Brown University. An accomplished extemporaneous preacher and orator who did not write out his talks, Manning left few published works. Three eighteenth-century sources are still more revealing than any twentieth-century works. Morgan Edwards, "Materials for a History of the Baptists in Rhode Island," *Collections of the Rhode Island Historical Society* 6 (1867): 301–80, was written about 1771 and is the best account of Manning's early life. Edwards's account of the founding of Rhode Island College is biased, but all subsequent interpretations have to deal with it. Isaac Backus's obituary of Manning, reproduced as "A Learned Baptist Founds an Ivy League College," in William G. McLoughlin, *Soul Liberty: The Baptists' Struggle in New England, 1630–1833* (1991), implies as much as it reveals. Franklin Dexter, ed., *The Literary Diary of Ezra Stiles* (1901), contains virulent attacks on Manning's character. Reuben Guild, *Life, Times, and Correspondence of James Manning, and the Early History of Brown University* (1864), is largely a collection of Manning's correspondence with commentary. William Sprague, "James Manning," *Annals of the American Pulpit*, vol. 6, *The Baptists* (1865), propagates its share of creative fiction but contains an informative letter from Rhode Island College graduate William Hunter. Walter Bronson, *The History of Brown University, 1764–1914* (1914), is capriciously selective in its use of sources. William G. McLoughlin, *New England Dissent, 1630–1833: The Baptists and the Separation of Church and State* (1971), follows Bronson on the founding of Rhode Island College but does an excellent job of placing Manning in the context of New England Baptists. An obituary is in the *Providence Gazette*, 6 Aug. 1791.

CHARLES L. DUNN

MANNING, Joseph Columbus (21 May 1870–19 May 1930), reformer and politician, was born in the hill country town of Lineville, Clay County, Alabama, the son of Henry Allen Manning, a merchant and Methodist minister, and Martha Burrough. A bright, devout boy, Manning grew up amid profound social and economic changes. The price of cotton, which had become a dominant upcountry crop, declined in the 1870s and 1880s. Supply merchants like Manning's father financed seeds and fertilizer at high rates of interest; many farmers fell into tenancy. As a result, a society once marked by a sense of equality among white landowners was increasingly stratified.

The same years marked the triumph of the Democratic party, dominated by "Black Belt" plantation interests but also supported by businessmen and officials in North Alabama. Democrats preached white supremacy and fiscal conservatism—each of which seemed irrelevant to restless farmers in debt-ridden counties like Clay, where few black people lived. Merchants, as Manning later wrote, looked upon their customers with "a feeling of political ownership." He added, that "was a thing I wanted to see smashed." In fact Independents, Greenbackers, and other third-party candidates sometimes won in the hill country. In statewide contests Democrats were able to "count out" opponents by fraudulent use of black votes.

As a boy, Joseph Manning sided almost instinctively with local Independents, probably to the dismay of his family. Working as a printer's devil for the county newspaper, he fell under the influence of its editor, a political freethinker. After attending the Florence Normal School (1886–1888), Manning worked for a

year as a traveling book agent in Texas—the ideological epicenter of agrarian revolt. In 1891 Manning went to Atlanta, where he worked as a journalist and was inspired by the radical agrarian Tom Watson. By 1892 he was a Populist, committed to currency inflation and to the overthrow of the Democratic party and convinced that the interests and rights of black and white "producers" were the same.

In the spring of 1892 the 22-year-old Manning returned to Alabama as chief organizer of the People's party, where his fiery stump-speaking earned him the nickname "Evangel." Methodism and Georgia populism had taught him how to rally the plain folk, but he was forced to work in the shadow of Reuben F. Kolb, a former state commissioner of agriculture who ran for governor as an insurgent Democrat in 1892 and 1894. Kolb was so popular that Populists (and Republicans) had little choice but to support him. Manning doubted Kolb's commitment to reform but was outraged to see him twice cheated out of office by ballot-box stuffers.

These frauds changed the complexion of state politics. Agrarians who might otherwise have campaigned for the Populist Omaha platform were forced instead to fight for "a free ballot and a fair count." Manning, who won election to the legislature from Clay County in 1894 and served one term, emerged as a strategist and voice of moderation, engineering a November 1894 convention that brought Kolb's supporters into the People's party. Likewise he headed a campaign to secure a U.S. Senate probe of Alabama politics. Election statistics in hand, Manning and his allies traveled to New York, Washington, and other cities; in New Orleans (1895) he founded a short-lived Southern Ballot Rights League. No investigation resulted, however, and in 1896 the People's party faded into the "Free Silver" wing of the Democrats. Unwilling to join the Democratic party he had long opposed, Manning became a Republican.

For the rest of his life Manning served as an informed critic of Democratic regimes. The Alabama Democrats' long-term response to insurgency was the constitution of 1901, which used a poll tax, understanding clause, and other devices to disfranchise nearly all black voters and many lower-class whites. Manning opposed the constitutional movement, which he saw as an effort to ensure "Black Belt" Democratic control. Though his attitude toward disfranchisement was not always consistent, he was generally a defender of black voting rights. As postmaster of Alexander City, Alabama (1900–1909), he caused a furor by insisting that black patrons be treated with respect. Meanwhile, in an effort to interest Republican presidents in regional issues, he was publishing pamphlets such as his *Rise and Reign of the Bourbon Oligarchy* (1904).

In this and other writings Manning sought to point out the hypocrisy of demagogues who, long after blacks had ceased to vote, used the cry of white supremacy as a means of camouflaging their neglect of other issues. Such tactics, he observed, corrupted white people and encouraged violence and oppression.

He stressed that the record of black people—whether measured in terms of literacy, property ownership, or respect for law—was outstanding for a people so recently enslaved. Likewise Manning demonstrated that Democratic election laws had reduced white voter participation across the South, cementing the power of courthouse cliques.

In 1909 Manning lost his postmastership and moved north, eventually settling in New York City. In 1909 he participated in the founding of the National Association for the Advancement of Colored People; he remained an active member and was a correspondent of several NAACP leaders, notably Walter S. White. In the last phases of his career he wrote for black newspapers such as the *Washington Bee*, lobbied Republican officeholders for civil rights legislation (including the Dyer antilynching bill), and denounced the second Ku Klux Klan. His health having failed by the late 1920s, Manning devoted himself to writing his memoirs. He had married Zoe Duncan in 1894. The couple had three sons and two daughters and later separated. Manning died in New York City.

Manning's story is one of courage in the face of defeat, but also one of growth. Unlike his former mentor, Tom Watson, Manning overcame the racial prejudices he had absorbed from his time, place, and culture. He died an exile from all he had once known but was not overwhelmed with bitterness. Ever optimistic, he predicted that a civil rights revolution would restore the voting rights of the plain folk. His *Fadeout of Populism* (1928) proclaims, "It is equally as impossible for the Constitution . . . to stand for one thing in the free states of the North . . . and another in the South . . . as it was impossible for the nation to continue, in Lincoln's time, half slave and half free."

• The largest concentration of Manning letters is in the William E. Chandler Papers, Library of Congress. Manning's other works include *Politics of Alabama* (1893); *Letting the South Alone* (1903); *Sectionalism: The Rise and Reign of the Southern Oligarchy* (1916); and *From Five to Twenty-Five: His Earlier Life as Recalled by Joseph Columbus Manning* (1929). Paul M. Pruitt, Jr., "Joseph C. Manning of Alabama: A Rebel against the Solid South" (Ph.D. diss., College of William and Mary, 1980), contains complete coverage of Manning's life. See also Pruitt, "A Changing of the Guard: Joseph C. Manning and Populist Strategy in the Fall of 1894," *Alabama Historical Quarterly* 40 (Spring and Summer 1978): 20–36, and "Defender of the Voteless: Joseph C. Manning Views the Disfranchisement Era in Alabama" *Alabama Historical Quarterly* 43 (Fall 1981): 171–85. See also Jerrell H. Shofner and William Warren Rogers, "Joseph C. Manning: Militant Agrarian, Enduring Populist" *Alabama Historical Quarterly* 29 (Spring and Summer 1967): 7–37, and William Warren Rogers, *The One Gallused Rebellion: Agrarianism in Alabama, 1865–1896* (1970).

PAUL M. PRUITT, JR.

MANNING, Marie (22 Jan. 1868–28 Nov. 1945), journalist and advice columnist, was born in Washington, D.C., the daughter of Michael Charles Manning, a retired military officer employed by the War Department, and Elizabeth Barrett. Her mother died when she was about six and her father before she was twenty. Although in modest circumstances, her family was well connected in Washington society, and she made occasional trips to England to visit her uncle, a captain in the British navy. Manning received the typical education of an upper-middle-class woman of the day. She was tutored privately in Washington, New York, and London and graduated from Miss Kerr's Finishing School in Washington about 1890. Concerned because she was exceptionally tall and lanky, her father had sent her to a ranch in the West to gain weight and improve her health as a teenager.

So intrigued by journalism that she had risked expulsion from Miss Kerr's by smuggling in sensational newspapers to read during nightly meditation, Manning seized a chance after graduation to write for Joseph Pulitzer's *New York World*, which epitomized "yellow journalism." This opportunity came her way when she found herself seated by accident at a dinner party beside *World* editor Arthur Brisbane, who invited her to contribute to the newspaper. Overcoming the objections of her guardian, she journeyed to New York, her "head full of the new idea of careers for women," she wrote in her 1944 autobiography, *Ladies Now and Then*. Journalism, she explained, looked more appealing than the life of an impoverished debutante who would "have to work from dawn to dark to try to round up some second lieutenant." Like other reportorial aspirants, Manning initially earned about $5 a week on "space rates," with her pay based on the amount of material she sold to the newspaper. She advanced to a regular job at $30 a week after gaining an interview that star reporters had failed to get with former president Grover Cleveland. When Brisbane left the *World* in 1897 to become editor of the *Evening Journal*, owned by William Randolph Hearst, Pulitzer's archrival, Manning, like a number of other staffers, followed Brisbane. Confined to an obscure office called the "Hen Coop" with two other women, she worked on the woman's page, interviewed celebrities, and wrote stories on murders from a woman's angle.

Acclaim came when Manning started the "Beatrice Fairfax" advice column on 20 July 1898. She proposed the column, the first of its type, after Brisbane appeared in the Hen Coop with letters from three women in desperate circumstances—one sought a job to support her children after being abandoned by her husband, another threatened suicide because her lover had left, and the third recounted domestic violence. "With the rashness of youth I suggested a new department and found the whole thing thrown in my lap," she recalled in an article in *Family Circle* (26 Jan. 1945). Since it was considered somewhat unseemly for women to write under their own names, she borrowed a pseudonym from Dante's "Beata Beatrix" and Fairfax County in Virginia, where her family had property. The column featured an idealized sketch of Manning in a high linen collar and promised she would advise "on the troubles of your heart." Although she made up a few letters to herself to start the column, her advice soon attracted up to 1,400 correspondents a day, mainly young people with courtship difficulties. Other newspapers hired their own lovelorn columnists, but the only one to rival Beatrice Fairfax was the widely syndicated "Dorothy Dix" (Elizabeth Meriwether Gilmer).

While she did not challenge conventional ideas of propriety, Manning avoided excessive sentimentality. She prided herself on wit and offered "large doses of common sense" to readers, as she put it in *Ladies Now and Then*; her philosophy was "dry your eyes, roll up your sleeves, and dig for a practical solution." Although the sophisticated professed to be amused by the column, its popularity testified to a public avid for guidance on personal relationships in an era when urbanization had weakened the traditional authorities of religion and the family.

In addition to writing as Beatrice Fairfax, who became celebrated in song and folklore, Manning continued as a feature writer for Hearst under her own name until her marriage in 1905 to Herman Edward Gasch, a Washington real estate dealer. Except for a brief period during World War I, she did not return to the column, which was continued by others, until 1929, when financial reverses forced her to resume full-time employment. During her almost quarter-century absence, she had two sons and wrote short stories, novelettes, and magazine articles similar to two earlier adventure novels, *Lord Allingham, Bankrupt* (1902) and *Judith of the Plains* (1903). Aware of legal inequalities facing women, she worked ardently for woman suffrage.

During the depression and World War II Manning covered women's news in Washington for the International News Service as well as writing the column, which by then was syndicated to 200 newspapers by King Features. A personal friend of Eleanor Roosevelt, Manning covered the first lady's press conferences for women only. During World War II Manning made the Fairfax column, at this point geared mainly to mature individuals with marital difficulties, a compendium of advice for service personnel and their families.

Just under six feet tall and weighing 170 pounds, Manning looked like an imposing grandmother in later years with her hair gathered into a bun high on the back of her head. She was a charter member of the Women's National Press Club and the American Newspaper Women's Club. She died at her Washington home.

A tough-minded woman of energy and initiative, Manning possessed an intuitive understanding that mass media could both entertain and instruct through interactive discussion of personal dilemmas. Through her column and by her own example, she encouraged women to better their conditions rather than to accept fate and play the roles of passive domestic victims.

• Manning's personal papers are in the possession of her son U.S. District Court judge Oliver Gasch of Washington, D.C. It is difficult to establish when she was born, since no governmental record can be found, and Manning herself apparently told people that she was several years younger than she actually was. According to Oliver Gasch, 1868 is recorded as her birth year in the baptismal records of St. Matthew's Catholic Church in Washington, D.C. Her book *Personal Reply*, a compilation of her World War II columns, was published in 1943. A rich source of biographical data is *Current Biography* (1944). Extensive quotations from the early column appear in Lynne Olson, "Dear Beatrice Fairfax . . . ," *American Heritage*, May–June 1992, pp. 90–97. A source for the World War II columns is "The Soldiers Told Beatrice Fairfax," *PIC*, 23 June 1942, pp. 40–42. For a contemporary view, see Ishbel Ross, *Ladies of the Press* (1936). Obituaries are in the *New York Times*, 30 Nov. 1945, the *Washington Times-Herald*, 29 and 30 Nov. 1945, and *Editor and Publisher*, 1 Dec. 1945.

MAURINE H. BEASLEY

MANNING, William Thomas (12 May 1866–18 Nov. 1949), Episcopal bishop of New York, was born in Northampton, England, the son of John Manning and Matilda Robinson. The family emigrated in order to farm in the United States, moving first to Nebraska (1882) and then to San Diego, California (1886). While in England, the Mannings were active in the Anglican church, an involvement that continued in the Protestant Episcopal Church in the United States of America. In April 1888 William Manning enrolled at an Episcopal school, the University of the South in Sewanee, Tennessee, where he prepared for the ordained ministry. Ordained a deacon in December 1889 he left Sewanee for a church in Memphis. He remained in touch, however, with Professor William Porcher DuBose, a man whom some have come to regard as the premier theologian of the nineteenth-century Episcopal church. Manning became a family friend, assisted DuBose with a writing project, and after ordination to the priesthood (Dec. 1891) and service at a church in Redlands, California, joined him on the faculty as professor of systematic divinity (1893–1894). Manning received his bachelor of divinity degree from Sewanee in 1894.

The focus of Manning's early career was parish ministry. Leaving Sewanee in 1895, he served churches in Cincinnati, Ohio; Lansdowne, Pennsylvania; and Nashville, Tennessee. He married Florence Van Antwerp in 1895 while he was serving Trinity Church in Cincinnati; they had two children. Manning met with particular success at Christ Church, Nashville (1898–1903), where he retired a $25,000 debt, organized a citywide preaching mission, and served as deputy to the General Convention of the Episcopal Church (1901).

In 1903 Manning accepted a call from Trinity Church, New York City, to serve as the vicar of St. Agnes' Chapel. In December of the following year the vestry added to this title that of assistant rector, an offer that induced him to decline his election as bishop of the new diocese of Harrisburg (Pennsylvania). When Morgan Dix, the rector of Trinity, died in 1908, the vestry elected Manning as his successor.

Trinity was the oldest and wealthiest church in the diocese of New York; to be named the parish's rector was to be recognized as a leader by the denomination.

Manning served on the Episcopal church's Board of Missions, represented his diocese at General Convention (1910, 1913), and declined a second election as bishop (Western New York, 1917).

At the General Convention of 1910, Manning joined with Bishop Charles Henry Brent, Robert Hallowell Gardiner (1855–1924), and others in calling for an ecumenical Faith and Order Conference, which would explore the issues of theology and ecclesiology that separated Christian churches. Manning traveled to the British Isles in 1912 to create support for the conference and in 1922 was elected president of the commission preparing for it. He represented the Episcopal church at the conference's first meeting (Lausanne, 1927), a gathering at which Brent presided. The conference would later become a commission of the World Council of Churches, which was founded in 1948.

In 1921 Manning accepted election as the bishop of New York, a position he would hold until retirement in 1946. As bishop he continued to play an active role at General Convention. Within his own diocese Manning initiated a building campaign for the partially constructed Cathedral of St. John the Divine, which led to the completion of the building's nave in 1941. He was an advocate of human rights, opposing racial segregation of churches and speaking against persecutions of Jews in Germany and the USSR at a 1933 rally in Madison Square Garden.

In his views of church order, Manning was a conservative high churchman. He regarded a literal succession of episcopal ordinations, connecting Jesus with present-day bishops, as necessary for a valid ministry, even though eminent Anglican scholars, such as B. H. Streeter, were at the time distancing themselves from historical claims about such a succession. Manning, though interested in ecumenical discussion, opposed the 1914 Panama Conference, which called for cooperative Protestant missions in Latin America. From his point of view the area was already provided with a valid ministry (i.e., one that made claims to apostolic succession) by the Roman Catholic church. Similarly, Manning issued an open letter in 1939 opposing union between Episcopalians, who claimed apostolic succession, and Presbyterians, who did not.

Manning spelled out his position on the fundamentalist-modernist controversy in the House of Bishops' 1923 letter on modernism and the Virgin Birth, which he drafted. Episcopalians, like many other Protestants, were seeking a proper relationship between the fruits of "modern" science and the traditional affirmations of the Christian faith. Manning attempted to balance the two by distinguishing intellectual assent from an attitude of devotion, which he characterized as an "entire surrender" that was "deeper and higher and more personal" than acknowledgment of mere facts. Manning believed that Christians could employ the disciplines of modern science in the study of religion so long as they maintained this deeper piety.

Manning was a defender of traditional family values, opposing liberalization of the Episcopal church's attitude on divorce and remarriage. He also supported American policy in World Wars I and II. He served as chaplain to the 302d Engineers prior to their departure for Europe in February 1918, and as early as 1935 he preached about the possibility of American involvement in a second European war. He died in New York City.

• The archives of the Episcopal Diocese of New York contain some of Manning's papers. His correspondence with Robert H. Gardiner concerning the World Conference on Faith and Order is housed at the General Theological Seminary in New York. A series of Manning's lectures on ecumenism delivered at Kenyon College in 1919 were published in 1920 with the title *The Call to Unity*. In the year after his retirement in 1946, Manning published *Be Strong in the Lord*, a collection of twenty-five sermons and addresses. W. D. F. Hughes's laudatory biography, *Prudently with Power: William Thomas Manning, Tenth Bishop of New York*, appeared in 1964. For a negative picture of the sometimes inflexible Manning, see Alexander Zabriskie *Arthur Selden Lloyd, Missionary-statesman and Pastor* (1942). For an account of his role in the drafting of the 1923 pastoral letter on modernism, see Hugh Martin Jansen, Jr., "Heresy Trials in the Protestant Episcopal Church, 1890–1930" (Ph.D. diss., Columbia Univ., 1965). Part six of *A History of the Parish of Trinity Church in the City of New York* (1962), written by Charles Thorley Bridgeman, details the years in which Manning served as Trinity's rector.

ROBERT W. PRICHARD

MAN RAY (27 Aug. 1890–18 Nov. 1976), artist and photographer, was born Emmanuel Radnitsky in Philadelphia, Pennsylvania, the son of Melach Radnitsky (later Max Ray), a tailor, and Manya "Minnie" Louria (or Lourie), both Russian-Jewish immigrants. In 1897 the family moved to Brooklyn. After high school young Emmanuel was awarded a scholarship to study architecture at New York University. Deciding to pursue a career as an artist, he attended classes at the National Academy of Design and at the Art Students League. He was temperamentally unsuited to the rigors of the academic styles favored by these institutions, however, and so enrolled in the Ferrer Center, where Robert Henri and George Bellows taught life drawing. It was around late 1911 or early 1912 that the Radnitsky family adopted the surname Ray. Man Ray, however, preferred to list his name as a single unit.

While taking classes at the Ferrer Center, Man Ray worked as a calligrapher and layout artist for a Manhattan publishing company. Frequenting Alfred Stieglitz's Gallery 291, Man Ray was exposed to the latest in modern art, both European and American. In 1913, at age twenty-three, he moved from his parents' home to an artists' colony in Ridgefield, New Jersey. His work from this period, landscapes painted with a brash, bright palette, was reminiscent of the work of the fauvists. At Ridgefield Man Ray met and in 1914 married Belgian poet Adon Lacroix. Together they published a small work, *Book of Divers Writings* (1915), that included poems by Lacroix and drawings by Man Ray. Guided by his wife's collection of French literature, particularly the works of Charles Pierre Baudelaire, Arthur Rimbaud, Stéphane Mallarmé, and the protodadaist Isidore Ducasse, Man Ray turned his thoughts to Paris.

Man Ray met French artist Marcel Duchamp during the latter's visit to New York in 1915. The two quickly established a friendship that would last until Duchamp's death in 1968. That same year Man Ray's first exhibition was held at the Daniel Gallery in New York. The next year, 1916, Man Ray painted his first major work, *The Rope Dancer Accompanies Herself with Her Shadows* (Museum of Modern Art, New York City). His second exhibition at the Daniel Gallery, which opened in 1916, included a number of works—such as *Self-Portrait*, constructed of an electric door bell mounted on canvas—that challenged the prevailing standards of even the most avant-garde American work of the time.

In the years between 1917 and 1921 Man Ray put aside painting in favor of three-dimensional objects of a sculptural nature. In many ways these works paralleled the iconoclastic work emerging out of the literary and artistic movement known as dada—begun in Zurich in 1916 for the purpose of negating all traditionally held values regarding art and culture—though Man Ray was not introduced to dadism by Duchamp until around 1920. Man Ray had earlier taught himself the rudiments of photography, and he now began to use the process to document his objects.

Having found a kindred spirit in dada, Man Ray hoped to foster its growth in the United States. In 1921, together with Duchamp, he began to publish the magazine *New York Dada*; it elicited little interest, however, and ceased publication after only one issue. Despondent by the lack of response to the magazine, Man Ray left for Paris—without his wife—in the spring of 1921. (The couple eventually divorced in 1937.) Greeted enthusiastically by the artists and poets who gathered at the Café Certa, Man Ray became a fixture in the Montparnasse section of Paris, where he moved in the circle of artists and poets that included Tristan Tzara, André Breton, Philippe Soupault, and Francis Picabia. Aware of his economic and cultural dependence—his French was basic at best—he avoided the political fractiousness of the dadaists, and his nonconfrontational personality enabled him to remain friends with them as well as with Breton and his cohorts, who subsequently became the core of the surrealist movement. Man Ray's first Paris exhibition, which opened in 1921 at the Librairie Six, consisted mostly of works he had brought from New York. A new work, *Le Cadeau*, consisting of a flatiron with fourteen tacks on its smooth surface, became a key icon both in Man Ray's oeuvre and in dada, as well as an embodiment of the emerging surrealism.

In late 1921 Man Ray began to use the photographic process he called "rayography": common objects such as combs, keys, and drinking glasses were placed directly on photosensitive paper, and lights were flashed on the objects; the developed image (called a rayograph) seemed to float somewhere beyond the plane of the paper itself. At the same time he also began to take portrait photographs of those in the Parisian art world.

Among the writers and artists who sat for him in his first years were James Joyce, Gertrude Stein, Henri Matisse, and Marcel Proust. As Man Ray's fame as a portraitist spread in the 1920s, his studio in Paris became a mandatory stop for travelers from America and other parts of Europe. Fashion photography assignments from the most important Parisian designers also became a staple of his work. Man Ray created a romantic style of fashion photography that sacrificed mundane realism in favor of surprising and sometimes shocking depictions of haute couture. His photographs appeared regularly during the 1920s and early 1930s in *Vanity Fair* and *Vogue*. By 1934, when his pictures began appearing in *Harper's Bazaar*, his career as a fashion photographer had reached its peak. The income from his fashion photography made Man Ray's life noticeably more comfortable, and he was able to build a New York bank account that would see him through later, less prosperous, times.

During his first months at Montparnasse Man Ray met the already celebrated gamine Kiki de Montparnasse (born Alice Prin). The two soon moved in together, and she became a key feature of his art. Serving as his model, Kiki was the subject of his well-known photographs "Le Violon d'Ingres" (1924) and "Noire et Blanche" (1926) as well as numerous portraits. The two remained a couple for only about six years but remained lifelong friends until Kiki's death in 1953.

In 1923 Tzara asked Man Ray to create a film for his planned dada-arts gala, and Man Ray improvised a two-minute blend of rayographs, photographs, and randomly exposed film that he ironically titled *Le Retour à la Raison* (The return to reason). The enigmatic film's debut was marred by a brawl among the dadaists that led to Breton's formal creation of the surrealist movement the following year. Cinema continued to intrigue Man Ray, and he made three more films: *Emak Bakia* (1926), *L'Étoile de Mer* (The Starfish; 1928), and *Les Mystères du Château de Dés* (The mysteries of the Château of Dice; 1929) before the advent of sound and the collaborative nature of film production discouraged him from further cinematic efforts.

In 1929, his relationship with Kiki having ended, Man Ray met Lee Miller, a former model for photographers Edward Steichen and Arnold Genthe. Miller became Man Ray's darkroom assistant and receptionist as well as his lover. During the three years that he and Miller worked together, Man Ray developed his "solarization" process in which negatives in the process of being developed are flashed with a bright light, creating a sort of halo effect around the main image. At the same time, an ever-widening social circle encompassed the couple as both participants and photographers. Miller's independent nature led her to leave Man Ray in 1932. Devastated by her departure, he threw himself into his work and created one of his best-known paintings, *A l'Heure de l'Observatoire—Les Amoureux* (also known as *The Lips*). This large painting of a pair of disembodied lips accompanied Man Ray on his travels and held a place of honor in many of his important exhibitions. Miller was also the subject of *Object Meant to Be Destroyed* (1932; later retitled *Perpetual Motif*), in which a photograph of her eye was affixed to a metronome. In later years Man Ray and Miller revived their friendship, and her husband, Roland Penrose, became an important supporter of his work.

Determined to deemphasize his work as a photographer, Man Ray worked on a number of different projects. In 1937 he published *Les Mains Libres*, a "surrealist travelogue" consisting of pen-and-ink drawings that, according to the title page, were "illustrated by the poems of Paul Éluard." In 1938 Man Ray participated in the Exposition Internationale du Surréalisme, the last formal gasp of the surrealist movement before its American exile during World War II. For the event, whose theme centered on altered store mannequins, he contributed a mannequin and acted as "master of lighting."

With the fall of France in 1940, Man Ray joined the exodus of artists to the United States. His companion of recent years, Adrienne "Ady" Fidelin, a dancer from Guadeloupe, chose to stay in France. His U.S. citizenship and New York bank account enabled him to escape to Spain, where he boarded a ship to New York with, among others, Salvador Dali. Not caring for the city of his childhood, Man Ray abandoned the group of exiled surrealists in New York and late in 1940 decamped to California. In Los Angeles he delivered a message from a New York acquaintance to Juliet Browner, a 28-year-old former artists' model then stranded on the West Coast. The two were immediately charmed with one another and moved to a Hollywood residential hotel together.

In Los Angeles Man Ray devoted his time entirely to painting. When visitors to his studio requested photographic portraits he told them, "I am not a photographer. I am a fautegrapher, I take a fautegraph, a false line. My true line is the pencil and the brush." Man Ray more formally repudiated the artistic nature of photography in his essay "Photography Is Not Art," which appeared in the April–October 1943 issue of the avant-garde journal *View*. In addition to working on new paintings, he re-created works he had left behind in Paris that he feared had been destroyed. Man Ray's first exhibition in the United States since leaving Paris was held at the Frank Perls Gallery in Los Angeles in 1941. His work was featured in a number of other exhibitions in southern California, but his paintings found few buyers. In 1946 he and Browner were married in a double ceremony with fellow surrealists Max Ernst and Dorothea Tanning. This would be his last relationship, and it, like the others, was childless.

Man Ray longed to return to France—"California is a beautiful prison," he once told his sister—and he and Browner moved there, permanently in 1951. Back in his beloved Paris, Man Ray began a new phase of his career, concentrating on painting and the creation of assemblages and filling his studio with these objects, among them *Miroir à Mourir de Rire* (Mirror to die laughing by; 1952), *Monument au Peintre Inconnu*

(Tomb of the unknown painter; 1953), and *Ballet Français* (1956). Participating in the Exposition inteRnatiOnale du Surréalisme (EROS), organized by André Breton and Marcel Duchamp in 1959, Man Ray reaffirmed his participation in the surrealist movement.

Numerous exhibitions of Man Ray's work were held throughout the world in the 1960s. He also began to create limited editions of his assemblages as well as his early dada sculptures, such as *Le Cadeau*. In the later 1960s he also lifted his self-imposed ban on photography and occasionally took portraits for friends and allowed his photography from earlier years to be exhibited. The increasingly fragile artist traveled to London in 1975 to attend the opening of an exhibition of his works at the Institute for Contemporary Art organized by the institute's founder-director and his longtime friend, Roland Penrose. Man Ray died the following year in his Paris studio.

Man Ray's varied career as a dadaist, a portrait, fashion, and fine art photographer, a sculptor, and a filmmaker continues to defy categorization, but his contribution to photography is perhaps his most lasting achievement. The major exhibition Perpetual Motif: The Art of Man Ray, organized in 1988 by the National Museum of American Art (Smithsonian Institution), focused on all aspects of his career and examined his contributions and lasting influence on twentieth-century art.

• Works by Man Ray are located in the Museum of Modern Art, New York; the Philadelphia Museum of Art; the National Museum of American Art, Smithsonian Institution, Washington, D.C.; the Yale University Art Gallery, New Haven, Conn.; and the Centre d'Art et de Culture Georges Pompidou, Paris. The Man Ray archive, which contains papers and the contents of his studio, is located in Paris. A photographic self-portrait taken in 1924 is owned by the National Portrait Gallery in Washington, D.C. *Self Portrait* (1963) is his idiosyncratic, meandering, and ultimately misleading autobiography. *Perpetual Motif: The Art of Man Ray* (1988), the catalog from the exhibition of the same name, is a valuable source of information on Man Ray's life and works. The major biography is Neil Baldwin, *Man Ray: American Artist* (1988). See also Kiki de Montparnasse's autobiography, *Souvenirs* (1929). An obituary is in the *New York Times*, 19 Nov. 1976.

MARTIN R. KALFATOVIC

MANSFIELD, Arabella (23 May 1846–1 Aug. 1911), the first American woman lawyer admitted to the bar, was born Belle Aurelia Babb, called "Arabella," near Burlington, Iowa, the daughter of Miles Babb and Mary Moyer, farmers. Her parents homesteaded at Sperry Station. Enticed by the California gold rush, Arabella's father left Iowa in 1850 and died when a mine caved in at the Bay State Mining Company, where he was superintendent. She attended rural schools and the Mount Pleasant, Iowa, high school when in 1860 her mother moved the family to that community. Mount Pleasant's leaders encouraged citizens to have progressive views, and Arabella's principal openly advocated abolition and universal suffrage.

Arabella enrolled at Iowa Wesleyan University, located in Mount Pleasant, in 1863, graduating three years later. Gifted at debate and classics, she was considered a brilliant student and delivered the valedictory address at commencement. She taught at Simpson College in Indianola, Iowa, from 1866 to 1868 before marrying John Melvin Mansfield, whom she had met in school, in 1868. They had no children. They both taught at Iowa Wesleyan; he was a professor of natural history, and she lectured on history and English. Together they studied law.

Arabella Mansfield began reading law with her brother, Washington Irwin Babb, after he passed the Iowa bar in 1867. She spent hours in his law office on the town square, absorbing legal information from his library. Confident that they had mastered the material, she and her husband applied to be admitted to the Iowa bar on 15 June 1869.

A liberal advocate of women's rights, Judge Francis Springer had jurisdiction of the district court and carefully selected examiners who would support professional women. Both Mansfields passed with high scores, which was, according to an unnamed Mount Pleasant attorney, the "best rebuke possible to the imputation that ladies cannot qualify for the practice of law" (Williams, p. 23). Stating that she had the intellect and character required to practice law, Springer admitted Arabella Mansfield to the bar, carefully interpreting the words "male" and "men" in the state statute to mean all humans.

Mansfield's milestone as the first American woman admitted to the bar received little press, nor did many people protest her accomplishment. A few editorials ridiculed both her and Springer, while others, written by luminaries such as Susan B. Anthony and Elizabeth Cady Stanton, celebrated her achievement. The *Mount Pleasant Journal* praised her as "a lady of a strong mind" but cautioned that "she must expect to be stared at, and remarked about on all occasions."

Despite their efforts, neither of the Mansfields ever practiced law. Arabella Mansfield said that she had studied law primarily for the "love of it." Both Mansfields continued teaching at Iowa Wesleyan, and Arabella earned a master's degree in 1870, then an LL.B. two years later. Some sources claim that she acted as principal of Mount Pleasant High School during this time. The Mansfields "were without question the most distinguished members of the Iowa Wesleyan faculty and important leaders of thought and action in the community" (Louis Haselmayer, "Belle A. Mansfield," *Women Lawyers Journal* 46 [Spring 1969]: 50).

Mansfield served as president of the Henry County Woman Suffrage Association and was a charter member and secretary at the Iowa Woman Suffrage Society state convention, which met in Mount Pleasant in 1870. She also joined the Iowa Peace Society. Touring southeastern Iowa's lecture circuit as "Belle Mansfield, Esq.," she spoke about government and women's rights. One reviewer commented that Mansfield's "lecture was a brilliant forensic display, her words coming with force and vehemence," presenting a "plain and suggestive argument as to 'what women should do.'"

By March 1870 the Iowa legislature removed the word "male" from attorney qualifications in the state's laws. The Mansfields toured Europe in 1873, and Arabella Mansfield studied at the École de Droit and the Sorbonne. She attended lectures about jurisprudence and visited London and Parisian courtrooms to learn more about European legal practices.

In 1879 the Mansfields moved to Greencastle, Indiana, where John Mansfield taught natural science at Asbury University (now DePauw University). John Mansfield suffered a mental breakdown around 1883, and Arabella Mansfield cared for him before he was institutionalized in Napa Valley, California, two years later. She paid all of his expenses until his death in 1894 and never spoke of his illness in public.

Mansfield taught history, music history, and aesthetics at DePauw but devoted her energy mostly to administrative matters as dean of women and dean of the schools of art and music. "Because of her singular energy, executive and business ability" (Williams, p. 24), Mansfield astutely made the schools financially solvent and self-supporting. Until shortly before her death, she also acted as registrar of faculty and preceptress of the women's dormitory where she lived.

Mansfield was active in Greencastle's Methodist congregation, teaching Sunday school and presenting Sunday lectures on art, literature, and religion. Busy with social and charity projects, she sought educational reform and equal opportunities for women. "She was the strongest and truest woman I have ever known," declared Bishop Edwin H. Hughes, president of DePauw. According to him, she was a "brave, patient, effective worker. Above all else she wrought out for herself in service a splendid character."

The university named a building Mansfield Hall, which later burned, but a portrait of her commissioned by her brother was salvaged. Mansfield spent summers in Mount Pleasant with her brother and his family, giving them presents, land, and investments. Although quite progressive, Mansfield embraced propriety, refusing to be seen in public without a bonnet. After her death, her heirs found that she had sixty hats, "all furbished and wearable," which proved the "true delineation of a decorous lady" (Williams, p. 54).

Even though she never practiced law, Mansfield retained her interest in legal proceedings. In 1893 she joined the National League of Women Lawyers (a predecessor of the National Association of Women Lawyers). At the Chicago World's Fair that year, the Congress of Woman Lawyers debated who was the first woman lawyer, Mansfield or Ada A. Kepley, the first female graduate of a law school in 1870. The group concluded Mansfield deserved the designation, noting that she had inspired early women lawyers throughout the country, including Mary B. Hickey, the first woman graduate of the University of Iowa Law School in 1873. Mansfield was "glad that her pioneering along this line has helped open up the way in which others are now achieving success" (Lelia J. Robinson, "Women Lawyers in the United States," *Green Bag* 2 [1890]: 20–21).

While traveling in Japan in 1909, Mansfield learned that she had cancer but continued working until just before her death. She died at her brother's home in Aurora, Illinois. Iowa Wesleyan hosted a centennial celebration of her admission to the bar in 1969.

• Mansfield's papers are in the archives of Iowa Wesleyan College, DePauw University, and Indiana United Methodist College. For further information on Mansfield see Aleta Wallach, "Arabella Babb Mansfield (1846–1911)," *Women's Rights Law Reporter* 2 (Apr. 1974): 3–5; M. Rondall Williams, "Nation's First Woman Lawyer," *Iowan* 15 (Fall–Summer 1966–1967): 23–24, 54; Cynthia Fuchs Epstein, *Women in Law* (1981); Jane M. Friedman, *America's First Woman Lawyer: The Biography of Myra Bradwell* (1993); and Karen Berger Morello, *The Invisible Bar: The Woman Lawyer in America 1638 to the Present* (1986).

ELIZABETH D. SCHAFER

MANSFIELD, Jayne (19 Apr. 1933–29 June 1967), actress, was born Vera Jayne Palmer in Bryn Mawr, Pennsylvania, the daughter of Herbert Palmer, an attorney, and Vera Jeffrey, a kindergarten teacher. Mansfield's father died of a heart attack when she was three, and after her mother married Harry Peers, an industrial sales agent, the family moved to Dallas in 1939. She graduated from Highland Park High School soon after marrying Paul Mansfield in May 1950. They had one child.

While attending the University of Texas at Austin in 1951, Mansfield decided to become an actress. The next year, her husband was drafted, and during his two years with the army she studied drama in Dallas and appeared in several plays on stage and local television. Following his discharge in 1954, they went to Hollywood so that Mansfield could pursue her dream of movie stardom. Her husband left her after six months, just before she landed minor roles in a television play and in a movie, *The Female Jungle* (1956). Determined to attract more attention, Mansfield dyed her hair platinum blond, flaunted her stupendous breasts, and affected an empty-headed manner complete with coos and squeals. She put herself on display in a series of publicity stunts, such as cavorting at a pool party for the 1955 movie *Underwater*—in which she had no role—in a bikini whose top conveniently fell off. This incident got her coverage in Hollywood trade publications and helped lead to the first of six photographic spreads in *Playboy* magazine, a six-month contract with Warner Bros., and small parts in *Illegal*, *Pete Kelly's Blues*, and *Hell on Frisco Bay*, all filmed in 1955. Despite her notoriety, Warner Bros. did not renew her contract.

Mansfield's show business career nevertheless reached new heights. She played her first major role in *The Burglar* (filmed in 1955 but released in 1957) and then starred on the New York stage in *Will Success Spoil Rock Hunter?* She became a hit on Broadway by playing a familiar character—a sexy but scatterbrained film star. During the play's run of almost a year, Mansfield shrewdly promoted herself through interviews and public appearances. She was so successful that the major press associations named her one of the ten most photographed Americans, *Life* magazine praised her as "Broadway's smartest dumb blonde," and Twentieth Century–Fox signed her to a film contract. But she earned neither plaudits nor box-office success for performances in *The Girl Can't Help It* (1956), an inane comedy in which she did little more than exhibit her breasts, the film version of *Will Success Spoil Rock Hunter?* (1957), *The Wayward Bus* (1957), and *Kiss Them for Me* (1957).

Although she lacked acting talent, Mansfield brilliantly played the role of movie star. She tantalized fans with clothing mishaps that left her breasts exposed, followed by outrageous explanations, such as "the dress did not behave like it did when I was standing straight" (*Variety*, 1 Jan. 1958, p. 50). She exploited her romance with Mickey Hargitay, a former Mr. Universe, for maximum publicity. Half the guests at their wedding in January 1958 were reporters, and thousands of fans mobbed the church. She and Hargitay moved into a Los Angeles mansion decorated mainly in pink, and photographers snapped pictures of her bathing in a heart-shaped tub. Mansfield and Hargitay had three children before their divorce in 1964. They also appeared together in a nightclub act and several dismal films, including *The Loves of Hercules* (1960), *Primitive Love* (1966), and *Spree* (1967). Mansfield's other midcareer films, *The Sheriff of Fractured Jaw* (1959), *It Takes a Thief* (1960), and *The George Raft Story* (1961), failed to gain much critical or popular success. American audiences saw an edited version of *Too Hot to Handle* (1959), a British film in which Mansfield played a nightclub singer, because censors ruled that her costumes were too revealing.

Once her contract with Twentieth Century–Fox expired in 1962, Mansfield's career declined. She appeared frequently on talk shows and at promotions, including everything from rodeos to supermarket sales. She also made two record albums, *Jayne Mansfield Busts Up Las Vegas* (1962) and *Shakespeare, Tchaikovsky and Me* (1963), on which she read romantic poetry to violin music. She continued to make movies, but the scripts got worse and her roles more tawdry. She created a scandal by appearing nude in *Promises, Promises* (1963) at a time when Hollywood production codes banned such exposure. Few American viewers saw several of the movies she made in Europe, including *Homesick for St. Paul* (1963), an East German production; *Panic Button* (1964), filmed in Italy; and *Dog Eat Dog* (1964), an Italian-German collaboration. In 1964 she married director Matt Cimber, with whom she had one child. With Cimber as costar, she filmed a pilot in 1965 for a television comedy series, but no network was interested. Her film career also reached its nadir. A brief performance in *The Loved One* (1965) did not make the final print. After two lame comedies, *The Fat Spy* (1966) and *Las Vegas Hillbilly* (1966), and a cameo appearance in *A Guide for the Married Man*

(1967), she tried to gain respectability with a dramatic role in *Single Room Furnished* (1968), a film directed by Cimber but unfinished at the time of her death. Reduced to performing in minor supper clubs, she was killed in an automobile accident near New Orleans. A posthumous exploitation film, *The Wild, Wild World of Jayne Mansfield*, was released in 1968.

Mansfield had a flair for publicity that made her a celebrity but that ultimately destroyed her career. She capitalized on the popularity of Marilyn Monroe by affecting a garish sexuality that simultaneously seemed naive. She was all exaggeration, however, with none of Monroe's wit or subtlety. "Nobody cares about a figure like 163," she often complained in referring to her professed IQ. "They're more interested in 40-21-35" (Saxton, p. 29). Mansfield knew how to exploit contemporary fascination with her measurements but not how to surmount it. In less than a decade her antic voluptuousness became cheap, lewd, silly, and stale. Unable to recast her image, she finally became its victim.

• The most reliable biography of Mansfield is Martha Saxton, *Jayne Mansfield and the American Fifties* (1975). Raymond Strait, *The Tragic Secret Life of Jayne Mansfield* (1974), is an account by her press agent, while May Mann, *Jayne Mansfield: A Biography* (1973), is based in part on alleged communications with Mansfield's spirit. Jocelyn Faris, *Jayne Mansfield: A Bio-Bibliography* (1994), contains detailed information about her career and an extensive bibliography. Guus Luijters and Gerard Timmer, *Sexbomb: The Life and Death of Jayne Mansfield* (1985), is a compilation of photographs with brief textual entries. James Robert Haspiel and Charles Herschberg, "Jayne Mansfield's Starlet Days," *Films in Review* 27 (June 1976): 321–35, provides a sympathetic analysis of her early career. Also useful are contemporary accounts of her activities, including "Star's Legend in the Making," *Life*, 23 Apr. 1956; "The Nudest Jayne Mansfield," *Playboy*, June 1963; and various articles in *Variety*. An obituary is in the *New York Times*, 30 June 1967.

CHESTER J. PACH, JR.

MANSFIELD, Joseph King Fenno (22 Dec. 1803–18 Sept. 1862), army officer, was born in New Haven, Connecticut, the son of Henry Mansfield, a merchant, and Mary Fenno. In 1817 young Mansfield entered the U.S. Military Academy, where his uncle Jared Mansfield was professor of natural and experimental philosophy. Graduating second in his class in 1822, he was commissioned second lieutenant in the Corps of Engineers. His first assignment was as an assistant to the Board of Engineers for Fortification, the panel of senior engineers that designed the program of seacoast defense—the foundation of the nation's defense system into the late nineteenth century. From 1825 to 1846 he divided his time between the construction of coastal fortifications, most notably Fort Pulaski, which defended the approach to Savannah, Georgia, and civil works, including the Cumberland Road and harbor improvements along the south Atlantic coast; during 1842–1845 he served as a member of the Board of Engineers for Fortification. He reached the rank of

captain in 1838 and that year married Louisa Maria Mather; they had five children, one of whom died in infancy.

Early in 1846 the War Department ordered Mansfield to Texas as chief engineer of Colonel Zachary Taylor's "army of occupation," and he accompanied Taylor's force on the march across the disputed zone between the Nueces and Rio Grande rivers. The army encamped on the north bank of the Rio Grande in late March, opposite the Mexican town of Matamoros. There Mansfield designed and supervised the construction of a star-shaped earthen fort named Fort Texas (later Fort Brown), intended to anchor the American position. In early May, soon after the opening clash of the Mexican War, Taylor marched with the bulk of his army to the coast in order to secure his supply line, leaving only 500 men to defend Fort Texas. Mexican batteries opened fire on the American bastion on 3 May, and Mexican forces crossed the river and began a siege. Demonstrating courage and professional skill, Mansfield helped direct the defense until Taylor's victories at Palo Alto and Resaca de la Palma on 8–9 May forced the Mexicans to withdraw. During the late summer of 1846 Mansfield participated in Taylor's invasion of northern Mexico. Prior to the attack on Monterrey in September, he reconnoitered the Mexican positions, and he was wounded while guiding an assault against the eastern defenses of the city. At the battle of Buena Vista in February 1847, he likewise distinguished himself through his reconnaissances and delivery of orders and dispatches. He received brevet promotions to major (May 1846), lieutenant colonel (Sept. 1846), and colonel (Feb. 1847) for his Mexican War achievements.

Resuming his regular engineering duties after the war, Mansfield served on the boards of engineers charged with planning both the Atlantic and Pacific Coast defenses and superintended the construction of Fort Winthrop, located in Boston harbor; he also worked on river improvements in Virginia. In 1853 Secretary of War Jefferson Davis, who had witnessed Mansfield's performance during the Mexican War, promoted him to colonel and inspector general—an advance, unprecedented in the old army, of three grades over his prior regular rank of captain. During the following eight years Mansfield traveled widely throughout the West, inspecting the scattered garrisons of the frontier army and submitting to the War Department detailed reports on training, discipline, and supply. On a tour of Texas in 1860–1861 he became concerned about the Texans' apparent preparations for secession, but his efforts to alert the administration were not heeded.

On 27 April 1861 the War Department assigned Mansfield to command the Military Department of Washington, D.C., and the following month he was promoted to brigadier general in the regular army. During the tense early stages of the Civil War he struggled to build up the defenses of the capital. On his initiative, Union forces advanced into Virginia, occupying Arlington and Alexandria and fortifying the south bank of the Potomac; according to Chief Engineer Joseph G. Totten, the Washington defenses may well have prevented disaster after the Federal defeat at the first battle of Manassas. By experience, however, Mansfield was a defense-minded engineer who questioned the battlefield reliability of inexperienced volunteers, and he advised caution in the face of popular pressure for a march on Richmond. During a reorganization of the army in August 1861 the administration merged the Department of Washington with General George B. McClellan's Department of the Potomac, thereby depriving Mansfield of an independent command. After a brief assignment to shore up Union defenses at Hatteras Inlet, North Carolina, he took charge of a brigade in Brigadier General John E. Wool's Department of Virginia, which incorporated much of the southeastern part of the state. During the early months of 1862 he commanded Federal troops at Newport News, and he took part in the capture of Norfolk in May; for most of the summer of 1862, his brigade occupied Suffolk, Virginia. In July he was advanced to major general of volunteers.

Unhappy with his relegation to a secondary command, Mansfield lobbied tenaciously for a combat assignment. In September 1862, just before the Confederate offensive into Maryland, the administration appointed him to head the Union Twelfth Corps, a unit recently added to McClellan's Army of the Potomac. Mansfield reached his new command on 15 September, as McClellan was preparing to block the Confederate advance near Sharpsburg, Maryland. In the battle of Antietam two days later, Mansfield's corps was ordered to bolster the collapsing right flank of the Union line, and the veteran engineer was fatally wounded while directing the deployment of his troops.

Mansfield was a highly respected career soldier whose fortification work, Mexican War exploits, and service as inspector general reflected the emerging professionalism of the antebellum army officer corps. His most important achievement was ensuring the security of Washington, D.C., during the critical early months of the Civil War.

• No collections of Mansfield's papers are known to exist. His military career is traced in George W. Cullum, *Biographical Register of the Officers and Graduates of the U.S. Military Academy at West Point, N.Y., from Its Establishment in 1802, to 1890* (1891). A biographical sketch and information on his family background may be found in Horace Mansfield, *The Descendants of Richard and Gilliam Mansfield Who Settled in New Haven, 1639* (1885). For his Mexican War service, see K. Jack Bauer, *The Mexican War, 1846–1848* (1974), and David Lavender, *Climax at Buena Vista: The American Campaigns in Northeastern Mexico, 1846–47* (1966). Several of his inspection reports have been published in Robert W. Frazer, ed., *Mansfield on the Condition of the Western Forts, 1853–54* (1963), and M. L. Crimmins, ed., "Colonel J. K. F. Mansfield's Report of the Inspection of the Department of Texas in 1856," *Southwestern Historical Quarterly* 42 (1939): 215–56, 351–87. Data on his Civil War service appear in U.S. War Department, *The War of the Rebellion: A Compilation of the Official Records of the Union and Confederate Armies* (128

vols., 1880–1901). For his death, see John M. Gould, *Joseph K. F. Mansfield, Brigadier General of the U.S. Army: A Narrative of Events Connected with His Mortal Wounding* (1895).

WILLIAM B. SKELTON

MANSFIELD, Portia (19 Nov. 1887–29 Jan. 1979), dance educator, choreographer, and camp director, was born Portia Mansfield Swett in Chicago, Illinois, the daughter of Edward R. Swett, a hotelkeeper, and Myra Mansfield. She received her early schooling in Winter Park, Florida, where the family moved in 1899, and, after another move, in New York City at Miss Morgan's School for Girls (1903–1906). As a child, she danced for her own pleasure and, occasionally, for hotel guests. Entering Smith College in 1906, she majored in philosophy and psychology but also was exposed to the Delsarte System of Expression and gravitated toward the physical education department. She was instrumental in organizing a dancing class at Smith. Classmates remembered her clouds of red hair, her lissomeness and grace, and her vivacity.

While at Smith, she met Charlotte Perry of Denver, who became her colleague and lifelong companion. After graduation in 1910 and a summer of dance study in Paris and Milan, Portia Swett enrolled in the ballet and character dance classes of Louis Chalif in New York and in the fall of 1910 set up a studio in Omaha, Nebraska, where she taught social dancing and organized cotillions.

Like many impressionable young dancers, she thrilled to performances by Anna Pavlova, Adeline Genée, and Ruth St. Denis. She continued to study: with Vernon Castle and Irene Castle on trips to New York, with Andreas Pavley and Serge Oukrainsky when she began in 1912 to teach at Miss Morgan's Dramatic School in Chicago (dividing her week between Chicago and Omaha).

With Perry, she planned a summer dancing camp in Colorado that would combine teaching and performing with the women's love of horseback riding and the outdoors. The first summer trial run was held in 1914 on rented property on Lake Eldora in Nederland, Colorado. In 1915, reportedly for $200, the two women bought a sizable tract of land in Strawberry Park outside of Steamboat Springs, Colorado, and themselves helped to construct the rustic Rocky Mountain Dancing Camp (later Perry-Mansfield). Mansfield, Perry, and Colorado residents from those early days have all recounted the mixture of bafflement, delight, and horror with which local ranchers viewed the scantily clad nymphs flitting about beneath the pines and aspens.

Mansfield and Perry taught in various eastern schools during the winters and continued their studies in dance. A 1923 brochure for the Steamboat Springs school and a winter camp the two had opened in 1917 in Carmel, California, offered training in ballet, Greek plastique, Spanish, Oriental, and "other Character Techniques"; improvisation, composition, and theory; riding and swimming. Perry taught drama, in which she had begun to be interested; she was to develop a theater program at Perry-Mansfield, to direct plays, and to become a notable teacher of acting.

In 1921 Portia Swett changed her name to Portia Mansfield, a name she believed was more appropriate for the small groups of dancers, Perry sometimes among them, that began to make public appearances as the Portia Mansfield Dancers. It was also in 1921 that Mansfield first provided choreography and costumes and sent four of her protégés on the vaudeville circuit to join the act of Hungarian violinist Ota Gygi and his ballerina wife, Maryon Vadie (the experience was documented by one of the dancers, Flavia Waters Champe, in *Innocents on Broadway* [1987]). At some point, four companies toured simultaneously. Reviews from 1924 of a group of Portia Mansfield Dancers list ten dancers, including one man. Publicity from vaudeville tours and concert appearances of the various companies indicates a repertory that blended the exotic with the exalted, including such titles as "A Picnic Day in Holland," "An Etruscan Screen" (praised as "a unique thing of lines and angles"), "Slave Dance," "Rhythmic Games," "Unfinished Symphony," and "Hymn of Joy" (Beethoven). In 1930 waning public interest in vaudeville caused Mansfield to disband her companies and concentrate on teaching—in New York and Baltimore during winters and during summers at the camp, by now officially called Perry-Mansfield.

In 1933 Mansfield received a master of arts degree from New York University and in 1953 (when she was in her sixties) a doctor of education degree from the same institution. Her dissertation topic was "Conchero Dancers of New Mexico," which included a film as part of the project. Mansfield had become interested in photography early in her career; several photographs by "Portia Swett" grace *Gymnastic and Folk Dancing* (five volumes published between 1923 and 1929 by Mary Wood Hinman, a noted Chicago teacher).

As the dance faculty at Perry-Mansfield expanded, many major figures in modern dance taught there, among them Doris Humphrey, Hanya Holm, José Limón, and Agnes de Mille. Mansfield developed her own form of rhythmic training, based on the ideas of Bess Mensendieck, Mabel Ellsworth Todd, and Lulu Sweigard about natural and healthy motions of the body. Mansfield's Body Mechanics and Fundamental Movement exercises are preserved on a 30-minute film by that title made probably in the late 1940s or early 1950s. Her *Sixty Exercises in Rhythmic Movement* were published in book form in 1939. An article she contributed to the *Journal of Health and Physical Education* in January 1935 put forth utopian ideas debunking "etiquette" and positing the growth of a "more real democracy" based on values inculcated in movement classes, among them, equality ("not kindness which might imply condescension"), safety first, culture, personal hygiene, gallantry, and temperance. Much later, in 1966, she contributed a series of articles to *Dance Magazine* on exercises for the elderly: "Help Them Move Young."

Mansfield and Perry continued to direct Perry-Mansfield and to teach there until 1965, when the camp was turned over to Stephens College, which had been granting college credit for studies there for several years. However, the next summer, with college friend and longtime colleague Helen Smith, Mansfield started a boys' camp on the nearby premises of the Whiteman School and operated it until 1976. In 1970 she was awarded the Governor's Award for her contributions to Colorado culture. In 1974 she received the American Camping Association's Honor Award for her fifty-year tenure at Perry-Mansfield.

Mansfield will not be remembered as a major choreographer or dancer but rather as an innovative force in dance education and a pioneer during the period that contributed to the development of what came to be known as modern dance. Perry-Mansfield provided a nurturing atmosphere for the gifted and famous who studied and taught there. She died in Carmel, California.

• Various films and publications by Portia Mansfield, as well as manuscripts and scrapbooks pertaining to her career and to Perry-Mansfield, are housed in the Dance Collection of the New York Public Library. Other memorabilia are preserved at Perry-Mansfield. Lucile Bogue, *Dancers on Horseback* (1984), chronicles Perry-Mansfield and the careers of its two founders. Mansfield is mentioned frequently in Flavia Waters Champe, *Innocents on Broadway* (1987). *A Divine Madness*, a videotape of reminiscences containing archival photographs and films by Mansfield, was completed at the time of her death. An obituary is in the *Steamboat Pilot*, 1 Feb. 1979.

DEBORAH JOWITT

MANSFIELD, Richard (24 May 1854–30 Aug. 1907), actor, was born in Berlin, Germany, the son of Maurice Mansfield, an English wine merchant who died when Richard was five, and Erminia Rudersdorff, an accomplished opera singer. Mansfield's mother's domineering tendencies led to a stormy relationship with her son. However, his difficult childhood and adolescence was partially offset by the cultural enrichment of travels through Europe, the kindness of his headmaster at Derby School, and the musical training provided by his mother.

After dividing his early years between England and Germany, in 1872 Mansfield accompanied his mother to Boston, where she established a residence. For a time he thought his future lay in commerce, and he clerked for family friend and prominent Boston merchant Eben D. Jordan. But he soon left to pursue a career in art, moving to London in 1877, both to study painting and to escape his mother.

Mansfield had been active in amateur theatricals in the Boston area, and, needing some means of support while in England, he found work on the music hall stage. Almost immediately he determined that the theater was his true calling. His vocal ability helped land him positions in two of D'Oyly Carte's Gilbert and Sullivan productions. For the next several years he traveled throughout England finding small roles to play, primarily in operettas.

Discouraged at his prospects in England, Mansfield returned to the United States in 1882 and performed on the musical stage in supporting roles. But his great break came on the dramatic stage. When J. H. Stoddart refused to play the lead role of Baron Chevrial in *A Parisian Romance* at New York's Union Square Theatre in January 1883, Mansfield was given the part. His portrayal of the profligate baron—especially his horrific death scene—became the sensation of the season. He bought the play and made it his starring vehicle for the next season on tour.

But this singular success did not assure stardom. Indeed, as most stars of that era discovered, the economics of the theater were unpredictable, and few players went through a career without financial reversals. In Mansfield's case this meant having a tour close prematurely on the road, having to temporarily surrender starring ambitions as part of a stock company, and later after acquiring a theater of his own having to soon lose it.

Still, Mansfield was fortunate in having his career coincide with the golden age of the American theater. Not only did scores of theatrical companies leave New York each year to tour the country, but the star system was firmly entrenched. Mansfield possessed a determination to be a star that was unusual even for his profession. "One thing is very distinct in my mind, and that is the impossibility and inadvisability of making an appearance here otherwise than as a star of the first magnitude," he wrote Augustin Daly in 1892, turning down the chance to appear with the company of the nation's leading theatrical manager. "I am exceedingly ambitious and I confess it." This ambition impelled Mansfield to produce a series of carefully chosen star vehicles beginning in the mid-1880s. His reemergence as a star came as a result of his portrayal of the title role in Archibald Gunter's *Prince Karl* in 1886 in Boston, which he took to New York and on tour in 1887. Thereafter, although enduring occasional financial setbacks and bouts of physical exhaustion, Mansfield belonged to the front rank of actor-managers.

During the next twenty-two years Mansfield put on twenty-seven plays and performed twenty-eight roles. He often alternated seasons of performing various plays in repertory with performing a single play for an entire season according to the theatrical custom of the day. He put great energy into seeking out challenging roles, not only performing the existing repertoire but also commissioning new plays. His most memorable roles displayed his dramatic stage effects. In *Dr. Jekyll and Mr. Hyde* (first performed in 1887 in Boston), perhaps his greatest crowd-pleaser, he effected a remarkable onstage transformation, portraying, as one critic put it, "a carnal monster of unqualified evil." *Beau Brummell* (1890), written by Clyde Fitch on Mansfield's commission, was sentimental fluff energized by the actor's moving portrayal of an English dandy's decline. His acclaimed *Cyrano de Bergerac* (1898) put financial concerns behind him; indeed, in the last decade of his life he was among the country's richest actors.

Although he kept Shylock in his repertoire through most of his career, Mansfield's most acclaimed Shakespearean role was Richard III. Oddly, considering his legendary ego, he never attempted Hamlet, Lear, Macbeth, or Othello, perhaps sensing a lack of depth in his art for the most profound of Shakespeare's characters. Although normally identified with the vigorous roles of costume drama, Mansfield championed the new realism of European drama, bringing the first George Bernard Shaw play to an American theater with his *Arms and the Man* (1894) and later staging the first American production of Henrik Ibsen's *Peer Gynt* (1906).

Mansfield also campaigned vigorously—if inconstantly—against the Theatrical Syndicate's attempts at monopolistic control of bookings. For a time in 1896–1897 he gave impassioned curtain speeches castigating the evils of the syndicate. Along with other leading stars, he helped organize and was elected president of the Association for the Promotion and Protection of the Independent Stage in the United States, a group dedicated to regaining independent control of their bookings. But the revolt was short-lived, largely because Mansfield soon defected to the syndicate. Minnie Maddern Fiske, who nearly alone carried on the struggle, explained (but did not forgive) Mansfield's betrayal as the action of a man haunted by his past struggles for stardom and determined to let nothing threaten it.

A theatrical proverb of the late nineteenth century quipped "There are good actors, bad actors, and Richard Mansfield." Mansfield's larger-than-life stage presence, his highly mannered approach to acting, his enormous ego, and his storied outbursts of temper resulted in a critical reputation that varied widely. Without question, however, he dominated the American stage in the decade and a half before his death. Often compared with Henry Irving, who contemporaneously presided over the English stage, Mansfield felt an acute burden to elevate the tone of the American theater. This self-imposed duty encouraged a nearly paranoid perception that others were out to besmirch his career. Even the great Irving, who had aided Mansfield in his early career, came to be viewed as an enemy. Mansfield's reputation as a troubled genius inspired novelist Thomas Wolfe to base a fictional character on him in *The Web and the Rock* (1939).

If Mansfield's public persona was tempestuous, he found domestic tranquility in marriage to his leading lady, Beatrice Cameron (whose given name was Susan Hegeman), in 1892. She retired from the stage following the birth of their only child in 1898. Even with this newfound happiness, Mansfield kept up his demanding schedule. He had suffered several bouts of what was diagnosed as nervous exhaustion during his career. In the spring of 1907 he became ill and was forced to cancel his tour. He never recovered and died in New London, Connecticut.

Mansfield must be counted among the most talented performers to grace the American stage. He sang and danced beautifully, wrote music, plays, and poetry, and was, by the prevailing theater standards of the day, an intellectual. Below average in height but powerful and athletic, he commanded the stage. Although he was respected as a performer, he never won the heart of the public as had Joseph Jefferson or Edwin Booth. Perhaps this was because of difficult temperament or that his greatest roles embodied unattractive characters. Mansfield's death, as contemporary critic Walter Prichard Eaton noted, represented the end of an era in the American theater. He stood in the great romantic tradition—costume dramas grandly performed—yet acknowledging the more subdued realism then coming to define American acting.

• Primary materials dealing with Mansfield's career can be found at the Library of Congress, Wilstach Collection; the Mansfield Scrap Book, Robinson Locke Collection; Billy Rose Theatre Collection, New York Public Library for the Performing Arts, Lincoln Center; and the Mansfield clippings, Shaw Collection, Harvard University Library. Biographies by contemporaries are Paul Wilstach, *Richard Mansfield, the Man and the Actor* (1908), and William Winter, *Life and Art of Richard Mansfield* (2 vols., 1910). An obituary is in the *New York Times*, 31 Aug. 1907.

BENJAMIN MCARTHUR

MANSHIP, Paul Howard (24 Dec. 1885–28 Jan. 1966), sculptor, was born in Saint Paul, Minnesota, the son of Charles Henry Manship, Jr., and Mary Etta Friend. Academically unmotivated, Manship did not complete high school, choosing instead to study art while supporting himself as a commercial artist. In 1905, in pursuit of further training, Manship moved to New York City, where he enrolled briefly at the Art Students League. He then secured an apprenticeship, lasting two years, with Solon Borglum, a well-established sculptor known for his expressive treatment of western American themes. After an additional year of formal academic training under sculptor Charles Grafly and others at the Pennsylvania Academy of the Fine Arts in Philadelphia, and another apprenticeship in New York with Isidore Konti, Manship won a three-year fellowship in sculpture from the American Academy in Rome.

Established in 1894, the American Academy was a profoundly conservative institution intended in part to combat what its founders believed to be the pernicious effects of modern Paris, by that time the art mecca for young Americans. Manship himself later admitted having had little desire to go to Rome, but, once there, he took full advantage of his surroundings. Abandoning the expressively modeled surfaces and prosaic subjects he had earlier favored, Manship turned to crisply articulated, glossy-surfaced interpretations of playful subjects from classical antiquity. In 1912, during his first trip to Greece, Manship discovered preclassical art—especially of the archaic period (600–480 B.C.)—little known or appreciated before major archaeological discoveries at Athens, Delphi, Olympia, and other sites during the late nineteenth century. Inspired above all by archaic sculpture and vase painting, Manship forged the distinctive style from which he would

never substantially depart, combining naturalistic anatomy with abstract treatment of details and stylized gestures informed by archaic art.

Manship's "archaistic" style, as critics promptly dubbed it, attracted considerable attention following the sculptor's return to New York in late 1912. Critics and patrons responded with enthusiasm to an art that appeared to combine aspects of modernism—particularly in the abstract treatment of hair and drapery—with an academic respect for fine craftsmanship and for tradition, however unfamiliar. In addition to Greek archaic art, Manship added to his eclectic mix of sources the art of the ancient Near East, early medieval Europe, and India. His favored material was bronze, but he also created many sculptures in marble. Wide exposure in solo and group exhibitions around the country, favorable reviews, numerous awards—including the Helen Foster Barnett Prize from the National Academy of Design in 1913 and 1917 (for *Centaur and Dryad* and *Dancer and Gazelles*, respectively), the Widener Memorial Gold Medal from the Pennsylvania Academy in 1914 (for *Duck Girl*), and a Gold Medal at the Panama-Pacific Exposition of 1915—and commissions from such well-established architects as Welles Bosworth and Charles Platt secured Manship's prominence and financial stability by the end of the decade. To meet the high demand for his work, Manship hired many assistants over the length of his career; among those in his studio between 1910 and 1920, Beniamino Bufano, Gaston Lachaise, and Reuben Nakian all enjoyed successful careers, though none followed Manship's artistic lead.

In 1921 Manship left New York for an extended stay in Europe with his wife, Isabel McIlwaine Manship, whom he had married in 1913, and his growing family (four children eventually). He traveled widely but made Paris his base, maintaining a studio there until 1937, though he returned to New York in 1926. By this period, archaism was all the vogue, and many writers held Manship—its most consistent and visible exponent—accountable for the sleek and palatable compromise with modernism, a novelty no longer. Archaism gained particular identification with the American Academy in Rome, owing both to Manship's prominence among its fellows and to his presence there as professor between 1922 and 1924 (though the position entailed no formal instructional duties). In fact, Manship had by that time begun to move away from the miniaturistic refinement of his earlier work toward a more simplified, streamlined form and mass, evident in his powerful *Diana* and *Actaeon* and in *Europa and the Bull*, all of the mid-1920s. Such works have prompted some to identify Manship's sculpture with art deco, a modern design movement having roots early in the twentieth century and flourishing during the 1920s and 1930s; however, Manship himself shunned this association because of its commercial connotations. In a break from his initial focus on work for the art marketplace, Manship also began to accept many commissions for monumental public sculpture, most notably the *Paul J. Rainey Memorial Gateway* for the New York Zoological Park (Bronx) and the *Prometheus Fountain* for Rockefeller Center, both completed in 1934, and *Moods of Time* and *Time and the Fates of Man* (sundial) for the 1939 New York World's Fair. Henry McBride, an unsympathetic critic, believed that Manship's work appealed to people obsessed with "getting their money's worth" (*New York Sun*, 7 Feb. 1925). Thus one of the Rockefeller Center architects explained why Manship had been chosen to design the major sculpture for the Plaza: "We know that he'll turn out a 100% professional job, capably modeled, brilliantly cast, in scale, and with waterworks that work. And furthermore, on the opening day Manship will be there with the cord in his hand all ready to unveil" (cited in Rosamund Frost, *Art News* 44 [June 1945]).

Manship's identification with the establishment is apparent from his election to leadership positions in several prominent, conservative professional associations. He served the National Sculpture Society as president (1939–1942), the National Academy of Design as vice president (1942–1948), and the American Academy of Arts and Letters as president (1948–1954). Additionally, Manship was a fellow of the American Academy of Arts and Sciences (elected 1931) and a member of the Smithsonian Fine Arts Commission (1931–1966) and the Federal Arts Commission (1937–1941). He was also corresponding member of the Academia Nacional de las Bellas Artes, Argentina, the Académie des Beaux-Arts, Paris, and the Accademia di San Luca, Rome. Throughout this period he had continued to receive honors for his art, including the Légion d'Honneur (1929); Diplome d'Honneur, Paris Exposition (1937); Medal of Honor, National Sculpture Society (1942); and the gold medal for sculpture, National Institute of Arts and Letters (1945). His solo exhibition at the Tate Gallery in 1935 united Manship with Rodin as the only non-Britons to be so honored during their lifetimes.

In his official capacity and in public lectures and writings, Manship promoted traditional ideas about art. He believed in the usefulness of the past, valued fine craftsmanship and technical expertise, emphasized the importance of collaboration among artists, and stressed the artist's obligation to create works the general public could understand. In short, he considered the artist a guardian of tradition, a missionary on behalf of beauty, and a public servant. Manship thus represented everything that modernists loved to hate, and his reputation plummeted with the rise of the American avant-garde by the 1940s. Although his productivity continued, Manship received far fewer commissions than previously; they included several sculptures for the American Military Cemetery at Nettuno, Italy (1952–1955) and a memorial to Theodore Roosevelt (1858–1919) for Roosevelt Island in Washington, D.C. (1964). He died in New York City.

Manship's fame and reputation, despite qualifications, were nearly unshakable from his artistic debut in the New York of 1913 to the 1930s, when his prominently situated public sculptures made him the most visible sculptor in America. The combination in his sculpture of naturalism and narrative legibility with archaism simultaneously evoked classicism and modernism—and proved irresistible to a patron class sophisticated enough to know that modern art could not be dismissed but not prepared to cast tradition to the winds. Manship's classicism appeared in his subject matter, ancient sources, and fine craftsmanship; together they connoted history and good taste. His modernism lay in the greater importance of form than subject to the effect of his works and in the provocative use of archaizing stylization. Manship, in sum, created an acceptable modernism for a broad public, a modern style that had recognizable ties to tradition. This was his original achievement, his invention.

Manship left the more than 700 sculptures and drawings in his personal collection to the Minnesota Museum of Art in Saint Paul and to the National Museum of American Art, Smithsonian Institution, in Washington, D.C. In addition to these major repositories, his work may be seen in the Museum of Fine Arts, Boston; the Art Institute of Chicago; the Los Angeles County Museum of Art; the Metropolitan Museum of Art, New York; the Philadelphia Museum of Art; the Saint Louis Art Museum; and many other public collections as well as in public sites in both the United States and Europe.

• Manship's papers (still privately held) have been microfilmed for the Archives of American Art, Smithsonian Institution. Books on the sculptor published during his lifetime include A. E. Gallatin, *Paul Manship: A Critical Essay on his Sculpture and an Iconography* (1917); Paul Vitry, *Paul Manship, Sculpteur américain* (1927); and Edwin Murtha, *Paul Manship* (1957), useful for its catalogue of 576 sculptures. Two books published in 1989, both titled *Paul Manship*, offer comprehensive assessments of the sculptor's life and work, along with excellent bibliographies; Harry Rand's is particularly sensitive to the formal qualities of Manship's sculpture, whereas John Manship's benefits from access that the sculptor's son had to unpublished, and generally unavailable, documents and photographs. Susan Rather, *Archaism, Modernism, and the Art of Paul Manship* (1993), is the first critical study of Manship's archaism and includes in an appendix the text of Manship's 1912 American Academy lecture, "The Decorative Value of Greek Sculpture," an important early document. An obituary is in the *New York Times*, 1 Feb. 1966.

SUSAN RATHER

MANTELL, Robert Bruce (7 Feb. 1854–27 June 1928), actor, was born in Irvine, Scotland, the third child of James Mantell, a baker, and Elizabeth Bruce. His English father moved the family to Belfast in 1859 to become the manager of a hotel frequented by theater folk. Schooled locally (he did not attend college), Robert became active in amateur theatricals as a teenager and made his professional acting debut with the stock company of the Theatre Royal at Rochdale in Lancashire, England, in 1876. He was chiefly influenced in his acting style by the Irish tragedian Barry Sullivan, who epitomized the old school of aggrandized reality in tragic acting, which survived in the English provinces after falling from fashion in London.

From 1877 through 1882 Mantell toured the provinces with a succession of companies, including those of Alice Marriott, a robust actress of the heroic Charlotte Cushman type; Charles Matthews, a light farceur with a proto-realistic style; Ellen Wallis, who had been Barry Sullivan's leading lady; and Dion Boucicault, the playwright and director. He also toured the United States for a season, playing featured roles for the highly respected Polish-American tragedienne Helena Modjeska. He generally won favorable reviews in these engagements; his Romeo to Wallis's Juliet prompted a London critic to name him one of the four best Romeos on the stage in 1882.

He returned to America in the fall of 1882 to play Jack Hearne in *The Romany Rye* at Booth's Theatre. A year later, opposite Fanny Davenport, he undertook the role that was to make him a star. As Loris Ipanoff in Sardou's *Fedora*, he "galvanized the house" (Robert Towse, *New York Post*, 2 Oct. 1883) with his natural, yet passionate acting, becoming *the* matinee idol in an era of matinee idols. (The soft, slouch hat he wore in the role has been called "fedora" ever since.) Immediately, he was much sought after, and he was subsequently directed in star vehicles by David Belasco and James Steele MacKaye. But Mantell's success as Loris Ipanoff was not repeated with these other roles, and he frequently changed managers.

For the next dozen years, he presented himself in a variety of contemporary (*Tangled Lives, Dakolar*) and older (*Monbars, The Corsican Brothers*) melodramas with middling success in New York and in the American provinces. His career was hindered by poor management, poor taste, and, crucially, domestic difficulties. In 1881 Mantell had married Marie Shand (stage name Sheldon), with whom he had three sons (one of whom drowned as an infant). They separated in 1892, commencing a bitter and protracted divorce proceeding that kept Mantell out of New York, the theatrical capital, for the next ten years, so that he would not be arrested as a bigamist. In 1895 he fathered a daughter with Charlotte Behrens, an actress in his company, whom he married the following year. Behrens died in 1898, and in 1900 Mantell married his then leading lady, Marie Booth Russell, and gained custody of his daughter. During this period, the press frequently carried stories of flagrant infidelities, Mantell's arrest for nonsupport, an alleged kidnapping of Mantell's daughter, bankruptcy proceedings, and other notorieties, which did little for his career. Within three months of Russell's death in 1911, he married actress Genevieve Hamper, forty years his junior; they had one son.

Shortly after the turn of the century, Mantell changed his billing from "The Eminent Romantic Actor" to "The Classic and Romantic Actor" and gradually introduced Shakespeare into his touring repertory. On 5 December 1904 he made his New York City Shakespearean debut, playing Richard III and Othel-

lo, as well as Bulwer-Lytton's *Richelieu*, to rave reviews—repeating his startling triumph as Loris Ipanoff twenty-two years previously. Once again managers sought to represent him, and again he chose poorly in William A. Brady, a colorful, erratic, and slightly disreputable prizefight promoter and producer of melodramas. Under Brady's flamboyant management Mantell in the next ten years became the most popular Shakespearean actor in America, but their association undermined the image of the dignified tragedian.

Until his death, Mantell crisscrossed the country with a touring company and boxcars of scenery, bringing Shakespeare (and a few potboilers like *Richelieu* and de la Vigne's *Louis XI*) to the largest cities and the smallest towns. Always more appealing to the gallery gods than to the kid-glove crowd, his annual New York City engagements ranged from three to twelve weeks when he was in his prime, though they trailed off to nothing in the 1920s. In the provinces, however, he remained extraordinarily popular until he could no longer go on, drawing packed houses at "$1.00 top" in his last season.

Mantell never achieved the cachet of the Edward H. Sothern and Julia Marlowe Shakespearean team, the magnetism of Richard Mansfield in his two successful Shakespearean roles, the critical acclamation of Walter Hampden as Hamlet or Cyrano, or even John Barrymore's notoriety. As a Shakespearean actor, he evidently reverted to the old-school style he had absorbed in the English provinces, and his performances were living repositories of ancient stage business, traceable back at least to the early eighteenth century. (He persisted in using the Colley Cibber adaptation of *Richard III*.) This style, at its best, was heroic, given to brilliant elocutionary and pantomimic effects, consciously picturesque, thrilling in its contrasts and rapid transitions of feeling. His large frame, square jaw, and stentorian voice amplified the desired effects. At its worst, his style could be stilted and overarticulated, relying on tradition rather than originality and emphasizing striking bits at the expense of a coherent whole and the star performance at the expense of ensemble play.

Mantell excelled in the more spectacular Shakespearean roles of Othello, Richard III, Shylock, Macbeth, and Lear. In the last three, especially, he was likely the best the American stage had to offer in his time. His Shylock avoided both of the contemporary stereotypes of the role: neither the unkempt, groveling, malicious usurer nor the sentimental, poignant, religious figure, Mantell's Shylock was emotional and impulsive, indulging himself in righteous and towering rage. His Macbeth grew beyond an early tendency to melodrama into a sustained, intelligent portrayal of great pathos. His Lear most resembled that of Edmund Kean: startling, frightening, almost unbearably poignant—he averted his eyes in shame during the entire recognition scene with Cordelia—and above all heroic. He gave over five hundred performances of Lear, more than any actor who has ever undertaken the role, and joins a handful of others (David Garrick, Edwin Forrest, and, in a lesser rank, Donald Wolfit and Morris Carnovsky) who could point to the role as the summit of their distinguished careers in the theater. He died on his estate in Atlantic Highlands, New Jersey.

• The Mantell-Hamper Collection in the Walter Hampden Memorial Library at The Players in New York City is the major repository for archival material on Mantell. The Folger Shakespeare Library in Washington, D.C., holds ten of Mantell's Shakespeare promptbooks and the largest collection of his letters. Mantell's original part books and additional promptbooks are held privately. The Theatre Collection of the Library & Museum of the Performing Arts in New York City contains a vast collection of clippings and photographs of Mantell, members of his company, and his contemporaries. The only biography is a romanticized and undependable account by Mantell's press agent Clarence J. Bulliet, *Robert Mantell's Romance* (1918). Autobiographies by two of Mantell's managers (William A. Brady, *Showman* [1937], and Augustus Pitou, *Masters of the Show* [1914]) provide colorful details. Useful accounts of the theater of the period include John Mason Brown, *Upstage: The American Theatre in Performance* (1930); Arthur Hornblow, *A History of the Theatre in America* (1919); John Rankin Towse, *Sixty Years of the Theater* (1916); and William Winter, *The American Stage of Today* (1910). Notable histories of acting, especially Shakespearean, include Edwin Duerr, *The Length and Depth of Acting* (1962); Bertram Joseph, *The Tragic Actor* (1959); Arthur Colby Sprague, *Shakespeare and the Actors* (1944); Garff B. Wilson, *A History of American Acting* (1966); and William Winter, *Shakespeare on the Stage* (1911–1916). Obituaries are in the *New York Times* and *New York World*, 28 June 1928, and the *New York Sun*, 27 June 1928; see also the *New York Times* editorial, 25 June 1928.

ATTILIO FAVORINI

MANTLE, Burns (23 Dec. 1873–9 Feb. 1948), theater critic and chronicler, was born Leroy Willis Mantle in Watertown, New York, the son of Robert Burns Mantle, a haberdasher, and Susan Lawrence, a music teacher. At age twelve Mantle began using the name of his recently deceased father. During his childhood, Mantle moved with his family to Denver, then briefly to Mexico, before they settled for several years in San Diego, California. Largely self-educated, his formal schooling was sketchy, and after the elementary grades he was tutored at home by his grandmother and mother. In San Diego, young Mantle began in the newspaper business as a delivery boy and, later, became a printer's apprentice at the *San Diegan*.

When his family returned to Denver in 1892, Mantle got a job as a linotype operator at the *Denver Post*. According to an oft-told story with slightly varying details, Mantle's career as a theater critic began by accident when a review, written in longhand by the *Post*'s regular critic Frederick W. White, was illegible to the linotype department. An avid theatergoer who had seen the production being reviewed, Mantle quickly wrote a substitute review, composing directly on the linotype machine. Impressed by the quality of Mantle's substitution, Frederick W. White asked the young linotypist to put together a weekly column of theater notes. To avoid being confused with Robert B. Mantell, a well-known actor of the period, Mantle used his middle name Burns as a professional name (friends continued to call him Robert or Bob). From 1898 to 1900 he was a reporter for the *Denver Times*, covering drama news and other subjects. After a brief stint as drama editor at the *Denver Republican*, he moved in 1901 to a similar position at the *Chicago Inter-Ocean* where he stayed until 1907. In that year he went to work for the *Chicago Tribune*, eventually becoming the paper's Sunday editor. Yet he was unhappy in this position because the theater remained his primary interest.

In September 1911, while in New York trying to sell features for the *Chicago Tribune* syndicate, Mantle learned that the *New York Evening Mail* needed a drama critic and agreed to review that evening's opening night performance of George M. Cohan's *The Little Millionaire*. Soon after Mantle was named the *Evening Mail*'s regular critic. He remained with the paper for eleven years, gaining a reputation as one of New York's most astute theater commentators. Uncomfortable with the title of "critic," Mantle considered himself a reporter or "professional playgoer." His reviews were noted for their lack of viciousness and infrequent use of clever bon mots, yet he believed a light, slightly flippant style was appropriate for daily newspaper reviewing. Mantle told the *New York Dramatic Mirror* in 1914 that the ideal theater critic "should be a combination of George Bernard Shaw, Arthur Wing Pinero, and George M. Cohan—authorities on literature, dramatic technique and what the public wants."

In 1922 Mantle moved to the *New York Daily News*, a tabloid newspaper founded three years earlier by the editors of the *Chicago Tribune*. Keeping in mind the typical "straphanger" reader of the *Daily News*, he established an easily apprehensible system of rating plays, assigning four stars to the finest productions and one-half of a star to the poorest, a much-imitated system. After seeing a performance, Mantle would go directly to the *Daily News* offices to write his review. Reflecting his beginnings as a linotypist, he kept his typewriter padlocked to prevent anyone from tampering with the keyboard and made it a point to meet printers' schedules. Fellow critic Ward Morehouse of the *New York Sun* called Mantle "a steadying critic, fair-minded and unsensational, and always aware of his responsibility to his readers" (*Matinee Tomorrow* [1949], p. 296).

The large number of plays opening on Broadway in the 1920s and the diminishing importance of star performers who could attract audiences even when appearing in below-par vehicles made newspaper reviews an increasingly powerful factor in determining a production's success. Mantle was wary of critics who abused this power by allowing personal biases to color their opinions. He expressed sympathy for actors and playwrights who had been raked over the coals by mean-spirited critics. When he retired from the *Daily News* in 1943, diminutive, soft-spoken Burns Mantle was regarded as the "dean of New York drama critics." He was succeeded by his long-time assistant John Chapman. In a letter to Chapman, the good-natured

Mantle told the younger man, "Broadway is your oyster. Open it. Season it with a dash of salt and a lot of pep—but go easy with the tabasco."

In addition to his duties as a daily newspaper critic, Burns Mantle served as editor of the *Best Plays* series from its instigation in 1919 through 1947. For these annual volumes, Mantle wrote condensed versions of what he thought were the ten best plays of the Broadway season. These condensations summarized plot business and repeated important dialogue. He also included a general essay on the current state of the New York theater, basic information about every play that had opened on Broadway that season, lists of award winners, and a theater world necrology. Mantle compiled two additional volumes, *Best Plays of 1899–1909* and *Best Plays of 1909 to 1919*. These volumes filled in most of the 25-year gap between the *Best Plays* series and George Odell's *Annals of the New York Theatre*, which chronicles the city's theater activity from its beginnings to 1894. After Mantle's death the *Best Plays* series continued under the editorship of John Chapman (later Louis Kronenberger, Henry Hewes, and Otis Guernsey) and was subtitled *The Burns Mantle Yearbook* in honor of its much-admired first editor. The prolific Mantle was also the author of *American Playwrights of Today* (1929), *Contemporary American Playwrights* (1938), and with John Gassner coedited *A Treasury of the Theatre* (1935). He frequently contributed articles to magazines such as *Good Housekeeping*, *Munsey's*, and *Theatre Arts Monthly*.

Married in 1903 to Denver native Lydia Sears, with whom he had a daughter, Mantle enjoyed gardening and golf, but theatergoing was his primary avocation as well as his occupation. The affable Mantle was among the first critics to be made a member of the Players Club, primarily an actor's organization. Mantle died at his home in Forest Hills, Queens, where he had lived for more than thirty years.

• Sources of information on Burns Mantle are Arthur John Krows, "Burns Mantle Separates Critics from Critics," *New York Dramatic Mirror*, 4 Mar. 1914; John Chapman, "Burns Mantle Ends Reviewing Career," *New York Sunday News*, 15 Aug. 1943; and "Mantle Emeritus," *Newsweek*, 23 Aug. 1943. See also a tribute to Mantle by fellow critic Brooks Atkinson in the *New York Times*, 10 Feb. 1948. Atkinson is also the author of the article on Mantle in the *Dictionary of American Biography*. Obituaries are in the *New York Daily News* and the *New York Times*, both on 10 Feb. 1948.

MARY C. KALFATOVIC

MANTLE, Mickey (20 Oct. 1931–13 Aug. 1995), baseball player, was born Mickey Charles Mantle in Spavinaw, Oklahoma, the son of Elvin "Mutt" Mantle, a lead and zinc miner, and Lovell Richardson, who had two children by a previous marriage. A fifth generation American, Mantle and his four younger siblings lived a hardscrabble life on a small farm where baseball became his boyhood passion. Tutored by his father, who like his father and two brothers had played semiprofessional baseball, Mantle, who was named after the famous Detroit Tigers catcher Mickey Cochrane, became a promising switch-hitting infielder. A versatile athlete, Mantle also played varsity basketball and football at Commerce (Okla.) High School. In 1946 a leg injury sustained in a football game developed into osteomyelitis and sidelined Mantle for a year, but in 1948 his prowess as a baseball player attracted major league scouts. Although most scouts were leery of Mantle's leg problems, Tom Greenwade of the New York Yankees saw a "17-year-old body that worked like a damn baseball machine." Upon graduating from high school in 1949, Mantle signed a Yankee contract and launched his professional baseball career by batting .313 with the Independence, Kansas, team of the Class D Kansas-Oklahoma-Missouri League. After being rejected by the military draft because of his leg injury, Mantle played shortstop for the 1950 Joplin, Missouri, team of the Class C Western Association. Despite making numerous fielding errors, his .383 batting earned him promotion to the Yankees in 1951. As a rookie bewildered by the glamour of New York City life Mantle required guidance on such basics as proper clothing and dietary habits. More important, Yankee officials had to rescue Mantle from unscrupulous exploiters who attempted to bilk him out of his salary earnings.

With the reigning champion Yankees the 19-year-old Mantle displayed outstanding running speed and batting ability, but his limitations at shortstop led to his speedy conversion to the outfield. Following an impressive debut, Mantle slumped and was sent to the Yankees' Kansas City club of the Class AAA American Association for further seasoning. Recalled in August, Mantle's lusty hitting helped the Yankees win a third straight league championship. The 1951 season launched Mantle's 18-year career with the Yankees during which he helped the team win 12 American League pennants and seven World Series titles. But Mantle's first World Series experience ended when he suffered a serious knee injury in the second game; deferring to Joe Dimaggio on a fly ball, Mantle caught his cleats on an uncapped drain in the outfield. It was the first of several serious injuries that marred his career. In its aftermath Mantle returned to Commerce and married Merlyn Johnson; subsequently they had four children.

In 1952 Mantle replaced DiMaggio as the team's center fielder. A pressurizing challenge for a twenty-year old, it was compounded by his father's death, which cast him as the financial supporter of seven dependents. By his own admission, his fear of cancer, which took his father and three male relatives all before the age of 40, prompted Mantle to take to drinking and carousing with teammates Whitey Ford and Billy Martin. But that season he batted .311 with 23 home runs, and his two home runs in the World Series enabled the Yankees to repeat as world champions. The following year, with Mantle batting .295 with 92 runs batted in, the Yankees won another league championship; then, with Mantle again driving two game-winning home runs, the Yankees won a record fifth consecutive World Series title.

Over the next five seasons the husky 5'11", 195-pound Mantle's offensive performance had his awed manager, Casey Stengel, describing him as the fastest and "best distance hitter . . . right or left" he had ever seen. Mantle was a continuing source of frustration to Stengel, who regarded him as an under-achiever who disregarded suggestions for improvement. Especially did Stengel fault his lack of dedication to rehabilitation regimens prescribed for his frequent injuries. Indeed, Stengel never placed Mantle on his personal all-star team. Unhampered by serious injuries, Mantle played in 737 games, batted .300 or better each year, and thrice led the league in home runs. In 1956, his best season, Mantle's Triple Crown feat of leading the majors with a .353 average, 52 home runs, and 130 RBIs won him the first of his three American League Most Valuable Player awards. A second came a year later on the strength of his .365 hitting, 34 home runs, and 94 RBIs. During this five-year span the Yankees won four more league pennants and two World Series titles, with Mantle becoming the highest-paid Yankee and, as the acclaimed "Commerce Comet," a national celebrity. However, such adulation was tempered by Mantle's displays of immature behavior and his continuing drinking and carousing.

Over the years 1960–1964, despite the enervating diversions and the debilitating effects of injuries, Mantle led the Yankees to a second skein of five consecutive league championships and two more World Series titles. In four of these seasons Mantle topped the .300 mark at bat while averaging 35 home runs a season. In 1961, as teammate Roger Maris hit 61 home runs to break Babe Ruth's seasonal record, Mantle hit 54 home runs. The following year, on the strength of his .321 batting average, 30 home runs, and 89 RBIs, Mantle won his third Most Valuable Player award. By then, however, a spate of injuries, complicated by his disdain for rehabilitation regimens, weakened both Mantle's knees and his throwing arm. After suffering a broken foot bone and knee damage in 1963, Mantle missed most of the playing season but returned in time to hit .314 with 15 home runs. The following year, Mantle's last good season, he batted .303 with 35 home runs and 111 RBIs. However, at the close of that season a major league scout rated him below average in running, throwing, fielding, and batting, although above average in power.

Mantle's last four years with the Yankees were pain-ridden, with nearly all the cartilage in his knees gone by 1967. Switching to first base, he never again batted .300 and his home run production slipped to 82 over these years. In 1968 he made his 16th and last All-Star Game appearance, and the following year he announced his retirement, admitting that "I just can't play anymore."

A legendary performer and a national hero, Mantle was paid a record $100,000 a season at the time of his retirement. Over his 18-year career he batted .298 with 536 home runs and 1,509 RBIs in regular season play, and he batted .257 with 18 home runs and 40 RBIs in 12 World Series appearances. Best known for his slugging, his 536 home runs (373 hit from the left side of the plate) ranked him third among all players in 1969. In 1953, when Mantle's home run at Washington's Griffith Stadium flew an estimated 565 feet, Yankee official Red Patterson grandiosely labeled it a "tape measure home run." However, Mantle claimed that a 620-foot home run he hit at Yankee Stadium was "the hardest I ever hit." In World Series competition he set longstanding records for home runs, scored runs (42), runs batted in, walks (43), strikeouts (54). Among his other feats, he led the American League in runs scored six times and his career total of 1,677 runs scored ranked third among American League players at the end of the twentieth century. A free swinger, Mantle struck out 1,710 times, but his total of 1,734 bases on balls ranked fifth among major league players at the end of the twentieth century. For his outstanding offensive performance, Mantle was elected to the National Baseball Hall of Fame in 1974.

Upon retiring from baseball, Mantle served as a part-time coach and batting instructor with the Yankees. But his retirement years were marked by moods of depression that he assuaged with alcohol. Exacerbating his problems were his separation from his wife, his dashed hopes of managing a major league team, and a failed fast food business venture that had him declaring bankruptcy in 1973. However, Mantle's popularity with baseball fans was so strong that during the last 15 years of his life he made far more money than he ever did in baseball. In 1982 his major source of income came from paid public appearances, and in 1983 he was paid $100,000 to do promotional work with an Atlantic City casino. For undertaking the casino work he was barred from any connection with major league baseball, but the ban was lifted two years later. By then royalties from his books and lucrative autograph-signing appearances at baseball collectors' shows enhanced his income. In 1993 he signed a $2.75 million contract with Upper Deck for the sale of autographed memorabilia.

But Mantle's worsening alcoholism reached such proportions that in 1994 he spent 32 days at the Betty Ford Center. The following June he was hospitalized for cirrhosis of the liver complicated by cancer and hepatitis. While hospitalized Mantle received a liver transplant that stirred allegations that he was favored over other waiting recipients. Ravaged by rapidly spreading cancer, Mantle died two months later in Dallas, Texas. His death and funeral were media events, and many tributes to his memory included the establishment of the Mickey Mantle Foundation for organ donor awareness.

It seems important to stress that Mantle was a "tragic hero" who was felled by both alcoholism and his own feelings of failure but who (ironically, perhaps) was a role model for millions of Americans growing up in the 1950s and 1960s. That Mantle's fans generally still adored him even after his problems were made public is a testament to the man.

• The National Baseball Library, Cooperstown, N.Y., has extensive clipping files on Mantle's life. Useful books on Mantle's baseball career include several autobiographies: *The Mickey Mantle Story* (1953); *The Quality of Courage* (1964); *The Education of a Baseball Player* (1967); *Whitey and Mickey: A Joint Autobiography of the Yankee Years*, with Joseph Durso (1977); *Mickey Mantle: The American Dream Comes to Life*, with Lewis Early (1994); *The Mick*, with Herb Gluck (1985); *All My Octobers*, with Mickey Herskowitz (1994); and *My Favorite Summer, 1956*, with Phil Pepe (1991).

Among numerous biographies of Mantle, David Falkner, *The Last Hero: The Life of Mickey Mantle* (1995), is outstanding. Other biographies include, By the Friends and Fans of Mickey Mantle, *Letters to Mickey* (1995); Mickey Herskowitz, *Mickey Mantle: An Appreciation* (1995); Dick Schaap, *Mickey Mantle, The Indispensable Yankee* (1966); Gene Schoor, *Mickey Mantle of the Yankees* (1959); Milton J. Shapiro, *Mickey Mantle, Yankee Slugger* (1962); and Al Silverman, *Mickey Mantle: Mr. Yankee* (1963). Myron Smith, Jr., *Baseball: A Comprehensive Bibliography* (1986), lists 153 articles and books on Mantle's career. For Mantle's career in the general history of major league baseball, see David Quentin Voigt, *American Baseball*, vol. 3 (1983). Among many obituaries in magazines and newspapers, see the *New York Times*, 14 and 15 Aug. 1995; the *Sporting News*, 21 Aug. 1995; and *USA Today Baseball Weekly*, 16–22 Aug. 1995.

DAVID Q. VOIGT

MANTOVANI (15 Nov. 1905–29 Mar. 1980), conductor, composer, and arranger, was born Annunzio Paolo in Venice, Italy, the son of Benedetto Bismark Paolo, a violinist and concertmaster at La Scala, and Iparia Manfrin Mantovani. His father, a principal violinist for Mascagni, Hans Richter, and Camille Saint-Saëns, had an opportunity to lead an Italian opera orchestra at Covent Garden in 1909. Three years later the family moved to London. The young Mantovani rejected a plan to pursue a career in engineering and enrolled at London's Trinity College of Music. He studied the piano before permanently settling on the violin. At the age of sixteen he took his mother's maiden name and began his professional career as a violinist with a restaurant group in Birmingham, England. He debuted playing the Max Bruch first Violin Concerto, op. 26.

Throughout the 1920s and 1930s Mantovani performed recitals and conducted orchestras in hotels, restaurants, clubs, and moving-picture houses. He formed his first orchestra in 1923 for the Midland Hotel in Birmingham, England, gave recitals at Wigmore Hall, and had the opportunity to satisfy as a teenager his ambition to play Saint-Saëns's Violin Concerto at Queen's Hall in London. In 1927 he became conductor of the Hotel Metropole's salon orchestra and regularly broadcast and recorded his concerts for the BBC. He formed the Tipica Orchestra in 1932 and broadcast a series of lunchtime performances from the famous Monseigneur Restaurant in Piccadilly, London. The same year he toured the British Isles and recorded for Regal Zonophone.

Mantovani became a British citizen in 1933 and on 4 August 1934 married Winifred Kathleen Moss. They had two children. Inspired by the creativity with

which Fritz Kreisler conducted the Arthur Hartman transcription of Debussy's *The Girl with the Flaxen Hair*, Mantovani switched from conducting classical music to popular music. He explained the challenge of conducting light music in a 1973 interview: "With the opera and symphony masterpieces you have substantial music that can survive a less than perfect or inspired performance. You have the great composer to fall back on. And you have more time to establish atmosphere, mood, color, and pace. With the short, light pieces that we play you have less to work with. And you have to accomplish everything in a matter of four or five minutes, maybe less" (Pleasants, p. 54). For years Mantovani worked in London's West End, orchestrating and conducting musicals such as *And So to Bed*, *Bob's Your Uncle*, *Lady Behave*, and Noël Coward's *Pacific 1860*, starring Mary Martin.

By 1950 Mantovani had become an international phenomenon, known for selecting, and holding onto, the best musicians. Yet success in the United States continued to evade him, despite his composing and recording of two hit songs in 1935 and 1936, "Red Sails in the Sunset" and "Serenade in the Night." In an effort to exploit the U.S. market, Mantovani experimented with various string arrangements that would allow him to add a personal style to familiar music. In 1951 he and arranger Ronald Binge combined lush strings, woods, and brass to create a Viennese "cascading strings" effect. The result was recognized as the "lush Monty-manner" (*Variety*, 12 Dec. 1956, p. 62).

Mantovani used this technique on a recording of "Charmaine," the theme song for the 1926 silent film classic *What Price Glory?* The single sold over a million copies, becoming his signature song and earning Mantovani the moniker "King of Strings." Other singles that sold over a million copies include "Wyoming," "Greensleeves," "Swedish Rhapsody," "Lonely Ballerina," and "Songs from the Moulin Rouge."

Mantovani signed with Coppicus, Schang & Brown, a division of Columbia Artists, and became as much a hit in North America as in Europe. From 1955 to 1966 he had twenty-eight albums in the U.S. Top 30. He became the first semiclassical artist to do one-night performances, covering as many as sixty cities in tours of seventy-two days. His program in the United States and Canada was a combination of symphony and jazz, with selections from Johann Strauss, Sigmund Romberg, Victor Herbert, Rudolf Friml, Richard Rodgers, and Morton Gould and "just enough of the commercial touch to sell it solidly to everybody" (*Variety*, 5 Oct. 1955, p. 51). His wide audience appeal meant mixing "mink and mouton, teenagers and annultants, homburgs and weathered snap-brims" (*Variety*, 4 Dec. 1963, p. 44).

In 1954 Mantovani and his orchestra accompanied artist David Whitfield to record "Cara Mia," which Mantovani had co-composed with Bunny Lewis. It sold over a million copies and stayed at the number one position on the United Kingdom's popular music charts for a record ten weeks. Mantovani received the Ivor Novello Award in 1956 as the artist who did the most for British popular music. In 1958 Franklin D. Roosevelt, Jr., general counsel for London, presented Mantovani with a gold disk at New York's Waldorf-Astoria Hotel for hitting the quarter-million mark eight times in the field of albums sold. Mantovani "outsold even the Beatles in some of that group's peak years in album unit terms" and claimed that the hard music produced by the Beatles and bands like them had helped create the demand for his easy listening alternative (*Billboard*, 12 Apr. 1980, p. 49).

By 27 April 1966 Mantovani had been with British Decca for twenty-five years, recorded over 1,000 tunes, and sold millions of disks. On 22 February 1967 the veteran British maestro was honored with a Presidential Award for his "unique and outstanding contribution to the field of recorded music" at the annual convention of the National Association of Recording Merchandisers in Los Angeles. On 18 March 1970 he won his seventh gold LP award. His *Golden Hits* album reached $1 million in sales in three years after it was released, coinciding with London's nineteenth annual "March Is Mantovani Month." In all he recorded more than fifty albums and sold more than 100 million records. His passions, aside from playing the violin and conducting, included playing bridge and buying exotic cars. He died in Tunbridge Wells, in Kent, England.

• Other notable Mantovani recordings include "Mexicali Rose," "La Cumparsita," "Dancing with Tears in My Eyes," and "It Happened in Monterey." For biographical sketches see Henry Pleasants, "Annunzio Paolo Mantovani, a Visit with the Palm-garden Toscanini," *Stereo Review*, Jan. 1973, p. 54. His music is discussed in T. Brown, "Mantovani Spearhead of Britain's Invasion," *Melody Maker*, 14 Nov. 1953, p. 3; "Mantovani's First U.S. Tour in 1955," *Variety*, 8 Dec. 1954, p. 47; "Mantovani 'Sound' Clicks in Canadian Concert Swing: Opens 32 City U.S. Tour," *Variety*, 5 Oct. 1955, p. 51; "Mink & Mouton and SRO at Lincoln Center for Mantovani Orchestra," *Variety*, 4 Dec. 1963, p. 44; and "Buffs Fill Philharmonic Hall to Hear Mantovani Play That Simple Melody," *Variety*, 30 Nov. 1966, p. 45. Donald Clarke mentions Mantovani briefly for his part in the British invasion of the American light music scene in *The Rise and Fall of Popular Music* (1995). Obituaries are in *Los Angeles Times*, 31 Mar. 1980; *Billboard*, 12 Apr. 1980; *Variety*, 2 Apr. 1980; and *Rolling Stone*, 15 May 1980.

BARBARA L. CICCARELLI

MANUELITO (1818?–1893), Navajo war and political leader also known as Ch'ilhaajinii (Black Weeds), was born probably near Bear's Ears, Utah, the son of Cayetano, a prominent war and political leader, and a Bit'ahni clan woman whose name is unknown. At age sixteen Manuelito married the daughter of Narbona, a major Navajo leader, and following Navajo tradition moved to his wife's camp. This was his first wife; he would later take several other wives, including a Mexican captive. The names of his wives and the total number of their children are unknown.

In 1834 he accompanied his father-in-law, who advocated making peace with local Mexican authorities, to talks in Santa Fe with the governor of New Mexico.

The following year he participated in the defeat of a Mexican slave raiding party at Washington Pass. Manuelito killed one of the raiders and was given the war name Hashkeh Naabaah (Angry Warrior).

In 1837, following the murder of a party of Navajos by the Hopis, Manuelito joined Ganado Mucho in an attack on Oraibi. Although he respected his father-in-law, Manuelito felt that the Navajos could trust neither the Mexicans nor the Pueblos. Thus he moved from Narbona's camp and joined the prowar Navajos living south of Sheep Springs, New Mexico. While still in his twenties, Manuelito became recognized as a *naat'aani* (chief) and one of the most clever and aggressive Navajo war leaders.

After the American occupation of New Mexico in 1846, Manuelito was one of the fourteen Navajo leaders who signed the Treaty of Bear Springs. The treaty committed the Americans to stop the Mexican slave raiders and return Navajo captives. Neither provision was enforced, and conflict between Navajos and Mexicans continued.

In 1851 Fort Defiance was established by the United States in present-day northeastern Arizona, the very heart of the Navajo country, in an attempt to bring peace to the region. Although Manuelito was antagonistic toward the Americans there were no immediate problems. In 1853 a party of Navajo leaders, including Manuelito, traveled to Santa Fe and met with Governor David Meriwether. The governor appointed Zarcillos Largos as "Captain" of the Navajos. Two years later Largos resigned, and Meriwether appointed Manuelito to take his place.

In spite of the presence of U.S. troops, raiding by and against the Navajos continued, and relations between the troops at Fort Defiance and the Navajos remained tense. In 1858 livestock belonging to Manuelito was shot by soldiers after the Navajos failed to follow the post commander's order to remove their animals from the vicinity of the fort. Subsequently Manuelito was replaced as "head chief" by Largos. Later that year open fighting broke out between the Navajos and the soldiers at Fort Defiance and continued throughout 1859 and 1860. In 1860 Manuelito led two minor attacks on the fort itself. In February 1861 a new peace treaty was negotiated, and Fort Defiance was abandoned. The start of the Civil War caused a further reduction of federal troops, and raiding by the Pueblos, Navajos, Mexicans, and Utes resumed on an unprecedented scale.

After the defeat of Confederate forces in New Mexico in 1863, U.S. general James Carleton decided to end the Indian problem in the territory by relocating the entire Navajo tribe to a small reservation on the plains of eastern New Mexico: the Bosque Redondo. There he intended to make large-scale farmers of the Navajos, who would be kept under military guard. Over 700 volunteers under Kit Carson invaded the Navajo country, killing anyone who resisted, destroying their fields and orchards, and seizing their sheep, cattle, and horses. Carleton encouraged the Utes and Pueblos as well as irregular groups of Mexicans and

Anglos to assist Carson by joining in the looting and carnage. During the winter of 1863–1864, thousands of frightened and starving Navajos surrendered to the troops at Fort Defiance, renamed Fort Canby. They were then marched under guard over 300 miles east to the Bosque Redondo. Eventually more than 8,500 Navajos made this trek.

While the majority of Navajos surrendered during the first winter, there were some holdouts. The most prominent was Manuelito. With his family, followers, and herds, he moved west to the valley of the Little Colorado, where in February 1865 a party of Utes discovered his camp and took most of his livestock. In the fall of 1865 another Ute party attacked his new camp near Black Mountain, killing or capturing most of his family. Manuelito and his surviving family and followers then moved to Grand Canyon. It was not until September 1866 that Manuelito surrendered to federal troops and was sent to Bosque Redondo. In June 1868 a new treaty was signed with the Navajo leaders, including Manuelito, allowing them to return to their homeland and providing a small reservation.

To assist the Indian agent in governing the new reservation, a twelve-member chiefs' council was established, with Manuelito as one of the members. The Navajos had been impoverished by the war, and government rations and livestock distributions were inadequate. Many Navajos soon resumed raiding in order to survive and rebuild their herds. The agent put pressure on the chiefs' council to stop the raiding and recover stolen stock. Manuelito took an active role in this campaign; he recovered stock and on one occasion killed a raider. To more effectively police the reservation in August 1872, the Navajo cavalry was organized, and Manuelito was placed in command. Within a year conditions had improved so dramatically that the Navajo cavalry was no longer needed.

During the 1870s the power of the chiefs' council increased as they took control over all the rations and goods given by the government to the tribe. These rations and goods were then distributed to the families and supporters of the chiefs. By playing the army against the Indian Service, they were able to control the agency and even had one agent who opposed them removed from office. In 1876 Manuelito visited Washington, D.C., and met with President Ulysses S. Grant. Many Navajos resented the growing power of the chiefs. In 1878 the chiefs and their supporters, particularly Ganado Mucho and Manuelito, found themselves the targets of Navajo witchcraft. Manuelito temporarily fled the reservation. The situation was resolved after the followers of the chiefs killed more than forty witches.

By the 1880s the influence of the chiefs was waning. Government issuance of rations and goods stopped in 1879. In 1884 a new Navajo police force was organized without reliance on the chiefs. While the chiefs' council, which still included Manuelito, survived, the group's importance was greatly diminished.

As a member of the council, Manuelito had become a strong supporter of education. One of his sons was in the first group of Navajo students sent to study at Carlisle Indian School in Pennsylvania in 1883, but he soon returned home sick and quickly died. Manuelito then turned against education and developed a drinking problem. He died at his home near Manuelito's Springs. For over forty years Manuelito was one of the most influential leaders of the largest and most powerful tribe in the southwestern United States.

• No definitive biography of Manuelito has been published. The best study is a short biographical sketch in Virginia Hoffman, *Navajo Biographies*, vol. 1 (1974), pp. 80–102. Other information on Manuelito can be found in Frank McNitt, *Navajo Wars* (1972); J. Lee Correll, *Through White Men's Eyes* (1979); and Garrick Bailey and Roberta Bailey, *A History of the Navajos* (1986).

GARRICK BAILEY
ROBERTA GLENN BAILEY

MANUSH, Heinie (20 July 1901–12 May 1971), baseball player, was born Emmett Henry Manush in Tuscumbia, Alabama. Little is known about his parents, only that his father had emigrated from Germany and that he died in 1924. Baseball was important to the family; Manush's older brother Frank had signed a professional contract, playing third base for the Philadelphia Athletics in 1908. Attempting to follow in his brother's footsteps, Manush played high school baseball before attending Massey Military Academy in Pulaski, Tennessee, for two years. Believing that he was not good enough to forge a career in professional baseball, Manush first worked in his brother's plumbing company in Burlington, Iowa, and then accepted a job as an apprentice pipe fitter in a Salt Lake City, Utah, refinery. While in Salt Lake, he played baseball for the company team and was discovered by scouts for the Detroit Tigers, who signed him to a professional contract in 1921.

After two minor league seasons in Edmonton and Omaha, Manush was promoted to the Tigers. In Detroit, the aggressive left-handed-hitting outfielder, who was always more of a line-drive hitter than a home run threat, joined an outfield featuring future Hall of Fame players Ty Cobb and Harry Heilmann. The young man from Alabama quickly earned a place for himself in this outfield by hitting .334 in 109 games. After successful seasons in 1924 and 1925, Manush hit .378, beating out Babe Ruth for the 1926 American League batting championship. However, in 1927 Manush slumped to .298 and had disagreements with new Tiger manager George Moriarty, who had replaced Cobb in that position. Following the 1927 season, the disgruntled outfielder was traded to the St. Louis Browns.

Manush flourished in a Browns uniform, equaling his career-high batting mark of .378 but losing the 1928 batting title to the Senator's Goose Goslin on the last day of the season. In 1928 he married Betty Lloyd. They had three children. In 1929 Manush continued to terrorize pitchers, finishing third in the American League with an average of .355. Following these two successful campaigns, Manush demanded a salary increase and was a holdout during spring training. Browns management responded to Manush's salary negotiations by dealing him to the Washington Senators forty-nine games into the 1930 season.

Manush played for the Senators from 1930 through 1935, contributing a .336 batting mark to the American League champion club in 1933. However, his only World Series appearance was less successful, as he managed only two hits for eighteen at bats during the 1933 fall classic. Nevertheless, Manush earned quite a bit of attention as he outfought other players to obtain the ball thrown out by Franklin Roosevelt to start the third game of the Series. In the fourth game, Manush was called out by umpire Charlie Moran on a close play at first base. A frustrated Manush charged the umpire, grabbing his bow tie, which was held in place by an elastic band, and popping it back onto his throat. Manush was immediately told to leave the game, but he only reluctantly retired after initially assuming his defensive position in left field. The incident marked the first time that a player had been ejected from a Series game since 1919, and Baseball Commissioner Kenesaw Mountain Landis, after first fining Manush fifty dollars, announced that hereafter the commissioner would have to be consulted before a player could be dismissed from a Series game.

Following a decline to a .273 batting mark in 1935, Manush was traded to the Boston Red Sox, where he was employed primarily as a pinch hitter until his release in late September. He was signed as a free agent by the Brooklyn Dodgers and hit .333 in his first National League campaign. However, after another spring training holdout, this time for a $1,000 salary increase, the Dodgers traded Manush to the Pittsburgh Pirates, where he finished his playing career in 1939.

From 1940 through 1945 Manush managed and played in the minor leagues, while from 1946 to 1948 he served as a major league scout for the Boston Braves and Pirates. Following the death of his wife in 1949, Manush devoted the next few years to raising their three girls. In 1953 and 1954 he returned to the major leagues as a coach for the Washington Senators. His last official affiliation with baseball was as a scout for the expanding Washington Senators in 1961 and 1962. In 1964 he was named to the Baseball Hall of Fame.

In very poor health during his later years, Manush died in Sarasota, Florida. In the *New York Times*, sportswriter Joseph Durso well summarized the baseball contributions of Manush, observing, "In an era of aggressive hitters in baseball, during the twenties and thirties, Henry Manush of Alabama was one of the most aggressive—and one of the most durable—compiling a .330 average during 17 seasons in both the American and National Leagues."

• For biographical information on Manush, see Martin Appel and Burt Goldblatt, *Baseball's Best: The Hall of Fame Gallery* (1980), and Ira L. Smith, *Baseball's Famous Outfielders* (1954). For Manush's statistics see the *Baseball Encyclopedia* or John Thorn and Pete Palmer, eds., *Total Baseball: The Ultimate Encyclopedia of Baseball* (1993). For baseball and Manush in the 1920s and 1930s, see John P. Carmichael, "Manush Recalls Outfield Cobb Couldn't Make," *Baseball Digest*, Sept. 1943, pp. 25–27; Franis Stann, "Manush's Return Stirs Memories," *Baseball Digest*, July 1953, pp. 80–83; and John J. Ward, "The Great Comeback of Manush," *Baseball Magazine*, Dec. 1937, pp. 297–98. An obituary is in the *New York Times*, 14 May 1971.

RON BRILEY

MANVILLE, Tommy (9 Apr. 1894–8 Oct. 1967), wealthy, talked-about playboy, was born Thomas Franklyn Manville, Jr., in Milwaukee, Wisconsin, the son of multimillionaire Thomas Franklyn Manville, an insulation manufacturer and founder of the Johns-Manville Corporation, and Clara Coleman. Manville's parents were divorced in 1909, at which time his father was given custody of him and his mother custody of his sister.

With both parents immersed in their self-centered lives, Manville sought and developed an attention-getting life-style of his own. He began with the usual pre-teen smoking and drinking, then the teenage stunts of running away from school, followed by a succession of low-paying, blue-collar jobs. But his real career began at age seventeen when he married for the first time. His wife, Florence Huber, was a chorus girl he had met five days earlier under a Broadway marquee. Ultimately, his life turned into an extraordinary cycle of marriage and divorce that became his only claim to celebrity. He took eleven wives, in thirteen marriages—he remarried twice—and was divorced from ten of them a total of eleven times. Once, he was widowed. His penchant was for pretty blonde chorus girls, most of whom he knew only briefly before marrying them, and he took great pride in selecting beautiful women.

The fact that Manville would become a career bridegroom was not immediately apparent. His first marriage lasted eleven years, although he and his wife lived separately from 1917 until their divorce in 1922. This was his longest marriage. The shortest—to wife number seven, Macie Marie "Sunny" Ainsworth, who had been married four times by her twentieth year—lasted only seven hours and forty-five minutes.

Manville's relationship with his father had long been rocky; repeated threats of disinheritance were followed by short-lived reconciliations. But on his father's death in 1925, Manville inherited about $10 million from a $50 million estate. He also had heavy courtship expenses not only before his numerous marriages, but before his many failed engagements, estimated by media sources to have numbered at least several dozen and possibly more than five hundred.

After receiving his inheritance, Manville lived in grand style in equally grand surroundings, a 28-room house on Long Island called "Bon Repos." It had a motion picture theater, a telephone switchboard in the master bedroom, and a security system worthy of Fort Knox because, despite his need for publicity, he sought privacy on his estate. Besides the burglar alarms, he employed armed guards, a public address system, and he often wore two pistols at his belt. He was of medium height and always well turned out. His prematurely gray, wavy hair made him easy to recognize and prompted him to ask police, who were regularly summoned to the estate during marital disputes, to call him "grandpappy."

His antics, outrageous behavior, and excesses kept "the marrying Manville," as he was tagged, in the public eye, giving him the attention he craved. At the time of his death Manville, who had no children, was still married to wife number eleven, Christina Erdlen, a former waitress who had divorced to marry him. She inherited the bulk of his estate, which consisted of $200,000, their home, automobiles, jewelry, and the income from trust funds that totaled slightly more than $1 million. Two codicils had been added to the will: (1) his stepdaughter, Dianna Ocker, his last wife's daughter, was the principal beneficiary when her mother died; (2) a previous codicil that willed $50,000 to his first wife, who was living alone in a New York hotel, was revoked. Manville died in Chappaqua, New York, where he had moved in 1955.

Although one might suspect that the Manville image and persona could have influenced popular culture, it appears to have been the other way round; William Randolph Hearst and F. Scott Fitzgerald's larger-than-life character Jay Gatsby seem to have influenced him.

• Manville's life history as well as explanations and examples of his escapades, which account for his notoriety, can be found in a clipping file, compiled by the defunct *New York Herald Tribune*, at the *New York Post*'s offices. Obituaries are in the *New York Times*, *Milwaukee Journal*, and *Milwaukee Sentinel*, 9 Oct. 1967. An article on Manville's will appeared in the *New York Times*, 24 Oct. 1967.

PATRICIA FOX-SHEINWOLD

MAPES, Charles Victor (4 July 1836–23 Jan. 1916), agricultural chemist, was born in New York City, the son of James Jay Mapes, an agriculturalist and analytical chemist, and Sophia Furman. His sister was Mary Mapes Dodge, the editor of the children's magazine *St. Nicholas* and author of the perennial favorite, *Hans Brinker; or, The Silver Skates*. When Mapes was eleven years old his family moved to a farm near Newark, New Jersey, on worn-out land that his father was rehabilitating as a demonstration of scientific agriculture. Here young Mapes acquainted himself with music, painting, and the written classics, as well as the sciences, the latter pursued in the small laboratory he installed in his room. He attended Harvard College and graduated in 1857.

Mapes's original aim was medicine, but for health and other reasons he was forced to abandon it for a career in commerce at the wholesale grocery house of B. M. and E. A. Whitlock and Co. in New York. In 1859 he and B. M. Whitlock began to manufacture agricultural implements and fertilizers in a factory near Newark. At the same time he assumed publishing re-

sponsibility for his father's journal, *The Working Farmer*. The factory produced the elder Mapes's patented nitrogenized superphosphate, the first complete artificial fertilizer marketed in this country, and sold imported fertilizers as well. Mapes's firm hoped to capture the market of the cotton-producing states of the South, but the Civil War intervened and the enterprise failed. In 1863 he married Martha Meeker Halsted; they had five children.

In 1874 Mapes began manufacture of specialty fertilizers that he formulated and tested himself. In this he was the first to market products for specific crops like Irish potatoes. These special-crop fertilizers were based on Mapes's own investigations of plant and soil requirements. Some of his conclusions, reflected in the nitrogen/phosphorus/potassium balance of his offerings, were that plants need different forms of food at different stages in their growth; that the sources of the critical chemical elements should be varied, rather than all from the same minerals; that when sugar and starch formation are important, potassium must be supplied as the carbonate or sulfate salt, not the chloride, as chloride inhibits growth of these carbohydrates; that in fruit crops, particularly oranges, two fertilizers are required, one for fruit growth, the other for the plant itself; and that corn should be treated as a nitrogen-fixing legume, not a standard grain. His finding on corn resulted in great economy, for it meant that farmers did not have to supply a nitrogenous fertilizer. In the course of his research Mapes worked for a time with Wilbur Olin Atwater, the Connecticut agricultural chemist who later set up the federal program of agricultural experiment stations. Together they performed hundreds of soil tests relating the mineral content of soils to the needs of plants grown in them; these tests were taken up and continued by a number of the state agricultural experiment stations. Mapes's pioneering work in fertilizers adapted to particular plant needs is his particular and permanent contribution to agricultural research.

In 1877 Mapes became vice president and general manager of the Mapes Formula and Peruvian Guano Company, of which he was the founder and later the president; he was president until his death. When the New York Chemical and Fertilizer Exchange was organized in 1888, Mapes became its first president. He was a member of the chemistry subsection of the American Association for the Advancement of Science and of the newly founded (1876) American Chemical Society. His published output included many articles in agricultural journals and pamphlets and the general articles "Some Rambling Notes of Agriculture and Manures" and "The Effects of Fertilizers on Different Soils" in the sixth (1879) and seventh (1879–1880) *Annual Reports of the New Jersey State Board of Agriculture*. Mapes died at his West Fifty-seventh Street home in New York City.

• Biographical material on Mapes is slender indeed. The *Report of the Class of 1857 in Harvard College* (1866, 1882, and 1910) contains some biographical information. For a glimpse of the business venture of 1859, see *Charles V. Mapes' Illustrated Catalog (for 1861) of Plows, and Other Agricultural Implements and Machines.* The obituary notices in *Science* and the *New York Times,* 24 Jan. 1916, run to only a few uninformative lines each.

ROBERT M. HAWTHORNE JR.

MAPES, James Jay (29 May 1806–10 Jan. 1866), chemist and writer, was born in Maspeth, New York, the son of Jonas Mapes, a merchant and importer, and Elizabeth Tylee. While at a boarding school on Long Island, Mapes lived for a time with the English reformer William Cobbett. As a scientist, however, he was largely self-taught.

In 1827 Mapes married Sophia Furman and opened his own mercantile business. The couple had four children and adopted two others. By 1834 Mapes advertised himself as a consulting chemist and became involved in numerous efforts to apply recent advances in chemistry to practical uses. He investigated the chemistry of sugar refining and dye making and the tempering of steel. He was among the first Americans to manufacture Epsom salts (magnesium sulfate) and synthetic tanning agents that replaced hemlock-based products. Though these techniques seemed to offer commercial potential, many of his enterprises failed. During the 1830s and 1840s Mapes earned much of his income as an expert on chemistry issues in patent cases.

Mapes was very active in efforts to popularize and promote science, which he considered vital both to a liberal arts education and as a strategy to establish American domestic industries. Mapes joined several of New York's learned societies, serving as secretary of the National Association of Inventors and president of the Mechanics' Institute of the City of New York. He received appointments as professor of chemistry and the natural philosophy of colors at the National Academy of Design and as professor of natural philosophy and chemistry applicable to the useful arts at the American Institute. Mapes also spent time with two early American scientific journals, as editor of the *American Repertory of Arts, Sciences, and Manufactures* from 1840 to 1842 and as assistant editor of the *Journal of the Franklin Institute* from 1842 to 1843.

In 1847 Mapes purchased a farm near Newark, New Jersey, and turned increasingly toward issues in agricultural chemistry. From 1849 to 1863 he was editor of the journal *Working Farmer.* Always an aggressive self-promoter, Mapes used the journal as a forum to advertise his innovations and services as well as to promote his vision of scientific agriculture. Above all, Mapes advocated deep plowing, careful attention to drainage, and heavy use of chemical fertilizers. Mapes offered classes and lectures for practicing farmers, opened his farm to Saturday tours, and lobbied legislators for increased governmental services for farmers, such as the establishment of a cabinet-level federal department of agriculture. He also promoted his innovative implements, like a root cleaner, a digging machine, and a horse hoe. His operation attracted several students, who spread his vision of agricultural improvement into the late nineteenth century.

Through his journal Mapes was probably the most aggressive promoter of fertilizers in the United States. He endorsed various systems of returning nutrients to the soils, including the recycling of sewage. By 1852 he had become the first American producer of superphosphate, a fertilizer commonly produced through the application of sulfuric acid to ground bones. The quality of Mapes's fertilizers soon became a controversial issue in agricultural circles; in 1855 a major dispute surrounded charges that Mapes simply ground and sold his fertilizer as Chilean guano. Though Mapes aggressively promoted the importance of chemistry in farm operations, the high prices that he charged for soil and fertilizer analyses and the inconsistent quality of his products probably played a role in farmers' long-lasting skepticism about the validity of agricultural chemistry.

Mapes combined careers in chemistry, agriculture, education, and business. His efforts to sell and promote chemical and agricultural chemical products were often controversial, however, reflecting the relatively rudimentary state of America's science in the early nineteenth century. Though his critics have labeled Mapes a quack, there is also reason to think that his efforts were sincere, if not always successful. At the time Mapes was a prominent member of America's intellectual community. He was a friend and colleague of Horace Greeley, John Ericsson, Samuel F. B. Morse, William Cullen Bryant, Peter Cooper, and Washington Irving. During the Civil War President Abraham Lincoln asked Mapes to review plans for the siege of Richmond.

Mapes died in New York City. Of his children, two became prominent figures. His eldest son, Charles V. Mapes, built the Mapes Company into one of the largest fertilizer businesses in the nation, and his daughter Mary Mapes Dodge became an editor of *St. Nicholas,* a children's magazine, and author of *Hans Brinker; or, The Silver Skates.*

• Mapes's own ideas and research results can be traced through the several journals with which he was associated, particularly the *Working Farmer* from 1850 to 1863. Published texts of several of his public speeches also survive, with an 1845 address on the value of science in a liberal arts education being especially influential. Mapes's personal papers apparently have not survived. Mapes's career has been summarized in several standard reference works, but the most complete biographical treatment is in William Haynes, *Chemical Pioneers: Founders of the American Chemical Industry* (1939). His agricultural career is discussed in a chapter of C. R. Woodward, *Development of Agriculture in New Jersey, 1640–1880* (1927). Two more recent works on the history of American agricultural chemistry also deal with Mapes. Margaret Rossiter, *The Emergence of Agricultural Science* (1975), is rather critical of Mapes's fertilizer products, while Richard Wines, *Fertilizer in America* (1985), is more sympathetic. An editorial published upon his death by Horace Greeley, *New York Daily Tribune,* 11 Jan. 1866, is especially favorable. An obituary is in the *New York Times,* 12 Jan. 1866.

MARK R. FINLAY

MAPHIS, Joe (12 May 1921–27 June 1986), country guitarist, was born Otis Wilson Maphis in Suffolk, Virginia. He came from a farming family and grew up in Cumberland, Maryland. His first musical engagements were as a rhythm guitarist and pianist with his father's square dance group, the Railsplitters. His guitar technique came from imitating square dance fiddle parts on the guitar. Maphis was also proficient on fiddle, mandolin, bass, and banjo, which earned him the nickname "King of the Strings."

After leaving home in 1938, Maphis went to Fredericksburg, Virginia, where he joined Blackie Skiles's Lazy "K" Ranch Boys on WFVA. In 1939 he moved to the "Old Dominion Barn Dance," broadcast on WRVA in Richmond, Virginia. Maphis next moved to WLW, Cincinnati, early in 1942, where he worked with Sunshine Sue Workman and her Rangers. After the Rangers disbanded, he moved to WLS in Chicago to play with the Corncrackers on the "National Barn Dance." After induction into the army, he trained in ordinance but served in the Special Services in the South Pacific between 1944 and 1946, leading his own band called the Swingbillies. Immediately after his discharge, he went back to WLS and then back to WRVA's "Old Dominion Barn Dance," where he led a group that was also called the Corncrackers. He played his first recording session on 12 December 1947, backing singer and harmonica player Salty Holmes on four titles for Decca Records.

In 1948 Maphis met Rose Lee Schetrompf, then one-half of the Saddle Sweethearts duet. In August 1951 they relocated to California and were married in Mexico the following year. They had four children. After working a short stint on popular singer's Cliffie Stone's "Hometown Jamboree," they became mainstays of a televized barn dance show, "Town Hall Party," broadcast on KTTV in Compton, California. It was hosted by cowboy star Tex Ritter in a format based on the Grand Ole Opry.

Television and radio work was high profile but low-paying, and it was only a sidebar to Maphis's daily work in the recording studios and dance halls in Bakersfield and Los Angeles. It was while he was working at the Blackboard Cafe in Bakersfield in 1952 that Maphis wrote the quintessential honky-tonk song, "Dim Lights, Thick Smoke and Loud, Loud Music." He recorded the first version of the song for Columbia Records that year. In his role as backing musician, Maphis played on teen star Ricky Nelson's first sessions for Imperial Records, as well as cowgirl belter Wanda Jackson's original version of "Silver Threads and Golden Needles." Maphis was offered the job of leading Nelson's band, but he turned it down in order to be able to meet his other commitments.

Maphis was the musician who popularized the double-neck Mosrite guitar built by Semie Moseley, one neck tuned an octave higher than the other. It was given to Maphis on stage at "Town Hall Party" in 1954, and Maphis used it to particularly good advantage on Jack Marshall's soundtrack to *Thunder Road*. Maphis

was also featured on Elmer Bernstein's *God's Little Acre* soundtrack.

Maphis remained on "Town Hall Party" until it folded in 1961. He and Rose Lee had already recorded a number of duet albums for Capitol, and, calling themselves "Mr. and Mrs. Country Music," they took their act on the road. After "Town Hall Party" went off the air, they gave up their home in the San Fernando Valley and toured the country in a motor home. The Maphises finally settled in Nashville in 1968 so that Joe could get session work in the studios there. Maphis continued to record for Starday Records, Mosrite Records, and then for CMH Records. Maphis died in Nashville.

Maphis was not only an accomplished musician in his own right, but he helped to encourage and give a first break to several other musicians, including guitarist Larry Collins (half of the Collins Kids, with whom Maphis worked on "Town Hall Party") and country singer Barbara Mandrell. Maphis's reputation in the flatpicking style was not only based on his extraordinary speed and dexterity, but also on the fluidity with which he played and the melodic quality that he brought to his solo work at any tempo. His influence was felt in rock 'n' roll as much as country music, and the "surf" style of electric guitar playing pioneered by Dick Dale, the Ventures, and others in the mid-1960s was based on Maphis's style. Maphis's cutting tone was an equally important element in his style and influenced the rock 'n' roll guitar players almost as much as his melodic conception and flatpicked style.

Maphis's original 1954 Mosrite double-neck guitar was donated to the Country Music Hall of Fame in Nashville. His song "Dim Lights, Thick Smoke, and Loud, Loud Music" is still a honky-tonk standard, and his composition "Fire on the Strings" is still considered a stern test of sheer speed on the guitar.

• There is no biography of Maphis. His career is best covered in two articles: Rich Kienzle, "Fire on the Strings," *Guitar Player*, Aug. 1981, and John Tynan, "Joe Maphis: Amazing Guitarist" *Country & Western Jamboree*, Nov. 1956.

COLIN ESCOTT

MAPPLETHORPE, Robert (4 Nov. 1946–3 Mar. 1989), photographer and artist, was born in Queens, New York City, the son of Harry Irving Mapplethorpe, an electrical engineer, and Joan Dorothy Maxey. Mapplethorpe attended Martin Van Buren High School in Queens and upon graduation entered Pratt Institute in Brooklyn. Originally studying advertising design, he later changed to a fine arts program. After a number of disruptions to his academic career and his father's refusal to fund further classwork, Mapplethorpe finally left Pratt in 1969, one course short of graduation.

Drafted by the U.S. Army in 1967, Mapplethorpe avoided induction by ingesting LSD before his psychiatric interview. Drug use would remain an integral part of his life. Also in 1967 Mapplethorpe first met Patti Smith, a poet and rock musician whose career and life became intimately entwined with his. Smith and Mapplethorpe became lovers and artistic collaborators. Moving to a brownstone in Brooklyn, the couple pursued a range of artistic forms, creating a miniature version of pop artist Andy Warhol's "Factory," where art became a 24-hour-a-day activity. Fearful of his parents' reaction, Mapplethorpe falsely claimed that he and Smith had married in California.

Mapplethorpe and Smith separated in 1968, although they remained friends. Mapplethorpe, who had denied his homosexuality up to this point, moved from Brooklyn to Manhattan at the time of the seminal Stonewall riots that energized the gay rights movement. Mapplethorpe began creating collages of photographs from gay pornographic magazines and incorporating homoerotic images into his art. A few months later, he and Smith again moved in together, this time living in a single room in the Chelsea Hotel.

While living at the Chelsea, Mapplethorpe met Sandy Daley. Under her tutelage Mapplethorpe was exposed to the photographs of Julia Margaret Cameron and Henry Fox Talbot. Daley introduced Mapplethorpe and Smith to the celebrated hangout Max's Kansas City, and the three soon collaborated on the film *Robert Having His Nipple Pierced*, which made its debut at the Museum of Modern Art in 1971. Mapplethorpe's first solo exhibition, consisting of often macabre collages, had opened in 1970, the artist's twenty-fourth birthday, at Stanley Amos's gallery in Chelsea.

In 1971 Mapplethorpe met John McKendry, curator of photographs at the Metropolitan Museum of Art. The two quickly became friends, and in addition to introducing Mapplethorpe to the world of New York's social elite McKendry gave Mapplethorpe a Polaroid camera, the format the photographer would use for his first works. That same year Mapplethorpe was introduced to Samuel Jones Wagstaff, Jr., the scion of a wealthy New York family and an art curator and collector. He and Wagstaff formed a complex relationship in which Wagstaff was lover, patron, father, teacher, pupil, and friend. Wagstaff's gift of a loft near SoHo relieved Mapplethorpe of financial worries.

Mapplethorpe's first solo exhibition of Polaroid photographs took place in the backroom space of the Light Gallery in New York City in 1973. The exhibition consisted of Mapplethorpe's three primary themes: portraits, flowers, and sex. In 1975 he produced the cover photograph for Smith's debut album, *Horses*. A chance encounter the next year introduced Mapplethorpe to SoHo gallery owner Holly Solomon. One of the few gallery owners to show contemporary photographs at that time, Solomon was impressed with Mapplethorpe's portrait work but dismissed his sex pictures as giving dignity to pornography. Solomon presented Mapplethorpe's exhibition of his photographs in 1977. Solomon's exhibit focused on his portrait work, and, consequently, Mapplethorpe arranged an exhibition of his more graphic work, Erotic Pictures, at an alternative SoHo artspace, The Kitchen. The two concurrent exhibitions served the dual purpose of establishing Mapplethorpe as a promising portrait photographer and setting the tone for his controversial career.

Between 1977 and 1979 Mapplethorpe's participation in and depiction of the homosexual sadomasochistic world intensified. He also developed the ability to eroticize his nonsexual images. Unhappy with the Holly Solomon Gallery, Mapplethorpe moved to the Robert Miller Gallery, where he and Patti Smith held a joint exhibition, Film and Stills, in 1979.

Over the next ten years Mapplethorpe's career reached ever higher levels of success. Numerous exhibitions, both in the United States and Europe, secured his position as one of the most important contemporary photographers. Prices for his works increased, and he continued his portrait work for a worldwide clientele. The range of Mapplethorpe's work began to expand in the early 1980s when he made a series of large-scale photographs of flowers and explored the form of female bodybuilder Lisa Lyon.

In late 1986 Mapplethorpe was diagnosed with AIDS. He continued a grueling schedule of exhibitions and photographic assignments, even as he was, by 1988, confined to a wheelchair. He shot the cover for *The Dream of Life* (1987), Patti Smith's first album in eight years.

On the death of Sam Wagstaff of AIDS in 1987, Mapplethorpe inherited nearly $7 million. He established the Robert Mapplethorpe Foundation the following year to further AIDS research as well as to support the art of photography. Also in 1988 the Whitney Museum of American Art organized a large retrospective of Mapplethorpe's photographs, including his portrait work (often of society or art world figures); floral still lifes; nude figure studies (particularly of the African-American male); and graphic depictions of the homosexual sadomasochism subculture. The exhibition was widely publicized and favorably reviewed in the popular press, with articles appearing in both *Time* and *Newsweek*. The next year Mapplethorpe died at the Deaconess Hospital in Boston where he had gone to receive an experimental AIDS treatment.

Although suffering only glancing contact with controversy during his life, the exhibition Robert Mapplethorpe: The Perfect Moment, organized by the Institute of Contemporary Art in Philadelphia in 1988, attracted nationwide attention. Soon after the photographer's death, the Corcoran Gallery of Art in Washington, D.C., canceled the exhibition for fear of losing funding from the National Endowment for the Arts. After the showing of The Perfect Moment at the Cincinnati Contemporary Arts Center in 1990, its director was tried but acquitted on obscenity charges. Although his flamboyant lifestyle and sometimes controversial subject matter tend to overshadow his work, Mapplethorpe's portrait photography and figure and floral studies made unique contributions to the art. Additionally, his darker world challenged many of the basic conceptions of what constituted art photography, opening the door for others.

• The Robert Miller Gallery in New York City was Mapplethorpe's dealer at the time of his death. Though many of Mapplethorpe's photographs are in private hands, examples of his work are in the Art Institute of Chicago, the Detroit Institute of Arts, and the Metropolitan Museum of Art, New York City. The Robert Mapplethorpe Foundation (New York City) is the repository of most of the photographer's negatives. Among the collections of his photographs are *Black Males* (1980), *Flowers* (1983), *Lady: Lisa Lyon* (1983), *Black Flowers* (1985), *Certain People: A Book of Portraits* (1985), *Black Book* (1986), and *Flowers* (1990). A controversial biography is Patricia Morrisroe, *Mapplethorpe: A Biography* (1995). Other works with biographical information include Richard Marshall, ed., *Robert Mapplethorpe*, the catalog to the Whitney Museum of Art exhibition (1988); and, Janet Kardon, ed., *Robert Mapplethorpe: The Perfect Moment* (1988). Ingrid Sischy, "White and Black," *New Yorker*, 13 Nov. 1989, pp. 124, 129–46, and Arthur C. Danto, "Robert Mapplethorpe," *The Nation*, 26 Sept. 1988, pp. 246–50, offer assessments of the photographer's career. An obituary is in the *New York Times*, 10 Mar. 1989.

MARTIN R. KALFATOVIC

MARA, Timothy James (29 July 1887–16 Feb. 1959), professional football team founder and owner, was born on New York City's Lower East Side, the son of Elizabeth Harris and John Mara, a New York City policeman who died before Mara's birth. Raised in poverty Mara quit public school at age thirteen to help support the family. While working as a newsboy along Broadway, he began to run bets for several New York bookmakers. Receiving 5 percent of the bookmakers' winnings on those bets, the young Mara soon gravitated full time into the world of bookmaking, which was then legal in New York. Later in life he remarked that he was attracted to bookmaking because bookmakers "seemed to dress the best and work the least of any people I knew."

Mara's quick wit, pleasant demeanor, and reputation for honesty won him a following among the New York gambling fraternity, and by 1921 he had set up shop in the enclosure at Belmont racetrack, also a legal practice in New York at that time. Mara prospered as a bookmaker. Although he booked bets on sporting events, he knew little about sports themselves, especially football, which he had never seen played. Consequently, it was something of a surprise when in 1925 Mara paid $500 for the New York franchise in the fledgling National League of Professional Football Clubs, the forerunner of the National Football League (NFL). At that time Mara is said to have remarked that "An empty store with chairs in it in New York City is worth $500."

Although Mara would be offered $1 million for the Giants in 1955, the team initially did poorly at the box office despite Mara's hiring of Bob Folwell, the former coach of the U.S. Naval Academy, to run the squad. However, a turning point for Mara—and for professional football in New York—occurred late in the 1925 season when he arranged for the Giants to play the Chicago Bears and their new halfback, the collegiate star Harold "Red" Grange who had just created a national sensation by leaving the University of Illinois for the Bears. On 6 December 1925 more than 70,000 fans jammed the Polo Grounds in New York City for the game and Mara netted $143,000, thereby finishing the season in the black.

More importantly for the long-term, this game helped to establish professional football in the country's largest market and began to legitimize Mara's franchise in the eyes of the city's sports fans. Previously, professional football had been largely confined to smaller midwestern cities such as Canton, Kenosha, Duluth, and Green Bay; now it had a viable representative in the nation's media capital. Although college football would continue to be more popular than professional football, Mara's Giants served to both enhance the status of the NFL and convince New Yorkers that professional football was a worthy attraction.

However, New York was such an important market that Mara's professional football monopoly in the city did not go unchallenged. Periodically rival football leagues surfaced, and on each occasion a team was placed in New York to compete against the Giants. In 1926 Grange and his manager, C. C. "Cash and Carry" Pyle, organized the American Football League with a team at Yankee Stadium featuring Grange as its star. A decade later, in 1936 and 1937, a revived American Football League reappeared in New York. Between 1946 and 1949 the All-America Football Conference fielded two New York football teams, the New York Yankees and the Brooklyn Dodgers. This competition hurt Mara financially, but on each occasion his Giants outlasted the upstart teams. Mara—and the NFL—maintained a monopoly on professional football in New York until the arrival of yet another American Football League and the New York Jets in 1960.

Under Mara the Giants proved to be an excellent team. Perhaps this was due to Mara's hands-off approach. He hired skilled men such as Steve Owen, who invented the umbrella defense against the pass, and Jim Lee Howell, whose defensive assistant coach Tom Landry developed the standard 4–3–4 defense (4 linemen, 3 linebackers, 4 defensive backs), and he let them alone. During his tenure as owner the New York Giants won three NFL titles (1934, 1938, 1956). In seven other seasons (1933, 1935, 1939, 1941, 1944, 1946, 1958) the Giants were runners-up. From 1925 until Mara's death, the Giants won 235, lost 136, and tied 24.

Despite his success, Mara never forgot his roots. In 1930, during the depression, New York mayor Jimmy Walker asked Mara to arrange an exhibition game between the Giants and a squad consisting of former Notre Dame stars. The promotion was successful, raising $115,000 for the city's Unemployment Relief Fund. Furthermore, in winning the game easily the Giants also demonstrated to the perhaps still skeptical New York fans that professional football was the equal of, if not superior to, college football.

From the day Mara purchased his franchise, he devoted most of his energies to his football club. The jovial Mara liked to joke that the Giants were built on "brute strength and ignorance—the strength of the players and my ignorance." Mara, who married Lizette Barclay in 1908, was later assisted by his two sons, John V. "Jack" Mara and Wellington T. Mara. The former served as president of the Giants from 1953 until his death in 1965; the latter became Giants president in 1965.

Among the early founders of the NFL, such as George Halas and George Preston Marshall, Mara was neither an innovator nor a visionary. Rather, he provided quiet, solid leadership and deserves credit for maintaining the NFL's presence in the country's largest city during the league's early, difficult years. As former Giant coach Allie Sherman remarked, "The Maras are a professional family."

In 1963 Mara was elected to the Professional Football Hall of Fame as one of its seventeen charter members. He died in New York City.

• The Professional Football Hall of Fame, Canton, Ohio, maintains a modest file consisting chiefly of newspaper clippings on Mara's career in professional football. Arthur Daley, *Pro Football's Hall of Fame* (1963), pp. 195–208, provides a sympathetic sketch of Mara's life. Another short piece covering Mara's first years with the Giants and emphasizing the colorful nature of early New York football is in Howard Roberts, *The Story of Pro Football* (1953), pp. 167–95. George Sullivan, *Pro Football's All-Time Greats* (1968), pp. 70–75, presents a short biographical sketch featuring Mara's founding of the Giants. Dennis J. Harrington, *The Pro Football Hall of Fame* (1991), pp. 329–331, focuses on Mara's establishment of the Giants and his struggle to remain solvent during professional football's early years. Jim Terzian, *New York Giants* (1973), an official history of the football team, discusses Mara's role in founding the Giants. Obituaries are in the *New York Times* and the *Washington Post*, 17 Feb. 1959. Sports columnist Arthur Daley published a retrospective of Mara's career in the *New York Times*, 18 Feb. 1959.

FRANK W. THACKERAY

MARABLE, Fate (2 Dec. 1890–16 Jan. 1947), musical director, pianist, and riverboat calliope player, was born in Paducah, Kentucky, the son of Elizabeth Lillian, who had taught music as a slave. His mother's maiden name and details about his father are unknown. According to jazz musician Clark Terry, Marable's real name was Marble.

Early on, Marable received strict training in music from his mother. In September 1907, at a time when he was shining shoes in a barber shop, the Streckfus family, owners of the Acme Packet Company, offered him a job on the excursion steamer *J.S.*, then in port at Paducah. For dances in the ship's ballroom Marable played piano in a duo with violinist Emil Flindt. Atop the ship he played the deafening steam calliope. A month later, at a riverboat parade for President Theodore Roosevelt, Marable manned the calliope to play "Turkey in the Straw" while Roosevelt danced a jig on top of the steamer *Mississippi*.

The dance band aboard the *J.S.* expanded to four pieces and flourished until the steamship burned to the water in 1910. Marable tried a carnival tour, but he disliked the work and resumed his association with the Streckfus line in 1911. Having replaced an African-American pianist, he remained a decade later the only African American in the Streckfus line's bands. Surprisingly, given the separation of riverboat audiences into white and black, the later separation of Streckfus bands into white and black, and wide-ranging racial tensions on the Mississippi, this integrated band seems not to have encountered problems in its reception, perhaps because of Marable's light complexion.

In a move toward the incipient jazz style, Marable in 1917 formed the Kentucky Jazz Band, using players from Paducah on the riverboat *St. Paul*, but he deemed the band musically inadequate. After working on the *St. Paul* as its intermission pianist, he recruited a new nine-piece band during the steamer's layover in New Orleans in the winter of 1918–1919. His Jazz Syncopators, soon to be called Fate Marable and his Jazz Maniacs, included Louis Armstrong, Johnny St. Cyr, Pops Foster, and Baby Dodds. A photo of the band, taken on the steamer *Sidney*, shows Johnny Dodds as well, but he was only a temporary replacement for clarinetist Sam Dutrey, Sr. In May 1919 the band took a train northward to join a black musicians' union and then began touring on the *St. Paul*, where Marable, a strict disciplinarian, gave Armstrong, St. Cyr, and Foster ongoing lessons in music-reading skills, general repertory, and professional musicianship. St. Cyr remained in the band until 1920, and Armstrong, Dodds, and Foster until 1921. According to St. Cyr, Marable himself grew bored of teaching his musicians and was given a vacation for the winter of 1920–1921.

Marable worked on several boats in the Streckfus line for another two decades. Among his bandsmen were saxophonist Gene Sedric, who later played with Fats Waller, and trumpeter Dewey Jackson, who subsequently directed his own groups on the steamers. When in 1927 the trumpeter received an offer to join Cab Calloway, Jackson's New Orleans Cotton Pickers became Marable's. Henry "Red" Allen was a member of this band in 1928–1929, as was bassist Al Morgan, who had joined Marable in 1926. By 1930 the band's name had been shortened to Fate Marable's Cotton Pickers. Later, his bands included saxophonists Tab Smith (1934) and Earl Bostic (1935–1936), with Marable in 1936 codirecting with Charlie Creath. Marable remained on the boats as a pianist in Creath's band until 1939, when he resumed directing his own band for trips to Pittsburgh. It was at this time that he discovered the pioneering string bassist Jimmy Blanton. According to his own version, Marable got in touch with Duke Ellington, who hired Blanton for his band. Marable's health and morale declined when he was fired in 1941. The details of what happened are unknown. He played in local clubs and made his home in St. Louis, where he died.

To work with Marable on the riverboats was to attend a floating conservatory of music. He was usually called the "leader," but since the musically knowledgeable Streckfus family handled financial matters and authorized hiring, as well as supervising the selection of musical repertory and some aspects of rehearsals, he more accurately should be called musical director. His acclaimed band with Armstrong reportedly played a wide variety of standard dance music scores exactly as written, yet this band was also said to have differed significantly from white bands on the Streckfus steamers and to have been the best on the river. There are no surviving recordings—Marable recorded two insignificant titles in 1924—and it must be inferred from oral testimony how strict reading and varied interpretation might be reconciled. Most probably, the band "jazzed up" standard arrangements by applying a tremendous sense of jazz rhythm to written music and by playing with jazz-oriented instrumental timbres. In doing so, Marable's band had a significant role in disseminating the sound of jazz northward from New Orleans.

• Marable's reminiscences form a portion of Beulah Schacht, "Story of Fate Marable," *Jazz Record* 42 (Mar. 1946): 5–6, 14 (repr. from *St. Louis Globe-Democrat*). Wilma Dobie, "Remembering Fate Marable," *Storyville* 38 (Dec. 1971–Jan. 1972): 44–49, offers memories of her friendship with Marable and excerpts from his unpublished autobiography. Peter Vandervoort II surveys Marable's life in "The King of Riverboat Jazz," *Jazz Journal* 23 (Aug. 1970): 12–13, 36. Clark Terry's assertion about Marable's surname appears in Dempsey J. Travis, *An Autobiography of Black Jazz* (1983), p. 459. David Chevan, "Riverboat Music from St. Louis and the Streckfus Steamboat Line," *Black Music Research Journal* 9, no. 2 (1989): 153–80, offers a scholarly survey of the subject, including further bibliography. Firsthand recollections of work with Marable are in Warren "Baby" Dodds and Lara Gara, *The Baby Dodds Story* (1959); Les Tompkins, "Personal Account: Henry 'Red' Allen," *Crescendo* 4, no. 7 (Feb. 1966): 16; Johnny St. Cyr, "Jazz as I Remember It, Part Three: The Riverboats," *Jazz Journal* 19 (Nov. 1966): 6–7, 9; Ed Crowder and A. F. Niemoeller, "St. Louis Jazzman" (Dewey Jackson), and Harry Dial, "Drums on the Mississippi," both in *Selections from the Gutter: Jazz Portraits from "The Jazz Record,"* ed. Art Hodes and Chadwick Hansen (1977), pp. 208–13; Peter Vacher, *Jazz Odyssey: The Autobiography of Joe Darensbourg* (1987), pp. 41–42; Pops Foster et al., *Pops Foster: The Autobiography of a New Orleans Jazzman* (1971), pp. 102–15; and Dial, *All This Jazz about Jazz: The Autobiography of Harry Dial* (1984). Armstrong's experience on the riverboats is summarized in James Lincoln Collier, *Louis Armstrong: An American Genius* (1983), pp. 76–81.

BARRY KERNFELD

MARACCI, Carmelita (1911–26 July 1987), dancer and teacher, was born in Goldfield, Nevada, the daughter of Joseph Maracci, a gambler and restaurateur, and Josephine Gauss. Early press biographies spelled her name variously ("Carmalita," for example) and put her birthplace in Montevideo, using its exotic allure as a publicity bid. Further complicating matters, the Goldfield city records were burned during a fire in the 1920s and, with them, all traces of her birth certificate.

Raised in California—first San Francisco, then Fresno—Maracci went to a private girls' school until age fifteen. Her remaining education was informal and autodidactic. A hothouse flower of an intellectual who studied everyone from Kierkegaard to Genet and pored over the music of Schubert, for example, she developed a keen social conscience and an unrelentingly critical eye for things aesthetic. Her resources were close at hand: a German mother from whom she absorbed every cultural tidbit lavished on her and an Italian father who was related to the bel canto singer Adelina Patti. She also took a single-minded attitude toward mastery of her art, sidestepping conventional ballet classes in favor of private study. This she did with Enrico Zanfretta, a maestro of the classical Cecchetti style, who engaged her in a particularly harsh, dismissive manner. He once came backstage after a Carnegie Hall performance and said, "Well, I think you've improved." Nonetheless, she built a technique that inspired her laughing ease; she commanded a small, perfect body with straight legs, highly arched feet, and natural turnout. *Entrechat huit* (rapid crossing of the feet in air, eight times per elevation) was a specialty, no less than virtuoso castenet playing, which she taught herself. The only other person she acknowledged as an influence was the South American dancer Helba Huara.

The few who actually saw Maracci, in New York appearances during the 1940s at the Ninety-second Street "Y" (an audience of liberal and cultural elite she considered choice) and other theaters, as well as on tour throughout the country, did not forget her: a fierce little figure whose powerful expression and thrilling ballet technique were forged into uniquely dramatic commentaries on life's large canvas.

New York Times dance critic John Martin called her "a phenomenon . . . [that one] in a generation manifestly destined for a great career" (27 June 1937). *Paris Soir* and the *Times* (London) (reporting from New York) also carried such notices. Her 1936 New York debut, which, by default, took place at the Y, was "spellbinding," according to dancer Marian McPherson. "She tore the house down with her 'La Cantina,' a seductive showstopper, but also left the audience (which included Martha Graham) awed by her serious pieces." In 1930 Lee Freeson, a rare books agent dealing only with the theater, encountered Maracci at her Los Angeles debut. "What she did was timeless," he said sixty-seven years later. "Today it would be seen as something new. One piece looked deceptively improvised and flirtatious, another plumbed the deepest sorrow. The contrasts were colossal." Maracci and Freeson lived together for twenty years before marrying in 1965. They had no children.

It was the subject matter of Maracci's interstylistic and interdisciplinary dances, not the fabulous facility, that invoked her fervor. By way of explaining what she called her "unplanned oblivion," she once said: "The terrain I traveled led me into Goya's land of terror and blood-soaked pits. So I danced hard about what I saw and what I lived. I was not an absentee landlord. I was one of the dispossessed" (quoted in Agnes de Mille, *The Book of the Dance* [1963]). In literal terms, she knew only privilege and doting parents and never encountered a land of terror with blood-soaked pits; hers was purely a case of identification with its victims, an overt rallying to their cause, an imaginative leap that, at its most profound, tapped a kinship based on *interior* terror and ravaged spirit.

Clearly, what she created for the stage reflected these sentiments—though not in the grand, revolutionary manner of an Isadora Duncan. Tyranny was a theme often referred to in her satiric vignettes. Seeing herself as an outsider, she shrank back from potential establishment patrons and allegedly turned down an offer from Antony Tudor and Anton Dolin (then influential members of Ballet Theatre, later called American Ballet Theatre) to dance the greatest dramatic challenge for a ballet dancer, *Giselle*. After attending a few rehearsals with her champions she withdrew from the work, saying of the lovelorn heroine, "I felt like an imbecile plucking petals from a daisy" (interview with Donna Perlmutter, Apr. 1985).

Nor would Maracci do any other repertory ballet or authentic Spanish dance. But her study of Carlotta Grisi, the legendary Italian romantic-era ballerina, apotheosized the period style with remarkable delicacy and purity of sentiment. In 1951, at the urging of her longtime friend and admirer Agnes de Mille, she staged for Ballet Theatre *Circo de España*, a dance suite rife with bullring metaphors. "It was a disaster," said the choreographer-dancer. "[Company director] Lucia Chase reneged on all her promises and I ended having none of the resources to put it right." So, too, did she blame de Mille for the failure, saying, "We ended up like dried roots fighting with each other" (interview with Perlmutter, Apr. 1985).

Thus her brief association with the company came to an end, as did all further stage appearances. She was unable to sustain the small troupe (formed in 1935) with which she toured; impresario Sol Hurok, who represented the crème de la crème of performing artists, dropped her because of an incident wherein she misperceived one roudy heckler as audience repudiation and refused to perform.

Despite her frustrated career as a performer, until 1985 students found their way to the self-exiled iconoclast—among them Jerome Robbins, Gerald Arpino, Erik Bruhn, Cynthia Gregory, and her most prized pupil, Allegra Kent. Charlie Chaplin recruited Maracci earlier as dancer-choreographer for the 1952 film *Limelight*. Of the near-oblivion that marked her stage career she said: "People call it a tragedy, but I say no. Keep that word for human suffering, for wars that kill the innocent, for the devastation of the poor and unwanted, for the corruption and cruelty that cause these things. Mine is no tragedy. If art could relieve misery, I'd gladly sacrifice it" (interview with Perlmutter, Apr. 1985). She died in Los Angeles, California.

A great innovator, Maracci boasted a theatrical daring second only to her depth of imagination. She flourished without the usual production trappings and, indeed, set the standard for a genre known as concert dancer. What she performed onstage went beyond physical virtuosity to the realm of satire and tragedy, equaling, without broad strokes or empty melodramatics, the substance of major authors and composers.

For all that, however, she materialized only briefly in the public view.

Maracci, a musician who could discuss the metaphysics of Beethoven's Opus 110 and who excoriated anyone with the bad taste to play such music as dinner party background, was proud of having appeared on the same Hurok concert series with the likes of Artur Schnabel and Pablo Casals—but could also appreciate an artful burlesque queen.

She wanted no part of spectacle or entertainment and refused to be, in her words, "a Dolly Dimples of the Dance," which is what she called fellow practitioners at their most objectionable. Hers was a higher artistic aspiration, one that railed against ignorance, pretension, and hypocrisy.

• Agnes de Mille, Maracci's friend for more than fifty years, offers a loving but not always accurate profile of Maracci in *Portrait Gallery* (1990). The Chicago dancer-choreographer Ruth Page studied with Maracci from the late 1930s through the early 1940s and took copious notes on the classes, which are published in Page's *Class: Notes on Dance Classes around the World* (1984). An obituary is in *Dance Magazine*, Nov. 1987, p. 33.

DONNA PERLMUTTER

MARAVICH, Pete (22 June 1947–5 Jan. 1988), basketball player, was born Peter Press Maravich in Aliquippa, Pennsylvania, the son of Peter "Press" Maravich, a basketball player and later coach, and Helen Gravor. From the beginning of his life basketball set the tone for Maravich. Born in Pennsylvania because his father played professionally for the Pittsburgh Ironmen of the Basketball Association of America, he grew up in the Carolinas because his father coached at Clemson and North Carolina State universities. To the satisfaction, if not the instigation, of his father, Maravich's childhood was consumed with basketball. Other children might take a teddy bear to bed; Pete slept with a basketball. Labeled "Pistol Pete" as an eighth grader by a reporter, he entertained at halftime of his father's games, showing off his shooting, dribbling, and ball-handling skills. His exploits as a player for Needham-Broughton High School in Raleigh, North Carolina, followed by a year in prep school, placed him in line for an athletic scholarship to a major university. He had almost decided to attend West Virginia University when his father accepted the job of head coach at Louisiana State University (LSU), apparently with an understanding that his son would be part of the deal.

If Maravich's first year at LSU marked his grand entrance into college basketball, it was a disaster for his father. During a time when freshmen were ineligible to play for the varsity, Press Maravich's team had a record of three wins and 23 losses, while the freshman squad compiled a 17–1 record. It was not uncommon for fans to watch Maravich play in the freshman game and then leave before the varsity game started. Standing 6'5", thin, and gangly, with a mop of brown hair and socks with no elastic that sagged below the ankles, Maravich quickly became the most recognizable player on the court. For a man of his size and build, he was remarkably agile, an exquisite dribbler, and a deft ballhandler. Most of all he was a master of clever and showy passing, such as blind passing and passing behind his back, between his legs, and between his opponent's legs. Maravich did everything with a flair; showmanship, he freely admitted, was his game.

Even so, Maravich's preeminence and lasting distinction came from an ability to score and especially to shoot the basketball. In each of his three varsity seasons, from 1967 to 1970, he averaged more than 40 points per game, ending with a general average of 44.2. He scored more than 50 points in 28 games, including 61 against Vanderbilt, 66 each against Tulane and Kentucky, and a high of 69 against the University of Alabama in 1970. He was on the All-American team and college basketball's leading scorer for all three years. He established 14 National Collegiate Athletic Association records, including highest point average and most points (3,667), all of which came before the adoption of the three-point field goal. He was college basketball's player of the year in 1970.

After graduating from LSU in 1970, Maravich began his career in the National Basketball Association (NBA), playing against a Milwaukee Bucks team that included Oscar Robertson and Lew Alcindor (Kareem Abdul-Jabbar); he ended it in 1980 with a Boston Celtics team that included Dave Cowens, Robert Parish, and Larry Bird. The Atlanta Hawks of the NBA—then a team of black starters a notch or two beneath title contenders—hoped that adding Maravich, a sensational white scorer (and a southern boy to boot) would pay huge dividends in both quality and attendance. To get Maravich the Hawks traded up in the 1970 NBA draft to get the third pick in the first round, then outbid the Carolina Panthers of the rival American Basketball Association. Maravich received a contract worth upward of $2 million, at the time the richest ever for a first-year player.

Maravich spent four years with the Hawks, after which he was traded in 1974 to an expansion team in New Orleans that wished to build around him. When the New Orleans Jazz moved to Utah in 1979, the new management used Maravich sparingly and then released him. He spent his final months as a substitute for the Boston Celtics in the season of 1979–1980.

In the course of this professional career Maravich established individual marks that were impressive, if not quite spectacular. He averaged 23.2 points his rookie year and ended eighth in scoring. He was fifth in scoring in 1973 with a 26.1 average, second in 1974 with 27.7, third in 1976 with 25.9, and in the season of 1976–1977 he led the league in scoring with an average of 31.1. In a game against the New York Knicks in 1977 he scored 68 points. His average of 24.2 points for ten years placed him among the top fifteen scorers in the NBA; his point total of nearly 16,000 did not. He was on the NBA All-Star team for five years and a member of the all-league team four times. In 1987 he was voted into the Naismith Memorial Basketball Hall of Fame, which honored both college and professional performers. In Maravich's case the distinction came predominantly from the college record.

Yet Maravich found that life as a professional produced valleys as well as peaks. His high salary and constant media attention produced resentment among teammates, as did his flair for shooting and flamboyant play. His father, with a six-year coaching record of 76–86, was fired by LSU two years after Maravich left, perhaps suggesting that he had the job mostly because of his son. Maravich's mother, who suffered with depression and alcoholism, committed suicide in 1974. Maravich himself suffered from occasional illness, problems with alcohol, and a serious knee injury in 1978 from which he never fully recovered.

Most disappointing from Maravich's perspective as a player was a failure to win a championship or even to play for teams with a winning record. His teams at LSU were mediocre, except for the last year when the record was 20–10, and never won a conference championship or played in the NCAA tournament. Only the conference champion qualified for the tournament during those years; but even had the field been expanded (as it later was) to include 32 and then 64 teams, only in Maravich's senior year would LSU possibly have received a bid. In his first nine years in the NBA Maravich played with only one team that had a winning record. The year he led the league in scoring his team won only 29 games. The Celtics of 1979–1980 won 61 games and a division title, but Maravich had little to do with it. Overshadowed by a veteran star (Cowens) and a new star (Bird), Maravich was released at the start of the 1980–1981 season by a Celtic team that would win the championship that year. Tired and uninspired, he retired at age 33.

Maravich spent his retirement in rural Louisiana a much-changed man. He became a "born-again" Christian and a convert to health foods—giving up first red meat and then all meat and fish. He supervised a construction business and gave occasional basketball seminars. Much of the time he devoted to his wife, Jackie Elliser, whom he had married in 1975, and two young sons and to spreading his messages of healthy eating and righteous living. At peace with himself, seemingly in the peak of health, he died at age forty of a heart attack in Pasadena, California, after playing in a pickup basketball game; he had traveled to California to appear on the religious radio show "Focus on the Family."

Maravich is remembered as a prolific scorer and exquisite showman both in college basketball and, if in somewhat less grandiose style, in the NBA. He attracted large crowds on both the professional and collegiate levels. But Maravich also reinforced the notion that basketball is a team game, and a team that relies heavily on one player, no matter how prolific and spectacular he might be, rarely, if ever, makes it to the top of its sport.

• Information on Maravich can be found at the Naismith Memorial Basketball Hall of Fame, Springfield, Mass. Maravich published an autobiography, *Heir to a Dream*, Darrel Campbell and Frank Schroeder (1987), a brief but indispensable account that documents the enormous influence of Maravich's father. Tom Saladino's *Pistol Pete Maravich* (1974) is a partial biography. Maravich's career in progress can be followed in sports magazines; examples include "The Upstaging of Pistol Pete," *Sports Illustrated*, 30 Mar. 1970, pp. 22–23, about his last collegiate game (in the National Invitation Tournament); "We Have a Slight Delay in Showtime," *Sports Illustrated*, 26 Oct. 1970, about his debut in the NBA; and "He's Shooting the Works," *Sports Illustrated*, 12 Nov. 1973, about Maravich's fast start in 1973. Information on the performance of Maravich's teams is in Zander Hollander, ed., *The Modern Encyclopedia of Basketball* (1973); Neil D. Isaacs, *All the Moves: A History of College Basketball* (1975); and *The Official NBA Basketball Encyclopedia* (1994). An obituary appears in *Time*, 18 Jan. 1988, p. 71.

ROSS GREGORY

MARBLE, Danforth (27 April 1810–13 May 1849), actor, was born in East Windsor, Connecticut, the son of William Marble and Mary (maiden name unknown), small furniture-business owners. In telling Yankee stories Marble liked to exploit the family name of Marble by claiming that they were true-blood New Englanders because they came from the *marble* state of Vermont, but whether his parents were actually born there it is not known. However, Marble was a Yankee to be sure, an important background in his career. After a rudimentary education, he started working in a dry goods store in Hartford and then as an apprentice to a silversmith in New York. These experiences taught him a good deal about the sharp trading practices and slick dealings of the resourceful Yankees, traits he worked into his first attempts at Yankee storytelling and in his career as a folk actor and comedian.

It was in 1831 at the Chatham Theatre in New York City that Marble began his stage career, first doing walk-ons as an amateur, and then, on 11 April 1831, playing Robin Roughhead in the farce *Fortune's Frolic*. He then played William in the drama *Black-Eyed Susan*, after paying the stage manager $20 for the privilege. At the Richmond Hill Theatre, also in New York, he attempted, unsuccessfully, Damon in *Damon and Pythias*. Still uncertain about his abilities and the line of acting he should pursue, he joined the S. Potter stock company in Norfolk, Virginia, and there he played a wide variety of roles. Soon back in New York, he told Yankee stories from real-life experiences, and he performed one or two Yankee characters at the Richmond Hill and Chatham theaters. He was so successful he decided that comedy was his line.

Dan's rise to stardom came quickly over a period of four years, from 1832 to 1836. He first joined the Charles R. Thorne company in New York City as a low-comedian and traveled west with the company along the Erie Canal, playing the towns along the way. At Buffalo he found work in the acting company at the Eagle Street Theatre under the management of Dean and McKinney, which began an association with Buffalo that lasted until his death. In November 1836 he married Anna Warren, the daughter of William War-ren of Philadelphia's Chestnut Street Theatre, a top-level connection.

In the four years before he achieved stardom at the Bowery and Park theaters in New York City, Marble built a solid reputation as a top-caliber comedian in engagements that extended from Buffalo to New Orleans—Columbus, Cincinnati, Pittsburgh, St. Louis, Memphis, and other river cities. Newspaper reports were most enthusiastic, with one reviewer declaring that "[n]o matter if you have a toothache, the headache, the heartache . . . [Marble's] cool, quiet deliberate nonsense . . . would make you laugh at a funeral." So successful was he in the West that it was only a short step to a debut as a star comedian at the Bowery Theatre in New York City on 1 May 1837 and shortly thereafter at the Park Theatre—all this while his chief competitor, George Hill, was performing in London. From this point forward the "new" Yankee comedian held a distinct place on the American stage. In 1844 Marble traveled to London to further enhance his reputation, performing at the Strand Theatre there on 30 September.

In America, Marble played everywhere to accolades. He had modeled his first Yankee on real life, he asserted, by remembering specific persons he had seen and patterning the character after them. How far he diverged from this intention can be known only through the eyes of the critics. What audiences saw, they tell us, was a broad, simply stated sentiment; his character was usually clever, even sly, akin to a practical joker. His constant motion and odd mode of expression could set the audience roaring. Other critics spoke of his openness and freshness, punctuated by a good deal of the bombast and rugged individualism of the frontier. Scenes of pathos and emotion he played quietly, which made them stand out sharply against his usual surefire comedy. Marble's later work seems to be marked by a more obvious playing that some thought was on the edge of vulgarity. As an astute actor, he probably changed with the times and the level and geographical location of the audiences he played to as he traveled America.

Like the other Yankee comedians before him, Marble was constantly on the lookout for acting pieces suitable to his special talents. In November 1836, in Buffalo, close to Niagara Falls, he first tried E. H. Thompson's *Sam Patch, the Yankee Jumper*, based on a real jumper of the falls in 1829. It proved so successful that Marble took it to New York City, first playing it at the Bowery Theatre in May 1938. So began Dan's "jumping career." Over Niagara Falls went Marble, a spectacular jump of forty feet against the painted drop of the falls, with a great splash (if well staged) when he disappeared through a stage trap to land on mattresses or a spring bed. A roar of applause at the courage displayed always followed. In London in 1844 some critics thought the melodrama contrived and ridiculous and Marble's jump laughable. But the staging there had been badly done. Back in America, audiences continued to love it, no matter what version of the play Marble acted, and there were several.

Marble added other characters to his list, which by 1838 included Jacob Jewsharp, Solomon Swap, Jonathan Ploughboy, and Deuteronomy Dutiful. Samson Hardhead, as he was called in one version of *The Backwoodsman; or, The Gamecock of the Wilderness*, is obviously a take-off on Davy Crockett. By 1842 Marble had added such pieces as *The Vermont Wool Dealer* and *Yankee Land; or, A Foundling of the Sea*, which Cornelius Logan had written or adapted for him. In *Yankee Land*, the main character, Lot, is an orphaned country boy, labeled a village half-wit, who outwits his guardian in a string of incidents and turns out to be the long-lost son of an English nobleman. This simple melodramatic plot structure exemplified Yankee comedy, where country backwardness overcame city slickness. Marble's early acting of Yankee characters drew upon the real Yankees he knew from his New England background, but his playing to audiences in the West probably broadened his Yankee to a more generalized folk character that might be labeled "Western Hybrid."

Marble died at the age of thirty-nine of cholera while traveling from St. Louis by riverboat to Louisville for his next theater engagement. Two years later Jonathan F. Kelly published a biography of Marble, the first to be written about a Yankee comedian. Through Kelly's recording of Marble's career we can piece together the vibrant life of what it meant to be a comedian in the first half of the nineteenth century; and when Marble's widow sold his repertoire to James McVicker for his theater in Chicago and for touring to theaters in Illinois and Iowa, we can see how the Yankee folk character made its way to California.

Marble's contribution to American comedy was much more than just his acting, for he extended the earlier satirical characterizations of the New England Yankee into one that could reflect not just one region, but all of America. He thus broadened the scope of American comedy, which soon began to include city types, like Mose the Fireman, and subsequently the ethnic characters played by Harrigan and Hart in the 1870s. To judge him by the plays that are extant misses the point, for Marble's theater came alive only in his playing and his arousal of audiences.

• Though inaccurate in some details, Jonathan F. Kelly [Falconbridge, pseud.], *Dan. Marble: A Biographical Sketch . . .* (1851), is the basic source. William Edward Dobkin, "The Theatrical Career of Danforth Marble: Stage Yankee" (available on tape; Ph.D. diss., Indiana Univ., 1970), is an excellent cross-check. The Lord Chamberlain's Collection, British Museum, London, has a record of his 1844 visit, as do the London newspapers for Oct.–Nov. 1844. Marble's life in the West is detailed in Noah Ludlow, *Dramatic Life as I Found It* (1880; repr. 1966). For the New York stage, see George Odell, *Annals of the New York Stage* (1927–1949), and Joseph Ireland, *Records of the New York Stage* (1866–1867). C. A. Logan's plays *Yankee Land* and *The Vermont Wool Dealer* were both published by Samuel French (n.d.). For a general review of Marble's work and a comparison to other actors of the New England folk character see Francis Hodge, *Yankee Theatre* (1964).

FRANCIS HODGE

MARBLE, Manton Malone (16 Nov. 1834–24 July 1917), journalist, was born in Worcester, Massachusetts, the son of Joel Marble, a teacher, and Nancy Coes. In 1840 the family moved to Albany, New York, where Marble attended secondary school. In 1855 he graduated from Rochester (N.Y.) University. While there he had been influenced by the Scottish Common Sense variation of philosophical idealism and by the Native American Whig politics of the Rochester *American*, at which he apprenticed. He entered journalism as an editor with two Boston papers, and in 1858 he joined the editorial staff of the New York *Evening Post*. In 1860 Marble was hired as night editor of the newly established New York *World*. Two years later, after the paper had survived several financial crises and management changes, he emerged as the chief editor. He secured financial backing from wealthy Democrats who wanted a daily newspaper to support their campaign in the midterm elections. Marble married Delia West in 1864; they had two children before she died in 1868.

During his editorship, Marble shaped the *World* into the organ of New York City's Democratic elite, which included S. L. M. Barlow, August Belmont, and Samuel J. Tilden. During the Civil War the *World* supported military victory over the Confederacy, praised General George B. McClellan and condemned President Abraham Lincoln's administration for its stance with regard to emancipation and its arbitrary arrests of political dissidents. In May 1864 the paper was briefly suspended by the military for printing a false story of defeatism in the White House. Later that year the *World* supported McClellan's successful bid for the Democratic presidential nomination. During the campaign the paper coined the word "miscegenation"—a reference to racial intermarriage—to mobilize whites against the idea of equal rights for African Americans. Still, throughout the war the paper's most consistent theme was opposition to centralized government.

After the war Marble sought to heal the wartime divisions in the Democratic party by opposing the policies of the Radical Republicans. When this strategy failed in the 1866 elections, resulting in the enactment of Radical Reconstruction, Marble counseled acceptance of black voting, anticipating that southern whites would "manage" the black vote. His strategy was undone, however, when southern blacks voted Republican. In 1868 Marble's candidate for the Democratic presidential nomination was Salmon P. Chase, who favored voting for blacks and amnesty for Confederates. But Chase lost out in the national convention, which was determined to nominate an opponent of reconstruction. In 1872 Marble supported an alliance between Democrats and Liberal Republicans only to see the Liberals nominate Horace Greeley, a candidate unacceptable to most Democratic voters because of his many years as a Republican and an abolitionist.

After the Democratic defeat in 1872 Marble gave up coalition building and emphasized party solidarity and loyalty. He became a steadfast supporter of Samuel J. Tilden, a wealthy corporation attorney and longtime party member. A member of the Manhattan Club, which he had helped to found to provide a home for upper-class, "swallow-tail" Democrats, Tilden concentrated on economic issues, especially advocating low tariffs and opposing the paper money or "greenback" currency issued during the war. Campaigning against the depression that had followed the panic of 1873 and the scandals of the Ulysses S. Grant administration, Marble and his party elected Tilden governor of New York in 1874. He supported Tilden's unsuccessful presidential candidacy, and after Tilden's nomination in 1876 Marble wrote the party platform, which again stressed the need for "reform."

In the meantime Marble had separated himself from journalism. During the postwar years he had built the *World* into a major regional daily, attaining a circulation that rivaled his major competitors. In 1866 he outmaneuvered both the Associated Press and James Gordon Bennett's *Herald* in a struggle to control news via the Atlantic cable. He successfully defied efforts by the Democratic party to subjugate the *World* to party discipline, and in 1868 he obtained financial control of the paper, realizing his dream of becoming an "independent and uncontrolled editor." He assembled an able editorial staff headed by William Henry Hurlbert and Ivory Chamberlain and supported by managing editor David Goodman Croly. But by 1875 his string of good luck had run out. Marble's record of party independence lost the *World* circulation among party regulars. The panic of 1873 and the ensuing depression caused large financial losses. In the fall of 1875 Marble put the paper up for sale, and the following year he sold it to railroad tycoon Thomas A. Scott.

Hoping to move from journalism to political office, Marble bid unsuccessfully for New York's gubernatorial nomination. He then worked for Tilden's presidential campaign. During the postelection dispute over crucial electoral votes, Marble traveled to Florida, where he was believed to have attempted to bribe a Republican member of the electoral board to certify the Tilden electors. But the evidence against him was inconclusive, and he was vindicated in the eyes of his friends.

In 1879 Marble married Abby Williams Lambard. They had no children of their own. Abby's wealth and his own means obtained from the sale of the *World* made them independently wealthy. He traveled frequently to Europe, first as a representative of the Grover Cleveland administration sent to determine sentiment for maintaining the gold standard. There he met Henri Cernuschi, an advocate of international bimetallism. For the rest of his active life Marble supported Cernuschi's theories, which proposed that all nations adopt gold and silver as their money standard and permit "free coinage" of both metals.

During the first Cleveland administration Marble promoted Cernuschi's views by writing the 1885 and 1886 *Treasury Reports* of Secretary of the Treasury Daniel Manning. Marble's efforts were thwarted, however, by three things: the determination of silver advocates to press for national legislation instead of an international agreement, Manning's resignation in February 1887, and Cleveland's decision to support tariff reform rather than currency reform. Frustrated and furious at Cleveland, who lost the presidency in 1888, Marble devoted his efforts to supporting David B. Hill's New York gubernatorial campaign, running on a "free silver" platform. Hill achieved a few promising successes but ultimately lost because he had hesitated to commit himself to Marble's theories and because international bimetallism had failed to develop substantial political support.

Marble actively pursued international bimetallism for a few more years during Cleveland's second term, but neither Cleveland nor the later standard-bearer William Jennings Bryan showed any interest. By the end of the century Marble was living in England, first in Brighton and then at Allington Castle in Kent, where he died.

Throughout his life Marble struggled to reconcile the values of genteel, upper-class culture and partisan politics. The first encouraged a politics of principle, by which independent persons of education and civic commitment determined government policies; the second advocated a politics that managed the mass of voters by organization and manipulated issues for popular effect. Learned, ambitious, and articulate, Marble risked much, and his efforts brought him many frustrations and failures that denied him the prominence he might have earned had he been simply a voice of independent comment or a political manipulator. More tellingly, however, he failed to gain distinction because the causes he advocated, especially with regard to emancipation, equal rights, and currency reform, ran counter to the major political forces of his time. Marble's newspaper career was essentially that of a political journalist; he was hard working, resourceful, and ambitious but was ultimately dependent on party patronage and his ability to articulate a consensus for his party's electorate.

• Marble's papers are in the Library of Congress. His own writings include *Freedom of the Press Wantonly Violated* (1864), a pamphlet attacking the Lincoln administration for suppressing the *World*, and *A Secret Chapter of Political History* (1878), which defends Marble's and Tilden's conduct during the disputed election of 1876. His views on journalism are recorded in Charles F. Wingate, ed., *Views and Interviews on Journalism* (1875). George McJimsey, *Genteel Partisan: Manton Marble, 1834–1917* (1971), is the most comprehensive biography. Mary Cortona Phelan, *Manton Marble of the New York World* (1957), focuses on Marble's political thought. J. M. Bloch, "The Rise of the New York *World* during the Civil War Decade" (Ph.D. diss., Harvard Univ., 1941), provides excellent information on the paper's financial history and political views up to 1868. Other historical and biographical works mention Marble but generally omit extensive comment on him. One exception is Herbert J. Bass, *"I Am a Democrat": The Political Career of David Bennett Hill* (1961), which details Marble's efforts to promote Hill as a presidential candidate supporting bimetallism.

GEORGE McJIMSEY

MARBURY, Elisabeth (19 June 1856–22 Jan. 1933), agent and theatrical producer, was born in New York City, the daughter of Francis Ferdinand Marbury, a prominent admiralty attorney, and Elizabeth McCoun. She attended private schools, but her most important education came in her father's office, where she read Blackstone's *Commentaries* and learned Latin at the age of seven. She saw a play every Friday, and by the time she was sixteen she had met Robert Louis Stevenson, Matthew Arnold, Emma Lazarus, and Henry James. Marbury also traveled to Paris and London, where she met Charles Darwin, Thomas Henry Huxley, and Herbert Spencer.

Marbury's socially active life was otherwise unremarkable until 1881, when, intrigued by the newly invented incubator, she used one to hatch 100 chicks in a bedroom of the family home in New York's Irving Place. She took the eighty-seven survivors to the family farm at Oyster Bay, Long Island, and began a thriving poultry-raising business that received a number of exhibition prizes. Marbury's 1885 society theatrical benefit raised $5,000 and brought her to the attention of producer Daniel Frohman, who suggested that she pursue a business career in the theater.

Following the death of her financially overextended father in 1887, Marbury acted on Frohman's suggestion. Observing that the visiting English novelist Frances Hodgson Burnett (author of *Little Lord Fauntleroy*) knew little of stage ways, Marbury volunteered her services and became Burnett's agent and personal manager. Marbury's next client was Frohman's brother Charles, cofounder of the syndicate that came to dominate American theater. Reading three to five plays daily and crossing the Atlantic to search for more, she soon provided Frohman with most of his material. In 1889 she coauthored *A Wild Idea*, a mildly successful one-act play. In 1888 Marbury had written *Manners: a Handbook of Social Customs* which reveals that, despite her own achievements, she continued to believe that, generally speaking, women belonged at home. She resolutely opposed the growing woman suffrage movement.

In 1884 at the Tuxedo Club, Marbury had met Elsie de Wolfe, a stylish, aspiring actress. The two began living together in 1887, an arrangement that continued for twenty-seven years. Impressed by de Wolfe's taste, Marbury urged her to become an interior decorator, a profession dominated by men. Although de Wolfe did not abandon the stage until 1904, Marbury remarked that they had "embarked on the turbulent sea of new careers for women" together. Often accompanied by Anne Morgan, the sister of banker J. P. Morgan, the two began to spend their summers in France, especially Versailles, where in 1903 Marbury purchased the Villa Trianon.

Marbury conceived of the theatrical royalty system in 1891 while stranded in Paris, after her share of a production's profits had been stolen. She approached Victorien Sardou, popular playwright and president of the French authors' society, and expressed her belief that authors would be better off taking a percentage of a play's gross profits instead of a flat fee. Sardou accepted her idea and agreed to make her the society's sole American and British representative. The works of Sardou, Edmund Rostand, and Georges Feydeau were thus introduced in the United States. Marbury estimated that the royalty system earned another client, Alexandre Bisson, $50,000 instead of $4,000. Twice decorated by the French government for service to French authors, Marbury wrote, "I have always found that events which seemed at the time disasters ultimately developed into positive blessings." Her British clients included Oscar Wilde, W. Somerset Maugham, Jerome K. Jerome, and George Bernard Shaw.

In 1907 Marbury helped to found New York's Colony Club, "the first all-around gathering place where women could exert their prerogatives as individuals." The colony was de Wolfe's first decorating commission. Marbury returned to personal management in 1913, working to extend the European success of Vernon and Irene Castle, the catalysts of the pre–World War I ballroom dancing craze. She acquired for the Castles a venue opposite New York's Ritz-Carlton Hotel, named it the "Castle House," and hired James Reese Europe's orchestra, the first "society" jazz band. The Castles' income increased fivefold; there followed a rooftop "Castles in the Air" and a "Castles on the Sea" on Long Island.

Marbury's career as a Broadway producer began in 1914, when she formed a partnership with F. Ray Comstock, who was already a successful producer of conventional musicals. She suggested a series of modern musical comedies with music written by Jerome Kern (better-known older composers would have cost too much). The resulting "Princess Theater Musicals," intended for a 299-seat theater, were based upon Marbury's manifesto, dictating casts of no more than thirty, including a twelve-woman chorus. The orchestra was limited to eleven members, and there were just two sets, one for each act. All stories were to take place in contemporary America, their "believable" characters caught in comic situations that, like the songs, were to arise naturally from the plot. Librettist Guy Bolton and lyricist P. G. Wodehouse completed the Princess team, which advanced the art of integrated musical comedy over the next thirty years.

In response to the prolonged rehearsals for *Nobody Home* (1915), the first Princess show (for which de Wolfe designed the sets), Marbury rejected the convention that denied "chorus girls" extra pay for long hours. Anticipating Actors Equity by a decade, she reclassified the women as "small part players," thus raising their salaries. In 1914 Marbury helped to establish the American Play Company. She wrote in 1915, "I am convinced that Mr [Cole] Porter is the one man of the many who can measure up to the standard set by the late Sir Arthur Sullivan. This looks like a boast, but watch him." After producing *See America First*, Porter's first show, Marbury gave up entrepreneurship, noting that her ventures into "musical comedy

. . . had met with considerable disappointment on the part of my friends."

In the early years of World War I Marbury's Villa Trianon became a hospital; Marbury worked for the French throughout the war. In 1917 she became a member of the mayor of New York's Women's Commission of National Defense. Marbury headed a women's committee supporting Democrat Al Smith's campaign for New York governor in 1918. Sent in 1919 to Europe by Secretary of the Interior Franklin Lane to oversee the welfare of American soldiers in France and Germany, Marbury continued this work for the Knights of Columbus. In 1920 she became a delegate to the Democratic National Convention and in 1928 a member of the Democratic National Committee. She fought Prohibition bitterly.

At 200 pounds, with a deep, foghorn voice, "Bessie" Marbury dressed "as mannishly as the era allowed" and smoked four to five packs of cigarettes a day. She never married, noting, "I never had a really good offer . . . I attracted all the lame ducks." Marbury died at her home in Sutton Place, perhaps New York's most desirable residential area. Jerome Kern's last show, *Very Warm for May* (1939), is partly based on Marbury's life, which Kern described as "dramatically vital."

• Marbury's autobiography is titled *My Crystal Ball* (1924), and de Wolfe's is titled *After All* (1935). Marbury's life, times, and contributions are treated in Gerald Bordman, *Jerome Kern: His Life and Music* (1980); Irene Castle, *Castles in the Air* (1958); Stanley Green, *Broadway Musicals: Show by Show* (1985); and Robert Kimball, ed., *Cole* (1971).

JAMES ROSS MOORE

MARBUT, Curtis Fletcher (19 July 1863–25 Aug. 1935), pedologist and geologist, was born near Verona, Lawrence County, Missouri, the son of Nathan T. Marbut and Jane Browning, farmers. He was educated in rural schools and the Cassville (Missouri) Academy. After teaching school in McDowell, Missouri, he entered the University of Missouri in 1885, completing his B.S. in 1889. He taught at the high school at Bethany, Missouri, for a year and worked for the Missouri Geological Survey from 1890 to 1893. He then entered Harvard to complete an A.M. in 1894. Continuing for another year, he wrote his doctoral thesis on the physiography of the Ozarks under William Morris Davis. Davis and Nathaniel Southgate Shaler inspired Marbut's lifelong interest in geographical science. Although Marbut completed residency requirements in 1894, finished his thesis in 1896, and (after it was tentatively approved by Davis) published it in late 1896, he never took the final oral examination for his doctorate. He studied abroad during 1899 and 1900, traveling over most of Europe, chiefly by bicycle, studying geology and landforms.

Marbut was appointed instructor in geology and mineralogy at the University of Missouri in 1895; he became an assistant professor in 1897 and was promoted to professor and curator of the Geological Museum

in 1899. He retained the last position until 1913. In addition, he was an assistant geologist in the Missouri State Geological Survey from 1890 to 1904. He was also director of the Soil Survey of Missouri from its inception in 1905 to 1913. He was made a cooperative agent of the Bureau of Soils of the U.S. Department of Agriculture in 1909 and 1910 for the purpose of making a reconnaissance survey of the soils of the Ozark Mountains. He was scientist in charge of the Soil Survey of the U.S. Department of Agriculture under changing titles from 1913 until his death, one year before his scheduled retirement. He also lectured at the graduate school of geography at Clark University from 1922 to 1935 and was a special lecturer at the University of Chicago.

Marbut was a member of a party sent to Central America in 1919 to survey the Guatemalan-Honduran border. There he made a study of the area's soils. In 1923 and 1924 he was a member of the Brazilian-American Rubber Survey, investigating possibilities for rubber development. Thereafter, with support from the American Geographical Society, he examined soils in the agricultural and ranching regions of Argentina. He was an organizer of the First International Soil Science Congress, held in Washington, D.C., in 1927, and led its transcontinental excursion. In 1930, with a grant from the American Geographical Society, he studied soils in Russia.

Marbut's reputation rests on his introduction of scientific pedology to the United States, his extensive soil surveys, and his longtime directorship of the U.S. Soil Survey during its formative years. Specifically, he is credited with merging the interests of agronomists and geologists in soil study through recognizing that soils result from interaction between climate, vegetation, and geology—not just from physical and chemical alteration of bedrock. In addition, he promoted use of soil profiles in classifying and understanding soil groups. Perhaps his most important work, *Soils of the United States*, appeared as Bulletin 96 of the U.S. Soil Survey in 1912; it was notable for introducing the idea of soil provinces. In 1920 he also translated the German edition of Konstantine Dimitriev Glinka's *Die Typen der Bodenbildung* (1914), originally published in Russian. Marbut's translation, published as *The Great Soil Groups of the World and Their Development* (1927), introduced American soil scientists to the fundamental principles developed in Russia. This revelation completely reoriented American soil science from an emphasis on mechanical analysis of surface soils to the study of soil profiles. The twelve map sheets of Marbut's "Soils" section of the *Atlas of American Agriculture* (1935) summarize the work of the Soil Survey from its founding in 1899. Marbut also published forty-seven journal articles.

Marbut was a fellow of the Geological Society of America and a charter member of the Association of American Geographers (president, 1924). As a member of the American Association for the Advancement of Science, he was chairman of Section O in 1926. He was elected a corresponding member of the Berlin

Geographical Society. He was chairman of the Fifth Commission of the International Soil Science Society on the genesis, classification, morphology, and mapping of soils, held in the Free City of Danzig in 1929. At the time of his death he was vice chairman of the national committee of the International Geographical Union; from 1931 to 1933 he was chairman of Committee III, land inventories and land classification, of the national land-use planning committee. He received the Cullum Medal of the American Geographical Society in 1930 for research conducted on African soils.

Marbut married Florence L. Martin of Cassville, Missouri, in 1891. They had five children. He died in Harbin, Manchukuo, en route to Peking, China, at the invitation of the Chinese government to conduct a study of Chinese soils.

• Basic sources of information include Charles E. Kellog, "Curtis Fletcher Marbut," *Science* 82, no. 2135 (1935): 267–68; *Geographical Review* 25 (1935): 688; Homer Leroy Shantz, "A Memoir of Curtis Fletcher Marbut," *Annals of the Association of American Geographers* 26 (1936): 113–23; H. J. Krusekopf, ed., *Life and Work of C. F. Marbut, Soil Scientist* (1942); and obituaries in *Nature* 136 (7 Sept. 1935): 365–66, and the *New York Times*, 26 Aug. 1935.

RALPH L. LANGENHEIM, JR.

MARCANTONIO, Vito Anthony (10 Dec. 1902–9 Aug. 1954), radical political figure and congressman, was born in East Harlem, New York City, the son of Sanario "Samuel" Marcantonio, an American-born carpenter, and Angelina deDobitis, a native of Italy. Though his father's skills allowed a relatively comfortable existence, Marcantonio imbibed radical politics at DeWitt Clinton High School from his history teacher, a one-time Socialist candidate for Congress and teachers' union organizer. Marcantonio organized a neighborhood rent strike while still a teenager and in 1921 was introduced to a kindred spirit, the president of the city's board of aldermen, Fiorello La Guardia. La Guardia became something of a surrogate father to Marcantonio. Despite stormy moments, their political and personal relationship lasted until La Guardia died.

After graduating from Clinton High School in 1921, Marcantonio entered New York University Law School. He received the LL.B. in 1925 only by special action of the faculty, having failed a prerequisite course twice in his senior year. Marcantonio's academic work had suffered because of his ambivalent commitment to the law as a career, extensive involvement in party politics, and volunteer work at Haarlem House, a settlement house for immigrants. At Haarlem House he met Miriam Sanders, whom he married in 1925. She was five inches taller, eleven years older, and born in Boston to an old WASP New England family. The marriage was not entirely happy, but it did last. The couple had no children.

In 1924 La Guardia, denied the Republican nomination and facing a stiff congressional reelection challenge, picked the 22-year-old law school student to be his campaign manager. Marcantonio, using Haarlem

House as a base, organized the Fiorello H. La Guardia Political Club, which grew to more than a thousand members. This gave the congressman and later his protégé an informal political "machine" independent of the Democrats and Republicans. After winning the election, both Italian mavericks returned to nominal affiliation with the Republican party.

The evolving demography of the Twentieth District in East Harlem shaped Marcantonio's political career. As polyglot as could be imagined, it had been a slum since the 1890s, dominated first by Irish immigrants, then by Jewish immigrants, and by 1930 by the largest Italian-American community in the country. By the 1940s Puerto Ricans and African Americans were an increasing presence. Like La Guardia, Marcantonio spoke Yiddish, Italian, English, and later Spanish to work the crowds. Toward the end of his life, Marcantonio was remembered as "the guy who brought the Puerto Ricans to New York." If he did not create the phenomenon, he certainly encouraged it by recruiting a Spanish-speaking staff to help the newcomers obtain all available benefits offered by the government.

Marcantonio cut a dashing figure in the 1920s. He was naturally pugnacious and did not hesitate to wade into crowds of hostile toughs recruited by the opposition. In between elections he ran La Guardia's local office while the congressman was in Washington. His careful attention to constituents' needs helped secure La Guardia's continued electoral success, and later it would get Marcantonio into office and keep him there.

La Guardia was swept out of office in the Franklin D. Roosevelt landslide election of 1932. Undaunted, he ran for mayor the next year and won. This created an opportunity for the 32-year-old Marcantonio, who easily won the Republican and City-Fusion party nomination, support from various anti-Tammany Democratic splinter groups, and the enthusiastic endorsement of New York's very popular mayor, to become one of only 103 Republicans to win election to Congress in 1934. Every two years like clockwork, despite bitter disagreements over various issues, La Guardia came out unreservedly for "Marc."

Part of Marcantonio's appeal to his constituents was his commitment to Roosevelt's New Deal. Indeed, sometimes he seemed more committed to fundamental change than the president himself, supporting, for example, the rights of miners and agricultural workers. He was allied with a small group of like-minded reformers under the informal leadership of Maury Maverick (D.-Tex.) in an unsuccessful attempt to drive the New Deal further to the left. He opposed the administration's defense bill in 1935, claiming it was immoral to spend money on weapons when ten million people were unemployed. He also opposed compulsory Reserve Officer Training Corps programs at colleges and universities. In 1935 he originally opposed the Social Security Act because he said it did not do enough. Convinced that fascism was growing in the United States, he criticized congressional attempts to restrict communism. His passion for civil liberties was not dogmatic, as illustrated by his call for strict repressive measures against the German-American Nazi Bund. Although originally supportive of the Neutrality Act of 1935–1937, he soon demanded an end to the arms embargo, because he wanted the United States to support the Loyalist government in the Spanish Civil War. Aware of the growing Puerto Rican constituency in his district, he denounced "American imperialism" against the island.

Although Marcantonio was more enthusiastic about the New Deal than his Tammany opponent, James Lanzetta, he lost his seat in the Democratic landslide of 1936. Thereafter he severed his ties to the Republican party leadership. However, he never abandoned his association with American Communist leaders, which would cost him the support of the influential International Ladies Garment Workers Union (ILGWU) and the newly formed American Labor party (ALP).

Marcantonio spent 1937 and 1938 repairing his political fences and planning a return to Congress. He succeeded in doing so by gaining the ALP nomination, either through La Guardia's intercession or because party elders recognized his popularity in the district. Still he knew that he could not win with only a third-party endorsement, so he decided to file for the Republican nomination over the vehement objections of the Republican county committee. His machine piled up enough signatures to force a primary and then enough votes to beat his conservative Republican rival. Running on both the GOP and ALP tickets, Marcantonio trounced Lanzetta in November 1938.

On his return to Washington, Marcantonio was dismayed to find the New Deal in retreat and increasing attention being given to foreign affairs. He had nothing to say about the Nazi-Soviet pact that August. When war came two weeks later, he followed the Communist party line by denouncing it as "an imperialistic war" and demanding American neutrality. In 1940 he was the only member of Congress to vote against expanding the U.S. Navy and Army Air Corps, and he also voted against the draft. His doctrinaire pacifism was no handicap in winning reelection that year, nor did he hesitate to oppose every effort by President Roosevelt to aid the allies, such as the Lend-Lease Act of 1940 and the destroyers for bases deal of September 1940. Only when German forces invaded Russia in June 1941 did he change his mind. By October he was calling for immediate and direct U.S. intervention in the war.

American participation in World War II brought Marcantonio to the height of his power and respectability. He supported virtually every war program proposed by the White House. Nevertheless, he continued to lobby for social justice at home, believing the cause of freedom to be indivisible. In 1941 he took up the cause of African-American civil rights. He unsuccessfully lobbied for a federal antilynching bill and succeeded in getting 218 representatives to sign a discharge petition to force a bill eliminating the poll tax (which disfranchised millions of black southerners) out of committee and onto the floor of the House for a vote. This bill passed the House in 1942 and each of several years thereafter only to be bottled up in the Senate. Later he used his parliamentary skills to ensure funding of the Fair Employment Practices Commission in the face of determined southern opposition, one of his few legislative victories.

In 1942 and again in 1944 Marcantonio performed the amazing feat of cross-filing and winning the ALP, Republican, and Democratic nominations. His 1944 victory occurred despite the gerrymandering of the historic Twentieth District out of existence by the Republican-controlled New York State legislature, which created a new and larger Eighteenth District in its place. Marcantonio's determined efforts on behalf of his constituents ensured his electoral victories. Efforts to smear him as a Red made little headway with voters concerned with bread and butter issues.

Marcantonio's affiliation caused him to be shunted into insignificant committees. As the years passed, he was even more marginalized. Despite the Allied victory in World War II, he continued to see the swastika in every rent increase, in every digit of inflation, in every effort to cut taxes, and in every antiunion outburst. In addition to his isolation on domestic issues, his enthusiasm for collaboration with the Soviet Union grew increasingly out of fashion in the Cold War. He objected without effect to the contempt of Congress citations filed against the Hollywood Ten, President Harry Truman's Loyalty Review Board, the Truman Doctrine, and the Marshall Plan, the last being to his mind a "war program." In 1948 he supported Henry Wallace's disastrous presidential bid. His own chances for electoral survival diminished when New York State revised its election laws to forbid cross-filing without the consent of the second party's county committee. Running only on the ALP line, Marcantonio won reelection in 1948. His political career ended in 1950, however.

When President Truman ordered U.S. forces into action to protect the freely elected South Korean government against Communist invasion in June 1950, Congress endorsed the decision almost unanimously, with Marcantonio the lone holdout. He castigated the South Korean government as tyrannical, blamed it for dividing the country, and defended the right of the Korean people to self-determination, even if they had to use Soviet tanks. He was universally jeered. Because of Marcantonio's unpopular opposition to the Korean War, leaders of the Republican, Democratic, and Liberal parties nominated the same opposition candidate by consent. Even Marcantonio could not prevail against those odds in such a climate.

The ex-congressman remained unconverted and unrepentant in defeat. He took on civil liberties cases, including his successful defense of radical African-American scholar and civil rights advocate W. E. B. Du Bois, who had been charged with not registering as an agent of a foreign power. In 1953 Marcantonio resigned form the virtually defunct ALP and formed his own political club in anticipation of running in the 1954 campaign as an independent. However, he died of a heart attack in New York City several months before the election. As a final insult to his memory, the Catholic archdiocese refused to permit his burial in consecrated ground.

Marcantonio was the most electorally successful radical in American political history, yet he sacrificed power for ideological purity, indulging his passion for political posturing. Never a card-carrying Communist, he nonetheless followed the party line rigidly. His constituents did not love him because of his pro-Communist positions but in spite of them. Unlike his mentor La Guardia, he never learned that there was a limit to how far a politician could travel from the mainstream and still accomplish important goals.

• Marcantonio's papers are deposited in the New York Public Library. For a collection of speeches and writings, see Annette Rubenstein, ed., *I Vote My Conscience* (1956). Biographies include Allan Schaffer, *Vito Marcantonio, Radical in Congress* (1966), and Gerald Myer, *Vito Marcantonio* (1989). An obituary is in the *New York Times*, 10 Aug. 1954.

DAVID M. ESPOSITO

MARCH, Alden (20 Sept. 1795–17 June 1869), surgeon and medical teacher, was born in Sutton, Worcester County, Massachusetts, the son of Jacob March and Eleanor Moore, farmers. After a brief career as a schoolteacher, he followed his elder brother David into medicine. In 1818–1819 he attended lectures by Dr. William Ingalls in Boston and in 1820 received a medical degree from Brown University.

March settled in Albany, New York, in 1820. His practice grew slowly, and he supplemented his income by teaching. He gave anatomical lectures, which, exceptionally for the time, used human cadavers, and from 1825 to 1835 he was professor of anatomy and physiology at the Vermont Academy of Medicine in Castleton. In 1824 he married Joanna Armsby. They had four children, two of whom survived to maturity. March's career was closely linked with that of his wife's younger brother, James H. Armsby, who had moved to Albany and received a medical degree from Vermont Academy of Medicine in 1833.

The Albany lectures grew, and in 1830 March delivered a "Lecture on the Expediency of Establishing a Medical College and Hospital in the City of Albany." The local medical profession opposed the creation of a medical school, as did the faculties of the two existing schools in New York State—the College of Physicians and Surgeons in New York City and the College of Physicians and Surgeons of the Western District in Fairfield, in central New York State. For some years, the idea seemed to have stalled, although March continued to offer more or less formal medical education and Armsby delivered popular scientific lectures. By 1837, March had enlisted the support of local physicians, and public backing for a medical school had grown to the point at which the city of Albany donated a building. A preliminary catalog was printed, and on 2 January 1839 Albany Medical College opened for sixteen weeks, a common term length for the time. The state legislature granted a charter to the college

that February. March became its president and professor of surgery, and Armsby became dean and professor of anatomy and physiology. A number of the local practitioners who earlier had opposed the creation of the college nevertheless joined its faculty. From the earliest days, March's teaching included "surgical clinics," which involved demonstration of the patient and his or her malady, followed immediately by the planned operation, all before the students. In a continuation of March and Armsby's efforts, in 1849 the Albany City Hospital was founded.

March's qualities of decisiveness and self-confidence were particularly valued before the 1846 introduction of anesthesia, when surgical procedures were performed on patients fully awake and speed and self-assurance were essential to any possibility of success. In his landmark paper on hip disease ("On Coxalgia, or Hip Disease," *Transactions of the American Medical Association* 6 [1853]: 479–506), March referred to the value of anesthesia in manipulation and reduction of hip dislocations. In that paper, he concluded that dislocation of the hip (in the absence of trauma) resulted from chronic degenerative disease of the joint. Because, according to the current teaching, dislocation caused the degeneration of the joint, March's hypothesis was slow to be accepted but eventually became universally so.

March's case records reveal the size of his surgical practice: although ten years of his career are missing, 7,124 operations are recorded between 1825 and 1869. In addition to his practice, he served as president of the Medical Society of the County of Albany in 1832–1833, and of the Medical Society of the State of New York in 1857. These societies shared the principal concern of organized medicine in the early nineteenth century—that of the quality of the education of doctors permitted to practice. The usual route to a medical career was some apprenticeship, perhaps a diploma or degree from an institution, then application to the local medical society for membership, which carried the legal right to practice. (Governmental bodies exercised no control or licensing.) Standards were nearly nonexistent, and schools feared that raising standards would drive potential students to less demanding institutions.

Several members of the Medical Society of the State of New York expressed concern that if the society were to raise its standards, aspiring physicians would go to other states for training. A leader of the movement to raise standards was Nathan Smith Davis, a physician from Chenango County in central New York State. March suggested to Davis that a national convention might address the issue successfully, and in 1845 a resolution of the society proposed a convention for "elevation of the standard of medical education in the United States." The national convention of delegates from several state medical societies was held in New York City in 1846 and led to the foundation of the American Medical Association in 1847; Davis is regarded as the founder. March was elected president in 1864 and devoted most of his presidential address to a discussion of, and a plea for, improvement of medical education (*Transactions of the American Medical Association* 15 [1864]: 65–76).

March was outwardly in good health until the spring of 1869, when after returning from the American Medical Association meeting in New Orleans, he suffered urinary retention and soon after died in Albany. The attending physicians, including Armsby, published the clinical details of the case and the autopsy findings, which showed massive enlargement of the prostate and long-standing bladder distention and hypertrophy (*New York Medical Journal* 10 [1869–1870]: 95–101). Charles A. Robertson, an Albany eye and ear specialist who was not on the best of terms with Armsby, published a searing indictment of the clinical care and autopsy, alleging improprieties and malpractice. Several rounds of acrimonious correspondence were published. Review of the facts and correspondence reveals no malpractice, although it is still true that autopsy findings frequently correct clinical impressions.

March influenced American medicine beyond what might be expected of a practitioner, however talented, in a small provincial city. The medical college and hospital he founded flourish; the American Medical Association continues to champion professional standards and education. March's vision of what was needed to advance the cause of medicine, and his successful alignment of his own career with that advancement, made him one of the most influential figures in nineteenth-century American medicine.

• March's professional and scientific papers, autograph correspondence, and memorials are in the Albany Medical College Archives, Albany, N.Y. Emerson Crosby Kelly drew on the March papers and other archives in "Development of Medical Education in Upstate New York: The Albany Area," *New York State Journal of Medicine* 55 (1955): 2664–68, and "The Doctors March to [*sic*] Armsby of Albany," *Bulletin of the History of Medicine* 30 (1956): 32–37. Richard T. Beebe, *Albany Medical College and Albany Hospital. A History: 1839–1982* (1983), discusses the foundation of these institutions and March's central role. Morris Fishbein, *A History of the American Medical Association 1847 to 1947* (1947), is a useful source. *Tribute to the Memory of Alden March, M.D., LL.D.* (1870), contains the funeral service, several memorial letters and notices, and a useful, complete review of March's professional practice and publications by James L. Babcock. Robertson's polemical "Review of the Report of 'Last Illness of Dr. Alden March,'" *New York Medical Journal* 10 (1869–1870): 355–74, was answered by March's physician James McNaughton in "Reply to Dr. C. A. Robertson's Review of the Report concerning the Last Illness of Doctor Alden March," *New York Medical Journal* 11 (1870): 85–95.

JEFFREY D. HUBBARD

MARCH, Fredric (31 Aug. 1897–14 Apr. 1975), actor, was born Ernest Frederick McIntyre Bickel in Racine, Wisconsin, the son of John F. Bickel, a successful manufacturer and devout Presbyterian, and Cora Brown Marcher. March was raised in a conventionally middle-class midwestern home. The youngest of four siblings, he was outgoing and popular in his childhood and adolescence. Charismatic and a natural leader,

March was elected president of his grammar school and high school classes and would be president of his senior class in college as well. He won a statewide public-speaking competition as a high school junior. The youthful March loved to recite at church bazaars and school entertainments and staged his own performances in the family's barn. In high school he attended theater regularly and saw Maude Adams play Peter Pan. At the University of Wisconsin March joined the debating team and performed in student theater; but, heeding the practical advice of his older brother, March majored in commerce, intending to work in finance after graduation.

March served stateside as a lieutenant in the artillery and an equestrian trainer in the U.S. Army during World War I. He moved to New York City after his discharge in February 1919, lured by a National City Bank scholarship designed to groom him for an overseas appointment. The program was suspended, however, and March soon found that working as a bank clerk bored him. During a period of convalescence following a burst appendix March devoted himself to a study of theater history and decided he was "ham enough" to try acting.

March pursued his long-delayed dream with the energy, discipline, and pragmatism that would mark his entire 53-year career as a performer. He had cheap publicity photos taken, found an agent, and began to work in 1920 as an extra in mob scenes for Paramount Studios for $7.50 a day. His broad-shouldered good looks led to sittings for commercial artists, who used his well-groomed image to sell hair tonic, shaving cream, shoes, and cravats. March made his Broadway debut on 23 December 1920 as Victor Hugo (a one-line role) in David Belasco's staging of *Debureau*. A series of gradually larger roles in Broadway and off-Broadway plays followed. March first attracted critical attention in *The Law Breaker* (1922), directed by John Cromwell, who became March's mentor and a lifelong friend. On Cromwell's advice the actor took "Fredric March" as his stage name in 1924. Under a personal contract with Cromwell, March's parts began to improve. His first Broadway lead was in 1926's *The Devil in the Cheese*.

In 1924 March married actress Ellis Baker, a niece of character actor Edward Ellis, but the couple divorced three years later. During a stint in summer stock in Denver, March married the company's leading lady, Florence Eldridge, on 30 May 1927. The newlyweds immediately embarked on an inaugural 132-city tour with the Theatre Guild Repertory Company, which for March led to a leading role in a comedy, *The Royal Family*, at Los Angeles's El Capitan Theatre. The performance won March a five-year contract with Paramount and enabled the couple to settle down. Their marriage was one of Hollywood's happiest; they later adopted two children and bought a forty-acre farm near New Milford, Connecticut.

The versatile March made twenty-nine of his sixty-nine sound films during these first five years in California. Although most of these were potboilers, his performances were consistently well received. March's resonant, stage-trained voice easily overcame the unforgiving microphones of early sound cinema. *The Dummy* (1929), one of Paramount's first talkies, was quickly followed by *The Wild Party* and *The Studio Murder Mystery* (also Eldridge's first film) in the same year. March earned his best notices for *The Royal Family of Broadway*, a 1930 reprise of the John Barrymore parody performance that had landed him his Hollywood contract. March received the first of his five Academy Award nominations for the part and won the next year for his dual title role in Rouben Mamoulian's *Dr. Jekyll and Mr. Hyde.*

The remaining years on March's Paramount contract were not entirely happy. He resisted playing inferior roles but risked suspension from the studio for his insubordination. *Smilin' Through* (1932), with Norma Shearer, shot while March was on loan to Metro-Goldwyn-Mayer, and three Paramount films—Cecil B. DeMille's *The Sign of the Cross* (1932), Ernst Lubitsch's *Design for Living* (1933), and a personal favorite of March's, *Death Takes a Holiday* (1934)—contain his best work of the period.

March refused Paramount's offer to renew his contract. In choosing to work as an independent actor outside the studio system, he paved the way for Cary Grant, Gary Cooper, and others who did the same. Few, however, matched March's skill in picking parts that suited his gifts for both drama and sophisticated comedy. He teamed with Shearer again in MGM's *The Barretts of Wimpole Street* (1934); played opposite Greta Garbo in MGM's *Anna Karenina* (1935); and made *Les Misérables* (1935) for Twentieth Century–Fox and *The Dark Angel* (1935), with Merle Oberon, for Sam Goldwyn.

The trio of films that March made in 1936 fared less well at the box office. Neither RKO's *Mary of Scotland*, directed by John Ford and costarring Eldridge and Katharine Hepburn, nor Twentieth Century–Fox's *The Road to Glory*, directed by Howard Hawks, did well, and *Anthony Adverse* was a flop for Warner Bros. Although the reputation of each film would grow in time, March, then nearing forty, felt he could not afford any more mistakes. March's powerful portrayal of alcoholic has-been Norman Maine in *A Star Is Born* in 1937 earned him a third Oscar nomination and consolidated his place as one of Hollywood's leading actors. *Nothing Sacred*, a seminal screwball comedy with Carol Lombard directed the same year by William Wellman, was also a huge box-office success. Selznick-International paid March $125,000 for each picture. *The Buccaneer* reunited March with DeMille for Paramount in 1938 and made March Hollywood's highest-paid actor and the fifth-highest salaried American at the time.

By the late 1930s March began a difficult transition to character parts on stage and screen. The Broadway production of *Your Obedient Husband* (1938), directed by Cromwell and costarring Eldridge, died after an embarrassing run of only eight performances. United Artists' *There Goes My Heart* (1938) was the first in a string of five lackluster films. March appeared with his wife in three plays: George S. Kaufman and Moss Hart's *The American Way* (1939), which succeeded modestly on Broadway; *Hope for a Harvest* (1941), which did not; and Thornton Wilder's *The Skin of Our Teeth* (1942), which won a Pulitzer Prize.

March's support for antifascist causes made him a target for investigation by the House Un-American Activities Committee in 1940; fortunately for his career, the committee concluded that March had allowed his name to be associated with organizations backed by Communists out of "humanitarian impulses." March performed for American troops on a 33,000-mile USO tour during World War II, while continuing to work in films and on stage. His best screen work of the period is *One Foot in Heaven* (1941) and *The Adventures of Mark Twain* (1944). March's sensitive portrayal of a battle-weary sergeant returning to civilian life in *The Best Years of Our Lives* (1946) won him critical praise, popular acclaim, and his second Oscar.

March received mixed reviews but another Oscar nomination for his role as Willy Loman in the screen version of Arthur Miller's *Death of a Salesman* (1951), a role he had declined when the play was produced on Broadway. But he did return to the stage in Eugene O'Neill's *Long Day's Journey into Night*, the Broadway event of the 1956 season, and won a Tony for his performance opposite Eldridge. By the 1960s March was widely regarded as a national treasure, receiving recognition and honors from the State Department, Congress, and President Kennedy. Judicious in choosing roles, he appeared in the film versions of the play *Inherit the Wind* (1960) and the novel *Seven Days in May* (1964).

March's final film role was Harry Hope in the American Film Theatre's adaptation of the Eugene O'Neill play *The Iceman Cometh* (1973). March's death from cancer in Hollywood shortly after was seen as the passing of a consummate craftsman whose acting, like that of friend and fellow Wisconsinite Spencer Tracy, set a standard of excellence for future generations. From modest beginnings as a romantic leading man, March had become an actor of vast range and depth. His gift for the subtleties of screen acting never compromised his abilities on the stage. Famed for his rendering of characters in states of psychological anguish, he was also a fine comic; he drew on his midwestern upbringing to inform his frequent portrayals of the quintessentially solid, sober middle-class American man. Always an actor first and a star second, March was celebrated for his self-effacing, unaffected style and respected by his peers for the dignity and devotion that marked his long and happy marriage and his commitment to the art and craft of film and stage acting.

• The Fredric March Papers are housed at the State Historical Society of Wisconsin in Madison; they include his film scripts, with his handwritten annotations. Biographical materials are at the New York Public Library for the Performing Arts at Lincoln Center in New York City. Biographies include Michael Burrows, *Charles Laughton and Fredric March* (1969); Lawrence J. Quirk, *The Films of Fredric March* (1971); and Deborah C. Peterson, *Fredric March: Craftsman First, Star Second* (1996). See also Richard Schickel, *The Stars: The Personalities Who Made the Movies* (1962); David Shipman, *The Great Movie Stars: The Golden Years* (1970); and Leslie Halliwell, *The Filmgoer's Companion* (1974). An obituary appears in the *New York Times*, 15 Apr. 1975.

BRUCE J. EVENSEN

MARCH, Joseph Moncure (27 July 1899–14 Feb. 1977), poet, writer, and screenwriter, was born in New York City, the son of Moncure March, an attorney, and Katherine O'Connell. March was educated at Lawrenceville, New Jersey, and at Amherst College, from which he graduated in 1920. His grandfather Francis Andrew March, an Anglo-Saxon scholar, philologist, and lexicographer, was only one of the March family members to attend Amherst; years later March vividly remembered sitting beneath his grandfather's portrait during chapel.

As a high school student at Lawrenceville, March began to write poetry, composing the ode for the class of 1916, of which he was a member. During his Amherst years March wrote poems and fiction for the *Monthly Literary Magazine*. Robert Frost fostered young March's interest in poetry, directing him away from free verse and insisting on the importance of form and balance in his work. After publishing independently a small pamphlet protesting Amherst classes, requirements, and administrative procedures, March enlisted in the U.S. Army at age eighteen. With volumes of John Keats and Percy Bysshe Shelley in his pack, March spent a year in the trenches of France; he was readmitted to Amherst and was commissioned in his senior year to write the Ivy Ode for the class of 1920.

March moved to New York City after college and married Cyra Thomas, a Vassar graduate, in 1921. One of his first jobs was on the editorial staff of the New York Telephone Company's *Telephone Review*. In 1925 and 1926 March served as the first managing editor of the *New Yorker*, until quarrels with Harold Ross led him to resign. While at the *New Yorker*, March contributed poetry and prose to the magazine; some of his verse contributions were reprinted in *Fifteen Lyrics* (1929). During the summer of 1926, separated from his first wife, unemployed, and on a $30-per-week salary from his father, March wrote the poem for which he is best known, *The Wild Party*.

The Wild Party has a self-descriptive title. It is a syncopated tale, or improvisation (March's own description of his poetry), in broken rhyming couplets and full of visual and musical description, of a late evening of drinking, sex, and murder in Greenwich Village, circa the summer of 1925. The poem's controversial stanzas kept it unpublished for several years. Although John Sumner, head of the New York Society for the Suppression of Vice, threatened to jail Dick Simon of Simon & Schuster if they brought out *The Wild Party*, Pascal Covici of Chicago published the poem in a limited edition of 750 copies in 1928. It created a sensation and was almost immediately more widely available in pirated editions. For the last legitimate American edition of *The Wild Party* released during his lifetime, that of 1968, March provided a long introduction, titled "A Certain Wildness" and covering his college years, his time in New York during the 1920s, and the process of creating the poem. The 1968 edition is expurgated; that of 1994, with illustrations by Pulitzer Prize–winning artist Art Spiegelman, is not. Shortly before March's death, a film version of *The Wild Party*, starring Raquel Welch as Queenie, was released.

March followed his success with *The Set-Up*, published in New York in late 1928. In the same verse style as *The Wild Party*, *The Set-Up* is the story of an African-American boxer, his best years in the ring lost to jail, who wins a long fixed bout instead of throwing it and pays for his last victory with his life. In 1949 *The Set-Up* was made into a critically acclaimed movie with—to March's horror, for he was not invited to work on the screenplay though he was in Hollywood at the time—Robert Ryan, a white actor, starring as the boxer.

Divorced from his second wife, Sue Wise, whom he had married in 1927, March married Peggy Pryor in Hollywood in 1931. (All of March's marriages were childless.) He and Peggy lived in Hollywood and New York for the rest of their lives, with March primarily employed as a journalist and screenwriter. His film credits include *Hell's Angels* (1930), the movie that launched Jean Harlow's career. From 1943 to 1945 March worked in Hollywood on documentary films for the State Department; from 1949 to 1964 he was back in New York, a writer and producer for MPO Productions. During the last decade of his life March returned to Hollywood, where he was a contributor of articles and reviews to the *New York Times Magazine*. He died in Los Angeles, California.

In 1977 James Farrell said that March had gone unremembered for two generations, but the 1994 resurrection of *The Wild Party* as a lost modernist classic, excerpted in the *New Yorker*, has reestablished March as a chronicler, like F. Scott Fitzgerald in prose and Peter Arno in art, of the Jazz Age.

• Amherst College maintains an alumni records file on March in the Amherst College Archives and Special Collections of the Frost Library. Additionally, the library of Lafayette College, Easton, Pa., has information on March's father and grandfather and their families. Biographical information about March can be found in his autobiographical essay, "A Certain Wildness," in Joseph Moncure March, *The Wild Party/The Set-Up/A Certain Wildness* (1968); Art Spiegelman, "Intoxicating Rhythm," in *The Wild Party: The Lost Classic by Joseph Moncure March* (1994); and James T. Farrell, "*The Wild Party* and *The Set-Up*," *New York Times Book Review*, 17 Apr. 1977, which also contains a tribute to March. For a review of the 1995 edition of *The Wild Party*, which mentions March's tenure at the *New Yorker* and his work with Robert Frost at Amherst, see the *New York Times*, 4 Jan. 1995. An obituary is in the *New York Times*, 16 Feb. 1977.

ANNE MARGARET DANIEL

MARCH, Peyton Conway (27 Dec. 1864–13 Apr. 1955), army officer, was born in Easton, Pennsylvania, the son of Francis Andrew March and Margaret Mildred Stone Conway. His mother was a great-granddaughter of Thomas Stone, a signer of the Declaration of Independence, and the sister of the famed writer and preacher Moncure D. Conway. His father, who taught at Lafayette College for fifty-one years, established an international reputation as a philologist. In his youth, March balanced studiousness with athletics. A classics major, he graduated from Lafayette in 1884 and entered the U.S. Military Academy a few weeks later. In his four years at West Point (1884–1888), he became acquainted with John J. Pershing, who was in the class of 1886. During the ten years between his graduation and the Spanish-American War, March did routine garrison duty as an artillery officer. In 1891 he married Josephine Smith Cunningham, with whom he had six children, one of whom died in infancy.

The war with Spain and the ensuing Philippine War gave March the opportunity to win distinction in battle. He organized the Astor Battery, which was financed by John Jacob Astor, and took it to the Philippines. In the battle of Manila, March led a charge against a blockhouse and gained the attention of Arthur MacArthur, who recommended him for a Medal of Honor. Although the recommendation was reduced eventually to a Distinguished Service Cross (awarded in 1920), MacArthur did not forget March and asked for him to serve as an aide after he had returned to the United States and disbanded his battery. After serving for some four months on Major General MacArthur's staff, First Lieutenant March joined the Thirty-third Volunteer Infantry Regiment as a major. From late October 1899 to January 1901 he participated in the guerrilla war in Luzon. In 1901, after several months of administrative and staff duty, he reverted to his permanent rank as a captain and returned to the United States.

For the next sixteen years, March continued to excel in both staff work and command assignments. As one of the first group of officers selected for the General Staff in 1903, March served with other outstanding officers such as George W. Goethals and Pershing. In 1904 he was one of the observers attached to the Japanese army in their war against Russia, but his wife's death in November of that year abbreviated his stay with the Japanese. He spent most of the five years from 1911 to 1916 as an adjutant general, which gave him the opportunity to learn about the records system and the general operations of the War Department. In October 1916 he went to the Mexican border to serve as the colonel in command of the newly created Eighth Field Artillery Regiment.

The American entry into World War I brought him promotion to brigadier and then major general as he was called to France to be the top artillerist in the American Expeditionary Forces (AEF). From July 1917 to February 1918 March trained the artillery in France and laid the plans for the other artillery organization to follow.

In the winter of 1917–1918, as the American war effort faltered, congressional leaders called for stronger leadership in the War Department. Secretary of War Newton D. Baker had attempted to supply this direction with three different officers as chief of staff as well as an advisory council of senior generals with indifferent success. Baker knew of March's reputation as an effective administrator, so he called March back to take over as chief of staff. On 4 March 1918 March became the acting chief of staff, and in May he became a full general.

While much of the organizational foundation was in place, March did create some new branches, including the Air Service, Chemical Warfare Service, and Tank Corps. His major contribution, however, was to give a firm, energetic, and decisive direction to the General Staff and the army, with the supremacy of the chief of staff unquestioned. He emphasized efficiency and brought into the War Department officers who could best carry out his aims, among them Goethals and Robert E. Wood. His zealousness and ruthless manner hurt feelings on Capitol Hill and in the army, including those of General Pershing, but he got results.

The major result was the accelerated shipment of American troops to France. Between the first of March and the end of the war in November, he oversaw the transportation of some 1.75 million men to the AEF. In contrast, only a quarter of a million American troops were in France when he became chief of staff. The importance of this massive reinforcement to the Allied cause cannot be underestimated. In early 1918 any hope of Allied victory depended on the rapid deployment of American manpower. Pershing had the framework in place to lead the vast number of men, but March supplied the leadership that got them there. In 1936 Secretary Baker lauded his contribution in speeding up the troop movement: "Your energy and drive supplied the days necessary for our side to win" (Coffman, p. 151).

For almost three years after the war, until 30 June 1921, March remained chief of staff. It then fell to him to supervise the bringing back of the AEF, the demobilization of the great force raised for the war, and the development of the postwar military establishment. The first two tasks were largely completed by the end of 1919, but the debate over reorganization of the army extended into 1920. March, with the backing of the secretary of war and President Woodrow Wilson, favored a peacetime army of 500,000—a force quadruple the size of the pre–World War I army. Caught up in antiadministration fervor as well as a strong revival of the American antimilitary spirit, Congress rejected this plan and in addition denied March permanent four-star rank for his high-handed ways during the war. In 1930, however, Congress gave all retired officers the highest rank they had held during the war, thus restoring March's four stars.

For the first five years of his retirement, March traveled extensively in Europe. He met and talked with national leaders and old adversaries, such as Field Marshal Paul von Hindenburg. He also married Cora

McEntee in 1923; they had no children. In 1953, two years before his death in Washington, D.C., he received from President Dwight D. Eisenhower a long overdue Thanks of Congress.

• The March papers are in the Library of Congress, although his record file as chief of staff remains in the National Archives. March's wartime memoir is *The Nation at War* (1932), and a biography is Edward M. Coffman, *The Hilt of the Sword: The Career of Peyton C. March* (1966).

EDWARD M. COFFMAN

MARCH, William (18 Sept. 1893–15 May 1954), writer and business executive, was born William Edward Campbell in Mobile, Alabama, the son of John Leonard Campbell, a timber cruiser, and Susan March. His childhood was spent in the small timber communities of West Florida and South Alabama, and his schooling ended at the age of fourteen when he began work in the office of a local sawmill. He left home at the age of sixteen for Mobile and obtained a position in a law office. He accumulated sufficient savings to put himself through a high school course of study at Valparaiso University (1913–1914) and subsequently to enter the law school of the University of Alabama as a special student (1914–1915). In 1916 he went to New York and became a subpoena server for a law firm.

In July 1917 he enlisted in the Marine Corps and served with distinction in France during 1918. He was wounded at Belleau Wood and participated in the Marine actions at Soissons, St. Mihiel, and the assault on Blanc Mont in the Argonne. He was awarded the Croix de Guerre, the Distinguished Service Cross, and the Navy Cross for gallantry.

He was discharged in August 1919 and returned to Mobile where, after a brief period in another law office, he became the personal secretary of John B. Waterman, president of the recently founded Waterman Steamship Corporation. Promotion swiftly followed. As traffic manager and ultimately a vice president of the company, he lived for varying periods in Mobile, Memphis, New York, Hamburg, and London. He began writing stories during time spent traveling in the Middle West between 1926 and 1928 and, using the pen name William March, had considerable success in getting these published in such little magazines as *Forum*, *Midland*, *Prairie Schooner*, *Pagany*, *Clay*, *Contempo*, and *Story*. Several of his stories were selected by Edward J. O'Brien for reprinting in his annual *Best Short Stories* anthologies. His first novel, *Company K* (1933), based on his Marine experiences, was greeted with much critical acclaim, both in the United States and England. His next two novels, *Come In at the Door* (1934), written while living in Nazi Germany, and *The Tallons* (1936), written in London, were not so well received. Two volumes of short stories, *The Little Wife and Other Stories* (1935) and *Some Like Them Short* (1939), deservedly attracted more favorable notices.

By 1939 he was a comparatively wealthy man, not through his literary output but because over the years he had acquired a considerable holding of stock in the rapidly expanding Waterman company. He resigned from his vice presidency, assured that he was financially secure enough now to devote all his time to writing. His finest full-length work, the novel *The Looking-Glass* (1943), an episodic psychological study of a large group of characters in a small country town in Alabama, was well received by the critics, if less so by the reading public. A volume of collected short stories, *Trial Balance* (1945), in many respects his most substantial work, confirmed him in the opinion of many critics as one of the best short-story writers of his generation.

He was incapacitated by an attack of acute depression in 1947, partly brought about as a result of a prolonged writer's block, and he returned to his roots in Mobile to recover. Unable to settle down to writing, he channeled his energies into acquiring a magnificent collection of modern French art, with particular emphasis on the work of Soutine, Rouault, and Modigliani. In 1950 he moved from Mobile to New Orleans and began writing again. His fifth novel, *October Island*, was published two years later. His last novel, *The Bad Seed* (1954), the horrifying story of Rhoda Penmark, an eight-year-old murderess, appeared a mere five weeks before his death. It became a sensational bestseller, a successful Broadway play (in an adaptation by Maxwell Anderson), a Hollywood film, and, in 1985, a TV movie. A lifelong bachelor, he died of a heart attack in New Orleans in the first house he had ever owned, purchased only a year before.

Although he was a master of irony and psychological insight, his work, other than his first and last novels, never really caught the imagination of the reading public and has never been given the attention and recognition it deserves. His work in the field of the short story is frequently anthologized, particularly the title story of his first collection. "The Little Wife," with its poignant understanding of the emotional uncertainties and fears of ordinary people, has become a classic in the genre.

• The principal collection of March manuscripts, letters, memorabilia, and emphemera is in the W. S. Hoole Special Collections Library, the University of Alabama, Tuscaloosa. The research papers of March's biographer, Roy S. Simmonds, have also been deposited in this library. Posthumously published works are *A William March Omnibus*, comp. Robert Loomis, with an introduction by Alistair Cooke (1956), and *99 Fables*, ed. William T. Going (1960). The biography by Simmonds is *The Two Worlds of William March* (1984). The bibliography is *William March: An Annotated Checklist*, comp. Roy S. Simmonds (1988). Important critical and biographical essays on March by William T. Going have appeared in his *Essays on Alabama Literature* (1975) and in the journal *Papers on Language and Literature* 13 (Fall 1977): 430–43; see also Robert Tallant, "Poor Pilgrim, Poor Stranger," *Saturday Review*, 17 July 1954, pp. 9, 33–34. Obituaries are in the *New York Herald Tribune*, *New York Times*, *New Orleans Times-Picayune*, and *Mobile Press Register*, all on 16 May 1954.

ROY S. SIMMONDS

MARCHBANKS, Vance Hunter, Jr. (12 Jan. 1905–21 Oct. 1988), aerospace surgeon, was born at Fort Washikie, Wyoming, the son of Vance Hunter Marchbanks, Sr., an army cavalry captain, and Mattie (maiden name unknown). Marchbanks, Jr., was influenced by the military career of his father, who was both a Spanish-American War and World War I veteran. A childhood operation inspired his "passion" for medicine. Marchbanks operated on cherries in his backyard, opening them up, removing the stones, and sewing shut the incision.

As an African American, Marchbanks encountered discrimination when he enrolled at the University of Arizona in 1927. Not allowed to live in the dormitories or participate in normal student activities, he lived in an off-campus boardinghouse. He ate in the railroad station restaurant, where he was expected to enter through the back door and was harassed; he often found cockroaches in his soup. Marchbanks graduated in 1931 and was accepted at the Howard University School of Medicine, where he met his future wife, Lois Gilkey, who was an undergraduate at Howard. He received his medical degree in 1937, then was an intern and resident in internal medicine at the Freedmen's Hospital in Washington, D.C., for two years.

Coping with discrimination, Marchbanks resolved: "I realized that if I stopped looking at the worse side and made an effort, I may be able to see the brighter side of things." His most frustrating experiences with discrimination occurred in the military, where he "experienced it his whole life." He hoped to become a flight surgeon. While serving at the Tuskegee, Alabama, Veterans Administration Hospital, Marchbanks heard that an Army Air Corps Flying School would be built at Tuskegee. A field surgeon at Maxwell Air Force Base in nearby Montgomery advised Marchbanks to apply to take an extension course at the School of Aviation Medicine at Randolph Field, Texas.

In 1941 Marchbanks, however, was assigned instead as a first lieutenant in the U.S. Army Medical Corps at Fort Bragg, North Carolina, where he endured "many unpleasant experiences." He later told another generation of black military doctors that "many of you younger physicians have had no such experiences because we paved the way by enduring those hardships and made it possible to abolish many of them."

By December 1942 Marchbanks had completed the Army Air Corps course in aviation medicine and was rated an aviation medical examiner. He was assigned to the station hospital at the Tuskegee Army Air Field, then transferred as a major with the 332d Fighter Group, known as the Tuskegee Airmen, to Selfridge Field, Michigan. He was the group's flight surgeon during campaigns in Italy, becoming one of the first black American flight surgeons and the first in the Air Force's Medical Service. He earned a Bronze Star. He also took classes on the medical aspects of atomic explosion and air base surgery.

Marchbanks's friendship with the Tuskegee Airmen resulted in his challenging military policy to discharge men who carried the sickle cell anemia trait. Sickle cell anemia is an inherited disease that primarily affects people of African and Mediterranean descent. Experts estimate that one of every twelve blacks carries the genetic trait. In a three-year study Marchbanks drew blood from the airmen and analyzed it. He published his results in the article "Sickle Cell Trait and the Black Airman," which helped prove that not everybody who carries the trait has the disease, and he convinced military authorities not to end the careers of black cadets who had the sickle cell trait.

In 1945 Marchbanks joined the 477th Composite Group of B-52 pilots at Godman Field, Kentucky, as group surgeon. A year later he held the same position at the Lockbourne Army Air Base in Ohio, where he had autonomy at his first station hospital. He applied for a commission in the army and was accepted on his second application, becoming the first black physician commissioned in the army. In 1949 Marchbanks was transferred to the Department of the Air Force when all segregated air force units were disbanded. He became group surgeon of the First Fighter Group at March Air Force Base in California, then of the Twenty-second Bombardment Group in Okinawa.

Marchbanks accumulated 1,400 hours of flight time during his tour of duty in Okinawa and Korea, where he flew three combat missions. Promoted to the rank of lieutenant colonel, he returned to Lockbourne in January 1951 as hospital commander and wing surgeon for the Ninety-first Strategic Reconnaissance Wing. Three years later he was assigned as deputy commander and chief of professional services at the Air Force Hospital in Nagoya, Japan. This 400-bed facility was the largest air force hospital in the Far East.

In 1955 Marchbanks was promoted to the rank of full colonel and named air force surgeon of Okinawa. He returned to the Strategic Air Command as hospital commander and division surgeon at Loring Air Force Base in Maine. At his various assignments, Marchbanks was a pioneer in aerospace medicine research and received two air force commendation medals for his research projects. He designed an oxygen mask tester, which the air force adopted as a standard item on air base equipment.

During "Operation Long Legs" in November 1957, Marchbanks accompanied a B-52 jet bomber crew on a 10,600-mile, nonstop flight from Florida to Argentina to New York. Spending almost twenty-three hours in the air, he tested the crew for signs of stress and fatigue. He observed that the adrenal hormone content in blood and tissue served as an index to the physical fatigue that often preceded fatal crashes. Marchbanks developed stress tests and a rating system to evaluate air crews in combat that were later adapted for astronaut training. He told colleagues, "Professionally this was my most rewarding assignment."

Marchbanks also developed a system to identify the remains of numerous casualties from multiple aircraft, as might be found in a war zone. National Aeronautics and Space Administration (NASA) officials cited this achievement as the reason he was selected as an aeromedical monitor and support physician for Project Mercury in 1960. While director of Base Medical Services at the 831 Tactical Hospital at George Air Force Base in California, he was loaned to NASA. As one of eleven specialists assigned to monitor astronaut John Glenn's vital signs for his orbital flight, Marchbanks prepared by studying electrocardiography at the School of Aviation Medicine at Brooks Air Force Base in Texas and familiarizing himself with Glenn's medical history. He also practiced monitoring the signs of the chimpanzee, Enos, during his orbit. Marchbanks traveled to the tracking station at Kano, Nigeria, and on 20 February 1962 Glenn, in the *Friendship 7*, became the first American to orbit the earth. During the three six-minute periods that Glenn passed over Africa, Marchbanks evaluated his respiration, temperature, and pulse, having the authority to terminate the mission if he detected extreme physical stress. "When he was up there, it was just routine for us," Marchbanks commented. "We'd been practicing and practicing. I'd studied his EKG for over a year. I hardly realized it was over until it was all over. It was like playing in a game and not realizing you had won until the end." Marchbanks was featured on the cover of *Jet* magazine's 21 December 1961 issue for his aerospace achievements.

While in Nigeria, Marchbanks visited a leper hospital and evaluated medical conditions. Shocked by the lack of books, he wrote physicians, medical schools, and publishers, asking them to donate medical texts to the country's primary medical training facility, the Hygiene School. Marchbanks collected hundreds of books for Nigeria.

Marchbanks retired from the air force in 1964 and accepted a research position as chief of environmental health services of Hamilton Standard, a division of the United Aircraft Corporation in Windsor Locks, Connecticut. He supervised medical and safety tests of spacesuits and life support systems for the Apollo moon missions and advised engineers building the equipment about physical and psychological factors crucial for success.

Marchbanks received numerous honors, including the William Alonzo Warfield Award from the Association of Former Interns and Residents of the Freedmen's Hospital. Accruing 1,900 flying hours in prop and jet aircraft, he collected medical data and published articles for military manuals and research publications. He focused on human reactions to speed, noise, and altitude during jet flight. In 1971 Marchbanks addressed the aerospace medicine section at the National Medical Association convention and presented an autobiographical account titled "The Black Physician and the USAF," which was later published in the *Journal of the National Medical Association* (64 [1972]: 73–74).

Marchbanks died in Hartford, Connecticut. He was buried with full military honors at Arlington National Cemetery. His widow and two daughters requested that memorials in his honor be donated to the Tuskegee Airmen Scholarship Fund.

• Articles on Marchbanks include "Col. Vance Marchbanks Slated for Medic Award," *Jet*, 4 May 1961, p. 27, and "Space Doctor for the Astronauts," *Ebony*, Apr. 1962, pp. 35–36, 38–40, 42. See also Herbert M. Morais, *The History of the Afro-American in Medicine* (1976).

ELIZABETH D. SCHAFER

MARCIANO, Rocky (1 Sept. 1923–31 Aug. 1969), heavyweight boxing champion, was born Rocco Francis Marchegiano in Brockton, Massachusetts, the son of Pierino Marchegiano, a shoe-factory worker, and Pasqualena Picciuto. He was considered the roughest kid in the neighborhood, although he was not overly pugnacious. A star athlete who hoped to become a major league baseball catcher, he dropped out of school at age sixteen when the baseball coach barred him from playing on a church team. Marciano then became a manual laborer while playing baseball on local semiprofessional teams. He was drafted into the U.S. Army in 1943 and was honorably discharged in 1946. Marciano kept his baseball dream alive until the spring of 1947, when a tryout with a Chicago Cubs minor league affiliate revealed that he lacked foot speed and a strong throwing arm.

Marciano had begun boxing competitively while in the army, mainly to avoid KP duty. He trained under Gene Caggiano, a local boxing promoter, and they signed an agreement early in 1948 stipulating that Marciano would retain Caggiano as his manager if he turned professional. Once Marciano became a professional boxer, however, he had nothing to do with Caggiano, who then sued Marciano. On 3 November 1950 the Plymouth County Court ruled that their contractual agreement was still valid, which would have entitled Caggiano to one-third of Marciano's earnings. However, on 16 July 1951 the state supreme court reversed the judgment.

Marciano had had one professional fight in 1947, while still an amateur, under the pseudonym Rocky Mack and earned $35 for a three-round knockout. In 1948 Rocky participated in the Golden Gloves and advanced to the All-East championship tournament. He had aspirations to box in the Olympics, but he broke a thumb in winning a New England AAU (Amateur Athletic Union) tournament that served as a trial for the Olympics. He then decided to turn professional and gave up his job as a digger for the gas company. Experts considered Marciano too old, too short, and too light, at 5'10" and 190 pounds, to become a successful heavyweight prizefighter.

Later in 1948 Marciano auditioned in New York with fight manager Al Weill and trainer Charley Goldman. They did not consider Marciano ready to be a top contender, but they liked his heart and his strong punch. Goldman found him a defenseless, upright, wild puncher with poor balance; he kept his legs too far apart, overstrode when punching, could not throw combinations, and relied too much on his powerful right fist. Goldman corrected Marciano's poor foot-work by tying his laces together, and he taught him how to fight from a crouch, slip punches, and utilize his left hand. Marciano was extremely well trained and took care of his diet. When working out with Goldman in New York he walked four miles just to get to the gymnasium. He was sent home to Brockton to hone his craft while he worked as a highway laborer. There he improved his stamina by running—often more than seven miles a day—and pounding the heavy bag to de-velop his power, avoiding the speedbag because of awkwardness. Marciano originally followed this regi-men with an hour of weightlifting; fearful of becoming muscle bound, however, he stopped lifting and swam laps instead.

Weill's stepson Marty became Marciano's manager of record, although his father was the "undercover manager." Weill was then the matchmaker for the In-ternational Boxing Club, and thus holding both posi-tions would have been a conflict of interest. Weill would become Marciano's official manager only in 1952, after he quit the IBC. Rocky's first professional bout under his own name came on 12 July 1948 in Providence, Rhode Island, for which he earned $40 for four rounds. Marciano mostly fought in Provi-dence, where he eventually had twenty-eight matches. His first big break came on 2 December 1949 when he won a second-round knockout over Pat Richards in his first semifinal bout (ten rounds) at Madison Square Garden.

Marciano became a top contender following his sixth-round knockout of Rex Layne at Madison Square Garden on 12 July 1951. His physical style in a very rough bout made him a popular favorite, and the crowd cheered him for twenty minutes after the match. However, Marciano's heavyweight title aspira-tions were dashed when the number-one contender, Joe Walcott, won the heavyweight title from Ezzard Charles. With a Charles-Walcott rematch scheduled, Marciano was matched against former champion Joe Louis, who was making a comeback in order to pay off tax debts. Weill opposed the bout, but Goldman be-lieved Marciano was ready to take on the aging Louis, who was a slight favorite. The fight took place on 26 October, with Louis receiving 45 percent of the purse and Marciano only 15 percent. Marciano won with an eight-round knockout, as youth, power, stamina, and hunger carried the day over experience and reach. With his victory over Louis, Marciano earned a title shot against Walcott, who at age thirty-eight was the oldest champion in boxing history to that time. In preparation for the bout, Marciano tuned up by de-feating light heavyweight contender Kid Matthews on 28 July 1952 at Yankee Stadium in New York City; the fight drew a crowd of 31,188 and earned Marciano $50,000.

The Marciano-Walcott championship match took place in Philadelphia on 23 September 1952, with Walcott a 3–1 favorite to win. The fight was attended by more than 40,000 spectators, who paid over $500,000. In addition, the bout was neither on home television nor on radio, but it was televised into fifty theaters in thirty cities, earning a profit of $125,000. The fight began poorly for Marciano, as he was knocked to the canvas for the first time in his career during the first round. In the sixth round the fighters' heads collided, cutting Marciano and blurring his vi-sion; he later claimed that Walcott's manager had rubbed ointment on the champion's gloves. By the thirteenth round Marciano was well behind in points, but he then knocked out Walcott with a short right. Experts have considered this Marciano's defining mo-ment. Having made a total of $100,000 from the bout, Marciano fought in a rematch with Walcott on 15 May 1953 in Chicago Stadium. This time Marciano scored a knockout after just 145 seconds of the first round, earning $166,000 while Walcott earned $250,000. Marciano had trained extraordinarily hard for this de-fense, sparring a remarkable 225 rounds. Such train-ing was not unusual for Marciano; he typically sparred 40 percent more than the average for a title bout.

On 17 June 1954 Marciano defended his title against the aged former champion Ezzard Charles before 47,585 at Yankee Stadium. Charles put forth a terrific performance, but he wearied after the fifth round and lost a split decision. A rematch on 17 September 1954 drew more than 34,000 to Yankee Stadium and gener-ated a $350,000 gate and $650,000 from ancillary rights. In the rematch Charles completely split Marci-ano's left nostril in the sixth round, and the doctors considered halting the bout. Marciano responded to the crisis by knocking out Charles in the eighth round. He earned a combined $450,000 for these two fights.

Marciano's final defense came on 20 September 1955 against light heavyweight champion Archie Moore. The fight brought a crowd of 61,574 to Yankee Stadium, with hundreds of thousands attending closed circuit television theaters. The fight grossed $2,248,117, then the second largest gate in boxing his-tory. Marciano was dropped to the canvas in the sec-ond round, but he survived to knock out Moore in the ninth round. According to Moore, "Marciano is far and away the strongest man I've ever encountered in almost twenty years of fighting." For this fight Marci-ano earned his largest purse of $468,374.

Marciano retired from boxing on 28 April 1956. He had lost his drive, had saved much of the $2 million earned from fights and personal appearances, and did not trust Al Weill, whose contract called for Weill to receive one-half of Marciano's earnings both in and out of the ring. Marciano had long felt that Weill was cheating him. He had also heard that Weill had scalped tickets worth thousands of dollars, without in-volving Marciano, and that Weill had skimmed $10,000 from the promotional costs of Marciano's title defense against Tom Cockrell on 16 May 1955.

Marciano enjoyed life in the fast lane ("If you want to live a full life then live dangerously"), disliked rou-tine, and was fascinated by the mobsters with whom he socialized and did business, such as Vito Genovese. He was a great hero to Italian Americans. Friends and acquaintances customarily gave him spending money, bought him dinner, and paid for his clothes. Parsimonious, Marciano never picked up checks. However, he was a poor businessman who made several bad decisions, including purchasing Florida swampland, investing substantial sums with loan sharks, and lending money at usurious rates on the street. Such transactions were never written down, and the death of a Cleveland loan shark reputedly cost him $100,000. He reputedly had over $2 million loaned out or stashed away in secret locations that have never been found.

In 1950 Marciano married Barbara Cousins, with whom he had one child and adopted a second. However, their relationship was strained by incompatibility. She was a homebody, while Marciano was constantly traveling, looking for business deals, making personal appearances (he was even paid for stepping into the ring when he attended boxing matches), and meeting beautiful women. He always stayed at friends' homes or hotels that offered him complimentary rooms.

In the mid-1960s Marciano turned down $2 million to fight Muhammad Ali (then known as Cassius Clay) when he could not get into fighting shape. In 1969 he participated in a computer tournament involving former champions that grossed about $1.7 million. For this endeavor he lost nearly 50 pounds, wore a toupee, and sparred eight hours of one-minute rounds with Ali to produce a marketable conclusion. Seven different endings were prepared, with the computer giving the victory to Marciano.

Marciano's professional record was 49–0. He was the victor in all six of his title defenses, and at the end of the twentieth century he was still the only undefeated heavyweight champion in boxing history. He left with a reputation for invincibility and for being particularly dangerous when hurt. A bruising fighter, Marciano was rated as the greatest slugger of all time with an 88 percent knockout record. A member of the International Boxing Hall of Fame, he was Fighter of the Year in 1952 and 1954. Marciano died when a private plane in which he was a passenger crashed near Newton, Iowa.

• For biographical information on Marciano, see Everett M. Skehan, *Rocky Marciano: Biography of a First Son* (1977), and Bill Libby, *Rocky: The Story of a Champion* (1971). His career was carefully followed by *Ring* magazine, which published the following articles: "Marciano Has Problems," Jan. 1953; Ted Carroll, "Food for Thought," Aug. 1953; Dan Daniel, "Power vs. Cleverness," Oct. 1953; and Lester Bromberg, "Crafty Seconds," Nov. 1954. For a controversial examination of Marciano's personal life, see William Nack, "The Rock," *Sports Illustrated*, 23 Aug. 1993, pp. 52–56ff. An obituary is in the *New York Times*, 1 Sept. 1969.

STEVEN A. RIESS

MARCOSSON, Isaac Frederick (13 Sept. 1876–14 Mar. 1961), journalist and author, was born in Louisville, Kentucky, the son of Louis Marcosson and Helen (maiden name unknown). When his father, a traveling salesman, became ill in a distant city, Marcosson voluntarily left high school for a job in a wholesale liquor firm; only sixteen years old, he contributed his five-dollar weekly salary to the family's support. However, his ambition was to become a full-time newspaperman, and soon he did freelance writing for the *Louisville Times*.

At age eighteen Marcosson became a cub reporter on the *Times*, covering local events ranging from fires to prizefights to hotel arrivals; this was his first opportunity to interview prominent people. Eventually, as assistant city editor and literary editor, he reported on political events and wrote book reviews, the latter gaining him the attention of authors and publishers. After nine years at the *Times* (1894–1903), in a position with no financial future, Marcosson left for New York City.

Through his friendship with Kentucky novelist James Lane Allen, Marcosson had earlier met Walter Hines Page, editor of the *World's Work*, a monthly publication of Doubleday, Page & Company; in August 1903 Page agreed to give him a two months' trial at the magazine. Marcosson soon became an associate editor, contributing as many as three articles per issue (some under pseudonyms), working with prospective authors, and handling book advertising. One of his proudest achievements was getting Mark Twain to submit material for an article featuring financier and Standard Oil executive Henry H. Rogers. During this period, Marcosson married his Louisville sweetheart, Grace Griffiths, who was in the last stages of tuberculosis; she died a week later.

In 1907 he abruptly left the *World's Work* after "an amiable difference" with Page over salary. He had already met George Horace Lorimer, editor of the *Saturday Evening Post*, while doing publicity for the Doubleday firm. From 1907 to 1910 Marcosson was financial editor of the *Post*, a position where his lack of fiscal knowledge was an asset, according to Lorimer, who wanted him to write for the average reader, using simple terms. To get the material for "Your Savings," a popular series of 124 unsigned articles, Marcosson made friends on Wall Street; early columns became the basis for his first book, *How to Invest Your Savings* (1907). Later he interviewed eight of the giants of industry for another series, "Wall-Street Men." At the same time, he wrote fillers for the *Post* and contributed monthly financial columns to *Pearson's* and *Success*, both under pseudonyms.

After a stint as associate editor of *Munsey's*, Marcosson returned to the *Post*, this time as a foreign correspondent. In 1915 he sailed for wartime England and soon was traveling steadily between America and Europe. British politicians David Lloyd George and Winston Churchill were among the first leaders he interviewed; later, he met U.S. General John Pershing, and went to France for talks with both Marshal Philippe Petain and Marshal Ferdinand Foch, supreme commander of the French forces. After a month with the British Army Service Corps, Marcosson returned to New York City, where he wrote a series of articles titled "The Business of War." Between 1917 and 1919, he published six books on war and wartime leaders. In his *Adventures in Interviewing* (1919), he explained, "I have always lived in an atmosphere of timeliness. I believe in making a record of people and events while they are alive and when the interest in them is keenest."

In the years following World War I, Marcosson traveled to Africa, South America, and the Orient, in addition to annual trips to Europe to continue interviewing heads of state and other world leaders for the *Post*. Between 1925 and 1928 alone, sixty-eight of his articles appeared in that weekly. He was especially proud of his meetings with Jan Smuts of South Africa, Leon Trotsky, Benito Mussolini, Kemal Ataturk, Emperor Hirohito, and Sun Yat-sen. He also conversed with kings, including Albert of Belgium and Gustav V of Sweden. Among his literary friends were James M. Barrie, Ellen Glasgow, O. Henry, H. G. Wells, and Mark Twain. And he claimed to have known every American president from William McKinley to Franklin D. Roosevelt. His extensive American lecture tours, under the aegis of the Pond lecture agency, were possible only because of his earlier, successful efforts to cure his stammering.

By the late 1920s "Marcosson's stories began to be more and more superficial," according to Lorimer's biographer, though the editor refused to drop him from the staff. Nevertheless, "Marcosson's kind of interviewing was gone forever." By the mid-1930s the man of "reportorial genius" whom Arthur Krock also called "the fairest-haired of all the protégés of George Horace Lorimer" began publishing elsewhere, most notably the *American Magazine*. After he became the official biographer of a murdered literary friend, publishing *David Graham Phillips and His Times* in 1932, he reportedly inherited $729,286 from Phillips's sister, Carolyn Frevert.

In 1931 Marcosson married Frances Barberey; they had no children. She died of cancer in 1936, soon after he left the *Post*. Thereafter, he concentrated on learning about the disease and its treatment, writing articles that appeared in such popular magazines as the *Reader's Digest*. He became director of public relations at New York City's Memorial Hospital; through this volunteer activity he met his third wife, Ellen Petts, who assisted him in writing corporate biographies. He married Petts in 1942; they had no children. Both his biography of Louisville editor Henry Watterson and his final volume, *Before I Forget*, are dedicated to her. Marcosson died in New York City.

His writings suffer from that "timeliness" which once gave them a sense of immediacy. They have a tone of self-congratulation for his ability to go through normally closed doors to meet the great men of the century; this hobnobbing with celebrities occasionally led him to believe that he influenced the course of history. Nevertheless, Marcosson attained his goal of making "the great of this earth become his journalistic quarry," and with colorful writing he made them come alive.

• Marcosson's papers (1899–1960) are at the University of Wyoming's American Heritage Center. They include correspondence, reviews of Marcosson's twenty-three books, *Post* articles, photographs, and book manuscripts. His three autobiographical volumes are *Adventures in Interviewing* (1919), *Turbulent Years* (1938), and *Before I Forget* (1959). See also his personal account, "Everything Is Possible," in the September 1921 issue of the *American Magazine*. Because Marcosson prided himself on never taking notes and apparently kept no personal diaries, the reader should be alert to numerous textual discrepancies and conflicting statements of fact, especially where the same incident appears in different volumes, written over a forty-year period. The Mark Twain episode is an example of these textual variations. See Mary Boewe, "Mark Twain Anonymous," *Kentucky Review* 9 (1989): 42–55. Marcosson's role at the *Post* is described in John Tebbel, *George Horace Lorimer and the Saturday Evening Post* (1948). An obituary is in the *New York Times*, 15 Mar. 1961.

MARY BOEWE

MARCOTTE, Léon Alexandre (15 May 1824–25 Jan. 1887), cabinetmaker and interior decorator, was born in Valognes, Manche, France, the son of Pierre Alexandre Marcotte, a lawyer, and Mélanie Julie Ringuet. He was educated as an architect at the École des Beaux-Arts in Paris and trained in the studio of Henri Labrouste, who designed the Bibliotheque Ste. Geneviève in Paris. Marcotte had been introduced into the world of cabinetmaking by the time that his sister married the Parisian *ébéniste* (cabinetmaker) Auguste-Émile Ringuet-LePrince, who was heir to a dynasty of French *ébénistes*. The house of Ringuet-LePrince suffered greatly as a result of the revolution of 1848, prompting Ringuet-LePrince to turn his attention to New York, where he had had a number of clients since the early 1840s. Ringuet-LePrince sent his brother-in-law Marcotte to New York, while Ringuet-LePrince remained in Paris, and a third man traveled between Europe and the United States to fill orders. The strong tie to Paris assured their New York clients of the very latest fashions and contributed to the early success of the firm there. In general, the furniture itself was made in New York, while decorative elements, including lighting fixtures, textiles, and wallpapers, were imported from France. The business, originally named Maison Ringuet-LePrince (1840–1849) and then Ringuet-LePrince and L. Marcotte (1849–1860), grew steadily. It gained exposure from its participation in the Great Exhibition at the Crystal Palace in London in 1851 and in the world's fair held at the newly constructed Crystal Palace in New York in 1853.

In the mid-1850s Marcotte was described as a smart, reliable man with much artistic taste; the company was worth $50,000 and employed 150 second-class hands (the second tier of skilled workers). During this time he furnished "Armsmear," the home of the gun magnate Samuel Colt in Hartford, Connecticut. Marcotte decorated the house in a variety of styles, choosing the Louis XV style for the parlor, with a more somber Renaissance Revival for the library and dining room. All of the furniture installed at Armsmear was custom-made.

In May 1859 Marcotte married Louise Marie de Rudder; they had three children. Marcotte's second extensively documented commission was the home of Ogden Codman, Sr., known as "The Grange," in Lincoln, Massachusetts. The house, now part of the Society for the Preservation of New England Antiquities, still retains its furnishings. When it was refurbished in 1862, the furniture was bought from stock in Marcotte's showroom in New York. Indeed, Marcotte never visited The Grange, and the decoration was supervised by Codman's brother-in-law, the architect John Hubbard Sturgis. A significant portion of Marcotte's business probably involved this kind of basic stock furniture, which could be upholstered to specifications and ornamented with additional carving or inlay and gilt-bronze mounts, which were available in a range of differing quality.

When Ringuet-LePrince retired in 1860, the firm's name was changed once again, to L. Marcotte & Co. (1860–1918); it was valued at more than $100,000. Its furniture and decorations were made according to most of the successive revival styles of the second half of the nineteenth century, although Marcotte himself is best known for his work in the Louis XVI style. His architectural training is evident in his furniture in general, which is marked by fine proportions. Ernest Hagan, a contemporary cabinetmaker in New York, wrote that L. Marcotte & Co. did "the very best work."

Marcotte counted many socially prominent New Yorkers among his clients, including John Taylor Johnston, the first president of the Metropolitan Museum of Art, whose Louis XVI–style ebonized and gilt-bronze mounted furniture has been in more recent times on exhibit in the museum's galleries. Henry Marquand, the second president of the Metropolitan Museum, also patronized Marcotte; a florid Rococo Revival center table made for Marquand's Madison Avenue house is in the collection of the Brooklyn Museum.

By 1874 L. Marcotte & Co. was doing $200,000 worth of business. The Philadelphia Centennial of 1876 marked a high point in Marcotte's career; he exhibited a library and a dining room that were hailed as "the best effort of [their] kind in the American Department." Two years later, in 1878, Marcotte won a gold medal for a cabinet at the Universal Exposition of Paris. The cabinet received a glowing review in the English publication *Art Journal*: "It is a work of very great merit and beauty. . . . Although a production of the new world, it competes with the very best work of the old" ([1878]: 144).

That Marcotte could compete not only with the long-established *ébénistes* of Paris but also his stiffest competition in the United States is proved by the commission he received in 1879 to decorate the house of Mr. and Mrs. Cyrus Hall McCormick of Chicago. Losing out to Marcotte were the prestigious firms Herter Brothers and Pottier and Stymus. Marcotte's mastery of contemporary styles was shown in the library and music room, both of which were decorated in the aesthetic style. The last documented Marcotte interiors are those for the Vanderbilt family in New York

City. One of the most exotic was the Moorish billiard room for the William K. Vanderbilt house at Fifth Avenue and Fifty-second Street, completed in 1883. Marcotte also received impressive commissions from William H. Vanderbilt for the decoration of the houses that he built for his daughters: Mrs. Margaret Vanderbilt Shepard and Mrs. Emily Vanderbilt Sloane, whose homes adjoined his residence at 640 Fifth Avenue.

Marcotte's reputation and patronage by the wealthy elite of New York lasted to the end of his life. Even though in the early 1880s he returned to Paris to live, he made frequent trips back to the United States. He died in Paris. The business continued under the name L. Marcotte & Co. until 1911 in Paris and until 1918 in New York. It still was awarded prestigious commissions, such as the one for furniture to be installed in the White House when McKim, Mead & White renovated the presidential residence at the turn of the century, yet after Marcotte's death the firm, lacking his artistic and business leadership, was not the same. According to an obituary published in the *American Carpet and Upholstery Journal* (Mar. 1887): "Marcotte . . . was without a doubt a master mind on interior decoration; twenty-five years ago he came here from France and immediately became the fashion. . . . He was a charming conversationalist, a man of easy manners and of high artistic sense."

• Collections that include Marcotte's correspondence or bills of the firm include the Ogden Codman Papers, Society for the Preservation of New England Antiquities, Boston; the James Colles Papers at the New York Public Library; the Samuel Colt Papers, Connecticut Historical Society; the R. G. Dun Ledgers, Baker Library, Harvard University; and the Cyrus Hall McCormick Collection at the Wisconsin Historical Society. See also Nina Gray, "Léon Marcotte: Cabinetmaker and Interior Decorator," *American Furniture* (1994): 49–72; Phillip Johnston, "Dialogues between Designer and Client, Furnishings Proposed by Léon Marcotte to Samuel Colt in the 1850's," *Winterthur Portfolio* 19, no. 4 (Winter 1984): 257–75; Marilynn Johnson et al., *Nineteenth Century America, Furniture and Other Decorative Arts* (1970); and Richard Nylander, "Documenting the Interior of Codman House: The Last Two Generations," *Old Time New England* 71, no. 258 (1981): 84ff. An obituary is in the *New York Daily Tribune*, 26 Jan. 1887.

NINA GRAY

MARCUS, Bernard Kent (1890?–16 July 1954), banker, was born in New York City, the son of Joseph S. Marcus, the founder of the Bank of United States, and Celia Cowen. Marcus graduated from Columbia University with a B.A. in 1911. He married Libby Phillips (marriage date unknown) and had three children.

Joseph Marcus founded the Bank of United States in 1913 with a capital of $100,000. The bank originally served a predominantly Jewish clientele of household savings depositors on the Lower East Side of Manhattan and had a reputation of conservative management. When Joseph Marcus died in July 1927, the bank had accumulated capital of $5 million and held deposits of just under $100 million. Bernard Marcus worked in the bank from its beginning, starting as a cashier and becoming a vice president in 1919. He became president of the bank after his father's death.

Marcus and his close associate Saul Singer acted rapidly to expand the bank through a series of incorporations and mergers. They also invested extensively in real estate developments. Marcus and Singer first incorporated the City Financial Corporation in September 1927; in June 1928 they incorporated the Consolidated Indemnity and Insurance Company. In December 1928 they formed their most noted affiliate, the Bankus Corporation. As in earlier affiliates, many of the officers and directors of the Bank of United States served in the same capacities in the Bankus Corporation. Their last major acquisition was the Municipal Bank and Trust Company and its affiliate, the Municipal Financial Corporation, in May 1929. To Marcus the Municipal Bank was an ideal target. It was the second largest bank in Brooklyn, a territory into which Marcus was eager to expand his banking empire. With this merger the Bank of United States directly and indirectly controlled fifty-seven branches, deposits worth $230 million, and total resources of more than $314 million.

Marcus and Singer engineered the merger of Municipal Bank and Trust Company by swapping Municipal Bank stock for Bankus–Bank of United States stock at a below-market price for Bankus stock. While legal, such a swap was financially risky. In a profit-taking move, former Municipal Bank shareholders began selling their Bankus–Bank of United States stock, driving down its price. To support the price of Bankus stock, Marcus and Singer began purchasing shares using funds from a syndicate of the directors of the Bank of United States, a cartel originally created in 1927 to trade City Financial Corporation stock.

Despite the efforts by Marcus and Singer to shore up the price of Bankus–Bank of United States stock, they were unable to buy enough shares to stem the fall. They next offered depositors of the Bank of United States the chance to buy shares and verbally promised to repurchase the shares if the price fell below $198. The price continued to fall, but Marcus and Singer failed to keep the repurchase agreement. Marcus and Singer finally decided that the bank's affiliates should purchase the stock with loans made by the bank itself.

The stock market crash of October 1929 drove down the price of Bank of United States stock farther, placing in default the loans made to the affiliates. New York State Banking Department examiners concluded in the summer of 1930 that the bank was nearing insolvency. The New York superintendent of banks, Joseph Broderick, decided that the only way it could be saved was to merge it with larger, healthier institutions. Unfortunately, reliable merger partners could not be located, owing in part to the complicated and suspicious maneuverings of Marcus and Singer to prop up the bank. On 10 December, while the New York Clearinghouse Association and the Federal Reserve Bank considered options to save the bank without a merger, substantial runs began at the bank's branches. The New York superintendent of banks took control of the bank's assets that evening, and the Bank of United States was declared insolvent on 11 December 1930.

Marcus and Singer were convicted in May 1931 of misapplication of an affiliate's funds and bank fraud involving phony accounting practices. They were sent to prison in March 1933 to serve terms of twenty-three months. Marcus returned to the business world in February 1935 as president and treasurer of General Capital Corporation; he filed for personal bankruptcy in 1937. Two years later he became vice president of Continental Factors Corporation. He later became president of Frackville Manufacturing Company, a maker of men's pajamas. According to Marcus's family, Governor Herbert Lehman pardoned Marcus six years after his release from prison. Marcus died at a resort near Hunter, New York.

Because the Bank of United States was the only major bank to fail in New York during the first wave of bank failures early in the depression, economists have devoted an unusual amount of research to its failure. Some economists have argued that the bank was basically solvent, but inaction on the part of the Federal Reserve and the New York Clearinghouse to provide liquidity was responsible for the failure. The inaction purportedly stemmed from anti-Semitism on the part of other Wall Street bankers who secretly wished that the bank would fail. Other experts have argued more recently that the failure was the result of imprudent and fraudulent banking practices. Having made an unwise investment in the Municipal Bank, Marcus then made a series of increasingly risky insider loans to keep his bank afloat rather than cutting his losses early. The evidence clearly is in favor of the mismanagement and fraud explanations, although Marcus appears to have been imprudent and too eager to expand his bank rather than intentionally criminal.

• On Marcus's life and career see Daniel Frederick Powell, *Depositors Paid in Full* (1931), and the *New York Times*, 26 Sept. 1937. M. R. Werner, *Little Napoleons and Dummy Directors* (1933), provides a detailed account of Marcus's and Singer's attempts to save the bank. Milton Friedman and Anna Schwartz, *A Monetary History of the United States, 1867–1960* (1963), argue that Federal Reserve inaction was responsible for the bank's failure. Two studies contend that mismanagement was responsible: Peter Temin, *Did Monetary Forces Cause the Great Depression?* (1976), and Paul Trescott, "The Failure of the Bank of United States, 1930: A Rejoinder," *Journal of Money, Credit, and Banking* (Aug. 1992): 384–99. Peter Garber and Steven Weisbrod, *The Economics of Banking, Liquidity, and Money* (1992), provide a concise economic analysis of the bank's failure. An obituary is in the *New York Times*, 18 July 1954.

JON R. MOEN

MARCUSE, Herbert (19 July 1898–29 July 1979), author, professor, and political activist, was born in Berlin, Germany, the son of Carl Marcuse, a prosperous merchant, and Gertrud Kreslawsky, the daughter of a wealthy German factory owner. Marcuse studied at the Mommsen Gymnasium in Berlin before World War I and served with the German army in the war. Transferred to Berlin early in 1918, he observed and sympathized with the German revolution that drove Kaiser Wilhelm II out of Germany and established a Social Democratic government.

After demobilization, Marcuse went to Freiburg to pursue his studies and received a Ph.D. in literature in 1922 for a dissertation on the German artist-novel ("Der deutsche Künstlerroman"). In 1923 he married Sophie Wertheim, with whom he was to have one child, and for a time he worked in Berlin as a bookseller. But by 1928 he was back in Freiburg, enrolled as a student of Martin Heidegger, whose influence in German philosophical circles was on the rise.

Marcuse soon began drawing together strands from different lines of thought, resulting in a type of Marxism colored by existential and phenomenological themes, which anticipated the work of the main exponents of existentialism and phenomenology of the post–World War II era. According to Marcuse, Marxist dogma regarding economics and the political sphere had led to a theory-laden paralysis that could only be alleviated by relating Marxism to contemporary cultural and social phenomena and to the existential needs of individuals. While socialist principles were meant to free society from the grip of capitalist exploitation, they also ought—in Marcuse's view—to liberate individuals from the narrow conventions of bourgeois life.

When Marcuse reviewed an edition of Karl Marx's previously unpublished "1844 Manuscripts" in 1932, he was one of the first to stress the importance of Marx's early philosophical perspectives on labor, human nature, and alienation, which were in line with Marcuse's own thinking at the time. For his *Habilitationsschrift* (qualifying publication for university employment), Marcuse turned to Hegel, in whom there was increasing interest among European philosophers, and wrote a study of the Hegelian categories of life and history, *Hegels Ontologie und die Grundlegung einer Theorie der Geschichtlichkeit* (1932; published in English as *Hegel's Ontology and the Theory of Historicity*).

In 1933, the year that Adolf Hitler came to power in Germany, the Institut für Sozialforschung (Institute for Social Research) in Frankfurt-am-Main offered Marcuse an appointment. The institute's aim was to develop a model of "critical theory" to counter more descriptive, empirical "traditional theory." A haven for interdisciplinary studies, the institute was well suited to Marcuse's outlook and interests, and he felt at home there. Several of his colleagues, including Max Horkheimer, Theodor W. Adorno, Leo Lowenthal, and Franz Neumann, were to remain lifelong friends of his.

Of Jewish birth and openly leftist in his politics, Marcuse was compelled to flee Nazism; his move to the United States in 1934 proved to be permanent. To his good fortune, however, Columbia University was able to house the Institute for Social Research, thus allowing Marcuse and other émigrés to sustain their intellectual projects begun in Europe. With *Reason and Revolution* (1941), the first significant treatise of his to appear in English, Marcuse carried forward his study of Hegel and Marx, demonstrating affinities in their thinking, and challenged the notion that Hegel's philosophy of state provided a rationale for German fascism, seeing it instead as part of a liberal constitutional tradition

Marcuse, a naturalized citizen since 1940, joined the U.S. Office of War Information as a senior analyst in the Bureau of Intelligence in December 1942 and prepared a report on ways that the mass media of the Allied countries could present images of German fascism. In March 1943 Marcuse transferred to the Office of Strategic Services (OSS), working until the end of the war in the Research and Analysis division of the Central European Branch. He and his colleagues wrote reports attempting to identify Nazi and anti-Nazi groups and individuals in Germany and drafted a civil affairs handbook that dealt with denazification. In September 1945, after the dissolution of the OSS, he moved to the State Department and was head of the Central European bureau until 1951, when he left government service following the death of his wife.

Marcuse received a Rockefeller Foundation grant to study Soviet Marxism, lecturing on the topic at Columbia in 1952–1953 and at Harvard in 1954–1955. Meanwhile, he undertook an intensive study of Sigmund Freud's writings, which led him to propose a philosophical nexus where Marxist and Freudian theories seemed to him to intersect logically. Using Freud's categories to provide a critique of bourgeois society, Marcuse attempted to adumbrate in *Eros and Civilization* (1955) a society in which repressive tendencies are held in check and the possibilities for self-fulfillment are enhanced. Critics generally thought well of the book, and it was to become an intellectual touchstone of sorts in the latter half of the 1960s, when the revolt against establishment culture was animated by utopian visions of individual liberation.

In 1955 Marcuse married Inge Werner, the widow of his friend Franz Neumann, who had died in an automobile crash the year before; this second marriage did not result in children. Marcuse's appointment to a faculty position at Brandeis University in 1958 coincided with the publication of his *Soviet Marxism*, which was notable for being a leftist's sharply critical examination of the USSR. Although he did not consider the Soviet Union incapable of reform, he saw much in the country's bureaucracy and culture that was at odds with his conception of Marxist theory. His view of how the USSR might evolve was borne out by the introduction of structural and organizational changes (*perestroika*) that caused Soviet Marxism to wither thirty years later.

In *One-Dimensional Man* (1964), perhaps his most important work, Marcuse turned his attention to the "ideology of advanced industrial society," in both its capitalist and socialist manifestations. As new forms of social control were being developed, so Marcuse argued, a "society without opposition" was emerging. Against the conformism engendered by mass media, ceaseless commercialization, and the constantly stimulated addiction to consumer goods of little intrinsic value, Marcuse counterpoised critical and dialectical thinking that could suggest a freer and happier form of culture and society. In *One-Dimensional Man* he also analyzed the integration of the industrial working class into capitalist society and new forms of capitalist stabilization, thus questioning the Marxist postulates for the revolutionary proletariat and the inevitability of capitalist crisis. Marcuse perceived in the struggles of the U.S. civil rights movement an exemplary form of oppositional thought and struggle. In response to all modes of repression and domination, he advocated a "great refusal." While U.S. involvement in the Vietnam War during the mid-1960s was radicalizing many younger people and abetting the growth of the counterculture, *One-Dimensional Man* gave expression to widespread feelings of social alienation and cultural discontent as well as to desires for a more liberated society and culture.

Having provoked fierce intellectual controversy over his views, Marcuse was forced to depart from Brandeis in 1965. He spent the remainder of his teaching career on the faculty of the University of California at San Diego. In a series of influential books and articles, including "Repressive Tolerance" (1965), *An Essay on Liberation* (1969), *Five Lectures: Psychoanalysis, Politics, and Utopia* (1970), and *Counterrevolution and Revolt* (1972), Marcuse contributed to the ideological underpinnings of New Left politics and expanded his critique of capitalist societies. A charismatic teacher, he nurtured students who rose in the academic world and further disseminated his ideas. During this time Marcuse became an international icon—in the words of *Time* magazine, the "guru of the New Left"—although the notoriety that he gained was ironic in light of his scathing assessment of the mass media as a corrosive agent of uncritical thought.

Following the decline of the New Left in the mid-1970s, Marcuse concerned himself to a large extent with questions of aesthetics. In *The Aesthetic Dimension* (1979), the last of his books, he argued for an "authentic art" that has the power to unshackle thought and feeling. He criticized, however, both Marxist aesthetics that celebrated "proletarian culture" and the "anti-art" movement of the time, which renounced the exigencies of aesthetic form. Within bourgeois art, Marcuse saw an admirable critical tradition that used aesthetic form to expose what was false or destructive in society and to envision a less repressed and repressive existence. He believed that the "aesthetic dimension" was a crucial component of an emancipated life.

Marcuse's second wife died in 1974, and two years later he married Erica Sherover. She was with him on his last trip to Germany when he died in Starnberg.

Primarily a philosopher, rather than an analyst of empirical data, Marcuse possessed a highly developed dialectical imagination that exemplified the kind of critical thinking espoused at the Institute for Social Research. Like others in the Frankfurt school of cultural criticism, such as Adorno and Horkheimer, he tended to conceptualize the world from the perspective of the social sciences; indeed, hostile critics denounced Marcuse's writing style as a morass of dense, obscure sociologese. Nonetheless, he was often prescient in his ruminations on social and cultural trends, and he provided a philosophical language for identifying the dynamics of both repression and emancipation. More than any other thinker in the tradition of critical theory, Marcuse had a direct impact on American culture. To the youth-oriented New Left during the 1960s, he was the exceptional elder whose views could be taken seriously; to political and social conservatives, he was anathema. Although he vanished from the popular American scene, Marcuse left an intellectual legacy of lasting import, having articulated the cultural pathologies of a "society without opposition."

• The Stadtsbibliothek in Frankfurt, Germany, holds Marcuse's papers. For analyses of his thought and influence, see Paul A. Robinson, *The Freudian Left: Wilhelm Reich, Geza Roheim, Herbert Marcuse* (1969; repr. 1990); Paul Breines, ed., *Critical Interpretations: New Left Perspectives on Herbert Marcuse* (1970); Vincent Geoghegan, *Reason and Eros: The Social Theory of Herbert Marcuse* (1981); Barry Katz, *Herbert Marcuse and the Art of Liberation: An Intellectual Biography* (1982); Douglas Kellner, *Herbert Marcuse and the Crisis of Marxism* (1984); and John Bokina and Timothy J. Lukes, eds., *Marcuse: From the New Left to the Next Left* (1994). The *New York Times* of 31 July 1979 has an obituary.

DOUGLAS KELLNER

MARCY, Henry Orlando (23 June 1837–1 Jan. 1924), physician, was born in Otis, Massachusetts, the son of Smith Marcy, a teacher, and Fanny Gibbs. An alumnus of Wilbraham Academy and of Amherst College, Marcy received his M.D. from Harvard medical school in 1863. That same year he married Sarah G. Wendell of Great Falls, New Hampshire; they had one child.

Marcy served in the Civil War as a medical officer of the Forty-third Massachusetts Volunteers, was medical director of Florida (1864), and under General Sherman's direction, was responsible for cleaning and renovating Charleston, South Carolina (1865). Between 1865 and 1869 he was an assistant in the Harvard medical school. He pursued postgraduate medical and surgical training in Berlin with Rudolf Virchow, in London with Spencer Wells, and in the summer of 1870 in Edinburgh with Joseph Lister, from whom he learned the principles and techniques of antiseptic surgery. By the time he returned to Boston in the autumn of 1870, he had decided to specialize in the diseases of women and soon became an active member of the Gynecological Society of Boston.

Marcy undertook the introduction of antisepsis at Massachusetts General Hospital, but Henry J. Bigelow, one of the ranking surgeons at the hospital, was unwilling to adopt it. Consequently, Marcy attached to his house in Cambridge a private hospital for women, where, for many years after 1880 he and his staff conducted microbiological research as well as practiced medicine and surgery according to Listerian technique.

Although Marcy later wrote that his failed attempt to introduce antisepsis had put him at odds with several members of the medical profession, a December 1883 sketch of Marcy in the *New England Medical Monthly* evaluated him as "an industrious student and systematic worker, . . . representative of the younger, active, progressive, liberal-minded men of his profession in America" (pp. 172–73). He was, for example, active in the Suffolk District Medical Society and the Massachusetts Medical Society, where he labored for the newly reorganized American Medical Association. He was active in the affairs of the AMA as vice president in 1880, a member of several of its committees, and president in 1891–1892. In 1883 he was elected president of the American Academy of Medicine, a society dedicated to the improvement of medical education in America. He lobbied extensively for the creation of a national board of health or of some other cabinet-level body that would foster a national health policy. He was a charter member and later president of the American Medical Editors Association and was a founding member of the American College of Surgeons. As a delegate to the 1881 International Medical Congress in London, he spoke in favor of antisepsis.

Civic affairs engaged Marcy as much as medical affairs. Even though Marcy maintained an office and practice in Boston, his hospital and house were in Cambridge, Massachusetts. He was always proud of his efforts in the planning of the Harvard Bridge, which connects Boston and Cambridge along Massachusetts Avenue; the Charles River Esplanade; and the erection of several buildings of the Massachusetts Institute of Technology on land he had sold to MIT.

In autobiographical memoirs, Marcy asserted that he had been Lister's first American pupil and that "in my enthusiasm I quite forgot that I was the pioneer in America of the new faith of the so-called antiseptic surgery" (*Transactions of the Southern Surgical Association* 33 [1921]: 31). His obituaries and biographical entries usually repeat these claims, but they cannot be accepted at face value. Before Marcy studied with Lister in the summer of 1870, other Americans, such as John Collins Warren in 1869, had visited Lister, and he had instructed them in his technique and had sent them supplies of his antiseptic dressings. Even before Marcy went abroad, articles had been published in American medical journals describing Lister's technique or the use of carbolic acid in surgical dressings. While some of these articles were transcriptions of reports from foreign medical journals, others were original contributions by American physicians or chemists.

If Marcy was not the first to introduce antisepsis into America, he nonetheless was its early and avid advocate. He published widely and often on the topic, conducted microbiological research in support of the underlying germ theory, sponsored the marketing of commercially prepared antiseptic dressings, and sought to extend its principles into wider issues of public health. To Marcy's contemporaries, Listerism was more than a debate over Louis Pasteur's germ theory or the acceptance of a carbolic acid spray; it included the substitution of carbolized animal tendons for the commonly used silk or metal sutures. Lister had found that, even in deep wounds, the body assimilated these tendons with little or no irritation or suppuration. After an extensive search, Marcy announced in the early 1880s that kangaroo (wallaby) tendons were best suited to the surgeon's needs; for many years thereafter, kangaroo tendons were widely used in surgery. At his death, fellow surgeons claimed that this discovery and his improvements in the surgical management of hernia were Marcy's most significant contributions to surgery.

After his first wife's death in 1910, Marcy married Mary E. Smeed of Batavia, New York, in 1912. They had no children. Marcy died at his home in Cambridge.

• If Marcy's personal papers exist, they are yet to be found. He published dozens of articles and books on topics such as antisepsis, germ theory, public health, sanitation, gynecology, and the history of medicine. A fairly complete bibliography of these works is found in the *Index Catalogue of the Surgeon General's Collection*, 1st ser., p. 601, and 2d ser., pp. 130–31. A. Scott Earle, ed., *Surgery in America: From the Colonial Era to the Twentieth Century*, 2d ed. (1983), contains Marcy's article "A New Use of Carbolized Catgut Ligatures" (*Boston Medical and Surgical Journal* 85 [1871]: 315) and a short assessment of his place in the development of American surgery. Obituaries are Frank C. Lewis, "A Tribute to Henry O. Marcy," *Journal of the American Medical Editors Association* 5 (1925): 16–19, and in the *Journal of the American Medical Association* 82 (1924): 226.

THOMAS GARIEPY

MARCY, William Learned (12 Dec. 1786–4 July 1857), governor of New York, secretary of war, and secretary of state, was born in Southbridge, Massachusetts, the son of Jedediah Marcy and Ruth Learned, farmers. He graduated from Brown University in 1808, paying for his education by teaching school. He traveled west to Troy, New York, where he read law and was admitted to the bar in 1811.

An ensign in the New York militia, Marcy was called to duty in the War of 1812; on the eve of his company's departure for Canada he married Dolly Newell, with whom he had three children before her death in 1821. After experiencing two minor skirmishes, he returned to Troy in 1812 to handle administrative duties, such as courts-martial, for the duration of the conflict. Following the war, he rose quickly in the peacetime militia to the rank of adjutant general by 1821. In the latter post he proposed reforms, including better training for officers and the removal of penalties for militiamen unable to afford weapons.

An admirer of Thomas Jefferson since boyhood and an ardent Democratic Republican, Marcy enmeshed himself in politics in heavily Federalist Troy, joining the Tammany Society and writing for the *Northern Budget* in Troy and the *Argus* in nearby Albany. The success of his party nationally enabled him to supplement his meager legal earnings with fees as federal tax assessor and deputy to the U.S. district attorney. In 1816, when Troy became a city, Marcy became its first recorder, performing some judicial and executive functions before his removal by Governor De Witt Clinton in 1818. Marcy was one of the original organizers of the Bucktail faction (later known as the Albany Regency) opposed to Clinton. He wrote a pamphlet in 1819 with Martin Van Buren promoting Rufus King for the U.S. Senate. With the triumph of his faction, Marcy returned as Troy's recorder, serving from 1821 to 1823.

Appointed state comptroller in 1823, Marcy moved permanently to Albany, where in 1824 he married Cornelia Knower, with whom he had three children. Marcy's six years as comptroller demonstrated his executive abilities. Not only did he perform the routine tasks of paying the state's bills and conducting tax sales, but he also invested state money to gain interest for the first time, scrutinized the bills for the Erie Canal to prevent overcharges, and rigorously examined the economic value of proposed internal improvements. Marcy was discussed as a possible candidate for governor in 1828, but Martin Van Buren, who wanted the post, prevailed. Van Buren appointed Marcy to the state supreme court in 1829. In two grueling years Marcy rendered close to 200 opinions. His most politically sensitive task was presiding over a trial of Masons in a special criminal court in western New York in 1830 during the anti-Mason movement. Although the trial resulted in no convictions, the anti-Masons respected Marcy's impartiality.

In 1831 the Democratic majority in the legislature elected Marcy to the U.S. Senate. The bank war and nullification crisis dominated his only session. Marcy served as chair of the Judiciary Committee but, disliking public speaking, seldom joined in debates. On one occasion, however, he defended Van Buren's use of patronage in New York when the latter's appointment as minister to Britain was under consideration, using the long-remembered phrase "to the victor belong the spoils."

In 1832 New York Democrats finally gave Marcy his long-coveted gubernatorial nomination, and he resigned his senate seat upon his election. During his three terms of office (1833–1838) repercussions from Andrew Jackson's veto of the Second Bank of the United States echoed through New York. When the bank contracted credit in 1834, Marcy successfully promoted a state bond issue to help the state's banks survive. A broker-style politician (and an investor in speculative enterprises), Marcy disliked the ideological extremes of outlawing banks or granting them special privileges. He acquiesced to the legislature's efforts to outlaw inflationary small note issue and adopt free (i.e., noncharted) banking. In the panic of 1837 he favored suspending laws that would have closed banks refusing to pay specie because of the dire economic consequences to debtors, and he advised Van Buren against removing government deposits from

banks. Despite his best efforts to find a middle position and promote party harmony, the Democrats factionalized on the banking issue, and Marcy was defeated for a fourth term by William Seward.

Beyond the banking controversy, Marcy as governor had also expanded the canal system, settled the New Jersey border dispute, established school district libraries, teacher training, insane asylums, and the first prison for women, and appointed the talented John A. Dix, Marcy's secretary of state, to conduct the first state geological survey. As radical abolitionism emerged, he condemned meddling in the affairs of southern states.

The panic had destroyed Marcy's hopes of becoming independently wealthy, and the triumph of the Whigs in politics left him with only the law, which no longer interested him, to support his family. In 1840 he eagerly accepted an appointment by Van Buren to serve on a commission in Washington examining claims of American citizens against Mexico. By 1842 most of the claims had been settled (although few payments were actually made to American citizens by Mexico).

When James K. Polk, a Democrat, won election as president in 1844, he offered Marcy the post of secretary of war in his cabinet. The move was controversial since Martin Van Buren, whom Polk had defeated for the nomination, blamed Marcy, and party conservatives on the bank issue, for his defeat. Believing radical (antibank) Democrats were weakening the party, Marcy denied them the patronage at his disposal, setting the stage for the later Free Soil insurgency under Van Buren.

Lacking experience in army matters, Marcy's administration at first appeared passive. He spent his time on pensions and Indian treaties, relying on General Winfield Scott's recommendations for legislation. When Polk's expansionistic foreign policy resulted in the Mexican War, however, his duties increased dramatically. Understanding the need for morale, efficiency, and discipline in the regular army, Marcy argued for the retention of the Whiggish high command of Zachary Taylor and Winfield Scott to head the war's major campaigns and opposed Polk's preference for appointing leading Democrats. As a surrogate for the commander in chief, however, Marcy also faced the venom of Scott and Taylor who suspected Polk's machinations and interpreted failure to receive timely reinforcements and supplies as a sign of administration treachery. Marcy ably defended his actions and explained the difficulties of provision and supply in letters that became public. His appointment and promotion of officers was generally seen as fair. While his belief that a campaign into Mexico's interior could never succeed proved wrong, his judgment in other areas was more sound, especially his strong insistence that Polk accept the treaty ending the war, negotiated by Nicholas Trist who had disobeyed Polk's order to break off negotiations and return home.

The quarrel over the extension of slavery into the territory acquired from Mexico led to Democratic defeat in 1848. Marcy, again driven back to the law, made restoring party harmony in New York his first priority. He himself considered slavery morally wrong but sanctioned by the U.S. Constitution. As a spokesperson for the conservatives, he sought common ground with the Van Burenite Free Soilers, deliberately saying little about the Compromise of 1850 in order to reassure them. His peacemaker role made him attractive to some as a presidential candidate in 1852, but hardline Democrats, under Daniel S. Dickinson, who believed the Free Soilers should be punished, actively worked against him. President Franklin Pierce, however, did name him to his cabinet as secretary of state.

Marcy, who had never been outside the United States, took over an understaffed, overburdened office. Pierce, to compensate for naming the cautious Marcy to the department, insisted that the principal diplomatic posts be given to extreme expansionists, such as Pierre Soulé in Spain. Marcy gave Young America nationalists in his party symbolic victories by issuing rules that American diplomats, if possible, wear business suits rather than court dress and that minor diplomatic positions be staffed only by Americans. He repudiated, however, the proposal in the Ostend Manifesto (written by the U.S. ministers to France, Spain, and England in 1854) that Spain be compelled to give up Cuba by force if necessary. Although in part responsible for the ministers' aggressiveness, Marcy realized in the end its disastrous effects at home and abroad and speeded the resolution of the initial dispute with Spain (over Cuban seizure of the *Black Warrior*).

Twenty-four treaties were negotiated during Marcy's tenure. The Gadsden Purchase added 30,000 square miles to the United States to facilitate a transcontinental railroad. The Marcy-Elgin Treaty (1854) was the first reciprocity treaty negotiated by the United States and allowed duty-free trade of fish and agricultural goods across the Canadian-American border as well as reciprocal fishing privileges and navigation of specified inland waters. Eleven of the treaties involved extradition. The Dallas-Clarendon Convention with Britain clarifying the Clayton-Bulwer Treaty of 1850 regarding Central America was defeated in the Senate. Most of the remaining treaties involved expanding American trade opportunities abroad or settling long-standing issues in dispute (for instance, Denmark's charging of dues for using the Danish Sound).

Four months after leaving office and exhausted by his labors, Marcy collapsed and died while vacationing at Ballston Spa, New York. In a long and varied career and at a time of extremes on many issues, he had consistently striven to exert a moderating influence on party politics.

• Marcy's papers are in the Library of Congress. See also the archives of the Department of State. A biography is Ivor Spencer, *The Victor and the Spoils* (1959). On diplomacy see Samuel Flagg Bemis, ed., *The American Secretaries of State and Their Diplomacy*, vol. 6 (1928), pp. 145–294, and Larry Gara, *The Presidency of Franklin Pierce* (1991). On his role in the Polk administration see Paul H. Bergeron, *The Presidency of James K. Polk* (1987). On New York politics see D. S. Alexander, *A Political History of the State of New York* (1906). An obituary is in the *New York Times*, 6 July 1857.

PHYLLIS F. FIELD

MARDEN, Charles Carroll (21 Dec. 1867–11 May 1932), philologist and university professor, was born in Baltimore, Maryland, the son of Jesse Marden and Anna Maria Brice. After completing his secondary education at Baltimore's City College high school, Marden remained in his hometown and entered Johns Hopkins University, from which he received an A.B. in 1889. Following graduation, he moved to Norfolk, Virginia, where he served as instructor in modern languages at Norfolk Academy during the academic year of 1889–1890. After spending the following year in Ann Arbor as an instructor in French at the University of Michigan, he returned to Johns Hopkins and entered graduate school. Under the mentorship of A. Marshall Elliott, one of the early American leaders in the study and teaching of modern languages, Marden received his Ph.D. in 1894 with a doctoral thesis titled *Phonology of the Spanish Dialect of Mexico City*. His study, the first by a North American of a Spanish-American dialect, was published in 1896. The following year he married Mary Talbott Clark of nearby Ellicott City; the couple had four children.

Eager to build on the pioneering work in foreign languages that his mentor Elliott had initiated at Johns Hopkins, Marden joined the faculty of his innovative alma mater immediately upon receiving his doctorate. There, he served successively as instructor and associate professor of Romance languages (1894–1900), associate professor of Spanish (1900–1905), and finally as full professor of Spanish—the first in this country—from 1905 until 1917.

While Marden never lost his original enthusiasm for the study of dialects, it was as an editor of ancient Spanish-language texts that he made his greatest scholarly contribution. In 1904 he published *Poema de Fernan Gonzalez*, in which he applied the standards of modern scholarship to a significant clerical epic from the Middle Ages; once again, he was the first American scholar to undertake such work. Marden's efforts netted him international acclaim that culminated in his election as a corresponding member of the Spanish Academy in 1907. After returning to his first area of interest in 1911 with the publication of "Notes for a Bibliography of American Spanish"—issued as part of a special Johns Hopkins commemorative of his mentor Elliott (*Studies in Honor of A. Marshall Elliott*, vol. 2 [1911], pp. 267–92)—Marden further secured his reputation with the publication of *Libro de Apolonio*. Issued in two volumes, the first volume (1917) reconstructed the poem by examining all known extant editions, while the second volume (1922) was a more literal rendering of the original manuscript.

During the completion of his groundbreaking scholarship, Marden assumed other burdens as well. A noted teacher in the tradition of his mentor, he inspired many students, both undergraduate and graduate, to develop and pursue their own philological interests. Following the death of Elliott in 1910, Marden assumed the duties of managing editor of *Modern Language Notes*, holding that position from January 1911 until December 1915. In the following year, Marden was named to the newly created Emery L. Ford Chair of Spanish at Princeton University. After dividing his time between Johns Hopkins and Princeton during the 1916–1917 academic year, he moved to Princeton in 1917, remaining there until his death.

While at Princeton, Marden continued to produce notable scholarship. In addition to the numerous articles and reviews that he contributed to the journals of his field, a chance discovery in 1925 resulted in perhaps his greatest work. While browsing through a secondhand bookstore in Madrid, Marden discovered a partial manuscript of the works of the earliest known Castilian poet, Gonzalo de Berceo. Realizing the importance of the fourteenth-century work, he presented the manuscript to the Royal Spanish Academy and prepared the text for publication. The result was his *Cuatro Poemas de Berceo*, which appeared in 1928. In February of that same year, Marden returned to Spain under the auspices of the Carnegie Foundation. After lecturing at various universities on international relations, Marden scoured the mountainous countryside of the province of Logrono in search of the remaining portions of the manuscript. Locating the remaining thirty-two folios in a remote village, he purchased the material and presented it to the academy. His additional efforts resulted in *Berceo: Veintitres Milagros*, which appeared in 1929.

In addition to his teaching duties at Princeton and his research, Marden also taught for several summers (between 1909 and 1928) at the University of Chicago. He published (with F. C. Tarr) *A First Spanish Grammar*, an elementary textbook, in 1926. He served as chief examiner in Spanish for the College Entrance Examination Board (1922–1924) and was a fellow of the Medieval Academy of America, as well as a member of the Hispanic Society. Honored by his designation as a knight commander in the Order of Isabel la Catolica, he also served on the executive council and editorial committee of the Modern Language Association of America before achieving his greatest honor—its presidency—in December 1931.

At the peak of his career and in the appearance of good health, Marden was working on a comprehensive examination of the *Alixandre* romance when he died in Princeton. One of the earliest American academics to apply the techniques of modern scholarship to modern languages, Marden continued the pioneering philological work that his mentor Elliott had initiated and made his own considerable contribution (both in teaching and in research) to the further development of the field.

• While some of Marden's correspondence remains scattered among various collections at the Johns Hopkins University archives in Baltimore, Md., and a collection of Spanish documents collected by him is held at the Princeton University archives, no organized body of his papers appears to have survived. Information on his life and career is scarce; the best sources remain anonymous obituary notices in *Publications of the Modern Language Association of America* 47 (Sept. 1932): 608–12, and *Romanic Review* (July–Sept. 1932): 281–82. An additional sketch was provided by H. C. Lancaster (with a bibliography by F. Courtney Tarr) in *Modern Language Notes*, Dec. 1932, pp. v–xi. Obituaries are in the *New York Times*, 12 May 1932, and the *Times* (London), 28 May 1932.

EDWARD L. LACH, JR.

MARÉCHAL, Ambrose (4 Dec. 1768–29 Jan. 1828), archbishop of Baltimore, was born at Ingré in the diocese of Orléans, France, the son of Ambroise Maréchal, a merchant, and Jeanne Grimault. Though destined by his parents for the study of law, Maréchal decided instead to become a priest. At the seminaries of Orléans and Bordeaux conducted by the Sulpicians he studied philosophy and theology, entering the Society of St. Sulpice in 1787. In the midst of the fury of the French Revolution he was ordained 25 March 1792 in the library of the Irish College in Paris and fled the following day to America. He said his first mass in Baltimore, where he had been sent by his Sulpician superiors to teach at St. Mary's Seminary, the first Catholic seminary in the United States.

For five years, however, Maréchal served as a missionary priest before teaching theology at St. Mary's Seminary and philosophy at Georgetown College in the District of Columbia. In 1803 he was recalled to France to teach at the Sulpician seminaries there. When the Society of St. Sulpice was temporarily suppressed in 1811, he seized the opportunity to return to Baltimore. There he was again employed as a teacher of theology at St. Mary's Seminary from 1812 to 1817, serving also in 1815 as president of St. Mary's College. Though he refused the bishopric of Philadelphia in 1816, he accepted the position of coadjutor bishop of Baltimore with right of succession the following year. On 14 December 1817 he was raised to the episcopacy as the third archbishop of Baltimore, Archbishop Leonard Neale having died in the interim, by Bishop John Cheverus of Boston.

At the prompting of the Holy See Maréchal submitted the first truly comprehensive report on the archdiocese of Baltimore and the Catholic church in the United States in general. Of the 100,000 Catholics in the nation, he reported, the greatest number by far could be found in Maryland, which state was also the most richly endowed in churches, priests, and religious orders. Although there was a shortage of priests everywhere, the most serious obstacles to the progress of the Catholic church in America, he claimed, were the schisms provoked by rebellious trustees. Two of the worst rebellions were in progress in Norfolk, Virginia, and Charleston, South Carolina, still parts of the archdiocese. In 1820, in an attempt to resolve these conflicts, the Holy See, without consulting Maréchal, dismembered the archdiocese by creating the dioceses of Richmond and Charleston, placing over them, and the diocese of Philadelphia, Irishmen. Maréchal, who had small regard for Irish ecclesiastics, objected vehemently to Rome, insisting that nominations to American sees should be left to the archbishop of Baltimore and his suffragan bishops.

Maréchal had also to contest the power of the Society of Jesus in Maryland derived from the considerable estates and the many churches the order controlled. When the Jesuits refused to continue a subsidy they had allowed the first two archbishops, both former Jesuits, Maréchal decided in 1821 to make an official, or *ad limina*, visit to Rome, the first archbishop of Baltimore to do so, to resolve this and the other controversies already mentioned. The Holy See acceded to almost all of his recommendations and requests. Maréchal practically dictated the terms of the papal brief *Non sine magno* of 1822, which laid out the rules for the settlement of trustee problems in the United States. Though he and his suffragan bishops were not given the right of nomination for new and vacant sees, they were allowed to submit three names from which the Holy See would choose. In lieu of a subsidy the archbishop of Baltimore was awarded the core of the Jesuits' most productive estate in Maryland. Maréchal was named an assistant to the pontifical throne and made a member of the Academy of Rome. At his request St. Mary's Seminary in Baltimore was raised to a pontifical university with the right to confer doctoral degrees. The most important consequence of the Roman visit, however, was the recognition of the role of the archbishop of Baltimore as spokesman for the Catholic church in the United States.

While many trustees outside Maryland remained refractory, those in Maryland willingly entered into legal agreements that bound them to the terms of *Non sine magno*. The Maryland Jesuits, however, refused to surrender the property awarded the archbishop. The quarrel would not be resolved in Maréchal's lifetime. Maréchal had also to face defiant Sulpicians, two of whom withdrew from the society in 1826 rather than close a second seminary at Mount St. Mary's in Emmitsburg, Maryland.

While he evidenced no temerity in his dealings with the Roman officials, Maréchal was cowed by the dynamic Irishman John England, named bishop of Charleston in 1820. Shortly after his arrival, England pressed upon Maréchal the necessity of a provincial council to resolve the problems and supply the needs of the Catholic church in the United States. Fearful perhaps of being overshadowed by the talented suffragan, Maréchal resisted the latter's persistent importunities to convoke a council. He showed little enthusiasm for the democratic constitution England had drawn for his own diocese with an evident hope that it would serve as a model for others. Although England viewed Maréchal's policies as attempts to impose French rule upon the preponderant Irish in America, they represented actually a continuation of Anglo-American dominance. Maréchal preferred Americans or Englishmen for American sees. Though a product of the *ancien régime*, Maréchal readily embraced such American principles as freedom of conscience and separation of church and state.

Although considered by many of his suffragan bishops as a man of mediocre talents, especially when compared with England, Maréchal proved to be an able administrator. As a result of the thoroughgoing visitations he conducted, he was better acquainted with the needs of the archdiocese than were his two predecessors and many of his successors. Unpretentious, Maréchal moved with as much ease among the lowly as among the elite of his flock. He was able in his last days to have a protégé, the English-born but Sulpician-trained James Whitfield, chosen as his successor despite an active promotion of the candidacy of Bishop England. Maréchal died in Baltimore.

• Archbishop Maréchal's papers are in the archives of the archdiocese of Baltimore. A scholarly biography is Ronin John Murtha, "The Life of the Most Reverend Ambrose Maréchal: Third Archbishop of Baltimore, 1768–1828" (Ph.D. diss., Catholic Univ. of America, 1965). See also Peter Guilday, *The Life and Times of John England: First Bishop of Charleston (1786–1842)* (2 vols., 1927); Thomas W. Spalding, *The Premier See: A History of the Archdiocese of Baltimore, 1789–1989* (1989); and Christopher J. Kauffman, *Tradition and Transformation in Catholic Culture: The Priests of Saint Sulpice in the United States from 1791 to the Present* (1988).

THOMAS W. SPALDING

MAREK, George Richard (13 July 1902–7 Jan. 1987), music writer and business executive, was born in Vienna, Austria, the son of Martin Marek, a dentist, and Emily Weisberger. Marek studied at the University of Vienna for two years beginning in 1918, then immigrated to the United States in 1920. He became an American citizen in 1925. The following year he married Muriel Hepner; the couple had one son. Marek's first job in the United States was with a milliner, first as a stock boy, and later in the ostrich-feather department, but he soon became involved in the advertising field. From 1930 until 1950 he was a vice president with the J. D. Tarcher Agency. In 1950, during his unsuccessful attempt to acquire RCA's advertising account for Tarcher, Marek was offered a position as manager of artists and repertory in RCA's Records Division; seven years later he became vice president and general manager of Victor Records.

As a boy in Vienna, Marek had developed a passionate love for opera; after his arrival in New York City he soon joined the ranks of standees at the Metropolitan Opera. He was largely self-taught as a musician, and this lack of formal training perhaps served him well in his crusade to share his love of classical music with the American public. Marek was a cofounder of the *Reader's Digest* Record Club, and he served as music editor of *Good Housekeeping* (1941–1957). He was for many years a panel member on the radio broadcasts of the "Metropolitan Opera Quiz."

Marek's tenure at RCA, 1950–1972, resulted in some pronounced changes in the marketing of classical music. Record jackets with colorful, attractive designs replaced the staid covers previously associated with so-called "serious" music. Recordings appeared for sale in drugstores and supermarkets in addition to record stores. Marek was responsible for the release of *Classical Music for People Who Hate Classical Music* in 1953. Although mood music, such as the Melachrino Strings, was popularized by Marek's division, he was also instrumental in promoting the recordings of pianists Gary Graffman and Artur Rubinstein and conductors Pierre Monteux and Fritz Reiner. His association with Arturo Toscanini covered that maestro's final years with the NBC Symphony. Marek was not a snob; he believed it was possible to popularize classical music with a wide audience by exposing that audience repeatedly to new and different sounds, thus changing their listening habits. Marek stated, "As the cigarette people believe, the habit is everything."

Marek's interest in bringing classical music to a wide audience is reflected in many of his books and articles. His columns for *Good Housekeeping*, for example, include such representative titles as "Quiz Kids' Favorite Music," "Most Popular Composers," and "Should I Read Books about Music?" As an author, opera and biography were Marek's two principal subjects. *Puccini: A Biography* (1951) set the pattern for later writings. Primarily devoted to a study of the composer's life, the volume is set in a cultural background. In it Marek makes extensive use of correspondence, some of it previously unpublished, but musical analysis is superficial at best, and although there is a partial bibliography, there are no footnotes or scholarly documentation. In *Richard Strauss: The Life of a Non-Hero* (1967), Marek attempted an objective view of the composer, discussing his artistic decline after the First World War and examining his dealings with the Nazi regime as well as his operatic triumphs and his close artistic relations with the librettist Hugo von Hofmannsthal. *Beethoven: Biography of a Genius* (1969) enabled Marek to draw on his own intimate knowledge of Vienna in sketching the composer's cultural milieu. Beethoven's correspondence and conversation books were cited extensively, the latter for the first time in a popular biography. *Gentle Genius: The Story of Felix Mendelssohn* (1972) leaves the reader with the impression that Marek was not entirely in sympathy with the composer or his music. *Toscanini* (1975) was Marek's only musical biography not written about a composer. The author's admiration for the conductor grew from their professional association in the early 1950s, and the book includes Marek's personal recollections. *Chopin* (1978) was coauthored with Maria Gordon-Smith, a native of Poland who provided Marek with the necessary background for the composer's earlier years.

In retirement Marek continued as a consultant to both RCA and the *Reader's Digest* Record Club. He died in New York City.

• Marek's enthusiasm for opera is reflected in some of his earliest publications: *A Front Seat at the Opera* (1948) and *Opera as Theater* (1962), as well as *The World Treasury of Grand Opera* (1957), which he edited. His interest in European cultural history resulted in *The Eagles Die: Franz Joseph, Elisabeth, and Their Austria* (1974) and *The Bed and the Throne* (1976), a book about Isabella d'Este.

PAULA MORGAN

MARES, Paul Joseph (15 June 1900–18 Aug. 1949), cornetist and trumpeter, was born in New Orleans, Louisiana, the son of Joseph Mares, Sr., an amateur trumpeter and dealer in fur pelts, and Louise Lacoste. A self-taught musician who never became proficient at reading music, Mares played while still in his teens at various venues in New Orleans, including the Bucktown Tavern on Lake Pontchartrain, with his childhood friends, clarinetist Leon Rappolo and trombonist Georg Brunis (born George Brunies). He also played with trombonist Tom Brown, whose band would later, in 1915, become perhaps the first white jazz band to play in Chicago. Shortly after he graduated from high school, patriotism prompted Mares to enlist in the marines in 1917, but although he was stationed in France, the war ended before he saw any action.

Returning to New Orleans, Mares soon joined the migration of New Orleans–born jazz musicians who found an audience for their music in Chicago. His summons came from the New Orleans drummer "Ragbaby" Stevens, who sent for Mares in 1919 after Abbie Brunis (Georg's brother) passed up the opportunity, preferring to maintain his taxi business instead. In Chicago, Mares worked with Stevens at Camel Gardens and later at Blatz's Beer Garden with Brunis and the Chicagoans Jack Pettis (saxophone), Elmer Schoebel (piano), Frank Snyder (drums), and Lou Black (banjo). An engagement on the SS *Capitol* took Brunis and Mares to Davenport, Iowa, where they were reunited with Rappolo. When the three returned to Chicago, they and others from the Blatz engagement, with bassist Arnold Loyocano, formed (under Mares's leadership) the Friar's Society Orchestra for an engagement at the Friar's Inn in 1921. The Friar's had had some previous success with New Orleans bands, and its manager, Mike Fritzel, was eager to capitalize on the popularity of New Orleans music, now being commonly referred to as "Dixieland." According to the historian William Russell in his interview for *Jazzmen* (conducted in 1938), the "regular band got off the stand. They [Mares and his band] got up and played 'Wabash Blues' and were hired on one number." Russell describes the Friar's as a medium-sized, cheaply painted room: "the hangout of the gangsters and the big money people in the rackets, all the people in the [*sic*] show business."

But the Friar's soon became the focal point for musicians as well, attracting the likes of Bix Beiderbecke and other midwesterners, and the band's popularity soon led to Mares's first and only recording sessions on the Gennett label, between August 1922 and March 1923. Now renamed the New Orleans Rhythm Kings

(NORK), they covered some of the titles ("Tiger Rag" and "Livery Stable Blues") recorded by the Original Dixieland Jazz Band five years earlier and also contributed a number of original compositions, including "That's A Plenty," "Weary Blues," "Tin Roof Blues," and "Wolverine Blues." In *Jazz Masters of New Orleans*, Martin Williams describes NORK's last session in March 1923 as "a much expanded group, including a saxophone section of three and, on certain titles, Jelly Roll Morton on piano, thus making it the first racially mixed jazz record date."

The Gennett recordings of Mares and the NORK served as an inspiration for the "Austin High School Gang" of white Dixielanders in the Midwest and contributed to the foundation for the so-called Chicago style, a brand of jazz marked by the two-beat feeling of ragtime and a greater emphasis on the soloist. But sustained success eluded them: in 1924 the group disbanded and Mares and Rappolo took an engagement in New York at a club in Greenwich Village. Thus the Gennett sides of 1922–1923 remain the best representation of Mares's and NORK's recorded work. Mares and Rappolo returned to New Orleans in 1924 and reorganized NORK with different personnel, including New Orleans trombonist Santo Pecora and a local rhythm section, for a January 1925 recording session for the Okeh label. A subsequent session for Victor in March of 1925 left Mares as the only remaining member of the original group, and with his career as a professional musician in decline, he joined his family in the fur enterprise.

The depression crippled the family business in the early 1930s and precipitated Mares's final return to Chicago, where he resumed on a much smaller scale the career he had abandoned less than ten years before. He could be heard sitting in with some former sidemen and younger musicians in small groups and jam sessions, but for all practical purposes his days in the music business were coming to an end. In 1935 Mares assembled the NORK for a recording session on the Okeh label: it was one of the company's last. The session was sponsored by the Mills Publishing Company, which hoped to benefit from the popularity of the earlier NORK tunes and to bring out two originals of Mares's: "Reincarnation," a slow blues, and "Land of Dreams," based on "Basin Street Blues." For this date, Mares called on drummer George Wettling, bassist Pat Pattison, guitarist Marvin Saxbe, clarinetist Omer Simeon, saxophonist Boyce Brown, pianist Jess Stacy, and trombonist Santo Pecora. This was one of Stacy's first recording dates, and the story is that Benny Goodman hired him after hearing these recordings.

By the late 1930s, Mares had opened the P&M New Orleans Barbecue restaurant (named for Paul and his wife, Marie) on Chicago's North Side. It soon became a popular hangout for musicians and the scene of popular jam sessions on Monday nights featuring leading jazz figures from both New Orleans and Chicago as well as some personnel from the Bob Crosby and Jimmy Dorsey orchestras. Soon after the Crosby orchestra moved to New York, however, the live music sessions faded and were eventually replaced by a juke box that featured some of Mares's earlier recordings. Mares worked in defense plants during the war years, and for a while he even closed up his restaurant. But he could be heard in jam sessions into the late 1940s and was even attempting to organize a group under his own name in Chicago at the time of his death from lung cancer.

The New Orleans Rhythm Kings was arguably the strongest white jazz band of the early 1920s. In true jazz tradition, and with their audiences unaware of it, they rehearsed right on the job. Their rhythmic drive and sense of rhythmic swing were inspired by the black organizations they heard in New Orleans and were unmatched by the rhythmic sense of any other white band of the period. Paul Mares was clearly their founder and, along with pianist Elmer Schoebel, their musical director. As a cornetist, Mares based his style on that of Joe Oliver and the other New Orleans musicians he had heard as a teenager. Contemporary accounts often speak of his "large, broad, yet rough tone," his ability to "swing," and his relaxed "legato" style—a marked departure from the then-current staccato approach and sometimes "hurried" rhythmic feeling that was characteristic of most midwestern jazz musicians and even the earlier all-white Original Dixieland Jazz Band. Although Mares's career as a full-time musician was relatively brief, he is remembered as the individual responsible for the New Orleans Rhythm Kings' influential although short-lived celebrity.

• Paul Mares's recordings as a leader span a thirteen-year period (1922–1935) and were originally issued on the Gennett, Victor, and Okeh labels under the titles *Friar's Society Orchestra* (1922), *New Orleans Rhythm Kings* (1923, 1925), and *Paul Mares Friar's Society Orchestra* (1935). The Gennett recordings of the New Orleans Rhythm Kings have been reissued on Riverside 12–202. Mares's and Rappolo's 1925 New Orleans recordings are included in the collection *Jazz Odyssey*, vol. 1, *The Sound of New Orleans (1917–1947)*, Col., C3L 30. Martin Williams, "N.O.R.K.," in *Jazz Masters of New Orleans* (1967; rev. ed., 1978), contains the most complete account of Mares and his sidemen. An early assessment of Mares's career appears in Dixon Gayer, "There Is a Chicago Style," *Down Beat*, 15 Feb. 1943, p. 4. More complete accounts were published following his death, including George Avakian, "Paul Mares: New Orleans Rhythm King," *Record Changer*, Nov. 1949, pp. 17, 31; and George Hoefer, "Mares Led Inspiring Crew" (includes discography), *Down Beat*, 23 Sept. 1949, p. 21. An interview with Mares's brother Joe Mares appears in Marjorie Roehl, "In the Swing with a Rhythm King," *New Orleans Times Picayune*, 14 June 1987.

CHARLES BLANCQ

MARETZEK, Max (28 June 1821–14 May 1897), opera impresario, conductor, and composer, was born Maximilian Mareczek in Brünn, Moravia (now Brno, Czechoslovakia). His formal education emphasized literature and the classics; he was also instructed on the piano and pursued general music studies. He enrolled at the University of Vienna at the age of seventeen, first to study medicine, then law (both professions were acceptable to his parents). He discarded both, however, and with the encouragement of the Austrian music historian and teacher Joseph Fischof turned his attention to music, his first love. His major field of concentration was composition, which he studied with the composer and conductor Ignaz Xaver Ritter von Seyfried. These studies resulted in his first major work, the opera *Hamlet*. Maretzek conducted its successful premiere performance in Brno on 5 November 1840; the opera met with some success elsewhere. Later in 1840 Maretzek was engaged to conduct at the opera house in Agram, Croatia; he subsequently held posts in Bamberg, Bavaria (where he was guest conductor), and Nancy, France. In late 1842, as a result of his growing reputation as a conductor and composer, Maretzek was invited to Paris, where he wrote ballet music for Carlotta Grisi and Lucille Grahn, finished a second opera (*Die Niebelungen*), commenced work on a third, and completed a set of songs that he dedicated to the duchess of Nemours. During this period he conducted opera and ballet; he also presented some of his own works—including the overture *Agnes Sorel*—at a Concert Vivienne.

While in Paris Maretzek came into contact with the young Hegelians, including Marx, Feuerbach, Bakunin, Heine, and Engels; although not a documented member of the group, Maretzek did contribute small music-related articles and reviews to their journal, *Vorwaerts*. It is possible that Maretzek's later goal in the United States—to provide the best opera to the people at the lowest possible cost—was influenced by his association with this group of intellectuals. In 1844 he was hired by George Lumley as choral director and assistant director at Covent Garden in London, where Maretzek gained valuable experience. In 1847 Louis Jullien engaged Maretzek as chorus master and Hector Berlioz as conductor in an unsuccessful attempt to establish English opera at Drury Lane Theatre. Maretzek's ballet *Les Genies du Globe* was the afterpiece to *Lucia di Lammermoor* on the opening night performance for this venture. The season collapsed shortly thereafter, leaving the musicians involved stranded and unpaid; Maretzek occupied himself by preparing choruses for Berlioz's occasional London concerts.

In September 1848 Maretzek arrived in New York, where he had been engaged as the conductor of the Astor Place Opera House; Edward R. Fry (the brother of composer William Henry Fry) was the director. After Fry's company failed in early March 1849 Maretzek took over as conductor and impresario; it was the first of his many American opera companies. From this period until he retired as an operatic manager in 1878, Maretzek's companies were a constant presence in the United States. His many troupes, the personnel and names of which changed frequently, were based primarily in New York City, but they were well known all over the continent, for they traveled and performed widely in the eastern United States as well as in Mexico and Cuba. Maretzek's efforts to establish opera in the United States were unequaled during this period, although the managers Maurice and Max Strakosch

and Bernard Ullman were strong competitors (and sometimes collaborators). During the mid-1850s there were operatic "wars" in New York between companies managed by these impresarii; in the same city during the 1870s there was a legendary "Battle of the Maxes" between troupes managed by Maretzek, at the Grand Opera House, and Max Strakosch, at the Academy of Music. Maretzek competed with the others for sponsorship and for the services of various operatic stars. A remarkably adroit manager, he constantly tinkered with the resources at his disposal, continually altering the bills to feature different combinations of performers and repertory, offering occasional grand operatic galas and other extravaganzas, deftly exploiting the press, and experimenting with various ticket-pricing schemes—all with the goal of attracting a large ticket-buying audience.

Maretzek was associated in the public mind primarily with Italian opera, but his troupes also mounted seasons of German and French opera in the 1860s and 1870s. Maretzek engaged many of the most prominent singers to appear in the United States during the period, including Clara Louise Kellogg, Minnie Hauk, Pauline Lucca, and Enrico Tamberlick. His troupes gave the American premiere performances of many important operas, including Verdi's *La Traviata*, *Rigoletto*, and *Don Carlos*, Meyerbeer's *Robert le Diable* and *Le Prophète*, and Gounod's *Romeo et Juliet*. Maretzek's most important contribution, however, was the firm establishment of opera on the American stage. He was profoundly interested in producing opera for audiences of various social and economic levels, and his troupes performed at New York venues as widely divergent as the Astor Place Opera House (identified in the public mind with the aristocracy) and both Niblo's and Castle Garden theaters (which catered to the working and middle classes). The activities of Maretzek's companies clearly laid the foundation for the later success of James Henry Mapleson's Italian Opera Company, which first performed in the United States in 1878, and of the New York Metropolitan Opera Company (founded in 1883). After Maretzek retired from operatic management in 1878 he continued to conduct, teach voice, and coach young American singers who aspired to operatic careers. His many contributions to the establishment of opera in the United States were recognized by his contemporaries when he was honored at a grand Golden Jubilee concert (commemorating the fiftieth anniversary of his conducting career) at the Metropolitan Opera House in February 1889; participants in the festivities included the conductors Walter Damrosch, Theodore Thomas, Anton Seidl, and Frank van der Stucken.

Maretzek remained an active composer throughout his life. He wrote piano compositions, songs, ballets, choral works, and operas, including the three-act *Sleepy Hollow; or, The Headless Horseman* (after Washington Irving), which was premiered at the New York Academy of Music in 1879. His two volumes of reminiscences, *Crotchets and Quavers; or, Revelations of an Opera Manager in America* (1855) and *Sharps and*

Flats: A Sequel to Crotchets and Quavers (1890), provide an engaging account of musical life in America during the 1850s, 1860s, and 1870s. He died at his home in Pleasant Plains, Staten Island, New York. He was survived by his wife, the contralto Apollonia Bertucca-Maretzek, a son and two daughters.

• A number of sources have useful information about Maretzek's career. Particularly valuable—although not completely reliable—are Maretzek's own autobiographical accounts, which have been published in a modern edition under the title *Revelations of an Opera Manager in 19th-Century America* (1968). Charles Haywood's introduction to this edition is useful and reliable. Waldemar Reick, "Max Maretzek: Impresario, Conductor and Composer," *Musical Courier* (22 June 1922): 6–7, 47, is an extensive sketch of his life and career. For information about Maretzek's career during the late 1840s and 1850s the best source is Katherine Preston, *Opera on the Road: Traveling Opera Troupes in the United States, 1825–1860* (1993), which includes a chapter that exhaustively explores the activities of Maretzek's Astor Place Opera Company of 1850–1851. There is frequent mention of Maretzek in the appropriate volumes of George C. D. Odell's *Annals of the New York Stage*. Other sources include Clara Louise Kellogg, *Memoirs of an American Prima Donna* (1913); H. E. Krehbiel, *Chapters of Opera* (1908); and Robert Grau, "Memories of Musicians of Other Days: Max Maretzek," *Musical Leader* 24, no. 26 (26 Dec. 1912): 30. Maretzek's obituary is in the *New York Times*, 15 May 1897.

KATHERINE K. PRESTON

MARGOLD, Nathan Ross (21 July 1899–16 Dec. 1847), attorney and political activist, was born in Jassy, Romania, the son of Wolf Margulies and Rosa Kahan. He was brought to the United States when he was two, grew up in Brooklyn, New York, and received his B.A. from the City College of New York in 1919. Margold studied law at Harvard University, serving as an editor of the law review and catching the attention of Professor Felix Frankfurter. Margold supported Frankfurter's efforts to diversify the law school's student body and shared Frankfurter's interest in social reforms such as racial justice and the labor movement. Margold received his LL.B. in 1923 and went into private practice in New York.

While an assistant U.S. attorney for the Southern District of New York from 1925 to 1927, Margold began teaching at Harvard Law School. Frankfurter and Dean Roscoe Pound proposed in 1926 that he be named to a five-year assistant professorship in criminal law, a move that started a battle that raged for two years. A large majority of the law school faculty voted for Margold, but Harvard President A. Lawrence Lowell felt that another Jewish reformer in addition to Frankfurter would be one too many, and Pound, wearied by his many battles with the administration, persuaded the faculty not to challenge Lowell. In 1928 Margold returned to New York and private practice.

In addition to his private work, he served as special counsel for the New York Transit Commission (1928–1929) and as legal adviser to the Pueblo Indian tribes on their land-title claims (1930–1931). He also wrote for law journals and edited *Cases on Criminal Law* (1928) with Joseph Henry Beale.

Margold's most important work was done between 1930 and 1933 as special counsel for the National Association for the Advancement of Colored People (NAACP). Hired at Frankfurter's suggestion to develop a plan to win equal rights for black children in southern public schools, Margold argued in his Report (1931) that the NAACP's projected taxpayers' suits in state courts would fail to eliminate separate schools. He noted that wherever state laws permitted or required segregated schools, black schools were unequally funded, and there was no available state remedy. He urged the NAACP to seek a declaration that the underfunding of black schools violated the equal protection clause of the Constitution's Fourteenth Amendment. The result would be to force the southern states either to raise and spend prohibitively large sums to improve black schools or move to an integrated school system. William Hastie later called the book-length Report the "Bible" of the NAACP's legal drive. It underlay the strategy successfully used by the NAACP in its school litigation from 1938 to 1950, which paved the way to the U.S. Supreme Court's decision in *Brown v. Board of Education* (1954), holding state-mandated segregated education unconstitutional.

Margold had less of an impact when he represented the NAACP before the Supreme Court in the case of *Nixon v. Condon* (1932). In *Nixon v. Herndon* (1927), the Court had held that a Texas all-white primary law violated the Constitution. The Texas legislature promptly shifted control of primaries from the state to party executive committees. The executive committee of the Democratic party, the one party of any importance in the southern states at that time, then declared its primaries open only to white Democrats. Margold argued in *Condon* that the executive committee was no more than a surrogate for the state, and the Court agreed. The victory was of little consequence, however, as the Texas Democratic convention, which could not easily be attacked as a state surrogate, met almost immediately after the Court ruled and voted to close its primary to all nonwhites.

Margold left the NAACP in 1933 to join numerous other Harvard Law School graduates who went to work for the New Deal, many of them at Frankfurter's urging. Margold's name was given to Harold Ickes, the new secretary of the interior, by Frankfurter and by Justice Louis Brandeis, who was as impressed as Frankfurter by Margold's legal abilities. Ickes, who shared Margold's interest in Native American affairs, hired him as solicitor of the Interior Department. Margold remained at Interior until 1942. Among his duties were chairing the Petroleum Administrative Board and the Labor Policy Board for the Petroleum Industry (1933–1934), both set up under the National Industrial Recovery Act. He also served as special assistant attorney general from 1933 to 1935.

President Franklin D. Roosevelt appointed Margold to the Municipal Court for the District of Columbia in 1942. He remained on its bench until 1945, when he was named a judge of the U.S. District Court in the District of Columbia, a position he held until he died of a heart attaack in Washington, D.C. Surviving him were his wife, Gertrude Wiener, whom he had married in 1927, and their son.

• The Margold Report, "Preliminary Report to the Joint Committee Supervising the Expenditure of the 1930 Appropriation by the American Fund for Public Service to the N.A.A.C.P.," is among the NAACP Papers in the Library of Congress. The New York Public Library's Margold papers contain another copy of the Report and other material about Margold. Information about Margold and the Report is in Richard Kluger, *Simple Justice* (1975); Mark Tushnet, *The NAACP's Legal Strategy against Segregated Education, 1925–1950* (1987); and Samuel Walker, *In Defense of American Liberties* (1990). An obituary is in the *New York Times*, 17 Dec. 1947.

PHILIPPA STRUM

MARGOLIS, Max Leopold (15 Oct. 1866–2 Apr. 1932), biblical scholar, was born in Meretz, part of the Russian province of Vilna, the son of Isaac Margolis, a rabbi and tutor, and Hinde Bernstein. He received a traditional Jewish education that acquainted him with both the sacred literature of Israel and with the interpretive methods that had been developed to deal with those texts. He excelled in formal and informal academic settings, where he received a fairly extensive introduction to secular and Christian literature. With the support of his maternal grandparents, he moved to Berlin, Germany, in the 1880s, where he enrolled in a prestigious Gymnasium and took highest honors in the study of the classics. At the same time, he came into contact with Reform Jews and Jewish practices, some of which he adapted to the more traditional Judaism in which he had been reared.

In 1889 Margolis followed the rest of his family to New York City, where he soon enrolled in Columbia College (now Columbia University), earning his M.A. in 1890 and his Ph.D. the following year. His dissertation, written in Latin, dealt with textual problems in the commentaries of the medieval Jewish scholar Rashi, and thereby represented the fruitful culmination of all of the various educational strands to which he had been exposed.

Margolis's first permanent academic appointment was to a post in biblical studies at Hebrew Union College (HUC) in Cincinnati, Ohio. Although he had wished to teach Talmud, in which he was naturally well versed, HUC's founder and president, Isaac Mayer Wise, urged him to accept the position in Bible with these words: "We have plenty of Talmud teachers, we have no Bible scholars among us Jews." Throughout his career at HUC (1892–1897 and 1905–1907), the University of California at Berkeley (1897–1905), and Dropsie College in Philadelphia, Pennsylvania (1909–1932) Margolis was a teacher of Bible, one of the very few Jewish scholars of his day to specialize in this area. From the beginning he drew on the vast resources of the various traditions, both Jewish and secular, in

which he had been educated. He clearly aligned himself with those who promoted and practiced critical approaches toward the biblical text. However, he strongly resisted what he viewed as radical critics of the Bible, who cast the ancient text and its authors in disrepute. He wrote a number of articles and books in which he exemplified his thoroughly Jewish and conservatively critical approach toward the Bible. In 1906 he had married Evelyn Goldwater Aronson in San Francisco, California; they had three children.

HUC was the educational flagship of the Reform movement in American Judaism and as such was a focal point of attention whenever theological or other controversies threatened to shake the movement. Margolis became embroiled in a bitter conflict over Reform attitudes toward Zionism. His attraction to the idea of rebuilding a Jewish homeland in Israel put him at odds with the majority of the Reform leadership of his day, which resulted in 1907 in his leaving HUC and the Reform movement itself. He spent the rest of his life, except for a year in Europe (1907–1908) and in Palestine (1924–1925), in Philadelphia.

Margolis was first drawn to Philadelphia by the offer to serve as editor in chief for the translation of the Bible for the Jewish Publication Society of America (JPS). In 1917 the JPS published this Bible, which was the Bible of English-speaking Jews for almost half a century thereafter. As editor in chief, he prepared the first draft for the translation of each book of the Hebrew Bible. He carefully modeled the language of his translation on the Revised Version of 1885, the first major revision of the King James Version since its appearance in 1611. At the same time, Margolis made sure that Christological interpretations, which had found their way into the Protestant King James Version, were eliminated and that traditional Jewish exegesis gained appropriate emphasis.

Margolis's books include *The Story of Bible Translations* (1917) and *The Hebrew Scriptures in the Making* (1922). But he is best remembered for *A History of the Jewish People* (1927), which he wrote along with Alexander Marx. Although he did not consider this a major piece of scholarship, this often reprinted volume was the introduction to the vast canvas of Jewish history for several generations of students. In it he gave witness to the sober intellectual viewpoint and careful writing that characterized all of his work.

Unknown to most of his contemporaries, Margolis devoted most of his scholarly efforts during the last twenty-five years of his life to a series of studies on the Septuagint, which was the Greek translation of the Old Testament prepared by the Jews of Alexandria, Egypt, in the third and second centuries BCE. Because the early church adopted the Septuagint as its Bible, there were few Jewish scholars of this text until the nineteenth century. In America, Margolis was a pioneer in this regard, and at the end of the twentieth century his judicious handling of the Septuagint, especially in the book of Joshua, commanded respect and continued to be reprinted.

Margolis was elected president of the Society of Biblical Literature for 1923. In his presidential address, he spoke of the need to concentrate on exegesis: "It is so easy to break up a text into atoms," he explained. "It is far more difficult to discern relevancy, continuity, coherence."

In many ways, those words can be applied to Margolis and the program he established for himself. While not demanding attention or asserting himself in a calculated fashion, he achieved a synthesis of Jewish and biblical studies that served as a model for his students and then for theirs. He demonstrated that it was possible to remain true to the high ideals of his religion and of the academy.

• Margolis's papers are in several formal and less formally organized archival collections. They are frequently cited in the only book-length study of him, Leonard Greenspoon's *Max Leopold Margolis: A Scholar's Scholar* (1987). This volume also includes a complete, partially annotated bibliography of Margolis's scholarly and popular publications, as well as references to several major unpublished manuscripts by Margolis. Still valuable, especially because of the essays by his former students and colleagues, is *Max Leopold Margolis: Scholar and Teacher*, ed. Robert Gordis (1952). His long association with the JPS is discussed in Jonathan D. Sarna, *JPS: The Americanization of Jewish Culture* (1989). Kimmy Caplan has published letters sent to Margolis by his father in *Zion* 58, no. 2 (1993): 215–40.

LEONARD GREENSPOON

MARIGNY, Bernard (28 Oct. 1785–3 Feb. 1868), Creole planter and politician, was born in New Orleans, Louisiana, the son of Pierre Enguerrand Philippe de Marigny de Mandeville, a Spanish army officer and rich landowner, and Jeanne Marie d'Estréhan, daughter of a distinguished family. He was christened Bernard Xavier Philippe de Marigny de Mandeville and grew up in the richest family in the French colony of Louisiana. When Marigny was fifteen his father died, at which time Lino de Chalmette, a relative, became his guardian. Already Marigny had developed into an unruly, spoiled young man, so addicted to gambling that Chalmette could not control him. Hence Marigny was dispatched to Pensacola, Florida, and placed in the care of a wealthy merchant named Panton, who found him so impossible that he immediately sent him back. Chalmette then sent Marigny to England, where he lived on an extravagant allowance, mingled with the best society, met Lord Byron, and continued his dissipated ways. Soon he was deeply in debt to London and Parisian gamblers. Returning to New Orleans after his eighteenth birthday, he came into possession of his entire fortune of $7 million but was compelled to liquidate a plantation in order to pay his creditors. Supposedly he maintained an entire street of houses on what he called "Rue de l'Amour" to shelter his numerous mistresses.

When Napoleon sold Louisiana to the United States in 1803, Marigny immediately pledged his services to the new government. A year later he was appointed to the staff of General James Wilkinson, who had come to New Orleans with Governor William C. C. Claiborne, and joined the Democratic party. Also in 1804 he married Mary Ann Jones, with whom he had two children before she died four years later. In 1810 he married Ann Mathilde Morales, with whom he lived unhappily; they had five children. He entered politics in 1810, winning election to the territorial legislature, and in 1812 was a delegate to the first Louisiana state constitutional convention. Until 1838 he was always a member of the legislature, and in 1845 he was at the second state constitutional convention. He also later ran for governor but was defeated. When General Andrew Jackson arrived at New Orleans in 1815 to defend the city against General Sir Edward Pakenham and his veteran British soldiers, Marigny headed a welcoming committee to greet him. More importantly, Marigny worked in the legislature to assist Jackson and helped convince the general to employ Jean Lafitte's pirates in defense of the city.

As he grew older, Marigny continued to live profligately, entertaining lavishly and gambling madly. It was rumored that Marigny, who was a close friend of John Davis, the gambling king of New Orleans, once lost $30,000 in a single night of wagering. He also spent money with abandon on objects of art, filling his houses with splendid portraits and other paintings, porcelains, lace, jewelry, and fine furniture. Journeying abroad on extravagant trips, he bought these art pieces without any consideration of cost, paying what the seller demanded and thinking it beneath his dignity to argue over a price. Although he inherited the wealth of his brothers and sisters as they died, in addition to his original portion of his father's estate, Marigny's fortune by 1839 was reduced to about $900,000, one-third of which he owed his creditors. Despite his extravagance, his economic misfortunes were not entirely his fault, for his plantations produced sugar, and tariffs had drastically reduced that commodity's value on world markets. In an attempt to restore his dwindling fortune, he traveled to France in 1830 to see if he could collect from King Louis Philippe a huge sum of money that his father had loaned the man when he visited New Orleans in 1798. Marigny and his young son, Antoine, were received warmly by the king and regaled with every favor except repayment of the debt. All Marigny got from the monarch was a gold snuff box and a promise that Antoine would be appointed to the military school at St. Cyr when he was old enough to apply. When Marigny's fortune was almost totally gone, his friends secured for him the position of registrar of conveyances to keep him from absolute penury.

In 1853 Marigny lost his job and was reduced to poverty because he had alienated too many political cronies with his extravagant life style and violent temper. That year he privately circulated a pamphlet denying any responsibility for his reduced circumstances. Living in a small house with one servant, he never saw any of his children or grandchildren, and he was largely ignored by New Orleans society. Hurt but too proud to let it show, he still occasionally threatened to avenge slights with a duel (he had fought nineteen during his lifetime). Moreover, he continued to live elegantly and to conduct himself imperiously. In 1854 he made a little money and proved he still had political influence by writing *Thoughts upon the Foreign Policy of the United States*, two copies of which were purchased by the House of Representatives. His life was almost untouched by the Civil War, for he was too old to get involved in arguments about secession and states' rights and had no material possessions to lose. He died after stumbling and striking his head on the pavement while taking his daily walk along the New Orleans street.

• Marigny's apologia is *Bernard Marigny, to His Fellow Citizens* (1853). Other contemporary information is in W. H. Sparks, *The Memories of Fifty Years* (1870). Informative books on Marigny's life are Grace Elizabeth King, *New Orleans: The Place and the People* (1895) and *Creole Families of New Orleans* (1921). Also useful are J. W. Cruzat, "Biographical and Genealogical Notes concerning the Family of Philippe de Mandeville, Écuyer Sieur de Marigny," Louisiana Historical Society, *Publications* 5 (1911), and Robert Tàllant, *The Romantic New Orleanians* (1950).

PAUL DAVID NELSON

MARIN, John (23 Dec. 1870–1 Oct. 1953), painter and etcher, was born John Cheri Marin in Rutherford, New Jersey, the son of John Cheri Marin and Annie Louise Currey. His mother died nine days after his birth, and his father, who has been variously identified as an investor, a textile merchant, and a public accountant, left their child in the care of the baby's maternal grandparents and his two maiden aunts, all of whom lived in the Currey home in Weehawken, New Jersey. Marin, who was ambidextrous, began to paint by age sixteen and surprised his family by his desire to be an artist. He studied mechanical engineering for eighteen months beginning in 1886 at the Stevens Institute of Technology and began his professional career in the field of architecture. From 1890 to 1892 he worked as a draftsman for four architects and from 1892 to 1897 ran his own firm and designed six residences in Union, New Jersey. Then, deciding on a career in the fine arts, he studied from 1899 to 1901 at the Pennsylvania Academy of the Fine Arts in Philadelphia—among his professors was Thomas Anshutz—and from 1903 to 1905 at the Art Students League in New York City. To further his education, Marin sojourned in Europe from 1905 to 1911 with one return visit in 1909–1910. In Paris, where he spent most of those six years, he briefly attended the Delecluse Academy and the Académie Julian.

A prolific artist whose subjects derived primarily from the landscape, Marin showed in his earliest watercolors of 1888 a use of transparent washes to suggest form, color, and reflective qualities of water. These watercolors—views of White Lake, Sullivan County, New York—reflect American impressionist characteristics typical of the generation of the 1880s and 1890s. In his watercolors from 1889 to 1893, he merged impressionist with tonal qualities to create a languorous mood.

In Paris Marin exhibited at the Salon d'Automne from 1907 to 1909 and at the Salon des Indépendants in 1907. In 1908 the French government purchased his oil *The Mills at Meaux* (1907). He was influenced primarily by late nineteenth-century artists, such as Bonnard, Vuillard, Signac, the Fauves, and, above all, James McNeill Whistler. Marin also traveled to Amsterdam, Venice, and London and while abroad, focused on etching. His scenes, mostly of European cities and monuments, were influenced by French printmaker Charles Meryon, but again they generally reflect a Whistlerian mode, as Marin absorbed the great expatriate's subjects and delicate atmospheric effects. Among Marin's luminous European watercolors, those painted in 1910 in the Austrian Tyrols, with their vaporous atmospheres, color nuances, lyrical linear rhythms, and oriental look reiterate Whistlerian influence. In Paris in 1909, through Edward Steichen, Marin met Alfred Stieglitz, who over the course of the next four decades influenced the development of Marin's artistic personality and celebrity. Marin, who became one of Stieglitz's coterie of modernists at his gallery, 291, had solo exhibitions there virtually every year from 1910 until Stieglitz's death in 1946.

In 1912, after returning permanently from Europe, Marin married Marie Jane Hughes, with whom he would have one child. By that time a new theme, New York City, had appeared in his oeuvre. His style also changed owing to various influences. By 1911 exposure to the works of Picasso and Cezanne at 291 led to Marin's involvement with cubist devices. Living in nearby New Jersey, he became as much associated with his etchings and Watercolors of the city—its skyscrapers, traffic, crowds, streets, the Hudson River—as with his rural studies of mountains, lakes, trees, and skies, some of which were painted in the Adirondacks. Marin had returned to America at a time when New York was in the midst of tremendous construction, and the immensity and excitement stirred his thoughts. He described his desire for his art to reach beyond the objective fact in regard to the growing metropolis. "I see great forces at work; great movements; the large buildings and the small buildings; the warring of the great and the small, the influence of one mass on another greater or smaller mass" (Marin, "Notes on 291," *Camera Work* 42 [Apr.–July 1913]: 18). The structures he re-created, whether famous buildings, churches, or thoroughfares in the city, displayed a new vitality and dynamism, which he expressed by filling the scenes with lines of various sorts.

The beat of the city and the presence there of modernist influences played a key role in the development of Marin's art in the second decade of the new century, when the disintegration of form and erratic linear rhythms dominated. His many etchings and watercolors of the Woolworth Building and the Brooklyn Bridge are, in their depictions of growing energy, similar, respectively, to the studies of St. Severin and the Eiffel Tower by Robert Delauney, whose orphism (an abstract style with color as its principal element) was a direct outgrowth of cubism. Debate regarding Marin's relationship to the futurists during these years centers around some stylistic affinities exhibited by the Italian group's application of cubism to express motion and modernity. Cubist works included in the Armory Show of 1913, in which Marin participated, as well as the presence in New York of Francis Picabia and Albert Gleizes during World War I, most probably contributed to Marin's shift toward abstraction.

By 1914 "ray lines," or staccato-like lines, began to appear in some of Marin's works as a means of conveying the energy of a site, whether in the city or country. Marin responded to the forces he sensed in an abstract rather than an anecdotal way by using these lines to delineate solid forms, such as buildings or trees, from adjacent areas, as if to show that both are in flux. Also in 1914, Marin first visited Maine. With the exception of trips to Taos, New Mexico, in 1929 and 1930, he spent every summer in Maine after 1920. The many seascapes he painted there until his death reflect an intimacy with the Atlantic. Like his urban scenes, Marin's Maine scenes show increasingly vigorous brushstrokes in striated, blotched, or wavy patterns. These denote, for example, clouds or sunlight to fortify a section or the shape of a composition; jagged short strokes also appear to describe the foliage of a tree; rounded lines capture the movement of a wave. His abstraction reached its peak after his participation in the 1916 Forum Exhibition, in which he saw paintings by several American artists who were working in the direction of nonobjectivity. Some of them, such as his friend Marsden Hartley, another in Stieglitz's celebrated group of artists, were more in touch with current trends, European movements, and theories than was Marin, and they inspired his pursuit of abstract ideals.

In the 1920s, when Marin was recognized as the preeminent watercolorist in the nation, remaining in that position for virtually the rest of his life, his work began to be characterized by a more closely integrated structure of interlocking planes, which created a precarious balance as his direct and close response to nature and the city continued with increasing abstraction. His personalized interpretations, whether rural or urban settings, combined land, sea, or architectural structures as points of departure. In his works, these elements do not lose their identity while the artist explores the total visual field for its abstract potential. For example, Marin developed and accentuated with heavy lines geometric patterns he saw in adjacent buildings. By imposing such design elements, he integrated his own glances and reflections with a sense of order. Balance and harmony were achieved by Marin's sensitive melding of realist and abstract tendencies. This integrated structure comprised writhing shapes, expressive linear washes treated in flat geometric forms or wave patterns, and rapid lines to describe trees, mountains, tidy Maine villages, even city sounds. His watercolors reached full strength in the brilliant palette of *Sun, Isles, and Sea* (1921), with its welter of brushmarks in bold colors forming streaks and blotches that recall the pulsations of nature's growth. To temper his exuberance for these images

and the energy he sensed in them, Marin developed, out of his cubist experiments, enclosure or framing devices. These emphatic outlines, as seen in *Deer Island, Maine* (1922), prevent his "movements" from sliding off the edges of the picture, tie disparate images and various forces within a scene, and affirm the flatness of the picture plane. Framing elements in *Lower Manhattan* (1922), with its collaged star on top of the since-destroyed Pulitzer Building and its many dense cubist passages, serve as a cap on a city about to explode with growth and power.

The 1930s were marked by increasing recognition of Marin as one of the great living masters of American art. During this period he used oil paint as if to experiment in those characteristics that are different from watercolor. By 1931 the ocean had become a major subject and would remain so for the rest of his life. *Rocks and Seas* (1932), with its churning and thickly applied paint evoking the movement of waves, typifies this interest. By the end of the decade he had painted the sea in all of its moods, grey as well as blue, rough as well as calm. Also in this decade, he pictured buildings, such as skyscrapers in *Mid-Manhattan 1* (1932), which indicate the persistence of his architectural experience, as well as churches in New Mexico and Delaware. Human subjects, appearing as parts of design schemes in the 1920s, became principal subjects starting around 1933. These figures reflect his continued interest in the movement of life around him, yet in the view of Sheldon Reich, the major Marin scholar, they constitute his weakest paintings. Reich considers Marin's figures to be rather flat and lacking in a sense of plastic awareness, with no underlying emphasis on their three-dimensional anatomical aspects. The Marin exhibition held in 1936 at the Museum of Modern Art was the first held outside the confines of Stieglitz's various galleries and, therefore, the first large-scale public viewing since Marin's return to the United States in 1911.

The 1940s was a period of triumph and sorrow. Marin's wife, with whom he had shared a close, rather isolated life, died in 1945; Stieglitz, the following year. Marin and Georgia O'Keeffe attempted but were unable to continue the gallery 291. By 1950 Marin was being represented by the Downtown Gallery, owned and operated by Edith Halpert. Because his work was constantly on display in a special room there, it was possible to view a small, frequently changing, and continuous retrospective of his paintings. Marin's oils and watercolors reached a greater freedom and expressiveness than ever in the 1940s. Increasingly abstract tendencies eliminated the previous rather naturalistic boundaries between various compositional parts such as sky and sea. In *Sea Fantasy, Maine* (1943) paint is rapidly scrubbed onto the canvas, and coarser brushwork delineates sea, cloud, and a figure in the sky. Without this rugged calligraphy, used to suggest nature's power, the canvas would almost be a total abstraction.

Ease and fluidity characterized Marin's final years. Pure painted line (an application of color devoid of textural effects and attempts to blend in other shades or tones), in serpentine forms or angular shapes, appeared around 1947, as an independent force and often formed a network of allover calligraphy symbolizing various forces or natural elements. Marin's desire to translate movement was realized in *The Written Sea* (1952), in which some of the oils were applied by forcing paint out of a syringe. These late expressionist works reflect the bolder and freer qualities that his painting had attained.

Marin, who had transformed watercolor into a major medium for artists, received many honors and tributes during the last years of his life. In 1948, a *Look* magazine survey of artists, curators, art critics, and museum directors selected him as the number one painter in the United States. The greatest watercolorist since Winslow Homer, Marin revealed in his late style a persistent response to the qualities of nature. This style bore visual affinities to the techniques of some abstract expressionists who rose to prominence during these same years, yet he was also interested in the visible world and attempted to express its growth, sounds, motions, and reflections. A prolific writer of letters, articles, and essays, Marin employed an individualistic style of punctuation—he eliminated commas and used dashes and capitalization for emphasis—that was comparable to his visual style. He wrote about himself, his family, his fishing, his neighbors, even his art. Marin died at his summer home in Cape Split, Maine.

• Photographs of Marin, exhibition catalogs, newspaper articles, correspondences, and Sheldon Reich's research materials are in the Archives of American Art, Washington, D.C. An extensive collection of Marin clippings is in the Whitney Museum of American Art. Art critic Dorothy Norman, a friend, edited *The Selected Writings of John Marin* (1949), which provides additional material to the 1931 volume edited for 291 by Herbert Seligmann, Marin's good friend and neighbor in Maine. The Norman volume, a compilation of Marin's writings and letters, particularly to Stieglitz, has facsimiles of Marin's original handwritten pages. Carl Zigrosser's *The Complete Etchings of John Marin* (1969) is the most renowned study of Marin's prints. The authoritative study of Marin is Sheldon Reich's *John Marin: A Stylistic Analysis and Catalogue Raisonne* (2 vols., 1970). The outstanding critical study is Ruth Fine's *John Marin* (1990). It is an indispensable, comprehensive, scholarly, and well-illustrated text. Fine, a curator at the National Gallery of Art, compiled a selected bibliography that provides critical information regarding Marin's writings, biographies, exhibition catalogs, and monographs. An obituary is in the *New York Times*, 2 Oct. 1953.

CAROL SALUS

MARION, Frances (18 Nov. 1888–12 May 1973), screenwriter, was born Marion Benson Owens in San Francisco, California, the daughter of Len Douglas Owens, an advertising executive, and Minnie Hall, a pianist. Her parents were divorced when she was ten, and Marion lived with her mother. She was suspended from elementary school when she was twelve for drawing satiric pictures of her teacher and was sent to St. Margaret's Hall, a private boarding school in San Mateo. At sixteen, she transferred to the Mark Hopkins Art Institute in San Francisco, affiliated with the University of California at Berkeley. The Art Institute was destroyed in the earthquake of 1906, as was much of her parents' wealth, and in October of that year Marion married her nineteen-year-old art instructor, Wesley de Lappe. She worked as an artist, illustrator, assistant and model for the photographer Arnold Genthe, and reporter for the *San Francisco Examiner*. She and de Lappe divorced in 1911; that November she married wealthy businessman Robert Pike, moving with him to Los Angeles where she painted posters for Morosco's theaters.

In 1914 Marion was hired as an actress and general assistant by Lois Weber, the foremost woman film director in Hollywood, and was given the stage name Frances Marion. The petite, chestnut-haired Marion had the looks to be an actress, but she preferred working on the other side of the camera, and from Weber she learned writing, cutting, and other technical aspects of filmmaking. Marion met Mary Pickford, acting with her in *The Girl of Yesterday* (1915) and then writing *The Foundling* for her, but the latter film was burned in a laboratory fire before it was released. Marion went to New York to write for William Brady, head of World Films; Pike sued her for divorce on grounds of desertion. At World she wrote six scenarios a month, was named head of the scenario department, and at $200 a week became the highest-paid writer in the business. In 1917 she reteamed with Pickford to write *Poor Little Rich Girl*, followed by *Rebecca of Sunnybrook Farm*, *The Little Princess*, and a series of films directed by Marshall Neilan that firmly established the star, the writer, and the director at the top of their fields.

Marion left Hollywood and a $50,000 annual salary to be assigned as a government war correspondent, writing and editing a film on women's contributions to the war effort in 1918. She was the first Allied correspondent to cross the Rhine after the Armistice. Before leaving for Europe she had met Frederick Clifton Thomson, an Army chaplain and champion athlete; she married him upon their return from the war in November 1919. They had two children, Fred, born in 1926, and Richard, adopted as a baby in 1927.

When Mary Pickford and Douglas Fairbanks married in 1920, they honeymooned together with Marion and Thomson in Europe; Marion then directed Pickford in *The Love Light*. Frances Marion directed or codirected several more films, but she lacked the desire and authoritarian will she felt a director needed. William Randolph Hearst offered to double her salary to $2,000 a week to write for Marion Davies, and for several years Marion freelanced for various studios, writing for Davies, Norma and Constance Talmadge, Colleen Moore, Alma Rubens, Ronald Colman, and Rudolph Valentino. She wrote *Humoresque* and *The Dramatic Life of Abraham Lincoln*, both winners of *Photoplay*'s Film of the Year award. For the producer Sam Goldwyn, Marion wrote *Stella Dallas* and Gary Cooper's first film, *The Winning of Barbara Worth*.

Thomson left the ministry after marrying the twice-divorced Marion, becoming a popular cowboy star known for promoting kindness to animals and action stunts that minimized violence. Marion wrote many of his scripts under her pseudonym, Frank M. Clifton. In 1926 she signed with MGM, working for Irving Thalberg and writing *The Scarlet Letter* for Lillian Gish, *Love* for Greta Garbo, and *The Cossacks* for John Gilbert.

On Christmas 1928 Thomson died of tetanus, and Marion was left to raise their small sons. After six months she returned to MGM and was assigned to write Garbo's first "talkie," *Anna Christie*, as well as *Their Own Desire* and *Let Us Be Gay* for Norma Shearer. In 1930 Marion became the first woman writer to win an Academy Award for writing achievement, with her original prison story, *The Big House*. That same year she married the film's director, George Hill. She stayed at MGM, reviving the career of her old friend Marie Dressler with *Min and Bill*. Marion won another Academy Award for *The Champ* in 1932 and returned to work with Mary Pickford on her last film as an actress, *Secrets*. Although not active politically, except for marching in suffrage parades, Marion used her position to help younger writers by being elected the first vice president and only woman on the board of the Screen Writer's Guild when it was founded in 1933. Her marriage to George Hill lasted less than a year, but they remained friends and were working together on *The Good Earth* in 1934 when he committed suicide.

Marion then took almost a year off from work, traveling with her children and reassessing her career. In the early years she had worked on the set with directors and helped in casting. In the new industry, women had been welcome at all levels, but as moviemaking became a big business, writers were more and more isolated. Marion made plans to enter into a multiyear agreement with Irving Thalberg to "write, direct and produce" exclusively with him, but his death in September 1936 abruptly ended the protection he had provided. MGM put her on a week-to-week contract, and, while she stayed with the studio off and on for another decade, she primarily "doctored" scripts and her name rarely appeared in the credits.

She turned to sculpting, painting, traveling, and writing novels to channel her creative energies and concentrated on raising her sons. Always looking ahead to her next project and actively involved with her multitude of friends, Marion died in Los Angeles. She was credited with writing 300 scripts and over 130 produced films.

• Marion donated a small portion of her personal papers to the University of Southern California Cinema Library. Marion wrote *Off with Their Heads: A Serio-Comic Tale of Hollywood* (1972), which she said was a story of her friends and not an autobiography; it contains relatively few facts about her own life. She published one book of short stories, *Valley People* (1935); a textbook, *How to Write and Sell Film Stories* (1937), and four novels, *Minnie Flynn* (1925), *Molly, Bless Her* (1937), *Westward the Dream* (1948), and *The Powder Keg* (1953). DeWitt Bodeen's essay on her in *Films in Review* was revised and lengthened for his book *More from Hollywood* (1977) and includes a filmography. See also Cari Beauchamp, *Creative Screenwriting* (Fall 1994), and Beauchamp's biography, *Frances Marion and the Powerful Women of Early Hollywood* (1997). Obituaries are in the *New York Times*, 14 May 1973, and in *Time* and *Newsweek*, both 28 May 1973.

CARI BEAUCHAMP

MARION, Francis (1732–26 Feb. 1795), revolutionary war soldier, was born in St. John's Parish, Berkeley County, South Carolina, the son of Gabriel Marion, a planter, and Esther Cordes. His grandparents were French Huguenots who had fled France in 1690 after the revocation of the Edict of Nantes and settled on the Santee River. He was the youngest of six children, a frail and puny lad until his twelfth birthday, after which he grew stronger. He received a modicum of education and at the age of sixteen joined the crew of a small schooner bound for the West Indies. On the return voyage, the vessel was rammed by a whale, and Marion, along with the rest of the crew, took to the jolly boat. After tossing about on the waves for a week, he and his mates were rescued by a passing ship, but not before two had died. Cured of any love for the sea, he settled down with his father on the latter's small plantation, and when the elder Marion died in 1750 he assumed management of the estate. In 1773 he became the owner of his own place, "Pond Bluff," near Eutaw Springs, where he made his home for the rest of his life.

Marion began his career as a soldier in 1756 when he enlisted in Captain John Postell's militia company. Five years later he joined Captain William Moultrie's militia as first lieutenant and marched with Lieutenant Colonel James Grant's British army against the Cherokee in upper South Carolina. He distinguished himself in a skirmish near the Indian town of Etchoe, leading a unit of thirty men against the main enemy position. In 1775, at the outbreak of the revolutionary war, he was elected as a delegate to the provincial congress of South Carolina, which voted to raise two state regiments and a body of cavalry to defend the colony against Great Britain. Marion was appointed captain of the Second Regiment (which soon became a Continental unit), and after helping to capture Fort Johnson, guarding the harbor at Charleston, he was promoted to major. The following year he played an important role in repulsing a British assault against Charleston, for which he was promoted to lieutenant colonel in the Continental army. Until 1779 he commanded Fort Moultrie on Sullivan's Island, near Charleston, then in October of that year took part in the patriot assault on Savannah. In early 1780 he broke his ankle and was furloughed home to recuperate, thus avoiding capture when Charleston fell to the enemy in May.

Recovered by July 1780, Marion joined General Johann de Kalb's army at Coxe's Mill, North Carolina, as it prepared to counter a thrust by Charles, Lord Cornwallis toward Virginia. Marion was dispatched immediately on a reconnaissance mission, and when he rejoined the main army de Kalb had been superseded by General Horatio Gates. Just before Gates's army was disastrously routed in the battle at Camden in mid-August, Marion was once more detached, this time under orders to sever British communications with Charleston. After the Camden debacle, and after General Thomas Sumter was defeated by the British at Fishing Creek shortly thereafter, Marion's little militia army was the only significant American force remaining in South Carolina. With this command, Marion, now promoted to brigadier general, commenced a campaign of harassment against British detachments, using strongly propatriot territory around Williamsburg as a base. Living on simple food such as hominy and sweet potatoes, striking swiftly at the enemy and then seeming to melt back into the swamps, he appeared almost superhuman to the British. For Marion, however, this mode of warfare was only the best he could do under the circumstances. His militiamen almost drove him crazy with their coming and going at will, and their "disappearing" act represented merely their mass desertion after a battle. And if Marion subsisted on simple food, it was solely because he could procure no better.

Nevertheless, over the next few months Marion gradually eroded British positions in South Carolina. In August and September he fought two fairly substantial skirmishes with Tories and British regulars. Three months later he unsuccessfully attacked Georgetown. Mostly, however, he harassed enemy supply lines, captured dispatch riders, and disrupted enemy recruiting parties. When Major General Nathanael Greene took command of America's southern armies in late 1780, Greene sent Colonel Henry Lee and his legion to assist Marion in a second unsuccessful assault on Georgetown. When Greene retreated northward in early 1781, Marion remained in the Pee Dee River region of northeastern South Carolina, fighting constantly to keep his little command from being destroyed by the British. After Greene's return to South Carolina in April, he sent Lee to cooperate with Marion in capturing Fort Watson, northwest of British-occupied Charleston. Then Marion took nearby Fort Motte on his own. He also carried out his third unsuccessful attack on Georgetown. Cooperating with Greene in August and September, he maneuvered brilliantly against Francis, Lord Rawdon before the battle of Eutaw Springs and in that battle commanded militia forces on the field. For the remainder of the war he was involved in desultory fighting, which ceased only when the British evacuated Charleston on 14 December 1782.

Even while the war continued, in 1781 Marion was elected to the state senate, remaining there more or less constantly until 1791, attempting to ameliorate harsh laws against Tories. Financially, he was practically bankrupted by the war, for Pond Bluff had been reduced to ruins by British forces. In 1784, to alleviate his sufferings, the legislature appointed him commandant of Fort Johnson, with an annual salary of £500.

Two years later, when he married Mary Esther Videau, a rich cousin, his salary, no longer needed, was reduced to a pittance, but he continued as commandant of the fort until 1790. That year, he served as a delegate to the state constitutional convention. When he died, childless, at Pond Bluff, he was buried in the family graveyard at his father's plantation, "Belle Isle." Remembered by his friends as a brave, simple, quiet, and courteous man, he was soon metamorphosed into the near-legendary "Swamp Fox" by his author friend and military compatriot Colonel Peter Horry and others.

• Collections of Marion papers are in the South Carolina Department of Archives, the South Carolina Collection, University of South Carolina, and the Henry L. Huntington Library, San Marino, Calif. Contemporary accounts of Marion's military services are Banastre Tarleton, *A History of the Campaigns of 1780 and 1781 in the Southern Provinces of North America* (1787); William Moultrie, *Memoirs of the American Revolution . . .* (2 vols., 1802); Henry Lee, *Memoirs of the War in the Southern Department of the United States*, ed. Robert E. Lee (1870); and John Drayton, *Memoirs of the American Revolution . . .* (2 vols., 1821). Among numerous biographies, the best are William Gilmore Simms, *The Life of Francis Marion* (1844); Robert D. Bass, *Swamp Fox: The Life and Campaigns of General Francis Marion* (1959); and Hugh F. Rankin, *Francis Marion: The Swamp Fox* (1973). Others are Peter Horry and Mason L. Weems, *The Life of Gen. Francis Marion, A Celebrated Partisan Officer in the Revolutionary War . . .* (1845), and William Dobein James, *A Sketch of the Life of Brig. Gen. Francis Marion and a History of His Brigade . . .* (1821). A good short sketch is George F. Scheer, "The Elusive Swamp Fox," *American Heritage* 9 (1958): 40–47.

PAUL DAVID NELSON

MARIS, Roger Eugene (10 Sept. 1934–14 Dec. 1985), professional baseball player, was born in Hibbing, Minnesota, the son of Rudolph Maras, Sr. (who changed the spelling of his family's last name in 1955), a railroad worker, and Anne Corrine "Connie" Sturbitz. The family moved to Grand Forks, North Dakota, and then to Fargo, North Dakota, where Maris became an all-around athlete. At Shanley High, a Catholic school, he played basketball, ran track, and excelled at football. In one game against Devils Lake, he scored five touchdowns, at that time a state record. In another, he set a national record, since broken, by returning four kickoffs for touchdowns.

Shanley did not have a baseball team, so Maris played in the local American Legion program. In 1950 he played in the outfield and pitched for the Fargo team that won the state championship. He hit .367 and was named the team's most valuable player. The following season he again starred offensively, but his team was unable to repeat as champion.

After high school, Maris had to decide whether to attend college and play football or sign a contract to play professional baseball. He visited the University of Oklahoma but turned down the offer of an athletic scholarship. "I realized then," he recalled, "that sitting in a classroom wasn't for me."

The Cleveland Indians and the Chicago Cubs had expressed interest in Maris while he was playing in the legion program, but after a tryout, the Cubs decided he was too small to play baseball. The Indians took a chance and signed Maris to a contract for 1953 that gave him a $5,000 bonus and promised $10,000 more if he made the major leagues.

Maris insisted that he be assigned to the Class C Northern League so that he could play his first season for the Fargo-Moorhead team. Despite the Indians' fear that he would not perform well in his home town, Maris hit .325 and won the league's rookie-of-the-year award. He advanced steadily through Cleveland's minor league system and along the way learned to play well defensively and to hit home runs by pulling the ball consistently.

After the 1956 season, during which Maris had played at Indianapolis, the Indians' highest-ranked minor league team, he married his high school sweetheart, Patricia Ann Carvell. They had six children.

Cleveland promoted Maris to the major leagues in 1957. He started the season strongly, but after sustaining two broken ribs in a collision at second base, his batting average tailed off to .235. He refused Cleveland general manager Frank Lane's request to play winter baseball in Latin America, and Lane resolved to trade him as soon as was practical. Midway through the 1958 season, he was dealt to the Kansas City Athletics.

Maris remained with Kansas City for a season and a half. He finished 1958 with respectable statistics and began 1959 with high expectations. An appendectomy sidelined him in May, but he returned to the lineup just three weeks later. Weak but determined, he played well and was selected to play in the year's second all-star game. For the season, he hit 16 homers, batted in 72 runs, and hit .273.

The New York Yankees, the American League's dominant team, had been interested in acquiring Maris for several years. On 11 December 1959 they traded for him in a seven-player deal. Maris protested that he did not want to leave Kansas City, where his family had made its home, but under baseball's rules he had no choice.

Maris established himself as an excellent addition to the New York roster early in the 1960 season. At six feet and 200 pounds, he hit with power and impressed his new teammates with his fielding. His Yankees debut was a true show: two home runs, a double, a single, and four runs batted in. Before the season was half over, he had amassed 25 homers, a total that invited some comparison with baseball's greatest slugger, Babe Ruth. New York manager Casey Stengel called Maris "fast, eager, ambitious, and full of pride. He is going to make a big difference to this club of ours." An August crash into an outfield wall put Maris on the disabled list, but the Yankees still came on to win the American League pennant. Maris finished with 39 homers, 112 RBIs, and a .283 batting average, good enough to earn the league's Most Valuable Player award.

The apex of Maris's major league career came in 1961 when he hit sixty-one home runs to surpass Babe Ruth's single-season record by one. Both Maris and his more illustrious teammate, Mickey Mantle, who hit 54, stayed abreast of Ruth's 1927 pace most of the season. Their pursuit of this hallowed record subjected both players, dubbed the M&M boys, to inordinate pressure on the field and extraordinary attention from a ravenous press.

Mantle bore up under this ordeal better than Maris, but a late September illness ended Mantle's chance to bypass Ruth. Maris persevered in the face of widespread resentment from fans and sportswriters jealously guarding Ruth's legacy. Maris insisted that he did not dwell on surpassing Ruth's mark, but he clearly was disturbed by the intense scrutiny his assault on the record created. He later recalled, "The sportswriters began ripping me apart and baseball was no longer fun. I dreaded coming to the park. I refused to talk to most of the reporters." Maris was further embittered by a controversial ruling by commissioner Ford Frick, Ruth's one-time ghostwriter. The American League had expanded by two teams in 1961 and lengthened its schedule from 154 to 162 games, and Frick declared that Ruth's record could be broken only by a player hitting 61 home runs in 154 or fewer games.

Maris did not hit his 60th home run until the Yankees' 159th game, and his 61st homer, against pitcher Tracy Stallard of the Boston Red Sox, did not come until 1 October in the last game of the year. Whether this performance broke Ruth's record or not is a question still debated in baseball circles, but in addition he led the league in RBIs, runs scored, and total bases. He captured a second consecutive MVP award and the Hickok Belt as the best professional athlete of the year.

Maris played five more seasons for the Yankees, but after 1962, when he hit 33 homers and had 100 RBIs, his yearly output declined because of injuries. In December 1966 he was traded to the St. Louis Cardinals, for whom he played dependably for two seasons as they won a pair of National League pennants. He retired in 1968 to operate a beer distributorship in Gainesville, Florida. For years he remained estranged from baseball, unable to forget the disaffection engendered during his record-setting season.

In 12 major league seasons, Maris hit .260 with 275 home runs and 851 RBIs. In addition to his two MVP awards, he was named Major League Player of the Year for 1960 by the *Sporting News*. He appeared in seven World Series and five all-star games but did not garner enough support from voting members of the Baseball Writers' Association of America to be elected to the Hall of Fame.

In 1983 Maris was diagnosed with lymphatic cancer. While undergoing treatment, including some experimental therapy, he made a long-delayed return to Yankee Stadium to see the retirement of his number and the unveiling of a plaque memorializing his achievement. He died in a Houston hospital.

• There are clipping files on Maris at the National Baseball Library, Cooperstown, N.Y., and at the *Sporting News*, St. Louis, Mo. Maris told his own story to sportswriter Jim Ogle in *Roger Maris at Bat* (1962). Later biographies include Maury Allen, *Roger Maris: A Man for All Seasons* (1986), and Harvey Rosenfeld, *Roger Maris: A Title to Fame* (1991). Both are highly eulogistic and argue that Maris should be elected to baseball's Hall of Fame. For a broader context, see Tony Kubek and Terry Pluto, *Sixty-One: The Team, the Record, the Men* (1987), and Ralph Houk and Robert W. Creamer, *Season of Glory: The Amazing Saga of the 1961 New York Yankees* (1988). Obituaries are in the *New York Times*, 15 Dec. 1985, and the *Sporting News*, 23 Dec. 1985.

STEVEN P. GIETSCHIER

MARKEL, Lester (9 Jan. 1894–23 Oct. 1977), journalist, was born in New York City, the son of Jacob Leo Markel, a prominent German-Jewish banker, and Lillian Hecht. Markel attended Townsend Harris High School, the College of the City of New York, and the Columbia School of Journalism, from which he received a bachelor of letters degree in 1914. Markel married Meta Edman on 3 April 1917; they had one daughter.

In college, Markel wrote and edited the *Northside News* in the Bronx. He joined the staff of the *New York Tribune* after he graduated and rose steadily as night city editor, night editor, and in 1919 assistant managing editor. In 1923 the publisher of the *New York Times*, Adolph S. Ochs, recruited Markel to run the faltering Sunday department of his newspaper. The two men worked out the arrangement in rolling chairs on the Atlantic City boardwalk. In a spectacular professional miscalculation, the *Tribune* let Markel get away in part because, in the words of its owner, "he is a Jew" (Kluger, p. 385).

During the next forty years Markel transformed the *Sunday Times* into one of the most influential and prosperous enterprises in American journalism. His small initial staff of five grew to more than eighty by the early 1950s. He improved the existing elements of the Sunday edition, such as the *New York Times Book Review* and the *New York Times Magazine*, and brought the arts, music, drama, radio (and later television) into one section. The Sunday edition added features on science, education, home furnishings, stamps, cameras, and a crossword puzzle in the *Magazine* during the 1930s and 1940s. The Sunday edition also carried current news and sporting events, but for Markel the main contribution of his part of the *Times* was the emphasis on news analysis. It took Markel more than a decade to establish the cornerstone of the revamped *Sunday Times*, the "News of the Week in Review," which debuted on 25 January 1935. In time it became "The Week in Review." This section allowed Markel to pursue what he called interpretive journalism. In his mind, "mere statements of fact, without interpretation of the meaning of facts, are meaningless" (*New York Times*, 24 Oct. 1977). For policymakers and politicians, "The Week in Review" became one of the indispensable aspects of their newspaper reading. The *New York Times Magazine* also served as an influential outlet for statements and commentary by powerful figures in the news. Markel's customary fee of $300 remained small by industry standards, but the chance to write for the *Times* brought him the writers he wanted. During Markel's heyday, there were two versions of the *New York Times*, the daily paper and the Sunday edition with Markel's unique stamp on it.

As an editor, Markel was a demanding perfectionist who insisted that everyone on his staff meet his standards of excellence. "I'm not looking for admiration," he said. "All I want is respect" (*Times*, 24 Oct. 1977). His medium height and wire-rimmed glasses gave Markel a meek appearance that belied his well-deserved reputation as a martinet. When roused to anger, as happened regularly in his office, his high-pitched voice dominated the eighth floor of the *Times* where the Sunday paper was assembled each week. In one *Times* anecdote, the ever-impatient Markel had two copy boys hold seats for him when a preview of a Marilyn Monroe movie, "Let's Make Love," did not provide reserved seats for critics. Always free with his comments about other colleagues, Markel bristled when the *Times* television critic, Jack Gould, reviewed unfavorably a program of news analysis that the *Times* produced in collaboration with National Educational Television. The show "News in Perspective" aired on a New York City station on 1 October 1963 and reflected Markel's interest in using television as a medium for news analysis. Markel's irate public response to Gould's negative notice received coverage in *Time* and *Newsweek*. As with so many of Markel's eruptions, the two men reconciled and their professional friendship endured.

In addition to his duties at the *Times*, Markel wrote extensively about the interaction of public opinion and the U.S. government. His books included *Background and Foreground* (1960) and *What You Don't Know Can Hurt You: A Study of Public Opinion and Public Emotion* (1972). He also edited the anthology *Public Opinion and Foreign Policy* (1949). He published many articles in the *New York Times Magazine* and other leading periodicals. Markel was an early pioneer in using television to reach a broader audience for the opinions of journalists. To the end of his life he remained interested in the potential of television as a means of educating the public.

After four decades at the *Times*, Markel had become an institution when Arthur Ochs "Punch" Sulzberger, Jr., was named publisher in 1963. The new executive regarded the existence of two newspapers within the same firm as "the Markel problem." He solved the dilemma in the summer of 1964 when he informed Markel that the newspaper would have only one editor in the future. Markel received an assignment to examine the future of the *Times* as a way of easing the transition to retirement. His formal departure from the paper came in 1968. For the last ten years of his life, Markel taught as a Distinguished Visiting Professor at Fairleigh Dickinson University, and consulted about television and news issues. His energy and interest in the news remained strong until he fell ill with cancer during 1977. He died in New York City. Despite Markel's abrasiveness, his colleagues recognized his editorial ability. "The trouble with Markel," said one of them about his insistence on numerous revisions, "is that he's always right" (*Times*, 24 Oct. 1977). Markel's achievement with creation of the *Sunday Times* proved his permanent legacy as a journalist, and the character of what he did to shape the newspaper was still evident in the *Times* years after his death.

• The Lester Markel Papers are at the State Historical Society of Wisconsin. Other Markel materials can be found at the Archives of the *New York Times*, which the newspaper operates in New York City, and in the Turner Catledge Papers at Mississippi State University. Markel did an oral history interview, the transcript of which is at the Oral History Research Office, Columbia University. "The Future of the Printed Word," *Vital Speeches of the Day*, 1 Apr. 1956, pp. 381–384, is representative of his magazine writing. For articles and books with information about Markel, see Meyer Berger, *The Story of The New York Times, 1851–1951* (1951); "Cactus Jack," *Time*, 11 Oct. 1963; Gay Talese, *The Kingdom and the Power* (1969); Turner Catledge, *My Life and The Times* (1971); Richard Kluger, *The Paper: The Life and Death of the New York Herald Tribune* (1986); and Joseph C. Goulden, *Fit to Print: A. M. Rosenthal and His Times* (1988). The *New York Times*, 24 Oct. 1977, has a lengthy obituary.

LEWIS L. GOULD

MARKEY, Lucille Parker Wright (11 Dec. 1888–24 July 1982), thoroughbred breeder, stable owner, and philanthropist, was born in Tolesboro, Kentucky, the daughter of John Winslow Parker, a wealthy tobacco grower, and Belle Owens. Little is known about her life before 1919, when she married Warren Wright, the president of his family's Calumet Baking Powder Company. A few years later Markey and her husband arrived at Calumet Farm, a trotting horse farm in Lexington, Kentucky, which was established by Wright's father. She would be intimately involved with Calumet Farm the rest of her life.

Markey gradually became familiar with the operations of Calumet, particularly so after 1931, when Wright inherited Calumet Farm and changed it to a thoroughbred breeding farm and stable. She became directly involved in thoroughbred breeding and racing and she assumed the responsibility of naming most of the horses produced by Calumet. At the beginning Calumet was unprofitable, and the Wrights considered putting the farm up for sale in 1939; Markey then hired Ben Jones as trainer, marking the rise of Calumet Farm to national attention.

From 1941 to 1961 Calumet Farm enjoyed unparalleled success, placing it at the top of the horse racing world. In 1941 Calumet had its first Triple Crown winner (winning the Kentucky Derby, the Preakness, and the Belmont Stakes) with Whirlaway, whose spectacular run set a track record of 2:01⅖ that remained unbroken for twenty-one years. Whirlaway was also the first horse to earn half a million dollars. Before 1950 Calumet had bred, raised, and raced four Kentucky Derby winners. After Whirlaway's win, Pensive

won the Derby in 1944. Calumet had its second Triple Crown winner in 1948 with the legendary Citation, who made racing history by winning $1 million and finishing in the money forty-four times in forty-five starts. The Seventy-Fifth Diamond Jubilee Kentucky Derby in 1949 was won by Calumet's Ponder.

Warren Wright died in 1950, leaving Calumet Farm entirely in Markey's capable hands. Two years later she married Gene Markey, a retired rear admiral and movie producer. She was actively involved with the farm, spending each spring and early fall at Calumet, summer in Saratoga, New York, and late fall and winter in Miami, Florida, to follow her racing stable. No matter where she was, Markey remained in almost daily contact with the trainer, guiding the direction of the farm. Under her firm leadership, Calumet Farm would produce four more Kentucky Derby winners between 1950 and 1968. Hill Gail won in 1952, followed in 1957 by Iron Liege. In 1958 the Derby was won by Tim Tam and ten years later it would be Forward Pass.

Markey hoped for one more Derby winner in 1978 with Alydar; the promising three-year-old had begun winning important races in the winter of 1977–1978, particularly the 1978 Blue Grass Stakes at Keeneland. Because of her failing health, the Blue Grass was the last race Markey was able to attend in person. She and her husband were driven to the rail by the homestretch to see Alydar win by thirteen lengths. There would not be another Derby winner, however; Alydar came in second and would go on to be the first Triple Crown runner-up.

Markey ran Calumet Farm with efficiency and economy. Unlike many other thoroughbred establishments, Calumet seldom lost money, managing in most years to cover any farm losses with the winnings of the racing stable. Under Markey, Calumet's horses earned the farm $26.4 million dollars in purses. It remained for many years the best known thoroughbred operation in the world.

Apart from horse racing, Markey enjoyed a substantial income from oil properties left her by her first husband. In the mid 1970s, because of the rapid rise in world oil prices and a change in her ownership of the Waddell oil and gas field in West Texas, her income multiplied almost ten times. With this newfound wealth, she made increased donations to The Bluegrass Boys' Ranch for underprivileged boys. Markey also made substantial charitable gifts for cancer research and education and for arthritis research. She died at Calumet Farm, leaving virtually her entire estate to be spent for the "support and encouragement of basic medical research," with all the money to be distributed within fifteen years of her death. In 1997 the trustees of the estate closed their operation after distributing over $500 million to American medical research institutions through the Lucille P. Markey Charitable Trust. The trust became an important model for private philanthropy on behalf of medical research.

• Very little has been written about Markey. A source on her early career is A. H. Auerbach's *Wild Ride* (1944). A short retrospective on Calumet Farm is "The Derby Is Old Hat In Calumet," *Sports Illustrated*, 17 Apr. 1978. An obituary is in the *New York Times*, 26 July 1982.

LOUIS J. HECTOR

MARKHAM, Edwin (23 Apr. 1852–7 Mar. 1940), poet, was born Charles Edwin Anson Markham in Oregon City in the Oregon Territory, the son of Samuel Barzillai Markham and Elizabeth Winchell, a rancher. Shortly after Markham's birth, his parents divorced, and he remained with his mother. In 1856 they moved to a ranch near Suisun, California, where Markham learned to do manual labor and from which his siblings gradually departed to escape their mother's oppressive presence. Markham himself ran away briefly in 1867, returning only when his mother agreed to help subsidize his education. He studied at California College in Vacaville, receiving teacher's certification, and subsequently at both San Jose Normal School and Christian College in Santa Rosa.

Markham began teaching in 1872 in Los Berros, California; in 1874 he moved to Coloma, where he was a popular and prominent figure. There he entered the first of his three marriages, wedding Annie Cox in 1875. They relocated to Placerville, California, where Markham was employed as a school administrator. At about the same time, Markham fell under the influence of Thomas Lake Harris, whom Joseph Slade describes as "a poet, spiritualist, socialist, and charlatan." Markham's interest in Harris's esoteric ideas shaped much of his intellectual and artistic development, and even in his earliest published poetry, which appeared in 1880, one can see the imprint of Harris's ideology.

Markham's first marriage failed in 1884, probably largely owing to his affair with Elizabeth Senter; Senter died in 1885, leaving Markham alone again. He soon entered another relationship, this time with Caroline Bailey, whom he subsequently married under duress in 1887. She moved out when Markham's mother joined their household, and she died in 1893. In Oakland in 1898 Markham married his third and final wife, Anna Catherine Murphy, with whom he had a son. Anna was Markham's "collaborator and editor" until her death in 1938.

Throughout the 1880s and 1890s Markham continued his teaching career and worked hard to establish himself as an important poetic voice. He published several individual poems and sought the insight of established literary figures such as Hamlin Garland and Ambrose Bierce regarding what direction he should take with his verse. Garland encouraged him to emphasize the realistic, while Bierce praised him for his idealism. Ultimately, however, Markham turned to his mystic beliefs and his interest in the difficulties of poor working people and crafted the poem that made him famous: "The Man with the Hoe."

"The Man with the Hoe" was a strong commentary on America's working class and their tribulations. Inspired by French artist François Millet's 1862 woodcut, also titled *The Man with the Hoe*, Markham's poem was first published in the *San Francisco Examiner* on 15 January 1899. The work vividly describes the oppressed day laborer and sends a challenge to the larger society as well:

> Bowed by the weight of centuries he leans
> Upon his hoe and gazes on the ground,
> The emptiness of ages in his face,
> And on his back the burden of the world.
> Who made him dead to rapture and despair,
> A thing that grieves not and that never hopes,
> Stolid and stunned, a brother to the ox?
> Who loosened and let down this brutal jaw?
> Whose was the hand that slanted back this brow?
> Whose breath blew out the light within this brain?

The poem was well received and spread almost immediately across the country. In line with the broad reform movements of its day, "The Man with the Hoe" sparked a great deal of controversy. Critic Edward B. Payne (1899) noted that the poem

appears to have everywhere stimulated thought upon social problems, and to have called out vigorous and diversified expressions of opinions all along the line of its course. . . . Clergy made the poem their text; platform orators dilated upon it; college professors lectured upon it; debating societies discussed it; schools took it up for study in their literary courses; and it was the subject of conversation in social circles and on the streets.

The success of "The Man with the Hoe," which was reprinted literally thousands of times in dozens of languages before Markham's death, paved the way for Markham's advancement and also became the title work of his first book of poetry, *The Man with the Hoe and Other Poems* (1899). Not all of the poetry in the volume is radical; indeed, Markham also turned to romantic treatments of much more common poetic subjects, as "A Prayer."

> Teach me, Father, how to go
> Softly as the grasses grow;
> Hush my soul to meet the shock
> Of the wild world as a rock;
> But my spirit, propt with power,
> Make as simple as a flower.
> Let the dry heart fill its cup,
> Like a poppy looking up;
> Let life lightly wear her crown,
> Like a poppy looking down,
> When its heart is filled with dew,
> And its life begins anew.

Definitely influenced by Markham's mysticism, the poem resonates much more with contemporary American verse and does not sound the strong call to reform of the volume's title piece; nevertheless, both critics and the general public were favorably impressed.

On the strength of his first book, Markham received a request to write a poem commemorating Abraham Lincoln's birthday in 1900. He first read "Lincoln, the

Man of the People" in New York before the celebration, and once again the newspapers picked it up and spread it across the nation. The poem was again well received, both in print and when Markham read it at the birthday ceremonies; he read it publicly again in 1922 at the dedication of the Lincoln Memorial. "Lincoln" did much to further strengthen Markham's growing reputation; Jack London compared Markham's poem favorably with Whitman's "O Captain, My Captain" and suggested that in the future, Markham's would be the poetic name most closely associated with the fallen leader's legacy.

In 1901 Markham published his second volume, *Lincoln and Other Poems*. After that first burst of creative output, Markham's productivity slowed dramatically. His third volume of poetry, *The Shoes of Happiness*, did not appear until 1915; his fourth, *The Gates of Paradise*, appeared in 1920, and his final book, *New Poems: Eighty Songs at Eighty*, was published in 1932. Between publications, Markham lectured and wrote in other genres, including essays and nonfiction prose. He also gave much of his time to organizations such as the Poetry Society of America, which he established in 1910. Throughout Markham's later life, many readers viewed him as an important voice in American poetry, a position signified by honors such as his election in 1908 to the National Institute of Arts and Letters. Despite his numerous accolades, however, none of his later books achieved the success of the first two.

The change in Markham's literary significance has been tied to the development of modernist poetry and his steadfast refusal to change to meet the increasing demands arising with the appearance of poets such as Ezra Pound, T. S. Eliot, and William Carlos Williams. Their emphasis on changes in literary forms and their movement away from social commentary and political topics made much of what distinguished Markham's verse dated. He gradually fell from critical favor, and his reputation never fully recovered.

Nevertheless, despite the critics' increasing disenchantment with him, Markham remained an important public figure, traveling across the nation and receiving warm praise nearly everywhere he went. At his home on Staten Island, his birthday was a local school holiday, and children marked the event by covering his lawn with flowers. The crowning glory came on Markham's eightieth birthday, when a number of prominent citizens, including President Herbert Hoover, honored his accomplishments at a party in Carnegie Hall and named him one of the most important artists of his age. In 1936 Markham suffered a debilitating stroke from which he never fully recovered; he died at his home on Staten Island, New York.

In his day Markham managed to fuse art and social commentary in a manner that guaranteed him a place among the most famous artists of the late nineteenth century. His reputation has faded because of the somewhat dated nature of his verse; nevertheless, he remains a notable figure for his contributions to American poetry. His work stands as an example of what American critics and readers valued near the turn of the century. His poetry offers insight into an important phase in the development of American letters.

• The most comprehensive collection of Markham's papers is the Markham Archives of Horrmann Library, at Wagner College, New York City, which includes all of Markham's library and correspondence as well as numerous unpublished manuscripts and other important resources. A number of doctoral dissertations have been done on Markham; the most helpful is Joseph W. Slade, "Edwin Markham: A Critical Biography" (Ph.D. diss., New York Univ., 1971); Slade also wrote the entry on Markham for the *Dictionary of Literary Biography*, vol. 54, which is noteworthy for its comprehensiveness. Other useful sources include Louis Filler, *The Unknown Edwin Markham: His Mystery and Its Significance* (1966) and "Edwin Markham, Poetry, and What Have You," *Antioch Review* 23, no. 4 (1963–1964): 447–59. Contemporary criticism of Markham's work is interesting and useful, particularly Edward B. Payne "The 'Hoe Man' on Trial," *Arena* 22, no. 1 (1899): 17–24, and Leonard D. Abbott, "Edwin Markham: Laureate of Labor," *Comrade* 1, no. 4 (1902): 74–75. For more recent criticism, see William R. Nash, "Edwin Markham," in *Whitman's and Dickinson's Contemporaries: An Anthology of Their Verse* (1996). An obituary is in the *New York Times*, 8 Mar. 1940.

WILLIAM R. NASH

MARKHAM, William (1635?–12 June 1704), colonial governor of Pennsylvania, was born in England. He was a cousin of William Penn, but his parents have not been definitively identified; his father was probably William Markham, a naval surgeon, and his mother was probably an older sister of Admiral Sir William Penn. Markham was twice married, first to Ann Wright, with whom he had one child, and in 1684 to Joanna Johnson, a sea captain's widow with whom he had no children. He apparently spent his early life in the city of Bristol. He entered the British navy late in the Commonwealth period and served for nearly twenty years.

Markham was commissioned deputy governor of Pennsylvania by William Penn in April 1681, shortly after Penn received his charter for the colony. Markham arrived in Pennsylvania in August and, although hampered by ill health, began the task of establishing the colony. He completed the first purchase of land from the Indians, and, after an extensive search, he selected the site for Philadelphia and began the distribution of lots in the town. He opened negotiations with Lord Baltimore to settle the boundary between Pennsylvania and Maryland but after learning that 40° north latitude, the southern limit of Pennsylvania decreed by the royal charter, lay farther north than Penn had supposed, he postponed resolving the issue until Penn could himself negotiate with the Maryland proprietor.

After Penn arrived in Pennsylvania in October 1682, bringing with him deeds from the duke of York for the Three Lower Counties (later Delaware), he installed Markham at New Castle as deputy governor of the Lower Counties. Markham also served briefly as an elected representative in the provincial council for New Castle County, then traveled to England late in the summer of 1683 as Penn's agent to argue the boundary dispute with Lord Baltimore. He returned to Pennsylvania in the spring of 1685 as both provincial and proprietary secretary. He represented Kent County, Delaware, in the provincial council in 1688–1689 and again served briefly as deputy governor of the Lower Counties in 1692–1693. Concern over the defenseless condition of Pennsylvania prompted Markham to accept service as lieutenant governor under Colonel Benjamin Fletcher in 1693–1695, when the British Crown temporarily revoked Penn's authority to govern Pennsylvania.

Penn's right to govern Pennsylvania was restored partially on the condition that he retain Markham as governor. Though increasingly burdened with ill health, Markham remained in office until Penn resumed personal government of Pennsylvania during his second visit to the colony (1699–1701). During Markham's tenure, 1695–1699, Pennsylvania was rent by political conflict within the Quaker political elite. His efforts to restore the provincial general assembly to the form that had been established in 1683, before the period of royal administration, led to conflict between the factions. One faction, led by David Lloyd, sought to enhance Quaker domination of the government in the face of the growing non-Quaker minority in the colony, and another, composed of former Quakers and Quakers disgruntled by their exclusion from power by the Lloyd faction, wished to retain the 1683 frame of government. In exchange for a grant of money for imperial defense, Markham acquiesced in the passage of a new frame of government by the 1696 assembly. The 1696 constitution, which bears Markham's name, solidified Quaker control of the assembly, at the expense of new, non-Quaker immigrants, by reducing representation and restricting the franchise. Although he was a lifelong Anglican, Markham came to accept the dominance of Quakers in the Pennsylvania assembly and began to work with them.

At the same time, Markham bore the brunt of attacks on the Pennsylvania government by the growing Anglican minority in the colony, who were assisted by such powerful allies as Governor Francis Nicholson of Maryland and customs and admiralty officials Edward Randolph, Robert Quary, and John Moore. The Anglicans in Pennsylvania made common cause with their discontented coreligionists in the Lower Counties, who complained that the Quaker-dominated assembly left their coastline defenseless and vulnerable to attack by pirates and enemy privateers at a time of war between England and France. The crux of the attack lay in charges that Pennsylvania was harboring pirates and illegally exporting colonial products to non-English ports in violation of the Navigation Acts. Markham was blamed by imperial authorities for the 1698 assembly's passage of the Act for Preventing Frauds, which attempted to circumvent the vice admiralty jurisdiction by providing that trials for violations of the Navigation Acts be heard by juries in local courts. He was accused of taking bribes from suspected pirates and was compromised when his son-in-law

was accused of piracy. When Penn returned to Pennsylvania in 1699, he removed Markham from office at the insistence of the imperial authorities.

Markham was the most steadfast supporter of Penn's interests for the first two decades of Pennsylvania's existence. His letters kept Penn informed on developments in the colony, and Penn, in turn, supported Markham when the assembly criticized him in 1689 for participating in the arrest of one of its members and when the provincial council complained in 1691 that Markham was "a chief upholder of loose Clubbs, w[hi]ch are to[o] much countenanced by his presence, even at unseasonable houres." Markham determined to accept the 1696 frame of government, which Penn never approved, in exchange for the assembly's passage of a supply bill designed to protect Penn's interests with the imperial authorities, who had insisted that Pennsylvania contribute to imperial defense as a condition of the restoration of Penn's government.

Markham seldom derived much profit from his multiple posts as both a provincial and a proprietary official, yet he loyally promised Penn that he would "with patience Indure the wringing Shooe." Penn was aware of the unprofitability of Markham's service, and this probably influenced him, initially, to believe the accusations that Markham had taken bribes from suspected pirates. After receiving a hurt and angry letter from Markham in 1697, Penn went to his cousin's defense. He accepted Markham's explanation that the alleged bribe was a bequest from a suspected pirate who had a home and family in Philadelphia and attributed his cousin's inadequate enforcement of the Navigation Acts to Markham's chronic ill health. Writing to the commissioners of the customs in 1700, Penn explained that Markham had been "so rudely handled with Gout" that he was virtually "a Prisoner to his own Chamber."

Although Markham remained in disfavor with the imperial authorities, in 1703 Penn recommended him to the board of trade for another appointment as governor of Pennsylvania. In the same year Penn tried to provide Markham with a source of income by issuing him a commission as register general of the province. The commission ultimately proved unenforceable, however, as it was disputed by the incumbent officeholder, and Markham died in Philadelphia before the conflict could be resolved.

• Letters to and from Markham are located in the Penn, Logan, and Chew manuscript collections, as well as in other collections, at the Historical Society of Pennsylvania. Many of the letters have been published in the *Pennsylvania Magazine of History and Biography* 90:314–52, 491–516; in Richard S. Dunn and Mary Maples Dunn, gen. eds., *The Papers of William Penn* (5 vols., 1981–1987); and in the microfilm edition of the *Papers of William Penn* (1975). Other important sources for Markham's career in Pennsylvania are Samuel Hazard, ed., *Minutes of the Provincial Council*, Colonial Records, vol. 1 (1852), and various volumes of W. Noel Sainsbury, ed., *Calendar of State Papers, Colonial Series, America and West Indies* for the years 1681–1685 and 1696–1703. Markham's role in Pennsylvania is also discussed in Gary B. Nash, *Quak-*

ers and Politics: Pennsylvania, 1681–1726 (1968). The most complete biography of Markham is in Craig W. Horle et al., *Lawmaking and Legislators in Pennsylvania: A Biographical Dictionary*, vol. 1: *1682–1709* (1991), pp. 525–32.

JEFFREY L. SCHEIB

MARKOE, Peter (1752?–30 Jan. 1792), poet and playwright, was born on St. Croix, Danish West Indies (now the Virgin Islands), the son of Abraham Markoe, a sugar plantation owner, and Elizabeth Kenny Rogers. Educated at Pembroke College, Oxford, and the Inns of Court in London, Markoe helped manage the family holdings on St. Croix but lived in Philadelphia after his father settled there around 1770. Peter Markoe apparently never married. Both Markoe and his father, while still Danish citizens, were officers in the Philadelphia City Cavalry, the "Light Horse," in the mid 1770s.

Markoe's interests turned early to literature. In his preface to *Miscellaneous Poems* (1787) he writes, "The following Collection of Poems, many of them written when I was very young, is submitted to the Judgment of the Public with all Deference and Respect." One poem is written as from a resident of St. Croix to General Van Roepstorf on his arrival as governor in 1771, and another is to Lady Clausen on her birthday, 1780. The ode is a favored form, including the initial poems of the collection to Faith, Hope, and Charity, the latter "sacred to the memory of William Penn, the Founder of Pennsylvania." "Harmony: An Ode for Music" commemorates General George Washington's birthday:

> The Muse a bolder strain in rapture pours;
> Plato and Dion both, she cries, are ours;
> Franklin the sage's true reward has won;
> Conquest and glory grace our Washington.
>
> (p. 29)

A long ode to the tragic genius of Shakespeare pays tribute to eleven plays as "Shakespeare's bold spirit seeks our western shores" (p. 27).

There are a few epigrams like this one, "On a beautiful Lady, with a loud voice":

> That Chloe should surprize our hearts,
> And quickly lose them—where's the wonder?
> Jove's lightning from her eyes she darts
> And from her tongue she rolls his thunder.
>
> (p. 22)

A poem, "To Mrs. C———R," requesting help in the courtship of "some fair one in Y[or]k," contains a rare personal reference: "And in beauty, I own, I'm deficient myself" (p. 10).

The Storm, a long political poem, was published anonymously in 1788 together with William Falconer's *The Shipwreck*. A play, *The Patriot Chief* (1784) and a comic opera, *The Reconciliation; or, The Triumph of Nature* (1790), were published but never performed. A classical tragedy in blank verse set in the ancient kingdom of Lydia, *The Patriot Chief* nevertheless reflects American political situations in 1784. Sis-

ter Mary Chrysostom Diebels believes that "the title character, Dorus the 'patriot chief,' is a deliberate tribute to Washington" (p. 13). *The Reconciliation* has gained attention as one of the earliest American comic or ballad operas. Seven airs set to existing tunes are interspersed with prose dialogue in two acts. The play ends with five songs, sung in turn by the principal characters, with this last general chorus:

> If fond of our friends and our kindred we prove,
> Our country may safely depend on our love.
> Then may true affection each bosom possess!
> 'Tis the parent of union! the source of success!

"Our country" receives more attention in two political satires, the poem *The Times* (1788) and *The Algerine Spy in Pennsylvania* (published anonymously in 1787), purporting to be letters written by an Algerian observing America in the 1780s.

In his own day Peter Markoe was known as Peter the Poet. His small body of work may in part be attributed to his reputation as a hard drinker. Family tradition has it that he died in Philadelphia at the age of forty.

• Sister Mary Chrysostom Diebels gives much useful information in *Peter Markoe (1752?–1792): A Philadelphia Writer* (1944). Patricia H. Virga, "The American Opera to 1790" (Ph.D. diss., Rutgers Univ., 1981), includes a chapter on Markoe's *The Reconciliation*. Brief biographical sketches of Markoe are included in several compilations, and his comic opera *The Reconciliation* is mentioned in many histories of American drama. Markoe's poetry is available on microfilm in *American Poetry, 1609–1900* (1976).

DORA JEAN ASHE

MARKOE, William Morgan (11 May 1892–6 Dec. 1969), Roman Catholic clergyman, was born in St. Paul, Minnesota, the son of James Markoe, a physician, and Mary Prince. Descended from a prominent French family whose fortune stemmed from a slave-served plantation in the West Indies, Markoe grew up in St. Paul. In September 1913, after a year of college at Saint Louis University, he entered the Jesuit Seminary in Florissant, Missouri, to study for the Catholic priesthood. Two years of intense religious training left little time for any extracurricular activity, but during the following two years of classical studies he volunteered to teach Bible lessons to black children in the neighborhood in his spare time. He matriculated at Gonzaga University in Spokane, Washington, from 1918 to 1921. He graduated with an M.A. in 1921.

Gradually Markoe felt a call to the religious ministry among blacks. He began to write articles on race questions for *America*, a magazine of opinion published by Jesuits in New York City. He also began to read widely in the black press. In reading his memoirs one gets the impression that he undertook this work with a sense of remorse that his family's fortune had been enhanced by the work of slaves. Markoe taught at St. Francis Mission School on the Rosebud (Sioux) Reservation in South Dakota from 1921 to 1923. Ministering to Native Americans had always been a major concern of the midwestern Jesuits, but Markoe had no enthusiasm for the work. He later wrote that he felt like a foreigner among the Sioux. He was never to feel that way among black people.

In 1923 he began theological studies at Saint Louis University. Segregated like all Missouri schools at that time, Saint Louis University bordered on a black neighborhood that had grown dramatically during World War I. Even though thousands of unchurched blacks lived directly east of campus, only three of the ninety Jesuit priests in St. Louis worked among the city's black residents.

As a seminarian Markoe taught religion to black children and prevailed on the Sisters of the Blessed Sacrament, a group of dedicated nuns founded by Mother Katherine Drexel, to open a school for these youngsters. Markoe also wrote fifty articles on race questions for various religious magazines; he was the only Jesuit to write on these issues for Catholic publications in the early twenties.

After completing his theology course in 1926, Markoe became pastor of the citywide black parish of St. Elizabeth, located twelve blocks east of Saint Louis University. Back in the 1860s Archbishop Peter R. Kenrick of St. Louis had allowed foreign-language groups to set up nonterritorial churches. In line with these, the archbishop had wanted Black Catholics to have their own citywide church, but he did not plan it as a segregated parish, which it later became.

The pastor of St. Elizabeth was not accorded the esteem that the other pastors enjoyed in the heavily Catholic city, but Markoe had the physical strength and the moral toughness to persevere in spite of public disesteem: He put out a monthly magazine, the *St. Elizabeth's Chronicle*; he spoke about his ministry to various white churches in the city; he organized a discussion club of black and white professionals—an unprecedented step in St. Louis; he began the "Interracial Hour" on Radio Station WEW; and he served on the board of directors of the St. Louis Urban League.

Markoe came to see himself and his two Jesuit colleagues—his brother John and classmate Austin Bork—as the only ones who cared, and he had little sympathy for other points of view. He ignored the work of the Divine Word Missionaries and individuals of other religious societies who came to work among St. Louis blacks. Markoe differed strongly with black leader Dr. Thomas Turner of Hampton Institute, who worked for a blacks-only national organization, the Federated Colored Catholics. Markoe believed that blacks needed white Catholic support. Nonetheless Markoe gave the welcoming address at the seventh annual convention of Federated Colored Catholics, hosted by St. Elizabeth's parish in St. Louis in September 1931. At the next annual convention the Federated Colored Catholics joined with white Catholics to form the National Catholic Interracial Federation. *St. Elizabeth's Chronicle* became the *Interracial Review*, the official organ of the new society.

Services for black Catholics in St. Louis steadily improved in the 1930s, with the opening of a Catholic

hospital for black patients, a retreat house for black men, and a high school for boys and girls. When the high school moved to St. Ann's, formerly a white parish, Markoe asked Archbishop John J. Glennon to allow him to locate the St. Elizabeth's operation there, as industrial plants and warehouses had displaced his parishioners. When, instead of St. Ann's, the archbishop assigned the ministry to a less satisfactory area, Markoe privately but vehemently disagreed with the archbishop's policies. Shortly thereafter Markoe's provincial superior assigned him to Mankato, Minnesota, in 1944, where he preached a provocative sermon that the local pastor thought too strong, and then to Denver in 1945.

After World War II American Jesuits began to devote more attention to issues of social justice. Markoe criticized their tardiness on racial questions and wrote an article for an in-house organ demanding that his colleagues face immediately the issue of miscegenation (*ISO Bulletin* 4 [Jan. 1947]: 2–3). His focus on miscegenation, rather than other areas of discussion such as employment and housing, caused editors generally to hesitate in publishing his work, which held back much good he might otherwise have accomplished.

Assigned to a traveling missionary team in 1949, Markoe spoke in predominantly white parishes for three years. After that he accepted a position with the Department of Theology at Marquette University. Focusing his attention on the tasks assigned, Markoe seemingly avoided his central interest, ministry to blacks. While at Marquette he completed his memoirs, and once a year he visited his former parishioners in St. Louis. Markoe retired from Marquette at age seventy but continued as a student counselor until shortly before his death in Milwaukee, Wisconsin. In 1947 Archbishop Joseph E. Ritter, Glennon's successor, integrated the city's 307 Catholic schools. The *Brown* decision integrating all American schools came seven years later. Although advances came slowly, progress was made in education, employment, housing, and health care. Markoe had played a significant part in paving the way for these advances.

• Markoe's memoirs (unpublished) are in the Jesuit Missouri Province Archives, St. Louis. "A Segregated City," in William Barnaby Faherty's *Rebels or Reformers? Dissident Priests in American Life* (1987), is a short account of Markoe's career. See also Jeffrey Smith, *From Corps to Core: The Life of John F. Markoe, Soldier, Priest and Pioneer Activist* (1977), about a brother of William Markoe, and Marilyn Nickels, "The Federated Colored Catholics: A Study of Three Variant Perspectives on Racial Justice as Represented by John LaFarge, William Markoe and Thomas Turner" (Ph.D. diss., Catholic Univ., 1975).

WILLIAM BARNABY FAHERTY

MARK TWAIN. *See* Twain, Mark.

MARLAND, Ernest Whitworth (8 May 1874–3 Oct. 1941), oilman and politician, was born in Pittsburgh, Pennsylvania, the son of Alfred Marland, an English-born industrialist, and Sara McLeod, his Scottish-born wife. Educated in private schools, Marland graduated from the University of Michigan School of Law in 1893. Too young to be admitted to the bar, Marland taught himself geology and went to the oil fields along the Pennsylvania–West Virginia border. There he made his first fortune in oil and just as quickly lost it when the panic of 1907 devastated the region's small, independent producers. In 1908 Marland left for Oklahoma. Passing over the fields already developed in the state's eastern counties, Marland ventured a hundred miles further west to the undulating plains near the village of Ponca City.

After drilling seven wells that turned up dry, Marland hit his first gusher in 1911, the first of many discovery wells that subsequently opened entire fields. Indeed Marland's drill bits opened the pool that lay at the heart of the fabulous midcontinent field. With one fabulous discovery following another, in 1920 he formed the Marland Oil Company, its headquarters in Ponca City, to oversee his expanding interests.

An oilman with the "Midas touch," Marland found oil everywhere he sought it: Texas, Kansas, California, and Mexico. Investing millions in the latest technologies, he developed a Ponca City refinery to integrate the company. By the mid-1920s Marland's crude oil supplied refineries across the nation as well as his own in Ponca City. (Standard Oil of New Jersey alone bought 30,000 barrels a day.) By 1928 the red triangle that designated "Marland Oils" appeared on more than 5,000 service stations, primarily in the Midwest, and Sealand Petroleum Company, a Marland subsidiary, distributed his products across Europe.

Marland's company was an exaggerated example of well-intended (and well-received) paternalism and, therefore, typified an important strand of industrialism between the world wars. Employing 6,000 people in Ponca City (roughly a third of the community's entire population), Marland insisted on paying not a "living wage" but a "saving wage." The company paid its employees' costs for life and health insurance, and its housing department built model housing and made it available to even the lowliest employee, the purchase financed with low-interest company loans. The same paternalism transformed Ponca City. Gifts from Marland of public buildings, schools, and recreation facilities rained down on the city—along with polo fields and a free public golf course. Every charity that needed money received it, including funds for every church in town and $150,000 for an American Legion orphanage. To the state Marland provided the money to build a student union with an athletic stadium at the University of Oklahoma. When the state built a governor's mansion, the money came from Marland.

Marland and his wife, Mary Virginia Collins, lived in a 22-room mansion that overlooked the public golf course and eighty acres of formal gardens. Married since 1903, the couple had borne no children but in 1916 adopted eighteen-year-old George Roberts and his sixteen-year-old sister, Lyde. The two were the children of Virginia Marland's sister in Flourtown, Pennsylvania. To house his growing family—and to live in a manner befitting his princely status—Marland ordered a new mansion built and set an army of European craftsmen to work on the $2.5 million project: a 55-room palace surrounded by 300 acres of landscaped gardens, lakes, polo fields, and grounds on which Marland and his executives would hunt (imported) foxes to the yelps of (imported) hounds. After Virginia Marland's death in 1926, Marland carried his new bride across the palace's threshold in July 1928. After a hasty annulment of the earlier adoption, Marland had married Lyde. She was twenty-eight; he was fifty-four. If many were shocked, Marland noticed not at all. The couple had no children.

Marland could not afford to be so oblivious to Wall Street. To finance his company's continuing growth (not to mention the generosities that he lavished on his employees, his community, and himself), Marland had borrowed $30 million from J. P. Morgan and his allies in 1923, pledging his personal stock holdings as security and giving the bankers what amounted to control of his company's executive board. In 1928 Morgan called in the loans, which Marland could not afford to pay. Morgan and the bankers then took over his stock, dismissed Marland, and had full control of the company, finally merging it with a small Colorado firm, Continental Oil Company. Overnight, "Conoco" replaced Marland's name on thousands of red triangles. Stunned by this rapid reversal and unable to pay even his new mansion's light bill—literally broke, he could not afford the $800 monthly bill—E. W. and Lyde Marland moved into a small outbuilding that had housed some of their craftsmen.

Marland then turned to politics. Denouncing the "wolves of Wall Street," he won Oklahoma's Eighth Congressional District seat in 1932, the first Democrat to do so. In 1934 he won Oklahoma's governorship with a then-record margin on his promise to "Bring the New Deal to Oklahoma." Although minor reforms came under his tenure—the state created a highway patrol and a planning and resources board, for example—his comprehensive plans for a "little New Deal" died a swift death, the victim of the conservative Democrats who firmly controlled the legislature. Stalemated and frustrated, Marland attempted in the middle of his gubernatorial term to take the U.S. Senate seat held by Thomas Pryor Gore in 1936. He placed last in the Democratic primary, well behind both Gore and Josh Lee, who went on to win the general election easily. A second senatorial campaign in 1938 was even more disappointing: Marland ran 147,000 votes behind Elmer Thomas, who won his third senatorial nomination and election. The fullest measure of his political decline came two years later, when Marland placed a distant third in a four-man field seeking the Democratic nomination to his old congressional seat.

Living again in an outbuilding of the mansion, Marland spoke of a new Marland Oil Company. Paralleling his political fall, one economic failure followed another. Deeply in debt, in 1941 he sold his one remaining resource, the still-unoccupied estate, to a religious order. For it, he received $66,000. He died in Ponca City, Oklahoma.

• The Oklahoma State Archives in Oklahoma City holds the official records of Marland's governorship; otherwise, none of his business or political papers is known to exist. The single published biography is John Joseph Mathews, *Life and Death of an Oilman: The Career of E. W. Marland* (1951). It is based largely on interviews with Marland and his associates but is written in a casual style and contains no bibliography. An obituary is in the *New York Times*, 4 Oct. 1941.

DANNEY GOBLE

MARLEY, Bob (6 Feb. 1945–11 May 1981), musician and political activist, was born Robert Nesta Marley in Nine Miles, St. Ann Parish, Jamaica, the son of Norval Marley, a British army officer, and Cedella Malcolm. After Norval Marley abandoned his family, Bob Marley grew up in extreme poverty, moving between Nine Miles and Kingston, finally settling in the rough ghetto of Trench Town.

When Marley and his mother moved to Trench Town in 1957, they shared a house in one of the government tenements, or "yards," with Thaddeus Livingston and his son, Neville O'Riley "Bunny" Livingston, who became Marley's constant companion. They dreamed of becoming musicians and eventually began spending time with Joe Higgs, who was widely regarded as one of the best singing teachers in Kingston. There Marley and Livingston met Winston Hubert McIntosh (Peter Tosh); the three learned to harmonize together and eventually formed a singing group called the Wailers.

The Wailers recorded their first singles in 1963, enjoying some local success. From then until Marley's death, the Wailers were a constantly evolving entity. The group repeatedly changed musical styles as the Jamaican music scene developed, moving from ska, rude boy music, and rock steady to island reggae and then beyond that to a fusion of rock and reggae that transformed the international music scene. As the group evolved, there were also personnel shifts, including Livingston's and Tosh's departure and the addition of the I-Threes, a female backup trio including Rita Anderson, whom Marley married in 1966 and with whom he had four children. (Marley also acknowledged having seven illegitimate children.) Most important, however, was the growing emphasis on Marley as a central figure in what had begun collectively.

The emphasis on Marley sprang partially from his charismatic personality and partially from his vision of the Wailers' importance. A devout Rastafarian, Marley believed that Ethiopian emperor Haile Selassie I was God incarnate and that Ethiopia was the true homeland for all people of color. Although the Rastafarians were well established in Jamaica before Marley grew famous, his international recognition provided new exposure for the tenets of his religion, and he used himself and the Wailers as vehicles for the Rasta message. Combining his songwriting and his performance style, Marley crafted an image as a Rasta prophet,

spreading their message of harmony and praising the power of Jah—the shortened version of "Jehovah," which Rastafarians regularly use to refer to Selassie. When, in 1978, one of Selassie's children gave Marley a ring that the emperor had worn, the prophet's anointing seemed complete.

As the Wailers, and Bob Marley and the Wailers, Marley and his associates produced ten albums in the 1970s, toured the world repeatedly spreading their Rasta message, and became a powerful force in Jamaican and international politics. Although Marley's day-to-day life resembled that of many other professional musicians, he always remembered his roots and acted on that memory. Biographer Stephen Davis notes that Marley regularly received supplicants from the ghetto in his compound on Jamaica's exclusive Hope Road, and he dispensed favors and money freely, thereby gaining a reputation as the friend and helper of Jamaica's poor.

His interest in and commitment to Jamaica's lower classes also appears in his participation in two politically significant concert events in Jamaica. The 1976 Smile Jamaica concert was originally conceived of as a benefit for the island poor. Shortly before the performance, however, the Jamaican government co-opted the concert, scheduled elections in its wake, and forced Marley into a situation that made it seem he was endorsing a particular candidate. In response to the "endorsement," assassins broke into the Marley compound, seriously wounding Bob Marley, Rita Marley, and Marley's manager, Don Taylor. After a brief period in seclusion, Marley and the Wailers performed at the concert, transforming their musical set into a stinging condemnation of their attackers. Even more important than the Smile Jamaica event was the One Love Peace Concert of 1978, at which Marley induced the rival leaders of Jamaica's warring political parties to join him onstage and to clasp hands. A powerful statement of unity in a country riven by violence and corruption, the moment remains almost mythical in its significance.

Marley's political activism increased as he addressed issues outside Jamaica, particularly efforts for African independence. Driven by his Rastafarianism and its emphasis on the sanctity of Africa for blacks, Marley actively supported African countries' efforts for freedom. One reward he received for this was an invitation to perform at the official celebration of Zimbabwe's independence in 1980; Marley was so honored by this invitation that he flew the Wailers there at his own expense as a gift to the new country.

After he returned from Africa, Marley embarked on a tour of America, where he was intent on reaching out to the African-American community, which had so far resisted the Rasta message. He collapsed on tour and was diagnosed with lung, stomach, and brain cancer, which he fought briefly and intensely. When he died in Miami, Florida, he was an international star whose words and music carried incredible political clout. Since his death, Marley has reached near-deity status in many parts of the world, and the presence and power of his music remains unabated.

• Two major biographies of Bob Marley are Stephen Davis, *Bob Marley* (1985), and Timothy White, *Catch a Fire: The Life of Bob Marley*, rev. ed. (1989). White's work assesses Marley's mysticism and provides a complete discography, which is notably absent in Davis's book. Davis's work describes the human Marley behind the myth. In addition to these books, Bruce Talamon, *Bob Marley: Spirit Dancer* (1994), provides some interesting insights into the man, as well as a number of useful photographs. Similarly, the liner notes for the CD box set *Bob Marley: Songs of Freedom* are a good starting place and offer other interesting artifacts as well.

WILLIAM R. NASH

MARLEY, John (17 Oct. 1907–22 May 1984), character actor, was born Mortimer Marlieb in New York City, the son of Russian immigrants Harry Marlieb, a vestmaker who loved classical music, and Ida Balterman, the "wise woman" who counseled her neighbors. Marley's early years were spent on the streets of Harlem, where he had to use his fists to survive. His drifting into dramatics was, as he later saw it, an alternative to joining a street gang. He probably completed the twelfth grade in school and took courses at the City College of New York. For the most part, however, he was self-educated. Having no formal training in acting, he acquired his skills by performing with shoe-string amateur groups. He told an interviewer, "I was working in experimental theatre, enjoying myself for seven years before I drew my first paycheck as an actor" (*Cleveland Plain Dealer*, 15 Dec. 1965). During these years he sold insurance.

His New York debut, at the age of thirty-two, was in a single-performance run of *Stop Press* (1939). Produced by the Acting Company, a loose association of unemployed performers, he played a newspaper reporter.

In World War II Marley served from 1942 to 1945 as a sergeant in the U.S. Army Signal Corps. During his tour in Algiers he wrote and performed over the radio for the American troops. Numerous celebrities appeared as guests on these eleven two-hour shows, including Marlene Dietrich, Humphrey Bogart, and Frank Sinatra.

Following the war, Marley returned to New York to a nightly show on ABC radio. Very soon his apartment on West Forty-fifth Street became a hangout for actors. Marley offered them not only his hospitality but his ideas and encouragement. He became recognized in the theatrical world as a mentor to young actors and playwrights.

His first break into the movies came when he was auditioned by the director Henry Hathaway for a role in the gangster film *Kiss of Death* (1947). Hathaway asked Marley, "Can you act?" Marley stared back out of his door, deep-set eyes, and in his cocky, slightly hoarse voice answered, "Sure, I'm a good actor" (*Cleveland Plain Dealer*, 25 Dec. 1968). The audition was complete. More supporting roles in such low-budget studio films followed, among them *My Six Convicts* (1952), *The Joe Louis Story* (1953), and *I Want to Live!* (1958).

Marley also appeared periodically on the New York stage. In 1948 Cheryl Crawford and Lee Strasberg collaborated on an off-Broadway production, *Skipper next to God*. Here Marley, the developing actor, came into firsthand contact with "the method," which Crawford and Strasberg taught at the Actor's Studio. The method relied heavily on introspection and improvisation, techniques already successfully exploited by Marley both as an actor and as a director.

Marley also played supporting roles in the New York productions of *An Enemy of the People* (1951), *Gramercy Ghost* (1951), *Compulsion* (1957), and *The Investigation* (1966). When not engaged in commercial theater, Marley regularly produced and directed plays for small theater groups in New York and California.

Though he was only 5′9″ in height, Marley's stage presence was one of rugged strength and latent energy. His dark, formidable eyebrows, his black, bushy hair—later turning to silver—his large nose, and his jutting, sharp jaw all combined to project a tough and nasty persona. However, he considered himself a character actor, and so, with a close shave, a pressed shirt, and a tie he became, as called for, a professional man, a fast-talking theatrical agent, or an ordinary man-next-door.

In the 1950s Marley, like so many other performing artists, found rich opportunities in the rapidly expanding medium of network television. Marley was cast in serious dramatic productions on "Studio One," "Pulitzer Prize Playhouse," and the "Ten Commandments" segment of "Heroes of the Bible," as well as in many popular series such as "The Twilight Zone," "Dr. Kildare," and "Gunsmoke."

He married Stanja Lowe, an actress, with whom he had three children. He divorced her in 1972 and married his second wife, Sandra Lee Ulosevich, a script supervisor, in 1975. They had one child.

As Marley approached sixty, his career came to full fruition. He landed a small but meaty role in *America, America* (1963), Elia Kazan's semiautobiographical film about immigrants to the United States. He was cast in a Stanley Kramer production, *A Child Is Waiting* (1963), and he appeared in *The Wheeler Dealers* (1963), the first of three roles in pictures directed by Arthur Hiller. Presently he found that he was able to be selective about his film roles and was also being recruited as a guest director by prestigious regional theaters. For the Pasadena Playhouse he directed *Send Me No Flowers* in 1962. Two years later he directed *Galileo* at the Baltimore Center Stage, returning the following year to direct *The Tavern*. For the Cleveland Play House he took on two socially conscious plays, *The Strong Are Lonely* (1967) and a new play, *The Day of the Lion* (1968). Local reviewers of these productions had high praise for Marley's perceptiveness and talent.

He gained further recognition in the role of Frankie Ballou in the comic western *Cat Ballou* (1965). John Cassavetes cast him as co-lead, with Lynn Carlin, in his independent black-and-white film *Faces*, released in London in 1968. In lieu of salaries, Marley and the others received shares in this production. *Faces* swept the awards that year at the 1968 Venice Film Festival, including the Best Actor award for Marley. Reviewers were divided over Cassavetes's "new wave" direction, some dismissing it as "home movies," but they unanimously praised the acting.

Marley also played in the top box-office attraction of 1970, *Love Story*, and as the father of the doomed heroine infused the film with badly needed authenticity. For this he received an Academy Award nomination as Best Supporting Actor. Soon afterward he gained further acclaim as Jack Woltz, the corrupt film producer in Francis Ford Coppola's *The Godfather* (1972).

Marley began to work even more steadily and eclectically. Several roles were in movies filmed in Canada; others were made specifically for television. He was cast as the appalled parent of young monsters in two horror films aimed at the teenage market and otherwise played mobsters, detectives, and a disreputable reporter. In the final decade of his life he performed in fifteen films, including *Blade* (1973), *Framed* (1975), *Hooper* (1978), and *Tribute* (1980). Perhaps his finest performance was in *On the Edge* (1986). This was a serious film about the challenges of mountain running directed by Rob Nilsson, whose style relied heavily on improvisation. The Marley character, Elmo Glidden, was singled out by a reviewer as "wise, crusty, compassionate, the hard-driving coach with a touch of poetry in his soul" (*New York Times*, 16 May 1986). The film was posthumously dedicated to Marley, who had died two years earlier in Los Angeles.

• There is no single source for information about Marley. The biographical entry in *Contemporary Theatre, Film, and Television* (1984), while informative, is incomplete and has several inaccuracies. The Cleveland Play House has a file of newspaper clippings on Marley from local newspapers. Playbills of plays directed by Marley can be found at Baltimore Center Stage, the Enoch Pratt Free Library, Baltimore, Md., and the Huntington Library, San Marino, Calif. Reviews of films in which Marley appeared are in the *New York Times* and in periodicals. Unfortunately, as a supporting actor, Marley is rarely mentioned. The Burns-Mantle *Best Plays* annual contains data on the plays in which Marley appeared and gives his name and role in the cast listings. Marley's widow, Sandra Marley, of Wilmington, N.C., has provided useful information and miscellaneous material. Useful obituaries of Marley are in the *New York Times*, 24 May 1984, and *Variety*, 30 May 1984.

ALBERT F. MCLEAN

MARLOWE, Julia (27 Aug. 1866–12 Nov. 1950), actress, was born Sarah Frances Frost in Upton Caldbeck, Cumberlandshire, England, the daughter of John Frost, a master shoemaker, and Sarah Hodgson (born Sarah Strong). At age four, Marlowe came to the United States with her family, settling in Cincinnati where they assumed the name Brough. Because of her parents' divorce and poverty, "Fanny Brough" received little formal education yet knew early that she wanted a life in the theater and began attending plays at age eleven. Her first acting job soon followed (1878) in the chorus of a juvenile opera company, touring for nine months in *H.M.S. Pinafore*. After the tour, she took various jobs, often working nights as an extra with traveling theater companies, occasionally seeing and performing with Edwin Booth, Lawrence Barrett, and Mary Anderson (1859–1940). In 1882 Marlowe caught the notice of Ada Dow, a veteran stock company actress who took the young actress to New York, where for three years she rehearsed plays and developed her rich contralto voice through singing lessons. She also chose her melodious stage name: Julia Marlowe.

In April 1887 Marlowe debuted in a two-week tour of small New England towns, playing Parthenia in *Ingomar*, Pauline in *The Lady of Lyons*, and Galatea in *Pygmalion*. Her New York debut in *Ingomar* was sparsely attended, but she received enthusiastic notices, leading to a week at the Star Theatre, where she launched her Shakespearean career as Viola in *Twelfth Night* and as Juliet. Her opening night audience for *Romeo and Juliet* included the Shakespearean scholar R. G. Ingersoll, who praised her performance, noting her intelligent delivery and calling her portrayal "the Shakespearean's Juliet." Her depiction of a complex Viola, ever pensive and lovely, reflected her years of personal study and her departure from tradition. Her Viola always revealed an undertone of melancholy, even in the lightest moments, even when winning her love. Her week at the Star Theatre left her with important admirers, Ingersoll and H. H. Furness among them, and was followed by a six-week tour of the West.

Resistant to joining a stock company, Marlowe hired Helena Modjeska's company for the 1888–1889 season, but it was a turbulent time: the experienced actors considered Marlowe an upstart. She refused direction from others, insisting on choosing her own plays, preparing her own stage texts, and directing her own productions. During this season she played the part of Rosalind in *As You Like It*, a role she loved despite the challenges of making the breeches disguise plausible. Furness commented that Marlowe was natural in every gesture, never overacting the breeches part, and that "the doublet and hose did not obliterate the duke's high-born daughter." At the age of twenty-three Julia Marlowe was recognized as an accomplished and innovative interpreter of Shakespeare on the American stage.

Over the next few years she expanded her repertoire with the roles of Beatrice in *Much Ado about Nothing* (1890), Constance in *The Love Chase* (1892), Imogen in *Cymbeline* (1893), and Letitia in *The Belle's Stratagem* (1893–1894). The purity and fidelity of Imogen always appealed to Marlowe, and she received abundant critical praise for her portrayal. Imogen exemplified to Marlowe the sort of role she sought and believed should be enacted on the stage: a morally strong woman who does not fall when tempted.

In 1894 Marlowe married fellow actor and occasional leading man Robert Taber, billing herself as Julia Marlowe Taber. She accommodated her husband's acting aspirations by performing a series of roles over the next few years, none of which suited her taste and style: Prince Hal in *Henry IV, Part One*, Lady Teazle in *The School for Scandal*, Miss Hardcastle in *She Stoops to Conquer*, Lydia Languish in *The Rivals*. The 1896–1897 season was their last, and they divorced in 1900.

Marlowe wanted to return to her beloved Shakespearean repertoire in 1897, but making a living proved difficult, and she was urged away from Shakespeare despite good critical reviews. She decided to give in temporarily to "the people who are not aware that Shakespeare is good entertainment" in the hopes that they would follow her back to the forest of Arden. She refused, however, to perform in modern, realistic plays, of a type that she called "problem plays" (those of George Bernard Shaw and Henrik Ibsen, for example), because they failed to meet her high moral standards for the stage. Instead, she chose a series of historical dramas and romances and met with instant financial success: *Countess Valeska* (1897–1898), *Colinette* (1898), *Barbara Frietchie* (1899), and her most popular, *When Knighthood Was in Flower* (1899–1901), a novel written by Charles Major and adapted for the stage for her by Paul Kestor. Having regained her financial independence, she planned a return to Shakespeare, but first, she needed the right leading man.

Marlowe saw Edward Hugh Sothern perform, and, impressed with his voice and intelligence, she suggested they plan a joint tour. Their first appearance together was on 19 September 1904 in Chicago in *Romeo and Juliet*, using her promptbook and direction. The tour also offered *Much Ado about Nothing* and *Hamlet*; they used Sothern's promptbook and direction for the latter. The partnership was successful and compatible, and they shared all of the burdens of managing tours and directing the plays. As their popularity and finances grew, they invested in scenery, costumes, musical accompaniment, and large numbers of supernumeraries, their performances becoming associated with a grand *mise-en-scène*. In the 1905–1906 season, they added *Taming of the Shrew* and *Merchant of Venice* to their repertoire. Marlowe's indomitable and quite likable Katherine again departed somewhat from stage tradition. At the end of the play, Katherine was clearly the tamer, glancing knowingly to the audience as she kisses Petruchio. While Marlowe's Portia was less convincing, Sothern shone with his terrifying and tragic portrayal of Shylock.

For two years Marlowe and Sothern worked apart, but they reunited in November 1909 to support the opening of the New Theatre in New York. Both endorsed the idea of a national theater devoted to the classics and believed that the New Theatre was such a project. They agreed to star in *Antony and Cleopatra*, a play chosen for them, but without their artistic control the production was a disaster. Severing their ties with the New Theatre, they renewed their own professional partnership and expanded their repertoire in 1910 with *Macbeth*. Critics doubted if Marlowe could make the transition from Juliet, Viola, and Ophelia to Lady Macbeth, but she felt the role very deeply. She played Lady Macbeth as still young and controlled by one dominating passion: love for her husband. Marlowe's business manager and biographer Charles E. Russell described her Lady Macbeth as neither a savage nor "an impetuous virago, ruling her husband to his ruin"; instead, her motive is a "great, mastering, compelling love." Her conception of the role was her own and resembled little that had been seen on the stage up until then.

In the summer of 1911, Marlowe and Sothern were quietly married in London, and they continued performing together until 1916, when they retired. In 1919, because of financial necessity, they returned to the stage every other season with their Shakespearean productions. The last new play they staged together was a revival of Marlowe's early favorite *Cymbeline*; it was also the play that revealed their day had passed. In October 1923 they opened an extravagant production of *Cymbeline* in New York, and while Shakespeareans in the audience applauded it as a masterpiece, postwar theatergoers and critics found the play and its pictorial staging tiresome. Her style and poetic interpretations, once considered innovative and forward-looking, by 1923 seemed outdated. Marlowe and Sothern withdrew *Cymbeline* after one week, and Marlowe retired at the end of the season. She clearly recognized that the increasing emphasis on psychological and physical realism would no longer accommodate the sweep and grandeur of her theatrical vision.

After her retirement in 1924, the couple lived abroad most of the time until Sothern died in 1933. Marlowe returned to the United States in 1939 and lived out her life at the Plaza Hotel in New York, never returning to the theater even as a spectator. She died in New York, and her ashes were buried next to Sothern's in Brompton Cemetery, London.

Julia Marlowe's career came at a transitional phase in the history of the American theater, a time when old traditions were fading yet new ones had not yet been established. The theater was filled with a diverse mixture of plays, players, and acting styles, ranging from the graceful, poetic style of Helena Modjeska, who starred in a classical repertoire, to the psychologically realistic style of Minnie Maddern Fiske, who championed the works of Ibsen. Marlowe's career coincided with this period of ferment and can best be understood in relation to the volatility of her theatrical environment. When compared with her immediate predecessors, such as Modjeska and Anderson, Marlowe seemed quite innovative, yet she never adapted to the new realism that emerged around the time of World War I. Very early she practiced some methods that were later associated with realistic acting (for example, developing a subtle, psychologically motivated portrayal of a character), but she was out of sympathy with the movement as a whole.

• Marlowe left her manuscripts and books to the New York Public Library and her costumes and theater memorabilia to the Museum of the City of New York. The Charles Edward Russell Papers in the Library of Congress also contain many of her letters. The most complete biography is Charles E. Russell, *Julia Marlowe: Her Life and Art* (1926). See also E. H. Sothern, *Julia Marlowe's Story*, ed. Fairfax Downey (1954), essentially an autobiography written by her husband as she told it to him. Marlowe wrote several articles on her roles and theories of acting. The best are "Reminiscences of an Actress," *Philharmonic*, July 1901, pp. 137–50; "The Essentials of Stage Success," *Theatre*, Dec. 1901, pp. 13–15; "The Future of the Historical Romance for the Stage," *Independent*, June 1902, pp. 1531–35; and "The Eloquence of Silence," *Green Book Magazine*, Mar. 1913, pp. 393–401. The best survey of Marlowe's Shakespearean roles is Charles H. Shattuck, *Shakespeare on the American Stage*, vol. 2 (1987). See also Edward Wagenknecht, *Seven Daughters of the Theatre* (1964). Richard A. Sogliuzzo, "E. H. Sothern and Julia Marlowe on the Art of Acting," *Theatre Survey* 11 (Nov. 1970): 187–200, and Patty S. Derrick, "Julia Marlowe: An Actress Caught between Traditions," *Theatre Survey* 32 (May 1991): 85–105, discuss Marlowe's career and acting style. An obituary is in the *New York Times*, 13 Nov. 1950.

PATTY S. DERRICK

MAROT, Helen (9 June 1865–3 June 1940), labor reformer and writer, was born in Philadelphia, Pennsylvania, the daughter of Charles Henry Marot, a publisher, and Hannah Griscom. She grew up in an enlightened and prosperous Quaker household, encouraged by her parents to be independent in her thoughts and actions.

After briefly working for the University Extension Service of Philadelphia in 1893, Marot worked as a librarian in Wilmington, Delaware. In 1897, along with her lifelong companion Caroline Pratt, she opened a private library in Philadelphia, specializing in radical periodicals and books. Two years later, she published her first book, *Handbook of Labor Literature* (1899). That same year, Marot began an investigation of Philadelphia garment workers. Part of the U.S. Industrial Commission's attempt to understand the conditions of labor, especially for the unskilled, this study gave Marot a firsthand look at the harsh work experiences many unskilled laborers faced.

In 1902 Marot conducted a similar study for the Association of Neighborhood Workers of New York, this time focusing on child labor. Her study led to the formation of the New York Child Labor Committee and, along with Florence Kelley and Josephine Goldmark, she lobbied the New York State assembly for laws limiting child labor. The Compulsory Education Act of 1903 was the result and served as a model for other states seeking to restrict child labor. After a year as secretary of the Pennsylvania Child Labor Committee, Marot returned to New York. In 1906 she joined the New York Women's Trade Union League (WTUL), serving as its executive secretary for the next seven years.

Founded in 1903, the national WTUL was a cross-class alliance that sought to organize women workers into existing unions. By early 1904, local branches had formed in New York, Chicago, and Boston. In New York, where one-third of the city's 350,000 women workers were engaged in manufacturing, the need for unions to protect these primarily unskilled workers was great. Working long hours for low wages under frequently dangerous conditions, these women were nonetheless seen as "unorganizable" by the male-dominated and craft-based American Federation of Labor. It was these women that the WTUL sought to organize, and as executive secretary of the New York branch Marot was a leader of this effort. At the same time, Marot joined with Kelley and Goldmark in collecting the data for the "Brandeis Brief," resulting in the historic *Muller v. Oregon* (1908) Supreme Court decision, which found the restriction of women's hours of labor to be constitutional based on their biological role as childbearers.

Marot also was active in organizing the growing number of women in the clerical field into the newly formed Bookkeepers, Stenographers and Accountants Union of New York. She herself was one of the first members of the union she helped create. However, it was during the 1909 strike of women garment workers, known as the Uprising of the Thirty Thousand, that Marot demonstrated her growing commitment to organizing the unskilled. The strike, which dragged on for months, won the workers shorter hours and slightly higher rates of pay but not union recognition. The women workers, primarily Russian Jews and Italian immigrants, were often divided on what the critical issues were, and the locals they formed, part of the International Ladies' Garment Workers Union, came to be dominated by the skilled male workers. Marot became increasingly frustrated by the divisions and growing dominance of the men. By 1911 she advocated that the New York WTUL concentrate its efforts on American-born workers. This position brought Marot into direct conflict with several of the working-class leaders of the league, including Pauline Newman and Rose Schneiderman. She resigned from her position as executive secretary in 1913 and turned to writing.

In 1914 Marot published *American Labor Unions* in which she examined the status of trade unionism. A committed Fabian socialist, she sought to present the views of the more radical part of the labor movement, particularly the Industrial Workers of the World (IWW), as well as the more conservative American Federation of Labor. For the WTUL, Marot had mostly words of praise despite her recent departure, writing that "the League has been persistent, strenuous, militant." However, Marot was most impressed by the work of the IWW, especially by its emphasis on direct action which Marot saw as serving "a more fundamental need of workers." She continued to write about the labor movement as an editor of the radical journal, the *Masses*, beginning in 1916 until 1917 when it was shut down by the U.S. government for its antiwar position. A year later, Marot went to work as a staff writer for the *Dial* and published her third and final book, *Creative Impulse in Industry* (1918). In her comparison of industrial education in Germany and the United States she argued for an American system based on efficiency and the recognition of the creative contribution of each worker to the process of production. Marot retired in 1920, after more than twenty years of publicizing the needs of the nation's unskilled workers, always remaining true to her particular brand of radical politics. She died in New York City.

• The annual reports of the New York WTUL (1906–1913) are useful sources for information about Marot's work in the organization. In addition to Marot's books and articles in the above-mentioned journals, see also Nancy Schrom Dye, *As Equals and As Sisters: Feminism, the Labor Movement, and the Women's Trade Union League of New York* (1980). On the radical Greenwich Village scene in which Marot lived, see Leslie Fishbein, *Rebels in Bohemia: The Radicals of the Masses, 1911–1917* (1982). An obituary is in the *New York Times*, 4 June 1940.

KATHLEEN BANKS NUTTER

MARQUAND, J. P. (10 Nov. 1893–16 July 1960), novelist, was born John Phillips Marquand in Wilmington, Delaware, the son of Philip Marquand, a civil engineer, and Margaret Fuller, a descendant of the American Transcendentalist and feminist writer. Marquand's father, once wealthy, became destitute in the financial crisis of 1907, and Marquand was sent to live with relatives at an ancestral home near Newburyport, Massachusetts, a seaside town at the mouth of the Merrimack River with which many of his fictions are identified. Two distinctive themes in his best novels, a romantic sense of loss and an almost mystical sense of place, can be traced to the decline of the family's fortunes and this childhood displacement.

After attending Harvard University on a scholarship, Marquand served in the U.S. Army in Europe during World War I. At war's end, he was employed briefly as a journalist for the New York *Tribune* and even more briefly at an advertising agency, neither position offering work to which he could imagine dedicating his life. In 1922, with *The Unspeakable Gentleman*, he began to publish popular romance novels. His first was followed by *The Black Cargo* (1925), *Warning Hill* (1930), and *Ming Yellow* (1935). He also wrote six detective novels during these years, each of them featuring Mr. Moto, a peripatetic Japanese sleuth; these books became a principal ingredient of Marquand's early success. Often his romances and mystery fictions were serialized in such popular magazines as the *Saturday Evening Post*. Starting in 1937, the Mr. Moto novels inspired Twentieth Century–Fox to produce eight films based on that character and starring Peter Lorre. This well-produced, modestly successful series concluded in 1939.

The Late George Apley, winner of the Pulitzer Prize for fiction in 1937, marked Marquand's breakthrough to critical acclaim. From that point onward, he was simultaneously regarded as both a serious writer and a popular one, and he played to two distinct, though sometimes overlapping, audiences.

In all of his writing he was the consummate craftsman, but certainly no experimentalist. His attitude toward his work is best summed up in a remark to an interviewer that writing seemed "the best means I could think of to be in business for myself." He considered Ernest Hemingway "boring" and William Faulkner "unreadable." He regarded James Joyce's *Ulysses* as "Hopeless! Absolutely hopeless," and, while he found himself in Paris (1926) during the heyday of the Lost Generation, he had no desire to associate or make common cause with Gertrude Stein or her coterie. A practitioner of the novel of manners, Marquand shared an affinity with earlier American writers such as William Dean Howells and Edith Wharton and their attachment to social distinctions as a theme. He also admired Flaubert and wished he could write a novel the equal of *Madame Bovary*, but until he wrote *Apley*, he was regarded by most critics as an immensely successful hack.

The acclaim for *Apley* was compounded when the novel was turned into a Broadway play in 1944 and into a Hollywood movie in 1947. Ironically, according to Marquand, he was advised to publish the novel under a pseudonym and told that "this sort of thing would ruin my market." A multitextured portrait of a Boston Brahmin and his city, *Apley* was described by the *New Yorker* as "the best-wrought fictional monument to the nation's Protestant elite that we know of" and "a detailed Valentine to a city—Boston." The novel purports to be a biography of George Apley, who has died shortly before the book opens. Told in the form of first-person letters, *Apley* is a unique satire of a traditional man whose priggishness is mediated by a sad self-awareness. As he declares to his grown son: "Everything I have done has amounted almost to nothing." Told largely in flashback, a Marquand trademark, *Apley* contains the author's recurring themes of a strong sense of place, a male narrator who yearns for the past but achieves painful self-knowledge in the present, and the unflattering reshaping that Marquand thought marriage worked on women.

His view of women in marriage may have derived, in part, from his unhappy marriages to Christina Sedgwick (1922–1935) and Adelaide Hooker (1937–1958), which were mirrored by distant relations with his five children. Both wives were wealthy and socially prominent. Marquand had an intense desire to know "the best people," and he took as much delight in memberships in exclusive clubs as he did in literary prizes. He never seemed able to decide whether it was artistic or social distinction he sought and whether he was the prototypical self-made man or of aristocratic lineage. Marquand became wealthy through his writing but apparently never wealthy enough and famous enough to recover from his youthful sense of loss and expulsion from an Edenic paradise. Late in his career he told interviewers: "I've been so warped and conditioned by life that I haven't found anything that will satisfy me."

Marquand is best remembered for his novels of American upper-class life and his ambivalent treatment of that milieu in small and telling detail. Novels such as *Wickford Point* (1938), *H. M. Pulham, Esquire*

(1941), *Point of No Return* (1949), and *Sincerely, Willis Wayde* (1955) reflected an unease with the rapid social and technological changes taking place in America and a yearning for an imagined, simpler past. As a highly prolific and best-selling author and a longtime member of the Book-of-the-Month-Club selection committee (1944–1960), he had an immense influence on the reading tastes of Americans in the 1940s and 1950s.

Marquand's popularity faded along with the world of manners and mores he portrayed so well. He may have been one of the last to write of the dominant White Anglo-Saxon Protestant culture before it began to be seen as merely one of many American cultures. The strength of his closely worked satires will endure, if only as texts that reflect the concerns of upper-class Americans in the first half of the twentieth century. His last and most autobiographical novel, *Women and Thomas Harrow* (1958), reworked the theme of a man coming to terms in adulthood with his youthful past, the women in his life, and thus with himself. Not long after the book's publication, Marquand died at Kent's Island, just outside Newburyport. It is not unfitting that his death came at the dawn of a new age of American ideas and values.

• The bulk of Marquand's correspondence and papers, as well as manuscripts of his novels, are to be found in the libraries at Yale, Harvard, and Boston University. The most interesting profile of Marquand was written by Philip Hamburger in the form of a parody of a Marquand novel; it appeared in consecutive issues of the *New Yorker* (29 Mar., 5 and 12 Apr. 1952) and then as a book, *J. P. Marquand, Esquire*. Three years earlier, Marquand was the subject of simultaneous *Time* and *Newsweek* cover stories in connection with the publication of *Point of No Return*, which, along with *The Late George Apley*, was the most critically praised of his novels. Stephen Birmingham, who as a novice writer was helped by Marquand, suggests in the very title of his *The Late John Marquand* (1972) how much the novelist, in spirit and manner, resembled his protagonists; at the end of Birmingham's biography is a chronological list of Marquand's major writings. Millicent Bell's *Marquand: An American Life* (1979), a full, scholarly treatment, is better at examining the complexities of Marquand's life and their effects on his work. A front-page obituary is in the *New York Times*, 17 July 1960.

PATRICIA M. ARD
MICHAEL AARON ROCKLAND

MARQUÉS, René (4 Oct. 1919–22 Mar. 1979), playwright, poet, and author, was born in Arecibo, Puerto Rico, the son of Juan Marqués Santiago and Pura Isabel Abreu, independent farmers. Marqués spent his childhood in a rural setting that was showing rapid changes toward modernity. Efficient mechanical devices were replacing traditional farming methods, and as a result, the island experienced two migrational patterns. As fewer men were needed for farmwork, families abandoned the countryside and sought opportunities in San Juan, the capital of the island, or they went to New York City. These radical changes became important motifs in Marqués's work, specifically in his transitional rural settings and in his strong ideological discourse.

Marqués responded in his work to the socioeconomic influences of a post–World War II Puerto Rican society. In 1942 he received a degree in agronomy from the College of Agronomy and Mechanical Arts in Mayagüez. He married Serena Velasco in 1943; they had three children before they divorced in 1954. Committed to farmwork, he worked for the Puerto Rican Department of Agriculture until 1946, when he left the island for Madrid to study theater. His first play, *El hombre y sus sueños* (The man and his dreams), belongs to this early, formative period. A year later, upon his return, he founded a small theater group in his native Arecibo and became a literary reviewer for various local journals and newspapers. In addition, he wrote another play, *El sol y los MacDonald* (The sun and the MacDonalds, 1950).

In 1949 Marqués traveled to New York to study drama at Columbia University with a Rockefeller Foundation fellowship. He wrote one play in English, *Palm Sunday*. He became exposed to American experimental theater as he traveled the country with university theaters. His experiences in New York, including encounters with the troubled lives of the Puerto Rican community there, marked his literary work deeply. Upon his return to the island, his theatrical experience led him to cofound in 1951 the Teatro Experimental del Ateneo Puertorriqueño, an experimental theater annexed to a distinguished institution of Puerto Rican literature. His association with New York continued through the years, including the premiere there of his best-known play, *La carreta* (The oxcart) in 1953. Another trip to New York in 1957 with a Guggenheim fellowship gave him the opportunity to write his first novel, *La víspera del hombre* (The eve of the man, 1959).

In 1955 Marqués published his first short-story collection, *Otro día nuestro* (Another day of ours). He continued writing short stories throughout his career and published them in distinguished Puerto Rican newspapers and journals. Eventually the stories appeared in book form as *En una ciudad llamada San Juan* (In a city named San Juan, 1960) and *Inmersos en el silencio* (Immersed in silence, 1976). The short stories in general follow themes similar to those of his plays, with preference for the existentialist anxieties of identity (national and personal), of death and time, and of more personal concerns, such as sexual dynamics.

International exposure came with a 1958 trip to Mexico City, where Marqués traveled as a member of the Puerto Rican delegation to the First Interamerican Biennial of Painting. He returned to the island and continued writing essays that showed a strong nationalist orientation toward Puerto Rico's relationship with the United States. (In 1952 Puerto Rico had signed an agreement with the United States that made the island an American "estado libre asociado," or commonwealth.) His play *Los soles truncos* (The fanlights) was performed in 1962 at the Latin American Theater Festival in Mexico. Official recognition of his talent came with his appointment as a professor of literature at the University of Puerto Rico in 1969.

Marqués's strong political ideals for the independence of Puerto Rico are best illustrated in his *Ensayos* (Essays, 1966). The volume includes pieces of literary criticism of contemporary Puerto Rican literature, with emphasis on sociological study of the role of the artist in a country dependent on American, and therefore foreign, aesthetics and political values. His theory of the "puertorriqueño dócil" (the docile Puerto Rican) incorporates a revision of Puerto Rican slave history; he points to that period (seldom discussed at the Puerto Rican national level) as pivotal to the understanding of traumatic conditions in modern Puerto Rico. This bold political position earned him both ardent followers and ardent detractors.

Marqués's most important contribution to Puerto Rican literature, however, is his powerful experimental theater. Influenced by classical trends such as Spanish Golden Age drama and contemporary American playwrights, his theater revitalizes Puerto Rican theater by bringing together aesthetics and ideology (usually a strong sociopolitical theme of interest to Puerto Ricans) by means of modern dramatic techniques of universal appeal. Such is the case of his masterpiece, *La carreta*. It presents a contemporary rural Puerto Rican family who have to migrate first to San Juan and later to New York City. In the process they face problems associated with industrialization and modernization. Their struggles are similar to those in other countries in development: ancient values clash with the newer ways of living in the big city and cause ruptures in cultural patterns. The changes are painful but ultimately necessary for the creation of a new society. For Marqués, however, in the specific case of Puerto Rico, the United States restricts the island in its handling of this new society, which Marqués characterizes as materialist and empty of national values.

An ardent nationalist, Marqués produced literature outstanding in its exploration of Puerto Rican themes. His work is not, however, merely a realistic reflection of characters of interest solely to Puerto Rican readers. In fact, it can be argued that Marqués's writing is closer to the highly experimental literature characteristic of Latin American writers of the 1960s and 1970s. He can also be considered a precursor in the use of more intimate themes such as issues of homosexuality. Marqués died in San Juan, Puerto Rico.

• For a biocritical overview of Marqués's narrative work, refer to Charles Pilditch, *René Marqués: A Study of His Fiction* (1976). Some major translations into English of Marqués's work are *The Oxcart* (1969), *The Fanlights* (1971), *The Docile Puerto Rican: Essays* (1976), and *The Look* (1983). An obituary is in the *New York Times*, 25 Mar. 1979.

RAFAEL OCASIO

MARQUETTE, Jacques (1 June 1637–18 May 1675), Jesuit Nicolas missionary and explorer, was born at Laon, France, the son of Nicolas Marquette, a municipal councillor, and Rose de la Salle. His family was of the minor nobility with a long history of military and governmental service. He began studies at the Jesuit college in Reims in 1646 and entered the Jesuits (Society of Jesus) at Nancy in 1654. His training as a Jesuit, which included philosophy and mathematics but little theology, was mainly at the University of Pont-à-Mousson. He taught between 1656 and 1664 at the Jesuit colleges at Auxerre, Reims, Charleville, Langres, and Pont-à-Mousson. In 1658 he petitioned the Jesuit general to be sent to the foreign missions. Immediately after his ordination to the priesthood at Toul in March 1666, his religious superiors assigned him to New France (Canada); he arrived at Quebec on 20 September.

One month later he was assigned to Trois Rivières to study the Algonquian language and the customs of Native Americans with the Jesuit Gabriel Druilletes. He was an apt pupil, learning to converse in six Indian dialects while working more than a year with Druilletes. After a brief return to Quebec, he set out from Montreal for the mission station at Sault Ste. Marie, where for a year and a half he worked as a missionary, mainly with the Chippewas. In August 1669 he was then assigned to a newer mission on the southwestern end of Lake Superior, the mission of the Holy Spirit at La Pointe, near today's Ashland, Wisconsin, where he tried to make converts among the Ottawas, Hurons, Potawatomi, Sioux, and others. He met members of the Illinois tribe, who told him about a great river that flowed southward. Fearing attacks by the Sioux against his mission at La Pointe, Marquette persuaded many of his converts to move to a new mission at Michilimackinac, Michigan, which he named Saint-Ignace.

In 1673 Marquette joined Louis Jolliet to search for and explore the great river now called the Mississippi. Leaving Michilimackinac, they shadowed the coast of Lake Michigan to modern-day Green Bay, Wisconsin, and then paddled up the Fox River to Portage, where they crossed over to the Wisconsin River, which took them down to the Mississippi near Prairie du Chien on 17 June. Marquette gave the river the name Rivière de la Conception. He, Jolliet, and five French and several Indian companions continued down the Mississippi until it joined with the Arkansas River. By then they were sure that it flowed into the Gulf of Mexico and not, as had been suspected, the Gulf of California. The expedition turned back, partly out of fear of meeting Spaniards, who might take them prisoner. During his voyage Marquette drew a map and kept careful notes in his diary about geography and Indian tribes they were seeing, believing that this information might be invaluable for later missionaries.

Returning, the explorers took a shorter route, up the Illinois River; they reached Lake Michigan at modern-day Chicago, then returned to the mission at the top of Green Bay, where Marquette continued his missionary work. While Jolliet was returning to report on the expedition at Quebec, his canoe overturned and his papers and records were lost. The accident gave greater importance to Marquette's diary.

Marquette tried to found a new mission of the Immaculate Conception, his third, at today's Utica, Illinois, in response to a promise to the Illinois Indians he had made when he stayed briefly at their large village there during his return with Jolliet, but his health was already failing. He and two other Frenchmen were the first white men to dwell at modern Chicago when they were forced to winter there (Dec.–Mar. 1674–1675) before returning to St. Ignace. The three then traveled up the eastern shore of Lake Michigan, but Marquette's health broke completely, and he died at modern Ludington, Michigan.

The expedition of Marquette and Jolliet not only informed Europeans about the unknown Mississippi heartland of North America, it also opened the way to later missionaries and to French colonization from Minnesota to Louisiana, which included a string of towns down the Mississippi from LaCrosse to New Orleans that still bear French names. A city in Michigan and a Jesuit university in Milwaukee are named after Marquette, and his statue stands in the Hall of Fame in Washington, D.C.

• Important archival materials on Marquette are at the Archives of the Archdiocese of Quebec and at the Collège Sainte-Marie in Montreal. The best modern biography is Joseph P. Donnelly, *Jacques Marquette, S.J., 1637–1675* (1968). More popular are Agnes Repplier, *Père Marquette, Priest, Pioneer, and Adventurer* (1929), and Raphael Hamilton, *Father Marquette* (1970). Hamilton has also studied Marquette's papers, *Marquette's Explorations: The Narratives Reexamined* (1970); these are printed in John G. Shea, *History and Exploration of the Mississippi Valley, with the Original Narratives of Marquette, Allouez, Membre, Hennepin and Anatase Donya* (1903). An eccentric study of Marquette is Francis Borgia Steck, *Marquette Legends*, ed. August Reyling (1960); Steck, for instance, argues that Marquette was not a priest.

JOHN PATRICK DONNELLY

MARQUIS, Albert Nelson (10 Jan. 1855–21 Dec. 1943), editor and publisher, was born on a farm in Brown County, Ohio, the son of Cyrenus G. Marquis and Elizabeth Redmon. His mother died in 1861; his father, in 1866. Marquis then went to live in nearby Hamersville with his maternal grandparents, who ran a general store and post office. He went to Brown County schools. When he was about sixteen, he and his younger brother ran away from their harsh grandfather to Kansas City, but when they soon heard that he was fatally ill, they returned home and ran the store themselves. They also collected tolls from people traveling along the private family road.

On turning twenty-one, Marquis moved to Cincinnati, where he sold books and established an advertising and publishing firm, which he called A. N. Marquis & Company. In 1884 he liquidated and moved to Chicago, where he established his company under its old name, resumed the publication of books, and traveled around the country seeking manuscripts. Also in 1884 he published the first Chicago business directo-

ry. Titled *Marquis' Hand-Book of Chicago: A Complete History, Reference Book and Guide to the City*, it was an enormous success and led to his issuance in the next fifteen years of similar directories of other big American cities. He later sold rights to his Chicago directory to the R. R. Donnelly Company. One of the most successful of Marquis's other publications was *The Animals of the World: Brehm's Life of Animals . . .* (1895), translated from the German of Alfred E. Brehm's *Thierleben* and with more than 500 excellent illustrations. Another success was an art portfolio of current stage celebrities, with brief biographies. In these works Marquis was aided by John William Leonard, who also edited publications by Marquis concerning the Klondike, Cincinnati, and Pittsburgh.

Marquis had already published special editions of city newspapers featuring biographies of civic, commercial, political, and cultural leaders; around 1894 he hit upon the idea of compiling a biographical directory of eminent Americans in all fields. An example was soon provided for him by the 1897 British *Who's Who*. Marquis developed the strategy of sending questionnaires to distinguished Americans and using their replies as the basis for brief and accurate sketches. His first volume in this venture was *Who's Who in America* (1899). It was a great success. New editions were published in 1901, 1904, and 1906, all edited by Leonard. Marquis himself edited the fifth and later volumes, and Leonard dropped out of sight around 1906. It is conjectured that the two men had political differences.

Marquis was always the one who decided which notables should be included and which excluded. Though availing himself of much good advice, he alone made the final choice of Americans important enough in the arts, the armed forces, education, government and politics, religion, and the sciences to merit inclusion. Significantly newsworthy persons also were considered. When a given questionnaire was completed and returned, a sketch was written and set in type; a proof was then sent to the biographee for correction and signed approval. No entry was published unless approval was obtained from the biographee. Although Leonard put himself in the first four volumes, Marquis, who was always modest and self-effacing, did not include himself until the seventh volume of *Who's Who* (1912–1913). Socially and politically conservative, Marquis rigorously avoided sports figures (on the grounds that physical prowess was not a reason for inclusion) and persons with any kind of political or criminal taint. Excluded also were divorced persons and men and women significant only because of illustrious ancestry. If an included subject should later be convicted of a crime, that person was dropped from subsequent volumes. For example, Albert Bacon Fall, President Warren G. Harding's secretary of the interior (1921–1923), was dropped after he was imprisoned in 1931–1932 for bribe-taking in connection with the Teapot Dome Scandal; and Richard Whitney, president of the New York Stock Exchange (1930–1935), was dropped after he was jailed in 1938 for embezzlement. Marquis never excluded notable persons, whether native or foreign-born, if they were members of minority racial, ethnic, or religious groups. For example, educator-writer W. E. B. Du Bois, poet Paul Lawrence Dunbar, and educator Booker T. Washington, among other distinguished African Americans, were all featured in Marquis's first *Who's Who* volume; and editor Edward William Bok, conductor-composer Victor Herbert, journal-author Jacob August Riis, and politician-editor Carl Schurz, among other foreign-born achievers, also appeared in various *Who's Who* volumes. Rumors to the contrary, it is not true that persons seeking the prestige of inclusion in Marquis's *Who's Who* ever successfully proposed their own names or bribed their way in, although many tried. Nor did anyone have to purchase a copy of *Who's Who* to gain admittance. Marquis's announced and sole criterion was talent and meritorious accomplishment.

In addition to successive general volumes of *Who's Who*, Marquis began to publish specialized volumes, with titles beginning *Who's Who* and continuing thus: *in California State, in Chicago, in Chicago and Illinois, in Chicago and Vicinity, in Commerce and Industry, in Latin America, in Law, in Massachusetts, in New England, in Pennsylvania, in Poetry in America, in the Central States, in the Clergy, in the East, in the Midwest, in the South, in the South and Southwest, in the West, in the Western Hemisphere, of American Women,* and *on the Pacific Coast.*

Marquis married the widowed Harriette Rosanna Gettemy Morgan in 1910. He incorporated his publishing firm in 1924, then sold control for $150,000 in 1926 but retained a 20 percent participation. In 1928 he and his wife moved from Chicago to nearby Evanston, Illinois. Marquis remained president of his company until 1937, was editor in chief until 1940, and served as editor emeritus thereafter, with headquarters in Indianapolis, Indiana, and offices in Chicago and Wilmette, Illinois. Marquis was a quietly sociable man who joined several conservative clubs, supported Republican party activities, stridently opposed the use of tobacco and alcohol, and with his wife joined the Congregational church in 1935. She died the following year. Dying eight years later in Evanston, Marquis, who had no children, bequeathed the bulk of an estate of slightly more than $600,000 (before taxes) to two close relatives and twenty-five friends and more distant relatives.

• Detailed biographical information on Marquis is in Cedric A. Larson, *Who: Sixty Years of American Eminence: The Story of Who's Who in America* (1958). An obituary is in the *New York Times*, 22 Dec. 1943.

ROBERT L. GALE

MARQUIS, Don (29 July 1878–29 Dec. 1937), columnist, short-story writer, and poet, was born Donald Robert Perry Marquis in Walnut, Illinois, the son of James Stewart Marquis, a country physician, and Virginia Whitmore. He attended local schools, lived with his mother while she ran a boardinghouse in Chicago

(1888–1889), and held various odd jobs (1893–1899) both before and after briefly attending Knox College (fall 1898).

After gaining experience writing for county newspapers, Marquis clerked in the Census Bureau in Washington, D.C. (1900); then he was a reporter in Washington and in Philadelphia (1900–1902). He moved to Atlanta, where from 1902 to 1907 he worked for the *Atlanta News* as associate editor and for the *Atlanta Journal* as an editorialist. He moved to Joel Chandler Harris's *Uncle Remus's Magazine* as associate editor and versatile writer (1907–1909).

Marquis married Reina Melcher, a freelance writer, in 1909 and moved a few months ahead of her to New York City, to become a part-time journalist and—after a struggle—a successful freelance writer. He published his first novel, *Danny's Own Story*, in 1912. Later that year the first major opportunity of his career came when he was allowed to originate his own column, "The Sun Dial," for the *New York Evening Sun*.

Marquis soon evolved into one of the best-known columnists New York ever produced. For a decade he wrote daily "Sun Dial" pieces for the *Sun*. In some of them—partly in parodic free verse—he introduced the immortal cockroach "archy" (who writes on Marquis's office typewriter but cannot manage capital letters or punctuation) and the oversexed cat "mehitabel" (whose dated motto is "toujours gai"). Marquis then moved to the *New York Tribune*, to write another column, "The Lantern" (1922–1925). Marquis ventured into drama with *The Old Soak*; its title character, a codger who likes alcoholic conviviality, had appeared in his "Sun Dial" column. The play enjoyed 325 performances on Broadway (1922–1923).

All was not happy for Marquis, however, then or later. He and his wife had a son and a daughter, but his son died at the age of five and his wife died two years later, in 1923. In 1926 he married Marjorie Vonnegut, an actress and theatrical director. He began writing irregularly for the movies in Hollywood in 1928 and had a heart attack the following year. In 1930 his play *Everything's Jake*, a sequel to *The Old Soak*, was a critical and popular disappointment. His daughter died in Hollywood in 1931. A year later Marquis felt humiliated when *The Dark Hours, Five Scenes from History* (published 1924), his profoundly serious play about the passion and crucifixion of Christ, closed on Broadway after eight performances in 1932. He had wanted the actor portraying Christ to remain offstage, with the audience only hearing his voice; however, Marquis's wife Marjorie, who directed the play, preferred to have the actor appear in person, and prevailed—perhaps unfortunately.

In his last years Marquis continued to work steadily. He assembled more Archy pieces for book publication and wrote other humorous sketches. He was happy when his final play, *Master of the Revels*, was produced at Union College (1935), but then he was felled by two final misfortunes. In 1936 he suffered a stroke that impaired his speech and his ability to walk, and a few months later his wife Marjorie died. When Marquis died in New York City a year later, he left an unfinished autobiographical novel, to be called *Sons of the Puritans*, dealing with small-town mores, rebellious youths, religion, politics, and war. Published in 1939 with Marquis's working notes, it inspired several reviewers to state that if completed, it would have been a major American novel.

Marquis deserves to be remembered for much more than famous Archy and Mehitabel. In addition to comic verse—not all of it involving the cockroach and cat—he also wrote five books of serious poetry, six collections of short stories, four novels, seven plays, six books of sketches, and much ephemeral material. In 1946 Christopher Morley assembled a representative anthology, *The Best of Don Marquis*; it includes Archy and Mehitabel material, *Old Soak* selections, short stories, satirical prose pieces, and serious and humorous verse. From this welter of writing, Marquis emerges as a deeply troubled man whose humor sprang less from joy than from sorrow. Marquis wanted to be both a lyricist and a free-verse spoofer, a romantic rebel and a moneymaking columnist. Contradictory also was his combination of orthodox Christian faith and an awareness of the appeal of nihilistic naturalism.

Marquis was close to the mark when he lamented that he would be remembered only as "the creator of a goddam cockroach." Of his non-Archy works, the best is *Hermione and Her Little Group of Serious Thinkers* (1916), which satirizes in deliberately goofy free verse a rich, liberated, but idiotic woman and her fellow faddists, who fancy that their vapid thoughts about literature, art, and philosophy are profound. A sample from Marquis's *Sonnets to a Red-Haired Lady* (1922) goes thus: "Will your Red Head shine for me through the dim / Damp shadows where I rub my soul and shiver / As I await old Charon's hydro-flivver?" In *Chapters for the Orthodox* (1934) Marquis laments materialism's threat to Christianity. *Out of the Sea* (produced in 1927) skillfully dramatizes the legend of Tristan and Isolde. *Master of the Revels* offers a credibly complex Henry VIII and assorted courtiers. But despite the energetic versatility hinted at here and in other works, the name Don Marquis will remain tightly linked to that of Archy and more loosely to that of Mehitabel, through whose hilarious comments their creator lambasted everything shoddy in his time.

• Marquis's papers are in the Huntington Library, San Marino, Calif.; the Houghton Library, Harvard University; the Butler Library, Columbia University; the Hampden Library, Players Club, New York City; the New York City Public Library; and the Library of Congress, Washington, D.C. Grantland Rice, *The Tumult and the Shouting: My Life in Sport* (1954), describes his friendship with Marquis. Edward Anthony, *O Rare Don Marquis* (1962), is a full-length biography; Lynn Lee, *Don Marquis* (1981), is biographical and critical. Christopher Morley, *Shandygaff . . .* (1919), evaluates Marquis as a satirist. Walter Blair and Hamlin Hill, *America's Humor: From Poor Richard to Doonesbury* (1978), discusses Marquis as a leader of a class of newspaper humorists. Useful also are Carl Van Doren, "Day In and Day Out: Adams, Morley, Marquis, and Broun: Manhattan Wits," *Century* 107 (Dec. 1923): 308–15; E. B. White, *The Second Tree from the Corner* (1954); Bernard DeVoto, *The Easy Chair* (1955); Hamlin Hill, "Archy and Uncle Remus: Don Marquis's Debt to Joel Chandler Harris," *Georgia Review* 15 (Spring 1961): 78–87; Norris W. Yates, *The American Humorist: Conscience of the Twentieth Century* (1964); and Louis Hasley, "Don Marquis: Ambivalent Humorist," *Prairie Schooner* 45 (Spring 1971): 59–73. An obituary is in the *New York Times*, 30 Dec. 1937.

ROBERT L. GALE

MARRANT, John (15 June 1755–Apr. 1791), minister and author, was born in the New York Colony to a family of free blacks. The names and occupations of his parents are not known. When he was four years old, his father died. Marrant and his mother moved to Florida and Georgia; subsequently Marrant moved to Charleston, South Carolina, to live with his sister and brother-in-law. He stayed in school until he was eleven years old, becoming an apprentice to a music master for two additional years. During this time he also learned carpentry. His careers in music and carpentry ended in late 1769 or early 1770, when he was converted to Christianity by the famous evangelical minister George Whitefield.

Over the next few years, Marrant converted many Native Americans, including members of the Cherokee, Creek, Choctaw, and Chickasaw nations. In 1772 he returned to his family for a short time. For the next three years Marrant worked as a minister in the Charleston area. There he saw a plantation owner and other white males whip thirty slaves for attending his church school.

With the onslaught of the revolutionary war, Marrant was impressed as a musician into the British navy in October or November of 1776. Not much is known of his exploits during this period besides the fact that he fought in the Dutch-Anglo War (1780–1784). As a result of his injuries, he was discharged in 1782.

Marrant eventually married. A listing in the New York City Inspection Roll of Negroes in 1783 cited a Mellia Marrant as "formerly the property of John Marrant near Santee Carolina"; this document also states that she "left him at the Siege of Georgetown." Apparently, his wife had been a slave; he bought and freed her in order to marry her. The same listing claimed that Mellia was aboard the *William and Mary* with her children Amelia and Ben, heading for Annapolis Royal, Nova Scotia. There is no evidence to support or deny that they were Marrant's children. The information in this record is all that is known of his marriage and offspring.

To further his opportunities, Marrant moved to London, England, living there between 1782 and 1785. In Bath on 15 May 1785, he was ordained a minister in the chapel of Selina Hastings, countess of Huntingdon and a supporter of the African-American poet Phillis Wheatley. During this time, despite being literate, Marrant told his story to Methodist minister William Aldridge, who later published it as *A Narrative of the Lord's Wonderful Dealings with John Marrant*, *a Black (Now Going to Preach the Gospel in Nova-Scotia) Born in New-York, in North-America* (1785). The narrative, in which Marrant describes his conversion and his life as a traveling minister, was so popular that it went through twenty editions by 1835. In 1785 S. Whitchurch and S. Hazard both published *The Negro Convert: A Poem; Being the Substance of the Experience of Mr. John Marrant, a Negro.*

In November 1785 Marrant moved to Birchtown, Nova Scotia, to minister to the black Loyalists who had emigrated there after the American Revolution. For the next two years he was persecuted and harassed by fellow ministers because he preached Calvinistic Methodism to whites, blacks, and Native Americans in Nova Scotia. Despite his persecution, he built a chapel in Birchtown, taught at the Birchtown school, preached to the congregation, and ministered in other towns. In late November 1786 Marrant gave up control of his school because of his exhaustion and decided to concentrate on being a traveling minister. He contracted smallpox in an epidemic in February 1787 and was ill for six months.

In Nova Scotia, Marrant lived a life of poverty and illness. In late January 1788 he moved to Boston, where he preached and apparently taught school. However, Marrant could not escape persecution. On 27 February 1789 he eluded a mob of forty armed men who were attempting to kill him because their girlfriends went to his Friday sermon. In March of that year he became a Freemason in the African Lodge. As a Freemason, Marrant gave a sermon at the Festival of John the Baptist; the sermon was published in 1789. On his way back to England, Marrant wrote his last journal entry on 7 March 1790. The journal was later published as *A Journal of the Rev. John Marrant* (1790), along with Marrant's sermon of a funeral service in Nova Scotia. The preface of the journal gave the publication date of 29 June 1790. Marrant died somewhere in England and is buried at Islington.

In his sermons, Marrant tried to teach people to love God through a comparison of biblical allegories and everyday life. For example, in his *Narrative*, Marrant's travels after his conversion are reminiscent of John the Baptist's sojourn in the wilderness. His theme is clear: let Jesus and God be your guides. This message is stressed when faith saves him from being executed by a Native-American nation: "I fell down upon my knees, and mentioned to the Lord his delivering of the three children in the fiery furnace, and of Daniel in the Lion's den, and had close communion with God. . . . And about the middle of my prayer, the Lord impressed a strong desire upon my mind to turn into their language, and pray in their tongue . . . which wonderfully affected the people" (Porter, p. 437).

In his short life, Marrant dedicated himself to helping others reach their religious potential. Through his published sermons and conversions, Marrant wanted to help humankind the best way he knew how: by giving them God's lessons. Even though he never reaped an earthly reward in his lifetime, his works stand as a model for religious colonial life.

• Marrant's contributions to African-American literature are discussed in Adam Potkay and Sandra Burr, eds., *Black Atlantic Writers of the Eighteenth Century: Living the New Exodus in England and the Americas* (1995); Blyden Jackson, *A History of Afro-American Literature*, vol. 1, *The Long Beginning, 1746–1895* (1989); William L. Andrews, *To Tell a Free Story: The First Century of Afro-American Autobiography, 1760–1865* (1988); and Dorothy Porter, *Early Negro Writing, 1760–1837* (1971). Henry Louis Gates, Jr., *The Signifying Monkey: A Theory of Afro-American Literary Criticism* (1988), argues that Marrant was the "first revisionist" of the black tradition for English literature. Roger Whitlow, *Black American Literature: A Critical History* (1973), claims that Marrant's *Narrative* is the second "slave narrative" published.

DEVONA A. MALLORY

MARRIOTT, John Willard (17 Sept. 1900–13 Aug. 1985), founder of the restaurant and hotel chain that bears his name, was born in Marriott, Utah, the son of Hyrum Marriott and Ellen Morris, farmers. In the town his grandfather established in 1854, the family, well off until after the First World War, was prominent in the Mormon church and the Republican party. At nineteen he left behind the hard life of farm work. For two years he served as a Mormon missionary in New England. While in the East he visited Washington and sought out members of Utah's congressional delegation known to sponsor promising young fellow Mormons. He hoped that political contacts would provide a suitable job, but when they failed he returned to Utah. There he worked his way through a junior college and then the University of Utah, receiving an A.B. in 1926. Concentrating more on earning money and on social activities than on academic pursuits, he was particularly successful as a salesman.

In 1927 Marriott decided to enter business for himself. With Hugh Colton, the younger brother of Utah congressman Don B. Colton, he bought the A&W franchise for Washington, a city where political connections could benefit them. He was attracted by the root beer chain, which had started in California a few years before, after observing its success in Salt Lake City and after a cousin had done well with its franchise in Fort Wayne, Indiana. With his business launched, he briefly returned to Utah to marry Alice Sheets, who had just graduated from the university where they had met. The couple had two children. When his partner returned to Utah in 1928, Marriott and his wife bought out his share, and together they operated the business.

From the very first, Marriott not only worked eighteen hours a day but also applied enterprise and modern management. Recognizing the seasonal nature of the soft-drink business, he obtained permission from A&W to introduce food service, and he renamed his small root beer stand The Hot Shoppe. He soon opened several more such restaurants in Washington, and on 10 July 1929 he officially incorporated the business in Delaware as Hot Shoppes, Inc., with plans for expansion beyond the city. Meanwhile, he gained valuable contacts after his widowed mother-in-law married Senator Reed Smoot, the senior Republican from Utah.

Marriott's expansion program followed the strategy of chain stores that aimed at high volume. With centralized management, he standardized operations and selected good locations. Like Howard Johnson's restaurant chain, the Hot Shoppes responded to demographic changes by locating outlets in suburbs and along highways. As the business grew, Marriott received encouragement, advice, and even financial support from Earl Sams, the president and later chairman of J. C. Penney, whom he met through a relative who was a vice president for the retail chain. Without collective bargaining, Marriott, like J. C. Penney, cultivated employee loyalty and good service by providing training and by promising opportunities for promotion.

While conservatively avoiding heavy debt burdens, Marriott steadily expanded his business. By putting air conditioning in the restaurants (1935), adding children's menus (1936), and starting to cater meals for airline flights from the Washington airport (1937), he raised gross annual sales before the Second World War to almost $1 million. During the war he developed new business by managing food services at factories and office buildings, and after the war Hot Shoppes expanded along major highways on the East Coast and in the West. To obtain capital, on 17 March 1953 the company publicly sold stock, though the family retained control. Four years later, with a new motel in Washington, it launched a profitable hotel division. In 1964 the corporate name changed to Marriott–Hot Shoppes, Inc., and Marriott turned over operations to the older of his two sons.

Success in business allowed Marriott and his wife to increase their involvements in Mormon affairs and Republican politics. During the late 1950s Marriott enjoyed a personal friendship with President Dwight D. Eisenhower, and his wife served on the Republican National Committee. In June 1960, a few months after civil rights activists began sit-in demonstrations at other restaurant chains in the South, the Hot Shoppes in Arlington, Virginia, became the first restaurants to breach the state's segregation law by serving customers without regard to race. Marriott supported George Romney, a fellow Mormon and friend since they met in Washington during the 1930s, in his Michigan gubernatorial elections and in his presidential bid in 1968. He then served as the committee chairman for both of President Richard Nixon's inaugural festivities. Marriott remained active in Mormon and other philanthropies until he died at the family's summer home near Wolfeboro, New Hampshire.

• The personal papers of J. Willard Marriott, Sr., and his wife, including some business records, are in the Manuscripts Division of the Marriott Library at the University of Utah. Robert O'Brien, *Marriott: The J. Willard Marriott Story* (1987), is an authorized biography that used Marriott's diaries. An obituary is in the *New York Times*, 15 Aug. 1985.

ALAN R. RAUCHER

MARSALA, Joe (4 Jan. 1907–3 Mar. 1978), jazz clarinetist and saxophonist, was born Joseph Francis Marsala in Chicago, Illinois, the son of Pete Marsala, a valve-trombonist. His mother's name is unknown. Starting on clarinet at age 15, Marsala was primarily self-taught, but in 1924 he started taking informal lessons from Johnny Lane, a local clarinetist and bandleader at the Friars Inn. Joe and his younger brother, Marty, a drummer and aspiring trumpet player, frequently stood outside nightclubs and dance halls to hear the hot jazz played within, but their own early playing seems to have been limited to the Jane Addams Hull House Band. It was at this time that Marsala first heard records by the great New Orleans clarinetists Leon Roppolo, Johnny Dodds, and Jimmie Noone, the masterful virtuoso who ultimately became his major influence. Throughout this period he also worked at a series of odd jobs: shoveling cinders off a freight car, clerking in a mail-order office, buying material for a shoe company, and working in a factory and a brass foundry. In 1926, on another of his day jobs, the delivery truck he was riding in crashed into a streetcar, causing him to be thrown through the windshield. The resulting facial lacerations left severe scar tissue that remained throughout his life.

As a musician, Marsala played locally with pianists Art Hodes and Dave Rose and in 1929 worked in Akron with New Orleans–born trumpeter Wingy Manone, after which he joined Nelson Maple's Leviathan Orchestra in Cleveland. Returning to Chicago, he spent nine months in Harold West's dance band and did occasional substitute work for Ben Pollack at the Chez Paree. Around 1931, Marsala signed on with a traveling circus band and barnstormed through Montana and the Dakotas, but in 1933, at the time of the Chicago World's Fair, he joined Manone's jazz group for an engagement at the Brewery Club overlooking the nearby fairgrounds. After sporadic freelancing in 1934, his career took a significant step ahead in the spring of 1935.

While Marsala was once again driving a truck in Chicago, Manone asked him to join his newly formed quartet for an engagement at the Hickory House in New York City. The group was very popular, thanks to Manone's hot swing vocals, and played to capacity crowds nightly. On 30 May 1936 the quartet participated in New York's first Swing Concert. A truly all-star occasion, the event was staged at the Imperial Theater and also featured Louis Armstrong, the Bob Crosby Bob Cats, Tommy Dorsey's Clambake Seven, Bunny Berigan, the Three Ts (Frank Trumbauer, Jack Teagarden, and Charlie Teagarden), Artie Shaw, Eddie Condon, Bud Freeman, Max Kaminsky, and many other top-ranking jazzmen. Manone also initiated a widely attended series of Sunday afternoon jam sessions at the Hickory House.

At the height of the combo's success, though, Manone decided to take off two months for a tour of vaudeville houses. In July 1936 Marsala was placed in charge of the music. He hired trumpeter Henry "Red" Allen as a temporary replacement for Manone and made other changes in personnel as well, including the substitution of guitarist Eddie Condon for the departing Carmen Mastren. Although not the showman that Manone was, Marsala nevertheless continued to do good business for the club, thus enabling him to play at other venues periodically and still have a job waiting for him upon his return. On some of these intermittent engagements he was able to hire his brother on trumpet, thereby introducing him to the New York fold. At both the Yacht Club and the short-lived Club McKenzie, Marsala used the same personnel but now with singer Red McKenzie as nominal leader and the occasional addition of trumpet star Bunny Berigan.

In December 1936 the Marsala-Condon group, sans McKenzie, played in Havana, Cuba, and Jamaica and for a short time afterward at the Paradise Restaurant on Broadway. Marsala returned to the Hickory House in March 1937 with essentially the same lineup but with one substantial difference. The group now included the attractive 24-year-old swing harpist Adele Girard, who had been playing at the Hickory House in the Three Ts, a jazz unit from the Paul Whiteman Orchestra. Marsala hired her immediately, and they were married in July.

On 5 November 1938 the BBC presented a special jam session transmitted via cable to England. Hosted by Alastair Cooke, the broadcast took place in the Viennese Room of the St. Regis Hotel in Manhattan, with Marsala chosen to assemble the musicians and organize the individual performances. In addition to himself, the participants included many of the jazzmen associated with Eddie Condon and the Greenwich Village and Fifty-second Street jazz clubs. Subsequent BBC specials featuring Marsala and other top jazzmen were broadcast from the Hickory House on 20 January and 18 August 1939. In the summer of 1939 Marsala started touring with a larger instrumentation, and for the next few years he alternated out-of-town big-band engagements with his residency at the Hickory House and occasional appearances at the Famous Door and Nick's. One such engagement in the summer and fall of 1942 was at the Log Cabin, a roadhouse in Armonk, New York, where his big band, with Girard as a featured soloist, was heard on nightly broadcasts.

Decreasing opportunities for work, problems with wartime gas rationing, and a shortage of qualified musicians caused Marsala to disband shortly after the Log Cabin engagement, and for the remainder of his active playing career he concentrated on small-band jazz exclusively. Following his 1948 departure from the Hickory House, he decided to abandon full-time playing. Between 1949 and 1954, he and his family, now including a daughter born in 1939, lived in Aspen, Colorado, where he ran jam sessions and opened an Italian restaurant. In 1954 they moved back to New York, where he formed a music publishing company, but in 1962 he left for Chicago to serve as vice president of Seeburg Music Corporation. After putting his publishing company under Seeburg's control, he remained with that firm until 1967, when its mob-affiliated owner was forced to sell the business to his debtors, allegedly to pay off gambling debts. On losing not only his job but his publishing rights as well, Marsala took his family to the West Coast in November 1967, where they moved around considerably before settling in Los Angeles. Although he had become increasingly depressed over the downward curve his career and finances had taken, Marsala had been playing on and off all this time, and his last known appearances were at jazz clubs and concerts in Hollywood in the early 1970s.

In addition to several jazz tunes, Marsala also wrote "Little Sir Echo" (1939), "Don't Cry, Joe" (1949), "And So to Sleep Again" (1951), and the score for a 1952 musical comedy, *I've Had It*, which enjoyed some local success in Aspen and Denver but never made it to Broadway. Although a gifted melodist, Marsala seemed to lack the necessary drive to become a successful songwriter. His best efforts in music were as an improvising jazz clarinetist, as is evidenced on the records he made from the mid-1930s on.

Starting in 1935 Marsala appeared on dozens of New York–based recording dates under the leadership of Manone, Berigan, Adrian Rollini, Sharkey Bonano, Leonard Feather, and others as well as under his own name from 1937 through 1945. He was especially well represented on records in the early and mid-1940s, when he appeared as an occasional guest on Eddie Condon's weekly broadcasts from Town Hall. Marsala also recorded with Wild Bill Davison and Yank Lawson at this time as well as leading his own dates featuring his wife and trumpet players Bill Coleman, Max Kaminsky, Billy Butterfield, Bobby Hackett, Joe Thomas, Dizzy Gillespie, Marty Marsala, and, on a 1957 comeback album, Rex Stewart. His last recorded performance was with Tony Bennett in 1965. He died in Santa Barbara, California.

Joe Marsala played with a highly personal tone that easily distinguishes him from other clarinetists who played in the same circles during the 1930s and 1940s. Taking Jimmie Noone as his model, he concentrated on developing a warm, moaning, blues-tinged sound that usually conveyed a sense of wistful sadness best exemplified in his playing of blues and ballads. Apart from practiced, Noone-like passages, he was less effective on faster tempos, but his rhythmic sense somehow carried him through. Some of his best and most representative work can be heard on "Swingin' on that Famous Door" (1935), "Cheatin' Cheech" (1936), "Wolverine Blues" (1937) "Jazz Me Blues" (1937), "A Good Man Is Hard to Find" (1940), "I Know that You Know" (1941), "Slow Down" (1941), "Chimes Blues" (1942), "Sweet Mama" (1942), "Walkin' the Dog" (1942), and "Lazy Daddy" (1942).

Marsala is more properly regarded as a stylist than an instrumental virtuoso, and during his peak years on Fifty-second Street his spirited, heartfelt improvisations were appreciated by a wide range of fellow clarinetists, from Pee Wee Russell and Barney Bigard to Benny Goodman and Artie Shaw. Since the early 1960s his unique style has been echoed in the playing of his only known disciple, clarinetist Bobby Gordon.

• No biographies of Marsala have yet been published, but a general view of his milieu and times can be found in William Howland Kenney, *Chicago Jazz: A Cultural History, 1904–1930* (1993); John Steiner, "Chicago," in *Jazz*, ed. Nat Hentoff and Albert McCarthy (1959); and Arnold Shaw, *52nd St.: The Street of Jazz* (1971). Autobiographies of his colleagues and contemporaries are even more helpful; see Wingy Manone, *Trumpet on the Wing* (1948); Eddie Condon, *We Called It Music* (1947) and *Eddie Condon's Scrapbook of Jazz* (1973); and Max Kaminsky, *My Life in Jazz* (1963). For additional personal references, as well as detailed overviews of the New York jazz scene of the mid-1930s, see Robert Dupuis, *Bunny Berigan: Elusive Legend of Jazz* (1993), and Robert Hilbert, *Pee Wee Russell: The Life of a Jazzman* (1993). Complete listings of Marsala's recordings, under both his name and others', are in Brian Rust, *Jazz Records, 1897–1942* (1982), and two works by Walter Bruyninckx, *Traditional Jazz Discography, 1897–1988* (5 vols., 1988), and *Swing Discography, 1920–1988* (13 vols., 1988).

JACK SOHMER

MARSH, Charles Wesley (22 Mar. 1834–9 Nov. 1918), inventor and manufacturer of a harvesting machine, was born on a farm in Northumberland County, Ontario, Canada, the son of Samuel Marsh and Tamar Richardson, farmers. Charles and his brother, William W. Marsh, farmed in De Kalb County, Illinois, at the time they invented and successfully operated a grain harvesting machine known as the Marsh harvester.

Marsh's parents worked as farmers in Northumberland County until Charles Wesley Marsh was eleven years old. They then sold their farm and began a planned move to Illinois. In route his father converted to the Second Adventist faith, and the family remained in Coburg, Canada, for four years before completing the trek to Illinois.

In Coburg, Charles Marsh attended St. Andrews School and then Victoria College. In 1849, at the age of fifteen, his family acquired a quarter-section (160 acres) of government land located near Shabbona and De Kalb in De Kalb County, Illinois. For the next ten years Charles and his family cleared the timber, broke the land, built a homestead, and farmed. Their major crop was wheat.

Cyrus McCormick (1832) and Obed Hussey (1833) each had developed a workable horse-drawn reaper. Before the development of these machines wheat and grain was laboriously harvested by hand sickles or cradles. In 1834 McCormick patented his reaper and, following improvements (patented in 1845 and 1847), he began mass production at a Chicago plant. In the 1850s, Charles and William Marsh improved on McCormick's design by creating an assisted mechanical binding device on the machine (which bundled and tied the sheaves) rather than having the grain dropped on the side or rear for gathering and binding by hand. They obtained a patent (no. 21,207) for their "reaping machine" on 17 August 1858. The Marsh reaper improved on the reaper developed by Cyrus McCormick by binding the grain on the machine and thus reducing required harvest labor by two or three persons.

Charles Marsh unsuccessfully attempted to manufacture twelve reapers in 1860, built only one workable model in 1861, and then in 1863 joined with Lewis Steward to manufacture the machines at a small plant in Plano, Illinois. They sold twenty-five reapers in 1864 and began enlarging their factory and licensing others in Illinois and Ohio. During the latter 1860s, Charles served two terms in the Illinois House of Representatives followed by one term (1870) in the state senate as a Republican. After selling the Plano factory, he organized the Sycamore Marsh Harvester Manufacturing Company in 1869, and in 1870 demonstrated his reaper in Austria and Hungary. His company prospered until 1876, when he sold a majority interest to J. D. Easter and Company and retired.

Unfortunately, Easter and Company failed the following year and Charles Marsh resumed control, but financial difficulties and the expiration of his patent and manufacturing licenses forced him to close in 1881. He then established the Marsh Binder Manufacturing Company in the factory at Sycamore, Illinois, but in 1884 that business failed as well.

The next year Marsh became editor of the *Farm Implement News*, a highly successful farm machinery trade journal. Marsh became president of the publishing company and retired as editor at the age of seventy. He was survived by his second wife, Sue Rogers, whom he married in 1881 (they had no children), and by the three children of his deceased first wife, Frances Wait, whom he married in 1860.

Although Marsh and others were significant pioneers in the development of the reaper-harvester machines, the manufacturing and business expertise of Cyrus McCormick ultimately caused the McCormick reaper and subsequently the McCormick-Deering harvester to dominate the field. Charles Marsh's career as an inventor and publisher is, however, exemplary of the energy and innovation that produced a revolution in American agricultural practices and yields during the nineteenth century.

• Secondary biographies and studies of Charles Wesley Marsh are no longer readily available, and the reader is advised to examine the sketch presented in *Dictionary of American Biography*, on which this essay relies heavily. Useful sources are C. W. Marsh, *Recollections* (1910); *Farm Implement News*, 14 Nov. 1918; and John T. Schlebecker, *Whereby We Thrive: A History of American Farming 1607–1972* (1975). An obituary is in *Farm Implement News*, 14 Nov. 1918.

HENRY C. DETHLOFF

MARSH, George Perkins (15 Mar. 1801–23 July 1882), scholar, politician, and diplomat, was born in Woodstock, Vermont, the son of Charles Marsh, a prominent lawyer, and Susan Perkins. The Marshes were among New England's aristocracy of Puritan intellectuals. Woodstock, unlike western Vermont of the free-spirited Green Mountain Boys, was a town of law-abiding, substantial settlers, conservative in religion and politics. George, in a milieu of book lovers, became an avid reader, although a lifelong eye ailment periodically forced him to turn from the printed page to the outdoor world. As a child, with his father or friends, he observed firsthand the effects of deforestation in early Vermont settlements, the decline of fish in the rivers, and the destruction of precious topsoil.

Graduating from Dartmouth College in 1820, Marsh became professor of the Greek and Latin languages at the American Literary, Scientific, and Military Academy (now Norwich University, Northfield, Vt.). However, teaching did not appeal to him, and his eye trouble reappeared. For the next four years, he studied law with his father and brother.

After being admitted to the bar in 1825, Marsh moved to Burlington. There he practiced law without enthusiasm, dabbled in politics without success, and entered business ventures, which ultimately ruined him financially. He made lasting friendships, and in 1828 he married Harriet Buel, who linked him with a prominent Burlington family and brought him happiness. They had two children. However, in 1833 the double tragedy of his wife's death from a heart condition and his elder son's death from scarlet fever sent Marsh into a period of deep sadness. Yet his inquiring mind and the energy of his work ethic saved his sanity, and the companionship of scholars at the University of Vermont, whose president was his cousin James Marsh, provided intellectual stimulation.

In 1835 Marsh was elected by an Anti-Mason/Whig coalition to the Supreme Legislative Council (then Vermont's upper house). In 1839 he married schoolteacher Caroline Crane, who became his beloved companion in a life of intellectual and artistic pursuits and public service. They had no children.

Vermonters sent Marsh to the Twenty-eighth Congress in 1843 as their Whig representative supporting protectionism and abolition. They returned him three successive times, as he spoke out for a high tariff to save their wool industry and against the annexation of Texas and the consequent war with Mexico. Committee work rather than debate appealed to Marsh's studious nature and inquisitive mind. On the Naval Affairs Committee he conducted technical inquiries, conferring with scientists while trying to avoid lobbyists. He and his colleagues on the Joint Committee of the Library of Congress persuaded Congress to raise the library's annual budget from $2,500 to $5,000. In urging the establishment of a national museum to house scientific collections and "give character, consistency, and unity to national science," he laid the foundation for the Smithsonian Institution (Lowenthal [1958], p. 80).

President Zachary Taylor rewarded Marsh's Whig loyalty with an appointment as minister to Turkey, where Marsh served from 1849 to 1854. His familiarity with twenty languages enabled him to deal with the many refugees from Europe's 1848 revolutions, and his keen observations on Turkish government and officials filled his diplomatic dispatches with important information. He had time to travel in the Middle East, studying humanity's effects on ancient landscapes.

Marsh was home between 1854 and 1861, coping with financial disasters from the failure of his wool en-terprises and the Vermont Central Railroad. In the winter of 1858–1859 he lectured at Columbia University on English language and literature; when the lectures were published, Marsh was acclaimed for his scholarship and contribution to American literature. A year later he gave lectures at Boston's renowned Lowell Institute (published as *The Origin and History of the English Language and of the Early Literature It Embodies*), technical discussions appreciated primarily by scholars that gained him fame but little money. Marsh served on Vermont's House, Fishing, and Railroad commissions, contributing his knowledge to proposals for fish restoration and preservation and to the design of Vermont's capitol building. His railroad commissioner's reports were studies in political economy and exposés of corporate irresponsibility. Again he gained respect, but his financial situation continued to mirror Vermont's nineteenth-century economic decline.

In 1861 President Abraham Lincoln appointed Marsh the first U.S. minister to the newly formed kingdom of Italy. No post was more appealing to the Marshes, and for twenty-one years they served in Turin, then Florence, then Rome. Marsh sympathized with the Risorgimento liberation movement and the recent unification of Italian states, and he admired the intellectual and artistic accomplishments of the Italians, "a civilized people" whom the United States should help. The Marshes enjoyed Italy's natural beauty as well as the cultural and social functions, whether with Europe's elite or Americans on the grand tour, that were a part of their life. The minister dealt with routine diplomatic matters of trade and immigration and with delicate issues, such as Giuseppe Garibaldi's march on Rome and his erroneous claim of U.S. citizenship. Marsh sought to dissuade European governments from intervening in the American Civil War. He worked to prevent sales of arms to the Confederacy and to facilitate arms sales to the Union.

Yet Marsh had time to complete his most important book, *Man and Nature: Physical Geography as Modified by Human Action*, a pioneering encyclopedic work on environment, conservation, and ecology. This book, states Vermont historian Charles T. Morrissey in *Vermont: A History* (1981), is "the most consequential message ever delivered by any Vermonter" (p. 188). First published in 1864, its message was original: "Man is everywhere a disturbing agent. Wherever he plants his foot, the harmonies of nature are turned to discord." Seventeen years earlier, Marsh had addressed the Rutland County (Vt.) Agricultural Society on this same theme, for Vermonters were experiencing that "discord." In *Man and Nature*, the theme assumed a worldwide dimension, based on Marsh's extensive travels and research. Marsh continued to improve on his book. Spending the summer of 1882 at Vallombrosa, the site of a forestry school near Florence, Marsh made additions to *Man and Nature* one morning and quietly died that evening.

Marsh hoped to promote reform, but the urgency of his message was not clear to an optimistic, expansionist America. Land-use policy was not deemed critical until the disastrous floods and soil erosion of the 1930s. In 1955 a conference of scholars at Princeton, New Jersey, honored Marsh; the "Marsh Festival" published an interdisciplinary source book, *Man's Role in Changing the Face of the Earth*, edited by William L. Thomas, Jr. In the latter half of the twentieth century, individuals and governments have accepted Marsh's challenge: man must and can function in harmony with nature.

• The George Perkins Marsh Papers (tens of thousands of items) in Special Collections, Bailey-Howe Library, University of Vermont, are the most important source; his diplomatic correspondence is in Diplomatic Dispatches from United States Ministers and Instructions of the Department of State (Turkey, Italy) at the National Archives. Indispensable is David Lowenthal, *George Perkins Marsh: Versatile Vermonter* (1958), with its 36-page bibliography of works by and about Marsh and 42 pages of notes locating sources. More recent is Jane Curtis et al., *The World of George Perkins Marsh, America's First Conservationist and Environmentalist: An Illustrated Biography* (1982). H. L. Mencken discusses Marsh's "Lectures on the English Language" in *The American Language: An Inquiry into the Development of English in the United States* (1936). Louis Mumford, *The Brown Decades: A Study of the Arts in America, 1865–1895* (1931), places Marsh at a critical time in American public conservation policy. Beginning in the 1950s Marsh received increasing attention in scholarly journals; see Lowenthal, "George Perkins Marsh on the Nature and Purpose of Geography," *Geographical Journal* 126 (1960): 413–17; R. F. Legget, "A Prophet of Conservation," *Dalhousie Review* 45 (1965): 34–42; M. J. Lacey, "Man, Nature, and the Ecological Perspective," *American Studies* 8 (1970): 13–27; Tom Daniels, "In Italy with Mr. and Mrs. George Perkins Marsh," *Vermont History* 47 (1979): 191–95, which treats us to a glimpse of life at the minister's Italian residence; D. M. Gade, "The Growing Recognition of George Perkins Marsh," *Geographical Review* 73 (1983): 341–44; and T. R. Cox, "Americans and Their Forests: Romanticism, Progress, and Science in the Late Nineteenth Century," *Journal of Forest History* 29 (1985): 156–69. An obituary is in the *New York Times*, 25 July 1882.

SYLVIA B. LARSON

MARSH, James (19 July 1794–3 July 1842), educator and philosopher, was born in Hartford, Vermont, the son of Joseph Marsh and Marion Harper, farmers. His paternal grandfather was the first lieutenant governor of the state. Marsh entered Dartmouth College in 1813 and found that he had a special intellectual interest in the Greek language and the ancient classics, but he also read widely on his own in English literature. He underwent a religious conversion in 1815 and made it a life purpose to connect religion with poetry and philosophy. That interest guided his early passion for Lord Byron and then William Wordsworth, and he wrote that "It is the poetry that, of all, I would prefer to make my habitual study." He graduated from Dartmouth and entered Andover Theological Seminary in 1817, determined to establish his religious beliefs on a firmer foundation. Andover had been established in 1808 in part by conservative dissenters from Harvard Unitarianism, and Marsh always stayed within the theological boundaries of Calvinism.

Marsh interrupted his studies at Andover to teach briefly at Dartmouth and then returned and finished his studies at Andover in 1822. The next year he began teaching at Hampden-Sydney College in Virginia and in 1824 became professor of Oriental languages. He found life in the South tolerably pleasant, but his letters from the college remark on his acute moral opposition to slavery, which he called "an intolerable weight" on the South. Marsh returned north to be ordained a Congregational minister in October 1824, two days before his marriage to Lucia Wheelock. Lucia Marsh died in 1828, and Marsh married her sister Laura in 1833.

In 1826 Marsh became president of the University of Vermont. He used his office to champion the cause of reform in American higher education and ranks with Philip Lindsley, Francis Wayland, and George Ticknor among critics who believed that American colleges must grow in the direction of greater liberality and practicality in their curricula. Marsh's continuing calls for an education that acknowledged the individuality of students and encouraged their intuitions and imaginations set him against the strict four-year curriculum and the emphasis on rote learning that prevailed almost everywhere in American higher education. Marsh's "Exposition of the Course of Instruction and Discipline in the University of Vermont," originally his outline of educational reform as presented to the corporation of the university, won expressions of approval from other college presidents and deserves notice as a major contribution to the reformist literature. It appeared the same year that Yale College issued its famous report of 1828 with its ringing defense of the traditional curriculum and pedagogy. Marsh's reforms at Vermont seem not to have lasted much beyond his presidency.

Marsh's ideas on education were of a piece with his new philosophical interests. He had been reading Immanuel Kant, but Kant's significance appeared only when Marsh encountered Samuel Taylor Coleridge's *Biographia Literaria* and his *Aids to Reflection*. Marsh enthusiastically prepared an American edition of *Aids* in 1829 and offered his own "Preliminary Essay" as an introduction of Coleridge to an American audience. Marsh conceded that Americans who knew Coleridge were likely to dismiss him as "mystical and unintelligible," but Marsh believed that Coleridge provided a new key to a spiritually fortified Christianity. His essay wanted above all to make that point. Here Marsh differentiated between the "understanding" and the "reason." Marking a continuation from Kant, Marsh associated the reason (not to be confused with the "rational" in the logical or deductive sense) with notions of freedom, morality, and God and designated this faculty as that which distinguishes human beings from the brutes. Essentially for Marsh, vindication of reason signified the reality of the spiritual, and he believed that Christianity greatly needed fortification by this principle. Marsh believed that Christian instructors who had recourse to Coleridge might better "prepare the way for the full and unobstructed influence of the Gospel" by removing other intellectual prejudices against it.

Marsh's edition of Coleridge offered another direct challenge to prevailing academic orthodoxy. He had long judged John Locke's epistemology inadequate and had little relish for the Scottish philosophers—Dugald Stewart especially—who had gained an ascendancy in American academic philosophy. In an 1829 letter to Coleridge, Marsh lamented how little influence the German thinkers had gained in the United States. The letter stated that Marsh believed that Coleridge was the key to gaining a hearing for an alternative philosophical system.

In the mid-1830s Marsh again had the occasion to take his religious views before the public. At that time Jedidiah Burchard, a practitioner of the strenuous revivalist techniques known as the "new measures," was winning converts in Vermont. Associated primarily with the career of Charles Grandison Finney in the Second Great Awakening, this revivalism caused considerable division in American Protestantism. Marsh added to it by using every opportunity to denounce Burchard. Disturbed that the Dartmouth faculty had endorsed Burchard, Marsh made his most elaborate case against the new measures in a letter to college president Nathan Lord. Above all, Burchard offended Marsh's neo-Calvinism. Burchard and Finney believed that religious conversions could be secured through natural causes. By use of psychological principles, that is, revivals could be "got up" by powerful preaching. Marsh distrusted these claims and the "barefaced quackery" that they produced among the most scandalous preachers. Marsh faulted the new measures because they left out the work of the Holy Spirit, the gospel, and the church. American revivalism, Marsh believed, had, in its triumphant self-confidence, dangerously weakened the idea of original sin.

Marsh resigned the presidency at Vermont in 1833, overburdened by administrative details for which he admitted he had no skills. Very much an intellectual person, Marsh often conveyed to contemporaries the personality of a recluse. He wrote of himself: "In a word, I was never made for society. The feelings that might flow spontaneously in solitude with my friends, are chilled, and all powers of sympathy destroyed, by the intercourse of the world" (Torrey, p. 61). But Marsh did flourish in small social and intellectual circles and often formed groups who convened to discuss literature and philosophy. After the death of his second wife in 1838, Marsh endured years of acute loneliness, sustained only by his intellectual work and his religious faith. He died of lung disease in Colchester, Vermont.

Marsh played a key role in laying the foundations of the Transcendentalist movement in the United States. Historian Perry Miller observed that with his edition of Coleridge's *Aids* Marsh "put into the hands of [Ralph Waldo] Emerson, [Theodore] Parker, [Bronson] Alcott and their group the book that was of the greatest single importance in the formation of their minds." Although Marsh judged Boston Transcen-

dentalism "a rather superficial affair," the key distinctions that Marsh made in his preliminary essay appeared as major points in Emerson's essay "The Transcendentalist" and Parker's essay "Transcendentalism."

• Relevant materials about Marsh, including correspondence, may be found in the Bailey-Howe Memorial Library of the University of Vermont, which also has a complete set of photocopies of the James Marsh Collection. A very useful biographical sketch of Marsh is *The Remains of the Rev. James Marsh, D.D., Late President, and Professor of Moral and Intellectual Philosophy, in the University of Vermont; with a Memoir of His Life* (1843; repr. 1971), written and comp. Joseph Torrey, a colleague and friend. Peter Carafiol's study, *Transcendent Reason: James Marsh and the Forms of Romantic Thought* (1982), is the most comprehensive review of Marsh's thought and his place in American intellectual history. John J. Duffy edited Marsh correspondence, much of it quite significant, in *Coleridge's American Disciples: The Selected Correspondence of James Marsh* (1973). An abbreviated version of Marsh's important "Preliminary Essay" in his edition of Coleridge's *Aids to Reflection* may be found in *The Transcendentalists: An Anthology*, ed. Perry Miller (1950). Scholarly books and articles about Marsh include Ronald Wells, *Three Christian Transcendentalists* (1943); John Dewey, "James Marsh and American Philosophy," *Journal of the History of Ideas* 2 (1941): 131–50; Marjorie Nicolson, "James Marsh and the Vermont Transcendentalists," *Philosophical Review* 34 (1925): 28–50; Duffy, "From Hanover to Burlington: James Marsh's Search for Unity," *Vermont History* 38 (1970): 27–48; Duffy, "Problems in Publishing Coleridge: James Marsh's First Edition of *Aids to Reflection*," *New England Quarterly* 43 (1972): 193–208; and Duffy, "Transcendental Letters from George Ripley to James Marsh," *Emerson Society Quarterly*, suppl. 50 (1970): 20–24.

J. DAVID HOEVELER

MARSH, John (5 June 1799–24 Sept. 1856), California ranchero and physician, was born in Danvers, Massachusetts, the son of John Marsh and Mary "Polly" Brown, farmers. After graduating from Phillips Academy in Andover, Massachusetts, in 1819, Marsh received his B.A. from Harvard in 1823. That year he accepted an appointment as a tutor at Fort St. Anthony (later Fort Snelling), in Michigan Territory. For two years Marsh taught school and studied medicine under the guidance of Edward Purcell, the post surgeon. Purcell died without giving his apprentice a certificate, but this did not prevent Marsh from successfully practicing medicine years later in California.

In 1824 Marsh became acting Indian subagent, which brought him into close contact with the Sioux. A gifted linguist, Marsh quickly learned the Sioux language and began writing a Sioux dictionary and grammar. He also married into the tribe, taking Marguerite Decouteaux as a common-law wife. The daughter of a Sioux mother and a French-Canadian father, Decouteaux helped Marsh complete his literary work. Entitled "Rudiments of the Grammar of the Sioux Language," Marsh's study was eventually published in 1831 as an appendix to Caleb Atwater's *Remarks Made on a Tour to Prairie du Chien*. Decouteaux lived with

Marsh for about seven years, until her death in 1831. the couple had one son.

In June 1825 Michigan territorial governor Lewis Cass appointed Marsh Indian subagent at Prairie du Chien, a major center of the North American fur trade. Here Marsh dealt not only with the Sioux but with the nearby Winnebago, Menominee, Chippewa, Sauk, and Fox as well. The favoritism he displayed for the Sioux soon led to conflicts with his superiors. So did his appointment in 1826 as justice of the peace for Crawford County. Marsh's two positions generated serious conflicts of interest that contributed to his dismissal as subagent in 1829. Marsh remained in Prairie du Chien as justice of the peace and opened a private trading post.

After the outbreak of the Black Hawk War in May 1832, Marsh helped raise and lead a force of Sioux and Menominee who fought alongside U.S. troops and Illinois militia against Chief Black Hawk's Fox and Sauk. In September Marsh participated in peace negotiations at Rock Island, Illinois, where he served as an interpreter for General Winfield Scott and signed the treaty ending hostilities. By the close of the war, Marsh had decided to leave Prairie du Chien and had resigned as justice. His departure became a flight when it was discovered that he had been illegally selling guns and ammunition to the Sioux. After a warrant was issued for his arrest, Marsh escaped south to St. Louis and then to Independence, Missouri, where he opened a store and saloon and competed in the flourishing trade on the Santa Fe Trail.

Bankruptcy and the discovery by federal authorities of his whereabouts forced Marsh to flee Independence on 15 June 1835. Heading southwest on the Santa Fe Trail toward the Mexican frontier, Marsh was captured by Comanche Indians and held captive for several days until he made yet another successful escape. Marsh settled temporarily in Santa Fe, where he spent three months learning Spanish before moving on to Los Angeles. Arriving in February 1836, Marsh managed to establish himself as the pueblo's only resident physician. Though very successful, Marsh left Los Angeles in September 1836 and made his way north to Yerba Buena (San Francisco). Desiring a land grant, Marsh underwent a nominal conversion to Catholicism and became a naturalized citizen of Mexico. Having thus qualified for land ownership, Marsh purchased "Rancho Los Meganos" from Jose Noriega in December 1837. Situated between Mount Diablo and the San Joaquin River, Marsh's estate covered about 17,000 acres. To stock his property, Marsh resumed his medical practice and collected his fees in cattle. This strategy, well suited to cash-poor and physician-starved Mexican California, enabled Marsh to engage successfully in the hide and tallow trade that dominated the territorial economy.

Although he supported various schemes to free California from Mexican control and was jailed briefly along with other Americans suspected of plotting a "Texas-style" revolution in the Isaac Graham affair of 1840, Marsh played no direct role in the American conquest of California. His chief contribution to U.S. expansion was his active promotion of American settlement in California before the Mexican War. In a series of well-publicized letters that included his influential missive to Lewis Cass on 20 January 1846, Marsh extolled the virtues of California. His publicity inspired the formation of the Bartleson-Bidwell party, the first organized wagon train of American settlers to head for California. Leaving Independence, Missouri, on 19 May 1841, the pioneers arrived at Marsh's rancho on 4 November, opening a steady trickle of migration that drew a thousand settlers across the California Trail by 1846.

The trickle became a flood with the discovery of gold in 1848. Marsh profited immensely during the gold rush, striking it rich at Park's Bar on the Yuba River in the summer of 1848. He then turned his attention to supplying the rapidly growing mining districts with food. Shipping beef, flour, pork, and butter from his landing on the San Joaquin, Marsh did a spectacular business that allowed him to expand his holdings. He eventually owned over 50,000 acres stocked with 6,000 head of cattle.

In 1851 Marsh married Abigail Smith Tuck, a schoolteacher and native of Massachusetts who had come to California in 1849. In 1852 Abigail gave birth to the couple's only child, a daughter. Unfortunately, Marsh was not able to enjoy his new family and great wealth for very long. In 1855 his wife died, and the next year Marsh was brutally murdered near Martinez, California, by three of his vaqueros in a dispute over wages.

Marsh's murder and its cause would not have surprised many of his contemporaries. After meeting him in 1841, John Bidwell wrote that Marsh "is perhaps the meanest man in California. . . . There is not an individual in California who does not dislike the man" (*A Journey to California, 1841* [c. 1843], p. 31). Bidwell's assessment is largely upheld by Marsh's biographer, George Lyman. Though Marsh possessed great courage, adventurousness, and intelligence, and seemed to genuinely love his two wives and children, his treatment of most other people revealed more negative character traits. Bitterness, greed, stinginess, and a violent temper too often governed his personality and ultimately stamped his public reputation.

• Marsh's papers are housed in the California State Library in Sacramento and the Bancroft Library at the University of California, Berkeley. Marsh's letter to Lewis Cass was reprinted in the *California Historical Society Quarterly* 22 (Dec. 1943): 315–22. Marsh's standard biography remains George D. Lyman, *John Marsh, Pioneer: The Life Story of a Trailblazer on Six Frontiers* (1931). See also Emily J. Ulsh, "Dr. John Marsh, California Pioneer, 1836–1856" (M.A. thesis, Univ. of Calif., Berkeley, 1924).

MICHAEL MAGLIARI

MARSH, Mae (9 Nov. 1895–13 Feb. 1968), actress, was born Mary Warne Marsh in Madrid, New Mexico, the daughter of Charles Marsh, a railroad company auditor, and Mary Warne. After the death of her father,

her mother moved the family to San Francisco, where they experienced the 1906 earthquake, and then to Los Angeles. While attending high school, Mae worked as a telephone operator.

Marsh's older sister, a movie actress using the name Marguerite Loveridge, worked with director D. W. Griffith at the Biograph Company. She introduced Marsh to Griffith, who hired her in 1912. Griffith gave Marsh the name Mae in order to facilitate his direction of films in which she and Mary Pickford both appeared. He told her: "We can't have two Marys in the company, so I'll call you Mae."

Lillian Gish, in her memoir *The Movies, Mr. Griffith, and Me* (1969), described Marsh as "a slight, red-headed girl with freckles, awkward and shy," who was "an actress from the heart." Gish stated: "I later told her that she was the only actress of whom I was ever jealous. Not only did she play the parts I thought I could play, but she was better in them than I could have been. And that hurt" (p. 97).

After several supporting roles, Marsh starred in *Man's Genesis* (1912). The leading Biograph actresses, Mary Pickford and Blanche Sweet, had declined the part because the heroine wore a grass skirt. Griffith then gave Marsh the lead in *The Sands of Dee* (1912) and began grooming her as Mary Pickford's replacement when she left for another studio in 1913.

Marsh also appeared in several films for Kalem Studios, and then she rejoined Griffith after he left Biograph for the Reliance-Majestic Film Company in 1913. Her first great role (and first screen credit) was in *Birth of a Nation* (1915), in which she played Flora, the "Little Sister." She entranced critics like Alexander Woollcott, who believed she possessed "the most exquisitely sensitive face the screen has found." Critics and the public also praised her work in Griffith's other masterpiece, *Intolerance* (1916), in which she played the wife of the condemned man in the modern episode. She attributed her success to Griffith, declaring: "I have seen *Intolerance* twenty times, I suppose, and it never occurs to me that 'the girl' in the modern episode is myself. It is all Mr. Griffith. When I watch her actions I am no more able to dissociate Mr. Griffith from them than I am able to watch the Babylonian spectacles without thinking of him" (quoted in Slide, p. 119).

Marsh's performances inspired Vachel Lindsay to write the poem "Mae Marsh, Motion Picture Actress," which was published in his *The Chinese Nightingale* (1917). Marsh declined his marriage proposal because he was "red-haired and funny-looking, and so much older." She stated that Lindsay's poem "didn't even phase me, partly because I had had other poems written about me and partly because I never knew that he was so famous to begin with" (Rosenberg and Silverstein, p. 211).

Marsh's success in *Intolerance* prompted Samuel Goldfish (later Goldwyn) to offer her a salary of $2,500 a week to join his newly created Goldwyn Company in 1917. Griffith, who had been paying her $85 per week, advised her to accept the offer. Marsh became the original "Goldwyn Girl," but most of her Goldwyn films were undistinguished and not very popular. She left after two years because "I was making bad pictures. . . . I was not having nearly the fun I had with the Griffith Company making good pictures. Still it made me very rich" (Rosenberg and Silverstein, p. 213).

On 21 September 1918 Marsh married Louis Lee Arms, a Goldwyn studio publicist. The couple had three children. After leaving Goldwyn, Marsh made several indifferently received films in Hollywood, toured England with the stage comedy *Brittie* (1921), and starred in two popular English films, *Flames of Passion* (1922) and *Paddy-the-Next-Best-Thing* (1923). She returned to work with Griffith in *The White Rose* (1923), in which she played a waitress seduced by co-star Ivor Novello. She costarred again with him in *The Rat* (1925), an English film based on a play Novello had written.

After *The Rat*, Marsh retired from the screen to spend more time with her family. Her husband became a land developer, invested her savings in California real estate, and filed for bankruptcy in the 1930s. Financial problems forced her to return to films, starting with *Over the Hill* (1932). Thereafter she appeared in dozens of films during the following three decades. She preferred small cameo roles rather than leads because she "didn't care to get up every morning at five o'clock to be at the studio by seven" and also because she had trouble memorizing lines. Many of her later films were with 20th Century–Fox, and she performed in films by most of Hollywood's major directors. She appeared in Joseph Mankiewicz's *The Late George Apley* (1946) and *A Letter to Three Wives* (1948), Raoul Walsh's *The Tall Men* (1955), and Andrew Stone's *A Blueprint for Murder* (1953), *Julie* (1956), and *Cry Terror* (1958). She preferred working with John Ford, whom she first met when he was an extra working with Griffith. He directed her in *The Grapes of Wrath* (1940), *Three Godfathers* (1948), *Sergeant Rutledge* (1960), *Two Rode Together* (1961), *Donovan's Reef* (1963), and *Cheyenne Autumn* (1964).

In 1955 the George Eastman House Festival of Fine Arts named her one of five outstanding actresses of the silent era (the others were Mary Pickford, Lillian Gish, Norma Talmadge, and Gloria Swanson). Her last film was *Arabella* (1967). After Marsh died in her home at Hermosa Beach, California, movie critic Pauline Kael wrote: "Mae Marsh died at seventy-two, but the girl who twists her hands in the courtroom scene of *Intolerance* is the image of youth-in-trouble forever."

• Some of Marsh's correspondence and other papers are in the D. W. Griffith Archive, Museum of Modern Art, New York. Marsh published a semiautobiographical work, *Screen Acting* (1921), and "What I Want to Do in My New Pictures," *Movie Weekly*, 23 Dec. 1922. "The Reminiscences of Mae Marsh" is an interview in the Popular Arts Project of the Oral History Collection, Columbia University. The Billy Rose Theatre Collection, New York Public Library for the Performing Arts, Lincoln Center, and the Harvard Theatre Collection, Harvard University, hold collections of her press clippings and photographs. She contributed an autobiographical chapter to Bernard Rosenberg and Harry Silverstein, eds., *The Real Tinsel* (1970). Her life and films are described in Anthony Slide, *The Griffith Actresses* (1973); Kalton C. Lahue, *Ladies in Distress* (1971); and Alexander Walker, *Stardom* (1970). See also Richard Schickel, *D. W. Griffith: An American Life* (1984), and Pauline Kael, "A Great Folly and a Small One," *New Yorker*, 24 Feb. 1968, pp. 102–7, reprinted in *Going Steady* (1970). Obituaries are in the *New York Times*, 14 Feb. 1968, and *Variety*, 21 Feb. 1968.

STEPHEN G. MARSHALL

MARSH, Othniel Charles (29 Oct. 1831–18 Mar. 1899), paleontologist, was born in Lockport, New York, the son of Caleb Marsh and Mary Gaines Peabody, farmers. Both parents descended from early settlers in New England, and his mother's brother, George Peabody, was a banker and philanthropist of international repute. With the death of his mother in 1834, Marsh was placed in the care of his aunt Mary Marsh. In 1836 his father married Mary Latten, and the Marsh children returned to live with them and a growing family of siblings. By 1839 the family was again living in Lockport, where Marsh was expected to help his father in running the family farm.

Marsh's habits of observing nature and collecting specimens were developed in Lockport's fields, woods, and Erie Canal excavation areas, which were rich in fossil specimens. Around 1845 he met Colonel Ezekiel Jewett, a field paleontologist and amateur geologist, who introduced him to a more systematic approach to making collections. When he was nineteen years old, he attended Lockport Union School, then tried teaching, and subsequently moved to Massachusetts. In 1851–1852 he received a partial settlement of property held in trust for him since his mother's death and decided to attend Phillips Academy in Andover. At Phillips he chose courses in mineralogy, geology, astronomy, and the classics as a preparation for college. He graduated from Phillips in 1856 as valedictorian and entered Yale College with the financial support of his wealthy uncle, George Peabody.

Marsh studied under notable Yale faculty, including James D. Dana (geology and natural history) and Benjamin Silliman, Jr. (chemistry). His undergraduate years at Yale intensified his enthusiasm for science, especially for vertebrate paleontology. Marsh's interest in paleontology fit well with the nineteenth century's emphasis on scientific classification and description and overlapped with the fields of earth science, zoology, botany, and geology. The work of geologist Charles Lyell, anatomist Richard Owen, and evolutionary biologist Charles Darwin captured the public's imagination as well as that of the scientific world. Marsh graduated in 1860, eighth in his class and Phi Beta Kappa, winning the Latin prize and a Berkeley scholarship for graduate study at Yale's Sheffield Scientific School. Continued financial support and encouragement from George Peabody enabled him to take advantage of the opportunity to continue his studies.

Marsh's first scientific paper appeared in November 1861, describing the gold fields of Nova Scotia; his second, in 1862, detailed Nova Scotian vertebrate remains. The second paper showed Marsh's leaning toward vertebrate paleontology and his thinking along genetic lines. Marsh received the master of arts degree from the Sheffield Scientific School in 1862 and immediately left for further study in Germany, where his instructors included the eminent paleontologist Heinrich E. Beyrich, zoologist W. K. H. Peters, and microgeologist C. G. Ehrenberg. During this time Marsh was actively preparing himself for a position as professor of paleontology at Yale, as well as curator of the Peabody Museum, the gift of his uncle to Yale College in 1863. His formal appointment as professor of paleontology (the first in the United States) at Yale was secured on 24 July 1866.

Marsh's most enduring legacy is the collections he acquired for the U.S. Geological Survey during his ten years as the government's first vertebrate paleontologist. The annual appropriation for this position enabled him to employ field collectors, laboratory preparation staff, artists, and other assistants at the Peabody Museum at Yale, resulting in a collection of great quantity and quality. Marsh insisted on having skeletons as complete as possible and became an expert in the art of constructing lifelike restorations of extinct dinosaurs, birds, and mammals.

Marsh was one of the earliest supporters of Darwin's theory of natural selection. His discovery of birds that had teeth and the complete sequence of American fossil horses helped to answer evolutionary questions and earned him the praise of Darwin and biologist Thomas Henry Huxley. His research on fossil vertebrates was published in more than 270 publications in which he described 496 species, 225 genera, 64 families, 8 suborders, 19 orders, and 1 subclass.

The 1870s and 1880s marked Marsh's most dramatic discoveries, as well as an epic feud with Edward Drinker Cope, another American paleontologist. Marsh and Cope disputed each other's digging rights to some of the same fields, claims of discovery, and the timing of discoveries in scientific circles as well as the public press. Much of Marsh's work at this time was conducted in the fossil fields of Colorado and Wyoming, where he discovered the remains of extinct vertebrates such as the horned Dinocerata and the elephantine brontotheres. Western Kansas was the site for his discovery of birds with teeth; "sea serpents," or mesasaurs; and pterodactyls. He helped identify and describe eighty new forms of dinosaurs and thirty-four new genera. These were the largest and most astonishing creatures known at that time, and Marsh began an extensive reform in their classification.

Marsh's scientific reputation was worldwide, and he served as president of the National Academy of Sciences for twelve years. Many of the fossil vertebrate specimens in the U.S. National Museum (Smithsonian Institution) came from his work with the U.S. Geological Survey. During the 1890s Marsh continued to publish paleontological research based on his superb collections, bringing much of his work together in *Dinosaurs of North America* (1896). In 1897 he received the Cuvier Prize, the highest award for a paleontologist, given every three years by the French Academy of Sciences. In 1898 he gave his personal collections to Yale University, which were claimed by Huxley to be unsurpassed. Marsh died at his home in New Haven, Connecticut. He had never married, and his will left his estate to the Peabody Museum, the National Academy of Sciences, and Yale University.

• Marsh's papers are in the Sterling Library at Yale University. Charles Schuchert and Clara Mae LeVene, *O. C. Marsh: Pioneer in Paleontology* (1940), is a general biography with an extensive bibliography. Marsh's scientific contributions are extensively covered in I. Bernard Cohen, ed., *The Life and Scientific Work of Othniel Charles Marsh* (1980), and Mark J. McCarren, *The Scientific Contributions of Othniel Charles Marsh: Birds, Bones and Brontotheres* (1993). Accounts of the Marsh-Cope feud are related in Elizabeth Noble Shor, *The Fossil Feud between E. D. Cope and O. C. Marsh* (1974). An obituary by Charles E. Beecher, *American Journal of Science*, 4th ser., 7 (1899): 403–28, also includes a bibliography.

NINA P. LONG

MARSH, Reginald (14 Mar. 1898–30 July 1954), artist and teacher, was born in Paris, France, the son of Fred Dana Marsh, a painter-muralist of modern industry and New York City skyscrapers, and Alice Randall, a painter of miniatures. In 1900 the family moved to exclusive Nutley, New Jersey. Marsh grew up in a home filled with his parents' art; reproductions of Rubens, Rembrandt, Titian, and Tintoretto; art books; brushes; canvases; and living models. He received no art instruction from his parents, however.

Marsh's biographer Lloyd Goodrich states, "He began to draw before he was three: locomotives, ships, skyscrapers, soldiers, policemen, everything" (*Reginald Marsh*, p. 18). Because his father inherited wealth, he stopped painting when Marsh was young, which caused Marsh to resent the rich and unproductive artists.

Summering in Sakonnet, Rhode Island (1907–1913), Marsh spent his time observing and engaging in activities along Narragansett Bay. In 1914 his family moved to New Rochelle, New York, and Marsh was sent to the Riverview Military Academy (1914–1915) and then to the Lawrenceville School (1915–1916), where he illustrated for the school *Annual*. In 1916 he enrolled in Yale University's art school, where he trained with William Sargeant Kendall. Marsh was an illustrator and art editor for the *Yale Record* and became a lifelong friend of incoming editor in chief William Benton, who became a publishing and advertising tycoon, a U.S. senator from Connecticut, and a Marsh patron.

After graduating from Yale with an A.B. in 1920, the witty, often shy Marsh moved to New York City, where he took drawing lessons from John Sloan from 1920 to 1921. Marsh considered himself an illustrator instead of a painter; he drew theater scenes, vaudeville acts, nightlife, and humorous everyday genres for *Vanity Fair* and *Harper's Bazaar*. In 1922, while taking lessons at the Art Students League, Marsh's graphic skills, humorous outlook, and evocative caricatural sense earned him a staff artist position for New York's *Daily News* (1922–1925), for which he drew illustrations of subway activity, Broadway and Bowery nightlife, street commotion, and "thousands of vaudeville acts."

Disdaining the works of old masters and businessmen, Marsh moved to Greenwich Village in 1922. He admired modernist paintings by Pablo Picasso, Paul Cézanne, Toulouse-Lautrec, Henry Rousseau, Henri Matisse, George Grosz, Charles Burchfield, and John Marin. By 1922 Marsh was an established graphic artist who designed and painted humorous stage curtains for *The Greenwich Village Follies* (1922–1929), and he wrote and illustrated articles about plays and movies for the *New Yorker* (1922–1925).

In 1922, wanting to expand his knowledge of art, Marsh again enrolled in classes at the Art Students League and studied with Kenneth Hayes Miller, George Bridgman, and George Luks. In the fall of 1923 Marsh married fellow student Elizabeth "Betty" Burroughs. Until their divorce in 1933, the couple lived in Flushing, Long Island, with Betty's father, painter Bryson Burroughs, and sculptor Edith Woodman Burroughs. The Burroughses encouraged Marsh's renewed interest in oil painting, as did sculptor Mahonri Young during Marsh's 1925 trip to Europe.

During 1927–1928 Miller taught Marsh basic principles of form and design and influenced him to paint inner-city subjects realistically and powerfully. Marsh's first paintings of New York City were executed in 1923, and he soon became well known for his unique, naturalistic style that showed raw, mean, dirty, crowded urban street scenes and views of alleys, subways, and the Battery filled with drunks and derelicts. So popular were his subjects, he was given exhibitions at the Valentine Dudensing Galleries in 1927, where he showed watercolors; the Weyhe Gallery in 1928; and the Whitney Studio Gallery in 1928, where he displayed etchings. In 1929 he moved to Fourteenth Street to be near Miller.

Wanting to paint contemporary urban life in the style of Rubens and Eugène Delacroix, Marsh developed a technique that closely copied the old masters' use of the translucent egg-yolk medium (egg tempera mixed with pigment and water and varnished) placed over gesso on wooden panels. Finding egg tempera easy to manipulate, Marsh fluently painted Bowery bums, downtown skyscrapers, and the inner-city rich and poor, and his work in the *New Yorker* and in gallery exhibitions became famous for its satire and its humanity.

During the Great Depression, Sloan's views of bread lines, Harlem streets, starving bums, prostitution, the homeless, and rundown theater districts were poignant glimpses of harsh reality. By the end of the depression, Marsh was painting voluptuous nudes and burlesque queens and plump ladies of the night who appeared on stage, city streets, and Coney Island beaches.

Wanting to draw the human body correctly, Marsh studied anatomy at the College of Physicians and Surgeons in New York City in 1931 and at Cornell University Medical College in 1934. His book *Anatomy for Artists* was published in 1945. In 1934 Marsh married painter Felicia Meyer, who became his model, and in 1937 the couple moved to Union Square. Marsh taught drawing and painting at the Art Students League from 1935 to 1949. In 1949 he was appointed head of the Department of Painting at the Moore Institute of Art, Science and Industry in Philadelphia.

Marsh's first one-man show was held at the Whitney Studio Club in 1924; from 1930 to 1954 the Frank Rehn Gallery of New York City was his primary dealer. His first major retrospective exhibition was held at the Whitney Museum of American Art in New York in 1955. He won many awards, including the prestigious gold medal from the American Academy of Arts and Letters.

Marsh was elected an associate of the National Academy of Design in 1937 and an academician in 1943. He was a member of the National Institute of Arts and Letters, the Society of American Etchers, and the Mural Painters. He executed murals for the U.S. Post Office building in Washington, D.C., and the Customs House rotunda in New York. In June 1954 Marsh was appointed art editor of the *Encyclopedia Britannica*.

Marsh died of a heart attack in Dorset, Vermont. In 1969 Felicia Marsh and Senator William Benton gave Marsh's etching and engraving plates to the Whitney Museum.

Marsh is remembered for his candid, truthful, realistic paintings and illustrations of New York City crowds, the burlesque, nightclubs, vaudeville, theaters, subways, and streets. He was a lifelong freelance illustrator for the *New Yorker*, *Esquire*, and other magazines. He is represented in many museum collections, including the Metropolitan Museum of Art; the Whitney Museum; the Wadsworth Athenaeum in Hartford, Connecticut; the Museum of Fine Arts, Boston; the Terra Museum of American Art, Chicago; and the Art Institute of Chicago.

• For a personal view, see Reginald Marsh, "A Short Autobiography," *Art and Artists of Today*, Mar. 1937, p. 8; Marsh, "Let's Get Back to Painting," *Magazine of Art*, Dec. 1944, pp. 292–96; "Reginald Marsh—Metropolitan Explorer," *Yale Record*, 25 Sept. 1935, pp. 15, 31–32; Norman Sasowsky, *Reginald Marsh: Etchings, Engravings, Lithographs* (1956). For exhibitions, see Whitney Museum of American Art, *Reginald Marsh* (1955), text by Lloyd Goodrich; Bernard Danenberg Galleries, *Aspects of New York by Reginald Marsh* (1969); and University of Arizona Museum of Art, Tucson, *A Retrospective Exhibition of Paintings, Watercolors and Drawings by Reginald Marsh* (1969), text by Edward Laning. For overview, see Lloyd Goodrich, *Reginald Marsh* (n.d.). For daily life, see "A Half-Day in the Studio of Reginald Marsh, Virile Painter of the American Scene," *American Artist*, June 1941, pp. 4–11. For style and subjects, see Lloyd Goodrich, "Reginald Marsh, Painter of New York in Its Wildest Profusion," *American Artist*, Sept. 1955, pp. 18–23, 61–63, and Alan Burroughs, "Reginald Marsh," *Creative Art*, Oct. 1931, pp. 301–05. For Whitney Studio Galleries, see Archives of American Art, Washington, D.C., file #NWH-5, and for Rehn Gallery exhibitions, see #NAAA2.

PATRICIA JOBE PIERCE

MARSH, Warne Marion (26 Oct. 1927–18 Dec. 1987), jazz tenor saxophonist, was born in Los Angeles, California, the son of Oliver T. Marsh, a cinematographer for MGM, and a violinist whose maiden name was Marionofsky. Marsh attended a private school in Hollywood and public schools in the San Fernando Valley. After taking up piano and accordion at age ten, he switched to alto saxophone at age thirteen and then to tenor sax at age fifteen. He also played tuba and bass clarinet in high school, while studying classical saxophone privately. He began playing professionally in 1944. The following year he worked with Hoagy Carmichael's Teenagers. He enrolled in music at the University of Southern California with the intention of becoming a Hollywood studio musician, but Charlie Parker's seminal bebop recording from 1945, "Ko-Ko," established instead a permanent devotion to jazz improvisation.

Drafted, Marsh served in the army from 1946 to 1947. Eventually he was stationed in New Jersey and was able to make frequent visits to New York City, where he was exposed to the teachings of pianist Lennie Tristano, who advocated a somewhat Europeanized conception of bop melody, with an emphasis on pitch rather than rhythm and a disdain for overtly emotional phrasing, and where he also strove to understand Parker's playing. The remainder of his life was a coast-to-coast shuttle between the comforts of home and the attractions of the New York jazz scene. He reenrolled at the University of Southern California and worked as a freelance musician in Los Angeles, but he soon returned to New York City, only to embark on a three-month cross-country tour with Buddy Rich's first big band.

Back in New York in 1948, he became one of Tristano's finest students and regular sideman, together with alto saxophonist Lee Konitz and guitarist Billy Bauer. In March and May 1949 Tristano's sextet made recordings that stand alongside Miles Davis's nonet sessions as the definitive examples of cool jazz: "Wow," "Crosscurrent," "Marionette," and "Sax of a Kind." These feature difficult and spectacularly well-rehearsed unison themes set to chord progressions of popular songs, but mimicking the melodic character of each man's improvisations. Although Marsh was not active as a composer, he and Konitz coauthored one such slithering new melody for "Sax of a Kind," based on the chord progression of "Fine and Dandy." At the session in May, Tristano's group also recorded two collectively improvised pieces, "Intuition" and "Digression," which were of no consequence at the time, but which retrospectively seem novel for having anticipated the free jazz era by nearly a decade. Despite Tristano's contributions to Marsh's identity and subsequent fame, the pianist and teacher also reenforced Marsh's impossibly high standard for technical perfection and excessively critical self-assessments, attitudes that would limit his playing permanently by causing him to refuse performing opportunities in which he apparently felt he could not play as well as he wanted to. Even during this period, while working intermittently with Tristano and Konitz (including the album *Lee Konitz with Warne Marsh*, 1955), he held daytime jobs out of music.

Returning to the Los Angeles area, Marsh formed a group with tenor saxophonist Ted Brown, pianist Ronnie Ball, bassist Ben Tucker, and drummer Jeff Morton (July 1956–Feb. 1957). Alto saxophonist Art Pepper sometimes played with the group and contributed to Brown's album *Free Wheeling* (Nov. 1956), which finds Marsh playing in what was for him an unusually forthright ballad style on "Crazy She Calls Me." His few other albums from this period include Pepper's *The Way It Was!* (on the tracks from Nov. 1956), pianist Joe Albany's *The Right Combination* (1957), and his own *Music for Prancing* (1957), with notable improvisations on "Ad libido" and "It's All Right with Me."

By December 1957 he was back in New York City, where he worked occasionally with Konitz and Tristano and recorded his albums *The Art of Improvising* (1959) and *Jazz from the East Village* (1960), but again he took undistinguished jobs out of music. He returned to Los Angeles in 1962. In 1964 he married Geraldine (maiden name unknown); they had two children. After another period in New York City, Marsh settled in Los Angeles in 1966. He mainly worked as a teacher at a music store in Pasadena, but he also recorded the album *Ne plus ultra* (1969), played in Clare Fischer's big band, and from 1972 to 1977 belonged to the group Supersax, which presented harmonized versions of Parker's improvisations. In 1975 and 1976 he teamed with Konitz for European tours and recordings.

For much of his career Marsh had been affiliated with instrumentalists—above all, Konitz—whose style coincided with his own, but he stepped out of this mold for excellent albums with tenor saxophonists Lew Tabackin (*Tenor Gladness*, Oct. 1976) and Peter Christlieb (*Apogee*, c. 1977) in which their emotive timbres and melodies, drawn from the approaches of diverse swing, rhythm-and-blues, and bop saxophonists, serve as a foil for his focused and ethereal approach. From this same period came his album *All Music* (1976), pianist Bill Evans's album *Crosscurrents* with Konitz and Marsh (1977), and his album *Warne Out* (1977), issued on Marsh's own record label, Interplay.

In 1978 Marsh moved to Ridgefield, Connecticut, and taught in New York City, while playing irregularly at the West End Café and the Village Vanguard. While on tour in Europe he made his last albums as a leader, including *Star Highs* (1982). In the mid-1980s he separated from his wife and finally settled in the Los Angeles area. He gave a concert late in 1987 at Mills College in Oakland, California, at the invitation of Anthony Braxton (a member of the Mills faculty and a saxophonist deeply devoted to Marsh's music). He died of a heart attack while performing "Out of Nowhere" with pianist Ross Tomkins's quartet at Donte's Jazz Club in North Hollywood, California.

Marsh epitomized the "cool" ideal in jazz. He produced a soft, detached, uniform tone quality throughout the tenor saxophone, and he favored the gentle articulation of fast-moving, even-noted melodies, thereby concentrating the listener's attention on heady pitch selection and irregularly phrased, undulating rhythm, disengaged from timbre and attack. He explored such melodies mainly via improvisation, but he also routinely played (and occasionally himself wrote) themes of a similar melodic character. This tightly defined sound is not an absolute constant in his recorded legacy, but it represents his dedicated ideal.

• Jean Delmas assesses Marsh's best-known work in "Tristano & ses fils: L'Archéologie du mythe," *Jazz hot*, no. 325 (Mar. 1976): 6–17. For interviews, see Laurent Goddet and Jean Delmas, "Warne Marsh," *Jazz hot*, no. 325 (Mar. 1976): 18–21; Les Tomkins, "The Warne Marsh Story," *Crescendo International* 14 (May 1976): 20–21, 23, continued as "Supersax, the Sound of Success, by Warne Marsh," 14 (June 1976): 16–17; Francis Davis, "Warne Marsh's Inner Melody," *Down Beat* 50 (1983): 26–28, repr. in Davis, *In the Moment: Jazz in the 1980s* (1986); and Whitney Balliett, "Jazz: A True Improviser," *New Yorker* 14 Oct. 1985, pp. 109–17, repr. in Balliett, *American Musicians: Fifty-six Portraits in Jazz* (1986). Also see Lee Hildebrand, "Tenor Saxophonist Warne Marsh: After 40 Years, Still Avant-Garde," *San Francisco Chronicle Datebook*, 18 Oct. 1987. Alun Morgan supplies a survey and recordings list to 1961 in "Warne Marsh," *Jazz Monthly* 7 (June 1961): 7–9. The recordings list was updated by Delmas in *Jazz hot*, no. 326 (Apr. 1976): 14–16, and Wim van Eyle, "Warne Marsh discografie," *Journal of Jazz Discography*, no. 1 (Nov. 1976): 5–10; no. 2 (June 1977): 2–3. Obituaries are in the *Los Angeles Times*, 19 Dec. 1987, and the *New York Times*, 20 Dec. 1987.

BARRY KERNFELD

MARSHAK, Robert Eugene (11 Oct. 1916–23 Dec. 1992), physicist, was born in the Bronx, New York, the son of Harry Marshak, a garment cutter and fruit peddler, and Rose Shapiro, a seamstress. After graduating from James Monroe High School at fifteen, Marshak attended City College for a semester before transferring to Columbia College, where he was awarded a Pulitzer scholarship, which provided $350 a year beyond tuition. While at Columbia he and a friend formed a physics club to learn more about the theory of relativity, which was not then taught to undergraduates. After graduating from Columbia in 1936, Marshak enrolled at Cornell University, where he worked in astrophysics with Hans Bethe, developing with him a theory of how stars produce energy through fusion reactions. He received a Ph.D. in 1939 at the age of twenty-two. That same year he began teaching at the University of Rochester. Taking a leave of absence during World War II, he worked at the Radiation

Laboratory at the Massachusetts Institute of Technology (1941–1943), at the Montreal Atomic Energy Laboratory (1943–1944), and at the Manhattan Project's Los Alamos, New Mexico, Scientific Laboratory, where he was deputy group leader in theoretical physics (1944–1946). In 1943 Marshak married Ruth Florence Gup; they had two children. In 1946 he helped found the 3,000-member Federation of Atomic Scientists and a year later, as its chair, lobbied for international control of atomic energy.

Like other American theoretical physicists of his generation, Marshak started his career when the quantum revolution (claiming that the allowed energies of atoms and molecules are at "quantized" [discrete] rather than continuous values) had gained acceptance; and the United States, by welcoming many of the theory's leaders who had fled Nazi Germany, had become a center of its study. Capitalizing on the advantages of his time and place and utilizing his own strengths, Marshak spent most of his life investigating the elementary objects of which all others are composed, as well as the forces between those elementary objects.

While at Rochester, Marshak established himself as a creative theoretical physicist and as an exceptionally influential teacher. In his theorizing in particle physics, particularly on weak interactions, he remained, in the words of his colleague Yuval Ne'eman, "much ahead of the advancing front." Intuitive and inspirational, he prompted his theory students to create advances in understanding, not just in improved calculational results. He guessed what particles might be responsible for certain forces and started students working in those areas. Like him, those he trained in theoretical physics helped their experimentalist colleagues with predictions and suggestions for new experiments.

Marshak, often working with students, made important contributions to particle physics in the late 1940s and 1950s. In particular, he made sense of puzzling experimental data by proposing, in 1947, that short-lived subatomic particles called mesons, first described in the 1930s and thought to be involved in the binding of protons and neutrons in the nucleus, actually consist of two species of particles, subsequently called pions and muons. The proposal not only clarified a decade of confusing experimental results, it also afforded physicists a new basis for understanding one of the most important physical problems—the nature of the so-called "strong force" that held particles together in the atomic nucleus. The exchange of mesons between protons and neutrons had been considered the source of nuclear binding energy; as it turned out only pions performed this function. Subsequently, a wealth of data was accumulated from experiments on the individual constituents of atomic nuclei. Marshak and his student Peter Signell showed that all of this data could be accounted for by a single force; the descendants of that force serve as a basis of the theory of nuclear forces and are used in calculating properties of atomic nuclei.

In 1957 Marshak made a second signal contribution to physics by developing with his colleague and former student E. C. G. Sudarshan a theory describing the spontaneous emission and absorption of electrons, muons, and other subatomic particles in nuclei. These emissions and absorptions, best exemplified by the spontaneous emissions of electrons in radioactive decay, were believed to be manifestations of a so-called "weak force," first postulated in the 1930s as one of the four fundamental forces in the universe (the others being gravity, electromagnetism, and the strong force). Earlier efforts to find a general and mathematically consistent treatment of weak interactions based on analogies with the equations governing electromagneticism had been confounded in 1956, with the suggestion that parity, a property analogous to electrical charge, was not conserved in weak interactions. This idea, experimentally confirmed in early 1957, launched several months of intense effort by theoreticians to understand the precise form of the equations governing weak interactions. Marshak and Sudarshan accomplished this in a paper presented at a conference in Padua, Italy, in September of that same year. Their theory was subsequently confirmed experimentally for all known manifestations of the weak interaction and served as a basis for a more comprehensive theory, developed in the early 1960s by Sheldon Glashow, Abdus Salam, and Steven Weinberg, unifying the physics of electromagnetism and weak interactions.

Exhibiting what his colleague Richard Wilson called "a nose and ear for the best people," Marshak attracted many of them to Rochester for the Rochester Conferences on high energy physics, which he inaugurated in 1950. These conferences, held in Rochester through 1957 and later at prominent research centers throughout the world, promoted cooperation between experimentalists and theorists and served as a meeting ground for American and foreign physicists. In 1955 he went to Washington, D.C., to secure visas for a number of Russian physicists, enabling them to participate in that year's Rochester Conference. The next year he and thirteen other American nuclear physicists attended the Moscow Conference on High Energy Particles.

Marshak left the University of Rochester in 1970 to take on what he called his "toughest assignment," the presidency of City College of the City University of New York. There his task was to maintain the school's distinguished reputation while providing education for the socially disadvantaged. Occurring during the student unrest of the 1970s and CUNY's period of open admissions, Marshak's nine-year presidency, as he later recalled, was an "unmanageable" but "challenging experiment in crisis resolution and human relations" (*Problems and Prospects*, p. x). Despite obstacles and the stroke he suffered during a campus crisis, Marshak raised $26.8 million in the private sector to rebuild the college's crumbling buildings and to make changes dictated by the times. These included reaching out to the Harlem community; adding departments in Black, Puerto Rican, Asian, and Jewish studies; establishing an Urban Legal Studies Program and a four-year School for Biomedical Education; and building a $2.5 million Center for the Performing Arts and a fourteen-story science building, which occupied a square block and was later named for him.

Marshak returned to physics research in 1979 when he became a distinguished professor at Virginia Polytechnic Institute, where he spent the remainder of his academic career, becoming an emeritus distinguished professor in 1987. While there he attracted 150 experts in frontier physics to an international conference, was awarded the J. Robert Oppenheimer Memorial Prize (1982), and became the president of the American Physical Society (1983). Under Marshak's presidency, that society called for nuclear arms reductions and stressed the need for arms control. Shortly before Marshak drowned at Cancun, Mexico, during a family celebration of the fiftieth anniversary of his marriage, it was announced that he was to be the first recipient of the Award for International Scientific Cooperation, presented by the American Association for the Advancement of Science.

Just before his death, Marshak had completed his eighth book, *Conceptual Foundations of Modern Particle Physics* (1993). During his career, he wrote forty-seven general articles and 180 specialized scientific articles, which appeared in *Physical Review* and other scholarly journals and conference reports.

During his important scientific career, Marshak contributed significantly to the effort to understand and develop a verified treatment of the forces that govern the interactions of subatomic particles. He was also instrumental in promoting the value to science of academic conferences, where colleagues could critique scholarship, rather than merely publishing it in a journal. The Rochester Conference that he started, later sponsored by the International Union of Pure and Applied Physics, in the late 1990s annually attracted 800 to 900 attendees, chosen by elaborate quota and invitational mechanisms. This unique conference has been called Marshak's greatest scientific legacy.

• Marshak's papers are at the Virginia Polytechnic Institute. Besides his last book, mentioned above, Marshak's works on physics include *Our Atomic World* (with E. C. Nelson and L. I. Schiff, 1946), *Meson Physics* (1952), *Introduction to Elementary Particle Physics* (with E. C. G. Sudarshan, 1961), and *Theory of Weak Interactions in Particle Physics* (with Riazuddin and Ciaran P. Ryan, 1969). He edited *Perspectives in Modern Physics: Hans Bethe Festschrift* (1966) and coedited (with R. C. Cool) *Advances in Particle Physics* (2 vols., 1968). For Marshak's years at City College, see his *Problems and Prospects of an Urban Public University: The City College of the City University of New York, 1970–1972* (1973); *Academic Renewal in the 1970s: Memoirs of a City College President* (1982), and "Dedicating Science Hall," *Addresses on the Dedication of Science Hall: The City College Papers*, no. 11 (1973?). See also "C.C.N.Y. Gets $2.5-Million Gift for a Center for Performing Arts," *New York Times*, 30 June 1971. The *New York Times* also carried "Physicist Named Head of C.C.N.Y" and "Scientist-Educator: Robert Eugene Marshak," 28 Feb. 1970; and "Physicists' Arms Stand Criticized," 7 May 1983. For biographical and bibliographical data, see E. C. G. Su-

darshan, ed., *A Gift of Prophecy: Essays in Celebration of the Life of Robert Eugene Marshak* (1994), and *Robert E. Marshak, 1916–1992: Tributes to His Memory, Rochester, New York, March 26, 1993* (1993). His obituary is in the *New York Times*, 25 Dec. 1992.

OLIVE HOOGENBOOM

MARSHALL, Andrew Cox (c. 1756–11 Dec. 1856), pastor and businessman, probably was born in Goose Creek, South Carolina. His mother was a slave and his father was the English overseer on the plantation where the family lived; their names are unknown. Shortly after Marshall's birth, his father died while on a trip to England, thus ending abruptly the Englishman's plans to free his family. Marshall, his mother, and an older sibling (whose sex is not revealed in extant records) were subsequently sold to John Houstoun of Savannah, a prominent public official.

Houstoun was the second of five masters Marshall had during his half century of servitude. Marshall became devoted to Houstoun, whose life he once saved, and the latter apparently grew fond of Marshall, for whose manumission he provided in his will. Nevertheless, when Houstoun, who had twice served as governor of Georgia and later as mayor of Savannah, died in 1796, the executors of his estate refused to honor the manumission provision. When they separated Marshall from his wife of nearly a quarter of a century (name unknown), selling them to different masters, Marshall rebelled by running away. This led his new master to cancel the purchase, but another purchaser, Judge Joseph Clay (1741–1804), was found. Judge Clay subsequently apprehended the runaway slave, who had sought refuge in the nearby environs. Marshall was never reunited with that wife. He was sold twice more, the last time to Richard Richardson, a Savannah merchant, who facilitated Marshall's manumission by loaning him the $200 needed to purchase his freedom (c. 1806).

After gaining his freedom, Marshall operated a very successful dray business that was patronized by Savannah's leading merchants. From this operation he earned sufficient income to repay Richardson; purchase the freedom of Rachel (his second wife), their four sons, a stepson, and his father-in-law; as well as build a home and rental property.

The person who influenced Marshall the most was his maternal uncle, Andrew Bryan, a slave preacher on Brampton Plantation, who founded First African Baptist Church there in 1788. In 1825 Marshall was called to the ministry of that church; he was installed the following year. In the ensuing thirty years, Marshall operated his dray business and also shepherded his flock with distinction. The same year Marshall was installed, the Sunbury Baptist Association, a biracial association to which First African Baptist belonged, invited him to preach to its annual convention. This marked the only time an African American ever received such an invitation. Less than five years after Marshall assumed the pulpit of that historic church, he lost his wife Rachel, who died in 1829.

By 1830 the membership of First African Baptist Church had reached 2,417, nearly double the size it was at the time of Bryan's death in 1812. A few years later, however, the church experienced a nasty schism when the Sunbury Baptist Association alleged that Marshall, in allowing Alexander Campbell to preach from his pulpit, had embraced the antislavery and theological views of the Disciples of Christ Church (Campbellites). Marshall was expelled from the Association in 1833 and was not allowed to return until he apologized in 1837. As a result of his expulsion, a majority of the deacons in First African Baptist Church, along with about 200 members (less than 10 percent of the total membership), left the church and founded Third African Baptist Church, which was renamed First Bryan Baptist Church after the Civil War.

Marshall's ministry achieved widespread recognition and attracted white visitors from throughout the nation and Europe. Several published favorable comments about his sermons. Sir Charles Lyell, commenting on a sermon he heard in 1846, said Marshall compared the probationary state of the pious to that of "an eagle teaching her newly fledged offspring to fly." Marshall assured the congregation that just as a mother eagle darts beneath her young eagle to keep it from hitting the ground while teaching it to fly, so does God rescue the pious whenever he or she is in danger. This is the first recorded instance of a black pastor preaching "An Eagle Feathereth Its Nest," a favorite sermon in black evangelical churches. In a sermon that Fredrika Bremer heard, Marshall asked his congregation, "Did He [Jesus Christ] come only to the rich?" He then answered his own question, "No! Blessed be the Lord! He came to the poor! He came to us, and for our sakes, my brothers and sisters." In his powerful expository style, Marshall, moreover, preached about sin, salvation, and punishment of the wicked—regardless of color (black or white) and legal status (slave or free). In the fiery style of the Great Awakening ministers, which black evangelical ministers retained long after that movement had died, Marshall preached to the hearts of his congregation, not to their heads. Hence his sermons were therapeutic to the black occupants of both the pulpit and the pews, because they were all in the same boat and had the same spiritual needs. As his fame spread, he was invited to preach in other cities, including New Orleans, and to give an address to the state legislature of Georgia (c. 1850). Marshall was the first African American to address that body.

Although Marshall never attended school, he did not allow this deprivation to hinder him. He never learned to write, but he taught himself to read and eventually assembled the largest black-owned library in antebellum Georgia. Under his leadership, First African Baptist Church, the oldest and largest Baptist church (black or white) in Savannah, remained the leading black church in the Lower South. It is said that over the span of his ministry Marshall baptized about 3,800 people, averaging nearly 127 annually; converted over 4,000; and married 2,000 persons. In addition to these achievements, Marshall was proud of serving as the coachman and manservant to George Washington during his visit to Savannah in the 1790s. In short, he was the most outstanding African American in antebellum Georgia.

It is small wonder that whites respected Marshall and blacks revered him, which was apparent in the eulogy in the local newspaper following his death in Richmond, Virginia. He was survived by Sarah, his third wife, whom he had married in the early 1830s, a son, and an adopted daughter. Marshall is buried in an impressive red brick vault in Laurel Grove Cemetery South (Savannah). Racially segregated, it was one of few black cemeteries in existence at that time.

• For additional information on Andrew Cox Marshall see Whittington B. Johnson, "Andrew C. Marshall: A Black Religious Leader of Antebellum Savannah," *Georgia Historical Quarterly* 69, no. 2 (1985): 173–92, and W. Harrison Daniel, "Andrew Marshall," in *Dictionary of Afro-American Slavery*, ed. Randall M. Miller and John David Smith (1988). For excerpts from two of Marshall's sermons see Sir Charles Lyell, *A Second Visit to the United States*, vol. 2 (1868), and Fredrika Bremer, *The Homes of the New World; Impressions of America*, vol. 1 (1853). J. P. Tustin, who knew Marshall personally, wrote about him from the view of a white southerner of that day, "Andrew Marshall, 1756–1856," in *Annals of the American Pulpit*, ed. William Sprague (1859). James M. Simms, who admired Marshall as a role model and was baptized by him, switched to Third African Baptist Church after Marshall's death and wrote *The First Colored Baptist Church in North America . . .* (1888) in support of that church's claim to be the oldest black church in North America. Emanuel K. Love, a pastor of First African Baptist Church in the late nineteenth century, countered Simms's claim in *History of the First African Baptist Church from Its Organization, January 20, 1788 to July 1st, 1888* (1888). Edgar G. Thomas was pastor of First African Baptist Church when he wrote *The First African Baptist Church of North America* (1925) in support of Love's position.

WHITTINGTON B. JOHNSON

MARSHALL, Arthur (20 Nov. 1881–18 Aug. 1968), ragtime composer and pianist, was born in Saline County, Missouri, to African-American parents, about whom very little is known. The Marshall family had relocated to Sedalia, Missouri, by the time Arthur was in grade school, where he befriended another budding musician, Scott Hayden. Noted ragtime pianist Scott Joplin lived with the Marshall family for a while, influencing the youngster's interest in ragtime; he also took private lessons in classical piano. Joplin is said to have introduced Marshall to the Maple Leaf Club (the inspiration for his own "Maple Leaf Rag") while Marshall was still in high school, and he is said to have performed there.

Marshall attended George R. Smith College, where he studied music and then obtained a teaching license. He worked at various parties and gatherings in St. Louis, as well as in the city's red-light district, where ragtime music was much in demand. In about 1901 he is said to have worked with a local minstrel troupe, McCabe's Minstrels, playing piano during their show's intermission. He probably married his first wife, Maude McAdams, at this time; details of their marriage are unknown. Hayden, Joplin, and Marshall spent much time together during this period, working together on a projected opera (*A Guest of Honor*) that was never produced, as well as critiquing each other's works and composing together.

Marshall and Joplin's collaboration, "Swipsey Cakewalk," was published by John Stark in 1900 and shows Marshall's predilection for folk melodies. As in his collaborations with Hayden, Joplin supplied the trio and probably helped give the entire work its formal structure.

In about 1906 Marshall left St. Louis and moved to Chicago because there were more performing opportunities there. Apparently either widowed or divorced, he married Julia Jackson in about 1907, and they had two daughters and a son. Most of his solo compositions were published while he was living in Chicago, although none were as successful as "Swipsey Cakewalk." "Lily Queen" (1907) was also credited to Joplin, who had arranged to have it published in New York but seems to have had no hand in its creation. Marshall published four other pieces with John Stark, who also published Joplin's works, through 1908.

In about 1910 Marshall returned to St. Louis, taking the prize for the best ragtime pianist at the contest sponsored by the Turpin family at the Booker T. Washington Theater. He worked for Tom Turpin at one of his bars for a while and continued to work St. Louis's bars and brothels through 1916. At that time, his second wife died, and Marshall relocated to Kansas City, abandoning his musical career. Sometime after 1917 he married for the third and final time; the name of his third wife is unknown.

Marshall's music was much in the style of his mentor Scott Joplin, with perhaps a little more folk flavoring than the elder composer used. Their "Swipsey Cakewalk" contains folkstyle melodies, reminiscent of the earlier "Cakewalk" style popularized in minstrel shows, although it is written in the four-part, formal, classical ragtime style that Joplin pioneered. The final part has the feeling of a barrelhouse ragtime stomp, the kind of music played in the bawdy houses throughout the South and West. Marshall only published five other rags during the heyday of the musical style from 1906 to 1908; unlike Joplin, Marshall actively performed his works and often incorporated crowd-pleasing devices into them, such as bluesy chords, slurred notes, and energetic endings (like the one heard in "Swipsey Cakewalk") that would bring a crowd to its feet.

Ragtime historians Rudi Blesch and Harriet Janis interviewed Marshall in the late 1940s for their landmark work *They All Played Ragtime* (1971); they also recorded him performing some rags for their small Circle label. Blesch and Janis printed three previously unpublished works by the composer ("Century Prize," "Missouri Romp," and "Silver Rocket") in their book;

a fourth work, "Little Jack's Rag," discovered after his death, was published in 1976.

• Marshall's life and career is documented in Dave Jasen and Trebor Jay Tichnor's *Rags and Ragtime: A Musical History* (1978). Edward A. Berlin, *King of Ragtime: Scott Joplin and His Era* (1994), also deals with Marshall. Marshall's works have not been republished in a single place or in a uniform "edition." Nor is there a single recording that contains all of his published or unpublished rags. Anthology recordings over the years have included his works, although none are currently available or in print.

RICHARD CARLIN

MARSHALL, Benjamin (1782–2 Dec. 1858), merchant and textile manufacturer, was born to a manufacturing family in West Riding, Yorkshire, England. At age sixteen he entered the cotton trade in Manchester. Seeking wider opportunity, in 1803 he sailed for America with his brother Joseph, arriving in New York in August. They brought a consignment of Lancashire cotton textiles with which to start an importing partnership; they soon opened a store at 10 Beekman Street. To pay for the imports the Marshalls began exporting raw cotton to the Lancashire mills, initially buying from New York middlemen. Benjamin soon recognized that they could simply buy directly at the source, in the South. Thus, Marshall started going south, principally to Georgia, for extended periods each winter, arranging purchases of cotton, pioneering a practice that later became standard among New York cotton exporters. Marshall also established an agent in New Orleans and bought several ships to engage in the southern coastal trade.

Among the Marshalls' neighbors in West Riding had been the Thompson family, owners of a woolen mill. In 1798 Francis Thompson had come to New York to import his family's woolens. When the Marshalls arrived in New York, they apparently made immediate contact with Thompson, who also did business on Beekman Street. Soon Thompson was also exporting cotton; Jeremiah Thompson, Francis's nephew, who had joined him in 1801, followed Marshall's lead, heading south to purchase cotton directly from planters. Other close business neighbors were Isaac and William Wright (Francis Thompson married Isaac's daughter and both families were Quaker). From 1807 Benjamin Marshall was involved in a variety of business activities with the Thompsons and the Wrights, including shared ownership of the sailing ships they all needed to carry their merchandise and cotton. Marshall's success permitted him to marry Niobe Stanton, daughter of the commander of one of the fastest of those ships, the *Pacific*, in 1813.

After the War of 1812, trade through New York harbor grew rapidly. Marshall, the Thompsons, and the Wrights had a thorough understanding of this burgeoning trade; they recognized that there was perhaps no greater obstacle to its continued expansion than the unreliability of shipping services. There were no common carriers; no ships sailed on a fixed schedule. Merchants either owned their own ships or had to seek out available space in ships of other merchants. Ships sailed only when they had a full cargo. Marshall is credited by some for first recognizing the opportunity, although others point to Jeremiah Thompson, and his partners moved to create the first scheduled service between New York and Liverpool. They already owned three fine ships; they acquired a fourth. On 27 October 1817 the *New York Commercial Advertiser* carried their first public announcement that they would dispatch a ship from each port on a fixed day every month, full or not; the *James Monroe* would sail from New York on 5 January 1818. Sail it did, at Marshall's insistence, in the teeth of a howling nor'easter.

The Black Ball Line—given that name because of the large black circle painted on the fore-topsail—used the large, swift ships, 400 to 500 tons each. Their captains were expected to drive them to the limit, which they did, averaging only twenty-three days on passages from Sandy Hook to Liverpool during the first nine years, with the fastest passage accomplished in 1822 in just fifteen days, eighteen hours. The westward passage, against the prevailing winds, averaged forty days. This intensive utilization of ships—each made three round trips a year—was a dramatic change from the typical pattern of one or occasionally two round trips a year. More important, for the first time merchants on both sides of the Atlantic could dispatch letters, orders for goods, and merchandise on a known schedule and know when they would arrive and when a response would be sent, a development with profound implications for the conduct of business.

Competition was slow to emerge; only in 1822 did a second line appear. Then the floodgates opened. By 1824 New York boasted dozens of packet services, to multiple European ports and to every significant American port. New York far outdistanced its rivals—Boston, Baltimore, and Philadelphia—absolutely dominating American foreign trade. The packet service was so efficient that the British gave up their own scheduled postal packet and sent Canadian mail via coastal packets to New York. The emergence of competing lines also helped drive naval architecture to design faster, larger ships, a process that eventually brought forth the great clippers.

In 1825 Marshall began to shift his interest from mercantile and shipping activities to manufacturing, probably motivated by the Tariff of 1824, which erected a significantly protective tariff barrier against long-dominant British imports. He considered building at Passaic Falls, New Jersey, but instead joined his brother Joseph and Benjamin Walcott to build a mill near Utica, New York. This New York Mill was in operation by late 1825. In 1826 Marshall and Joseph established the Hudson River Print Works (Hudson was later renamed Stockport, New York) and the Mount Ida Mill in Troy, New York. He later bought additional mills in Middlebury, Vermont, and in North Adams, Massachusetts. He personally managed the print works, among the first printing mills in America.

In 1833 Marshall sold his remaining interest in the packet line to Joseph, and in 1834 Marshall ended his partnership with Joseph and took sole control of the New York Mill. Benjamin Marshall took the mills near Troy and the Mount Ida and the Hudson River plants. Thereafter he lived in Troy, becoming one of its leading citizens. About 1840, using ingenious tunneling, he developed waterpower along the Poestenkill Creek; mills making paper, hardware, cotton goods, tapestry, and velvet carpets soon lined the waterway.

Marshall served as president of one of Troy's banks, of the Troy & Schenectady Railway, and of Mrs. Emma Willard's Female Seminary. He had lost his wife in 1823, and their only child, a son, died of mental disease about 1847; in 1848 he endowed the Marshall Infirmary in Troy, which was incorporated 20 June 1851 and later renamed the Marshall Sanitarium. Marshall himself served as its first president. He died in Troy.

• There are some original legal papers relating to Marshall in the Charles Linsley Papers at the Sheldon Museum Research Center, Middlebury, Vt. A good discussion of Marshall and the singular importance of the packet is Robert G. Albion, *Square Riggers on Schedule* (1938), which includes an excellent discussion of sources and a bibliography. He covers the same material in *The Rise of New York Port: 1815–1860* (1939). Conrad P. Wright's unpublished "Origins and Early Years of the Transatlantic Packet Ships of New York, 1817–1835" (Ph.D. diss., Harvard Univ., 1932) also provides some excellent detail not available elsewhere. William R. Bagnall, *The Textile Industries of the United States* (1893), has the only substantial information on Marshall's investments in textiles. There is some additional information on Marshall in Joseph A. Scoville, *The Old Merchants of New York City*, vols. 4 and 5 (1872).

FRED CARSTENSEN

MARSHALL, Benjamin Howard (5 May 1874–19 June 1944), architect, was born in Chicago, Illinois, the son of Caleb H. Marshall, a successful miller and commercial baker, and Celia F. LeBaillie. After attending the Harvard School in Chicago, Marshall worked briefly as a clothing designer for Clement, Bane & Company before joining the architectural firm of Horatio R. Wilson and Oliver W. Marbel in 1892 as a clerk. Marbel died in 1895, and Marshall, who was largely self-taught, became Wilson's partner.

Wilson and Marshall's buildings were mainly middle-class flats and high-quality residences, augmented occasionally by better buildings, all in Chicago. The most notable was the Iroquois Theater, designed in 1900, the scene of a famous and tragic fire in 1903.

In 1902 the partnership was dissolved and Marshall took the first of many trips to Europe. In 1905 he married Mary Elizabeth Walton; the couple had three children. From 1905 until 1924 Marshall's partner was Charles E. Fox, who handled Marshall & Fox's technical tasks. Overall, Marshall's output ran to more than three hundred buildings, including more than sixty mansions and country houses, the most prominent extant one being B. A. Eckhart's, at 1530 North Lake Shore Drive (1914). A strikingly original design, the Eckhart mansion was for many years the site of the

Polish consulate in Chicago. Other extant buildings include one church (Emmanuel Episcopal, La Grange, 1925), two banks (notably the Lakeshore National Bank, 1921), and numerous commercial and light-industrial buildings, including the Steger (1909), the Chicago, Burlington, & Quincy Railroad (1911), the Horn and Hardart Bakery and Commissary (1917), Popular Mechanics (1922), and, in Milwaukee, Northwest Mutual Life Insurance (1911). Other designs ranged from New York to Los Angeles and from Havana to Philadelphia, but the Chicago buildings were and remain the most important.

Marshall's enjoyment of the theater and of flamboyant, extravagant living were combined in his spectacular studio, perched above his Lake Michigan yacht harbor in Wilmette (1921, destroyed). It had drafting rooms for forty-five and a family suite, including studios for a son and a daughter. Crammed with antique and exotic furnishings brought from around the world, the public areas included his studio, which could quickly be converted into a theater, a banquet hall, or the famous party room. Protected by a retractable glass roof were an adjacent tropical garden and swimming pool.

Marshall's fame rested on three building types: theaters, hotels and country clubs, and apartments. Of his theaters (he designed fourteen, most of them in Chicago), the only Chicago survivor is the Blackstone Theatre (1910). Marshall designed twenty-nine hotels, clubs, and similar buildings for social life. They include Chicago's Blackstone Hotel (1908) on the South Side and the Drake (1919), whose construction on the North Side marked the definitive shift there of Chicago's fashionable and wealthy "bluestocking" set. Another south-to-north march is marked by the succession of the South Shore Country Club (first phase, 1906; main building, 1915) to the Edgewater Beach Hotel (first phase, 1915). Its expansion culminated in the only extant part of the building, the Edgewater Beach Apartments (1927).

Marshall's most enduring legacy may well be his luxury apartment buildings. For several decades these provided the model followed in Chicago for the design of their peers and lessers in their segregation and disposition into three zones of public entertainment rooms, private bedroom and bathroom suites, and service spaces, including kitchen and maids' rooms. Other aspects not adaptable to less expensive buildings included the suites of grand entertainment rooms, the high quality of the extensive interior architectural finishing, and the incorporation of newly developed mechanical devices to facilitate lavish living—for example, an automobile turntable in the porte cochere in 199 East Lake Shore Drive, or a weathertight garden room connecting a reception room, parlor, and dining room in 1100 North Lake Shore Drive. Marshall's buildings established the architectural and urban character of Chicago's Gold Coast facade since five of the eight buildings, including the Drake Hotel, on East Lake Shore Drive were his while on the drive's north stretch the oldest two apartment buildings, which

were most important in defining what would follow, also were his. The Raymond (1900, destroyed) was the first and 1550 North State Parkway (1911) the grandest both of his and of Chicago's apartments. Surviving in Hyde Park is 5825 Blackstone (1909), a representative of the best of his three- and four-story buildings. Marshall was both architect and sole or principal owner of many of these buildings. He began this practice when he used his father's money to build 1100 North Lake Shore Drive (1905, destroyed), a risky venture because it was the first high-rise apartment building among the lakefront mansions.

Marshall's practice was undermined by the collapse of building activity after the stock market crash of 1929. His practice was sustained mainly by work for the national chain of Thompson "quick eateries," which he had begun designing in 1915. In 1936, after he did the last two, in Philadelphia, of a total of thirty-nine or more, he closed his practice and sold and moved out of his studio. He died in Chicago before building activity resumed after World War II.

Construction following that long hiatus would take the shape of the new, sleek, slick forms for tall modernist buildings with which, beginning in 1928, Marshall had flirted in some unbuilt schemes. Always before that he had followed the traditional classical styles that had gained new popularity at the 1893 Chicago World's Columbian Exposition and that had dominated the imagery in the Chicago envisaged in the seminal *Plan of Chicago* (1909), by Daniel H. Burnham and Edward H. Bennett. Like other practicing architects of his generation, as well as their clients, Marshall benefited from increased opportunities to learn a more canonic classicism through easier travel and the improved architectural education informing the profession and its publications. The classicism of most of his earlier buildings, such as the brick, stone, and mansarted Blackstone Hotel, was generally French, while the work after the Drake Hotel, with its colorful interiors and carved, classically detailed limestone exterior, all based on Renaissance motifs, was generally Italian, although for buildings associated with leisure and recreation, the balconies, terraces, and colorful stucco exteriors and the spacious, ornamented interiors suggested generalized Mediterranean or Spanish forms. When called for, a Gothic, Tudor-based brick and stone architecture also appeared in his work. Marshall's eclectic output represents the high achievement of the generation that inherited the American Renaissance from men like Burnham, Augustus Saint-Gaudens, and Stanford White, whose sgraffito busts Marshall had placed on the auto court entrance facade of his studio.

• Materials from Marshall's office, including account books, working drawings, and some studies, especially of interiors, are in the Architecture Library, University of Texas, Austin; see Carl J. Sterner, "The Marshall-Walton Papers," *Library Chronicle of the University of Texas at Austin*, n.s., 9 (1978): 61–65. The only thing to appear in print under Marshall's name is brief, "Architecture of an Expanding Metropolis and Some of Its Towers," in *Chicago: The World's Youngest Great*

City (1929). The only extensive treatment of Marshall's career, which includes a nearly complete list of his buildings and major projects and several illustrations, is Carroll William Westfall, "Benjamin Henry [lapsis for Howard] Marshall of Chicago," *Chicago Architectural Journal* 2 (1982): 8–27. An obituary is in the *Chicago Daily Tribune*, 20 June 1944.

CARROLL WILLIAM WESTFALL

MARSHALL, Catherine (27 Sept. 1914–18 Mar. 1983), biographer and novelist, was born Sarah Catherine Wood in Johnson City, Tennessee, the daughter of John Ambrose Wood, a Presbyterian minister, and Leonora Whitaker. She grew up in the South in her father's parsonages. The family never had much money; she later remembered her father's buying groceries from week to week on credit. Nevertheless, she maintained, her parents instilled in her a sense of helping those with less money and of spiritual richness. Catherine Wood graduated from Agnes Scott College with a B.A. in history in 1936. She enjoyed writing during her college years and planned to write and teach after graduation. These plans were changed, however, by her marriage in the fall of 1936 to Peter Marshall, minister of the Westminster Presbyterian Church in Atlanta.

A Scottish immigrant whose sermons attracted much of Atlanta's Presbyterian community, Marshall was twelve years older than the bride he dazzled and, by her account, inspired. Immediately after their marriage he took over the pastorate of the prestigious New York Avenue Presbyterian Church in Washington, D.C. Paul Boyer has noted that "from the first day of her marriage to the last, Catherine Marshall's identity was shaped by her role as a minister's wife" (p. 707). She was observed carefully in her wifehood, both by her husband's congregation and by Peter Marshall himself, who expected his spouse to be a sweetly supportive housewife and careful mother to their son, cleaving to his traditional view of womanhood while he devoted himself to his many pastoral duties.

From 1943 to 1945 Catherine Marshall took to her bed with tuberculosis, later claiming that her illness and its eventual cure were "spiritual as well as physical." During her time in retreat from the world she returned to her writing. In 1947 her husband's busy schedule picked up even more when he was asked to serve as chaplain of the U.S. Senate. In January 1949 the overworked Peter Marshall died of a heart attack, leaving her to support herself and their son.

Soon realizing that God had yet more work for her to do, Catherine Marshall edited several of her husband's sermons into a book, *Mr. Jones, Meet the Master* (1949). When asked for another such book she produced instead a biography of her husband, *A Man Called Peter*. Published in 1951, the book stayed on the bestseller list for three years. A. Powell Davis wrote in the *New York Times* (7 Oct. 1951):

It can scarcely be claimed that any man's wife is well equipped to be his most objective biographer. In the present case this does not matter, since objectivity is not essential in portraying a beloved person for a multitude of others who also loved him. Catherine Marshall writes extremely well. Those who do not accept her religious viewpoint will nevertheless admit that she presents it with grace and charm.

The book, which Marshall helped adapt into Twentieth Century-Fox's most successful film of 1955, perfectly suited popular reading tastes of the decade. The biography, like the film of the same name, presented a charming, religious man with a talented yet self-effacing wife. According to *Something about the Author* (vol. 2), "when seven Russian journalists visited the United States in 1955, one of them claimed that he didn't believe that Catherine Marshall existed. He had been so impressed by the story of her life that he thought she was the creation of American propaganda." In 1957 Marshall continued her own life story in *To Live Again*, which described her efforts to cope with her husband's death and to find new meaning in her life through spiritual writing. In 1959 she married Leonard LeSourd, editor of the inspirational periodical *Guideposts* magazine. Once more she took on the role of housewife, remaining in their home in Westchester County to care for her three stepchildren while LeSourd went to his New York office every day. In a later autobiography, *Meeting God at Every Turn* (1981), she described her adjustment to this regime and her desire for LeSourd to take on his full duties as spiritual head of the household. Nevertheless, she never again stopped writing, and the couple found help to run the house. Marshall continued to write spiritual books and articles. From 1958 to 1960 she served as women's editor for the *Christian Herald*, and from 1960 on she acted as "roving" editor for *Guideposts*. She and LeSourd eventually set up their own publishing company, Chosen Books.

In 1967 Marshall produced *Christy*, a novel based on her mother's experience as a teacher and missionary in Appalachia. The book sold more than four million copies. She and LeSourd spent their last years together in Florida, where she died, in Boynton Beach.

• The best sources on Catherine Marshall's life are her three autobiographical works cited above. Numerous profiles were written about her, including one in *Newsweek*, 4 Apr. 1955. Paul Boyer, "Minister's Wife, Widow, Reluctant Feminist: Catherine Marshall in the 1950s," *American Quarterly* 30 (Winter 1978): 703–21, nicely analyzes Marshall's housewife-vs.-author dilemma. Obituaries are in the *New York Times*, 19 Mar. 1983, and *Christianity Today*, 22 Apr. 1983. The *Saturday Evening Post* ran memorial pieces in Apr. 1987.

TINKY "DAKOTA" WEISBLAT

MARSHALL, Christopher (6 Nov. 1709–4 May 1797), pharmacist and revolutionary leader, was born in Dublin, Ireland. His parents' names are unknown. He received a classical education in England and developed an interest in chemistry. Marshall, a Quaker, married Sarah Thompson in 1735; they had three sons. His second marriage to Abigail, a Philadelphia Quaker, ended with her death in 1782. After moving to Philadelphia in 1727, Marshall started a pharmaceutical company. He was a religious man and in 1758 served as one of Philadelphia's overseers of the poor.

Marshall conducted his pharmacy business in 1729 at the sign of the Golden Ball at Front and Chestnut streets. In 1735 he continued the business on Chestnut near Second Street. His sons Christopher, Jr., and Charles became his partners in 1765 and took over the business in 1772. Christopher, Jr., an apothecary, druggist, botanist, and chemist, turned over the active, day-to-day management of the business to Charles. The firm sold drugs, chemicals, and paint.

Marshall retired in 1774 and became active in revolutionary affairs. He served on several revolutionary committees and kept a diary from 1774 to 1781. On the Philadelphia Committee of Inspection and Observation (1774–1775) he obtained supplies for the military and determined violations of the nonimportation agreement. He participated in the Provincial Conference of 1775. In March 1775 Marshall was chosen as one of twelve managers of a company "set on foot for making woollens, linen, and cotton." John Adams thought Marshall "an excellent Whig." He was appointed to the Philadelphia Council of Safety in December 1776 and to the Lancaster Council of Safety in October 1777. On the Philadelphia Council of Safety he helped obtain housing and supplies for sick and wounded soldiers brought to the city. In Lancaster he chaired a price-fixing committee in 1779 and helped provide food and clothing for Pennsylvania troops. A Constitutionalist, Marshall opposed the Republicans and defended the 1776 Pennsylvania Constitution.

The Quakers disowned Marshall for his part in the Revolution. He complained that the Friends met almost daily "to defeat the pacific proceedings of the Continental Congress," urged its members to withdraw from county committees "under penalty of excommunication," and warned citizens against "usurpation of power." After the skirmishes at Lexington and Concord, Marshall thought the "stiff Quakers" appeared ashamed of their opposition. The Provincial Conference at Carpenters' Hall in June 1776, which included Marshall, called for a convention on 18 July 1776 to form a new government "on the authority of the People only." Marshall petitioned the assembly in December 1777, "to call out the whole force of this State immediately . . . to attack General Howe . . . ruin his army, and rid the colonies of such cruel monsters." Marshall helped form the Philadelphia Society of Free Quakers in 1781. Among the first members were Moses Bartram, Clement Biddle, Elizabeth Claypoole, Lydia Darragh, Timothy Matlack, Benjamin Say, and Samuel Wetherill, Jr.

When General Howe took Philadelphia in 1777, Marshall escaped to Lancaster. He was a very conscientious man who deplored frivolity during the trying times of the Revolution. He recorded many aspects of the people's daily life in his personal writings. He documented the war-inflated prices demanded for common objects at a public sale in February 1780: frying pan, £25; saw, £37.10; razor, £20; eyeglasses, £19; a

walnut eight-day clock, £210. With prices so high, he complained, it was time for a "Bedlam" to be built in Lancaster. Despite the gradual influence of abolitionism, racism was common in Lancaster, a fact that Marshall deplored. The Marshalls hired two free blacks, a housekeeper and a laborer, but when the housekeeper died, Marshall could find no one to help bury her. Indignant, he denounced the racist attitudes of his community: "O what a wretched place. . . . Full of religious professions but not a grain of love or charity." He invited all "the Negros in Lancaster" to her funeral. Marshall also condemned entertainment during wartime. In his diary he criticized the people who drank wine and punch, ate cakes, danced, and sang until 4:00 A.M. on 31 January 1778, and he denounced "a great number of Fobs, fools, &c. of both sexes, old and young" for attending a ball on 20 February 1778.

Despite being disowned by the Society of Friends for his support of the Revolution, Marshall remained faithful to Quaker religious principles. After the Revolution Marshall moved back to Philadelphia, where his sons developed the nation's first large-scale pharmaceutical and chemical manufacturing company. In 1786 they started the production of ammonium chloride, used as an expectorant, muriate of ammonia, and Glaubers salt, used as a laxative. The Marshalls also continued to import large quantities of chemicals, compounds, plants, herbs, and other items in a large pharmacopoeia, including antimony, Peruvian bark, mercury, and tartar. His son Charles was chosen as the first president of the Philadelphia College of Pharmacy in 1821. Marshall died in Philadelphia.

• Marshall's "Diaries and Notes, 1774–1793," "Letterbook, 1773–1778," and "Waste Book, Accounts with the Continental Congress, 1776" are at the Historical Society of Pennsylvania. The most complete published version of Marshall's diary is William Duane, Jr., ed., *Extracts from the Diary of Christopher Marshall, Kept in Philadelphia and Lancaster, during the American Revolution, 1774–1781* (1877). On his pharmacy career, see Brooke Hindle, *The Pursuit of Science in Revolutionary America* (1956). On his political influence, see Richard Alan Ryerson, *The Revolution Is Now Begun* (1977), and Jerome H. Wood, Jr., *Conestoga Crossroads* (1979). An obituary is in *Claypoole's American Daily Advertiser*, 6 May 1797.

RODGER C. HENDERSON

MARSHALL, Clara (8 May 1847–13 Mar. 1931), physician and educator, was born in Chester County, Pennsylvania, the daughter of Pennock Marshall and Mary Phillips, Quakers and abolitionists. Education, medicine, and the advancement of women were intertwined themes throughout Marshall's life. She recalled in later years that prominent educators and physicians from the community often visited her family's home when she was a child. As a young woman and before entering medical school, Marshall taught school in Chester County.

In 1871 Marshall enrolled in the Woman's Medical College of Pennsylvania, where in 1874, while still a student, she was made auxiliary instructor in materia medica and pharmacy. After graduation in 1875 she became instructor, and in 1876 professor, of materia medica and general therapeutics, a post she held for thirty years. In 1888 she was elected dean of the faculty, remaining in that position until 1917. During her career as professor and dean she also maintained a medical practice in Philadelphia and authored numerous medical articles.

Marshall's career spanned a period of intensive efforts to gain educational and administrative opportunities for women in organized medicine, and to improve the quality of medical education in the United States. Her insistence on excellence in the qualifications of women medical students and physicians was a leitmotif struck early in Marshall's career. She attended medical school for a full four years at a time when few medical schools in the country required even a three-year course of study. After graduating she became the first woman to enter the Philadelphia College of Pharmacy, where she studied in 1876. At the National American Woman Suffrage Association meeting in 1898, she delivered a talk in which she stressed the need for women of wealth to endow women's medical schools, not only to improve the curriculum but also to ensure that only the "thoroughly well prepared" were admitted.

Marshall both expounded the advancement of women in medicine and actively sought positions herself in previously all-male institutions. In 1882 she was elected to the staff of the obstetrical department of the Philadelphia General Hospital at Blockley, one of the first two women so elected. It was, however, as dean of the Woman's Medical College of Pennsylvania that Marshall had her greatest impact. In this position she oversaw a significant upgrading of admissions requirements; an extension of the curriculum, in 1893, to its mandatory four-year length; the increase in clinical opportunities for medical students; and in 1904 the opening of a teaching hospital wholly owned and administered by the college. The establishment of a teaching hospital paved the way for the college's Class A rating and did much to ensure its survival during the critical period from 1905 to 1910, when the Flexner study of U.S. medical schools exposed schools' shortcomings and placed the continuance of some substandard institutions in jeopardy.

Marshall was described by those who knew her as a woman of energy, enthusiasm, clarity of vision, and an "intelligent appreciation of the problems that confronted her." She never married. For part of her time in Philadelphia she shared a home with her older sister, Helen Marshall, a teacher. She died in Philadelphia.

• Manuscripts and a bibliography of some of Marshall's writings, as well as correspondence and minutes from her tenure as professor and dean of the Woman's Medical College of Pennsylvania and other papers related to her work, are in the Archives and Special Collections on Women in Medicine, Medical College of Pennsylvania. Genealogy and newspaper clippings on the Marshall family are at the Chester County Historical Society. Marshall's writings include *The Woman's Medical College of Pennsylvania: An Historical Outline* (1897)

and nine articles on medical topics in various medical journals in the 1880s and 1890s. Obituaries are in the *New York Times*, 15 Mar. 1931; the *Philadelphia Evening Bulletin*, 16 Mar. 1931; and the *Daily Local News* of Chester County, Pa., 14 Mar. 1931.

SANDRA L. CHAFF

MARSHALL, Daniel (1706–2 Nov. 1784), Baptist pastor and itinerant preacher, was born in Windsor, Connecticut, the son of Thomas Marshall and Mary Drake, prosperous farmers. According to his son Abraham, Marshall received no formal education, was "religiously educated by respectable and pious parents," joined the local Standing Order Congregational church at the age of about twenty, and served as a deacon there for almost twenty years. He was a prosperous farmer by occupation. In 1742 he married Hannah Drake, who died shortly after the birth of their only child. In 1747 he married Martha Stearns, sister of the famous Separate Baptist leader, Shubal Stearns. The couple had ten children, all but one of whom survived their father.

Coming under the influence of revivalist George Whitefield about 1745, Marshall became a Separate Congregationalist, a group considerably more evangelistic and charismatic than members of the Standing Order. Expecting the imminent end of history, for about eighteen months (c. 1751–c. 1753) he preached among the Mohawks at "Onnaquaggy" (perhaps near modern Binghamton, N.Y.). When threatened by the impending French and Indian War, he moved with his family for a brief period to "Connogogig" (perhaps in modern Franklin County, Pa.).

A momentous move came in 1754 when he went to Frederick County, Virginia, there finally becoming a Baptist. Apparently Marshall had displayed Baptist leanings about 1743 (the year that Separate Baptists arrived in Connecticut), and his second wife surely contributed to his spiritual pilgrimage. According to early Baptist historian Morgan Edwards, the Marshalls joined the Mill Creek Church (located in what is now Berkeley County, W.Va.), and he was licensed to preach. Accompanied by Shubal Stearns and others, Marshall moved to North Carolina, helping to initiate the Sandy Creek Baptist Church of Guilford (now Randolph) County in 1755. The following year he was the founding pastor of Abbott's Creek Baptist Church of Guilford (now Davidson) County and was soon ordained to the ministry. In 1758 he participated in forming the Sandy Creek Baptist Association, comprised of nearby church leaders united for fellowship and encouragement. As a Separate Baptist pastor and evangelist, he influenced at least seven men in North Carolina and Virginia to enter the ministry and directly assisted in the formation of at least five Baptist churches in those colonies.

About 1760 Marshall became founding pastor of the Beaver Creek Baptist Church of Fairfield County, South Carolina, and later founding pastor of Stephen's Creek Baptist (now Big Stevens) Church in Edgefield County. For a decade he lived in South Carolina, influencing at least seven men to enter the ministry and assisting in the formation of at least thirteen Separate Baptist churches. Doubtless he was instrumental in founding the Congaree Baptist Association in 1771.

Having already established branches of the Stephen's Creek Church in nearby Georgia, Marshall made one last move in 1771 and became, in 1771 or 1772, the founding pastor of Kiokee Baptist Church, St. Paul's Parish (now Columbia County), the first continuing Baptist church in Georgia. He apparently also retained his connection with Stephen's Creek. At the age of sixty-five he was the patriarch among Georgia Baptist preachers. He took at least sixteen younger men under his wing as spiritual sons, instructing them in Baptist doctrine and methods of church growth. Of the 104 known Baptist churches organized in Georgia during the eighteenth century, a large portion of them trace their origins to Marshall or one of his junior colleagues.

Marshall was sensitive to the issue of religious liberty and the American cause. About 1770 he was arrested for conducting a non-Anglican service of worship while visiting in Georgia. Four years later he temporarily opposed the anti-British Tondee Resolutions—perhaps only because of procedural concerns—but soon thereafter showed himself to be a vigorous patriot. The revolutionary war virtually paralyzed organized Baptist life in Georgia. Only Marshall and some of his assistants remained in the area throughout the struggle. At times he was chaplain for nearby troops, and once he was detained by British authorities because of his preaching.

After the conflict was over, some members of the state legislature expressed an interest in supporting all Christian denominations by taxation. Favoring religious liberty, Marshall and his colleagues founded the Georgia Baptist Association in October 1784, with Marshall as first moderator. His death at his residence near Appling, Columbia County, Georgia, came before the objectionable legislative act was passed in February 1785. Three months later the association composed a lengthy Remonstrance in opposition and sent it to the legislature. Marshall must be given part of the credit when the act was ignored.

Marshall's contemporaries characterized him in varying ways. His son Abraham spoke of his father's holy zeal, meekness, and patience but then admitted that his gifts "were by no means above *mediocrity*." The historian Edwards, also a friend, said, "His success is surprising when we consider that he is a man of no bright parts nor eloquence nor learning. Piety, earnestness and honesty are all he can boast of "; "he is a weak man, a stammerer, & no schollar."

Evidence exists that Marshall owned an undetermined amount of land in Virginia and South Carolina and at least 400 acres in Georgia, but apparently he held no slaves. He left an estate "of considerable value." He was a farmer and preacher but, in light of his travels and advancing age, probably much of the actual farming was done by his sons. Located near Ap-

pling, Georgia, the Marshall Historical Site was dedicated in 1984.

It is remarkable that Marshall's second wife, Martha Stearns Marshall, was a preacher in her own right. One early admirer commented, "Without the shadow of an usurped authority over the other sex, Mrs. Marshall, being a Lady of good sense, singular piety, and surprizing elocution, has, in countless instances, melted a whole concourse into tears by her prayers and exhortations!" Further, for the first sixty-one years of its life, the Kiokee Baptist Church had as its pastor Marshall, then his son Abraham, and later his grandson Jabez. Seldom is such a ministerial dynasty on record in Baptist circles.

• Early sources are two in number. Most complete is the sketch prepared by Marshall's son Abraham Marshall, "Biography of the Late Rev. Daniel Marshall," first printed in *Analytical Repository* 1 (May–June 1802): 23–31, and reprinted by numerous later historians. Morgan Edwards produced materials on Virginia, North Carolina, South Carolina, and Georgia, in 1771–1772, containing information about Marshall. These may be consulted in E. B. Weeks and M. B. Warren, eds., *Materials towards a History of the Baptists* (2 vols., 1984), although the transcriptions should be checked against the original manuscripts found at the Colgate Rochester Divinity School, Rochester, N.Y., and the South Carolina Baptist Historical Society, Greenville.

More recent careful studies of Marshall are James D. Mosteller, *A History of the Kiokee Baptist Church in Georgia* (1952); and Waldo P. Harris III, "Daniel Marshall: Lone Georgia Baptist Revolutionary Pastor," *Viewpoints: Georgia Baptist History* 5 (1976): 51–64, and "Locations Associated with Daniel Marshall and the Kiokee Church," *Viewpoints: Georgia Baptist History* 6 (1978): 25–46. One recent comprehensive summary essay that is also useful is Gregory L. Hunt, "Daniel Marshall: Energetic Evangelist for the Separate Baptist Cause," *Baptist History and Heritage* 21 (Apr. 1986): 5–18.

ROBERT G. GARDNER

MARSHALL, Eli Kennerly, Jr. (2 May 1889–10 Jan. 1966), pharmacologist and physiologist, was born in Charleston, South Carolina, the son of Eli Kennerly Marshall, a retail (shoe) merchant, and Julia Irene Brown. Marshall obtained his B.S. at the College of Charleston in 1908 and his Ph.D. in chemistry at Johns Hopkins University in 1911. In 1912 he studied with the physiologist Emil Abderhalden in Halle, Germany. At Johns Hopkins Medical School he was assistant in physiological chemistry (1911–1914), successfully beginning a research career with the development of an enzymatic method for the determination of urea that was subsequently used for the study of the distribution in the organism and excretion of urea. From 1914 to 1917 he was associate in pharmacology with the pharmacologist John J. Abel, who convinced him to study medicine and became his lifelong model of a highly educated experimental researcher. In 1917 Marshall earned his M.D. from Johns Hopkins, became associate professor of pharmacology, and married psychiatrist Alice Berry Carroll. The couple had three children. From 1917 to

1919 he was commissioned for toxicological work on mustard gas at the Chemical Warfare Service in Washington, D.C.

Marshall was chairman and full professor of pharmacology at Washington University in St. Louis, Missouri, from 1919 to 1921. He devised a method to measure cardiac output in animals that he extended to humans. In 1923 he visited with renal physiologists in Britain, Denmark, the Netherlands, and France. His earlier work on urea was a starting point for a decade of studies on urine formation in the kidney. His major contribution to renal physiology was his proof of a direct transfer into the urine of substances (tubular secretion) in addition to the two transfer processes known at that time (filtration and reabsorption). This discovery, made by the use of dyes as tracers and methods of comparative physiology, was not accepted by the leading kidney physiologists until much later, though it proved to be pathbreaking. From the summer of 1926 on, Marshall also did research on renal urine formation at the Mount Desert Island Biological Laboratory in Maine. In 1928 he succeeded William Henry Howell in the chair of physiology at Johns Hopkins.

In 1932 Marshall was offered the Johns Hopkins chair of pharmacology (and experimental therapeutics), which had been held for almost forty years by Abel. This brought Marshall back into pharmacology and opened his most successful period. A study of physiological and pharmacological regulation of respiration (1937) disclosed new mechanisms and showed the danger of giving oxygen or carbon dioxide to victims of overdoses of morphine or barbiturates. His most original work was on antibacterial chemotherapy with the then new sulfa drugs (1936–1942). In 1937 he devised an analytical method for these drugs, which was used for the study of their absorption, distribution, excretion, and metabolism in animals and humans. The method was improved by A. Calvin Bratton, Jr., one of Marshall's coworkers, in 1939 and came to be known as the Bratton-Marshall reaction. These processes determined the duration and intensity of a drug's action. Marshall used the time-courses of drug concentrations in blood as a rational basis for establishing effective dosage schemes. This was a new approach, improving on the traditional practice of giving patients standard doses based on "clinical experience." He also studied the toxicity of these drugs and in 1939 devised methods, later widely used, for the assessment of their chemotherapeutic activity in disease models in animals. Furthermore, he produced an injectable sulfa drug, sodium sulfanilamidopyridine, and another one, sulfanilguanidine, that remains and acts in the intestinal tract. Marshall warned that "the use of drugs in sick human beings before adequate toxicologic and pharmacologic investigation on animals is available can only impede true progress and lead to unnecessary human suffering and death" (*Journal of the American Medical Association* 112 [1939]: 352).

During World War II Marshall was one of the leaders of the U.S. Malaria Program (1941–1945). He improved testing methods for antimalarial drugs using the avian disease equivalent and quinine as a standard. His concept of dosage schedules based on the time-course of blood concentration led to the successful use of the synthetic antimalarial, atabrine (later given the generic name quinacrine), and thus to protection of U.S. armed forces in the South Pacific theater. Studies similar to those made with sulfa drugs were carried out with the new antibiotics, penicillin and streptomycin (1946–1948). In his final years at Johns Hopkins he worked on potential anti-inflammatory drugs and made important contributions to the metabolism of ethyl alcohol and chloral hydrate (1949–1955). Throughout his career in pharmacology he cooperated with clinicians and was instrumental in shaping a new discipline, later called clinical pharmacology.

Marshall served as editor of the *Journal of Pharmacology and Experimental Therapeutics* (1932–1938) and as president of the American Society for Pharmacology and Experimental Therapeutics (1942). After retirement from Johns Hopkins in 1955, he served as consultant for the University of Florida, the National Cancer Institute, the Mount Desert Island Biological Laboratory, and for pharmaceutical firms. He died in Baltimore, having authored some 160 research papers and a score on the history of chemotherapy, on the theoretical basis of science, on financial support of medical research, and on J. J. Abel.

Marshall is remembered as a serious and straightforward person of absolute integrity, a well-organized and systematic researcher and teacher. As was rarely achieved in the twentieth century, he was active and successful in three medical fields: biochemistry, physiology, and pharmacology. According to historians of medicine at Johns Hopkins, "Marshall's work was original in theory and practice, and he stands in bold relief as a principal architect of the scientific age of chemotherapy" (Harvey et al. [1989]: 258). His concepts, which marked the beginning of a new branch of pharmacology, later called pharmacokinetics, have largely influenced both the safe and effective use of drugs and the scientific development of pharmacology in the second half of the twentieth century. Clinical pharmacologist Richard M. Weinshilboum observed that "perhaps most important, Marshall pioneered the use of a quantitative approach . . . based on . . . the use of blood drug level measurements, first for establishing dosages and later for laying the conceptual foundation for pharmacokinetics. . . . This 'new pharmacology,' . . . based on the application of quantitative principles of basic pharmacology in the clinical realm, played an important role in the development of the National Institutes of Health after World War II" (Weinshilboum, p. 483). Marshall's work was successfully carried on by men like James A. Shannon and B. B. Brodie at the National Institutes of Health, an institution that stands for the dramatic development of medical research in the second half of the twentieth century.

• An autobiographical sketch and other papers by and on Marshall are at the Alan Mason Chesney Archives of the Johns Hopkins Medical Institutions. All of Marshall's major fields of research are represented in his review articles: on renal physiology, see *Physiological Reviews* 6 (1926): 440–84 and 14 (1934): 133–59; on sulfa drugs, *Physiological Review* 19 (1939): 240–69, and *Annual Review of Physiology* 3 (1941): 643–70; on antibiotics, *Journal of Pharmacology and Experimental Therapeutics* 92 (1948): 43–48; on malaria, in *A Survey of Antimalarial Drugs, 1941–1945*, vol. 1, ed. F. Y. Wiselogle (1946), pp. 59–71; and on alcohol and chloral hydrate, *Bulletin of the Johns Hopkins Hospital* 97 (1955): 395–404. Most of Marshall's individual publications are listed in Thomas H. Maren's memoir in National Academy of Sciences, *Biographical Memoirs* 56 (1987): 313–52. Other biographies and assessments are Marcel H. Bickel, "Eli K. Marshall, Jr. (1889–1966): From Biochemistry and Physiology to Pharmacology and Pharmacokinetics," *Drug Metabolism Reviews* 28 (1996): 311–44, and A. McGehee Harvey, "The Story of Chemotherapy at Johns Hopkins: Perrin H. Long, Eleanor A. Bliss, and E. Kennerly Marshall, Jr.," *Johns Hopkins Medical Journal* 138 (1976): 54–60. See also Thomas B. Turner, *Heritage of Excellence: The Johns Hopkins Medical Institutions 1914–1947* (1974); Richard M. Weinshilboum, "The Therapeutic Revolution," *Clinical Pharmacology and Therapeutics* 42 (1987): 481–84; and Harvey et al., *A Model of Its Kind*, vol. 1, *A Centennial History of Medicine at Johns Hopkins* (1989), pp. 257–58.

MARCEL H. BICKEL

MARSHALL, Frank James (10 Aug. 1877–9 Nov. 1944), chess player, was born in New York City, the son of Alfred George Marshall, a flour mill salesman, and Sarah Ann Graham. His family moved to Montreal when he was twelve, and at age fifteen Marshall won the Montreal Chess Club Championship. He returned to New York in 1896 and won the Brooklyn Chess Club championship in 1899. Marshall was poorly educated, and while he spoke some French and German, his command of written English was poor. He never attended college.

After his relatively minor successes in the United States, Marshall traveled to Europe in 1899 to try his luck in the much stronger European tournaments. Not skilled enough or well enough known to merit a place in the premier tournament in London, Marshall entered the "Minor" tournament, which he won, ahead of Jacques Mieses and Georg Marco. This victory was sufficiently prestigious to earn him a place the following year in the international tournament held in Paris. Although he only tied for third place, Marshall beat world champion Emanuel Lasker, an impressive accomplishment. After only one more tournament, in Vienna in 1902, where he shared second place, Marshall began a string of exceptional international successes. He won an international tournament in Cambridge Springs, Pennsylvania, in 1904, ahead of Emanuel Lasker. First places in Scheveningen in 1905, Nuremberg in 1906, Düsseldorf in 1908, New York in 1911, and Havana in 1913, ahead of the young star José Raul Capablanca, confirmed his place as one of the strongest players in the world. After qualifying for the world championship match in 1907, Marshall

lost to defending champion Emanuel Lasker, 3.5–11.5. Marshall also tied for first place in premier tournaments in Amsterdam in 1911, Budapest in 1912, and Paris in 1914.

Marshall defeated defending champion Jackson Showalter in a match played for the U.S. championship in 1909 and successfully defended his title against Edward Lasker, defeating him 9.5–8.5 in a match in 1923. He voluntarily relinquished the title in 1936 to allow the replacement of a match system with an invitational tournament championship. In other matches, Marshall defeated Adolf Teichmann, David Janowski, Jacques Mieses, and Oldrich Duras. As captain and player for the U.S. Chess Olympiad teams of 1930, 1931, 1933, 1935, and 1937, Marshall was instrumental in bringing home four U.S. gold medals. Marshall's best individual Olympiad performance was at Folkestone, England, in 1933, where he scored seven out of ten points to win the Second Board Prize, given for the best performance among all second-ranked players.

A dominant personality in the American chess scene, and especially in New York City, Marshall, along with his wife Caroline D. Krauss, whom he married on 6 January 1905 and with whom he had one son, founded the Marshall Chess Club in 1915, which continued to operate in Greenwich Village at the end of the twentieth century. Marshall died of a heart attack after collapsing on the street on his way home from a chess event in Jersey City, New Jersey.

In style an exponent of the Romantic school, Marshall favored open, attacking positions. In his autobiography, he compares his style to that of boxer Jack Dempsey: "I have always liked wide open games and tried to knock out my opponents with a checkmate as quickly as possible. I subscribe to the old belief that offense is the best defense." In his later years he was characterized by *Life* magazine as "a preoccupied old gentleman who looks like a Shakespearean actor, smokes strong cigars and always takes a pocket board to bed with him" (29 Jan. 1940). The Marshall gambit, a popular and aggressive variation of the Ruy Lopez opening, is named after him.

• Marshall's autobiography, *My Fifty Years of Chess* (1943), reprinted as *Marshall's Best Games of Chess* (1960), was actually ghostwritten by Fred Reinfeld; a chatty, engaging account of his life, it includes 140 annotated games. Marshall did write *Chess Swindles* (1914) and *Comparative Chess* (1932). The most comprehensive biography of Marshall is Andy Soltis, *Frank Marshall, United States Chess Champion* (1994). Articles on Marshall appear in Harry Golombek, *Golombek's Encyclopedia of Chess* (1977), and David Hooper and Kenneth Whyld, *The Oxford Companion to Chess* (1984). Marshall's papers are housed at the Marshall Chess Club in Manhattan. An obituary appears in the *New York Times*, 10 Nov. 1944.

ELIZABETH ZOE VICARY

MARSHALL, George Catlett, Jr. (31 Dec. 1880–16 Oct. 1959), soldier and statesman, was born in Uniontown, Pennsylvania, the son of George Catlett Marshall, Sr., a businessman distantly related to Chief Justice John Marshall, and Laura Bradford. Marshall spent an unexceptional childhood in Uniontown. In 1897 he was admitted to the Virginia Military Institute in Lexington, where he first exhibited his leadership abilities and was selected first corporal, sergeant, and captain of the cadets. Soon after graduation in 1901 he applied for and on 2 February 1902 received a commission in the U.S. Army as a second lieutenant. Nine days later he married Elizabeth Carter Coles. They remained happily married until her death in 1927 but had no children.

From 1902 to 1916 Marshall served in the Philippines twice and on a series of army posts in the continental United States. More important than these standard assignments were those with the volunteer state militia, which developed his ability to work with civilians, and his appointment in 1906 to the Infantry-Cavalry School at Fort Leavenworth, which was on the cutting edge of the major reforms taking place within the army. He exhibited a talent for staff work, graduated first in his class, qualified for a second year at the Staff College, and in 1908 was appointed an instructor. Because of his abilities as a staff officer, he was also appointed aide-de-camp to Generals J. Franklin Bell and Hunter Liggett between 1913 and 1916 and often assumed responsibilities far beyond those normally associated with his rank. Indeed, his promotion in the small U.S. Army was extremely slow despite his outstanding record; only in 1907 did he become a first lieutenant and only in 1916 a captain.

U.S. entry into World War I the following year provided Marshall with new opportunities, but owing to his unique managerial abilities and reputation, they all involved staff work rather than field command. Assigned to the staff of the First Infantry Division, he was one of the first American soldiers to land in France in 1917. Over the next year he played a major role in training U.S. forces and helped plan the counterattack at Cantigny against the 1918 German spring offensive. He came to the attention of General John J. Pershing, head of the American Expeditionary Forces, and in mid-1918 was assigned to the operations staff of Pershing's general headquarters. Marshall assumed major responsibilities in planning the two great American offensives of the war: St.-Mihiel and the Meuse-Argonne. By the armistice in November he was chief of operations for the U.S. First Army with the temporary rank of colonel and had become one of Pershing's most valued tactical and logistical experts. He had also developed an extraordinary ability to organize and operate within Allied commands and had been recommended by Pershing for promotion to brigadier general.

The end of the war precluded that promotion, and in 1920 Marshall reverted to the rank of major. He became one of Pershing's postwar aides, however, and thereby once again assumed responsibilities far beyond his official rank. This was especially true from 1921 to 1924, when Pershing was army chief of staff and Marshall his virtual executive. Pershing in turn became Marshall's powerful mentor and supporter, introducing him to politico-military affairs at the highest level and promoting his protégé in whatever ways possible. Those ways were quite limited in the small interwar army, however, and for most of these years Marshall's talents went largely unused and unrewarded.

In 1923 Marshall was promoted to lieutenant colonel and in the following year was assigned to the Fifteenth Infantry Regiment in Tientsin, China. In July 1927 he returned to Washington, D.C., as instructor at the National War College. The sudden and unexpected death of his wife of a heart condition in September of that year put him into a deep depression, from which he gradually emerged via total absorption in a new and pivotal assignment: head of the Infantry School at Fort Benning, Georgia. He undertook a revolution in the training of U.S. Army officers, emphasizing simplicity, innovation, and mobility. In the process he created what would become the U.S. high command during World War II: 200 future generals passed through Fort Benning during Marshall's 1927–1932 tenure, including such luminaries as Omar N. Bradley, J. Lawton Collins, Matthew Ridgway, Walter Bedell Smith, and Joseph W. Stilwell. Midway through this tenure, in 1930, Marshall married Katherine Tupper Brown, a widow with three children.

Between 1932 and 1936 Marshall received promotion to colonel, commanded army posts in Georgia and South Carolina, worked closely with the newly established Civilian Conservation Corps, and was senior instructor to the Illinois National Guard in Chicago. In 1936 he finally received promotion to brigadier general and was given command of the Fifth Infantry Brigade at Vancouver Barracks in the state of Washington. In all of these positions he continued to exhibit exceptional managerial competency and skill with civilians. In 1938 he was recalled to Washington, D.C., to head the War Plans Division of the Army general staff. Within a few months he was promoted to deputy chief of staff, and in April 1939 President Franklin D. Roosevelt selected him to succeed General Malin Craig as chief of staff. The selection was a surprise to many in light of Marshall's relative lack of seniority and recent outspokenness with the president. (Marshall believed that Roosevelt's desire to focus rearmament on aircraft production was an unbalanced and unwise approach, and said so.) In addition, there was the marked contrast between Marshall's very formal and FDR's informal manner. However, Marshall had been strongly supported by Pershing and had impressed presidential adviser Harry Hopkins as well as Roosevelt himself.

Marshall officially assumed his responsibilities and was promoted to permanent major general and temporary full general on 1 September 1939, the same day Germany invaded Poland to begin World War II. His next two years were dominated by efforts to convince both the president and Congress of the threat this conflict posed to the United States and the subsequent need to create a large and balanced armed force. The efforts with Congress were successful, especially after the German conquest of France in the spring of 1940. Marshall quickly developed a reputation for honesty as well as competence, with numerous congressmen willing to give him what they would not give the president. Their passage of the first peacetime draft and billion-dollar defense bills during the spring and summer of 1940 provided Marshall with the resources he desired, and by late 1941 his army had expanded from its 1939 level of fewer than 175,000 to 1.4 million men. By that time his staff was planning further expansion to more than 8 million for service in Europe should the nation officially enter the war.

Working closely with the chief of naval operations, Admiral Harold R. Stark, Marshall also won presidential approval in 1941 for a "Europe first" strategy in conjunction with Great Britain should the United States find itself at war with Japan as well as Germany; secret staff conversations that year resulted in Anglo-American agreement to concentrate initially on defeating Germany. Throughout 1940–1941, however, Marshall also struggled, often unsuccessfully, to halt Roosevelt's proclivity to overcommitment. Particularly noteworthy and frustrating were disagreements over how aggressively to oppose Japan in the Pacific and whether scarce supplies should be allocated to the army or to potential allies under lend-lease.

After Pearl Harbor Marshall's sphere of activity expanded enormously. So did his accomplishments and stature. He reorganized the War Department in early 1942 and soon became the leading figure in the newly formed U.S. Joint Chiefs of Staff and Anglo-American Combined Chiefs of Staff organizations. He also attended all ten Anglo-American and three Anglo-Soviet-American summit conferences during the war and gradually emerged as Roosevelt's key military adviser. Marshall played a major role in the critical decision taken soon after Pearl Harbor to apply the principle of unity of command to all British and American ground, naval, and air forces and in developing and promoting the U.S. strategic plan for decisive cross-Channel operations in northern France rather than Mediterranean operations as British Prime Minister Winston S. Churchill and his military advisers preferred. Marshall was defeated in this Anglo-American debate in 1942, and as a result Allied forces invaded French North Africa in November of that year and Sicily and Italy in 1943. He did succeed in winning British support for a 1944 cross-Channel assault, however, which culminated in the decisive Normandy campaign of that year.

Although many had assumed Marshall would himself command this operation, by late 1943 he had become irreplaceable to Roosevelt not only as army chief but also as his most effective spokesman with Congress, unofficial leader of the Joint Chiefs, "first among equals" within the Combined Chiefs, and one of the president's closest and most trusted advisers. Roosevelt was nevertheless willing to give Marshall the command if the chief of staff requested it, but as a matter of principle Marshall refused to do so. Consequently the president selected Marshall's protégé,

General Dwight D. Eisenhower, who had commanded Anglo-American forces in North Africa, Sicily, and Italy, on the grounds that he "could not sleep at ease" with Marshall out of Washington. This exercise in self-denial only added to the Marshall legend, and in 1944 Congress awarded him a fifth star and the title General of the Army. In that same year *Time* magazine selected him its "Man of the Year" and labeled him "the closest thing to 'the indispensable man'" (3 Jan. 1944, p. 18). To Churchill he was by war's end the "true 'organizer of victory,'" and to President Harry S. Truman he was "the greatest military man that this country has ever produced."

Rather than allow him to retire after victory, Truman in November 1945 asked Marshall to become special presidential emissary to China in an attempt to avert civil war between the Nationalists and the Communists. Marshall's prestige and diplomatic ability led to some success at first, but in late 1946 his mediation effort collapsed. The task was probably impossible under any circumstances, but the U.S. policy of trying to play impartial mediator while simultaneously providing the Nationalists with military supplies only compounded the difficulties.

Marshall's failure in China did not diminish his prestige. Facing a hostile Republican Congress as postwar relations with the Soviet Union rapidly deteriorated, Truman recalled Marshall from China and nominated him to become secretary of state in early 1947. Marshall was approved by the Senate Foreign Relations Committee with no hearings and no opposition and by the full Senate on the same day. For the next two years he presided over one of the most important, creative, and controversial periods in the history of both the State Department and U.S. foreign policy.

That period witnessed the full emergence of the Cold War and the acceptance by the United States of a major role in international affairs. Marshall's key responsibilities were to help define the U.S. role, win public support for it, and restructure the State Department to implement it. He managed to accomplish all of these tasks during his two-year tenure while simultaneously attending numerous international conferences, including two long sessions of the Council of Foreign Ministers and one of the United Nations General Assembly in Europe as well as two inter-American conferences in South America, which culminated in the Rio Pact and the Organization of American States in 1947–1948.

Marshall was assisted in the State Department by an extraordinary group of subordinates, most notably Dean G. Acheson, who would succeed him as secretary of state, and George F. Kennan, whom he appointed to head the new Policy Planning Staff. The main problem, they all agreed, was European hunger and despair, not a Soviet Union that would merely take advantage of the situation. Soviet expansion did need to be "contained," as Kennan would publicly argue, but the main U.S. weapon in this containment should be economic assistance to check the Soviets by alleviating Europe's deeper problems. At Harvard

University on 5 June 1947, Marshall invited the European nations to coordinate their efforts and request such assistance from the United States. That request, eventually amounting to more than $13 billion, passed Congress after an extensive and successful campaign by Marshall to win public and Republican support. Officially entitled the European Recovery Program and commonly known as the Marshall Plan, it succeeded in helping to economically revive and integrate the nations of Western Europe, including the western occupation zones of Germany.

The Marshall Plan also helped to solidify the growing East-West split on the European continent, however, and to bring the Soviet-American confrontation to the brink of war—most notably after the 1948 Communist coup in Czechoslovakia and Soviet blockade of the western sections of Berlin. The American responses included not only the successful Berlin airlift but also U.S. membership in a formal alliance with Canada and Western Europe—the North Atlantic Treaty Organization. Plans also proceeded for the creation of a Federal Republic in the western zones of Germany. Marshall played major roles in the initiation, congressional approval, and implementation of all these dramatic policies for Europe, even though many did not reach fruition until after he left office.

Marshall and his subordinates were less successful in other parts of the world, particularly in the Middle East, where they opposed the creation of Israel as counterproductive to U.S. interests, and in China, where they opposed continued aid to the corrupt and ineffective Nationalists. Domestic politics precluded presidential agreement to such policy recommendations, however. Marshall was thus overruled by the president on Israel and forced to support continued funding of the Nationalist Chinese in order to win Republican support for the European Recovery Program. He managed to keep such financial support limited, however, and to continue to focus on a Europe-first policy in the Cold War.

In late 1948 and early 1949 Marshall underwent major surgery to remove a kidney and resigned as secretary of state. After his recovery he agreed to head the American Red Cross, but the outbreak of war in Korea in 1950 led Truman to call him out of his semiretirement and nominate him to be secretary of defense. By this time the anticommunist hysteria known as McCarthyism had already begun, and although Marshall was confirmed in September, he was clearly a target because of his ties to the Roosevelt and Truman administrations as well as his policies throughout the 1940s, particularly his opposition to continued funding of the Nationalist Chinese. The hysterical charges against him increased substantially when in late 1950 the Communist Chinese successfully counterattacked against the advancing U.S. forces in Korea, and the administration decided to pursue a limited war strategy focused only on returning to the thirty-eighth parallel. In 1951 Marshall recommended and publicly defended before Congress the removal of Far Eastern commander General Douglas MacArthur for the in-subordination of refusing to accept this policy. After the storm of controversy had receded, he announced his resignation in September 1951. The first professional soldier to be so honored, he was awarded the Nobel Peace Prize in 1953 for his European Recovery Program. He spent his remaining years in long-desired retirement at his homes in Leesburg, Virginia, and Pinehurst, North Carolina, until a series of strokes required his hospitalization in 1959 at Walter Reed Army Hospital in Washington, where he died. He was buried in Arlington National Cemetery in Virginia.

Despite the political attacks during the McCarthy era, Marshall's reputation has both survived and grown in the years since his death. He is considered the architect and organizer of the Allied victory during World War II and of U.S. policies during the early years of the Cold War. In addition to his accomplishments as World War II army chief of staff, Cold War secretary of state, and Korean War secretary of defense, Marshall was recognized as one of the foremost defenders of civilian control of the military and a key definer of the proper role for the military in a democratic society. Throughout his career he also exhibited extraordinary personal integrity. As a result he became the model of the selfless public servant, the greatest soldier-statesman since George Washington.

• The voluminous papers and taped reminiscences of Marshall and many of his associates are housed in the George C. Marshall Research Library and Museum adjoining the Virginia Military Institute campus in Lexington, Va. Three volumes of these papers have been published under the editorship of Larry I. Bland as *The Papers of George Catlett Marshall* (1981–1991). Many of Marshall's official papers can also be found in the regular chronological and the World War II special conference volumes of the State Department's *Foreign Relations* series. The full China mission report has been published as *Marshall's Mission to China* (2 vols., 1976).

Despite numerous lucrative offers, Marshall refused to publish any memoirs after his retirement and even attempted to destroy all copies of a manuscript he had written after World War I. Those efforts were unsuccessful, however, and a copy of the manuscript was found and published many years after his death as *Memoirs of My Services in the World War, 1917–1918* (1976). Marshall is also the focal point of memoirs by his second wife, Katherine Tupper Marshall, *Together: Annals of an Army Wife* (1946), and by his goddaughter, Rose Page Wilson, *General Marshall Remembered* (1968). In 1956–1957 Marshall did agree to a series of oral history interviews with his official biographer. Twenty-five years later these were published as Bland, ed., *George C. Marshall: Interviews and Reminiscences for Forrest C. Pogue* (1991).

Marshall's papers and tapes provided much of the raw material for Forrest C. Pogue's authorized biography, *George C. Marshall* (4 vols., 1963–1987). This is clearly the best and most comprehensive study available, and it supersedes all earlier biographies—most of which dealt only with portions of Marshall's life and only superficially. Two brief but complete biographies have been published since the appearance of Pogue's final volume: Edward Cray, *General of the Army: George C. Marshall, Soldier and Statesman* (1990), and Mark A. Stoler, *George C. Marshall: Soldier-Statesman of the Ameri-*

can Century (1989). See also the dual biography by Thomas Parrish, *Roosevelt and Marshall: Partners in Politics and War* (1989). An obituary is in the *New York Times*, 17 Oct. 1959.

MARK A. STOLER

MARSHALL, George Preston (11 Oct. 1896–9 Aug. 1969), professional football team owner, was born in Grafton, West Virginia, the son of T. Hill Marshall, a newspaper publisher and businessman, and Blanche Preston Sebrell. Marshall's family moved to Washington, D.C., when he was a child, and he always regarded himself as a Washingtonian. As a young man, he ignored his family's more conventional business interests and gravitated toward show business. He appeared as a stock player in a number of productions and then served as manager of several theaters in Baltimore and Washington. In 1920 he married Elizabeth Mortensen, a Ziegfeld Follies girl, whom he divorced in 1935; they had two children.

In 1918 Marshall inherited the family laundry business, building it into a major operation with fifty-seven outlets before he sold it at a considerable profit in 1945. Despite his conventional business success, his real love was show business. Although he never returned to the theater, he applied the promotional talents he learned there to the world of professional sports.

In 1932 Marshall joined a syndicate that paid $1,500 for the defunct Pottsville, Pennsylvania, football franchise; the team was transferred to Boston, where it entered the National Football League (NFL) as the Boston Braves. A year later, Marshall, now sole owner after his partners dropped out in the face of mounting losses, changed the team's nickname to the Redskins and scheduled its games at Fenway Park, home of the Boston Red Sox baseball team. Despite these changes, the Redskins continued to founder at the box office.

After the team won the NFL's Eastern Division in 1936 with 7 wins and 5 losses, Marshall moved the championship game against the Green Bay Packers from Boston to New York's Polo Grounds to attract a larger crowd. A year later, he shifted the franchise to Washington, D.C., where the Redskins found a permanent home. Marshall's decision to relocate was influenced by his second wife, the screen actress Corinne Griffith, whom he married in 1936 and divorced in 1957.

Marshall was instrumental in revising the rules of professional football. At NFL meetings in 1933 he persuaded his fellow owners to accept a number of changes designed to make the game more high-scoring and wide-open. To stimulate the passing game, a slimmer, more easily thrown football was introduced, and forward passing from anywhere behind the line of scrimmage was allowed (previously forward passing had been restricted to five yards behind the scrimmage line). Additional changes made the field goal more important by moving the goal posts from the back of the end zone to the goal line.

Even more important than rules changes, Marshall introduced structural alterations to the league. To increase fan interest and revenues, he convinced his fellow owners in 1933 to split the NFL into two divisions, with the winner of each division meeting to determine the league champion. He drew up a set schedule for the league, replacing the haphazard scheduling that reflected the NFL's barnstorming origins. He also is credited with creating the Pro Bowl, the NFL's all-star game, first played in 1951.

Marshall's showmanship left an indelible mark on professional football. He played a major popularizing role in creating a glittering spectacle rather than a mere game. He invented the spectacular half time show, which in the case of his own team invariably featured the Redskin Marching Band, a gaudily dressed ensemble with a signatory fight song, "Hail to the Redskins." Marshall is reputed to have said: "Football without a band is like a musical without an orchestra." He was the first owner to develop an extensive regional radio network to broadcast his team's games, and he later extended the network to include television broadcasts. Every NFL team subsequently modeled its radio and TV networks on his originals.

A crusty, irascible, self-centered man, Marshall was considered a bigot by many. When accused of anti-Semitism, he responded that he loved Jews, "especially when they're customers." On his failure to sign African Americans for the Redskins, he remarked: "We'll start signing Negroes when the Harlem Globetrotters start signing whites." In fact, his Redskins were the last professional football team to employ African-American players. Although African Americans had played in the modern NFL since 1946, Marshall refused to sign black players until 1962. He attributed his reluctance to integrate the club to the team's ties with the South, claiming that blacks playing for the Redskins would alienate southern fans and harm his radio and television revenues. Only after the federal government brought considerable pressure on him by threatening to deny his team access to D.C. Stadium (now Robert F. Kennedy Stadium) did Marshall relent and add African Americans to the roster.

The Redskins enjoyed great success during the NFL's early years. Led by quarterback Sammy Baugh, who signed out of Texas Christian University in 1937, the team won five more Eastern Division titles (1937, 1940, 1942, 1943, 1945) and two NFL championships (1937, 1942). Although the Redskins remained a top box office attraction, the team's performance after 1945 declined and remained mediocre during the rest of Marshall's life. Critics attributed the falloff to his unwillingness to sign blacks, his frequent hiring and firing of coaches, and his legendary stinginess, which alienated many players. In 1963 he was chosen as one of seventeen charter members of professional football's Hall of Fame. He died in Washington, D.C.

In 1969 Pete Rozelle, the NFL commissioner, eulogized Marshall as a strong and energetic man whose "fertile imagination and vision brought vital improvements to the structure and presentation of the game."

• Information on Marshall is contained in the George Preston Marshall File at the Professional Football Hall of Fame, Canton, Ohio. An informative biographical sketch appears in Arthur Daley's *Pro Football's Hall of Fame* (1963), pp. 209–21. Howard Roberts, *The Story of Pro Football* (1953), pp. 196–204; Myron Cope, *The Game That Was* (1970), pp. 113–19; and George Sullivan, *Pro Football's All-Time Greats* (1968), pp. 75–80, provide additional insights into his career and personality. Dennis J. Harrington, *The Pro Football Hall of Fame* (1991), pp. 332–34, covers Marshall's role in transferring the Redskins to Washington, D.C., and emphasizes his promotional skills. Robert H. Boyle, "All Alone by the Telephone," *Sports Illustrated*, 16 Oct. 1961, profiles him in his last years. Jack Clary, *Washington Redskins* (1974), an official team history, discusses his role in building the Redskins. The best account of his clash with federal authorities over integration is Thomas G. Smith, "Civil Rights and the Gridiron: The Kennedy Administration and the Washington Redskins," *Journal of Sport History* 14 (Summer 1987): 189–208. Obituaries are in the *New York Times, Washington Post, Los Angeles Times,* and *Washington Star,* all 10 Aug. 1969, and the *Sporting News,* 23 Aug. 1969. In a feature article, sportswriter Bob Addie evaluates Marshall's career, *Washington Post,* 10 Aug. 1969.

FRANK W. THACKERAY

MARSHALL, Humphrey (1760–26 June 1841), senator and historian of Kentucky, was born near Warrenton, Fauquier County, Virginia, the son of John Marshall and Mary Quisenberry, farmers. He received his education from family and private tutors at home and at the neighboring plantation of his uncle Thomas Marshall, the father of Chief Justice John Marshall.

At age eighteen Marshall joined Colonel Thomas Marshall's Virginia artillery regiment as a cadet. He left this militia service with the rank of captain in 1781, upon the expiration of his three-year enlistment, and the following year he was awarded 4,000 acres in Kentucky as a military land bounty. Marshall visited Kentucky in 1781 and returned to the region the following year as a deputy surveyor for Fayette County. He resided initially in Lexington and subsequently lived in Bourbon, Woodford, and Franklin counties. He established a farm at Leestown, adjacent to Frankfort, naming his home "Glen Willis." The substantial fees in land for his surveying duties and land speculation made Marshall one of the largest landowners in Kentucky. He acquired 97,316 acres, and he was sharply criticized for charging double fees on occasion. By law, patentees had to pay up in twelve months or lose their lands, providing opportunity for Marshall to then lay claim to the forfeited property.

Marshall studied law in Kentucky and became a practicing attorney. In 1784 he married his first cousin Mary (she often signed her name Anna Maria) Marshall, daughter of Thomas Marshall. They had three children, one of whom was killed by lightning in infancy.

Few men on the frontier had greater staying power in politics than Marshall, even though he embraced unpopular views. At one time or another he was the most hated man in Kentucky. He hurled biting insults at other politicians but usually came out ahead because

of his strong sense of being a gentleman and his wit, forcibly displayed by pen and oratory. His views on issues, while unpopular, often proved correct in the long run. A member of the Danville conventions of 1787 and 1789, he opposed the separation of Kentucky from Virginia until land titles and statehood were guaranteed. Attending the Virginia convention to ratify the U.S. Constitution in June 1788, Marshall was one of three of the fourteen Kentucky delegates who voted in favor of adoption, calculating that under a strong central government Kentucky would be admitted to the Union and the Mississippi River would be opened for American navigation.

Marshall became a bitter enemy of General James Wilkinson, whom he accused, along with John Brown, Benjamin Sebastian, and Harry Innes, of being involved in a "Spanish conspiracy" to detach Kentucky from the United States. He was correct as to Wilkinson and Sebastian but probably was wrong concerning the other two. Marshall denounced the scheme of the French minister Edmond Charles Genet to enlist George Rogers Clark and other Kentuckians to attack Spanish New Orleans.

Serving in the Kentucky House of Representatives from 1793 to 1794, Marshall introduced legislation simplifying the assessment and taxation of lands. Defeating John Breckinridge by a narrow vote in a legislative election for U.S. senator, Marshall served in the Senate from 4 March 1795 to 3 March 1801. Most Kentuckians were Democratic Republicans, but Marshall was a Federalist to the last. His vote for the Jay Treaty was extremely unpopular in Kentucky. Marshall was burned in effigy and stoned, and a mob seized him for the purpose of ducking him. Approaching the water, Marshall told the rioters that, since Baptists allowed their converts to tell of their experience before being immersed, he should have the same right. He so enthralled the crowd for half an hour in explaining his reasons for voting for the treaty that his hearers shouted his praise. Marshall also unsuccessfully tried to have the Senate pursue censorship measures equally against both Federalist and Republican newspapers.

Marshall was the first to expose the alleged conspiracy of Aaron Burr. Joseph Hamilton Daviess, Marshall's brother-in-law, failed in an attempt to obtain an indictment of Burr for treason in a Kentucky court. Marshall was again a member of the state legislature in 1807–1809 and in 1823, being defeated in 1810 and 1813. In January 1809 the bad blood between Marshall and Henry Clay, who had been chief counsel at the Burr hearing, came to a boiling point. Marshall cast the only vote against the legislature's condemnation of British violation of American maritime rights, and he also was one of only two delegates to oppose Clay's resolution that the legislators be required to wear homespun clothes. Marshall, attired in a British-made suit, accused Clay of demagoguery and of lying. Although a fight between the two men on the floor of the legislature was broken up, Clay challenged Marshall to a duel. The encounter took place at Shippingport, Indiana, across the Ohio River from Louisville, on 9 January 1809. One bullet slightly wounded Clay in the right thigh, and another grazed Marshall at his navel.

On 26 June 1810 Marshall began publishing the *American Republic*, the only Federalist newspaper in Kentucky. It was shortly afterward renamed the *Harbinger*. Marshall continued publishing the journal until 1825, when he sold it. The new owner issued the paper as the *Constitutional Advocate*. Fittingly Marshall's newspaper had at its masthead a rattlesnake coiled, ready to strike. In 1812 he published the *History of Kentucky*, which appeared again in 1824 in a two-volume edition. The work, the first formal and comprehensive history of the state, was valued by later historians for its wealth of information on all aspects of Kentucky's past, including its culture. If biased and controversial, Marshall's history gives colorful descriptions of people and events. In 1814 a suit for defamation brought by Judge Innes against Marshall for material appearing in the newspaper, the *Western World*, resulted in a compromise agreement that neither man would write or publish anything casting aspersions on the other. Marshall, in the 1824 revision of his *History*, did not enlarge on his derogatory remarks on Innes but retained the adverse comments of the earlier edition, because that book had been printed before the trial.

Marshall's wife died in 1824, and during his last years Marshall, who was becoming paralyzed, resided with his son, Judge Thomas A. Marshall, in Lexington. Humphrey Marshall died in Lexington.

Marshall's outspokenness alienated many Kentuckians, but his courage and intellectual ability won the grudging respect of many. In religion, notes his biographer, "He was not only an avowed disbeliever in all forms of revealed religion, but an active and aggressive enemy to them." Marshall was, in Kentucky, much like a Tory in Virginia during the American Revolution.

• The Kentucky Historical Society, Frankfort, has the Marshall Family Collection, which contains Humphrey Marshall's letterbook and miscellaneous legal and land documents. A sympathetic biography of Marshall is A. C. Quisenberry, *The Life and Times of Hon. Humphrey Marshall* (1892). The relationship between Marshall and Clay is in James F. Hopkins and Robert Seager II, eds., *The Papers of Henry Clay*, vols. 1–8 (1959–1984). For Marshall's political career, see George Chinn, *Kentucky: Settlement and Statehood, 1750–1800* (1975), which has a biographical sketch on pp. 599–606; Patricia Watlington, *The Partisan Spirit: Kentucky Politics, 1779–1792* (1972); Lowell H. Harrison, *Kentucky's Road to Statehood* (1992); and Lewis Collins, *History of Kentucky*, rev. Richard H. Collins (2 vols., 1874; rev. ed. 1966). William Littell, *Littell's Political Transactions* (1806; repr. 1926), answers Marshall's charges that certain Ky. leaders were involved in efforts to separate Ky. from the United States. For the "Spanish conspiracy," see Thomas M. Green, *The Spanish Conspiracy* (1891; repr. 1967), and Elizabeth Warren, "Benjamin Sebastian and the Spanish Conspiracy in Kentucky," *Filson Club Quarterly* 20 (1946): 107–30. A brief commentary on Marshall's *History of Kentucky* is Howard

Meredith, "The Historical Thought of Humphrey Marshall: A Note on Frontier Historicism," *Filson Club Quarterly* 47 (1973): 349–54. A death notice is in the *Louisville Daily Journal*, 9 July 1841.

HARRY M. WARD

MARSHALL, Humphry (10 Oct. 1722–5 Nov. 1801), nurseryman and botanist, was born in Chester County, Pennsylvania, the son of Abraham Marshall, a prosperous Quaker farmer, and Mary Hunt, daughter of one of the first settlers in Pennsylvania. With limited opportunities for education, the boy went to school only until his twelfth year, then worked on his father's farm until he was old enough to be apprenticed to a stonemason.

In 1748 Marshall married Sarah Pennock; they had no children. Following the marriage, Marshall took over the management of his father's farm and gave serious attention to self-education by reading widely in natural history and astronomy. When it became necessary to enlarge his father's house, where he and his wife also lived, he built a small greenhouse adjoining it to accommodate the more delicate plants he was beginning to collect. After his father's death in 1767, when he came into a comfortable inheritance, he erected a grist mill on the estate and began collecting indigenous American plants and seeds for shipment to Europe. The death of his cousin John Bartram in 1777 left him the principal supplier of American botanical material for the growing European market. Most of his shipments went to England and France, but some also were sent to Holland.

With the skills he had learned as an apprentice, Marshall built a stone house at Marshallton and surrounded it with a botanical garden that was both a nursery for his business and a horticultural retreat. There he developed a collection of exotics obtained by exchange with English garden enthusiasts such as Peter Collinson and John Fothergill, and he stocked his garden as well with native trees, shrubs, and other plants, some of which he obtained by exchange with American botanists such as Samuel Kramsh and Henry Muhlenberg. Fothergill, in gratitude for the seeds and plants he received, also sent Marshall a reflecting telescope, a microscope, and a thermometer. From the second story of Marshall's house projected a small observatory, where he made astronomical observations, principally on sun spots. He forwarded notes on these observations to both the American Philosophical Society and the Royal Society; the latter published them in its *Philosophical Transactions* (64 [1774]: 194–95). He also took an active role in community affairs, serving for a time as county treasurer.

Marshall is best remembered for his only book, *Arbustum Americanum: The American Grove*, begun about 1780 but not printed until the end of 1785 and then only with the offer of a subsidy by his friend Samuel Vaughan and the agreement of the American Philosophical Society, to whose members it was dedicated, to take forty copies. It sold so poorly that Marshall never carried out his plan to issue a second volume on the herbaceous plants. The book, which described American forest trees and shrubs, was the first volume of descriptive botany published in America by a native-born author, but its title was marred, with the first word misprinted as *Arbustrum*. Translations appeared in 1788 both in Paris and Leipzig, but both English and French commentators supposed the author to be an Englishman. More recently its title has led to the misapprehension that Marshall's garden was only an arboretum.

The *Arbustum* collected information from many authors and also included Marshall's own observations. In it, plants are listed alphabetically by the scientific name of the genus, though the Linnaean classes and orders also are given. The genera are characterized, and each species is described—all in English. Following many of the descriptions are a few words on the medical or economic uses of the plants. The most extensive discussion (pp. 125–26) is that of Marshall's curious belief that timber cut "in the spring of the year . . . and also in the third or last quarter of the moon's age" proves to be "much more durable than when cut at any other time." He explained this by the theory that sap "has a kind of monthly circulation," said to be "ascending in the moon's decrease, but descending in the increase." The book also served as a sales catalog for trees and their seeds available from Marshall's botanical garden.

Marshall's first wife died in 1786, and in 1788 he married Margaret Minshall, who long survived him. They had no children. As he grew older, Marshall came to rely more and more on the assistance of his nephew, Dr. Moses Marshall, who acted much in the role of the son he never had. In 1785 he tried to find financial support to send Moses Marshall and William Bartram to explore the westernmost parts of the nation. When this failed, Moses Marshall undertook a botanical tour from Pittsburgh south through the back country of South Carolina in 1789.

Although he was never wholly blind, cataracts greatly hampered Humphry Marshall's vision during his last years. In a bid to restore his sight, he underwent an operation at the hands of Caspar Wistar called couching, which consisted of inserting a needle to push the lens of the eye down below the line of sight; the surgery was not wholly successful. Marshall died in Marshallton, Pennsylvania.

• Most of what is known about Marshall comes from the correspondence gathered in William Darlington's *Memorials of John Bartram and Humphry Marshall . . .* (1849), to which Darlington contributed a substantial biographical sketch. As was his custom, Darlington did not hesitate to abridge many of the letters, nor did he print all of those known to him. A barrelful of Marshall's papers was destroyed in the twentieth century. The bulk of the surviving correspondence is at the Historical Society of Pennsylvania (HSP), and business papers and a few letters are at the Chester County Historical Society. The William L. Clements Library owns a number of letters written to Marshall. Supplemental to Darlington is John W. Harshberger, "Additional Letters of Humphry Marshall, Botanist and Nurseryman," *Pennsylvania Magazine of History and Biography* 53 (1929): 269–82, which gives a calendar of the HSP letters and indicates which of them were included by Darlington in his *Memorials of John Bartram and Humphry Marshall*. Joseph Ewan's introduction to the 1967 reprint of *Arbustum Americanum* is an important assessment of the book's place in the history of botany in America. See also Louise Conway Belden, "Humphry Marshall's Trade in Plants of the New World for Gardens and Forests of the Old World," *Winterthur Portfolio* 2 (1965): 106–26.

CHARLES BOEWE

MARSHALL, James Wilson (8 Oct. 1810–10 Aug. 1885), discoverer of gold in California, was born in the vicinity of Marshall's Corner in present-day Mercer County, New Jersey, the son of Philip Marshall, a coach and wagonmaker, and Sarah Wilson. He was educated in private schools, and under the tutelage of his father, he became a wheelwright and carpenter; he also learned something about lumbering and sawmills. Seeking adventure and fortune, he started west in 1834. A shortage of funds forced brief stops in Crawfordsville, Indiana, and Warsaw, Illinois, where he earned money as a carpenter before moving on to Omaha. There he worked as a wheelwright and entered the employment of the American Fur Company, which had a trading post at nearby Bellevue. When the Platte Purchase near Fort Leavenworth was opened for settlement, he preempted and subsequently purchased 140 acres and gained a frontage on the east bank of the Missouri River. Plagued by fever and illness, he sold the land and livestock in 1844 and joined an overland emigrant group en route to Oregon, arriving at Fort Vancouver before the end of the year.

Early the next summer, he went to California with the James Clyman party and by mid-July was at Sutter's Fort, where he was employed by Johann Augustus Sutter as a carpenter and wheelwright. From Samuel J. Hensley, Marshall purchased almost two square leagues of land out of the Aguas Nieves grant. His ranch was in the northern part of the Sacramento Valley, with Butte Creek flowing along its eastern border. Marshall stocked the ranch with cattle and erected a cabin. In 1846 he joined the Bear Flaggers in their revolt against Mexico, and when the Stars and Stripes were raised in California, he fought in the California Battalion. At the end of the fighting, he made his way north from San Gabriel and found that his place had been pillaged and his cattle and horses either had been stolen or had strayed away.

Sutter reemployed him, and the two men became partners in the construction of a sawmill on the South Fork of the American River in the Coloma Valley. While Sutter financed construction, Marshall oversaw the building and the operation of the mill, which was built on Indian land wholly outside the boundaries of Sutter's Mexican land grant. As the sawmill neared completion, Marshall picked up gold in the millrace on 24 January 1848. An effort was made to keep the discovery quiet for a time, but that was impossible. By late spring the stampede was on. Sutter sold his interests in the sawmill, and the new partners of Marshall did a splendid business in 1849 and 1850, but thereafter operations virtually ceased and the mill was gradually dismantled or fell into disrepair. Marshall's preemption claim was ignored, and Sutter's place was overrun by prospectors and miners. Neither of the two men profited from the gold discovery.

Marshall embarked on prospecting adventures. A believer in Spiritualism, he thought the spirits would guide him to rich gold deposits. This never happened, and he repeatedly returned to his carpentry skills as a reliable way of supporting himself. In 1853 he sold the ranch that he had acquired from Hensley and later bought fifteen acres on the slope of a hill on the south side of the town of Coloma. There he built a cabin and began growing grapes and making wine. While he received recognition for the quality of his fruit, he found that the vineyard was too small to yield a livelihood. His cabin was destroyed by fire in 1862, and he was convinced that it was the work of an arsonist who wished to destroy his valuable papers, especially those documenting him as the first discoverer of gold in California. There had been some challenges to his claim, and he became bitter over the attempt to rob him of the honor as he had been robbed of his land claim on the South Fork. Ruefully, he noted that the discoverer of gold in Australia had been liberally rewarded by both the British and Australian governments, whereas by contrast, he had lost all.

As a veteran of the Mexican War, he applied for and received in 1865 a bounty land warrant for 160 acres, but he never took up land. In 1871 when he became stranded in Kansas City, Missouri, en route to New Jersey to visit his aged mother and three surviving sisters, he paid a delinquent hotel bill with the warrant. He seems never to have applied for a veteran's pension. As his poverty deepened, friends attempted to help by arranging lecture tours and by having his life story published. Marshall was a disaster on the platform, however, and George Frederic Parsons's *The Life and Adventures of James W. Marshall* was full of hokum and sold poorly. In 1872 the state of California granted Marshall a pension but refused to renew it in 1878 because he was seen too frequently in the saloons.

As seen daily about Coloma and Kelsey, "Marshall was an unattractive and awkward appearing man, shabbily dressed, careless in his personal habits, inclined to be morose and moody, embittered toward the world, quite willing to let his belief in spiritualism guide his activities, yet an ingenious person, honest, kind-hearted, sometimes industrious, and faithful—a strange character in all" (Gay, p. 340).

Marshall died in Kelsey, where he had interests in mining property and where he had been residing since the late 1860s. The body was taken to Coloma, three miles distant, for burial atop the hill where he had once cultivated grapes and where a tall monument was dedicated in his honor in 1890. It depicts Marshall holding a piece of gold in the open palm of his right hand; the index finger of his left hand points to the spot on the South Fork of the American River a half-mile away where he picked up the first piece of gold that electrified the world.

• Theressa Gay, *James W. Marshall, the Discoverer of California Gold: A Biography* (1967), brings together the widely scattered and fragmentary source material relating to Marshall.

MARY LEE SPENCE

MARSHALL, John (24 Sept. 1755–6 July 1835), fourth chief justice of the United States, was born near Germantown, Prince William (now Fauquier) County, Virginia, the son of Thomas Marshall and Mary Randolph Keith. The eldest of fifteen children, John Marshall grew up in the foothills of the Blue Ridge Mountains. His father was a planter of middling circumstances whose success in land speculation made him one of the leading men of Fauquier, then a frontier county. His mother, a clergyman's daughter, was related to such "first families" of Virginia as the Randolphs and the Lees. Thomas Marshall superintended his son's education, giving him, as John Marshall recalled later, "an early taste for history and for poetry." As the youth's "only intelligent companion," the elder Marshall "was both a watchfull parent and an affectionate instructive friend" (Adams, ed., p. 4).

At age fourteen Marshall spent a year at a school in Westmoreland County, followed by a year of study at home with the local parish priest who temporarily resided with the family. These two years were the extent of Marshall's formal schooling before the outbreak of the War of Independence, during which he acquired the rudiments of a classical education and was able to begin reading Horace and Livy. As important as formal instruction was Marshall's exposure to the informal "curriculum" of the colonial Virginia gentry, an unexcelled practical school for training future American statesmen. Through observing his father in his various roles as surveyor, justice of the peace, sheriff, vestryman, militia leader, and burgess of the county, Marshall acquired the values and habits of a Virginia gentleman and gained admittance to the most famous ruling class America has produced.

At the onset of hostilities with Great Britain, Marshall put aside the classics and Sir William Blackstone's *Commentaries on the Laws of England* (1765–1769), which he apparently had begun to read before the war. When war broke out, he took up arms, first as an officer of the county militia, then as an officer in the Virginia line of the Continental army. He participated in the battles of Brandywine Creek, Germantown, Monmouth, and Stony Point. He also survived the harsh winter's encampment at Valley Forge in 1777–1778. The war was a formative experience, for he associated "with brave men from different states who were risking life and everything valuable in a common cause . . . and was confirmed in the habit of considering America as my country, and congress my government" (Adams, ed., pp. 9–10).

During an interlude in the war, in the spring and summer of 1780, Marshall attended a course of lectures on law and natural philosophy at the College of

William and Mary. The newly appointed professor of law was George Wythe, Thomas Jefferson's law mentor and an eminent judge. Wythe's lectures occurred twice a week over several months, supplemented by monthly moot court exercises and individual tutorial sessions. The term at William and Mary constituted Marshall's only formal study of law, but at the time formal instruction was not the ordinary means of legal education. Law was a practical profession, for which most aspirants prepared by apprenticeship to a practicing attorney. Marshall's law course with Professor Wythe supplemented his own self-education, which began before and certainly continued after his college attendance.

Whatever mastery of the law Marshall had gained by the time he left the college in the summer of 1780 was sufficient to qualify him for a law license. Full of ambition and talent to match, he rapidly ascended the professional ladder, particularly after moving permanently to Richmond, the state capital, in 1784. There he joined the small fraternity of lawyers who practiced in the superior courts of the state. By the end of the 1780s his reputation placed him at the top of the bar, and his income grew commensurately. In 1783 he married Mary Willis Ambler, known to him throughout his life as "dearest Polly," a daughter of the state treasurer. They had ten children, of whom five sons and a daughter survived to adulthood.

In 1782 Marshall was elected to the House of Delegates, the first of several terms he served as a legislator during that decade. The questions agitating the public mind in those years, he later recalled, were "paper money, the collection of taxes, the preservation of public faith, and the administration of justice. . . . The state of the Confederacy was also a subject of deep solicitude." On these issues Marshall followed the lead of James Madison, "the enlightened advocate of Union and of an efficient federal government" (Adams, ed., pp. 7–8). All the important public questions of the 1780s were subsumed in the debate over the Constitution in 1787 and 1788. Marshall actively participated in this debate, most importantly as a delegate to the state ratifying convention of June 1788. His principal contribution to the cause of ratification was a speech defending the judiciary article, in the course of which he assumed that courts would have power to pronounce invalid a law that was contrary to the Constitution. If Congress "were to make a law not warranted by any of the powers enumerated, it would be considered by the Judges as an infringement of the Constitution which they are to guard: They would not consider such a law as coming under their jurisdiction. They would declare it void" (Johnson et al., eds., vol. 1, p. 277). Thus did the future chief justice give early expression to the idea that judges should be guardians of the Constitution.

From the time the new government went into effect in 1789 until his judicial appointment twelve years later, Marshall made occasional forays into the public arena that gained him further valuable experience in constitutional dialectics. Pressed to run for Congress or to accept a federal office, including appointments as attorney general and associate justice of the Supreme Court, he resolutely declined all such offers. He could not yet afford to give up his lucrative law practice, which expanded to include business in the new federal courts. Politics constantly beckoned during the decade of the 1790s, however, as divisions over financial and foreign policy gave birth to an opposition party, the Republicans, led by Jefferson and Madison. There was never any question that Marshall, whose association (through his father) with George Washington dated from before the Revolution, would remain unswervingly loyal to the president.

Marshall's role as defender of the administration and unofficial leader of the Federalist party in Virginia first became public in the summer of 1793, when he drew up a series of resolutions condemning the conduct of French minister Edmond Genêt, who in defiance of American neutrality attempted to fit out privateers in American ports to attack British shipping. He also published pseudonymous newspaper pieces praising the president and his neutrality policy. Two years later Marshall again found himself in the midst of partisan warfare, this time over the controversial commercial treaty with Great Britain negotiated by John Jay. Jay's Treaty provoked such bitter opposition that for a time it appeared the House of Representatives would withhold appropriations to implement the treaty. Marshall, now back in the state legislature, boldly defended the treaty's constitutionality, and at a public meeting in Richmond he persuaded a majority to adopt resolutions in favor of giving full effect to the treaty. The House subsequently voted the necessary appropriations. These efforts attracted notice beyond the borders of Virginia, as an account of Marshall's speech in the legislature was published widely in newspapers. Early in 1796 he went to Philadelphia to make his only appearance as a lawyer before the Supreme Court, arguing the celebrated "British debts" case, *Ware v. Hylton*, which he lost. In Philadelphia Marshall was cordially received by leading northern Federalists, such as Fisher Ames, Theodore Sedgwick, and Rufus King.

Having turned down several federal offices, Marshall in June 1797 accepted President John Adams's appointment to a commission, which included Charles Cotesworth Pinckney and Elbridge Gerry, to settle outstanding differences with the revolutionary Republic of France. Although the mission failed because the French refused to enter into negotiations until the United States agreed to a loan and payment of a bribe to high officials of the revolutionary government, it proved to be a personal triumph for Marshall. His dispatches reporting the commissioners' steadfast refusal to compromise American sovereignty and independence and detailing the intrigues and insulting behavior of the wily French foreign minister Talleyrand (Charles-Maurice de Talleyrand-Périgord) and his anonymous agents, "X," "Y," and "Z," created a sensation when published in the newspapers back home.

On arriving in New York in June 1798, Marshall was acclaimed a national hero.

Soon thereafter, at General Washington's urging, Marshall became a candidate for Congress. From December 1799 to May 1800 he served in the Sixth Congress, distinguishing himself in the debates of that notable session as a formidable spokesman for the Adams administration. In March 1800 he delivered the greatest speech (apart from his judicial opinions) of his career, a defense of the president's conduct in handing over an accused murderer, who claimed to be an American seaman impressed into British service, to British authorities. Marshall presented a masterly defense of the president's action as properly within the sphere of the executive's authority to carry out the terms of national treaties.

For this great forensic effort, Adams rewarded Marshall with a place in his cabinet. From May 1800 through the remainder of Adams's term, Marshall served as secretary of state. Though he administered that department for less than a year, he made a valuable contribution, notably in forwarding negotiations with Great Britain concerning prerevolutionary debts owed to British subjects. Besides carrying out his official duties, he acted as Adams's confidential adviser, drafting the president's annual message to Congress and counseling him on the numerous judicial appointments that marked the final days of his presidency. Among the latter was the chief justiceship of the United States, made vacant by the resignation of Oliver Ellsworth. Adams's first choice, Jay, who had served as the first chief justice, declined. Not wishing to delay further and risk letting the appointment fall to his Republican successor, Adams tendered the appointment in person to Marshall, who "was pleased as well as surprized, and bowed in silence" (Adams, ed., p. 30). He was confirmed by the Senate on 27 January 1801, a little more than a month before he administered the oath of office to President Jefferson.

Marshall was a happy choice to fill the highest judicial office in the land. Intermittent though it was prior to 1801, his participation in public life occurred at times and places that in retrospect appear to have been nicely calculated to prepare him for his role on the Supreme Court. In the area of public law, and constitutional law in particular, his training could not have been better. He came to the bench thoroughly versed in the political processes and workings of the federal and state governments; he understood as well as anyone the nature and boundaries of legislative, executive, and judicial power. "Experience of men and affairs" in various public offices "doubtless reinforced a temperament to which abstract theorizing was never congenial," wrote a twentieth-century judge who admired Marshall's "hardheaded appreciation of the complexities of government, particularly in a federal system" (Kurland, ed., p. 145).

It is clear, too, that Marshall could not have effectively led the Court without a sound grasp of law acquired over nearly twenty years of practice in the state and federal courts. Contrary to popular myth, which portrays the chief justice as wanting in legal learning, Marshall's proficiency in the science was worthy of one who occupied his high judicial station. Close associates acknowledged his profound and comprehensive knowledge of English common law and equity jurisprudence, the foundation upon which American law grew and developed. The chief justiceship, observed an associate, was "the very post where weakness and ignorance and timidity must instantly betray themselves and sink to their natural level" (Story, p. 373).

Along with a solid knowledge and understanding of law, Marshall was endowed with a first-rate mind that could simultaneously grasp a subject in its entirety, analyze its constituent parts, and understand their relation to the whole. Contemporaries marveled at his quick and discerning comprehension, his extraordinary ability to extract the essence of law from particular cases. The clear, precise, mathematical quality of his mind was reflected in legal arguments and opinions that moved progressively from premise to conclusion with the logic and rigor of a geometric proof, omitting all superfluous matter. An abundance of charm and sociability also served him well as chief justice. During Court terms the justices roomed and boarded together, and professional and social life blended into one. In the convivial atmosphere of the dinner table or in conversation over a glass of Madeira, the chief was able to achieve a working consensus among his brethren. An engaging intellectual humility enabled him to defer, when necessary, to the superior learning of others. As much as he commanded respect by his own formidable intellect, the key to Marshall's leadership lay in his openness to argument and persuasion, his willingness to subordinate his own views if necessary to obtain a single opinion of the Court. If the Court most often spoke through the chief justice, the opinion was the product of collaborative deliberation, carried out in a spirit of mutual concession and accommodation.

Marshall not only presided over the Supreme Court but also sat on the U.S. circuit courts for Virginia and North Carolina. For more than three decades he marched to the rhythms of various court seasons: winters in Washington to attend the Supreme Court and spring and fall circuits in Richmond and Raleigh. Enjoying unusually good health until late in life, the chief justice was present at every Supreme Court term and rarely missed a circuit throughout his long career.

The dominant theme of Marshall's early years on the bench was conflict between the federal judiciary and the new Republican political majority that controlled the legislative and executive branches. Among the first acts of the new Congress was the repeal of the Judiciary Act of 1801, which abolished in one stroke the host of new judgeships, the so-called "midnight judges," filled by Adams's appointees. Despite serious reservations about the constitutionality of this action, Marshall and his fellow Supreme Court justices acquiesced in the repeal.

On the other hand, in the case of *Marbury v. Madison* (1803), which arose directly out of the refusal of the Jefferson administration to deliver a commission to a justice of the peace appointed by Adams, the Court sternly rebuked the executive for failing to perform its duty. This was the first occasion in which the Supreme Court pronounced a law of Congress unconstitutional, though the most controversial aspect of the case at the time was the Court's alleged meddling in the affairs of the executive department. *Marbury* was followed soon after by the impeachment and conviction of a federal judge and the impeachment of Supreme Court associate justice Samuel Chase, notorious for using his judicial pulpit to air his highly partisan Federalist views. The Senate's acquittal of Chase early in 1805 signified a triumph of moderation, however, and introduced a period of accommodation, if not harmony, between the judicial and political branches. Conflict did break out anew during the celebrated treason trial of Aaron Burr, which took place in Marshall's circuit court in Richmond in the summer of 1807. By then the concept of an independent judiciary had more or less gained general acceptance. Subjected to occasional verbal assaults, the federal judiciary not only survived intact but in subsequent years consolidated its independence and expanded its powers.

After 1807 relations between the administration and the judiciary improved, reflecting changes in court personnel and a shared commitment to upholding national power. In return for dutifully enforcing the government's embargo policy, the judiciary received timely support from Madison's administration when the state of Pennsylvania openly resisted the Supreme Court's decree in *United States v. Peters* (1809). Fortified by this endorsement of federal judicial power against an assertion of states' rights, the Supreme Court in 1810 for the first time nullified a state law as repugnant to the Constitution. The same case, *Fletcher v. Peck*, was also the first of a line of decisions interpreting the contract clause of the Constitution.

During his first decade on the bench, Marshall announced several characteristic themes of his constitutional jurisprudence. In the landmark *Marbury* opinion, he sought to define the "province of the judiciary" by positing a distinction between the spheres of "law" and "politics," according to which the judiciary refused to take jurisdiction over "questions, in their nature political" and confined itself to deciding upon the legal rights of individuals. The separation of law and politics was the fundamental proposition underlying Marshall's jurisprudence, one that in attenuated form continues to influence our perception of the Supreme Court as an institution elevated above and insulated from the political arena. In contending that withholding Marbury's commission was "violative of a vested legal right," the chief justice introduced another resonant theme, namely the idea that judicial power is peculiarly charged with protecting the "vested rights" of individuals, rights deemed so fundamental as to be beyond the control of government in ordinary circumstances.

Marbury is most celebrated for invalidating a law of Congress—specifically Section 13 of the Judiciary Act of 1789, which authorized the Supreme Court to issue writs of mandamus to government officers. The Court held this provision to be void on the ground that it enlarged the Court's original jurisdiction beyond the terms prescribed by the Constitution. Marshall justified this assertion of "judicial review" on the simple but profound idea that the Constitution was a "law," created by the American people acting in their highest sovereign capacity, that judges were bound to uphold and enforce in preference to an ordinary statute. In 1803 the doctrine of judicial review was neither novel nor highly controversial, having gained increasing acceptance among the American people during the previous two decades. Marshall merely reaffirmed the doctrine as founded in the joining together of the ideas of popular sovereignty and fundamental law in a written constitution. His principal contribution as chief justice was to solidify the practice of judicial review by adapting the methods of common law interpretation to the task of expounding the Constitution.

For Marshall, judicial review did not imply any claim to judicial supremacy or monopoly in interpreting the Constitution. Legislative and executive constructions of that instrument, he did not deny, must prevail in all cases that did not take the form of a legal dispute to be decided in a court of law. He acknowledged, moreover, that a court would have to be persuaded beyond a reasonable doubt before pronouncing a law void. As employed by the Marshall Court, judicial review was primarily a defensive weapon to preserve the independence of the judiciary, to resist encroachments by the states on the national government, and to protect private rights against infringement by acts of government (mainly state). Except for *Marbury*, the Marshall Court exercised judicial review exclusively against acts of the state legislatures.

Most of Marshall's great constitutional opinions occurred between 1810 and 1824, years in which the Court enjoyed remarkable stability and harmony. Although by 1811 five Republican appointees had joined Marshall on the bench, party affiliations among the justices were virtually meaningless. The Court's internal unity, fostered by the chief justice's effective leadership and by agreement on basic values embodied in the Constitution, was the precondition of its rise to preeminence as the guardian of the fundamental law and the umpire of the American federal system.

Chief Justice Marshall invoked judicial review to restrict state sovereignty in two broad categories of cases. In one a state law was declared to have violated a specific constitutional prohibition or restraint on state power; in the other the law was held to be incompatible with federal supremacy. In the first category the prohibition against laws "impairing the Obligation of Contracts" supplied the Court with its principal weapon for protecting the vested rights of individuals. Under Marshall's expansive reading, the contract clause performed a function similar to that later undertaken by the Fourteenth Amendment and by the application of the Bill of Rights to the states. Before the twentieth century the Bill of Rights restrained only the federal government, as Marshall himself declared in one of his last opinions, *Barron v. Baltimore* (1833). Yet to a remarkable degree his broad reading of the contract clause succeeded in making the original Constitution serve as a "bill of rights for the people of each state," protecting them from the acts of their state governments.

Fletcher was the first of a series of opinions in which Chief Justice Marshall brought state legislation within the contract clause's prohibition. In disallowing an act of the Georgia legislature that rescinded the state's sale of its vast "Yazoo" lands to various land companies, he held that the term *contract* embraced public grants of land. In *Dartmouth College v. Woodward* (1819) he brought corporate charters within the clause's protection, striking down the New Hampshire legislature's attempt to revoke the college's colonial charter and reorganize that institution as a state university. In *Sturges v. Crowninshield* (1819) the chief justice declared that state bankruptcy laws discharging a debtor from full liability unconstitutionally impaired the obligation of contract. The offending law in this case was retrospective, enacted after the contract had been executed. Marshall insisted that prospective bankruptcy laws were also unconstitutional, but a majority of the Court upheld such laws in *Ogden v. Saunders* (1827). In a powerful opinion, his only dissent in a constitutional case, the chief justice contended that the prohibition was expressed in general and comprehensive terms, that it proscribed all bankruptcy laws, no matter when adopted, and that the obligation of contract was founded in nature, not on the laws of civil society.

The cumulative effect of Marshall's contract clause decisions was to fortify the practice of judicial review based on written fundamental law. According to his understanding of the doctrine, unwritten principles of "natural justice" could never provide a satisfactory rationale for judicial annulment of a law. As a judge Marshall strove to reconcile text-based judicial review with natural law, testing statutes against the standard of a written constitution while finding in that text—notably the contract clause—ample protection for fundamental rights. In applying this clause to public grants, corporate charters, and bankruptcy laws, the chief justice denied that he was enlarging its scope beyond what the framers of the Constitution intended. That intention, he insisted, could only be derived from the actual words of the instrument. The general language of the contract clause manifested an intention to embrace not only the particular evils contemplated at the time the Constitution was adopted but also unforeseen cases that might arise as a result of legislative ingenuity. The application of the clause to such cases depended on what Marshall called a "fair construction" of the Constitution. Although he had no doubt that the purpose of the clause was to impose a great barrier to state interferences with vested rights of property and contract, he never regarded it as a general prohibition against unwise or obnoxious laws. As shown by *Providence Bank v. Billings* (1830), which upheld a tax imposed on a state-chartered bank, he rejected specious arguments that would have severely hampered the ability of state governments to perform their functions.

In addition to giving a broad reading to the prohibitions on state power, Chief Justice Marshall employed with equal effect the principle of national supremacy to limit state sovereignty. His leading "federalism" decisions were *McCulloch v. Maryland* (1819), which upheld Congress's power to charter a national bank while invalidating a state law laying a tax on the bank; *Cohens v. Virginia* (1821), which articulated an enlarged conception of federal judicial power while reaffirming the Supreme Court's appellate jurisdiction over state judiciaries; and *Gibbons v. Ogden* (1824), which expansively defined Congress's power to regulate interstate commerce while striking down a New York law creating a monopoly over steamboat navigation on the state's waters.

In these opinions Marshall presented a masterly statement of constitutional nationalism, advancing a series of propositions that ultimately became settled principles of American constitutional law. The Constitution, he premised, was the constituent act of the people of the United States, not a compact among sovereign states. It created a real government, one of enumerated powers yet supreme within the sphere of action allotted to it. As merely a general outline, designating only the important objects, this instrument was to be construed in an enlarged or liberal sense, not in a restrictive sense appropriate to a detailed legal code. The grant of enumerated powers was to be understood as conferring upon the general government ample discretion to choose the means for executing its express powers. The Constitution also conferred upon the federal judiciary broad jurisdiction to decide cases arising under the Constitution and laws of the United States and imposed the duty of preserving federal law as the "supreme law of the land." The Supreme Court was accordingly empowered not only to nullify state laws that were repugnant to federal law but also to overrule decisions of state courts that failed to preserve federal supremacy.

By upholding the exercise of national power, striking down state laws, and asserting a supervisory role over the state courts, Chief Justice Marshall roused the spirit of antifederalism and states' rights, nowhere with greater intensity than in his own state of Virginia. Led by Judge Spencer Roane of the Virginia Court of Appeals, critics accused the Court of converting a government of limited powers into a "consolidated" government, reducing the states to nullities. The censures of *McCulloch*, in particular, so alarmed Marshall that in the spring and summer of 1819 he took the unprecedented step of defending that opinion in a series of pseudonymous essays for the press. The aftermath of *McCulloch* and *Cohens* saw periodic attempts in Congress to curb the powers of the federal judiciary. That none of these measures succeeded signified an underlying agreement among the American people to preserve the integrity of the institution.

This consensus (clear enough in retrospect, if not to Marshall and his brethren) did not, to be sure, spare the Court from occasional political controversy. During the last decade of his tenure, Marshall continually met with serious challenges to his vision of union and national power and of the role of the Supreme Court as arbiter of the Constitution. Whether by coincidence or for reasons of political expediency, the Supreme Court began to render decisions more favorable to state power. In *Willson v. Blackbird Marsh Company* (1829), a commerce clause case, and again in *Providence Bank v. Billings*, a contract case, the Court upheld the state law in question. In his last constitutional opinion, *Barron v. Baltimore*, Marshall ruled that the Bill of Rights restricted only the federal government, not the state governments.

The internal unity of the Court also began to break down during the last years, a reflection of the chief's diminishing hold over a Court that was also changing with the addition of new members. Not only did separate and dissenting opinions appear more frequently, but after 1830 the justices' communal living arrangements came to an end. Even when the Court did strike down state laws, as in *Craig v. Missouri* (1830) and in *Worcester v. Georgia* (1832), Marshall was unable to restore the old harmony. The latter case, in which the rights of the Cherokee Indians clashed with the asserted sovereignty of the state of Georgia, underscored the impotence of the Supreme Court to check determined political majorities.

The erosion of the Court's unity coincided with and seemed to be symptomatic of a larger crisis of union that overshadowed Marshall's final years on the bench. Nothing portended the mortality of the Constitution and the Union more ominously than the doctrine of "nullification," by which the states claimed the right to declare federal laws unconstitutional and nullify their operation. Marshall regarded this idea as so "extravagant in itself, and so repugnant to the existence of Union between the States" that he could scarcely "believe it was seriously entertained by any person." At the height of the nullification crisis in 1832, the aging jurist confided that he was yielding "slowly and reluctantly to the conviction that our constitution cannot last." He foresaw the end of a Union that had "been prolonged thus far by miracles."

Although his health began to fail after he reached the age of seventy-five, Marshall's intellectual powers remained undiminished to the day he died. In the fall of 1831 the chief justice underwent successful surgery in Philadelphia for the removal of bladder stones. He recovered so quickly that a month later he was able to hold circuit in Richmond. Not long after, however, his beloved Polly died, leaving him to mourn her loss for the few years remaining of his life. In June 1835, suffering from a liver ailment, Marshall again sought medical treatment in Philadelphia. He died in that city a few weeks later.

Marshall's life from 1801 to 1835 was by no means all courts and cases. Attending five relatively short Court terms a year left ample time for other pursuits and avocations. In the midst of the judiciary crisis of his first years in office, Marshall composed *The Life of George Washington*, a massive life and times of the late general published in five volumes between 1804 and 1807. He always regretted having written the *Life* in such great haste and allowing it to be rushed into print without sufficient time for revision. The preparation of an abridged second edition occupied his attention for much of the rest of his life. A historian and writer himself, Marshall was fond of literature and looked forward to a retirement in which he would "read nothing but novels and poetry." He took delight in Jane Austen and recommended her as "pleasing, interesting, equable, and yet amusing."

Nor did judicial duties prevent Marshall from answering an occasional call to public service on behalf of his state. In 1812 the legislature appointed him chairman of a commission to survey a water and land route to connect the eastern and western regions of the state. After leading an expedition to the falls of the Kanawha River (in present-day W.Va.), he prepared a report that became a landmark in the history of internal improvements in Virginia. At the age of seventy-four, in 1829, Marshall participated in the Virginia constitutional convention. There he proved to be an able and impassioned defender of the principle of judicial independence, having "grown old in the opinion, that there is nothing more dear to Virginia, or ought to be dearer to her statesmen."

In addition to long summer vacations in the mountains, Marshall spent many idle hours at his farm just outside Richmond. In town he enjoyed the company of a close circle of family and friends, regularly hosting lawyers' dinners in his home and attending Saturday meetings of the Barbecue Club, where he liked to imbibe punch laced with brandy, rum, and Madeira and display his skill at pitching quoits. Secure in his place as a member of the Virginia gentry, Marshall exuded warmth and good humor in his personal and social relations. In his unaffected modesty, polite but informal manner, plain attire, and easy familiarity with social inferiors, he fully lived up to the ideal of a republican gentleman. More so than Jefferson, his great democratic rival, he possessed the common touch. A frequent sight in Richmond was the chief justice, basket in hand, doing the family marketing.

The events of his last years, which in his darker moments made Marshall despair for the future of the Union and the Constitution, undoubtedly cast a shadow that obscured from his view the great accomplishments of his judicial statesmanship. Under his leadership the Supreme Court evolved into a far more powerful institution than it had been in 1801. It successfully assumed its peculiar function as the preeminent interpreter and guardian of the Constitution and as the arbiter of conflicts arising from the clash of federal and state sovereignties. In a series of notable opinions, Marshall construed the Constitution so as to give full effect to the enumerated powers conferred on the federal government and to the restraints and prohibitions placed on the state governments. He articulated a constitutional vision that in the late nineteenth and twentieth centuries facilitated the creation of the mighty nation-state the United States became. Yet consolidation of national power was not his conscious design. Marshall did not seek to enlarge federal powers by construction but to enable the general government to operate effectively, with supreme authority within its assigned sphere. His constitutional jurisprudence was essentially defensive in character, not looking to build up a powerful federal state but to protect and defend the general government against persistent antifederal forces that imperiled the "more perfect Union" formed by the Constitution of 1787.

• Marshall's surviving correspondence is scattered among many collections, the largest of which is at the College of William and Mary. *The Papers of John Marshall*, ed. Herbert A. Johnson et al. (8 vols., 1974–1995), is a comprehensive annotated edition of correspondence, legal papers, and miscellaneous papers. Still useful printed collections of correspondence include Charles C. Smith, ed., "Letters of Chief Justice Marshall," *Proceedings of the Massachusetts Historical Society*, 2d ser., 14 (1900): 320–60, and Charles Warren, "The Story-Marshall Correspondence (1819–1831)," *William and Mary Quarterly*, 2d ser., 21 (1941): 1–26. Marshall's autobiographical letter to Joseph Story, written in 1827, has been separately published in *An Autobiographical Sketch by John Marshall*, ed. John Stokes Adams (1937). An invaluable guide to Marshall documents is Irwin S. Rhodes, *The Papers of John Marshall: A Descriptive Calendar* (2 vols., 1969). Marshall's Supreme Court opinions were originally published in William Cranch, *Reports of Cases Argued and Adjudged in the Supreme Court of the United States (1801–15)* (9 vols., 1804–1817); Henry Wheaton, *Reports of Cases Argued and Adjudged in the Supreme Court (1816–27)* (12 vols., 1816–1827); and Richard Peters, Jr., *Reports of Cases Argued and Adjudged in the Supreme Court of the United States, from 1828–1843, Inclusive* (17 vols., 1828–1843), which were later incorporated into the ongoing official *United States Reports*. Among numerous anthologies of his principal opinions, the most comprehensive is Joseph P. Cotton, Jr., ed., *The Constitutional Decisions of John Marshall* (2 vols., 1905). Albert J. Beveridge, *The Life of John Marshall* (4 vols., 1916–1919), is woefully dated but remains the classic life and times. A more recent full-length biography is Jean Edward Smith, *John Marshall: Definer of a Nation* (1996). The best short biography is Francis N. Stites, *John Marshall: Defender of the Constitution* (1981). See also Philip B. Kurland, ed., *James Bradley Thayer, Oliver Wendell Holmes, and Felix Frankfurter on John Marshall* (1967). For a portrait of Marshall's mind see Joseph Story, "A Discourse upon the Life, Character, and Services of the Honorable John Marshall," in *John Marshall: Life, Character, and Judicial Services*, vol. 3, ed. John F. Dillon (3 vols., 1903). The most thorough study of Marshall's thought is Robert Kenneth Faulkner, *The Jurisprudence of John Marshall* (1968). See also Charles F. Hobson, *The Great Chief Justice: John Marshall and the Rule of Law* (1996).

CHARLES F. HOBSON

MARSHALL, Louis (7 Oct. 1773–Apr. 1866), physician and college president, was born Lewis Marshall on the family estate, "Oak Hill," in Fauquier County, Virginia, the son of Colonel Thomas Marshall, a military leader and surveyor, and Mary Randolph Keith. Louis, the eleventh of fifteen children, was a brother of Chief Justice John Marshall. In 1785 the family moved to the "Buckpond" estate, in Woodford Coun-

ty, Kentucky. During 1793–1794 Marshall studied medicine in Philadelphia and then departed for medical and literary studies in Edinburgh (1794–1795) and medical and surgical training in Paris (1795–1798). Meanwhile, he changed his name to the French, "Louis."

A curious account of Marshall's Paris days has been carried by most biographers. The story depicts Marshall being taken up with the French Revolution, participating in the storming of the Bastille, being arrested, languishing in prison for some time, being condemned to death, and then gaining release through the efforts of his brothers, John and James, American envoys to Paris. Although John Marshall was in Paris from 1797 to 1798, Leonard Baker notes that "in all of the John Marshall correspondence while he was in Paris, there is no reference to any brother, and it is difficult to accept that he could see his brother Louis after a separation lasting years and rescue him from prison without mentioning it in a letter" (*John Marshall: A Life in Law* [1974], p. 293). Nothing confirms this "Paris" account, although Marshall may have encountered the law as the consequence of his duels ("He was a dead-shot and an accomplished swordsman, and possessed wonderful coolness and nerve in a fight" [Ruffner, p. 93]). Since Louis Marshall "would never suffer any one to refer to his career in Paris" (Paxton, p. 69), the truth may never be known about what actually happened.

Back in Kentucky, Marshall practiced medicine and "attained the name of the most learned and successful physician in the State" (Paxton, p. 69). In 1800 he married Agatha Smith, receiving the Buckpond estate as a wedding gift. The Marshalls had five boys and one girl. Marshall continued the practice of medicine through at least the late 1810s. At some point, however, he put aside his medical instruments in favor of setting up Buckpond Academy, offering a classical education for Kentucky's favored sons. William Paxton, whose stepmother was Marshall's niece, notes that "he was a fine linguist, and well read in science, history, philosophy. . . . He was a strict disciplinarian—severe and dogmatic in his style" (p. 69).

In 1830 Marshall became the fourth president of Washington College (now Washington and Lee University) in Lexington, Virginia. There at one time enrollment had reached sixty-five students, but for the previous three years fewer than twenty had attended. Opposing the existing traditional format, Marshall implemented a permissive disciplinary routine and a self-paced tutorial system similar to his own Edinburgh experience—a striking contrast to his rigorous disciplinary procedures while teaching at Buckpond. This four-year educational experiment failed for various reasons, not the least of which was a continuing battle with Henry Ruffner. Ruffner had been acting president of Washington College, was the sole faculty member when Marshall arrived, and was displaced as the professor of languages by Marshall. As a result of their conflicting personalities and philosophies, in the words of Ruffner's son, "War, of course, was inevitable" (Ruffner, p. 2). The following year, attendance increased to thirty-nine, but in 1832 another drastic downturn precipitated the board's inquiry into making curriculum changes. Soon even the trustees did not support Marshall, and at one point they held back his paycheck. Defeated and discouraged, Marshall left Virginia at the end of the school year in 1834, without a word of explanation, to return to his Kentucky scholars at Buckpond. Ruffner then resumed the duties of president.

Marshall, the first non-clergy president of Washington, had conducted himself there as a faithful Presbyterian and firm believer in Christianity even though he had been a religious skeptic during his early years. He gave the Sunday morning lecture, normally reserved for a ministerial member of the faculty, usually to expound his favorite topic, biblical prophecy. His studies led him to fix the date for when the world would come to an end, which turned out to be the year of his own demise. Marshall was active in the American Bible Society, the American Colonization Society (antislavery), and the temperance movement.

A few years after leaving Washington College, Marshall became Morrison Professor of Languages at another Presbyterian school, Transylvania University in Lexington, Kentucky, where he served as acting president from 1838 to 1840. Little is known of his tenure there. Apparently he remained a faculty member until his wife died in 1844. Subsequently he traveled extensively among his relations, tutoring their children during each stay. At about the age of ninety, Marshall confided in a former student, "My son Tom said to me not long ago, 'Father, you argue as well as you ever did'" (Buchanan, p. 60). He died at Buckpond.

Although Marshall was not a typical scholar—he left no writings—his natural talents were reported by a contemporary, Hugh A. Garland, to "surpass those of his illustrious brother, the Chief Justice" (Buchanan, p. 7). A good number of Marshall's students, including Robert Breckenridge, George B. Crittenden, General Basil Duke, and Colonel Alex McClung, became prominent leaders of public life. He was an innovator and committed to individualized instruction, yet, as Paxton sums up his reputation, "he was more feared, than respected—more admired than loved" (p. 71).

• Marshall's papers are in the Southern Historical Collection, University of North Carolina at Chapel Hill. The most thoroughly researched treatment of Marshall's life is William Buchanan, "Louis Marshall, M.D., His Administration as President of Washington College" (master's thesis, Washington and Lee Univ., 1941), which purports to "incorporate everything about him that can be brought to light." The earliest available biographical sketch of Marshall, *The Marshall Family* (1885), is by a relative, William M. Paxton, who first met "Uncle Louis" in 1835. (Paxton is the original source of the Paris story.) The most extensive account of Marshall's Washington College experience, focusing solely on his first two years, is in *The Washington and Lee Historical Papers*, no. 6, *The History of Washington College, 1830–1845* (1904), by William H. Ruffner, son of Marshall's chief rival (this particular account is freely excerpted from personal papers left by

Ruffner, Sr., and thus does not provide complete objectivity). The work includes an eight-page biographical sketch of Marshall, his wife, and their children.

KLAUS D. ISSLER

MARSHALL, Louis (14 Dec. 1856–11 Sept. 1929), lawyer and Jewish communal leader, was born in Syracuse, New York, the son of Jacob Marshall and Zilli Strauss, poor German-Jewish immigrants. His father, at first a porter and peddler, ended up in the hide and leather business. A graduate of Syracuse High School, Marshall read law for two years in a local law office. In 1876 he left to attend Columbia University Law School in New York City, where he completed the two-year curriculum in one year. Admitted to the bar on 1 January 1878, he joined the Syracuse law firm headed by William C. Ruger, later chief judge of New York State. In 1894 he returned to New York City at the invitation of his classmate Samuel Untermyer to create the law firm of Guggenheimer, Untermyer and Marshall. He continued as a partner in the firm for the rest of his life.

In 1895 Marshall married Florence Lowenstein, with whom he had four children before her death in 1916. His eldest son, James, was a lawyer and civic leader in New York City and a leader in Jewish communal affairs. His second son, George, was an economist and conservationist. His youngest son, Robert, was prominent in the U.S. Forest Service and Office of Indian Affairs. His daughter, Ruth, was married to Jacob Billikopf, a leader in Jewish social work and community organizations.

Although Marshall was active as a business and corporate lawyer, it was his expertise and activity in constitutional law that brought him national renown. Arguing more cases before the U.S. Supreme Court than any contemporary, Marshall was a firm and passionate defender of civil rights. Many of his cases were argued without remuneration, as matters of public interest. Among these were *Pierce v. Society of Sisters* (1925), in which an antiparochial school law in Oregon was ruled unconstitutional; *Nixon v. Herndon* (1927), in which a state statute excluding black voters from political primaries was adjudged unconstitutional; and *Luria v. United States* (1913), in which the Court ruled that naturalized citizens enjoy the same rights as native-born Americans. He also argued cases involving attempts to prevent Asians from owning land along the Pacific Coast, residential segregation of racial and religious groups, wildlife conservation, alien immigration, and workmen's compensation. One of his defeats was in the Leo Frank case in 1915. Frank, a Jewish businessman in Atlanta, Georgia, had been unjustly convicted in 1913 of murdering an employee. Marshall argued that the state court had been intimidated by a prejudiced mob, but the Supreme Court, with Justices Oliver Wendell Holmes (1841–1935) and Charles Evans Hughes dissenting, ruled against him. Ultimately, however, the Court adopted the dissenting opinion.

Marshall's intense conviction that legal and human rights were universal and indivisible led him to champion unpopular minorities. In the era of hysterical antibolshevism following World War I, Marshall was a prime defender of five Socialists who had been elected to the New York State Assembly but who were refused their seats on grounds of disloyalty. He fought many legal battles for black Americans and was an active member of the board of directors of the National Association for the Advancement of Colored People. He was also involved with the defense of American Indians and Haitians.

Marshall's legal eminence was early recognized in New York State, where he was appointed or elected to three constitutional conventions: in 1890, 1894, and 1915. Although he was considered for an appointment to the U.S. Supreme Court in 1910, it did not materialize. Marshall never sought public office himself but was generally a loyal supporter of the Republican party. In 1902 Mayor Seth Low appointed him as a member of a commission to investigate living conditions in the Lower East Side, New York City's crowded immigrant quarter, resulting in the correction of police and judicial abuses. During a major strike by 70,000 cloakmakers in New York in 1910, Marshall served as mediator, framing a famous "Protocol" that not only settled the strike but served as a model for other industries. A lifelong partisan of governmental protection of the environment and, in particular, of the Adirondack Forest Preserve, Marshall led in the establishment of the New York State College of Forestry at Syracuse University.

Marshall's leadership in American Jewish communal affairs was such that, especially during the last two decades of his life, American Jewry was said to have lived under "Marshall law." Marshall was the chief spokesman for the wealthy, assimilated German-Jewish elite who dominated Jewish communal affairs during the late nineteenth and early twentieth centuries. This became evident during the successful campaign in 1911 to abrogate the United States–Russian Commercial Treaty of 1832, under which the czarist government discriminated against American Jews, refusing them admission to Russia. Marshall and his associates, including the financier Jacob Schiff, mounted a skillful campaign, mobilizing congressional allies and public opinion, until President William Howard Taft was persuaded to notify the Russians that the treaty would be terminated. Marshall's ascendancy was recognized in 1912 when he became president of the American Jewish Committee, a post he held until his death. In this, his "principal and favorite office," he led a brilliant and determined struggle to prevent the imposition of increasingly restrictive laws designed to limit immigration to the United States. Marshall did this both because he believed in America's traditional open door policy and because of the desperate plight of East European Jews and others during and after World War I. Unfortunately, he succeeded only in delaying and modifying the restrictionist policy, which was swept along on a tide of nativism.

During World War I, Marshall spent much time in a running battle with newer groups in the Jewish community who wished to establish a more democratic American Jewish Congress in preparation for postwar peace negotiations. He also served as president of the American Jewish Relief Committee and helped organize the American Jewish Joint Distribution Committee, supporting the latter's postwar relief efforts, which included the establishment of agricultural settlements for poor Jews in the new Soviet Union. In 1919 Marshall joined the Jewish delegation at the Versailles Peace Conference, where he played a key role as mediator between the various factions. His efforts were crucial in obtaining national minority status for Jews in several of the new East European states established by the peace treaties.

At home, Marshall fought vigorously against a resurgence of anti-Semitism during the 1920s. Perhaps the most dangerous manifestation was the dissemination of the *Protocols of the Elders of Zion*, a European import that described an alleged Jewish plot to control the world. In 1920 the widely distributed *Dearborn Independent*, owned by Henry Ford, embarked on a crusade to popularize the *Protocols*. Marshall sought, without success, to prevent the publication of the *Protocols* and to dissuade Ford from pursuing his policy. Behind-the-scenes pressure and influential intermediaries did not seem to work. Finally, in 1927, after lawsuits and boycott threats, Ford agreed to sign an apology to the Jews, the text of which was prepared by Marshall.

Dedicated to Jewish religion and education, Marshall served (1916–1929) as president of Temple Emanu-El in New York, the leading Reform Jewish congregation in the United States. Earlier, he had clashed with Stephen S. Wise who was turned down in 1905 for the post of rabbi at Emanu-El. The rivalry between these two strong-willed men continued and was later reflected in Wise's leadership of the American Jewish Congress. Although personally a Reform Jew, Marshall believed that there was only one Judaism. Thus, he supported Orthodox religious and educational institutions and, from 1902, was chairman of the board of directors of Conservative Judaism's main institution, the Jewish Theological Seminary of America.

Although opposed to political Zionism, Marshall accepted the goal of the Balfour Declaration in 1917 that a Jewish national home be established in Palestine. Marshall was a non-Zionist rather than an anti-Zionist. He was realistic enough to understand that restricted immigration to the United States made it necessary to support Zionist efforts to establish Jewish settlements in Palestine. Consequently, during the 1920s he worked with Chaim Weizmann, leader of world Zionism, to establish a *modus vivendi* that would bring influential non-Zionists into an alliance with Zionists for the support of the Palestine Jewish community. These efforts culminated in August 1929 when an agreement was reached in Zurich, Switzerland, for the establishment of the Jewish Agency. Marshall's fatal illness and death due to an abscess of the pancreas a few weeks later in Zurich prevented full implementation of the agreement, but an important principle had been achieved. Leading American Jewish non-Zionists would henceforth cooperate with the Zionists in supporting the Jews of Palestine.

Marshall's leadership of the American Jewish community coincided with the greatest period of mass immigration. Although he represented the old Jewish establishment, Marshall displayed remarkable sensitivity to the aspirations of the newcomers. He learned Yiddish as an adult and supported moderate Americanization activities. Recent historians regard Marshall as one of the two or three preeminent American Jewish leaders of the twentieth century. On his seventieth birthday, Supreme Court Justice Benjamin Cardozo said of Marshall: "One feels that somehow he has been transformed into a great civic institution, coordinating the energies and activities of many men, so that with all his intensely human traits he has acquired in his own life, a new and, as it were, a corporate personality. He is a great lawyer; a great champion of ordered liberty; a great leader of his people; a great lover of mankind."

• The major collection of Louis Marshall's papers is located at the Hebrew Union College–Jewish Institute of Religion's American Jewish Archives in Cincinnati, Ohio. Charles Reznikoff edited a two-volume selection from Marshall's extensive correspondence, *Louis Marshall: Champion of Liberty* (1957), with a lengthy biographical introduction by Oscar Handlin. Morton Rosenstock, *Louis Marshall, Defender of Jewish Rights* (1965), deals with his leadership in the Jewish community. Jerome C. Rosenthal's unpublished Ph.D dissertation (Univ. of Cincinnati, 1983) deals with "The Public Life of Louis Marshall." See also Lucy S. Dawidowicz, "Louis Marshall's Yiddish Newspaper," *Jewish Social Studies* 25 (Apr. 1963): 102–32; David G. Dalin, "Louis Marshall, the Jewish Vote and the Republican Party," *Jewish Political Studies Review* 4 (Apr. 1992): 55–84; and Herbert Parzen, "Louis Marshall, the Zionist Organization of America, and the Founding of the Jewish Agency," in *Michael*, vol 3., ed. Lloyd P. Gartner (1975). An informative obituary by Cyrus Adler is in the *American Jewish Year Book* 32 (1930–1931), pp. 21–55.

MORTON ROSENSTOCK

MARSHALL, Robert (2 Jan. 1901–11 Nov. 1939), environmentalist and social activist, was born in New York City, the son of Louis Marshall, a renowned Jewish and civil rights leader, and Florence Lowenstein. He was strongly influenced by his father, who besides being an ardent defender of Jewish and other minorities' civil rights, was an avid art collector, philanthropist, and defender of wilderness preservation in the Adirondack Mountains of upstate New York. Marshall was educated at the Ethical Culture School in New York and then studied forestry at the New York State College of Forestry at Syracuse University (receiving a bachelor's degree in 1924) and the Harvard Forest in north-central Massachusetts. He earned his master's degree in forestry from Harvard in the spring of 1925. Somewhat obsessed with the early American explorers

and wishing to reenact their adventures, he had, by the time he was twenty-four, climbed all forty-six of the Adirondack "high peaks."

From 1925 to 1928, Marshall, who was known as "Bob," worked for the U.S. Forest Service conducting tree-growth research on both sides of the Idaho-Montana border. During this time he became well known within the Forest Service for his twenty- to forty-mile hikes on days off and for ardently adopting the minority position within the agency that large tracts of the national forests should remain roadless and undeveloped. He became known also for his zany sense of humor, well illustrated by a detailed study he conducted of lumberjacks' eating habits and usage of profanity. When in December 1929 *Social Forces* magazine published the resulting parody of social science research, its readers learned such startling facts as that "an average of 136 words, unmentionable at church sociables, were enunciated every quarter hour by the hardy hewers of wood."

Marshall spent the fall of 1928 to the spring of 1930 at Johns Hopkins University in Baltimore, Maryland, where he obtained a Ph.D. in plant physiology and "more or less" ran the Johns Hopkins Liberal Club. Marshall's father died in 1929, and Marshall inherited a substantial amount of money, enabling him to be financially independent for the rest of his life. He spent the summer of 1929 exploring an unmapped portion of Alaska's Brooks Range, accompanied only by a gold seeker named Al Retzlaff. A year later—beginning in August 1930—he spent another twelve and a half months continuing to explore and map the same region and conducting a sociological study of the 100 or so inhabitants of the region. His headquarters for the sociological study was a tiny mining settlement called Wiseman. The area he explored and mapped included much of what later became Gates of the Arctic National Park. His Brooks Range explorations, which included two subsequent trips in 1938 and 1939, resulted in a posthumous book, *Arctic Wilderness* (1956; 2d ed., *Alaska Wilderness*, 1970), the first maps of the region, and some 164 names for geographical features eventually adopted by the U.S. Geological Survey. His sociological study resulted in a popular book, *Arctic Village*, which was a *Literary Guild* selection for June 1933.

Marshall spent from autumn 1931 to May 1933 writing *Arctic Village* and another book, *The People's Forests* (1933), which advocated a total takeover by the federal government of all forestlands in the country. By this time, Marshall had become an avowed socialist. He was also very active in many liberal, civil rights, and civil liberties causes. He served, for example, as chairman of the Washington branch of the American Civil Liberties Union, was active in the Tenants Unemployed League, and was arrested in March 1933 for participating in a United Front demonstration. Meanwhile he did freelance work for the Forest Service and campaigned for wilderness preservation. An article he had published in 1930 for *The Scientific Monthly* called "The Problem of the Wilderness" had aroused much interest among natural resource professionals and outdoor enthusiasts, and Marshall spent much time in the early 1930s making contacts with such people, who shared his wilderness love.

Throughout most of the 1930s Marshall was based primarily in Washington, D.C. From 1933 to 1937 he worked for the U.S. Bureau of Indian Affairs, under its liberal commissioner John Collier, as head of that agency's forestry division. While in this position, he convinced Collier and Interior Secretary Harold Ickes to declare some 4.8 million acres on thirteen reservations off limits to federally assisted development—in essence creating Indian reservation wilderness areas. He also began a relentless personal campaign to convince his friends and acquaintances in the Forest Service to expand that agency's fledgling system of "primitive areas." In 1935 he was the primary organizer and founder of the Wilderness Society, thus fulfilling his desire to create, as he had written in "The Problem of the Wilderness," an organization "of spirited people" who would "fight for the freedom of the Wilderness." Marshall personally financed much of the society's activities until his death in 1939.

In May 1937 Marshall accepted a position as chief of the division of recreation and lands for the U.S. Forest Service. In this position, he stepped up his personal campaign for Forest Service wilderness preservation. On summer inspection tours of western national forests, he often hiked across large roadless areas, then circled these areas on maps, and formally urged local and regional Forest Service officials to preserve them. These maps of Marshall's influenced the evolution of the Forest Service's primitive area system for several decades after his death, indeed up until the Wilderness Act of 1964 created the National Wilderness Preservation System.

Marshall died in his sleep on a train before reaching his thirty-ninth birthday; he never married. A police autopsy gave the cause of death as leukemia and arteriosclerosis. His primary contributions were as an Alaskan explorer, early environmentalist, and inspirational figure to later wilderness advocates. During the time of his active wilderness crusade (roughly 1933–1939), the U.S. Forest Service added some 5.4 million acres to its primitive area system; many areas added after 1939 had also been advocated by Marshall. His brainchild, the Wilderness Society, emerged as a leading environmental voice in the second half of the twentieth century. His chief aim was to rescue the opportunity for an ancient human experience, which he believed was enormously enriching. He spoke as much for himself as others when he wrote that for some, "the enjoyment of solitude, complete independence, and the beauty of undefiled panoramas is absolutely essential to happiness" ("The Wilderness as a Minority Right," *Forest Service Bulletin*, 27 Aug. 1928).

• The primary collection of Marshall's papers is at the Bancroft Library, University of California-Berkeley. There are smaller Marshall collections at the American Jewish Archives, Cincinnati, Ohio; the Franklin D. Roosevelt Library, Hyde Park, N.Y.; and the Moon Library, State University of New York, College of Environmental Science and Forestry, Syracuse. Revealing articles by Marshall not mentioned in the text include "Recreational Limitations to Silviculture in the Adirondacks," *Journal of Forestry* 23 (Feb. 1925): 173–78; "Impressions from the Wilderness," *The Living Wilderness*, Autumn 1951, pp. 10–13; "Public Forestry or Private Devastation?" *New Republic*, 27 June 1934, pp. 176–78; and "The Universe of the Wilderness Is Vanishing," *Nature Magazine*, Apr. 1937, pp. 235–40. A book-length biography is James M. Glover, *A Wilderness Original: The Life of Bob Marshall* (1986). See also Roderick Nash, *Wilderness and the American Mind* (1967); Peter Wild, *Pioneer Conservationists of Eastern America* (1986); and Jim Dale Vickery, *Wilderness Visionaries* (1986). Obituaries are in the *New York Times*, 12 Nov. 1939; the *Nation*, 2 Dec. 1939, p. 635; and the *New Republic*, 27 Dec. 1939, p. 289.

JAMES M. GLOVER

MARSHALL, S. L. A. (18 July 1900–17 Dec. 1977), soldier, reporter, and historian, was born Samuel Lyman Atwood Marshall in Catskill, New York, the son of Caleb Carey Marshall, a bricklayer, and Alice Medora Beeman. The family moved in 1912 to Niles, California, and Samuel, at age twelve, was involved in Hollywood productions as a child extra. He worked in Western Essanay Studio productions, including the "Bronco Billy" features. In 1914 the Marshalls moved to El Paso, Texas, where Samuel finished high school. He entered the Texas College of Mines (later the University of Texas at El Paso) but did not finish his college education. Becoming caught up in World War I, he joined the U.S. Army in 1917.

Marshall's on-again, off-again association with the army began in the Ninetieth Infantry Division. He saw action at Ypres, St.-Mihiel, Meuse-Argonne, and the Soissons sectors. In 1919 he earned a commission, becoming a lieutenant while still in France. He later claimed to be the youngest officer in the army. He joined the National Guard and left the army in September 1919 to return to Texas, securing a job as the sports editor on the *El Paso Herald*. In 1927 he moved to Michigan to further pursue his career in journalism, joining the staff of the *Detroit News*. While with this newspaper, Marshall became a nationally known polo journalist, wrote a humor column, and covered military affairs in Latin America. When Fascist aggression began to cast shadows in Europe, Marshall began to drift further into military reportage and commentary. In 1936–1937 he covered the Spanish Civil War. In 1940 he published the first of almost thirty books, a volume foretelling the coming German army method of offensive warfare, *Blitzkrieg*. It was timely and sold well, so in 1941 Marshall followed it up with another, *Armies on Wheels*. His writings brought him to the attention of Secretary of War Henry Lewis Stimson and paved the way to a resumption of his uniformed service.

On America's entry into World War II, Marshall found himself a major in the Office of War Information, a position not to his liking because it was too far from battle. Wrangling a job in the newly established Army Historical Office, he managed to draw duty in the Pacific with the task of recording the U.S. Army offensives in the Marshall and Gilbert islands. He was promoted to lieutenant colonel and was writing the overall history of these campaigns when an incident occurred that ever after drove his focus to the individual soldier's story and the dynamics of combat at the small unit level. He was talking to a soldier about a recent action when, by chance, another soldier chimed in with a different version of the same event. Marshall, realizing he might be able to discover what really happened, was intrigued. He began to conduct collective interviews with individuals and groups, squads, platoons, and on occasion entire companies. Prior to the 1944 Normandy invasion, he was transferred to the European theater of operations, and he began using his after-action interview techniques in an entirely new setting.

Marshall later extended his interviews to the other side of the lines. Elevated by the army to colonel and chief historian of the European theater, he conducted talks with top-level German military officers. Collecting information from his many World War II interviews, he published *Men against Fire* (1947). Although the American public had little interest in yet another book about the war, resulting in poor sales, the work sparked a lively debate among army officers. In his book, Marshall claimed that fewer than 25 percent of American infantrymen fired their weapons in a firefight.

After World War II Marshall returned to newspaper work in Detroit, Michigan. However, in 1948 he was briefly recalled to active duty with the U.S. Army's growing European headquarters activities. He was again put in uniform for the Korean War. At this time he began interviewing for twin purposes, providing the army with fresh field combat data with which to improve battlefield performance and providing himself with material for commercial books. His best two books from the Korean War are *The River and the Gauntlet* (1953) and *Pork Chop Hill* (1956). The latter was made into a notable Hollywood film.

The dates of Marshall's first two marriages are unknown. His first wife was Ruth Elstner, with whom he had one child. The date of her death is not known. His second wife, Edith Ives Westervelt, died in 1952. In 1954 he married Catherine Finnerty. They had three children, and Catherine brought one child to the family from a previous marriage.

Marshall's fame grew internationally, and although he retired with the rank of reserve brigadier general in 1960, he continued to be influential in army affairs. After interviewing a number of Israeli soldiers and officers, he produced two books, *Sinai Victory* (1958) and *Swift Sword* (1967). The first of these dealt with the 1956 Arab-Israeli War and the second with the 1967 conflict, and both have been highly prized by the Israeli army. Marshall's services continued to be in demand by the U.S. Army as a speaker before military audiences, an after-action interviewer, and a writer of combat reports. He made numerous trips to Vietnam War battlefields and produced another string of books. He died in El Paso, Texas.

Marshall was one of the better-known members of a distinguished American genus, the reporter–military historian. He thus joined Stephen Crane, Douglas Southall Freeman, Allan Nevins, and Walter Millis, all journalists and historians of America's military endeavors.

• Marshall's personal papers are at the University of Texas, El Paso. His uncompleted autobiography was finished by his wife Catherine after Marshall's death and is the best account of his life, *Bringing Up the Rear* (1979). His influence on the U.S. Army is treated in an official publication, Major F. D. G. Williams, *SLAM: The Influence of S. L. A. Marshall on the United States Army* (1990), which contains a list of his publications. An extensive obituary is in the *New York Times*, 18 Dec. 1977.

ROD PASCHALL

MARSHALL, Thomas Alexander (15 Jan. 1794–15 Apr. 1871), jurist, lawyer, and legislator, was born near Versailles, Woodford County, Kentucky, the son of Humphrey Marshall, a Kentucky legislator and later U.S. senator, and Mary Marshall, a sister of Chief Justice John Marshall. Marshall was educated at Joshua Fry's academy in Mercer County, Kentucky, and at Yale College, from which he graduated with a B.A. in 1815. He returned to Kentucky, where he married Eliza Price, a sister-in-law of statesman Henry Clay, in 1816; the couple would have five children.

After reading the law, Marshall was admitted to the bar in 1817. He practiced in Frankfort until 1819, when he moved to Paris, Kentucky. In 1827 and 1828 he served one-year terms as a representative to the Kentucky legislature, where he generally voted against the Jacksonian party. He served two terms in Congress, from 1831 to 1835, failing to secure reelection only in 1834. As a congressman he supported the National Republican (ultimately Whig) party on most issues, including defense of high tariffs and the Bank of the United States. He especially endorsed efforts to compensate revolutionary war veterans, a crusade that he spearheaded as chairman of the House committee on revolutionary claims.

Governor James T. Morehead appointed Marshall to the Kentucky Court of Appeals in March 1835. It was as a member of the state's highest court that he achieved his most lasting significance, especially in cases involving slavery. Indeed, the court unofficially seems to have designated him its chief opinion writer on the subject. His most important opinions in this regard were issued in the companion cases of *Graham v. Strader* (1844) and *Strader v. Graham* (1847), which concerned the legal effect of a slave's residence in a free state—one of the most divisive legal issues of the antebellum United States. Some free-state courts emancipated slaves whose owners voluntarily took them into their jurisdictions. In these cases three slave-musicians had obtained passage on a steamboat to escape to the North; their master sued the boat owner for their value under a Kentucky statute that established steamboaters' liability for runaways. The boat owner argued that the African Americans in question were not slaves because their master had allowed them to spend time in the free states of Ohio and Indiana. A unanimous court, through Marshall, rejected this argument and in both cases ruled for the slaveowner on the grounds that a temporary residence in a free state followed by a return to the slave state did not emancipate the slaves. Marshall's were the first major opinions from a slave-state court to support the right of a master voluntarily to employ his slaves in a free state for a short time and then return with them to a slave state, where they would remain slaves. In 1850 the U.S. Supreme Court upheld Marshall's opinions, although in so doing Chief Justice Roger B. Taney fashioned a more explicitly proslavery argument, paving the way for the Court's notorious decision in *Dred Scott v. Sandford* (1857).

In *Maria v. Kirby* (1851), Marshall wrote the opinion for a unanimous court in a decision denying that a black woman's temporary residence in the free state of Pennsylvania had emancipated her; Marshall ignored the fact that a Pennsylvania circuit court judge had declared her to be a free person in part because Pennsylvania statutes seemed to provide freedom for slaves in transit. This ruling, as explained by Marshall, refused to honor the statutes and proceedings of a neighboring state, a denial entirely in keeping with mainstream American law practice. Nevertheless, Marshall's court did rule in favor of slaves seeking emancipation by virtue of permanent residence in free states, a position that was decidedly more libertarian than that of the high courts of many other slave states.

Because Kentucky's constitution of 1850 provided for an elected judiciary, Marshall sought and secured election to the court of appeals in 1851. He failed to win reelection to the court in 1856 in part because he was a member of the American party in a year in which Democrats made sweeping gains. During much of his initial sojourn on the court (1836–1849) he also served as professor of law at Transylvania University in Lexington, where he resided from 1836 to 1857. On his retirement from the court he moved to Chicago to practice law but soon returned to Louisville, Kentucky, where he opened another law office.

During the Civil War, Marshall supported the Union and served in the Kentucky General Assembly from 1863 to 1865. As a house member he expressed his growing disenchantment with the antislavery policies of the federal government by opposing the ratification of the Thirteenth Amendment and switching his allegiance to the Democratic party. He also joined hands with other Democrats to oppose alleged encroachments of the Union army on Kentucky citizenry and to support resolutions asking for an end to martial law in the commonwealth and for the removal of African-American troops from the state. In February 1866, to fill a vacancy created by the death of William Sampson, Governor Thomas Bramlette appointed Marshall chief justice of the court of appeals (a posi-

tion he also held from 1847 to 1851 and from 1854 to 1856). But, because he was successfully branded as having been a Unionist during the war, he failed to win a regular term to that tribunal in the August 1866 elections. He practiced law in Louisville until his death there.

Marshall performed his most important public service as a state court judge. While his most significant opinions contributed only modestly to the increasingly controversial problem of the rights of slaveowners who temporarily took their slaves to free states, Marshall nevertheless enjoyed the respect of his countrymen and fellow jurists. His obituary in the *Louisville Courier-Journal* (17 Apr. 1871) described him as one of the two most influential Kentucky jurists of his time.

• No single body of Marshall papers exists. The *Kentucky House Journals* (1827, 1828, 1863–1865) and the *Congressional Debates* (1831–1835) furnish evidence of his legislative record; the *Kentucky Reports* (1835–1856 and 1866) contain his judicial opinions. *The Kentucky Encyclopedia* (1992) contains a useful biographical sketch. Paul Finkelman, *An Imperfect Union: Slavery, Federalism, and Comity* (1981), places Marshall's principal judicial opinions on slavery in their historical context. W. M. Paxton, *The Marshall Family* (1880), offers useful genealogical information.

ROBERT M. IRELAND

MARSHALL, Thomas Riley (14 Mar. 1854–1 June 1925), governor of Indiana and vice president of the United States, was born in North Manchester, Indiana, the son of Daniel M. Marshall, a physician, and Martha Patterson. From 1856 to 1860 the Marshall family lived in Illinois, Kansas, and Missouri before returning to Indiana. Marshall grew up in the village of Pierceton, attended school in Warsaw, and completed high school in Fort Wayne. At Wabash College he concentrated on the classics and was elected to Phi Beta Kappa. He graduated in 1873. He read law under the direction of Judge Walter Olds in Fort Wayne and was admitted to the bar in Columbia City, a nearby county seat town, on his twenty-first birthday. For thirty-three years he was a country lawyer, taking every kind of case, civil and criminal. He won a reputation for persuasive speaking when addressing juries. In 1895 he married Lois Irene Kimsey. He and his wife took prominent roles in the Presbyterian church, and Marshall held high offices in the Masonic Lodge.

Like his father, Marshall was a lifelong Democrat. He liked to say that Stephen A. Douglas and Samuel J. Tilden were his heroes, for they accepted electoral decisions that had unfortunate consequences for their own careers in order to spare the nation irreparable harm. While at Wabash he spoke in Democratic campaigns and continued to do so throughout his life. He ran unsuccessfully for prosecutor in 1880 and for some time resisted suggestions that he run for other offices. When friends in 1906 urged him to run for Congress, he refused but told them he would like to be governor. The movement to elect him to that office began in the following year. When the state Democratic convention convened in 1908, he had support only among delegates from northern Indiana. The real contest seemed to be between Samuel M. Ralston, the choice of the leader of the Democratic state organization Thomas Taggart, and L. Ert Slack, who was backed by Taggart's many opponents. When Taggart realized that Ralston could not be nominated, he threw his support to Marshall, who won the nomination on the fifth ballot.

The Indiana campaigns of 1908 were hard fought. William Jennings Bryan, for the third time the Democratic presidential nominee, spoke in Indiana several times, and Marshall traveled throughout the state, later saying he gave the same speech 169 times. He declined financial support from the state Democratic committee and borrowed to pay expenses. This decision was wise, for several groups hoping to influence him wanted to provide funds. The temperance issue overshadowed other questions. As the campaign got underway, the incumbent Republican governor, J. Frank Hanly, complicated matters for Marshall and his Republican opponent, Congressman James E. Watson, by securing a county option law from a special session of the general assembly. Marshall himself had overcome a drinking problem several years before and had been a speaker at temperance meetings, but he was convinced of the wisdom of his party's contention that the power to decide whether or not to permit the sale of alcoholic beverages should reside in townships rather than larger county units. He directed his sharpest remarks at ministers determined to impose prohibition but won much support from both "drys" and "wets." Marshall won the election by a margin of 14,809 votes in a total vote of 712,000. The Democrats won a majority in the state house of representatives, but holdover senators denied them a majority in the senate. They elected the lieutenant governor and the superintendent of public instruction, but the Republicans retained other high elective offices. The Democrats secured eleven of Indiana's thirteen congressional seats but failed to carry the state for Bryan and his Indiana running mate John W. Kern.

As governor, Marshall was sometimes described as a "progressive with the brakes on," but his leadership was vigorous, especially after the 1910 election gave the Democrats majorities in both houses of the legislature. Marshall's reforms included new taxes and regulations for railroads, telegraphs, and telephone companies. New laws regulated employers' liabilities and limited the use of child labor. Other laws supplemented the Pure Foods Act passed by Congress in 1906. The legislature in 1911 replaced Hanly's county option with township option. Marshall gave particular attention to finances, thwarting the attempts of legislators to transfer money from the state's sinking fund to its general fund, a move that he believed might allow unnecessary spending. The governor also introduced an audit of the books of all public officials by two certified public accountants, one from each party. While Marshall often advised restraint when recommending reform legislation, he urged bold constitutional changes. He and his closest associates wrote a new constitu-

tion that simplified the amending process and provided for a larger house of representatives and a larger supreme court. The general assembly, following the governor's lead, voted to submit the new constitution to the voters, bypassing the amendment procedure of the existing constitution. A Marion County circuit court judge promptly stopped the referendum with an injunction, and the state supreme court upheld his action. The Marshall constitution had failed, but the reputation of its principal author as a progressive had been enhanced. The governor of Indiana was in an excellent position for a strong showing as a favorite son at the 1912 Democratic National Convention in Baltimore.

After Governor Woodrow Wilson of New Jersey won the Democratic presidential nomination, his leading supporters advised supporting Marshall for the vice presidency. Wilson did not know that the leader of his forces in Baltimore, William F. McCombs, had already promised the vice presidency in return for the Indiana delegation's votes for Wilson's nomination. Wilson described Marshall as "a very small calibre man." Indiana, however, was a doubtful midwestern state, and its governor could carry its electoral votes and possibly the votes of neighboring states. By a logic similar to that which had led to other Indiana vice presidential nominations, Marshall was given the nomination. Marshall campaigned in the Middle West and in New England. A speech in Portland, Maine, was something of a sensation. He urged revisions of the tariff so drastic that the result would have been free trade. It was feared that he would drive Louisiana sugar growers and other southern groups that relied on tariff protection into Theodore Roosevelt's Progressive party, but that did not happen.

As vice president Marshall for a time continued to startle people with his speeches. Addressing a Jefferson Day dinner in New York on 12 April 1913, he warned that the nation could face "socialism or paternalism" if the tendency of some men to amass "vast fortunes was not curbed." Surely the vice president was a dangerous radical, some individuals charged. Thereafter Marshall was more circumspect and took greater care to adjust his public statements to the president's policies. After the sinking of the *Lusitania* in May 1915 he went even farther than Wilson in calling for continued American neutrality in the European war. This time his moderation aroused controversy.

Despite the prominence the press gave to Marshall's comments about controversial questions, he believed that presiding over the Senate was his most important function. He mastered its rules and tried to treat senators of both parties impartially. When he lectured for the Chautauqua organization he told critics that presiding over the Senate was only a part-time job. After he left office he said that he had had to earn money for some speeches or "steal, or resign." In truth his expenses were burdensome. The Marshalls lived in a hotel and yet did their full share of official entertaining.

In 1924 Marshall told Mrs. Edith Wilson that he had no letters he had exchanged with the president and could not give her a detailed account of his association with Wilson as she had requested, for his "public services simply consisted in representing the president upon social and formal occasions which have nothing to do with his real life work." While Marshall never was one of Wilson's close advisers, his role during the administration's second term was often of considerable importance. American entry into World War I meant more social responsibilities for the Marshalls, including dinners and receptions for visiting foreign dignitaries and speeches for Liberty Loan drives. When Marshall, in the spring of 1918, told the president that he intended to open the Indiana Democratic Convention with a call for nominations of men dedicated to winning the war who would support the president and that he would refrain from attacks on Republicans, Wilson said such a speech would not do. The president thought that a hard-hitting partisan speech was in order. Marshall spoke in Indianapolis as Wilson wished, and when he was campaigning for the Democratic senatorial candidate in Wisconsin, he again followed the president's lead, severely criticizing the Republican party and its candidate, Irvine L. Lenroot. The partisan strategy backfired, contributing to Lenroot's victory. In the Senate the Republicans ended up with a majority of one, enough to organize that body's committees, including the Foreign Relations Committee, which considered the Versailles treaty and the attached covenant of the League of Nations.

The most important period of Marshall's service as vice president began when the president went to Paris for the peace conference and continued to the end of the administration. In the president's absence, he presided over cabinet meetings but took no part in decisions. Wilson's subsequent illness required all the forbearance Marshall possessed. He said nothing that indicated willingness to assume presidential power, although many individuals thought he should do so. He presided over the Senate's debates on the Versailles treaty and the league covenant with his usual impartiality. When asked his views, he supported the president, but little doubt exists that he favored acceptance of ratification with the Senate's reservations. He assumed onerous new social duties, acting as official host for the visits of the Belgian royal family and the Prince of Wales.

As the 1920 presidential campaign began, Marshall considered running for the Democratic nomination but abandoned the idea when delegates gathering for the convention showed no interest. After the inauguration of President Warren G. Harding, he returned to Indianapolis to practice law occasionally while giving most of his attention to making speeches and writing syndicated articles. Continuing in the Democratic party leadership, he accepted appointment to the Federal Coal Commission by President Harding. He died in Washington while on commission business.

Since Marshall's death, his humorous comments about the vice presidency and his aside to a Senate secretary, "What this country needs is a really good five-cent cigar," have often been recalled, but other aspects of his career have been largely forgotten. This is unfortunate, for even his speeches, which included his wittiest remarks, were essays of substance and ideas. His service as governor was distinguished. In his difficult role as Wilson's vice president, he made few mistakes and conducted himself with tact and grace.

• Marshall's papers are in the Indiana State Library and the Indiana State Archives. Marshall dictated his memoirs shortly before his death, and they were published as *The Recollections of Thomas R. Marshall Vice-President and Hoosier Philosopher: A Hoosier Salad* (1925) soon after he died. They contain insights more important than the subtitle may lead one to expect. Charles M. Thomas published *Thomas Riley Marshall: Hoosier Statesman* (1939), for which he interviewed and corresponded with Marshall's wife and several other people who had known the vice president, supplementing the Marshall papers substantially. Keith S. Montgomery, "Thomas R. Marshall's Victory in the Election of 1908," *Indiana Magazine of History* 53 (1957): 147–66, is an excellent study of a complicated campaign. Clifton J. Phillips, *Indiana in Transition: The Emergence of an Industrial Commonwealth 1880–1920* (1968), studies Marshall's career before the vice presidency as part of the political history of the Progressive Era. Arthur S. Link, *Wilson: The Road to the White House* (1947), explains Marshall's nomination for the vice presidency. An obituary is in the *New York Times*, 2 June 1925.

CALVIN D. DAVIS

MARSHALL, Thurgood (2 July 1908–24 Jan. 1993), civil rights lawyer and U.S. Supreme Court justice, was born Thoroughgood Marshall in Baltimore, Maryland, the son of William Canfield Marshall, a dining-car waiter and club steward, and Norma Arica Williams, an elementary school teacher. Growing up in a solid middle-class environment, Marshall was an outgoing and sometimes rebellious student who first encountered the Constitution when he was required to read it as punishment for classroom misbehavior. Marshall's parents wanted him to become a dentist, as his brother did, but Marshall was not interested in the science courses he took at Lincoln University in Pennsylvania, from which he was graduated with honors in 1930. He married Vivian "Buster" Burey in 1929; they had no children.

Unable to attend the segregated University of Maryland Law School, Marshall enrolled in and commuted to Howard University Law School, where he became a protégé of the dean, Charles Hamilton Houston, who inspired a cadre of law students to see the law as a form of social engineering to be used to advance the interests of African Americans. After graduating first in his class from Howard in 1933, Marshall remained in Baltimore, where he opened a private law practice and struggled to make a living during the depression. Marshall was active in the Baltimore branch of the National Association for the Advancement of Colored People (NAACP), and in 1936 Houston persuaded both the NAACP board and Marshall that Marshall ought to join him in New York as a staff lawyer for the NAACP. After Houston returned to Washington in 1938, Marshall remained and became the chief staff lawyer, a position he held until 1961.

Early in his Baltimore practice Marshall had decided to attack the policies that had barred him from attending the state-supported law school. Acting under Houston's direction, Marshall sued the University of Maryland on behalf of Donald Murray. The Maryland state court's 1936 decision ordering the school to admit Murray because the state did not maintain a "separate but equal" law school for African Americans was the first step in a two-decade effort to undermine the constitutional basis of racial segregation. Over the next fourteen years, Marshall pursued his challenge to segregated higher education through two main areas. In *Missouri ex rel Gaines v. Canada* (1938), a case Houston developed and argued, the U.S. Supreme Court directed the University of Missouri to either admit Lloyd Gaines to its law school or open one for African Americans. The attack culminated in Marshall's case of *Sweatt v. Painter* (1950), in which the Supreme Court held that the law school Texas had opened for African Americans was not "equal" to the well-established law school for whites.

The cases that the Supreme Court decided under the name *Brown v. Board of Education* constituted Marshall's main efforts from 1950 to 1955. Assembling a team of lawyers to develop legal and historical theories against segregation, Marshall had his greatest triumph as a lawyer in *Brown* (1954), in which the Supreme Court held that segregation of public schools by race was unconstitutional. In the 1896 case of *Plessy v. Ferguson*, the Supreme Court had upheld segregation, saying that segregation was a reasonable way for states to regulate race relations and that it did not "stamp [black Americans] with a badge of inferiority." Examining the background of the Fourteenth Amendment, Marshall's team concluded that the amendment's framers did not intend either to authorize or to outlaw segregation. From this research Marshall came to the conclusion that under modern conditions, given the place of education in twentieth-century life, segregated public education was no longer reasonable. Marshall also relied, though less heavily, on arguments based on modern psychological research showing that, *Plessy* notwithstanding, segregation did in fact damage the self-images of African-American schoolchildren. During oral arguments Marshall occasionally stumbled over technical and historical details, but his straightforward appeal to common sense captured the essence of the constitutional challenge: "In the South where I spend most of my time," he said, "you will see white and colored kids going down the road together to school. They separate and go to different schools, and they come out and they play together. I do not see why there would necessarily be any trouble if they went to school together."

There was trouble, however, as officials in the Deep South engaged in massive resistance to desegregation. Marshall argued the case of *Cooper v. Aaron* (1958), which arose after Arkansas governor Orval Faubus sought to circumvent desegregation by closing four Little Rock schools on the first day of class. Marshall pointed out that Faubus's attempts to thwart the Supreme Court directive in *Brown* threatened fundamental American ideas about the rule of law, and he asked the Court to assert its constitutional authority by directing Little Rock officials to reopen and racially integrate the schools. Marshall told the justices that a ruling in favor of Faubus would be tantamount to telling the nine black boys and girls who had endured harassment and intimidation at Little Rock's Central High School throughout the 1957–1958 school year, "You fought for what you considered democracy and you lost. . . . go back to the segregated school from which you came." Again the Supreme Court agreed with Marshall, and in August 1959 the schools reopened in line with federal desegregation orders.

A gregarious person who was always ready to use an apt, humorous story to make a point, Marshall traveled throughout the segregated South to speak to teachers and NAACP members, and in the 1940s and 1950s he became a major civil rights leader. By the mid-1950s his role as a civil rights leader had superseded his work as an attorney and he had become a widely sought-after speaker and fundraiser. He also was active in the Episcopal church and the Prince Hall Masons. His wife died of lung cancer in February 1955, and the following December he married Cecilia Suyatt, a secretary in the NAACP's national office; they would have two children, both boys.

Fending off attacks on the NAACP, its lawyers, and its members as well as attempting to push desegregation forward took a toll on Marshall. His travels kept him away from his family, and his NAACP salary, even when supplemented by gifts from wealthy white members, was inadequate to provide a college education for his sons. To ease the financial burden and make more time for his family, and because he could see that the civil rights movement was shifting away from the legal strategies he favored toward more direct-action tactics with which he was uncomfortable, in 1961 Marshall accepted an appointment to the U.S. Court of Appeals for the Second Circuit (in New York). Political maneuvering delayed his confirmation for nearly a year, after which he served on the Second Circuit for five years. His opinions were solid but hardly path-breaking. Aware of his lack of experience in business and tax law, which constituted an important portion of the Second Circuit's business, Marshall took guidance from Judge Henry Friendly in those areas.

In 1965 President Lyndon Johnson named Marshall U.S. solicitor general, the government's chief lawyer before the Supreme Court. Although neither said so explicitly, both Johnson and Marshall expected that Johnson would name Marshall to the U.S. Supreme Court as soon as possible. In 1967 Johnson manipulated Justice Tom Clark into resigning from the Court by naming his son Ramsey Clark attorney general, and that same year, saying it was "the right thing to do, the right time to do it, the right man and the right place," Johnson named Marshall to be the first African-American Supreme Court justice.

Marshall joined a Court that was dominated by liberals, but within five years the Court's composition had changed dramatically following the retirement of Chief Justice Earl Warren and the deaths of Justice Hugo Black and Justice John Marshall Harlan. Instead of being active in the coalition that determined the Court's positions, Marshall found himself in a beleaguered minority that opposed the more conservative justices appointed by Richard Nixon and Ronald Reagan. Marshall rarely got the opportunity to write important majority opinions, even when his liberal colleagues led by William J. Brennan were able to cobble together a majority, because such opinions had to appeal to one or two of the justices who were significantly more conservative than Marshall, and Marshall was relatively uncompromising on matters he cared about.

Marshall's repertoire of stories endeared him to nearly every one of his colleagues, although initially some conservatives, including Lewis F. Powell, were put off by what they saw as Marshall's failure to approach the job with appropriate seriousness. Marshall did delight in puncturing what he took to be Chief Justice Warren Burger's pomposity, occasionally greeting Burger with, "What's shakin', Chiefy baby?" Yet most of Marshall's colleagues came to understand that he used his stories, often about the experiences of black Americans in the nation's court system, to make points about the cases the justices were considering. At the time of his retirement in 1991, Marshall brought more experience as a practicing lawyer to the Court than did any of his colleagues, and he often urged them to take more account of courtroom realities than of abstract deliberations about the Constitution.

Court watchers, particularly those who were unsympathetic to Marshall's positions on constitutional issues, criticized him for delegating too much of his work to his law clerks. Familiar with numerous aspects of the law from his experiences on the court of appeals and as solicitor general, Marshall had a facility for quickly determining the main thrust of each party's contentions and for deciding what result to reach. He would provide a sketchy outline of what an opinion should say; after that, the law clerks did substantially all of the opinion drafting in his chambers, as was the case in other chambers as well. Marshall did not edit his clerks' drafts as closely as other justices did, but he rejected drafts that did not capture the substance or the intensity of his views, and thus the guidance he gave made the opinions his own.

Marshall's most important contribution to constitutional doctrine was his "sliding-scale" theory of the Fourteenth Amendment's guarantee of equal protection of the laws, which he stated in most detail in dissenting opinions in *Dandridge v. Williams* (1970) and *San Antonio Independent School District v. Rodriguez* (1973). The Court's stated doctrine distinguished between two "tiers" of judicial scrutiny. One tier involved "suspect" classifications, such as race or "fundamental" interests; statutes using those classifications received strict scrutiny and rarely were upheld. The other tier contained all other statutes; statutes in this category simply had to have a "rational basis" and rarely were struck down. As the Court grappled with more and more cases involving discrimination against women, aliens, and nonmarital children, and cases dealing with the provision of public assistance, Marshall pointed out that the rigid two-tiered approach was inadequate, because for one thing, it failed to take account of variations in the importance of different interests; perhaps even more important, it failed to describe the outcomes of the Court's cases. Marshall proposed that the Court adopt an approach that openly balanced the importance of the goals the government was trying to achieve, the nature of the interest(s) affected, and the character of the group adversely affected by the classifications of a given statute. Although the Court did not expressly adopt Marshall's suggestion, some of its decisions seemed implicitly to do so, and many scholars believe that his analysis was more representative of the Court's decision making than was the doctrine that the Court claimed to be applying.

Beyond his specific doctrinal contributions, Marshall provided a voice on the Court, and in the Court's internal deliberations, for black Americans and others with few champions. After he retired, several of his colleagues said that Marshall's opinions had brought the real world into the Court's deliberations. When the Court, in upholding a federal filing fee for bankruptcy (*United States v. Kras* [1973]), suggested that it should not be difficult for a poor person to set aside about $2 a week to pay the fee, Marshall became indignant, writing in his published opinion, "No one who has had close contact with poor people can fail to understand how close to the margin of survival many of them are."

Marshall drew on his experience as a criminal defense lawyer when he argued that in all cases capital punishment is a form of cruel and unusual punishment barred by the Constitution. After the Court rejected that proposition in *Gregg v. Georgia* (1976), Marshall continued to express his disagreement; his dissents often asserted that the fair administration of justice was compromised in death penalty cases, particularly when defendants facing death sentences had received inadequate legal assistance.

Marshall's overall approach to constitutional law combined Charles Hamilton Houston's view that it is a form of social engineering with a pragmatic grasp of courtroom and practical realities. For example, he refused to deem that the police practice of arresting drunks was unconstitutional, in part because he believed that society had not instituted a better method of dealing with the problem than to lock up drunks until they were sober. He was willing to endorse large-scale reforms through constitutional law, as in attempts to effect desegregation and to rid the law of the death penalty, because *Brown* had taught him that a bold Supreme Court pronouncement often had an indirect but lasting impact on social practices.

Feeling the effects of age, and having lost his closest ally on the Court when Brennan retired in 1990, Marshall announced his retirement on 27 June 1991. The Court was substantially more conservative when Marshall left than when he arrived. During his tenure the nation's political system had drifted to the right; so had the Court. Marshall never was able to act as a social engineer on behalf of African Americans and others who had made up the New Deal and Great Society political coalition; instead he came to occupy a different role on the Court, that of the great dissenter.

Earlier on the day of his retirement Marshall filed his final dissent. In *Payne v. Tennessee* a majority of the Court overruled the controversial decision in *Booth v. Maryland* (1987) and allowed prosecutors to introduce statements about the personal impact that a murder had had on the victim's family and friends. Beginning with the statement "Power, not reason, is the new currency of this Court's decisionmaking," Marshall's dissent bitterly criticized the majority opinion. Although the Warren Court, whose work Marshall had endorsed and contributed to during the 1960s, was not averse to overruling precedents, Marshall believed that those cases were different: old rules that either did not work or were inconsistent with later developments had been displaced. In *Payne*, by contrast, Marshall believed that the only change that had taken place between 1987 and 1991 was the makeup of the Court. To have constitutional law turn on the personalities of the judges was, in Marshall's view, inconsistent with the ideal of the rule of law.

Marshall died at Bethesda Naval Hospital in Maryland. Many tributes noted that he would have deserved a major place in histories of constitutional law even had he not served on the Supreme Court, because his efforts as chief lawyer for the NAACP in leading the Court to restructure constitutional law with regard to race was as important a contribution as any in modern history. Marshall made fewer contributions to constitutional law as a justice, largely because he was not part of the Court's more conservative majority, but his passionate voice for the poor and for African Americans resonated in his dissenting opinions, and he remained an inspiration to those who believed in the possibility of achieving justice through the Constitution.

• Marshall's professional papers are collected in the NAACP Papers and the Thurgood Marshall Papers, both in the Manuscript Division of the Library of Congress. Each collection contains a small number of personal papers as well. For his professional life, see Mark Tushnet, *Making Civil Rights Law: Thurgood Marshall and the Supreme Court, 1936–1961* (1994) and *Making Constitutional Law: Thurgood Marshall and the Supreme Court, 1961–1991* (1997). Richard Kluger, *Simple Justice* (1975), is a comprehensive study of *Brown v. Board of Education*. Carl Rowan, *Dream Makers, Dream Breakers: The World of Justice Thurgood Marshall* (1993), and Michael Davis and Hunter Clark, *Thurgood Marshall: Warrior at the Bar, Rebel on the Bench*, rev. ed. (1994), contain personal anecdotes, some of which are not entirely accurate. Symposiums containing personal recollections and evaluations of Marshall's career were published in the *Stanford Law Review* 44 (Summer 1992): 1213–99, and *Texas Law Review* 71 (May 1993): 1099–1130. Major obituaries are in the *New York Times* and the *Washington Post*, both 25 Jan. 1993.

MARK TUSHNET

MARSTON, William Moulton (9 May 1893–2 May 1947), psychologist and comic book creator, was born in Cliftondale, Massachusetts, the son of Frederick William Marston, a wholesale merchant, and Annie Dalton Moulton. Marston married Elizabeth Holloway in 1915, and the couple had five children, four of whom survived infancy. He graduated from Harvard University with an A.B. in 1915 and enrolled in the Harvard Law School the same year. Marston later claimed he "had the luck to discover the so-called Marston Deception Test, better known as The Lie Detector" while he was still an undergraduate. He was certainly one of the lie detector's most energetic publicizers, and the publication of his 1917 paper on the "Systolic Blood Pressure Symptoms of Deception" (*Journal of Experimental Psychology* 2: 117–63) is generally regarded as an important event in the instrument's history. Conducted in the Harvard psychological laboratory under the supervision of Hugo Münsterberg, whose interests included criminology, Marston's research resulted in a brief appointment to the U.S. Army's Psychological Division.

In 1918 Marston received an LL.B. and was admitted to the Massachusetts bar, becoming a Boston legal aid attorney. By 1921 he had obtained a Ph.D. in psychology from Harvard and the following year began to teach as a professor of legal psychology at the American University in Washington, D.C. Although the 1923 *Frye v. U.S.* case in the Court of Appeals of the District of Columbia ruled Marston's deception test inadmissible in court on the grounds that it had not yet been accepted by the majority of the scientific community, it nevertheless established the legal criteria for the admissibility of new scientific evidence. The following year Marston traveled to New York City to work as a psychologist for the National Committee for Mental Hygiene. Between 1925 and 1926 he was assistant professor of psychology and philosophy at Tufts College, and between 1926 and 1929 he lectured in psychology at Columbia and New York Universities.

During the 1920s, Marston worked on a variety of psychological topics, such as the detection of deception and his theory of the existence of primary emotions, and on philosophical problems concerning materialism and vitalism, and the nature of consciousness. This research resulted in the publication of more than a dozen academic journal articles and was summarized in his first book, *Emotions of Normal People* (1928). As a result of his experiments on the personality characteristics of "blondes, brunettes and red-heads," Marston was offered the position of director of public service at Universal Pictures in 1929. His task was to ascertain audience emotional reactions to motion pictures and to advise the producers accordingly. During his year in Hollywood he also lectured in psychology at the University of Southern California.

Between 1931 and 1932 Marston was visiting professor of psychology at Long Island University. With his wife and C. D. King, he wrote *Integrative Psychology: A Study of Unit Response* (1931), in which he ambitiously proposed that the four "elementary unit responses" of Dominance, Compliance, Submission, and Inducement could transform psychology into a rigorously scientific discipline. Marston's last academic positions were as lecturer in psychology at the New School of Social Science and the Rand School (1933–1934).

During the 1930s, Marston increasingly devoted himself to activities in keeping with his flamboyant personality: writing articles on popular psychology for mass circulation magazines such as *Cosmopolitan* and *Reader's Digest*; working for the short-lived Hampton, Weeks and Marston advertising agency (1931–1932); and appearing in advertisements for razor blades with his lie detector (the device showing that a Gillette blade was less emotionally upsetting for a man who was shaving than a competitor's blade). In his capacity as "consulting psychologist—a new sort of creature who seems to combine the advisory functions of the old-time pastor and country doctor" (*Harvard Class of 1915 25th Anniversary Report*, p. 481), he also advocated the lie detector as a solution to "marital or other domestic problems" (*Look*, 6 Dec. 1938, p. 16). In 1932 he published a novel, *Venus with Us: A Tale of the Caesar*. A succession of popular inspirational psychology works quickly followed: *You Can Be Popular* (1936), *Try Living* (1937), and *March On! Facing Life with Courage* (1941). Marston's *The Lie Detector Test* (1938) was also written for a popular audience, an attribute noticed by contemporary reviewer Fred E. Inbau, who dismissed it as "practically useless as a guide" to the field (*Journal of Criminal Law, Criminology and Police Science* 29 [1938]: 307).

In 1937 Marston predicted that "within a hundred years the United States" would witness "the beginning of a sort of Amazonian matriarchy" (*New York Times*, 11 Nov. 1937). He believed that psychology had discovered the true facts of the female nature and that society would eventually discover them too, resulting in a society in which women's talents would be recognized. Four years later, he encouraged this development by creating the first female comic book superhero character: Wonder Woman. "I fully believe I am hitting a great movement now under way," he wrote on 23 February 1941 to Sheldon Mayer, the editor of All-American Comics, "the growth in power of women." Wonder Woman also personified Marston's knowledge of psychology. She carried a lie detector—a "Golden Lasso of Truth"—and wore "Bracelets of Submission." Reminding the Amazons of the "folly of submitting to men's domination!," the bracelets expressed Marston's philosophy of freedom. The destructive and masculine notion of unconstrained liberty, according to Marston, needed to be replaced with a notion of freedom based on feminine "love allure" and

submission to "loving authority." "The world needs peace, security, an aristocracy of altruism," he wrote in 1942, "a new set of social values based upon what one individual can do for others and not upon what he can take away and keep for himself."

Marston devoted the last six years of his life to writing the stories for *Wonder Woman*. In 1944 he became the vice president of the Brunswick School, Connecticut. His last book, a collaboration with J. H. Feller, was a biography of *F. F. Proctor, Vaudeville Pioneer* (1943). Although Marston's own vaudevillian sensibility and tireless self-promotion invoked criticism from his academic contemporaries, his enthusiastic populism led him to create one of American popular culture's most enduring icons. He died in Rye, New York, of cancer.

• Marston's letters and scripts pertaining to *Wonder Woman* are in the Special Collections Department of the Smithsonian Institution Libraries. A brief autobiographical sketch is in the *Harvard Class of 1915 25th Anniversary Report*, pp. 480–82. Marston's academic publications are listed in Carl Murchison, ed., *The Psychological Register*, vol. 3 (1932). The most comprehensive modern analysis is Geoffrey C. Bunn, "The Lie Detector, *Wonder Woman* and Liberty: The Life and Work of William Moulton Marston," *History of the Human Sciences* 10, no. 1 (1997): 91–119. See also Matthew Hale, *Human Science and Social Order: Hugo Münsterberg and the Origins of Applied Psychology* (1981), and Donald S. Napoli, *Architects of Adjustment: The History of the Psychological Profession in the United States* (1981). An obituary is in the *New York Times*, 3 May 1947.

GEOFFREY C. BUNN

MARTEL, Charles (5 Mar. 1860–15 May 1945), chief developer of the Library of Congress classification scheme, was born Karl David Hanke in Zurich, Switzerland, the son of Franz Hanke, an antiquarian bookseller, and Maria Gertrud Strässle. Martel felt his true education came from daily association with his father's outstanding general reference library of more than 250,000 volumes. He also completed the Gymnasium course in Zurich and attended courses at the University of Zurich in 1876–1877 before emigrating to the United States in late 1879 or early 1880. He became an American citizen in 1887 under the name Charles Martel. From 1880 to 1892, Martel worked as a teacher, farmer, accountant, and estate manager in Kentucky, Missouri, Nebraska, and Iowa. He also served as a public library volunteer.

Martel chose librarianship as a full-time career in March 1892 when he joined the staff of the Newberry Library in Chicago. His bibliographic knowledge and linguistic skills led to rapid success, and he held several positions during his five years at the Newberry, including cataloger and head of the Departments of Arts and Letters (1893–1896) and Early Printed Books and Manuscripts (1896–1897). He also learned the fundamentals of library classification and formed a lifelong personal and professional friendship with J. C. M. Hanson, who left the Newberry in 1893 to become head cataloger at the University of Wisconsin in Madison.

In September 1897 Librarian of Congress John Russell Young appointed Hanson to head the Library of Congress's new Catalogue Department. Hanson convinced Young to hire Martel as his assistant, effective 1 December 1897. When Martel joined Hanson, the Library of Congress, according to their colleague William Warner Bishop, acquired a cataloging and classification team "which has never been equaled anywhere."

The new Library of Congress building was opened on 1 November 1897, and its enormous collection of nearly 800,000 volumes, the largest in the country, filled the halls of the new building. The books were classified according to an increasingly unsatisfactory Baconian system of forty-four classes of knowledge, originally devised by Thomas Jefferson and then gradually modified throughout the nineteenth century. Martel's first task was to analyze the old system to see if any of it might be salvaged. His conclusion, reported to Librarian Young, was negative: "everything must be worked over anew."

Martel rejected the use of any classification systems then in existence and began devising his own eclectic system, using in part the expansive classification ideas developed by librarian Charles A. Cutter. Books were assigned to main classes designated by capital letters, such as J for political science and Z for bibliography, and subclasses were expressed by numbers. Martel applied his new scheme to Chapter 38 (literature and bibliography) of the old system and worked quickly, for *Class Z, Bibliography and Library Science* was completed by mid-1898. Over 6,000 volumes were added to the new Class Z shelflist.

After Class Z was completed, Librarian Young decided that additional staff was needed before full-scale reclassification could continue. Martel never stopped classification work, but Hanson was soon busy with cataloging changes of an equally fundamental nature. In later years Hanson always rejected credit for the Library of Congress classification scheme, as he explained in a 1915 letter to Librarian of Congress Herbert Putnam: "Soon after 1898 I was forced to give almost all my time to the cataloguing, leaving the details of the classification to Mr. Martel."

In May 1898, in a cooperative undertaking with the Copyright Office, the Catalogue Department began preparing book entries for copyright deposits for the *Catalogue of Title-Entries*. Two months later, the Government Printing Office began printing, on three-by-five-inch cards, fifty copies of each entry from the *Catalogue*, enabling the Library of Congress to establish a new card catalog for the public and two card catalogs for the cataloging staff. This innovation and Martel's classification work were the fundamental elements in the new national bibliographic system soon to be established by the Library of Congress, particularly through the printing, sale, and distribution of catalog cards to other libraries that would begin in 1901.

Young died in early 1899. Reclassification work was officially suspended in April 1899 when Herbert Putnam, former director of the Boston Public Library, became librarian of Congress. Putnam asked Hanson and Martel to again reassess the possibility of using a classification scheme already in existence, recognizing the potential advantages of uniformity if a standard system could be adopted. Martel, with Hanson's support, continued his opposition to adopting Melvil Dewey's Decimal Classification System or any other classification scheme currently in use. He argued that the Library of Congress needed a new system that was based on the special characteristics of its own comprehensive collections. By the end of 1899 Putnam was reasonably certain that a new classification system had to be devised, but he still was not convinced that Martel's system was the best solution.

In spite of Putnam's continuing uncertainty, in January 1901 Martel and five assistants began reclassifying the old Chapter 4, America, into the new Classes E and F, American History. In May 1901 Putnam sent Martel and William P. Cutter, chief of the library's Order Division, on one last trip to consult with other librarians about the possibility of revising other systems for Library of Congress use. The trip made it clear that other classification schemes, including the Dewey decimal system, were too inflexible and confining for use by a national institution with a large and rapidly growing scholarly collection. Putnam finally agreed to the full development of Martel's more adaptable and expansive system. In 1905, addressing the American Library Association, Putnam expressed his disappointment, not with Martel's scheme, but with the library's failure to find an existing system it could use: "We considered long, but . . . have proceeded to construct a system of our own, and have thus added one more crime to the calendar."

Thus Martel was responsible not only for the philosophical base for the Library of Congress classification system, but also, with Hanson's help, for convincing Putnam that the Library of Congress required its own classification system, one suited to the special needs of the nation's largest library collection.

Martel continued to supervise and modify the library's classification work. Class E appeared in 1901, and during the next thirty years all the other schedules were completed except for K (Law), which was not developed until after his death.

In 1900 Martel married Emma McCoy Haas, of Woodstock, Virginia. They had one child. After his wife's death in 1906, Martel concentrated his interests on the Library of Congress and its bibliographic work. He was a quiet and self-effacing man who was happily devoted to his work and to instructing others. Putnam often referred to Martel as "a marvel of modest scholarship."

Martel also made a major contribution in descriptive cataloging. Hanson left the Library of Congress in 1910 to become director of the University of Michigan Library, and Martel was named chief of the library's Catalog Division in 1912. He skillfully guided the development of uniform cataloging rules and established the Library of Congress cataloging as authoritative. In 1928 he rejoined his colleagues Bishop and Hanson as part of a Carnegie Endowment team that helped the Vatican Library reorganize and establish modern cataloging procedures.

In 1930 an executive order from President Herbert Hoover exempted Martel from mandatory retirement, citing his "irreplaceable knowledge of the collections of the Library of Congress and his rich bibliographical and technical experience." A special position was created for him: Consultant in Cataloging, Classification and Bibliography. Martel did not retire until 1 May 1945, forty-eight years after he joined the library's staff. He died two weeks later in Washington, D.C.

• Martel's official Library of Congress correspondence is in the Library of Congress Archives in the Manuscript Division, Library of Congress. Martel wrote several summaries of his work at the Library of Congress. They include "Classification: A Brief Conspectus of Present Day Practice," *Library Journal* 36 (1911): 410–16; "Cataloging 1876–1926," *Library Journal* 51 (1926): 1065–69; and "The Library of Congress Classification," in *Essays Offered to Herbert Putnam*, ed. William Warner Bishop and Andrew Keogh (1929). The most detailed account of Martel's early years is James B. Childs, "Charles Martel," *Encyclopedia of Library and Information Science*, vol. 17, Allen Kent et al. (1976). His contribution to bibliography and librarianship is outlined in Leo E. LaMontagne, *American Library Classification, with Special Reference to the Library of Congress* (1961), and Francis Miksa, *The Development of Classification at the Library of Congress*, University of Illinois, Graduate School of Library Science Occasional Paper no. 164 (1984). Also useful is William Warner Bishop, "The Library of Congress, 1907–1915," *Library Quarterly* 18 (1948): 1–25. An obituary by Martel's friend and colleague J. Christian Bay is in *Library Journal* 70 (1945): 589.

JOHN Y. COLE

MARTIN, Alexander (c. 1740–2 Nov. 1807), revolutionary soldier and political leader, was born in Hunterdon County, New Jersey, the son of Hugh Martin, a Presbyterian minister, and Jane Hunter. Both parents were of Irish descent. Educated at the College of New Jersey (now Princeton University), he received A.B. and A.M. degrees in 1756 and 1759, respectively. After a sojourn in Virginia as a tutor, he settled in Salisbury, Rowan County, North Carolina, about 1760. He acquired property there and in Guilford County (now Rockingham County) along the Dan River. He became a merchant and, by appointment of Governor William Tryon, a public official, serving successively as justice of the peace and deputy king's attorney for Rowan County in the 1760s.

As a royal appointee, Martin became embroiled in the Regulator controversy sweeping the piedmont counties. Under-represented in the assembly, the westerners believed themselves to be victims of the greed and dishonesty of colonial officials, especially extortionate lawyers, judges, and tax collectors. The Regulators sought to prevent the transaction of official business by mob action, both threatened and real. At the September 1770 session of Hillsborough court, an

angry crowd disrupted the proceedings and severely whipped several lawyers and colonial functionaries, Martin among them. When a similar situation arose in March 1771 at the Rowan court, Martin, John Frohock, and a few others met the Regulators and offered conciliation. The negotiators signed an agreement to return excessive legal fees and to arbitrate other divisive matters. An angry Governor Tryon sarcastically denounced the agreement and its authors, declaring their actions "unconstitutional, Dishonorable to Government and introductive of a practice the most dangerous to the peace and happiness of Society" (Tryon to Frohock and Martin, 5 Apr. 1771). On 16 May 1771 Tryon and the militia defeated and scattered the Regulators at the battle of Alamance.

About 1770 Martin settled his widowed mother and his siblings on his Dan River property, naming his plantation there "Danbury." Although he retained his Salisbury holdings, his interest turned to Guilford County. He studied law and was admitted to the North Carolina bar in 1772. Soon thereafter he began a long period of public service. He was a Guilford County delegate to the colonial assembly in 1773–1774, was judge of the Salisbury court of oyer and terminer in 1774, and represented Guilford in the Second Provincial Congress in April 1775. An active patriot, Martin was a member of the Third Provincial Congress, a body that appointed him lieutenant colonel of the Second North Carolina Continental Regiment. In an ensuring winter campaign, the regiment fought Tories in western South Carolina and at Moore's Creek Bridge in February 1776. Having been appointed colonel in May 1776, Martin led his regiment in the defense of Charleston. Subsequently the Second North Carolina joined General George Washington in the Pennsylvania campaign. After having been engaged at Brandywine, Martin and the regiment played a controversial role in the battle of Germantown. In the recriminations that followed, Martin was accused of cowardice, reportedly having hidden in a hollow tree as the tide turned against North Carolina troops in the vanguard of the American assault. Tried and acquitted by an ensuing court-martial, he resigned his commission in November 1777 and returned to North Carolina.

For most of his post-military life, Martin held a succession of offices in state and national government. He was state senator for Guilford County in 1778–1782, 1785, and 1787–1788 and for Rockingham County in 1804–1805. He was Speaker in every session except that of 1778–1779 and 1804. Moreover, he was a member of the state's Board of War and Council Extraordinary in the tumultuous last years of the Revolution. These powerful bodies coordinated North Carolina's military efforts. After acting as chief executive when Thomas Burke, the sitting governor, was captured by the British, Martin was elected by the general assembly to six terms as governor (1782, 1783, 1784, 1790, 1791, 1792), serving the constitutional limit of three consecutive terms on two occasions. Perhaps his elective successes were attributable to his acknowledgement that the governor was subordinate to the general assembly.

As governor he proposed clemency for Tories; promoted public education, economic development, and internal improvements; advocated public support for Protestant ministers; and favored greater powers for the national legislature. In December 1786 he was elected to the Confederation Congress but resigned without attending a session. Martin was one of five North Carolina delegates to the Constitutional Convention of 1787. A moderate Federalist, he made no recorded contributions to the constitutional process and left Philadelphia before the resulting document was signed. Elected to the U.S. Senate in December 1792, he aligned himself with the Jeffersonians in opposition to Federalist foreign policy but supported the Alien and Sedition Acts—votes that probably cost him reelection in 1798. As a senator his principal interest was advocacy of public legislative sessions. On his return to North Carolina, he settled at Danbury. He served in the legislature of 1804 as a senator and died at his home three years later. Martin never married but had a son, Alexander Strong Martin, whom he acknowledged in life and in his will.

Martin was sophisticated, honest, and trustworthy. A moderate in politics, he was a master of conciliation. Although he had no great ability, he was extremely popular with his fellow citizens as his unusually long public career attests.

• A number of disparate sources are available to Martin scholars. For factual data see James McLachlan, *Princetonians, 1748–1768, a Biographical Dictionary* (1976); Francis B. Heitman, *Historical Register of Officers of the Continental Army during the War of Revolution* (1914; repr. 1967); John L. Cheney, Jr., *North Carolina Government* (1975); and *Raleigh Register and N.C. State Gazette*, 19 Nov. 1807. For substantive information about his career see William S. Powell et al., *The Regulators in North Carolina* (1971); *Colonial Records of North Carolina* (10 vols., 1886–1890); and *State Records of North Carolina* (16 vols., 1895–1905). See also Francis Nash, *Governor Alexander Martin: An Address* (1908), and Elizabeth Winston Yates, "The Public Career of Alexander Martin" (M.A. thesis, Univ. of North Carolina, Chapel Hill, 1943).

MAX R. WILLIAMS

MARTIN, Anne Henrietta (30 Sept. 1875–15 Apr. 1951), suffragist and feminist essayist, was born in Empire City, Nevada, the daughter of William O'Hara Martin, a state senator, merchant, and Reno bank president, and Louise Stadtmuller. She attended Bishop Whitaker's School for Girls in Reno, then the University of Nevada (1892–1894), where she received a B.A. in history. After a second B.A. in 1896 and an M.A. in history in 1897, both from Stanford University, she founded the history department at the University of Nevada and headed it until 1899. From 1899 to 1901 she continued her studies at Chase School of Art, Columbia University, and the Universities of Leipzig and London; she then lectured in art history at Nevada until 1903.

Family crisis, combined with her later experience in the English suffrage movement, transformed the student who in 1896 had responded lukewarmly to Anna Howard Shaw and Susan B. Anthony's suffrage speeches in Stanford Chapel. Returning from Europe for her father's funeral in 1901, Martin tried to prevent mismanagement of his estate by his partners and her brothers but was thwarted by her mother's deference to male authority. This experience, she later reflected, "suddenly made a feminist of me! . . . I found that I stood alone in my family against a man-controlled world." For the next few years she traveled in Europe and Asia and experienced the women's revolution in England from 1909 to 1911. Attracted to the militant suffrage strategies of Emmeline Pankhurst, Martin was arrested in the melee erupting from the "Black Friday" deputation on 18 November 1910 protesting the prime minister's announcement that consideration of woman suffrage would be delayed. She became a Fabian Socialist and expressed her social concerns in essays and stories under the name Anne O'Hara.

Martin returned to Nevada in the fall of 1911 eager to apply her English experiences to ratification of the suffrage amendment recently passed by the state legislature. Elected chair of the Nevada Equal Franchise Society (NEFS) in February 1912, she organized an exhausting campaign over sparsely populated deserts and mountains that convinced male voters to enfranchise women on 3 November 1914. Success propelled her into the national movement as a speaker and executive committee member of both the National American Woman Suffrage Association (NAWSA) and the more militant Congressional Union (CU). After the NEFS reorganized as the Nevada Women's Civic League in 1915 under Martin's leadership, it followed her sympathies with the CU, though some Nevada suffragists continued to find its strategies too militant and its structure too undemocratic.

In 1916 the CU separated from NAWSA to mobilize women's voting power and elected Martin to chair the National Woman's Party (NWP), its political organization in the twelve states where women could vote. When the CU combined its voting and nonvoting organizations in 1917 to form the NWP, Alice Paul became the chair while Martin served as vice chair, a featured speaker, and head of the legislative department, which lobbied for a federal amendment. Committed to militant tactics, she helped organize voting women in the West in 1916 to challenge Democrats, including President Woodrow Wilson, because they had failed to invoke party discipline to secure a federal suffrage amendment. On 14 July 1917 she was arrested for picketing the White House and sentenced briefly to the Occoquan Workhouse, a women's facility in Virginia.

Martin's vision of political equality transcended suffrage to include equal representation for women at every level of politics. Her candidacies for the U.S. Senate in 1918 and 1920 constituted the logical next step in "a campaign that is destined to give woman her place in the political affairs of the nation." Her campaign manager, Mabel Vernon, and others who suspended their national suffrage activities to help understood themselves to be involved in a new level of struggle. As an Independent, Martin searched for language, style, and issues that would animate women as political actors outside the framework of the traditional political parties. Her platforms calling for legislation to provide better working conditions for both men and women and the nationalization of railroads and public utilities alienated wealthy suffragists, however, demonstrating that the suffrage movement had united women with different class interests. Martin supported the federal control of land and natural resources to protect farmers, miners, and laborers; amnesty for conscientious objectors and political prisoners; prohibition; and the Sheppard-Towner Bill to improve the welfare of mothers and infants. After World War I she opposed the League of Nations. Nevertheless, in each of the two elections Nevada voters gave her 20 percent of the vote.

Between her 1918 and 1920 campaigns Martin wrote a series of articles in *Good Housekeeping* on the Sheppard-Towner Bill. These articles spawned more than a decade of essays in American and British magazines, including the *Nation*, the *New Republic*, the *Independent*, *Current History*, *New York Times Magazine*, *Reconstruction*, *Sunset*, *Time and Tide*, and *English Review*. In these essays Martin urged women to form autonomous political organizations, and she articulated harsh critiques of male domination in politics, employment, education, professional training, and even women's magazines. She favored support networks for women seeking political office similar to the Women's Local Government Society in England, arguing that: "Women must support women until they win approximate equality in government. . . . Then we can forget sex, and establish human qualifications as the standard." Women who failed to see the logic of this strategy, she explained, suffered from an "inferiority complex" caused by man's power to interpret woman's experience.

Martin, who never married, moved in 1921 to Carmel, California, to maintain a home for her mother. From there she kept a critical distance from activities organized by eastern women. NWP lobbying efforts, she argued, used antiquated forms of influence when the vote had created new options for women's political power. She denounced Carrie Chapman Catt for organizing the League of Women Voters to educate women for citizenship instead of taking direct political action, and she warned women who joined the mainstream political parties that they succeeded only in creating "ladies auxiliaries" and not equal political partnerships.

A member of the Women's Peace Party since 1915, Martin served on the national board of the Women's International League for Peace and Freedom from 1926 to 1936 and as western regional director from 1926 to 1931. She was a delegate to its world conferences in Dublin (1926) and Prague (1929) but resigned in 1936, citing weak and ineffective national leadership, whereupon she joined the People's Mandate to Governments to End War. Reflecting on world affairs between the world wars, she claimed that "another world catastrophe" would only be prevented by "the functioning of women *as women* in government, on a fifty-fifty basis with men, not imitating them but 'giving their differences' to life and to the state." Martin continued to lecture on government and women's rights until shortly before her death in Carmel.

Near the end of her life, Martin recalled her fifty years of women's rights advocacy and exclaimed, "Equality for women is a passion with me" (Martin, unpublished autobiography, p. 3). A prominent suffrage leader in Nevada and the nation, her advocacy for political equality went far beyond suffrage in her pioneer campaigns for the U.S. Senate, in her essays exploring the roots of inequality and the development of women's political networks, and in her organizational work for peace. Martin's vision of equality was broader and her analysis of inequality deeper than that of most of her contemporaries. Her actions and words continued the political dialogue long after women had won the vote, a dialogue that would resonate powerfully with subsequent generations of women who shared Martin's passion for equality.

• Anne Martin's complete papers, including the manuscript of her unpublished autobiography, correspondence, and other materials related to suffrage and her senatorial campaigns, are in the Bancroft Library at the University of California, Berkeley. The Nevada Historical Society, Reno, has the two sketchbooks Martin produced while a student at Bishop Whitaker's School. Other collections containing significant related material include the National Woman's Party Papers, Library of Congress, and the Women's International League for Peace and Freedom Papers, Swarthmore Peace Archive. Oral history interviews with Alice Paul, Mabel Vernon, and Sara Bard Field, Regional Oral History Office, University of California, Berkeley, and several interviews in the Oral History Project, University of Nevada, offer additional perspectives. Among Martin's significant writings are "Women's Inferiority Complex," *New Republic*, 20 July 1921, pp. 210–12; "Woman's Vote and Woman's Chains," *Sunset*, Apr. 1922, pp. 12–14; "English and American Women in Politics," *New York Times Magazine*, 5 Nov. 1922, pp. 12–13; and "Feminists and Future Political Action," *Nation*, 18 Feb. 1925, pp. 185–86. She also wrote a well-known NAWSA pamphlet with Mary Austin, *Suffrage and Government: The Modern Idea of Government by Consent and Woman's Place in It, with Special Reference to Nevada and Other Western States* (1914), and, more than thirty years later, an often-quoted reflection, "The Story of the Nevada Equal Suffrage Campaign: Memoirs of Anne Martin," *University of Nevada Bulletin* 42 (Aug. 1948): 4–19. The only biography is Anne Bail Howard, *The Long Campaign* (1985). See also Ann Warren Smith, "Anne Martin and a History of Woman Suffrage in Nevada, 1869–1914" (Ph.D. diss., Univ. of Nevada, 1976), and Kathryn Anderson, "Practical Political Equality for Women: Anne Martin's Campaigns for the U.S. Senate in Nevada, 1918 and 1920" (Ph.D. diss., Univ. of Washington, 1978). An obituary is in the *Reno Evening Gazette*, 16 Apr. 1951; the newspaper also ran a feature summarizing her political career on 21 Apr. 1951.

KATHRYN ANDERSON

MARTIN, Artemas (3 Aug. 1835–7 Nov. 1918), mathematician, was born in Steuben County, New York, the son of James Madison Martin and Orenda Knight Bradley, farmers. Martin received little formal education as a child and no college education. He attended the district school for three terms and spent a few months at the Franklin Academy when he was seventeen. This education introduced him to algebra, geometry, and trigonometry. At eighteen he began submitting solutions to problems posed in the Pittsburgh *Almanac* and in the *Saturday Evening Post*'s "Riddler Column." Throughout his life, he continued to publish solutions to problems in periodicals such as *Clark's School Visitor* (later *Schoolday Magazine*), *Illinois Teacher*, *Iowa Instructor*, *National Educator*, and the *American Mathematical Monthly*. He also contributed to several British publications, including *Lady's and Gentleman's Diary*, *Messenger of Mathematics*, and *Quarterly Journal of Mathematics*, among others. In 1870 he served as the editor of the "Stairway Department" of *Clark's School Visitor*, and he edited the *Normal Monthly*'s department of higher mathematics from 1875 to 1876. In his writings and problem-solving, Martin dealt mostly with Diophantine analysis, probability, elliptic integrals, logarithms, and properties of numbers and triangles.

In 1877 Martin founded the *Mathematical Visitor*, a periodical he hoped would encourage interest in mathematics among amateurs. Not only did Martin write many of the articles in the *Visitor* himself, he also did the typesetting and printing of all but the first three issues. The same year that he began the *Visitor*, Yale University awarded Martin an honorary A.M. He expanded his publishing responsibilities in 1882 with the establishment of another journal, *Mathematical Magazine*. Like the *Visitor*, this publication dealt with mathematical problems and their solutions. The last number of the *Visitor*, dated January 1894, appeared in October 1895, and the *Mathematical Magazine* was published officially until September 1910. In the years following the founding of the journals, Martin received two more honorary degrees, a Ph.D. from Rutgers University in 1882 and an LL.D. from Hillsdale College in 1885.

Until 1885 Martin lived in Pennsylvania, earning his living farming, chopping wood, and drilling oil wells, with the exception of four winters spent teaching in district schools. In 1881 he turned down an opportunity to be professor of mathematics at the Normal School in Warrensburg, Missouri. He accepted a position as librarian for the United States Coast and Geodetic Survey (USCGS) in Washington, D.C., in 1885, becoming a computer in the survey's Division of Tides in 1898.

While working for the USCGS and publishing his journals, Martin presented his paper "On Fifth Power Numbers Whose Sum Is a Fifth Power" at the International Mathematical Congress of 1893. The congress, held at the World's Columbian Exposition in Chicago, featured presentations of papers (many *in absentia*) by such world-renowned mathematicians as David Hilbert, Hermann Minkowski, Heinrich Maschke, and Eliakim Hastings Moore.

Martin belonged to the New York (later American) Mathematical Society, the Mathematical Association of America, the London and Edinburgh Mathematical Societies, the Société Mathématique de France, the Deutsche Mathematiker-Vereiningung, and the Circolo Matematico di Palermo. He was also a Fellow of the American Association for the Advancement of Science.

An avid book collector, Martin accumulated a large library of mathematical and miscellaneous works. His contemporaries considered his collection of American arithmetic and algebra texts to be one of the largest and finest of its kind. He drew on his knowledge of these works in his *Notes on the History of American Text-Books on Arithmetic*, written with J. M. Greenwood (1899). He left his mathematics collection as well as his numerous books on such subjects as botany, natural history, and poetry to the American University. Martin died in Washington, D.C. He had never married and had no children.

Martin's contributions to American mathematics, although not in the form of important original research, received recognition and appreciation from his peers. Through his publications, he furthered public interest in mathematical work. His lack of formal education did not seem to hinder his ability to communicate mathematically. As B. F. Finkel wrote in a biographical sketch of Martin for the *American Mathematical Monthly* Martin "has that rare and happy faculty of presenting his solutions in the simplest mathematical language, so that those who have mastered the elements of the various branches of mathematics, are able to understand his reasoning" (p. 111).

• The Special Collections of the American University contain Martin's library as well as his papers, including notebooks in which he wrote out mathematical problems and descriptions of books that he owned or planned to purchase. For Martin's paper presented at the International Mathematical Congress, see E. H. Moore et al., eds., *Mathematical Papers Read at the International Mathematical Congress Held in Connection with the World's Columbian Exposition Chicago 1893* (1896). B. F. Finkel's biographical sketch appeared in the *American Mathematical Monthly* 1 (Apr. 1894): 109–11. See also Florian Cajori, *The Teaching and History of Mathematics in the United States* (1890), and David Eugene Smith and Jekuthiel Ginsburg, *A History of Mathematics in America before 1900* (1934). Obituaries are in *Science*, 22 Nov. 1918, and the *American Mathematical Monthly* 26 (Feb. 1919).

PATTI W. HUNTER

MARTIN, Billy (16 May 1928–25 Dec. 1989), baseball player and manager, was born in Berkeley, California, the son of Alfred Martin, a musician, and Juvan Salvini Pisani. (Questions surround his given name; some sources say it was Alfred Manuel Pesano or Pisani; other sources claim it was Alfred Manuel Martin, Jr.) Martin's parents separated shortly before Martin was born, and in 1929 his mother married Jack Downey, who worked at assorted jobs. Martin described his childhood in Berkeley as rough, and he would later consider it a reason for his many physical altercations as an adult. Known as "Billy" from an early age, he developed into a fine teenage baseball player. In 1946 he signed with the Oakland Oaks of the Pacific Coast League, managed by Casey Stengel. After season-long stints with minor league teams in Idaho Falls, Idaho (1946), and Phoenix, Arizona (1947), Martin played for the Oaks in 1948 and 1949. In 1949 Stengel became the manager of the New York Yankees of the American League, and at the end of that season the Yankees, acting on Stengel's strong recommendation, purchased Martin's contract. In October 1950 Martin married Lois Elaine Berndt; they had one daughter before divorcing in 1953.

Having played sparingly for the Yankees in 1950 and 1951, Martin blossomed as the team's second baseman in 1952, playing in 109 games and batting .267. However, he became better known for his hard-nosed, hustling style of play. This style was most evident in the seventh game of the 1952 World Series between the Yankees and the Brooklyn Dodgers. In the seventh inning, with the Yankees ahead 4–2, the Dodgers loaded the bases with two out and Jackie Robinson at the plate. Robinson hit an infield pop fly to Yankees first baseman Joe Collins. However, the prevailing wind affected the ball such that Collins appeared to lose sight of it. With no other fielder in the vicinity, Martin rushed in and made a knee-high catch that ended the inning and won the series for the Yankees.

In 1953 Martin played in a career-high 149 games for the Yankees and again stood out in the World Series. In the Yankees' four-games-to-two victory over the Dodgers, he batted .500 with 12 hits in 24 at-bats, setting a World Series record for most hits in a six-game series; he batted in the series-winning run; and he earned the series' Most Valuable Player award. Martin then served in the U.S. Army, missing all of the 1954 season and most of the 1955 season; he played in twenty games for the Yankees at the end of the 1955 season, and his return sparked a successful late run at the American League pennant.

During his playing career with the Yankees, Martin, who exhibited a "work hard and play hard" attitude, developed a taste for the nightlife of New York City and caroused regularly with his teammates, particularly Mickey Mantle and Whitey Ford. On one such occasion, in May 1957, Yankees players met at the Copacabana nightclub in New York to celebrate Mantle's birthday. There the players became involved in a brawl in which a delicatessen owner from the Bronx received a concussion and a fractured jaw. Yankees general manager George Weiss wrongly held Martin responsible for the fracas, and on 15 June 1957 Martin was traded to the Kansas City Athletics in a multi-player transaction.

Martin spent the remainder of his playing career in a journeyman capacity. Between June 1957 and his retirement as a player in 1961, he played for six teams: Kansas City (1957), the Detroit Tigers (1958), the Cleveland Indians (1959), the Cincinnati Reds (1960), the Milwaukee Braves (1961), and the Minnesota Twins (1961). His final career numbers include a .257 batting average, with 64 home runs and 333 runs batted in over 1,021 games. In five World Series appearances he batted .333, with five home runs and 19 runs batted in over 28 games. However, Martin never played in the postseason after being traded by the Yankees, and his earlier accomplishments as a team leader and sparkplug became overshadowed by a growing number of brawls on and off the field—likely because of his general temperament but possibly because of his continued drinking. In October 1959 Martin married Gretchen Winkler, a flight attendant; they had one son.

Upon his retirement as a player, Martin continued to work for the Minnesota Twins, first as a scout (1962–1964), then as their third base coach (1965–1967), and finally as the manager of their minor league team in Denver, Colorado (1968). In 1969 he became the manager of the Twins, beginning a successful yet stormy major league managing career. That year, under Martin's leadership, the Twins improved from the 79–83 record of the previous year to a 97–65 record, winning the American League's Western Division championship in the first year of divisional play in major league baseball. Despite this success, Martin's drinking and brawling caught up with him. In August 1969 he engaged in a fistfight with Twins pitcher Dave Boswell outside a bar in Detroit, after which Boswell received twenty stitches to close lacerations on his face. The Twins fired Martin at the end of the season, claiming that he had violated club policies, but his altercation with Boswell probably accelerated the process.

In 1971 Martin took over as the manager of the Detroit Tigers, who had finished with a 79–83 record the previous season. That year the Tigers improved to 91–71 and earned second place in the American League Eastern Division, and in 1972 the Tigers won the Eastern Division title with an 86–70 record. The Tigers grew tired of Martin's fractious behavior, however, and near the end of the 1973 season, with the team headed for a third-place finish in the division, Martin was fired. Before the season ended he was hired by the Texas Rangers, and Martin's managerial pattern continued. The Rangers improved from a 57–105 record and a last-place finish in 1973 to an 84–76 record and second place in 1974 under Martin, who won manager of the year honors from the Associated Press. However, in September of that year Martin assaulted the Rangers' traveling secretary after they disagreed about the idea of the Rangers' wives forming a club; and he again engaged in disputes with ownership, which resulted in his termination in July 1975.

Martin's managerial career would reach new highs and new lows with the Yankees. His tumultuous tenure as the Yankees' manager began when majority owner George Steinbrenner hired him on 2 August 1975. The following year, Martin's Yankees won the American League pennant, their first since 1964, before being swept by the Cincinnati Reds in the World Series. In 1977, when Steinbrenner acquired free-agent outfielder Reggie Jackson (whose self-regard often rankled others), the team seemed in disarray; during a nationally televised game at Boston's Fenway Park in June 1977, Martin and Jackson nearly came to blows in the dugout. Despite the clash of egos, giving rise to the epithet the "Bronx Zoo," the Yankees pulled together to win the league championship and then the World Series in six games over the Los Angeles Dodgers.

In 1978 Martin's marriage to Gretchen Winkler ended in divorce. During the baseball season that year, the Yankees battled to catch the Boston Red Sox, who had established a substantial lead in the American League Eastern Division. In July of that year Martin, sitting in a bar and feeling particularly disgusted with both Jackson and Steinbrenner, blurted out to reporters, "One's a born liar and the other's convicted"—the latter comment a reference to Steinbrenner's 1974 conviction on charges of illegal contributions in connection with Richard M. Nixon's 1972 presidential campaign. As a result, Steinbrenner forced Martin to resign immediately and replaced him with Bob Lemon. Incredibly, four days later Steinbrenner announced to a Yankee Stadium crowd that Lemon would manage only through the end of the 1979 season and that Martin would return as manager in 1980. In the midst of these distractions, the Yankees repeated as world champions under Lemon, but when the team struggled again in 1979, Steinbrenner replaced Lemon with Martin in June of that year. The stalwart catcher Thurman Munson's death in a plane crash that August ended whatever dreams the Yankees had of returning to postseason play for a fourth consecutive year. In October Martin got into a fight in a bar with a Minneapolis marshmallow salesman, for which Steinbrenner fired him.

In 1980 the Oakland Athletics, who had finished in last place with a 54–108 record the year before, hired Martin as their manager. By combining aggressive offense, steady defense, and shrewd management of his pitching staff, he created what became known as "Billyball." The result, again, was substantial improvement in a short period of time. The A's achieved an 83–79 record and a second-place division finish in 1980, and the following year, in the split-season format resulting from a protracted players' strike, the A's won the American League's Western Division playoff before losing to the Yankees in the league championship series. When the team's pitching failed in 1982—possibly because Martin had overused his starters—he considered informal offers from Steinbrenner to return to New York; the decision was clinched when the A's fired him in October. A month later Martin married Heather Ervolino; the marriage ended in divorce four years later.

In 1983 Martin began the first of three short stints as the Yankees manager. He was fired by Steinbrenner in September 1983, as the Yankees headed for a third-place finish in the division; he was rehired in April 1985 to replace Yogi Berra, then fired again at the end of the 1985 season; then, after two years broadcasting Yankees games, he was hired again in 1988 and fired one last time in June 1988. That same year he married Jill Guiver. The revolving-door saga of George and Billy became the stuff of comedy between the two men at press conferences and in commercials, but it did nothing to raise the Yankees beyond the status of contenders during the 1980s, and it embarrassed the players and fans alike. While Steinbrenner apparently was motivated both by a deep respect for Martin's managerial ability and fiery competitiveness and by the public attention that hiring Martin would generate, Martin retained an everlasting loyalty to the Yankees that dated back to his playing career. Regardless, both possessed strong personalities that inevitably broke down the working relationship each time.

Martin finished his managerial career with a won-lost record or 1,258–1,018, five division championships won with four different teams, two league championships, and a World Series championship. In recognition of his contributions to the club, the Yankees retired Martin's uniform number 1 in August 1986. The best measure of his success was his ability to mold previously mediocre or bad teams into contenders by motivating average players and being an expert strategist. But his abrasive personality invariably antagonized the star players and the ownership of every team he managed, and as a result, during a managerial career that spanned twenty years, he never held a particular job for more than three years. In addition, the chronic drinking, brawling, and miseries with women took their toll on Martin and made him something of a tragic figure.

On Christmas Day 1989 Martin died of massive internal injuries sustained when his pickup truck slid off the road and slammed into a culvert outside his home near Binghamton, New York. The driver of the truck was William Reedy, a longtime drinking buddy of Martin's, and newspaper accounts stated that both men had been drinking before they entered the truck.

• Martin wrote an autobiography with Peter Golenbock titled *Number 1* (1980); he then worked with Phil Pepe on a second book, *Billyball* (1988). Two biographies offer the fullest accounts of Martin's life, although they differ concerning historical details: Golenbock, *Wild, High and Tight: The Life and Death of Billy Martin* (1994), and David Falkner, *The Last Yankee* (1992). Martin's career statistics as both a player and a manager are in John Thorn and Pete Palmer, eds., *Total Baseball*, 3d ed. (1993). A player's account of the Yankees under Martin's first tenure as manager is Sparky Lyle and Golenbock, *The Bronx Zoo* (1979).

BROOKS D. SIMPSON
MATTHEW E. VAN ATTA

MARTIN, Everett Dean (5 July 1880–10 May 1941), social psychologist, social philosopher, and adult educator, was born in Jacksonville, Illinois, the son of Buker E. Martin, a tobacconist, and Mollie Field. Martin earned his B.A. from Illinois College in Jacksonville in 1904. In 1907 he graduated from McCormick Theological Seminary and was ordained as a Congregational minister. That same year he married Esther W. Kirk; they had three daughters. Martin held pastorates in Lombard, Illinois (1906–1908), Dixon, Illinois (1908–1910), and Des Moines, Iowa, where he was a minister of the First Unitarian Church (1910–1914). In 1915 he divorced his wife, married Persis E. Rowell, and, as result of his marital problems, was forced to resign from the ministry. He had one son with Rowell, but this marriage also ended in divorce. In 1931 he married his third wife, Daphne Crane Drake.

Martin had begun his writing career in Des Moines, where in 1914 he began writing featured columns for the *Des Moines Register and Leader*. After moving to New York City, he found work as a writer for the *New York Globe*. But scandal followed Martin east, and he was forced to leave his job on the *Globe* as well.

In 1916 Martin began his long association with the People's Institute of New York City, a center for adult education that had been founded by Charles Sprague Smith in 1897. Initially appointed as a lecturer in social philosophy, Martin in 1917 became director of the Cooper Union Forum, a series of public lectures held at Cooper Union but offered through the People's Institute. In the same year he also became the assistant director of the institute and undertook as his first task the development of the institute's School of Philosophy. This school grew directly out of the interest provoked by Martin's own lectures and students' desires for more in-depth study of philosophical issues. Martin became director of the institute in 1922.

Martin's tenure at the People's Institute was marked by a shift from the progressive reform ethos of an earlier era, to offerings shaped by his particular humanist philosophy. Utilizing the resources of New York's intellectual community, Martin organized lecture series, small group discussions, and study groups on a wide variety of topics. Martin brought to the institute a wide range of speakers, including Fiorello LaGuardia, Amy Lowell, Frederick Lewis Allen, A. A. Berle, and Clifton Fadiman. His own Friday evening lectures attempted to take often abstruse material and make it available to a wide and heterogeneous audience. His audiences were large, often totaling more than 1,000 people. Topics included such titles as "Human Nature in Modern Civilization," "The New Liberalism: A Study in the Changing Outlook of Social Philosophy," and "Psychology—What It Has to Teach You About Yourself and the World You Live In."

Although Martin used the People's Institute programs to both develop and reflect his ideas about education, it was primarily through his writings that he became well known. Martin authored twelve books on social psychology, social philosophy, and politics. Starting with his first book, *The Behavior of Crowds* (1920), Martin laid out his concern with the state of modern life. In particular, he feared the demagoguery of the masses and saw education and the cultivation of the individual as the only way to safeguard against the threat of the crowd. This book was most notable for its use of psychological theory to explain mob behavior.

Because of his work on crowds and his fear of mobs, Martin has been criticized as an exponent of antidemocratic thought. Yet Martin clearly remained committed to a Jeffersonian democratic ideal, one emphasizing rationality, human excellence, restraint, and individual responsibility. Martin undoubtedly believed in an intellectual elite, but he was also committed to the attainment of rational discourse in order to solve social problems. Thus he disdained the view that revolution could bring about true social change. Only discussion and dialogue could truly ameliorate social conditions. His work with the People's Institute brought him into daily contact with the poor and with immigrants, and he steadfastly defended his students, praising them in the highest possible terms.

Martin was best known for his defense of liberal education, which he saw as an antidote to both the irrationality of the crowd and the power of propaganda. His humanist defense of liberal education, most cogently stated in *The Meaning of a Liberal Education* (1926), made special reference to the needs of workers and to the kinds of education offered outside of traditional educational agencies. Martin believed that adults seeking a liberal education were striving to move beyond the boredom of their work and to transcend their everyday lives.

Although hundreds of people attended its lectures throughout the 1920s, the People's Institute found it increasingly difficult to raise funds. The deficit was covered by the philanthropic donations of the Laura Spelman Fund of the Rockefeller Foundation and, most importantly, by the Carnegie Corporation through the American Association for Adult Education. In the 1930s the Carnegie Corporation withdrew funding and persuaded Cooper Union to take over the institute. In 1934 the People's Institute closed, and Martin became head of the Department of Social Philosophy at Cooper Union. He left Cooper Union in 1936 to become a professor in the Department of Social Philosophy at Claremont Graduate School in Claremont, California, where he remained until his death. While at the People's Institute, Martin had been involved in a number of other adult education activities. He was a founding member of the American Association for Adult Education (AAAE) in 1926 and served as its president in 1937. He was also a key adviser to the Carnegie Corporation, which funded the AAAE and, through it, a wide variety of adult education activities, from 1926 until his death. In addition, he served as lecturer in social psychology at the New School for Social Research in New York City and as an instructor in social psychology at the Brookwood Workers College in Katonah, New York. From 1919 until 1922 he chaired the National Board of Review of Motion Pictures.

• Martin's papers are located at the Everett Dean Martin Collection, the Ella Strong Denison Library, Scripps College, Claremont, Calif. The People's Institute papers can be found at the New York Public Library and at the Cooper Union Library. Robert Bruce Fisher, "The People's Institute of New

York City, 1897–1934: Culture, Progressive Democracy, and the People" (Ph.D. diss., New York Univ., 1974), covers Martin's work with the institute and effectively analyzes his philosophy. Some short studies of Martin and analyses of his work include Michael Day and Donald Seckinger, "Everett Dean Martin: Liberal in Adult Education," *Journal of Thought* 24, nos. 1 and 2 (Spring/Summer 1989): 26–40, and Harold Stubblefield, *Towards a History of Adult Education in America* (1988). For Martin's historical significance in the social psychology of the crowd, see Gordon W. Allport, "The Historical Background of Social Psychology," in *Handbook of Social Psychology*, vol. 1: *Theory and Method*, ed. Gardner Lindzey and Elliot Aronson (1985). A more thorough discussion of his contribution on crowd psychology may be found in Stanley Milgram and Hans Toch, "Collective Behavior: Crowds and Social Movements," in *The Handbook of Social Psychology*, Vol. 4: *Group Psychology and Phenomena of Interaction*, ed. Lindzey and Aronson, 2d ed. (1969).

AMY D. ROSE

MARTIN, François-Xavier (17 Mar. 1764–10 Dec. 1846), jurist and author, was born in Marseilles, France. Little is known of his childhood, except that he was educated for the priesthood. He immigrated to Martinique in 1782, and two years later to New Bern, North Carolina. There he supported himself successively by teaching French, becoming a typesetter, shop foreman, and ultimately owner of a printing office, which published a daily newspaper as well as school books and novels, some of which were his own translations from the French. While owning and running the printing establishment, Martin also studied law and was admitted to the North Carolina bar in 1789. The legislature commissioned him to publish a digest of state laws and cases (1792–1794). He also published *Cases in the Court of King's Bench during the Reign of Charles I* (1793), *Notes of a Few Decisions of the Superior Courts of the State of North Carolina* (1797), his own translation of Pothier's *A Treatise on Obligations* (1802), and his *History of North Carolina* (1806–1807). Also in 1806 he was elected to the North Carolina legislature.

In 1809 President James Madison appointed Martin a federal judge for the Mississippi Territory and one year later transferred him to the Territory of Orleans. His knowledge of French and English as well as of common and civil law traditions was of great value in the new territory. He became the first attorney general of the new state (1813), and two years later he was appointed as judge of the Supreme Court of Louisiana (the judges of this court were not styled "justices" until after the constitution of 1845 went into effect) and chief judge in 1836. He served the court for thirty-one years.

When Martin began his tenure as judge of the supreme court, Louisiana law was in a state of chaos. The *Digest of the Civil Laws Now in Force in the Territory of Orleans* (1808) was a compilation of existing civil law, which necessitated knowledge of Roman, French, and Spanish law as well as English common law and its American variations. Martin was instrumental in ordering and reconciling the various legal conflicts that resulted, carefully selecting the best elements from each system. Because common law devalued the use of precedents to support judicial decision, Martin used elements from French, Spanish, and Roman law to gain the judicial discretion he needed to support his decisions. He was not always appreciated for his efforts to harmonize legal customs with the reality of American rule. In 1819 he wrote a decision that required all judicial proceedings to be held in "the language of the Constitution"—English. This ruling included "family meetings," a specialized gathering of relatives provided for in the *Digest* held before a justice of the peace or notary public for the purpose of making decisions concerning the affairs of minors or others legally incapable of handling their own affairs. The ruling caused such resentment among the French-speaking population that in 1822 a prominent member of the New Orleans bar and a member of the legislature, Christobel de Armas, introduced a resolution before the Louisiana legislature calling for Martin's impeachment. The resolution failed.

Despite his duties as judge and later chief judge of the Supreme Court of Louisiana, Martin continued writing and publishing when he moved to the state. He wrote and printed a two-volume *History of Louisiana* (1827–1829), which noted Louisiana historian Charles Gayarré critiqued as at best a recitation of facts "as lifeless as the minutes and records of proceedings in a court of justice" (*Fernando de Lemos* [1872], p. 246). This defect later became an asset in the most valuable contribution of Martin's publishing career, his *Louisiana Reports*, the first law reports in the state. These reports reviewed decisions of the Superior Court of the Territory of Orleans from 1809 to 1812 and the Supreme Court of Louisiana from 1813 to 1830 and were especially important in Louisiana, where aspiring attorneys had to acquire familiarity with French, Roman, Spanish, and American law operating in Louisiana's mixed system. Martin was not ashamed to use his position for personal financial gain. In 1816 and 1818 he persuaded the Louisiana legislature to pass laws requiring the state government to purchase copies of his digests and reports from him. Although such arrangements were not unusual in the antebellum period, Martin possessed a single-minded determination to amass a fortune.

During his years in Louisiana, Martin acquired extensive holdings in real estate. He lived in an abstemious and miserly manner; contemporaries noted that his house and his appearance were equally unkempt. Martin never married; he owned one slave who attended to his personal needs. Devoted to his work and the accumulation of a fortune, he had use for neither humor nor leisure. As a speaker he was neither polished nor pleasant and was described as "dry as a hardbaked brickbat." In 1838 his sight failed, but he continued his work as chief judge, writing his decisions in a wooden box to guide his hand. Although his infirmity impeded the flow of cases heard by the court, and a huge backlog of cases waiting to be heard continued to grow, he staunchly resisted attempts by other members of the court to reform the court's procedures and clear the docket. He went to France in 1844 to seek a cure. When he failed to find one, he returned to New Orleans, where he died. The Louisiana Constitution of 1845, which went into effect the year of Martin's death, sought to resolve the problem of an elderly and infirm bench by limiting judges' terms to eight years rather than life appointments.

Even in death Martin was to have an impact on Louisiana law. Just before his unsuccessful visit to France, he executed an olographic (a civil law term meaning entirely in his own handwriting) will in which he left his entire estate of $400,000 to his brother, Paul Barthelemy Martin. The attorney general of Louisiana filed a motion to have the will invalidated on the grounds that Martin was blind and was physically incapable of writing out his own will. Whether Martin left the estate to a brother in Louisiana to avoid inheritance taxes was also at issue. A New Orleans notary testified that Martin had brought him documents in his own handwriting to be notarized quite often; the case went to the Supreme Court of Louisiana, which declared the will valid. The ruling limited the state's power to tax inheritance and also established the principle that the blind could make olographic wills.

Although Martin may have remained on the supreme court longer than he was capable of being an effective member, his efforts to report and explain Louisiana's complex mix of law remains a valuable contribution to the state's rich legal traditions.

• Martin left no papers other than his publications. Memorials to him are by William Wirt Howe in Martin's *History of Louisiana* (1882) and in William Draper Lewis, *Great American Lawyers*, vol. 2 (1907). The controversy surrounding his will can be found in Warren M. Billings, "A Judicial Legacy: The Last Will and Testament of François-Xavier Martin," *Louisiana History* 25 (Summer 1984): 277–88, and a summary of his life is in Henry Plauché Dart, "The History of the Supreme Court of Louisiana," *Louisiana Reports* 133 (1913): 6–37. One of his colleagues on the court, Henry A. Bullard, wrote an obituary that appears in *Louisiana Reports*, 1 Robinson (1846): vii–viii.

JUDITH SCHAFER

MARTIN, Franklin Henry (13 Jul. 1857–7 Mar. 1935), surgeon, organizer, and editor, was born on a farm near Ixonia, Wisconsin, the son of Edmond Martin and Josephine Carlin, farmers. Martin's father died in the Union army in 1862. Five years later his mother remarried, and young Martin was put under the care of his maternal grandparents. After passing the teacher's examination, he taught at several village schools.

When Martin finally decided on a career in 1876 he read medicine with William Spalding, an esteemed surgeon in Watertown, Wisconsin. As Martin's medical knowledge grew, Spalding occasionally asked for Martin's help with patients. Spalding, impressed by both Martin's alertness and his skill and persistence at memorizing Sir Erasmus Wilson's *System of Human Anatomy* (1843), urged him to enter medical school. On the advice of Nicholas Senn, one of the leading

surgeons in Chicago, Martin enrolled in the Chicago Medical College (now the Northwestern University Medical School) in 1877 and received his M.D. in 1880. After an internship at Chicago's Mercy Hospital, where he was exposed to aseptic surgery, he began his career in 1881 as an ophthalmologist in private practice. However, he soon switched to gynecology, where he remained for the next thirty-five years. Martin's growing experience and knowledge of aseptic surgery made possible much of his later innovative surgery.

Isabelle Hollister and Martin were married in 1886; they had no children. Isabelle became a great help to her husband, translating medical literature from the French, bringing his financial records and business practices into order, advising him on important decisions, and making sure that he took sufficient time away from his work. Martin referred to Isabelle as his "gyroscope."

Martin served on the staff of the South Side Dispensary (1883–1888) and as professor of gynecology at the Polyclinic Hospital and Medical School (1886–1888). However, he and several others became displeased with the Polyclinic's lack of enterprise and interest in new methods and resigned to found the Post-Graduate Medical School and Hospital, where they could provide more relevant experience for medical practitioners. Martin also devoted time and effort to charitable work, becoming one of the founders of Charity Hospital. For many years he served as gynecologist at the Woman's Hospital.

At neurologist Daniel R. Brower's neurological clinics in Chicago, Martin became interested in the use of electrical currents in medicine. Several of his early papers and his first book, *Electricity in Gynecology* (1890; 2d ed., 1891), resulted from this area of research.

Martin did pioneering experimental surgical work during 1897–1899 in transplanting the ureters from the bladder to the intestines so that organ could be removed. He also developed and reported on successful methods for treating uterine fibroids in humans. This led to his second book, *Treatment of Fibroid Tumors of the Uterus* (1897). Martin's third major book, *A Treatise on Gynecology*, appeared in 1903.

However, Martin was at his best in founding, promoting, and leading medical organizations. In 1888 he became president of the Chicago South-Side Medico-Social Society, an organization founded by Martin in 1883 to motivate him and other young members to prepare scientific papers for effective presentation before a group. In 1895 he was elected chairman of the American Medical Association's Section on Obstetrics and Diseases of Children, the association's largest section. He later served as president of the Chicago Gynecological Society (1895) and the American Gynecological Society (1919).

Martin shifted his locally based organizational efforts to the national level in 1904 when he proposed the idea of a new surgical journal run by surgeons, rather than a commercial publisher. With the strong support of John B. Murphy, a widely known surgeon, this journal, *Surgery, Gynecology, and Obstetrics*, made its appearance in 1905, and it remains an outstanding journal today. Martin, editor in chief for the rest of his life, retained 51 percent of its ownership for himself and Isabelle. In 1908 he began a British edition, and in 1912 he initiated the section *International Abstracts of Surgery*.

In 1910 Martin organized the Clinical Congress of Surgeons of North America to provide a forum for demonstrations by practicing surgeons. The annual meetings of the congress became larger each year, and Martin and the other officers were faced with the problem of surgeons they deemed incompetent obtaining the imprimatur of membership in the congress. This problem was solved in 1913 by Martin's founding of the American College of Surgeons; he became its secretary-general that year. An up-to-date surgeon in his own operations and the ensuing care, he realized that only a solidly based and tightly knit organization could encourage and enforce the standards he believed were necessary then and for the future. The college concentrated on the ethical and professional standards of practice, while the American Board of Surgery (founded in 1937) certified the qualifications of the individual surgeon. The American College of Surgeons' program sought to improve the practices of both surgeons and hospitals. A surgeon applying for fellowship, in addition to meeting educational and training requirements, had to submit 100 case histories for evaluation. A hospital also had several requirements, one of the most important being the creation and maintenance of a medical records department. Some within the American Medical Association looked unfavorably upon the college as an attempt by surgeons to speak for all of medicine. The college has done valuable work in several areas, especially in the standardization and improvement of hospitals. In 1917, when he reluctantly agreed to become the salaried full-time director-general, he had to give up his surgical practice. In 1919 the college took over *Surgery, Gynecology, and Obstetrics* as its official journal. Martin served as the college's president in 1928–1929.

In World War I Martin soon became convinced that the United States would ultimately have to become involved. He set up the Committee of American Physicians for Medical Preparedness in April 1916. He then provided, at Surgeon General William Crawford Gorgas's request, lists of physicians to be medical reserve officers. Martin was invited by President Woodrow Wilson to become a member of the Council on National Defense's Advisory Commission and General Medical Board. During the war Martin did much traveling in the United States and Europe to organize, promote, and improve a variety of medical, surgical, and public health functions. He established the Volunteer Medical Service Corps and, near the end of the war, was promoted to colonel. Martin was decorated by the United States, Great Britain, and Italy.

After the war Martin remained away from surgical practice but kept himself busy. He continued as editor of *Surgery, Gynecology, and Obstetrics* and as a member of the college's board was active in its programs. Impressed by Gorgas's work in preventive medicine and health education, Martin helped establish the Gorgas Memorial Institute of Tropical and Preventive Medicine in 1921. He traveled widely, often with his wife, and wrote several books about these trips. The Martins had spent their winters in Arizona for some years before he suffered a coronary thrombosis and died in Phoenix. According to author Loyal Davis, the red-haired Martin was "a dreamer, an enthusiast, a driver . . . dynamic, [and] Indian-erect." Although genial and kindly to his close friends, Martin appeared to many as austere, pompous, and aggressively ambitious. An accomplished and creative surgeon, Martin also made his name as an editor and a founder and leader of organizations.

• The American College of Surgeons houses a large collection of Martin's private papers. Primary sources are Martin's autobiography, *The Joy of Living* (2 vols., 1933), and Loyal Davis's *Fellowship of Surgeons: A History of the American College of Surgeons* (1960). Martin's *Fifty Years of Medicine and Surgery* (1934) is a considerable abridgment of his two-volume work. An obituary is in the *Chicago Tribune*, 8 Mar. 1935.

WILLIAM K. BEATTY

MARTIN, Glenn Luther (17 Jan. 1886–4 Dec. 1955), aviation pioneer and aircraft manufacturer, was born in Macksburg, Iowa, the son of Clarence Y. Martin, a hardware and farm implements salesman, and Arminta "Minta" De Long, a former schoolteacher. His family moved to Liberal, Kansas, in 1888, then, in 1895, to Salina, where Martin would eventually begin working in carriage and bicycle shops. Martin's mother played a significant role in his life; she actively supported him in his aeronautical ventures, and, as he never married, they were completely devoted to each other. Martin left high school after his sophomore year to take bookkeeping classes at Kansas Wesleyan Business College. In 1905 the family moved to Santa Ana, California, where the young Martin opened a successful Ford and Maxwell automobile dealership.

Martin's aviation career began in 1907 with glider experiments. His first attempt at powered flight in the summer of 1908 failed, but on 1 August 1909 he managed to get his second airplane into the air, becoming only the fourth man in the United States—behind the Wrights and Glenn Curtiss—to fly. He immediately opened an airplane factory, which in 1911 had been incorporated as the Glenn L. Martin Company, and by 1912 was employing 165 workers, with capitalization at $100,000.

To support his aeronautical ventures, Martin took to barnstorming. He was nicknamed the "Flying Dude" because of his stylish flying attire, an all-black outfit that included leather helmet, gloves, coat, and boots. Between 1910 and 1915 he toured the United States, competing with other fliers for awards and records. At the same time, he began building dual-control training aircraft and experimenting with hydroplanes. In 1912 he won national acclaim with a record-setting flight from Newport Beach, California, to Santa Catalina Island and back in his new hydroplane. The demonstration soon led to orders for Martin aircraft from the United States military and from foreign governments. In 1915 he had a brief shot at movie stardom, when he played the role of a flying villain in the Mary Pickford film *The Girl of Yesterday*.

During World War I, Martin joined Thomas A. Edison's Naval Consulting Board to appraise new military inventions. In 1916, as part of an attempt by Wall Street investors to consolidate aircraft development in the United States, Martin merged his company with the New York–based Wright syndicate, assuming the vice presidency of the new corporation. The merger stripped Martin and his company of all design and aircraft manufacturing operations. Within a year he resigned and formed a new Glenn L. Martin Company in Cleveland, Ohio. In 1918 he designed and built a bomber for the U.S. Army, eventually known as the MB-2. Introduced too late to see action in the war, this plane was used by General William "Billy" Mitchell during his famous bombing tests on a captured German battleship in 1921. However, the enormous costs of developing the bomber gave Martin a lifelong reputation as a high-cost producer. He was underbid on a second production run and nearly went bankrupt.

In 1929 Martin relocated his plant to Middle River, Maryland, near Baltimore. Here, in 1931, he unveiled his revolutionary B-10 bomber. An all-metal monoplane with a top speed of 200 miles per hour—nearly twice that of early bombers—the B-10 could easily outrun existing fighter aircraft. Accolades for his achievements poured in, including an invitation to deliver the Wilbur Wright Memorial Lecture at London's Royal Aeronautical Society in 1931. In 1933 the army ordered forty-eight B-10s. He also was awarded the Robert J. Collier Trophy in 1933. Despite the success of the B-10, economic difficulties forced Martin to seek a Reconstruction Finance Corporation loan to stave off bankruptcy in 1934. A second large order from the army in 1935 and foreign sales finally put the company back on its feet.

In 1935 Martin introduced the M-130 "China Clipper," a large four-engine flying boat, for use by Pan American Airlines on their trans-Pacific flights. As World War II broke out, Martin introduced the B-26 Marauder, a new high-speed twin-engine bomber. Faster than most fighter planes, the B-26 was a difficult airplane to fly. Eventually structural modifications and new pilot-training programs overcame many of the problems, and the B-26 provided outstanding service in all theaters of operations during the war.

During the war Martin sat on the Aircraft War Production Council, serving as its president in 1943. He also established both the Minta Martin Aeronautical Endowment at the Institute of Aeronautical Sciences in New York and the Glenn L. Martin College of Engineering and Aeronautical Science at the University of Maryland. Martin's fortunes began to slide, however, after the war. Anticipating a huge market for commercial aircraft, he developed the 2-0-2, a twin-engine medium-range transport. Unfortunately the commercial market did not develop as he expected, and few orders came in. The crash of a 2-0-2 in August 1948, together with reports of poor workmanship, led to financial losses amounting to $37 million. In 1949 Martin lost control of his company to Chester Pearson, the 42-year-old vice president of Curtiss-Wright. Martin remained as chairman of the board until 1952, when he was named honorary chairman. On 14 March 1953 his life was shattered by the death of his mother at the age of eighty-nine. He never recovered from the shock and died at his farm near Chestertown, Maryland, a few years later.

Glenn Martin's career spanned the creation of the aircraft industry in the United States, from its beginnings in garages and small workshops to mass production in huge plants employing thousands of workers. At the time of his death, his company was beginning to experiment with both rocketry and satellite technologies. His progressive ideas pertaining to the need for high-speed bombers played a primary role in the development of the Army Air Corps's strategic bombing policies. Martin's companies also provided a training ground for many of the industry's future leaders, including Donald W. Douglas, Sr., and Lawrence Bell. Another associate, William E. Boeing, had been a student at Martin's flying school. At his passing, Martin left an estate valued at $14 million.

• An extensive collection of Martin's papers, company records, and memorabilia is held by the Library of Congress. A smaller collection of secondary biographical material can be found at the National Air and Space Museum of the Smithsonian Institution. The only biography of Martin is Henry Still, *To Ride the Wind: A Biography of Glenn L. Martin* (1966). An examination of Martin, his companies, and their place in the development of the aircraft and aerospace industries can be found in Wayne Biddle, *Barons of the Sky: From Early Flight to Strategic Warfare, the Story of the American Aerospace Industry* (1991). Specifics concerning business and labor conditions at the Glenn L. Martin Company between the two world wars are in Jacob Vander Meulen, *The Politics of Aircraft: Building an American Military Industry* (1991). An obituary is in the *New York Times*, 5 Dec. 1955.

JOSEPH E. LIBBY

MARTIN, Henry Newell (1 July 1848–27 Oct. 1896), physiologist, was born in Newry, County Down, Ireland. Details about his parentage are unknown except that his father was a congregational minister. Martin received his medical and scientific training at University College, London (D.Sc., 1872), and Cambridge University (D.Sc., 1875). He studied with and served as assistant to leading British physiologists William Sharpey, Michael Foster, and Thomas Huxley. In 1875 Daniel Coit Gilman, president of the Johns Hopkins University, which would open the following year in Baltimore, Maryland, was in Europe seeking faculty members for the new institution, where graduate training and research would be the focus. An influential champion of scientific education and research, Huxley was largely responsible for Martin's selection as the University's first professor of biology.

At Johns Hopkins, Martin inaugurated in 1876 an innovative program of advanced instruction in physiology and provided his graduate students and associates with a stimulating atmosphere in which to undertake biological research. Martin's 1878 marriage to Hetty Cary Pegram, the widow of a Confederate officer, facilitated his entry into Baltimore society. The couple had no children.

By the early 1880s, Martin had assembled an outstanding group of productive young scientists at Johns Hopkins, which included William K. Brooks, William T. Sedgwick, Henry Sewall, and William H. Howell. In less than a decade Martin's department at Hopkins was widely acknowledged as the best place in America for advanced instruction and research in physiology. Reflecting the influence of his teacher Michael Foster, the predominant theme of Martin's research was circulatory physiology.

With Howell and Frank Donaldson, Jr., Martin developed the first isolated mammalian heart preparation by perfusing blood through the organ after it had been removed from an experimental animal. In 1928 American physiologist Walter Meek characterized this achievement as "possibly the greatest single contribution ever made from an American physiological laboratory." Martin and his associates used their isolated heart preparation to gain new insight into circulatory dynamics. Anticipating conclusions drawn decades later by physiologists Otto Frank and Ernest Starling, Martin's associates claimed in an 1884 paper that it was the diastolic pressure in the ventricle that determined cardiac output. Subsequently, researchers in Europe and the United States adapted Martin's isolated heart preparation for their studies of cardiac physiology. This approach led to many important discoveries in cardiovascular physiology and pharmacology.

Like his mentor Thomas Huxley, Martin sought to popularize science. He began teaching a Saturday biology course for schoolteachers in 1879. Two years later the first of several editions of his popular college textbook *The Human Body* appeared. Shortly after his arrival in the United States, Martin began to give demonstrations to Baltimore medical students and deliver public lectures in biology. With Henry Bowditch of Harvard and Horatio Wood of the University of Pennsylvania, he served as an American editor of Foster's *Journal of Physiology* when it was first published in 1878. Martin also inaugurated the journal *Studies from the Biological Laboratory of the Johns Hopkins University*, which appeared irregularly beginning in 1879.

By the age of forty Martin was a recognized leader in the emerging discipline of experimental physiology. He was elected a Fellow of the Royal Society in London and was chosen to deliver the society's prestigious Croonian Lecture in 1883. That same year Johns Hopkins acknowledged Martin's success by constructing for him a spacious and well-equipped biological laboratory building. When the American Physiological Society was founded in 1887, Martin served as secretary-treasurer and was influential in defining the character of the new organization.

During the mid-1880s Martin's life and career entered a period of decline. In 1883, after his new laboratory had opened, Martin became the target of a malicious and sustained attack by antivivisectionists who objected to animal experiments undertaken by him and his pupils. Meanwhile, his senior assistants took faculty positions elsewhere as opportunities arose for physiologists in some of the nation's universities. Their departures left Martin to teach introductory courses and supervise much of the routine laboratory work. This limited the time he had to devote to research and to the supervision of advanced pupils and caused Martin great consternation.

By 1891 Martin, a sensitive and temperamental man, had become an alcoholic and was suffering from painful peripheral neuritis that led to morphine addiction. His decline accelerated the following year when his wife died. As Martin's alcoholism-related absences became more frequent and prolonged, the officers of Johns Hopkins realized that he could not play the important role they had envisioned for him in their medical school, which was scheduled to open in 1893.

After his physician, William Osler, urged him to resign, Martin returned in the spring of 1894 to England, where he hoped to resume some physiological studies in his friend Edward Sharpey-Schafer's laboratory. He never regained his health and died at Burley-in-Wharfedale, Yorkshire, England. During the course of his brief career, Martin made important scientific discoveries and played a major role in the professionalization of American physiology.

• Important correspondence between Martin and Gilman is in the Daniel Coit Gilman Papers, Johns Hopkins University. Among Martin's major works are *The Human Body: An Account of Its Structure and Activities* (1881) and a collection of his most important papers, *Physiological Papers* (1895). Biographical sketches of Martin include W. Bruce Fye, "H. Newell Martin: A Remarkable Career Destroyed by Neurasthenia and Alcoholism," *Journal of the History of Medicine and Allied Sciences* 40, no. 2 (1985): 133–66, and "H. Newell Martin and the Isolated Heart Preparation: The Link between the Frog and Open Heart Surgery," *Circulation* 73, no. 5 (1986): 857–64; C. S. Breathnach, "Henry Newell Martin (1848–1893 [*sic*]): A Pioneer Physiologist," *Medical History* 13 (1969): 271–79; and A. McGehee Harvey, "Fountainhead of American Physiology: H. Newell Martin and His Pupil, William Henry Howell," *Johns Hopkins Medical Journal* 136 (1975): 38–46. An intimate account of Martin and his laboratory by one of his earliest pupils and his successor is William Henry Howell, "Early Days in the Biological Laboratory," Howell papers, Alan M. Chesney Archives, the Johns Hopkins Medical Institutions. Martin's laboratory is described (and illustrated) in "The Biological Laboratory of the Johns Hopkins University," *Science* 3 (1884): 350–54. See also chapter four of Fye, *The Development of American Physiology: Scientific Medicine in the Nineteenth Century* (1987).

W. BRUCE FYE

MARTIN, Homer Dodge (28 Oct. 1836–12 Feb. 1897), landscape painter, was born in Albany, New York, the son of Homer Martin, a carpenter, and Sarah Dodge. Martin's school studies ended at age thirteen, when he began work in his father's carpentry shop. He later worked in a relative's architectural office, but he maintained a passion for drawing landscapes. When Martin was sixteen years of age, the sculptor Erastus Dow Palmer convinced Martin's father to let Martin develop his painting ability. In 1861 Martin married Elizabeth Gilbert Davis, who wrote literary criticism for the *Leader*, the *Round Table*, and the *Nation*; they had two sons. Martin had incorporated his future wife's initials with his own and the date of 30 July 1860 (to mark their engagement) in his first major commissioned painting, *The Old Mill* (1860, Georgia Museum of Art).

Martin tried to enlist during the Civil War but was rejected because of poor eyesight. His only direct association with the war came through his early landscapes—in the collections of his mentor, Palmer, and his patron, the Reverend Elias L. Magoon—that were exhibited in the Albany Sanitary Bazaar Exhibition, benefiting the U.S. Sanitary Commission, in February 1864. He was indirectly associated with the war through his friendship with Winslow Homer, whose on-the-spot war sketches appeared regularly in *Harper's Monthly*.

In 1864 Martin visited the Adirondacks in northern New York State for the first time, and the area became his principal American landscape subject. His painting of *The Ausable Valley and Mount Marcy*, the highest peak in the region, served as his initiation fee into New York City's Century Club in 1866. The following year he won his first critical acclaim as an American landscape artist by appearing in Henry Tuckerman's *Book of Artists*, in which the author commented on Martin's lake scenes (very likely Adirondack in subject), noting their "decided and progressive merit and character." The near photographic character of one of these lake scenes—*Upper Ausable Lake* (1868)—compares closely with an 1880 photograph of the same area by Seneca Ray Stoddard. Despite his topographical precision, Martin's paintings are known for their poetic and tonal qualities.

Martin was elected an associate member of the National Academy of Design in 1868 and a full member in 1875. (For his initiation requirement, he painted Winslow Homer's portrait.) Three years after his election to full membership, he defied the academy by becoming a founding member of the more "modern" Society of American Artists.

In the summer of 1876 Martin visited London and was a house-guest of James McNeill Whistler. Martin's awareness of Whistler's *Nocturnes*, in which Whistler flattened out conventional pictorial space, can be seen in his own English paintings such as *Evening on the Thames*, which was exhibited in 1879. Shortly after that English visit, Martin received critical acclaim for his use of color, "a scheme of color [that] is altogether his own, full of luminousness and purity" (Samuel Benjamin, *Art in America* [1880], p. 106). In addition to encouraging Martin's experiments in color, Whistler must also have directed him toward the watercolor medium, for Martin's first watercolors are of the St. Lawrence River in 1879.

Martin returned to England in 1881 on commission from *Scribner's* to illustrate Rose Kingsley's article on George Eliot's Warwickshire. By the time the article appeared in print in 1885, the Martins were happily ensconced in Villerville, Normandy, France. Their five-year residency there came about from a chance invitation offered by William J. Hennessy, an English artist who was then living in Normandy. Their sojourn in France is described by Elizabeth Martin "as the most tranquil and satisfactory period in our life together" (Martin, p. 27). Homer Martin's best-known French painting, *Harp of the Winds* (1895), was executed in the United States, to which he had returned in 1886. It depicts a view of the small town Quilleboeuf on the River Seine.

Besides his many paintings of the Seine, Martin also painted Newport, Rhode Island, with its glimpses of the Atlantic Ocean. Writing to Russell Sturgis from St. Paul, Minnesota, where the Martins had moved in 1893 to live with their eldest son, he said he "missed the ocean with a special longing." His last painting, completed in St. Paul, was of Newport. (Martin's Newport patron was James Stillman, and his other connection to the town was his lifelong friend John La-Farge.) Martin died in St. Paul.

Martin's greatest fame came after his death, when in 1913 *Mussel Gatherers*, his famous French landscape, sold for an astronomical $9,000. Around the same time, the popular press also became interested in Martin's work because of the piggy-back publication of two books: Frank Jewitt Mather's *Homer Martin, Poet in Landscape* (1912) and Dana Carroll's *Fifty-Eight Paintings by Homer D. Martin* (1913). National focus on Martin's work prior to the sale of *Mussel Gatherers* had been on a 1908 lawsuit involving the sale of two allegedly forged Martin paintings.

Adirondack Scenery (1895) is Martin's greatest painting. He himself said of it: "I have learned to paint at last" (Martin, p. 49). It melds his two stylistic characteristics: realism and poetic expressionism. The painting is based on his *Source of the Hudson* (1869); the twenty-six year interim transformed a realistic Adirondack landscape into an "elegiac" one (Virgil Baker, *American Painting* [1960], p. 602). It is a color painting rooted in the real; it juggles color and space and goes far beyond being a "picture" with a foreground, middleground, and background. It is not an illusion of reality; it is a painting. In this sense, it is a truly modern painting that can be "experienced" by the viewer.

In his later years, the visual problem that had prevented him from enlisting during the Civil War had become a matter of serious proportions, causing him to have great difficulty seeing to paint or to write. Part of the problem can be attributed to cataracts. The effect on his painting is evident in his loosening technique, in which he sometimes laid on color heavily with a palette knife, resulting in jewelled mosaics of paint that serve as a kaleidoscope through which the viewer perceives the "real" world.

In 1926 Mantle Fielding called Martin "the first American impressionist." Later he was rightfully disassociated from that term after intense art-historical work on American Impressionism. Better to remain with Mather's estimation of him as a "poet in landscape," a sentiment earlier expressed by Samuel Isham in *The History of Modern Painting* (1905), when he wrote of the continuum in Martin's work despite its change from conventional realism to an emotionally charged realism approaching expressionism, noting that there was no change in the "real essentials (the feeling for the relations of mass, for the exact difference of tone between the sky and the solid earth [and] the sense of subtle color)." In his work as well as in his person, Homer Dodge Martin was a "loner," an American landscape painter of intense individualism who cannot be pigeonholed.

• Critical unpublished Martin material lies in three collections of his and Elizabeth Gilbert Martin's letters from 1872 to 1908. The majority of the Homer Martin letters are written to Brownell (1874-1895), and are in the Rare Book Library, Princeton University. The other major holding is the collection of Martin's letters to Thomas B. Clarke (1893–1897) in both the Thomas B. Clarke and Charles W. Hart Papers in the Archives of the American Art, Smithsonian Institution. The archives also house all of Elizabeth Martin's correspondence with William Macbeth from 1897 to 1908. (Macbeth was the dealer for Martin's work after his death.) The principal published material on Martin includes his wife's *Homer Martin: A Reminiscence* (1904), published by William Macbeth; Frank Jewett Mather, *Homer Martin: Poet in Landscape*, privately printed in 1912 by Frederic Fairchild Sherman, a Martin collector; and Dana Carroll, *Fifty-Eight Paintings by Homer D. Martin*, privately printed by Sherman in 1913. *Fifty-Eight Paintings* is essentially a picture-book and is invaluable as a photographic document. See also Patricia C. F. Mandel, "Homer Dodge Martin: American Landscape Painter, 1836–1897" (Ph.D. diss., New York Univ., Institute of fine Arts, 1973); Mandel, "The Stories Behind Three Important Late Homer D. Martin Paintings," *Archives of American Art Journal* 13, no. 3 (1973): 2–8; and Mandel's entry on Martin's *Mountain View in Saranac, 1868* in *Fair Wilderness, American Paintings in the Collection of the Adirondack Museum* (1990). Further material specifically related to Martin research can be found in Mandel's continuing, photographically documented, unpublished catalog raisonné of Martin's entire oeuvre. This five-volume work, begun in 1966, includes full bibliographical references and stylistic notes on nearly five hundred works; it records those cited but not seen or located.

PATRICIA F. MANDEL

MARTIN, John Alexander (10 Mar. 1839–2 Oct. 1889), journalist, army officer, and governor of Kansas, was born in Brownsville, Pennsylvania, the son of James Martin, a justice of the peace, boardinghouse keeper, and postmaster, and Jane Montgomery Crawford. He attended public school in Brownsville and at age fifteen was apprenticed as a printer on the town newspaper, the *Clipper*. He became local editor and printshop foreman before moving to Pittsburgh in 1857, where he worked briefly on the *Commercial Journal*. That same year he moved to Atchison in Kansas Territory. He spent several months working for the *Squatter Sovereign*, which had been the territory's most vitriolic proslavery newspaper, before purchasing it in February 1858. A staunch antislavery, free soil man, Martin changed the paper's name to *Freedom's Champion*. It later became the *Daily Champion* and then the *Atchison Champion*.

The paper provided Martin with a power base from which to begin a successful career in the Free State movement and the nascent Republican party. Although only twenty years old and ineligible to vote, he was a delegate to the Osawatomie convention, which organized the Republican party in Kansas in 1859. On 5 July of that year he was elected secretary of the Wyandotte constitutional convention. In 1860 he was secretary of a railroad convention in Topeka that was dedicated to bringing rail lines into the state. When the first state legislature was organized in 1861, he was elected to the state senate. Throughout most of his remaining years, Martin kept active in the Republican party, serving frequently as chairman of the Atchison County Central Committee and as a member of the state central committee. He was Kansas's national committeeman from 1868 to 1884, secretary of the Republican National Committee from 1880 to 1884, and a delegate to national nominating conventions in 1860, 1868, 1872, and 1880.

On 27 October 1861 Martin resigned from the state senate to be mustered into the Union army as a lieutenant colonel of the Eighth Kansas Volunteer Infantry Regiment, which he helped raise. He served as provost marshal of Leavenworth in early 1862 and accompanied his regiment to Corinth, Mississippi, in March. On 1 November 1862 he was promoted to colonel and made provost marshal at Nashville, Tennessee, for six months. A member of the Army of the Cumberland, he took part in its principal engagements. He fought at Perryville and Lancaster, Kentucky, in the campaigns against rebel forces at Tullahoma and Chattanooga, in the battle of Chickamauga, the siege of Chattanooga, the storming of Missionary Ridge, and the campaign in East Tennessee during the winter of 1863–1864. In the campaign from Chattanooga to Atlanta, he commanded one of the units that chased John B. Hood's forces. Colonel Martin took charge of the Third Brigade, First Division, Twentieth Army Corps on the second day at Chickamauga and was made commander of the First Brigade, Third Division, Fourth Army Corps in August 1864, where he remained until mustered out of the service on 17 November 1864. He was breveted brigadier general of volunteers for gallant and meritorious service.

After the Civil War Martin returned to Atchison where in addition to editing the *Champion*, he became active in a variety of military, political, and civic affairs. He was elected mayor in 1865 and was appointed as the city's postmaster for the next twelve years. He served as the first commander of the Department of

Kansas, Grand Army of the Republic veterans' organization, and was a member of the Loyal Legion. Congress named him to the Board of Managers of the National Soldiers' Home, and at the time of his death, he was its vice president. He was a member and vice president of the U.S. Centennial Commission, president of the state Editors' and Publishers' Association, and one of the founders of the *Kansas Magazine* and the Kansas State Historical Society, of which he also served as president. In 1871 he married Ida Challis; they had four children.

Martin's main passion was to be governor. Republicans nearly nominated him in 1878, but they chose the dark horse, prohibitionist John P. St. John. At the time Martin was ardently opposed to the temperance movement. In 1884, when the party did nominate and help elect him governor, he supported the law and became one of the more effective enforcers of the state's constitutional ban on the manufacture and sale of alcoholic beverages. He was easily reelected in 1886.

During Martin's tenure, Kansas sustained a period of unprecedented growth and prosperity, even though his last year in office witnessed the beginning of the drought and recession that spawned the farmers' revolt of the 1890s. Governor Martin recognized that local governments had overspent on railroad subsidies, and he was able to secure legislation limiting somewhat the extent of future indebtedness by counties, cities, and townships, although the step occurred too late to affect matters much. He also championed equalization of tax assessment, legal and judicial reform, and highway improvements, and he established a school for feeble-minded youth in Winfield and a state-operated silk farm in Peabody. The silk farm was to bolster the efforts of silk producers in twenty Kansas counties before 1900. Unfortunately, competition with the cheaper labor of foreign countries eliminated this industry, and the state silk station was closed by the turn of the century.

Many of Martin's ideas anticipated the Progressive Republican movement in Kansas, and he was the tacit leader of the party's reform faction during the 1880s. He advocated a state corporation law to attack business abuses and the monopoly problem. He played a role in helping secure for women the right to vote in school, school bond, and municipal elections. He supported governmental organization, adding several boards and commissions to state government, including the Board of Health, the Board of Pardons, the Board of Pharmacy, the Board of Dentistry Examiners, the Bureau of Labor Statistics, and a Board of Arbitration for labor disputes. His second term was beset with labor problems stemming from strikes along various Kansas railroad lines by the Knights of Labor. He used the militia, which was reorganized into the Kansas National Guard, to keep order. He was also forced to deal with a number of county seat struggles, including the "Stevens County War" of 1887.

Martin died suddenly at his home in Atchison from what the *Topeka Daily Capital* (3 Oct. 1889) said were "various diseases." The *Topeka State Journal* (2 Oct.

1889) claimed he succumbed to typhoid fever, while Sol Miller, editor and publisher of the *Kansas Chief* (10 Oct. 1889), stated that the governor's excessive cigar smoking was the main contributor to his demise. He was honored with one of the largest funerals ever held in the state. Martin was not a demonstrative man but was mentally quick, studious, and thorough. He was even-tempered and friendly. During his life he was perhaps the most respected and well liked Republican leader in Kansas, and in death he became one of its most venerated by the generations that knew him.

• A few of Martin's personal papers are at the Kansas State Historical Society (KSHS), as are his gubernatorial papers. See Martha B. Caldwell, ed., "Some Notes on the Eighth Kansas Infantry and the Battle of Chickamauga: Letters of Col. John A. Martin," *Kansas Historical Quarterly* 13 (May 1944): 139–45. KSHS has microfilm copies of the *Champion*. He published *A Military History of the Eighth Kansas Veteran Volunteer Infantry* in 1869 and a volume of *Addresses* in 1888, which may also be found at KSHS. A variety of excellent short biographies exist, including the entry by James C. Malin, the famous Kansas historian, in the *Dictionary of American Biography* and entries in Frank W. Blackmar, ed., *Kansas: A Cyclopedia of State History*, vol. 2 (1912), and William E. Connelley, ed., *A Standard History of Kansas and Kansans*, vol. 2 (1918). A good overview of his early career is Matthew A. Raney, "The Early Political and Military Career of Governor John Alexander Martin of Kansas" (M.A. thesis, Kansas State Univ., 1991). For detailed discussions of labor union difficulties consult Edith Walker, "Labor Problems during the First Year of Governor Martin's Administration," *Kansas Historical Quarterly* 5 (Feb. 1936): 33–53, and Dorothy Leibengood, "Labor Problems in the Second Year of Governor Martin's Administration," *Kansas Historical Quarterly* 5 (May 1936): 191–207. Robert Bader, *Prohibition in Kansas: A History* (1986), has considerable information on Martin and that topic. An obituary is in the *Topeka State Journal*, 2 Oct. 1889.

ROBERT S. LA FORTE

MARTIN, John Joseph (2 June 1893–19 May 1985), dance critic, was born in Louisville, Kentucky, the son of William Joseph Martin, a railroad purchasing agent, and Cara Steinberg, a singer. In childhood, Martin studied violin and piano; he once recalled that he knew the operettas of Gilbert and Sullivan before he knew his prayers. He considered becoming a musician but turned to theater, performing in amateur theatrics during high school and college. He studied classics at the University of Louisville and graduated at the age of eighteen. Martin began his professional career in the theater as an actor in the Chicago Little Theater from 1912 to 1915.

During World War I, Martin served in the U.S. Army Air Force Signal Corps; he was about to be sent overseas when the armistice was declared in November 1918. Earlier that year he had married Hettie Louise Mick, an actress from Chicago; they had no children.

From 1919 to 1922 Martin served as a press agent and a writer-editor for the *Dramatic Mirror*, a trade publication; he worked as a director at the Chautauqua program in Swarthmore, Pennsylvania, in 1923. Martin joined Richard Boleslavsky's Laboratory Theater as executive secretary in 1924 and remained with the company until 1927, performing administrative duties. In this group, he met dancer Elsa Findley, who was teaching Dalcroze Eurhythmics (a form of music training in movement), and she introduced him to Olin Downes, music critic at the *New York Times*.

While Martin was struggling to make a living in theater, American modern dance was developing at a rapid pace. In the twenties, such dancers as Martha Graham, Doris Humphrey, Charles Weidman, and Helen Tamiris began experimenting with new styles of dance, a reaction against classical dance and Denishawn, the school of Ruth St. Denis and Ted Shawn, which provided eclectic training for American dancers but was rather derivative of exotic forms of dance. At the *New York Times*, Downes covered dance performances as well as musical events. However, by 1926 (the year Graham gave her first solo concert), he felt that he could no longer keep up with the rapid growth of dance events. He asked Findley if she knew of anyone who could cover dance for the paper, and she recommended Martin. He was hired for an initial trial period of six months. His first review in the *Times*, on 27 November 1927, began: "The amazing growth of art consciousness of the American people during the last twenty years or so is nowhere more clearly manifested than in the field of dance."

Martin joined the full-time staff of the *Times* in October 1928 and continued to write for the paper for thirty-five years. His position as the first full-time dance critic on New York's premier paper gave him enormous influence. During this period of change and growth in American dance, Martin was instrumental both in championing and shaping that evolution. He came to be known as the dean of American dance critics.

The development of a uniquely American art form was Martin's passion. He was called an "aesthetic patriot" by one friend. He sought to create an audience for the new style of dance, an audience that could participate with active interest in performance and in the growth of the artists.

Along with writing for the *Times*, Martin lectured widely, establishing a series of introductory courses and lecture-demonstrations in dance theory and history at the New School for Social Research in New York City (1931–1934) and participating in the Bennington College Summer School of Dance in Bennington, Vermont (1934–1937). His lectures for the New School were published as *The Modern Dance* (1933), a work that offers a theory of modern dance and its relation to other arts. He considered modern dance a "point of view"—emphasizing individuality and revealing both authentic personal experience and connection to the current world. Martin's other books are *America Dancing* (1936), *Introduction to the Dance* (1939), *The Dance* (1946), *World Book of Modern Ballet* (1952), *John Martin's Book of the Dance* (1963), *Sybil Shearer* (1968), and *Ruth Page: An Intimate Biography* (1977). His arti-

cles appeared in a wide range of magazines, including *Theater Arts* and the *American Scholar*. Throughout the thirties he also wrote and directed plays. He helped to organize the American Dance Festival (which grew out of the summer dance course at Bennington and began at Connecticut College in New London in 1948) and the New York High School of the Performing Arts. Martin also encouraged the creation of the Capezio Awards, which recognized significant contributions to the field of dance.

By the 1950s American dance was attracting widespread public enthusiasm and support, owing in part to Martin's role as an advocate and educator in the field. Paradoxically, Martin was at the same time increasingly disappointed with the state of dance in the United States. In 1955 he wrote an article challenging modern dancers to assess their directions and principles, commenting that they were "still trading on the achievements of two or three masters," and moving in ever-narrowing circles. In response, his own writing was criticized for being too judgmental and not sufficiently descriptive.

During a trip to the USSR with his wife in 1956, Martin became fascinated by the dynamism, grand scale, and brilliance of the Russian dancers. When Martin retired from the *Times* in 1962 he received an outpouring of appreciation; in 1969 he was given the Capezio Award, citing him as "apostle and arbiter, critic and counselor, fighter and friend for the dance in America." The New York Public Library for the Performing Arts created an exhibition in his honor in 1974, the first time the writing of a dance critic had been so exhibited.

Between 1965 and 1970 Martin lived in California, teaching at the University of California, Los Angeles, and winning praise from his students for his sensitivity, inspiration, warmth, and wealth of knowledge.

Martin returned to the East Coast in 1971, and for the remainder of his life he shared a home in Saratoga, New York, with Zachary Solov, ballet dancer, choreographer, and longtime friend. Martin died in Saratoga. Later that year a memorial service was held at the New York Public Library for the Performing Arts. On that occasion Martha Graham commented, "John Martin was such a delight and holy terror in our lives. . . . he created a world of challenge for all dancers; [he] prodded us to seek the truth and to present it as daringly as we could."

A broad range of interest characterized Martin's work. His reviews discuss the aesthetics and the practicalities of dance—working conditions, dance training, the need for film and notation archives, dance history and dance books, and specific performances. He was interested in the entire field, including ballet, musical theater, folk dances of all cultures, and modern dance, which he considered the most expressive of American art forms. His writing was direct, nontechnical, and nonelitist. He wrote from a mental rather than a physical viewpoint, and he did not like to describe movement. In 1933, for example, he wrote of Graham:

It is worthy of being recorded that on a May night in the middle of the week a large audience sat in absorbed silence watching a program of dances which has seldom had a peer for depth of substantiality and concentration of method; furthermore, there was no indication that these dances were considered unintelligible because of their subjectivity or eccentric because of their having pushed still farther to the left the boundaries of radicalism. Here, indeed is a dancer whose audience does her credit (*New York Times*, 14 May 1933).

Martin's work provides an invaluable picture of the decades during which dance became an established art form in the United States and during which American dance influenced the field of dance worldwide. His concern was to educate the public to support dance as a serious art, believing that dance could give people a nobler and richer life.

• Martin's personal papers and belongings are in the possession of Zachary A. Solov, Martin's heir and the executor of his estate. The New York Public Library of the Performing Arts Dance Collection lists items by and about Martin along with numerous clippings and photos.

Besides the books mentioned above, Martin's important writings include "The Dance Completes a Cycle," *American Scholar* 12 (Spring 1943): 205–15. Most major books on dance published since 1930 refer to Martin. In particular, see A. Chujoy and P. W. Manchester, eds., *Dance Encyclopedia* (1949), pp. 606–7; Murray Louis, *Inside Dance* (1980), pp. 23–27, 41; and Sali Ann Kriegsman, *Modern Dance in America: The Bennington Years* (1981), which quotes extensively from Martin's reviews. In addition, see Jack Anderson, "Pioneer of Dance Criticism," *New York Times*, 12 June 1983; Doris Hering, "Meet John Martin," *Dance Magazine*, Nov. 1952, pp. 20–23, 38–39, 45; Lincoln Kirstein, "In Appreciation: John Martin," *Dance News*, Sept. 1962, p. 3; Dorothy G. Madden, "A Question and a Challenge," *Dance Observer*, June–July 1957, pp. 85–86; Ernestine Rothschild, "John Martin at School," *Dance Magazine*, Jan. 1968, p. 39; Robert Sabin, "Dance Critics in America: John Martin," *Dance Observer*, June–July 1946, pp. 72–73; and Walter Terry, "Walter Terry Interviews John Martin," *Dance Magazine*, Jan. 1956, pp. 36–39, 66, 68–69. Also see Thomas B. Herthel, "John Martin, Dance Critic" (Ph.D. diss., Cornell Univ., 1966), and Diane Hottendorf, "Criticism in the Art of Dance: An Analysis of John Martin's Reviews in the *NY Times*, 1928–1962" (Ph.D. diss., UCLA, 1976).

An obituary is in the *New York Times*, 21 May 1985. *Ballet Review* 16 (Spring 1988) contains a synopsis of the memorial meeting held after Martin's death.

AANYA ADLER FRIESS

MARTIN, John Sella (Sept. 1832–Aug. 1876), minister and abolitionist, was born into slavery in Charlotte, North Carolina, the son of Winnifred, a mulatto slave, and the nephew of his mother's owner. He had one sister. In an eighteen-year period he was sold eight times. Martin taught himself to read and write. In 1856 he used those skills and his employment as a boatman on the Mississippi River to escape to Cairo, Illinois.

Martin settled in Chicago, where in 1856 he met May Ann Shadd and began his abolitionist career. That same year Shadd appointed him as an agent for the *Provincial Freeman*. He eventually moved to Detroit, where he spent nine months studying for the ministry. Martin worked diligently toward perfecting his speaking ability. He quickly earned a reputation for being a natural orator.

Martin served briefly in 1858 as minister of the Michigan Street Baptist Church in Buffalo, New York, before moving on to Boston. Boston was a major center of black activism, with a number of individuals participating visibly in antislavery work. Martin was one of the few ministers who did so.

The pastor of Boston's Tremont Temple, the Reverend Isaac Smith Kalloch, invited Martin to temporarily fill his pulpit in 1859. Kalloch's church was one of the few integrated churches in Boston. That same year Martin became pastor of the First Independent Baptist Church, also known as the Joy Street Baptist Church. The church was also called "abolition church" because it was the site of local antislavery gatherings and black community organizations.

While serving at this church, Martin developed his reputation as a powerful orator and militant antislavery speaker. He endorsed slave insurrections, noting that the only difference between the American Revolution and John Brown's act was that for once someone had used their resources for black men instead of white men. Martin once stated that it was providential that he was born on the same day that Nat Turner was hanged. He envisioned himself as a replacement for Turner and often made him the subject of his speeches.

Martin took issue with Frederick Douglass's assertion that slaves were apathetic and cowardly and would not fight for their freedom. Martin argued in public addresses and in articles in the *Liberator* that blacks had not fully participated in John Brown's raid because they had learned hard lessons about the treachery of white men. Blacks felt that they could not trust whites, even when a white person came as a deliverer. Martin also supported the African Civilization Society's emigration program as a legitimate response to America's racist obstinacy, although he would abandon his emigrationist stance just prior to the Civil War.

Martin was an ardent defender of black people, particularly when accusations were made regarding laziness and the inability to learn. He believed that there was no such thing as natural inferiority. The allegation of black inferiority was a red herring concocted to confuse the issue of equality.

In 1861 Martin traveled to Britain to help build support for the Union. In 1862 he returned to Boston with $2,500 to purchase his sister and her two children from a Georgia plantation. After some time, he was able to buy their freedom. He eventually resigned as pastor of Joy Street Baptist and took a position with a congregation near London. He used the opportunity to continue his travels and garner support for the Union cause.

Martin returned for a brief time to the United States in 1864, becoming pastor of Shiloh Presbyterian Church in New York City. His transition from Baptist to Presbyterian was facilitated by his association with the Congregationalist chapel in London.

While Martin was living in New York, Abraham Lincoln was assassinated. Martin was appalled at the treatment given to blacks who wanted to participate in the funeral procession march. Many blacks gathered at his church to protest the actions of the city's governing board that had barred blacks from participating. Although the War Department insisted that blacks be allowed to participate, they were placed so far back in the line that Lincoln's coffin had left the city by the time they joined the procession. Martin wrote a letter to the editor of the *New York Evening Post* denouncing the racist actions of the council, but the paper refused to print it.

Martin began work with the American Missionary Association (AMA) in 1864. He traveled to Britain on a fundraising mission on its behalf. Between 1864 and 1868 he was able to raise thousands of dollars to aid freedmen in the South. As a result of his success, he was put in charge of the AMA's solicitation efforts for all of Europe.

Returning to the United States in 1868, Martin became pastor of the Fifteenth Street Presbyterian Church in Washington, D.C. He became actively involved in the black labor movement, serving as editor of the *New Era*, the official journal of the Colored National Labor Union. He was also elected to the Executive Board of the National Colored Convention.

Between 1870 and 1876 Martin had difficulty finding stable employment. Consequently, he found himself struggling financially. He was appointed as a special agent with the post office in Mobile, a position he held for only a few months. In 1870 he moved to New Orleans, where he worked with the black Republicans in Louisiana. He was named coeditor of the Republican paper the *New National Era*. After the paper merged with another in 1873, Martin was unemployed.

Martin eventually found a position in 1874 as a Treasury Department special agent in Shieldsboro, Mississippi. He held the position for a short time, then moved back to New Orleans. He went to Massachusetts briefly to live with his wife Sarah, whom he had married in 1858, and their daughter, but he returned to New Orleans in 1876. His family had not lived with him on a permanent basis since they had resided in Washington in 1868–1870.

Martin was frequently beset with painful urinary infections. He also had attacks of pleurisy, neuralgia, ague, liver disorder, and catarrhal fever. These ailments often immobilized him and interrupted his work and travel schedule. To relieve his pain and symptoms, he was given prescriptions for opium and laudanum, drugs to which he became addicted. He was found by a servant in his bedroom in New Orleans suffering from irregular breathing. Next to his bed was a half-empty vial of laudanum. Efforts to revive him failed, and he died soon afterward. Autopsy reports revealed little as to the actual cause of death. The evidence suggests that, because of his financial prob-

lems, inability to find work, and estrangement from his family, Martin became despondent and committed suicide.

• There is very little written about John Sella Martin. A brief biographical sketch appears in a footnote in C. Peter Ripley, ed., *Black Abolitionists Papers*, vol. 5 (1985). There are also references to him scattered throughout the volume as well as vol. 3. There is a letter to the editor of the *New York Evening Post* and a portrait. Jane H. Pease and William H. Pease, *They Who Would Be Free* (1974), also contains several references to Martin, as does Benjamin Quarles, *Black Abolitionists* (1969).

MAMIE E. LOCKE

MARTIN, Joseph William, Jr. (3 Nov. 1884–6 Mar. 1968), Speaker of the U.S. House of Representatives, was born in North Attleboro, Massachusetts, the son of Joseph William Martin, Sr., a blacksmith, and Catherine Keating. Educated in the public schools, he was graduated from North Attleboro High School in 1902. The second oldest of eight children, he turned down an opportunity to attend Dartmouth College to help support his family.

At age six Martin began to work, assisting his father in the blacksmith shop and selling newspapers. In high school he worked for the North Attleboro *Leader* as a copyboy, handpress operator, and reporter. After graduation he worked as a full-time reporter, first for the *Leader*, then for the Attleboro *Sun*, supplementing his income by selling articles to other papers and playing semipro baseball. In 1908 he and nine local businessmen purchased the North Attleboro *Evening Chronicle*, and he became its publisher and editor. Over time he bought his partners' interests in the paper. He purchased the A. T. Parker Insurance Agency in 1918, and in 1944 he bought the weekly Franklin (Mass.) *Sentinel*. He owned both newspapers and the insurance agency for the remainder of his life.

Martin's career in elective politics began with his election as a Republican to the Massachusetts State House of Representatives in 1911. He served three one-year terms in the house (1912–1914) and three one-year terms in the state senate (1915–1917). While serving as secretary of the Joint Rules Committee he became a protégé and friend of its chairman, Senate president Calvin Coolidge. Not a candidate for reelection in 1917, Martin, to help heal a party split in 1922, became executive secretary of the state Republican committee (1922–1925) and manager of U.S. senator Henry Cabot Lodge's successful reelection campaign.

Martin was elected to the U.S. House of Representatives in 1924, serving from 1925 to 1967. An economic conservative, he was prototypical of a small-town businessman from a congressional district composed of small towns and medium-sized cities. Its major industries, textiles and jewelry, were owner operated, not unionized, and supportive of protective tariffs. He began his congressional career by supporting, at the request of President Coolidge, the successful bid of Representative Nicholas Longworth (Ohio) for the House Republican leadership and Speakership. Appointed to the House Rules Committee in 1929, Martin automatically became a member of the Republican steering committee that assisted the Speaker in setting up the Republican legislative program. Following the death of Speaker Longworth and the loss of the Republican majority in the House in 1931, Martin supported the election of Representative Bertrand H. Snell (N.Y.) as minority leader; Martin was assistant whip from 1931 to 1933. In 1933 Snell appointed him to the unofficial position of assistant minority leader, a post he held until 1939. Beginning on 21 March 1933 with a critical speech on the House floor, the strongly partisan Martin became a vigorous and consistent opponent of President Franklin D. Roosevelt's New Deal.

In 1939 Martin was elected House minority leader and held that office or the Speakership until 1959. His use of the whip organization, an enlarged steering committee, special committees to research issues and lead opposition on the House floor, the research facilities of the Republican National Committee, and frequent conferences of House Republicans to discuss issues, made the Republicans more effective opponents of the New Deal. A congressional technician, Martin helped forge a bipartisan anti–New Deal conservative coalition with southern Democrats. Contemporary observers quickly noted his success; indeed, fifty-three Washington correspondents rated him the ablest congressman in a *Life* magazine poll (20 Mar. 1939). Although Martin and the House Republicans supported the Roosevelt administration's military measures in World War II, they continued to oppose Roosevelt's domestic programs and after 1945 President Harry S. Truman's Fair Deal.

On 3 January 1947, following the Republicans' success in the 1946 congressional elections, Martin was elected Speaker of the House of the Eightieth Congress (1947–1949). A strong Speaker, he led his colleagues through personal persuasion but noted in his autobiography that "no Republican went on an important committee without my approval" (*First Fifty Years*, p. 181). He supported legislation to limit the power and influence of organized labor and the federal government, including the Labor Management Relations Act of 1947 (Taft-Hartley) and the Revenue Act of 1948 that slashed income tax rates. Administration proposals he deemed in the national interest such as the National Security Act of 1947, which unified the armed forces and created the Central Intelligence Agency, and the Marshall Plan (1947), which helped reconstruct a war-ravaged world, received his support. With the Republicans' loss of the House in the 1948 elections, Martin, as minority leader from 1949 to 1953, used the same tactics to oppose Truman that he had used against Roosevelt. He sought to achieve partisan advantage on almost all issues; thus, he solicited a letter from General Douglas MacArthur critical of Truman's Korean War policies and read it on the House floor on 5 April 1951. Truman then relieved MacArthur of his commands.

When Republicans won control of the presidency and both houses of Congress in the 1952 elections, Martin, once again elevated to Speaker during the Eighty-third Congress (1953–1955), found this responsibility less enjoyable than during the Eightieth Congress because "I had loyally to follow President Eisenhower and assume the responsibility of getting his program through the House" (*First Fifty Years*, p. 229). He worked hard to pass the president's program, looking to the White House for policy decisions. In June 1953 he used his influence with his congressional colleagues to send a bill extending the excess profits tax to the House floor over the objections of Ways and Means chairman Daniel A. Reed (N.Y.) because Eisenhower wanted it passed. Martin's time as Speaker proved short-lived as the Democrats regained the House majority in the 1954 elections. During his last four years as minority leader (1955–1959), Martin continued to push the president's program in the House, sometimes drawing on his friendship with Speaker Sam Rayburn (D.-Tex.) to enact legislation. On 6 January 1959, however, he was defeated for reelection as minority leader by Representative Charles A. Halleck (Ind.), who promised his colleagues to challenge more vigorously the Democrats on the House floor and forcefully present Republicans' views to the White House. Without power during his last eight years in the House, Martin was defeated in the 1966 Republican primary by Margaret M. Heckler. He died two years later in Hollywood, Florida.

In addition to his House service, Martin was active in national Republican politics. With the exception of 1932, he attended all Republican National Conventions from 1916 to 1964 and was permanent chairman of five between 1940 and 1956. He was a presidential elector in 1920. In 1936 he was eastern campaign manager for the Republican presidential nominee Alfred M. Landon. He chaired the National Republican Campaign Committee that assisted GOP candidates for the U.S. House from 1937 to 1939. Republican presidential nominee Wendell Willkie selected him as his campaign manager in 1940; Martin chaired the Republican National Committee during 1940–1942.

For thirty years a member of the House Republican leadership (the last twenty as either minority leader or Speaker), Martin played a major role in mid-twentieth-century national politics. A conservative bachelor, he believed that if one diligently followed values such as hard work, thrift, sobriety, and personal initiative, one would succeed as he had. He thought individuals would be better served if the government simply left the economy alone. This is the basis for his opposition to the liberal reform programs of Roosevelt and Truman. It was not a systematized conservatism. He was a congressional technician who led his colleagues through personal persuasion. Whenever the president was a Democrat, Martin and his colleagues would plan how to best oppose the White House program, although at times he offered alternatives. With a Republican president, he loyally assumed the responsibility of pushing the president's program through the House.

• Martin's papers are in the Joseph W. Martin, Jr. Institute for Law and Society at Stonehill College, North Easton, Mass.; the institute supplements his papers with copies from collections of his contemporaries. His autobiography, as told to Robert J. Donovan, *My First Fifty Years in Politics* (1960; repr. 1975), is an excellent source of information. Additional information on Martin and his family can be found in Edward E. Martin, with the assistance of James J. Kenneally, *Down Memory Lane* (1980). Carlisle Bargeron, *Joe Martin: An American Story* (1948), is a brief campaign biography. Information on how Martin led House Republicans for twenty years, along with a bibliography, are in William A. Hasenfus, "Managing Partner: Joseph W. Martin, Jr., Republican Leader of the United States House of Representatives, 1939–1959" (Ph.D. diss., Boston College, 1986). An excellent bibliographical source is Donald R. Kennon, ed., *The Speakers of the U.S. House of Representatives: A Bibliography, 1789–1984* (1986). Obituaries are in the *New York Times* and the *Washington Post*, both 8 Mar. 1968.

WILLIAM A. HASENFUS

MARTIN, Josiah (23 Apr. 1737–13 Apr. 1786), last royal governor of North Carolina, was born in Dublin, Ireland, the son of Colonel Samuel Martin, a prominent Antigua sugar planter, and Sarah Wyke Irish. Originally intended for a commercial or a legal career, Josiah Martin was educated in England and Antigua and briefly studied law in the Inner Temple of the Inns of Court before deciding, against his family's wishes, to enter the military. Beginning with the island militia in 1754, in three years Martin became an ensign in the Fourth Regiment of Foot. During the Seven Years' War Martin, now a lieutenant, participated in a military expedition in 1758 against Martinique and Guadeloupe and in the conquest of Canada. Near the end of the war, on 24 December 1762, he was commissioned a lieutenant colonel in the Twenty-second Regiment of Foot.

While in North America Martin spent time at "Rockhall," the Long Island, New York, estate of his uncle Josiah Martin. He married his first cousin Elizabeth Martin in 1761; they had eight children. He was assigned to the Sixty-eighth Regiment on Antigua in 1764 and the next year was named to the island's council. By 1769 Martin's health had so deteriorated that he sold his commission and began seeking civil employment in some colonial post in America. Through the influence of his half brother Samuel Martin of London, who was a member of Parliament and had held positions in the Treasury Department, Josiah Martin was appointed governor of North Carolina on 14 December 1770.

Arriving in New Bern on 12 August 1771, Martin found a province torn by the recent back-country Regulator rebellion and plagued by the growing rift between the legislature and the governor over taxes, the courts, the legislative quorum, and the appointment of officials. These issues, magnified by the developing revolutionary crisis challenging the royal prerogative in all of the colonies, would overwhelm the favorable reputation that preceded him to the colony. Colonial official Samuel Johnston (1733–1816) reported in 1771 that "we hear a very amiable Character of him and are not uneasy at the approaching change." Within a few years Martin had become, according to historian Robert D. W. Connor, "one of the chief factors that drove the colony headlong into rebellion and revolution." The characterization of Martin by historians as mediocre, unimaginative, and obsequious toward superiors is balanced by his enthusiasm, conscientiousness, loyalty, and honesty. Martin's record is no worse than those of other royal governors of the period, and in many ways he was more active than others in attempting to quell the growing rebellion. That he did not succeed may be attributed more to the failure of the ministry in England to comprehend the strength of the rebellion than to his own ideas and efforts.

Martin began his tenure with an extensive three-month tour through the colony, and he and his wife were received cordially everywhere. He wrote that in the back country the requested meetings with the ex-Regulator leaders did "open my eyes exceedingly" to the "rapine and extortion" of the county clerks, officials, and attorneys; but efforts to alleviate the colonists' plight were blocked by the provincial power structure and submerged in the much more threatening revolutionary conflict.

The key issue propelling North Carolina toward revolution was the refusal of the Crown to allow "foreign attachment," the legal attachment by North Carolina creditors of colonial property owned by British citizens to secure the payment of a local debt. The general assembly's refusal to pass a court law without "foreign attachment" resulted in the demise of the province's court system after 1773. Governor Martin's effort to establish special criminal courts was stymied by the assembly, which would not fund them. The court conflict, which brought both civil and criminal processes to an end, greatly aggravated the turbulence of the last years before the Revolution.

In North Carolina the constitutional crisis came to a head at New Bern in August 1774, when the revolutionary leaders openly defied the governor by holding a provincial congress that replaced the disintegrating royal authority with a government of local and provincial committees. When confronted by the New Bern Committee of Safety over the control of the palace cannon, Martin, who had no military support, fled to the protection of Fort Johnston and the naval vessels in the Cape Fear River, arriving there on 2 June 1775. Over the next six weeks the patriot militia closed in on the fort, forcing Martin to retreat to the ship *Cruizer*. Martin conceived a plan to regain control of the province by a rising of Loyalists among the back-country ex-Regulators and the Cape Fear Highland Scot community, where he had considerable support. London promised the aid of an expeditionary force of British regulars. The Loyalists rallied in January under the command of General Donald MacDonald at Cross Creek and began their march on Wilmington, but the British support did not arrive until well after the destruction of the Loyalist army at the battle of Moore's Creek Bridge on 27 February 1776. Accepting that royal government could not be restored in North Carolina at that time, Martin left with the British fleet.

In the summer of 1776 Martin joined his family on Long Island, where they had been for the past year, remaining there in semiretirement. His wife died in October 1778, and in 1779 he was asked to accompany Sir Henry Clinton's invasion of South Carolina. After the fall of Charles Town (now Charleston) in May 1780, Martin volunteered to serve with Lord Cornwallis in the conquest of the Carolinas, and at the rout of the Americans at the battle of Camden in August, Cornwallis wrote that Martin had "behaved with the spirit of a young volunteer." Following the subsequent British invasion of North Carolina in September, Martin called for a Loyalist rising. The British defeat at Kings Mountain a few days later, however, precipitated a withdrawal from the state. In January 1781 Cornwallis reentered North Carolina in pursuit of General Nathanael Greene's command, and Martin endured the privations of the winter southern campaign. Greene's army escaped to Virginia across the Dan River in February, and the state was proclaimed to be under royal control. Greene immediately returned to North Carolina, and although the battle of Guilford Courthouse (15 Mar. 1781) was a tactical victory for Cornwallis, the heavy British casualties forced him to retreat to Wilmington and eventually to leave the state for Virginia. Martin participated in the fighting at Guilford, but his health again broke; he left the army at Wilmington and sailed for Long Island.

Resigning his governorship, Martin took his children to London in 1781. Other than his advocacy on the behalf of fellow Loyalists seeking compensation for their losses, Martin lived his remaining years quietly in London, where he died.

• The extensive Martin papers in the Manuscript Collections, British Museum, are invaluable for details on Martin's personal life. The bulk of his official papers have been published in William L. Saunders, ed., *The Colonial Records of North Carolina*, vols. 8–10 (1890), and Walter J. Clark, ed., *The State Records of North Carolina*, vols. 15–24 (1898). A contemporary view of him is in Janet Schaw, *Journal of a Lady of Quality*, ed. Evangeline W. Andrews (1921). Biographical information is in Vernon O. Stumpf, *Josiah Martin: The Last Royal Governor of North Carolina* (1986); E. Alfred Jones, *American Members of the Inns of Court* (1924); and Richard B. Sheridan, "The West Indian Antecedents of Josiah Martin, the Last Royal Governor of North Carolina." *North Carolina Historical Review* 54 (July 1977): 253–70. Useful for background is Lindley S. Butler, *North Carolina and the Coming of the Revolution, 1763–1776* (1976).

LINDLEY S. BUTLER

MARTIN, Lillien Jane (7 July 1851–26 Mar. 1943), psychologist, was born in Olean, New York, the daughter of Russel Martin, a merchant, and Lydia Hawes. She was sent to the Olean Academy, which she entered at the unusually early age of four. Her early academic interests included mathematics, surveying, physics, and

chemistry. She was also influenced by the psychological insights of Watt and Locke in their respective treatises, *On the Human Mind* and *Essay concerning Human Understanding*. At sixteen, short of money, Martin curtailed her studies and began teaching in an Episcopal girls' school near her new home in Racine, Wisconsin, where her family had moved. She soon moved to Omaha, Nebraska, and found a similar teaching job at an Episcopal girls' school there.

In 1876 Martin applied to Vassar. She received a full scholarship, including expenses. Graduating in 1880 with a B.A., Martin took a teaching position at Indianapolis High School in Indiana, where she taught physics and chemistry. For two summers she did graduate work at the University of Iowa, focusing on plant physiology. After nine years in Indianapolis she was offered a position as vice principal and head of the science department at the Girls' High School in San Francisco, California. In the summer of 1894, inspired by a book by the French psychologist Théodule Ribot, Martin decided to quit her teaching job and study psychology at the University of Göttingen in Germany. At the time, very few women were permitted to study at the university, and doing advanced work in science was especially rare. She studied at Göttingen under George Elias Müller, receiving a Ph.D. in 1898 after four years. During this time she also interned at a Swiss psychiatric institution, studying techniques of hypnotism. She co-wrote with Müller *Zur Analyse der Unterschiedsempfindlichkeit* (Toward an analysis of sensitivity differentials) (1899), which focuses on problems of successive judgments and is considered a classic of psycho-physics. It studies the way that subjects make mental comparisons by asking which of two weights held at different times is heavier. Martin and Müller found that rather than remembering the weight of the first object and making a direct mental comparison to the second, subjects tended to judge both weights against predetermined notions of heaviness and lightness.

Returning to the United States in 1899, Martin was invited by her old friend, now president of Stanford University, David Starr Jordan, to teach there as an assistant professor of psychology. She accepted but spent every second summer until her retirement in Germany doing further study and writing four volumes of technical psycho-physics in German. Promoted to associate professor in 1909, full professor in 1911, and executive head of the psychology department in 1915, Martin became the first woman to attain that status in any department at Stanford. She retired as professor emeritus the following year at age sixty-five.

Her retirement did not last long. After only a few months, Martin moved to San Francisco and opened a private practice as a psychologist while simultaneously working in mental hygiene clinics. In 1920 she opened the first mental hygiene clinic for normal preschool children in the United States at Mount Zion Hospital in 1920. A growing interest in the concerns of the elderly, initially prompted by her interactions with a cranky grandparent of one of her clinic's young patients, led Martin to establish the country's first geriatric counseling center in 1929. She developed methods to train the elderly who had grown incapable of caring for themselves to relearn living skills and regain their independence. Individually designed exercise programs were prescribed to each client after extensive diagnostic interviews. Systematizing these teaching methods, Martin also trained other counselors in their prescription and implementation.

An intensely independent woman, Martin was an irrepressible adventurer. She toured Russia alone at age seventy-eight. Also at seventy-eight she learned to drive, persevering through the fifty lessons it took to pass the test, and then drove across the United States three years later. At age eighty-seven, she traveled for six months in South America. When arthritis caused her hands to tremble uncontrollably, she taught herself touch typing. Martin, who never married, had a long-term companion, Fidelia Jewett. Martin died in San Francisco.

Professionally, Martin is best known for her work in gerontology, especially in the area of psycho-physics. She also developed experimental methods to measure abstract, imageless thought, attempting to determine the difference in strength and quality between remembered and imagined images. Her work supported the argument that all thought is not necessarily derived from sensory experience. She also proved that the clarity of a remembered visual image is not necessarily indicative of the strength of nonvisual memory connected to it. This was an important finding for gerontology because it suggested that the less distinct mental pictures formed by the elderly do not imply a general mental degeneration nor an impaired ability to function. This work built off the ideas of Osward Külpe, a professor at the University of Bonn, whose division of thought into cognitive contents and cognitive acts, separating the sensory content of thought from its structural and interrelational aspects, laid the groundwork for the development of theories involving imageless thought. In recognition of her findings, Martin was awarded an honorary Ph.D. from Bonn in 1913, the first such degree ever given to an American psychologist. She also published significant work in the fields of hypnotism, memory, the psychology of humor, and the psychology of aesthetics.

• There is no collection of her personal papers as most were destroyed at her request. Besides those works noted above, Martin wrote *Memory vs. Imagination* (1911), *The Function of an Image in Memory and Imagination* (1913), *An Experimental Contribution to the Investigation of the Subconscious* (1915), *Personality as Revealed by the Content of Images* (1916), *Mental Hygiene* (1917), *Mental Hygiene; Two Years' Experience of a Clinical Psychologist* (1920), and *The Work of a Mental Hygiene Clinic for Pre-School Age Children* (1921). Two nontechnical accounts of her work written by Martin in collaboration with Clare DeGrunchy are *Salvaging Old Age* (1930) and *Sweeping the Cobwebs* (1933). The best source for information on her life is Miriam Allen deFord, *Psychologist Unretired: The Life Pattern of Lillien J. Martin* (1948). Criticism of some of her professional work can be found in Edward Bradford Titchener, "Professor Martin and the Perky Experiments," *American Journal of Psychology* 26 (Jan. 1913). See also Robert S. Woolworth, *Experimental Psychology* (1938). Obituaries are in *Psychological Review* 50 (July 1943), *American Journal of Psychology* 56 (Nov. 1943), *American Sociological Review* 7 (June 1943), and the *New York Times*, 28 Mar. 1943.

ELIZABETH ZOE VICARY

MARTIN, Luther (Feb.? 1748–8 July 1826), lawyer and politician, was born near New Brunswick, New Jersey, the son of Benjamin Martin and Hannah (maiden name unknown), farmers. Luther Martin graduated from the College of New Jersey (later Princeton University) in 1766. For the next three years he served as schoolmaster at the Queen Anne's County Free School on Maryland's Eastern Shore. During this time Martin began studying law with books borrowed from a local attorney.

In 1770, Martin moved farther down the Eastern Shore to Somerset County, where he began reading law in the office of Samuel Wilson. After a few weeks, however, he accepted a position as superintendent of the Onancock Grammar School in Accomack County on Virginia's Eastern Shore. There he remained until the fall of 1771, when he passed the Virginia licensing examination for the bar. Following a six-month tour of the western regions of Virginia, Maryland, and Pennsylvania in 1772 in search of a place to set up a law practice, Martin returned to Somerset County to find that the three most active lawyers in the area had recently died. He therefore decided to practice law on the Eastern Shore. In debt when he left teaching, Martin's energy and brilliance quickly gained him a large law practice. Within two years he claimed an annual income of about £1,000 pounds, an enormous sum for the day. Much of his early practice was before Virginia courts, but Martin soon built a reputation in Maryland as well.

As engrossed as he was in building his law practice, Martin could not ignore the critical state of affairs between the colonies and Britain. Like much of the lower Eastern Shore, Somerset County had a large Loyalist population. Martin, however, identified with the patriot cause. He opposed British efforts to tax the colonies and to regulate colonial trade more closely, and he became an early proponent of the necessity of declaring independence. In 1774, Somerset County patriots elected Martin to the local Committee of Observation, a group charged with the responsibility of enforcing the resolves of the Continental Congress and promoting the patriot cause. He was also elected as one of the county's delegates to the extralegal Maryland Convention, which began meeting in June 1774 in an effort to coordinate the colony's opposition to British imperial policies. Martin missed the first two of these conventions, probably because of the press of legal business, but he attended the third, held in Annapolis in December 1774.

Maryland's first state constitution, adopted in November 1776, established the office of attorney general, to be appointed by the governor and council. After their first two choices declined the honor, the governor and council accepted Martin's offer to assume the post. He held the office from 1778 until 1805 and again from 1818 until 1822. After being appointed attorney general, Martin moved from the Eastern Shore to Baltimore Town. There he became a member of the Baltimore Light Dragoons, described by the *Maryland Journal & Baltimore Advertiser* (19 June 1781) as "an elegant Corps consisting of 50 respectable gentlemen" who equipped themselves as a cavalry unit. Martin's war experience, however, was limited to a few weeks during the summer of 1781, when the Baltimore Light Dragoons were ordered south to reinforce the marquis de Lafayette in the Virginia campaign against Lord Cornwallis. The unit apparently saw no action, and Martin may have returned home early to attend to pressing business in the attorney general's office.

In December 1783, Martin married Maria Cresap, daughter of Captain Michael Cresap of Oldtown, on the western Maryland frontier. They had five children, including three who reached adulthood.

After the war, Martin's private law practice prospered, and he became recognized as the leading member of the Maryland bar. He also continued serving as attorney general. When the framers of Maryland's first state constitution created the office, they did not expect the attorney general to be more than a lawyer the governor and council could turn to when they needed legal advice. Because of his legal prowess and long tenure in the office, Martin is credited with shaping the office of attorney general and making it a distinct and essential part of state government.

The Maryland General Assembly elected Martin a delegate to Congress in 1784, but he was too busy with his public and private legal business to attend. Three years later the assembly elected him one of Maryland's five delegates to the Philadelphia convention called to revise the Articles of Confederation. In Philadelphia, Martin's extensive legal knowledge and his commitment to preserving a role for small states made him a leader among the delegates who opposed James Madison's Virginia Plan. Its proposal for proportional representation in both houses of the legislative branch would, Martin argued, create a "system of slavery, which bound [the small states] hand and foot." Martin helped frame the small states' alternative, the New Jersey Plan. This proposal called for amending the Articles of Confederation to give Congress more power, but it preserved the single vote per state feature of the original Articles. After the defeat of the New Jersey Plan, Martin gave a long, impassioned speech, which stretched over two days, defending the sovereignty and independence of the individual states and denouncing the national government implicit in the Virginia Plan. Appointed a member of the committee charged with resolving the issue of representation in Congress, Martin supported the resulting Connecticut compromise even though "he did not like many parts of it."

Later in the convention Martin introduced what became the "supremacy clause," although he opposed the amended provision as it finally appeared in article 6 of the proposed Constitution. Martin argued against the need for inferior federal courts, saying that the federal Supreme Court would provide sufficient check on any errors the state courts might commit. When the convention turned to the executive department, Martin sought to limit the president to a single term. He also proposed that the president be indirectly elected by electors, the method finally adopted by the convention. As the weeks passed, Martin became convinced that the constitution taking shape would create a strong national government that would effectively abolish state governments and jeopardize individual rights. He prepared a bill of rights for the consideration of the convention but never introduced it because he could find no one to support him. Martin left the convention before it ended, determined to fight ratification of the proposed Constitution in Maryland.

Martin detailed his reasons for opposing the proposed Constitution in an exhaustive report delivered before the Maryland General Assembly in November 1787 and published in newspapers and in pamphlet form under the title *The Genuine Information*. Connecticut Federalist and fellow convention delegate Oliver Ellsworth, writing under the pen name "The Landholder," criticized Martin's behavior at the convention, especially the length of his speeches. Martin responded with a volley of letters published in the critical weeks leading up to Maryland's vote for delegates to the state's ratification convention.

The danger of the proposed Constitution, in Martin's opinion, was that it would replace a federal system, in which the states protected the rights and liberties of their citizens, with a strong national government empowered to act directly on individuals. He wrote in his first "Address" to the citizens of Maryland:

[N]o *greater powers* ought to be given "than *experience has shewn to be necessary*, since it will be *easy to delegate further power* when *time* shall dictate the *expediency* or *necessity*; but powers *once bestowed* upon a government, should they be found ever so *dangerous* or *destructive* to freedom, *cannot be resumed or wrested from government*, but by *another revolution*.

Martin argued that a bill of rights "to serve as a barrier between the general government and the respective states and their citizens" ("Address No. II") needed to be added to the Constitution before it was ratified because once the government was operational its supporters would never agree to limitations on its power. Furthermore, Martin urged his fellow citizens not to be rushed into ratifying a document that was fundamentally flawed, asking them to "reject the advice of those *political quacks*, who . . . would urge you *rashly to gulp down* a constitution, which, in its present form, unaltered and unamended, would be as certain death to your liberty, as *arsenick* could be to your bodies" ("Address No. III").

Martin was one of only twelve Antifederalists among the seventy-six delegates elected to Maryland's ratification convention, which met in Annapolis in late April 1788. Martin attended the convention, but a severe sore throat prevented him from participating in the debate. Even if he had been well, nothing he could have said would have changed the outcome. With such a large Federalist majority in the convention, the Antifederalists knew they could not defeat the proposed Constitution outright. Instead, they focused on the need for a bill of rights and attempted to submit for the convention's consideration a list of twenty-two amendments designed to protect individual liberties and to preserve a role for the states in the new national government. The Federalist majority would not allow the proposed bill of rights to be considered and even refused to debate the Antifederalists on the merits of the Constitution. Instead, they sat in stony silence until the Antifederalists gave up in frustration. The convention then approved the Constitution on 28 April 1788, by a vote of sixty-three to eleven.

Martin paid a political price for his opposition to the Constitution. In 1791, James McHenry (1753–1816), a Federalist member of Maryland's delegation to the Philadelphia convention, responded to President George Washington's request for a nominee to be the first federal district attorney for Maryland by noting that Martin was "the best qualified man in the state." But Martin's extreme Antifederalism, McHenry added, made him "the last person who merits the appointment."

Martin's Antifederalism soon waned, however. The adoption of the federal Bill of Rights in 1791 removed many of his objections to the Constitution, and the way the federal government took shape under the administrations of Washington and John Adams (1735–1826) impressed him. Martin had always championed republican government, which to him meant a government limited in geographic extent in which a restricted electorate would select as their representatives men they knew to be of high ability and virtue. He saw the more democratic political philosophy championed by Thomas Jefferson, which advocated expanding the electorate to all free white males, as a greater threat to liberty than a strong central government, properly tempered by a bill of rights. Jefferson's democracy, Martin claimed, would replace "true republicanism" with "mobocracy."

Martin's animosity toward Jefferson had a personal dimension as well. Discussing the American Indians in 1785 in his *Notes on Virginia*, Jefferson described Martin's father-in-law as "a man infamous for the many murders he had committed on those much-injured people." After his wife died in 1796, Martin determined to honor her memory by clearing her father's name. In a series of published letters, Martin challenged Jefferson to prove his claim; he also gathered evidence that suggested the allegations were false. Jefferson was unable to verify his statement, but he refused to admit the error, and Martin had to be satisfied with crowing that Jefferson's charge had "no other

foundation but the fanciful reveries of a philosophical imagination."

Martin appears to have begun drinking heavily after his wife's death, and by 1800 his alcoholism was attracting public notice. He was lonely, his legal practice was enormous and demanding, and he faced a serious problem with his fourteen-year-old daughter, Eleonora, who had fallen in love with Richard Reynal Keene, Martin's law clerk. Martin forbade the courtship, but in 1802 the two defied him and eloped. Martin took his anger to the press, airing his grievances against Keene in letters that he then had reprinted in a pamphlet entitled *Modern Gratitude* (1802).

Jefferson's election as president in 1800 set the stage for Martin to vent his political and personal animosity toward him in a national forum. His brilliant defense of Supreme Court associate justice Samuel Chase in his impeachment trial before the U.S. Senate in 1805 deterred the Republicans' efforts to reshape the federal judiciary by impeaching Federalist judges. Martin again thwarted Republican ambitions, and the personal wishes of Jefferson himself, when he successfully defended Aaron Burr (1756–1836) at his treason trial in Richmond in 1807. In a letter to George Hay, Jefferson suggested that Martin be criminally charged as part of the Burr conspiracy so as to "put down this unprincipled & impudent federal bull-dog." To Martin, however, Burr's acquittal proved "that in America there are lawyers who cannot be intimidated by fear of presidential vengeance, nor by the frenzy of a deceived, misguided people."

Martin's defense of Chase and Burr brought him national prominence and made him a Federalist hero. The acclaim affected Martin little, however, and he remained principally occupied with his busy law practice. He maintained his large private law practice, continued his appellate work before the state court of appeals, and, from 1813 to 1816, served as chief judge of the Baltimore criminal court. Reappointed attorney general of Maryland in 1818, Martin appeared before the U.S. Supreme Court in 1819 in the landmark *McCulloch v. Maryland* case to argue for the state's right to tax federally chartered banks. Martin lost the *McCulloch* decision, and it proved to be his last major court appearance. In August 1819 Martin suffered a stroke that permanently impaired his mental capacities.

Martin lived seven years longer, unable to support himself and dependent upon others for his care. He had earned vast sums during his long legal career but, through personal intemperance and generosity to friends, was at the end reduced to poverty. In 1822, in gratitude for his long service to the state and in recognition of his preeminent position in the Maryland bar, the General Assembly passed an unprecedented resolution requiring every practicing lawyer in Maryland to pay five dollars annually toward Martin's support. Less than one year after the resolution passed, Aaron Burr learned of Martin's plight and took him into his home in New York, where he remained until his death.

Martin's brilliance as a lawyer, as well as his eccentricities and boorish behavior, elicited frequent comment from his contemporaries. One person who knew him well, Henry M. Brackenridge, described Martin's voice as "thick and disagreeable, his language and pronunciation rude and uncouth." A fellow Marylander, U.S. Supreme Court chief justice Roger Brooke Taney, remembered in his *Memoirs* that Martin's clothes seemed to be a "compound of the fine and the coarse, and appeared never to have felt the brush." He wore shirts with broad, ruffled cuffs long after they had gone out of style, Taney added, and they were "dabbled and soiled, and showed that they had not been changed for a day or more." Martin also frequently appeared in court drunk, earning himself the appellation, "Lawyer Brandy Bottle." Yet Taney acknowledged that Martin was the greatest member of the Maryland bar of his day, noting that he was a "profound lawyer" who "never missed the strong points of his case."

• There is no large collection of Martin papers, although a number of letters are scattered among the collections of the Maryland Historical Society in Baltimore, and the Maryland State Archives in Annapolis has many official papers documenting his public career. The autobiographical fifth number of *Modern Gratitude* (1801) is the source for much of the information on Martin's early life and career. His arguments against the proposed U.S. Constitution are detailed in *The Genuine Information* (1787), reprinted in Max Farrand, ed., *Records of the Federal Convention of 1787* (4 vols., 1911–1937), specifically volume 3, and in his four addresses to the citizens of Maryland, published in the *Maryland Journal* in Mar. and early Apr. 1788, which can be found in John P. Kaminski and Gaspare J. Saladino, eds., *Commentaries on the Constitution, Public and Private*, vol. 4, in *Documentary History of the Ratification of the Constitution*, vol. 16 (1986). The only full biography of Martin, Paul S. Clarkson and R. Samuel Jett, *Luther Martin of Maryland* (1970), is a fine volume full of detail. Some additional information, including a few corrections to items in the Clarkson and Jett volume, can be garnered from the biographies of Martin that appear in James McLachlan, *Princetonians, 1748–1768: A Biographical Dictionary* (1976), and Edward C. Papenfuse et al., *Biographical Dictionary of the Maryland Legislature, 1635–1789* (1985).

GREGORY A. STIVERSON

MARTIN, Mary (1 Dec. 1913–3 Nov. 1990), actress, was born Mary Virginia Martin in Weatherford, Texas, the daughter of Preston Martin, an attorney, and Juanita Presley, a violin teacher at the Weatherford Seminary (later renamed Weatherford College). Martin studied violin and took voice lessons. Her first public appearance, at age five, was at a fireman's ball where she sang, "Where the Apples Grow on the Lilac Tree." At age twelve she gave her first singing recital while a girlfriend accompanied her on the violin. She sang for local churches, women's clubs, and men's fraternal organizations. Movies captivated her, and she emulated her favorite stars.

When she was fourteen years old she met Benjamin Hagman. She started dating him during her last year in high school. To stop this blossoming romance, Martin's parents sent her to the Ward Belmont finishing school for young ladies in Nashville, Tennessee. But after two months her parents relented and permitted her to marry Hagman at Hopkinsville, Kentucky, in 1930 on her seventeenth birthday. Hagman was twenty-one. They had one child, Larry Martin Hagman, who later followed his mother into a successful acting career. Benjamin Hagman became an accountant and lawyer.

At age eighteen Martin opened a dance school in Weatherford; to stay ahead of her students, she commuted to Fort Worth for dancing classes. At age nineteen she went to Hollywood to study at the Fanchon and Marco School of the Theater. In 1936 she returned to Hollywood aiming to become a movie star. For two years she auditioned without success. She occasionally sang on the Don Lee radio network and the Buddy Rogers radio program. She had her first serious singing job, at $40 a week, at the Cinegrille Room, a popular Hollywood night spot. In 1937 Martin's father got her a divorce-in-absentia from Hagman.

The turning point in Martin's career occurred when she was booked to sing at the Trocadero, then Hollywood's top nightclub. Broadway producer Lawrence Schwab saw her there and brought her to New York, where he helped her get a role in Cole Porter's *Leave It to Me*. The play opened on 9 November 1938 at the Imperial Theater on Broadway; that week *Life* magazine pictured Martin on its cover. Paramount Pictures signed her to a movie contract. With the possible exception of *The Great Victor Herbert*, her films for Paramount were undistinguished.

While with Paramount she met Richard Halliday, a story editor at the studio's New York offices. They married in 1930 in a civil ceremony in Las Vegas. Theirs was one of the most successful marriages in show business. Halliday became Martin's manager, agent, consultant, and some-time producer. They had one daughter. Halliday encouraged Martin to concentrate on stage work. Her first Broadway starring role was in *One Touch of Venus*, written by Kurt Weills, Ogden Nash, and S. J. Perlman; it was directed by Elia Kazan and co-starred John Boles. The play, which opened on 7 October 1945 and ran through 567 performances, established Martin as a foremost Broadway star. In 1945 Martin and Boles took *Venus* on a countrywide tour for a year.

After *Venus* Martin co-starred with Yul Brynner in *Lute Song*, a lyrical play based on an ancient Chinese legend. It opened at the Plymouth Theater on 6 February 1946 and had 142 performances. That spring Martin sailed to England with her husband and two children to star in Noël Coward's production of his play *Pacific 1860*. This was not the only association she had with Coward. In 1952 they performed together, just the two of them, at a large benefit at the Café de Paris in London. In 1955 they did a ninety-minute television special in the United States.

In 1946 Martin wanted to star as sharpshooter Annie Oakley in Irving Berlin's *Annie Get Your Gun*. She lost the role to Ethel Merman but persuaded Joshua

Logan to cast her in that part for the national touring company. She toured with it for eleven months during 1947–1948, then repeated the tour in 1957.

Martin is best known for her performance as Nellie Forbush from Little Rock, Arkansas, in *South Pacific*, a musical play based on James Michener's *Tales of the South Pacific*. It costarred Ezio Pinza in the role of the planter Emile de Becque. The script was written by Logan, who also directed it, and Leland Hayward. Richard Rodgers and Oscar Hammerstein wrote the music and the lyrics. The play opened at the Majestic Theater in New York on 7 April 1949 and ran for two years, followed by a one-year run at the Drury Lane Theatre Royal in London. Brooks Atkinson found Martin's performance "full of quicksilver, pertness and delight . . . She sings with skill and good nature . . . particularly delightful—the stomping jubilee of 'I'm Gonna Wash That Man Right Outa My Hair' and blowing out the walls of the theater with the rapture of 'I'm in Love with a Wonderful Guy' (*New York Times*, 8 Apr. 1949).

Returning from England Martin was in no hurry to choose a new vehicle for herself. She unwisely turned down many scripts, including *Oklahoma!*, *Kiss Me Kate*, *My Fair Lady*, *Fanny*, and *Mame*. But she made her mark on television with a new genre, the one-night spectacular. It was Leland Hayward's concept. He cast Martin and Ethel Merman in one of early television's greatest successes. It was broadcast live and not taped. Martin sang, danced, and hosted the show. Jerome Robbins directed, Oscar Hammerstein enacted a scene from Thornton Wilder's *The Skin of Our Teeth*, and Marian Anderson sang the "Battle Hymn of the Republic."

Martin's stage career resumed with *Dancing in the Streets*, which closed in Boston, and *Kind Sir*, with Charles Boyer, which had a limited run on Broadway from 4 November 1953 to 27 March 1954, a total of 166 performances. The reviews were lukewarm. Her next play was *Jennie*, based on the life of actress Laurette Taylor, but it never reached Broadway. In 1954 she was cast in *Peter Pan*. Martin regarded it as her definitive role and the most important thing she had ever done in the theater. It ran on Broadway in 1956 and 1957. Jerome Robbins directed and Cyril Ritchards co-starred. Martin did various productions of *Peter Pan* until 1960, when she played it on television in its third and last production. This version was taped and reaired successfully to a new audience in 1989. In 1955 Martin toured abroad for the Department of State in *The Skin of Our Teeth*. In 1958 and 1959 she toured in *Music with Mary Martin*, backed by a thirty-piece orchestra, and *Magic with Mary Martin*. She also toured with a show specially designed for children, *Three to Make Music*. It included scenes from *Peter Pan* and *Cinderella* and a short revue with a clown and an orchestra.

In 1959 Martin opened in another landmark of the American theater. She created the role of Baroness Maria von Trapp in *The Sound of Music*, with songs by Rodgers and Hammerstein. The show ran for two years. To Martin's great disappointment she was not chosen to enact the role on the screen. Although Martin was a superstar of the Broadway stage, she had only a marginal career in Hollywood.

For a long time Martin and Halliday paid many visits to Brazil, a country that held a special attraction for them. They fell in love with a piece of the countryside, purchased the land, and built a large farm. In 1962 they settled on the farm, and Martin became a fashion designer while there. Her enterprise stirred interest in the United States. *Women's Wear Daily*, the leading trade paper in the garment industry, sent a photographer and a writer to report on the collection. Jack Paar visited twice to do segments for television specials that aired in 1965 and 1971.

In 1965 Martin toured Japan, South Korea, South Vietnam, and England in *Hello Dolly!* for the Department of State. On 6 December 1966 she opened in a new play, *I Do! I Do!*, at the Forty-sixth Street Theater in New York. David Merrick produced, Gower Champion directed, and Robert Preston co-starred. The Martin-Preston musical ran for one year on Broadway and another year on tour. It was to be Martin's last legitimate play. The doctors ordered her to stop working due to exhaustion.

After Halliday died in 1973, Martin moved to California. She lived near her son and kept another house at Rancho Mirage in Palm Springs near her closest friend, Janet Gaynor, a film star of the 1930s. In 1981 Martin performed with her son in England on the occasion of the Queen Mother's eightieth birthday celebration. In 1982 first lady Nancy Reagan invited Martin to a White House dinner reception for the president of Brazil and his wife. The Brazilian government had long recognized Martin's passionate attachment to the country. Three years earlier, in 1979, Ambassador Pinhiero had awarded her a special medal from the government at a dinner ceremony held in her honor at the Brazilian Embassy.

During the 1970s and 1980s Martin went on numerous talk shows and signed copies of her autobiography. She also designed a line of bed sheets and towels for the Fieldcrest Mills. In 1980 she became a cohost of the half-hour television show "Over Easy." It was seen by six million viewers weekly on about 250 public television channels. Many of her friends performed on her show, including Ethel Merman, Florence Henderson, Pearl Bailey, Van Johnson, Maxine Andrews, Jimmy Stewart, Betty Ford, and Bob and Dolores Hope.

In 1986 Martin and musical theater star Carol Channing were cast in straight dramatic roles in James Kirkwood's play *Legends*, about two aging actresses. The play enjoyed a successful tour, but it never went to New York.

Martin traveled to New York in 1989 to participate in a television tribute to Richard Rodgers. That year she also received the Kennedy Center Lifetime Achievement Award. It was preceded by a brief ceremony in the Oval Office, where President Ronald Reagan pinned medals on the year's honorees. Martin died at her home in Rancho Mirage.

• Mary Martin wrote a charming, albeit chronologically and thematically rather bewildering autobiography, *My Heart Belongs* (1976), which she published after her husband's death. James Watters, *Return Engagement* (1984), is a biography of Martin. Barry Rivadue, *Mary Martin* (1991), is a bio-bibliography of the actress. James Robert Parish, *Hollywood Songsters* (1991), devotes a chapter to Martin. An obituary is in the *New York Times*, 5 Nov. 1990.

SHOSHANA KLEBANOFF

MARTIN, Roberta (12 Feb. 1907–18 Jan. 1969), gospel pianist, composer/arranger, and singer, was born Roberta Evelyn Winston in Helena, Arkansas, the daughter of William Winston and Anna (maiden name unknown). One of six children in the Winston household, Roberta showed an early proclivity for music. When only a toddler, she climbed onto the piano bench and picked out melodies that she had heard. This interest and talent was nurtured by her oldest brother's wife, who became her first piano teacher.

When Roberta was ten years old, her family moved from Arkansas and settled in Chicago. Roberta continued her piano studies with Mildred Bryant Jones in standard keyboard literature and pointed her career toward that of concert pianist or professional accompanist. She graduated from Wendell Phillips High School and was encouraged by Jones to pursue a career in music. Why Roberta chose "Martin" as her surname is not known.

Martin began playing for churches at an early age. Her first experience was at Pilgrim Baptist Church, where she served as pianist for the Sunday school. In 1932 she was invited by Thomas A. Dorsey (the father of gospel music) and Theodore R. Frye to accept the position of pianist for the Ebenezer Baptist Church junior choir. Dorsey and Frye, longtime friends, worked together as pianist and director, respectively, for the Ebenezer adult choir. They had heard of Martin's talent and wanted her to play for the younger choir. She was apprehensive because this choir of young people sang only gospel songs. She auditioned with the one gospel song that she knew and was immediately hired.

Dorsey and Frye encouraged and guided Martin in her development of a gospel style of piano playing. In 1933 they assisted her in organizing her first gospel group, the Martin-Frye Quartet, which included singers Robert Anderson, James Lawrence, Norsalus McKissick, Eugene Smith, and Willie Webb. This group was renamed the Roberta Martin Singers in 1936. By this time Martin had worked with choirs enough to know what type of sound she wanted. In the 1940s she made the quantum leap of combining male and female voices. She was a pioneer in the formulation of a mixed-voice choir. According to Pearl Williams-Jones, "The unique harmonic sound created by this particular voicing was mellow and smooth, with dynamic nuances that ebbed and flowed and a timing that was almost imperceptibly 'behind' the beat" (Rea-

gon, p. 258). Martin's first female singers were Bessie Folk and Delois Barrett Campbell. Other talented singers were added later. Martin chose outstanding singers who could perform as soloists as well as blend in ensemble. This was the beginning of the Roberta Martin "sound," which in the mid-1940s was called "classic gospel." Martin's group established the sound benchmark against which future gospel choirs would be measured.

Another of Thomas Dorsey's protégés, Sallie Martin (no relation to Roberta Martin), helped to popularize gospel music through her singing, composing, arranging, and development of choruses. The two Martins operated as a team very briefly and called their chorus the Martin and Martin Gospel Singers. This merger did not last long because neither woman wanted to risk being overshadowed by the other. Dorsey, however, recognizing the talent of both Martins, promoted a gospel singing contest between the two groups. The contest was held at DuSable High School and played to a full house. The fifteen-cent admission charge did not dissuade hundreds from attending and set a precedent of paid admission for gospel concerts that continues today.

In 1939 Roberta Martin expanded her career to include music publishing. She had learned the business from Dorsey, who was the first publisher of gospel sheet music. Martin's publishing company thrived because those who heard her group wanted to purchase the arrangements so that they could sing them in their church choirs. Songwriters took their songs to Martin for arranging and publishing because they knew that the music would sell. The oral tradition of gospel music with its florid piano ornamentation and vocal improvisation is not easily committed to notation. This fact generated a need for recordings to supplement live performances. Roberta Martin's Singers recorded on the Apollo and then the Savoy labels, winning several gold records for extraordinary sales. People would attend the concerts and purchase the sheet music and recordings so that they could imitate the Roberta Martin sound in their singing.

Because Martin was a trained musician who could read, write, and arrange music, she began to compose gospel songs and also arrange songs written by others. She arranged songs for other gospel greats, including James Cleveland, Lucy Smith Collier, Willie Webb, and Robert Anderson. Martin's first composition, written in 1943, was the familiar *Try Jesus He Satisfies*. During the 1940s the Roberta Martin Singers traveled widely and established a reputation as one of the most outstanding gospel choirs in the nation.

In 1947 Martin married James Austin and started a family. She decided to leave the travel circuit so that she could raise their son properly. She turned over the management of the group to Eugene Smith, who was best known for his narrative song introductions during concerts. Lucy Smith Collier, Martin's stepdaughter and protégé, having sung with the group and closely observed Martin's playing style, replaced her as group pianist. Austin focused his energies on the financial management of their publishing business so that Martin could spend time with their son and continue her gospel songwriting and arranging. Her compositions include "God Is Still on the Throne," "Have You Found a Friend," "He's Always Right There," "I Don't Mind," "Is There Anybody Here," "I'm Just Waiting on the Lord," "Let It Be," "No Other Help I Know," and "Teach Me Lord."

The Roberta Martin Singers continued to draw huge audiences on their tours. They headlined at the Los Angeles World's Greatest Gospel Caravan in 1959, received the annual Thomas A. Dorsey award in New York in 1962, served as featured group at the New York Coliseum in 1963, and sang at Italy's Spoleto Festival of Two Worlds in 1963.

After thirty years of singing together, the group retired in 1966. During the Martin era the Singers performed on radio and television and in major concert halls, stadiums, and churches at home and abroad. Individuals who had sung with Martin's groups went on to forge for themselves prominent positions in the musical world. Chief among these were Archie Davis, who traveled widely as guest soloist with the Billy Graham Crusades; Dinah Washington, who was called "Queen of Rhythm and Blues"; James Cleveland, a prolific gospel singer and composer, who was dubbed "Crown Prince of Gospel"; and Della Reese, who was nominated for a Grammy Award in gospel music in 1987 and who enjoyed success in the popular music field.

When Martin died in Chicago, more than 50,000 mourners attended her memorial service. During her lifetime she composed approximately 70 songs and arranged and published approximately 280. After Martin's death James Austin continued the still thriving Roberta Martin Publishing Company to ensure that her songs would remain accessible. In 1981 a Black History Month tribute was paid to Roberta Martin for her contributions to gospel music. This event was held at the Smithsonian Institution and included a concert series of Martin's songs sung by nine former Singers and a colloquium featuring gospel scholars and colleagues of Martin. This tribute to Roberta Martin served to highlight the legacy as performer, composer/arranger, and pianist that she left to the gospel community and the world.

• The most comprehensive discussion of Martin's life and works is in *Roberta Martin and the Roberta Martin Singers: The Legacy and the Music*, ed. Bernice Johnson Reagon and Linn Shapiro (1981). This booklet serves as a report of the 6–8 Feb. 1981 colloquium and reconstruction concert series based on Martin's music. A selected discography of Martin's recordings is included. Bernice Johnson Reagon, ed., *We'll Understand It Better By and By: Pioneering African American Gospel Composers* (1992), includes an overview of the Smithsonian Research Project on gospel music and a comprehensive section on Roberta Martin (pp. 255–306). A discography and annotated bibliography provide important information for those seeking additional resources. Horace Clarence Boyer, "The Gospel Song: A Historical and Analytical Survey" (master's thesis, Univ. of Rochester, Eastman School of Mu-

sic, 1964), includes recorded interviews and correspondence with Martin and other gospel artists. Irene V. Jackson, "Afro-American Gospel Music and Its Social Setting with Special Attention to Roberta Martin" (Ph.D. diss., Wesleyan Univ., 1974), offers extensive biographical information about Martin and a list of gospel music from 1938 to 1965. Anthony Heilbut, *The Gospel Sound: Good News and Bad Times* (1985), serves as a general history of gospel music that is written in a conversational style. The introduction begins with the funeral of Martin and notes that her obituary did not appear in either the *New York Times* or *Jet Magazine*. Several brief references are made to Martin throughout the book.

MARY FRANCES EARLY

MARTIN, Sara (18 June 1884–24 May 1955), blues and vaudeville singer, was born Sara Dunn in Louisville, Kentucky, the daughter of William Dunn and Katie Pope. Nothing is known of her youth. Based in Chicago, she traveled in vaudeville from around 1915.

While performing in New York City clubs and cabarets, Martin was discovered by songwriter and publisher Clarence Williams, who arranged to have her record "Sugar Blues" for the OKeh label in October 1922. According to Williams's wife, singer Eva Taylor, pianist Fats Waller was supposed to play at the session but never showed up, and Williams himself accompanied Martin. "Sugar Blues" proved to be a big hit anyway, and Martin subsequently became the most popular blues and vaudeville singer on OKeh Records; she eventually recorded more than 120 titles for the label. She recorded "Achin' Hearted Blues" in November and four additional titles with Waller in December 1922, including "'Tain't Nobody's Bus'ness If I Do." (These were Waller's first disc recordings; he had earlier made piano rolls.)

Martin recorded mainly in New York City, but for performances in theaters, clubs, and casinos she toured widely throughout the eastern and midwestern states during the 1920s, joining blues musician W. C. Handy on the Theater Owner's Booking Association vaudeville circuit in 1923. At some point she presented a family act with her three-year-old son and her banjo-playing husband, William Myers; the date of their marriage is unknown. For an October 1923 recording of "Graveyard Dream Blues" she was accompanied by Williams's jazz group, which included reed player Sidney Bechet. That same month OKeh initiated a series of duos by Martin and Sylvester Weaver, the first down-home blues guitarist to record.

In 1927 Martin sang with Williams's band on radio in New York City, and she performed with Taylor in Atlantic City, New Jersey, and in New York City in the musical comedy *Bottomland*. She also appeared in the film *Hello Bill* (c. 1927). Late in 1928 she made her last recordings, still with Williams's band and with King Oliver as cornetist. On "Death Sting Me Blues," her best-known title, Martin utilizes a harsh timbre, a fast, prominent vibrato, and sliding blue notes—all typical of many classic female blues singers—but she takes an oddly mannered approach to pronunciation, delivering the blues as if she were affecting an upper-class dialect. Martin married Hayes Withers in 1929;

nothing is known of the ending to her previous marriage or of additional children.

Martin continued to appear in theaters and clubs until 1931. At this point several sources have her leaving secular music to begin an affiliation with gospel musician Thomas A. Dorsey in Chicago, but Dorsey's musical partner from 1932 to 1939 was Sallie Martin, not Sara. If she worked at all with Dorsey around 1932, it was a brief and unsuccessful venture. Martin left music, holding unspecified jobs in New York City before establishing a nursing home in Louisville, Kentucky, in the 1940s. She died in Louisville.

Billed as "the colored Sophie Tucker," Martin was one of the first female blues and vaudeville singers to record, and she reached a large audience throughout the 1920s. However, her music has found little lasting appeal by comparison with that of such contemporaries as Ma Rainey, Bessie Smith, and Ethel Waters. Writer Derrick Stewart-Baxter reported that "on stage she was a fine showwoman and held her audience in the palm of her hand. Unfortunately, she was unable to put this across on record" (p. 80).

• Little is known of Martin. The most reliable source of information is Sheldon Harris, *Blues Who's Who: A Biographical Dictionary of Blues Singers* (1979). A brief anonymous article, "Sara Martin," appeared in *Living Blues*, no. 52 (Spring 1982): 23. Beyond that, one can only extract isolated information from "Looking Back with Eva," *Storyville*, no. 14 (Dec. 1967–Jan. 1968): 24; Ronald Clifford Foreman, Jr., "Jazz and Race Records, 1920–1932: Their Origins and Their Significance for the Record Industry and Society" (Ph.D. diss., Univ. of Illinois, 1968); Robert M. W. Dixon and John Godrich, *Recording the Blues* (1970); Derrick Stewart-Baxter, *Ma Rainey and the Classic Blues Singers* (1970); Daphne Duval Harrison, *Black Pearls: Blues Queens of the 1920s* (1988); Michael W. Harris, *The Rise of Gospel Blues: The Music of Thomas Andrew Dorsey in the Urban Church* (1992); and Laurie Wright, *"Fats" in Fact* (1992).

BARRY KERNFELD

MARTIN, William Alexander Parsons (10 Apr. 1827–17 Dec. 1916), missionary educator to China, was born in Livonia, Indiana, the son of William Martin, a Presbyterian minister and educator, and Susan Depew. His father personally educated Martin to become a missionary. In 1842 he matriculated at Indiana University, where Chancellor Andrew Wylie imbued him with the concept of Manifest Destiny (the United States' mission to take science, liberal principles of government, and Christianity to the people of Asia). After receiving his A.B. in 1846, Martin studied for the ministry at New Albany Theological Seminary in New Albany, Indiana. In 1849 he married Jane Van-Sant of Abington, Pennsylvania. Ten days later the couple sailed for China, where their only child was born.

In China, the Overseas Mission Board of the Presbyterian Church posted Martin as itinerant preacher to its mission in Ningbo. While studying the Ningbo dialect, Martin developed a phonetic script that he used to translate religious texts and to write school

textbooks. In 1853 Martin used semiliterate Chinese to write *Evidences of Christianity*, employing traditional Chinese concepts to present the Christian gospel. This popular Christian apologia was republished in a number of editions, including a Japanese edition.

Martin won few converts at Ningbo besides the mission's employees. He partially attributed his failure to China's reactionary Manchu rulers and official state ideology, which legitimized the position of the ruling elite and condemned Christianity as a heterodox religion. This led Martin to support the rebellion of quasi-Christian Taipings and to advocate the West's use of arms to open China to Christianity and "progress." In response to Britain's defeat of China in the Arrow War of 1858, the United States sent William Reed to China to negotiate a new bilateral treaty with the Qing government. Martin served as Reed's translator, a position that enabled him and Reed's secretary, Samuel Wells Williams, to insert a clause in the treaty guaranteeing Christians throughout China the freedom of worship.

After a two-year leave in the United States, Martin returned to China in 1862 with a new strategy: work from the top down, attack only those aspects of Chinese culture directly in conflict with Christian doctrine, and use science and Western law to give prestige to Western culture while clearing away Chinese "superstitions." Underlying Martin's new strategy was the assumption that Western science and liberal thought were universal truths, inseparable from Christianity, and that the Chinese could therefore not accept one without the other.

Martin translated Henry Wheaton's *Elements of International Law* into Chinese, and in 1863 he presented this translation to the Zongli Yamen, China's newly established ministry of foreign affairs. Consequently, China would for the first time use international law to settle a dispute with a foreign power when it forced Prussia to pay an indemnity for violating China's territorial waters. Thereafter, officials of the Zongli Yamen frequently consulted Martin on international affairs.

In 1863 Martin started a mission in Beijing with a chapel and a school. But the mission made little progress, and Martin soon closed the school for lack of students. The next year he agreed to teach English for two hours a day at the Tongwen Guan, an interpreters' school attached to the Zongli Yamen. Shortly thereafter the Zongli Yamen expanded the Tongwen Guan into a college and appointed Martin first as professor of political economy and international law and then as president of the college. From 1869 (when he resigned his mission position to assume the college presidency) until 1895 (when he resigned the presidency for reasons of health), Martin gradually developed the Tongwen Guan into a respected college.

Throughout the Tongwen Guan's existence, court officials restricted its ability to recruit first-rate students and made sure the school remained at the margins of China's regular education system. Nonetheless, under Martin's guidance, the school fulfilled its official objective of training interpreters and lower-level officials to staff China's first overseas legations and some domestic offices. The school also translated Western books on international law and science for Chinese government officials. In addition, from 1872 to 1875 Martin personally published *Peking Magazine*, a secular journal devoted to bringing the best in modern science and liberal thought to China's ruling elite.

As part of his cultural strategy for mission work, Martin also sought to raise the West's understanding of the principles of Chinese history and life. He wanted to prepare the West for the day when China abandoned the old imperial system and joined the community of nations. Thus, from 1862 on Martin frequently delivered lectures on China to Western audiences and published his lectures in various journals. He republished these lectures in *The Lore of Cathay* and other books that were well received in the United States and Europe.

Japan's defeat of China in the war of 1894–1895 forced the Qing court to recognize the importance of Western learning. Two years later this led the Guangxu emperor to open the Imperial University, modeled after the Tongwen Guan, with Martin as dean of the foreign faculty. In 1900 the dowager empress Cixi encouraged bands of anti-Christian, antiforeign Boxers United in Righteousness to rid Beijing of all foreigners. After sacking the university, they laid siege to the foreign legation quarter, where Martin had taken refuge. After a joint expeditionary force of Western troops lifted the siege, an angry Martin castigated Cixi and the Chinese government and called on the Western powers to partition China into spheres of influence. Two years later the chancellor of the Imperial University dismissed Martin, along with the rest of the foreign faculty, as part of preparations to reopen the university.

Although Martin had converted very few Chinese to Christianity throughout his stay in China, when plans for a new university headed by Martin failed to materialize, the Presbyterian mission board appointed Martin "honorary missionary" with no set duties. Thereafter, he semiretired in Beijing where he continued to discuss mission policy and write about conditions in China until his death.

• Martin's letters and reports to the Presbyterian Board of Foreign Missions in New York (1849–1869, 1905–1916) are in the Presbyterian Historical Society Archives and Library in Philadelphia. Other letters by Martin are at the American Bible Association in New York City; the Henry Francis du Pont Collection of Winterthur Manuscripts at the Eleutherian Mills Historical Library in Greenville, Del.; the Fryer Collection at the Bancroft Library, University of California, Berkeley; and the W. D. Whitney Collection and the Samuel Wells Williams Family Collection at the Sterling Memorial Library, Yale University.

The most comprehensive collection of Martin's articles is *The Lore of Cathay; or, the Intellect of China* (1901). In *A Cycle of Cathay* (1896), *Siege in Peking* (1900), and *The Awakening of China* (1907) Martin reminisces on his experiences and comments on conditions in China. Ralph R. Covell, *W. A. P. Martin: Pioneer of Progress in China* (1978) contains the most complete listing of Martin's works, and Norma Far-

quhar provides an annotated bibliography of his published works in "A Bibliography of the Writings of W. A. P. Martin," *Papers on China* 10 (1956): 128–41.

Covell's book is the most complete modern assessment of Martin. Two other useful biographies are Peter Duus, "Science and Salvation in China: The Life and Work of W. A. P. Martin," *Papers on China* 10 (1956): 97–127, and Jonathan Spence, *To Change China: Western Advisers in China, 1620–1960* (1969). For an assessment of the Tongwen Guan see Knight Biggerstaff, *The Earliest Modern Government Schools in China* (1961). Obituaries are in the *New York Times*, 24 Dec. 1916, and the *Chinese Recorder* 48 (Feb. 1917).

ERNST SCHWINTZER

MARTINEAU, Harriet (12 June 1802–27 June 1876), author, was born in Norwich, England, the daughter of Thomas Martineau, a textile manufacturer, and Elizabeth Rankin. The family was Unitarian, republican, and laissez-fairist, and these traditions shaped both Harriet's early thinking and her implicit belief in natural law and the rights of the individual. Although her education was inferior to that given her brothers, it was more rigorous than was customary for girls of the period. In adolescence she developed a hearing disorder that left her permanently hard of hearing, but, despite this disability and her inferior status as a woman in the nineteenth century, she made her living as a writer and earned an international reputation doing so.

Martineau's authorship began modestly enough with contributions to the *Monthly Repository*, a vehicle for Unitarian opinion. Between 1829 and 1832 she became the journal's leading writer. Her *Monthly Repository* articles were reprinted in 1836 as *Miscellanies*, but by then provincial anonymity was behind her. It was with the publication of *Illustrations of Political Economy* (1832–1833) that she received wide recognition. In *Illustrations* (published in twenty-five separately bound installments) she used fiction to popularize the principles and virtues of free trade and to denounce protectionism. Through these little tales, readers on both sides of the Atlantic became familiar with the economic theories of Adam Smith, David Ricardo, and James Mill.

After completing *Illustrations*, she spent two years touring the United States, a country that symbolized for her democracy and the free enterprise system. Journeying by riverboat, canal barge, train, horseback, and stage, she traversed some 10,000 miles. She was entertained in the homes of the wealthy and prominent but sought to avoid only "partial intercourse with the nation," making a special point of meeting ordinary folk, in fishing boats and country stores, on the porches of bordinghouses, on college campuses, and behind the plow. She had set out on her odyssey to the United States of America anticipating that in this new republic the people would be living up to the ideals manifested in their Declaration of Independence. But while she was pleased to find no "hereditary humbug," she was disappointed to note that the country was still feudal when it came to the relationship between white and black Americans.

Following her return to England, she published *Society in America* (3 vols., 1837) and *Retrospect of Western Travel* (3 vols., 1838). In the latter she painted a coherent and vivid portrait of the United States and its peoples. The former publication provided commentary on the political, religious, social, and economic structures of Jacksonian America. *Society in America* and *How to Observe Morals and Manners* (1838)—the latter set out a primitive sociological methodology—are considered to be forerunners of modern sociology.

It was her intent in *Society in America* "to compare the existing state of society in America with the principles on which it was professedly founded." While in *Democracy in America* (1835) her contemporary Alexis de Tocqueville examined theories of democracy and their application in America, Martineau used the principles of democracy as criteria of judgment. Impressed as she was with the independent spirit of Americans and the belief that the principles of democracy would ultimately triumph, she was nevertheless disappointed to find that the tyranny of the majority could be as pernicious as the tyranny of the aristocracy ever was, that the free enterprise system encouraged "a sordid love of gain," that one individual's freedom too often encroached upon the liberties of others, and that instead of demonstrating "moral independence," politicians were on the whole subservient to public opinion. Furthermore, she concluded that as long as slaves and women were excluded from citizenship, the government could not truly reflect the will of the majority. Perceiving a strong parallel between the enslavement of black Americans and the subjugation of women, Martineau emphatically addressed both issues in *Society in America*.

Already an expressed opponent of slavery, Martineau while in America joined the New England Anti-Slavery Society and the American Anti-Slavery Society. She would later argue forcefully against the institution of slavery in *Society* as well as in articles published in America in the *National Anti-Slavery Standard* and in England in the *Edinburgh Review*, the *Westminster Review*, and the *Daily News*. In 1838 she was made an honorary member of the Massachusetts Anti-Slavery Society, and, although too ill to attend at the time, she was elected as a delegate to the International Anti-Slavery Convention held in London in 1840. Despite support for the South in England, she remained a strong voice for the Union and championed the cause of emancipation throughout the Civil War. Writing to her in 1855, the abolitionist leader William Lloyd Garrison commented, "At the risk of social outlawry, popular contempt and indignation, and pecuniary loss . . . [you] have ever . . . been the unflattering championess of justice, humanity and freedom on a world-wide scale."

Throughout her long literary career, Martineau supported equity for women in education, marriage, the workplace, and the ballot box. Though some of these ideas had first been expressed in early *Monthly Repository* articles, they crystallized when she came to America. In *Society* she wrote of women's education

and marital status, of the role of religion in their lives, and of working women (especially the operatives in Waltham and Lowell), and, long before there was a recognizable women's rights movement, she included a chapter in *Society* titled "The Political Non-existence of Women." The powers of government were not "just," she concluded, if they were "not derived from the consent of the governed" (*Society*, vol. 1, p. 199).

Despite two prolonged periods of ill health (1839 to 1844 and 1852 to her death in 1876), Martineau's many publications and extensive private correspondence remain a tribute to the Victorian work ethic, dedication, and industry. For in addition to works cited here and in the bibliography, and to numerous articles published in major contemporary journals, Martineau was also chief editorial writer for the *London Daily News*. She contributed more than 1,600 editorials, letters, and obituaries from 1852 to 1866. Besides the topics already mentioned, she articulated a wide range of domestic and foreign subjects, including political, legal, and prison reform; public health; working-class housing; national education; factory legislation; the Anti-Corn Law League; the Indian Mutiny of 1857; the Crimean War; and Imperial policy in Ireland, India, and the colonies. It was during this period too that she published *Letters on the Laws of Man's Nature and Development*, with Henry Atkinson (1851). In the *Letters* she publicly rejected traditional theology and avowed a pseudo-scientific agnosticism for which she was criticized by the public and ostracized by members of her family.

Unafraid of embracing and promoting potentially controversial or unpopular opinions, Martineau made it "my business . . . to speak out with absolute freedom what I have thought and learned" (*Autobiography*, vol. 1, p. 133). While she always had her share of detractors, even Martineau's worst critics could not help but admire her courage and integrity. When writing of her in the latter part of the nineteenth century, John Morley, a prominent Liberal member of Parliament, said she "had a sure eye for social realities; a moral courage that never flinched; a strong judgment within its limits; a vigorous self-reliance both in opinion and act; . . . a splendid sincerity; a magnificent love of truth" (*Critical Miscellanies*, vol. 3 [1909], pp. 176–77).

After a lifetime of earning her living by the pen, Martineau was forced by ill health to give up writing in 1866. She never married, but to the end she enjoyed the companionship of devoted relatives and friends. She died in her home in Ambleside in the Lake District of England. Sometimes didactic and more often than not controversial, her worth to her contemporaries was that she had provided them with timely commentary on the events and issues of their era. It is this same contemporaneity that makes her work significant for the modern historian.

• The chief collections of Martineau's correspondence are at the Manchester College Library and the Bodleian Library, Oxford; the University College Library, Dr. Williams's Library, and the British Museum, London; Trinity College Library and Cambridge University Library, Cambridge; and the extensive and well-cataloged collection in the University of Birmingham Library. In the United States, Martineau correspondence can primarily be found in the Boston Public Library; the Beineke Library, Yale; the University of California Library, Berkeley; and the Houghton Library, Harvard. No study of Martineau is complete without her *Autobiography*, written in 1855 but published posthumously in 1877. In addition to the works already cited in the text, her other important publications include *The History of England during the Thirty Years' Peace, 1816–1846* (2 vols., 1849–1850), a social and political history of her own times; a highly praised translation of Auguste Comte's *Positive Philosophy* (3 vols., 1853); the hit novel *Deerbrook* (3 vols., 1839); and *Eastern Life Past and Present* (3 vols., 1848), a vivid account of her travels in Egypt and the Middle East. Joseph B. Rivlin published a comprehensive listing of Martineau's works, "Harriet Martineau: A Bibliography of Her Separately Printed Works," in *Bulletin of the New York Public Library* 50 (1946) and 51 (1947). A catalog of her *Monthly Repository* articles can be found in Francis E. Mineka, *The Dissidence of Dissent: The Monthly Repository, 1806–1838* (1944). R. K. Webb's catalog of her *Daily News* articles is available in the Library of Congress, the Boston Public Library, and the British Newspaper Library. An anthology of Martineau's feminist writings is *Harriet Martineau on Women* (1985), ed. Gayle Graham Yates. Scholarly works on Martineau include R. K. Webb, *Harriet Martineau: Radical Victorian* (1960); Valerie Kossew Pichanick, *Harriet Martineau: The Woman and Her Work, 1802–1876* (1980); Valerie Sanders, *Reason over Passion* (1986), on Martineau's works of fiction; Deidre David, *Intellectual Women and Victorian Patriarchy: Harriet Martineau, Elizabeth Browning and George Eliot* (1987); and Susan Hoecker-Drysdale, *Harriet Martineau, First Woman Sociologist* (1994).

VALERIE KOSSEW DUNN

MARTÍNEZ, Esteban José (9 Dec. 1742–28 Oct. 1798), Spanish naval officer and explorer of the northwest coast of North America, was born in Seville, Spain, of unknown parentage. At thirteen years of age, Martínez entered a three-year program at Seville's marine Semenario de San Telmo. During the 1760s he served in several merchant ships on voyages from Spain to the Americas. In 1770 he married Gertrudis González. Transferred to duty on Mexico's Pacific Coast, in 1773 he was a second pilot in the naval department of San Blas that supplied Baja California and Sonora and was home base to the naval vessels that had begun to explore the California coast.

When the Spanish government received reports of Russian voyages from Kamchatka into American waters, Viceroy Antonio María Bucareli of New Spain appointed Juan Pérez in 1773 to command the frigate *Santiago* on a reconnaissance expedition, which departed San Blas in 1774, to high latitude with Martínez as his second officer. The voyage failed to reach further north than the stormy waters north of the Queen Charlotte Islands and anchored off Nootka Sound on Vancouver Island without landing a party to claim sovereignty, but nevertheless, unlike most officers, Martínez became a determined advocate of a major Spanish role in the North Pacific. He expressed enthusiasm for the Haida and Nootka peoples, the great nat-

ural harbors, and the potential forest and mineral resources, and he believed from published sources that there was a navigable Northwest Passage through the continent linking the Pacific and Atlantic oceans.

While Spain dispatched expeditions in 1775 and 1779 that penetrated Alaska waters, Martínez returned to routine supply missions that took him to San Diego, Monterey, and San Francisco. In 1786 he encountered at Monterey the French expedition led by the Comte de la Pérouse and learned about possible new Russian moves southward to Nootka Sound. Fearing encroachments into California waters, in 1788 the Crown dispatched Martínez with the frigate *Princesa* and Gonzalo López de Haro with the packet *San Carlos* to sail as far north as sixty-one degrees latitude. Beginning at Prince William Sound and reaching as far west as Unalaska Island, the Spaniards met Russian fur traders and natives, landed surreptitiously to claim sovereignty, and kept detailed reports. The expedition was successful, and Martínez warned his government about a possible Russian naval plan to establish in 1789 a post at Nootka Sound. However, during the voyage Martínez exhibited a hot temper, instability, and quarrelsome characteristics that provoked some officers to complain about his consumption of alcohol and question his fitness for senior command.

Notwithstanding his doubts about Martínez, Viceroy Manuel Antonio Flórez of New Spain had no other experienced commander available. Based on information gathered in 1788, the viceroy ordered a new expedition for 1789 that would anticipate the suspected Russian advance. Reports of the arrival in Chilean waters of two American ships commanded by John Kendrick and Robert Gray bound for the Northwest Coast appeared to confirm the danger to Spanish sovereignty. Martínez's instructions were to establish a temporary post at Nootka Sound in modern British Columbia and to be firm but to avoid violence with foreigners. Anchoring on 5 May 1789, the Spaniards had no real idea about the rapid development of the transpacific fur trade in sea otter pelts that had opened after Captain James Cook's 1778 visit to the coast. Without any Russian presence, Nootka Sound emerged as a veritable entrepôt for British, American, and other foreign traders. Finding Kendrick's expedition at Nootka, Martínez befriended the Americans, who gave information about the native cultures and British trading activities. Occupying Yuquot (Friendly Cove), which was the summer village site of Chief Maquinna's people, the Spaniards interrupted normal activities and dislocated the native role as middlemen in supplying furs to British and American traders.

After seizing and later releasing the *Ifigenia Nubiana*, a British vessel masquerading under the Portuguese flag from Macao, Martínez constructed a small fort, planted gardens, and sought to develop friendly relations with the natives. Real trouble commenced on 2 July with the arrival of the *Argonaut* commanded by James Colnett from Macao, who insisted that he had orders from England to erect a permanent settlement. The presence aboard *Argonaut* of Chinese craftsmen, artillery pieces, a small ship in frame, and other supplies lent credence to Colnett's claims. Polite diplomacy soon degenerated into shouting matches between two irascible commanders who lacked adequate translators. When during one argument Colnett grasped his sword and denigrated Spain, Martínez ordered him arrested and proceeded to capture his ship and crew. A few days later, the Spaniards detained the British trading vessel *Princess Royal*. In the midst of this discord, a harried Martínez ordered a musket fired at a native chief in his canoe who sided with the British prisoners and refused to refrain from yelling insults. By misfortune, the shot killed the chief, presenting British propagandists with ideal material to condemn Spain and its agent Martínez. With British seamen imprisoned at San Blas, Mexico, both nations became entangled in the Nootka Sound Controversy. In London, pamphleteers blackened Martínez's reputation and drummed up war fever.

Having lost its French military ally to revolution, the Spanish government was eager to avoid war over an isolated North Pacific post. Martínez remained at Nootka until the end of October 1789, hoping for supplies and reinforcements that would make the establishment permanent. When no word came, he abandoned the port and returned to San Blas. Embarrassed Mexican officials had to organize another expedition in 1790 to reoccupy Nootka Sound. This time, more senior naval officers were available, and Martínez served as second in command. He returned to Spain in 1791, but in 1795 he was back in Pacific waters to serve the California supply vessels. On one of these expeditions Martínez died at Loreto in Baja California.

Although something of an eccentric dreamer, Martínez's real problem was that his designs for Pacific empire did not fit the aspirations of his impecunious nation. While in other circumstances Martínez might have been proclaimed a visionary, many Spaniards viewed him as wildly impractical or, even worse, as a violent hothead. In fact, Martínez read James Cook's journal, maintained a regimen of hygiene and good diet aboard his vessels, and thought deeply about how Spain could benefit from possession of the Northwest Coast. He proposed permanent occupation of the Northwest Coast based upon four presidios similar to Monterey and sixteen missions, a fleet of sloops built of coastal timber, the export of lumber and masts to Asia, a monopoly company to pursue the fur trade with China, settlement of the Hawaiian Islands, development of grain and livestock industries in California, and stimulation of the Mexican economy to produce textiles, copper, and clothing for the native trade. He envisioned a lumber and fur trade that would produce surpluses to finance the import of Asian luxury products and mercury needed in the Mexican mining industry to refine silver ores. Such schemes as these, based on Martínez's firsthand observations of Russian and British trading activities, went well beyond the reality of late eighteenth-century Spanish pretensions. Once it was obvious that there was no navigable Northwest Passage, Martínez's ambitious schemes could be discarded. In 1795, after signing conventions with Great Britain, Spain withdrew permanently from the Northwest Coast. In evaluating Martínez, many Spanish observers and later historians dismissed the explorer or accepted an indelibly negative view based on contemporary propaganda. If like so many other early Pacific explorers he exhibited personality quirks and eccentricities, Martínez was also a committed proponent of Spanish Northwest Coast development and transpacific empire.

• Martínez's unpublished journals and correspondence are in the Archivo General de la Nación (Mexico City), the Archivo General de las Indias (Seville, Spain), and the Archivo Histórico Nacional (Madrid). The journal of his 1789 voyage has been published in Spain by the Consejo Superior de Investigaciones Científicas, Instituto Histórico de Marina, *Colección de Diarios y relaciones para la historia de los viajes y descubrimientos*, vol. 6, *Esteban José Martínez* (1964). Modern assessments may be found in Herbert K. Beals, *Juan Pérez on the Northwest Coast* (1989), Warren L. Cook, *Flood Tide of Empire: Spain and the Pacific Northwest, 1543–1819* (1973), and Michael Thurman, *The Naval Department of San Blas: New Spain's Bastion for Alta California and Nootka, 1767–1798* (1967). For an overview, see O. H. K. Spate, "Paradise Found and Lost," in *The Pacific since Magellan*, vol. 3 (1988).

CHRISTON I. ARCHER

MARTINY, Philip (19 May 1858–26 June 1927), sculptor, was born in Strasbourg, Alsace, France, the son of Philip Martiny and Katherine Blacke. His first professional experience came as apprentice to the elder Martiny, an ornamental carver. Young Martiny next became an assistant to Eugene Dock, a decorative carver who had studied at the École des Beaux-Arts in Paris. Martiny therefore began his career by being trained in decorative carving as a craftsman in a workshop rather than as a student in an art school where one was taught to make figurative sculpture from live models and antique casts. His art retained an ornamental quality throughout his career, and it was for such work that he became famous.

About 1878 Martiny immigrated to the United States, and in New York City he found employment as a carver. In 1882, while he was executing some carvings for the Cornelius Vanderbilt II mansion on Fifth Avenue, his abilities were noted by Augustus Saint-Gaudens, who was then on the threshold of becoming the most celebrated American sculptor of the late nineteenth century. Seeing in Martiny an artistic talent not exhibited by his other carvers at the Vanderbilt mansion, Saint-Gaudens asked him to become his assistant. The reserved, controlled style of Saint-Gaudens could not subdue Martiny's natural penchant for exuberant decorative form, but through Saint-Gaudens Martiny met the members of the prestigious architectural firm of McKim, Mead & White—a most fortuitous contact for the young sculptor. In 1889, when Saint-Gaudens was asked to model the George Washington Inaugural Centennial Medal, he declined, saying he had no time. However, he then offered to design it for free if Martiny received the commission, which he did.

Martiny established his own studio in New York in the late 1880s but first gained national prominence in Chicago in 1893 at the World's Columbian Exposition. From McKim, Mead & White he received a commission to produce eighty-three huge angels, forty large eagles, and sixteen heroic figural groups to adorn the firm's enormous Agricultural Building at the fair. These pieces were made of staff (plaster and straw) and have long since disappeared, but photographs of them reveal Martiny's movement away from the restrained style of Saint-Gaudens toward a decorative baroque grandeur.

Typical of Martiny's work are the sculptures he made for the new Library of Congress in Washington, D.C. (1898), where his lively, decorative figures adorn the newel posts and balustrades of the grand stairway. Martiny's special flair was given further display in one of the centerpieces of the Pan-American Exposition held in Buffalo, New York, in 1901—the Fountain of Abundance, the main motif of which was a festooned maiden attended by lively *putti*. At the Louisiana Purchase Exposition (Saint Louis, 1904), the sculptor's group of Apollo and the Muses became the decorative focal point atop the Festival Hall while two of his quadriga adorned the New York State Building. Martiny was twice married, first to a German woman, Hermine Horning, with whom he had four children and, second, to a French woman, Yvonne Flouret, whom he married in 1902 and with whom he had eight children.

Among the memorials that deserve mention are the Soldiers' and Sailors' Monument (1899) in Jersey City, New Jersey; the statue of Vice President Garrett Hobart (1902) in Paterson, New Jersey; and, following the First World War, Martiny's doughboy statues for Abingdon Square in Greenwich Village and for Chelsea Park in New York City. For the Hall of Records in New York, Martiny produced, from 1903 to 1908, a great number of allegorical figures in granite, and for the Old District of Columbia Public Library he created a sculptural group titled *The Light of Knowledge*, in form similar to the group he had made in 1899 for the Atlanta Public Library. His style here was typically exuberant with richly modeled surfaces and profuse decorative detail. His marble figure of Confucius (1899) was one of the many to adorn the Appellate Court Building in New York City. To celebrate the triumphant return of American soldiers and sailors after World War I, Martiny's staff group *Our Allies* was placed atop the famous skyscraper the Flatiron Building in New York in 1919.

Martiny was elected to the Society of American Artists in 1891, became an associate of the National Academy of Design in 1902, and belonged to the Architectural League of New York, the National Sculpture Society, and the National Arts Club. The robust baroque grandeur and decorative quality of his style were ideally suited for many of the most important Beaux-Arts architectural projects of his day. But in 1921 a paralyzing stroke put an end to his career, although he lived for another six years before a second stroke claimed his life in New York City.

• The Archives of American Art in Washington, D.C., has an annotated list of Martiny's works, compiled by his grandson Raymond J. Linder. To the same repository Linder gave an assortment of about 150 items, including newspaper clippings, letters, photographs, and a sketchbook. Several Martiny letters are among the Adolph Weinman Papers, also at the Archives of American Art. Martiny's life and career were first chronicled in Lorado Taft, *History of American Sculpture* (1903), pp. 452–56, and reviews of his work are in Wayne Craven, *Sculpture in America* (1968; rev. ed., 1984), pp. 473–75. He receives brief mention in Homer Saint-Gaudens, ed., *Reminiscences of Augustus Saint-Gaudens* (1913); Charles H. Caffin, *American Masters of Sculpture* (1903); and Adeline Adams, *The Spirit of American Sculpture* (1929). An obituary is in the *New York Times*, 27 June 1927.

WAYNE CRAVEN

MARTLAND, Harrison Stanford (10 Sept. 1883–1 May 1954), pathologist, was born in Newark, New Jersey, the son of William Henry Martland, a physician, and Ida Carlyle Bucklish. He received a B.S. from Western Maryland College in 1901 and an M.D. from Columbia University in 1905. Martland interned for eighteen months at New York City Hospital, also known as Metropolitan Hospital. In 1907–1908 he was assistant pathologist at the Russell Sage Institute of Pathology, a research division of the Metropolitan Hospital laboratory.

In 1909 Martland was appointed pathologist for the city of Newark and Newark City Hospital, and he served in these positions until 1953. At various times, he was the pathologist for several medical institutions in the Newark metropolitan area. He also maintained a private practice as a consultant in internal medicine, especially for cases of syphilis.

During World War I Martland was director of laboratories of the Bellevue Medical College unit, in charge of the military hospital in Vichy, France, and consulting pathologist at the Vanderbilt Hospital in Paris. He subsequently obtained the rank of colonel in the U.S. Army Medical Corps Reserves.

Martland did his most important scientific work in the mid-1920s. In 1925 he investigated the mysterious deaths of several workers in an Orange, New Jersey, watch factory, all of whom had suffered from "jaw rot," a condition that had caused them to lose their teeth and, sometimes, their jaws. The disease was common among dial painters who applied luminous paint containing radium to clock and watch dials to make them glow in the dark. About eight hundred women had worked in the plant from the time it opened in 1913.

Some dentists, chemists, and physicians suspected that the women had developed jaw rot as a result of their contact with the radioactive paint, but the diagnosis was disputed by several medical authorities who were employed by the U.S. Radium Corporation, which manufactured the watches, to investigate the matter. Martland learned that before applying the paint the workers would bring the brush they were using to a fine point by applying it to their lips. On the basis of clinical reports and autopsy findings, he determined that the women had died from aplastic regenerative anemia caused by the ingestion of minute amounts of a radioactive compound (radium-mesothorium). Furthermore, he found evidence of radioactive substances in radium painters with advanced illnesses and in workers who appeared to be in good health. Martland also autopsied a company chemist who had died from radiation poisoning, but he delayed in releasing his report in return for the company's help in educating him about radiation. In December 1925 he published the first scientific paper on the medical aspects of industrial radiation poisoning in the *Journal of the American Medical Association*: "Some Unrecognized Dangers in the Use and Handling of Radioactive Substances."

In his long career as a pathologist Martland made several other important discoveries. He demonstrated that most deaths from cardiovascular syphilis resulted from lesions of the aorta and aortic valves rather than from syphilitic infection of the heart muscle (1925–1930). And he provided evidence that punch-drunkenness in prizefighters was a serious medical condition, a type of concussion caused by rupture of tiny blood vessels in the brain (1928).

In 1925 Martland was appointed county physician of Essex County, New Jersey, an office that had been established in 1917 to replace the outdated coroner system for inquiring into suspicious deaths. The coroner system allowed a jury of laypeople to determine the cause of death in sudden, unusual, or unexplained fatalities. At the time, only New York and a few other cities used medical examiners to conduct medicolegal investigations. It was as a coroner that Martland had investigated the deaths of the radium painters.

Martland believed that the county physician plan, while an improvement over the coroner system, was flawed because it still allowed the use of a jury of laypeople to determine the cause of death in certain cases. In order to raise the standards of the county's medicolegal investigations to the level of the nation's most progressive cities, Martland requested the New Jersey state legislature in 1927 to establish the office of chief medical examiner of the county of Essex, which he headed until 1953. In 1933 Martland was appointed assistant professor of forensic medicine at New York University College of Medicine (Bellevue Medical College) and remained on the faculty, advancing to full professor in 1935, until his death. In these positions he pioneered the field of forensic medicine and helped establish the professional medical examiner system, which empowers the medical examiner—a physician (preferably a forensic pathologist)—to perform an autopsy when the cause of death is suspicious or unexplained, without holding an inquest.

Martland helped make Newark City Hospital a respected scientific and teaching hospital. His museum of pathology and his laboratory drew national attention and attracted medical students seeking internships and physicians wanting postgraduate instruction (which was offered under the sponsorship of New York University College of Medicine in the years 1941–1945). In 1945 the Essex College of Medicine was founded, and Martland agreed to accept the chair of pathology and bacteriology; the school closed in 1946.

In the years following his original investigation of the radioactive poisoning of radium painters, Martland made several other important discoveries in the field of atomic medicine that established his reputation as one of the world's leading authorities on the subject. Most important, he discovered that persons exposed to radium were at grave risk of developing bone sarcomas. During World War II procedures he had developed for safeguarding workers against radiation poisoning were used by the Manhattan Project at Oak Ridge, Tennessee, where work was proceeding on the controlled fission of the uranium atom. Despite the enormous amount of radiation produced by the work, only two deaths were attributed to radioactive contamination.

Martland's last important scientific work was on deaths from beryllium poisoning among workers engaged in the manufacture of fluorescent lamps. On this project he worked with Henry Brodkin, a consultant to the New Jersey Department of Labor, in 1948. As a result of this work, the states adopted rules and regulations governing the use of the mineral in industrial plants.

Martland married Myra Cee Ferdon in 1910, and they had two children. He belonged to a reading group in New York City devoted to the study of detective novels and wrote an essay on the forensic pathologist as medical detective, which was published as volume 3 of the New York Academy of Medicine's *Lectures to the Laity* (1938). He suffered his first stroke in 1951 and another in the fall of 1953, shortly after he retired and moved to his daughter's home in New York City, where he died a few months later.

• Martland's life is recounted by his student and colleague Samuel Berg in *Harrison Stanford Martland, M.D.: The Story of a Physician, a Hospital, an Era* (1978). Contrasting accounts of Martland's role in uncovering the radiation poisoning of the radium dial painters are offered in William D. Sharpe, "The New Jersey Radium Dial Painters: A Classic Case in Occupational Carcinogenesis," *Bulletin of the History of Medicine* 52 (1979): 560–70, and Claudia Clark, "Physicians, Reformers, and Occupational Disease: The Discovery of Radium Poisoning," *Women and Health* 12, no. 2 (1987): 147–67. A bibliography of Martland's writings is in Francis R. Ginley, "Harrison Stanford Martland, 1883–1954: Personal Recollections," *Academy of Medicine of New Jersey Bulletin* 15 (Dec. 1969): 204–13. An obituary is in the *New York Times*, 2 May 1954.

STUART GALISHOFF

MARTY, Martin (12 Jan. 1834–19 Sept. 1896), Benedictine monk and missionary, was the son of Jacob Alois Marty, a shoemaker and church sexton, and Elizabeth

Reichlin. He was born in Schwyz, Switzerland, and baptized Aloysius. His earliest education was at Jesuit schools in Schwyz and later at Fribourg. When the Jesuits were expelled from Switzerland in 1848, Marty entered a monastic community, the Benedictine College of Einsiedeln, taking the religious name "Martin." He was professed a monk in 1855 and ordained to the priesthood in 1856.

Especially adept at languages and music, Marty taught a variety of subjects at the abbey school and developed a reputation as a stirring preacher for the pilgrims who came to Einsiedeln to visit the famous image of the Virgin Mary. The task of translating the *Annals of the Propagation of the Faith* from French into German ignited his interest in missionary work. In 1860 he was appointed superior of the floundering monastic community of St. Meinrad in southern Indiana, a daughter-house of Einsiedeln. He arrived in late September 1860 and reopened the school and founded the town of St. Meinrad. His efforts made the community an important center of theological instruction in the region. In 1870 St. Meinrad was raised to the status of an independent abbey, and Marty was installed as its first abbot in 1871.

President Ulysses S. Grant adopted a "peace policy" that transferred administration of Indian affairs from the Interior Department to private religious denominations. In 1876 the Bureau of Catholic Indian Missions sent Abbot Marty to the Sioux reservation of Standing Rock in the Dakota Territory to explore the possibility of sending monks from St. Meinrad to work with the Indians. Yearning for more missionary work and perhaps a bit restive at the fairly prosperous St. Meinrad, Marty agreed to bring Benedictines to the Great Plains. He devoted the rest of his life to missionary endeavors among the Indians, becoming proficient in the Siouan language and translating prayers and hymns. Indeed, he enjoyed such respect among the Sioux that he was one of the few whites permitted to approach Chief Sitting Bull, the powerful medicine man, after the battle of the Little Big Horn. In 1877 Marty was made vicar general for the Indian missions in Nebraska and the Dakota Territory, and in 1879 he was chosen vicar apostolic of the newly established vicariate of the vast Dakota Territory. On 1 February 1880 he was consecrated a bishop.

Marty's labors corresponded with a steady influx of settlers into the Dakota Territory, and the numbers of priests and religious orders increased rapidly. When the territory was divided into states, Marty was assigned as bishop to the new diocese of Sioux Falls, South Dakota. He continued to have a high standing with the Plains Indians, and he played a successful role in defusing the tensions that developed in the wake of the massacre of Indian men, women, and children at Wounded Knee on 29 December 1890. Marty sponsored the first Catholic Indian Congress at Standing Rock during the week of 4 July 1891, a unique amalgam of the Indian annual hunting encampment and Catholic sacramental celebration and catechetical instruction. In January 1895 he was transferred from Sioux Falls to the diocese of St. Cloud, Minnesota, where he died.

• Many of Marty's papers were burned by the family, but important sources can be found in the Archives of St. Meinrad Abbey, St. Meinrad, Ind., and Conception Abbey Archives, Conception, Mo. Moreover, the abbey archives of Einsiedeln contain important information. Marty's most important literary work is *Dr. Johann Martin Henni: Erster Bischof und Erzbischof von Milwaukee* (1888). Ildephons Betschart, *Der Apostel der Siouxindianer Bischof Martinus Marty, O.S.B., 1834–1896* (1934), contains much helpful information. This is also true of Robert F. Karolevitz, *Bishop Martin Marty: "The Black Robe Lean Chief"* (1980). Joel Rippinger has produced two excellent articles that place Marty in the context of the historical and cultural forces of his time, "Martin Marty: Monk, Abbot, Missionary, and Bishop," *American Benedictine Review* 33 (Sept. 1982): 223–40, and "Martin Marty: Monk, Abbot, Missionary, and Bishop, Missionary to the Indians," *American Benedictine Review* 33 (Dec. 1982): 376–93. Important secondary material can be found in Francis Paul Prucha, *American Indian Policy in Crisis: Christian Reformers and the Indian, 1865–1900* (1976); and Albert Kleber, *History of St. Meinrad Archabbey, 1854–1954* (1954).

STEVEN M. AVELLA

MARVEL, Carl Shipp (11 Sept. 1894–4 Jan. 1988), organic and polymer chemist, was born in Waynesville, Illinois, the son of John Thomas Marvel and Mary Lucy Wasson, farmers. Although he was expected to become a farmer, Marvel was encouraged by his mother to attend college and by an uncle, a former high school teacher, to study science because future farmers would require a knowledge of science for their work. In 1911 Marvel entered Illinois Wesleyan University, where during his junior year, he discovered his forte—synthesizing organic compounds. Developing a "library of smells," he used his nose as an "infrared spectroscope" for recording the odor of every organic compound available to him.

After receiving both a B.A. and an M.S. in 1915, Marvel entered the University of Illinois at Urbana on a scholarship to study chemistry, still intending to return to farming. There his ability to exceed the standard course load, work late hours, and sleep until just before the dining hall closed in the morning earned him the nickname "Speed," which he used throughout his career, even in official correspondence.

In 1917–1918 Marvel worked in the Organic Chemical Manufactures Unit, a university division founded by faculty member Clarence Derick in 1916, which produced organic chemicals previously imported from Germany before World War I. The work of this unit resulted in the founding in 1921 of the journal *Organic Syntheses*. Nearly 20 percent of the 264 chemical preparations described in Collective Volume 1 (1932) of that journal were submitted or checked by Marvel. In 1919 Marvel, having discovered that he enjoyed synthesizing organic compounds more than farming, returned to full-time graduate studies and received his Ph.D. from Illinois in 1920. Because industrial jobs were then scarce, he remained at Illinois, becoming an instructor in 1920, associate in 1921, assistant professor in 1923, associate professor in 1927, professor of organic chemistry in 1930, and research professor of organic chemistry in 1953. With Roger Adams and Reynold C. Fuson, he made Illinois's organic chemistry program preeminent in the United States. After retiring in 1961 he became professor of chemistry at the University of Arizona. Following his second retirement, in 1978, he continued working almost daily in his laboratory with a small group of postdoctoral fellows, until the summer before his death in Tucson. Marvel married Alberta Hughes, a librarian and former high school English teacher in 1933; they had a son and a daughter.

Marvel's first sixty or seventy articles dealt largely with preparative organic chemistry such as syntheses of amino acids, organometallic compounds, and acetylenes, but he soon moved into the areas of rearrangements, free radical chemistry, magnetic susceptibility, hydrogen bonding, stereoisomerism, structure of organomercury and organophosphorus compounds, and most important, polymers. He not only was the first American university chemist to study the synthesis, structure, and mechanism of formation of synthetic polymers, but he also introduced several generations of research students, postdoctoral students, and colleagues to polymer science. He also significantly influenced the increasing industrial research on polymers and made polymer chemistry a popular field of study in numerous academic laboratories.

Marvel's close study of polymers began after he became a consultant for E. I. Du Pont de Nemours & Co., one of the world's largest chemical firms, in 1928. Over the next sixty years he gave Du Pont 19,000 consultations. Beginning in 1933 he determined the structure of copolymers of sulfur dioxide and α-olefins and developed initiators for their preparative polymerization reactions. In 1937 he began to study the polymerization mechanism and structure of vinyl polymers, which led to the preparation and polymerization of many new monomers. When the Japanese disrupted the flow of natural rubber supplies from India, Ceylon, the Malay Peninsula, and the Dutch East Indies during World War II, Marvel headed a group of as many as 100 chemists on the U.S. government's program to produce synthetic rubber. During the next decade this experience enabled him to synthesize a large series of new polymers. After traveling to Germany as part of a technical intelligence team, he developed a German process for producing synthetic rubber at low temperatures for U.S. industry.

While synthesizing heat-resistant polymers for the government's space program, Marvel developed the technique of cyclopolymerization, an addition polymerization that leads to the introduction of cyclic (ring) structures into the main chain of the polymer. He synthesized polymers with repeating rigid heterocyclic, or benzenoid, groups in the main chain as well as polybenzimidazoles (PBIs, polymers with repeating benzimidazole groups), one of the most important developments in high-temperature polymers in the 1960s. PBIs, introduced in 1980 for use in suits for fire

fighters and astronauts as substitutes for potentially carcinogenic fiberglass and asbestos, became the first synthetic fibers to be produced commercially in almost a decade.

In his spare time, Marvel was an avid bird watcher and became an accomplished ornithologist. He succeeded in identifying almost all 650 species of American birds and wrote two ornithological books, *Unusual Feeding Habits of a Cape May Warbler* (1928) and *The Blue Grosbeak in Western Ontario* (1950).

Active in the American Chemical Society, in which he held many offices, including president (1945), Marvel received numerous domestic and foreign honors and awards. During his almost three-quarter-century research career he wrote more than 500 articles and four books, and he held fifty-two patents. Despite his voluminous research Marvel considered teaching his greatest contribution: 176 students earned their doctorates under his tutelage, and 150 postdoctoral fellows worked with him. A list of his students reads like a "Who's Who" of American chemistry. According to former American Chemical Society president Charles C. Price, "Marvel exerted an extraordinary influence on American chemistry. He stood at the center of its transformation from a small and provincial enterprise to a world-renowned, technologically rich, and continuously innovative science."

• An extensive oral history interview with Marvel by Leon Gortler and Charles C. Price is in the Othmer Library at the Chemical Heritage Foundation, Philadelphia, Pa., which also houses ninety-three boxes of Marvel's manuscripts, letters, research reports, books, photographs, and awards. Autobiographical accounts of his life and work, which include historical material on American organic and polymer chemistry, are "Autobiography," in *Contemporary Topics in Polymer Science*, vol. 1: *Macromolecular Science: Retrospect and Prospect*, ed. R. D. Ulrich (1978), pp. 133–41; "My 69 Years of Chemistry," *CHEMTECH* 10 (Jan. 1980): 8–11; "The Development of Polymer Chemistry in America—The Early Days," *Journal of Chemical Education* (July 1981): 535–39; and J. E. Mulvaney, "Interview with Carl S. Marvel," *Journal of Chemical Education* (Oct. 1976): 609–13. Biographical articles are Burton C. Anderson, "'Speed' Marvel at Du Pont," *Journal of Macromolecular Science—Chemistry* A21 (1984): 1665–87; Herman Mark, "The Contribution of Carl (Speed) Marvel to Polymer Science," *Journal of Macromolecular Science—Chemistry* A21 (1984): 1567–1606; Peter J. T. Morris, "Carl Shipp ('Speed') Marvel (b. 1894)," in Morris's *Polymer Pioneers: A Popular History of the Science and Technology of Large Molecules* (1986), pp. 61–63; Ward Worthy, "Carl Marvel: An Extraordinary Influence on American Chemistry," *Chemical and Engineering News* 66 (25 Apr. 1988): 20–22; Morris, "Carl S. Marvel and Synthetic Rubber Research at Illinois," *Beckman Center News* (Fall 1988): 8–11; and George B. Kauffman, "'Speed' Marvel: American Organic Pioneer and Patriarch," *Today's Chemist* (Oct. 1989): 10–13.

GEORGE B. KAUFFMAN

MARVIN, Charles Frederick (7 Oct. 1858–5 June 1943), meteorologist, was born in Putnam, later a portion of Zanesville, Ohio, the son of George Frederick Adams Marvin, a railroad baggage master, and Sarah

Anne Speck. He attended the public schools in Columbus and earned a degree in mechanical engineering at the Ohio State University in 1883. He married Nellie Limeburner in 1894; they had three children. She died in 1905. In 1911 he married Retta Mabel Bartholow. After her death in 1932, he married Sophia A. Beuter in the same year. Neither marriage produced children.

While in college Marvin was an assistant in the mechanical (scientific) laboratory and, following graduation, became an instructor in mechanical drawing and an assistant in the physics laboratory. In 1883 he passed the U.S. Civil Service examination and was named junior professor, effective 1 September 1884, in the Office of the Chief Signal Officer of the Army, which became the civilian U.S. Weather Bureau in 1891.

Marvin's initial assignment was to formulate a revised series of tables for the calculation of humidity from the sling psychrometer, by using dry and wet bulb temperature readings taken at the various levels of Pikes Peak. In 1888 he was placed in charge of the Instrument Division, a position he held for the next twenty-five years in the Signal Service and Weather Bureau. Here Marvin developed new or improved apparata for the recording of rainfall, sunshine, air pressure, soil temperature, and evaporation as well as tables and other instructions for better measurement of the depth density and amount of snowfall, indication of river stages at a distance, and determining accurate measurements of solar radiation in standard units. He also perfected the measurement of cloud velocity, direction, and height. Through his efforts, the Weather Bureau seismograph, first at Washington, D.C., and later in Chicago and Northfield, Vermont, began, in 1914, to maintain the nation's only continuous and systematic recording of earthquake activity. By 1911 he had built kiosks for the display of these various instruments at weather stations and at public locations in twenty-nine cities. In spite of crude and inadequate facilities in Washington, D.C., in 1891 Marvin carried out experimentation on water and the maximum pressure at temperatures below the freezing point, results later confirmed by Swedish and German experiments.

In the early 1890s Marvin turned his attention to the systematic investigation of the upper air via devices launched in kites. In order to achieve higher flight angles, these kites had to be of increased strength and efficiency but with less weight than earlier models. With Marvin's assistance in determining the appropriate kite weight, improving the recording instruments that were placed in the kites, and developing reeling devices that used piano wire, which later were copied in Europe and elsewhere, the Weather Bureau opened sixteen kite observation stations. Marvin's essay "Mechanics and Equilibrium of Kites" was awarded a prize of $100 offered by the pilot Octave Chanute through the New England Aeronautical Society.

According to longtime colleague W. J. Humphreys, Marvin labored on the measurement of wind velocity from early in his career until long after his retirement.

In the 1880s he discovered that the readings of the Robinson Anemometer, a pre-1870 wind movement recorder, were affected by both wind gusts and the moment of inertia of the apparatus. The development of wind measurement seemed to fascinate Marvin the most of all his diverse studies and inventions, and he contributed to its further improvement.

While still in charge of instrumentation, in 1909 Marvin designed a system of lightning protection for the White House, which was adopted there and also for various other local buildings. From 1894 to 1902 he also taught meteorology at George Washington University.

In 1913, when the head of the Weather Bureau was dismissed for a scandal involving the misuse of funds, Marvin was recommended as the new chief. When Marvin was appointed, on 4 August, the *New York Times* commented that science had won out over politics, even though it remained to be seen whether Marvin could handle the administrative headaches. Another paper praised the fact that the appointment had gone to the real man behind the Weather Bureau's success.

Marvin's predecessor's malfeasance left a stigma that made it difficult for Marvin to gain adequate appropriations. Nevertheless, during Marvin's tenure as bureau chief, meteorological aid to the new field of aviation increased, and conditions and wages improved somewhat for bureau employees. During World War I, the Weather Bureau trained meteorologists for the Army Signal Corps, and 25 percent of bureau personnel entered military service. Federal hurricane and river-flood services were dramatically increased by Marvin. The fire-weather service (fighting forest fires), begun during World War I, also survived and flourished. Not so lucky in gaining funds were the services that provided frost warnings and forecasting of severe storms. Though existing and even expanded services were given to aviation, especially after the 1926 Air Commerce Act, studies of the upper air were not yet sophisticated enough to allow for notable advancement until late in the 1930s. Nevertheless, special forecasts and data were provided for the many airmail and pioneering flights of the era and for such famous pilots as Octave Chanute and Charles Lindbergh. Marvin's studies of past weather data frequencies later provided valuable information for Allied bombing missions in World War II.

Presidents Herbert Hoover and Franklin D. Roosevelt retained Marvin for over five years beyond the usual age for retirement, but in January 1934 Roosevelt appointed a new chief. Marvin stayed on as professor to complete his fifty years of service with the organization.

In retirement Marvin continued his meteorological interests and the promotion of calendar reform. For the latter he offered a thirteen-month year of twenty-eight days each, always starting on a Sunday and with an extra day at the end of the year. Marvin contended it was superior to our current year with months of varying length. He was a delegate to Geneva in 1931 for the International Conference on Simplification of the Calendar. He also belonged to and held positions in a number of other national and international organizations, including the presidency of the American Meteorological Society in 1926 and membership in the National Advisory Committee for Aeronautics. His many honors included his 1928 knighting by Norway's King to the Order of St. Olaf for services by the Weather Bureau to the Arctic explorations of Roald Amundsen.

Marvin's chief claim to fame rests on his widespread invention and perfection of meteorological and other scientific instruments and the implementation of these apparata to daily use. Quiet, unassuming, fair and frank, a man of great integrity, Marvin used his good judgment and stability to keep science above politics. Attending only the required social functions, he spent his free time enjoying the classics, opera, photography, hiking, and travel. He was an Episcopalian, though not a very active one, but he often read the Bible. One daughter recalled often hearing his calculator in operation during the night as her father pondered his many scientific problems. Marvin died in Washington, D.C.

• Limited materials on Marvin's life are located in the many records, publications, and correspondence of the U.S. Army Signal Service and the U.S. Weather Bureau (now the National Weather Service). Scattered individual items on his genealogy, an autobiographical note dated 1913, and several letters were made available by the family. Marvin's publications include a coauthored book, with Moses Cotsworth, *Moses, the Greatest of Calendar Reformers* (1927); a pamphlet, *Barometers and the Measurement of Atmospheric Pressure* (1941); and numerous articles in a wide variety of prestigious scientific journals and official publications, especially the *Monthly Weather Review*. For a thorough assessment of his scientific inventions and leadership of the Weather Bureau, see Donald R. Whitnah, *A History of the United States Weather Bureau* (1961). The most helpful obituary is in *Science*, 2 July 1943.

DONALD R. WHITNAH

MARVIN, Cornelia (26 Dec. 1873–13 Feb. 1957), librarian and social reformer, was born in Monticello, Iowa, the daughter of Charles Elwell Marvin and Cornelia Moody. Her father's business failure and her mother's tuberculosis led the family to relocate in Tacoma, Washington, where she completed her secondary education in 1891. In 1893, a year after her mother's death, Marvin moved to Chicago and became a "mother's helper" while she took extension courses through the University of Chicago. A motivated student, Marvin confided to her sister: "I am afraid I worship 'culture'—and 'knowledge' combined as much as some do money." Although she dreamed of becoming a literary critic or dramatist, Marvin, who "resolved to be a bachelor so I won't have a family to rear," felt obliged to assist her siblings while they attended college. By September 1894, Marvin had persuaded her father to provide the $500 she needed to attend the recently established Library School at the Armour Institute of Technology. She envisioned library school as a way to enter the work force quickly, earn money to help her siblings, and then pay for her own college education.

Marvin and eighteen other women studied under the inspirational direction of Katharine Sharp (director of the library school at the Armour Institute, later the University of Illinois Library School), who compared the library to the church in its ability to do good. During that year Marvin distributed home libraries in the Chicago stockyards district, where she worked with Mary McDowell and encountered Jane Addams and Florence Kelley. During her year at Armour, she discovered a challenging profession in need of her inquisitive mind and unlimited energy.

Foregoing the second year of library school, Marvin accepted an appointment as an assistant at Armour in 1895 and soon became an instructor in reference and bibliography. In 1897 the library school became part of the University of Illinois in Urbana, and Marvin became librarian of the Scoville Institute of Oak Park, Illinois. During the summers of 1897 and 1898, she replaced Sharp as director of the Wisconsin Library Commission Summer School of Library Training. The proliferation of small public libraries created a growing demand for such instruction. By 1899, Marvin had accepted a full-time appointment as library instructor for the Wisconsin Library Commission. Her experiences in the state often referred to then as the "laboratory of democracy" provided her with a political and social ideology that remained with her throughout her life.

Marvin moved to Salem, Oregon, in 1905 to become secretary of the newly created Oregon Library Commission. The position paid less than Marvin had earned in Wisconsin, but she welcomed the opportunity to work in a state where virtually everything—in terms of library development—needed to be accomplished. As she recalled at the dedication of the Oregon State Library Building thirty-four years later, the commission had "neither books, quarters, traditions, nor financial support beyond the state appropriation of $1,200 a year. . . . The field was clear before me." Additionally, the state had no school, county, or traveling libraries, and there were no tax-supported free public libraries outside Portland.

Marvin made many tours of the state by horse-drawn stage to survey library conditions, before implementing the most desirable programs from the Wisconsin system. She focused on the commission (and later the state library) as the center from which libraries would be sent, "ennobling character, opening vision, and widening horizons." At this time Oregon was a hotbed for the discussion of political and social issues, and often the commission represented the sole source of information. Traveling libraries became a vehicle for the dissemination of information on such issues as sex education, temperance, and capital punishment.

During her incumbency as secretary of the state library commission (1905–1913) and then as Oregon state librarian (1913–1928), Marvin gained the support of many influential politicians for her work. Under her guidance the state library became a leader in initiating and advancing general access to the best books. Although she served as a vice president and council member and on several committees of the American Library Association, Marvin increasingly distanced herself from the national association. When she compared the reality of pioneer conditions in Oregon with the projects of this increasingly bureaucratic professional association, Marvin came to believe that her energies could be better spent at the local and state level. During World War I, Marvin described the expenditures on camp libraries and book drives as a "tremendous mistake" but at the same time made use of patriotic rhetoric to keep fiction out of the state library by adopting the slogan "No New Fiction until after the War." She preferred to be active in the Pacific Northwest Library Association, believing that "a small association that is alive is more important for our people than the larger one."

Upon her resignation from the state library in 1928, Marvin married former Oregon governor Walter M. Pierce. They had maintained a discreet relationship for a number of years without marrying, which would have forced Marvin to give up her influential position as state librarian. A registered Republican, Cornelia Marvin Pierce nearly became a candidate for Congress in 1932 but instead decided to support her husband's campaign for the same position. In addition to campaigning for him (one of her frequently given speeches was entitled "Why I, a Republican, Support Roosevelt"), she also served as an adviser and speech writer. During his ten years in Congress, she served as his private secretary.

Cornelia Marvin Pierce served as a member of the Oregon State Board of Higher Education from 1931 until 1935, when she resigned because of the impracticability of attending meetings from the distance of Washington, D.C. She also served as a regent of the Oregon Normal Schools. Following Walter Pierce's defeat in 1942, the couple retired to a farm near Salem, but their last years together were marred by an unfortunate dispute with Pierce's daughters (from a previous marriage) over property that Cornelia had purchased and owned in her name only. Although the couple's relationship remained warm, the daughters sued her for a portion of the farm holdings after their father passed away in 1954. The case remained in litigation until the day after Cornelia Marvin Pierce's death, when it was decided in her favor. She died in Oregon.

Cornelia Marvin Pierce, a woman of strong convictions and great energy, devoted her life to improving the human condition. By occupation a librarian, she was in reality a public servant with a firm grasp of public affairs and a commitment to social reform, education, and politics. Her tireless dedication had inspired many others to enlist in her causes.

• Cornelia Marvin's papers that cover her work for the state library commission and as state librarian are preserved in the Oregon State Archives, Salem. Her personal papers, interfiled with the Walter M. Pierce Papers, are located in the Special Collections Division of the University of Oregon, Eugene. For Walter M. Pierce's letters to Marvin, consult the Pierce papers at the Oregon Historical Society, Salem. The most complete modern assessment is Melissa Ann Brisley, "Cornelia Marvin Pierce: Pioneer in Library Extension," *Library Quarterly* 38 (Apr. 1968): 125–53. See also Dorothy Johansen, *The Library and the Liberal Tradition* (1959), and Wayne A. Wiegand, "Oregon's Public Libraries during the First World War," *Oregon Historical Quarterly* 90 (Spring 1989): 39–63.

JOANNE E. PASSET

MARVIN, Lee (19 Feb. 1924–29 Aug. 1987), actor, was born in New York City, the son of Lamont Walter Marvin, an advertising executive, and Courtenay (maiden name unknown), a fashion magazine editor. Marvin referred to his childhood as sheltered, spent among his parents' Waspy, upper-crust set. He ran away from home at the age of four and was not found for two days. "I wasn't having any too much discipline even then," he later quipped. By age sixteen he had been "booted" out of a dozen prep schools throughout the East, often for the offense of smoking. At St. Leo's in Florida he was expelled for throwing a roommate out of a second-floor window. His father, recalling Lee's childhood, said that "he was a wild, harmless, innocent, crazy kid. Between us, though, there never was a period of misunderstanding."

In 1942 Marvin asked his father's permission to drop out of school and join the U.S. Marines. Lamont, who had been an officer during World War I, approved and reenlisted himself. Lee's only sibling, Robert, also enlisted. As a soldier in "I" company of the fourth division of the Twenty-fourth Marines, Marvin saw action in twenty-one landings in the Pacific. Serving as a point man and sniper, the 6′3″ corpsman was wounded during the invasion of Saipan in 1944. A bullet severing the sciatic nerve took him out of the war for thirteen months of hospitalization. He said years later, "up to that time I was playing it tough, but then I knew you had to be tough to survive. The most useless word in the world is 'help.'"

Marvin returned to his parents' second home in Woodstock, New York, and trained to become a stenographer. In boredom he became a plumber's apprentice. While he was repairing a clogged toilet at Woodstock's little theater, a director seeking a walk-on replacement gave him his first role. The granite-faced, steely-eyed youth then began a career in summer stock. By 1948 he had moved to Greenwich Village and with financial support from the GI bill was studying at the dramatic school of the American Theater Wing. Among his more influential instructors was the Russian émigré Andrea Jalinski, who guided him over a period of eighteen months.

Until 1951 Marvin played small off-Broadway roles, toured with road companies, and acted in more than two hundred television productions. Then he caught the eye of film director Henry Hathaway, who brought him briefly to Hollywood for a bit part in the Gary

Cooper comedy *You're in the Navy Now* (1951). Returning to New York, he gained critical notice in the role of Hallam in the Broadway production of *Billy Budd* (1951). After completing two national road company tours in other plays, he took the advice of his agent, Meyer Mishkin, and moved to California to pursue a film career. He appeared in small parts in as many as eight films a year, mostly forgettable fare such as *Gun Fury* and *Glory Brigade* (both 1953). In 1952 he married Betty Ebeling, a UCLA music graduate. The marriage, which lasted twelve years, produced four children.

Early in Marvin's 75-film career, the former Marine honed a screen image as a hard-boiled, violence-prone loner, a characterization that easily lent itself to both gangster and serviceman roles. He became memorable as the sadistic, coffee-splashing gunman who disfigures Gloria Grahame's face in *The Big Heat* (1953). He also gave sharp definition as a boozy, sociopathic motorcycle gang leader in *The Wild One* (1954). As Marvin's career ascended he often played supporting roles for such established names as Spencer Tracy, Humphrey Bogart, John Wayne, and Vivien Leigh. He once noted that "the job of an actor who's playing number two is to make number one look a hell of a lot better than he is." His intelligence and instincts were such that he frequently rose above inferior material to thrill audiences. In recalling *Violent Saturday* (1955), film critic Judith Crist wrote, "You realize, watching this performance, that Marvin stood distinct and apart from the maudlin melodrama swirling around him."

Marvin's first breakthrough was to receive star billing alongside Randolph Scott in the 1956 western *Seven Men from Now*. Two years later he received an Academy Award nomination as best supporting actor opposite Montgomery Clift in the Civil War epic *Raintree County*. In 1957 Marvin began a three-year stint as Lieutenant Frank Ballinger, a toughened, world-weary homicide detective in an elite Chicago police department, in the NBC television drama "M-Squad." The program, which Marvin produced as well as starred in, ranked third in the Nielsen ratings among suspense dramas and was the highest syndicated television show of its time. Marvin described the role as "no broads, no mother, no sleep, no eat, just a dumb, fair cop." Tiring of the daily grind, in 1960 he returned to film, appearing opposite John Wayne in three back-to-back productions. In the most notable, *The Man Who Shot Liberty Valance* (1962), he portrayed a brutal killer described by a *Rolling Stone* writer as being "in some kind of private, soul-killing hell" (3 Sept. 1981). The film is a cult classic, as are *The Killers* (1964), *Point Blank* (1967), and *The Dirty Dozen* (1967).

Marvin hit his prime in 1965 in two films in which his characterizations brought almost unanimous critical acclaim. In *Ship of Fools*, an adaptation of the Katherine Anne Porter novel, he played Tenny, a washed-up, alcoholic ex-baseball player. Particularly memorable was a drunken monologue in which he tragicomically described the torture of being unable to

hit a curve ball. "He's a childlike adult," Marvin said in describing the role, "a little afraid, trying to work out values in his own way, a little like me." The second critically acclaimed film, a farcical western in which he played both good guy Kid Shelleen and villainous Tim Straun, was described by *Newsweek* as "one of the high water marks of American film comedy." *Cat Ballou* earned Marvin an Academy Award as best actor in 1965 and showed audiences that, by displaying a gift for comic timing and physical humor, the actor had a far broader range than previously imagined. Twenty-one films followed; among the more intriguing were *The Iceman Cometh* (1973) and *The Big Red One* (1980). "Bogart started out pretty much as I did—a heel, all bad," Marvin told *Life* magazine in 1965. "Then, as audiences warmed to him he became good-bad. Finally he was all good." In 1969 St. Leo's College, which had expelled Marvin as a youth, awarded him an honorary doctor of fine arts degree and named a dormitory after him.

After Marvin's first marriage ended he moved in with Michele Triola, a singer who had a small part in *Ship of Fools*. The relationship lasted for six years, until, in 1970, he married Pamela Feeley, a childhood sweetheart from Woodstock. While Triola and Marvin were together she changed her name legally to Marvin, and in 1972 she initiated a lawsuit against the actor for $1.8 million, alleging that he had agreed to share his earnings with her. *Marvin v. Marvin* became the landmark "palimony" case, raising publicly for the first time the question of whether unmarried couples had binding shared property rights. The court's 1979 decision went against the singer.

Marvin maintained a well-deserved reputation as a boozer and carouser until he moved from Malibu to Tucson, Arizona, in 1975 and gave up drinking. For years, meditative time, as a recovering alcoholic, was spent deep-sea fishing aboard his 56-foot yacht *Blue Hawaii*, which he annually sailed to Australia. Between 1975 and 1986 he appeared in nine films. One of his more notable performances was a grizzled, world-weary infantry sergeant in *The Big Red One* (1980). His last film was *Delta Force* (1986). In mid-August 1987 Marvin was hospitalized at the Tucson Medical Center because of a run-down condition resulting from a flu cold. He steadily worsened until, with his wife at his side, he died of a heart attack.

A *Time* magazine review of *The Dirty Dozen* perhaps best described Marvin's hold on audiences: "Using little more than a twitch of an eye or cheek muscle he transmits a chilling, below-the-surface hint of authority and brutality."

• Clippings on Marvin can be found in the Billy Rose Theatre Collection at the New York Public Library for the Performing Arts, Lincoln Center. See also Donald Zec, *Marvin* (1980). An obituary is in the *New York Times*, 31 Aug. 1987.

DON STEWART

MARVIN, William (14 Apr. 1808–9 July 1902), jurist, was born in Fairfield, Herkimer County, New York, the son of Selden Marvin and Charlotte Pratt, farmers.

Shortly after Marvin was born the family moved to Tompkins County, New York. He attended district schools and Homer Academy in Tompkins County. When he was fifteen years old he began teaching at a district school near his home. The next two years he taught in Phelps, New York, returning in the summers to work on the family farm.

When Marvin turned eighteen he left home, "determined to cut loose from my brothers, and seek my own fortune in my own way" ("Autobiography," p. 181). He taught elementary school in Maryland and read law under an attorney in Frederick. In 1830 he was admitted to the Maryland bar. He then returned to Phelps and clerked another three years for Thomas Smith after he discovered that New York would not honor his Maryland credentials. Following his admittance to the New York bar in May 1834, Marvin opened his own law office in Phelps.

In December 1834 legal business took Marvin to Florida. While in St. Augustine he became friends with several of the territory's leaders, including Joseph White, Florida's delegate to Congress. In 1835, when the office of U.S. attorney for the southern district of Florida became vacant, White recommended Marvin to President Andrew Jackson. In addition to his official duties, Marvin established a lucrative private law practice in Key West, from which he earned enough to invest substantially in Florida real estate. Marvin also became involved in territorial politics, representing Monroe County in the Legislative Council for two terms and serving as a delegate to the St. Joseph Constitutional Convention, which drafted Florida's first state constitution.

On 11 March 1839, President Martin Van Buren appointed Marvin as judge of the southern district of Florida. Marvin served as territorial judge until 3 March 1845, when Florida achieved statehood. The new state legislature elected Marvin to the circuit court in Key West, but he declined the office because he hoped to be appointed as federal judge for the district of Florida. When Isaac Bronson, another territorial judge, received the nomination, Marvin resumed private practice in Key West. In 1846 he married Harriette Newell Foote, who died two years later, six months after the birth of their only child. In 1847 Marvin returned to the bench when Congress divided the state into two judicial districts, necessitating the appointment of an additional judge.

The primary judicial business conducted in Key West concerned the maritime salvage industry. The treacherous conditions off the coast of Florida caused numerous shipwrecks, creating the need for salvors to rescue property before it was damaged. Virtually everyone on the island was engaged in some aspect of the wrecking business, and the court annually awarded hundreds of thousands of dollars to salvors. As both a territorial and federal judge Marvin earned a reputation as a jurist who successfully balanced the needs of a local economy based on the salvage industry with the interests of large commercial shippers and marine insurance companies. Professional salvors were often re-

garded as greedy opportunists, but Marvin was able, as he explained in the case of the *Alabamian* (1839), to "teach a moral lesson to the professional wreckers upon this coast [by] rewarding good conduct . . . with a generous liberality, and by withholding this liberality when these virtues are wanting" (*Federal Cases*, vol. 1, p. 283). Marvin's careful supervision was largely responsible for elevating the salvage industry from virtual piracy to a legitimate and vital enterprise. Marvin's experiences made him a leading expert on admiralty and maritime law, and he published *A Treatise on the Law of Wreck and Salvage* in 1858.

Holding court in the only population center in south Florida, Marvin worked in relative isolation until the advent of the Civil War, which he characterized as "the saddest period of my life" ("Autobiography," p. 214). The New York native actively opposed secession, but he was also a slaveowner and a Democrat whose loyalties were torn between his duty to uphold the Constitution and his love for his adopted state. In 1861, after Florida seceded from the Union, every federal official in Key West resigned except for Marvin and the collector of customs. Union troops quickly occupied the island, however, and secured Marvin's post. Thus Marvin's court was the only federal court to operate continuously in a seceded state throughout the Civil War. Nevertheless, Marvin's southern sympathies still caused concern among some military officials, and when he criticized General David Hunter, the commanding officer on Key West, Hunter accused Marvin of treason. Only Hunter's removal to another command prevented Marvin's arrest. He remained on the bench until 1863, primarily adjudicating prize cases that arose from the capture of vessels attempting to run the Union blockade.

In 1863 Marvin resigned and moved to New York City because his health had been "impaired by long residence in a hot climate, mental anxiety, and overwork" ("Autobiography," p. 214). Two years later he accepted President Andrew Johnson's invitation to return to Florida as provisional governor of the state until a new civil government could be established. Marvin was a popular choice among former Confederates because of his long association with the state and his Democratic loyalties, while his lengthy federal service made him acceptable to the leaders of the military occupation.

Marvin spent most of his term traversing the state, lecturing Floridians about the adjustments that Reconstruction would require. He urged former slaves to exercise their freedom prudently. "You must not think because you are as free as the white people, that you are their equal," he told an audience in Marianna, "because you are not" (quoted in Shofner, p. 39). He advised white audiences of the absolute necessity of granting full legal equality to African Americans as a prerequisite for readmission to the Union, but he ardently opposed the enfranchisement of blacks. "If the colored race in this country can be fully and fairly protected in the exercise and enjoyment of their newly acquired rights of freedom," he counseled the 1865 state constitutional convention, "they will be a quiet and contented people, unambitious of . . . any participation in the affairs of the government" (John Wallace, *Carpetbag Rule in Florida* [1888], pp. 14–15). Based on Marvin's assurances that the president and Congress expected nothing more, the convention adopted a very conservative document that granted blacks basic civil rights but reserved for whites the right to vote, hold office, and serve on juries.

On 29 December 1865, with civil government restored in Florida, the state legislature elected Marvin to the U.S. Senate. Despite the endorsement of several northern senators, who vouched for Marvin's character and loyalty, the Senate refused to seat Marvin because Radical Republicans were dismayed with Florida's conservative approach to Reconstruction. Disenchanted with politics and the law, Marvin returned to New York. In 1866 he married Elizabeth Riddle Jewett, and they retired to her family home in Skaneateles, New York, where he tended his garden and wrote several books until his death there.

After Marvin left Florida he remained one of the state's most popular governors, but his tenure was unexceptional. He had little influence over Reconstruction policy, and his refusal to press for more than token protections for the ex-slaves virtually ensured that Congress would demand even greater concessions from former Confederates in the state. Marvin's accomplishments as an admiralty judge, however, had a more lasting impact. Using his authority to regulate salvors, shippers, and insurers, Marvin fashioned a broad commercial policy that facilitated the economic development of the state and the nation.

• Marvin left no papers, but in 1892 he recorded several reminiscences that were later published as "The Autobiography of William Marvin," ed. Kevin E. Kearney, *Florida Historical Quarterly* 36 (Jan. 1958): 179–222. Nearly seventy of Marvin's written opinions in admiralty salvage cases are located in *Federal Cases* (30 vols., 1894–1897). In addition to his treatise, Marvin also published *A System of General Average* (1866) and two editions of *The Authorship of the Four Gospels* (1884, 1885). For an analysis of Marvin's judicial service see Kermit L. Hall and Eric W. Rise, *From Local Courts to National Tribunals: The Federal District Courts of Florida, 1821–1990* (1991). Contrasting interpretations of Marvin's tenure as governor are provided by William Watson Davis, *The Civil War and Reconstruction in Florida* (1913), and Jerrell H. Shofner, *Nor Is It Over Yet: Florida in the Era of Reconstruction, 1863–1877* (1974).

ERIC W. RISE

MARWEDEL, Emma Jacobina Christiana (27 Feb. 1818–17 Nov. 1893), kindergarten reformer, was born in Münden, in the Kingdom of Hanover (now Germany), the daughter of Heinrich Ludwig Marwedel, a district assistant judge, and Jacobina Carolina Christiana Brokmann. Little is known of Marwedel's early life. Both of her parents died during her youth; the death of her mother left her with the task of caring for her younger brothers and sisters. The death of her father gave her the additional responsibility for earning her own living. Details of her schooling are not known, but she seems to have been chiefly self-educated.

Probably as a means of supporting herself, Marwedel studied kindergarten pedagogy, either with the founder of this field, Friedrich Froebel, or with his widow, Luise Levine Froebel. Friedrich Froebel had designed kindergarten pedagogy as a new form of early childhood education based on the development of the child's native potential for intellectual, physical, and social development (as metaphorically expressed in the name "kindergarten" or "child-garden"). He believed that women were best equipped by nature to teach small children, and he set up the first institutions for the training of kindergarten teachers. The kindergarten, which developed in Germany outside the public school system under private sponsorship, was associated with German liberal and feminist movements.

Marwedel also took an interest in the problems of working women. During the 1860s her investigation of this topic involved extensive travel in Western Europe and resulted in a book in 1868 on girls' vocational schooling, *Why Do We Need Female Industrial Schools and How Shall They Be Established?* (Warum bedürfen wir weibliche Gewerbeschulen und wie sollen sie angelegt sein?). An active feminist, she was appointed in 1865 to the first executive committee of a new national organization devoted to the rights and advancement of women, the General German Women's Association (Allgemeiner Deutscher Frauenverein). In 1867 she became the director of a school of industrial arts for girls in Hamburg.

In 1867 Marwedel met American social reformer Elizabeth Palmer Peabody, who had traveled to Germany to encourage some of Froebel's German disciples to establish kindergartens in the United States. Peabody, who later asserted that Marwedel had introduced her to authentic Froebelian kindergarten theory, persuaded Marwedel that the United States provided the most favorable environment for the development of the kindergarten. Marwedel immigrated to the United States probably around 1870. Having failed in her first attempt to found an industrial training school for girls (in Brentwood, N.Y.), she moved in 1871 to Washington, D.C., where she established a kindergarten (known as the German-American Kindergarten), a vocational school, and a training institution for kindergarten teachers. The success of these schools, which by 1874 enrolled ninety-five pupils, attested to the high regard for German educational theories in the United States during these years and especially to the commitment of American educators to the training of American teachers in Froebelian methods.

Although well established in Washington, Marwedel was nonetheless reluctant to settle there, for she aspired to spread the kindergarten idea to places where it was as yet unknown. She responded in 1876 to a call issued by the Froebel Union of New England for a teacher to found kindergartens in California. Aided by philanthropist Caroline Severance, Marwedel moved in 1876 to Los Angeles, where she founded the California Model Kindergarten and the Pacific Model Training School for Kindergartners. Among the first students of the training course was Kate Douglas Smith (later Wiggin), who spread Marwedel's influence through a notable career as author, educator, and kindergarten activist.

In 1878 Marwedel moved her kindergarten and training school to Oakland, California, apparently because the Los Angeles venture had not been a financial success. Such financial instability was typical of many early kindergartens, which were founded entirely under private auspices and subsisted on tuition fees and the donations of supporters. In 1879 she moved again to Berkeley, where she founded an institution known as the Pacific Kindergarten Normal School. In 1880 she moved her school to San Francisco, presumably because by this time she had been appointed to the board of directors of the San Francisco Public Kindergarten Society, founded in 1878 by New York social reformer Felix Adler. The society, which promoted kindergarten education as an important means of integrating immigrant children into mainstream American society, set up free kindergartens in order to educate the children of the poor. Marwedel also became the first president of another such organization, the California Kindergarten Union, in 1879.

Marwedel probably retired from teaching in 1886; her later years were devoted to writing and public lecturing. Her best-known work, *Conscious Motherhood; or, The Earliest Unfolding of the Child in the Cradle, Nursery, and Kindergarten*, was published in 1887. Marwedel's writings linked Froebel's theories, which emphasized the child's spiritual nature, with the physiologically oriented approach developed by the new field of child psychology. She strongly promoted the ideas of German psychologist Wilhelm Preyer, who linked the physical development of children to their emotional and intellectual development. She portrayed child rearing as a complex and scientifically based task that required education, both for mothers and for professional child-care workers. Improved child rearing, she asserted, would lead to the end of crime and class tensions and the beginning of a new and harmonious social order. She called for improvements in the economic, social, and legal status of women, to whom this vital work of social regeneration was entrusted. Her theories were both more scientifically sophisticated and more explicitly feminist than those of most American kindergarten educators of her era.

Marwedel's total dedication to the cause of educational and social reform left her little energy to devote to her own physical or economic well-being. She never married or had children. She died in San Francisco of a condition then known as "senile gangrene," probably caused in part by malnutrition and overwork.

Because of her impractical and idealistic personality and her limited knowledge of the English language and American culture, Emma Marwedel experienced much frustration and failure. Nonetheless, she made an important contribution to both the institutional and

the theoretical basis of early childhood education in the United States. Later developments, such as the incorporation of kindergarten classes into public school systems and the reform of educational methods in accordance with theories of child psychology, owe much to Marwedel's work. She helped to develop Froebelian methods to suit the conditions of urban schools. Along with a few other kindergarten teachers from Germany, she trained a generation of American-born educators who gained national and international prominence. She helped progressive urban reformers, especially women, recognize that early childhood education was a key to social reform and asserted the dignity, importance, and complexity of professional training for women in that field.

• A biography of Marwedel is Fletcher Harper Swift, *Emma Jacobina Christiana Marwedel: Pioneer of the Kindergarten in California* (1932). Recollections of Marwedel are in Kate Douglas Wiggin, *My Garden of Memory: An Autobiography* (1923), and in *Letters of Elizabeth Palmer Peabody: American Renaissance Woman*, ed. Bruce Ronda (1984). Further information on Marwedel's career in the context of the American kindergarten movement is in Earl Barnes, "Emma Marwedel," in Committee of Nineteen, *Pioneers of the Kindergarten in America* (1924); Agnes Snyder, *Dauntless Women in Early Childhood Education, 1856–1931* (1972); Nina Vandewalker, *The Kindergarten in American Education* (1908); Michael Steven Shapiro, *Child's Garden: The Kindergarten Movement from Froebel to Dewey* (1983); and Barbara Beatty, "A Vocation from On High: Kindergartning as an Occupation for American Women," in *Changing Education: Women as Radicals and Conservators*, ed. Joyce Antler and Sari Biklen (1990).

ANN TAYLOR ALLEN

MARX, Alexander (29 Jan. 1878–26 Dec. 1953), historian and librarian, was born in Elberfeld, Germany, the son of George Marx, a merchant and banker, and Gertrude Simon. The family moved to Königsberg when Alexander was seven, and he received an intensive secular and Jewish religious education. After graduating from the Gymnasium, he spent a year in Halberstadt engaged in rabbinic studies under the tutelage of the renowned Rabbi Joseph Nobel. Between 1896 and 1903 Marx studied at the universities of Berlin and Königsberg and at the Orthodox Rabbinical Seminary in Berlin. He received his Ph.D. from the University of Königsberg in 1903.

During his student years in Berlin, Marx attended lectures offered by Moritz Steinschneider at a private institution, the Veitel-Heine Ephraim Institute. Steinschneider was considered one of the founders of modern Jewish scholarship and the father of scholarly Hebrew bibliography. Marx became his favorite student, and a deep friendship developed between the two men. Marx was influenced by Steinschneider to such an extent that A. S. W. Rosenbach, the great American book dealer and bibliophile, remarked many years later: "Europe had its Steinschneider, America now has its Marx."

Although Steinschneider exerted the most profound influence on Marx's scholarly work and on his contributions as a librarian, Marx was also indebted to his other teachers, prominent historian Abraham Berliner, philologist Jacob Barth, and rabbinic scholar David Hoffmann, rector of the Orthodox Rabbinical Seminary in Berlin. In 1905 Marx married Hoffmann's daughter, Hanna; they had two children.

In 1898 Marx traveled to England in order to study Hebrew manuscripts in connection with his work on a critical edition of an ancient Hebrew work of chronology, the *Seder Olam*. While in England, he visited Solomon Schechter in Cambridge. When Schechter assumed the presidency of the Jewish Theological Seminary of America in New York City in 1902, his first concern was to assemble an outstanding faculty. Young Marx had made a great impression on Schechter, and he invited Marx to become a professor of history and librarian at the newly reorganized institution. Marx arrived in New York City in 1903 and for the following half century served the seminary in his dual capacity. He also played a leading role in various American Jewish academic and cultural organizations, including the Jewish Publication Society, the American Academy for Jewish Research (president, 1931–1933), and the American Jewish Historical Society.

Marx's contributions as historian and as librarian are thoroughly intertwined. During his tenure as librarian at the seminary, his main goal was to amass an extensive collection of primary sources, medieval manuscripts, archival documents, and early printed books. Much of his own historical research made use of such primary sources. Under his direction, the seminary library grew into one of the largest and finest depositories of Jewish manuscripts and books in the world. In addition to collecting books, manuscripts, and documents, Marx was also concerned with the preservation of Jewish art and ceremonial objects. The Jewish Museum in New York City had its origins at the library and was under Marx's direction until the 1940s. Authors of many important works in Jewish studies acknowledge their reliance on the rich resources of the seminary library and Marx's help. His annual reports about new acquisitions and library activities contain a wealth of original bibliographical and historical information about rare Hebrew books and manuscripts. These reports were collected and published in 1977 in *Bibliographical Studies and Notes on Rare Books and Manuscripts in the Library of the Jewish Theological Seminary of America*. Marx was the author of many other bibliographical studies, some concerning the discovery and description of hitherto unknown books and others embracing wider topics, such as "Illustrated Haggadahs," "The Literature of Hebrew Incunabula," "Notes on the Use of Hebrew Type in Non-Hebrew Books, 1475–1520," and "The Choice of Books by the Printers of Incunabula" (in "*To Dr. R.*" [1946]).

As a historian, Marx studied ancient, medieval, and early modern Jewish history; he was interested in the literary, cultural, social, political, and economic aspects of the history of the Jews. One of his first publications, a 1903 edition of chapters 1–10 of the ancient

Hebrew *Seder Olam*, is a model of a text-critical edition. In numerous articles, Marx published and analyzed texts relating to Jewish history in Spain, Italy, Germany, Bohemia, and Moravia, among other places. His most notable contributions include "Untersuchungen zum Siddur des Gaon R. Amram; I. Die handschriftliche Überlieferung" (*Jahrbuch der Jüdischen Literarischen Gesellschaft* 5 [1907]), "The Expulsion of the Jews from Spain," "Maimonides and the Scholars of Southern France," "Astrology among the Jews in the Twelfth and Thirteenth Centuries," "A Jewish Cause Célèbre in Sixteenth Century Italy," and "A Contribution to the History of the Jews in Cochin."

Marx summarized his views on Jewish history in "Aims and Tasks of Jewish Historiography" (*Publications of the American Jewish Historical Society* 26 [1918]). He rejects the concentration on the "monotonous description" of agonies suffered by Jews in the Middle Ages (the "lachrymose" conception of Jewish history) and also wants to limit the preoccupation with literary history. He advocates a balanced treatment in which "constitutional, social and economic history" takes its rightful place. He also demands that Jewish history be placed in the framework of general history of all the countries where Jews had lived, believing that it must become an "organic part of the history of the world."

Besides his bibliographical and historical studies, Marx wrote numerous biographies of medieval and modern Jewish personalities, such as Saadia Gaon, Rashi, Maimonides, Moritz Steinschneider, David Hoffmann, Mayer Sulzberger, and Solomon Schechter. These concise biographies are based on primary and secondary sources and, in the case of modern subjects, on personal acquaintance.

The crowning achievement of Marx's work as a historian is his one-volume *History of the Jewish People* (coauthored with Max L. Margolis [1927]). Avoiding a preoccupation with literary history, it is, rather, "a history of the entire people, of the mass," focusing primarily on economic and social concerns. Within a relatively limited space, this work has come to be a very frequently consulted reference book because of the reliability of its information, which it presents in a continuous narrative.

Marx saw himself as a link between the Old and the New Worlds. He helped to develop centers of Jewish scholarship in the United States, utilizing the knowledge he had acquired as a student of outstanding European scholars. He took advantage of his many personal and family connections with the Jewish scholarly establishment in Western and Central Europe in order to facilitate the transfer of ideas, people, and books from the threatened and disintegrating centers of European Jewish learning to the United States. As a teacher, as a scholar, and particularly as the man who almost single-handedly was responsible for making the library of the Jewish Theological Seminary of America into one of the most important collections of Hebraica and Judaica in the world, Marx was one of the most significant scholars in Jewish studies in the United States in the first half of the twentieth century.

Marx died in New York City. His brother, Moses, was a bibliographer and librarian, and his sister, Esther, was married to Nobel Prize–winning Israeli novelist S. Y. Agnon.

• Alexander Marx's papers, including his extensive correspondence, are in the library of the Jewish Theological Seminary. Many of Marx's bibliographical studies, essays, and biographies are included in his *Studies in Jewish History and Booklore* (1944) and *Essays in Jewish Biography* (1947). During his lifetime, two Festschriften were published in his honor: David Frankel, ed., *Sefer Ha-Yovel: A Tribute to Professor Alexander Marx . . . on Completing Forty Years of Distinguished Service as Librarian of the Jewish Theological Seminary of America* (1943) and *Alexander Marx Jubilee Volume on the Occasion of His Seventieth Birthday* (2 vols., 1950), which includes a bibliography of his writings compiled by Boaz Cohen and biographical appreciations by Rebekah Kohut and Solomon Goldman. Abraham S. Halkin's article, "Alexander Marx," in *American Jewish Year Book*, vol. 56 (1955), assesses his importance as a historian. See also Menahem Schmelzer, "Alexander Marx (On the Occasion of the 100th Anniversary of His Birth)," in *Jewish Book Annual*, vol. 35 (1977–1978), pp. 123–27. His role in the growth of the library of the Jewish Theological Seminary is discussed in detail in Herman Dicker, *Of Learning and Libraries: The Seminary Library at One Hundred* (1988). See also Dicker, ed., *The Mayer Sulzberger–Alexander Marx Correspondence, 1904–1923* (1990). Obituaries include Adolf Kober, *History Judaica* 16 (1954); Louis Finkelstein, *Proceedings of the Rabbinical Assembly of America* 18 (1954); and H. A. Wolfson et al., *Speculum* 29 (1954).

MENAHEM SCHMELZER

MARX, Louis, Sr. (11 Aug. 1896–5 Feb. 1982), toy manufacturer, was born in Brooklyn, New York, the son of Jacob Marx, a tailor and the proprietor of a modest drygoods establishment, and Clara Lou (maiden name unknown). Jacob Marx's business never proved entirely successful, and the family enjoyed few extras. Working hard to improve himself, a trait he would exhibit throughout his life, Louis Marx graduated from high school in just three years at age fifteen. Before 1915 German toymakers supplied the largest portion of the American toy market. World War I, however, greatly reduced the availability of German playthings and encouraged the development of domestic toy manufacturing. Marx's initial exposure to the toy business began on the eve of this expansion.

In 1912 Marx found a position as an errand boy with Ferdinand Strauss, "The Toy King," who was widely acknowledged then as the founder of the mechanical toy industry in America. Strauss proved a valuable teacher and benefactor. In 1916 the elder toymaker dispatched Marx to his plant in East Rutherford, New Jersey, expecting Marx to learn the manufacturing process there. Satisfied with the young man's progress, Strauss promoted his trainee to manager of the facility. While manager, Marx reworked a Strauss toy horn into a party favor—a noisemaker in the guise of a lapel flower. Over time, turning older designs into

new playthings would become a favorite Marx strategy. In this instance the item sold so well that Strauss promoted Marx to director.

But by 1917 Strauss's relationship with Marx had begun to deteriorate. Besides factories, the toy manufacturer's holdings included four New York City retail stores in railroad terminals located throughout the city. Marx saw these shops as only tangential to the business of manufacturing playthings in quantity and thus a waste of managerial effort and capital. At a Strauss board of directors meeting, the controversial nature of Marx's stand became evident. When Marx alone voted to sell, Strauss fired him.

In 1919, together with his brother Dave, Marx incorporated as Louis Marx & Co., Inc., an independent toy design firm. Their strategy and forte involved improving on inexpensive playthings manufactured by competitors that were sold in chain stores; they would either find some way to make the same toy more cheaply or add a new feature at no additional production cost. After securing a store order, Marx would then contract with a third party to produce the desired playthings.

Starting in 1921, however, the partners manufactured their own toys. When Strauss grew insolvent, Marx purchased from him patterns for two tin playthings—"Zippo the Climbing Monkey" and the "Alabama Coon Jigger," a mechanical minstrel—and obtained space in an old Strauss factory to produce them. Other makers viewed the brothers' plans as sheer folly. The Strauss patents had lapsed, and after over two decades of sales, most makers assumed that little demand for these toys remained.

Marx proved his critics wrong. As he had done previously, Marx modified the old Strauss toys, this time creating larger, more colorful versions. The brothers sold more than sixteen million monkeys and jiggers, and by 1922 Louis Marx had become a millionaire. In 1928 Marx triumphed again when he devised the "Yo-Yo," based on a traditional Filipino toy.

Despite his successes, Marx reacted cautiously at first, concluding that capital costs were too high to justify expansion. But during the Great Depression, bankruptcies made affordable facilities more available. Marx established two manufacturing concerns in Pennsylvania—one in Girard, the other in Erie—and a third factory in Glendale, West Virginia. Also during this period, Marx established a plant in England and began producing toys overseas.

After World War II, consumer affluence and a baby boom greatly increased consumer demand for playthings, and Marx took full advantage by constructing some of the most up-to-date, fully mechanized plants in the industry. As early as 1946, Marx's prolific assembly lines earned him comparisons to Henry Ford, but his methods also resembled those of Andrew Carnegie. Like Carnegie, Marx would replace even new machinery with more efficient equipment if doing so would increase output. A pioneer manufacturer of plastic toys, Marx also boosted production and reduced costs by utilizing this cheaper material in place of tin or wood.

And yet for all of his innovations, in other respects Marx resisted change. Convinced that few truly original toy ideas remained, Marx continued to redesign older playthings, not only his own but also those of other manufacturers, altering them just enough to avoid paying royalties. "When they copy you, it's piracy," he once said. "When you copy them, it's competition."

And while Marx sometimes incorporated licensed television characters into his designs—comedian Milton Berle as a wind-up toy and fictitious astronaut "Tom Corbett" as the subject of a play set, for example—he also reacted slowly to developments in television advertising. Indeed, Marx engaged in little direct marketing of any kind. As late as 1955, his advertising expenditures totaled a scant $312. Instead, to merchandise his toys Marx relied largely on the great retail chains—J. C. Penney, Montgomery Ward, Woolworth, and Sears—together with the free publicity that celebrity status afforded him.

In *Time* magazine—as in the December 1955 cover story—*Reader's Digest*, and *Life*, Marx related his theories on the place of toys in the lives of young consumers. He opposed the development of "educational toys," declaring them unrealistic and blaming them for later classroom disinterest. By providing children with educational toys, he believed, adults rushed youngsters to maturity, depriving them of the singular joys of childhood. Marx called on parents to give inexpensive playthings frequently as tangible and reassuring examples of affection.

During the 1940s and 1950s, contemporaries credited Louis Marx with manufacturing more toys than any other producer in the United States. In 1941 roughly 600 toy makers each manufactured an average of $200,000 worth of playthings. Marx kept his sales figures a secret, but industry observers estimated that Marx produced one-sixth of the $120 million worth of toys made. By 1955 Marx increased his share of the domestic market, amassing more than $50 million in gross sales, 10 percent of the U.S. market. In 1972, with his children unwilling to assume control of the company, Marx sold his firm to the Quaker Oats Company for $52 million. During the 1970s, mismanagement caused Marx toy sales to decline precipitously. In 1976 Quaker Oats sold most of Marx to Dunbee-Combex. Liquidated piecemeal after Dunbee-Combex-Marx declared bankruptcy in 1980, Marx operations in United States ceased altogether during 1983. Marx died in White Plains, New York.

Marx married twice. During the mid-1940s, his first wife, Renee Freda Marx (marriage date unknown), died of cancer but not before the couple had four children. One of his daughters, Patricia, married Daniel Ellsberg, later charged in the theft of the Pentagon Papers. Marx's second marriage to showgirl Idella Ruth Blackadder (date unknown) produced four more children. Well known for his generosity, Marx gave as many as a million toys each year to poor children. He also contributed to other causes but favored cancer-related charities.

Despite Marx's past notoriety, scholars have largely ignored him. Collectors, however, highly prize his toys. Marx's place in social, cultural, and business history remains significant. Due in part to the substantial output of his factories, the American toy industry maintained worldwide predominance.

• A full-length biography of Louis Marx, Sr., has yet to be published. Maxine A. Pinsky, with MaryAnn S. Suehle, ed., *Greenberg's Guide to Marx Toys, Volume I: 1923–1950* (1988), provides the most complete treatment of Marx's life. Eric J. Matzke, *Greenberg's Guide to Marx Trains*, vol. 1 (1989), also is useful. Other works especially helpful in reconstructing Marx's early years and career are "Louis Marx: Toy King," *Fortune*, Jan. 1946, pp. 122–25, 127, 163–64; "Toys and the King," *Time*, 5 Nov. 1951, pp. 110–11; and "The Little King," *Time*, 12 Dec. 1955, pp. 92–96. Marx explains why certain playthings appeal to children and then harangues "educational toys" in Herbert Brean, "Top Toymaker's Buying Guide," *Life*, 23 Nov. 1959, pp. 119–20. Marx also gives his opinion on "educational toys" in J. P. McEvoy and Peggy McEvoy, "Talk with a Toy King," *Reader's Digest*, Jan. 1955, pp. 125–28. In "Successors Couldn't Match His Genius, So Louis Marx's Toy Empire Crumbled," *Wall Street Journal*, 8 Feb. 1980, p. 6, Cynthia Saltzman explains why eventually the Marx toy company declined. Obituaries are in the *New York Times*, 6 Feb. 1982, and *Time*, 15 Feb. 1982.

LAWRENCE F. GREENFIELD

MARX BROTHERS, comedy team, comprised Leonard "Chico" Marx (22 Mar. 1887–11 Oct. 1961), Adolph (later Arthur) "Harpo" Marx (23 Nov. 1888–28 Sept. 1964), and Julius Henry "Groucho" Marx (2 Oct. 1890–19 Aug. 1977), three of five sons of Samuel Marx and Minna "Minnie" Schönberg, German-Jewish immigrants who settled in New York City in the mid-1880s. Of the younger brothers, Milton "Gummo" Marx (1897–21 Apr. 1977) appeared on stage with the group, but he eventually retired to become the team's manager. The youngest, Herbert "Zeppo" Marx (25 Feb. 1901–30 Nov. 1979), played the earnest straight man on the stage and in the early films and operated a theatrical agency, and he too occasionally managed the group's affairs.

Sam Marx's business was in the tailoring trade, but he frequently served as the family cook and housekeeper. His cooking prowess earned him the family nickname "Frenchie." Early in his sons' careers he prompted audiences as the "laugh starter." Anonymously seated in the middle of the theater, Sam would immediately begin laughing at their antics. But it was their mother who was the driving force that led them onto the burlesque and vaudeville stages and who over the years constantly fought for bookings in the most popular theaters. She had initially wanted her sons to become career musicians and gradually introduced them to the stage individually and in pairs, playing instruments, singing, and portraying bit parts. Minnie's father had played a musical instrument, and her connection to the stage was through her brother Al Shean (originally Schönberg), half of a highly popular vaudeville comedy team, Gallagher and Shean.

The Marx Brothers began their careers at a time of deep hostility toward immigrant groups from southern and eastern Europe. Their nicknames—given to them during a poker game in their vaudeville period—as well as their dialogue and distinct costumes were inspired by the ethnic character of American culture.

The brothers began performing early in childhood. Chico, the oldest, was a piano player plugging songs for music companies and was the most ambitious in upgrading the brothers' career by demanding higher billings. His stage persona was an Italian who dressed in a pointed hat, seedy velvet jacket and tie, baggy pants, and deadpan face. A gentle and playful demeanor offset Chico's parody of a mixture of English and Italian words and phrases. Crazy sequences flowed from his straight expression as Chico's face rarely betrayed his next offbeat move. In his roles he was the pickpocket, the short-changer, and the plot-thickener. Chico played the piano and delighted audiences when he jabbed his right hand index finger at the keyboard like a pistol.

Harpo's moniker derived from his love of the harp. A self-taught performer, he played the instrument on the stage and in films with a dreamy tenderness, his eyes rolling upward in quiet reverence. Dressed in a battered plug hat, wild-mopped flaming red wig, checkered shirt and tie, flappy trench coat and underslung pants, Harpo let his humor flow from his muteness and adroit miming. His comedic presence was highly physical and his stage inventiveness legendary. "Most people have a conscious and a subconscious," he said of his farcical impulses. "Not me. I've always operated on a subconscious and a sub-subconscious." Because of his ability to translate silence into action, Harpo's parts were rarely scripted. "How can you write for Harpo?" griped playwright George S. Kaufman when he was writing their play *The Cocoanuts*. "What do you put down on paper? All you can say is, 'Harpo enters.' From that point on, he's on his own!" Harpo extended his clownishness through a combination of large saucerlike eyes and a childlike smile that gave the impression of an impish waif. Performing with puckish glee, he kept everyone off-balance by beeping an old-fashioned bulb car horn as he chased women and piqued men, snipping an item of clothing with a pair of scissors kept hidden in his coat, shaking stolen cutlery secreted in an oversized raincoat, mouth-whistling with fingers, throwing his leg into someone's arms, and darting around in acts of mischievous delight.

Groucho was the most celebrated of the brothers, and his stage persona became the most recognized in entertainment. He dressed in a tie and draping suit and had dark, unsettled eyebrows that moved up and down above frame-rimmed glasses and a thick, darkly-painted mustache that eventually became a permanent feature much later in life. He had a loping walk and deployed a cigar as a prop. His comedy poured out in a rapid staccato style of delivery that combined a devilish manipulation of words with wiseacre repartee. According to Harpo, a compelling urge to get "a laugh every second" drove Groucho to make puns on lines that were already puns; at other times he would create jokes about the show and the performance rather than conform to the plot. More often than not, even his silliest pun or non sequitur contained a meaningful connection. Several of his comments have become classics, such as his refusal to join the exclusive Commonwealth Club of Los Angeles: "I refuse to belong to any club that would have me as a member." His defiance of authority was displayed in his response to the U.S. Customs' Declaration of Purchase upon return from an overseas trip: next to "occupation" he wrote, "Smuggler," and to the queries of where foreign goods were bought and for how much he put down, "Wouldn't you like to know?" Consequently, the Customs inspector examined the entire contents of the family's baggage, a situation that worsened when Groucho loudly whispered to his wife, "What did you do with the opium? Do you still have it on you?" At his last birthday party, when he turned eighty-seven, he raised a glass of pink lemonade and bantered, "I'm as young as the day is long, and this has been a very short day. Nothing lasts forever."

Billed as the "Three" or "Four Nightingales" in the early part of their career, the brothers appeared week after week in small towns and cities across the country in revues and skits for fifteen years. In 1919 they had their first "legitimate" musical show, *The Cinderella Girl*, billed as "A Merry Melange of Mirth, Melody, and Music." It opened in Battle Creek, Michigan, at the height of the influenza epidemic that was decimating the country, and closed three days later. They rebounded in *I'll Say She Is* (1923–1925), billed as "The Laughing Revue" that eventually made its way to Broadway, and was followed by their breakthrough show *The Cocoanuts* (1925–1928). While their next production, *Animal Crackers* (1930), had a comparatively short Broadway run, it further solidified the brothers' reputations as among the most unusual and innovative comedians in the country.

Following their Broadway triumphs, the brothers moved to Hollywood. Over a twenty-year period they made eleven pictures, in the early years under contract to Paramount Pictures, then moving to Metro-Goldwyn-Mayer (MGM), where for several years they were guided by the brilliant Irving Thalberg, head of production. At Paramount, their first movies, in 1929 and 1930, respectively, recreated the Broadway hits *The Cocoanuts* and *Animal Crackers*, which propelled them to national prominence. These were followed in rapid succession by *Monkey Business* (1931), *Horsefeathers* (1932), and *Duck Soup* (1933); *Duck Soup*, a semi-surrealist parody about war, is regarded by many as their finest film. Their sole foray into political satire, it was not a particular success at the box office.

At MGM, the Marx Brothers made a series of films, including *A Night at the Opera* (1935) and *A Day at the Races* (1937), several of which were praised by critics as minor classics. Among their later films were *Room*

Service (1938), *Go West* (1940), *The Big Store* (1941), and, after World War II, *A Night in Casablanca* (1946) and *Love Happy* (1950). Despite the extraordinary popularity of their films, one critic observed that celluloid never truly captured the essence of their comedic personas: "The Marx Brothers have never been in a picture as wonderful as they are."

Some of the most proficient comedy writers in the first half of the twentieth century wrote for them. Besides Kaufman and Morrie Ryskind, the brothers worked with material from the songwriting team of Bert Kalmar and Harry Ruby, the ingenious gagster Al Boasberg, and the satirical essayist S. J. Perelman. They drove writers and directors to distraction with their script mutations and on-stage capers. One well-known screenwriter, Herman J. Mankiewicz, counseled Perelman, who had just agreed to write for them: "I hate to depress you, but you'll rue the day you ever took the assignment. This is ordeal by fire. Make sure you wear your asbestos pants."

Although the brothers' performances were based on a prepared script, they constantly improvised, and their frenetic pace created a wildly improbable and illogical experience. "We never did stop ad-libbing," wrote Harpo in his autobiography. "No two performances were quite the same." Routines changed nightly, to the chagrin of their writers. "You should see *Cocoanuts* sometime, Morrie," said Kaufman to Ryskind, "It's not what we wrote." Constantly challenging each other heightened the brothers' zaniness. During a performance of *The Cocoanuts*, Harpo suddenly asked a chorus dancer to run screaming across the stage. She complied, and Harpo tore after her in full pursuit, leaping and honking his bulbous car horn. Undaunted by the interruption, Groucho extemporaneously exclaimed, "First time I ever saw a taxi hail a passenger." Harpo quickly chased her back across the stage, trying to catch his brother off-guard. Groucho, peering over his glasses, pointedly declared, "The nine-twenty's right on time. You can always set your clock by the Lehigh Valley." The chase subsequently became a running gag in many of their skits.

The brothers' frolics at the Hollywood studios were as celebrated as their film performances. Even awe and respect for the powerful Thalberg did not prevent the brothers from taking him to task when he kept them waiting for appointments. On one occasion they smoked cigars and blew the smoke under his office door until he came out choking to investigate, whereupon they stuck their feet in his door until he consented to let them enter. At another time, they waited until the secretary left for the day, then moved her desk in front of Thalberg's door, collected all the heavy steel filing cabinets and piled them on top and departed. It took Thalberg an hour to escape from his office, and he rarely kept them waiting again.

A constant rollicking energy characterized the way the brothers meshed madcap capers with word play. Scenes unfolded in a cascade of seeming nonsense, yet they usually contained a meaningful connection. Typical was their punning in the film *Duck Soup*:

Groucho: Chicolini, give me a number from one to ten.
Chico: Eleven.
Groucho: Right.
Chico: Now I ask you one. What is it has a trunk, but no key, weighs 2,000 pounds, and lives in the circus?
Prosecutor: That's irrelevant.
Chico: A relephant! Hey, that's the answer! There's a whole lotter elephants in the circus.
Minister: That sort of testimony we can eliminate.
Chico: Atsa Fine. I'll take some.
Minister: You'll take *what?*
Chico: Eliminate. A nice cool glass eliminate.

Representing the powerless, they spoofed the upper classes, their expensive dress and fine manners, and their sacred institutions. In *Horsefeathers*, as the president of Huxley College, Groucho zeroed in on college athletics and student behavior:

Groucho: Where would this college be without football? Have we got a stadium?
Professors: Yes.
Groucho: Have we got a college?
Professors: Yes.
Groucho: Well, we can't support both. Tomorrow we start tearing down the college.
Professors: But, Professor, where will the students sleep?
Groucho: Where they always sleep. In the classroom.

The brothers lampooned the aristocratic practice of the African safari, poking fun at the great white hunter's elevated sense of superiority and ridiculing his endless quest for animal trophies. In *Animal Crackers*, dressed in boots, riding pants, and pith helmet, Groucho as Captain Spaulding is carried into a Park Avenue reception on an African sedan chair supported by four Nubians. Describing his arduous experience, he proudly declares, "Up at six, breakfast at six-thirty, and back in bed at seven. . . . One morning I shot an elephant in my pajamas. How he got in my pajamas I'll never know."

Each of the brothers married and had children. Chico was twice married, first in 1916 to Betty Karp, with whom he had a daughter. After their divorce he married Mary De Vithas in 1958. They had no children. In 1936 Harpo married Susan Fleming, an actress; they adopted four children. Groucho was married several times. In 1920 he married Ruth Johnson, a dancer; they had two children before divorcing in 1942. He then married Kay Gorcey in July 1945. They had one child and divorced in 1950. Four years later Groucho wed Eden Hartford. They had no children and divorced in 1969. In 1971 Groucho met Erin Fleming, who was his companion and manager until his death. Gummo in 1929 married Helen Von Tilzer, the widow of composer Russell Von Tilzer; they had one son together and he adopted her child from her previous marriage. Finally, Zeppo married Marion Benda in 1927. They adopted two sons before divorcing in 1954. In 1959 he wed Barbara Blakely; he adopted her son from a previous marriage, and they divorced in 1973. Three years later Barbara Marx married entertainer Frank Sinatra.

By mid-century the brothers had terminated their film career, yet in retirement continued performing individually and in pairs. Chico starred in the road company of *The Fifth Season* in 1956, and he and Harpo played a successful engagement at the Palladium Theatre in London in 1949. They also made appearances on television shows and contributed at benefits. Groucho hosted the highly rated quiz program "You Bet Your Life," broadcast first on radio and then on television for eleven years, becoming the perennial top-rated show on NBC. Chico, Groucho, and Harpo all died in the Los Angeles area, and Zeppo and Gummo died in Palm Springs, California.

The brothers' wild theatricality on stage and in films transformed major elements of American comedy. They created a brand of anarchistic comedy that lampooned the social structure of American society, upsetting cherished values by questioning and skewering authority and tradition. That irreverent attitude gave voice to the experience of millions of first-generation citizens who grappled daily with the vicissitudes of an expanding urban, industrial culture.

To an extent the brothers' attraction rested on a clownish pretense as well. Groucho preposterously feigned being a lover and parodied officious leaders such as the president of a supposedly august institution; Chico caricatured an Italian-American hustler; Harpo faked a spirited muteness. Consequently, their particular brand of humor played an important acculturating role by mediating between divergent groups and undercutting animosities. Their influence, moreover, extended beyond the country. When a prominent French absurdist playwright, Eugène Ionesco, was asked about the greatest influence on his work, he gave the names of the Marx Brothers.

• There have been a variety of works about the Marx family. Salient are Kyle Crichton, *The Marx Brothers* (1950); Allen Eyles, *The Marx Brothers: Their World of Comedy* (1966); Paul Zimmerman, *The Marx Brothers at the Movies* (1968); and particularly Joe Adamson, *Groucho, Harpo, Chico, and Sometimes Zeppo: A History of the Marx Brothers and a Satire on the Rest of the World* (1973). A charming, informative autobiographical work is by Harpo Marx, written with Rowland Barber, *Harpo Speaks!* (1961). There are numerous works on Groucho. Especially pertinent is his own collection of letters and informative details, *Groucho and Me* (1959), and an embracing recollection by his son Arthur Marx, *Life with Groucho* (1954); see also *Love, Groucho: Letters from Groucho Marx to His Daughter Miriam*, ed. Miriam Marx Allen (1992). Highly useful is Hector Arce, *Groucho* (1979). Obituaries for Chico, Harpo, Gummo, Groucho, and Zeppo are in the *New York Times*, 12 Oct. 1961, 29 Sept. 1964, 22 Apr. 1977, 20 Aug. 1977, and 1 Dec. 1979, respectively.

JOSEPH BOSKIN

MASARYK, Charlotte Garrigue (20 Nov. 1850–13 May 1923), first First Lady of Czechoslovakia, was born in Brooklyn, New York, the daughter of Rudolph Garrigue—a man of Huguenot descent who had lived in Denmark and Germany and had established the Germania Fire Insurance Company after his bookstore in Brooklyn burned—and Charlotte Lydia Whiting, who was touched by liberating, unorthodox Transcendentalist ideas. Garrigue, who was called Charlie by her ten siblings, was christened a Unitarian because her paternal grandparents were members of that church. When she was four years old, she moved with her parents to a large house in the Bronx. Hoping to become a concert pianist, Garrigue went to Leipzig, Germany, to study when she was seventeen years old. She stayed with the Goering family, for whom her father had worked in the book business before coming to the United States. After three years of study, Garrigue returned home with her dream shattered; prolonged piano practice had permanently damaged her hand. While instructing others in piano and studying mathematics, she corresponded regularly with the Goering family. She returned to Leipzig in 1876 after they had piqued her curiosity with descriptions of Thomas Masaryk, who was boarding with them. The son of a Slovakian serf, Masaryk was a university sociology student and a private tutor.

Finding that they shared a devotion to rational thought and a faith in the spiritual qualities of all human beings, Garrigue and Masaryk soon set aside time to study and discuss books together. Among these was John Stuart Mill's *Subjection of Women*, which Garrigue later translated into Czech, bolstering the women's movement in Czechoslovakia. Masaryk was especially impressed by Garrigue's love for mathematics, desire for precise knowledge, deep religious feeling, and unshakable belief in immortality. Calling her intellect magnificent, he declared it better than his own.

When Garrigue left Leipzig to visit friends, before returning to the United States, Masaryk proposed marriage to her in a letter, and she immediately agreed to marry him. After arriving back in New York, she was injured during the winter of 1878 in a carriage accident with runaway horses. By the time Masaryk reached her side, she had recovered, and they were married on 15 March 1878 in the double living room of her Bronx home. Rudolph Garrigue was not opposed to his new son-in-law, who had taken Garrigue as his own middle name, but he was shocked when Masaryk asked him for financial assistance. He reluctantly agreed to furnish his daughter with a monthly allowance to supplement what Masaryk would receive from a poor-paying university teaching job in Vienna.

Charlotte Masaryk remained in Vienna until 1882. That year she and her children, who eventually numbered five (although one died in babyhood), joined her husband in Prague, Bohemia, which was part of the Austro-Hungarian Empire. Because Thomas Masaryk was prominent in the movement to restore the Czech language, he had been hired the year before to teach philosophy in the half of Charles University, where Czech was to be used. Along with her husband, Masaryk became a striking personality in Prague. She learned the Czech language, became an ardent patriot, and studied Czech literature, music, and history. Even though her reading gave her an excellent literary background, music remained her first love. Her research and writing championed and popularized the music of

Bedrich Smetana, the Czech nationalist composer, to the extent that a post–World War I edition of his works was dedicated to her as the "true friend of Smetana's genius" (McKinney, p. 89). During ten "fairy tale come true" summers, with their children in the country, Charlotte and her husband continued their research and writing (Alice Masaryk, p. 40). At first these summers were spent in Klobouky, Thomas Masaryk's parental hometown in Moravia, and later on a farm in Bystrička.

Considering the birth of Czechoslovakia more important than her own comfort or the needs of her family, Masaryk twice refused to consider her husband's decision to immigrate to the United States. The first of these crises followed the overwhelming hostility toward him after his 1884 refusal to accept forgeries of ancient manuscripts perpetrated to bolster Czech identity. The second one followed his 1890 attack on anti-Semitism when Leopold Hilsner, a poor Jew accused of committing a ritual murder, was condemned to death. When his stand in the Hilsner case made her husband a target both in the university and in the country at large, Masaryk accompanied him to his classroom, knowing that her presence would shield him from being murdered, and when angry anti-Semitic students demonstrated outside her home, threatening her family, she addressed them until they dispersed.

Concerned with social problems, Masaryk worked in the Czech women's movement and in 1905 joined the Social Democratic party rather than her husband's Realist party. The next year she demonstrated with workers demanding free and equal suffrage and the secret ballot. Her tutoring made her husband "the most influential male intellectual involved with the woman's movement" (Skilling, p. 127). He later declared, "I am only a peddler of my wife's opinions" on women's rights and admitted that she had authored *Polygyny and Monogyny*, one of his major statements favoring equality for women (Skilling, p. 115). Their older daughter Alice was among Prague's first generation of girls to receive a higher education.

Until World War I Masaryk worked with her reformer husband to educate the Czech people for democracy by helping them overcome their prejudice and intolerance. "Without her," he later declared, "I wouldn't have had a clear sense of . . . my political task" (Polák, p. 42). In 1891 he was elected by the Young Czech party to the Austro-Hungarian parliament in Vienna, where he served two years before resigning. In 1907 Masaryk and her husband came to the United States to attend the International Congress of Religious Liberals in Boston, and that same year he was returned to the Vienna parliament by the Realist party. Thomas Masaryk's opposition to the aggressive Austro-Hungarian policy in the Balkans made the incubating "Czech nation great and noble throughout the world" (Skilling, p. 141). By proving that Austro-Hungarian officials had forged documents to justify the empire's annexation of Bosnia-Herzegovina he became internationally renowned and locally reviled.

When World War I broke out in 1914 Thomas Masaryk escaped to Italy and then to Switzerland with his younger daughter Olga. After declaring war on the Austro-Hungarian Empire on 6 July 1915 in the name of the not-yet-founded Czech nation, he joined the Allied powers and worked in other countries to gain recognition for the Czechoslovakian National Council. Back in Prague, Charlotte Masaryk was persecuted by Austro-Hungarian authorities, who had sentenced her husband to a traitor's death. Under constant surveillance, she purposely did not know where his writings were hidden nor did she accept news about his work abroad, lest those bringing her information be imprisoned. On the theory that they knew the whereabouts of Thomas Masaryk's writings, Alice Masaryk and Hana Benešová, the wife of Masaryk's associate Eduard Beneš, were questioned for two weeks in Prague and then sent to a Vienna prison, where Alice was incarcerated for eight months before American friends gained her release.

During that fearful period when she was harassed in Prague, Charlotte Masaryk, a lone, ill woman suffering from heart disease and depression, maintained her courage. Despite grief over her older son Herbert (who had died from typhus while working in a Galician refugee camp) and worry over her younger son Ján (who was captured while attempting to flee to the United States and was drafted into the army), she gave Alice, when she was in prison, "the strength to go on" by writing her nearly a hundred wonderfully supportive letters (Alice Masaryk, p. 70).

In 1918 the new nation that Thomas Masaryk had fathered was recognized by France, England, and the United States. Two years later under its new constitution, he was elected its first president and reelected in 1927 and 1934. Too ill to participate fully in the victory she had helped win, Masaryk died at their summer home in Lany, near Prague.

Her husband realized that Charlotte Masaryk's uncompromising political positions and her utter truthfulness greatly influenced his own development. She moderated the scope of his original designs, making it possible for him to accomplish concrete reforms. "Neither golden letters nor marble monuments," Czech poet Oldra Sedlmayer declared, "can express the moral contribution, the price in human suffering which that daughter of free America paid in the life and work of our president" (McKinney, pp. 91–92).

• Alice Garrigue Masaryk, *Alice Garrigue Masaryk, 1879–1966: Her Life as Recorded in Her Own Words and by Her Friends* (1980), contains many of her mother's letters and is an excellent source, as is Stanislav Pólak, *Charlotta Garrigue Masaryková* (1992). H. Gordon Skilling, *T. G. Masaryk: Against the Current, 1882–1914* (1994), has considerable information. See also "Brooklyn's First Lady of Czechoslovakia," in Donald W. McKinney, *When the Pulpit Starts to Creak* (1992); Roman Szporluk, *The Political Thought of Thomas G. Masaryk* (1981); George J. Kovtun, *Masaryk and America: Testimony of a Relationship* (1988); and George J.

Kovtun, ed., *The Spirit of Thomas G. Masaryk (1850–1937): An Anthology* (1990). A short obituary is in the *New York Times*, 14 May 1923.

OLIVE HOOGENBOOM

MASCHKE, Heinrich (24 Oct. 1853–1 Mar. 1908), mathematician, was born in Breslau, Germany, the son of a prominent pharmacist. Maschke entered the University of Heidelberg in 1872, having already resolved to study mathematics. He attended lectures there for several semesters, taking calculus from the noted mathematician, Leo Königsberger, before the mandatory year of service in the Prussian army necessitated his return to Breslau. He continued his studies at his hometown university, and, after his tour of duty, moved on to Germany's premier institution for mathematical research, the University of Berlin. There, he studied with several of the leading mathematicians of the nineteenth century, most notably, Karl Weierstrass, Leopold Kronecker, and Ernst Eduard Kummer. In 1878 Maschke passed the state teachers' examination, a necessary prerequisite for a career in secondary teaching, and in 1880 he earned a doctoral degree in mathematics from Göttingen University.

Because salaried German university positions were at this time in short supply, Maschke fell back on his Gymnasium (or secondary school) teaching credential and in 1880 secured a position in mathematics at the Luisenstädtische Gymnasium in Berlin. By all accounts, Maschke proved effective in the classroom, but the twenty-hour-a-week schedule and the thoroughly elementary level of the instruction ultimately convinced him that he should seek another career.

This conviction grew stronger after the 1886–1887 academic year, which he spent on sabbatical in Göttingen. Together with his friend, the mathematician Oskar Bolza, he attended Felix Klein's lectures on the theory of algebraic equations. Both Maschke and Bolza also participated in a weekly private seminar at Klein's home, during which they worked to extend some of the ideas Klein had presented in 1884 in his influential work linking the symmetry of the icosahedron to the solution of fifth-degree equations. Maschke, in particular, benefited from Klein's tutelage and published his first important piece of mathematical research in 1887.

Maschke continued his highly calculational work on finding the invariants of various specific types of linear substitution groups after his return to the Luisenstädtische Gymnasium in the fall of 1887 and published further results the following year. By 1889, he had finally decided to leave secondary teaching, still longing for a university position. That year his friend Bolza had left Germany for the United States and had landed a three-year appointment at Clark University. Maschke thought he might follow Bolza's lead, but Bolza cautioned him that academic positions were also scarce in America. In order to prepare himself for a marketable and presumably more satisfying career than secondary teaching, Maschke combined his final year at the Gymnasium (1889–1890) with coursework in electrical engineering in Charlottenburg and, in the winter semester of 1890–1891, completed his technical studies in Darmstadt.

Maschke left for the United States in the spring of 1891 and quickly secured a position as an electrician at the Weston Electric Company in Newark, New Jersey. Just before his departure he married Theresa (maiden name unknown); they had no children. One year later, thanks to the shrewd negotiations of his friend Bolza, Maschke got and accepted an offer of an assistant professorship at the newly founded University of Chicago. When that school opened in October 1892, Maschke joined Bolza and departmental head Eliakim Hastings Moore in what would very quickly become the country's foremost department of mathematics. These three men organized and coordinated the Mathematical Congress held in conjunction with the World's Columbian Exposition in Chicago in 1893, the first international mathematics meeting in America. They also participated actively in the Chicago section of the American Mathematical Society, which they had founded in 1897, and Maschke served on the council of the AMS from 1902 to 1905 and as the organization's vice president in 1907.

In addition to participating in these broader activities, Maschke came into his own as a mathematical researcher during his years at Chicago. After a period of adjustment both to the demands of university teaching and to the rigors of mathematical research, he returned to his previous work on the theory of finite groups of linear substitutions. His new approach, however, was decidedly more abstract, less computational, and more focused on general theorems than on results about specific groups. In particular, he proved the so-called cyclotomic theorem for linear substitution groups in 1898. One year later, he published the demonstration of his most famous result, now known as "Maschke's theorem," a key result in the structure theory of algebras. He spent the years after 1900 principally engaged in a new line of research in differential geometry.

Maschke also enjoyed success in Chicago as a teacher of advanced students. Although only five graduates earned their doctoral degrees under his supervision, virtually every student trained at Chicago took his courses, which ranged in topic from the theories of algebraic surfaces and substitution groups to potential theory and electricity. The slow and deliberate peace at which he delivered his classroom lectures and the care he took to ensure that his auditors were following the mathematics under discussion distinguished markedly his teaching from that of his colleagues Bolza and Moore.

Maschke was promoted to the rank of associate professor in 1896 and to full professor in 1907. He died in Chicago from complications encountered during an emergency surgery. Although neither a prolific nor an exceptionally dynamic mathematician, Maschke made solid and lasting contributions to algebraic research, especially in the closing years of the nineteenth century. Moreover, he joined with colleagues Moore and

Bolza in establishing much of the institutional framework crucial for the support of a research-level community of mathematicians in the United States.

• Assorted correspondence between Maschke and Felix Klein is in the Klein Nachlaß at the Niedersächsische Staats- und Universitätsbibliothek, Göttingen. The papers of William Rainey Harper, first president of the University of Chicago, in the Joseph Regenstein Library at the University of Chicago, contain several letters from Maschke to members of the university. Among Maschke's most important works are "Ueber die quaternäre endliche, lineare Substitutionsgruppe der Borchardt'schen Moduln," *Mathematische Annalen* 30 (1887): 497–515; "Aufstellung des vollen Formensystems einer quaternären Gruppe von 51840 linearen Substitutionen," *Mathematische Annalen* 33 (1888): 317–44; *Mathematical Papers Read at the International Mathematical Congress Held in Connection with the World's Columbian Exposition Chicago 1893*, ed. E. H. Moore et al. (1896); "Ueber den arithmetischen Charakter der Coefficienten der Substitutionen endlicher linearer Substitutionsgruppen" *Mathematische Annalen* 50 (1898): 492–98; and "Beweis des Satzes, dass diejenigen endlichen linearen Substitutionsgruppen, in welchen einige durchgehends verschwindende Coefficienten auftreten, intransitiv sind," *Mathematische Annalen* 52 (1899): 363–68. On Maschke's life, see Oskar Bolza, "Heinrich Maschke: His Life and Work," *Bulletin of the American Mathematical Society* 15 (1908): 85–95, and "Zur Erinnerung an Heinrich Maschke," *Jahresbericht der Deutscher-Mathematiker Vereinigung* 17 (1908): 345–55, both of which include a bibliography and discussion of most of his works. Maschke's role in the early American mathematical community is detailed in Karen Hunger Parshall and David E. Rowe, *The Emergence of the American Mathematical Research Community 1876–1900: J. J. Sylvester, Felix Klein, and E. H. Moore* (1994). An obituary is in the *Chicago Tribune*, 2 Mar. 1908.

KAREN HUNGER PARSHALL

MASLIANSKY, Zvi Hirsch (6 June 1856–11 Jan. 1943), Yiddish preacher, was born in Slutzk, a province of Minsk, Belorussia, the son of Rabbi Chaim Masliansky and Rebecca Popok. He was educated in the yeshivas of Mir and Volozhin and received rabbinical authorization from Rabbis Isaac Elchanan Spektor of Kovno and Samuel Mohilever of Bialystock. In 1875, while still a student, he married Yetta Rubinstein, with whom he had six children.

Masliansky spent the early years of his career as a teacher and preacher in Eastern Europe where he worked enthusiastically for the nascent Zionist cause. While he was the principal of a Jewish school in Pinsk (1882–1890), Masliansky influenced Chaim Weizmann, future first president of Israel. Recognized by his fellow *Hibbat Zion* (Lovers of Zion) colleagues as their most effective orator, Masliansky was encouraged to travel throughout Russia and spread the modern Jewish nationalist creed. In 1894 czarist authorities banished Masliansky for promoting Zionism, and he immigrated to the United States by way of a Western European and English lecture tour. Masliansky soon assumed a pioneering role in the American Zionist movement. From 1900 to 1910 he was a vice president of the Federation of American Zionists and in 1915 was elected to the American Jewish Congress. In

these and other Jewish communal activities Masliansky displayed a willingness unique among Orthodox leaders to cooperate with both Reform and secular Jews.

Masliansky's comfort with, and trust in, Jews with different theological orientations also was evident in his other life-long effort: helping immigrant Jews acculturate without abandoning their basic ancestral traditions. In 1898, when the German-American Jewish leaders who operated the Educational Alliance settlement house on New York City's Lower East Side recognized the cultural heritage of their East European clients, Masliansky readily accepted their call to be the alliance's first Yiddish lecturer. From 1902 to 1905 Masliansky found common cause with Louis Marshall in editing the *Yiddishe Welt* (Jewish World), an organ dedicated to encouraging rapid acculturation, and between 1910 and 1922 he served on the executive committee of the Kehillah (Jewish Community) of New York City, which united Jews of varying ethnic and ideological persuasions to advance the cause of Americanization.

Masliansky was most enthusiastic about efforts specifically within the Orthodox community to synthesize American values and religious traditions. He was a charter member both of the Union of Orthodox Jewish Congregations of America (1898–) and of the ephemeral Jewish Ministers Association of America (1916–c. 1920), organizations dedicated to making Jewish religious services and education more popular among Americanized immigrants. In the 1920s Masliansky expressed his dedication to Jewish education through his leadership of the Yeshiva of Borough Park. He died at his home in Brooklyn, New York.

• Masliansky's views can be best studied through two volumes of his Yiddish orations, *Masliansky's Droshos fir Shabbosim un Yomim Tovim* (1908–1909), published in English as *Sermons by Reverend Zevi Hirsch Masliansky* (1926), and his memoirs, *Masliansky's Zichrones for Fertzig Yahr Leben un Kemfen* (1924), published in English as *Masliansky: Forty Years of Life and Struggle* (1924). The most reliable biographical sketch of Masliansky is based on information that he provided. See "Biographical Sketches of Jews Prominent in the Professions, etc. in the United States," *American Jewish Year Book* (1904–1905), p. 152.

JEFFREY S. GUROCK

MASLOW, Abraham Harold (1 Apr. 1908–8 June 1970), psychologist and humanistic psychologist, was born in New York City, the son of Rose Schlosky and Samuel Maslow, Russian-Jewish immigrants from Kiev. His father was in the barrel-repair business. Maslow described his shy, depressed, lonely, and self-reflective childhood as neurotic. He felt unloved by his parents and oppressed by anti-Semitism in school. He married a cousin, Bertha Goodman, in 1928; they had two children. He earned a B.A. (1930), M.A. (1931), and Ph.D. (1934) in psychology from the University of Wisconsin–Madison.

Maslow was a teaching fellow in psychology (1934–1935) at his alma mater. Having failed to secure a regular faculty position because of the depression and latent anti-Semitism in universities, he worked as a research assistant (Carnegie fellow) for Edward L. Thorndike at Teachers College, Columbia University (1935–1937). From 1937 to 1951 he was associate professor at Brooklyn College. In 1951 he was instrumental in the establishment of the psychology department at Brandeis University, which he chaired for ten years. Next, Maslow was a visiting fellow at Western Behavioral Sciences Institute in La Jolla, California (1961–1962) and received a fellowship from the Fund for Advancement of Education for 1967–1968. During his last year, 1969–1970, he was a resident fellow at the W. Price Laughlin Charitable Foundation in Menlo Park, California.

Behavioristic studies of animals permeated Maslow's graduate research, which was carried out under the supervision of Harry Harlow at the primate laboratory of the University of Wisconsin–Madison. His early research interests in the emotion of disgust in dogs and in learning among primates led to a doctoral dissertation titled "The Role of Dominance in the Social and Sexual Behavior of Infra-human Primates" (1936), in which he proved that primates dominate one another by visual intimidation, not physical aggression.

Maslow's postdoctoral encounters in New York City, during World War II, with the neo-psychoanalysts Karen Horney, Alfred Adler, and Erich Fromm; the anthropologist Ruth Benedict; the Gestalt psychologists Max Wertheimer and Kurt Koffka; and other European intellectuals who fled the war, such as Kurt Goldstein, had a profound impact on his intellectual development.

During his first years of teaching at Brooklyn College and upon the inspiration of Adler, Maslow shifted the focus of his research on the psychological phenomenon of dominance from primates to college women. He realized that the image of human nature presented by behavioristic psychology and psychoanalysis was overly pessimistic and distorted primarily because of its overreliance on pathological case studies. Thus Maslow came to concentrate his life research on what he thought were rather psychologically healthy human beings. Under the influence of the Gestalt concept of holism and the growth hypothesis of Kurt Goldstein, and focusing on human motivation, he formulated a humanistic view of human nature and studied its implications for education, management, social psychology, ethics, and philosophy of psychology. In so doing Maslow spearheaded a research initiative and laid a theoretical framework that, on his suggestion, came to be known as the "third force" in psychology (the other forces being behaviorism and psychoanalysis) or humanistic psychology. In the late 1950s and 1960s he was also instrumental in the institutionalization of humanistic and transpersonal psychologies; the latter studied mystical experiences, meditation, spiritual issues, unitive consciousness, transcendence of the self, and related topics and experiences.

Although Maslow was recognized in the early 1950s as a talented experimental and comparative psychologist, as he began exploring unconventional psychological subjects he was ostracized by the psychological community. Blaming this situation on the dominance of behavioristic approaches, he found it increasingly harder to publish his research. As a result he began contacting like-minded discontented psychologists who experienced the same difficulties and in 1954 compiled a list of about 125 names for the purpose of exchanging mimeographed copies of their writings. Over the years the mailing list grew, and in the early 1960s the people on this list became the first subscribers to the *Journal of Humanistic Psychology*, which Maslow and Anthony Sutich founded in 1961. In 1962 the Association for Humanistic Psychology was established, also with the help of Sutich. Discontented with the theory and practice of orthodox behavioristic psychology, this group of psychologists emerged, under Maslow's leadership, as distinct within the profession, seeking the construction of a separate set of theories and research, that is a humanistic psychological paradigm. In so doing they contributed to the dismantling of the monopoly of behaviorism over midcentury American psychology.

Maslow was not the founder of humanistic psychology in the same sense that, for example, Freud founded psychoanalysis. There were various trends within humanistic psychology, such as the psychoanalytical, existential, phenomenological, hermeneutical, Gestalt, and other minor and more esoteric perspectives. The growth hypothesis view of human nature of Maslow and Carl Rogers, another founder of humanistic psychology, however, served as an early catalyst for the constitution of the humanistic school or system of psychology.

Central to Maslow's understanding of human nature was the assertion that the organism contained an instinctoid inner core holding in potential the unfolding of the person's process of becoming. He was, however, careful to avoid the pitfalls of biological determinism—a psychological perspective that he extensively criticized. The organismic potential for growth was only a sort of biological "raw material" that had to be nurtured by the cultural environment and developed and actualized by the idiosyncrasies of the individual's will and choices. Culture in this context should foster synergetic conditions that encourage a process of self-discovery and subjective actualization of the instinctoid human nature. A prime subject of study in psychology, suggested Maslow, should be the values that induce "good-growth-toward-self-actualization." The conviction that human nature is fundamentally trustworthy, self-governing, and self-protective permeates Maslow's psychological thought. If only provided with an environment that fosters self-discovery and freedom of expression, people will grow in the right direction.

The failure to satisfy the needs associated with the instinctoid urges of the inner core of the human organism results in physical and psychological sickness and frustration. Such sickness and frustration, in turn, are responsible for what is so-called evil behavior. If the first and most basic physiological needs related to personal and species survival are not satisfied, then all subsequent needs are pushed aside. If fulfilled, however, higher needs, such as the need for safety and security, love and belongingness, and self-esteem arise. At the top of Maslow's hierarchy of needs is self-actualization: the desire to fully actualize one's potential, and encompassing deep curiosity about natural wonders and the meaning of our existence, the need for meaningful work, responsibility, creativity, and justice. Toward the end of his life Maslow believed that there was yet a higher, transcendental need centered on cosmic mysteries and evident in the realm of religion and symbols where individuals transcend themselves. In this context Maslow's research led him to conclude that self-actualizers often have peak-experiences or moments of intense bliss and intuitive understanding that significantly transform their lives. Upon this realization he was instrumental in the establishment of transcendental psychology.

That Maslow did eventually attain a high degree of professional recognition is indicated by the positions he held in professional societies and the editorial functions he performed. He was president of the Massachusetts, the New England, and the American (1967–1968) psychological associations and also president of the Personality and Social Psychology and the Esthetics divisions of the American Psychological Association. He served on the editorial boards of sixteen scholarly journals, including the *Journal of Individual Psychology*, the *Journal of Humanistic Psychology*, the *Journal of Creative Behavior*, and the *Review of Existential Psychology and Psychiatry*. Abraham Maslow died in Menlo Park, California.

• Maslow's papers are in the Archives for the History of American Psychology at the University of Akron, Ohio. Useful archival material may also be found in the Humanistic Psychology Archives at the University of California, Santa Barbara. Maslow's extensive bibliography is in the *Journal of Humanistic Psychology* 10, no. 2 (1970): 98–110. Jammy Scheele compiled an exhaustive index to that bibliography in *Registers Referring to the Complete Works by A. H. Maslow* (1978), published in Delft, the Netherlands; a copy is available at the University of Wisconsin–Madison. Maslow's *Motivation and Personality* (1954; rev. ed., 1970), his most famous work and now a classic in psychology, comprises the seminal papers of his views on motivation, including "A Theory of Human Motivation," first published in 1943. In *Toward a Psychology of Being* (1962) he placed his thought in the context of the emerging humanistic paradigm in psychology. *Religion, Values and Peak-Experiences* (1964) expanded this paradigm to the understanding of religious experiences and the field of ethics and digressed into the phenomena of peak-experiences often associated with self-actualization. He ventured into the field of management and industrial psychology in *Eupsychian Management* (1965) and into the field of the philosophy of science, with a focus on psychology, in *The Psychology of Science* (1966). *The Farther Reaches of Human Nature* (1971), published posthumously, consists of essays published individually during the 1960s on the subjects of health and pathology, creativeness, values, education, society, cognition, and transcendental psychology. Also published posthumously was his diary, *The Journals of Abraham Maslow*, ed. Richard J. Lowry (1979).

Edward Hoffman, *The Right to Be Human: A Biography of Abraham Maslow* (1988), is authoritative. Other biographical references are Richard J. Lowry, *A. H. Maslow: An Intellectual Portrait* (1973); Bertha G. Maslow, comp., *Abraham H. Maslow: A Memorial Volume* (1972); Frank G. Goble, *The Third Force: The Psychology of Abraham Maslow* (1970); Willard B. Frick, *Humanistic Psychology: Interviews with Maslow, Murphy and Rogers* (1972); and Roy J. deCarvalho, "A History of the 'Third Force' in Psychology," *Journal of Humanistic Psychology* 30 (1990): 22–44. Colin Wilson, *New Pathways in Psychology: Maslow and the Post-Freudian Revolution* (1972), places Maslow's humanistic psychology in the context of the history of western psychology, as do deCarvalho's two volumes, *The Growth Hypothesis in Psychology: The Humanistic Psychology of Abraham Maslow and Carl Rogers* (1991) and *The Founders of Humanistic Psychology* (1991).

ROY J. deCARVALHO

MASON, Alpheus Thomas (18 Sept. 1899–31 Oct. 1989), political scientist, biographer, and author, was born at Snow Hill on Maryland's eastern shore, the son of Herbert William Mason and Emma Leslie Hancock, farmers. Although lacking in formal training, Mason's father was a student of life and politics and pressed education on his son. In particular, he pushed his son to excel as a public speaker and helped him to win several oratorical prizes in school. Mason's mother had a lasting influence on her son. Although she only finished seventh grade, like his father, she was a first-rate teacher and a perfectionist through and through. She instilled in her son the idea that nothing was "good enough" until it reached the acme of perfection. Her persistence and perfectionism were traits that her son inherited and admired.

Mason received his A.B. from Dickinson College in 1920. While at Dickinson he became friends with Professor Patterson, with whose encouragement he wrote a long paper and qualified for an honors course. Mason's papers contained references to constitutional interpretation, stimulated by a 1914 book by Johns Hopkins University president Frank Goodman. Mason also took a course in government using a textbook written by W. F. Willoughby, the second McCormick Professor of Jurisprudence at Princeton. He then entered Princeton University as a graduate student in the Department of Economics but gravitated almost immediately to Professor Edward S. Corwin's course in constitutional interpretation. Before the end of his first year he claimed to have "discovered my career." Although Mason became a protégé of Corwin, a man whose mind he said was "the best I had ever encountered," Mason wrote in later years that "Corwin's primary concern was with institutions, mine with men. He wrote exclusively with public documents. My main interest was in private papers, including those of Supreme Court justices."

Mason was awarded an A.M. from Princeton in 1921. After receiving a Ph.D. from Princeton in history and politics in 1923, he taught political science for two years at Duke University. His Ph.D. dissertation was published as *Organized Labor and the Law with Special Reference to the Sherman and Clayton Acts* (1925).

Mason returned in 1925 to Princeton, where he joined the faculty. He held the prestigious McCormick Professorship, ranked among the most influential professorships in Princeton's history, until his retirement in 1968, when he was named McCormick Professor of Jurisprudence Emeritus. In 1934 he married Christine Este Gibbons; they had one child.

Mason, a prolific writer, was fascinated by the law and the influence of law and judges, especially those of the U.S. Supreme Court, on American life. His first biography, *Brandeis: A Free Man's Life* (1946), on Supreme Court Justice Louis D. Brandeis, was on the bestseller list for five months in 1947. In 1956 his biography of Chief Justice Harlan Fiske Stone, *Harlan Fiske Stone: Pillar of the Law*, was awarded the American Liberty and Justice Award in the field of history and biography and earned Mason a Guggenheim Fellowship. In 1965 he published *William Howard Taft: Chief Justice*, which also made the bestseller list. In reviewing Mason's biography of Taft, John P. Frank, himself a Supreme Court biographer, observed that "the book is a remarkable achievement for Professor Mason, who stands forth as the country's foremost judicial biographer. . . . This intriguing and thoroughly workmanlike job makes Mason the only major biographer of three Justices in American history. This could have been done only by prodigious effort and skill, and puts every lawyer, historian, and political scientist deeply into his debt" (*Michigan Law Review* [Dec. 1965]).

Mason wrote or shared the writing of at least twenty-two books on law, political science, and the Constitution, including *American Constitutional Law*, with William M. Beaney (1954); *Security through Freedom* (1955); *In Quest of Freedom*, with Richard H. Leach (1959); *The Supreme Court in a Free Society*, with Beaney (1959); *The Supreme Court: Palladium of Freedom* (1962); *Free Government in the Making* (1965); and *The Supreme Court from Taft to Burger* (1979).

As the nation's foremost judicial biographer Mason received numerous awards. In 1957 he was awarded a $5,000 prize in history and biography from the American Library Association and from 1960 to 1963 was the recipient of a Rockefeller Foundation Study Award. He was made a McCosh Faculty Fellow by Princeton in 1963–1964.

After his retirement from Princeton, Mason taught at fifteen different institutions between 1968 and 1980, including Cambridge University in England, Hebrew University in Jerusalem, Dartmouth, Yale, Harvard, and Johns Hopkins. He received several honorary degrees, including one from Princeton. In 1974 the Princeton University Alumni Council awarded its Outstanding Alumni Award for service to Princeton to Mason, the first faculty member to be so honored.

A fellow of the American Academy of Arts and Sciences, Mason was also a member of the American Political Science Association, serving as its vice president; Phi Beta Kappa; Sigma Alpha Epsilon; and the Presbyterian church. A recognized perfectionist, Mason delivered his last lecture at Princeton in 1968 to an audience composed of a full enrollment of his students, as well as visitors, undergraduates, colleagues, and local Princeton residents, and received a standing ovation that did not end until after he left the room.

Mason died at his home in Princeton. Each of his biographies of the three U.S. Supreme Court justices stands out as preeminent in the field of American judicial biography, as they did during his lifetime, marking Mason as America's foremost judicial biographer.

• Mason's works not cited above include *The Supreme Court from Taft to Warren* (1958), *The States Rights Debate: Antifederalism and the Constitution* (1964), and *Corwin on the Constitution: Essays in American Constitutional History*, with Gerald Garvey (1964). An obituary is in the *New York Times*, 1 Nov. 1989.

EUGENE C. GERHART

MASON, Charles (24 Oct. 1804–25 Feb. 1882), lawyer and jurist, was born in Pompey, New York, the son of Chauncey Mason and Esther Dodge, farmers. He entered the U.S. Military Academy at West Point in 1825 and graduated in 1829 first in a class whose members included Robert E. Lee and Joseph E. Johnston. Assigned to the Engineering Corps, Mason served as an assistant professor of engineering at West Point for two years. In 1831 he resigned from the army and read law. He practiced for two years at Newburgh, New York, and then for two years in New York City. There he contributed to the *New York Evening Post*, serving for a year as managing editor when William Cullen Bryant was in Europe. In 1836 Mason traveled briefly in the West, and in April 1837 Governor Henry Dodge appointed him as public prosecutor for Des Moines County, Wisconsin Territory. After his marriage to Angelica Gear in August 1837, he moved to Burlington, Iowa, where he bought and managed a large farm. Devoted to his wife and family, Mason suffered several personal tragedies. Two of his three children died in infancy, and two of his grandchildren also succumbed to childhood diseases.

Following the organization of the territory of Iowa in 1838, President Martin Van Buren appointed Mason the chief justice of the territorial supreme court, and he held this position until several months after the admission of Iowa to the Union in December 1846. He presided over a variety of cases, the case load growing parallel to the rapid increase in population, and as the chief legal officer of the territory he had great latitude in shaping the territory's legal code. Of the opinions that he wrote, the most important concerned the legal status of a Missouri slave, Ralph (later Ralph Montgomery), who sued for his freedom by virtue of his residence in Iowa Territory on the grounds that the Northwest Ordinance prohibited slavery in the territory. Mason's opinion relied on the Missouri Compromise of 1820 and affirmed that, when Ralph became a resident of Iowa, his owner lost the right of property in him. In the case *In re Ralph* (1839), Mason concluded for the court, "When the slave-owner illegally restrains a human being of his liberty, it is proper that the laws, which should extend equal protection to men of all colors and conditions, should exert their remedial interposition."

Among Mason's many other opinions, two are noteworthy. In the first, he dealt with the question of squatters on the public lands. When Congress organized the territory of Iowa, perhaps as many as 25,000 people without title were settled on the public domain, and accordingly innumerable land transactions among these people were of doubtful legality. In his opinion in *Hill v. Smith et al.* (1840), upholding the legality of these transactions, Mason wrote that Congress could never have intended to "disturb the peaceable and industrious husbandman whose labor was adding so much to the public wealth, changing the barren wilderness into fertile fields, and calling into almost magic existence whole states and territories, whose prosperity and power are constantly adding so much to the strength and glory of the nation."

This same flexible and commonsense attitude toward the law characterized his views on the technicalities of the law. While he affirmed that the law should give every accused the right to prove innocence, he did not intend the law to "open an aperture through which guilt and innocence may alike escape with impunity." In espousing such views of the "common sense of mankind," he reaffirmed an interpretation of the law associated with the frontier at the expense of the details embodied in the precedent of the English common law.

When Iowa became a state in 1846, Governor Ansel Briggs appointed Mason head of a commission to draft the first code of the state. The Code of 1851, including as it did some 3,367 sections printed in 469 pages, was a tribute to Mason's skill and knowledge. The code embodied his views as chief justice of the territorial supreme court: direct and clear language and common sense, mixed with a high respect for the law. One of the striking features of the code was its organization based not on alphabetical arrangement but on an analysis of the subject matter of law. This structure in four parts—public law, private law, civil procedure, and criminal law—was preserved in subsequent codes.

At the close of his service for the territory and the state, Mason was elected county judge of Des Moines County in 1851 and practiced law in Keokuk. He was appointed federal commissioner of patents in 1853, resigning in 1857 to become a member of the first Iowa State Board of Education. Mason gradually shifted his legal career to Washington, D.C., where he became a prominent patent lawyer. Although he flirted with politics, as a Democrat in a world that was becoming increasingly associated with the new Republican party, Mason found himself out of favor with the electorate. He declined the Democratic nomination for governor of Iowa in 1861, lost an election for a position on the state supreme court, and was defeated for the governorship in 1867. As a loyal antiwar Democrat, he served on the National Central Committee in 1864 and was a delegate to the nominating conventions of 1868 and 1872. Following his retirement from political life, his main interest was the specie issue, in connection with which he wrote *A Plan for Specie Resumption* (1874), advocating a restoration of the gold dollar, albeit adjusted for inflation. He remained convinced that the president and Congress would eventually embrace his views on the matter. After his wife's death in 1873, Mason lived with his daughter, Mollie, who married George Collier Remey, a naval officer.

Mason was more than six feet in height, thin, and of erect bearing, as befitted a graduate of the U.S. Military Academy. His mind was orderly and deliberate, appropriate to his training and career as a lawyer. He tended to reticence, but with his family and close friends he was cheerful and possessed of a sense of humor. He was abstemious in personal habits, never drank, and did not smoke. He was careful of his money, but at the same time he assisted many young people in need, including artists. Mason traveled widely throughout Western Europe, and his letters convey an inquiring mind concerned with the fine arts and literature. In declining health, he spent the last years of his life with his daughter's family in Washington and on their farm outside Burlington, Iowa. He died at his home in Iowa.

• The State Historical Society of Iowa has several Mason diaries. Among the printed sources, the most important are George H. Yewell, "Reminiscences of Charles Mason," *Annals of Iowa*, 3d ser., 5 (1901): 161–76, 251–71; Emlin McClain, "Charles Mason—Iowa's First Jurist," *Annals of Iowa*, 3d ser., 4 (1900): 595–609; and Yewell, "The Yewell Portrait of Charles Mason," *Annals of Iowa*, 3d ser., 2 (1895): 161–73. An obituary is in the *Burlington Hawkeye*, 26 Feb. 1882.

MALCOLM J. ROHRBOUGH

MASON, Charlotte Louise (18 May 1854–15 Apr. 1946), patron of writers and artists, was born in Princeton, New Jersey, the daughter of Peter Quick and Phoebe Van der Veer, farmers. Eighteen months after her mother's death in 1864, her father married Catherine Jane Pumyea.

Nothing of Mason's life is known until her marriage in 1886 to a widower named Rufus Osgood Mason, a prominent New York physician twenty-four years her senior. Although often listed in the *Social Register* and *Elite Directory*, the Masons shared views that were somewhat unorthodox for the time. Mason's husband was an early experimenter in the use of hypnosis and telepathy for medical treatment, influenced in part by his wife's interest in mystical and psychic phenomena. Their only child was a daughter from Dr. Mason's first marriage.

Four years after her husband died in 1903, Mason's sole published work, "The Passing of a Prophet: A True Narrative of Death and Life," appeared in the *North American Review*. With its references to the "sex ideal" and the "womb of the Earth-Mother," and its assertion that earthly existence is but "a formative, experimental phase" in "preparation for the rebirth into a larger life," the article elucidated some of Mason's more unconventional beliefs.

Widowed at forty-eight but extremely well-to-do, Mason soon established herself as a benefactor and patron, seeking to assist needy writers and artists, particularly those involved in some aspect of the primitive. Her first known protégé was Natalie Curtis, one of the earliest ethnomusicologists to study and record the music and songs of Native Americans. Curtis did not acknowledge Mason's patronage when her research was first published as *The Indians' Book* (1907), perhaps because Mason had insisted on anonymity. But a later edition, one year after Curtis's accidental death in 1921, paid tribute to "Mrs. Osgood Mason, whose help made possible the original undertaking, and without whose continued devotion the present edition could never have been accomplished." Although some have claimed that Mason also "lived for years among the Plains Indians," there is no evidence that she ever gave up the comforts of her midtown Manhattan apartment for any such extended periods of time.

It is probably no coincidence that when Curtis shifted her attention from Native Americans to African Americans—to research Negro spirituals and secular songs at the Hampton Institute—Mason was doing likewise. Working through Alain Locke, a professor of philosophy at Howard University and editor of the influential anthology, *The New Negro* (1925), Mason soon established herself as "Godmother" (a title she relished) to many of the most promising writers and artists of the Harlem Renaissance.

In 1927 Langston Hughes, for instance, was ushered by Locke into Mason's penthouse on Park Avenue, where he was captivated by (as he later wrote) "one of the most delightful women I had ever met, witty and charming, kind and sympathetic, very old and white-haired, but amazingly modern in her ideas, in her knowledge of books and the theater, of Harlem, and of everything then taking place in the world" (Hughes, p. 312). Mason was similarly attracted to Hughes and agreed to pay the writer a monthly stipend of $150 in addition to numerous other benefits such as packages of food, an apartment in New Jersey, theater tickets, evening clothes, the use of her limousine, writing paper and the services of a typist, and even financial support for his foster brother. In return, Hughes was expected to correspond with "Godmother" almost daily, serve occasionally as her escort, and follow her directions about what culture he should absorb and what literature he should produce. By December 1930, however, tensions that had been building between patron and protégé came to a head. Mason argued that Hughes should write only about topics relating to what she saw as his "great link with the primitive"; he wanted to move in a more political direction. The sundering of their relationship proved so traumatic for Hughes that even ten years later he would become physically ill at the thought of their last half-hour together.

Mason's patronage of Zora Neale Hurston followed a similar pattern. Introduced by Locke in 1927, Hurston received $200 a month from Mason as well as the use of an automobile and movie camera to collect African-American folklore in the South, and later she was given the use of an apartment in New Jersey in which to do her writing. During a five-year period, before Hurston severed her ties with Mason in 1932, she received approximately $15,000 in financial assistance. In return, Hurston was required (like Hughes) never to reveal the identity of her patron and was likewise expected to maintain a close spiritual and psychic bond with her "Godmother."

Other protégés, all procured for Mason by Locke, included novelist Claude McKay, folklorist Arthur Huff Fauset, musician Hall Johnson, painters Aaron Douglas and Miguel Covarrubias, sculptor Richmond Barthé, and Louise Thompson, a writer and educator who served for a time as secretary to both Hughes and Hurston. Mason also helped to underwrite the Negro Art Institute and Harlem Museum of African Art. It is estimated that her financial contributions to the writers and artists of the Harlem Renaissance totaled $75,000.

Although Mason has been praised for sharing her wealth, her motives and her obsession with the primitive have been criticized by some as essentially racist. According to this interpretation, Mason condescendingly treated her protégés like children: she commanding from an antique throne-like chair, they sitting uncomfortably on footstools. However, it should also be noted that Mason's interest in Native Americans and African Americans seems consistent with her earlier beliefs in the mystical world. Contending that whites had been corrupted through over-civilization and the oppression of other races, Mason genuinely sought spiritual nourishment and inspiration from the "native harmony" of American Indians and blacks.

Increasingly debilitated by arthritis, Mason relied heavily for many years on two close family friends, the poet Katherine Garrison Chapin Biddle and her younger sister, Cornelia Van Auken Chapin, a sculptor. When Mason became unable to write legibly, they maintained her correspondence and other matters. After falling and injuring herself in February 1933, Mason entered New York Hospital, where she had a room overlooking the East River. She remained in the hospital until her death thirteen years later.

• Several of Mason's notebooks and extensive correspondence with Alain Locke and Zora Neale Hurston (and to a lesser extent, Claude McKay and Aaron Douglas) are in the Alain L. Locke Papers, Moorland-Springarn Research Center, Howard University. Some of Mason's letters to and from Langston Hughes are in the James Langston Hughes Papers, James Weldon Johnson Collection of Negro Arts and Letters, Yale University. The most detailed information on her life is in the autobiographies and biographies of the major Harlem Renaissance figures she patronized. See, for example, Langston Hughes, *The Big Sea* (1940); Zora Neale Hurston, *Dust*

Tracks on a Road (1942); Faith Berry, *Langston Hughes: Before and Beyond Harlem* (1983); Arnold Rampersad, *The Life of Langston Hughes* (2 vols., 1986–1988); and Robert E. Hemenway, *Zora Neale Hurston: A Literary Biography* (1977). Other useful sources include Ardie Sue Myers, "Relations of a Godmother: Patronage during the Harlem Renaissance" (M.A. thesis, George Washington Univ., 1981); David Levering Lewis, *When Harlem Was in Vogue* (1981); and Ralph D. Story, "Patronage and the Harlem Renaissance: You Get What You Pay For," *College Language Association Journal* 32 (1989): 284–95. Mason achieved much of the anonymity and obscurity that she seems to have sought, even avoiding a published obituary in the *New York Times*.

JAMES I. DEUTSCH

MASON, Daniel Gregory (20 Nov. 1873–4 Dec. 1953), composer, writer, and teacher, was born in Brookline, Massachusetts, the son of Henry Mason, president and co-founder of Mason and Hamlin Company, and Helen Augusta Palmer. The youngest of four sons, Mason spent an idyllic childhood in a comfortable suburban home so saturated with music that it became for him, as he reflected in his autobiography, "the most vivid thing in the world." When Mason was twelve he moved with his family to Boston and in 1891 entered Harvard University, graduating in 1895.

After a brief tour of Europe the summer following his graduation, Mason moved to New York City, where he pursued studies in composition with Percy Goetschius, orchestration with George W. Chadwick, and piano with Arthur Whiting. While in New York, Mason fell under the influence of his uncle William Mason, a pianist of considerable renown, and through him made a number of distinguished musical acquaintances, including the composer Edward MacDowell.

In 1896 financial pressures as well as fragile health forced Mason to leave New York. The ensuing six years proved bleak ones for Mason personally and professionally as he sought to reconcile his practical need for an income with his long-held desire to pursue a life as a composer. From 1902 to 1904 he taught English at Princeton University. In the end Mason combined his literary and musical skills and began to write about music. His first book, a compilation of previously published articles, *From Grieg to Brahms*, was published in 1902. It led to further work as a public lecturer for the New York Board of Education, which became for him a lifelong project to educate the general public about music.

Mason married Mary Lord Taintor, his eldest brother's former wife, in October 1904. Although Taintor had four children from her first marriage, she and Mason had no children together. Mason's second book, *Beethoven and His Forerunners*, was published in 1904, and *The Romantic Composers* appeared two years later. His appointment in 1905 as lecturer in the music department at Columbia University as well as his post as editor of a new magazine, *Masters in Music*, finally afforded Mason financial stability.

The summer of 1907 found Mason in a position to take a brief break from teaching and lecturing and to turn his attention toward composition. With his Quartet for Piano and Strings, written over a succession of summers between 1907 and 1911, Mason believed he was at last on his way to a life as a composer.

In 1910 Mason was elevated to the rank of assistant professor at Columbia University, where he stayed until he retired thirty-two years later. At his wife's urging, he took a sabbatical leave in 1913 to study composition in France with Vincent d'Indy, the only contemporary French composer whom Mason admired and whom he had met on a previous trip to Europe in 1901.

Mason's writings during this new period of creativity reflect his compositional concerns. In *Contemporary Composers* (1918) he included a chapter on music in the United States and outlined the possibility of using folk music as the basis for a national school of composition, an idea he was later to reject. He outlined his creative principles of independence, spontaneity, workmanship, originality, universality, and fellowship in a series of six lectures, published in 1925 as *Artistic Ideals*. Shortly thereafter, between 1926 and 1928, Mason wrote what was to become his best-known composition, the festival overture *Chanticleer*. Ironically, its exuberant character makes it also his most stylistically uncharacteristic work. The majority of Mason's music reflects a consistently conservative composer who sought to emulate the restraint, balance, and proportion he saw in the great composers of the Austro-German tradition; Bach, Beethoven, and Brahms. He wrote mostly chamber music, favoring the formal principles of classicism and Romanticism. His music, often subjected to repeated revision, is highly disciplined and meticulously crafted.

Mason repeatedly tackled the issues surrounding American music in his writings from the 1920s and 1930s. In *The Dilemma of American Music* (1928) he rescinded some of his earlier notions and declared that the way to develop a rich American artistic tradition was not through a common "nationalist" style but through "an elastic eclecticism of individual choice." He expanded this idea in a letter to John Tasker Howard, in which he stated that American composition was "necessarily eclectic and cosmopolitan, and that the kind of distinctiveness to be looked for in it is individual rather than national." In *Tune In, America* (1931), however, Mason appeared significantly less tolerant of the cosmopolitan face of contemporary American music and strongly denounced what he saw as extravagant "alien" influences threatening American artistic integrity.

In 1929 Mason was appointed MacDowell Professor and head of the music department at Columbia, a position he held until 1940. His autobiographical *Music in My Time* was published in 1938, the same year he was elected to the National Institute of Arts and Letters. He retired fully from Columbia in 1942 and in 1950 moved with his wife to Greenwich, Connecticut, where he died after a period of ill health.

• Mason's papers are held in the special collections department of Butler Library at Columbia University. This collection includes roughly 2,000 items, including books, papers, manuscript letters, business papers, scrapbooks, and music sketch books. For a list of Mason's published writings, see Boris Schwarz, "Daniel Gregory Mason," *New Grove Dictionary of American Music*, vol. 13 (1986). Sister Mary Justina Klein, *The Contribution of Daniel Gregory Mason to American Music* (1957), and Ralph B. Lewis, *The Life and Music of Daniel Gregory Mason* (Ph.D. diss., Univ. of Rochester, 1959), are good sources for information on Mason and include biographical summaries, lists of Mason's compositions and writings about music, and bibliographies. For contemporary sketches of Mason, see Olin Downes, "An American Composer," *Musical Quarterly* 4, no. 1 (Jan. 1918): 35–36, and Burnet Tuthill, "Daniel Gregory Mason," *Musical Quarterly* 34, no. 1 (Jan. 1948): 46–60.

ANDREA KALYN

MASON, Edith (22 Mar. 1891–26 Nov. 1973), operatic soprano, was born Edith Marjory Barnes in St. Louis, Missouri, the daughter of Baron Steuben Barnes, a successful grain commodities trader, and Eva Salisbury, a college professor who taught after her husband's untimely death in 1899. In early childhood Edith exhibited an interest in singing and was beguiled by the musical theater, but it was not until 1908, when she heard Geraldine Farrar and Enrico Caruso in *Madama Butterfly* while on an excursion from Miss Wright's private school in Bryn Mawr, Pennsylvania, that she determined to pursue a career in opera. Her first vocal training was at the H. Thane Miller School in Cincinnati, Ohio, where it became apparent that her voice had unusual promise. Upon graduation she studied for two years in Paris, first with Spanish tenor Enrico Bertran and then more significantly with the famous baritone Victor Maurel. She returned to the United States in 1910 and was briefly married to Dexter Somes, whom she divorced in February 1911. She then enrolled in the New England Conservatory of Music in Boston, where she made notable progress under the guidance of Arnoldo Conti, who was also principal conductor of the Boston Opera Company.

Edith made her operatic debut as Nedda in the Boston Opera Company's 7 January 1912 matinee of *Pagliacci*, substituting on only two days' notice for the indisposed Carmen Melis. Though she had never sung on an operatic stage before, she scored a triumph, and impresario Henry Russell signed her to a contract for that season and the next.

Edith left the Boston Opera Company early in 1913 when she married Norman Mason, an artist and amateur tenor and the scion of a prominent family in Highland Park, Illinois. After a half year's stay in Buenos Aires, the two returned to Paris, where they had originally met, and Edith Mason resumed her vocal career, studying with famed tenor Edmond Clement, whom she credited for her fine free vocal technique. Upon his recommendation Mason sang in Nice and then in Monte Carlo, where her Marguerite and Juliette won commendation. Eager to expand her repertoire, she studied in Milan with retired singers Salvatore Cottone and Vittorio Vanzo, making such progress that

the Municipal Opera of Marseilles signed her to a contract for twenty-two roles in the fall of 1914. However, World War I intervened and she returned to America.

After a successful audition at the Metropolitan Opera, she joined the company for the 1915–1916 season and made a highly acclaimed debut as Sophie in *Der Rosenkavalier*. Before the season's end she had sung forty performances of such roles as Papagena, Marzelline, Gretel, and Micaela, the latter with her youthful idols Farrar and Caruso. She was also studying once again with her former teacher Victor Maurel. Her second season at the Metropolitan was equally prestigious—one of her roles was the Prioress in the world premiere of DeKoven's *The Canterbury Pilgrims*—but she left the company on the pretext of seeking wider operatic opportunities. At this time her romantic liaison with conductor Giorgio Polacco became public, and both their respective mates sued them for divorce.

Undaunted, Mason and Polacco won great favor in their debut season with the Ravinia Opera during the summer of 1917. That fall Mason sang for several months with the Sigaldi Opera Company in Mexico, and for the next two seasons she and Polacco toured with the Bracale Opera Company in Latin America. In 1919 they married and spent the better part of a year in Paris, where Mason garnered praise for her roles as Manon, Marguerite, Juliette, and Margherita. She had almost completed her preparation of Louise with the composer Gustav Charpentier when her mother's fatal illness brought her back to the United States. After Eva Barnes's death in August 1920, Mason went into seclusion for several months.

Lasting fame and fortune awaited both Mason and Pollaco when Mary Garden, newly appointed director of the Chicago Opera Company, added their names to the 1921–1922 roster. Assigned what would become her favorite role, that of Cio-Cio San in Puccini's *Madama Butterfly*, Mason spent the summer working with the composer on her interpretation, and her performance on 16 November was a revelation. Both critics and the public showered her with such superlatives that she reigned for the next twenty years as one of Chicago's leading sopranos.

Mason, however, did not limit herself to the operatic scene in Chicago. She sang with almost all of the Chicago Opera tours and concertized frequently throughout the nation. In 1923 she sang Mimi with great success at La Scala, and four years later she returned to sing Gounod's Marguerite under Toscanini's baton. From 1924 to 1928 she was a major artist in the Brunswick Record Company's Hall of Fame series. Although these recordings captured every nuance of her beautiful voice, few of them represented her vast repertoire of forty-one roles. In 1925 Mason gave birth in Milan to her only child, Graziella, though her marriage to Polacco became so difficult that she divorced him in July 1929. Three months later she married prominent orthopedic surgeon Maurice Bernstein.

For the 1930 spring season at Covent Garden, John Barbirolli invited Mason to participate, but a throat malady marred much of her singing during the two-month stay. Nor was her marriage to Bernstein prospering, and in May 1931 she won a decree of annulment. Soon after, she and Polacco reconciled. They returned to Europe where Mason, making her first appearance at the 1932 Maggio Musicale Fiorentino, sang Margherita in Boito's *Mephistopheles*. On a visit to Switzerland they remarried. Mason returned the next year to the May Festival, singing Nanetta in Verdi's *Falstaff*, followed by a lengthy tour of the major Italian opera houses. When the Chicago Opera reopened its doors after a year's hiatus because of lack of funds, Mason sang Cio-Cio San and Marguerite. At Toscanini's request she studied the role of Violetta in 1934 and reaped genuine success in Chicago, Italy, and New York. Early in 1935 she toured with Isaac Van Grove's opera/ballet group. That summer at the Salzburg Festival she sang Nanetta under Toscanini's direction, and in the fall she made a triumphant return to the Metropolitan after an eighteen-year absence.

From 1936 on Mason limited her number of operatic appearances, though her beautifully realized conception of Desdemona brought her rave notices. Unfortunately, her second marriage to Polacco was deteriorating, and in 1937 she sued him for divorce. The following year she married financier William Ragland, which became the happiest of her marriages and lasted until her death.

On 27 November 1941 Mason sang her operatic farewell as Mimi at the Chicago Opera and her final concert at Chicago's Grant Park the next summer. For ten years she was on the faculty of DePaul University and taught singing privately as well. In 1944 she embarked on a highly popular lecture tour, advertised as "Edith Mason Speaking," but in the postwar years she retired, dividing her time between her villa in Cortina d'Ampezzo and Chicago. Her last appearance in public was as an honored guest at the Farewell Gala to the old Metropolitan Opera House in 1966. Her health declined soon after and she and Ragland moved to San Diego, where she died.

• In the May 1991 issue of the *Record Collector*, pp. 91–121, there is a comprehensive article on Mason's life and career, as well as a detailed discography written and compiled by Edward Hagelin Pearson. His liner notes for the Romophone compact disc release *Edith Mason* (81009–2) provide a brief summary of her career. An earlier article by Arthur Knight is in the *Record Collector*, 10, no. 4: 75–87. Mary Jane Matz's "All Pepper," *Opera News*, 18 Mar. 1967, pp. 26–27, offers an interesting portrait of the singer. The 1966 hour-long radio interview with Studs Terkel from Chicago's FM station, WFMT, is available on the audiocassette *Edith Mason Memorial Issue* (Crest CC751). Mason's complete recordings from 1924 to 1928 have been reissued on a compact disc (Romophone 81009-2). An obituary is in the *New York Times*, 27 Nov. 1973.

EDWARD HAGELIN PEARSON

MASON, F. Van Wyck (11 Nov. 1901–28 Aug. 1978), author of suspense and historical novels, was born Francis Van Wyck Mason in Boston, Massachusetts,

the son of Francis Payne Mason and Erma Coffin. He spent much of his childhood in Europe, where his grandfather was in the diplomatic corps. He left school to work as an ambulance driver in France during World War I but obtained his B.S. from Harvard in 1924. He planned a diplomatic career but after his father's death instead started his own business, importing rugs, embroideries, and antique books he found on buying trips in Europe and North Africa. In 1927 he married Dorothy Louise Macready. They had two children.

According to Mason, he began writing after meeting an old college professor at the Harvard Club. John Gallishaw remembered his former student's essays and encouraged Mason to take a writing course he was then giving. From 1928 on he made a living writing magazine articles and novels. Mason recalled in the 1940s: "I set about learning by writing in the most popular vein, presumably the easiest vein. Instead of trying to write opera I wrote jazz. My first markets were the pulp magazines. That was in 1928 when there was money for all of us, and in that first year of writing I earned $18,000."

In 1930 Mason published his first mystery novel, *Seeds of Murder*, which features his most popular and enduring hero, Captain (later Major and then Colonel) Hugh North of U.S. Army Intelligence, who stars in twenty-six of Mason's books. North originally acts as a traditional, American-based sleuth but soon changes his ambience to one of international intrigue. The series is described in *Twentieth-Century Crime and Mystery Writers*:

Stripped to their essential detective structure, the novels involve a problem for North to solve which includes a series of murders and a puzzle to unravel. This may be a message to be deciphered, the true meaning of a word or phrase, or the location of a treasure, all of which become keys to the larger mystery. The vivid background based on careful research and Mason's own travels is part of the appeal of the stories.

Mason seems to have liked the idea that North was modeled on his creator. North operates in the sort of sophisticated environment favored by Mason himself, who prided himself on his social connections and chic pursuits—big game hunting, riding, polo. As well as the Hugh North books, Mason produced numerous short stories and more than thirty novels. (He also used the pen names Geoffrey Coffin, Frank W. Mason, and Ward Weaver.) Many of his novels are based on characters and events in (mostly American) history, with emphasis on adventure and the military. *Captain Nemesis* (1931) and *Cutlass Empire* (1949), for example, re-create the experiences of pirates—cast, like North and Mason's other detectives, in the heroic mold. Mason was proud of the research that made his novels heavily detailed, although he tried to balance reading pleasure and education. He explained:

I have written . . . both the historical books and the "North" series with the intention of informing as well as entertaining people. The historical books are designed to remedy the deplorable lack of imagination with which history is taught in most of our schools. The "North" books are intended to keep reminding the public that security is obtainable only at the price of vigilance. (Warfel, *American Novelists of Today*)

Mason spent time between the wars in the National Guard. Between 1942 and 1945 he served as an army intelligence officer and historian; he spent the last two years of the war working with the Allied Expeditionary Forces and, according to one journalist, "saw a good deal of General Eisenhower, whom he compare[d] on many counts to George Washington."

After the war Mason returned to writing, turning out exciting stories with brave, elegant heroes regularly and easily. Mason never worried very much about his writing style, explaining:

Novelists are up against such tough competition for a reader's attention, what with newspapers full of news, hell popping on the radio, movies to see and automobile drives to go on, that I doubt whether pretty phrases sell many books. There is still a respect for the very polished kind of writing, of course, and that's fine. But I wonder how many people have a go at a book in order to savor the prose. I believe the majority prefers a well-plotted, fast-moving yarn, with plenty of incident. (van Gelder, *Writings and Writers*)

In 1956 Mason moved to Bermuda. His wife died in 1958, and that same year he married Jeanne-Louise Hand. He continued to write until his death off the coast of Bermuda. One critic observed of him, "His own development as a writer may be charted in the North books: from pulp thrillers to smooth, professional entertainment."

• Van Wyck Mason's papers are at Boston University. A colorful and productive author, he has been profiled numerous times, most extensively in Henry R. Warfel, *American Novelists of Today* (1951); Robert van Gelder, *Writers and Writing* (1946); and Lesley Henderson, ed., *Twentieth-Century Crime and Mystery Writers*, 3d ed. (1991). See also John K. Hutchen, "People Who Read and Write," *New York Times Book Review*, 15 Feb. 1948. Obituaries are in *Time*, 11 Sept. 1978, and the *New York Times*, 6 Nov. 1978.

TINKY "DAKOTA" WEISBLAT

MASON, George (1725–7 Oct. 1792), planter and revolutionary statesman, the son of George Mason (c. 1629–c. 1686), a planter, and Ann Thomson. He was probably born at Dogue's Neck (now called Mason Neck) in the northern part of Stafford County, Virginia, now Fairfax County. Both his namesake father and grandfather had been important planters and sometimes controversial public men in the Potomac River Valley. His mother was the daughter of Stevens Thomson, an English barrister who served as attorney general of Virginia from 1703 until his death early in 1713. Mason's father drowned in an accident in 1735, leaving his strong-willed and self-reliant mother to manage the large estate. George Mason remained in Virginia for a private education, which he obtained in

part in the library of his guardian, the noted legal scholar John Mercer, who owned the finest book collection in northern Virginia. A man of strong opinions and emotions, Mercer's personality and interests were in some measure reflected in those of George Mason.

In 1750, Mason married Anne Eilbeck, daughter of William Eilbeck, a merchant of Charles County, Maryland. They had nine children, three of whom died in infancy before Anne Eilbeck Mason died in 1773. About 1754 Mason began the construction of his country home, "Gunston Hall," which overlooked the Potomac River in Fairfax County. William Buckland, the craftsman who finished the hall in 1758, combined in it the grace and symmetry of Georgian architecture with an intimate and livable quality that distinguishes it from all other surviving colonial Virginia homes. Gunston Hall is one of the jewels of eighteenth-century Virginia architecture.

Mason was a private man who preferred the comfort and security of his study and his formal boxwood garden to the confusions and compromises of public life. He was also plagued with chronically poor health. Although a vestryman for Truro Parish and a justice of the peace for Fairfax County for most of his adult life, Mason was not happy when sharing responsibility and often did not attend meetings. He was not without ambition, though, and in 1758 he was elected to the House of Burgesses. The few short meetings between 1758 and 1761 constituted the whole of his legislative experience before the American Revolution.

Mason nevertheless became well known to Virginia's political leaders. He was remarkably well informed on matters of law and commerce and particularly on western affairs. In 1752 he became treasurer of the Ohio Company, one of the largest of the land companies attempting to gain title to large tracts of western lands with the hope of selling small plots to settlers and making large profits in the process. Early in the 1770s he made a study of colonial charters and laws in order better to inform himself of the legal rights of the Ohio Company and to be prepared to counter the competing claims of other companies. His unpublished "Extracts from the Virginia Charters, with Some Remarks Upon Them" from this period has been called an important state paper, but in reality it was a private memorandum that clearly exhibits Mason's skill in analyzing legal and political issues.

Mason gave strong support to the protests that Virginians and other colonial leaders made against British policies during the Stamp Act crisis, and he admired the eloquence and skill with which Patrick Henry stepped to the front of the Virginia opposition. In a public letter of 6 June 1766 addressed to the merchants of London, he gave strong voice to the claim of fair and equal treatment for the colonies. In 1769, following the adoption of the Townshend Duties, Mason prepared the draft of a nonimportation association intended to force British merchants to join the colonists in demanding repeal of the taxes. Mason's friend and neighbor, George Washington, introduced the draft in a meeting of former burgesses in Williamsburg and secured its adoption. At the same time, Thomson Mason, Mason's younger brother, writing under the pseudonym "A British American," published in the *Virginia Gazette* a powerful series of supportive letters that probably reflected his brother's opinions.

In the summer of 1774 George Mason composed, and Washington secured, the adoption by the assembled gentlemen of Fairfax County of resolutions condemning the Coercive Acts and laying out the American position with respect to the imperial crisis. In the summer of 1775 the voters of Fairfax County selected Mason to take Washington's place in the third of the five Virginia conventions that met between the summers of 1774 and 1776. For the first time Mason took a leading role on the colony's public stage. His reputation had preceded him, and he improved his standing by helping a few experienced legislators take control of the session when it bogged down in confusion and indecision. The other delegates wanted to send Mason to the Continental Congress to succeed Washington, and it was only by the most earnest entreaties, appealing to his colleagues to permit him to care for his motherless children, that he persuaded them not to. The convention nevertheless elected Mason the ranking member of the Virginia Committee of Safety. Illness forced him to be absent from the committee during the autumn of 1775, and he also missed the Fourth Convention that met in December 1775 and January 1776.

In April 1776 Mason was elected to the last of the conventions. By then, he and most of the other leading Virginians had accepted the necessity of declaring independence, and Mason spent the spring studying forms of government and corresponding with Richard Henry Lee, who was in Philadelphia, and deep in conversations on the same subject with George Wythe of Virginia and John Adams (1735–1826) of Massachusetts, among others. Because of ill health, Mason arrived at the convention almost two weeks late, after the other delegates had voted unanimously for independence and created a committee "to prepare a Declaration of Rights and such a plan of government as will be most likely to maintain peace and order in this colony and secure substantial and equal liberty to the people." The president of the convention, Edmund Pendleton, added Mason to the committee, and within a few days wrote that "The Political Cooks are busy in preparing the dish, and as Colonel Mason seems to have the Ascendancy in the great work, I have sanguine hopes it will be framed so as to Answer it's end, Prosperity to the Community and Security to Individuals." Mason wrote the initial drafts for both the Declaration of Rights, which the convention unanimously adopted on 12 June 1776, and the first constitution of the independent Commonwealth of Virginia, which the convention unanimously adopted on 29 June 1776. Edmund Randolph (1753–1813) recalled later that several members introduced drafts that disclosed "the ardor for political notice rather than a ripeness in political wisdom." Mason's drafts, however, "swallowed up all the rest by fixing the grounds and plan, which after great discussion and correction were finally ratified."

By "correction," Randolph meant enlargement. Mason's draft for the Declaration of Rights laid out the basic principles of republican government as he conceived them, together with clauses affirming the right to jury trials in civil and criminal cases and a declaration in favor of religious toleration. The committee and the convention added other guarantees of individual liberties, such as freedom of the press, protections against general warrants, and bans on excessive bail and cruel and unusual punishments. Mason was regarded as the principal author of the Declaration of Rights and considered it to be his most important work. The Virginia Declaration of Rights was one of the most important and influential public papers of 1776.

Mason's draft for the first constitution of Virginia provided for separation of the legislative, executive, and judicial branches of government, prohibited plural office holding, and lodged the greatest share of power in the popularly elected lower house of the assembly. He regarded executive excesses as the greatest threat to individual and public liberties.

Mason served in the General Assembly during the Revolution, the longest period of public service of his career. He retained his interest in western affairs and was a member of a committee in 1777 and 1778 that prepared instructions for George Rogers Clark prior to Clark's campaign in the Ohio Valley that secured for Virginia and the United States effective control over what became known as the Old Northwest, the region in which the Ohio Company had heavily invested.

Mason retired from legislative politics at the end of the revolutionary war. He was then engaged in long-running feuds with other members of the Fairfax County court over the location of the county courthouse and the administration of the affairs of the county and of the town of Alexandria. These and other arguments exposed a contentious side of his personality. Perhaps it was in part the effect of chronic poor health, but it was also a result of his uncompromising style and his confidence in the soundness of his judgments. Despite continued ill health, he married in April 1780 a fifty-year-old spinster, Sarah Brent, daughter of George Brent of Stafford County.

Mason attended the Mount Vernon Conference of 1785, which was formed ostensibly to discuss commercial problems. The legislature then named him a delegate to the follow-up Annapolis Conference of 1786, but for some reason he was not notified in time to attend. In 1787 the assembly appointed Mason one of the Virginia delegates to the Constitutional Convention in Philadelphia, which continued the work of the Mount Vernon and Annapolis conferences. Mason made the trip, the only time during his life that he ever traveled beyond the immediate vicinity of the Potomac River and Chesapeake Bay. As an advocate of a strengthened national government, Mason became disillusioned when the convention decided in favor of an executive not answerable to the legislature, a strong and independent judiciary, and provisions that threatened the supremacy of the state governments over the national government. Mason criticized those decisions and also unsuccessfully moved that a declaration or bill of rights be added to the Constitution. Mason refused to sign the Constitution, declaring angrily, according to James Madison's notes, "that he would sooner chop off his right hand than put it to the constitution as it now stands."

Mason prepared a memorandum entitled "Objections to This Constitution of Government," which he later industriously circulated. It began, "There is no Declaration of Rights," and contained more than a dozen serious substantive objections to individual clauses in the Constitution. One that he pointedly condemned was the provision that allowed the slave trade to remain open for twenty years. Along with the pamphlet signed, "Federal Farmer," Mason's "Objections" were some of the most widely read and discussed critiques of the Constitution.

George Mason returned to Virginia in ill humor. The rigidity of his views and his increasingly belligerent personality produced an intolerance and intemperance in his behavior that surprised and angered Madison, with whom he had worked closely at the beginning of the convention, and Washington, who privately condemned Mason's actions during the ratification struggle.

Mason moved unsuccessfully to bring about a second national convention to rewrite the Constitution into a form he could accept, and by the time the Virginia Ratification Convention met in Richmond in June 1788, Mason had emerged as one of the leaders of the opposition. He had so alienated his neighbors that he stood no chance of being elected in Fairfax County and instead stood for, and barely won, a seat from neighboring Stafford County. During the convention, Mason argued to no avail for amendments to make the Constitution conform to his own ideas, and was joined by the other leading opponents of ratification, Patrick Henry and William Grayson, who waged the principal battle. After the convention ratified the Constitution, it adopted a report that Mason helped prepare calling for structural changes in the Constitution and the addition of specific guarantees of individual liberties. This soothed the feelings of some opponents of the Constitution but not Mason's. He left the ratification convention at the end of June 1788 in almost as bad a humor as he had left the Philadelphia convention at the end of September 1787. Even the subsequent adoption of the Bill of Rights did not reconcile Mason to the Constitution, which he believed had perverted the principles of legislative and state supremacy and destroyed the balance of powers.

George Mason declined a seat in the U.S. Senate in 1790, citing illness. He died at Gunston Hall.

• Mason's letters and recorded speeches in the conventions of 1787 and 1788 are in Robert A. Rutland, ed., *The Papers of George Mason, 1725–1792* (3 vols., 1970); other important family and plantation records, including the family Bible, are in the library at Gunston Hall; the best modern biographies are Helen Hill Miller, *George Mason, Gentleman Revolutionary* (1975), which concentrates on his public life, and Pamela C. Copeland and Richard K. MacMaster, *The Five George Masons, Patriots and Planters of Virginia and Maryland* (1975), which concentrates on his private and family life; important recent reassessments include Peter R. Henriques, "An Uneven Friendship: The Relationship between George Washington and George Mason," *Virginia Magazine of History and Biography* 97 (1989): 185–204, and Brent Tarter, "George Mason and the Conservation of Liberty," *Virginia Magazine of History and Biography* 99 (1991): 279–304.

BRENT TARTER

MASON, George Walter (12 Mar. 1891–9 Oct. 1954), automobile industry executive, was born in Valley City, North Dakota, the son of Simon Mason and Annie Simons. Mason got involved in automobiles and mechanics at an early age. In 1907 he found after-school work as a volunteer mechanic at the local Maxwell automobile dealer in Valley City, and soon the dealer signed him on as a paid salesman and demonstrator of Maxwell cars. The young Mason also developed an avid interest in motorcycles, racing them for one season on dirt tracks in North Dakota. In the summer of 1908 he worked for a Buick dealer and also ran his own small motorcycle dealership and tire-vulcanizing business.

In 1909 Mason entered the University of Michigan's engineering school. As a college student, Mason developed a unique and ambitious way of paying for his education: he maintained a dealership for Briggs-Detroiter automobiles in his hometown of Valley City, a demanding but feasible task because during that era automobile sales were strictly seasonal, with a rush during spring and summer that tapered back sharply in the fall and winter months. Mason capitalized on his experiences as both a businessman and an auto mechanic to request from the University of Michigan administration a new course of study, combining three years of mechanical engineering with a final year of business administration. (The University of Michigan had no school of business administration at the time.) Mason's academic precedent set a pattern that endured, as engineering students thereafter were strongly encouraged to take business courses.

After receiving his B.S. degree in 1913, Mason went to Detroit and embarked on a series of jobs in the automobile industry. He first joined the Studebaker Corporation, and in 1914 he became a layout and design engineer at the Dodge Brothers plant. The following year he assumed work as a purchasing agent for the American Automobile Trimming Company. In 1916 he moved to Waukegan, Illinois, for a year with the Wilder Tanning Company, controlled by Dodge.

During World War I Mason served as a coordination specialist at the Rock Island Arsenal in Illinois. Working as a civil service appointee of the Army Ordinance Department's Central Planning Division, Mason supervised production of all war materials at the arsenal. After the war Mason went to New York, where he was in charge of business extension for the Irving National Bank of New York. In 1921 Mason returned to Detroit to work as an executive for the Maxwell-Chalmers Corporation, which Walter Chrysler was reorganizing. When the Chrysler Corporation was formed in 1924, Mason served as assistant to the vice president in charge of manufacturing and he supervised production of the Chrysler car, which was an instant success when it hit the market and quickly established Chrysler as a powerful new salient in the automobile industry.

Despite his success at Chrysler, Mason was restless, and in 1926 he left to become vice president and general manager of Copeland Products of Detroit, a leading manufacturer of electric refrigerators, which were becoming popular among consumers. Elected president the following year, Mason left in 1928 to become president of Kelvinator, the pioneer refrigerator company. Mason led Kelvinator with spectacular results. He revamped the company's manufacturing and sales techniques, and within eight years he quadrupled its production, a remarkable feat during the Great Depression. His work won Mason widespread respect and recognition in American business, and in 1936 Charles Nash offered him the presidency of Nash Motors Company in Kenosha, Wisconsin, one of many automobile manufacturing companies that were struggling during the Great Depression. Instead of abandoning Kelvinator, in 1937 Mason negotiated a merger of the Nash and Kelvinator companies, with himself as president and Nash as chairman of the board of the new Nash-Kelvinator company. By 1940 the company was finally a financially profitable enterprise.

During World War II the Nash-Kelvinator company manufactured helicopters, propellers, binoculars, aviation instruments, and automobile and ship parts. During and after the war, Mason also sent to Europe five-pound bags of coffee, which had become a scarce commodity overseas. After the war Mason was a prominent fundraiser for the University of Michigan's multimillion-dollar Phoenix project, which was dedicated to the peaceful use of atomic power.

In 1946 Mason was elected president of the Automobile Manufacturers Association (AMA), a post he held until his death in 1954. This position allowed Mason to begin a close business relationship with George Romney, who was managing director of the AMA. Mason eventually brought Romney to Nash-Kelvinator.

In 1948 Charles Nash died, and Mason succeeded him as chairman of the board, while also being reelected president. The following year the company introduced an all-new Nash car, the Airflyte, which featured radical aerodynamic styling. Airflyte sales in 1950 totaled 160,000, which was a company record, propelling Nash into position as one of the nation's top ten automakers.

Mason was resolved to have Nash introduce a small car that would help the company secure a stable market niche in the face of stiff competition from Detroit's Big Three automakers. Thus in 1950 he presided over the introduction of the Nash Rambler, which became the first small car in the United States to enjoy substantial sales. The car became Nash's flagship product and allowed the company to remain profitable. Mason also guided the production of the low, two-seat Nash-Healey sports car that debuted in 1950. The Nash-Healey, which resulted from a serendipitous encounter between Mason and British sports car builder Donald Healey aboard the *Queen Elizabeth* ocean liner, was built in England.

After the war Mason began to streamline Nash-Kelvinator's production operations and began to court the few remaining independent automobile companies for a possible merger. He had the prescience to foresee an imminent shakedown in the American automobile industry; he realized that the postwar boom in automobile sales would someday level off, and he wanted the independents to pool their research, design, and manufacturing programs so as to give them the same production and cost advantages that the Big Three automakers enjoyed. Mason even had a name already in mind for a new company—American Motors—but first had to find an independent receptive to his merger plans.

In 1948 Mason approached both the Packard and Hudson automobile companies with offers of a merger, but both spurned him. Cars were still selling briskly in 1948, and both companies believed that they could continue along healthily as independents. But events soon convinced them otherwise. A price war broke out between Ford and Chrysler in 1954, weakening the competitive sales positions of the independents. The previous year Hudson's financial health was battered by the failure of its new model, the Jet. Although Mason preferred to merge with Packard, the company had proved reluctant to be wooed, so he turned to Hudson instead, which in its anemic position had become eager to merge. In May 1954 Mason's efforts came to fruition when Nash-Kelvinator and Hudson were officially merged to form the American Motors Corporation (AMC), the fourth largest automaker in the United States with assets of almost $200 million. It was the biggest merger in the history of the American automobile industry, much larger than the 1953 merger of Willys-Overland and Kaiser Motors, and set an example that the Studebaker and Packard automobile companies followed when they merged later in 1954. Mason became president, chief executive officer, and chairman of the board of AMC, positions he held at the time of his death just five months later. George Romney was named executive vice president.

As president and CEO of AMC, Mason moved quickly to husband resources, slash costs, and put the new company on a competitive footing. (As one condition of a merger between Nash and Hudson, Mason had insisted that Hudson abandon its unsuccessful Jet car.) He consolidated manufacturing by moving Hudson assembly lines from Detroit to the Nash manufacturing plants in Milwaukee and Kenosha, Wisconsin, and he ordered that the same body be used for both Nash and Hudson cars.

Even after Nash merged with Hudson, Mason continued to believe that America's independent automakers would eventually perish unless they pooled their resources to form a larger, combined corporation, thus creating a "Big Four" among American automakers. He still pursued the dream that AMC would combine with two other independent automakers, Studebaker and Packard, and as a prelude to such a merger Mason convinced Packard president James Nance to take over the financially troubled Studebaker company, a merger that took place in October 1954. Later that month, on a fishing trip in Wyoming, Mason suddenly took ill with pneumonia. He died shortly afterward in Detroit. With him died the dream of creating a merger between the Studebaker-Packard Corporation and AMC.

Mason enjoyed the outdoors and pursued several outdoor sports, including duck hunting and fly fishing. He often flew his own airplane during his hunting and fishing trips, as well as on business trips. He served on the board of trustees and as a treasurer of Ducks Unlimited, an organization dedicated to the preservation and propagation of wild ducks. After his death it was revealed that he had bequeathed a fourteen-mile-long tract of land along the Au Sable River (near Grayling, Michigan) to the Michigan State Department of Conservation, so that the people of Michigan could enjoy the land and the trout fishing the area offered. Mason and his wife, Florence, had two sons and two daughters.

• The National Automotive History Collection of the Detroit Public Library maintains a file on Mason. A profile of Mason is Kent Sagendorph, "George Mason: Monumental Man of Michigan," *Inside Michigan*, Jan. 1955, pp. 19–22. A description of Mason's attempts to secure a merger between Nash-Kelvinator and Hudson can be found in Patrick Foster's *American Motors: The Last Independent* (1993). Obituaries are in *Newsweek* and *Time*, 18 Oct. 1954, and in the *Detroit Free Press* and the *New York Times*, 9 Oct. 1954.

YANEK MIECZKOWSKI

MASON, James (15 May 1909–27 July 1984), actor, was born James Neville Mason in Huddersfield, Yorkshire, England, the son of John Mason, an affluent textile merchant, and Mabel Hattersley Gaunt. In 1928, after completing his primary education at Windermere Preparatory School and Marlborough College, Mason enrolled at Cambridge University, pursuing a degree in the classics, the mandatory course of study required of those seeking a position in the Indian Civil Service. As with many entering university, Mason discovered what were to him new cultures, perspectives, and ideas. He not only changed his course of study, to architecture, but he also received his introduction to the dramatic arts, as a member of the chorus in a production of *Bacchae* during his first summer term. He continued to be active in college dramatics and, after receiving one of only three first-class degrees awarded in architecture in 1931, sought a professional acting career.

With the exception of his portrayal of Brutus in William Shakespeare's *Julius Caesar* in 1934 at the Gate Theatre in Dublin, Ireland, Mason's work as a stage actor was of little note. His motion picture debut was in 1935 in a film directed by Al Parker titled *Late Extra*, a critical and box-office failure. Mason continued to work in motion pictures, obtaining small roles in several undistinguished films. In 1937 he formed Gamma Productions with cameraman and film director Roy Kellino and his wife Pamela, the daughter of an executive of the Gaumont-British film company (Mason wed Pamela Kellino in February 1941; they had two children.) Their production, *I Met a Murderer*, written by the trio and starring Mason, received some favorable reviews but was a financial disaster. The film was scheduled for general release in 1939, but when Britain declared war on Germany in September of that year movie theaters in Britain were closed for three months.

Mason became an international star at the age of thirty-five, seven films later, with a role that was to become his trademark for several years. As the marquis de Rohan in Leslie Arliss's *The Man in Grey* (1943) and in several films that followed, Mason became known as "the man you love to hate," playing villainous roles that took advantage of his dark good looks. So popular was Mason in these roles that in 1943 he was voted actor of the year by *Picturegoer* magazine.

At the height of his box-office success, Mason became the subject of much controversy. As a conscientious objector, he refused to register for military service because, as he states in his autobiography, his "abhorrence of war as a means of settling international economic and political difference . . . and the glib acceptance in wartime of an alien code which we would quite properly condemn in the intervals of peace." He also became alienated from the British film industry and movie audiences because of several articles that he wrote critical of the industry and its production practices.

Mason and his wife Pamela immigrated to the United States in 1946. Though the notoriety of his British films preceded him, the start of Mason's film career in Hollywood was as uneven as his start was in England. His first moderate success was not until 1951, in the role of German tank commander Field Marshall Rommel in 20th Century–Fox's war film *The Desert Fox* (1951). He repeated the role in *The Desert Rats* (1953) and was well received in another role that he had also played before—Brutus, this time in the Metro-Goldwyn-Mayer production of *Julius Caesar* starring John Gielgud and Marlon Brando, also in 1953.

In 1954 Mason accepted a part previously turned down by film stars Cary Grant, Humphrey Bogart, James Stewart, and Montgomery Clift: Norman Maine in *A Star Is Born*. Starring opposite Judy Garland in the Warner Bros. remake of the 1932 film *What Price Hollywood?* Mason earned his first and only Academy Award nomination for best actor, although the award was given to Brando for *On the Waterfront*.

Despite his performances in *A Star Is Born* and in the popular Disney film *20,000 Leagues under the Sea* (1954), Mason became known primarily as a character actor, appearing in such films as *Island in the Sun* (1956), noted for its depiction of interracial romance, and Alfred Hitchcock's *North by Northwest* (1959). One of his most noted roles, as Humbert Humbert in Stanley Kubrick's *Lolita*, based on Vladimir Nabokov's novel, was produced in 1962. Between films, Mason also worked in television, hosting two drama series, "The James Mason Show" and "Lux Video Theater."

After eight more films and a divorce from his wife in 1965, Mason received his second Academy Award nomination—this time for his supporting performance as James Leamington in *Georgy Girl* (1966). Once again he lost, this time to Walter Matthau for *The Fortune Cookie*.

Mason continued to work actively in film, and in 1969, while shooting the film *Age of Consent*, he met Australian actress Clarissa Kaye, whom he married in 1971. He received his last Oscar nomination, once again for best supporting actor, for the 1982 film *The Verdict*, directed by Sidney Lumet. Of Mason, the renowned director said, "I always thought he was one of the best actors who ever lived. Whatever you gave him to do, he would take it, assimilate it and then make it his own. . . . He was always expected to be good on camera, and so nobody ever bothered to notice how good he was every time" (Morley, p. 142). Mason died in Lausanne, Switzerland, where he had made his home for twenty-two years.

• Mason's autobiography is *Before I Forget* (1981). A biography is Sheridan Morley, *James Mason: Odd Man Out* (1989), and a filmography is Clive Hirschhorn, *The Films of James Mason* (1977). See also Ronald Haver, *"A Star Is Born": The Making of the 1954 Movie* (1988).

FRANCES K. GATEWARD

MASON, James Murray (3 Nov. 1798–28 Apr. 1871), U.S. representative, U.S. senator, and Confederate diplomat, was born in Georgetown, District of Columbia, the son of John Mason, a businessman and farmer, and Anna Maria Murray. He was a grandson of revolutionary era statesman George Mason. He studied under private tutors and in the Georgetown public schools and graduated from the University of Pennsylvania at Philadelphia in 1818. He completed his legal education in 1820 at the College of William and Mary in Williamsburg, Virginia. He subsequently practiced in the Shenandoah Valley town of Winchester.

In 1822 Mason married Elizabeth Margaretta Chew, a member of the wealthy, powerful Chew clan of Philadelphia. They returned to Winchester, where Mason purchased a home they called "Selma." They had eight children. Though he would be a fervent defender of the peculiar institution, he did not become a plantation owner nor invest heavily in farmlands and slaves but did own a small number of house servants.

While the Masons were not extremely wealthy, they maintained a comfortable lifestyle at Selma.

Mason was elected to the Virginia State House of Delegates and served from 1826 to 1831. He also served in the 1829 Virginia constitutional convention, where, despite his Tidewater antecedents, he favored apportioning representation in the state legislature by white population alone, so as not to accord disproportionate power to districts with large numbers of slaves. Because of his support of Democrats Andrew Jackson and Martin Van Buren, he was elected to the Twenty-fifth Congress of the United States on 4 March 1837. After serving only one term in Congress, he broke with the Democratic leadership over tariff legislation. The Democratic party refused to nominate him and accused him of forming an alliance with the Whigs. Upon the death of U.S. senator Isaac S. Pennybacker and after moderating his view on the tariffs, however, Mason was selected in 1847 to complete the unexpired term. He was reelected to the Senate in 1850 and 1856 and continued to serve as a Virginia senator until 28 March 1861. Joining John C. Calhoun's "mess," he became a leading spokesman for southern interests. He read the critically ill Calhoun's final speech to the Senate during the compromise debate of 1850. Although popular with southern legislators, Mason never achieved national prominence, and Senate leadership was assumed by more moderate southerners.

Unlike most political leaders from the Upper South, Mason strongly believed that slaveholders' rights could not be protected within the Union and supported the radical secessionist leadership of the South. In Mason's view, the industrializing North, corrupted by banking interests, threatened the southern way of life. A strict constructionist, he was the author of the Fugitive Slave Law of 1850 and believed slavery should be expanded into the territories without restrictions. In 1850 he refused to join Robert Toombs, Howell Cobb, William L. Yancey, and other southern moderates and instead allied himself with Robert Barnwell Rhett and other obstructionists, who refused any concessions to the antislavery element in Congress in the interest of a compromise on the issue of slavery in the territories. By that time Mason did not wish to preserve a Union that rejected southern values and leadership, and he was prepared to secede from the Union. In 1856 he was similarly outspoken in his commitment to lead Virginia out of the Union if the newly formed Republican party was successful in electing John C. Frémont as president.

Early in 1860, with Mason serving his tenth year as chairman of the Senate Foreign Relations Committee, Dudley Mann, a member of the first diplomatic delegation appointed by the fledgling Confederacy, traveled to Washington to seek his advice before departing for Europe. After a thorough briefing on the new Confederate Constitution, Mason expressed to Mann his disappointment that he was unable to do more, at that time, than voice his expectation that Virginia would soon join the Confederacy.

With the Confederate bombardment of Fort Sumter on 12 April 1861 and Lincoln's subsequent call for volunteers to suppress the southern rebellion, Mason and other secessionists persuaded Virginia to join the rebellion. Mason's fellow Virginian, R. M. T. Hunter, with whom he had shared accommodations while both were in Washington, was appointed Confederate secretary of state. Hunter immediately determined that only permanent diplomatic representatives might obtain European recognition of the Confederacy. Mason, because of his experience as chairman of the Senate Foreign Relations Committee and his close friendship with President Jefferson Davis, and John Slidell of Louisiana were appointed to fill the permanent positions in London and Paris respectively. The newly appointed diplomats, along with an entourage of family, secretaries, and friends, passed through the Union blockade bound for Europe aboard the *Theodora* on 12 October 1861. They safely reached Cuba and, after a brief stay, departed for Europe aboard the British ship *Trent*.

On 8 November 1861 Captain Charles Wilkes, commander of the U.S. frigate *San Jacinto*, stopped and boarded the *Trent* on the high seas. Wilkes, without direct orders, had been searching for the two Confederate diplomats, and he ordered Mason and Slidell seized and removed from the *Trent*. The boarding of a neutral British ship and the removal of persons under the protection of the British flag provoked a strong diplomatic response from England. The British demanded the return of Mason and Slidell and a public apology from the U.S. government. After a tense cabinet meeting on 25 December 1861, Secretary of State William H. Seward persuaded President Lincoln to release the two southerners to prevent armed intervention by the British. Mason and his colleague were returned to British custody on 2 January 1862, and they proceeded to Europe. The "*Trent* affair," one of the major diplomatic incidents during the American Civil War, elevated Mason to international recognition.

Upon his arrival in London, Mason immediately sought British recognition of the Confederacy. He organized a group of British sympathizers into the famous "Confederate lobby," which pressed for favorable action for the southern cause in Great Britain throughout the war. Lord John Russell, the British foreign secretary, refused to accept Mason as an official representative or to meet with him in any official capacity. Russell's decision offended the prideful Mason, who frequently made inappropriate and provocative comments about his exclusion from official diplomatic circles.

Confederate operatives, led by Mason, met with limited success by raising much needed financial support through various means, particularly the $3 million Erlanger bond issue released on the open market in March 1863. He also coordinated the legal obstruction that allowed the construction and escape of the Confederate raiders *Florida* and *Alabama*. Mason failed to overcome a growing antislavery mood or the realities of the emerging power politics in Europe and ultimately failed in his diplomatic mission to obtain European recognition or intervention on behalf of the South.

When the Confederacy collapsed in 1865, Mason was isolated from his home and family. His wife and children fled to Montreal, Canada, where Mason joined them in April 1866. They rented a house in Niagara Falls, Canada, where a number of southern exiles resided. Finally in 1868 Mason was able to make his initial trip back to Virginia. His health failing, he wished to return his family to a friendly environment. Depressed and bitter that battles around Winchester had destroyed Selma, Mason purchased a cottage near Alexandria that he named "Clarens." Mason died there.

• The James Mason Papers in the Manuscript Division of the Library of Congress contain correspondence from the Civil War years. Virginia Mason, *The Public Life and Diplomatic Correspondence of James M. Mason* (1906), written by his daughter, contains selected personal letters. His official diplomatic correspondence is included in *The Official Records of the Union and Confederate Navies in the War of the Rebellion*, ser. 2, vol. 3 (30 vols., 1894–1922). The Confederate State Department Papers ("Pickett Papers"), Library of Congress, contain correspondence between Mason, Slidell, and other operatives in Europe. For a good overview of the *Trent* incident, see Norman B. Ferris, *The "Trent" Affair: A Diplomatic Crisis* (1977). On Mason's diplomatic role more generally, see E. D. Adams, *Great Britain and the American Civil War* (1924); Frank L. Owsley, *King Cotton Diplomacy: Foreign Relations of the Confederate States of America* (1936); D. P. Crook, *The North, the South, and the Powers* (1974); Brian Jenkins, *Britain and the War for the Union* (2 vols., 1973); and Howard Jones, *Union in Peril: The Crisis over British Intervention in the Civil War* (1972).

CHARLES M. HUBBARD

MASON, James Tate (20 May 1882–20 June 1936), surgeon, was born in Lahore, Orange County, Virginia, the son of Claiborne Rice Mason and Mary Moore Woolfolk. He trained in medicine at the University of Virginia, graduating in 1905, and he completed a surgical internship in Philadelphia in 1906. He then found a position as a ship's doctor on the steamship *President* and traveled to Seattle, arriving in 1907. He was attracted to the Pacific Northwest and found employment as a company doctor for the Pacific Coast Coal Company. He married Laura DeWolfe Whittlesey in 1912; they had two sons and one daughter. In 1911 he was elected as the county coroner and introduced significant reforms in that office, instituting the practice of photography in coroners' investigations. After two successful terms as county coroner, Mason in 1916 was appointed as the chief of the King County Hospital, serving in that capacity through the end of the First World War (1916–1920).

The epidemic of Spanish influenza that struck the Northwest in late September 1918 exposed a severe shortage of hospital beds in Seattle. Mason, in partnership with several colleagues, founded the Mason Clinic. Under Mason's leadership these physicians planned to build a combined hospital and clinic building to promote their specialty group practice. Completed in 1920, the Virginia Mason Hospital was unique for its time and was modeled on the principle of group practice exemplified by the Mayo Clinic. The six-story fireproof steel and concrete building commingled acute and ambulatory care, with its entire first floor devoted to physicians' offices. Upper floors contained lab and X-ray facilities, specialty procedure rooms, and, for fee-for-service and contract patients, a mixture of private rooms and wards. By 1929 the Mason Clinic and Virginia Mason Hospital had seventeen practicing specialists, several interns, and a special program in the treatment of diabetes.

While Mason was introducing this new mode of medical practice in Seattle, his surgical career was winning him recognition at the state and national level. Throughout the 1920s he published papers based upon his clinical experiences, including a frank evaluation of goiter surgery titled "Mistakes in One Hundred Thyroidectomies," delivered before the Seventy-first Annual Session of the American Medical Association (AMA) in New Orleans. By mid-career he was a consulting surgeon of the U.S. Marine Hospital at Seattle, the American Mail Line, the Alaska Steamship Company, and the Northern Pacific Railway Company; he was also a fellow of the American College of Surgeons and a member of the American Surgical Association, the American Association for the Study of Goiter, and the Western, Southern, and Pacific Coast Surgical Associations. In the 1920s he became active in national medical politics, serving as the secretary of the AMA section on general and abdominal surgery from 1923 to 1926 and as an elected member to the AMA House of Delegates from 1928 to 1934.

In 1935, at the peak of his professional life, Mason was elected president of the AMA. The midst of the depression was a troubled time for organized medicine, and the AMA meetings of the mid-1930s were characterized by debates over the financing and delivery of medical care. In order to run for national office, Mason was forced to relinquish several lucrative medical contracts to the King County Medical Service Bureau, run by the local medical society. He did so reluctantly, and the transfer of business severely damaged the financial conditions of the Virginia Mason Hospital and Clinic. Throughout the last months of 1935, president-elect Mason toured the nation, but the traveling and speechmaking exhausted him, and he was hospitalized. In May 1936, as the Kansas City meeting of the AMA convened, Mason listened on the radio from his hospital bed as the delegates read a message relaying the "affectionate regard of American medicine" for him. In early June an AMA representative traveled to his bedside to award him the Presidential Medal of the association. Just three weeks later he died in Seattle of a stroke after leg amputation for a blood clot.

Mason was long remembered in the Pacific Northwest as a local doctor who achieved national prominence. Throughout his career, Mason embodied the ambivalence of the medical profession over the growing phenomenon of prepaid group practice. As a former coal company doctor and contract practitioner, he felt that specialty group practice was a valuable and efficient way to practice, and he built a hospital and clinic devoted to this principle. Yet in a speech delivered after his election as the president of the AMA in the economically troubled mid-1930s, Mason warned against the dangers "that would lie ahead with the adoption of various ill considered health insurance schemes," noting that "the stress of economic necessity is the greatest force that is sapping the roots of our system of medical ethics today" (*Journal of the American Medical Association* 106 [16 May 1936]: 1695. Throughout his career he remained concerned with the quality and efficiency of medical care, founding one of the premier group practices of the Pacific Northwest and using his influence as a highly regarded surgeon to argue for the establishment of an American board of surgery. Always the consummate gregarious clinician, Mason received notes of appreciation for decades from patients he had first seen in the coal camps of western Washington.

• Several of Mason's surviving papers and ephemera are in the possession of Tate Mason, Jr., in Seattle, Wash. The most important of Mason's published papers include "Impressions Received from a Visit to Some Eastern Surgical Clinics," *Northwest Medicine* 6 (Aug. 1914): 246–48; "Mistakes in 100 Thyroidectomies, with Description of New Method of Thyroid Cauterization in Treatment of Exophthalmic Goiter," *Journal of the American Medical Association* 75 (17 July 1920); "Clinical Symptoms and Treatment of Exophthalmic Goiter," *Journal-Lancet* 50 (1 Dec. 1930): 583–86; and "Conservative Treatment of Cholecycstitis," *Journal of the American Medical Association* 99 (19 Sept. 1932): 891–93. A complete bibliography of his published works is listed in George Aaron Williams, "J. Tate Mason, M.D. (1882–1936): His Contributions to the History of Medicine in the Pacific Northwest," (M.A. thesis, Univ. of Southern California, Jan. 1953). For background on the Virginia Mason Hospital and Clinic, see "Virginia Mason Medical Center: Fifty Years of Serving, 1920–1970," *Virginia Mason Hospital Review* (Spring 1970); and Alan E. Nourse, *Virginia Mason Medical Center: The First Fifty Years* (1970). A detailed obituary is in the *Seattle Times*, 21 June 1936.

NANCY ROCKAFELLAR

MASON, Jeremiah (27 Apr. 1768–14 Oct. 1848), lawyer and U.S. senator, was born in Lebanon, Connecticut, the son of Jeremiah Mason, a prominent farmer, and Elizabeth Fitch. In his later life Mason lamented his lack of formal education until age fourteen—only three months for each of three winters. Compensating with two years of disciplined study, he entered Yale in 1784 and graduated in 1788 with great skill in forensic disputation. While at Yale he observed trials in New Haven, which inspired him to become a lawyer. He studied briefly with Simeon Baldwin in Connecticut, but seeing few career opportunities there, he moved to Vermont in 1789. There he read law with Stephen Row Bradley, who allowed his student to share in the practice and its income. In June 1791, Mason was admitted to the Vermont bar, but the better reputation of the New Hampshire bar caused him later that year to move to Portsmouth in Rockingham County, New Hampshire, where he gained admission to the bar. In 1799 he married Mary Means, with whom he had eight children. By 1805 he had become the acknowledged leader of the New Hampshire bar, challenged only by Daniel Webster, with whom Mason enjoyed a lifelong friendship.

Mason remained steadfastly committed to the practice of law, seldom venturing into other pursuits. After three years as attorney general of New Hampshire from 1802 to 1805, he resigned because the salary was unacceptably low. He served as a Federalist U.S. senator from 1813 to 1817 and also spent several terms in the New Hampshire legislature, but he refused several judicial appointments, including the chief justiceship of New Hampshire, again because the salary was inadequate. He also served as president of the Portsmouth branch of the Bank of the United States during the Jacksonian Bank War (1831–1832). Mason stayed at Portsmouth until 1832, when he moved to Boston where professional fees were higher.

The New Hampshire phase of the Dartmouth College litigation was Mason's most celebrated case. Jeremiah Smith and Webster teamed with Mason in representing the Dartmouth College trustees in their resistance to the state's takeover of the college in 1816. Mason's two-hour argument before the New Hampshire Superior Court, found fully only in Timothy Farrar's report of the case, was a powerful, traditional due-process, rule-of-law argument against summary deprivation of private property. A judicial hearing, Mason argued, and not legislative enactment, was the proper method for determining whether private rights could be deprived. He argued that the 1816 New Hampshire legislation violated the due process clause of the New Hampshire constitution and the contract clause (Article One, section 10) of the U.S. Constitution. Webster acknowledged using Mason's argument in successfully arguing the case on appeal to the U.S. Supreme Court in 1819.

Early-nineteenth-century lawyers referred to the Rockingham County bar as an arena of giants. It was a severe school of practice among lawyers who were more concerned with justice for their clients than kind treatment for their opponents. Certainly Mason, at six feet seven inches, was physically impressive. His intellectual powers were just as impressive. In this arena of giants, wrote William Plumer Jr., Mason was "the Ajax or Agamemnon, towering head and shoulders above the rest" (p. 179). His skill as a defense lawyer, especially in cross-examination, his deep familiarity with the common law and local New England customs, and his plain-spoken addresses to juries made him formidable. Webster called him a "cause-getting man" (Curtis, p. 90).

Mason is a transitional figure in the development of American law. He and Jeremiah Smith were responsible for professionalizing the law in New Hampshire by successfully introducing respect for the technicalities of the law. Such mastery and the power of his personality, his compelling logic, capacity for hard work, and legendary sarcasm made him one of the finest of early-nineteenth-century lawyers. All who opposed him or witnessed him in court testified to his power. Webster was so impressed by Mason at Portsmouth that he modified his style of argument by removing some ornamentation; Joseph Story had much the same response. Exceptionally skillful at local and state law, Mason was also an astute constitutional lawyer, although he never argued before the U.S. Supreme Court. His *Dartmouth College* argument demonstrated this, and his last reported case was an 1839 constitutional law case, *Boston Water Power Company v. Boston and Worcester Railroad*, involving the question of eminent domain and whether government grants may be taken under it. Webster declared, "If you were to ask me who was the greatest lawyer in the country, I should answer John Marshall; but if you took me by the throat and pinned me to the wall and demanded my *real* opinion, I should be compelled to say it was Jere. Mason" (Bell, p. 506).

In the autumn of 1848, Mason took his wife to Mt. Auburn cemetery in Portsmouth and picked a burial spot. Two weeks later he died of a stroke in Boston, Massachusetts.

• The Jeremiah Mason Papers are at the library of the New Hampshire Historical Society, Concord. Mason's autobiography covering his life to 1797 and a good collection of his letters, many to his wife, are in G. S. Hillard, ed., *Memoir, Autobiography and Correspondence of Jeremiah Mason* (1873). A review of Hillard's *Memoir* is G. J. Clark, ed., *Memoirs of Jeremiah Mason* (1873). General biographical information for his life after 1797 is in W. D. Lewis, *Great American Lawyers*, vol. 3 (1907); C. H. Hill in *American Law Review*, Jan. 1878; and Charles H. Bell, *Bench and Bar of New Hampshire* (1894). Francis N. Stites, *Private Interest and Public Gain: The Dartmouth College Case, 1819* (1972) offers a description and analysis of Mason's role in that controversy. Mason's *Dartmouth College* argument occupies forty pages in Timothy Farrar, *Report of the Case of the Trustees of Dartmouth College against William H. Woodward* (1819). There are references to Mason in biographies of his contemporaries and colleagues, including William Plumer, Jr., *Life of William Plumer*, ed. A. P. Peabody (1857; repr. 1969); Lynn W. Turner, *William Plumer of New Hampshire, 1759–1850* (1962); Maurice G. Baxter, *Daniel Webster and the Supreme Court* (1966); Robert Ernst, *Rufus King: American Federalist* (1968); and Claude M. Fuess, *Rufus Choate: The Wizard of the Law* (1928).

FRANCIS N. STITES

MASON, John (c. 1600–30 Jan. 1672), soldier and magistrate, was born in England of unknown parents. Little is known of his early life except that he saw military service in the Netherlands. He migrated to the Massachusetts Bay Colony sometime before 2 July 1633. He was appointed captain of the Dorchester militia shortly after his arrival, and he was one of the founders of Windsor, Connecticut, in 1635.

Mason is best known for his role as commander of the Connecticut forces in the Pequot War (1636–1637). The Pequots had already laid siege to the English settlement at Fort Saybrook on the Connecticut coast when Wethersfield settlers, despite earlier promises to the contrary, seized lands from the local Sequin Indians. Their sachem, Sowheag, went to the Pequots for help. In late April 1637 the Pequots attacked Wethersfield, killing nine and taking two young girls as prisoners. The attack spurred the colony's leaders to action. Mason organized a force of 80 Connecticut militia, 20 Massachusetts militia under Captain John Underhill, 100 Mohegans and other local Indians led by the Mohegan sachem Uncas, and 500 Narragansett Indians to invade Pequot territory. Rather than move down the Pequot River (now the Thames River) and attack the principal Indian stronghold directly, Mason approached from Narragansett country to the east, ensuring himself the element of surprise. He also decided to attack the lesser Pequot village on the Mystic River rather than the main fortress on the Thames. Underhill and Lieutenant Lion Gardiner, the commanding officer at Saybrook, raised some objections, but both lent their support after the expedition's chaplain spent a night in prayer and contemplation and endorsed the new strategy.

On the night of 25 May Mason moved his force to the circular, palisaded fort that served as the Pequot village, and the men quietly surrounded it. They attacked at dawn. Mason himself recounted in his *Brief History of the Pequot War*, "We had formerly concluded to destroy them by the Sword and save the Plunder," but when he began to encounter resistance he decided to burn the entire village. He later claimed that 150 Pequot warriors had arrived at the fort the day before the attack, necessitating the more drastic strategy. Some historians question the presence of the additional warriors and judge Mason's actions even more harshly, but his own description of the subsequent events leaves no doubt of the suffering the Indians experienced: "And indeed such a dreadful Terror did the Almighty let fall upon their spirits that they would fly from us and run into the very Flames where many of them perished." God himself, Mason noted, "laughed at the Enemies of his People, made them a fiery Oven. . . . Thus did the Lord judge among the Heathen, filling the Place with dead Bodies!" The soldiers killed those who managed to escape the flames, and their Indian allies did the same to those who escaped the English. The Narragansetts, however, had withdrawn after Mason had announced his plan to attack the village and not the main Pequot fort; they were shocked at the colonists' intent, while Mason accused them of cowardice. Certainly the English enjoyed an insurmountable advantage; in just minutes, about 700 Pequots died. Only seven survived to be captured, and perhaps half a dozen escaped.

Mason was promoted to major after the war, and the Massachusetts General Court commissioned him to write a history of the conflict. An edited version of this work was published, without attribution, by Increase Mather in 1677 as part of his *Relation of the Troubles Which Have Hapned in New England.* . . . In 1736 the Puritan minister Thomas Prince published the full version, with a preface, as *A Brief History of the Pequot War*. Mason became an important figure in Connecticut politics over the next three decades, serving as deputy to the general court from 1637 to 1642, as magistrate from 1642 to 1660, as deputy governor from 1660 to 1669, and as an assistant from 1669 to 1672. He also served as chief military officer for the colony for much of this time, and he handled Indian relations for both Connecticut and for the New England Confederation. Married twice, he had one child with his first wife, who died in 1638, and seven children with his second wife, Anne Peck, whom he had married in 1639. Mason died in Norwich, Connecticut.

Mason's life and career remind us that many inhabitants of early New England migrated to the region for more than just religious reasons. A contemporary described him as "full of Martial Bravery and Vigour." For Mason and many others, the New World, even New England, offered opportunities for adventure and political and economic opportunity not available in England. His actions in the Pequot War remind us, most graphically, of the cruelty that sometimes accompanied Puritan self-righteousness.

• The histories written by Mason and other participants remain indispensable sources, despite their obvious biases. They have been collected in Charles Orr, ed., *The History of the Pequot War: The Contemporary Accounts of Mason, Underhill, Vincent and Gardiner* (1897). The relevant portions of the following works contain important information on Mason: Francis Jennings, *The Invasion of America: Indians, Colonialism, and the Cant of Conquest* (1975); Alden T. Vaughan, *New England Frontier: Puritans and Indians, 1620–1675* (1965); Douglas Edward Leach, *Arms for Empire: A Military History of the British Colonies in North America, 1607–1763* (1973); John E. Ferling, *Struggle for a Continent: The Wars of Early America* (1993); Neal Salisbury, *Manitou and Providence: Indians, Europeans, and the Making of New England, 1500–1643* (1982); and Steven T. Katz, "The Pequot War Reconsidered," *New England Quarterly* 64 (June 1991): 206–24.

RONALD P. DUFOUR

MASON, John Young (18 Apr. 1799–3 Oct. 1859), planter-lawyer, politician, and diplomat, was born at "Homestead," the family plantation in Greensville County, Virginia, the son of Edmunds Mason and Frances Ann Young, both descendants of landed southern Tidewater families. An excellent student, young Mason graduated from the University of North Carolina in 1816, read law with Judge Griffin Stith in Southampton County, and then attended the law school of Judge Tapping Reeve in Litchfield, Connecticut. Admitted to the Virginia bar in 1819, he began his practice in Greensville County but moved to Southampton County following his marriage in 1821 to Mary Ann Fort, the daughter of a wealthy planter. They had eight children. Mason practiced law in the courts of Greensville, Brunswick, and Sussex counties as well as Southampton, attended the Episcopal church, and became a member of the Masonic Order. Eventually the couple owned the 2,000-acre plantation "Fortsville" that extended from Southampton into

Greensville and Sussex counties, a townhouse in Richmond, and a plantation in Mississippi. In the 1820s and the 1830s Mason prospered. The census of 1830 lists him as the owner of forty-eight slaves in Southampton County alone. While he later sent sixty slaves to Mississippi, he still held eighty-three in Virginia in 1850.

Most of Mason's adult life was spent in public service. Soon after moving to Southampton, he was elected to the Virginia General Assembly, where he sat in the House of Delegates from 1823 until 1827. He was then elevated to the state senate, where he remained for the next four years. During this time he also served as commonwealth's attorney for Greensville County and as a delegate to the constitutional convention that met in 1829–1830. Virginia politics during these years placed a heavy emphasis on personal characteristics, and Mason revealed quickly the even temper and convivial nature that marked his career. Like most Jeffersonian Republicans in the Old Dominion, especially those from the Southside, Mason was a supporter of the Doctrines of '98—states' rights and strict construction of the Constitution—when he served in the general assembly. In the Virginia constitutional convention of 1829–1830, he was an opponent of democratic reforms, such as the expansion of the suffrage and the reapportionment of the legislature in line with the distribution of white population.

From 1831 to 1837 Mason served three terms in the U.S. House of Representatives, where he became chairman of the Committee on Foreign Affairs and championed "Spread Eagle" diplomacy and an interest in Texas. He was a staunch supporter of Andrew Jackson on all matters except the Force Bill, drawn up in response to South Carolina's efforts to nullify federal law and which he, like most Virginia Democrats, opposed. In 1835 he showed a modesty uncharacteristic of a Southside planter in stepping aside to allow his college friend James K. Polk to become Speaker of the House.

Mason resigned his seat in Congress in 1837 to accept a judgeship on the General Court of Virginia, and in 1841 he was elevated to the federal bench by Martin Van Buren. However, he returned to Washington three years later, when fellow conservative Virginian, President John Tyler, who had broken with the Whig party, called on this ideologically compatible Democrat to join his makeshift "no-party" cabinet as secretary of the navy. Mason was the only member of Tyler's cabinet retained by Polk, who was elected in 1844, and he obliged his old collegiate and political friend first as attorney general and then during the Mexican War as secretary of the navy. Mason was an ardent expansionist and an advocate of Texas annexation as a member of Tyler's cabinet. His commitment to Manifest Destiny combined with their long friendship led Polk to retain Mason in his cabinet and to look to him for advice. The Virginian helped Polk draft his constitutionally orthodox vetoes of the Reviver and Harbors Bill and the French Spoliation Claims Bill. The president often used the tactful Mason as a go-between to smooth ruffled feathers of congressional leaders of both parties.

From 1849 to 1853 Mason returned to private life and was chosen by the Democratic assembly to be president of the James River and Kanawha Company, Virginia's major state-supported internal improvement company. During this time he was elected as a delegate to the constitutional convention of 1850–1851 and was made the presiding officer.

While Mason consistently sustained the administrations of Jackson, Van Buren, and Polk and thus the basic policies that defined the American democracy in the 1830s and 1840s, he continued to oppose the democratization of the constitution of the Old Dominion. As president of the reform convention of 1850–1851, Mason spoke against the hostility between the eastern and western portions of the state and in favor of compromise, but in the end he voted against the document that expanded the suffrage, reformed representation to accommodate the white population in the West, and made most state and local offices elective. His position represented that of his Tidewater constituency, which rejected the constitution in the 1851 referenda.

Because of Mason's activity as a Democratic party spokesman and a presidential elector in 1852, Franklin Pierce appointed him as the American minister to France. By the 1850s Mason's faith in states' rights had evolved into a defense of southern rights, incorporating the dream of a Caribbean empire, which he had earlier advocated in the Polk cabinet. Along with James Buchanan and Pierre Soulé, the American ministers to England and Spain, Mason authored the belligerent Ostend Manifesto that asserted the right of the United States to seize Cuba by military force if Spain refused to sell the island or possibly freed the slaves, thus endangering American national interest. Although he was closely associated with the rapacious Democrats whom Pierce loosed upon Europe and who were vaguely associated under the "Young America" umbrella, Mason chose to deal with the French court on its own terms. He circumvented the order of Secretary of State William Marcy to dress as a republican and was able to ingratiate himself to Louis-Napoléon. Most of Mason's initial mission to France was devoted to defending the hotspur Soulé and defusing his quarrels.

A jaundiced nineteenth-century journalist writing in *Harpers* characterized Mason as a man "whose long official career was a marvel to everyone who knew him well and a piece of good luck at which he himself was much astonished." He was basically an intelligent compromiser who overvalued the good life. A more sympathetic observer described him as having a "commanding presence, kindly heart and good head" but added that Mason was "portly, indolent, and fond of comfort." Senator Thomas Hart Benton, who knew him well, said that Mason "only required having his stomach full of oysters and his hands full of cards to be perfectly happy." Surely he was easygoing and fun-loving, but at crucial points in cabinet meetings his inattention to detail and his uncritical reliance upon subordinates made him seem inept and uninformed if not incompetent. He was overly indulgent of his wife, who loved their house in Richmond, and of his daughters, who enjoyed their role in the frivolous aspects of life in Paris. He gave lavish parties at the French court, plied Louis-Napoléon with Virginia hams, tobacco, and potables, and managed to fritter away his huge estate. When Mason died suddenly in Paris, he left his wife and eldest son Lewis—who had tried vigilantly to manage the family's holdings in Virginia and Mississippi during the 1840s and 1850s—bankrupt, at the mercy of his creditors, and living on family largess.

• The Mason Family Papers are at the Virginia Historical Society, and Mason's papers are at the Library of Congress. A contemporary sketch is in the *Richmond Whig*, 6 Nov. 1850. Frances Leigh Williams, "The Heritage and Preparation of a Statesman, John Young Mason, 1799–1859," *Virginia Magazine of History and Biography* 75 (1967): 305–30, provides information on Mason's family background and early life. Daniel W. Crofts, *Old Southampton: Politics and Society in a Virginia County, 1834–1869* (1992), reviews Mason's life and surroundings, and Robert P. Sutton, *Revolution to Secession: Constitution Making in the Old Dominion* (1989), includes a brief sketch along with a discussion of the conventions in which Mason participated. *The Diary of James K. Polk during His Presidency, 1845 to 1849*, ed. Milo M. Quaife (4 vols., 1910); T. N. Parmelee, "Recollections of an Old Stager," *Harpers New Monthly Magazine* 48 (Dec. 1873–May 1874): 254, 740; and Charles Sellers, *James K. Polk, Continentalist, 1843–1846* (1966), include many references to Mason's activities in the cabinet. Mason's diplomatic activities are discussed in Amos Aschbach Ettinger, *The Mission to Spain of Pierre Soulé, 1853–1855* (1932), and Robert E. May, *The Southern Dream of a Caribbean Empire, 1854–1861* (1973). Obituaries are in the *Richmond Enquirer*, 18 Oct. 1859, and the *Baltimore Sun*, 17 Oct. 1859.

WILLIAM G. SHADE

MASON, Lowell (8 Jan. 1792–11 Aug. 1872), music educator and composer, was born in Medfield, Massachusetts, the son of Johnson Mason, a businessman, and Catherine Hartshorn. Mason was educated in Medfield schools and singing schools, where he learned to read music. He took an active interest in music and at age sixteen conducted his church choir. Largely self-taught, he played many instruments and as a teenager led a local band. Nonetheless, he intended to become a businessman and not a musician, as he saw no future for himself in music, which offered little opportunity for a livelihood.

Finding no business opportunities locally, Mason moved to Savannah, Georgia, in 1813. There he worked first in a dry goods store and later at a bank. Continuing his musical pursuits, Mason taught in local singing schools, studied composition with Carl Frederick Abel, a gifted German immigrant, and served as organist and choir director at the Independent Presbyterian Church. Mason married Abigail Gregory of Westborough, Massachusetts, in 1817; they had four children. He also compiled and published his first tunebook, *The Boston Handel and Hay-*

dn Society Collection of Church Music (1822). An immediate success, the book appeared in successive editions through 1839.

Mason moved to Boston in 1827 and attained prominence as a church musician and educator. From 1827 to 1832 he was the president and music director of the Boston Handel and Haydn Society. Between 1827 and 1851 he also served as organist and choir director at Boston's Hanover, Park, Essex, Bowdoin, and Winter Street Congregational churches. Mason developed his choirs into major performing groups. Using church facilities, he taught music to choir members and others, often free of tuition, to improve the quality of church music.

In 1833 Mason helped establish the Boston Academy of Music, Boston's first comprehensive music school. The academy enrolled 1,700 students for class and private instruction its first year, and enrollments grew steadily thereafter. In 1834 the academy pioneered annual teacher conventions, consisting of two weeks of summer training for music teachers and choir directors. Mason also taught at the Perkins Institute for the Blind (1832–1836), in private schools in Boston, and at Andover Theological Seminary (1836–1844), where he established the first church music course in an American Protestant seminary.

During his lifetime, Mason published over 100 separate works, including textbooks, hymnals, Sabbath school books, sheet music, and sacred and secular choral music anthologies. Mason's pedagogy is delineated in the *Manual of the Boston Academy of Music* (1834), a work Mason traced to various sources, including Johann Heinrich Pestalozzi and his followers. Many of Mason's publications became bestsellers, rendering him wealthy and influential in musical circles.

Mason believed that music should be part of the public school curriculum. As early as 1826, he argued that the improvement of church music is impossible unless children are taught music as they are taught to read. One goal of the Boston Academy of Music was to institute curricular music. To that end, Mason proved to be politically astute in working with academy and civic leaders.

To demonstrate that public school students could benefit from music instruction, Mason taught vocal music, without pay, at Hawes Grammar School in 1837–1838. The success of his teaching led the Boston School Committee to pass a landmark resolution on 28 August 1838 authorizing the hiring of music teachers for the public schools. Over time, school districts across the nation instituted music programs in their curricula, following Boston's example.

Mason was the first teacher hired under the 1838 resolution. He taught and hired associate teachers in the Boston public schools until 1851. Concurrently, he advanced teacher training by organizing music conventions, and in 1853 he joined with George F. Root and William Bradbury in establishing the New York Normal Musical Institute, a three-month training session for teachers. Mason's contemporaries praised his masterful teaching. Horace Mann invited Mason to teach at the annual Mann Institutes for Teachers beginning in 1845. Surviving letters from Mann testify to Mason's extraordinary skill, both in teaching music and in exemplifying the art of teaching. An avid collector of music and books on music, Mason built an extensive library. It was bequeathed to Yale University, where it remains a rich legacy for scholars.

Mason had spent seven months in Europe in 1837, and he returned there for fifteen months in 1852–1853. While traveling, he attended dozens of concerts, recitals, and church services and met many leading musicians. Mason's travel writings offer unique glimpses into contemporary music culture.

A lifelong advocate of congregational singing, Mason composed and arranged about 1,700 hymn tunes. Among the best known are Bethany ("Nearer, My God, to Thee"), Olivet ("My Faith Looks Up to Thee"), Dennis ("Blest Be the Tie That Binds"), and Hamburg ("When I Survey the Wondrous Cross"). During his retirement in Orange, New Jersey, Mason continued to compose and arrange, develop his music library, and participate in church music programs and teachers' conventions and institutes. Mason died at his home in Orange. His lasting contributions include his leadership and example as a music educator and an advocate of teacher training, his composing of beloved hymn tunes, his role in the revival of congregational singing, his writings, and his music library.

• Publications by and about Mason are described in Carol A. Pemberton, *Lowell Mason: A Bio-Bibliography* (1988). *A Yankee Musician in Europe: The 1837 Journals of Lowell Mason*, ed. Michael Broyles (1990), offers insights into Mason's thinking and into his era. The definitive biography is Pemberton, *Lowell Mason: His Life and Work* (1985). An unpublished biography by Henry Lowell Mason, Mason's grandson, is at the Beinecke Rare Book and Manuscript Library, Yale University. Mason's role in establishing public school music is described in Pemberton, "Critical Days for Music in American Schools," *Journal of Research in Music Education* 36 (Summer 1988): 69–79. Pemberton summarizes Mason's contributions to church music in "Praising God Through Congregational Song: Lowell Mason's Contributions to Church Music," *Hymn* 44 (Apr. 1993): 22–30. Essays addressing several aspects of Mason's career are featured in *The Quarterly: A Journal of Music Teaching and Learning* 3 (Fall 1992), an issue entirely devoted to Mason.

CAROL A. PEMBERTON

MASON, Lucy Randolph (26 July 1882–6 May 1959), labor activist and social reformer, was born at "Clarens," on Seminary Hill near Alexandria, Virginia, the daughter of Landon Randolph Mason, an Episcopal minister, and Lucy Ambler, a reformer. A direct descendant of George Mason, author of the Virginia Bill of Rights, and James Murray Mason, Confederate ambassador to Great Britain, Mason's pedigree included the oldest and most prominent families of the South. However, she and her four siblings grew up in modest circumstances, and the family finances did not permit her to finish high school. From 1904 to 1914, Mason worked as a stenographer at a Richmond law firm.

In 1914 Mason became the industrial secretary of the Richmond Young Women's Christian Association (YWCA), the first person to hold that position in a southern state. At the YWCA Mason developed her interest in labor causes, particularly those affecting wage-earning women. Not for the first time, her social standing helped her get away with controversial stands, such as organizing support for an all-female strike at a local company. She became an active member of the Union Label League, which encouraged shoppers to buy union-made products. In 1917 Samuel Gompers named Mason the Virginia chairman of the Committee on Women in Industry of the wartime National Advisory Committee on Labor.

After her mother's death in 1918, Mason resigned from the YWCA to care for her ailing father, until his death in 1923. Supported during this period by her brother John, Mason volunteered as president of the Richmond Equal Suffrage League and its successor the Richmond League of Women Voters. Like many suffragists, Mason argued that women had a special role to play in reforming society and that they needed the vote to help frame laws that served reform ends, especially the "humanizing of industrial processes." In 1923 Mason resumed her paid work for the Richmond YWCA as its general secretary, a position she held until 1932.

Inspired by the example of her parents, Mason's social activism was fueled by profound religious convictions. "If I had been a man," she once told a journalist, "I would have become a minister." Throughout her career, she invoked the principles of Christianity to demand justice for all of "God's children," whether black or white, male or female, rich or poor. Believing that "religion includes both one's relationship to God and to man," Mason cherished the social gospel ideal of creating "God's Kingdom on earth" (Salmond, p. 5). These ideas underpinned her efforts to improve the political and economic status of African Americans. In addition to fighting a Richmond segregation ordinance, Mason served on a biracial Negro Welfare Survey Committee in 1928 that led to the formation of the Richmond Urban League, whose Economic Committee Mason chaired. She also continued to lobby for state laws abolishing child labor and improving conditions and wages for women workers.

Mason's activism was sustained by loving relationships with like-minded women, which blurred the boundary between the personal and the professional in Mason's life. Perhaps her most intense partnership was with Katherine Gerwick, a national YWCA officer. Gerwick's sudden death in 1927 devastated Mason, who never married, and triggered her interest in spiritualism, the belief that the dead could communicate with the living.

Mason's activities in Virginia brought her to the attention of Florence Kelley of the National Consumers' League (NCL), a prominent labor reform group. For several months in 1931, the NCL paid Mason's salary as head of the fledgling Southern Committee on Women and Children in Industry, during which time Mason promoted progressive labor bills and wrote a groundbreaking pamphlet, *Standards for Workers in Southern Industry* (1931). In 1932 Mason moved to New York City to succeed Kelley as the NCL's general secretary.

Mason led the NCL as it enjoyed a resurgence of influence during the New Deal years. Mason made the promotion of labor and social welfare legislation in the southern states one of the NCL's highest priorities, and she forged fruitful ties among southern liberals, labor officials, and government administrators. While testifying in support of a federal Fair Labor Standards bill at congressional hearings in 1937, Mason met John L. Lewis, president of the Congress of Industrial Organizations (CIO), whose strategy of organizing across boundaries of skill, race, and sex impressed her. At fifty-five, she became a southern public relations representative for the CIO.

Mason served as a "roving ambassador" for the CIO in the South for sixteen years, from the heady promise of the late 1930s through the war, the postwar reaction, and the frustration of the "Operation Dixie" drive (1946–1953). Using many of the ideas and methods she had developed at the YWCA and the NCL, Mason acted as an "interpreter" for the labor movement, addressing southern college classes, church groups, social workers, and civic clubs to explain the goals of the CIO. Mason drew upon her extensive contacts among southern ministers, journalists, academics, and politicians in an effort to offset deep-seated southern hostility to unions and to interracial organizing. When the CIO met violence, Mason helped protect workers and organizers by publicizing civil liberties violations, often asking friends in the Roosevelt administration to intervene.

Mason played a vital role in the development of southern liberalism, through her involvement with the Southern Policy Committee, the Southern Conference for Human Welfare, and the Southern Regional Council. She also was an active officer of the Southern Summer School for Women Workers and the Highlander Folk School. Mason retired in 1953 after writing a well-received memoir, *To Win These Rights* (1952). She died in Atlanta, Georgia.

Throughout her career, Mason argued that recognizing the interdependence of economic and political democracy was essential to reforming the South and the nation. She insisted that political democracy was withering in the absence of "industrial democracy," and that successful labor reform in the South depended on eliminating the race and sex barriers that kept workers in competition. Although her hopes for southern unions were not fulfilled, Mason ranks high among the southern liberals who gave the New Deal a toehold in the South and helped to sow the seeds for the civil rights movement.

• Mason's papers are at the Perkins Library, Duke University, Durham, N.C. In addition to those cited above, Mason's publications include *The Divine Discontent* (1912), a pamphlet on woman suffrage; "Southerners Look at the South," *North Georgia Review* (Fall–Winter 1938–1939): 17–18, 40; "The CIO and the Negro in the South," *Journal of Negro Education* 14 (Fall 1945): 552–61; and "I Turned to Social Action Right at Home," in *Labor's Relation to Church and Community*, ed. Liston Pope (1947). For a detailed biography of Mason, see John Salmond, *Miss Lucy of the CIO* (1988). On her Richmond years, see Betsy Brinson, "'Helping Others to Help Themselves': Social Advocacy and Wage-Earning Women in Richmond, Virginia, 1910–1932" (Ph.D. diss., Union Graduate School, 1984). For Mason's work in the mid-1930s, see Landon Storrs, "Civilizing Capitalism: The National Consumers' League and the Politics of Fair Labor Standards in the New Deal Era" (Ph.D. diss., Univ. of Wisconsin–Madison, 1994). John Glen, *Highlander: No Ordinary School, 1932–1962* (1988), and Linda Reed, *Simple Decency and Common Sense: The Southern Conference Movement, 1938–1963* (1991), document Mason's contributions to important southern liberal groups. Many historians have written about Mason's work with the CIO, including Barbara Griffith, *The Crisis of American Labor: Operation Dixie and the Defeat of the CIO* (1988), and Steve Fraser, *Labor Will Rule: Sidney Hillman and the Rise of American Labor* (1991). Obituaries are in the *Atlanta Constitution*, 7 May 1959, and the *New York Times*, 8 May 1959.

LANDON R. Y. STORRS

MASON, Max (26 Oct. 1877–23 Mar. 1961), mathematical physicist, was born in Madison, Wisconsin, the son of Edwin Cole Mason, a businessman and public accountant, and Josephine Vroman. Although his parents named him Charles Max Mason, he never used his first name even on official correspondence, going instead by Max. Mason did his undergraduate work at the University of Wisconsin. He had intended to study engineering but changed to mathematics after Charles Sumner Slichter, professor of mathematics and later dean of the graduate school at the university, encouraged his interest in the subject. Mason received his B.Litt. in 1898 and spent the next academic year teaching mathematics at the high school in Beloit, Wisconsin. At the same time, he coached the track team, led the school orchestra, and trained the debating club.

In the autumn of 1900 Mason began graduate work at the University of Göttingen in Germany. He wrote his dissertation on boundary values of differential equations under renowned mathematician David Hilbert and received his Ph.D. magna cum laude in 1903. In subsequent years, Mason published research on differential equations and on the calculus of variations. He taught mathematics at the Massachusetts Institute of Technology in 1903–1904 and then at Yale University's Sheffield Scientific School from 1904 until 1908. In 1904 he married Mary Louise Freeman, with whom he had three children.

The University of Wisconsin hired Mason as an associate professor of mathematics in 1908. He held this position for one year. He then joined the physics department as a full professor, having acquired an interest in mathematical physics while teaching a few courses in that department. Warren Weaver, one of Mason's students, considered him an excellent teacher who "had a great and lasting influence on a large number of graduate students. The mediocre ones found him pretty tough, but the really good ones almost worshiped him" (Weaver, p. 217).

Between 1917 and 1919 Mason took a leave of absence from the university to serve as a member of the submarine committee of the National Research Council. During this time he invented a sonar submarine-detecting device known as the multiple-variable, or "M-V," tube. These tubes consisted of sets of sound receivers, which were mounted on the outside of a ship below the water line, and transmitters that focused the sound inside the ship. The device allowed the crew to determine the location of a submarine or other ship producing the noise. Mason supervised the production and installation of his invention while working at the Naval Equipment Station in New London, Connecticut. According to an associate at the time, Louis B. Slichter (son of Charles Slichter), Mason's "contributions were critical in all aspects of these problems, in acoustical theory, and in mechanical and naval engineering. The short time required to bring this detector into service is almost complete evidence of the energy and ability which Mason concentrated upon this problem" (Weaver, p. 217).

After the war, Mason continued his research in physics, focusing on electromagnetic field theory. He published *The Electromagnetic Field*, written with Warren Weaver, in 1929. In 1925 he left his position at Wisconsin to become the president of the University of Chicago. The first president of the university from outside its faculty, Mason helped to establish close ties between the institution and the city of Chicago. During his three years as president, Mason successfully campaigned to increase the university's endowment and building funds and spoke extensively on educational subjects. In an article for *World's Work*, he discussed the importance of private universities. Because of their freedom from political control, Mason believed that such institutions had "the duty of experimentation in educational method, and the duty to promote higher standards of productive scholarship" (June 1928).

After his wife's death in 1928, Mason left Chicago and became the director of the Rockefeller Foundation's newly organized Division of Natural Sciences, with the understanding that he would assume the foundation's presidency when George Edgar Vincent retired from the position. Mason headed the foundation from 1930 until 1936. His interest in behavioral research and in the cooperation between the physical and the biological sciences contributed to an increased emphasis on psychiatry in the foundation's Division of Medical Sciences and to a program in experimental biology in its Division of Natural Sciences.

In 1936 Mason moved to California to become the chair of the California Institute of Technology's observatory council and a member of its executive council. As chair of the observatory council, Mason directed both the administrative and technical aspects of the construction of the Mount Palomar Observatory, which was completed in 1948. From 1945 until 1951

he served on the institute's board of trustees. In 1938 he married Helen Schermerhorn Young. A year after her death in 1944, Mason married Daphne Crane Drake. He had no children in either of these marriages.

During World War II Mason advised the Naval Research Laboratory on scientific aspects of defense against submarines, while also heading a committee appointed by the National Academy of Sciences. With funds from the Rockefeller Foundation and from the National Defense Research Committee, he studied problems related to the water-entry of projectiles and to the sinking rate of depth charges in order to improve the effectiveness of anti-submarine attacks.

Mason retired in 1949 and moved with his third wife to Claremont, California, where he taught science courses at the Claremont Colleges in 1948–1949 and continued to return to Caltech for special occasions. Over the course of his career, he had become a member of the National Academy of Sciences, the American Mathematical Society, the American Physical Society, the Deutsche Mathematiker-Vereiningung, and the Circolo Matematico di Palermo. He died in Claremont.

Mason combined creative research with the capacity to teach and direct the work of others. His colleagues respected both his scientific pursuits and his administrative abilities. He also foresaw the need to combine scientific progress with concern for society. As he wrote in the preface to Edward Price Bell's *Europe's Economic Sunrise* (1927), "Unless man can set his social house in order, . . . all his knowledge of natural law, so dearly bought, will but serve to bring him the quicker to disaster."

• Records from Mason's university presidency are included in the University Presidents' Papers at the University of Chicago. The archives of the Rockefeller Foundation contain some of Mason's correspondence, his office diaries, and other materials documenting his presidency. The American Institute of Physics also holds some of his papers. Mason's dissertation is titled "Randwertaufgaben bei gowöhnlichen Differentialgleichungen," and his publications include "Zur Theorie der Randwertaufgaben," *Mathematische Annalen* 58 (1903): 528–44; "Green's Theorem and Green's Functions for Certain Types of Differential Equations," *Transactions of the American Mathematical Society* 5 (1903): 220–25; and "Submarine Detection by Multiple Unit Hydrophones," *Wisconsin Engineer* 25 (1921): 75–77, 99–102, and 116–20. Consult Warren Weaver, "Max Mason," *Biographical Memoirs*, vol. 37 (1963), pp. 205–36, for the most complete biography and a list of Mason's publications and speeches. See also Neil M. Clark, "Learn How to Play and You Will Know How to Live," *American Magazine*, June 1926, pp. 32–33 and 161–66, and Frederick Palmer, "Which Way America?" *World's Work*, June 1928, pp. 196–97. An obituary is in the *New York Times*, 24 Mar. 1961.

PATTI WILGER HUNTER

MASON, Otis Tufton (10 Apr. 1838–5 Nov. 1908), ethnologist and museologist, was born in Eastport, Maine, the son of John Mason, a sea trader, and Rachel Thompson Lincoln. The father suffered financial reversals when Mason was a child and moved the family several times before again becoming prosperous and settling in 1849 at Woodlawn Plantation in Fairfax County, Virginia. A devout Baptist with certain advanced ideas, John Mason provided schools for his workers' children and sent his own children to them. Otis Mason went on to study at Columbian College (now George Washington University) in Washington, D.C., where he earned an A.B. in 1861, an A.M. in 1862, and a Ph.D. in 1879.

In 1862 Mason married Sarah E. Henderson, the daughter of a local judge. They had three daughters. Mason became the principal of the preparatory school at Columbian College. In 1884 he became professor of anthropology at Columbian, teaching fourth-year students, and starting in 1892 he headed a graduate department of anthropology at the same institution.

For special study, Mason inclined towards the culture history of the eastern Mediterranean; he was especially interested in the people of the Bible. When he approached Joseph Henry, secretary of the Smithsonian Institution, concerning this subject, Henry and his assistant Spencer F. Baird persuaded Mason to study American Indian cultures instead. In doing so, they offered him the opportunity to enter a wide open field for academic work.

In 1872 Mason became a collaborator in ethnology at the Smithsonian. Along with his work with the institution's collection, Mason published instructions for the collection of ethnographic and archaeological artifacts; he also reported worldwide anthropological work in *Harper's Annual Record of Science and Industry*, the *American Naturalist*, and the *Annual Report of the Smithsonian Institution*. Mason also undertook the preparation of exhibits for the Centennial Exposition at Philadelphia in 1876.

Having acquired many specimens from the Philadelphia exposition, the Smithsonian established the United States National Museum. In 1884 Mason was appointed its curator of ethnology. His work with Columbian College then became secondary, and his life became almost entirely devoted to the study, exhibition, and description of the specimens under his care. He read exhaustively, corresponded widely, visited many museums in North America and abroad, and studied at first hand the manufacture and use of many types of objects and the ways in which they were preserved and exhibited in museums. Most of his publications derived directly or indirectly from this work and involved cross-cultural studies of activities such as agriculture, transportation, and child carrying, and investigations of specific types of artifacts.

Mason was strongly influenced by evolutionary ideas of the German Gustav Klemm. This work offered a detailed outline for the classification of ethnographic objects from any culture. In addition, it argued for exhibiting specimens of a given class so that, in theory, they progressed through all stages of development from the most primitive examples to the most sophisticated and modern. Such an exhibit, it was argued, would reflect the various stages through which human groups advanced in their cultural development. In 1887 Franz Boas strongly challenged Mason's use of this evolutionary frame. Boas argued that theory should be deferred in favor of data collection, and for exhibits he favored those based on ethnic groups.

Mason himself valued exhibits based on ethnic groups; he used them to demonstrate the influence of geography in determining the particular expression of a people's state of development. This was the basis of dioramas he arranged for the Columbian World's Exposition in Chicago in 1893. In addition he put forth a method for exhibiting both the material objects of given cultures and man's evolutionary development in a single installation.

As a vice president of the American Association for the Advancement of Science in 1877 and again in 1884, Mason presided over Section H, at that time the only national organization devoted to anthropology. In 1879 he was a founder of the Anthropological Society of Washington and served as its president in 1893–1895. Also in 1879 he was a founder of Washington's intellectual Cosmos Club. In 1890 he became a member of the United States Board of Geographic Names. In 1902 he was appointed acting head curator of the Department of Anthropology of the United States National Museum and later that year he became the head curator. Mason died in Washington, D.C.

Mason's contributions can perhaps be most appreciated if he is considered as an ethnologist with a specialty in museology. He was significantly involved in developing theories and methods of ethnological exhibits. His greatest and most enduring work, however, was probably the Smithsonian ethnological collection itself. As its first curator, Mason provided direction and much of the hands-on work for that large, sometimes very inclusive, and, in contrast to many others, well-documented collection. Furthermore, Mason's patient and persistent research in his collection is clearly indicated by his many publications on material culture. The best example is his masterpiece, "American Indian Basketry: A Study of a Textile Art Without Machinery" (*Annual Report of the United States National Museum*, 1900).

In the field of anthropology as a whole, Mason's recognition of the importance of environment to culture connects him to a topic that has become very important in the field. He also played important roles in the early organization of anthropology, being a leader in its learned societies and a significant figure in the early development of its bibliographic tools.

• Mason's papers are at the Smithsonian Institution. Its National Anthropological Archives holds several sets of papers, mostly research notes and correspondence concerning his research. The archives also has material connected to Mason's exhibits, especially photographs and labels. The Smithsonian Institution Archives (SIA) has collections of papers consisting of responses to Mason's request for information about American archaeological sites and letters of 1889 written in Europe, where Mason was studying museum techniques. In addition, the SIA has several other files that include Mason's materials. The George Washington University Library has a few documents concerning Mason's career as a teacher.

A work with biographical information is Carol Beth Hetler, "Otis Tufton Mason and the Organizing of Washington Anthropology, 1870–1895" (M.A. thesis, George Washington Univ., 1978). Mason's career is placed in the context of anthropological development in general and its development at the Smithsonian in particular in Curtis Hinsley, *Savages and Scientist: the Smithsonian Institution and the Development of American Anthropology, 1846–1910* (1981), republished as *The Smithsonian and the American Indian: Making a Moral Anthropology in Victorian America* (1994). Obituaries by Mason's friends and close associates include Walter Hough, *American Anthropologist*, n.s. 10 (1908): 661–67; Aleš Hrdlička, *Science* 28 (1908): 746–48; and Charles D. Walcott, *Annual Report of the Smithsonian Institution* (1909): 32.

JAMES R. GLENN

MASON, Richard Barnes (16 Jan. 1797–27 July 1850), army officer and military governor of California, was born in Fairfax County, Virginia, the son of George Mason (1753–1796) and Elizabeth Mary Ann Barnes Hooe, planters. Although his family was prominent—his grandfather, George Mason (1725–1792), had been a member of the Constitutional Convention—young Mason's father died before he was born, and an elder brother inherited the family estate. In 1817 Mason received a commission as second lieutenant of infantry in the U.S. Army and embarked on a lifelong military career. Promoted to captain in 1819, he served at garrisons in the Old Northwest and earned a reputation as a stern disciplinarian. At Fort Howard in 1821 he was nearly killed when a soldier, whom he had struck for making an impertinent remark, shot him in the chest with a load of pigeon shot.

Mason commanded a company in the Black Hawk War of 1832, and he saw action at the battle of Bad Axe Creek in southwestern Wisconsin, where the army crushed Black Hawk's band of Sauks and Foxes. During the following year, he was appointed to the rank of major in the newly formed Regiment of Dragoons, the first mounted regiment in the regular service since the War of 1812. Throughout the 1830s and early 1840s Mason was stationed at garrisons along the eastern edge of the Great Plains, and he took part in expeditions to gather topographical information and intimidate the Plains tribes into submission. In the years before the Mexican War, he commanded Fort Gibson in the present state of Oklahoma, a key post for administering the eastern Indians resettled in the West as a result of Indian removal. He married Elizabeth Margaret Hunter, with whom he had two children. (The date of their marriage is unknown.)

During the spring of 1846, about the time of the outbreak of war with Mexico, the War Department ordered Mason to New York on recruiting duty, and in June he was promoted to the rank of colonel and commander of the First Dragoon Regiment. In November 1846 he embarked on a naval vessel for California, where he was to relieve Brigadier General Stephen Watts Kearny as commander of the motley United States forces that had wrested that territory from the Mexicans. Arriving in San Francisco in February 1847, Mason encountered a confused and unstable political situation. A succession of military officers had governed the territory since its seizure the previous July. Their authority was poorly defined, however, and the occupation had been plagued by a power struggle between Kearny and Lieutenant Colonel John C. Frémont. Mason carried instructions from the War Department that clearly established Kearny's right to act as governor. In May 1847 both Kearny and Frémont left the region, and Mason assumed the combined military command and governorship, a position he was to hold for nearly two years. From the start Mason made clear that his regime was a military one, resting on the army's wartime authority to rule a conquered people, and that he would exercise all appointive, administrative, and judicial powers within the territory. Nevertheless, he demonstrated a sensitivity to Mexican concerns about U.S. rule by provisionally retaining a great part of the Mexican legal system. He also continued the use of alcaldes—municipal officials who exercised a range of judicial and administrative functions at the local level—though he appointed most of them rather than sanctioning elections.

As military governor, Mason faced a host of problems—insufficient funds, civil-military tensions, disputed land claims, American-Indian unrest, chronic lawlessness, and potential insurrection by the Hispanic Californians. Moreover, the discovery of gold in 1848 brought an avalanche of fortune-seekers to the territory and a wave of desertions from his already thinly stretched military force, leaving him with few troops to back up his authority. Out of necessity as well as conviction, Mason assumed the role of a neutral caretaker, holding the line until Congress installed a civilian government. He refused to ratify land titles until the adoption of a permanent court system. Although his secretary of state, Lieutenant Henry W. Halleck, drafted a law code for the territory, the governor hesitated to order it into effect without congressional authorization. During the summer of 1848 Mason toured the gold fields near Sacramento. His detailed report to the adjutant general, which described the overnight fortunes made by the gold-seekers, appeared in newspapers around the world and helped fuel the gold craze. In contrast to many officers stationed in California, however, the veteran commander resisted the temptation to speculate in land or otherwise enrich himself, as he thought such action would compromise his official position.

In August 1848 the arrival of news of the Treaty of Guadalupe Hidalgo presented Mason with a dilemma. The end of the war seemed to remove the legal foundation of his military regime, yet Congress, wrestling with the question of the status of slavery in the western territories, was slow to establish a civilian government. The governor relaxed some aspects of military rule, including the collection of revenue as a military contribution, and permitted local elections of alcaldes. Nevertheless, he faced a rising tide of civilian complaints about his failure to establish a permanent law code and legitimize land claims, and some argued that he did not provide sufficiently for the public protection. Much to Mason's relief, the administration replaced him as governor with Lieutenant Colonel Bennet Riley, and he left the territory in early May 1849. He took command of Jefferson Barracks, outside St. Louis, where he died of cholera.

In his strong sense of duty and his refusal to take sides in civilian political disputes, Mason exhibited the emerging professionalism of the army officer corps in the antebellum era. William Tecumseh Sherman, who served as Mason's chief of staff in California, described his old commander in his memoirs as stern but "honest to a fault, he was the very embodiment of the principle of fidelity to the interests of the General Government. He possessed a native strong intellect, and far more knowledge of the principles of civil government and law than he got credit for."

• A small collection of Mason's correspondence as governor is preserved at the Bancroft Library, University of California, Berkeley. A great deal of his official correspondence as governor is published in 31st Cong., 1st Sess., House Executive Document no. 17. For Mason's family background and pre–Mexican War career, see Pamela C. Copeland and Richard K. MacMaster, *The Five George Masons: Patriots and Planters of Virginia and Maryland* (1975), and Carolyn T. Foreman, "General Richard Barnes Mason," *Chronicles of Oklahoma* 19 (1941): 14–36. Mason's governorship is covered in Theodore Grivas, *Military Governments in California, 1846–1850; With a Chapter on Their Prior Use in Louisiana, Florida and New Mexico* (1963), and Neal Harlow, *California Conquered: War and Peace on the Pacific* (1982). William T. Sherman includes many insights into Mason's character and administration in *Memoirs of Gen. W. T. Sherman* (1890).

WILLIAM B. SKELTON

MASON, Samuel (c. 1750–July 1803), outlaw and pirate, was born in Virginia of unknown parents. Virtually nothing is known of his early life, although historian Samuel Draper noted that he was "connected by ties of consanguinity with the distinguished Mason family of Virginia, and grew up bad from his boyhood." Mason first appeared in historical records during the American Revolution, during which he served as a captain in the Ohio County, Virginia (now West Virginia), militia. He fought in several engagements against Native Americans in 1777 and served at Fort Henry in the upper Ohio Valley until the autumn of 1779. Retiring from active service, he retained his captaincy in the militia until at least May 1781 and apparently also ran a tavern in the vicinity of present-day Wheeling, West Virginia.

Prosperous enough by this time to own slaves, he had also begun a criminal career at some time prior to the war by stealing horses in Frederick County, Virginia. Following the Revolution, he drifted down to what is today eastern Tennessee and occupied (in squatter fashion) some cabins belonging to General John Sevier. There Mason and a band of companions apparently engaged in petty thievery and otherwise made such a nuisance of themselves that Sevier sum-

marily evicted them. By 1787 Mason was in western Kentucky, possibly to claim a land grant that was a reward for his wartime service. Although he had signed a petition in 1790 (along with 114 other "respectable citizens") urging the creation of Logan County in what is today southwestern Kentucky, his veneer of respectability was apparently insufficient to sustain him in the community, and by 1794 he had removed to Henderson, Kentucky, where he dwelt among "horse thieves, rogues, and outlaws." In 1795 a disagreement between Mason and the local constable, John Dunn, led to Mason (with four others) physically attacking Dunn in ambush and leaving him for dead. While making his headquarters in Henderson County, Mason, his family, and his gang also stole slaves and were parties to at least one murder.

By 1797 Mason and his ensemble had moved once again, to Cave-in-Rock, Illinois. A large natural cave that overlooked the Ohio River in Hardin County, Illinois, the site was long noted as a haven for criminals as well as a temporary shelter for travelers. Numerous river pirates preyed on the slow-moving flatboats that brought settlers and supplies down the river during the period, and Mason ranked among the most successful of the lot. Operating under the alias of Wilson, he opened "Wilson's Liquor Vault and House for Entertainment" in the cave to lure unsuspecting passersby. The site offered an excellent long-distance view of the river in both directions, thereby giving Mason and his associates early warning of both potential victims and militias sent to curtail Mason's activity. Some flatboats were lured to shore by the use of a man or woman (posing as a stranded settler) hailing the boats from the riverbank as they passed. While some of the captured crewmen were killed to ensure their silence, Mason always promoted himself as a robber who only killed when necessary. As a result he frequently forced his victims to join his gang in lieu of murdering them.

Ever restless and fearing the repercussions that were likely to follow his growing notoriety, Mason moved his operation southward, establishing a base on Wolf Island in the Mississippi River (about twenty-five miles south of the mouth of the Ohio). In March 1800 he applied for and received a passport to the Spanish-held western bank of the Mississippi in New Madrid, Missouri. This passport, he hoped, not only would allow him to purchase land in Spanish-held territory but also would allow him to concentrate his operations on the eastern (American) side of the river and use the western bank as a safe haven. In the latter part of his career Mason continued to rob riverboats on the Mississippi and also turned highwayman by expanding his operations to the Natchez Trace. Using agents in places like Natchez to inform him concerning movements of mule trains on the trace, Mason plundered trade moving through the two major thoroughfares of the Mississippi Valley.

Mason's continued notoriety led to his capture at Little Prairie, Missouri (about thirty miles south of New Madrid), in January 1803. Along with his four sons, a daughter-in-law, three grandchildren, and a man with several aliases (John Taylor, John Setton, and Wells), he was questioned at length by the Spanish commandant Don Henri Peyroux de la Coudreniere. Don Henri then sent the band under guard to his superior in New Orleans, Intendant Manuel Salcedo. After arriving downriver, the gang was questioned by Salcedo. Although unable to prove any criminal activity within Spanish territory, the intendant suspected that infractions had been committed on the American side, and arrangements were made to turn Mason over to the American authorities in Natchez. Leaving New Orleans by boat, the party traveled upriver until a broken mast forced a repair stop and provided Mason with his chance. On 26 March 1803 Mason grabbed a rifle from his captors and escaped with the rest of his band, with Captain Robert McCoy dying during the attempt from gunshot wounds. News of Mason's escape traveled quickly, and a reward of $1,000 was soon offered by the Americans for his recapture. Sometime in July 1803 Mason was killed by two members of his gang, John Setton and James May. The two men cut off Mason's head and attempted to collect the reward money in Mississippi but were recognized as members of the gang and were put on trial. During the trial it came to light that John Setton was actually the notorious Wiley "Little" Harpe, who with his reputed brother Micajah "Big" Harpe had cut a murderous swath through Kentucky and Tennessee several years earlier. Following the trial, the two men were executed by hanging on 8 February 1804 at Old Greenville (no longer in existence), Jefferson County, Mississippi. The disposition of Mason's gang is unclear, but he was survived by his wife (name and date of marriage unknown) and four sons.

During his years of operations on the Ohio and Mississippi rivers and the Natchez Trace, Mason was a widely known and feared individual. His gang made early journeys through these regions more perilous.

• Some of Samuel Mason's correspondence has survived and is held with the papers of Samuel Draper at the Wisconsin State Historical Society, Madison, and a manuscript in French of his trial at New Madrid is held by the Mississippi Department of Archives and History, Jackson. The best secondary source of the life and career of Samuel Mason remains Otto A. Rothert, *The Outlaws of Cave-in-Rock* (1924).

EDWARD L. LACH, JR.

MASON, Stevens Thomson (27 Oct. 1811–4 Jan. 1843), lawyer and politician, was born in Leesburg, Virginia, the son of John T. Mason, a lawyer, and Elizabeth Moir. Mason moved to Kentucky with his family when he was still very young. To aid the family finances, he dropped out of Transylvania University in 1828 to work as a clerk. In 1830 Mason moved to Detroit after President Andrew Jackson appointed his father secretary of the Michigan Territory. In 1831, shortly after John Mason resigned his post, Jackson commissioned the nineteen-year-old Stevens T. Mason his father's replacement. At about the same time,

Michigan territorial governor Lewis Cass was appointed secretary of war, leaving the young Mason acting governor.

Mason's appointment caused "considerable excitement" in Michigan, and a petition to the president was circulated demanding the secretary's removal. The signers were particularly critical of Mason's youth, claiming that the appointment was "in the highest degree derogatory to the freemen over whom he is thus to be placed." Mason responded to his critics by publishing a public statement that "was at once both so temperate and free from arrogance that it went far towards turning feelings of opposition to kindly sympathy." The arrival in Detroit of a new territorial governor, George P. Porter, on 17 September 1831, further reduced criticism. By June 1832, when Mason's selection was officially confirmed by the U.S. Senate, opposition "had quite faded away."

When Porter was out of the territory—including during the Black Hawk War in 1832, which was fought in the western part of the Michigan Territory (present-day Wisconsin)—Mason served once again as acting governor. After Porter's death on 6 July 1834 and the Senate's rejection of Porter's replacement, Mason, as acting governor, took charge of the effort to make Michigan into a state. On 12 January 1835, declaring Michigan had a "right" to be admitted to the Union, Mason asked the legislative council to call a constitutional convention, although Congress had rejected Michigan's request to hold one. On 11 May 1835 ninety-one elected delegates assembled in Detroit; in forty-five days they drafted a constitution for the proposed state. While not a delegate, Mason is credited with convincing the delegates to adopt a more liberal provision on the convention's "most bitter" question—the right to vote.

As the constitution was being written, Mason led the struggle with Ohio over a 500-square-mile strip of land that included the community of Toledo. The border dispute, known as the Toledo War, stemmed from Michigan's claim—derived from the ordinance of 1787—to the mouth of the Maumee River, which was to be a terminus for a proposed canal connecting the Great Lakes with the Ohio River. Michigan's call for a constitutional convention led Ohio to annex the strip. Describing Ohio's annexation as "unjustifiable" and "high-handed," Mason declared, "We are the weaker party, it is true, but . . . we cannot fail to maintain our rights against the encroachments of a powerful neighboring State." Michigan retaliated with the Pains and Penalties Act, which made it illegal for Ohio residents to exercise official jurisdiction in the disputed territory.

When warned by U.S. Secretary of State John Forsyth that the U.S. government might "force" a compromise with Ohio if the act was not repealed, Mason threatened to resign if President Jackson would not support him. Jackson did not pursue Mason's resignation but sent commissioners to resolve the matter. After meeting with Mason and the governor of Ohio they proposed a compromise that favored Ohio. In August

1835, as Michiganians and Ohioans skirmished along the border, Mason convened the legislative council to consider the proposed compromise. The council rejected the measures, and Mason sent a note to the president that concluded, "The General Government may expect a serious collision. . . . The consequences attending such a state of things are deeply to be regretted, but they must rest with those who might prevent their occurrence."

On 29 August, citing Mason's overzealous defense of Michigan's rights, Jackson fired the young governor. In early September, unaware of Jackson's decision, Mason joined a large contingent of Michigan militia headed for Toledo to prevent Ohio from symbolically establishing jurisdiction over the strip by convening a session of the Court of Common Pleas.

The firing of Mason ended the Toledo War but not Michigan's quest to become a state. Without receiving federal authorization, Michigan voters on 5 October 1835 elected Mason governor, chose a congressman and a state legislature, and overwhelmingly approved the state constitution. With federal authorities still not recognizing Michigan statehood, Mason promised cooperation with the newly appointed territorial governor and urged all Michiganians "to await with patience the final recognition of our equal sovereignty" by Congress. After debating for six months, Congress passed the Northern Ohio Boundary Act in June 1836. The bill gave the Toledo Strip to Ohio and offered Michigan the western Upper Peninsula and immediate statehood. On 28 September 1836 delegates gathered in Ann Arbor to consider the measure and rejected the compromise. A month later, as the impact of the decision—including the estimated loss of $500,000 that Michigan would have received when the surplus in the federal treasury was divided among all states—became known, Wayne County Democrats persuaded Mason to call another convention. In mid-December a second convention approved the compromise providing for statehood. Although some members expressed concern with the extralegal nature of the December convention, Congress allowed Michigan to enter the Union.

With statehood finally achieved in January 1837, Mason's career reached its zenith. As land sales in and migration to Michigan boomed, there was much excitement over new methods of transportation. Mason recommended that the state borrow money and buy stock in private companies building railroads and canals, but the legislature passed legislation committing the state to build three major railroads and two canals. To finance the building, Mason was authorized to negotiate a loan of $5 million "secured by the faith and credit of the state." Meanwhile, in 1838 he married Julia Phelps, and the couple would have three children.

The effects in Michigan of the nation's worsening economy and the criticism of how he negotiated the internal improvements loan led to harsh attacks on Mason, leading him not to seek reelection for a third term in 1839. In 1841, his political career ruined in Michi-

gan, Mason moved his family to New York City, the home of his wife. There he began a law career that was cut prematurely short when he contracted pneumonia and died.

• Mason's papers are located in the Burton Historical Collection, Detroit Public Library, Detroit, and the William L. Clements Library, University of Michigan, Ann Arbor. Biographies include Lawton T. Hemans, *Life and Times of Stevens T. Mason* (1930), and Kent Sagendorph, *Stevens Thomson Mason* (1947).

ROGER L. ROSENTRETER

MASON, Walt (4 May 1862–22 June 1939), poet, humorist, and journalist, was born in Columbia, Ontario, Canada, the son of John Mason, a wool dyer, and Lydia Campbell. Mason worked at his father's woolen mill and as a farmhand during his boyhood and attended school only sporadically. He detested mathematics but later claimed to have memorized all the poetry in his readers. Orphaned by the age of fifteen, he moved to Port Hope, Ontario, where he worked for a year and a half at a hardware store, earned low wages, and met with little success. In 1880 he sailed across Lake Huron to upstate New York, where he again worked as a farm laborer, hoeing beans, "the poorest fun I ever struck."

The first half of Mason's working life proved to be itinerant and erratic. He worked as a migrant laborer, stopped briefly in Ohio and then Illinois, and finally settled in St. Louis, Missouri, where he found work as a typesetter, the first of his many jobs in the newspaper business. He sent some material to the *Hornet*, a humor magazine in that city, and was employed for "writing gems of thought, reading proofs, sweeping the floors, and generally making myself useful." When the *Hornet* ceased publication, Mason found himself unable to secure another job in publishing, and so he migrated to Kansas, where he once again worked as an agricultural laborer, this time for three years.

In 1885 Mason landed a job with the *Atchison (Kans.) Globe*. Here he distinguished himself by racing about the town gathering local news stories to compete with the wire services of the *Globe*'s competitors. After Atchison he joined the *State Journal* in Lincoln, Nebraska, and subsequently a series of local papers in Omaha, Beatrice, and other Nebraska towns. For the next twenty-two years Mason would follow the career path of the many itinerant reporters, printers, and "paragraphers" in the rural Midwest: "From that time forward I was chasing myself over the country, and was connected with newspapers in a dozen cities," Mason later recalled, "but always had the idea that the next town would be a little better, and kept moving around." While on the staff of the *Lincoln Journal*, Mason met Willa Cather, then a University of Nebraska student doing freelance work. In 1931 Mason recalled, "I was praising a great American poet whose name has been a household word since the days of our grandfathers, and she said that most of his stuff was trash, and that this country had produced only one great poet,

Whitman. Such blasphemy almost moved me to tears. . . . It took me a long time to realize that my own judgment was slightly out of gear." This anecdote illustrates Mason's populist leanings in literature and disdain for what he considered "highbrow" art.

During his stint in Lincoln, Mason began a lifelong friendship with William Jennings Bryan, then a young attorney. Mason "wrote a number of paragraphs about William," and Bryan apparently never forgot; one of Mason's books of poems would later bear a testimonial from the famous orator. The acquaintance also led to a brief job in 1892–1893 as a columnist with a new Democratic newspaper, the *Evening News* in Washington, D.C. Mason, whose homespun persona was not inauthentic, confessed to feeling extremely uncomfortable in Washington society: "I had but recently escaped from the Kansas cornfields and this was my first contact with high society, and my misery was so great that I kept on sweating as though that were my specialty." Moreover, the panic of 1893 led to salary reductions and layoffs at the paper. Mason, sensing that the time was right to move on, returned to Nebraska to resume the life of a migrant farmworker and itinerant journalist. In that same year he married Ella Foss in Wooster, Ohio. Their first child, a son, died in infancy. In the 1910s they adopted their only other child, a daughter.

The Pulitzer Prize–winning editor William Allen White, Mason's lifelong friend, in his obituary for Mason recounted Mason's repetitive cycle of getting a newspaper job, succeeding at it, neglecting it for drink, losing the job, and sobering up. He made a number of attempts to recover; one of these resulted in his 1892 Associated Press article "Rum Reminiscences" and his 1893 book *The Man Who Sobered Up.* Probably at the insistence of his wife, he twice traveled to Kansas City and took the "Keeley cure," a grueling therapy involving complete withdrawal, purgation, and a spartan diet, only to relapse later. In 1906, deserted by his wife, he tried the cure once more. Then White gave Mason a chance on the *Emporia* (Kansas) *Gazette.*

The reporter-poet's arrival in Emporia—in a buckboard wagon drawn by a pinto pony and bearing a typewriter bolted to it—later became part of the turnabout success story that was a large part of Mason's fame. White supplied Mason's needs on account in order to deprive the latter of money for liquor. Mason sent for his wife, got his books out of storage, and set about redeeming himself. William Lewis White, White's son, recorded, "Eventually it must have been the rewards of national fame which relieved him of the need to get drunk." That fame came largely through daily prose poems that he wrote for the last thirty years of his life. Early in Mason's stay in Emporia, he was asked to write some filler for the front page; this he did in the form of a poem urging church attendance. The poem, though written in rhyme and meter, was condensed to paragraph form to save space; these metrical prose poems became Mason's characteristic form. This first piece garnered much positive response from readers, and on Decoration Day 1908, Mason wrote

"The Little Green Tents," which would become his best-known poem: "The little green tents are built of sod, And they are not long, and they are not broad, But the soldiers have lots of room; And the sod is part of the land they saved, When the flag of the enemy darkly waved, The symbol of dole and doom." The poem was not copyrighted and so was printed by papers across the nation at the time and for many Decoration Days afterward.

Soon Mason wrote a daily poem for the front page of the *Gazette*. In 1909, largely through the urging and mediation of White, the George Matthew Adams Syndicate signed Mason and began offering the poems; eventually more than two hundred papers in the United States and abroad carried the poet's "Rippling Rhymes." The writer developed a reputation as the best-paid poet in the country (an assertion that *Poetry* magazine repeated in its obituary). "I have established the poetry business on a firm basis, and have fixt prices," Mason declared in a 1914 interview, "just like the phonograph-manufacturers." The Adams syndicate, in one advertising insert, trumpeted Mason's verses as a "Tonic to 10,000,000," and the ad goes on to explain his success: "Long ago he decided on his key . . . *for the people.*" Many of his poems are humorous, but many of the most popular offered inspiration or preached optimism and hard work. "Uncle Walt," as he became known to a devoted following, went on to publish seven books of verse. Although Mason was primarily known for his poems, he also wrote short humorous prose paragraphs. For instance, "The Fat One," as Mason styled himself, wrote of golf, "I see no sense in walking all over a pasture to drive a ball into nine or eighteen holes. Why not have one hole in the back yard and drive the ball into it eighteen times, saving all the walking?"

In 1920, ostensibly due to the poet's rheumatism, Mason and his family moved from Emporia to La Jolla, California, where he and his wife lived the rest of their lives. Mason continued to write daily verses until his health failed him, but by the time of his death, all his books were out of print. Although many obituaries recalled the poet with nostalgic fondness, the taste for newspaper poetry of the type purveyed by Mason, James Whitcomb Riley, Eugene Field, or T. A. Daly had waned by the late 1930s.

In the 1910s, however, Mason's name was undoubtedly a household word in white America. In 1915 William Dean Howells wrote Mason, "Dear Uncle Walt: Your Horse Sense hast lightend already many a heavy hour of those that weigh upon the heart between 3 and 5 in the morning, and if I live, it will lighten many more." Theodore Dreiser claimed, "Walt Mason has entertained me on many a dreary railroad journey," and the Rippling Rhymes seem to have found their way onto many trains as well as into many poetry scrapbooks, common household possessions at the time. Mason's popularity, the accessibility of his verse (in both content and distribution), and his affirmation of dominant American values led William Allen White to dub his colleague "the poet laureate of American democracy." In 1920 the *Emporia Gazette* reprinted what it claimed was a letter from a sergeant in the medical corps, writing from the Western Front in 1918. The sergeant describes a soldier, who, upon having his legs destroyed in an artillery attack, affirmed, "If I was Walt Mason I'd say I was damn lucky it wasn't my hands, as I couldn't roll a cigarette." When the soldier died, the sergeant claims, he was clutching a notebook filled with Mason's poems.

Mason was almost as celebrated for his rags-to-riches, drunkenness-to-sobriety, farmhand-to-poet life story, his expensive house and cars, and his obsessive work habits as he was for his writing. In any event, Mason offers a fascinating case study in the divergence from a "mass poetry" that flourished around World War I and the poetic tastes later propagated in U.S. universities, where his name is seldom heard. He is also the embodiment of a defensiveness on the part of popular literary culture against highbrow art—a defensiveness that the rise of modernist poetics exacerbated. "The modern newspaper poets are doing more to brighten the world and make it a good place to live in than all the extinct poets in the Hall of Fame or Westminster Abbey ever did," Mason claimed. This statement offers a succinct credo of most American poetry readers of the late nineteenth and early twentieth centuries.

• Biographical information on Walt Mason and many contemporary assessments of his work are in the Walt Mason Collection at the Lyon County Historical Society, Emporia, Kans. Mason's books of poems are *Uncle Walt, the Poet Philosopher* (1910), *Business Prose-Poems* (1911), *Walt Mason, His Book* (c. 1911, 1916), *Uncle Walt's Philosophy: A Little Collection of Prose Poems* (1912), *Rippling Rhymes to Suit the Times, All Sorts of Themes Embracin'; Some Gay, Some Sad, Some Not So Bad, as Written by Walt Mason* (1913), *"Horse Sense" in Verses Tense* (1915), and *Fifty-two Sermons* (1918?). Obituaries are in *Poetry*, Aug. 1939, and *Time* and *Newsweek*, both 3 July 1939.

JOSEPH HARRINGTON

MASON, William (2 Sept. 1808–21 May 1883), inventor and manufacturer, was born in Mystic, Connecticut, the son of Amos Mason, a blacksmith, and Mary Holdredge. At age six he moved with his family to Stonington. Seven years later he went to work as an apprentice spinner in a cotton mill in nearby Canterbury, and at age sixteen he moved to Lisbon, Connecticut, where he worked in a textile factory as an operator and mechanic. He became so adept at repairing machinery that a year later his employer put him in charge of setting up the machinery in a new cotton mill in East Haddam. On his return to Lisbon, he worked in the mill's machine shop until his apprenticeship was completed in 1828.

Over the next four years Mason worked for a textile mill in New Hartford, New York, painted portraits, made fiddles, and held several odd jobs. During this period he returned to Canterbury, where he developed a power loom for making diaper cloth as well as a loom for weaving damask tablecloths. Having received a patent for the diaper loom in 1832, he began that same year to manufacture this device in a rented machine shop in Willimantic. In 1833 he went to work for Asell Lampear, owner of a machine shop in Killingly, and invented the ring frame, a device for spinning cotton thread whereby the yarn was twisted and stretched around a ring while being wound onto a bobbin. In 1835 Mason moved to Taunton, Massachusetts, where he affiliated himself with Crocker and Richmond, manufacturers of cotton-mill machinery, and began making his ring frames in increased quantities. In 1837 he designed a device for speeding up the operation of the ring frame; he also became manufacturing foreman for Leach and Keith when this firm acquired the assets of Crocker and Richmond. In 1840 he patented his first self-acting mule, a device that permitted the spinning and winding of yarn onto multiple spindles. The subsequent introduction of a competitive design led him to patent a much-improved self-acting mule six years later. This invention was received with great enthusiasm by American yarn manufacturers because it reduced their reliance on English mule spinners, skilled laborers whose relative scarcity resulted in high wages and an independent manner that had irritated their employers for years. When Leach and Keith went bankrupt in 1842, he purchased the company machine shop and began building on a large scale his self-acting mule as well as a variety of other pieces of cotton-mill machinery.

Over the next ten years Mason also became involved in the manufacture of tools, blowers, furnaces, gears, shafts, and printing presses. In 1844 he married Harriet Augusta Metcalf, with whom he had three children. In 1847 he founded and became the first president of the Machinists' National Bank in Taunton, a position he held for ten years.

In 1852 Mason responded to a downturn in the demand for textile machinery by converting part of his facilities to the manufacture of railroad locomotives. The next year the company's first locomotive, a 4-4-0 "American" type named the *James Guthrie*, was delivered to the Jefferson Railroad in Indiana. Unlike his competitors, Mason concerned himself with the aesthetic appearance of the locomotive as well as its functionality. Within a short period the straight, clean lines that he gave his locomotives were adopted by other builders of the American type, as were such design improvements as the horizontal arrangement of cylinders, the spread truck (whereby the distance between the two front axles was increased considerably), well-balanced driving wheels with cast-iron centers, and the spliced or divided frame. Other innovations, such as the development in 1871 of a double-ended, or "bogie," engine, and the introduction in 1875 of the Walschaerts valve motion for regulating the supply of steam to a cylinder, were not readily accepted by the railroading community, although the Walschaerts did become popular in the early twentieth century.

During the Civil War, Mason dedicated much of his company's manufacturing capacity to the production of Springfield rifles for the Union army. In 1873 he consolidated all of his manufacturing interests into the Mason Machine Works, of which he served as president until his death. He died in Taunton.

• Mason's contributions to textile manufacturing are discussed in Anthony F. C. Wallace, *Rockdale: The Growth of an American Village in the Early Industrial Revolution* (1980). His contributions to railroad manufacturing are discussed in Angus Sinclair, *Development of the Locomotive Engine* (1907; repr. 1970). Obituaries are in the *Boston Daily Advertiser*, 22 May 1883, and the *Railroad Gazette*, 1 June 1883.

CHARLES W. CAREY, JR.

MASON, William (24 Jan. 1829–14 July 1908), musician and composer, was born in Boston, Massachusetts, the son of Lowell Mason, a professional musician, and Abigail Gregory. Having shown his musical talent at an early age, Mason at age seven began to accompany on the organ the church choir his father directed. About 1845 Mason began to study piano at the Boston Academy of Music and published his first piano composition, *Deux Romances sans paroles*, op. 1. In 1846 he made his professional debut as a pianist in a concert of the Boston Academy of Music, followed in the next two years by programs in Boston and other cities. With his father and others he edited several tunebooks of sacred and secular music in this period.

In 1849 Mason sailed to Europe where he studied with Ignaz Moscheles, Moritz Hauptmann, and Ernst Friedrich Richter in Leipzig, and beginning in August 1850, with Alexander Dreyschock in Prague. In April 1853 Mason arrived in Weimar to study piano with Franz Liszt, remaining more than a year.

In July 1854 Mason returned to the United States. After successful recitals in Boston, New York, and New England, he made a concert tour of twenty recitals in two months, probably the first such tour in the United States that consisted entirely of piano music. Although he was well received, Mason found the life of a touring concert pianist not to his liking.

In 1855 Mason settled in New York City to pursue a career of performing, teaching, and composing. In October he began his tenure as organist at the Fifth Avenue Presbyterian Church. There and at other churches he was celebrated for his improvisational skills. At this time he also organized a chamber music group consisting of himself and a string quartet. Later known as the Mason-Thomas Quartette (after Theodore Thomas), it was critically acclaimed, giving concerts through 1868. During this period Mason published several of his piano compositions. He composed at a regular, moderate pace throughout his career. On 12 March 1857 Mason married Mary Isabella Webb of Boston, the daughter of his father's musical associate, George James Webb. They had three children.

In 1867 the first of several pedagogical works by Mason was published, *A Method for the Piano-forte*, coauthored by E. S. Hoadley. Mason had his first experience of teaching in a normal music school in 1870, and his participation was the first time piano and piano pedagogy instruction had been given on a significant scale. His wife Mary died in Paris in 1880, when the Masons were completing a lengthy trip through Europe.

During the 1880s Mason was active in the Music Teachers National Association, reading papers to annual meetings and serving on committees. In 1887 he became the first president of the American Vocal Music Association, organized to use the tonic sol-fa system to increase musical proficiency in the United States. In 1890 Mason journeyed again to Europe, a trip that included a visit with Edvard Grieg in Norway. Mason's most famous pedagogical work, *Touch and Technic*, op. 44, was published in 1889. In 1899 Mason's seventieth birthday was celebrated in Steinway Hall, New York. He died in New York City.

• The largest holdings of Mason materials are in the Newberry Library, Chicago; Yale University's John Herrick Jackson Music Library; Columbia University's Butler Library; the New York Public Library's Performing Arts Research Library, Lincoln Center; and the Library of Congress. His instrumental works include over fifty piano works, including "Amitié pour amitié," op. 4 (1854), "Badinage" for piano four hands, op. 27 (1869), "Dance Antique," op. 38 (1882) and "Capriccio fantastico," op. 50 (1897). They also include his "Serenata" for piano and cello, op. 39a (1882). Collections edited by Mason that include his glees, part songs, and hymn tunes are *The Social Glee Book* (with S. A. Bancroft, 1847), *Fireside Harmony* (1848), *The Melodist* (with G. J. Webb, 1850); and *Asaph; or, The Choir Book* (with L. Mason, 1861). Additional writings include *A System for Beginners* (with E. S. Hoadley, 1871), *A System of Technical Exercises for the Piano-forte* (1878), and *A Primer of Music* (with W. S. B. Mathews, 1894). Kenneth Graber lists about eighty keyboard works edited or arranged by Mason (see below).

Mason published an autobiography, *Memories of a Musical Life* (1901; repr. 1970). A chronology of his life can be found in Kenneth Graber, *William Mason (1829–1908): An Annotated Bibliography and Catalog of Works* (1989).

HARRY ESKEW

MASSASOIT (1600?–1661), leader of the Wampanoag Indians who was also known as Great Chief, Woosamequin, Ousamequin, and Yellow Feather, was born near the site of Bristol, Rhode Island, and lived in Pokanoket near Motaup, or Mount Hope, near the southern end of the peninsula of Rhode Island. Nothing is known of his parents or his youth. Though Massasoit was not warlike, his sphere of influence extended over present-day New England from approximately Cape Cod, Massachusetts, to Narragansett Bay. Governor John Carver of Plymouth Colony and John Smith titled Massasoit "king of the country." The Wampanoags were skilled horticulturalists, fishermen, hunters, and gatherers.

On 22 March 1621 Massasoit and some sixty warriors accompanied Samoset and Squanto to meet English colonists at Plymouth. The dignitaries promised peace and amity, a promise Massasoit never broke. Massasoit formally made a friendship treaty including a land cession to King James I of England the same month. Remarking, "Englishmen take that land, for none is left to occupy it. The Great Spirit . . . has swept its people from the face of the earth," Massasoit assigned "empty" land to the settlers. An epidemic of smallpox had depopulated the eastern shore from Penobscot to Narragansett Bay. In December 1621 Massasoit participated in the famous thanksgiving feast with Plymouth colonists in celebration of their first year of survival in America, a survival that would have been impossible without aid from the Wampanoags under Massasoit. In 1622 another smallpox epidemic (the "great sickness") decimated the Wampanoags. When in 1623 Massasoit fell seriously ill, English colonist Edward Winslow and others hurried to his side. They nursed him to a remarkable recovery with goose soup and herbal concoctions. A grateful Massasoit told them about an impending attack on an English plantation by neighboring tribes.

The alliance with the English settlers initially brought profit and wealth to Massasoit and his tribe in contrast to neighbors such as Miantonomo of the Narragansetts and Uncas of the Mohegans. Massasoit's influence rose as he acquired access to guns, horses, and European manufactured goods. He paid for these goods with Wampanoag ancestral lands. Massasoit remained friendly toward the English until his death. For example, Massasoit found Englishman John Billington lost in the woods and helped him return to the colony; another time Massasoit bartered two French prisoners to Captain Thomas Dermer. Massasoit tolerated Christian missionaries such as John Eliot setting up "Praying Towns" for Indian converts, although he himself never converted.

Until the end of his life Massasoit crisscrossed New England on diplomatic missions to prevent or stop hostilities among the diverse peoples of his land. During hostilities in 1632 involving neighboring Narragansetts, Massasoit sided with the English against the Narragansetts and resided in Plymouth for protection and diplomacy. He returned to Plymouth in 1634 to maintain good relations. In 1636 the Puritans scattered the few Pequot survivors of the 1636 Pequot War among Massasoit's Wampanoags and two neighboring tribes, thereby virtually exterminating the Pequot tribe, a lesson not lost to Massasoit and the remaining Indian tribes. In 1638 Massasoit traveled to Boston on a mission to placate the English, carrying with him eighteen precious beaver skins. In 1642 he visited John Winthrop. Massasoit never gave up hope of peaceful coexistence with the English.

Massasoit had three sons and two daughters. Before his death he asked the English general court in Plymouth to name his older boys and successors Wamsutta Alexander and Metacom Philip (later also known as "King Philip"). The latter became a foe of the English during King Philip's War (1676) after Massasoit's painfully carved diplomatic channels had proven to be dead ends.

• For more information on Massasoit, see John Collier, *Indians of the Americas* (1947); Frederick Dockstader, *Great North American Indians* (1977); *John Eliot's Indian Dialogues:*

A Study in Cultural Interaction, ed. Henry W. Bowden and James P. Ronda (1980); and Marcia Sewall, *People of the Breaking Day* (1990).

KATJA MAY

MASSEE, May (1 May 1881–24 Dec. 1966), editor and producer of children's books, was born in Chicago, Illinois, the daughter of Charlotte Maria Bull and Francis Spink Massee. When she was five, Massee's family moved to Milwaukee, a German colony at the time. She did well in high school and before age eighteen completed a teaching program at the Milwaukee Normal School (later named the State Teacher's College); she had to lie about her age to receive her certificate. Between 1901 and 1902 she taught elementary school, then worked at a library in White Water, Wisconsin. In 1904 she enrolled at the Wisconsin Library School in Madison.

After two years in Chicago as an assistant librarian at the Armour Institute, Massee had plans to organize the libraries of western Illinois. Before she could follow through, however, Theresa West Elmendorf, the first woman president of the American Library Association (ALA), persuaded her to work at the Buffalo (New York) Public Library. Massee was head of the children's department from 1905 to 1910. Based on what she learned about "what the children themselves really like and want to read," she lectured around the country. Massee believed the nation's cultural values could be established through children's books. Once such books represented every type of American, they would be truly American. The growing number of public libraries with children's rooms allowed all children access to this education. Massee wrote that the United States has "fewer bookstores in proportion to the reading public than any other country on record but we have more public libraries. And it is to the growth of public libraries with children's rooms and their demand for more and better books that we owe the rapid increase in children's book publishing" (*Publisher's Weekly*, Aug. 1938, p. 673). In 1913 Massee accepted a job in Chicago as editor of *The Booklist*, the ALA's approval list of children's books for booksellers and librarians.

In 1923 Massee accepted Samuel Alexander Everitt's offer to lead Doubleday's children's book department, only the second in the country. Her first objective was to discard the "juvenile" label for children's books, which she believed discouraged all readers, children and adults, from enjoying children's literature. Determined constantly to challenge the expectations of authors, booksellers, librarians, and readers, Massee took a hand in every aspect of production, from content to illustrations and jacket. She believed the "dress of [the] book should exactly fit and enhance the text. . . . And there came to be such important things to say with pictures, type, paper and cloth that the book-designer grew in importance, too" (Miller, p. 202). The first book produced under her direction was Charles Falls's *The ABC Book*. With its unusual woodcut color illustrations, it was a quick success, confirming Massee's "originality, balance of interests, humor, good taste, daring in production and book patterns" (Bechtel, p. 213). Massee was open to any innovation that would promote children's books. She welcomed new methods of production, such as offset lithography, and endorsed the making of iconographic films based on children's books, an idea proposed to her by Morton Schindel of Weston Woods Studios. Her interest in new techniques led her to employ illustrators from France, Germany, Hungary, Russia, and Scandinavia. Included on Massee's book list are the picture books of Boris Artzybasheff, Elizabeth MacKinstry, Marie Hall Ets, James Daugherty, Maud and Miska Petershams, Ingri and Edgar Parin D'Aulaires, Ludwig Bemelmans, and Zhenya Gay, among others. One author, Elizabeth Cleveland Miller, explains that Massee "wasn't interested in the 'foreign' as a picturesque dressing for a story; she wanted to *use* the foreign to broaden the minds of young Americans—to prove to them that there was more than one way of skinning a cat, and, though methods varied, all were worthy of respect and interest" (*Horn Book*, p. 223). In 1928, after Massee had been publishing children's books for only six years, reviewer Rowe Wright commented that Massee required no introduction because "everyone who is in anyway interested in the trade or in libraries knows her and . . . knows her sincerity and her enthusiasm for good books" (p. 1334).

In 1932 the depression had its effect on the field of children's books, resulting in the termination of the department at Doubleday and of Massee's position. However, she quickly returned to the field when on 1 January 1933 Harold Guinzburg, the president of Viking Press in New York, established a junior books department and asked her to be editor. Massee vowed to help produce "books that will make young Americans think and feel more vividly, make them more aware of the world around them and more at home in the world within, more able to give something to their generation and thoroughly to enjoy the giving" (Duff, p. 186). Massee soon gained a reputation as a "real" editor, one who could recognize talent and nurture it. When on 4 June 1959 she became the first woman member of the American Institute of Graphic Arts, inscribed on her gold medal were the words, "Her Guidance Awakens Inspiration." Her years of work resulted in the publication of numerous beautiful books, nine Newbery Medals, and four Caldecott Medals. In 1950 the Women's National Book Association presented her with the Constance Lindsay Skinner Medal for her contribution to children's books, and on that occasion Eleanor Roosevelt spoke in her honor. Although she retired from Viking Junior in 1960, Massee remained advisory editor until her death at her home in New York City. She never married.

• In 1972 a library collection in Massee's honor opened at Emporia State University in Kansas. The collection includes all material pertinent to publishing books for children and a

reconstruction of Massee's Viking office. For an inventory of the contents of the collection, see the published catalog, *The May Massee Collection* (1979). Annis Duff gives an overview of the organization and opening of the collection in "This Was the Dream: The Dedication of the May Massee Collection," *Wilson Library Bulletin*, Oct. 1972, pp. 186–91. For several articles written by Massee and about Massee beginning in 1923, see Robin Gottlieb, *Publishing Children's Books in America, 1919–1976: An Annotated Bibliography* (1978). Summaries of her achievements include Rowe Wright, "Women in Publishing: May Massee," *Publishers' Weekly*, 29 Sept. 1928, pp. 1334–35, and Louise Seaman Bechtel, "May Massee, Publisher," and Bertha Mahoney Miller, "Children's Books in America Today," both in the July/Aug. 1936 issue of the *Horn Book Magazine*, which is completely devoted to May Massee and includes fifty pages of praise by authors, illustrators, designers, and librarians. Reactions to her death and lifetime achievement can be found in *Publishers' Weekly*, 2 Jan. 1967 and 20 Feb. 1967.

BARBARA L. CICCARELLI

MASSEY, Raymond (30 Aug. 1896–29 July 1983), actor, was born Raymond Hart Massey in Toronto, Ontario, Canada, the son of Chester Daniel Massey, a business executive, and Anna Vincent. Massey's father was president of the Massey-Harris Company, a leading farm implements manufacturer. His elder brother, Vincent, became the first Canadian-born governor general of Canada. Massey was educated at the Upper Canada Preparatory School, St. Andrew's College, Appleby School in Oakville, Ontario, and the University of Toronto. He served in World War I as a captain in the Canadian field artillery (1915–1919) and saw combat on the Western Front and in Siberia; he was wounded twice in Belgium. After the war he studied at Balliol College, Oxford (1919–1921), but he left without taking his final examinations.

Returning to Canada, Massey worked for the family firm, but having a love of theater instilled in him by his mother and confirmed by undergraduate acting at Oxford, he participated in amateur productions. Determined to go on the stage, he went back to England and joined the Everyman Theatre Company, making his debut as an American sailor in Eugene O'Neill's *In the Zone* at the Winter Gardens Theatre, New Brighton, in 1922. A short-lived West End debut in *Glamour* in 1922 was followed by a run of three hundred performances as a juvenile in the comedy *At Mrs. Beam's* in 1923. While playing two small roles in the big hit of 1924, George Bernard Shaw's *Saint Joan*, Massey developed the other side of his theatrical talent, directing Sunday night performances of plays for various stage societies. In 1926 he and two partners took a lease on the Everyman Theatre in Hampstead and entered management, achieving artistic acclaim but little financial success. After a year, he returned to full-time acting, earning plaudits in two short-lived H. M. Harwood plays in which he demonstrated his abilities as a character actor, *The Transit of Venus* (1927), as an Eastern potentate, and *The Golden Calf* (1927), as a Jewish financier. He then starred opposite Noël Coward in S. N. Behrman's comedy *The Second*

Man (1928), and he played Coward's original role in a successful revival of *The Constant Nymph* (1928). In 1931 he directed four major plays, all hits, among them *Five Star Final* (retitled *Late Night Final* for Britain), in which he also acted as the ruthless newspaper editor.

By the early 1930s Massey was a recognized member of the English theatrical world, both as an actor and director. In 1931 he made his Broadway debut in Norman Bel Geddes's controversial production of *Hamlet*, which ran for only a few weeks. Back in England, Massey directed and starred in two new plays by Keith Winter, *The Rats of Norway* (1933) and *The Shining Hour* (1934). Both were successes. In 1936 he made his first major impact on American theater as the embittered New England farmer in *Ethan Frome*. Then, after six months in London in 1938 as vaudevillian Harry Van in Robert Sherwood's antiwar play *Idiot's Delight*, he returned to New York where in that same year he appeared as Abraham Lincoln in Sherwood's *Abe Lincoln in Illinois*. It was the role that changed his life. The *New York Herald Tribune* declared it "one of the classic characterizations of our time." The play won both the Pulitzer Prize and the New York Drama Critics' Award. It was filmed in 1940 with Massey re-creating his stage role and becoming for millions the incarnation of the Great Emancipator, visually resembling the photographs and illustrations of Lincoln and imbuing the part with dignity, humanity, and a Christlike sense of destiny. Massey received an Academy Award nomination for his performance. He played Lincoln again on stage in 1957 in Norman Corwin's unsuccessful dramatization of the Lincoln-Douglas debates, *The Rivalry*, and he appeared in a cameo in *How the West Was Won* (1962).

Massey was always a striking presence both on stage and on film, a tall, lean, saturnine figure with a uniquely twisted mouth and piercing eyes. With this appearance went an ability to project an almost palpable intensity, which allowed him to play with equal conviction dedicated visionaries and brooding fanatics. It is no coincidence that just as he played Lincoln twice on film, he also twice played the abolitionist John Brown, depicted as a single-minded and murderous fanatic, in *Santa Fe Trail* (1940) and *Seven Angry Men* (1957).

Intensity too was the keynote of the gallery of memorable characters that Massey played in films in the 1930s. In Britain he appeared to excellent effect as Sherlock Holmes in *The Speckled Band* (1931), the French revolutionary Chauvelin in *The Scarlet Pimpernel* (1934), King Philip II of Spain in *Fire Over England* (1937), and Cardinal Richelieu in *Under the Red Robe* (1937). In Hollywood he was the definitive Black Michael in *The Prisoner of Zenda* (1937), and he was impressive as the French governor of Manikura, tormented by a conflict between duty and natural justice, in *The Hurricane* (1937). But perhaps the most memorable of all his 1930s film performances was the dual role of John and Oswald Cabal, who are really one, the idealized leader of the scientific "new order" in Alexander Korda's futuristic epic *Things to Come* (1936). Massey's is one of the towering performances of British cinema—inspired, intense, visionary.

It was his success as Lincoln that led Warner Brothers to sign him for two pictures a year in 1941, a deal that lasted fifteen years and resulted in eighteen films. After the successes of the 1930s, however, the films of the 1940s and 1950s were for the most part anticlimactic. Massey's own view that "I have forgotten most of those Warner pictures. . . . I have a blurred impression of acting one heavy after another, a procession of tedious villainy" is correct. His Hollywood career was largely a succession of one-dimensional Nazi villains, western bad guys, and sinister Oriental potentates. There were a few exceptions: the sympathetic husband of a deranged Joan Crawford in *Possessed* (1947), a despotic newspaper tycoon in *The Fountainhead* (1949), and James Dean's stern father in *East of Eden* (1954).

During these largely unmemorable movie years, Massey found his real artistic fulfillment on the stage. During World War II he costarred with Katharine Cornell in Shaw's *Candida* and *The Doctor's Dilemma*, and after the war he successfully revived *Pygmalion* on Broadway. In 1942 he had served for a year as a major in the Canadian army adjutant general's office before being invalided out. In 1944 he became a naturalized U.S. citizen and starred in a USO tour of *Our Town*.

In 1952 Massey appeared with Judith Anderson and Tyrone Power in a highly successful dramatized reading of Stephen Vincent Benét's *John Brown's Body*, directed by Charles Laughton. It enjoyed a nine-month tour. He made his last appearance on Broadway in 1958 as the elderly actor Mr. Zuss in Archibald MacLeish's *J.B.* But he enjoyed an Indian summer as an actor playing the crusty but wise and kindly Dr. Gillespie in the Metro-Goldwyn-Mayer television series "Dr. Kildare" (1960–1966). It brought him worldwide celebrity and affection. From the mid-1960s onward, however, he suffered from increasingly crippling arthritis; after a final stage appearance, as the wheelchair-bound poet Nonno, in *The Night of the Iguana* (1975), he retired from acting. He wrote two volumes of autobiography. Earlier, he had adapted Bruce Hamilton's novel *The Hanging Judge* for the stage (1952) and had played the leading role in a television adaptation.

Massey was married three times, first to Margery Fremantle, daughter of Admiral Sir Sydney Fremantle, in 1922. They had one son and were divorced in 1929. He next married the English actress Adrianne Allen (1929). They had two children, Daniel and Anna, who both became distinguished British actors; Massey and Allen were divorced in 1939. Finally, he married an American in 1939, Dorothy Ludington Whitney. Massey died in Beverly Hills, California.

• Massey wrote two volumes of autobiography, *When I Was Young* (1977) and *A Hundred Different Lives* (1979). His film career is discussed in Jeanne Stein, "Raymond Massey," *Films in Review* 13 (1963): 389–402. An obituary is in the *New York Times*, 30 July 1983.

JEFFREY RICHARDS

MASSINE, Léonide (8 Aug. 1895–15 Mar. 1979), dancer and choreographer, was born Leonid Fedorovich Miasin in Moscow, Russia, the son of Fedor Afanasievich Miasin, a French horn player in the Bolshoi Theater orchestra, and Evgenia Nikolaevna Gladkova, a soprano in the Bolshoi Theater chorus. His name was changed to Massine by Serge Diaghilev after he joined the Ballets Russes company. Massine was the youngest of five children. Raisa, his only sister, was closest to Leonid in age and was his frequent playmate. Their youthful relationship is significant, as Massine would eventually incorporate childhood games and dances into his own ballets. The two especially enjoyed folk dances, and Massine recalled that he often amused himself alone as a child inventing his own dances. Although his parents were both in the performing arts, they did not assume that Leonid would follow them in his own career. One of his mother's friends saw him dancing alone and suggested that his parents enter him in the Bolshoi Theater School to be trained as a dancer. He was accepted on a one-year trial in 1903 and then given permanent status in 1904.

Massine promptly fell in love with the world of the Bolshoi Theater. His slight build, dark coloring, and skill aided him in winning his first role: the dwarf, Chernomor, in the opera *Ruslan and Ludmila* by the Russian composer Mikhail Glinka. The role required not much more than wearing an exotic costume and huge false beard, but it was the first of many professional appearances for Massine as a child actor at the Maly and Bolshoi theaters in Moscow. It was also the first of his lifelong appearances in character roles made famous through his interpretive gifts. He also appeared in ballets at the Bolshoi but by age fifteen found the plays more interesting and the actors more intelligent than their ballet counterparts. Except for Tchaikovsky, Massine considered ballet music second-rate.

Typical of his lifelong dedication to improving his own education, Massine began to study the violin and painting while a young teenager. He also devoted himself to reading Dostoevsky, an unusual pursuit for a dance student. Massine admired the personality of Aleksandr Gorsky, the Bolshoi Theater's leading choreographer at the time, but felt that he could not transmit his ideas to his dancers, move big groups across the stage, or choreograph dances in authentic foreign styles. These were all to become central concerns of Massine's mature work.

Massine graduated from the Bolshoi School in 1912 and joined the Bolshoi company. In 1913 he danced the Tarantella in *Swan Lake*. Serge Diaghilev, director of the Ballets Russes company, was in the audience. Fokine, Diaghilev's leading choreographer, was planning a ballet, *La Légende de Joseph*, based on the biblical story. Seeing Massine in *Swan Lake* led Diaghilev

to select him to be Joseph. At first, not willing to leave Moscow or to end his successful theater career, Massine decided to reject the offer. He then abruptly changed his mind, moved to Paris to join the ballet, and thus created a new life for himself.

The ideal of Diaghilev's company was a fusion of the arts. By taking an immediate interest in educating Massine, Diaghilev further developed Massine's remarkable curiosity and keenness for learning. Massine saw that ballet for Diaghilev was a collaboration of artists steeped in European culture. Through Diaghilev, Massine had the opportunity to work with leading figures in the Paris art world. He also traveled to Monte Carlo, where he studied with Enrico Cecchetti, a ballet master whose impact on the art created an eponymous technique. At the premiere in Paris in 1914, Massine's role as Joseph was a success even though the ballet was not. It gave Massine sudden stardom, but he still sought to improve his technique. He found that the academic ballet he had learned in the Bolshoi School was not enough to meet the demands of Fokine's style, inspired in part by the freer movement of Isadora Duncan.

In his work both as a dancer and choreographer, Massine always sought the most complete expression of character, music, and theme by including the finest work not only in dance but also in music, painting and design, and literary and philosophical thought. Even as a young man, Massine was never content to be the tool of his directors and mentors. His artistic contributions went beyond the guidelines and suggestions laid out by Diaghilev. This was especially apparent in his use of major symphonic works for his choreography; Diaghilev preferred obscure or newly commissioned music. Massine also developed his work further by his accurate use of traditional dance from various cultures. Scholarly in his preparation, Massine differed from most choreographers in his interest in and knowledge of arts other than dance and his willingness to study.

In 1914, as World War I began in Europe, Nijinsky, Diaghilev's leading male dancer, and most of the Ballets Russes company were in America. This gave Massine the opportunity to work with the modern composer Igor Stravinsky and the designer Mikhail Larionov and to experiment in new choreography. Massine created his first ballet, *Le Soleil de Nuit* (later called *Midnight Sun*), in 1915. In it the Russian dances and games of his childhood appear as the basis of the choreography. The music was by Nikolai Rimsky-Korsakov.

In his first four years as a choreographer, Massine produced a surprising number of ballet masterpieces that pushed the art form into new areas. In 1917 he presented *Les Femmes de Bonne Humeur* (The Good-Humored Ladies) with music by Domenico Scarlatti, and *Parade*, a collaborative work with costumes and sets by Pablo Picasso and Jean Cocteau and music by Erik Satie. *Les Femmes de Bonne Humeur* incorporated the Italian *commedia dell'arte* style of masked players representing character types. In the production Massine created and performed the first of many roles that no one has been able to fill adequately after him because of his stage presence and precisely choreographed characterization. In *Parade*, Cocteau's stage innovations, Picasso's immense, painted flats, carried as though they were costumes, and Satie's idiosyncratic score with Cocteau's requests for the sounds of typewriters, sidewalk puddles, and carnival barkers were hard for the Parisian public to accept at the time, but the ballet enjoyed popular revivals in the 1990s.

La Boutique Fantasque (The Fantastic Toyshop), the story of a shop whose toys come to life, was produced in 1919. The characterizations of the shopkeeper, assistant, Russians, Americans, dolls, and even poodles are presented in careful detail. Its version of cancan, danced by Massine and Lydia Lopokova, became one of the most celebrated dances in ballet history. The artist André Derain made his first efforts as a theater designer in this ballet; the music was by Gioacchino Rossini, arranged by Ottorino Respighi.

During World War I, Massine studied Spanish classical and folk dance in Seville. *Le Tricorne* (The Three-Cornered Hat) was the result, premiering in London in 1919. Massine's accomplishment was incorporating the true movement and rhythm of the dances into ballet without giving them a false prettiness. The music by Manuel de Falla and the costumes by Picasso also were true to their folk origins.

Massine's last work for Diaghilev's company during this period of their association was a new version of *Le Sacre du Printemps* (The Rite of Spring). Massine's version had its premiere at the Paris Opera in December 1920. Nijinsky had choreographed the original version, set to music by Stravinsky and a scenario by Stravinsky and Nikolai Roerich, in 1913. Massine rechoreographed this controversial work. The primitive-sounding music with its complicated and jagged rhythms supported the creation of modern movements to express the ancient story of a community sacrificing a young woman. Latter-day dance enthusiasts have engaged in pointless debate over which was the superior version of the dance. Massine's was not adequately recorded, and Massine would not involve himself in the debate. His version, unlike Nijinsky's, was a great success when first performed. The chief choreographic element was the use of the dancer's weight to create an earthbound look and shape to the movement, the opposite of the ethereal look of classical ballet and its appearance of airborne lightness. The use of weighted movement was a basic element of modern dance, and Massine understood its usefulness in creating dramatic tension and expression.

Massine and Diaghilev had a personal falling out in 1921 that led Massine to other work. He formed his own company and produced several works for the "Soirees de Paris," organized by Count Etienne de Beaumont. These included *Salade*, choreographed to music by Darius Milhaud; *Mercure*, with music by Satie and decor by Picasso; and *Le Beau Danube*, with music by Johann Strauss; all appeared by 1924. Diaghilev convinced Massine to rejoin his company after these successes, and the second engagement with Diaghilev lasted from 1925 to 1928.

Massine's second time with the Ballets Russes produced still more experiments with modern movement, novel themes, and contemporary composers. *Zéphire et Flore* (Zephyr and Flora) had its premiere in 1925. Massine's collaborators were the cubist artist Georges Braque, who created the costumes and decor, and the composer Vladimir Dukelsky. Dukelsky was very taken by jazz, and this influenced the dance as well as the score. *Les Matelots* (The Sailors) also had its premiere in 1925. It was the first in what has become a tradition of lighthearted dances about three sailors on the town. The music was by Georges Auric. A Soviet-inspired ballet, *Le Pas d'Acier* (The Dance of Steel), with music by Sergei Prokofiev, had its premiere in 1927. In it the dancers took on the angular, abrupt movements of machinery, expressing fear of automation and the encroaching era of the machine. This, too, began a thematic tradition in dance.

While still with Diaghilev's company, Massine also worked as dancer-choreographer for the London Cochrane Revues from 1925 through 1926. In 1930 he revived *Le Sacre du Printemps* for the League of Composers, starring the modern dancer Martha Graham. He also choreographed for the Ida Rubinstein ballet company from 1929 through 1931.

In 1932 Colonel Wassily de Basil began his own Ballets Russes de Monte Carlo, and Massine joined the company as ballet master in 1933. During this period, he choreographed three of his symphonic ballets, *Les Présages* (Destiny, 1933), choreographed to Tchaikovsky's Fifth Symphony; *Choreartium*, choreographed to Brahms's Fourth Symphony; and *Symphonie Fantastique* (*Épisode de la Vie d'un Artiste*, 1936) to the Symphonie Fantastique, op. 14, by Hector Berlioz. *Les Présages* had its premier in Monte Carlo and soon thereafter in London; the other two were first performed in London.

Although these works were among Massine's greatest accomplishments, they have been the least appreciated. They embodied his understanding of music of the greatest scope and complexity and his concern with deep questions of humanity such as human destiny, the common man and warfare, the sources of creativity, and the ethos of artists. In these ballets Massine demonstrated his mastery of music, theme, and movement. Massine's fusion of the arts reached for a unity of art and understanding on a scale as grand as human aspirations. Such an achievement of detail and nuance in movement within a large-scale production and incorporating the movement of large groups of dancers has rarely been attempted. Massine, like any artist creating work on a grand scale in his own idiom, needed an open-minded and educated audience willing to transcend the more familiar categories of ballets.

However, the reception by reviewers was mixed: the music reviewers could not appreciate the ballet movements, and the ballet reviewers could not understand his use of music. When Massine's first symphonic ballet, *Les Présages*, appeared, the music critics paid little attention as Tchaikovsky was then out of favor. The attitude toward Brahms at the time was quite the contrary: the critics took him very seriously and mounted an attack on the choreographer who dared dance to this music. In another affront to the accepted way to do things, the ballet used modern dance technique derived from the work of Mary Wigman, the German pioneer of Expressionist dance.

Dance writers Adrian Stokes and Arnold Haskell and the music critic Ernest Newman championed the abstract ballet, *Choreartium*. Audiences in London applauded *Choreartium*, but the critics panned it until Newman, music critic for the London *Sunday Times*, wrote a series of articles defending it as a great work. Newman's authority was sufficient to silence the other writers, although he may not have converted them. In New York, audiences did not like or understand *Les Présages*, which had been the main success of the London season, and *Choreartium* received no critical praise but was well received by the audience at the Metropolitan Opera House. Leopold Stokowski, the great conductor in Philadelphia, admired Massine's work and understood his artistic and musical accomplishment. He gave *Choreartium* its most important seal of approval by conducting its performances at the Philadelphia Academy of Music in 1935.

Symphonie Fantastique created less controversy, as the choreography closely followed the setting described by Berlioz for his symphony. Massine's other major symphonic ballets included *Seventh Symphony* (1938), a work based on creation myths set to Beethoven's Seventh Symphony; *Nobilissima Visione* (*Saint Francis*, 1938) based on a scenario by Massine and the composer, Paul Hindemith; *Rouge et Noir* (1939), choreographed to Dmitri Shostakovitch's First Symphony, with decor by Henri Matisse; and *Labyrinth* (1941), with a scenario based by Salvador Dali on the legend of Theseus and Ariadne, choreographed to Schubert's Seventh Symphony, with decor by Dali.

Massine choreographed more than one hundred ballets. He worked with other companies including René Blum's Ballet Russe de Monte Carlo in 1938 and New York's Ballet Theatre in 1942–1943. He toured with his own company, Ballet Russe Highlights in 1945–1946. His work continued to grow through his use of the best music and the widest variety of human concerns and expressions, from the frivolity of *Gaîté Parisienne* (1938), known for its cancan to Offenbach's music, to the religious inspiration of *Laudes Evangelii* (1952), a ballet based on a scenario by Giorgio Signorini with music from the thirteenth century adapted by Valentino Bucchi and first performed in the Church of San Domenico, Perugia. In keeping with his lifelong interest in innovations, Massine also made three important films: *The Red Shoes* (1946), *The Tales of Hoffmann* (1951), and *Carosello Napolitano* (1954).

Massine's personal life encompassed several marriages and homes in several nations. He was proud to have become a naturalized American citizen and frequently commented that his son, Leonide, Jr., was born in the same year he became an American. Massine married three dancers. Vera Clark, known as Vera Savina, and Massine married in 1921 and divorced in 1924. He married Eugenia Delarova in 1928, and that marriage ended in divorce when he married Tatiana Orlova in 1939. With his third wife, Massine had two children, Tatiana and Leonide, Jr., both of whom became dancers. Massine also married Hannelore Holtwick (date of marriage unknown), with whom he had two sons. In 1922 he bought a group of three tiny islands in the Mediterranean, known collectively as Isole dei Galli, and established his studios and family villas there.

In his later years Massine traveled a great deal and worked in both the United States and Europe. He encouraged his son's choreography and urged him to follow his own instincts, to "avoid excessive symmetry," and to study history, literature, and painting in order to broaden his art. His work in Europe after the late 1940s included freelance choreographic work for the Sadler's Wells Ballet in London and the Ballets des Champs-Élysées in Paris. He also formed the Ballet Europe for the festival in Nervi in 1960. His work began to be revived in Europe in the 1960s, sometimes with his direct participation. The American ballet companies followed in the 1970s and 1980s as interest spread. In the United States, for example, Massine helped to reset some of his important works such as *Parade* and *Pulcinella* for the Joffrey Ballet and *Gaîté Parisienne* for the Cleveland Ballet and American Ballet Theatre.

Massine continued his dedication to the study and presentation of dances of specific cultures with those of American Indians, and he presented lecture-demonstrations on the subject throughout the world. Demonstrating the value of the traditional arts of Native Americans to fine arts at this time was revolutionary, both in the context of the world of classical ballet and the larger society.

In his autobiography, Massine cites his textbook on choreography as an accomplishment as important to him as his work in the theater. The result of many years of theoretical analysis of the essentials of choreography, including a study of rhythm and time, he continued his work on the book while a guest teacher of choreography at the Royal Ballet School in London in 1969, and the text was published in 1976. He made a trip to California in 1977 at the invitation of Merriem Lanova, director of Theater Ballet of San Francisco. While continuing to travel and work, he spent increasing amounts of time on Galli, where he worked to reconstruct a fourteenth-century tower and made plans to build a large music room. He died in 1979 in Weseke bei Borken, Germany.

Massine's influence as an American artist came in several ways. By contributing choreography and performances to American companies and dancers he added his international prestige to American dance at a time when its vigor and invention were gaining recognition both at home and abroad. His work with artists as diverse as Martha Graham and Leopold Stokowski gave dance itself attention as a significant art form, a spur to creative thought and new perspectives on the world. His approach to music and his expressive style were eclipsed in the United States during his lifetime by growing abstraction in dance. Renewed attention to his work in the late 1980s gave him new legitimacy, and in 1989 *New York Times* writer Anna Kisselgoff pointed out ways in which his technique was a source for the choreographers George Balanchine and Frederick Ashton, both highly regarded at that time.

As a dancer, Massine's greatest accomplishments were his own performances, celebrated not only for his technique but also for his stage presence. No one has been able to duplicate his delicate and precise characterizations, though his ballets have been revived and kept in active repertory. As a great performer, it is possible to memorialize him only through audience accounts. He was best known and won universal admiration for his character roles in lighthearted ballets. He made an unusual contribution to the art of ballet through his unification of the roles of actor, dancer, and musician. His reputation suffered sometimes in assessments by those who prefer discrete categorization of the arts, and, among contemporaries early in his career, those who were displeased when he left Diaghilev. His curiosity, energy, and dedicated self-education, along with prodigious talents, made him a great artist. His gifts of understanding several art forms and his willingness to study outside his own cultural sphere allowed his work to transcend narrow definitions of dance. He sought to explore the broadest sense of the human comedy and in order to do so expanded the realm of dance theater, music, and movement.

• Massine's own works include his autobiography, *My Life in Ballet* (1968), and *Massine on Choreography: Theory and Exercises in Composition* (1976). Taped interviews of Massine are in the Oral History Archive of the Dance Collection, New York Public Library for the Performing Arts, Lincoln Center. Another interview is in John Gruen, *The Private World of Ballet* (1970). A full-length biographical work is Vincente García-Márquez, *Massine: A Biography* (1995). Useful information about Massine and the ballet world is found in Arnold Haskell, *Diaghilev: His Artistic and Private Life* (1935), and Richard Buckle, *Diaghilev* (1979). Memoirs of other dancers are a colorful source, including Lydia Sokolova, *Dancing for Diaghilev* (1989), and *Diaghilev and the Ballets Russes* (1970), written by Boris Kochno, Diaghilev's private secretary. Gordon Anthony, *Massine: Camera Studies* (1939), includes an appreciation by Sacheverell Sitwell and offers visual records of Massine's unique presence and Sitwell's appraisal of his greatness. An obituary is in the *New York Times*, 17 Mar. 1979.

LESLIE FRIEDMAN

MASSING, Hede Tune (1899–8 Mar. 1981), Communist spy and later Federal Bureau of Investigation informant, was born to a Polish-Austrian couple. Hede's mother was the daughter of a prominent Polish rabbi, while her father was a circus acrobatic rider. When Hede was a young girl, the family moved to the United States and lived in Massachusetts and New York City. Massing's father tried to start a catering business but failed.

The family returned to Austria, where Massing went to finishing school. She then attended a fine arts conservatory and studied drama. At seventeen she met her future husband Gerhardt Eisler in the Cafe Herrenhof in Vienna. She was a vibrant young actress with radical views, and he was a charismatic, revolutionary playwright. They had a passionate romance and married in 1920 after moving to Berlin. Eisler had been a lieutenant in the German army during World War I but was demoted for spreading Marxist propaganda among the troops. Soon he became part of the international Soviet intelligence network, or the apparat. He eventually oversaw all Soviet espionage operations in the Far East and in the United States.

In Berlin Massing pursued acting while Eisler wrote Communist editorials. Their social life involved only fellow Communists. In 1923 Massing fell ill and went to live with friends outside Berlin. She and Eisler drifted apart as his radical activities kept him supposedly too busy to visit. Soon she started seeing wealthy Communist publisher Julian Gumperz. They fell in love and lived together. Her sister Elli moved in with Massing and Gumperz, and so did Gerhardt Eisler after he lost his job. Elli and Eisler became lovers, but Massing was happy with this arrangement.

In 1926 Massing and Gumperz went to New York City, where Massing met other Communists and applied for and was granted full American citizenship. After the papers came through, she returned to Germany in 1928 to be with Gumperz, who worked at Frankfurt's Institute of Social Research. There she met Paul Massing, a doctoral student in agricultural economics. They fell in love, and she left Gumperz. Whether Hede and Paul were ever legally married is not known, although Hede did adopt Massing as her last name.

Paul Massing took a job teaching at Moscow's International Agrarian Institute, while Hede stayed in Berlin until Paul could find living quarters for them. During this time she renewed her friendship with the Soviet spy Richard Sorge, who introduced her to "Ludwig" (Ignace Poretsky, *alias* Ignace Reiss), head of Soviet secret police operations in Europe. Meeting Ludwig began Hede's initiation into espionage. She learned to locate "safe" apartments for agents and to set up "maildrops" where messages could be exchanged. Then she traveled to Moscow to join Paul. In 1932 the couple returned to Germany and began recruiting new agents for Ludwig. They believed that spying for the Soviet Union was fighting fascism. Throughout the early 1930s Hede used her American passport to get Jews and Communists out of Nazi Germany and into Russia and Czechoslovakia, where they would presumably be safe. Paul was arrested in Hitler's anti-Communist purges and sent to a concentration camp, where he remained a secret member of the Soviet apparat.

Hede Massing threw herself into her work. Ludwig arranged for her to work as a Soviet agent in the United States, which her U.S. citizenship facilitated. She received warm welcomes from Gerhardt Eisler, who was on Communist work in the Midwest, and from Communists in the New York and Washington, D.C., areas. American Communists admired her as a Jewish German refugee and as an antifascist journalist. When Paul was released, he joined her in the United States and taught economics while she continued her espionage work. Hede got governmental data from Washington contacts and relayed it to her superiors in Paris, who then passed it to Moscow. In this line of work, Hede later claimed, she was an agent handler for Alger Hiss and Noel Field—both State Department employees.

In 1937 Paul was recalled to Moscow, and Hede went with him. They learned that Ludwig, their former superior, had left the secret service and had been purged by Joseph Stalin. As Ludwig's agents, they were in danger. The Massings were closely interrogated and kept under surveillance. They did not then understand that Paul had been summoned because Stalin was purging the European antifascist apparat as part of secret agreements with Adolf Hitler that would culminate in the short-lived Nazi-Soviet Pact. Hede, as a valuable American-based spy, would not have been in danger had she remained in the United States when Paul was called to Moscow. While held in the Russian capital, Hede and Paul threatened to go to the U.S. embassy and were allowed to leave the country.

By 1938 the Massings had learned more about Stalin's purges and Ludwig's execution. This disillusioned them with secret work and severed their obedience to Stalin. In 1947 the FBI contacted Hede Massing for information about Gerhardt Eisler, and she began describing the vast Soviet intelligence networks of which she had been a part. She became an FBI expert witness against Eisler, who fled to Eastern Europe to avoid charges of passport fraud and contempt of Congress.

During Alger Hiss's second perjury trial in 1950, Massing was the only witness to corroborate Whittaker Chambers's testimony that Hiss was a Communist spy. She said that she had met Hiss at Noel Field's home and bantered with him over which part of the apparat Field should belong to. Hiss denied her charges but was found guilty of perjury and sentenced to five years in prison.

After testifying for the government, Massing provided her services to the Central Intelligence Agency. Her autobiography, *This Deception*, was published in 1951. Reviled by liberals and leftists during the early Cold War, Massing faded into obscurity during later years. She died in New York City. Upon learning about her death, anti-Communist journalist Ralph de Toledano wrote, "She had lived when Communism seemed to hold out a promise. She had survived the ordeal by fire of being a witness against the world's great evil." When she died, he said, "part of an era went with her."

• Hede Massing's autobiography, *This Deception* (1951), is the best source of information on her life, focusing on her participation in prewar Soviet espionage rings throughout the United States and Europe. Informative profiles of Massing are in several works dealing with Soviet espionage networks and the Cold War. One of the more recent and informative is Stephen Koch, *Double Lives: Spies and Writers in the Secret Soviet War of Ideas against the West* (1994). Flora Lewis, *Red Pawn: The Story of Noel Field* (1965), focuses a great deal on Massing while trying to explain Field's choices and draw conclusions about his alleged espionage career. This work suffers from the fact that Lewis was not allowed access to then-classified information about Field that was later released. Allen Weinstein utilized newly declassified materials in his *Perjury: The Hiss-Chambers Case* (1978), which speculates about Massing's contacts in the worldwide Communist intelligence apparat and about whether Massing really knew Alger Hiss as a spy. Overall, Weinstein believes Massing's testimony. Former FBI agent Robert Lamphere and coauthor Tom Shachtman's *The FBI-KGB War: A Special Agent's Story* (1986) provides an American Cold Warrior's perspective on Massing and her life's choices. Obituaries are in the *New York Times*, 9 Mar. 1981, and the *National Review*, 17 Apr. 1981.

VERONICA WILSON

MASTER JUBA. *See* Lane, William Henry.

MASTERS, Edgar Lee (23 Aug. 1869–5 Mar. 1950), poet and lawyer, was born in Garnett, Kansas, the son of Hardin Wallace Masters, a lawyer, and Emma J. Dexter. Though his father had moved the family briefly to Kansas to set up a law practice, Masters grew up in the western Illinois farmlands where his grandparents had settled in the 1820s. He was educated in the public schools in Petersburg and Lewistown (where he worked as a newspaper printer after school) and spent a year in an academy school hoping to gain admission to Knox College. Instead of entering college, he read law with his father and, after a brief stint as a bill collector in Chicago, formed a law partnership in 1893 with Kickham Scanlan.

Over the next ten years he expressed his Populist views in a series of essays and plays, written under the pseudonym Dexter Wallace. In 1898 he married Helen M. Jenkins, the daughter of a Chicago lawyer; they had three children. In 1903 he joined Clarence Darrow's law firm, where he defended the poor over the next eight years. Some dozen plays and books of poems during this period are undistinguished, serving mostly as political tracts and verse exercises. Extramarital affairs and an argument with Darrow unsettled his personal and professional life from 1908 to 1911, when he went into law practice on his own.

In 1914 Masters began a series of poems about his boyhood experiences in western Illinois, published (under the pseudonym Webster Ford) in *Reedy's Mirror* (St. Louis). This was the beginning of *Spoon River Anthology* (1915), the book that would make his reputation and become one of the most popular and widely known works in all of American literature. In "The Genesis of Spoon River" (*American Mercury,* Jan. 1933), Masters recalls how his interest turned to "combinations of my imagination drawn from the lives of the faithful and tender-hearted souls whom I had known in my youth about Concord, and wherever on Spoon River they existed." Though he would never equal the achievement or fame of *Spoon River Anthology,* he continued publishing poetry, novels, essays, and biographies for nearly thirty years. The amount and wide range of his production far exceeded its quality, by most accounts, and Masters's place in twentieth-century American literature is still debated.

There is no doubt about the impact of *Spoon River Anthology.* Critical reception ranged from English critic John Cowper Powys's view that Masters was "the natural child of Walt Whitman" to Ezra Pound's proclamation that "at last, America has discovered a poet." Perhaps more impressive was the book's enormous popularity with nonspecialist readers, an achievement that has outlasted the ups and downs of many a literary reputation in the academic canons. *Spoon River Anthology* is a series of poignant and often sardonic graveside monologues that capture small-town America, midwestern values, and the angst of modern life. Representatives of the community from librarians to preachers bare their souls; poets and atheists speak their minds; women drop their polite-society guard; corruption is exposed. "Petit, the Poet," speaks for Masters when he laments those who prefer trivial formalities, while "Homer and Whitman roared in the pines." Needless to say, these monologues upset fundamentalists, "patriots," and political and literary conservatives and earned Masters a place in what would come to be called "the revolt from the village." These at once caustic and loving short poems began a lifelong celebration of the region that can be traced through *The New Spoon River* (1924) and in some three dozen lyrical and nostalgic poems published in various books and now collected in *The Enduring River: Edgar Lee Masters' Uncollected Spoon River Poems,* edited by Herbert K. Russell (1991). *Spoon River Anthology* has been adapted for the stage, and music has been added, and demand for the book and the dramatic adaptations has continued. The work was to earn the Spoon River poet a reputation as a one-book author, a distinction that understandably annoyed so diverse and prolific a writer.

Masters never did match the success of the original *Spoon River*—even in *The New Spoon River* or in several volumes of poems set on the Illinois prairies—*Songs and Satires* and *The Great Valley* (1916), *Toward the Gulf* (1918), *Starved Rock* (1919), and *The Open Sea* (1921). In *Domesday Book* (1920) and *The Fate of the Jury* (1929) he drew upon his legal career to create courtroom poems indebted to Robert Browning's dramatic monologues. His later poetry reflects the wide range of his interests—from the pithy *Lichee Nuts* (1930) to the lengthy Shelleyan narratives *The Serpent in the Wilderness* (1933), *Invisible Landscapes* (1935); and *The New World* (1937). His celebration of the midwestern landscape continued even in the later poetry he wrote while living in New York. *Poems of People* (1936) and *More People* (1939), as well as *Illinois Poems* (1941) and *Along the Illinois* (1942), are character

sketches and tributes to the land and the prairie myths. In 1942 he again expressed his sense of place in *The Sangamon,* a well-received volume in the Rivers of America series.

In the 1920s and 1930s Masters also tried his hand at fiction and biography. The novels—*Mitch Miller* (1920), *Skeeters Kirby* (1923), and *Kit O'Brien* (1927)—are mostly about growing up in Illinois and have gained little repute. The biographies are either adulatory, as in *Vachel Lindsay: A Poet in America* (1935) and *Whitman* (1937), or controversial, as in *Lincoln: The Man* (1931) and *Mark Twain: A Portrait* (1938). Masters saw biography as a form of revisionist history and set out to correct prevailing misconceptions about America's heroes and values. For much of his life he was a political and social outsider. His father had been a liberal in rural conservative Illinois, a Democrat in Republican territory. Masters often expressed contempt for the small-mindedness that hurt his father, a theme carried through in his own later populism as well as in literary values that went against the grain of mainstream opinion. He described himself as committed to "the Democratic creed of 1896 and 1900," standing with "Americanism and Democracy as against European domination and Toryism."

In the years of his greatest notoriety for *Spoon River,* Masters's personal life was less fortunate. While trying to balance two careers as lawyer and writer, he suffered a lingering and near-fatal bout of pneumonia. In 1923 he experienced a bitter divorce and moved to New York, where he practiced law for some years. After a literary tour of the country in 1925, he published *Selected Poems* (1925), a collection that drew deserved attention for its variety. In 1926 he married Ellen Coyne. They lived in New York, though later her teaching required that they live apart at times. Masters retired to the Chelsea Hotel to write a series of biographies as well as an autobiography covering his boyhood years and his career up to 1917. *Across Spoon River: An Autobiography* (1936) is blunt and cranky about a life he saw as largely "scrappy and unmanageable." Emphasizing life on his grandfather's farm, his school days, his political battles, the workday world, and the growth of a poet's mind through wide reading, the book is a valuable record of Masters's work habits and offers considerable insight on his position as a critic and his place in American literature.

Retired and not in the best health, Masters moved with his wife to her teaching positions in North Carolina and Pennsylvania. Throughout the 1940s he received several literary awards, including the Poetry Society of America medal, the Shelley Memorial Award, and the Academy of American Poets Fellowship. He died in Melrose, Pennsylvania and is buried in Oakland Cemetery in Petersburg, Illinois.

Masters is a transitional figure in American literary history. The Spoon River poems are distinctly modern, leading one to forget that he composed poems on the deaths of Whitman and Browning. He was comfortable with nineteenth-century long narrative poems but also contributed much to the development of the modern idiom. For over four decades he celebrated the prairie landscapes, the people of Illinois, and the values of his midwestern heritage. Though what he called "soul fatigue" drove him away from the loneliness of the prairie towns he both satirized and praised, in his later poems he still pictured himself choking with unfulfilled longing, reaching to the sky for his kite floating above the hills of Mason County.

As a biographer, Masters took the historical figures out of "the dust bins" and tried to "correct" the country's "vast mendacity" with a "sane record of men and affairs." He has been underrated as a critic and commentator on American culture, particularly in the tradition of Whitman as against the more dominant *Wasteland* and imagist schools. Much of his literary career reflects the marginalization of midwestern opinion and influence in light of eastern establishment power and control. Masters bemoaned what he felt was the takeover of the "Knickerbocker schools" of poetry after the death of Whitman; when Romanticism was out of favor, he argued for the universality of regional values and for Shelleyan poetry and politics. He once described his poems as following either the "cyclopean eye" of realism or the "dreaming eye" of mysticism. The poems and essays of this lawyer who hid poetry behind law books (he said the law and poetry were like "oil and water") may yet gain new attention from cultural historians and intertextual critics. Masters's attempt to balance two very different careers no doubt hurt his law practice and his books, though he once suggested that "if I had lived a cloistered life I should not have learned much besides books." Masters sought space for his own work in a closed critical environment and, in the process, challenged the assumptions upon which literary canons had been formed.

• Most of Masters's manuscripts and his letters are in the Humanities Research Center at the University of Texas at Austin. The University of Chicago and the Newberry Library (Chicago) also house some materials. *Across Spoon River* was reissued by the University of Illinois Press in 1991. Two useful bibliographies are John T. Flanagan, *Edgar Lee Masters: The Spoon River Poet and His Critics* (1974), and Frank K. Robinson, *Edgar Lee Masters: An Exhibition in Commemoration of the Centenary of His Birth* (1970). Several interviews with Masters that provide new insights on American life and letters are in the *University Review* 4 (Summer 1935); the *Providence Evening Bulletin*, 4 May 1936; *Dun's Review*, Apr. 1940; and the *New York Times Book Review*, 15 Feb. 1942. There is no full-length biography. Biographical information is in Gertrude Claytor, "Edgar Lee Masters in the Chelsea Years," *Princeton University Library Chronicle* 14 (Autumn 1952): 1–29; Herb Russell, "Edgar Lee Masters' Final Years in the Midwest," *Essays in Literature* 4 (Fall 1977): 212–20; Hardin W. Masters, *Edgar Lee Masters: A Biographical Sketchbook about a Famous American Author* (1978); Hilary Masters, *Last Stands: Notes from Memory* (1982); John H. Wrenn and Margaret H. Wrenn, *Edgar Lee Masters* (1983); and Marcia Lee Masters, *The Wind around the Moon and Other Poems* (1986). For critical assessment, see Willis Barnstone's introduction to *The New Spoon River* (1924); Charles E. Burgess,

"Edgar Lee Masters: The Lawyer as Writer," in *The Vision of This Land*, ed. John E. Hallwas and Dennis J. Reader (1976); August Derleth, *Three Literary Men* (1963); Bernard Duffey, *The Chicago Renaissance in American Letters: A Critical Study* (1954); Ernest Earnest, "Spoon River Revisited," *Western Humanities Review* 21 (Winter 1967): 59–65; Lois Teal Harley, *Spoon River Revisited* (1963); Dale Kramer, *Chicago Renaissance: The Literary Life in the Midwest, 1900–1930* (1966); Ronald Primeau, *Beyond Spoon River: The Legacy of Edgar Lee Masters* (1981); Max Putzel, *The Man in the Mirror: William Marion Reedy and His Magazine* (1963); Herbert K. Russell's introduction to *The Enduring River;* Louis Untermeyer, *American Poetry since 1900* (1923); and Michael Yatron, *America's Literary Revolt* (1959). An obituary is in the *New York Times*, 6 Mar. 1950.

RONALD PRIMEAU

MASTERS, Sybilla (?–23 Aug. 1720), inventor and merchant, was the daughter of William Righton, a mariner and merchant, and Sarah (maiden name unknown). Her exact birthdate and birthplace are not known, but she may have been born in Bermuda. Her name is recorded also as Sabella or Isabella. Her parents were Quakers. By 1687 her father had emigrated from Bermuda to Burlington in the colony of West Jersey, where he purchased a plantation on the Delaware River.

Masters's name first appears in New Jersey court records in 1692, when she served as a witness for her father. Sometime between 1693 and 1696 she married Thomas Masters, also a Quaker, who had left Bermuda for Philadelphia about 1685; they had four children. A merchant, Masters's husband invested his profits from overseas trade in real estate in the Northern Liberties area of Philadelphia; he also built a plantation and a summer home, "Green Spring," in Philadelphia. In addition to being a successful merchant, he served simultaneously as an alderman of Philadelphia and as the city's mayor (1707–1708) and later as a provincial councilor (1720–1723)—appointments that offer evidence of the prominent status that he and Masters held among influential Quaker aristocrats during Philadelphia's early years.

Masters's mechanical ingenuity led her to secure patents for two inventions. Although both patents were granted under her husband's name because of contemporary English law forbidding the granting of patents to women, she did receive due credit in the patent descriptions as the inventor. To initiate the process of securing her patents, Masters notified the Quaker meeting on 24 June 1712 that she intended to go to London, and she obtained a certificate of good standing from the meeting to take with her. Her first patent (no. 401), issued in London on 25 November 1715, was purportedly the first granted to any person in the American colonies (Needles, p. 286). This patent describes a device consisting of a long cylinder with mechanisms to drive two series of heavy pestles into continuous rows of mortars; it was to be used for crushing corn by a stamping process instead of the usual grinding process, and it included troughs for drying the corn. Powered either by horse or water, the device produced "Tuscarora Rice," a corn meal that Masters offered for sale in Philadelphia as a cure for consumption. Masters's husband had acquired the Governor's Mill in 1714, and he used it to produce larger quantities of the meal until declining sales led him to convert the mill for other purposes. Masters secured her second patent (no. 403), also in London, on 18 February 1716. This patent outlined a method of weaving palmetto leaves, chips, and straw for covering and adorning hats and bonnets. After her husband secured a monopoly for importing palmetto leaf from the West Indies, Masters opened a shop in London, where she sold hats and bonnets as well as child-bed baskets.

Masters had returned to Philadelphia by 25 May 1716. By 15 July 1717, following her husband's petition, the Provincial Council had granted permission to record and publish her patents in Pennsylvania. Masters died three years later, probably in Philadelphia.

• Frederick B. Tolles, *Meeting House and Counting House: The Quaker Merchants of Colonial Philadelphia, 1682–1763* (1948), adds valuable contextual information about Masters's life and times. Ethlie Ann Vare and Greg Ptacek, *Mothers of Invention: From the Bra to the Bomb: Forgotten Women and Their Unforgettable Ideas* (1988), has a copy of mechanical drawings from Masters's first patent. An important article to consult is Samuel H. Needles, "The Governor's Mill, and the Globe Mills, Philadelphia," *Pennsylvania Magazine of History and Biography* 8 (1884): 285–90, which reproduces Masters's drawings and provides detail about her husband's purchase and bequest of the Governor's Mill.

FAYE A. CHADWELL

MASTERSON, Bat (26 Nov. 1853–25 Oct. 1921), frontier lawman and sportswriter, was born Bartholomew Masterson in Henryville, Quebec, Canada, the son of Thomas Masterson, a farmer, and Catherine McGurk. The name Bart was corrupted to Bat in his early years. He later assumed the name William Barclay, and it was as William Barclay "Bat" Masterson that he became a well-known frontier figure. The Masterson family entered the United States about 1861 and began a ten-year westward trek with stops in New York, Illinois, and Missouri before settling in Sedgwick County, Kansas, in June 1871. The seven Masterson children received limited formal education in one-room schoolhouses along the way.

In the fall of 1871 Masterson and his elder brother Edward left home to hunt buffalo on the plains of western Kansas. The following summer they contracted to grade a section of railroad for the Atchison, Topeka & Santa Fe (AT & SF), then building into Dodge City, Kansas. When their subcontractor employer cheated the brothers of their earnings, Masterson confronted him before a crowd in the Dodge City depot and collected the money at gunpoint. In June 1874 at Adobe Walls in the Texas Panhandle he was one of twenty-eight buffalo hunters who withstood an attack and siege by several hundred Indians. During the ensuing Red River War (1874) Masterson served as a civilian scout. On 24 January 1876 he shot and killed an army corporal in a dancehall fracas at Sweetwater (later Mobeetie), Texas. A woman was also killed, and Masterson was seriously wounded in the melee. These episodes formed the genesis of Masterson's renown as a quick-shooting man of determination and courage, a reputation that would assume legendary proportions.

After recovering from his gunshot wound, Masterson served intermittently as a Dodge City policeman. In July 1876 he joined the gold rush to Deadwood, South Dakota, but got only as far as Cheyenne, Wyoming, where he devoted his time to gambling, a profession he would pursue for the next quarter-century. Back in Dodge City in November 1877, he was elected sheriff of Ford County, which at the time encompassed most of western Kansas. Within weeks the 24-year-old sheriff gained distinction by capturing outlaws who had attempted a holdup of the AT&SF train near Dodge City. In April 1878 Edward Masterson, city marshal of Dodge, was shot and killed by rampaging cowboys and died in his brother's arms.

Defeated for reelection in 1879, Masterson turned again to the gambling tables and visited Leadville and other booming Colorado mining camps. In 1880, at the request of his friend, Texas gambler and gunfighter Ben Thompson, he went to Ogallala, Nebraska, and spirited away Thompson's brother Billy, who had been threatened with lynching after being wounded in a gunfight. The following year Masterson was in Tombstone, Arizona, gambling and assisting another close friend, Wyatt Earp, in law enforcement. Masterson returned to Dodge City in April 1881 to support another brother in a difficulty and took part in a shooting affray in the town's main plaza, an affair that greatly diminished his popularity in the town. In 1882 he ran a gambling operation in Trinidad, Colorado, and served a year as city marshal. His reputation as a resourceful and fearless friend continued to grow when in 1882 he engineered the release of gambler Doc Holliday from Denver authorities before Holliday could be extradited to Arizona and in 1883 when he enlisted Earp and other gunmen in a campaign to protect Luke Short's gambling interests in Dodge. About this time he and a vaudeville performer, Emma Walters, began a common-law marriage. They had no children.

For the next twenty years Masterson maintained a residence in Denver, where he had interests in various saloons and gambling halls, including the landmark Palace Variety Theater and Gambling Parlors. He left on frequent gambling junkets and ran a gambling house at Creede, Colorado, during the 1892 mining boom. There and at other wild camps his presence was said to have had a quieting influence. He developed a strong interest in prize fighting, which was controlled and promoted by the gambling fraternity during this period, and attended most of the major bouts, often acting as an official. In 1899 he was president of the Olympic Athletic Club in Denver, where he promoted and refereed prizefights. He also authored a sports column in a weekly Denver paper.

Masterson left Denver in 1902 for New York City. He began writing on sports for the *Morning Telegraph*, a breezy New York daily specializing in sporting and theatrical news. In 1905 President Theodore Roosevelt (1858–1919) appointed him deputy U.S. marshal for the southern district of New York, a position he held concurrently with his newspaper job for four years. At the request of Alfred Henry Lewis, author of a 1905 novel based on Masterson's life, Masterson wrote a series of six articles under the title "Famous Gunfighters of the Western Frontier," which were published during 1907 and 1908 in Lewis's monthly, *Human Life*. His column "Masterson's Views on Timely Topics" appeared three times a week in the *Morning Telegraph*, and he became nationally recognized as a leading boxing authority. His column often contained pithy comments on life in general that revealed a sardonic view of the world. On 25 October 1921 he wrote, "Those who argue that everything breaks even in this old dump of a world of ours . . . hold that because the rich man gets ice in the summer and the poor man gets it in the winter, things are breaking even for both. Maybe so, but I'll swear I can't see it that way." He suffered a heart attack and died at his desk in his New York City office while writing his column.

• Masterson's articles in *Human Life* have been collected and reprinted in W. B. (Bat) Masterson, *Famous Gun Fighters of the Western Frontier* (1982), annotated and illustrated by Jack DeMattos. For the most complete study of Masterson's life, see Robert K. DeArment, *Bat Masterson: The Man and The Legend* (1979). A less detailed biography is Richard O'Connor, *Bat Masterson* (1957). Alfred Henry Lewis, *The Sunset Trail* (1905), is an early fictional treatment. George G. Thompson, *Bat Masterson: The Dodge City Years* (1943), details one period of Masterson's life. Nyle H. Miller and Joseph W. Snell, *Why the West Was Wild* (1963), reprints contemporary newspaper items concerning Masterson's Kansas activities. Jack DeMattos, *Masterson and Roosevelt* (1984), deals with the relationship and correspondence between the western gunfighter and the president.

ROBERT K. DeARMENT

MATAS, Rudolph (12 Sept. 1860–23 Sept. 1957), surgeon, was born on a plantation near Bonnet Carré, Louisiana, the son of Spanish immigrants Narciso Hereu y Matas, a pharmacist and physician, and Teresa Jorda. Matas's father, who spent 1864–1865 in Paris studying ocular surgery, successively moved his family to Brownsville, Texas; Matamoros, Mexico; Paris, France; Barcelona, Spain; and back to New Orleans. Matas attended school in all these places and became fluent in English, Spanish, and French. In 1875 he entered St. John's Collegiate Institute in Matamoros, where he studied medicine with his father and assisted part time in a pharmacy. After graduating in 1877, he enrolled in the medical department of the University of Louisiana (later Tulane University), and in 1878 he was awarded a two-year student residency in the New Orleans Charity Hospital.

Matas's excellent academic record and his knowledge of languages led his university professor Stanford E. Chaillé, chair of the Yellow Fever Commission, to appoint him as clerk and interpreter to the Yellow Fever Commission sent to Cuba by the National Board of Health in 1879. There he came to know George M. Sternberg, later surgeon general of the army, and Carlos J. Finlay, the Cuban physician who in 1881 recognized the mosquito *Aedes aegypti* as the vector of yellow fever. Matas, the only physician to appreciate the significance of this work, translated and published Finlay's findings in the *New Orleans Medical and Surgical Journal* in February 1882, almost twenty years before the Yellow Fever Commission headed by Walter Reed (1901–1902) demonstrated the validity of the mosquito theory.

Following his graduation from medical school in 1880, Matas embarked on a medical career that rapidly brought him national and international fame. In 1883 he assumed the editorship of the distinguished *New Orleans Medical and Surgical Journal*. Having already acquired a reputation as an excellent physician, Matas turned with success to surgery. His appearance on the scene coincided with the introduction of the antiseptic and aseptic techniques that were to reduce the danger from secondary infections. While at the beginning of his career, abdominal, thoracic, and neurosurgeries were seldom if ever performed, within twenty-five years no section of the body was considered inoperable.

In 1884 Matas was appointed demonstrator of anatomy in the Tulane Medical School. Within ten years, partly in response to newspaper and public pressure, he was elected professor and chairman of the department of surgery. In the meantime he helped found the New Orleans Polyclinic, one of the early postgraduate schools for physicians. He was a pioneer in the development of local, regional, and spinal anesthesia and in the intravenous use of saline solutions and serums for the treatment of shock, hemorrhage, and collapse. He also made major contributions in the areas of thoracic, intestinal, and cranial surgery. These included developing a catgut ring for making end-to-end sutures of severed intestines and devising an apparatus and the necessary technique for preventing lung collapse following resection of the chest wall (intralaryngeal insufflation).

The operative procedure for which Matas is best known, the endoaneurysmorrhaphy, vascular surgery for the treatment of aneurysms, was first performed early in his career. In 1888 he was called on to treat a young patient suffering from an aneurysm of the brachial artery resulting from a gunshot wound. After unsuccessfully trying compression and ligation of both the proximal and distal sides, Matas boldly opened the aneurysm. On removing the clotted blood, he found three openings from which other blood vessels were supplying the aneurysm. In the emergency he disregarded traditional teaching and closed the orifices inside the aneurysmal sac with fine sutures. The patient, to the attending surgeons' surprise, made a complete recovery. In 1915 the greatest physician of the early twentieth century, Sir William Osler, urged young British army surgeons to read the section on aneurysms in William Williams Keen, Jr.'s *Surgery* "by that modern Antyllus, my old and valued friend, Rudolph Matas of New Orleans."

During World War I Matas, who was appointed major in the Medical Reserve Corps, organized a Tulane unit (Base Hospital No. 24) and directed an officers' school for intensive training in the treatment of war fractures and military surgery. He served as vice president of the American Medical Association (1931–1932), as president of the American Surgical Association (1909) and the American College of Surgery (1924–1925), and was an active member of many other organizations. His numerous honors included the Henry Bigelow Medal from the Boston Medical Society (1926) and membership in the French Legion of Honor, the Orders of Alfonso XII and Isabella the Catholic of Spain, and the Order of Public Instruction in Venezuela.

Matas had an attractive personality and was beloved by his patients and students. In a day when the medical profession was not noted for erudition, he was well educated, read voraciously, and was exceedingly articulate. He had a retentive memory and, when faced with an emergency while operating, would give a recitation of the ways in which his predecessors had met the problem. In 1895 he married Adrienne Goslee Landry, a widow with two children; the couple had one stillborn child.

For most of the thirty years following his retirement Matas maintained a consulting practice. He had a keen interest in medical history and began gathering materials for a history of medicine in Louisiana. Although beset by various ills in his early nineties, he remained clear in mind until the year before his death in New Orleans. He left behind a trust fund for the preparation of a history of medicine in Louisiana and bequeathed the bulk of his estate to the Tulane University School of Medicine.

Matas was one of the outstanding surgeons of his day and ranks among the world's major medical figures for his pioneering work in the fields of vascular, abdominal, and thoracic surgery; spinal anesthesia; and the use of intravenous fluids. His many national and international honors and awards speak for his standing among his contemporaries. His work helped lay the basis for the rapid advances in surgery during the twentieth century.

• The Howard-Tilton Library of Tulane University has the Matas papers, which consist of forty-nine boxes of correspondence, lecture and clinical notes, diaries, and miscellaneous items. Among his more important articles are "Traumatic Aneurism of the Left Brachial Artery . . . ," *Medical News* 53 (27 Oct. 1888): 462–63; "Intralaryngeal Insufflation for the Relief of Acute Surgical Pneumothorax," *Journal of the American Medical Association* 34 (9 June 1900): 1371–75, 1468–73; and "Local and Regional Anesthesia," *American Journal of Surgery* 25 (July–Aug. 1934): 189–96, 362–79. Matas's own account of his early life is in his introduction to Pedro Puliulacho Oliva, *Ulcers of the Legs* (1956). The most detailed account of his personal life is in Isadore Cohn and Hermann B. Deutsch, *Rudolph Matas* (1960). See also John Duffy, ed.,

The Rudolph Matas History of Medicine in Louisiana, vol. 2 (1962). An obituary is in the *Orleans Parish Medical Society Bulletin*, 11 Nov. 1957.

JOHN DUFFY

MATCHEKEWIS (?–c. July 1805), Ojibwa war leader and chief of a village at Cheboygan, Michigan, east of Fort Michilimackinac. He was also known as Mashipinashiwish (Damn Bad Bird). Nothing is known about his place of birth or his parents. He emerges from obscurity as the leader of the attack upon Fort Michilimackinac during the American Indian revolt against the British in 1763, a rebellion prompted by various Indian grievances, including the price of trade goods and concern that the British were restricting supplies of arms and ammunition to the Indians in order to destroy them. The Indians appeared before the fort on 2 June and played a game of ball while some of their women walked through the gates carrying weapons under their clothes. During the match the ball was purposely struck into the fort, and the warriors streamed after it, seized weapons from their women, and fell upon the surprised British garrison. Manned by thirty-five men, Fort Michilimackinac was the largest of nine forts that fell during the uprising.

The war ended in 1764, and in succeeding years Matchekewis appeared as an ally of the British, visiting the Indian superintendent Sir William Johnson in Johnstown, New York, in 1768 to affirm the support of his people. Although the chief was briefly imprisoned at Michilimackinac in 1771 upon suspicion of murdering a trader, he understood the importance of maintaining good relations with the British who continued to control the Indian trade of the Northwest, even after the War of American Independence. In 1774 he was among those who welcomed to Michilimackinac its new commander, Captain Arent Schuyler De Peyster, and throughout the revolutionary struggle he was at the service of the Crown. He accompanied General John Burgoyne's march into New York in 1777, and in the uncertainty created by the American capture of Vincennes, Indiana, in 1779 Matchekewis steadied Indian loyalties at councils in Detroit, L'Arbre Croche, and Fort St. Joseph at present-day Niles, Michigan. These activities suggest the British belief in the chief's widespread influence among the Ojibwas, Ottawas, and Potawatomies of Michigan.

In efforts to restore Britain's credibility on the upper Mississippi, Captain Emanuel Hesse led an expedition against the Spanish capital of upper Louisiana, St. Louis, Missouri, in 1780. Matchekewis helped recruit warriors for the campaign and accompanied it as the premier Indian spokesman. Unfortunately, St. Louis withstood the British–Indian attack in May, and many of the tribesmen scattered, raiding across the countryside. This failure did not discourage Matchekewis from continuing to fuse British and Indian interests for the duration of the war, although after its close he voiced discontent at the lack of provisions being made available to former allies.

Matchekewis's activities are obscure during the postrevolutionary period, but he apparently supported the Indian confederacies that tried to hold the country north of the Ohio from the encroaching United States. He was, however, among the first significant leaders to seek peace with the Americans after the Indians' defeat at Fallen Timbers in August 1794 and the increasingly obvious inability of the British to offer effective aid. In December 1794, while with some forty Ojibwas, Ottawas, Potawatomies, Sacs, and Miamies, he met the French-Canadian trader Antoine Lasselle northwest of Fort Wayne, Indiana, and was persuaded by him to treat with Major General Anthony Wayne at Fort Greenville, Ohio. Preliminary articles of peace were signed by these Indians at Greenville on 21 January 1795. Matchekewis also attended the final negotiations, signing the Treaty of Greenville on 3 August 1795 and agreeing to the cession of most of Ohio to the United States in return for treaty annuities. The chief was one of the more prominent speakers at the treaty and additionally ceded Bois Blanc Island at Mackinac to ensure American goodwill. In 1796 he was named as one of several important chiefs to be entertained in Philadelphia and to be met by President George Washington, but he was too ill to make the journey.

Matchekewis continues to appear in British records up to the close of the eighteenth century, but his end, as his beginning, is obscure. His son, also called Matchekewis, said that the chief died during a treaty council on the Maumee, and presumably indicated the negotiations at the so-called "Fort Industry" at Swan Creek, in the summer of 1805. Described as a striking man in his prime, tall and heavy, Matchekewis was an important figure in the maintenance of British influence among the Lakes Indians during the revolutionary period.

• References for Matchekewis's career are thin and scattered. Most are noted by David A. Armour, "Madjeckewiss," *Dictionary of Canadian Biography* 5 (1983): 567–68. Lyman C. Draper, "Notice of Matchekewis, Captor of Mackinaw," *Wisconsin Historical Collections* 7 (1876): 188–94, draws together some reminiscences about the chief. Details of Matchekewis's negotiations with Wayne are contained in the Anthony Wayne Papers, Historical Society of Pennsylvania, Philadelphia, for 1794 and 1795 (he appears there as Mashipinashiwish).

JOHN SUGDEN

MATEER, Calvin Wilson (9 Jan. 1836–28 Sept. 1908), Presbyterian missionary in China, was born in Mechanicsburg, Pennsylvania, the son of John Mateer and Mary Diven. The family lived in various locations in central Pennsylvania. His parents were staunch Presbyterians, and his mother consecrated six of her seven children for missionary work. All six offered themselves to the Board for Foreign Missions of the Presbyterian Church in the U.S.A., and four were accepted and served in China.

Lacking funds to finance his education, he taught school for several years, and in 1855, the year he joined the Presbyterian church, he convinced the faculty of Jefferson (now Washington and Jefferson) College, in Canonsburg, Pennsylvania, to accept him as a member of the junior class. When he graduated in 1857, he was asked to deliver the valedictory but demurred in favor of a classmate who had been hoping to deliver it. Upon graduation, he served for two years as principal of Beaver Academy in Pennsylvania, increasing its enrollment from twenty to ninety pupils. He graduated from Western Theological Seminary in Delaware, Ohio, in 1861 and was ordained the same year. He served a church in Delaware, Ohio, until 1863. He married Julia Ann Brown in 1862; they had no children. His appointment by the Presbyterian Board of Foreign Missions was confirmed shortly after their marriage. Having heard that learning Chinese would be extremely difficult for a man his age, Mateer refused assignment to Canton, but the board refused his requests for an assignment to Japan, Africa, or India. He finally agreed to go to Shantung.

The Mateers and the Reverend and Mrs. Hunter Corbett set sail for China on 3 July 1863, while the battle of Gettysburg raged near his family's home. The sea voyage, with wretched food and an incompetent captain, against whom they filed a lawsuit in Shanghai, took six months, and their journey, in a second vessel, finally ended in a shipwreck on the China coast. The Mateers reached their home in Tengchow in January 1864. Mateer's brothers John and Robert subsequently joined them in the mission work in Shantung. After the death of his first wife in 1898, Mateer married Ada Haven, a missionary of the American Board Commissioners Foreign Missions in Peking in 1900.

In China, Mateer quickly realized the importance of an excellent command of the language and worked diligently at acquiring it. He also recognized that schools were sorely needed and began a small one. Overcoming opposition from both mission colleagues and Chinese, he managed to write the textbooks and construct the scientific apparatus the students needed. His scientific tools ranged from those used for dentistry to electrical devices. By 1880 the school had become Tengchow College, termed the best of the nineteenth-century Christian colleges in China. The college eventually received the support of the English Baptist mission and became the nucleus of the ecumenical Shantung Christian College, also known as Cheeloo.

Recognizing the need for all missionaries to be fluent in Chinese, he spent more than a year traveling through central China collecting idioms and recording the sounds of the various dialects of the language. The result was his *Mandarin Lessons*, well known for its explanation of Chinese synonyms and its idioms. Later editions of the work were revised by his wife, who was skilled in Mandarin. He also published *Primary Lessons in Mandarin*. At the 1890 mission conference in Shanghai a committee was formed to translate the Bible into the Mandarin colloquial. Mateer was the committee's chairman, serving until his death. He resigned as president of Tengchow College in 1898 to devote his time to the translation.

Mateer was a frequent contributor of articles to the *Chinese Recorder*. He was a powerful preacher in both English and Chinese and early in his career had itinerated throughout Shantung. With John Nevius he published the *Nevius-Mateer Hymnal*, translating many hymns himself. Mateer possessed an extremely strong character and was often stern and severe with those who disagreed with him. Numerous medical doctors, sent by the Presbyterian Board of Foreign Missions, left the mission because Mateer found them wanting. He died of peritonitis at Tsingtao.

• A biography by Daniel W. Fisher, *Calvin Wilson Mateer: Forty-five Years a Missionary in Shantung, China*, appeared in 1912; see too Fisher's *Character Building in China: The Life Story of Julia Brown Mateer* (1912). Mateer, along with his Southern Baptist colleagues in Shantung, T. P. Crawford and Lottie Moon, is the subject of Irwin T. Hyatt, Jr., *Our Ordered Lives Confess* (1976). See also *Annual Reports of the Board of Foreign Missions of the Presbyterian Church in the U.S.A., 1863–1908*.

KATHLEEN L. LODWICK

MATHER, Cotton (12 Feb. 1663–13 Feb. 1728), Puritan minister, was born in Boston, Massachusetts, the son of Increase Mather, a Puritan minister, and Maria Cotton. The marriage of Increase Mather and Maria Cotton continued the union of two great New England families. Richard Mather, father of Increase, had married John Cotton's widow, Sarah Hawkridge Story Cotton, in 1656; Maria Cotton was the daughter of John and Sarah Cotton. Cotton Mather believed that he was chosen to provide leadership in the Puritans' errand into the wilderness. His parents' character and conduct reinforced this feeling. His mother was in all but formal designation the head of the Mather household, taking care of virtually all the day-to-day responsibilities while her husband spent his days in his study. Increase Mather much preferred immersion in his books to making pastoral visits or performing the mundane duties of a minister.

Cotton Mather sensed his father's large expectations for himself before he was told of them. The intensity of his father's faith also affected him, providing a model of the life of a deeply pious man. Increase Mather's moods, his frequent depression, and his terrible nightmares when Cotton was a boy contributed to his son's early piety and seriousness. Cotton Mather showed signs of his faith before he was three years old, and he learned to pray almost at the time he learned to speak. In these early years it was his practice to make up his own prayers. He also learned to read before his formal schooling began. In school his precocity appeared at once—he soon proved able to read Latin and Greek with ease. When he was eleven, he could take notes in Latin on the sermons he heard, which of course were preached in English.

Mather was not quite twelve when he entered Harvard (1674). He did not have an easy time in the college—his studies were not a problem, but his relations with other students were. All were older than he, and they seem to have tormented him. The stutter he had developed could not have made his life easier. He was converted at Harvard, but the process of his conversion was conventional, as he suffered the doubts that often plagued the unregenerate. He lost the stutter in his youth, but he never fully escaped the feelings of his own sinfulness. At times these feelings would break in upon his spirit, even when he was an old man. Only strenuous prayer would relieve his conviction of sin and worthlessness.

Shortly after his graduation in 1678, he began preaching in nearby churches. He received the M.A. from Harvard at eighteen and five years later was ordained in his father's church, Boston's Old North. They served together until Increase Mather's death in 1723.

Cotton Mather married three times. His first marriage was to Abigail Phillips of Charlestown in 1686. She was not quite sixteen; they had nine children. She died in 1702. The next year Mather married Elizabeth Hubbard, a widow. They had six children; she died in 1713. These marriages were happy, for both women were emotionally stable and deeply religious, but Mather's third wife, Lydia Lee George, whom he married in 1715, showed signs of instability a few years into the marriage. Her rages, almost always directed at her husband, frightened and depressed him. He also felt humiliated by her behavior; she left him for a short period of time, and word of their unhappiness soon spread throughout Boston. What made these years even more distressing were the obligations he unwittingly assumed through the financial arrangements of the marriage. For several years creditors threatened to reduce him to poverty, and only the help of loyal—and wealthy—members of his church saw him through.

Cotton Mather's life and career centered on his church and New England. The pulpit he shared in the Old North Church (Boston's Second Church) was a center of religious intensity through the preaching of the two Mathers. By the early years of the eighteenth century, the congregation numbered around 1,500, about 400 in full communion. Cotton Mather favored the Half-Way Covenant (1662), the agreement by which baptism was extended to the children of baptized adults who had not experienced conversion and therefore were denied the Lord's Supper, as communion was called in the Congregational churches. But he supported his father's opposition to opening up this sacrament to all who led moral lives and who made a profession of faith in the articles of Christianity. Open communion had become the cause of Solomon Stoddard, the great Puritan minister of Northampton, Massachusetts. The Mathers considered Stoddard's position a betrayal of the "New England Way," the conception of the New Testament church that the Puritans had established in America.

Much of Cotton Mather's preaching over the course of his life was in the service of the original mission of the founding generation, as he understood it. Such service for him entailed an immense effort to convert sinners as well as to nourish believers and to fight off challenges to the Puritan errand, as the mission was sometimes called.

Stoddard presented daunting opposition in the 1670s and 1680s. In the 1680s there was also a severe challenge from England, as the government sought to force Massachusetts Bay to acknowledge its allegiance to the Crown. For this purpose the Crown sent Sir Edmund Andros, who arrived in December 1686 to govern New York and New Jersey as well as New England. Andros brought changes—a claim that Anglicans should worship openly and in a Congregational meetinghouse in Boston at that. He also dispensed with the elected houses of the legislature in Massachusetts and challenged the basis of land titles, requiring owners to pay fees to repatent land that they owned. In 1688 Increase Mather sailed to England with the intention of obtaining relief for his colony. Cotton Mather remained behind, feeling very much alone.

Later in 1688 the Glorious Revolution deposed King James II in favor of William and Mary. Soon thereafter, in April 1689, Boston revolted against Andros. Although he remained mostly behind the scenes, Cotton Mather seems to have been an important actor in this revolution, which saw Andros arrested and the government taken over mostly by the Puritans he had replaced. Cotton Mather wrote the *Declaration of the Gentlemen, Merchants, and Inhabitants of Boston and the County Adjacent*, which justified the rebellion. His father returned with the new governor, Sir William Phips, in May 1692, bearing a new charter that for several years kept power in Puritan hands.

Soon after Increase arrived, the outbreak of witchcraft in Salem Village threatened the entire province. Cotton Mather played an important role, but he did not instigate the affair. Four years earlier, he had been drawn into the case of some of the children of John Goodwin, a Boston craftsman. In the summer of 1688 these children began to show signs of being bewitched, undergoing what they described as attacks by demons and apparitions invisible to those who watched. The local magistrates were soon called in, along with a physician and local ministers. Cotton Mather served as more than an observer, for he and his wife took Martha Goodwin, then thirteen years old, into their house and after months of careful nurture enabled her to recover.

The Salem crisis was much larger and eventually saw hundreds arrested and twenty executions. Mather was torn by the upheaval. He had no doubts that witches were abroad in Salem and elsewhere, but he felt uneasy at the methods followed by the court. The proceedings were disorderly, sometimes so much so that the adolescent girls who made most of the charges were out of control. They shrieked, shouted, and sometimes fainted, and soon accused citizens of high social standing. The court seemed willing to accept their charges almost without question for several months. The use of evidence called "spectral testimony"—the belief that an apparition responsible for carrying out the Devil's wishes reflected the willing agreement to witchcraft by the person represented by the specter—was especially disturbing. Cotton Mather opposed the use of such evidence, but his opposition was muted and ineffectually conveyed to the court. Publicly he justified the proceedings—most dramatically in his famous book *Wonders of the Invisible World* (1692), which combined with the general understanding that he favored the prosecutions brought attacks on him by Robert Calef and others. When the crisis finally ended, Cotton Mather's reputation was tarnished and a terrible blow had been delivered to the public's morale.

For a few years after the Salem witchcraft episode, the Mathers' political influence remained fairly strong. But decline was probably inevitable—the new charter set Massachusetts on a new course of religious toleration, and it opened the way for all landowners, rather than church members, to participate in political life. Cotton Mather disliked the new arrangements, but he called for transatlantic cooperation among all Protestant believers, and he and Increase made their peace with Benjamin Colman, the Congregational minister of the Brattle Street Church who had denied that a true church required a covenant among its members. Father and son continued to take an active interest in church disputes and provincial politics until their deaths, alternately supporting or opposing governors based on either their religious policies or more personal, factional considerations.

Cotton Mather's internal life—his religious devotions—grew more intense in these years, and this life had never been placid. He seems to have felt even more guilt over his own imperfections (though he acknowledged none over Salem), but he also received much satisfaction from private experiences that included occasional visits from angels. His own religious practices followed his increasing interest in the spirit and became more enthusiastic as he grew older.

Some of Mather's obsession with the spiritual side of religion can be seen in the *Magnalia Christi Americana*, though parts of that work, which may be his greatest published book, appeared in other forms—for example, as sermons and short biographies—before publication of the complete version in 1702. Mather conceived of the *Magnalia* in 1693. It appeared in two volumes and was printed in England because no American printer could take on such a large project—about 800 folio pages in double columns. The *Magnalia* was divided into seven books or parts: one on the early history of New England, the others providing short sketches of the lives of governors, ministers, the history of Harvard, Puritan modes of worship, instances of remarkable providences in New England, and an account of various afflictions visited on New England. It is not easy to classify—it is at once a work of piety and dogma and a work of scholarship with an emphasis on history, biography, and institutions. Mather had at his disposal manuscript diaries and letters of early Puritans, sermons, oral testimony, and much more. His intention was to preserve and revive the sense of New England's mission. He also intended to demonstrate that literature and learning could flourish in America. The *Magnalia* is, among other things, the production of a self-conscious literary intelligence.

During at least several of the years given to the *Magnalia*, Mather also worked on his immense commentary on scripture, the "Biblia Americana," which contained six long manuscript volumes and has never been published. In a sense it was never finished. Mather seems to have added to it during the years of the eighteenth century. While he pored over these massive works, he also wrote many pietistic tracts and corresponded with English and German pietists. In certain respects *Bonifacius: Essays to Do Good* (1710) is an expression of what he called the "new piety"; in other respects, it was a manual of conduct addressed to various groups in society. As such it was a tacit admission that the old conception of a New England as a united society in the service of God could not be maintained. Society and religious faith had been shattered in the experience of the New World.

It may seem paradoxical that while Cotton Mather became more spiritual he also began contributing accounts of natural phenomena in America to the Royal Society. These were his "Curiosa Americana"—the works of God in America—letters describing the flora and fauna in the New World. Many of these letters dealt with medical matters, especially the plants used in American medicine, including a cure for syphilis that he learned of from the Indians. The Royal Society published many of these efforts, and elected him to its membership in 1713.

Mather studied and wrote about nature in a religious spirit, confident that his findings would redound to the glory of God. The climax of his scientific work came in *The Christian Philosopher* (1721), a book that fell into the category of "natural theology," science in the service of religion. In this book, Mather's knowledge of European science is displayed with liberal citations of the great scientists of his time.

The year of the publication of the *Christian Philosopher* saw the eruption of the controversy over inoculation for smallpox in Boston. Cotton Mather's advocacy of inoculation was at the heart of this upheaval, which involved Dr. William Douglass and Zabdiel Boylston, also called doctor though he had little medical training, James Franklin's *New England Courant*, both Mathers, and other Boston ministers.

Inoculation entailed the use of untreated pus taken from those infected with smallpox; it was not modern vaccination. When cases of the disease appeared in spring 1721, Cotton Mather, who had learned of inoculation from the *Transactions of the Royal Society*, urged Dr. Boylston to use the new method to prevent the spread of the disease. Boylston did so in spite of opposition from Dr. Douglass and much of the town. A nasty fight ensued with James Franklin's *New England Courant* weighing in with the critics of inoculation. Six people of the 247 inoculated died, and since Boylston did not isolate his patients, inoculation may have contributed to the spread of the infection. By the summer of the next year the worst of the conflict—and the epidemic—was over. Mather never admitted to any regrets, but the affair revealed that antiministerial feelings were common and not far from the surface in Boston. Mather's account of the smallpox episode is most fully expressed in *The Angel of Bethesda*. His medical understanding and his knowledge are explained in this work, which contains much on other diseases and their remedies. (The book was not published until 1972, when it received a careful editing.)

Mather's last publications were directed to ministers; they were *Manuductio ad Ministerium* (1726), a manual of practical and inspirational instructions, and the *Ratio Disciplinae Fratrum Nov-Anglorum*, also published in 1726 though written much earlier, a history of church practice and worship in the Congregational churches.

Any assessment of Cotton Mather must recognize his deep religious belief, his immense learning and scholarship, and his leadership in New England. He had a kind of genius. He also had a sense that he had been called to serve his God and New England. The last great member of a Puritan dynasty, he made mistakes, he sometimes failed to explain his purposes, but he left a legacy of a life of ceaseless striving in the service of Puritanism and New England.

• Mather papers are found in several collections in the United States and England. The major collections are in the American Antiquarian Society (Worcester, Mass.) and the Massachusetts Historical Society (Boston). A superb bibliography of his works is Thomas J. Holmes, *Cotton Mather: A Bibliography of His Works* (3 vols., 1940). Kenneth Silverman, ed., *Selected Letters of Cotton Mather* (1971), is valuable, as is Mather's *Diary* (2 vols., 1912; repr. 1957). For the context of Mather's life, see Perry Miller, *The New England Mind: The Seventeenth Century* (1939; repr. 1954) and *The New England Mind: From Colony to Province* (1953). Excellent biographies are David Levin, *Cotton Mather: The Young Life of the Lord's Remembrancer, 1663–1703* (1978), and Kenneth Silverman, *The Life and Times of Cotton Mather* (1984). For Mather's theology, see Richard F. Lovelace, *The American Pietism of Cotton Mather: Origins of American Evangelicalism* (1979); and for his religious thought and experience, see Robert Middlekauff, *The Mathers: Three Generations of Puritan Intellectuals* (1971).

ROBERT MIDDLEKAUFF

MATHER, Frank Jewett, Jr. (6 July 1868–11 Nov. 1953), writer, art collector, and museum director, was born in Deep River, Connecticut, the son of Frank Jewett Mather, a lawyer, and Caroline Arms Graves. An 1889 graduate of Williams College, Mather received his Ph.D. in English philology and literature from Johns Hopkins University in 1892. As an undergraduate he had caught the chronic virus of art collecting, and by 1892 he had begun his studies of Italian painting. After a year of study in Berlin Mather returned to Williams to teach Anglo-Saxon and Romance languages from 1893 to 1900, taking a year off for study in Paris.

In 1901 Mather temporarily changed careers to become a journalist, in retrospect a happy move in that it allowed him to develop a prose style qualitatively rare among his peers. He served as assistant editor of the

Nation, as editorial writer with the *New York Evening Post*, and as art critic for the latter paper in 1904–1906 and again in 1910–1911. That his interest in scholarship remained firm is suggested by his service as American editor of London's *Burlington Magazine*, in 1904–1906.

In the fall of 1903 Mather wrote his fiancée from Madrid that the Spanish painter Velasquez "trusted his eye, and he trusted life," a characterization as apt for Mather's own critical writing in these years. In 1905 he married Ellen Suydam Mills, with whom he had two children.

In 1906, in the wake of Mather having experienced serious illness, the Mather family moved to Italy. There Mather freelanced, becoming one of the first correspondents to cover the devastating Messina earthquake of 1908. It was probably in Italy that he met Allan Marquand, founder of the Department of Art and Archeology at Princeton University. Appealing to Mather's unabated interest in Italian art and his former enjoyment of academics, Marquand persuaded Mather to accept appointment at Princeton in 1910 as the first Marquand Professor of Art and Archaeology.

In 1912 Mather published two books that demonstrated his range as a thinker and a writer: *Homer Martin, Poet in Landscape*, an art historical study, and *The Collectors*, a collection of short stories, one of which contains a sketch of his friend Bernard Berenson. In March 1913 Mather published a brilliant review of the Armory Show in the *Independent*. Recognized as a distinguished commentator on culture, he was given an honorary degree by Williams College later that year.

Beyond a prolific production of scholarly articles on problems in European and American art, Mather wrote a number of books intended for the general reader, of which the *History of Italian Painting* (1923, 1938) is the best known, having served tourists and students alike for a quarter century. In 1927 he published *Modern Painting*, a book marked by both an essentially nineteenth-century respect for the classical tradition and an unease with what he saw as unbridled excesses of the modern imagination. *Venetian Painters* followed in 1936, and *Western European Painting of the Renaissance* in 1939.

In addition to broad surveys, Mather wrote specialized monographs (*Portraits of Dante*, 1921; *The Isaac Master*, 1932), a drama (*Ulysses in Ithaca*, 1926), a work on aesthetics (*Concerning Beauty*, 1935), and two sets of collected critical essays (*Estimates in Art*, 1916 and 1931). This last volume grew out of work on "The American Spirit in Art," a 1927 volume he co-authored with Charles Rufus Morey and William James Henderson in the series *The Pageant of America*. The 1931 *Estimates* arguably contains Mather's most prescient and enduring critical judgments, in elevating Albert Pinkham Ryder, Thomas Eakins, and Winslow Homer above the easier visions of John Singer Sargeant and James McNeill Whistler.

Although this production attests to the contemplative side of Mather, he was by temperament an activist. Late in life he recalled his service as an ensign in the naval reserve in World War I as among the most interesting years of his life. From there he went on to build a schooner, the *Four Winds*, and in World War II he tried unsuccessfully, at over age seventy, to re-enlist in the navy!

Indeed, Mather's career took an activist turn when in 1920 he began twenty-seven years of service on the Smithsonian Art Commission, a distinguished panel that advised on the development and disposition of the nation's art collections. Given Mather's decades of collecting (everything from first editions of Melville to Japanese sword guards), Princeton turned to him in 1922 to direct its art museum, a post he held until 1946, thirteen years beyond his designation as professor emeritus. He established the core of the museum's holdings through institutional purchase and generous personal donations, primarily in old master European and American paintings and drawings. Always outspoken and no friend of the protocols of academic decorum, the tenure of "the Skipper" as director seems never to have been viewed as becalmed by his colleagues.

Mather's last working decades saw him in residence at his Bucks County farm, "Three Brooks," where he enjoyed, as he put it, "the mixed blessing of alfalfa, goats, and Japanese beetles." There he led the active and contemplative life, re-reading Cicero and reading Gide for the first time when not tending the goats.

Today, Mather's contributions seem to vary in importance. He was the dean of American art critics, highly influential in both artistic and literary circles, and the leading prize for art criticism in America today (awarded by the College Art Association) bears his name. On the other hand, his art historical writing is largely dated in both fact and judgment, though highly interesting as a document of the earlier years of art history in America. His role as a collector in the history of the American university and college museum is secure. At his death his qualities as a teacher, combining great breadth with memorable language, were recalled by former students, who referred to him as "a wise and humane spirit," and "a mind with range and velocity."

When asked in his last year if there were one more book he would like to write, he replied "The Memoirs of an Unplanned Life." Mather died in Princeton, New Jersey.

• "A Private Life," a biography written by Mather's father, is at the Archives of Princeton University, as is correspondence between Mather and many other notable literary and artistic figures. Important documents are also at the Princeton University Department of Art and Archaeology Archives and the Archives of American Art in New York City. See also Marilyn Aronberg Lavin, *The Eye of the Tiger: The Founding and Development of the Department of Art and Archaeology, 1883–1923, Princeton University* (1983), and H. Wayne Morgan, *Keepers of Culture: The Art-Thought of Kenyon Cox, Royal Cortissoz and Frank Jewett Mather, Jr.* (1989). An obituary is in the *New York Herald Tribune*, 12 Nov. 1953.

A. RICHARD TURNER

MATHER, Increase (21 June 1639–23 Aug. 1723), Puritan minister, was born in Dorchester, Massachusetts, the son of Richard Mather, Dorchester's minister, and Katherine Holt, both of Lancashire, England. Increase was the youngest of five sons, four of whom also became ministers. His father was among the most prominent religious leaders of early Massachusetts, and Increase was raised in a family of considerable social eminence. From the age of twelve he lived in Boston in the home of John Norton, another prominent minister and scholar, and in 1656 he received a B.A. from Harvard College. Mather went to England the next year. He followed two older brothers, Samuel and Nathaniel, who had established themselves in Puritan churches of the Interregnum and stayed in England and Ireland to play important parts in the later development of English dissent. Increase earned an M.A. at Trinity College, Dublin, in 1658 and then held several church appointments until after the Restoration. He returned to Massachusetts in 1661.

On 6 March 1662 Mather married Maria Cotton, daughter of New England's best-known clergyman, John Cotton. Their first child, a son, was born 12 February 1663 and was named Cotton Mather after his grandfather. Two more sons and seven daughters lived to maturity. In the summer of 1662 Mather attended the synod that produced the Half-Way Covenant. As early as the 1650s Puritans observed a decrease in new admissions to their churches. The Half-Way Covenant allowed baptism for the infant grandchildren of members of the Congregational churches, even if neither of the children's immediate parents had experienced new birth or been admitted to a church. Mather opposed the Half-Way Covenant, even though his father had taken a leading role in promoting it. By adopting this position Increase Mather publicly opposed his father and allied himself with the lay members of the churches, who generally disliked their ministers' innovation, and with the lay members' deputies in the General Court. These became political alliances that Mather held for the rest of his life.

In 1664, while the division over the Half-Way Covenant was festering and after great hesitation, Mather allowed himself to be ordained a teacher at the North Church or Second Church in Boston. He was to remain there for almost sixty years. He at once became involved in a struggle over his authority vis-à-vis a founding lay member, John Farnum, who soon joined a Baptist meeting. Mather stood at the forefront of the effort to keep Baptists out of Massachusetts and maintain a narrow religious uniformity in New England. By the end of the decade the Half-Way Covenant had caused a schism in the First Church of Boston, an uproar in the House of Deputies, and the creation of Boston's more liberal Third Church, and, incidentally, had led to the death of Richard Mather. All of these circumstances, together with the early death of his brother Eleazar, then minister at Northampton, caused Increase Mather to suffer a life-threatening depression from which he emerged in 1672 a changed person.

Mather recorded his spiritual struggles during two years of emotional illness in an autobiography intended for his children and not published until 1962. In it he revealed how he had gained confidence about his own salvation ("I have prevayled! I have prevayled!") and a conviction of New England's place in world history that had heretofore been lacking in him and generally in his generation. Starting in 1670 Mather joined that small number of ministers who began to redefine the New England errand. His first major contribution to this vision was a biography of his father, *The Life and Death of That Reverend Man of God, Mr. Richard Mather* (1670), written in part to assuage his feelings of guilt at having opposed his father over the Half-Way Covenant.

In this innovative work Increase created an image he was to use frequently in describing New England's beginnings. The reasons for Richard Mather's coming to New England "are of weight . . . ," he wrote, "because Posterity may thereby see what were the swaying Motives which prevailed with the First-Fathers of N. E. to venture upon that unparallel'd Undertaking, even to Transport themselves, their Wives and Little ones, over the rude Waves of the vast Ocean, into a Land which was not sown." Increase equated his father's motives for sailing to America with those of all the founders. These motives now became the very raison d'être of Massachusetts. In the next few years he elaborated on New England's errand through sermons that insisted on the colony's special relationship to God: "This is Immanuel's Land . . . ," and "Christ as Mediator is the Father of the new world."

The Increase Mather who emerged thus in 1670–1672 became over the next twenty years the leading voice of American Puritanism. During that period he published forty-six books, some of them single sermons, others collections of eight or ten, and still others books of doctrine, theology, natural science, and history. At the outbreak of King Philip's War in September 1675, he articulated a providential interpretation of the war, explaining it as a punishment from God for the colony's sin. He proposed a strict moral code enacted into a new law titled "Provoking Evils" that condemned tavern going, the unlicensed sale of alcohol, frivolous travel on Sundays, and "the evil pride in Apparell." He wrote a history of the war, but it was less successful than a more secular history by a competitor, William Hubbard. Mather unsuccessfully challenged the governing magistrates to enforce the stricter sumptuary laws. After the war he used a fire in Boston in 1677 and a smallpox epidemic in 1678 to reinforce his providential interpretation of events.

In 1679 Mather succeeded in getting the General Court to call the Reforming Synod, the last of the four synods that marked the course of Massachusetts's Puritan period. This occasioned an early disagreement between Mather and Solomon Stoddard. Stoddard was ready to welcome people to the Lord's Supper without their having had a definite experience of regeneration. Mather opposed any change in the traditional requirement of a public testimony to an experience of new birth. Samuel Willard (1640–1707), minister at the Third Church, Boston, sided with Stoddard, presaging a new flexibility about the conversion experience that had been central to the Puritan understanding of election. The report of the synod, written by Mather, is better known for his passionate denunciation of the growing moral indifference in the colony.

During the early 1680s Increase Mather was at the peak of his influence in a colony still miraculously independent of all outside authority. In 1680 he encouraged the widespread adoption of collective covenant renewals by congregations and led his North Church in a renewal of its commitment to its own principles. He supported Willard's continued attack on Baptists, and in 1681 and 1682 he used the appearance of comets to preach and write about the natural world: *Heavens Alarm to the World* (1681), *Kometographia* (1683), *Doctrine of Divine Providence*, and *An Essay for the Recording of Illustrious Providences* (both 1684). In the course of these studies Mather read widely in contemporary astronomy. As a consequence of this interest in science Mather and Samuel Willard organized the Boston Philosophical Society (1683), modeled on the Royal Society of London, but it was short-lived. Mather became increasingly active in the affairs of Harvard College. He was appointed a nonteaching fellow and member of the corporation in 1675, refused the presidency in 1681, and finally accepted it pro tempore in 1685 on condition that he continue to live in Boston and serve as teacher of his North Church. As president, Mather revised the college curriculum by restoring Greek and Hebrew studies and emphasizing the Bible and Christian writing instead of Roman authors as the sources of ethics. He rewrote the college laws after years of slack leadership to require residence in the dormitories, presence at meals, and regular attendance at all lectures and recitations. He strictly forbade hazing of young students by the seniors.

One of Mather's most important influences on seventeenth-century Boston was his encouragement of the press. He was instrumental in establishing John Foster (1648–1681) as the first printer in Boston (1675) and then provided him with a steady flow of books to print. Heretofore all New England printing had been done at nearby Cambridge. Foster, a philomath, printed an annual almanac in competition with the Cambridge press, introduced Mather to astronomy, and began to print maps and illustrate books with woodblocks of his own creation. Mather, for his part, expanded his own flow of book manuscripts, and by distributing gift copies to colleagues across New England and in old England too, Mather spread his version of New England's providential history far and wide. Boston became the literary metropolis of Anglo-America, a position it would keep well into the nineteenth century.

In the ten years following King Philip's War, when Mather was achieving intellectual and religious leadership, developments in England began to threaten the Puritan colony's independence. The royal charter of 1629 had given the Massachusetts Bay Company authority to govern its own affairs, as long as it did not contravene English law. That same year some Puritan stockholders of the company changed their purpose from a commercial enterprise to a civil society in which they planned to live. They took the royal charter with them to New England, and using its grant of self-government the Puritans were able to govern New England for years without interference from home. After Edward Randolph reported in 1676 how independent they had become, the Crown sought ways to bring the Puritans back under its authority. It decided to revise the charter, and in 1683 it asked Massachusetts to return the original charter voluntarily. In 1683 Mather edited and helped publish a number of written arguments against voluntary submission, and early in 1684, twenty years after starting his regular preaching career, he gave his first political speech. He spoke in town meetings to the freemen of Boston and urged resistance to London's request. Politics now became a central concern of Mather's public life.

The Crown succeeded in vacating the charter in English courts and created a new form of government for all northern colonies called the Dominion of New England. In December 1686 Sir Edmund Andros arrived to be governor-general of this new entity. It soon included all the English colonies from Maine to New Jersey. Andros, who was a professional soldier, had already served as lieutenant governor of New York, which at that time did not have any form of representative government. The new Dominion of New England did not have elected legislatures either, and more than fifty years of political tradition in Massachusetts was ignored. Besides governing without an elected legislature, Andros was arrogant in his relations with Puritan leaders, scornful of Puritan religion, and indifferent to basic institutions like town meetings. When James II issued a Declaration of Indulgence (1687) that suspended penal laws against dissenters, Mather believed the king might restore the old charter. Mather sailed for England with the blessings of his church to plead Massachusetts's case at court.

For the next four years, from May 1688 to March 1692, Increase Mather maneuvered his way among the centers of power in London. In the spring and early summer of 1688 he exulted over three apparently successful audiences with James II but then was dismayed when the Glorious Revolution occurred and James fled to France. Quickly siding with the revolution, Mather soon (8 Jan. 1689) had an interview with William of Orange. Mather's introduction to the new court came from a staunch ally of the old Puritan cause, Lord Philip, fourth Baron Wharton. Mather had equally important support in Parliament from Sir Henry Ashurst, son of a wealthy London merchant alderman and now a member of the House of Commons. Once he understood that the judicial ruling against the original charter would not be reversed, Mather hoped to have the charter restored by an act of Parliament. In June 1689 he learned of the rebellion that had taken place in Boston on 18 April. Governor Andros and allies like Joseph Dudley and Edward Randolph were imprisoned. Mather was successful in persuading William III that this was not rebellion against him, but rather against the old government of James II. The bill that might have restored the charter failed when Parliament was dissolved, and when new elections went against the Whigs, Mather lost hope of having the old charter restored. He now turned his energies toward obtaining a new charter that would contain the privileges of the old one.

It was an uphill fight against Lord Treasurer Danby, who was president of the Committee for Trade and Plantations, and its secretary, William Blathwayt, both of whom were Tories, royalists, and strongly in favor of direct control of the colonies from London. An added difficulty developed when Andros, Dudley, Randolph, and others arrived from Boston in March 1690. The charges of misgovernment laid against them by the interim government in Boston would be heard by the Committee for Trade and Plantations. Thomas Oakes and Elisha Cooke (1637–1715), who along with Mather and Sir Henry Ashurst had been named agents for Massachusetts, also arrived from Boston. Those four together were to plead Massachusetts's case. Cooke in particular disagreed with Mather over their legal strategy, and the four agents were unable to make the colony's charges against Andros, Dudley, and Randolph stick. Those men went free (May 1690) to resume their careers in colonial government. Over the objections of Cooke, who insisted on a return of the original charter, Mather, Ashurst, and Oakes petitioned the king for a new colonial charter. A draft was prepared under Mather's supervision by the fall of 1690 and was sent by William III to the Committee for Trade and Plantations for review early in 1691.

Meanwhile, through all these political ups and downs, Increase Mather had made wide acquaintance among the dissenting ministers around London. He preached in innumerable dissenting churches and held many conversations with men like Dr. William Bates, John Flavel, and the dean of Puritan divines, Richard Baxter. Mather's brother Nathaniel was already living in London and active in a movement to unite the Presbyterian and Congregational ministries. Increase actively supported this union, which took form in a document titled "Heads of Agreement Assented to by the United Ministers in and about London, Formerly Called Presbyterian and Congregational." Although in England the union soon fell apart, Increase Mather's part in it was important to his later reputation in New England and influential in the growing tolerance among Massachusetts churches at the opening of the next century.

In the spring of 1691 Mather saw his draft for a new charter for Massachusetts thrown out in favor of one drawn up on instructions from Secretary Blathwayt. At every stage Mather was assiduous in representing the interests of the colony. Several details, like the inclusion of Plymouth, can be directly attributed to him. The new charter provided for a governor appointed by the Crown and a house of representatives elected by the people. The governor and the lower house shared in choosing the upper house or council. Mather took great pride in this unique but cumbersome arrangement, for he saw it as an ultimate protection of the people's rights. The franchise for the lower house was given to freeholders, not church members as had been the case under the old charter. A freehold franchise had already been sought by the townsmen themselves in Massachusetts. Mather was asked to nominate the first governor to serve under the new charter—testimony to his reputation in London—and he nominated Sir William Phips. Phips, who grew up in Boston, was knighted in 1687 for recovering sunken Spanish treasure in the Caribbean. At the outbreak of war with France in 1690 he led a fleet of armed merchantmen on a successful attack on Port Royal. Back in Boston he was elected a magistrate in the interim government. In 1691 he was in London, where he and Mather were close allies. Mather chose to nominate him partly because William III was known to want a governor who could lead troops against the French, but the choice soon backfired on Mather when Phips proved to be a coarse and bullying officeholder.

Mather sailed for Massachusetts in March 1692 after an absence of four years. When he arrived in Boston in May, the Salem witch hunt was in full cry. He was slow to intervene, but later that summer at the request of other ministers he wrote a criticism of the use of spectral evidence, *Cases of Conscience Concerning Evil Spirits* (1692), which was important in bringing the trials to a stop. His son Cotton simultaneously wrote a book supporting the trials, *Wonders of the Invisible World* (1692), which Mather approved of in an introduction, thus straddling one of the most troublesome moral issues in New England Puritan history. Increase Mather's ambivalence about the witchcraft trials did nothing to harm his career during his lifetime but greatly damaged his later reputation.

The ten years following his return to Boston were tumultuous ones. Many people, led by Elisha Cooke, resented the new charter and blamed Mather for selling out the old Puritan colony. Governor Phips behaved outrageously, and Mather felt obliged to defend him until he was recalled to England. Mather's presidency of Harvard College became the focus of political controversy. Before the old charter was lost the college had been under the supervision of the legislature. Now Mather tried to get a royal charter for the college, like Oxford and Cambridge. His motive was partly prestige but also to protect the college and his own actions as president from local interference. Mather's political enemies, Elisha Cooke chief among them, opposed taking ultimate authority for the college out of the colony, and they tried repeatedly to force Mather out of the presidency by demanding that he reside at the college in Cambridge, which would have meant giving up his church.

While campaigning for a royal charter, Mather also moved to rid Harvard of the latitudinarianism that had developed in his absence. Latitudinarianism was a mood of broad-minded tolerance that in England after the Civil War displaced much of the earlier rigid, puritanical morality. When Mather was in England the two tutors he had left in charge, John Leverett (1662–1724) and William Brattle (1662–1717), had openly turned to latitudinarian books and principles. Mather forced them out in 1698, and they and their friends then founded the Brattle Street Church in Boston as a clear alternative to the traditional Congregational churches. They invited Benjamin Colman to be its minister. Colman had grown up in Mather's North Church, but after attending Harvard he had gone to England and imbibed the full latitudinarian style. On the advice of his Boston friends, who anticipated the opposition, Colman had himself ordained in a Presbyterian church in England. Increase Mather furiously attacked the new church in *Order of the Gospel* (1700) but could not prevent this breach in traditional Congregationalism. At the turn of the century Mather clearly represented the conservative end of a new religious spectrum. Mather's defense of the new colonial charter, on the other hand, placed him at the forward-looking end of the political spectrum. Although Mather remained proud of his role in drafting the charter, under which Massachusetts was governed until independence, his most determined political enemy, Elisha Cooke, at last succeeded in forcing him to resign the presidency of Harvard College in 1701.

The next six years brought an end to Mather's direct participation in Massachusetts politics and his final separation from the college. This chain of events began when Joseph Dudley was appointed governor-general in 1702. Dudley was a wealthy son of one of the colony's founders and a Tory who had cooperated with Andros during the Dominion of New England. After 1690 Dudley held several positions in colonial government outside Massachusetts and won the respect and confidence of influential patrons in England, including Secretary Blathwayt. At first Mather hoped to get on well with a man who had been raised in his own church, but it soon became clear that Dudley was too much an Anglican in religion and a Tory in politics for Mather to be an ally. In 1706 a scandal broke over Dudley's trading with the enemy in the French war (Queen Anne's War, 1702–1713). Cotton Mather took a leading part in an effort to have Dudley recalled, but the governor survived the attempt, partly by ingratiating himself with the Massachusetts House of Representatives by restoring the original 1650 charter to Harvard College. For a moment it looked as if Increase might once more be chosen president, but instead the overwhelming vote went to John Leverett. With that Increase Mather withdrew both from active politics and from the college.

Mather was more successful in his leadership of the New England churches. In 1705 Benjamin Colman, now securely ensconced in the Brattle Street Church, tried to persuade the Cambridge Association, a regional association of ministers organized in part by Cotton Mather, to adopt rules that would have given the colony's ministers a veto over whom individual congregations could ordain. Increase Mather saw in this a blow to the autonomy of every congregation, an autonomy that had been at the heart of the Congregational church since its inception. He blocked Colman's proposal then and for the next ten years, keeping Massachusetts from taking the direction Connecticut took in the Saybrook Platform of 1708. When Solomon Stoddard argued for a Presbyterian form of national church as early as 1700, Mather and his son Cotton were quick to publish their objections. Stoddard was an experimenter, and Increase Mather was not. For all their differences the two men remained strong admirers of each other. In Boston Mather exerted strong and on the whole successful force for the traditional Congregational church described in the Cambridge Platform until the end of his life. In 1717 he did finally relax his opposition to a Baptist congregation that in any event had existed in Boston for decades.

In 1714 Maria Mather died. The next year Increase, now seventy-six, married Ann Lake Cotton. She was the widow of Maria Mather's nephew, her brother Seaborn's son, who had been named John Cotton after his grandfather.

Mather continued to turn out books on a variety of religious subjects. He published forty volumes, mostly sermons and collections of sermons, in the first two decades of the eighteenth century alone. He wrote his last controversial piece in 1721, when he published a short argument in support of his son Cotton's use of inoculation during a smallpox epidemic. Increase died in Boston two years later. An immense funeral procession including virtually every important public figure in Boston made its way to the burial grounds on Copp's Hill, where the Mather grave remains.

Increase Mather's life had its greatest influence on that half century in New England that followed the deaths of the founders, a time when the first generation to be born in America reached maturity. In that social environment Mather was a powerful force for continuity. From his opposition to the Half-Way Covenant in 1662 to his opposition to Benjamin Colman in 1717 Mather was consistent in his defense of the doctrine and church polity spelled out by his father's generation. In this entire period he never wavered from supporting the lay worshippers of those congregations against assumptions of better-educated classes that they knew better. That position often set him at odds with the ruling magistrates. When compromise with the government of England became inevitable, he devoted himself to salvaging what he could of Massachusetts's old freedoms. His enormous outpouring of books stimulated and fed Boston's early publishing industry to a commanding lead in Anglo-America. Beyond his influence on New England's institutions, his spiritual and intellectual leadership gave unmistakable shape to the faith and ideas of his time.

• Most of Increase Mather's papers are held by the American Antiquarian Society, Worcester, Mass., which also holds a large part of Mather's library. Other important manuscript repositories are the Massachusetts Historical Society (which also holds the records of the North Church), the Boston Public Library, and the Harvard College Archives. Of the unpublished manuscript materials the most important are the diaries from 1664 to Mather's death, at the American Antiquarian Society. Many sermon books are also there. Published primary material (in addition to Mather's own books) is extensive. Cotton Mather's biography of his father, *Parentator* (1724), can be supplemented by *The Autobiography of Increase Mather*, ed. Michael G. Hall (1962). Mather's biography of his father, Richard, and Cotton's biography of Increase have been published together, *Two Mather Biographies: "Life and Death" and "Parentator"*, ed. William J. Scheick (1989). A large selection of Mather letters is available in the *Collections of the Massachusetts Historical Society*, 4th ser., vol. 8 (1866). The Mather family Bible record of Increase's children is published in an important secondary work, Chandler Robbins, *History of the Second Church, or Old North, in Boston* (1852).

The number of books Mather wrote during his lifetime is enormous. The indispensable guide to them is Thomas J. Holmes, *Increase Mather: A Bibliography of His Works* (1930). This work describes 175 complete works and many more introductions and prefaces. All these early publications are available in microform in *Early American Imprints, First Series (Evans) 1639–1800*.

The full-length biography by Michael G. Hall, *The Last American Puritan: The Life of Increase Mather* (1988), supersedes Kenneth B. Murdock, *Increase Mather: The Foremost American Puritan* (1925). Robert Middlekauf examines the thought of Richard, Increase, and Cotton Mather in *The Mathers: Three Generations of Puritan Intellectuals, 1596–1728* (1971). Mather's place in American literature is described in Mason I. Lowance, Jr., *Increase Mather* (1974).

MICHAEL G. HALL

MATHER, Kirtley Fletcher (13 Feb. 1888–7 May 1978), scientist and liberal activist, was born in Chicago, Illinois, the son of William Green Mather, a railroad ticket agent, and Julia Sabrina King. Neither parent attended college, but they encouraged Kirtley's interest in science and appreciated his chance, in high school, to take a course in earth science that required frequent field trips. Raised a liberal Baptist, Mather saw no conflict between biblical revelation and the concept of human evolution.

During the summer after completing high school he worked in a barbed-wire factory for $3.75 a week, a sum paltry enough to make him sympathetic to unskilled labor thereafter but aware of his immediate need of further education. He sought it first at the University of Chicago, but because his grandparents considered it "godless," after two years he transferred to Denison, a small college in Granville, Ohio, home of the Ohio Baptist Convention. It had many attractive female students (with one of whom, Marie Porter, he fell deeply in love) and a gifted professor, Frank Carney, whose difficult course "Geographic Influences," in essence a treatment of human ecology, helped determine Mather's professional career. Soon aware of Mather's potential, Carney gave him the chance, hardly ever awarded an undergraduate, of reading a paper based on his own research at the 1908 meeting of the Ohio Academy of Science, and of having it published.

After graduating in 1909, Mather returned to the University of Chicago for graduate study. By the spring of 1911 he was given his first teaching assignment, a course in historical geology. His major professor, Wallace Atwood, not only directed his doctoral dissertation in geology but chose him as his associate for summer fieldwork in Colorado for the U.S. Geological Survey. In 1912 Mather married Marie, with whom he had three children. That same year he became a full-time teacher, first at the University of Arkansas and later, in 1915, at Queen's University in Ontario. During World War I he was named geological assistant to General John Pershing, but his appointment papers were misplaced and he served, instead, as captain in the Army Reserve Corps. In 1918 the *Atlantic Monthly* published his "Parables from Paleontology," a statement of his firm belief that organic evolution and "survival of the fittest" are compatible with the doctrine of Christian brotherhood. If any one public statement embodies Mather's distinctive merging of religious and scientific concepts, this is unquestionably it.

The year 1918 also marked his return to Denison, which he loved so well that he declined every offer to teach elsewhere until, in 1924, he could not resist one from Harvard. He spent the next thirty years in Cambridge, teaching advanced courses, conducting seminars, directing dissertations, chairing the department of geology, gaining local fame as a public speaker, playing an active role in national and international associations, and even, from 1934 to 1941, directing the Harvard summer school. He was also gaining notoriety as a participant in liberal causes, some of them highly controversial. In July 1925, after only one year at Harvard, he volunteered his services to the group defending John Scopes at his trial in Dayton, Tennessee. The presiding judge would not let him read a 23-page statement of how geology supports evolution and the earth's antiquity. But he was able to help, as secretary of the Scopes Scholarship Fund, by collecting about $4,000 to finance the further education Scopes needed for his eventual career as a petroleum geologist.

Ten years later, when the General Court of Massachusetts ruled that nobody could teach in that state without signing an oath of allegiance, Mather was among the few who would not sign. He asserted in 1935 that "the real danger democracy faces is a result of the increase of undemocratic tactics in the guise of democratic ideals." He eventually did sign, however, after Harvard's president, fearful of losing his services, privately urged him to do so; but he added a rider that he also supported the Declaration of Independence. Mather's assertion about the oath would be borne out when, in 1950, Senator Joseph R. McCarthy declared that a tenth of those listed in *American Men of Science* were "openly associated with Communist groups" and named seven of them, including Mather. It was a typical McCarthy ploy, easily dismissed by all who knew that eminent American scientists often conferred with their Soviet counterparts.

Retirement from Harvard at age sixty-five brought no letup in Mather's multiple activities. He continued his contributions, on both scientific and cultural subjects, to periodicals as different as the *Nation*, the *American Scholar, Bulletin of the Atomic Scientists*, and *Educational Horizons*, until they reached a lifetime total of more than 250. Books he reviewed—at incredible speed—totalled roughly 1,200. His own books were of two kinds, laboratory manuals and sourcebooks of particular value to students and teachers, and books for general readers. Three were published early in his career—*Old Mother Earth* (1928), *Science in Search of God* (1928), and *Sons of the Earth* (1930)—and two followed his retirement, *The World in Which We Live* (1961) and *The Earth beneath Us* (1964). The latter, his "bestseller," won two awards and was translated into French, German, Dutch, and Italian; it was reissued by Mather with extensive revisions in 1975, when he was eighty-seven.

Retirement also meant more freedom to travel, with two major overseas trips deserving mention. In 1960, as his wife's diary reports in detail, Mather traveled through France to Geneva and then Scandinavia on YMCA business and was the honored guest at both the Royal Society's Tercentery Celebration in London and the Twenty-first International Geological Congress in Copenhagen. Four years later the couple circled the earth, partly as sightseers but also to attend meetings in Bombay, Delhi, Teheran, Cairo, Singapore, Manila, Tokyo, and Honolulu. In 1971 they settled for good in Albuquerque, New Mexico, where Mather continued his reading, writing, teaching—at the University of New Mexico—and lecturing at the request of any local group. His final public address, in November 1976, was a throwback to the summer of 1925, "The Scopes Trial and Its Aftermath." By then he had been a widower for five years, but in 1977 he was married again, to Muriel Williams, in a joyous wedding among old friends at Harvard. The next year he died in Albuquerque of a massive stroke.

A direct descendant of Increase and Cotton Mather, Kirtley Mather inherited their intellectual powers but not their harsh theology. They could not have anticipated the merging of science and religious spirit that made him a living synergism, and a happy one at that. A highly respected scientist and an inspiring teacher, his breadth of human knowledge suggests a Renaissance man, while his keen sense of perspective made him able to respond with civility even when attacked.

• Mather's scrapbooks and other primary documents are preserved in the archives of Denison University, Granville, Ohio, deposited there by Dr. LeRoy Seils, a member of the Denison faculty, and his wife, one of Mather's daughters. Mather's harmonizing of revelation and evolution is clearly stated in his "Parables from Paleontology," *Atlantic Monthly*, 1918, pp. 35–43. The Scopes trial prompted Mather to write "Evolution on Trial," which he read on WNAC, 11 Dec. 1925, and published in the *Harvard Alumni Bulletin* 28 (1926): 446–50. For a detailed account of the trial, see L. S. deCamp, *The Great Monkey Trial* (1968). A detailed biographical sketch is by Kennard B. Bork of the Department of Geography and Geology at Denison, "Kirtley Fletcher Mather's Life in Science and Society," *Ohio Journal of Science* 82

(1982): 74–95. A Mather son-in-law, Dr. Sherman Wengerd, wrote an obituary on Mather for the *Bulletin of the American Association of Petroleum Geologists* 62 (1978): 2337–40.

WILLIAM PEIRCE RANDEL

MATHER, Richard (1596–22 Apr. 1669), Puritan minister, was born in Lowton, near Liverpool, in Lancashire, England, the son of Thomas Mather, an artisan and small businessman, and Margaret Abrams. Richard Mather received most of his formal education in a grammar school in nearby Winwick, where he learned Latin and Greek. At fifteen he began teaching school in Toxeth Park, some twenty miles from Lowton. He matriculated in Brasenose College in 1618; he was much older than most freshmen at Oxford. Mather left Oxford after less than a year when he was summoned to become a minister in the Church of England in Toxeth Park. He was ordained in March 1619 in a ceremony presided over by the bishop of Chester. The bishop, according to a story told later, asked Mather, who was reputed to be a very holy man, to pray for him. The bishop did not know what lay behind the reputation. Richard Mather indeed was a man of strong faith. He had been converted while living (1611–1618) with the pious family of Edward Aspinwall. The family was also of Nonconformist beliefs, and Richard Mather was anything but an orthodox clergyman. He believed that the organization of the Church of England was flawed because it was not formed around a covenant of believers. He rejected most of its ceremonies as unscriptural, and he defied the authority of the bishop by refusing to wear a surplice. His unorthodox convictions, which eventually would result in his suspension, also made for difficulty in his personal life. In these first years of his ministry of the church in Toxeth Park, he courted Katharine Holt; her father did not regard Mather's religious qualifications with favor and forbade the couple's marriage. He finally relented, and Richard Mather and Katharine Holt married in 1624. Katharine Mather bore six children, all male; five lived into adulthood, and four became ministers. The best known of these four was Increase Mather, the father of Cotton Mather. Katharine Mather died in 1655; shortly afterward Richard married Sarah Cotton, the widow of the Reverend John Cotton.

Richard Mather's Puritan convictions became known to his superiors in the diocese, and after an investigation he was suspended from his church in 1633. A few months later influential friends succeeded in getting him restored to the pulpit, but he refused to conform and the next year was suspended again. This time there was no hope of getting the suspension lifted. When his friends had interceded for him they were asked by the archbishop's visitor how long he had been a minister. They answered, "fifteen years." The next question was how long he had worn the surplice. They answered that he had never worn it. "'*What*' (said the visitor, swearing as he spake it) '*preach fifteen years and never wear a Surpless? It had been better for him that he had gotten Seven Bastards'*" (Increase Mather, p. 11).

Without prospects in England, Mather sailed with his family for Boston, Massachusetts, in spring 1635. He was soon offered the pulpits of several churches and chose Dorchester. There, after the initial failure of candidates for membership to persuade ministers from nearby churches that their faith was sound, the Dorchester Church was gathered. Mather's faith was not questioned, and he preached in the church for the rest of his life. In many ways his service there did not depart from the ordinary round of a minister's calling. He preached, administered the sacraments, catechized children, and watched over his flock.

But Mather was neither an ordinary man nor an ordinary minister. Early on he took the lead in establishing the Congregational system in Massachusetts and defended it against all critics. The Massachusetts Puritans were nonseparating Congregationalists; that is, they considered their churches to be within the Church of England. But the English church was flawed and corrupt, while their own were institutions purged, so far as possible to human beings, of their flaws and evils. Nonseparating Congregational churches were formed by covenants, agreements among members who had given evidence of their conversion experiences. As "a company of the faithful gathered out of the world," as a commonly repeated description put it, a Congregational church administered the sacraments only to those who were deemed qualified and disciplined its members when their sins were uncovered. Each church enjoyed a high measure of autonomy—there were no bishops, no hierarchy over the Congregational churches. Such officials were not known to New Testament churches, the Puritans said, and they were not having any in Massachusetts.

Mather defended this system whenever it was challenged. Several of the most pressing criticisms came from Charles Herle, a Presbyterian who preached before the long Parliament, and Samuel Rutherford, another Presbyterian and a Scot who opposed the independence the nonseparating Congregationalists claimed for their churches in New England. Herle and Rutherford attacked the New England idea of the particular church, especially its autonomy; they argued for an organization in which each church was under a synod. Their model was the Presbyterianism of Scotland. Mather answered both critics in works published in London—*A Reply to Mr. Rutherfurd* (1647), and with the Reverend William Tompson, *A Modest and Brotherly Answer to Mr. Charles Herle* (1644). Fuller expositions of Congregational theory were made in two powerful works, both published in 1643: *An Apologie for Church Covenant* and *Church Government and Church Covenant Discussed in Answer to Two and Thirty Questions*. In all of these efforts, Mather laid out the scriptural basis for Congregational institutions while insisting that the New England churches remained within the great tradition of the Church of England before it began the backsliding of recent years.

The power of Mather's interpretation impressed his colleagues in New England, and in 1646 they assigned him the task of pulling together the leading tenets of Congregational church government and discipline for the synod that met in Cambridge. In 1649 the synod issued the definitive statement regarding these matters for the first generation in New England in *A Platform of Church Discipline Gathered Out of the Word of God*. Mather composed most of this *Cambridge Platform*, as it was called, under the direction of his fellow ministers.

The *Cambridge Platform* remained silent on the question of what was to be done by the churches about children born of marriages in which neither husband nor wife was a member in full communion. The children of members were baptized, and later, if they could give a "relation" of their conversion experience, were admitted as members in full communion. That meant that they could vote in church affairs and could receive the Lord's Supper (as Puritans usually called Holy Communion). Not long after the establishment of New England, Puritans discovered that many of their baptized children were not experiencing conversion, but they were marrying and having children. The question then arose concerning these unbaptized children—should they in turn be baptized even though their parents were not full members? A negative decision, Mather perceived at once, would open the prospect of failed churches. They could not sustain themselves without members, and the effects of such a decision on children and their parents would be devastating. The children, lacking baptism, would fall outside church supervision and discipline. Turning them away would be tantamount to consigning them to eternal damnation.

In 1657 Mather and a majority of his colleagues proposed a solution that, once it was adopted by a synod in 1662, was called the Half-Way Covenant. Under its terms the unbaptized children of halfway members would receive baptism and thereby come under the discipline of churches. Though they would be denied voting rights and the Lord's Supper, they would be regarded with hope. As halfway members, like their parents, their chances of conversion presumably would be greater within the churches than outside them. Richard Mather argued vigorously for this solution. Though most ministers agreed with him, one important one did not—his son Increase. But even Increase, by now a powerful figure in New England Congregationalism, could not resist forever the pleas of his father for the children of the land, and before Richard's death Increase gave his support to the new practices.

Much of Richard Mather's published writing dealt in controversy, and he was skillful in argument. One work that was not controversial was the *Bay Psalm Book*, the short title of *The Whole Book of Psalms Faithfully Translated into English Metre* (1640). Mather and his colleagues John Eliot, the famous missionary to the Indians, and Thomas Welde translated the Psalms in meters suitable for singing in Congregational churches.

Richard Mather did not possess the originality of his greater colleagues John Cotton and Thomas Hooker, ministers of churches in Boston and Hartford, respectively. Nor was his scholarship as profound or his prose as compelling. Yet he clearly had his colleagues' respect and the regard of his generation. His steadiness and his unostentatious style made him ideal for the role he played. He was always a determined man who felt his calling in powerful ways. His was a generous spirit, a spirit that made him especially sensitive to the fears of parents for their children. The solution he championed on behalf of unbaptized children brought into conjunction his concern for the young and his abiding interest in the Congregational churches of New England. He died in Dorchester, Massachusetts.

• Richard Mather's important papers are in the American Antiquarian Society, Worcester, Mass. The standard bibliography of Richard Mather's works is Thomas J. Holmes, *The Minor Mathers: A List of Their Works* (1940). The only full, modern biography is Richard Burg, *Richard Mather of Dorchester* (1976), which is unsatisfactory on many points. Robert Middlekauff, *The Mathers* (1971), provides an account of Mather's intellectual life, his religion, and biography. Increase Mather's *The Life and Death of that Reverend Man of God, Mr. Richard Mather* (1670), is still valuable for many aspects of Mather's life. For ecclesiastical background, Williston Walker, *The Creeds and Platforms of Congregationalism* (1893; repr. 1960), contains indispensable documents. Perry Miller, *Orthodoxy in Massachusetts, 1630–1650* (1933), explains Nonseparating Congregationalism. Edmund S. Morgan, *Visible Saints* (1963), revises Miller in certain points.

ROBERT MIDDLEKAUFF

MATHER, Samuel (30 Oct. 1706–27 June 1785), clergyman, was born in Boston, Massachusetts, the son of Cotton Mather, the renowned Puritan minister, and Elizabeth Clark. He attended the North Grammar School and received a degree from Harvard College in 1723.

If Richard Mather, Mather's great-grandfather, is considered the founder of the "Mather dynasty" in New England after his emigration from England in 1630, Mather represents the end of that dynasty and its political and theological influence in New England. Mather had an undistinguished career characterized by controversy and ill will towards his parishioners. In this respect only, his ministerial life resembled the stressful career of his contemporary, Jonathan Edwards of Northampton, Massachusetts. Mather began preaching at Castle William, the fortress in Boston, where he remained chaplain until 1732. In 1733 he married Hannah Hutchinson, sister of Thomas Hutchinson who later became royal governor of Massachusetts.

In 1732 Mather moved to the Second Church in Boston, where he was unenthusiastically chosen pastor by a marginal vote of 69 out of 112 votes. A decade later, in 1741, the congregation challenged his doctrinal positions and, according to historian Kenneth Murdock, accused him of "improper conduct." The

cause of the charge is unclear. In fact, a lengthy investigation by a committee of the church failed to prove any specific charges; nevertheless, Mather was dismissed shortly before Christmas 1741 with one year's severance pay. The faithful in his congregation moved with him, some ninety-three of his parishioners; they established a new church where he remained for the rest of his career.

The majority's dissatisfaction may have come from Mather's sermonizing. Mather was not successful as a preacher, and by his later years attracted only twenty or thirty to his sermons. A conservative Old Light theologian, Mather was spurned by the rising majority of New Lights, followers of Jonathan Edwards, who demanded the emotional preaching and lay control characteristic of the Great Awakening. Possibly because of poor preaching, Mather failed to produce anything like the record of publications his father and grandfather had realized. The author of twenty short books or pamphlets, he is primarily noted for his formulaic biography of his father, the *Life of the Very Reverend and Learned Cotton Mather* (1729), published shortly after his father's death. This hagiographic treatment follows the characteristic pattern of transforming the realities of the Puritan divine's experience into a saint's life and is hardly an objective account of the subject's experience.

Mather was a scholarly minister and avid book collector; his library was one of the greatest in New England. He was unable, however, to use his position to exert influence in social and political affairs, as had his father and grandfather. While it is unfair to contrast Mather with his illustrious ancestors, he represents a significant shift away from the theocratic power enjoyed by the Mather dynasty during the first two generations toward a more secular extension of the future family influence in affairs of business. Thus while the theological Mathers died out with Samuel Mather, later generations of the family entered a changing America to become almost as successful in the arena of business and commerce.

• For more on Mather and his family see Michael G. Hall, *The Last American Puritan: The Life of Increase Mather, 1639–1723* (1988), Mason I. Lowance, Jr., *Increase Mather* (1974), Robert Middlekauff, *The Mathers: Three Generations of Puritan Intellectuals, 1596–1728* (1978), H. E. Mather, *The Lineage of Rev. Richard Mather* (1890), and J. H. Tuttle, "The Libraries of the Mathers," American Antiquarian Society, *Proceedings* 20 (1910).

MASON I. LOWANCE, JR.

MATHER, Samuel (7 July 1851–19 Oct. 1931), industrialist and philanthropist, was born in Cleveland, Ohio, the son of Samuel Livingston, a financier and founder of mining companies, and Georgiana Pomeroy Woolson. Mather attended public schools in Cleveland and took college-preparatory classes at St. Mark's School in Southboro, Massachusetts. He had planned to enter Harvard University in the fall of 1869 but was badly injured in an explosion that occurred on 14 July 1869 at the Cleveland Iron and Mining Company in

Ishpeming, Michigan, which his father owned and where he was working for the summer. Mather convalesced for two years—much of that time as an invalid—and then embarked on a lengthy trip through Europe. In the fall of 1873 he returned to Cleveland Iron and Mining, where over the following eight years he learned the iron-mining business. In 1881 he married Flora Amelia Stone, with whom he would have four children.

In 1883, after another long trip abroad, he joined James Pickands and Jay C. Morse in founding Pickands, Mather & Company, an iron-mining operation. The firm's first venture was the operation of two mines in Wisconsin's Marquette range that produced for fifteen months at a combined annual output of nearly 27,000 tons of iron ore. In 1884 the firm, along with Joseph Sellwood, leased the Colby mine in the recently discovered Gogebic range, also in Wisconsin; within three years it was producing more than a quarter million tons of ore. The firm ultimately leased eight mines in the Gogebic range, and by the year of Mather's death they were averaging a combined annual output of 2.5 million tons. In 1887 the partners expanded into the Menominee range of Ohio. That year they became sales agents for the Pewabic mine, two years later they acquired an interest in the Hemlock mine, and subsequently they prospected in the area of the Iron River Valley.

The mining business, like other heavy industries at the turn of the century, underwent a period of rapid expansion. Mather's mining empire grew steadily in tandem with the ever-increasing demand for cheap energy sources. In the ensuing years, iron ore deposits were discovered and developed into many successful mines, among them the Chandler mine in the Vermilion range in Minnesota, from which more than eleven million tons of ore were extracted. Shortly after iron ore was discovered in the Mesabi range in 1890, the partners extended their operations into what became the greatest deposit of ore in the Lake Superior region, eventually acquiring ten mines and shipping almost eight million tons annually from its Mesabi operations alone. In 1896, following Pickands's death, Mather became senior partner, a position he held until his own death. By that time, Pickands, Mather & Co. was operating more mines in the Lake Superior region than any other organization, shipping about fourteen million tons of ore annually and employing some thirty-six hundred workers.

Mather's enterprise, partly as a result of its phenomenal growth, underwent a period of transition, and his holdings were vertically integrated with associated business enterprises. In a rapidly growing industry, suppliers of intermediate services, such as lake or rail transportation, are sometimes unable to expand quickly enough to meet the needs of the producer of final goods. Indeed, a principal argument for the superiority of vertical integration over other forms of corporate structuring is the potentially greater ability of the large firm to implement innovation, especially large-scale innovations capable of dynamic transformation. Thus,

in connection with its mining operations, Pickands, Mather & Co. owned a fleet of forty-nine freighters that were used to transport iron ore and Minnesota grain eastward and Pennsylvania coal and other commodities westward. The firm also operated, through its affiliates, docking facilities, a steamship company, pig iron blast furnaces at several Great Lake cities, and coal mines in Pennsylvania and West Virginia. Mather exercised many of the prerogatives of the emerging corporate state, especially in terms of exerting influence, and his control extended well beyond the companies he owned. He was an executive of many mining firms and a director of a multitude of mining and allied firms, all of which supported the activities of his core businesses, as well as numerous banks.

The Mathers not only played a major role in the industrial development of northern Ohio, they also were known for their philanthropic endeavors. Samuel Mather himself reportedly contributed more than $7 million to several community-based organizations in Cleveland. Given the high risks associated with mining operations, one of his primary interests was the support of medical education and hospitals. He became a member of the board of managers of the private Cleveland City Hospital in 1875, was made a trustee in 1884, and in 1889 was elected president, a post he held until his death. In 1914 he, along with several other prominent citizens, purchased land near Western Reserve University for the construction of a medical center. Mather contributed the funds to build and endow the center's first building, the new School of Medicine of Western Reserve University. Later, in 1927, he donated $1 million as seed money to raise the $8 million that was necessary to complete the project. An incorporator of the American National Red Cross, he was a member of its central committee and of the executive committee of the Cleveland chapter. During World War I he raised $4.5 million for the Red Cross and financed the sending of a unit of Lakeside Hospital (the former Cleveland City Hospital) to France. In 1920 he reorganized the Cleveland Red Cross war council into the Cleveland Community Fund, which he served for the rest of his life, donating to it generously. Also in 1920, the people of Serbia recognized him with the Serbian Cross of Mercy, and in 1922 France bestowed a similar honor, awarding him the Cross of the Legion of Honor, both for his contributions during the war.

Since the days of Puritan divine Cotton Mather, one of Samuel Mather's ancestors, American benefactors had believed that charity, if improperly administered, weakened the self-reliance of the recipient. In the late nineteenth century, charity reformers such as Mather tried to make philanthropy more efficient by introducing a system intended to prevent assistance from going to the undeserving. As an alternative to indiscriminate benefaction—the bread line method of giving aid—Mather (and many of his contemporaries) offered the case work method, through which the particular situation of each recipient was investigated. Mather viewed philanthropy as a kind of tax to be paid by the wealthy, and he directed his resources toward treating the ills of the underclass by providing poor people in his community with opportunities to live a better life and by teaching them the virtues of self-reliance, self-respect and self-control. Toward those ends he established the Community Chest, a fund that was supported by a $1.6 million trust established in 1930. He was a trustee of the Goodrich Social Settlement, which had been founded by his wife. In 1897 he donated funds for a 53-acre summer camp associated with the Hiram House, a settlement house that provided services for Jewish immigrants; later, in 1903, he financed the expansion and outfitting of the organization's building in Cleveland. Among the many Cleveland-area charities that Mather and his wife supported were the Children's Aid Society, the Home for Aged Women, the Visiting Nurse Association, and the Floating Bethel and City Mission (later part of the Cleveland Associated Charities). Mather also gave generously to the Case Library Association, the Cleveland Orchestra, the John Huntington Art and Polytechnic Institute, and the Kelley Art Foundation. In part because of his contributions to local charities, the city awarded him its inaugural Cleveland Medal for Public Service in 1924.

In addition, Mather served as a trustee of Western Reserve University for forty-five years and, from 1914 until his death, as vice president of the board of trustees, a position earned in large measure because of his continued contributions to the institution. His wife and children also made significant contributions to the university, providing funds for the first women's dormitory, Hayden Hall, and two other buildings for the College of Women, which was later renamed the Flora Stone Mather College of Western Reserve University.

Mather was a prominent member of the Protestant Episcopal church and a Republican. At his death, in Cleveland, he was the richest man in Ohio. However, the depression made the immediate settlement of his estate impossible, and as market conditions slowly improved, many of his heirs contested provisions in the will. Because many changes had been made to his will in the last year of his life, some bequests (including one to Western Reserve University) were invalidated. Like a latter-day Federalist, Mather exercised a business and philanthropic acumen that was dedicated to the advancement of progressive ideals. He understood that in order to expand the nation's greatness it was necessary to preserve avenues of opportunity. Like others of his generation, Mather concluded that it was the duty of powerful private interests to promote the political, moral, and material empowerment of those less advantaged.

• The Mather family papers are located in the Case Western Reserve University Archives and the Western Reserve Historical Society. Other biographical information can be found in Bruce Bowlus, "Samuel Mather, 1851–1931, " *Hayes Historical Journal* 10, no. 1 (1990): 44–46, 64–68; H. E. Mather, *Lineage of Rev. Richard Mather* (1890); and Ernest H. Rankin, "The Mathers of Marquette and Cleveland, 1857," *Inland Seas* 24, no. 3 (1968): 193–201. A good corporate history is Joan Kloster, "Pickands Mather and Company: The Early Years," *Anchor News* 20, no. 4 (1989). Obituaries are in the *Cleveland News* and the *Cleveland Press*, both 19 Oct. 1931.

CHRISTOPHER D. FELKER

MATHER, Samuel Livingston (1 July 1817–8 Oct. 1890), industrialist, was born in Middletown, Connecticut, the son of Samuel Mather, a businessman, and Catherine Livingston. Mather was a member of the first graduating class of Wesleyan University in 1835. During the years after college he transacted business on behalf of his father and later went into business on his own in New York City. During this time he also made two trips to Europe.

Mather's father was a member of the Connecticut Land Company and the son of one of the company's founders. The company was authorized by the state to purchase and resell land in the Western Reserve, the area in northeastern Ohio that Connecticut had reserved for its citizens in exchange for ceding western land claims to the federal government in 1786. In 1843 Mather went to Cleveland, Ohio, as a land agent, representing his father and several others with interests in the reserve, to oversee the sale of land. Shortly after settling in Cleveland, Mather was admitted to the bar in Ohio, but he never practiced law.

In 1844 surveyors in Marquette County, Michigan, reported finding significant iron deposits in the area. Subsequent explorations of the area led to the discovery of the Jackson Mine in Negaunee as well as other iron deposits. Mather soon became convinced that the area would one day become a major source of industrial raw materials, and he began to invest his efforts and capital into developing the area as well as persuading other local investors to invest in what was still a speculative venture.

Mather helped found the Cleveland Iron Mining Company in 1849. First organized under a special Michigan charter, the company began to buy land and explore for iron ore in the Marquette iron district bordering Lake Superior. It soon opened its first mine, but operations were hampered by the lack of facilities and severe winter weather. In 1853 the company reorganized in Ohio with Mather as one of the incorporators. The second iron company in the area to organize, Cleveland Iron Mining became both the most successful and one of the chief companies on the Michigan upper peninsula. The company built railroads and docks in the area while shipping 3,000 tons of ore during its first four years of operation. When the Sault Ste. Marie canal system opened in 1855, relieving a major transportation obstacle, the company sent the first shipment of ore through the canal that August on the brigantine *Columbia*.

A member of the company's board of directors since its founding and its first secretary and treasurer, Mather was elected president in 1860, serving in that office until his death. He played a major role in helping the company survive the panic of 1857, first by securing needed financing from banks in Boston and New York City and then by helping to devise a temporary "iron money" exchange system used by the company in the mining ranges. In 1869 the company started its own fleet of ore carriers, and as surfacing mining was depleted in the 1880s, the company pioneered the development of an underground mining system. In 1889 Mather contracted for a fleet of steel steamers, the first owned by any of the Great Lakes mining companies. He also initiated negotiations to purchase controlling interest in the Iron-Cliffs Company, a firm on adjoining property that owned more than 50,000 acres of land in the best mining area in Michigan. The companies merged in 1891, becoming Cleveland-Cliffs Iron Company.

Mather was a driving force in the development of the iron industry in northeastern Ohio and in making the city of Cleveland a controlling center in the industry. As president of the company Mather was a leader in organizing, planning, and financing the new and venturesome industry. He combined a conservative, cautious, and careful nature with the ability to calculate risks, balance them against opportunities, and make decisions accordingly. He operated the company on the foundations of sound finances and orderly and realistic planning so that throughout even the early years of constant capital expenditure he remained certain of the company's eventual success.

Mather served as secretary and director of Marquette Iron Company; as president of Cleveland Boiler Plate Company, American Iron Mill Company, and McComber Iron Company; and as a director of Bancroft Iron Company, New York, Pennsylvania & Ohio Railroad Company, and Merchants National Bank and its successor, Mercantile National Bank.

A man of medium height, erect and portly, Mather earned a reputation for honesty, integrity, loyalty, and fair-mindedness. He always displayed unfailing cheerfulness and mirth along with a keen sense of humor. He was a generous contributor to many charities and was active as an officer of Trinity (Episcopal) Cathedral for more than forty years. Held in profound respect by both his friends and the public, he sought neither active involvement in politics nor public celebrity.

Mather was married twice. In 1850 he married Georgiana Pomeroy Woodson, and they had two children. After his first wife died in 1853, Mather married Elizabeth Gwinn in 1856 and had one child with her. Mather died in Cleveland.

• A portion of Mather's correspondence is included in the Samuel Mather Family Papers at the Western Reserve Historical Society in Cleveland. Harlan Hatcher, *A Century of Iron and Men* (1950), discusses Mather's importance in the early development of the Cleveland Iron Mining Company and the iron ore industry on the Great Lakes. For information concerning Mather's company importance see *The Cleveland-Cliffs Iron Company: An Historical Review of this Company's Development and Resources Issued in Commemoration of Its Seventieth Anniversary* (1920), published by the company, as well as newspaper articles on Cleveland-Cliffs housed in the Cleveland Press Collection at Cleveland State University. Biographical profiles of Mather are included in George Weiss,

America's Maritime Progress (1920); Samuel P. Orth, *A History of Cleveland, Ohio* (1910); James Harrison Kennedy, *A History of the City of Cleveland* (1897); and Miriam Cramer, "Biographical Sketches of Early Clevelanders" (manuscript at Western Reserve Historical Society), though all say similar things and begin to sound too much alike. Obituaries are in the *Cleveland Press* and the *Cleveland Plain Dealer*, both 9 Oct. 1890.

WILLIAM BECKER

MATHER, Stephen Tyng (4 July 1867–22 Jan. 1930), organizer and director of the National Park Service, was born in San Francisco, California, the son of Joseph Wakeman Mather, a business merchant with ties to the borax industry, and Bertha Jemima Walker. A descendant of Richard Mather, a prominent Puritan minister in seventeenth-century Massachusetts, Stephen attended Lincoln Grammar School and Boys' High School in San Francisco and graduated from the University of California, Berkeley, in 1887. After college, he moved to the East Coast and worked as a reporter for the *New York Sun* for five years. In 1893 he married Jane Thacker Floy; they had one daughter. After his marriage, with his family and opportunities for advancement in mind, Mather joined his father in the borax business as an advertising and sales promotion manager at the Pacific Coast Borax Company in New York.

Mather proved exceptionally talented at marketing and publicity, especially given that his boss, Francis Marion "Borax" Smith, was notoriously cheap and insisted that Mather generate publicity without an advertising budget. Using skills honed in his days as a reporter, he helped Borax Smith make the brand name Ten Mule Borax synonomous with borax in the United States. But by 1903 he had worked himself into a state of near nervous exhaustion. As he was convalescing in a sanatorium, Smith decided to stop paying his salary. Mather resigned and joined another former Smith employee in a borax refining company the two had begun in 1898, the Thorkildsen-Mather Borax Company of Chicago. In the next five years, Mather and his partner aquired new borax supplies, another refinery, many of Smith's old business accounts, and a modest fortune. In 1923 Mather became the president of the Sterling Borax Company, the successor to Thorkildsen-Mather.

Business, however, was not Mather's only concern, and it was his commitment to good works and his love of the outdoors that defined the latter portion of his life. A Republican and progressive, Mather was active in the settlement movement and several political reform groups in Chicago and a member of the Sierra Club. In 1904 he hiked the Swiss Alps, and the following year he climbed up the icy side of Mount Rainier with the Sierra Club. He credited such experiences not only with making him into a committed mountaineer but also with inspiring ideas to improve national parks in the United States. In contrast to European parks, Mather found that American parks had poorly maintained trails and roads and no protection from private lumber and cattle interests. In 1914, after hiking in the High Sierra, he wrote the secretary of interior, Franklin K. Lane, who was an old college friend, to complain about the management of American parks. Lane, who coincidentally was looking for someone to administer the parks, invited Mather to come to Washington, D.C., and "run them yourself" as assistant to the secretary of the interior. Two years later he became the first director of the National Park Service, an agency created by Congress as a result of his persistent prodding.

Upon taking his position, Mather faced a dual problem. Congress refused to appropriate funds for park improvements until there was public interest, but public interest promised to lag until publicity and improvements made the parks more accessible. The only public access to Yosemite, for example, was an old privately owned toll road that had fallen into serious disrepair, but Congress could not approve federal funds to repair a private road. Mather's response to this dilemma was characteristic of the way he commonly combined private support, public resources, and his own administrative and financial means to aid the cause of the parks. Mather arranged to purchase the road for $15,500, raised one half of the money through subscriptions, contributed the balance himself, then donated the road to the U.S. government.

As director of the national parks, Mather created order where formerly there had been none. Before he took over the nation's fourteen national parks, administration was divided among the Departments of Interior, Agriculture, and War, and there were no uniform standards for defining or protecting the parks. In his first years as director, he set new official standards for defining national parks as areas scenically the finest of their kind and created an organized system for maintaining them. At the same time he lobbied for congressional funding and protection for the parks against industrial use. Using old newspaper connections and skills honed during his days in the borax business, Mather employed the natural splendor of the parks to sell congressmen, editors, and contributors on the need to establish new national parks and protect old ones by organizing and leading regular camping expeditions. His office successfully defeated several local initiatives to use national park resources for private use, most notably plans to flood areas of Yellowstone to create irrigation reservoirs for Idaho and Montana farms. Although Mather arranged to have a few areas of less importance removed from the roster of national parks, he also expanded the park system to include such important additions as the Grand Canyon, Zion, Bryce Canyon, Mount McKinley, Grand Teton, Hawaii, Lassen Volcanic, Shenandoah, and the Great Smoky Mountains.

Often described in terms of his warmth, sincerity, and enthusiasm, Mather's efforts in Congress and among private interests were exceptionally well received. He repeatedly succeeded in increasing the amount of interest and funding the parks received from Congress. At the same time, he negotiated successfully with railroad executives for better tourist accommodations, more advertising, and more train routes leading to national park approaches. Nor did Mather's efforts focus exclusively on national parks. He was also an important founder of the state park movement to protect natural landmarks and recreation areas. In 1921 he organized a National Conference on State Parks, which became a permanent organization.

In 1928 Mather suffered a stroke and was forced to retire. Two years later he died in Brookline, Massachusetts. His extraordinary contributions to the cause of preservation are commemorated today on plaques in most of the national parks. The memorials credit Mather with creating the policies that protect the parks for future generations and proclaim proudly that "there will never come an end to the good that he has done."

• Robert Shankland, *Steve Mather of the National Parks* (1951), based on papers made available by Mather's family, provides an exceptionally thorough account of Mather's early career and all his efforts as the director of the national parks. Also useful are Alfred Runte, *National Parks: The American Experience (1979)*, and a biography of the park's assistant director during Mather's tenure, Donald C. Swain, *Wilderness Defender: Horace M. Albright and Conservation* (1970). Obituaries are in the *New York Times*, 23 and 24 Jan. 1930.

MICHELLE BRATTAIN

MATHER, William Williams (24 May 1804–25 Feb. 1859), geologist, was born in Brooklyn, Connecticut, the son of Eleazar Mather, a proprietor of a temperance hotel, and Fanny Williams. Little is available about his early life and education. Mather developed an interest in chemistry after taking up medical studies in Providence, Rhode Island. He became proficient at chemical analysis of minerals and mineral ores before he entered the West Point Military Academy in 1823. Chemistry and mineralogy were among the subjects studied by cadets at that time. Mather graduated from West Point in 1828 and accepted a commission as a second lieutenant in the U.S. Army. After a brief posting to Fort Jessup, Louisiana, in 1829 he was reassigned to West Point as acting assistant professor of chemistry, mineralogy, and geology.

During Mather's six-year tenure at West Point, he wrote *Elements of Geology for the Use of Schools* (1833), in which he offered a succinct list of thirty "principal facts of geology" and argued that geology is a science of facts from which theories must be cautiously erected. Mather was critical of both sides in reviewing the conflict between Neptunists (followers of the German geologist Abraham Gottlob Werner, who believed in the aqueous origin of primary rocks) and Plutonists (followers of the Scottish geologist James Hutton, who believed in an igneous origin). He pointed out that the former theory was interwoven with hypothetical points not widely demonstrable outside Werner's homeland, and the latter promoted deductions often carried farther than the facts warranted. The book concludes with a chapter on the history of geology and a plea to prospective geologists to carefully accumulate facts before theorizing. A growing interest in geology and especially mineral resources developed during this period in the United States, and the subject was widely included in college curricula. In 1830 Mather married his cousin, Emily Maria Baker; they had six children.

During a recess in his instructional duties at West Point in 1833, Mather taught geology at Wesleyan University in Connecticut. In 1835 he was assigned to topographical duty in the Wisconsin Territory as assistant geologist to explorer George W. Featherstonhaugh. Mather's contribution to the government report issued in 1836 (Senate Document no. 333) was a description and map of the St. Peter's River valley in Minnesota. Late in 1835 Mather was promoted to the rank of first lieutenant and ordered to Fort Gibson, Oklahoma. A year later he resigned from the army in order to devote his career exclusively to geology.

Mather's most important assignment came in 1836 with his attachment to the New York Geological Survey. As the geologist of the first of four districts, he was responsible for surveying Long Island and the Hudson River valley. Survey work continued until 1841, and his final report was published in *Geology of New York*, pt. 1 (1843). Although Mather cited the Taconic System and the divisions of the New York System as promoted by geologist Ebenezer Emmons in *Geology of New York*, pt. 2 (1842) for the second district, he refused to accept Emmons's contention that the Taconic System represented primordial rocks. He asserted, instead, that the Taconic rocks exposed in the first district were actually metamorphosed rocks from the Champlain Division, the basal division of the New York System. Emmons's claim for the antiquity of the Taconic System was later strengthened on the basis of fossils collected in Washington County, within Mather's district. Neither geologist was entirely right or wrong. New York's first district did contain rocks with fossils older than anything previously described at that time, but many of the other rocks ascribed to Emmons's Taconic System were truly younger rocks affected by metamorphism.

Part of Mather's 1843 report is devoted to the erratic boulder and till deposits of Long Island. In 1840 the Harvard naturalist Louis Agassiz had promoted the idea that such deposits were the product of continental glaciation. Mather objected to Agassiz's glacial theory on the grounds that the flat lands of the United States presented an insufficient slope to induce the motion of an ice sheet. Mather adopted the interpretation that erratic boulders were drop stones carried by ice that floated well away from glaciers before melting. Data on the distribution of erratic boulders and other glacial features are so complete in Mather's 1843 report that later geologists were able to use his carefully recorded facts to reconstruct the backbone of Long Island as the terminal moraine of a great continental ice sheet.

While working for the New York Geological Survey in 1837, Mather agreed to take charge of the Ohio Geological Survey, which functioned under his supervision with a staff of six geologists until 1840. He also undertook a geological reconnaissance of Kentucky, which that state authorized in 1838–1839. The coal resources of Ohio and Kentucky figured prominently in Mather's official reports for the states, which were in 1838 and 1839, respectively.

After completion of the Ohio survey in 1840, Mather purchased a tract of land around Pigeon Roost near Jackson, Ohio, where he made his home in 1841. From 1842 to 1845 he served as professor of natural science at nearby Ohio University in Athens, Ohio. He also served as that institution's vice president for a year in 1845 and again in 1847 and as acting president in 1845. In 1846 he was professor of chemistry, mineralogy, and geology at Marietta College in Marietta, Ohio. From 1850 to 1854 Mather served the Ohio State Board of Agriculture as its agricultural chemist and corresponding secretary.

In 1851, after the death of his first wife, Mather married Mary Harris Curtis; they had one child. During the rest of his life, Mather remained active as a geological engineer, mostly conducting mineral surveys for various railroads. He died in Columbus, Ohio.

Mather is remembered as one of the early professional geologists who emerged during the first half of the nineteenth century as products of the government support that many states invested in their geological surveys. He consistently strived not only to increase the bounds of geological knowledge but also to apply that knowledge to economic development. A good example of Mather's efforts, his experiments on the extraction of bromine from the salt works at Athens, Ohio, appear in "On Bromine and Iodine in the Ohio Salines" (*American Journal of Science* 49 [1845], p. 211). The improved efficiency of his methods resulted in the establishment of a new bromine industry, which remained active long after Mather's death.

• Details on Mather's life and career are in an anonymous biography in *Popular Science Monthly* 49 (1896): 550–55, and a biography by Charles H. Hitchcock in *American Geologist* 19 (1897): 1–15, which includes a complete list of Mather's geological publications. A sketch of Mather with emphasis on his contribution as an early American writer on the history of geology is given by George W. White in *Isis* 64 (1973): 197–214. The impact of Mather's survey work in New York, Ohio, and Kentucky is summarized in George P. Merrill, *The First One Hundred Years of American Geology* (1924).

MARKES E. JOHNSON

MATHEWS, Cornelius (28 Oct. 1817?–25 Mar. 1889), author and editor, was born in Port Chester, New York, the son of Abijah Mathews, a cabinetmaker, and Catherine Van Cott. Little is known about Mathews's childhood. No diaries, letters, or articles exist before the mid-1830s. However, according to Trows New York Directory, his family moved from Westchester County to Manhattan, and Mathews resided for the rest of his life in various locations in lower Manhattan. He attended Columbia University from 1830 to 1832. In 1833 he transferred to the College of the City of New York, now known as New York University. The Reverend James Mathews, a relative of the family, was the chancellor of the newly established college. Cornelius Mathews received his A.B. degree in the first graduating class of 1834, and, at the commencement ceremony held at the Middle Dutch Church of New York, he gave a speech titled "Females of the American Revolution." Mathews was admitted to the bar in 1837 and practiced law for a short time. He became the first president of the university's alumni association in 1846. For a Eucleian Society meeting he presented his speech "Americanism—What Is It?" (1845), later published in the *Morning Express* (31 Mar. 1855), and at an alumni dinner he spoke about authors and authorship.

Writing and not the law was Mathews's true vocation, and the topics of Americanism and authorship most interested him and shaped his career. In the late 1830s, he was a member of the Tetractys Club, a group composed of Evert A. Duyckinck, Duyckinck's brother George, and Alfred A. Jones. During the tempestuous 1840s and 1850s, these New Yorkers spawned the literary and political movement called "Young America." Each through his writings advocated that a national literature be nurtured and developed in America.

Mathews was a prominent and vocal proponent of international copyright who wrote about it and spoke of it as often as he could. He drew attention to the business practices of American publishers who would reprint pirated editions of popular European writings without duly compensating the authors and were reluctant to publish American authors, whom they would have to pay for their work. As an editor of *Arcturus: Journal of Books and Opinions*, as a contributing writer for the *Literary World*, and in other periodicals of the day, Mathews argued for mutual recognition of copyright by the countries of the world. In February 1842, during a dinner to honor Charles Dickens, Mathews delivered an impromptu speech on the subject.

Mathews's somewhat abrasive nature and staunch support of his cause earned him the nickname "the Centurion." It also generated many unflattering caricatures of him in the works of James Russell Lowell, Thomas Frederick Briggs, Oliver Wendell Holmes, and Henry Wadsworth Longfellow. Perry Miller in *The Raven and the Whale* (1956) described Mathews as "a man who excited among his contemporaries a frenzy of loathing beyond the limits of rationality" (p. 80). On the other hand, Miller also says that Mathews was "almost the only man of letters outside of New England who gave serious thought to the problem of the new direction in which an American artist might develop, who sought vistas untenanted by Irving, Bryant and Cooper" (pp. 79–80). To this end Mathews began writing essays, short stories, poems, novels, and plays, each of which has a uniquely American flavor. In his lecture "The Better Interests of the Country in Connection with International Copyright," delivered in 1843, Mathews stated that America's books should be as "rugged as the mountains and cataracts among which they were produced."

Mathews tried to capture this spirit. In his epic fantasy *Behemoth: A Legend of the Moundbuilders* (1839), he depicts a race that predates the Native Americans and draws his descriptions from ethnological resources available during his time. He followed this with *Wakondah: The Master of Life. A Poem* (1841), in which a Native American spirit appraises the state of the country after the demise of his people. Mathews also wanted to highlight the injustices and vagaries of the political system of the nineteenth century and so wrote his political satire, *The Career of Puffer Hopkins* (1842), and his collection of poetry, *Poems on Man, in His Various Aspects under the American Republic* (1843). Other novels center on New York. *Big Abel and Little Manhattan* (1845) tells of the fanciful redistribution of the island of Manhattan between the descendants of Chief Manahatta and Henry Hudson. *Moneypenny; or, The Heart of the World* (1849–1850) and *Chanticleer: A Thanksgiving Story of the Peabody Family* (1850) center on family and relationships among residents of the state of New York. After the mid-1850s, Mathews published little of his own work. Instead he became involved in editing the Native American myths transcribed by Henry Rowe Schoolcraft, a prominent ethnologist and head of the U.S. Bureau of Indian Affairs. This work first appeared as *The Indian Fairy Book from the Original Legends of Henry Schoolcraft* (1856) and was reprinted through the 1870s with a substantial addition of two tales in 1877. At that time, its title changed to *The Enchanted Moccasins and Other Legends of the American Indians Compiled from Original Sources.*

Mathews also wrote plays set in America. *The Politicians* (1840) is a satire on New York politics; it was never produced. *Jacob Leisler, the Patriot Hero; or, New York in 1690* (1848) depicts colonial New York. It ran for twenty-seven performances in 1848 at New York's Bowery Theatre. *Witchcraft* illustrates a mother and son's relationship during the Salem witch trials. One of Mathews's most favorably received plays, it was produced in 1846 at the Walnut Street Theatre in Philadelphia and in 1847 at the Bowery Theatre in New York. *Calmstorm, the Reformer* (1853) relates the story of a man who returns to the wilderness after his disappointment with society. It was never produced.

Concurrently with his literary and dramatic works, Mathews acted as editor and publisher for various weekly and monthly journals. In 1841 he and Evert A. Duyckinck cofounded *Arcturus*, in which Mathews first serialized his novel *The Career of Puffer Hopkins*. This first journal folded after a year and a half. He went on to contribute articles, reviews, and poems to the *Literary World*. In 1847 Mathews edited *Yankee Doodle*, a humorous journal modeled on *Punch*, and pursued his theatrical interests with two journals, the *Prompter* and the *Prompter's Whistle*. In his later years he was the editor of the *New Yorker Magazine* (1858–1876).

We know very little of Mathews's personal life except that he was a bachelor and a faithful correspondent who kept in contact throughout his life with such figures as William Gilmore Simms, Elizabeth Barrett Browning, and Evert A. and George L. Duyckinck. From an account of his niece, Frances Aymar Mathews, daughter of his younger brother Daniel A. Mathews, we know he spent time with her and that he regaled her with stories of literary luminaries he had known. One story tells of Mathews being present in 1844 or 1845 the night Edgar Allan Poe wrote the first verses of "The Raven." He also chronicled for the *Literary World* (1850) the first meeting of Nathaniel Hawthorne and Herman Melville during an informal picnic in the Berkshires.

Mathews died in New York City. In his final years, he would still come to the offices of the *New York Dramatic Mirror*, where he had last been an editor, to stay in contact with the events of the theater that he had always enjoyed. His novels, poems, and plays give a unique depiction of urban life in the nineteenth century. Soon after his death the international copyright law was passed in 1891.

• Mathews's papers are in the Duyckinck Family Papers in the New York Public Library's Manuscript and Rare Book Collection, the Gratz Collection in the Historical Society of Pennsylvania, and the Houghton Library at Harvard University. A contemporary biographical sketch appears in *The Cyclopaedia of American Literature*, ed. Evert A. Duyckinck (1877). Perry Miller, *The Raven and the Whale* (1956), places Mathews in the context of the New York literary scene in the mid-1800s. Allen F. Stein, *Cornelius Mathews* (1974), and Donald J. Yannella, Jr., "Cornelius Mathews: Knickerbocker Satirist" (Ph.D. diss., Fordham Univ., 1971), focus on his career and literary works. Obituaries are in the *New York Dramatic Mirror*, 6 Apr. 1889, and in the *New York Times*, 27 Mar. 1889.

LISA M. CESARANI

MATHEWS, George (30 Aug. 1739–30 Aug. 1812), soldier, frontiersman, and governor of Georgia, was born in Augusta County, Virginia, the son of John Mathews, an Irish immigrant. His mother's name is not available. Little is known of his early life, but in 1757 he commanded a company of volunteers fighting against the Indians on the Virginia frontier. In 1762 he married Anne Paul, with whom he is thought to have had eight children. That same year he established himself as a merchant in Staunton, Virginia, and during the next decade he served as a vestryman, justice of the peace, tax collector, and sheriff in Augusta County. In 1776 he was elected to the House of Burgesses. Later that year he joined the army under George Washington and in 1777 was promoted to colonel. Wounded and captured at Germantown, he was held prisoner until 1781, when, in an exchange, he rejoined the army under General Nathanael Greene. He served out the war with Greene in the southern campaign.

In 1784 Mathews purchased land on the Broad River in Georgia, where he settled with a number of Virginians. He was appointed brigadier general in the militia and in January of 1787 chosen governor by the general assembly. He served a year in that post and in March of 1789 became a member of the first federal

Congress under the new U.S. Constitution, an office he held until 1791. A Jeffersonian Republican in his politics, he was once again chosen governor in 1793. During his second administration the Yazoo Act was passed, under which bribed legislators released between 35 and 50 million acres of land to private companies for some $500,000. Although Mathews was not implicated in the corruption as so many in government were, he did sign the bill, and his reputation suffered. In this term as governor Mathews was faced with the threat of a major Indian war on the frontier, a threat made greater when Elijah Clarke took an army of irregular volunteers into Indian territory and set up the "Trans-Oconee Republic." Mathews responded by sending troops under General Jared Irwin against the irregulars. By the fall of 1794 Clarke had fled the area, and the settlements he established had been destroyed.

Mathews's first wife had died, and in 1790 he married Margaret Reed, a widow from Staunton. In 1793 she returned to Virginia against his wishes, and when she asked him to come get her, he refused. They remained separated until 1797, when the legislature granted them a divorce. Later he married a third time, probably to Harriet Flowers, a Mississippi widow.

In 1798 Mathews was nominated by President John Adams as first governor of the Mississippi Territory, but the appointment was withdrawn amid rumors of unsavory land speculation. Outraged, Mathews traveled to Philadelphia to confront the president, but his temper cooled when his son was given a federal appointment. During the next decade he withdrew from public life, became wealthy as a land speculator, and reportedly lived in a simple log cabin he had built earlier in Wilkes County.

In 1810, apparently at the suggestion of Georgia senator William H. Crawford, Mathews was approached to open discussions with Spanish officials in West Florida about the possibility of that province being delivered to the United States. His subsequent negotiations came to naught, but from what he saw of the region, Mathews became convinced that all of Florida should be under U.S. jurisdiction. Others thought so as well, and in 1811 President James Madison secretly authorized Mathews to move into Florida and stir up secession sentiment among Americans living there. Mathews went and began working with English-speaking Spanish subjects in the province. He planned to combine converts from that group with volunteers from Georgia and other recruits and with that army wrest Florida from Spain. Initially his plan seemed to be working. On 17 March 1812 this irregular force, with help from Georgia and from American gunboats stationed on the St. Marys, took Fernandina in the name of the United States. They then began expanding their holdings and moving south until, in early June, they were at the gates of St. Augustine. At that point Mathews learned that, having no desire to alienate Spain with war against Britain on the horizon, the administration had disavowed his scheme.

This disavowal was a bitter blow to Mathews. Even a private letter from Secretary of State Monroe praising his zeal (while wishing his methods were more "restrained") was not enough to salve his wounded pride. He waited a week for his anger to abate, but when it did not, he decided to go to Washington and confront the president. He was on his way when he fell ill at Augusta and died. At the beginning of his trip, he had sworn that in Washington he'd "be dam'd if he didn't blow them all up"—he might not have succeeded, but everyone believed he would have tried.

• Most of Mathews's papers are in the Library of Congress, Washington, D.C., and the Georgia Department of Archives and History, Atlanta. Other papers relating to his activities are in the *Papeles procedentes de la Isla de Cuba*, Archivo General, Seville, and in the Pickering papers at the Massachusetts Historical Society. Some information is found in biographical directories such as James F. Cook, *Governors of Georgia* (1979). See also Joseph Burkholder Smith, *The Plot to Steal Florida: James Madison's Phony War* (1983); G. Melvin Herndon, "George Mathews, Frontier Patriot," *Virginia Magazine of History and Biography* 77 (July 1977): 307–28; and Paul Kruse, "A Secret Agent in East Florida: General George Mathews and the Patriot War, 1811–1812," *Journal of Southern History* 18 (May 1952): 285–302.

HARVEY H. JACKSON

MATHEWS, John (1744–26 Oct. 1802), politician and governor of South Carolina, was born in Charlestown (now Charleston), South Carolina, the son of John Mathews, a planter, and Sarah Gibbes. Mathews began his public career in 1760, when he was commissioned an ensign (and later a lieutenant) to fight in the Cherokee War. In 1764 he studied law at Middle Temple in London and, upon completing his degree, returned to South Carolina to begin his practice. He was admitted to the South Carolina bar on 22 September 1766. In the same year he married Mary Wragg, daughter of William Wragg, and soon moved to his 600-acre "Uxbridge" plantation on the Ashley River. There they had their only child, a son.

Shortly afterward, Mathews began his extensive political career. From 1767 to 1768 he represented St. Helena Parish in the Twenty-seventh Royal Assembly and in 1772 represented St. John Colleton Parish in the Thirtieth Royal Assembly. In 1775 and 1776 he was elected to represent St. George Dorchester Parish in the First and Second Provincial Congresses and later served four terms in the South Carolina State General Assembly from 1776 to 1782, primarily representing Dorchester. During the latter part of his second term (6 Dec. 1776 to 12 Sept. 1777), he further led the general assembly as Speaker.

In 1778 the general assembly of South Carolina appointed Mathews a delegate to the Continental Congress, where he frequently voted with the nationalists. He favored the impost amendment of 1781, adhered to a strict interpretation of the Articles of Confederation, and proposed that George Washington be given dictatorial powers as commander in chief. In addition, he became a liaison between Congress and the southern department. He was instrumental in appointing Nathanael Greene general of the southern army and

thwarted secret plans to sacrifice Georgia and the Carolinas to the British in exchange for the independence of the northern colonies. He resigned his Continental post in January 1782, when the famous Jacksonborough assembly elected him governor.

As the state's second governor, Mathews carried out three notable acts. He oversaw British withdrawal from Charleston, granted a stay for British merchants, and established an initial peace with the Cherokee. The Jacksonborough assembly was controlled by representatives from back-country and low-country parishes. Its members were bitter about the participation of British Loyalists in the revolutionary war, and in February 1782 they attempted to pay off state debts by confiscating the estates of Loyalists. When the British prepared to evacuate Charleston six months later, Mathews agreed not to extend the confiscation acts in exchange for the return of American slaves under the control of British general Alexander Leslie. Mathews was criticized for this action by members of his privy council, because he did not attempt to recover other types of property stolen by the British. Leslie agreed to the measure, however, and on 10 October 1782 signed with Mathews a "Treaty Respecting the Slaves within British Lines, British debts, [and] Property Secured by Family Settlements." In addition, British merchants living in Charleston requested permission from Governor Mathews to remain in the city for eighteen months after the British evacuated in order to sell their wares and collect debts. Instead Mathews granted the merchants a six-month stay, during which time they undercut established prices, maintained a virtual monopoly, and amassed large profits. In a close political battle, the legislature decided to extend Mathews's agreement with the merchants until 1 June 1784, much to the chagrin of Carolina merchants attempting to compete but to the advantage of planters benefiting from the lower prices offered by the British. In a final act during his one-year term as governor, Mathews met with the chiefs of the Cherokee nation, gave them necessities and a small quantity of goods on the state's account, and recommended that the general assembly appoint commissioners to negotiate peace and establish trade with the Cherokee. Unilateral treaties with the Indians violated the Articles of Confederation, but Mathews rationalized his inconsistency by lobbying Congress for a federal treaty. On 4 March 1784 Congress negotiated such a treaty with the Indians.

When Mathews's governorship ended in 1782, the South Carolina legislature appointed him chancellor of the court of equity. He returned to the state general assembly, representing the election district of St. Philip and St. Michael in the sixth, seventh, and eighth general assemblies from 1785 to 1790. In the state's ratifying convention of 1788, he voted in favor of the federal Constitution and maintained his disposition toward a strong central government.

Mathews served as judge of the court of equity from 1791 until he retired from public life in November 1797. His private interests included horse breeding and acting as a trustee for the College of Charleston.

After the death of his first wife, Mathews married Sarah Rutledge in 1799. They had no children. Mathews was a capable politician who worked to protect South Carolina during the revolutionary war and to restore it after the war. He died in Charleston.

• Mathews's personal manuscripts are found in Paul Smith, ed., *Letters of Delegates to Congress* (1976–); R. W. Gibbes, *Documentary History of the American Revolution*, vols. 2 and 3 (1855–1857); and *South Carolina Historical and Genealogical Magazine* 17 (Jan. 1916): 11–12, and 27 (Apr. 1926): 69–72. For the historical context of Mathews's life see David Ramsay, *History of South Carolina* (1809); Edward McGrady, *The History of South Carolina under the Royal Government* (1899) and *The History of South Carolina in the Revolution* (1902); Charles G. Singer, *South Carolina in the Confederation* (1941); H. James Henderson, *Party Politics in the Continental Congress* (1974); Jerome Nadelhaft, "Ending South Carolina's War," *South Carolina Historical and Genealogical Magazine* 80 (Jan. 1979): 50–64; and Christopher Lee, "The Transformation of the Executive in Post-Revolutionary South Carolina," *South Carolina Historical and Genealogical Magazine* 93 (Apr. 1992): 89–93. John B. O'Neall, *Biographical Sketches of the Bench and Bar of South Carolina* (1859), provides a specimen of Mathews's legal writing.

KEITH DOUGHERTY

MATHEWS, John Joseph (16 Nov. 1894–11 June 1979), Native-American writer and Osage council member, was born in Pawhuska, Osage Nation in Indian Territory (later Oklahoma), the son of William Shirley Mathews, an Indian trader, and Pauline Eugenia Girard, a mixed-blood Osage. Mathews grew up on the reservation, learning to speak the tribal language, although somewhat haltingly, and was included on the 1906 tribal allotment roll. He enrolled at the University of Oklahoma in 1914, but his studies were interrupted for nearly three years after he volunteered for service in the army during World War I. He served part of his enlistment in Europe as a flight instructor in the aviation section of the Signal Corps. After the war he returned to the university and graduated in 1920 with a degree in geology.

Between 1920 and 1923 Mathews studied natural science at Oxford University. He declined the Rhodes scholarship awarded him, preferring to pay for his own education with money he received as an original allottee of the Osage mineral estate that produced vast quantities of oil and natural gas during the 1920s. After receiving a B.A. from Oxford, he enrolled briefly at the School of International Relations in Geneva, Switzerland, and wrote articles on the League of Nations for the *Philadelphia Ledger*. After traveling in Europe and North Africa, Mathews returned to the United States, settling in California, where he worked in real estate until 1929, when he returned to Oklahoma.

Mathews erected a cabin on his land allotment in a forested area a few miles from Pawhuska, Oklahoma, and lived there alone until he married a non-Indian, Elizabeth Palmour Hunt, in 1945; they had no children, but she had a son from a previous marriage. He frequently entertained guests and took numerous hunting trips in the Rocky Mountain states. In 1932

the first of his five books was published by the University of Oklahoma Press, *Wah' Kon-Tah: The Osage and the White Man's Road*. It was selected by the Book-of-the-Month Club and sold well enough to inspire Mathews to write a novel, *Sundown* (1934), one of the first works of fiction by a Native American. The story of its mixed-blood protagonist, who struggles with identity problems and the sudden oil wealth of the Osages, closely parallels Mathews's own youth.

In 1934 Mathews was elected to the first of two successive four-year terms on the eight-man tribal council. He was often cast in the role of tribal spokesperson because of his education and sophisticated knowledge of the world. Mathews was instrumental in maintaining a degree of council control over the Osage mineral leases and in securing governmental assistance for the tribe during the depression years.

Mathews devoted his adult years to two pursuits: a solitary literary career and public service on behalf of the Osages. *Talking to the Moon* (1945), Mathews's third book, chronicled the years in his forest cabin and has been compared to Henry David Thoreau's *Walden*. His last work, *The Osage: Children of the Middle Waters* (1961), was a comprehensive history of his people. He died in Pawhuska.

• Although there is no significant collection of Mathews's papers, he figures prominently in the records of the Osage Agency located at the Federal Records Center in Fort Worth, Tex. The University of Oklahoma Library's Western History Collections have a file of correspondence between Mathews and Savoie Lottinville, his editor, as part of its University of Oklahoma Press Collection. While there is no book-length biography of Mathews, he has been the subject of articles by a variety of scholars, including Terry P. Wilson, "Osage Oxonian: The Heritage of John Joseph Mathews," *Chronicles of Oklahoma* 59 (Fall 1981): 264–93; Guy Logsdon, "John Joseph Mathews—A Conversation," *Nimrod* 16 (Apr. 1972): 70–79; and Garrick Bailey, "John Joseph Mathews," in *American Indian Intellectuals: 1976 Proceedings of the American Ethnological Society*, ed. Margot Liberty (1978). An obituary is in the Oklahoma City *Daily Oklahoman*, 11 June 1979.

TERRY P. WILSON

MATHEWS, Joseph McDowell (26 May 1847–2 Dec. 1928), surgeon and medical editor, was born in New Castle, Henry County, Kentucky, the son of Caleb M. Mathews, a lawyer and jurist, and Frances S. Edwards. Educated at the New Castle Academy, Mathews began his medical preceptorship in his home town under his brother-in-law, William B. Oldham. Beginning in 1865 he attended two sessions of medical lectures at the Kentucky School of Medicine in Louisville, Kentucky, obtaining his M.D. in 1867 from the University of Louisville Medical Department, during a brief consolidation of the schools. Following graduation he returned home and began the general practice of medicine with his former preceptor. He remained there for five years, but desiring to practice in a larger community, he moved to Louisville. He married Sallie E. Berry of Midway, Woodford County, Kentucky, in 1877; they had no children.

Having become interested in colon and rectal diseases, in 1877 Mathews made a brief tour of surgical clinics at medical centers in New York City. It confirmed his impression that there was a profound lack of interest among the medical profession in these diseases. He corresponded briefly with William Allingham, proctologic surgeon at St. Mark's Hospital, London, England, and spent several months there in 1877 and 1878 in observation and study.

Soon after his return from London in 1878, Mathews received his first academic appointment, at the Hospital College of Medicine in Louisville as lecturer on diseases of the rectum. The following year he resigned this appointment to accept another at the Kentucky School of Medicine, as professor of surgical pathology and diseases of the rectum. In 1880 he was named professor of surgery at the same institution, remaining for seventeen years. Under his direction, the first separate department of proctology in an American medical college was established there in 1883; both medical students and practitioners received instruction in it.

Mathews began a career as an editor of medical journals when he joined with Dudley S. Reynolds in 1879 to establish the short-lived *Medical Herald* in Louisville (2 vols., 1879, 1880). Later Mathews founded the first medical journal devoted to proctology, *Mathews' Medical Quarterly* (1894–1896); it was soon enlarged in scope under the title *Mathews' Quarterly Journal of Rectal and Gastro-Intestinal Diseases* (Jan. 1897–Apr. 1898). In 1898 it became the *Louisville Journal of Surgery and Medicine*, the official organ of the Louisville Surgical Society. Another merger and title change occurred, and Mathews continued as editor of the *Louisville Monthly Journal of Medicine and Surgery* until volume 13 was completed in 1906.

Mathews wrote a textbook on proctology, *Diseases of the Rectum, Anus, and Sigmoid Flexure* (1892), with two revised editions (1896, 1903). At the request of his students he also wrote a small book, *How to Succeed in the Practice of Medicine* (1902).

Well-known in both the lay and professional communities, Mathews rose to leadership positions at local, state, and national levels, serving as president of the Kentucky Medical Association (1898), of the American Medical Association (1899), of the Mississippi Valley Medical Association, and of the American Medical Editors Association. In June 1899 a dozen pioneers in proctology founded the American Proctologic Society, electing him its first president; he served again in 1913. He was an active member and president of the Louisville Surgical Society and the Louisville Clinical Society. He also served for a decade as president of the Kentucky State Board of Health (1896–1906). In addition, writing was a skill Mathews used to great advantage throughout his lifetime. He was also an able speaker, known as something of an orator.

Mathews and his wife made an around-the-world tour in 1912, and upon their return he retired from practice. They moved to Los Angeles, California, and, except for four years in Seattle, Washington, they remained there for the rest of their lives. Mathews died in Los Angeles.

Mathews helped to establish the specialty of proctology in the United States, focusing the attention of his colleagues on a neglected area of medical practice. His contributions to medical journalism during the late nineteenth century and early twentieth century were important, particularly for his inauguration of a specialty journal for proctology. Although it could not survive, serving so few interested practitioners, it continued as the *Louisville Journal of Surgery and Medicine*, with proctology still receiving special attention.

During an era of major medical advances in the diagnosis, treatment, and prevention of disease, Mathews was instrumental in the dissemination and effective use of new knowledge. His talent for organizing others toward effective group action were repeatedly manifested during his service to the Kentucky State Board of Health and to numerous medical societies.

• An associate, Granville S. Hanes, published a biographical sketch of Mathews in *Transactions of the American Proctologic Society for 1929* (1930): 1–3. Another brief sketch, unsigned, appeared in *History of Ohio Falls Cities and Their Counties*, vol. 1 (1882), pp. 458–59. Ten of Mathews's publications are listed in the *Index-Catalogue of the Library of the Surgeon General's Office, U.S. Army*, vol. 8 (1887), p. 711, and 2d ser., 10 (1905), p. 262. Obituaries are in the *Journal of the American Medical Association* 91 (15 Dec. 1928), and *Kentucky Medical Journal* 27 (Feb. 1929).

EUGENE H. CONNER

MATHEWS, Shailer (26 May 1863–23 Oct. 1941), theologian and educator, was born in Portland, Maine, the son of Jonathan Bennett Mathews, a merchant, and Sophia Lucinda Shailer. Though his grandfather was a prominent Baptist minister in Portland, young Mathews manifested only lukewarm interest in pursuing a similar career. Still, after graduating from Colby College in 1884, he attended Newton Theological Institution for three years. He graduated in 1887 and was licensed to preach, but he neither sought ordination nor engaged in pastoral activities. Preferring the vocation of teaching, he accepted positions at Colby, first as professor of rhetoric and then of history and political economy. Between 1890 and 1891, in the middle of his seven-year stint at Colby, Mathews pursued graduate studies in history at the University of Berlin. During that time he also married Mary Philbrick Elden; they had three children.

In 1894 Mathews accepted an invitation from the Divinity School at the University of Chicago, despite misgivings that his training did not qualify him for such a post. Between 1894 and 1908 he nevertheless excelled in the classroom, first as a professor of New Testament history and interpretation and then in historical and comparative theology. In 1908 he became dean of the seminary and served in that capacity until his retirement in 1933. At various times during his years at the University of Chicago, he also served as editor of the *World Today* (1903–1911) and *Biblical World* (1913–1920), two journals produced on the campus to further the causes of biblical criticism and liberal theological thought.

As professor and dean, Mathews played a central role in creating and nurturing the "Chicago School" of modernist theology, as did Shirley Jackson Case and William Rainey Harper. All three scholars regarded Christian ideas as a series of responses to various cultural contexts, formulations derived from practical experience rather than from some orthodoxy based on outmoded climates of opinion. Thus seen as historically conditioned, all doctrines were to be understood as products of different time periods, each with its own needs, angle of vision, and answers. Ideas were useful only insofar as they addressed contemporary issues; as time went on, the accumulated layers of truth formed what Mathews termed "generic Christianity." The challenge to modern Christians, as he saw it, was to forge new truths that spoke meaningfully to contemporary humanity. Rather than parrot phrases that relied on revelation or outdated metaphysics for authority, he sought to incorporate the norms of modern science into Christian theology and to rephrase Christian attitudes within an intellectual context dominated by naturalism and an awareness of the limits of physical data. Doctrine understood historically could thus be applied to contemporary human problems, especially within rubrics determined by scientific and socioeconomic considerations.

Despite holding radical theological convictions that virtually abandoned much of traditional Christianity, Mathews continued to appreciate the practical value of local churches. He saw them not as guardians of timeless dogma but as social agencies that could help people adjust their priorities in an industrial society. In this regard Mathews was an early proponent of the Social Gospel. Influenced by studying Richard T. Ely's economics and Washington Gladden's sermons, Mathews advocated applying Christian principles to social problems. He was the author of more than twenty books, and his notable 1879 volume on the social teachings of Jesus urged churches to embrace social reform as part of their responsibility. It was hailed by Social Gospel leader Walter Rauschenbusch as an outstanding effort in the movement.

In a more tangible expression of his concern that churches should take effective action instead of mouthing musty credos, Mathews served as president of the country's largest interdenominational agency interested in social reform, the Federal Council of Churches, from 1912 to 1916. After World War I and the emergence of neo-orthodoxy as a new theological trend, he remained a staunch liberal in thought and action. He persevered in urging vigorous organization and efforts to help cure social and economic problems. Evangelicals and other conservatives attacked his views as being more concerned with saving society than with saving souls. But with his perception of each generation's need to seek its own truth, Mathews accepted such criticisms and returned the compliment by pillorying the static beliefs of conservatives as useless in modern times. After a vigorous retirement filled with a great deal of writing, Mathews died in Chicago, where he was cremated and buried in a Unitarian cemetery.

• A large collection of Mathews's papers, consisting of correspondence, administrative records, lecture notes, and materials related to publications, is housed in the University of Chicago archives. Of his many works, the most important are *Gospel and the Modern Man* (1910), *The Faith of Modernism* (1924), *The Atonement and the Social Process* (1930), *The Growth of the Idea of God* (1931), *Immortality and the Cosmic Process* (1933), and *New Faith for Old: An Autobiography* (1936). Studies of modernism at Chicago that feature information about Mathews are Joseph H. Jackson, *Many but One* (1964), and Charles H. Arnold, *Near the Edge of Battle* (1966). An obituary is in the *New York Times*, 24 Oct. 1941.

HENRY WARNER BOWDEN

MATHEWS, W. S. B. (8 May 1837–1 Apr. 1912), music educator, was born William Smythe Babcock Mathews in London, New Hampshire, the son of Samuel S. Mathews, a Methodist minister, and Elizabeth Stanton Babcock. (His second given name was originally spelled "Smith.") Encouraged by his mother to study music, Mathews was largely self-educated, a fact that might account for his failure to obtain a permanent teaching position in a college or university. He was broadly educated, however, reading widely in philosophy as well as in music, and his own success in self-education may account for his efforts to establish procedures by which others could become self-educated. In 1857 he married Flora Swaim, with whom he had seven children. In 1910, as an elderly widower, he married his business associate Blanche Dingley.

Mathews's reputation stems from a broad definition of the term music education. He was not among those turn-of-the-century emerging public school music educators; rather, his role as educator was to inform through his writings music supervisors, elementary grade teachers, rural piano teachers, and lay individuals about performance standards and about music and musicians. By 1859 he had become a regular correspondent for Dwight's *Journal of Music*. Ten years later he became the editor of Lyon and Healy's *Musical Independent*, a position he held for two years. He also edited the *Journal of School Music* for a year (1908–1909) and *Music* for a decade (1892–1902). He was an associate editor and frequent author (137 articles) for *Etude* beginning in 1884 and continuing until one year before his death, a period of enormous growth and influence in music for the journal. He also had editorial responsibilities for the *Song Messenger of the Northwest*, the *New York Musical Gazette*, and the *Christian Advocate*. In addition to writing extensively for the journals he edited, he contributed to at least eight other journals, producing at least five hundred articles, about half of which were on piano teaching and learning. His emphasis was on piano pedaling practices, memorization, and ear training. He wrote musical criticism for three newspapers in Chicago and wrote, coauthored, or contributed to more than thirty books and teaching methods.

Mathews followed in his father's evangelical footsteps as he attempted to convert musicians and nonmusicians alike to a stronger belief in the importance and value of music. For him, promoting music as art was an all-encompassing occupation for which he felt a passionate calling. He stated in *Music: Its Ideals and Methods* (1897) that music as art is almost a religion, and he certainly spoke truly for himself.

Mathews's first teaching experiences were influenced by Lowell Mason and George F. Root, two pioneer school music educators. Mason introduced public school music into American education when in 1837 the Boston School Committee took the radical step of hiring him to teach music at the grammar school level. Mason created training methods for music teacher education and was a prolific composer of Protestant hymn tunes. Root helped Mason organize the first Normal Musical Institute for training teachers (1853) and wrote musical compositions designed to be performed in the schools and in the community. (The Civil War song "Tramp, Tramp, Tramp, the Boys Are Marching" is from his pen.) After the 1860s Root gave up the teachers' classes to devote himself to publishing and writing.

Though Mathews was initially interested in singing, he soon (in the mid-1860s) turned from singing to the piano, believing the piano to be the equal of the voice but "weaker than a string quartet." He systematized the piano pedagogy of Mason's son William Mason, and throughout his life he worked at the grading and classifying of piano repertoire for teaching. William Mason, during his lifetime considered the dean of American piano teachers, created piano teaching methods that emphasized the importance of musical forms and the need to understand form in order to perform musically. Mathews developed and applied these ideas in his extensive writings and teaching.

Mathews was one of the first individuals to give serious and systematic attention to pedagogy. He believed that even exercises should be performed with attention to their musical qualities and that no more than one-third of practice time should be devoted to technical studies. He believed that the rather unmusical technique books of Carl Czerny, Louis Kohler, Louis Plaidy, and their ilk commanded too much respect from piano teachers. His emphasis in teaching was on comprehension of the musical work as a whole: performers should be aware of how musical ideas were transmitted through melody, rhythm, and harmony.

Mathews also promoted listening to and appreciating music. His book *How to Understand Music* (1888) was widely used. The book had a self-study orientation; it was designed as part of a three-year extension course with examinations to document musical accomplishment. (Taking extension courses to learn music was influenced by the popular Chatauqua movement.) Many of Mathews's ideas foreshadowed twentieth-century music appreciation approaches. He emphasized the importance of feeling and imagination and suggested that the point of study of music was to acquire a knowledge *of* music, not knowledge *about* mu-

sic. He emphasized perceiving, comparing, and concluding, a three-step process similar to more recent pedagogical ideas that promote perceiving, reflecting, and judging. (This is not to say that Mathews is still an influence in the area of music appreciation, an area that has undergone many transformations since his time.) In Mathews's emphasis on the primacy of form he stressed the elements of unity, symmetry, and contrast. He believed that musical form was continually evolving: for instance, musical composition based on unity was perfected by Bach, and the fugue, the highest example of a work composed on a single idea, reached its ultimate expression in his fugues. The next musical development was the sonata, which in the hands of Haydn, Mozart, and Beethoven utilized contrast and symmetry to achieve coherence and great expressiveness. Schumann, creating large works that contained numerous short pieces, was able to carry contrast farther than any of his predecessors. Wagner abandoned the classical forms altogether, returning to the principles of Bach by achieving unity through the use of leitmotifs (leading motives), distinctive short melodies that recurred throughout a musical work and gave it coherence.

Mathews's history of music, *A Hundred Years of Music in America* (1889; repr. 1970), is notable for its extensive inclusion of contemporary American musicians and may be the best source for information on some relatively unknown musicians (composers and performers) who at the beginning of the twentieth century appeared to have potential. Mathews had high standards and deplored the musical sloppiness he observed in teachers and performers. "The larger number of teachers in the country at large, until very recently, were imperfectly qualified for their work and we cannot wonder that the public has not been ready for class teachers of music" (*A Hundred Years of Music in America*, pp. 536–37). His interest in teaching probably stemmed from his commitment to upgrade musical standards. Teaching for him was not a high art but neither was it drudgery or ignoble. He focused on the feeling and meaning of music while holding firmly to the attainment of skill in music reading and memorization. He was careful not to overemphasize knowledge, continually insisting that music was too much eye, not enough ear; too much finger, not enough touch. Touch was an important piano teaching concept for him; using a loose wrist while playing also received emphasis. His interest in ear training was reinforced by the expertise of his second wife, who collaborated with him in his composing, teaching, and publishing endeavors. The point of music teaching for him was to ensure that musical concepts were "in the ear."

In promoting standards, Mathews was an active supporter of E. M. Bowman in the formation of the American College of Musicians (1884), whose purpose was to improve the quality of music teachers, especially those belonging to the Music Teachers' National Association. A Chicago-based professional organization, the college had an examination system that was the essential part of membership in the organization.

When the college ceased giving examinations Mathews continued to promote a similar examination system in connection with his extension and correspondence work. In cities where several students were using his correspondence courses he formed student extension clubs to promote musical intelligence and to educate a class of students for whom listening and performing the greatest music would be a delight.

Mathews's purpose in founding the *Journal of School Music* in 1908 was a further effort to raise the standards of music. He knew that there were music supervisors who had good ideas they had obtained from experience but whose ideas were not being adequately disseminated to the classroom teacher—the key to music instruction. The problem he foresaw was that the teaching of music was becoming divided into two camps: those who championed music reading and those who believed that reading was secondary to rote singing. Mathews suggested that he was a neutral party and that the journal would carry articles advocating both positions. He believed that although the level of American musical culture was rising, there still remained questions about a systematic progression in pedagogy.

Mathews continued to be productive and influential to the end of his life. In his last two years he continued to work at making piano instruction more systematic and was a primary consultant to the Columbian Conservatory of Music (Arts Publication Society) in revising their four-year correspondence course. His efforts at self-teaching and self-examination were not as successful with others as they had been with himself; however, thousands of readers absorbed his reports on music and musicians, studied the elements of music through his books, and were influenced by his emphasis on deriving meaning from the greatest musical literature. He died in Denver.

Based on his own history of music, Mathews viewed his primary contribution as that of promoting an understanding of music through the education of teachers and audiences. His livelihood came from his successful career as a private piano teacher and church musician; his importance lies in the fact that for forty-three years he was a national voice from Chicago speaking about music education in the broadest sense.

• Four volumes of Mathews's papers are in the Newberry Library in Chicago. *The Great in Music, a Systematic Course of Study in the Music of Classical and Modern Composers* (1900–1902) is a good example of his contribution to extension courses. Mathews's *Graded Materials for the Piano* (1895) exemplifies his efforts to explain William Mason's piano teaching. His scholarship is best reflected in his editing of *A Hundred Years of Music in America* (1889) and his editorship of the *Journal of School Music* (1908–1909). Two dissertations on Mathews have been completed: R. W. Groves, "The Life and Works of W. S. B. Mathews (1837–1912)" (Ph.D. diss., Univ. of Iowa, 1981), and J. W. Clarke, "Prof. W. S. B. Mathews (1837–1912): Self Made Musician of the Gilded Age" (Ph.D. diss., Univ. of Minnesota, 1983). Clarke provides a more thorough analysis of Mathews's many journal articles. Mathews's long affiliation with William Mason is described in John Draper's doctoral dissertation, "Life and Works of William Mason" (Harvard Univ., 1920).

RICHARD COLWELL

MATHEWSON, Christy (12 Aug. 1880–7 Oct. 1925), baseball player, manager, and executive, was born Christopher Mathewson in Factoryville, Pennsylvania, the son of Gilbert B. Mathewson, a gentleman farmer, and Minerva J. Capwell. His parents were religiously conservative. Mathewson enjoyed many advantages as a result of his family's affluence. He attended Keystone Preparatory Academy and went on to Bucknell College in 1898 on an academic scholarship. While there he became an All-American in football and excelled in baseball and basketball. He also played baseball for a number of local semiprofessional baseball clubs before becoming a professional player in 1899 with the Taunton, Massachusetts, team. During the summers of 1898 and 1899, Mathewson also played for Honesdale to earn extra spending money for school. Mathewson married Jan Stoughton; they had one son.

Mathewson developed a unique pitch called his "fadeaway" that became his bread-and-butter pitch; it worked a lot like a screwball. With his size, strength, and special pitch, he became a pitcher to be feared when the game was on the line.

Mathewson joined the New York Giants of the National League midway through the 1900 season. The Giants purchased his contract from Norfolk, Virginia, of the Virginia League, where he had put together a 20–2 record. Mathewson went on to pitch in the major leagues for seventeen years, compiling an impressive record that ranks him among the all-time pitching leaders in baseball history.

Mathewson compiled a record of 373–188, for a .665 winning percentage. This victory total placed him high on the all-time win list and the list of highest winning percentages. He completed 435 of the 634 games he started, pitching an astonishing 4,782 innings. He struck out 2,502 batters while walking only 838. Eighty of his complete games were shutouts. His career ERA of 2.12 was led by an astounding 1.14 ERA in 1909, when he posted a record of 25–6. For twelve consecutive years, Mathewson won more than 20 games—evidence that his pitching was consistently excellent.

Mathewson led the National League four times in win total, with a high of 37 in 1908 that included 12 shutouts. He led the league five times in ERA and another five times in strikeouts, with a high of 267 in 1903. Mathewson also pitched two no-hitters, one against St. Louis in 1901 and another against Chicago in 1905. Both were also shutouts (5–0 and 1–0, respectively). Mathewson's World Series record was only 5–5 in 11 games, 10 of which he completed. His World Series ERA is 1.15. His most impressive achievement was his four World Series shutouts, three of which were in a span of five days against Philadelphia in

1905. (This is a record that many experts doubt will ever be broken.)

Mathewson was always considered a true gentleman of the game of baseball. He was a star among stars during the first years of the twentieth century, but he was also a devoted family man who was genuinely well liked and respected; these qualities enhanced his stature as a national idol.

In 1916 Giants manager John McGraw traded Mathewson to the Cincinnati Reds so that Mathewson could continue his baseball career as a manager. Mathewson pitched one game for the Reds (which he won) before taking over as the team's manager for the 1916 and 1917 seasons. He steered the Reds to 164 wins and 176 losses, ending in fourth place both years. In 1918 he enlisted in the army, becoming a captain and serving in the Gas and Flame Division in France. There he was exposed to poisonous gases and forced to leave military service. He suffered from tuberculosis as a result of this experience. After leaving the service in 1919, he rejoined the Giants as a coach until 1920. Then he retired to Saranac Lake, New York, to try to recuperate from his tuberculosis. In 1923 the Boston Braves made him the organization's president as a publicity stunt (Mathewson could no longer work regularly). He finally succumbed to his disease in Saranac Lake, depriving thousands of fans of their American hero and role model.

Mathewson's greatness was recognized in 1936, when he was elected to the National Baseball Hall of Fame as one of the "Five Immortals"—along with Ty Cobb, Walter Johnson, Babe Ruth, and Honus Wagner—that made up the first group of inductees. His manager John McGraw called him the greatest pitcher ever.

• The National Baseball Library in Cooperstown, N.Y., has an extensive file on Mathewson and his achievements. His own *Pitching in a Pinch*, with John N. Wheeler (1912; repr. 1994) reveals his views on pitching in the major leagues. Mathewson's statistics are compiled in *The Baseball Encyclopedia*, 9th ed. (1993); and *Total Baseball*, ed. John Thorn and Pete Palmer, 4th ed. (1995). Mathewson's contributions to baseball are discussed in David Q. Voigt, *American Baseball*, vol. 2 (1970). Ray Robinson, *Matty: An American Hero* (1993), examines Mathewson's role as an American hero for many fans, young and old alike. Information on the working relationship between Mathewson and his manager, John Mc-Graw, is provided in Charles C. Alexander, *John McGraw* (1988). See also Joseph M. Wayman, "The Matty-Alex Tie," *Baseball Research Journal* 24 (1995): 25–26; and Dick Thompson, "Where Matty Learned His Fadeaway," *Baseball Research Journal* 25 (1996): 93–96. Obituaries are in the *New York Times*, 8, 9, 10, and 11 Oct. 1925.

LESLIE HEAPHY

MATLACK, Timothy (28 Mar. 1736?–14 Apr. 1829), merchant and brewer, was born in Haddonfield, New Jersey, the son of Timothy Matlack, a merchant and brewer, and Martha Burr Haines; both of his parents were Quakers who moved to Philadelphia in 1746. Timothy, Jr., however, remembered that he went to Philadelphia in 1744 and resided with a Quaker elder

in 1749. He married Ellen Yarnall, the daughter of the Quaker preacher Mordecai Yarnall, in 1758; they had five children. In the 1760s and 1770s he was first a merchant and then a brewer, businesses that apparently he had established himself.

Matlack loved horse racing and cockfighting, activities in which he mingled with all classes and races. A hardy, convivial, and combative man, he neglected his hardware business and fell into debt. In July 1765 the Philadelphia monthly meeting disowned him. He was thrown into debtors' prison, and his release was obtained by Quakers, who often reminded him of their generosity and his unacceptable associations with lower classes and African Americans. During the revolutionary war, Matlack savagely caned two Quakers who had criticized his son for taking up arms. This "Fighting Quaker" was a "main Spring" in 1781 in the formation of the Society of Free Quakers, mostly Quakers who had resigned or been disowned.

The outbreak of war in 1775 witnessed Matlack's emergence as a politician who became one of Pennsylvania's most powerful leaders. The radicalism of Matlack and several other political neophytes (James Cannon, Thomas Paine, and Thomas Young) drew Pennsylvania toward independence and ended in the drafting of a most democratic state constitution. Matlack's political philosophy was uncomplicated. He asserted that government was instituted first to protect "personal liberty and safety" and second "the possession and security of property." "The first great principle" of American government was that "all men are born free and equal," a belief that drove his opposition to slavery. (He criticized Quakers for dragging their heels on abolition.) He believed that trial by jury was a "sacred" right, "citizen-soldiers" (the militia) ensured America's safety, and great wealth was an evil.

In May 1775 Matlack was appointed clerk to Charles Thomson, secretary of the Second Continental Congress, and in October he became a storekeeper of military supplies. As clerk, he probably copied the Declaration of Independence on parchment. In 1775 and 1776 he sat on two successive Philadelphia committees of inspection and observation, each numbering 100 men, and served on the second's policy-making subcommittee. In the latter half of 1775, Matlack became colonel of the Fifth (Rifle) Battalion of Philadelphia Associators, campaigning in New Jersey after the battle of Trenton. He was a delegate to the provincial conference (June 1776) that called a convention to draft a state constitution. As a delegate to the convention and a member of eight convention committees (July–Sept. 1776), Matlack helped to draft the democratic constitution and declaration of rights. The convention appointed him to the prestigious state council of safety.

The constitution's unpopularity caused Matlack and other Philadelphia Constitutionalists to be defeated in the first election for the single-house assembly under the new constitution, but in November 1776 the assembly elected him its secretary. In March 1777 he obtained his most important post, secretary of the supreme executive council. Other offices followed: keeper of the great seal, 1777; keeper of the register of those attainted for treason, 1778; keeper of the register of forfeited estates, 1779; trustee of the University of Pennsylvania, 1779; and delegate to the Second Continental Congress, 1780. During the late 1770s Matlack wrote newspaper articles attacking James Wilson, a leader of the state Republicans, the opponents of the constitution, and the high-living general Benedict Arnold. The articles were signed "T.G." for "Tiberius Gracchus." His opponents rendered the initials "Tim Gaff." For parts of 1777 and 1778 he lived in Lancaster, where Pennsylvania's government retreated after the British occupied Philadelphia.

In January 1780 Matlack was elected to the American Philosophical Society (with such luminaries as George Washington, John Adams, and Thomas Jefferson), and in March he gave the annual oration, extolling the virtues and blessings of agriculture. From 1781 to 1783 he was one of the society's secretaries, and in succeeding years he addressed it on several scientific topics. Matlack was a director of the Republican-dominated Bank of North America in 1781 and 1782, and he kept the minutes of board meetings.

This "upstart," "demogogue," "course Courteor," and "Villun" made enemies in his mercurial rise, and in March 1783 the Republican-controlled assembly charged that, because he had mismanaged public funds, he was "unworthy of public trust or confidence." The supreme executive council asked him to resign, which he did immediately. Court proceedings were begun against him, but in the summer of 1784 the council of censors, a constitutional body meeting to determine whether the state constitution had been preserved inviolate, ruled that the actions taken against Matlack were unconstitutional. In December the Constitutionalist-dominated assembly agreed, annulling the proceedings against him.

Matlack never again exercised great political power, and for a time he had difficulty making a living. In 1784 he went into business in New York City but returned to Philadelphia later that year. His career and fortunes began to revive in 1789, when he was appointed one of three commissioners to determine how to make the Delaware River more navigable; the next year he was one of three "to explore the western waters." Under the new Republican-sponsored state constitution (1790), Matlack, whose occupation was listed as "scrivener" in the 1790 federal census, became clerk of the state senate in December 1790, remaining in that post until March 1800. His first wife having died in 1791, Matlack was married in 1797 to the widow Elizabeth Claypoole Copper by Episcopal bishop William White in Philadelphia's Christ Church. Two years later the Matlacks moved to Lancaster, the new state capital, and in April 1800 Matlack was made state master of the rolls, responsible primarily for recording laws, acts, resolutions, and patents; he retained this office until it was abolished by the state legislature in 1809. In Lancaster, Matlack tended his substantial garden and orchards and lived in "easy circumstanc-

es." During these years he presented several papers to the Philadelphia Society for Promoting Agriculture. By 1810 Matlack was back in Philadelphia. One of the city's "warmest Democrats," he was an alderman, 1813–1818, and prothonotary of the district court of Philadelphia city and county, 1817–1822. He died in Holmesburg, Pennsylvania, his residence for several years.

• The standard source is A. M. Stackhouse, *Colonel Timothy Matlack, Patriot and Soldier* (1910), which reprints Matlack's American Philosophical Society published oration. Another revealing document written by Matlack is his 11 Jan. 1817 letter to William Findley on the abolition of slavery in Pennsylvania, printed in the Massachusetts Historical Society Collections, 2d ser., no. 8 (1826): 183–92. John F. Watson, *Annals of Philadelphia* (1830), has many Matlack reminiscences. For Matlack's role in Pennsylvania politics, see Robert L. Brunhouse, *The Counter-Revolution in Pennsylvania, 1776–1790* (1942); Richard A. Ryerson, "*The Revolution Is Now Begun": The Radical Committees of Philadelphia, 1765–1776* (1978); and Steven Rosswurm, *Arms, Country, and Class: The Philadelphia Militia and "Lower Sort" during the American Revolution, 1775–1783* (1987). For Matlack's occupations and officeholding, see John Hill Martin, *Martin's Bench and Bar of Philadelphia* (1883), and J. Thomas Scharf and Thompson Westcott, *History of Philadelphia, 1609–1884* (3 vols., 1884). For his service as secretary of the supreme executive council, see *Minutes of the Supreme Executive Council of Pennsylvania, from Its Organization to the Termination of the Revolution* (1852–1853). For his revolutionary activities, see William Duane, ed., *Extracts from the Diary of Christopher Marshall, Kept in Philadelphia and Lancaster during the American Revolution, 1774–1781* (1877). For his social activities, see Jacob Cox Parsons, ed., *Extracts from the Diary of Jacob Hiltzheimer of Philadelphia, 1765–1798* (1893). And for his tenure as a congressman, see Paul H. Smith, ed., *Letters of the Delegates to Congress, 1774–1789* (1976–).

GASPARE J. SALADINO

MATSON, Ralph Charles (21 Jan. 1880–26 Oct. 1945), and **Ray William Matson** (21 Jan. 1880–12 Sept. 1934), surgeons and pioneers in the treatment of pulmonary tuberculosis, were born in Brookville, Pennsylvania, the sons of John Matson and Minerva Brady, farmers. The Matsons received their M.D.s from the University of Oregon Medical College in 1902. They were interns and resident physicians at Good Samaritan Hospital in Portland from 1902 to 1905.

As was typical for the times, both Matsons did postgraduate study abroad. Ralph Matson studied at Cambridge University and St. Mary's Hospital, London (1906); at London one of his coworkers in the bacteriology laboratory was Alexander Fleming, the discoverer of penicillin. He also studied at the University of Berlin, the University of Vienna, the Academy of Medicine (Düsseldorf, Germany) during 1911–1912, and at Victoria Park and St. Mary's hospitals (London) and the University of Vienna (1923–1925). Ray Matson did postgraduate study at the University of Vienna (1909, 1914, 1920, 1925), the University of London (1909), and the University of Paris (1919).

The death of the Matsons' father from tuberculosis perhaps influenced the choice of their professional medical specialty. In 1909 Ralph Matson became bacteriologist and Ray Matson became pathologist at the Portland Open Air Sanatorium, which was founded in 1905 as the first tuberculosis institution in the Pacific Northwest. At this institution, following a regimen instituted at Saranac Lake in New York state, fresh air, exercise, and special diet were prescribed for the patients. In 1912 the Matsons became the permanent staff doctors and co–medical directors of this sanatorium. Ralph would stay in this position until 1925, Ray until 1934. In 1913 at the sanatorium the Matsons introduced the X-ray machine and induced artificial pneumothorax therapy to collapse one or both lungs with air, both firsts in the Pacific Northwest. Probably it was in the same year that the Matsons and Marr Bisaillon established the first specialized tuberculosis practice in Portland.

Both Matsons served in World War I. Ralph Matson went to Europe in 1916 with the Harvard University Surgical Team that was associated with the Royal Army Medical Corps. He worked in a mobile laboratory close to the front to study the treatment of war wounds, especially chest wounds complicated by empyema (pus in the pleural cavity). His services were recognized with an award of the French Legion of Honor. When the United States entered the war, both Matsons became majors in the Army Medical Corps. Ray Matson gained further insights into lung problems as a gas officer with the Ninety-first American Division in France. Both Matsons were chief medical examiners and tuberculosis specialists at Camp Lewis, Washington, from late 1917 to 1919. From 1919 to 1920 Ralph Matson was chief of staff at Fitzsimmons General Hospital in Denver where he led a training program for medical officers in the diagnosis of tuberculosis.

In Germany after the war, Ralph Matson learned the technique of thoracoplasty (surgery to reshape the thorax permanently to compress the lung). In 1932 the two brothers and Bisaillon performed the first thoracoplasty in the Pacific Northwest at the Portland Open Air Sanatorium. In 1914 the Matsons had begun doing a surgical procedure to interrupt one phrenic nerve to paralyze the diaphragm in order to limit motion of a diseased lung, an operation they had learned in Europe and which they introduced at the sanatorium. The Matsons and Bisaillon also took the lead in the Pacific Northwest in using pneumothorax therapy and pioneered in the treatment of one of its common complications, tuberculosis empyema, through injecting oil (oleothorax) or certain chemicals in the space around the lung. Ralph Matson was one of the first surgeons in the United States to use intraplural pneumolysis, a procedure in which adhesions limiting the collapse of a lung, and thus the efficacy of pneumothorax treatment, could be divided by cautery.

Other operations that Ralph Matson pioneered in the Pacific Northwest were pulmonary resections (removal of part or all of the lung) in the treatment of lung cancer and severe lung infections and the operation to create an extrapleural space at the top of the lung to collapse cavities there. The space so created could be maintained by periodic refills of air or ping-pong balls or gauze packing surrounded by plastic film. The Matsons' influence on the treatment of tuberculosis was spread through their articles on pneumothorax, phrenic nerve surgery, and oleothorax and through Ralph Matson's presence at the University of Oregon Medical School, where he excelled at teaching.

The reputation of the Matsons was recognized both in the United States and abroad through the many distinctions they received. Ralph Matson was a founding member in 1917 of the American Association for Thoracic Surgery and a fellow of many scientific societies. He was a vice president of the National Tuberculosis Association and an editor of *Diseases of the Chest*. Ray Matson was president of the Portland Academy of Medicine, a vice president of the National Tuberculosis Association, and a vice president of the American Clinical and Climatological Association. Ralph Matson married Adeline Ferarri in 1907; they had one child before they divorced. He married Chiara DeBona (or de Bona) in 1923; this union produced no children. In 1907 Ray Matson married Carolyn Holmes; they had no children.

The personalities of the twin brothers contributed to their influence as administrators, surgeons, and teachers. They had flair, courage, and energy. They played polo, steeplechased, drove fast cars, and flew airplanes. Even Ray Matson's accidental death, and that of a young female companion, in the fiery wreckage of their sports car was sensational. Yet in time much of the Matsons' work—as is inevitable in the process of scientific advance—became obsolete with the discovery of new drugs, beginning in 1944 with streptomycin, that essentially made intraplural pneumonolysis and pneumothorax no longer of concern. Both brothers died in Portland.

• The most comprehensive account of the Matsons' life and work in the context of the history of the treatment of tuberculosis is John E. Tuhy, *Annals of the Thoracic Clinic* (1978). Olof Larsell, *The Doctor in Oregon* (1947), also provides a contextual basis for Ralph Matson's career. More technical surveys of their accomplishments are in Allen K. Kraus, "Ray William Matson, 1880–1934," *American Journal of Tuberculosis* 31 (1935): 250–53, and James T. Speros, "Ralph Charles Matson: 1880–1945," *Diseases of the Chest* 11 (1945): 687–88.

GORDON B. DODDS

MATSUNAGA, Spark Masayuki (8 Oct. 1916–15 Apr. 1990), representative and senator from Hawaii in the U.S. Congress, was born in Kukuiula, Kauai, Hawaii, the son of Kingoro Matsunaga and Chiyono Fukushima, plantation workers. Educated in Hawaii's public schools from 1931 to 1934, he worked while a student as a stevedore and warehouseman and upon graduation spent three years as a bookkeeper and sales clerk. Matsunaga then attended the University of Hawaii, obtaining his Ed.B. in 1941. While at the university, he served in the ROTC for two years and after graduation was commissioned a second lieutenant in the U.S. Army Reserve. Matsunaga volunteered for active service in World War II and was assigned to the 100th Battalion in July 1941. His unit, composed entirely of Nisei (Japanese Americans), was organized to show support for the U.S. cause and loyalty of Japanese born in America through its bravery in combat. After being wounded twice, he was released from active service as a captain in December 1945. For his valor, he was awarded the Purple Heart with Oak Leaf Cluster, the Bronze Star, an Army Commendation Medal, and numerous theater ribbons. In 1948 he married Helene Hatsumi Tokunago; they had five children. Matsunaga enrolled at Harvard law school and obtained his J.D. in 1951.

Matsunaga returned to Hawaii after law school and served as a city and county of Honolulu assistant public prosecutor from 1952 to 1954. He then entered private practice, also undertaking postgraduate studies at Northwestern University's Traffic Institute in 1957 and Lawyers Postgraduate Clinics of Chicago, Illinois, in 1958. Simultaneously, Matsunaga made his first bid for public office in 1954 as a liberal Democrat and served as a representative in the legislature of the Territory of Hawaii from 1954 to 1959, acting as majority leader in 1959. The Democratic landslide of 1954 in which he was first elected ended a half-century of Republican domination guided by representatives of the "Big Five," the large corporations associated with the development of Hawaiian sugar.

In 1962 Matsunaga was elected as an at-large candidate to the U.S. House of Representatives. After 1970, when Hawaii was divided into two congressional districts, he represented Hawaii's First Congressional District, receiving strong backing from the International Longshoremen's Union and from Oriental voters. His district included Pearl Harbor, Waikiki Beach, the University of Hawaii, and Oahu's light industries and canneries, which represented Hawaii's defense, tourism, and manufacturing interests. CINC-PAC (Commander in Chief, Pacific Area Command), command headquarters for the Pacific, Fort Shafter and Schofield Barracks, Hickam Air Force Base, the headquarters of the Pacific Air Command, and the Marine Corps Air Station at Kaneohe were within his district. Federal military expenditures in Hawaii were the largest single source of income for Hawaii in the 1960s and 1970s during the war in Vietnam. Because of Hawaii's key military role in the Pacific, Matsunaga's campaigns used slogans like "In the Forefront for Hawaii and the Nation" and "Keep Hawaii Strong in Congress," and his voting record indicated a strong focus on the prosperity of Hawaii.

Matsunaga was a prime mover behind the passage of the Sugar Act in 1971, which allocated quotas to Hawaii and other sugar-producing states to sell raw sugar above the world market price: as a result, Hawaii received more than $9 million in sugar subsidies that year. For labor, Matsunaga was able to bring in federal contracts for harbor improvements and improved benefits for federal employees. Whenever his Hawaiian

constituents visited Washington, D.C., they were usually treated to lunch in the Capitol and a photograph with Matsunaga on the Capitol steps. He served on both the Agricultural Committee and the important Rules Committee, where he wielded exceptional power. As House majority leader Hale Boggs stated in 1971, "It's getting to the point where you have to see Sparky Matsunaga to get a bill passed around here." He garnered an impressive legislative track record by becoming a cosponsor of many bills before they were voted on in the Rules Committee. His endorsement gained the bills' support from "middle of the road people," since he had a reputation "as having liberal tendencies, but was not a radical," as judged by Sarah Jane Glazer in a biographical sketch written for Ralph Nader's congressional project (p. 15). Matsunaga's book *Rulemakers of the House* (1976) is a definitive work explaining the evolution of the House Rules Committee and the changes he was able to make in that important group. For instance, he obtained a rule authorizing the majority to call a meeting of the committee without the chairman's consent, and another rule set a regular meeting date for every Tuesday. These changes prevented the committee's chairman from killing a bill simply through his absence or inaction, a strategy that had often served as a conservative roadblock to liberal legislation. Matsunaga understood the importance of rules and mastered them to secure support for his programs. He also valued his membership on the Agriculture Committee because, he said, "sugar is the life-blood of Hawaii."

His congressional voting record indicated that he voted with the Democratic majority 88 percent of the time and with a bipartisan majority 81 percent. One notable bill he introduced in 1971 was the repeal of Title II of the Internal Security Act, under which 110,000 Japanese had been interned on the West Coast during World War II. Repeal, he said, would remove the "blot on the pages of our nation's history" and lessen the chance for "self-styled extremist leaders . . . to escalate confrontation, foment arrest, violence and even revolution." Matsunaga also introduced legislation (1971–1972) to establish ethnic studies in American universities in order to combat racism and generate a "more harmonious, patriotic, and committed populace." He spoke out for adoption of the Environmental Quality Education Act (1970) to provide courses in ecology for high school, elementary, and adult education programs. Matsunaga was an opponent of the war in Vietnam and introduced one of the earliest resolutions for withdrawal (1966) and, after 1966, voted to cut off funds to Vietnam. He was a critic of nuclear testing and dispatched a personal plea to President Richard Nixon to halt the Cannikin test of 1971. Nevertheless, he voted in favor of a strong U.S. defense system, so as to continue the military funds distributed to Hawaii.

Sparky Matsunaga was elected to the Senate in 1976 with a plurality of 54 percent and in 1980 and 1986 with pluralities of 80 percent reflecting Hawaii's heavy concentration of Democratic voters. In the Senate, in

1977, he cast the deciding vote in favor of Senator Robert Byrd as majority leader, was rewarded with a seat on the influential Finance Committee and, later, on the Energy and Natural Resources Committee, where he served as vice chair of the research and development subcommittee. He was noted for his interest in the development of alternative energy sources and introduced several bills encouraging the use of water, solar, and wind power. He was also keenly interested in the nonmilitary uses of outer space and introduced bills encouraging U.S.–Soviet joint cooperation in space exploration, which culminated in the writing of his 1986 book, *The Mars Project*. In 1980 he served as chairman on the Commission for a National Academy of Peace and Conflict Resolution, which traveled all over the country gathering testimony on the feasibility of establishing a national peace academy. This resulted in 1984 in the establishment of the U.S. Institute for Peace in Washington, D.C., an important source of funding for peace research in the United States.

Matsunaga's hobbies included writing poetry, for which he won an award from the International Poetry Institute; reading; and playing the harmonica. An Episcopalian, he helped organize the Brotherhood of St. Andrew's Cathedral in Honolulu. Because of his peace endeavors he was awarded the B'nai B'rith International Peace Year Award in 1986.

After his death, in Toronto, the Institute for Peace at the University of Hawaii in Honolulu was renamed the Spark M. Matsunaga Institute for Peace. The two peace institutes associated with Matsunaga are fitting reminders of a distinguished war veteran turned congressional politician.

• Matsunaga's papers are in the Spark M. Matsunaga Peace Foundation, University of Hawaii at Manoa. Biographical sketches can be found in the *Biographical Directory of the American Congress, 1774–1971* (1971); David Watumull, ed., *Prominent People of Hawaii* (1988); and Sarah Jane Glazer, *Spark M. Matsunaga, Democratic Representative From Hawaii*, written for the Ralph Nader Congress Project, Citizens Look at Congress (1972). Spencer Rich, "Sugar Act: Grower Prop or Congressman Swindle?" *Washington Post*, 30 May 1971, and *Hawaii Economic Review*, Mar.–Apr. 1971, p. 5, contain information on Matsunaga's sugar policies. An obituary is in the *New York Times*, 16 Apr. 1990.

BARBARA BENNETT PETERSON

MATTESON, Tompkins Harrison (9 May 1813–2 Feb. 1884), painter and illustrator, was born in Peterboro, Madison County, New York, the son of John Matteson and Hadassah Bliss. He was raised in Morrisville, New York, where his father became sheriff in 1815. He learned the rudiments of drawing and painting from Abe Antone, a Native American held in the Morrisville jail on a charge of murder. In return for the art materials that the young Matteson procured for him, the prisoner allowed the boy to look on as he worked.

Matteson began to paint professionally in Hamilton, New York, where he was involved with a theatrical troupe. On tour with the company in 1834, he visited Sherburne, New York, where he eventually settled. He studied briefly with Alvah Bradish, a portrait painter from Manlius, New York. Sometime in the mid- to late 1830s Matteson went to New York City and enrolled in the antique class at the National Academy of Design. In 1839 he returned to western New York and painted portraits in Sherburne, Auburn, and Geneva, where he lived after his marriage to Sarah Elizabeth Merrill. Matteson's portraits of John M. Messinger, Newton Messinger, and Charlotte Messinger (all in the collection of the Oneida Historical Society) date to this period. His first biographer, Henry T. Tuckerman, wrote that Henry Dwight, Jr., formerly of Geneva, but who was living in New York City by 1841, was responsible for persuading Matteson to pursue his art in New York, where opportunities for study as well as patronage were greater. Consequently, Matteson opened a studio in New York City in 1841. Three of his paintings were exhibited that year at the National Academy. Their titles, *The Village Doctor*, *The Novel Reader*, and *The Travelling Tinker*, suggest that with single-figure compositions Matteson had begun an evolution from portraitist to genre painter.

Matteson came to the attention of genre painter and banknote engraver Francis William Edmonds, who urged the American Art Union to purchase Matteson's *The Spirit of '76*, a full-blown genre picture combining domestic and patriotic themes. It depicted a young man bidding farewell to his family as family members help him prepare to go to war. The picture was exhibited at both the Art Union and the National Academy in 1845, and its success essentially determined the course Matteson's subsequent career would take. From then on Matteson was known for historic themes full of patriotic virtue. Many of his paintings were sold as engravings or used as textbook illustrations, so they became familiar national icons to a mass audience.

While in New York Matteson began his career as an illustrator. In 1846 and 1847 he provided illustrations for the periodicals *Whig Review*, *Columbian Lady's and Gentleman's Magazine*, and *Sartain's Union Magazine of Literature and Art*. He provided the original art for books published by George F. Cooledge and Brother of New York, including *The Life of Benjamin Franklin* (1848), *Life of Nathaneal Greene* (1849), and *The Complete Works of William Shakespeare* (1851), and he also worked for other publishers in New York, Philadelphia, and Buffalo. He collaborated principally with wood engraver Alexander Anderson.

After establishing a fine reputation in the art capital of the United States, Matteson purchased a home in Sherburne and moved there permanently in 1850. He was an outstanding citizen who provided service in a number of capacities outside his profession. Immediately after settling in Sherburne he became chief engineer and foreman of the Sherburne fire department, positions he held for twenty-five years. He served as president of the board of trustees of the Union Free Schools of Sherburne and worked tirelessly for improvement of the schools. In 1855 he was elected to the New York State Legislature.

Matteson's art career flourished. He sent pictures to New York City for exhibition and sale, and he sold paintings upstate as well. Among his patrons were Henry M. Mygate, Gilbert Davidson, and William D. White, all of Albany, and Mortimer Conger of Waterville, New York. He painted a number of works for New York art dealer William Schaus, including *Signing the Contract on Board the Mayflower* (1853), *The First Sabbath of the Puritans*, *Perils of the Early Colonists*, and *Santa's Workshop* (1856). His work was exhibited at the National Academy throughout the 1840s and in 1860, 1868, and 1869; he became an associate member of the academy in 1848. His paintings were also exhibited at the Brooklyn Art Association, the American Institute of the City of New York (1856), the Utica Art Association (1867), and the American Society of Painters in Water Colors (1873). He also lent a painting to the exhibition held in Albany in 1864 for benefit of the U.S. Sanitary Commission.

In addition to creating historic themes, Matteson painted scenes of domestic genre set in homes or farmyards. *Now or Never* (1849, Parrish Art Museum, Southampton, N.Y.) shows a young woman dozing by an open window, her suitor gazing at her and contemplating whether or not to kiss her while her aged parents tend the hearth in the background. *Caught in the Act* (1860, Vassar College Art Gallery, Poughkeepsie, N.Y.), which depicts the punishment meted out to a mischievous young boy, in theme and composition owes a debt to the work of Edmonds. *At the Stile* and *Hop Picking* (1862, Munson-Williams-Proctor Institute, Utica, N.Y.), depict farm life in a bucolic manner. Tuckerman praised Matteson's work from this period as "well fitted to charm rural households."

In the 1870s Matteson painted works of allegorical, religious, and literary themes, including *The Triumph of Freedom*, an allegory on the triumph of the Union and the abolition of slavery as a result of the Civil War, which Matteson also rendered as a bas-relief carving, his only known sculpture. A Sherburne newspaper reported on 24 May 1873 that viewable in Matteson's studio were *Jacob's Dream*, *Daniel in the Lion's Den*, *Falstaff's Bath*, and a scene from *The Tempest*.

Matteson taught art in his Sherburne studio in the 1850s. His most famous pupil, Elihu Vedder, offered a fond recollection of the artist in his autobiography, *The Digressions of V* (1910):

Matteson was remarkable for being a self-made man who had made a good job of it. Somewhat stately and precise in manner, but kindly and with a fine sense of humor, he had turned out a gentleman in spite of very adverse circumstances. . . . He wore a steeple-crowned hat and a short mantle, and was not adverse to being called the pilgrim painter. For one of his favorite subjects was the pilgrim, either departing or arriving . . . [He] must have been, with his large family, in very straitened circumstances; yet he never complained nor allowed it to be seen. . . . I tell all this, to leave a little record of a man I loved, respected and admired.

Matteson lectured to agricultural societies in Sherburne and Oxford, New York. In 1865 he was elected president of the Chenango Agricultural Society. Matteson died in Sherburne.

Whether the themes he painted resulted from personal choice or publishers' commissions, Matteson painted subjects of such great importance to our national life, representing either significant historical events, such as *Captain Glen Claiming the Prisoners after the Burning of Schenectady, N.Y.*, *Washington Crossing the Delaware*, and *Custer's Last Shot*, or pictures representing democratic ideals, such as *Justice's Court in the Backwoods* (1850, New York State Historical Association, Cooperstown, N.Y.), *Spirit of '76*, and *The Triumph of Freedom*. As many of his important pictures received wide distribution through book illustrations or engravings, Matteson's work has had an effect in shaping the popular concept of a national identity.

• For a biography of the artist and an estimate of his work by a contemporary, see Henry T. Tuckerman, *Book of the Artists: American Artist Life* (1867). *Thompkins [sic] H. Matteson, 1813–1884* (1949) quotes many contemporary references to the artist, including the discussion in Tuckerman, Matteson's obituary from the Sherburne newspaper, and newspaper reviews of his work. For a discussion of Matteson's work as an illustrator plus a listing of books illustrated by him, see Princeton University Library, *Early American Book Illustrators and Wood Engravers, 1670–1870* (1958).

CYNTHIA SEIBELS

MATTHEW, Wentworth Arthur (23 June 1892–3 Dec. 1973), leader of a black Jewish sect, was born in St. Marys or in Spooner's Village in the British West Indies, the son of Joseph Matthew and Frances M. Cornelius. Matthew always claimed that he was born in an African country (usually reported as Lagos, Nigeria) and that he arrived in New York City by way of the British West Indies. However, according to his naturalization application, he was born in the British West Indies and in 1913 immigrated as a carpenter to the United States from St. Kitts. It probably was there that he married Florence Docher Liburd, also from the British West Indies, with whom he had four children. He supported his family by performing a variety of odd jobs.

In 1919, according to Matthew, he founded the Commandments Keepers Church of the Living God, the Pillar and Ground of the Truth and the Faith of Jesus Christ, and became the minister of the congregation. In 1921 the Commandments Keepers church was officially incorporated. Initially its members practiced a mixture of Christian and Jewish rituals but as a result of criticism voiced mainly by Jewish visitors to the temple and by his closest rival, "Rabbi" Arnold J. Ford, Matthew began to divest his church of its Christian elements. He called himself rabbi, claiming that he had been trained at the Hebrew Union College in Cincinnati and had a Ph.D. in sociology from the University of Berlin. No evidence has been found to substantiate these claims. He probably learned Hebrew from an immigrant Jewish teacher who also initiated him into the rituals of Jewish worship. During the 1930s Matthew placed more and more emphasis on the assertion that he and his largely West Indian followers were descended from an ethnic group of black Jews known as the Falashas, who lived around Gondar in Ethiopia. His links with this African country were further accentuated when, in 1931, Arnold Ford, who had left for Ethiopia the year before together with his followers, sent Matthew his ordination papers from Addis Ababa.

Thanks to growing interest in his sect on the part of Jewish immigrants who had fled from Europe, Matthew and his followers began to receive more and more publicity. Articles and photo reports on the group appeared in newspapers and magazines throughout the 1930s, enabling Matthew to refine the image he wished to present to the outside world. In 1942 he published the so-called *Minute Book*, in which he set out the profession of faith, the history, and the organization of the Commandments Keepers Congregation.

Matthew repeatedly stressed the importance of education, and he founded a school through which he taught his followers himself. In the decades after the Second World War disciples trained by Matthew set up "houses of worship" in the various boroughs of New York City. Directly after the war, Matthew and some of his followers bought land on Long Island, where he intended to set up a resident community, with an orphans' home and a home for elderly people. The project never got off the ground, but Matthew was successful at founding several branches outside of New York City, including one in Youngstown, Ohio. In 1962 his own synagogue, originally located at 29 West 131st Street, moved to a large building on the corner of West 123d Street and Mount Morris Park, where the Commandments Keepers continue to reside. Also at this time, Matthew changed the official name of the Commandments Keepers, as laid down in the incorporation papers of 1921, because he felt that it was not in keeping with the Jewish principles of his congregation: henceforth it was to be known as the Commandments Keepers Ethiopian Hebrew Congregation of the Living God, the Pillar and Ground of Truth.

A gifted speaker who could hold the attention of an audience for hours, Matthew had an exceptional talent for firing his listeners' enthusiasm. Occasionally he also wrote short, mainly propagandistic, articles. In 1958, for example, the *New York Age* published a series of eight pieces by Matthew called "The Truth about Black Jews and Judaism in America," in which he examined the articles of faith and the origins of his followers. In the *Malach* (Messenger), a periodical published by the congregation at irregular intervals during the period 1965–1967, Matthew and several of his disciples wrote about the history of the movement, publicizing the various activities of the Ethiopian Hebrew Congregation.

During the 1950s and 1960s Matthew was in frequent touch with representatives of the Jewish community. At the instigation of Rabbi Irving J. Block of the white Brotherhood Synagogue in Manhattan, he put forward a second formal application—the first one, submitted in 1931, had been rejected—for admission to the New York Board of Rabbis. This, too, was rejected, since the rabbis did not recognize his credentials. Block repeatedly lent his support to the black Jewish congregations, while the Hatzaad Harishon (First Step), a mixed group of black and white Jews founded in 1964, also worked to reinforce the bonds between the two communities, organizing children's camps, scholarships, and the like for white Jewish children and Matthew's followers. The idea behind these efforts was to reach some level of integration, something Matthew was not too keen on, fearing that it would mean the end of the carefully fostered identity of the black Jews.

In the late 1960s and early 1970s a disappointed Matthew turned his back on the Jewish community. Several years before his death he appointed as his successor his grandson David Dore, who had studied at Yeshiva University in New York City. From then on, Matthew appeared only rarely in his house of worship before his death in Harlem Hospital. Matthew is not buried in a Jewish cemetery, as a number of his followers have claimed, but in the Afro-American section of the Frederick Douglass Memorial Park on Staten Island.

• The American Jewish Archives in Cincinnati holds the papers of Rabbi Irving Block, which include a few letters by Matthew. Newspaper clippings and magazine articles can be found in the vertical files of the Schomburg Center for Research in Black Culture, New York Public Library, and in the Blaustein Library of the American Jewish Committee, both in New York City. Matthew's writings include the *Minute Book of the Commandments Keepers Congregation of the Living God, the Pillar and Ground of the Truth* (1942) and "The Truth about Black Jews and Judaism in America," *New York Age*, 17, 24, and 31 May; 1, 14, 21, and 28 June; and 5 July 1958. The most extensive research devoted to Matthew and his congregation has been conducted by Howard M. Brotz, whose master's thesis (1947) can be found at the University of Chicago library. See also Brotz's "Negro 'Jews' in the United States," *Phylon* 13 (1952): 324–37, and *The Black Jews of Harlem: Negro Nationalism and the Dilemmas of Negro Leadership*, 2d ed. (1970), pp. 15–59. Other useful publications include Roi Ottley, *New World A-Coming: Inside Black America* (1943), pp. 137–50; A. Dobrin, "A History of the Negro Jews in America" (unpublished paper, City College of the City University of New York, 1965), pp. 27–36; H. Waitzkin, "Black Judaism in New York," *Harvard Journal of Negro Affairs* 1, no. 3 (1967): 12–44; A. Ehrman, "Explorations and Responses: Black Judaism in New York," *Journal of Ecumenical Studies* 8, no. 1 (1971): 103–14; and G. Berger, *Black Jews in America: A Documentary with Commentary* (1978), pp. 86–107.

J. F. HEIJBROEK

MATTHEW, William Diller (19 Feb. 1871–24 Sept. 1930), paleontologist, was born in Saint John, New Brunswick, Canada, the son of George Frederic Matthew, a customs house official and an authority on geology, and Katherine Diller. His father, an amateur, conducted important studies on the geology and invertebrate fossils of New Brunswick. Young Matthew took an interest in his father's activities and participated in fieldwork. Encouraged by his family, he entered the University of New Brunswick in 1887, completing a bachelor's degree two years later. In 1889 he moved to the United States to begin graduate work in geology at Columbia University's School of Mines. Matthew's interest focused on geology and invertebrate paleontology, but in 1894 a course with Henry Fairfield Osborn shifted his attention to vertebrate paleontology. Completing his Ph.D. in 1895, he was hired as Osborn's assistant in the Department of Vertebrate Paleontology of New York's American Museum of Natural History. Matthew would spend more than thirty years in that department, eventually becoming curator, before leaving in 1927 to become professor of paleontology at the University of California at Berkeley. He married Kate Lee in 1905; they had three children.

Matthew was primarily a vertebrate paleontologist and made many contributions to that field. Throughout his career he conducted fieldwork in western fossil beds almost annually and helped develop the large collection of fossil mammals at the American Museum. Most of Matthew's publications were technical descriptions and classifications of fossil vertebrates, and his work redefined the understanding of the evolution of several orders and families of extinct mammals.

Matthew took an interest in theoretical problems pertaining to vertebrate paleontology and evolutionary biology. In the early twentieth century, most paleontologists had abandoned Darwinism in favor of other theories of evolution. The data of the fossil record seemed to indicate regular, cumulative patterns of change, and, according to many scientists, suggested that rather than natural selection the inheritance of acquired characteristics or nonmaterial, teleological forces controlled evolution. Matthew was one of the few who opposed such interpretations. He was a committed Darwinian and defined the evolution of fossil mammals in terms of the natural selection of random variations and adaptation to environmental conditions. By the 1920s Matthew, equating the variations found among fossils in the field with the mutations described by experimental biologists, called on paleontologists to heal the split between laboratory and field biology and to take seriously the work of Mendelian geneticists. Matthew's views led to controversies with Osborn but influenced Matthew's colleague George Gaylord Simpson, an assistant at the American Museum who later helped integrate paleontology with population genetics and Darwinian theory.

Matthew was best known for his work on the origin and geographical distribution of animals. His work drew on the ideas of Charles Darwin and Alfred Russel Wallace, the codiscoverer of evolution by natural selection, who had interpreted biogeography in terms of distribution of plants and animals across geological and geographical regions similar to those on today's earth. However, many early twentieth-century scientists challenged those views and explained biogeography on the basis of extended land bridges, sunken con-

tinents, and drifting landmasses. Matthew opposed those ideas. His most famous work, "Climate and Evolution" (1915), was an extended argument for the northern origin and dispersal of vertebrates and the permanence of continents and ocean basins. While some contemporaries criticized his interpretation, it was widely accepted by vertebrate biologists and paleontologists and provided a framework for distributional studies through the 1940s.

Through his fieldwork and attention to geological questions, Matthew also contributed to the understanding of stratigraphy and the relative age of the earth. His trips to western fossil beds resulted not only in the collection of fossil specimens but detailed descriptions of geological formations and faunal relations that surpassed anything previously done in American vertebrate paleontology. He devoted much attention to establishing both the biological and the geological age differences between archaic and modern families of fossil mammals. Through that work he helped define the Paleocene epoch of geological time; he also became involved in two major scientific controversies. One concerned the boundary between the Cretaceous and Tertiary periods of geological time, a line that scientists had traditionally designated by defining the Cretaceous as the last age of the dinosaurs, and the Tertiary as the beginning of the age of mammals. In the 1910s, when some scientists challenged that interpretation by claiming that dinosaurs had persisted into the Tertiary, Matthew emerged as a leading opponent to the challenge and helped establish a compromise position that eventually resolved the issue. He played a similar role in an international controversy over stratigraphy. Whereas most European and North American scientists had defined South American faunas as descendants of northern faunas, in the 1890s the Argentine paleontologist Florentino Ameghino inverted that interpretation. Ameghino defined Patagonia as the center of vertebrate evolution and dispersal and maintained that South American faunas and geological horizons antedated those elsewhere. His theory, which provoked a worldwide reaction, was refuted by Matthew, who pointed out that Ameghino's reliance on a southern origin of animals had resulted in serious misinterpretations of evolutionary lineages and geological ages.

At the American Museum, Matthew worked to make the findings of paleontology accessible to the public. He participated in many field trips and frequently wrote popular articles on dinosaurs, fossil mammals, and other extinct animals. As curator of the museum's vertebrate paleontology program, he helped develop popular exhibits of extinct animals. Working with Osborn and the artist Charles R. Knight, Matthew directed and participated in the creation of innovative skeletal displays and large murals of prehistoric life that dominated the museum's halls into the 1980s. Although Matthew disagreed with Osborn's linear view of evolution, he participated in the design and construction of displays of horses, elephants, and humans that emphasized that interpretation and became standard in museums, textbooks, and other educational venues. Matthew died in Berkeley, California.

Some of Matthew's work has not stood the test of time. Interpretations from plate tectonics have replaced his belief in the northern origin of vertebrates and permanent land masses and ocean basins. Over the years scientists and the public have criticized American Museum displays, and in the 1990s those exhibits were revamped. Yet during the first half of the twentieth century Matthew stood out as one of the world's leading paleontologists, a scientist whose knowledge of mammalian fossils and biostratigraphy was unrivaled and whose views on evolution and biogeography had a profound impact.

• The two principal collections of Matthew's papers are in the archives of the Department of Vertebrate Paleontology, American Museum of Natural History, and in the Bancroft Library, University of California, Berkeley. Other small collections include letters in the archives of the New Brunswick Museum and in the Witmer Stone Collection, archives of the Academy of Natural Sciences of Philadelphia. Many of Matthew's letters to his wife were published in Charles L. Camp, "The Letters of William Diller Matthew," *Journal of the West* 8 (1969): 263–90, 454–76. Matthew's major publications are "Climate and Evolution," *Annals of the New York Academy of Sciences* 24 (1915): 171–318; *Outline and General Principles of the History of Life* (1930); "Paleocene Faunas of the San Juan Basin, New Mexico," *Transactions of the American Philosophical Society* n.s., 30 (1937): 1–510. The most recent and extensive biography of Matthew is Edwin H. Colbert, *William Diller Matthew, Paleontologist: The Splendid Drama Observed* (1992). Matthew's work is also discussed in Ronald Rainger, *An Agenda for Antiquity: Henry Fairfield Osborn and Vertebrate Paleontology at the American Museum of Natural History, 1890–1935* (1991); William King Gregory, "A Review of William Diller Matthew's Contributions to Mammalian Paleontology," *American Museum Novitiates* no. 473 (1931): 1–23; and Henry Fairfield Osborn, "Memorial of William Diller Matthew," *Bulletin of the Geological Society of America* 42 (1931): 55–95.

RONALD RAINGER

MATTHEWS, Ann Teresa (1732–12 June 1800), a founder of the first Roman Catholic religious order for women in the United States, was born in Charles County, Maryland, the daughter of Joseph Matthews, a planter, and Susannah Craycroft. Her last name is also seen as Mathews, but both her father's will and the record of her profession refer to her as Ann Matthews. Joseph Matthews died when Ann was two. He left his wife and three children a modest estate that included a 345-acre farm and two slaves. Ann's mother remarried, to Edward Clements, by the time Ann was nine.

The Matthews family was Roman Catholic. The Calverts had founded Maryland as a haven for Roman Catholics, but after the Protestant Revolution of 1689 the Maryland government imposed severe restrictions, including a ban on Catholic churches and schools. Jesuit priests ministered privately to Catholics and established a clandestine academy for boys, but those who wanted a college education or who desired to enter a religious order still had to go to Europe.

In 1754 Ann Matthews sailed for Belgium to enter the convent of the Discalced Carmelites at Hoogstraet. The life of the Carmelites centered on contemplation and communal prayer. The order's strict discipline included a ban on wearing shoes ("discalced" means barefoot, or without shoes).

The Carmelites had established an English-speaking convent in Antwerp in 1619 to serve the daughters of recusant British families. They founded two more English-speaking carmels in Lierre and Hoogstraet later in the century. Women from British colonies, many of them from Maryland, began joining these carmels in the 1740s. In September 1754, Matthews received the religious habit of the Carmelites at Hoogstraet and assumed the name Bernardina Teresa Xavier of St. Joseph. The next year she made her profession. After completing her novitiate, she remained at the Hoogstraet convent as mistress of novices. In 1771, her fellow religious elected her prioress of the Hoogstraet convent.

With American independence, the new Maryland government removed the religious strictures against Roman Catholics. Sister Bernardina's brother Ignatius, a Jesuit priest in Maryland, urged her to return to the state to establish a carmel for Catholic women.

After several years of planning and fundraising, Sister Bernardina left Hoogstraet in April 1790 to return to Maryland to found a Carmelite convent. Accompanying her was Clare Joseph Dickinson, an English-born sister from the Antwerp carmel, and her brother William's two daughters, who in 1786 had taken religious vows at their aunt's convent in Hoogstraet. Two Jesuit priests traveled with the women—Father Robert Plunkett, an Englishman, who was going to America as a missionary, and Father Charles Neale, a Maryland-born cousin of Sister Bernardina who since 1780 had been chaplain to the Antwerp Carmelite convent. Father Neale would be the chaplain and confessor to the new American carmel.

The sisters took the precaution of donning secular dress before boarding the ship. They celebrated mass secretly in the middle of the night in Father Neale's private cabin, considering it prudent to keep their religious practices a "profound Secret" from the Protestant captain and crew. Despite their efforts, when they arrived in Tenerife in the Canary Islands their ship's captain told another captain their "history in full." Within a few hours everyone on the island knew that the "Brothers" passengers included "4 nuns [that] had Escaped from their Monastery & 2 priests running away with them" (FitzGerald, vol. 2, p. 61).

In early July 1790 the ship carrying the Carmelites reached New York. By 20 July the sisters were at "Chandler's Hope," Father Neale's boyhood home in Charles County, Maryland. The next day they resumed wearing their religious habits and formally began Carmelite life in America. Chandler's Hope proved too small for a convent, and the nuns accepted an offer from a Roman Catholic landowner, Baker Brooke, of a house and land further up the Port Tobacco River. This house became the first convent for Roman Catholic women in the United States and served the Carmelites until the order moved to Baltimore in 1831.

Although Carmelites lived in cloistered communities that dealt sparingly with the wider world, the new American bishop of the Roman Catholic Church, John Carroll, asked the Carmelites to open a school. Because a public vocation violated the order's rules, Carroll had to petition the Vatican for a dispensation to enable the Maryland Carmelites to teach. The sisters at Port Tobacco refused, however, preferring to maintain their contemplative life. While they were unwilling to go out into the world, the Maryland Carmelites did welcome and train women who came to them in search of a religious vocation. Four novices joined the Port Tobacco carmel in 1794, and by 1800 the community numbered fourteen nuns.

Mother Bernardina served as prioress of the Maryland carmel during its first ten years. Little is known about her during these years, but she had been a much-loved prioress in Hoogstraet and the Maryland carmel's success suggests she was an effective founder and leader of the new community. Two years after the settlement, Bishop Carroll wrote that the Carmelites had been "a salutary example to the people of the vicinity, and their singular piety has moved even non-Catholics to admiration" (Guilday, p. 490). The fact that both she and Father Neale, the chaplain of the Maryland carmel, were native Marylanders with extensive family connections among the Catholics in southern Maryland was important to the Carmelites' success in America. Relatives and friends provided financial support, as well as many of the first novices who joined the community.

Mother Bernardina died at the Port Tobacco convent in Charles County, Maryland. Clare Joseph, cofounder with Mother Bernardina of the Carmelite order in the United States, succeeded her as prioress of the Port Tobacco carmel.

• Records and artifacts from the founding years of the Carmelite order in America, including some items belonging to Bernardina, are preserved at the Baltimore Carmel. Letters from Bernardina to Bishop John Carroll are in the archives of the Archdiocese of Baltimore. Many manuscripts and artifacts relating to the founding years of the Carmelites in America were displayed at Loyola College during the order's bicentennial year and are described in *Carmel 200: Baltimore Carmel Archival Exhibit*, the catalog published for the 11–17 Aug. 1990 exhibit. Another bicentennial anniversary publication is Constance FitzGerald, ed., *The Carmelite Adventure*, Carmelite Sources, vol. 2 (1990), which includes Clare Joseph's diary of the founding voyage to America in 1790 and a facsimile of Bernardina's profession in 1755. Bernardina's own brief account of the founding voyage, from the archives of the Carmelite Convent at Lanherne, England, is printed in Peter Guilday, *The Life and Times of John Carroll* (1922), pp. 488–89.

GREGORY A. STIVERSON

MATTHEWS, Artie (15 Nov. 1888–25 Oct. 1958), musician and educator, was born in Braidwood, Illinois. His parents' names are unknown. He spent his childhood in Springfield, Illinois, where his family moved when he was a young child. Matthews expressed an early interest in music, and historical accounts credit his mother as his first piano teacher, although he later took lessons from local teachers. A trip to St. Louis, Missouri, in 1904 exposed Matthews to the major African-American performers of ragtime, the dominant popular music of the time. Upon returning to Springfield, Matthews learned ragtime from local performers.

Sometime in 1907 or 1908, Matthews settled in St. Louis, where he remained for the next seven or eight years, with some excursions to Chicago. While there he studied theory, arranging, composition, and organ at the Keeton School of Music. He developed into an excellent pianist, composer, and arranger, and his reputation led to his being sought by a variety of writers and publishers of music, including Barrett's Theatorium and publisher John Stark. He functioned as arranger for the first published song with "blues" in the title, singer Baby Seals's "The Baby Seals Blues" (1912). Matthews also served as musical director for Turpin's Booker T. Washington Theater, where he was responsible for composing and arranging the music for the many variety and vaudeville shows appearing weekly.

During his time in St. Louis, Matthews made outstanding contributions with his own compositions in the genres of blues and ragtime. His blues composition "The Weary Blues" (1915) was very popular and has become an American standard. Matthews also composed a series of five ragtime compositions known as *The Pastime Rags*. They are recognized as "classics" in the tradition of ragtime composition and feature innovative and advanced approaches. For instance, "Pastime Rag #4" features dissonant clusters and atonal segments, while "Pastime Rag #1" introduces a walking bass line in strain C. Matthews made significant contributions to refining and extending the melodic, harmonic, and rhythmic approaches to ragtime composition and performance. In their book *The Art of Ragtime*, Schafer and Riedel spoke of *The Pastime Rags* as constituting "a compendium of ragtime techniques."

In 1915 Matthews moved to Chicago, where he was active as a church organist and studio teacher. In 1916 he settled permanently in Cincinnati, Ohio, accepting a position as organist and choir director for the St. Andrew's Episcopal Church. While serving in these capacities, Matthews continued to expand his musical skills and knowledge. He studied organ and theory with Professor W. S. Sterling of the Metropolitan College of Music and Dramatic Arts, receiving a diploma in 1918. In 1920 he married Anna Howard; they had no children.

While Matthews was able to pursue his musical education, he recognized that racism and segregation denied such opportunities to many other African Americans in Cincinnati. In order to provide music education for African Americans that would develop talent and open up new career opportunities, Matthews and his wife—also an accomplished musician and educator—established the Cosmopolitan School of Music in Cincinnati in 1921. The school was divided into four departments of instruction: applied music (performance), theoretical music, music education (public school music), and speech and dramatic art. The school also offered a course in the history of Negro music. The Cosmopolitan School of Music became one of the best-equipped and best-staffed private music schools in the area. Its highest enrollment was over 150 students, including many who were working toward a college degree.

Along with operating the Cosmopolitan School of Music, Matthews was a leader and activist in the Cincinnati community. He likewise continued to work as a composer and arranger. In 1922 he established the Cosmopolitan School of Music Press and published *Ethiopia*, a religious anthem for voices and organ (piano) or orchestra with a nationalistic theme similar to those expressed by other African-American artists of the Harlem Renaissance era. In 1924 he served as musical director for Marian Anderson's first Cincinnati recital. In 1928 he pursued advanced studies in music at New York University and in 1929 became choral director for the Cincinnati Public Recreation Commission, a position he kept for seventeen years. The decade of the 1920s also saw Matthews begin a thirty-year service as secretary-treasurer for the African American Musicians' Union, Local 814. He continued his involvement with African-American sacred music by serving as choir director and organist for various black church congregations.

Despite the death of Anna Howard Matthews in July 1930, the Cosmopolitan School of Music became a major music education institution, establishing cooperative links with Wilberforce University and Knoxville College, both historically black institutions of higher education. Matthews's efforts included gaining the support of sensitive whites in the Cincinnati community. In 1934 a series of meetings between Matthews, the Race Relations Committee of the Cincinnati Women's City Club, and administrators at the University of Cincinnati resulted in an agreement that placed the Cosmopolitan School of Music on the university's accredited list of affiliated music schools. This agreement afforded African Americans attending the Cosmopolitan School of Music the opportunity to earn a bachelor of music education, thus enabling them to pursue careers in music education. Matthews experienced a personal tragedy when his second wife, Beryl Winston, and their unborn child died during childbirth in September 1935, just fifteen months after their marriage.

In 1938 Matthews's contributions were recognized when Wilberforce University conferred an honorary doctor of music degree on him. That same year Matthews was active in establishing Cincinnati's annual summer "Festival of Negro Music," which continued until the mid-1950s and featured such artists as Paul Robeson, Clarence Cameron White, R. Nathaniel Dett, and Todd Duncan. Matthews served as organizer and music director for these events.

In the 1940s Matthews served as musical director for local African-American World War II patriotic events, arranged music for the Cincinnati Symphony Orchestra and Cincinnati Summer Opera, and continued his music evolution through summer studies at Northwestern University. In December 1951 Matthews married for a third time, to Hazel Anderson. They had one child, a son. During this decade, Matthews continued to direct and lead the Cosmopolitan School of Music and serve the black church as organist, choral director, and minister of music until his death in Cincinnati.

Artie Matthews's legacy reflects his multidimensional capacities. He was a pioneering and innovative composer and pianist who created some of the most significant ragtime music of the twentieth century. For over three and a half decades, Matthews's Cosmopolitan School of Music provided musical training and education for hundreds of African Americans, thus providing career opportunities as performers, arrangers, composers, and educators. His achievements are all the more significant because they were accomplished in the face of overt racial prejudice.

• Matthews's papers are in the possession of his family and not accessible to the public. The most important source for his St. Louis years is Rudi Blesh and Harriet Janis, *They All Played Ragtime* (1950). For more information concerning his ragtime contributions, see Peter Gammond, *Scott Joplin and the Ragtime Era* (1976); David A. Jasen and Trebor Jay Tichenor, *Rags and Ragtime* (1978); and John Hasse, *Ragtime: Its History, Composers, and Music* (1985). See Rudi Blesh, *Classic Piano Rags* (1973), for the complete *Pastime Rags*. See W. P. Dabney, *Cincinnati's Colored Citizens* (1926), and Frank M. Fox, "Artie Matthews: A Cincinnati Legend," *The Classic Rag*, Feb. 1978. pp. 5–7, for Matthews's Cincinnati years. An obituary is in the *Cincinnati Enquirer*, 28 Oct. 1958.

LEONARD L. BROWN

MATTHEWS, Brander (21 Feb. 1852–31 Mar. 1929), author, scholar, and teacher, was born James Brander Matthews in New Orleans, Louisiana, the son of Edward Matthews, a prosperous broker in cotton, real estate, and railroads, and Virginia Brander. Educated privately in Europe and in New York City, where his father settled the family when Matthews was seven, he received his B.A. (1871) and M.A. (1874) from Columbia College. In 1873 Matthews married British actress Ada S. Smith; they had one daughter. That same year, he completed a law degree at Columbia, in preparation for managing the fortune he would inherit. However, when the financial panic of 1873 destroyed the family wealth, Matthews was left largely free to pursue his literary interests, particularly his enthusiasm for the theater. Although he worked for several years as a lawyer in his father's New York City office, he devoted what time he could to studying, writing, and reviewing drama. "From my youth up, my strongest literary ambition was to write plays," Matthews recalled in his autobiography, *These Many Years* (1917). His concerns with structure and technique, derived from his study of French neoclassical drama and nineteenth-century French comedy, would become lifelong preoccupations, influencing Matthews's conceptions of fiction and poetry as well.

He served his dramatic apprenticeship in the 1870s, doing English adaptations of light French plays. The next two decades, Matthews authored original plays, solely and in collaboration with others. Six of his plays were performed in New York and two of these were produced throughout the country for several seasons. He also wrote theater and book reviews, articles on European (particularly French) and American drama, and short fiction for various magazines, including *Galaxy*, *Appleton's Journal*, *Scribner's Monthly*, the *Critic*, and *Saturday Review*. His best efforts in fiction emerged in three forgotten but creditable volumes of brief, vivid episodes set in New York City: *Vignettes of Manhattan* (1894), *Outlines in Local Color* (1898), and *Vistas of New York* (1912); Matthews termed them "sketches" or "etchings."

Matthews also wrote literary criticism. His *French Dramatists of the Nineteenth Century* (1881) was the first scholarly examination, in French or English, of the emergence of romantic drama in France. Highly regarded, the book went through five editions in Matthews's lifetime. *Pen and Ink: Papers on Subjects of More or Less Importance* (1888) reflects his growing interest in fiction and in poetry. With fellow drama critic Laurence Hutton, he edited *Actors and Actresses of Great Britain and the United States, from the Days of David Garrick to the Present* (1886), a five-volume work blending biography, criticism, and anecdote, calculated to make theater more familiar and appealing to American audiences.

By the 1890s Matthews was the leading American authority on drama. Asked in 1891 to offer literature courses at his alma mater, he was named professor of literature at Columbia the next year. In December 1893 a celebration in his honor was given in New York City by some of the nation's foremost literary figures, including William Dean Howells, *Century* editor Richard Watson Gilder, and Mark Twain, who delivered the evening's final speech. In 1899 Columbia established for Matthews the chair of professor of dramatic literature, the first such position in an American college or university; he would hold the title until his retirement in 1924. Literary life became for him the source of social life and social action as well. Matthews was a member of various literary clubs in New York and London, including the Athenaeum, to which Matthew Arnold proposed his membership. Throughout the last decade of the nineteenth century and the first quarter of the twentieth, he was an outspoken advocate of international copyright, of simplified spelling, and of organizations promoting the development and appreciation of American letters. Matthews served as president of the Modern Language Association (1910) and of the National Institute of Arts and Letters

(1913), as well as chancellor of the American Academy of Arts and Letters (1922–1924).

Despite these broadening professional responsibilities, Matthews remained an active scholar and teacher. He wrote a popular text for high school students, *An Introduction to the Study of American Literature* (1896). Like the earlier *Actors and Actresses of Great Britain and the United States*, it was a mixture of biography and anecdote, and it sold 250,000 copies in the twenty-five years following its initial publication. Other works coming from his courses were *The Development of the Drama* (1903), *A Study of Versification* (1911), and *Suggestions for Teachers of American Literature* (1925). In *The Tocsin of Revolt, and Other Essays* (1922), Matthews expressed his hostility to modernist experimentation and its "amazing slovenliness of craftsmanship."

After retirement, Matthews published little. The title piece of his final volume, *Rip Van Winkle Goes to the Play, and Other Essays on Plays and Players* (1926), is an apt expression of his situation in the teens and twenties—he had indeed fallen out of touch. When Matthews died, in New York City, the *New York Times* characterized him as "one of the last of the 'eminent victorians.'" Today he is recalled only as one of the defenders of James Fenimore Cooper derided by Mark Twain. However, Matthews deserves a less dubious reputation as a pioneer in American theater criticism.

• Matthews's manuscripts and papers are in the Butler Library at Columbia University. His works include *His Father's Son; a Novel of New York* (1895), *The Action and the Word; a Novel of New York* (1900), and *A Confident Tomorrow; a Novel of New York* (1900), and several volumes of short fiction, including *A Family Tree, and Other Stories* (1889), *Tales of Fantasy and Fact* (1896), and, with H. C. Bunner, *In Partnership: Studies in Storytelling* (1884). Many of his plays also were published, but all are long forgotten. His theater commentary includes *The Theaters of Paris* (1880), *A Study of the Drama* (1910), *Molière, His Life and His Works* (1910), *Shakspere as a Playwright* (1913), *On Acting* (1914), and *A Book about the Theater* (1916). His most important work on fiction is *The Philosophy of the Short Story* (1901). He also wrote perceptive pieces on *vers de société* or "familiar verse," a light but intricate poetic form often following complex French patterns; among these essays are "Two Latter-Day Lyrists," one of the selections from *Pen and Ink: Papers on Subjects of More or Less Importance* (1888); and "Familiar Verse" from *Gateways to Literature and Other Essays* (1912).

For his importance as a critic and scholar of drama, see William Peterfield Trent, "Brander Matthews as a Dramatic Critic," *International Monthly* 4 (1901): 289–93; and Jack E. Bender, "Brander Matthews, Critic of the Theatre," *Educational Theatre Journal* 12 (1960): 169–76. For overviews of Matthews's contributions to the theory and practice of short fiction, see Blanche Colton Williams, *Our Short Story Writers* (1920); and Edward J. O'Brien, *The Advance of the American Short Story*, rev. ed. (1931). Obituaries are in the *New York Times*, 1 Apr. 1929, and *Scribner's Magazine*, June 1929, pp. 82–87.

WILLIAM J. HUG

MATTHEWS, Burnita Shelton (28 Dec. 1894–25 Apr. 1988), women's rights activist and the first woman federal trial judge, was born in Copiah County, Mississippi, the daughter of Burnell Shelton, a plantation owner and county official, and Lora Drew Barlow. The only girl in a family of five children, Matthews aspired to follow her older brother to law school, but when her mother died when she was sixteen her father sent her to study piano and voice at the Cincinnati Conservatory of Music. He said he thought she would be "happier doing what women did down there in Mississippi." For a few years she supported herself by teaching music in public schools in Texas, Georgia, and Mississippi, and in 1917 she married her high school sweetheart, Percy Ashley Matthews, now a Washington lawyer; the couple did not have children.

When the United States entered World War I, Matthews took a Civil Service Exam for a clerkship. In 1918 she accepted a job at the Veterans Administration in Washington, D.C., and enrolled in evening classes at the National University Law School (subsequently merged with George Washington University). She earned an LL.B. in 1919, LL.M. and M.P.L. degrees in 1920 and was admitted to the bar of the District of Columbia in 1920 and to the bars of Mississippi and the U.S. Supreme Court in 1924.

Once in Washington, Matthews joined the National Woman's Party (NWP), picketing the White House for woman suffrage and stuffing envelopes with equal enthusiasm. Her concern for equal rights for women was to be lifelong, and prior to her appointment to the federal bench it was closely intertwined with her legal work. When she was refused employment with the VA as a lawyer on the basis of her sex, she opened her own practice, specializing in real estate transactions. At times she was in practice with another NWP member, Laura M. Berrien, and with Rebekah Greathouse.

After passage of the Suffrage Amendment in 1920, Matthews turned her attention to the Equal Rights Amendment (ERA) and to lifting legal barriers against women in the states. Repeatedly asked by Alice Paul to volunteer her time to look up legal discrimination against women by the states, in the late fall of 1921 she requested and received a retainer to oversee the NWP's Legal Research Department. There she directed a massive research project to create a legal digest of the laws of every state; each included an assessment of the legal position of women in the state, the labor laws affecting women employees, and a report analyzing the state constitution as its language pertained to women. She drafted corrective legislation to remedy inequities for women; NWP members submitted her drafts to state legislatures. Among those enacted were the law removing the disqualification of women as jurors in the District of Columbia; laws eliminating a preference for males over females in inheritance in Arkansas, the District of Columbia, and New York; acts giving teachers equal pay regardless of sex in Maryland and New Jersey; and a South Carolina law allowing married women to sue and be sued without joinder of husbands. She also drafted the 1931 and 1934 amendments to the national laws extending the citizenship rights of women, and in 1935 she wrote an *amici curiae* brief in *Morehead v. Tipaldo*, asking the Supreme Court to declare the New York State minimum wage law unconstitutional as discriminating against women.

Matthews spoke and wrote extensively on inequities in the legal status of women and in favor of the ERA; many of her articles were published in the NWP journal, *Equal Rights*. After the ERA was introduced into successive Congresses, she was a frequent witness before congressional committees, testifying on legal aspects of the amendment.

As counsel for the NWP and adjacent property owners in opposition to litigation brought by the United States in 1927 to acquire property across the street from the Capitol as the site for a new Supreme Court building, she argued that the NWP building was of historic value as the "Old Brick Capitol" from the era of President James Monroe. She failed to stop the destruction of the NWP's headquarters but won a generous settlement that enabled the NWP to purchase historic "Belmont House" on Capitol Hill. Also in the 1920s Matthews represented newspaper correspondent Ruby A. Black and won a ruling from the State Department establishing the precedent that a woman who does not change her name at the time of her marriage does not need to assume her husband's name to obtain a passport.

An active participant in organizations of women lawyers, Matthews was president of the Women's Bar Association of the District of Columbia (1925–1926) and of the National Association of Women Lawyers (1934–1935). During 1934–1935 she also served as associate editor of the *Women Lawyer's Journal*. From 1933 to 1939 she taught the law of evidence at Washington College of Law (now part of the American University).

A massive lobbying effort by women nationwide, and a personal visit to President Harry S. Truman by India Edwards, head of the Women's Division of the Democratic National Committee, secured the appointment of Matthews as the first woman in the United States to serve as a federal district judge. Her recess appointment to the District of Columbia district took effect on 21 October 1949; she received a permanent appointment from Truman, after Senate confirmation, on 7 April 1950. Matthews took senior judge status in 1968 but never resigned from the bench; she accepted assignment to the Court of Customs and Patent Appeals in 1969 and 1970 and heard her final district court case at age eighty-eight. Her husband died in 1969.

On becoming a judge, Matthews curtailed her public activities on behalf of the Equal Rights Amendment, believing it improper for a judge to attempt to influence the passage of legislation that she might later be called on to interpret. Matthews, however, continued her personal crusade to advance the position of women by selecting only female law clerks, "to show her confidence in women."

Among the cases she thought noteworthy were *Monroe v. United States* (1956), *Kyne v. Leedom* (1958), *United States v. Wise* (1962), *Fitzgerald v. Hampton* (1972), *United States v. McSurely* (1972), and

Evans v. Sheraton Park Hotel (1974). She presided over a number of major trials, including the 1957 bribery trial of James R. Hoffa, at which the Teamsters Union leader was acquitted and during which Matthews's life was threatened. Senator Joseph R. McCarthy and singer Paul Robeson also appeared in her court.

Of Matthews as a judge, her law clerk Betty Poston Jones wrote in 1974, she "combines a brilliant mind with splendidly reliable instincts and a great deal of common sense. A leader, not a follower, she has never been reluctant to administer the law as she sees it, even when she has stood alone. It is legend that she has been the least 'reversed' judge on the district court" (Introduction to *Pathfinder*, p. v). Her portrait was the first of a woman judge to hang in the District of Columbia Courthouse (1973). She died in Washington, D.C., and was buried in Copiah County, Mississippi.

Although Matthews was less visible than some other women leaders in the postsuffrage period, her contributions to improving the legal status of women were substantial and lasting. As a jurist, she was capable and respected, and by her example and her nurturing of young women attorneys she improved the atmosphere for the next generation of women on the bench.

• Judge Matthews meticulously documented her professional career in ten scrapbooks and other papers donated to the Schlesinger Library, Radcliffe College; she placed personal and family papers at the Mississippi Department of Archives and History, Jackson. Microfilms of the scrapbooks are available at the American University and at the Mississippi Department of Archives and History as well as at Schlesinger Library. Many letters and reports are included in the micropublication of the *Papers of the National Woman's Party, 1913–1974* (1979) and in the papers of other members of the NWP, including Jane Norman Smith and Emma Guffey Miller, also at Schlesinger Library. Her oral history, *Pathfinder in the Legal Aspects of Women*, was recorded by Amelia R. Fry in 1973 as part of the Suffragists Oral History Project of the Regional Oral History Office, the Bancroft Library, University of California, Berkeley; appendices to the oral history include a few articles and speeches by and about Matthews. There is a brief biography by Lee Berger Anderson in *Women Lawyers Journal* 59 (Summer 1973): 92–94, and "Leader of Women's Rights Movement Recalls Suffrage Fight and Appointment to Bench," *Women Lawyers Journal* 71 (Summer 1985): 6–10, reprints an interview with Judge Matthews from the March 1985 issue of *The Third Branch: Bulletin of the Federal Courts*. Obituaries are in *The New York Times* and the *Washington Post*, 28 Apr. 1988.

PATRICIA MILLER KING

MATTHEWS, Francis Patrick (15 Mar. 1887–18 Oct. 1952), secretary of the navy, was born in Albion, Nebraska, the son of Patrick Henry Matthews, a merchant, and Mary Ann Sullivan. Although his father died when Matthews was eleven, he was able to complete his secondary schooling in Albion and then work his way through Creighton University in Omaha by waiting on tables and doing janitorial chores. He graduated in 1910 and completed his legal studies at Creighton three years later. Matthews was admitted to the bar in 1913 and practiced law in Omaha, where he became a partner in the firm of Frandenburg and Matthews. He was also active in several business ventures. In 1914 he married Mary Claire Hughes; they had six children.

Although he lost heavily in the 1929 stock market crash, Matthews was able to rebuild his assets while continuing to devote time to civic endeavors, partisan politics, and public service. He served on the Nebraska State Board of the Knights of Columbus and later as supreme knight (1939–1945); was counsel for the Reconstruction Finance Corporation in the Nebraska-Wyoming region; was an officer in the U.S. Chamber of Commerce; and was active in the United Service Organizations during World War II, becoming a USO vice president. In 1944 he traveled extensively in Europe and North Africa to organize relief work in liberated areas. Already well known to many leading Democrats, he was named by President Harry S. Truman in 1946 to the fifteen-member Civil Rights Committee chaired by Charles E. Wilson. An ardent anticommunist, Matthews chaired a special U.S. Chamber of Commerce study group to prepare a report, publicly released in 1946, on communist infiltration in the United States. Matthews helped carry the Nebraska delegation for Truman at the 1948 Democratic National Convention, and Truman appointed him secretary of the navy the following year.

At the time of Matthews's appointment, the Defense Department was in turmoil. Secretary of Defense Louis Johnson had imposed a controversial program of financial austerity that was sure to antagonize one or more of the three armed services and its partisans in Congress and the media. Navy leaders had earlier accepted cutbacks in other areas to secure funding for the construction of a supercarrier larger than any that had been built during the Second World War. The new carrier in turn would have made possible the use of a new generation of aircraft. In April 1949, however, Johnson canceled construction of the carrier, the keel of which had already been laid, prompting Secretary of the Navy John Sullivan to resign in protest. At Johnson's behest, Matthews was nominated to replace him. Johnson and Matthews had known each other in Democratic party affairs, and it was assumed they would work well together. Candidly admitting he knew next to nothing about maritime matters, Matthews was dubbed "the rowboat secretary" by the press.

Instead of dwelling on the cancellation of the supercarrier, Matthews sought to defend other naval programs and publicly emphasized the importance of the navy to the national defense. The postwar navy maintained powerful forces in the Atlantic, the Pacific, and the Mediterranean; was opening more opportunities for women and for blacks; and was improving its capabilities in antisubmarine warfare. Matthews's assertions, however, failed to reassure senior naval aviation officers, who openly criticized the civilian leaders of the defense establishment. During hearings held by the House Armed Services Committee in the fall of

1949 on the procurement of the air force's new B-36 bomber, naval officers identified the many shortcomings of the bomber and questioned the wisdom of relying on the capability of the B-36 to deliver nuclear weaponry while ignoring the need to modernize naval aviation by funding the supercarrier. Matthews was particularly chagrined when Chief of Naval Operations Louis Denfeld, the navy's top uniformed officer, broke with Defense Department policy and joined other naval officers in criticizing the B-36 program. Matthews's predicament stemmed, in part, from his aloof administrative style. Thus, while Secretary of the Air Force Stuart Symington worked closely with air force officers in preparing the air force's position at the hearings, Matthews had remained uninvolved in the preparation of the navy's case by uniformed officers. Consequently, Matthews was unaware of the depth of resentment many naval officers felt about the funding of the B-36 and the cancellation of the supercarrier. Some of these points were made during congressional testimony; even greater bitterness surfaced in letters leaked by senior naval officers to the press. The whole affair became known as the "revolt of the admirals."

In his own testimony, Matthews did seek to call attention to the needs of naval aviation. In the main, however, he endorsed Johnson's leadership of the Defense Department. Much of what Denfeld and other officers subsequently stated therefore appeared to contradict the points Matthews had made. Once the hearings had been concluded, Matthews gained permission to transfer Denfeld to a command in London, England. In response, Denfeld retired effective 1 March 1950 and soon authored three articles that appeared in the popular magazine *Collier's*. In them Denfeld accused Johnson and Matthews of vindictiveness and of favoring the air force, whose leaders, he claimed, seemed to be motivated in part by hostility toward naval aviation.

Matthews was fortunate in obtaining as Denfeld's successor the astute Forrest Sherman, an experienced carrier officer, who handled himself adroitly in Washington. Matthews was thus able to maintain his loyalty to Johnson and to the principle of unification of the armed services. Even before the Korean War began in June 1950, the navy had received overwhelming approval from the House Armed Services Committee to fund the modernization of many existing ships and to construct the first nuclear submarine. Johnson concurred with these increased appropriations. Once the Korean War began, the navy had the opportunity to remind Americans and official Washington of its prowess in amphibious operations and in delivering supplies, and also of the versatility of carrier aviation. With Johnson now gone from the cabinet, Sherman, who had held back on the supercarrier while he studied the various proposals for its design, sought and received approval for the new carrier in early 1951. By this time Matthews had come to appreciate the navy's need to have its own trained public relations specialists at a high level. Morale within the navy improved, as did Matthews's reputation.

Matthews, however, unwittingly antagonized President Truman early in the war by remarking in a speech in Boston that he could foresee the possibility of initiating preventive war against the communist powers. Several observers speculated that Matthews's own tenure as secretary of the navy was in jeopardy. Matthews nevertheless retained his position until June 1951, when, with Johnson long since gone from office, Truman offered Matthews the post of ambassador to Ireland, which Matthews accepted. He died while on a visit to Omaha, Nebraska.

Little in Matthews's previous experience had prepared him for leadership of the navy. At a time when defense funds were being slashed, the air force, which alone had the capability to use atomic weapons, seemed to be getting much of what it wanted. Legitimate questions could be—and were—raised about placing excessive reliance on the atom bomb while slighting America's capability to use conventional weapons. Matthews's failure to pay heed to public relations and to ascertain the thoughts of naval officers on troublesome issues placed him in a bad light during the 1949 hearings, where he seemed at odds with the navy's ranking officers. Once Matthews gained more understanding of his role and of the navy's needs, he received more respect from both the leadership of the Congress and the naval service.

• Matthews's papers are at the Harry S. Truman Library in Independence, Mo. The most important source is Paolo E. Coletta, "Francis P. Matthews," in *American Secretaries of the Navy*, vol. 2, *1913–1972*, ed. Coletta (1980). Denfeld's three articles are "Reprisal: Why I Was Fired," *Collier's*, 18 Mar. 1950; "The Only Carrier the Air Force Ever Sank," *Collier's*, 25 Mar. 1950; and "The Nation Needs the Navy," *Collier's*, 1 Apr. 1950. E. B. Potter, *Admiral Arleigh Burke: A Biography* (1990), and Jeffrey G. Barlow, *Revolt of the Admirals: The Fight for Naval Aviation, 1945–1950* (1995), provide two of the most illuminating secondary accounts of the episode. On the important theme of Matthews's anticommunism see Peter Irons, "American Business and the Origins of McCarthyism: The Cold War Crusade of the United States Chamber of Commerce," in *The Specter*, ed. Robert Griffith and Athan Theoharis (1974). An obituary is in the *New York Times*, 19 Oct. 1952.

LLOYD J. GRAYBAR

MATTHEWS, Harrison Freeman (26 May 1899–19 Oct. 1986), career diplomat, was born in Baltimore, Maryland, the son of Henry Clay Matthews, a merchant, and Bertha Belknap Freeman. His childhood years were spent alternating between the comfort of a fine home in Baltimore during the cold months and an equally comfortable family farm in nearby Cockeysville during the warm months. He studied history and international law at Princeton, earning a B.A. in 1921 and an M.A. the following year. He completed his formal studies with a year at l'Ecole Libre des Science Politiques in Paris in 1923. In 1925 he married Elizabeth Luke, with whom he had two children.

During Matthews's thirty-eight years with the U.S. Foreign Service he was frequently near the center of pivotal and, at times, world-changing events. Although his presence was often obscured by the imposing personalities of the statesmen with whom he worked, his subtle influence was significant. After a rather typical beginning in the Foreign Service with an entry-level post at Budapest in 1924, he was moved to Bogota, where, in 1927, he began to cultivate some expertise in Latin American affairs. In 1930 this experience gained for him a coordinating role in Washington over the State Department's Colombian and Cuban desks. After serving as assistant chief of the Latin American division from 1931 to 1933 he was transferred to Havana, where he became an early advocate of the ascending General Fulgencio Batista.

In 1937 Matthews was transferred to Europe, a continent with which he would be associated for the remainder of his career. In 1939, after serving under William Bullitt in Paris, he was dispatched to Spain to open relations with Francisco Franco's regime. Back in Washington when Germany began its western thrust in 1940, Matthews was in a position to provide critical information about France and French ability to withstand an invasion. After his return to France he was ordered to follow the French government to Vichy to provide guidance to a new deputy ambassador. While there he successfully worked with the U.S. ambassador, Admiral William D. Leahy, to discourage the government of Marshall Henri Philippe Pétain from conceding so much to Germany as to hamper a liberating Allied offensive in North Africa. In 1941 Matthews was brought back to Washington before being reassigned to London. Called to the White House two weeks after the United States entered World War II, he participated in a high-level meeting with Franklin Roosevelt, Winston Churchill, and Harry Hopkins. At that meeting Matthews provided critical insight into the likely reaction of the French to the anticipated Allied offensive in North Africa. En route to his London post he saw to the discreet transmission of plans for this potential offensive to the isolated Vichy government. He later accompanied General Dwight Eisenhower's entourage to Gibraltar, where he participated in the plans for the North African effort and helped to draft the so-called Clark-Darlan Agreement that provided for the cooperation of French forces.

In 1943 Matthews returned to Washington as director of European affairs and the next year joined Deputy Secretary of State Edward Stettinius in England to discuss plans for postwar Europe. He assisted in the preparations for, and participated in, the Yalta Conference of 1945. At that conference Matthews articulated for the U.S. delegation the American position on postwar Europe. This included the question of structure and form for the provisional government of Poland and for Allied plans for a defeated Germany. Matthews was part of a three-member committee that drafted a surrender clause for Germany granting the Allies wide latitude for Germany's disarmament, demilitarization, and dismemberment. He attended all of the Big Three meetings at Yalta, produced one of the most reliable records of those meetings, and

helped to persuade Roosevelt that France should participate in the occupation and administration of postwar Germany. After the European war ended Matthews helped to prepare for and took part in the Potsdam Conference with Secretary of State James Byrnes. He also joined most of the high-level postwar meetings, including those of the Council of Foreign Ministers.

As one of the professional diplomats close to the center of U.S. policy formulation, Matthews's influence over America's position in the developing Cold War was noteworthy. From his office at the State Department, he watched in frustration as the Soviet Union defaulted on pledges for the postwar political structure of Eastern Europe. After initially advocating attempts to redeem U.S.–Soviet cooperation, he soon joined Byrnes to call for a rigid nonconciliatory policy toward the communist power. In 1947 Matthews was named chair of the State-War-Navy Coordinating Committee that reestablished a working relationship between the Department of State and the Pentagon. While serving in that capacity he offered critical support for deliberations over the substance and implementation of the European Recovery Plan. Also in 1947 President Harry Truman named him ambassador to Sweden, where he struggled unsuccessfully during the next two years to bring that nation into the emerging North Atlantic Treaty Organization (NATO). In 1950 Secretary of State Dean Acheson called him to Washington to serve as deputy under secretary of state, the first Foreign Service officer to hold that rank. While in that position he attended all substantive meetings on the Korean War and resumed his role as liaison between the Department of State and the Pentagon. In 1953 he was named secretary of state ad interim between the resignation of Acheson and the installation of John Foster Dulles.

After continuing briefly under Dulles in Washington as deputy under secretary, Matthews served as ambassador to the Netherlands from 1953 to 1957 and ambassador to Austria from 1957 to 1962. One of the first American diplomats to attain the rank of career ambassador, a position created in 1956, Matthews expended much of his time and energy at The Hague balancing Dutch irritation over U.S. intrusion in Indonesian affairs with Washington's desire to build up Dutch forces in NATO. Among his last duties with the Foreign Service was the preparation for and hosting of the Vienna Summit for Nikita Khrushchev and John Kennedy in 1961. He retired from the Foreign Service the following year but soon joined the Board of National Estimates at the behest of the Central Intelligence Agency and served simultaneously as the American chairman of the Permanent Joint Board on Defense, Canada–United States, for the remainder of the decade. Matthews's first wife had died in 1955. Two years later he had married Helen Lewis Skouland, with whom he had no children. She died in 1966, and the next year he married Elizabeth Bluntschli. They had no children. Matthews spent the last years of his life pursuing the fruits of well-deserved retirement and died in Washington.

• Much of Matthews's official correspondence, notes, and memoranda can be found in the appropriate volumes of the *Foreign Relations of the United States*. Because Matthews's career parallels the emergence of the United States as a super-power, it is an invaluable reflection of U.S. diplomacy in the twentieth century. Unfortunately, the best source for such an investigation of his career is a privately published memoir titled *Memories of a Passing Era* (1973) that is not readily accessible. An oral history record is available on Matthews from the *Truman Library Oral History Collection*. The memoirs and diaries of the presidents and secretaries of state from the administration of Franklin Roosevelt to that of John Kennedy also are useful as are more general works such as Hugh De Santis, *The Diplomacy of Silence* (1980). For official documents, see the H. Freeman Matthews–John D. Hickerson Files in Record Group 59 and the regional and international conference, commission, and advisory files in Record Group 43 at the National Archives, Washington, D.C. An obituary is in the *New York Times*, 21 Oct. 1986.

DONALD A. RAKESTRAW

MATTHEWS, Herbert Lionel (10 Jan. 1900–30 July 1977), journalist, was born in New York City, the son of Samuel Matthews and Frances Lewis. Little is known of his childhood. After high school, during World War I, he enlisted as a private in the Army Tank Corps but was disappointed that the war was over by the time he reached France. He returned to New York and entered Columbia University, where he studied romance languages and medieval history. His interest in journalism developed slowly. After graduating with an A.B. in 1922, he joined the *New York Times* as a stenographer in the business department. Working nights, Matthews worked days on postgraduate work at Columbia, earning a yearlong fellowship in Italy to study medieval history, philosophy, and the works of Dante during 1925 and 1926. When he returned to the *Times*, he was assigned to the news department as a secretary. Showing a talent for writing, he advanced to reporter and, later, to the cable desk. In 1929 Matthews was chosen to represent the *Times* on a Far East junket to study Asian politics. In 1931 he married Nancie Edith Cross, an English-woman with whom he would have two children, and became a *Times* correspondent in Paris. There he began a career that would make him one of the most controversial journalists in history.

Knowing Italian, Spanish, and French allowed Matthews to move easily about pre–World War II Europe. At first an admirer of fascism, Matthews traveled with Benito Mussolini's troops when they conquered Ethiopia in 1935. He was often the only American reporter with the Italian troops, giving *New York Times* readers the most extensive battle accounts. But Matthews's sympathy for Mussolini caused American editors to doubt his cables and exposed him to accusations of biased reporting. It was his first long-distance fight with his editors in New York over whether his reporting could be trusted. The editors sympathized with Ethiopia, causing them to discount Matthews's

predictions of an Italian victory. When Mussolini's troops prevailed, Matthews wrote nonstop for eleven hours and filed the longest single story published to that time by the *Times*.

The fight with his editors, however, continued the next year when Matthews, by this time disillusioned with fascism, reported—with Ernest Hemingway and Martha Gellhorn, among others—on the Spanish Civil War from the Loyalist side. Before long he was being accused by Catholics in and out of the newsroom of being a communist. The war pitted Spain's leftist government against the rebel right-wing forces of Francisco Franco, who had the support of the Catholic church and of fascist Italy and Germany. The civil war became an international cause and a warm-up for World War II. Catholic leaders in New York criticized Matthews's reporting from Spain, and Catholic editors at the *Times* doubted his cables (Salisbury, pp. 452–53). From his exclusive, eyewitness report that Italian bombers and tanks had entered the war on Franco's side, the *Times* deleted all references to Italian troops, thereby delaying public recognition that the civil war had expanded to include foreign troops.

Matthews went on to produce distinguished reporting from Italy and India during World War II, after which, from 1945 to 1949, he headed the *Times* London bureau. Accusations of biased reporting continued to plague his career but not in some quarters. Hemingway, for one, described Matthews as the "straightest, the ablest and the bravest correspondent, a gaunt lighthouse of honesty" (quoted in Talese, p. 54). His reporting did indeed prove to be accurate, yet Matthews himself never claimed to be objective, arguing instead that a war correspondent ought to be honest about his biases. "In condemning 'bias,'" Matthews wrote in *The Education of a Correspondent*, "one rejects the only factors which really matter—honesty, understanding and thoroughness. A reader has a right to ask for all the facts; he has no right to demand that a journalist or historian agree with him" (p. 69). In other words, he argued, a journalist should report with both his head and his heart. Within the context of his reportage, Matthews made his biases clear to readers, but he always strove for honesty and accuracy in his reporting of facts. His stories weren't distrusted, except by those readers and editors who disagreed with his interpretation of events. Overall, history has proven him to have been a brilliant journalist whose reports were usually correct and never intentionally wrong to support his personal biases. Although often at odds with some of his editors, he was protected at the *Times* by his close friendship with publisher Arthur Hays Sulzberger and by the admiration of several key staff members, such as A. M. Rosenthal, who rose through the paper's ranks, eventually becoming managing editor in 1968.

In 1949 Matthews returned to New York to write editorials for the *Times* but remained controversial. In 1957 he pretended to be a vacationing American in order to enter Cuba for a clandestine interview with Fidel Castro, then a rebel leader presumed dead. By verifying that Castro was alive, his reports bolstered the revolution and gave Americans their first insight into the man who would become the Marxist dictator of Cuba. Castro insisted to Matthews that he was fighting for a democratic Cuba. When, however, he took power and declared his allegiance to the Soviet Union, critics accused Matthews of having been duped or, worse, collaborating with him. Later, in his book *The Cuban Story* (1961), Matthews argued that although the democratic ideals of the Cuban revolution had not borne fruit, it was in part American antagonism toward him that had pushed Castro to join the communists.

For decades Matthews remained the only American reporter with access to Cuba, but his reputation kept the news department of the *Times* from publishing his reports on the country. His writing on Cuba was confined to the editorial pages. In 1965 he wrote the first *Times* editorials challenging U.S. policy in Vietnam and called for a negotiated settlement. The editorials legitimized antiwar sentiment and helped erode President Lyndon Johnson's support.

After Matthews retired in 1967, he settled in Adelaide, Australia, where he died. During his career Matthews wrote numerous books on international politics and, often risking his life in battle, produced dispatches with stunning details as well as reasoned analysis. One *Times* historian sized up Matthews as a reporter "deeply concerned about [war's] victims, and this concern, together with his sense of history and hypocrisy, brought a dimension and edge to his reporting that was involving and memorable." He was not one who "played it safe with the official version," and his reports provoked readers to "extravagant praise or scorn" (Talese, p. 54). Matthews entered journalism to describe events "as a mere spectator," without moral judgment; ironically, he is remembered primarily as a journalist who, as he wrote, ultimately believed that the task of "true journalism . . . is not mere chronology . . . but placing the event in its proper category as a moral act and judging it as such" (*Education*, pp. 21 and 11).

• There is a collection of Matthews papers at Columbia University. The best biographical material, though it concerns only Matthews's adulthood, is his memoir, *Education of a Correspondent* (1946). His other major works are *Eyewitness in Abyssinia* (1937), *Two Wars and More to Come* (1938), *The Fruits of Fascism* (1943), *Assignment to Austerity*, with Edith Matthews (1950), *The Yoke and the Arrows* (1957; rev. ed. 1961), and *A World in Revolution* (1971). On Cuba see Jerry W. Knudsen, *Herbert L. Matthews and the Cuban Story*, Journalism Monographs (Feb. 1978), and the bibliography therein. His career is also examined in Phillip Knightley, *The First Casualty: From the Crimea to Vietnam: The War Correspondent as Hero, Propagandist, and Myth Maker* (1975); Gay Talese, *The Kingdom and the Power: The Story of the Men Who Influence the Institution That Influences the World, the New York Times* (1969); and Harrison E. Salisbury, *Without Fear or Favor: The New York Times and Its Times* (1980). An obituary is in the *New York Times*, 31 July 1977.

JAMES L. AUCOIN

MATTHEWS, Joseph Brown (28 June 1894–16 July 1966), political activist, was born in Hopkinsville, Kentucky, the son of Burrell Jones Matthews, a businessman and member of the Kentucky legislature, and Fanny Wellborn Brown, a former schoolteacher. When he was an early teenager the family moved to Lexington. In 1915 Matthews graduated from Asbury College in Wilmore, Kentucky. Ordained as a Methodist minister that year, he served as a missionary in Java, teaching indigenous Chinese nationals. A gifted linguist, he translated over 200 hymns into Malay and edited a Malay paper. In 1917 he married Grace Doswell Ison, a fellow missionary; the couple had four children.

Upon returning to the United States in 1921, Matthews earned a B.D. from Drew University (1923), an S.T.M. from Union Theological Seminary (1924), and an M. A. from Columbia University (1924). His master's thesis centered on Sanskrit and Persian elements in Malay. After serving a parish in Bound Brook, New Jersey, for two years, he became professor of Hebrew and the history of religion at Scarritt College for Christian Workers in Nashville, Tennessee, in 1924. Far too radical for the college's trustees and particularly outspoken in favoring racial integration, Matthews resigned his teaching and ministerial position in 1927, after which he taught at two black universities, Fisk in Nashville and Howard in Washington, D.C.

In June 1929 Matthews was appointed one of the two executive secretaries of the pacifist Fellowship of Reconciliation (FOR), and that November he joined the Socialist party. The end of capitalism, he believed, meant the end of war. In December 1933, in protest against the FOR's refusal to sanction class warfare, Matthews resigned his FOR post.

While never a member of the Communist party, Matthews sought to unite all left-wing groups, including, he later said, "Socialists, Stalinists, Lovestonites, Musteites, Trotskyists, and even the I.W.W. [Industrial Workers of the World] and the Socialist Labor Party." He wrote for an equally wide variety of radical journals, including the *New Leader*, *World Tomorrow*, *Soviet Russia Today*, *Daily Worker*, *New Masses*, *Revolutionary Age*, and *Labor Age*. Later Matthews claimed membership in twenty-eight Communist front organizations, holding offices in fifteen. In 1933, for example, he became the first national chairman of the American League against War and Fascism, the leading Communist front in the United States, but resigned within half a year following a Communist-inspired riot at New York's Madison Square Garden. Such activities caused the Socialist party to suspend him for a year. His books included *Traffic in Death—A Few Facts Concerning the International Munitions Industry* (1934), a denunciation of the arms industry; with Ruth Elanda Shallcross, *Partners in Plunder: The Cost of Business Dictatorship* (1935), an indictment of the profit system, the "pro-business" New Deal, and the "pro-capitalist" churches; and *Guinea Pigs No More* (1936), in which he combined his critique of mass advertising with, for the first time, an attack on the Communist party and Soviet economy.

In early 1934 Matthews became vice president of Consumers' Research, an organization that sought to warn buyers of hazardous, poisonous, and shoddy goods. That year he divorced his wife, and in 1936 he married his coauthor, Shallcross. In 1935 three temporary employees were dismissed from Consumers' Research. They protested to the National Labor Relations Board, which ordered their reinstatement, and the employees of Consumers' Research called a strike. Suddenly the leading U.S. advocate of the Popular Front was being attacked by the *Daily Worker* and was convicted by a left-sponsored mock trial held in New York City. Matthews later recalled entering a process of political detachment for two years, during which time he experienced "an ethical revulsion against the Communist movement." In June 1938 he resigned from Consumers' Research.

That August Matthews testified extensively before the House Un-American Activities Committee (HUAC), chaired by Martin Dies. He appeared so knowledgeable that he was appointed the committee's chief investigator and staff director, holding that position from late 1938 until 1945. Though the committee focused primarily on Communist groups, it also investigated Fascist and pro-Japanese organizations. Matthews interrogated witnesses, prepared many committee reports, wrote many of Dies's speeches and magazine articles, and was ghostwriter for Dies's book, *The Trojan Horse in America* (1940). In 1938 Matthews published a rambling autobiography, *Odyssey of a Fellow Traveler*.

After leaving HUAC, Matthews was hired by John A. Clements Associates, the Hearst Corporation public relations firm, as a consultant on communism, in which capacity he maintained files on 500,000 individuals affiliated, so he claimed, with front organizations. In 1949, after another divorce, he married Ruth Inglis; they had no children. In June 1953 Joseph R. McCarthy, chairman of the Senate Permanent Subcommittee on Investigations, appointed Matthews the subcommittee's executive director. Matthews had just published an article in the July 1953 issue of the *American Mercury*, by then a monthly of the radical right edited by Clements. Entitled "Reds and Our Churches," the article claimed in its lead sentence, "The largest single group supporting the Communist apparatus in the United States today is composed of Protestant clergymen." Though he affirmed the loyalty of "the vast majority of American Protestant clergymen," Matthews charged that over the past seventeen years some 7,000 were "party members, fellow-travelers, espionage agents, party-line adherents, and unwitting dupes." The article evoked an immediate rebuke from President Dwight D. Eisenhower and led to Matthews's forced resignation from the subcommittee.

During the 1950s, Matthews frequently wrote for the *American Mercury*, which listed him as a contributing editor. During the 1960s he contributed to the John Birch Society's periodical, *American Opinion*,

and the conservative *National Review* added his name to its masthead. In his last years, he was research director of the Church League of America, an arch-rightist body that maintained dossiers on suspected radicals. He died in New York City.

• Matthews's widow donated voluminous papers concerning political activism from 1920 to 1960 to Duke University. Much Matthews material is in the papers of the Fellowship of Reconciliation, Swarthmore College Peace Collection. In addition to the books listed in the text, Matthews also wrote *Christianity the Way* (1929), a collection of speeches on race. The most thorough account is Nelson L. Dawson, "From Fellow Traveler to Anticommunist: The Odyssey of J. B. Matthews," *Register of the Kentucky Historical Society* 84 (1986): 280–306. For a sensitive treatment, see Murray Kempton, "O'er Moor and Fen: J. B. Matthews and the Multiple Revolution," in *Part of Our Time: Some Monuments and Ruins of the Thirties* (1955). For a critical account, see Paul Hutchinson, "The J. B. Matthews Story," *Christian Century* 70 (29 July 1953): 864–66 . For a eulogy, see Howard Rushmore, "Mr. Anti-Communist," *American Mercury* 76 (May 1953): 79–86. A superior treatment of Matthews's flirtation with pacifism is in Charles Chatfield, *For Peace and Justice: Pacifism in America, 1914–1941* (1971). An obituary is in the *New York Times*, 17 July 1966.

JUSTUS D. DOENECKE

MATTHEWS, Mark Allison (23 Sept. 1867–5 Feb. 1940), fundamentalist minister and civic reformer, was born in Calhoun, Georgia, the son of Mark Lafayette Matthews, the owner of a carriage shop and factory, and Malinda Rebecca Clemmons. His once prosperous family suffered serious reversals when the carriage shop, factory, and home were burned to the ground by the marauding armies of William Tecumseh Sherman during their march to the sea from Chattanooga to Atlanta. In later years, the economic fortunes of the family were further diminished by the burgeoning of modern machinery with its manufacture of more products—carriages and wagons included—at lesser cost than the labors of skilled craftsmen, such as Matthews's father. Furthermore, the loss of good health, a result in part of the family's financial problems, made its impact on both parents and children. Of twelve children, only Mark Allison and one sister lived to maturity.

Matthews's education was meager partly because the war and Reconstruction disrupted the educational system. He attended Calhoun Academy, graduated from the short-lived Gordon County University, and studied theology with a private tutor, J. B. Hillhouse of Calhoun Academy, who also served as minister of the small Presbyterian church in Calhoun. Having been converted at the age of thirteen, Matthews was ordained at the age of twenty to the ministry of the Presbyterian Church in the United States, a regional southern denomination. He succeeded Hillhouse as pastor of the Presbyterian church in his hometown and remained there from 1888 to 1893. Two other pastorates followed: Dalton, Georgia (1893–1896) and Jackson, Tennessee (1896–1902). At Jackson he studied law and in 1900 passed the bar examination. Even from this early time he studied law to make his struggle against social corruption more effective.

Early in 1902 Matthews accepted a call to the First Presbyterian Church of Seattle. The city, just fifty years old, was a seaport of 80,000, flourishing after the Alaskan Gold Rush of 1897. By 1910 the population nearly tripled, aided by railroads and steamship trade with Asia. Matthews and Seattle would grow up together. He was installed by the Presbytery of Puget Sound on 2 February 1902 as pastor of a young congregation with many debts. He served the congregation thirty-eight years and saw it grow from 400 to about 9,000 members; it became the largest Presbyterian church in the country. Matthews became a household name in Seattle and in much of the Pacific Northwest.

While in Seattle, Matthews was admitted to the Seattle Bar Association and to practice before the U.S. Supreme Court. He was examined for the Supreme Court by Chief Justice William Howard Taft sometime between 1921 and 1930, Taft's years of service on the tribunal. Matthews married Grace Owen Jones, the daughter of one of his associate ministers, in Seattle in 1904. They had two children.

Matthews was a Calvinistic fundamentalist in theology, save for his denial of belief in a literal hell; an authoritarian leader; and a civic and social reformer. His fundamentalism dovetailed with his devotion to evangelism: fundamentalism with its emphasis on religious salvation only through faith in Christ; evangelism with its provision of a method whereby that faith might be expressed. Shortly after going to Seattle, Matthews held several evangelistic campaigns in his own church and served as his own evangelist. Within a year the congregation doubled its membership; within two years it doubled again. By 1907 it constructed a new church building to house its parishioners. This was an institutional church designed to minister to the whole person, and it contained not only an enlarged sanctuary but also recreational rooms, a miniature art gallery, libraries, and a track on the roof for bicycling and running. Matthews extended his outreach by founding twenty-eight branch churches from which grew eight permanent congregations, including the University Presbyterian Church and the Japanese Christian Church. In 1917 he founded the Bible Institute of Seattle, a school designed to train primarily laity who wished to enter full-time Christian work but were unprepared for admission to college or seminary and preferred not to give several years to formal study. He also led in establishing in 1927 radio station KTW, the first church-owned and operated radio station in the country and the pioneer station of the Pacific Northwest. Matthews declared that from its inception the station had been dedicated to "unselfish service . . . the preaching of the Gospel of Jesus Christ and . . . the defending of the Constitution of the United States." He kept a tight hand over all these activities and organizations, reserving to himself the superintendency of the Sunday school and the leadership of worship without assistance from thirteen pastoral associates.

From the earliest days of his ministry, Matthews believed that the minister should not simply sound an evangelistic note and proclaim the premillennial second coming of Jesus but should also seek to correct individual and social wrongs. He ranged widely in his pronouncements. As a civic reformer Matthews fought against municipal corruption, especially in the Skid Road section where gambling, prostitution, and the abuse of alcohol flourished. In 1910 he led a campaign that forced the mayor out of office for allegedly tolerating such conditions, and soon afterwards he brought charges of bribery and failure to enforce the law against the chief of police, who was sentenced to five years in prison. On the more positive side, Matthews and his congregation founded the Anti-Tuberculosis Society of Seattle, a major hospital that became associated with the Medical School of the University of Washington, the Child's Welfare and Humane Society, the Voter's League of Washington, and the first kindergartens in Seattle.

Matthews's pulpit pronouncements on social issues were wide-ranging. He supported senior citizens, arguing that people did their best work between the ages of fifty-five and eighty-five. He favored cremation of the dead, supported socialized medicine, encouraged mandatory agricultural education for young men, and argued that in coeducational schools and colleges one-third of the faculty should consist of "the brainiest women" available. In 1910 he spoke against granting suffrage to women, but in 1919 he reversed himself, probably because he realized that women would support his causes. He did, however, oppose the ordination of women as contrary to biblical teaching; he also thought that it would force thousands of men out of work. Ever civic-minded and practical, he recommended a new seawall for the city "at the waterway of Smith's Cave and ending about one block below the Moran ship yards . . . [and reaching] out 150 feet from Railroad Avenue." As an American patriot, he supported the First and Second World Wars, believing neutrality was impossible. He saw Hitler as a madman and wrote him to suggest he relinquish power to preserve world peace. Two generalizations may be made about Matthews's social views: social reform did not take the place of personal conversion or, as he called it, regeneration; and the harsh realities of World War I did not chill his commitment to social change. To the very end he advocated the expansion, beautification, and evangelization of Seattle. "No man," he said, "has ever been insane enough to try to control, or suggest or influence my utterances."

Matthews's admirers considered him an outstanding preacher. The *Post Intelligencer* of Seattle commented that he "had a greater hand in shaping the destinies of Seattle during the thirty-eight years of his pastorate than any other single person." His critics saw him as a sensationalist and a perennial disturber of the peace, theologically rigid, unfair to his enemies and dominating in his personality. He remained important because of his influence on a major American city and section of the country and as an illustration of variation within the ranks of the fundamentalists: he was much more given to civic and social reform than most of his conservative colleagues.

When Matthews died in Seattle, the mayor of the city and the governor of the state of Washington were honorary pallbearers at his funeral. Civic leaders dedicated a statue of Matthews in Denny Park in his honor, paying tribute to "the tall pine of the Sierras" who was intoxicated with visions of a new Seattle as well as with the ultimate hope of the new Jerusalem.

• Primary sources for Matthews's life are his papers, which include scrapbooks, newspaper clippings, sermons, some correspondence, and books (largely collections of sermons). These materials are in the Manuscript Division, Suzzallo Library, at the University of Washington, Seattle. Matthews's best-known book was *The Second Coming of Christ* (1918). For secondary sources see E. P. Giboney and Agnes M. Potter, *The Life of Mark A. Matthews* (1948); C. Allyn Russell, "Mark Allison Matthews: Seattle Fundamentalist and Civic Reformer," *Journal of Presbyterian History* 57 (Winter 1979): 446–66; and George W. Dollar, *A History of Fundamentalism in America* (1973).

C. ALLYN RUSSELL

MATTHEWS, Nathan, Jr. (28 Mar. 1854–11 Dec. 1927), mayor of Boston, Massachusetts, was born in the West End of Boston, the son of Nathan Matthews, a real estate agent, and Albertine Bunker. He received an elite education, graduating from Harvard College in 1875. After two years of postgraduate study in political economy at the University of Leipzig in Germany, he graduated from Harvard Law School in 1880 and opened a Boston legal practice, specializing in trusts and real estate. In 1883 he married Ellen Bacon Sargent; they had two children. A Democrat by family habit, Matthews joined the Democratic party revival in Massachusetts, inspired by Grover Cleveland's presidential victory in 1884, and moved swiftly into the leadership ranks of the state party. In 1888 he helped to organize the Young Men's Democratic Club of Massachusetts, an energizing political force in the state, and became chairman of the executive committee of the party's State Committee two years later. Together with political allies Josiah Quincy (1859–1919) and Patrick Collins, he worked hard to meld the Yankee and Irish-American factions of the party into functional cohesion despite troubling cultural divisions between them. He also befriended politically potent Boston Democrats like Patrick Maguire, leader of the city's Irish political machine, and Henry M. Whitney, an influential rapid transit magnate.

On the strength of these connections as well as his talent for fundraising and enlisting new voters for the party, in 1890 Matthews was tapped by Maguire to run for the Boston mayoralty. He swept into office with an unprecedented majority, becoming at age thirty-six the youngest mayor in the city's history thus far. Reelected in 1891, 1892, and 1893, he brought to city hall a brisk and somewhat intimidating executive authority, combining tight business efficiency with a broad grasp of the growing city's metropolitan needs.

A lawyer friend, who helped him expose fraud and overpricing in Boston's coal gas monopoly in 1893, later wrote of him in a private memorandum, "Matthews is a man of wonderful ability, far-seeing and a great master of motives and details" (George Fred Williams, diary notes, 10 Sept. 1895, Williams papers, Massachusetts Historical Society).

The most celebrated of Matthews's mayoral initiatives was the elaborate planning that went into the first leg of Boston's underground transit system, the first subway in the United States, its construction finally getting under way shortly after Matthews left office. Another intractable long-term city problem, water supply, neared eventual solution when he persuaded the state to create a metropolitan water system, though its completion awaited the early twentieth century. Meanwhile Matthews expedited the completion of Boston's sprawling new park system, the "emerald necklace" that landscape architect Frederick Law Olmsted (1822–1903) had begun designing in the late 1870s.

Matthews used his expertise in real estate development and his command of municipal budgeting to cobble cost efficiency with the rudiments of a city planning program. He was applauded for coordinating suburban growth with street, sewer, and water extensions, transit facilities, and environmental amenities. And he was the first mayor to exploit fully the potential of Boston's new charter of 1885 to consolidate executive control over the city's governance. However, the sudden onset of a depression in 1893 exposed the limits of his municipal reform vision. With unemployment lurching toward 20 percent among the city's wage workers, he struggled to provide municipal jobs for the party faithful during the harsh winter of 1893–1894 and sponsored a private sector Citizen's Relief Committee to ease misery among the "worthy poor." Fearing the "insidious encroachment of socialism," he refused to spend public funds "for the sole purpose of furnishing work for the unemployed" (*Proceedings of the Common Council of Boston, 1894*, p. 4). Hard times stunted Matthews's reformist energies, ruined his reputation in the city's ward headquarters and union halls, and crippled his career in elective politics. As the party coalition he had earlier helped to mobilize began to come apart, he left office in January 1895 to resume his law practice. In 1896 he bolted his party over the presidential nomination of William Jennings Bryan to support the Gold Democratic ticket.

A decade later Matthews began his final contribution to Boston governance as an organizer of the city's Good Government Association, which labored to expose mismanagement at city hall under Mayor John F. Fitzgerald. Under sharp political pressure, Fitzgerald authorized a special governance investigation by a blue-ribbon Finance Commission, chaired by Matthews himself. The commission's recommendations, issued in 1909, inspired charter reforms, which, in line with Matthews's long-standing priorities, greatly enhanced and clarified the executive authority of the mayor at the expense of the city council. Fitzgerald's subsequent reelection under the new charter ironically confirmed the bruising power transfer from Yankee to Irish-American domination in Boston politics, a transition that Matthews had strived to moderate in earlier years.

Matthews spent his last years quietly practicing law in Boston, lecturing on government at Harvard (1909–1911), and serving from 1913 to 1923 as chairman of the water supply board of Salem and Beverly, cities near his rural estate in the village of Hamilton, Massachusetts. In 1914 he published *Municipal Charters*, which further enhanced his reputation as a reformer and municipal expert. He died in Boston.

The patterns in Matthews's political career meshed with the changing fortunes of the Democratic party in Massachusetts and the nation: impressive vigor and promise in the 1880s, followed by moments of substantial if prudent reform achievement, and sudden party fracture and collapse thereafter. His municipal reform agenda anticipated the Progressive era's stress on executive centralization to contain factional impulses in the urban electorate's street-corner leadership. He understood Boston's structural problems as well as any Yankee politician of his day and applied his austere intelligence to solving some of them before economic and ethno-cultural realities forced him from power.

• The Nathan Matthews Papers at Littauer Library, Harvard University, span the years 1885 to 1893. Matthews's valedictory address as mayor, *The City Government of Boston* (1895), provides valuable insights. Robert A. Silverman, "Nathan Matthews: Politics of Reform in Boston, 1890–1910," *New England Quarterly* 50 (Dec. 1977): 626–43, is a nicely balanced appraisal. Geoffrey Blodgett, *The Gentle Reformers: Massachusetts Democrats in the Cleveland Era* (1966), also tracks Matthews's career. Obituaries are in the *Boston Evening Transcript* and the *New York Times*, both 12 Dec. 1927.

GEOFFREY BLODGETT

MATTHEWS, Stanley (21 July 1824–22 Mar. 1889), U.S. Supreme Court justice, was born in Lexington, Kentucky, the son of Thomas J. Matthews, a college professor, and Isabella Brown. Matthews graduated from Kenyon College (Ohio) in 1840, studied law in Cincinnati, and moved to Columbia, Tennessee, where he was admitted to the bar and was active in Democratic politics. In 1844 he returned to Cincinnati, espoused antislavery principles, and, despite that unpopular stance, was elected a judge of the Ohio Court of Common Pleas, where he served from 1851 to 1853. Matthews continued to practice law and was elected to the Ohio State Senate, serving from 1855 to 1857. From 1858 through 1861 he was U.S. attorney for the Southern District of Ohio. In that office, despite his hostility to slavery, he prosecuted a man who had assisted the escape of two fugitive slaves.

Matthews married Mary Ann Black in 1843. They had eight children, of whom five survived to adulthood. The death of three sons in an 1857 scarlet fever epidemic led Matthews to discard the rationalist Unitarianism of his youth for a fervent, though liberal, Calvinist Presbyterianism. Mary Ann Matthews died in 1885, and he married Mary Theaker in 1887.

In 1861 Matthews joined the Republican party and volunteered for military service. He was commissioned lieutenant colonel of the Twenty-third Ohio Volunteer Infantry and then colonel in the Fifty-first Ohio Volunteer Infantry. He was provost marshal of Nashville and a brigade commander at Lookout Mountain and Chickamauga. He resigned from the army in 1863 when he was elected judge of the Ohio Superior Court, where he sat until 1865.

Back in private practice, Matthews prospered, representing railroads and other corporate interests. He became active in Republican politics and ran unsuccessfully for the U.S. House of Representatives in 1876. In 1877 he argued the cause of his college and army friend Rutherford B. Hayes before the electoral commission. Matthews also helped engineer the Wormley Compromise of 1877, which resolved the disputed 1876 presidential election on the basis of Republican pledges to terminate what was left of military Reconstruction. This assured a return of Democratic control in the southern states. The former opponent of slavery seemed untroubled that this action abandoned the freedpeople of the South to domination by vengeful, racist regimes, who within a generation would impose Jim Crow, economic servitude, political disfranchisement, and the political ideology of white supremacy. Republicans in control of the Ohio legislature elected Matthews to the U.S. Senate, where he served until 1879 and, characteristically out of step with his party, supported greenbacks and silver.

In 1881 President Hayes nominated Matthews to the Supreme Court, but the nomination proved politically controversial and languished in the Judiciary Committee. Democrats bore a grudge over his political role in the 1876–1877 negotiations and considered him Hayes's crony because the two men were related by marriage. Hard money proponents resented his support for silver, while reformers of either party viewed his lucrative railroad practice suspiciously. Newly elected president James A. Garfield resubmitted the nomination, and Matthews was confirmed by a margin of one vote in 1881. He sat until his final illness in 1888 forced him off the bench and died in Washington, D.C., the next year.

Though Matthews served only seven years and was little differentiated ideologically from his brethren on the Court, several of his opinions have lasting significance. In *Yick Wo v. Hopkins* (118 U.S. 356, 373–374 [1886]), Matthews struck down a facially neutral San Francisco ordinance regulating the licensing of laundries on the grounds that it was discriminatorily applied to exclude Chinese laundrymen. "Though the law itself be fair on its face, and impartial in appearance, yet," he wrote, "if it is applied and administered by public authority with an evil eye and an unequal hand," it violated the Fourteenth Amendment's equal protection clause. Despite the memorable trope and realistic approach of this passage, the equal protection clause thereafter lapsed into a coma from which it did not awaken until after World War II. Yet *Yick Wo* remained a valuable precedent for voiding laws that were valid on their face but unequally enforced.

Matthews's opinion in *Hurtado v. California* (110 U.S. 516 [1884]) was significant not because of innovation or doctrine, but because it opened a question that required eighty years of contentious debate on the Court to resolve. He upheld a California criminal procedure whereby proceedings against the defendant could be begun by an information filed by the attorney general, rather than by an indictment. This raised the issue of the extent to which the Fourteenth Amendment "incorporated" the first eight amendments of the Bill of Rights as limitations on the power of the states. Matthews's *Hurtado* opinion began the approach of selectively incorporating particular provisions one at a time, rather than the total incorporation approach later advocated by Justice Hugo L. Black.

Matthews's holding in *Ex parte Crow Dog* (109 U.S. 556, 571 [1883]) followed the precedent established by Chief Justice John Marshall of respecting the quasi-sovereign status of American Indian tribes. Preventing extension of territorial court jurisdiction over tribal Indians, whom he described as "members of a community, separated by race, by tradition, by the instincts of a free though savage life," Matthews sought to preserve the authority of tribal law on the reservations. Unfortunately, this only encouraged pressures for enactment of the Major Crimes Act (1885) and the Dawes Act (1887), which denigrated tribal sovereignty and substituted a policy of forced assimilation and dependency.

In *Poindexter v. Greenhow* (114 U.S. 270, 288 [1885]), Matthews anticipated the inroad bulldozed into the Eleventh Amendment by the later case of *Ex parte Young* (1908) by drawing a distinction between states, immune from suit by citizens of other states under the Eleventh Amendment, and a state's agent, who could be sued because he was "stripped of his official character." Matthews was similarly in advance of doctrinal development in his last significant opinion, which struck down an Iowa prohibition statute on the grounds that it interfered with interstate commerce even though Congress had not legislated on the subject, a concept later known as the "dormant commerce power" doctrine (*Bowman v. Chicago and Northwestern Railway Co.*, 125 U.S. 465 [1888]).

Stanley Matthews was esteemed by his contemporaries for legal acumen and remembered affectionately by former enemies such as Senator George Edmunds, who had opposed his nomination to the Supreme Court, for "the gentleness of his disposition, the affability of his conduct."

Matthews was one of the more progressive jurists on a Court that was beginning to formulate doctrines, such as substantive due process, that were hostile to state regulatory power. His realistic approach in *Yick Wo* was far in advance of its time and marked one of the few occasions before 1950 when the equal protection clause was enforced to protect racial minorities. In his seven years of service on the Supreme Court, Matthews left an enduring mark on American public law.

• Matthews's papers are held in the Cincinnati Historical Society (wartime correspondence to his wife) and the Rutherford B. Hayes Library in Fremont, Ohio. Louis Filler wrote a brief sketch, more insightful into its subject's pre-Court career than into his juristic contributions, "Stanley Matthews," in *The Justices of the United States Supreme Court, 1789–1969: Their Lives and Major Opinions*, comp. Leon Friedman and Fred L. Israel, vol. 2 (1969–1978), pp. 1351–61. Also for Matthews's pre-Court years, see William R. Wantland, "Jurist and Advocate: The Political Career of Stanley Matthews, 1840–1889" (Ph.D. diss., Miami Univ.). Contemporary opinions of Matthews's personality and abilities are collected in *Proceedings of the Bench and Bar of the Supreme Court of the United States: In Memoriam Stanley Matthews* (1889). Charles T. Greve contributed a genre piece, "Stanley Matthews," which drew largely on the *Proceedings*, in *Great American Lawyers: The Lives and Influence of Judges and Lawyers*, ed. William D. Lewis, vol. 7 (1907–1909), pp. 395–427.

WILLIAM M. WIECEK

MATTHEWS, Thomas Stanley (16 Jan. 1901–4 Jan. 1991), magazine editor and memoirist, was born in Cincinnati, Ohio, the son of Paul Clement Matthews, an Episcopal priest, later bishop of New Jersey, and Elsie Procter, an heiress of a founder of the Procter & Gamble Company. His grandfather Stanley Matthews was a U.S. senator and Supreme Court justice. Matthews's early schooling was in Glendale, Ohio. He subsequently attended the Park Hill School in Hampshire, England, and Shattuck Academy in Faribault, Minnesota. After graduation from St. Paul's School in New Hampshire, Matthews enrolled at Princeton University in 1918, receiving a B.A. degree with a major in English in 1922. He received an A.B. from New College, Oxford, in 1924. The following year he married Juliana Stevens Cuyler; they had four sons.

Matthews was hired in 1925 by the *New Republic*, a weekly journal of opinion, as a proofreader and production assistant and soon became assistant editor. Matthews later wrote in his distinguished autobiography, *Name and Address* (1960), that he "never intended to be a journalist; I meant to be a great writer. I was pretty sure, even at the age of twenty-three, that you couldn't be both." Noted critic Gertrude Himmelfarb called the book "a commentary on the achievement of success and the simultaneous loss of identity" (p. 83).

Matthews wrote occasional book reviews under the tutelage of Edmund Wilson. "I have a distinct recollection of his saying once, with a sigh, that I was now able to write a sentence, though still pretty wobbly on my paragraphs," Matthews wrote in his autobiography. "He considered me good enough, at any rate, to use as a guided missile against certain popular writers whose reputations he felt should be deflated." Matthews was given a page in the *New Republic* to unleash his iconoclastic prose. When a writer threatened to horsewhip him for his published remarks, Matthews recalled that he had his "first intimation of the power of the press, and a dim inkling of its true nature." He continued to contribute signed and unsigned editorial material, developing a satirical, periodical, impressionistic style under the guidance of A. R. Orage, a British journalist who offered evening writing classes. Matthews became an associate editor at the *New Republic* in 1927.

In 1929 he joined Henry R. Luce's *Time* magazine and contributed to its books, religion, and press sections while working as night editor. He wrote in his autobiography that the difference between the *New Republic* and *Time* was a "contrast between scholarly, distinguished men and smart, ignorant boys." The books page soon became his primary responsibility, and he wrote occasional cover stories on literary subjects such as the publication in the United States of James Joyce's *Ulysses* and T. S. Eliot's *The Waste Land* and *Four Quartets*. He also wrote novels, including *To the Gallows I Must Go* (1931) and *The Moon's No Fool* (1936).

In 1937 Matthews was appointed assistant managing editor at *Time*, in charge of the art, theater, books, religion, music, and cinema sections. He was promoted to national affairs editor in time to cover the 1940 presidential election. In 1942 he became executive editor. For several months he was based in the London bureau, returning to New York as managing editor in 1943. He was appointed editor in 1949, although Luce continued to exercise editorial authority.

Tensions between Matthews and Luce increased during the 1952 presidential election. Although Luce and most of his senior management associates supported the Republican party candidate, Dwight D. Eisenhower, Matthews supported and advised the Democratic candidate, Adlai E. Stevenson, a close friend and former Princeton classmate. Matthews contended in his autobiography that the "distortions, suppressions and slanting" of the magazine's political reports during the election compromised journalism ethics. After a writer submitted a cover story on Stevenson that Matthews considered a "clumsy but malign and murderously meant attack," he vowed to resign. Luce, however, persuaded him to go to England to study the possibility of *Time*'s publishing a British edition of the magazine. After reporting to Luce that the magazine could quickly show a profit, and expecting to become its first editor, Matthews was shocked to receive a cable canceling the project. *Time* had elected to start another magazine, *Sports Illustrated*, instead. Matthews's reply found its way into the New York press: "Why did you keep me standing on tiptoes if you weren't going to kiss me?" He resigned soon after and remained in England to write and to study at Oxford. He received an M.A. in 1968. After the death of his wife in 1949, Matthews had married writer Martha Gellhorn in 1954. The marriage ended in divorce. He married Pamela Firth Peniakoff in 1964. He died in Cavendish, England.

Matthews was a prolific and versatile writer. He edited *Selected Letters of Charles Lamb* (1956). His other works include *The Sugar Pill: An Essay on Newspapers* (1957); *O My America! Notes on a Trip* (1962); *The Worst Unsaid: A Book of Verse* (1962); *Why So Gloomy?* (1966), verse; *Great Tom: Notes towards the Definition of T. S. Eliot* (1974); *Jacks or Better: A Narrative* (1977), published in England as *Under the Influence* (1979); *Angels Unawares: Twentieth-Century Portraits* (1985); *Sorry about That* (1986); *No Problem, OK?* (1987); and *Mind Your Head* (1988). He also reviewed books for the *New York Times* and contributed reports, reviews, and essays to a number of publications, including *Forum, New English Weekly, Harper's, Atlantic, American Scholar, Vogue, New Yorker, Saturday Evening Post, Life, The Guardian, Observer*, and others.

Matthews presided over the day-to-day management of *Time* when it was at the height of its influence during the later years of World War II and the early Cold War era. Although he was always ambivalent about his profession, he claimed he had tried to act on the belief that journalism could be "a crude but fairly effective means of keeping a democracy awake and self-conscious." As he left *Time*, however, he was less certain. He said he had attempted, but failed, during his managing editorship "to root out *Time*'s notorious technique of innuendo." He was, however, credited by colleagues with adding greater depth to the magazine and improving its style, while developing a reputation as a stern editor. This was particularly so in his development of some of *Time*'s most celebrated writers, such as James Agee, John Hersey, and Whittaker Chambers. In an article for *Saturday Review* (16 Apr. 1966), Matthews recalled a commentary Agee wrote after the atomic bomb attacks on Japan: "When people tell me about '*Time* style' or assert that *Time* was always written in some form of pidgin English, I remember Agee—and this piece in particular."

The writing that Matthews did after he left *Time* enabled him to reflect on his career and expand his literary interests. His autobiography and personal essays are filled with charitable, humorous, and sometimes harsh portraits of friends and colleagues such as Stevenson, Robert Graves, Wilson, Luce, and Agee. His ironic, lyrical reflections about his privileged upbringing, family, profession, and religion show a personal struggle for self-understanding and an ultimately unrealized search for narrative truth. "I set out to become a first-rate man, or at any rate a good one," he wrote, "and instead turned into—me."

• Matthews's papers, including a considerable number of letters, are at Cavendish Hall, Cavendish, Suffolk, England. They are expected to be transferred eventually to Princeton University. Matthews's various autobiographical works are basic sources; they include "The Reminiscences of Thomas S. Matthews" (1958), which are in the Oral History Collection of Columbia University. Information about Matthews's career with *Time* and his relationship with Luce and other colleagues is available in Robert T. Elson, *The World of Time Inc.: The Intimate History of a Publishing Enterprise*, vol. 1: *1923–1941* (1968), vol. 2: *1941–1960* (1973), and, by Curtis Prendergast, vol. 3: *1960–1980* (1986). See also W. A. Swanberg, *Luce and His Empire* (1972); Roy Hoopes, *Ralph Ingersoll* (1985); James L. Baughman, *Henry R. Luce and the Rise of the American News Media* (1987); and Thomas Griffith,

Harry and Teddy: The Turbulent Friendship of Press Lord Henry R. Luce and His Favorite Correspondent, Theodore H. White (1995). Of the many reviews of Matthews's *Name and Address*, see especially Gertrude Himmelfarb, "Anonymity, 'Time,' and Success," *Commentary*, July 1960, pp. 83–86. Obituaries are in the *New York Times*, 6 Jan. 1991, the *Washington Post*, 7 Jan. 1991, *Time*, 14 Jan. 1991, and *The Times* (London), 12 Jan. 1991.

PAUL G. ASHDOWN

MATTHIESSEN, F. O. (19 Feb. 1902–1 Apr. 1950), educator, literary critic, and scholar, was born Francis Otto Matthiessen in Pasadena, California, the son of Frederic William Matthiessen, Jr., and Lucy Orne Pratt. Matthiessen's grandfather had emigrated from Germany to La Salle, Illinois, founded the Western Clock Corporation (later the Westclox Corporation), and died in 1918, leaving an estate of approximately $10 million. Matthiessen's father was spoiled as a youth and unsettled as an adult, became a spendthrift and a philanderer, deserted his wife and their four children in 1907, and was divorced in 1915. Matthiessen's mother lived with her children during some of these years in her father-in-law's La Salle home.

Matthiessen attended the Polytechnic School in Pasadena and then from 1914 to 1918 the Hackley School in Tarrytown, New York. He served very briefly in the Royal Canadian Air Force in 1918 and entered Yale University in 1919. He not only was an excellent student, taking classes in Greek and Latin, but was also active in student journalistic endeavors, plays, and other social events. He was a member of clubs devoted to religion and liberal politics. He was profoundly influenced while still an undergraduate by attending lectures delivered by Norman Thomas and Eugene V. Debs and by reading *The Acquisitive Society* by R. H. Tawney (1920). After graduating with an A.B. in 1923, Matthiessen studied at New College, Oxford, as a Rhodes scholar. While there he joined the Oxford Labour Club and remained interested in the cause of organized labor. After being awarded a B.Litt. in English in 1925, he returned to the United States and enrolled as a graduate student at Harvard University. He quickly earned an M.A. in 1926 and a Ph.D. a year later. He never sought to publish his 1925 Oxford thesis, "Oliver Goldsmith as Essayist and Critic," but he revised his Harvard dissertation for publication as *Translation: An Elizabethan Art* (1931).

Matthiessen was an English instructor at Yale from 1927 to 1929. While there, he wrote his first book in the field of American literature. It was *Sarah Orne Jewett* (1929), an unconventionally impressionistic study of the local-colorist from South Berwick, Maine. In the course of research for this work, Matthiessen came to admire the people and the scenery of coastal Maine. Jewett was distantly related to Matthiessen's mother, who died in 1925 while he was abroad. In 1929 Matthiessen returned to Harvard. He admired and added prestige to an undergraduate honors program there that stressed the interrelationship of history and literature. He also improved the quality of Harvard's already fine tutorial system. Rising steadily in the ranks, he was an instructor and tutor (1929–1930), assistant professor (1930–1934), associate professor (1934–1942), and professor of history and literature thereafter.

Although he taught courses and tutored his students in the forms of drama, Shakespeare, and criticism of poetry, his most influential teaching was in the field of American literature, as were his publications. The list of students that directly benefited from his teaching both at Yale and at Harvard and who went on to distinguished academic careers is extensive. As for his publications, totals are most impressive: he wrote ten books and edited five others; in addition, he wrote twenty-seven articles, contributed thirteen essays to collaborative works and anthologies, and published seventy-three reviews, in many of which he touched on more than one book each. Matthiessen never slighted administrative, committee, and other responsibilities in academe. His most significant such work was as head tutor at Harvard's Eliot House (1931–1933), chairman of the board of tutors in history and literature (1931–1948), president of the Harvard Teachers' Union (1940–1942, 1946–1947), trustee of the Samuel Adams School of Social Studies (1944–1948), and influential member of a committee at Harvard that encouraged the study of American civilization through an interdepartmental program.

Matthiessen was an unusually complex person—an avowed and active Christian, a democratic socialist, a theoretical pacifist, and a homosexual. He led an intense life outside university walls. His Harvard colleagues included Bernard DeVoto, Howard Mumford Jones, Perry Miller, Samuel Eliot Morison, Kenneth B. Murdock, Ralph Barton Perry, Arthur Schlesinger, Jr., and Theodore Spencer. He was a bright and gracious host, especially shining during annual Christmas Eve parties that he held in his Boston apartment. He also served energetically in the Massachusetts Civil Liberties Union. He was remembered as strongly urging his homosexual colleagues to keep their academic, political, and private activities distinct and separate.

His most intimate friend was Russell Cheney, a painter whom he chanced to meet on an ocean liner in 1924. The two men fell in love almost immediately, bought a house together in Kittery Point, Maine, and enjoyed each other's companionship for more than twenty years. When they were apart, Matthiessen, calling himself "Devil," and Cheney, calling himself "Rat," kept up a daily correspondence that eventually totaled some 1,400 letters by Matthiessen and some 1,700 by Cheney. Cheney periodically fought alcoholism, once in 1938 so unsuccessfully that he expressed a desire to die; Matthiessen, because of his own resulting nervousness and insomnia, had himself admitted to a mental sanatorium in Waverly, Massachusetts (26 Dec. 1938–13 Jan. 1939). International political dislocations occasioned by World War II, which Matthiessen, who was rejected when he tried to enlist in the Marine Corps, watched from the sidelines while attempting to teach and write productively, caused renewed bouts of bleak melancholy. Cheney died in July 1945; Matthiessen never completely recovered from the loss and ever after fought hard against loneliness. In addition, he grew increasingly discontent with administrative procedures and decisions at Harvard and at one point even considered resigning from the Harvard faculty and teaching at nearby Brandeis University. He was a visiting professor at Princeton University and at Kenyon College in 1946. In 1947 he published *Russell Cheney, 1881–1945: A Record of His Work*, written partly in their old Kittery Point summer home.

In 1947 Matthiessen was saddened by the death of his father, with whom he had recently become reconciled to a degree. In the summer of 1947 he taught in Austria at the first Salzburg Seminar on American Civilization and then that fall at Charles University in Prague, Czechoslovakia. His students, who came from seventeen countries, idolized him, and he felt that he was helping to heal wounds of many sorts caused by the war. His high hopes for the Czech regime he admired, however, were destroyed in the early 1948 Soviet-led coup, during which Czech president Eduard Beneš was ousted, Foreign Minister Jan Masaryk, whom Matthiessen had met and respected, was apparently murdered, and communism smothered all hopes of democracy in Czechoslovakia for almost half a century. The publication later in 1948 of Matthiessen's *From the Heart of Europe*, a journal-like book containing guardedly optimistic comments on international social, political, labor, and cultural problems of the postwar world, was ill timed and served, among few other uses, to give ammunition to his political opponents both in and out of academe. Conservatives despised him for his liberalism, and many leftist friends even rebuked him for being soft on Stalinism. The most damaging sentence in *From the Heart of Europe* is probably the one that begins "I accept the Russian Revolution as the most progressive event of our century." Matthiessen only made matters worse for himself by campaigning for Henry Agard Wallace's Progressive party candidacy for president in 1948 as a member at large of the party and by giving one of the nominating speeches at the party convention in Philadelphia in July.

During his last two years, Matthiessen felt intellectually more isolated and personally lonelier. President Harry S. Truman's 1947 order to investigate the loyalty of government employees was being carried out, as was his containment doctrine aimed at blunting the advance of communism in Europe; at the same time, the fulminations of Senator Joseph McCarthy, distressing to intellectuals of almost all persuasions, were particularly repugnant to Matthiessen. Nor did it ultimately help that the next subject Matthiessen chose for critical treatment was Theodore Dreiser, a theoretical Communist whose political opinions were in many ways similar to Matthiessen's but whose general philosophy of life—that we are all hopeless victims of cosmic forces beyond our ability to control—Matthiessen remained a little too idealistic ever to accept. By

March 1950 he had completed a draft of his book on Dreiser, was dissatisfied with it, and had not fully revised it. On the evening of 31 March, after visiting the home of his friend Kenneth Murdock, Matthiessen checked into a Boston hotel, went to a room on the twelfth floor, left carefully written notes, and jumped from the window to his death. In one note he explained that he was exhausted, had been severely depressed for years, regarded himself as useless to his profession and to his friends, and felt oppressed by current international tensions.

Matthiessen's major publications are *The Achievement of T. S. Eliot: An Essay on the Nature of Poetry* (1935; rev. ed., 1947), *American Renaissance: Art and Expression in the Age of Emerson and Whitman* (1941), *Henry James: The Major Phase* (1944; based largely on lectures Matthiessen gave at the University of Toronto in the fall of 1944), *The James Family: Including Selections from the Writings of Henry James, Senior, William, Henry, and Alice James* (1947), and *Theodore Dreiser* (1951). Matthiessen's finest editorial work is in Henry James, *Stories of Writers and Artists* (1944), *The Notebooks of Henry James*, coedited with Kenneth B. Murdock (1947), and *The Oxford Book of American Verse* (1950). Fifty of his short pieces were posthumously published in *The Responsibilities of the Critic: Essays and Reviews by F. O. Matthiessen*, edited by John Rackliffe (1952).

In his study of Eliot, Matthiessen showed that the works of Dante, the English metaphysical poets, the French symbolists, and Charles Baudelaire inspired Eliot's own verse. He also explained that Eliot regarded awareness of tradition as the means of organically unifying the past and the present not only historically but also artistically, with the result that love of great literature can be a spiritual experience.

Matthiessen's *American Renaissance*, his greatest scholarly accomplishment, sought to ignite in Americans in that dangerous year of 1941 (and beyond) a renewed awareness of the democratic values, under attack by totalitarian forces, in the works of Ralph Waldo Emerson, Henry David Thoreau, Walt Whitman, Nathaniel Hawthorne, and Herman Melville. The first three, especially Whitman, he generally saw as representing American idealism and optimism; the last two, though often more gloomy, as prescribing faith in democracy and Christianity as a means of healing America's troubled psyche. To underscore the positive, Matthiessen ended his book with nine vigorous chapters on Whitman. Perhaps better than Matthiessen's arching thesis are his separate content-and-style explications, often rich and ranging, of the masterworks of his five principal authors. As if to prove Eliot's theory that individual talents are influenced by tradition, Matthiessen wrote especially well on continuity in works by Hawthorne, Henry James, and Eliot. Inevitably, *American Renaissance* has been subject to no little adverse critical commentary and a few revisionist attacks for both its final optimism and its omissions. Nevertheless, it stands securely as a monumental example of American literary scholarship at its best.

Matthiessen's choice of James and Dreiser as authors to analyze in great depth is curious. In *Henry James: The Major Phase*, Matthiessen demonstrates his view of James not as a deracinated American expatriate writing abroad, as he had been seen too often, but as a preeminent literary artist whose notebooks and meticulous rewriting show his commitment to art, whose final novels are formal masterpieces of great complexity and moral seriousness, and whose *American Scene* should be better known. *The James Family* is a richly detailed family biography; it includes selections of formal and informal written work by the four Jameses considered, together with insightful editorial commentary. Making Dreiser the subject of what became his final book may have been a mistake for Matthiessen, who must have found his subject's works dreadfully depressing. Matthiessen's book stresses Dreiser's economic, political, and social philosophy and weakly—if understandably—slights Dreiser's awareness of the fierce power of sex in most relationships. Matthiessen skillfully regards Dreiser's massive descriptions as an attempt to counter mutability in all things human. Viewed as a whole, *The Responsibilities of the Critic* demonstrates Matthiessen's abiding preoccupation with the American past, with the best of modern poets, and with the most challenging historians and critics of American literature.

Matthiessen is of almost unparalleled significance as a cultural critic of mid- and late nineteenth- and early twentieth-century America. He combined respect for Christian and socialist values and a keen knowledge of the history of ideas in America with a skillful use of close textual and formalistic explication. His best works are distinguished by a lucid style, a somber tone, and an abiding profundity.

• Many of Matthiessen's working papers are in the Harvard University Archives; several manuscripts and his European journals are in the Houghton Library at Harvard. Many of his other papers are in the Library of Congress and in libraries at the Universities of Connecticut, Michigan, and Pennsylvania and Yale. *Rat & the Devil: Journal Letters of F. O. Matthiessen and Russell Cheney*, ed. Louis Hyde (1978), details the two men's friendship. Paul M. Sweezy and Leo Huberman, eds., *F. O. Matthiessen, 1902–1950: A Collective Portrait* (1950), contains tributes by thirty-four friends. Matthiessen's critical accomplishments are discussed at length in Giles B. Gunn, *F. O. Matthiessen: The Critical Achievement* (1975), which also contains a full bibliography of his publications; Frederick C. Stern, *F. O. Matthiessen: Christian Socialist as Critic* (1981); and William E. Cain, *F. O. Matthiessen and the Politics of Criticism* (1988). Kermit Vanderbilt, *American Literature and the Academy: The Roots, Growth, and Maturity of a Profession* (1986), and Vincent B. Leitch, *American Literary Criticism from the Thirties to the Eighties* (1988), place Matthiessen in context. Edward L. Schapsmeier and Frederick H. Schapsmeier, *Prophet in Politics: Henry A. Wallace and the War Years, 1940–1965* (1970), presents Wallace's political opinions, which resemble Matthiessen's closely. An obituary is in the *New York Times*, 2 Apr. 1950.

ROBERT L. GALE

MATTINGLY, Garrett (6 May 1900–18 Dec. 1962), historian and educator, was born in Washington, D.C., the son of Leonard H. Mattingly, a civil servant and engineer, and Ida Roselle Garrett. Educated in the public schools of the capital, and from age 13 in those of Kalamazoo, Michigan, he originally considered applying to the U.S. Military Academy at West Point and becoming an army officer. On graduating from high school, he served during 1918 and 1919 as a sergeant in the Forty-third Infantry and Fifteenth Division. Afterward he entered Harvard College, where he took his A.B. summa cum laude in 1923. While still an undergraduate, he studied in France at Strasbourg and Paris and in Florence, Italy, with the aid of a Sheldon traveling fellowship. Two years spent working in a New York City publishing house persuaded him to enter graduate school at Harvard. Mattingly received his M.A. in 1926, then began his academic career at Northwestern University in Evanston, Illinois, teaching history and literature. There he formed a close personal and professional friendship with writer Bernard Devoto that would endure until the latter's death in 1955. They corresponded frequently, exchanging advice concerning literary style and historical narration. Each would dedicate a book to the other, and Mattingly was to vigorously defend his friend's reputation as an author and critic in *Bernard Devoto: A Preliminary Appraisal* (1938).

In 1928 Mattingly married Gertrude L. McCollum, a teacher; the couple had no children. That same year Mattingly accepted a position at Long Island University in Brooklyn, New York, where he would remain until 1942. While continuing to teach, Mattingly resumed his education at Harvard, earning a doctorate in 1935 for his dissertation "Eustache Chapuys and the Spanish Ambassadors in England, 1488–1536." He had developed a strong interest in the sixteenth century as an undergraduate and had come under the influence of Roger B. Merriman, a specialist in the history of the Spanish Empire.

Aided by a Guggenheim Fellowship, he spent the academic year 1937–1938 doing intensive research in continental and English archives. A scrupulous scholar, he taught himself several foreign languages as well as the difficult sixteenth-century script so as to gain firsthand knowledge of the documentary sources. He generally disdained secondary accounts, preferring to draw his own conclusions about contentious historical issues. Mattingly incorporated many of his archival discoveries in a volume prepared for the Calendar of State Papers series issued by the British Public Record Office, *Further Supplement to Letters, Dispatches, and State Papers Relating to the Negotiations between England and Spain* (1940).

Synthesizing the material that he had patiently gathered, Mattingly produced his *Catherine of Aragon* in 1941. More than a biography of Henry VIII's unfortunate first wife, the book untangled the intricate strands of diplomacy conducted by the major powers and demonstrated how royal marriage and divorce were linked to diplomatic alliances, wars, religion, and the everyday lives of common people. Mattingly's stately prose, the result of endless polishing, resembled traditional nineteenth-century narrative. So, too, did his deft word portraits of the figures, major and minor, involved in great affairs of state. In addition to describing their physical appearance and character, he provided psychological insights into their behavior so that they emerged as three-dimensional personalities. Generally praised by critics, the volume was chosen as a selection of the Literary Guild.

World War II interrupted Mattingly's academic career. From 1942 to 1945 he served in the U.S. Naval Reserve as a lieutenant commander, but he spent most of his service in Washington, D.C., instructing intelligence officers. Mattingly learned much about naval operations that would later prove useful in his scholarship. At war's end he received a Guggenheim Fellowship that enabled him to resume his research abroad.

In 1946 he accepted a teaching post at Cooper Union in New York City, where he remained for two years. Mattingly then joined the faculty of Columbia University, becoming the William R. Shepherd Professor of European History in 1959. There lectures attracted a large following, impressing students with his depth of knowledge and lively teaching style. "With head cocked, his arms sweeping out generous arcs," a friend later recalled, "he talked in a flow of words, witty, gay, and serious, about sailing ships and men, herbs and spices, full-bodied wines and rich cheer, about tapestries and paintings, music and poetry, [and was] at his most dazzlingly Renaissance" (*American Historical Review* [Apr. 1963]: 907).

At Columbia Mattingly produced two volumes that established him as a major historian. *Renaissance Diplomacy* (1955), which he considered his most important work, thoroughly explained how diplomatic relations developed from the fifteenth through the seventeenth centuries, paying special attention to the evolution of the ambassadorial corps. The book was well researched, citing documentary sources in five foreign languages, and was written in a sprightly style that appealed to the general reader.

Even more successful was *The Armada*, published in 1959. Originally conceived in 1940 during the battle of Britain, this volume brilliantly recounted the destruction of the "invincible" Spanish fleet by superior English seamanship and foul weather. As in *Catherine of Aragon*, Mattingly's analysis took in events across Europe, integrating the Armada expedition into the wide network of diplomatic relations. Framed by the execution of Mary, Queen of Scots, and the murder of the French duke of Guise, the narrative was written in purple prose but a royal purple, which read like historical fiction. Hailed enthusiastically by critics, the book achieved bestseller status as Book-of-the-Month Club and History Book Club selections. It also won Mattingly a special citation from the Pulitzer Prize committee in 1960.

Buoyed by this success, Mattingly planned two other books, one on the Italian Renaissance, the other on the growth of European civilization. But his career was soon cut short. Mattingly died in Oxford, England, while teaching at Oxford University as George Eastman Visiting Professor. His death ended the career of a historian whose conscientious scholarship, complemented by brilliant writing, gave his work enduring value.

• Mattingly's papers are in the Columbia University Library. His numerous letters to Devoto are preserved at the Stanford University Library. An autobiographical statement appears in the twenty-fifth anniversary report of the Harvard class of 1923, published in 1948. Mattingly expressed admiration for Roger B. Merriman in "The Historian of the Spanish Empire," *American Historical Review* (Oct. 1948). A festschrift edited by Charles H. Carter, *From the Renaissance to the Counter-Reformation: Essays in Honor of Garrett Mattingly* (1965), contains appreciations of Mattingly as a teacher and scholar. See also Robert M. Kingdon, "Garrett Mattingly," *American Scholar* (Summer 1982), for a student's recollections. Obituaries are in the *New York Times*, 20 Dec. 1962; *American Historical Review* (Apr. 1963); and *Political Science Quarterly* (Sept. 1963).

JAMES FRIGUGLIETTI

MATZELIGER, Jan Earnst (15 Sept. 1852–24 Aug. 1889), inventor, was born in Paramaribo, Surinam (Dutch Guiana), the son of Carl Matzeliger, a Dutch engineer in charge of government machine works for the colony, and a native Surinamese mother. At the age of ten, Matzeliger began serving an apprenticeship in the machine works. In 1871 he signed on to the crew of an East Indian merchant ship and set out to seek his fortune overseas. After a two-year voyage, he landed at Philadelphia, where he probably worked as a cobbler. In 1877 he settled in the town of Lynn, Massachusetts, the largest shoe-manufacturing center in the United States. His first job there was with the M. H. Harney Company, where he operated a McKay sole-stitching machine. He also gained experience in heel-burnishing, buttonholing, machine repair, and other aspects of shoe manufacture. Later, he was employed in the shoe factory of Beal Brothers. In his spare time Matzeliger drove a coach, studied to increase his proficiency in the English language, and painted oils and watercolors (mostly landscape scenes). After covering rent and other essentials, his small earnings went into the purchase of books, including such useful reference tools as *Popular Educator* and *Science for All*.

At the time, a major challenge facing the shoe industry was how to improve the technique of "lasting"—or connecting the upper flaps to the soles of the shoe. Lasting was still done entirely by hand, an arduous process that slowed production. Several lasting machines had been tried without success. With characteristic zeal, Matzeliger took up this challenge, which had eluded the best mechanical minds. He spent long evening hours in his garret room experimenting and building models. In March 1883 he finally received Patent No. 274,207 for his "Lasting Machine." With sole and upper positioned on a lath, the machine alternately drove tacks, rotated the shoe, and pleated the leather—an automated replication of the manual technique. Two years later he ran a successful factory test in which, over the course of a day, his machine lasted a record seventy-five pairs of shoes (a handlaster could produce no more than fifty in a ten-hour period). With further improvements, it lasted up to 700 pairs a day. This invention, dubbed the "niggerhead," came into universal use in the shoe industry. (It is unclear how the machine acquired its name. The term "niggerhead," applied in several contexts at the time was used in the apparel industry to designate a type of fabric.)

Matzeliger's "dark complexion" made him stand out among his mostly white fellow workers, and his reception by the community varied. A religious man, he tried without success to join the local Unitarian, Episcopal, and Catholic churches. In 1884 he was accepted into the Christian Endeavor Society, the youth wing of the North Congregational Church. He was active in the society's Sunday school and fundraising work. His diligence, polite bearing, and easygoing personality endeared him to those whose minds had not been completely closed by racial prejudice. Among his circle of friends were the younger group of factory workers and members of the Christian Endeavor Society. He never married.

Although he remained active in the developing shoe machinery technology, and was awarded four related patents between 1888 and 1891, Matzeliger's financial benefit from the work was relatively modest. He sold the patents to his backers for $15,000 worth of stock in their company. By the end of the century, this company had become part of the United Shoe Machinery Corporation. Matzeliger's patents provided a nucleus of economic strength for the corporation in its early years. Matzeliger was long since gone, however, having died of tuberculosis. At the time of his death he was being cared for by friends at his home in Lynn. Three of his five patents were granted posthumously.

• The most thorough treatment of Matzeliger's life and career is Sidney Kaplan, "Jan Earnst Matzeliger and the Making of the Shoe," *Journal of Negro History* 40 (Jan. 1955): 8–33. Kaplan's article cites numerous primary sources, including contemporary accounts in the *Lynn News* and other newspapers; MS Minute Book of the Young Peoples' Society of Christian Endeavor of the North Church of Lynn, Lynn Public Library; and Last Will and Testament of Jan Earnst Matzeliger, 15 Apr. 1889, Probate Office, Essex County, Mass. A small collection of correspondence, photographs, and other materials compiled by Kaplan is preserved in the Manuscript Division of the Moorland-Spingarn Research Center, Howard University. See also Dennis Karwatka, "Against All Odds," *American Heritage of Invention and Technology* 6, no. 3 (Winter 1991): 50–55, and Louis Haber, "Jan Earnst Matzeliger," in *Black Pioneers of Science and Invention* (1970), pp. 25–33. A book for younger readers is Barbara Mitchell, *Shoes for Everyone: A Story about Jan Matzeliger* (1986).

KENNETH R. MANNING

MAUCHLY, John William (30 Aug. 1907–8 Jan. 1980), physicist and inventor, was born in Cincinnati, Ohio, the son of Sebastian Jacob Mauchly, a physicist, and Rachel Scheidemantel. The family moved from Cincinnati to the Maryland suburbs of Washington, D.C., after his father, who had been teaching physics at the University of Cincinnati, took a job at the Department of Terrestrial Magnetism (DTM) at the Carnegie Institution of Washington. That department was a leading center for research in terrestrial magnetism and would become famous for research in high-energy physics in the following decades. Mauchly recalled visiting his father there often as a youth. Significantly, the DTM's study of the earth's magnetic field required the sorting and analyzing of large quantities of statistical data gathered from stations around the world. Mauchly's later efforts to employ computing machines for the analysis of weather phenomena echoed that style of work.

In 1925 Mauchly enrolled in an engineering curriculum at Johns Hopkins University in Baltimore and after two years transferred directly into the school's graduate course of study in physics (he never received a bachelor's degree). In 1930 he married Mary Augusta Walzl; the couple had two children. He received his Ph.D. in physics in 1932. Although he was a gifted student, finding a teaching position in those years was difficult. In 1933 he took a job at Ursinus College in Collegeville, Pennsylvania, where he became, in his words, a "one-man physics department." He had a heavy teaching load but also pursued research in weather phenomena, a topic that inevitably brought him up against a need for numerical calculation. Mauchly explored a variety of avenues to mechanize these calculations, including methods of calculating with vacuum tube circuits instead of the mechanical cams, wheels, and levers that the calculators of the day used. The sheer number of calculations required for weather analysis demanded that some way be found to calculate quickly. Electronic circuits, though difficult to design and plagued by reliability problems owing to burned-out tubes, offered a way to do that.

Mauchly intensified his efforts at using vacuum tubes after meeting Professor John V. Atanasoff of Iowa State College, who was working on a computing machine. In 1941 he visited Atanasoff in Iowa. That same year he also enrolled in a course at the University of Pennsylvania's Moore School of Electrical Engineering to learn more about electronics. Soon thereafter he left his teaching post at Ursinus to become an instructor at the Moore School. There he met J. Presper Eckert, with whom he would eventually build the electronic computer known as ENIAC (Electronic Numerical Integrator and Computer). It was clear that Mauchly was focusing his efforts on the feasibility of electronic methods, and his visit to Iowa probably helped sharpen that focus. In any case, it was Mauchly whose drive and energy was essential in bringing the ENIAC, and with it electronic computers, into being.

In 1942 Eckert and Mauchly submitted their proposal to the U.S. Army for an electronic computer. The proposed use of the instrument was not to do weather research, but to solve a more urgent wartime problem of computing firing tables for the many types of ordnance being developed and sent to the front. At the Moore School, alongside some specialized mechanical equipment, was a group of women—called "computers"—who laboriously turned out these tables assisted only by desk calculators. After the death of his first wife in 1946, Mauchly married Kay McNulty, one of the Moore School's "computers." They had five children.

After some bureaucratic delays the army approved the proposal and construction began in 1942. The ENIAC was completed late in 1945, at a cost of around half a million dollars. The formal dedication in February 1946 marked the beginning of the computer age. One of the first problems the ENIAC took on had to do with the design of the hydrogen bomb, the details of which were being hammered out by scientists at Los Alamos, New Mexico. (At that time only Moore School people knew enough about the ENIAC to program it, but none had the required security clearance. The Los Alamos scientists had to remove all evidence pointing to the nature of the problem when they gave the ENIAC team the equations to be solved. Contrary to folklore, the ENIAC did not assist in the design of the atomic bombs that ended World War II.) The army then used it for ballistics work, after moving it to the Ballistics Research Laboratory in Aberdeen, Maryland, where it operated reliably into the mid-1950s.

In 1947, after a disagreement with the University of Pennsylvania over the rights to the ideas contained in the ENIAC, Mauchly and Eckert left to form the Electronic Control Company, which later became the Eckert-Mauchly Computer Corporation. Its goal was to design and build a computer for commercial customers: the UNIVAC (Universal Automatic Computer). But the company could not raise enough cash in advance because many experts in applied mathematics, physics, and the commercial world, including many who were working on other computer projects, believed that no more than a few of these machines would be necessary to satisfy the world's needs. For them the computer was like a wind tunnel or a cyclotron: an expensive piece of scientific apparatus that was of use only to those few researchers who required one for their work. Unlike most specialists in the field, Mauchly saw that the electronic digital computer was not simply a replacement for human beings equipped with desk calculators or punched-card tabulators. He realized that the ability to alter its program in effect could transform a computer into a variety of machines, each tailored for a specific task.

In February 1950 the company was purchased by Remington Rand, for which it became the Eckert-Mauchly division. In 1951 the company introduced the UNIVAC and found a few customers, most notably the U.S. Census Bureau, General Electric, and several branches of the U.S. Defense Department. Those sales inaugurated commercial computing in the United States and laid the foundation for the present-day Unisys Corporation. The sales were also the spur that drove the IBM Corporation to transform itself from a maker of accounting machines to an aggressive marketer of electronic computers. The UNIVAC was not a financial success for either Eckert and Mauchly or for Remington Rand, but it was a technical tour de force that proved that electronic computers could be used in a commercial setting. Mauchly continued to promote this invention, although increasingly he was removed from the technical decisions of the company. Part of that was the result of an investigation of his alleged communist background during the McCarthy era. The allegations were later found to be groundless, but the company was denied his talents at a time when perhaps they were most needed. He did, however, lead an effort to make the UNIVAC easier to use by initiating the development of computer languages that relieved the user from having to learn the arcane codes and rules demanded by the UNIVAC's circuits.

Mauchly left most of the details of computer design to Eckert and a cadre of talented engineers; programming and software support were provided by people such as Grace Murray Hopper, a UNIVAC employee in the early 1950s. But without his unshakable faith in the potential of this new invention, it is unlikely the others would have accomplished what they did.

Mauchly left Remington Rand in 1959 (by this time Remington Rand had merged with Sperry, to form Sperry Rand). He formed a computer consulting company and continued to be active in the field. His later years were clouded by poor health, probably aggravated by a patent dispute over his role as a co-inventor of the ENIAC. Mauchly felt that his and Eckert's place in history was being unfairly challenged by attorneys, whose real goal was to prevent Sperry from collecting royalties on the basic patents that he helped secure. In 1973 a judge ruled the original ENIAC patents invalid, in part because of Atanasoff's work prior to Mauchly's. It should be noted that some technical details concerning the ENIAC's design and construction had been disclosed to the public at the unveiling in 1946, and this fact might have given the court sufficient reason to invalidate the patent anyway. Shortly before his death in Abington, Pennsylvania, Mauchly worried that the court case would forever cloud his and Eckert's reputation, for he believed that he and Eckert were to computing what the Wright Brothers were to aviation. Many agree with him, although some historians insist that Atanasoff receive a measure of credit as well.

Mauchly always saw his work as that of developing a tool to aid his research on weather forecasting. He lived to see the computer industry become a powerful force in American society, but he did not live to see the rapid spread of personal computer use in the daily lives of ordinary people. As that has happened, some historians have shifted their emphasis away from the nuances of technical invention to the problem of bringing an invention to market. The growth of Silicon Valley, and the desire to re-create that entrepreneurial climate elsewhere, has added a new dimension to Mauchly's achievements as an entrepreneur, not as an inventor or a geophysicist. His greatest legacy may be his role in bringing the computer out of its narrow place as a mathematical aid to scientists or engineers and into a place where it serves nearly every facet of modern, information-based society.

• Mauchly's papers are deposited at the Van Pelt Library of the University of Pennsylvania. The Charles Babbage Institute at the University of Minnesota has a copy of the transcript, depositions, and documents introduced as evidence at the *Honeywell v. Sperry Rand* trial, during which Mauchly gave extensive testimony. The best record of Mauchly's ideas on electronic computation is found in the materials prepared for a course he helped organize on "Theory and Techniques for Design of Electronic Digital Computers: Lectures Given at the Moore School, 8 July–31 August, 1946" (4 vols., 1948). For information about early computers and Mauchly's role in their invention, see Nancy Stern, *From ENIAC to UNIVAC* (1981); Paul Ceruzzi, *Reckoners: The Prehistory of the Digital Computer, 1935–1945* (1983); and Alice R. Burks and Arthur Burks, *The First Electronic Computer: The Atanasoff Story* (1988).

PAUL E. CERUZZI

MAULE, Thomas (c. 1645–1724), Quaker polemicist and merchant, was born near Coventry, England. Little is known of his family background. At age twelve, he emigrated to Barbados, where he apparently learned tailoring. One of the many poor settlers uprooted by the sugar revolution that was transforming the island's economy, in 1666 he moved to New England. After a brief stay in Boston he settled in Salem among the town's Quaker minority, in his words, "a people of few words and good works."

By the time of Maule's arrival, the worst of the persecution of the Society of Friends was over. Some Salem Quakers, especially long-term residents, were treated with tolerance, even grudging respect, but they nonetheless endured sporadic harassment. Salem's tradition of alternating accommodation and antagonism among competing religious and social groups fundamentally shaped Maule's outlook as a citizen and a writer. As early as May 1669 he was whipped for asserting that the local Puritan pastor, John Higginson, "preached lies and that his doctrine was of the devil." In 1672 the selectmen warned him, along with other immigrants, that the town had not granted him a right of inhabitantship, meaning the right to public support in case of personal emergencies. However, that same year the town hired him as bell ringer and caretaker of the meetinghouse, a part-time post usually given to legal inhabitants in financial difficulty. Thus Maule, in his early years in Salem, was both opponent and client of the town's Puritan leadership, an ambivalent position shared by other Quakers as well.

In 1670 he married Naomi Lindsey, a Quaker; they had eight children. Naomi died around 1707. In 1713 he married British Quaker Sarah Kendall; they had three children.

Maule prospered in commercial Salem initially through the town's Quaker economic network and his Barbadian connections. By 1674 he was a retail shopkeeper and owned a brickyard. By the late 1680s he was a merchant engaged in the Atlantic trade. On the local tax lists for 1689 and 1699, Maule appears among the wealthiest 3 percent of Salem residents. Also, after 1680, he gained enough respectability to hold minor town offices such as overseer of highways and constable. However, unlike other prominent Salem merchants, he never held higher office. Maule invested a portion of his growing wealth and influence in supporting the Society of Friends throughout New England. After the last legal disabilities against the Quakers were removed under the Dominion of New England, the short-lived Stuart experiment in centralized regional government, Maule built Salem's first Quaker meetinghouse on his own land in 1691.

During the 1690s Maule emerged as an influential Quaker apologist and became embroiled in legal tangles that ultimately made him an important figure in the history of the pursuit of American civil liberties. Inspired by James II's Declaration of Indulgence (1687), by the rapid political changes in New England, and by the increasing number of local Quaker converts, Maule wrote a pamphlet attacking Puritan orthodoxy. However, he delayed publication at the request of Rhode Island Quakers who in 1689, during the Glorious Revolution, feared heightening regional religious tensions.

In the aftermath of the orthodox Puritans' attempt to govern the Massachusetts Charter of 1691 and the Salem witchcraft crisis, Maule could no longer hold his peace. In 1695, Maule's pamphlet, *Truth Held Forth and Maintained*, expanded from the earlier draft, was published by William Bradford of New York, presumably because no Massachusetts printer would accept it. Its major theme was a defense of the Quaker doctrines of the Inner Light and continuing revelation. Maule also attacked the "Hireling Teachers" of Puritan orthodoxy, claiming that their persecution of Quakers and abuse of Indians had provoked God into unleashing Satan's power during the witchcraft episode. Although he expected to be tried for heresy, Maule was, in fact, merely indicted in December 1695 for distributing the book without a license.

Preceding the trial of John Peter Zenger by some forty years, Maule's case was probably the first criminal action involving freedom of the press in Anglo-America. Indeed, his defense was based primarily on the right of Englishmen to a free press and of merchants to sell books like other commodities. After a complex series of legal actions, a Salem jury, whose foreman was a fellow Barbadian immigrant, found him innocent in November 1696. The next year Maule published a second pamphlet, *New England's Persecutors Mauled with Their Own Weapons*, recounting his experiences and reiterating his denunciations of the Puritan clergy. His last work in 1703 was a defense of traditional Quaker doctrine against the Pennsylvania Quaker reformer, George Keith, who sought closer theological agreement between the doctrine of the Inner Light and the general Protestant commitments to scriptural authority and the atonement of the historical Christ.

Maule died in Salem. His writings, which generated much contemporary controversy, were significant in that they introduced a strong but respectable dissenting perspective on religion and government in Massachusetts during the era when the colony was becoming a royal province.

• The most complete biography is Matt Bushnell Jones, "Thomas Maule, the Salem Quaker, and Free Speech in Massachusetts Bay, with Bibliographic Notes," *Essex Institute Historical Collections* 72 (Jan. 1936): 1–42. See also the entry on Maule by James W. Schmotter in *American Writers before 1800: A Biographical and Critical Dictionary*, ed. James A. Levernier and Douglas R. Wilmes (1983). For a good sense of the milieu, see Arthur J. Worrall, *Quakers in the Colonial Northeast* (1980), especially pp. 46–54; and Jonathan M. Chu, *Neighbors, Friends, or Madmen: The Puritan Adjustment to Quakerism in Seventeenth-Century Massachusetts Bay* (1985), especially pp. 125–63.

RICHARD GILDRIE

MAURER, Alfred Henry (21 Apr. 1868–4 Aug. 1932), painter, was born in New York City, the son of Louis Maurer, an illustrator for Currier and Ives, and Louise (or Louisa) Stein. Growing up in New York City, "Alfy," as he was known to family and friends, showed an early interest in art. Leaving Public School 58 at the age of sixteen, he joined his father's lithographic firm of Heppenheimer and Maurer in 1884. While continuing to work as a professional artist designing cigar and soap labels, he attended classes at the National Academy of Design and also took private lessons from Edgar Ward.

In 1897, with savings from nearly ten years of work as a commercial artist, Maurer sailed for Europe, eventually settling in Paris. Briefly studying at the Académie Julian, he continued to work in the conservative, naturalistic style for which his studies had trained him. Exhibiting at the Paris Salons of 1899 and 1900, Maurer received his first major professional recognition in 1901 when he won the Carnegie Institute's gold medal and $1,500 for *An Arrangement* (1901, Whitney Museum of American Art). His work was soon recognized at both American and European juried exhibitions, such as the Pan-American Exposition (Buffalo, 1901, bronze medal), the St. Louis Exposition (1904, silver medal), and the Liege Exposition (Belgium, 1905, third medal).

In 1904, however, Maurer's aesthetic began to change. Meeting Gertrude and Leo Stein soon after their arrival in Paris, Maurer regularly attended the Steins' "Saturday Soirées." Surrounded by the work of Cézanne, Lautrec, Picasso, and Matisse and with the general feeling of aesthetic revolt in the Parisian air, Maurer was converted to the "modern" style of painting. According to Max Weber, Maurer did not, however, attend Matisse's school between 1906 and 1909. Exhibiting at the revolutionary Salon d'Automne in 1905, Maurer made his final break with his earlier, naturalistic style, prompting his friend, the American sculptor Mahonri Young, to say, "From that day on, he painted like a wild man. He was never the light-hearted, gay Alfy we had known." A work from around this time, *Landscape with Red Tree* (c. 1907–1908, John C. Marin Collection), is an example of Maurer's experimentation with the bold colors and techniques of the Fauves.

This change, however, cut Maurer off from the financial rewards and critical praise his work had previously won him. Although opportunities for exhibiting his new work were rare, by 1909 Maurer was fully immersed in the Fauvist landscape. In that same year Alfred Stieglitz offered Maurer and John Marin a joint show in New York at Stieglitz's Photo-Secession Gallery, the famous "291" gallery. Charles Caffin, writing in *Camera Work* ("The Maurers and the Marins at the Photo-Secession Gallery," no. 27 [July 1909]: 41), said of Maurer's work, "You may even observe in some of them . . . a dripping application of the color, and the leaving of portions of the ground apparent between the masses of color." Maurer also participated in Stieglitz's exhibition, *Younger American Painters*, in 1910 and had a one-man show at Folsom Galleries in New York in 1913. In this same year, Maurer also showed three works, *Landscape*, *Old Faience*, and *Autumn* (all c. 1912), at the Armory Show, controversial because of its exhibition of the latest modern works from Europe and America. The art press, not yet ready to accept the modern movement that had recently arrived from Paris, criticized Maurer's pieces, lamenting the unfortunate change in his work. J. F. Chamberlin, writing in the *New York Evening Mail* (3 Apr. 1909), said of Maurer's work, "Two or three, indeed, possess strong indications of an intense feeling for the beauty of dazzling light, and for big, splended forms in nature. But here is one which has in the foreground a great gob of color; what is it? A bursted tomato? A fireman's hat? A red rock? A couple of people under an umbrella? Nobody can make it out."

Though disapproving of the change in his son's artistic style, Maurer's father continued to support him in Paris until the outbreak of World War I. In August 1914 Maurer returned to his parents' home, where he would live for the rest of his life. Maurer's flight from Paris was likely motivated by the events in Europe. Louis Maurer's threats of cutting off his financial support might also have influenced his decision. Regardless of his reason, in his rapid departure, Alfred Maurer left behind a studio full of paintings that were eventually sold for back rent, most of which were subsequently lost. Gertrude Stein also claimed that Maurer (who never married, citing reasons of economy) regretfully left behind a French mistress.

From 1914 to 1924 Maurer led a quiet life, marked only by the 1917 death of his mother, with whom he was particularly close, and infrequent exhibitions. Soon after returning to the United States, Maurer began summering at "Shady Brook" in Marlboro-on-the-Hudson; he also visited his longtime friend, the painter Arthur Dove, in both Connecticut and Long Island. In 1917 Maurer displayed his work at the first annual exhibition of the Society of Independent Artists, a group with which he exhibited each year for the remainder of his life; Maurer was also elected a director of the society in 1919.

Maurer's work during this time was becoming increasingly abstract, blatantly exhibiting the influence of the cubist movement. These works, such as *Abstract Still Life* (c. 1919, Hirshhorn Museum and Sculpture Garden), with its analysis of forms, also illustrate his movement away from pure color. It was one of these works that the book and art dealer Erhand Weyhe purchased in 1922. Two years later Weyhe purchased all of Maurer's work from the previous ten years (well over 200 works) and presented a selected exhibition of his purchase that same year. Although both the purchase and exhibition were briefly covered in the art press, Maurer did not return to public attention until 1928, when his exhibition at Weyhe Gallery led critics to praise his work for the first time since his conversion to abstraction and hail him as an early American modernist. The *Chicago Evening Post* called Maurer a "talented artist and born experimenter," whose works had "taken on a richness and a vibrance and freedom of handling" (3 Apr. 1928).

The year 1928 was critical for Maurer. A painful prostate condition slowed his production, and the exhibition at Weyhe's would be his only one until 1931. The year also saw the rediscovery of his father as an artist. As the last living Currier and Ives artist, the elder Maurer became a popular human interest story. In his many press interviews, Louis Maurer took the opportunity to deride his son's modern art, and on 26 January 1931, the day Alfred Maurer's last exhibition closed, Louis Maurer's first one-man show opened with critics calling him "America's Oldest Living Artist."

In April 1932 Maurer's health improved after surgery for his prostate condition. The next month Louis Maurer died, ending Maurer's contentious relationship with his father. Moving into his father's downstairs bedroom, Maurer received callers, and his friends described him as cheerful, apparently recovering well from both his surgery and his father's death. Consequently, Maurer's friends were shocked when he hung himself in the door frame of his old bedroom.

In his last years Maurer completed a number of significant cubist works, many of which were depictions of female heads, including *Twin Heads* (c. 1930, Whitney Museum of American Art) and *Head in Window* (c. 1928–1930, Salander–O'Reilly Galleries). Among his other later cubist works are *Four Heads* (1930, Hirshhorn Museum and Sculpture Garden) and *George Washington* (1932, Portland Art Museum).

Shortly after Maurer's suicide, Lewis Mumford of the *New Yorker* called Maurer "one of the handful of genuine moderns who really felt their abstractions as experience" (17 Nov. 1934). Maurer's pioneering work in abstract painting has been increasingly recognized since his death. Likewise, in an essay in the catalog for Maurer's memorial exhibition, Robert Ulrich Godsoe wrote, "I consider Alfred Maurer to have been the greatest American painter of all time" (*Works of the Late Alfred Maurer*, Uptown Gallery [1934], p. 1).

This assessment was echoed much later in the *New York Times* by Hilton Kramer, who placed Maurer "unequivocally in the first rank of the American painters of his generation" (25 Mar. 1973).

• Maurer's works are represented in the collections of the Smithsonian Institution (Hirshhorn Museum and Sculpture Garden and the National Museum of American Art); the University of Nebraska, Art Galleries; and the Brooklyn Museum, among others. Selected letters are in the microfilm collections of the Archives of American Art at the Smithsonian Institution. For a biography see Elizabeth McCausland, *A. H. Maurer* (1951). McCausland was also the author of the catalog *A. H. Maurer, 1868–1932* (1949), which accompanied the first major exhibition of his work at the Walker Art Center in Minneapolis. The major retrospective of Maurer's work organized by the National Collection of Fine Arts (now National Museum of American Art, Smithsonian Institution) produced *Alfred H. Maurer, 1868–1932* (1973). Salander–O'Reilly Galleries in New York City published two catalogs of selected works, *Alfred H. Maurer, 1868–1932: Modernist Paintings* (1983) and *Alfred H. Maurer (1868–1932): The Cubist Works* (1988). See also the exhibition catalog from the Bernard Daneberg Galleries, *Alfred Maurer and the Fauves: The Lost Years Rediscovered* (1973). Obituaries are in the *New York Times* and the *New York Herald-Tribune*, both 5 Aug. 1932, and in *ArtNews*, 13 Aug. 1932, p. 8.

MARTIN R. KALFATOVIC

MAURER, James Hudson (15 Apr. 1864–16 Mar. 1944), socialist politician and labor official, was born in Reading, Pennsylvania, the son of James R. Maurer, a shoemaker, and Sarah Lorah. James endured a difficult childhood. His father, a strict Lutheran, died of smallpox in 1872. His mother remarried soon after, but his stepfather proved stern and abusive. Poverty cut short James's formal education. After just fourteen months at public school, without the ability to read or write, he was forced to seek work to supplement the family's income. He labored as a newsboy, farm laborer, factory operative, and, at age sixteen, machinist's apprentice. During his apprenticeship Maurer learned to read and developed an interest in politics and economics. In 1880 he joined the Knights of Labor and the Greenback party. In 1881, after moving to nearby Pottstown, Maurer rose through the ranks of the Knights, eventually becoming district master workman for the Schuylkill Valley. In 1886 he married Mary J. Missimer; they had two children. In 1891 the family returned to Reading.

After a series of failed business ventures in the 1890s, Maurer focused his enormous energies on trade unionism and socialism. In 1901 he became a delegate to the Central Labor Union of Reading. In that same year he joined the recently formed Socialist party of America and ran for the state legislature in 1902. Although he failed in this bid for office, in 1904 he was elected to the party's national executive committee. In 1906 Maurer ran on the Socialist ticket for governor of Pennsylvania, garnering a respectable 26,000 votes. In 1910 he gained national attention by becoming Pennsylvania's first Socialist state legislator.

Maurer served three terms in the state legislature, during which he fought for a variety of labor and reform laws. His most notable success came in 1915 when he led the fight to secure Pennsylvania's first workers' compensation act. He also pressed for child labor restrictions, industrial safety regulations, and old-age pensions. As a Socialist, Maurer was outspoken in his opposition to U.S. involvement in World War I.

Maurer was elected to the presidency of the Pennsylvania State Federation of Labor in 1912, a position he held until 1928. He transformed the federation into a powerful political lobby for prolabor legislation. Although a Socialist, he upheld the American Federation of Labor's principle of nonpartisanship. Under his direction, the state federation supported all prolabor candidates regardless of party affiliation.

From 1921 to 1929 Maurer served as the first director of the Workers' Education Bureau of America, an agency originally intended to popularize the need for industrial unionism. In 1928 and 1932, when the Socialist party backed Norman Thomas for president, Maurer served as Thomas's running mate. In 1934 Maurer ran unsuccessfully on the Socialist ticket for the U.S. Senate. This proved to be his last campaign. In 1936 he resigned from the party's national executive committee to protest the party's united front strategy, which he regarded as a trend toward communism. Upon retirement, Maurer wrote his autobiography, *It Can Be Done*, published in 1938. He died in Reading. Maurer is best remembered as a soft-spoken but indefatigable champion of progressive unionism and moderate socialism.

• Secondary sources on Maurer are limited. See, for example, David A. Shannon, *The Socialist Party of America* (1955); Henry G. Stetler, *The Socialist Movement in Reading, Pennsylvania* (1943); and Gary M. Fink, ed., *Biographical Dictionary of American Labor* (1984), pp. 399–400. An obituary is in the *New York Times*, 17 Mar. 1944.

CRAIG PHELAN

MAURIN, Peter Aristide (9 May 1877–15 May 1949), cofounder of the Catholic Worker Movement, was born in Oultet, France, the son of Jean Baptiste Maurin, a farmer, and Marie Pages, who later died in childbirth. At age fourteen, Maurin received his certificate d'études from a local school and continued his studies in Mende at the Personnat St. Privat sponsored by the Christian Brothers. Maurin entered this religious congregation and professed first vows in September 1895, using the name Brother Adorator Charles. A Christian Brother for nine years, he was particularly influenced by the order's belief that teachers should become, for their students, models of sacrifice, devotion, and concern for the poor. Maurin read widely and joined a study group that discussed contemporary issues, in particular the notion that politics, history, literature, and religion could provide avenues for social reform. Although he was a brother in a religious order, Maurin was required to serve in the French

army. He was assigned to the 142d Infantry Regiment of Mende at Lodève from November 1898 until September 1899, for several weeks in 1904, and again in 1907.

Before professing perpetual vows in the Congregation of the Christian Brothers, Maurin withdrew and joined Le Sillon (The Furrow), an activist group whose goal was to see that the Catholic church played an important role in France's becoming a republic infused with Christianity. During his six-year involvement with Le Sillon, Maurin's philosophy of social activism began to emerge. He believed that social change begins with a change of heart inspired by religious principles, which ultimately would transform society into a Christian environment. Le Sillon's loose structure and its strategies of teaching, debating, and indoctrination were to serve for him as the prototype for the Catholic Worker Movement.

Maurin arrived in New York City in 1909 and traveled to Canada with a fellow Frenchman to begin a homestead in Saskatchewan. Unable to work the land alone after his friend was killed during a hunting trip, Maurin left Canada and wandered across the United States, working on the railroad, doing many odd jobs, and even being arrested twice for vagrancy. Throughout this phase of his life there is no mention of any association with the Catholic church. Because French translators were needed during World War I, Maurin opened a school in Chicago to give French lessons. He taught there for eight years before moving to Woodstock, New York, to be a teacher.

Although there are no recorded details, Maurin experienced in Woodstock a religious conversion that led him to practice again the tenets of Catholicism after a ten-year period of noninvolvement. His behavior apparently changed; he stopped charging for language lessons and instead requested that pupils give him whatever they thought his instruction was worth. In addition, he began writing his "Easy Essays," which conveyed his philosophy of life, and used them to teach French. In exchange for food and lodging Maurin took a job as a handyman at a summer camp run by Father Joseph B. Scully in Mount Tremper, New York. Here Maurin read and thought, refining and writing the essays that formed the basis for his program of social action.

Maurin's plan contained four components for the renewal of society:

1. To spread the message of the social teachings of the Catholic church, which affirmed the dignity of all people and spoke out against human abuses of all kinds.
2. To practice the corporal and spiritual works of mercy through houses of hospitality, which provided safe housing, food, and clothing.
3. To hold roundtable discussions of his principles called "the clarification of thought seminars."
4. To establish farming communities known as "agronomic universities" in order to reduce unemploy-

ment and simultaneously to make workers into scholars and scholars into workers.

Eager to implement this program of social reform, Maurin frequently proselytized in Manhattan's Union Square in the hope of finding someone who could make his ideas a reality. In December 1932 he met Dorothy Day, a recent Catholic convert and former socialist and journalist. Their association first resulted in the "Catholic Worker" news sheet distributed on 1 May 1933 and later spawned the movement of the same name. With Maurin's four-point program as its touchstone, the Catholic Worker Movement was to spread across the country by the early 1940s. Its first house of hospitality, the Teresa-Joseph House, was opened in December 1934, in New York City, and a communal farm under the movement's aegis was established in 1935 at Huguenot on Staten Island. Maurin's role in the movement was that of an itinerant teacher, proclaiming his message to engender support from anyone who would listen to him. In 1944 a stroke reduced his active involvement in his life's work. The years that followed were spent at the communal farms at Easton, Pennsylvania, and later at the Maryfarm in Newburgh, New York, where he died.

• Marc Ellis, *Peter Maurin: Prophet in the Twentieth Century* (1981), is a biography with a good treatment of Maurin's philosophy. Anthony Novistsky, "The Ideological Development of Peter Maurin's Green Revolution" (Ph.D. diss., 1969, SUNY-Buffalo), is a thorough account of Maurin's ideology and its impact on the movement. Arthur Sheehan, *Peter Maurin: Gay Believer* (1959), is an extensive biography. See also Brendan A. O'Grady, "Peter Maurin the Propagandist" (Ph.D. diss., Univ. of Ottawa, 1954). Dorothy Day writes about Maurin; see in particular *The Long Loneliness* (1952) and *Loaves and Fishes* (1963). William Miller's books, *A Harsh and Dreadful Love: Dorothy Day and the Catholic Worker Movement* (1972) and *Dorothy Day: A Biography* (1982), David O'Brien's *American Catholic and Social Reform* (1968), and Michele Aronica's *Beyond Charismatic Leadership: The New York Catholic Worker* (1987) contain information about Maurin and his ideology. Maurin's writings are collected in *Easy Essays* (1936) and *Catholic Radicalism* (1949); the latter was revised as *The Green Revolution and Radical Christian Thought*, ed. Chuck Smith (1971). The most complete information about Maurin is located in the Catholic Worker archives housed at Marquette University.

MICHELE TERESA ARONICA

MAURY, Antonia Caetana De Paiva Pereira (21 Mar. 1866–8 Jan. 1952), astronomer, was born in Cold Spring, New York, the daughter of Mytton Maury, a clergyman, naturalist, and editor of *Maury's Geographical Series*, and Virginia Draper. Maury was the granddaughter of John William Draper, a physician and early photographer of the moon and the solar spectrum, and the niece of Henry Draper, also a physician and the first to photograph a stellar spectrum. Educated in part by her father, Maury went on to graduate from Vassar College in 1887, with honors in astronomy,

physics, and philosophy. Her professors included the pioneering American woman astronomer Maria Mitchell.

After graduation, Maury went to work at the Harvard College Observatory, then directed by Edward C. Pickering. Pickering was much intrigued by stellar spectroscopy and had just discovered that the spectral lines of the star Mizar were double on one photographic plate but single on others. He reasoned that Mizar was actually a pair of stars, which were too far away to be seen individually. The orbital motion of the stars led to the changes in spectra. Such stars are now called spectroscopic binaries; Mizar was the first one found. Maury determined its period and in 1889 discovered the second known spectroscopic binary, Beta Aurigae.

After the death of Henry Draper in 1882, his widow, Annie Palmer Draper, had lent his telescope to the Harvard Observatory and provided funds for the reduction of photographs of stellar spectra. To carry out the work, Pickering hired Williamina Fleming, a Scottish immigrant with no special training in physics or astronomy. Fleming catalogued the spectra of over 10,000 stars, publishing the *Draper Catalogue of Stellar Spectra* in 1890. To obtain more detailed spectra, Pickering and his assistants placed three or four prisms in front of the Draper refractor. Maury was assigned the task of classifying the spectra of several hundred bright stars in the Northern Hemisphere that were photographed in this way. She found Fleming's classification scheme inadequate for the task. More specifically, Maury placed classes of stars in a somewhat different order than that used by Pickering and Fleming. Her colleagues at Harvard and elsewhere adopted this change. Maury also subdivided stars of early spectral types into three subclasses, designated *a*, *b*, and *c*. The *a*-stars had normal lines; *b*, hazy lines; and *c*, sharp lines. Intermediate subclasses were called *ab* and *ac*.

Developing an independent classification scheme required time and slowed the efficient reduction of data favored by Pickering and Fleming. Maury, who wanted to understand astronomy, suggested that she should learn the calculus, but she did not. Pickering grew impatient with the slow pace of Maury's data reduction, particularly when she left the observatory from time to time with her task unfinished. The catalog finally was published in 1897 as volume 28, part I, of the *Annals* of the Harvard College Observatory.

While Maury puzzled over the spectra of stars in the Northern Hemisphere, Annie Jump Cannon, also of the Harvard College Observatory, examined photographs of bright stars from the Southern Hemisphere. Cannon's spectral classification scheme, like that of Fleming, made no distinction among stars according to the sharpness of their spectral lines. This simpler scheme was generally adopted at Harvard. In 1905, however, the Danish astronomer Ejnar Hertzsprung argued that class *c* stars were unusually luminous compared to other stars of the same spectral type. Such stars would later be designated as supergiants when compared to normal giant stars (still fainter stars were called dwarfs). Hertzsprung urged that Harvard continue to include this subclassification in its catalogs, but Pickering declined to do so. In more recent years, subclassifications like those introduced by Maury have been widely adopted.

Maury left Harvard in 1896 and spent the next two decades teaching and lecturing at Cornell University and elsewhere. Returning to Harvard in 1918, she resumed her study of the orbits of spectroscopic binaries. She became particularly intrigued by one of these stars, Beta Lyrae, and examined over 300 spectra of it, seeking to understand the behavior of the atmospheres of the component stars. Her paper on the subject was published in 1933 as "The Spectral Changes of Beta Lyrae" (*Annals of the Harvard College Observatory* 8, no. 8). Even after she left Harvard in 1935, she continued to visit annually until 1948 to check new data about Beta Lyrae against her predictions.

Maury was elected to the Council of the American Association of Variable Star Observers in 1921 and to the Royal Astronomical Society in 1922. She received the Annie Jump Cannon Prize of the American Astronomical Society in 1943. In addition to astronomy, her interests included ornithology and the conservation of historic sites and natural resources. For three years after her retirement from Harvard, she tended the collections at the Draper Park Observatory Museum, the former home of the Drapers in Hastings-on-Hudson, New York. She continued to live in Hastings-on-Hudson until her death in a hospital in Dobbs Ferry, New York. She never married or had children.

• Scattered correspondence of and relating to Maury survives in the papers of Edward C. Pickering and of Harlow Shapley in the Harvard University Archives. Her major work on spectral classification was "Spectra of Bright Stars . . . ," *Annals of the Harvard College Observatory* 28, pt. 1 (1897). General discussions relevant to Maury's work are Dorrit Hoffleit, "The Evolution of the Henry Draper Memorial," *Vistas in Astronomy* 34 (1991): 107–62; Bessie Z. Jones and Lyle G. Boyd, *The Harvard College Observatory* (1971); and Pamela E. Mack, "Straying from Their Orbits: Women in Astronomy in America," in *Women of Science*, ed. G. Kass-Simon et al. (1990), pp. 72–116. A brief obituary by Dorrit Hoffleit is in *Sky and Telescope* 11 (1952) 106.

PEGGY ALDRICH KIDWELL

MAURY, Dabney Herndon (21 May 1822–11 Jan. 1900), soldier and writer, was born in Fredericksburg, Virginia, the son of Captain John Minor Maury, a U.S. naval officer, and Eliza Maury, who was John Maury's first cousin. After the death of their father in 1828, Dabney and his brother lived with their uncle Matthew Fontaine Maury. Dabney graduated in 1842 from the University of Virginia. He next studied law at the university and under a judge at Fredericksburg. Preferring a military career to one in the law, Maury entered West Point and graduated thirty-seventh of a class of fifty-nine in 1846. He was commissioned a second lieutenant in the Regiment of Mounted Rifles. With that unit, Maury served in the Mexican War and received a brevet as first lieutenant for gallant and meritorious conduct at the battle of Cerro Gordo. A

Mexican musketball shattered his left arm, permanently crippling it, and he returned to the United States to recuperate. In 1856 Maury married Nannie Mason; they had three children.

During the years prior to the Civil War, Maury held a number of positions in the army. He served from 1847 to 1852 as a professor and instructor at West Point. Then he spent four years on the frontier in Texas. Next Maury was superintendent of the cavalry school at Carlisle Barracks, Pennsylvania, until 1860. Finally, as a captain, he was assistant adjutant general of the Department of New Mexico. He resigned his commission in May 1861, when he learned of the secession of his native state, and the War Department dismissed him on 25 June. Maury traveled to Richmond, where in July he received commissions as a captain of cavalry in the regular Confederate army, colonel of cavalry in the Virginia state forces, and lieutenant colonel in the provisional army. On 19 July the War Department assigned him as adjutant general to General Joseph E. Johnston at Manassas, but on 23 August he was reassigned as adjutant general to Major General Theophilus H. Holmes, commander of the Department of Fredericksburg.

Maury remained on Holmes's staff until February 1862. He then was promoted to colonel and ordered to become chief of staff to Major General Earl Van Dorn, who had just been placed in command of the Trans-Mississippi Department. Maury performed outstanding service at the battle of Elkhorn Tavern (Pea Ridge), 7–8 March. For his conduct, he received a promotion to brigadier general on 18 March to rank from 12 March. He accompanied Van Dorn's Army of the West to Corinth, Mississippi, and in late April was placed in command of a brigade in Major General Samuel Jones's (1819–1887) division. During the evacuation of Corinth, Maury had charge of the army's rear guard. He was given command of a division in the Army of the West in June and led his men in the battles of Iuka, 19 September, and Corinth, 3–4 October. Major General Sterling Price praised him highly for his role in the latter engagement. Maury was promoted to major general on 4 November and took his division to Vicksburg the next month.

After commanding at Snyder's Bluff, north of Vicksburg, for several months, Maury went in early April 1863 to support Major General William W. Loring's forces defending Fort Pemberton. On 15 April President Jefferson Davis ordered Maury to Knoxville to assume command of the Department of East Tennessee. Less than two weeks later, however, the War Department ordered him to Mobile, Alabama, where he replaced Major General Simon B. Buckner (1823–1914) as commander of the District of the Gulf. Maury assumed the latter position on 19 May and held it until the end of the war. In June 1863 Maury's command was upgraded to a department, but it was redesignated as a district within the Department of Alabama, Mississippi, and East Louisiana in January 1864. Federal naval vessels bombarded Fort Powell in Mississippi Sound in February and March 1864, but its defenders successfully withstood the attack. On 26 July Maury assumed temporary command in Meridian, Mississippi, of the Department of Alabama, Mississippi, and East Louisiana and held that position until Lieutenant General Richard Taylor (1826–1879) assumed command on 6 September. In August, during Maury's absence from Mobile, the operations known as the battle of Mobile Bay occurred. That campaign resulted in the destruction of the small Confederate naval force in Mobile Bay and the capture by Union forces of Fort Morgan, Fort Gaines, and Fort Powell at the bay's entrance.

Maury again exercised temporary departmental command from 22 November to 11 December while Taylor was away in Georgia. Federal forces moved against the eastern defenses of Maury's district in late March 1865. After the capture of Spanish Fort on 8 April and Fort Blakely the next day, Maury ordered an evacuation of Mobile. He left the city with his army's rear guard on 12 April. When his forces reached Meridian, they were formed into an infantry division in Taylor's army. Maury and his men surrendered at Cuba Station, Alabama, on 8 May.

After a brief visit to New Orleans, Maury returned to Virginia, opened the Classical and Mathematical Academy for boys in Fredericksburg, and taught there for a time. Then he moved to New Orleans to become an express agent. Shortly afterward he purchased land in nearby St. Tammany Parish and operated a naval stores manufacturing establishment. The latter enterprise failed, and Maury returned to New Orleans. There in 1868 he organized the Southern Historical Society to preserve the Confederacy's archives. In 1873 the society relocated to Richmond, Virginia. Maury served as the chair of its executive committee until 1886. President Grover Cleveland appointed Maury as U.S. minister to Colombia, and he held that post from 1885 to 1889. When he returned to the United States, Maury lived with his son in Peoria, Illinois, where he died.

As commander of the Confederate District of the Gulf, Maury proved a competent and trustworthy general. He supervised the construction of Mobile's defenses and was selfless when called on to send men or supplies to other points of the Confederacy. Maury recognized the city's place in the Confederacy's overall war strategy and acted accordingly. He deserves credit for accepting his role in a relatively inactive theater of operations and performing his job most capably.

• Many of Maury's official papers are in the National Archives. Maury published his memoirs as *Recollections of a Virginian* (1894). His service as commander of the District of the Gulf is analyzed and described in Arthur W. Bergeron, Jr., *Confederate Mobile, 1861–1865* (1991). An obituary from the Richmond (Va.) *Dispatch*, 14 Jan. 1900, was reprinted as "Dabney Herndon Maury," Southern Historical Society, *Papers* 27 (1900): 335–49.

ARTHUR W. BERGERON, JR.

MAURY, Matthew Fontaine (14 Jan. 1806–1 Feb. 1873), naval officer and oceanographer, was born near Fredericksburg, Virginia, the son of Richard Maury and Diana Minor, farmers. In 1811 the family settled on a farm near the frontier village of Franklin in Central Tennessee. Matthew Fontaine Maury, who is usually known by all three of his names, attended country schools in the area, but in 1818 he enrolled in Harpeth Academy at Franklin. One of his older brothers was a naval officer, and in 1825 Maury received a midshipman's warrant in the U.S. Navy. During the next nine years he sailed to Europe, around the world on the USS *Vincennes*, and to the Pacific coast of South America. While on a leave of absence in 1834 he married Ann Hull Herndon. A devoted family man and largely self-educated, Maury took a great interest in the educations of his eight children.

Maury wrote *A New Theoretical and Practical Treatise on Navigation* in 1836. This general and popular text for naval officers, in which Maury emphasized the need for the collection of data on winds and ocean currents, established his reputation as an author on scientific and technological subjects. That year he was promoted to lieutenant. In 1837 he was appointed as astronomer on a U.S. Navy exploring expedition to the Pacific, but dissatisfied with the command on this venture, Maury requested reassignment to harbor surveys in the southeastern United States. Using the pseudonym Harry Bluff, he wrote articles criticizing the previous naval administration. These articles and others, which he signed "From Will Hatch to his old messmate Harry Bluff," were published in 1838 in the *Richmond Whig and Public Advertiser*. Maury's articles proposed reforms, including establishment of a naval academy, which was later founded at Annapolis. In 1839 Maury's right leg was injured in a stagecoach accident, leaving him permanently handicapped. He continued writing pieces critical of the naval establishment, which were published in the *Southern Literary Messenger* under various pseudonyms, but his identity was revealed by an article of July 1841 signed "A Brother Officer."

Under a navy administration more favorable to his interests, Maury was in 1842 appointed superintendent of both the Depot of Charts and Instruments of the Navy Department in Washington, D.C., and the Naval Observatory. In 1854 these institutions were consolidated as the U.S. Naval Observatory and Hydrographic Office, with Maury in charge. In his professional work he concentrated on hydrology and meteorology and conducted research on winds and currents. He published *Wind and Current Chart of the North Atlantic* (1847); *Abstract Log for the Use of American Navigators* (1848), which was reissued in 1850 as *Notice to Mariners*; and *Explanations and Sailing Directions to Accompany the Wind and Current Charts* (1851), which was published in eight subsequent editions. On the basis of the application of data in these publications, great savings were effected in sailing time between ports on the Atlantic. Maury next extended his methods to other oceans. At first he used old log books, but soon he requested that naval officers and masters of commercial vessels send in reports of their voyages on forms he had specially prepared for the purpose. At an international oceanographic meeting in Brussels in 1853, Maury persuaded other maritime nations to adopt his methods.

At his headquarters in Washington, Maury now received information from all parts of the world, with which he revised his earlier charts and compiled new ones of routes not previously covered. For example, following the California gold rush he produced charts that, along with other technological advances, reduced the sailing time from New York to San Francisco from the previous average of 180 days to about 130 days. A proportionate savings of time was accomplished for other voyages. The proposed tracks might deviate considerably from great circle routes (the shortest distance between points on the globe) but took into account prevailing and seasonally changing winds and currents. Maury was offered memberships in scholarly associations, was honored by foreign governments, and was given an award from merchants and underwriters in New York City acknowledging the economic value of his work.

In 1855 the U.S. Congress called a secret meeting of a navy board to assess naval efficiency. Surprisingly, the board assigned Maury to a leave of absence, though he was to continue his duties as head of the Naval Observatory. He protested and, assisted by friends, newspapers, and resolutions passed by the legislative bodies of several states, was restored to active service in 1858 and promoted, retroactively, to commander. In the meantime, Maury had written *The Physical Geography of the Sea* (1855), in which he laid the foundations of the modern science of oceanography.

Following the outbreak of the American Civil War, Maury, out of loyalty to the region where he was born and grew up, joined the Confederate States Navy. With the rank of commander, he was assigned to harbor defense duties, including designing and laying mines. In 1862 he was sent to England to enlist aid for the South. Overseas he obtained ships for the Confederacy and experimented with electric mines. In 1865 he was on his way back to North America when, in Havana, Cuba, he learned of the surrender of the Confederate States. Rather than return home, Maury went to Mexico to initiate colonization of exiled Confederates under the patronage of Emperor Ferdinand Maximilian. Colonization proved unsuccessful, so Maury returned to England, where he wrote several geography textbooks. The British raised a large sum of money by public subscription and presented it to Maury for his scientific contributions. He returned to the United States in 1868, where he became professor of meteorology at the Virginia Military Institute in Lexington, Virginia. He died there four years later and eventually was buried in Richmond.

Some of Maury's practical work was partly superseded as steamships replaced sailing vessels on the world's oceans. His deep-sea soundings proved useful in the laying of a transatlantic cable, but not enough data could be collected by these methods to make a satisfactory, general map of the sea floor at that time.

Nevertheless, many of his contributions to the knowledge of the oceans and to scientific education endure. Several memorials have been erected in his honor, especially in the South. For his pioneering work in oceanography, Maury well merits the appellation "the Pathfinder of the Seas."

• The largest collections of Maury materials are at the National Archives and the Library of Congress in Washington, D.C. Letters, papers, and other records related to Maury are scattered among various smaller collections, including those at the Public Record Office, London, the University of Virginia, the Virginia State Library, the Virginia Historical Society, Virginia Military Institute, and the Confederate Museum, Richmond. Maury's own publications, in addition to those noted in the text above, include *On the Saltiness of the Sea* (1852), *The Amazon and the Atlantic Slopes of South America* (1853), and *Physical Survey of Virginia* (1868). His writings are listed in Ralph M. Brown, "Bibliography of Commander Matthew Fontaine Maury," *Bulletin of the Virginia Polytechnic Institute* 37 (Oct. 1944). The earliest biography is by Maury's daughter Diana F. M. Corbin, *A Life of Matthew Fontaine Maury* (1888). Others are Jaquelin A. Caskie, *Life and Letters of Matthew Fontaine Maury* (1928); Hildegard Hawthorne, *Matthew Fontaine Maury: Trail Maker of the Seas* (1943); Columbus O'D. Iselin, *Matthew Fontaine Maury: Pathfinder of the Seas* (1957); Patricia Jahns, *Matthew Fontaine Maury and Joseph Henry: Scientists of the Civil War* (1961); Frances L. Williams, *Matthew Fontaine Maury: Scientist of the Sea* (1963); and Janice J. Beatty, *Seeker of Seaways: A Life of Matthew Fontaine Maury* (1966).

NORMAN J. W. THROWER

MAVERICK, Mary (16 Mar. 1818–24 Feb. 1898), pioneer, was born Mary Ann Adams in Tuscaloosa County, Alabama, the daughter of William Lewis Adams and Agatha Strother, planters. Her parents, whose forebears had settled near Boston in the eighteenth century, were recent arrivals to frontier Alabama at the time of her birth. She grew up on their plantation, was educated locally, and at the age of eighteen met and soon afterward married a lawyer named Samuel Augustus Maverick, who was fifteen years her senior.

Sam Maverick was also from a pioneering Alabama family. Sometime around 1830 he had settled in San Antonio, where he became a leader in the movement to secure the independence of Texas from Mexico. Maverick played a major role in the Texas revolution that broke out in 1835, and he was one of the signers of the territory's declaration of independence in March 1836. That summer, on a visit to his family in Alabama, he met Mary Ann Adams and married her some weeks later. The couple eventually had ten children, of whom four died in childhood. Shortly after their wedding, Mary began keeping the diary that would later earn her a place in Texas history.

Because there was still political unrest in San Antonio, the couple remained with relatives in Alabama and South Carolina for more than a year. Finally, in early December 1837, Sam and Mary, together with their infant son, Samuel Jr., began their journey by wagon to Texas, accompanied by Mary's younger brother and several slaves, and arrived in San Antonio in January 1838.

Maverick owned land and a small stone house at the corner of Main and Soledad streets, near the center of the town. In the months after the family's arrival, Maverick enlarged the house and erected other buildings on the property, which extended to the banks of the San Antonio River. Mary had a second son, Lewis, in the spring of 1839; he is remembered as the first Anglo-American to be born and reared in San Antonio.

While Sam pursued his career as a lawyer and politician—he later served in both the republic's congress and the state legislature—Mary was responsible for the day-to-day running of the household, which included not only her children but also a number of servants and slaves that she had to instruct and supervise. Her daily life and that of other upper-class women in San Antonio could hardly be called arduous, however, at least in comparison with the experiences of their sister pioneers of the Great Plains and other regions of the American West, where settlers endured extreme physical hardships. In San Antonio winters were not harsh and domestic help was abundant.

In many ways, life in San Antonio more closely resembled that of the southern plantations where Mary Maverick and many of the other settlers had spent their childhoods. To her credit, Mary Maverick recognized that hers was a privileged existence, which she described in her diary as "a lazy life of ease." The San Antonio settlers had created an attractive landscape of flowering plants and fruit trees, which flourished in the temperate climate. Food was abundant, Spanish-style structures of adobe and stone provided comfortable housing, and both women and men could indulge their tastes for expensive clothing and furnishings. There were frequent parties and balls, and the long summers were filled with picnics and swimming.

There were dark sides to life in San Antonio, however: malaria and cholera, as well as less exotic diseases, plagued the settlement—"fevers" took the lives of several Maverick children—and there was an ever-present threat of raids by both Native Americans and Mexican soldiers. The men of the settlement bore the major responsibility for confronting these dangers, as well as the nuisance of continually losing property: mules and gear were frequently stolen by Indians, and the Mavericks lost their share. Sometimes these raids threatened the peacefulness of domestic life: in one memorable incident, which occurred in March 1840, several Comanche warriors fleeing a skirmish at the courthouse ran into the Maverick home and apparently threatened the children, but the invaders were driven away by the female cook.

Mary Maverick's life was disrupted two years later, in the spring of 1842, when increasing incursions by the Mexican army led her husband to move the family to a safer site some fifty miles to the northeast, near La Grange and the Colorado River. That September her life was further disrupted when her husband was one of fifty male settlers seized by pro-Mexican mercenar-ies and taken to a prison east of Mexico City. Appeals by U.S. authorities led to the release of Sam and the other Americans in March 1843, but only after the prisoners had endured six months of forced labor.

The desire for safety led Sam Maverick to move his family again, this time south to the Gulf Coast. After living in Decrows Point, near Matagorda, for several years, Sam bought a large ranch in the area following the annexation of Texas to the United States in the summer of 1845. The family remained there, raising both cattle and vegetables, until 1847, when they returned to their San Antonio residence, which had been heavily damaged in their absence. Three years later they moved to their last home, a new stone dwelling across from the Alamo.

In addition to his activities as a lawyer and legislator, Sam Maverick also entered the cattle business. In 1854 he bought the Conquista ranch, forty-five miles south of San Antonio, and moved his herds there from his much smaller spread in Matagorda. At Conquista he sought to establish a major cattle-raising operation, but because his cows were not branded they were frequently stolen by neighboring ranchers, who marked them with their own brands. Sam Maverick's association with the cattle business earned his name a permanent place in the English language: other ranchers called unbranded cows "mavericks," and eventually the name was applied to anyone "outside the herd," human as well as animal.

These and other incidents were duly recorded by Mary Maverick in her diary, which she kept until 1881. In its pages she detailed not only the dangers and travails of the Mavericks and other settlers, but also described her daily activities, recorded current events, and noted the behavior, customs, and dress of her fellow settlers. During the Civil War, Mary recorded not only life in San Antonio but also the experiences of four Maverick sons who fought with the Confederate army.

After Sam Maverick died in the fall of 1870, Mary remained at their home near the Alamo. She continued her diary until 1881, when she presented the manuscript to her children and grandchildren. The remainder of her life was uneventful, and she died in San Antonio. At her death she was remembered as the matriarch of the Maverick clan, which had become one of the leading families of Texas.

In 1920 Maverick's memoirs were edited and privately published by a granddaughter, Rena Maverick Green. The document was immediately recognized as a valuable record of nineteenth-century Anglo life in frontier Texas, and it has earned Maverick a minor but lasting place in western American history.

• The Eugene C. Barker Texas History Center, a division of the Center for American History at the University of Texas, Austin, has an extensive collection of documents relating to the Maverick family, including a typescript of Mary Maverick's diary and a first edition of the *Memoirs*. The original diary is in the possession of family members. It is published as *Memoirs of Mary A. Maverick*, ed. Rena Maverick Green (1921; repr. 1989). For biographical information on Mary

Maverick, see "Recorder of Texas Life: Mary Adams Maverick," in *Women in Texas: Their Lives, Their Experiences, Their Accomplishments* (1992), by Ann Fears Crawford and Crystal Sasse Ragsdale. See also *Samuel Maverick, Texan: 1803–1870* (1952), Rena Green's biography of her grandfather; and Dee Brown, *The Gentle Tamers: Women of the Old West* (1958). Birth and death dates and other data on the Maverick family are in Frederick C. Chabot, ed., *With the Makers of San Antonio: Genealogies of the Early Latin, Anglo-American, and German Families* (1937), which can be found in the collections of the Daughters of the Republic of Texas Library in San Antonio. Relevant information on the early history of Texas can be found in John Edward Weems, *Dream of Empire: A Human History of the Republic of Texas, 1836–1846* (1971).

ANN T. KEENE

MAVERICK, Maury (23 Oct. 1895–7 June 1954), politician and government administrator, was born Fontaine Maury Maverick in San Antonio, Texas, the son of Albert Maverick, a real estate investor, and Jane Lewis Maury. His grandfather, Sam Maverick, a rancher, was a signer of the Texas Declaration of Independence in 1835 and mayor of San Antonio. When he refused to brand his cattle—contrary to prevailing custom—"maverick" became embedded in the English language as a term designating a stray. Maury Maverick lived within this tradition.

He entered Virginia Military Institute in 1912, but after one year he left for the University of Texas where, with interruptions, he studied for the next three years. In 1916 he was admitted to the Texas State Bar and joined a law practice in San Antonio. But when the United States entered the First World War in 1917, Maverick enlisted in the army and was commissioned as a lieutenant. In 1918 he was sent to France, where he saw action in some of the heaviest fighting undertaken by American forces. At St. Mihiel and the Argonne he was severely wounded, receiving the Purple Heart and a Silver Star for gallantry.

After recovering from his wounds, Maverick returned to San Antonio and the practice of law. In 1920 he married Terrell L. Dobbs, with whom he had two children. After two years he tired of the law and went into the construction business. He also became involved in local politics and was a vocal opponent of the Ku Klux Klan. Throughout the 1920s he espoused the rights of minorities, especially the Spanish-speaking people of San Antonio. With the stock market crash of 1929 he assumed an active role in local relief programs. He won election as tax collector of Bexar County in 1929 and again in 1931. An enthusiastic Democrat, he supported Franklin D. Roosevelt for the presidency early on and after 1933 became an avid New Dealer. With assets such as a well-known name in Texas and a reputation as a friend of the underdog, he won a seat in the U.S. House of Representatives in 1934. Much of his political base was among Mexican Americans. Maverick forced the U.S. Census Bureau to reverse a long-standing policy and count them as whites rather than as Negroes in his district.

In Congress Maverick lived up to his name. He became one of the administration's most fervent advocates and supported virtually all of the New Deal's programs. He also organized a group of insurgent House liberals who became known as the Mavericks. Unlike most southerners, he was a strong supporter of civil rights and consistently endorsed antilynching legislation. Alone among many from his region, he enthusiastically backed Roosevelt's court-packing plan in 1937. In addition, although he defended the Neutrality Act of 1935, after 1937 he was a strong supporter of the president's foreign policies. He had emerged from the First World War an avowed pacifist, but the rise of fascism in the 1930s led him to reevaluate his position. Thus he argued vehemently for the president's 1938 rearmament proposals, for the construction of 50,000 planes, and for closer collaboration with Great Britain.

Maverick's strong views usually aroused controversy. His pronounced liberalism and his independence were anathema to many Texas Democrats, including Vice President John N. Garner, and he was defeated in the primary when he sought reelection to the House in 1938. Maverick was not easily intimidated, however. In the following year he ran for the mayoralty of San Antonio and was elected on a Fusion ticket, with significant support from Mexican Americans, blacks, and the Congress of Industrial Organizations. Although he advanced a comprehensive program to improve public housing and public health, conservatives stymied his efforts. When he permitted an avowed Communist to speak in the San Antonio Municipal Auditorium, opponents accused him of being a Communist himself and blocked his reelection in 1941.

During the next decade Maverick held various administrative positions in the federal bureaucracy. In 1941 he was appointed to the Office of Price Administration, where he evaluated controls in overseas possessions and territories. From there he moved to the Office of Production Management in the following year. When the president transformed that agency into the War Production Board in April 1942, Maverick became a vice chairman in charge of the division of government requirements. He served in that capacity until January 1944, when he was selected to head the new Smaller War Plants Corporation. In this post he sought to secure a greater volume of war contracts for small businesses. Maverick viewed himself as a true Jeffersonian democrat, opposed to centralization of power in business. Thus, he favored decentralization of the economy, supported antitrust policies fervidly, and urged a more prominent role for small business in the American economy. Until 1946, when he left the federal bureaucracy, Maverick was a passionate advocate of small business who sought to shape the government's disposal of war plants in accordance with his Brandeisian views.

For eight years after he left public service in 1946, Maverick practiced law in San Antonio. He made several attempts to win public office, but all were unsuccessful, largely because his bluntness had won him more enemies than friends. He died in San Antonio.

Maverick held to his liberal views throughout his life. It could be argued that he was ahead of his contemporaries by at least one generation. He was a dedicated civil libertarian and advocate of minority rights. He was a strong proponent of antitrust policies and competition who championed the cause of small business. He was a prophetic publicist who called for greater economic diversification in the western states and an end to their colonial economic dependence on the East. He also urged more extensive federal planning to attain full employment and economic prosperity along lines subsequently followed by both Democratic and Republican administrations. However, his unorthodoxy and brashness often alienated powerful political interests, and consequently his influence as a public servant was circumscribed. He nonetheless deserves recognition as a significant advocate of traditional liberalism in a rapidly developing corporate society.

• Maverick's papers are at the Eugene C. Barker Texas History Center of the University of Texas at Austin. Extensive files of Maverick's correspondence can be found in records at the National Archives in Washington, D.C., notably in those of the Office of Production Management, the War Production Board, and particularly the Smaller War Plants Corporation. Maverick wrote an autobiography, *A Maverick American* (1937), and discussed his views in *In Blood and Ink* (1939). A full biography is Richard B. Henderson, *Maury Maverick* (1970). Maverick's World War II career is discussed in Gerald D. Nash, *World War II and the West: Reshaping the Economy* (1990). A noteworthy obituary is by Alistair Cooke in the *Manchester Guardian*, 9 June 1954.

GERALD D. NASH

MAVERICK, Samuel (1602?–1676?), colonist, was born in Devonshire, England, the son of the Reverend John Maverick, a clergyman in the Church of England, and Mary Gye. He was one of the earliest settlers of Massachusetts, arriving prior to the mass migration of English Puritans that began in 1630. He moved to New England sometime in 1624 as part of the attempt by Sir Fernando Gorges to settle New England. Maverick married Amias Cole Thompson about 1628. They had three children. Maverick became the first white inhabitant of Noddle's Island, land that was granted to him by the colonial government in 1633. Most descriptions of Maverick picture him as a generous and hospitable man, but he never became an influential person in the Massachusetts Bay Colony because he was Anglican. Although not a Puritan, he did take the freeman's oath on 2 October 1632. He was heavily involved in colonial trade and sought to encourage the development of Boston and Massachusetts Bay. He joined with the Puritan authorities in several commercial ventures designed to promote growth in the colony, such as the 1635 venture to Virginia to purchase corn and other supplies. He remained almost a year in Virginia, engaging in a variety of trading schemes designed to benefit Boston. After his return to Massachusetts in 1636, Maverick continued to support the colony's growth. He also made substantial contributions to the refortification of Castle Island in 1646. Maverick's good relations with the Puritan leadership, however, were shaky from the beginning and did not last.

Maverick first clashed with the colonial government in 1641 when he was fined for harboring a man and woman accused of "illicit conduct." His original fine of £100 was eventually reduced to £20, but further conflicts erupted in later years. In 1646 Maverick was one of a group of seven men who petitioned the Massachusetts General Court to grant them their rights as Englishmen, which they claimed were denied them as members of the Church of England. Their complaint centered on their ineligibility for public office while still having to serve in the militia and to pay taxes. The petition was denied by the colonial legislature as unlawful, and the men who signed it were fined for their actions. Maverick was fined £10. The petitioners appealed to Parliament for redress of their grievances, but nothing came of the request because of the English civil war. Maverick and some of the other petitioners were arrested in 1647 for their attempt to appeal to Parliament. Maverick was imprisoned for twelve days and fined £150. Feeling that he had been treated unjustly, he petitioned on three occasions to have his fine reduced or canceled. Finally, in 1650, his fine was reduced to £75, half the original amount. In 1648 Maverick had deeded his property on Noddle's Island to his son to avoid its confiscation, but following the reduction of his fine, he sold the property and apparently left the Massachusetts Bay colony.

Maverick never forgave the leaders of Massachusetts Bay for this treatment. Following the restoration of the monarchy in 1660, he traveled to England to complain to imperial authorities and to request that a royal commission be appointed to visit New England to settle outstanding disagreements and "reduce the English to due obedience." While in England, Maverick wrote *A Briefe Discription of New England and the Severall Townes Therein* (1660) in order to help royal authorities in their efforts to control the Puritan government of Massachusetts. On 25 April 1664 Charles II acceded to Maverick's request, appointing four commissioners charged with "reducing the Dutch in or near Long Island" and with investigating concerns about religious issues and the denial of English liberties in the colonies of New England. The commissioners were Colonel Richard Nichols, Sir Robert Carre, George Cartwright, and Maverick himself. Boston authorities, however, refused to recognize the commissioners' jurisdiction, and the commission accomplished little. The government of Massachusetts Bay requested that the commission be recalled as unjustified and unnecessary, making particular reference to Maverick as an "enemy" of the colony. Maverick sought diligently to create some success out of the efforts of the commission, but he was unable to produce any improvements for those who, like himself, enjoyed few political rights because of their religion. The royal commission was finally recalled in 1665, but this did not mark the end of Maverick's service to the

Crown. He continued to represent the royal government while remaining in the colonies. Deciding that Boston was no longer a hospitable place to live, Maverick moved to New York. Sometime before 1669 he received a house in New York City from the duke of York as a gift for his loyalty to the king. Maverick remained in New York until his death, sometime between 1670, when Samuel Maverick last appears in historical records, and 1676, when a deed showed his house belonging to his daughter Mary. He apparently died in New York City.

As one of the first settlers of the Boston area, Maverick should have been an influential person among the early settlers of Massachusetts. The primary cause for his failure to gain influence was his membership in the Church of England. Although well liked by many, Samuel Maverick was not a part of the ruling elite of the colony. He is thus remembered primarily for the times he challenged the Puritan leadership rather than for his contributions to the growth and development of the colony.

• Maverick's *Briefe Discription* is reprinted in the *New England Historical and Genealogical Register*, Jan. 1885, pp. 34–48. Letters to the Winthrops are reprinted in *Collections of the Massachusetts Historical Society*, 4th ser., 7 (1865): 307–20; letters to the earl of Clarendon are reprinted in *Collections of the New York Historical Society* 2 (1869): 19–74. Other sources include Charles Francis Adams, *Three Episodes of Massachusetts History* (1892); Victor F. Casaburi, ed., *A Colonial History of East Boston* (1975), which is based on William H. Sumner, *A History of East Boston* (1858); *The New England Historical and Genealogical Register*, Apr. 1894, pp. 207–9, and Apr. 1915, pp. 157–59; and *Winthrop's Journal, 1630–1649*, ed. James Kendall Hosmer (1946).

CAROL SUE HUMPHREY

MAVERICK, Samuel Augustus (23 July 1803–2 Sept. 1870), politician and landowner, was born in Pendleton, South Carolina, the son of Samuel Maverick, the owner of "Montpelier" plantation, and Elizabeth Anderson. He received his early education locally and then attended Yale College, from which he received his B.A. in 1825. Afterward, he studied law in Winchester, Virginia, then returned to Pendleton, where he was admitted to the bar in 1829 and practiced law.

Maverick left South Carolina after dueling with a man who had jeered his father because of a speech he had delivered criticizing John C. Calhoun's nullification doctrine. Maverick first managed a plantation in Alabama but soon moved on to Texas in search of new opportunities. He arrived in 1835 and considered locating along the coast, but pressed on to San Antonio. He was in San Antonio when a Texas army, under Stephen F. Austin, laid siege to the city, and he was placed, along with others, under arrest by General Martín Perfecto de Cós, who had been sent to Texas in September 1835 to instigate resistance to the rule of Antonio López de Santa Anna. Held captive until 1 December, he was released on the promise that he would return to the United States. But he instead joined the Texas army and subsequently served as a guide for one of the divisions of General Edward Burleson's small force that attacked the city on 5 December. He also was present when Cós surrendered on 9 December 1835.

Maverick was still in San Antonio when, in 1836, contrary to orders to abandon the site, Jim Bowie and others fortified the Alamo, an old Spanish mission in that town. Maverick became a member of the garrison and remained there until he was sent to the Texas Convention at Washington-on-the-Brazos, arriving on 3 March 1836, just in time to sign the Texas Declaration of Independence. He served in the convention until it adjourned and then returned to Alabama. In August he married Mary Ann Adams, whom he had met at Tuscaloosa. For almost a year they remained with Maverick's father in South Carolina, where in 1837 they had their first of seven children. The couple finally moved to Texas in January 1838, settling at San Antonio, despite its openness to Mexican attack, rather than on land Maverick owned at Cox's Point on Matagorda Bay. Maverick ran successfully for mayor of that city and served from 8 January 1839 to 8 January 1840.

During the Mexican invasion of Texas by General Santa Anna in 1842, Maverick moved his family from San Antonio; but he was captured by Adrian Woll on 11 September 1842 when he returned for district court. Maverick was sent with other prisoners to the castle of Perote, near Mexico City, where he remained incarcerated until 30 March 1843, when he secured his release with the aid of Waddy Thompson, U.S. minister to Mexico. While in prison, having entered the race before his capture, he was elected as Bexar County's representative in the Seventh Congress of the Republic and then reelected to the eighth. Because of his imprisonment he was able to attend only the sessions of the latter body.

In 1844 Maverick moved to Matagorda County, Texas, where he ranched and was elected a member of the first Texas legislature, but he returned to San Antonio in 1847. He was elected to the fourth legislature's extra session in 1853 and served continuously in that body until 2 November 1862. He also served in the house in the fourth and fifth legislatures and then in 1855 began two terms in the state senate. During the seventh legislature he served as president pro tempore ad interim and spoke out against William Walker's filibustering expedition to Nicaragua. In 1859 he returned to the house for the eighth and ninth legislatures. In state politics Maverick was generally a loyal Democrat, although in 1859 he supported Sam Houston, who had broken from the regular faction of the party to run for governor on a platform encouraging strong support for the Union; he ran for the legislature from Bexar County on Houston's Union Democratic ticket.

Despite his many political activities, Maverick's primary success was as a land speculator. During his life he acquired approximately 385,000 acres of land in some thirty different counties within the state and was one of the wealthiest Texans both before and after the

Civil War. He was a rancher of only modest talent, but he was skilled in land transactions and spent much of his time on the frontier running land surveys.

Although not a strong proponent of secession, Maverick attended the state secession convention, and, when it became clear that the state would secede, he voted with the majority. On 6 February 1861 the Texas Committee of Public Safety named Maverick along with three other commissioners to demand the surrender of supplies and posts belonging to the Federal government on the Texas frontier. They secured these from General David E. Twiggs. Thereafter, although his sons served in the Confederate army, Maverick played no active role in the state or Confederate government. He was engaged, however, in efforts within San Antonio to put down anti-Confederate sentiment and activities, including bringing charges against suspected disloyalists before the Confederate Military Commission at San Antonio.

After the war Texas provisional governor Andrew J. Hamilton personally requested Maverick's pardon from President Andrew Johnson after Maverick reminded him that he had opposed secession, even as a youth in South Carolina, and had never supported slavery, although in 1860 he had owned eighteen slaves. He received his pardon, but unlike many other prewar Unionists, he did not shift political allegiances to the Republican party. Instead, he helped reorganize the Democratic party, joining John H. Reagan, Ashbel Smith, and others in calling for the party's first postwar convention in January 1868. Much of his political effort during this period focused on preventing the Republicans from dividing the state, which would have adversely affected his land holdings. Maverick died in San Antonio.

• Maverick's correspondence can be found in the Samuel A. Maverick Papers at the American History Center, University of Texas, Austin. Many of these papers have been published in *Samuel Maverick, Texan: 1803–1870, a Collection of Letters, Journals and Memoirs*, ed. Rena Maverick Green (1952), and *Memoirs of Mary A. Maverick*, ed. Green (1989). The best study of Maverick and his wife is Paula M. Marks, *Turn Your Eyes toward Texas: Pioneers Sam and Mary Maverick* (1989).

CARL H. MONEYHON

MAXCY, Jonathan (2 Sept. 1768–4 June 1820), college president and Baptist minister, was born on his father's Attleborough, Massachusetts, estate, the son of Levi Maxcy, a member of the colonial Massachusetts legislature, and Ruth Newell. The youngest of his three brothers was Virgil Maxcy, who would later serve as a member of both houses of the Maryland legislature; solicitor of the U.S. Treasury; and charge d'affaires to Belgium. Jonathan Maxcy prepared at Wrentham Academy and in 1783 entered Rhode Island College (renamed Brown University in 1804), where he studied the Scottish rhetoricians, whose writings the college president, James Manning, had introduced into the curriculum. At the 1787 commencement, Maxcy graduated with highest honors

and presented "A Poem on the Prospects of America." He was almost immediately hired as tutor and librarian at Rhode Island College, a position he held until April 1791. Baptized in 1789 at the First Baptist Church in Providence, Rhode Island, by Reverend Manning, Maxcy studied for the ministry and was licensed to preach on 1 April 1790. In 1791 he married Susannah Hopkins; they had ten children, six of whom survived infancy.

Maxcy assumed the pulpit of the First Baptist Church in 1790 and the following year was ordained its minister and appointed Rhode Island College's first and only divinity professor and a trustee. When, on 7 September 1792, Maxcy was elected president pro tempore of the college to succeed Manning, who had died in July 1791, he resigned his pulpit and became probably the youngest college president of the era. In 1793 Jonathan Trumbull painted his portrait as "preacher of the First Baptist Society of Providence." Formally elected the college's second president in September 1797, Maxcy also taught oratory and belles lettres and published nine sermons, four commencement addresses, and three orations. In 1801 Harvard College awarded him the doctorate of sacred theology.

In September 1802 Maxcy became the third president of Union College in Schenectady, New York, where he taught logic, ethics, and oratory, and later classics. Preferring a warmer climate for his health, he accepted, in April 1804, the offer of a $2,500 annual salary to become the first president of South Carolina College in Columbia (later the University of South Carolina). On the recommendation of Richard Furman, a Baptist minister in Charleston and a patron of Brown University, "easy-going South Carolina" had imported "a Rhode Island Baptist who had had a meteoric career" (Hollis, p. 33). Maxcy and Furman shared similar religious and political beliefs—both were Baptists and Federalists—and a commitment to education.

When the college opened in January 1805 with nine students, Maxcy, professor of belles lettres, criticism, and metaphysics, was one of only two professors; he also served on the board of trustees. Although there were frequent faculty turnovers, additional professorships were established: logic and moral philosophy (1809) and chemistry (1811) were later followed by chairs of law and political economy. Courses in natural philosophy and mineralogy were also added, but advanced Greek and Latin were dropped. The trustees insisted in 1813 that juniors and seniors study theology, while Maxcy emphasized the importance of ordering the leading European literary journals. In 1810 the trustees required the president to submit semiannual reports on the courses offered and on student progress. Although the college's academic standards were fairly rigorous, an 1818 student committee application for membership in Phi Beta Kappa, which was endorsed by President Maxcy and Secretary of War John C. Calhoun, was declined.

Student discipline became an "omnipresent nightmare" and threatened Maxcy's presidency. The strict regulations that the college tried to maintain on the 126 students enrolled in 1813 conflicted "with prevailing *mores* of South Carolina society." To curb disorderly students, the faculty imposed suspensions, but only the trustees could mandate expulsions, a responsibility they seldom exercised. When Maxcy's efforts to tame the students with chapel speeches failed, he was charged by the trustees' investigating committee in April 1813 "with many and great derelictions of duty." Such censure was "the most painful occurrence of my life," Maxcy replied on 24 April, since he was "not conscious of having given just cause." He defended himself effectively, and the trustees ceased to consider the charges. They nevertheless bypassed his authority by requiring the faculty to submit weekly reports to their standing committee. Maxcy also asked the trustees to appoint a committee to attend final examinations, since in the absence of spectators student oral exhibitions were "reduced to private exercises, and the beneficial effects contemplated from them are not realised."

In chronically ill health, Maxcy was confronted in February 1814 by a liquor-fueled student rebellion aimed at the strict professor George Blackburn, which necessitated the town militia's intervention. After investigation by the trustees' standing committee, student ringleaders were expelled. The performances of Maxcy and three other professors were judged adequate, but Blackburn was forced to resign. Maxcy's declining health, however, led to faculty criticism and a trustee resolution for his dismissal in November 1815. Following his self-defense, the trustees tabled the resolution until November 1816. It was never reintroduced, probably because of improved campus conditions and better meals at the compulsory commons. In 1817 the legislature reelected Maxcy to the college's board of trustees. By the time of his death, the legislature had financially supported the college's expansion from one to seven buildings. Maxcy died in Columbia of unspecified chronic ill health.

In his eulogy in the college chapel, Reverend Robert Henry, classical scholar and professor of logic and moral philosophy, noted that "as teacher, Dr. Maxcy enjoyed a reputation, higher, perhaps than that of any other President of a College in the United States." By raising academic standards gradually, Maxcy had, according to Henry, rendered "a wilderness of mind" in South Carolina "productive in all the best fruits of Science and Taste; of Virtue and Patriotism." In December 1827 the student Clariosophic Society (of which Maxcy was a founder and first honorary member) dedicated, with Masonic honors, the Maxcy Monument in the center of the campus.

Maxcy influenced three colleges in three different sections of the nation, but his imprint was deepest on South Carolina College. He steered the new college as it developed academic standards and the curriculum and often bore the brunt of criticism as it tried to discipline unruly students. Although more teacher than scholar, Maxcy demonstrated in his textbook *Principles of Rhetorick and Criticism* (1817) the place of rheto-

ric in the collegiate curriculum. His sermons, like *The Existence of God Demonstrated from the Works of Creation* (1795), were described by one contemporary, Romeo Elton, as having "made his hearers feel the grasp of his intellect, and subdued them by his logical arguments, his profound reasoning, and his deep pathos" (p. 16). One of Maxcy's legacies to future generations of Americans was his religious toleration. He called no one a heretic for exercising his "full liberty of opinion" in religious matters and censured no one except for immoral conduct. Indeed, he firmly believed that doctrinal consensus was not required either to maintain a Christian society or to achieve salvation. Maxcy was thus one of the strong voices for religious toleration in his era.

• The South Caroliniana Library in Columbia has thirty-two documents, chiefly Maxcy's reports to either the board or a committee of the trustees of the University of South Carolina, a number of his published sermons, addresses, and orations, and his portrait by Jonathan Trumbull. The minutes (1805–1820) both of the faculty and of the trustees are in the university archives. For nineteenth-century reprints of Maxcy's sermons, addresses, and orations, see [anon.], *Sermons, Essays, and Extracts, by Various Authors; Selected with Special Respect to the Great Doctrine of Atonement* (1811); and Romeo Elton, *The Literary Remains of the Rev. Jonathan Maxcy, D.D. . . . with a Memoir of His Life* (1844). See Clifford K. Shipton, ed., *Early American Imprints*, 1st ser.: *1639–1800* (1956–1983), based on Charles Evans's Numbers 1–49197, and Shipton, ed., *Early American Imprints*, 2d ser.: *1801–1819* (1964–1983), keyed to Ralph R. Shaw and Richard H. Shoemaker, comps., *American Bibliography: A Preliminary Checklist* (1958–1966), for Readex microfiche reproductions of various sermons, lectures, and papers.

For contemporary assessments, see Robert Henry, *An Eulogy on Jonathan Maxcy, D.D., Late President of the South Carolina College: Pronounced in the Chapel of That Institution, on Wednesday Evening the 6th December, 1820* (1822), and Maximilian La Borde, *History of the South Carolina College, from Its Incorporation December 19, 1801, to November 25, 1857, including Sketches of Its Presidents and Professors* (1859; 2d ed., 1874). Daniel Walker Hollis, *South Carolina College*, vol. 1 of *University of South Carolina* (1951), is the most comprehensive recent analysis. Of interest is Patrick Greig Scott, "Jonathan Maxcy and the Aims of Early Nineteenth-Century Rhetorical Teaching," *College English* 45 (Jan. 1983): 21–30. Also helpful are John C. Hungerpiller, "A Sketch of the Life and Character of Jonathan Maxcy, D.D.," *Bulletin of the University of South Carolina*, no. 58 (July 1917); and Thomas Healey Fearey, "Jonathan Maxcy, Third President of Union College (1802–4)," *Union Alumni Monthly* 10 (Sept.–Oct. 1921): 363–68, 11 (Nov. 1921): 19–22, and 11 (Dec. 1921): 51–54.

MARCIA G. SYNNOTT

MAXIM, Hiram Percy (2 Sept. 1869–17 Feb. 1936), inventor and radio pioneer, was born in Brooklyn, New York, the son of Hiram Stevens Maxim, an inventor, and Louisa Jane Budden. In his memoir, *A Genius in the Family* (1937; movie adaptation, *So Goes My Love* [Paramount, 1946]), Percy recalled a childhood dominated by his eccentric father, who was trying to perfect the incandescent bulb before Edison. Scandal involving a mistress drove the elder Maxim to England in

1881, where he invented the machine gun, became a director of the Vickers Sons and Maxim armaments firm, and received a knighthood. A sense of loss spurred the son to become an inventor like the father he never saw again. Graduating at age sixteen from Boston Tech (later MIT) in 1886, Percy worked as an engineer for various electrical companies. A passion for bicycles led to his building a crude but original gasoline motor in his spare time.

In 1895 Maxim became the fourth American (after engineers Charles and Frank Duryea and Elwood Haynes) to propel a vehicle with a gasoline engine. The Pope Manufacturing Company, later the Electric Vehicle Company, hired Maxim to build the Columbia series of electric and gasoline-powered automobiles in Hartford, Connecticut. Success encouraged Maxim in 1898 to marry Josephine Hamilton, the daughter of a Maryland governor; they had two children. Maxim's *Horseless Carriage Days* (1936) details the experiments that made Hartford the first capital of the automobile industry. His design, which featured a front-mounted engine, three-speed power-train, and steering wheel on the left, set standards for American cars. In 1907 he quit the Electric Vehicle Company, angered by its use of a spurious patent to extract royalties from other car manufacturers.

In 1908 Maxim drew on his experience with exhaust systems to invent the rifle silencer. The baffle-lined cylinder screwed onto the barrel to reduce the gun's report dramatically. When the Maxim Silencer Company began to market it, the reaction of a public fearful of criminals carrying concealed weapons was hysterical. Maxim actually sold only sporting versions, and only until 1930. Maxim's company also devised mufflers, baffles, and acoustic resonators to mute the sound of steam, gasoline, and diesel engines. More than any other person, Maxim enabled Americans to live amid the noise of industrialization. Fascination with sound led to an early interest in radio, although his contributions had less to do with technological innovation than with his organization of the nation's amateur radio operators. In 1914 he founded the American Radio Relay League to conduct research, establish a national network for communication during disasters, and lobby for a democratic allocation of the spectrum. In 1925 he founded the International Amateur Radio League to unite the world's ham radio operators and helped pass multinational legislation to safeguard noncommercial wavelengths.

Maxim's fascination with photography and motion pictures led him on a dare to write a screenplay for the popular film actress Pearl White in 1921 (produced as *The Virgin Paradise*) and to establish the Amateur Cinema League in 1926. He also wrote a syndicated column for newspapers and a book on astronomy, *Life's Place in the Cosmos* (1933), for popular audiences. His last major invention, in 1928, was a seawater desalination process that is still in use. In his later years, deeply-felt civic and professional responsibilities increasingly claimed his energies. He lectured widely on technology as an agent of democracy as well

as on the need to make it accessible. He was the force behind building a municipal airport for Hartford and sat on the Hartford Aviation Commission from 1922 to 1933. He also served as a lieutenant commander in the naval reserve and as an officer in local and national engineering and scientific societies. He died in La Junta, Colorado, revered by radio operators around the globe.

• Maxim's automotive notebooks; records of the Maxim Silencer Company; notes and manuscripts for speeches, articles, and books; volumes of newspaper clippings; filmscripts; and extensive photographs can be found in the Maxim Collection at the Connecticut State Library in Hartford. The most useful biographical information is in Percy Maxim Lee and John Glessner Lee, *Family Reunion: An Incomplete Account of the Maxim-Lee Family History* (1971). See also Alice Clink Schumacher, *Hiram Percy Maxim: Father of Amateur Radio, Car Builder and Inventor* (1970). Clinton B. De Soto, *Two Hundred Meters and Down: The Story of Amateur Radio* (1936), and the Jan.–May 1964 issues of *QST* detail Maxim's contributions to early radio. Allan Nevins, *Ford: The Times, the Man, the Company* (1954), briefly discusses Maxim's automobiles. Obituaries are in the *New York Times* and the *New York Herald Tribune*, 18 Feb. 1936.

JOSEPH W. SLADE

MAXIM, Hiram Stevens. *See* Maxim, Sir Hiram.

MAXIM, Sir Hiram (5 Feb. 1840–4 Nov. 1916), engineer and inventor, was born Hiram Stevens Maxim near Sangersville, Maine, the son of Isaac Weston Maxim, a mill operator, and Harriet Boston Stevens. The boy learned woodworking and mechanics from his father and showed an early aptitude for invention by building a chronometer, a tricycle, and a better mousetrap, which exploited the mouse's energy against itself. His family's poverty, unhappy apprenticeships to carriage-makers, and a contentious disposition led Maxim at age twenty to break with his parents. Migrations around Maine, New York State, and Quebec as a carpenter, prizefighter, bartender, and painter provided colorful exploits later recounted in *My Life* (1915). Maxim became exempt from Civil War conscription when two brothers joined the Union army, but four decades later critics of his weapons business charged him with draft-dodging.

In the fall of 1863 Maxim joined his uncle, Levi Stevens, in Fitchburg, Massachusetts, an industrial center. Maxim helped Stevens move his brass foundry into a machine shop vacated by Sylvanus Sawyer, inventor of novel rifled cannon and shells, whose designs Maxim studied. Stevens built locomotive boilers and steam engines, but he also made gas generating machines to light interiors. When Maxim designed a better generator, he quarreled with Stevens over ownership and tried to market the machine with Oliver Drake, a precision instrument manufacturer in Boston. In 1866 Maxim spent a few months at the Boston machine shop of Charles Williams; there Thomas Edison patented his first invention, Alexander Graham

Bell invented the telephone, and Maxim and Edison saw a crude electric light built by Moses Farmer.

In 1867 Maxim married Louisa Jane Budden, with whom he had three children. That same year, Maxim moved to New York City to work for the Novelty Iron Works, where he experimented with "flying machine" propellers and a steam-powered yacht. In 1869 the Maxim Gas Machine Company began to sell his gas generator, meters, valves, pumps, lamps, and locomotive headlights throughout the United States and Central America. Conscious that electricity held more promise than gas, Maxim also began to build arc lights and generators. In 1878 investors formed the United States Electric Lighting Company to market these devices, while Maxim tried to beat Edison in the race to perfect an incandescent bulb. Although Maxim's bulbs lacked a sealed vacuum, his filaments and voltage regulators were superior to Edison's; in 1880 Maxim installed his bulbs in the Equitable Life Assurance Company on Broadway, the first commercial building in the United States to be electrically illuminated. When Maxim's competition with Edison threatened to bankrupt his company, the directors hired Charles Flint, a celebrated trust-builder, to merge United States Electric Lighting with the firm of Edward Weston, another electrical power pioneer. Flint sent Maxim abroad, ostensibly to find European patents to outflank Edison's. The International Exposition of 1881 in Paris awarded both Maxim and Edison the Legion of Honor for their electrical achievements, but angry over his defeats by Edison, Maxim chose to begin a new career.

Abandoning his family—he would marry Sarah Haynes in 1888—Maxim settled in London to perfect a truly automatic weapon, on the advice that he could make money with an invention that would "enable Europeans to cut each other's throats with greater facility." The prototype machine gun of 1884 spewed 660 .45 caliber shells per minute. The principle—in which the detonation of a belt-fed cartridge hurls a breechblock back against a spring with sufficient force to eject the spent shell, load the next, and fire a succession of others—remained the basis of the more than 100 million automatic weapons built in the twentieth century. Maxim took out patents on every conceivable version of the mechanism. He also chambered the weapon for .303 caliber shells, added a water-jacket for cooling, designed a versatile tripod, and moved on to the 37mm automatic "pom-pom," aerial bombs, cannon, and torpedoes. With his brother Hudson, Maxim compounded a smokeless powder that improved the gun's ammunition; the two argued over credit for the formula, and Hudson, returning to America, became a bitter rival. Albert Vickers, an English armaments manufacturer, bankrolled the Maxim Gun Company, then merged it with the Anglo-Swedish Nordenfelt Company in 1888. That year Maxim turned to artificial flight. Lord Kelvin and other scientists helped Maxim test a three and one-half ton, steam-powered, triple-winged aircraft mounted on railroad tracks. On 31 July 1894, at Baldwyn's

Park, Kent, Maxim and two passengers achieved a powered flight of 600 feet before crashing. Maxim never devised a means of control, and thus made few contributions beyond wing and propeller design to manned flight, although he stimulated enthusiasm for aircraft more than any individual before the Wrights and recorded his experiments in *Artificial and Natural Flight* (1908).

The machine gun extended the reach of Britain's empire by enabling battalions of British troops to destroy whole armies in Africa and India. The Sudan campaigns (1896–1898) and the battle of Omdurman (1898) led to gun orders from around the world, absorption of Maxim-Nordenfeldt into Vicker's Sons and Maxim in 1896, and a knighthood for Maxim in 1901. A frequent visitor to Monte Carlo, he published a pamphlet, *Monte Carlo: Facts and Fallacies* (1904), on the mathematical odds in roulette. A lifelong study of mosquitos produced a primitive but theoretically important steam-powered sonar system, described in Maxim's *A New System for Preventing Collisions at Sea* (1912). A lifelong affliction with bronchitis led to an effective steam-inhaler. When an admirer accused him of "prostituting his talents on quack nostrums," Maxim replied that he could "stand the disgrace." A growing eccentricity took the form of diatribes against clerics, published as *Li Hung Chang's Scrap-Book* in 1913, and climaxed with his arrest for pelting Salvation Army workers in London with a peashooter. He died at his estate in West Norwood, aware of the astronomical numbers of troops slaughtered in the global conflict called "the machine-gun war."

• Some of Maxim's papers, diaries, records, articles, and books, volumes of newspaper clippings, and photographs can be found with the papers of his son, Hiram Percy Maxim, in the Maxim Collection at the Connecticut State Library in Hartford; the patents and designs of his weapons, aircraft, and sonar inventions, together with the commercial records and daybooks of his various companies in England are in the Vicker's Sons and Maxim archive at Cambridge University. Joseph W. Slade, "The Man Behind the Killing Machine," *American Heritage of Invention and Technology* 2, no. 2 (Fall 1986): 18–25, provides a comprehensive overview of Maxim's life and career. Personal information is contained in Hiram Percy Maxim's memoir of his father, *A Genius in the Family* (1936); in Clifton Johnson's transcription of Hudson Maxim's autobiographical remarks, *Reminiscences and Comments* (1924); and in Percy Maxim Lee and John Glessner Lee's *Family Reunion: An Incomplete Account of the Maxim-Lee Family History* (1971). P. Fleury Mottelay, *The Life and Work of Sir Hiram Maxim* (1920), provides a record of important inventions but little on his life. A biased and incomplete account of Maxim's rivalry with Edison is in Francis Jehl, *Menlo Park Reminiscences* (1937); more balanced is Harold C. Passer, *The Electrical Manufacturers, 1875–1900* (1953). John Ellis, *The Social History of the Machine Gun* (1975), offers insight on the significance of Maxim's weapon. Dolf L. Goldsmith, *The Devil Paintbrush: Sir Hiram Maxim's Gun* (1989), is the standard work on technical specifications of various models; and John Dick Scott, *Vickers: A History* (1962) is the best source on Maxim's industrial experience.

JOSEPH W. SLADE

MAXWELL, Augustus Emmet (21 Sept. 1820–5 May 1903), jurist and legislator, was born in Elberton, Georgia, the son of Simeon Maxwell, a planter, and Elizabeth Fortson. When he was two years old, the family moved to Green County, Alabama. After attending country schools, in 1836 Maxwell began study at the University of Virginia; he left school briefly because of vision problems but he graduated from the university in 1841.

While in Charlottesville, Maxwell met Sarah Roane Brockenbrough, whom he married in 1843. They moved to Alabama, where he was admitted to the bar. In 1845 they moved to the new state of Florida, where Sarah's brother, William Henry Brockenbrough, was a congressional delegate. Maxwell opened a law office in Tallahassee and was the first person to be admitted to practice before the Supreme Court of Florida. His young wife died in 1847, leaving their three children.

In public life Maxwell made good use of his connections, securing appointments as attorney general and secretary of state in Governor William D. Mosely's cabinet. Although during this period the Whig party dominated Florida politics, Maxwell staked his political fortunes with the Democrats and soon found success. In 1847 he was elected to the Florida house of representatives, and two years later he moved to the state senate. In 1852 he became the first Democrat to be elected to Congress from Florida. In 1853, on his way to Washington, Maxwell detoured to Pensacola to marry Julia Hawks Anderson, the daughter of Florida Supreme Court Chief Justice Walker Anderson. The couple subsequently had five children.

Maxwell was well received by Democrats in the nation's capital. The Washington *Union*, a party organ, called him "one of that gallant brand of sterling young democrats now in Congress who have contributed so much . . . to elevate the character of the House of Representatives, and to give confidence to the masses of our party in its continued ascendancy" (quoted in the *(Tallahassee) Floridian and Journal*, 8 July 1854). Maxwell also found support among Florida Democrats, who reelected him in 1854. Nevertheless, he ended his congressional career after two terms, announcing that a "duty too controlling to be resisted, bids me relinquish a public service in which I cannot continue with due regard to private responsibilities" (*Floridian and Journal*, 9 Feb. 1856). Maxwell apparently did not enjoy political life in Washington, where he eschewed the machinations of career politicians and participated little in legislative debates that did not bear directly on Florida concerns. He moved his family to Pensacola, where he built his plantation, Oakfield. He did not abandon government service, however, handling the financial affairs of the Pensacola Naval Yard as a navy agent.

As the nation moved along the road to disunion, Maxwell supported secession. No opponent of slavery, in Congress he had urged passage of the Kansas-Nebraska Act. When Union troops seized Pensacola in 1862, the Maxwells escaped to their new plantation near Evergreen, Alabama, which they named Rebel Haven. Meanwhile, Confederate troops used the house at Oakfield as a headquarters. Confederate authorities also seized the rails and rolling stock of the Alabama and Florida Railroad, of which Maxwell had been president.

In 1862 Maxwell was elected to the Confederate senate. One of his legislative priorities was the elimination of speculation on goods. After Governor John Milton called for an end to the "villainous traffick" in the "prime necessities of life," Maxwell proposed price controls on all goods, but the Confederate congress rejected his plan out of fear that such a policy would discourage production altogether (Wilfred Buck Yearns, *The Confederate Congress* [1960], p. 133). By 1864, as a Northern victory began to look inevitable, Maxwell voiced support for negotiating an armistice with the Union, but he never actively participated in the Confederate peace movement.

After the war Maxwell returned to Pensacola, where he was surprised to see his plantation home still standing. As a reward for his service, Governor David Walker appointed him to the state Supreme Court in 1865. Maxwell resigned only a year later to resume the presidency of the Alabama and Florida Railroad Company, which was attempting to rebuild. He also returned to the practice of law, opening an office with Stephen R. Mallory, former secretary of the Confederate navy. Much of their litigation grew out of the chaos and destruction left in the wake of the Civil War. Their first client, for example, sought to establish his claim to several properties after legal documentation of ownership had burned during the Union occupation of Pensacola.

Maxwell continued to support Democratic politics. In 1877 he represented the Tilden electors in *quo warranto* proceedings to dismiss Republican claims to presidential victory in Florida. That same year, after Democrats regained nearly every state office, Governor George Drew rewarded Maxwell with an appointment to the circuit court in Pensacola. Maxwell resigned in 1885 to form a new law partnership with Stephen R. Mallory, Jr. He also represented Escambia County in the 1885 state constitutional convention, where he chaired the committee on the executive department.

In 1887 Maxwell returned to the Florida Supreme Court when Governor Edward A. Perry appointed him chief justice. When the state's new constitution, which called for judicial elections, took effect in 1888, Florida voters retained Maxwell. The constitution provided for six-year terms, but in order to stagger the terms it provided that the first justices elected would draw lots to determine their tenure. Maxwell drew the two-year term. In a similar lottery, he lost his seat as chief justice to George P. Raney.

When Maxwell's term expired, he returned to Pensacola to practice law with his son, Evelyn, with whom the justice had lived since his second wife died in 1886. When Evelyn was appointed circuit judge in 1896, his father retired from the law. In 1902 Evelyn moved to Tallahassee after being elected to the Supreme Court, and Maxwell moved to Chipley, Florida, to live with his son-in-law, Francis C. Wilson. He died in Chipley, remembered primarily as one of the last two surviving members of the Confederate Senate. Despite his service as a state legislator, congressman, Confederate senator, and state Supreme Court justice, Maxwell left no lasting contributions to the law and jurisprudence of Florida or the nation. Nevertheless, his peripatetic career had allowed him to participate fully in the state's development from statehood through the turn of the century.

• Maxwell left no papers, but some useful information can be found in the Maxwell Family Biographical File at the Pensacola Historical Society; see especially the biographical sketch by Adelaide Bell. The most complete published account of Maxwell's life is in Walter W. Manley et al., *The Supreme Court of Florida and Its Predecessor Courts, 1821–1917* (1997). Useful memorials and obituaries are in *Florida Reports* 45 (1903): xvi–xvii; the *Pensacola Daily News*, 6 May 1903; and the *New York Herald*, 7 May 1903.

ERIC W. RISE

MAXWELL, Elsa (24 May 1883–1 Nov. 1963), international hostess, songwriter, and newspaper columnist, was born in a theater box during a touring company's performance of *Mignon* in Keokuk, Iowa, the daughter of James David Maxwell, an insurance salesman and part-time journalist, and Laura Wyman. Her childhood was spent in a modest flat situated among the elegant homes on San Francisco's Nob Hill. A disappointment there at age twelve may have influenced her later party giving. A neighbor, the wealthy senator James G. Fair, hosted a gala party for his daughter Theresa; Maxwell watched the preparations from her window with great anticipation. When her mother announced that the Maxwells were not invited because they lacked the proper social background, the young girl was bitterly unhappy.

Although Maxwell had less than two years of formal schooling, her father taught her to read when she was five and gave her access to his large library. Because he was the West Coast theater critic for the *New York Dramatic Mirror*, he also took her to many concerts and plays. Exposed to quality music at an early age, Maxwell discovered that she could play the piano by ear, a talent that later helped her gain access to fashionable society.

When her father died in 1905, Maxwell and her mother were left poor. After the great earthquake of 1906 Maxwell's opportunities in her hometown were rather limited; she therefore joined a touring Shakespeare company headed by the actress Constance Crowley. In March 1907, stranded in New York City at the close of the company's tour, Maxwell took a job playing piano in a nickelodeon theater. She also performed at private parties, sold her first song, "The Sum of Life," for ten dollars, and at one such party, given by the actress Marie Doro, met Dorothy Toye, a vaudevillian singer with a multi-octave voice that was much in demand. Toye hired Maxwell as her accompanist

for a South African tour. When Toye left for England, Maxwell could not afford to travel with her until Doro sponsored Maxwell's passage; the two women were reunited in London in 1908. Their subsequent tours took Maxwell back to South Africa in 1909, where she stayed on alone, performing and writing for the *State*, a magazine.

Aboard ship in 1912 Maxwell met Dorothy "Dickie" Fellowes-Gordon, a wealthy Englishwoman who would be a lifelong friend and benefactor. The two women roomed together in London, where Maxwell began in earnest a songwriting career.

In the summer of 1915, as the war in Europe intensified, Maxwell and Gordon sailed to New York. There Maxwell wrote the music and lyrics for a suffragette opera entitled *Melinda and Her Sisters*, which opened on 18 February 1916 but was only moderately successful. Her other main interest during this era was to promote the entry of the United States into World War I; she lectured frequently for this cause.

Maxwell also continued to entertain at society parties as an unpaid pianist. She was introduced at one society event to Millicent Hearst (the wife of William Randolph Hearst), who would also become her close friend and benefactor.

As much as she enjoyed New York society, Maxwell was drawn to Paris to witness the peace conference at the end of World War I. In 1919 she had achieved such social acceptance at the Ritz Hotel, where she often resided while in France, that she hosted an elegant dinner there for England's secretary of foreign affairs, Arthur Balfour. This party, one of her early triumphs, gained Maxwell a reputation throughout England and France as an imaginative and amusing hostess.

Throughout the early 1920s, with Dickie Gordon as her sponsor, Maxwell's fame increased, especially among expatriates in Paris and English royals. The 1920s were also the years in which she experimented with unique ideas for entertainment. She was particularly fond of costume balls and devised several variations on the standard theme, hosting "come as your opposite" and "come as the person you least like" parties. In 1927 she created some civil disturbances in Paris with her scavenger hunts (a form of entertainment she claimed to have invented). Maxwell also promoted the murder-mystery party. She was very successful at this genre of specialized entertainment, which sometimes took weeks to organize effectively. Her imagination and affable personality made Maxwell an outstanding international hostess: entertaining the bored rich of Europe, she filled a special need. Among her other major occupations during the 1920s were her work to design and promote the Lido in Venice in 1925 and the Le Sporting hotel and casino in Monte Carlo in 1927.

By the fall of 1929, feeling she had been away from the United States for too long, Maxwell returned to New York. The stock market crash and subsequent depression meant fewer grand parties and entertainments and, as a result, Maxwell focused more on lecturing and journalism. In Hollywood during the 1930s she was a script consultant for David O. Selznick. Beginning in 1938 she also acted in five films (both features and shorts) loosely based on her own adventures; none was a success, but she showed herself to be a moderately good comedian in the short *Riding into Society* (1940).

Maxwell's stay in Hollywood also launched her career as a syndicated gossip columnist for the Hearst newspapers in 1940. A disagreement with William Randolph Hearst over her liberal political comments led her to quit. She then wrote for the *New York Post* for about eight years. She later resumed writing for the Hearst papers when Hearst died and his son inherited the newspaper dynasty. Beginning in 1942 Maxwell also hosted a fifteen-minute weekly radio program called "Elsa Maxwell's Party Line," on which she interviewed celebrities and repeated gossipy anecdotes from her own social career. This program was at its peak of popularity during the 1940s. A memoir, *My Last 50 Years*, was published in 1943.

In the years after World War II Maxwell found a new medium in television. When she appeared on "The Jack Parr Show" she was an instant hit with her humorous anecdotes and brash candor. Her autobiography, *R.S.V.P.: The Elsa Maxwell Story* (1954), was well received. Maxwell herself best summed up her successful career as a hostess in *R.S.V.P.* In it, Maxwell, who never married or had a home of her own, maintained that her hefty figure and plain facial features had aided her. "There are certain compensations for overweight women," she wrote. "Men do not suspect them and other women do not fear them as competition." But above all, it was Maxwell's imaginative way of inventing herself and her energetic pursuit of amusing others that resulted in her remarkable career as an international hostess.

Maxwell died in a Manhattan hospital.

• The extensive profile of Maxwell in Janet Flanner, *An American in Paris* (1940), is personal and detailed but slightly inaccurate. Maxwell was interviewed by Rose Heylbut for *Etude*, Aug. 1942, p. 509. An obituary and related article are in the *New York Times*, 2 Nov. 1963 and 13 Nov. 1963.

PATRICIA E. SWEENEY

MAXWELL, Martha Ann Dartt (21 July 1831–31 May 1881), naturalist, was born in Dartt's Settlement, Pennsylvania, the daughter of Spencer Dartt and Amy Sanford, farmers. Her father died shortly afterward, and when she was ten years old, her mother married Spencer's first cousin, Josiah Dartt, a scholarly man who became an important mentor and guide. Moving westward, the Dartts followed family members to Illinois and then Wisconsin, eventually settling in Baraboo. Although funds were scarce, Dartt's parents wanted her to continue her education, and in 1851 she entered Oberlin College, the first American school to admit women to regular college classes and to award them the A.B. degree. Dartt's Oberlin years were perhaps the happiest of her life, forming and strengthening her commitment to learning and reform. Forced

by lack of money to leave Oberlin in late 1852, she soon was given a chance to attend Lawrence University, another early coeducational school, in Appleton, Wisconsin. Baraboo businessman James A. Maxwell, a widower twenty years her senior with six children, asked her to accompany his eldest son and daughter to Lawrence; in return, he would pay her expenses. Soon James's true motivation became clear—he wanted to marry her, and thus she became Martha Dartt Maxwell on 30 March 1854 in Appleton. They had one child.

Always reform minded, Maxwell supported temperance and abolition movements in Baraboo. By the late 1850s, however, her husband had lost most of his money, and Maxwell and he set out for the Pikes Peak goldfields in 1860. For two years they both prospected around Central City, Colorado, while Maxwell also ran boardinghouses. In early 1861 she bought a "ranch claim" near Denver, where she encountered a German taxidermist who helped determine her life work. A mysterious figure, the man was among several claim jumpers who tried to take over the Maxwell property. Maxwell was intrigued by his mounted birds, telling her Wisconsin relatives on 1 January 1862 that she wished "to learn how to preserve birds & other animal curiosities in this country" (Maxwell Papers, quoted in Benson, p. 70).

Later in 1862, Maxwell returned (without her husband) to Baraboo, where she mounted some birds and mammals for the Baraboo Collegiate Institute. In 1867 she decided to settle with her daughter Mabel in Vineland, New Jersey, an idealistic community that attracted reformers of all sorts, especially temperance adherents. Early in 1868 James came to Vineland and persuaded Maxwell and Mabel to return to Baraboo; in February the reunited family left Wisconsin for Boulder, Colorado, where James's business interests were then centered. Soon Maxwell began collecting natural history specimens in earnest and contributing exhibits to local and territorial agricultural fairs. Realizing that to be a successful naturalist she needed more training, she appealed for help to the Smithsonian Institution and began fruitful relationships with ornithologist Robert Ridgway and Assistant Secretary Spencer Baird.

In June 1874 Maxwell opened the Rocky Mountain Museum on the second floor of a business block in Boulder. Here "cabinets of curiosities" designed both to inform and to entertain augmented the museum's centerpiece—birds and mammals arranged in a re-creation of their natural habitat. Although innovative and popular, the museum did not pay its way, and in late 1875 Maxwell moved it to Denver, where she hoped to attract more customers.

Just after Maxwell had relocated, however, the Colorado Centennial Commissioners asked her to represent the territory at the 1876 Philadelphia Centennial Exposition. Her exhibit along one wall of the Kansas-Colorado Building featured a comprehensive display of mounted specimens on a mountain landscape. Visitors and reporters flocked to the exhibit, intrigued not only by the naturalistic displays but by the "Colorado huntress" who had prepared them.

To capitalize on her Centennial triumph, Maxwell and her half-sister Mary wrote *On the Plains, and among the Peaks; or, How Mrs. Maxwell Made Her Natural History Collection* (1878), dedicated to Spencer Baird and published under Mary Dartt's name. Appended were a "Notice of Mrs. Maxwell's Exhibit of Colorado Mammals" by noted naturalist Elliott Coues and "Mrs. Maxwell's Colorado Museum Catalogue of the Birds" by Robert Ridgway. Coues's contribution included descriptions of Maxwell's rare black-footed ferrets, while Ridgway's catalog contained an account of "Mrs. Maxwell's owl" (*Otus asio maxwelliae*). "I name this new form in honor of Mrs. M. A. Maxwell," he wrote, "not only as a compliment to an accomplished and amiable lady, but also as a deserved tribute to her high attainments in the study of natural history" (*On the Plains*, p. 236).

Although *On the Plains* received good reviews, sales were slow, and Maxwell continued to seek financial security and a measure of personal fulfillment. After the Centennial she had briefly exhibited her collection in Washington, D.C., and at the "Permanent Exhibition" in Philadelphia that had evolved from the Centennial. Still remaining separated from her husband in Boulder, she settled early in 1880 in Brooklyn, New York, planning to establish a combined "bathhouse-museum" at Rockaway Beach, Long Island. By this time, however, her health was failing; she died at Rockaway Beach the next year, probably of ovarian cancer.

Thus ended the life of this woman naturalist-taxidermist who made significant contributions to the development of museum habitat groups. Modern scientists recognize Maxwell as the first woman ornithologist to have a subspecies she herself discovered named for her and as the first woman field naturalist who collected and prepared her own specimens. Museum historians acknowledge her as an early exponent of habitat exhibits in natural history museums. Writing in the *Proceedings of the American Association of Museums* (vol. 9, 1915), University of Colorado Museum Curator Junius Henderson said that her work represented "one of the earliest efforts in America to exhibit the animals of a large area in an imitation of their natural environment." Few of her specimens survive in museum collections, but her work continues to live in numerous photographs and in *On the Plains*.

• Most of Maxwell's papers are in the Colorado Historical Society, Denver, although some remain in family hands. Significant correspondence with Smithsonian officials can be found in the Smithsonian Institution Archives. The account she wrote with her half-sister Mary, *On the Plains, and among the Peaks*, an important source of factual information, also indicates to some degree how Maxwell wanted to be perceived. A detailed contemporary biography can be found in the *History of Clear Creek and Boulder Valleys, Colorado* (1880). Mabel Maxwell Brace, *Thanks to Abigail* (1948), is a reminiscence by Maxwell's daughter that provides a crucial perspective on the mother-daughter relationship. Maxine Benson, *Martha Maxwell, Rocky Mountain Naturalist* (1986), is a modern critical biography. For young readers see Jane Valentine Barker and Sybil Downing, *Martha Maxwell: Pioneer Naturalist* (1982).

MAXINE BENSON

MAXWELL, William (1766 or 1767?–10 Sept. 1809), pioneer printer, newspaper editor, and office holder, was long thought, based on statements made by his descendants, to have been born about 1755 in New York or New Jersey, the son of William Maxwell, an immigrant from Scotland. Current scholarship infers a probable birth date of 1766 or 1767 from a contemporary newspaper obituary and suggests several additional mid-Atlantic states (Pennsylvania, Delaware, Maryland) as possible places of origin. Little is known of Maxwell's early life, including his mother's identity. Although he is reputed to have served as a revolutionary war soldier, his participation has not been confirmed by extant military records.

Maxwell began his printing career in Lexington, then the capital of Kentucky. The second printer known to have worked in the state, he was preceded at Lexington by John Bradford, official printer to the commonwealth and editor of the *Kentucky Gazette*. Uncertainty as to the exact date of Maxwell's westward migration has invited speculation that he may have issued an anonymous prospectus that appeared in the *Gazette* in 1787 for *Holland's Essay*, never published. Nevertheless, there is no direct evidence of Maxwell's work in Lexington until 1793. A bill dated Delaware, 1792, that was presented to the administrators of Maxwell's estate after his death suggests that he may have made purchases for his trip west at that time.

In 1793 Maxwell is known to have printed two pamphlets in Lexington, both issued in response to a local controversy in the Presbyterian church. *A Process in the Transilvania Presbytery, &c.*, clergyman Adam Rankin's defense of his dissenting views on psalmody, was followed by the related *A Narrative of Mr. Adam Rankin's Trial*. Maxwell appears to have had at least one partner, for the two imprints bear the names "Maxwell & Cooch" and "W. Maxwell & Co.," respectively. With this same Cooch, of whom nothing is known, Maxwell also advertised for subscribers to a newspaper, to have been called the *Kentucky Centinel*. Cancellation of the planned newspaper was announced in the fall of 1793, probably in anticipation of Maxwell's intended move to Cincinnati. His subscription agent, James H. Stewart, remained in Lexington and later became Kentucky's third printer.

The difficulty of competing with Bradford in Lexington and the publishing opportunities presented by the recently settled Northwest Territory probably inspired Maxwell's move to Cincinnati, seat of the territorial government. On 9 November 1793 he issued the first number of the *Centinel of the North-Western Territory*, thereby establishing himself as the pioneer printer in the territory. In his salutation to the public, Maxwell explained, "The *Printer . . .* having arrived at *Cincinnati*, he has applied himself to that which has been the principal object of his removal to this country, the Publication of a *News-Paper*." Bearing the motto "Open to all parties—but influenced by none," Maxwell's frontier weekly appeared regularly and was generally deserving of its self-proclaimed political impartiality. In 1794 he married Nancy Robins (or Robbins), with whom he had nine children, all of whom survived him.

In 1795 Maxwell successfully presented a proposal to the territorial legislature to print its collected laws, previous editions of which had been published in Philadelphia by Childs & Swaine. The resulting *Laws of the Territory of the United States North-West of the Ohio*, subsequently known as the *Maxwell Code*, was published in 1796 in an edition of 200 official and 800 additional copies, which Maxwell sold by advance subscription in his newspaper. (Nancy Maxwell is frequently credited with the binding of the *Maxwell Code*.) Maxwell also advertised the publication of another work in the *Centinel* in 1796, *On the First Settlement of the North-West Territory*, by John Cleves Symmes, but no copies are known to exist.

In early June 1796 Maxwell abandoned his printing career, selling the *Centinel* to Samuel and Edmund Freeman, who changed its name to the *Freeman's Journal*. In 1795 Maxwell had been appointed Cincinnati's second postmaster, a position he continued to hold until 1797. In 1799 he left Cincinnati and settled on land near Dayton on the Little Miami River in what is now Greene County, where he devoted himself to raising livestock and the pursuit of a succession of political offices. While serving as representative from Hamilton County at the first meeting of the Ohio General Assembly in Chillicothe in 1803, Maxwell was instrumental in drafting legislation for the creation of Greene County from parts of Ross, Wayne, and Hamilton counties. That same year the legislature appointed him one of three associate judges for the county, an office he held only briefly before resigning to become sheriff. Sheriff of Greene County from 1803 until 1807, Maxwell was also active during these years in the local militia. Commissioned captain in 1804, major in 1805, and lieutenant colonel in 1806, he was commonly referred to as "Colonel Maxwell" by the time of his death three years later, probably on his farm in Greene County, where he was buried. Maxwell's pioneering role in the westward expansion of the press and his years of service as a public official helped to foster Ohio's transition from territory to statehood.

• The most complete run of the *Centinel* (9 Nov. 1793–4 or 11 June 1796) is at the Cincinnati Historical Society; the Ohio Historical Society possesses the only known copy of the first issue. Abstracts of individual issues and an index are provided in Karen M. Green, *Pioneer Ohio Newspapers, 1793–1810* (1986). A full-length study is Robert Oldham, "William Maxwell (1755?–1809): Pioneer Printer" (M.A. thesis, SUNY Oneonta, 1975). August Brunsman, *A Brief Monograph on the Life and Works of William Maxwell* (1993), provides a modern introduction. C. B. Galbreath, "The First Newspaper of the Northwest Territory: The Editor and His Wife," *Ohio Archaeological and Historical Quarterly* 13 (1904): 332–49, is an important early source, based partly on inter-

views with Maxwell's descendants; an interview with Maxwell's widow is provided in P. S. Hamin, "Auld Lang Syne of Ohio," *Xenia Gazette*, 26 Jan. 1869. See Walter Sutton, *The Western Book Trade: Cincinnati as a Nineteenth-Century Publishing and Book-Trade Center* (1961), on Maxwell as a forerunner of later developments in the Ohio Valley book trade, and Jesse J. Currier, *The Beginnings of Ohio Journalism* (1942), on his journalistic role. An obituary is in the Cincinnati newspaper *Liberty Hall*, 13 Sept. 1809.

MANON THÉROUX

MAXWELL, William Henry (5 Mar. 1852–3 May 1920), educator, was born in Stewartstown, County Tyrone, Ireland, the son of John Maxwell, a noted scholar, preacher, and Presbyterian pastor, and Maria M. Jackson. Maxwell entered the Royal Academical Institution in Belfast and then Queen's College, Galway, where in 1872 he received an A.B., taking first place in classics and English. While teaching at the Royal Academical Institution and Ladies' Collegiate Institute, Maxwell pursued graduate studies in philosophy and political science at Queen's College, earning an M.A. in 1874. Failing to secure financial assistance for legal studies, Maxwell immigrated to New York in 1874.

Lacking the political patronage needed to obtain a teaching position, Maxwell instead worked as a reporter for the *New York Tribune* and later the *Herald*. He then became assistant editor of the weekly *Metropolitan* and finally managing editor of the *Brooklyn Times* in 1877. In that year he married Marie Antoinette Folk, with whom he had three children, one of whom died in infancy. His articles in the *Times* on school conditions brought him to local notice, and in 1881 Maxwell was appointed a lecturer in the Brooklyn evening schools. In 1882 he was appointed associate superintendent in Brooklyn. Chosen superintendent in 1887, he was reelected three times.

As Brooklyn's superintendent, Maxwell's prominence as an educator was established in New York and beyond. Absorbed in the elite reform currents of the late nineteenth century, he was a strong advocate of professionalization and centralization. He demanded that credentials rather than political influence govern the selection of teachers. He sought to move the curriculum away from rote memorization, supported manual and vocational training, and helped make the Brooklyn high school system the model for that of Greater New York. Maxwell was also recognized as an author and lecturer. He was a founding associate editor of the *Educational Review* and was the author of a widely used series of English grammar and composition texts whose sales totaled 300,000 in the 1898–1899 school year alone. He was the recipient of numerous honors, including the presidency of the National Education Association in 1905.

When Brooklyn became part of the consolidated New York City in 1898, Maxwell was chosen as superintendent of schools for a six-year term, a post to which he was reelected three times. He advocated a common education for all at the elementary level and the expansion of New York's underdeveloped high school system. Maxwell supported many turn-of-the-century progressive educational trends, including commercial and industrial education, special education for exceptional students, accelerated English-language training for immigrants, music and drawing instruction, inexpensive school lunches and medical care, kindergartens, junior high schools, and free lectures for adults. He was a firm opponent of corporal punishment and child labor. He truly made his mark as a systematizer. Under him New York teachers saw enhanced training, higher standards for licensing, and improved compensation. Maxwell, who had found his own entrance into teaching frustrated by politics, crusaded for the use of civil service methods in hiring, assignment, and promotion. His crowning achievement was the consolidation of the superintendent's control over the public schools under the city's revised 1902 charter and in particular his control over the board of examiners, which had sole authority in personnel matters.

Despite his antipathy toward the "evil influence" of politics on schools, Maxwell's own political adroitness let him survive as head of the Brooklyn and New York schools for more than three decades. He was certain of the correctness of his own policies and brooked little opposition to the paternalistic control he exerted over New York's school system. Maxwell battled frequently with the board of estimate, which oversaw the school system's finances and sought to constrain his expansive plans. His imperious style earned him little love from fellow administrators and the teaching rank and file. Maxwell was "a classic and royal type" who adopted a "high-horse manner towards those whom he called 'my subordinates'" ("A Life of Superintendent Maxwell," *School and Society* 40, no. 1019 [7 July 1934]: 35). The clearly sympathetic *New York Tribune* characterized him as "a sort of benevolent educational dictator," a man who "ruled" rather than led the school system.

In 1912, at the height of his powers, Maxwell was feted at Carnegie Hall in celebration of his twenty-five years at the helm of the schools of Brooklyn and New York. Subsequently, opposition from a strong school board president and from a mayor bent on reducing school costs by implementing the "Gary plan" for platoon schools undercut some of Maxwell's authority, as did support for the Gary plan by business and the conservative press. Maxwell, who was at heart a classicist, opposed the Gary plan (named after the Indiana city where it was introduced), which was an effort to unify general and vocational education, more efficiently use school facilities, and better integrate the schools into their surrounding communities by transforming schools into social centers. The centerpiece of the plan was its scheduling system, which, by maximizing the use of playgrounds, gymnasiums, and assembly halls (in addition to classrooms), permitted schools to accommodate twice as many students as traditional schools. In failing health, Maxwell took a leave of absence in April 1915 and worked only infrequently

thereafter. By a special act of the legislature, in January 1918 he was elected superintendent emeritus. He died at his home in Flushing, New York. In January 1928 a large memorial statue in bronze, depicting a seated Maxwell in flowing robes above a massive plinth, was presented by the Maxwell Memorial Society to the American Museum of Natural History (AMNH).

In 1918 the *Brooklyn Citizen* wrote, "It would perhaps be somewhat misleading to characterize Mr. Maxwell as an educational reformer, but it is certainly not misleading to place him high on the list of the most enlightened educators of the past thirty odd years" (Maxwell, *The Election . . . as City Superintendent of Schools Emeritus*, p. 71). Maxwell is remembered as a dynamic administrator rather than a profound educational theorist. With a forceful personality he organized, led, and adapted New York's underdeveloped school system to meet the needs of industrial society in the early twentieth century. The first and so far the longest-serving of Greater New York's school superintendents, he charted a course for the city's public schools that remained largely fixed until the 1960s.

• No single collection of Maxwell's papers exists, but scattered correspondence is in the Municipal Archives of the City of New York, particularly the Mayor's Papers. His writing in the *Educational Review* continued irregularly after he gave up his editorship there in 1896. Much of Maxwell's most important writing is in his superintendent's reports and in the annual reports and journals of the Brooklyn and New York City Boards of Education. A valuable collection of Maxwell's addresses, essays, and official reports is *A Quarter Century of Public School Development* (1912). William H. Maxwell, comp., *The Election of William H. Maxwell as City Superintendent of Schools Emeritus* (1918), is a collection of official pronouncements and laudatory statements upon the superintendent's retirement. A book-length hagiographic biography by Samuel P. Abelow, *Dr. William H. Maxwell: The First Superintendent of Schools of the City of New York* (1934), is based largely on official records and newspaper reports. More useful, though brief, is John Vincent Mooney, Jr., "William H. Maxwell and the Public Schools of New York City" (Ph.D. diss., Fordham Univ., 1981), which also draws heavily from newspapers and official documents. Mary I. MacDonald, "Dr. Maxwell as an Educator" (Ph.D. diss., New York Univ., 1923), contains a valuable bibliography of Maxwell's writings. Diane Ravitch, *The Great School Wars: New York City, 1805–1973* (1974), fits Maxwell's superintendency into the broader progressive educational and political currents of the period. The Maxwell statue resided in the Education Wing of the AMNH until the 1970s, when it was dismantled and moved to storage. Obituaries are in the *New York Evening Post*, 3 May 1920, and the *New York Tribune*, 4 May 1920.

KEVIN J. SMEAD

MAY, Abigail Williams (21 Apr. 1829–30 Nov. 1888), reformer and philanthropist, was born in Boston, Massachusetts, the daughter of Samuel May, a deacon, hardware merchant, and woolen manufacturer, and Mary Goddard. Both parents were abolitionists. May attended various Boston schools, and in her late teens she and seven other girls started a reading program that included Plato, Spenser, and Dante. In 1851 May, who thought it was a woman's responsibility to prepare for some type of work as a provision against hardship, studied at Boston's newly opened School of Design where she later became a member of the governing committee. May never married, but in 1853, when her youngest brother Frederic's wife died at the birth of their first child, May assumed responsibility for her niece's health and education.

Like many in her family, May was influenced by her first cousin, the prominent Unitarian clergyman Samuel Joseph May. Her oldest brother, the Reverend Samuel May, Jr., also inspired May's abolitionist sentiments. Another first cousin was the pioneering social worker Abigail May Alcott. May took an interest in Bronson Alcott's "conversations" and had a close relationship with the novelist Louisa May Alcott. She admired writer-philosopher Ralph Waldo Emerson and was in tune with the mystical Transcendental thought of the time and place. The charismatic Reverend Theodore Parker aroused May's compassion, leading her to her first charitable work of teaching sewing to impoverished young women.

From 1856 to 1879 May was a visitor for Boston's Provident Association. She was an enthusiastic homeopathist and once said that she would rather "die under homeopathic than live under allopathic treatment"; in 1859, however, she helped found and became secretary of the obstetrics clinic of the New England Female Medical College under the newly appointed chair of obstetrics, Marie E. Zakrzewska. In 1860 May delivered the hospital's first annual report, which her friend and colleague Ednah Dow Cheney described as "an admirable paper,—full, concise, and tender in feeling" (pt. 2, p. 12). May's experience was useful when in 1861 she joined the newly formed U.S. Sanitary Commission and became secretary of the executive committee of its New England Women's Auxiliary Association. The following year she was chosen as chairperson. May was tireless in her work during the Civil War, distributing more than $1 million in supplies and traveling aboard a hospital transport ship to determine at first hand the soldiers' needs. She remained chair until the association was dissolved in 1866 and was referred to as "Chair" for the rest of her life. With the end of the Civil War, May took up the cause of the emancipated slaves. She remained active in the New England Freedmen's Aid Society until 1873 and was a supporter of the Normal and Industrial Institute at Tuskegee, Alabama, founded by her friend Booker T. Washington.

May and many contemporary female abolitionists believed that women's conditions were similar to those of slavery. May diverted more and more time and energy to improving women's status, and in 1868 she and her friends, women's rights activists Julia Ward Howe and Cheney, helped create the New England Women's Club, of which May was one of the chief advocates of education for women. She helped establish the Horticultural School for Women in 1868 (later becoming its president) and was one of the four women who were the first to be elected to the Boston School Committee in 1873. A dispute over whether women could serve on the committee involved the city solicitor and the state supreme court. It was resolved through a special act passed by the Massachusetts legislature in 1874. In the same year May joined the executive committee of both the New England and Massachusetts woman suffrage associations, later becoming vice president of each, in 1881 and 1882, respectively.

May was not reelected to the Boston School Committee when her second term expired in 1878. To secure a permanent role for women in school suffrage, the Massachusetts School Suffrage Association was formed and the Committee of Conference [sic] of Women Voters of Boston was created with May as "chairman." In 1879 the association was formally organized with May as president and Cheney as vice president. The association was nearly disbanded because of the group's "opposition to the influence of Catholicism in schools," but May "calmly and strongly expressed her view of the importance of the position of the association," which convinced the board unanimously to reconsider. They "determined to go on with renewed zeal and courage." In ill health in 1888, May retired "the unserviceable timber taking a place on the board."

In 1879 Governor Talbot had appointed her a member of the State Board of Education. She was delighted in the appointment, took particular interest in the normal schools, and "felt that she was working at the very source of good influence." The Normal School at Framingham was of special interest, and her portrait hangs in a building named for her. In 1880 she joined the Massachusetts Society for the University Education of Women (she was its president from 1884 to 1886) and that year became the first president of the Women's Auxiliary Conference of the American Unitarian Association, a position she held until 1886. From 1875 to 1885 May was an active member of the Association for the Advancement of Women.

An able executive as well as a reformer who challenged women to lead socially significant lives whether in the domestic or public sphere, May donated vast amounts of time and energy to various charitable causes and often offered financial assistance to pupils and schools. Living in an intellectually charged time, she was modest in nature and attire. She remained in Boston throughout her life. When her father died in 1870, she took on responsibility for her mother's care. With her mother's death in 1882 went her strength. She died of an ovarian cyst in the Massachusetts Homeopathic Hospital in Boston.

• May's papers are in the Schlesinger Library at Radcliffe College; other letters are in the Sophia Smith Collection at Smith College and the Boston Public Library. A full account of her life is Ednah Dow Cheney's *Memoirs of Lucretia Crocker and Abby W. May* (1893). Obituaries are in the *Boston Transcript*, 1 Dec. 1888; the *Christian Register* (Boston), 6 Dec. 1888; the *New York Times*, 2 Dec. 1888; the *New York Tribune*, 2 Dec. 1888; and the *Women's Journal*, 8, 15 Dec. 1888.

MARK R. WILLIAMS

MAY, Andrew Jackson (24 June 1875–6 Sept. 1959), U.S. congressman, was born in Langley, Kentucky, the son of John May and Dorcas Conley. After being educated in Floyd County schools, he entered Southern Normal University Law School in Huntington, Tennessee, graduating in 1898. After admission to the bar, he practiced law. He married Julia Grace Mayo in 1901; they had three children.

From 1901 to 1909 he served two terms as Floyd County prosecuting attorney. He then pursued a business career, eventually becoming president of the Beaver Valley Coal Company. May subsequently served from 1925 to 1926 as special judge of the Johnson and Martin County Circuit Court. In 1930 he was elected to the U.S. Congress from Kentucky's Tenth District. Because he was elected a full term before many Democrats who swept the field in 1932, he was able to acquire seniority over them. In 1938 he became chairman of the House Military Affairs Committee, replacing Alabama congressman Lister Hill.

May, who unlike many other Democrats had not been elected on President Franklin D. Roosevelt's coattails, did not support the president's economic recovery measures and later became a leading critic of the Tennessee Valley Authority (TVA). Originally a moderate, he became increasingly conservative and harshly criticized what he regarded as radical tendencies in New Deal programs. After failing in his attempt to block all TVA legislation in his Military Affairs Committee, in 1939 he sponsored a bill in the House restricting TVA operations to certain counties in Alabama and Mississippi, reducing a bond issue authorized by the Senate from $100 million to $61.5 million, and placing restrictions on future agency activities that TVA supporters protested were designed to destroy the "power yardstick" idea, whereby the TVA's cheap public power production was used as the yardstick against which the cost of private power production was measured. The passing of May's bill was clearly a victory over the powerful faction supporting the TVA in Congress and in his view helped restore public confidence in the electric utility industry. While continuing his attacks on the TVA and the Roosevelt administration, May pushed for increased military expenditures as World War II began, in line with Roosevelt's 1940 preparedness strategy, and he was a firm supporter of Roosevelt's Lend-Lease Act, passed by Congress in 1941. Nevertheless, he sought to embarrass the administration by demanding the court-martial of army and navy commanders in Hawaii after the attack on Pearl Harbor, even suggesting that "when General Short and Admiral Kimmel come up for court-martial, I'm in favor of holding a shooting match." Also that year he and three other Democrats joined the Republicans on the Military Affairs Committee in issuing a report critical of inefficiency in the war production industry.

May's effectiveness as a congressman came to a sudden end in 1946 when Senator James M. Mead of New York launched an investigation of war contract procurement and May's alleged association with an Illi-

nois munitions firm headed by Henry M. Garsson. May, it was charged, had steered $78 million in war contracts to Garsson and his associates. In July, while under subpoena to appear before Mead's committee (up until that time he had repeatedly refused to appear) to answer charges of bribery, he suffered a heart attack, rendering him unable to appear. After a short hospital stay, he returned to Kentucky to run for reelection but was defeated. After the Mead committee turned the matter over to the Justice Department, on 23 January 1947 a federal grand jury indicted May, Henry Garsson, and Murray Garsson on charges of conspiracy to defraud the government. Although May pleaded not guilty, testimony in his 47-day trial uncovered that he had accepted bribes in excess of $53,000. On 3 July the three defendants were convicted of conspiracy, May on charges of taking bribes, and the Garssons of paying them. All appeals to higher courts were denied. May was sentenced to up to two years in prison, serving from December 1949 to September 1950, when he was released for his "outstanding institutional record." He spent the remainder of his life practicing law in Prestonsburg, Kentucky. Continuing to protest his innocence, he was granted a full pardon by President Harry Truman in 1952. He died in Prestonsburg.

• There is no collection of May papers. Material on May is in Estes Kefauver and Jack Levin, *A Twentieth-Century Congress* (1947), and Denis Brogan, *Politics in America* (1954). Both *Time* and *Newsweek* covered his indictment, trial, conviction, and release. On the Mead committee hearings, see the *Nation*, 3 Aug. 1946. An obituary is in the *New York Times*, 7 Sept. 1959.

MARIAN C. MCKENNA

MAY, Morton Jay (13 July 1881–17 May 1968), department store executive, was born in Denver, Colorado, the son of David May and Rosa Shoenberg. His father, a German immigrant, had opened a dry goods store in Irwin, Colorado, a mining town, shortly before May's birth. Within a few years the elder May, in partnership with his brothers-in-law, had six stores in the Rocky Mountain states. In 1888 he shifted the firm's headquarters to Denver. The company then began to expand to other areas of the country.

Morton May, one of four children, grew up in Colorado, went to school in Denver, and attended the University of Colorado until 1901. He had already begun learning his father's business, doing menial jobs while a student. Upon leaving school he worked his way up through sales and managerial positions. In 1903, when his father moved the growing company's headquarters to St. Louis, he left the May Company store in Cleveland and went to work in the family-owned Famous store in St. Louis. In 1909 he married Florence Goldman, with whom he had two children. She died in 1938.

In 1910 his father dissolved the partnership with his brothers-in-law and incorporated. Morton May became a member of the board. Beginning in 1912, the company started another period of expansion, which accelerated after May became president in 1917. When his father, who had been chairman of the board, died in 1927, May became chief executive officer as well as president.

May Company was one of the first chains to develop large branch stores. By 1968 there were fifteen May Company stores in Los Angeles, seven in Cleveland, and six Famous-Barr stores (the result of merger) in St. Louis. The company also steadily acquired other department store chains, thus gaining more branches. There were four Kaufman stores in Pittsburgh; fourteen Hecht stores in Baltimore and Washington, D.C.; and twelve O'Neil stores in Akron. Other stores were acquired: William Taylor, Son and Company in Cleveland; Strouss-Hirshberg Company in Youngstown; G. Fox in Hartford; and Meir and Frank in Portland, Oregon.

May followed the practice of operating the stores he acquired across the country under their various names (rather than having them all carry the May Company title) and did not use central purchasing techniques for his stores as a group, instead delegating substantial responsibilities to individual buyers at the local level. His stores, which were identified with lower- and middle-income customers, prospered during the Great Depression of the 1930s in part because they sold a basic and lower-priced line of goods, which that large group of customers could afford. In 1939, toward the end of the Great Depression, he built the famous store on Wilshire Boulevard in Los Angeles that was featured on Jack Benny's radio program. That store departed from the traditional emphasis of the company and appealed to higher middle- and upper-income customers.

May's career reflected the history and development of retail merchandising in the United States, particularly in the department store and chain store fields. Entering merchandising at the end of the nineteenth century, he took part in the transformation of dry goods stores (which carried mainly textiles and clothing) into department stores (which sold a much larger line of products, including such items as furniture).

In addition to realizing the benefits of scale through the growth of individual stores and the broadening of the merchandise base, May also expanded the number of units. By the time of his death, the family company owned eighty stores in nine states and the District of Columbia. With annual sales of $1 billion, the company was the fourth largest chain in the United States, rivaling Sears Roebuck, J. C. Penney, and Federated Department Stores.

In his later years May became active in community affairs. Although he was Jewish, he spent considerable time raising money for St. Louis University, a Catholic institution, and for this Pope John XXIII awarded him the Knighthood in the Order of Pope St. Sylvester—the oldest papal order—in 1959. May also founded the Morton J. May Foundation.

In 1951 May gave up the presidency of the May Company to his son, Morton David May, whom he had groomed to take over, but he remained chief executive officer until 1957 and chairman of the board until 1967. He appeared at his eleventh-floor office at the company headquarters—the main Famous-Barr store in St. Louis—nearly everyday until his death. He died in Clayton, Missouri.

• An obituary for Morton May is in the *New York Times*, 18 May 1968.

CARL RYANT

MAY, Rollo (21 Apr. 1909–22 Oct. 1994), psychoanalyst, was born Reece May in Ada, Ohio, the son of Earl Tittle May, a field secretary for the Young Men's Christian Association, and Matie Boughton. His family moved to Michigan when May was a child. The second oldest of six children, May grew up feeling closer to his father than to his mother, and he was awkward and shy in school. May attended Michigan State College but transferred to Oberlin College after *The Student*, the college magazine he had helped to start, ran an editorial that criticized the state legislature. May earned a bachelor of arts degree from Oberlin in 1930, majoring in English with a minor in Greek history and literature. He then went to Greece and taught for three years at the American College at Salonika. While in Greece, May took time off to attend seminars given in Vienna, Austria, by the psychoanalyst Alfred Adler. By the time May returned to the United States in 1933, he was eager to pursue the greater questions of life; like many American psychologists before and after him, he was drawn to the ministry as well as to psychology and so he enrolled at Union Theological Seminary in New York City.

After taking time off to help his siblings in the wake of his parents' divorce, May worked as a counselor to male students at Michigan State College. He then reentered Union Theological Seminary, where he studied under the existentially minded theologian Paul Tillich and earned a bachelor of divinity degree in 1938. That same year he married Florence De Frees, with whom he would have a son and twin daughters. He preached for two years at a Congregational church in Verno, New Jersey, before coming to the conclusion that he was better suited to the practice of psychology. Around the same time his first two books were published, *The Art of Counseling: How to Gain and Give Mental Health* (1939) and *Springs of Creative Living: A Study of Human Nature and God* (1941).

May's personal strengths and weaknesses were put to a supreme test in his early thirties, when he contracted tuberculosis. During this period he fortified himself with the philosophy of living in the moment and of finding personal freedom through the acceptance of his situation. He spent eighteen months in a sanitarium in upstate New York but left before the treatment could be ruled a complete success, apparently believing that his life or death was more dependent on his will and attitude than on the particulars of his treatment.

After leaving the sanitarium, May entered the doctoral program in psychology at Columbia University and in 1949 graduated with a Ph.D., awarded with highest honors. His dissertation, soon published as *The Meaning of Anxiety* (1950), would have a great impact on the development of a new, humanistic, more client-centered—some would say more human-centered—type of psychology that would come fully into its own during the 1960s and 1970s. May and his first wife were divorced in 1969, and he subsequently married Ingrid Schöll. They too were divorced, in 1978, and in 1989 he married Georgia Lee Miller Johnson.

In 1948 May joined the faculty of the William Alanson White Institute of Psychiatry, Psychoanalysis, and Pschyology in New York City. His colleagues there were receptive to his maverick ideas and approaches to therapy—so considered by behavioristically oriented psychologists as well as psychoanalysts—and within a decade he had become the training and supervisory analyst of the institute. He also served as a lecturer at the New School for Social Research (1955–1976) and as an adjunct professor of clinical psychology at New York University. These academic affiliations enabled May to branch out and further the development of his particular brand of psychology. He was a visiting professor at Harvard, Princeton, and Yale and by the time of his official retirement in the late 1970s had become one of the most powerful voices in American psychology.

May was one of the most important writers in the field of humanistic psychology during the second half of the twentieth century. Among his most influential books were *Man's Search for Himself* (1952), *Psychology and the Human Dilemma* (1967), *Love and Will* (1969), *Power and Innocence: A Search for the Sources of Violence* (1972), and *The Courage to Create* (1975). In all of his works May sought to emphasize the spiritual and practical power that human beings can bring to bear in facing their problems. Though acknowledging the cruelty inherent in many of life's experiences, he nonetheless set forth a practical spiritual philosophy that spoke to the worthiness, dignity, and personal power of each person. Several therapists shared his views, notably psychiatrist Viktor Frankl, who wrote *Man's Search for Meaning* (1963). May continued to write until his death in Tiburon, California, having lived to see a humanistic type of psychology become more acceptable than exceptional in the United States.

An early convert to many of the theories proposed by European existentialists, May helped to introduce these concepts into the American psychological mainstream both through his practice and his many books. Influenced in these endeavors by his traditionally American identity, May advocated a humanistic blend of trust in a divine plan, belief in one's capabilities, and resilience in the face of adverse circumstances. Never an indulgent optimist, he nevertheless offered a guarded message of hope through which everyday people could become more heroic in their own lives by fighting the demons of physical and mental illness, poverty, and painful circumstances. If May's philosophy injected religion into psychology, it was a distinctly secular religion, one focused on the exigencies of this life. The humanistic, client-centered approach that May fostered continues to influence psychologists, social workers, therapists, and others who provide counseling to those trying to find their way through difficult situations.

• May's papers are at the archives of the University of California at Santa Barbara. Among the numerous magazine profiles on May are ones in the *New York Post*, 25 Nov. 1972, and the *New York Times Magazine*, 28 Mar. 1971. Journal articles include Roy J. DeCarvalho, "The Humanistic Ethics of Rollo May," *Journal of Humanistic Psychology* 32, no. 1 (1992): 7–18; James F. Bugental, "Outcomes of an Existential-Humanistic Psychotherapy," *Humanistic-Psychologist* 19, no. 1 (1991): 2–9; and Heinz L. Ansbacher, "Alfred Adler's Influence on the Three Leading Cofounders of Humanistic Psychology," *Journal of Humanistic Psychology* 30, no. 4 (1990): 45–53. An obituary is in the *New York Times*, 24 Oct. 1994.

SAMUEL WILLARD CROMPTON

MAY, Samuel Joseph (12 Sept. 1797–1 July 1871), Unitarian minister and radical reformer, was born in Boston, Massachusetts, the son of Joseph May, a merchant, and Dorothy Sewall. May graduated from Harvard College (1817) and Harvard Divinity School (1820) and filled pulpits in Connecticut, Massachusetts, and New York. In 1825 he married Lucretia Flagge Coffin, the daughter of a Boston merchant. Rearing their four children preoccupied his wife, but it also allowed her time to improve her French and learn Italian and promote the temperance cause.

Early in his career, May proved to be a successful advocate of Unitarianism and worked tirelessly as a missionary for the American Unitarian Association. During the 1820s, his promotion of the peace, temperance, and anti–capital punishment movements, but especially education reform, established May's national reputation. Throughout his life, May championed racially and sexually integrated free public education. He zealously advanced the educational theories of the Swiss reformer Johann Pestalozzi, hired Connecticut's first female elementary school teacher, assisted the great education reformer Horace Mann in founding a common school system in the state, and in 1842 became president of the Lexington, Massachusetts, Normal School.

A chance meeting with William Lloyd Garrison in 1830 drew May into the abolitionist movement. At great personal cost—alienating family, friends, and professional colleagues in the Unitarian ministry over his antislavery principles—May joined Garrison in founding the radical antislavery movement and helped organize the New England Anti-Slavery Society (1832), the American Anti-Slavery Society (1833), and the Garrisonian peace organization, the New England Non-Resistance Society (1838). A model antislavery agent, May lectured throughout the North, published scores of antislavery pamphlets and addresses, and helped modernize the agency system of the antislavery societies. He was one of the few whites to work closely with black abolitionist leaders and made the idea of racial equality central to his antislavery appeal. May defended Prudence Crandall's Canterbury, Connecticut, school for young black women against racist opposition in the early 1830s, and he admitted the Lexington Normal School's first black student. Having become a leading figure in western New York's underground railroad, he helped plan in 1851 the rescue of the fugitive slave William "Jerry" McHenry.

May also was a pioneer in the women's rights movement and became the nation's first clergyman to advocate female suffrage. His *Rights and Condition of Women* (1846), popular in the United States and Great Britain, defended women's right to vote and sought to recast the nation's definitions of masculinity and womanhood. May's defense of the rights of working women in Syracuse, New York, led him into the cause of radical economic reform. His call for a complete revision of all laws regarding capital and labor included advocacy of a soak-the-rich income tax and a complete redistribution of national wealth.

Despite his peace principles, May saw the Civil War as the only opportunity to end slavery and urged the Lincoln administration to crush the rebellion. He formed one of the first freedman's aid societies and spent his remaining years promoting Radical Reconstruction, women's rights, education reform, and Unitarianism. His memoir, *Some Recollections of Our Antislavery Conflict* (1869), recounted the early years of Garrisonian abolitionism, sought to defend the egalitarian goals of Radical Reconstruction, and is noteworthy for its discussion of black abolitionists. May died in Syracuse, New York.

• Most of May's personal letters were accidentally destroyed after his death, but many survive in collections at the Massachusetts Historical Society and the Rare Book Room of the Boston Public Library and in the Samuel Joseph May Anti-Slavery Collection at Cornell University. Any study of May should begin with the *Memoir of Samuel Joseph May* (1874), which includes a short autobiography, a diary, and commentary by many of his close friends. A great deal of information about his relationship with William Lloyd Garrison and the antislavery movement can be found in Walter Merrill and Louis Ruchames, eds., *The Letters of William Lloyd Garrison* (6 vols., 1971–1979). Among other important writings of May's are *A Discourse on Slavery in the United States* (1832); *The Right of Colored People to Education, Vindicated: Letters to Andrew T. Judson* (1833); "Slavery and the Constitution," *Quarterly Antislavery Magazine* 2 (Oct. 1836): 73–90; and *The Second Revolution* (1855). The only biography of May is Donald Yacovone, *Samuel Joseph May and the Dilemmas of the Liberal Persuasion, 1797–1871* (1991).

DONALD YACOVONE

MAYBANK, Burnet Rhett (7 Mar. 1899–1 Sept. 1954), politician and businessman, was born in Charleston, South Carolina, the son of Joseph Maybank, a physician, and Harriet Lowndes Rhett. By birth, Maybank was a member of Charleston's aristocracy and inherited a place in two of South Carolina's oldest and most distinguished families. The Maybanks were an integral part of the Low Country plantation life in South Carolina, and the Rhetts were among the earliest settlers in Charleston. Robert Barnwell Rhett, Maybank's great-grandfather, was the architect of South Carolina's secession from the Union in 1861, and Maybank was also related to five governors of the state.

Maybank received his preparatory education at Porter Military Academy in Charleston and graduated with a B.S. from the College of Charleston in 1919. His college education was interrupted in 1917, when he enlisted as an air cadet in the U.S. Naval Reserve. His brief military career consisted primarily of training exercises, and when World War I ended he returned to finish his senior year in college. In 1923 he married Elizabeth de Rossett Myers; they had three children. His first wife died in 1947, and he married Mary Randolph Pelzer Cecil in 1948; they had no children. Upon graduating from college, Maybank worked as a cotton broker and exporter for a cotton export firm owned by his uncle. He later served as general manager of the firm, working in this profession until 1938.

Although successful in business, Maybank became captivated by public service. A lifelong Democrat, he entered politics for the first time in 1927, when he was elected to a four-year term as alderman in Charleston. He rose to mayor pro tempore in 1930 and, with the support of prominent businessmen in the city, was elected mayor of Charleston in 1931, serving until 1938. As mayor, Maybank brought order to the city's finances and balanced the budget. He cut his own salary from $6,000 to $3,600, reduced taxes, and got federal support for slum clearance, public housing, and unemployment. He was effective in guiding work relief and funds for civic improvements. He used a Works Progress Administration grant to restore the historic Dock Street Theater, and other grants went to such improvements as the city docks and a city incinerator. During this period Maybank was a member of the State Board of Bank Control (1932–1933) and was chairman of the South Carolina Public Service Authority (1935–1939), a state-sponsored power project on the Santee River. This project, known as the "little TVA," successfully controlled floods and provided hydroelectric power for the state. He was a conservative supporter of President Franklin Roosevelt's New Deal, favoring public works and job programs. A personal friend of Roosevelt and Harry Hopkins, Maybank was an occasional guest at the White House, and Roosevelt visited Charleston on several occasions between 1935 and 1940.

With the favorable publicity from the Santee project, a strong political base in Charleston, and support from his mentor, U.S. senator James F. "Jimmy" Byrnes, Maybank announced for governor and won election in 1938. As governor, Maybank tried unsuccessfully to create an adequate state police force, but he did supervise a vigorous prosecution of the criminal element in the state. He strictly enforced liquor and gambling statutes and, in a courageous move, used all his power to fight the revived Ku Klux Klan. He nonetheless was a firm believer in white supremacy and opposed any federal intervention in racial matters, including a federal antilynching law. He did, however, favor some expanded economic opportunities for blacks and tried to improve the quality of black schools in the state.

In January 1941 President Roosevelt appointed Byrnes to the U.S. Supreme Court. Maybank won a special election to fill Byrnes's Senate seat in September 1941, defeating former governor Olin D. Johnston with 56.6 percent of the vote. In 1942 Maybank was elected to the full six-year term, and in 1948 he was reelected without opposition.

In the Senate Maybank considered himself an "interventionist" in foreign policy. He supported legislation providing for the prosecution of World War II and favored U.S. participation in the United Nations and the International Bank. In domestic policies he generally supported the goals of the Democratic party and in the Seventy-ninth Congress voted with the party majority 82 percent of the time. He adhered to his racial views by joining southerners in fighting the anti–poll tax bill and the Fair Employment Practices Commission. When the U.S. Supreme Court gave blacks the right to vote in South Carolina Democratic primary elections, Maybank campaigned to have the ruling reversed. In 1946 he voted for abolition of the Office of Price Administration and supported the Taft-Hartley Labor Law, voting to override President Harry Truman's veto. Maybank was chairman of the Banking and Currency Committee during 1949–1952. He piloted through the Senate the 1949 Banking and Currency Housing Act, which stimulated home construction and included slum clearance and public housing projects. The *New York Times* quoted Maybank as saying, "If there ever was a bipartisan housing bill for the good of the poor people of this country, this is that bill" (26 Feb. 1949). Maybank was also chairman of the Senate Appropriations Committee (1951–1954) and served on the Armed Services Committee (1944–1954).

In addition to his senatorial duties, Maybank, who sponsored the bill making Fort Sumter a national monument, was a member of the American Battle Monuments Commission and a member of the Board of Visitors to the U.S. Naval Academy. From 1940 to 1944 he was a member of the Democratic National Committee. Maybank died unexpectedly of a heart attack at his summer home in Flat Rock, North Carolina. Byrnes told the *New York Times*, "The state has lost an able public servant and I have lost a dear friend" (2 Sept. 1954).

• Extensive manuscript holdings are in the Maybank collection at the College of Charleston, Charleston, S.C. His gubernatorial and senatorial papers, some 12 volumes and 50,000 items, are at the South Carolina Department of Archives in Columbia, S.C. Marvin L. Cann, "Burnet Rhett Maybank and the New Deal in South Carolina, 1931–1941" (Ph.D. diss., Univ. of North Carolina, 1967), covers his terms as mayor and governor but not his Senate career. *Memorial*

Services for Senator Maybank (1955) consists of tributes to his life and career by those who knew him well. Articles on Maybank include Edward B. Talty, "A New Leader in the New South: South Carolina's Governor Burnet Rhett Maybank Emerges from a Background of Charleston Aristocracy as the Champion of Liberal Political Philosophy," *Christian Science Monitor*, 30 Mar. 1940, p. 2; "Production: Arms—Sooner or Later," *Newsweek*, 17 Dec. 1951, p. 22; and "The Southern Delegation: Portraits of the Reluctant Rebels Who Hold Harry Truman in Political Hostage," *Fortune*, Feb. 1952, pp. 85–87. Another useful source is Roy Glashan, *American Governors and Gubernatorial Elections, 1775–1975* (1975). Obituaries are in the *New York Times*, 2 Sept. 1954, and *Newsweek*, 13 Sept. 1954.

JULIAN M. PLEASANTS

MAYBECK, Bernard Ralph (7 Feb. 1862–3 Oct. 1957), architect, was born in New York City, the son of Bernhardt Maybeck, a furniture maker, and Elisa Kern. He received abundant cultural stimulus as a youth living in the New York household of his grandfather, Christian Kern, where a number of German-American intellectuals gathered on an informal basis. After briefly attending the City College of New York (c. 1880), Maybeck worked for the stylish interior design firm Pottier & Stymus. He joined Pottier's Paris office in 1881, leaving the next year when he gained admission to the École des Beaux-Arts. Upon returning to New York in 1886, he joined the office of Carrère & Hastings, which though newly formed was fast gaining a national reputation.

After a brief and unsuccessful attempt at establishing an independent practice in Kansas City, Missouri, Maybeck moved to San Francisco in 1890, holding minor jobs that seldom lasted for more than a few months. Steady employment finally came when he was appointed instructor of drawing at the University of California, Berkeley, in 1894, a position he held until 1903. Of greater consequence was his conception of a master plan for the university. From 1896 to 1899 Maybeck orchestrated a two-stage international competition for the plan. The competition was probably the most ambitious of its kind yet held in the country and was influential in advancing both campus planning and the ideals of the City Beautiful movement.

While at the university, Maybeck began to receive commissions for modest-size houses. The extent of such work was sufficient for him to open an office in San Francisco in 1902. Soon thereafter, his brother-in-law, Mark White, became a partner, concentrating on technical aspects of the work. Maybeck's wife, the former Anne White, whom he had married in 1890 and with whom he had two children, played a key role in managing the office. The firm of Maybeck & White continued through the late 1930s, during which time its character and orientation changed little. The office had only a few assistants; most commissions were for houses, and most of them were relatively small, inexpensive dwellings situated in Berkeley or nearby East Bay communities. The work itself was highly varied. Designs could be formal and grand or utterly casual and unpretentious. Ornament could be employed to the brink of lavish excess or not at all. Forms were sometimes tight and contained, yet on other occasions they were varied and accretive. The plan could have axial or circuitous sequences; the spaces themselves might be open and flowing, or they might be tightly defined. Divergent qualities often were combined in a single scheme. Maybeck continuously experimented. He developed numerous designs as if no precedent existed, yet the results always imparted a sense of longstanding tradition.

By the late 1900s Maybeck's multifaceted explorations began to coalesce in a remarkable series of synthetic designs, including houses for Leon Roos in San Francisco (1909–1910) and Guy Hyde Chick in Berkeley (1914–1915). Arguably his masterwork was the First Church of Christ, Scientist, Berkeley (1910–1912), where the lavish decorative program inside is mostly structural and which from the street scarcely appears to be a building at all. Maybeck's Palace of Fine Arts (1913–1915) for the Panama-Pacific International Exposition in San Francisco ranks among the most unconventional museums designed before the 1940s. The gallery proper is a shed; the "building," as it is perceived, consists almost entirely of independent ornamental conceits that are as rigorously composed as they are theatrically displayed.

Throughout his practice, Maybeck sought to design large public complexes, but he never again saw one realized as grand as the Palace of Fine Arts. The closest he came was in the commercial sphere, with two sumptuous sales and service facilities for Packard dealer Earle C. Anthony in San Francisco (1926–1927) and Oakland (1928–1938), which suggest antique ruins preempted by doyens of the machine age. On the other hand, Principia College (1930–1938), in Elsah, Illinois, Maybeck's last major commission and the largest of his career, evokes an English hamlet, its fabric an understated backdrop for academic pursuits.

After designing Principia, Maybeck closed his office, though he continued working out of his Berkeley house for several years. In 1951 he received the Gold Medal of the American Institute of Architects. After a long, contented retirement among friends, Maybeck died, one year after his wife, in Berkeley.

Maybeck stands as one of the most inventive, individualistic, and ultimately enigmatic American architects of his time. Though trained in the French academic tradition and deeply rooted in nineteenth-century European eclecticism, he drew from historic precedent in a more freewheeling manner than most architects and continually altered and defied convention. He also drew heavily from the European vernacular sources that inspired contemporary leaders of the Arts and Crafts movement, but unlike them he sought to reconcile such precedent with classicism. Throughout his long career, Maybeck never lost a childlike affection for fantasy. At the same time, he considered no problem in architecture too trivial or mundane to warrant meticulous attention. Fluent in three languages, well read in literature, well versed in architectural the-

ory, and well traveled abroad, Maybeck nonetheless had a demeanor that seemed homespun.

• An extensive collection of Maybeck's surviving office records is at the Documents Collection, College of Environmental Design, University of California, Berkeley. A large amount of material pertaining to Principia College is housed at that institution. The most detailed account of Maybeck's career is Kenneth Cardwell, *Bernard Maybeck: Artisan, Architect, Artist* (1977). See also William H. Jordy, *American Buildings and Their Architects: Progressive and Academic Ideals at the Turn of the Twentieth Century* (1972); Richard Longstreth, *On the Edge of the World: Four Architects in San Francisco at the Turn of the Century* (1983); Esther McCoy, *Five California Architects* (1960); Sally Woodbridge, ed., *Bay Area Houses* (1976); and Jacomena Maybeck, *Maybeck: The Family View* (1980).

RICHARD LONGSTRETH

MAYER, Alfred Marshall (13 Nov. 1836–13 July 1897), physicist, was born in Baltimore, Maryland, the son of Charles Frederick Mayer, a lawyer, and Eliza C. Blackwell. Intrigued by mechanical devices and physical phenomena, Mayer wanted to enroll in a program of engineering and physics after he completed his preparatory education at St. Mary's College, Baltimore. His father was unsympathetic, however, and intended for him to study law; when Alfred would not relent, the senior Mayer elected not to send him to college at all. At the age of sixteen, therefore, Mayer went to work as a machinist, a task at which he excelled. Two years later he established himself as a consulting chemist to mining and manufacturing firms, and in 1855 he perfected a device for creating carbonic acid. After receiving a recommendation from Joseph Henry, the noted American physicist and secretary of the Smithsonian Institution, the University of Maryland appointed Mayer as professor in physics and chemistry in 1856.

When Mayer learned of the newly established Charless Professorship in the Physical Sciences at Westminster College in Fulton, Missouri, he applied for the position. Once again endorsed by Henry, he obtained the appointment in 1859. An excellent teacher, he used numerous illustrations and demonstrations, many of his own devising, to enhance students' understanding in physics and chemistry. Although highly respected by his students and colleagues, Mayer failed to win reappointment after the academic term ended in June 1861. He thought the decision was politically motivated, but at least in part, the trustees believed that his absence from the city at the end of the term and his earlier vow to join a military regiment if Maryland seceded from the Union suggested possible abandonment of his duties. Whether or not the young professor's political views mattered to the Westminster trustees is unknown, but Mayer did sympathize with the slaveholding states; he referred to President Abraham Lincoln as a "black republican fanatic." Maryland chose not to secede, however, and Mayer never enlisted. In 1863 he traveled to France and studied physics at the University of Paris for eighteen months.

After the Civil War, the Pennsylvania College of Gettysburg (later Gettysburg College) appointed Mayer as the Ockershausen Professor of Physical Science, a position he held from 1865 to 1867. In 1865 he married Katherine Duckett Goldsborough; they had one child. In 1866 the Lutheran *Evangelical Quarterly Review* published Mayer's "God in Nature," an argument that the nature of physical phenomena, such as the atomic structure of matter and the effects of heat and freezing on water, reveals "a Unity in the design of the Physical Universe that testifies to the creation of One Supreme Intelligence." At that time Mayer was apparently a nominal Lutheran, but during his days at Westminster College he had expressed sympathy with "the New School of Presbyterians." Later in his life, in response to the theory of evolution by natural selection, he averred that he was an agnostic.

Although Mayer enjoyed his association with Pennsylvania College, he found his teaching load so time consuming that he could do little research. Therefore, in 1867 he accepted a professorship of physics at newly founded Lehigh University in Bethlehem, Pennsylvania, which offered greater promise for fulfillment of his desire to conduct experiments and to publish. Between 1867 and 1870 he published nine scientific articles, including reports of two experiments in magnetism and, under the auspices of the U.S. Nautical Almanac Office, a pioneering study of the solar eclipse of 7 August 1869, in which he made use of photographs he had taken of the phenomenon. In addition, in 1867 and 1868 he published a six-part series, "Lecture-Notes on Physics," in the *Journal of the Franklin Institute*; the series appeared soon thereafter as a book of the same title. Mayer's wife died in 1868, soon after the birth of their son. In 1869 Mayer married Maria Louisa Snowden; they had two sons, both of whom died young. Mayer's first son, Alfred Goldsborough Mayer (who later changed the spelling of his surname to Mayor), became a renowned marine zoologist.

In 1871 Mayer became professor of physics at Stevens Institute of Technology in Hoboken, New Jersey. Its superior laboratories and equipment motivated him to a higher level of productivity, and during his first decade there he published thirty-five articles and three books. Among his most important research was a series of studies of sound, which established his reputation as perhaps the leading American authority on that subject. Mayer also conducted experiments in magnetism, electricity, and heat conduction. His inventions during that period include the topophone (a device for determining the position of a source of sound) and an advanced heliostat (an instrument for reflecting sunlight in a fixed direction). In 1873 he traveled to Britain, where he received the attention of that country's leading physicists.

Mayer did not confine his writing to professional journals, however; he possessed a strong desire to popularize physics and to motivate boys to learn to conduct basic experiments in sound and light. In 1872 he presented a lecture on "The Earth, a Great Magnet," which was published as a book under the same title later in the same year. Five years later he coauthored a work for juveniles, *Light: A Series of Simple, Entertaining and Inexpensive Experiments in the Phenomena of Light, for the Use of Students of Every Age*, and in 1878 he published a book on sound with a similar subtitle. Mayer also wrote the chapter on sound for a physics textbook for secondary schools (1891) and published several articles in encyclopedias and the popular press. His ingenious experiments with magnetized needles placed in corks and suspended in water under a strong "super-imposed magnet," for the purpose of "illustrating the action of atomic forces," contributed to the development of the atomic theory.

During the period from 1881 to 1889 Mayer was relatively unproductive in scholarly publication, turning most of his attention instead to writing about game shooting and fly fishing. In addition to writing popular articles on those subjects, he edited *Sport with Gun and Rod in American Woods and Waters* (1883). By 1890, however, he had returned in earnest to his research in physics, and from then until his death he conducted many more experiments and published seventeen articles, most of them in the *American Journal of Science*.

Although he had very little formal training, Mayer earned a lasting place in the annals of physics. Honored by election to the National Academy of Sciences at the age of thirty-six, he made important contributions to physics at a time when the United States was emerging as a leader in science. Among his seventy-four scientific publications were several pioneering studies, especially on sound. After an illness of several months, Mayer died at his home outside Maplewood, New Jersey.

• The major collections of Mayer's manuscripts are in the Manuscripts and Archives Section of the New York Public Library (notebooks and correspondence) and in the Special Collections Department, E. S. Bird Library, Syracuse University, which contains Mayer family items, correspondence, a diary, and a scrapbook. Letters are also in the Mayer Family Papers, Maryland Historical Society Library, and in the Hyatt and Mayer papers, Department of Rare Books and Special Collections, Princeton University Library. A good synopsis of Mayer's scientific contributions is in his obituary in *American Journal of Science*, 4th ser., 4 (1897): 161–64. The most comprehensive sketch of Mayer's life and work is Alfred G. Mayer and Robert S. Woodward, "Biographical Memoir of Alfred Marshall Mayer, 1836–1897," National Academy of Sciences, *Biographical Memoirs* 8 (1916): 243–72; the close personal association of the authors with the subject and their knowledge of his professional work results in both useful insights and a perhaps exaggerated admiration. This memoir provides the most complete bibliography of Mayer's publications, though it contains some minor mistakes and omits a few items. An obituary is in the *New York Times*, 14 July 1897.

LESTER D. STEPHENS

MAYER, Arthur Loeb (28 May 1886–14 April 1981), motion picture exhibitor, art film importer, and cinema historian, was born in Demopolis, Alabama, the son of Simon M. Mayer, a small-businessman, and Rachel Bernheim. Although born into an affluent German Jewish family in the South, Mayer spent most of his youth in New York City where his mother moved after his father's death. Mayer attended private secondary schools and graduated with honors from Harvard College in 1907. An uncle introduced him to aspiring movie mogul Sam Goldfish, who hired Mayer as an assistant and trained him in motion picture publicity and ballyhoo. By the time Goldfish took the name Sam Goldwyn immediately before U.S. involvement in World War I, Mayer moved to work for the most profitable of the early movie theater chains, Chicago's Balaban & Katz. He never worked for, nor was he related to, MGM executive Louis B. Mayer.

In 1926 Balaban & Katz merged with Hollywood's Paramount studio, and Mayer found himself employed by the world's most powerful motion picture combine. Based in New York City, where Paramount operated its international film distribution and ran its nationwide chain of theaters, he worked his way up the bureaucracy in the theaters side. He tutored under Paramount's legendary theater mogul, Sam Katz; through the late 1920s Mayer helped run the world's largest chain of movie theaters, Paramount-Publix.

The Great Depression dimmed Paramount's luster, and in 1933 Mayer exited along with the rest of the Katz regime that was blamed for the decline in theater attendance. Hard times forced Mayer to take on management of a rundown Times Square cinema, the Rialto, which he made into what he later described as a mecca for "M pictures—mystery, mayhem, and murder." Amid the bustle of Broadway, the Rialto catered almost exclusively to sailors and soldiers on leave and to young males from all five boroughs. Mayer continually invented new ways of promoting his movie shows. When he booked *The Jungle Princess* (1936) he re-created a tropical jungle in the lobby, full of mangy lions, moth-eaten tigers, stuffed birds, and an occasional live monkey swinging from a papier-mâché tree. He sought to improve on the titles of his "B" films; *A Son Comes Home* (1936) became *From Gangland a Son Comes Home*. Newspaper advertisements screamed: "How would you like to see your own burial?" Popular hits were brought back in pairs—for example, *Dracula* (1931) and *Frankenstein* (1931).

Mayer kept his contacts with mainstream movie operations, and during World War II he volunteered to help organize and operate the industry's War Activities Committee. In the process he helped distribute thousands of films to the military to be shown on a 16mm process that recently had been invented and marketed by Kodak. Mayer did his job so well that he was called on also to serve as a consultant to the secretary of war and to the chairman of the American Red Cross on international distribution of motion pictures. After the war Mayer was appointed chief of the motion picture branch of the military government in occupied Germany to help de-Nazify the German film industry. He served four years.

Mayer began his second career after World War II when he and Joseph Burstyn, who also had gained experience in international distribution, formally entered the film import and distribution business. Mayer used this position to spark interest across the United States in art films from abroad. Thanks to the Mayer-Burstyn Film Corporation, filmgoers in the United States were able to see Roberto Rossellini's *Open City* (1945) and *Paisan* (1946), Vittorio De Sica's *Bicycle Thief* (1949), and other classics of postwar Italian neorealism. Mayer-Burstyn also carried the legal fight for First Amendment protection of cinema to the U.S. Supreme Court; in the famous "Miracle" case (named for Rossellini's film *The Miracle*) the Court declared in 1952 that the movies were a form of expression equal to written or spoken language. From 1946 through 1960 Mayer helped make the movies truly an international art form.

Simultaneously, Mayer began a third career as a writer and educator. He regularly penned columns for *Saturday Review*, the *Reporter*, *Theater Arts*, *Harper's*, and a host of specialized film magazines. His two most famous books are *Merely Colossal*, a memoir of his days working for Paramount and at the Rialto, and *The Movies*, with Richard Griffith, a pioneering history of film. Mayer wrote for a serious film audience; he became an impassioned voice against censorship of movies, for educational use of documentary film, and for the movies as an art form.

In 1961, contemplating retirement, Mayer was approached by officials of Brandeis University to teach a course on the history of film. This proved a success, and in time Mayer took on lectureships in cinema history at Dartmouth College, Stanford University, and the University of Southern California. Students loved his ability as a raconteur and his skill at blending analysis of complex films with anecdotes about the "old days of the Hollywood studio system."

Mayer married Lillie Stein in 1931 and survived her by one year. Lillie Mayer loved the cinema as much as her husband and established her own career as a film reviewer. One son, Michael, became an attorney advising filmmakers, while another, Peter, made art films. Mayer's home always remained New York City, where he died.

Mayer played a minor role in the history of Hollywood, but a major one in advocating the serious consideration of film as an art. He helped establish a market in the United States for imported art films. His writings argued the case for good films to serious thinkers of the post–World War II era.

• Mayer repeated many of the same stories from his memoir in an interview found in Bernard Rosenberg, *The Real Tinsel* (1970). Some of his influential essays are "Premature Obituary," *Harper's*, July 1944; "Post-War Preambles: IV, Films for Peace," *Theater Arts*, Nov. 1944; "An Exhibitor Looks at Hollywood," *Screen Writer*, June/July 1948; "Documentary Film," *Saturday Review*, 13 Nov. 1948; "Disquiet on the Western Front," *Theater Arts*, May 1950; "Are Movies Better Than Ever?," *Saturday Review*, 17 June 1950; "Myths and Movies," *Harper's*, June 1951; "Hollywood Verdict: Gilt but

Not Guilty," *Saturday Review*, 31 Oct. 1953; "A Movie Exhibitor Looks at Censorship," *Reporter*, 2 Mar. 1954; "Hollywood: Save the Flowers," *Saturday Review*, 29 Mar. 1958; "Hollywood's Favorite Fable," *Film Quarterly*, Winter 1958; "From Bernhardt to Bardot," *Saturday Review*, 27 June 1959; "The Origins of United Artists," *Films in Review*, Aug.-Sept. 1959; "Growing Pains of a Shrinking Industry," *Saturday Review*, 25 Feb. 1961; "How Much Can Movies Say?," *Saturday Review*, 3 Nov. 1962; and "The New Film Frontier," *Saturday Review*, 5 Oct. 1963.

DOUGLAS GOMERY

MAYER, Louis Burt (1885?–29 Oct. 1957), motion picture producer, was born Lazar Meir, probably in the Ukrainian town of Dumier, the son of Jacob Meir and Sarah Meltzer, Jewish laborers. Some sources claim that he was born in the Byelorussian city of Minsk or a small Lithuanian village near Vilnius. Equally uncertain is the date of his birth, which some sources give as 1882, but which Mayer later claimed patriotically was 4 July 1885. Mayer's family immigrated first to New York City around 1887 and to Saint John, New Brunswick, five years later.

After leaving school in his early teens, Mayer joined his father's small scrap-metal business, then moved to Boston in January 1904 in search of better prospects. Within five months he married Margaret Shenberg, the daughter of a cantor; they had two daughters. Around this time the infant motion picture industry was growing rapidly, moving out of vaudeville houses and into converted storefronts known as nickelodeons.

Sensing economic opportunity and frustrated with salvage and scrap metal, Mayer purchased a dilapidated burlesque hall in Haverhill, north of Boston, and reopened it as a 600-seat movie theater in November 1907. He displayed acumen in his management, employing an all-female orchestra and an ever-changing schedule of films at an admission charge of ten to twenty-five cents (five cents for children) in a wholesome environment. He thereby established himself as a successful theater owner, grossing $25,000 in his first year of operation.

Using his profits to expand, Mayer swiftly gained control of other theaters in the area. In 1914 he organized his own distribution company to ensure a steady supply of films for his exhibition outlets. The next step was film production, which Mayer entered initially by creating the Metro Pictures Corp. in 1915, and after moving to Los Angeles in 1918, having left Metro, through his own independent production unit.

Mayer's success in all three components of the film industry—exhibition, distribution, and production—attracted the attention of Marcus Loew, the owner of Loew's theaters and Metro Pictures, who was negotiating the purchase of the Goldwyn studio. Loew needed an experienced executive to oversee the films that would be produced by the newly combined Metro-Goldwyn company and appointed Mayer in 1924 to serve as vice president in charge of production at the studio. Mayer and Loew had decided to rename the studio Metro-Goldwyn-Mayer to honor the new exec-

utive. Mayer remained the head of production at MGM for the next twenty-seven years.

Under Mayer's leadership, MGM grew by the mid-1930s to become the best-known Hollywood studio, boasting more than 4,000 employees and twenty-seven sound stages on 168 acres in Culver City. Until production was curtailed by World War II, MGM averaged forty-seven feature films a year, headlined by its famous roster of "more stars than there are in heaven." Of course, Mayer was not solely responsible for MGM's success. At Loew's headquarters in New York, Nicholas Schenck kept a close watch on company finances. In California, Mayer was assisted by the so-called "boy wonder" of the industry, Irving Thalberg, until his untimely death in 1936. Nevertheless, it was Mayer who received much of the credit and a salary that for nearly a decade made him the highest paid individual in the United States. During the depression year of 1937, for instance, he earned $1.3 million.

During this peak period "L. B." (as Mayer was known) was both admired and feared. To some he seemed so charming and sincere that he could "convince an elephant that it was a kangaroo." But others found him coldly calculating, vindictive, and tyrannical. No one could complain, however, that Mayer lacked energy or shirked his responsibilities. Typically, he worked from 8 A.M. to 9:30 P.M. in a steady round of telephone calls, business conferences, and film screenings. Although Mayer personally favored films that were wholesome and sentimental, such as the Andy Hardy series, his own family relations had begun to deteriorate by the mid-1930s, as his wife suffered from what was termed melancholia and lived for a time in a Massachusetts sanitarium. On the eve of their fortieth wedding anniversary in 1944, Mayer moved out of their Santa Monica home. A formal divorce came in 1948, and Mayer was remarried later that year to Lorena Danker. They had no children, although Danker had a daughter from a previous marriage.

By 1950 the Hollywood studios were in decline owing to a combination of factors, including the competition of television and the effects of a Supreme Court ruling in 1948 that would eventually force production companies like MGM to separate from theater chains like Loew's. Looking to boost MGM's profits, Schenck had hired Dore Schary from RKO, hoping he would become a "new Thalberg." However, Schary's promotion of realistic dramas with controversial themes inevitably clashed with Mayer's sentimental romanticism. When Mayer told Schenck that it was "either me or Schary," Schenck picked Schary, and Mayer resigned in August 1951. In the years that followed Mayer tried new ventures sporadically but without much enthusiasm. Still bitter over his departure from MGM, he attempted in early 1957 to gain control of Loew's through a complicated stock maneuver, but the effort failed. Mayer died soon afterward in Los Angeles.

• Mayer did not leave personal papers, but the Metro-Goldwyn-Mayer studio records are in the Cinema-Television Library and Archives of Performing Arts at the University of Southern California. Certain details of Mayer's life differ according to his various biographers, each of whom claims to know the true story. The most reliable, albeit with contrasting opinions of their subject, are Bosley Crowther, *Hollywood Rajah: The Life and Times of Louis B. Mayer* (1960); Gary Carey, *All the Stars in Heaven: Louis B. Mayer's M-G-M* (1981); and Charles Higham, *Merchant of Dreams: Louis B. Mayer, M.G.M. and the Secret Hollywood* (1993). Other useful sources, based on personal contact with Mayer, include Samuel Marx, *Mayer and Thalberg: The Make-Believe Saints* (1975), and Irene Mayer Selznick (Mayer's younger daughter), *A Private View* (1983). An obituary is in the *Los Angeles Times*, 30 Oct. 1957.

JAMES I. DEUTSCH

MAYER, Maria Gertrude Goeppert (28 June 1906–20 Feb. 1972), physicist, was born in Kattowitz, Germany (now Katowice, Poland), the daughter of Frederich Goeppert, a pediatrician, and Maria Wolff. Maria Goeppert grew up in the university town of Göttingen, Germany, where her father became a professor of pediatrics at the University of Göttingen in 1910. With his encouragement, she became interested in science and mathematics at an early age and enrolled in the same university in 1924 to study mathematics.

Göttingen in the 1920s was one of the world's best universities, boasting of such great mathematicians and physicists as David Hilbert, Max Born, and James Franck. In 1927 Maria Goeppert switched from mathematics to theoretical physics after attending Born's seminars. With Born she studied the exciting new quantum mechanics that was being developed by Werner Heisenberg and Born himself. She spent one term in 1928 in England at Cambridge University, where she not only improved her English but also attended lectures by the great experimental physicist Ernest Rutherford. In 1930 she completed her dissertation under Born on a theory of the double photon process—the probability of the emission of two light quanta in a single atomic transition—and received her Ph.D. from Göttingen. The same year she married Joseph E. Mayer, an American chemical physicist who had come to work with Franck, and together they moved to Baltimore, where he accepted an appointment in chemistry at the Johns Hopkins University. She became a U.S. citizen in 1933 and gave birth to two children.

Because of nepotism rules and the traditional emphasis on experimental physics at American universities, Maria Mayer, a theoretician, received only a nominal appointment as a "volunteer associate" at Johns Hopkins. Nevertheless, with support from her husband and other faculty members, especially theoretical physicist Karl Herzfeld, she did engage in active research on applying quantum mechanics to chemical physics, the solid state, and other subjects. For several summers she also went back to Göttingen to work with Born. Later when Franck joined Johns Hopkins, and Edward Teller, another friend from the

Göttingen days, came to George Washington University in nearby Washington, D.C. she renewed collaboration with them, too. At Johns Hopkins, she also had her first graduate student, Robert G. Sachs, with whom she studied the new nuclear physics and published a joint paper on the subject in 1938. She impressed her students with both her ability to use mathematics to solve physical problems quickly and her "well organized, very technical, and highly condensed" (Sachs, pp. 316–17) occasional graduate lectures.

In 1940 the Mayers went to Columbia University, where Joseph Mayer became associate professor of chemistry. The same year they completed a book, *Statistical Mechanics*. Maria Mayer received no offer from Columbia, although Harold Urey, head of the chemistry department, asked her to give some classes as a lecturer. Mayer continued her research in physics, now with the support and guidance of Enrico Fermi, a pioneer in modern physics who was then at Columbia. At Fermi's suggestion, Mayer fruitfully investigated the chemical properties of several transuranium elements through the use of quantum mechanics.

Like many other American women, Mayer was employed in a real job for the first time during World War II. In December 1941 she began to teach, part time, a science course at Sarah Lawrence College in Bronxville, near New York. Then in the spring of 1942 she took another part-time job in Urey's Substitute Alloy Materials Laboratory at Columbia, which, as part of the Manhattan Project, was aimed at separating uranium 235 from natural uranium for the making of the atomic bomb. In this work she made ample use of her expertise in chemical physics. She first explored, with a team of scientists, the possibility of separating isotopes such as U-235 by photochemical reactions, which proved not very promising (at least not until the invention of the laser in the 1960s). She then studied the thermodynamic properties of uranium hexafluoride for the gaseous diffusion and photochemical separation methods of making U-235. During the war, she also worked with Teller on problems related to the development of the thermonuclear weapon, entailing a stay of several months in Los Alamos, New Mexico.

In February 1946 the Mayers moved again, to the University of Chicago, where Joseph Mayer assumed professorships in both the chemistry department and the new Institute for Nuclear Studies. Nepotism rules once again prevented a regular position for Maria Mayer; she became a voluntary associate professor of physics in the institute. The position allowed her to participate in all university activities, including lecturing to classes and supervising graduate students. With the arrival of Fermi, Franck, Urey, Teller, Willard Libby, the Mayers, and other prominent scientists, Chicago soon became a center of nuclear physics and chemistry in the world. During this period, Maria Mayer continued to work with Teller on the thermonuclear project, first at the Metallurgical Laboratory of the Manhattan Project, and then at its successor, the

Argonne National Laboratory, which the University of Chicago managed for the new Atomic Energy Commission. When Sachs came to head Argonne's theoretical physics division in 1946, he offered his former professor a regular, albeit half-time, paid job as a senior physicist. In this especially stimulating environment, Maria Mayer began to study nuclear physics seriously and soon made her own major contribution, the nuclear shell model.

Mayer first became interested in the shell structure of nuclei when she collaborated with Teller on a cosmological model of the origin of the chemical elements. The project involved compiling a list of available isotopes—atoms with the same number of protons but differing numbers of neutrons in their nuclei—of the elements and their "abundances." A higher abundance of an isotope indicated that it had a more stable nuclear structure than others. In collecting and analyzing the data, Mayer found a pattern in that nuclei with "magic numbers" of 2, 8, 20, 28, 50, 82, or 126 neutrons or protons were unusually stable. It immediately led her to think of a shell structure of the nucleus analogous to the shell structure of the atom itself.

The shell model of the atom portrays it as a planetary system, consisting of a nucleus, positively charged, and with one or more electrons, negatively charged and spinning around the nucleus and on their own axes, like the planets around the sun. According to quantum mechanics, there are only certain discrete energy levels (shells or orbits) for an electron to occupy, and only certain numbers of electrons can occupy each level. If an atom fills each of its shells with the maximum number of electrons, it becomes stable. This is the case with the inert gases, whose atomic numbers (numbers of electrons) are 2, 10, 18, 36, 54, and 86. In studying the nuclei, several other physicists before Mayer had also speculated about a shell structure on similar but less firm evidence. Most nuclear physicists, however, discounted the shell model on the ground that the interactions among protons and neutrons within the small nucleus are so strong that the internal structure of the nucleus must be radically different from that of the atom. The prevailing liquid-drop model of the nucleus treated it as a homogeneous mass of materials, rather than a collection of discrete particles.

A near novice in nuclear physics, Mayer nevertheless persisted in constructing a shell model, through the use of quantum mechanics, to make sense of her magic numbers. In this, she was aided by her husband and, above all, Fermi. Her various calculations failed to yield the desired results, however, until one legendary moment when Fermi, leaving Mayer's office after a long discussion on the subject to take a phone call, asked her the crucial question, "Is there any indication of spin-orbit coupling?" "When he said it," Mayer later recalled, "it all fell into place." Familiar with electrons' spin-orbit coupling in her earlier research and proficient in the mathematics of quantum mechanics, Mayer proceeded to calculate how protons or neutrons spinning and orbiting in different directions could

have different energy levels and thereby allow, in a manner analogous to the atomic structure, only the magic numbers of them to occupy each level.

Mayer's spin-orbit-coupling shell model of nuclear structure soon gained acceptance by the scientific community, partly because it was independently and simultaneously discovered by a team led by Hans D. Jensen at the University of Heidelberg in Germany. Mayer later collaborated with Jensen in writing a book, *Elementary Theory of Nuclear Shell Structure* (1955), to explain their work. In 1963 Mayer and Jensen were awarded the Nobel Prize in physics (shared with Eugene P. Wigner) for their theory. (Wigner earlier had worked on the nuclear structure, but he won the prize mainly for his application of group theory in particle physics.) She was the second woman in history, after Marie Curie in 1903, to win that prize.

In 1960 Maria and Joseph Mayer made their last move, this time to the University of California at San Diego, where she became, for the first time, a full-time professor in physics and he a professor in chemistry. Unfortunately, she suffered a stroke shortly after arriving in San Diego and had health problems thereafter, although she continued to teach and conduct research until her death. She died in San Diego.

Maria Goeppert Mayer, through her scientific research, especially her shell model of nuclear structure, made a great contribution to human understanding of nature and, by her example, served to inspire many women in science.

• Maria Goeppert Mayer's papers are deposited in the Special Collections of the Library of the University of California, San Diego. Robert G. Sachs, "Maria Goeppert Mayer," *National Academy of Sciences of the United States of America Biographical Memoirs* 50 (1979): 311–28, provides useful biographical information and a bibliography. Joan Dash, *A Life of One's Own: Three Gifted Women and the Men They Married* (1973), accounts Mayer's personal and family life based on interviews with Maria and Joseph Mayer. Karen E. Johnson, "Maria Goeppert Mayer: Atoms, Molecules and Nuclear Shells," *Physics Today* 39 (Sept. 1986): 44–49, traces Mayer's scientific contributions and her route to the nuclear shell model. An obituary is in the *New York Times*, 22 Feb. 1972.

ZUOYUE WANG

MAYER, Oscar Gottfried (10 Mar. 1888–5 Mar. 1965), meat packer, was born in Chicago, Illinois, the son of Bavarian immigrants Oscar Ferdinand Mayer, also a meat packer, and Louise Christine Greiner. The local meat market and sausage factory that his father and two uncles operated in Chicago would become Oscar Mayer and Company, and it was at the meat market that Mayer began to learn the business at an early age. At six, though he had to stand on an upturned tub to reach the counter, he learned to link sausages. After graduating from Robert Waller High School in Chicago in 1905, he entered Harvard, where he wrote for the *Harvard Advocate* and developed literary and other cultural interests that he maintained throughout his life.

Graduating in 1909 with a degree in engineering and a knowledge of industrial methods, Mayer joined his father's company and became secretary, director, and general manager in 1912, vice president in charge of operations in 1921, and president of the firm when his father retired in 1928. From the beginning he pioneered methods of meat processing and packaging that became standard in the industry. In his first three years in the company he invented several devices, including a lard-tub washer and a casing flusher, and a process for packaging sausage in cardboard cartons. In 1913 he married Elsa Stieglitz; they had four children.

In 1919, to expand the company's markets outside the western Great Lakes area, he led in its acquisition of a farmers' cooperative packing plant in Madison, Wisconsin, and its development as the company's biggest facility. After World War II the company acquired plants in Philadelphia, Los Angeles, and Davenport, Iowa, and in 1961 it purchased controlling interest in a packing house in Caracas, Venezuela.

When Mayer became president of the company in 1928 it employed 900 and had annual sales of $21.5 million. Under his leadership, the company grew until it employed 8,500 and had annual sales of $220.3 million when he retired as president in 1955. This success was due to skillful advertising made possible by Mayer's ability to anticipate changes caused by new developments in retailing. With the introduction of supermarkets, for example, he realized that customers would be affected by the loss of the friendly neighborhood butcher whose advice on meat selection they had trusted. He saw that with the butcher's replacement by the commercial meat-packer, a company's success would depend on customers' recognition of easily identified brands and confidence in their quality. In 1929, therefore, the company introduced wieners with an identifying band around every fourth wiener, and in 1944, with the development of equipment for automatically banding wieners, they could be distributed with an advertising slogan—"Look for the yellow band on every wiener"—which was designed to build confidence in "a wiener with a conscience."

Because Oscar Mayer and Company had remained a family business, with 85 to 89 percent of its stock owned by family members and thus with less pressure to pay dividends, it was possible to invest more than half the profits in capital expansion and research. Under Mayer's leadership the company developed equipment for meat packaging familiar to modern consumers. These included a linker that automatically wrapped sausages in standard lengths, a stripper that produced skinless wieners by removing the cooking casing, a machine that encased liver sausage in plastic tubes closed with a metal ring, and in 1950 the Slice-Pak, which vacuum-packed sliced meats in plastic. The vacuum-sealed packaging of sausage and wieners was introduced in 1960 after a $1.5 million six-year development program. All this pioneering equipment, manufactured by The Kartridg Pak Company, a subsidiary of the firm, was leased to other companies.

Although profit margins are low in the meat-packing industry and although Oscar Mayer and Company was ninth in volume among American packers in Mayer's last years, it was first in profit margin. Its market research made it possible to predict the demand for its products with remarkable accuracy and to keep production slightly below demand to eliminate losses due to unloading "distress merchandise." The company's brilliant advertising campaigns and its development of local distribution centers, with adequate refrigeration facilities and resident sales staffs maintaining prices set by the company, also contributed to the company's profits.

Mayer retired as president of the firm in 1955, but he remained chairman of the board until his death. His career included many philanthropic activities, and he established and headed the Oscar Mayer Foundation to provide assistance to many medical and educational institutions. His achievements as an engineer and industrialist, his sense of responsibility for the welfare of his company's customers and employees, his philanthropy, his activity as an amateur astronomer, and his broad interests in the arts are reflected in the creed that he outlined in *A Plan for Living*, which he delivered as a commencement address at Beloit College in 1956: "Life-long personal development, generous consideration for others, due service to society." In 1959, fifty years after joining Oscar Mayer and Company, he was honored by the American Meat Institute as one of his industry's great pioneers. He died in Evanston, Illinois.

• Oscar Mayer and Company published its history as *Oscar Mayer: The Company* (1975). Further information on its development may be found in "How a Smaller Packer Does Better than the Giants," *Business Week*, 22 Nov. 1958; "The Meat Packers: To Oscar Mayer's Taste," *Newsweek*, 14 Nov. 1960; and "Wurst for Wares," *Time*, 12 Apr. 1968. See also the company's house organ, *The Link*, Spring 1965. An obituary is in the *New York Times*, 6 Mar. 1965.

ROBERT L. BERNER

MAYES, Edward (15 Dec. 1846–9 Aug. 1917), educator and lawyer, was born in Hinds County, Mississippi, the son of Daniel Mayes, a lawyer, and Elizabeth Rigg. He enrolled at Bethany College in Virginia (now W.Va.) in 1860, but he left at the beginning of the Civil War and returned to the family home near Jackson to manage a clothing store. When the Union forces captured the city in 1863, he and his widowed mother moved to Carrollton, where he taught school and studied law. The following year he enlisted in the Confederate army and served as a private in a regiment of Mississippi cavalry until the end of the war.

Mayes entered the University of Mississippi at Oxford in the fall of 1865 and received a bachelor of arts in 1868 and a bachelor of law in 1869. In May 1869 he married Frances Eliza Lamar, the daughter of his law professor, L. Q. C. Lamar. They had seven children. Mayes taught English at the university during the 1869–1870 school year and then moved to Coffeeville to practice law. After his father-in-law's election to Congress in 1872, Mayes moved back to Oxford and took over Lamar's law practice.

In 1877 Mayes accepted an appointment to the chair of law at the university and held it for the next fourteen years. In recognition of his legal attainments, Mississippi College, in Clinton, awarded him the LL.D. in the mid-1880s. Following the discontinuance of the office of university chancellor in 1886, the board of trustees ordered the faculty to elect a chairman to assume the responsibilities of the post. Mayes, the unanimous choice for the chairmanship, subsequently won widespread acclaim for his successful defense in 1880 of a state law to compensate the university for the loss of funds that had been set aside for its endowment in the 1840s; the legislature had invested the funds from the sale of the university's original land grant in bonds of a state bank that later failed. Mayes's response to those who challenged the university's entitlement to the state indemnity received extensive coverage in the newspapers and the pamphlet *The State University: A Reply by Professor Edward Mayes to Senator J. Z. George* (1887).

In 1889, seeking to modernize the educational structure of the university, Chairman Mayes recommended the replacement of most of the faculty and a major reorganization of the curriculum. The changes included the establishment of independent schools that offered more extensive courses, a wider selection of electives, and fellowships to encourage graduate students to pursue their higher educational goals. Despite opposition to the proposals, the board of trustees not only approved them but also reestablished the chancellorship, as Mayes had recommended, and elected him to the office. To stimulate more interest in the university and increase its enrollment, the chancellor toured the state to publicize the benefits of the reforms. The legislature granted the chancellor's requests for funds to build a library and to renovate dormitories and faculty residences. Governor Robert Lowry recognized Mayes as "a thorough scholar and a cultured gentleman" who inaugurated important changes that gave the university "new life and vigor" (Lowry and McCardle, p. 425).

Chancellor Mayes also played an active role in the cultural and political activities of the state. In 1890 he led in the reestablishment of the Mississippi Historical Society and served as its president. He also represented the state at large at the constitutional convention of 1890 and drafted many of the provisions in the new constitution. Recognized as "the best authority in the convention on educational matters" (*Tupelo Journal*, 26 Sept. 1890), Mayes served on the Education Committee and chaired the Committee on the Bill of Rights and General Provisions. Instrumental in the construction of the legal framework for white political supremacy, he devised an electoral plan that gave voters in the more heavily populated white counties a reserve power over the election of the governor and other state executive officials, effectively limiting the power of black voters (*Mississippi Constitution* [1890], arts. 5, 13).

Mayes's display of ability at the convention attracted national attention and enhanced his reputation as a lawyer. It also influenced his decision to change careers. In the summer of 1891, feeling that he had accomplished his main educational objectives, he informed the university trustees of his plans to resign. He remained in the chancellor's post until the end of the year and then moved to Jackson to practice law.

After establishing a law firm in the state capital, Mayes served for a number of years as counsel for the Illinois Central and Yazoo and Mississippi Valley Railroads. He handled numerous cases in the state courts and often assisted in important railroad litigation before the U.S. Supreme Court. When Millsaps College in Jackson added a law department in 1895, Mayes became the dean of its faculty and occupied the post until his death. Naturally modest and retiring, he never sought political honors, but he served as a Democratic presidential elector in 1900. He subsequently declined an appointment to the state supreme court and two offers of reappointment to the chancellorship at the university. He served on the board of trustees of the Mississippi Department of Archives and History from 1903 until his death.

A reputable author, Mayes completed his *History of Education in Mississippi* in 1891, although it was not published until 1899. He also wrote chapters on legal and educational history for the two volumes of Goodspeed's *Biographical and Historical Memoirs of Mississippi* (1891). His most notable literary achievement was the biography of his distinguished father-in-law, *Lucius Q. C. Lamar: His Life, Times and Speeches, 1825–1893* (1896). He also won acclaim for *Ribs of the Law* (1909), a collection of his lectures that was used primarily as a textbook for beginning law students.

Mayes died at his home in Jackson. His wife had preceded him in death. In an obituary, the *Jackson Clarion-Ledger* (10 Aug. 1917) recognized him as "Mississippi's foremost jurist, a literary man of note, and the most highly esteemed citizen of the Capital City." In an address at the University of Mississippi Law School in 1938, R. V. Fletcher, vice president and general counsel of the Association of American Railroads, chose as his subject "Edward Mayes: The Ideal Lawyer," noting: "Mr. Mayes was never a judge, nor . . . was he a frequent contributor to the pages of law reviews. His fame rests upon his work as a teacher and administrator . . . and the record of his brilliant career at the Mississippi bar, of which, for more than forty years, he was the pride and glory."

• In the absence of any known collection of Mayes's papers, the extant Miss. newspapers of the period are the best primary sources for details of his career. An anonymous typewritten biographical sketch and a printed copy of a speech, "Christianity versus Anarchy" (1887), are in the archives at the University of Mississippi. Two articles by Mayes are "Origin of the Pacific Railroads and Especially of the Southern Pacific," *Publications of the Mississippi Historical Society* 6 (1902): 307–37; and "Charles Betts Galloway," *Publications of the Mississippi Historical Society* 11 (1910): 21–30. Three of his works that were published posthumously are *Genealogical*

Notes on a Branch of the Family of Mayes (1928), *Genealogy of the Family of Longstreet* (1928), and *Genealogy and History: A Branch of the Family of Lamar* (1935). He also supervised and wrote comments in *Banking and Commercial Statutes of Mississippi: From the Code of 1906 and the Legislative Acts of 1908, 1910, 1912, 1914 and 1916*, comp. T. H. Dickson (1916). Biographical material is in the *Historical Catalogue of the University of Mississippi, 1849–1909* (1910), and Dunbar Rowland, *Courts, Judges, and Lawyers of Mississippi, 1798–1935* (1935). See Robert Lowry and William H. McCardle, *A History of Mississippi* (1891), and Rowland, *History of Mississippi: The Heart of the South*, vol. 2 (1925), for observations about his public career; and Allen Cabaniss, *The University of Mississippi: Its First Hundred Years*, 2d ed. (1971), and David G. Sansing, *Making Haste Slowly: The Troubled History of Higher Education in Mississippi* (1990), for recent assessments of his leadership.

THOMAS N. BOSCHERT

MAYES, Herbert R. (11 Aug. 1900–30 Oct. 1987), magazine editor, was born Herbert Raymond Mayes in New York City, the son of Herman Mayes and Matilda Hutter. He was reared in a Harlem tenement, and in his autobiography he wrote, "My parents were native New Yorkers of average and unvarying normality." Mayes's formal education ended in 1915 when his father died and he was forced to withdraw from Townsend Harris High School after only one semester to help support his family. After working as a secretary and stenographer, he was hired in 1920 to edit *Inland Merchant*, a trade magazine with a circulation of 13,000 for small-town general stores. From 1924 to 1927 Mayes edited *Good Looks Merchandising*, a trade paper for cosmetics salespeople published by the Western Newspaper Union.

Mayes joined the Hearst Corporation in 1927 as managing editor of the trade magazine *American Druggist*. Early in his career, he made a small splash in scholarly circles as the author of a famously fraudulent biography of the juvenile writer Horatio Alger, Jr. "As anyone who has read my book is aware," Mayes later explained, "I made Alger out to be a pathetic, quite ridiculous character." Although written in debunking style, *Alger: A Biography without a Hero* (1928) was "accepted pretty much as gospel," and, in the vacuum of verifiable sources, it became the basis for virtually all information about Alger's life until Mayes publicly acknowledged his hoax in 1973. "Why it was not recognized for what it was supposed to be baffled the publisher and me," he wrote. In 1930 Mayes married Grace Taub, with whom he had two children.

In 1934, after writing an investigative article about the pharmaceutical industry, the Hearst Corporation promoted Mayes to editor of *Pictorial Review*, one of the most important women's magazines of the period. He soon began successfully to experiment with the standard format of the magazine, replacing lengthy serializations of fiction with a booklength novel complete in one issue. The change was both popular with readers and critically acclaimed.

Promoted to managing editor of *Good Housekeeping* in 1938 and to editor the next year, Mayes soon revived the moribund magazine. He again redesigned its format, replacing serial fiction with shorter stories by prominent writers such as Sinclair Lewis, John P. Marquand, Somerset Maugham, Edna Ferber, John Cheever, and Evelyn Waugh. Mayes later collected some of this fiction in a pair of anthologies, *Twenty-Five Stories from Good Housekeeping* (1945) and *Editor's Choice: 26 Stories from Good Housekeeping* (1956). To maintain the reputation the magazine enjoyed for its service to consumers, Mayes constructed additional kitchens, an engineering department, a new chemistry laboratory, a textile laboratory, a children's center, and a sewing and needlework department. Under his direction, the magazine became one of the most popular and profitable magazines in the country, and Mayes enjoyed virtual autonomy in its management. In the early 1950s, for example, Mayes refused to print an article critical of Robert Hutchins, the chancellor of the University of Chicago, whom Richard Berlin, president of the Hearst Corporation, believed was a Communist.

In 1958, however, Mayes was abruptly fired in a dispute with Hearst executives, including Berlin. A few weeks later he was hired to edit *McCall's*, owned by Norton Simon, Inc. Once again, he oversaw dramatic innovations in its format, particularly in the use of color photography. Likewise, he increased the calibre and quantity of its articles. Among the contributors to *McCall's* during Mayes's tenure as editor were John Steinbeck, Herman Wouk, Anne Morrow Lindbergh, Salvador Dali, and Clare Booth Luce. Under his stewardship, *McCall's* soon overtook both *Good Housekeeping* and the venerable *Ladies' Home Journal* in profitability. Between 1958 and 1963 circulation increased by nearly 3 million to over 8.2 million, and advertising revenue more than doubled to nearly $42 million over the same period. For his efforts Mayes received the Editor of the Year Award from the Magazine Editors Council in 1960.

In 1961 Mayes assumed the presidency of the McCall Corporation, with annual revenues of $100 million. In this office he oversaw the publication of fifty-three magazines, including *Redbook* and *Saturday Review*. He formally retired as editor of *McCall's* in 1962 and as president and CEO of the McCall Corporation in 1965. However, he remained as a consultant to Norton Simon in 1966, and he guest-edited the March and April 1969 issues of *McCall's* in an attempt to revive its flagging popularity.

With his final retirement from editorial duties in 1969, Mayes moved to London, and from 1970 to 1972 he sent an occasional column on English topics to the *Saturday Review*. In 1975 he returned to the United States. During the final years of his life he weighed investment opportunities in magazine properties and wrote his autobiography, *The Magazine Maze: A Prejudiced Perspective* (1980). Mayes died at his Manhattan apartment.

More than any other editor of his generation, Mayes was responsible for transforming American women's magazines. Not only did he change their look and format, he revised their content to reflect the interests of middle-class and professional women at mid-century; he believed they should serve the readers' interests, not his own. Mayes also solicited new fiction by the best and best-known contemporary writers rather than continuing to print "slick" or sentimental romance, the staple of such magazines as *Ladies' Home Journal*. During his tenure as editor, too, he increased the prestige of the "Good Housekeeping Seal of Approval" by sponsoring extensive testing so that it became a genuine badge of consumer merit. During a career spanning nearly fifty years, according to the *New York Times*, he "built a reputation as one of the country's most respected magazine editors."

• The most significant biographical sources are John Tebbel's "The Remarkable Mr. Mayes," *Saturday Review*, 8 Oct. 1960, and Mayes's autobiography. For details about Mayes's biography of Alger see Gary Scharnhorst with Jack Bales, *The Lost Life of Horatio Alger, Jr.* (1985). See also "Herbert R. Mayes: The Absolute Editor," *Folio: The Magazine for Magazine Management* 20 (Mar. 1991); and Mayes's essays "Notes on Creative Editing," *Writer* 78 (Feb. 1965), and "Henry R. Luce," *Saturday Review*, 18 Mar. 1967. An obituary is in the *New York Times*, 1 Nov. 1987.

GARY SCHARNHORST

MAYHEW, Experience (27 Jan. 1673–29 Nov. 1758), Congregational missionary, was born at Chilmark, on Martha's Vineyard, the son of John Mayhew, a Congregational clergyman, and Elizabeth Hilliard. Experience Mayhew was the great-grandson of Thomas Mayhew (1593–1682), the original patentee of Martha's Vineyard and the pioneer of the island's mission to the Indians of the local Pawkunnawkutt federation, an Algonquin-speaking branch of the Wamponoags. Since he had "learnt the Indian language by rote, as I did my mother tongue, and not studying the rules of it as the Lattin tongue is comonly learned," Mayhew took up mission work among the Indians on the island in March 1694, soon after his father's death. Mayhew's mission was supported by funds from the Society for the Propagation of the Gospel in New England (also known as the New England Company), and he labored as a lay missionary rather than as an ordained pastor. The SPG repeatedly urged the Indian congregations on the Vineyard to ordain Mayhew as their pastor, but the Indian converts preferred to call Native-American pastors instead.

Mayhew's leadership of the Indian congregations on the island was the golden age of the Vineyard mission. Although Mayhew led no particular congregation, he nevertheless had general oversight of the island's Indian congregations and controlled the incoming support funds from the SPG. By 1704 he was able to report to the SPG that, of the 1,500 adults on Martha's Vineyard and Nantucket, there were only two pagan families; and he deeply impressed the SPG's representatives with the degree of acculturation to English ways that he fostered among the Indians. Samuel Sewall found that the congregation at Gay Head Neck had "upward of an Hundred Men & Women besides Chil-

dren" in attendance for Mayhew's preaching, "many of them well habited." Similarly, Benjamin Colman cited Mayhew's mission work in 1719 as an exception to the poor success of other New England Indian missions: "There only are the Natives humaniz'd and civiliz'd that I know of, and brot to cloathe, work, and live like us."

In addition to his preaching and pastoral work, Mayhew was also one of three New Englanders (along with Grindal Rowson and Samuel Danforth) employed to translate English-language theological works into Indian dialects. Mayhew translated numerous sermons, tracts, and catechisms and published a large-scale translation of the Psalms, *The Massachuset Psalter* (1710), for the use of Indian congregations. The SPG also directed him to undertake missions to the Pequots and Mohegans in Connecticut in 1713 and 1714, which he described to the society in two detailed journals. He also defended the integrity of Indian land titles (as well as his own family land interests) on Martha's Vineyard before the General Court of Massachusetts.

Mayhew's lengthy missionary career was untroubled by dissension, apart from his anxiety over the "spreading of ye Anabaptistical Notions" among the Indians, until the Great Awakening burst upon New England in the 1740s. Mayhew looked upon the Awakening with its itinerant evangelists, radical Calvinism, and separatistic churchmanship, as a disruptive influence on the Vineyard and in New England. In 1741 he published a defense of conventional New England communion practices in *A Right to the Lord's Supper*, following it three years later with *Grace Defended in a Modest Plea for an Important Truth*, a detailed response to Jonathan Dickinson's *A Display of God's Special Grace* (1742). Replying to Dickinson, a New Jersey Presbyterian, Mayhew admitted that he differed "from most that are in the Calvinian scheme" and questioned Calvinist teaching on original sin, limited atonement, and predestination. His aim, however, was not so much the obliteration of Calvinism as the moderation of its most objectionable features, so that "such as are disposed to *Arminianism* among us, would be more inclined to receive our doctrine."

Mayhew, however, was disinclined to take an active role in the post-Awakening controversies. Although he withdrew from membership in the Indian congregations in 1715 to join the English congregation at Tisbury, he remained active in mission work and frequently assisted the pastor of the English congregation until his death from a stroke at Tisbury. He was married twice, first to Thankful Hinckley (1671–1706) in 1695 and then to Remember Bourne in 1711, who died in childbirth on 2 March 1722. Of his six children, three graduated from Harvard. Jonathan Mayhew became an articulate and celebrated Boston minister; Experience Mayhew delivered the charge at his ordination in 1747. Zechariah Mayhew (b. 1718) was ordained in 1767 to continue the family's mission work on Martha's Vineyard for yet another generation. Even though Experience Mayhew never attended college, he was offered a Harvard M.A.; he refused it, but Harvard awarded it anyway on 3 July 1723.

• A small collection of Mayhew's letters is contained in the Mayhew family correspondence at Boston University. Mayhew published only a few sermons, but he published a large collection of spiritual narratives of Christian Indians in *Indian Converts; or, Some Account of the Lives and Dying Speeches of a Considerable Number of the Christianized Indians of Martha's Vineyard* (1727). His 1713 and 1714 missionary journals were published in England in *Some Correspondence between the Governors and Trustees of the New England Company* (1896). Mayhew's "Letter on Indian Languages," written in 1722 to explain the intricacies of the Martha's Vineyard Indian dialect (and to compare it to the Natick, Pequot, and Mohegan dialects), was published in *The New England Historical and Genealogical Register*, vol. 39 (1885). The most important sources on Mayhew are his biographical entry in *Sibley's Harvard Graduates*, vol. 7 (1945) and two brief sketches in *The New England Historical and Genealogical Register*, vol. 13 (July 1859) and the *American Quarterly Register* (May 1843). Accounts of Mayhew's mission work can also be found in William Kellaway, *The New England Company, 1649–1776* (1961); Charles M. Segal and David C. Stineback, *Puritans, Indians, and Manifest Destiny* (1977); and James Axtell, *The Invasion Within: The Contest of Cultures in Colonial North America* (1985).

ALLEN C. GUELZO

MAYHEW, Jonathan (8 Oct. 1720–9 July 1766), Congregational minister, was born at Chilmark on Martha's Vineyard, Massachusetts, the son of Experience Mayhew, a clergyman and missionary to Indians, and Remember Bourne. Descended from several generations of Martha's Vineyard proprietors, young Mayhew removed to the more cosmopolitan setting of Boston, where he thrived at the crossroads of brisk controversies. He graduated with honors from Harvard College in 1744. During the ensuing three years he occasionally taught school and studied theology at his alma mater. In 1747 he received ordination and accepted a call from the West Congregational Church in Boston, a position that he occupied for the next nineteen years. In 1756 he married Elizabeth Clarke; the couple had three children, of which only one lived to adulthood.

Mayhew early showed little concern about accepting orthodox opinions for their own sake. His independent turn of mind was so pronounced at the beginning of his career that several Boston ministers feared he would preach unsound doctrine and introduce questionable religious tenets into the local culture. For those who treasured adherence to received ideas, this is precisely what he did. For those who advocated rational religion with practical guidelines for ethical progress, Mayhew became a champion in his day of liberal Christianity. Along with his colleague Charles Chauncy, Mayhew set the tone for discussing the reasonableness of Christian tenets and the practical benefits of its behavioral standards. The basis on which he constructed this ministerial tutelage was the Bible read from a rationalistic perspective common among those who comprised the Age of Enlightenment. In this view

the plain teachings of Scripture were clear and free for all to accept; truth had intrinsic value and needed no theological school to lend it greater authority.

The school against which Mayhew argued was Calvinism. Instead of accepting doctrines formulated in the past, he maintained that human reason validated the essentials of revealed truth. In that context he affirmed belief in a single Godhead and rejected trinitarian concepts. Refusing to deify Jesus because that would detract from God's supremacy, Mayhew also declined to lower Jesus to a mere human level. In earnest sermons that were printed and read on both sides of the Atlantic, he extolled Jesus as the preexistent mediator between divine perfection and human failings, a moral exemplar whose sacrificial death enhanced the plan of salvation by vindicating the glory of God's Law. Such theological reasoning was largely ahead of its time, and Mayhew may be said to have laid some of the intellectual foundations of what later became the Unitarian denomination.

Another Calvinist staple that Mayhew's cast of mind would not accept had to do with free will. His affirmation of human agency in spiritual matters paralleled his espousal of free inquiry and private judgment of ideas. According to Calvinists, salvation was a process of unconditional election that touched sinners whose utter depravity robbed them of effective volition. Mayhew rejected any doctrine of reprobation or spiritual incapacity. Such tenets were unscriptural, he said; they paralyzed any effort at moral reform, and they blasphemed a benevolent God by portraying him as vengeful. Whether debating against traditionalists of the New Divinity, such as Samuel Hopkins, or Great Awakening preachers, such as George Whitefield, he rejected notions that an all-powerful grace rescued a few helpless beings from multitudes of the damned. He never tired of defending free will as an element in God's created order. He stressed a sober religion of human effort, a search for God's help obtained through good works and virtuous habits. Mayhew's published sermons bear titles such as "Discourse Occasioned by Earthquakes" (1755), "God's Hand in Public Calamities" (1760), and "The Nature and Extent of Divine Goodness" (1763).

Outspoken whenever a principle was concerned, Mayhew entered debates over political questions as well as religious ones. Several of his printed sermons nurtured incipient patriotism in the colonies. He produced, for instance, learned discourses against unlimited submission to political power, especially that of Charles I. Those ideas formed some of the theoretical framework for subsequent American revolutionary efforts. Another treatise defended the right to disobey unjust laws. He upheld basic liberties in the face of arbitrary rule and justified taking over reins of government to preserve fundamental freedoms. Men were bound to obey a king who ruled justly, he acknowledged, but if royal authority proved to be tyrannical, citizens had the right to resist oppression in the name of civil liberty. His famous address, "The Snare Broken" (1766), embodied public satisfaction over repeal of the Stamp Act that occurred shortly before his death.

Another running battle that Mayhew conducted with gusto concerned the Society for the Propagation of the Gospel in Foreign Parts (SPG). This British organization had been founded to conduct evangelical work among African Americans and Native Americans. But by 1750, SPG officials had deviated from their early purpose and had sent Anglican missionaries to parts of New England already settled with Congregationalist churches. In three vigorous, caustic pamphlets Mayhew railed at SPG efforts to evangelize an already Christian people. Anglican infiltration was just a preliminary to introducing bishops of England's established church, he charged. And from there it was only a short step to further political subservience under Crown officials.

Mayhew's ardent liberalism in religion and politics was consistent with the intellectual freedom and governmental philosophy produced in the Age of Reason. He advanced those principles in sermons and tracts, but his death in Boston from complications of a cerebral hemorrhage came before such ideals reached their zenith in this country. His fellow citizens mourned his early demise and honored Mayhew as a genial colleague, spirited controversialist, pastoral leader, and firm patriot.

• Mayhew's few papers are among the 140 surviving items of his distinguished family archived at Boston University. Many of his sermons were printed singly as commemorations of solemn occasions. Several collections include *Seven Sermons* (1749; repr. 1969); *Sermons* (1755); *Christian Sobriety* (1763); and *Sermons to Young Men* (2 vols., 1767). An early biography is Alden Bradford, *Memoir of the Life and Writings of Jonathan Mayhew* (1838), although a much better, more recent one is Charles W. Akers, *Call unto Liberty: A Life of Jonathan Mayhew, 1720–1766* (1964). Additional material is in John Corrigan, *The Hidden Balance: Religion and the Social Theories of Charles Chauncy and Jonathan Mayhew* (1987).

HENRY WARNER BOWDEN

MAYHEW, Thomas (1593–25 Mar. 1682), New England merchant and proprietor of Martha's Vineyard and Nantucket, was born in St. John the Baptist parish, Tisbury, Wilshire, England, the son of Matthew Mayhew and Alice Barter, farmers. Though his exact date of birth is uncertain, he was baptised on 1 April 1593. Mayhew was an established merchant (mercer) and free commoner when in 1631 he accepted the agency of Matthew Cradock of London to manage properties in Medford, Massachusetts, and to engage in trade and shipbuilding. A man of restless energy, he easily handled his responsibilities, although perhaps not well, also finding time to chair a committee of the General Court on a town dispute, probate a will, advise on docks in Charlestown, and build corn and lumber mills that soon brought "great profit." He was elected a freeman in 1634. In 1634 or 1635 business with Cradock took him to London, where he also married Jane (Gallion?) Paine, who cared for his son by a previous marriage, Thomas Mayhew, Jr., the future

missionary; together they had an additional four children. In New England again he returned to Medford (probably to wind up his work for Cradock). Mayhew then moved to Watertown, where he was a farmer, shipbuilder, and merchant and served as a selectman and a representative to the General Court until 1645. Official and trading matters took him north to Salem and Newbury, and south to Plymouth and Barnstable.

Mayhew's search for opportunities culminated in 1641 when he secured Martha's Vineyard, Nantucket, Elizabeth Islands, and other islands as a proprietorship, from Sir Ferdinando Gorges and Lord Sterling, presumably to succeed them as sovereign landowner. The grant permitted him to transfer his business operations there. With the help of colonists from Watertown under the leadership of his young son Thomas, a settlement was planted, farms selected, and whaling begun. In 1646 Mayhew took personal charge, possibly because of rivalry among planters, and by the mid 1650s he was addressed regularly as governor, ruling with six other settlers and adopting a form of government similar to that of Massachusetts. Sometime before 1658 he took full power into his own hands, a decision that may have been affected by the tragic drowning of his missionary son when the ship on which he was riding was lost at sea on a voyage to England.

The death occurred at a particularly critical moment. Mayhew was forced not only to find a worthy successor to his son for missionary leadership but also to handle problems arising from unsettled politics in England and estate litigation by the Gorges heirs that challenged his title as proprietor. In 1664 James, the duke of York, bought out proprietary rights from the Gorges heirs, and Martha's Vineyard became part of New York when the Dutch colony was seized. Even though controversy over title persisted for years, Mayhew and his friends held local power. Indian policy was put into the hands of John Cotton of Boston and then assumed by reliable Christian natives. Mayhew's grandson Matthew and other relatives assisted him in running his businesses and the government, which were often intermixed. Success in Indian policy helped later shield the colony from the bloodshed of King Philip's War.

In 1671 negotiations with New York officials confirmed Mayhew's distribution of land titles and possession of political authority. He was proclaimed governor for life, presumably to share power with relatives and settlers of Edgartown and Tisbury. But Mayhew was unwilling to broaden the basis of authority, and a rebellion of Dutch and English settlers erupted in 1673 that removed him and his friends from office. The revolt was also part of general unrest over English rule elsewhere in the New York colony. With the help of English soldiers, however, Mayhew was soon restored to office, as were other English authorities in New York as well. Mayhew used the opportunity to oppress his enemies. Through his grandson, relatives, and friends he controlled the courts and militia; he used this power to seize estates, impose fines, and disenfranchise enemies. The oppression continued for years, surviving even beyond Mayhew's death at Martha's Vineyard. Mayhew disregarded pressure from New York officials, and the abuses lingered under Matthew Mayhew, his successor, until Martha's Vineyard was annexed to Massachusetts in 1690 as part of the political settlement of the Glorious Revolution. The Mayhew family, in spite of its loss of political control, multiplied in numbers and retained its modest wealth on the islands.

• A few of Mayhew's papers are in the Massachusetts Historical Society and the Massachusetts Archives. See also the printed *Records of the New Plymouth Colony in New England* (12 vols., 1855–1861) and the *Records of the Governor and Company of Massachusetts Bay* (5 vols., 1853–1854). The best general history of Mayhew's activities on Martha's Vineyard is in Charles E. Banks, *The History of Martha's Vineyard* (3 vols., 1911–1925; repr. 1966), which includes considerable discussion of the amazing Mayhew family in volume one and a genealogy in volume three. Lloyd C. M. Hare has corrected some of Banks's impressions in his *Thomas Mayhew: Patriarch to the Indians* (1932). Also consult John Eliot, *Tears of Repentance: A Further Narrative of the Progress of the Gospel amongst the Indians* (1653), for a contemporary view of missionary activity.

JOHN A. SCHUTZ

MAYHEW, Thomas, Jr. (1621–1657), missionary and settler of Martha's Vineyard, was born in Southampton, England, the son of Thomas Mayhew, a merchant and proprietor of Martha's Vineyard. (His mother's name is unknown.) Thomas accompanied his father to Medford, Massachusetts, in 1631 and was educated in Medford and Watertown schools. He was tutored for the ministry with training in the classics and languages. Instead, he first assisted his father in operating their corn and timber mills. In 1641 he shared his father's proprietorship of Martha's Vineyard (known then variously as "Noepe" or the "Isle of Capswack") and took the first colonists there. He was a farmer and an early trader with the Indians. Until his father arrived in 1646 to assume personal charge of the property, Mayhew was sole agent, but he was anxious to work with the Indians. His marriage in 1647 to Jane Paine, his father's stepdaughter from his second marriage, brought six children who were responsible in coming years for the increase of the Mayhew family in the Vineyard.

At first, Mayhew, as agent for his father, developed the property, whaling, and trade, but he became most interested in the welfare of the local Indians (Pawwaws), learned their languages, and studied their customs. By the time his father joined him at the Vineyard, Mayhew had become so concerned about the Indians' spiritual and physical health that he was preaching to them, teaching the youth, and using home remedies to cure their ills. By 1651 he counted 199 conversions. "There are now two meetings kept every Lord's day, the one three miles and the other about eight miles off my house. . . . This winter I intend, if the Lord will, to set up a school to teach Indi-

ans to read viz, the children, and also any young men that are willing to learn."

When Henry Whitfield, a local minister, visited him in 1650, Mayhew and his family were living in dire poverty, and Mayhew himself was taciturn. "I could get but little [information] from him; but after, I understood from others how short things went with him; and how he was many times forced to labour with his own hands. . . . The truth is, he will not leave the work, in which his heart is engaged."

Through such visitors Mayhew's missionary work, together with that of John Eliot near Boston, attracted the attention of sympathetic Englishmen who sent gifts at first, then provided stipends for him, his Indian assistants, and a schoolmaster, Peter Folger. Mayhew also joined Eliot in publishing observations on their work with the Indians, permitting a few letters to be included in the pamphlets. By 1657 his reputation had spread widely. He was called a "Worthy gentleman" who was providing an "almost inexpressible labor, and vigilant care for the Good of the Indians." This annalist, Thomas Prince, counted "many hundred men and women added to the Christian Society" through Mayhew's efforts. Most of the remaining Pawwaws were influenced by the Christianized Indians and were satisfied apparently that they were being treated fairly. Mayhew used natives to spread his influence—Hiacoomes as a pastor, John Taskanash as a teacher, and John Nahnose and Joshua Monatchegin as ruling elders.

Mayhew lived frugally, perhaps entirely on his English stipend and from what his father provided. He was undoubtedly devoted to the welfare of his Indian converts, but his work fitted as well into the purposes of the proprietorship, which valued the trade and docility of the Indians. His remarkable success, nonetheless, was recognized by occasional visitors. In November 1657 he set out for England, probably to secure greater support from London friends, but the ship, with all of its passengers, was destroyed by heavy seas. He left the burden of continuing the missionary work on his father, who was perplexed at first by the responsibility. Jane Mayhew and her young family were not of much immediate help. In 1667 she married Richard Sarson, a settler who was a supporter of the governor; she was soon the mother of two additional children. Both Matthew and John, her older sons, were added to the governor's staff. John became his father's successor as an ordained missionary. Despite the untimely accident that cut short his career, Mayhew was recognized as a devoted friend of the Indians, leaving them "more civilized than anywhere else in New England."

• Apparently no personal letters from Mayhew have survived, but a few letters used to promote his missionary endeavors were prepared for John Eliot and published in *Tears of Repentance* (1653), and for Edward Winslow, *The Glorious Progress of the Gospel* (1649). The most informative general history of Martha's Vineyard is Charles E. Banks, *History of Martha's Vineyard* (3 vols., 1911; repr. 1966). Henry Whitfield, *A Farther Discovery of the Present State of the Indians of New England* (1865) is a reprinting of the contemporary account, which discusses Mayhew's missionary activities. Lloyd C. M. Hare, *Thomas Mayhew: Patriarch to the Indians, 1593–1682* (1932), a biography of the missionary's father, is an enlightening account of the family.

JOHN A. SCHUTZ

MAYNARD, Horace (30 Aug. 1814–3 May 1882), congressman and postmaster general of the United States, was born in Westboro, Massachusetts, the son of Ephraim Maynard, a wheelwright, and Diane Cogswell. His father was a lifelong resident of Westboro, and both parents were members of old Puritan families. Graduated in 1838 from Amherst College as valedictorian, young Maynard moved to Knoxville, Tennessee, to accept a position as tutor in the preparatory department of East Tennessee College (now the University of Tennessee). In 1840 he married Laura Ann Washburn; they had seven children. In 1841 he was promoted to professor of mathematics and natural and moral philosophy at the university, but he left academics to study law with Judge Ebenezer Alexander. Admitted to the bar in 1844, Maynard soon established an enviable reputation in his profession.

An active Whig, Maynard was a delegate to his party's 1852 national convention in Baltimore and served as a presidential elector for Winfield Scott. In 1853 he was a candidate for Congress, but, having referred to the people as "the common herd" in one of his essays, he was defeated by the Democrat William M. Churchill. A presidential elector for Millard Fillmore in 1856, Maynard finally won election to the House of Representatives as an American (Know Nothing) in 1857 and was reelected in 1859. His firm Unionist convictions led him to become one of the organizers of the 1860 Constitutional Union party convention, which nominated John Bell and Edward Everett.

The secession crisis created a difficult situation for Maynard. When he met Stephen A. Douglas in the summer of 1860, Maynard suggested that a special House committee with one representative from each state be established to deal with the crisis, a course that was taken in December 1860. Occupying a middle ground, he supported the proposed Crittenden Compromise to create a dividing line between slavery and freedom at 36° 30′, declared that he saw no reason why the Union could not continue half free and half slave, and strongly urged the North to listen to the grievances of the South and remove the causes of discontent. At home, he valiantly campaigned against secession, supported Unionists regardless of party, and cooperated with fellow Whigs like William G. Brownlow as well as Democrats like Andrew Johnson, whom he had opposed for years.

Maynard's efforts were crowned with success in East Tennessee, which voted against secession, but the state as a whole joined the South. In August 1861 he won reelection to Congress against a Confederate opponent, only to be forced to flee to the North immediately afterward. In Washington, together with Johnson, Maynard became one of the principal advocates of a Union campaign to liberate East Tennessee, a course of action he ceaselessly urged on the Lincoln administration. In 1863 Johnson, then military governor of Tennessee, appointed him attorney general.

After the reconquest of East Tennessee, Maynard returned home. Active in the movement to reconstruct the state, in April 1865 he was a candidate for U.S. senator but was defeated by Johnson's son-in-law David Patterson. In August 1865 Maynard was reelected to his seat in Congress; however, when the House met on 4 December, the clerk refused to call his name, and he was not seated until the readmission of Tennessee in July 1866. Thereafter he was a Radical Republican, voting with this faction on all important issues on Reconstruction and retaining his seat in 1866 and 1868. By this time the conservatives had regained control of the legislature, and they sought to end Maynard's career by gerrymandering his district. Running for congressman-at-large in 1872, Maynard succeeded in defeating both of his opponents, General Benjamin F. Cheatham and ex-president Johnson. Two years later, however, despite equivocation on the pending federal Civil Rights Bill, he lost the race for governor to James D. Porter.

In 1875 President Ulysses S. Grant appointed Maynard minister resident to the Ottoman Empire. He served in Constantinople until May 1880, when President Rutherford B. Hayes elevated him to the cabinet as postmaster general. He retained this position until the end of the Hayes administration in 1881, when he retired to Knoxville. An unsuccessful candidate for the Senate that year, he resumed his legal career until his death in Knoxville.

An active Presbyterian, Maynard served as an elder of the Second Presbyterian Church in Knoxville from 1849 to 1882. He also engaged in literary endeavors, composing while still an undergraduate an essay on the legends about a pond in his hometown. Under the pseudonym Zadock Jones, he contributed frequently to the *Knoxville Press* and, under his own name, wrote articles for his university's magazine.

Maynard was tall and of commanding build. With his dark eyes and straight black hair parted on the left side and combed back over his ears, he looked so swarthy that the students dubbed him "the Narragansett." His cold and suspicious nature prevented him from becoming truly popular, but he was an effective Unionist whose support of the national cause was a faithful reflection of the sentiments of the majority of his East Tennessee constituents.

• Some Horace Maynard Papers are at the University of Tennessee, Knoxville. Brief sketches may be found in Mary Utopia Rothrock, ed., *The French-Broad Holston Country* (1946); James Park, *The Life and Services of Horace Maynard* (1903); Oliver P. Temple, *Notable Men of Tennessee* (1912); and *The Papers of Andrew Johnson*, ed. LeRoy P. Graf et al. (1967–). Further information is contained in *Amherst College Biographical Record, 1963; Biographical Record of the Graduates and Non-Graduates of the Classes of 1822–1962* (1963); Charles Henry Hunt, *The Numismatic and Antiquarian Society of Philadelphia: Necrology for 1882* (1883); *Vital Records of Westboro,*

Mass. to the End of the Year 1849 (1903); and E. O. Jameson, *The Cogswells in America* (1884). See also F. Wayne Binning, "The Tennessee Republicans in Decline, 1869–1876," *Tennessee Historical Quarterly* 39 (Winter 1980): 471–84, and 40 (Spring 1981): 61–84. Obituaries are in the *Knoxville Daily Tribune*, 5 May 1882, and the *New York Tribune*, 4 May 1882.

HANS L. TREFOUSSE

MAYNARD, Robert Clyve (17 June 1937–17 Aug. 1993), journalist, editor, and publisher, was born in the predominantly African-American Bedford-Stuyvesant section of Brooklyn, New York, the son of Samuel C. Maynard, a lay preacher and the owner of a small trucking firm, and Robertine Isola Greaves. His parents, who had immigrated from Barbados in 1919, encouraged personal expression in their six children and believed in Robert's aspiration to be a writer from the time he was eight years old. Maynard attended Boys' High School in Brooklyn until, at the age of sixteen, he dropped out of school to become a reporter for the *New York Age*, a local African-American weekly. At nineteen he moved to Manhattan, where he supported himself doing odd jobs and as a freelance writer, with the encouragement of James Baldwin and Langston Hughes. During a stint as a reporter for Baltimore's *Afro-American News* he sent out 320 applications for jobs on mainstream newspapers, but although his freelance work got him a few interviews he was rejected when his race became known. One editor told him frankly that his publisher would shoot him if he hired a black man.

In 1961 Maynard was hired by the *York (Pa.) Gazette and Daily* as a police and urban affairs reporter. His beat came to include a wide range of national news, including the civil rights movement in the South. In 1966 he was awarded a one-year Nieman fellowship to study journalism at Harvard University, and he returned to become the night city editor at the *Gazette*. In 1967 he became the *Washington Post's* first African-American national correspondent. A five-part series he wrote on racial unrest, covering five major cities, was widely reprinted and won him a national reputation during his first year at the *Post*. His personal experience and contacts gave him a vantage point that lent his reporting unique authority. As Howard Simons, managing editor of the paper, noted, "He gave us eyes and ears that we lacked somewhat in black affairs in this country" (quoted in *Newsweek*, 24 Sept. 1979). At that time only about 300 of the estimated 40,000 newspaper writers, editors, and photographers in the United States were nonwhite, and Maynard was outspoken on minority hiring practices in journalism. In 1972 he was selected to join *New York Times* reporter Earl Caldwell to codirect a summer program in journalism for minorities sponsored by the Ford Foundation at Columbia University. That same year he began to work part time as a senior editor for the African-American monthly *Encore*, and he was made ombudsman and assistant editor of the *Post*. As White House correspondent, he was selected as one of the three questioners in the debate between President Gerald Ford and candidate Jimmy Carter in 1976.

Maynard married Nancy Hall Hicks, a science and medical writer for the *New York Times*, in 1975; the couple had two children (Maynard also had a daughter from an earlier marriage). In 1977 he and his wife left Washington for the Berkeley campus of the University of California, to help found the Institute for Journalism Education as part of Berkeley's graduate program in journalism. The nonprofit institute, modeled on the program he had codirected at Columbia, established Jobnet, a service that found employment for minority journalists. The network was credited with placing more than 600 students in newspaper jobs by the time of Maynard's death. In 1982 it was estimated that one-fourth of all nonwhite newspaper employees hired that year were graduates of the institute.

Soon after founding the institute, Maynard became an affirmative-action consultant to the Gannett Company, the country's largest newspaper chain, and in 1979 he became the first African American to lead a major U.S. metropolitan daily when he was made editor of Gannett's *Oakland (Calif.) Tribune*. He redesigned the paper, whose circulation had fallen from 200,000 to fewer than 170,000 between 1977 and 1979, but he was unable to make it profitable. When the Gannett Company sought to buy a local television station and wished to simplify the procedure by divesting itself of the paper, Maynard took ownership of the *Tribune*. In 1982 he thus became the first African American to own a major daily newspaper. The price was $22 million, and Maynard financed it entirely by loans on the paper's real estate holdings and from the Gannett Company. He struggled to keep the paper afloat, increasing its local coverage in an effort to make it more responsive to community concerns, but it continued to lose money. The *Tribune's* circulation sank to 121,000 in 1992, and Maynard was forced to sell the paper to the Alameda News Group. He returned to work with the Institute for Journalism Education and continued promoting the cause of equal opportunities for minority journalists until his death of prostate cancer in Oakland, California.

Maynard began writing a weekly column the year he assumed the editorship of the *Tribune* and increased its frequency to semiweekly six years later. Touching on a wide variety of subjects, from family anecdotes to international affairs and social issues, the popular feature was distributed nationally by the Universal Press Syndicate, and a collection of the columns, edited by his daughter Dori, was published in 1995 as *Letters to My Children*. Maynard also appeared regularly as a television commentator on several national news programs and served on the board of directors of the Associated Press, the American Society of Newspaper Editors, the National News Council, the Oakland Chamber of Commerce, and the Pacific School of Religion. He was a member of the Pulitzer Prize committee and received honorary degrees from six institutions of higher learning.

Known for his ebullient personality and his brimming confidence, Maynard was described by Paul Cobb, an Oakland community activist, as being to journalism what Jackie Robinson was to baseball. He dedicated his working life to the cause of racial equality in his field, and his obituary in the *New York Times* noted that, in addition to the professional honors he received, "he won more praise for his efforts to help minority youths follow him into journalism." He stated his mission clearly in his last public speech, in May 1993, when he affirmed, "This country cannot be the country we all want it to be if its story is told by only one group of citizens. Our goal is to give all Americans front-door access to the truth."

• Maynard's career is discussed in *Newsweek*, 24 Sept. 1979, p. 80, and 16 May 1983, p. 93; the *New York Times*, 1 May 1983, 5 June 1985, 6 Feb. 1989, 22 June 1990, and 15 Aug. 1991; *Time*, 16 May 1983, p. 85; and the *Christian Science Monitor*, 16 June 1983 and 22 Aug. 1986. See also Pamela Noel, "Robert Maynard: Oakland's Top Newsman," *Ebony*, June 1985. Obituaries appear in the *New York Times*, *Newsday*, and the *Washington Post*, all 19 Aug. 1993.

DENNIS WEPMAN

MAYO, Amory Dwight (31 Jan. 1823–8 Apr. 1907), Unitarian clergyman and educator, was born in Warwick, Massachusetts, the son of Amory Mayo and Sophronia Cobb. Mayo enrolled at Amherst College in 1843. However, during his freshman year, illness forced him to leave school. For a short time he taught at district schools, but interest in the ministry led him to begin studying theology with Rev. Hosea Ballou II. By 1846 Mayo was an ordained Universalist minister with his first congregation in Gloucester. Mayo's preaching style, according to his parishioners, was appealing, enlightening, and spiritually uplifting, and his popularity led to ever-increasing church attendance. Mayo's health, however, was unsteady, sometimes preventing him from delivering church services. Nevertheless, many of his sermons were collected in his works *The Balance; or, Moral Arguments for Universalism* (1847) and *Graces and Powers of the Christian Life* (1853). These books provided continued Christian growth and spiritual illumination both for his congregation and future Christians.

In 1846, while serving as minister at Gloucester, Mayo married Sarah Edgarton, who was noted in the church for her literary accomplishments. Sarah died only two years after their marriage. In 1853 Mayo married Lucy Caroline Clarke. Mayo had five children.

In October 1854 Mayo resigned his pastoral duties at Gloucester, responding to an invitation to become pastor of the Independent Christian Church in Cleveland, Ohio, where he served for the next two years. This appointment was less fruitful than he expected, and in 1856 he relocated to Albany, New York, where he ministered at the Division Street Unitarian Church until 1863. In that year he moved once again, accepting a position as preacher of the Church of the Redeemer in Cincinnati, Ohio. Also in 1863, while residing in Cincinnati, he accepted a position as nonresident professor of administration and church polity at Meadville Theological School (Pa.), a position he maintained for the next thirty-five years.

Initially, the Meadville Seminary faculty consisted of three resident and five nonresident instructors. Among other duties, Mayo delivered an annual course of twelve to fifteen lectures on principal denominational creeds and their varied methods. He also discoursed on religious reform and policy. After 1883 Mayo delivered these lectures on a triennial basis.

In 1872 Mayo left Cincinnati to preach at the Church of the Unity in Springfield, Massachusetts. He retained his position in Springfield until 1880, when he resigned from active ministerial duties and devoted more time to writing and lecturing.

In 1880 Mayo's interests became more directed toward educational pursuits. He had been interested in education since his ministerial work in Albany and had served on both the Cincinnati and Springfield school boards. He had also served as a leader of the Christian Amendment movement, which advocated a provision in the Constitution affirming the right to teach the Bible in public school. With his move to Boston in 1880 his interest in education, particularly education in the South, became a driving force. For the next twenty years Mayo devoted himself to advancing southern education, traveling an estimated 200,000 miles. He lectured, delivered sermons, and consulted numerous southern educators. Since most of his lecturing and counseling were provided gratis, Mayo was forced at first to depend on an annual grant from the American Unitarian Association and later on contributions from friends and well-wishers. Owing to his behavior and personality, he was usually well received by blacks, poor whites, and members of the middle class. From 1880 to 1885 Mayo, between travels, served as associate editor of the *New England Journal of Education* and as chief editorial writer for the *National Journal of Education*.

At the request of Dr. William T. Harris, U.S. commissioner of education, Mayo dedicated himself to writing the history of American common schools. The work was uncompleted at his death. Between 1893 and his death, Mayo was listed as lecturer of education at Berea College, Kentucky. His lectures on various aspects of southern educational problems and reforms and the educational condition of southern blacks and whites were given during frequent visits to Berea. Mayo died at his home in Washington, D.C.

Mayo was a man of vision and Christian character. During his life, he created two separate careers; either of these callings could have allowed him to carve a place for himself in American history. As a minister, his sermons and books, besides providing spiritual enrichment, were instructive in moral and ethical behavior. Later in life, as an educational researcher and promoter, he conducted a 26-year campaign of lecturing, interviewing, visiting, preaching, and writing in behalf of public schooling for both races within the South.

• The Frederick Huidekoper Papers, which contain letters and journals about Mayo and the Meadville Theological School, are located at the Crawford County Historical Society (Meadville, Pa.) and the Meadville-Lombard Theological School Library (Chicago, Ill.). Mayo left a legacy of pamphlets, sermons, magazine and journal articles, and published works. A partial listing of his works includes *Selections from the Writings of Mrs. Sarah C. Edgarton Mayo: With a Memoir by Her Husband* (1849); *Symbols of the Capital; or, Civilization in New York* (1859); *Religion in the Common Schools* (1869); *The Bible in the Public Schools*, with Thomas Vickers (1870); *Talks with Teachers* (1881); *Industrial Education in the South* (1888); and *Southern Women in the Recent Educational Movement in the South* (1892). One of the best sketches of Mayo's life is by his son Arthur Dwight Mayo in "The Mayo Family in the United States," vol. 1, ed. Chester G. Mayo (1927), typewritten in the Library of Congress. Another excellent biographical sketch is in Laura S. Hersey, *Gloucester Universalist Newsletter*, Dec. 1992. Richard Eddy, *Universalism in Gloucester, Mass.* (1892), is a brief yet important source relating to Mayo's years as pastor of the Gloucester Universalist Church. Francis A. Christie, *Makers of the Meadville Theological School, 1844–1894* (1927), offers an interesting history of the Meadville Seminary with, however, the noticeable absence of information relating to Mayo. Obituaries are in the *Unitarian Year Book*, 1 July 1907; the *Christian Register*, 18 Apr. 1907; and the *Washington Evening Star*, 9 Apr. 1907.

C. E. LINDGREN

MAYO, Charles Horace. *See* Mayo, William James, and Charles Horace Mayo.

MAYO, Frank (18 Apr. 1839–8 June 1896), actor and author, was born in Boston, Massachusetts, the son of now unknown Irish parents about whom Mayo remained silent (perhaps because he was embarrassed about his poverty-stricken heritage). Although it is probable that Mayo received some basic elementary school education, little is known about his life up to age fourteen, when he left Boston by ship bound for California, hoping to strike it rich in the aftermath of the gold rush. Finding no success in the gold fields, Mayo wandered into theatrical life in San Francisco in 1855 or 1856, at first working at a variety of behind-the-scenes tasks and walk-on parts before advancing to speaking roles by July 1856. As a teenager, Mayo received valuable experience in a variety of roles and theatrical companies in California, for the most part in San Francisco but often touring through the mining country, acting in support of such stars as Laura Keene, Charles Wheatleigh, and Junius Brutus Booth. By age nineteen Mayo had begun to attract newspaper attention for his acting and had even received a benefit performance. Although he participated in numerous performances of Shakespeare's dramas, his first notable successes came in supporting roles as villain or hero in sensational melodrama.

In May 1859 Mayo married Mary D. Bryan in San Francisco; the couple had four children, of whom three lived to maturity. By March 1863 Mayo had become leading man at Mcguire's Opera House in San Francisco. In the same year, he appeared in Virginia City, Nevada, in the midst of silver fever and met the young journalist Samuel Clemens (Mark Twain), beginning a friendship that would extend through Mayo's career.

Knowing that real theatrical success would come only in the eastern United States, Mayo secured the position of leading man at the Boston Theater in 1865. For a year and a half Mayo acted a variety of roles from Shakespeare (he played Iago to Edwin Booth's Othello) to sensational melodrama; but his greatest success was in the role of Badger in *The Streets of New York*, a play that centers on the conflicts between rich and poor in American society. As Badger, Mayo portrayed an ordinary bank clerk, streetwise, clever, and unpretentious, whose inherent morality and common sense snare the rich villain while underscoring the character advantages of poverty. Convinced that true stardom would require more exposure than he could receive in Boston, Mayo began touring widely with a variety of companies (most of which he created and managed). He performed many roles but relied more often than not on his role as Badger to assure a full house and financial success.

While managing and starring in a theater in Rochester, New York, in 1872, Mayo obtained rights to a play by Frank Hitchcock Murdoch, *Davy Crockett*. This play became synonymous with Mayo's career and proved both a blessing and a curse. Mayo rewrote much of the play over the years to suit his style and at the same time turned it into the nineteenth century's most popular American drama on western themes. The play centers on young Davy's love for a girl above his station, his protection of her from a pack of wolves in a blizzard, and his eventual winning of his sweetheart after he daringly rescues her during her wedding from men of villainous intent. Although melodramatic, the play features a hero with common sense, valor, great physical strength, and rustic humor. Mayo brought to the role a fine voice, rugged good looks, physical vitality, insight into western American manners and movements, and a studied naturalness to his acting—which, as Fike notes, "appeared deceptively simple, but was the result of much practice." The play became his mainstay for the next twenty-two years, often being paired with *The Streets of New York* in Mayo's nationwide tours. With his resulting financial success, Mayo bought an estate in Canton, Pennsylvania, building an elaborate Victorian house with extensive furnishings and grounds.

Whenever Mayo attempted to abandon *Davy Crockett*, thinking that it was narrowing his range and hampering his artistic success, he would return to the drama as the surefire remedy to the financial problems created by his growing family and his own material needs. Before long, the identification of the actor with his role became so complete that the public began to confuse the player with his character. Mayo became depressed, according to W. A. Lewis, when a man in Buffalo said to him: "I don't suppose you'll ever play anything else but Mayo, Mr. Crockett?"

Eventually, however, in the late 1880s and early 1890s, the play began to lose its audience, except in smaller cities and outlying areas of the country. With a star now over fifty, gray haired and fuller of figure, attempting to play the young Davy Crockett involved in a budding romance, the drama seemed less than convincing to many observers.

Finally, in 1894, after a chance meeting with Mark Twain on a New York street, Mayo spent months adapting Twain's latest work of fiction, *Pudd'nhead Wilson*, for the stage. This play, Mayo's last great success, was staged in early 1895 in Hartford, Connecticut, and later in New York City. Mayo's adaptation was carefully crafted and included some helpful dramatic twists missing from the novel. Mayo himself played the title role of the Pudd'nhead, bringing to the part a careful underplaying that heightened the humor of the play. An immensely successful nationwide tour followed, which took Mayo as far west as San Francisco. While playing in Denver, Mayo was continuously bothered with abdominal pain, but he refused medical help. He died of heart failure en route by train from Denver to Omaha, where he was to appear in four performances of the play prior to ending his exhausting tour. He was buried in the West Laurel Hill Cemetery in Philadelphia.

Although Mayo rewrote and adapted several works into his own stage versions over the years, his major success was as an actor in roles and plays with peculiarly American traits. He excelled at portraying characters with traits of common sense, plain speech, down-to-earth humor, and physical strength. Although he often acted well in classical and European roles, he would not have attained true star status had it not been for his characterizations of Badger, Davy Crockett, and Pudd'nhead Wilson.

• Some diaries and correspondence, especially letters to Mayo, are in the New York Public Library. The Libraries of Performing Arts in New York City have a variety of Mayo posters, photographs, and play manuscripts. The Mayo adaptation of Murdoch's *Davy Crockett* can be found in Barrett Clark's *America's Lost Plays*, vol. 4 (1940). Mayo recalls the details surrounding his adaptation of Twain's *Pudd'nhead Wilson* in an article in *Harper's Weekly*, 22 June 1895. The best full-length study of Frank Mayo is the unpublished dissertation by Duane Joseph Fike, "Frank Mayo: Actor, Playwright, and Manager" (Univ. of Nebraska, 1980). An unpublished M.A. thesis by Norman Leslie Earle, "Frank Mayo—American Actor" (California State Univ., 1972), is also available. Moving reminiscences with valuable information about Mayo's personality and attitudes are found in an article by W. A. Lewis, "Frank Mayo—Man and Artist," *Theater Magazine*, June 1906, pp. iii and 149–51. A short summary of Mayo's career is given in Richard Moody, *America Takes the Stage* (1955). Informative obituaries of Mayo are in the *New York Times*, 9 June 1896, and the *Philadelphia Inquirer*, 10 June 1896.

DELMER DAVIS

MAYO, George Elton (26 Dec. 1880–7 Sept. 1949), professor, was born in Adelaide, Australia, the son of George Gibbes Mayo, a successful realtor, and Henrietta Mary Donaldson. In 1899 Mayo's parents persuaded him to begin medical studies at the University of Adelaide, but lacking enthusiasm for the subject, he

failed. After trying again at the University of Edinburgh and St. George's Hospital in London, in 1903 he abandoned medical schooling altogether. Seeking a fresh start, Mayo became a clerk in a West African gold mine, but his health soon deteriorated. In 1904 he returned to England, where he wrote for a newspaper, worked as a proofreader, and taught at the Working Men's College in London for a year. Mayo's slender earnings made him unhappily dependent on his father's assistance. In 1905 he sailed back to Australia and worked for several years in a print shop. In 1907 he again entered the University of Adelaide, this time studying philosophy and psychology, and in 1911 received, with honors, a B.A. in philosophy. Whether Mayo later received an M.A. from Adelaide is unclear.

Mayo became a lecturer in 1911 at the University of Queensland in the fields of logic, psychology, ethics, metaphysics, and economics. In 1913 he married Dorothea McConnel; they had two daughters. Mayo became head of the philosophy department in 1914 and in 1918 was promoted to professor. During this period he gave psychoanalytical treatment to neurotics and especially concentrated on the stress disorders suffered by soldiers in World War I. He also immersed himself in the writings of psychoanalyst Sigmund Freud on the societal causes of neuroses, sociologist Emile Durkheim on industrialization as a cause of anomie, and psychologist Pierre Janet on distortion of reality as a common condition. His well-attended public lectures on applying psychology to social problems received a wider audience in *Democracy and Freedom* (1919), in which he noted that democracy may stifle freedom because politicians twist truth for their own ends. Freedom, he argued, requires the collaborative efforts of business and labor leaders who are trained in understanding the psychological causes of social unrest. Mayo's *Psychology and Religion* (1922) maintained that behavior is often shaped by present or previous emotional distress and that, therefore, a turn to religion in adulthood is a means of escape from psychological anxieties.

Despite his accomplishments, Mayo was uncomfortable at Adelaide. He felt that his colleagues did not sufficiently appreciate his work and that it lacked adequate financial support by the university. Unable to find more attractive employment in Australia, Mayo departed for the United States in 1922. Arriving in San Francisco, he unsuccessfully tried his hand at lecturing, journalism, and personnel work. Within a month his luck turned when he was introduced to the secretary of the National Research Council, Vernon Kellogg, who liked Mayo's ideas on the psychological causes of industrial unrest; to the officers of the newly established Personnel Research Council in Washington, D.C.; and to Beardsley Ruml, director of the Laura Spelman Rockefeller Memorial (later the Rockefeller Foundation), who planned to fund efforts to solve social problems with objective, scientific methods. Mayo reinforced the beliefs of these individuals that professional personnel researchers could perceive issues and solutions neutrally, favoring neither workers nor management.

With Ruml's endorsement and funding, Mayo joined the University of Pennsylvania's Department of Industrial Relations in 1923. His studies of labor turnover in Philadelphia textile mills focused on the theme that uncooperative work actions resulted from psychopathology (for example, hostility to one's father) combined with faulty work conditions (such as inadequate rest pauses). He theorized that industrial problems could not, therefore, be solved without uncovering their underlying psychological causes. When no employer in the plants that Mayo examined was willing to let him try out his ideas, Ruml helped him relocate.

Ruml subsidized an associate professorship for Mayo in 1925 at the Harvard Business School. Its dean, Wallace Donham, hoped that Mayo would contribute to changing business management into a profession that was grounded in science and assigned Mayo to the new, Rockefeller-funded Harvard Fatigue Laboratory. In 1927 Mayo met the personnel director of Western Electric (AT&T's production arm), who invited Mayo to visit the relay-assembly test-room experiment at the Hawthorne Works in Chicago. AT&T officials soon asked Mayo to advise the Hawthorne manager in charge of the relay test room, which contained five young women assembling electromagnetic telephone relay switches. From 1928 to 1932 data from the relay assembly room were collected in detail on output in relation to rest pauses, illumination, and pay schemes, as well as the assemblers' conversations or other activities. Although related experiments, including a massive program of interviewing supervisors and workers, were later conducted, the relay test room captured Mayo's analytical interest and became the most famous of the Hawthorne studies. Studying all of the test room records, Mayo passed them on to his students and associates and commented on their meaning. His influence on others' published interpretations of the Hawthorne experiments gave birth to a new perspective on industrial behavior: human relations, which took its most significant form in Fritz J. Roethlisberger and William J. Dickson, *Management and the Worker* (1939).

In his *The Human Problems of an Industrial Civilization* (1933), Mayo proposed that rapid industrialization had fostered social disintegration that reached into the workplace, and that to cope with this condition, administrators must understand the underlying, psychological causes in order to achieve collaboration. His *The Social Problems of an Industrial Civilization* (1946) argues that to counteract the socially destructive effects of swift industrialization, workplace and political administrators must learn to recognize and respond to widespread psychological distress; indeed, their social skills must match their technical abilities. *The Political Problems of an Industrial Civilization* (1947), Mayo's final book, restates the belief that people's fundamental needs for stable conditions and firm social relationships are best satisfied by membership in enduring groups at the workplace; by responding to people's real needs, political and industrial leaders can counter widespread feelings of social isolation and develop cooperative relations.

After retiring from Harvard in 1947, Mayo spent his final years in England. He remained intellectually vigorous, continuing to publish on industrial human relations. He died in Guildford, Surrey, England.

From the 1940s on, numerous ideas for industrial reform have been indebted to the human relations perspective that Mayo fostered, such as improving supervisors' people skills, job enrichment, worker participation, self-directed work groups, values-defining leadership, and strong organizational cultures. In contrast to "behaviorist" theories (for example, scientific management or other rational-choice outlooks), which emphasize tangible motivators (such as pay), a psychological approach to industrial problems assumes that employees will productively respond to psychological incentives such as a friendly work group, interesting job, or the chance to contribute ideas. While not as psychoanalytically grounded as Mayo would have preferred, the human relations viewpoint continues to be heard and debated in industrial psychology, sociology, and management.

• Mayo's papers are in the Baker Library, Harvard Business School, and the State Library, Adelaide, Australia. Richard C. S. Trahair, *The Humanist Temper: The Life and Work of Elton Mayo* (1984), is a fine biography with a complete list of Mayo's writings. For detailed description of the Hawthorne experiments and Mayo's role in their interpretation, see Richard Gillespie, *Manufacturing Knowledge: A History of the Hawthorne Experiments* (1991). For a review of the experiments in light of critics' assessments, see Henry A. Landsberger, *Hawthorne Revisited: Management and the Worker, Its Critics and Developments in Human Relations in Industry* (1958).

CURT TAUSKY

MAYO, Henry Thomas (8 Dec. 1856–23 Feb. 1937), naval officer, was born in Burlington, Vermont, the son of Henry Mayo and Elizabeth Eldredge. His father was the captain of a merchant ship engaged in trade on Lake Champlain. Mayo entered the U.S. Naval Academy at Annapolis, Maryland, when he was only fifteen years old and graduated in 1876. After a cruise in Asian waters, he was promoted to ensign and was assigned to duty with the U.S. Coast and Geodetic Survey for work in Puget Sound. In 1881 he married Mary Caroline Wing; they had two children. Between 1882 and 1885 Mayo was with the *USS Yantic*, and during this period he was involved in the 1883 rescue of the stranded polar expedition led by the soldier and explorer Adolphus Washington Greely.

Promoted to lieutenant (junior grade) in 1885, Mayo returned to survey work in 1886. From 1895 until the Spanish-American War in 1898 he was the navigator aboard the hydrographic survey ship *Bennington*. He did not see active operations during the war with Spain, but during the conflict he carried out the first scientific survey of Pearl Harbor in Hawaii. Mayo was promoted to lieutenant commander in 1899 and to commander in 1905.

Despite his lack of combat experience, Mayo began to move quickly up the navy's career ladder. In 1907–1908 he commanded the *Albany*. Promoted to captain, he served a year as secretary of the Lighthouse Board and then commanded the armored cruiser *California*. In 1911 he was given command of a major navy facility, the Mare Island Navy Yard in California. While he was there, Mare Island was inspected by the secretary of the navy, Josephus Daniels. Daniels was impressed with Mayo and ordered him to Washington to assist in personnel matters. Thereafter Mayo rose even more rapidly. He was soon promoted to rear admiral, by-passing several officers senior to him. Requesting sea duty and a command, Mayo was given both; in 1912 Daniels sent him to the Naval War College at Newport, Rhode Island. Mayo then took command of a division of the Atlantic Fleet in December 1913.

In 1914 Mayo's name, already known in the navy, began to be familiar throughout the Western Hemisphere. Laying just off the port of Tampico, Mexico, with two U.S. battleships and other vessels, Mayo was intent on protecting American lives and property in the midst of an armed insurgency. On 9 April a boat's crew from his flagship, the *Dolphin*, landed in Tampico to purchase some gasoline and was arrested by poorly informed Mexican troops. After the sailors were detained for about an hour, Mexican authorities responded to an American protest and returned the boat and crew with profuse apologies. Mayo would not have it. He insisted on a public apology, disciplinary action against the errant officers, and a 21-gun Mexican salute to the American flag. The Mexicans agreed to all but the 21-gun salute, and a serious U.S. confrontation with Mexico emerged. President Woodrow Wilson supported Mayo and ordered the seizure of the customhouse at Veracruz by other elements of the Atlantic Fleet. Mayo's snap decision over the adequacy of an apology was no small part of the subsequent American intervention in Mexico, actions that ultimately resulted in General John J. Pershing's 1916 punitive expedition.

Some characterize Mayo as a high-handed militarist who brought on an unnecessary period of animosity between the United States and Mexico, but such a judgment is surely shallow. Having just left a high-level assignment in Washington, Mayo likely knew the Wilson administration was at odds with the Mexican government and concerned about American commercial interests, particularly the extensive oil investments in a chaotic Mexico. It is clear that President Wilson backed Mayo, whose action probably merely set in motion forces that were bound to be unleashed in any event. His most notable contribution to the American story, therefore, is being in tune with Washington's desires at a critical turn in U.S.–Mexican relations.

Mayo was promoted to temporary vice admiral in June 1915 and was given command of the Atlantic Fleet's battleship squadron. A year later he became the commander of the Atlantic Fleet with the tempo-

rary rank of full admiral. In September 1917 he represented the United States at the London Naval Conference to coordinate Allied naval strategy against the Central Powers after the country assumed belligerency status in the First World War. Mayo remained as commander of the Atlantic Fleet throughout the war and up to January 1919, when his command became the U.S. Fleet. In June 1919 he reverted to his permanent rank of rear admiral and assumed duties on the General Board. Mayo retired from the navy in December 1920. From 1924 until 1928 he served as governor of the Philadelphia Naval Home. He died in Portsmouth, New Hampshire.

• Mayo's career is summarized in his U.S. Navy Service Record, Bureau of Navigation Files, Records of Officers, National Archives and Records Administration. The highlights of Mayo's career are placed in context in several passages of Robert W. Love, *History of the U.S. Navy* (1992). The incident at Tampico is analyzed in Robert E. Quirk, *An Affair of Honor: Woodrow Wilson and the Occupation of Veracruz* (1962). An extensive obituary is in the *New York Times*, 24 Feb. 1937.

ROD PASCHALL

MAYO, Katherine (24 Jan. 1867–9 Oct. 1940), writer, was born in Ridgeway, Pennsylvania, the daughter of James Henry Mayo, a mining engineer, and Harriet Elizabeth Ingraham. Mayo and her family moved regularly as her father pursued mining opportunities. She was educated at private schools in Boston and Cambridge, Massachusetts, where she lived between 1883 and 1888. Her family then moved to Atlantic Highlands, New Jersey. After finishing school, Mayo pursued studies in colonial history on her own.

In 1892 Mayo's career as a writer began when she sold *Life* magazine a sketch for five dollars. She also contributed an article to the *New York Evening Post* in 1894, supposedly using the pseudonym Katherine Prence for some of her publications. In 1899 she traveled with her father who was searching for gold in Dutch Guiana. During this time, Mayo wrote about a range of subjects, including life in Dutch Guiana, for magazines like *Atlantic Monthly* and *Scribner's Magazine*. Meanwhile, she was collecting samples of native insects to sell to the *Entomological News* of Philadelphia and collecting indigenous people's relics to sell to Harvard's Peabody Museum. Mayo spent eight years in Dutch Guiana, occasionally contributing magazine pieces about the native people of South America. Following extensive travels as the fact-finding research assistant for Oswald Garrison Villard of the *New York Evening Post*, Mayo helped Villard prepare *John Brown* (1910). Villard became a mentor to Mayo, influencing her to use her journalistic skills as a social reformer. Mayo also assisted Horace White, editor in chief of the *New York Post* until 1903, with his work, *Life of Lyman Trumbull* (1913).

In September 1910 Mayo met orphaned heiress M. Moyca Newell. Newell became her lifelong, inseparable friend, giving Mayo the financial security to follow her writing interests. The two traveled across the globe—to Panama, the Philippines, Europe, and India gathering information for Mayo's books. In 1921 they also established a recreational center and club in New York City, the British Apprentice Club, for young cadets in the British merchant navy.

The murder of a paymaster or supervisor in August 1913 at Newell's estate, Maaikenshof, in Bedford Hills, New York, prompted Mayo to write her first book. A historical study of the Pennsylvania State Police, *Justice to All* (1917) was influential in helping to establish the New York State Police and probably established the muckraking style that Mayo used throughout her later career. Theodore Roosevelt even contributed the book's introduction. This topic intrigued Mayo, and she wrote two additional books on the state police, *The Standard Bearers* (1918) and a collection of true stories of the state police, *Mounted Justice* (1922).

Her obituary in the *New York Times* describes Mayo as "a woman who ranged the earth in pursuit of what she regarded as facts, only to find that they often became causes." Mayo's next cause was the Young Men's Christian Association (YMCA), which had been heavily criticized in the United States during the American participation in World War I for the handling of its funds during its overseas war operations. Mayo restored the YMCA's reputation in *That Damn Y* (1920). Mayo traveled to the Philippines in 1923 to study firsthand the island's customs, culture, and people. This trip's result, *The Isles of Fear* (1925), was first published serially in the *New York Evening Post*. It outlined Mayo's strong opposition to the Philippines' being granted independence. Her most controversial book, *Mother India* (1927), concluded that India, like the Philippines, was not ready for independence. Mayo focused her criticism on the Hindu country's custom of child marriage and demonstrated her outrage at what she considered the sexual exploitation of women. Considered sensationalist, *Mother India* was burned in India as well as in New York City. Mahatma Gandhi, whom Mayo befriended and interviewed while visiting India, even entered the fray, denouncing the book as untruthful in its depiction of Indian social conditions. There were strong reactions in the West about the conditions Mayo described and negative responses from India regarding Mayo's status as an outsider commenting on India's social problems. The numerous negative responses to her work included such book-length pieces as Lala Lajpat Rai's *Unhappy India* (2d ed., 1928), Dhan Gopal Mukerji's *A Son of Mother India Answers* (1928), Kamakshi Natarajan's *Miss Mayo's Mother India: A Rejoinder* (3d ed., 1928), and C. S. Ranga Iyer's *Father India* (1927).

Mayo wrote three more books on India: *Slaves of the Gods* (1929), short stories about the country; *Volume II* (1931), which documents findings in *Mother India*; and *The Face of Mother India* (1935), which includes further findings about the system of child marriage. However, none of these books gained the notoriety of *Mother India*. Mayo published two other books, *Soldiers What Next!* (1934), which studies the pension

plan of American veterans, and *General Washington's Dilemma*, which focuses on a little-known incident of the Revolutionary War. An Episcopalian and a Republican, Mayo was a member of the Society of Mayflower Descendants and the New York City Cosmopolitan Club. She was working on yet another book about the international narcotics trade at the time of her death in Bedford Hills, New York.

Katherine Mayo's extensive travels and her career as an independent researcher resulted in several books and numerous essays on a multitude of topics. Her crusades for the facts covered controversial political and social issues, including law enforcement, the conditions of women in India, and the independence of the Philippines.

• A collection of Mayo's papers are housed in the Sterling Memorial Library, Yale University. For information on the controversy surrounding *Mother India*, consult the early Indian viewpoint of Manoranjan Jha, *Katherine Mayo and India* (1971). For a dynamic debate with good detail about the controversy, consult the following articles in *South Asia: Journal of South Asian Studies*: William W. Emilsen, "Gandhi and Mayo's *Mother India*," 10, no. 1 (1987): 69–81; P. Athiyaman and A. R. Venkatachalapathy, "On Gandhi, Mayo, and Emilsen," 12, no. 2 (1989): 83–88; and Emilsen's final response, "A Note on Mayo, Athiyaman and Venkatachalapathy," 12, no. 2 (1989): 89–90. An obituary in the *New York Times* on 10 Oct. 1940 provides excellent details about Mayo's life and a photo. An editorial in the *Times* on 11 Oct. 1940 provides further insight into her reputation as a writer.

FAYE A. CHADWELL

MAYO, Margaret (19 Nov. 1882–25 Feb. 1951), actress and playwright, was born Lillian Slatten on a farm near Brownsville, Illinois, the daughter of Warren Slatten and Elizabeth Cavender. When her parents separated she accompanied her mother to Portland, Oregon. She was educated at the Convent of the Sacred Heart in Salem, Oregon, and at a girls' school in Fox Lake, Wisconsin. In her early teens, in order to escape the attentions of an elderly suitor, Margaret left her mother's home in Portland and, with her mother's consent, went to New York to look for work. Although she had no particular intention of going into the theater, she won a walk-on role in *Thoroughbred* at the Garrick Theatre in 1896. Taking the stage name Margaret Mayo, she continued to act for the next seven years, mostly in minor roles on tour but also appearing in a major role, Susan in *Because She Loved Him So*, at Madison Square Theatre in 1899.

Mayo met Edgar Selwyn in 1897, when they toured together in William Gillette's *Secret Service*; they were married in 1901. (The marriage was childless.) In 1902 they appeared together in a six-week run of Augustus Thomas's *Arizona* in London. Tall and handsome, Selwyn became a successful leading man in New York; petite blond Mayo felt that she was better suited to character parts. Hoping to play the role of Cigarette, in 1901 she wrote a one-act dramatization of Ouïda's novel *Under Two Flags*, which she later expanded to five acts. She never got to appear in it, as another version starring Blanche Bates was produced at about the same time, but Mayo eventually sold her script, and it was widely used by stock companies.

After appearing with Grace George in *Pretty Peggy* at the Herald Square Theatre in 1903, Mayo received two playwriting commissions from George: a dramatization of Mrs. Humphrey Ward's novel *The Marriage of William Ashe* (produced in 1905) and an American adaptation of the French farce *Divorçons* (produced in 1913), which was published as *Cyprienne*. Both were successful enough to justify her retirement from the stage in order to write. In 1903 she won a widely publicized and carefully monitored wager that she could write a four-act play within twenty-four hours after being given a premise on which to base the plot. The resulting play, *The Mart*, was never produced.

Although Mayo's 1907 dramatization of Upton Sinclair's *The Jungle* was unsuccessful (she considered it her only failure on the stage), that same year she enjoyed her first major success, the sentimental *Polly of the Circus*. The play had been rejected by every manager in New York and had remained unproduced for several years, until it came to the attention of producer Frederic Thompson, whose weakness for circus themes and search for a vehicle for actress Mabel Taliaferro led him to produce it. A favorite of road companies for many years, the work was made into a silent film starring Mae Marsh in 1917 and was remade in 1932, starring Clark Gable. With royalties from *Polly of the Circus* the Selwyns built a house named "Tumble In" at Harmon-on-the-Hudson, New York. Over the years Mayo designed and built a number of houses there ("probably no one but Miss Mayo ever made sleeping porches for their servants"), establishing it as a community of theater people. By 1910 Mayo's mother had come to live with the Selwyns and eventually had her surname legally changed to Mayo.

In 1908 Selwyn quit acting to become a playwright, and a friendly rivalry developed between husband and wife. Each sought the other's advice and usually rejected it. They fought regularly but were known as one of the theater's happiest couples and among the least changed by success. They collaborated on one work, the book for the 1912 musical *Wall Street Girl*. Together they made frequent trips abroad: to Spain in 1908, to Greece in 1909, to the Holy Land in 1911, and to England and France in 1913–1914. Their return passage from this last trip was booked on the ill-fated *Titanic* until a last-minute change in plans took them to Paris instead.

Mayo's greatest hit, *Baby Mine* (1910), was inspired by a news story asserting that three thousand deluded husbands in Chicago were fondling infants whom they had not fathered. The play is a farce about a wife who borrows a baby to win back her estranged husband and ends up juggling several babies. Produced at Daly's Theatre by William A. Brady (who was surprised to learn that it was original work rather than an adaptation of a French play), it ran 287 performances. Within a few months of the play's opening Mayo remarked, "There are 'Baby Mine' dolls and 'Baby Mine' hats. The baby elephant at the Hippodrome is named 'Baby Mine,' and I am told there are 'Baby Mine' cocktails, but the thing that interests me most, of course, are the 'Baby Mine' dollars" (Apr. 1911, p. 873). *Baby Mine* was soon translated into French, Russian, and Japanese, among other languages, and was produced around the world. A film version was made in 1928, and a musical version, *Rock-A-Bye-Baby*, appeared in 1918. Of Mayo's many other plays, the most successful was the farce *Twin Beds* (1914), which she wrote with playwright Salisbury Field.

In 1917 Mayo became head of the scenario department for Goldwyn Pictures Corporation, the studio established that year by her husband and Samuel Goldfish (later Goldwyn). She resigned after a year to head a unit of the Overseas Theatre League, the first to take a program of entertainment to American doughboys in the trenches in France in World War I. For that tour (late summer/fall 1918) she devised a light satire called *Somewhere in America*, which linked several vaudeville specialty acts. Mayo's own role was that of "a flighty young person who has the dance craze and can't dance. This leads up to a burlesque dance specialty with Roland Young" (*Detroit News*, 20 July 1918). After the war she served as treasurer of the American Committee for Wounded Allies Relief Fund.

Divorced from Selwyn in 1919 Mayo moved into "The Crest," one of several houses she built in Harmon-on-the-Hudson and the one in which she spent the rest of her life. Although she lost her wealth in the stock market crash of 1929, she retained extensive real estate holdings in Harmon and Croton, New York. For ten years she was involved in litigation with the city of New York over Croton Dam, and in 1939 the court of appeals upheld a lower court decision against her. But she did win a suit to prevent New York Central from building more railroad tracks near her house. The townspeople regarded her as their guardian angel. In the last years of her life Mayo's main interests were spiritualism and animals. Her house was overrun with eighteen cats and three dogs. As a result of a spine fracture suffered while playing with her dogs, she became an invalid three years before her death in Ossining Hospital in Ossining, New York.

• An extensive clippings file on Mayo is in the Billy Rose Theatre Collection of the New York Public Library for the Performing Arts at Lincoln Center. Also see Edgar Bruno, "A Story-ized Review of *Twin Beds*," *Green Book*, Nov. 1914, pp. 940–47; The Mirror Man, "A Successful Playwright," *New York Dramatic Mirror*, 23 July 1910, p. 5; Mary Morgan, "A Wedded Pair of Successful Playwrights," *Theatre Magazine*, Oct. 1910, pp. 103–4; Rennold Wolf, "The Romance of the Selwyns," *Green Book*, Oct. 1913, pp. 616–26; Margaret Mayo, "My Most Successful Play," *Green Book Album*, Apr. 1911, pp. 871–74; "The Screen Wins Margaret Mayo," *Theatre Magazine*, Oct. 1917, pp. 248, 250, 252; "Every Time She Builds a House She Writes a Play," *Every Week*, 15 Nov. 1915, p. 18; and "Margaret Mayo," *McClure's Magazine*, Sept. 1912, pp. 597–99. The most complete listings of her plays and scenarios are in *Who Was Who in the Theatre 1912–1976.* An obituary is in the *New York Times,* 26 Feb. 1951.

FELICIA HARDISON LONDRÉ

MAYO, Mary Anne Bryant (25 May 1845–21 Apr. 1903), farmer and Grange leader, was born to James Bryant and Ann Atmore on their pioneer farm near Battle Creek, Michigan, in Convis Township of Calhoun County. She spent her entire life in that immediate vicinity. After graduating from Battle Creek High School, she taught in a district school until 1865, when she married Perry Mayo, who had just returned from fighting the Civil War. The couple shared the work of farming in Marshall Township, reared two children, and also found time to continue their own studies, which was especially important to them after Mary Mayo encountered a high school classmate who "presumed, as I had married a farmer, about all I had to do . . . was to work hard and make lots of good butter." Unwilling to accept that stereotypical limitation, the Mayos sought intellectual opportunities in neighborhood Farmers' Institutes, the Grange, and a Chautauqua Reading Circle.

Mary Mayo attained some local prominence by 1877, when she read a paper on "A Higher Standard of Culture for Housekeepers" to a Farmers' Institute in Marshall, Michigan. Mayo urged farm women to study morality, history, and children and all of their interests during time that they saved by simplifying and rationalizing housework; that theme dominated Mayo's later public speaking and writing. At about the same time, both Mayos became leaders in their county Grange, which the organization called its Pomona level. She wrote reports of the county's edifying programs that dealt with subjects including farm operations, nutrition, efficient housekeeping, and the moral cultivation of children. Her reports of the meetings appeared in the *Grange Visitor,* the official organ of the Michigan State Grange, and she also sent the *Visitor* many essays of her own on a wide range of moral and domestic topics. Her favorite themes included reading for children; ways of reducing household labor; and simplification of diets, notably by omitting pies in favor of good, plain Michigan apples. What may have been her earliest *Visitor* essay reminded mothers to give their sons "instructive reading matter" lest they be corrupted by "sensational, blood and thunder trash."

By 1882 Mayo was traveling outside of her immediate neighborhood to organize Granges and speak about farm women's housework, child rearing, and the need to escape drudgery by simplifying all of their tasks and doing them efficiently. In 1884 she ventured a county eastward by herself while Perry Mayo worked the farm; encouraged by the result, she then toured several counties, beginning a career of lecturing and Grange recruiting and organizing that finally took her throughout the state of Michigan and into parts of neighboring Ohio and Indiana. Deputy lecturer of the Michigan State Grange for fifteen years, lead-

er of its Woman's Work Committee for twelve years, and state Grange chaplain for most of the same period, she was the most prominent Grange woman in Michigan and one of the best known in the order nationally.

Mary Mayo took no recorded interest in the long campaign that finally put the Grange on record in favor of woman suffrage. Instead, she focused on relieving farm women of some of the pressures of the enormous amount of work they had to do in their homes, as well as on their moral and educational duties to children, their responsibility to attract children to Grange activities, and their charitable opportunities. Mayo's most strongly emphasized charity was the "Fresh Air" project, which brought city children and women to farms for summer vacations. She also campaigned for the establishment of a practical, domestic curriculum for women at the Michigan Agricultural College, now Michigan State University; agitation by the Grange and women's clubs finally moved the college to establish a "Women's Course of Study" in 1897. The dormitory called Mary Mayo Hall, dedicated in 1931, memorializes her contribution to women's education at the university. That reward came long after her death at home from a painful disease.

• A number of Mayo's manuscript letters and speeches are in the University Archives and Historical Collection at Michigan State University; most of her published writing appeared in the *Grange Visitor,* which can also be consulted at Michigan State University. Jennie Buell, *One Woman's Work for Farm Women* (1908), is a short biography based largely on the author's acquaintance with Mayo. See also James Bryant, "More Than Hard Work and Good Butter," *Michigan History* 65 (July/Aug. 1981): 32–36, and Donald B. Marti, *Women of the Grange: Mutuality and Sisterhood in Rural America, 1866–1920* (1991.)

DONALD B. MARTI

MAYO, Sara (26 May 1869–7 Mar. 1930), physician and humanitarian reformer, was born Sara Tèw Mayo on a plantation in Catahoula Parish, Louisiana, near the town of Vidalia, the daughter of George Spencer Mayo, a lawyer, and Emily Tèw. After the death of her parents, Sara spent her early years in New Orleans at the home of her father's cousin, Judge William Brainerd Spencer. After receiving her primary education in the city's public schools, she attended Millwood High School in Jackson, a town north of New Orleans close to the Mississippi border. As a child, Sara showed an interest in nursing and medicine by constantly ministering to her dolls and pets. Determined to become a physician, she applied to Tulane University Medical School but was rejected. Undeterred, she left for Philadelphia, where she entered Woman's Medical College, graduating in 1898. She then returned to New Orleans, where she was to practice medicine for the next thirty-two years.

Shortly after entering practice, Mayo joined a group of women physicians who were contributing their services to Kingsley House, a settlement house with a free clinic. In February 1905, four of them, Mayo, Elizabeth Bass, Cora M. Bass, and Susanna Otis, were proposed for membership in the Orleans Parish Medical Society. Although they had received their medical training in excellent medical schools, the society continued its policy of refusing to accept women as members. Women physicians in New Orleans were also denied access to the city's hospitals. Outraged by this treatment and aware from her work in the settlement house of the lack of medical care for poor women, Mayo sought to solve both problems by organizing a dispensary and hospital for women and children. At the turn of the century, outpatient clinics for the poor, or dispensaries, were common in all cities. On 8 May 1905, in a small four-room house supplied rent-free by Susanna Otis, the New Orleans Dispensary for Women and Children was opened with Mayo as president. In addition to Mayo, the original staff members were Otis, Clara Glenk, Elizabeth Bass, Cora Bass, and a female dentist, Blanche Tassy. Shortly thereafter, two other women physicians, Edith Loeber and Clotilde Jaquet, joined the staff.

On the opening day, the dispensary had total assets of $25 and treated eight patients. News of the dispensary spread rapidly, however, and a total of 3,760 patients were treated the first year. For those who could afford it, a small fee was charged. Men were treated only on an emergency basis, and the dispensary was open to all races. During the first year, people in the neighborhood gathered driftwood for the furnace and contributed tallow candles and kerosene lamps. According to one observer, male physicians reacted to the dispensary "with tolerant shrugs where comment was kindest."

The growing number of patients required a larger building, and, assisted by the generosity of the *New Orleans Daily Delta*, which contributed the receipts from the sale of one day's edition, the dispensary moved into a two-story building in March 1908. By this time, the dispensary had added beds for inpatients and had been renamed the New Orleans Hospital and Dispensary for Women and Children, commonly known as the Women's Hospital. Several of the attending physicians eventually began giving most of their time to their private practices, but Mayo continued to spend her mornings at the dispensary caring for gynecological and obstetrical cases. She served as president of the institution for two years, then took over the duties of treasurer for the rest of her career. Under her leadership, in 1907 the hospital began offering care to patients in their homes by establishing a District Nursing Service, consisting of five practical day nurses and one night nurse. Mayo was also instrumental in persuading the state and city to contribute to the annual expenses, which had grown to approximately $10,000 per year by 1911.

In March 1911, Mayo was awarded the *Daily Picayune* Loving Cup for the year 1910 for her services to the community, and in particular for her work with the hospital and dispensary. She was also appointed by Mayor Martin Behrman to the board of the Sickles Commission, a group designed to raise a permanent fund for social welfare purposes. Mayo apparently had a major voice in determining the outlays from this fund. In 1915 she reported that the fund had spent $1,500 for prescriptions for the poor and that the agency was considering opening a second dispensary.

The recognition gained by Mayo and other women physicians in New Orleans finally led the Orleans Parish Medical Society in 1913 to admit them to membership. In addition to her private practice and her work with the Women's Hospital, Mayo was a staff member of St. Anna's Asylum for Destitute Women and Children, Touro Infirmary, and Baptist Hospital.

Mayo was a warm, generous person, known as "Uncle Doc" to her nieces and nephews and as "Daisy" to her patients in the early years of the dispensary. She never married, lived thriftily, and shared a home with her half sister, Virginia Mayo. Her entire life was devoted to her private medical practice and her work for the sick poor, and she remained active until her death. In recognition of her leadership, in 1948 the institution she had promoted was renamed the Sara Mayo Hospital.

• As far as is known, Sara Mayo left no papers. Some information can be gleaned from the C. C. Bass Collection and the Physicians' File in the Rudolph Matas Medical Library of Tulane University. The Bass collection contains a short typescript biography of Mayo based on information provided by Florence Dymond, Mayo's secretary. Mary Gehrman and Nancy Ries, *A History of Women in New Orleans* (1988), provides a brief biography. A summary of Mayo's efforts to join the Orleans Parish Medical Society is given in A. E. Fossier, *History of the Orleans Parish Medical Society, 1878–1928* (1930). The best sources for her career are the New Orleans newspapers: *Daily Picayune*, 15 Mar. 1908, 24 May 1910, 26 Mar. and 24 May 1911, and 16 Apr. 1913; *Times-Picayune*, 27 Apr. 1915, 8 Mar. 1930, 12 Oct. 1948, 7 July 1949, and 20 July 1969; *New Orleans Item*, 12 May 1909, and 10 May 1948. Her death was recorded in *Journal of the American Medical Association* 94 (1930): 1162.

JOHN DUFFY

MAYO, Sarah Carter Edgarton (17 Mar. 1819–9 July 1848), author and poet, was born in Shirley, Massachusetts, the daughter of Joseph Edgarton, a manufacturer, and his second wife, Mehitable Whitcomb. The tenth of fifteen children born to Joseph Edgarton, Sarah was raised in a harmonious and financially comfortable family. Although extremely shy, she excelled at the local district school, particularly enjoying the study of poetry, geography, astronomy, and botany. Her earliest literary endeavors included acrostics for school friends and descriptions of nature. Sarah attended the Westford Academy for one semester and at age seventeen joined the Universalist church of her parents. Despite her limited formal education, she attained considerable facility as a writer while still a teenager.

Under the name Sarah C. Edgarton, Mayo first submitted poems, essays, and stories for publication at the age of sixteen to relieve her family's financial reversals. She found a receptive market for her work in various denominational publications, most notably the Boston

Universalist and Ladies' Repository, the preeminent New England periodical for women during the middle decades of the nineteenth century. Like other magazines of its era for women, the *Universalist* was dedicated to its readers' moral and literary edification. Mayo and her fellow contributors eschewed theological speculation and disputation and instead emphasized virtuous sentiments and actions. These qualities also characterize Mayo's didactic children's tales, *The Palfreys* (1838), which was aimed at grade-school children, and *Ellen Clifford; or, The Genius of Reform* (1838), which evidently was aimed at adolescents. Mayo may also have written the anonymously published *Tales and Sketches by a Christmas Fireside* (1838).

In 1839, at the invitation of its publisher, Abel Tompkins, and its editor, Henry Bacon, Mayo became an associate editor of the *Universalist*, a position she retained through 1842. In the May 1839 issue, in which her editorship was announced, Mayo promised to further female education and intellectual development by encouraging readers to adopt a disciplined program of reading, meditation, and domestic virtue. In fact, the most persistent theme in Mayo's writing, both fictional and nonfictional, is women's fulfillment through intellectual development. Many of Mayo's tales, comments Ann Douglas, depict "Young women who find lovers, social status, and personal significance through a well designed course of reading" (p. 62). According to a letter by Bacon, Mayo was responsible for writing both original works and book notices for the *Universalist* but was spared "the care of superintending" the journal generally or the performance of "any of the editor's drudgery" (Bacon, p. 87). Mayo wrote prolifically for the *Universalist* between 1839 and 1846, providing sentimental poetry and fiction, and essays on social, religious, and moral themes. From 1840 until her death, Mayo also edited the highly popular Universalist gift annual, *The Rose of Sharon: A Religious Souvenir*.

Fatigued by her responsibilities as editor and writer, Mayo complained to a correspondent in 1840 of "working on a treadmill of poetry for the dear admiring public" (Mayo, p. 36). Yet Mayo took up new projects. She not only published two collections of poems, *Spring Flowers* (1840?) and *The Poetry of Woman* (1841), but also wrote several flower books, a popular literary form in the mid-nineteenth century. The first of these was *The Flower Vase* (1843), a traditional flower-language book combining prose discussions of flower symbolism and sentimental poetry. It was followed by *Fables of Flora* (1844), a collection of flower fables written either by herself or John Langhorne, the English popular poet and translator who published flower tales under the same title in 1771. *The Floral Fortune-Teller* (1846) provided directions for an elaborate game involving flower symbolism and poetry, principally passages from Shakespeare. Both *The Flower Vase* and *The Floral Fortune-Teller* saw multiple editions. With her earnings, Mayo helped support

her own family and completely financed the Harvard education of her talented younger brother, John.

Meanwhile Mayo strove to improve her education. She found intellectual companionship and support in her friendships with two Universalist poets, Julia H. Scott and Charlotte A. Jerauld. Mayo honored Scott by publishing a memoir and collection of Scott's poems in 1843 and gathered materials for a similar memorial for Jerauld, a project never completed because of Mayo's own untimely death. Mayo was also encouraged in her intellectual pursuits by the brother whose education she had secured. Although she studied French and Latin on her own, he instructed her in German and made works in the Harvard library available to her. Mayo was an avid and serious reader of belles lettres and scientific literature throughout her brief life. In the 1840s she read and commented on works by Carlyle, Spenser, Wordsworth, Shelley, Keats, Dickens, Dana, Irving, Emerson, Channing, Cousin, de Staël, Sand, Schiller, and Goethe among many others. Unfortunately, Mayo's wide and sophisticated reading made her frustrated and dissatisfied with her own work, which included verse translations of classical and modern authors. Mayo lamented to a correspondent in 1841: "There is such an unattainable excellence constantly before me in the writings of the great and gifted, that my pen falters in every line it would trace. My versification is all tame, spiritless; my prose seems either too simple, or too artificial" (Mayo, p. 70). Similar discouragement about her writing permeates an 1842 letter in which Mayo feared that "instead of giving pleasure to [her] friends, [she would] only weary them with hackneyed thoughts and feeble expressions" (Mayo, p. 73).

In 1846 she married Amory Dwight Mayo, a Universalist clergyman who later became a Unitarian educator and author. The couple moved to Gloucester, Massachusetts, where she spent the last two years of her life. During these years, the previously productive Mayo wrote a small number of poems and sketches, some for the *Rose*, others for a literary and religious magazine she planned to publish with her brother. The magazine venture was abandoned when John died unexpectedly in October 1847. One of the last literary projects on which Mayo worked was an autobiographical novel tracing the spiritual development of a woman from childhood to middle age. Dejected about her efforts, she destroyed all but a few fragments of the work. Mayo devoted the last months of her life to the care of her ailing husband and her infant daughter born in September 1847. She died in Gloucester after a brief illness the following July.

Despite her considerable intellectual achievements and her early success as an author and editor of publications for women co-religionists, Mayo's timidity and limited formal education discouraged her from seeking a broader audience and sometimes paralyzed her efforts to write altogether. Using her beloved flower imagery, Mayo described herself as a "shrinking, simple thing, grown up like a weed without care or cultivation . . . too conscious of [her] infirmities" (Mayo,

p. 39). Under more favorable circumstances, her intellectual gifts might well have blossomed.

• The primary source of information about Sarah C. E. Mayo's life and work are A. D. Mayo, *Selections from the Writings of Mrs. Sarah C. Edgarton Mayo; with a Memoir* (1849), and Mrs. E[liza] A[nn] Bacon, *Memoir of Rev. Henry Bacon* (1857). Studies of Mayo's work in relation to that of other religious writers of her time include Ann Douglas, *The Feminization of American Culture* (1977; repr. 1988), and David S. Reynolds, *Faith in Fiction: The Emergence of Religious Literature in America* (1981), pp. 96–101. For a discussion of the *Universalist*'s cultural influence, see Bertha Monica Stearns, "New England Magazines for Ladies, 1830–1860," *New England Quarterly* 3 (Oct. 1930): 627–56, esp. 632–35. An obituary is in the *Boston Transcript*, 13 July 1848.

JEANNE M. MALLOY

MAYO, William James (29 June 1861–28 July 1939), and **Charles Horace Mayo** (19 July 1865–26 May 1939), physicians and surgeons and cofounders of the Mayo Clinic, were born, respectively, in Le Sueur and Rochester, Minnesota, the sons of William Worrall Mayo, a physician, and Louise Abigail Wright. When William (who went by Will) was nearly three years old, the family moved to Rochester, where his father had been appointed a Civil War examining surgeon for the enrollment board of the first Minnesota district, headquartered in the city. By the time Charles (who went by Charlie) was born, their father had established a medical practice in Rochester and was on his way to becoming a medical leader in southeast Minnesota and, later, the state. As the brothers grew they were naturally drawn into helping their father—driving and taking care of his horses, performing housekeeping duties in his office, and later, assisting in elementary ways with patient care. Also, by seeing their mother sometimes act as their father's first assistant and use her skills to set bones, they acquired an early awareness of shared responsibility in caring for the sick.

While their mother taught them botany and astronomy, the latter as observed through her telescope, the Mayo brothers were also influenced by their father's informal instruction, which was augmented by his substantial library and microscope. Instead of completing public school, the boys attended a private training school in Rochester to further their knowledge of science and languages. Thus it is not surprising that when the time came for advanced training the brothers chose medicine.

Will Mayo entered the University of Michigan Medical School in the fall of 1880. Modeled after Harvard's pioneer program, Michigan's new medical curriculum was a graded three-year program with entrance requirements. The university's new hospital offered students clinical experience for the first time. Will was not a notable student, but he became an assistant in surgery and an underdemonstrator in anatomy. His physiology professor, Henry Sewall, predicted that Will and two classmates, Franklin Mall and Walter Courtney, would never succeed in medicine. Sewall's

assessment was later proven wrong when each of the three achieved national prominence. After graduating on 28 June 1883, Dr. William J. Mayo returned home to enter practice with his father.

Before Charlie Mayo left for medical school two years later, the family reviewed the opportunities, and Northwestern University in Chicago was chosen. Like Michigan, it had a three-year program, but its students were not limited to one hospital or staff; they were welcomed at several Chicago-area clinics and hospitals where physicians had different approaches to the practice of medicine. Charlie was an average student but was noted for his ability to find interesting operations in the city to observe. Graduating on 27 March 1888, Dr. Charles H. Mayo returned home to join his father and brother in the growing Doctors Mayo practice.

The Mayo brothers' medical training included instruction in Joseph Lister's new antiseptic techniques for minimizing wound and surgical infection. The revolutionary approach was then in the process of being accepted by American physicians. The brothers traveled individually to New York City to see its clinical applications as demonstrated by Arpad Gerster. From the first, they used Lister's antiseptic methods in the operating room of the newly opened Saint Marys Hospital in Rochester. The hospital was completed in 1889 by the Sisters of Saint Francis, a charitable Catholic order. Its construction had been pushed by Mother Alfred Moes, the order's leader, after a devastating tornado hit Rochester in 1883. She enlisted the elder Mayo and his sons to plan and staff it. By the early 1900s the Mayo brothers' interest and success in surgery had led to several hospital expansions to house facilities assigned primarily to surgical treatments.

The Mayo brothers' specialization in general surgery paralleled the growth of surgical therapy in the United States. With the advent of antiseptic techniques, the interior of the human body could be safely opened, and this enabled surgeons to deal with a variety of internal disorders involving the stomach, the gallbladder, the lungs, and the central nervous system. Initially working as a team, the Mayo brothers developed techniques that attracted increasing numbers of patients and visiting physicians to their operating rooms. Anxious to improve their skills, each of them interrupted their work for separate annual study trips to learn from other progressive surgeons, including Charles McBurney, Howard A. Kelly, and William S. Halsted, among others. Astute observers, the Mayo brothers always acknowledged the elements of their procedures that had been developed elsewhere. Over time the brothers began to concentrate on different parts of the body. Whereas Will focused on pelvic and abdominal surgery, Charlie handled eye, ear, nose, throat, bone and joint, brain, nerve, and neck surgery. Will became well known for surgeries involving the stomach and gallbladder and Charlie, especially so, for surgery of the thyroid gland.

As patient numbers increased, the Mayo brothers

added medical staff to their office practice in order to assist them in the diagnosis of patients needing surgery. Their father now semiretired, the brothers assumed direction of the firm's daily operation. In consultation with his brother, Will in particular was involved in handling financial and personnel matters. By the turn of the century the Mayo family practice had evolved into a limited partnership, with the brothers retaining ownership. More diagnostic staff was only the first in a series of changes instituted by the brothers. By that time, scientific developments had made laboratory medicine a dependable adjunct to medical therapy. Aware of these advancements, the brothers either trained or recruited personnel to incorporate laboratory instruments and techniques that would enhance Mayo patient care. These efforts were further advanced with the institution of research activities in 1905. The same year the first of a number of surgeons personally trained by the brothers began helping with the increasing surgical work. At about the same time, the brothers also employed specially trained business and service personnel so that the medical staff could concentrate on caring for patients.

Under the brothers' watchful eyes, the pioneer Mayo private group practice of medicine emerged, having followed no developmental plan and bearing some resemblance to groups in public medicine. Described by Will as a "scientific cooperation for the welfare of the sick," the Mayo group integrated the skills of various specialists, an approach that greatly influenced the way medical treatment is delivered in the United States. By 1914 the Mayo private group practice was informally called "Mayos' Clinic" by visiting physicians and patients. With the dedication that year of the first specially designed building for the group, the name Mayo Clinic was formally adopted.

In the meantime, the brothers had begun to concentrate on educational as well as clinical concerns. In 1906 they helped visiting physicians form a surgeons club, through which informal discussions were held following surgical clinics conducted by the Mayos at Saint Marys. After he was appointed a regent of the University of Minnesota in 1907, Will began to learn about graduate medical education needs. Eight years later, encouraged by university leaders, the brothers established the pioneering graduate clinical medicine program in the United States, the Mayo Foundation for Medical Education and Research (later the Mayo Graduate School of Medicine, Mayo Foundation). Initially the foundation offered advanced degrees through the University of Minnesota for studies completed at the Mayo Clinic in Rochester. Implementation of the Mayo graduate program was contested by some medical school faculty who apparently were concerned about its potential effect on the school. Surprised, the brothers tried to allay their fears and despite bitter opposition completed university affiliation in 1917. The brothers' initial endowment was $1.5 million, the bulk of their life savings; in 1934 they brought the amount up to $2.5 million.

As World War I raged in Europe, the Mayo brothers were prominent in medical preparedness. Early medical reservists, they served on the General Medical Board of the U.S. Council for National Defense in 1916. After the United States entered the war the brothers alternated duty in the Surgeon General's office in Washington, D.C.

Before ending surgery in the late 1920s, the Mayo brothers provided for the continuation of the Mayo Clinic by establishing, in 1919, the Mayo Properties Association, a charitable organization (later the Mayo Association and then the Mayo Foundation). After endowing it with all the properties and assets of the Mayo Clinic, the brothers placed themselves and their colleagues on salaries. To oversee the clinic's operation, a board of governors was created. The brothers led its deliberations until their retirement in 1932. The honors and membership certificates received by the brothers cover the walls of a clinic room, and they served as president of many national medical and surgical associations of their day, including the American College of Surgeons (Will from 1917 to 1919, Charlie in 1924–1925), the American Medical Association (Will in 1905–1906, Charlie in 1916–1917), the American Surgical Association (Will in 1913–1914, Charlie in 1931–1932), and the Western Surgical Association (Charlie in 1904–1905).

In retirement the brothers enjoyed travel and their homes in Rochester and Tucson, Arizona. Both were married to women from Rochester. Will had been married to Hattie May Damon since 1884. Of their five children, three died in infancy, and two daughters married clinic surgeons. Charlie had married Edith Maria Graham in 1893. A trained nurse, she taught the sisters how to be nurses after Saint Marys Hospital opened. Two of Charlie's eight children died young, and two sons joined the Mayo Clinic. The Mayo brothers died within two months of each other, Charlie in Chicago and Will in Rochester.

• Clippings, photographs, and miscellaneous papers of the Mayo brothers are housed in the Mayo Foundation Historical Collection in Rochester, Minn. Will published some 575 articles; Charlie, some 413 articles. The titles of these are reproduced in *Physicians of the Mayo Clinic and the Mayo Foundation* (1937). Helen Clapesattle, *The Doctors Mayo* (1941), is a classic study, complete with extensive bibliographic notes. Clark W. Nelson, *Mayo Roots: Profiling the Origins of Mayo Clinic* (1990), presents some new facts.

CLARK W. NELSON

MAYO, William Starbuck (15 Apr. 1811–22 Nov. 1895), author and physician, was born in Ogdensburg, New York, the son of Obed Mayo, a shipbuilder, and Elizabeth Starbuck. Descended from the first minister of Boston's North Church, Rev. John Mayo, on his father's side and the Nantucket whaling and merchant Starbuck family on his mother's, Mayo attended an academy in Potsdam and, choosing a career in medicine, first studied under two local physicians and then attended the College of Physicians and Surgeons in New York. After completing his medical studies in

1832, Mayo practiced for a few years in Ogdensburg, but after suffering from ill health he took a tour of Spain and the Barbary Coast of North Africa. These travel experiences were the material on which Mayo based most of his subsequent work as an author. After his travels, Mayo relocated his medical practice to New York and began to write professionally. In 1851 he married Helen Stuyvesant. They had no children.

Mayo's literary career has been consistently linked to that of Herman Melville; antebellum critics often favorably compared Mayo to Melville, while twentieth-century literary scholars have used Mayo's work to demonstrate the relative strengths of Melville's early writings. Mayo's first novel, *Kaloolah; or, Journeyings to the Djébel Kumri*, was published in 1849 and went through four editions before the year was out. The *Democratic Review* called *Kaloolah* "the book of the season" and suggested that Mayo was "at once among the most successful American authors." Like Melville's *Typee* (1846) and *Omoo* (1847), the narrative of *Kaloolah* joined exotic travel and romance with a veneer of ethnographic and naturalist fact to generate its plot of adventure in North Africa. Also like its 1849 counterpart, Melville's *Mardi*, *Kaloolah* presented a philosophical commentary on antebellum American society through its depiction of a utopian nation, in this case Framazugda, an imaginary white African society of order and plenty ruled by an intellectual elite. The hoaxlike presentation of the novel as a found manuscript (Mayo presented himself as the editor of the manuscript, but his claim is contradicted by the fact that the early life of the narrator, named Jonathan Roemer, closely follows Mayo's biography) recalls Edgar Allan Poe's *The Narrative of A. Gordon Pym* (1838). In addition, the racialist fantasy of *Kaloolah*'s comparison of a "white African" order to the slavery and violence of North African tribes and city-states resembles the racial splits of Poe's polar navigation adventure narrative. Twentieth-century scholars have seen the earlier chapters of *Kaloolah*, which recount Roemer's (and Mayo's) family history of whalers on Nantucket and a tale of a whale that destroys a ship hunting it, as possible source material for Melville's *Moby-Dick* (1851).

In 1851 Mayo published his popular historical novel, *The Berber; or, The Mountaineer of the Atlas*. As with his first novel, *The Berber* grew out of Mayo's travel experiences, but this time he transposed them into a narrative of adventure in seventeenth-century Spain and North Africa. The complicated story of *The Berber* follows an English merchant's twin sons, who are separated in childhood. One is brought up as a Barbary pirate, but they are reunited to pursue adventure in the Atlas mountains. The adventure is augmented by a romance plot that leads to the twins' marriage to lovely Spanish and Moroccan maidens. In 1851 Mayo also published *Romance Dust from the Historic Placer*, a collection of short stories that similarly combined history, romance, and nautical adventure. In 1872 Mayo published *Never Again*, a novel that departed from his other works by taking the domestic

scene of New York as its locale. Transferring the familiar adventure, intrigue, and romance narrative elements to postbellum New York social life, *Never Again* sets its hero against villainous immigrants and the prevailing social atmosphere of New York wealth, which the narrator describes as "a tornado of greed."

Like the exotic Algerian milieu of his earlier writings, *Never Again* depicted a setting with which Mayo was familiar. His marriage into the wealthy Stuyvesant family placed him in the social world of upper-class New York and turned him into a man of leisure. In the intervening years, Mayo pursued financial interests (including an ill-fated purchase of oil rights in Italy) and advocated design changes in the building of warships during the Civil War in his published letter *To the Hon. Gideon Welles* (1862). He died in New York City.

The critical comparison of Mayo to Melville, while limiting to both writers, is also instructive. Like Melville, Mayo adapted his travel experiences to the antebellum literary market's demand for exotic foreign setting and adventures substantiated by at least a veneer of fact. While Melville first accepted, then struggled against this demand, seeking greater control in his more ambitious later novels, Mayo's works do not show the same struggle against market demands but still reveal an engagement with the writer's place in antebellum American culture. In *Kaloolah*, antebellum New York comes up for repeated attack in comparison with Mayo's utopian Framazugda, a nation in which only literary men are deemed qualified to be elected to public office. Though Mayo's works can be seen as characteristic embodiments of the popular generic forms of nineteenth-century American literature, his writings reveal an interest in issues such as American imperialism, racialist discourses, the changing social landscape of American life, and the writer's authority and status within American society—issues that also motivated much of the work of Mayo's more famous contemporaries such as Melville, Poe, and Nathaniel Hawthorne.

• Scattered letters of Mayo can be found in the New York Public Library, Butler Library at Columbia University, and the New-York Historical Society Library. His literary works and career have been studied almost exclusively in relation to Herman Melville's, where consideration has been less on the content of Mayo's texts than on their possible reflection in Melville's. Examples include Arthur Hobson Quinn, *American Fiction* (1936); Luther S. Mansfield and Howard P. Vincent's edition of *Moby-Dick* (1952); Perry Miller, *The Raven and the Whale* (1956); and Cecil D. Eby, Jr., "William Starbuck Mayo and Herman Melville," *New England Quarterly* 35 (1962): 515–20. Notable reviews of Mayo's work can be found in *United States Magazine and Democratic Review* 25 (1849): 91–92 and *Literary World* 4 (1849): 532–33. An obituary is in the *New York Tribune*, 23 Nov. 1895.

JOHN EVELEV

MAYO, William Worrell (31 May 1819–6 Mar. 1911), physician and surgeon, was born near Manchester, England, the son of James Mayo, a skilled artisan, and

Anne Bonselle. He studied physics and chemistry at Owens College, Manchester, under John Dalton. Sources disagree on the details of his early medical education; however, he may have worked as an apprentice at the Manchester Infirmary, as well as briefly in London and Glasgow. For reasons that remain unclear, Mayo left England for the United States in 1845, before he had qualified for a medical license. His early employment in the United States included working in New York City as a chemist at Bellevue Hospital. He headed west in 1847, ending up in Lafayette, Indiana, where he briefly became a partner in a tailor shop, and in the summer of 1849 he began to study medicine under Dr. Eleazer H. Deming, a prominent Lafayette physician. That autumn, Mayo entered Deming's Indiana Medical College at LaPorte. Owing to his medical education in England, he completed the program quickly.

After graduating in 1850, he returned to Lafayette, where he worked prescribing and dispensing at Hart's Drugstore. He left this work in May 1852 after a dispute over his payment and took up practice with Dr. Deming. In 1851, in Galene Woods, Michigan, Mayo married Louise Abigail Wright, a native of Syracuse, New York. They had four children. In the autumn of 1853, Mayo followed Deming to the University of Missouri in St. Louis; in 1854 he received a second M.D. from that institution.

Later that year, Mayo moved his family to St. Paul in the Minnesota Territory. At that time Minnesota, one of the far western outposts of the American frontier, was reported to have a healthier climate than Indiana and was experiencing boom growth. Mayo's skills as a competent physician earned him a flourishing practice and positive reputation, not diminished by his tendency to neglect—and fail to collect—many of his professional fees. Beyond his own practice, Mayo became quite active in organizing the first board of commissioners of St. Louis County, locating the county seat on land where the city of Deluth eventually developed. He volunteered to take the census of St. Louis County in 1855, not an easy task on the frontier, and in 1856 he settled his family on a farm in Cronan's Precinct, near Le Sueur, and moved into the latter town in 1859. Finding his physician's income insufficient to support his growing family, Mayo worked during the spring and summer of 1860 on board a Minnesota River steamboat with future railroad builder James J. Hill.

In 1862 Mayo was surgeon to a relief force that suppressed a Sioux uprising in the Mississippi valley. In spring 1863 Mayo was appointed the army's examining surgeon for the enrollment board of the first Minnesota district. The office was located in Rochester. He moved his family there in January 1864 and quickly became the area's leading surgeon and physician.

Mayo helped found both the Olmstead County Medical Society in 1868 and the Minnesota State Medical Society in 1869. He served as the latter society's president in 1873 and contributed articles to its organ, *Transactions*. The technical nature of these articles demonstrate Mayo's skills and capacity for careful observation. One of the first western physicians to use a microscope diagnostically, he was also responsible for several medical innovations. The most notable of these came in 1871, when he designed a clamp to be used during laparotomies for ovarian tumor. He inspired a number of acquaintances to pursue medical careers, including Henry (later Sir Henry) Wellcome, who had been working as a prescription clerk at a Rochester dentist's office. In the winter of 1869–1870 Mayo returned to Bellevue Hospital in New York to take postgraduate courses in medicine for several months.

In 1883 a cyclone hit Rochester, Minnesota, killing twenty-two people and injuring many others. Mayo was called upon to take charge of the emergency hospital. In this capacity he was assisted by the recently arrived sisters of the Order of St. Francis. When Mother Alfred Moes, the order's superior, approached Mayo with the idea of creating a hospital in Rochester, he initially opposed the plan because he believed it would be a financial failure. Not to be deterred, Mother Alfred managed to extract a promise from Mayo that, were the order to raise enough money for a hospital, he would take charge of it. This they did; in 1887 Mayo selected a site for the building and traveled to eastern hospitals with his son William to examine their architectural designs.

St. Mary's Hospital opened on 1 October 1889, when Mayo was seventy years old and preparing to retire from practice. He appointed himself consulting physician and surgeon of the hospital, and his two sons, Charles and William Jr., served as staff physicians. As their practice grew, they invited other physicians to join their team. Eventually, this expanded practice became known as the Mayo Clinic.

In his later years, with his sons taking on most of the surgical duties, Mayo found time to travel the world—his last journey was made when he was eighty-seven—and to continue his active involvement in politics. Although his political career was uneventful, he served at both the municipal and state level: as mayor of Rochester (1882), as alderman (1885–1889), and as state senator (1890–1894). Mayo died in Rochester. He was survived by his wife and three of his children.

Mayo helped to organize several local medical societies, served in politics, was a medical innovator, helped to organize the early medical staff of the St. Mary's Hospital, and played a seminal role in creating what would become the Mayo Clinic. The example of experimentation and innovation he presented to his peers and progeny set a standard for the clinic's work.

• Few records of Mayo's life remain. The most extensive biographical study of the Mayo family is Helen Clapesattle, *The Doctors Mayo* (1941), which contains an extensive set of bibliographical notes. Clapesattle's records challenge some of the details of Mayo's early life, such as those found in standard reference works. Clapesattle's research is convincing, and her interpretation prevails here. The bulk of Clapesattle's records for the book are at the Mayo Clinic, but access to most Mayo family records at the clinic is restricted. Other biographical treatments include Louis B. Wilson, "Wm. Worrell Mayo: A

Pioneer Surgeon of the Northwest," *Surgery, Gynaecology and Obstetrics* 44, no. 5 (1927), and Frank J. Jirka, *American Doctors of Destiny* (1940). Obituaries are in the *Journal of the Minnesota State Medical Association and the Northwestern Lancet* (15 Mar. 1911) and the *Minneapolis Morning Tribune*, 7 Mar. 1911.

DANIEL MALLECK

MAYOR, Alfred Goldsborough (16 Apr. 1868–24 June 1922), marine zoologist, was born Alfred Goldsborough Mayer near Frederick, Maryland, the son of Alfred Marshall Mayer, a physicist, and Katherine Duckett Goldsborough. During his formative years he displayed a keen interest in natural history and exceptional skill in drawing and coloring animals, especially butterflies and moths. His father was determined, however, that young Alfred would study mechanical engineering at Stevens Institute of Technology, where he was a professor of physics. After graduating in 1889, Mayor served as assistant in physics at Clark University and later at the University of Kansas, but he resigned from the latter in 1892 in order to do advanced study in zoology at Harvard University.

Under the direction of Charles B. Davenport, Mayor concentrated his first scientific work upon color patterns in butterflies and moths, and in 1896 and 1897 he published two monographs on that subject in the *Bulletin of the Museum of Comparative Zoology*, for which he drew and colored all of the figures. Meanwhile, his superb talent for drawing and his remarkable knowledge of natural history caught the eye of Alexander Agassiz, the director of the Museum of Comparative Zoology, who urged him to focus on the hydromedusae and scyphomedusae, or jellyfishes, and the ctenophores, or comb jellies. Mayor readily mastered the art of depicting those organisms and soon established himself as a leading authority on their habits and physiology. Invited to accompany Agassiz on major collecting expeditions to the Bahamas and Cuba (1892–1893), the Great Barrier Reef of Australia (1896), and the Fiji Islands (1897–1898), Mayor also collected specimens at various sites along the Atlantic coast, including the Tortugas Keys. Between 1894 and 1899, as author or coauthor with Agassiz, he published four important articles on medusae in the *Bulletin of the Museum of Comparative Zoology*. He also drew the 145 figures and the thirty-six colored plates for those articles. In 1895 Agassiz appointed Mayor the curator of the radiate collections in the Museum of Comparative Zoology, and in 1897 Harvard took the extraordinary step of awarding the honorary degree of Sc.D. to Mayor.

In 1900 Mayor married Harriet Randolph Hyatt; they had four children. Already the author or coauthor of sixteen articles and monographs by the time of his marriage, Mayor came to the attention of the trustees of the Brooklyn Institute of Arts and Sciences, who appointed him in 1900 the curator of natural history of its museum and a member of the executive committee of its Department of Zoology. In 1902 Mayor assumed the position of president of the Department of Zoology, and in 1903 he became the curator in chief of the Brooklyn Museum. Zealous in building the collections in natural history and in promoting the museum, Mayor was a notably effective administrator. In addition, he continued to conduct original research, and from 1901 to 1904 he published six substantial articles, including three in the museum's *Science Bulletin* and one in its *Memoirs*. Mayor also completed the manuscript of *Sea-Shore Life*, published in 1905 by the New York Zoological Society. Intended for a general audience, *Sea-Shore Life* included more than 100 illustrations and photographs by Mayor.

When Mayor learned in 1902 that the Carnegie Institution of Washington intended to establish a marine laboratory, he launched a campaign to direct the interest of the institution's trustees toward a site in the Tortugas Keys. In 1903 he stepped up his campaign by soliciting the support of leading marine biologists, touting the Tortugas Keys in *Science* magazine, and sending a persuasive proposal to the Carnegie Institution trustees. Mayor also coveted the directorship of the proposed laboratory, and he won it when the trustees decided in December 1903 in favor of his proposal.

Within two months after officially assuming his new position on 1 June 1904, Mayor had arranged for two prefabricated buildings to be erected on the north end of Loggerhead Key and for a specially designed yacht to be provided for trawling and dredging. By April 1905 the laboratory was in full operation, with Mayor and eight other scientists at work on various projects. During the following seventeen years, Mayor worked diligently to make the Tortugas Marine Biology Laboratory a major center of research, and he succeeded to a remarkable degree. Through his efforts, a considerable number of scientists worked at the laboratory, and an impressive number of their papers were published—most but not all in *Papers from the Tortugas Laboratory of the Carnegie Institution of Washington* (later titled *Papers from the Department of Marine Biology of the Carnegie Institution of Washington*) or, particularly in the case of Mayor himself, through special publications of the Carnegie Institution. From his earliest to his final years with the laboratory Mayor continued to study medusae, but by 1914 he was also doing important work on the ecology of coral reefs, using Carnegie Institution funding for expeditions to Tahiti, Samoa, and Australia, as well as to Caribbean ports. Indeed, Mayor was a pioneer in the study of coral-reef ecology and in the use of quantitative methods in his studies. Perhaps better known, however, are his classic works on jellyfishes and comb jellies. In 1910 the Carnegie Institution published his three-volume *Medusae of the World*, which contained 735 pages of text, 428 text figures, and seventy-six exquisitely rendered plates. Two years later, the institution published his *Ctenophores of the Atlantic Coast of North America*. More than seventy of Mayor's taxa of medusae and ctenophores are currently valid.

By 1910 Mayor had begun to search for a more suitable place to locate the Carnegie marine laboratory, since the site on Loggerhead Key, although ideal for the study of tropical fauna, was hampered by isolation, a brief season for collecting, and vulnerability to tropical storms. In fact, in 1910, 1917, and 1919 hurricanes did extensive damage to the laboratory's facilities. Mayor continued to operate the laboratory during the years of the First World War. An ardent patriot, he became so obsessed over the Germanic origin of the name Mayer that he had it legally changed to Mayor in August 1918. Ready to assist his country, Mayor taught a course on navigation in 1918 at Princeton University, where he held an adjunct appointment in 1910–1911 and from 1915 until his death; in 1918 he also published *Navigation, Illustrated by Diagrams* for prospective naval officers.

Elected to membership in the National Academy of Sciences in 1916, Mayor was active in the affairs of numerous scientific organizations. He was the author or coauthor of approximately 100 publications. By 1917 he was suffering from tuberculosis, but he continued his scientific work, even submerging in a diving hood to study coral reefs at Samoa in 1918, 1919, and 1920. The disease began to worsen in 1920, and during the spring of 1922 he had to spend a month in a sanatorium in Tucson, Arizona. Despite his illness, Mayor returned to the Tortugas laboratory in May 1922; he died there, his body found in the shallow waters of Loggerhead Key where he had apparently passed out and drowned. A bronze tablet, designed by his widow, an artist, was erected in his memory on Loggerhead Key in 1923. It is the sole vestige of the marine laboratory, which closed in 1939.

• Major collections of Mayor's papers are in the American Philosophical Society Library, the Brooklyn Museum, the Carnegie Institution of Washington, the New York Public Library, Princeton University, and Syracuse University. Important correspondence to or from Mayor can also be found in the Alexander Agassiz Collection in the Museum of Comparative Zoology, the Joseph A. Cushman Collection in the Paleobiology Division, U.S. National Museum of Natural History, and various collections in the Smithsonian Institution Archives. Mayor's activities as director of the Tortugas Marine Biology Laboratory, including information on scientific expeditions on behalf of the Carnegie Institution of Washington, are given in the institution's *Yearbooks* (1902–1924). The most comprehensive bibliography of Mayor's publications is in Charles B. Davenport, National Academy of Sciences, *Biographical Memoirs* 21 (1926): 1–11. To place the origins of the Tortugas laboratory in context, see Frank R. Lillie, *The Woods Hole Marine Biological Laboratory* (1944), and James D. Ebert, "Carnegie Institution of Washington and Marine Biology: Naples, Woods Hole, and Tortugas," *Biological Bulletin*, supp., 168 (June 1985): 172–82. Brief sketches of Mayor and his role in the Tortugas laboratory are in Joseph J. Betz, "Pioneer Biologist," *Sea Frontiers* 11 (Sept.–Oct. 1965): 286–95, and Patrick L. Colin, "A Brief History of the Tortugas Marine Laboratory and the Department of Marine Biology, Carnegie Institution of Washington," in *Oceanography: The Past*, ed. M. Sears and D. Merriam (1980).

LESTER D. STEPHENS

MAYS, Benjamin Elijah (1 Aug. 1894 or 1895–28 Mar. 1984), educator, college president, and civil rights activist, was born near Rambo (now Epworth), South Carolina, the son of Hezekiah Mays and Louvenia Carter, tenant farmers who had been enslaved. Benjamin, the youngest of eight children, grew up in the rural South when whites segregated and disfranchised African Americans by law (he himself was not allowed to vote until 1945, when he was fifty-one years old). His first childhood memory was the 1898 Phoenix Riot in South Carolina where, he recalled, white vigilantes murdered his cousin.

At an early age Mays developed an "insatiable desire" for education. Extreme racial inequality, however, marked the South's segregated education system. In 1900, for example, African Americans, 55 percent of South Carolina's population, received only 2 percent of the appropriations for higher education. By the age of seventeen Mays had been in school no more than four months a year. To continue his schooling, he had to grapple with racial discrimination, poverty, and his own father, who wanted him to remain on the farm. In 1916 Mays graduated valedictorian from the high school of the black South Carolina State College at Orangeburg and became engaged to Ellen Harvin, a fellow student.

Struggling against a culture that devalued African-American intellect, Mays determined to receive the best education possible and to prove to himself that he could compete successfully with whites. Mays decided to attend a northern college, but his first choice, Holderness School in New Hampshire, rejected him because of his race. A year later Bates College in Lewiston, Maine, accepted his application. In 1920 Mays graduated from Bates and married Harvin, who was then teaching home economics at Morris College in Sumter, South Carolina; she died in 1923. After leaving Bates, Mays applied to Newton Theological Seminary, but again was refused because he was black. Instead Mays attended the University of Chicago. He continued to encounter racism; many cafes close to campus refused to serve African Americans. Three semesters later the president of Atlanta's Morehouse College, John Hope, enticed Mays away from Chicago with an offer of a teaching position at Morehouse. From 1921 until 1924 Mays taught algebra and mathematics and for one year was acting dean at the all-male Morehouse. He also was the pastor of the Shiloh Baptist Church; he had been licensed for the ministry in 1919 and ordained in 1921.

During these years Mays kept alive his dream of earning an advanced degree. He left Morehouse after three years to continue his work at the University of Chicago. In 1925 Mays completed his M.A. He contemplated pursuing a Ph.D. at Chicago but instead decided to teach English at his high school alma mater, South Carolina State. There he met Sadie Gray, and in the summer of 1926, while both of them conducted graduate work at the University of Chicago, Mays married Gray. Because South Carolina State prohibited married couples from working together, the newlyweds accepted jobs with the National Urban League. Mays had no children from either of his marriages.

As the executive secretary of the National Urban League in Tampa, Florida, Mays labored to improve the poor conditions for African Americans in housing and employment. Especially effective in reaching out to delinquent African-American youths, he made sure that they were sent to the Urban League rather than the home for juvenile offenders. Mays and his wife exceeded their job requirements by helping Tampa's African-American community build self-esteem. By challenging the humiliating system of segregation, however, the Mayses angered many whites. Expecting to be fired for failing to abide by the status quo, they resigned from the Urban League in 1928.

The couple moved to Atlanta, where Mays assumed a position as the secretary for the National Young Men's Christian Association, working with African-American students in Alabama, Georgia, South Carolina, Tennessee, and Florida. One of Mays's outstanding accomplishments was the partial integration of the YMCA in the North and the South. In 1930 Mays left the YMCA to accept an offer from the Institute of Social and Religious Research, a Rockefeller-affiliated agency, to conduct a study of African-American churches in the United States. Mays and a fellow minister, Joseph W. Nicholson, researched 609 urban congregations and 185 rural churches and in 1933 published the results as *The Negro's Church*.

The intellectual rigors of research renewed Mays's lifelong quest to earn a doctorate; in 1931 he returned to the University of Chicago. In addition to studying, Mays protested discrimination on campus by fighting for equal seating at public events and equal housing in the dormitories. In the summer of 1934, after finishing his coursework, he accepted a position as the dean of the School of Religion of Howard University in Washington, D.C. His success there brought him recognition and invitations to various speaking engagements, permitting him to travel overseas for the first time in his life. Traveling taught Mays that prejudice was a worldwide problem, as he observed discrimination against people of color in other countries. With foreign leaders such as Mahatma Gandhi of India, Mays discussed strategies to effect nonviolent social change and reduce discrimination. In 1935, at the age of forty, Mays earned his Ph.D. from the University of Chicago School of Religion.

After six years at Howard, Mays accepted an offer on 31 May 1940 to become president of Morehouse College. At that time severe problems plagued the university. It had lost almost $1 million of endowment money, had low morale, and was poorly situated among the colleges that formed the Atlanta Affiliation. Mays's leadership helped transform the school. In his twenty-seven years as president, he supervised donations of more than $15 million and oversaw the construction of eighteen buildings, elevating the school's status as a liberal arts college. Mays boosted the student body's morale as well, especially with his popular Tuesday morning talks with students. In the talks Mays always encouraged Morehouse men to be strong and accept nothing less than equality.

One student inspired by Mays's tenacious stand against racial discrimination was Martin Luther King, Jr. Mays's outstanding oratorical skills and broad social vision left a deep impression on King. Their friendship, begun when King entered college, continued until his assassination in 1968. Impressed by Mays's sermons at Morehouse, King often stayed afterward to discuss thorny issues with him, and these meetings soon blossomed into regular discussions in Mays's office. Both Mays and King shared a commitment to nonviolent social change. When King won the Nobel Peace Prize in 1964, Mays, to the dismay of conservative whites and King's black rivals, organized a successful citywide celebration in Atlanta. At King's funeral four years later, Mays gave the eulogy.

Mays's relentless stand against segregation earned him scorn from many sources. Nominated in 1961 to the Civil Rights Commission by President John F. Kennedy, Mays was denied confirmation by the Senate because he advocated integration, viewed by a majority of legislators as a violation of "impartiality." Because of his active opposition to segregation and disfranchisement during the 1930s and 1940s, conservatives charged Mays (and others who struggled for civil rights) with being Communists. Mays's opponents cited the Georgia Committee on Education's 1958 report, *Communism and the NAACP*, which listed thirty-one "Communist activities" in which Mays had participated.

Supposedly subversive were Mays's membership in the Southern Conference for Human Welfare in 1947–1948, his support of the American Crusade to End Lynching, his chairmanship of a conference on discrimination in higher education for the Southern Conference Educational Fund, and his very active leadership in the National Association for the Advancement of Colored People (NAACP). Mays was no Communist; indeed, his deep Christian commitment made him unsympathetic to what he perceived as "Godless Communism." Mays also drew fire from conservative civil rights leaders for his criticisms of the U.S. war with Vietnam. Mays never hesitated to speak out and pursue what he thought was right.

Although president of an urban college, Mays felt a commitment to African Americans living in the countryside. He often spoke at rural congregations and felt a particular duty to rural children. The importance of Mays as a role model to African-American students is illustrated by the naming in 1953 of the small, rural black school in Pacolet, South Carolina, the Ben E. Mays High School. This school also honored Mays by naming a day each school year in his honor, and Mays always attended the accompanying ceremony. He also continued his ties to his alma mater, South Carolina State, acting as president of the alumni association. Mays believed in treating everyone fairly. "The test of good religion is not how we treat our peers and those above us," he wrote in his autobiography, *Born to Rebel*, "but how we treat those beneath us, not how we treat the man highest up, but how we treat the man farthest down. . . . the real test of my religion would be how I treat the man who has nothing to give me—no money, no social prestige, no honors."

After Mays retired as president of Morehouse College in 1967, he served for twelve years as chair of the Atlanta school board and tirelessly sought to rectify inequalities that African-American children endured. Active in national as well as local politics, Mays advised President Jimmy Carter, who thought of Mays as his friend, critic, and adviser, especially on issues of civil rights. To that end, Mays never stopped agitating for racial equality. In *Born to Rebel*, Mays wrote, "I worked all my life as if eternity was in every minute."

Committed to improving life for African Americans, Mays found religion to be essential to the task. His unwavering faith in God gave him strength to fight segregation and oppression. "The Christian," Mays stated in his autobiography, "cannot excuse himself by saying, 'I cannot go against tradition; I cannot buck the mores; I cannot jeopardize my political, social, or economic future.' The true Christian is a citizen of two worlds. Not only must he answer to the mores, but he must give an account to God." His religion also gave him a forgiving attitude toward the perpetrators of racism. The "chief sin of segregation," he maintained in *Born to Rebel*, "is the distortion of human personality. It damages the soul of both the segregator and segregated. . . . It is difficult to know who is damaged more—the segregated or segregator."

Mays produced many outstanding scholarly works, publishing seven books and authoring numerous articles. He was especially successful in exploring the relationship between black religion and race relations in two influential works, *The Negro's Church* and *The Negro's God, as Reflected in His Literature* (1938). In another book, *Seeking to Be Christian in Race Relations* (1957), Mays argued that the slave spirituals comprised the origins of the nonviolent protest tradition in the African-American community. In 1971 Mays published *Born to Rebel: An Autobiography*, an invaluable contribution to the study of American race relations.

Throughout his life Mays felt a keen sense of alienation and grievance. Segregation affected blacks and whites so deeply that Mays "never felt that any white person in Greenwood County [his native county] or in South Carolina would be interested in anything I did." Yet in 1981 the state erected a granite monument in his home county, a monument larger than that honoring another native, Preston Brooks, a white U.S. representative who in 1856 caned Republican abolitionist senator Charles Sumner. Although Mays witnessed much racist violence during his lifetime, his life demonstrated the efficacy of nonviolent social change and the tenacity of African Americans to win equal rights in the country of their birth. In the end, the nation and the South celebrated Mays and the life he led. He was awarded forty-nine honorary degrees, his portrait was hung in the South Carolina State House in Columbia in 1980, and he was inducted into the South Carolina Hall of Fame in 1981. He died in Atlanta.

• The Moorland-Spingarn Research Center at Howard University houses the majority of Mays's papers. A few papers are at the South Caroliniana Library at the University of South Carolina. More than forty boxes of uncataloged Mays papers sit in the chaplain's office at Morehouse College. Mays also published *A Gospel for the Social Awakening: Selections, Edited and Compiled from the Writings of Walter Rauschenbusch* (1950), *Disturbed about Man* (1969), *Lord, the People Have Driven Me On* (1981), and *Quotable Quotes of Benjamin E. Mays* (1983). For an historical overview of Mays's life, see Orville Vernon Burton's foreword to *Born to Rebel* (repr. 1987). On Mays's role as an educator, see Barbara Levinson, "Three Conceptions of Black Education: A study of the Educational Ideas of Benjamin Elijah Mays, Booker T. Washington, and Nathan Wright, Jr." (Ph.D. diss., Rutgers Univ., 1973); Dereck Joseph Rovaris, "Developer of an Institution: Dr. Benjamin E. Mays, Morehouse College President, 1940–1967" (Ph.D. diss., Univ. of Illinois, Urbana-Champaign, 1990); Doris Levy Gavins, "The Ceremonial Speaking of Benjamin Elijah Mays: Spokesman for Social Change, 1954–1975" (Ph.D. diss., Louisiana State Univ., 1978); and Edward A. Jones, *A Candle in the Dark: A History of Morehouse College* (1967).

For the crucial role religion played in Mays's development, see his works "I Have Been a Baptist All My Life," in *The Baptists Tell Their Story*, ed. John S. Childers (1964); "Why I Believe There Is a God," in *Why I Believe There Is a God: Sixteen Essays by Negro Clergymen* (1965); and "The New Negro Challenges the Old Order," in *Sketches of Negro Life and History in South Carolina*, ed. Asa H. Gordon (1929). Also see Richard I. McKinney, "The Black Church: Its Development and Present Impact," *Harvard Theological Review* 64, no. 4 (Oct. 1971).

For Mays's importance to the civil rights movement and to the spiritual development of Martin Luther King, Jr., see Lerone Bennett, Jr., "The Last of the Great Schoolmasters," *Ebony*, Dec. 1977, pp. 74–79, and Thomas J. Mikelson, *The Negro's God in the Theology of Martin Luther King, Jr.* A week-long conference on Mays was held at Morehouse College in Feb. 1995 and resulted in a collection of essays edited by Lawrence E. Carter, Sr., *Walking Integrity: Benjamin Elijah Mays: Mentor to Generations* (1996). An obituary is in the *New York Times*, 29 Mar. 1984.

ORVILLE VERNON BURTON

MAYS, Carl William (12 Nov. 1893–4 Apr. 1971), baseball player, was born in Liberty, Kentucky, the son of William Henry Mays, a farmer and Methodist minister, and Louisa Callie. At some point the family moved to Missouri. After his father died in 1904 young Carl helped around the farm, but records indicate that he had four years of high school in Mansfield, Missouri. Meanwhile he learned to play baseball with his seven siblings, and he became good enough to play semiprofessionally. He received his first professional opportunity with Boise of the Western Tri-State League in 1912. The next year he pitched for Portland, Oregon, in the Northwestern League, then Providence, Rhode Island, in the International League. His 1914 record for Providence was 24 wins and only eight losses. That performance earned him a promotion to the Boston Red Sox of the American League in 1915.

Mays was a winner from the start. In his first season he led the league in saves with seven, won six games, and lost five. In 1918 he led the league in shutouts with eight and complete games with 30, out of the 33 games he started. In his first four years, 1915 through 1918, his record was a more than satisfying 67–40. But in 1919 Mays's tough, competitive nature began to damage him. His earned run average was still below 3.00, but he was not winning many games, and he publicly blamed poor fielding by the Red Sox. Angered at a sniping spectator, Mays threw a baseball at him, a cardinal baseball sin. When his own catcher hit him in the back with an errant throw, Mays walked off the field and demanded a trade, saying he could not win with Boston players. The New York Yankees immediately purchased his contract, but Ban Johnson, the American League president, nullified the trade on the grounds that Mays should be disciplined first. The case reopened an ongoing issue of those days—the amount of power the league president should have relative to the owners. The New York State Supreme Court overruled Johnson, and Mays moved to New York. Also in 1919, Mays married Frederika Marjorie Madden.

The following year Mays became involved in baseball's worst tragedy. The Yankees were playing Cleveland in New York, and Mays was pitching. A pitch, usually reported as being in the strike zone, hit the Indians' shortstop, Ray Chapman, in the temple. Chapman died a few hours later, the first case of its kind in major league history. Reactions to Chapman's death were intense and varied. Mays was sorry, but he denied any malice; Chapman, he declared, had "lunged out of the batter's box." Mays also swore that he had thrown an ordinary fast ball, not some strange, unusual pitch. This comment referred to Mays's pitching style, which involved the use of the "submarine pitch," released just above ground level. Mays had used this different yet legal pitch for several years, and Chapman was certainly familiar with it. Several teams threatened but did not institute boycotts against Mays, who went into seclusion for a few days. In his defense Yankees management pointed out that Mays was only seventh in the league in the number of hit batters. Officially, baseball exonerated Mays from blame, and in time the matter was in a fashion forgotten.

The tragedy did not seem to affect Mays's baseball performance. In 1920 his record was 26–11, and again he led the American League in shutouts. In 1921 he did even better, with a 27–9 record, while leading the league in games, innings pitched, and saves. Mays was the Yankees' best pitcher as they won their first pennant. In 1923, however, the Yankees had a surplus of younger pitchers and used Mays sparingly in the World Series. He was traded the next year to the Cincinnati Reds.

With the Reds Mays became the biggest winner again, winning 20 and losing nine. He did little in 1925 but came back again in 1926, compiling a record of 19–12 and leading the National League in complete games with 24. But he was being used less and less, and in 1929, his final year in the major leagues, he was 7–2 for the New York Giants.

In 15 major league seasons Mays won 207 games and lost 126. He pitched in five World Series; his earned run average was a fine 2.20, although his record was only 3–4. Playing for Boston in the 1918 World Series, he and Babe Ruth each defeated the Chicago Cubs twice without a loss, with Mays allowing only one run in each game. After being released by the Giants in 1929, Mays pitched two years of minor league baseball and then retired. In later years he scouted for several major league teams and ran a boys' baseball camp. In 1932 his wife died, and in 1939 he married Esther Ugstad.

Mays's record must be classified as exceptional yet puzzling. He was the first man to lead both major leagues in complete games in a single season and the first man to win twenty games in one season in each league. He had superb seasons and a few lackluster seasons. He often had trouble with management, including that of teams he once respected, and he had many enemies. But he was a fierce competitor and the man a team wanted as pitcher in the proverbial clutch.

Mays died in El Cajon, California, after several weeks of pneumonia. He left two adult children.

• Information is less available on Mays than on other players; however, there is a file on him at the National Baseball Library, Cooperstown, N.Y. Very thorough documentation of his baseball statistics is in John Thorn and Pete Palmer, eds., *Total Baseball*, 3d ed. (1993). Gene Karst and Martin J. Jones, Jr., *Who's Who in Professional Baseball* (1973), has a good biographical sketch. A few, unusual details of Mays's life are provided in Mike Slatzkin, *The Ballplayers* (1990). Mays's version of Chapman's death is in his article "My Attitude towards the Unfortunate Chapman," *Baseball Magazine*, Nov. 1920. An obituary is in the *New York Times*, 6 Apr. 1971.

THOMAS L. KARNES

MAYSLES, David Carl (10 Jan. 1932–3 Jan. 1987), documentary filmmaker, was born in Boston, Massachusetts, the son of Philip Maysles, a postal clerk, and Ethel Epstein, a grammar school teacher. Maysles spent his childhood in Dorchester, a working-class, predominantly Irish-Catholic Boston neighborhood. Both his parents had immigrated to the United States from Russia as young children and were devoted to American ideals of upward mobility. His mother had been one of the "Saturday Evening Girls," a group of immigrant children given a classical education in the arts, sponsored by a Boston philanthropist. Ethel Maysles's devotion to the arts exerted a lifelong influence on her two sons and a daughter. In 1939 the Maysles family moved to Brookline, a middle-class Boston suburb, where Ethel Maysles became the first Jewish teacher in the community's public schools.

David Maysles attended public schools in Boston and Brookline. He financed his education at Boston University partly by selling Avon products and graduated with a degree in business administration in 1953. He spent two years in the U.S. Army, serving at the Military Intelligence School in Oberammergau, Germany. He then worked as a production assistant for

Milton Greene on two Marilyn Monroe vehicles, *The Prince and the Showgirl* (1956) and *Bus Stop* (1956), but he found Hollywood-style filmmaking unsatisfying. With his older brother, Albert, Maysles hitchhiked across the United States and traveled by motorcycle from Munich to Moscow. During these trips the brothers developed their curiosity about life stories and forged a close artistic partnership.

Their first joint film production, *Youth in Poland*, was broadcast in the United States on NBC in 1957 and opened the way for the Maysles brothers to join a group of young, innovative journalists who were making experimental documentaries in the Living Camera series for Time, Inc., under the leadership of Robert Drew. Al became one of several exceptional cameramen in the unit, while David Maysles worked as a correspondent on projects such as *Adventures on the New Frontier* (1961). Using lightweight, mobile cameras, portable recorders, directional microphones, and high-speed film, Drew and his colleagues were among the pioneers of a new film style called cinéma vérité or—an expression the Maysles favored—direct cinema. This form eschewed voice-over narration, interviews, and staged action, instead forming an allegiance with the possibilities and demands of an essentially observational documentary style. It reflected a 1960s urge to merge the real world with the traditional arts through media. When the Drew Organization was officially formed, the Maysles brothers declined to join; instead in 1962 they founded their own production company, Maysles Film, Inc., based in New York City.

David Maysles, according to his brother, was a "beautiful kid" with a "pure, love-me" nature. Personal charm, a lifelong interest in meeting strangers, a nonjudgmental attitude, and a special attraction to people with the "gift of gab" helped make Maysles a successful documentary producer. The Maysles brothers always operated as a filmmaking team, despite consistent divisions in work tasks. David recorded sound and supervised the editing, while Al was the cameraman. They shared business responsibilities and routinely financed their more personal projects by producing corporate promotional films and reality-based commercials. These personal projects had common goals, which colleague Ellen Hovde described as "pushing in film terms towards a novel of sensibility rather than a novel of plot." Most of the Maysleses' documentaries focused on celebrated individuals and on an American infatuation with fame: *Showman* (1962, with movie producer Joseph E. Levine), *What's Happening: The Beatles in the U.S.A.* (1964, re-released as *The Beatles: The First U.S. Visit* in 1992), *Meet Marlon Brando* (1965), *With Love from Truman* [Capote] (1966), *Journey to Jerusalem* (1968, with Leonard Bernstein), *Gimme Shelter* (1970, with the Rolling Stones), four films with the artist Christo: *Valley Curtain* (1974), *Running Fence* (1978), *Islands* (1986), and *Christo in Paris* (1990), *Muhammed and Larry* (1980, with boxers Ali and Holmes), *Vladimir*

Horowitz: The Last Romantic (1985), and *Ozawa* (1985).

Three notable exceptions to a focus on the famous were *Salesman* (1968), *The Burkes of Georgia* (1976), and *Grey Gardens* (1976). In *Salesman* the Maysleses returned to the Irish Boston of their boyhood and followed four Bible salesmen on their rounds. The result, later included in the National Film Registry, was the Maysleses' most celebrated film, a classic study of the centrality of selling in American life. *The Burkes*, set in rural poverty, was included in a six-part series on the American family produced by Paul Wilkes. *Grey Gardens* examined the intense relationship between Edith Bouvier Beale and her middle-aged daughter, Edie, two eccentrics secluded on their East Hampton estate. The frankness of *Grey Gardens* struck an emotional chord with audiences. It was criticized as exploitation and also praised as important, revelatory nonfiction.

A project close to Maysles's heart, begun in the late 1960s and tentatively titled *Blue Yonder*, remained unfinished at his death. Intended as a family biography featuring the filmmakers, their beloved mother, and two male heroes—their cautious father and a daring older cousin, a fighter pilot who died at the age of twenty-six—the documentary was stymied by the limitations of a cinema style dedicated to recording life as lived, rather than life as remembered.

The Maysles brothers remained bachelors into their forties; they both married in 1976 and began their own families in middle age. David Maysles married Judith Verhagen; they and their son and daughter lived in Manhattan, with a summer home in the Hamptons. Maysles suffered a stroke in late December 1986 and died in New York.

In interviews throughout his career Maysles addressed two criticisms commonly lodged against cinéma vérité documentaries: voyeurism and a failure to meet a supposed promise of objectivity. In an interview with James Blue he considered mutual respect and a "solid relationship with the people you're filming" as the central means of avoiding voyeurism and "objectivity" a bogus goal: "There is no such thing as being strictly objective in anything that is at all artistic. The objectivity is just a personal integrity: being essentially true to the subject and capturing it essentially."

Although never active contributors to documentary theory, the Maysleses' best work anticipated and influenced two important documentary trends of the 1980s and 1990s: a recognition of the political dimensions of family life and a reflexive acknowledgment of the filmmaking process within the film text. Their experiential style was imitated by many realist fiction filmmakers, but the Maysleses' greatest contribution to cinema was their ability to share an abiding fascination with the complexity and ambiguity of human personality.

• Interviews with David and Albert Maysles by James Blue, *Film Comment* (Fall 1965), and G. Roy Levin, *Documentary Explorations* (1971), consider the Maysleses' working methods, goals, and sensibilities. Interviews with colleagues Charlotte Zwerin (in Alan Rosenthal, *The New Documentary in Action: A Casebook in Film Making* [1971]) and Ellen Hovde (in Rosenthal, *The Documentary Conscience* [1980]) provide further insight into the Maysleses' procedures and projects. A paperback published in 1969, with an introduction by Harold Clurman and production notes by Howard Junker, offers background and a full transcript of *Salesman*. Stephen Mamber, *Cinema Verite in America: Studies in Uncontrolled Documentary* (1974), and P. J. O'Connell, *Robert Drew and the Development of Cinema Verite in America* (1992), are comprehensive analyses of cinéma vérité and the place of the Maysles brothers within that documentary tradition. Obituaries are in the *New York Times*, 4 Jan. 1987, and the *Boston Globe*, 5 Jan. 1987.

CAROLYN ANDERSON

MAYTAG, Frederick Louis (14 July 1857–26 Mar. 1937), manufacturer, was born in Elgin, Illinois, the son of Daniel William Maytag and Amelia Tonebon, farmers. His father was then farming in Cook County, but he soon moved to another farm in Clay County and then again to Mattoon, Illinois, to open a grocery store. Frederick Maytag, then eight years old, worked as a delivery boy. In 1866 his father traded the grocery for a quarter section in Marshall County, Iowa. This he soon sold, buying a half section near Laurel, Iowa, not far from Newton. By age thirteen Frederick had learned to manage the farm and help supervise his nine siblings, as his father was by then often absent, working as a carpenter on building projects. It is thus not a surprise that Maytag estimated he received merely twenty-two months of formal schooling.

At age sixteen Maytag began doing contract threshing work; he found it profitable enough to do the same for the next six harvests. At age twenty-one, given a team of horses by his father, he bought a wagon and contracted to haul coal to township school houses during the winter. In January 1880 McKinley & Bergman, a farm machinery dealer in Newton, offered Maytag $50 a month to work as a salesman. He worked for two seasons; in the fall of 1881, with $800 of his own money and $2,700 borrowed from his father, he bought out McKinley, and the firm became Maytag & Bergman. The following September he married Bergman's younger sister, Dena, with whom he eventually had four children. In 1890 he sold his interest in the implement company, purchasing the W. R. Manning lumberyards, which were then operating in three towns. In 1894 he took in A. K. Emerson as a partner, finally selling his interest in 1904 to W. E. Denniston.

Maytag's motivation for moving away from the lumber business was his involvement with a new venture. In 1892 Maytag saw an exciting new invention, George Parsons's band cutter and self-feeder attachment for threshers. Parsons soon invited Maytag to participate in manufacturing and marketing his invention; they incorporated in March 1893. During the first year the attachment sold well, but many failed when used. Maytag thus learned the difference between "sold and satisfied." It was also clear that one partner had to manage the business full time, and

since Maytag was the choice, beginning in January 1894 it became his primary concern.

Maytag immediately put customer satisfaction and product quality ahead of all other concerns, insisting that Parsons offer high quality and dependability. With this policy in place, all twenty-eight thresher manufacturers soon purchased and resold the Parsons cutter and feeder as part of their own machines. Maytag also learned that providing maintenance to customers ate up profits made on sales to manufacturers. But he also noticed that around Austin, Minnesota, Parsons attachments never seemed to need servicing. Investigating, he discovered the reason: in that region a brilliant young mechanic, Howard Snyder, was providing the crucial services. In 1898, Maytag brought Snyder to the company headquarters in Newton, where he became head of the experimental department in 1912, plant superintendent during World War I, and vice president in 1921. Snyder made signal contributions in both product design and manufacturing processes, helping achieve Maytag's commitment to quality and dependability.

As Parsons prospered under Maytag's direction, the company added numerous products, including a hay press, a corn husker and shredder, and buggies. In November 1907, looking for a product to offset the seasonal slack in production of farm implements, Maytag began manufacturing a hand-operated washing machine. It was logical development: two Newton firms, including his brother-in-law's, were already making washers. In 1909, the year Maytag bought out his partners and created the Maytag Company, he added a new design that permitted the washer to be run with a power take-off and that added a wringer.

Maytag gave active management of the company to his sons in 1910 and moved to Chicago. In 1911 the company introduced a washer with an electric motor and the first reversible swinging wringer. Because electricity was then available only in limited areas, the company developed a washer run with a gasoline motor, introduced in 1915. That critical year was the first in which sales of washers surpassed the total sales of farm implements, and it was the year Maytag himself, having failed in automobile and railroad ventures, resumed a central role in company management. It was also the year when, at the urging of one of his sons, the company undertook its first national advertising campaign, one that had an immediate, dramatic impact on sales.

The engine that Maytag developed, a half-horsepower, two-cycle design, was the product around which the Maytag legend for quality perhaps first emerged. Quality standards were so rigorous that 94 percent of a production run was once rejected simply because compression was slightly below the promised level. A variety of manufacturers, from Sweden to the Philippines and China, adopted the widely admired engine, making Maytag for a time the largest small engine producer in the world. In 1919 the Maytag Multimotor was used to build the first power lawn mowers.

In 1922 Snyder perfected the Gyrafoam washer, which relied on violent water action to clean rather than on traditional rubbing methods. This product, a revolutionary change in design offering distinctly superior results, carried the company in just four years from thirty-eighth place and losing money (with annual sales of $2.5 million) to first place, $54 million in sales, and large profits. In 1921 Maytag stepped down as president, remaining as chairman of the board; he left an enduring legacy of devotion to quality and dependability in company products and an excellent marketing organization with high morale among its myriad retailers. Maytag remained deeply involved, but his primary continuing interest was radio advertising. In 1924 he sponsored a vocal ensemble, the Maytag Troubadours, and then experimented with daily afternoon "Household Talks" and a thirty-minute evening entertainment program. In 1928 stations in six major cities began carrying "The Maytag Happiness Hour." In 1935 Maytag sponsored broadcasts of University of Iowa football games, with announcer (and later U.S. president) Ronald "Dutch" Reagan.

Maytag was a politically active Republican, serving in the Iowa state senate from 1902 to 1912, for six years on the Newton city council as mayor from 1923 to 1925, and in 1925 as Iowa's first director of the state budget. Maytag made numerous gifts, especially in Newton, where he funded a public park and swimming pool, the Young Men's Christian Association building, and aid for local schools and hospitals. He died in Los Angeles, California.

• The Maytag Company, headquartered in Newton, Iowa, has extensive original Maytag material. A. B. Funk, *Fred L. Maytag: A Biography* (1936), which was privately printed, offers a detailed personal history, and Robert Hoover, *An American Quality Legend: How Maytag Saved Our Moms, Vexed the Competition, and Presaged America's Quality Revolution* (1993), offers a broader if somewhat unconventional business history. A long article on Maytag is "He Could Have Worked Harder," *Nation's Business*, May 1937, p. 112; and there are numerous book chapters on the company, such as the one in *Everybody's Business*, ed. Milton Moskowitz et al. (1990).

FRED CARSTENSEN

MAYWOOD, Augusta (5 Mar. 1825–3 Nov. 1876), ballerina, was born Augusta Williams in New York City, the daughter of the theatrical actors Henry Williams and Martha Bally. After her parents' marriage ended in 1828 and her mother's remarriage, Augusta took the surname of her stepfather, Robert Campbell Maywood. The manager of Philadelphia's Chestnut Street Theatre, he claimed credit for enrolling her in her first ballet lessons with Paul H. Hazard, a former Paris Opéra dancer. Maywood and her rival, Mary Ann Lee, studied together for two years before making their dance debut at Mrs. Williams's benefit performance. On 30 December 1837, Maywood appeared as Zoloe, the dancing *bayadère*, in François Auber's ballet-opera *La bayadère*. The twelve-year-old girl "caused a sensation among the veteran playgoers," who were "aston-

ished at her excellence" (*Philadelphia Public Ledger*, 10 Jan. 1838). Following her triumph, she traveled to New York City for a February debut at the Park Theatre. Critics were once again "astonished" by her talents and praised her "high degree of perfection" (*Spirit of the Times*, 6 Jan. and 17 Feb. 1838). The writer in *The Spirit of the Times* advised that "by all means should she go abroad at once, and commence a most diligent and thorough course of study of her art. If Miss Maywood . . . will but persevere to go through with all the indispensable drudgery, her career must inevitably prove brilliant and lucrative" (17 Feb. 1838).

Not long after, the young Maywood sailed off to France with her mother and enrolled in classes at the Paris Opéra with two of the greatest ballet teachers that France, the ballet capital of the world, had to offer. Jean Coralli, creator of *Giselle* and ballet master at the Opéra, was praised by the *Gazette musicale de Paris* for developing her into "one of the most original and most piquant dancers that one can imagine." In her other classes with Joseph Mazillier, *premier danseur* at the same institution, she galvanized her peers out of their complacency. Within less than two years she was invited to make her debut at the Opéra, a signal honor for this foreign youngster who had come from, as the poet Théophile Gautier termed it, the land of savages. For her debut performance at the Opéra on 11 November 1839, Coralli composed a special solo for her in *Le Diable boiteux*. Over and over again the words "original," "eccentric," and "astonishing" were applied to this "prodigy" whose athletic leaps challenged those of the two greatest male dancers of that century, Antoine Paul and Jules Perrot. Some compared her unconventional dance style to the movements of wild animals and called her a "wild doe," a "lively gazelle," or a "jaguar" (*Revue et Gazette Musicale de Paris*, 14 Nov. 1839).

Maywood was quickly appointed to the Opéra at a generous salary and appeared in other Coralli ballets, including *La Tarentule* and *La Gipsy*, star vehicles for the great Fanny Elssler. She danced in various opera divertissements and in two revived ballets, Louis-Jacques Milon's *Nina, ou La Folle par amour* and Jean Dauberval's *La Fille mal gardée*. The next season she was cast in *Le Diable amoureux*, which was to become the ballet sensation of the fall 1840 season.

Now fifteen years old, Maywood had tasted the glamour of being a star at the Opéra for a year. Her stepfather, for whom she harbored a lifelong aversion, was impatient for her to come home so he could earn some returns on his investment, but his plans were thwarted. Her favorite dancing partner, Charles Mabille, had become more than her onstage cavalier and made a bid to become her life partner as well. In 1840 the two made headlines across the Atlantic when they decided to elope and missed the performance, the latter an unforgivable sin that was to cost Maywood her Opéra contract.

After a series of engagements in the south of France at Lyon and Marseilles, where their daughter was born in 1842, the husband-and-wife team was appointed leading dancers at Lisbon's opera house. Maywood's interpretation of *Giselle* was praised for her "passion, agility, and grace" (quoted in Artur Michel, "Great American Ballerina," *Dance Magazine*, Nov. 1943, p. 30). Other ballets in her repertoire included *La Gipsy*, *Le Diable amoureux*, and the first one she ever danced in America, *La bayadère*. Maywood's marriage ended in 1845 when the ballerina allegedly eloped with yet another of her dancing partners and, after the birth of her second child, made her debut at Vienna's Kärntnerthor Theater as *Giselle*.

In Vienna she worked again under Fanny Elssler, but this time took on Elssler's leading roles, including that of Jules Perrot's *La Esmeralda*. After the birth of a son, in 1847 she followed Elssler to Italy, which was to become her home for the next twelve years and the scene of her greatest artistic triumphs. At La Scala, Maywood replaced Elssler as Margherita in Perrot's *Faust*. The newspaper *Il Trovatore* (26 Sept. 1855) extolled this "sublime" artist, whose "fanatic" partisans were said to respond with ecstatic fervor to her dancing.

Known as "the Queen of the Air" for her bravura technique and lauded as "the greatest dancer of the age" (*Il Trovatore*, Aug. 1855), she appeared in scores of Italian opera houses, major and minor, where her popularity was such that appearances had to be booked years ahead. She preferred to keep a tight rein on artistic matters and traveled with her own company, which included a ballet master, dancers, and costumes—an arrangement that was common in the United States, where there was a scarcity of trained dancers, but unique to Europe. Her most popular dramatic role was *Rita Gauthier*, with music by Verdi and plot adapted from *La Traviata*. She also staged a balletic version of *Uncle Tom's Cabin*, one of the few links to her American roots. In 1858 Maywood married Carlo Gardini and retired (they separated after three years). The next year she returned to Vienna, where she became director of an academy that included a ballet school; ten years later she was engaged as ballet mistress at a well-known theater.

Augusta Maywood was a brilliant shooting star whose prodigious talents shone only briefly across the American skies; however, her thirty years in Europe provided the perfect backdrop for her to achieve her potential. She earned rank as Italy's *celebrita danzante et mima assoluta* and won enduring fame as one of the greatest Romantic ballerinas. She died of smallpox in Leopoldville, Austria (now Lvov, Poland).

• An analysis of Maywood's early career in Paris and Philadelphia can be found in Maureen Needham [Costonis], "The Wild Doe: Augusta Maywood in Paris," *Dance Chronicle* (1994): 123–48. Marian Hannah Winter is the first dance historian of note to discuss the significance of Maywood's career in "Augusta Maywood," *Chronicles of the American Dance*, ed. Paul Magriel (1948), pp. 119–37; Parmenia Migel traces Maywood's career throughout Europe in *The Ballerinas: From the Court of Louis XIV to Pavlova* (1972), pp. 179–93.

MAUREEN NEEDHAM

MAZAKUTEMANI, Paul (1806?–6 Jan. 1885), Wahpeton Dakota known for his oratorical skill and pro-white stance in the Dakota War of 1862, was born probably at Lac qui Parle, Minnesota, the son of a Mdewakanton man and Old Eve, a Wahpeton woman. His Indian name translates as Shoots Iron [Gun] as He Walks; he was also known as Little Paul.

Mazakutemani was raised as a typical hunter and warrior but became one of the first Wahpetons to receive an education in Dr. Thomas Williamson's school at Lac qui Parle. In 1838 he was converted to Christianity and later joined Williamson's mission church (Presbyterian). In the mid-1850s he was elected president of the Hazelwood Republic, a farming group of Christianized Dakotas who were under the sponsorship of missionary Stephen R. Riggs near Yellow Medicine Agency.

Mazakutemani became famous in 1857 when he along with John Other Day and another comrade rescued Abbie Gardner from the Inkpaduta band. He was honored by territorial governor Samuel Medary in St. Paul (27 June 1857) and said in part,

The American people are a great people—a strong nation; and if they wished to, could kill all our people, but they had better judgment, and permitted the Indians to go themselves and hunt up the poor girl. . . . We believed . . . that we would be killed ourselves; but . . . we desired to show our love to the white people.

When government authorities coerced the Dakotas into making a punitive expedition against Inkpaduta's band in August 1857, Mazakutemani was chosen as their speaker: "I am not a chief among the Indians . . . [but] the white people have declared me a chief, and I suppose I am able to do something."

Thereafter Mazakutemani was the leading speaker for the Wahpeton tribe. In 1858 he was a member of the Dakota delegation to Washington. He initially objected to the sale of the northern half of the reservation, feeling that it would deprive his people of timber and bring whiskey sellers closer. However, the sale of the land was forced upon the Dakota leaders, and he signed the treaty.

By 1860 Mazakutemani was the single most prominent leader of the pro-civilization movement among the Wahpetons. During the Dakota War of 1862 against the United States, he was appointed speaker of the upper Dakota soldiers' lodge. He used his position to frustrate the prosecution of the war. In several councils he spoke strongly against the war and of his desire to have the mixed-blood and white captive women and children released. In one speech he derided the warriors, concluding, "I am ashamed of the way you have acted toward the captives. Fight the whites if you desire to, but do it like brave men. Give me the captives and I will carry them to Fort Ridgely." Captive Samuel Brown noted that Mazakutemani was not deterred "from expressing himself without any fear whatever." Thomas Robertson called him "the man of the hour."

Mazakutemani entered into secret communications with Colonel Henry Sibley during the war. He wrote on 15 September 1862, "I have tried to do all that I could to get the captives free. . . . But Little Crow won't give them up." When the hostile faction was finally defeated, Mazakutemani remained at "Camp Release" with those who wished to surrender. He was the first to greet Sibley: "I have grown up like a child of yours. With what is yours, you have caused me to grow. . . . With a clean hand I take your hand."

Afterward Mazakutemani served as a scout under Major Robert Rose at Fort Wadsworth, South Dakota, and was in charge of the Twin Lakes scout camp. It was said, perhaps with some exaggeration, that the scouts killed more hostile Dakotas than Sibley's army did during his campaigns. In 1866 Mazakutemani received $500 for his services to the whites during the war and returned to farming.

Mazakutemani's later years were devoted to his eldership of a Dakota church. He was a featured guest speaker on 30 September 1871 before the Presbyterian Synod at Rochester, Minnesota. He described his work in this way: "I try to carry a candle into the dark corners. Where I go, I speak of the Savior and the way of salvation." He also spoke at a Dakota mission convention in Minneapolis in the fall of 1873. In 1880 he wrote his reminiscences, which were translated and published by Stephen R. Riggs. He died at the Sisseton Reservation and was buried at Long Hollow.

Mazakutemani was a notable Dakota orator and a leader in the pro-Christian "civilization" movement. He tried to free the captives taken during the Dakota War of 1862 and was thus a hero to both the whites and the antiwar Dakotas. Riggs considered him a native orator, a fine diplomatist, and a splendid manager of Indians.

• A short autobiographical account is in Stephen R. Riggs, trans., "Narrative of Paul Mazakootemane," *Minnesota Historical Collections* 3 (1880): 82–90; a short biography is in Thomas Hughes, *Indian Chiefs of Southern Minnesota* (1927). Several of Mazakutemani's speeches are in Mark Diedrich, comp., *Dakota Oratory* (1989), and *St. Paul Weekly Pioneer*, 6 Oct. 1871. An account of the treaty making of 1858 is in Barbara T. Newcombe, "'A Portion of the American People,'" *Minnesota History* 45 (1976): 83–96. Mazakutemani's letter to Sibley is in Isaac Heard, *History of the Sioux War and Massacres of 1862 and 1863* (1863). Other information can be found in Gary C. Anderson and Alan Woolworth, eds., *Through Dakota Eyes* (1988), and Stephen R. Riggs, *Mary and I* (1880).

MARK F. DIEDRICH

MAZZEI, Philip (25 Dec. 1730–19 Mar. 1816), physician, merchant, and agent of Virginia during the American Revolution, was born Filippo Mazzei in Poggio-a-Caiano, Italy, the son of Domenico Mazzei, a tradesman, and Maria Elisabetta di Guissepe del Conte. He studied medicine in nearby Florence, and in 1755 he joined the practice of a Dr. Salinas in Smyrna, Turkey. By year's end he took passage for England as a ship's doctor. Shortly after his arrival in London in 1756, he began an import-export business that enjoyed moderate success for the next sixteen years.

In 1772 Mazzei returned to Tuscany with plans for an agricultural venture in America. Upon approval of the grand duke, he collected grape and olive cuttings and recruited a number of peasant viticulturists to accompany him. In 1773 he arrived in Virginia, purchased a property next to Thomas Jefferson's "Monticello" that he called "Colle," and made the first large planting of vinifera grapes in the colonies. Mazzei married Marie Hautefeuille Martin, a widow, in 1774. They had no children.

Mazzei quickly became Jefferson's friend and associate and was active in the social and political life of Albemarle County. In 1775 he joined in the forcible removal of arms from the governor's palace and entered the local militia as a private. Mazzei's draft "Instructions of Freeholders of Albemarle County to Their Delegates in Convention" was used by Jefferson when he attempted to revise the Virginia constitution. Mazzei also published essays in the *Virginia Gazette* and in Italian journals, explaining and defending the American struggle for liberty.

In 1779 Governor Patrick Henry appointed Mazzei as Virginia's agent in Europe, instructing him to seek loans from Tuscany and other countries. En route to Europe, Mazzei was captured by a British privateer and held in New York for several months. He had jettisoned his papers upon his capture, thus, he finally arrived in Europe lacking the credentials to carry out his mission. In any case, Benjamin Franklin, whom Mazzei had known during his London years and who disapproved of separate states seeking foreign loans, foiled Mazzei's efforts on Virginia's behalf whenever he could. Nevertheless, Mazzei continued his money-raising efforts, interspersed with regular written reports to Virginia's governor and with the publication of his pamphlets and newspaper essays on behalf of the American cause. His continued advocacy of that cause in Europe brought praise from John Adams and confirmed Jefferson's high opinion of Mazzei as "a zealous Whig."

Returning to Virginia in 1783, Mazzei found that Colle had been used to house prisoners of war; the vineyard and orchard were destroyed. With Virginia's payments for his European services, he purchased a property in Richmond and plunged back into public life. In mid-1784 he was a prime mover and organizer of the Constitutional Society, whose purpose was "preserving and handing down to posterity . . . pure and sacred principles of liberty." Members were to write regular papers on public policy, which the society was to collect and publish in popular forums. Mazzei offered the first two. In one he proposed strong sumptuary laws to encourage frugality and republican morals. In the other he strongly opposed the issuance of paper money.

He now sought a consular post where he could put his European and business experience to use, but Congress did not permit naturalized citizens to hold official positions abroad. When Jefferson was appointed minister to Paris, Mazzei sent him long letters of advice and information about the leading figures in the French government, with whom he had worked when he was Virginia's agent. The next year he decided to go to Paris himself and left the United States for good in June 1785.

In Paris he rejoined the circle of figures in the government and the salons who had been supporters of America. He continued to seek employment from Jefferson or any other American agency, with no success. Despite that, he asked Jefferson's advice and approval for every one of his endeavors as long as Jefferson was minister in Paris. In 1788 he published in French the four-volume *Political and Historical Researches on the United States*, which corrected the factual errors and anti-American prejudices of similarly titled volumes by Gabriel Bonnot de Mably and Guillaume-Thomas-François de Raynal. Well received in France, Mazzei's work was translated into German.

In the same year Mazzei accepted an appointment as correspondent to Stanislas II, king of Poland, a position that was changed to chargé d'affaires in 1789. His copious correspondence with Stanislas included commentary on American and European political life as well as counsel about the new Polish constitution of May 1791.

When the French Revolution began, Mazzei remained close to leaders like the marquis de Lafayette and the marquis de Condorcet. He joined a group of moderate constitutional monarchists to form the Society of 1789 and became its corresponding secretary. Dismayed by the radical turn of the revolution, in 1791 he accepted Stanislas's invitation to come to Warsaw as a privy councilor. Upon the second partition of Poland in 1792, he retired from that post and settled in Pisa, Italy.

His first wife having died in 1788, Mazzei married Antonia Antoni in 1796; they had one child. No longer active in public life, he continued a wide correspondence with political and intellectual figures in a half-dozen countries. Preeminent among these were his mentors and friends from his Virginia days. Jefferson's letter of 24 April 1796 was highly critical of Federalist "monarchical" tendencies and suggested that President George Washington was easily manipulated by his advisers. Mazzei gave copies to friends, and it was then published with varied content in European and American newspapers. The "Mazzei Letter" created a storm of criticism for Jefferson, but the event did not shake their friendship. In 1805 Jefferson commissioned Mazzei to recruit Italian sculptors for work on the new Capitol building in Washington, D.C.

In 1813 Mazzei published *Memoirs of the Life and Peregrinations of the Florentine, Philip Mazzei*. Despite that title, in many documents of that era he still signed himself, "Philip Mazzei, Citizen of the United States of America." The notices in the American press after his death in Pisa seemed to confirm that identification, and during bicentennial celebrations of American independence, the U.S. Postal Service issued a stamp with the legend, "Philip Mazzei, American Patriot."

• For Mazzei's papers see M. M. Marchione, *Philip Mazzei: The Comprehensive Microform Edition of His Papers, 1730–1816, with Guide and Index* (1982). All the documents in this microfilm edition are on deposit at the American Philosophical Society, Philadelphia. See also Marchione et al., eds., *Philip Mazzei: Selected Writings and Correspondence* (3 vols., 1983). Several of Mazzei's books have been translated, including *My Life and Wanderings* (Memorie della vita e delle peregrinazioni del fiorentino Filippo Mazzei), trans. E. Scalia and Marchione (1980); and C. D. Sherman, ed., *Philip Mazzei: Researches on the United States* (Recherches historiques et politiques sur les Etats-Unis de l'Amérique septentrionale) (1976). On the famous "Mazzei Letter," see H. R. Marraro, "The Four Versions of Jefferson's Letter to Mazzei," *William and Mary Quarterly*, 2d ser., 22 (Jan. 1942): 18–29.

STANLEY J. IDZERDA

MAZZUCHELLI, Samuel Charles (4 Nov. 1806–23 Feb. 1864), Catholic priest, missionary, and educator, was born in Milan, Italy, the son of Luigi Mazzuchelli, a merchant, and Rachele Merlini. He came from a distinguished Lombard family of long-remembered artists, scholars, merchants, and public servants. After his education in Milan and Lugano, Switzerland, the youth believed himself called to religious life in the worldwide Order of Preachers, or Dominican friars, founded by St. Dominic. After secondary schooling Mazzuchelli entered the novitiate of the order and made his studies in Rome at the ancient Basilica of Santa Sabina on the Aventine. As a youth of twenty-two he came to the United States, one of the earliest Italian immigrants, to serve in a role little known among the Mazzuchellis: that of a Catholic missionary.

The young man was welcomed by the frontier bishop of Ohio, Edward Dominic Fenwick, to the river town of Cincinnati, "Queen City of the West." He then studied English and theology in a log cabin priory at Somerset, Ohio, and was ordained a priest at the age of twenty-three. Sent on mission to the northwest frontier in 1830, his first lone ministry centered at Mackinac Island near the Canadian boundary and reached out to all of present-day Wisconsin and upper Michigan. The young Mazzuchelli's life began to merge with and to influence a society of many cultures on the frontier of the Old Northwest. These included the Menominee, Winnebago, Ottawa, and Chippewa natives; the French Canadian fur traders and voyageurs; American officials; and soldiers at five forts, from Sault Ste. Marie at the Canadian border down the roadless wilderness to Prairie du Chien on the upper Mississippi River.

Mazzuchelli lived for months at a time among the native peoples, eager to learn from them and bring them knowledge of the gospel while respecting their cultures. He wrote later of their families and way of life, their religion, their love for children and respect for the elderly, their skill at rice gathering, ice fishing, and making maple syrup. He opened a school in 1834 at Green Bay, Wisconsin, for the Menominees and attempted to establish one for the Winnebagoes, insisting on three principles not then encouraged by U.S. agents for Indian Affairs: use of the native language, rather than English; employment of native teachers; and not separating children from their families. His plan included adult education, but this was left unrealized for lack of the expected government grants for education. On behalf of all the tribes he protested to Congress against the tribal removal policy of the Jacksonian government, reminding his congressman that native families regretted leaving their homes as much as he did. In 1833 in Detroit Mazzuchelli published a small prayerbook for the Winnebago, similar in format to the popular New England primer. It was a first among publications in the Sioux tongue. He also published an 1834 Chippewa calendar for the natives, the first item ever printed in Wisconsin.

In 1835 Mazzuchelli was assigned to serve with settlers moving into the upper Mississippi Valley and later assisted Bishop Mathias Loras. He worked first among the lead miners, centered at Galena and Dubuque, in a milieu as rough—and sometimes gainful—as the later gold mines in California. As families arrived from the East and the South by way of the Great River, Father Mazzuchelli cooperated with pioneers of various faiths to establish their first towns in Iowa, Wisconsin, and northwest Illinois. They looked to him to help form Christian communities and build churches, cherishing his gift for architecture and his willingness to work side by side with them in the stone quarry or woodworker's cabin. With their collaboration he initiated forty parish foundations, from Mackinac Island on the north to Keokuk, Iowa, on the south. When the territories of Michigan, Wisconsin, and Iowa began to take permanent shape and sought statehood, the priest worked with their civic leaders, who in 1836 invited him to be chaplain and speaker of the first Wisconsin legislature.

In 1844 Mazzuchelli wrote, for the Italian people, an account of his experiences in the United States, including descriptions of the Menominee and Winnebago peoples and the early pioneers. Called *Memorie* (Memories), the volume covered only his first fourteen years in the United States. It offered readers insights concerning the people of a young nation hardly known to his fellow Italians, including their democratic government, the influence of the press, the frontier religions, government policy concerning religion, and the advantages of American separation of church and state.

Realizing keenly the need for education on the frontier, Mazzuchelli provided institutions and teachers for the settlers from primary through secondary classes and college. He founded Sinsinawa Mound College for men in southwest Wisconsin Territory in 1846, which gave degrees until its close at the end of the Civil War. At the same location in 1847 he invited young women to join a nucleus of dedicated teachers to staff district and parish schools. These became the first Sin-

sinawa Dominican Sisters. With steady growth of membership they expanded their ministry to open St. Clara Academy in 1854, which led to the founding of other high schools and two colleges: Rosary in River Forest, Illinois, and Edgewood in Madison, Wisconsin. From 1850 to 1864 Mazzuchelli remained pastor of several parishes, directed St. Clara Academy, and guided the Dominican sisters, especially by writing a "Rule" for their way of life. Mazzuchelli died in Benton, Wisconsin.

Public witness to Mazzuchelli's great-hearted ministry has been given throughout the late nineteenth and twentieth centuries by descendants of the people who knew him to the sixth generation. Their remembrance and testimony has emphasized the conviction that Mazzuchelli was a man of heroic kindness, wisdom, and courage: a model of unselfishness. That continuing vox populi has led, since the centenary of his death in 1964, to petitions that officials of the Catholic Church recognize Mazzuchelli as a believable hero, an American saint. The first step in that recognition took place in July 1993 when Pope John Paul II declared him worthy of the title "Venerable."

• No papers of Mazzuchelli are extant. His memoirs are available in Maria Michele Armato and Mary Jeremy Finnegan, trans., *The Memoirs of Father Samuel Mazzuchelli* (1967). His career is discussed in Jo Bartels Alderson and J. Michael, *The Man Mazzuchelli* (1974), and Mary Nona McGreal, *Samuel Mazzuchelli O.P.: A Kaleidoscope of Scenes from His Life* (1973; repr. 1994).

MARY NONA MCGREAL

MCADIE, Alexander George (4 Aug. 1863–1 Nov. 1943), meteorologist, was born in New York City, the son of John McAdie, a printer, and Anne Sinclair. After attending public schools in New York City, McAdie earned an A.B. and an A.M. from the College of the City of New York in 1881, where he studied atmospheric phenomena. At the time the U.S. Army Signal Corps, which was in charge of the weather service for the federal government, was looking for young scientists to fill its ranks. McAdie responded to the call and was accepted. He spent the first half of 1882 in training at Fort Myer in Arlington, Virginia. He was then sent to Harvard to study meteorological physics, receiving his second A.M. in 1885.

During his time in Cambridge, McAdie met MIT student Abbott Lawrence Rotch, who established the Blue Hill Meteorological Observatory in 1884. McAdie was offered the post of observer, but he declined. He visited Blue Hill, however, in 1885, 1891, and 1892 to study atmospheric electricity using kites. This was a pioneer approach to the study of aerial phenomena, one that was a valuable alternative to the more costly balloon flights in use at the time. Instruments could easily be attached to the kite and lifted to an altitude sufficient to measure barometric pressure, wind directional shifts, and other phenomena.

After leaving Harvard, McAdie served as an assistant in the Physical Laboratory of the Signal Service in

Washington, D.C. His service there was briefly interrupted by a stint as observer at the St. Paul observatory in Minnesota during the winter of 1887–1888. A year later he resigned from the laboratory and taught physics and meteorology at Clark University in Worcester, Massachusetts. In 1891 he returned to Washington to join the newly established U.S. Weather Bureau, where he remained until 1895. He met and married Mary Randolph Browne in 1893; they had no children.

In 1895 McAdie moved to the San Francisco office of the bureau, where he remained for eighteen years. In 1903 he became a professor of meteorology at the California section of the Climate and Crop Service, where he was also its director, and in 1906, following the San Francisco earthquake, he founded the Seismological Society of the Pacific.

McAdie was offered and accepted an appointment in 1913 as director of the Blue Hill Observatory, which had by then become affiliated with Harvard University. He later became the first person to hold the Abbott Lawrence Rotch Chair in Meteorology. During his tenure he urged the adoption of scientific units and standard annotations in meteorology, emphasizing in particular the value of the metric system, the kilobar, and the "kelvin kilograd" scale—all of which were logical changes, but were abandoned in favor of established practices. During World War I, McAdie trained ensigns for a North Atlantic weather service and commanded the officers of the aerographic section overseas. In fact, McAdie invented the term "aerography" in 1916, defining it as the science of the structure of the atmosphere. He recognized the necessity of accurate weather predictions for aviation and suggested that pilots be provided with cross sections of weather patterns along air routes.

Following his retirement from Harvard in 1931, McAdie moved to Virginia where, although no longer actively involved in meteorology, he communicated new ideas to friends—including the possibility of harnessing atmospheric electricity for power production. While he did not contribute many new discoveries to meteorological science, he expanded its scope by advocating standardization of measure units. He also presided over various scientific groups, including the Astronomical Society of the Pacific (1912) and the Seismological Society of America (1915–1916), of which he was the founder. His writing also distinguished him from others in his field with its poetic and powerful style. Among his sixteen books and more than 400 articles, his best works include *The Principles of Aerography* (1917), a textbook written for his students, and *Cloud Formations as Hazards in Aviation* (1929). He also produced early studies on how smoke pollutes the atmosphere.

McAdie's background, often described as that of a "gentleman scientist," points to his varied interests, which ranged from meteorology to military tactics, electricity, aviation, and seismology. His capacity for switching from advanced scientific discourse to "layman's English" made his scientific writings quite popular, as he interwove witticisms with scientific facts. This style made him more recognizable to the public than many other scientists and helps explain the great affection expressed to him upon his retirement. He died in Elizabeth City, Virginia.

• A biographical sketch and a complete bibliography of McAdie's publications is in Mary R. B. McAdie, ed., *Alexander McAdie: Scientist and Writer* (1949). Ronald Whitnah, *A History of the United States Weather Bureau* (1961), and Roy Popkin, *The Environmental Science Services Administration* (1967), both contain material that help place McAdie in context.

GUILLAUME DE SYON

MCADOO, William Gibbs (31 Oct. 1863–1 Feb. 1941), railroad executive, secretary of the treasury, and U.S. senator, was born in Marietta, Georgia, the son of William Gibbs McAdoo, Sr., and Mary Faith Floyd. His father served in the Tennessee state government and as attorney general in Knoxville before the Civil War. In 1863 his parents moved to Georgia intending to reside on his mother's family plantation, but bleak prospects forced them to stop in Marietta and then settle in Milledgeville, the old state capital and McAdoo's childhood home. During the last years of the war, McAdoo's father fought in Georgia as a Confederate officer. Like many southerners McAdoo's parents never recovered financially after the war, but they tried to replace material advantage with intellectual pursuits. His mother published several romantic novels of the Old South, and both parents wrote essays and book reviews for the local press. McAdoo's father struggled to find work in Milledgeville before securing a professorship at the University of Tennessee in 1877 and moving the family back to Knoxville.

As a young man McAdoo exhibited the worldly ambition his father lacked. In 1882 he left his studies at the University of Tennessee to accept a position as deputy clerk of the U.S. Circuit Court in Chattanooga. An early interest in politics led him to the 1884 Democratic National Convention in Chicago, where he served as an alternate delegate from his home district. He took advantage of his position as court clerk to study law and passed the bar examination in 1885. That year he married Sarah Houstoun Fleming; they had six children. As a lawyer he helped promote the Chattanooga segment of a proposed rail line and in return became the local counsel for the Richmond & Danville Railroad, a position he used to learn the fundamentals of the business. In 1889 he invested his entire savings of $25,000 in the reorganized Knoxville Street Railway Company, which he served as president. Using funds solicited from a Philadelphia bank, he built the company into one of the first electrified city railways, but his operation tumbled into receivership in 1892 because he had overreached his financial resources and the available technology.

McAdoo then moved his family to New York City and started a fledgling business selling railroad bonds and other securities. He gained considerable expertise in the financial conditions of the major rail lines. While riding daily on the overcrowded ferries shuttling commuters across the Hudson River into Manhattan, McAdoo recognized that a railway tunnel would vastly improve the service. When he discovered that a half-finished shaft lay abandoned under the river, he gathered all the financial and engineering data available on the former project and in 1901 started a relentless campaign to secure investors to resurrect the Hudson tunnel. Eight years and $70 million later he completed twin tunnels under the river that connected by subway to the midtown lines. The undisputed success of the "McAdoo Tunnels" made him a local celebrity and established him as one of the financial and political leaders of the city.

As president of the Hudson and Manhattan Railway (later Railroad) Company, McAdoo earned a reputation for progressive management of a public utility. Adopting the policy "the public be pleased" in deliberate opposition to the "public be damned" behavior of other railway operators, he sacrificed high profits for steady growth, tried new ideas like women-only cars, and insisted on equal pay for male and female employees. As a proponent of business reform, he made the Hudson and Manhattan a showcase for safe, efficient operation and earned unprecedented public support.

In 1910 McAdoo became an active supporter of Woodrow Wilson's New Jersey gubernatorial campaign and in 1912 was in the forefront of a grass-roots effort to nominate Wilson for president. During that contest McAdoo served as an able Wilson lieutenant and took full control of the campaign for a brief time at the Democratic convention. Although he disclaimed any ulterior motive for his efforts, he accepted Wilson's offer of a cabinet position with alacrity. Having proven himself as a railroad executive, McAdoo was an acceptable if not obvious choice for secretary of the treasury. He won Senate approval despite the financial community's fears of his progressive record and penchant for independent action. His first wife died in 1912, and in 1914 he married Eleanor Wilson, the president's daughter. They had two children.

McAdoo presided over a virtual revolution in the management of the nation's money supply and a dramatic increase in the economic power of the federal government. Beginning with tariff reform, banking regulation, and a personal income tax, he helped implement much of Wilson's New Freedom program, allegedly designed to wrest the country from the grip of monopoly. As a major architect of the Federal Reserve System, he assured his position as one of the most influential of the country's Treasury leaders. Similarly, he helped set up a federal farm loan program that sought to protect the nation's agricultural mortgages from the ravages of the market. Never an ideologue, McAdoo negotiated a workable combination of public and private control of the nation's currency, although he consistently irritated leading financiers by refusing to seek their counsel in formulating his plans. One contemporary newswriter asserted, "When Secretary McAdoo walks in Wall Street he carries his hat on his head—not in his hand" (Broesamle, p. 146). Still, McAdoo's background as a successful corporate executive brought an unprecedented business sense to his government work, and he ran the Treasury Department as efficiently as he had the Hudson and Manhattan Railway.

External events magnified McAdoo's personal strengths as he took charge of important aspects of the only economy capable of ensuring an Allied victory in Europe during World War I. In addition to coordinating massive loans to the European powers, he pushed for the creation of the U.S. Shipping Board to maintain transatlantic traffic and was responsible for creating and promoting the successful Liberty Loan campaigns, which generated almost $17 billion from the American public in less than two years. Furthermore, when the nation's railroad system threatened to grind to a halt under the strain of the wartime economy, Wilson approved a government takeover of the network and appointed McAdoo as director general of the railroads. In this position McAdoo in 1918 successfully coordinated conflicting lines, eliminated the backlog of shipments, and intervened on behalf of railway employees to increase wages and improve working conditions. As this activity suggests, McAdoo's tireless efforts and his practical attitude were vital to America's successful role in the war at a time when government officials and the heads of private industry were forced by circumstance to work together and coordinate their activities on an unprecedented level.

Overall, McAdoo was a dedicated and innovative public servant, but years of intense effort left him physically drained and financially insecure. Family obligations coupled with the expenses of his government position made it difficult for him to live on his official salary. For this reason he resigned from the cabinet three days after the signing of the armistice in November 1918, fulfilling his promise to stay throughout the war.

Once out of office McAdoo plunged into his legal practice in an effort to rebuild his financial situation. Some political analysts considered him a potential Democratic nominee for the 1920 presidential election. Wilson was unwilling to substantiate rumors that his son-in-law had become the "crown prince" of the party, and McAdoo was averse to seeking the nomination while Wilson was still in office. McAdoo also realized that his cabinet record and support of Prohibition made any political success as a resident of New York doubtful. With this in mind, he positioned himself for the next election by moving to California and aligning with the progressive wing of the Democratic party there.

This strategy enabled McAdoo to begin the 1924 campaign as a strong favorite for the Democratic presidential nomination. Running as a strict prohibitionist and preaching against the evils of Wall Street and the East Coast political machines, he intended to succeed William Jennings Bryan as the champion of the agrarian West. Ironically, information from a Senate investigation forced him to fend off charges of personal corruption in January 1924, when the public learned that he had recently performed legal work on a large retainer for Edward L. Doheny, the Los Angeles oilman implicated in the unraveling Teapot Dome oil scandal. McAdoo was also branded as a supporter of the Ku Klux Klan because he refused to alienate his southern constituency by disavowing the Klan. After this prelude, the 1924 convention in New York City turned into an embarrassing spectacle that left the delegates deadlocked between McAdoo and New York governor Alfred E. Smith. After sixteen days and 103 ballots, the party finally settled on John W. Davis as a weak compromise.

Despite this catastrophe, McAdoo proved his resiliency and persistence when he resurrected his political life and in 1932 won a U.S. Senate seat from California as a staunch supporter of Franklin D. Roosevelt's New Deal. McAdoo's election was well timed to take advantage of his record as a politician who could respond appropriately to a crisis. In particular, the worsening depression and the threat of civil unrest demanded government intervention and highlighted McAdoo's previous experience during the First World War. For that reason, he was most helpful in the early years of the New Deal when the Roosevelt administration took immediate action to stabilize the economy and head off the threat of more radical alternatives. In 1934 his second marriage ended in divorce, and in 1935 he married Doris Cross. They had no children. Defeated for reelection in 1938, McAdoo died in Washington, D.C.

Despite his abilities, McAdoo could never completely overcome the contradictions that ruined his presidential chances in 1924. Ultimately, his practicality and nonideological approach to politics led many to mistrust his motives. This was especially true in the 1920s when his list of legal clients included large corporations, wealthy industrialists, and California socialites. Although publicly McAdoo was known for being forthright and somewhat aloof, he had an easy sense of humor and a long list of friends. He also earned a reputation as a daredevil when it came to speed and was involved in a number of serious automobile crashes at a time when the nation had yet to embrace the new mode of transportation.

• McAdoo's private papers and those of Eleanor Wilson McAdoo are among the manuscripts of the Library of Congress and provide an extensive record of his public life. McAdoo's autobiography, *Crowded Years: The Reminiscences of William G. McAdoo* (1931), ghostwritten by W. E. Woodward, is an engaging but unreflective review of his life intended for the popular press. For McAdoo's own description of his work on the Hudson and Manhattan Railroad see William G. McAdoo, "The Soul of a Corporation," *World's Work*, Mar. 1912, 579–92. For an early appraisal of his career and personality see Burton J. Hendrick, "McAdoo and the Subway," *McClure's Magazine*, Mar. 1911, 485–99. His political position in 1920 is analyzed in Mark Sullivan, "McAdoo's Chances for the Democratic Nomination," *World's Work*, May–Oct. 1923, 193–201. Mary Synon, *McAdoo: The Man and His Times: A Panorama in Democracy* (1924), is a highly embellished campaign biography written by a former Treasury employee. The best critical source is John J. Broesamle, *William Gibbs McAdoo: A Passion for Change, 1863–1917* (1973), which was intended as the first volume of a multivolume work and therefore covers McAdoo's career only to America's entrance in World War I. For an appraisal of McAdoo's role in the 1924 election see Herbert A. Gelbart, "The Anti-McAdoo Movement of 1924" (Ph.D. diss., New York Univ., 1978). An obituary is in the *New York Times*, 2 Feb. 1941.

MARTIN R. ANSELL

MCAFEE, Robert Breckinridge (18 Feb. 1784–12 Mar. 1849), historian and statesman, was born on the banks of the Salt River, four miles from Harrodsburg, Kentucky, the son of Robert McAfee and Anne McCoun. His father, one of Kentucky's earliest explorers and settlers, was killed in 1795 while taking a load of goods to New Orleans. Since his mother had already died, McAfee was left in the care of his brother Samuel and his father's executors, James McCoun and John Breckinridge. Just before his father's departure for New Orleans, young McAfee had moved to Lexington to attend school. For much of the time between 1795 and 1797 he studied at Transylvania Seminary, but in November 1797 money problems forced his return to his brother's home.

McAfee was fond of reading and had acquired a library of about fifty books by the time he left Lexington. Back on the Salt River, he again attended a local school and joined a debating society, where he learned public speaking. In 1799 he moved to Danville, Kentucky, to attend Mahan's School. While in Danville, physician Ephraim McDowell offered him room and board if he would study medicine. He declined because he had already determined to become a lawyer. John Breckinridge then offered him the use of his law office and books, and in January 1800 he began to read law with Breckinridge. He completed his studies in September 1801, when he received a license to practice law, although he was not yet eighteen.

McAfee moved back to his brother Samuel's, where he remained until March 1805. He then took up residence in his old family home, where he lived for the remainder of his life. In 1807 he married Mary Cardwell, with whom he had several children, most of whom did not survive to adulthood. His law practice grew slowly, since he lived so far from town, and he was continually pressed for money until his father's estate, which had been tied up in lawsuits over conflicting land claims, was finally settled in favor of the McAfees in 1820.

A Jeffersonian Republican, McAfee made a speech in 1803 in favor of the acquisition of Louisiana and prepared to go there if troops were needed. In 1804 he began to write historical sketches of the early settlements in Kentucky. He was elected to the Kentucky House of Representatives in 1810 and continued there until 1815.

McAfee entered the army at the beginning of the War of 1812, and in 1813 he was commissioned captain in Colonel Richard M. Johnson's regiment. He commanded the largest company in that regiment at the victorious battle of the Thames on 5 October 1813. During the war, he kept a journal, which later served as the basis for his book, *The History of the Late War in the Western Country* (1816).

In 1819–1820 McAfee again served in the Kentucky house. The following year, he was elected to the state senate, where he remained until 1824, when he was elected lieutenant governor on the Relief party ticket with Joseph Desha as governor. At the time of this election, Kentucky was experiencing the political and economic furor known as the Old Court–New Court struggle. The state had passed debtor relief laws, which the Kentucky Court of Appeals had struck down. Relief partisans passed a bill in 1824 reorganizing the court system by abolishing the old court of appeals and creating a new one. The old court refused to step aside, and for a time the state had rival courts of appeals, which caused a state of anarchy bordering on civil war. By 1825, however, supporters of the old court had won control of the Kentucky house, which in November passed a bill repealing the new court legislation. When the bill went to the senate, where McAfee presided, he broke a tie vote, thereby killing the repeal bill. At the following election, old court partisans won control of the senate and proceeded to repeal the new court act.

In 1829 McAfee was nominated for Congress but declined to run. He returned to the Kentucky house for 1830–1832 and in the latter year served as a delegate to the Democratic National Convention, which nominated Andrew Jackson. In 1833 Jackson appointed him chargé d'affaires to Colombia, a post he held until 1837. He again served in the Kentucky Senate from 1841–1845 and in 1842 was on the Board of Visitors of the U.S. Military Academy at West Point. A dedicated Presbyterian, for many years he was active in the New Providence Church in Mercer County. He died at his home. Despite years of public service, perhaps his most lasting contribution can be found in his journals and historical writings, which detail much about the early years of Kentucky settlement through the War of 1812.

• A collection of McAfee's papers, including minutes of an 1824 meeting he chaired that proposed exploration of the earth's polar regions, is located at the Kentucky Historical Society, Frankfort. Published transcriptions of McAfee's accounts of his family's settlement on the Salt River and his journal of the War of 1812 include "The Life and Times of Robert B. McAfee and His Family and Connections: Written by Himself," *Register of the Kentucky Historical Society* 25 (1927): 4–37, 111–43, 215–37; "The McAfee Papers: Book and Journal of Robt. B. McAfee's Mounted Company, in Col. Richard M. Johnson's Regiment, from May 19th, 1813, Including Orders, &c.," *Register of the Kentucky Historical Society* 26 (1928): 4–23, 107–36, 236–48; and "The History of the Rise and Progress of the First Settlement on Salt River and Establishment of the New Providence Church," *Register of the Kentucky Historical Society* 29 (1931): 1–17, 117–32, 231–45. For the McAfee family genealogy, see Neander M.

Woods, *The Woods-McAfee Memorial* (1905). On the Old Court–New Court struggle, see Arndt M. Stickles, *The Critical Court Struggle in Kentucky, 1819–1829* (1929).

MELBA PORTER HAY

MCALEXANDER, Ulysses Grant (30 Aug. 1864–18 Sept. 1936), soldier, was born in Dundas, Minnesota, the son of C. P. McAlexander and Margaret Tilton, farmers. His father, a former Union lieutenant in the Civil War, named his first son for the Federal officer he most admired. The family moved to Kansas, and McAlexander earned an appointment to the U.S. Military Academy at West Point, New York, in 1883. Graduating with the class of 1887, he was commissioned as a second lieutenant of infantry. That year he married May Skinner; they had one son.

During his early military career, McAlexander was a professor of military science and tactics at Iowa Wesleyan University from 1891 to 1895. In 1898 he participated in the Spanish-American War in Cuba, rising to the rank of captain of volunteers. In the Santiago campaign he was cited for gallantry in action. Promoted to captain in the regular army in 1899, he fought in the Philippine insurrection from 1900 until 1902, the first of three tours in the Philippines. He was again professor of military science and tactics, this time at Oregon State Agricultural College, before returning to the Philippines, 1905–1906. In 1905 he published *History of the Thirteenth Regiment, U.S. Infantry.* The second Philippine tour was followed by a general staff assignment from 1906 to 1907. Promoted to major in 1911, he spent 1912–1915 in the Philippines, then rose to lieutenant colonel in 1916.

On the eve of U.S. entry into World War I, McAlexander returned to Oregon State Agricultural College. He was swept up in the preparedness movement in 1916, detailed to duties as an instructor and inspector with the Oregon National Guard. A month after Congress declared war, he was promoted to full colonel and given command of the Eighteenth Infantry Regiment, which he accompanied to France, arriving on 26 June 1917. Soon assigned to inspector general duties, he remained with that office until May 1918, when he returned to troop command.

McAlexander's moment of glory came a year after he arrived in France, in July 1918. In command of the Thirty-eighth Infantry, he was thrown with his regiment into the teeth of an all-out German offensive, the second battle of the Marne. On 15 July the Imperial German Army had crossed the River Marne along a fifty-mile front, advancing about four miles from the river, except in the sector held by McAlexander's troops near Moulins. The Thirty-eighth held its ground, a slight wooded rise, despite the withdrawal of units on both of the regiment's flanks. In the face of repeated German assaults, McAlexander and the Thirty-eighth Regiment clung to their battered position for twenty-one hours. After McAlexander was wounded, the Thirty-eighth was ordered to withdraw, but the regiment had gained enough time for Allied reinforcements to arrive on the scene to begin a steady reversal of their opponent's advance. McAlexander, despite his wound, refused to be evacuated, and a week later he was wounded again.

McAlexander's action near Moulins helped set up one of the early American victories and was widely heralded. It occurred when the fighting qualities of U.S. forces was still at issue, and champions of America's participation in the war and officers responsible for U.S. battlefield performance were quick to seize on this defensive feat as an example of American battlefield proficiency. General John J. Pershing, commander of the American Expeditionary Force, later labeled the action "one of the most brilliant pages in the annals of military history." The official dispatch of the day lionized the unit and its leader, claiming the Germans had been halted and thrown back and had suffered the loss of some 200 prisoners. McAlexander's name was prominently mentioned in the press release, and the popular press subsequently referred to him and his regiment as the "Rock of the Marne." For this action and his subsequent conduct, McAlexander was showered with decorations, including the highly coveted U.S. Distinguished Service Cross and Distinguished Service Medal, the French Legion of Honor with croix de guerre, and the Italian Croce di Guerra. Elevated to brigadier general, McAlexander commanded the 180th Brigade of the 90th Division during the rest of the war.

McAlexander was promoted to major general on 21 July 1924 and retired the next day. His wife died on 18 June 1928, and six months later he married Grace Palmer Craig. They had no children. Settling in Portland, Oregon, he waged an unsuccessful campaign for the Republican gubernatorial nomination in 1934. He died in Portland.

General McAlexander's contribution to his country was a display of bravery and battlefield competence at the right moment. Prior to the second battle of the Marne, the Allies made a serious effort to disperse U.S. troops among British and French units. This would have been humiliating for American soldiers, and it could have deprived the United States of a proper place in the peace settlement. Pershing, backed fully by President Woodrow Wilson and Secretary of War Newton D. Baker, stubbornly resisted persistent pressure from the Allies to subordinate the American army to their command. The "Rock of the Marne" provided a solid case in point why Americans should fight within U.S. units and in an American-controlled sector.

• McAlexander's papers are housed at the Oregon State University Archives. His military career is detailed in George W. Cullum, *Biographical Register of the Officers and Graduates of the U.S. Military Academy*, vols. 4–8 (1901–1940). His World War I Marne campaign exploits are detailed in Historical Division, Department of the Army, *U.S. Army in the World War, 1917–1919*, vol. 5 (1948), and John J. Pershing, *My Experiences in the World War, 1917–1919*, vol. 1 (1931). An extensive obituary is in the *New York Times*, 19 Sept. 1936.

ROD PASCHALL

MCALMON, Robert Menzies (9 Mar. 1895–2 Feb. 1956), writer and publisher, was born in Clifton, Kansas, the son of John Alexander McAlmon, a Presbyterian minister, and Bess Urquhart. McAlmon spent an unsettled boyhood in a succession of small towns in eastern South Dakota. In 1913 he entered the University of Minnesota but withdrew after one semester. He then roamed the upper Midwest working on surveying and grain-harvesting gangs and as a reporter and copywriter; he later based many short stories on these experiences. Moving to Los Angeles with his mother after his father's death (1917?), he enrolled at the University of Southern California. But a desultory student, believing that college stifled rather than encouraged creativity and critical thinking, he never earned a degree.

Enlisting in the army in March 1918, McAlmon learned to fly and edited the Rockwell Field (San Diego) newspaper. After his discharge he edited and contributed articles and poems to a flying magazine called *The Ace*. In March 1919 Harriet Monroe published six of his poems about flying in *Poetry*, marking the start of his literary career. Early in 1920, feeling restless and dissatisfied (as he would throughout his life), he quit a good job as a court reporter and left Los Angeles for New York, stopping briefly in Chicago to visit Monroe and the poet Emanuel Carnevali.

Arriving in Greenwich Village without money or connections, McAlmon took a job posing nude for art classes at Cooper Union. There, he met the expressionist painter and poet Marsden Hartley, who introduced him to William Carlos Williams. For the next thirty years Williams would be McAlmon's closest friend and his literary champion. Sharing the view that modern writing should be above all clearly expressed direct perceptions of experience, McAlmon and Williams founded *Contact* magazine, whose first issue (Dec. 1920) stated their credo: "For native work in verse, fiction, criticism or whatever is written we mean to maintain a place, insisting on that which we have not found insisted upon before, the essential contact between words and the locality that breeds them, in this case America." Heeding their call for idiomatic American writing, Ezra Pound, Wallace Stevens, Marianne Moore, H.D., Kay Boyle, and Glenway Wescott, among others, published poetry and criticism in *Contact*'s four issues. McAlmon transmuted his bohemian days into a short roman à clef, *Post-Adolescence* (1923).

In September 1920, through Williams, McAlmon met the English writer Bryher (Annie Winifred Ellerman) who was in New York with her lover-companion H.D. When, after returning from five months in California, Bryher proposed a convenient marriage to him, McAlmon shocked his friends by accepting. They were married on 14 February 1921 and departed for England shortly afterward. McAlmon got from this nominal marriage not only notoriety that persisted even after they divorced in 1926, but financial and artistic independence since Bryher was the daughter of English newspaper and shipping magnate Sir John Ellerman. Charged by some with crass opportunism,

McAlmon insisted in his memoirs that he "had married a girl under her writing name" and therefore had no inkling of her great wealth.

When McAlmon arrived in London, he began a twenty-year expatriate odyssey that would influence the course of modern literature. Within months, in London and Paris, he befriended Wyndham Lewis, searched out T. S. Eliot, had *Explorations* (poems and prose sketches) (1921) published by Harriet Weaver's Egoist Press, became James Joyce's regular drinking companion, was one of the first Americans to frequent Sylvia Beach's Shakespeare and Company bookstore, and found time to complete a volume of stories appropriately titled *A Hasty Bunch* (1922). "He dominated whatever group he was in. Whatever café or bar McAlmon patronized at the moment was the one where you saw everybody," Beach recalled in *Shakespeare and Company* (1959). Perhaps his money as much as his galvanic personality attracted hangers-on, of whom expatriate Paris had a plentiful supply.

From 1921 until 1929 few British or American writers who came to Paris escaped McAlmon's ken, and many received his material or literary help. In 1922, with the aid of a munificent cash gift from his father-in-law, McAlmon established the Contact Publishing Company to publish work, like his own, that commercial publishers eschewed. Foremost among those benefiting from McAlmon's largess was Ernest Hemingway, whom McAlmon met for the first time in Rapallo, Italy, in February 1923. Later that year McAlmon financed Hemingway's first trip to Spain and published his first book, *Three Stories and Ten Poems*. Their friendship soured over the years, and by 1929 they had become bitter enemies.

Pound praised *A Hasty Bunch* in *The Dial* (February 1922) for "show[ing] . . . the American small town in hard and just light, no nonsense, no overworking, no overloading . . . in the American spoken language." McAlmon followed up with more stories in *A Companion Volume* (1923) and a loosely plotted autobiographical novel, *Village* (1924), which traces the vicissitudes of a small prairie town over a fifteen-year period. Now among the vanguard assaulting genteel literature, he was recognized as the most promising young expatriate American writer in Paris, a title he was soon to lose to Hemingway. In their early writing, McAlmon and Hemingway mined the same territory, but whereas McAlmon presented his diamonds rough, Hemingway cut and polished.

In 1925 McAlmon brought out *Distinguished Air (Grim Fairy Tales)*, three thematically related stories exploring "hand-me-down, quick order, bargain variety, wholesale" gay and straight sex in chaotic Weimar Berlin, which he had visited in 1921. "Miss Knight," McAlmon's most original and perhaps best story, recounts the tribulations of Charlie Knight, an aging transvestite prostitute, whose confused sexual identity McAlmon evokes by interchanging masculine and feminine nouns and pronouns. A bisexual who probably became exclusively homosexual in middle age,

McAlmon wrote other stories and novels in this vein, none of which were published.

The Portrait of a Generation (1926) is an ambitious poem attempting to convey, through a montage of imagistic lyrics and narrative contemporary voices, the sterile mechanization of modern life. His quasi-epic poem *North America, Continent of Conjecture*, illustrated by Hilaire Hiler, appeared in 1929. Harriet Monroe criticized its disunity and fragmentation, while Louis Zukofsky lauded its "objectification."

McAlmon never stopped writing, but he published nothing after 1929 except for his memoirs, a story, several poems against fascism, and a short appreciation of Williams. In 1932 Crosby Continental Editions reprinted a selection of stories culled from little magazines entitled *The Indefinite Huntress and Other Stories*, and in 1937 avant-garde publisher New Directions put out *Not Alone Lost*, selected poems, the only one of McAlmon's books to be published in the United States during his lifetime. It received mostly negative reviews. McAlmon completed *Being Geniuses Together*, a memoir of his life abroad, in 1934, but he had to wait until 1938 before Secker & Warburg agreed to publish it after considerable excising. Its salty frankness alienated some old friends like Joyce but captivated recent ones like Katherine Anne Porter. McAlmon's best-known book, *Being Geniuses Together* has proved indispensable for any study of expatriate life and writing in the 1920s.

McAlmon's Contact Publishing Company folded in 1929, but from 1923 till its demise he was the leading expatriate publisher in Paris. As both his contemporaries and literary historians have affirmed, he performed invaluable service for modern letters by publishing writing too daring in subject, style, and language for commercial publishers. Among the Contact Editions are Bryher's *Two Selves*, H.D.'s *Palimpsest*, Hartley's *Twenty-Five Poems*, Robert M. Coates's *Eater of Darkness*, Djuna Barnes's *Ladies Almanack*—and three touchstones of modern American literature: Williams's *Spring and All*, Hemingway's *Three Stories and Ten Poems*, and Gertrude Stein's *The Making of Americans*. *The Contact Collection of Contemporary Writers* (1925) broke new ground by amalgamating both traditional and experimental British, Irish, and American writing. Ironically, McAlmon saw many of those he published become famous while his own writing would be forgotten except by a small band of partisans.

During the 1930s McAlmon drifted in Europe, with sojourns in the United States and Mexico. Trapped in Paris by Germany's swift conquest of France, he finally was able to come home in the fall of 1940, via Lisbon, after his family provided money and exerted political influence. He lost almost all of his books and papers, and he contracted tuberculosis from the harsh conditions under German occupation on top of years of heavy drinking and frenetic living. Thereafter, he worked for his brothers' surgical supply company in Phoenix and El Paso until retiring to Desert Hot Springs, California, in 1951. There he died, remembered only by his family and a few unforsaking friends.

• McAlmon's papers are in the Beinecke Rare Book and Manuscript Library, Yale University. The Morris Library, Southern Illinois University, also holds a collection of memorabilia. Sanford J. Smoller, *Adrift among Geniuses: Robert McAlmon, Writer and Publisher of the Twenties* (1975), is a full-length study of his life and work in the context of his times. It provides a bibliography of his publications and critical and biographical sources through 1972. Since that year some of McAlmon's writings have been reprinted: "Birds Foredoomed" (poem), *Pembroke Magazine* 6 (1975) (*Pembroke Magazine* 8 [1977] also published three of his letters to Norman Macleod); *A Hasty Bunch*, with afterword by Kay Boyle (1977); *North America, Continent of Conjecture* (1983); and three University of New Mexico Press reissues, each ed. with intro. by Edward N. S. Lorusso: *Village: As It Happened through a Fifteen Year Period* (1990), *Post-Adolescence: A Selection of Short Fiction* (1991), and *Miss Knight and Others*, with foreword by Gore Vidal (1992).

As for secondary studies documenting McAlmon's associations and contributions during the twenties, Hugh Ford, *Published in Paris: American and British Writers, Printers, Publishers in Paris, 1920–1939* (1975), fully discusses McAlmon's publishing activities; Barbara Guest, *Herself Defined: The Poet H.D. and Her World* (1984), offers insights into McAlmon's marriage to Bryher and his relationship with H.D.; Paul Mariani, *William Carlos Williams: A New World Naked* (1981), elaborates on McAlmon's friendship with Williams; *The Selected Letters of Ernest Hemingway, 1917–1961*, ed. Carlos Baker (1981), contains revealing letters to and about McAlmon. Jeffrey Meyers, *Hemingway: A Biography* (1985); Kenneth S. Lynn, *Hemingway* (1987); and Michael Reynolds, *Hemingway: The Paris Years* (1989), chronicle McAlmon's dealings with Hemingway. Of the three accounts, Reynolds's is the most balanced and sympathetic to McAlmon. Humphrey Carpenter draws heavily from McAlmon's long article "Truer Than Most Accounts" (*The Exile* 2 [1927]) and *Being Geniuses Together*, and he accords him a central place in *Geniuses Together: American Writers in Paris in the 1920s* (1988). James K. P. Mortenson ascertains that McAlmon's correct date of birth is 9 Mar. 1895 in "Robert McAlmon's Birth Date," *American Notes and Queries* 22, no. 3–4 (1983): 47.

SANFORD J. SMOLLER

MCANALLY, David Rice (17 Feb. 1810–11 July 1895), Methodist clergyman and editor, was born in Grainger County, Tennessee, the son of Charles McAnally, a Methodist minister and sheriff, and Elizabeth Moore. David was educated in the county school and in a private academy. In 1828 he was licensed to preach, and the next year he was admitted into the Holston Conference of the Methodist Episcopal church. In 1831 McAnally was ordained a deacon, and in 1833 he became an elder. He married Maria Ann Patton Thompson in December 1836 in Abingdon, Virginia; they had three children. After her death in 1861, he married Julia Reeves in 1871; they had no children.

For fourteen years, McAnally served appointments in Tennessee, North Carolina, and Virginia. He was elected president of the East Tennessee Female Institute in Knoxville in 1843, a position he held for eight years. During the period he served as a trustee of the Deaf and Dumb School in Knoxville and as an associate editor of the *Highland Messenger*, published in Asheville, North Carolina. Through his interest in the common-school system, McAnally became associated with Horace Mann and other educational reformers. On 25 December 1851 he became editor of the *St. Louis Christian Advocate*, a post he filled until his death except for a few brief absences. He also founded the First Methodist Church in Carondelet, Missouri, in 1857.

The *St. Louis Christian Advocate*, which McAnally edited for more than forty years, had been founded in 1850. The Methodist Episcopal Church, South authorized its annual conferences to create such a publication in that year. Under McAnally's leadership, this weekly publication of four large pages had 7,000 subscribers by 1858. By printing stories of general contemporary interest as well as religious material, plus a featured section titled "News of the Week," the influence of the paper grew. McAnally was able to persuade the St. Louis and Missouri conferences of the denomination to fund the establishment of a book and publishing company in connection with the paper. Through editorials and personal addresses, he was also able to convince both conferences to support the creation of a college, which was chartered by the state in 1855. Located in Fayette and named Central College, McAnally's dream was that it be a "college of highest grade" with a special emphasis on the education of young men who might become ministers. The school opened in 1857, and while the Civil War forced its closure, it reopened in the fall of 1868. In 1962 its name was changed to Central Methodist College.

Before the Civil War, the editorial position of the *St. Louis Christian Advocate* defended slavery without praising it, endorsed state's rights, and subsequently approved the secession of the southern states. This brought McAnally under suspicion for subversive and treasonable statements. His articles in April–May 1861 titled "The Times," "The Duty of Christian Men," and "The Time for Prayer"—in which he admonished the people of Missouri to remain home, cultivate family relations, and pray for peace—did not spare him from arrest on 21 April 1862 and imprisonment in the Myrtle Street Military Prison. A military commission examined the *Advocate* and suppressed the paper, but McAnally was placed on parole that lasted until 19 November 1865. The book and publishing company narrowly escaped confiscation as a property of the Methodist Episcopal Church, South, but both the *Advocate* and book concern were reopened following the war. By the 1880s McAnally was a strong advocate for the reunion of southern and northern Methodists.

McAnally was known as a man of principle, a powerful preacher, a journalist, and an author with a national reputation. His leadership in conference and denomination is evident in his election to the General Conferences of 1854, 1858, 1866, and 1870. Interested in the affairs of church, state, and nation, although not an intellectual, he was a keen observer and recorder of events, and his work provides valuable information on his times. He also helped fix the place of Methodism in Missouri and beyond through his published works. These included *A Sketch of the Life and Character of Martha Laurens Ramsey* (1853); *A Statement of Facts . . . on the Subject of Slavery* (1856); *Life and Times of the Rev. William Patton* (1858); *Life and Times of the Rev. Samuel Patton* (1859); *The Life and Labors of the Rev. E. M. Marvin* (1878); *Linguistic Curiosities* (1879); *Doctrine of Sanctification* (1880); *The Future Life: Certainty and Character* (1880); and *History of Methodism in Missouri* (1881). He died in St. Louis, Missouri, and is buried in Bellefont Cemetery.

• There is a collection of McAnally materials in the St. Louis Public Library, St. Louis, Mo. Helpful sources include "David Rice McAnally," *Encyclopedia of World Methodism*, vol. 1 (1974); Marcus L. Gray and Ward Baker, *The Centennial Volume of Missouri Methodism* (1907); William M. Leftwich, *Martyrdom In Missouri*, vol. 1 (1870); William H. Lewis, *The History of Methodism in Missouri* (1890); *Minutes of the Annual Conferences of the Methodist Episcopal Church, South* (1895); James P. Pilkington, *The Methodist Publishing House* (2 vols., 1965); Richard N. Price, *Holston Methodism: From Its Origin to the Present Time* (1908); Frank C. Tucker, *The Methodist Church in Missouri, 1798–1939* (1966); and A. Sterling Ward, "Glimpses of Our History Found in the *St. Louis Christian Advocate* of 1851–1854," *Methodist History* (Jan. 1964): 37–39. Obituaries are in the *Knoxville Journal*, 13 July 1895, and the *St. Louis Republic*, 12 July 1895.

FREDERICK V. MILLS, SR.

MCANDREW, William (20 Aug. 1863–28 June 1937), educator and editor, was born in Ypsilanti, Michigan, the son of William McAndrew, a furniture manufacturer, and Helen Walker, an obstetrician and the first female physician in the state of Michigan. His parents, both Scottish immigrants, were active in local reform causes, supporting forums where they hosted such activists as Susan B. Anthony and John B. Gough.

McAndrew received his A.B. from the University of Michigan in 1886 and was elected to Phi Beta Kappa. Upon graduation he became superintendent of the St. Clair, Michigan, schools and was associated with the *Detroit Free Press*. In 1889 he accepted a teaching post at Hyde Park High School in Chicago, becoming principal shortly thereafter. He was dismissed in 1891 when he refused to graduate a book publisher's son who had not fulfilled the prescribed course of study. After working briefly for the Great Northern Railway, in 1892 McAndrew was named principal of the Pratt Institute's high school in Brooklyn, New York. There he served until 1898, when he became principal of the Israel Putnam School in Brooklyn. During this period McAndrew also wrote features for the *Brooklyn Daily Eagle*. He had married Susan Irvine Gurney, daughter of a Congregationalist clergyman, in 1893; they had three children.

In 1902 the New York City public schools selected McAndrew to organize what became Washington Irving High School, a technical school training girls in both academic and manual subjects. At this time

McAndrew's rise to prominence in progressive educational circles began, initially as an advocate of industrial education. Declining the Detroit superintendency in 1912, McAndrew became an associate superintendent of the New York City public schools in 1914. He continued to promote industrial education and led the school system's abortive effort to introduce "Gary Plan" platoon schools. Progressive supporters of the Gary Plan like McAndrew sought to unify general and vocational education, more efficiently use school facilities, and better integrate the schools into their surrounding communities, thereby promoting the Americanization of immigrants. During the postwar period McAndrew crusaded for "civic education," shifting his emphasis to the need for training in "American ideals" as exemplified by the nation's founding documents. Writing for such publications as the *Outlook*, *World's Work*, *School and Society*, and the *Educational Review* (of which he became editor in 1923), McAndrew merged the nationalistic fervor of the postwar years with progressive educators' calls for the creation of a broader community in which schools played a central role.

For McAndrew progressive educational reform meant not merely the Deweyan notion of schooling as education for life but also the operation of the schools along business lines. He promoted separating the schools from politics and encouraging efficiency through "close supervision" of teachers by expert administrators. McAndrew also advocated the use of hierarchical management techniques as seen in factories and business offices and increased use of educational research and measurement tools. Possessing a management style described as brusque, domineering, and undiplomatic, McAndrew carried great liabilities into the highly political world of school management. Yet McAndrew—who received an M.Pd. (master of pedagogy) from the State Normal College at Ypsilanti in 1916—was self-assured enough to eschew as a vanity the honorific title of "Doctor" almost universally applied to men in his position.

In 1924 McAndrew became superintendent of Chicago's public schools. An outsider to Chicago school politics, his methods and policies endeared him to few beyond middle-class reformers who agreed with his efficiency goals and a business elite who wanted schools to supply a more tractable labor force. McAndrew alienated many local politicians, for whom the schools traditionally had been an extension of the local political structure, through his attempts to wrest control of school administration from elected officials and place it in the hands of an administrative elite. The Chicago Teachers Federation, having initially favored McAndrew, withdrew its support after he undercut the authority of teachers' councils. Although the councils had enjoyed an important advisory voice in school management for years, McAndrew refused to meet with them and did away with paid council meetings during the school day. McAndrew's support for intelligence testing, his unilateral imposition of junior high schools, his call for the Gary system in elementary schools, and his increasingly remote and bureaucratic management system further alienated the teaching corps.

As an appointee of reform Democratic mayor William E. Dever, McAndrew was the favorite target of former mayor "Big Bill" Thompson in the latter's attempt to regain office in 1927. Branded "the stool pigeon of King George" in Thompson's "America First" mayoral campaign, McAndrew faced spurious charges of introducing pro-British texts into the Chicago schools. When Thompson returned to city hall, a compliant school board brought charges of insubordination against McAndrew, now bereft of any broad base of support. McAndrew was suspended, and a lengthy and sensational trial before the Board of Education, described in the *New York Times* (27 Oct. 1927) as "a mixture of vaudeville burlesque and broadest farce," ensued. McAndrew was found guilty and dismissed in March 1928, despite the fact that his term had expired two months earlier. The decision was later overturned on appeal, a moral victory for McAndrew, who had since returned to New York.

After his dismissal McAndrew continued as editor and book reviewer for the *Educational Review*. He wrote and lectured widely on the subjects of educational administration and citizenship education. He was also the author and editor of a number of books and reports, most notably *Social Studies: An Orientation Handbook for High-School Students* (1935). The recipient of many honors and a member of numerous organizations and clubs, including the Masons, McAndrew served as president of the Department of Superintendence of the National Education Association in 1925 and was a past president of the New York Schoolmasters' Association. He died in Mamaroneck, New York. While most noted for his role as the foil in "Big Bill" Thompson's jingoistic attack on the administration of Chicago's schools, McAndrew also represented and led a generation of progressive school reformers who were concerned as much with the mechanics of efficient public school administration as with the content and social role of public school instruction.

• There are no collected papers of William McAndrew, and only scattered items exist in other collections. More useful are the various reports, authored by McAndrew, published by the Brooklyn, New York City, and Chicago boards of education. Although the periods of McAndrew's life and work before and after his Chicago superintendency in particular remain to be fully explored, Arthur Tavardian, "Battle over the Chicago Schools: The Superintendency of William McAndrew" (Ph.D. diss., Loyola Univ. of Chicago, 1992), deals with McAndrew in Chicago but provides little analysis and a limited bibliography. Useful on the Chicago period is George S. Counts, *School and Society in Chicago* (1928). Counts turned McAndrew's analysis of school politics on its head by arguing for a greater role for politics in school management. Julia Wrigley, *Class Politics and Public Schools: Chicago 1900–1950* (1982), and David John Hogan, *Class and Reform: School and Society in Chicago, 1880–1930* (1985), each have valuable sections on McAndrew's progressive educational politics in Chicago, although they approach the intersection of progressive ideology and social class differently. Obituaries are in the *New York Times*, the *New York Sun*, the *New York Herald Tribune*, the *New York World-Telegram*, and the *Chicago Daily Tribune*, 29 June 1937.

KEVIN J. SMEAD

MCARTHUR, Duncan (14 Jan. 1772–28 Apr. 1839), governor of Ohio and congressman, was born in Dutchess County, New York, the son of John McArthur and Margaret Campbell. Unlike many of the early Jeffersonian Republican leaders of south-central Ohio, McArthur was neither from Virginia nor a comfortable background. Following the death of McArthur's mother, his father migrated from New York to western Pennsylvania in 1780. There McArthur learned the life of a backwoodsman. By the early 1790s, he was serving in military expeditions (most particularly, the one led by Josiah Harmar) against the American Indians in the Northwest Territory and looking for work along the river. The key moment in his early career came when he met the Virginia-born land speculator Nathaniel Massie.

In the spring of 1793, McArthur traveled with Massie's surveying party into the Scioto Valley as a chain bearer. Scouting American Indian activities and learning the arts of land surveying from Massie occupied the next few years. After the Treaty of Greenville (1795) reduced the threat of American Indian attack, McArthur moved in February 1796 to some land near Chillicothe. Like Massie, he took advantage of the fact that the Virginia Military District was not federal land and thus exempt from the surveying procedures outlined in the Land Ordinance of 1785. The commonwealth had issued warrants for land in the district to its revolutionary war veterans. Many of them sold the warrants to speculators while others hired men to locate and survey their claims. McArthur did the latter for a commission of 20 percent of the land he located; he also bought and sold warrants. Through hard work, a willingness to gamble, and a single-minded pursuit of profit, McArthur accumulated over 90,000 acres and became one of the wealthiest landowners in Ohio.

McArthur had a two-story stone mansion built on his estate, "Fruit Hill," in 1805. He had married Nancy McDonald in February 1796. While he could read and write, McArthur had no desire to acquire the trappings and style of a gentleman. He encouraged the education of his children and supported his wife's piety (although he had little interest in religion himself), but he never lost the gruff and cantankerous manner he had developed in his youth, particularly when it came to legal disputes over land.

McArthur's political career began with his election to the Ohio House of Representatives in 1804 and continued the next year with his elevation to the state senate, in which he served eight consecutive terms and was Speaker in 1809 and 1810. In 1812 he was elected to Congress but resigned in April 1813 because of his military activities. McArthur had been chosen a militia colonel in 1806, as much a recognition of his service in the 1790s as of his economic standing; two years later, he had become a major general. In 1812 McArthur had participated in General William Hull's campaign against Canada as a colonel of a militia regiment. He had served with distinction, despite the surrender of the army, and later testified at Hull's court-martial. This led to McArthur's March 1813 appointment as a brigadier general in the U.S. Army. He proved to be a solid officer but was impatient with the handling of the war by his superiors. In 1814 he succeeded William Henry Harrison as commander of the army in the Northwest.

After the war, McArthur returned to Fruit Hill and his diverse agricultural and business interests. He served in the Ohio House in 1815–1816, 1817–1818 (Speaker), and 1826–1827, and he served in the state senate in 1821–1822, 1822–1823, and 1829–1830. McArthur was a member of Congress from 1823 to 1825 and was narrowly elected governor of Ohio in 1830. His last campaign, an 1832 race for Congress, ended in his defeat by one vote by William Allen (1803–1879), who would marry one of McArthur's daughters and inherit his estate.

In 1819 the Englishman William Faux and former governor Thomas Worthington ran into McArthur while walking. Faux described Worthington's neighbor as "dirty and butcherlike and very unlike a soldier in appearance, seeming half savage, and dressed as a backwoodsman." The two Ohioans exchanged brief greetings, after which Worthington compared McArthur to Andrew Jackson: "he is fit only for hard knocks and Indian warfare." It was true that McArthur was a tough customer with a reputation for protecting his interests at all costs, but that unrefined determination made him one of the most powerful men in early Ohio.

McArthur was a staunch supporter of National Republican candidates in the 1820s and was a Whig in the 1830s. He made little effort to hide the fact that he was in public service as much to protect his interests as anything else. He was straightforward in his defense of the utility of banks, particularly the Second Bank of the United States. More spectacularly, he lobbied throughout the 1820s to receive compensation for land claims he held in the upper Little Miami Valley; in May 1830 Congress granted him $80,000 in return for giving up his claim to 14,000 acres. If his economic interests sometimes hurt him politically (in his 1824 defeat for reelection to Congress, for example), he prospered nonetheless. In 1832 he had over $29,000 loaned out at interest in Ohio and close to $2,800 in Kentucky.

McArthur's political legacy was meager. His significance today lies in the ways in which his life illustrates the symbiotic relationship between political power and economic development in the early American Republic. McArthur may have appeared to Faux to be a rude frontiersman, but he was in actuality an astute, hard-nosed entrepreneur who personified the spirit of nineteenth-century commercial enterprise as much as the character of the eighteenth-century backwoods. Mc-Arthur apparently suffered a serious injury in 1830. He died at Fruit Hill.

• The Duncan McArthur Papers are in the Library of Congress; they are one of the largest and most valuable sources on early Ohio economic and political development. There are some papers in the Ross County (Ohio) Historical Society and many letters from McArthur in the papers of other early Ohioans in the Ohio Historical Society in Columbus. John McDonald, *Biographical Sketches of General Nathaniel Massie, General Duncan McArthur* (1838), is an important memoir by someone who knew McArthur. See also David M. Massie, *Nathaniel Massie, A Pioneer of Ohio* (1896). The best study of land speculation in the Scioto Valley is William T. Hutchinson, "The Bounty Lands of the American Revolution in Ohio" (Ph.D. diss., Univ. of Chicago, 1927). See also Andrew R. L. Cayton, *The Frontier Republic: Ideology and Politics in the Ohio Country, 1780–1825* (1986); Alfred Byron Sears, *Thomas Worthington, Father of Ohio Statehood* (1958); William T. Utter, *The Frontier State, 1803–1825* (1942); and Francis P. Weisenburger, *The Passing of the Frontier: 1825–1850*, vol. 3 of *The History of the State of Ohio*, ed. Carl F. Wittke (1941).

ANDREW CAYTON

MCARTHUR, John (17 Nov. 1826–15 May 1906), soldier, businessman, and public servant, was born in Erskine Parish, on the River Clyde, in Renfrewshire, Scotland, the son of John McArthur and Isabella Neilson, who anticipated that he would become a Presbyterian divine. But he opted for employment in his father's blacksmithery. In 1849—one year after he married a neighbor, Christine Cuthbertson—he emigrated to the United States, joining his brother-in-law, Carlile Mason, in Chicago. McArthur and Cuthbertson had seven children. After working for several years as a boilermaker and having accumulated some capital in 1854 McArthur entered into partnership with Mason as owner-manager of the Excelsior Ironworks, manufacturing "steam boilers, engines, and iron work of every description." Buying out Mason, from 1858 to 1861 McArthur was sole operator of the business.

McArthur was active in Scot fraternal organizations and the militia. Joining the Chicago Highland Guards as a third lieutenant, by 1861 he had become its captain. On 3 May 1861 he was named colonel of the Twelfth Illinois Infantry, a ninety-day regiment, which was organized at Springfield. McArthur and his men were rushed by rail to help garrison Cairo, a key city at the confluence of the Ohio and Mississippi rivers, where they learned the art of soldiering. On 1 August the unit was reorganized and reenlisted as a three-year regiment.

McArthur and his regiment early became associated with Brigadier General Ulysses S. Grant's command, participating in expeditions from Cairo to Belmont and Charleston, Missouri, on 2 and 4 September, and to Paducah on 5 and 6 September 1861. He was posted at Paducah until 4 February 1862 and played an active role in expeditions organized and sent by Brigadier General C. F. Smith to threaten Columbus, Kentucky, on several occasions, the first time in early November in conjunction with Grant's attack on Belmont.

McArthur, now leading a brigade, was at Fort Heiman on 6 February 1862 and in the fight for Fort Donelson, where he and his troops were the first to meet the enemy during their bold attempt to roll back the right flank of Grant's investing army. Although compelled to give ground, McArthur was commended for his courage and skill.

The tall, brawny, tight-lipped Scot, having earned the confidence of General Grant, as well as that of his troops, was promoted to brigadier general on 21 March 1862. At Shiloh, on Sunday, 6 April, McArthur and brigade stood tall, posted between the Peach Orchard and the Tennessee River, athwart the route the Confederate right wing must take if their bold plan to seize Pittsburg Landing and drive Grant's army into the Snake Creek bottom was to succeed. Before they were driven from their position, the Confederates had lost their leader—General Albert Sidney Johnston—and vital time. Among the casualties in this fighting was McArthur, who was seriously wounded in the foot.

Some six weeks later McArthur, having recovered from his wounds, returned to duty and assumed command of a brigade in Brigadier General Thomas J. McKean's Sixth Division. McArthur led his unit in the closing days of the Corinth siege. In mid-July McKean was detached and sent to Benton Barracks and did not return until 20 September. During his absence, McArthur led the Sixth Division and accompanied Grant's column to Iuka but was not actively engaged in the 19 September fighting. He initiated the battle of Corinth on 3 October and was slowly forced back, and at nightfall he took position in the inner works. McArthur resumed command of the Sixth Division on 6 October, the Confederates having retreated following their 4 October repulse, and pursued the rebels as far as Ripley. McArthur's role at Corinth was commended by army commander William S. Rosecrans, while General McKean spoke of his zeal and ability.

McArthur retained the Sixth Division in the reorganization incident to Rosecrans's reassignment and the disbandment of the Army of the Mississippi. He and his division marched with Brigadier General Charles S. Hamilton's Left Wing, Army of the Tennessee, on Grant's soon-to-be-aborted southward thrust down the Mississippi Central Railroad. The organization of the Army of the Tennessee into wings was scrapped on 22 December 1862, and McArthur and his Sixth Division became part of Major General James McPherson's XVII Corps. Early in February 1863 McArthur and his troops moved by boat from Memphis to Lake Providence, Louisiana, to work on a canal.

McArthur's three brigades, tied down guarding supply depots and wagon trains, did not arrive before the fortifications guarding Vicksburg's eastern approaches until 19 May. Troops of his Second Brigade suffered heavy losses in their 19 and 22 May assaults. McArthur was diverted from siege operations on 23 June to command a provisional division of the force under Major General William T. Sherman that Grant had constituted to prevent the army assembled by General Joseph E. Johnston from storming across Big Black River and relieving Vicksburg. Following the 4 July surrender of Vicksburg, McArthur guarded Sherman's supply lines as he advanced and laid siege to and captured Jackson. After Sherman's return from Jackson in the fourth week of July, McArthur took position at Big Black Bridge and then went on leave.

Returning from furlough, McArthur established his headquarters in Vicksburg. Among the projects undertaken by his division was construction of Fort Grant, as the defenses guarding the approaches to the Vicksburg enclave were designated. McArthur was responsible for the post and defenses of Vicksburg while General McPherson participated in Sherman's Meridian Expedition (3 February–6 Mar. 1864). After McPherson returned to Vicksburg, having succeeded Sherman as commander of the Army of the Tennessee, he began assembling his troops at Huntsville, Alabama. McArthur remained in Mississippi, retaining responsibility for security of the Vicksburg enclave. He was absent from Vicksburg from 4 to 21 May, beating up the country northeast of Vicksburg, between the Yazoo and Big Black rivers, wreaking havoc on the Mississippi Central Railroad at Vaughan and skirmishing with rebel horse soldiers.

McArthur was transferred to Georgia and on 5 August placed in charge of troops guarding the Western & Atlantic Railroad, Sherman's lifeline, from Big Shanty to the Chattahoochie and protecting the Marietta and Vining's Magazines. Twice—in mid-August and again in early October—McArthur was challenged by Confederates. Major General Joseph Wheeler's horse soldiers broke the railroad at Acworth during their August raid before crossing the Etowah, and, in the days immediately following General John B. Hood's crossing of the Chattahoochie, McArthur fought him at Big Shanty.

In October McArthur rushed to Missouri, where he reported to Major General A. J. Smith, whose "10,000 Israelites" had been diverted to that state to cope with Major General Sterling Price's columns that had threatened St. Louis. He reached Sedalia on 3 November after the crisis had passed and assumed command of the First Division, XVI Corps. Hood's army poised for an invasion of middle Tennessee; McArthur and his troops were sent to Nashville, landing there on 30 November. McArthur and his division were in the forefront in the decisive battle of Nashville. He ordered the charge that sent his men scrambling up Shy's Hill on 16 December in the surge that shattered the hinge of the Confederate line and precipitated the retreat by Hood's army that did not stop until it reached northeast Mississippi. In recognition of his "conspicuous gallantry and efficiency" at the battle of Nashville, McArthur was brevetted major general of volunteers to rank from 15 December.

McArthur and his division departed Eastport, Mississippi, on 7 February by boat and reached New Orleans two weeks later. Landing on the east side of Mobile Bay, after a twelve-day investment he and his troops occupied Spanish Fort and moved next against Blakely. Mobile surrendered on 12 April and the next day McArthur started for Montgomery, reaching there on 25 April. Ten days after the Confederate troops in the region surrendered at Citronelle, Alabama, McArthur moved his headquarters to Selma, where he remained until mustered on 24 August 1865.

McArthur's business career soured in the two decades following the Civil War. He was unsuccessful in reestablishing his foundry; the Great Chicago Fire of 1871 swept the city while he was commissioner of Public Works (1866–1872); and while he was city postmaster (1873–1877), $73,000 of federal monies for which he was responsible were lost when the bank in which they were deposited failed. To make good this loss cost much of his personal capital. The loss of two ships in the early 1880s caused the failure of the Chicago & Vert Island Stone Company, with which he was associated as a major stockholder and official. Retiring from business in the mid-1880s, McArthur continued his active involvement in the Presbyterian church, the Grand Army of the Republic, the Loyal Legion, the Society of the Army of the Tennessee, and St. Andrew's Society until his death in Chicago.

• For more information on McArthur, see Edwin C. Bearss, "McArthur's May Expedition against the Mississippi Central Railroad," *Journal of Mississippi History* 28 (Feb. 1966): 1–14; *War of the Rebellion: A Compilation of the Official Records of the Union and Confederate Armies* (128 vols., 1880–1901); and J. Ezra Warner, *Generals in Blue: Lives of the Union Commanders* (1964), pp. 288–89. Obituaries are in the *Chicago Chronicle*, 6 Oct. 1906, and the *Chicago Daily News*, 26 Aug. 1906.

E. C. BEARSS

MCARTHUR, John, Jr. (13 May 1823–8 Jan. 1890), architect, was brought at the age of ten from Bladenock, his birthplace in Scotland, to Philadelphia, Pennsylvania, by his builder uncle of the same name. (To differentiate between them, the architect added the "Jr." to his own name. Nothing is known of his parents.) Apprenticed to his uncle, McArthur attended evening classes at Carpenter's Hall and studied drawing and design at the Franklin Institute. He married Matilda Prevost, had four children, and lived in an elaborate house of his own design (1864) at 4201 Walnut Street. He was Presbyterian.

McArthur's first competition-winning design was for the Philadelphia House of Refuge for white children (1848), and in the following year he made extensions to the Philadelphia Hospital (originally built in 1755 by Isaac Holden). During the early 1850s he designed an almshouse at Wilmington, Delaware, and the Farmer's Bank and a Presbyterian church at New Castle, Delaware.

Isaiah Rogers, a major American architect in the thirty years prior to the Civil War, had established the precedent for hotel design in Boston to replace the traditional eighteenth-century inn, and McArthur continued this pattern in Philadelphia with Italianate designs for the Girard (1852), La Pierre House (1852, later renamed the Lafayette), and the Continental (1858–1860), this last hotel with a steam elevator. McArthur's Greek Doric Presbyterian Church at Media, Pennsylvania, was dedicated in 1855, and his own West Spruce Presbyterian Church in Philadelphia—basically Gothic but with Romanesque and classical detailing—was in use by 1859. He designed commercial iron-fronts for William Weightman and the J. E. Caldwell store on Chestnut Street (1860) adjacent to his Continental Hotel. In 1861 he became the first president of the Philadelphia Institute of Architects.

During the Civil War, McArthur was attached to the Quartermaster General's Department in Philadelphia, where he designed twenty-four temporary U.S. hospitals. The largest of these, the 3,600-bed Mower in Philadelphia, covered twenty-seven acres, having fifty wings radiating from an oval-planned corridor. After the war, in 1866, McArthur was appointed architect to the Navy Department, and in 1871 he became superintendent of public buildings for the Treasury Department. (The Treasury paid for, supervised, and superintended all federal buildings.) In this capacity he oversaw the construction of the Philadelphia Post Office and Court House (1874–1884), designed by Alfred Bult Mullett, the supervising architect of the Treasury Department, with sculptures by Daniel Chester French in the Second Empire style, which was adapted from Napoleon III's France.

McArthur's greatest competition-winning commission (1869) was for the Philadelphia City Hall (now the Municipal Court Building). Though most of it was built between 1871 and 1881, it was not completed until 1907 at a cost of well over $24 million. It is the largest extant example of the French Second Empire style in the United States and among the most distinguished anywhere, with sculpture, interior decor, and architecture complementing each other.

The last twenty-five years of McArthur's life were mostly devoted to the Philadelphia City Hall, but he also designed the Public Ledger Building (1866), the Luzerne County Prison (1867–1870), the state hospital at Danville (1870), Pardee Hall at Lafayette College, Easton (1871–1873), and a small Presbyterian children's hospital for Philadelphia (1888).

• The Philadelphia Free Library has numerous scrapbooks illustrating works of McArthur by building type, and many prints are available at the Historical Society of Pennsylvania, Philadelphia. The Philadelphia Municipal Building has an extensive archive, the state hospital at Danville has twenty original drawings, and the Philadelphia Hospital has twenty-two original drawings, including six by McArthur and Collins. The most complete overview of his work is Lawrence Wodehouse, "John McArthur, Jr. (1823–1890)," *Journal of the Society of Architectural Historians* 28 (Dec. 1969): 271–83, and of his most famed building is John Maass, "The Philadelphia City Hall, Monster or Masterpiece," *American Institute of Architects' Journal* 43 (Feb. 1965): 23–30. Obituaries are in

American Architect and Building News 27 (1890): 35; *Architect and Building* 12 (18 Jan. 1890): 25; and the *Philadelphia Public Ledger*, 9 Jan. 1890.

LAWRENCE WODEHOUSE

MCARTHUR, William Pope (2 Apr. 1814–23 Dec. 1850), hydrographer and naval officer, was born in Ste. Genevieve, Missouri, the son of John McArthur and Mary Linn, occupations unknown. He was appointed a midshipman in the U.S. Navy on 11 February 1832 and spent his early years on the South Pacific Station. He was promoted to passed midshipman on 23 June 1837 and then attended the Naval School at Norfolk. Upon completion, he reported to naval lieutenant Levin M. Powell's expedition to the Everglades, a special group of sailors, soldiers, and militiamen using small boats and canoes to operate against the Indians in south Florida during the Second Seminole War (1835–1842).

McArthur's scientific interest was piqued by the expedition's civilian topographical engineer Joseph E. Johnston. Johnston had earlier resigned his army commission to study civil engineering. While waiting for a reappointment to the army, he volunteered for this duty, and the two men became friends. McArthur was an acting lieutenant of one of the units going into the interior. On 15 January 1838, at the headwaters of Jupiter River, they encountered the Seminoles. In the ensuing engagement McArthur was seriously wounded, and later he was sent to the Naval Hospital in Norfolk. There he met Mary Stone Young, the daughter of the superintendent of the hospital; they married in 1838. The McArthurs had five children.

The war brought a number of naval vessels and army transports to Florida's coast. In 1836 the West India Squadron conducted several hurried, partial coastal surveys of Florida's west coast. Later Lieutenant Raphael Semmes, USN, lost his steamer, the *Lieutenant Izard*, while attempting to bring troops and supplies up the Withlacoochee River because of inadequate charts. Superintendent Ferdinand R. Hassler, U.S. Coast Survey, became aware that the Florida charts in use were based on surveys made by George Gauld for the British Admiralty in 1773–1775. In 1840 he accepted the services of Lieutenant Powell to command, and McArthur to serve, on the *Consort* "for the rectification of positions and soundings of the eastern coast and harbors of the Gulf of Mexico." On 8 September 1841 McArthur was promoted to lieutenant. After the survey he returned to naval duty, but in mid-1844 he rejoined the Coast Survey as a lieutenant commanding the *Vanderbilt*. For the next four years he gathered hydrographic data during the summer months and spent his winters in Washington, D.C., reducing his observations for the draftsmen. His shipboard duties included observing the set and velocity of currents in Narragansett Bay, surveying the Virginia and Maryland coasts of Chesapeake Bay, and sounding for shoals in Delaware Bay.

In the fall of 1848 Superintendent Alexander Dallas Bache assigned McArthur to make the first U.S. survey of the Pacific Coast. McArthur took passage for Panama while his ship, the *Ewing*, sailed around South America. The isthmus was a lawless region filled with adventurers headed for California's gold fields. Because he spoke Spanish, local authorities asked him to lead a vigilance committee of Americans and Panamanians in a demonstration of force to reestablish order, which he did. On the Pacific side he found the *Humboldt* anchored off Taboga Island loaded with emigrants and no captain. McArthur agreed to take the *Humboldt* to San Francisco for its owner. He assumed command of the *Ewing* when it arrived in September 1849.

McArthur recommended Mare Island in San Pablo Bay, twenty-five miles northeast of San Francisco, for the site of the Pacific Squadron's navy yard. When some of his sailors threw an officer overboard and made off for the gold fields, McArthur rescued the officer, captured the men, and convicted them of mutiny. But he could not begin his survey immediately because the price of supplies exceeded his allotted finances, sailors were deserting to pan for gold, and his health was deteriorating under an attack of fever of a malignant type. In December he sailed to the Sandwich (Hawaiian) Islands to rectify his problems by recruiting additional sailors, by keeping his present crew from deserting, and by escaping the rainy weather that was so debilitating to his health. McArthur paid an official visit to King Kamehameha III, who reciprocated by entertaining him at a royal function. Returning to the West Coast early in 1850, he began his reconnaissance on 3 April. Ultimately he completed a successful survey of the coast from Monterey to the Columbia River. He compiled an outline of the coast noting the headlands, bays, rivers, and soundings, and he discovered important errors in earlier charts of the West Coast. In November he was ordered to Washington, D.C., to take command of a new steamer for the 1851 season. McArthur took passage on the *Oregon* for the isthmus and en route suffered a fatal attack of dysentery just before the ship reached Panama. He was buried on Taboga. In one of his last letters he had summed up his work saying, "My fame (if any be merited) will rest upon this reconnaissance" (Lewis A. McArthur, p. 258). In 1851 the Coast Survey published his *Notices of the Western Coast of the United States*. In 1876 the U.S. Coast Survey commissioned the schooner, *McArthur*, in his honor.

• Lewis A. McArthur, "The Pacific Coast Survey of 1849 and 1850," *Quarterly of the Oregon Historical Society* 16 (Sept. 1915): 244–74, has the most complete development of his grandfather's life. The superintendent of the Coast Survey's annual reports to the secretary of the treasury for the years 1844–1847 provide details of his hydrographic duties, as does Senate Executive Doc. 6, 30th Cong., 1st sess., and Senate Executive Doc. 6, 35th Cong., 2d sess. Panama and the voyage of the *Humboldt* are described by Julius H. Pratt, who was a passenger on the *Humboldt*, in "California by Panama in '49," *Century Magazine*, Apr. 1891, pp. 901–17; chapter 5, "First Attempt," of George E. Buker, *Swamp Sailors* (1975), relates McArthur's brief role in the Second Seminole War.

GEORGE E. BUKER

MCAULIFFE, Anthony Clement (2 July 1898–11 Aug. 1975), soldier, was born in Washington, D.C., the son of John Joseph McAuliffe, the chief of the stenographic section of the Interstate Commerce Commission, and Alice Katherine Gannon. Anthony McAuliffe was raised in Washington, D.C., where he first experienced military life as a 14-year-old cadet in the Reserve Officer Training Corps. He entered the U.S. Military Academy at West Point in 1917; his accelerated wartime class graduated in November 1918 but was recalled to complete the course as student officers and graduated a second time in June 1919. McAuliffe was in the top tenth of the class of 284. As a field artillery officer, McAuliffe spent the interwar years in routine assignments in the United States and Hawaii and remained a lieutenant for sixteen years. He married Helen Willet Whitman in August 1920; they had two children. After promotion to captain in 1935, McAuliffe attended Command and General Staff College at Fort Leavenworth, Kansas, and two years later the Army War College at Carlisle Barracks, Pennsylvania.

Promotions began to quicken on the eve of the Second World War, and McAuliffe advanced to brigadier general by 8 August 1943. He became the division artillery commander of the newly formed 101st Airborne Division at Camp Claiborne, Louisiana. In this position he saw combat in the Normandy invasion and Operation Market Garden in Holland.

In December 1944 McAuliffe was in temporary command of the 101st Airborne while the division commander, Major General Maxwell Taylor, was in the United States. On 16 December the Nazis launched their Ardennes offensive, better known as the Battle of the Bulge. The only reserve forces in the theater were the two airborne divisions of the XVIII Airborne Corps, the 82d and the 101st. Supreme Headquarters Allied Expeditionary Forces (SHAEF) ordered McAuliffe to get the division to the critical Belgian road junction at Bastogne and to block attacking German forces from passing to the west. McAuliffe assembled the division staff and said, "All I know of the situation is that there has been a breakthrough and we have got to get up there."

McAuliffe quickly got the division to Bastogne by every means available. Joining forces with the Combat Command of the Tenth Armored Division already in Bastogne and receiving permission to take command of any units withdrawing through the area, the force in the village was larger and considerably stronger in firepower than the original division. By 19 December the division was patrolling and digging in around the village.

McAuliffe determined that the key to holding Bastogne was building and maintaining strong defensive positions and countering attacks on the perimeter with a mobile reserve of armor and infantry teams. By nightfall on 20 December the last road connecting the division with American forces had been cut; the division would remain surrounded by the Germans until 26 December. During this period there were dozens of attacks, counterattacks, and desperate situations, but

the defining moment in McAuliffe's career came on 22 December, when Nazi officers approached Bastogne under a flag of truce with a message from the German commander demanding that the division surrender to avoid its complete destruction. When McAuliffe received the note he read it, laughed, and said, "Aw, nuts!" The staff discussed whether to reply, and McAuliffe said, "I don't know what to tell them." His G-3, Lieutenant Colonel Harry W. O. Kinnard, spoke up, saying that McAuliffe's original reaction would be hard to beat. The staff prepared the message "NUTS!" and McAuliffe signed it. The German emissaries translated but did not understand the slang; their American escort translated it into more formal language and sent the enemy delegation back to their lines. Word of the general's audacious and flippant response in such desperate circumstances quickly spread through the command and raised morale during the rest of the period of encirclement.

Until 23 December bad weather prevented aerial resupply of Bastogne as well as close air support of the division against armored attacks. Ammunition stocks quickly shrank, creating a growing problem, as did the lack of proper medical facilities. On the twenty-third, skies cleared enough that 144 tons of supplies were dropped. At the same time, the Fourth Armored Division was fighting its way up from the south to relieve Bastogne. Nonetheless, there remained difficult fighting on Christmas Day. McAuliffe's leadership was evident in his mimeographed Christmas message to the embattled soldiers, drafted by Kinnard. It described the German surrender demand and his response, wished the soldiers a merry Christmas, and continued:

What's merry about this, you ask? We're fighting—it's cold—we aren't home. All true, but what has the proud Eagle Division accomplished with its worthy comrades? . . . Just this: We have stopped cold everything that has been thrown at us from the north, east, south and west. . . . These units, spearheading the last desperate German lunge, were heading straight west for key points when the Eagle Division was hurriedly ordered to stem the advance. How effectively this was done will be written in history; not alone in our Division's history but in world history. . . . We continue to hold Bastogne. By holding Bastogne we assure the success of the Allied armies.

Armored relief forces broke through to Bastogne on 26 December. Although severe fighting continued around Bastogne into January, the spirited defense and particularly McAuliffe's inspired response to the surrender demand made the encirclement an event that will live forever in American military history.

McAuliffe went on to command the 103d Infantry Division through the Siegfried line and into Austria to link up with the Fifth Army in Italy. After the war, he was ground forces adviser during the Bikini tests of the atomic bomb. He was appointed head of the army's Chemical Corps in 1949; served as deputy chief of staff for operations in 1953; acted as commanding general of the Seventh Army (Europe) from 1953 to 1955; and held the post of commander in chief of the U.S. Army (Europe) in 1955. McAuliffe retired a full general in 1956. Later he served as vice president and director of American Cyanamid Company until his retirement in 1962. He died at the Walter Reed Army Medical Center in Maryland.

General McAuliffe had a successful, distinguished career, which was elevated to the singularly noteworthy at the siege of Bastogne. His command there and particularly his irreverent response to the surrender demand brought him to prominence.

• A personal account of the siege of Bastogne is in the transcript of an oral history interview of Lieutenant General Kinnard in the Kinnard papers at the archives of the U.S. Army Military History Institute, Carlisle Barracks, Pa. There is no complete biography of McAuliffe. Details of his life are in *Current Biography 1950* (1950), and in Sidney Shalett, "McAuliffe Says 'Nuts' to the Atom," *Saturday Evening Post*, 29 June 1946, pp. 20, 94–96. The best accounts of the siege of Bastogne are found in S. L. A. Marshall, *Bastogne* (1946), Hugh M. Cole, *The Ardennes: Battle of the Bulge* (1965), and Charles B. MacDonald, *A Time for Trumpets: The Untold Story of the Battle of the Bulge* (1985). An obituary is in the *New York Times*, 14 Aug. 1945.

K. E. HAMBURGER

MCAULIFFE, Christa. *See* Challenger Shuttle Crew.

MCAULIFFE, Leon (3 Jan. 1917–20 Aug. 1988), steel guitarist, was born William Leon McAuliffe in Houston, Texas. The names of his parents are not known. As a youngster McAuliffe became fascinated with the "Hawaiian" style of guitar playing that he heard on the radio and on recordings, such as those by popular recording artist Sol Hoopi. Because many players in this style used steel-bodied instruments, the style was also known as "steel guitar." By the time he was fifteen, McAuliffe had formed his first group, colorfully named the Waikiki Strummers, and they landed local radio jobs, playing Hawaiian-flavored music along with country, jazz, and blues numbers. Two years later he was invited to join the Light Crust Doughboys, a local band sponsored by a flour company and organized by the company's public relations representative, W. Lee O'Daniel. McAuliffe recorded with them at the Chicago session in 1933 and soon after became a full-time member, settling in Fort Worth. Meeting Bob Dunn, another popular steel guitar player, McAuliffe decided to electrify his instrument to gain the loud, sharp sound that Dunn had achieved.

In March 1935 McAuliffe was brought to the attention of Bob Wills, a band leader who had been with the Light Crust Doughboys before McAuliffe was in the band. Wills had broken away to form his own group, the Texas Playboys. McAuliffe joined Will's group and settled in Tulsa, Oklahoma, at the time the group's home base. He became a featured performer on Wills's recordings from the mid-1930s through the early 1940s, when Wills moved to California to embark on a movie career. McAuliffe's solos were often introduced by Wills colorfully shouting, "Take it away, Leon." McAuliffe also is credited with adapting a blues recording originally made by guitarist Sylvester Weaver and renaming it "Steel Guitar Rag," which became one of Wills's most popular numbers. In the movies Wills and McAuliffe played supporting roles in films by Tex Ritter and Russell Hayden as well as appearing in several musical shorts.

McAuliffe left the band to become a flight instructor in World War II; he was stationed with Tex Beneke, who had previously played tenor saxophone with Glenn Miller. The duo formed their own band and began performing western swing with a big-band sound. The band got a radio job in Tulsa and signed with Columbia Records, scoring an immediate top-ten country hit with McAuliffe's instrumental "Panhandle Rag." Known as the Cimarron Boys (after a local ballroom), the band included brass and reeds as well as twin fiddles, giving it a unique sound. By the early 1960s a new version of the band was again recording, this time for McAuliffe's own Cimarron label, and had minor country hits with "Cozy Inn" (1961) and a cover of Bob Wills's classic, "Faded Love" (1962). McAuliffe abandoned recording and performing in the mid-1960s, as his style of music faded in popularity, and purchased small radio stations in rural Arkansas.

However, interest in western swing music began to grow again in the early 1970s. Wills returned to the recording studio, and McAuliffe performed with him on his last sessions in 1973. He joined the reunited Texas Playboys for a series of recordings and tours through the late 1970s and also recorded on his own. Although less active in the 1980s, he continued to perform, record, and teach until his death.

• Bob Wills's career, including Leon McAuliffe's contributions to the band, is documented in Charles Townsend, *San Antonio Rose* (1976). McAuliffe can be heard playing on many of Wills's 1930s recordings, including *The Essential* (Columbia/Legacy 48958). His band recordings of the late 1940s and early 1950s have been collected on Columbia Historic Edition (1984). See also Jimmy Lathem, *The Life of Bob Wills: The King of Western Swing* (1987), and Tom Dunbar, *From Bob Wills to Ray Benson: A History of Western Swing Music* (1988). Gary Ginell, "The Development of Western Swing," *JEMF Quarterly* 20, no. 74 (Fall/Winter 1984): 58–67, discusses the addition of the steel guitar to western swing bands.

RICHARD CARLIN

MCAVOY, May (18 Sept. 1901–26 Apr. 1984), silent screen actress, was born in New York City. Her father ran a successful livery stable on Park Avenue on the site of what is now the Waldorf-Astoria Hotel. McAvoy quit high school at age fifteen to become a model, ultimately making the transition to acting in silent films. She began by appearing in small roles in features shot in New York. In 1917 McAvoy made her debut as an ingénue in *Hate*, billed as Mae McAvoy. She subsequently appeared in a series of popular films including *To Hell with the Kaiser!* (1918), *Mrs. Wiggs* *of the Cabbage Patch* (1919), *The Way of a Woman* (1919), *Man and His Woman* (1920), *The Devil's Garden* (1920), and *The Truth about Husbands* (1920). By this time McAvoy had become well known, and her popularity was assured when she had a major personal success in *Sentimental Tommy* (1921), an adaptation of a James M. Barrie story.

McAvoy's triumph in *Sentimental Tommy* led to her being signed to an exclusive contract with Paramount Pictures in 1921. She appeared in a successful string of hits, the best of which included *A Private Scandal* (1921), *Morals* (1921), *A Homespun Vamp* (1922), *The Top of New York* (1922), *Clarence* (1922), *Her Reputation* (1923), and *Only 38* (1923). After two years with Paramount, McAvoy, who was not always satisfied with the quality of scripts she was receiving, bought out the remainder of her contract because she refused to appear scantily clad in the Cecil B. DeMille epic, *Adam's Rib* (1923). As an independent star, McAvoy was more successful than she had been under studio contract. Her selection of projects was tasteful, and the films were usually of high quality, most particularly *The Enchanted Cottage* (1924), costarring Richard Barthelmess; the drama *Tarnish* (1924); *Lady Windermere's Fan* (1925), directed by Ernst Lubitsch and costarring Ronald Colman; and *Ben-Hur* (1926), playing opposite Ramon Navarro and Francis X. Bushman.

McAvoy was a petite and wide-eyed brunette, highly photogenic and exuding sex appeal combined with an air of innocence and charm. In a review of one of her films, writer Carl Sandburg described her as "a star-eyed goddess." Similar epithets were written about her screen image throughout the remainder of the silent era, and she was generally recognized as one of Hollywood's brightest talents. McAvoy commanded top salaries and was extremely popular with moviegoing audiences.

In 1927 McAvoy signed a contract with Warner Bros., and following a few undistinguished silent roles she was assigned to appear in Samson Raphaelson's *The Jazz Singer*, to be directed by Alan Crosland. The film was planned as an attempt to popularize the use of synchronized sound in feature films (short subjects had occasionally featured sound since the early 1920s). Warner Bros., fearing that the public needed encouragement to accept sound, decided to include musical segments in *The Jazz Singer*, which had originally been a popular stage drama starring Georgie Jessel. When Jessel proved difficult about salary, Warner's turned to the outstanding star of the musical stage, Al Jolson, to costar with McAvoy. Although often considered the "first talking picture," *The Jazz Singer* was, in fact, part silent and part sound (McAvoy only appeared in the silent portions of the film). *The Jazz Singer*, however, can certainly be credited with popularizing sound and making it seem to reluctant Hollywood studio executives a viable commercial product. As a result of the success of *The Jazz Singer*, Jolson became the first important star of the sound era. According to Herbert G. Goldman, Jolson was so grateful for McAvoy's support during the making of the film that he presented her with a diamond-encrusted cigarette case. McAvoy was appreciative but refused to accept what she thought was an inappropriately expensive gift. The cultural significance of *The Jazz Singer* is incalculable, and McAvoy's fine performance in it provides an opportunity to see her on screen, since so many of her earlier films, like most silent pictures, are rarely shown.

McAvoy continued in sound pictures through 1928 in *If I Were Single*, *The Terror*, and *The Lion and the Mouse*, all of which seemed to expose that McAvoy was ill suited to talkies. As Richard Barrios writes in *A Song in the Dark*, his history of the early primitive days of sound film, McAvoy played opposite distinguished stage actor Lionel Barrymore in *The Lion and the Mouse*, and "in juxtaposition with the vocal skill of Lionel Barrymore, she was clearly and audibly in trouble." Of her performance in *The Terror*, Dorothy Parker noted that one line of McAvoy's dialogue came out, "I am thick of thutth thilly antickth." Throughout the remainder of her life, McAvoy denied the story that her lisp made her a casualty of the arrival of sound, and, in fact, surviving prints of the film do not confirm Parker's criticism. Following *The Terror*, McAvoy did appear in two 1929 sound films, *Stolen Kisses* and *No Defense*, but Parker's criticism had been expounded by other critics and the damage was done. Warner Bros. dropped McAvoy in 1929, presumably because of her steadfast refusal to take voice lessons. She retired with a minimum of fanfare to marry Maurice G. Cleary, a businessman and theatrical agent, with whom she had one son.

McAvoy lived away from the spotlight for the subsequent decade, but following her divorce from Cleary, she signed a contract with Metro-Goldwyn-Mayer in 1940. She remained with the studio until the mid-1950s. She had high hopes for a revival of her career, but to her intense disappointment, she was only given bit roles and extra parts. This work did, however, provide her with a comfortable living. McAvoy's late film appearances include *Two Girls on Broadway* (1940), *Ringside Maisie* (1941), *Luxury Liner* (1948), *Mystery Street* (1950), *Executive Suite* (1954), and *Gun Glory* (1957). After this second career wound down in the late 1950s as the studio system declined, McAvoy retired again, living quietly in Los Angeles, where she died.

• For information on McAvoy, see Richard Lamparski, *Whatever Became Of . . . ?*, 3d ser. (1970); DeWitt Bodeen, *More from Hollywood: The Careers of 15 Great American Stars* (1977); Robert L. Carringer, ed., *The Jazz Singer* (1979); Ephraim Katz, *Film Encyclopedia* (1979); Herbert G. Goldman, *Jolson: The Legend Comes to Life* (1988); James Fisher, *Al Jolson: A Bio-Bibliography* (1994); Leslie Halliwell, *The Film Encyclopedia* (1994); and Richard Barrios, *A Song in the Dark: The Birth of the Musical Film* (1995). An obituary is in the *New York Times*, 3 May 1984.

JAMES FISHER

MCAVOY, Thomas Timothy (12 Sept. 1903–5 July 1969), priest, archivist, and historian, was born in Tipton, Indiana, the son of Charles Edward McAvoy, a merchant, and Nora Bernardine Walsh. He graduated from the University of Notre Dame in 1925, made final profession of vows in the Congregation of Holy Cross (C.S.C.) that same year, and was ordained a priest in 1929. He taught high school Latin and English from 1929 to 1932, offered courses in American history at Notre Dame from 1933 to 1935, and received a Ph.D. in history from Columbia University in 1940. He was appointed university archivist at Notre Dame in 1929, chairman of the department of history ten years later, and managing editor of the *Review of Politics* in 1942. He served as department chairman until 1960 and as archivist and managing editor until his death.

At the time of McAvoy's appointment in 1929, the Notre Dame archives housed approximately 300,000 documents, chiefly official records of various Catholic dioceses in the United States and personal papers of Catholic lay and clerical leaders. Most of these had been collected by an earlier Notre Dame librarian and historian, James F. Edwards, but the documents were unorganized and many still unboxed. McAvoy set about organizing these collections for scholarly use, assisted in the late 1930s by students supported by grants from the National Youth Administration. He also undertook to compile indexes of several important nineteenth- and early twentieth-century American Catholic periodicals and to calendar the archives' major manuscript collections, typing on index cards succinct but detailed summaries of each individual document. At the time of McAvoy's death, these indexes and calendars, available for scholarly research, filled more than 900 file drawers.

McAvoy also added significant new collections to the archives. In addition to the papers of prominent Notre Dame professors and administrators, he acquired the personal papers of Civil War general William T. Sherman, Ohio senator Thomas Ewing, Franklin Roosevelt adviser Frank Walker, Democratic National Committee chairman Paul Butler, and the official records of Catholic organizations such as the Christian Family Movement, the Liturgical Arts Society, and the Young Christian Students. Undoubtedly his most significant acquisitions were microfilmed copies of U.S. records in the archives of the Vatican's Congregation for the Propagation of the Faith (the agency overseeing developments in the American church until 1908) and in the archives of several European organizations sending financial and other assistance to American Catholics—the Society for the Propagation of the Faith of Paris and Lyons, the Leopoldine Society of Vienna, and the Ludwig Mission Society of Munich. Church historian John Tracy Ellis called McAvoy's archives "the richest and most systematically ordered manuscript collections in American Catholic history to be found anywhere in the United States" (*Catholic Historical Review* 55 [Oct. 1969]: 560).

A prolific writer, McAvoy authored five books, more than seventy-five scholarly articles, and 200 book reviews, chiefly in American Catholic church history. He wrote on Catholicism in the Midwest—*The Catholic Church in Indiana, 1789–1834* (his doctoral dissertation, 1940), *The History of the Catholic Church in the South Bend Area* (1953), and "The Le Bras Approach to the History of the Diocese of Fort Wayne" (*Indiana Magazine of History* 52 [Dec. 1956]: 369–82)—and on the history of Notre Dame—"Notre Dame, 1919–1922: The Burns Revolution" (*Review of Politics* 25 [Oct. 1963]: 431–50), and *Father O'Hara of Notre Dame: The Cardinal-Archbishop of Philadelphia* (1967).

McAvoy focused his major attention, however, on what he called the "Catholic minority" in the United States, the small group of English Catholics who settled chiefly in Maryland and Pennsylvania in colonial days, whose numbers were augmented over time through waves of immigration and who developed unique American Catholic characteristics through continuing interaction with America's dominant Protestant culture. The growth and development of this Catholic minority were traced in detail by McAvoy in *A History of the Catholic Church in the United States*, published posthumously in 1969. McAvoy's most influential book, and the one for which he was awarded the John Gilmary Shea Prize of the American Catholic Historical Association in 1957, was *The Great Crisis in American Catholic History, 1895–1900*, a detailed study of the so-called "Americanist" heresy. It was McAvoy's contention that the liberal theological views condemned by the Vatican under the name "Americanism" in 1899 were not held by American church leaders at all but only by more radical European leaders, chiefly in France, who were misinformed about Catholic practices in the United States.

As chairman for twenty-one years (1939–1960), McAvoy developed Notre Dame's department of history into one of its most respected academic units. He attracted highly esteemed professors to the faculty, strengthened academic requirements, increased the number of undergraduate majors sevenfold, and inaugurated a doctoral program in 1945.

Because of a noticeable speech impediment, McAvoy was not a successful classroom lecturer, but he was a dedicated mentor of graduate students and introduced scores of young scholars to the study of American Catholicism. He insisted on extensive research, especially in archival sources, on historical judgments founded solidly on scholarly evidence, and on clear and precise writing. He had early formed the habit of writing at least a paragraph every day, and he urged this practice on his students. He could be overly critical and short of patience, especially when confronted by what he considered incompetence, but he shared his time and expertise generously with serious scholars seeking his assistance. He was an effective and strong-willed administrator and an outspoken champion of historical studies in the liberal arts curriculum. He died in his archives office, working alone over a long holiday weekend.

• The major collection of McAvoy manuscripts and correspondence is preserved in the University of Notre Dame Archives. In addition to the works cited above, McAvoy's most significant writings include "The Catholic Church in the United States between Two Wars," *Review of Politics* 4 (Oct. 1942): 409–31; "American Catholics and the Second World War," *Review of Politics* 6 (Apr. 1944): 131–50; "The Formation of the Catholic Minority in the United States, 1820–1860," *Review of Politics* 10 (Jan. 1948): 13–34; "Bishop John Lancaster Spalding and the Catholic Minority (1877–1908)," *Review of Politics* 12 (Jan. 1950): 3–19; "The Role of History in the Catholic Liberal Arts College," *Catholic Educational Review* 48 (Oct. 1950): 505–15; "Manuscript Collections among American Catholics," *Catholic Historical Review* 37 (Oct. 1951): 281–95; "The Catholic Minority in the United States, 1789–1821," *Historical Records and Studies* 39–40 (1952): 33–50; "A New Technique: Writing Religious History," *University of Portland Review* 8 (Apr. 1955): 9–17; "American Catholics: Tradition and Controversy," *Thought* 35 (Winter 1960): 583–600; and "Catholic Archives and Manuscript Collections," *American Archivist* 24 (Oct. 1961): 409–14. McAvoy published a brief autobiographical article in Walter Romig, ed., *The Book of Catholic Authors*, 6th ser. (1966?), pp. 253–62. His work is also discussed in J. Douglas Thomas, "Interpretations of American Catholic Church History: A Comparative Analysis of Representative Catholic Historians, 1875–1975" (Ph.D. diss., Baylor Univ., 1976) and "A Century of American Catholic History," *U.S. Catholic Historian* 6 (Winter 1987): 25–49; Philip Gleason and Charlotte Ames, "Catholic Americana at Notre Dame," in *What Is Written Remains*, ed. Maureen Gleason and Katharina J. Blackstead (1994); Richard Gribble, "Thomas T. McAvoy, C.S.C.: Historian, Archivist, Educator" (in possession of Thomas E. Blantz); and Francis J. Weber, "Thomas T. McAvoy, C.S.C.: Historian of American Catholicism," *Indiana Magazine of History* 64 (Mar. 1968): 15–24. An obituary is in the *South Bend Tribune*, 7 July 1969.

THOMAS E. BLANTZ

MCBETH, Susan Law (1830–26 May 1893), Presbyterian missionary to American Indians and author, was born in Scotland to Alexander McBeth, a stonemason, and Mary Henderson. In 1831 the family immigrated to the United States, settling in Wellsville, Ohio. Her father became an elder in the newly founded Wellsville Presbyterian Church, and the family may have helped runaway slaves, a widespread practice among midwestern Presbyterians. Sue (as she generally called herself) graduated from the Steubenville Female Seminary in 1854 and taught at schools in Wellsville and Iowa and at Fairfield University in Iowa.

McBeth's vocation, however, lay elsewhere. Her life spanned most of the "Great Century" of Protestant missions. Stimulated by the revivals of the Second Great Awakening, Protestants organized foreign missionary societies to carry to "heathen" everywhere the blessings of Christian civilization: the gospel, intertwined with idealized forms of American life. Cooperating with the U.S. government, evangelicals also focused on American Indians, "our own heathen," as a Presbyterian pamphlet called them.

As a young girl, McBeth had fantasized about becoming a missionary to the American tribes, and in 1860 she achieved her wish. The Board of Foreign Missions (BFM) of the Presbyterian Church in the United States of America (Old School) sent her as a teacher to Goodwater Academy in the Choctaw Nation of present-day Oklahoma. Like other evangelical missionary societies, the BFM combined a near-absolute intolerance of "savage" cultures with an equally intense belief in the capacity of individual Indians to reject their past and to become citizens of Christian civilization. McBeth too possessed such ethnocentric but racially egalitarian beliefs. The diary she kept as a young teacher, however, reveals a less judgmental and more intellectually curious approach to Indian culture than she would show in later life. She especially enjoyed teaching Choctaw girls. But hardly had her work begun than the Civil War broke out, shattering the BFM southern Indian mission. As she returned home amid the signs of war, she noted bemusedly that "God works in a mysterious way His wonders to perform."

During the Civil War McBeth served with the United States Christian Commission in the Jefferson Barracks military hospital in St. Louis. Tracts she wrote for soldiers were published in book form as *Seed Scattered Broadcast; or, Incidents in a Camp Hospital* (1869). Florence Nightingale contributed an introduction to an English edition that appeared in 1871. In the late 1860s McBeth helped found a settlement home for young women and became engaged, but her fiancé died before the couple could be married. During these deeply testing years she suffered a stroke that permanently incapacitated one of her legs, yet she completed a manuscript history of the Choctaw mission, which has been lost.

In the early 1870s McBeth returned to the Indian field during the period of President Ulysses S. Grant's "peace policy." To establish more just relationships with the tribes, the government invited Catholic and Protestant churches to nominate agents and teachers among the Indians. The BFM participated in the ambitious experiment, and in 1873 a more worldly wise and perhaps more embittered McBeth took a position as a teacher at a government school on the Nez Perce reservation at Lapwai, Idaho. Although the Nez Perce war of 1877 again forced her to flee, she soon returned under the direct commission of the BFM. She delighted in the name *pika*, the mother, which she claimed the Indians called her. The Nez Perces, she wrote in 1886, "are *all* my children."

McBeth's dedication and combative personality embroiled her in disagreements, even with other missionaries, including her sister Kate, who arrived in 1879 and remained with the Nez Perce mission until her death in 1915. Complex disputes wracked the tribe, involving traditionalists, agents, missionaries, and Indians more willing to selectively adapt white ways, and the McBeths became actively involved in many of them. Indeed, by championing one group of Presbyterian converts against another, Sue McBeth helped produce division within her own church. She left the reservation in 1885 at the behest of the agent and the BFM, settling finally in the nearby village of Mt. Idaho. There, until the end of her life, she continued her special task: the training of Nez Perce men for church eldership, ordination, and leadership among their own and other Indian peoples. At least ten students (her "boys") became Presbyterian ministers. During this period she also wrote "Dictionary and Grammar of the Nez Perce Language" (Smithsonian Institution National Anthropological Archives Manuscript 2487, 1873–1893).

Fellow Presbyterians Sheldon Jackson and the "martyred" Marcus and Narcissa Whitman, killed by Cayuse Indians in 1847, perhaps achieved greater national fame among evangelical Protestants. But the small, lame Sue McBeth also became an inspirational figure to many in the Protestant missionary movement. Sue and Kate McBeth provided crucial assistance to Alice C. Fletcher, the renowned anthropologist who surveyed the Nez Perce reservation so that the land could be divided into individual farms and the "surplus" land sold according to the stipulations of the General Allotment Law (Dawes Act) of 1887. Benefiting from hindsight, some historians claim that the long-term results of this allotment process were highly detrimental to the Nez Perces.

McBeth denied that she was a woman's rights advocate and attempted to inculcate traditional Presbyterian gender roles, which mandated that Nez Perce husbands should farm and some should preach but that their wives should keep the home. Yet she possessed a fierce sense of independence and, ironically, demonstrated how the mission field could sometimes offer radically expanded opportunities to women: had she been on the home front during these decades, she would not have had the opportunity to train male Presbyterian ministerial candidates.

In her missionary goals for Indians, McBeth was broadly representative of her nineteenth-century BFM colleagues and indeed of most evangelicals in other denominations. In her faith, intelligence, and drive she was an extraordinary individual, and, at least during her later decades, she was an extraordinarily difficult colleague to work with. Intensely focused on her chosen method of saving Indians and on tribal intrigues, she wrote long, often anguished letters to BFM headquarters in New York. In these letters she thrilled to the victories of the Lord and battled against all, regardless of personal relationship, race, sex, or creed, who opposed her understanding of His cause.

• Sue McBeth's letters from the Choctaw and Nez Perce mission fields are in the American Indian Correspondence, Library of the Presbyterian Historical Society, Philadelphia. *American Indian Correspondence: The Presbyterian Historical Society Collection of Missionaries' Letters, 1833–1893* (1979) is on microfilm. Other collections include the Idaho State Historical Society, Boise; the library of the University of Idaho, Moscow; the Holland Library of Washington State University, Pullman; the Graduate Theological Union Library, San Anselmo, Calif.; the Oklahoma Historical Society, Oklahoma City; and the Schlesinger Library, Radcliffe College, Mass. See also Hope Holway, "A Report on Research on the Record of Sue McBeth, Missionary," *Chronicles of Oklahoma* 44 (Summer 1966): 222–25. McBeth's publications not mentioned in the text are her diary, *Chronicles of Oklahoma*, ed. Anna Lewis (Sept. 1939, Dec. 1939, and June 1943), and "Our Indian Sisters," *Woman's Work for Woman* 15, no. 7 (July 1885): 223–24. See also Kate McBeth, *The Nez Perces since Lewis and Clark* (1908), and Mary M. Crawford, *The Nez Perces since Spalding: Experiences of Forty-One Years at Lapwai, Idaho* (1936).

A carefully researched biography is Allen Conrad Morrill and Eleanor Dunlap Morrill, *Out of the Blanket: The Story of Sue and Kate McBeth, Missionaries to the Nez Perces* (1978). See also Michael C. Coleman, *Presbyterian Missionary Attitudes toward American Indians, 1837–1893* (1985) and "Christianizing and Americanizing the Nez Perce: Sue L. McBeth and Her Attitudes to the Indians," *Journal of Presbyterian History* 53, no. 4 (Winter 1975): 339–61.

For Nez Perce perceptions, see McBeth's pupil James Hayes, *Called to Evangelize* (n.d.); Albert Moore, *Pi-Lu-Ye-Kin: The Life History of a Nez Perce Indian*, ed. Anthony E. Thomas (1970; microfilm 1972); and Allen P. Slickpoo, Sr., *Noon Nee-Me-Poo (We the Nez Perces): Culture and History of the Nez Perces*, vol. 1 (1973). For a broader sense of Indian responses see Michael C. Coleman, *American Indian Children at School, 1850–1930* (1993).

MICHAEL C. COLEMAN

MCBRIDE, F. Scott (29 July 1872–23 Apr. 1955), clergyman and reformer, was born Francis Scott McBride in Carroll County, Ohio, the son of Francis McBride, an iron molder, and Harriet Miller. After studying at Mechanicstown (Ohio) Academy and Indiana State Normal School, he received a B.S. in 1898 from Muskingum College in New Concord, Ohio. Three years later he graduated from Pittsburgh Theological Seminary. He had interrupted his education periodically to teach school in Carroll County.

After being ordained in the United Presbyterian church in 1901, McBride received his first pastorate in Kittanning, Pennsylvania. That year he married Geraldine Van Fossen; they would have three children. While serving in Kittanning, McBride paid off the church's debt, reconstructed its building, and tripled the size of the congregation. In 1909 he moved to the Ninth Avenue United Presbyterian Church in Kittanning, Illinois. There he began the temperance work that was to become the focus of his professional life. As chair of the county temperance organization, an affiliate of the Anti-Saloon League of America, he led an intensive campaign that managed to send two "dry" representatives to the state legislature—the first ever elected in the county.

In 1912 McBride became a full-time employee of the Anti-Saloon League. After a year as district superintendent of the state league in Springfield, he moved to Chicago to become state superintendent. His vigorous lobbying and political organizing helped elect a temperance sympathizer as Speaker of the state legislature and got a number of temperance laws passed, including Illinois's ratification in 1917 of the Eighteenth Amendment to the U.S. Constitution, which established national Prohibition.

In 1924 McBride was elected general superintendent of the Anti-Saloon League of America, headquartered in Westerville, Ohio. Soon after he took office, the Federal Council of Churches of Christ in America produced a report acknowledging Prohibition's many failures. This represented a blow to the league's claim to speak for all Protestant churches. McBride, who was a member of the council, succeeded in persuading the organization's board to disavow the report, but the episode presaged the growing disillusion with Prohibition that the league would face in the years ahead. One group within the league, led by Ernest Cherrington, argued that the organization should turn from compulsion to persuasion and concentrate on educating the young instead of harassing established drinkers. McBride and his allies, on the other hand, favored the league's traditional, more militant and evangelistic approach.

The best-known member of the militant camp (considerably overshadowing McBride) was Wayne Wheeler, who had played an important role in the drafting and passage of the Eighteenth Amendment and who now served as the league's legislative superintendent, based in Washington. Wheeler exerted formidable influence in Congress, in part because his close ties to the Treasury Department's Prohibition Bureau gave him control over thousands of patronage jobs, which he could trade for favorable votes on temperance legislation. Shortly after Wheeler died in 1927, the conflict between the league's two factions came to a head. McBride was narrowly reelected general superintendent in 1928 but was forced to accept a new department of education and propaganda headed by Cherrington. Officially the league would now, as McBride put it, "fight the demon rum on two fronts—that of force and that of persuasion." Nevertheless, McBride's reelection and the organization's unwillingness to disavow Wheeler's strong-arm tactics in Congress signified that the more militant wing retained much of its power. McBride moved the league headquarters to Washington and continued most of Wheeler's activities himself, particularly the fight to protect the Eighteenth Amendment against repeal. "Among the ideals of the present day, few are more nearly right basically than Prohibition," wrote McBride in 1928.

Under McBride's leadership the league helped persuade both the Democratic and Republican parties to support Prohibition in their 1928 platforms. When the Democratic candidate, Alfred E. Smith, repudiated this position, McBride mobilized the league to campaign vigorously for Smith's opponent, Herbert Hoover, under the slogan "A dry president in 1928." The league also worked with its state affiliates to support hundreds of local temperance candidates from both parties. At the same time McBride lobbied Congress continuously, pressing for stiffer antiliquor regulations and tighter enforcement. Repealing Prohibition, he warned, would increase "drunkenness, misery, crime, lunacy, and death." A reporter during this period described him as "dynamic, raw-boned, gaunt, clean-shaven, six feet tall, with a full head of unruly black hair."

Contributions to the league had begun to decline as soon as the battle for national Prohibition was won in 1919, and by the end of the 1920s they were falling even more sharply, as the public grew disillusioned with the actual workings of Prohibition. The league's revenue was further eroded by the failing economy after the stock-market crash of 1929. But McBride remained stubbornly—even misleadingly—upbeat, resisting all proposals for compromise and insisting as late as 1931 that the league was "in a better position today than ever before."

In a notable break with the past, both Democratic and Republican platforms in 1932 included a recommendation that Prohibition be resubmitted for a national vote. In March 1933 Congress went further still and voted to repeal the Eighteenth Amendment; by December of that year repeal had received the necessary ratification in the states, and America's experiment with national Prohibition was over. McBride held his ground, however, observing in 1934 that "the tide is beginning to turn" and predicting a year later that Prohibition would be back within a decade. In 1936 he resigned from the national superintendency of the league, though he remained on the administrative committee for the rest of his life and headed the league in Pennsylvania from 1936 to 1943. He remained active in church affairs as well, serving as vice moderator of the general assembly of the United Presbyterian church (1934–1935) and moderator of its Illinois synod (1944–1945). He died at his winter home in St. Petersburg, Florida.

McBride took his place at the head of the Anti-Saloon League when the battle to achieve national Prohibition had already been won and the practical difficulties of enforcing the law were beginning to emerge. His unwillingness to consider any compromise on Prohibition may have eased the way for repeal. Yet he must be credited for the intensity of his struggle to keep America dry and for his unswerving conviction that he was fighting for the prosperity and the soul of the nation.

• McBride's papers are housed at the Ohio Historical Society. Correspondence with him appears in the Oscar G. Christgau Papers and in the Papers of the American Council on Alcoholism, both in the Michigan Historical Collection, Bentley Historical Library, University of Michigan, Ann Arbor. For an expression of McBride's views on Prohibition, see his article, "The Official View of the Anti-Saloon League," *Current History* 28, no. 1 (Apr. 1928): 1–4. See also "The New Policy of the Anti-Saloon League," an unsigned article in *Literary Digest* 96, no. 1 (7 Jan. 1928): 8–9. McBride's career in the league is discussed in Larry Engelman, *Intemperance: The Lost War against Liquor* (1979), and Andrew Sinclair, *Prohibition: The Era of Excess* (1962). An obituary is in the *New York Times*, 24 Apr. 1955.

SANDRA OPDYCKE

McBRIDE, Henry (25 July 1867–31 Mar. 1962), art critic and writer, was born in West Chester, Pennsylvania. Little is known about his early life except that his parents were Quakers and that McBride's first job after graduating from high school was writing and illustrating seed catalogs for a local nursery. By 1887 he had saved $200 and moved to New York City to study art. He attended the Artists' and Artisans' Institute for four years under iconoclast John Ward Stimson, then continued his studies at the Art Students League, eventually teaching at both organizations.

In 1900 McBride approached the Educational Alliance, a settlement house on the Lower East Side, with an offer to organize an art department. McBride served as its director and also taught life-drawing classes. In 1901 he also became director of the School of Industrial Arts at Trenton, New Jersey, where he taught three days each week for five years. The monotony of this work wore on him, however, and around 1905 he left the United States to live and travel abroad.

McBride began his writing career at the age of forty-six, joining the staff of the *Sun* (formerly the *New York Sun*) as an assistant to art critic Samuel Swift just in time to publish an unsigned piece on the historic Armory Show of 1913. After Swift resigned that same year, McBride took over and for the next thirty-seven years wrote the paper's weekly art reviews, described by writer Lincoln Kirstein as "unmatched in this country for their charm, perception and urbanity." Although the *Sun* did not enjoy the prestige of the *New York Times* or the *Herald Tribune*, where conservative art critics Edward Alden Jewell and Royal Cortissoz wrote, respectively, McBride's columns had enormous influence over contemporary opinion and the development of the New York art world.

McBride became known for his wit and humor. As one profile opined, he "belonged to a generation that realized that his audience could best be instructed or converted if they were entertained." In addition, his friendships with many contemporary artists lent a delightfully intimate note to his columns. For example, lamenting his lackluster response to the art shows of December 1922 he noted, "There seemed to be no occasion to send a telegram to Charlie Demuth, at Lancaster, Pa.: 'Mustn't Miss It. Come At Once,' except possibly in the case of his own show at Daniel's and that, of course, he had seen already." Yet McBride was gracious, even to artists whose work he disliked, as in his review of painter Robert Henri's 1931 retrospective: "It becomes my painful duty to confess that, in my opinion, the memorial show to the work of the late Robert Henri at the Metropolitan Museum is not a triumph."

McBride brought many prominent artists, including Demuth, painter John Marin, sculptor Jo Davidson, and painter Georgia O'Keeffe, their first critical acclaim and actively promoted their work. He also generated greater appreciation of past masters, for example, encouraging his friend Bryson Burroughs, curator at the Metropolitan Museum of Art, to hold a retrospective exhibition in 1917 of the work of nineteenth-century artist Thomas Eakins. McBride's glowing review of the exhibition helped to revitalize interest in the then-forgotten artist's career.

Through Mrs. Burroughs, McBride met writer Gertrude Stein, and he became a frequent visitor to her home in Paris, where he met cubist painters Pablo Picasso, Georges Braque, and Juan Gris and many others. He printed a poem by Stein in his column and encouraged her to present her work in America. In return, Stein composed a poetic portrait of McBride entitled "Have They Attacked Mary. He Giggled. (A Political Caricature)" (1916). Many of McBride's other friends created portraits of him, including painter Florine Stettheimer, sculptor Jo Davidson, printmaker Peggy Bacon, watercolorist Jules Pascin, painter Margaret Zorach, sculptor Gaston Lachaise, and composer Virgil Thomson.

In addition to his work for the *Sun*, from 1920 to 1929 McBride wrote for *Dial* magazine, a monthly compendium of the best in American literature and culture. His first article focused on Walter Arensberg's art collection, still hanging in Arensberg's West Sixty-seventh Street apartment where McBride was taken by painter Marcel Duchamp. Duchamp was also responsible for designing and publishing the first compilation of McBride's writings, *Some French Moderns Says McBride* (1923).

In 1930 McBride was appointed editor of the magazine *Creative Arts*, for which he wrote "The Palette Knife" editorial section each month. By then, however, he was in his sixties, and this work on top of visiting thirty to forty exhibitions each week for his *Sun* columns proved to be too much, and he left *Creative Arts* after only two years. McBride continued to write essays for various exhibitions, such as *Matisse* (1930), *John Marin* (1936), *Charles Demuth Memorial Exhibition* (1937), *Florine Stettheimer* (1946), and *George Bellows* (1957).

In 1949 M. Knoedler Galleries held an exhibition honoring the 82-year-old McBride and his influence on the modern art world. In an introduction to the catalog, Lincoln Kirstein wrote: "For forty years Henry McBride has been one of the half dozen serious writers in America who has humorously drawn time's attention to half a dozen serious artists." Nonetheless, the following year the *Sun* merged with the *World Telegram*, and the new owners decided that an art critic was no longer needed. McBride was fired. He was immediately hired by *Art News* to write a monthly essay, which he did for the next five years, as well as occasional reviews. In a 1955 profile in *Art in America*, Charlotte Devree remarked that McBride had "kept his dash. He has written and still writes like a man who doesn't mind committing himself and would a good deal rather be wrong than dull."

For the last twenty-five years of his life, McBride was cared for by his companion, Maximilian H. Miltzlaff, dividing his time between a room at the Herald Square Hotel in New York and a small home in Pennsylvania. He died quietly in New York City. At his death, Alfred Frankfurter, publisher of *Art News*, wrote: "His professional career was one that forever was opening eyes and lifting aside curtains—with grace and an inevitable sense of proportion, for Henry was literally of the antique species called gentleman."

• McBride's papers are at the Beinecke Rare Book and Manuscript Library at Yale University and are also available through the Archives of American Art, Smithsonian Institution, Washington, D.C. *To Honor Henry McBride* is the catalog that accompanied the exhibition of the same name held at M. Knoedler Galleries; Lincoln Kirstein's essay for that catalog was later reprinted as the quasi-preface to *The Flow of Art* (1975), a compilation of some of McBride's *Sun* articles. Profiles appeared in *Art in America*, Oct. 1955, and in *Apollo*, Mar. 1978. Obituaries are in the *New York Times*, 1 Apr. 1962, and *Art News*, May 1962.

JULIE MELLBY

MCBRIDE, Katharine Elizabeth (14 May 1904–3 June 1976), educator, was born in Philadelphia, Pennsylvania, the daughter of Thomas Canning McBride, a mechanical engineer, and Sally Hulley Neals. She received her B.A., M.A., and Ph.D. in psychology from Bryn Mawr in 1925, 1927, and 1932, respectively. She also did research at Columbia University (1928–1929). She joined the Bryn Mawr faculty in 1935, holding the positions of lecturer in education (1935–1936), assistant professor of education and psychology (1936–1938), and associate professor of education and psychology (1938–1940). Her early publications included *Aphasia: A Clinical and Psychological Study*, with Theodore H. Weisenburg (1935), and *Adult Intelligence: A Psychological Study of Test Performances*, with Weisenburg and Anne Roe (1936). From 1940 to 1942 she was dean at Radcliffe College. In 1942 she became Bryn Mawr's fourth president at the age of thirty-seven, a position she held for twenty-eight years. Arriving at a time when college life was dominated by war preparations, she also led the school through the Cold War and a period of student unrest associated with the war in Vietnam.

McBride presided over a period of significant expansion at Bryn Mawr. Enrollment grew, particularly at the graduate level, and the curriculum was enlarged by several new majors and interdepartmental studies at the graduate level. The college's physical plant also expanded during her administration with the construction or acquisition of many new buildings, including major expansions of the science center, a new library building, and two new dormitories, including Erdman Hall, designed by the noted Philadelphia architect Louis Kahn.

The state of education in the United States was McBride's chief concern. In a 1960 speech titled "Education: The Decade Ahead," delivered at the American Association of University Women Women's Forum, she stated, "What is new is a greatly increased dependence of society on education, so great that we shall be hard pressed to provide for those who can absorb very little education." She also noted the need for specialization and concentrated training. In the Horace Mann lecture in 1971 in Pittsburgh, Pennsylvania, she acknowledged that the college student population had nearly doubled in the preceding decade and voiced her concern that students from all income groups have the opportunity for higher education, stating, "The real

question will increasingly become how open access can be achieved."

McBride was an advocate of academic and individual freedom. In 1959 she urged a U.S. Senate subcommittee not to require loyalty oaths of students seeking federal student loans. Later she withstood pressure from legislators and the local community to withdraw the appointment of Herbert Aptheker, a member of the National Committee of the American Communist party, to teach black history at Bryn Mawr.

McBride also participated in many national, state, and local organizations concerned with education policy. She served on the National Science Foundation (chair, 1951–1953), the American Council on Education (chair, 1955–1956), the Delaware Valley Educational Television Corporation, the Board of Trustees of the Educational Testing Service (chair, 1952–1953, 1957–1958, 1963–1964), the College Entrance Examination Board (executive committee chair, 1949–1952), the Institute of International Education, the American Association of University Women, the Philadelphia Commission of Higher Education, the Commission of the Carnegie Foundation on the Future of Higher Education, and the American Council of Learned Societies, among others. She was appointed by President Dwight D. Eisenhower to the Committee on Education beyond High School in 1956. In 1959 she joined the board of the New York Life Insurance Company, becoming one of America's first women to serve on the board of a commercial, rather than academic, organization. She remained on the board until her death. Governor William Scranton appointed her to the Pennsylvania State Board of Education (1963–1967). She was also a trustee of seven educational facilities, including the University of Pennsylvania and Radcliffe.

As chair of the State Council on Higher Education's Committee on a Master Plan for Higher Education in Pennsylvania from 1963 to 1967, McBride participated in the design of the state's first plan to ensure adequate higher education resources through orderly growth and approved funding for the state community college system.

McBride received the Gold Medal of the National Institute of Social Sciences (1963), the Gimbel Award (1961), the Humanitarian Award of the Philadelphia Society of Clinical Psychologists (1970), and Bryn Mawr College's M. Carey Thomas Award (1960). She died in Bryn Mawr, Pennsylvania.

McBride devoted her life to the advancement of teaching and research and the welfare of her students at Bryn Mawr. Poet Marianne Moore (Bryn Mawr College, class of 1909), wrote of her:

O fortunate Bryn Mawr with her creatively unarrogant
    President
unique in her exceptional unpresidential constant:
a liking for people as they are.

• McBride's papers are in the Archives of Bryn Mawr College. See "Bryn Mawr College Head Hailed by Marianne Moore," *Philadelphia Inquirer*, 2 Mar. 1967. Other information can be found in "Memorial Minute for Katharine Mc-Bride," published by the College Entrance Examination Board (10 Oct. 1976), and "Resolution of the General Faculty in Memory of Katharine E. McBride," in the faculty minutes of Bryn Mawr College (22 Sept. 1976).

LORETT TREESE

MCBRIDE, Mary Margaret (16 Nov. 1899–7 Apr. 1976), radio talk show pioneer and writer, was born in Paris, Missouri, the daughter of Thomas Walker Mc-Bride, a farmer, and Elizabeth Craig. Through the intervention of a wealthy great-aunt she attended boarding school with the understanding that McBride would become a teacher at the school upon graduation from college. After one year at the University of Missouri, McBride decided she would rather be a writer. Her benefactor withdrew her financial support, but McBride worked to stay in school and earned a bachelor of journalism degree in 1919.

McBride started working as a reporter for the *Cleveland Press* in Ohio, then briefly worked as an assistant to the publicity director of the Interchurch World Movement in New York City in 1920. She returned to reporting in 1920 as a features writer for the *New York Evening Mail*. In 1924 she left the paper to become a freelance writer. Highly successful, she became one of the busiest women freelancers of the day. During the next ten years she wrote for such national publications as the *Saturday Evening Post*, *Cosmopolitan*, *McCall's*, and the *Ladies' Home Journal*. Starting in 1926, she also wrote or cowrote a number of books. In 1929 she paired with her friend Helen Josephy to write *Paris Is a Woman's Town*, an erstwhile travel guide for women that was more a gossipy description of designers, restaurants, and places to stay and see. This was followed by similar volumes on London, New York City, and Germany.

In 1930 McBride published a journalistic biography of lawyer and diplomat Dwight W. Morrow, which led to her writing a series of "star" biographies for Star Library Publications. In 1932 she churned out the life stories of Constance Bennett, Clark Gable, Greta Garbo, and Robert Montgomery. In 1934 she was hired by the New York City radio station WOR to host a women's show under the pseudonym Martha Deane, a folksy grandmother. After a few weeks, she decided it was too difficult for a 35-year-old single woman to maintain the deception. "Oh what's the use?" she asked. "I can't do it! I've mixed up all those grandchildren I've invented. I'm not a grandmother. I'm not even married. I made that up and it doesn't sound real because it isn't. The truth is I'm a reporter who would like to come here every day and tell you about the places I go, people I meet. Write me if you like that. But I can't be a grandmother any more!"

McBride's listeners loved her, and she built a loyal following. She remained at WOR until 1937 when she switched to the Columbia Broadcasting System (CBS) to host a show under her own name. In 1941 the National Broadcasting Company (NBC) lured her away with the promise of an unprecedented 45-minute daily

show. It was here that she honed her signature formula of a thirty-minute interview paired with fifteen minutes of ad-libbed chat, household tips, recipes, and commercial endorsements.

During her heyday, McBride had a daily listening audience of more than six million, mostly women, who were unusually loyal fans. During World War II, when the U.S. government asked citizens for scrap paper, McBride donated more than three million fan letters that she had stored in a warehouse. She received over 1,000 pieces of mail a week, a number that often jumped to 5,000 when she had discussed something controversial on her show. She was also a consummate saleswoman. Her listeners knew that anything "Mary Margaret" had endorsed was something they could trust. If she did not try an advertiser's product herself, she hired an independent laboratory to test the product's claims. Only then would she endorse it. She also had a down-home yet lyrical style, and her descriptions of food often made people drool.

McBride was also an insightful interviewer who over the years hosted such diverse guests as Eleanor Roosevelt, President Harry S. Truman, Queen Elizabeth II, Tibet's Dalai Lama, and such entertainers as Bob Hope, Orson Welles, and Jimmy Durante. Her popularity allowed her to enjoy journalistic coups, as well. She was the first reporter to interview General Omar Bradley after the surrender of Germany. One of her aides spotted him in line for her show—his wife was a fan. He was invited in and was that day's impromptu guest. Part of McBride's allure, though, was that she would invite anyone interesting to speak on her show. She often had guests ranging from zookeepers, interior designers, and plumbers to the more unique hog callers, bell ringers, and flagpole sitters.

When McBride celebrated her tenth anniversary in radio with a full-house show in New York's Madison Square Garden, First Lady Eleanor Roosevelt said of her, "I always rejoice when a woman succeeds. And when one succeeds superlatively, as you have done, Mary Margaret, it helps us all." Her fifteenth anniversary show was held to a packed audience in New York's Yankee Stadium.

In 1950 McBride switched to the American Broadcasting Company (ABC), where she remained for four years before her semiretirement in 1954. She retired to West Shokean, New York, and broadcast three times a week from WGHG, a Kingston, New York, radio station. In 1960 the New York Herald-Tribune Radio Operation picked her show up for syndication, and she worked for it until her death in West Shokean. In the final years of her life, she often broadcast from her own living room.

McBride was a member of the Author's League, the New York Newspaper Woman's Club, Query, Heterodoxy, and the Women's City Club. She received the Haitian National Order of Honor and Merit, a special medal of honor from the city of Vienna, a special recognition from the Virgin Islands, and in 1950 the One World Award. In her lifetime, Mary Margaret Mc-Bride was America's "first lady of radio." She was not the first person to host a radio talk show, but her format and technique of dropping any kind of persona were unique. Because of these qualities, she was the most successful radio personality of her own time. Extremely popular with her fans, McBride became part of their families. When she died, she was mourned as a favorite aunt, for many had forgotten that she was really just a reporter.

• McBride published several autobiographical works, including *How Dear to My Heart* (1940), *America for Me* (1941), *A Long Way from Missouri* (1959), and *Out of the Air* (1960). Her other books include *Jazz*, with Paul Whiteman (1926); *Charm: A Book about It and Those Who Have It, for Those Who Want It*, with Alexander Williams (1927); *London Is a Man's Town (But Women Go There)*, with Helen Josephy (1930); *New York Is Everybody's Town*, with Josephy (1931); *Beer and Skittles: A Friendly Guide to Modern Germany*, with Josephy (1932); *Here's Martha Deane* (1936); *Tune in for Elizabeth: Career Story of an Interviewer* (1954); *Harvest of American Cooking* (1957); *Encyclopedia of Cooking: America's Most Complete Cook Book* (1959); and *The Growing Up of Mary Elizabeth* (1966). In addition, she edited *How to Be a Successful Advertising Woman: A Career Guide for Women in Advertising, Public Relations, and Related Fields* (1948), authored a daily newspaper column for the Associated Press, "Mary Margaret McBride Says," from 1953 to 1976, and was the editor of the woman's page for the Newspaper Enterprise Association of New York City from 1952 to 1953. See also Joseph Gustaitis's brief assessment of McBride's role in radio. "Prototypical Talk Show Host," *American History Illustrated* (1993), vol. 28. Obituaries are in the *New York Times* and the *Washington Post*, 8 Apr. 1976, *Newsweek*, 19 Apr. 1976, and *Current Biography*, June 1976.

MARGARETTE R. CONNOR

MCBRYDE, John McLaren (1 Jan. 1841–20 Mar. 1923), agriculturist, educator, and college president, was born in Abbeville, South Carolina, the son of John McBryde, a successful cotton factor, and Susan McLaren. His parents immigrated to the United States from Scotland around 1820. After receiving a classical education at local schools, McBryde entered South Carolina college in Columbia, where he received lectures from John Le Conte (1818–1891) and Joseph Le Conte, who inspired in him a love of science. From Columbia, McBryde went to the University of Virginia, where he was studying at the outbreak of the Civil War.

In 1861 McBryde joined the Confederate forces as a volunteer. He served with P. G. T. Beauregard at the first battle of Manassas before being transferred to the cavalry on James Island. There he contracted typhus fever and was invalided home. To continue his service for the South, McBryde joined the Treasury Department of the Confederacy in Richmond, where he did very well. In 1863, at twenty-two years old, he was appointed head of a division of the war tax office. In the same year he married Cora Bolton, with whom he had eight children, six of whom survived.

After the war McBryde farmed in Buckingham County, Virginia, for two years before moving to a thousand-acre farm nearer to Charlottesville in Albemarle County. He resumed his interest in scientific agriculture with special attention to agricultural chemistry and botany. He also became very involved in the local farming organizations, writing articles on farming and founding farmers' clubs. Through this activity he became sufficiently well known that in 1879 he was appointed professor of agriculture and botany at the University of Tennessee.

Having established a strong agricultural department in Tennessee, McBryde accepted an appointment to an agricultural chair in 1882 at South Carolina College in Columbia. Almost immediately upon arrival he was made acting president. At the earliest opportunity, in 1883, this appointment was voted permanent. Four years later McBryde turned down the presidency of the University of Tennessee. In the same year the South Carolina legislature promoted the college to a university and gave it the necessary funding to develop an agricultural and mechanical school and experiment stations. This greatly pleased McBryde, who supervised the experiment stations directly, initiating work on the planting and fertilizing of cotton.

Unfortunately, in the early 1890s a political storm in the state resulted in the university being downgraded to a college once more, and the agricultural department was moved to Clemson. In 1891 McBryde accepted the presidency of the Agricultural and Mechanical college of Virginia (now Virginia Polytechnic Institute). With less than one hundred students, the school was in poor shape. In his sixteen-year tenure McBryde managed to reinvigorate the college, increasing its student body to more than seven hundred. Within two months of assuming his position, McBryde made a report to the board of visitors that called for a complete restructuring of the institution. Working with the 1862 Land-Grant Act and its companion legislation of 1890, McBryde determined to improve the polytechnic's standards, streamline admissions procedures, and focus more clearly on the technical aspect of the Land-Grant Act. He dealt with the need for a "liberal" education by offering nominal courses in the liberal arts and by a very broad interpretation of the word "liberal." He said:

In my opinion, a well planned course of scientific study, thoroughly taught in the laboratory and lecture room, can be made to give some of the elements of a liberal education, the development of the observing facilities, the strengthening of the power of inductive reasoning, accuracy of method and statement and love of truth. (quoted in DiCroce, p. 207)

During his tenure at Virginia Polytechnic, McBryde was offered the position of assistant secretary of agriculture under President Grover Cleveland, and he was elected to the presidencies of Sweet Briar Institute and the University of Virginia. All of these offers he refused. In 1907 he retired and was made professor emeritus of the Virginia Polytechnic Institute and awarded the degree of doctor of science. Five years later he was awarded the McMaster Medal by the University of South Carolina in recognition of his distinguished service to his native state. McBryde died at his son's home in New Orleans. He was buried in Blacksburg, Virginia.

• McBryde's papers are at the South Caroliniana Library at the University of South Carolina and also at the University of North Carolina, Chapel Hill. The best biography is still that in Lyon G. Tyler ed., *Men of Mark in Virginia: Ideals of American Life*, vol. 3 (1907). Information on his work at Virginia Polytechnic Institute is in Deborah M. DiCroce, "Ut Prosim—The Balance of Liberal and Useful Education in the American Land-Grant University: A Case Study of Virginia Tech" (Ph.D. diss., William and Mary, 1984). An obituary is in the *New Orleans Times-Picayune*, 21 Mar. 1923.

CLAIRE STROM

MCBURNEY, Robert Ross (31 Mar. 1837–27 Dec. 1898), general secretary of the Young Men's Christian Association of Greater New York, was born of Scotch-Irish parentage at Castle-Blaney, County Monaghan, in the Protestant province of Ulster, Ireland. A physician and surgeon, his father was an officer in a local Presbyterian church and was known for his hostility toward Roman Catholicism. His mother, whose maiden name was Ross, was a Wesleyan Methodist.

In 1854 Robert McBurney arrived in New York, where he worked as a clerk in a hat shop until 1861 when the business failed. He also became active as a layman in church work and led noon prayer meetings at North Dutch Church. Soon after his arrival in New York, he came in contact with the Young Men's Christian Association (YMCA). Founded in 1852, the New York association became one of the direction-setting associations within the North American YMCA movement. Originally a British organization established in London in 1844, the first YMCA on American soil was founded in Boston in 1851.

For more than three decades McBurney was one of the driving forces in the North American YMCA movement. In 1862 he became the librarian of the New York YMCA, and in 1863 he was elected its director and recording secretary. In 1864 he left the position but was called back in April 1865. In 1866 the New York YMCA moved from its quarters in the Bible House to its new building on Fourth Avenue and Twenty-third Street. Based on McBurney's own plans, the $487,000 construction became the model for YMCA buildings all over the country for decades.

Under McBurney's leadership, the New York YMCA expanded vastly and became one of the leading associations in the whole movement. The association inaugurated specialized work for railroad men and men of German and French ancestry. In 1875 Cornelius Vanderbilt agreed to provide two rooms in the basement of Grand Central Station for the New York YMCA's work with railroad men. In 1887 the first building for railroad men opened its doors. A German branch was organized in 1881, and a French branch followed in 1889. Altogether, McBurney witnessed the addition of fourteen new branches to the YMCA of New York. At the time of his appointment in 1862, the New York YMCA had 150 members and occupied three small rented rooms. The annual budget amounted to $1,700. In 1898, the year of McBurney's death, the New York YMCA carried out its programs at fifteen locations in the city, owning nine buildings and spending annually $175,000.

McBurney became one of the central figures in the YMCA's statewide work in New York and was involved with the International Committee, the central governing body of YMCAs in North America. In 1866 and 1867 he was called to be the leader of the first two state conventions, and in 1869, 1870, and 1875 he was chosen president of the YMCA state convention of New York. At the 1866 Albany convention of YMCAs of North America, McBurney led in the effort to locate the International Committee in New York and to establish state and provincial organizations. He was elected a full member of the International Committee in 1869. In 1874 he was elected president of the international convention at Dayton but declined the position.

Within the YMCA, McBurney devoted his attention to the interests and concerns of the general secretaries, YMCA's executive officials. He developed the executive character of the position of general secretary through his own leadership. In 1871 he was chosen the first president of the first General Secretaries Conference, and he helped to found the YMCA's International Training School at Springfield, Massachusetts, for secretaries in 1885. But despite his advocacy of the role and importance of the general secretaries within the YMCA movement, he opposed the elevation of their needs and concerns over the association's purpose.

In the later years of his life, McBurney focused on the YMCA's missionary work overseas. In 1889 he was appointed the first chair of the International Committee's subcommittee on foreign-mission work. He continued to fill that post until 1895. During his years as chairman, he always insisted that the YMCA never conduct missionary work independently or in competition with the churches.

Among McBurney's most important contributions to conservative association policy was his support for the so-called Evangelical Test. A compilation of New Testament phrases that the YMCA considered central tenets of orthodox Protestant doctrine, the test was designed to keep the YMCA firmly tied to the Protestant churches. Signing the test was to be a prerequisite for entering active, voting membership and for holding office in the YMCA and was aimed at excluding Catholics, Unitarians, and all members of non-Christian religions from active membership. At the 1869 Portland, Maine, convention of the YMCA, delegates resolved to require local associations' Committees of Management and all active YMCA members to sign the Evangelical Test. By 1885 McBurney and Cephas Brainerd, secretary of the International Committee, had succeeded in convincing most associations to adopt the test. Privately, McBurney later recognized that the Evangelical Test posed a barrier to the YMCA's attempts to reach workingmen, many of them immigrants, who belonged to non-Protestant churches. However, it was only in 1933 that the National Council of the YMCA ruled to permit local associations to autonomously determine the requirements for active membership. In 1939 the YMCA abandoned the test completely.

Although McBurney took a conservative position on many aspects of association policy, in some matters he was ahead of his time. When McBurney introduced chess into the halls of the New York YMCA in 1870, games were controversial within the association. But not all his efforts were crowned with success. When he tried to introduce sex education into the YMCA's program in 1883, he faced universal rejection from his association peers.

McBurney's personal life itself was the cause for some muted controversy within association circles. Men in positions of religious leadership, like McBurney, were expected to get married. Although the obituaries eulogize McBurney for his personal commitment, at the time some voices within the YMCA criticized prominent leaders like McBurney, Richard Cary Morse, and Richard Weidensall for their failure to marry. McBurney died at Clifton Springs, New York.

During the thirty-six years of his involvement with the YMCA, McBurney became one of the most important leaders of the association on the city, state, and national levels. He is remembered as one of the makers of YMCA history.

• McBurney's papers and materials pertaining to his life and career and his relation to the YMCA are in the YMCA of the USA Archives at the University of Minnesota, St. Paul. A full account of his life is Laurence Locke Doggett, *Life of Robert R. McBurney* (1902). A short biographical sketch is "Robert R. McBurney," *New York Railroad Men* 4 (May 1891): 135–38. For McBurney's career in the context of the history of the YMCA, see C. Howard Hopkins, *History of the Y.M.C.A. in North America* (1951); Richard C. Morse, *My Life with Young Men: Fifty Years in the Young Men's Christian Association* (1919); and Morse, *History of the North American Young Men's Christian Associations* (1919). The issue of marriage in relation to YMCA leaders is discussed in John D. Wrathall, "Provenance as Text: Reading the Silences around Sexuality in Manuscript Collections," *Journal of American History* 79 (June 1992): 165–78. Obituaries are in the *New York Times*, 28 Dec. 1898, and the *Intercollegian* 21 (Feb. 1899): 111–12.

THOMAS WINTER

MCCABE, Charles Cardwell (11 Oct. 1836–19 Dec. 1906), Civil War chaplain and Methodist Episcopal bishop, was born in Athens, Ohio, the son of Robert McCabe, a tailor, and Sarah Robinson. At age fifteen, McCabe worked on a small farm in Mt. Pleasant, Iowa, and, by age sixteen, clerked in a store in Cedar Rapids, Iowa. In 1854 he enrolled at Ohio Wesleyan University, Delaware, Ohio, where his uncle, Lorenzo Dow McCabe, was a distinguished professor; he withdrew from school in 1858 but graduated with a B.A. in 1860 and was accorded on honorary M.A. in 1864.

After withdrawing from the university, McCabe taught at a small country school and then became principal of the high school in Ironton, Ohio. "My young friends, I am a Christian," he said as he introduced himself and emphasized the Golden Rule as his modus operandi. During his two years there, he married Rebecca Peters, an iron manufacturer's daughter, in 1860. They had one son, John P. McCabe.

As the Civil War broke out, McCabe, via rousing speeches, helped raise the 122d Regiment of Ohio Volunteer Infantry for the northern army. He had been ordained deacon in the Methodist Episcopal church by Bishop Matthew Simpson, 23 September 1860, at Gallipolis, Ohio, and elder by Bishop Thomas A. Morris, 7 September 1862, at Zanesville, Ohio. By 8 October 1862, McCabe was serving as chaplain of the 122d Ohio Infantry.

Chaplain McCabe set up his regimental church, held protracted services, wrote letters for soldiers, and prepared newspaper articles. Staying behind to help the regimental surgeon, W. M. Houston, as the 122d retreated after the battle of Winchester, McCabe, according to military reports, was captured on 15 June 1863 and turned over to Major General Jubal A. Early. Although chaplains and surgeons had been released upon capture, Early sent McCabe to Libby Prison, Richmond, Virginia, saying, "You are a preacher, are you? . . . Well, you preachers have done more to bring on this war than anybody and I'm going to send you to Richmond . . . They tell me you've been shouting 'On to Richmond' for a long time, and to Richmond you shall go" (Bristol, p. 125).

In his lecture, "The Bright Side of Life in Libby Prison"—first delivered for Sunday school children and thus with tempered images of a horrific reality—McCabe related anecdotes of his months in prison. He and other prisoners dealt with their circumstances by telling jokes, following the news, teasing Rebels with patriotic songs, holding lectures and concerts, and organizing a university. Inmates taught French, German, Spanish, Latin, Greek, algebra, geometry, philosophy, and religion (Parker, p. 45). During his last six weeks there, McCabe nearly died of typhoid, but, according to military records, he was paroled 17 October 1863.

Although ill health forced him to resign his chaplaincy on 8 January 1864, he joined the United States Christian Commission on 29 March 1864. A "brotherhood of Good Samaritans" sprung from the Young Men's Christian Association, its delegates followed Federal armies into the South, helped chaplains and surgeons, distributed food, clothing, medicines, and literature, and held revival services. With no "misgivings about war as an instrument of politics" (Ferguson, p. 419), this patriotic, evangelistic McCabe was back where he loved to be—at the front.

By this time, McCabe was closely associated with Julia Ward Howe's "Battle Hymn of the Republic." Having noticed it in the February 1862 *Atlantic Monthly*, he had memorized it and sung it in his rich baritone at public gatherings. He taught it to his soldiers of the 122d Ohio and fellow inmates at Libby. Abraham Lincoln had enjoyed McCabe's rendering of it so much that McCabe sang it in connection with Lincoln's funeral and burial in Chicago and Springfield, Illinois, respectively. Ultimately, Howe thanked McCabe in a 1904 letter for his role in fostering her song's popularity.

After the war, McCabe was appointed pastor of Spencer Chapel in Portsmouth, Ohio. His service there, however, was not long-lived. Church leaders already had been attracted by his charisma and fundraising ability. "I seemed doomed to raise money," he once wrote (Bristol, p. 164). After two years, McCabe joined Alpha J. Kynett in 1868 to head the Church Extension Society. First, as financial agent and then, as assistant corresponding secretary, McCabe promoted church building throughout the American West. As McCabe's biographer affirmed, "Very rarely have these two qualities, the financial and the evangelistic, been so conspicuously united in one secretary" (Bristol, p. 235).

When McCabe learned that the infidel Robert G. Ingersoll had scoffed that "churches are dying out all over the land," McCabe, using the title of a hymn, quickly wired his opponent: "'All hail the power of Jesus' name.' We are building more than one Methodist church for every day" (Bristol, p. 259). Consequently, McCabe wrote an allegory, like Bunyan's *Pilgrim's Progress*, titled *Dream of Ingersollville*, in which he parodied atheism's moral emptiness and ineffectiveness. In one comic conclusion, he imagined Ingersoll himself giving up his scheme of unbelief and frantically seeking preachers to come and hold revival services.

McCabe was elected corresponding secretary of the Missionary Society in 1884, and by 1887 Methodism had reached "a [yearly] million for missions" (Ross, p. 31). His Libby Prison lecture and "Battle Hymn" were effective fundraisers, too. Yet, his understanding of people's benevolent giving was that the heart was "the only true basis" (Bristol, p. 324).

In 1896 McCabe was elected to the general superintendency. Although bishops traveled at large, Fort Worth, Texas, was his first episcopal residence. Not a parliamentarian, McCabe often used extemporaneous singing and revivalistic preaching to ease conference business. Many who had played down his election, saying that he was "not bishop timber" (Bristol, p. 363), recanted their criticisms because of his sensitivity, impartiality, enthusiasm, cheerfulness, and courage.

In an episcopal tour of Mexico, he challenged bull fighting as cruel and immoral. He traveled to South America twice and felt tormented with desire to help establish churches and schools in this "land which had so long been neglected by the whole Protestant Church!" (Bristol, p. 382). Also, in December 1902, McCabe became chancellor of American University, Washington, D.C.

McCabe's last benevolent mission was an attempt to help the Methodist Episcopal Church of Torrington, Connecticut, pay off a $10,000 mortgage by preaching there on 9 December 1906. The next morning, he fell ill in New York City and died in New York Hospital.

• The Commission on Archives and History of the Ohio West Conference of the United Methodist Church, Ohio Wesleyan University, Delaware, Ohio, has some McCabe family papers. McCabe's papers generated during his service at the Church Extension Society (1868–1884) and the Missionary Society (1884–1896) are kept by the General Commission of Archives and History of the United Methodist Church in Madison, N.J. A stenographer's transcription of McCabe's "The Bright Side of Life in Libby Prison"; *Dream of Ingersollville*; and *A Glance Backwards*, an 1886 pamphlet history of the Church Extension Society, are cited in Frank Milton Bristol, *The Life of Chaplain McCabe, Bishop of the Methodist Episcopal Church* (1908). McCabe's memoir, written by Joseph B. Hingeley, is found in the *Journal* of the Twenty-fifth Delegated General Conference of the Methodist Episcopal Church, which was held in Baltimore, Md., 6 May–1 June 1908.

See also Charles M. Stuart, "Charles Cardwell McCabe," *Methodist Review* 90 (Jan. 1908): 8–19; Isaac Crook, "Reminiscences of Bishop McCabe," *Methodist Review* 90 (Mar. 1908): 210–22; Charles Wright Ferguson, *Organizing to Beat the Devil: Methodists and the Making of America* (1971); William E. Ross, "The Singing Chaplain: Bishop Charles Cardwell McCabe and the Popularization of the 'Battle Hymn of the Republic,'" *Methodist History* 28, no. 1 (Oct. 1989); William Warren Sweet, *The Methodist Episcopal Church and the Civil War* (1912); chapter 14, "Methodism North and South in the Civil War," in Sweet, *Methodism in American History* (1933); James W. May, "The War Years," Walter W. Benjamin and Leland Scott, "The Methodist Episcopal Church in the Postwar Era," and Martin Rist, "Methodism Goes West," in *The History of American Methodism*, vols. 2–3, ed. Emory Stevens Bucke (1964); "122nd Ohio Volunteer Infantry," in Whitelaw Reid, *Ohio in the War: Her Statesmen, Generals, and Soldiers* (1895); and Sandra V. Parker, *Richmond's Civil War Prisons* (1990).

DUANE W. PRISET

MCCABE, Thomas Bayard (11 July 1893–27 May 1982), international businessman and government official, was born in Whaleyville, Maryland, the son of William Robbins McCabe, a banker, and Beulah Whaley. McCabe received his early education in Whaleyville and then entered Wilmington Academy in Dover, Delaware, in 1907; three years later he entered Swarthmore College, from which he received his A.B. in economics in 1915. After graduating from Swarthmore, McCabe joined the Scott Paper Company of Chester, Pennsylvania, earning $15 a week as a salesman until U.S. entry into World War I. McCabe served in the U.S. Army from 1917 to 1919, rising from the rank of private to captain.

After the war, McCabe rejoined Scott Paper, and the company rapidly promoted him. He rose from assistant sales manager (1919–1920) to sales manager (1920–1927, joining the company's board of directors in 1921, to vice president (1927) and then to president (1927–1962). From 1962 to 1968 he served as chairman and chief executive officer. He remained on the board of directors until his retirement in 1980. McCabe accomplished somewhat of an economic miracle for Scott Paper. When he joined the company in 1916 it operated only one mill that employed 500 workers. By the time McCabe retired in 1980, Scott Paper had become a multinational business with more than sixty plants worldwide staffed by a total of 40,000 employees; in 1980 it posted sales of more than $2.3 billion. McCabe married Jeannette Laws in 1924; they had three sons, including Thomas, Jr., who also became a noted international businessman.

Given McCabe's successful business career, it was not surprising that the U.S. government called on his services. Even though McCabe always described himself as a middle-of-the-road Republican, his government career flourished under the Democratic administration of Franklin D. Roosevelt. In 1938 the Senate confirmed McCabe as a director of the Federal Reserve Bank of Philadelphia; the next year he became chairman of the board, a post he held until 1949. In 1940 he became a member of the Business Advisory Council of the Department of Commerce, which he chaired from 1944 to 1945. Also in 1940 he served as an assistant to the Council for National Defense. He became deputy director of the Division of Priorities in the Office of Production Management in 1941 and deputy lend-lease administrator that same year; during World War II he served in various other posts for the federal government, including an assignment as commissioner of army-navy liquidation and as a special assistant to the State Department.

In 1948 McCabe was named chairman of the board of governors of the Federal Reserve System and manned that Washington, D.C., position until 1951. He worked with President Harry S. Truman to reform the then Federal Reserve practice of supporting government securities, a practice that McCabe said "feeds the fires of inflation." McCabe preferred an open market tied to the general economy of the country. He arranged an acceptable compromise with President Truman in which the government supported some securities but did not support others. When he left his post in 1951, McCabe said that the Federal Reserve had "maintained its integrity" for it had not been victimized by the temporary winds of politics.

McCabe also engaged in civic work throughout his long career. From 1954 to 1968 he chaired the board of trustees of the Eisenhower Exchange Fellowships Program. In the late 1950s he chaired the Rockefeller Brothers Fund, to which he submitted a report titled "The Challenge to America: Its Economic and Social Aspects," wherein he made educated guesses about the issues that would concern Americans in the future. McCabe served as a governor of the New York Stock Exchange from 1960 to 1963. From 1962 to 1970 he also chaired the board of trustees of the Marketing Science Institute; further, throughout his career he held many positions for the U.S. Chamber of Commerce and was awarded its Medal of Merit in 1946. He became a member of the International Chamber of Commerce and headed the American delegation to its 1947 meeting in Montreux, France. He also received a host of honorary degrees.

In retirement McCabe spent most of his time at his farm in Berlin, Maryland, near his home town. He enjoyed rising early to go duck hunting or to go fishing or surf-casting on the ocean. His retirement was cut short, however. He died at his home in Swarthmore, Pennsylvania.

• The National Archives has various files relating to McCabe's years of public service, and Swarthmore College has a collection of his personal papers. For more information see Philip S. Klein and Ari Hoogenboom, *History of Pennsylvania* (1980), and John B. Trussell, *Pennsylvania History and Biography* (1989). An obituary is in the *New York Times*, 28 May 1982.

JAMES SMALLWOOD

MCCAINE, Alexander (c. 1768–1 June 1856), clergyman and a founder of the Methodist Protestant Church, was born in Dublin, Ireland. His parents' names are unknown, and details of his youth and education are not available. He was raised in the Roman Catholic faith and planned to enter the priesthood of that church but never did. In 1787 McCaine immigrated to the United States, landing in Charleston, South Carolina. Soon after his arrival he was attracted to the Methodists and experienced conversion under the persuasive preaching of William Hammett, who later separated from the Methodist Episcopal church because he did not agree with the authority that resided in the episcopal office.

McCaine felt called to the Methodist ministry and began to preach in Charleston. In 1797 he was admitted on trial to the Methodist itinerancy. Two years later he was ordained deacon and admitted to full membership in the Methodist Conference. In 1801 he was ordained elder. McCaine served circuits in the Carolinas and Virginia. His outstanding ability to proclaim the Christian message came to the attention of Bishop Francis Asbury, the premier leader of early American Methodism, who invited McCaine to travel with him when he itinerated in McCaine's region. In 1799 Asbury wrote to McCaine praising his "piety, conscience, and honor."

In 1806 McCaine withdrew from the active itinerant ministry of the Methodist Episcopal church in order to educate his children. After the death of his wife Kitnel (maiden name unknown) in 1815, he was persuaded by Asbury to reenter the itinerancy. Thereafter, he served circuits in the Virginia and New York Annual Conferences until 1821, when he left the itinerant ministry to become the headmaster of a boys' school in Baltimore. McCaine was elected secretary of the 1820 General Conference, the chief legislative body of the church, a testimony to the high regard in which he was held by the leaders of the church since he had not even been a delegate to the conference.

During the first three decades of the nineteenth century there was an attempt to make the Methodist Episcopal church more democratic. This reflected a democratic spirit abroad in the nation that resulted in the election of Andrew Jackson to the presidency in 1828.

A reform party in the church proposed that lay people be given an official voice in church governance, that presiding elders be elected (rather than appointed by bishops) to superintend the church's work, and that local preachers be granted clergy rights similar to those accorded itinerating preachers. "Reformers" were especially active in the Baltimore Annual Conference. McCaine was one of their most able proponents. He set forth arguments for reform in *The History and Mystery of Methodist Episcopacy* (1827), *A Defence of the Truth* (1829), and *Letters on the Organization and Early History of the Methodist Episcopal Church* (1850). He was also a regular contributor to the Reformers' monthly publication, *Mutual Rights*, which began in 1824.

McCaine believed that the chief culprits in preventing the necessary reforms in the Methodist Episcopal church were the itinerant clergy, especially the bishops. He held that the office of bishop was an illegitimate development in the church and contrary to the intentions of its founder, John Wesley. After all, McCaine argued, Wesley had written to Asbury asking by what authority he accepted the title bishop. Wesley asserted, "Men may call *me* a knave or a fool, a rascal, and I am content; but they shall never, by my consent, call me a *bishop*." According to McCaine it was time to eliminate the episcopal office and make the church more democratic.

The Reformers held conventions in Baltimore on 15 November 1827 and 12 November 1828, at which McCaine was a prominent presence. On 2 November 1830 they met to form a new denomination, the Methodist Protestant church. McCaine was a member of the committee that drafted the new church's constitution and discipline. In the following years he was a traveling evangelist, preaching mainly in the southern states. In 1842 he was elected a delegate to the General Conference from the South Carolina Annual Conference. The slavery question was debated at this General Conference, which recommended that each Annual Conference devise its own rules on the matter. McCaine was one of many who defended slavery. He published his views in a pamphlet, *Slavery Defended from the Scripture against the Attacks of the Abolitionists*, in which, as the title indicates, he was an apologist for slaveholding as defensible from biblical texts. Slavery, he argued, was not a sin as the abolitionists taught. In 1853 he was elected by the Alabama Annual Conference as a delegate to the 1854 General Conference but was unable to attend because of ill health. McCaine's last years were spent living with his children; he died at the home of his daughter in Augusta, Georgia.

McCaine is recognized as one of the founders of the Methodist Protestant church. He was one of its most creative, articulate, and striking personalities. He has been described as a person of "indomitable will, clear convictions, honest to the core," but excessively impetuous, a trait that occasionally caused embarrassment to him and his friends (Drinkhouse, vol. 2, p. 401). He led the church through its break with episcopal Methodism and provided significant leadership to the denomination during the earliest years of its life.

• Biographical information is in Thomas Henry Colhouer, *Sketches of the Founders of the Methodist Protestant Church* (1880); Ancel Henry Bassett, *A Concise History of the Methodist Protestant Church from its Origin, with Biographical Sketches* (1877); and Edward J. Drinkhouse, *History of Methodist Reform and the Methodist Protestant Church* (1899). An obituary is in the *Augusta (Ga.) Daily Constitutionalist*, 3 June 1856.

CHARLES YRIGOYEN, JR.

MCCALL, John Augustine (2 Mar. 1849–18 Feb. 1906), insurance executive, was born in Albany, New York, the son of John A. McCall, a politician, and Katherine MacCormack. After receiving his early education in the Albany public schools, he entered the Commercial College (a business school), from which he graduated in 1865. His father, a local ward leader for the Democratic party, then obtained a bookkeeping position for his son at the Albany assorting house for state currency. McCall left this position in 1867 for a similar one with the local office of the Connecticut Mutual Life Insurance Company. In 1870 he married Mary I. Horan of Albany, with whom he was to have seven children, and in the same year took the job of clerk in the actuarial branch of the New York State Department of Insurance. In 1872 McCall assumed control of the statistical work within the department and in November was appointed examiner of companies.

In 1876 McCall was named deputy superintendent of insurance for New York State, and he soon attracted attention for his vigorous investigations of life and fire insurance companies. Although his 1877 investigation of Metropolitan Life revealed no wrongdoing, in 1879 McCall accused the officers of Knickerbocker Life of perpetrating one of the "most stupendous frauds in the history of life insurance." During his tenure in office eighteen life insurance companies were declared insolvent and were thereby restricted from conducting business in the state. Further investigations resulted in the indictment and subsequent conviction (on charges of perjury) of numerous officers of the Security, American Popular, and Continental Life insurance companies.

As a result of his diligence, McCall was appointed superintendent of insurance by Governor Grover Cleveland on 16 April 1883. A popular choice for the position, with the benefit of broad bipartisan support, McCall remained in the post until 26 December 1885, when he resigned to assume the duties of comptroller of the Equitable Life Assurance Society. His work within the industry that he had once overseen with such vigor attracted positive attention from rival New York Life, which after the resignation of William H. Beers unanimously elected McCall to succeed him as president in February 1892.

At the time of his own election, McCall insisted on the election of George Perkins to the position of third vice president; he continued to work closely with his subordinates. The early years of his administration were most notable for the structural change effected in the field agent force of New York Life. The old general agency system (wherein agents were hired by and worked for what were essentially contractors, with little direct contact with the home office) was abandoned and replaced by the district office system. It allowed greater assistance to the field staff by the home office and also proved more effective in curbing agent turnover and abuses such as rebating (the practice of returning a portion of insurance premiums to the purchaser), which had provided immediate sales volume to the general agents at the expense of long-term continuity in business. Along similar lines, company vice president Darwin P. Kingsley developed the "Nylic" system, wherein agents were financially rewarded for writing insurance policies that stayed in force.

New York Life continued to grow and prosper under McCall's leadership. Company income more than tripled, and business development continued overseas amid occasionally difficult conditions (the company went so far as to invite a German investigative team to the home office to mollify various concerns regarding its operations). In a development that many leading insurance executives came to regret, close relationships developed among the so-called "Big Three" insurers (New York Life, Equitable, and Mutual Life); McCall even became a director of Metropolitan Life in 1896.

The growth in and concentration of wealth within the life insurance industry had received outside scrutiny in years past, and at the height of the Progressive Era (with its "muckrakers"), an internal squabble at the Equitable brought unwanted attention to the industry. Egged on by the press, the New York State legislature moved in 1905 to launch an investigation that focused on the activities of the largest life insurance firms. The Armstrong committee (as the hearings came to be known), featuring future Supreme Court justice Charles Evans Hughes as its counsel, relentlessly questioned several leading life insurance executives. Testifying before the committee, McCall (appearing without counsel) acknowledged the receipt of a personal low-interest (1.5 percent) loan from the Metropolitan. It was further revealed that political financial contributions had been made to the Republican party during the presidential elections of 1896, 1900, and 1904 and that these payments had been disguised on the books. When Hughes asked McCall whether he thought that these actions were matters for the trustees of New York Life, McCall replied, "No, if I haven't got judgment under those circumstances to make a decision, I am not worthy to be president of the company." Even more damning was the revelation that McCall, on his own initiative, had paid almost $1.2 million—nearly all of it unaccounted for—to Andrew Hamilton, a flamboyant Albany lobbyist. Hamilton, who had also lobbied on behalf of other life insurance companies, was unavailable for scheduled testimony; he had departed for France prior to the hearings and had pleaded ill health as an excuse against his return.

While admitting that $235,000 of the money remitted to Hamilton belonged to New York Life, McCall also promised to reimburse the company if Hamilton failed to do so. After Hamilton's subsequent failure to repay, McCall covered the debt by transferring his own life insurance and by disposing of a residence in Elberon, New Jersey.

McCall consistently denied wrongdoing during the investigation; he claimed that the huge expenditures were needed to protect insurers against legislative harassment. He contended that "three-fourths of the insurance bills introduced in the United States are blackmail bills." Resigning as president of New York Life at the end of 1905, McCall was a man broken in both health and spirit. Shortly following his resignation he succumbed to cancer of the liver while at the resort community of Lakewood, New Jersey.

McCall rose from modest circumstances to preside over solid growth and substantial internal change at New York Life, only to see his career end under the scrutiny of state-sponsored investigation—the same type of scrutiny he had once conducted so effectively on behalf of the state of New York. His career stands as an example of the possibilities as well as the pitfalls that existed in American business at the turn of the century.

• The papers of John A. McCall are held at the New York Life Archives, New York City. The best source of information on his life and career is Lawrence F. Abbott, *The Story of NYLIC: A History of the Origin and Development of the New York Life Insurance Company from 1845 to 1929* (1930). Another good source of information on his career is Marquis James, *The Metropolitan Life: A Study in Business Growth* (1947). The Armstrong committee investigation receives coverage in R. Carlyle Buley, *The American Life Convention, 1906–1952* (1953). An obituary is in the *New York Times*, 19 Feb. 1906.

EDWARD L. LACH, JR.

MCCALL, Samuel Walker (28 Feb. 1851–4 Nov. 1923), lawyer, congressman, and governor of Massachusetts, was born in East Providence, Pennsylvania, the son of Henry McCall and Mary Ann Elliott. In 1853 his father moved the family to Mount Carroll, Illinois, where Henry McCall manufactured stoves and farm machinery and speculated in prairie land. After the panic of 1857 forced him to close his factory and brought him to the brink of financial ruin, he took up farming and became prosperous again. Young Samuel attended public schools before entering Mount Carroll Seminary. When that school was converted into an academy for young women in 1867, he acted upon the suggestion of a neighbor and enrolled at the New Hampton Literary and Biblical Institution in New Hampton, New Hampshire. He completed his secondary education there and matriculated at Dartmouth College in 1870. A superior student, McCall excelled in the classics and won election to Phi Beta Kappa. Outside the classroom, he gained notoriety as editor of the *Anvil*, one of the first student newspapers to comment boldly on state, national, and world affairs.

After graduating in 1874 McCall chose to remain in New England rather than accept an offer to study law in the Chicago office of former Illinois senator Lyman Trumbull. He received his legal education with prominent firms in Nashua, New Hampshire, and Worcester, Massachusetts, and was admitted to the Massachusetts bar in 1875. Later that year McCall moved to Boston and opened an office in conjunction with a former Dartmouth classmate. He also continued to work as a journalist, using his evenings to write articles on current affairs for newspapers and magazines. In 1881 he married Ella Esther Thompson. They settled in Winchester, Massachusetts, and had five children.

In 1887 McCall was elected as a Republican to the Massachusetts House of Representatives. He emerged from the ranks of the conservative majority party as a mild reformer by sponsoring legislation that ended imprisonment for debt in the state except in the case of fraud. Reelected in 1888, McCall was named chair of the Judiciary Committee. That same year he and two other prominent Republicans, William Barrett and Henry Parkman, purchased the *Boston Daily Advertiser*. McCall served as the paper's editor in chief for two years and was a state ballot law commissioner from 1890 to 1892. Returning to the Massachusetts House in 1892, he authored a pioneering corrupt practices act, which defined the purposes for which money could be expended in election campaigns and prescribed penalties for violations of the law. Later in 1892 McCall was elected to Congress from the Eighth District, defeating by 992 votes the incumbent Democrat John Forrester Andrew, the son of legendary Civil War governor John Albion Andrew. Even though he was always at a disadvantage in elections because he lived in the smallest town in his district, McCall was returned to office nine times by substantial margins. He won 74 percent of the vote in 1896 and 89 percent in 1904.

McCall had a routinely conservative voting record and initiated little legislation in the U.S. House, but his occasional deviation from the dictates of the Republican leadership and considerable ability as a debater earned him a reputation as something of a maverick. In 1897 he separated himself from other Bay State congressmen and the majority of his party by declaring that Dingley Tariff duties were too high and detrimental to the national economy. From his seat on the House Ways and Means Committee (1899–1913), McCall remained a voice of moderation on tariff policy.

Even more notable was McCall's opposition to some of the imperialist foreign policies of the administration of President William McKinley. One of only six House members who voted against the resolution for war with Spain in 1898, he also subsequently criticized the annexation of the Philippines and favored free trade with Puerto Rico and reciprocity with Cuba. However, McCall was not a strong anti-imperialist.

He supported the annexation of Puerto Rico and the Platt amendment, which gave the United States the right to intervene in Cuban affairs, and he did not join House Speaker Thomas B. Reed of Maine and Senator George Frisbie Hoar of Massachusetts in condemning the war waged against Filipino guerrillas (1899–1901).

During the Theodore Roosevelt and William Howard Taft administrations, McCall maintained his position as a "man of independence with conservative Progressive leanings." He embraced the Elkins Act of 1903, which prevented railroads from giving rebates to large industrial concerns and stifling competition, but assailed the Hepburn Act's authorization of the Interstate Commerce Commission to fix railroad rates as a "heated center of despotism destructive of the last appearance of individual freedom." He was one of only seven congressmen who voted against the Roosevelt-backed measure in 1906. McCall also spoke against a successful Democratic–progressive Republican effort to weaken conservative House Speaker Joseph G. Cannon of Indiana by removing him from the Committee on Rules in 1910. Addressing the House, McCall asked his colleagues to ignore anti-Cannon muckrakers, whom he called "a gang of literary highwaymen" who were "willing to assassinate a reputation in order to sell a magazine." Although Cannon was voted off the Rules Committee, he was able to remain Speaker until the end of his term. At the same time McCall seemed to be upholding standpattism, he also backed national corrupt practices legislation, the direct election of senators, and woman suffrage, all of which were high on the progressive agenda.

McCall turned down an offer to succeed William Jewett Tucker as president of Dartmouth in 1908. He told the college's trustees that their offer flattered and tempted him, but politics had become his life, and he would "be a sorry soldier to weigh causes and to decide at this moment to step out of the ranks." When he finally chose to leave the House in 1913, it was to run for the seat of Senator Winthrop Murray Crane, who was retiring. McCall led Congressman John W. Weeks after three days of balloting in the Republican state legislative caucus but could not capture the necessary two-thirds majority. On the fourth day he was greatly disappointed when the caucus opted for the more reliably conservative Weeks, who was then formally elected by the legislature.

McCall returned to the political wars in 1914 as the Republican nominee for governor of Massachusetts. He lost to the incumbent, Democrat David I. Walsh, by the narrow margin of 11,815 votes. A Progressive party candidate received 32,145 votes and probably caused McCall's defeat. Nominated again in 1915, McCall worked to heal the breach between GOP conservatives and the Progressives, most of whom had been Republicans prior to 1912. He saw to it that his party's platform endorsed a constitutional convention to reorganize state government and gave voice to other issues of concern to Progressives. As a result, McCall won the support of Progressive leader Charles Sumner Bird and went on to beat Walsh by 46,573 votes. He won reelection by landslides in both 1916 and 1917. Calvin Coolidge was elected lieutenant governor on McCall's ticket in 1915, 1916, and 1917.

As governor, McCall made good on his promise to the Progressives by calling for the first state constitutional convention in sixty years to change a "hydra-headed system with a minimum of responsibility." The proposal was placed before the voters by the legislature and approved in 1916. When it met the following year, the convention agreed to a modest array of reforms, including a reduction of state commissions and the adoption of the initiative and referendum, biennial elections, and a state budget system.

The constitutional convention proved the high point of McCall's gubernatorial years. His plans for a state insurance program, an extension of old-age pensions, the abolition of capital punishment, and the construction of a governor's residence all expired in the legislature in 1917. Most of the rest of McCall's governorship was taken up with war emergency measures. Although popular, he was not viewed as a successful state executive by many contemporary observers. To his friend Moorfield Storey and others, McCall was not the man of action the job required. They believed his reflective nature and oratorical skills were better suited to a legislative setting.

McCall announced his intention to challenge the renomination of his bitter rival Weeks early in 1918 but ultimately withdrew from the race. In the ensuing election contest, McCall angered his party by refusing to support Weeks against the Democrat Walsh. Further complicating matters was the presence in the campaign of Thomas W. Lawson, a wealthy independent candidate whose daughter was married to McCall's son. Weeks subsequently lost the Senate seat to Walsh by 19,191 votes, 2,794 fewer than Lawson's overall total. McCall's 1918 apostasy effectively ended his political career. His nomination to the U.S. Tariff Commission by President Woodrow Wilson was blocked by the Republican-controlled Senate in 1920.

McCall practiced law and wrote extensively in his last years. A regular commentator for the *Atlantic Monthly*, he strongly supported Wilson and scathingly rebuked the Senate for its rejection of the Versailles Treaty and the League of Nations in 1920. Having authored well-received biographies of his congressional mentor Reed and Pennsylvania Radical Republican Thaddeus Stevens, McCall was at work on a life of Daniel Webster at the time of his death in Winchester.

• In addition to *Thaddeus Stevens* (1898) and *The Life of Thomas Brackett Reed* (1914), McCall published *The Business of Congress* (1911), *The Liberty of Citizenship* (1915), and *The Patriotism of the American Jew* (1922). His articles include "Power of the Senate," *Atlantic Monthly*, Oct. 1903, pp. 433–42, and "Again the Senate," *Atlantic Monthly*, Sept. 1920, pp. 395–403. The official record of McCall's governorship is Henry F. Long, comp., *Messages to the General Court, Official Addresses, Proclamations and State Papers of Governor Samuel Walker McCall, 1916–1918* (1919). Lawrence B. Evans, *Samuel W. McCall: Governor of Massachusetts* (1916), is an admiring biography. Informative articles are Lawrence

Shaw Mayo, "Memoir of Samuel Walker McCall," *Massachusetts Historical Society Proceedings* 57 (Oct. 1923–June 1924): 503–12; and W. Cameron Forbes, "Samuel Walker McCall," in *Later Years of the Saturday Club*, ed. Mark Antony DeWolfe Howe (1927). See also Moorfield Storey's untitled tribute to McCall in *Massachusetts Historical Society Proceedings* 57 (Oct. 1923–June 1924): 186–90; Samuel Leland Powers, *Portraits of a Half Century* (1925), a memoir by McCall's Dartmouth classmate and former law partner; and Brent Walth, *Fire at Eden's Gate: Tom McCall & the Oregon Story* (1994), a biography of a McCall grandson who served as governor of Oregon. McCall's political career is covered in Michael E. Hennessy, *Four Decades of Massachusetts Politics, 1890–1935* (1935); Richard B. Sherman, "Progressive Politics in Massachusetts, 1908–1916" (Ph.D. diss., Harvard Univ., 1959); and Donald R. McCoy, *Calvin Coolidge: The Quiet President* (1967). Obituaries are in the *Boston Herald* and the *Boston Evening Transcript*, both 5 Nov. 1923.

RICHARD H. GENTILE

MCCALLA, Bowman Hendry (19 June 1844–7 May 1910), naval officer, was born in Camden, New Jersey, the son of Aulay McCalla, a bank clerk, and Mary Duffield Hendry. With his parents dead before he was thirteen years old, McCalla's two older sisters enrolled him in a Moravian school that enforced discipline. When fifteen, he supported himself by working as a store clerk. He was too young to enlist in the army at the beginning of the Civil War but old enough to be nominated to the U.S. Naval Academy in 1861. After completing the three-year wartime course, he served in both sailing ships and steamers and saw much of the world. In 1871, while studying torpedoes in Newport, he met Elizabeth Hazard Sargent, whom he married in 1875; they would have four children.

In the normal rotating career pattern, McCalla served at sea from 1865 to 1874, at the Naval Academy from 1874 to 1878, at sea from 1878 to 1881, and then for six years as assistant chief of the Bureau of Navigation. While in the bureau, in 1885 he was chosen to lead an expedition to quell revolutionary disturbances in Panama. He was also considered radical for demanding reforms that he thought would improve his service—that promotion be based on merit rather than seniority, that the engineer corps and line officers be merged, that a naval officer rather than a political appointee head the Navy Department, and that the navy adopt a naval general staff. The first two reforms became effective while he remained on duty until 1906. The merging in 1899 of the engineer and line officer worked well. The engineer was granted wardroom privileges, respect as an officer, and duty on deck, while the line officer learned about the machinery that provided the ship's power. The naval secretary, however, remained a political appointee, and the Office of the Chief of Naval Operations created in 1915 cannot be considered to be a general staff.

In 1890, while commanding a ship, with his sword McCalla slightly slashed a drunken and unruly crewman, John E. Walker, for which he received a court of inquiry and a court-martial. The latter suspended him from rank and duty for three years but allowed him to retain his present number on the list of commanders while so suspended. Not until March 1900, owing much to Elizabeth McCalla's efforts, would President William McKinley grant him a complete pardon for striking Walker.

From 1893 to 1897 McCalla served as the equipment officer at the Mare Island, California, Navy Yard. His otherwise fine record was marred when he settled an argument with a civilian contractor by knocking him down. In September 1897 he was given command of the light cruiser *Marblehead*. As he had with the other ships he commanded, McCalla had the crew learn how to conduct landing operations, apply first aid, and swim.

Although he was in his mid-fifties, the years 1898–1900 were McCalla's "fighting years," for he served in the Santiago campaign of the Spanish-American War, participated in the pacification of Filipino insurgents, and led the retreat of the allied forces that failed to reach and defend their legations in Peking (Beijing) during the Boxer Rebellion. In the first, on 11 May 1898, he cut the cables connecting Havana and Europe. On 7 June he captured Guantánamo Bay, from then on used as a logistic support base by U.S. warships. In the subsequent Sampson-Schley controversy that grew out of the Santiago campaign, he supported William T. Sampson. In the second, during November and December 1899, he cleared Filipino insurgents from the north and west coasts of Luzon and had his seamen cooperate with U.S. Army forces in chasing insurgents from a town four miles inland. In the third, he led the allied retreat from Peking to Tientsin, 15–24 June, even though he was wounded three times (in a thigh, a foot instep, and an ankle).

McCalla's last seagoing billet was as executive officer of the *Kearsarge* (BB-5), 1901–1903; his last shore billet, in the rank of rear admiral, was as commandant at Mare Island. Following the great San Francisco earthquake of 1906, he had many wounded citizens brought to his hospital and in addition sent food, water, tents, and marines to patrol the city against looting. He retired later that year. He died in Santa Barbara, California. If on the one hand McCalla was a perfectionist unable always to curb his terrible temper, on the other hand he proved his valor in battle and sought to improve conditions in his navy with respect to promotion, personnel administration, organization, and amphibious operations.

• McCalla's heirs donated his manuscript autobiography to the Library of Congress. Also helpful are the papers of naval officers William H. Emory, George C. Remey, Joseph K. Taussig, John G. Walker, John C. Watson, and William V. Pratt, all in the Manuscript Division, Library of Congress. Other primary sources include the *Report of Commander McCalla upon the Naval Expedition to the Isthmus of Panama* (1885) and the *Annual Report of the Secretary of the Navy* (for the years 1864–1906). A full-scale biography is Paolo E. Coletta, *Bowman Hendry McCalla: A Fighting Sailor* (1979), which derives in part from McCalla's manuscript autobiography. Pertinent information on McCalla's combat experiences can be found in A. S. Daggett, *Americans in the China Relief Expedition* (1903); Herbert H. Sargent, *The Campaign of Santiago* (3 vols., 1907); and Herbert W. Wilson, *The Downfall of Spain: The Naval History of the Spanish-American War* (1900). First-person accounts include Naval Cadet C. E. Courtney Journal, in "Navy in China," *All Hands Book Supplement* (Oct. 1956): 59–63; John T. Myers, "Military Operations and the Defense of Peking," U.S. Naval Institute *Proceedings* 28 (Sept. 1902): 541–51; and Joseph K. Taussig, "Experiences during the Boxer Rebellion," U.S. Naval Institute *Proceedings* 53 (Apr. 1927): 403–20. Helpful in understanding McCalla's desire to improve naval administration is Bradley A. Fiske, *From Midshipman to Rear-Admiral* (1919).

PAOLO E. COLETTA

MCCALLUM, Daniel Craig (21 Jan. 1815–27 Dec. 1878), engineer, builder, and railroad manager, was born in Johnstone, Renfrewshire, Scotland, the son of a tailor, and emigrated as a child with his parents, whose names are unknown, to Rochester, New York. After an elementary school education he worked his way from carpenter and builder to become a distinguished architect and engineer. The date of his marriage to Mary McCann is unknown; they had three sons.

In 1851 McCallum invented and patented the inflexible arched truss, which dominated the subsequent building of timber bridges in the United States and is described in his *McCallum's Inflexible Arched Truss Bridge Explained and Illustrated* (1859). This invention made McCallum a wealthy man and led to a distinguished career in bridge building mixed with railroad administration. In 1852 he moved to New York, where he associated with Samuel Roberts, the engineer who built the High Bridge over the Harlem River. McCallum was general superintendent of the New York and Erie Railway from 1855 to 1856 and spent 1858–1859 building bridges in the American West and in South and Central America with his McCallum Bridge Company as well as consulting for the Atlantic and Great Western Railway.

On 11 February 1862 Secretary of War Edwin Stanton marshaled McCallum's talents for the Union war effort, appointing him director and superintendent of the newly established U.S. Military Rail Roads (USMRR), organized to administer railroads in the occupied South. Stanton appointed McCallum to the rank of colonel attached as aide-de-camp to the commander in chief, thus directly responsible to Stanton. McCallum's quasi-military hierarchy of local railroad operators likewise held sufficient rank to deal effectively with the military hierarchy in the field should rank become an issue in directing the military railroads.

For a time McCallum was titular head of a divided domain, since the talented and efficient Herman Haupt was in the field, running the railroads of Virginia, while J. B. Anderson was running the railroads in the occupied territories of the West. Haupt was responsible for creating the Construction Corps, which achieved fame for its feats of construction in the field. For a time this division of authority worked, with McCallum remaining in the North, organizing the operations of the military railroads in the field. It was not until early 1864 that McCallum assumed total control and active command in the field, with Anderson removed for incompetence, upon McCallum's insistance, and Haupt departing under controversial circumstances.

By war's end McCallum's conquered and constructed domain exceeded 2,000 miles of rail line, spreading throughout the South. His organization established a reputation for efficiency in Union service perhaps rivaled only by the navy and the Sanitary Commission. The most celebrated achievement of the military railroads was in support of William T. Sherman's Atlanta campaign. The Construction Corps followed Sherman into the field, performing remarkable feats of laying rail and building trestles to keep supplies flowing to his army. McCallum was brevetted brigadier general 24 September 1864 and major general 13 March 1865. His report presented to the 1866 Congress was published that year as *United States Military Railroads*, one of the important historical documents to come out of the war.

In the first war to experience the extended strategic use of railways, McCallum's military railroads constituted the greatest leap into modern warfare. There had been limited use of railroads before the Civil War to move troops and supplies to the field of operations, and arguably the French, to some degree, had integrated railroads into strategic planning to move troops to the front during the War of Italian Independence in 1859. But there was no precedent for the scale and nature of Civil War practice. In particular there was no precedent for the operational use of the railroad in the field. The U.S. Army had from the 1830s made limited use of railroads to move troops, most notably in the war with Mexico, and there was some antebellum speculation about the strategic use of railroads, but the scope, geographical scale, and strategy of the Civil War pushed the use of railroads beyond what anybody anticipated. Most notably, the Union decision to wage the first modern total war deep in the enemy's territory depended upon railroads, in coordination with traditional animal-drawn field transportation, as an integral part of field operations.

McCallum's place in the military development of the railroad probably is most accurately described as a shared vision between the frequently interlocked worlds of professional military officers and railroad management with respect to the strategic potential of railroads. From Montgomery Meigs, the talented Union quartermaster general, through field commanders, and from political-military leadership through railroad managers, awareness grew that railroads had an unprecedented strategic role to play in the American Civil War. The leadership of McCallum, and before him Haupt, in developing the USMRR was an exceptional case of this vision bringing together modern industrial development and modern warfare.

Following the war McCallum worked briefly as inspector of the Union Pacific Railroad but soon returned with his family to Brooklyn. He published a volume of poetry, *The Water Mill and Other Poems*, in 1870. He died in Brooklyn and was buried in Rochester, N.Y.

• McCallum's personal papers are collected in the National Archives. For McCallum's bridge patent see Senate, 32d Cong., 1st sess., 1859, S. Ex. Doc. 118. Good scholarly studies of his USMRR are Robert Edgar Riegel, "Federal Operation of Southern Railroads during the Civil War," *Mississippi Valley Historical Review* 9 (1922): 126–38, and Eva Swantner, "Military Railroads during the Civil War," *Military Engineer* 21 (1929): 310–16, 434–39, 518–26, and 22 (1930): 13–21. Indispensable for details of the railroads that came under McCallum's authority and their use, construction, mileage, and rolling stock is Charles E. Fisher, "The United States Military Railroads," *Railway and Locomotive Historical Society* no. 108 (1963): 49–79. For the operation of Virginia railroads under Union control see the thorough analysis by Angus James Johnston, *Virginia Railroads in the Civil War* (1961). Johnston's bibliography is a valuable guide to unpublished manuscript sources on McCallum and the USMRR. Also valuable for the Virginia railroads is Herman Haupt, *Reminiscences of General Herman Haupt* (1901). For the place of McCallum in the larger picture of Civil War railroads see George Edgar Turner, *Victory Rode the Rails* (1953), and Thomas Weber, *The Northern Railroads in the Civil War, 1861–1865* (1952). See also U.S. War Department, *The War of the Rebellion: A Compilation of the Official Records of the Union and Confederate Armies* (128 vols., 1880–1901).

EDWARD HAGERMAN

MCCANN, Alfred Watterson (9 Jan. 1879–19 Jan. 1931), journalist, radio commentator, and crusader for pure food, was born in Pittsburgh, the son of Michael McCann, a printer and engraver, and Maria (maiden name unknown). He attended the University of Chicago and was graduated in 1899 from Pittsburgh's Duquesne University, where he accepted a faculty position teaching English and mathematics after graduation. In 1905 he married Mary Carmody of Pittsburgh; they had five children.

As a youngster McCann suffered from an ailment that doctors attributed to poor nutrition; he related it to impure food. Throughout his life the study of nutrition was his avocation. In 1911 McCann's first writings on nutrition and impure food appeared in the *New York Press* and in the *New York Evening Mail*. Government-led pure-food reform was coming too slowly for McCann, so he took his own program for reform to the public by writing "The Pure Food Movement," which appeared in the *New York Globe* in October 1912.

In 1912 McCann left teaching to become the *Globe's* food editor, and during the next ten years gained a reputation for his nutrition consciousness and pure-food campaigns. He wrote articles and series for the newspaper protesting adulterated foods and brand misrepresentation, and castigated public officials whom he accused of graft-taking in permitting the sale of such foods. He investigated various industries connected to food production, from bakers, canners, and packers to shippers and dairies. He crusaded against the chemical treatment of meats and the use of coal tar dyes in the manufacture of confectionery.

McCann also railed against the use of inferior-grade eggs in cakes and called for the end of the sale of stale fish and their unhygienic route to market. He added fruits, honey, and jams to his crusade, employing the same successful methods to get them delivered to market more hygienically. Through his urging of its nutritional value, he helped to popularize whole wheat bread in the United States. McCann was often arrested for libel but was never convicted. He appeared frequently in court, obtaining many convictions against food adulterators.

McCann returned to school to earn a law degree from Fordham University in 1917. He wrote and published *Starving America* (1913); *Vital Questions and Answers Concerning 15,000,000 Defective Children* (1913); *Thirty Cent Bread* (1917), a war emergency food book espousing the advantages of cornmeal; *This Famishing World*, a book revealing the value of mineral salts; *The Science of Eating* (1918), a revision of *Famishing World*; *God—or Gorilla* (1922), an anti-evolution book; *The Science of Keeping Young* (1926); and *Greatest of Men—Washington* (1927), an inspirational and laudatory book on the founding father.

In 1923 he began McCann Laboratories to test food products and to serve as a base for a consumer-reporting and endorsement system. He appeared in many advertisements endorsing products that his company had thoroughly tested. In the early 1920s he advocated lowering the prices of foods to levels that he believed were fairer to consumers. In 1928 McCann wrote for the *New York Mirror* and began a one-hour, four-times-weekly syndicated radio show with WOR in New York City; he died of a heart attack one hour after broadcasting one of his shows.

McCann's many outlets for disseminating his pure-food crusade—newspaper articles, books, advertisements with McCann Laboratories endorsements, and radio broadcasts—built a large following. In spite of critics who called McCann a faddist for his unrelenting attacks on impure foods, he was widely acknowledged for his campaigns in the public interest for high-quality comestibles. Along with others who crusaded to improve the public food supply, McCann's efforts led to government regulation of food industries and enactment of consumer-protecting pure food laws.

• A portrait of McCann can be found in *World's Work* (Oct. 1923) and additional biographical information is in Marlen E. Pew, "Shop Talk at Thirty," *Editor & Publisher* (24 Jan. 1931) and in an obituary appearing in the same issue. An obituary also appears in the *New York Times*, 20 Jan. 1931.

EDWARD E. ADAMS

MCCARRAN, Patrick Anthony (8 Aug. 1876–28 Sept. 1954), U.S. senator, was born in Reno, Nevada, the son of Patrick McCarran, a rancher, and Margaret Shay. The only son of Irish Catholic immigrants, McCarran spent much of his childhood on his family's sheep ranch. He attended the University of Nevada in Reno, excelling more at athletics and debate than in his schoolwork. An injury to his father forced McCarran to withdraw from the university to run the family ranch, but his interest in politics and the law already had been sparked.

Soon after returning to the ranch in 1901, McCarran became involved in local politics. In 1902 he won a place in the state legislature as a Democrat-Silverite. In 1903, in separate Protestant Episcopal and Roman Catholic ceremonies, McCarran married Martha Harriet Weeks; they had five children. An established politician defeated McCarran in a 1904 contest for a state senate seat. That loss, combined with his passing of the bar examination, convinced him to abandon ranching and to move to Tonopah, a mining boom town in central Nevada. There he won election as Nye County district attorney in 1906. Always willing to strike out on his own, McCarran quickly made powerful enemies within his state's Democratic party. His unsuccessful challenge to an incumbent Democrat in the U.S. House of Representatives in 1908 only widened the split.

After his 1908 defeat, a disappointed McCarran moved his family back to Reno. He soon prospered as one of the state's leading defense attorneys, practicing from 1909 to 1912 and from 1919 to 1932. A powerful and emotional speaker, McCarran overwhelmed juries with his oratory when his rigorous legal arguments failed. He took many controversial cases, but none brought him more fame than the scandalous 1920 divorce of actress Mary Pickford from Owen Moore.

Although neither the legal profession nor his Democratic party backed him enthusiastically, McCarran's popular reputation earned him election to the Nevada Supreme Court in 1912. He served from 1913 to 1918. The bench, however, could not contain McCarran's ambition. Ignoring provisions of the state constitution that barred justices from running for elective office, he launched in 1916 a disastrous challenge against an incumbent fellow Democrat for the nomination for U.S. senator. Two years later he was defeated in a reelection bid for his supreme court seat, largely because he had alienated many powerful Democrats.

Undeterred, McCarran ran for the U.S. Senate again in 1926 and 1932. The first attempt failed, but the second succeeded. He used organization, hard work, and luck to secure the Democratic nomination despite the hostility of the party's leadership. McCarran then rode Franklin Roosevelt's coattails to a narrow victory in the general election.

Even as a freshman, McCarran demonstrated keen insight into the mechanics of power on Capitol Hill. He relied on diligence, patronage, and seniority to build an independent political base in the Senate and to construct a network of loyal appointees in Nevada. Since the federal government owned about 97 percent of Nevada's land, McCarran's maneuvers in Washington permitted him to have an influence in his home state equaled by few of his Senate colleagues. He developed a statewide political machine, which, along with his ability to funnel government funds to Nevada, guaranteed he would not be challenged seriously for reelection in 1938, 1944, or 1950. His personal accumulation of power, however, undermined the Democratic party in Nevada.

In the Senate McCarran cultivated his reputation as a lone wolf. McCarran set the tone for his national career in his first speech on the Senate floor, criticizing a bill proposed by President Roosevelt. His vocal resistance to Roosevelt's 1937 "court packing" plan garnered national attention and earned the wrath of the White House. Already a critic of domestic affairs, McCarran then opposed President Roosevelt's interventionist policies toward Germany and Japan. Although McCarran's brand of isolationism had many sympathizers before the United States entered World War II, it played poorly during the war years of 1941–1945, reinforcing his image as a parochial politician who placed Nevada's interests above those of the country.

Despite his declining national status, McCarran's seniority won him the chair of the Judiciary Committee in 1943. This gave him a direct hand in about 40 percent of the Senate's legislative business, which had to pass through his committee. McCarran also headed subcommittees that allocated funds to the State, Justice, and Commerce Departments and that oversaw foreign aid. He used these seats to become, even his enemies acknowledged, one of the most influential senators of the next decade.

Untamed by power, McCarran continued to chart an independent course. He consistently blocked the legislative goals of Democratic presidents Roosevelt and Harry Truman. In 1949, for example, McCarran named a segregationist to lead the Judiciary Subcommittee on Civil Rights, stalling all efforts at reform. Despite his opposition to the priorities of Democratic presidents, McCarran remained a party member. When asked why, he explained how Senate seniority rules worked to his favor, "I can do more good by staying in the Democratic party and watching the lunatic fringe—the Roosevelt crowd" (Steinberg, p. 89).

McCarran's suspicion of and hostility toward liberals underpinned his anti-Communist crusade of the late 1940s and early 1950s. He repeatedly insisted that naive Americans promoted the Communist cause under the guise of liberalism. To root out such threats, he sponsored the 1950 Internal Security Act, which passed over President Truman's veto. Commonly called the McCarran Act, the law required the registration of all Communist action groups, a vaguely defined category. Those affiliated with suspect organizations could be denied passports, fired from defense-related jobs, and even deported. The law also authorized the creation of camps to detain subversives in a national emergency. The McCarran Act undermined civil liberties by restricting rights based on political belief rather than on specific action. In so doing, McCarran reflected and magnified the anti-Communist fears of postwar America.

As chair of the recently established Internal Security Subcommittee, McCarran conducted public hearings similar to those being held by his more famous red-hunting contemporary, Senator Joseph McCarthy. During the summer of 1951, for instance, McCarran presided over an investigation of the Institute of Pacific Relations, a liberal think tank focusing on Asian affairs. At the time, he forged a covert liaison between the subcommittee and the Federal Bureau of Investigation. McCarran blamed U.S. government officials associated with the institute, notably Far Eastern expert Owen Lattimore, for the 1949 Communist victory in the Chinese civil war. In 1952 the senator pressured the Truman administration to indict Lattimore for perjury. Lattimore was never convicted, as judges found the indictment tainted. McCarran's efforts contributed to a purge of Asian experts at the State Department, which some analysts later blamed for American troubles in Vietnam.

In 1952 McCarran's Cold War concerns produced significant but limited immigration reforms. The McCarran-Walter Act established provisions for the screening of subversives coming into the United States. The law also repealed a 1790 act that prevented nonwhites from becoming naturalized U.S. citizens, in part as acknowledgement of the patriotism of Japanese-American soldiers during the Second World War. Finally, the act partially lifted the practice of racial exclusion in immigration policies, permitting one hundred immigrants annually from select Asian countries. Although McCarran staunchly opposed immigration from non-European lands, he recognized the symbolic importance of this issue in the Cold War. By ensuring a small quota for Asian immigrants, McCarran and other proponents sought to portray the United States as a bastion of freedom in the world without substantially altering the nation's ethnic composition. President Truman vetoed the measure because of its continuation of national quotas, but Congress overrode his veto.

McCarran's power began to erode substantially in 1952. In Nevada the rapid growth of Las Vegas undermined the senator's grip on state politics. He was tarnished during an ugly public squabble with opponents in Las Vegas when his close links to the state's gambling interests were revealed. At the same time, McCarran further strained his relationship with the Democratic party by disavowing the 1952 Democratic nominee for president, Adlai Stevenson. When Republicans won control of the Senate in the autumn elections, McCarran lost his committee leadership. Isolated from the Democrats, he was also ignored by the new Republican majority. Even while his power crumbled, however, he remained influential in the Senate. McCarran stalled efforts to censure Senator McCarthy through the summer of 1954, but the tide had turned against him even on this issue. The Senate subsequently voted to condemn McCarthy for "conduct unbecoming a U.S. senator."

McCarran's health deteriorated rapidly under the strain, and he died while campaigning in Hawthorne, Nevada. A Republican delivered his eulogy, and only one of his Democratic Senate colleagues made the trip to Nevada for his funeral.

Despite his controversial political career, McCarran illustrated well the influence of seniority and patronage in the mid-twentieth-century Senate. A cantankerous independent, he nevertheless became one of the most powerful members of both Congress and his party. Overall, McCarran astutely used his authority to bring federal resources to Nevada, to block liberal reforms, and to lead an anti-Communist crusade during the early Cold War years.

• The major collection of McCarran's papers is at the Nevada Historical Society in Reno. The papers of Eva Bertrand Adams, an important and longtime McCarran aide, are in the University of Nevada, Reno, Library's Special Collections Division. For a sample of McCarran's anti-Communism, see his interview, "Communist Threat inside the U.S.," *U.S. News and World Report*, 16 Nov. 1951, pp. 24–30. Jerome E. Edwards chronicles the senator's life, focusing on his role in Nevada politics, in *Pat McCarran: Political Boss of Nevada* (1982). A detailed and extremely sympathetic biography was written by the senator's daughter, Sister Margaret Patricia McCarran, "Patrick Anthony McCarran," *Nevada Historical Society Quarterly* 11 (Fall–Winter 1968): 5–66, and "Patrick Anthony McCarran, Part II," *Nevada Historical Society Quarterly* 12 (Spring 1969): 5–75. Alfred Steinberg authored a more objective article, "McCarran: Lone Wolf of the Senate," *Harper's*, Nov. 1950, pp. 89–95. Gary May exposes the excesses of McCarran's attacks on the Institute of Pacific Relations in *China Scapegoat: The Diplomatic Ordeal of John Carter Vincent* (1979). Robert Newman, *Owen Lattimore and the "Loss" of China* (1992), chronicles McCarran's role as chair of the Senate Internal Security Subcommittee and its investigation of the Institute of Pacific Relations. Christopher Gerard analyzes the impact of McCarran's anti-Communism on the State Department in "On the Road to Viet Nam, 'The Loss of China Syndrome': Pat McCarran and J. Edgar Hoover," *Nevada Historical Quarterly* 37 (Winter 1994): 247–62. An obituary is in the *New York Times*, 29 Sept. 1954.

PETER G. FELTEN

MCCARROLL, Marion Clyde (8 May 1891–1 Aug. 1977), newspaper editor and columnist, was born in East Orange, New Jersey, the daughter of Helen Fredericka Stoughton Loomis and James Renwick McCarroll, an importer of leather goods. She attended the Beard School and was graduated from Wellesley College in 1914 with a bachelor's degree in English. McCarroll started out as a social worker and taught at a school for retarded children near Philadelphia. A summer clerical job at the *New York Tribune* led her instead to a career in journalism. In 1914–1915 she worked as a reporter for the *Ridgewood News* in New Jersey, then moved in 1920 to the *New York Commercial*, where she ultimately received her own column, "Women in Business." In the course of her work for the *Commercial*, she became the first woman to whom the New York Stock Exchange issued a press card.

In the mid-1920s she worked for the *New York Evening Post* and the *New York Sunday World*, using slightly different bylines at the two papers by arrangement with her editors. One of her favorite pieces at the *Post*, for which she thought up her own assignments, was an article that began, "A woman should make her first airplane flight with a woman pilot." She lived up to her words by taking, and writing about, a trip in the early 1930s with aviatrix Ruth Nichols in a small two-seater plane. She noted in 1964 that the plane had "had about the same dimensions as a canoe and was as wide open as a canoe, too!" She was proud of her pathbreaking career. In 1926 McCarroll married a fellow writer from the *Commercial*, Ormond Lynn Booth, who died in 1933.

In the 1930s McCarroll moved from journalism to public relations, representing first the New York Museum of Science and Industry and then Rockefeller Center. After her husband's death she shared an apartment for many years with a Wellesley classmate, Jean Corwin, who worked in New York as a doctor. In 1941 McCarroll returned to what she considered "the real newspaper field," accepting a post as women's editor for King Features Syndicate. Four years later, on the death of Marie Manning Gash, she inherited the "Dear Beatrice Fairfax" advice column. Although the arrangement was supposed to be temporary, McCarroll found she liked the column, which she wrote until her retirement in 1966, editing the women's page at the same time.

McCarroll's tenure as Beatrice Fairfax transformed advice columns from puffy "advice to the lovelorn" sections of newspapers to forums for earnest efforts to help readers solve their problems. In an article in the July 1954 *Wellesley Alumnae Magazine*, McCarroll explained that she had at first taken the Beatrice Fairfax persona lightly. Over time, however, she found the column to be a serious challenge. Treating it as a genuine journalistic assignment, she did research on readers' problems and kept files on individuals and agencies who could aid her and her correspondents. In an article in the Wellesley alumnae magazine in 1954 she explained:

In all cases where ordinary intelligence, common sense and humanity are not enough—and sometimes they really are enough, as my correspondence files readily demonstrate—I refer the letter writers, wherever possible, to some person or some social service organization near them which can supply on-the-spot counseling and such practical help as may be indicated. In this, I work closely with national social service organizations.

McCarroll answered each letter personally and found that her jobs as women's-page editor and advice columnist for King Features balanced each other nicely.

In her spare moments McCarroll worked on two books. *Suzanne of Belgium* (1932), illustrated by Suzanne Silvercruys Farnam, told of Farnam's escape from Belgium as a girl in World War I and her subsequent career as an artist in the United States. *Summer Cookbook* (1954) drew on McCarroll's experience as a leisure editor to describe easy-to-cook dishes and menus. She also spent time at her summer home in Bradford, Vermont.

In 1952 McCarroll was honored with a "Woman of Achievement" award from Theta Sigma Phi, the national journalism sorority (now Women in Communications). In 1966 eye troubles forced her to retire from journalism. She moved to Ridgewood, New Jersey, and shared a home with her sister and brother until ill health in 1970 forced her to move into a nursing home in Allendale, New Jersey, where she died.

The first modern advice columnist, Marion McCarroll in her "Beatrice Fairfax" writings paved the way for later journalists like Dear Abby and Ann Landers. Applying common sense as well as well-honed research skills, McCarroll took readers' problems seriously and brought a social-service approach to their concerns.

• Wellesley College has files on McCarroll that include clippings, lists of courses taken, questionnaires she filled out, and updates that this active alumna sent to her class. An obituary is in the *New York Times*, 5 Aug. 1977.

TINKY "DAKOTA" WEISBLAT

MCCARTAN, Edward Francis (16 Aug. 1879–20 Sept. 1947), sculptor, was born in Albany, New York, the son of Michael McCartan, an Irish immigrant merchant of limited means, and Anna Hyland. McCartan began to draw instinctively at age five or six and by age ten had modeled a lion in clay. In his teens he entered Pratt Institute in Brooklyn, New York, and studied with Herbert Adams. He enrolled at the Art Students' League in New York City in the fall of 1901 to study sculpture with George Grey Barnard and Hermon Atkins MacNeil and drawing with Kenyon Cox and Bryson Burroughs. McCartan supported his widowed mother, who had moved to New York City, by assisting Adams, MacNeil, Karl Bitter, Isidore Konti, Francois Tonetti, J. Massey Rhind, and other sculptors who appreciated his proficiency at enlarging monumental and architectural sculpture.

Through Rhind, McCartan received the commission for a statue of Benito Juarez for Mexico City, which he completed in 1906. With the proceeds from that job he traveled to Paris, where he entered the École des Beaux-Arts studio of Jean Antoine Injalbert on 30 March 1907. He stayed for three years, making frequent visits to the Louvre to see antique and Renaissance sculpture. McCartan also became well acquainted with the statuary at Versailles. The sculpture of Jean Goujon, Clodion, and Jean Antoine Houdon exerted a lasting influence on McCartan. He exhibited at the salons in Paris but later destroyed most of his early sculptures. Although McCartan expressed enthusiasm about the work of Rodin during his stay in Paris, Rodin's impact on McCartan's sculpture was short lived. Only one work, *The Kiss* (Albright-Knox Gallery), a marble group of a nude female kissing a child, echoes Rodin's style. McCartan began *The Kiss* in Paris in 1908 but did not finish it until 1924.

McCartan returned to New York in February 1910 and for a year helped Adams on the McMillan Fountain for Washington, D.C. He again assisted MacNeil, Rhind, Konti, and Tonetti before opening his own studio in New York in 1913. In 1914 McCartan began

teaching at the School of Beaux-Arts Architects (later called Beaux-Arts Institute of Design), where he trained many American sculptors to create ornament for neoclassical buildings. Such work was consistent with McCartan's artistic philosophy, which recognized that sculpture should be decorative and allied with its surroundings.

McCartan created architectural sculpture for the New York Central building (New York City, 1928), the New Jersey Telephone building (Newark, c. 1928), and the Department of Labor Building (Washington, D.C., 1934). He also produced a work of monumental sculpture, the *Eugene Field Memorial* for Lincoln Park in Chicago, which won the medal of honor at the exhibition of the Architectural League of New York in 1923. But McCartan was far more prolific in the production of mythical woodland creatures that he intended for placement in gardens, where the floral surroundings created a natural home for his sylvan figures. In this genre the love and mastery of elegant line and graceful form that McCartan had acquired from the study of French eighteenth-century sculpture served him especially well.

From the National Academy of Design in 1912 McCartan won the Helen Foster Barnett Prize for Sculpture (for the best work by a sculptor under thirty-five) for *Fountain*, a naiad atop a turtle with a large basin from which water pours. He won the Wilder Gold Medal at the Pennsylvania Academy of the Fine Arts in 1916 for his *Spirit of the Woods*, a slender, dancing bacchante holding a baby in her outstretched hands—a composition reminiscent of Frederick Mac-Monnies's infamous *Bacchante and Infant Faun*. McCartan's *Pan*, which was influenced by MacMonnies's *Pan of Rohallion*, was exhibited at the National Academy of Design in 1913 and the Panama-Pacific Exposition in San Francisco in 1915. His *Dancing Satyr* (c. 1915) and *Girl with Goat* (c. 1920) were also widely acclaimed. McCartan's mature style is fully evident in the *Nymph and Satyr* (Century Association, 1920). Art historian Beatrice Proske discerned that "the forms are purified and the lucid composition polished to a glowing brilliancy of line. The few ornamental passages, the hair, the basket of fruit, and the satyr's wreath are finished with sparkling clarity of detail" (Proske, p. 230).

McCartan created his best-known work, *Diana with a Hound*, in 1923. In this signature piece he crystallized his conception of the ideal nude in the spirit of Clodion and Jean Goujon. The svelte huntress strides forward while restraining her lean hound, who leaps ahead at her side. She twists to resist his pressure on the leash and extends the bow in her left hand to keep her balance, thus framing the primary view of her exquisite torso as her muscles tighten in response to the dog. The interplay of human and animal energy and forward and backward movement create a tension visible throughout the softly modeled forms of the goddess's nubile body. The gilded leash, bow, and the crescent moon on Diana's tiara highlight the refined composition, which ranks as McCartan's masterpiece and one of the most beautiful nudes in the history of art. It was exhibited at the National Sculpture Society exhibition in 1923 and in 1925 at the Concord Art Association, where it won a medal of honor. The first bronze cast of the two-foot-tall sculpture was purchased by the Metropolitan Museum of Art, and a heroic-scale version was completed for a Connecticut garden in 1930.

In the 1920s McCartan also produced *Dionysus* (1923), a muscular youth with a panther at his feet; the work won the McClees Prize when it was exhibited at the Pennsylvania Academy of the Fine Arts in 1931. The sculpture was enlarged, remodeled, gilded, and placed in Brookgreen Gardens at Murrells Inlet, South Carolina, in 1930. Like *Diana*, its anatomical accuracy, lyrical lines, and graceful pose echo French eighteenth-century sculpture. *Isolute* (1926), a larger-than-life nude with a fawn, marks McCartan's shift from naturalistic modeling to bolder, more simplified forms. His *Bather* (Pennsylvania Academy of the Fine Arts, 1935) is the best example of this phase of his career. In this standing figure McCartan concentrated on form rather than line, and a hint of archaism is evident.

McCartan spent several months in 1936 as a visitor at the American Academy in Rome. In the late 1930s McCartan, a heavy smoker, began to suffer from emphysema. His creativity decreased, and he received few new commissions except portraits, but he continued to teach. He became head of the Rinehart School of Sculpture at the Maryland Institute in Baltimore in 1943. McCartan never married, and he died, bankrupt, in New Rochelle, New York. The National Sculpture Society paid his funeral expenses.

• About one hundred items of McCartan's correspondence (1924–1947), primarily concerning the National Institute of Arts and Letters and the American Academy of Arts and Letters, are in the American Academy of Arts and Letters Library. An interview with McCartan is in the Dewitt M. Lockman Collection of Interviews with American Artists, New-York Historical Society. The best source on McCartan is Janis Conner and Joel Rosenkranz, *Rediscoveries in American Sculpture: Studio Works, 1893–1939* (1989). Royal Cortissoz, "The Sculpture of Edward McCartan—The Winter Academy," *Scribner's Monthly*, Feb. 1928, pp. 236–44, is insightful, particularly regarding the essence of McCartan's style. See also Cortissoz, *The Painter's Craft* (1930); and Agusta Owen Patterson, "Edward McCartan, Sculptor," *International Studio* 83 (Jan. 1926): 27–31. Beatrice Gilman Proske, *Brookgreen Gardens Sculpture* (1943) illuminates McCartan's garden statuary; and George Gurney, *Sculpture and the Federal Triangle* (1985) discusses McCartan's role in the Department of Labor Building architectural sculpture.

MICHAEL W. PANHORST

MCCARTHY, Charles (29 June 1873–26 Mar. 1921), civil servant and reformer, was born in Brockton, Massachusetts, the son of John McCarthy, an enginetender in a shoe factory, and Katherine O'Shea Desmond, a domestic servant who also maintained a boardinghouse for immigrant laborers. At the age of nineteen, after working at numerous occupations while reading vociferously, McCarthy was admitted to Brown University as a special student. There he distinguished himself academically and athletically, and became the first Brown player to score touchdowns against both Harvard and Yale. He also developed a long-lasting friendship with the team's student trainer, John D. Rockefeller, Jr., and earned the respect of such eminent scholars as J. Franklin Jamieson and E. Benjamin Andrews. The former, who became his mentor, recalled that McCarthy was "forever asking questions and storing his mind with knowledge concerning all sorts of conditions of men, their occupations, their amusements, their ways of thinking."

After receiving a Ph.B. from Brown in 1896, McCarthy spent a year teaching and coaching at the University of Georgia. In 1899 he entered graduate school in political economy at the University of Wisconsin, where he studied under Richard E. Ely, Fredrick Jackson Turner, and Charles Homer Haskins. In his own words, McCarthy, "a wandering student, seeking knowledge, came knocking at the gates of the great University of Wisconsin, and it took me in, filled me with inspiration, and when I left its doors, the kindly people of the state stretched out welcoming hands and gave me a man's work to do." His doctoral dissertation, "The Anti-Masonic Party," won the Justin Winsor Prize of the American Historical Association in 1902, two years after McCarthy received a Ph.D. at Madison.

In 1901 McCarthy married Louise Howard Schreiber; they had one child. That same year, on Turner's recommendation that his student was a "digger after truth," the Wisconsin Free Library Commission appointed McCarthy as the first director of the Legislative Reference Library, a post that he held until his death. In that capacity, McCarthy labored to provide Wisconsin lawmakers with as much information as possible, in the form of statutes, reports, books, articles, pamphlets, speeches, newspaper accounts, and other documents, to aid them in drafting legislation. His aim was "to make a working library of the greatest practical value to members of the legislature and to state departments." McCarthy and his "boys and girls" compiled clipping files and scrapbooks filled with material gathered from all over the United States as well as other parts of the world on every topic that might conceivably become the subject of legislation.

Under McCarthy, the library's "bill-drafting department," which prided itself on its apolitical, technical approach, wrote virtually every piece of legislation that earned Wisconsin its reputation as a highly progressive state. But the overwhelmingly progressive nature of the legislation, combined with McCarthy's outspoken advocacy of forward-looking measures and politicians, caused conservatives to call for the abolition of the "progressive bill factory" in 1914. McCarthy managed, nevertheless, to weather the storm by convincing incoming governor Emanuel Philipp of his value and objectivity. In presenting McCarthy an honorary doctorate in 1913, Brown University President William Faunce proclaimed that the recipient proved that an "athlete may be a scholar and the scholar may shape life and law."

During that same period, McCarthy served on a number of appointed commissions that drafted plans for the reform of the Wisconsin economy and society. Chief among these were the revitalization of the University of Wisconsin extension division, the establishment of civil service, the revamping of rural education, the creation of "continuation schools" for vocational/technical education, the adoption of workmen's compensation, and the development of a comprehensive Industrial Commission. In close collaboration with agrarian reformers Gifford Pinchot and Sir Horace Plunkett, McCarthy tirelessly championed such causes as agricultural education in rural schools, farmers' cooperatives, and state financing for marginal farmsteads.

A close adviser to Wisconsin progressive governors Robert M. La Follette, Sr., and Francis McGovern, McCarthy also served as consultant to Presidents Theodore Roosevelt and Woodrow Wilson, and several other states' governors. By 1910 he had turned the Legislative Reference Library into a training school for public servants and a model for emulation by other states. He also taught political science at the University of Wisconsin from 1905 to 1917 and was the guiding force behind the State Board of Public Affairs, an ambitious effort at comprehensive social planning. The publication of McCarthy's *The Wisconsin Idea* in 1912, with an introduction by Theodore Roosevelt, made McCarthy and Wisconsin synonymous with progressive reform, even though it was, by its author's own admission, sketchy and skewed. His most famous publication, *The Wisconsin Idea* provides many useful insights into McCarthy's character, personality, and philosophy.

In 1914 McCarthy was appointed director of the U.S. Commission on Industrial Relations, established in 1912 and chaired by labor lawyer Francis "Frank" P. Walsh, which was empowered "to seek to discover the underlying causes of dissatisfaction in the industrial situation and report its conclusions thereon." Differences in temperament, philosophy, and methodology between Walsh and McCarthy, however, which were exacerbated by the latter's ongoing communication with his college classmate Rockefeller, led to McCarthy's "resignation" in March 1915.

During the war years, McCarthy served on the Wisconsin State Council of Defense as a "dollar a year" man for the Food Administration, which was headed by Herbert Hoover, and as an intelligence gatherer for the War Labor Policies Board under Felix Frankfurter. In 1918 he ran unsuccessfully as the Democratic candidate for the U.S. Senate from Wisconsin. Worn out by years of overwork and self-denial, McCarthy went to Prescott, Arizona, to convalesce from a sore throat and stomach pains; he died there from peritonitis after an operation for perforated stomach ulcers. He became the only appointed official ever to lie in state in the Wisconsin Capitol.

• The Charles McCarthy Papers are housed in the archives division of the State Historical Society of Wisconsin at Madison. *McCarthy of Wisconsin* (1944), written by McCarthy protégé Edward A. Fitzpatrick, is an uncritical but valuable source on the subject's work and life. Marion Casey, *Charles McCarthy, Librarianship and Reform* (1981), examines the relationship between the Legislative Reference Library and the progressive reform movement in Wisconsin and in the nation. Irish agrarian reformer Sir Horace Plunkett, a frequent correspondent and collaborator on agricultural causes, supplies a European perspective in "McCarthy of Wisconsin," *Nineteenth Century and After* 77 (June 1915): 1335–47. Other helpful sketches are in the *New Republic*, 27 Apr. 1921; the *Wisconsin State Journal*, 27 Mar. 1921; *American School*, May 1921; and the *Wisconsin Library Bulletin*, Apr.-May 1921.

JOHN D. BUENKER

MCCARTHY, Joe (21 Apr. 1887–13 Jan. 1978), baseball player and manager, was born Joseph Vincent McCarthy in the Germantown section of Philadelphia, the son of Benjamin McCarthy, a construction contractor, and Susan Connolly Bradley. His father was killed on the job when McCarthy was three years old, so the boy went to work at an early age in a textile mill to help support the family. McCarthy developed a lifelong passion for sports, especially baseball and boxing, and gained local renown as a semipro ball player. Although he never went to high school, he attended Niagara University near Niagara Falls, New York, on a baseball scholarship from 1905 to 1906.

McCarthy began his professional career in 1907 in the Tri-State League (Class B), but he ended the season playing in the Class D Inter-State League. A .314 batting average in 1908 led to his promotion to the American Association, the highest-ranked minor league. He performed at every infield position except first base, and he even played in the outfield for two clubs. Weak hitting brought a demotion to Wilkes-Barre of the Class B New York State League in 1912, but his keen understanding of the game led to his being named the club's playing manager in 1913. Assigning himself exclusively to second base, he posted a career-high .325 batting average, earning promotion to Buffalo of the International League in 1914. In 1916 he signed with Brooklyn of the Federal League, but when that league folded before the season opener, he joined the Louisville Colonels of the American Association.

A solid but unexceptional performer who hit .300 only twice, McCarthy realized that he would never reach the major leagues as a player ("I wasn't much of a hitter, and I didn't have good speed either"), and he began to concentrate on developing his managerial skills. He served as player-manager for Louisville from 1919 through 1921 and, after leading the Colonels to their first AA pennant in 1921, retired as an active player. He soon became recognized as perhaps the finest manager in the minor leagues, and after the Colonels won another AA pennant in 1925 he was hired by William Wrigley, Jr., to take over the last-place Chicago Cubs of the National League.

During twenty years in the minors McCarthy developed the managerial style and technique that made him the most successful major league manager of his era and arguably the best in baseball history. He immediately established himself as the unquestioned (task)master of the Cubs by getting rid of the team's malcontents, including the hard-drinking and unreliable star pitcher, Grover Cleveland Alexander, thus earning the nickname "Marse Joe" from Harry Neily of the *Chicago Evening American*. Under McCarthy's strong and disciplined leadership, the Cubs improved to fourth place in his first two seasons, finished third in 1928, and won the league title in 1929, only to lose to Philadelphia in the World Series four games to one. The team was a contender again in 1930, ultimately finishing second, two games out of first, but the thin-skinned McCarthy resented the persistent criticism from fans and press for the 1929 World Series disappointment. With the consent of the Chicago front office, he began negotiations with the New York Yankees, and in September 1930 the Cubs announced his resignation.

McCarthy took over the Yankees in 1931 fully aware of its stature as the premier team of the 1920s. Since 1921 the Yankees had won the American League pennant six times, twice posting three consecutive titles, while finishing second twice. He knew that winning was mandatory, but simply winning was not enough for him. He saw himself as responsible for creating the fabled Yankee "image." On the field, he insisted on precision in executing the fundamentals of batting, fielding, and baserunning and the primacy of teamwork over individual achievement. Off the field, he insisted that players conduct themselves with dignity, and he required them to wear coats and ties in public. "Yankee Pride" was his motto, and he constantly reminded players: "You are a Yankee!"

The team finished second in McCarthy's first year, but in 1932 the Yankees won the pennant and defeated the Cubs in four straight games in the World Series. The Yankees finished second each of the next three seasons, playing well despite the personal resentments and challenges to his authority by players who disliked the hiring of an "outsider" to lead the club. Tensions were especially deep between McCarthy and Babe Ruth, who had campaigned for the manager's job. The two men rarely spoke, and the normally strict McCarthy made no attempt to discipline his free-spirited outfielder. Tensions came to a head when Ruth, his playing days nearly over, demanded the club fire McCarthy and hire him as manager. When the Yankees released Ruth in February 1935, McCarthy gained complete control.

The result was the most spectacular record in major league history. Over the next eight years the Yankees won seven American League titles (1936–1939, 1941–1943) and six World Series (1936–1939, 1941, 1943). They almost went eight-for-eight, finishing third in 1940, only two games out of first. From 1936 to 1939 the team won more than 100 games three times and averaged a stunning 102 wins per season. The 1939 team, which followed 106 wins (a winning percentage of .702) in the regular season with a fourth consecutive World Series title by sweeping Cincinnati in four games, has been judged by some baseball historians to be equal to, if not better than, the famous "Murderer's Row" 1927 Yankees led by Ruth and Lou Gehrig.

McCarthy's fortunes changed abruptly. With a roster depleted of talent by World War II, his team slipped to third place in 1944 and fourth in 1945. More significantly, Larry MacPhail, Sr., became president of the club in 1945 and immediately began to interfere with player personnel decisions and to publicly criticize the team and its manager. Although the Yankees improved as players returned from the war, McCarthy, who had been suffering for two years from a stomach ailment exacerbated by his heavy drinking, resigned on 24 May 1946, with the team in second place. He came out of retirement to lead the Boston Red Sox to second place in 1948 and 1949. Both pennant races were photo finishes. In 1948 Boston tied with Cleveland but lost a one-game playoff; in 1949 the Red Sox finished one game behind the Yankees. On 23 June 1950, with the team mired in fourth place, McCarthy retired for good, spending the rest of his life on a 61-acre farm in Amherst, New York, a suburb of Buffalo, with his wife, Elizabeth "Babe" McCave, whom he had married in 1921; they did not have children. He died in a Buffalo hospital.

Generally regarded as one of the greatest managers in baseball history, McCarthy's record is unequaled. In twenty-four major league seasons his teams won nine league championships and seven World Series titles; his career (.615) and World Series (.698) winning percentages were unexcelled. Most remarkable, no team of his ever finished out of the first division. In fifteen full seasons with New York, the Yankees finished first eight times, second four times, third twice, and fourth once; his winning percentage of .627 was unmatched. He led the American League to four victories in seven All-Star games. In 1929 he became the first manager without major league playing experience to win a league championship, and in 1932 he became the first to win titles in each league. He was also the first to win four consecutive World Series.

Despite his achievements, McCarthy's managerial ability was often underestimated. A low-key as well as no-nonsense personality, he confined his leadership to the dugout and clubhouse. He never engaged in histrionics on the field and infrequently challenged umpires, and then only on rules interpretations; he was ejected only twice with the Yankees. Although possessing a keen sense of humor, McCarthy was a reserved individual who not only shunned publicity but was self-effacing in explaining his team's success: "Get the players and keep them happy" was his stated formula for winning. Consequently, the public accorded him faint praise when his teams won and unfairly blamed him when they lost. His reserved demeanor coupled with jealousy over his success led to the charge that he was a "push-button" manager whose success was the inevitable byproduct of extraordinarily talented teams. In fact, McCarthy consistently had a dramatic impact on the performance of players and teams throughout his managerial career. In addition to having a firm grasp of the strategic nuances of the game, he was a master at handling players, and his clubs always exhibited remarkable teamwork and mastery of fundamental playing techniques. The Cubs finished second in 1930 under McCarthy's tutelage, as the talented but undisciplined Hack Wilson hit .356 and set the National League record for home runs (56) and the major league record for runs batted in (190); with McCarthy gone in 1931, Wilson reverted to old habits, his statistics plummeted, and the Cubs dropped to third place. Conversely, the Yankees finished third in 1930 but rose to second the next season under McCarthy. New York was in second place when he resigned in 1946, then declined the rest of the season and finished a distant third. Similarly, McCarthy took over a Boston team that had finished third the previous season and led them to two straight second-place finishes, failing to win the pennant each year by the narrowest of margins; after he resigned, the Red Sox slipped to third place and would ultimately drop to sixth before regaining respectability.

McCarthy was a square shooter who earned the respect of players not only with his knowledge of the game, but also with his candor and his practice of confining criticism to private discussions. He was very close to most of his players and praised by all. Joe DiMaggio recalled that "There wasn't a day that someone on the Yankees didn't learn something from McCarthy," and shortstop Phil Rizzuto noted: "He would never say anything behind a player's back and he would never second-guess his men. He was very strict, but very, very fair." Tommy Henrich flatly stated: "I played under three great managers—McCarthy, [Bucky] Harris, and [Casey] Stengel—and I have to put McCarthy at the top of the list." Temperamental Ted Williams of the Red Sox, a perfectionist who rarely handed out compliments, was of the same opinion: "McCarthy was the best manager I ever worked for. The man knew what he was doing and he knew the right moves." Even those who disliked him, like Yankee pitcher Joe Page, conceded his ability: "I hate his guts, but there never was a better manager." Baseball writers, with whom McCarthy had never curried favor, agreed: In 1957 Joe McCarthy was elected to baseball's Hall of Fame, the first person enshrined solely for achievements as a manager.

• The National Baseball Library, Cooperstown, N.Y., has an extensive clippings file on McCarthy. For personal reminiscences, see Donald Honig, *The Man in the Dugout* (1977), pp. 80–95, and Joe McCarthy, "An Old Yankee Manager Recalls the Joy of His Job," *New York Times*, 25 Sept. 1977. For assessment of his managerial career, see Edward G. Barrow, "The Greatest Manager," *Collier's* 125 (1950): 28–29ff., and Arthur Mann, "Of McCarthy and Men," *Baseball Magazine* 71 (1943): 365–67, as well as chapters in Ed Hurley, *Managing to Win* (1976), Jim Bouton, *"I Managed Good, But Boy Did They Play Bad"* (1973), and Edwin Pope, *Baseball's Greatest Managers* (1960). For managerial career statistics, see Macmillan's *Baseball Encyclopedia*, 9th ed. (1993), and John Thorn and Pete Palmer, *Total Baseball*, 3d ed. (1993). Context for his Yankee years is provided by Frank Graham, *The New York Yankees: An Informal History* (1943). Obituaries are in the *New York Times*, 14 Jan. 1978, and the *Sporting News*, 28 Jan. 1978.

LARRY R. GERLACH

MCCARTHY, Joseph (14 Nov. 1908–2 May 1957), U.S. senator, was born Joseph Raymond McCarthy on a dairy farm near Appleton, Wisconsin, the son of Timothy McCarthy and Bridget Tierney, farmers. At age sixteen McCarthy quit school to begin a poultry business on rented land. When a bitter winter killed most of his flock, he returned to high school in the fall of 1929 and crammed four years of work into two semesters. In 1930 he enrolled in Marquette University, a Jesuit institution in Milwaukee.

McCarthy financed his education with earnings from odd jobs and all-night card games at neighborhood taverns. "One should play poker with him to really know him," a friend wrote, "but in case you do, it would be my advice to . . . get some big bank to back you. He raises on poor hands and always comes out the winner." McCarthy also boxed at Marquette as a heavyweight. At six feet tall and 200 pounds, "Smiling Joe" became a crowd favorite who took tremendous punishment in the ring in stride.

McCarthy earned a law degree from Marquette in 1935 and moved back to the Appleton area to begin his political career. After running unsuccessfully for district attorney on the Democratic ticket, he set his sights on the circuit judgeship, a nonpartisan office that allowed him to run free of party affiliation. The incumbent, Edgar Werner, had been in office for more than twenty years, and expecting another easy victory, he did not bother to campaign. McCarthy, however, visited every farm and business in the district. He also misrepresented Werner's age and salary, making him appear older and richer than he was. McCarthy won by 4,000 votes.

At age twenty-nine, McCarthy became the youngest and most controversial judge in Wisconsin. The local press criticized him for granting "quickie" divorces to political supporters, and the state supreme court censured him for destroying crucial evidence in a price-fixing case. Yet McCarthy was a popular jurist, described by lawyers and constituents as evenhanded and approachable. The longtime court reporter in Appleton claimed that "Joe was the sharpest on legal evidence of any judge I have ever worked for." McCarthy's rulings were rarely reversed on appeal.

In 1942 McCarthy joined the marines. Though exempt from military service as a judge, he concluded that front-line action would be essential for political advancement once the fighting stopped. He spent World War II as an intelligence officer in the Pacific, debriefing combat pilots who returned from bombing runs over Japanese-held islands. McCarthy embellished his record, portraying himself as a "tail-gunner" who flew dangerous missions against the Japanese. He claimed to have fired the most bullets of any marine in history and to have suffered a war wound when his plane crash-landed in flames. In fact, McCarthy flew only a handful of safe missions in the tail-gunner's seat, strafing islands already abandoned by the Japanese. His war wound was the result of a hazing incident aboard a troop ship. Yet, as often happened with McCarthy, the truth got lost in a maze of changing numbers and claims. In 1944 he spoke of 14 bombing runs over "enemy" territory; that figure rose to 17 in 1947 and to 32 in 1951. A few years later he received at his own request the Distinguished Flying Cross, which was awarded for 25 missions in combat.

In 1946 McCarthy challenged Robert M. La Follette, Jr., the popular three-term incumbent, in Wisconsin's Republican senatorial primary. Like the overconfident Judge Werner, La Follette did not aggressively campaign. With the field wide open, McCarthy crisscrossed the state, posing as a war hero and berating La Follette, who was then fifty-one, for failing to enlist. "TODAY JOE McCARTHY IS HOME," his campaign flyers emphasized. "He wants to SERVE America in the SENATE. Yes, folks, CONGRESS NEEDS A TAIL-GUNNER."

McCarthy narrowly defeated La Follette by 5,000 votes, but a few months later he buried his Democratic opponent, Howard McMurray, in a pile of baseless charges. Using a tactic that soon made him infamous, McCarthy accused the liberal McMurray of accepting Communist support. He won in a landslide.

McCarthy's early Senate years gave signs of trouble to come. He earned the nickname "Pepsi Cola Kid" for his tireless efforts to aid the soft drink industry's campaign to decontrol the price and supply of sugar following World War II. He raised eyebrows by criticizing the U.S. Army's prosecution of Nazi troops involved in the massacre of American prisoners during the Battle of the Bulge—an obvious ploy, some suspected, to win favor among Wisconsin's large German-American population. Angry colleagues accused McCarthy of lying, insulting fellow members, and ignoring the Senate's cherished folkways. Before long Senate leaders removed him from the Banking Committee and reassigned him to the lowly District of Columbia Committee.

McCarthy needed an issue to salvage his failing career. On the evening of 7 February 1950 he delivered a political stump speech before a Republican women's group in Wheeling, West Virginia, decrying "Communist influence" in the Truman administration. By then the subject was familiar. Indeed, large chunks of McCarthy's speech had been lifted from a recent address by Republican congressman Richard Nixon. But McCarthy added a paragraph that catapulted him to national prominence. "While I cannot take the time to name all of the men in the State Department who have been named as members of the Communist Party . . . ," he said, "I have here in my hand a list of 205 . . . names that were known to the Secretary of State and who nevertheless are still working and shaping the policy of the State Department."

McCarthy had no such list. Furthermore, he had little expertise about communism in the federal government. The figure 205 came from an outdated letter that had been compiled by a 1946 House committee based on a "preliminary loyalty screening" of 3,000 State Department employees. As of July 1946, "damaging information" had been uncovered in 284 cases, and 79 people had been discharged. Presumably the 205 were still employed by the State Department. McCarthy had no idea how many of them had been fired since 1946, nor did he know what the "damaging information" entailed.

McCarthy's charges in February 1950 commanded press attention, and the public was aroused. In the months before McCarthy's Wheeling speech, Cold War tensions had reached a boil. China had recently fallen to the Communists in 1949, while the Russians had successfully tested an atomic bomb in August 1949. The previous month Alger Hiss had been found guilty of perjury, and Klaus Fuchs, a British scientist on the Manhattan Project, had confessed to sending atomic secrets to the Soviet Union. McCarthy seemingly produced a simple explanation for these disturbing events. The Communists were "winning" the Cold War, said McCarthy, because of the actions of disloyal government officials. In addition, the Truman administration had failed to dismiss "known" Communists.

McCarthy's allegations made him an instant celebrity. His face adorned the covers of *Time* and *Newsweek*, while the cartoonist Herblock coined the word "McCarthyism" to describe his reckless ways. Early public opinion polls showed about 40 percent of the people agreeing that McCarthy's charges were "a good thing for the country," and that figure rose above 50 percent in the coming months. As expected, prominent Republicans rallied to his side. Privately, Senator Robert A. Taft of Ohio dismissed McCarthy as a fraud, yet Taft encouraged him to keep attacking the Truman administration, saying, "If one case doesn't work out, try another."

McCarthy needed no prodding. Following the outbreak of the Korean War in 1950, with American troops battling Communist forces in Asia, his message took on special force. At one time he claimed to have uncovered the "top Russian spy" in the United States, Sinologist Owen Lattimore. As the 1952 presidential campaign approached, he called Secretary of Defense George C. Marshall a traitor, mocked Secretary of State Dean Acheson as the "Red Dean of Fashion," and described President Truman as a drunkard, adding, "The son-of-a-bitch should be impeached." During the 1952 campaign, McCarthy claimed, falsely, that the Communist *Daily Worker* had endorsed the Democratic presidential nominee Adlai Stevenson. And he made the ugly slip, "Alger . . . I mean Adlai," on several occasions.

Easily reelected in the Republican landslide of 1952, McCarthy became chairman of the Senate Committee on Government Operations and its Subcommittee on Investigations. With the authority to hire staffers, hold hearings, issue subpoenas, and publish final reports, the senator became a major force on Capitol Hill. For the key position of chief counsel, he selected Roy Marcus Cohn, an abrasive young attorney from Manhattan who had served as a prosecutor in the Julius and Ethel Rosenberg spy trial. Cohn possessed boundless energy and excellent contacts within the Federal Bureau of Investigation (FBI), which provided him access to classified files. A bachelor for most of his life, McCarthy married Jean Kerr, his political assistant, in 1953. The couple adopted a daughter.

In 1953 Cohn and McCarthy held hearings on "Communist influence" throughout the federal government. Their targets included the Voice of America, the Government Printing Office, and the Foreign Service. These hearings proved disastrous. Without uncovering any Communists, they served to undermine government morale, damage numerous reputations, and make America look sinister in the eyes of the world. Not surprisingly, Republican criticism of McCarthy began to build, because the senator was now attacking a bureaucracy controlled by his own party. Many expected President Dwight D. Eisenhower to step in and silence McCarthy.

Though Eisenhower despised the senator, he chose not to confront him. He believed that a fight with McCarthy would divide Republicans into warring camps and demean the presidential office. Time and again, he told his aides, "I just will not—I *refuse*—to get into the gutter with that guy."

In the fall of 1953, however, McCarthy's subcommittee initiated fateful hearings into subversive activity in the U.S. Army. The subcommittee's first allegation—that a Communist spy ring existed at Fort Monmouth, New Jersey, headquarters of the Army Signal Corps—at first brought a panicked response from Army secretary Robert Stevens, who suspended more than forty of Monmouth's top engineers as "security risks." One was accused of signing a nominating petition for a Socialist candidate in 1940 and another of having a "close and continuing association" with his brother, who had "attended a rally at Yankee Stadium at which Paul Robeson spoke."

By 1954 Cohn and McCarthy were attacking the army for "coddling Communists" within its ranks. At one hearing, McCarthy angrily browbeat a decorated officer who had served under Eisenhower in World War II. "You should be removed from any command," the senator told General Ralph W. Zwicker. "Any man . . . who protects Communists is not fit to wear that uniform." Eisenhower was furious, while Secretary Stevens claimed that Cohn was harassing the military to win preferential treatment for a close friend and part-time McCarthy staffer named G. David Schine, who had recently been drafted into the army.

In April 1954 the Senate decided to investigate the feud between the army and McCarthy. At Eisenhower's insistence, Republican leaders agreed to televise the hearings. The president believed that the cameras would capture the real McCarthy in ways the printed word could not. Huge crowds packed the Senate Caucus Room and forty million people followed the action on radio and television. Lasting thirty-six days, the army-McCarthy hearings overshadowed events of greater importance, such as the Supreme Court's decision to end public school segregation in *Brown v. Board of Education* (1954) and the French military defeat at Dien Bien Phu.

The president's instincts proved correct. The American people did not like the McCarthy they saw in action. His windy speeches, his frightening outbursts, and his crude personal attacks created the impression of a bully out of control. The highlight of the hearings came on 9 June, when McCarthy impugned the loyalty of a young attorney who worked in the law firm of army counsel Joseph Welch. "Until this moment, Senator, I think I never really gauged your cruelty or your recklessness," Welch responded with perfect contempt. "Have you no sense of decency, sir? At long last, have you left no sense of decency?" The audience burst into applause. More importantly, Senator Ralph Flanders introduced a resolution calling for McCarthy's censure, and a special Senate committee chaired by Arthur Watkins conducted hearings that eventually recommended reprimanding McCarthy.

In December 1954 the Senate voted to censure McCarthy for bringing that body "into dishonor and disrepute." The vote was 67–22, with only Republican conservatives opposed. Many viewed the censure as a sign that Cold War tensions had eased, if only a bit. The Korean War was over, and Stalin was dead. McCarthy himself faced oblivion and disgrace. Reporters and colleagues ignored him, and his influence disappeared. He spent his final days in the Senate a lonely figure, drinking heavily and railing against those who had deserted his cause. McCarthy died, virtually alone, of acute hepatitis (inflammation of the liver), caused by alcoholism, at the naval hospital in Bethesda, Maryland.

• The Joseph McCarthy Papers at Marquette University are closed to researchers. The best biographies are Richard Rovere, *Senator Joe McCarthy* (1959), and David M. Oshinsky, *A Conspiracy So Immense: The World of Joe McCarthy* (1983). A solid study of McCarthy as a local figure is in Michael O'Brien, *McCarthy and McCarthyism in Wisconsin* (1980). McCarthy's Senate career is superbly covered in Robert Griffith, *The Politics of Fear* (1970). For McCarthy as a political figure, see Richard Fried, *Men against McCarthy* (1976). Valuable information about the senator's relationship with journalists is in Edwin Bayley, *Joe McCarthy and the Press* (1981). For a good account of McCarthy and the Catholic church, see Donald Crosby, *God, Church, and Flag* (1978). The most provocative overview of the domestic Cold War and the meaning of McCarthyism is Stephen Whitfield, *Culture of the Cold War* (1991). An obituary is in the *New York Times*, 3 May 1957.

DAVID OSHINSKY

MCCARTHY, Mary (21 June 1912–25 Oct. 1989), writer and critic, was born in Seattle, Washington, the daughter of Roy McCarthy, a lawyer, and Therese Preston. McCarthy was the oldest of four children and the only girl. Her parents died of the flu during the epidemic of 1918. In *Memories of a Catholic Girlhood* (1957) McCarthy recalls a childhood of indulgence with her parents, followed by a life of penury and regimentation under the guardianship of her uncle Myers and aunt Margaret Shriver. The Shrivers raised the children in Milwaukee, Wisconsin, with strict discipline, frequent beatings, and few friends. McCarthy notes that her wealthy paternal grandparents, who lived only two blocks away, seemed unaware of the children's living conditions or of how little of the money they gave for their needs was used for that purpose.

When she was eleven, McCarthy's maternal grandparents, the Prestons, took her back to Seattle to live with them. Her grandfather showed little interest in her three younger brothers, placing them in boarding schools. McCarthy did not see her brothers again for six years.

Despite the trauma of her parents' death and the Shrivers' cruelty, McCarthy told an interviewer in 1984 that "I had a lot of fun doing that book" (*Memories of a Catholic Girlhood*), comparing memories with her brother, actor Kevin McCarthy, and that, by noting her guardians' and grandparents' comic attributes, she was able to use "laughter" as a "remedy for self-pity."

Throughout her childhood, McCarthy took refuge in Catholicism, but, although she was schooled in convents and considered herself a devout Catholic, she tried to call attention to herself as a teenager by pretending to have lost her faith. Questioned about her claim, she found that she had in fact done so. She remained an atheist.

In 1929 McCarthy went east to Vassar. Although she was thrilled to be there, she was bored by her classes except for English. At Vassar she first read John Dos Passos's *The 42nd Parallel*, which she said "radicalized" her politically. Further reading led her to the *New Republic*, in which she later published her first book reviews. McCarthy and several other students started the short-lived literary magazine *Con Spirito*, in protest against the *Vassar Review*, which would not publish their work.

McCarthy married actor Harold Johnsrud soon after her graduation from Vassar in 1933. They lived in New York, where Johnsrud worked at a variety of theatrical jobs while trying to get his plays produced. McCarthy's prolific writing career began with three reviews for the *New Republic*, followed by dozens of reviews for the *Nation*. Since reviewing paid poorly, she supplemented the couple's income by typing. She was unhappy with Johnsrud, whom she later said she did not love. She divorced him in 1936 to marry a man with whom she had been having an affair, only to realize that she did not want to marry her lover, either.

Following her divorce from Johnsrud in 1936, McCarthy went to work as an editorial assistant for Covici-Friede, a New York publishing house. Through acquaintances she made there, her commitment to the intellectual left solidified. Like many others in her circle, McCarthy separated herself from communism, seeing herself as an anti-Stalinist in the light of the Moscow treason trials of 1936–1938. She joined Philip Rahv, with whom she had been living since the summer of 1937, and several other anti-Stalinists in reviving the literary journal *Partisan Review*; the first issue was published in December 1937. Originally a Communist publication, the *Partisan Review* now insisted on its independence from political ties. McCarthy served as an editor for its first year and continued to write its theater reviews for the next twenty-five years. Collections of essays from her "Theatre Chronicle" column were published in several editions, including *Sights and Spectacles, 1937–1956* (1957) and *Mary McCarthy's Theatre Chronicles, 1937–1962* (1963).

Through her work on the *Partisan Review*, McCarthy met literary critic Edmund Wilson, who was a frequent contributor. They were married in February 1938 and had one son. McCarthy credited Wilson with her turn to fiction writing. He hired a sitter for their child and limited visitors so that she could work. When he decided she should try fiction, he shut her in a room to write a story. McCarthy wrote "Cruel and Barbarous Treatment" while thus confined; it was published in the *Southern Review* in 1939 and became the opening chapter in her first novel, *The Company She Keeps* (1942), a bildungsroman based largely on her own experiences.

McCarthy separated from Wilson in 1945, claiming that he beat her throughout their marriage. Wilson countered with charges of violence from his wife. They were divorced in 1946. Despite the turbulence of their marriage and their bitter divorce, McCarthy and Wilson remained in contact and were able to cooperate in their son's upbringing.

McCarthy taught at Bard College in New York during 1945–1946. Although she left Bard because teaching allowed her no time to write, she loved her work there. "At Bard," she said, "I acquired a literary conscience." Mary also taught at Sarah Lawrence College in the winter of 1948. In the meantime, she had moved in with Bowden Broadwater, a reporter for the *New Yorker*; they married in 1946.

McCarthy continued to be politically active during this period; in 1948, along with several friends, she began the "Europe-America Groups." The groups' purpose was to discuss political and cultural issues with European intellectuals and to "provide some center of solidarity with and support for intellectuals in Europe," as their manifesto states. Out of this work grew *The Oasis*, McCarthy's 1949 novel about a utopian intellectual community that ultimately fails.

In *The Groves of Academe* (1952) McCarthy experimented with writing from the characters' points of view. This contrasted with her previous fiction, in which she used essentially her own acerbic voice. She wrote in her characters' voices thereafter, although she found the technique limiting. *Groves*, which was written during the Joseph R. McCarthy era of anti-Communist investigations and right-wing political reactions, involves a professor who, when fired, claims falsely to be a Communist and the victim of a witch-hunt.

McCarthy drew heavily on real life in her fiction, from the autobiographical episodes in *The Company She Keeps* to the portraits of New Englanders in *A Charmed Life* (1955), drawn from the town of Wellfleet, where she and her husband lived. As her husband foresaw, the residents of Wellfleet were so upset by the novel that the Broadwaters felt compelled to move away. Although McCarthy believed that "the relation between life and literature . . . is one of mutual plagiarism," she maintained that she used real people as models only, transforming them in her novels to suit her fictional purposes.

McCarthy spent August through December 1955 doing research in Venice for an art book. The project became *Venice Observed* (1956), which sparked her lasting interest in art. She then published an architectural history, *The Stones of Florence* (1959). To do this work she spent several years dividing her time between winters in New York and the rest of the year in Europe. Her time away from the States contributed to her growing estrangement from Broadwater. They were divorced in 1961.

In 1960 McCarthy traveled on a speaking tour of Eastern Europe as part of a State Department authors' series. She had an affair with James West, the diplomat who arranged her itinerary in Poland; they married in 1961. McCarthy stayed with West for the rest of her life. Their marriage was to be the only one during which, she said, she had no affairs.

The Wests lived primarily in Paris, where West was reassigned, until McCarthy's death. West's three children often spent weekends and summers with them. They purchased a house in Maine in the early 1970s and spent summers there until West retired in 1980; from then on, they divided the year between Europe and Maine.

It was not until the publication of *The Group* in 1963 that McCarthy became famous outside intellectual circles. McCarthy summed up *The Group* in the plan for it that won her a Guggenheim fellowship. From the eight women's points of view in the novel "are refracted . . . all the novel ideas of the [1930s and 1940s] concerning sex, politics, economics . . . a 'true history' of the times despite the angle or angles of distortion." "For these girls," McCarthy later said in response to criticism that the book was full of clichés, "clichés precede experience." The book's detailed look at birth control practices and women's love affairs caused considerable scandal, as did McCarthy's earlier "The Man in the Brooks-Brother's Shirt," in *The Company She Keeps*, in which a woman has an affair with a stranger on a train. McCarthy spent eleven years working intermittently on *The Group*.

The Group was an instant bestseller, despite McCarthy's reluctance to help publicize it. She believed print interviews "cannot help vulgarizing a writer because the part of himself that writes is invisible." She did, however, consent to be interviewed by Jack Paar on television's "Tonight Show." Published in August 1963, *The Group* topped the *New York Times* bestseller list the last week in September and remained number

one through January 1964. Over 190,000 hardcover copies of the book have been sold in the United States; estimated hardcover and paperback international sales exceed five million copies. A 1966 film version of *The Group* stars Candace Bergen.

McCarthy's political commitment of the mid-1930s influenced the rest of her life. Some of its more obvious manifestations included her visits in the 1960s to both North Vietnam and South Vietnam, which resulted in the books *Vietnam* (1967) and *Hanoi* (1968). She also wrote about the Watergate affair, which led to the resignation of President Richard M. Nixon, in *The Mask of State: Watergate Portraits* (1974).

McCarthy's last novel, *Cannibals and Missionaries*, was published in 1979. In the novel, terrorists hijack a plane, planning to gain publicity by taking a group of liberals hostage. But they discover that a group of wealthy art collectors is also on board. The ensuing plot revolves around their efforts to ransom the collectors for their artwork. As McCarthy said in her initial notes for the novel, it "is about values—exchange values," and thus it makes the point that works of art are often valued more highly than people.

In 1980 McCarthy published *Ideas and the Novel*, in which she critiqued what she saw as modern novels' preoccupation with "showing" at the expense of plot and ideas and their contrast with the "fascination of ideas" in nineteenth-century novels.

Occasional Prose (1985) collected McCarthy's book reviews and essays from the *New York Times*. Her last book, *How I Grew*, was published in 1987. She meant this to be the first of a three-volume "intellectual autobiography." But *How I Grew*, which covers the same period as *Memories of a Catholic Girlhood*, was not well received. She also returned to teaching each fall at Bard, where she held a chair of literature from 1986.

In addition to her prolific writing career, McCarthy enjoyed several close friendships with other intellectuals. Along with the "P.R. Boys" of the *Partisan Review*, which included Dwight Macdonald and Philip Rahv, and Edmund Wilson, McCarthy befriended Italian novelist Nicola Chiaromonte and political writer Hannah Arendt. She was particularly close to Arendt, whose controversial *Eichmann in Jerusalem* (1963) McCarthy defended in the *Partisan Review*. She edited Arendt's *The Life of the Mind* after Arendt's death in 1975.

McCarthy's uninhibited statements frequently caused problems. Friends and acquaintances often resented her fictional portrayals of them, and critics decried her writing about such things as women having affairs. Yet, as biographers and critics have noted, McCarthy's controversial works and her insistence on honesty in her writing expanded the restrictions on what could be written about. Her outspokenness also resulted in a libel lawsuit brought by Lillian Hellman, of whom she had said, "every word she writes is a lie," in a television interview show. (Hellman died before the lawsuit was brought to court.)

In a 1966 interview Edwin Newman asked McCarthy if she thought critics were "unfair" to label her "acid, pitiless . . . and corrosive." McCarthy responded that if women writers are "at all satirical" they are "identified with cats," while "a man writer can be infinitely more savage, ruthless, et cetera and not be classified under . . . these epithets."

McCarthy's other fiction includes a collection of stories, *Cast a Cold Eye* (1950), and a novel, *Birds of America* (1971). Some essays were collected in *On the Contrary* (1961) and in *The Writing on the Wall and Other Literary Essays* (1970) in addition to *Occasional Prose*. McCarthy received the National Medal for Literature and the Edward MacDowell Medal, both in 1984. She died in New York City.

• McCarthy's papers, including manuscripts and typescripts, are at Vassar College. Her other books include *Medina* (1972), about the trial of Captain Ernest Medina, who was involved in the My Lai massacre during the Vietnam War; *The Seventeenth Degree* (1974), a collection of her previously published *Medina*, *Hanoi*, and *Vietnam*; and *The Hounds of Summer and Other Stories* (1981). Major secondary sources include Carol Brightman, *Writing Dangerously: Mary McCarthy and Her World* (1992), and Carol Gelderman, *Mary McCarthy: A Life* (1988). See also Doris Grumbach, *The Company She Kept: A Revealing Portrait of Mary McCarthy* (1967); Irvin Stock, *Mary McCarthy* (1968); and Barbara McKenzie, *Mary McCarthy* (1966). Carol Gelderman, ed., *Conversations with Mary McCarthy* (1991), is a collection of previously published and televised interviews. There is a brief biographical sketch and interview in *Contemporary Authors* (1986).

KATHY D. HADLEY

MCCAUSLAND, John (13 Sept. 1836–22 Jan. 1927), Confederate general, was born in St. Louis, Missouri, the son of John McCausland, a merchant, and Harriet Kyle Price. His parents died within a month of each other in 1843, leaving young John and his brother to the care of their grandmother. When she died six years later the two boys were taken to the village of Henderson in the Kanawha Valley of western Virginia, where they were raised by a widowed aunt.

After receiving a basic education at a local academy, McCausland entered the Virginia Military Institute (VMI) in 1853. He studied mathematics and engineering, the latter subject taught by Thomas J. Jackson, and graduated first in his class in 1857. In 1859 he returned to VMI as assistant professor of mathematics under Jackson and assistant professor of artillery tactics.

When the Civil War broke out, McCausland recruited and became the colonel of the Thirty-sixth Virginia Infantry, which saw service in western Virginia. Later McCausland and his regiment were transferred to General Albert Sidney Johnston's army in Kentucky. His command was one of the few units to escape from Fort Donelson when it fell to besieging Union forces in February 1862. Afterward McCausland operated in western Virginia under various commanders. Because of his tenacity in battle his men dubbed him "Tiger John."

At the battle of Cloyd's Mountain on 9 May 1864, Brigadier General Albert Gallatin Jenkins was mortally wounded, and McCausland assumed command of his cavalry brigade and was subsequently promoted to the rank of brigadier general. In this capacity he gained fame in the South and notoriety in the North.

When a numerically superior Union force under Major General David Hunter threatened to capture Lynchburg in mid-June 1864, McCausland was conspicuous in the town's defense. His command helped hold off the Federals for three days until a larger force under Lieutenant General Jubal Early arrived, forcing Hunter to retreat into western Virginia. For his services, the grateful citizens of Lynchburg presented McCausland with a gold engraved sword, a pair of silver spurs, and a new horse.

Next, McCausland and his brigade accompanied Early's army of fewer than 20,000 men down the Shenandoah Valley and across the Potomac into Maryland. Along the way Early sent McCausland to Hagerstown, Maryland, where on 6 July 1864 he skirmished with Union cavalry in the streets and then demanded a ransom from its citizens. Early wanted Hagerstown to be ransomed for $200,000, ostensibly to reimburse civilians in Virginia for damages incurred by Union depredations there under Hunter. However, in his excitement, McCausland, the former math teacher, missed a decimal point when he wrote the ransom demand and asked for only $20,000, which was promptly paid.

On 9 July 1864 McCausland led his brigade in bloody action at the battle of Monocacy, Maryland. By the end of the day Early's forces had driven the Union army of Major General Lew Wallace off the field. Within a few days Early's invading force was at the gates of Washington, D.C., probing the Union defenses north of the city. McCausland and his men scouted ahead as far as Georgetown. The timely arrival of Union reinforcements into Washington forced Early to break off his attempt to capture the capital and withdraw.

When Early returned to Virginia he found that General Hunter had returned and had committed more depredations against civilians, including burning a number of private homes. Early said later, "I came to the conclusion it was time to open the eyes of the people of the North to this enormity, by an example in the way of retaliation." Chambersburg, Pennsylvania, was selected as the site to be ransomed or burned, and McCausland was picked to lead the raid with his brigade and another under Brigadier General Bradley Johnson. The total strength of the force numbered approximately 2,800 men.

McCausland's force crossed the Potomac near Clear Spring, Maryland, on 29 July 1864. After a number of skirmishes with Union cavalry, the Confederates arrived at Chambersburg early the next morning. McCausland and his staff entered Chambersburg and demanded to see the town fathers. When they could not be found, he issued the ransom demand of $100,000 in gold or $500,000 in greenbacks to a crowd of citizens that was gathered. The town could not pay and did not take the ransom demand seriously. By mid-morning the entire place was in flames. The fire destroyed more than 500 structures and caused nearly $1 million in property damage. A more controversial aspect of the raid was the drunkenness and looting that occurred. McCausland's second in command, Johnson, was very critical of the raid, reporting that "everything in the catalog of infamy but rape and murder" had occurred.

With the town still in flames, McCausland led his force back toward the Potomac. At Hancock, Maryland, a mutiny almost ensued among the Maryland Confederate troops when McCausland issued orders to ransom that town or burn it. The arrival of pursuing Union cavalry forced the Confederates to mount up and head toward Cumberland, Maryland, another target of the raiders because it was a key point on the Baltimore and Ohio Railroad. A hastily gathered Union force was able to repulse McCausland's attack. Accordingly, McCausland led his command to the Potomac River and, after a sharp fight at Oldtown, Maryland, crossed the river into West Virginia. After another unsuccessful attempt to capture an important railroad center, this one at New Creek, he withdrew to the perceived safety of Moorefield, West Virginia.

At Moorefield, on 7 August 1864, McCausland's command was overtaken by Union cavalry bent on revenge for Chambersburg. The Confederates were routed, and more than 400 were taken prisoner. Subsequently, McCausland led his command in the final Confederate operations in the Shenandoah Valley. In March 1865 McCausland and his brigade joined Robert E. Lee's Army of Northern Virginia at Petersburg, Virginia, and participated in the Appomattox campaign. Refusing to formally surrender, McCausland led the few hundred men that composed the remnant of his brigade through Union lines to Lynchburg. There, what was left of his command was disbanded.

McCausland surrendered to Federal authorities near Charleston, West Virginia, and was paroled. However, he found the political climate in the new state of West Virginia unfriendly to former Confederates. He also heard of an indictment against him in Pennsylvania for the burning of Chambersburg and of a War Department order for his arrest. He fled first to Canada, then to the British Isles, and later to France. He became an officer in the French army, serving in Mexico until the fall of Emperor Ferdinand Maximilian.

Like most Confederates who had gone into exile, McCausland soon longed to return to the United States. In 1868 he returned to West Virginia after receiving assurances from the government that he would not be prosecuted. He bought land in Mason County in the Kanawha Valley and began the life of a gentleman farmer.

In 1878 he married Charlotta Hannah, a union that produced four children. His wife died in 1891 at the age of forty. McCausland never remarried and spent the remainder of his life somewhat of a recluse at his estate. When he passed away at his home in Mason County, West Virginia, only one other former Confederate general survived. Even in death McCausland could not escape the bitter feelings that still existed sixty-five years after the war. Some obituaries in northern newspapers referred to him as the "Hun of Chambersburg."

• Very little has been written by or about McCausland. The McCausland Family Letters at the Library of the Virginia Military Institute provide some information. McCausland wrote "The Burning of Chambersburg" for *The Annals of the War*, ed. Alexander K. McClure (1878) and granted an interesting interview in his last years for the *West Virginia Review* (Apr. 1926). A book-length biography of the general is Michael J. Pauley, *Unreconstructed Rebel: The Life of General John McCausland C.S.A.* (1992). For a detailed account of the Chambersburg raid see Ted Alexander, "McCausland's Raid and the Burning of Chambersburg" (master's thesis, Univ. of Maryland, 1988). An excellent account of Early's raid and McCausland's role in it is Benjamin F. Cooling, *Jubal Early's Raid on Washington: 1864* (1989). A number of unit histories have been written about regiments in McCausland's brigade. The most useful is Robert J. Driver, Jr., *14th Virginia Cavalry* (1988).

TED ALEXANDER

MCCAW, James Brown (12 July 1823–13 Aug. 1906), hospital administrator and educator, was born in Richmond, Virginia, the son of William Reid McCaw, a third-generation physician, and Ann Ludwell Brown. Having apparently opted for a career in medicine at an early age, McCaw completed his premedical studies at Richmond Academy and then enrolled in the medical school of the University of the City of New York (now New York University), where he studied with the renowned surgeon Valentine Mott. He received an M.D. in 1843 and returned to Richmond, where he opened a private medical practice and remained for the rest of his life. In 1845 he married Delia Patteson, with whom he had nine children, three of whom also became physicians. In 1858 he took on the additional duties of professor of chemistry and pharmacy at the Medical College of Virginia (MCV).

In 1861, after the battle of First Manassas, 6,000 Confederate sick and wounded were sent to Richmond, where they were cared for in a makeshift hospital housed in some unfinished buildings on Chimborazo Hill. After serving as the hospital's administrator for about six months, McCaw was about to join a cavalry unit when Samuel P. Moore, the Confederate army's surgeon general, requested that he continue in his duties at the hospital and expand its facilities. In 1862 Chimborazo Hospital was organized as an independent military post, and McCaw, who remained a civilian for the war's duration, was appointed its commandant and surgeon in chief.

The hospital eventually acquired a thirty-man garrison and 8,400 beds, which were distributed equally among five separate hospitals or divisions. Each division contained thirty individual buildings or wards that could accommodate up to sixty patients apiece as well as its own well, soup house, icehouse, and bathhouse. In addition to the five divisions, Chimborazo ran its own post office, bakery, brewery, dairy farm, and cemetery and employed a labor force of more than 250 slaves. There was a chronic shortage of drugs and medical supplies as well as of trained nurses. The sheer press of his administrative duties apparently caused McCaw to neglect his recordkeeping; Moore often chided him for carelessness and inaccuracy in his reports and accounts. Nevertheless, under McCaw's direction, over 90 percent of the 76,000 patients treated at Chimborazo Hospital survived. This record is even more impressive when one considers that it was achieved before the development of antibiotics and the principles of antisepsis.

During the war McCaw taught at MCV on an adjunct basis and helped to train more than 400 medical students for military service. He further contributed to the South's war effort by serving as first vice president of the Association of the Army and Navy Surgeons of the Confederate States from 1863 until the war's end and by editing all fourteen issues of the association's organ, the *Confederate States Medical and Surgical Journal*. The only medical journal ever published in the Confederacy, it focused on military medicine and mostly contained articles by Confederate surgeons describing unusual or difficult procedures in traumatic surgery. In 1864 he became a director of the Women's Relief Society of the Confederate States, a group concerned primarily with providing maimed servicemen with artificial limbs.

After the war McCaw returned to MCV in his former capacity and in 1869 became its professor of the practice of medicine. He also served as dean of the faculty for twelve years. In 1883, wearied by constant criticism from state government officials and several members of the board of directors regarding the quality of the college's training and disgusted by dissension between the faculty and the board of visitors, he retired from MCV. He later served as president of the board of visitors and continued to practice medicine privately until 1901.

McCaw played a prominent role in state and local medical affairs both before and after the war. He co-edited the *Virginia Medical and Surgical Journal* and its successor, the *Virginia Medical Journal*, from 1854 to 1859; the *Maryland and Virginia Medical Journal* in 1860; and the *Virginia Clinical Record* from 1871 to 1873. In 1870 he presided over the convention that reestablished the Medical Society of Virginia. In 1876 he became a member of the board of directors of Pinel Hospital, which specialized in the treatment of alcoholics and mental patients. In 1879 he became a consultant to the Richmond Eye, Ear, and Throat Infirmary and Dispensary, a free clinic for the city's poor, and in 1889 he began contributing his services free of charge to the indigent residents of the Sheltering Arms Hospital. He also served as president of the Richmond Academy of Medicine. A great patron of music and the arts, he presided for a number of years over the Mozart Society of Richmond. He died in Richmond.

During the Civil War, McCaw administered effectively and efficiently what was at the time the largest military hospital that had ever existed. He also contributed to the advance of medicine in Virginia as an editor and educator.

• McCaw's papers have not been located. His published works include "Remarks on the Uses and Effects of Sulphate of Quinine," *Stethoscope* 2 (1852): 665–80, and "Sick Headache," *Virginia Medical Journal* 8 (1857): 34–39. McCaw's contributions are discussed in Frank Stoddard Johns and Anne Page Johns, "Chimborazo Hospital and J. B. McCaw, Surgeon-in-Chief," *Virginia Magazine of History and Biography* 62, no. 2 (Apr. 1954): 190–200; Wyndham Blanton, *Medicine in Virginia in the Nineteenth Century* (1933); and Horace Herndon Cunningham, *Doctors in Gray* (1958). Obituaries are in the *Richmond Times-Dispatch*, 14 Aug. 1906, and the *Old Dominion Journal of Medicine and Surgery* 5, no. 3 (Aug. 1906): 65–66.

CHARLES W. CAREY, JR.

MCCAW, Walter Drew (10 Feb. 1863–7 July 1939), army medical officer, was born in Richmond, Virginia, the son of James Brown McCaw, a physician and former Confederate medical officer, and Delia Patteson. Because of his son's precocity, McCaw's father hired a tutor to guide McCaw through the work of the average undergraduate curriculum, which enabled him to finish his studies in half of the time that he would have spent in college. He then attended the Medical College of Virginia, from which he received an M.D. in 1882. He earned a second M.D. from the College of Physicians and Surgeons in New York City in 1884. He never married.

After receiving a commission as lieutenant in the U.S. Army Medical Department on 20 August 1884, McCaw served for fourteen years at various western posts and received a promotion to captain in 1889. After the start of the Spanish-American War in 1898, he accompanied the army's V Corps to Cuba and participated in the battle that preceded the surrender of Santiago. For his gallantry in that action, he was awarded the Silver Star in 1932, the year that the medal was authorized. Like so many others in the invasion force, he contracted a virulent form of malaria while in Cuba and was evacuated to Camp Wikoff on Montauk Point, Long Island, New York. With the rest of the survivors of the V Corps, he remained quarantined at Camp Wikoff until authorities were convinced that they were not carrying yellow fever (the fact that mosquitos transmitted this disease was not known at the time).

In 1899 McCaw was assigned to serve in the Philippine Islands after the outbreak of the Philippine Insurrection and was promoted to major in February 1901. When Robert M. O'Reilly became surgeon general in 1902, he made McCaw one of his three assistants in Washington, D.C. McCaw's responsibilities included making up the surgeon general's annual reports and often serving as head of the medical examining boards that selected medical officers for the army's Medical Corps. He also became head of the Museum and Library Division of the Surgeon General's Office and served in this capacity for twelve years. He led the struggle to gain adequate space for both the museum and the library and presided over the move of the army's medical museum into new and larger quarters. From 1902 to 1905 he assumed the additional responsibilities of professor of military hygiene at the Army Medical School, where aspiring young medical officers were trained in military medicine, and from 1904 to 1913 was also professor of military and tropical medicine. Medical officer Alexander Taylor Cooper wrote in his autobiography that, as a teacher, McCaw was "a finished scholarly gentleman" and "gave a good course as far as didactic lectures were concerned." In January 1909 McCaw was promoted to lieutenant colonel and in May 1913 to colonel.

Most of McCaw's professional publications were written during the time that he was in Washington, among them the booklet *Walter Reed, a Memoir* (1904) published by the Walter Reed Memorial Association and articles based on his experiences in the Spanish-American War and in the tropics. When army rules were changed to forbid retaining individual medical officers for long periods in assignments within the United States, he was sent in 1914 to serve in the Philippines as chief surgeon of the Division of the Philippines. In 1915 he was placed in command of the division hospital in Manila. In 1916–1917 he was returned to the United States and appointed department surgeon for the Southern Department during the mobilization along the border with Mexico.

After the outbreak of World War I, McCaw was sent to France, where from March to October 1918 he served in the office of the chief surgeon for the American Expedition Force and was made assistant to the chief surgeon when Brigadier General Merritte W. Ireland became chief surgeon in April 1918. In October 1918, when Ireland succeeded William C. Gorgas as surgeon general, McCaw became chief surgeon of the American Expeditionary Force, despite intense competition from Gorgas's chief assistant in Washington. McCaw was promoted to brigadier general in March 1919 and served as chief surgeon for the American Expeditionary Force until July 1919. Upon his return from France he was assigned to Washington, D.C., where he served as an assistant to the surgeon general and from 1919 to 1923 as commandant of the Army Medical School. He retired in February 1927.

Although highly regarded by subordinates and peers alike, McCaw was one of a group of bright and successful medical officers who, while they served their country long and well in positions of leadership in both war and peace, never achieved the position of surgeon general. The value of his services was widely recognized, however, and he received many honors, not only from the United States but from France, Great Britain, and Italy, including the Distinguished Service Medal, the Silver Star, and honorary membership in the Royal Society of Medicine. He died in Woodstock, New York. In the obituary by his friend and fellow Virginian Jefferson Randolph Kean, McCaw is credited with "a mind so quick and penetrating that nothing was too difficult for it." Kean add-

ed, however, that a "mild pessimism . . . made him sometimes shoot below the mark."

• Many of McCaw's professional papers for the period 1904–1913 are held in two collections at the National Library of Medicine in Bethesda, Md. Among his journal articles on topics in military medicine are "The Medical Service of an Army in Modern War," *Journal of the Association of Military Surgeons* 16 (1905): 334–49; "Aggressive War against Typhoid Fever," *Old Dominion Journal of Medicine and Surgery* 8 (1909): 248–56; and "Typhoid Vaccination No Substitute for Sanitary Precautions," *Public Health Reports* 34 (1919): 605–21. McCaw declined the contribution of his autobiography to a collection of autobiographies and biographies of medical officers now held by the National Library of Medicine, responding to the request by sending in a brief, humorous poem. References to McCaw can be found in Jefferson Randolph Kean's memoirs and in the papers of some of his other contemporaries, among them Alexander Taylor Cooper, whose autobiography, like that of Kean, is at the National Library of Medicine. Kean's "Walter Drew McCaw, M.D., Brigadier General, U.S. Army, Retired," *Military Surgeon* 85 (1939): 334–35, is more a brief and affectionate memoir than a true obituary. A more conventional obituary is in the *Journal of the American Medical Association* 113 (1939): 437.

MARY C. GILLETT

MCCAY, Winsor Zenic (26 Sept. 1871–26 July 1934), comic strip artist, animator, and editorial cartoonist, was born in Spring Lake, Michigan, the son of Robert McCay, a lumberman and real estate agent, and Janet Murray. McCay cited 1871 as the year of his birth, but his gravestone cites 1869, and other sources cite 1867. Since his birth record may have been destroyed in a fire, the exact year may remain unknown. In addition to public education, in 1888 McCay studied business at Cleary's Business College in Ypsilanti and took private art lessons with John Goodison of the Michigan State Normal School, who taught him the geometric bases for effective use of perspective in drawing, lessons he would later put to extraordinary use.

In 1889 McCay moved to Chicago, where he had to work rather than continue his art studies, and one of his jobs for the National Printing and Engraving Company was to produce woodcuts to illustrate theatrical productions and circuses. That same year McCay moved to Cincinnati on his own to work as a designer and poster painter for Kohl and Middleton's Vine Street Dime Museum, modeled after P. T. Barnum's famed New York freak emporium. All of this work in posters, banners, woodcuts, and advertising art schooled McCay in the uses of bold outline, fantasy, and the grotesque, characteristics of his later art. McCay met the teenage Maude Dufour in Cincinnati, and they eloped in 1891. The couple had two children.

The *Cincinnati Commercial Tribune* hired McCay as a staff artist in 1898. At the *Tribune* he illustrated a variety of features and drew his first editorial cartoons, and he also began to contribute freelance cartoons to *Life*, the national humor periodical in New York. In 1900 he joined the staff of the *Cincinnati Enquirer*, for which he drew his first Sunday color comics page in

1903, *A Tale of the Jungle Imps*, illustrating forty-three poems by George Randolph Chester about how animals adapt to survive in the jungle, partly a parody of Rudyard Kipling's *Just So Stories* (1902) and Darwinian ideas.

On the strength of *Life*'s interest in his work, McCay decided late in 1903 to move to New York, where he found a position with James Gordon Bennett, Jr., who published several newspapers. For Bennett, he created the comic strip *Little Sammy Sneeze* in July 1904, a feature about the cataclysmic effects of a little boy's irresistible sneezes, and another comic strip in January 1905, *Hungry Henrietta*, about the devastating results of an infant's insatiable appetite. Both carried normal childhood functions into areas of humor and fantasy through extreme exaggeration. McCay's most popular feature for Bennett begun in 1904 was *Dream of the Rarebit Fiend*, each installment concerned with some monstrous nightmare suffered as a consequence of eating rarebit cheese sandwiches before retiring. This was an adult series often dealing with morbid and sensational themes. Both *Little Sammy Sneeze* and the *Dream* series were collected into books in 1905, and the *Dream* strips inspired a silent film comedy by Edwin S. Porter in 1906.

McCay's strong interests in dreams, childhood, fantasy, and nightmares were brought together in a fortunate conjunction that became on 15 October 1905 the Sunday full-page color comic strip *Little Nemo in Slumberland*. In an incredibly complex and richly detailed style, drawing heavily from the entire history of illustration and the Art Nouveau movement, but indebted to no specific influence, and dealing with the psychological subtexts of dreams that Freud had only recently begun to uncover in his research, McCay produced a comic strip unlike any other before or since. With a nominal story line about a little boy named Nemo who answers a summons to Slumberland to play with the daughter of King Morpheus, over the next twelve years McCay would elaborate on a variety of themes, moving between fantasy and reality and the concerns of the subconscious, in a series of the best-drawn and most subtly suggestive comic strip pages to appear in the newspaper. *Little Nemo in Slumberland* became the basis for a popular operetta in 1908 with music by Victor Herbert; the pages have been reprinted in lavish anthologies in the United States and Europe; and in 1992 a feature-length film adaptation, based on a concept by Ray Bradbury, was made in Japan and released in the United States.

McCay provided a major stimulus for another budding form of visual culture when he became interested in animation as an adjunct to his successful career as a vaudeville stage sketch artist. He spent four years completing the thousands of individual drawings for his first short feature completed in 1911, *Little Nemo*, using characters from his strip. *The Story of a Mosquito* followed in 1912, but the third film in 1914 became a milestone in animation history. *Gertie the Dinosaur* features a lively anthropomorphic creature that has continued to charm audiences since her first appearance on the screen. By investing an animal, albeit an extinct one, with a distinct personality, McCay established the model to be successfully followed by Walt Disney, Paul Terry, Walter Lantz, and generations of animators. Other films followed, including *The Sinking of the Lusitania* in 1918, the first effort to apply animation to a historic current event. After 1921, however, McCay abandoned animation partly because he felt that purely commercial interests were beginning to exploit the art form. The remainder of his career was largely devoted to skillful illustration and editorial cartoons for the Hearst syndicate. The editorial cartoons are powerfully rendered statements about the problems of modern society from a conservative point of view, many of them appearing alongside the editorials of Arthur Brisbane.

A slender, neatly dressed, and handsome man, McCay was shy and reserved in spite of his frequent appearances on stage and in the prologues to his animated films. He was a devoted family man, but he spent nearly all of his waking hours at the drawing board. While he drew rapidly, he never compromised the exhaustive and careful detail that characterized his work. McCay died in New York City. His legacy is a body of work that continues to inspire illustrators, animators, cartoonists, and artists in all fields of the visual arts.

• The standard biographies of McCay are Judith O'Sullivan, "The Art of Winsor Z. McCay" (Ph.D. diss., Univ. of Maryland, 1976), and John Canemaker, *Winsor McCay: His Life and Art* (1987). Other sources include the essays on McCay in Maurice Horn, ed., *The World Encyclopedia of Comics* (1976); Ron Goulart, ed., *The Encyclopedia of American Comics* (1990); Richard Marschall, *Great American Comic Strip Artists* (1989); Judith O'Sullivan, *The Great American Comic Strip* (1990); and M. Thomas Inge, *Comics as Culture* (1990).

M. THOMAS INGE

MCCLAIN, Emlin (26 Nov. 1851–25 May 1915), judge and legal educator, was born in Salem, Ohio, the son of William McClain, a teacher and farmer, and Rebecca Harris. In 1855 the family moved to Iowa and settled near Tipton, Cedar County, where McClain's father farmed, administered the local schools, and taught at the teachers' institute. After the Civil War the family moved to Iowa City and Des Moines, where his father operated preparatory schools.

For eight years McClain was educated at home by his mother. He attended the academy at Wilton before entering the preparatory department of the State University of Iowa in 1866. By 1871 he had completed both the science and classics curricula. He received a B.A. in 1872 after a further year of study, during which he also taught at the Iowa City Academy.

McClain graduated from the university's law department in 1873 after a year's study and delivered an honor address at commencement. He clerked at a law firm in Des Moines, then worked as secretary for U.S. senator George G. Wright (partner in his law firm) in Washington, D.C., from 1875 to 1877. McClain then returned to private practice in Des Moines, where he lived with his parents. In 1879 he married Ellen Griffiths; they had three children.

McClain rose to prominence in the state bar with the publication of *Annotated Statutes of Iowa* (2 vols., 1880; supp. 1884; 2d ed., 1888; supp. 1892). The only consolidated compilation of the state laws since 1873 and the only annotated edition, this work was made an official source of state law by legislation enacted in 1882. He also published *Iowa Digest* (2 vols., 1887; supp. 1893, 1898, 1904), which summarized all reported state and federal cases from Iowa. Recognized as an authority on state law, he was selected by the Iowa Senate in 1894 to serve on the Code Commission, created to draft a comprehensive new code. With its adoption, McClain was retained to provide complete official annotations. Using his own annotated statutes as a model, he prepared official annotations for supplements in 1902, 1907, and 1913.

In 1881 McClain became a professor of law in the State University of Iowa law department, where he lectured on various topics, including criminal law, the Iowa code, and constitutional law. With the expansion of the law school curriculum to two years in 1884, he began to teach international law, conflict of laws, contracts, insurance, and chattel mortgages. McClain was named vice chancellor in 1887 and chancellor of the law department in 1890. As an administrator, he supervised improvement in the quality of entering law students and completed the transition to a full-time resident faculty.

An untiring scholar, McClain published *A Treatise on the Criminal Law* (2 vols., 1897) and contributed articles on diverse subjects such as law, legal history, and legal education to *American Encyclopedia*, *Cyclopedia of Law and Procedure*, *Harvard Law Review*, *Yale Law Journal*, *Columbia Law Review*, and other journals. He also wrote a text for nonlaw students, *Constitutional Law in the United States* (1905; 2d ed., 1910).

Through the early 1890s McClain adopted the lecture method in his teaching, employing treatises as texts and publishing his own outlines for his students on elementary law (1887), carriers (1889), bailments (1890), chattel mortgages (1890), remedial law (1890), and sales (1891). In 1891 he commenced publication of the *Law Bulletin*, which posed various hypothetical-fact situations for law students. Eventually, however, he embraced the newer case method of instruction and published materials that employed that method, including *A Selection of Cases on the Law of Carriers* (1893; 2d ed., 1896), *A Selection of Cases on Constitutional Law* (1900; 2d ed., 1909), and *A Selection of Cases on the Law of Bailments and Carriers* (1914).

Active in the state bar, which he helped revive in 1894 after more than a decade's inactivity, McClain served from 1894 to 1912 as chair of the bar's Committee on Legal Education. Under his leadership the committee professionalized the study of law, mandating a three-year postsecondary curriculum as prerequisite for practice. He joined the American Bar Association (ABA) in 1889 and played an active role in its Special Committee on Uniform State Laws and the Committee on Classification of the Law. A founding member of the ABA Section on Legal Education, he helped found the Association of American Law Schools and was its president in 1902.

McClain was elected as a Republican to the Iowa Supreme Court and served as a justice from 1901 to 1906. He was reelected for 1907–1912 and served as chief justice for the years 1906 and 1912. His opinions were characterized by concise statement of legal issues, clear organization, and attention to judicial authority from other states. Respecting the role of trial juries, he held in a series of railroad-crossing cases in 1901–1904 that injured persons who had failed to look and listen were not automatically barred from recovery, but the jury should consider their contributory negligence in deciding if they were entitled to damages.

In 1913 McClain resumed teaching, taking a position at Stanford but returning to Iowa the next year as dean of the law school. Plagued by allergies, he sought to leave Iowa in the summer and taught as a visitor at the Universities of Chicago (1905, 1906) and Wisconsin (1907).

McClain's painstaking annotations and digests of Iowa law made the state's growing body of cases and statutes accessible to practitioners. An energetic legal scholar and judge, he played a signal role in the movement to professionalize legal education. His high academic standards helped both the Iowa bar and the university rise to a position of national prominence in law that they have retained ever since. In his teaching and scholarship he helped assure the geographical spread of the case method in legal education. He was a charter member of Phi Beta Kappa at Iowa. McClain died in Iowa City, Iowa.

• The McClain family donated his papers to the University of Iowa. The Historical Manuscripts Collection of the Special Collections Department (main library) holds ten volumes of his diaries (1869–1908), some correspondence (1869–1913), manuscripts of speeches on painting, and clippings. Papers relating to his work at the university are held at the University of Iowa Archives. The State Historical Society of Iowa in Iowa City also holds a large collection of his papers. Contemporaneous accounts of his life and work are Jacob Van der Zee, "Emlin McClain," *Iowa Law Bulletin* 1 (1915): 157–79; Eugene Wambaugh, "Emlin McClain: A Great Teacher of Law," *Iowa Law Bulletin* 1 (1915): 180–82; and Horace E. Deemer, "Emlin McClain: 1851–1915," *Proceedings of the Twenty-first Annual Session of the Iowa State Bar Association* (1915). His obituary is in the *New York Times*, 26 May 1915.

MICHAEL H. HOFFHEIMER

MCCLAIN, Leanita (1951–28 May 1984), journalist, was born in Chicago, Illinois, the daughter of Lloyd McClain, a clothing factory employee, and Elizabeth (maiden name unknown). She grew up on the south side of Chicago in the Ida B. Wells public housing project. Her parents stressed obedience and achievement and taught her that she was not to consider the "projects" a place where they would spend their lives. "We were brought up knowing we would not have to raise our children there," she later recalled. McClain attended local schools, including an all-girls public high school. As a young girl she was beset by identity problems, most stemming from her physical appearance. She claimed an African-American, Native-American, and Caucasian heritage. Her mother was an albino, and Leanita was by all accounts a lovely young woman with freckles and a light complexion, green eyes, and with hair naturally streaked blonde. However, writings from her mid-teens indicated a girl not sure of her worth, and acutely aware of "so much hate and contempt among people." Her mother taught her to type, and her father taught her to sew. Following completion of high school, she attended Chicago Teachers College (later Chicago State University) and graduated with a B.A. in education in 1972. She then obtained her master's degree from Northwestern University's Medill School of Journalism in 1973.

During her time at Medill, McClain took a job in 1970 as a classified-ad taker at the *Chicago Tribune*. Upon graduation she was made a cub reporter. She later was made a copy editor as well as photo editor and editor of an opinion section of the *Tribune*. In 1974 she married fellow journalist Clarence Page; they had no children.

In 1980 McClain garnered national attention by submitting a column to *Newsweek* magazine's 30 October issue. Printed in the "My Turn" feature section and titled "The Middle-Class Black's Burden," she clearly showed how she was caught between the white-dominated world of professional journalism and her need to be cared about for who she was, not who the world thought she should be: "I am burdened daily with showing whites that blacks are people. I am, in the old vernacular, a credit to my race . . . though many have abandoned me because they think that I have abandoned them. . . . I assuage white guilt. I disprove black inadequacy." Thereafter, she received several promotions, going from an occasional columnist to a weekly columnist. In 1981 McClain and her husband separated and she attempted suicide. She began a relationship that culminated in her having an abortion, a grave contradiction from a woman who openly wanted children in her life. She, moreover, felt guilty because she lived in the mostly white North Side of Chicago. Yet she continued to write her columns.

In 1982 McClain was made a member of the editorial board of the *Tribune* as their specialist in minority and urban affairs. She was the first black and the first woman to achieve that status. That year she became one of nine editorial writers, and in 1983 she was made a twice-weekly columnist. In "How Chicago Taught Me to Hate Whites," McClain, writing about the victory of Harold Washington, Chicago's first black mayor, called the campaign a "race war." She was bitterly disappointed by her white colleagues' reaction to the victory of a black man and was tired of what she called "the voice of this evil . . . the voice going on about 'the blacks' this, 'the blacks' that. . . . It would make me

feel like machine-gunning every white face on the bus" (*Washington Post*, 24 July 1983).

The furor over McClain's column went on for weeks. The white-controlled city council called for her resignation from the *Tribune*. She also received hate mail and threatening phone calls. Her elderly father was quoted at the time as saying, "She told the truth."

McClain moved to a new home on the integrated South Side. She appeared as a guest on television broadcasts and in spring of 1984 taught a journalism seminar at Howard University. Yet in private she was moody, subject to crying jags and making late-night phone calls to friends. She became withdrawn when in her office, not really sure who were her supporters. On Memorial Day weekend in Chicago, she committed suicide, taking an overdose of antidepressants. Some colleagues blamed McClain's death on the stresses of racism; others blamed it on personal problems. In her newspaper columns she left behind no simple answers.

Despite McClain's short life and even shorter career as a journalist, she is responsible for creating a state- and citywide dialogue on ethnic relations in Chicago. Her teaching at the Medill School of Journalism spurred many black students to choose journalism as a career, and she broke barriers based on gender and ethnicity at the *Chicago Tribune*. Her insistence on focusing on Chicago's race-related problems guaranteed that media organizations in Chicago continued to bring the ethnic dialogue to the public arena.

• A posthumous collection of McClain's essays and articles is *A Foot in Each World*, ed. Clarence Page (1987). Obituaries are in the *Washington Post* and the *Boston Globe*, both 31 May 1984.

MARIA ELENA RAYMOND

MCCLATCHY, Charles Kenny (1 Nov. 1858–27 Apr. 1936), newspaper editor and publisher, was born in Sacramento, California, the son of James McClatchy, a journalist and newspaper publisher, and Charlotte McCormack. McClatchy's father emigrated from Ireland in 1842 and was hired by Horace Greeley's *New York Tribune*. At Greeley's urging, the elder McClatchy and his Canadian-born wife moved in 1848 to booming California, where he founded the *Sacramento Bee*. Charles McClatchy grew up in his father's newspaper office, once remarking that he had "a lifetime familiarity with the smell of printer's ink, with the intimate feel of the scissors and the clinging aroma of the paste pot" (McClatchy, p. xiii). He officially joined the paper in 1875 after a year's attendance at Santa Clara College. Upon his father's death, McClatchy became editor of the paper in January 1884, signing his popular column "C. K." His brother Valentine Stuart took over as business manager. The following year C. K. married Ella Kelly, with whom he had three children. In 1922 the McClatchy brothers founded the *Fresno Bee* and in Sacramento began one of the first commercial California radio stations, where they experimented with a "newspaper of the air." The brothers split over policy differences in 1923, and C. K. became the sole owner of the newspapers and radio station. His company, McClatchy Newspapers, added the *Modesto Bee* newspaper and radio stations in Reno, Nevada, and Fresno, Bakersfield, and Stockton, California.

McClatchy inherited his father's passion for journalism and reform politics. He became a leading spokesman in California for the Progressives, aligning himself with California reform governor and later U.S. senator Hiram Johnson. In a tribute after McClatchy's death, Senator Johnson wrote that "no cause, however poor, no citizen, however humble, called upon [McClatchy] in vain. . . . He would fight as hard to preserve a shade tree as to drive a rogue from office" (McClatchy, pp. vii–viii). A crusader against the powerful Southern Pacific Railroad and gas and electric companies that dominated politics in California, McClatchy was noted for his courage and honesty in opposing private interests that controlled public utilities and corrupted local and state governments. His editorials were influential during the successful 1910 political reform movement in California state government. In 1934 the *Sacramento Bee* won the Pulitzer Prize for public service in recognition of its crusade against political corruption in Nevada.

McClatchy's papers also were important voices in northern California in defense of human rights and Progressive social legislation, collective bargaining for workers, direct election of U.S. presidents and senators, and U.S. entry into World War I. They opposed Prohibition, bigotry, the League of Nations (because he distrusted European leaders), and concentrations of power and wealth.

McClatchy's independence of thought was evident in his response to the celebrated case of Tom Mooney, a labor activist and radical leftist convicted in the 1916 bombing of the San Francisco Preparedness Day political parade in San Francisco that killed ten bystanders. Mooney's case gained international notoriety among leftists and liberals as an example of unjust prosecution. While McClatchy was always a strong supporter of organized labor and a tireless critic of the private utility companies that were blamed for Mooney's alleged persecution, he remained adamant in his belief that Mooney was guilty. McClatchy wrote that Mooney did not "symbolize labor," as his supporters claimed, but symbolized nothing "but murder."

While known for his Progressive allegiance, McClatchy was in practice a political independent. In 1924 he worked for Progressive party candidate Robert La Follette, but in 1928 and 1932 he supported Democratic candidates Alfred E. Smith and Franklin D. Roosevelt, respectively. In earlier times, he had registered and voted Republican.

McClatchy's newspaper column, first titled "Notes" and later "Private Thinks," revealed its author's passionate, humane character and well-trained intellect. He often commented on the role of the press, once excoriating editors who feared showing leadership on controversial public issues, assigning them as much

use to humanity and to God "as a jellyfish quivering on the July sands." He argued that aggressive, enterprising journalism was the best way for a newspaper publisher to ensure financial success. McClatchy admired Joseph Pulitzer of the *St. Louis Post-Dispatch* but disliked fellow Californian William Randolph Hearst, whom he ridiculed and called "that irrepressible chameleon." McClatchy's columns showed breadth of learning, commenting knowledgeably on politics, education, the environment, crime and punishment, literature, foreign affairs, and the theater, which was his lifelong love outside of newspapers.

In his private life, McClatchy, a Catholic, was a devotee of Shakespeare, Charles Dickens, and the Bible. His custom-designed bookplate incorporated all three and the words, "These are enough." After McClatchy died at his ranch near Sacramento, his daughter Eleanor succeeded him as head of McClatchy Newspapers.

McClatchy's influence as a newspaper publisher and columnist was regional, but his professional integrity gained him national recognition. His commentaries on the role and responsibilities of journalists, as well as the example provided by his exemplary career, spoke to the higher ideals and standards for an entire industry.

• The California State Library in Sacramento has a clipping file on the McClatchy family. Eleanor McClatchy and Roy V. Bailey, eds., *Private Thinks by C. K.* (1936), offers some biographical material and collects many of McClatchy's newspaper columns and other writings. See also George E. Mowry, *The California Progressives* (1951). An obituary is in the *New York Times*, 28 Apr. 1936.

JAMES L. AUCOIN

MCCLAUGHRY, Robert Wilson (22 July 1839–9 Nov. 1920), warden and prison reformer, was born in Fountain Green, Illinois, the son of Matthew McClaughry and Marry (maiden name unknown). McClaughry attended Monmouth College in Illinois, receiving a B.A. in 1860. On 17 June 1862 he married Elizabeth C. Maiden, with whom he had five children. Two months after marrying Elizabeth, McClaughry became a private in the 118th Illinois Infantry. During the sectional conflict, McClaughry served in the Army of the Tennessee for two years and the payroll department for one, advancing to the rank of major in December, 1862. Mustered out of the army in October 1865, McClaughry returned to Illinois, taking a job as Hancock County Clerk.

In 1874 McClaughry was appointed warden of the Illinois State Penitentiary at Joliet. His appointment came at a propitious moment in the development of America's penal history. By the early 1870s the country was experiencing a new prison reform movement that placed a renewed emphasis on reformatory measures over retribution as the primary goal of incarceration. The movement also stressed parole programs, indeterminate sentences, graded classification of convicts, and the establishment of adult reformatories.

McClaughry served as warden of Joliet for sixteen years from 1874 to 1888 and again from 1897 to 1899. Dating back to the founding of its first state prison at Alton in 1827, Illinois had always lagged behind the more vanguard reformatory penitentiaries of the Northeast. McClaughry used his position as warden at Joliet to connect Illinois to the emerging currents of penal reform and acquired a reputation as one of the nation's leading wardens. Through attending the various meetings of the newly formed National Prison Association (founded in 1870) McClaughry became acquainted with the luminaries of the new prison reform movement, who included Enoch Cobb Wines, Richard C. Vaux, and Zebulon R. Brockway.

By the early 1880s McClaughry had developed his own complex reform plan for overhauling Illinois' approach to incarceration. Influenced by his connection with the National Prison Association and the reformatory measures instituted by Brockway at the Elmira adult reformatory, McClaughry called for separating hardened from novice criminals and establishing a grade system in which convicts would progress through various levels until they obtained parole. In addition prisons would provide religious and vocational education and organize a Prisoners' Aid Society to help discharged convicts find housing and employment.

Although McClaughry failed to implement most of these reforms at Joliet, he did succeed in introducing the use of new scientific technologies into prison management schemes. In 1885 Joliet became one of the first penitentiaries in the nation to photograph incoming convicts. McClaughry also sought to develop a uniform, reliable, and centrally located convict database that prison officers throughout the country could access to distinguish between habitual and occasional offenders. The Wardens' Association for the Identification of Habitual Criminals, which McClaughry worked to create between 1886 and 1887, did just that. As the first secretary of the organization, McClaughry was responsible for introducing the Bertillion method of recording a convict's physical features, and Joliet became the first national repository of Bertillion records. As warden, McClaughry also employed new social science techniques, compiling detailed case histories of convicts in order to uncover crime's root causes and develop successful classification and treatment programs. These new approaches to identifying and understanding criminal behavior reflect the growing influence of scientific practice in organizing reform measures.

By the late 1880s McClaughry had created a name for himself as one of the nation's leading wardens. Over the next twelve years he parlayed this success into a series of jobs at fledgling institutions where he was responsible for implementing his scientific practices and reformatory regimes. In 1888 McClaughry left Joliet to become superintendent of the new Pennsylvania Industrial Reformatory at Huntington, and in 1891 he left Huntington to become Chicago's chief of police. In 1893 McClaughry, who was a lifelong Re-

publican, left that post and, at the request of the newly elected Democratic governor, John P. Altgeld, took over as superintendent of the newly formed Illinois State Reformatory. A new Illinois governor, John Rielly Tanner, this time a Republican, persuaded McClaughry in 1897 to return to his old post as warden of Joliet. McClaughry's final position came as the warden of the newly formed federal penitentiary in Leavenworth, Kansas. Appointed warden by President William McKinley in 1899, McClaughry served at Leavenworth until his retirement in 1913.

McClaughry believed that by implementing his reform schemes, "our prisons will become places which teach men, by rational exercise of all their God-given faculties, how to live by honest industry, and in obedience to law." Middle-class reformers like McClaughry no doubt believed his own rhetoric. However, the idea that penal institutions could be used to inculcate middle-class values such as thrift, obedience, and respect for authority reveal the deep-seated class bias in nineteenth-century reform thought about crime and punishment.

The reality of late nineteenth-century prison life differed dramatically from the lofty rhetoric expressed by men like McClaughry. The fact was that McClaughry maintained order at Joliet not through a "humane system of discipline," as he professed, but by brutal and capricious punishments that included random beatings; the tortuous shower bath, where convicts repeatedly had their heads forced under water until they lost their breath; and the chaining of convicts standing up to their cell doors until they collapsed. The desire to maintain order and the necessity of eking out some form of economic self-sufficiency mainly determined McClaughry's approach to prison management. The internal governing of prison life was more often dictated by the concerns of private businessmen working convict labor inside the prison walls for profit than it was by any plan to implement reformatory measures. Even McClaughry complained at one point that, in reality, the Joliet penitentiary was nothing more than "a vast manufacturing establishment."

By the turn of the nineteenth century McClaughry reached the pinnacle of his profession. As the warden of the new federal penitentiary at Leavenworth, McClaughry oversaw the development of a key institution in an emerging national prison system. In 1899 he became only the second warden ever to be appointed president of the National Prison Association, and he was reappointed president for the next congress. While he never achieved the national recognition or subsequent scholarly attention as Brockway, by the turn of the century McClaughry had emerged as "the best Republican governor in the country" (McKelvey, p. 194). McClaughry retired from public life in 1913. In 1915, a year after his first wife died, he married Emma F. Maiden. He died in Joliet.

• No known collection of McClaughry's papers exist. However, as warden of various institutions, McClaughry had to file annual or biannual reports to state legislatures and to

Congress, many of which were published. In particular see *Reports of the Commissioners of the Illinois State Penitentiary* (1874–1886). Also see McClaughry, "The Registration and Identification of Criminals," pp. 15–17; "Discussion of the Bertillion System," pp. 18–31; and the "Address of Warden McClaughry" pp. 75–78; as well as the minutes of the first meeting of the Wardens' Association, pp. 7–15, all included in *The Proceedings of the Annual Congress of the National Prison Association of the United States, held at Toronto, September 10–15, 1887* (1889). Three notable secondary sources that discuss elements of McClaughry's career as a prison reformer are: Blake McKelvey, *American Prisons* (1977); Alexander Pisciotta, "A House Divided: Penal Reform at the Illinois State Reformatory, 1891–1915," *Crime and Delinquency* (Apr. 1991): 165–85, and Pisciotta, *Benevolent Repression* (1994).

HENRY KAMERLING

MCCLELLAN, George (23 Dec. 1796–8 May 1847), anatomist and surgeon, was born in Woodstock, Connecticut, the son of James McClellan, a respected farmer and schoolteacher, and Eunice Eldredge. His Scottish forebears were fighting Highlanders and American revolutionary patriots. McClellan received his preliminary education at Woodstock Academy, where his father was headmaster. He excelled academically, with a preference for mathematics and language. In 1812 he entered the sophomore class of Yale College, from which he graduated in 1816. During the latter part of his college course he placed himself under the preceptorship of Dr. Thomas Hubbard, a prominent Connecticut surgeon. In 1817 he went to Philadelphia, where he became a private student of Professor John Syng Dorsey and matriculated at the Medical School of the University of Pennsylvania.

As a medical student McClellan's brilliance was manifested by his extensive reading, hard clinical work, and unusual interest in anatomy and surgery. He served extracurricular time as a resident student in the Philadelphia Almshouse. There he gained experience in performing autopsies and in operating. At graduation in 1819 his thesis was "Anatomy of Arteries." The following year he married Elizabeth Brinton, daughter of a prominent Philadelphia family; they had two children. One son, George B. McClellan (1826–1885), was general of the Union Army of the Potomac during the early years of the Civil War. The other, John Hill Brinton McClellan, was a physician.

McClellan went immediately into practice in Philadelphia and became an instant success. So many young men engaged him as a preceptor that he opened a private school, to which he added three colleagues to diversify the teaching. This led him to plan for a second medical school in Philadelphia, a project strongly opposed by the University of Pennsylvania. Unable to obtain a charter from the state legislature, he and his colleagues petitioned Jefferson College in Canonsburg, Pennsylvania, to use its charter in establishing a medical department in Philadelphia. By this strategy the Jefferson Medical College was instituted under his leadership on 30 October 1824; he was its first professor of anatomy and surgery.

The University of Pennsylvania made a protest to the state legislature in January 1826 in the form of a memorial to prevent the fledgling Jefferson Medical College from granting the M.D. diploma. In March Jefferson's first graduating class was ready to receive the M.D., but the legislature still had not voted its approval. On 6 April 1826 McClellan learned that the decisive vote was to take place the next day. He immediately set out by horse and buggy for Harrisburg, ninety-six miles away. With a quick change of horses in Lancaster, McClellan reached his destination in less than twenty-four hours. He arrived in time to make an impassioned plea before the legislature, which voted in favor of Jefferson Medical College. McClellan and his colleagues, all young men, were daring to compete in Philadelphia against the dominant and oldest medical authority in the country, the University of Pennsylvania.

McClellan's greatest contribution to medical education was to offer practical clinical instruction directly from patients in a collegiate setting. His lectures were delivered extemporaneously and with an exuberance that communicated immediately with every member of the class. Because he worked in a period before anesthesia and antisepsis, his surgery was rapid and crude by today's standards. He performed all the operations in current use at home and abroad and was the first in the United States to remove the parotid gland. McClellan was not a writer, but he did contribute a few articles to several of the existing medical periodicals. He edited John Eberle's *Theory and Practice of Physic* and wrote a one-volume surgery text, *Principles and Practice of Surgery* (completed by his son John and published in 1848, one year after his death).

In a dispute with the board of trustees, McClellan was dismissed from Jefferson Medical College in 1839. He promptly obtained a charter from the state legislature for another medical school in Philadelphia, this one associated with Pennsylvania (now Gettysburg) College. In another quarrel he resigned his final professorship in 1843 and spent his remaining years in private practice. He died suddenly from a perforation of the sigmoid colon.

The founder of two medical schools, McClellan is also notable for introducing practical clinical instruction to students directly from patients and as a daring surgeon and anatomist who worked before the advent of anesthesia and antisepsis.

• Personal papers, correspondence, and other materials are in the archives of Thomas Jefferson University. Two biographical portraits, available at the archives, are G. McClellan, "Dr. George McClellan," *Jeffersonian* 14 (Feb. 1913): 1–6, and W. Darrach, "Memoir of George McClellan, M.D.," in *A Lecture Introductory to the Course of the Theory and Practice of Physic in the Medical Department of Pennsylvania College* (1847), pp. 1–10. On the founding of Jefferson Medical College, see Frederick B. Wagner, Jr., "The Making of a Medical School," *Jefferson Medical College Alumni Bulletin* (Winter 1980): 16–18, and *Thomas Jefferson University: Tradition and Heritage* (1989), pp. 509–13. An account of Mc-

Clellan's educational approach can be found in S. M. Schultz, "The Surgical Lectures of George McClellan," *Surgery, Gynecology, and Obstetrics* 172 (May 1991): 401–6.

FREDERICK B. WAGNER, JR.

MCCLELLAN, George B. (3 Dec. 1826–29 Oct. 1885), general and presidential candidate, was born George Brinton McClellan in Philadelphia, Pennsylvania, the son of George McClellan, a physician, and Elizabeth Steinmetz Brinton. After two years at the University of Pennsylvania, he entered the U.S. Military Academy at age fifteen. Four years later he graduated second in the class of 1846.

The Mexican War began that year, and the company of engineers to which McClellan was assigned served briefly with the army of Zachary Taylor in northern Mexico before becoming part of Winfield Scott's army advancing from Veracruz to Mexico City. McClellan served ably throughout the campaign, winning two brevet promotions.

After the war, McClellan spent a good deal of his time on the frontier with various army expeditions. He surveyed the passes of Washington's Cascade Mountains in search of a possible route for a transcontinental railroad. An apparent favorite of Secretary of War Jefferson Davis, McClellan was sent in 1854 as a military attaché with the frigate *Columbia* to the Dominican Republic to spy out its defensive arrangements and locate a site for a possible future U.S. naval base. The following year he was sent with two much older officers as part of the U.S. military commission to observe the Crimean War. The assignment allowed him to observe the world's leading armies in action and to assess the impact of the new rifle-musket, with its longer range, on battlefield conditions. The report he wrote for the War Department earned him high praise, though its observations were for the most part drawn from the writings of British officers who had been much closer to the fighting front than McClellan had ventured.

Upon his return to the United States, McClellan faced a future of monotonous service under hidebound superiors at dusty and isolated frontier outposts. It was not an appealing prospect. Despite promotion to captain on 3 March 1855 and a reputation as one of the army's most promising young officers, he resigned in 1857 and took a position as superintendent of the Illinois Central Railroad. The pay and amenities were vastly better than he had enjoyed in the military, but McClellan found the life of a railroad executive unsatisfying. He attempted to get back into the army and seriously considered joining a filibustering expedition bound for Mexico to support Benito Juárez. Such plans went nowhere, so he remained in railroading and played an important role in helping the hard-pressed Illinois Central weather the financial stress created by the panic of 1857.

Throughout the 1850s McClellan kept up his efforts to win the hand of Mary Ellen Marcy, daughter of a superior officer during his army days. The parents were willing, but Mary Ellen was not and flatly turned him down. Instead she favored his old West Point roommate, A. P. Hill, until her father forbade that match. Persistence paid off for McClellan, and he finally wed Mary Ellen in 1860. They had two children. Shortly thereafter George left the Illinois Central and became a superintendent of the Ohio & Mississippi Railroad, simultaneously moving his residence from Chicago to Cincinnati.

In politics, McClellan had been a Whig, but he rejected all forms of antislavery agitation and so during the 1850s became a staunch Democrat and a supporter of Stephen A. Douglas. Like Douglas, he opposed secession and had no hesitation about fighting to preserve the Union. He hoped to be appointed commander of the volunteer forces of his native state, and when a commission was not immediately forthcoming from Pennsylvania, he set out for Harrisburg to see about it. On the way, he accepted the invitation of Ohio governor William Dennison to stop by Columbus and discuss military affairs. When he did, the governor offered him command of Ohio's troops, and McClellan accepted.

The Ohio commission meant that McClellan's first assignment, once he and his men came into U.S. service, was the contest for what is today West Virginia. The region contained the vital tracks of the Baltimore & Ohio Railroad, and its Union-loyal majority desired to split from the secessionist government in Richmond. The Confederate government was able to make only the feeblest of efforts to hold this mountainous district, and troops under McClellan's command won celebrated skirmishes at Philippi, Rich Mountain, and Corrick's Ford, extinguishing Confederate hopes in the region. Though he was not present on the battlefields of these small successes, McClellan appeared to be a victorious general at a time when the nation badly needed one.

After the disastrous defeat of the Union's major advance on Richmond at the first battle of Bull Run (Manassas) on 21 July 1861, Abraham Lincoln felt compelled to remove the defeated commander, Major General Irvin McDowell. For a replacement he turned to McClellan, summoning him to report to the capital at once. McClellan arrived in Washington in the aftermath of the defeat and found the troops there disorganized, demoralized, and ill equipped. He set about immediately to restore their spirits and put them back into fighting trim. In that much, at least, he succeeded. By autumn the forces around Washington, collectively known as the Army of the Potomac, were thoroughly equipped and drilled and devoted to their commanding general. McClellan cut an imposing martial figure at reviews, superbly mounted and uniformed and riding with consummate skill. As his troops cheered wildly, he would doff his cap with a debonair flourish that seemed to convey soldierly camaraderie. The men loved him.

Although the press and politicians had at first been as enamored of McClellan as his soldiers continued to be, that changed by late autumn 1861. Patience wore thin as week after week of favorable campaigning weather passed with no advance and Confederates continued to hold positions within sight of the unfinished Capitol dome. Some in Congress and the press began to clamor for action. Lincoln tried to persuade McClellan to move, or at least to say when he would, but without avail. McClellan came to be contemptuous of Lincoln, referring to him privately as a "baboon" or a "gorilla." The president endured the 35-year-old general with remarkable patience, even after he grossly snubbed Lincoln and Secretary of State William Seward when they came to see him at his Washington home. When McClellan complained that he was hamstrung by the presence of the U.S. Army's top general, the aged Winfield Scott, Lincoln eased Scott into retirement, and McClellan took over the role of general in chief as well as commander of the Army of the Potomac. "I can do it all," he confidently asserted.

Yet he did nothing but continue to perfect his grand army. In late December 1861 he suffered a bout of typhus and remained confined to his quarters for some time. Lincoln, who had begun to speak seriously of "borrowing" the army if McClellan did not plan on using it, summoned a council of its top generals to discuss what to do next. A weak but furious McClellan tottered to the meeting but still refused to reveal his intentions.

McClellan was beginning to exhibit one of his greatest flaws as a general, a fundamental lack of nerve. This was displayed in the fact that he habitually insisted that the enemy greatly outnumbered him, when in fact the opposite was the case. Like all generals, McClellan received a plethora of raw intelligence material, some false, some true. The general's job was to sift through it and gain some sort of grasp on the truth. Instead, McClellan, probably driven by a compulsive fear of failure, consistently accepted the highest, wildly unrealistic figures for the enemy's numbers. Paralyzed by fear of this phantom army and fixating on the real but relatively minor problems of his own powerful army, McClellan delayed.

Lincoln's continued prodding elicited from the general a plan to transport his army by water down Chesapeake Bay to land at Urbanna, Virginia, at the mouth of the Rappahannock River, flanking the Confederate army and probably taking both it and Richmond. Strategically the plan had much to commend it and may even have been brilliant. If it worked as McClellan planned, it would make Virginia's west to east river system work for him rather than against him. Difficult river crossings would be minimized, supply lines would be kept relatively short and secure, and the Union would utilize its naval superiority to turn the Confederates' strategic flank. McClellan aimed to force their retreat and possible destruction without the high casualties that the rifle-musket, which he had seen in action in Crimea, could inflict on a general incautious enough to launch his troops in a head-on assault. McClellan seemed to return his soldiers' affection (or maybe it was just his lack of nerve coming out again), and he was ever alert to means of sparing their lives. In

any case, the indirect approach by Chesapeake Bay appealed to every fiber of his generalship.

Yet if the plan was brilliant strategy, well suited to McClellan's personality, it was also atrocious politics. It would remove the chief Union army from its position covering Washington, D.C., theoretically, at least, leaving the way open for a bold Confederate counterstroke that might take the national capital. The worst of it was that all this came at a time when Republicans in Washington were beginning to wonder if McClellan, the pro-Union but proslavery Democrat, was not a traitor who actually wanted the rebels to win the war. Lincoln warned his general of the existence of such attitudes, but McClellan, true to form, only saw this as a further affront to his dignity.

With grave misgivings, Lincoln consented to McClellan's bold plan for a waterborne movement, provided the general would leave behind enough troops to guarantee the safety of Washington. At the same time, however, the president relieved McClellan of his duties as general in chief, leaving him the command only of the Army of the Potomac.

The boldest of plans may become bland and pointless if delayed long enough or carried out slowly enough. While McClellan continued to dally, the Confederates withdrew from Centerville, Virginia, to a position closer to Richmond, completely wrecking McClellan's cherished scheme. McClellan was also the object of considerable criticism and ridicule when the abandoned Confederate positions revealed the relative weakness of their force. Remarkably, he clung to his bizarre overestimate of opposing strength. Still fertile in strategic resources if not always resolute or realistic in executing them, the young general modified his plan into a landing further south, at Fort Monroe at the tip of the peninsula between the York and the James rivers. At long last, during late March and early April, he transported his enormous army down Chesapeake Bay.

Difficulties started immediately. By this time McClellan was convinced that Lincoln and other politicians in Washington wanted him to lose, thus prolonging the war until they could make it an abolitionist crusade. He saw the proof of this perfidy in their efforts to goad him into action before he was ready. The suspicion of treason had thus become mutual, and it came to a head in a misunderstanding about just how many troops were to be left in the immediate Washington vicinity. Believing McClellan had disregarded his orders to leave enough troops behind to protect the capital, Lincoln withheld more than 40,000 of the somewhat over 140,000 men that McClellan had planned to take to the peninsula. Republicans in Congress and in the cabinet saw McClellan's intent to take them as treason. McClellan saw Lincoln's withholding of them in the same light.

In this frame of mind McClellan approached the ridiculously undermanned Confederate fortifications at Yorktown near the end of the York-James Peninsula and decided he was vastly outnumbered, when just the opposite was the case. He settled down to a lengthy siege, precisely what the Confederates needed in order to bring up more troops. McClellan's timid opponent, Confederate general Joseph E. Johnston, retreated to the outskirts of Richmond, followed cautiously by McClellan. Massive pressure from Confederate president Jefferson Davis finally obliged Johnston to launch a counterattack. The resulting battle of Fair Oaks was inconclusive except for the wounding of Johnston and his replacement by the aggressive Robert E. Lee.

Throughout June 1862 McClellan continued his inordinately slow and cautious approach to the Confederate capital and complained to Washington that he needed more men. McClellan's prewar army assignment had been that of an engineer, and much of the action he had observed in the Crimea stemmed from siege operations. He felt relatively confident with this slow but sure mode of warfare and resolved to take his time tightening the vice on Richmond. Meanwhile, Lee prepared a counterstroke, and on 26 June the audacious Confederate began his attack. McClellan's troops fought well and fended off the assault, but fearing a Confederate threat to his flank, McClellan determined to fall back and simultaneously to shift his base of supplies from White House, at the head of the York River, to Harrison's Landing on the James River. It was a very complicated maneuver to make in the face of an aggressive and skillful foe like Lee, who tried through a week of heavy fighting to cut the Federals off from their base. With undeniable skill, McClellan succeeded in his plan, and his troops severely punished the attacking Confederates. Nevertheless, he had been forced farther away from Richmond, and the fighting, known as the Seven Days' battles, could only appear as a serious defeat for him. Frustrated and humiliated, McClellan angrily vented his suspicions about the politicians in Washington in a telegram to Secretary of War Edwin M. Stanton. "You have done your best to sacrifice this army," he seethed. But the startled army telegrapher who received the message at the War Department deleted the offending sentence, concealing from the Lincoln administration just how bitter McClellan had become.

Safely back in Harrison's Landing, McClellan proposed another long delay while he refitted his troops. When Lincoln came down from Washington to inspect the army, McClellan gave him a letter advising that the war be waged along political lines acceptable to McClellan's fellow northern Democrats—no harsh measures such as confiscation of rebel property; no foraging of foodstuffs from rebellious civilians by hungry Union troops; no burning of houses or barns in retaliation for guerrilla attacks; and, most especially, no emancipation. Rather, the Union war effort should be a chivalrous contest of soldier against soldier on the battlefield, with no attempt to make an impact on southern society at large.

Once again, McClellan was being hopelessly obtuse politically. It simply was not that kind of war anymore, and McClellan's own failure, in allowing himself to be driven back from the gates of Richmond by an inferior force, had done as much as anything to convince a frustrated northern government and populace that just such hard measures were necessary. In fact, Lincoln was even then planning emancipation as a next step in expanding both the means and the ends of the conflict. He read the letter and said nothing.

Returning to Washington, Lincoln began drawing units of the Army of the Potomac out of McClellan's camp at Harrison's Landing and transferring them to northern Virginia for inclusion in a new force called the Army of Virginia, commanded by Major General John Pope. Lee's brilliance on the battlefield, Pope's incapacity, and perhaps also the uncooperativeness of McClellan and some of his loyal officers contributed to the Army of Virginia's defeat at the second battle of Bull Run (Manassas) late in August. McClellan was quoted as suggesting that, as far as he was concerned, Pope could "get out of his scrape."

Lee followed up his victory by invading Maryland, threatening Washington and other cities. In the crisis, Lincoln restored McClellan to command of the Army of the Potomac, into which the erstwhile Army of Virginia was now reincorporated. Aided by the providential discovery of a copy of Lee's detailed plan of campaign, McClellan had the opportunity to annihilate the Confederate Army of Northern Virginia as it moved into Maryland. He knew not only the precise location of Lee's units but also that Lee had boldly divided his army into several segments that could now be gobbled up piece by piece. Yet McClellan moved too slowly, and the opportunity slipped away. He did, however, succeed in catching Lee with his back to the Potomac River just above Antietam Creek in Maryland. If easy victory was no longer possible, a hard-fought but annihilating triumph definitely still was. On 17 September 1862 the two armies clashed in the bloodiest single day of the war. Outnumbering Lee perhaps 2 to 1, McClellan imagined the odds reversed and held about 40 percent of his force in reserve all day. Lee in desperation used every last man he had and still came within a hairbreadth of total defeat three different times during the day. McClellan's uncoordinated attacks allowed Lee to shift his scant forces to meet one crisis after another. Either better coordination on McClellan's part or the commitment of even half his reserves would almost certainly have crushed Lee. Instead, the Confederate general retreated into Virginia with his army intact, to Lincoln's immense disgust. McClellan, by contrast, was quite satisfied with his own performance. "Those in whose judgment I rely," he boasted in a letter to his wife, "tell me that I fought the battle splendidly and that it was a masterpiece of art." Clearly, his ability for self-delusion had progressed beyond mere overestimation of the enemy's numbers.

When the Army of the Potomac sat idle for days after the battle, Lincoln again visited McClellan to prod him to action, without success. On 6 October Lincoln issued a peremptory order for an advance against Lee. McClellan ignored it, complained of the condition of his army, and called for more of everything, especially troops and time. It was nearly three weeks before the army crossed the Potomac. By that time, however,

Lincoln's seemingly inexhaustible patience had finally run down to one last chance. If McClellan allowed Lee to get his army out of the Shenandoah Valley, into which it had retreated after the battle of Antietam, and onto the east side of the Blue Ridge, he was through. By 5 November just that had occurred, and Lincoln sent orders relieving McClellan of command of the Army of the Potomac and ordering him to New Jersey, where his wife was staying with her parents in Trenton. The man who had once reveled in the title "Young Napoleon" never received another army assignment.

McClellan sought and obtained the Democratic party's 1864 presidential nomination, but the convention was dominated by Peace Democrats, or Copperheads, who wrote a platform calling the war a failure and demanding an immediate armistice, with vague reference to a possible, though in reality highly unlikely, future restoration of the Union by peaceful negotiation. McClellan, in his letter accepting the nomination, tried unsuccessfully to distance himself from this extreme position, emphasizing his determination to continue the war until the Union was restored. The people, however, perceived McClellan and the Democrats, not without reason, as the party of peace and disunion. In the event, major Federal victories during the fall of 1864, particularly the capture of Atlanta, made a mockery of the Democratic platform and helped ensure McClellan's defeat by a landslide. Vote totals among soldiers were even more starkly against him, even in the Army of the Potomac that once idolized him.

On election day, before the results were known, McClellan wrote out his resignation from the army. He could live comfortably on the wealth produced by his stockholdings in the Ohio & Mississippi Railroad. Disgusted with the electoral decision of the American people, he left the country in January 1865 and traveled in Europe for three years. Returning to the United States and settling in New Jersey, he did engineering consulting and amassed considerable wealth. In 1877 he was elected governor of New Jersey and served a single three-year term marked by frugal, conservative policies. During his later years, he made several extended trips to Europe with his family. He died apparently of heart failure at his home in Orange, New Jersey.

McClellan remains hard to assess. As commander of the Army of the Potomac, he was perhaps the only man in the country who could have won the war in an afternoon, but he was also one of the few who could have lost it in that span. The accomplishment of denying so formidable an opponent as Lee his goal of crushing the Army of the Potomac in the Seven Days' battles was not without merit, but its credit to McClellan was interred long before the general's bones were laid to rest. Missed opportunities have haunted his posthumous standing. Whatever McClellan may have accomplished in avoiding the disasters he so dreaded, his reputation as a general fell victim to his own failings. Although on at least two occasions he had the power to reach forth his hand and end the war during the summer of 1862, timidity palsied that hand, and the killing went on for another two and a half years. Ironically, his failure of nerve ensured the adoption and full implementation of the hard war policies he deprecated, including emancipation. His squeamishness for the lives of his soldiers doomed them to added years of combat; had their beloved general been less solicitous, tens of thousands of them would have survived the war. Gifted with a brilliant intellect, McClellan also had personal charm and a remarkable ability to win the affection not only of his soldiers but of nearly everyone who came into contact with him. Even those who later became disgusted with his policies had to acknowledge his winning ways and likable personality. His ability as an organizer and motivator of troops was equally impressive.

Yet McClellan's self-confidence proved a hollow shell inhabited by little more than imperious self-will and preening vanity. He seemed unable or unwilling to apply his remarkable intelligence in new ways or in the face of unforeseen circumstances. His plans often had much merit to them, but he lacked the toughmindedness to see them through to victory. Until the Civil War, he had never known failure, and its prospect seemed to paralyze him. He can only be seen in the light of irony: in his determination to make failure in war impossible, he made it for himself inevitable.

• Many of McClellan's Civil War papers are in *The War of the Rebellion: A Compilation of the Official Records of the Union and Confederate Armies* (128 vols., 1880–1901). *McClellan's Own Story*, ed. William C. Prime (1887), written in part by the general himself, is in some ways as damaging to his reputation as the works of his critics, with its revelation of his conceit and self-delusion. The definitive biography of McClellan is Stephen W. Sears's excellent but highly critical *George B. McClellan: The Young Napoleon* (1988). Kenneth P. Williams's massive *Lincoln Finds a General* (1949–1959) contains an even harsher, somewhat one-sided attack. Warren W. Hassler, *General George B. McClellan: Shield of the Union* (1957), is a more sympathetic account by one of McClellan's few defenders among modern historians, while Hamilton J. Eckenrode and Bryan Conrad, *George B. McClellan: The Man Who Saved the Union* (1941), is, as its title suggests, even more enthusiastic and somewhat of a counterweight to Williams. Sears has also written on McClellan's two greatest campaigns, *Landscape Turned Red: The Battle of Antietam* (1983) and *To the Gates of Richmond: The Peninsula Campaign* (1992), and has edited *The Civil War Papers of George B. McClellan* (1989). Older biographies of McClellan include William Starr Myers, *General George Brinton McClellan: A Study in Personality* (1934). The difficult relationship between Lincoln and McClellan receives considerable attention in T. Harry Williams, *Lincoln and His Generals* (1952). Insightful and highly readable accounts of the general's Civil War service are in Bruce Catton, *Mr. Lincoln's Army* (1951), and John C. Waugh, *The Class of 1846* (1994), which also deals with McClellan's West Point days. David E. Long, *The Jewel of Liberty* (1994), is a study of the 1864 presidential election.

STEVEN E. WOODWORTH

MCCLELLAN, George Brinton (23 Nov. 1865–30 Nov. 1940), educator, author, and mayor of New York City, was born in Dresden, Saxony, the son of Civil

War general George Brinton McClellan and Mary Ellen Marcy. McClellan attended St. John's Boarding School in Sing Sing, New York. He then entered Princeton University in 1882. Upon graduating with an A.B. in 1886, he spent two years traveling in Europe. Afterward, he reported for New York daily newspapers, including the *Herald*, the *World*, and the *Morning Journal*, and attended the New York Law School. In 1889 McClellan joined the New York City political machine Tammany Hall, eventually rising to a leading position within the organization, which awarded him the post of treasurer of the Brooklyn Bridge from 1889 to 1893. In 1889 McClellan married Georgiana Louise Heckscher; they did not have children. From 1885 to 1888 he was also a first lieutenant in the New York state militia. He was admitted to the bar in 1892 and went into practice.

During the 1890s political achievements came in rapid succession for McClellan because of his famous name. He presided as president of the Board of Aldermen for New York City from 1892 to 1894, and he was a delegate to the Democratic National Conventions from 1890 to 1903. In 1894 he was elected to Congress, serving from 4 March 1895 until 21 December 1903. During his terms as congressman, he labored on several committees, including Military Affairs, Pensions, and Ways and Means, and he fought against American imperialism and high tariffs. In 1900 McClellan was considered as a vice presidential candidate and in 1904 as a presidential contender. On both accounts, his ties with Tammany, which was under fire from the anti-Boss reformers, and his limited national exposure ruled against his rise to national prominence.

In 1903 McClellan was selected by Tammany Hall boss Charles F. Murphy to run for mayor of New York City. He easily defeated Republican Seth Low, the incumbent mayor. McClellan's initial term as mayor lasted two years, and he won a second term for four years in 1905. During an age of progressive reform, he acted out of a self-confessed noblesse oblige. Concentrating on internal improvements, he accomplished his main task of securing a water supply for the city from the water systems in the Catskills. New York City also saw development in roads, schools, hospitals, bridges, docks and ferries, rapid transit, and a new municipal building under McClellan. All this came at a cost. The city's debt increased dramatically during his two terms. In 1906 McClellan vigorously attacked gambling, prostitution, and corruption, and several city officials consequently lost their jobs. These actions completed his split with Boss Murphy, after which McClellan stepped up his reform efforts and futilely attempted to form an alternative political force to Tammany. Thereafter, the Tammany Hall organization worked diligently to fight McClellan on every front, effectively ending his political career. Moreover, William Randolph Hearst and his newspapers marred McClellan's second term with unrelenting attacks. Hearst, who had opposed McClellan in the 1905 mayoral election, charged McClellan with voter fraud and political corruption, earnestly working to force a recount through legislation. Hearst could not prove the charges, and the courts ruled the bill unconstitutional, much to McClellan's relief.

After retiring in 1909, McClellan occasionally lectured on public affairs at Princeton, as he had begun to do as mayor. He also briefly joined a New York law firm, but he preferred academia. He became a professor of economic history at Princeton in 1912, remaining until 1931. At the outbreak of World War I, McClellan lost popularity because of his sympathetic view of the German position. He urged the United States to aid both sides in ending the war. During a 1915 trip to Germany, he described his visit for the *New York Times* in a series of letters, which were collected into one volume, *The Heel of War*, in 1916. Nevertheless, when President Woodrow Wilson declared war on Germany in 1917, McClellan enlisted in the U.S. Army as a major in the Ordnance Department and saw action in the battle at Meuse-Argonne. His enlistment restored his reputation.

Upon his discharge, Colonel McClellan returned to Princeton. Becoming an expert on Italian history and knowledgeable in the arts, he wrote three more books, *The Oligarchy of Venice* (1904), *Venice and Bonaparte* (1931), and *Modern Italy* (1933). During a visit to Italy, he was impressed with Benito Mussolini's government and its assault on Ethiopia, which he compared to America's 1846 invasion of Mexico. After retiring from Princeton in 1930, he moved to Washington, D.C., where he was renowned for his fine art collection and dinner parties. McClellan was an incorporator and vice president of the American Academy in Rome, a patron of the American Museum of Natural History, and a fellow in perpetuity at the Metropolitan Museum of Arts. He was also a life fellow at the Royal Economic Society and belonged to the American Economic Association. Toward the end of his life, McClellan worked on his memoirs, *The Gentleman and the Tiger: The Auto-biography of George B. McClellan, Jr.* (1956), which was published sixteen years after his death and covered his life until approximately his retirement. He died in Washington, D.C.

McClellan was a nineteenth-century aristocratic gentleman who sought to contribute to the common good. He spent his life trying unsuccessfully to vindicate his father, "who was the finest man he knew." McClellan provided New York City with an artistic, stable, honorable mayor in contrast to the typical Tammany mayors previous to him. He is not a historical immortal, but his story is a critical example of the conflicts between machine politics and progressive reform during this period.

• McClellan's personal papers are in the Library of Congress. A *New York Times* article, "M'Clellan's Six Years," 31 Dec. 1909, provides much information about him. During his terms as mayor, the various New York newspapers frequently ran articles about him with varying degrees of value. See also Alfred Connable and Edward Silberfarb, *Tigers of Tammany: Nine Men Who Ran New York* (1967). An obituary is in the *New York Times*, 1 Dec. 1940.

DENNIS ADAMS

MCCLELLAN, John Little (25 Feb. 1896–27 Nov. 1977), U.S. senator, was born in Sheridan, Arkansas, the son of Isaac Scott McClellan, a sharecropper, teacher, and lawyer, and Belle Sudduth. With no college preparation, McClellan studied for the bar exam under his father's tutelage. He passed in 1913, and at the age of seventeen, with special permission from the state legislature, became the youngest member of the Arkansas legal profession. He often faced his father in court. Enlisting in the U.S. Army during World War One, he attained the rank of first lieutenant in the Aviation Section of the Signal Corps and served entirely in the United States until discharged in 1919.

Moving to Malvern, Arkansas, that same year, McClellan established his own law office and became city attorney (1920–1926) and state prosecuting attorney (1927–1930). Desiring national political office, he won election to the U.S. House of Representatives and served from 1935 to 1939. Campaigning for the U.S. Senate in 1938, he failed to unseat Senator Hattie Caraway, President Franklin D. Roosevelt's choice, but he impressed many with his dogged campaigning skills. In 1942 he won the first of six terms to the Senate.

Colleagues most often described McClellan as dour, grimly owlish, unsmiling, and burly. A glimpse into his personal life reveals a man who suffered Job-like tragedies, beginning with his mother's death when he was still an infant. His first marriage in 1913 to Eula Hicks, with whom he had two children, ended in a rancorous divorce in 1919. In 1922 he married Lucille Smith; they had two children before her sudden death in 1936. In 1937 he married Norma Myers Cheatham, with whom he had one child. In 1943 a son died while serving in World War II, in 1949 another son was killed in an auto wreck, and a third son died in a plane crash in 1958.

McClellan grounded his legislative career in southern Democratic conservatism. "I did not become a senator," he recalled, "to transfer the United States into a socialistic, paternalistic state" (*Washington Post*, 29 Nov. 1977). Although he favored most of Roosevelt's New Deal and supported labor with his vote for the 1935 Wagner Act, by World War Two he increasingly endorsed limits to the federal government. He opposed the "Fair Deal" of Harry S. Truman, insisting it would bankrupt the country.

McClellan first gained national prominence during the 1950s hearings chaired by Wisconsin senator Joseph McCarthy. As the ranking minority member of the committee, he at first acquiesced in McCarthy's inquisition. In January 1954, as McCarthy grew wilder in his accusations, McClellan led a boycott of public sessions by fellow Democrats. When his party gained control of Congress in 1955, he assumed chairmanship of the committee and formulated new procedures that protected witnesses' rights. In contrast to McCarthy, McClellan appeared to be the paragon of logic and fairness.

Turning the nation's attention from fears of communism to the improprieties of labor unions, McClellan's Committee on Improper Activities in the Labor or Management Fields uncovered abuses of power by labor leaders, fraudulent elections, racketeering, and ties to organized crime. In 1957 television audiences were mesmerized as labor officials took the Fifth Amendment more than 300 times during the 270 days of public hearings. Robert Kennedy, chief counsel for the committee, described McClellan as "the most devastating cross-examiner I ever heard" (Schlesinger, p. 171). Investigations led to the enactment of the 1958 Welfare and Pension Plans Disclosure Act and the 1959 Landrum-Griffin Act, which regulated who could hold union leadership positions, monitored union elections, and offered a "bill of rights" for union rank and file. Probes of organized crime ensued. In 1963 McClellan's committee documented the workings of La Cosa Nostra, a national crime syndicate. Once again the nation riveted its attention to the televised hearings as Joseph Valachi, a member of the crime ring, detailed the daily operations of the crime world.

McClellan consistently and staunchly opposed civil rights legislation. He signed the 1956 Southern Manifesto, which urged states to resist federally mandated integration of public schools. During the 1957 Little Rock Central High School crisis, he attempted to mediate between President Dwight Eisenhower and Governor Orval Faubus. Unable to broker a middle path, he vehemently denounced the president's introduction of federal troops. Opposing the 1964 Civil Rights Act and the 1965 Voting Rights Act, he insisted that such legislation would create an uncontrollable federal bureaucracy that would "destroy the rights and personal liberties of all the people" (*Congressional Record*, 14 Apr. 1964, p. 7872).

Insisting that the Supreme Court, in decisions such as *Miranda v. Arizona* (1966) and *Escobedo v. Illinois* (1964), hampered law enforcement, McClellan pushed for tougher criminal penalties and broader police powers. In 1966 he began an effort to modernize the U.S. criminal code that culminated in the passage of a new law code in 1978. Blaming domestic unrest on agitators who fostered raised expectations among urban poor, he supported the 1968 Omnibus Crime Control and Safe Street Acts, which he hoped would empower police to deter violence and crime.

In foreign policy, McClellan balanced his beliefs in fiscal responsibility and a strong defense. During the Truman administration he had supported the Marshall Plan and military aid to Greece and Turkey. He had also favored economic and military assistance to South Korea and South Vietnam as they resisted communism. However, his patience thinned as the Vietnam struggle wore on, and he eventually supported President Richard Nixon's Vietnamization policy. By 1973 he opposed escalating the conflict into Laos or Cambodia. Unlike his Arkansas colleague, Senator J. William Fulbright, he increasingly opposed economic foreign aid. In 1974, as chair of the powerful Senate Appropriations Committee, he sought to slash more than $3 billion from the Pentagon budget.

Continuing to be equally conservative in fiscal policy, McClellan objected to massive outlays of federal funds for school programs under President Lyndon Johnson's "Great Society." He voted against such programs as Model Cities, Headstart, job training, subsidies for mass transit, and the creation of the Department of Health, Education, and Welfare. However, if a proposal aided Arkansas or the rural South economically, McClellan usually favored it. He supported federal aid for school construction in 1955 and also endorsed the 1965 Elementary and Secondary Education Act. He labored for over two decades with Senator Robert Kerr of Oklahoma to obtain more than a billion dollars in federal funds for the Arkansas River Navigation project, which made Little Rock, Arkansas, and Tulsa, Oklahoma, seaports. He also successfully lobbied for the industrial development of Arkansas and pushed for federal assistance through the Arkansas Industrial Development Commission, which helped lure more than 700 new industries to the state.

In November 1977 deteriorating health forced McClellan to announce he would not seek reelection in 1978. "All my political ambitions have been fully achieved," he announced. He died a week later in Little Rock. Although he amassed considerable personal wealth while in the U.S. Congress, he also funneled millions of dollars into the Arkansas economy. Colleagues respected his tenacious yet fair investigations. Few senators in the twentieth century were more powerful.

• McClellan's papers are collected at Ouachita Baptist University in Arkadelphia, Ark., and include helpful scrapbooks of newspapers and journal clippings kept by his staff. His *Crime without Punishment* (1962) reveals his perceptions of the labor union and organized crime hearings. Good political assessments are Richard Harris, "Annals of Legislation: The Turning Point," *New Yorker*, 14 Dec. 1968, pp. 70–179; "The Senate: Man behind the Frown," *Time*, 27 May 1957, pp. 21–24; Al Tofler, "John McClellan's Trial by Ordeal," *Coronet*, Aug. 1959, pp. 68–75; "How Riots Are Stirred Up: Interview with Senator McClellan," *U.S. News and World Report*, 6 May 1968, pp. 68–71; and Shellie Sachs and Mark Green, "John McClellan," in *Citizens Look at Congress* (1972). For insights into McClellan's investigative techniques see Arthur M. Schlesinger, Jr., *Robert Kennedy and His Times* (1978); Arthur A. Sloan, *Hoffa* (1991); and David M. Oshinsky, *A Conspiracy So Immense: The World of Joe McCarthy* (1983). Obituaries are in the *New York Times*, *Washington Post*, and *Arkansas Gazette*, 29 Nov. 1977.

RANDY FINLEY

MCCLELLAND, Robert (1 Aug. 1807–30 Aug. 1880), politician and secretary of the interior, was born in Greencastle, Pennsylvania, the son of John McClellan [*sic*], a physician, and Eleanor McCulloh. He taught school before graduating from Dickinson College in 1829 and two years later was admitted to the bar in Chambersburg. He practiced law in Pittsburgh before emigrating to Monroe, Michigan, in 1833. He was a member of the convention that drafted Michigan's first state constitution in 1835, serving on the Judiciary Committee. Two years later he married Sarah E. Sabine of Williamstown, Massachusetts.

McClelland was elected as a Democrat to the state legislature in 1838 and was chosen Speaker in 1843, the same year he took a seat in the U.S. Congress. He served three terms in the House and was an active member of the Commerce Committee. Despite his support of the presidential aspirations of Lewis Cass, a fellow Michiganite and moderate Democrat, McClelland voted for the Wilmot Proviso and a bill introduced by Joshua Giddings abolishing slavery in the District of Columbia. He also backed John Quincy Adams in his struggle against the "gag rule" during the right of petition debates. In 1848 McClelland was a delegate to the Democratic National Convention that nominated Cass and subsequently traveled to Pennsylvania in a vain attempt to persuade David Wilmot not to endorse the insurgent Free Soil party candidate, Martin Van Buren. He served as Cass's chief lieutenant in Michigan during the ensuing campaign, choosing not to seek a fourth congressional term.

McClelland returned to private law practice and in 1850 was appointed to the Board of Regents of the University of Michigan. He attended the second state constitutional convention, chairing the Legislative Committee, and presided over the Michigan Democratic convention that endorsed the Compromise of 1850. He was instrumental in healing the breach within the party's ranks caused by the slavery extension controversy. In 1851 McClelland was elected governor for the one-year interregnum created by the new constitution, and he was reelected to a full term the following year, defeating Whig candidate Zachariah Chandler. He was a delegate to the Democratic National Convention in 1852 and resigned the governorship in 1853 to become secretary of the interior under Franklin Pierce.

McClelland was an effective department head. The *New York Times* (27 Mar. 1853), which supported the Whigs, acknowledged that McClelland was "sober in his judgment, moderate in his politics, and equally moderate in his abilities. . . . as he is neither ambitious nor proscriptive, he will probably make a useful and efficient Secretary of the Interior." That department had been created in 1849 by combining four bureaus: the Indian, Land, Patent, and Pension offices. The Interior Department itself had no building, so McClelland worked out of the Patent Office. He was a demanding taskmaster. A stickler for detail and a man of stern integrity, he brought needed reform and order to the department. Clerks were required to labor diligently and avoid distractions, and McClelland made an effort to root out the corruption endemic to the Indian, Land, and Pension bureaus. His annual reports focused on the need for more American Indian reservations and shifting annuities from cash payments to goods, liberalizing "pre-emption" rights of squatters, expanding land grants to encourage settlement and railroad construction, hiring more Patent Office clerks, and guarding against pension frauds and limiting stipends to the truly needy. President Pierce accepted these recommendations, but Congress was generally unresponsive, opposing land grants to railroads in particular.

Nevertheless, McClelland's tenure at the Interior Department was a success. He presided over an Indian Bureau that negotiated fifty-two treaties, acquired 174 million acres of land, and administered to the needs of 300,000 Indians. Almost 94 million acres of land were sold or distributed as military bounties or other grants, the number of patent applications rose from 2,500 to 4,000 per year, and nearly 14,000 individuals received annual pensions averaging close to $100. As a member of the cabinet, McClelland took a stand on the important issues of the day. He did not promote the Kansas-Nebraska Bill but opposed Jefferson Davis's subsequent call for the removal of federal troops from "Bleeding Kansas." The president sided with McClelland. Pierce, however, rejected McClelland's advice and sanctioned the Gadsden Purchase treaty.

The emergence of the Republican party in the Old Northwest signaled the end of McClelland's political career. He joined Cass in campaigning for James Buchanan to succeed Pierce, but the Democrats failed to carry Michigan. Following Buchanan's inauguration, McClelland retired to Detroit and resumed his law career. He urged compromise as the Civil War approached and did not play a public role during the conflict. He took part in drafting the third state constitution in 1867 and the following year was a delegate to the Democratic National Convention. McClelland suffered several strokes during the final years of his life and died at his Detroit home, survived by his wife and two daughters.

McClelland belonged to the moderate wing of the antebellum Democratic party. He served Cass faithfully, acting more as a surrogate son than political protégé. After a brief flirtation with free soil principles, he endorsed compromises in a futile effort to ease sectional tensions. McClelland's accomplishments, notably as secretary of the interior, were due to his work ethic and rectitude. In the words of one acquaintance, he was "pure and unsullied." Honest and meticulous, his personality was better suited to bureaucratic administration than rough-and-tumble politics.

• Scant sources pertain to McClelland's life and public career. Some of his papers are in the Burton Historical Collections of the Detroit Public Library; the William L. Clements Library at the University of Michigan, Ann Arbor; and the Library of Congress. The best study of McClelland's contributions as secretary of the interior is Roy Franklin Nichols, *Franklin Pierce: Young Hickory of the Granite Hills*, rev. ed. (1958). A more recent work, Larry Gara, *The Presidency of Franklin Pierce* (1991), relies heavily on Nichols. Contemporary reactions to McClelland's death and obituaries are in *Pioneer Collections: The Report of the Pioneer Society of the State of Michigan* 4 (1883): 454–57; the *Detroit Evening News*, 30 and 31 Aug. 1880; and the *Detroit Free Press*, 1 Sept. 1880.

WILLARD CARL KLUNDER

MCCLENDON, James Julius (16 Mar. 1898–20 Apr. 1982), physician and civil rights activist, was born in Rome, Georgia, the son of Benjamin McClendon, who died when James was very young, and Louisa Buckner. With the assistance of siblings, he graduated from Atlanta University (1921) and by his own efforts earned an M.D. at Meharry Medical College (1926). He then moved to Detroit, interned at black-owned Dunbar Hospital, and served as a staff member of Hutzel Hospital for nearly fifty years. Assisting patients of all classes, "Doc Mac" never refused treatment to the poor. He cofounded the Fairview Sanatorium and served on several black and white staffs, including those of Parkside and Woman's Hospital. In 1932 he married college graduate Irene Hunter Scruggs; the couple had two daughters. McClendon actively participated in the Second Street Baptist Church and St. Antoine Street Young Men's Christian Association.

McClendon also became a recruiter for the local National Association for the Advancement of Colored People (NAACP) and, beginning in 1937, served as its president. He led the organization for eight successive years, establishing its first office, hiring its first executive secretary (Gloster B. Current), and expanding its membership from 3,000 to nearly 25,000. Combining his organizational skills, Current's relentless energy, and the city's importance as a center of defense production during World War II, McClendon forged one of the most effective chapters in NAACP history.

McClendon's presidency covered three interrelated yet distinct periods. From 1937 to 1942 he addressed issues associated with the depression and, increasingly, preparedness at home. His call for an end to police brutality resulted in the resignation of one police commissioner, and his request that blacks be represented in the selective service process caused the statewide appointment of fourteen black board members. He pressed less successfully for greater inclusion of blacks in civil service, while protesting the treatment of black soldiers at nearby Fort Custer. Perhaps most significant, he broadened the base of the NAACP to reach across ideological lines within the black community and embraced trade unionism for black workers; he also reinforced the national office's 1941 support of the United Automobile Workers' effort to organize Ford Motor Company.

In 1942 McClendon helped form the Citizen's Committee on Sojourner Truth, headed by Reverend Charles A. Hill, and provided it with seed money, financial oversight, and office facilities, as well as legal advice from the national office. This collective, biracial effort overcame white opposition, which included a localized riot that forced all levels of government into action. The riot came on 29 April 1942, when military and police forces moved black defense workers into the 200 federally-funded units named after famed abolitionist Sojourner Truth. The conflict also revealed escalating white resistance to black demands for a wartime "Double V"—a victory abroad against fascism and a victory at home against fascists.

The housing controversy ushered in the second phase of McClendon's presidency during which the focus on wartime issues of housing and employment deepened. The NAACP continued to provide space and funding for Hill's committee, which transformed itself in name and emphasis from housing to defense jobs. Increasingly, however, McClendon and his board expressed concern over Hill's ties to communist-connected members of the National Negro Congress and leftist unionists seeking more militant action in behalf of the black masses and on the labor front. In a December 1942 showdown for control of the NAACP, he handily defeated write-in candidate Hill, opened the board to union representation, and severed all ties with the jobs committee. He also permitted board members more influence and gave executive secretary Current greater responsibility.

McClendon's second period ended with the worst race riot of the war, which began on 20 June 1943 and claimed thirty-four lives, injured 765 persons, and destroyed $2 billion in property. He began his third presidential phase in the wake of this devastation and charges by white officials that actions by the NAACP and black journalists had instigated the bloodshed. He jousted with Wayne County prosecutor William E. Dowling of the governor's riot committee, and Mayor Edward J. Jeffries, Jr., whose reelection he publicly opposed that fall. But he failed on all fronts, including his call for a grand jury to investigate the upheaval and promote a more positive atmosphere for race relations.

Thereafter, McClendon pressed for action, although less militantly than before. Like most leaders of both races, he feared another outburst. He criticized the newly formed Mayor's Interracial Committee only when necessary and cooperated with local groups to redress wrongs, most notably in black housing. In this atmosphere of status quo politics and racial tension, his chapter doubled its membership, but like other private and public organizations, it could not resolve socioeconomic issues exacerbated by war.

When McClendon stepped down from his eight years as president in December 1945, he left a legacy that reached back to Frederick Douglass. He grew up believing that reform required cooperation among blacks and conflict with whites. Active on the campus of NAACP cofounder W. E. B. DuBois and his own classmate, future NAACP executive secretary Walter F. White, he became a full-blown neoabolitionist in Detroit. There he advocated democratic ideals, such as biracial housing, believing the end of segregation and discrimination necessary for true racial progress. Throughout the war, he spoke and acted boldly, though hardly recklessly, urging blacks to fight for their rights and fulfill their responsibilities as citizens. He pressured officials, joined coalitions, financed committees, sponsored conferences, and—despite NAACP policy—endorsed political candidates. An aristocratic member of the Talented Tenth, he adjusted to wartime circumstances by continuing to adopt various tactics and strategies as the situation required.

McClendon retired as chapter president, but never left the NAACP, serving on its national board of directors until his death. A member of several medical associations, he continued his practice, and between 1965 and 1971 he became a member and president of the Detroit Board of Health. He also remained active as an investor in ventures like Wayne County Better Homes. When he died in Detroit, the local Young Men's Christian Association, state medical society, and alma maters had already recognized and honored him. As "Mr. NAACP," he had linked the struggle for racial equality of one generation with that of another.

• Biographical materials on McClendon are scarce, but his years as president of the Detroit NAACP can be reconstructed from various sources: NAACP Branch Files and General Office Files, Library of Congress, Washington, D.C.; Detroit NAACP Collection, Gloster B. Current Collection, and Dr. James J. McClendon Verticle File, Archives of Labor and Urban Affairs, Detroit, Mich.; and articles in the *Detroit Tribune* and *Michigan Chronicle* (1937–1945). McClendon wrote little himself, but several historians have included him in studies of issues that affected black Detroiters of his era. Richard W. Thomas, *Life for Us Is What We Make It: Building Black Community Detroit, 1915–1945* (1992), and Alan Clive, *State of War: Michigan in World War II* (1978), mention McClendon briefly; the latter also contains an overview of race relations, particularly in Detroit, during the years of McClendon's NAACP leadership. August Meier and Elliott Rudwick, *Black Detroit and the Rise of the UAW* (1979), and Dominic J. Capeci, Jr., *Race Relations in Wartime Detroit: The Sojourner Truth Housing Controversy of 1942* (1984), provide more extensive coverage on his role in those and related events. An overview of McClendon's first five years as NAACP president and an obituary, respectively, appear in the *Michigan Chronicle*, 10 Oct. 1942, and *Detroit News*, 23 Apr. 1982.

DOMINIC J. CAPECI, JR.

MCCLENDON, Rose (27 Aug. 1884–12 July 1936), actress, was born Rosalie Virginia Scott in Greenville, South Carolina, the daughter of Sandy Scott and Tena Jenkins. Around 1890 the family moved to New York City, where her parents worked for a wealthy family as a coachman and a housekeeper, respectively. An avid reader, McClendon and her brother and sister were educated at Public School No. 40 in Manhattan. Although she admitted to having no inclinations for the stage at this time, as a child she participated in plays at Sunday school and later performed in and directed plays at St. Mark's African Methodist Episcopal Church. In 1904 she married Henry Pruden McClendon, a licensed chiropractor and Pullman porter for the Pennsylvania Railroad. The couple had no children and McClendon was content as a housewife for a number of years while also active in the community and at St. Mark's.

In 1916 McClendon received a scholarship to attend the American Academy of Dramatic Art at Carnegie Hall, studying acting under Frank Sargent and others. Three years later McClendon made her professional theatrical debut at the Davenport Theatre in New York during the 1919–1920 season, appearing in John

Galsworthy's *Justice* with the Bramhall Players. For the next fifteen years McClendon appeared in almost every important drama about black life that was produced in New York, which earned her the title of the "Negro race's first lady."

McClendon gained some critical attention in a touring production of *Roseanne* (1924), which starred Charles Gilpin, but it was the small role of Octavie in Lawrence Stallings and Frank Harling's *Deep River* that first brought McClendon critical success and the acknowledgment of her peers. The play opened on 21 September 1926 in Philadelphia and on 4 October moved to New York City. As Octavie, McClendon entered and walked slowly down a grand staircase and exited through a garden—all without saying a word. Of her performance, critic John Anderson of the *New York Evening Post* said McClendon created "out of a few wisps of material an unforgettable picture" (5 Oct. 1926). In Philadelphia, director Arthur Hopkins convinced Ethel Barrymore to "watch Rose McClendon come down those stairs," and Barrymore later referred to McClendon's performance as "one of the memorable, immortal moments in the theatre" (*Journal of Negro History*, Jan. 1937).

On 30 December 1926 McClendon appeared as Goldie McAllister in Paul Green's Pulitzer Prize–winning play *In Abraham's Bosom* for the Provincetown Players at the Provincetown Theatre, which also starred Abbie Mitchell and Julius Bledsoe. The play was a success and ran for 277 performances. A revival was staged after the Pulitzer was awarded. In 1928 McClendon played Serena in Dorothy and DuBose Heyward's *Porgy*. The play had an extended run of 217 performances in New York, after which McClendon toured with the show across the country and abroad. McClendon was called "the perfect Aristocrat of Catfish Row" and won critical acclaim for her role. In 1931 she played Big Sue in Paul Green's *House of Connelly*, the first production of the Group Theatre. The production, which opened 23 February 1931, starred Franchot Tone and Morris Carnovsky and was sponsored in part by the Theatre Guild. *House of Connelly* was an immediate success and became an important part of the Group Theatre's contribution to American theater. In 1932 McClendon took the role of Mammy in *Never No More*, and for the 1933 season she played various roles in the radio series "John Henry, Black River Giant."

In 1935 McClendon played Cora in Langston Hughes's *Mulatto*, which premiered at the Vanderbilt Theatre in New York on 24 October. *The Oxford Companion to American Theatre* asserts that the play itself was inferior but succeeded on the strength of McClendon's performance. Doris Abramson expressed a similar sentiment and praised McClendon, saying, "This great Negro actress brought power and dignity to the role" (*Negro Playwrights*, p. 79). The New York critics agreed. Brooks Atkinson called her "an artist with a sensitive personality and a bell-like voice. It is always a privilege to see her adding fineness of perception to the parts she takes" (*New York Times*, 25 Oct. 1935).

The show ran 373 performances, a record for a play by a black author. However, ill health forced McClendon to leave the cast a few months after the opening. She died of pneumonia a year later in New York City.

Beyond her own acting, McClendon was deeply concerned with the state of the black theater art, and she used her influence to promote it during what became known as the Harlem Renaissance. She directed productions for the Harlem Experimental Theatre, founded in 1928, and helped found in 1935 the Negro People's Theatre, which through McClendon's guidance became incorporated into the Federal Theatre Project's Black Unit in Harlem. McClendon also served on the advisory board of the Theatre Union, a nonprofit producing company founded in 1932 to produce socially significant plays at popular prices. She saw the theater as an important medium for depicting a true picture of African-American life. She hoped the Federal Theatre Project support would produce quality black actors and writers.

As one of the great actresses of her time, McClendon became a strong symbol for black theater at a time when African Americans were just gaining their theatrical voice; indeed, when McClendon first appeared on the stage, blacks were not yet allowed into theater audiences. In the year after her death, the Rose McClendon Players were organized by Dick Campbell in memory of her vision for the black theater. While the company faltered after the Second World War, it launched the careers of numerous artists who would make their mark in the postwar American theater—her vision fulfilled.

• The Rose McClendon scrapbook and clippings are in the Schomburg Collection of the New York Public Library. McClendon is included in *Notable American Women*, vol. 2 (1971), and *The Oxford Companion to American Theatre* (1984). Additional information on McClendon is in Doris Abramson, *Negro Playwrights* (1969); Frederick Bond, *The Negro and the Drama* (1940); and Edith J. R. Isaacs, *The Negro in the American Theatre* (1947). See also a biographical sketch in *Crisis*, Apr. 1927. Obituaries are in the *New York Times*, 14 July 1936; the *Journal of Negro History* (Jan. 1937), and the *Afro-American* and *New York Amsterdam News*, both 18 July 1936.

MELISSA VICKERY-BAREFORD

MCCLENNAN, Alonzo Clifton (1 May 1855–4 Oct. 1912), black physician and professional leader, was born in Columbia, South Carolina, the orphaned son of unknown parents. As with many African Americans of the post–Civil War era, it was Reconstruction that gave McClennan a chance at larger life. In 1872, at the height of the movement in South Carolina (and thanks to the influence of a guardian-uncle), he became a page in the black-dominated state senate. There he won the notice and friendship of influential legislator Richard H. "Daddy" Cain. That fall Cain ran successfully for Congress, and in 1873, after McClennan passed a competitive examination, Cain appointed his young protégé to the U.S. Naval Academy.

Only the second African-American student to enter Annapolis, McClennan, who was light enough to pass for white but never denied his race, found that the navy had made no accommodation to the new racial ethic of Reconstruction. From midshipmen and officers alike the young South Carolinian met savage hatred and the most blatant injustice. Goaded into minor infractions (or falsely accused of them), McClennan was dealt the severest punishments, including several months' confinement on a training ship and a court-martial (whose judgment was stayed by his patron Cain). Soon McClennan's life at Annapolis was so desperately lonely that his one joy was the nightly visit of the black servant who cleaned his boots and tidied his room. After three terms, only his worry about letting down his people kept him from quitting. Finally, in January 1874, two sympathetic faculty members not only urged him to resign but also promised to help him enroll elsewhere. He then decided he could withdraw with honor.

But the hound of racism was still in pursuit. Following a brief stint at Wesleyan Academy in Massachusetts, McClennan returned home to Columbia in 1875 to take advantage of the recent integration of South Carolina College. His timing could not have been worse: a year later General Wade Hampton's "Red Shirts" ousted the Republican regime. One consequence was a resegregation of the college and the resignation of all its blacks. Once again, McClennan was on the hunt for a place to complete his degree, which he was now determined to take in medicine.

Fortunately, Howard University Medical School, just ending its first decade, wanted the determined young South Carolinian badly enough to offer him a scholarship. Finally, blond, blue-eyed McClennan could pursue his training without harassment or unusual notice. His record, however, did get attention: in 1880 he completed the surgery program with distinction (as well as acquiring a degree in pharmacy) and was ready to let down his bucket among his people. He set up practice first in Columbia but soon shifted to Augusta, Georgia, where he not only began to earn his way out of poverty but also found a wife. In 1883 he married Veronica Ridley, who, like her husband, could also have passed for white. They had two daughters.

In 1884 McClennan made his final move—to Charleston—and was soon enjoying a substantial income. Two things likely accounted for his remarkable rise (and a lifestyle that included a large home and a black domestic). The first was the existence in Charleston of a large black middle class; the second was his physiognomy and coloring. As under slavery, lightness of skin still translated into social standing and popularity in African-American communities. McClennan's daughters, who took pride in their father's Caucasian features, likely reflected the community view. Yet there was nothing elitist about him. Unlike the storied black plutocrat who turned his back on his race to curry favor with whites, McClennan sought only to serve his people. Colleagues may have found

him dictatorial in pushing his professional agenda, but there was no denying its usefulness or his sincerity.

Its first major component was the state's first Negro nurse training school, begun by McClennan in 1896. One of many responses to nursing reforms begun at the Johns Hopkins Hospital only a few years before, his school was more than just a reaction to professional need. With just a few black doctors in Charleston and no access for black people to existing hospitals (except the city hospital, where African Americans faced overcrowding and indifferent attention), McClennan's efforts to supply trained black nurses for home care met a critical community need. Plus, Charleston had a ready supply of underemployed young women to furnish a corps of students. What the school did not have was a clinical setting where students could practice and apply their book skills. Neither the private white hospitals (including that of the state medical college) nor the city hospital or poor house would accept black students. When, finally, local government rebuffed his appeal for aid (at the very moment it was funding a white school), McClennan went to the black community for help. From meager resources, money began to trickle in—from individual gifts, community dances, food sales—until by 1897 there were sufficient funds to buy and improve a frame house on Cannon Street to accommodate ten students.

But the community-owned Cannon Street Hospital served more than novice nurses. Its twenty-four patient beds offered care not only to local blacks but also to those from throughout the Low-Country as well as from states as far north as Virginia. Open to all city physicians—who donated their services—the hospital also provided rare clinical experience to doctors. But McClennan, the hospital director and surgery chief, saw the facility reaching far beyond its patients and staff; he wanted to extend health and medical education to the whole state. To that end, in 1899 he founded (and edited) the *Hospital Herald*, a monthly newsletter filled with information and advice for mothers, doctors, nurses, the sick, and the well. It also carried constant appeals for money; once the hospital's founding moment passed, contributions from hard-pressed blacks tailed off. To meet operating and debt-retirement expenses its medical staff and trustees had little choice but to dig deeper into their own pockets.

McClennan never slackened in his commitment. By 1906 he had even won some funding from city government. Though there never was enough funding to equip the hospital adequately (McClennan had to outfit the operating room himself) or to give patients the kind of modern care whites enjoyed, the most important thing was to keep Cannon Street Hospital in business. If blacks got less than they should have, they got far more than they would have without McClennan's efforts. Moreover, no matter how sharp the money pinch, McClennan never turned away a patient for lack of funds. Yet, while staggering under the burden of a continually failing institution, McClennan found energy to tackle other professional problems. In 1897 he joined a handful of colleagues in creating the Palmetto Medical, Dental, and Pharmaceutical Association, the state's first organization for black health professionals, and by 1900 had served as its president for one year. But a lifetime spent battling high odds had taken its toll, and at age fifty-seven McClennan died in Charleston, still working for his hospital and his people.

A black version of the rags-to-riches tale, his story is at once instructive and substantial. It mirrors the ambiguity and ultimate tragedy of Reconstruction, and it also reflects the near-heroic labors of southern blacks to create from scant resources—and against an intense racism—the institutions they needed to survive.

• A small collection of McClennan's papers are housed at the Amistad Research Center at Tulane University. Of special value is "A Pace Maker," a daughter's recollection of McClennan's life. The Rockefeller Archive Center in Tarrytown, N.Y., has a 1906 account of McClennan's hospital, and the Waring Historical Library at the Medical University of South Carolina in Charleston holds a nearly complete collection (1899–1901) of McClennan's *Hospital Herald*. His Annapolis period is thoroughly detailed by Willard B. Gatewood, Jr., in "Alonzo Clifton McClennan: Black Mid-shipman from South Carolina, 1873–1874," *South Carolina Historical Magazine* 89 (Jan. 1988): 24–29; while E. H. Beardsley, *A History of Neglect: Health Care for Blacks and Mill Workers in the 20th Century South* (1987), explores the handicaps and achievements of southern black doctors of McClennan's era.

E. H. BEARDSLEY

MCCLERNAND, John Alexander (30 May 1812–20 Sept. 1900), politician and soldier, was born near Hardinsburg, Kentucky, the son of John A. McClernand, a physician, and Fatima Cummins Seaton. His father died when McClernand was four, and he was raised by his mother in and near Shawneetown, Illinois, where he attended school and studied law. Admitted to the bar in 1832, he soon enlisted in the Black Hawk War, from which he returned to Shawneetown to practice law, edit the *Gallatin Democrat and Illinois Advertiser*, and enter politics. Elected to the Illinois House of Representatives for the first of three terms in 1836, he met Representative Abraham Lincoln, elected two years earlier, who was as ardent a Whig as McClernand was a Democrat.

The Illinois legislature held a galaxy of future political stars, including Stephen A. Douglas, already a Democratic leader. McClernand soon established a reputation for oratorical flamboyance and Democratic orthodoxy. In 1840 and 1842 he won additional terms in the general assembly and, also in 1842, election to the U.S. House of Representatives for the first of four consecutive terms. McClernand took a commanding role among Illinois House Democrats only after Douglas won election to the Senate in 1847. McClernand supported the Mexican War, opposed the Wilmot Proviso, and assisted Douglas with both the Compromise of 1850 and the land grant for the Illinois Central Railroad. Discouraged by his own failure to follow Douglas to the Senate in 1849, McClernand attributed his

defeat by James Shields to the diminished political power of extreme southern Illinois. In 1843 he had married Sarah Dunlap, daughter of the wealthy and influential James Dunlap, and in 1851 McClernand moved to Jacksonville and entered into land speculation with his father-in-law. In 1856 he moved to Springfield to practice law. When incumbent congressman Thomas Harris died in 1858 just after his re-election, McClernand won the scramble for the seat. After an eight-year absence he returned to Congress (5 Dec. 1859) from a different district and came close to winning the Speakership. In 1854 McClernand had broken with Douglas in opposition to the Kansas-Nebraska bill, but by the end of the year he had resumed this traditional alliance. He loyally supported Douglas's 1860 presidential campaign.

When the Civil War began, McClernand followed Douglas's patriotic course and resigned from Congress to accept appointment from Lincoln as brigadier general of volunteers. Commanding a brigade at the southern tip of Illinois at Cairo, he came under the command of Brigadier General Ulysses S. Grant, his immediate superior for nearly two years. With Grant, McClernand steamed down the Mississippi River to attack Confederate forces at Belmont, Missouri, an inconclusive battle, after which both sides claimed the victory that neither deserved. In February 1862 Grant launched his Tennessee River campaign with the capture of Fort Henry on the Tennessee River then advanced to the far stronger Fort Donelson on the Cumberland River. There Grant besieged a Confederate force of 21,000 with his own 15,000 while awaiting reinforcements and gunboats. The Union gunboats suffered a repulse on 14 February, and the following day Confederate forces broke through McClernand's division on the Union right. Grant rallied his troops, pushed the Confederates back to their fortifications, and tightened his grip on Donelson, compelling the acceptance of his terms of "unconditional surrender" the next day. The capture of some 15,000 Confederates, the first major Union victory of the war, brought acclaim and promotion to major general for both Grant and McClernand. McClernand's congratulatory orders to his own men, claiming too much for his own brigade, foreshadowed his doom.

McClernand was at Shiloh when Confederate forces surprised Grant on 6 April, pushing his army to the banks of the Tennessee River. Grant turned defeat into victory on the second day of fighting. McClernand's congratulatory orders, again self-aggrandizing and aimed at Illinois voters, angered Grant and other generals, including William T. Sherman, rebuked by implication. The initial surprise brought such severe criticism of Grant that McClernand's boasting seemed to have sinister implications.

In the fall of 1862 McClernand began to press Lincoln for independent command by using threats of northwestern disaffection and promises of new regiments of Democrats. Gaining grudging assent, McClernand returned to Illinois to recruit. General in Chief Henry W. Halleck, a protector of Grant and

Sherman, funneled the new regiments down the Mississippi, stranding McClernand in Illinois. McClernand protested inactivity but improved his leisure with his marriage on 30 December 1862 to Minerva Dunlap, sister of his late wife. The newlyweds steamed downriver in search of an army. McClernand found that Sherman, repulsed at Chickasaw Bayou, proposed an attack on Arkansas Post, fifty miles above the Mississippi on the Arkansas River. McClernand consented, and the Confederate position there fell on 11 January. Grant called the expedition a "wild goose chase" before he learned that Sherman had planned the victorious campaign. At the end of January Grant, the only general in the department who ranked McClernand, took personal command of the army at Milliken's Bend, giving McClernand command of the XIII Corps, one of three composing the army menacing Vicksburg. McClernand took to subordination ungraciously enough to irritate his fellow corps commanders Sherman and Major General James B. McPherson, to say nothing of Grant. With Vicksburg encircled on 22 May, Grant launched the second of two frontal assaults. By claiming that his forces had achieved considerable success, McClernand lured Grant into committing more troops to a hopeless endeavor. When McClernand issued yet another windy congratulation to his own corps on 17 June, neglecting to obtain prior approval at headquarters, Grant sent him home in disgrace. McClernand protested loud and long to Washington, but cheers of rejoicing over Vicksburg's surrender (4 July) drowned out the howls from Springfield.

Restored to command of the XIII Corps in February 1864, McClernand joined the ill-fated Red River campaign of Major General Nathaniel P. Banks, a botched enterprise that destroyed what military reputation McClernand retained. He resigned as of 30 November 1864 and returned to Democratic politics. With Republicans dominant and Grant triumphant, McClernand found his political path blocked. President Andrew Johnson twice (1867, 1868) nominated McClernand as minister to Mexico; twice Grant vigorously and successfully opposed confirmation. McClernand served as Sangamon County circuit judge (1870–1873), as chairman of the Democratic National Convention (1876), and by appointment of President Grover Cleveland, as a member of the Utah Commission. He did not write his memoirs, especially unfortunate because few had more to tell and more time available to tell it. McClernand died in Springfield, survived by his widow and four children.

Overshadowed politically by Douglas and militarily by Grant, McClernand's ambitions exceeded his abilities. Although he was a competent soldier, his resentment of West Pointers and relentless self-aggrandizement infuriated his superiors and led to his downfall.

• The Illinois State Historical Library has a large collection of McClernand papers, an unpublished biography written by Joseph Wallace (1865), and another attributed to Adolph Schwartz (1873). The library also houses a collection of research materials on McClernand assembled by Philip L. Shutt. Victor Hicken, "From Vandalia to Vicksburg: The Political and Military Career of John A. McClernand" (Ph.D. diss., Univ. of Illinois, 1955), remains the best introductory study. Also useful are Arthur Charles Cole, *The Era of the Civil War 1848–1870, The Centennial History of Illinois*, vol. 3 (1919), and Bruce Catton, *Grant Moves South* (1960). A lengthy obituary is in the Springfield *Journal*, 20 Sept. 1900.

JOHN Y. SIMON

MCCLINTIC, Guthrie (6 Aug. 1893–29 Oct. 1961), director and producer, was born in Seattle, Washington, the son of cousins both surnamed McClintic, Edgar Daggs and Ella Florence. His father worked in the Seattle Assay Office and wanted his only child to become a lawyer. McClintic wanted to be an actor. When he was age twelve, he followed a group of actors through a stage door and was entranced by the backstage atmosphere. He stayed to watch the rehearsal and returned every Saturday for matinees. His father objected to his interest in theater, resulting in bitter quarrels. His father relented when McClintic graduated from high school in 1910, and he sent him to the American Academy of Dramatic Art in New York City.

McClintic's first professional engagement was in 1912 as the Artful Dodger in a touring company of *Oliver Twist*. When his acting career did not flourish, he took a position in 1913 as a stage manager for producer Winthrop Ames. He arrived at the first rehearsal ignorant of his duties, and the director, George Foster Platt, gave him neither instructions nor a copy of the play. The leading actress, Julia Dean, recognizing his plight, offered her own script and a lunch-hour lesson in stage management.

Ames next invited McClintic to stage manage a revival of Clyde Fitch's *The Truth* that he was directing. "There I was," McClintic recalled, "sitting at his elbow across the prompt table, writing down his directions and absorbing as much as the days gave. This was the beginning of my theater doctorate—or apprenticeship. . . . It was to continue eight more years" (*Me and Kit*, p. 125). McClintic assisted Ames in casting, conducting rehearsals, reading scripts, and scouting for new talent. He returned to acting briefly for a season with Grace George's company in 1915 but realized that he was not suited to be an actor. "I was a misfit— too odd a personality . . . the prospect of directing seemed more logical" (*Me and Kit*, pp. 154–55).

In 1917 McClintic read a notice by Heywood Broun in the *New York Tribune* that an actress in the play *Plots and Playwrights* was "a dead-white, young American Duse." Intrigued, he attended a performance. "Her voice was lovely," McClintic wrote, "she moved with ease and grace; there was a haunting mystic quality about her. . . . I wrote beside her name on my program, 'Interesting, monotonous, watch'" (*Me and Kit*, p. 160). The actress was Katharine Cornell, and McClintic married her four years later. He became the guiding force in her career as her director and producer, and she starred in his most notable successes. In the meantime McClintic married the English actress Estelle Winwood. They separated in 1919 and were divorced in 1921.

McClintic received a medical exemption for a "wretchedly inadequate heart" when the United States entered World War I. While Ames was in Europe organizing entertainment for the troops, McClintic took a leave of absence to direct *She Would and She Did* (1917) for another producer. His first effort on his own closed during its tryout in Washington, D.C. He decided to gain more directing experience away from New York and in 1920 took a summer position with Jesse Bonstelle's Detroit stock company. "I had the feeling that dialogue could overlap, as it does in reality—that the grouping of furniture in a stage drawing-room could have a greater reality without every piece facing front, and at the same time be more fluid and easier to act on, and around; that it was possible to say a line with one's back to the audience—these and many more that were theories to me I wanted to test" (*Me and Kit*, p. 189).

Cornell was in the company, and McClintic directed his future wife for the first time in Austin Strong's *Heaven*. They were married in 1921 as their respective careers blossomed. They had no children. Cornell opened in *A Bill of Divorcement* in her first starring role on 10 October 1921. McClintic, with financial backing from Ames, began rehearsals for his first independent New York production, A. A. Milne's *The Dover Road*. It opened on 23 December to lavish praise from the critics. Alexander Woollcott welcomed McClintic's debut as a producer and director in the *New York Times*: "As the American theater's poverty is most conspicuous in the matter of directors, his advent takes on the nature of an occasion" (24 Dec. 1921).

In 1925 McClintic directed Cornell for the first time on Broadway in *The Green Hat*, which ran for three years. With two exceptions he directed every play she appeared in afterward. Their most important collaboration was *The Barretts of Wimpole Street*, with Cornell as producer. The production opened in New York on 9 February 1931 and played 370 performances. Then, in repertory with *Romeo and Juliet* and *Candida*, it went on a 17,000-mile tour in 1934, before reopening for twenty-four performances in New York the following year. It played to army audiences in Europe in 1944, again in New York in 1945, and on a tour of the northwestern United States in 1946.

For decades McClintic was a shaper of the twentieth-century American theater. His sensitivity for spotting and nurturing talent contributed to the careers of young actors, including Tyrone Power, Gregory Peck, Kirk Douglas, Ethel Waters, Maureen Stapleton, Burgess Meredith, Marian Seldes, Julie Harris, and Judith Anderson. He helped playwright Maxwell Anderson emerge from a period of failures to create his most important works, *Winterset* (1935), *High Tor* (1937), and *Key Largo* (1939). The Broadway stage was dominated by light entertainments when McClintic began his career. He expanded its scope by presenting serious drama and the classics in productions that ap-

pealed to a popular audience. These included Sidney Howard's *Yellow Jack* (1934); *Romeo and Juliet* (1934); *Hamlet* (1936), with John Gielgud, Judith Anderson, and Lillian Gish; *The Three Sisters* (1942), with Cornell, Anderson, and Ruth Gordon; *Antigone* (1946); *The Playboy of the Western World* (1946); *Antony and Cleopatra* (1947); *Medea* (1949), with Anderson; and *The Dark Is Light Enough* (1955).

McClintic directed his last production in 1955. Although never formally retired, he spent most of his last years at his home on a bluff above the Hudson River. He produced *Dear Liar* for his wife in 1960 and was a consultant to director Jerome Kilty. He died in Palisades, New York.

• McClintic's anecdotal memoir, *Me and Kit* (1955), concentrates on his early years. John K. Tillinghast, "Guthrie McClintic, Director" (Ph.D. diss., Indiana Univ., 1964), is a comprehensive overview of his career and contains a complete listing of his productions. Katharine Cornell's *I Wanted to Be an Actress* (1938) and her biography, Tad Mosel, *Leading Lady* (1978), are useful sources. See also Frances Robinson, "Remembering Mr. McClintic," *New York Times*, 5 Nov. 1961. An obituary is in the *New York Times*, 30 Oct. 1961.

ARNOLD WENGROW

MCCLINTOCK, Barbara (16 June 1902–2 Sept. 1992), geneticist, was born in Hartford, Connecticut, the daughter of Thomas Henry McClintock, a physician, and Sara Handy. McClintock spent most of her early years in semirural Brooklyn, New York. As a child she was a tomboy, demonstrating early in her play the traits of independence and total absorption that were to characterize her later work in genetics.

In 1919, after an early graduation from Erasmus Hall High School, McClintock entered the College of Agriculture at Cornell University. She soon found herself drawn to the study of biology, especially the fields of genetics, cytology (the study of cells), and botany. After earning a B.S. in 1923, she continued at Cornell as a graduate student, working on the cytogenetics of maize (corn). She simplified and refined a technique for preparing corn cells so that their chromosomes could be examined under the microscope. Through a series of acute microscopic observations, she was able to identify each of the ten chromosomes based on its size and shape, and to describe the pattern of bands that appear along their length. In her doctoral work she used these techniques to correlate groups of traits that were inherited together to specific chromosomes. She received an M.A. in 1925 and was appointed an instructor at Cornell after earning a Ph.D. in botany in 1927.

McClintock continued her work in the lab of Rollins A. Emerson, which was at this time a center of maize cytogenetics. Here she found support and encouragement as part of a group of promising young geneticists known as the Cornell corn group. Her colleagues included Marcus Rhoades, who would remain a lifelong friend, and George Beadle, who won a Nobel Prize in 1958 for his work in molecular biology. In the 1920s genetics was in what is now considered its classical period. Mendel's laws, which describe the patterns by which genes are inherited, had been rediscovered. Cytological studies had revealed that chromosomes, tiny filaments visible in the nuclei of dividing cells, obeyed these same patterns of inheritance. But while it was generally accepted that genes must be located on chromosomes, definitive proof was lacking. In 1931 McClintock and graduate student Harriet Creighton published a paper providing the final piece of evidence for the presence of genes on chromosomes. This paper established her as a geneticist possessing both a talent for theory and extraordinary powers of observation.

Even though McClintock had received recognition among geneticists for her work with maize, for the following decade she was unable to find a permanent academic position. The Great Depression had forced universities to cut back, and few positions then existed for a woman as a career scientist. Between 1931 and 1933, with support from a fellowship from the National Research Council, she worked in labs at Cornell, the University of Missouri, and California Institute of Technology. In 1933 a Guggenheim Fellowship sent her briefly to Germany, where she worked with geneticist Richard B. Goldschmidt. After two more years at Cornell on a Rockefeller Foundation grant, she finally received an appointment as assistant professor at the University of Missouri. Here she continued her work in cytogenetics, experimenting with mutations in chromosomes broken by X-rays. However, after five years it was clear that she was not well suited for her role on the teaching faculty. Conflicts with the university administration and a lack of promotion led her to take a permanent leave of absence in 1941.

That year her fortunes turned. Through the efforts of Marcus Rhoades, McClintock obtained a one-year position at the Cold Spring Harbor Laboratory on Long Island. After two months the position was made permanent. Here she began a series of investigations into mutations and chromosome anomalies in maize. In 1944 she was elected a member of the National Academy of Sciences, only the third woman to receive such an honor. Later that year she became the first woman elected president of the Genetics Society of America.

In 1944 McClintock began the work for which she is best known: the discovery of transposable genetic elements, or transposons. In earlier studies with maize, she had noted a type of mutation that did not occur randomly, but came at a constant and characteristic rate. This suggested that some regulatory mechanism was controlling the rate of mutation. Microscopic examination of the nuclei of cells from these plants showed that sections of their chromosomes had changed position. After six years of carefully planned experiments and intensive cytological observations, she was able to unravel a complex system of genetic controls that enabled maize to regulate the activity of its genes by transposing portions of its chromosome.

In 1950 McClintock published a brief account of this work and presented her findings at a Cold Spring Harbor Symposium a year later. However, her research was not well received. The idea that parts of chromosomes could jump around seemed unlikely to geneticists, who regarded the chromosome as highly stable. In addition, McClintock's control mechanisms were exceedingly complex, and many in her audience simply could not understand her ideas. Nevertheless, she continued with her research, uncovering even more genetic regulatory systems. When the focus of genetics shifted from classical genetics to molecular biology in the 1950s, it became more common to study the DNA of simple organisms like bacteria or viruses. McClintock's studies relied on simple microscopy—analyzing visible changes in banding patterns on the chromosomes of maize. Compared to molecular genetic research, her techniques seemed quaint and outmoded. Although she continued to publish papers, and made several additional attempts to gain the interest of her colleagues at symposia, she found few who would listen.

After 1960 McClintock's work began to receive some recognition as molecular biologists discovered cases of genetic regulation and gene transposition in other organisms. It was not until the late 1970s, however, that her research was fully embraced by the scientific community. In 1970 she was awarded the National Medal of Science, and in 1983 she won the Nobel Prize for physiology or medicine. Although she formally retired in 1967, she continued working with maize until her death in Huntington, New York.

• McClintock's most important papers are collected in Nina Fedoroff and David Botstein, eds., *The Dynamic Genome: Barbara McClintock's Ideas in the Century of Genetics* (1991). This volume, published in celebration of her ninetieth birthday, includes a collection of essays in her honor written by her friends and colleagues, as well as a complete list of her publications. The biography by Evelyn Fox Keller, *A Feeling for the Organism: The Life and Work of Barbara McClintock* (1983), includes a summary of her research and an analysis of the reception given to her by the scientific community. For a relatively nontechnical explanation of McClintock's discoveries by the same author, see "McClintock's Maize," *Science* 81 (Oct. 1981): 55–58.

WILLIAM J. LAMBERTS

MCCLINTOCK, Emory (19 Sept. 1840–10 July 1916), actuary and mathematician, was born in Carlisle, Pennsylvania, the son of the Reverend John M'Clintock, a clergyman and professor of mathematics and classics at Dickinson College, and Caroline Augusta Wakeman. The young McClintock went to school for the first time at age thirteen; he then attended Dickinson College (1854–1856) and Yale (1856–1857) before transferring to Columbia. He received his A.B. in 1859 and his A.M. in 1862, from Columbia, and he taught mathematics there as a tutor during the 1859–1860 academic year. Becoming interested in chemistry, he studied it in Paris in 1860 and in Göttingen in 1861. In 1862 he returned to the United States intending to volunteer for military service in the Civil War, but illness prevented his entry into the Union army. He served as U.S. Consular Agent in Bradford, England, from 1863 to 1866, after which he worked in a private banking firm in Paris until 1867. Returning to the United States, McClintock worked as an actuary for the Asbury Life Insurance Company of New York (1867–1871) and the Northwest Life Insurance Company of Milwaukee, Wisconsin (1871–1889), before joining the Mutual Life Insurance Company of New York. There he was a vice president and trustee from 1906 to 1911, and upon retiring he remained a consulting actuary from 1911 until 1916.

McClintock was highly regarded in both the mathematical and actuarial communities. He served as second president of the New York Mathematical Society (later the American Mathematical Society) from 1890 to 1894, and he was a founder (1889) and president of the Actuarial Society of America from 1895 to 1897. In addition, he was a fellow of the Institute of Actuaries in London (1892) as well as a corresponding member of the Association des Actuaires Belges (1896) and of the Institut des Actuaires Français (1896).

McClintock's principal contributions to mathematical research center on two major topics. The first was treated in his "An Essay on the Calculus of Enlargement" (1879), in which he sought to develop a unified theory of the calculus of finite differences and the differential calculus. This led him to restate difference equations as differential equations of infinite order, and subsequently he considered interpolation and expansion theorems in his theory. His second area dealt with methods of solving quintic algebraic equations (1884, 1885, 1898). In both of these topics his interest was computational rather than conceptual, and his colleagues greatly admired his clear vision and manipulative skill. However, his major mathematical contribution was in his early participation in the American Mathematical Society. There he was of great help in establishing the *Bulletin of the American Mathematical Society* and *Transactions of the American Mathematical Society*; contemporary accounts have suggested that his role was not limited to merely advice but also extended to financial assistance (very likely including corporate support from his company). It is known that he made substantial donations to the society's library. In any case, his reputation was such that in 1903, when *American Men of Science* conducted a poll of the leaders of American science, he was ranked nineteenth out of eighty in mathematics.

McClintock's research contributions to actuarial sciences were probably more important than his pure mathematical work. Between 1868 and 1877 he published some thirty technical papers, and he became a recognized authority on actuarial mathematics. He edited and enlarged the *Interest Tables Used by the Mutual Life Insurance Company of New York for the Calculation of Interest and Prices of Stocks and Bonds for Investment* (1889, 1904), originally prepared by William H. C. Bartlett; and his essay, "On the Effects of Selection—An Actuarial Essay," won him second prize in an 1892 competition held by the Institute of Actuaries in London. As president of the Actuarial So-

ciety of America, he instituted examinations for membership in the society. However, his greatest service to the actuarial community was through his service as a champion and spokesman for the insurance community. The period of business expansion at the close of the nineteenth century was rife with dealings that were both unscrupulous and fraudulent. These dealings centered on businesses in which minority influences were without influence, as well as businesses in which stock ownership and interlocking directorates enabled some individuals to manipulate corporations to their personal advantage. In particular, these practices occurred in many insurance companies. In 1905, when public antagonism and distrust toward insurance companies was rampant, the New York state legislature instituted an insurance investigative committee, called the Armstrong Committee after its chairman, Senator William W. Armstrong. McClintock gave extensive testimony before this committee, which both defused the issues and led to substantive insurance reforms. He was so effective that a year later, when difficulties arose with foreign insurance companies doing business in Great Britain, he testified before a committee of the House of Lords; again his expert knowledge and integrity instilled confidence and helped to resolve the problem.

McClintock was a natural leader who not only inspired and stimulated his colleagues but also served as a stabilizing influence and an initiator of reforms. He brought confidence to his causes, and in doing so he made significant contributions to both the mathematical and actuarial communities. He was married twice: an early marriage to Zoe Darlington of Yorkshire, England, produced one son, and in 1890 he married Isabella Bishop of New Brunswick, New Jersey. He died in his home in Bay Head, New Jersey.

• McClintock's views on the role of the American Mathematical Society in encouraging research and setting standards of excellence are contained in his retiring presidential address, "The Past and Future of the Society," *Bulletin of the American Mathematical Society* 1 (Jan. 1895): 85–94. The most complete biographical notice, by Raymond C. Archibald, is in the *American Mathematical Society Semi-Centennial Publications* 1 (1938): 112–17; this contains a complete list of publications and a portrait. An obituary by Thomas S. Fiske is in the *Bulletin of the American Mathematical Society* 23 (May 1917): 353–57; an obituary is also in the *New York Times*, 11 July 1916. A subsequent letter in the *New York Times*, 19 July 1916, discusses McClintock's services toward insurance reform.

JOSEPH D. ZUND

MCCLINTOCK, John (27 Oct. 1814–4 Mar. 1870), clergyman and educator, was born in Philadelphia, Pennsylvania, the son of John McClintock, a retail dry goods merchant, and Martha McMackin. Although McClintock showed much promise in classical languages during six years at the University of Pennsylvania's grammar school, he was removed at age fourteen to work in his father's store. In 1830 he began two years as a bookkeeper for the Methodist Book Concern in New York City.

A conversion experience during revival meetings at New York City's Allen Street Methodist Church in 1831 intensified his religious commitment and also renewed his interest in higher education. In September 1832 McClintock entered Wesleyan University, but within a week an intestinal illness sent him home. Upon recovery, he entered the University of Pennsylvania, and although the term had already started, he was able to excel. He progressed rapidly, completing his college course in three years. During his final year, he also carried heavy responsibilities as a Methodist local preacher to small churches in New Jersey. After graduating in July 1835, he became pastor of a Methodist congregation in Jersey City, New Jersey. Within a year, however, throat and chest ailments impaired his health. Warned by physicians to choose other employment, he became assistant professor of mathematics at Dickinson College in Carlisle, Pennsylvania, in September 1836. Later that year he married Caroline Augusta Wakeman; two of their three children survived to adulthood.

McClintock was promoted to full professor in 1837 and remained at Dickinson until 1848. His teaching responsibilities shifted in 1839 to classical languages. In 1845, with George Crooks, he began a series of Greek and Latin textbooks that introduced to the United States new methods of language instruction using practice exercises rather than memorization only. He collaborated in 1848 with Charles E. Blumenthal on a translation of the German theologian August Neander's *Life of Jesus Christ*, which had been written in 1837 as a reply to *Life of Jesus* (1835), David Friedrich Strauss's controversial biography of Jesus. Poor health, however, intermittently hampered his work. At times his throat malady made solid food or speech impossible; by the late 1840s, he feared that his heart was damaged as well. Physicians tried various remedies or recommended rest and travel. When he was able, McClintock preached in Methodist pulpits; in April 1840 he was ordained as an elder in Burlington, New Jersey.

McClintock vigorously opposed slavery. In 1841 he wrote, "It seems to me that the Church can do only one thing in regard to so heinous a crime as slavery, namely, to bear her testimony against it, and use all her influence for its extirpation" (Crooks, p. 128). He decried the annexation of Texas, and during 1847 he penned antislavery articles for the *Christian Advocate*, a prominent Methodist weekly. In June 1847 the arrival in Carlisle of two Maryland slaveowners pursuing fugitives raised local tempers. McClintock was not a participant in the violence that left one slaveowner badly beaten, but he was arrested and charged with having incited the attack; a jury acquitted him in August 1847. His own evaluation was that "my human and Christian sympathies were openly exhibited on the side of the poor blacks, and this gave mortal offence to the slaveholders and their *confreres* in the town" (Crooks, p. 158).

In 1848 McClintock became editor of the *Methodist Quarterly Review* and moved to Jersey City to be closer to the New York editorial office. After his wife's death in March 1850 and his remarriage in October 1851 to Catherine W. Emory, the widow of his friend and colleague Robert Emory, he resided in New Brunswick; two years later, he moved back to Carlisle with the hope that his health would improve. In 1853 he and James Strong began to edit a twelve-volume *Cyclopaedia of Biblical, Theological, and Ecclesiastical Literature* (1867–1881), three volumes of which were published before McClintock's death.

McClintock's editorship of the *Methodist Quarterly Review* gave him an opportunity to influence American Methodism; his intent was to make it more fully engaged with modern thought. McClintock, whose own thinking was inspired by Romantics like Samuel Taylor Coleridge and Thomas Carlyle, opened the *Review* to a wide range of opinion and moved it into the front ranks of American denominational quarterlies. McClintock was not himself a scholar of first importance, but as an editor he greatly facilitated both the exchange of ideas and the initiation of personal correspondence and meetings among those who were. For example, he played a key role in American discussions of Auguste Comte's positivism. Although McClintock loathed Comte's epistemology and his priestly Religion of Humanity, he believed that the French thinker raised valid, inescapable questions about the certainty and limits of human knowledge. The *Methodist Quarterly Review* carried frequent articles on positivism during the 1850s, including an important series by George Frederick Holmes (1820–1897) that brought McClintock into correspondence with leading American positivists and with Comte himself. Subsequently, McClintock helped to raise money in the United States on Comte's behalf and served as an intermediary between him and his American readers. McClintock's broad-minded editorial policy was controversial. Some complained that the *Review* was too intellectual or that it ventured too often into topics unconnected or even contrary to the denomination's religious concerns; others resented McClintock's continuing crusade against slavery. Subscriptions declined, and in 1856 McClintock lost his editorship.

In 1857 McClintock became minister of St. Paul's Methodist Church in New York City. His theology, reflecting that of Friedrich Schleiermacher, was experience-based and Christ-centered. In the pulpit, he avoided scholarly contention; the mark of a good sermon was to set forth Christ crucified in "simplicity" and "godly sincerity" (Crooks, p. 267). From 1860 to 1864 he pastored the American Chapel in Paris; in addition to his religious duties, he was credited with promoting and interpreting to Europeans the Union cause in the Civil War.

When he returned to the United States, McClintock served again at St. Paul's in New York City. After a year, however, his failing health prevented continuation. He retired to Germantown, Pennsylvania, and then to New Brunswick, New Jersey, where he devoted himself to writing and occasional preaching. In January 1866 he met with President Andrew Johnson (1808–1875) to urge suffrage for the freedmen.

McClintock was chosen by the General Conference to chair the 1866 centenary celebration of American Methodism. In response to its fundraising, business leader Daniel Drew offered to endow a Methodist seminary if McClintock would become its first president. Drew Theological Seminary (which in the next century expanded to become Drew University) opened in November 1867 in Madison, New Jersey. McClintock served as its head until he died in Madison.

• The largest collection of McClintock papers is at Emory University, with smaller portions at Dickinson College and Drew University. Compilations of his sermons and classroom lectures appeared posthumously as *Living Words; or, Unwritten Sermons* (1871) and *Lectures . . . on Theological Encyclopaedia and Methodology* (1873). In addition to the publications previously mentioned, McClintock prepared an *Analysis of Watson's Theological Institutes* (1842) for students, edited *The Life and Letters of Stephen Olin* (1853) and *Sketches of Eminent Methodist Ministers* (1853), and prepared an American edition of an earlier British translation of Laurence Bungener's *History of the Council of Trent* (1855). Researchers should begin with George R. Crooks, *Life and Letters of the Rev. John McClintock* (1876). Additional information is in Charles D. Cashdollar, "Unexpected Friendship: John McClintock and Auguste Comte," *Pennsylvania Magazine of History and Biography* 105 (Jan. 1981): 85–98. An obituary is in the *New York Times*, 5 Mar. 1870.

CHARLES D. CASHDOLLAR

MCCLOSKEY, John (10 Mar. 1810–10 Oct. 1885), Roman Catholic bishop and first American cardinal, was born in Brooklyn, New York, the son of Patrick McCloskey, a clerk, and Elizabeth Harron, recently arrived Irish immigrants. In 1817 the family moved to New York City, and John entered Thomas Brady's Classical School. A member of St. Peter's Church in St. Patrick's parish, he came under the influence of his pastor, John Power, and Power's assistant, Jesuit Peter Malou. After his father died in 1820, McCloskey became the ward of Cornelius Heeney, a wealthy philanthropist who arranged for McCloskey to be admitted to Mount St. Mary's College in Emmitsburg, Maryland, in September 1821. After completing the college course he continued at Mount St. Mary's as a seminarian and was ordained to the priesthood by Bishop John Dubois at St. Patrick's Cathedral on 12 January 1834. He had the distinction of being the first native of New York State to enter the diocesan priesthood. For several months he taught philosophy at the diocesan seminary in Nyack, New York, but after it burned to the ground that summer, McCloskey left New York and spent three years studying at the Gregorian University in Rome, also traveling extensively throughout Europe, England, and Ireland.

When he returned to New York City in 1837, Bishop Dubois appointed him pastor of St. Joseph's Church on Sixth Avenue, where he faced determined opposition from lay trustees who believed they should have made his appointment. By combining gentle persuasion with appeals to authority, McCloskey was able to defuse the explosive situation and served successfully as pastor for seven years. In 1841, Bishop John Hughes made him the first president of St. John's College (later Fordham University), which he organized in one year and then resigned his post. On 10 March 1844 he was consecrated an auxiliary bishop of New York with right of succession. As an understudy to the dynamic Bishop Hughes, McCloskey kept a low profile but was extremely influential in the conversions of James Roosevelt Bayley, who later would become archbishop of Baltimore, and Isaac Hecker, who later would found the Paulists; he formally received Bayley into the church in 1842 and Hecker in 1844. In 1847 he became the first bishop of Albany, New York.

Throughout his seventeen-year tenure in Albany, McCloskey was an active and energetic bishop. He built a cathedral, increased the numbers of churches and priests, and worked with Archbishop Hughes in creating a new provincial seminary, St. Joseph's, in Troy, New York. As bishop of the state capital, he used his proximity to the legislature to work for the repeal of the Putnam Law, which made it illegal for Catholic bishops to bequeath church property to their successors, thereby ensuring the use of a trustee system. Although his efforts did not meet with immediate success, ultimately the law was repealed. In his quiet, conservative way, McCloskey cultivated the admiration of many prominent New York politicians, including Horatio Seymour, Thurlow Weed, Erastus Corning, and Rufus King, who was appointed emissary to the Holy See.

After Hughes died in January 1864, McCloskey was transferred to New York City and on 21 August was formally installed as archbishop in Old St. Patrick's Cathedral. McCloskey continued construction of the new St. Patrick's Cathedral on Fifth Avenue and dedicated the magnificent Gothic structure on 25 May 1879. As archbishop he warned Irish-American Catholics against becoming involved in the Fenian Movement and its plans of armed assault against Canada. At Vatican Council I (1869–1870), McCloskey was part of the "inopportunist" faction that opposed a definition of papal infallibility, but when the issue came to a vote he cast his ballot in the affirmative.

On 15 March 1875, Pope Pius IX named him a cardinal, the first American to be so honored. Unable to cross the Atlantic in time to attend the formal consistory in Rome, on 27 April he received the cardinal's red biretta from his former convert, now Archbishop James Roosevelt Bayley of Baltimore. That September he went to Rome to take possession of Santa Maria sopra Minerva, his titular church, and to pay his respects to the pope. When Pius IX died in 1878, McCloskey wanted to participate in the papal conclave that elected Pope Leo XII, but he arrived too late. The timing of papal elections continued to be a problem for American cardinals until 1922, when Pope Pius XI lengthened the time between the death of a pope and the meeting of the electors.

Because of ill health, McCloskey received a coadjutor, Bishop Michael A. Corrigan of Newark, who was appointed in 1880. McCloskey withdrew more and more from diocesan activities but reemerged in September 1883 in order to convene a meeting of the bishops of the state of New York. Moreover, in 1884 he successfully petitioned the U.S. Department of State for assistance in protecting the North American College in Rome from confiscation by the Italian government. He died at Mount-Saint-Vincent-on-Hudson and was buried in St. Patrick's Cathedral.

• The archives of the Archdiocese of New York and the Diocese of Albany contain McCloskey's papers. See also John M. Farley, *The Life of John, Cardinal McCloskey, First Prince of the Church in America, 1810–1885* (1918), and Florence D. Cohalan, *A Popular History of the Archdiocese of New York* (1983).

STEVEN M. AVELLA

MCCLOSKEY, William George (10 Nov. 1823–17 Sept. 1909), Catholic bishop, was born in Brooklyn, New York, the son of George McCloskey and Ellen Kenny. After study from 1846 to 1852 at Mount St. Mary's Seminary in Emmitsburg, Maryland (and a brief attempt at the study of law in New York City), McCloskey was ordained a Catholic priest of the archdiocese of New York on 6 October 1852. Following a short time of parish ministry, he returned to Mount St. Mary's to serve as professor and eventually seminary rector. In March 1860 McCloskey arrived in Rome to become the first rector of the newly established American College (Seminary). He held this post until 1868, when he was removed from office after several American bishops criticized his ability to manage the college's finances effectively. McCloskey apparently had been unsuccessful in drawing either contributions or students from America in the Civil War years and in its aftermath.

In 1868 McCloskey arrived in Louisville, Kentucky, after appointment as bishop of that diocese by Pope Pius IX. His tenure was to last forty-one years and would be marked by the same authoritarian tendencies that had been in evidence in his headship at the American College in Rome. During his Louisville years, he oversaw the building of nearly one hundred churches and other institutions in the diocese; the number of Catholics and of priests under his administration more than doubled in this same period.

The daily press in Louisville described the new bishop as "a tall and commanding figure with handsome round face and hair tinged irongray," who was "charming and courtly in manner and dress." For his fastidiousness in style, McCloskey was dubbed "the Lord Chesterfield of the American Catholic Church" by twentieth-century American Catholic historian James Hennesey.

The years of McCloskey's episcopacy in Louisville were turbulent. He quarreled frequently with the priests in his diocese over finances as well as what many of them perceived to be arbitrary reassignment from parish to parish. The difficulties extended to several religious communities within his jurisdiction as well when he attempted to interfere with their internal affairs and regulations. These communities included such teaching sisterhoods as the School Sisters of Notre Dame and the Ursulines. Several appeals to authorities in Rome resulted in the overturning of McCloskey's decisions; but Rome made no attempt to remove the prelate from office, though authorities did dispatch an investigator in 1871 who exonerated the bishop.

Most notably, McCloskey placed the Motherhouse of the Sisters of Loretto under an interdict (suspension of Mass and sacraments) over an insurance dispute in the summer of 1904. After a vigorous protest from Mother Praxedes of the Loretto community and with the support of Abbot Edmund Obrecht of the nearby Abbey of Gethsemani, the penalty was lifted after two weeks.

McCloskey attended the Third Plenary Council of Baltimore in 1884, but took no outstanding part. At the First Vatican Council, he at first opposed the definition of papal infallibility on the grounds that its timing was not opportune. But at the final ballot, he voted in favor of it.

Disputes decreased as McCloskey aged. By the time of his death in Louisville, he was the oldest Catholic bishop in the United States and was eulogized in standard obituary quotations by several Catholic bishops as a steadfast and faithful leader. Even in his obituary in the *Louisville Courier-Journal*, however, one of his most revered priests (George Schuhmann) continued to describe the bishop as "inflexible."

McCloskey is significant as a striking example of the growing tendency of the bishops in several American Catholic dioceses in the generations after the First Vatican Council (1869–1870) to become more Roman, centralized, and authoritarian in administrative style. Ironically, the very Roman authority that McCloskey represented would frequently overturn his decisions on appeals from his subjects, indicating a lively dialectic of ecclesiastical power in this era.

• For primary sources, see McCloskey files in archives of the Archdiocese of Louisville and the Archdiocese of Cincinnati. See also Clyde F. Crews, "American Catholic Authoritarianism: The Episcopacy of William George McCloskey," *Catholic Historical Review* 70 (Oct. 1984): 560–80. Obituaries are in the *Louisville Courier-Journal*, 17 and 18 Sept. 1909.

CLYDE F. CREWS

MCCLOY, John Jay, Jr. (31 Mar. 1895–11 Mar. 1989), lawyer, banker, and diplomat, was born in Philadelphia, Pennsylvania, the son of John Jay McCloy, a claims officer for an insurance firm, and Anna May Snader. McCloy's father died just before McCloy's sixth birthday. Left with a modest bequest, Anna McCloy learned hairdressing and developed a wealthy clientele to support herself, John, and her two spinster sisters. In summers Anna followed her clients to their vacation homes in the Adirondack Mountains, where John worked as a chore boy at resorts and taught tennis, a sport in which he excelled. Tennis opened doors for him for many years, as did his mother's clients and his father's business associated.

Upon graduation from the Peddie Institute of Hightstown, New Jersey, in 1912, McCloy enrolled at Amherst College and received a bachelor's degree cum laude in 1916. He then entered Harvard Law School. His legal education was interrupted in May 1917 by service with the U.S. Army during World War I. Commissioned as a provisional second lieutenant, he arrived in France in July 1918 to serve as operations officer with a field artillery brigade that saw limited action. At the end of the war, he served with the American army of occupation before returning in the fall of 1919 to Harvard, where he received his law degree in 1921.

Advised not to practice law in Philadelphia because he lacked a prestigious family background, McCloy went to New York to become an associate in the firm of Cadwalader, Wickersham, and Taft. This immediately put him among the elite. Taft was the brother of former president William Howard Taft, and Wickersham had been the president's attorney general. McCloy's bachelor status, tennis proficiency, and particularly his genial personality also helped him establish friendship with many people who had or would have prominent positions in the nation's affairs.

Impressed by the status of their clients, the quality of their work, and the opportunity to travel abroad, McCloy moved to the firm of Cravath, Henderson, & de Gersdorff in 1924. Continuing his work in corporate law, he spent considerable time in Europe assisting financial ventures intended to rebuild economies destroyed by the world war. In 1930 he married Ellen Zinsser; they had two children. He was counsel for Schechter Poultry in *Schechter Poultry Corporation v. the United States* (1935), a famous case in which the Supreme Court declared Franklin Roosevelt's National Industrial Recovery Act unconstitutional. Throughout the 1930s McCloy was occupied in a prodigious effort to secure compensation for Bethlehem Steel for a 1916 explosion at a munitions depot on Black Tom Island in New York Harbor. Despite two unsuccessful efforts before the World Court, he persisted and won the case in 1939, demonstrating that the explosion was sabotage ordered by the German government.

His experience with the Black Tom case, his concern about growing Nazi militarism, and his friendship, only casual to that point, with Secretary of War Henry Stimson led to McCloy's appointment as a consultant to Army Intelligence in 1940. He had never voted for a Democratic presidential candidate, not even in 1936, when Alf Landon ran as an isolationist. Yet in 1941 McCloy became assistant secretary under Stimson, also a Republican. McCloy was active on several fronts, notably in support of lend-lease legislation, for which he served as Stimson's spokesman in lobbying Congress. His years in Europe and his many friends there had convinced McCloy that the United States must not abandon Europe.

When the United States became involved in the conflict, McCloy's duties as assistant secretary of war were broad. He played a central role in a number of the most controversial episodes of U.S. war making. After Pearl Harbor was bombed, hysteria swept the nation, and even such persons as California attorney general Earl Warren and journalist Walter Lippmann advocated interning Japanese Americans until the war's end. McCloy concurred, and the executive order mandating this action gave the War Department responsibility for administering the program, which was assigned to McCloy. Although the program was clearly unconstitutional, he acted promptly to implement it. At the same time, he moderated its application by seeking exemptions for a few individuals and furloughs for thousands to work outside the camps and successfully advocated creation of an army regiment composed of Nisei, native-born Japanese Americans. The regiment endured the most casualties and gained the most decorations of any regiment.

The Nazi death camps were the focus of a second controversy. In early 1944 the Allies had substantial evidence that Nazi Germany was operating camps to exterminate European Jewry. McCloy, who, like many others, was slow to grasp the dimensions of the Holocaust, was among those consulted about sending Allied bombers to destroy Auschwitz and railroads servicing it. On the advice of military officers, McCloy agreed that the bombing proposal was not practical. To do so would kill innocent Jews and divert military resources, thus delaying victory, the most effective avenue to stop the atrocities. Accordingly, he became a target of those criticizing the Allies for not acting more decisively to end the Holocaust by bombing Auschwitz. Subsequent assessment indicated that such a raid was feasible. Yet if Auschwitz had been attacked, the Nazis might have expanded their other means of slaughtering Jews. As with the internment policy, the controversial decision not to bomb was not based on McCloy's advice alone.

McCloy's contention, expressed in the debate about internment of Japanese Americans, that the Constitution was only a piece of paper when the security of the nation was at stake was evident in other ways. He demonstrated his willingness to encroach further upon civil liberties in 1941, when, despite Attorney General Robert Jackson's opposition, he prodded the Justice Department to expand its use of wiretapping, to conduct unlimited searches, and even to steal potential evidence in the pursuit of suspected saboteurs.

McCloy had become convinced by his dogged work in the Black Tom case that espionage was a fact of international relations and that the United States must develop an intelligence capability. He participated in the creation of the Office of Strategic Services, forerunner of the Central Intelligence Agency. He was also involved in the establishment of the United Nations, construction of the Pentagon, and planning for the Dumbarton Oaks Conference and for the war crimes tribunals. He headed the committee that was the predecessor to the National Security Council, and he attended the Potsdam Conference. As chairman of the army's Advisory Committee on Negro Troop Policy, McCloy resisted the pleas of civil rights leaders to end segregation. His views gradually changed. In November 1945, before he left the War Department, he proposed ending segregation in the military.

In the closing days of World War Two, McCloy was among those the new president, Harry Truman, turned to for policy recommendations. McCloy and others unsuccessfully advised that the Japanese be warned that an unprecedented weapon, meaning the atomic bomb, would be used on them if they did not surrender. McCloy's advice with respect to Europe was more influential. His and Stimson's view prevailed that Germany should not be stripped of its industrial capacity and reduced to a pastoral economy as recommended by Secretary of the Treasury Henry Morgenthau.

In January 1946 McCloy joined the law firm of Milbank, Tweed, Hope, Hadley, and McCloy as a named partner, renewing an association from his teen years with the Rockefeller family, whose legal affairs were handled by this firm. After gaining additional powers for the position, in February 1947, he became president of the International Bank for Reconstruction and Development (later the World Bank), one of the agencies created to restore economies destroyed by the war. Strapped by a lack of resources at the bank, he lobbied the U.S. Congress to approve the Marshall Plan, which would provide government funds for European reconstruction in contrast to reliance on private sources, as was the case after World War One. McCloy's tenure at the World Bank was disappointing. Upon arranging the appointment of his successor, he left to assume the post for which he became best known.

In June 1949, a few weeks after the Soviets lifted the Berlin blockade, McCloy replaced General Lucius Clay as military governor of Germany. Two months later, when the three western zones of Germany were combined as the Federal Republic of Germany, he become U.S. high commissioner for occupied Germany. His wife, who had no visible role in his work before, utilized her fluent German in appearances throughout West Germany and became popular with Germans.

McCloy and his British and French counterparts retained control over key policy areas, but their primary duty was to assist in the establishment of a democratic government in the Federal Republic. Its first chancellor, the reserved, acerbic Konrad Adenauer, was a sharp contrast to the open, friendly McCloy. Yet the two soon found common ground in discontinuing the dismantling of German industry and granting the Federal Republic additional authority at a rate frowned upon in Washington, London, and Paris as well as in Moscow. The chancellor and the high commissioner were each seen as the lap dog of the other by their respective constituents.

Together McCloy and Adenauer laid the foundation for West Germany's integration into the combined economies and military forces of Western Europe. Achieving economic cooperation was facilitated by McCloy's longtime friendship with Jean Monnet, the central figure in integration efforts, but negotiations were complicated by the emergence of different plans and by acrimony among the French, British, and Americans over the prospect of a rearmed Germany. McCloy and Adenauer agreed on the necessity of linking West Germany, economically and militarily, to Western Europe, but many Germans complained that this would delay reunification. The Schuman plan, the first critical step on the path to economic integration, was enacted during McCloy's tenure as high commissioner. Military integration, which was much more contentious, came years later.

A less flattering aspect of McCloy's administration was covert intelligence operations that utilized the services of hundreds if not thousands of former Nazis, including Klaus Barbie, Reinhard Gehlen, and Franz Six, each of whom was notorious for brutality during the Third Reich. The extent of McCloy's detailed knowledge of these matters was never ascertained, but he unquestionably knew of and encouraged monetary support by the Central Intelligence Agency of anti-Soviet politicians, publications, and programs, such as highly publicized conferences of intellectuals. De-Nazification efforts, which were more extensive in the American zone of occupation than in the British and French zones, were scaled down in the face of the Soviet military and espionage threats that seemed particularly ominous with the 1950 outbreak of war in Korea. McCloy touched off a political conflagration when late that year and early the next he reduced the sentences of dozens of ex-Nazis convicted at the Nuremburg war trials, including Alfried Krupp, head of his family's industrial empire. These grants of clemency were condemned across the world except in West Germany, where McCloy was derided for not being more lenient.

McCloy left Germany in 1952. Some expected President Dwight Eisenhower to appoint him secretary of state. When that did not materialize, McCloy became chairman of Chase National Bank, renewing his ties with the Rockefellers, and arranged the merger that created the Chase Manhattan Bank. Beyond his banking duties, he served on the board of directors of several firms, cofounded the American Council on Germany, and was chairman of the Council on Foreign Relations (1953–1970) and of the Ford Foundation (1953–1970).

While he never again held a full-time government post, he continued to serve and advise presidents. After declining to serve as President John Kennedy's secretary of defense, McCloy agreed to develop an arms control and disarmament policy for the new president. Faced with substantial disagreement within the administration, McCloy's preference prevailed: the process would be step-by-step within the context of international law, not immediate disarmament. With the creation of the Arms Control and Disarmament Agency in October 1961, McCloy returned to his law practice while chairing the President's Advisory Committee on Disarmament, a part-time assignment. During the Cuban Missile Crisis in 1962, Kennedy called on McCloy to head a team that worked out details for withdrawing Soviet missiles from Cuba. After Kennedy's assassination in 1963, McCloy, with his decade-long work on the Black Tom conspiracy, became the most qualified member of the Warren Commission. He was instrumental in fleshing out a compromise conclusion of the findings. He always defended the report while conceding that in hindsight he would have changed portions of the investigation.

Later in the decade, despite his reservations about American military involvement in Vietnam and his refusal to be America's chief envoy in Saigon, McCloy joined others in supporting President Lyndon Johnson's expansion of military operations there. He became a member of the Committee for an Effective and Durable Peace in Asia, which was regularly consulted by Johnson in the mid-1960s. His views were also solicited by President Jimmy Carter in the 1970s regarding Cuba, the Panama Canal Treaty, arms control, Germany, and China, and he was among those who urged the president to grant asylum to the shah of Iran.

Until the end of his days, McCloy was the object of both abuse and praise. Though he was criticized for his role in the Japanese-American internment program and for his defense of U.S. policy in Vietnam, he never second-guessed himself or his colleagues. He died in Stamford, Connecticut.

• McCloy's papers are at Amherst College. McCloy's lectures were published in two books, *The Challenge to American Foreign Policy* (1953), based on his 1953 Edwin Godkin Lectures at Harvard, and *The Atlantic Alliance: Its Origin and Its Future* (1969), derived from his 1968 Benjamin F. Fairless Memorial Lectures at Carnegie-Mellon University. McCloy also published three articles, "The Great Military Decisions," *Foreign Affairs* 26, no. 1 (Oct. 1947), "The Lesson of the World Bank," *Foreign Affairs* 27, no. 4 (July 1949), and "Balance Sheet and Disarmament," *Foreign Affairs* 40, no. 3 (Apr. 1962). A full-length biography of McCloy is Kai Bird, *The Chairman* (1992), which is based on interviews with McCloy and about 100 associates and includes a lengthy bibliography. Also valuable but narrower in scope is Thomas Alan Schwartz, *America's Germany: John J. McCloy and the Federal Republic of Germany* (1991). Erika J. Fischer and Heinz-D. Fischer, eds., *John J. McCloy, an American Architect of Postwar Germany: Profiles of a Trans-Atlantic Leader and Communicator* (1994), is a collection of seventeen pieces, some written specifically for this book, by various German scholars and officials and includes McCloy's personal diary for the period he was high commissioner. Walter Isaacson and Evan Thomas, *The Wisemen: Six Friends and the World They Made* (1988), traces the intersecting careers of McCloy, Dean Acheson, Charles Bohlen, Averell Harriman, George Kennan, and Robert Lovett from youth to the middle 1980s. See also Alan Brinkley, "Minister without Portfolio," *Harper's*, Feb. 1983, pp. 30–46.

THOMAS P. WOLF

MCCLUNG, Clarence Erwin (5 Apr. 1870–17 Jan. 1946), biologist, was born in Clayton, California, the son of Charles Livingston McClung, a civil and min-

ing engineer, and Annie Howard Mackey. McClung's family moved about a great deal because of his father's profession. Only for his high school years did they settle in Columbus, Kansas, where McClung became interested in science, surveying, and pharmacy. In 1890 he enrolled in the University of Kansas School of Pharmacy, receiving a Ph.G. in 1892. He enrolled in the College of Liberal Arts there in 1893, receiving his B.A. in 1896, an M.A. in 1898, and a Ph.D. in 1902. As a graduate student, he was appointed as assistant professor of zoology in 1898, and in 1901 he was promoted to associate professor and head of the Department of Zoology. While at Kansas he married Anna Adelia Drake in 1899, with whom he had two children.

Further appointments at Kansas included curator of the paleontological collections (1902–1912), acting dean of the medical school (1902–1906), and professor of zoology (1906–1912). In 1912 he moved to the University of Pennsylvania, remaining there until he retired in 1940. Then followed an acting chairmanship at the University of Illinois in 1940–1941 and another in 1943–1944 at Swarthmore College. He also served as a trustee at the Marine Biological Laboratory at Woods Hole, Massachusetts, beginning in 1913; as chair of the Zoology Committee of the National Research Council in 1917; and as chair of the new Division of Biology and Agriculture of the National Research Council in 1919. In addition, he held a full complement of memberships in professional societies, serving as president of the American Society of Zoologists in 1914 and of the American Society of Naturalists in 1927 and as managing editor of the *Journal of Morphology* (1920–1946).

McClung spent the summer of 1898 visiting William Morton Wheeler's lab at the University of Chicago, where he studied spermatogenesis in *Xiphidium fasciatum*, a grasshopper, to complement Wheeler's own work on oogenesis. McClung identified what he called an "accessory chromosome" in the male, one which the female did not have. With cytological studies of chromosomal behavior, McClung suggested that the accessory chromosome determines sex—a topic of much debate at the time. McClung thought that it might do so in insects, though he felt that environmental factors may play a determining role as well, especially for humans. He also spent a semester visiting Edmund Beecher Wilson's lab at Columbia University, thus extending his discussions of chromosomal importance and sex determination.

In fact, McClung had miscounted the number of chromosomes; further studies revealed that females, not males, have the accessory chromosome that determines sex. However, by identifying the accessory chromosome and adding his voice to that of German cytologist Hermann Henking to suggest that chromosomes determine sex, he also provided evidence that chromosomes at least help to determine characteristics and thus to effect heredity from parent to offspring.

Sex determination, and particularly the role of chromosomes, became the focus of Wilson's research at

Columbia as well as that of American cytologist Nettie Stevens. By 1905 they had each independently shown that, for most animals they had studied, the female has two accessory, or sex-determining, chromosomes and the male one. This varied in some species, but it demonstrated the importance of the accessory chromosome and raised the possibility of studying that chromosome in more detail to discover what other characteristics it might determine. McClung's work, with its suggestive hypotheses and imperfect data, helped to stimulate a research program that became one of the most productive in the next few decades. McClung continued his own work on chromosomes, on the respective importance of heredity and development, and on microscopic techniques. He worked carefully and was recalled by one student as "an artist in everything he does." He died in Swarthmore, Pennsylvania.

• McClung's most important published works are "Notes on the Accessory Chromosome," *Anatomischer Anzeiger* 20 (1901): 220–26; "The Accessory Chromosome: Sex Determinant?" *Biological Bulletin* 2 (1902): 43–84; "A Comparative Study of Chromosomes in Orthopteran Spermatogenesis," *Journal of Morphology* 25 (1914): 651–749; and "The Cell Theory—What of the Future?" *American Naturalist* 74 (1939): 47–53. The most complete biographies of McClung are Garland E. Allen, "Clarence Erwin McClung," in *Dictionary of Scientific Biography* (1970), and D. H. Wenrich, "Clarence Erwin McClung," *Journal of Morphology* 66 (1940): 635–88, the latter written for McClung's seventieth birthday. Articles written about him during his lifetime are in *Bios* 11 (1940): 141–55.

JANE MAIENSCHEIN

MCCLURE, Alexander Kelly (9 Jan. 1828–6 June 1909), newspaper publisher and politician, was born in Sherman's Valley, Pennsylvania, the son of Alexander McClure and Isabella Anderson, farmers. He received his education from his parents and at local schools. He "got no further than long division and never learned how to phrase a sentence" (*Chicago Daily Tribune*, 7 June 1909). At age fourteen, he went to work as a tanner's apprentice. McClure entered the newspaper trade in his teens, first in Perry County and then as the publisher of the *Juniata Sentinel* (Mifflintown, Penn.) in 1846. His purchase of the Chambersburg *Franklin Repository* in 1852 gave him influence within the state's Whig party. He married Matilda S. Gray that same year; they had at least one child, a son.

McClure was the Whig candidate for auditor general in 1853 but was defeated. He read for the law and won admission to the bar in 1856. By the mid-1850s he had become active in the newly organized Republican party. Outspoken on the slavery question, he was a delegate to the party's national convention in 1856. Elected to the Pennsylvania House of Representatives in 1857, he was twice reelected in 1858 and 1859. In 1860 he was elected to the Pennsylvania Senate.

The Republican National Convention in 1860 brought McClure greater political recognition. Long identified as an opponent of Simon Cameron, an important figure in the Pennsylvania Republican organization, McClure could only get a place on the state's delegation to the Republican National Convention by pledging to support his old foe Cameron. Once at the party conclave, the young editor and his allies on the delegation played key roles in winning the state's vote for Illinois's Abraham Lincoln rather than New York's William Seward. As a reward for having backed the winner, McClure became chairman of the Republican state committee in the autumn of 1860, helped elect Andrew G. Curtin as governor, and was an important organizer and campaigner of the People's party, the name under which the Republicans and their anti-Democratic partners campaigned in Pennsylvania. The coalition won the state for Lincoln in November.

During the Civil War McClure took a leading role as chairman of the state senate committee on military affairs in generating statewide support for the war effort. Accepting a commission from President Lincoln as a U.S. assistant adjutant general in 1862, he placed seventeen regiments in the field. McClure endorsed Lincoln throughout the war. In later life he often recalled in lectures and in print his close dealings and personal exchanges with the president. While his Civil War links with Lincoln were genuine, and McClure's service was important to the Union cause in Pennsylvania, his personal relationship with the president got closer in the retelling. Lincoln's secretary, John Hay, was skeptical about McClure's exaggerated claims of intimacy with Lincoln. He called McClure one of the "professional liars" who had "written several volumes of reminiscences of Lincoln with whom I really think he never had two hours' conversation in his life" (Dennett, p. 136).

McClure remained active in Republican affairs throughout the 1860s. He supported Curtin for reelection in 1863 and served as a delegate to the Republican National Convention in 1864. That same year he won election to the Pennsylvania house again and helped Lincoln carry the state in the presidential contest. His health and his personal finances suffered as a result of his wartime exertions. McClure traveled in the West to regain his health and that of his wife and son during 1867; his book, *Three Thousand Miles through the Rocky Mountains* (1869), became a popular source about the West. As a delegate to the Republican National Convention in 1868, McClure supported Ulysses S. Grant and once again worked to put Pennsylvania in the GOP column.

Residing in Philadelphia from 1868 onward as a practicing lawyer (the disposition of his newspaper is unknown), McClure became more and more disenchanted with the direction of the Pennsylvania Republicans under Cameron's leadership. When his friends did not receive patronage support from the Grant administration, McClure sought to defeat the president for reelection. He backed the Liberal Republicans and their unsuccessful presidential candidate, Horace Greeley.

McClure gained a seat in the Pennsylvania Senate as an independent Republican in 1873. He ran for mayor of Philadelphia on a reform platform a year later but lost by 900 votes. His active career as an office seeker ended, and he began publishing the *Philadelphia Times* in 1875. His editorials attacked the political partisanship with which he was now disenchanted. He married Cora M. Gratz in 1879; they had no children. (It is not known what happened to his first wife.) Over the next decade, McClure moved more steadily toward the Democrats. By 1884 he was closely allied with Congressman Samuel J. Randall in negotiations that helped Grover Cleveland win the Democratic presidential nomination. He became a confidant of Cleveland who sought McClure's advice on subjects such as the 1887 annual message that set the strategy for the president's unsuccessful reelection bid.

During the 1890s, as the southern and western Democrats flirted with the inflationary doctrine of free silver, McClure wrote in favor of the gold standard. This ideological commitment and the waning power of the Cleveland Democrats moved him back toward the Republican party under William McKinley. He also championed the cause of Admiral William S. Schley in his well-publicized dispute with Admiral William Sampson over naval tactics and leadership during the battles with the Spanish navy off the coast of Cuba in the war with Spain in 1898. As further evidence of his renewed ties with the Grand Old Party, McClure advised the influential Republican leader in Pennsylvania, Matthew S. Quay, in state and municipal campaigns. McClure devoted himself to volumes of reminiscences in which his own part in events received prominent attention. He sold his interest in the *Philadelphia Times* in 1901 and retired with a comfortable fortune. However, he lost his money in the stock market within a few years. With the aid of former political enemies, he received an appointment as prothonotary (law clerk) of the Supreme Court of Pennsylvania, a lifetime appointment that brought him a generous annual salary of $12,000. He died at his farm in Wallingford, Pennsylvania, after a brief illness.

McClure's abundant reminiscences have made him a frequently cited source for the political history of the second half of the nineteenth century. He captured the spirit of the time effectively, but a careful assessment of his true role in the politics of his day remains to be published.

• McClure's personal papers did not survive him, but letters from him are in the Simon Cameron, Grover Cleveland, John Covode, Abraham Lincoln, Edward McPherson, John Nicolay, and Thaddeus Stevens papers, Manuscript Division, Library of Congress, and in the Fitz-John Porter Papers, Military History Institute, Carlisle Barracks, Penn. McClure wrote extensively about his own life, including *Lincoln and the Men of War Times* (1892), *Addresses, Literary, Political, Legal, and Miscellaneous* (1894–1895), *Colonel Alexander McClure's Recollections of Half a Century* (1902), and *Old Times Notes of Pennsylvania* (1905). For his early political career, see William H. Russell, "A. K. McClure and the People's Party in the Campaign of 1860," *Pennsylvania History* 28 (Oct. 1961): 335–45, and William E. Gienapp, *The Origins of the Republican Party, 1852–1856* (1987). Allan Nevins, *Gro-*

ver Cleveland: A Study in Courage* (1932); Tyler Dennett, *John Hay: From Poetry to Politics* (1933); and James A. Kehl, *Boss Rule in the Gilded Age: Matt Quay of Pennsylvania* (1981), deal with McClure's later career. Obituaries in the *Chicago Daily Tribune*, the *New York Tribune*, and the *New York Times*, all 7 June 1909, contain relevant biographical data on McClure.

LEWIS L. GOULD

MCCLURE, George (1770–16 Aug. 1851), soldier and public official, was born near Londonderry, Ireland. His ancestors had left Scotland for religious reasons in the seventeenth century. Working as a carpenter, at the age of twenty he decided to immigrate to the United States. He entered the new nation at Baltimore with only extra clothes and a chest of tools. After two years he set off on foot to see more of the country. In Pennsylvania he read an advertisement offering good pay to craftsmen who would come to Bath in western New York. En route to Bath, McClure passed through uninhabited land and crossed streams that had not yet been bridged. He joined a crew of thirty men tasked by an agent for a large landed interest to build houses as fast as they could in an attempt to hurry up settlement. In 1795 he married Eleanor Bole of Derry, Pennsylvania. After she died, he married Sarah Welles in 1808.

McClure, on his own time, tried anything that seemed to promise a profit. He bought land for 25 cents an acre, shipped barrel staves down the streams to Baltimore, 300 miles away, and got into trade. He lost thousands of dollars to debtors who slipped over into Canada but recouped some of his losses. Selling his carpenter's tools, McClure turned altogether to enterprise. Since credit was easy on the frontier and cash scarce, he built a flour mill and a sawmill and installed a carding machine. When it became unprofitable to ship wheat, he established a distillery and shipped the whiskey. He sent droves of cattle by land to Philadelphia, shipped flour by river flatboat to Baltimore, and built a substantial trade with the Seneca Indians by learning their language.

Success as a frontier entrepreneur paralleled a public career. McClure was at some time a justice of the peace, at another time a judge. At all times he remained unwavering as a radical temperance man and as an opponent of the extension of slavery. As a brigadier general in the New York militia, McClure served in the War of 1812 and took part in General Alexander Smyth's aborted campaign on the Niagara frontier in the late fall of 1812.

In September 1813, at the head of a brigade of 2,000 militiamen, McClure reported to Major General James Wilkinson at Fort George, on the Niagara frontier. He urged Wilkinson to lead an attack on the key British position, Burlington Heights, at the head of Lake Ontario. Wilkinson declined, instead following orders from Secretary of War John Armstrong to go with his troops to Sackets Harbor at the other end of the lake. On 30 October Major General William Henry Harrison arrived from the West, and McClure also urged him to attack Burlington Heights. Harrison agreed but received orders from Armstrong to take his forces and go to Sackets Harbor, where Armstrong was concentrating the army for an attack down the St. Lawrence to Montreal and Quebec.

McClure decried this strategy, which left him in the lurch. He found himself in command at Fort George, but his militia had served their contracted three months and returned to the United States. He had sixty regulars, most of them the sick left behind by Harrison, forty volunteers, and a band of Canadians who sided with the United States with which to defend the fort. The area for three miles around the fort was virtually stripped, so supplies had to come from Fort Niagara, across the river.

Colonel John Murray was approaching with 378 British regulars as well as some volunteers and Indians. McClure and a council of his officers decided that they must abandon Fort George. McClure himself determined that he must destroy the village of Newark, lying about a mile away toward the lake, on the grounds that Newark would sustain the British force and threaten Fort Niagara across the river. Armstrong on 4 October had written that defense of his area "may render it proper to destroy the town." McClure took this as his authority, but one of his colonels, Cyrenus Chapin, violently disagreed with the destruction.

Newark at this time had 400 residents and 300 buildings, including large stores, hotels, and two churches. At dusk on 10 December McClure notified the townspeople that he would burn their dwellings the next day. Snow was deep and the temperature was near zero. True to his word, at 1:00 P.M. on 11 December, he sent Joseph Willcocks, a Canadian with sympathies for the United States, with three companies carrying torches to burn down the village. One large usable barracks remained intact, and 1,500 tents were left standing, leaving some shelter for the British army.

McClure crossed over to Fort Niagara and then left for Buffalo to try to raise volunteers and to entreat the administration to send regulars. He described the militia as little better than an "infuriated mob" and Chapin as an "unprincipled disorganizer." Since the militia refused to serve any longer under him, he turned the command over to Amos Hall.

The British revenged Newark several times over. Murray captured Fort Niagara, inflicting heavy losses. British detachments then devastated all the small towns on the American bank of the Niagara River. Finally they burned both Black Rock and Buffalo. The Niagara Valley fell totally under British control.

McClure is noted in all histories of the War of 1812 because of his destruction of Newark. In some Canadian versions he is a monster; in most American histories, a failure. The 1813 winter campaign terminated his military career. Armstrong shifted all blame to McClure for abandoning Fort George and above all for burning Newark. In a booklet published in 1817 McClure struck back, charging Armstrong with error after error that prolonged the war in the West.

McClure overcame the onus of his military debacle and became a respected citizen. He returned to his enterprises, served as sheriff of Steuben County, New York, in 1815, and completed three terms in the New York legislature. In 1834 he moved to Elgin, Illinois, where he lived as a responsible citizen until his death there.

• For George McClure's account of the Niagara frontier campaign, see his *Causes of the Destruction of . . . the American . . . Towns on the Niagara Frontier* (1817). Also see G. H. McMaster, *History of the Settlement of Steuben County New York* (1835); William Kirby, *Annals of Niagara* (1927); and John K. Mahon, *War of 1812* (1972).

JOHN K. MAHON

MCCLURE, Robert Alexis (4 Mar. 1897–1 Jan. 1957), army officer, was born in Mattoon, Illinois, the son of George Hurlbert McClure, a railroad manager, and Harriet Julia Rudy. His mother remarried after George's death, and the family moved to Madison, Indiana. He attended the Kentucky Military Institute at Lyndon, Kentucky, graduating in 1915. Lured by the Orient, McClure traveled to the Philippines and joined the Philippine Constabulary as a junior officer, serving from 13 July 1916 to 9 August 1917. The constabulary had close relations with the U.S. Army, and under the manpower pressures of World War I, the army accepted even more recruits than usual from the Philippine military. Among them was McClure, who enlisted as a second lieutenant and was promoted to first lieutenant the same day.

Lieutenant McClure was assigned garrison duty with the U.S. Thirty-first Infantry on the Philippine island of Luzon until the fall of 1917, when he transferred to similar duty at Tientsin, China, with the Fifteenth Infantry. In China McClure met Marjory Leitch, whom he married on 11 November 1918, the day an armistice ended World War I, which the young officer had spent entirely in these Far Eastern assignments. The McClures would have two sons. McClure, now two years a captain, returned to Philippine duty in the summer of 1920. With the exception of a few months' temporary duty in the United States, McClure remained in the Philippines until late 1921, when he was seconded to the Twenty-ninth Infantry, a demonstration unit attached to the Army Infantry School at Fort Benning, Georgia. Thus began a long interval of interwar tours at various army schools, where McClure proved so adept a student that he was repeatedly retained as an instructor. Assignments included the Infantry School; the Cavalry School; the Command and General Staff School, where he took the prestigious two-year course, finishing in June 1932 and remaining as instructor; and the Army War College (1935–1936), where McClure, now a major, spent four additional years as a teacher and as executive officer, or second in command, of the facility.

McClure received promotion to lieutenant colonel in August 1940 and spent the final months of peace at San Francisco's Presidio base as personnel officer for the Fourth Army. He then went to London as assistant military attaché. Quickly elevated to senior attaché, he served additional duty as liaison to various European governments in exile there, including Greece, Poland, Czechoslovakia, Holland, Belgium, and Norway. Promoted to colonel in December 1941 and brigadier general just three months later, in the fall of 1942 McClure was reassigned to the Allied Force Headquarters that was preparing to invade French North Africa through Algeria and Morocco. As intelligence chief for that command, he supervised the collection and assembly of data on the opposing forces and political characteristics of the region. Following the North African invasion, McClure went to Algiers in December 1942 as chief of information and censorship, most importantly monitoring the activities of journalists in his area. McClure received a Distinguished Service Medal for his work in that post and returned to London in November 1943 to help plan press policy for the Normandy invasion. Six months later he was appointed chief of psychological warfare at the Supreme Headquarters Allied Expeditionary Forces (SHAEF) in charge of programs to induce the desertion of German soldiers, help break German morale, and undermine Germany's will to fight. General McClure continued to direct psychological warfare activities throughout the remainder of the war and for two years afterward. Following the war his main task, using similar techniques, became to reorient or "denazify" the German press. McClure returned to the United States in June 1947 to hold posts in military civil affairs planning. In January 1949 he was assigned as assistant commander of the Fourth Infantry Division at Fort Ord, California. It was the first troop command McClure had held since the 1920s.

When the army established a staff section at Washington headquarters level to control all psychological warfare functions in September 1950, McClure became its first chief. In that capacity McClure played a formative role in setting up war plans opposing the Soviet Union that provided for avoidance of attacks against people of certain nationalities and ethnic groups in the hope of promoting internal dissension within the Soviet Union. McClure also motivated the army to create regular units for field operations called psychological warfare battalions. Contributing to the interest in unconventional warfare that led to formation of the Special Forces (Green Berets), he argued that the army possessed greater capacity for information operations and psychological warfare than even the State Department. During the Korean War (1950–1953) many such psychological operations occurred, and McClure was also instrumental in establishing the concept of "voluntary repatriation," under which Chinese Communist prisoners held by United Nations forces would be returned to China only if they wished to go. In March 1953 McClure was sent to Teheran, Iran, as chief of the U.S. Military Assistance Advisory Group in that country, but there is no evidence that he had any part in the coup d'état sponsored there by the Central Intelligence Agency five months later. McClure was promoted to major general in the summer of 1955 and retired on 31 May 1956, intending to make his home in Carmel, California. En route across the United States, however, McClure was stricken while visiting at Fort Huachuca, Arizona, and died there of a coronary thrombosis.

• As far as is known, the McClure papers remain in possession of the family. No biography has yet been published, apart from standard reference sources. See Harry C. Butcher, *My Three Years with Eisenhower* (1946), and Irving Dillard, *The Development of a Free Press in Germany* (1949). For McClure's influence on unconventional warfare, see Alfred H. Paddock, Jr., *U.S. Army Special Warfare: Its Origins* (1982). An obituary is in the *New York Times*, 5 Jan. 1957.

JOHN PRADOS

MCCLURE, Samuel Sidney (17 Feb. 1857–21 Mar. 1949), editor and publisher, was born in Frocess, County Antrim, Ireland, the son of Thomas McClure, a farmer and then a Glasgow shipyard worker, and Elizabeth Gaston. McClure, the eldest of four sons, was very bright, loved school, and read voraciously. His father was killed in a shipyard accident when the boy was eight. A year later his mother migrated with her sons to Indiana, where four of her siblings were living. She married a farmer in Valparaiso in 1867 and had four more children. McClure enjoyed high school, but when his stepfather died in 1873, he and his brothers returned to work the farm. In 1874 he entered Knox College, in Galesburg, Illinois, where he was enrolled for eight years, interrupted by work and a trip home to Ireland with his mother. While in college, he edited the *Knox Student* and established the Western College Associated Press. After graduating in 1882, he got a job in Boston with Colonel Albert A. Pope, the famous bicycle manufacturer, who persuaded him to establish and edit a monthly magazine about cycling, to be financed by Pope. The *Wheelman* appeared in August 1882 and was enthusiastically received. McClure was launched. In 1883 he married Harriet Hurd, the daughter of one of his Knox professors. The couple had four children and adopted one more child.

The year 1884 was momentous for McClure. When Pope merged his *Wheelman* with *Outing*, McClure briefly coedited the new magazine, which was called *Outing*. He then obtained a job with a New York printing firm, became a junior editor of the *Century*, soon quit, and announced the formation of his own literary syndicate. By much pluck and travel, and a little prevaricating, he gathered publishable stories and poems from a few writers and promises from newspaper editors to publish the items—each editor to pay a small fee but all to publish. The first editors to sign on were in St. Paul and San Francisco. McClure went into debt, often felt desperate, and had to cajole writers into waiting for their pay. Neophytes were willing to do so because it was hard for some of them to get published at all. By mid-1885 McClure was in the black. His first authors were of three sorts: established figures, those unremembered later, and his own discoveries. By 1887, with his college friend John Sanborn

Phillips, who had worked with him on the *Wheelman*, in the office as his reliable business manager, McClure was able to visit Europe in search of talent. (Later, he did so almost annually.)

In 1892 he decided to found his own monthly magazine, for two purposes: to outsell, by keeping the price down, the *Atlantic*, *Century*, and *Harper's Weekly*, all of which were more expensive, and to promote literary realism in a vast readership of ordinary subscribers. He had 2,000 unpublished manuscripts in his syndicate files, which could go into his new periodical. *McClure's Magazine*, ultimately an enormous success, began in 1893 under adverse circumstances. The financial panic of that year froze the currency system, and many of McClure's syndicate debtors could not meet their obligations to him. He sold future advertising space to his old employer Pope and also offered stock in the magazine, two substantial investors being Henry Drummond, the well-to-do scientist-theologian, and Arthur Conan Doyle, the famous fiction writer, both of whom happened to be on tour lecturing in the United States and published through McClure. A major coup was McClure's hiring Ida M. Tarbell, whom he first met in Paris in 1893 when she was doing research there. He persuaded her to write a biography of Napoleon, which he serialized in *McClure's* in 1894–1895. Next, he published installments of her biography of Abraham Lincoln in two parts (1895–1896, 1898–1899). It was published in book form (2 vols., 1900) by McClure and Frank Nelson Doubleday, who had been associates since 1897 and who issued a hundred or so books in 1899. Doubleday left McClure to form his own successful house with Walter Hines Page, which began publishing in 1900. Doubleday had been rendered uneasy when the mercurial McClure made an offer—quickly vacated—to buy the publishing house of Harper & Brothers in 1899. McClure rebounded in 1900 by establishing McClure, Phillips & Company, to publish books.

By this time, *McClure's* was carrying a greater quantity of advertising than any other magazine in the world and could boast the following authors, among many others: Gertrude Atherton, Rex Beach, Ned Buntline, Stephen Crane, Bret Harte, Joel Chandler Harris, O. Henry, Julia Ward Howe, Owen McMahon Johnson, Myra Kelly, Rudyard Kipling, Jack London, John Ruskin, Robert Louis Stevenson, Charles Algernon Swinburne, Booth Tarkington, and Emile Zola—most of whom McClure knew personally. The magazine also published excellent short biographies of eminent persons and fascinating articles on animals, exploration, and scientific discoveries. Its poetry section was its weakest feature. Circulation figures are truly remarkable: first issue, 8,000 copies; 1894, 30,000; 1895, 175,000; 1896, 250,000; 1899, 360,000.

McClure was a genius at assembling talented staffs, but he was also an exasperating leader. In addition to Tarbell, notables who worked closely with him included Ray Stannard Baker, Joseph Lincoln Steffens, and—as poetry editor—Witter Bynner. McClure's manuscript reader was Viola Roseboro', who was both loyal and uncanny in recognizing talent in unknown writers. She first spotted O. Henry, Damon Runyon, and Booth Tarkington, among others, including Bynner himself, who later signed A. E. Housman and William Butler Yeats to publish in *McClure's*. Its January 1903 number has been called the most important single issue in the history of early twentieth-century periodical publication. It included Baker's "The Right to Work: The Story of Non-striking Miners," Steffens's "The Shame of Minneapolis," and the third installment of Tarbell's exposé of the Standard Oil Company. These three writers, soon joined by others that McClure recruited, fought against the victimizing of ordinary people by corrupt politicians, industrialists, bankers, church officials, and labor leaders. Muckraking had burst upon the public consciousness and would continue as a forceful intellectual movement considerably beyond McClure's personal interest in it.

In 1906, with his magazine circulation at 400,000, McClure planned to reorganize and expand his concerns yet again. This time he failed to consult his associates. He envisioned the development of more modern distribution facilities, the publication of textbooks and reference books, and the establishment of an insurance company, a bank, employee housing, and a charitable foundation. Most of his staff, many of whom were stockholders in his company, rebelled at his dictatorial decision making. So he bought out Phillips, at which point Steffens, Tarbell, and a few others also left him and, with Phillips, purchased and began to improve the *American Magazine*, which had been *Leslie's Monthly Magazine* and then the *American Illustrated Magazine*. In 1907 McClure, with his magazine circulation peaking at almost a half-million, started to build a huge plant on Long Island at an enormous cost overrun—eventually to a reported $700,000. His magazine sales fell because of the panic of 1907 and despite new muckrakers, including Will Irwin and C. P. Connolly, who wrote, respectively, about city combinations of vice, commerce, and politics, and about corruption in Montana politics and mining.

By 1911 McClure was in poor health and also on a perilous financial slide. Years of slick maneuvering had not helped permanently. After rejecting other options, he was forced to sell his magazine to a combination. It had been formed by Frederick Lewis Collins, the editor of *Woman's Home Companion*, and Cameron Mackenzie, McClure's trusted son-in-law and a competent editor and author, with financial help from Holland Duell, an attorney who had married into a wealthy family. McClure was told that he could remain as editor at an annual salary of $25,000. But in 1912 he was ousted as editor and was given a token stipend of $10,000 a year.

McClure engaged his associate Willa Cather to ghostwrite his life's story, which was called simply *My Autobiography* and was published in 1914. During the same year, his old magazine suspended publication. He became editor of the pro-German newspaper the *New York Evening Mail* from 1915 to 1917. Soon after

World War I began, he joined Henry Ford's Peace Ship pilgrimage, which in 1915 sailed to several European ports in Ford's noble but fruitless attempt to halt hostilities. McClure jumped ship in Copenhagen, later explaining, lamely, that he went with Ford only out of personal friendship. He proceeded alone to Germany in 1916 on a fact-finding mission, returned to New York, and visited England that summer, where he was initially regarded as pro-German. After a quick trip to France, he returned home, lectured on peace efforts, and published *Obstacles to Peace* (Mar. 1917), in which he blamed blundering politicians in general for the war but mainly indicted German leaders. McClure acted as editor again of the moribund *McClure's* from 1921 through 1924, but in name only. (It was sold to Hearst's International Publications in 1925 and disappeared five years later.)

The remaining decades for McClure were tragic. In 1926 he had an audience with Benito Mussolini, arranged for a series of articles on him, agreed to pay Mussolini's mistress lavishly for her cooperation, and sold the results to the *Saturday Evening Post* at a profit. He was not the only former muckraker impressed by the efficiency of antidemocratic tyrants. He was personally devastated by his wife's death in 1929, and he was professionally disgusted by criticism of his part in the muckraking movement, notably by alleged distortions in Steffens's 1931 autobiography. Although McClure had a home in Brookfield Center, Connecticut, he spent his last years mostly in a New York hotel, living in part on the charity of relatives and friends. He died in a Bronx hospital. In his prime, McClure was a phenomenally vigorous and hard-hitting editor whose publications benefited numerous specific authors and innumerable fellow citizens.

• Most of McClure's widely scattered correspondence is in the Alderman Library at the University of Virginia, the Butler Library at Columbia, the Houghton Library at Harvard, the Howard-Tilton Memorial Library at Tulane, the Lilly Library at Indiana University, and the Reis Library at Allegheny College. McClure's *My Autobiography* is not completely reliable. The fullest biography is Peter Lyon, *Success Story: The Life and Times of S. S. McClure* (1963). *All in the Day's Work* (1939), Ida M. Tarbell's autobiography, contains valuable information about her work with McClure. James Woodress, *Willa Cather: A Literary Life* (1987), details Cather's professional relationship with McClure. Frank Luther Mott, *A History of American Magazines, 1885–1905* (1957), summarizes the history and contents of *McClure's Magazine*. Harold S. Wilson, *"McClure's Magazine" and the Muckrakers* (1970), discusses McClure's role in the early days of the muckraking movement. Robert Miraldi, *Muckraking and Objectivity: Journalism's Colliding Traditions* (1990), considers McClure's competing concerns with objectivity, activism, and circulation figures. Obituaries are in the *New York Times*, with portrait, and the *New York Herald Tribune*, both 23 Mar. 1949.

ROBERT L. GALE

MCCLURG, James (1746–9 July 1823), physician and delegate to the Federal Convention of 1787, was born in Elizabeth City County, Virginia, the son of Walter McClurg, a British naval surgeon (mother's name unknown). His father had been sent to Hampton, Virginia, to open a hospital for inoculation against smallpox. Since the practice of inoculation had been introduced into the American colonies only a few years earlier, this was probably the first hospital of its kind in America.

After graduating from the College of William and Mary in 1762, McClurg studied medicine at the University of Edinburgh and earned his doctor of medicine there in 1770. He then studied for a time in Paris and London, where he came into contact with many of the scientific pioneers of the Enlightenment. In 1772 he published *Experiments upon the Human Bile and Reflections on the Biliary Excretion*, which furthered medical knowledge of the functions of human intestines and earned him a European reputation. It was translated into several languages. He returned to Virginia in 1773 and established a medical practice in Williamsburg. During the American Revolution he served as a surgeon to the American navy at Hampton, and in 1777 he was named physician general and director of hospitals for Virginia's military forces. In 1779 he married Elizabeth Selden, the daughter of a prominent lower James River planter and slaveowner. That same year he was chosen to fill the newly created chair of anatomy and medicine at the College of William and Mary, a post he held until 1783, when he moved to Richmond.

There is good evidence of McClurg's engaging personality, and his contacts with the scientific Enlightenment during his stay in Europe no doubt won him respect among Virginia's elite. In 1782–1783 James Madison (1751–1836), then a delegate to the Continental Congress, advocated the appointment of McClurg to succeed Robert R. Livingston (1746–1813) as secretary of foreign affairs for the United States. The move did not succeed, but it was a sign of the respect that McClurg was earning in Virginia's political circles. In 1784 he was appointed to the Council of State, a body that advised the governor, where he served until 1794.

In the spring of 1787, after Patrick Henry and Richard Henry Lee declined to serve in the Philadelphia Convention, the House of Delegates placed McClurg on the Virginia delegation. Madison later admitted in his notes on the Federal Convention that he had "actively promoted" McClurg's candidacy. Madison no doubt knew McClurg as a staunch advocate of strong central government who would be a dependable ally in the convention.

McClurg's federalist sympathies became evident early in the convention. On 8 June, when the convention was debating the broad outlines of Madison's Virginia Plan, McClurg supported a proposal to give the national legislature a veto over state laws. This was too extreme a measure for the majority of delegates; Virginia was one of only three states that voted in favor of it.

McClurg took the convention floor on only two occasions. Both dealt with the executive, which McClurg maintained should be both strong and independent. After the convention determined that there would be a single "Executive Magistrate" chosen by the "National Legislature," it was proposed that the term of office should be seven years, with ineligibility for a second term. When ineligibility was deleted by a vote of 6 states to 4, McClurg moved to strike out seven years and insert "during good behavior." Because the executive was to be chosen by the legislature, McClurg argued, he would be forever dependent upon it for reelection. Since judges were to hold office "during good behavior" in order to render them independent, McClurg thought the same principle ought to apply to the executive. When it was objected that a life tenure for the executive risked the establishment of a monarchy, McClurg replied that he "was not so much afraid of the shadow of monarchy as to be unwilling to approach it; nor so wedded to Republican Govt. as not to be sensible of the tyrannies that had been & may be exercised under that form." The convention was not persuaded, and his motion lost by a vote of 4 states to 6 (Virginia among the "ayes").

Three days later, 20 July, McClurg was still fretting about the powers of the executive. He asked the convention how the executive was to enforce the laws. Was it to be given a military force for the purpose, for instance, or would it be dependent on the cooperation of state militias? The convention decided to leave this tricky issue up to the Committee of Detail. It was McClurg's last appearance. A few days later he left the convention and returned to Virginia.

McClurg resumed his medical practice and returned to public life only once more, serving as mayor of Richmond in 1801–1802. He was elected president of the state medical society in 1820 and 1821. He died in Richmond.

• Sketches of the life of James McClurg can be found in J. B. McCaw, *A Memoir of James McClurg, M.D.* (1854), and in H. A. Kelly and W. L. Burrage, *American Medical Biographies* (1920). For his role in the Federal Convention see Max Farrand, *The Records of the Federal Convention* (3 vols., 1911). His correspondence with Madison is in Robert A. Rutland, ed., *The Papers of James Madison*, vol. 10 (1962). For the political milieu of Virginia in McClurg's time see Norman K. Risjord, *Chesapeake Politics, 1781–1800* (1978).

NORMAN K. RISJORD

MCCLURG, Joseph Washington (22 Feb. 1818–2 Dec. 1900), congressman and governor of Missouri, was born in St. Louis County, Missouri, the son of Joseph McClurg, an ironmaker, and Mary Brotherton. His father died when McClurg was seven, and his mother sent him to Pittsburgh, Pennsylvania, to be raised by relatives. Originally named Joseph Edwin McClurg, at age thirteen he legally adopted Washington as his middle name in honor of the man on whose birthday he had been born. Shortly thereafter he rejoined his mother in Xenia, Ohio, where he attended the local academy. From 1833 to 1835 he enrolled at Oxford College (later Miami University). He then taught school for a year in Carroll Parish, Louisiana.

From 1837 to 1839 McClurg served as a deputy under his uncle, James Brotherton, who had become sheriff of St. Louis County. He moved to Columbus, Texas, in 1839 and was employed as clerk of the circuit court for the next two years, during which time he studied law and was admitted to the bar. En route to Texas he had stopped briefly at a boardinghouse in Farmington, Missouri, where he met Mary Catherine Johnson, daughter of the proprietress. An active correspondence followed, and they were married in 1841, soon after he returned to Missouri; they had eight children. With the help of his wife's stepfather, William D. Murphy, McClurg established a mercantile business at Hazelwood, Webster County, in the heart of the Missouri Ozarks. In addition he prospected a number of lead mines in the vicinity during the 1840s and built two smelters to produce lead bars for exportation to markets as distant as St. Louis and New Orleans. He also established a profitable connection with the James Iron Works at Maramec, Missouri.

In April 1849 McClurg organized a party of two dozen wagons and headed for the California gold rush. He settled at Georgetown, where he opened a mercantile store to furnish goods for the nearby miners. He returned to Missouri two years later and moved to Linn Creek in Camden County to go into business with his father-in-law and brother-in-law. McClurg, Murphy, Jones, and Company became a major merchant-distributor of all kinds of trading goods throughout the upper Ozarks region, including beef and pork processed at its own slaughterhouse. By 1860 the company was carrying $100,000 in stock and had $300,000 in accounts receivable.

McClurg was elected in 1861 to the state convention called to determine Missouri's course regarding secession, which he strongly opposed. When war broke out, he organized and equipped seventeen companies of local men, known as the Osage Regiment of Missouri Volunteers, and became colonel of the Eighth Cavalry, Missouri Militia, a unit designated for duty on the home front. As guerrilla warfare broke out along the western border of Missouri and penetrated the Ozarks region, McClurg became a strong supporter of the developing emancipation movement in the state. He served as temporary chairman of the state convention called by B. Gratz Brown in June 1862 to promote that cause and the following November was elected as an Emancipationist to Congress, where he served three terms. He favored immediate action with some form of apprenticeship for the newly freed slaves. He freed his own slaves, inherited from his wife, who had died in 1861, in the fall of 1863, keeping some in his employ while helping others hire out to neighbors. Not all of his neighbors supported McClurg's views, however, and twice during the war, his business fell victim to raids from pro-southern guerrillas, who attacked and burned his storehouses at Linn Creek.

In Congress McClurg quickly joined forces with the Radicals led by Thaddeus Stevens of Pennsylvania. In the early political maneuvering of 1864, McClurg, with other Missouri Radicals, leaned toward Secretary of the Treasury Salmon P. Chase as a Republican presidential candidate to replace Abraham Lincoln. When Conservative Unionist congressman General Frank Blair launched an attack on Chase on the floor of the House, McClurg responded by accusing Blair of corruption in dispensing liquor and tobacco to his troops. Blair ridiculed McClurg in return and demanded an investigation, which proved his innocence. The enmity between the two men would carry over into postwar Missouri politics.

When the Radicals gained control of the Missouri state government in the election of 1864, McClurg supported their revision of the state constitution at the hands of Charles D. Drake. This document strongly proscribed former Confederates while seeking to promote a number of social and economic reforms including immediate emancipation, establishment of public education for both blacks and whites, and the establishment of an immigration agency. Aided by a stringent test oath (which required that former Confederates and their sympathizers state that they had never sympathized with the South let alone actively supported it) and registry law (which left it up to local Radical appointees to determine who should be eligible to vote under these provisions), McClurg was elected governor in 1868 by a 20,000-vote margin. As governor he sought to promote equal albeit segregated educational opportunities for both black and white students and supported woman suffrage. Much of his administration was embroiled in controversy over the removal of proscriptions against the former Confederates and the enfranchisement of the state's blacks. With the passage of the Fifteenth Amendment in the spring of 1870, the Missouri legislature decided that the reenfranchisement of former Confederates could be safely considered and proposed a constitutional amendment to that effect. Although McClurg generally supported the move, he refused to give it official party sanction in his reelection campaign that fall, leading to a split in the Missouri Radical Union party and the emergence of the Liberal Republicans. Helped by the Democrats' not nominating a candidate of their own, the Republican leader, Brown, defeated McClurg in the election.

McClurg retired to Linn Creek and resumed his mercantile business and mining and smelting enterprises. He also became involved in steamboat operations on the Osage River. In June 1886 he joined a son-in-law, who had homesteaded in South Dakota, but returned to Lebanon, Missouri, in the summer of 1887, where he made his home for the remainder of his life. He was appointed registrar of the Federal Land Office at Springfield during the Benjamin Harrison administration (1889–1893). He died on his daughter's farm near Lebanon.

• McClurg's papers are included in the Draper-McClurg Collection, which is in private hands. A microfilm copy is available at the Western Historical Manuscripts Collection at the University of Missouri at Columbia. Lynn Morrow, "Joseph Washington McClurg: Entrepreneur, Politician, Citizen," *Missouri Historical Review* 78 (Jan. 1984): 168–201, is based on this collection. A five-page autobiography, written in May 1863, can be found in the Charles Lanman Collection within the Western Historical Manuscripts Collection. Helpful biographical sketches are C. C. Draper, "Joseph Washington McClurg," in *The Messages and Proclamations of the Governors of the State of Missouri*, vol. 4, ed. Floyd C. Shoemaker and Grace G. Avery (1924); and James S. Botsford, "Gov. Joseph W. McClurg and His Administration," *Missouri Historical Review* 6 (July 1912): 182–91.

WILLIAM E. PARRISH

MCCOLLUM, Elmer Verner (3 Mar. 1879–15 Nov. 1967), biochemist, was born near Fort Scott, Kansas, the son of Cornelius Armstrong McCollum, a farmer, and Martha Catherine Kidwell. A typical upbringing on a lonely farmstead in the Midwest was offset by McCollum's mother, who insisted that the family move to a farm near Lawrence, Kansas, so that her two sons could obtain formal schooling. McCollum completed both his undergraduate and master's degrees at the University of Kansas in 1903 and 1904, respectively, with chemistry as his principal interest. He obtained his doctorate from Yale University in 1906 with the dissertation "Researches in Organic Chemistry." He worked as a postdoctorate fellow for another year, taking courses in physiology and physiological chemistry with Lafayette B. Mendel, Russell Chittenden, and others at Yale's Sheffield Scientific School. He also did laboratory research in protein and amino acid chemistry with Thomas B. Osborne for six months at the Connecticut Agricultural Experiment Station.

Upon Mendel's recommendation, McCollum was employed by the Wisconsin Agricultural Experiment Station in Madison in July 1907 to do chemical analyses of food, blood, and excreta of cows restricted to feed from single plant sources, a long-term experiment being conducted to determine the nutritional characteristics of corn, wheat, and oats. Although the experiment showed significant differences in the cattle, McCollum despaired of ever finding chemical differences in feeds, which seemed too complex. A literature search showed him that other investigators had tried similar experiments with smaller animals such as mice, rabbits, and rats. Operating on the biological fact that mature white rats reproduce in twenty-one days, McCollum inaugurated the first white rat colony devoted solely to nutritional study in January 1908. He believed that using live animals with short life spans and rapid reproductive rates would provide better answers to the problems of adequate nutrition. Two of McCollum's mentors at Yale, Osborne and Mendel, started their own rat colony in 1909 and within ten years there were hundreds of such colonies in the United States alone. McCollum was the first to systematize the principle of biological analysis in nutritional studies, that is, the feeding of living animals to determine the differential value of foods.

These investigations, focused on animal requirements of proteins, fats, carbohydrates, and minerals, soon led McCollum to confirm the work of Osborne and Mendel showing that proteins varied widely in their ability to support normal growth and maintenance. And, until 1912, McCollum, like other researchers, believed that all fats were alike in nutritional value. In that year, however, he discovered that he was wrong about fat nutrition. In 1913 he and colleague Marguerite Davis published the first paper demonstrating that something in butter fat not present in olive oil made rats grow ("The Necessity of Certain Lipins in the Diet during Growth," *Journal of Biological Chemistry* 15 [1913]: 167–75). McCollum had discovered vitamin A. By 1916 additional research by McCollum and others showed that there were at least two such substances that the experimental animals needed, and McCollum named the first fat-soluble A and the second water-soluble B. Thus was born the alphabetical nomenclature of the vitamins, organic chemical substances required by living organisms in only trace amounts.

In 1917 McCollum became head of the Department of Biochemistry in the new School of Public Health and Hygiene at Johns Hopkins University in Baltimore, a position he held until his retirement in 1944. At Hopkins he continued his researches in nutrition, contributing much to the elaboration of vitamin D as well as widening the understanding of vitamins in animal nutrition. He also conducted investigations into the roles of various mineral salts such as phosphorus, iron, zinc, magnesium, and manganese in animal diets.

The results of McCollum's work also appeared outside scientific journals. He was a regular nutrition contributor to *McCall's Magazine* for many years and wrote articles for other periodicals aimed at the general public. The first edition of his book, *The Newer Knowledge of Nutrition*, was published in 1918 (the fifth and last edition appeared in 1939). Another of his books, *A History of Nutrition* (1957), is one of the best texts for the nonspecialist to learn a great deal about nutrition. In addition, McCollum's belief that scientific discoveries should be translated to the public at large resulted in his appointment to many advisory panels and committees on nutritional well-being. He was an outspoken advocate of the dairy industry and a fervent opponent of the enrichment of breads with synthetic vitamins and minerals, believing rather that the addition of nonfat milk solids, brewer's yeast, and wheat and corn germs would better improve the nutritional value of flour and bread. Until the end of his life, McCollum held that "natural foods" were better than diets supplemented with synthetic substances.

When Elmer McCollum died in Baltimore, he was survived by his second wife, Ernestine Becker McCollum, and by the five children of his first marriage, which had taken place in 1907 and had ended in divorce in 1944. He was a member of the National Academy of Sciences, the American Society of Biological Chemists, and the American Institute of Nutrition. McCollum pioneered the use of biological analysis as the principal tool to measure and evaluate many of the characteristics of adequate nutrition and received nu-

merous awards, medals, and honorary degrees as testimony to his achievements.

• There are no known repositories of McCollum's notebooks, correspondence, or plan books. Some correspondence is found in scattered locations such as the Thomas B. Osborne Files at the Connecticut Agricultural Experiment Station (New Haven); History File, Department of Biochemistry, University of Wisconsin (Madison); and the library of the University of Kansas (Lawrence). McCollum's autobiography, *From Kansas Farm Boy to Scientist* (1964), lacks a definitive picture of the author's attainments.

McCollum's contributions are exemplified by such publications as McCollum and Marguerite Davis, "Observations on the Isolation of the Substance in Butter Fat Which Exerts a Stimulating Influence on Growth," *Journal of Biological Chemistry* 19 (1914): 245–50; McCollum, Nina Simmonds, and William Pitz, "The Relation of the Unidentified Dietary Factors, the Fat-soluble A, and the Water-soluble B, of the Diet to the Growth Promoting Properties of Milk," *Journal of Biological Chemistry* 27 (1916): 33–43; McCollum, Helen T. Parsons, Paul G. Shipley, and Edwards A. Park, "Studies on Experimental Rickets. I. The Production of Rachitis and Similar Diseases in the Rat by Deficient Diets," *Journal of Biological Chemistry* 45 (1921): 333–41; and McCollum and Elsa R. Orent, "Effects of Deprivation of Manganese in the Rat," *Journal of Biological Chemistry* 92 (1931): 651–78.

The best biographical sketch is Harry G. Day, "Elmer Verner McCollum, 1879–1967," National Academy of Sciences, *Biographical Memoirs* 45 (1974): 262–335. A highly personal sketch is Agatha A. Rider, "Elmer Verner McCollum—A Biographical Sketch (1879–1967)," *Journal of Nutrition* 100 (1970): 1–10. An evaluation of McCollum's experimental work at the University of Wisconsin is found in Stanley Leonard Becker, "The Emergence of a Trace Nutrient Concept through Animal Feeding Experiments" (Ph.D. diss., Univ. of Wisconsin, 1968).

STANLEY L. BECKER

MCCOMAS, Louis Emory (28 Oct. 1846–10 Nov. 1907), politician and judge, was born on a farm near Williamsport, Washington County, Maryland, the son of Frederick C. McComas, a farmer and merchant, and Catherine Angle. After attending the public schools of Williamsport, he studied for three years at St. James' College, a private academy, then completed his schooling at Dickinson College in Pennsylvania, graduating with high honors in 1866. Although McComas did not serve in the military, he was still touched by the Civil War. In 1863 his father was one of several prominent western Marylanders arrested and briefly held as a hostage by Confederate general Jubal Early. Years later, as a congressman and senator, McComas helped settle the claims of Maryland Unionists for property damages inflicted by Confederate troops, worked to preserve the Antietam battlefield under government auspices, and seemed to revel in sharp exchanges with southern Democratic legislators. In 1866, however, he applied his energies to the study of law. He read law for two years in Cambridge and Hagerstown, Maryland. He was admitted to the Washington County bar in 1868 and practiced in Hagerstown until 1892, serving as the senior partner in the firm of L. E. and F. F. McComas for most of those years.

McComas was an able lawyer but was best known for his national service as a legislator and jurist. He was the first public official to hold a seat for several terms in Congress, then win a federal judicial appointment with lifetime tenure, leave the federal court to enter the Senate, and subsequently receive a second life term seat on the federal bench. In 1875 he married Leah Humrichhouse. They had one daughter who survived to adulthood. An orthodox and scrupulously loyal Republican, McComas ran for Congress in 1876, losing by fourteen votes. In 1882 he was elected to the first of four consecutive terms in the House of Representatives, where he served from 1883 to 1891. Although never a leader among congressional Republicans, McComas quickly established himself as a frequent and energetic debater. Most notable in that regard was his success in overriding a presidential veto by Grover Cleveland to obtain a Civil War pension for one of his constituents. Beyond his efforts on behalf of his state, McComas also demonstrated a talent for the technical challenges of legislation. He offered an amendment that clarified the intent of the Contract Labor Law of 1884 and, as part of his special interest in the administration of the District of Columbia, arranged for the preparation of a workable criminal code for the District. His primary achievements in the House were nevertheless oratorical rather than legislative and reflected his deep Republican loyalties. He offered a rejoinder to Democratic calls for the unlimited coinage of silver currency that later circulated as a campaign document and, in 1890, vigorously supported Henry Cabot Lodge's Force Bill that proposed federal supervision of southern congressional elections. After his spirited defense of the Force Bill, McComas provoked a sympathetic demonstration in the House gallery by saying to Richard Bland of Missouri, "I denounce you and those like you, because in the Southern States you do not treat the black men and the white men alike" (*Congressional Record*, 51st Cong., 1st sess., 28 June 1890, p. 6679).

After four terms representing a district that he described as "about 'a tie'" in its party divisions, McComas was defeated for reelection in 1890, partly because of his vote that year for the protectionist McKinley Tariff. He attended the Republican National Convention as a delegate in 1892 (he served again in 1900 and 1902) and was named secretary of the Republican National Committee for the 1892 campaign. After the 1892 election, President Benjamin Harrison appointed him associate justice of the Supreme Court of the District of Columbia. McComas performed his judicial duties with dignity and probity, remaining on the bench until he entered the U.S. Senate in March 1899.

Elected by one of Maryland's infrequent Republican-controlled legislatures to take the place of the powerful Democrat Arthur Pue Gorman, McComas loyally served the interests of his party during his six-year Senate tenure. In 1901 he left Washington and hurried to Annapolis to fight Democratic efforts to disfranchise black Maryland voters, most of whom were Republicans. On the floor of the Senate, aside from steering money toward the Naval Academy and the Baltimore Customhouse, McComas was most adamant in his advocacy of Republican foreign policy during the period of imperial expansion that followed the war with Spain. He served on the Committees for Puerto Rico and the Philippines, in each case helping to craft legal systems that bound those territories to the interests of the United States. In May 1902, when reports of American atrocities committed during the war against Filipino nationalists were aired by Senate Democrats, McComas delivered an impassioned defense of the American military and civil administration of the Philippines, comparing Republican policy there favorably to the ballot restrictions and flurry of lynching that disgraced the American South. Similarly, after Theodore Roosevelt's administration quickly recognized the revolutionary Panamanian republic and moved to secure a canal route across its territory, McComas swiftly acted to defend Roosevelt from Democratic critics. "What quixotic scruples constrain Senators to delay for years the fulfillment of our pledge to the world to excavate the great canal?" he asked, adding that the "Republican Administration was right in Hawaii, right in Cuba, right in Porto [*sic*] Rico, right in the Philippines, and . . . is right again in the Panama incident" (*Congressional Record*, 58th Cong., 2d sess., 4 Jan. 1904, pp. 430, 432).

McComas also taught law and foreign policy at Georgetown University Law School and was a trustee of Dickinson College beginning in 1875. He retired from the Senate in 1905, and in return for his loyalty, Roosevelt appointed him an associate justice of the federal Court of Appeals of the District of Columbia. He served in that position until his death. His first wife died in 1904, and in 1907 he married Hebe Harrison Muir. He had just returned from Europe with her at the time of his death in Washington, D.C.

• McComas left no collection of papers. A brief letter of his is in the James Morrison Harris Papers at the Maryland Historical Society, Baltimore. The best summary of his life is in Thomas J. C. Williams, *A History of Washington County Maryland*, vol. 2 (1906). The *Congressional Record*, 1883–1891 and 1899–1905, is the best guide to his legislative career. A detailed obituary is in the *Baltimore Sun*, 11 Nov. 1907.

THOMAS R. PEGRAM

MCCOMB, John, Jr. (17 Oct. 1763–25 May 1853), architect, was born in New York City, the son of John McComb, Sr., a builder and architect, and Mary Davis. The father, who began his career as a bricklayer, was a city surveyor of New York from 1784 to 1792 and was active in the General Society of Mechanics and Tradesmen, serving as secretary from 1787 to 1791. Trained under his father, McComb first appears as an architect in 1790, when he submitted designs for Government House in New York, the proposed residence for the president of the United States.

For the next thirty-five years he practiced architecture in New York, becoming the leader of the profession there. McComb combined with a late colonial style a strong element of the refined neoclassicism pioneered in England by Robert Adam and characterized by attenuated proportions, delicate classical decoration, and enjoyment of unusual room shapes. During the first quarter of the nineteenth century, he garnered many major public and private commissions, making his brand of neoclassicism the dominant style in the city. This perhaps explains New York's reluctance to adopt the Greek revival manner, which only became popular there about 1825, seven years or so after its triumph in Philadelphia and a quarter century after its first appearance there. His unexecuted designs, beginning with those for Government House and continuing throughout his career, are often more adventurous, with, for example, a greater profusion of round, oval, and octagonal spaces, than those carried out for his predominantly conservative clientele.

Among his works of the 1790s were a series of lighthouses at Cape Henry, Virginia (1792), Montauk, New York (1795), and Eaton's Neck, New York (1797–1798); houses for such prominent Federalists as Rufus King [1755–1827] (1795) and John B. Coles (1797–1799) in New York and for Dominick Lynch in Clausen's Point, New York (c. 1797); and designs for New York's Tontine City Tavern (c. 1793–1795). In 1792 he married Elizabeth Glean, with whom he had three children. She died in 1817, and in 1821 he married Rebecca Rockwell.

McComb's most important opportunity came in 1802 when, together with Joseph François Mangin, a French emigré, he won the competition for New York City Hall. Although Mangin had conceived and drawn the submitted designs, McComb alone was appointed architect for the building. McComb executed the edifice, modifying Mangin's original French neoclassical conception with his own English-inspired style, and designed most of the interior. The work was completed in 1812. McComb was probably selected as the supervising architect because of his greater previous activity as an architect in New York and his connections with prominent New Yorkers such as his former client John B. Coles, who was a member of the New York Common Council that made the appointment.

During this time McComb built a number of other significant works, including The Grange, Alexander Hamilton's (1755–1804) country house in New York (1801–1802); Queen's Building at what is now Rutgers University (1808–1811); Washington Hall, the New York headquarters of the Federalists' Washington Benevolent Society (1809–1814); and three notable New York churches: St. John's Episcopal Chapel (1803–1807, with his brother Isaac); Cedar Street Presbyterian Church (1807–1808), and Murray Street Presbyterian Church (1811–1812).

McComb's closeness to the conservative, especially Federalist, forces in New York would seem to be confirmed by a list of his clients, who included not only Hamilton and King but many others of this group, as well as Abraham Blauvelt of New Jersey, a rabid Federalist editor who was chairman of the Queen's College building committee, and by McComb's selection as architect for the party's headquarters, Washington Hall. His Federalist contacts probably also helped him to triumph in the New York City Hall competition over Benjamin Henry Latrobe (1764–1820), who was supported by the leading Democratic Republican in New York, Aaron Burr (1756–1836). McComb's essentially conservative executed buildings could be seen as a manifestation of this Federalist ethos.

During the last twelve years before his retirement from active practice in 1826, he was responsible for Alexander Hall at Princeton Theological Seminary (1815–1817) and, in New York, for the headquarters of the American Bible Society (1822–1823), the American Tract Society (1825–1826), and Bleecker Street Presbyterian Church (1825–1826). In 1817 he was approached about a joint appointment with Charles Bulfinch as architect for the U.S. Capitol, succeeding Latrobe, but in the end Bulfinch was appointed alone. During this period and later McComb was street commissioner of New York (1813–1821), inspecting and offering suggestions for roads; a New York agent for the commissioner of public buildings in Washington (c. 1815–1819); a member of the American Academy of Fine Arts (1816–1828), as well as a member of its board (1817–1828) and its treasurer (1820–1824); a longtime member of the General Society of Mechanics and Tradesmen (from 1787) and its president in 1818; a director of the Mechanics Bank (1820); a member of the board of governors of New York Hospital (1832); and a trustee (1816–1825) and deacon (1827–1853) of the Brick Presbyterian Church. By 1826 he largely retired from the practice of architecture, and in that year he declined election as an academician of the American Academy of Fine Arts, stating in a letter to Alexander Robertson that "a number of years has elapsed since I attempted to make a finished drawing = having laid aside my pencil except occasionally to make working plans" (AAFA Papers, New-York Historical Society). No buildings by him after this date are known, but he continued to list himself as an architect in city directories most of the years until 1837. After his career in architecture ended he attended to his extensive investments, joined a partnership as a merchant, and in 1829–1830 was president of the La Fayette Insurance Company. He continued to live in New York until his death.

• The principal collections of drawings and documents by McComb are at the New-York Historical Society. The most complete study of his career and his architecture is Damie Stillman, "Artistry and Skill in the Architecture of John McComb, Jr." (M.A. thesis, Univ. of Delaware, 1956). See also Agnes Addison Gilchrist, "John McComb, Sr. and Jr., in New York, 1784–1799," *Journal of the Society of Architectural Historians* 31 (1972): 10–21; Gilchrist, "Notes for a Catalogue of the John McComb (1763–1853) Collection of Architectural Drawings at the New-York Historical Society," *Journal of the Society of Architectural Historians* 28 (1969): 201–10; and Damie Stillman, "New York City Hall: Competition and Execution," *Journal of the Society of Architectural Historians* 23 (1964): 129–42.

DAMIE STILLMAN

MCCONE, John A. (4 Jan. 1902–14 Feb. 1991), government official, was born John Alex McCone in San Francisco, California, the son of Alexander J. McCone, a manufacturer, and Margaret Enright. He attended high school in Los Angeles and received a B.S. in engineering from the University of California at Berkeley in 1922. McCone then worked at the Llewellyn Iron Works in Los Angeles, first as a riveter and boilermaker and then as a superintendent. In 1933 he became executive vice president and director of Consolidated Steel Corporation, with which Llewellyn had previously merged.

In 1937 McCone embarked on a business partnership that made him a multimillionaire in less than a decade. He joined with Stephen Bechtel, a college classmate and son of a construction magnate, to form the Bechtel-McCone Corporation in Los Angeles. With McCone as its president, the firm specialized in the design and construction of oil refineries, power plants, and other industrial projects. McCone married Rosemary Cooper in 1938. They had no children. During World War II Bechtel-McCone produced military aircraft at a plant in Alabama. The partners also joined in four shipbuilding ventures that prospered as American industry geared up for the war effort. McCone left the partnership after the war, becoming president and sole proprietor of the Joshua Hendy Iron Works, a Los Angeles shipping firm, in 1945.

McCone's experience as a wartime industrialist brought him into contact with government officials and led to a postwar career in public service. In 1947 President Harry Truman appointed him to the Air Policy Commission, which recommended the creation of an independent air force. McCone served in 1948 as a special adviser to James V. Forrestal, secretary of the newly created Department of Defense, and two years later was appointed undersecretary of the air force. An early believer in the military potential of guided missiles, McCone urged the development of a missile program under a single director. President Truman rejected the plan, which later critics saw as a lost opportunity to give the United States an early lead in missile development over the Soviet Union. McCone returned to private life in 1951 but occasionally advised President Dwight D. Eisenhower on defense and other matters.

In 1958 Eisenhower named McCone to head the Atomic Energy Commission (AEC). The new chairman successfully implemented the "Atoms for Peace" initiative, which promoted civilian uses of nuclear power. He concluded agreements with both the Soviet Union and Euratom, a consortium of Western European countries, for shared nuclear research. McCone failed, however, to secure a treaty with the Soviet Union to end the testing of nuclear weapons. Early in his tenure, the chairman warned that the United States would continue its own nuclear tests unless the Soviet Union agreed to a one-year ban. The Soviets refused, and the treaty remained elusive.

McCone, a lifelong Republican, left office in 1961, when John F. Kennedy succeeded Eisenhower in the White House. He returned to government service, however, in less than a year, this time as director of central intelligence. In April 1961 the Central Intelligence Agency (CIA) had backed right-wing expatriates who invaded Cuba at the Bay of Pigs. The failure of the invasion left the CIA in official disfavor and internal disarray. McCone took office in November 1961 and replaced Allen Dulles, an Eisenhower appointee whom Kennedy blamed for the Cuban debacle. McCone revived morale within the agency, instituted management reforms, and emphasized the gathering and analysis of information over covert operations. His first wife died in 1961, and the following year he married Theiline McGee Pigott.

The single most important event of McCone's tenure at the CIA was the Cuban missile crisis in 1962. That summer the agency received information regarding new activity by the Soviet military in Cuba, and McCone warned that the Soviets might be preparing to install nuclear missiles on the island. In October, photographs taken by U-2 reconnaissance planes confirmed the director's hunch. McCone served on the "Excom" (executive committee) of top advisers who decided U.S. policy during the crisis. Like the president, the CIA chief initially favored military action against Cuba, but he came to support the naval blockade eventually decided upon by the Excom. The crisis was defused when the Soviets agreed to dismantle the missile sites. Shortly thereafter, McCone created a new division within the CIA, called the Directorate for Science and Technology, to oversee the collection of intelligence by reconnaissance planes, satellites, and other technical means.

In contrast to his prominent role in the Cuban missile crisis, McCone chafed at his inability to influence policy regarding Vietnam. In 1963 he opposed plans for a U.S.–backed coup against South Vietnamese president Ngo Dinh Diem, believing the consequence would only be further instability. The coup went forward, with the results that the CIA chief had predicted. After Kennedy was assassinated, McCone found himself increasingly alienated from President Lyndon Johnson, who did not wish to hear skeptical CIA assessments of the situation in Vietnam. The final straw for McCone came in early 1965, when Johnson approved a bombing campaign against North Vietnam and an active combat role for American troops in the South. The CIA director was no dove—indeed, he criticized the air strikes as "not sufficiently severe"— but he feared Johnson's policy would leave the United States "mired down in combat in the jungle in a military effort that we cannot win, and from which we will have extreme difficulty in extracting ourselves." McCone penned that assessment in early April 1965 and retired by the end of the month.

Back in private life, McCone returned to management of his shipping company, which he sold in 1969, and became a director of International Telephone and Telegraph Corporation (ITT). He chaired a commission appointed by California governor Edmund G. Brown, Sr., to study the causes of the 1965 riots in Watts. In 1973 McCone was called before the Senate Foreign Relations Committee to testify about reports that, three years earlier, he had offered the CIA $1 million of ITT's money to help defeat Salvador Allende, the Socialist candidate for president in Chile. (Allende won the election but was assassinated in 1973.) McCone claimed the money was intended only for social and agricultural reform. In 1987 he received the Presidential Medal of Freedom. He died at his home in Pebble Beach, California.

McCone is chiefly remembered for his tenure at the CIA. Observers have generally ranked him as one of its best directors, citing his revival of the agency after the Bay of Pigs and his emphasis on its intelligence-gathering functions. McCone is also noteworthy for his role in the Cuban missile crisis and for his early skepticism regarding escalation of American involvement in Vietnam.

• McCone's official papers from his tenure at the AEC and the CIA are available in RG 326 and RG 263, respectively, of the National Archives, Washington, D.C. An oral history and a collection of papers relating to his chairmanship of the AEC are at the Eisenhower Library, Abilene, Kans. Another oral history is at the Eisenhower Administration Project, Columbia University; and the Institute of International Studies at the University of California, Berkeley, produced "Reflections" (1988), a videotaped interview with McCone. For a generally positive assessment of McCone's leadership of the CIA, see John Ranelagh, *The Agency: The Rise and Decline of the CIA* (1986), and Ray S. Cline, *Secrets, Spies and Scholars: Blueprint of the Essential CIA* (1976). More negative evaluations are in Rhodri Jeffreys-Jones, *The CIA and American Democracy* (1989), and Thomas Powers, *The Man Who Kept the Secrets: Richard Helms and the CIA* (1979). An obituary is in the *New York Times*, 16 Feb. 1991.

STEPHEN A. WEST

MCCONNELL, Francis John (18 Aug. 1871–18 Aug. 1953), Methodist clergyman and bishop, was born near Trinway, Ohio, the son of Israel H. McConnell, a Methodist minister, and Nancy Jane Chalfant. Because of his father's itinerant ministry, McConnell studied in public schools in Norwalk and Elyria, Ohio, and Indianapolis, Indiana, before attending preparatory schools at Ohio State University in Columbus and Phillips Academy in Andover, Massachusetts. He graduated from Ohio Wesleyan University with an A.B. in 1894. Later that year, he entered the School of Theology at Boston University and worked as a student pastor in West Chelmsford, Massachusetts. In March 1897 he married Eva Hemans Thomas; they had three children.

McConnell received an S.T.B. in 1897 from Boston University, where he was influenced by Borden Parker Bowne, Boston's preeminent professor of philosophy, who held that ultimate reality in the universe was personal. While he was Bowne's graduate student, McConnell became the pastor of the Methodist Episcopal Church in Newton Upper Falls, Massachusetts (1897) serving there until he was awarded a Ph.D. by Boston University in 1899.

McConnell next served at the Methodist Episcopal Church in Ipswich, Massachusetts (1899–1902), and at Harvard Street Methodist Episcopal Church in Cambridge, Massachusetts (1902–1903). In 1903 he moved to the New York Avenue Methodist Episcopal Church in Brooklyn, New York. While serving there, he declined an invitation to become dean of Boston University's school of theology but in 1909 accepted the presidency of DePauw University, a liberal arts college in Greencastle, Indiana, affiliated with the Methodist church. During these years, he published his first important books, *The Divine Immanence* (1906), a theological essay, and *Christian Focus* (1911) and *The Increase of Faith* (1912), collections of lectures and sermons.

In 1912 McConnell was elected a bishop of the Methodist Episcopal church and was assigned to Denver, Colorado, where he became chairman of the radical and unofficial Methodist Federation for Social Service. Although he was increasingly prominent as a spokesman for radical social Christianity, his first important book after his election to the episcopacy was *Personal Christianity* (1914). In 1920 he moved to Pittsburgh and chaired the commission of the Interchurch World Movement, which investigated the 1919 labor strike at United States Steel. The commission report redirected national attention from the alleged radicalism of the strike's leaders to working conditions, including the industry's twelve-hour work day.

In his eight years at Pittsburgh, McConnell published *Living Together* (1923), *Is God Limited?* (1924), *The Christlike God* (1927), *Humanism and Christianity* (1928), and *Borden Parker Bowne* (1929). These works discussed the nature of God as revealed in Jesus Christ and restated personalism's reconciling the reality of evil with the claim that God is both loving and omnipotent. He argued that God wills the good but voluntarily limits himself and allows evil to exist for the sake of human freedom.

In 1928 McConnell became bishop of the New York area and was elected president of the Federal Council of Churches, an important ecumenical alliance of Protestant denominations. Shortly thereafter, however, he was accused of heresy by religious conservatives for advocating the theory of evolution. McConnell was acquitted by a church tribunal in 1929. During the depression, he continued to defend the interests of organized labor and the unemployed, as suggested by his books, *Human Needs and World Christianity* (1929) and *The Prophetic Ministry* (1930). In 1928 and 1932 McConnell supported the campaigns of the Socialist party presidential candidate Norman Thomas. He gave the Lyman Beecher lectures at Yale, which were published as *The Prophetic Ministry*. During a tour of India in 1931, he gave the Barrows lectures, which were published as *The Christian Ideal and Social Control* (1932). In 1932–1933 he was a visiting professor at Columbia University. As an ardent defender of the Spanish Loyalist cause in the mid-1930s, McConnell continued to advocate democratic socialism in *Christianity and Coercion* (1933) and *Christian Materialism* (1936). When he was accused of being a Communist by the Jersey City Chamber of Commerce in 1940, liberal Methodists rallied to demand an apology.

In 1942 McConnell lectured at Garrett Biblical Institute and Drew University; these talks were published as *A Basis of the Peace to Come* (1942) and *Evangelicals, Revolutionists, and Idealists* (1942), which outlined the religious liberal's hopes for a postwar world. He retired as bishop of the New York area in 1944 but returned to active service in 1948 to preside over the Portland, Oregon, episcopal area. He died in Lucasville, Ohio. A model of the intellectual as church administrator, McConnell was one of the best-known liberal Protestant leaders of his time.

• The primary collection of Francis John McConnell Papers is in the Archives of Indiana Methodism at DePauw University. The United Methodist Archives at Drew University, the National Council of Churches, and the archives of episcopal areas over which McConnell presided also have some of his papers. In addition to *By the Way: An Autobiography* (1952), see Harris Franklin Rall, ed., *Religion in Public Affairs* (1937); Paul A. Carter, *The Decline and Revival of the Social Gospel: Social and Political Liberalism in American Protestant Churches, 1920–1940* (1954); Judge Neal Hughley, *Trends in Protestant Social Idealism* (1948); Donald B. Meyer, *The Protestant Search for Political Realism, 1919–1941* (1960); and Robert Moats Miller, *American Protestantism and Social Issues, 1919–1939* (1958). An obituary is in the *New York Times*, 19 Aug. 1953.

RALPH E. LUKER

MCCOOK, Alexander McDowell (22 Apr. 1831–12 June 1903), soldier, was born in Columbiana County, Ohio, the son of Daniel McCook, a lawyer, and Martha Latimer. Of Scotch-Irish descent, he was the highest ranking of the fourteen "Fighting McCooks" who soldiered for the Union during the Civil War. This included his father, his seven brothers, and five cousins. Two of his brothers, Daniel, Jr., and Robert Latimer, and his first cousin, Edward Moody McCook, also became generals.

Alexander graduated from the U.S. Military Academy in 1852, having taken five years to complete the four-year course. He was commissioned a brevet second lieutenant in the Third U.S. Infantry and was posted to Newport Barracks, Kentucky. After a brief tour at Jefferson Barracks, McCook was ordered to New Mexico Territory, where he served from 1853 until 1857. Promoted to second lieutenant on 30 June 1854, he participated during the year in a scouting expedition into the Apache country. In 1855, while on duty as a commissary officer, he took the field with Company H, First Dragoons, to pacify the Utes and Apaches and saw action in the White Mountains, southeast of Las Lunas. As chief of guides, he accompanied the Gila Expedition of 1857 and on 27 June participated in a fight with the Apaches on the Gila River.

McCook, following a leave, reported for duty as assistant instructor of infantry tactics at the U.S. Military Academy on 12 February 1858; he was promoted to first lieutenant in December 1858. On 24 April 1861 he was ordered to Columbus, Ohio, and charged with mustering into federal service the regiments being raised by Ohio under President Abraham Lincoln's call for 75,000 volunteers. Three days later he assumed command of the First Ohio Infantry Regiment, a ninety-day unit; his commission as colonel of volunteers was postdated to 16 April.

McCook and his regiment reached Washington, D.C., in late April and were assigned to the brigade commanded by Brigadier General Robert Schenck, posted at Four Mile Run in Arlington County, Virginia. McCook first met Confederates in a fight at Vienna on 17 June. On 21 July he was engaged in the battle of First Manassas, seeing action at Lewis' Ford and the Stone Bridge, and was breveted a major for gallant and meritorious service. He was mustered out on 2 August 1861; eight days later he was commissioned a colonel of the First Ohio Infantry, a three-year regiment.

McCook was made a brigadier general of volunteers to rank from 3 September 1861 and was placed in command of a brigade posted on Kentucky's Nolin Creek in the Department of the Cumberland. In mid-December, McCook, now commanding a division in the Army of the Ohio, advanced and took possession of Munfordville. There he remained until the fourth week of February, when he and his troops advanced to and occupied Nashville. Although no combat was involved, on 3 March McCook was breveted a lieutenant colonel for his noble service at the capture of Nashville.

McCook and his division reached Pittsburg Landing at daybreak on 7 April and were active participants in the second day's fight at Shiloh, earning for McCook a brevet as colonel and a commendation from Major General Don Carlos Buell. He participated in the advance on and the siege of Corinth (29 Apr.–30 May). Buell in June wheeled his army east and advanced on Chattanooga, and, by 19 July, McCook, now leading two divisions, had reached Battle Creek, twenty-five miles west of the "Gateway City." The Confederates turned the tables on Buell and a race for Louisville was on. The federals won the race, and when Buell again took the field, McCook, promoted major general to rank from 17 July, led the army's First Corps. At Perryville, on 8 October, McCook was caught in the vortex of a savage Confederate attack, and his corps was mauled.

Before the end of the month, Major General William S. Rosecrans had replaced Buell, and the Army of the Ohio was reorganized and redesignated the Army of the Cumberland. McCook and his command—now known as the Right Wing of the Fourteenth Corps—returned to Tennessee and in early November took position at Nashville. McCook and two divisions of his corps were savaged by the Confederates and pursued for several miles at Stones River on 31 December before fierce resistance by his third division slowed the rebel surge and helped turn defeat into victory.

On 14 January 1863 Rosecrans reorganized his army following the occupation of Murfreesboro, and McCook assumed command of the Twentieth Corps. The army again took the field on 23 June, and at Liberty Gap (24–27 June), McCook engaged the foe and was first to enter Tullahoma on 1 July. After a six-week pause, Rosecrans moved forward again on 16 August. McCook, on the right, crossed the Tennessee River at Bridgeport and Bellefont, and pushed on into northwest Georgia. At Chickamauga, McCook with two of his three divisions engaged the rebels in and west of Viniard's Farm on 19 September. At midday the next day, McCook and the two divisions with him on the Union right were routed and swept from the field. As a result of the Union defeat and retreat into Chattanooga, McCook was relieved of his command on 28 September and ordered to report to Indianapolis, preparatory to facing a court of inquiry, which convened in Nashville on 29 January and adjourned on 23 February 1864. The court exonerated McCook of any responsibility for the disaster that followed the Confederate breakthrough, but found that in leaving the field to go into Chattanooga he had made a judgmental error.

The court had acted, but McCook's actions at Perryville, Chickamauga, and particularly Stones River, led to the conclusion that he was not a prudent corps commander. Consequently, he never again led large numbers of troops in the field. While at his home in Dayton, Ohio, awaiting orders, McCook was called to Washington, then threatened by Lieutenant General Jubal A. Early's army. Reaching the city on 10 July, McCook reported to the War Department and was placed in charge of the troops guarding the northern approaches to Washington. On the next afternoon his forces skirmished with the rebels in front of Fort Stevens, and on 12 July he was there when President Lincoln visited the fort and came under fire. He remained on duty in the Department of Washington until 16 July, when he returned to Dayton.

It was 23 November before McCook next received orders to report to duty to Major General Philip H. Sheridan, who commanded the Middle Military Division. Sheridan, who had led a division under McCook at Stones River and Chickamauga, was unenthusiastic about receiving McCook, but yielded to pressure from Lieutenant General Ulysses S. Grant, and on 10 December Sheridan directed McCook to report to Major General Lewis Wallace's Baltimore headquarters. McCook, as Wallace's second in command, had few responsibilities.

On 9 March McCook assumed command of the District of Eastern Arkansas, headquartered at Helena. His stay in Arkansas was brief; on 26 April he was ordered to St. Louis to accompany a joint congressional committee investigating Indian affairs in New Mexico, Colorado, and Utah Territory. While in Arkansas,

McCook had received two brevets for gallantry and meritorious service in the U.S. Army: the first to brigadier general for action at Perryville and the second to major general for duty in the field during the Civil War. After the war McCook served on the western frontier for most of the time until his retirement on 22 April 1895 as a major general.

McCook married twice. In 1863 he married Kate Phillips of Dayton, Ohio, with whom he had three daughters. After his first wife died in 1881, he married Annie Colt of Milwaukee. McCook died in Dayton and was buried in Cincinnati.

• Letters received from McCook by the Commission Branch of the Adjutant General's Office are in the National Archives, M-1064. For additional information on McCook, see George W. Cullum, *Biographical Register*, vol. 2 (3d ed., 1895); *War of the Rebellion: A Compilation of the Official Records of the Union and Confederate Armies* (128 vols., 1880–1901); Whitelaw Reid, *Ohio in the War*, vol. 1 (1868); Henry Howe, "The Fighting McCooks," *The Scotch-Irish in America*, Proceedings and Addresses in the Sixth Genealogical Congress (1894); and Ezra J. Warner, *Generals in Blue: Lives of the Union Commanders* (1964), pp. 294–95. Obituaries are in the *Ohio State Journal* (Columbus), 13 June 1903, and the *Army and Navy Journal*, 20 June 1903.

E. C. BEARSS

MCCOOK, Edward Moody (15 June 1833–9 Sept. 1909), politician, lawyer, and soldier, was born in Steubenville, Ohio, the son of John McCook, a physician, and Catharine Julia Sheldon. After being educated in the Steubenville public schools, McCook moved to Minnesota in 1849. When news of the highly publicized gold strikes in Colorado began to sweep the country, McCook was one of the fifty-niners involved in the rush to the new gold fields. He settled in the mining camp of Central City, where he amassed a respectable fortune. Moreover, he began to practice law and was elected to the Kansas legislature in 1859, when Colorado was still part of Kansas Territory. McCook was also a leader in the movement that led to the creation of Colorado as a separate territory on 28 February 1861, a month after Kansas became a state.

McCook held staunch pro-Union views, and after Fort Sumter fell in April 1861 he joined the Kansas Legion in Washington, D.C. McCook, the eldest of four sons, came from a family that achieved such exceptional recognition during the Civil War that they became known as "the fighting McCooks." McCook's success in delivering dispatches to General Winfield Scott through hostile Confederate lines in Maryland won him the rank of lieutenant in the cavalry. His military record in the Union campaigns of 1862–1863 led to promotions at Shiloh, Perryville, and Chickamauga. After serving as a cavalry officer in eastern Tennessee, he became a brevet lieutenant colonel. On 27 April 1864 McCook was elevated to brigadier general of volunteers and given command of the cavalry of the Army of the Cumberland. His most distinguished exploit occurred a few months later when he prevented General John B. Hood, who was in command of Con-

federate troops at Atlanta, from receiving badly needed reinforcements from the south. McCook's cavalry
sweep behind Hood's position destroyed Confederate
trains, cut rail lines, and took large numbers of prisoners before he rejoined the main Federal force at Marietta, Georgia. His successful campaign was regarded
as paving the way for the fall of Atlanta and William T.
Sherman's subsequent march to the sea. McCook was
rewarded with ranks of brevet brigadier general of the
U.S. Army and major general of volunteers.

At the end of hostilities, McCook served briefly as
the military governor of Florida. He resigned his military commission in 1866 to become U.S. minister to
Hawaii until President Ulysses S. Grant gave him an
opportunity to return to Colorado as the territory's
new governor in 1869. Grant's appointment, like so
many made in the western territories during the late
nineteenth century, was regarded by many Coloradans
as yet another example of spoils politics. Consequently, McCook's return to the Colorado political scene
was marred by charges that his military reputation and
his friendship with Grant were his only qualifications
for the position. Nevertheless, the new governor made
some substantial contributions to the territory's
growth. He helped open up agricultural and mineral
lands in Colorado by moving some of the Ute Indians
from their coveted territorial tribal lands to Utah. He
promoted railroad building, organized Colorado's
school system, and encouraged the building of the waterworks for Denver. He was, like so many western
territorial governors, a great booster and advocate for
economic development. At his suggestion, the Colorado Territorial Board of Immigration was organized to
attract new citizens to the bustling mining commonwealth, and he even bucked a strong nativist sentiment
by advocating Chinese immigration as a source of
cheap labor for the territory.

Despite McCook's accomplishments, his governorship remained controversial. He was accused of playing spoils politics, as Grant had been, and of nepotism
and fraud. He and his brother-in-law, James B.
Thompson, were accused of making a net profit of
more than $22,000 from a governmental contract to
supply cattle and sheep to the Utes, in which a distant
relative made the actual bid to conceal McCook's improper participation. The controversy grew to such an
extent that some of the worthwhile proposals he advocated, such as woman suffrage, were rejected because
of his support. One result of this partisanship was the
development of an anti-McCook faction in the Republican party, which launched an investigation into his
administration. The allegations that resulted were
publicized in Washington by Colorado's territorial
delegate, Jerome Chaffee. As a result of Chaffee's revelations and angry petitions from many Coloradans,
Grant removed McCook in 1873 and replaced him
with Samuel Elbert, who had been Colorado's first territorial secretary.

But in keeping with his reputation as a fighter, Mc-
Cook hurried to the nation's capital to protest his innocence. Grant, who was easily persuaded by old friends

and colleagues, finally relented, and in 1874 he removed Elbert and restored McCook to office. This action enraged Colorado Republicans to such a degree
that the party split in the 1874 election, allowing the
outnumbered Democrats to capture the office of territorial delegate, the territory's only voice in Congress.
McCook's second term lasted less than a year. Grant,
anxious to restore party harmony, replaced him with
the less controversial and more popular John Routt,
who successfully promoted statehood for Colorado in
1876.

After he left public life, McCook continued his business enterprises throughout the West and abroad. At
one time his investments in mining and other ventures
made him the largest taxpayer and real estate owner in
Colorado. He was married twice, having two sons by
his first marriage and two daughters by his second.
His first wife, whom he married in 1865, was Mary
Thompson, whose charm and attractiveness were assets to his political career. As Colorado's first lady, she
gained national attention by fainting in the arms of the
territory's most dazzling visitor, Grand Duke Alexis of
Russia, during his much publicized 1872 visit to the
West to hunt buffalo. After his first wife's death on 12
May 1874, McCook married Mary McKenna of Colorado. McCook died in Chicago.

• A small collection of McCook's personal correspondence is
in the Books and Manuscripts Department of the Colorado
Historical Society. Primary materials relevant to his Colorado
governorship are in the Division of State Archives and Public
Records of Colorado; the Western History Department of the
Denver Public Library; and the University of Colorado at
Boulder, University Libraries, Archives. Secondary sources
dealing with all phases of his career include Richard D.
Lamm and Duane A. Smith, *Pioneers and Politicians: 10 Colorado Governors in Profile* (1984); Smith, *Rocky Mountain
West, Colorado, Wyoming, and Montana* (1992); Carl Abbott,
Colorado: A History of the Centennial State (1976); and Stephen J. Leonard and Thomas J. Noel, *Denver: Mining Camp
to Metropolis* (1990). For valuable but biased information
about the controversies of McCook's governorship, see Frank
Hall, *History of the State of Colorado* (1891). A more objective
assessment of McCook is in Wilbur Fisk Stone, ed., *History
of Colorado* (1918). Essential facts about McCook's war record are in *The War of the Rebellion: A Compilation of the Official Records of the Union and Confederate Armies* (128 vols.,
1880–1901). An informative obituary is in the *Denver Times*,
10 Sept. 1909.

ROBERT W. LARSON

MCCOOK, Henry Christopher (3 July 1837–31 Oct.
1911), naturalist, was born in New Lisbon, Ohio, the
son of John McCook, a physician, and Catharine Julia
Sheldon. His early years were spent in the public
schools of Ohio, where he taught briefly before entering Jefferson College at Canonsburg, Pennsylvania.
He received his A.B. in 1859 and entered the Western
Theological Seminary in Pittsburgh in 1860. The same
year, he married Emma C. Herter from New Lisbon;
they had two children before her death in 1897. Ordained in the Presbytery of Steubenville, Ohio, in
1861, McCook left his ministerial calling shortly there-

after to help raise the Forty-first Regiment of Illinois Volunteers. As one of the "fighting McCooks," he entered the Civil War in the service of the Union, mustered into the Forty-first Regiment as a first lieutenant, F Company, on 7 August 1861, subsequently serving his unit as chaplain.

McCook's active ministerial career began in 1862 at the Presbyterian church of Clinton, Illinois (1862–1864), and continued with city mission work in St. Louis, Missouri (1864–1869). In January 1870 McCook accepted a call to be pastor of the Seventh Presbyterian Church of Philadelphia. He became involved in the civic life of the city, organizing the Presbyterian Hospital, serving on various boards such as the Presbyterian Historical Society, and editing that society's journal. During McCook's pastorate the Seventh and Sixth churches merged to become the Tabernacle Presbyterian Church (1873) with one of the city's largest congregations. Indulging his lifelong interest in symbolism and heraldry, McCook designed many of the architectural details for a new church building, including emblems and scriptural texts incorporated into the edifice. He also designed the seal of the Presbyterian General Assembly and the flag of the city of Philadelphia. In 1893 he designed the original seal for the Wistar Institute of Anatomy and Biology.

McCook's national reputation rests on his credentials as a scientific observer and investigator in the field of entomology, with a particular interest in ants and spiders. Selecting an area of study in which few Americans had specialized, he first focused on the natural history and social habits of ants. His first scientific article appeared in 1876, followed by the studies *Mound-making Ants of the Alleghenies* (1877) and *The Honey Ants of the Garden of the Gods and the Occident Ants of the American Plains* (1882). From 1876 until 1907 McCook authored more than twenty books and papers on spiders, most of them published in the *Transactions of the American Entomological Society* and the *Proceedings of the Academy of Natural Sciences*. Preferring to study specimens in their natural setting, McCook made forays into the country for two months each summer and during whatever leisure time his pastoral and civic duties allowed, observing the creatures both day and night. His principal work, the three-volume *American Spiders and Their Spinning Work* (1894–1899), was the result of sixteen years of study in the field and is filled with illustrations developed from his personal sketches. While taking care to write with scientific accuracy and detail, McCook produced works in his later years that he hoped would be of educational value to children and the general public. *Old Farm Fairies: A Summer Campaign in Brownie-land against King Cobweaver's Pixies* (1895) and *Nature's Craftsmen: Popular Studies of Ants and Other Insects* (1907) were works in a lighter style, demonstrating his ability to turn a technical subject into an engaging piece. In 1875 he became a member of the Academy of Natural Sciences of Philadelphia, where he exhibited his collections of specimens and was actively involved with other members of the scientific community, such as Joseph Leidy, Edward Drinker Cope, Angelo Heilprin, and Harrison Allen. For eight years (1882–1900) he served as one of two vice presidents of the organization. Entering the American Entomological Society in 1877, he was its vice president (1884–1893) and president (1898–1900). Lafayette College awarded him the doctor of divinity in 1880 and the doctor of science in 1888; Washington and Jefferson College, his renamed alma mater, conferred the doctor of laws on McCook in 1902.

In 1898 McCook was detached from his reserve position as chaplain of the Second Regiment, Pennsylvania Volunteers, and sailed for Cuba with the National Relief Commission, which he had helped to organize. The commission's assignment was the reorganizing of civil hospitals and the care of sick and wounded soldiers from the Spanish-American War. During this time he began the work of identifying and designating the graves of American soldiers who had died on the island. *Martial Graves of Our Fallen* (1899) was published by McCook and detailed the experiences of the commission as they worked in the heat of a tropical climate to identify and rebury remains and place gravestones.

In 1899 McCook married Mrs. Eleanor D. S. Abbey. In December 1902 he resigned as pastor of Tabernacle Presbyterian and retired in ill health to Devon, Pennsylvania, but he continued as an active member of the Entomological Section of the Academy of Natural Sciences. He died at his home in Devon.

• Many of McCook's letters, sketches of specimens, and publications are in the archives of the Academy of Natural Sciences of Philadelphia; the Wistar Institute also has a small collection of his correspondence. Sketches of his life include P. P. C., "Henry Christopher McCook," *Entomological News* (1911): 433–38, and Henry Skinner, "Henry C. McCook Memorial," *Journal of the Presbyterian Historical Society* 6, no. 4 (1911): 97–150, which includes a complete bibliography of his publications.

NINA P. LONG

MCCORD, James Iley (24 Nov. 1919–19 Feb. 1990), Presbyterian minister, educator, and ecumenical statesman, was born in Rusk, Texas, the son of Marshal Edward McCord, a carpenter, and Jimmie Oleta Decherd. McCord earned a B.A. at Austin College in 1938. He attended Union Theological Seminary in Virginia from 1938 to 1939, but received a B.D. and M.A., respectively, from Austin Presbyterian Theological Seminary and the University of Texas in 1942. That year he was ordained by the Presbytery of Brazos of the Presbyterian Church, U.S. (southern). While studying at Harvard from 1942 to 1943, he served as pastor of the Westminster Presbyterian Church, Manchester, New Hampshire. In Austin, he pastored University Presbyterian Church from 1944 to 1945 and was adjunct professor of systematic theology at the seminary. From 1945 to 1949 he was dean and professor of theology at the seminary. The next year he studied at the University of Edinburgh and then returned to Texas to serve University Church from 1952 to 1954 and to fill the post of dean and professor of systematic theology at the seminary from 1952 to 1959. He was also instructor in philosophy and professor of Bible at the University of Texas from 1954 to 1958. In 1939 he married Hazel Gertrude Thompson of Sherman, Texas, and they had three children: Vincent, Alison McCord Zimmerman, and Marcia McCord Verville.

In 1959 McCord became the fourth president of Princeton Theological Seminary and a professor of theology; he filled both positions for twenty-four years. Noted for his commitment to the Reformed tradition, he enhanced the seminary's role in world theological circles, enlarged its ecumenical commitments, and introduced a program of continuing education. During his tenure the student body more than doubled (many of the new students were from Eastern Europe and the Third World), a world class faculty increased by one-third, and the endowment increased sixtyfold. Twenty-six faculty chairs were endowed, the Speer Library became one of the world's finest theological libraries, and Ross Stevenson housing, Erdman Hall, and Charlotte Rachel Wilson apartments were added. During these years, McCord lectured or preached in several theological seminaries and churches in Great Britain, Netherlands, Canada, Czechoslovakia, and South America as well as the United States. For twenty-five years he chaired the Editorial Council of *Theology Today* (Princeton). He edited *Supplementa Calviniana* (1961), and coedited *Service in Christ* (1966), *Marburg Revisited* (1966) and the *Phenomenon of Convergence and the Course of Prejudice* (1964), all of which emphasized the Reformed faith, biblical witness, and the importance of ecumenical dialogue. He was a frequent contributor to the *Interpretation*, the *Ecumenical Review*, the *Reformed and Presbyterian World*, the *Presbyterian World*, and others. The creation of the Center For Theological Inquiry, a research center for creative interchange among scholars, of which he served as chancellor from 1983 to 1989, was a major accomplishment.

McCord's ecumenical activity was evident in 1948 and 1954 when he represented his denomination respectively at the Geneva and Princeton General Councils of the World Alliance of Reformed Churches. In 1954 he became a member of the executive council of that body, and from 1958 to 1960 he chaired the North American Area of the World Alliance, which he continued to serve until 1977. From 1977 to 1982, McCord was president of the World Alliance of Reformed Churches and is largely responsible for the uniting of Reformed and Congregational Churches throughout the world. He participated in the organization of the World Council of Churches in Amsterdam in 1948 and subsequently served on the Council of Faith and Order. As chairman of the Consultation on Church Union from 1961 to 1963, he was a key figure in efforts to unite ten Protestant denominations. From 1978 to 1980, he was president of the Association of Theological Schools in the United States and Canada and the United Board for Christian Higher Education in Asia from 1983 to 1986 and chairman of Christian Ministry in National Parks in 1987.

Throughout his career McCord's outstanding abilities were recognized. The University of Texas twice awarded him the Charles Oldwright Fellowship in philosophy and Harvard made him a Henry B. Rogers Fellow in Philosophy. Many institutions bestowed honorary doctorates upon him among which were the University of Geneva (1958), Debrecen Reformed Theological Faculty, Hungary (1967), United Protestant Theological College, Cluj, Rumania (1974), and Yale University (1987). In 1986 McCord was presented the Templeton Foundation Prize for Progress in Religion. He died in Princeton, New Jersey.

• The James I. McCord Papers, 1944–1989, are in Luce Library Special Collections Department of Princeton Theological Seminary. The Presbyterian Historical Society Archives (Philadelphia, Pa.) file on McCord is valuable. The *Princeton Seminary Bulletin* no. 2 (July 1990): 119–32; *Theology Today* 47, no. 2 (July 1990): 120–21; *Reformed World* 41, no. 1 (Mar. 1990): 1; *Time*, 11 Apr. 1960, pp. 56, 58, 27 Oct. 1961, pp. 62, 65, and 27 Apr. 1962, p. 75, all provide vital information. Wilbert Forker, ed., *The Templeton Foundation Prize for Progress in Religion* (1988), and *Who Was Who In America* (1993), are essential sources.

FREDERICK V. MILLS, SR.

MCCORD, Louisa Susannah Cheves (3 Dec. 1810–23 Nov. 1879), writer, was born in Charleston, South Carolina, the daughter of Langdon Cheves, a lawyer, and Mary Elizabeth Dulles. Her early schooling took place from 1819 to 1829 at Grimshaw's School in Philadelphia, where Langdon Cheves was president of the Bank of the United States. McCord's formal education was chiefly confined to learning French, but when McCord's father discovered her hiding behind a door where her brothers' tutor was teaching mathematics, he gladly allowed her to study the classics and mathematics with them. Also formative in her early life was contact with her father's colleagues who discussed politics and economics stimulating her interest in the place of women and the status of the South.

In 1840 Louisa Cheves married a politically active attorney, David James McCord, a widower with ten children. They lived at her plantation at "Lang Syne," near Fort Motte, South Carolina. The McCords had three children; but apparently McCord was most ambitious for her son, Langdon, in whom she hoped her own denied political career would be fulfilled. In an essay printed in the *Southern Quarterly Review* in April 1852, she said that "woman was made for *duty*, not for *fame*; and so soon as she forgets this great law of her being, . . . she throws herself from her position, and thus, of necessity, degrades herself."

Barred from political life, she turned to writing, one of the few acceptable activities for an upper-class southern woman. She began writing seriously in 1848 by translating Frédéric Bastiat's *Sophismes Économiques*. Her background in French and economics produced a well-received work. A collection of poems, *My Dreams*, appeared that same year. *My Dreams* emphasized her unfulfilled ambitions and persistent discontent through extended metaphors in poems with such titles as "The Comet," "The Firefly," and "The Falling Star." Her unconventional role later as a writer on political economy, women's rights, and slavery distinguished her from the "typical" white woman of the planter class. Despite demanding obligations of her large family and the management of Lang Syne with at least 200 slaves, she wrote for leading southern periodicals such as the *Southern Quarterly Review* and *DeBow's Review*. She was best known for articles popularizing free trade, defending the religious and economic justification for slavery, and arguing that women belong in the home. Her work was sometimes published anonymously or simply initialed L. S. M. She sought credibility from an objectively political view and, as Elizabeth Fox-Genovese has said, as a "latter-day Roman matron" writing for an enlightened audience. She drew parallels between slavery and a woman's lot but challenged the wisdom of reforming nature's laws. McCord was one of a few who supported the views of Josiah Nott, a southern doctor who based his defense of slavery on the laws of nature. She agreed with Nott that physical and biological differences in slaves, as well as in women, precluded true equality.

McCord's writing bridged two worlds. O'Brien and Moltke-Hansen call her a "strong critical voice [that] neither betrayed femininity in the eyes of men nor critically extended woman's sphere beyond existing conventions." Her best-known work, *Caius Gracchus* (1851), a five-act tragedy in blank verse, strongly paralleled tensions between North and South, her vicarious ambitions for Langdon, and her own subordinated political plans. *Caius Gracchus* fused in Caius McCord's husband and son and presented in Cornelia, his mother, an idealized portrait of herself. Caius is defender of the common people against the greed of Roman senators who wish to appropriate public lands. Cornelia serves as the wise mother who gives savvy political advice to her idealistic son. The text is embedded with classical allusions and symbolism, reflecting McCord's extensive education.

After the death of her husband in 1855, McCord shifted her energies to Langdon's education. Then, during the Civil War, she armed and clothed her son's military company. At about this time her friend Mary Boykin Chesnut observed that McCord "has the intellect of a man and the perseverance and endurance of a woman." McCord was elected president of the Soldier's Relief Association and of the Lady's Clothing Association in 1861. When her son died in 1862 from wounds received at the second battle of Manassas (Bull Run), McCord dedicated herself to arming, clothing, nursing, and feeding soldiers in the military hospital housed in dormitories across from her house at South Carolina College in Columbia. After the war McCord moved to Cobourg, Ontario, Canada, for two years to avoid taking the required oath of allegiance to the federal government. In 1867 she complied for economic reasons and returned to Charleston, where she died.

McCord's synthesis of social, political, and economic views, according to Eugene Genovese and Elizabeth Fox-Genovese, was neither "original nor technically sophisticated" in thinking. Nonetheless, she persisted in her elitist prosouthern views and saw herself and her slaveholding contemporaries as duty-bound keepers of the Christian code. Within her own milieu, McCord stood as a classic defender of the conservative antebellum South amid a larger shift toward inevitable and irreversible change.

• Many of the McCord/Cheves papers are in the South Carolina Historical Society in Charleston and in the South Caroliniana Library, University of South Carolina, Columbia. Two early works are helpful: Jessie Melville Fraser, *Louisa C. McCord*, Bulletin of the University of South Carolina, no. 91 (1920), and Margaret Farrand Thorp, *Female Persuasion: Six Strong-Minded Women* (1949). For a contemporary view, see Mary T. Tardy, *The Living Female Writers of the South* (1872). Mary Boykin Chesnut, *A Diary from Dixie*, ed. Ben Ames Williams (1950), and C. Vann Woodward's more recent *Mary Chesnut's Civil War* (1981) are particularly helpful as edited primary sources. See also Eugene Genovese and Elizabeth Fox-Genovese, "Slavery, Economic Development and the Law: The Dilemma of the Southern Political Economists, 1800–1860," *Washington and Lee Law Review* 41 (1984): 1–29. Michael O'Brien and David Moltke-Hansen provide a focused analysis of *Caius Gracchus* in *Intellectual Life in Antebellum Charleston* (1986). Mary Margaret Johnston, "The Exceptional Case: Louisa McCord and Antebellum Southern Thought" (M.A. thesis, Queens Univ., Ontario, 1987), contains an extensive bibliography. For a broader perspective see Elizabeth Fox-Genovese, *Within the Plantation Household: Black and White Women of the Old South* (1988).

BARBARA KRALEY YOUEL

MCCORKLE, Samuel Eusebius (23 Aug. 1746–21 Jan. 1811), Presbyterian minister and educator, was born near Harris's Ferry in Lancaster County, Pennsylvania, the son of Irish immigrants Alexander McCorkle and Nancy Agnes Montgomery, farmers. In 1756 the McCorkle family relocated to Rowan County, North Carolina, settling on a farm near the town of Salisbury. Upon the family's move to North Carolina, McCorkle took up classical studies, first under the Reverend Joseph Alexander and then under the tutelage of the Reverend David Caldwell. In 1768 McCorkle enrolled at the College of New Jersey (now Princeton University) to study for the ministry. There he came under the influence of John Witherspoon, who taught a modified Calvinism that elevated the role of reason in the Christian life and placed greater confidence in human nature while still professing adherence to the doctrine of original sin and total depravity. McCorkle embraced Witherspoon's teachings and graduated with an A.B. in 1772.

After graduation McCorkle spent two years teaching school and studying for the ministry with his uncle, Rev. Joseph Montgomery, in New Castle, Delaware. The New York Presbytery licensed him to preach in 1774. McCorkle itinerated as a probationer minister in western Virginia before accepting, in 1776, a call to return to his home church, Thyatira Church, in North Carolina. That year he married Margaret Gillespie; they had ten children, four of whom died in childhood, and owned six slaves.

McCorkle, like most Presbyterian ministers, supported the American Revolution. On 24 July 1786 he preached "A Sermon for the Anniversary of American Independence." Citing Esther 9:20–21, which recounts Mordecai instituting the festival of Purim to celebrate the Jews' liberation from the evil designs of Haman, McCorkle weaved together the themes of liberty, education, and religion as he called upon his listeners to join him in commemorating the "day of our deliverance." He began "first with religion, not only on account of her superior importance: but influence on all the rest. Religion promotes learning and liberty, in one word it exalts a nation."

The themes of religion, learning, and liberty secured by republican virtue characterize the rest of McCorkle's career. Convinced that ignorance and impiety lay at the root of virtually all of humanity's troubles, he merged learning with faith in both the church and the classroom. Reason alone was inadequate, for it led to deism. A conversion experience remained central to the development of a life of piety. Although he expressed concern over the bodily excesses that sometimes accompanied revivals, McCorkle desired the renewal of believers and new converts engendered by these events. A large revival in 1802 eventually led to a split in Thyatira Church. McCorkle, while cautious of the potential for physical excess, supported the event as a work of God.

McCorkle promoted learning at every opportunity. He frequently encouraged his people to study the Scriptures at home, instituted weekly Bible classes to assist their efforts, and created a church lending library. He served several years as a trustee of Liberty Hall Academy in Charlotte (1777–1780?) and later as president and teacher at nearby Salisbury Academy (1784–1791). In 1794 McCorkle and the Thyatira congregation opened Zion-Parnassus Academy, a school intended to prepare young men for university education.

McCorkle is perhaps best remembered for his efforts to establish the University of North Carolina. In 1784 he first drafted a proposal to establish a state university. In 1789, when the legislature finally chartered the University of North Carolina, McCorkle was appointed to the board of trustees. He served as a tireless promoter and fundraiser for the institution, outlining his vision for the school in *A Charity Sermon*, first preached in 1793 and published in 1795. On 12 October 1793 he delivered the dedication speech for the laying of the cornerstone of Old East, the university's first building, reminding his listeners, "'Except the Lord do build the house, they labor in vain that build it.'" Despite his enthusiasm and efforts on behalf of the school, McCorkle's early efforts with the university were marked by controversy, especially with fellow trustee William R. Davie. The heart of their debate centered over the nature of the curriculum the new university should offer. Davie's blueprint focused on the sciences and modern languages, which, McCorkle

argued, would elevate reason at the expense of rectitude. Instead, McCorkle favored one similar to his classical background that was devised to inculcate piety and moral discipline in the student body. With that goal in mind, his list of twenty-seven rules to govern student life, initially adopted by the board of trustees, advocated a wide range of activities, from morning prayers to weekly lectures on morality and religion. In 1795 the trustees appointed McCorkle to head the faculty as professor of moral and political philosophy and history. He also assumed on a temporary basis, some executive duties until a president of the university was appointed. When McCorkle suggested a counteroffer that would ensure him adequate compensation upon setting aside presidential duties, Davie succeeded in opposing the recommendation. Thereafter McCorkle increasingly inveighed against the university's slide toward rationalism. In 1801 he severed ties with the young institution, leaving with a reputation as an embittered man.

McCorkle suffered assorted health problems during the last decade of his life. A stroke in late 1805 prevented him from regularly taking the pulpit. He died at his farm in Rowan County, North Carolina.

• A number of McCorkle's published sermons survive, and the Special Collections room of the William Perkins Library of Duke University contains six manuscript sermons as well as a collection of sermon notes. What remains of McCorkle's journal is at the Archives of the Presbyterian and Reformed Churches, Montreat, N.C. Early source material includes S. C. Alexander, "An Historical Address, Delivered at the Centennial Celebration of Thyatira Church, Rowan County, N.C., October 19, 1855," (Salisbury, N.C.); Eli W. Caruthers, "Samuel Eusebius McCorkle, D.D., 1774–1811," in *Annals of the American Pulpit*, ed. William B. Sprague (1859); and William Henry Foote, *Sketches of North Carolina*, 3d ed. (1966). A full-length biography is James F. Hurley and Julia Goode Eagan, *The Prophet of Zion-Parnassus: Samuel Eusebius McCorkle* (1934). More recent treatments include Thomas T. Taylor, "Samuel E. McCorkle and a Christian Republic, 1792–1802," *American Presbyterians: Journal of Presbyterian History* 63 (Winter 1985): 375–85; Wesley Frank Craven's entry in *Princetonians, 1769–1775: A Biographical Dictionary*, ed. Richard A. Harrison (1980); the William R. Enger and Taylor entry in *Dictionary of North Carolina Biography*, vol. 4, ed. William S. Powell (1991); and Robert M. Calhoon, "Samuel E. McCorkle and James S. Ferguson: Ideology, Religion, and Higher Education in North Carolina," Presidential Address, Historical Society of North Carolina, Oct. 1995.

KURT BERENDS

MCCORMACK, Arthur Thomas (21 Aug. 1872–7 Aug. 1943), physician and health officer, was born near Howard's Mill, Nelson County, Kentucky, the son of Joseph Nathaniel McCormack, a physician and health officer, and Corinne Crenshaw. Growing up in Bowling Green, Kentucky, McCormack graduated with a B.A. from Ogden College in 1892, attended the University of Virginia in 1892–1893, and received the M.D. from Columbia University College of Physicians and Surgeons in 1896. After completing a year's internship at Paterson General Hospital (Paterson, N.J.)

in 1897, McCormack had the unusual experience of being licensed to practice medicine by his own father, whose practice in Bowling Green he then joined.

McCormack served as health officer of Warren County (1897–1908), assistant secretary of the Kentucky State Board of Health (1898–1912), and surgeon general, Kentucky National Guard (1900–1908). During the years 1908 to 1912, together with his father and an associate, Lillian H. South, he established and operated St. Joseph's Hospital in Bowling Green, a 42-bed institution that in its day was the only hospital between Louisville and Nashville. He became a member of the Kentucky Medical Association in 1897, served as its secretary from 1907 to 1943, and was the founder and editor of the *Kentucky Medical Journal* from 1901 to 1943. Beginning in 1908 he was a frequent member of the American Medical Association's House of Delegates for more than three decades.

Commissioned a first lieutenant in the U.S. Army Medical Reserve Corps (MRC) in 1911, McCormack was promoted to major when the United States entered World War I in 1917 and assigned command of Base Hospital No. 59 at Camp Greenleaf, Georgia. Before the unit sailed for the European theater, however, he was ordered to succeed Surgeon General William C. Gorgas as health officer of the Panama Canal Zone for the duration of the war at the rank of lieutenant colonel. There he supervised completion of the Ancon (Gorgas) Hospital near Panama City and controlled an outbreak of meningitis aboard the Japanese vessel *Anyo Maru*, for which he received the gratitude of the emperor. Later, after advancing to colonel in the MRC, he helped organize the Medical Veterans of the World War, which subsequently merged with the Association of Military Surgeons. Following the outbreak of World War II, though in failing health, McCormack spent an increasing amount of time in Washington as an adviser to several government agencies. At his death, it was widely commented in the medical press that he had been a casualty of the conflict.

The medical press also noted that McCormack's death marked the end of a 64-year father-son dynasty unparalleled in the history of American medicine and public health. The senior McCormack, as executive officer of the Kentucky State Board of Health since 1883, wrote the state's modern medical practice statutes, reorganized its medical profession, and brought the two together as a force for public welfare. The passage of leadership to his son during the second decade of the twentieth century coincided with the application of bacteriology to disease problems on a large scale. Whereas Joseph Nathaniel McCormack established a framework for public health in Kentucky, Arthur Thomas McCormack built on it an elaborate structure for policy development and administration.

Founder and dean of the University of Louisville School of Public Health (1919–1930), the younger McCormack became secretary of the Kentucky State Board of Health after his father's death in 1922, serving continuously in that position and as state commissioner of health from 1936 to 1943. Under his leadership, and with financial assistance from the Rockefeller Foundation, major advances were made against diverse infections such as malaria, tuberculosis, trachoma, and hookworm. His vigorous efforts in behalf of maternal and child welfare, especially in the poorer counties of eastern Kentucky, were instrumental in establishing the Kentucky Committee for Mothers and Babies in 1925 and, subsequently, the famous Frontier Nursing Service (FNS).

In 1928 nurses on horseback in military-type uniforms served families in an area of 250 square miles, charging fees of a dollar per person per year (payable in kind or labor) for all nursing care and five dollars for obstetrical cases. In cooperation with the state board of health the nurses also gave hookworm treatments, inoculated against typhoid and diphtheria, and chlorinated wells. During the next five years, under McCormack's guidance, the FNS's range increased to 800 square miles, covering parts of Leslie, Perry, Clay, and Bell counties, and the scope of its activities broadened to include generalized public health nursing. In 1940, among 120 county jurisdictions in Kentucky, eighty-six had full-time health departments, an achievement that placed McCormack among the nation's leading state health officers. For his contributions to medicine and public health he was elected president of the Conference of State and Provincial Health Authorities of North America in 1927, the American Public Health Association in 1937, and the Southern Medical Association in 1940. He was also a founder and diplomate of the American College of Surgeons.

Besides an indefatigable zest for public service, McCormack was also known for his magnetic personality and genuine warmth in personal relations. He was reputed to be a raconteur without peer, altogether genial and affable in manner, and a man who, with a wink and a smile, won the confidence of skeptics and the respect of adversaries. Playing cards and relaxed gatherings were his favorite leisure activities, and his memberships in social and fraternal organizations were as numerous as his public and professional ones. McCormack had married Mary Moore in 1897; they had four children. The couple divorced, and in 1924 he married Jane Teare Dahlman. They had no children. McCormack died in Louisville.

• McCormack's papers are held in Special Collections, Kornhauser Health Sciences Library, University of Louisville. His work as an editor and writer on medicine and public health may be seen in the *Kentucky Medical Journal* and in *Bulletins* of the Kentucky State Board of Health for the appropriate years. He was also the author of *A Course in Physical Education for the Common Schools of Kentucky* (1920). See also Medical Historical Research Project of the Work Projects Administration for the Commonwealth of Kentucky, *Medicine and Its Development in Kentucky* (1940); James G. Burrow, *AMA: Voice of American Medicine* (1963); John H. Ellis, *Medicine in Kentucky* (1977); and Broadus B. Jackson, "A History of Public Health Administration in Kentucky, 1920–1940" (Ph.D. diss., Indiana Univ., 1963). Useful obituaries and eulogies include *Journal of the American Medical Association* 122

(1943): 1201; *Kentucky Medical Journal* 41 (1943): 289–90; and *Supplement to the Kentucky Medical Journal* 42 (1944): 215–50.

JOHN H. ELLIS

MCCORMACK, John (14 June 1884–16 Sept. 1945), singer, was born John Francis McCormack in Athlone, Ireland, the son of Andrew McCormack, a foreman in the woolen mills, and Hannah Watson. Although poor, the family managed to send John to a local Marist Brothers' school, where his natural singing ability was recognized, and he received his first formal musical training. He excelled in academics as well and won scholarships that enabled him to attend the Diocesan College of the Immaculate Conception of Summer Hill at Sligo, where he gave his first public performances during school concerts. At his graduation in 1902, he won first prizes in languages and mathematics but failed to secure a scholarship to the Dublin College of Science to pursue these studies.

Later that year McCormack relocated to Dublin to prepare for the civil service examinations only to be discovered as a musical talent. Singing and accompanying himself on the piano, he was overheard by a neighbor who arranged for an audition with Vincent O'Brien, the director of the Marlborough Street Cathedral Choir. O'Brien became the young tenor's first teacher, eventually offering him his first professional position with the Marlborough choir in 1903.

In May 1904 McCormack won the gold medal at the Dublin Feis Ceoil, a national Irish cultural festival. The following month the tenor made his first trip to the United States, where he performed at the St. Louis Exposition with soprano Lily Foley. During this visit he made his first recordings on cylinders for Edison Bell and the Gramophone Company. Returning to Ireland, McCormack was encouraged to study voice more seriously. He went in 1905 to Milan, where he studied with Vincenzo Sabatini and made his debut in *L'Amico Fritz* on 13 January 1906 in Savona under the stage name of "Giovanni Foli."

Upon his return to Ireland in 1906, McCormack married Lily Foley; they had two children of their own and adopted another. The couple moved to London to facilitate McCormack's career. However, he encountered a profound lack of interest in his talents and spent months auditioning and filling engagements in minor venues. In February 1907 he received an invitation to perform at an Arthur Boosey "Ballad Concert." This first performance was so successful that another was scheduled for the next month. These appearances gained him a Covent Garden audition and an October 1907 debut as Turiddù in Mascagni's *Cavalleria Rusticana*. At age twenty-three McCormack became what was then the youngest tenor to have sung a principal role with the company. The 1907–1908 season at Covent Garden included appearances as the Duke of Mantua in Verdi's *Rigoletto* and as Don Ottavio in Mozart's *Don Giovanni*. During the same period McCormack toured the British Isles with Fritz Kreisler and made

his oratorio debut as tenor soloist in Mendelssohn's *Elijah*.

Oscar Hammerstein heard McCormack at Covent Garden and arranged for his American operatic debut as Alfredo in Verdi's *La Traviata* on 10 November 1909 with the Manhattan Opera Company. When the company shut down in 1910, McCormack toured Australia with Nellie Melba in Italian operas. On 29 November 1910 he debuted with the Metropolitan Opera, again as Alfredo. In 1914 Lilli Lehmann invited him to perform Don Ottavio at the Salzburg Festival, but the outbreak of World War I brought plans for the event to a halt. Until 1919 McCormack continued to appear with opera companies in Chicago, Boston, and Philadelphia. However, the tenor had already begun to see success on the concert stage, and by his own choice his operatic roles became more infrequent. He made his final operatic appearance with the Monte Carlo Opera in 1923.

His application for U.S. citizenship in 1914 and his support of Irish nationalism alienated him from the British public throughout World War I. However, McCormack won American audiences with his appearances, many of which benefited various American war charities, and he raised hundreds of thousands of dollars in Liberty Bond sales alone. In June 1919 McCormack became a naturalized citizen, and the period that followed saw the beginning of the tenor's brilliant concert career and his meteoric rise in popularity.

Although he was often criticized by the musical establishment for his programming of popular songs and Irish ballads, McCormack's concerts were enormously successful among the wider public audience. Houses were often sold out, creating such a tremendous demand for tickets that it is believed the Irish-born tenor was the first artist to have audiences seated on the stage. In a single season he gave twelve sold-out concerts in New York City, alternating between the Hippodrome and Carnegie Hall. Those who could not hear him in the concert halls could hear him on recordings of favorite selections from his recitals. Sales from recordings of songs like "When Irish Eyes Are Smiling," "Mother Machree," and "I Hear You Calling Me" totaled more than $2 million. McCormack continued to make recordings until 1942.

McCormack's concertizing expanded further, climaxing in a return to England in June 1924 for a Queen's Hall concert. After his ten-year absence, McCormack was received warmly and with much acclaim. He appeared throughout the British Isles until well after his "official" retirement in 1938.

McCormack continued to build an American career with his broadcasts on "The Victor Hour," which began on 1 January 1925, and his motion picture debut in *Song o' My Heart*, released in 1929. These ventures served to gain for him a larger following in the United States, even after he returned to Ireland in 1938.

McCormack made his final American concert appearance in Buffalo, New York, in March 1937. He planned to retire after a performance in London in November 1938, a farewell recital in the Royal Albert

Hall before an audience of 9,000. However, he returned to the stage the next year to raise funds for the war effort. It is believed that McCormack never regained his health after collapsing at a benefit for the British Red Cross early in 1945. He eventually contracted pneumonia, from which he died at his home outside Dublin.

During his lifetime McCormack enjoyed numerous honors. In 1920 he was named vice president of the Irish Royal Academy of Music, and in 1933 he received the Laetare Medal from the University of Notre Dame. He was given the title of count by Pope Pius XI, was chevalier of the French Legion of Honor, and held decorations from the Orders of the Holy Sepulchre and St. Gregory the Great. In a tribute to the endurance of his stature as an artist, in 1984 the postal services of both the United States and Ireland issued stamps commemorating the centennial of his birth.

• McCormack's autobiography, *John McCormack: His Own Life Story* (1918; repr. 1973), was transcribed by Pierre V. R. Key. Lily F. McCormack, *I Hear You Calling Me* (1949; repr. 1979), offers a great deal of information on his life and career. Releases of historical recordings include *John McCormack Recital* (1981) and *Great Singers: Previously Unpublished Recordings* (1985), which provide examples of McCormack's vocal abilities. Leonard Strong, *John McCormack: The Story of a Singer* (1941; repr. 1949), Raymond Foxall, *John McCormack* (1964), and Gordon Ledbetter, *The Great Irish Tenor* (1978), are nicely complemented by the remembrances of Charles Wagner (McCormack's manager), *Seeing Stars* (1940), and Gerald Moore (the singer's last accompanist), *Am I Too Loud?* (1962). James Cartwright and Paul Worth, *John McCormack: A Comprehensive Discography* (1986), includes a foreword by Gwendolyn McCormack-Pyke and is the definitive work in this genre.

STEPHANIE TINGLER

MCCORMACK, John William (21 Dec. 1891–22 Nov. 1980), Speaker of the U.S. House of Representatives (1963–1971), was born in South Boston, Massachusetts, the son of Joseph H. McCormack, a stonemason, and Mary E. O'Brien. When his father died, John left school at age thirteen to support his mother and two younger brothers. After studying law on his own, McCormack was admitted to the bar in 1913 and started a small practice. In 1920 he married Harriet Joyce of South Boston, who gave up a promising career as a contralto with the Metropolitan Opera. Although childless, the marriage became a Washington legend; the McCormacks had dinner together every evening until Harriet's death in 1971.

Unlike many other Boston neighborhoods, South Boston did not have a single dominant political organization, thus permitting McCormack and others to launch their political careers pretty much on their own. An excellent public speaker, McCormack made the rounds of community organizations, becoming a familiar figure in this heavily Irish–working-class and Democratic party bastion. He first ran for public office in 1917, winning election as a delegate to the Massachusetts Constitutional Convention, although he re-

signed the post when he enlisted as a private in the army. McCormack remained stateside during World War I, and he was elected to the first of three consecutive one-year terms in the Massachusetts House of Representatives in 1919. He entered the Massachusetts Senate in 1923 and served as the leader of the Democratic minority in 1925–1926; while in the state legislature he fought repeal of protective legislation for women and children employed in factories and against Prohibition. In 1926 McCormack unsuccessfully challenged the veteran Democratic incumbent, James A. Gallivan, in the South Boston–Dorchester–Roxbury congressional district. When Gallivan died in 1928, McCormack defeated eight rivals in the special election to fill the district's vacant seat; he never faced serious opposition in subsequent elections.

In the U.S. House, McCormack quickly became an intimate of Democratic leader John Nance Garner of Texas, with whom he shared a strong sense of party loyalty and a passion for poker. Garner's appointment of the relatively junior McCormack to the powerful Ways and Means Committee in 1931 heralded the alliance of rural southerners and big-city northerners that captured the White House for the Democrats in 1932 and provided solid majorities for the New Deal until 1937.

McCormack's reputation for protecting party interests led to his appointment as chairman of the Special Committee on Un-American Activities in 1934. Although the sponsor of the resolution creating the committee, Samuel Dickstein (D-N.Y.), had intended it as a measure directed against Nazi and anti-Semitic organizations, McCormack focused the committee's attention on the Communist party. As a devout Roman Catholic and firm believer in the American faith in individualism, freedom, capitalism, and opportunity, McCormack despised communism with a passion. (This attitude later made him a strong proponent of the Cold War containment policy and of continued American involvement in Vietnam.) Nonetheless, McCormack ran the panel with a due regard for the rights of those under investigation and in 1935 produced a report that led to the enactment in 1938 of legislation requiring the registration of all agents distributing propaganda on behalf of a foreign power.

McCormack's support of Texan Sam Rayburn over New Yorker John J. O'Connor in the contest to be House majority leader in January 1937 broke O'Connor's grip on the northern, urban, Irish vote in the Democratic caucus and helped carry Rayburn to victory. Three years later, when Rayburn became Speaker, McCormack enjoyed his backing and that of President Franklin D. Roosevelt in his successful bid for the majority leadership. For the next twenty-two years McCormack labored in Rayburn's shadow, earning a reputation for both partisanship and a willingness to compromise. The two men, positioned at the center of the Democratic party in the 1940s and 1950s, strategically as well as ideologically, advanced a moderately liberal platform embracing limited expansion in coverage of and spending on social welfare programs as well as marginal action on civil rights.

McCormack and Rayburn, despite their very different backgrounds, worked well together because of their shared attachment to the Democratic party and to the House of Representatives as an institution. By contrast, although McCormack and John F. Kennedy were both of Irish descent and natives of the Bay State, their relationship proved far less congenial. Separated by more than a quarter-century in age, by wealth and education, and by the younger man's White House ambitions, they could find little common ground. McCormack only reluctantly endorsed Kennedy's abortive attempt to capture the vice presidential nomination in 1956, and he ultimately supported Kennedy's presidential aspirations in 1960 largely because he had little choice. In 1962 McCormack's nephew and the president's youngest brother waged a bitter primary contest for the Democratic senatorial nomination, with Edward Kennedy prevailing.

McCormack's ascension to the Speakership in January 1962, following Rayburn's death the previous November, created additional tensions with President Kennedy. Rayburn had had little success in getting southern Democrats to back the president's more expansive liberal agenda, including a cabinet-level Department of Urban Affairs and Housing, health insurance for the elderly, and federal aid for education, and McCormack, despite his long ties with southern congressmen, fared no better. Also, McCormack, the first Roman Catholic to be Speaker, helped defeat Kennedy's aid to education bill because it contained no assistance for parochial schools.

McCormack forged a good relationship with Lyndon Johnson when Johnson became president following Kennedy's assassination. The Texan's old-style politicking meshed perfectly with McCormack's techniques, and Johnson's Great Society programs received prompt House approval from 1964 to 1966.

But McCormack's bland and aging leadership came under increasing fire from his House colleagues. The Speaker's defense of the seniority system and his unwillingness to challenge the power of committee chairmen led Richard Bolling (D-Mo.) in October 1967 to urge McCormack to retire at the end of the 1968 session. The Speaker ignored Bolling's call, but at the start of the new Congress in 1969 he was challenged for the Speakership by Morris Udall (D-Ariz.). Although McCormack retained the post by a 178-58 vote in the Democratic caucus, his support for President Richard M. Nixon's Vietnam policies and his resistance to institutional change in the House continued to rankle liberal Democrats. In early 1970 Jerome Waldie (D-Calif.) introduced a motion of no-confidence in the Speaker, which the caucus defeated 192-23.

By the time of the Waldie motion, however, McCormack's days as Speaker were numbered. In 1969 McCormack's reputation had been tarnished by disclosures that a top aide and a friend had used the Speaker's office to influence a government agency on behalf of a private client. McCormack denied any personal wrongdoing, and none was proven. Still, the episode raised further doubts about his leadership, and in May 1970 McCormack announced that he would retire from the House at the end of the year. His nine years as Speaker placed him second only to Rayburn in the length of his tenure.

McCormack spent much of the first year of his retirement in Washington caring for his ailing wife; after her death in December 1971, he returned to Boston. Aside from appearances at ceremonial occasions, McCormack led a quiet life in the decade before his death.

• McCormack's congressional office files are at the Boston University Library; mainly dealing with constituent matters, they offer little insight into McCormack's leadership role. They might be supplemented by the Sam Rayburn Papers at the Rayburn Library in Bonham, Tex. McCormack prepared oral histories for the John F. Kennedy and Lyndon B. Johnson libraries. A brief and affectionate account of his life is Paul M. Wright, *John W. McCormack* (1985). For a historian's understanding portrayal of the urban neighborhood in which McCormack grew up and represented in Congress, see Thomas H. O'Connor, *South Boston: My Home Town* (1988). The only extended scholarly treatment of a portion of McCormack's career is Lester I. Gordon, "John McCormack and the Roosevelt Era" (Ph.D. diss., Boston Univ., 1976). His chairmanship of the Special Committee on Un-American Activities is discussed in Walter Goodman, *The Committee* (1968), and Philip L. Cantelon, "In Defense of America: Congressional Investigations of Communism in the United States, 1919–1935" (Ph.D. diss., Indiana Univ., 1971). McCormack is mentioned frequently in the memoirs of his two immediate successors as Speaker, Carl Albert, *Little Giant* (1990), and Tip O'Neill, *Man of the House* (1987). Richard Bolling criticized McCormack's leadership in *House Out of Order* (1965) and *Power in the House* (1968). Ronald M. Peters, Jr., *The American Speakership* (1990), presents an academic's view. *Current Biography* featured McCormack in 1943 and 1962, and the Boston *Globe* and the *New York Times* ran lengthy obituaries, 23 Nov. 1980.

MARK I. GELFAND

MCCORMACK, Joseph Nathaniel (9 Nov. 1847–4 May 1922), physician and health officer, was born near Howard's Mill in Nelson County, Kentucky, the son of Thomas McCormack, a farmer and merchant, and Elizabeth Brown. The sixth of sixteen children, he attended local schools until the outbreak of the Civil War, when, with two brothers in Confederate service, he began to work on the farm and in his father's store. McCormack aspired to become a doctor, and he prepared himself by studying Latin, mathematics, literature, and history. In 1868 he enrolled in the medical department of Miami University of Ohio in Cincinnati, and in 1870 he received his M.D. Following a year's internship at Cincinnati Hospital, he returned home to marry Corinne Crenshaw and to enter the practice of medicine. Their only child, Arthur Thomas McCormack, would one day succeed to his father's eminence in the field of public health.

As a fledgling country doctor, McCormack battled epidemic cholera and yellow fever in 1873 and exhibited a special talent for surgery. After moving to Bowling Green, Kentucky, in 1875, he successfully performed a then-uncommon Cesarean section, winning him the recognition of leading surgeons and an M.D. *ad eundum* from the University of Louisville. In another daring operation, he resected the gut of an intestinal gunshot victim and saved the patient's life. The youngest physician in the community, McCormack gained further recognition by his selfless care of the sick and dying during severe yellow fever epidemics in 1878 and 1879, events that marked a turning point in his career.

During the Danville meeting of the Kentucky State Medical Society in May 1879, McCormack listened as Samuel David Gross, an elder statesman of American surgery, urged physicians to heed the higher calling of preventive medicine, then understood as public hygiene. For meritorious service during the epidemics, Governor Luke P. Blackburn, a physician, appointed McCormack to the newly created Kentucky State Board of Health in 1880. In 1882, after studying public health organizations and methods in London and Edinburgh, he became the board's secretary and state health officer, a position he held actively until 1912. A supporter of the short-lived National Board of Health (1879–1883) and the early Sanitary Council of the Mississippi Valley (1879–1884), he also served in various capacities with the American Public Health Association, the National Conference of State Boards of Health, the National Conference of State Licensing and Examining Boards, and the International Quarantine Commission.

In Britain McCormack had learned that a well-educated and well-organized medical profession was prerequisite to the successful formulation and administration of public health policy. In the Kentucky of the 1880s, and in most of the United States, medical education, licensure, and organization suffered from a half-century's deterioration, and quackery dominated the field of medical practice. In city, town, and village, sanitary conditions were appalling and infectious diseases rampant. Against fierce opposition, McCormack waged a vigorous campaign for effective licensure. This struggle resulted in the 1888 enactment of Kentucky's first medical practice statute, the first in the nation to unify licensure of allopathic, homeopathic, and eclectic physicians. The law was greatly strengthened in 1892 by an amendment establishing the principle of state interest in competent medical practice. Further revision of licensure requirements in 1904 raised standards of medical education in the state well before the Flexner *Report on Medical Education in the United States and Canada* of 1910.

Responding to McCormack's energetic leadership as state health officer and secretary of the state medical society, Kentucky physicians supported his extensive legislative measures through new county and municipal boards of health. McCormack also used public health initiatives during the 1890s to resurrect old county medical societies and to establish new ones. At the Paducah meeting of the state medical society in 1898, he presented what proved to be an effective plan for reorganizing the medical profession to increase its political power. Already well known professionally outside Kentucky for his accomplishments there, McCormack rose to a position of national leadership in the American Medical Association, which was then foundering on the same problems with which he had had demonstrable success. "No event in the social history of American medicine," writes the premier historian of the AMA, "is more important than the selection in 1900 of the magnetic secretary of the Kentucky State Board of Health to organize the medical profession" (*Organized Medicine*, p. 16).

Led by McCormack, the AMA's Committee on Reorganization presented its plan to the St. Paul convention in 1901 to bring all licensed physicians (a designation later expanded to include sectarian practitioners) into membership under professional discipline. Beginning in 1902, as the AMA's official organizer, McCormack traveled the length and breadth of the land for a decade, tirelessly addressing medical groups as well as mixed audiences of physicians and laity on the principles of public health and professional welfare he had learned in Europe. A man of less physical stamina and missionary zeal could hardly have endured his schedule. His itinerary for the period of 30 April to 26 May 1906, for example, included thirty-eight speeches, most of them given in two towns on the same day.

An imposing figure and eloquent speaker, McCormack skillfully linked public and professional interests in addresses such as "What the People Should Know about the Doctors and What the Doctors Should Know about Themselves" and "The New Gospel of Health and Long Life." He used down-home phrasing and biblical metaphor to convey in evangelical style the message that the interests of society might best be served by first serving the interests of the profession. In 1900 the AMA had enrolled only 8,400 of the nation's 100,000 allopathic physicians. When McCormack rested his labors in December 1911, AMA membership exceeded 70,000, a number reflecting the absorption of formerly shunned sectarians and declining medical school enrollments. By 1920, when membership reached 83,338, the AMA stood at the threshold of an era of unprecedented economic and political power.

In 1912 McCormack relinquished executive authority in the Kentucky State Board of Health to his son, although he remained active in the board's affairs until his death in Louisville. A communicant of the Episcopal church, he avoided the label of party in politics. His personal reputation was that of a devoted husband and father, a charming, affable gentleman of refinement and culture. A contemporary described him as "a distinguished and most useful man of medicine. . . . [T]here was at all times no man more fully abreast of his era, more completely in the medical movement" (*Louisville Herald*, 5 May 1922).

• McCormack's official and personal papers are held by the Kentucky State Board of Health and the Kornhauser Health Sciences Library, University of Louisville, respectively. His writings on medicine and public health are in numerous publications including the bulletins of the Kentucky State Board of Health, the *Kentucky Medical Journal*, the *Journal of the American Medical Association*, the *American Public Health Association Reports*, and the *American Journal of Public Health*, to mention but a few. In retirement he edited a compilation of essays and documents titled *Some of the Medical Pioneers of Kentucky* (1917). See also Medical Historical Research Project of the Work Projects Administration for the Commonwealth of Kentucky, *Medicine and Its Development in Kentucky* (1940); James G. Burrow, *AMA: Voice of American Medicine* (1963) and *Organized Medicine in the Progressive Era: The Move toward Monopoly* (1977); John H. Ellis, *Medicine in Kentucky* (1977); and Broadus B. Jackson, "A History of Public Health Administration in Kentucky, 1920–1940" (Ph.D. diss., Indiana Univ., 1963). Useful obituaries include the *Kentucky Medical Journal* 21 (Jan. 1923): 1–74, and the *Louisville Courier-Journal* and *Louisville Herald*, both 5 May 1922.

JOHN H. ELLIS

MCCORMICK, Anne Elizabeth O'Hare (16 May 1882?–29 May 1954), political journalist, was born in Wakefield, Yorkshire, England, the daughter of American parents, Thomas J. O'Hare, a life insurance regional manager who deserted the family, and Teresa Beatrice Berry, a poet and journalist. There is some discrepancy regarding the exact year of her birth, some sources listing it as 1880. McCormick grew up in Columbus, Ohio, and graduated in 1898 from St. Mary of the Springs Academy, a convent school that later became a college. Following her mother's footsteps as a poet and a writer for a national Catholic weekly, *Catholic Universe Bulletin*, McCormick served as its associate editor.

After her marriage in 1910 to Francis J. McCormick, a Dayton engineer and importer of industrial equipment, McCormick resigned her editorship and traveled with her husband on European business trips. She wrote freelance articles for *Catholic World*, *Reader Magazine*, the *Saturday Evening Post*, and *Atlantic Monthly*. In 1921 she sent a "timid note" to Carr V. Van Anda, managing editor of the *New York Times*, asking if she could send him some news stories from overseas. Van Anda agreed, and her *New York Times Magazine* articles began appearing as impressionistic pieces about European countries in the aftermath of World War I.

The *Times*'s irascible editor Lester Markel often had McCormick rewrite a piece several times. Her writing style caused the men on the copy desk to call her "Verbose Annie" until she honed her skills so well that her columns went to press untouched. What amazed everyone was how she was able to get the interviews she did, when so many *Times* foreign correspondents could not. James Reston said that her ability to gain access was due to her "sheer gift of personality" and her intelligence. Clifton Daniel recalled that after World War II, when he offered the usual courtesies when McCormick came into Bonn, she politely refused, and "the next thing I knew, she had an appointment with everyone in town."

Her early stories covered the rise of fascism in Italy. Although other journalists dismissed Benito Mussolini as just "an upstart Milanese newspaper editor," McCormick understood his appeal. After hearing him give a particularly stirring political speech, she wrote, "Italy has heard its master's voice." After 1925, she wrote exclusively for the *Times*, with the exception of a 1933–1934 series on Europe in the *Ladies' Home Journal*.

From the day he became the *Times*'s publisher in 1896, Adolph S. Ochs fought to deny women the vote and keep them out of the newsroom. His daughter Iphigene, who secretly supported the suffrage movement, was appointed to the *Times* board of directors and along with her husband became friends with Anne McCormick. After Ochs died in 1935, Iphigene's husband, Arthur Hays Sulzberger, the new publisher, appointed McCormick to the editorial board. As the only woman to have gained such status, at the *New York Times*, she received Sulzberger's directive, "You are to be the 'freedom' editor. It will be your job to stand up on your hind legs and shout whenever freedom is interfered with in any part of the world" (*The World at Home*, p. x).

McCormick did just that with three columns a week on world affairs. She began by contributing unsigned columns, as was the practice in 1936. By February 1937 she had her own regular byline column. She became one of the four great political columnists of the time: Walter Lippmann and Arthur Krock wrote on national affairs, and McCormick and Dorothy Thompson wrote on world affairs. McCormick culled vast knowledge from the European upheavals, the people affected, and the most influential political leaders. Her colleagues noted that "she had the uncanny knack of being where the news was breaking" (*New York Times*, 30 May 1954): she was in Rome when Neville Chamberlain, Britain's prime minister, called on Mussolini; she was in the British Parliament when Chamberlain finally gave up on his policy of appeasement toward the Nazi-Fascist axis; she was in eastern Czechoslovakia when it declared its short independence and when the Germans authorized the Hungarians to occupy it.

Her goal was to capture the essence of people and reveal how their minds worked. She brought to the *Times* the personalities and thinking of such world leaders as Léon Blum, Adolf Hitler, Harry Truman, Dwight Eisenhower, and Franklin D. Roosevelt. Roosevelt broke his rule of "no exclusive interviews" for her yearly requests of "tea and conversation." She wrote her insights of their last interview some three weeks before he died on 12 April 1945. She said about Roosevelt, "Small and shortsighted as he sometimes was in his political deals at home, his 'farsight' was keener than that of any statesman of his time. So was his instinct for reading the minds of men. People everywhere trusted him above all others because he was their representative in the high councils of the world" (*New York Times*, 22 Apr. 1945).

McCormick's technique was to listen carefully and seldom take notes because "it made people too cautious." She would absorb facts and figures and take in the mood of the persons and places. Her manner was said to be modest but energetic, quiet but intelligent. Her grasp of the world's knottiest problems was penetrating. In 1936 she wrote, "All the rulers of Europe have shriveled or aged during the past few years. On the faces of Mussolini, Hitler, Stanley Baldwin, even the rotating governors of France, strain and worry have etched indelible lines. Caught off-guard, when they are alone they are tired and baffled men who have paid a heavy price for power" (*New York Times*, 21 June 1936). About Franklin Roosevelt in 1936 she wrote, "Mr. Roosevelt is a unique figure in the modern world: the one statesman this writer has seen who seems able to relax" (*New York Times*, 21 June 1936).

Few journalists were so honored in their own time. Her 1937 Pulitzer Prize was awarded for correspondence at a time when there was only one award for both domestic and international reporting. She also received the 1939 Woman of the Year award from the National Federation of Business and Professional Women. She won countless other awards, such as the Women's National Press Club Achievement Award in 1945, and received honorary degrees from sixteen universities. After the war she served as a delegate to the United Nations Educational, Scientific and Cultural Organization (UNESCO) Conferences in 1946 and 1948.

After she died in New York City President Eisenhower acknowledged her unusual ability to explain the complex issues of world events. He said, "Mrs. McCormick was a truly great reporter, respected at home and abroad for her keen analysis and impartial presentation of the news developments of our day." In the *Times* James Reston wrote, "She had all the qualities of a good reporter—vitality, curiosity, intelligence, courage and something more, a rare fit of sympathy for all sorts of people . . . a religious conviction which enabled her to see things in the ultimate perspective of life itself."

• McCormick's papers are in the New York Public Library and include her correspondence, her lectures, and clippings of her articles. She wrote *The Hammer and the Scythe: Communist Russia Enters the Second Decade* (1928). Her friend Marion Turner Sheehan edited two collections of her columns, *The World at Home: Selections from the Writings of Anne O'Hare McCormick* (1956) and *Vatican Journal, 1921–1954* (1957). For substantial references to McCormick's journalism, see Julia Edwards, *Women of the World* (1988); Nan Robertson, *The Girls in the Balcony: Women, Men, and the New York Times* (1992); and Ishbel Ross, *Ladies of the Press: The Story of Women in Journalism by an Insider* (1936). An obituary is in the *New York Times*, 30 May 1954.

BETTY HOUCHIN WINFIELD

MCCORMICK, Cyrus Hall (15 Feb. 1809–13 May 1884), inventor and businessman, was born in Rockbridge County, Virginia, the son of Robert McCormick, an inventor and farmer, and Mary Ann Hall. As a youth, McCormick received very little formal schooling. He spent many hours in the workshop of his father, who invented a clover huller, blacksmith's bellows, a hydraulic power machine, and other labor-saving devices. For twenty years McCormick's father tried to build a reaping machine, but like many other inventors, he was unsuccessful. In 1831, at the age of twenty-two, McCormick constructed a reaper, based on principles completely different from those used by his father. Although crude in design, this machine employed the features basic to all subsequent reapers. After several public trials of his new machine, McCormick took out a patent on it in 1834. For the next few years, however, he was primarily preoccupied with the family iron works. But when the panic of 1837 crippled the business and brought significant debts, McCormick again turned his attention to improving and manufacturing his reaper.

In 1844 sales of McCormick's reaper, all built at the family blacksmith shop at Walnut Grove, reached fifty. After experimenting with constructing machines in Brockport, New York, and Cincinnati, Ohio, McCormick consolidated his manufacturing in Chicago in 1847, having recognized the city's potential as a commercial center because of its potential for rail and water transport and its proximity to the grain fields of the Midwest and Plains states. The company he formed in Chicago was called McCormick and Gray, becoming McCormick, Ogden, and Co. in October 1848. His main competitor during these years was Obed Hussey, whose machine was better for mowing (cutting grass) but not as good for reaping (cutting grain) as McCormick's. A reaper had a divider to separate the grain to be cut from the adjacent grain, a reciprocating cutting blade, a reel to pull the grain to be cut against the blade, and a platform to catch the severed grain.

After McCormick's basic patent expired in 1848, he was involved until the end of his life in many legal battles. He spent much time and money on this litigation, which featured such prominent lawyers as Abraham Lincoln, William Seward, Edwin Stanton, and Roscoe Conkling as counsels either for or against him, but his legal efforts brought him little benefit. Only a few of his improvements made after 1831 remained protected; his basic design passed into the public domain.

McCormick's genius lay more in his ability to manufacture and promote farm implements than in his talent as an inventor. A shrewd organizer, he bested his competitors through the use of mass production, creative advertising, public demonstrations of the quality of his machines, warranties, and consumer financing. He also developed a large group of traveling salesmen who worked primarily on commission. As a result, during the 1850s McCormick's reaper became well known throughout the United States while competition in reapers increased quickly and dramatically. By 1860 more than 100 companies were making reapers, but McCormick was outdistancing all rivals, selling about 5,000 machines a year.

By winning the Council Medal, the highest prize awarded at the Great Exhibition of 1851 in London, McCormick's reaper was introduced to Europe. Between 1855 and 1880 it earned major prizes at world fairs in Paris, London, Hamburg, Lille, Vienna, Philadelphia, and Melbourne. Despite these honors and extensive efforts to sell reapers in Europe—some by McCormick himself, who spent much time in England and on the Continent during the 1860s and 1870s—overseas sales did not become profitable until after 1876. During the 1880s large numbers of reapers were sold abroad, especially in Canada, Russia, New Zealand, Australia, and Argentina.

Always looking for ways to improve his product, McCormick led the way in developing an automatic self-raking device, a hand-binding harvester, a wire-binder, and a twine-binder. When the great Chicago fire of 1871 destroyed his factory, the 62-year-old entrepreneur, who was already very wealthy, built a larger one. Despite the hordes of grasshoppers, and the bad weather that plagued the Plains states, and the opposition of the Grangers, who wanted to buy farm machinery in large lots at low cash prices directly from manufacturers, thereby eliminating both credit and salesman's commissions, his company greatly expanded production and sales during the next four years. Aided by good harvests, high prices for grain, improved transportation, and mushrooming settlement of the Plains states, McCormick's company, by the mid-1880s, was selling over 50,000 machines a year, employing 1,400 workers at peak times, and making unparalleled profits. The business, which for many years was primarily managed by two of Cyrus's brothers Leander J. McCormick and William S. McCormick and eventually by his son Cyrus Hall McCormick, Jr., continued to grow steadily after the inventor's death in 1884 and in 1902 merged with several other firms to form the International Harvester Company.

In 1879 McCormick was elected to the French Academy of Sciences on the grounds that he had "done more for the cause of agriculture than any other living man." Like other major technological innovations, the reaper profoundly changed the pattern of human activity and interaction. Because wheat and other grains had to be harvested within one or two weeks of when they ripened, before the invention of the reaper a farmer could plant only as much acreage as his entire family and perhaps a couple of seasonal laborers could cut and store in this amount of time. Using a reaper, a farmer could harvest as much wheat in a day as he could in two weeks using sickle and cradle. The reaper therefore led to larger farms, improved fields (as farmers removed rocks and stumps to facilitate reaping), higher yields, and lower labor costs, and it helped to motivate hundreds of thousands of Americans to move west and begin new farms. By making agricultural production much more efficient and reducing labor demands in agriculture, it contributed to an increased work force for business and industry. Moreover, it helped the North to win the Civil War by releasing many men from farming to serve in the army, by providing England with wheat to offset the South's cotton exports to that country (which early in the war threatened to cause England to support the South), and by enabling the North to sell large amounts of grain to Europe and pay its military bills.

In addition to his business activities, McCormick was very involved in the affairs of the Presbyterian church and the Democratic party. Before 1861 he thought that these two organizations held the greatest hope for holding the nation together. After 1865 McCormick worked through these agencies and others to reduce intersectional hatred and to heal the nation's wounds. His large donation to a struggling Presbyterian seminary in New Albany, Indiana, in 1859 led to its relocation in Chicago later to become the McCormick Theological Seminary. For many years thereafter he was actively involved in the life of the seminary, contributing additional funds, helping to select professors, and prodding the institution to remain faithful to Old School Calvinism. He fought against the reunion of the Old School and New School branches of the Presbyterian church, accomplished in 1870, because he believed that New School theology was not fully orthodox. His dislike for the New School also sprang from the denomination's practice of taking stands on "political" issues, especially its opposition to slavery in the 1840s and 1850s. On the other hand, he strongly supported reunion of the northern and southern branches of the Presbyterian church, which had split at the onset of the Civil War. His desire to promote Old School Calvinism led him to acquire the *Presbyterian Expositor* in 1860 and the *Interior* in 1872. Under his leadership, the *Interior* became a very respected and influential Presbyterian periodical. McCormick's political connections, wealth, prestige, and involvement in theological debates made him a significant force in the Presbyterian church between 1855 and his death.

In 1864 McCormick ran as the Democratic candidate for Congress from the First District of Illinois (losing to the Republican) and in 1876 was seriously considered as the party's vice presidential candidate. The combination of Republican electoral strength in the state and McCormick's candidness about and unwillingness to compromise on many issues prevented him from winning political office. He also chaired Illinois's Democratic state central committee (1872 and 1876) and served on the Democratic National Committee (1872 to at least 1876).

In addition to contributing liberally to what eventually became McCormick Theological Seminary in Chicago and to the Democratic party, McCormick also supported other educational institutions (especially Washington and Lee College and Union Theological Seminary in Virginia), the Chicago YMCA, and Presbyterian foreign and domestic missions. Like most other wealthy businessmen, he was besieged by requests for financial assistance, especially by fellow Virginians after the Civil War ended. According to one estimate, McCormick gave away about $550,000 of his $10 million fortune, of which about $450,000 went to enterprises associated with the Presbyterian church.

McCormick's tremendous success as an inventor and entrepreneur was due in large part to his personality and his philosophy of life. Raised in a strict Presbyterian home, he embodied throughout his life the Protestant work ethic. A tenacious, driven, and innovative man, his life was dominated by his business activities. He did not marry until 26 January 1858, when he was nearly fifty, and even a wife and as many as five children did not moderate his custom of working as much as fourteen hours a day. His wife, Nettie Fowler McCormick, who became well known herself as a philanthropist, expanded the inventor's interests, broadened his social circle, and discussed many business decisions with him. After they married, they divided their time among homes in Chicago, the ideal location for their manufacturing; New York City, the center of their financial affairs; and Washington, D.C., the site of their legal battles. A born competitor, McCormick was preoccupied with defeating his rivals, solving difficult mechanical problems, and overcoming the obstacles of nature, new markets, and litigation. Although he actively sought popularity and praise, McCormick was not willing to sacrifice his integrity or his principles to gain status or success. He died in Chicago.

His inventive genius, willingness to take risks, organizational skills, business ingenuity, and persistence enabled McCormick to design and market machines that helped to transform agriculture in the nineteenth century, making it much more capital-intensive, efficient, and productive. The farm implements he developed and creatively merchandised contributed to a revolution in agriculture that has allowed the world's food supply to keep pace with its explosive population growth.

• McCormick's papers, as well as those of other family members, relevant contemporary agricultural and scientific periodicals, newspapers, reports of world fairs, court records, and the records of the McCormick Reaper companies are in the libraries of the McCormick Historical Association and the Nettie F. McCormick Biographical Association in Chicago. Leander J. McCormick, *Family Record and Biography* (1986), is a useful primary source. R. B. Swift analyzes the historical debate over rival claims in "Who Invented the Reaper?" *Implement Age*, 15 Apr. 1897. R. G. Thwaite, *Cyrus Hall McCormick and the Reaper* (1909), and H. N. Casson, *Cyrus Hall McCormick, His Life and Work* (1909; repr. 1972), are important early assessments. William T. Hutchison's two volumes, *Cyrus Hall McCormick: Seed-Time, 1809–1856* (1930) and *Cyrus Hall McCormick: Harvest, 1856–1884* (1935), both reprinted in 1968, use family letters and papers extensively and contain a wealth of information about all the major aspects of McCormick's life. L. J. Halsey, *A History of the McCormick Theological Seminary* (1893), describes McCormick's involvement with the seminary. Walter W. Moore, "Historical Address in Appreciation of the Life and Work of Cyrus Hall McCormick," in *McCormick Theological Seminary Historical Celebration* (1910), provides a good overview of all the major aspects of McCormick's career and contribution. Cyrus McCormick (a grandson), *The Century of the Reaper* (1931), provides an account of his forebear's work, the McCormick Harvesting Machine Company, and the International Harvester Company.

GARY SCOTT SMITH

MCCORMICK, Cyrus Hall, Jr. (16 May 1859–2 June 1936), manufacturer, was born in Washington, D.C., the son of Cyrus Hall McCormick, an inventor and manufacturer of the reaper, and Nancy Maria "Nettie" Fowler. He spent his early years in New York City and London and traveling in Europe. However, when the great Chicago Fire of 1871 destroyed the McCormick reaper factory, the family moved permanently to Chicago to look after company affairs probably at his mother's insistence. Cyrus attended public schools in Chicago and began learning the reaper business by taking dictation for his father and observing frequent discussions about the implement trade.

McCormick's father, who had little patience with formal education, did not want McCormick to attend college. In the summer of 1877 McCormick, aged eighteen, successfully demonstrated a reaper in England and then handled important business negotiations, including one with Junius S. Morgan. This confirmed his father's opinion that he was ready to come to work full time. But his mother was insistent; aided by the fortuitous arrival of James W. McCosh—the president of the College of New Jersey (now Princeton University), an eminent Presbyterian minister, and a family friend—McCormick proceeded to college. To satisfy the elder McCormick, McCosh designed a special two-year curriculum, and McCormick graduated in 1879 with a special diploma.

Upon graduating, McCormick immediately joined his father in the management of the McCormick Harvesting Machine Company. He quickly demonstrated his business skills (indeed, he was a more decisive businessman than his father), a fact that brought the long-simmering tension between his father and his father's brother Leander to a head. Leander and his son Robert Hall were soon ejected from the company; McCormick later bought out their one-quarter interest. McCormick quickly involved himself in virtually every aspect of the business, from factory production and sales to experimental work. He personally took new designs into the field for testing.

In 1884, at the death of his father, McCormick, just shy of twenty-five, became the company president (although he always made decisions in close consultation with his mother). Under his leadership, the McCormick Company recaptured clear leadership in the grain-harvesting industry during the 1880s. In 1889 he married Harriet Hammond; they had three children. In 1890 the heads of all the harvester manufacturers met in Chicago to negotiate a merger of their companies into a single trust, the American Harvester Company. McCormick played a leading role in this effort, and he was projected as the president of the new company. It collapsed at the last minute, largely because several owners feared giving up control.

The failure of that consolidation effort led to particularly intense competition during the 1890s and ended with only six major producers left; McCormick was decisively in the lead, holding almost half the world market. During the decade the company had introduced the first successful corn harvester, built its own state-of-the-art twine mill (to produce consistent, high-quality binder twine for its machines), and developed an extensive, profitable foreign business.

In 1902, after several failures to merge with or buy the second-ranked Deering Company, McCormick agreed to merge his company into International Harvester, so named by Morgan partner George W. Perkins to reflect his ambition for the new company. The merger brought together the five leading harvester producers: McCormick, Deering, Champion, Milwaukee, and Plano. Perkins skillfully avoided the issue of who would control the new company by creating a voting trust, with Perkins, McCormick, and a Deering as trustees. McCormick was named as the president of the new $120 million corporation. Perhaps more important, McCormick, with 46 percent of the initial stock distribution and with the help of John D. Rockefeller (who was connected to the McCormicks by marriage), quickly secured over half the stock; when the voting trust ended, McCormick's interests would be in control.

McCormick pushed expansion, both domestic and foreign. The merger itself had added a major steel plant in South Chicago, iron ore mines in Minnesota, and coking coal mines in Kentucky. In 1903 International Harvester bought its one principal remaining competitor, the Osborne Company; in 1905 the company bought a mower factory in Sweden and then, over the next few years, added factories in Canada, France, Germany, and Russia. In 1910 International Harvester became the leading tractor manufacturer, in 1914 it introduced the combined harvester-thresher, and in 1918 it became a full-line implement manufacturer with the introduction of its own line of plows. It developed a large henequen plantation in Cuba to supply adequate fiber with which to make twine for binders and hay balers, and in 1923 farm machinery design was transformed when International Harvester introduced the power takeoff. McCormick himself took a special interest in developing model farms and pushing research on new designs.

McCormick confronted several serious challenges to the continued existence of International Harvester. The first arose from the Deerings. Once they realized that the McCormicks held a majority interest, they threatened to take back their assets forcibly. They then apparently tried to instigate a federal antitrust suit in 1907, building on the successful antitrust suit brought against the "Harvester Trust" in Arkansas and Missouri. In 1912 the U.S. government filed an antitrust suit against the company, which it won in 1914. In response, International Harvester divided itself into a firm owning new product lines and handling foreign sales, which was exempt from the suit, and a domestic firm for the harvester business and U.S. marketing.

The legal threats also made McCormick reluctant to replace managers he considered inadequate because he feared they would seek revenge by testifying against the company. But with World War I, Attorney General Thomas W. Gregory cut short appeals by arranging a consent decree, in which the company disposed of minor properties and consolidated its brand names. Another Federal Trade Commission investigation after the war led to a second suit in 1923, but in 1927 the Supreme Court found for the company, declaring that only actual control and not potential power to control markets was forbidden. In the meantime, Deere & Company had emerged as a full-line competitor, Henry Ford had challenged International Harvester with his Fordson tractor, and International Harvester's share in the harvester market itself had declined by almost half.

As the president of International Harvester, McCormick made important contributions in developing employee benefits. In 1908 the company established the Employee Benefit Association, which provided accident benefits, and an employee pension system. In 1910 the company made the accident compensation system comprehensive, an approach later used in state legislation. In 1919 the company added a system of employee representation to help negotiate wages, hours, and working conditions.

On 1 January 1919 McCormick assumed the position of chairman of the board; his brother Harold succeeded him as the president. He resigned as the chairman in 1935, remaining a director until his death. Company employment during his tenure rose to as many as 50,000 worldwide, and capital stock rose to $250 million in 1933, with assets of $348 million.

In 1917 President Woodrow Wilson appointed McCormick to a special diplomatic mission to Russia, headed by Elihu Root. McCormick gave liberally to the Young Men's Christian Association; in 1925, with his two sons, he also gave $1 million to the Chicago Young Women's Christian Association to memorialize his first wife, Harriet Hammond. He established the Elizabeth McCormick Memorial Fund to aid child welfare, in memory of his only daughter, who died in 1905 at age twelve. After the death of his first wife in 1921, he married Alice Marie Hoit, his former secretary in 1927; they had no children. He served as a director of the Presbyterian Theological Seminary (formerly McCormick Theological Seminary), to which he gave major gifts in 1905 and 1927, and as a trustee for the Field Museum of Natural History and Princeton University. The French awarded him an order of "Merite Agricole." He was very interested in music and skillful enough to compose several pieces, which were performed publicly. McCormick died at "Walden," his country estate, in Lake Forest, Illinois.

• The State Historical Society of Wisconsin has an enormous collection of McCormick family and business records, which contains much original correspondence from, to, and about McCormick. William T. Hutchinson, *Cyrus Hall McCormick*, vol. 2 (1935; repr. 1968), offers the most comprehensive information about his youth and early business career. Cyrus McCormick III, *The Century of the Reaper* (1931), is an admiring history of the McCormick family, the McCormick Company, and International Harvester written by McCormick's son. Additional material is available in Stella V. Roderick, *Nettie Fowler McCormick* (1956), and Gilbert A. Harrison, *A Timeless Affair: The Life of Anita McCormick Blaine* (1979). In addition, see Fred V. Carstensen, *American Enterprise in Foreign Markets* (1984), and "'. . . a dishonest man is at least prudent': George W. Perkins and the International Harvester Steel Properties," *Business and Economic History* 9 (1981): 87–102, for a business history of McCormick-International Harvester to 1914 and the tensions arising from the merger in 1902.

FRED CARSTENSEN

MCCORMICK, Edith Rockefeller (31 Aug. 1872–25 Aug. 1932), philanthropist, socialite, and patron of the arts and psychiatry, was born in Cleveland, Ohio, the daughter of John D. Rockefeller, Sr., an industrialist, and Laura Celestia Spelman. She spent her youth in Cleveland and New York City, where the family moved in 1880. In addition to attending the Rye Female Seminary, Edith received private tutoring and learned to play the cello. Unusually gifted and endowed with a strong scholarly inclination, she had mastered three foreign languages by the time she was ten years old.

On 26 November 1895 Edith married Harold Fowler McCormick, the son of Cyrus Hall McCormick. The couple had five children, two of whom died at an early age. A third child nearly died from appendicitis while McCormick herself was undergoing treatment for tuberculosis of the kidney. McCormick's marriage was problematic. Although he was adoring of his wife in letters to friends and family, Harold McCormick's social background may have led him to be oblivious to the emotional needs of others, leading him to neglect his wife. McCormick always had to compete with her husband's overprotective mother and sister for his attention and affection. Harold McCormick also had extramarital affairs that were widely known in Chicago circles.

McCormick took a great interest in philanthropy. Throughout her life, she helped people in financial difficulties, always trying to conceal the fact that she had been the benefactor. In 1899 she provided funding that the city had failed to provide to staff Chicago's newly created juvenile court system. She also became a patron of the arts, giving to the Art Institute of Chicago, and instituting the Chicago Grand Opera Company with her husband. After the death of their son John, the McCormicks founded the John McCormick Institution for Infectious Diseases and endowed the *Journal for Infectious Diseases*. With the support of the institution's funding, researchers at Johns Hopkins University later discovered the bacterium that causes scarlet fever.

To the outside observer, McCormick's personality must have been difficult to comprehend. Opinionated and temperamental, she was obsessed with manners and household procedures. Although she was given to frequent moods of somberness and despair, she was eager to entertain and was described as vivacious by some who knew her. She suffered from nervous disorders throughout her lifetime. In 1913 she went to Zurich, Switzerland, into the psychiatric care of Carl Jung. Refusing to leave during the war, she stayed in Zurich until 1921. She turned from patient to lay analyst and saw patients for several hours daily. In 1916 she provided funding for the Psychological Club, a place for analyst trainees to meet and exchange insights and to discuss the problems they encountered in their treatments.

While in Zurich, McCormick continued her philanthropic work. Her generosity toward local residents led the government to exempt her car from gas rationing. When the Germans released fifty-nine American sailors from the *Yarrowdale*, she provided for the sailors and gave them spending money for the way home. She also supported many artists who had escaped from neighboring war-torn countries to Zurich in neutral Switzerland. McCormick generously funded many of them by anonymously setting up accounts in their names. Her most prominent protégé was James Joyce. In 1919, after eighteen months of funding, he was able to publish *Ulysses* shortly after she discontinued the allowance.

On one occasion, McCormick's philanthropic efforts took an adventurous turn: in 1917 a French fighter pilot crashed in Switzerland. In line with the Swiss policy of neutrality, Swiss officials interned the pilot. One night, the guard let the pilot wander off, and he escaped in a fast motor boat to France. It turned out that McCormick had bribed the guard to let the pilot escape and probably also had arranged for the boat to be there.

By the end of the war, McCormick was troubled by personal and financial difficulties. During 1919 and 1920 she had borrowed increasing amounts of money against her trust fund. She owed taxes, and she had lost money in business deals. Moreover, her husband, who had become infatuated with the Polish singer and actress Ganna Walska, filed for a divorce in 1921. After the divorce took effect that year, McCormick continued to entertain with great aplomb but also invested increasing amounts of time and money into philanthropic efforts. She gave money to the Chicago Zoo and began a project to provide affordable housing.

Her attempt to partake in the real estate boom of the 1920s and provide affordable housing on a 200-acre site in Highland Park—together with her continued philanthropic giving—proved to be financially taxing. Discussions over McCormick's management style, personnel policy, and her financial generosity toward her business partners further undermined her financial solvency. She did not have a lucky hand with business investments. In 1920 her outstanding debts amounted to $812,000. In addition, the same year McCormick lost $339,000 on a business investment involving a chemical process for treating wood. Throughout her life, her brother John D. Rockefeller, Jr., intervened with advice and money. He estimated

MCCORMICK • 915

before her death that his sister needed $332,000 per annum to cover expenses and bills, mostly consisting of back taxes.

By 1932 her health had begun to fail. She had to undergo treatment for cancer and, under pressure from her brother, John D. Rockefeller, Jr., moved into the Drake Hotel to cut back on expenses. Despite her somewhat erratic character, McCormick had won the affection of many Chicagoans, and thousands lined the roads to the cemetery when her coffin passed by.

• McCormick's papers and correspondence are in the Rockefeller Family Archives at the Rockefeller Archive Center in Pocantico Hills, North Tarrytown, N.Y. The papers of her husband, Harold Fowler McCormick, located in the McCormick Collection of the State Historical Society of Wisconsin, however, contain no correspondence with Edith. See Margaret Hafstead, ed., *Guide to the McCormick Collection of the State Historical Society of Wisconsin* (1973). The best source on McCormick's life is Clarice Stasz, *The Rockefeller Women: Dynasty of Piety, Privacy, and Service* (1995). See also the more dated Allan Nevins, *Study in Power: John D. Rockefeller, Industrialist and Philanthropist* (2 vols., 1953); Aline B. Saarinen, *The Proud Possessors: The Lives, Times, and Tastes of Some Adventurous American Art Collectors* (1958); and Wayne Andrews, *The Battle for Chicago* (1946). McCormick is briefly mentioned in John Ensor Harr and Peter J. Johnson, *The Rockefeller Conscience: An American Family in Public and in Private* (1991). After McCormick's death, many of her personal belongings were sold; for a catalog, see *Collection of the Late Edith Rockefeller McCormick* (1934). Obituaries are in the *New York Times* and *Chicago Tribune*, both 26 Aug. 1932.

THOMAS WINTER

MCCORMICK, Jim (1856–10 Mar. 1918), baseball player and manager, was born James McCormick in Scotland, the son of James McCormick and Rose Lowrey. His family immigrated to the United States when he was a child and settled in Paterson, New Jersey. Little is known about his youth, and even his exact date of birth is unknown. In 1873 he and a boyhood friend, future Baseball Hall of Fame player and manager Mike "King" Kelly, started a baseball club in Paterson. In 1876 McCormick was the Paterson club's pitcher. The stocky righthander joined the Columbus, Ohio, Buckeye team in the International Association in 1877 and won six of twelve decisions.

McCormick first played in the major leagues in 1878 with the Indianapolis Browns of the National League. With a handlebar mustache and 215 pounds on a 5'10½" frame, McCormick did not present an athletic appearance. However, he recorded an estimated 1.69 earned run average (official ERA statistics were not kept), won five games, and lost eight on a weak team. When the Indianapolis team ceased operations after the season, McCormick signed with the Cleveland Spiders in the National League as the "change pitcher," or second hurler, behind Bobby Mitchell. Only 23 years old in 1879, he was appointed team "captain" or manager. McCormick made himself the primary pitcher, starting 60 of Cleveland's 82 games and logging 546 innings. Playing on the weakest hitting team in the league and one of the poorest defensively, he won 20 games but lost 40. The 1880 Spiders were a much improved team at bat and in the field. Manager McCormick penciled his name in as starter a league-leading 74 times. He also led the league with 72 complete games, 657⅔ innings, and 45 victories, and his 45–28 record might have been even better with more run support. Cleveland was shutout in ten of his defeats, and on 12 June he lost 1–0 to Worcester when John Lee Richmond pitched the major league's first perfect game. McCormick batted .246 and occasionally played the outfield.

In 1881 McCormick relinquished the managerial role to focus entirely on pitching. He led the league with 57 complete games, but his won and lost record fell to 26–30. The following year McCormick had the dubious distinction of becoming the first pitcher to lose four consecutive opening-day games for the same team. He managed the Spiders through their first four games and losses, then turned the skipper's reins over to second baseman Fred Dunlap. The big righthander proved his durability by recording league highs of 68 games, 65 complete games and 595⅔ innings pitched, and 36 wins. He posted a 2.37 ERA that season. He won 28 games and lost 12 in 1883 while posting a league leading 1.84 ERA. In 1884 McCormick had lost 22 of 41 decisions when he, catcher Charles Briody, and shortstop Jack Glasscock jumped to the Cincinnati Outlaw Reds of the Union Association in August for $1,000 each. McCormick won 21 and lost only 3 and led Union Association pitchers with a 1.54 ERA.

When the Union Association folded, McCormick signed with the Providence Grays of the National League in 1885. After losing three of four starts he was picked up by Cap Anson's Chicago White Stockings and won 20 of 24 starts as Chicago edged the New York Giants for the National League pennant. In the postseason championship series with the American Association champion St. Louis Browns, McCormick split four decisions, and the seven-game series ended with the teams knotted at three wins each plus a tie. He won his first 16 games for the 1886 White Stockings on his way to 31 victories and 11 defeats. McCormick lost the second game of the championship series with St. Louis 12–0. A sore arm prevented him from pitching any other games in the series.

In 1887, because McCormick broke club rules about drinking and wanted more money, Chicago sold his contract to the National League's Pittsburgh Alleghenies. As the number-two hurler behind Pud Galvin, he won 13 and lost 23. His .243 batting average was better than that of three everyday Allegheny players. The next season Pittsburgh tried to reduce his salary, reasoning that neither he nor the Alleghenies were coming off good years. In good health and only 32 years old, McCormick chose to quit. Pittsburgh kept him on their reserve list for several seasons, preventing McCormick from returning with another team. He returned to Paterson and operated a small diner for many years. McCormick married, probably in 1883;

he had a son and a daughter. McCormick died of cirrhosis of the liver in Paterson.

While few know of McCormick today, he was one of the dominant pitchers of the early golden age of baseball. Only Pud Galvin and Tim Keefe won more games before 1890 than McCormick's 265. McCormick lost 214 games. From 1879 to 1884 he averaged 539 innings pitched per season. He pitched 494 games, and his 466 complete games place him among the all-time leaders. In 4,275⅔ innings McCormick struck out 1,704 batters and walked 749. He hurled 33 shutouts and his earned run average is calculated to be 2.43. He had 491 hits and a respectable .236 career batting average.

• The National Baseball Library in Cooperstown, N.Y., has a file on McCormick. Shorter biographies are found in Michael Shatzkin, ed., *The Ballplayers* (1990); and the Society of American Baseball Research, *Nineteenth Century Stars* (1989). For complete statistical information on McCormick's playing career and managerial record see Rick Wolff, ed., *The Baseball Encyclopedia*, 9th ed. (1993); Paul MacFarlane, ed., *The "Sporting News" Daguerreotypes of Baseball* (1981); and John Thorn et al., eds., *Total Baseball*, 5th ed. (1997). An obituary is in the *Paterson, N.J., Evening News*, 11 Mar. 1918.

FRANK J. OLMSTED

MCCORMICK, Katharine Dexter (27 Aug. 1875–30 Dec. 1967), social activist and philanthropist, was born in Dexter, Michigan, the daughter of Wirt Dexter, a prominent Chicago corporate attorney, and Josephine Moore, a schoolteacher. Katharine was born in her grandparents' mansion, Gordon Hall, in the village founded by her grandfather, Judge Samuel William Dexter. In 1889 her father suffered a fatal heart attack in her presence. Following the death of her brother from meningitis in 1894, she and her mother, supported by their inheritance, relocated to Boston.

Katharine's family had long been advocates of higher education and had unbroken ties to Harvard University and Harvard Law School dating back to the seventeenth century. Katharine chose an education in science, however, and matriculated at the Massachusetts Institute of Technology in 1900 after studying there for three years as a special student. In 1904 she received a degree in biology, the first woman to earn a science degree from MIT. She had planned to become a surgeon but gave that up to marry a childhood friend, Stanley McCormick, the youngest son of Cyrus McCormick and comptroller of International Harvester. The two were married at the Dexter family chateau in Lake Geneva, Switzerland, in September 1904. They had no children.

A year into their marriage, Stanley McCormick was disabled by mental illness, later diagnosed as schizophrenia. In May 1906 he was forced to resign from International Harvester, and in 1909 he was declared legally incompetent. His illness was to shape some of the public service and social activism that would fill the remainder of McCormick's life.

In 1909 McCormick spoke at the first outdoor rally for woman suffrage in Massachusetts. She quickly became a key figure in the woman suffrage movement as vice president and treasurer of the National American Woman Suffrage Association. McCormick provided key funding for the association's publication, the *Woman's Journal*, and lobbied the Massachusetts state legislature. During World War I she contributed to the Women's Committee on Defense Work of the U.S. Council of National Defense.

For the next several years McCormick organized much of Carrie Chapman Catt's effort to gain ratification for the Nineteenth Amendment. Through this work she met other social activists, including American birth control proponents Mary Dennett and, in 1917, Margaret Sanger. In 1920 McCormick cofounded the League of Women Voters with Carrie Chapman Catt and became its first vice president.

Throughout the 1920s McCormick and Sanger worked together on birth control issues. McCormick smuggled diaphragms from Europe to New York for Sanger's Clinical Research Bureau. A reception for the delegates attending the 1927 World Population Conference was held at McCormick's Lake Geneva chateau. In 1927 McCormick, who had continued to seek help for her husband from psychologists and psychiatrists, turned to endocrinology. She established the Neuroendocrine Research Foundation at Harvard Medical School, where it was hoped that research into the adrenal gland would find the cause of schizophrenia. She also subsidized the journal *Endocrinology*.

In the 1930s and 1940s McCormick continued to support and fund those causes that fulfilled her interests in social activism and her scientific training. Her largess was always coupled with a close attention to the goals and means of the projects she supported. She made frequent trips from her home in Boston to Santa Barbara, where her husband lived with custodial care on a family estate. In 1947 he died at the age of seventy-three, and McCormick no longer supported the Neuroendocrine Research Foundation, which closed its offices, its work having never developed a treatment for schizophrenia. She spent the next three years liquidating her husband's $33 million estate to pay $23 million in inheritance taxes.

In 1950 McCormick began to search for worthy recipients who could benefit from her husband's fortune. In response to her inquiry, Sanger replied that there remained a great need to discover a method of contraception for women besides the diaphragm. In 1951 McCormick visited Gregory Goodwin Pincus, who, since the 1930s, had been conducting research on the role of hormones in the female reproductive cycle. She discussed with him her hope that a safe, effective oral contraceptive could be developed through laboratory research. Pincus's work on progesterone was encouraging, but his employer G. D. Searle seemed doubtful of the eventual marketability of a contraceptive.

On 8 June 1953 McCormick and Sanger met with Pincus at the Worcester Foundation for Experimental

Biology, a nonprofit Massachusetts laboratory. McCormick provided $20,000 on that occasion, and, in response to budgets presented by Pincus, she gave $150,000 to $180,000 a year for the remaining fourteen years of her life. McCormick provided more than money. She kept in almost daily contact with Pincus's lab, taking an active role in setting research directions. Although Sanger wanted McCormick to fund a number of approaches to the problem, McCormick concentrated her funds and attention on Pincus's work. In 1954 McCormick and Pincus convinced John Rock, a distinguished Harvard gynecologist, to oversee human trials of a pill that Pincus developed. Small-scale testing began that year, and large-scale clinical trials were conducted in Puerto Rico between 1956 and 1958. In 1959 Searle applied to the Food and Drug Administration (FDA) for approval to market the pill as an oral contraceptive. In May 1960 the FDA approved the first birth control pill for sale in the United States. McCormick had provided virtually all of the $2 million for the cost of development and the field trials. Pincus's book, *The Control of Fertility* (1965), contained this dedication: "This book is dedicated to Mrs. Stanley McCormick because of her steadfast faith in scientific inquiry and her unswerving encouragement of human dignity." She continued funding new birth control research throughout the 1960s.

McCormick viewed her medical philanthropy as a memorial to her husband. In the 1960s she extended her generosity in his name to her alma mater, MIT, where the Stanley McCormick women's dormitories were built to allow MIT to increase female enrollment. McCormick died in Boston. Her will provided $5 million to the Planned Parenthood Federation of America, which funded the Katharine Dexter McCormick Library in New York City. An additional $1 million went to Pincus's Worcester Foundation for Experimental Biology. Through her personal and financial support Katharine McCormick contributed to the success of the movement for woman suffrage, the founding of the League of Women Voters, the cause of higher education for women, and, her greatest legacy, the production of an oral contraceptive.

• Photographs of McCormick and papers related to her work at the Massachusetts Institute of Technology are held in the Historical Collections, Archives, and Special Collections Library at MIT. The McCormick Family Papers, State Historical Society of Wisconsin, are closed to the public. Biographical information is in Moira Reynolds, *Women Advocates of Reproductive Rights: Eleven Who Led the Struggle in the United States and Great Britain* (1994). Her suffrage work is described in Elizabeth Cady Stanton et al., *History of Woman Suffrage*, vols. 5–6 (1900–1922), and her work with the birth control movement is addressed by Albert Maisel, *The Hormone Quest* (1965), and James Reed, *The Birth Control Movement and American Society: From Private Vice to Public Virtue* (1978; rev. ed., 1984).

STEVEN L. TUCK

MCCORMICK, Leander James (8 Feb. 1819–20 Feb. 1900), farm implement manufacturer, was born in Rockbridge County, Virginia, the son of Robert Mc-

Cormick, a farmer and inventor, and Mary Ann Hall. He was educated in an old-field school and also by private tutors. His father was an active inventor, and Leander came to love mechanics while working with his father and his oldest brother Cyrus Hall McCormick, who demonstrated the first successful mechanical grain reaper in 1831. Leander was involved with building early reapers and plows in a blacksmith shop on the farm. In the early 1840s, when Cyrus began developing the reaper business, Leander and his father built at least seventy-five reapers for sale in Virginia. In the mid-1840s he helped Cyrus perfect a seat for the raker, which was responsible for raking the cut gravel off the reaper platform, an improvement that vastly improved the machine's efficiency. The U.S. Commissioner of Patents declared it to be "the crowning glory of the machine." Leander then developed a seat for the driver (who had previously ridden one of the draft horses). The seat was movable so it could be adjusted to preserve balance of the machine, which rode largely on a bull wheel. He also improved the design, removing a supporting post that interfered with the uncut grain as it came onto the platform. In October 1845 Leander married Henrietta Maria Hamilton; they had four children.

In 1847 Cyrus persuaded Leander to move to Cincinnati to superintend construction of 100 McCormick reapers at the A. C. Brown foundry. In 1848, when Cyrus consolidated all reaper production in Chicago, Leander moved there, and in 1849 he took charge of manufacturing in the C. H. McCormick Company reaper factory; he would superintend production of McCormick harvesters for the next thirty-one years. In 1852, 1853, and 1854, Leander again contributed useful improvements in design details, helping establish the McCormick reaper as the national leader.

Cyrus persuaded a second brother, William Sanderson McCormick, to join his company, taking responsibility for general administration and sales. During the 1850s, as the company enjoyed great success, Leander and William worked on annual contracts, earning a fixed salary. Leander increasingly believed that the arrangement was unfair, failing to recognize the contributions that he and William made to the substantial profits the company earned. On 1 November 1859, Cyrus signed a twelve-year agreement that gave each brother a one-quarter share of the profits and renamed the company C. H. McCormick & Brothers.

Cyrus was virtually absent during the years of the Civil War, living in London after 1862, a situation that led to a new agreement in 1864 giving Leander and William each one-quarter ownership. But this period also saw a rapid decline in the company's standing; it fell from a dominant position, with more than half of the total market, to that of a regional company, with sales concentrated only in Illinois and three nearby states and as little as 5 percent of the market.

With the end of the Civil War, Cyrus returned to America but chose to live in New York, leaving much of the responsibility with Leander (William had died in 1865). The firm also again changed its name, to

C. H. McCormick & Company, with Leander retaining a quarter interest. In 1871 the great Chicago Fire destroyed the McCormick factory. Though Cyrus—enormously wealthy even without his reaper company—might have abandoned the business, his wife, Nettie Fowler, insisted on rebuilding, a process in which Leander played a central role. In 1872 the company opened a much expanded factory in Chicago. The company was again restructured in 1874, with a new five-year contract, and renamed C. H. & L. J. McCormick, with Leander and his son Robert Hall McCormick owning together one quarter.

In the next few years the company rebuilt its position, largely under the leadership of Nettie Fowler and a new general manager, E. K. Butler, who reorganized and extended the sales organization. Leander continued in his capacity as factory superintendent, with Hall (as Robert Hall was called) working as his assistant. The presence of Hall greatly intensified long-standing tension between Leander and Cyrus—a tension already evident in the 1850s—that was openly expressed in 1862 in a confrontation in London that led to Leander's walking out on Cyrus and immediately returning to Chicago. Cyrus had wanted to exclude Hall from the company in 1874; Hall for his part was unwilling simply to work as his father's assistant, increasingly involving himself in patent issues, an arena for which he was ill suited and in which he came into frequent conflict with Cyrus's own specialist.

When Hall in 1877 joined a partnership to manufacture threshers, raising the possibility that he and Leander might become direct competitors, and Leander and Hall refused to assign to the company potentially significant patents they owned, a confrontation was unavoidable. In late 1879, in a last-ditch effort at compromise, the company was incorporated as The McCormick Harvesting Machine Company, with Leander as a vice president and Leander and Hall sharing a one-quarter interest. But the antipathy between the brothers, Cyrus's deep dislike and distrust of Hall, and the emergence of the young Cyrus Hall McCormick, Jr., who had begun working full time in the company office in mid-1879 and had immediately distinguished himself, led to a final break in 1880. On 18 February 1880, Cyrus read to the board a bill of complaint against Leander and Hall, accusing them of breach of contract and disloyalty. On 14 April the board declared Leander's and Hall's positions vacant and adopted a resolution of censure (it was later formally excised from the minutes). In 1889, Cyrus, Jr. bought out Leander and Hall's interest for $3.5 million.

Upon leaving the McCormick company, Leander, with Hall's assistance, spent much time and energy seeking to give his father Robert—rather than his brother Cyrus—credit for inventing the reaper. He published *Memorial of Robert McCormick* (1885), a set of recollections that he had gathered over many years from neighbors in Virginia. In the book he claimed that Cyrus had essentially stolen his father's ideas, and in an affidavit written shortly before his death, Lean-

der claimed that Cyrus had little mechanical ability and that Leander himself had provided the inventive imagination to improve Robert's original design into a commercially successful reaper.

About 1870 Leander engaged Alvan Clark & Sons, of Cambridgeport, Massachusetts, to construct for him the largest refracting telescope in the world, twenty-six inches in diameter; he then presented this telescope and $18,000 for an observatory to house it to the University of Virginia. From 1891 on focused on managing his massive real estate investments in Chicago. He also amassed a notable collection of paintings, and after careful research he published a family genealogy, *Family Record and Biography* (1896). He died in Chicago.

Scholarship has tended to minimize Leander James McCormick's contribution to the development of the McCormick Company and the harvester industry. But he in fact sustained the company in the face of years of neglect by Cyrus Hall McCormick, and by 1880 he had helped bring the company back to prominence, laying the foundation for dramatic growth over the next two decades and the eventual creation of International Harvester.

• The State Historical Society of Wisconsin has an enormous collection of McCormick family and business records that contain a great deal of original correspondence from, to, and about Leander James McCormick. William T. Hutchinson's massive two-volume *Cyrus Hall McCormick* (1930, 1935; repr. 1968) offers the most comprehensive information about Leander's relationship with his brother and the McCormick business interests, as well as Leander's effort to give his father credit for developing the reaper. Leander's grandnephew (Cyrus's grandson), Cyrus McCormick, wrote *The Century of the Reaper* (1931), an admiring history of Cyrus H. McCormick, Sr., and the McCormick Company. Norbert Lyons responded with a highly partisan, pro-Leander book, *The McCormick Reaper Legend* (1955). Additional material on Leander is available in Stella V. Roderick's *Nettie Fowler McCormick* (1956) and Gilbert A. Harrison's *A Timeless Affair: The Life of Anita McCormick Blaine* (1979).

FRED CARSTENSEN

MCCORMICK, Medill (16 May 1877–25 Feb. 1925), publisher and U.S. senator, was born Joseph Medill McCormick in Chicago, Illinois, the son of Robert Sanderson McCormick, a diplomat, and Katherine Van Etta Medill, the daughter of *Chicago Tribune* publisher Joseph Medill. After attending Ludgrove, just southwest of London, England, and Groton School, Groton, Massachusetts, Medill attended Yale University, from which he graduated in 1900. Heir apparent to the *Tribune*, McCormick immediately began work on the paper, starting as a police reporter. In 1901, as a war correspondent, he covered the Philippine insurrection, participating in the Samar campaign. He served the paper in various capacities, becoming particularly active in its business and advertising sections. By 1907 he was vice president, secretary, and treasurer of the Tribune Company. A year later he was elected vice president of the American Newspaper Publishers Association. Until 1907 he was also copublisher of the *Cleveland Leader*, founded by his grandfather, and its afternoon affiliate, the *Cleveland News*.

In 1903 McCormick married Ruth Hanna, who became a prominent figure in Republican ranks, an appropriate role for the daughter of the extremely powerful Ohio senator Mark Hanna. They had three children. Soon after their marriage, McCormick revealed himself as a manic-depressive, subject to nervous breakdowns and increasingly dependent upon alcohol. In 1908 and 1909 he went to Europe, where he became a patient of noted psychoanalyst Carl Jung. By 1915 he might have stopped drinking but, in order to control depression, probably continued to experiment with drugs.

In 1909 McCormick left the *Tribune* world for good. His brother Robert Rutherford McCormick and cousin Joseph Medill Patterson assumed the paper's direction. In 1911 McCormick joined the new Progressive party, led by Wisconsin senator Robert M. La Follette, though he soon switched his allegiance to his close friend Theodore Roosevelt. Because of his intimate knowledge of the publishing industry, he directed party publicity and from 1912 to 1914 was vice chairman of the Progressive National Committee. When in 1912 Roosevelt became the Progressive ("Bull Moose") presidential candidate, McCormick directed the party's western campaign.

That same year McCormick was elected to the Illinois House of Representatives, leading some twenty-seven Progressives who possessed the balance of power there. In 1914 he was one of only two Progressives returned to office. That year, again a war correspondent, he went to Mexico, where he was twice arrested, once as a spy. Writing for *Harper's Weekly*, he defended the American decision not to recognize Victoriano Huerta. In 1915 he resigned from the Progressive party's executive committee and started to vote with the Republicans, saying that the outbreak of World War I and economic recession had destroyed the Progressive movement. In 1916 he was made chairman of the Illinois State Republican Convention and was elected delegate at large to the national party convention.

That year, running as a Republican, McCormick was elected representative at large from Illinois. During the campaign he attacked the Democratic tariff, military, and fiscal policies. President Woodrow Wilson, he said, was a "rotten" administrator and a "wretched" executive. From late August until mid-October 1917 he toured battlefields in Italy and France, where he was almost injured by a trench bomb. Upon returning, he warned of total defeat within a few weeks, for soon the Allies, he said, could no longer supply American forces from their own diminishing armaments. "Win the war the quickest way and damn the expense," his report summarized.

In 1918 McCormick entered the Illinois Republican senatorial primary, running against Chicago mayor William Hale "Big Bill" Thompson and Congressman George Edmund Foss. He was endorsed by Roosevelt at the Springfield State Fair, undoubtedly a factor in

gaining a plurality of 50,000 votes. Stressing Democratic "mismanagement" of the war, he defeated incumbent James Hamilton Lewis by 53,000 votes.

While in the Senate McCormick became most prominent as a leading "Irreconcilable," strongly opposing the Versailles treaty and American membership in the League of Nations. He coordinated tours for the League for the Preservation of American Independence, himself speaking on the organization's behalf. The treaty, he claimed, simply rewarded the victors, thereby paving the way for a "new imperialism" and future wars. Because Germany would have to pay indemnities, he said, it would be unable to buy American farm products, which in turn would create an agricultural depression in the United States. He attacked Britain for not granting the Irish home rule, claimed that Japanese diplomacy had marked thirty-five years of "consistent perfidy and aggression," and accused the League of Nations of being in reality a "super-state." Not above a touch of nativism, he warned of "Hindoo janitors in our offices and apartments [and] . . . Chinese craftsmen driving rivets, joining timbers, laying bricks in the construction of our buildings." At one point he said he would "very readily vote for a League which does not threaten the peace and security which is ours through geographical isolation."

While in Congress, McCormick pushed budget reform, legislation that bore fruit in 1921 when Congress established a Bureau of the Budget partially modeled on a system he had fostered in Illinois. He worked for home rule in Chicago, fighting the Republican machine led by the triumvirate of Thompson, the mayor's campaign manager Fred Lundin, and Governor Len Small. He sought to abolish the Department of the Interior and to create the departments of public works and public welfare. He introduced the child labor amendment to the Senate, being handpicked by labor leader Samuel Gompers; its passage, McCormick said, was worth more to him than occupying the White House. He fought for adjusted compensation for veterans, sought to eliminate useless navy yards, endorsed civil government for the U.S. protectorates of Haiti and Santo Domingo, and called for a waterway from the Great Lakes to the Illinois Valley and the Mississippi River. In 1922 he chaired the Republican senatorial campaign committee, personally directing the speaking program.

In the Republican primary of 1924, McCormick was defeated by former governor Charles S. Deneen by fewer than 6,000 votes out of 800,000 votes cast. Depressed by his defeat, he committed suicide, dying in Washington, D.C.

• No McCormick papers per se exist, though Kristie Miller holds the McCormick family papers, which are quite valuable. Miller's biography of Medill's wife, *Ruth Hanna McCormick: A Life in Politics, 1880–1944* (1992), offers the most thorough treatment of Medill himself. For McCormick's journalistic role, see Lloyd Wendt, *Chicago Tribune: The Rise of a Great American Newspaper* (1979). Belle C. La Follette and Fola La Follette offer detail on McCormick's role in the early Progressive movement in their *Robert M. La Follette*

(1953), written from the perspective of the Wisconsin senator. For McCormick's isolationism, see Ralph A. Stone, "Two Illinois Senators among the Irreconcilables," *Mississippi Valley Historical Review* 50 (1963): 443–65, and Stone, *The Irreconcilables: The Fight against the League of Nations* (1970). For superior obituaries, see the *New York Times* and the *Chicago Tribune*, 26 Feb. 1925.

JUSTUS D. DOENECKE

MCCORMICK, Nettie Fowler (8 Feb. 1835–5 July 1923), businesswoman and philanthropist, was born Nancy Maria Fowler in Brownsville, Jefferson County, New York, the daughter of Melzar Fowler and Clarissa Spicer, general merchants. In infancy Nettie Fowler lost her father; her mother ran the family business until her death, when Nettie was seven. Nettie was then raised by her maternal grandmother in the family of her uncle, a prosperous merchant and temperance activist; both guardians were local philanthropists. Between 1850 and 1855, she was educated at three seminaries, one year each at Falley Seminary of Fulton, New York; Emma Willard's Troy Female Seminary; and Genesee Wesleyan Seminary, Lima, New York. She did not earn a diploma. For a short period (1855–1856) she taught school in Clayton, New York. Her journal (c. 1850–1878) indicates that her early training in Methodism and Calvinism fostered pious habits of mind and a commitment to Christian charity, moral duty, and the work ethic as well as to the practice of introspection and self-education, along lines acceptable for women of her class. In the Puritan tradition, as applied by Cotton Mather and secularized by Benjamin Franklin (1706–1790), she compiled a list of "Rules for Right Living," a practice encouraged by Cyrus Hall McCormick, whom she met while visiting Chicago in 1857. Cyrus McCormick, inventor of the mechanical reaper and an ardent old-school Presbyterian, was more than twice her age. They were married in 1858.

Nettie McCormick's subsequent rise into high society created the defining tension of her life: the requirements of antimaterialist, womanly self-denial set against the attractions of great wealth and secular individualism. Her duty to submit to her husband likewise conflicted with her need to take active care of him. Although Cyrus insisted that as her husband he would be "under your control and influence," neither strong-willed person found submission acceptable. In keeping with her habitual self-criticism, Nettie seldom recorded her pleasure or contentment; her journal documents the trials of the marriage. Through the period of childbearing (five of seven children survived infancy), she was often lonely and frustrated and experienced periods of illness (chest pains and periodic deafness), which at the time suggested neurasthenia. For treatment, she tried the water cure, a popular form of medical therapy using cold water in a variety of applications. Although critical of her husband, she tended to blame herself and to demand constant self-improvement. Cyrus's business and political commitments often took him away from the family; on

lengthy journeys he insisted that she accompany him without the children. "If men in business were no more careful in the discharge of their commercial obligations than they are in the discharge of their more solemn obligations to their children, their credit would be ruined," she later wrote (28 Oct. 1877).

Disharmony notwithstanding, the McCormicks had a productive business relationship. Nettie assumed the role of silent partner early in the marriage. Cyrus was accustomed to nap after dinner and then to write business letters with Nettie late into the night, a practice that made her well acquainted with the details of his affairs. In 1871, after the Chicago fire, Nettie, then age thirty-six, began to take a visible role in the business. When the McCormick Harvesting Machine plant was destroyed, Cyrus intended to retire. Nettie, however, insisted that the plant be rebuilt and full production resumed and that he continue to work together with her. His decision to comply was made "principally under my influence," which, she wrote in her journal, Cyrus referred to as "whip and spur" (29 June 1872). Nettie oversaw construction of the new plant. Increasingly she asserted her authority over the business, guiding her husband's investments and shaping new policies and ventures. The International Harvester Company was ultimately the product of her efforts to consolidate the farm machine industry. After minor surgery in 1878, Cyrus never returned to work in his former capacity; Nettie took control of the company, of which she was untitled director before and after Cyrus's death in 1884. A talented businesswoman, Nettie justified the pursuit of wealth as a means toward public stewardship. The profit motive was acceptable, but not as an end in itself; constrained by the demands of business and family, she often noted that she "ought to do a great deal of good to the poor, the homeless, and the orphan" (22 Oct. 1862).

Nettie's career as a benefactor began early in the marriage, when she joined the Women's Presbyterian Board of Missions; during the Civil War she offered charity to victims on both sides. She extended her influence over Cyrus from business to philanthropy. He became the principal donor to the McCormick Theological Seminary in Chicago to restore conservatism to the Presbyterian church (she allowed the seminary to be liberalized after his death), and she persuaded him to put money into the Young Men's Christian Association and other charities.

After her son Cyrus finished his studies at Princeton, Nettie gradually handed him control of the McCormick company, where she remained an active adviser. Henceforth she dedicated herself to philanthropy. During the settlement of her husband's estate, she and her son gave away $475,000, approaching the total amount her husband had given in his lifetime; between 1890 and 1923, she gave more than $8 million, nearly half of which went to educational institutions, most notably Dubuque College and Seminary, Jamestown College (N. Dak.), McCormick Theological Seminary, Stanley McCormick School (N.C.), Tusculum College (Tenn.), Washington and Lee College

(Va.), and Princeton University. In addition to being the principal donor to the Presbyterian church, its seminaries, colleges, and missions, she gave money to orphanages, schools, colleges, hospitals, relief agencies, and individuals of a wide range of affiliation, including the American Indian Institute, the YMCA and YWCA, the Chicago Home for Incurables, and Thornwell Orphanage (Tenn.). She was particularly generous to poorly endowed schools and colleges in the rural Midwest, West, and South. Her commitment to educational innovation for the sake of public welfare was shaped by her acquaintance with John Dewey and Francis Parker; her preferred charities fostered moral and intellectual growth, promoted individual development and social responsibility, and provided health care and relief for victims of war and disaster. Among great philanthropists of the turn of the twentieth century, Nettie McCormick is distinguished by her quiet independence. She was not an affiliate of organized social housekeeping; she did not promote her own name or business connections. Self-effacing, meticulous in the details of management, and resolutely private, she exemplified in her work the careers of many nineteenth-century women who as wives or widows held silent partnership in family business. Nettie Fowler McCormick died in Lake Forest, Illinois.

• Nettie McCormick's papers are in the McCormick manuscript collection, State Historical Society of Wisconsin, Madison. An important source is Charles O. Burgess, *Nettie Fowler McCormick: Profile of an American Philanthropist* (1962). For a romantic interpretation, see Stella Virginia Roderick, *Nettie Fowler McCormick* (1956). For discussion of Nettie's life in the context of her husband's career, see Herbert N. Casson, *Cyrus Hall McCormick* (1909); William T. Hutchinson, *Cyrus Hall McCormick: Seed-Time, 1809–1856* (1930) and *Cyrus Hall McCormick: Harvest, 1856–1884* (1935); and Cyrus McCormick, *The Century of the Reaper* (1931). Obituaries and information about settlement of the estate are in the *Chicago Tribune*, 6, 10 July, 8 Aug., and 31 Oct. 1923.

SUSAN ALBERTINE

MCCORMICK, Robert Rutherford (30 July 1880–1 Apr. 1955), newspaper editor and publisher, was born in Chicago, Illinois, the son of Robert Sanderson McCormick, a diplomat, and Katharine "Kate" Van Etta Medill, the daughter of Joseph Medill, the longtime editor and publisher of the *Chicago Tribune*. McCormick attended Ludgrove, a preparatory school in England, where he developed a strong sense of patriotism and even hung an American flag over his bed. His classmates respected his support of his country, yet it added to his already solitary existence. At the age of twelve McCormick transferred to Elstree. In 1899 he graduated from Groton preparatory school in Massachusetts, where he was a schoolmate of Franklin Delano Roosevelt, who became his political and philosophical nemesis later in life.

McCormick attended Yale, and for the first time he became "one of the boys" (Morgan and Veysey, p. 55), making friends and participating in social affairs. His devotion to the United States intensified during his college days, and he engaged in campus political activities, siding with the majority of his classmates in support of the Republican party. At Yale he took up polo, a sport he would enjoy throughout his adult life. Without thoughts of going to work for the *Tribune*, he turned his attention toward the law. He graduated in the spring of 1903 with a liberal arts degree and made plans to attend Northwestern University Law School the following fall.

Meanwhile, the *Chicago Tribune* was being run by McCormick's uncle, Robert W. Patterson, Jr., who was married to Kate McCormick's sister Elinor. Both McCormick's older brother Medill and his cousin Joseph Patterson had worked for the *Tribune* but moved on to other jobs away from Chicago. The elder Patterson assumed command of the paper after the death of Joseph Medill in 1899 and was glad to have the paper to himself.

Perhaps needing the continued support of the *Tribune* or persuaded by Patterson (in an effort to keep another Medill grandson out of the business), Republican leader Fred Busse approached McCormick in the spring of 1904 about running for alderman of the Twenty-first Ward. He left Northwestern and won the election, serving a two-year term. Alderman McCormick became highly visible to the public. Standing six feet, four inches tall, dressed in tailored clothes or occasionally polo attire, he stood out among his colleagues. Not only recognized for his sense of style, McCormick was also viewed as honest, hardworking, and able to see across party lines for the best interest of the city. His service on the city council so impressed Busse and other party leaders that in 1905 they chose him as the party's candidate for the Chicago Sanitary District presidency. He served a five-year term on this important project, which created an outlet for Chicago's sewage.

During the time he served as president of the sanitary district, McCormick was also a member of the law firm of McCormick, Kirkland, Patterson, and Fleming. Though he had not received his law degree, he was admitted to the bar in 1908. He might have continued his law practice if not for the death of Patterson in 1910 and the prospect of the *Tribune*'s being sold to a competitor. McCormick, who had become involved in the paper in a nonpaying position (he served as treasurer before his uncle's death), appealed to his cousin Joseph Patterson's sense of family obligation, and the two men decided to take over the paper.

McCormick and Patterson were an odd couple—Bertie was ever the conservative, and Joe was a socialist. However, they had a successful working relationship that led the *Tribune* from third in circulation among Chicago's eight dailies to first within seven years. At first, the two men worked on separate aspects of the paper. Patterson worked as Sunday editor and developed new features such as a beauty column, an advice column, and comic strips (including "Andy Gump," "Moon Mullins," and "Little Orphan Annie"), and McCormick headed the business department. One of the first financial concerns he faced was the soaring cost of newsprint. He realized that if the *Tribune* could manufacture its own newsprint, it could save money. Canada seemed the best place to set up shop because an import duty on Canadian newsprint had been dropped by Congress. McCormick took advantage of this change, acquiring cutting rights and building paper mills in Quebec and Ontario.

From the beginning of their association with the *Tribune*, McCormick and Patterson left the managing of the paper to James Keeley, who for the most part remained in control of the editorial page. When Keeley asked to be promoted to editor and publisher, his request was denied; he left the paper in 1914. Rather than fill the vacated position with another outsider, McCormick and Patterson decided to share the editorship, alternating monthly. This led to editorials that were as varied as the cousins' personalities and politics. After gaining active control of the paper, McCormick and Patterson added "The World's Greatest Newspaper" to the masthead.

By 1915 McCormick had given up his political and legal aspirations and was committed to making the *Tribune* worthy of its new slogan. War was raging in Europe, so Europe was where he planned to be. In addition, Kate McCormick arranged through the Russian ambassador, a longtime family friend, for her son to travel to Russia as a war correspondent. Thinking a military title would add to his credibility overseas, McCormick asked Illinois governor Ed Dunne, another friend of the family, to appoint him an officer in the Illinois National Guard. Dunne agreed, and McCormick became a colonel.

In 1915 Colonel McCormick married Amie Irwin Adams, a divorcée eight years his senior; the couple did not have children. Kate McCormick was adamantly opposed to the union and had earlier offered her son $50,000 to give up Amie. In England, McCormick's first stop on his European venture, he tried using his clout to get on the front line, but he was not successful. He then went to France and called upon yet another family friend, Foreign Minister Théophile Delcassé, who permitted him to go to Arras to see the German atrocities. On his return to England, McCormick secured passage to the British front on the European mainland. It was here that McCormick learned the meaning of true courage. "Physical courage," he said, "varies with the individual but it can be improved, like piano playing and polite conversation, and is a more desirable accomplishment for a man than either" (Morgan and Veysey, p. 138).

From Western Europe, McCormick continued to Russia and toured the front line, taking notes that led to the publication of his first book, *With the Russian Army* (1915). McCormick would eventually write six other books. Returning to Chicago, he became somewhat of a celebrity in part because of the release in city theaters of newsreels he had taken while in Russia and a lecture series he conducted at the request of the U.S. military.

Since the outbreak of war, both McCormick and Patterson had voiced opposition to America's involvement. But, in 1916, when America's own border was threatened by Mexican bandits, the coeditors supported President Woodrow Wilson's plan to invade. Wilson named General John J. Pershing to head the effort, and McCormick volunteered for the First Illinois Cavalry, a National Guard unit; he was elected major. He promised *Tribune* employees that if they volunteered, their jobs would be secure and wages would be paid during their service. When the guard was called to the border, McCormick was ready. He had managed to acquire machine guns for his men, a first for the U.S. Army.

McCormick criticized others in industry who did not support his position of preparedness, and he specifically targeted Henry Ford. According to an employee, Ford threatened his workers with loss of employment if they went to the border. In response to McCormick's attack, Ford brought a libel suit with the aim of exacting $1 million in damages. Even though Ford prevailed in court, he was awarded only six cents. This turn of events solidified McCormick's belief in a free press, a cause he championed vigorously throughout his career.

McCormick returned to Chicago in the fall of 1916. On 2 April 1917 President Wilson asked Congress to declare war on Germany. By this time, the *Tribune* supported America's entry into the war. McCormick once again urged volunteers to come forward. Again serving under Pershing, he went to France and saw battle at Cantigny. During his military service, he stayed current with events at the *Tribune* by corresponding with his business manager, Bill Field. By the end of the war, McCormick rose in rank to colonel and had received a Distinguished Service Medal. He returned to the United States before Patterson (now a captain), who continued in combat.

Back at the *Tribune*, McCormick made good on his promise to implement Patterson's idea of launching a tabloid newspaper in New York modeled on the *London Daily Mirror*. In 1919 the *New York Daily News* was established, and Patterson assumed its direction, although operating from Chicago. Patterson became more involved with the *News* and less involved with the *Tribune* and by 1925 he had relocated to New York. He assumed full command of the *News*, while McCormick remained in Chicago, now sole editor and publisher of the *Tribune*. Both men enjoyed tremendous success in their new posts. The *Daily News* became the top-selling paper in the country, and the *Tribune* achieved the largest circulation of a standard-sized newspaper. Unfortunately, another postwar effort by the cousins was not as successful. In 1924 they had launched a weekly magazine, *Liberty*, intended to compete with the *Saturday Evening Post*. It never surpassed the *Post*'s popularity and never earned a profit. Abandoned in 1931, it cost the Tribune Company almost $14 million.

During the 1920s McCormick spoke out against Prohibition and continued to advocate smaller government and isolationism. He used the paper as a vehicle to "clean house" in local politics and was successful in helping to force former mayor and longtime rival William Hale Thompson to restore more than $1 million to the city treasury. Though his critics stressed his isolationism and accused him of having no vision for the future of the country (even calling him "the greatest mind of the fourteenth century"), McCormick expressed opinions that appealed to many readers, and the *Tribune*'s circulation continued to grow.

In 1924 McCormick founded Chicago radio station WGN, the call letters standing for World's Greatest Newspaper. He did not consider radio a threat to the newspaper industry, but rather a way of attracting readers. He thought that if listeners heard a news summary on the radio, they would want to read the *Tribune* for more details. Years later, McCormick himself appeared on the radio, broadcasting his memoirs on Saturday nights during the intermission of a popular show.

In the 1930s McCormick rallied opposition to Franklin D. Roosevelt, his former Groton schoolmate, and insisted on addressing him informally, writing letters to him with the salutation, "Dear Frank." So strong was McCormick's dislike of the New Deal that he called it "totalitarianism" or "communism." His biggest gripe was with the NRA (National Recovery Administration) headed by former *Tribune* reporter Harold Ickes, who became second only to Roosevelt on the *Tribune*'s list of anathemas. McCormick blamed Roosevelt personally for maneuvering the United States into World War II (he was opposed to the president's willingness to give moral and financial support to the British) and denounced America's involvement until after Pearl Harbor.

In 1939 Amie (now Amy) McCormick died and was buried on the family estate, which McCormick had named "Cantigny" when he returned from his war service. In 1944 he married Maryland Mathison Hooper, an old family friend; they too did not have children.

McCormick remained a staunch Republican in the 1940s, supporting Wendell Willkie for president in 1940 and Thomas Dewey in 1944, but he became discouraged with the party's inability to produce what he considered a viable candidate. He thought the party should seek new leadership, and in 1948 he supported Senator Robert A. Taft of Ohio for the presidential nomination. Taft, however, was defeated in the primary by Dewey, and Dewey in turn was defeated in the election by the incumbent, Truman. Truman was McCormick's least favorite postwar politician, and in an editorial appearing in the *Tribune* on 11 June 1948 McCormick denigrated the president: "Mr. Truman has added his name to the long list of political crooks and incompetents who have regarded *The Tribune* as first among their foes" (Gies, p. 226). After Truman won the election, he posed for the now famous photograph holding the *Chicago Tribune* flaunting the headline "Dewey Defeats Truman."

In the 1950s McCormick's frustration with the Republican party led to his proposal to start a new political party, the "American party." He urged readers to vote for neither Dwight D. Eisenhower nor Adlai Stevenson and to focus instead on getting "patriotic candidates" elected to Congress (*New York Times*, 2 Apr. 1955). But McCormick's battles had mostly been fought at this point; his health steadily declined. He underwent prostate surgery twice and suffered from liver problems as well. Despite his doctor's warnings, he refused to give up scotch, which he referred to as "one of the few pleasures in my life" (Morgan and Veysey, p. 461). In 1953 he caught pneumonia. He then underwent surgery for abdominal adhesions and never fully recovered. He died at his home in Wheaton, Illinois.

As one of the great publishers in American history, McCormick sparked controversy and intrigue among his readers, peers, and the public at large for five decades. During his tenure with the *Tribune*, he was often ridiculed for his seemingly antiquated way of thinking, yet he did not waver from his belief in isolationism. He was openly hostile to both Roosevelt and Truman and a strong opponent of the New Deal, organized labor, and other liberal causes. With a renown that was worldwide, he made an unquestionable impact on American journalism. He died just days after fellow publishing giant Joseph Pulitzer had, leading President Dwight D. Eisenhower to say, "American journalism has lost the services of two of its outstanding publishers. Although frequently on opposite sides of public issues, both were staunch champions of a free press so essential to our freedoms" (*New York Times*, 2 Apr. 1955).

• Robert McCormick's private papers are on reserve at the *Chicago Tribune* and are not available for public use. Besides *With the Russian Army*, McCormick's books include *The Army of 1918* (1920), *Ulysses S. Grant, the Great Solider of America* (1934), *The Freedom of the Press* (1936), *How We Acquired Our National Territory* (1942), *The American Revolution and Its Influence on World Civilization* (1945), and *The War without Grant* (1950). Even his former war correspondents turned biographers Gwen Morgan and Arthur Veysey did not have access to *Tribune* records during their research for their book, *The Life and Times of Col. Robert R. McCormick: Poor Little Rich Boy (and How He Made Good)* (1985). Microfilm files of the *Chicago Tribune* are available at the Library of Congress; included are copies of McCormick's radio memoirs, which can also be found in *Memoirs* (made up of transcripts of a series of radio addresses, 1952–1954). Other full-length accounts of the colonel's life include Joseph Gies, *The Colonel of Chicago* (1979), Frank C. Waldrop, *McCormick of Chicago* (1966), and Richard Norton Smith, *The Colonel: The Life and Legend of Robert R. McCormick, 1880–1955* (1997). A detailed obituary is in the *New York Times*, 2 Apr. 1955.

LISABETH G. SVENDSGAARD

MCCORMICK, Ruth Hanna (27 Mar. 1880–31 Dec. 1944), congresswoman and political leader, was born in Cleveland, Ohio, the daughter of Marcus Alonzo "Mark" Hanna, a businessman and politician, and Charlotte Augusta Rhodes. In 1896 Mark Hanna, Republican national chairman, managed William McKinley's presidential campaign, in which Ruth participated. Hanna was elected to the U.S. Senate in 1897, and Ruth worked as his private secretary on Capitol Hill. Her marriage in 1903 to Joseph Medill McCormick of the *Chicago Tribune* newspaper family was also a political event, attended by President Theodore Roosevelt, who was eager for Hanna's endorsement. The McCormicks had three children.

In Chicago Ruth and Medill McCormick took part in progressive reform activities. They lived for a time at the University of Chicago Settlement House behind the stockyards. Ruth was active in the Consumers' League and the Women's Trade Union League and worked for better labor-management relations in the women's division of the National Civic Federation. By 1912 Medill had left the newspaper to enter politics, and both McCormicks campaigned for Roosevelt's Progressive party. Roosevelt, commenting on the couple to a friend, remarked, "My money's on the mare."

Medill was elected to the state legislature in 1912, and Ruth McCormick joined him in Springfield to lobby for a suffrage bill, the first passed east of the Mississippi, granting women the right to vote in presidential and municipal elections. When Alice Paul, who headed the Congressional Committee of the National American Woman Suffrage Association, became too controversial, Ruth McCormick was chosen to replace her. McCormick disapproved of Paul's campaign against the Democrats, who had failed to pass a suffrage amendment. She worked instead at the state level to elect prosuffrage members to Congress. In 1918 the Republican party named her chair of their new National Women's Executive Committee to attract women voters.

Medill McCormick was elected to the U.S. House of Representatives in 1916 and to the U.S. Senate in 1918, defeating the Democratic whip, James Hamilton Lewis. Medill McCormick was among the Republican "Irreconcilables" who blocked America's entry into the League of Nations. Ruth McCormick and her friend Alice Roosevelt Longworth lobbied members of Congress in their salons.

After passage of the Nineteenth Amendment in 1920, the Republican party reorganized itself to include eight women among the 21-member executive committee, with McCormick in charge of the central division. She thought women should join the major political parties, arguing that organizations like the Woman's party or the League of Women Voters diluted women's political strength. For this reason, and to help Medill win reelection in 1924, Ruth McCormick organized Republican women's clubs throughout Illinois, which claimed over 200,000 members by the end of the decade. Medill McCormick was narrowly defeated in the primary by Charles S. Deneen, who was elected in November. In February 1925, just before his Senate term expired, Medill, who had been subject to depression all his life, committed suicide.

Although Ruth McCormick had other occupations, such as a dairy farm in Byron to provide safe milk for city children, newspapers and a radio station in Rockford, and later a ranch in Colorado, she liked to say that politics was her profession. In 1928 she ran for one of two seats for congressperson at large from Illinois. (Some states, instead of redistricting, added seats "at large," representing the entire state.) Although some voters were opposed in principle to a woman legislator, many hoped she would be free of the factionalism of Illinois politics. She waged a vigorous grassroots campaign and easily triumphed over seven male opponents.

Soon after taking office in the spring of 1929, McCormick began to campaign for the Senate in 1930. Even though her statewide constituency would be the same, more opposition existed to a woman senator. Former Progressive Hiram Johnson thought women in the Senate would lead to its "thorough breakdown and demoralization." McCormick drew upon the African-American community and organized labor and denounced Deneen for his support of the World Court, which, like the League of Nations, was unpopular in Illinois. In the April primary she soundly defeated Deneen, the man who had defeated her husband, to become the first woman to win a Senate nomination by a major political party. However, she lost in the Democratic landslide of 1930, ironically, to Lewis.

In 1932 McCormick married Albert Gallatin Simms of New Mexico, a former fellow congressman; they had no children. She moved to Albuquerque and, although she campaigned for Alf Landon in 1936, was less active in politics than in civic works, such as founding the Manzano and Sandia schools for girls and supporting the arts.

After the death of her son in 1938, McCormick reentered the political fray. In the fall of 1939 she became the principal manager of Thomas Dewey's 1940 presidential campaign. Dewey was young and little known outside of New York and New England, and McCormick was well connected and experienced. Typical was Raymond Clapper's observation in the *Washington Daily News* (11 Apr. 1940): "She is the only real big-time politician in the crowd. . . . She is the political brains and carries the load in organizing the campaign." Dewey agreed with McCormick on the need to keep the United States out of the European war. As the international situation worsened, the convention turned to Wendell Willkie, an internationalist. Although Dewey distanced himself from McCormick in 1944 because of her isolationism, she continued to work for him, insisting: "I will always be active in party affairs. . . . It is my inheritance and my conviction. . . . It is my right and my pleasure." She died in Chicago.

McCormick had the background and determination to take advantage of new opportunities for women in electoral politics in the first half of the twentieth century. As a leader in the suffrage movement and the Republican party as well as a successful campaigner, she attracted large numbers of women into partisan politics.

• McCormick's papers are in the Hanna-McCormick collection in the Manuscripts Reading Room of the Library of Congress. Kristie Miller, *Ruth Hanna McCormick: A Life in Pol-*

itics 1880–1944 (1992), is a full-length biography. See also Miller, "Ruth Hanna McCormick and the Senatorial Election of 1930," *Illinois Historical Journal* 81, no. 3 (Autumn 1988): 191–210; Miller, "Of the Women, for the Women, and by the Women," *Chicago History* 24, no. 2 (Summer 1995): 58–72, on the Woman's World's Fair; and Hope Chamberlin, *A Minority of Members: Women in the U.S. Congress* (1973). A contemporary assessment is in Raymond Moley, *27 Masters of Politics: In a Personal Perspective* (1949). Obituaries are in the *Rockford Register-Republic*, the *Chicago Tribune*, and the *New York Times*, 1 Jan. 1945.

KRISTIE MILLER

MCCORMICK, Samuel Black (6 May 1858–18 Apr. 1928), Presbyterian clergyman and educator, was born in Westmoreland County, Pennsylvania, the son of James Irwin McCormick, a physician and classical scholar, and Rachel Long. His early education began at home and continued at Washington and Jefferson College in Washington, Pennsylvania, from which he graduated with highest honors in 1880. For the next two years he supported himself by teaching Greek at his alma mater and by instructing younger students at the Canonsburg Academy. In his free time he studied law with his uncle Henry H. McCormick, the U.S. district attorney for the western district of Pennsylvania. He was admitted to the Allegany County Bar in 1882. In September of that year, McCormick married Ida May Steep; they had four children. The couple moved to Denver, Colorado, in 1883, where McCormick opened a law practice with R. D. Thompson.

After four years, McCormick gave up his law career to become a minister. Returning to Pennsylvania, he entered the Western Theological Seminary in Allegany, supporting himself by teaching English literature and rhetoric at the Western University of Pennsylvania until he graduated from the seminary in 1890. The Presbytery of Allegany ordained McCormick that same year and assigned him to the Central Presbyterian Church in Allegany. While the pastor of Central, McCormick taught at the seminary and served on its board of directors. After four years there he was called to serve at the First Presbyterian Church in Omaha, Nebraska, where he worked for three years. From 1897 to 1904 McCormick was the president of Coe College in Cedar Rapids, Iowa, a small and unorganized but growing school.

Evidence of McCormick's effective leadership at Coe promoted his invitation in 1904 to become the chancellor of the Western University of Pennsylvania. He accepted the chancellorship only on the condition that the trustees would support his planned expansion of the school.

In the first six years of McCormick's tenure, the university purchased its dental school and the medical department and stock of the West Penn Medical College. Its name was changed from the Western University of Pennsylvania to the University of Pittsburgh in 1908. This change was made to better indicate the geographic location of the school and the population it served, to distance the school from associations with the University of Pennsylvania, and to avoid its existing undignified acronym WUP (pronounced "whup"). The School of Economics (later renamed the School of Business Administration), the School of Education, and the summer school were established. Lastly, in the first years of McCormick's leadership, the school purchased a new 48-acre site in downtown Pittsburgh and held a nationwide contest to design the campus's proposed thirty buildings. During McCormick's tenure in office, six of the major buildings were constructed.

In the later years of McCormick's chancellorship, the school raised academic standards, established a system of tenure, obtained state money for expansion and maintenance, and secured an endowment from the Mellon Institute of Industrial Research. Enrollment grew from 800 to 6,000 students. McCormick's tenure was marked by the unprecedented power given to deans of schools and heads of departments. The small but growing university gained national recognition through its excellence in athletics, notably its football team. During World War I, McCormick oversaw the university's training of students as automobile and gas engine mechanics for service in the war industry and the compulsory military training required of all male college students. McCormick resigned in January 1920, citing his age and decreasing energy as the primary reasons.

McCormick's historical significance rests on his service to the University of Pittsburgh, which involved the overseeing of many enormous changes and enlargements to the school. In addition to his service at the university, McCormick spent his later years as a member of the committee for the revision of the confession of faith of the General Assembly of the Presbyterian church, a director of the Western Theological Seminary, a trustee of the Carnegie Foundation for the Advancement of Teaching, and a member of the Pittsburgh Chamber of Commerce. He died at his home in Caraopolis Heights, near Pittsburgh.

• McCormick is mentioned in the *University of Pittsburgh Bulletin: The Celebration of the One Hundred and Twenty-fifth Anniversary* (1912), and in the *Biographical and Historical Catalog of Washington and Jefferson College* (1902). For information on his contribution to the university, see Robert C. Alberts, *Pitt: The Story of the University of Pittsburgh, 1787–1987* (1986). Obituaries are in the *Pittsburgh Record*, June 1928, and the *Pittsburgh Post-Gazette*, 19 Apr. 1928

ELIZABETH ZOE VICARY

MCCOSH, James (1 Apr. 1811–16 Nov. 1894), philosopher and educator, was born in Patna, southwestern Scotland, the son of Andrew McCosh and Jean Carson, farmers. The family was prosperous and lived in a large home. The couple had seven children, but after the death of an older brother in 1811, James was the only surviving male. Andrew, a religious man who led the family in evening Bible readings, died when James was nine.

McCosh studied at Glasgow University from 1824 to 1829. He boarded with a cousin in that expanding metropolis and saw many of the social ills of Scotland, which later influenced his ministry. Upon completion of his studies at Edinburgh, McCosh prepared for the ministry at the University of Edinburgh. There he was influenced by Thomas Chalmers, who held the Chair of Divinity and was one of the powerful forces in the Scottish evangelical movement. McCosh graduated from Edinburgh in 1834 and the next year was called to the Abbey Church in Arbroath where he began his ministerial career.

The Church of Scotland was then undergoing a schismatic period in which a popular evangelical movement was challenging the authority of the Moderates. The latter group, born of Scotland's rational Enlightenment in the eighteenth century, had moved Scottish Presbyterianism out of its Calvinist mold. Moderates in the Church owed their control to the Patronage Act of 1712, which was challenged by the evangelicals. At Arbroath and then at Brechin, where he headed the West Church after 1839, McCosh became an organizer of the evangelical movement, headed in that area by Thomas Guthrie. Evangelicals wanted to remove the influence of both the state and the wealthy patrons in the Church of Scotland. When their efforts failed in the courts, they used the occasion of the 1843 General Assembly meeting to sever their connections to the Church. McCosh joined the hundreds of schismatics who went on to establish the Free Church of Scotland. In the meantime, McCosh strengthened his ties to the Guthrie family. He courted Isabella Guthrie, the daughter of Thomas's older brother, Alexander. The couple married in 1845; they had five children.

Amid a busy life as parish preacher, McCosh made time to read philosophy, an effort that led to the publication of his first book, *The Method of the Divine Government* (1850). The book summarized the religious phase of McCosh's intellectual career as it endeavored to demonstrate how nature reveals divine intelligence. *Divine Government* was essentially a book of evidence, somewhat in the tradition of William Paley, but it supplemented external evidence of design with internal evidence—conscience, will, and emotion. This introspective methodology, very much in the Scottish philosophical tradition of the eighteenth century, gave the book its neo-Calvinist quality, which reflected McCosh's role in the evangelical ministry.

Divine Government won a large following for McCosh and led to his appointment to Queen's College in Belfast, Ireland. From 1852 to 1868 he was a professor of logic and metaphysics at that institution. At Belfast, McCosh wrote his most important philosophical works, including *The Intuitions of the Mind, Inductively Investigated* (1860), and *An Examination of Mr. J. S. Mill's Philosophy* (1866). In these works McCosh sought to extend Scottish Common Sense philosophy, especially as expressed by Thomas Reid, into the mid-nineteenth century. He made revisions of the Scottish philosophers' realism as he sought to define a middle position between empiricism, as in the philosophy of Thomas Brown, on the one hand, and several neo-Kantian formulations of idealism on the

other. Particularly troublesome to McCosh were the recent writings of Sir William Hamilton, professor at Edinburgh, who had become controversial through his contention that because we can know one thing only as related to another thing, we can have no concept of an unrelated whole, or essence. Hamilton thus defended only a negative idea of the absolute, insisting that the concept cannot be positive notion of the mind, that the absolute is, in essence, inconceivable. McCosh and other religious-minded thinkers read the dangerous implications of this notion, and in rebuttal they sought to secure the absolute as a positive concept, intuitively perceived. But McCosh also argued that intuitions do not overreach reality, but instead build in conjunction with experience.

McCosh's book was widely read, especially in the United States. He was a familiar name when he toured America in 1866 and spoke in St. Louis to the General Assembly meetings of both the Old Side and New Side factions of the Presbyterian church. The groups were beginning to repair their schism of 1837 and McCosh appeared as a reconciler in the denomination. Two years later the College of New Jersey (later Princeton) named McCosh its new president, the same year in which the Presbyterian Reunion occurred.

At Princeton McCosh inherited a college long affiliated with the conservative side of the Presbyterian denomination. Despite the college's separation from Princeton Theological Seminary after 1812, the faculty was dominated by Calvinists, and the president of the board of trustees was Charles Hodge, the formidable Calvinist theologian. One issue that McCosh approached cautiously was evolution. He had studied and written on science, and his book *Typical Forms and Special Ends in Creation* (1856), coauthored with George Dickie, anticipated his agreement with the evolutionary hypothesis. But his accommodation did not sit well with some faculty and trustees. McCosh continued to write on evolution and is generally considered one of the first American Protestants to attempt a reconciliation of science and religion with respect to the evolutionary hypothesis. He insisted that Princeton students accept the facts of science, and although he conceded the plausibility of natural selection, he did not rule out a spiritual intervention in evolution.

McCosh's inaugural address at Princeton outlined his intention to expand the college's curriculum by introducing modern subjects. He especially wanted to strengthen the offerings in science. McCosh, however, did not endorse the more open elective system that Charles W. Eliot introduced at Harvard in 1869. On two occasions McCosh engaged Eliot in public debate about the much-agitated questions concerning the new directions in American higher education. Though many thought that he and Noah Porter of Yale represented the conservative position, McCosh insisted that the elective system was faulty because it did not require that students be educated in modern science. McCosh also insisted, however, on the imperative of religious instruction in the curriculum. Generally, at

Princeton, he moved in both directions, making some key faculty appointments in the sciences—Cyrus Fogg Brackett and Charles Augustus Young—and other disciplines, but perpetuating an evangelical ethos reminiscent of his Scottish years. Strict moral supervision of students was maintained, and McCosh even encouraged religious revivals on campus to stay the tide of student rowdiness.

McCosh moved to make Princeton a less provincial college. The new faculty appointments broke a pattern of hiring mostly Princeton graduates. McCosh traveled around the country to set up admissions tests for prospective students and otherwise promote the college and expand its geographical base. He also visited affluent Presbyterian churches in the eastern cities to gain new financial support for the college. His recourse to wealthy businessmen thus tied the direction of the school to the hopes of individuals who wanted Princeton to be an institution of national influence. McCosh also proposed alumni representation on the board of trustees, but did not secure that change until 1885.

By 1882 the McCosh reforms had become more controversial. Some of the trustees feared he was weakening Princeton's religious identity, and a few decried his agreement with evolution. He offered to resign but yielded to a request for continued service. Partly to fortify his position politically, in the 1880s McCosh filled faculty appointments with his former students, including William Berryman Scott and Henry Fairfield Osborn (1857–1935). He also believed that the new educational directions of the college would be secured by recent Princeton graduates who had, with McCosh's encouragement, undertaken further training in Europe. These students were the group McCosh proudly called "me bright young men."

McCosh's pride and egotism were traits for which he was often remembered at Princeton. In the 1870s he saw Princeton through an ambitious building program and often, when showing visitors the campus, said, "that's mine, I built it." McCosh's temper was equally visible, and all the more formidable as it was conveyed by a heavy Scottish brogue. But most agreed that his bark was worse than his bite, and McCosh's gestures of kindness and encouragement were equally remembered. The most loyal of the McCosh students were those who caught his vision of a modern Princeton and worked in different capacities to realize it. Isabella McCosh was a nurse to Princeton students for twenty years, and the university infirmary was later named for her.

McCosh retired from the presidency of the university in 1888 but remained in Princeton until his death. Conservative trustees prevailed in naming Francis L. Patton to succeed McCosh. Increasingly, however, as the Patton administration foundered, a movement succeeded in raising enough money to induce Patton to leave office in 1902. Most of those who worked for Patton's defeat were products of the McCosh era who wanted Princeton to break from narrow doctrinal and denominational affiliations. The insurgents included faculty member Woodrow Wilson, who had been a McCosh student in the class of 1879, and Moses Taylor Pyne, another member of the class of 1879, who was Princeton's first alumni trustee.

• McCosh's papers are in the Department of Rare Books and Special Collections at Princeton University. In addition to McCosh's writings cited above, see his *The Supernatural in Relation to the Natural* (1862), *Christianity and Positivism* (1871), *The Scottish Philosophy, Biographical, Expository, Critical, From Hutcheson to Hamilton* (1875), and *The Religious Aspect of Evolution* (1888). William Milligan Sloane's *The Life of James McCosh: A Record Chiefly Autobiographical* (1896), is the work of a historian at Princeton during McCosh's presidency. The standard biography is J. David Hoeveler, Jr., *James McCosh and the Scottish Intellectual Tradition: From Glasgow to Princeton* (1981).

J. DAVID HOEVELER, JR.

MCCOY, Elijah (27 Mar. 1843–1929), inventor, was born in Colchester, Canada West (now Ontario), the son of George McCoy and Mildred Goins, former slaves who had escaped from Kentucky. In 1849 his parents moved the family to Ypsilanti, Michigan, where Elijah began attending school. In 1859 he went to Edinburgh, Scotland, to undertake an apprenticeship as a mechanical engineer; he stayed there five years.

Unable to obtain a position as an engineer after he returned to the United States, McCoy began working as a railroad fireman for the Michigan Central Railroad. This position exposed him to the problems of steam engine lubrication and overheating. Locomotive engines had to be periodically oiled by hand, a time-consuming task that caused significant delays in railroad transport of commercial goods and passengers. Poorly lubricated locomotives also used more fuel than those that were efficiently lubricated.

McCoy began his career as an inventor by first examining and improving the lubrication of stationary machines. On 23 June 1872 he patented "an improvement in lubricators for steam engines," the first of his automatic lubrication devices for use on stationary engines. The rights for this patent were assigned to S. C. Hamlin of Ypsilanti. McCoy received several additional patents for improvements in lubricators that were all for use on stationary engines and on steam engines for ships.

In 1882 McCoy began receiving patents for lubricators specifically designed for railroad locomotive engines. His hydrostatic lubricator for locomotives made quite an impact. Largely constructed of brass, the lubricators, approximately twelve inches in height, had valves that fed the oil to the engine and that regulated the steam pressure. These lubricators were assigned to Charles and Henry Hodges and were manufactured by the Detroit Railway Supply Company. The money McCoy received from these patent assignments he used for further studies of the problems of lubrication.

McCoy continued to receive patents for improvements to his hydrostatic lubricator, and railroad officials soon took note. Despite that other locomotive lubricators were on the market, McCoy's lubricators sold well. He became an instructor in the correct installation and maintenance of his lubricators and also served as a consultant for several lubricator manufacturing companies, such as the Detroit Lubricator Company.

In 1915 McCoy patented a graphite lubricator, specifically designed for use on the newly introduced "superheater" locomotive engines. Because of the extreme temperatures of the steam, it was difficult to control and regulate the supply of oil with which the superheater engines were lubricated. McCoy's new lubricator relied on the use of a solid lubricant, graphite, combined with oil that solved this problem. The basic design was economical and simple with few moving parts. The amount of lubricant was controlled by an equalizing valve that regulated the flow of oil and graphite over the engine cylinder. One enthusiastic customer reported that his locomotive made thirteen round trips between Chicago and the Mississippi River, and when the engine was examined it was in "perfect condition." On these trips the amount of oil used for lubrication was reduced by one-third to one-half, and the amount of coal was reduced by four to six tons. McCoy considered the graphite lubricator to be his greatest invention.

The Elijah McCoy Manufacturing Company, located in Detroit, was established in 1916 to sell the graphite lubricator. But apparently McCoy was only a minor stockholder; the company went out of business a few years after it began. Many questions remain about the extent to which McCoy himself profited from his own inventions. McCoy could have become a very wealthy man given the commercial success of his lubricator design. But many of his patents were quickly assigned to others, and he merely served as a figurehead for the company bearing his name.

McCoy married Mary E. Delaney, his second wife, in 1873. They later moved to Detroit, where she became a well-known civil rights and women's rights activist and clubwoman. The McCoys were very close, and after her death in 1923 Elijah McCoy's health began to deteriorate. Never a very sociable man, he began to withdraw from the world around him. In 1928 he was committed to Eloise Infirmary, suffering from senile dementia, and he died there. By the time of his death he had received at least fifty patents, many held in foreign countries and virtually all of them in the area of engine lubrication.

Many historians think that another one of McCoy's enduring legacies is the phrase "the real McCoy." The quality of his lubricators was so outstanding in comparison to the many other lubricators on the market that railroad inspectors and engineers are said to have challenged their crews as to whether they had installed "the real McCoy" instead of less effective lubricators.

• Biographical materials on McCoy tend to contain widely varying dates. The best sources of information are Albert P. Marshall, *The "Real McCoy" of Ypsilanti* (1989); Robert C. Hayden, *Eight Black American Inventors* (1972); and Aaron Klein, *Hidden Contributors: Black Scientists and Inventors in America* (1971).

PORTIA P. JAMES

MCCOY, Frank Ross (29 Oct. 1874–4 June 1954), soldier and diplomat, was born in Lewistown, Pennsylvania, the son of Thomas Franklin McCoy, an attorney, and Margaret Eleanor Ross. Inspired by his father's volunteer service in both the Mexican War and the Civil War, McCoy decided at an early age to become a soldier. Appointed to West Point, McCoy graduated with the class of 1897 and was commissioned a second lieutenant of cavalry. One year later, he was deployed to Cuba with the expedition that was mounted to liberate that island from Spanish rule. On 1 July 1898 McCoy was wounded at Kettle Hill. Following convalescence in the United States, he returned in 1899 to Cuba, where he became an aide and staff officer of General Leonard Wood, the American military governor. McCoy became extraordinarily devoted to Wood and was soon the general's protégé and closest confidant.

After the Cuban military government dissolved in 1902, McCoy accompanied Wood on the latter's subsequent posting as governor of the Moro Province in the Philippines. For four years, McCoy participated in an often brutal effort to pacify the Moros; in October 1904 he led a daring expedition that tracked down and killed the notorious chieftain Datto Ali. His return to the United States in June 1906 coincided with an outbreak of severe unrest in Cuba, which generated pressure for a second American intervention. When Secretary of War William Howard Taft was dispatched to negotiate between Cuba's warring factions, he requisitioned McCoy to assist him. American efforts to broker a settlement failed, and Taft placed himself at the head of an American-run provisional government to rule Cuba. Judge Charles E. Magoon soon succeeded Taft, but McCoy stayed on to assist the new governor. After completing this assignment, McCoy was detailed to the White House, where he spent two years as senior military aide to President Theodore Roosevelt. After an interval of troop duty, McCoy in 1911 rejoined Leonard Wood, now the army chief of staff in Washington. During this time McCoy became fast friends with Henry L. Stimson, then serving his first tour as secretary of war.

In 1915 McCoy again returned to troop duty, commanding a cavalry squadron assigned to patrol a stretch of the Rio Grande. With Mexico convulsed by revolution, McCoy's troops skirmished periodically with raiders crossing the border. Following Pancho Villa's attack on Columbus, New Mexico, in March 1916, President Woodrow Wilson dispatched additional reinforcements to the region, and McCoy became chief of staff of a composite force of 30,000 regulars and National Guardsmen, an experiment that allowed him to test concepts of military preparedness that Wood was promoting nationwide. Among these concepts were the raising of a citizen army, vice one composed exclusively of regulars; the training of large units (division-size and greater) for large-scale operations; and the development of a pool of trained reservists, especially officers, available for mobilization in an emergency. When tensions along the border eased, McCoy found himself on the move again: in February 1917 he became military attaché in the newly reopened American embassy in Mexico City. Chief among his responsibilities was the coordination of intelligence activities that were directed at assessing German influence and intentions in Mexico. With U.S. entry into World War I in April, however, McCoy lobbied for immediate reassignment from Mexico and by June was en route to France.

Throughout the build-up of the American Expeditionary Forces in France, McCoy remained in AEF general headquarters there, serving as secretary of the general staff for military commander John J. Pershing. During the major battles of 1918, however, he commanded first a regiment and then a brigade with distinction and ended the war a brigadier general. After the armistice, McCoy remained in France to direct redeployment operations for the AEF. On the eve of returning to the United States in August 1919, he was detailed as chief of staff of the American Military Mission to Armenia, which had been created by President Woodrow Wilson to consider the advisability of the United States accepting a mandate for Armenia. Headed by Major General James G. Harbord, the mission spent the autumn of 1919 crisscrossing Turkey and Transcaucasia. Following his return to Paris, the mission released its findings, the so-called Harbord Report, which called for an American mandate to encompass not only Armenia but Turkey, Georgia, and Azerbaijan as well. With the tide of American isolationism already rising, the recommendation garnered virtually no support.

In early 1920 McCoy returned to the United States and joined Wood's staff during the latter's unsuccessful effort to win the Republican nomination for the presidency. The following year McCoy was posted to the Philippines as chief of staff of the Wood-Forbes Commission, created by President Warren G. Harding to determine whether the islands were ready for independence. Stated Republican policy opposed Philippine independence, and the commission reported accordingly. When Harding subsequently asked Wood to stay on in the islands as governor general, Wood accepted contingent on McCoy being attached to his staff. As a result, McCoy remained in Manila, a key figure in the so-called cavalry cabinet—Wood's chosen instrument for reversing the erosion of American authority that had occurred during the tenure of the previous governor general. In 1923 McCoy was on leave bound for China when a great earthquake struck Tokyo, killing some 150,000; without orders, he immediately sailed for Japan and took charge of the highly visible American relief effort mounted in the wake of the disaster. In 1924 he married Frances Judson, a niece of Leonard Wood; the couple had no children.

McCoy's return to the United States in 1925 initiated a sequence of assignments in which increasingly senior military commands alternated with duty as a diplomatic troubleshooter, usually at the behest of Stimson, who was soon to become secretary of state. McCoy directed the American supervision of Nicaraguan elections during 1927–1928, chaired an international commission that attempted unsuccessfully in 1929 to settle a dispute between Bolivia and Paraguay over control of Chaco Boreal, and served throughout 1932 as the American member on the Lytton Commission, formed by the League of Nations to investigate Japan's invasion of Manchuria the year before. Although his close connections with various prominent Republicans dampened the demand for his diplomatic skills once Franklin Roosevelt became president in 1933, McCoy's military career continued to prosper. During the 1930s he held a succession of key military appointments, which culminated in the command of First Army, headquartered at Governor's Island, New York.

In October 1938 McCoy retired from the army as a major general. From 1939 to 1945 he was president of the New York–based Foreign Policy Association, a nominally nonpartisan organization that generally favored U.S. intervention in World War II and supported internationalist policies. Twice during the Second World War McCoy was recalled to active duty, first serving on the Roberts Commission that investigated the attack on Pearl Harbor and later presiding over the military courts that in 1942 convicted eight captured German saboteurs.

In October 1945 President Harry S. Truman appointed McCoy chairman of the Far Eastern Advisory Commission (later renamed the Far Eastern Commission) to coordinate allied policy toward occupied Japan. Though frustrated by the commission's lack of authority and by the opposition of General Douglas MacArthur, the supreme allied commander in Tokyo, McCoy continued in this capacity until his final retirement in November 1949. He died in Washington, D.C., and was buried at Arlington National Cemetery.

Theodore Roosevelt once described McCoy as "the best soldier I ever laid eyes on" ("The Army's McCoy," *Literary Digest* 121 [25 Apr. 1936]). At the time of his death, the *New York Times* praised him as "one of the best soldiers this country has produced." Yet McCoy left no distinctive legacy and was soon all but forgotten. A man of high character and formidable talent, McCoy's most outstanding quality may have been his amiability. Friendships acquired throughout the course of his long life grew to form a large and diverse network. Time and again, these personal connections provided the lubricant that enabled McCoy to move easily between several distinct realms—traditional military service, colonial administration, high-level diplomacy, and the world of politics. Prominent friends like Wood and Stimson sponsored McCoy's own advancement, and he repaid them by acting as their agent in enterprises great and small. In serving his friends well, this versatile and self-effacing soldier-diplomat also served his country with admirable effectiveness.

• The principal collection of McCoy's papers is in the Library of Congress. The most complete biographical treatment is A. J. Bacevich, *Diplomat in Khaki: Major General Frank Ross McCoy and American Foreign Policy, 1898–1949* (1989). An obituary is in the *New York Times*, 6 June 1954.

A. J. BACEVICH

MCCOY, Horace Stanley (14 Apr. 1897–15 Dec. 1955), novelist and screenwriter, was born in Pegram, Tennessee, the son of James Harris McCoy, a railroad conductor, and Nancye Holt. In 1899 McCoy's father moved his family to Nashville. McCoy quit school at the age of sixteen and took a series of odd jobs to supplement his father's modest income.

In World War I McCoy served in France as a member of the American Air Service. He was wounded in action and, after being discharged, worked variously as a reporter, sportswriter, and editor for the *Dallas Dispatch* and the *Dallas Journal*.

In 1921 McCoy married Loline Shere; they had one child. During the early 1920s McCoy began writing fiction. He published numerous stories in *Black Mask*, which became, under editor Joseph T. Shaw, a training ground for writers of the hard-boiled school of fiction. McCoy also produced fiction for the *Dallasite*, an arts magazine for which he was editor.

When the *Dallasite* folded in 1930, McCoy, who was divorced in 1928, struck out for Hollywood, where in 1933 he found work as a scriptwriter at Columbia Studios. During that same year, he married Helen Vinmont, with whom he had two children. For the next two years, McCoy, in addition to working as a screenwriter, was busy converting his short story "Marathon Dance" into his first novel, *They Shoot Horses, Don't They?* (1935). The story is told in flashback by Robert Syverten as a death sentence is being pronounced on him for the murder of Gloria Beatty, his partner in a dance marathon. Gloria is McCoy's greatest creation. A midwesterner like Robert, she once sought fame and fortune in Hollywood. She has destroyed Robert's optimism through her relentless cynicism and persuaded him to shoot her to end her misery. The animal metaphor of the novel's title, illustrating Robert's rationale for killing Gloria, is an apt reference to the subhuman level to which the dance contestants fall. The novel, an impressive depiction of the dark underside of Hollywood during the depression, exposing a milieu that undermined human dignity and destroyed dreams of success, remains McCoy's best-known work. A film adaptation, directed by Sidney Pollack, appeared in 1969.

After being rejected by many American publishers, McCoy's second novel, *No Pockets in a Shroud*, was published in England in 1937. McCoy's days as a reporter provided material for his story of Michael Dolan, a crusading journalist in a small southwestern town who, after exposing a fascist, klanlike organiza-tion, is murdered. The novel was generally well received and marked the beginning of interest in McCoy abroad.

McCoy's next novel, *I Should Have Stayed Home* (1938), is a return to the depression setting of Hollywood in the thirties. The book examines two jobless extras, Ralph Carston and Mona Matthews, both of whom struggle through a series of misfortunes. But lacking the claustrophobic dance-hall setting and self-conscious literary approach of *Horses*, the book proves to be less effective than its predecessor.

For the next ten years McCoy wrote little fiction, and, though somewhat disillusioned with screenwriting, he produced scripts for numerous B movies, most of which were produced by Paramount. But McCoy's reputation had unexpectedly grown in Europe after World War II, especially in France, where some of his novels began appearing in the legendary *série noire*, a French paperback series known for its stylized black covers. McCoy's sudden acclaim overseas encouraged him to begin work on a new novel. *Kiss Tomorrow Good-Bye* (1948), described by its author as a "psychological story of a pathological killer," disrupts the crime genre by inverting its usual trappings. Ralph Cotter, alias Paul Murphy, who became a criminal by choice and not by way of environmental failure, is a shadowy, contradictory, and complex character, more romantic intellectual than calculating professional, whose downfall is the result of his own private demons and not the machinations of an impersonal law force. McCoy intended his book to be, as Thomas Sturak notes, "the acid test of his creative genius and artistic talents." Written in lyrical prose that stretches the limits of hard-boiled realism, McCoy's fourth novel demonstrates his unresolved lifelong conflict between artistic ambition and a desire for popular success. A film version starring James Cagney appeared in 1950. Since then the movie's reputation has grown, often being cited by film scholars as an important film noir of the period.

McCoy returned to screenwriting, and in 1952 he produced his most notable screen credit, for Nicholas Ray's *The Lusty Men*, a somber tale of rodeo people complete with characteristic McCoy meditations on self-delusion, success, and failure. That same year, the rodeo became the subject of another McCoy-scripted film, Budd Boetticher's *Bronco Buster*. Also in 1952, McCoy sold a script to Hal B. Wallis Productions. A medical story, filmed as *Bad for Each Other* in 1954, the scenario also provided the basis for McCoy's novel *Scalpel*, published in 1952. McCoy's only hardcover success, it is the story of army surgeon Tom Owen, who, despite profound doubts about his medical competence, attempts to scale the heights of Pittsburgh's high society by servicing the rich in private practice. Seeming to be a clearcut example of the slick medical story bestseller, *Scalpel* nonetheless reveals several McCoy trademarks, especially obsessions with personal masks and problems of identity.

In 1952 Paramount released the McCoy-written *Turning Point*, but his fragile health after a series of heart attacks made it impossible for him to complete any later projects, including a novel, *The Hard Rock Man*, and a movie he planned to direct. He died in Hollywood of heart failure.

Though McCoy was once considered to be a peer of the masters of hard-boiled fiction—Dashiell Hammett, Raymond Chandler, and James M. Cain—he is virtually unknown today. Yet he contributed much to a literary trend whose tough language and frank subject matter revolutionized crime fiction. At the same time, he was also a bold and original prose stylist whose intuitively crafted fiction eludes critical labels. McCoy may best be seen as a precursor of the *roman noir* writers such as David Goodis and Jim Thompson, whose paperback originals of the 1950s—inward dramas often featuring introspective, unhinged, or contradictory characters resembling those of Horace McCoy—also inhabit a zone between serious and popular literature.

• McCoy's agent, Harold Matson, became his literary executor after his death, but the current location of McCoy's papers is unknown. Some letters are in private hands. None of McCoy's five novels is currently in print. The most comprehensive critical study is John T. Sturak, "The Life and Writings of Horace McCoy, 1897–1955" (Ph.D. diss., UCLA, 1966). See also Mark Winchell, *Horace McCoy* (1982); Thomas Sturak, "Horace McCoy's Objective Lyricism," in *Tough Guy Writers of the Thirties*, ed. David Madden (1968); and Tom Newhouse, "Horace McCoy's Introspective Gangster," *Clues*, Spring–Summer 1985, pp. 15–31. A brief discussion of McCoy may be found in Geoffrey O'Brien, *Hardboiled America* (1981), pp. 79–81. McCoy's name often appears in studies of better-known crime writers such as Chandler, Hammett, and Cain, though his accomplishments barely constitute a footnote in such contexts. More frequently, perhaps, one may discover references to McCoy in studies of film noir, since McCoy is considered an important influence on vision, story material, and narrative technique. See Foster Hirsch, *The Dark Side of the Screen: Film Noir* (1981), pp. 41–43; and Paul Schrader, "Notes on Film Noir," *Film Comment* 8, no. 1 (Spring 1972): 8–13. A discussion of McCoy as a screenwriter may be found in David Wilt, *Hardboiled in Hollywood* (1991). An obituary is in the *New York Times*, 17 Dec. 1955.

THOMAS NEWHOUSE

MCCOY, Isaac (13 June 1784–21 June 1846), Baptist missionary, surveyor, and U.S. Indian agent, was born near Uniontown, Pennsylvania, the son of William McCoy, a clergyman. His mother's name is unknown. When he was six years old, his family moved to Kentucky, where he attended public schools. At nineteen he married Christiana Polke, who had strong religious convictions and missionary spirit and became his dedicated partner throughout his life. They had thirteen children.

In 1804 the newlywed couple moved to the Indian territory near Vincennes, Indiana, where McCoy became a self-educated Baptist minister. Here he learned of the desperate condition of the Indians and decided to devote his missionary efforts to them. In 1817 he was formally appointed missionary to the Indians in the valley of the Wabash, working among first the Wea and then the Miami. He later established missions among the Potawatomi and the Ottawa in the Michigan Territory.

As the white frontier moved toward his missions, McCoy was forced to relocate twice, and as soon as he had established his Carey Mission at Niles, Michigan, white interference made the site untenable. These experiences led McCoy in mid-1823 to formulate the idea of a permanent Indian country, west of Missouri, where the Indians, removed from the detrimental influence of white settlers, might gradually adapt to Christian civilization. Under his plan the federal government was to provide suitable land on which each Indian would receive a plantation, and all denominations were to send their missionaries to teach the Indians Christian civilization so that they might enjoy the "privileges of men and the prospects of a settled home," without disturbance of bad whites or heathen Indians.

In early 1824 McCoy traveled to Washington, D.C., to personally present his plan to the Baptist Board of Missions and Secretary of War John C. Calhoun. This trip marked the shift in his career from a missionary to a political lobbyist. From then on McCoy pushed his plans before Congress, the administration, the Baptist Board of Missions, and the public, while his subordinates managed the missions he nominally headed.

McCoy favored a policy of negotiation that respected the tribes' right to ratify or to reject removal treaties, but he came to be convinced that removing the Indians from the lands east of the Mississippi was the only way to save them. McCoy's proposal of an Indian state called for the consolidation of all the Indians in the West and the dissolution of the tribal organization. Calhoun fully supported his plan, but some critics doubted whether a unified community could be formed among Indians of different tribes, with different languages, and in different states of civilization.

One year after he published *Remarks on the Practicability of Indian Reform* in 1827, clearly setting forth his idea, he induced the Baptist Triennial Convention to present a memorial to Congress and to print and distribute his pamphlet. In 1828 he was also appointed to a commission to manage the removal of the Ottawa and the Miami to the West. By 1829 McCoy had not only pressured the Baptist Convention into endorsing his plans, but he also began an eight-month campaign swing throughout the East Coast to win support for Indian removal.

McCoy came to support Andrew Jackson's removal policy, although he criticized its emphasis on removal rather than colonization. Following the passage of the Indian Removal Bill, which was signed by Jackson in May 1830, McCoy was commissioned to survey the boundaries of the domains assigned to the various Indian tribes. The survey party, consisting of twenty-four persons, including two of his sons, Dr. Rice McCoy and John C. McCoy, and President Jackson's nephew John Donelson, conducted exploration in

Kansas and Oklahoma and located and surveyed the western lands for most of the emigrant tribes.

Although he agreed that President Jackson's removal policy was "the most judicious and humane policy" for an aboriginal population, McCoy insisted that the government should take one additional step and establish an Indian territory. He vigorously argued that the establishment of a "regular Territorial government" for the Indian country (which he called "Aboriginia") was "essential" to the "future prosperity" of the transplanted Indians. In order to solve disputes among neighboring emigrant tribes and between the emigrant and indigenous Indians, McCoy urged the need for bringing the Indians together in a council. His plan was to unite all of the tribes into a single "body politic" that could become an integral part of the United States and that would be governed by a superintendent, the position he himself hoped to secure, appointed by the president.

In 1832, when John Bell introduced a bill in the House calling for the War Department to submit "a plan for the government of the Indians," McCoy fully supported its passage. He published and printed 700 extra copies, at his own expense, of his *Address to the Philanthropists in the United States*, which enthusiastically endorsed the plan of congregating the Indians in a western territory.

Several proposals to establish an Indian state, which McCoy ardently advocated, were in fact introduced in Congress, but all failed to pass. One of the most significant was the bill of 1834, which established boundaries for an Indian territory west of Arkansas and Missouri, in which the tribes were to organize a confederate government to handle their internal affairs. The territory was to be eventually admitted as a state. The bill was opposed by whites, who questioned the right of the United States to organize such a government for Indians, and by the Indians, who were not willing to accept a confederate government. In 1838 McCoy also worked closely with Senator John Tipton, his personal friend and a former Indian agent from Indiana, who had been converted to McCoy's views since 1836. The bill Tipton proposed, calling for the organization of the Indian territory, passed the Senate, but it did not come before the House.

Throughout the 1830s McCoy devoted most of his time to the formal organization of the Indian territory. When all the proposals he supported failed, he turned his attention to the promotion of peaceful relations between emigrant and indigenous tribes in the Indian territory.

Because McCoy had worked more as a removal agent employed by the federal government than as a missionary, the Baptist Board finally dismissed him in 1842. Shortly thereafter he founded the American Indian Mission Association in Louisville, Kentucky, where he served as its first corresponding secretary and general agent until he died in Louisville. The association, however, never flourished, just like his plans for an Indian state, which was reviewed repeatedly in the 1840s and 1850s but failed to materialize.

• Isaac McCoy's correspondence and journals (38 vols.) are in the archives of the Kansas State Historical Society, Topeka. His main published works are *Remarks on the Practicability of Indian Reform, Embracing Their Colonization* (1827), *Address to the Philanthropists in the United States . . . on the Condition and Prospects of the American Indians* (1832), *Periodical Account of Baptist Missions within the Indian Territory, for the Year Ending December 21, 1836* (1837), *Annual Register of Indian Affairs within the Indian (or Western) Territory* (1835–1838), and *History of Baptist Indian Missions* (1840). Major secondary works on McCoy and his accomplishments include Annie H. Abel, *The History of Events Resulting in Indian Consolidation West of the Mississippi* (1908); R. Pierce Beaver, *Pioneers in Mission: The Early Missionary Ordination Sermons, Charges, and Instructions: A Sourcebook on the Rise of American Missions to the Heathen* (1966); Robert F. Berkhofer, Jr., *Salvation and the Savage: An Analysis of Protestant Missions and American Indian Response, 1787–1862* (1972); Emory J. Lyons, *Isaac McCoy: His Plans and Work for Indian Colonization* (1945); Ronald N. Katz, *American Indian Policy in the Jacksonian Era* (1975); George A. Schultz, *An Indian Canaan: Isaac McCoy and the Vision of an Indian State* (1972); Schultz, "Isaac McCoy, 1784–1846," in *History of Indian-White Relations*, ed. Wilcomb E. Washburn (1988), p. 662; and Bernard W. Sheehan, *Seeds of Extinction: Jeffersonian Philanthropy and the American Indian* (1973).

YASUHIDE KAWASHIMA

MCCOY, Joseph Geiting (21 Dec. 1837–19 Oct. 1915), businessman, was born near Springfield (Sangamon County), Illinois, the son of David McCoy and Mary Kilpatrick, farmers. Joseph McCoy attended Knox College at Galesburg (1857–1858). In 1861 he married Sarah Epler; they had seven children.

Before his marriage, McCoy had raised and traded mules, and in 1861 he commenced buying "western" cattle and fattening them on local grains for the Chicago slaughter market, a booming enterprise into which his two older brothers had preceded him. During the Civil War, Joseph McCoy expanded his activities by fattening hogs and sheep. In 1867 he joined his brothers' cattle brokerage firm William K. McCoy & Brothers. While a member of that firm, McCoy conceived the notion of a remote cattle market for Texas livestock.

Largely isolated during the Civil War, Texas cattle had proliferated while slaughter cattle counts elsewhere, both North and South, had been decimated by wartime demand. In 1866 many enterprising Texans tried to connect $2 cows with $40 markets by driving upwards of 260,000 Longhorns in search of buyers, many of them following the Shawnee Trail into Missouri. Before the war both Missouri and Kansas had quarantined themselves against "Texas" or "tick fever" (piroplasmosis), a pestilence carried by southern cattle. Northern herds were vulnerable to the fever, not having been immunized as Longhorns had by centuries of exposure to the offending microbe, *Babesia bovis*. As the malady reappeared in the wake of the first trail drives in 1866, Missouri farmers and lawmen began blocking trails, confiscating or killing suspect animals, and otherwise impeding the path to railhead-markets. So difficult was the long drive north that most Texans resolved not to try again in 1867.

After Kansas amended its quarantine law that year to permit Texas cattle to traverse the state west of the sixth principal meridian, an area then mostly unsettled, McCoy grasped the idea, as he later put it, "of opening up an outlet for Texas cattle." He persuaded Kansas Pacific Railroad officials to provide sidings and other facilities at Abilene, Kansas, a six-year-old prairie hamlet where McCoy had acquired 250 acres, and to pay him a commission of $5 for every carload of cattle shipped from his pens, which, along with a hotel and offices, he erected on his land. He also printed handbills to attract Texans, advising drovers to follow a trader's trace, Jesse Chisholm's trail, northward from the Canadian River in Indian Territory past Chisholm's trading post at the confluence of the Little Arkansas and Arkansas rivers (present-day Wichita, Kans.) to Abilene, about ninety miles away.

No more than a score of trail drives, aggregating an estimated 35,000 cattle, responded in 1867, but, as the word spread, Abilene quickly became the principal terminus of the famed Chisholm Trail. Over the ensuing five years upwards of two million animals filled McCoy's pens before being shipped eastward, mostly for slaughter. With the $200,000 he is said to have earned in commissions, he bought more land, erected more buildings, and became Abilene's first mayor, hiring Wild Bill Hickok as town marshal to maintain law and order among cowboys, gamblers, prostitutes, and other disreputable elements who were attracted to Kansas's first cow town.

In 1869 the railroad reneged on its agreement with McCoy, and as the cattle trade shifted to other Kansas settlements, he sold his Abilene holdings and pursued a variety of other endeavors. He wrote *Historic Sketches of the Cattle Trade of the West and Southwest* (1874), a mostly third-person autobiographical account that railed against the railroad. He also designed stockyards at Newton, Kansas (1871); sold wrought-iron fences in Wichita and promoted its stockyards (1872); operated a cattle commission company in Kansas City, Kansas (1873–1881); gathered statistics on range and ranch cattle traffic for the U.S. government (1880–1881); collected taxes in Indian Territory for the Cherokee nation (1881); was a grocer, real estate agent, commodity speculator, cattle broker, and feed and flour store operator in Wichita (intermittently, 1885–1899); became an Oklahoma territorial promoter and unsuccessful Democratic nominee as territorial delegate to Congress (1890); served as a U.S. Treasury agent in the Pacific Northwest to detect opium smuggling (1893); and worked as a cattle inspector in the Kansas City Stock Yards (1894). Retiring in 1900, he resided in Wichita until 1914 when, in failing health, he moved to Kansas City to live with one of his daughters, a physician.

McCoy, who is widely recognized as the originator of the cattle-trailing industry, died in Kansas City and was buried in Wichita.

• McCoy's *Historic Sketches of the Cattle Trade of the West and Southwest* (1940 ed.) was thoroughly edited and documented by Ralph P. Bieber, whose introduction offers the best synopsis of McCoy's life yet published. McCoy's "Historic and Biographical Sketch," *Kansas Magazine* 2 (Dec. 1909): 45–55, also penned as third-person narrative, adds a few details to his life. Don D. Walker, *Clio's Cowboys* (1981), disparages McCoy and his book. Far more helpful is William E. Unrau, "Joseph G. McCoy and Federal Regulation of the Cattle Trade," *Colorado Magazine* 43 (1966): 32–41. Obituaries are in the Kansas City *Journal*, 20 Oct. 1915, and Wichita *Eagle*, 20, 21 Oct. 1915.

JIMMY M. SKAGGS

MCCRACKEN, Emmett Branch (9 June 1908–4 June 1970), basketball player and coach, was born in Monrovia, Indiana, the son of Charles McCracken and Ida Williams, farmers. McCracken, known by his middle name, Branch, graduated from Monrovia High School in 1926 and entered Indiana University the same year. He received a B.S. in 1930 and an M.S. in 1935, both in physical education. McCracken earned varsity letters at Indiana for three years of play (1927–1930). At that time Indiana competed in the Western Conference, a forerunner to the Big Ten, and McCracken was named to the all-conference first team each season and as the conference's most valuable player in 1928. In his senior year, 1929–1930, he set a conference scoring record and was a Helms Foundation All-America selection. At 6'4" and 195 pounds—big for that era—he was one of the first players to dominate a game by virtue of his size. In addition, he played football for Indiana, although he reputedly had never seen a game before arriving at the university. His height made him an effective end, and he lettered all three years that he played, earning all-conference honors in 1929.

In the fall of 1930 McCracken began an eight-year stint as head basketball coach at Ball State Teachers College (now Ball State University) in Muncie, Indiana. In his first weeks there he met Mary Jo Pittenger, the daughter of the college president. They were married in 1931 and had one child. His successful tenure at Ball State included 93 wins, 41 losses, and selection as the nation's outstanding small college coach in 1932 and 1938.

To augment his salary, McCracken played for the Fort Wayne Hoosiers of the professional American Basketball League (ABL) during the 1930–1931 season, earning $30 per game. He and the Hoosiers went to the league championship series, where they lost to the Brooklyn Visitations. In November 1931 the league folded, a victim of the depression and an unsavory reputation for its rough style of play.

Following the 1937–1938 season, Everett Dean (who had been McCracken's college coach) left Indiana to take the coaching position at Stanford, and McCracken was hired as his successor; no other candidates were considered. In twenty-five years as head basketball coach at Indiana (1938–1943; 1946–1965), McCracken's teams won 364 games, lost 174, and captured national championships in 1940 and 1953. His teams won Big Ten championships in 1953, 1954, and 1958 and tied for the title in 1957.

McCracken, who was often called by his nicknames "Big Bear," "Mac," or "Sheriff," built his coaching success around a strategy that incorporated a fast-break offense and a tenacious defense. He emphasized physical conditioning that gave his players the speed and stamina to wear out opponents. As a result, scoring levels increased at Indiana, and other college coaches adopted his style of play. In the 1940 National Collegiate Athletic Association (NCAA) championship game in Kansas City, Indiana beat Kansas 60–42, a high point total for the time that stood as a record until 1951; Indiana's victory margin of eighteen points was not exceeded until 1968.

From 1943 until 1946 McCracken performed wartime service in the U.S. Navy, attaining the rank of commander. He spent a year in preflight school, then was assigned to the Pacific theater for two years, where he managed recreation facilities and taught stress management (then called "relaxation") in the Philippines.

In 1947, a year after returning to Bloomington, McCracken ignored official Big Ten disapproval, and, with the support of the Indiana University president, Herman B. Wells, recruited Bill Garrett, a black player from Shelbyville, Indiana. Although black athletes had been playing football and running track in the conference for some years, the supposedly more intimate nature of basketball had served as a color bar, and Garrett, a three-year letterman who graduated in 1951, was the first black to play basketball for Indiana and in the Big Ten.

Turning down an offer to take the head coaching job at UCLA in 1947, McCracken signed a ten-year contract at Indiana, which provided a first-year salary of $7,500 that increased to $11,500. He received a $1,000 bonus for winning the national championship in 1953, and his contract was adjusted so that the payment was incorporated into his base pay. Throughout these years McCracken's salary was among the highest of Big Ten coaches. In 1957 he signed another ten-year contract, accompanied by a promotion to the rank of professor. The athletic department supported the promotion by pointing to McCracken's *Indiana Basketball* (1955), an instructional book on his style of coaching. The department characterized it as a "contribution to the literature of basketball" and noted McCracken's professional reputation in the United States and abroad as well as the "high quality" of his teaching. McCracken's international reputation derived from basketball clinics he conducted at U.S. Army bases in Japan, Okinawa, and the Philippines in 1951. Two years later, the Department of Defense had invited him to run similar clinics in Germany, Austria, and France.

McCracken's coaching record earned him election to the Helms Foundation Basketball Hall of Fame in 1957. For his years as a player in high school and at Indiana University, he was chosen for the National Basketball Hall of Fame in 1960 and the Indiana Basketball Hall of Fame in 1963.

In 1965 McCracken was named the Knute Rockne Foundation Coach of the Year for turning a team that had won 9 and lost 15 the year before into a winner (18–5) by using a zone press defense that sharply contrasted with Indiana's former style. Two games before the end of the season, he announced his retirement. While the announcement surprised many, McCracken may have presaged his retirement in 1963 when he said that recruiting problems and pressure from alumni were "beginning to bother [him]" and that "boys are a lot harder to handle now than they were 25 years ago." He was replaced as coach by a former player, Lou Watson, but he continued to work for the university as an administrator and teacher until his death in Indianapolis.

In his twenty-five years as Indiana's head basketball coach McCracken was regarded as a skillful strategist, whose emphasis on speed and defense changed the nature of the college game. A dynamic individual who had so much difficulty staying on the bench during games that friends provided him with a seat belt as a joke, he was an excellent motivator who cared about the academic performance of his players and took pride in the fact that most of them graduated and went on to successful careers.

• The Indiana University archives has a McCracken file that contains newspaper and magazine clippings, a few letters and university documents, and some basketball programs. McCracken's career is lauded in Ray Marquette, *Indiana University Basketball* (1975), written for Indiana fans. The early history of professional basketball is told in Robert W. Peterson, *Cages to Jump Shots* (1990). A lengthy obituary tracing his career and including reminiscences of former players is in the *Bloomington Herald*, 4 June 1970. A *New York Times* obituary appeared on 5 June 1970.

JOHN E. FINDLING

MCCRACKEN, Jack (11 June 1911–5 Jan. 1958), basketball player and coach, was born John McCracken in Chickasha, Oklahoma. Little is known about either his parents or his early life. In 1925 McCracken entered Classen High School in Oklahoma City, Oklahoma, where he played for Henry (Hank) Iba, who would become one of basketball's coaching legends. After a sparkling high school career, which included a second place finish in the 1929 National High School Basketball Tournament held in Chicago and 1929 High School All-American honors, McCracken accompanied Iba to Maryville, Missouri, to play for Maryville Teachers College (later Northwest Missouri State University). During McCracken's three years at Maryville the Bobcats compiled a perfect 31–0 record in 1930–1931, and in 1932 they lost in the championship game of the Amateur Athletic Union (AAU) tournament in Kansas City, Missouri, to the Wichita Henry Clothiers on a last-second shot, 15–14.

During the tournament McCracken, who made the All-American team, caught the eye of William N. "Bill" Haraway, who was organizing a basketball team in Denver, Colorado, that could compete at the championship level. As the vice president and divisional manager of the Piggly-Wiggly grocery store chain, Haraway offered McCracken a job working in his warehouse and playing on his basketball team. Two Maryville teammates, Robert "Duck" Dowell and Tom Merrick also joined the "Pigs," as they were affectionately known in Denver. While the revamped "Pigs" began to improve, the team lacked a big man to stabilize the team. In the 1934 AAU tournament Haraway spotted Robert Gruenig, a former Chicago high school star playing for the Lifschultz Fast Freighters of Chicago. Subsequently, Haraway offered Gruenig a job with Piggly-Wiggly, which had merged with Safeway, and in 1934–1935 the McCracken-Gruenig era began. (The Denver team would go through several name changes during the course of McCracken's career, being called the Denver Safeways [1936–1938], the Denver Nuggets [1939–1940], the Denver Legion [1941–1943], the Denver Legion–Ambrose Jellymakers [1943–1944], and the Denver Ambrose Jellymakers [1944–1949].)

By the time the 6′8″ Gruenig joined the team, the McCracken legend was well established. In 1935 Robert Gamzey, a *Denver Post* sportswriter, wrote that the 6′3″ guard "is generally ranked as one of the two greatest players in the game (Chuck Hyatt is the other)." Excited about their team's prospects, Denver sports officials persuaded the AAU to move its national tournament from Kansas City to Denver. In 1935 and 1936, however, the Denver team failed to move beyond the quarterfinal round of the AAU tournament. Denver sports writers began to write that an "unshakeable jinx" cursed the fortunes of the city's basketball team. In 1937, however, Denver shook its curse and defeated the powerful Phillips 66ers, 44–38, to win the AAU crown. That season McCracken and Gruenig won AAU All-American honors.

After Denver lost in the championship game of the 1938 tournament, McCracken became the team's player-coach. The following year Denver won the championship for a second time by edging the Phillips 66ers, 25–22. The headlines of the *Denver Post* read, "Jack McCracken Is Denver's Sports Hero," and the adulation McCracken received following the championship game helped to secure his place as a Denver sports legend. In that game Gruenig, nicknamed "Ace" by McCracken, held Phillips's great center, Joe Fortenberry, to one basket and led all Denver scorers. By 1940 the *Denver Post* described "Ace" as "the greatest scoring threat in basketball. Gruenig has no peer when it comes to wheeling off the post with either hand."

In 1940 Denver lost to the Phillips 66 Oilers in the championship game. After failing to make the championship round in 1941, Denver won its third and final AAU championship in 1942, crushing Phillips 45–32. Gruenig scored 20 points in this game, a record for a championship game at that time, and was high scorer for the tournament with 87. McCracken, still the playing coach and now affectionately called the "old man," joined Gruenig on the AAU All-American team.

The impact of World War II gave a strange twist to the Gruenig-McCracken relationship. After the 1942

season Denver did not field a regular season team. McCracken, who had worked for the Phillips 66 division in Denver, became a player-coach for the 66ers when the oil company transferred him to Bartlesville, Oklahoma. Two weeks before the 1943 AAU tournament, the Denver American Legion put together a team of Gruenig, Bob Doll, a former star at the University of Colorado, and several undergraduates from the varsity. With only two weeks of practice Denver beat the University of Wyoming Cowboys 41–33 in the semifinals of the AAU tournament. This victory was especially sweet for Denver because several weeks later Wyoming defeated Georgetown to win the NCAA championship. In the 1943 AAU championship game Phillips 66 trounced Denver 57–40, a game that McCracken sat out because of a broken leg.

McCracken and Gruenig were reunited in 1943, when McCracken moved back to Denver, and they would play together for five more seasons. Their teams made it to the final games of the AAU tournament in 1944 and 1945, only to lose to Phillips 66. They had to settle for third-place finishes in 1946 and 1947. After the latter season the Nuggets elected to revamp their team and to turn to younger players. Oddly enough, Gruenig and McCracken, who both had threatened retirement for years, joined some other aging Denver players to form the Murphy-Mahoney Graybeards. To the absolute delight of the fans the Nuggets and Graybeards met in the semifinal round of the 1948 AAU tournament. The Graybeards, who were sentimental favorites, did not disappoint their fans as they took the younger Nuggets into overtime, only to lose 60–56. Gruenig scored 24 and made the All-America team for his last time as he scored 108 points, a personal tournament career high. McCracken retired after the 1948 tournament and never returned to basketball. He remained in Denver and worked in automobile sales. He and his wife, Charlotte, had two sons.

In November 1957 McCracken, along with Gruenig, was among the first inductees to the Helms Amateur Basketball Hall of Fame in Los Angeles, California. Two months later McCracken died in Denver from a heart attack. Jack Carberry, the influential sports editor of the *Denver Post*, wrote that McCracken "was in large measure the one who made the Mile High City the AAU basketball capital of the world." McCracken's strength was his ability to control the tempo of the game, and Carberry described him as "the most relaxed player ever to take the floor." Frank Haraway, sportswriter for the *Denver Post*, wrote that "no other athlete enjoyed as nearly complete adoration of the sports public as McCracken." The McCracken mystique, Haraway explained, came from a blend of "his poker face, his jug ears, his slow drawl with a cracking wit, his deliberate saunter down the basketball floor, and his incomparable flick of the wrist long shots." In 1962 McCracken was elected to the Naismith Memorial Basketball Hall of Fame in Springfield, Massachusetts; Gruenig joined him the following year. In 1968, amid much emotion, their friends and admirers celebrated their memory by inducting them posthumously as a single entry in the Colorado Sports Hall of Fame. In death, as in life, McCracken and Gruenig were inseparably linked in the minds of Denver's sports community. Twelve years later Northwest Missouri State University named McCracken and Henry Iba its first inductees in the university's hall of fame.

• An overview of the AAU tournament is found in Adolph H. Grundman, "Pigs, Jellymakers, and Graybeards," *Colorado Heritage*, Autumn 1994, pp. 35–43. A brief summary is Frank Haraway, "McCracken, Gruenig Always Stars," *Denver Post*, 26 Feb. 1968. Also useful are Frank Haraway, "Jumpin Jack McCracken Dead," *Denver Post*, 6 Jan. 1958, and Jack Carberry, "The Second Guess," *Denver Post*, 6 Jan. 1958.

ADOLPH H. GRUNDMAN

MCCRACKEN, Joan (31 Dec. 1917–1 Nov. 1961), dancer and actress, was born in Philadelphia, Pennsylvania, the daughter of Franklin T. McCracken, a sportswriter for the Philadelphia *Public Ledger*, and Mary W. Humes. She began studying ballet as a child under the tutelage of Catherine Littlefield and as one of the first scholarship students at George Balanchine's newly formed School of American Ballet in New York City. In 1935 McCracken became a member of Littlefield's Philadelphia Ballet, with which she performed for four years, appearing in operas, new American ballets, and on a 1937 European tour. McCracken moved to New York City in 1940 and danced with the corps de ballet at Radio City Music Hall. In 1942 she joined Eugene Loring's Dance Players, with which she performed in New York City and on tour throughout the United States.

McCracken's Broadway career began in 1943, when choreographer Agnes de Mille cast her as a dancer in *Oklahoma!* and in so doing discovered her comedic talents. A member of the dancing ensemble in this landmark musical, McCracken achieved notoriety for a comic fall she performed in the "Many a New Day" dance: she did a high leg extension to the side, collapsed to the floor, and then quickly stood up, smiling divinely, as if she had done absolutely nothing at all out of the ordinary. She created such a comic sensation opening night that the program was quickly amended to include McCracken's billing as "The Girl Who Falls Down." De Mille (telephone interview, 29 Apr. 1990) hailed McCracken as a ravishing talent, a natural actress with bewitching good looks and crackerjack dance technique.

In 1944 McCracken portrayed herself in *Hollywood Canteen*, a film musical in which many celebrities made cameo appearances in a loosely constructed story about entertaining American servicemen. McCracken performed in a comic dance sequence that included pantomime, ballet, and jitterbug movements that displayed her technical prowess as a dancer and her pixie cuteness, an adorable quality that critics generally found charming and enthralling but that some later found cloying. She also performed a featured role in the 1947 film musical *Good News*. Though she was

given ample opportunity in the film to display her acting ability, critics lamented that McCracken's terpsichorean gifts were not aptly tapped.

In between, McCracken returned to Broadway to play featured roles in the musicals *Bloomer Girl* (1944) and *Billion Dollar Baby* (1945), revealing her talents as an actress and, to a lesser degree, a singer. The February 1946 *Theatre Arts* magazine commented on her extraordinary "versatility" and her "engaging, piquant personality" as well as her remarkable dance technique. McCracken won a Donaldson Award for each of these performances.

McCracken continued to develop her acting talents through studies with Sanford Meisner and Herbert Berghof and work with Lee Strasberg at the Actor's Studio in New York. She garnered critical praise for her dramatic roles in the Experimental Theatre's *Galileo* (1947) and the Broadway productions of *The Big Knife* (1949) and *Angel in the Pawnshop* (1951). In addition, McCracken continued to perform in musical productions, including the 1950 Broadway revue *Dance Me a Song*, the 1951 national tour of the musical *Peter Pan*, in which she played the title role, and the 1953 Broadway musical *Me and Juliet*.

McCracken performed in summer stock theaters throughout the country and appeared in war-effort variety shows and numerous magazine advertisements. She also acted featured roles in several television dramas, starred in the 1952 series "Claudia: The Story of a Marriage," and appeared on the "Ed Sullivan Show" in 1953. Her final ballet appearance was dancing the lead role of the cowgirl in de Mille's *Rodeo* on a 1955 tour with Ballet Theatre. Her final stage appearance was in the 1958 off-Broadway play *The Infernal Machine*.

McCracken married novelist Jack Dunphy in 1941 and director-choreographer Bob Fosse in 1952. Both marriages were childless, and both ended in divorce.

McCracken was a charismatic performer who possessed a rare combination of talents. Moreover, she represented a new, American-style ballet dancer. She was exuberant, tiny, and theatrical, with an athletic energy that did not recall ballet's aristocratic European origins. Reflective of the artistic climate of her times, McCracken came of age as a dancer just as American ballet was emerging as a new style to be defined largely by the work of Balanchine. It is only fitting that McCracken made her performing debut dancing for Balanchine in the inaugural performance of the first troupe of student dancers organized to perform his choreography in the United States. Moreover, as a charter member of Littlefield's Philadelphia Ballet and of Loring's Dance Players, McCracken worked in companies committed to developing new ballets by American choreographers based on native themes, rather than reproducing the European classics. Furthermore, she made her Broadway debut in the seminal American musical *Oklahoma!*, dancing the work of de Mille, who seasoned ballet with American folk dance flavors.

In addition to her contributions as a performer, McCracken was responsible for nurturing Fosse's career. It was she who convinced him to extend his artistic focus beyond that of a mere hoofer. She encouraged him to study drama and music as well as movement, enabling him to conceive and design whole productions and providing the foundation for his later successes as a Broadway and film director-choreographer. McCracken also helped many Broadway dancers develop their acting careers during the 1950s by conducting dramatic coaching sessions: one of the participants was actress Shirley MacLaine, who has credited McCracken for discovering her acting talents.

Friends and colleagues, including dancers Danya Krupska, Irene Zambelli Silverman, and Buzz Miller, have described McCracken as ambitious, narcissistic, aloof, amusingly witty, and naturally vaudevillian. Generally uninterested in social and political affairs, she was nevertheless well versed in all the arts, including music, literature, and painting as well as dance and drama; yet she sometimes seemed to exist in a private, whimsical world. McCracken suffered from diabetes throughout her life and was diagnosed with heart disease in 1954, at which point she was advised to discontinue dancing. She devoted the last few years of her life to painting and performing dramatic roles; it is suspected that she suffered from depression during this time. She spent her final year as a virtual recluse in her home on Fire Island and died of a heart attack in New York City.

• McCracken can be seen in the films *Hollywood Canteen* and *Good News*, and she can be heard on the original Broadway cast recordings of *Bloomer Girl* and *Me and Juliet* and on the soundtrack recording of *Good News*. Scrapbooks of clippings and photographs kept by McCracken's mother are in the Billy Rose Theatre Collection at the New York Public Library for the Performing Arts at Lincoln Center. The library's Dance Collection also has clippings, programs, and photographs. McCracken expresses her own ideas about dance and film in her "Thoughts While Dancing," *Dance Magazine*, Apr. 1946, pp. 16, 41. An obituary is in the *New York Times*, 2 Nov. 1961.

LISA JO SAGOLLA

MCCRACKIN, Josephine (25 Nov. 1838–21 Dec. 1920), writer and conservationist, was born in Westphalia, Prussia, the daughter of Georg Woempner (or Wompner), a former member of the Hanoverian army and a civil-service surveyor for Prussia, and Charlotte Hartman. The Woempner family emigrated to the United States in 1846 when Josephine was eight, settling in St. Louis. She was educated privately and in convent schools. Georg Woempner died in 1854, and about this time her older brother left for the California goldfields. Josephine, her younger sister, and her mother continued to live in St. Louis.

Sometime during the Civil War, Josephine met James Clifford, then serving in the First Missouri Cavalry. They were married, but the exact date and place of the marriage is not clear; it could have been as early as November 1863 or as late as November 1864 and may have taken place in St. Louis, Brooklyn, or Baltimore. Wherever and whenever it occurred, the marriage was bigamous for James Clifford, who had married Margaret Dillon under his real name, James Ingram, in 1851. James and Josephine spent the first years of their marriage in Washington, D.C., where Josephine worked in the Dead Letter Office of the district post office. The couple had no children.

In March 1866 James Clifford was given an appointment as a lieutenant in the Third Cavalry and ordered to New Mexico. In New Mexico he became more and more erratic and abusive in his behavior, threatening and inflicting violence on his wife and her pets, including a beloved horse that he killed. Finally, and only with the help of the post commander and other army members, Josephine was able to leave James in 1867. She joined her mother and brother in California, and to support herself she taught German in various San Francisco schools. Though she was a practicing Catholic, Josephine applied for and was granted a divorce by a California court in 1869. Later that year she became an editorial assistant to writer Bret Harte and placed her first story in the magazine he edited, the *Overland Monthly*. "Down among the Dead Letters" was based on Josephine's job in Washington, D.C. Like most of her work, "Down among the Dead Letters" is filled with exact description and includes a bit of romantic mystery.

For a time Josephine lived in the same house as the Harte family. Harte encouraged her to write about her experiences in New Mexico and to base some of her fiction in that locale. Although she wrote stories set in Europe as well, much of her fiction does focus on the West, and, especially after her former husband died, she reworked her experiences as an army wife in her fiction. In the 1870s her stories were published in the *Overland Monthly*, the *Lakeside Monthly*, *Harper's*, and other magazines. She became part of the literary circle around Harte and the *Overland Monthly*, counting among her friends writer Ambrose Bierce and poet Ina Coolbrith. She was somewhat unsure of her own talent and modest in her self-appraisals, but her stories were full of incident and plots that appealed to the popular taste for narrative and melodrama. Her first collection of fiction, *Overland Tales*, was published in 1877. Although Josephine was able to place much of her fiction, this writing never brought very much money, and she had to work hard at journalism as well.

In 1882 Josephine visited friends in Arizona, where she met Jackson McCrackin. They were married the same year. The couple returned to California, building a ranch in the mountains near Santa Cruz. Josephine called the ranch "Monte Paraiso" and was apparently very happy in the new marriage and her new home. Her second collection of short stories, *Another Juanita*, was published in 1893. In 1899 a fire destroyed both the ranch and a nearby redwood forest. The fire, caused by careless logging practices, awakened Josephine McCrackin to the dangers facing the redwoods, and she began to write passionately in whatever venues she could in defense of the trees and on other conservation topics. Typical of her style in her conservation writings is this passage from "About the Big Basin," published in the *Overland Monthly* in August 1900: "Fire, however, is not the worst enemy of the redwood; a greater enemy, and more dangerous, is the greed, the rapacity, the vandalism, which would hack and cut and mutilate the grandest, the most magnificent forest that can be found on the face of the globe, the Redwood Forest of the Big Basin."

With other equally concerned Californians, McCrackin formed the Sempervirens Club of California, dedicated to saving the redwood forests. She also helped to found the Ladies' Forest and Song Bird Protective Society and was active in the California State Humane Association and the Audubon Society. Most of her writing after this time focused on conservation topics, though a third collection of stories, *The Woman Who Lost Him*, was published in 1913.

Jackson McCrackin died in 1904, and Josephine was left with many debts. She continued to work as a journalist, writing for the *Morning Sentinel* in Santa Cruz and the *Mercury Herald* in San Jose as late as 1919 (as reported in the *American Literary Yearbook* of that year). She died in Santa Cruz.

• The California State Library in Sacramento has a collection of manuscripts, correspondence, and other material relating to McCrackin. Biographical sketches have relied on George W. James, "The Romantic History of a Remarkable Woman—Josephine C. McCrackin," *National Magazine*, Mar. 1912, pp. 795–800, and Bertha Snow Adams, "A Seventy-six-year-old Woman Reporter," *American Magazine*, June 1915, p. 51. Cheryl Foote, "'My Husband Was a Madman and a Murderer': Josephine Clifford McCrackin, Army Wife, Writer, and Conservationist," *New Mexico Historical Review* 65 (Apr. 1990): 119–224, focuses on McCrackin's experiences as a battered wife but also argues for a higher estimation of McCrackin's literary skills. An obituary is in the *Santa Cruz Sentinel*, 22 Dec. 1920.

JoAnn E. Castagna

MCCRADY, Edward (19 Sept. 1906–27 July 1981), biologist and university president, was born in Canton, Mississippi, the son of Edward McCrady, an Episcopal priest, and Mary Ormond Tucker. Descended from an old South Carolina family distinguished in law, politics, religion, and science, McCrady graduated with a degree in classics from the College of Charleston in 1927. In 1928 he joined the staff of the Highlands Art Museum (N.C.) after the Gibbes Museum of Art in Charleston sent him to do graduate work in Japanese at Columbia University. Though tempted to study both theology and medicine, he switched to biology for his master's degree, which he received from the University of Pittsburgh in 1930. That same year he married Edith May Dowling, whom he had met during his summer studies at Woods Hole, Massachusetts. They had four children.

After earning his biology doctorate from the University of Pennsylvania in 1933, McCrady became a research scientist at the Wistar Institute, which published his *Embryology of the Opossum* (1938). For his

work in otolaryngology McCrady attained an international reputation. He had just completed a season of lectures at the Sorbonne when he was elected chair of biology at the University of the South in Sewanee, Tennessee, a post that was first held by his grandfather, John McCrady, who had succeeded Louis Agassiz at Harvard. During World War II McCrady taught physics to naval officer candidates at Sewanee. After the war, his reconstruction of a Pleistocene jaguar skeleton (*Panthera* [*Jaguarius*] *augusta*), discovered during cave explorations near Sewanee, was accepted by the Smithsonian Institution, where he was invited to lecture for a summer. During these years McCrady supplemented his income by painting portraits, the best known being that of Thomas Lynch, a signer of the Declaration of Independence, which now hangs in the governor's mansion in Columbia, South Carolina. In 1948 he became senior biologist for the Atomic Energy Commission at Oak Ridge, advancing to chief of the Biology Division in 1949. At Oak Ridge he lectured on radioisotopes to postdoctoral students and used the AEC's mass spectrometers to pursue research on the age of the universe.

In 1952 he was elected the eleventh president (vice chancellor) of the University of the South after acting in that post the previous year. His twenty-year administration was the longest in the school's history. Continuing self-education, aided by his prodigious reading, universal curiosity, and an encyclopedic memory, ultimately qualified McCrady to lecture in virtually every discipline of the liberal arts. He played regularly as an orchestral violinist, composed occasionally, and published translations of Greek and Latin classics. Entertaining and articulate, he received innumerable invitations to lecture before religious groups, learned societies, conferences, and scholastic institutions. In his travels to study firsthand the chief universities of Europe and Russia, McCrady eventually encircled the globe. He presided over the Southern Association of University Presidents and served on widely varied boards (e.g., the Institute for American Universities in Aix-en-Provence and the United States Air University in Colorado). He served five terms on the Executive Council of the Episcopal Church (1956–1971). Under his leadership, Sewanee's endowment increased tenfold. In finance and administration he leaned heavily on his self-effacing but devoted friend, the mathematician Gaston S. Bruton, for whom he created the office of provost. McCrady supported and strengthened the *Sewanee Review*, the oldest literary-critical quarterly in the United States, founded in 1892.

Although an enthusiastic sportsman, McCrady strongly objected to the professionalization of college athletics, which he considered a perversion of academic goals. In McCrady's view, only meritorious students should win scholarships, and he believed that athletes should be able to quit teams without losing financial aid. His diplomacy guided Sewanee through the controversies by which it became in 1953 the South's first private, all-white institution to admit a black student, a year before the U.S. Supreme Court's decision in *Brown v. Board of Education* and while integration was still illegal in Tennessee.

After retirement in 1971, McCrady was named Brown Foundation Fellow, which allowed him to teach his favorite science-and-religion course without additional duties. Thereafter he alternated semesters between Sewanee and the College of Charleston, lecturing primarily on the same subject. In the last year of his life he was a research consultant at the Centre for Immunological Biology at Victoria Hospital in East Grinstead, Sussex, England, where he resumed embryological studies and lectured on the trophoblast. His magnum opus, *Seen and Unseen: A Biologist Views the Universe*, was published posthumously in 1990, condensed from 900 to 350 pages by his son Edward, also a biologist. In addition to writing this book, McCrady said he enjoyed most helping to establish in 1957 the Sewanee Summer Music Center and to see to the completion of All Saints' Chapel at the center of the campus. He was iconographer for most of the stained glass in the chapel, and he designed in detail the clerestory and rose windows, vaulting, narthex, chancel, and tower, which he added to the already existing nave. Since it was finished in 1959, the tower, designed specifically to house the Leonidas Polk Memorial carillon, then third largest in the world, has been the central adornment of Sewanee's campus.

McCrady was notable for his versatility. While president of the small but complicated university, he was de facto mayor of the town. In those combined capacities, he oversaw a 10,000-acre forested domain, with water and sewer systems, fifty miles of paved roads, sixteen lakes, and a general store, and he was responsible for fire and police protection. He gave hands-on planning, participation, and supervision to numerous activities. Through it all, he remained a teacher (one course a year), a poet, a research scientist and explorer (of Tennessee caves), a practicing portrait painter, a musician (violinist), a composer (one symphony), a popular speaker (from parish groups to national conventions of the Episcopal church to the American Medical Association), and an architect, drawing plans for five major sandstone buildings on campus. More was constructed during his administration than in the previous history of the institution. McCrady's most formidable achievement was bringing to its highest pinnacle the academic excellence of an institution that, to date, has been the intellectual home of six generations of his family.

• A full collection of McCrady's speeches and papers is housed in the University Archives at Sewanee. His first published work (by the Wistar Institute c. 1935) was *The Ear of the Opossum as Related to Human Hearing* (exact title uncertain). In addition to his magnum opus, McCrady wrote several dozen articles for professional journals. See also Moultrie Guerry, with Arthur Ben Chitty and Elizabeth N. Chitty, *Men Who Made Sewanee* (1981), and Hodding Carter, "The Amazing Gentleman from Sewanee," *Saturday Evening Post*, 28 Mar. 1953, pp. 28–29ff.

ARTHUR BEN CHITTY

MCCRAE, Thomas (16 Dec. 1870–30 June 1935), physician, was born in Guelph, Ontario, Canada, the son of David C. McCrae, a cattle breeder and town leader, and Janet Eckford. He grew up in Guelph and received an A.B. in biology (1891), M.B. (1895), and M.D. (1903) from the University of Toronto. He then served an internship at Toronto General Hospital and studied briefly in London, Edinburgh, and Göttingen. In 1899 McCrae, like other outstanding students of Toronto's highly respected medical professors R. Ramsay Wright and James Graham, joined William Osler, a leader of the younger generation of physicians and professor of medicine at the new Johns Hopkins Hospital, as a resident medical officer and later became instructor (1901) and associate professor (1906) in the department of medicine. In 1912 he was appointed professor of medicine at the Jefferson Medical College in Philadelphia, where he became Magee Professor in 1917 and remained until his death. He was Lumleian Lecturer at the University of London in 1924 and president of the American Association of Physicians in 1930.

McCrae was one of a cadre of academic physicians at the turn of the century who built their careers primarily as clinical teachers, practicing the new hospital-oriented "scientific" medicine exemplified in Osler's landmark textbook *The Principles and Practice of Medicine* (1892). Unlike earlier generations of physicians who became medical teachers because of their reputations as practitioners, or subsequent generations, whose academic distinctions derived from their scientific research, McCrae's generation developed careers as clinical assistants to such professorial leaders as Osler, taking on the labor intensive duties of teaching the techniques of physical examination to the new classes of college-educated men enrolling at the elite medical colleges. Working very much to Osler's model, McCrae taught at the bedside and in the amphitheater, emphasizing methods of diagnosis and concentrating on the common diseases physicians would see in their practices.

McCrae wrote extensively on clinical subjects and, as one of Osler's trusted students, assisted with the editing of new editions of *The Principles and Practice of Medicine* (1912–1935) and the multiauthored *Modern Medicine: Its Theory and Practice* (edited by Osler, 1907–1928). His contributions to these volumes seem to have been principally the preparation of notes summarizing the medical literature for Osler's use in revision and editorial work on the submissions to *Modern Medicine*. After Osler's death in 1919, McCrae was sole editor of the *Principles and Practice* until his own death, maintaining the book's general approach and organization while updating diagnostic and therapeutic details. During his stewardship, the book continued to be a preeminent medical school text, although newer "physiologically" oriented texts were beginning to displace the older clinical works.

While at Hopkins, McCrae began collecting, abstracting, and indexing the clinical records of the hospital's medical inpatients. This eight-year task eventually (in 1908) created the first modern medical records library, an institution that eventually became a nation-wide requirement for hospital accreditation and, by allowing the systematic scholarly analysis of clinical experience with specific diseases, was one of the great research and educational tools of twentieth-century medicine.

McCrae was a quiet, methodical man who had few interests outside of medicine and was described by colleagues as a "slave to duty," devoting nearly all his waking time to his medical work. Although he was considered an able clinician, sometimes sharing with his Baltimore colleagues William S. Thayer (later Osler's successor as professor of medicine at Hopkins) and Thomas B. Futcher Osler's less pressing consultations, he deliberately limited his clinical consulting work to avoid being "run by it," preferring instead to spend his time reading and writing medicine. At Jefferson, he continued to teach and write, coming to be known as a careful and dedicated, but demanding, teacher. In 1908 he married Osler's niece Amy Gwyn; they had no children. He died in Philadelphia.

Although not himself an innovator in medical education or practice, McCrae educated over his long career a generation of physicians in Baltimore and Philadelphia in the remarkable combination of clinical observation and thoughtful analysis that is associated with William Osler. In addition, his organization of hospital records by diagnosis allowed the systematic analysis of clinical experience in the hospital and became the principal method for writing and publishing "clinical reviews" in which the early nineteenth-century French physician P. C. A. Louis's "numerical method" could be fruitfully applied both to define the "natural history" and complications of diseases and to assess medical therapeutics.

• McCrae's papers have not been collected. University records and newspaper clippings are on file at the University of Toronto Archives. Scattered letters are in the Alan M. Chesney Medical Archives at the Johns Hopkins Medical Institutions. A memoir by his friend and colleague, medical historian Archibold Malloch, is in *Annals of Medical History*, n.s., 8 (1936): 371–75. A brief biographical summary, with two photographs, appears in *Thomas Jefferson University: Tradition and Heritage*, ed. Frederick B. Wagner, Jr. (1989), pp. 245–47. Wagner has also written an interesting description of McCrae's professorial work at Jefferson, "The Career and Strange Terminal Illness of Professor Thomas McCrae" (unpublished, held by Wagner, 1993). McCrae is mentioned in several places in Harvey Cushing, *The Life of Sir William Osler* (1925), as a close junior associate of Osler's and an informal member of the Osler household during Osler's years in Baltimore. Materials concerning McCrae's organization of the medical records "History Room" at Hopkins are in his biographical file at the Chesney Archives, and discussed briefly in A. M. Harvey et al., *A Model of Its Kind*, vol. 1, *A Centennial History of Medicine at Johns Hopkins* (1989), p. 35. Obituaries are in *Toronto Mail and Empire*, 1 July 1935; *Lancet*, 13 July 1935; and *Journal of the American Medical Association* 105 (July 1935): 105.

PAUL J. EDELSON

MCCREA, Jane (?1752–27 July 1777), folk heroine, was born in Somerset County, New Jersey, the daughter of James McCrea, a Presbyterian minister, and Mary Graham. The family name is variously spelled as M'Crea, M'Kray, and MacCrea. Within a year of her birth her mother died, and her father soon remarried. Following the death of her father in 1769 she moved with her brother John McCrea, a lawyer and Princeton graduate, to Argyle, in Washington County, New York. When the Revolution came the family was divided in its loyalties with John becoming a colonel in the Continental army.

Here the facts of the McCrea story become hopelessly blurred by the combination of history, martyrdom, and romantic myth that surrounded Jane's death and transformed the meaning of her life.

As the story goes, Jane McCrea met and fell in love with David Jones. Jones, also from a New Jersey family who moved to the Hudson River valley, joined up with General John Burgoyne's forces in the summer of 1777. The British strategy was to divide New England from New York State by dispatching forces from Canada through the Champlain Valley and down the Hudson to New York while at the same time sending British, Loyalist, and a variety of allied Indian forces around Lake Ontario near Lake Erie and across New York State through the Mohawk Valley. The plan was to combine forces along the Hudson at a major battlefield, at which time the victory would both cut off New York from its New England troop supply and defeat the rebel forces.

In the midst of this military endeavor McCrea and Jones were to rendezvous and marry. A fabled letter from David was to signal McCrea's secret leaving of her brother's house. Although McCrea was from a family that strongly supported the Revolution, she chose to meet her lover. But this was not to be. As McCrea left John's house to wait for Jones at the home of Sarah Fraser Campbell McNeil, the McNeil's home was attacked by British allied Indians. Both women were captured, and McCrea was killed.

The story of McCrea's death is said to have spread through the revolutionary troops around Burlington and New York, and it became a symbol of the brutality of the Indians allied with the British and of the British lack of control. In these stories McCrea is a beautiful young woman with extraordinarily long and luxuriant hair. She is well educated and from a family of means and patriotic intent. Dressed in finery in anticipation of her meeting and wedding with Jones, she was brutally cut down. In some versions she was dragged from her horse, in most, scalped, in others axed to death or shot. Often sexual foul play is suggested. As word spread of her demise, irate revolutionaries converged at Saratoga (Sept.–Oct. 1777). On the battlefield the name of Jane McCrea was allegedly heard from the incensed troops. The battle was won, and Saratoga became the turning point of the war. Jane McCrea was Saratoga's only heroine.

There is no doubt that Jane McCrea lived and died. Several accounts of her death appear in the colonial newspapers of Connecticut and New York. American general Horatio Gates protested McCrea's death to Burgoyne and used the event to his political advantage. Edmund Burke protested General Burgoyne's use of Indian troops on the floor of Parliament. Lieutenant William Digby refers to McCrea's death in his journal "Some Account of the American War between Great Britain and the Colonies" (in James Phinney Baxter, ed. *The British Invasion from the North: The Campaigns of Generals Carleton and Burgoyne from Canada, 1776–1777* (1887). But from the first accounts, McCrea's story became muddled. Even the details of her physical and mental attributes became altered, with her hair being variously described as everything from blond to red to black.

The year following her death, in a poem titled "A Tragical Death of Miss Jane M'Crea," written by the Reverend Wheeler Case, who described blood "gushing forth from all her veins" and "her scalp torn from her head," the poet asks, "Is this that blooming fair? Is this McCrea? / This was appointed for her nuptial day . . . / Oh, cruel savages! What hearts of steel! / O cruel Britons! who no pity feel!" The Connecticut poet Joel Barlow asked artist John Vanderlyn for a set of illustrations to his epic poem *The Columbiad* (1807). In it, after the defeat at Saratoga, he imagined David Jones running through the woods in search of his beloved: "Swift thro the wood paths frenetic springs," calling her name while Mohawks "Drive the descending ax" through her face. Philip Freneau, in "American Independent and Her Everlasting Deliverance from British Tyranny and Oppression" (1809), found the maiden "all breathless, cold and pale, / Drenched in her gore."

The new republic's first artists and historians added more spice to the story and spread it further. The most famous visual representation of Jane McCrea was painted by John Vanderlyn as the *Death of Jane McCrea* (1803–1804). Its popularity and frequent reproduction has symbolized Indian savagery and made McCrea a central exhibit of propaganda purporting Indian (in this case supposedly Mohawk) violence against innocent white women. Other representations in the same mode appeared in the nineteenth century and include Asher B. Durand's *The Murder of Miss McCrea* (1839), lithographs by Nathaniel Currier (1846), and a depiction on the battle monument relief at Saratoga.

In Michel René Hilliard-d'Auberteuil's patriotic novel, *Miss McCrea: A Novel of the American Revolution* (1784), McCrea became the heroine of a novel about the Revolution first published in Europe and then in the United States. Here McCrea's lover, renamed Captain Belton, is a Tory, and her father, who supports the Revolution, admonishes her for her lack of patriotism and bad choice. Her first biographer, David Wilson, memorialized her as a romantic heroine in *The Life of Jane McCrea, with an Account of Burgoyne's Expedition in 1777* (1853). Unable to find a real letter of Jones's Wilson made one up and included it in his narrative. In his version, although Jones is a Tory,

McCrea's love for him, although wrongheaded, is understandable.

Although McCrea received a good deal of attention from such nineteenth-century historians as Benson J. Lossing, Charles Neilson, Asa Fitch, William L. Stone, and George Bancroft, these scholars repeated most of the earlier mix of legend and history with continual variations on the theme of the tragic romantic heroine.

McCrea's legend persisted throughout the nineteenth century but has been, with the exception of local history, largely forgotten in the twentieth century. Whereas the American Revolution, unlike the French Revolution, has practically no heroines, it is important to ask why McCrea, a victim rather than a heroine, and in fact a victim who loved a Tory, becomes one of the few women to enter the folklore about the founding of the Republic. McCrea's story appears to be a cautionary tale both for women and for men about women's place and their options in the new Republic. Besides highlighting Indian savagery, her story demonstrates women's weakness, and their need for masculine protection, and their inability to make correct romantic decisions at a time when those decisions involved a patriotic component. McCrea's choice of a Tory lover is interpreted in much of the folklore as an inability to use her independence properly. Her perceived poor choice comes at a time when the issue of independence from the Mother Country along with the wider role of women in politics was linked in the writings of Abigail Adams, Judith Sargent Murray, and others, and by the rhetoric of liberty itself. In the uncertain days of the early Republic, the fact that women might choose their mates was a new but accepted feature of life, transformed from the days when a parent, usually the father, determined the marriage of his daughter. In this new world, the death of Jane McCrea signaled how wary the Founding Fathers, historians, artists, and writers were about the newly emerging freedom of the founding daughters.

• Primary cultural material on Jane McCrea, much of it legendary rather than factual, is in the Fort Edward Historical Association and Old Fort House Museum, Fort Edward, N.Y. The earliest, longest, and best recounting of the McCrea narrative as history is James Austin Holden, "Influence of the Death of Jane McCrea on Burgoyne Campaign," *Proceedings of the New York Historical Association* 12 (1913): 249–310. Other secondary material on McCrea and her legend includes Lewis Leary's introduction to Michel René Hilliard-d'Auberteuil's *Miss McCrea: A Novel of the American Revolution* (1784; repr. 1958); Samuel Y. Edgerton, Jr., "*The Murder of Jane McCrea*: The Tragedy of an American Tableau d'Histoire," *Art Bulletin* 58 (Dec. 1965): 481–92; and "*The Murder of Jane McCrea* and Vattemare's System of International Exchange," *Bulletin of the Fort Ticonderoga Museum* 11, no. 6 (1965): 336–42. Jay Fliegelman discusses McCrea as a cultural heroine in *Prodigals and Pilgrims: The American Revolution against Patriarchal Authority, 1750–1800* (1982). The best treatment of McCrea as a cultural icon is June Namias, "Jane McCrea and the American Revolution," in *White Captives: Gender and Ethnicity on the American Frontier* (1993). For a Canadian perspective of McCrea as a Canadian heroine, see Grace Tomkinson, "Jane McCrea: A Martyr of the Revolutionary War," *Dalhousie Review* 49 (Autumn 1969): 399–403. For work on women in the Revolution see Linda K. Kerber, *Women of the Republic: Intellect and Ideology in Revolutionary America* (1980), and Mary Beth Norton, *Liberty's Daughters: The Revolutionary Experience of American Women, 1750–1800* (1980).

JUNE NAMIAS

MCCREA, Joel (5 Nov. 1905–20 Oct. 1990), actor and rancher, was born Joel Albert McCrea in South Pasadena, California, the son of Thomas P. McCrea, an executive with the Los Angeles Gas and Electric Company, and Lou Whipple. When he was nine, his father moved the family to the rural community of Hollywood, California, where McCrea attended local schools. Education and work were both stressed in the McCrea household. During the school year Joel delivered the *Los Angeles Times* to his neighbors, including movie mogul Cecil B. DeMille. In summers he worked as a stable boy, ranch hand, and teamster. His love of horseback riding literally carried him into his first movie appearance. While pleasure riding in a canyon near his home, McCrea came upon the filming of a Ruth Roland serial. He paused to observe, as he frequently did in these instances, and noticed that the director was having difficulty getting the male lead to perform a riding maneuver correctly. A confident horseman, McCrea quickly offered his services. The director accepted and gave him $2.50 a day to perform the riding chores of the lead actor.

McCrea's formal training as an actor began at Pomona College in 1924 (he graduated in 1928). One of his classmates was the daughter of movie director Sam Wood. When Wood went to Pomona to direct a Marion Davies comedy, *The Fair Coed* (1927), he asked McCrea to serve as an extra. Wood would later be instrumental in opening other Hollywood doors for McCrea. He recommended McCrea to Gloria Swanson, who found him "too handsome" for the supporting roles she was casting. However, she referred him to William LeBaron, who gave him a small role in *The Jazz Age* (1929). Although McCrea's career appeared to be gaining momentum, he had already decided that acting would only be a means to an end. His first love was ranching, and he hoped to use money from his acting to fulfill his dream of owning a working ranch.

In 1929 DeMille gave McCrea a supporting role in *Dynamite*, one of MGM's first "talkies." However, his major break came when he was cast as the hero in an RKO film, *The Silver Horde* (1930), quickly followed by a highly acclaimed performance in the Will Rogers feature *Lightnin'* (1930). McCrea would later note that, besides his father, Rogers was the most influential person in his life. "He was a man of such integrity and such sanity and dignity," McCrea stated, "that it was an example you had to be stupid not to follow."

Throughout most of the 1930s McCrea was cast primarily in romantic dramas and a few action films. The typecasting would yield mixed results for his career. On the one hand, as a romantic lead, McCrea frequently found himself taking roles that had been declined by two other prominent male actors, Cary Grant and Gary Cooper. Yet, on the other, McCrea, by assuming their discarded roles, was given the opportunity to work with some of Hollywood's most talented directors and leading ladies.

In 1933 McCrea starred with Ginger Rogers in a romantic comedy, *Chance at Heaven*. After the film the actress remarked that McCrea was "one of the nicest, warmest, most generous-of-heart men in the world, he truly loves everybody." That same year he appeared with Barbara Stanwyck for the first time. They would go on to make several features together, including *Gambling Lady* (1934), *Banjo on My Knee* (1936), *Internes Can't Take Money* (1937), *Union Pacific* (1939), and *Great Man's Lady* (1941). However, his favorite actress turned out to be Frances Dee, whom he met on the set of *The Silver Cord* (1933). They married the year they met, shortly after starring together in *One Man's Journey*. Also in 1933 McCrea fulfilled his dream of owning a working ranch. He bought 1,000 acres in the Conejo Valley west of Los Angeles. He and his wife would go on to appear together in McCrea's first western, *Wells Fargo* (1937), and then *Four Faces West* (1948), before she retired in 1954. They had three children.

McCrea's status as a major box-office draw was established in 1940 by his performance in Alfred Hitchcock's *Foreign Correspondent*. This appearance was followed by his first collaboration with director Preston Sturges (*Sullivan's Travels*, 1941). He and Sturges would make two other films together, *The Palm Beach Story* (1942) and *The Great Moment* (1944). It was McCrea's work with Sturges, especially *Sullivan's Travels*, in which his versatility and range as an actor was fully demonstrated. In particular, under Sturges's direction, McCrea's affable cowboy image was exchanged for that of a wise-cracking, low-key comic. As such, McCrea usually found himself at the center of a film's narrative in that he was constantly responding to the antics and activities of those around him. In such roles, McCrea demonstrated a keen sense of comedic timing and pacing that had not been explored in his previous films.

In 1946 McCrea starred in Paramount's western *The Virginian*, a film based on the Owen Wister novel of the same name. The financial and critical success of this film turned McCrea into one of the genre's top performers. Subsequently, he would go on to star in a number of westerns throughout the late 1940s and 1950s, including *Ramrod* (1947), *Colorado Territory* (1949), *Stars in My Crown* (1950), *Saddle Tramp* (1950), *Stranger on Horseback* (1955), *Wichita* (1955), *The First Texan* (1956), *Trooper Hook* (1957), *Cattle Empire* (1958), and *Gunfight at Dodge City* (1959).

In the late 1950s McCrea became interested in television. He agreed to do a series, "Wichita Town," for producer Walter Mirisch, with whom he had previously worked on the film *Wichita*. However, the television series had an even greater appeal for McCrea—it offered him the opportunity to work with his oldest son, Jody. Unfortunately, the series never garnered a large enough audience and was canceled after the first season. For the next few years McCrea enjoyed working on his ranch.

In 1962 McCrea was lured back to the big screen by Sam Peckinpah's *Ride the High Country*, which paired McCrea with another cowboy legend, Randolph Scott. The two men, both in the twilight of their careers, lent a certain poignancy to their portrayals of aging gunfighters. Afterward McCrea retired for eight years until his oldest son convinced his father to star in his production, *Cry Blood, Apache* (1970). After this appearance McCrea served as narrator of several documentaries, including *The Great American Cowboy* (1974), *George Stevens: A Filmmaker's Journey* (1984), and *The Rise and Fall of an American Dreamer* (1990).

After a career that spanned more than three decades and included more than eighty films, McCrea devoted the last twenty years of his life to being a full-time rancher. He also spent a great deal of time writing. He contributed to the books *The Great Cowboy Stars of Movies and Television* (1979), by Lee O. Miller, and *The Conejo Valley: Old and New Frontiers* (1989), by Carol Bidwell. A member of the Cowboy Hall of Fame, McCrea was also a recipient of the Hollywood Westerner Hall of Fame award. He died in Woodland Hills, California.

• A biography, more historical than analytical, of McCrea is Tony Thomas, *Riding the High Country* (1991). Treatments of McCrea and his work are in the *International Dictionary of Films and Filmmakers*, vol. 3 (1984), and William K. Everson, *The Hollywood Western* (1992). For other information see Jimmie Hicks's two-part article, "Joel McCrea" in *Films in Review*, Sept.–Oct. 1991, pp. 315–23, and Nov.–Dec. 1991, pp. 392–403; and Scott Berg, "Joel McCrea: A Ranch for the Star of *Sullivan's Travels*," *Architectural Digest*, Apr. 1994, pp. 220–25, 285. Obituaries are in the *Los Angeles Times* and the *New York Times*, 21 Oct. 1990.

GINGER CLARK

MCCREADY, Benjamin William (28 Oct. 1813–9 Aug. 1892), physician, was born in New York City, the son of Thomas McCready and Margaret Miller, occupations unknown. His parents were wealthy enough to send him to New York High School, and after graduating he entered an apprenticeship with John Broadhead Beck, a medical practitioner who was professor of materia medica and botany at the city's College of Physicians and Surgeons. At Beck's encouragement he sought a medical degree from the college and graduated in 1835. His high class standing then helped to secure for him a prestigious year-long post as house physician at New York Hospital.

McCready's initial and, in the long run, most enduring renown came after the New York Medical Society announced in 1835 that the next subject for one of its prize essays would be "the influence of trades, professions and occupations in the United States on the production of disease" ("On the Influence" [1837]: 85). Thereby calling attention to the health consequences of changing economic circumstances in Jack-

sonian America, the prize committee was probably influenced by the 1831 appearance of Englishman C. Turner Thackrah's book on a similar topic. McCready's mentor Beck may have encouraged him to participate, since Beck chaired the prize committee. McCready received the $50 prize for an essay of sixty pages in 1837, when twenty-three years old. After appearing in the *Transactions of the Medical Society of the State of New York* in 1837, McCready's sixty-page essay became the first extensive American publication on occupational diseases.

At a time when the orthodox medical profession was under attack from sectarians for its elitist and rationalist claims, McCready's piece articulated a more egalitarian approach to medical knowledge and to clientele that better harmonized with Jacksonian democracy's creeds. Drawing much of his information from workers themselves, McCready presented simple associations between some thirty-one occupations and various diseases. He asserted causal links such as impure air, overcrowding, intemperance, climate, and geography, whose perception did not require specialized skills. He upheld agriculture as the healthiest pursuit and attributed "the pale and unhealthy appearance of our population" to the urbanization, manufacturing, and "speculation" that comprised the dual, ongoing revolution of market and industry in the United States.

At the same time McCready reaffirmed the moral and epistemological authority of orthodox medicine by suggesting that it could alleviate the worst consequences of these changes. Reflecting the unquestioned assumptions of his time, he viewed as unavoidable the few ailments such as lead colic and the dust-related maladies that he could attribute to specific industrial processes; ironically, these diseases would become the primary targets of twentieth-century industrial hygiene. For McCready, however, ignorance and vice were responsible for the great majority of the ills associated with occupations. The physician could remedy these causes by inculcating basic physiological principles among workers and the rest of the populace, by promoting "professorships of physiology in our literary colleges, and popular lectures and popular books," as well as by instructing individual patients (*On the Influence* [1943; repr. 1972], p. 129). Conveniently, education would also render the public less susceptible to quackery and better able to recognize the truths of medical orthodoxy.

McCready's prize-winning essay, the product of a fleeting medical curiosity about the wider circumstances of the working class in the mid-nineteenth century, brought him little sustained attention from his contemporaries. He went on to a career as practitioner and teacher that yielded few additional literary efforts, though he maintained the twin devotion to the poor and marginal members of society and to orthodox medicine that he had voiced in his essay. He served on the medical staff of several dispensaries and of the Tombs, a New York prison. In the 1850s he wrote a series of popular articles for the *New York Tribune* on the poor physical condition of runaway slaves. McCready also played a role in the efforts of the city's physicians to improve professional status by organizing medical societies, including the New York Medical and Surgical Association in 1835 and the New York Academy of Medicine in 1847, of which he became a charter member. He had his first teaching experience at the New York City College of Pharmacy, where he spoke out against pharmaceutical quackery. McCready was associated with Bellevue Hospital beginning in 1848; he subsequently became the first professor of materia medica and therapeutics at the medical college established there in 1861. He also pioneered an alliance between physicians and a burgeoning insurance industry by serving for twenty years as chief medical examiner of the Washington Life Insurance Company of New York City.

McCready was married twice, the first time to Margaret Doyle of New York City and the second to an Englishwoman, Jane Gall. Altogether, he had four children. The dates of his marriages, what happened to his first wife, and the number of children with each are unknown. He died in New York.

McCready's primary significance lies in his unique early nineteenth-century depiction of the hazards faced by American workers. The tensions within his prize-winning essay itself suggest how the limited physician interest in occupational maladies during this era arose out of professional insecurities; for McCready himself, pursuit of this interest gave rise to a career-long project of sustaining medical orthodoxy through intraprofessional reform.

• A few surviving manuscripts and lectures of McCready's are in the New York Academy of Medicine. His famous essay was first published as "On the Influence of Trades, Professions, and Occupations in the United States in the Production of Disease," *Transactions of the Medical Society of the State of New York* 3 (1837): 91–150. It was later reprinted as *On the Influence of Trades, Professions, and Occupations in the United States in the Production of Disease* (1943; repr. 1972), which contains an introductory essay by Genevieve Miller (pp. 1–30) that covers most of the known details of McCready's life. Other secondary sources include Carey P. McCord, "The Second Ramazzini Oration; Benjamin William McCready, M.D. (1813–1892) and His Essay . . . ," *Industrial Medicine* 16 (Nov. 1947): 535–38, and obituaries in the *Medical Register of New York, New Jersey and Connecticut, 1893–94*, vol. 31 (1893), pp. 310–11, and the *New York Medical Examiner, 1891–92*, vol. 1, pp. 150–51.

CHRISTOPHER C. SELLERS

MCCULLERS, Carson (19 Feb. 1917–29 Sept. 1967), novelist, short-story writer, and playwright, was born Lula Carson Smith in Columbus, Georgia, the daughter of Lamar Smith, a jewelry store owner, and Vera Marguerite Waters. Lula Carson, as she was called until age fourteen, attended public schools and graduated from Columbus High School at sixteen. An unremarkable student, she preferred the more solitary study of the piano. Encouraged by her mother, who was convinced that her daughter was destined for greatness,

Carson began formal piano study at age nine but was forced to give up her dream of a career as a concert pianist after a childhood case of rheumatic fever left her without the physical stamina necessary for the rigors of practice and a concert career. While recuperating from this illness she began to read voraciously and to consider writing as a vocation. In 1934 she sailed from Savannah to New York City, supposedly to study piano at the Juilliard School of Music but actually to pursue her secret ambition. Working various jobs to support herself, she studied creative writing at Columbia University and Washington Square College of New York University. Back in Columbus in the fall of 1936 to recover from a respiratory infection, she was bedridden several months during which time she began work on her first novel, *The Heart Is a Lonely Hunter*. Her first short story, "Wunderkind," was published in the December 1936 issue of *Story* magazine, edited by Whit Burnett, her former teacher at Columbia.

In September 1937 Carson married James Reeves McCullers, Jr., a native of Wetumpka, Alabama, whom she met when he was in the army stationed at Fort Benning, near her hometown. In April 1938 she submitted an outline and six chapters of *The Heart Is a Lonely Hunter* to Houghton Mifflin and was offered a contract and a $500 advance. The book was published in June 1940. The story of a deaf mute to whom the lonely and isolated people of a southern town turn for silent solace, the novel included the themes of loneliness and isolation that recur in much of McCullers's work. The novel was an immediate and much-praised success. Rose Feld's *New York Times* review was typical of the positive response to the power of the young author's work: "No matter what the age of its author, 'The Heart Is a Lonely Hunter' would be a remarkable book. When one reads that Carson McCullers is a girl of 22 it becomes more than that. Maturity does not cover the quality of her work. It is something beyond that, something more akin to the vocation of pain to which a great poet is born. Reading her, one feels this girl is wrapped in knowledge which has roots beyond the span of her life and her experience."

Reflections in a Golden Eye, McCullers's second novel, first appeared in *Harper's Bazaar* in August 1940 and was published in book form by Houghton Mifflin in 1941. Readers who expected a book like the author's first novel were shocked by the troubling story of voyeurism, obsession, repressed homosexuality, and infidelity set on a peacetime army base. *Reflections in a Golden Eye* received a mixed critical reception, and its author faced ridicule from the people of her hometown who saw negative reflections of themselves in the maladjusted characters of the novel.

The years 1943 to 1950 saw the publication of what many consider McCullers's finest creative work. *The Ballad of the Sad Cafe*, the lyrical story of jealousy and obsession in a triangular love relationship involving an amazonlike Miss Amelia, a hunchbacked midget Cousin Lymon, and an ex-convict Marvin Macy, set in a small southern mill town, appeared in the August 1943 *Harper's Bazaar*. The work was later published by Houghton Mifflin in an omnibus edition of the author's work, *"The Ballad of the Sad Cafe": The Novels and Stories of Carson McCullers* (1951). March 1946 saw the publication of McCullers's fourth major work, *The Member of the Wedding*, the story of a lonely adolescent girl, Frankie Addams, who wants to find her "we of me" by joining with her older brother and his bride. McCullers's theatrical adaptation of the novel opened on Broadway in 1950 to near-unanimous acclaim and enjoyed a run of 501 performances. This adaptation proved to be her most commercially successful work.

The final fifteen years of McCullers's life saw a marked decline in the writer's health and in her creative output. Bedridden by paralysis from a series of debilitating strokes, McCullers was devastated by the failed production of her second play, *The Square Root of Wonderful*, which closed after only forty-five performances on Broadway in 1957, and the mixed reception of her final novel, *Clock without Hands* (1961). Her final book-length publication was a book of children's verse, *Sweet as a Pickle and Clean as a Pig* (1964). At the time of her death she was at work on an autobiography, "Illumination and Night Glare." A more encouraging event in her final years was the success of Edward Albee's 1963 adaptation of *The Ballad of the Sad Cafe*, which enjoyed a Broadway run of 123 performances.

The marriage to Reeves McCullers was the most supportive and destructive in the author's life. From its beginning it was plagued by the partners' shared difficulty with alcoholism, their sexual ambivalence (both were bisexual), and the tension caused by Reeves's envy of Carson's literary successes. Moving to New York in 1940 when *The Heart Is a Lonely Hunter* was published, Carson and Reeves divorced in 1941 but reconciled and remarried in 1945. While living near Paris in the early 1950s, Reeves tried to convince Carson to commit suicide with him. Fearing for her life, Carson fled to the United States. Remaining behind, Reeves committed suicide in a Paris hotel room in November 1953. Carson and Reeves did not have any children.

During a separation from Reeves in 1940, Carson moved into a house in Brooklyn Heights owned by George Davis (literary editor of *Harper's Bazaar*) and shared with the British poet W. H. Auden. This house, located at 7 Middagh Street, became the center of a bohemian literary and artistic constellation including Gypsy Rose Lee, Benjamin Britten, Peter Pears, Richard Wright, and Oliver Smith. In the spring of 1941 Carson and Reeves, who were temporarily reconciled, both fell in love with the American composer David Diamond. This complicated love triangle led to Carson and Reeves's second separation and found articulation in the love-triangle theme in McCullers's novella *The Ballad of the Sad Cafe* and her novel/play *The Member of the Wedding*. Following her father's sudden death in August 1944, Carson with her mother and sister moved to Nyack, New York, where her mother purchased a house. McCullers spent most of the rest of her life in this house on the Hudson River.

McCullers's life was blighted by a series of cerebral strokes caused by her childhood case of rheumatic fever. The first stroke in February 1941 temporarily impaired her vision and caused debilitating head pains. The second and third occurred in Paris in the fall of 1947. These strokes temporarily destroyed the lateral vision in her right eye and permanently paralyzed her left side. Depressed by her declining health and her marital difficulties, she attempted suicide in March 1948 and was briefly hospitalized in a psychiatric clinic. On 15 August 1967 McCullers suffered her final cerebral stroke. Comatose for forty-seven days, she died in the Nyack Hospital. McCullers was buried in Nyack's Oak Hill Cemetery on the banks of the Hudson River. A memorial service was held at St. James's Episcopal Church in New York City on 3 October 1967.

Assessing McCullers's stature in American arts and letters, Virginia Spencer Carr wrote, "Critics continue to compare and contrast McCullers with Eudora Welty, Flannery O'Connor, and Katherine Anne Porter, whom they generally consider to be better stylists in the short form than McCullers. They tend to rank McCullers above her female contemporaries as a novelist. McCullers herself had a keen appreciation of her own work without regard to the sex of those with whom she was compared." In an appraisal of her life and work accompanying McCullers's front-page obituary in the 30 September 1967 *New York Times*, Eliot Fremont-Smith wrote of the impact of her first novel in what could also be an assessment of McCullers's lasting influence:

It is not so much that the novel paved the way for what became the American Southern gothic genre, but that it at once encompassed it and went beyond it. . . . The heart of this remarkable, still powerful book is perhaps best conveyed by its title, with its sense of intensity, concision and mystery, with its terrible juxtaposition of love and aloneness, whose relation was Mrs. McCullers's constant subject. . . . Mrs. McCullers was neither prolific nor varying in her theme. . . . This is no fault or tragedy: to some artists a vision is given only once. And a corollary: only an artist can make others subject to the vision's force. Mrs. McCullers was an artist. She was also in her person, an inspiration and example for other artists who grew close to her. Her books, and particularly 'The Heart,' will live; she will be missed.

In addition to the New York Drama Critics Circle and Donaldson awards for her play *The Member of the Wedding* (1950), McCullers also received two Guggenheim fellowships (1942, 1946), an Arts and Letters Grant from the American Academy of Arts and Letters and the National Institute of Arts and Letters (1943), and various other awards and honors. McCullers was inducted into the National Institute of Arts and Letters in 1952.

• The most extensive collection of McCullers's manuscripts, correspondence, and miscellaneous papers is the Carson McCullers Collection at the Harry Ransom Humanities Research Center at the University of Texas. There is also a significant collection of materials by or related to McCullers in the Special Collections Library of Duke University. McCullers's short stories, poems, essays, reminiscences, and reviews are published in collections, including *Collected Short Stories and the Novel "The Ballad of the Sad Cafe"* (1961); the posthumously published *The Mortgaged Heart*, ed. and with an introduction by McCullers's sister Margarita G. Smith (fiction editor of *Mademoiselle* magazine) (1971); and *Collected Stories of Carson McCullers*, ed. Virginia Spencer Carr (1987). Biographies and critical studies of McCullers include Carr, *The Lonely Hunter: A Biography of Carson McCullers* (1975) and *Understanding Carson McCullers* (1990); Richard M. Cook, *Carson McCullers* (1975); Dale Edmonds, *Carson McCullers* (1969); Oliver Evans, *The Ballad of Carson McCullers: A Biography* (1966), Lawrence Graver, *Carson McCullers* (1969); Judith Giblin James, *Wunderkind: The Reputation of Carson McCullers, 1940–90* (1995); Margaret B. McDowell, *Carson McCullers* (1980); Margaret Sue Sullivan, "Carson McCullers, 1917–1947: The Conversion of Experience" (Ph.D. diss., Duke Univ., 1966); and Louise Westling, *Sacred Groves and Ravaged Gardens: The Fiction of Eudora Welty, Carson McCullers, and Flannery O'Connor* (1985). McCullers bibliographies include Adrian M. Shapiro et al., *Carson McCullers: A Descriptive Listing and Annotated Bibliography of Criticism* (1980), which contains an exhaustive listing of McCullers's work and an annotated bibliography of writing about McCullers, and Robert F. Kiernan, *Katherine Anne Porter and Carson McCullers: A Reference Guide* (1976). An excellent bibliographical summary of McCullers's writing, unpublished manuscripts and letters, biography, and criticism is Virginia Spencer Carr and Joseph R. Millichap, "Carson McCullers," in *American Women Writers: Bibliographical Essays* (1983).

CARLOS L. DEWS

MCCULLOCH, Ben (11 Nov. 1811–7 Mar. 1862), Confederate general, was born in Rutherford County, Tennessee, the son of Alexander McCulloch, a soldier and farmer, and Frances LeNoir. He spent his early years working his father's land. He had little formal schooling but became an avid reader. A natural woodsman, McCulloch hunted with the legendary Davy Crockett.

In 1835, at the urging of Crockett, Ben and his brother Henry Eustace moved to Texas, which was then a province of Mexico. McCulloch joined the Texas rebellion in the following year and fought at the battle of San Jacinto, where he was praised by his commander, Sam Houston, for outstanding bravery and skill as an artillerist.

After the rebellion, McCulloch left the army and settled in the town of Gonzalez. In 1839 he was elected to the Congress of the Republic of Texas, but his fame in Texas would come to rest more on his achievements as an Indian fighter than on his accomplishments as a lawmaker. As one of the first of the legendary Texas Rangers, formed in 1842 to protect Texas's border from Mexican incursions and its settlements from Commanche raids, McCulloch seemed to have hit upon the profession best suited to his gifts. Described by contemporaries as taciturn, perfectly controlled, and especially cool under fire, McCulloch drew the attention of General Zachary Taylor as Taylor began his 1846 campaign in northern Mexico during the Mexican War.

Because of their intimate knowledge of the terrain, companies of the Texas Rangers—including McCulloch's—were invited to join Taylor's force as he moved toward Monterrey and a showdown with General Antonio López de Santa Anna at Buena Vista. Though Taylor disapproved of their proneness to excessive violence, he valued the rangers' services in forward scouting and in providing critical information on the size and disposition of Santa Anna's army. He singled out McCulloch for special praise.

Following the war he joined the gold rush to California, but like so many others he failed in the quest for great wealth and returned to Texas in 1852. In 1853 President Franklin Pierce appointed him a federal marshal for Texas, a post he held until the spring of 1859. The year before, President James Buchanan had sent him to Utah to assist in settling problems related to the Mormons.

McCulloch achieved his greatest stature as soldier during the Civil War. He supported the secession movement in Texas despite his long association and friendship with Governor Sam Houston, a staunch Unionist. As ranking officer in the soon-to-be Confederate army of Texas, he accepted the surrender of Federal troops in San Antonio in February 1861. The following May, Confederate president Jefferson Davis appointed him brigadier general to command regiments recruited from Texas, Louisiana, and Arkansas. His charge was to defend his base in Arkansas and the Indian Territory to the west and to assist Confederate forces in Missouri as they fought to control that pivotal border state.

McCulloch's brigade figured in two major battles in the western theater. In the first, McCulloch joined forces with Missouri Confederate leader Sterling Price to confront a Union army moving toward Arkansas under the aggressive Nathaniel Lyon. The battle that followed on 10 August 1861 at Wilson's Creek in southwestern Missouri was one of the bloodiest in the early years of the war. The Federals were forced to retreat, but McCulloch's performance was at best mixed. Despite commanding a numerically superior force, he had unwisely permitted Lyon to seize the offensive, and as a result his army was nearly driven from the field in the first hours of battle. McCulloch eventually rallied his men and won the day but at a huge cost in human life. The second major battle in which McCulloch fought occurred in northwestern Arkansas six months later. It involved much larger forces than had been engaged at Wilson's Creek and ended in defeat for the southern forces. Their loss in the battle of Pea Ridge on 7–8 March 1862 cost the Confederates Missouri and seriously endangered their control of Arkansas. The battle also resulted in McCulloch's death, as he was shot through the heart while, characteristically, leading a charge against heavily fortified Union positions.

• There are no known collections of McCulloch papers. Victor M. Rose, *The Life and Services of General Ben McCulloch* (1888), is an early and mostly laudatory biography. The most recent full-scale treatment is Thomas Cutrer, *Ben McCulloch and the Frontier Military Tradition* (1993). Accounts of his life in Texas and during the Mexican War may be found in T. R. Fehrenbach, *Lone Star: A History of Texas and the Texans* (1968), and Walter P. Webb, *The Texas Rangers: A Century of Frontier Defense* (1965). The following works examine his brief career in the Confederate army: Albert E. Castel, *General Sterling Price and the War in the West* (1968); William Shea and Earl Hess, *Pea Ridge: Civil War Campaign in the West* (1992); Michael B. Dougan, *Confederate Arkansas: The People and Policies of a Frontier State in Wartime* (1976); Robert U. Johnson and Clarence C. Buel, eds., *Battles and Leaders of the Civil War* (4 vols., 1884–1887), vol. 1, pp. 298–303, 314–34; and *The War of the Rebellion: A Compilation of the Official Records of the Union and Confederate Armies* (128 vols., 1880–1901), ser. 1, vol. 3, pp. 104–7, and vol. 8, pp. 283–301.

KENNETH B. SHOVER

MCCULLOCH, Catharine Gouger Waugh (4 June 1862–20 Apr. 1945), lawyer and social reformer, was born in Ransomville, New York, the daughter of Abraham Miller Waugh and Susan Gouger, farmers. The family moved to New Milford, Illinois, when Catharine was five years old. At the age of sixteen, she declined an offer to work as a schoolteacher in a nearby district. Instead, she entered the Rockford (Illinois) Female Seminary, graduating in 1882. For the next year and a half, she traveled throughout Illinois speaking on behalf of temperance. In 1884 she began to study law in the Rockford law firm of Marshall and Taggart, and the following year she entered Union College of Law in Chicago, forerunner of the law school of Northwestern University. She graduated from law school and was admitted to the Illinois state bar in 1886.

After graduation, Waugh sought a position as a law clerk in Chicago. She brought with her letters of recommendation from both professors and judges who knew her. "I sailed out inflated with enthusiasms and confidence in my own abilities," she later wrote. She soon learned, however, that at that time Chicago was not a hospitable place for an aspiring woman lawyer. She answered every advertisement for a law clerk but encountered only resistance. Finally giving up her search there, she felt that "there was no place on earth for a young woman just graduated from law school" (McCulloch, "Women as Law Clerks," n.d., Dillon Collection, Schlesinger Library, Radcliffe College).

Waugh then returned to Rockford and opened a solo law practice, eventually attracting enough paying clients to support herself and to make it possible for her to offer free legal services to many poor women. Through her practice, she learned more about the legal status of women and became increasingly interested in reform work on women's behalf, specifically suffrage and temperance. In 1888 she completed her thesis, "Woman's Wages," and received both a B.A.

degree and an M.A. degree from Rockford College. In that same year, the Winnebago County Prohibition party nominated her as its candidate for state attorney. Also in 1888 she attended the meeting of the International Council of Women in Washington, D.C., and helped form the International Women's Bar Association.

From 1888 to 1890, Waugh was a member of the Equity Club, a national correspondence club of women lawyers. The club members' letters to one another explored a broad range of professional and personal issues confronting women lawyers of the day. One such issue was the question of whether philanthropy and reform had a place in a woman lawyer's practice. Despite receiving advice from male lawyers that she should concentrate exclusively on building her professional career, Waugh remained committed to charity work for poor women clients and was an active public speaker on behalf of a number of women's reforms, including temperance, suffrage, and women's legal rights.

Another concern of the members of the Equity Club was the question of marriage and its place in the life of a woman lawyer. Waugh believed that if a husband was "progressive enough to be proud that his wife was a lawyer," marriage would not hinder the woman lawyer in her work (letter to the Equity Club, 8 Nov. 1890, quoted in Drachman, p. 192). In 1890 Catharine married such a husband, law school classmate Frank McCulloch, who was supportive of her professional aspirations as well as her political concerns. Anna Howard Shaw, a leading female minister and suffragist, performed the wedding ceremony. The couple spent their honeymoon in South Dakota, where Catharine had agreed, prior to making wedding plans, to conduct a series of lectures for local suffrage groups. After returning to Chicago, she joined her husband's law firm, which they renamed McCulloch and McCulloch. Although many of her fellow Equity Club members feared that marriage was an obstacle for an aspiring woman lawyer, in McCulloch's case marriage provided the key to her entry into the Chicago legal establishment that had so fiercely excluded her only a few years before. Almost immediately McCulloch took on the responsibilities of motherhood as well. Between 1891 and 1905 she had four children.

From 1890 until 1912, McCulloch was legislative superintendent of the Illinois Equal Suffrage Association and became a popular speaker on behalf of suffrage throughout the Midwest. In 1910 she contributed to the growing popularity and momentum of the suffrage movement by organizing motor tours to spread the message of suffrage to remote towns and villages throughout the state. She was also an active member of the National American Woman Suffrage Association (NAWSA), serving as both legal adviser and its first vice president. Deeply committed to the suffrage movement in her own region of the country, she helped to found the Mississippi Valley conference in 1912 to bring together suffrage leaders in the Midwest. After the federal suffrage amendment passed in

1920, McCulloch joined NAWSA's descendant, the League of Women Voters, and served until 1923 as the chair of its Committee on Uniform Laws Concerning Women.

McCulloch also continued to work for other legal rights for women. In 1899 she published the book *Mr. Lex*, a fictional account of the legal disabilities of wives and mothers. The popularity of the book helped persuade the Illinois legislature in 1901 to pass a bill drafted by McCulloch to give wives equal guardianship rights with their husbands over their children. In 1905 the legislature passed another of her bills, this one to raise the age of consent for women from fourteen to sixteen years of age.

McCulloch remained professionally active in addition to undertaking reform work and meeting domestic responsibilities. She was elected justice of the peace for the Chicago suburb of Evanston in 1907 and 1909 and served as master in chancery of the Cook County Superior Court. She was president of the Women's Bar Association of Illinois from 1916 to 1920. In 1929 she and her husband published *A Manual of the Law of Will Contests in Illinois*. McCulloch was also active in a broad spectrum of women's organizations, including the Woman's Christian Temperance Union, the Chicago Commons Settlement House, the Illinois Woman's Democratic Club, and the Women's City Club of Chicago. In addition, she was an active alumna and trustee of Rockford College.

In 1940, the year of their fiftieth wedding anniversary, the McCullochs were named "Senior Counsellors" by the Illinois Bar Association in honor of their many years in the legal profession. Catharine McCulloch died in Evanston. Admired and respected widely for her wit, grace, and accomplishment, she stood as proof to many women and men of her day that women could be successful in both their personal and their public lives.

• The McCulloch papers are in the Dillon Collection, Schlesinger Library, Radcliffe College. McCulloch's Equity Club letters and a biographical essay are in Virginia G. Drachman, *Women Lawyers and the Origins of Professional Identity* (1993). See also Nancy Cott, "Women as Law Clerks: Memoir of Catharine G. Waugh," in *The Female Autograph*, ed. Domna Stanton (1984); Frances E. Willard and Mary A. Livermore, eds., *A Woman of the Century* (1893), p. 485; and James B. Bradwell, "Women Lawyers of Illinois," *Chicago Legal News*, 2 June 1900. An obituary is in the *New York Times*, 21 Apr. 1945.

VIRGINIA G. DRACHMAN

MCCULLOCH, Hugh (7 Dec. 1808–24 May 1895), banker and secretary of the treasury, was born in Kennebunk, Maine, the son of Hugh McCulloch, a merchant and shipbuilder, and Abigail Perkins. After studies at Thornton Academy, McCulloch entered Bowdoin College in 1824 but left in his sophomore year because of illness. He taught school from 1826 to 1829 and then read law in Kennebunk and Boston. Having decided that the prospects for a young lawyer would be greater in the West, he headed for Indiana

and opened a law practice in the frontier community of Fort Wayne in the summer of 1833. His career direction soon changed when the recently chartered State Bank of Indiana established a branch at Fort Wayne in 1835, and he accepted the directors' offer to become the branch's cashier and manager. Despite his acknowledgment that he had "no practical knowledge whatever of banking," McCulloch quickly adapted to the financial world and served as head of the Fort Wayne branch and as a director of the State Bank until its charter expired in 1857, whereupon the directors of the new Bank of the State of Indiana chose him as president. Both banking systems were among the most solid in the country, and the second, through McCulloch's prudent management, was one of the few to weather the panic of 1857 without suspending specie payments.

In 1838, McCulloch married Susan Man, a native of Plattsburg, New York, who had come to Fort Wayne to establish a girls' school two years earlier. Bright, talented, and devout, Susan became involved in the temperance and other antebellum reform movements. In dedicating his memoirs to her, McCulloch described her as his "helpmate" in "the fullest sense of the word," and during their fifty-seven years together, the couple had four children. While Susan McCulloch was a New School Presbyterian, Hugh McCulloch remained nonsectarian with broadly humanitarian beliefs; at the same time, he had a streak of more orthodox piousness that often cropped up in his views on finance and politics.

Coming from a Federalist–National Republican political lineage, McCulloch described himself as "an original Henry Clay Whig" who supported all elements of Clay's American System, although he had misgivings about the high protective tariff, which he saw as detrimental to the country's commercial interests. When the Whig party disintegrated in the mid-1850s, McCulloch joined the new Republican party and was quietly antislavery, though like many conservative former Whigs he lamented the spiraling sectional controversy that divided the nation. Still, he saw the differences between North and South as irreconcilable and believed that only war could curb the aggressive and expansionist slave power.

As the war began, McCulloch continued to head the Indiana banking system and in 1862 he lobbied against creating a national banking system, which he saw as "greatly prejudicial to the State banks." The following year, however, Congress passed an amended version of the bill, which satisfied McCulloch's objections, and he accepted an invitation from Secretary of the Treasury Salmon P. Chase to become comptroller of the currency for the new system and moved to Washington to organize the National Currency Bureau. Working with Chase and then William Pitt Fessenden when Chase resigned in 1864, McCulloch was instrumental in getting the banking network off to a solid start. When Fessenden resigned in March 1865, McCulloch agreed to Abraham Lincoln's offer of the

Treasury portfolio, and he continued under Andrew Johnson's administration.

McCulloch later characterized his four years as secretary as "laborious and thankless." In the years after the Civil War, the United States faced a host of pressing and intertwined financial issues, with a bewildering array of bipartisan and regional divisions between soft and hard money interests, protectionist and free traders, manufacturing and financial interests, and agrarians and industrialists. At base, the government had to establish policy for handling the huge war debt of $2.85 billion and begin to work its way back to the resumption of specie payments—to make the national paper currencies created during the war convertible at par into gold. Forced to abandon the gold standard in late 1861, the North had resorted to non-specie-backed paper money—most notably $450 million in United States Notes, commonly known as "greenbacks." While the greenbacks had legal tender status, they had quickly depreciated, and by the war's end one-dollar notes were worth only about sixty-seven cents in gold. To this situation McCulloch brought a lifelong abhorrence of "perpetuated debt" and an abiding faith in the absolute necessity, indeed morality, of a well-secured, convertible paper currency. "There is," he intoned in his memoirs, "no real money but gold and silver."

Given his classical monetary views, McCulloch firmly believed that the only quick path to resumption was to contract the volume of greenbacks until they reached parity with gold. In a major address at Fort Wayne in October 1865, and in his report to Congress in December, he asked for authority to withdraw greenbacks from circulation "as rapidly as it could be done, without affecting injuriously industry and trade." Fearing the adverse impact of a too-rapid contraction, in April 1866 Congress refused to give McCulloch unrestricted discretionary power. It limited greenback contraction to $10 million in the first six months and to no more than $4 million in any one month thereafter. Chafing at the limitation yet working cautiously, McCulloch managed to retire about $44 million of the $400 million in circulation before Congress cut off further contraction in 1868. While his actions had the nearly solid backing of the larger eastern bankers and merchants, opposition to contraction of the popular currency stiffened among western bankers, industrial capitalists, and most protectionist manufacturing interests, especially during the economic recession of 1867–1868. McCulloch's own party was sharply split on the issue between the orthodox gold standard, free-trade conservatives like himself, and the more entrepreneurial, speculative, and protectionist wing of the party, which included many Radical Republicans. Some Republicans maintained that as the country "grew up" to the volume of paper money, it would gradually appreciate to par with gold; others argued with McCulloch's timing and thought it more important to refinance the debt first. Through it all McCulloch stood his ground, determined and independent, although perplexed at times by the "unrea-

sonable apprehension" that eventually stopped further contraction.

Similarly, McCulloch constantly urged Congress to increase revenues to service the debt and to refund it into lower-interest bonds. In the absence of congressional action, he was able to consolidate many short-term and high-interest securities into "five-twenties," a series of bonds redeemable in five years and payable in twenty, bearing 6 percent interest in gold. During the latter part of his tenure, McCulloch vigorously opposed the argument of western soft money interests that the principal of the five-twenties should be paid in depreciated greenbacks as well as the recommendation of Johnson himself that interest payments on the bonds be withheld and applied to the principal. Shortly after McCulloch left office, Congress sustained his position with passage of the Public Credit Act, pledging the government's faith to pay off the principal as well as the interest on the bonded indebtedness in coin; it later refunded the five-twenties and other series into longer-term, lower-interest securities.

Although McCulloch tried to divorce politics from his work at the Treasury, his support for Johnson's reconstruction policy greatly complicated his job during this highly politicized period. While he was not blind to Johnson's shortcomings, particularly his intemperate stump-style speeches, McCulloch shared Johnson's strict constructionist views and once referred to Radical Republicans as "Constitutional tinkers." He clashed with Radicals such as Senator Charles Sumner of Massachusetts over the appointment of revenue agents in the South, and he earned lasting Radical enmity for his opposition to suffrage for the newly freed blacks. Finally, McCulloch thought the Radical-led effort to remove Johnson from office in 1867–1868 was "purely political" and not constitutionally justified. In short, his political and financial positions often brought a buffeting from all sides; "the palm of being the 'best abused' man in the country," he wrote in late 1868, now belonged to him rather than Johnson.

Having also crossed Ulysses S. Grant during the Johnson impeachment imbroglio, McCulloch had no place in the Grant administration, which began in March 1869. The following year he joined New York financier Jay Cooke to open Jay Cooke, McCulloch and Company as the London branch of the financier's empire. Although the branch survived the parent company's failure in the panic of 1873, it was soon dissolved, and McCulloch joined a syndicate involved in refunding southern state debts. His retirement into the world of private finance was interrupted only when he again accepted the Treasury portfolio late in President Chester A. Arthur's term and helped him close out his administration. After serving from October 1884 to March 1885, McCulloch retired to his farm, "Holly Hill," a few miles outside Washington, where he wrote his memoirs and died quietly.

On balance, historians have argued that as secretary, McCulloch was too inflexible, too concerned with the welfare of northeastern financial interests, and too little aware of the need for an adequate circulating medium in the currency-starved South and the expansionist West. In the evaluation of Robert Sharkey, McCulloch had a "rigid, conservative, and essentially unimaginative mind" (p. 59), and as Irwin Unger has noted, his stubborn advocacy of forced contraction perhaps even hurt the hard money cause by "identifying resumption with the remorseless burning of the people's money" (p. 403). Still, McCulloch kept the sanctity of the public credit and specie resumption at the forefront of the postwar financial debate, and his advocacy of conservative fiscal practices prevailed in the long run as the debt was refunded and effectively serviced, and resumption was finally achieved in 1879.

• The primary collections of McCulloch's papers are at the Manuscript Division of the Library of Congress and the Lilly Library, Indiana University. His memoirs, *Men and Measures of Half a Century* (1888), are a notable conservative Republican perspective on the middle period, and his financial arguments can be found in his *Addresses, Speeches, Lectures, and Letters upon Various Subjects* (1891) and in his lengthy *Annual Reports of the Secretary of the Treasury, 1865–1868, 1884*. Although there are no major biographies, valuable for his Indiana years are Raymond J. Reece, "Hugh McCulloch Moves West," *Indiana Magazine of History* 32 (1936): 95–105, and Charles R. Poinsatte, *Fort Wayne during the Canal Era, 1828–1855: A Study of a Western Community in the Middle Period of American History* (1969). Still offering a solid overview of his years as secretary is Herbert S. Schell, "Hugh McCulloch and the Treasury Department, 1865–1869," *Mississippi Valley Historical Review* 17 (1930): 404–21. Providing a larger context for his actions and more critical of his contractionist, hard money views are Robert P. Sharkey, *Money, Class, and Party: An Economic Study of Civil War and Reconstruction* (1959), and Irwin Unger, *The Greenback Era: A Social and Political History of American Finance, 1865–1879* (1964). A full obituary is in the *New York Times*, 25 May 1895.

TERRY L. SEIP

MCCULLOCH, Oscar Carleton (2 July 1843–10 Dec. 1891), clergyman and reformer, was born in Fremont, Ohio, the son of Carleton Graves McCulloch, a druggist, and Harriet Pettibone. McCulloch was brought up in a strongly orthodox Presbyterian family and accepted, until some years later, the doctrines of strict Calvinism.

McCulloch graduated from Eastman Business College in 1864 and immediately secured a clerk position in Springfield, Illinois, for the state government. In 1865 he moved to Chicago to become a salesman for a wholesale drug company. In that capacity he traveled widely in the southwestern and far western states. Though successful as a salesman, McCulloch became dissatisfied with his career and began to take up religious work in his free time. He talked to men in bars and poolrooms about religious questions and volunteered in church missions and in the Chicago branch of the YMCA. In 1867 he resigned from the drug company and entered the Chicago Theological Seminary, from which he graduated in June 1870. That September he married Agnes Buel; they had two children.

McCulloch's career as a minister began in 1870 at the First Congregational Church in Sheboygan, Wisconsin. From the beginning, his sermons presented liberal religious beliefs that he had developed as a student. Though not recognized as an early leader of the Social Gospel movement, McCulloch was an exponent of its principal tenet, social justice. His underlying message was that anything that concerned the welfare of the individual concerned the church. He preached on business ethics, child labor, and the relation of capital to labor. McCulloch's liberal preaching brought many new members to the church in Sheboygan but also provoked criticism from leading congregants. With the membership divided over his controversial leadership, McCulloch accepted a "call" in 1877 to the Plymouth Congregational Church in Indianapolis. In 1878, four years after his first wife's death, McCulloch married Alice Barteau. They had three children.

At his second church, McCulloch developed a series of secular programs open to members and nonmembers of the church. These included the Plymouth Savings and Loan Association, the Plymouth Book Club, a library, a boys' orchestra, a gymnasium, and an annual concert and lecture series. He hoped that these programs, the first of their kind in Indiana and among the first in the country, would make Plymouth Church into a "people's church" and a "people's college." As in Sheboygan, his preaching and activism attracted many new members to his church.

McCulloch believed that his role as a minister required him to identify with the life and concerns of the wider community. He became involved with existing private and public benevolent agencies in Indianapolis and played an instrumental role in creating new programs and agencies, such as the Charity Organization Society, Children's Aid Association, and a visiting nurse service. McCulloch formulated and lobbied for acts that created the Indiana Board of State Charities and the State Board of Children's Guardians in all townships having a population of more than 75,000. He advocated that the Children's Guardians law be operative in all counties of the state, but this was not enacted until 1901. He also served on a number of the boards' committees. Outside of Indiana, he was an important early leader of the National Conference of Charities and Correction, and his national recognition as an authority on the organization of charities led to his being called on to help promote societies of associated or organized charities in Cincinnati, Milwaukee, and Denver.

Unlike his contemporary Washington Gladden, recognized as the most influential leader of the Social Gospel, McCulloch was not a prolific writer. His chief works included *The Open Door*, a selection of his sermons and prayers that was compiled by his widow and published posthumously, and *The Tribe of Ishmael*, a study of hereditary pauperism. He also published a number of articles, lectures, and book reviews in the local press and in religious journals and other periodicals. He died in Indianapolis of Hodgkin's disease.

• McCulloch's *Diaries* (14 vols., 1877–1891), are in the Indiana Division of the Indiana State Library in Indianapolis. They contain, in addition to his entries, numerous newspaper clippings, leaflets, programs, and announcements of social agencies and of the two churches with which he was connected. See also Alexander Johnson, "Oscar Carleton McCulloch," *Charities Review* 1 (1892): 97–104; *Proceedings of the National Conference of Charities and Correction, 1879–1892* (1899); and Jacob Piatt Dunn, *Greater Indianapolis: The History, the Industries, the Institutions, and the People of a City of Homes* (2 vols., 1910). Obituaries are in the Indianapolis *News* and the Indianapolis *Sentinel*, 11 Dec. 1891. A memorial is H. D. Stevens, "Oscar Carleton McCulloch—A Memorial Tribute," *Unitarian* 7 (1892): 55–60.

GENEVIEVE C. WEEKS

MCCULLOUGH, John (14 Nov. 1832–8 Nov. 1885), actor and theater manager, was born in Blakes, Londonderry, Ireland, the son of James McCullough, an indigent farmer, and Mary (maiden name unknown). After Mary's death, James and his four children (three daughters and a son) emigrated at different times in the late 1840s to the United States, John arriving in the spring of 1847. Illiterate and poor, he made his way to Philadelphia, where he apprenticed in the business of a cousin, who was a chair maker. In 1849 he married Letitia McLain of Germantown, Pennsylvania; they had two sons (James and William). He taught himself to read and write and pursued his trade for a period of years. A fellow workman introduced him to the plays of Shakespeare, and McCullough subsequently joined an amateur dramatic society and undertook elocution lessons with Lemuel White, the teacher of the tragedian Edwin Forrest.

McCullough made his professional stage debut at Philadelphia's Arch Street Theatre as Thomas in *The Belle's Stratagem* on 15 August 1857. His first starring role during his three years there was Astralagus in *King of the Alps* on 28 June 1858. E. L. Davenport, a respected actor-manager, hired him for the 1860–1861 season at the Atheneum in Boston. He returned to Philadelphia in 1861 for a season at the Walnut Street Theatre, only to interrupt that engagement to tour with his hero and model, Edwin Forrest. He first appeared with Forrest in Boston in October 1861 as Pythias to the latter's Damon—the title roles of John Banim's popular piece. His association with and purported imitation of Forrest attracted both positive and negative attention from critics for his entire career.

McCullough spent the next five years touring with Forrest's company, playing such Shakespearean roles as Laertes, Macduff, Iago, Edgar, Cominius, and Richmond to Forrest's Hamlet, Macbeth, Othello, Lear, Coriolanus, and Richard III. He also played second leads in the repertory of heroic American (and some British) melodramas that were Forrest's trademark: *Metamora*, *The Gladiator*, *Jack Cade*, *The Broker of Bogota*, and Sheridan Knowles's *Virginius*. In May 1866 McCullough arrived with Forrest in San Francisco to play an engagement with the stock company at Maguire's Opera House. It was here that Forrest reportedly advised McCullough to cease imitating

his style and to settle in the West. McCullough was to retain San Francisco as his base of operations for the next eleven years.

Through the end of 1868 McCullough performed at Maguire's and other local theaters, gradually building his repertory as a heroic leading man and winning the respect of the San Francisco critics, who had been initially cold to him. He performed at Maguire's with Lawrence Barrett in 1868, a combination successful enough to encourage their collaboration as actor-managers of the new California Theatre. Erected by William C. Ralston, head of the Bank of California, the California Theatre aimed to be the rival of any theater in America, and its management assembled a considerable company from among local actors and others brought in from the East. The California Theatre Stock Company debuted on 18 January 1869 with Bulwer-Lytton's *Money*, McCullough playing the lead role. (Barrett did not perform until February, when he appeared in Selby's *The Marble Heart*.)

McCullough and Barrett comanaged the California Theatre until the summer of 1870, when the latter withdrew as a partner. McCullough had initially invested $12,000 for his share of the lease and bought out Barrett for $5,000. Independently, McCullough continued the policy that he and Barrett had developed. On the one hand, McCullough maintained the high quality of the local stock company, himself often performing the lead roles in the standard pieces that he had learned under Forrest. On the other hand, he negotiated to engage visiting stars in their recent hits or the classical repertory. Thus, San Francisco audiences were able to see Frank Mayo as Davy Crockett, E. A. Sothern as Lord Dundreary in Tom Taylor's *Our American Cousin*, and Edwin Booth, acknowledged as the greatest American actor of his time, in a round of Shakespearean roles.

In 1877 McCullough also took Baldwin's Theatre in San Francisco under his management. But despite some successful programming, renovations to the theaters, and innovative marketing (McCullough sold choice tickets for Booth's engagement at auction), he fell victim to the erratic California economy. The lingering effects of the 1876 recession took their toll at the box office, and in the latter half of 1877 McCullough yielded all his management responsibilities, selling his interests in both theaters and departing San Francisco with a debt of $55,000. His Hamlet on 27 August 1877 was his final role at the California Theatre.

Although management had consumed much of his energy from 1869, McCullough continued to establish his reputation as a studious and traditional actor, eager to improve his craft, in starring tours across the United States. In September 1869 he had briefly played Othello to Booth's Iago in New York City and returned to Booth's Theatre in May 1874 to do star turns in *Hamlet*, *Damon and Pythias*, Bulwer-Lytton's *Richelieu*, *The Gladiator*, and *The Stranger* (adapted from Kotzebue). He added to his repertory in the latter half of the 1870s, gradually winning the grudging admiration of critics in the East who had earlier disparaged the rough and boisterous style they imagined he had developed in the Far West. He apparently benefited from studying a more subdued style of elocution with Steele MacKaye, the chief American proponent of Francois Delsarte's theories of actor training. Even so, McCullough remained most successful in the more robust roles of classical tragedy and melodrama: Virginius (which became the role he was most identified with), Lear, Othello, Coriolanus, Richelieu, Metamora, Spartacus, Rolla in R. B. Sheridan's *Pizarro*, and Lucius Brutus in *The Fall of Tarquin*.

His reputation and skills reached a peak in 1877–1883, during which time he played annual engagements in New York City. Most of these were successful and staged at prestigious theaters such as Booth's and the Fifth Avenue (though his 1883 run was at Niblo's Garden, indicating a decline in status). In 1881 he played a month at the Drury Lane in London, winning mild praise as an "actor of the people" for his Othello and Virginius. Even during this period of eminence, his muscular style (following, still, the manner of Forrest) had almost as many detractors as supporters.

Chief among the latter was the moralistic, conservative, Harvard-educated William Winter, who wrote for the *New York Tribune* from 1865 until 1909. Allowing for Winter's unquestioning approval of the moral intent of McCullough's repertory ("if acting ever could do good the acting of McCullough did" [*Shadows of the Stage*, p. 191]) and of his training under the esteemed Forrest, Winter gives a fair enough account of McCullough's strengths and limitations as an actor. McCullough's physical appeal—a powerful build, "Roman" features, and a trumpet-toned voice—signified not only to Winter but to McCullough's many admirers a noble presence, high-mindedness, virtuous strength, integrity, and depth of character. Whether he deliberately chose roles to exploit these natural traits or whether the roles became the filter through which his own character was viewed is difficult to determine. But, in any case, this performing persona combined with his offstage generosity, good humor, and sociability to forge an attractive public image.

Among Shakespearean roles he was most successful in Lear, Othello and the rarely performed Coriolanus. Initially, he played Nahum Tate's Restoration-era adaptation of *King Lear*, only later restoring the semblance of the Shakespearean text that was the norm of the nineteenth-century stage. (He also used Colley Cibber's *Richard III* and Garrick's *Katharine and Petrucchio*.) Even then, he retained the hoary traditions of banging down the first act curtain with the cursing of Goneril and the second with a tumultuous exit on "O, Fool, I shall go mad!" Winter felt that he realized the full pathos of the role and made a fine distinction between the agony of a man while going mad and the vacant, heedless condition of one who has lapsed into madness. J. Ranken Towse, the other major New York critic of the period, acknowledged the theatrical effectiveness of McCullough's Lear but said it lacked grandeur and subtlety. As Othello, McCullough emphasized the spirituality of the Moor's love of Desdemona, manly tenderness, and a "massive serenity" (Winter's phrase) suddenly disturbed by tempests of emotion. Towse found the performance crude and unimaginative, though he admired McCullough's depiction of patrician pride, courage, and contempt as Coriolanus.

McCullough's signature role Virginius—like Othello and Lear—hinged upon the destruction of a defenseless woman as the result of the actions of the man expected to protect her. That McCullough won praise for his moral grandeur and paternal agony in his display of Virginius (under extreme circumstances) stabbing his daughter to death says much about the performance of masculinity on the late nineteenth-century stage. Sympathy was deflected from the female victim, and masculinity was associated with virtuous strength, even when fatally applied, as feminity was associated with innocent weakness.

Suffering from the advanced stages of syphilis, McCullough gave his final performance 29 September 1884 at McVicker's Theatre in Chicago in *The Gladiator*. After a period of confinement in the Bloomingdale (N.Y.) Insane Asylum, he died at his home in Philadelphia.

• Letters, promptbooks, and clippings related to McCullough are held in major collections including the Harvard Theatre Collection; the Folger Shakespeare Library; the Billy Rose Theatre collection at the New York Public Library for the Performing Arts, Lincoln Center; and the Walter Hampden Memorial Library at the Players, New York City. A biography is Susie C. Clark, *John McCullough as Man, Actor and Spirit* (1905), but see also Bruce E. Woodruff, "Genial John McCullough" (Ph.D. diss., Univ. of Nebraska, 1984). William Winter wrote extensively about McCullough in *Shadows of the Stage* (1892–1895), *Other Days* (1908), and *Vagrant Memories* (1915). Garff B. Wilson, *A History of American Acting* (1966), devotes a section to McCullough and his followers. McCullough is referenced in such standard works as Stephen Archer, *American Actors and Actresses: A Guide to Information Sources* (1983); Ronald Moyer, *American Actors and Actresses, 1861–1910: An Annotated Bibliography of Books Published in the United States in English from 1861 to 1976* (1979); Donald Mullin, *Victorian Actors and Actresses in Review: A Dictionary of Contemporary Views of Representative British and American Actors and Actresses, 1837–1901* (1983); Weldon B. Durham, *American Theatre Companies, 1749–1887*; and Barnard Hewitt, *Theatre U.S.A., 1665–1957* (1959). Obituaries are in the *New York Times* and the *Boston Transcript*, both 9 Nov. 1885, and the *New York Clipper*, and the *New York Dramatic Mirror*, both 14 Nov. 1885.

ATTILIO FAVORINI

MCCURDY, Richard Aldrich (29 Jan. 1835–6 Mar. 1916), insurance executive, was born in New York City, the son of Robert H. McCurdy, a prosperous dry goods merchant, and Gertrude Mercer Lee. He grew up in New York City in well-to-do surroundings before entering Harvard College in 1852. Leaving undergraduate studies after two years, he then entered Harvard Law School, from which he graduated in 1856. McCurdy immediately gained admittance to the New York bar and that same year married Sarah Ellen Little of Boston, Massachusetts; the couple eventually had three children.

After forming a legal partnership with William Betts, Jr., and Lucius Robinson, McCurdy practiced law in New York City for a number of years. In 1860 he became an attorney for the Mutual Life Insurance Company of New York, of which his father had been a director for many years. Growing rapidly in professional stature, he was appointed in the following year as transfer agent for the issuing and countersigning of New York State equities and with the advent of the Civil War became a U.S. draft commissioner as well. Following the end of hostilities in 1865, McCurdy became both a director and vice president of Mutual Life. As vice president, McCurdy took an active role in opposing the issuance of so-called tontine life insurance policies (a speculative type of policy that, through deferment of dividends, offered the policyholder the potential—often unrealized—for enormous financial gains) by Mutual's competitors.

McCurdy's rise in the management ranks of Mutual coincided with a period of rapid growth in the life insurance industry at large and of intense competition for new business among the so-called Big Three companies (Mutual, Equitable, and New York Life). By the mid-1880s Mutual lost its leadership position to Equitable, and McCurdy joined with others in the company in urging the adoption of more aggressive efforts on the part of Mutual, including the issuance of deferred dividend, or "semitontine," policies. Shortly after the decision was reached to enter the highly profitable semitontine market, Mutual president Frederick S. Winston died and was soon replaced by McCurdy.

Assuming his new duties in 1885, McCurdy blasted his predecessor's preoccupation with capital accumulation and investment at the expense of business expansion, complaining that Mutual "had gradually been converted into a loan and trust institution with a life insurance branch, instead of . . . a life insurance company" (Keller, p. 128). Vowing to return Mutual to its former position, he soon used the new semitontine policy to great effect. New business more than doubled during the first three years of McCurdy's administration, and in the twenty years that he ran Mutual assets increased from $103 million to $470 million, while insurance in force rose from $351 million to $1.5 billion. Proving as flexible in his attitudes toward trust companies as he was toward tontine insurance, McCurdy also took leading roles in the formation of the United States Mortgage and Trust Company (1893) and the Guaranty Trust Company (1896). He also invested heavily (using—and making little distinction between—his own and Mutual's funds) in other institutions, such as the National Bank of Commerce and the Morristown (N.J.) Trust Company.

McCurdy was autocratic and even arrogant in his style; when Mutual charged policyholders who had joined the military during the Spanish-American War extra premiums, McCurdy defended his company's actions, stating, "Whatever sympathetic interest we may feel for the defenders of our country in time of war, as a business proposition they are not worth any special effort to secure their patronage" (Keller, p. 55).

An era of nearly uninterrupted growth, however, came to a halt in 1905. In that year, prompted by years of rumors and policyholder complaints, as well as a high-level squabble among the management at Equitable, the New York state legislature convened the Armstrong Committee to investigate conditions and practices within the life insurance industry. As the head of one of the largest life insurance firms, McCurdy was among those called to testify before the committee.

Led by counsel Charles Evans Hughes, the Armstrong Committee conducted a thorough investigation and extracted extensive testimony from key industry figures. No figure emerged from the proceedings more devastated than McCurdy. While the investigation revealed an industry rife with nepotism, excessive salaries, and declining dividends for policyholders in the face of lavish company expenditures for entertainment and political lobbying efforts, McCurdy compounded his (and Mutual's) problems with his testimony. Seventy years old, he responded to questions in an often barely audible whisper, while his tone veered from evasiveness to outright petulance. Giving the impression of a man who knew little of his firm's internal workings, he drew outright ridicule from the press with his claim that life insurance companies existed not to make money but as "a great beneficent missionary institution . . . an eleemosynary institution, to a very large extent, I have always believed all my life, and I believe it today" (Buley, p. 216). Hughes, after noting that McCurdy earned $150,000 a year (that figure combined with the salaries of other employed family members reached $500,000), retorted, "As a missionary enterprise . . . the question goes back to the salaries of missionaries" (Buley, p. 216).

McCurdy resigned as president during the investigation, pleading poor health. His departure did not end his troubles, however, as he was soon sued by the trustees of Mutual for the recovery of $6 million that he allegedly owed the company (a settlement was reached in 1909 for $750,000 in cash; the suit itself was discontinued in 1910). McCurdy, after living in France during the years 1906–1907, returned to the United States and his estate in Morristown, New Jersey, in 1908. He died there after living the balance of his life in obscurity.

The real contributions of McCurdy toward the creation of today's Mutual of New York have long been overshadowed by his participation in the Armstrong investigation. While other insurance industry executives participated in many of the same activities that landed McCurdy in trouble, his arrogant and inept handling of the controversy ensured that his would be the name most associated with the controversy.

• The papers of Richard Aldrich McCurdy are held at the History Factory in Chantilly, Va. His life and career received coverage in R. Carlyle Buley, *The American Life Convention 1906–1952: A Study in the History of Life Insurance* (2 vols., 1953), and in Morton Keller's excellent overview, *The Life Insurance Enterprise, 1885–1910: A Study in the Limits of Corporate Power* (1963). Obituaries are in the *New York World* and the *New York Times*, both 7 Mar. 1916.

EDWARD L. LACH, JR.